THE STATESMAN'S YEAR-BOOK

1996–97

Man hat behauptet, die Welt werde durch Zahlen regiert: das aber weiss ich, dass die Zahlen uns belehren, ob sie gut oder schlecht regiert werde. GOETHE

Editors

Frederick Martin	1864–1883
Sir John Scott-Keltie	1883–1926
Mortimer Epstein	1911/27–1946
S. H. Steinberg	1946–1969
John Paxton	1963/69–1990
Brian Hunter	1990–

THE STATESMAN'S YEAR-BOOK

A STATISTICAL, POLITICAL AND ECONOMIC ACCOUNT
OF THE STATES OF THE WORLD
FOR THE YEAR

1996–1997

EDITED BY

BRIAN HUNTER

MACMILLAN

Published annually since 1864
133rd edition first published 1996 by
THE MACMILLAN PRESS LTD
London and Basingstoke

Associated companies in Auckland, Delhi, Dublin, Gaborone, Hamburg, Harare, Hong Kong, Johannesburg, Kuala Lumpur, Lagos, Manzini, Melbourne, Mexico City, Nairobi, New York, Singapore, Tokyo

British Library Cataloguing in Publication Data
Statesman's year-book.–1996-1997
1. Social conditions–Serials
909.82'8'05 HN1

ISSN 0081-4601
ISBN 0-333-65573-7

Typeset in Great Britain by
A. J. LATHAM LIMITED
Dunstable, Bedfordshire

Printed in England by BPC Hazell Books Ltd
A member of
The British Printing Company Ltd

PREFACE

In the title of this edition the term 'Historical' is replaced by 'Political and Economic'. Although the 133 volumes of the STATESMAN'S YEAR-BOOK constitute valuable historical material, the primary aim of each annual volume is to present a survey of the statistical, political and economic data of the world at a given moment, and the new wording is intended to proclaim the scope of this survey more explicitly.

A Topic Finding List has been introduced to assist readers in identifying the section of text containing the data they seek. Other innovations include the relocation of Russia and the other countries in the Commonwealth of Independent States (CIS) to the general A–Z sequence, the CIS as an institution moving to Part I: International Organizations; the addition of entries for the International Telecommunications Satellite Organization and the South African Development Community; and the quotation of currency exchange rates for the German mark as well as the American dollar and pound sterling.

In our last edition the Human Development Index (HDI) for 1992 was added to the masthead of each country. The HDI has been devised by the UN Development Programme as a socio-economic measure of national progress. It combines the factors of longevity (based on expectation of life), knowledge (based on adult literacy and mean years of schooling) and standard of living (based on real GDP per capita adjusted for local cost of living), and is expressed as a three-figure decimal on a scale descending from 1 to 0. The index not only measures the achievement of each country, but also provides the possibility of a synchronic comparison between countries, since a 'world rank' is also given. Although the updated HDI in this edition still relates to 1992, it has been adjusted to take account of a major revision in its formulation introduced by the UN Development Programme in 1994. The aim of this revision was to widen and stabilize the indicators used to permit a more meaningful record of countries' development through time.

The editor would like to express his warmest thanks to all his colleagues for their work in the preparation of this edition, and to the many specialist correspondents throughout the world whose contributions ensure its reliability and topicality.

Correspondents should note that the STATESMAN'S YEAR-BOOK OFFICE has changed its address once again this year as indicated below.

B.H.

THE STATESMAN'S YEAR-BOOK OFFICE,
THE MACMILLAN PRESS LTD,
25 ECCLESTON PLACE,
LONDON SW1W 9NF

WEIGHTS AND MEASURES

On 1 Jan. 1960 following an agreement between the standards laboratories of Great Britain, Canada, Australia, New Zealand, South Africa and the USA, an international yard and an international pound (avoirdupois) came into existence. 1 yard = 91·44 centimetres; 1 lb. = 453·59237 grammes.

The abbreviation 'm.' signifies 'million(s)' and tonnes implies metric tons.

LENGTH		**DRY MEASURE**	
Centimetre	0·394 inch	Litre	0·91 quart
Metre	1·094 yards	Hectolitre	2·75 bushels
Kilometre	0·621 mile		
		WEIGHT—AVOIRDUPOIS	
LIQUID MEASURE			
Litre	1·75 pints	Gramme	15·42 grains
Hectolitre	22 gallons	Kilogramme	2·205 pounds
		Quintal (= 100 kg)	220·46 pounds
		Tonne (= 1,000 kg)	0·984 long ton; 1·102 short tons
SURFACE MEASURE		**WEIGHT—TROY**	
Square metre	10·76 sq. feet	Gramme	15·43 grains
Hectare	2·47 acres	Kilogramme	32·15 ounces; 2·68 pounds
Square kilometre	0·386 sq. mile		

BRITISH WEIGHTS AND MEASURES

LENGTH		**WEIGHT**	
1 foot	0·305 metre	1 ounce (= 437·2 grains)	28·350 grammes
1 yard	0·914 metre	1 lb. (= 7,000 grains)	453·6 grammes
1 mile (= 1,760 yds)	1·609 kilometres	1 cwt. (= 112 lb.)	50·802 kilogrammes
		1 long ton (= 2,240 lb.)	1·016 tonnes
		1 short ton (= 2,000 lb.)	0·907 tonne
SURFACE MEASURE		**LIQUID MEASURE**	
1 sq. foot	9·290 sq. decimetres		
1 sq. yard	0·836 sq. metre	1 pint	0·568 litre
1 acre	0·405 hectare	1 gallon	4·546 litres
1 sq. mile	2·590 sq. kilometres	1 quarter	2·909 hectolitres

CONVERSION OF UNITS

To convert from	*To*	*Multiply by*
acre	hectare	0·4047
barrel (oil)	cu. metre	0·159
bushel (imperial)	litre	36·37
bushel (US)	litre	35·24
carat	gramme	0·2
cu. foot	cu. metre	0·028317
cu. metre	cu. foot	35·315
foot	metre	0·3048
gigawatt-hour	kilowatt-hour	1,000,000
hectare	acre	2·471
hundredweight (long)	kilogramme	50·802
hundredweight (short)	kilogramme	45·359
inch	millimetre	25·4
kilogramme	pound	2·2046
kilometre	mile (statute)	0·62137
megawatt	kilowatt	1,000
metre	foot	3·2808
mile (nautical)	kilometre	1·852
mile (statute)	kilometre	1·6093
millimetre	inch	0·03937
ounce (troy)	gramme	31·103
pound	kilogramme	0·45359
register ton	cu. metre	2·832
sq. kilometre	sq. mile	0·3861
sq. mile	sq. kilometre	2·590
per sq. mile	per sq. kilometre	0·3861
ton (long)	tonne (metric)	1·016
ton (short)	tonne (metric)	0·9072
tonne	barrel (oil)	7·33

ABBREVIATIONS

Abbreviations of the names of organizations also appear in the index.

The three-letter groups in parentheses after the names of currencies are the codes of the International Standardization Organization (ISO).

ACP	African Caribbean Pacific
Adm.	Admiral
b.	born
bbls.	barrels
bd	board
Brig.	Brigadier
bu.	bushel
Cdr	Commander
CEFTA	Central European Free Trade Area
CFA	Communauté Financière Africaine
CFP	Comptoirs Français du Pacifique
c.i.f.	cost, insurance, freight
C.-in-C.	Commander-in-Chief
CIS	Commonwealth of Independent States
cu.	cubic
CUP	Cambridge University Press
cwt	hundredweight
D.	Democratic Party
DWT	dead weight tonnes
ECOWAS	Economic Community of West African States
EEA	European Economic Area
EEZ	Exclusive Economic Zone
EMS	European Monetary System
ERM	Exchange Rate Mechanism
f.o.b.	free on board
ft	foot/feet
G7 Group	Canada, France, Germany, Italy, Japan, UK, USA
GDP	gross domestic product
Gen.	General
GNP	gross national product
GRT	gross registered tonnes
ha	hectare(s)
HDI	Human Development Index
ind	independent(s)
K	kindergarten
kg	kilogramme(s)
kl	kilolitre(s)
km	kilometre(s)
kW	kilowatt
kWh	kilowatt hours

ABBREVIATIONS—*contd.*

lb(s)	pound(s) (weight)
Lieut.	Lieutenant
m.	million
Maj.	Major
MW	megawatt
NRT	net registered tonnes
OUP	Oxford University Press
oz.	ounce(s)
PAYE	Pay-As-You-Earn
R.	Republican Party
SADC	Southern African Development Community
SDR	Special Drawing Rights
sq.	square
SSI	Supplemental Security Income
TAFE	technical and further education
TBVC	Transkei, Bophuthatswana, Venda, Ciskei
TV	television
Univ.	University
VAT	value-added tax
vfd	value for duty

CONTENTS

Comparative Statistical Tables

Part I: International Organizations

Other International Organizations

Part II: Countries of the World A–Z

COMPARATIVE STATISTICAL TABLES

WHEAT [2]

Countries	Area (1,000 ha) Average 1979-81	1990	1993	1994	Production (1,000 tonnes) Average 1979-81	1990	1993	1994	Ranking by production
Argentina	5,245	5,797	4,754	5,042	8,060	11,014	9,604	10,680	14
Australia	11,440	9,218	8,891	8,400	14,468	15,066	16,877	16,480	8
Bulgaria	986	1,163	1,268	1,320	3,881	5,292	3,681	3,788	24
Canada	11,386	14,098	12,377	10.919	20,430	32,098	27,232	23,350	6
China	28,930	30,754	30,236	30,501*	59,196	98,232	106,390	101,205*	1
Egypt	577	821	912	887	1,844	4,266	4,833	4,437	21
France	4,473	5,148	4,515	4,591	22,362	33,312	29,252	30,652	5
Germany	2,340	2,430	2,395	2,435	11,229	15,242	15,767	16,480	9
Hungary	1,187	1,221	986	1,059	4,800	6,198	3,021	4,874	20
India	22,364	23,502	24,431	24,437	34,550	49,850	56,762	59,131	3
Iran	5,858	6,278	6,807	6,800 [1]	5,843	8,012	10,732	11,500*	13
Italy	3,373	2,773	2,299	2,299	8,989	8,109	8,126	7,805	16
Kazakhstan [3]	—	14,070	12,750	12,620	—	16,197	11,585	9,052	15
Mexico	723	933	874	802	2,754	3,935	3,582	4,171	23
Morocco	1,673	2,719	2,310	3,050	1,500	3,614	1,573	5,523	19
Pakistan	6,865	7,845	8,300	8,030	10,760	14,316	16,157	15,213	10
Poland	1,525	2,281	2,477	2,407	4,189	9,000	8,243	7,658	17
Romania	2,154	2,209	2,282	2,411	5,371	7,290	5,314	5,991	18
Russia [3]	—	24,244	24,666	22,146*	—	49,596	43,500	32,094	4
Spain	2,628	2,005	2,025	1,994	4,510	4,759	4,989	4,311	22
Syria	1,383	1,341	1,385	1,553	1,878	2,070	3,626	3,703	25
Turkey	9,208	9,432	9,716	9,600	17,058	20,000	21,000	17,500	7
Ukraine [3]	—	7,558	5,748	4,507	—	30,374	21,831	13,857	11
UK	1,434	2,013	1,759	1,811	8,116	14,033	12,890	13,164	12
USA	28,898	28,038	24,998	24,998	66,229	74,473	65,210	63,141	2
World total	*234,891*	*231,721*	*222,497*	*215,921*	*437,543*	*592,918*	*564,065*	*527,982*	

* *Unofficial figures.* [1] FAO estimates. [2] Includes spelt. [3] Does not include spelt.

RYE

Countries	Area (1,000 ha) Average 1979-81	1990	1993	1994	Production (1,000 tonnes) Average 1979-81	1990	1993	1994	Ranking by production
Argentina	199	101	73	85 [1]	169	95	64	79	21
Austria	105	93	74	77	327	396	292	292*	10
Belarus	—	917	1,011	833*	—	2,652	2,901*	2,200*	4
Canada	362	341	161	186	636	599	319	394	8
China	733	600 [1]	500 [1]	500 [1]	1,167	900 [1]	700 [1]	570 [1]	6
Czech Republic	—	—	67	79	—	—	256	276	12
Denmark	59	109	79	88	221	545	356	423	7
Estonia	—	66	62	25*	—	178	123	56*	23
France	121	65	45	45	368	236	177	176	17
Germany	1,203	1,056	662	722	3,828	3,989	2,984	3,451	3
Greece	4	20	19	18*	7	36	42	42*	25
Hungary	72	92	68	90	117	232	113	193	16
Kazakhstan	—	772	528*	335*	—	843	835*	264	13
Latvia	—	131	188	56	—	324	341	112	19
Lithuania	—	168	231	203*	—	470	434	380*	9
Poland	2,970	2,314	2,213	2,436	6,166	6,100	4,992	5,300	2
Portugal	166	95	72	65	128	97	67	59	22
Romania	33	40 [1]	26	29	65	89	40	43	24
Russia	—	7,989	5,976	3,904*	—	16,431	9,166*	5,994*	1
Slovakia	—	—	23	31	—	—	69	96	20
Spain	219	207	170	155	239	274	300	220	14
Sweden	58	71	46	39	197	335	230	173	18
Turkey	439	158	147	130 [1]	558	240	235	195	15
Ukraine	—	517	499	477	—	1,260	1,180	942	5
USA	295	152	291	164	474	259	263	283	11
World total	*15,045*	*16,549*	*13,450*	*11,012*	*23,930*	*37,838*	*26,869*	*22,588*	

* Unofficial figures. [1] FAO estimates.

BARLEY

Countries	Area (1,000 ha) Average 1979-81	1990	1993	1994	Production (1,000 tonnes) Average 1979-81	1990	1993	1994	Ranking by production
Australia	2,539	2,556	3,638	3,400	3,278	4,108	6,995	6,670	9
Belarus	—	1,029	1,115	1,290*	—	2,908	3,165*	2,700*	16
Canada	4,631	4,529	4,159	4,092	11,199	13,441	12,972	11,690	3
China	1,295	1,150	1,400 [1]	1,400 [1]	3,133	3,000	3,500*	3,200*	14
Czech Republic	—	—	636	640	—	—	2,419	2,419	18
Denmark	1,580	901	709	700	6,250	4,987	3,369	3,446	13
Finland	579	486	458	506	1,421	1,720	1,679	1,858	19
France	2,670	1,756	1,623	1,404	10,997	10,020	8,981	7,637	6
Germany	2,971	2,613	2,201	2,069	12,158	13,992	11,006	10,902	4
Hungary	265	297	429	423	848	1,369	1,138	1,558	24
India	1,802	991	903	887	2,020	1,486	1,506	1,621	23
Iran	1,727	2,628	1,960	2,100 [1]	1,558	3,548	3,058	3,100 [1]	15
Kazakhstan	—	6,660	6,972	6,044*	—	8,500	7,149	5,497	11
Morocco	2,190	2,415	2,151	2,582	1,712	2,138	1,027	3,720	12
Poland	1,362	1,174	1,168	1,032	3,563	4,200	3,255	2,686	17
Romania	833	749	637	551	2,321	2,680	1,553	1,661	22
Russia	—	13,723	15,479	16,383*	—	27,235	26,843*	27,079*	1
Saudi Arabia	7	77	221	324*	8	361	1,420	1,800*	20
Spain	3,520	4,359	3,499	3,602	6,571	9,410	9,532	7,596	7
Sweden	678	468	420	473	2,323	2,123	1,671	1,661	21
Syria	1,220	2,729	2,169	1,894	1,129	846	1,553	1,482	25
Turkey	2,846	3,321	3,464	3,400	5,480	7,300	7,500	7,000	8
Ukraine	—	2,712	4,215	5,902	—	9,169	13,550	14,509	2
UK	2,333	1,516	1,164	1,106	10,058	7,911	6,038	5,862	10
USA	3,214	3,047	2,733	2,698	8,838	9,192	8,665	8,165	5
World total	*81,244*	*73,961*	*74,282*	*73,512*	*153,790*	*177,670*	*169,140*	*160,810*	

* Unofficial figures. [1] FAO estimates.

OATS

Countries	Area (1,000 ha) Average 1979-81	1990	1993	1994	Production (1,000 tonnes) Average 1979-81	1990	1993	1994	Ranking by production
Argentina	353	324	287	303	431	431	600	436	16
Australia	1,201	1,044	997	950	1,386	1,530	1,649	1,650	5
Austria	93	62	53	49	298	244	191	200*	25
Belarus	—	360	309	377*	—	806	871*	752*	11
Brazil	76	193	266	290	77	178	261	310	20
Canada	1,501	1,154	1,341	1,511	2,993	2,692	3,549	3,699	2
Chile	84	78	68	58	151	205	202	202	24
China	400	400 [1]	400 [1]	400 [1]	600	600 [1]	700 [1]	720 [1]	12
Czech Republic	—	—	70	76	—	—	263	208	22
Denmark [2]	40	24	31	40	166	102	138	206	23
Finland	444	453	331	334	1,183	1,463	1,202	1,150	8
France	525	218	174	166	1,850	848	726	685	13
Germany	855	473	359	392	3,347	2,105	1,731	1,663	4
Italy	223	157	144	145	433	298	372	369	19
Kazakhstan	—	382	549	645	—	610	802	822	10
Norway	108	129	105	99	424	601	380	388	18
Poland	1,082	747	642	618	2,387	2,100	1,493	1,243	7
Romania	57	144	364	334	57	234	554	494	15
Russia	—	9,032	8,402	8,329	—	12,326	11,556	10,748*	1
Spain	453	349	326	346	527	519	400	402	17
Sweden	461	368	322	341	1,635	1,584	1,295	991	9
Turkey	199	137	134	130 [1]	350	270	245	230	21
Ukraine	—	486	510	604	—	1,303	1,479	1,385	6
UK	142	107	92	109	587	530	479	606	14
USA	3,743	2,406	1,539	1,627	7,234	5,189	3,001	3,336	3
World total	*25,643*	*21,152*	*19,335*	*19,749*	*40,958*	*39,130*	*35,647*	*33,735*	

* Unofficial figures. [1] FAO estimates. [2] Including mixed grain.

MAIZE

Countries	Area (1,000 ha) Average 1979-81	1990	1993	1994	Production (1,000 tonnes) Average 1979-81	1990	1993	1994	Ranking by production
Argentina	2,895	1,672	2,503	2,421	9,333	5,047	10,901	10,246	8
Brazil	11,430	11,394	11,868	13,745	19,265	21,348	30,051	32,487	3
Canada	1,039	1,062	985	955	5,904	7,066	6,501	7,043	11
China	19,986	21,483	20,769	20,575*	60,720	97,158	102,700	103,550*	2
Egypt	800	830	829	731	3,159	4,799	5,039	4,833	14
France	1,773	1,561	1,848	1,666	9,627	9,291	14,843	13,040	5
Germany	122	229	331	345	753	1,552	2,656	2,446	19
Hungary	1,270	1,082	1,264	1,204	7,022	4,500	4,044	4,761	15
India	5,887	5,954	6,133	6,000*	6,486	9,073	9,653	10,500*	7
Indonesia	2,761	3,158	2,940	3,040	4,035	6,734	6,460	6,617	11
Italy	956	768	927	916	6,590	5,864	8,029	7,661	10
Kenya	1,273	1,449	1,308	1,450 [1]	1,714	2,290	1,748	2,970*	18
Mexico	6,836	7,341	7,536	7,853	11,866	14,640	18,648	18,499	4
Nigeria	443	1,500 [1]	1,600 [1]	1,600 [1]	599	1,832	2,300 [1]	2,000 [1]	24
North Korea	690	710 [1]	600 [1]	600 [1]	2,198	4,400 [1]	2,940	2,140*	23
Philippines	3,267	3,820	3,260	3,136*	3,174	4,854	4,798	5,400*	13
Romania	3,226	2,467	3,066	2,990	10,218	6,810	7,988	9,300	9
South Africa	4,298	3,475*	3,662	3,904	11,322	8,709	9,668	11,811	6
Spain	450	473	265	342	2,227	3,042	1,633	2,266	21
Tanzania	1,350	1,631	1,824	1,629*	1,762	2,445	2,282	2,159*	22
Thailand	1,412	1,545	1,218	1,200*	3,103	3,772	3,300	3,800*	17
Turkey	583	515	550	450*	1,263	2,100	2,500	1,850	25
USA	29,661	27,094	25,464	29,508	192,084	201,532	160,954	256,629	1
Yugoslavia	—	—	1,389	1,400*	—	—	4,002	4,724	16
Zimbabwe	1,097	1,150	1,401	1,305	1,829	1,994	2,562	2,300	20
World total	*125,636*	*127,422*	*126,869*	*131,528*	*420,408*	*479,140*	*470,354*	*569,557*	

* Unofficial figures. [1] FAO estimates.

RICE (Paddy)

Countries	Area (1,000 ha) Average 1979-81	1990	1993	1994	Production (1,000 tonnes) Average 1979-81	1990	1993	1994	Ranking by production
Bangladesh	10,310	10,435	10,056	9,850*	20,125	27,377	26,925	27,537	4
Brazil	5,932	3,947	4,421	4,446	8,533	7,421	10,108	10,499	9
Burma	4,684	4,760	5,487	6,477	12,637	13,969	16,760	19,057	6
Cambodia	1,154	1,400	1,824	1,700 [1]	1,248	2,155	2,383	1,800	22
China	34,323	33,519	30,746	30,373 [1]	145,629	191,589	177,700	178,251*	1
Colombia	428	521	386	408	1,831	2,117	1,590	1,679	23
Egypt	416	436	539	579	2,376	3,167	4,161	4,582	13
India	40,091	42,596	42,202	42,034	74,557	111,953	117,052	118,400	2
Indonesia	9,063	10,502	11,013	10,646	29,570	45,179	48,181	46,245	3
Iran	434	524	588	620	1,394	1,981	2,281	2,700*	17
Japan	2,384	2,074	2,139	2,212	13,320	10,499	7,834	11,918	8
North Korea	660	750	600 [1]	600 [1]	2,917	5,330	2,940 [1]	2,104 [1]	20
South Korea	1,230	1,244	1,135*	1,160 [1]	6,780	7,722	5,315	7,056*	12
Laos	722	638	539	639	1,025	1,491	1,251	1,653	24
Madagascar	1,182	1,165	1,209	1,180	2,055	2,420	2,400	2,360	19
Malaysia	722	678	668*	665*	2,053	2,026	2,031*	2,040*	21
Nepal	1,275	1,455	1,450 [1]	1,450	2,361	3,502	3,100*	3,496	16
Nigeria	517	1,289	1,676*	1,688*	1,027	2,500	3,400 [1]	3,857*	15
Pakistan	1,981	2,113	2,187	2,190	4,884	4,891	5,992	3,995	14
Peru	132	185	178	238	587	966	968	1,391	25
Philippines	3,513	3,319	3,282	3,350*	7,747	9,319	9,434	10,150*	10
Sri Lanka	819	828	820	825 [1]	2,093	2,538	2,570	2,582	18
Thailand	8,986	8,792	9,160	8,482	16,967	17,193	19,440	18,447	7
USA	1,345	1,142	1,147	1,336	6,968	6,968	7,081	8,972	11
Vietnam	5,579	6,028	6,500	6,500 [1]	11,808	19,225	23,500	24,500	5
World total	*143,703*	*146,688*	*146,867*	*146,542*	*393,949*	*521,140*	*527,103*	*534,701*	

* Unofficial figures. [1] FAO estimates.

MILLET

Countries	Area (1,000 ha) Average 1979-81	1990	1993	1994	Production (1,000 tonnes) Average 1979-81	1990	1993	1994	Ranking by production
Bangladesh	61	90	86	84	40	67	63	63	24
Burkina Faso	803	1,150	1,200 [1]	1,250 [1]	390	449	763	800 [1]	6
Burma	179	168	205	206	80	126	144	156	18
Chad	360	488	567	621	182	168	234	321	11
China	3,981	2,279	2,000 [1]	1,800 [1]	5,790	4,576	3,961 [1]	3,001 [1]	3
Côte d'Ivoire	64	80	85 [1]	85 [1]	37	47	80*	81	22
Ethiopia	226	280	235 [1]	215 [1]	203	273	272 [1]	233 [1]	13
Ghana	182	124	204	200 [1]	117	75	198	150 [1]	19
India	17,845	15,120	13,401	14,700*	9,189	10,470	8,644	10,330	1
Kazakhstan	—	781	527	363*	—	940	233	130	20
Mali	643	1,213	1,280	1,280	461	737	691	905	5
Nepal	122	199	200 [1]	225	121	232	232 [1]	246	12
Niger	3,011	3,100	4,675	4,900 [1]	1,311	1,113	1,430 [1]	1,725 [1]	4
Nigeria	2,366	4,350	3,700 [1]	3,500 [1]	2,496	5,136	3,800 [1]	3,600 [1]	2
Pakistan	509	491	303	488	255	196	126	210 [1]	15
Russia	—	1,936	1,464*	1,007*	—	1,946	1,128*	482*	10
Senegal	932	865	974	936	555	505	657	548	8
Sudan	1,098	662	1,069	2,924*	436	85	221	483*	9
Tanzania	450	178	325	340*	360	200	210	218*	14
Togo	121	143	150	140 [1]	44	58	75	75	23
Uganda	297	373	404	412	473	560	652	659	7
Ukraine	—	194	197	179	—	338	294	158	17
USA	89	155	150 [1]	150 [1]	107	180	180 [1]	180 [1]	16
Zambia	34	59	53	72	22	32	37	63	25
Zimbabwe	353	233	300	315	153	143	95	95	21
World total	*37,644*	*35,759*	*34,707*	*37,710*	*25,465*	*29,478*	*25,331*	*25,982*	

* Unofficial figures. [1] FAO estimates.

SORGHUM

Countries	Area (1,000 ha) Average 1979-81	1990	1993	1994	Production (1,000 tonnes) Average 1979-81	1990	1993	1994	Ranking by production
Argentina	1,866	689	717	641	5,641	2,016	2,839	2,160	7
Australia	548	380	427	495	1,084	946	548	933*	10
Brazil	81	138	125	151	172	236	251	290	23
Burkina Faso	1,051	1,250	1,300 [1]	1,350 [1]	620	751	1,228	1,200 [1]	8
Cameroon	374	513	500 [1]	510 [1]	301	350	390 [1]	400 [1]	19
Chad	414	439	523	576	210	280	306	379	21
China	2,828	1,571	1,425 [1]	1,326 [1]	7,034	5,777	5,612*	4,915*	3
Colombia	220	273	202	223	488	777	631	680	13
Egypt	172	134	146	154	644	630	779	717	12
Ethiopia [2]	1,048	750	840 [1]	790 [1]	1,419	787	1,079 [1]	1,109 [1]	9
France	75	67	83	48	332	264	507	266	24
Ghana	223	215	310	315 [1]	140	136	328	260 [1]	25
India	16,361	12,370	12,943	12,800*	11,380	11,878	11,803	12,500*	2
Mali	434	809	1,006	1,016	341	531	694	903	11
Mexico	1,491	1,818	1,157	1,298	4,991	5,978	4,085	3,169	6
Niger	822	1,000	2,237	2,300 [1]	347	286	305 [1]	420 [1]	18
Nigeria	2,683	4,000	4,000 [1]	4,000 [1]	3,284	4,185	4,800 [1]	4,000 [1]	4
South Africa	215	247	170	161	540	275	478	432	17
Sudan	3,054	2,759	4,684	6,234*	2,273	1,180	2,386	3,498*	5
Tanzania	713	380	642	664*	543	368	719	478*	14
Thailand	220	188	146	183 [1]	237	250	208	300*	22
Uganda	175	240	255	260	312	360	382	390	20
USA	5,273	3,678	3,608	3,629	19,157	14,562	13,569	16,638	1
Venezuela	227	176	154	209	365	376	367	446	15
Yemen	622	507	457	448	616	441	465	444	16
World total	*44,891*	*40,447*	*41,574*	*43,718*	*65,525*	*56,716*	*57,111*	*60,951*	

* Unofficial figures. [1] FAO estimates [2] Includes teff.

CRUDE OIL RESERVES AND PRODUCTION

Countries	Proven reserves (1m. bbls.) [1] 1993	1994	Production (1,000 bbls. per day) 1980	1990	1993	1994	1995 [1]	Rank in 1995
Algeria*	9,200	9,200	1,106	1,207	1,200	1,190	1,205	16
Argentina	1,570	1,570	491	485	583	658	726	19
Australia	1,768	1,615	382	577	497	501	630	21
Brazil	3,030	3,600	187	656	669	698	745	18
Canada	5,292	5,096	1,762	1,959	2,179	2,227	2,386	10
China	24,000	24,000	2,113	2,771	2,900	2,939	2,994	6
Ecuador	1,600	2,014	204	284	350	374	385	23
Gabon*	730	730	174	275	300	318	344	24
Indonesia*	5,779	5,779	1,576	1,398	1,466	2,506	1,476	14
Iran*	92,860	92,860	1,467	3,148	3,681	3,625	2,029	4
Iraq*	100,000	100,000	2,646	2,055	481	567	650	20
Kuwait* [2]	96,500	96,500	1,664	1,161	1,868	2,026	2,029	13
Libya*	22,800	22,800	1,830	1,372	1,411	1,415	1,476	15
Mexico	51,298	50,925	2,130	2,974	3,133	3,070	3,075	5
Nigeria*	17,900	17,900	2,058	1,838	2,067	2,068	2,059	12
Norway	8,806	9,284	527	1,697	2,374	2,701	2,902	7
Oman	4,483	4,700	283	660	775	812	864	17
Qatar*	3,729	3,729	471	396	449	447	474	22
Saudi Arabia* [2]	260,342	261,203	9,900	6,459	8,177	8,085	8,083	2
USSR/CIS	57,000	57,000	12,109	11,464	7,843	7,097	2,994	3
UAE*	98,100	98,100	1,709	2,122	2,252	2,245	2,246	11
UK	4,144	4,554	1,647	1,880	2,039	2,584	2,672	9
USA	24,682	23,745	10,170	8,915	8,647	8,455	8,371	1
Venezuela*	62,650	63,330	2,165	2,150	2,374	2,506	2,657	8
World total	*997,042*	*999,124*	*62,866*	*64,876*	*65,039*	*65,753*	*66,656*	

* Member of OPEC. [1] Estimates. [2] Includes share of Neutral Zone (all allocated to Saudi Arabia, Aug. 1990–Jan. 1991).

MARITIME LIMITS (IN MILES)

State	*Territorial Sea*	*Jurisdiction over fisheries (measured from the baseline of the territorial sea)*
Albania	12 (1976)	—
Algeria	12 (1963)	—
Angola	20 (1975)	200 (1975)
Antigua and Barbuda	12 (1982)	200 (1982) [1]
Argentina	12 (1991)	200 (1991) [1]
Australia	12 (1990)	200 (1979)
Bahamas	12 (1991)	200 (1977)
Bahrain	3	—
Bangladesh	12 (1974)	200 (1974) [1]
Barbados	12 (1977)	200 (1979) [1]
Belgium	12 (1987)	up to median line (1978)
Belize	12 (1992)	200 (1992) [1]
Benin	200 (1976)	—
Brazil	12 (1988)	200 (1988)
Brunei Darussalam	12 (1983)	200 (1983) (or median line)
Bulgaria	12 (1951)	200 (1987) [1]
Burma	12 (1988)	200 (1977) [1]
Cambodia	12(1969)	200 (1979) [1]
Cameroon	50 (1974)	—
Canada	12 (1970)	200 (1977)
Cape Verde	12 (1977)	200 (1977) [1]
Chile	12 (1986)	200 (1986) [1]
China	12 (1958)	200 (1992) [1]
Colombia	12 (1978)	200 (1978) [1]
Comoros	12 (1976)	200 (1982) [1]
Congo	200 (1977)	—
Costa Rica	12 (1982)	200 (1975) [1]
Côte d'Ivoire	12 (1977)	200 (1977) [1]
Cuba	12 (1977)	200 (1977) [1]
Cyprus	12 (1964)	—
Denmark (including Faroe Islands and Greenland)	3 (1966)	200 (1977)
Djibouti	12 (1979)	200 (1979) [1]
Dominica	12 (1981)	200 (1981) [1]
Dominican Republic	6 (1967)	200 (1977) [1]
Ecuador	200 (1966)	—
Egypt	12 (1958)	200 (1983) [1]
El Salvador	200 (1983)	—
Equatorial Guinea	12 (1984)	200 (1984) [1]
Ethiopia	12 (1953)	—
Fiji	12 (1977)	200 (1981) [1]
Finland	4 (1956)	12 (1975) (or agreed boundary)
France	12 (1971)	200 (1977) [1] (except Mediterranean)
Gabon	12 (1986)	200 (1986) [1]
Gambia	12 (1969)	200 (1978)
Germany	3 [2]	200 (1977)
Ghana	12 (1986)	200 (1986) [1]
Greece	6 (1936)	200 (1986) [1]
Grenada	12 (1978) [3]	200 (1978) [1]
Guatemala	12 (1976)	200 (1976) [1]
Guinea	12 (1980)	200 (1980) [1]
Guinea-Bissau	12 (1978)	200 (1978) [1]

[1] Exclusive Economic Zone. [2] In the Baltic Sea; off the former GDR, 12 miles; in the German Bight, at least 12 miles; area defined by coordinates. [3] 10 miles for aviation purposes.

MARITIME LIMITS (IN MILES)—*contd.*

State	*Territorial Sea*	*Jurisdiction over fisheries (measured from the baseline of the territorial sea)*
Guyana	12 (1977)	200 (1977)
Haiti	12 (1972)	200 (1977) [1]
Honduras	12 (1965)	200 (1951) [1]
Iceland	12 (1979)	200 (1979) [1]
India	12 (1967)	200 (1977) [1]
Indonesia	12 (1957) [2]	200 (1980) [1,7]
Iran	12 (1959)	[8]
Iraq	12 (1958)	—
Ireland	12 (1988)	200 (1977)
Israel	12 (1990)	—
Italy	12 (1974)	—
Jamaica	12 (1971)	—
Japan	12 (1977)	200 (1977)
Jordan	3 (1943)	—
Kenya	12 (1971)	200 (1979) [1]
Kiribati	12 (1983)	200 (1983) [1]
Korea (North)	12 (1967)	200 (1977) [1]
Korea (South)	12 (1978)	12
Kuwait	12 (1967)	—
Lebanon	12 (1983)	—
Liberia	200 (1976)	—
Libya	12 (1959)	—
Madagascar	12 (1985)	200 (1985) [1]
Malaysia	12 (1969)	200 (1984) [1]
Maldive, Republic of	12 (1975)	(1976) [1,3]
Malta	12 (1978)	25 (1978)
Mauritania	12 (1988)	200 (1988) [1]
Mauritius	12 (1977)	200 (1977) [1]
Mexico	12 (1972)	200 (1976) [1]
Monaco	12 (1973)	(1985) [9]
Morocco	12 (1973) [4]	200 (1981) [1,4]
Mozambique	12 (1976)	200 (1976) [1]
Namibia	12 (1990)	200 (1990)
Nauru	12 (1971)	200 (1978)
Netherlands	12 (1985)	200 (1977)
New Zealand	12 (1977)	200 (1978) [1]
Nicaragua	(1979) [5]	200 (1979) [5]
Nigeria	30 (1971)	200 (1978) [1]
Norway	4 (1812)	200 (1977) [1]
Oman	12 (1977)	200 (1981) [1]
Pakistan	12 (1976)	200 (1976) [1]
Panama	200 (1967)	—
Papua New Guinea	12 (1977)	200 (1978) (offshore waters)
Peru	(1947) [5]	200 (1947) [5]
Philippines	[6]	200 (1978) [1]

[1] Exclusive Economic Zone.
[2] The territorial sea of Indonesia is measured by straight lines surrounding the archipelago.
[3] Territorial limits and economic zone defined by geographical co-ordinates.
[4] Limits with opposite or adjacent states to be fixed by agreement, failing which median line principle to apply.
[5] Sovereignty and jurisdiction over the sea, its soil and subsoil up to 200 miles.
[6] The territorial sea of the Philippines is determined by straight base-lines joining appropriate points of the outermost islands forming the Philippine archipelago in accordance with Treaties of 1898, 1900 and 1930 (1961).
[7] 200 mile exclusive fisheries zone established 1985.
[8] Outer limits of the superjacent waters of the continental shelf. 50-mile fishing zone in the Sea of Oman (1973).
[9] Half way to Corsica.

MARITIME LIMITS (IN MILES)—*contd.*

State	*Territorial Sea*	*Jurisdiction over fisheries (measured from the baseline of the territorial sea)*
Poland	12 (1978)	to be determined by international agreement (1978)
Portugal	12 (1977)	200 (1977) [2]
Qatar	12	[1]
Romania	12 (1956)	200 (1986) [2]
Russia [9]	12 (1982)	200 (1982) [2]
St Kitts and Nevis	12 (1984)	200 (1984) [2]
St Lucia	12 (1984)	200 (1984) [2]
St Vincent and the Grenadines	12 (1983)	200 (1983) [2]
São Tomé and Principe	12 (1978)	200 (1978) [2]
Saudi Arabia	12 (1958)	[6]
Senegal	12 (1985)	200 (1985) [2]
Seychelles	12 (1977)	200 (1977) [2]
Sierra Leone	200 (1971)	—
Singapore	3 (1878)	—
Solomon Islands	12 (1978)	200 (1986)
Somalia	200 (1972)	—
South Africa	12 (1977)	200 (1977)
Spain	12 (1977)	200 (1978) [2] (except Mediterranean)
Sri Lanka	12 (1977)	200 (1977) [2]
Sudan	12 (1987)	—
Suriname	12 (1978)	200 (1978) [2]
Sweden	12 (1980)	up to equidistance line with neighbouring states
Syria	35 (1981)	—
Tanzania	12 (1989)	200 (1989) [1]
Thailand	12 (1966)	200 (1980) [2]
Togo	30 (1977)	200 (1977) [2]
Tonga	12 (1978) [3]	200 (1978)
Trinidad and Tobago	12 (1969)	200 (1986) [2]
Tunisia	12 (1973)	—
Turkey	[7]	200 (1986) [1]
Tuvalu	12 (1984)	200 (1984) [2]
Ukraine [9]	12 (1982)	200 (1984) [2]
United Arab Emirates	3 [4]	[5]
UK	12 (1987)	200 (1977)
USA	12 (1988)	200 (1983) [2]
Uruguay	200 (1969)	—
Vanuatu	12 (1978–82)	200 (1978–82) [2]
Venezuela	12 (1956)	200 (1978) [2]
Vietnam	12 (1977)	200 (1977) [2]
Western Samoa	12 (1971)	200 (1980) [2]
Yemen [8]	—	—
Yugoslavia	12 (1979)	—
Zaïre	12 (1974)	200 (1992)

[1] Limited by agreement by the outer limits of the superjacent waters of the continental shelf or by a median line (1974).
[2] Exclusive Economic Zone.
[3] 1978 legislation not yet in force.
[4] Sharjah, 12 miles.
[5] Limits to be defined by agreement, failing which median line to apply (1980).
[6] Outer limits of the superjacent waters of the continental shelf.
[7] 6 Aegean (1964), 12 Black Sea and Mediterranean.
[8] Situation under review following unification.
[9] Limits as determined for the former USSR.

The table above is reproduced from a survey prepared by the FAO.

Further Reading

Attard, D. J., *The Exclusive Economic Zone in International Law.* Oxford, 1987
Booth, K., *Law, Force and Diplomacy at Sea.* London, 1985
Buzan, B., *Seabed Politics.* New York, 1976
Churchill, R. R. and Lowe, A. V., *The Law of the Sea.* Manchester, 1988
Janis, M. W., *Sea Power and the Law of the Sea.* Lexington, 1977
Luard, E., *The Control of the Sea-Bed.* London, 1974
Moore, G., *Coastal State Requirements for Foreign Fishing. FAO Legislative Study No. 21.* 3rd revision, Rome, 1988
Sangar, C., *Ordering the Oceans: The Making of the Law of the Sea.* Univ. of Toronto Press, 1987
UN. *Law of the Sea: a Select Bibliography.* 1991

CHRONOLOGY

1995

April

3 *Burundi* Massacre of more than 400 reported in Gasorwe region of north-east Burundi.
Sudan Newly formed Southern Sudan Independence Movement joins ceasefire.

4 *EU* European Monetary Institute publishes first annual report.
Ukraine Government of Prime Minister Ievheni Marchuk dismissed after no-confidence vote.

5 *Ethiopia* Economic agreement signed with Eritrea.

7 *UN* Berlin conference on climate change adopts Berlin Mandate to combat global warming.

8 *Chad* Koibla Djimasta elected Prime Minister by Higher Transitional Council.
South Africa Inkatha Freedom Party implements threat to boycott Constitutional Assembly.

8–9 *Zimbabwe* Ruling Zimbabwe African National Union-Patriotic Front (ZANU-PF) wins fourth successive election victory.

9 *Liechtenstein* Referendum approves participation in European Economic Area.
Peru President Fujimori re-elected for second term in presidential elections.

10 *China* Death of veteran leader Chen Yun.

12 *Central African Republic* Gabriel Koyambounou appointed Prime Minister after resignation of Jean-Luc Mandaba.
Mozambique Formation of Mozambique Communist Party (Pacomo).

13 *Finland* 5-party coalition government under Paavo Lipponen, leader of Finnish Social Democrat Party, sworn in.

14 *USA* President Bill Clinton confirms candidature in 1996 presidential election.

16 *Canada* Fishing dispute with EU settled.

17 *Estonia* Coalition government of Centre Party and centre-left Coalition Party and Rural Union Party sworn in.

18 *Bolivia* Government declares 90-day state of siege in face of civil unrest.

19 *Sri Lanka* Truce between government and Tamil separatist forces collapses.
USA Over 150 killed by bomb in Oklahoma City.

22 *Cyprus* Rauf Denktaş re-elected President of self-proclaimed Turkish Republic of Northern Cyprus.
Iceland New centre-right coalition government formed under Prime Minister David Oddsson.
Rwanda UN estimates more than 2,000 killed in Ribeho refugee camp.

23 *France* Lionel Jospin, socialist candidate, wins most votes in first round of presidential elections.
Italy Centre-left parties win 40·5% of total vote in regional elections.

24 *Malaŵi* Formal opening of trial of former President Hastings Banda on murder charges.

CHRONOLOGY—*contd.*

1995		
April	24–25	*Malaysia* Ruling 14-party coalition wins landslide victory in general election.
	25	*Niger* Agreement ending 4-year conflict signed by government and Tuareg rebels.
		Nigeria National Constitutional Council adopts draft constitution with rotating presidency but postpones return to civilian rule.
	27	*Sierra Leone* Head of state Captain Valentine Strasser lifts ban on political parties.
	29	*Kazakhstan* President Nursultan Nazarbaev wins referendum extending his presidency to year 2000.
	30	*Bosnia-Hercegovina* Ceasefire agreed in Dec. 1994 expires.
		Iran US announces total ban on all trade and investment in Iran.
May	1	*Russia* Heavy fighting in Chechen capital of Grozny.
	1–2	*Croatia* Croatian forces retake part of land held by Serbs since 1991.
	2	*Cuba* Agreement signed with USA regulating immigration policies.
	4	*Turkey* Turkish troops leave northern Iraq after offensive against Kurdistan Workers' Party
		UK Major losses for ruling Conservative Party in local authority elections.
	5	*Burma* Thai forces launch cross-border attack on guerrilla camp.
		Ethiopia First multi-party legislative elections.
		Slovakia Constitutional crisis after Slovak National Council's no-confidence vote in President Mihal Kováč.
	7	*France* Jacques Chirac wins presidential election.
		Kenya New political party formed by, among others, conservationist Richard Leakey.
	8	*Philippines* President Fidel Ramos claims fresh mandate after congressional elections.
	10–24	*Northern Ireland* First ministerial-level talks for 23 years between UK government and leaders of Sinn Féin.
	11	*Nigeria* Moshood Abiola, self-declared winner of aborted 1993 presidential elections, rejects bail terms of military government.
		UK Report of Nolan committee on standards in public life recommends 'radical overhaul'.
	12	*Nuclear Non-Proliferation Treaty (1968)* Review and extension conference agrees to extend treaty indefinitely.
	14	*Argentina* President Carlos Menem re-elected in presidential and congressional elections.
		Belarus Referendum gives overwhelming support to closer cultural and economic links with Russia.
	15	*Burundi* Temporary suspension of humanitarian relief in face of escalating violence.
	16	*Bosnia-Hercegovina* Escalation of fighting in Sarajevo area.
		Poland Złoty floated on international currency markets as part of move to free-market economy.

CHRONOLOGY—*contd.*

1995

May 17 *Iran* Rial devalued and strict foreign currency exchange controls introduced.

North and South Korea First independent joint ventures agreed since division of Korean peninsula in 1953.

18 *France* New Prime Minister Alain Juppé announces cabinet.

19 *Thailand* Collapse of 4-party coalition government.

20 *Eritrea* New regional administrative structure approved by National Assembly.

21 *Belgium* General and regional elections largely confirm position of ruling Christian-Socialist coalition.

22 *New Zealand* Government of Prime Minister Jim Bolger and largest Maori tribal federation sign compensation agreement for seizure of land in nineteenth century.

Sri Lanka President Chandrika Kumaratunga confirms collapse of peace talks with Tamil separatists.

24 *Brazil* Military seize 4 state oil refineries in 4-week strike by oil workers.

25 *Bosnia-Hercegovina* NATO air strike against Serb ammunition dump near Pale.

Lebanon Prime Minister Rafik Hariri reappointed after resignation and names new Cabinet.

27 *Japan* Extraordinary national convention of Social Democratic Party of Japan votes to dissolve party and form a new one.

29 *Jordan* Opposition conference banned.

June 1 *Greece* Parliament ratifies UN Convention on Law of the Sea.

4 *Turkey* Ruling True Path Party clear winner in local elections.

6 *Japan* Compromise agreement within ruling coalition government on wording of Diet resolution to mark 50th anniversary of end of Pacific War.

8 *Canada* New Democratic Party loses power to Progressive Conservative Party in Ontario.

Ghana Controversial value-added tax, imposed in April, suspended.

9 *Ukraine* Dispute with Russia over former Black Sea fleet settled.

11 *Guinea* First multi-party elections give absolute majority to Party of Unity and Progress led by President Lansana Conté.

12 *North Korea* Agreement reached with USA on implementation of Oct. 1994 nuclear accord.

13 *Nepal* King Birendra's dissolution of Parliament pending Nov. elections provokes opposition protest.

14 *Bosnia-Hercegovina* Major Bosnian government offensive against Bosnian Serb forces besieging Sarajevo.

Russia Chechen rebels attack Budennovsk in Russian Federation territory.

15 *Somalia* Gen. Muhammad Farah Aidid, recently ousted as leader of Somali National Alliance, proclaims himself president.

Uruguay General strike called to oppose government plan to reduce cost of state pensions.

CHRONOLOGY—*contd.*

1995		
June	15–17	*G7* Annual economic summit agrees to co-ordinate fresh action against global unemployment.
	17	*Angola* Constitution revised to permit 2 vice-presidents; Jonas Savimbi, leader of UNITA, appointed one.
	18	*Bosnia-Hercegovina* UN forces effectively withdraw from Bosnian Serb territory after release of hostages by Bosnian Serb forces.
		Burundi Security measures, including nationwide curfew, media censorship and ban on demonstrations, imposed in response to escalating violence.
	19	*Hungary* President Árpád Göncz elected for second 5-year term.
	19–20	*Mercosur* Presidential summit of the Latin American common market countries dominated by dispute between Brazil and Argentina over import quotas.
	20	*Australia* Finance Minister Kim Beazley elected Deputy Prime Minister.
		Grenada New National Party defeats ruling National Democratic Congress in general election.
		Uganda Constitutional Assembly votes to retain current system of non-party government.
	22	*Nicaragua* Accord on constitutional reform agreed by President Violeta Barrios de Chamorro and National Assembly.
		UK Prime Minister John Major resigns as leader of ruling Conservative Party in order to precipitate party leadership contest.
	23	*Belgium* Jean-Luc Dehaene reappointed Prime Minister after May 21 general election.
	25	*Burundi* Resignation announced of Finance Minister Jean-Marie Ngendahayo.
	26	*Egypt* Attempted assassination of President Hosni Mubarak in Ethiopian capital of Addis Ababa.
		UN 50th anniversary celebrations in New York marred by prospect of major financial crisis and calls for reform.
	26–27	*EU* Summit of heads of state and government agrees to implement monetary union by Jan. 1, 1999.
	26–28	*OAU* 31st annual summit of heads of state and government.
	27	*Nigeria* Government lifts ban on political activity imposed in Nov. 1993.
		Qatar Crown Prince Shaikh Hamad bin Khalifa Al-Thani takes over as Amir from his father in bloodless coup.
		South Korea Ruling Democratic Liberal Party heavily defeated in local elections.
	29	*New Zealand* New United New Zealand Party formed.
		Spain Several senior ministers resign in phone-tapping scandal.
July	1	*EU* Schengen Convention for abolition of frontier controls implemented by 7 signatories.
	2	*Thailand* New coalition government formed after general election, led by Chart Thai party.

CHRONOLOGY—*contd.*

1995

July 4 *India* Abduction of 5 foreign nationals by separatist group in Kashmir.

Nicaragua Official publication of amendments to constitution ends conflict between executive and legislature.

UK Prime Minister John Major wins first-round victory in Conservative Party leadership contest and reshuffles Cabinet.

4–7 *CARICOM* 16th annual summit.

5 *Iraq* Government acknowledges to UN existence of biological weapons programme.

6 *Venezuela* Civil liberties suspended in June 1994 restored.

8 *Argentina* President Carlos Menem sworn in for second 4-year term.

9 *Sri Lanka* Massive government offensive against Tamil separatists.

10 *Burma* Release of opposition leader Aung San Suu Kyi from house arrest.

11 *Algeria* Failure of talks between government and banned opposition Islamic Salvation Front (FIS).

Bosnia-Hercegovina Bosnian-Serb forces capture Srebrenica, UN-designated 'safe area' and Moslem enclave.

Vietnam US announces establishment of full diplomatic relations.

12 *Chad* Prime Minister Koibla Djimasta proclaims nationwide ceasefire.

13 *Italy* Government of Prime Minister Lamberto Dini wins vote of confidence on pension reform.

16 *Malaŵi* President Bakili Muluzi names his Cabinet.

23 *Japan* Government of Tomiichi Murayama suffers major losses in upper house elections.

Turkey Grand National Assembly approves 16 constitutional amendments extending democratic rights.

25 *Ecuador/Peru* Agreement for demilitarization of disputed border area.

France Bomb on Paris Metro kills seven.

26 *Armenia* New Cabinet announced by Prime Minister Grant Bagratyan after first parliamentary elections since independence.

EU Europol Convention signed on drug trafficking and illegal immigration.

29–30 *ECOWAS* 18th annual summit of heads of state and government.

30 *Zambia* Breakaway Zambia Democratic Congress formed as leadership challenge to President Frederick Chiluba.

31 *France* National Assembly approves major constitutional amendments.

Spain Supreme Court rules for a review of evidence involving Prime Minister Felipe González Márquez in 'dirty war' against Basque ETA separatists.

Aug. 2 *Saudi Arabia* King Fahd announces new Cabinet, most significant government reorganization since 1975.

CHRONOLOGY—*contd.*

1995

Aug. 3 *Afghanistan* Russian cargo aircraft hijacked by Taliban fighters.

4 *Italy* Chamber of Deputies gives final approval to pension reform plan.

5 *Ecuador/Peru* Agreement on resumption of trade.
Sri Lanka President Chandrika Kumaratunga announces devolution plans intended to end civil war with Tamil separatists.

9 *Bosnia-Hercegovina* US peace initiative based on territorial division proposed.
Croatia Croatian government forces recapture region of Krajina from Bosnian Serbs.
Iraq Defection of Lieut.-Gen Hussein Kamel Al Majid, Minister of Minerals and son-in-law of President Saddam Hussein.

11 *Middle East* Taba Declaration, interim agreement reached in Israeli-Palestinian negotiations.

13 *India* One of 5 Western hostages in Kashmir found dead..

15 *São Tomé and Príncipe* Bloodless military coup topples President Miguel Trovoada and Prime Minister Carlos de Graça.

16 *Colombia* President Ernesto Samper declares 90-day state of emergency.

17 *Bermuda* Referendum decisively rejects independence from UK; resignation of Prime Minister Sir John Swan, replaced by David Saul.
France Bomb explosion near Arc de Triomphe injures 17.
Rwanda UN arms embargo lifted.

18 *Madagascar* Compromise agreement including new Cabinet ends period of tension between President Albert Zafy and Prime Minister Francisque Ravony.

19 *Liberia* Peace agreement signed between 6 main factions in civil war.
Mexico Resignation of president of ruling Institutional Revolutionary Party after poor showing in gubernatorial elections.

20 *Zaïre* Government begins expelling refugees from Rwanda and Burundi.

22 *Ethiopia* New constitution formally instituted with proclamation of Federal Democratic Republic of Ethiopia and election of Negaso Gidada as President.
Haiti Repeat first round of voting in legislative and municipal elections endorses populist Lavalas movement.
Togo Main opposition Action Committee for Renewal ends nine-month boycott of National Assembly.

24 *China* Expulsion of US citizen and human rights activist Harry Wu Hongda.

25 *France* Resignation of Alain Madelin as Minister of Economy and Finance.

28 *Bosnia-Hercegovina* Bosnian Serb shell kills 37 in Sarajevo market place.
Nepal Supreme Court orders reinstatement of Parliament, unconstitutionally dismissed in June.

CHRONOLOGY—*contd.*

1995

Aug. 28 *Northern Ireland* Resignation of James Molyneaux as leader of Ulster Unionist Party.
Rwanda Prime Minister Faustin Twagiramungu dismissed by President Pasteur Bizimungu.
SADC Annual meeting of heads of state and government is first to be hosted by South Africa.

29 *Georgia* Assassination attempt made on head of state Eduard Shevardnadze.
Kazakhstan New constitution approved by 89% of voters in referendum.

31 *Rwanda* New Cabinet appointed with Pierre-Céléstin Rwigyema as Prime Minister.
Slovakia Kidnapping of President Mihal Kováč's son.

Sept. 1 *Liberia* 6-member Council of State formally inaugurated; announces transitional government on Sept. 3.

4 *UN* Opening of Fourth UN World Conference on Women in Beijing.

5 *French Pacific* French nuclear bomb test provokes fierce protest.

6 *Pakistan* Controversial dismissal of Punjab Chief Minister Mian Manzoor Ahmed Wattoo.

8 *Bosnia-Hercegovina* Geneva meeting between main protagonists and 5-member Contact Group signs agreement covering basic principles of a peace accord.

11 *Bosnia-Hercegovina* Bosnian government troops launch offensive against Serb-held areas of Bosnia.
Mexico Government and Zapatista National Liberation Army sign accord.

12 *Sri Lanka* Renewed government offensive against Tamil separatists.

13 *Macedonia* Interim accord with Greece on mutual relations.

13, 16 *India* Cabinet reshuffled by Prime Minister Narasimha Rao.

17 *Haiti* Lavalas coalition supporting President Jean-Bertrand Aristide gains most seats in second round of elections.
Hong Kong Elections to Legco endorse pro-democracy parties.
Madagascar Referendum approves presidential power to appoint or dismiss prime minister.

21 *Japan* Social Democratic Party decides to disband and re-form as a new party.

22 *Uganda* New constitution enacted.

22/23 *EU* Informal meeting of heads of state and government dominated by discussions on issue and timing of European Monetary Union (EMU).

26 *Yugoslavia* Foreign ministers of Bosnia, Croatia and Yugolsavia, meeting in New York, agree further basic principles for peace accord.

27 *Afghanistan* President Burhanuddin Rabbani offers unconditional peace talks to Taliban fighters threatening to attack Kabul.

CHRONOLOGY—*contd.*

1995

Sept. 27–30 *North and South Korea* Third round of bilateral talks end in stalemate.

28 *Middle East* Israel and Palestine Liberation Organization sign interim agreement providing for expansion of Palestinian self-rule on West Bank.

Oct. 1 *Latvia* General election produces fragmented parliament.

Nigeria Announcement of 3-year extension of military rule.

Portugal Socialist Party gains most seats in general election, but no overall majority.

3 *French Pacific* South Pacific Forum suspends links with France in protest at further nuclear bomb tests.

Macedonia President Kiro Gligorov seriously injured in assassination attempt.

5 *Bosnia-Hercegovina* 60-day ceasefire announced.

Comoros Collapse of attempted military coup.

Latvia Coalition government formed led by right-wing Zigerists' Party.

9 *Japan* Resignation of Justice Minister Tomoharu Tazawa.

11 *Ecuador* Vice-President Alberto Dahik Garzoni resigns and flees to Costa Rica.

Estonia Collapse of centre-left coalition and resignation of Prime Minister Tiit Vahi.

12 *Austria* Collapse of ruling coalition government over budget negotiations.

Burundi Major Cabinet reshuffle after earlier split in ruling coalition,

Portugal Socialist Party forms minority government under António Guterres, ending 10 years rule by Social Democratic Party.

13 *EU* Latvia formally applies for membership.

Madagascar Resignation of Prime Minister Francisque Ravony.

Philippines Peace agreement signed with military dissidents.

14 *Pakistan* Attempted pro-Islamic military coup confirmed.

15 *Iraq* Referendum approves further 7-year term of office for President Saddam Hussein.

16 *Bolivia* Lifting of state of siege imposed in April.

Haiti Official announcement of the resignation of Prime Minister Smarck Michel.

16–19 *Bangladesh* General strike paralyses country in opposition attempt to force early general election.

18 *Colombia* Constitutional Court declares unconstitutional the presidential state of emergency decree issued in August.

19 *Romania* Nationalist Greater Romania Party leaves coalition government.

20 *NATO* Resignation of Secretary-General Willy Claes, to stand trial on corruption charges in Belgium.

21 *Japan* Major protest march in Okinawa against US military presence.

CHRONOLOGY—*contd.*

1995

Oct. 22 *Netherlands* Coalition government agrees major constitutional reforms.

UN More than 150 world leaders celebrate 50th anniversary in New York and agree to reform UN institutions.

Tanzania Disputed outcome to presidential and legislative elections.

23 *Argentina* First meeting of President Carlos Menem and UK Prime Minister John Major since the end of the Falklands war in 1982.

24 *China* Resumption of dialogue with USA.

25 *Spain* Proposed 1996 budget rejected by lower house of Cortes.

26 *Estonia* Tiit Vahi forms new coalition government.

Italy Failure of right-wing parties to gain no-confidence vote against government of Lamberto Dini.

Sri Lanka Whole country placed on war footing in escalation of offensive against Tamil separatists.

27 *Peru* Debt agreement announced with 250 creditor banks.

29 *Croatia* Ruling Croatian Democratic Union wins most votes in legislative elections.

30 *Canada* Quebec narrowly votes to remain within Canadian federation in referendum.

31 *Turkey* Caretaker government appointed under Tansu Çiller of the centre-right True Path Party.

Nov. 1 *Yugoslavia* Peace talks open in Dayton, Ohio.

Nigeria Death sentence on oppositionist writer Ken Saro-Wiwa.

3 *Russia* President Yeltsin relinquishes control of 4 key ministries after second heart attack.

4 *Israel* Assassination of Prime Minister Yitzhak Rabin.

5 *Poland* President Lech Wałesa emerges as favourite in first round of presidential election.

6 *UK* Parliamentary defeat of Prime Minister John Major on disclosure of MP's outside earnings..

9 *Sudan* Rebels of Sudan People's Liberation Army advance on southern capital of Juba.

10 *NATO* Former Dutch Prime Minister Ruud Lubbers forced to withdraw candidacy for post of Secretary-General after failing to secure US backing.

Nigeria World protest at hanging of Ken Saro-Wiwa.

Sweden Resignation of Deputy Prime Minister Mona Sahlin.

UN Children's agency UNICEF suspends aid to educational programmes in Islamic militant controlled areas of Afghanistan.

11 *Nigeria* Commonwealth summit suspends Nigeria from Commonwealth membership.

12 *Croatia* Serbs agree to restoration of Eastern Slavonia to Croatia.

EU Study group charged with setting agenda for reform of EU aims and adminstration produces inconclusive report.

Guatemala Victory for Alvaro Arzú of the National Advancement Party (PAN) in first round of presidential elections.

CHRONOLOGY—*contd.*

1995

Nov. 13 *Commonwealth* New Zealand summit adopts Millbrook Programme, establishing democratic norms for member states.
Saudi Arabia Bomb explodes outside US-run training centre for Saudi National Guard.

14 *USA* Government workers sent home after President Bill Clinton and Congress fail to agree 1995–96 budget.

15 *France* Prime Minister Alain Juppé announces reforms to health and social security system to cut government welfare expenditure.

17 *Algeria* Victory for President Liamine Zeroual in first parliamentary election since cancelled election of 1991.

19 *APEC* Third summit of Asia-Pacific Economic Co-operation forum reaffirms commitment to trade liberalization.
Poland President Lech Wałęsa defeated by former communist Aleksander Kwasniewski in presidential election.

20 *EU* Rejection of proposed oil embargo on Nigeria.
Spain Conservative People's Party makes substantial gains in Catalan parliamentary election.
Sri Lanka Government troops enter rebel-held city of Jaffna.

21 *Yugoslavia* Bosnia, Croatia and Serbia agree to a US-brokered peace plan ending 4 years of war.

22 *Israel* Shimon Peres sworn in as Prime Minister.
South Africa First draft of new constitution released.

24 *France* Strikes in protest at social security reform cripple country.

25 *Lebanon* Parliament extends term of President Elias Hrawi by three years.

27 *Côte d'Ivoire* Ruling Democratic Party wins absolute majority in second multi-party general election.
Middle East Israel and Syria make first move toward dialogue at conference in Barcelona of EU and Mediterranean countries.

28 *Egypt* President Mubarak's National Democratic Party wins substantial majority in parliamentary elections amid claims of ballot-rigging.
Slovakia President Mihal Kováč signs controversial law making Slovak the sole state language.

Dec. 1 *Iraq* Dissidents promised support against President Saddam Hussein by King Hussein of Jordan.
NATO Spanish Foreign Minister Javier Solana named Secretary-General.

2 *Taiwan* Ruling Nationalist Party wins but loses ground in parliamentary elections.

4 *Estonia* Application for EU membership presented.
Sweden Finance Minister Göran Persson nominated as Social Democratic party leader.
UN USA announces intention to leave UN Industrial Development Organization.

5 *South Korea* Former President Roh Tae Woo formally indicted on corruption charges.

CHRONOLOGY—*contd.*

1995
Dec. 7 *China* Chinese authorities enthrone their own candidate as Tibetan Panchen Lama, rejecting choice of exiled Dalai Lama.

11 *Israel* Israeli troops leave West Bank city of Nablus after 28 years of occupation.

12 *Bosnia-Hercegovina* Release of 2 French pilots held captive by Bosnian Serbs.

13 *Turkey* European Parliament assents to customs union.

14 *Yugoslavia* Formal signing of peace deal in Paris.
Germany Resignation of Justice Minister Sabine Leutheusser-Schnarrenberger.

15 *Burundi* Red Cross suspends relief operations after wave of attacks on agency offices.
EU Madrid summit of heads of state and government confirms a timetable for single European currency, to be named the 'euro'.
Nigeria Shell consortium signs major contract to build natural gas plant despite protests at death of minority-rights activists.
Turkey Rebel Kurdistan Workers' Party declares unilateral ceasefire and seeks peace talks.

16 *Israel/Syria* Israel and Syria agree to resume intensive peace talks.

17 *Austria* Chancellor Franz Vranitzky's Social Democrat party retains power in general election.
Russia Communist Party makes significant gains in parliamentary elections.

18 *Haiti* René Préval of outgoing President Jean-Bertrand Aristide's Lavalas Party wins presidential election.
Spain Prime Minister Felipe González agrees to lead Socialist Party in early March election.
Yemen Eritrea seizes Red Sea island of Greater Hanish from Yemen.

27 *Bosnia-Hercegovina* Withdrawal of Serb frontline forces around Sarajevo completes first peace deadline.

29 *UK* Defection to Liberal Democrats of Conservative MP Emma Nicholson reduces Conservative parliamentary majority to five.

30 *Italy* Government of caretaker Prime Minister Lamberto Dini resigns.

1996
Jan. 1 *Saudi Arabia* Crown Prince Abdullah takes over day-to-day government from ailing King Fahd.

2 *Austria* Resignation of Finance Minister Andreas Staribacher after nine months in office.
Egypt Resignation of Prime Minister Atef Sedki, succeeded by deputy Kamal El Ganzouri.

3 *Bosnia-Hercegovina* Serb officials detain 16 Bosnian citizens despite ceasefire.

5 *Japan* Resignation of Prime Minister Tomiichi Murayama, leader of left-wing coalition.
Lithuania Resignation of Defence Minister Linas Linkevičius and Foreign Minister Povilas Gylys.
Russia Resignation of liberal Foreign Minister Andrei Kozyrev.

CHRONOLOGY—*contd.*

1996

Jan. 7 *India* April general election announced.
USA Compromise budget proposals end longest-ever government shutdown.

8 *France* Death of former President François Mitterand.

9 *Russia* Chechen insurgents seize 3,000 civilian hostages in Russian town of Kizlyar.

11 *Japan* Ryutaro Hashimoto, leader of Liberal Democratic Party, elected Prime Minister by ruling coalition.

12 *Italy* Resignation of Prime Minister Lamberto Dini.
South Korea Former President Chun Doo Hwan charged with accepting bribes.

14 *Portugal* Socialist former mayor of Lisbon Jorge Sampaio elected President.

15 *Greece* Resignation of Prime Minister Andreas Papandreou due to ill health.

16 *Sierra Leone* Head of state Captain Valentine Strasser overthrown and replaced by deputy, Gen. Julius Maada Bio.

18 *Greece* Costas Simitis chosen as new Prime Minister.
India 3 ministers resign in bribes scandal.

21 *Middle East* Yasser Arafat, leader of Palestinian Liberation Organization, elected President of the Palestinian Authority in Gaza and the West Bank.

22 *Bahrain* Opposition leader Shaikh Abdul Amir Al-Jamri arrested.

24 *UK* Mitchell Report on Northern Ireland recommends peace talks should proceed simultaneously with the disarmament of paramilitary factions.
Poland Resignation of Prime Minister Józef Oleksy over allegations that he once spied for the USSR.
Russia Release by Chechen rebels of some civilian hostages.

25 *Colombia* Opposition Conservative Party withdraws support from government of President Ernesto Samper.

26 *China* Official establishment of Preparatory Committee to determine government of Hong Kong after 1997 restitution of sovereignty.

27 *Niger* President Mahamane Ousmane overthrown in military coup.

28 *India/Pakistan* Heavy fighting along disputed border in Kashmir.

29 *French Pacific* France announces end of current series of nuclear tests.

30 *Sri Lanka* Suicide bomber kills sixty.

31 *Aegean* End of 4-day confrontation between Greece and Turkey over Imia-Kardak group of islets.
Bosnia-Hercegovina Election by special assembly established under peace agreement of Croat and Moslem ministers to run federated Bosnia.

Feb. 1 *Italy* Antonio Maccanicio asked to form new government.
Sudan Withdrawal of US embassy staff from Khartoum.

CHRONOLOGY—*contd.*

1996

Feb. 4 *Bosnia-Hercegovina* Military withdrawal from 'areas of transition' agreed under Dayton Plan.

6 *Morocco/Spain* Agreement to build tunnel under the Strait of Gibraltar to link Europe and Africa.

Taiwan US deploys naval presence in face of military build-up on mainland China.

7 *Poland* New left-wing coalition government under Włodzimierz Cimoszewicz sworn in.

8 *Bosnia-Hercegovina* Bosnian Serb forces suspend contacts with NATO-led peace-keeping force.

Lithuania Prime Minister Adolfas Sleževicius dismissed by presidential decree for involvement in financial scandal.

9 *Spain* Suspension in relation to Belgium of parts of Schengen Accord in protest at Belgian failure to extradite suspected Basque rebels.

UK Massive bomb explosion in London's Docklands signals end of IRA ceasefire.

11 *Israel* Prime Minister Shimon Peres brings forward general election date to end of May.

15 *Colombia* President Ernesto Samper charged with funding presidential campaign with proceeds of drug trade.

Russia President Yeltsin announces intention to seek second term; Communist Party names Gennadi Zyuganov as its presidential candidate.

UK Publication of Scott Report into supply of arms to Iraq.

16 *Bangladesh* Ruling Bangladesh Nationalist Party wins clear victory in general election.

Italy President Scalfaro dissolves parliament and calls elections for 21 April.

18 *Bosnia-Hercegovina* Meeting in Rome of Croatian, Moslem and Serb leaders reinforces peace process.

19 *EU* Draft blueprint for European reform envisages abolition of single-country veto.

France Constitutional amendment enacted setting limits to welfare spending.

Russia Last Chechen hostages freed.

21 *Saudi Arabia* King Fahd resumes full government powers after illness.

USA Pat Buchanan wins primary in New Hampshire, first step in nomination of Republican presidential candidate.

22 *Bosnia-Hercegovina* Mass Serb exodus from Sarajevo in advance of restitution of Bosnian government rule.

UK Conservative parliamentary majority reduced to two.

23 *Iraq* Murder of returning defector Gen. Hussein Kamel Al Majid, President Saddam Hussein's son-in-law.

25 *Bosnia-Hercegovina* Serb forces evacuate civilians from areas of Sarajevo to pass to Moslem-Croat federation.

Cuba 2 American-owned private light aircraft shot down by Cuban fighters.

Equatorial Guinea First presidential elections in 25 years.

CHRONOLOGY—*contd.*

1996

Feb. 25 *Israel* Palestinian suicide bomber kills twenty-six.
Sierra Leone Rebel Revolutionary United Front and government meet for first talks after 5 years of civil war.

27 *USA* Millionaire Steve Forbes is surprise victor in Arizona primary.

28 *Council of Europe* Russia becomes 39th member.

29 *Bosnia-Hercegovina* Siege of Sarajevo officially ends as Moslem-Croat federation takes control of agreed areas of city.

March 1 *Israel* Rejection of offer by Hamas militant Islamic organization of conditional truce.
Russia Mikhail Gorbachev announces candidacy in June presidential election.

2 *Australia* Liberal-National opposition coalition, led by John Howard, gains landslide victory over Paul Keating's Labor Party in general election.

3 *Hong Kong* British Prime Minister John Major announces visa-free access to Britain for over 2m. Hong Kong Chinese after reunification with China.
Iran Opposition Iran Freedom Movement announces boycott of forthcoming general election.
Israel Militant Hamas group claims responsibility for suicide bomb killing eighteen on Jerusalem bus.
Spain Conservative Popular Party, led by José Maria Anzar, defeats ruling Socialists in general election but fails to win overall majority.
Turkey 2 main secular parties, True Path and Motherland, agree coalition with alternating Prime Ministers.

6 *USA* Senator Bob Dole wins key primaries in battle for Republican Party presidential nomination.

7 *Austria* Social Democrats and People's Party renew coalition agreement.
Russia Chechen rebels take control of part of disputed city of Grozny.

12 *China* New live-ammunition military exercises off Taiwanese coast.
Turkey Parliament accepts government programme put forward by new coalition.
Zimbabwe Opposition leader Ndabaningi Sithole withdraws from forthcoming presidential election.

13 *Middle East* World powers meet at Egyptian summit to revive flagging peace process.

14 *Iran* Inconclusive first round of parliamentary elections.

15 *Sierra Leone* Ahmad Tejan Kabbah of People's Party wins presidential elections to end military rule.

19 *Australia* Paul Keating resigns as leader of Labor Party.
Benin Former dictator Ahmed Kerekou returned to power in presidential election.
Bosnia-Hercegovina Formal reunification of Sarajevo.

CHRONOLOGY—*contd.*

1996

March 20 *Sudan* Military leader Lieut.-Gen. Omar al-Bashir and his supporters confirmed in power in parliamentary and presidential elections.

21 *EU* British beef banned after UK government announcement of possible link between bovine spongiform encephalopathy (BSE; 'mad cow disease') and Creutzfeldt-Jakob disease in humans.

UK John Major announces election to a Northern Ireland forum.

24 *Aegean* New Turkish Prime Minister Mesut Yilmaz offers Greece unconditional talks on future of the Aegean.

Taiwan President Lee Teng-hui gains significant victory for pro-independence movement in first-ever elections.

Germany State elections give boost to Chancellor Kohl's Christian Democrat-Free Democrat coalition government.

25 *South Pacific* USA, Britain and France sign treaty declaring South Pacific a nuclear-free zone.

26 *EU* France and Germany agree on formation of new exchange rate mechanism to apply to members not joining the single European currency.

27 *Bangladesh* Prime Minister Begum Khaleda Zia steps down prior to fresh elections in May.

29 *EU* Opening of heads of government conference in Turin.

Sierra Leone Peaceful handover of power by military rulers to elected government led by President-elect Ahmed Tejan Kabbah.

31 *Bangladesh* Caretaker government appointed under Habibur Rahman.

Russia Unilateral ceasefire ordered in Chechenia.

TOPIC FINDING LIST

Information about each country is presented in a standardized framework of **SECTIONS, Sub-sections,** and *Paragraphs* as follows:

Title heading

KEY HISTORICAL EVENTS

TERRITORY AND POPULATION

CLIMATE

[MONARCH]*

CONSTITUTION AND GOVERNMENT: *National flag, National anthem, Local Government*

DEFENCE: Army, Navy, Coastguard, Air Force

INTERNATIONAL RELATIONS: Membership

ECONOMY: Policy, Budget, Currency, Banking and Finance, Weights and Measures

ENERGY AND NATURAL RESOURCES: Electricity, Oil and Gas, Minerals, Agriculture, Forestry, Fisheries

INDUSTRY: Labour, Trade Unions

FOREIGN ECONOMIC RELATIONS: Commerce, Tourism

COMMUNICATIONS: Roads, Railways, Civil Aviation, Shipping, Telecommunications, Cinemas, Press

SOCIAL INSTITUTIONS: Justice, Religion, Education, Health, Social Security and Welfare

DIPLOMATIC REPRESENTATIVES

Further Reading

* The heading varies according to the nature of the monarchy, e.g. 'Ducal House' (Luxembourg), 'Royal House' (Denmark).

Additional headings are used in the extended coverage given to the United Kingdom and the United States, and also in some countries where appropriate, e.g. **Water** *under* **ENERGY AND NATURAL RESOURCES** *for desert countries, and 'European Parliament' under* **CONSTITUTION AND GOVERNMENT** *for EU members. The headings are also used with suitable modifications for states, provinces and dependencies.*

TOPIC FINDING LIST—*contd.*

LOCATION OF SPECIFIC TOPICS BY HEADINGS

A

abortions	**TERRITORY AND POPULATION**
academic staff	**SOCIAL INSTITUTIONS: Education**
administrative divisions	**TERRITORY AND POPULATION, CONSTITUTION AND GOVERNMENT:** *Local Government*
agriculture	**ENERGY AND NATURAL RESOURCES: Agriculture**
air forces	**DEFENCE: Air Force**
airlines	**COMMUNICATIONS: Civil Aviation**
airports	**COMMUNICATIONS: Civil Aviation**
alphabets	**TERRITORY AND POPULATION**
ambassadors	**DIPLOMATIC REPRESENTATIVES**
animal products	**ENERGY AND NATURAL RESOURCES: Agriculture**
anthems	**CONSTITUTION AND GOVERNMENT** *National anthem*
aquaculture	**ENERGY AND NATURAL RESOURCES: Fisheries**
area	**TERRITORY AND POPULATION**
armed forces	**DEFENCE**
average wage	**INDUSTRY: Labour**

B

banknotes	**ECONOMY: Currency**
banks	**ECONOMY: Banking and Finance**
bibliographies	**Further Reading**
births	**TERRITORY AND POPULATION**
book production	**COMMUNICATIONS: Press**
books of reference	**Further Reading**
borders	**TERRITORY AND POPULATION**
broadcasting	**COMMUNICATION: Telecommunications**
budget	**ECONOMY: Budget**
buses	**COMMUNICATIONS: Roads**

C

cabinets	**CONSTITUTION AND GOVERNMENT**
calendar	**ECONOMY: Weights and Measures**
canals	**COMMUNICATIONS: Shipping**
capital cities	*Title heading,* **TERRITORY AND POPULATION**
cars	**COMMUNICATIONS: Roads**
censuses	**TERRITORY AND POPULATION**
central banks	**ECONOMY: Banking and Finance**
central statistical offices	**Further Reading**
churches	**SOCIAL INSTITUTIONS: Religion**
cities	**TERRITORY AND POPULATION**
citizenship	**TERRITORY AND POPULATION**
civil aviation	**COMMUNICATIONS: Civil Aviation**
climate	**CLIMATE**
coastguard	**DEFENCE: Coastguard**
coinage	**ECONOMY: Currency**
colleges	**SOCIAL INSTITUTIONS: Education**
commerce	**FOREIGN ECONOMIC RELATIONS: Commerce**
conscription	**DEFENCE**

TOPIC FINDING LIST—*contd.*

TOPIC FINDING LIST—*contd.*

TOPIC FINDING LIST—*contd.*

TOPIC FINDING LIST—*contd.*

TOPIC FINDING LIST—*contd.*

ADDENDA

ADDENDA

All dates are 1996 unless stated otherwise

AUSTRALIA. The 38th Parliament was elected on 2 March. In the House of Representatives the Liberal Party (LP) gained 75 seats; the Australian Labor Party (ALP), 49; the National Party (NP), 19; independents, 5. An LP-NP coalition government was formed. *Cabinet: Prime Minister,* John Howard (LP). *Deputy Prime Minister and Minister for Trade:* Tim Fischer (NP). *Treasurer:* Peter Costello. *Minister for Primary Industries and Energy:* John Anderson. *Environment, Leader of the Government in the Senate:* Robert Hill. *Communications and the Arts:* Richard Alston. *Industrial Relations:* Peter Reith. *Social Security, Minister assisting the Prime Minister for the Status of Women:* Jocelyn Newman. *Foreign Affairs:* Alexander Downer. *Industry, Science and Tourism:* John Moore. *Defence:* Ian McLachlan. *Transport and Regional Development:* John Sharp. *Health and Family Services:* Dr Michael Wooldridge. *Finance:* John Fahey. *Employment, Education, Training and Youth Affairs:* Amanda Vanstone. *Outer Ministry: Minister for Immigration and Multicultural Affairs:* Philip Ruddock. *Science and Technology:* Peter McGauran. *Schools, Vocational Education and Training, Minister assisting the Prime Minister for the Public Service:* Dr David Kemp. *Assistant Treasurer:* Jim Short. *Resources and Energy:* Warwick Parer. *Small Business and Consumer Affairs:* Geoff Prosser. *Family Services:* Judi Moylan. *Defence Industry, Science and Personnel:* Bronwyn Bishop. *Attorney-General and Minister for Justice:* Daryl Williams, QC. *Sport, Territories and Local Government:* Warwick Smith. *Veterans' Affairs:* Bruce Scott. *Aboriginal and Torres Strait Islander Affairs:* John Herron. *Administrative Services:* David Jull. The leader of the Opposition is Kim Beazley (ALP).

Following a by-election in Queensland in Feb. the state of the parties in the Legislative Assembly was: ALP, 44; NP, 29; LP, 15; ind, 1. A new NP-LP coalition government was formed in Feb.: *Premier,* Rob Borbridge. *Deputy Premier, Treasurer, Minister for Arts:* Joan Sheldon. *Attorney-General:* Denver Beanland. *Minister of Education:* Bob Quinn. *Public Works, Housing:* Ray Connor. *Economic Development, Trade:* Doug Slack. *Transport, Main Roads:* Vaughan Johnson. *Police, Corrective Services, Racing:* Russell Cooper. *Environment:* Brian Littleproud. *Local Government, Planning:* Di McCauley. *Health:* Mike Horan. *Training, Industrial Relations:* Santo Santoro. *Natural Resources:* Howard Hobbs. *Mines, Energy:* Tom Gilmore. *Emergency Services, Sport:* Mick Velvers. *Tourism, Small Business, Industry:* Bruce Davidson. *Families, Youth, Community Care:* Ken Lingard. *Primary Industries, Fisheries, Forestry:* Trevor Perrett. The leader of the Opposition is Peter Beattie (ALP).

Following a state election held in Tasmania on 24 Feb. the state of the parties was: LP, 16; ALP, 14; Greens, 4; ind, 1. A minority LP government was formed on 15 March, comprising: *Premier, Treasurer, Minister for State Development:* Tony Rundle. *Deputy Premier, Minister for Education and Vocational Training, Arts, Sports and Recreation:* Sue Napier. *Police and Public Safety, Forests, Mines:* John Beswick. *Transport, Energy, Inland Fisheries:* Thomas Cleary. *Finance, Public Sector Employment, Industrial Relations, Leader of the Government in the House:* Ron Cornish. *Attorney General, Justice, Tourism, Workplace Safety:* Ray Groom. *Environment, Land Management:* Peter Hogman. *Status of Women, Community Development, Local Government, Multicultural Ethnic Affairs, Aboriginal Affairs:* Denise Swan. *Community and Health Services:* Peter McKay. *Primary Industries and Fisheries, Racing:* Bill Bonde.

A state election was held in Victoria on 30 March.

AUSTRIA. Following the elections of 17 Dec. 1995 the Social Democratic Party (SPÖ) and the People's Party (ÖVP) concluded an agreement to govern as a coalition in March. The *Chancellor* is Dr Franz Vranitzky (SPÖ), the *Vice-Chancellor,* Wolfgang Schüssel (ÖVP). The *Speaker* is Heinz Fischer (SPÖ).

BANGLADESH. Parliamentary elections were held on 15 Feb.; turn-out was less than 10% owing to opposition calls for a boycott. The Bangladesh National Party won an absolute majority of seats. Habibur Rahman (b. 1930) became *Prime Minister.*

BELARUS. On 2 April the Presidents of Belarus and Russia signed a treaty providing for political, economic and military integration, creating the nucleus of a potential future 'Commonwealth of Sovereign Republics'. The agreement establishes a Supreme Council comprising the Presidents, Prime Ministers and Speakers of both countries.

BENIN. The first round of presidential elections on 3 March was won by President Nicéphore Soglo with 35·69% of votes cast against 2 opponents. At the run-off with President Soglo on 18 March Mathieu Kerekou (b. 1934) was elected *President* by 52·49% of votes cast.

BURKINA FASO. Kadré Desiré Ouédraogo became *Prime Minister* on 6 Feb.

COMOROS. A first round of Presidential elections took place on 6 March; turn-out was 64%. There were 15 candidates. Mohamed Taki Abdoulkarim (b. 1936; National Union for Democracy in Comoros) gained 21·28% of votes cast; Abbas Djoussouf (Forum for National Renewal), 15·71%. A run-off round was held on 16 March; turn-out was 62%. Abdoulkarim was elected *President* by 64·29% of votes cast, and sworn in on 25 March.

EQUATORIAL GUINEA. Presidential elections were held on 25 Feb. It was announced that President Nguema Mbasogo had been re-elected by 99% of votes cast. Elections for the National Assembly were held on 26 Feb.

IRAQ. Parliamentary election were held on 24 March. The Ba'ath Party gained a majority of seats.

ITALY. Parliamentary elections were held on 21 April. There were 1,574 candidates. The Olive Tree Alliance gained 284 seats in the Chamber of Deputies and 157 in the Senate with 41·2% of the national vote, the Freedom Alliance 246 and 116 with 37·3%, the Northern League 59 and 27 with 37·3%, the Refounded Communists 35 and 10 with 8·6%. In the Chamber of Deputies minor parties won 6 seats. In the Senate the Pannella List won 27 seats and minor parties won 4.

SOUTH KOREA. Paraliamentary elections were held on 11 April. 1,389 candidates stood. The electorate was 31,526,918; turn-out was 63·9%. The New Korea Party won 139 seats with 34·5% of votes cast; the National Congress for New Politics, 79 with 25·3%; the United Liberal Democrats, 50 with 16·2%; the Democratic Party, 15 with 11·2%; independents, 16 with 11·9%.

PERU. Alberto Pandolfi Arbulú became *Prime Minister* on 3 April.

SOUTH AFRICA. Trevor Manuel (ANC) became *Minister of Finance*, Alec Erwin (ANC) *Trade and Industry* and Jay Naidoo (ANC) *Posts, Telecommunications and Broadcasting* on 28 March. The Reconstruction and Development Programme portfolio was merged with the Ministry of Finance.

SPAIN. Parliamentary elections were held on 3 March. 67 parties presented candidates. The electorate was 24,985,343; turn-out was 78·06%. In the Congress of Deputies the Popular Party (PP) won 156 seats with 38·2% of votes cast (141 with 34·8% in 1993); the Spanish Workers' Socialist Party (PSOE), 141 with 37·4% (159 with 38·8%); the United Left Coalition (IU), 21 with 10·5% (18 with 9·5%);

Convergence and Union (CiU, Catalan nationalists), 16 with 4·6% (17 with 4·9%); Basque Nationalist Party (PNV), 5 with 1·2% (5 with 1·2%); Canarian Coalition (CC), 4 with 0·8% (4 with 0·9%); Galician Nationalist Bloc, 2 with 0·8%; Herri Batasuna (Basque separatists), 2 with 0·7% (2 with 0·8%); Esquerra Republicana de Catalunya, 1 with 0·6% (1 with 0·8%); Eusko Alkartasuna (Basque separatists), 1 with 0·4% (1 with 0·6%); Valencian Union, 1 with 0·3% (1 with 0·5%). In the Senate PP gained 132 seats; PSOE, 96; CiU, 11; PNV, 6; IU, 2; CC, 2; 6 other parties, 1 seat each.

The *Speaker* of the Congress of Deputies is Federico Trillo (PP).

On 5 May José María Aznar (b. 1953; PP) was sworn in as *Prime Minister* and formed the following government: *Deputy Prime Minister, Minister for the Prime Minister's Office:* Francisco Alvárez Cascos (PP). *Deputy Prime Minister, Minister for the Economy and Finance:* Rodrigo Rato (PP). *Foreign Affairs:* Abel Matutes (PP). *Interior:* Jaíme Mayor Oreja (PP). *Justice:* Margarita Mariscal de Gante (ind). *Defence:* Eduardo Serra (ind). *Agriculture and Fisheries:* Loyola de Palacio (PP). *Development:* Rafael Arías Salgado (PP). *Education and Culture:* Esperanza Aguirre (PP). *Labour and Social Affairs:* Javier Arenas (PP). *Industry:* Josep Piqué (ind). *Public Administration:* Mariano Rajoy (PP). *Health:* José Manuel Romay (PP). *Environment:* Isabel Tocino (PP).

SUDAN. At the elections on 22 March Lieut.-Gen. Omar al-Bashir was re-elected *President* by 75% of votes cast.

SWEDEN. A new Social Democratic government was formed in March which included: *Prime Minister:* Göran Persson. *Foreign Minister:* Lena Hjelm-Wallén. *Finance:* Erik Asbrink. *Labour:* Margareta Winberg. *Defence:* Thage G. Peterson. *Agriculture:* Annika Aahnberg. *Commerce:* Björn von Sydow. *Interior:* Jörgen Andersson. *Social Affairs:* Margot Wallström. *Industry:* Anders Sundström. *Culture:* Marita Ulvskog. *Environment:* Anna Lindh.

TAIWAN. At the presidential elections on 23 March turn-out was 76%. President Lee Teng-hui (b. 1923) was re-elected against 3 opponents by 54% of votes cast.

UNITED KINGDOM. Mrs Marina Mowatt, daughter of Princess Alexandra, was separated from her husband Paul Mowatt on 11 April. Proceedings for the divorce of Prince Andrew, Duke of York, and Sarah, Duchess of York, were begun in court on 17 April.

PART I

INTERNATIONAL ORGANIZATIONS

THE UNITED NATIONS (UN)

The United Nations is an association of states which have pledged themselves, through signing the Charter, to maintain international peace and security and to co-operate in establishing political, economic and social conditions under which this task can be securely achieved. Nothing contained in the Charter authorizes the organization to intervene in matters which are essentially within the domestic jurisdiction of any state.

The UN Charter originated from proposals agreed upon at discussions held at Dumbarton Oaks (Washington DC) between the USSR, the USA and the UK from 21 Aug. to 28 Sept., and between the USA, the UK and China from 29 Sept. to 7 Oct. 1944. These proposals were laid before the UN Conference on International Organization, held at San Francisco from 25 April to 26 June 1945, and (after amendments had been made to the original proposals) the Charter was signed on 26 June 1945 by the delegates of 50 countries. Ratification of all the signatures had been received by 31 Dec. 1945. (For the complete text of the Charter *see* THE STATESMAN'S YEAR-BOOK, 1946, pp. xxi–xxxii.)

The United Nations formally came into existence on 24 Oct. 1945, with the deposit of the requisite number of ratifications of the Charter with the US Department of State. The official languages are Arabic, Chinese, English, French, Russian and Spanish.

Headquarters: United Nations, New York, NY 10017, USA.

Flag: UN emblem in white centred on a light blue ground.

Membership. Membership is open to all peace-loving states whose admission will be effected by the General Assembly upon recommendation of the Security Council. The table below shows the 185 member states.

The principal organs are: 1. The General Assembly. 2. The Security Council. 3. The Economic and Social Council. 4. The Trusteeship Council. 5. The International Court of Justice. 6. The Secretariat.

1. **The General Assembly** consists of all the members. Each member has 1 vote. The General Assembly meets regularly once a year, commencing on the third Tuesday in Sept.; the session normally lasts until mid-Dec. and is resumed for some weeks in the new year if required. Special sessions may be convoked by the Secretary-General if requested by the Security Council, by a majority of members or by 1 member concurred with by the majority of the members. The Assembly also meets in emergency special session. It elects a President for each session.

The work of the General Assembly is divided between 6 Main Committees, on which every member state is represented. These are: Disarmament and International Security Committee (First Committee); Economic and Financial Committee (Second Committee); Social, Humanitarian and Cultural Committee (Third Committee); Special Political and Decolonization Committee (Fourth Committee); Administrative and Budgetary Committee (Fifth Committee); Legal Committee (Sixth Committee).

In addition there is a General Committee charged with the task of co-ordinating the proceedings of the Assembly and its Committees; and a Credentials Committee. The General Committee consists of 29 members, comprising the President of the General Assembly, its 17 Vice-Presidents and the Chairmen of the 6 Main Committees. The Credentials Committee consists of 9 members, elected at the beginning of each session of the General Assembly. The Assembly has 2 standing committees—an Advisory Committee on Administrative and Budgetary Questions, and a Committee on Contributions. The General Assembly establishes subsidiary and *ad hoc* bodies when necessary to deal with specific matters. These include: Special Committee on Peace-keeping Operations (34 members), Human Rights Committee (18 members), Committee on the peaceful uses of outer space (61 members),

Conciliation Commission for Palestine (3 members), Conference on Disarmament (38 members), International Law Commission (34 members), Scientific Committee on the effects of atomic radiation (21 members), Special Committee on the implementation of the declaration on the granting of independence to colonial countries and peoples (24 members) and UN Commission on International Trade Law (36 members).

The General Assembly may discuss any matters within the scope of the Charter, and, with the exception of any situation or dispute on the agenda of the Security Council, may make recommendations on any such questions or matters. For decisions on important questions a two-thirds majority is required, on other questions a simple majority of members present and voting. If the Security Council, because of lack of unanimity of the permanent members, fails to exercise its primary responsibility for the maintenance of international peace and security in any case where there appears to be a threat to the peace, breach of the peace or act of aggression, the General Assembly shall consider the matter immediately with a view to making appropriate recommendations to members for collective measures, including in the case of a breach of the peace or act of aggression the use of armed force when necessary, to maintain or restore international peace and security.

The General Assembly receives and considers reports from the other UN organs. The Secretary-General makes an annual report to it on the work of the organization.

2. **The Security Council** consists of 15 members, each of which has 1 vote. There are 5 permanent and 10 non-permanent members elected for a 2-year term by a two-thirds majority of the General Assembly.

Retiring members are not eligible for immediate re-election. Any other member of the United Nations may be invited to participate without vote in the discussion of questions specially affecting its interests.

The Security Council bears the primary responsibility for the maintenance of peace and security. Decisions on procedural questions are made by an affirmative vote of 9 members. On all other matters the affirmative vote of 9 members must include the concurring votes of all permanent members (in practice, however, an abstention by a permanent member is not considered a veto), subject to the provision that when the Security Council is considering methods for the peaceful settlement of a dispute, parties to the dispute abstain from voting.

For the maintenance of international peace and security the Security Council can, in accordance with special agreements to be concluded, call on armed forces, assistance and facilities of the member states. It is assisted by a Military Staff Committee consisting of the Chiefs of Staff of the permanent members of the Security Council or their representatives.

The Presidency of the Security Council is held for 1 month in rotation by the member states in the English alphabetical order of their names.

The Security Council functions continuously. Its members are permanently represented at the seat of the organization, but it may meet at any place that will best facilitate its work.

The Council has 3 standing committees. The Committee of Experts on Rules of Procedure, the Committee on Council Meetings away from Headquarters and the Committee on the Admission of New Members. In addition, from time to time, it establishes *ad hoc* committees and commissions.

Permanent Members: China, France, Russia, UK, USA. Russia took over the seat of the former USSR in Dec. 1991.

Non-Permanent Members: Botswana, Germany, Honduras, Indonesia and Italy (until 31 Dec. 1996); Chile, Egypt, Guinea-Bissau, South Korea, Poland (until 31 Dec. 1997).

3. **The Economic and Social Council** is responsible under the General Assembly for carrying out the functions of the UN with regard to international economic, social, cultural, educational, health and related matters. It may also make arrangements for consultation with international non-governmental organizations and, after consultation with the member concerned, with national organizations.

It consists of 54 member states elected by a two-thirds majority of the General Assembly for a 3-year term. Retiring members are eligible for immediate re-election. Each member has 1 vote. Decisions are made by a majority of the members present and voting.

The Council nominally holds 2 sessions a year, and special sessions may be held if required. The President is elected for 1 year and is eligible for immediate re-election.

The Economic and Social Council has the following commissions:

Regional Economic Commissions: ECE (Economic Commission for Europe. Geneva); ESCAP (Economic and Social Commission for Asia and the Pacific. Bangkok); ECLAC (Economic Commission for Latin America and the Caribbean. Santiago, Chile); ECA (Economic Commission for Africa. Addis Ababa). ESCWA (Economic Commission for Western Asia. Baghdad). These Commissions have been established to enable the nations of the major regions of the world to co-operate on common problems and also to produce economic information.

11 functional commissions on: Crime and Criminal Justice; Social Development; Human Rights; Narcotic Drugs; Science and Technology for Development; Status of Women; Statistics; Sustainable Development; Human Settlements; New and Renewable Sources of Energy and Energy for Development; Population and Development.

The Economic and Social Council has the following standing committees: The Committee on Non-Governmental Organizations; the Committee for Programme and Co-ordination; the Committee on Natural Resources, the Committee for Development Planning; the Committee of Experts on the Transport of Dangerous Goods.

Other special bodies are the International Narcotics Control Board and the Administrative Committee on Co-ordination to ensure (1) the most effective implementation of the agreements entered into between the United Nations and the specialized agencies and (2) co-ordination of activities.

4. **The Trusteeship Council.** The Charter provides for an international trusteeship system to safeguard the interests of the inhabitants of territories which are not yet fully self-governing and which may be placed thereunder by individual trusteeship agreements. These are called trust territories.

All the original 11 trust territories had become independent or joined independent countries by 1994. The Trusteeship Council consisted of the member administering trust territories, the USA and the permanent members of the Security Council. Since 1994 it meets only on an extraordinary basis as needed.

5. **The International Court of Justice** was created by an international treaty, the Statute of the Court, which forms an integral part of the United Nations Charter. All members of the United Nations are *ipso facto* parties to the Statute of the Court.

The Court is composed of independent judges, elected regardless of their nationality, who possess the qualifications required in their countries for appointment to the highest judicial offices, or are jurisconsults of recognized competence in international law. There are 15 judges, no 2 of whom may be nationals of the same state. They are elected by the Security Council and the General Assembly sitting independently. Candidates are chosen from a list of persons nominated by the national groups in the Permanent Court of Arbitration established by the Hague Conventions of 1899 and 1907. In the case of members of the United Nations not represented in the Permanent Court of Arbitration, candidates are nominated by national groups appointed for the purpose by their governments. The judges are elected for a 9-year term and are eligible for immediate re-election. When engaged on business of the Court, they enjoy diplomatic privileges and immunities.

The Court elects its own *President* and *Vice-President* for 3 years and remains permanently in session, except for judicial vacations. The full court of 15 judges normally sits, but a quorum of 9 judges is sufficient to constitute the Court. In 1993 the Court formed a 7-member *Chamber for Environmental Matters.* It may further form chambers of 3 or more judges for dealing with a particular case or particular categories of cases. Mohammed Bedjaoui (Algeria) and Stephen M. Schwebel (USA) are, respectively, President and Vice-President of the Court until 1997.

Competence and Jurisdiction. Only states may be parties in cases before the Court, which is open to the states parties to its Statute. The conditions under which the Court will be open to other states are laid down by the Security Council. The Court exercises its jurisdiction in all cases which the parties refer to it and in all matters provided for in the Charter, or in treaties and conventions in force. Disputes concerning the jurisdiction of the Court are settled by the Court's own decision.

The Court may apply in its decision: *(a)* international conventions; *(b)* international custom; *(c)* the general principles of law recognized by civilized nations; and *(d)* as subsidiary means for the determination of the rules of law, judicial decisions and the teachings of highly qualified publicists. If the parties agree, the Court may decide a case *ex aequo et bono*. The Court may also give advisory opinions on legal questions to the General Assembly, the Security Council, certain other organs of the UN and a number of international organizations.

Procedure. The official languages of the Court are French and English. All questions are decided by a majority of the judges present. If the votes are equal, the President has a casting vote. The judgment is final and without appeal, but a revision may be applied for within 10 years from the date of the judgment on the ground of a new decisive factor. No court fees are paid by parties to the Statute.

Judges. The judges of the Court, elected by the Security Council and the General Assembly, are as follows:

(1) To serve until 5 Feb. 1997: Stephen M. Schwebel (USA), Mohammed Bedjaoui (Algeria), Mohamed Shahabuddeen (Guyana), Vladlen S. Vereshchetin (Russia).

(2) To serve until 5 Feb. 2000: Rosalyn Higgins (UK), Gilbert Guillaume (France), Andrés Aguilar Mawdsley (Venezuela), Christopher G. Weeramantry (Sri Lanka), Raymond Ranjeva (Madagascar).

(3) To serve until 5 Feb. 2003: Shigeru Oda (Japan), Géza Herczegh (Hungary), Shi Jiuyong (China), Carl-August Fleischhauer (Germany), Abdul G. Koroma (Sierra Leone).

If there is no judge on the bench of the nationality of a party to a case, that party has the right to choose a person to sit as judge for that case. Such judges take part in the decision on terms of complete equality with their colleagues.

The Court has its seat at The Hague, but may sit elsewhere whenever it considers this desirable. The expenses of the Court are borne by the UN.

Registrar: Eduardo Valencia-Ospina (Colombia).

6. **The Secretariat** is composed of the Secretary-General, who is the chief administrative officer of the organization, and an international staff appointed by him under regulations established by the General Assembly. The Secretary-General, the High Commissioner for Refugees and the Managing Director of the Fund are appointed by the General Assembly.

The Secretary-General acts as chief administrative officer in all meetings of the General Assembly, the Security Council, the Economic and Social Council and the Trusteeship Council.

The financial year coincides with the calendar year; accounting is in US dollars. Budget for 1996–97, US$2,610m. Assessments on member states constitute the main source of funds. These are in accordance with a scale specified by the Assembly, and determined primarily by the country's national income, in the range 25%–0·01%.

Secretary-General: Boutros Boutros Ghali (b. 1922; Egypt) appointed 1 Jan. 1992 for a 5-year term.

The Secretary-General is assisted by Under-Secretaries-General and Assistant Secretaries-General.

MEMBER STATES OF THE UN

The 185 member states as at Feb. 1996, with percentage scale of contribution and year of admission:

	% contri-bution	*Year of admission*		*% contri-bution*	*Year of admission*
Afghanistan	0·01	1946	Georgia	0·16	1992
Albania	0·01	1955	Germany	8·94	1973
Algeria	0·16	1962	Ghana	0·01	1957
Andorra	0·01	1993	Greece [1]	0·37	1945
Angola	0·01	1976	Grenada	0·01	1974
Antigua and Barbuda	0·01	1981	Guatemala [1]	0·02	1945
Argentina [1]	0·48	1945	Guinea	0·01	1958
Armenia	0·08	1992	Guinea-Bissau	0·01	1974
Australia [1]	1·46	1945	Guyana	0·01	1966
Austria	0·85	1955	Haiti [1]	0·01	1945
Azerbaijan	0·16	1992	Honduras [1]	0·01	1945
Bahamas	0·02	1973	Hungary	0·15	1955
Bahrain	0·02	1971	Iceland	0·03	1946
Bangladesh	0·01	1974	India [1]	0·31	1945
Barbados	0·01	1966	Indonesia	0·14	1950
Belarus [1]	0.37	1945	Iran [1]	0·60	1945
Belgium [1]	0·99	1945	Iraq [1]	0·14	1945
Belize	0·01	1981	Ireland	0·20	1955
Benin	0·01	1960	Israel	0·26	1949
Bhutan	0·01	1971	Italy	4·79	1955
Bolivia [1]	0·02	1945	Jamaica	0·01	1962
Bosnia-Hercegovina	0·04	1992	Japan	3·95	1956
Botswana	0·01	1966	Jordan	0·01	1955
Brazil [1]	1·62	1945	Kazakhstan	0·26	1992
Brunei Darussalam	0·02	1984	Kenya	0·01	1963
Bulgaria	0·10	1955	Korea (North)	0·04	1991
Burkina Faso	0·01	1960	Korea (South)	0·80	1991
Burma	0·01	1948	Kuwait	0·20	1963
Burundi	0·01	1962	Kyrgyzstan	0·04	1992
Cambodia	0·01	1955	Laos	0·01	1955
Cameroon	0·01	1960	Latvia	0·10	1991
Canada [1]	3·07	1945	Lebanon [1]	0·01	1945
Cape Verde	0·01	1975	Lesotho	0·01	1966
Central African Rep.	0·01	1960	Liberia [1]	0·01	1945
Chad	0·01	1960	Libya	0·21	1955
Chile [1]	0·08	1945	Liechtenstein	0·01	1990
China [1]	0·72	1945	Lithuania	0·11	1991
Colombia [1]	0·11	1945	Luxembourg [1]	0·07	1945
Comoros	0·01	1975	Macedonia	0·01	1993
Congo	0·01	1960	Madagascar	0·01	1960
Costa Rica [1]	0·01	1945	Malawi	0·01	1964
Côte d'Ivoire	0·01	1960	Malaysia	0·14	1957
Croatia	0·10	1991	Maldives	0·01	1965
Cuba [1]	0·07	1945	Mali	0·01	1960
Cyprus	0·03	1960	Malta	0·01	1964
Czech Republic [3]	0·32	1993	Marshall Islands	0·01	1991
Denmark [1]	0·70	1945	Mauritania	0·01	1961
Djibouti	0·01	1977	Mauritius	0·01	1968
Dominica	0·01	1978	Mexico [1]	0·78	1945
Dominican Republic [1]	0·01	1945	Micronesia	0·01	1991
Ecuador [1]	0·02	1945	Moldova	0·11	1992
Egypt [1]	0·07	1945	Monaco	0·01	1991
El Salvador [1]	0·01	1945	Mongolia	0·01	1961
Equatorial Guinea	0·01	1968	Morocco	0·03	1956
Eritrea	0·01	1993	Mozambique	0·01	1975
Estonia	0·05	1991	Namibia	0·01	1990
Ethiopia [1]	0·01	1945	Nepal	0·01	1955
Fiji	0·01	1970	Netherlands [1]	1·58	1945
Finland	0·61	1955	New Zealand [1]	0·24	1945
France [1]	6·32	1945	Nicaragua [1]	0·01	1945
Gabon	0·01	1960	Niger	0·01	1960
Gambia	0·01	1965	Nigeria	0·16	1960

	% contribution	Year of admission		% contribution	Year of admission
Norway [1]	0·55	1945	Spain	2·24	1955
Oman	0·04	1971	Sri Lanka	0·01	1955
Pakistan	0·06	1947	Sudan	0·01	1956
Palau [2]	...	1994	Suriname	0·01	1975
Panama [1]	0·01	1945	Swaziland	0·01	1968
Papua New Guinea	0·01	1975	Sweden	1·22	1946
Paraguay [1]	0·01	1945	Syria [1]	0·05	1945
Peru [1]	0·06	1945	Tajikistan	0·03	1992
Philippines [1]	0·06	1945	Tanzania	0·01	1961
Poland [1]	0·38	1945	Thailand	0·13	1946
Portugal	0·24	1955	Togo	0·01	1960
Qatar	0·04	1971	Trinidad and Tobago	0·04	1962
Romania	0·15	1955	Tunisia	0·03	1956
Russia [1, 4]	5·68	1945	Turkey [1]	0·34	1945
Rwanda	0·01	1962	Turkmenistan	0·04	1992
St Kitts and Nevis	0·01	1983	Uganda	0·01	1962
St Lucia	0·01	1979	Ukraine [1]	1·48	1945
St Vincent and the Grenadines	0·01	1980	United Arab Emirates	0·19	1971
			UK [1]	5·27	1945
San Marino	0·01	1992	USA [1]	25·00	1945
São Tomé and Principe	0·01	1975	Uruguay [1]	0·04	1945
Saudi Arabia [1]	0·80	1945	Uzbekistan	0·19	1992
Senegal	0·01	1960	Vanuatu	0·01	1981
Seychelles	0·01	1976	Venezuela [1]	0·40	1945
Sierra Leone	0·01	1961	Vietnam	0·01	1977
Singapore	0·14	1965	Western Samoa	0·01	1976
Slovakia [3]	0·10	1993	Yemen	0·01	1947
Slovenia	0·07	1991	Yugoslavia [1, 5]	0·11	1945
Solomon Islands	0·01	1978	Zaïre	0·01	1960
Somalia	0·01	1960	Zambia	0·01	1964
South Africa [1]	0·34	1945	Zimbabwe	0·01	1980

[1] Original member. [2] Contribution to be determined.
[3] Pre-partition Czechoslovakia (1945–92) was an original member.
[4] As USSR, 1945–1991. [5] Excluded from the General Assembly 1992.

Further Reading

Yearbook of the United Nations. New York, 1947 ff.—*United Nations Chronicle.* Quarterly
Monthly Bulletin of Statistics.—General Assembly: Official-Records: Resolutions.—Reports of the Secretary-General of the United Nations on the Work of the Organization. 1946 ff.—*Charter of the United Nations and Statute of the International Court of Justice.—Official Records of the Security Council, the Economic and Social Council, Trusteeship Council and the Disarmament Commission.—Demographic Yearbook.* New York.—*Basic Facts about the United Nations.* New York [Various years].—*Statistical Yearbook.* New York, 1947 ff.—*Yearbook of International Statistics.* New York, 1950 ff.—*World Economic Survey.* New York, 1947 ff.—*Economic Survey of Asia and the Far East.* New York, 1946 ff.—*Economic Survey of Latin America.* New York, 1948 ff.—*Economic Survey of Europe.* New York, 1948 ff.—*Economic Survey of Africa.* New York, 1960 ff.—*United Nations Reference Guide in the Field of Human Rights.* UN Centre for Human Rights, 1993.
Baehr, P. R. and Gordenker, L., *The United Nations in the 1990s.* 2nd ed. London, 1994
Bailey, S. D. and Daws, S., *The United Nations: a Concise Political Guide.* 3rd ed. London, 1994
Baratta, J. P., *United Nations System* [Bibliography]. Oxford and New Brunswick (NJ), 1994
Durch, W. J., *The Evolution of UN Peacekeeping: Case Studies and Comparative Analysis.* New York, 1993
Luard, E., *The United Nations: How It Works and What It Does.* 2nd ed. London, 1994
Osmanczyk, E., *Encyclopaedia of the United Nations.* London, 1985
Parsons, A., *From Cold War to Hot Peace: UN Interventions, 1947-94.* London, 1995
Ratner, S. R., *The New UN Peacekeeping: Building Peace in Lands of Conflict after the Cold War.* London, 1995
Roberts, A. and Kingsbury, B. (eds.) *United Nations, Divided World: the UN's Roles in International Relations.* 2nd ed. Oxford, 1994.
Simma, B. (ed.) *The Charter of the United Nations: a Commentary.* OUP, 1995
Williams, D., *The Specialised Agencies of the United Nations.* London, 1987

UN Information Centres. Millbank Tower, 21st Floor, London SW1P 4QH; Public Inquiries Unit, Department of Public Information, Room GA-57, United Nations, New York, NY 10017.

UNITED NATIONS SYSTEM

There are 14 major UN programmes and funds devoted to achieving economic and social progress in the developing countries.

The *United Nations Development Programme* (UNDP) is the world's largest agency for multilateral technical and pre-investment co-operation. It is the funding source for most of the technical assistance provided by the UN system, and had 93 country programmes in 1992–96 with distributed resources of US$4,194m., and was supporting some 6,000 projects. UNDP assistance is provided only at the request of governments and in response to their priority needs, integrated into overall national and regional plans. Its activities are funded mainly by voluntary contributions outside the regular UN budget.

Administrator: James Gustave Speth (USA).

UNICEF, established in 1946 to deliver post-war relief to children, now concentrates its assistance on development activities aimed at improving the quality of life for children and mothers in developing countries. During 1991, UNICEF was working in over 110 countries with a child population of some 1,300m., concentrating on basic services for children and maternal health care, nutrition, water supply and sanitation and education. *The State of the World's Children Report*, published annually by UNICEF, has helped to spread acceptance by local and national leaders of a strategy for child health and nutrition which UNICEF estimates could save the lives of 7m. children. UNICEF has focused on popularising four primary health care techniques which are low in cost and produce results in a relatively short time. These include: Oral rehydration therapy to fight the effects of diarrhoeal infections, which kill some 4m. children each year; expanded immunization against the 6 most common childhood diseases; child growth monitoring, and promotion of breast-feeding. The World Health Organization and UNICEF work closely together, providing training, equipment and the services of health care professionals. UNICEF is the world's largest supplier of vaccines and the 'cold chain' equipment needed to deliver them, as well as oral rehydration salts.

Executive Director: Carol Bellamy (USA).

The UN Population Fund (UNFPA) carries out programmes in over 130 countries and territories. The Fund's aims are to build up capacity to respond to needs in population and family planning; to promote awareness of population problems in both developed and developing countries and possible strategies to deal with them; to assist developing countries at their request in dealing with population problems. More than 25% of international population assistance to developing countries is channeled through UNFPA.

Executive Director: Dr Nafis Sadik (Pakistan).

Humanitarian relief to refugees and victims of natural and man-made disasters is also an important function of the UN system. Among the organizations involved in such relief activities are the Office of the UN Department of Humanitarian Affairs (UNDHA), the Office of the UN High Commissioner for Refugees (UNHCR), the UN High Commissioner for Human Rights and the UN Relief and Works Agency for Palestine Refugees in the Near East (UNRWA).

UNRWA was created by the General Assembly in 1949 as a temporary, non-political agency to provide relief to the nearly 750,000 people who became refugees as a result of the disturbances during and after the creation of the State of Israel in the former British Mandate territory of Palestine. 'Palestine refugees', as defined by UNRWA's mandate, are persons or descendants of persons whose normal residence was Palestine for at least 2 years prior to the 1948 conflict and who, as a result of the conflict, lost their homes and means of livelihood. UNRWA has also been called upon to assist persons displaced as a result of renewed hostilities in the Middle East in 1967. The situation of Palestine refugees in south Lebanon was of special concern to the Agency in 1984 which has carried out an emergency relief programme in that area for Palestine refugees affected in the aftermath of the Israeli invasion of Lebanon in 1982. Its activities have the consent of the Israeli government.

Over 2m. refugees are registered with the Agency which provides education, health care, supplementary feeding and relief services. Education and basic health care account for over 80% of the Agency's budget, which is financed by voluntary contributions from Governments.

The Agency's mandate is renewed at intervals by the UN General Assembly.

The *Office of the United Nations High Commissioner for Refugees (UNHCR)* was established by the UN General Assembly with effect from 1 Jan. 1951, originally for 3 years. Since 1954, its mandate has been renewed for successive 5-year periods.

The work of UNHCR is humanitarian and non-political. UNHCR concerns itself with refugees who have been determined to come within its mandate under its Statute, namely, any person who, 'owing to well-founded fear of being persecuted for reasons of race, religion, nationality, or political opinion, is outside the country of his nationality and is unable or, owing to such fear or for reasons other than personal convenience, is unwilling to avail himself of the protection of that country; or who, not having a nationality and being outside the country of his former habitual residence, is unable or, owing to such fear or for reasons other than personal convenience, is unwilling to return to it', and with persons in analogous circumstances whom it assists under the terms of the 'good offices' resolutions adopted by the General Assembly.

The High Commissioner is elected by the General Assembly and follows policy directives given by the General Assembly or the Economic and Social Council, mainly through the Geneva-based Executive Committee of the High Commissioner's Programme.

International protection is the primary function of UNHCR. Its main objective is to promote and safeguard the rights and interests of refugees. In so doing UNHCR devotes special attention to promoting a generous policy of asylum on the part of Governments and seeks to improve the legal status of refugees in their country of residence. Crucial to this status is the principle of *non-refoulement*, which prohibits the expulsion from or forcible return of refugees to a country where they may have reason to fear persecution. It also helps them to cease being refugees through the acquisition of the nationality of their country of residence when voluntary repatriation is not possible. UNHCR pursues its objectives in the field of protection by encouraging the conclusion of intergovernmental legal instruments in favour of refugees, by supervising the implementation of their provisions and by encouraging Governments to adopt legislation and administrative procedures for the benefit of refugees.

UNHCR is often called upon to provide material assistance (i.e. the provision of food, shelter, medical care and essential supplies) while durable solutions are being sought. Durable solutions generally take one of 3 forms: voluntary repatriation, local integration or resettlement in another country.

Although at the beginning of 1995 the refugee population worldwide had decreased to 14·5m. the total number of persons of concern to UNHCR had risen to 27·4m. (non-refugees included internally displaced persons, or persons in a refugee-like situation, but who have not crossed an international border). The humanitarian crisis provoked in 1994 by the flight of over 2m. Rwandans and Burundians in the African Great Lakes region continued to fester. Zaïre, host to the largest population of Rwandan refugees, forcibly repatriated a number of them, while Tanzania, a country of asylum for African refugees since before independence, sealed its border against further arrivals. Southern Africa, in contrast, saw the successful completion in June 1995 of the voluntary repatriation of 1.6m. Mozambicans. In the former Yugoslavia the displaced person population was estimated at 3.5m. in early 1995. A US-brokered peace accord gave hope, but the return of displaced persons to 'ethnically cleansed' areas remained problematic. In the former Soviet Union the UNHCR assisted 210,000 persons who had fled the Russian advance into Chechnya by escaping to neighbouring Ingushetia and Daghestan. Afghan refugees, who began to leave their country after its invasion by Soviet forces in 1979, continued to constitute the largest refugee caseload of concern to UNHCR, with 2·7m. persons hosted by Iran and Pakistan. Some 200,000 Burmese Moslem refugees had repatriated from Bangladesh since Sept. 1992, and 50,000 remained in camps in Bangladesh.

In Dec. 1995, the UNHCR's Executive Committee comprised 50 Member States. UNHCR expenditure in 1994 amounted to US$1,170m.
Member countries' contributions are voluntary.

The UNHCR was awarded the Nobel Peace Prize in 1955 and 1981.

Headquarters: Case Postale 2500, 1211 Geneva 2 dépôt, Switzerland.
UK Office: Millbank Tower, 21st Floor, London, SW1P 4QP.

High Commissioner: Sadako Ogata (till Dec. 1998).

A post of *High Commissioner for Human Rights* was established by consensus of the General Assembly on 20 Dec. 1993. The High Commissioner is nominated by the UN Secretary General for a 4-year term renewable once. The Commission has 53 members and elects a *Subcommission on Prevention of Discrimination and Protection of Minorities.* The Commission co-ordinates all UN human rights activities and receives complaints of violations which may be made confidentially.

High Commissioner: José Ayala Lasso (Ecuador; appointed Feb. 1994).

INTERGOVERNMENTAL AGENCIES RELATED TO THE UN

The intergovernmental agencies related to the UN by special agreements are separate autonomous organizations which work with the UN and each other through the co-ordinating machinery of the Economic and Social Council. 16 of the agencies (ILO, FAO, UNESCO, WHO, IBRD, IDA, IFC, IMF, ICAO, UPU, ITU, WMO, IMO, WIPO, IFAD and UNIDO) are 'Specialized Agencies' within the terms of the UN Charter, and report annually to the Economic and Social Council.

GATT was absorbed into the World Trade Organization on 1 Jan. 1995. The IAEA was established in 1957 under the aegis of the UN and reports annually to the General Assembly.

INTERNATIONAL ATOMIC ENERGY AGENCY (IAEA)

Origin. The IAEA came into existence on 29 July 1957. Its statute had been approved on 26 Oct. 1956, at an international conference held at UN Headquarters. A relationship agreement links it with the UN. It had 123 member states in 1996.

Functions. (1) To accelerate and enlarge the contribution of atomic energy to peace, health and prosperity throughout the world, and (2) to ensure that assistance provided by it or at its request or under its supervision or control is not used in such a way as to further any military purpose. In addition, under the terms of the Non-Proliferation Treaty, the Treaty of Tlatelolco and the Treaty of Rarotonga, to verify states' obligation to prevent diversion of nuclear fissionable material from peaceful uses to nuclear weapons or other nuclear explosive devices.

The IAEA gives advice and technical assistance to developing countries on nuclear power development, on nuclear safety, on radioactive waste management, on legal aspects of the use of atomic energy, and on prospecting for and exploiting nuclear raw materials; in addition it promotes the use of radiation and isotopes in agriculture, industry, medicine and hydrology through expert services, training courses and fellowships, grants of equipment and supplies, research contracts, scientific meetings and publications. During 1994 there were 1,192 operational projects. This total comprised 1,114 projects continued from 1993, as well as newly-approved core projects for the start of the biennial cycle and 47 training courses, 17 Reserve Fund projects and 1 UN Development Programme Project. These activities involved 3,205 expert assignments while 2,785 persons received training abroad. The IAEA has research laboratories in Austria and Monaco. At Trieste, the International Centre for Theoretical Physics was established in 1964 which is now operated jointly by UNESCO and IAEA.

In Dec. 1994, a total of 199 safeguards agreements were in force with 118 states. Safeguards are the technical means applied by the IAEA to verify that nuclear equipment or materials are used exclusively for peaceful purposes. IAEA safeguards cover more than 95% of the civilian nuclear installations outside the 5 nuclear-weapon states (China, France, Russia, UK and USA). All nuclear-weapon states have opened all (Russia, UK, USA) or some (China, France) of their civilian nuclear plants to IAEA safeguards inspection. Installations in non-nuclear-weapon states under safeguards or containing safeguarded material at 31 Dec. 1994 were 207 power reactors, 167 research reactors and critical assemblies, 12 conversion plants, 40 fuel fabrication plants, 6 reprocessing plants, 11 enrichment plants, and 508 other installations.

Organization. The Statute provides for an annual General Conference, a Board of Governors of 35 members and a Secretariat headed by a Director-General.

Headquarters: Vienna International Centre, PO Box 100, A-1400 Vienna, Austria.

Director-General: Hans Blix (Sweden).

INTERNATIONAL LABOUR ORGANIZATION (ILO)

Origin. The ILO, established in 1919 as an autonomous part of the League of Nations, is an intergovernmental agency with a tripartite structure, in which representatives of governments, employers and workers participate. It seeks through international action to improve labour conditions, raise living standards and promote productive employment. In 1946 the ILO was recognized by the United Nations as a specialized agency. In 1969 it was awarded the Nobel Peace Prize. In 1995 it numbered 173 members.

Functions. One of the ILO's principal functions is the formulation of international standards in the form of International Labour Conventions and Recommendations. Member countries are required to submit Conventions to their competent national authorities with a view to ratification. If a country ratifies a Convention it agrees to bring its laws into line with its terms and to report periodically how these regulations are being applied. More than 6,000 ratifications of 176 Conventions had been deposited by mid-1995. Machinery is available to ascertain whether Conventions thus ratified are effectively applied.

Recommendations do not require ratification, but Member States are obliged to consider them with a view to giving effect to their provisions by legislation or other action. By the end of 1995 the International Labour Conference had adopted 183 recommendations.

Organization. The ILO consists of the International Labour Conference, the Governing Body and the International Labour Office.

The Conference is the supreme deliberative organ of the ILO; it meets annually at Geneva. National delegations are composed of 2 government delegates, 1 employers' delegate and 1 workers' delegate.

The Governing Body, elected by the Conference, is the executive council. It is composed of 28 government members, 14 workers' members and 14 employers' members.

10 governments of countries of industrial importance hold permanent seats on the Governing Body: Brazil, China, Germany, France, India, Italy, Japan, Russia, UK and USA. The remaining 18 government seats were, at the end of 1994, held by Argentina, Australia, Chile, Congo, the Czech Republic, Ghana, Iran, Kenya, Mexico, Nicaragua, Niger, Norway, the Philippines, Qatar, Romania, Tunisia, Venezuela and Zimbabwe.

The Office serves as secretariat, operational headquarters, research centre and publishing house.

The ILO budget for 1996–97 amounted to US$579·5m.

Activities. In addition to its research and advisory activities, the ILO extends technical co-operation to governments under its regular budget and under the UN

Development Programme and Funds-in-Trust in the fields of employment promotion, human resources development (including vocational and management training), development of social institutions, small-scale industries, rural development, social security, industrial safety and hygiene, productivity, etc. Technical co-operation also includes expert missions and a fellowship programme. In 1994, US$113m. was spent on technical co-operation.

In 1994 the technical services offered by the ILO to its tripartite constituents came under scrutiny leading to a re-affirmation of technical co-operation as one of the principal means of ILO action. In 1994 the process of implementing the new Active Partnership Policy made significant progress and the 14 multidisciplinary advisory teams began to engage ILO constituents in a dialogue centred on the identification of Country Objectives to form the basis of the ILO's contribution.

The International Labour Conference (Geneva, June 1995) adopted a Convention and a Recommendation on safety and health in mines.

Labour inspection services are a vital part of national mechanisms for enforcement of law at the workplace. ILO Standards in this field cover most sectors of economic activity, with the exception of non-commercial services. The Conference filled this gap by extending the existing labour inspection Convention no. 81 to this sector, adopting a protocol to the instrument.

In 1960 the ILO established in Geneva the International Institute for Labour Studies. The Institute specializes in advanced education and research on social and labour policy. It brings together for group study experienced persons from all parts of the world—government administrators, trade-union officials, industrial experts, management, university and other specialists. The International Training Centre of the ILO, in Turin, was set up in 1965 to lead the training programmes implemented by the ILO as part of its technical co-operation activities. Member States and the UN system also call on its resources and experience. A UN Staff College was established on the Turin Campus in 1996.

Headquarters: International Labour Office, CH-1211 Geneva 22, Switzerland.
Director-General: Michel Hansenne (Belgium).
Chairman of the Governing Body: Yvon Chotard (France).
London Branch Office: Vincent House, Vincent Square, London, SW1P 2NB.

The ILO has regional offices in Abidjan (for Africa), Bangkok (for Asia and the Pacific), Lima (for Latin America and the Caribbean) and Geneva (for Arab States and Europe).

Further Reading

Publications: Regular periodicals in English, French and Spanish include the *International Labour Review, Labour Law Documents, Bulletin of Labour Statistics, Year Book of Labour Statistics, International Labour Documentation, Official Bulletin* and *Labour Education, World of Work.*

Annual publications: *Yearbook of Labour Statistics; World Labour Report; World Employment.*

FOOD AND AGRICULTURE ORGANIZATION OF THE UNITED NATIONS (FAO)

Origin. The International Conference on Food and Agriculture in May 1943, at Hot Springs, Virginia, set up an Interim Commission in Washington in July which planned the Organization. The Constitution was signed on 16 Oct. 1945 in Quebec City.

Aims and Activities. In 1995 174 countries were members. In 1991 the EU became a member as a 'regional economic integration organization'. Puerto Rico has associate membership. The aims of FAO are to raise levels of nutrition and standards of living; to improve the production and distribution of all food and agricultural products from farms, forests and fisheries; to improve the living conditions of rural populations; and, by these means, to eliminate hunger. One of FAO's priority objectives is to encourage sustainable agriculture and rural development, a long-term strategy for the conservation and management of natural resources. FAO's other great priority is ensuring availability of adequate food supplies, maximizing stability in the flow of supplies and securing access to food by the poor. The People's Participation Programme promotes the involvement of rural people in decision-making and the policy-making and activities affecting their lives.

In carrying out these aims, FAO promotes investment in agriculture, better soil and water management, improved yields of crops and livestock, agricultural research, and the transfer of technology to developing countries. FAO promotes the conservation of natural resources and the rational use of fertilizers and pesticides. It combats animal diseases, promotes the development and sustainable utilization of marine and inland fisheries and the growth of agriculture, and encourages the sustainable management of forest resources. Technical assistance is provided in all these fields and others such as nutrition, agricultural engineering, agrarian reform, development communications, remote sensing for climate and vegetation, and the prevention of post-harvest food losses. FAO also works to maintain global biodiversity with particular emphasis on the genetic diversity of crop plants and domesticated animals, essential for stable agricultural production.

Special FAO programmes help countries prepare for, and provide relief in the event of, emergency food situations, in particular through the setting up of food reserves. The Special Programme for Food Security through Food Production in Low-Income Food-Deficit Countries, launched in 1994, is designed to assist target countries to increase food production and productivity as rapidly as possible, primarily through the widespread adoption by farmers of available improved production technologies and with emphasis on high potential areas. FAO largely provides support for the global co-ordination of the Programme and helps attract funds. The Emergency Prevention System for Transboundary Animal and Plant Pests and Diseases (EMPRES), established in 1994, strengthens FAO's existing contribution to prevention, control and eradication of diseases and pests. The first two EMPRES priorities are locusts and rinderpest. The Global Information and Early Warning System provides current information on the world food situation and identifies countries threatened by shortages to guide potential donors.

The Organization also has a major rôle in the collection, analysis and dissemination of information on agricultural production, including commodities.

FAO sponsors the World Food Programme (WFP) with the UN; WFP uses food commodities, cash and services contributed by member States of the UN to back programmes of social and economic development, as well as for relief in emergency situations.

Finally, FAO acts as a neutral forum for the discussion of issues and advises governments on policy. It convenes international conferences such as the 1992 International Conference on Nutrition, organized with the WHO.

Finance and Administration. The FAO Conference, composed of all members, meets every other year to determine the policy and approve the budget and work programme of FAO. The Council, consisting of 49 member nations elected by the Conference, serves as FAO's governing body between Sessions of the Conference. The budget for the 1996–97 biennium is US$650m., representing a decline over the previous biennium. The budget of FAO's Regular Programme, financed by contributions from member governments, covers the cost of the Organization's secretariat, its Technical Cooperation Programme (TCP) and part of the costs of several special programmes.

The technical assistance programme, however, is funded from extra-budgetary sources. The single largest contributor is the United Nations Development Programme (UNDP), which in 1994 accounted for US$81·3m., or 30% of field project expenditures. Increasingly important are the trust funds that come mainly from donor countries and international financing institutions, totalling US$160·5m., or 58% of technical assistance funds. FAO's contribution under its TCP was some US$33·6m., or 12%. FAO's total field programme expenditure for 1994 was an estimated US$275·4m. In 1994 there were 1,862 field projects in operation, 38% in Africa, 25% in Asia and the Pacific, 13% in Latin America and the Caribbean, 12% in the Near East, 4% in Europe and 8% interregional or global.

The Director-General has a renewable 6-year mandate.

Headquarters: Viale delle Terme di Caracalla, 00100 Rome, Italy.
Director-General: Jacques Diouf (b.1938; Senegal; from 1994).

Further Reading

FAO publications include: Ceres (bi-monthly) 1968 ff; *Unasylva* (quarterly) 1947 ff; *FAO Annual Review* 1971 ff; *The State of Food and Agriculture* (annual), 1947 ff.; *Animal Health Yearbook* (annual), 1957 ff.; *Production Yearbook* (annual), 1947 ff.; *Trade Yearbook* (annual), 1947 ff.; *FAO Commodity Review* (annual), 1961 ff.; *Yearbook of Forest Products Statistics* (annual), 1947 ff.; *Yearbook of Fishery Statistics* (in two volumes); *FAO Fertilizer Yearbook; FAO Plant Protection Bulletin* (quarterly); *Rural Development* (annual).

UNITED NATIONS EDUCATIONAL, SCIENTIFIC AND CULTURAL ORGANIZATION (UNESCO)

Origin. A Conference for the establishment of an Educational, Scientific and Cultural Organization of the United Nations was convened by the government of the UK in association with the government of France in 1945. UNESCO came into being on 4 Nov. 1946.

Functions. The purpose of UNESCO is to contribute to peace and security by promoting collaboration among the nations through education, science and culture in order to further universal respect for justice, for the rule of law and for the human rights and fundamental freedoms which are affirmed for the peoples of the world, without distinction of race, sex, language or religion, by the UN Charter. As part of its basically ethical purpose it has the task of constructing the defences of peace in the minds of human beings. The third Medium-Term Plan for 1990-95 established UNESCO's policy and strategy, giving priority to the development of human and natural resources and communication and the World Decade for Cultural Development (1988-97).

Activities. The education programme has 3 main objectives: The extension of education; the improvement of education; and life-long education for living in a world community.

To train teachers specialized in the techniques of fundamental education UNESCO has established regional and sub-regional offices for education in Beirut, Bridgetown, Bucharest (higher education), Caracas, Dakar, Harare, Kuwait and Santiago. UNESCO seeks to promote the progressive application of the right to free and compulsory education for all and to improve the quality of education. UNESCO also seeks to promote international scientific cooperation. It encourages scientific research designed to improve living conditions. Science co-operation offices have been set up in Cairo, Jakarta, Nairobi, New Delhi, Montevideo and Venice.

In the field of communication, UNESCO endeavours, by disseminating information, carrying out research and providing advice, to increase the scope and quality of press, film and radio services throughout the world.

In the cultural field, UNESCO assists member states in studying and preserving both the physical and the non-physical heritage of each society. In 1972 the General Conference adopted the Convention concerning the Protection of the World Cultural and Natural Heritage under which a list of sites and monuments of exceptional interest and universal value whose protection is the responsibility of all mankind has been drawn up.

In the social sciences UNESCO helps in the development of research and teaching facilities and focuses on questions concerning peace, human rights, philosophy, youth and development studies.

Organization. The organs are a General Conference (composed of representatives from each member state), an Executive Board (consisting of 51 government representatives elected by the General Conference) and a Secretariat. The 26th general conference in Oct.–Nov. 1991 amended its constitution by consensus, making the members of the Executive Board direct representatives of their countries. UNESCO had 185 members in 1995. The UK and the USA are not members.

National commissions act as liaison groups between UNESCO and the educational, scientific and cultural life of their own countries.

Budget for 1994–95: $455,490,000.

Headquarters: UNESCO House, 7 Place de Fontenoy, Paris.
Director-General: Federico Mayor Zaragoza (Spain).

Further Reading

Periodicals. Museum (quarterly, English and French); *International Social Science Journal* (quarterly, English and French); *Impact of Science on Society* (quarterly, English and French); *Unesco Courier* (monthly, English, French and Spanish); *Prospects* (quarterly, English, French and Spanish); *Copyright Bulletin* (twice-yearly, English and French); *Unesco News* (English and French); *Nature and Resources* (quarterly, English, French and Spanish).

WORLD HEALTH ORGANIZATION (WHO)

Origin. An International Conference, convened by the UN Economic and Social Council, to consider a single health organization resulted in the adoption on 22 July 1946 of the constitution of the World Health Organization. This constitution came into force on 7 April 1948.

Structure. The principal organs of WHO are the World Health Assembly, the Executive Board and the Secretariat. Each of the 190 member states has the right to be represented at the Assembly, which meets annually in Geneva. The 31-member Executive Board is composed of technically qualified health experts designated by as many member states elected by the Assembly. The Secretariat consists of technical and administrative staff headed by a Director-General. Health activities in member countries are carried out through regional organizations which have been established in Africa (regional office, Brazzaville), South-East Asia (New Delhi), Europe (Copenhagen), Eastern Mediterranean (Alexandria) and Western Pacific (Manila). The Pan American Sanitary Bureau in Washington serves as the Regional Office of WHO for the Americas.

Functions. WHO's objective, as stated in the first article of the Constitution is 'the attainment by all peoples of the highest possible level of health'. As the directing and co-ordinating authority on international health it establishes and maintains collaboration with the UN, specialized agencies, government health administrations, professional and other groups concerned with health. The Constitution also directs WHO to assist governments to strengthen their health services, to stimulate and advance work to eradicate diseases, to promote maternal and child health, mental health, medical research and the prevention of accidents; to improve standards of teaching and training in the health professions, and of nutrition, housing, sanitation, working conditions and other aspects of environment health. The Organization also is empowered to propose conventions, agreements and regulations and make recommendations about international health matters; to revise the international nomenclature of diseases, causes of death and public health practices; to develop, establish and promote international standards concerning foods, biological, pharmaceutical and similar substances.

Methods of work. Co-operation in country projects is undertaken only on the request of the government concerned, through the 6 regional offices of the Organization. Worldwide technical services are made available by headquarters. Expert committees whose members are chosen from the 55 advisory panels of experts meet to advise the Director-General on a given subject. Scientific groups and consultative meetings are called for similar purposes. To further the education of health personnel of all categories, seminars, technical conferences and training courses are organized and advisors, consultants and lecturers are provided. WHO awards fellowships for study to nationals of member countries.

Activities. The main thrust of WHO's activities in recent years has been towards promoting national, regional and global strategies for the attainment of the main social target of the Member States for the coming years: 'Health for All by the Year 2000', or the attainment by all citizens of the world of a level of health that will permit them to lead a socially and economically productive life.

Almost all countries indicated a high level of political commitment to this goal, and guiding principles for formulating corresponding strategies and plans of action were prepared.

The 48th World Health Assembly which met in May 1995 approved a programme budget of US$1,900m. for the global work of the WHO in 1996–97. During the 47th World Health Assembly, in May 1994, decisions taken during its annual session included the restoration to South Africa of its full rights and privileges, suspended for the past 30 years.

The Assembly adopted numerous resolutions on public health issues including:

Emergency and Humanitarian Action. The Assembly recognized that disaster reduction is an integral part of sustainable development. Each country should strengthen its capacity to protect its people. Member states are urged to include disaster reduction and emergency preparedness in their national development plans and make special national budgetary allocations for this purpose.

Intensified Co-operation with Countries in Greatest Need. The Assembly recognized poverty as the most fundamental obstacle to health and development, as well as a permanent menace to world peace. The international community is asked to mobilize additional resources for health development in countries in greatest need in co-ordination with WHO.

Reproductive Health; WHO's Role in the Global Strategy. Having acknowledged reproductive health as a central component of women's health, the Assembly urged the Director-General to pursue his efforts to increase resources for strengthening reproductive health in the context of primary health care, including family health. An important action to be undertaken is the promotion of ethical practices in the human reproduction field to protect the health and human rights of individuals in different social and cultural settings.

New, Emerging, and Re-emerging Infectious Diseases. There was much concern at the lack of co-ordinated global surveillance to monitor, report and respond to new emerging and re-emerging infectious diseases, which are on the increase. WHO was asked to strengthen the active surveillance of infectious diseases, ensuring early detection of outbreaks and their prompt identification, as well as to foster applied research.

Control of Diarrhoeal Diseases and Acute Respiratory Infections. These remain the 2 major causes of child mortality, accounting, together with malaria, measles and malnutrition, for 7 out of 10 deaths in children under 5 years in the developing world. The Assembly endorsed the integrated management of the sick child as an essential tool for reaching the 1990 Summit goal for the reduction of childhood mortality by 50% by the year 2000.

An International Strategy for Tobacco Control. The Assembly requested the Director-General to develop an international instrument such as guidelines, a declaration, or an International Convention on Tobacco Control to be adopted by the UN, taking into account existing trade and other conventions and treaties. The Assembly also commended the ICAO response to ban smoking on all international flights as of 1 July 1996.

Renewing the Health for All Strategy. The Assembly requested the Director-General to take the necessary steps for renewing the Health for All strategy by developing a new holistic global health policy based on the concepts of equity and solidarity. In addition, the Director-General was requested to redefine WHO's mission and to take the necessary measures for WHO to secure high level political endorsement of a health charter based on the new global health policy.

Health Days. World Health Day is observed on 7 April every year, and is used to promote awareness of a particular health topic (poliomyelitis in 1995). The theme chosen for 1996 World Health Day is Healthy Cities with the slogan 'Healthy Cities for Better Life'. World No-Tobacco Day held on 31 May 1995 had 'Tobacco costs more than you think' as its theme. The slogan for 1996 World No-Tobacco is 'Sports and the Arts without Tobacco'. 'World AIDS Day' was celebrated on 1 Dec. 1995 with 'Shared Rights, Shared Responsibilities' as its slogan.

Headquarters: Avenue Appia, CH-1211 Geneva 27, Switzerland.
Director-General: Dr Hiroshi Nakajima (Japan).

Further Reading

Annual Report on World Health. 1995 ff.
World Health Forum (from 1980, quarterly: Arabic, Chinese, English, French, Russian and Spanish)
Bulletin of WHO (quarterly, 1947–51; 6 issues a year from 1978; bilingual English/French, Arabic, Russian; selection in Chinese)
International Digest of Health Legislation (quarterly, from 1948; English and French)
World Health. 1957 ff. (6 issues a year; English, French, German, Russian and Spanish; and 4 issues a year. Arabic and Farsi)
Health and Safety Guides, 1987 ff.
International Statistical Classification of Diseases and Related Health Problems. 10th revision, vols. 1–3. 1992–94
WHO Technical Report Series, 1950 ff. (Arabic, Chinese, English, French, Russian, Spanish)
WHO AIDS series, 1988 *ff.* (Arabic, Chinese, English, French, Russian, Spanish)
Public Health Papers, 1959 ff. (Arabic, Chinese, English, French, Russian, Spanish)
World Health Statistics Annual (from 1952; English, French and Russian)
World Health Statistics Quarterly (monthly, 1947–76 then quarterly; bilingual English/ French)
Weekly Epidemiological Record (from 1926; bilingual English/French)
WHO Drug Information (from 1987, quarterly; English and French)

INTERNATIONAL MONETARY FUND (IMF)

The International Monetary Fund was established on 27 Dec. 1945 as an independent international organization and began financial operations on 1 March 1947; its relationship with the UN is defined in an agreement of mutual co-operation which came into force on 15 Nov. 1947. The first amendment to the IMF's articles creating the special drawing right (SDR; ISO code, XDR) took effect on 28 July 1969. The second amendment took effect on 1 April 1978. The third amendment came into force on 11 Nov. 1992; it allows for the suspension of voting and related rights of a member which persists in its failure to settle its outstanding obligations to the IMF.

The capital resources of the IMF comprise SDRs and currencies that the members pay under quotas calculated for them when they join the IMF. An increase of almost 60% in IMF quotas became effective in Nov. 1992. As a result, members' quotas rose to SDR 144,800m. (about US$202,000m.) in 1994. The initial quotas of members which have joined the IMF since 30 April 1992 account for SDR 6,600m. of the quota increase. Members' quotas are linked to their drawing rights on the IMF under both regular and special facilities, their voting power, and their share of SDR allocations. Every IMF member is required to subscribe to the IMF an amount equal to its quota. An amount not exceeding 25% of the quota has to be paid in reserve assets, the balance in the member's own currency. The members with the largest quotas are: 1st, the USA; joint 2nd, Germany and Japan; joint 4th, France and the UK.

The IMF is authorized under its Articles of Agreement to supplement its resources by borrowing. In Jan. 1962, a 4-year agreement was concluded with 10 industrial members (Belgium, Canada, France, Germany, Italy, Japan, Netherlands, Sweden, UK, USA) who undertook to lend the IMF up to US$6,000m. in their own currencies, if this should be needed to forestall or cope with an impairment of the international monetary system. Switzerland subsequently joined the group. These arrangements, known as the General Arrangements to Borrow (GAB), have been extended several times and were renewed in Oct. 1992 for 5 years from 26 Dec. 1993. In early 1983 agreement was reached to increase the credit arrangements under the GAB to SDR 17,000m.; to permit use of GAB resources in transactions with IMF members that are not GAB participants; to authorize Swiss participation; and to permit borrowing arrangements with non-participating members to be associated with the GAB. Saudi Arabia and the IMF have entered into such an arrangement under which the IMF will be able to borrow up to SDR 1,500m. to assist in financing purchases by any member for the same purpose and under the same circumstances as in the GAB. The changes became effective by 26 Dec. 1983. The IMF has also borrowed from member countries and official institutions for 2 oil facilities, a supplementary financing facility and to finance enlarged access by members.

Purposes: To promote international monetary co-operation, the expansion of international trade and exchange rate stability; to assist in the removal of exchange restrictions and the establishment of a multilateral system of payments; and to alleviate any serious disequilibrium in members' international balance of payments by making the financial resources of the IMF available to them, usually subject to economic policy conditions to ensure the revolving nature of IMF resources.

Activities. Each member of the IMF undertakes a broad obligation to collaborate with the IMF and other members to ensure orderly exchange arrangements and to promote a system of stable exchange rates. In addition, members are subject to certain obligations relating to domestic and external policies that can affect the balance of payments and the exchange rate. The IMF makes its resources available, under proper safeguards, to its members to meet short-term or medium-term payments difficulties. The first allocation of SDRs was made on 1 Jan. 1970 with five SDR allocations since then. SDRs in existence now total SDR 21,400m. To further enhance its balance of payments assistance to its members the IMF established a compensatory financing facility on 27 Feb. 1963, temporary oil facilities in 1974 and 1975, a trust fund in 1976, and an extended facility for medium-term assistance to members with special balance of payments problems on 13 Sept. 1974. In March 1986, it established the structural adjustment facility to provide assistance to low-income countries. In Dec. 1987, the IMF established the enhanced structural adjustment facility (ESAF) to provide further assistance to low-income countries facing high levels of indebtedness. In Aug. 1988, the compensatory and contingency financing facility was established, succeeding the compensatory financing facility; the new facility provides broader protection to members pursuing IMF-supported adjustment programmes. In April 1993 the IMF established the systemic transformation facility (STF) to assist members facing balance of payments difficulties arising from severe disruptions in their trade and payments arrangements attributable to a shift from trading at non-market prices to multilateral, market-based trade. Because of the importance of continuing concessional ESAF support, the IMF is studying the options for continued financing and adaptation of the ESAF.

The Interim Committee of the Board of Governors on the International Monetary System and the Joint Ministerial Committee of the Boards of Governors of the World Bank and the IMF on the Transfer of Real Resources to Developing Countries (Development Committee) were established at the 1974 Annual Meetings and held their initial meetings in Jan. 1975. They meet twice a year. Details of the reform of the international monetary system were incorporated in the second amendment of the IMF's Articles of Agreement, effective April 1978. In order to oversee the compliance of members with their obligations under the Articles of Agreement, the IMF is required to exercise firm surveillance over their exchange rate policies.

Organization. The highest authority is the Board of Governors on which each member government is represented. Normally the Governors meet once a year, although the Governors may take votes by mail or other means between Annual Meetings. The Board of Governors has delegated many of its powers to the 24 executive directors in Washington, who are appointed or elected by individual member countries or groups of countries. Each appointed director has voting power proportionate to the quota of the government he or she represents, while each elected director casts all the votes of the countries represented.

The managing director is selected by the executive directors and serves as chairman of the Executive Board, but may not vote except in case of a tie. The term of office is for 5 years, but may be extended or terminated at the discretion of the executive directors. The managing director is responsible for the ordinary business of the IMF, under the direction of the executive directors, and supervises a staff of about 2,100. There are 3 deputy managing directors.

There were 181 members of the IMF as of Dec. 1995.

Headquarters: 700 19th St. NW, Washington, D.C., 20431. Offices in Paris and Geneva.

Managing Director: Michel Camdessus (France).

Further Reading

Publications. Summary Proceedings of Annual Meetings of the Board of Governors.—Annual Report of the Executive Board.—Selected Decisions of the International Monetary Fund and Selected Documents.—International Financial Statistics (monthly).—*IMF Survey* (biweekly).—*Balance of Payments Statistics.* Washington, monthly.—*IMF Staff Papers* (four times a year). Washington, from Feb. 1950.—*IMF Occasional Papers.—IMF Pamphlets.—IMF Economic Reviews* [of the economies of member countries].—*Annual Report on Exchange Arrangements and Exchange Restrictions.* Washington, 1950 ff.—*Finance and Development.* Washington, from June 1964 (quarterly).—*Direction of Trade Statistics.* Washington (quarterly). *IMF World Economic and Financial Surveys* (including the semi-annual *World Economic Outlook).* Washington. *Government Finance Statistics Yearbook. The International Monetary Fund, 1945–65: Twenty Years of International Monetary Co-operation.* 3 vols. Washington, 1969.—de Vries, M. G., *The International Monetary Fund, 1966–1971: The System Under Stress.* 2 vols. Washington D.C. 1976.—*The International Monetary Fund 1972–1978: Co-operation on Trial.* 3 vols. Washington D.C., 1985

Humphreys, N. K., *Historical Dictionary of the International Monetary Fund.* Metuchen (NJ), 1994

James, H., *International Monetary Cooperation since Bretton Woods.* OUP, 1996

Salda, A. C. M., *The International Monetary Fund.* [Bibliography) Oxford and New Brunswick (NJ), 1993

INTERNATIONAL BANK FOR RECONSTRUCTION AND DEVELOPMENT (IBRD; WORLD BANK)

Conceived at the Bretton Woods Conference, July 1944, the Bank began operations in June 1946. Its purpose is to provide funds and technical assistance to facilitate economic development in its poorer member countries.

The Bank obtains its funds from the following sources: Capital paid in by member countries; sales of its own securities; sales of parts of its loans; repayments; and net earnings. The subscribed capital of the Bank amounted to $176,438m. at 30 June 1995. A resolution of the Board of Governors of 27 April 1988 provides that the paid-in portion of the shares authorized to be subscribed under it will be 3%. At 30 June 1995 authorized capital stock totalled $184,050m. Outstanding medium- and long-term borrowings had reached $104,507m. by 30 June 1995. The Bank is self-supporting. Its net earnings for year ending 30 June 1995 amounted to $1,354m.

By 30 June 1995 the Bank had made 3,794 loans totalling $266,251m. in 127 of its 178 member countries. Lending was for the following purposes: Agriculture and rural development, $45,904m.; education, $13,218m.; energy, $53,916m.; environment, $1,213m.; financial sector, $28,806m; industry, $16,829m.; mining, $3,119m.; multi-sector, $25,123m.; population, health and nutrition, $4,180m.; public-sector management, $4,995m.; social sector, $755m.; telecommunications, $4,850m.; transportation, $39,615m.; urban development, $11,826m.; water supply and sewerage, $11,914m. In order to eliminate wasteful overlapping of development assistance and to ensure that the funds available are used to the best possible effect, the Bank has organized consortia or consultative groups of aid-giving nations for many countries. Consultative groups include those for Bangladesh, Belarus, Bolivia, Bulgaria, Egypt, Ethiopia, Jordan, Kazakhstan, Kenya, Kyrgyzstan, Macedonia, Malaŵi, Mauritania, Moldova, Mozambique, Nicaragua, Pakistan, Peru, Romania, Sierra Leone, Tanzania, the [Palestinian] West Bank and Gaza

Strip, Zambia, Zimbabwe and the Caribbean Group for Co-operation in Economic Development. The Bank furnishes a wide variety of technical assistance. It acts as executing agency for a number of preinvestment surveys financed by the UN Development Programme. Resident missions have been established in 64 developing member countries as well as regional offices for East and West Africa, the Baltic States and South-East Asia, primarily to assist in the preparation and implementation of projects. The Bank maintains a staff college, the Economic Development Institute in Washington, DC, for senior officials of the member countries.

Headquarters: 1818 H St., NW, Washington, DC, 20433, USA. *European office:* 66 avenue d'Iéna, 75116 Paris, France. *London office:* New Zealand House, Haymarket, SW1Y 4TE, England. *Tokyo office:* Kokusai Building, 1–1, Marunouchi 3-chome, Chiyoda-ku, Tokyo 100, Japan.
President: James D. Wolfensohn (b. 1934; USA).

Further Reading

Publications. Annual Reports. 1946 ff.—*Summary Proceedings of Annual Meetings.* 1947 ff.—*The World Bank & International Finance Company.* 1986.—*The World Bank Atlas.* 1967 ff.—*Catalog of Publications,* 1986 ff.—*World Development Report.* 1978 ff.
Nelson, P. J., *The World Bank and Non-Government Organizations: the Limits of Apolitical Development.* London, 1995
Salda, A. C. M., *World Bank:* [Bibliography]. Oxford and New Brunswick (NJ), 1993
Wilson, C. R., *The World Bank Group: A Guide to Information Sources.* New York, 1991

INTERNATIONAL DEVELOPMENT ASSOCIATION (IDA)

A lending agency which came into existence on 24 Sept. 1960. Administered by the World Bank, IDA is open to all members of the Bank.

IDA makes loans at 0%–1% interest to countries with an annual *per capita* GNP of less than US$866 (1995 rate). IDA credits are made to governments only. It had committed $90,078m. for 2,593 development projects in 91 countries by 30 June 1995. Its resources consist of subscriptions and general replenishments from its more industrialized and developed members, special contributions, and transfers from the net earnings of the Bank.

In the triennial budget 'IDA10', covering July 1993–June 1996, the USA reduced its contributions by 40%, causing a shortfall of US$23,700m. Canada and Germany have also reduced their contributions. 'IDA11' covers July 1996–June 1999.

INTERNATIONAL FINANCE CORPORATION (IFC)

The Corporation, a member of the IBRD (World Bank), was established in July 1956. Paid-in capital at 30 June 1995 was $1,900m., subscribed by 168 member countries. In addition, it has retained earnings of $1,700m. IFC supplements the activities of the World Bank by encouraging the growth of productive private enterprises in developing member countries. Chiefly, IFC makes investments in the form of subscriptions to the share capital of privately owned companies, or long-term loans, or both. The Corporation will help finance new ventures and assist established enterprises to expand, improve or diversify. It also provides a variety of advisory services to public and private sector clients.

During 1994–95, the IFC approved US$2,900m. in financing for its own account 213 private-sector projects in 67 developing countries.

President: James D. Wolfensohn (b. 1934; USA).
Headquarters: 1850 I St., NW, Washington, D.C., 20433, USA.

Publications. Annual Reports. 1956 ff.—*What IFC Does.* 1988,—*How to Work with IFC,* 1988

INTERNATIONAL CIVIL AVIATION ORGANIZATION (ICAO)

Origin. The Convention providing for the establishment of the ICAO was drawn up by the International Civil Aviation Conference held in Chicago in 1944. A Provisional International Civil Aviation Organization (PICAO) operated for 20 months until the formal establishment of ICAO on 4 April 1947.

The Convention on International Civil Aviation superseded the provisions of the Paris Convention of 1919 and the Pan American Convention on Air Navigation of 1928.

Functions. It assists international civil aviation by establishing technical standards for safety and efficiency of air navigation and promoting simpler procedures at borders; develops regional plans for ground facilities and services needed for international flying; disseminates air-transport statistics and prepares studies on aviation economics; fosters the development of air law conventions. As an administrative arm of the UN Development Programme it provides technical assistance to states in developing civil aviation programmes.

Organization. The principal organs of ICAO are an Assembly, consisting of all members of the Organization, and a Council, which is composed of 33 states elected by the Assembly, for 3 years, and meets in virtually continuous session. In electing these states, the Assembly must give adequate representation to: (1) states of major importance in air transport; (2) states which make the largest contribution to the provision of facilities for the international civil air navigation; (3) those states not otherwise included whose election will ensure that all major geographical areas of the world are represented. The main subsidiary bodies are: The Air Navigation Commission, composed of 15 members appointed by the Council; the Committee on Joint Support of Air Navigation Services; the Personnel Committee; the Finance Committee; the Committee on Unlawful Interference; the Technical Co-operation Committee; the Air Transport Committee, all of the foregoing committees being open to Council members; and the Legal Committee, on which all members of ICAO may be represented. There are 183 members. Budget for 1996: US$50,340,000; 1997: US$52,191,000; 1998: US$54,596,000.

Headquarters: 1000 Sherbroke St. West, Montreal, Quebec, Canada H3A 2R2.
President: Dr Assad Kotaite (Lebanon).
Secretary-General: Dr Philippe Rochat (Switzerland).

Annual Report of the Council. (Arabic, English, French, Russian, Spanish)
ICAO Journal (10 times a year in English, French, Spanish; quarterly in Russian)

UNIVERSAL POSTAL UNION (UPU)

Origin. The UPU was established on 1 July 1875, when the Universal Postal Convention adopted by the Postal Congress of Berne on 9 Oct. 1874 came into force. In 1994 there were 189 member countries.

Functions. The aim of the UPU is to assure the organization and perfection of the various postal services and to promote, in this field, the development of international collaboration. To this end, the members of UPU are united in a single postal territory for the reciprocal exchange of correspondence.

Organization. The UPU is composed of a Universal Postal Congress which usually meets every 5 years, a Council of Administration consisting of 41 members which meets annually and is responsible for supervising the affairs of the UPU between Congresses, a Postal Operations Council which consists of 40 members, and an International Bureau, which functions as the permanent secretariat.

A Specialized Agency of the UN since 1948, the Union is governed by the Constitution of the UPU adopted at the 1964 Vienna Congress, and amended by the 1969 (Tokyo), 1974 (Lausanne), 1984 (Hamburg), 1989 (Washington) and 1994 (Seoul) Additional Protocols.

Budget for 1996: 33,376,400 Swiss francs.

Headquarters: Weltpoststrasse 4, 3000, Berne 15, Switzerland.
Director-General: Thomas E. Leavey (USA).

Further Reading

Acts of the Universal Postal Union: revised in Washington in 1989 and annotated by the

International Bureau. vols 1–4.—*The Postal Union* (quarterly, Arabic, Chinese, English, French, German, Spanish, Russian).—*The UPU: Its Foundation and Development.* Berne, 1991.

INTERNATIONAL TELECOMMUNICATION UNION (ITU)

Origin. In 1932, at Madrid, the Union decided to merge the Telegraph Convention adopted in 1865 and the Radiotelegraph Convention adopted in 1906 into a single International Telecommunication Convention. It also decided to change its name to International Telecommunication Union to better reflect all its new responsibilities. The ITU has been governed since 1 Jan. 1984 by the International Telecommunication Convention adopted in Nairobi in 1982. A constitution and convention were adopted at Nice in 1989. This will come into force after 55 members have ratified it.

Functions. (1) to maintain and extend international co-operation for the improvement and rational use of telecommunications of all kinds, as well as to promote and to offer technical assistance to developing countries in the field of telecommunications; (2) to promote the development of technical facilities and their most efficient operation with a view to improving the efficiency of telecommunication services, increasing their usefulness and making them, so far as possible, generally available to the public; (3) to harmonize the actions of nations in the attainment of those ends.

Organization. The ITU consists of the Plenipotentiary Conference, Administrative Conferences, the Administrative Council of 46 members, and of 5 permanent organs (the General Secretariat, the International Frequency Registration Board, and 2 international consultative committees, one for radio and one for telephone and telegraph and the Telecommunications Development Bureau).

185 countries were members in 1995.

Budget, 1995: 164m. Swiss francs.

Headquarters: Place des Nations, CH-1211 Geneva 20, Switzerland.
Secretary-General: Dr Pekka Tarjanne (Finland).

INTERNATIONAL TELECOMMUNICATIONS SATELLITE ORGANIZATION (INTELSAT)

Origins. Intelsat was founded in 1964 to own and operate the world-wide commercial communications satellite system.

Membership and Funding. In 1995 there were 136 member states. Costs are borne by members in proportion to their usage of the system.

Objectives. Intelsat provides international telephone and TV services, a digital data transmission service (Intelnet), a business service (IBS) and domestic telecommunications services.

Organization. Representatives of member states' governments meet every other year in the *Assembly of Parties to the Agreement* to consider policy. Practical aspects of the system are dealt with at the annual *Meeting of Signatories*. There is a 27-member Board of Governors.

Director-General: Irving Goldstein (USA).
Headquarters: 3400 International Drive NW, Washington DC 20008–3098, USA.

WORLD METEOROLOGICAL ORGANIZATION (WMO)

Origin. A Conference of Directors of the International Meteorological Organization (set up in 1873), meeting in Washington in 1947, adopted a Convention creating the World Meteorological Organization. The WMO Convention became effective on 23 March 1950, and WMO was formally established on 19 March 1951, when the first session of its Congress was convened in Paris. An agreement to bring WMO into relationship with the United Nations was approved by this Congress and came into force on 21 Dec. 1951 with its approval by the UN General Assembly.

Functions. (1) To facilitate world-wide co-operation in the establishment of networks of stations for the making of meteorological observations as well as hydrological or other geophysical observations related to meteorology, and to promote the establishment and maintenance of meteorological centres charged with the provision of meteorological and related services; (2) to promote the establishment and maintenance of systems for the rapid exchange of meteorological and related information; (3) to promote standardization of meteorological and related observations and to ensure the uniform publication of observations and statistics; (4) to further the application of meteorology to aviation, shipping, water problems, agriculture and other human activities; (5) to promote activities in operational hydrology and to further close co-operation between meteorological and hydrological services; and (6) to encourage research and training in meteorology and, as appropriate, to assist in co-ordinating the international aspects of such research and training.

Organization. WMO is an inter-governmental organization of 176 member states and 5 member territories responsible for the operation of their own meteorological services. Congress, which is the supreme body of WMO, meets every 4 years and approves policy, programme and the budget, and adopts regulations. The Executive Council meets at least yearly to prepare studies and recommendations for Congress and supervises the implementation of Congress resolutions and regulations. It has 36 members comprising the President and 3 Vice-Presidents of WMO, Presidents of the 6 Regional Associations (Africa, Asia, South America, North and Central America, South-West Pacific, Europe) and 26 members elected in their personal capacity. There are 8 Technical Commissions composed of experts nominated by members of WMO.

A permanent Secretariat is maintained in Geneva with 3 regional offices for Africa, Asia and the Pacific, and the Americas.

Budget for 1996–99: 255m. Swiss francs.

Secretary-General: G. O. P. Obasi (Nigeria).
Headquarters: Case postale No. 2300, CH-1211, Geneva 2, Switzerland.

Publications. WMO Bulletin. (quarterly; in English, French, Russian and Spanish).—*WMO Annual Report* (in English, French, Russian and Spanish).

INTERNATIONAL MARITIME ORGANIZATION (IMO)

Origin. The International Maritime Organization, until 1982 known as Inter-Governmental Maritime Consultative Organization (IMCO), was established as a specialized agency of the UN by a convention drawn up at the UN Maritime Conference held at Geneva in 1948. The Convention became effective on 17 March 1958 when it had been ratified by 21 countries, including 7 with at least 1m. gross tons of shipping each. The IMO started operations in 1959.

Functions. To facilitate co-operation among governments on technical matters affecting merchant shipping, especially concerning safety at sea; to prevent and control marine pollution caused by ships; to facilitate international maritime traffic. The IMO is responsible for convening international maritime conferences and for drafting international maritime conventions. It also provides technical assistance to countries wishing to develop their maritime activities.

Organization. The IMO had 152 members (and 2 associate members) in 1995. The Assembly, composed of all member states, normally meets every 2 years. The Council of 32 member states acts as governing body between Assembly sessions. The Maritime Safety Committee deals with all technical questions relating to maritime safety. It has established several sub-committees to deal with specific problems. There is a secretariat.

The IMO is depositary authority for international conventions regulating maritime affairs.

Headquarters: 4 Albert Embankment, London SE1 7SR.
Secretary-General: William O'Neil (Canada).

IMO News

WORLD TRADE ORGANIZATION (WTO)

Origin. The General Agreement on Tariffs and Trade (GATT) entered into force on 1 Jan. 1948. Its 23 original signatories were members of a Preparatory Committee appointed by the UN Economic and Social Council to draft the charter for a proposed International Trade Organization. Since this charter was never ratified, the General Agreement remained the only international instrument laying down trade rules. In Dec. 1993 there were 111 contracting parties and a further 22 countries applying GATT rules on a *de facto* basis. On 15 April 1994 trade ministers of 125 countries signed the final act of the GATT Uruguay Round of negotiations at Marrakesh, bringing the WTO into being on 1 Jan. 1995. The object of the act is the liberalization of world trade. By it member countries undertake to apply fair trade rules covering commodities, services and intellectual property. It provides for the lowering of tariffs on industrial goods and tropical products, the abolition of import duties on a variety of items, the progressive abolition of quotas on garments and textiles, the gradual reduction of trade-distorting subsidies and import barriers, agreements on intellectual property and trade in services. (For details of GATT *see* THE STATESMAN'S YEAR-BOOK, 1994–95, pp. 25–28).

Functions. Members are required to accept the results of the Uruguay Round talks in their entirety, and subscribe to all the WTO's agreements and disciplines. There are no enforcement procedures, however; decisions are ultimately reached by consensus.

Organization. A 2-yearly ministerial meeting is the ultimate policy-making body. A 110-member *General Council* has some 30 subordinate councils and committees. The *Dispute Settlement Body* was set up to deal with disputes between countries. Appeals against its verdicts are heard by a 7-member *Appellate Body* sitting for 60 days a year. In 1996 it was composed of representatives of Egypt, EU, Japan, New Zealand, Philippines, USA and Uruguay. Dispute panels may be set up *ad hoc*, and objectors to their ruling may appeal to the *Appellate Body*, whose decision is binding. Refusal to comply at this stage results in the application of trade sanctions. Each appeal is heard by 3 of the *Appellate Body* members. Before cases are heard by Dispute Panels there is a 60-day consultation period.

The previous GATT Secretariat now serves the WTO.

To assist the trade of developing countries, GATT established in 1964 the *International Trade Centre* (since 1968 operated jointly with the UN, the latter acting through the UN Conference on Trade and Development) to provide information and training on export markets and marketing techniques.

The WTO has no resources of its own other than its operating budget. Budget for 1996: 115m. Swiss francs.

Director-General: Renato Ruggiero (b. 1930; Italy).

Headquarters: Centre William Rappard, 154 rue de Lausanne, 1211 Geneva 21, Switzerland.

WORLD INTELLECTUAL PROPERTY ORGANIZATION (WIPO)

Origin. The Convention establishing WIPO was signed at Stockholm in 1967 by 51 countries, and entered into force in April 1970. In Dec. 1974 WIPO became a specialized agency of the UN. WIPO took over the functions of the United International Bureaux for the Protection of Intellectual Property (BIRPI), established in 1893 to administer the affairs of the 2 principal international intellectual property treaties – the Paris Convention for the Protection of Industrial Property of 1883 and the Berne Convention for the Protection of Literary and Artistic Works of 1886.

Functions. WIPO is responsible for the promotion of the protection of intellectual property throughout the world. Intellectual property comprises two main branches: Industrial property (chiefly in inventions, trademarks and industrial designs) and copyright and neighbouring rights (chiefly in literary, musical, artistic, photographic and audiovisual works). WIPO administers various international treaties, of which the most important are the Paris and Berne Conventions.

In 1995, 2 new international treaties, the Eurasian Patent Convention, and the Protocol relating to the Madrid Agreement concerning the International Registration of Marks, came into force. Operations under these started on 1 Jan. 1996 and 1 April 1996 respectively

WIPO carries out a programme of activities to promote the protection of intellectual property, including a substantial programme of development co-operation for the benefit of developing countries. As regards standard-setting, WIPO prepares new treaties concerning the protection of intellectual property and undertakes the revision of existing treaties administered by the Organization. It carries out studies on issues in the field of intellectual property that could be the subject of model laws or guidelines for implementation at the national or international levels and maintains international registration services (patents, trademarks, industrial designs, appellation of origins and audio-visual works). The WIPO Arbitration Center resolves disputes between private parties.

Membership of WIPO is open to any state which is a member of at least one of the unions created by the Paris Convention and the Berne Convention and to other States which are members of the UN organizations, are party to the Statute of the International Court of Justice, or are invited to join by the General Assembly of WIPO. Membership of the unions is open to any state. The number of member states was 157 in 1996.

Organization. WIPO has 3 governing bodies: the *General Assembly* (countries members of WIPO, provided they are members also of the Paris and/or Berne Unions), the *Conference* (all countries members of WIPO) and the *Co-ordination Committee* (countries elected among the membership of WIPO and the Paris and Berne Unions). The conference, among its functions, adopts the biennial budget and establishes the biennial programme of legal and technical assistance. In addition, the Paris and Berne Unions have Assemblies and Executive Committees with functions similar to those of the WIPO bodies in respect of the biennial budgets and programmes of the Unions.

The executive head of WIPO is the Director General, who is elected by the General Assembly.

The *WIPO Permanent Committees for Development Co-operation Related to Industrial Property* and *Related to Copyright and Neighbouring Rights* plan and review activities in the said fields; the *WIPO Permanent Committee on Industrial Property Information* is responsible for intergovernmental co-operation in industrial property documentation and information matters such as the standardization and exchange of patent documents.

The budget for 1996–97 was Sw. Fr. 300m.

WIPO had an international staff of 517 in 1996, nationals of 64 countries. Its working languages are Arabic, English, French, Russian and Spanish.

Director-General: Dr Arpad Bogsch (USA).
Headquarters: 34, chemin des Colombettes, 1211 Geneva 20, Switzerland.

Further Reading

Periodicals. Industrial Property and Copyright (monthly, also in French; bi-monthly, in Spanish).—*PCT Gazette* (weekly, in English and French)—*PCT Newsletter* (monthly)—*International Designs Bulletin* (monthly, in English and French)—*Les Marques Internationales* (monthly)—*Intellectual Property in Asia and the Pacific* (quarterly).

INTERNATIONAL FUND FOR AGRICULTURAL DEVELOPMENT (IFAD)

The establishment of IFAD was one of the major actions proposed by the 1974 World Food Conference. The agreement for IFAD entered into force on 30 Nov. 1977, and the agency began its operations the following month. By the end of Sept. 1994 the Fund had invested US$4,548·3m. in financing 429 projects in 106 developing countries. IFAD's purpose is to mobilize additional funds for agricultural and rural development in developing countries through projects and programmes directly benefiting the poorest rural populations while preserving their natural resource base. In line with the Fund's focus on the rural poor, its resources are being made available mainly in highly concessional loans as well as grants.

Organization. The highest body is the *Governing Council*, on which all 158 member countries are represented. Operations are overseen by an 18-member Executive Board (with 17 alternate members), which is responsible to the Governing Council. The President of IFAD is chair of the Executive Board.

President: Fawzi H. Al-Sultan (Kuwait).
Headquarters: 107 Via del Serafico, Rome, 00142, Italy.

UNITED NATIONS INDUSTRIAL DEVELOPMENT ORGANIZATION (UNIDO)

Origins. UNIDO became an autonomous organization within the UN Secretariat in 1966, superseding the Centre for Industrial Development which had been operating since 1961. Its General Conference in 1975 recommended its conversion to a UN Specialized Agency, and this was achieved in 1986. Its 1993 General Conference approved a recommendation for the reform and revitalization of the Organization. 169 countries were members in 1995. In Dec. 1995 the USA gave notice of its intention to withdraw at the end of 1996.

Activities. According to its Constitution which entered into force in 1985 UNIDO's principal aim is to promote industrial development in the developing countries. Activities concern the formulation of industrial development policies, introduction of modern technical and managerial methodology, collaboration with UN regional economic commissions and technical and economic assistance, advice and financing. Support activities (studies and services) and special programmes are undertaken.

Organization. The General Conference meets every 2 years to determine policy and approve the budget. It consists of representatives of all member states. The 53-member governing body (33 members from developing countries) is the *Industrial Development Board*, elected for 4 years by the General Conference. The General Conference also elects a 27-member Programme and Budget Committee for 2-year terms of office, and appoints a Director-General for a 4-year term.

UNIDO had 990 employees in 1995. Its original budget for 1995-96 was for not more than US$157m., but the announcement of US withdrawal in 1996 caused a reconsideration of funding.

Director-General: Mauricio de María y Campo (Mexico; till 1 April 1997).
Secretariat: POB 300, A-1400 Vienna, Austria.

THE COMMONWEALTH

The Commonwealth is a free association of sovereign independent states, numbering 53 at the beginning of 1996. There is no charter, treaty or constitution; the association is expressed in co-operation, consultation and mutual assistance for which the Commonwealth Secretariat is the central co-ordinating body.

The Commonwealth was first defined by the Imperial Conference of 1926 as a group of 'autonomous Communities within the British Empire, equal in status, in no way subordinate one to another in any aspect of their domestic or external affairs, though united by a common allegiance to the Crown, and freely associated as members of the British Commonwealth of Nations'. The basis of the association changed from one owing allegiance to a common Crown, and the modern Commonwealth was born in 1949 when the member countries accepted India's intention of becoming a republic at the same time continuing 'her full membership of the Commonwealth of Nations and her acceptance of the King as the symbol of the free association of its independent member nations and as such the Head of the Commonwealth'. There were (1995) 16 Queen's realms, 30 republics, and 5 indigenous monarchies in the Commonwealth. All acknowledge the Queen symbolically as Head of the Commonwealth.

The Queen's legal title rests on the statute of 12 and 13 Will. III, c. 3, by which the succession to the Crown of Great Britain and Ireland was settled on the Princess Sophia of Hanover and the 'heirs of her body being Protestants'. By proclamation of 17 July 1917 the royal family became known as the House and Family of Windsor. On 8 Feb. 1960 the Queen issued a declaration varying her confirmatory declaration of 9 April 1952 to the effect that while the Queen and her children should continue to be known as the House of Windsor, her descendants, other than descendants entitled to the style of Royal Highness and the title of Prince or Princess, and female descendants who marry and their descendants should bear the name of Mountbatten-Windsor. The Royal Style and Titles of Queen Elizabeth are: In *Antigua and Barbuda* 'Elizabeth the Second, by the Grace of God, Queen of Antigua and Barbuda and of Her other Realms and Territories, Head of the Commonwealth'. In *Australia*: 'Elizabeth the Second, by the Grace of God Queen of Australia and Her other Realms and Territories, Head of the Commonwealth'. In the *Bahamas*: 'Elizabeth the Second, by the Grace of God, Queen of the Commonwealth of the Bahamas and of Her other Realms and Territories, Head of the Commonwealth'. In *Barbados*: 'Elizabeth the Second, by the Grace of God, Queen of Barbados and of Her other Realms and Territories, Head of the Commonwealth'. In *Belize*: 'Elizabeth the Second, by the Grace of God, Queen of Belize and of Her Other Realms and Territories, Head of the Commonwealth'. In *Canada*: 'Elizabeth the Second, by the Grace of God of the United Kingdom, Canada and Her other Realms and Territories Queen, Head of the Commonwealth, Defender of the Faith'. In *Grenada*: 'Elizabeth the Second, by the Grace of God, Queen of the United Kingdom of Great Britain and Northern Ireland and of Grenada and Her other Realms and Territories, Head of the Commonwealth'. In *Jamaica*: 'Elizabeth the Second, by the Grace of God of Jamaica and of Her other Realms and Territories Queen, Head of the Commonwealth'. In *New Zealand*: 'Elizabeth the Second, by the Grace of God Queen of New Zealand and Her Other Realms and Territories, Head of the Commonwealth, Defender of the Faith'. In *Papua New Guinea*: 'Elizabeth the Second, Queen of Papua New Guinea and Her other Realms and Territories, Head of the Commonwealth'. In *Saint Christopher and Nevis:* 'Elizabeth the Second, by the Grace of God, Queen of Saint Christopher and Nevis and Her other Realms and Territories, Head of the Commonwealth'. In *Saint Lucia*: 'Elizabeth the Second, by the Grace of God, Queen of Saint Lucia and of Her other Realms and Territories, Head of Commonwealth'. In *Saint Vincent and the Grenadines*: 'Elizabeth the Second, by the Grace of God, Queen of Saint Vincent and the Grenadines and of Her other Realms and Territories, Head of the Commonwealth'. In *Solomon Islands*: 'Elizabeth the Second by the Grace of God Queen of Solomon Islands and of Her other Realms and Territories, Head of the Commonwealth'. In *Tuvalu*: 'Elizabeth the Second by the Grace of God Queen of Tuvalu and of Her other Realms and Territories, Head of the Commonwealth'. In the *United Kingdom*: 'Elizabeth the Second, by the Grace of God of the United Kingdom of Great Britain and Northern Ireland and of Her other Realms and Territories Queen, Head of the Commonwealth, Defender of the Faith'.

A number of territories, formerly under British jurisdiction or mandate did not join the Commonwealth: Egypt, Iraq, Transjordan, Burma, Palestine, Sudan, British Somaliland, South Cameroons, and Aden. 3 countries, Ireland in 1948, South Africa in 1961 and Pakistan in 1972, left the Commonwealth. Fiji's membership lapsed with the emergence of its Republic in 1987. Pakistan was re-admitted to the Commonwealth in 1989, South Africa in 1994. Nigeria was suspended in 1995 for violation of human rights.

Nauru and Tuvalu are special members, with the right to participate in all functional Commonwealth meetings and activities but not to attend meetings of Commonwealth Heads of Government.

Member States. The following are the member countries, with their dates of independence, and, where appropriate, the date on which they became republics: *United*

Kingdom; *Canada* 1 July 1867[1]; *Australia* 1 Jan. 1901[1]; *New Zealand* 26 Sept. 1907 [1]; *South Africa* 11 Dec. 1931 (Republic on 31 May 1961); left Commonwealth 31 May 1961, re-admitted 1 June 1994; *India* 15 Aug. 1947 (Republic on 26 Jan. 1950); *Sri Lanka* 4 Feb. 1948 (Republic on 22 May 1972); *Ghana* 6 March 1957 (Republic on 1 July 1960); *Malaysia* 31 Aug. 1957 as Federation of Malaya, 16 Sept. 1963 as Federation of Malaysia; *Cyprus* 16 Aug. 1960 (Republic on independence; joined Commonwealth on 13 March 1961); *Nigeria* 1 Oct. 1960 (Republic on 1 Oct. 1963); suspended Nov. 1995; *Sierra Leone* 27 April 1961 (Republic on 19 April 1971); *Tanzania*–Tanganyika 9 Dec. 1961 (Republic on 9 Dec. 1962), Zanzibar 10 Dec. 1963 (Republic on 12 Jan. 1964), United Republic of Tanganyika and Zanzibar 26 April 1964; renamed United Republic of Tanzania 29 Oct. 1964; *Western Samoa* 1 Jan. 1962 (joined Commonwealth on 28 Aug. 1970); *Jamaica* 6 Aug. 1962; *Trinidad and Tobago* 31 Aug. 1962 (Republic on 1 Aug. 1976); *Uganda* 9 Oct. 1962 (Republic 8 Sept. 1967, second republic 25 Jan. 1971); *Kenya* 12 Dec. 1963 (Republic on 12 Dec. 1964); *Malaŵi* 6 July 1964 (Republic on 6 July 1966); *Malta* 21 Sept. 1964 (Republic on 13 Dec. 1974); *Zambia* 24 Oct. 1964 (Republic on independence); *The Gambia* 18 Feb. 1965 (Republic on 24 April 1970); *Maldives* 26 July 1965 (Republic on independence, joined Commonwealth on 9 July 1982); *Singapore* 16 Sept. 1963 as a state in the Federation of Malaysia, 9 Aug. 1965 as an independent state and republic not part of Malaysia; *Guyana* 26 May 1966 (Republic on 23 Feb. 1970); *Botswana* 30 Sept. 1966 (Republic on independence); *Lesotho* 4 Oct. 1966; *Barbados* 30 Nov. 1966; *Nauru* [2] 31 Jan. 1968 (Republic on independence); *Mauritius* 12 March 1968 (Republic on 12 March 1992); *Swaziland* 6 Sept. 1968; *Tonga* [3] 4 June 1970; *Bangladesh* seceded from Pakistan as Republic 16 Dec. 1971, recognized by United Kingdom 4 Feb. 1972 (joined Commonwealth on 18 April 1972); *Bahamas* 10 July 1973; *Grenada* 7 Feb. 1974; *Papua New Guinea* 16 Sept. 1975; *Seychelles* 29 June 1976 (Republic on independence); *Solomon Islands* 7 July 1978; *Tuvalu* 1 Oct. 1978; *Dominica* 3 Nov. 1978 (Republic on independence); *Saint Lucia* 22 Feb. 1979; *Kiribati* 12 July 1979 (Republic on independence); *Saint Vincent and the Grenadines* 27 Oct. 1979; *Zimbabwe* 18 April 1980 (Republic on independence); *Vanuatu* 30 July 1980 (Republic on independence); *Belize* 21 Sept. 1981; *Antigua* and *Barbuda* 1 Nov. 1981; *Saint Kitts and Nevis* 19 Sept. 1983; *Brunei* [2] 1 Jan 1984; *Pakistan* 15 Aug. 1947 (Republic on 23 March 1956); left Commonwealth 30 Jan. 1972, re-admitted 1 Oct. 1989; *Namibia* 21 March 1990 (Republic on independence); Cameroon, Nov. 1995 (Former French part republic on independence, federal republic incorporating former British part 1 Oct. 1961); Mozambique Nov. 1995.

[1] These are the effective dates of independence, given legal effect by the Statute of Westminster 1931.

[2] Nauru had been first a Mandate, then a Trust territory.

[3] Brunei and Tonga had been sovereign states in treaty relationship with the UK, whereby the UK was responsible for the conduct of external affairs and had a consultative responsibility for defence.

Dependent Territories and Associated States. There are 15 British dependent territories, 7 Australian external territories, 2 New Zealand dependent territories and 2 New Zealand associated states. A dependent territory is a territory belonging by settlement, conquest or annexation to the British, Australian or New Zealand Crown.

United Kingdom dependent territories administered through the Foreign and Commonwealth Office comprise, in the Far East: Hong Kong; in the Indian Ocean: British Indian Ocean Territory; in the Mediterranean: Gibraltar; in the Atlantic Ocean: Bermuda, Falkland Islands, South Georgia and the South Sandwich Islands, British Antarctic Territory, St Helena, St Helena Dependencies (Ascension and Tristan da Cunha); in the Caribbean: Montserrat, British Virgin Islands, Cayman Islands, Turks and Caicos Islands, Anguilla; in the Western Pacific: Pitcairn Group of Islands. The Australian external territories are: Coral Sea Islands Territory, Cocos (Keeling) Islands, Christmas Island, Heard Island and McDonald Islands, Norfolk Island, Australian Antarctic Territory and the Territory of Ashmore and Cartier Islands. The New Zealand dependent territories are: Tokelau and Ross Dependency. The New Zealand associated states are: Cook Islands and Niue.

While constitutional responsibility to Parliament for the government of the British dependent territories rests with the Secretary of State for Foreign and Commonwealth Affairs, the administration of the territories is carried out by the Governments of the territories themselves.

Aims and Conditions of Membership. Membership involves acceptance of certain principles and is subject to the approval of other member states. In the Harare Declaration of 1991 these principles were defined as political democracy, human rights, good government and the rule of law. Commitment to these principles was made binding as a condition of membership at the 1993 Heads of Government meeting in Cyprus. The Millbrook Action Programme of 1995 aims to support countries in implementing the Harare Declaration, providing assistance in constitutional and judicial matters, running elections, training and technical advice. Violations of the Harare Declaration will provoke a series of measures by the Commonwealth Secretariat, including: Expression of disapproval, encouragement of bilateral actions by member states, appointment of fact-finders and mediators, stipulation of a period for the restoration of democracy, exclusion from ministerial meetings, suspension of all participation and aid and finally punitive measures including trade sanctions. An 8-member *Ministerial Action Group* may be convened by the Secretary-General to deal with violations.

British Government Department. With effect from 17 Oct. 1968, the Secretary of State for Foreign and Commonwealth Affairs is responsible for the conduct of relations with members of the Commonwealth as well as with foreign countries, and for the administration of British dependent territories.

Commonwealth Secretariat. The Commonwealth Secretariat is an international body at the service of all 51 member countries. It provides the central organization for joint consultation and co-operation in many fields. It was established in 1965 by Commonwealth Heads of Government and has observer status at the UN General Assembly.

The Secretariat disseminates information on matters of common concern, organizes and services meetings and conferences, co-ordinates many Commonwealth activities, and provides expert technical assistance for economic and social development through the multilateral Commonwealth Fund for Technical Cooperation. The Secretariat is organized in divisions and sections which correspond to its main areas of operation: International affairs, economic affairs, food production and rural development, youth, education, information, applied studies in government, science and technology, law and health. Within this structure the Secretariat organizes the biennial meetings of Commonwealth Heads of Government, annual meetings of Finance Ministers of member countries, and regular meetings of Ministers of Education, Law, Health, and others as appropriate.

To emphasize the multilateral nature of the association, meetings are held in different cities and regions within the Commonwealth. Heads of Government decided that the Secretariat should work from London as it has the widest range of communications of any Commonwealth city, as well as the largest assembly of diplomatic missions.

The Commonwealth Secretary-General, who has access to Heads of Government, is the head of the Secretariat which is staffed by officers from member countries and financed by contributions from member governments.

Flag: Royal blue with the emblem of a globe surrounded by 50 rays, all in gold.

Headquarters: Marlborough House, Pall Mall, London, SW1Y 5HX.
Secretary-General: Emeka Anyaoku (Nigeria).

Further Reading

The Commonwealth Year-Book, HMSO, Annual
The Cambridge History of the British Empire. 8 vols. CUP, 1929 ff.
Austin, D., *The Commonwealth and Britain*. London, 1988

Chan, S., *Twelve Years of Commonwealth Diplomatic History: Commonwealth Summit Meetings, 1979–1991*. Lampeter, 1992
Hall, H. D., *Commonwealth: A History of the British Commonwealth*. London and New York, 1971
Judd, D. and Slinn, P., *The Evolution of the Modern Commonwealth*. London, 1982
Keeton, G. W. (ed.) *The British Commonwealth: Its Laws and Constitutions*. 9 vols. London, 1951 ff.
Larby, P. and Hannam, H., *The Commonwealth*. [Bibliography]. Oxford and New Brunswick (NJ), 1993
McIntyre, W. D., *The Significance of the Commonwealth, 1965–90*. London, 1991
Moore, R. J., *Making the New Commonwealth*. Oxford, 1987

COMMONWEALTH OF INDEPENDENT STATES (CIS)

The Commonwealth of Independent States is a community of independent states which proclaimed itself the successor to the Union of Soviet Socialist Republics in some aspects of international law and affairs. The member states are the founders, Russia, Belarus and the Ukraine, and 9 subsequent adherents: Armenia, Azerbaijan, Georgia, Kazakhstan, Kyrgyzstan, Moldova, Tajikistan, Turkmenistan and Uzbekistan. The common affairs of the CIS are conducted on a multilateral, inter-state basis rather than by central institutions. It provides a framework for military, foreign policy and economic co-ordination.

HISTORY. Extended negotiations in the Union of Soviet Socialist Republics (USSR) in 1990 and 1991, under the direction of President Gorbachev, sought to establish a 'renewed federation' or, subsequently, to conclude a new union treaty that would embrace all the 15 constituent republics of the USSR at that date. According to a referendum conducted in March 1991, 76% of the population (on an 80% turn-out) wished to maintain the USSR as a 'renewed federation of equal sovereign republics in which the human rights and freedoms of any nationality would be fully guaranteed'. In Sept. 1991 the 3 Baltic republics – Estonia, Latvia and Lithuania – were nonetheless recognized as independent states by the USSR State Council, and subsequently by the international community. Most of the remaining republics reached agreement on the broad outlines of a new 'union of sovereign states' in Nov. 1991, which would have retained a directly elected President and an all-union legislature, but which would have limited central authority to those powers specifically delegated to it by the members of the union.

A referendum in the Ukraine in Dec. 1991, however, showed overwhelming support for full independence, and following this the 3 Slav republics (Russia, Belarus and the Ukraine) concluded an agreement on 8 Dec. 1991 establishing a Commonwealth of Independent States (CIS) with its headquarters in Minsk. The USSR, as a subject of international law and a geopolitical reality, was declared no longer in existence, and each of the 3 republics individually renounced the 1922 treaty through which the USSR had been established.

The CIS declared itself open to other former Soviet republics, as well as to states elsewhere that shared its objectives, and on 21 Dec. 1991 in Almaty a further declaration was signed by representatives of the 3 original members and of 8 other republics: Armenia, Azerbaijan, Kazakhstan, Kyrgyzstan, Moldova, Tajikistan, Turkmenistan and Uzbekistan. The declaration committed those who signed it to recognize the independence and sovereignty of other members, to respect human rights including those of national minorities, and to the observance of existing boundaries. Relations among the members of the CIS were to be conducted on an equal, multilateral basis, but it was agreed to endorse the principle of unitary control of strategic nuclear arms and the concept of a 'single economic space'. Members pledged themselves to discharge the obligations that arose from the international treaties and agreements to which the USSR had been a party. In a separate agreement the heads of member states agreed that Russia should take up the seat at the United Nations formerly occupied by the USSR, and a framework of inter-state and inter-government consultation was established. Following these developments Mikhail Gorbachev resigned as USSR President on 25 Dec. 1991, and on 26 Dec. the USSR Supreme Soviet voted a formal end to the treaty of union that had been signed in 1922 and dissolved itself.

INSTITUTIONS. The 'supreme organ' of the CIS, according to the agreement concluded in Almaty on 21 Dec. 1991, is a *Council of Heads of States*; associated with its work is a *Council of Heads of Government.* At a summit meeting of heads of all the states except Azerbaijan in July 1992, agreements were reached on the formation of a CIS peacekeeping force, the establishment of an economic arbitration court and a way to divide former Soviet assets abroad, and some progress was made towards the creation of economic co-ordinating structures. At their subsequent meeting in Jan. 1993 Russia, Belarus, Armenia, Kazakhstan, Kyrgyzstan, Turkmenistan and Uzbekistan agreed on a charter to establish a defence alliance, an economic co-ordination committee and an inter-state court. 3 participants (Ukraine, Moldova and Tajikistan) agreed only to a declaration that any state would be free to sign the charter in future, and that an inter-state bank should be set up.

On 24 Sept. 1993 Russia, Armenia, Azerbaijan, Belarus, Kazakhstan, Kyrgyzstan, Moldova, Tajikistan and Uzbekistan signed an agreement to form an economic union, with Ukraine and Turkmenistan as associated members. Georgia signed some provisions.

A summit meeting in Dec. 1993 set up a *Council of CIS Foreign Ministers.* In March 1994 the CIS was accorded observer status in the United Nations.

In Dec. 1993 the *CIS Inter-State Bank* was set up to facilitate multilateral clearing of CIS inter-state transactions with a starting capital of 5,000m. rubles. Members' contributions, based on their share of foreign trade turn-over in 1990: Russia, 50%; Ukraine, 20·7%; Belarus, 8·4%; Kazakhstan, 6·1%; Uzbekistan, 5·5%; Moldova, 2·9%; Armenia, 1·8%; Tajikistan, 1·6%; Kyrgyzstan, 1·5%; Turkmenistan, 1·5%.

The former USSR railway network is administered by the *CIS Railway Council* through operating authorities set up in 1991 in each member country.

Meeting in July 1992 representatives of the defence and foreign ministries of member states agreed on the creation of a peacekeeping force ('white helmets') to be deployed in intra-CIS conflicts at the request of member states, and with the consent of the parties to the conflict. CIS members contribute to this force in proportion to the size of their armed forces; the commander is appointed on each occasion by the CIS heads of state.

In 1993 the office of C.-in-C. of CIS Joint Armed Forces was replaced by that of Chief of Joint Staff for Co-ordinating Military Co-operation.

In Oct. 1994 a summit meeting established the *Inter-Government Economic Committee* to be based in Moscow. Members are all CIS states except Turkmenistan. Its decisions are binding if voted by 80% of the membership. Russia commands 50% of the voting power and the other 10 members combined, 50%. The Committee's remit is to co-ordinate energy, transport and communications policies. A *Payments Union* was also agreed to regulate payments between member states with non-convertible independent currencies.

The *administrative centre* is in the Supreme Soviet, Minsk, Belarus.

WORLD COUNCIL OF CHURCHES

The World Council of Churches was formally constituted on 23 Aug. 1948, at Amsterdam, by an assembly representing 147 churches from 44 countries. By 1995 the member churches numbered over 330, from more than 100 countries.

The basis of membership (1975) states: 'The World Council of Churches is a fellowship of Churches which confess the Lord Jesus Christ as God and Saviour according to the Scriptures and therefore seek to fulfil together their common calling to the glory of the one God, Father, Son and Holy Spirit.' Membership is open to Churches which express their agreement with this basis and satisfy such criteria as the Assembly or Central Committee may prescribe. Today more than

330 Churches of Protestant, Anglican, Orthodox, Old Catholic and Pentecostal confessions belong to this fellowship.

The World Council was founded by the coming together of several diverse Christian movements. These included the overseas mission groups gathered from 1921 in the International Missionary Council, the Faith and Order Movement founded by American Episcopal Bishop Charles Brent, and the Life and Work Movement led by Swedish Lutheran Archbishop Nathan Söderblom.

On 13 May 1938 at Utrecht a provisional committee was appointed to prepare for the formation of a World Council of Churches. It was under the chairmanship of William Temple, then Archbishop of York.

Assembly. The governing body of the World Council, consisting of delegates specially appointed by the member Churches. It meets every 7 or 8 years to frame policy and to consider some main theme. The Assembly has no legislative powers and depends for the implementation of its decisions upon the action of the member Churches. Assemblies have been held in Amsterdam (1948), Evanston (1954), New Delhi (1961), Uppsala (1968), Nairobi (1975), Vancouver (1983) and Canberra (1991). The Eighth Assembly is scheduled to be held in Harare in 1998. In between assemblies, a 150-member Central Committee meets annually to carry out the assembly mandate, with a smaller 28-member Executive Committee meeting twice a year.

Presidents: Prof. Anne-Marie Aagaard (Denmark), Bishop Vinton Anderson (USA), Bishop Leslie Boseto (Solomon Islands), Ms Priyanka Mendis (Sri Lanka), His Beatitude Parthenios of Alexandria (Egypt), Rev. Dr Eunice Santana (Puerto Rico), His Holiness Pope Shenouda (Egypt), Dr Aaron Tolen (Cameroon).

WCC programmes are organized from headquarters in Geneva, Switzerland, by a staff of 270 and a range of supervisory committees drawn from member churches. The 4 programme units are:

(i) Unity and Renewal – continuing the search for visible unity - Ecclesial Unity: Faith and Order; Lay Participation towards inclusive Community; Renewal through Worship and Spirituality; Ecumenical Theological Education. With other Units: Biblical/theological reflection on *koinonia*, theology of life and *diakonia.*

(ii) Churches in Mission: Health, Education Witness – focusing on Mission and Evangelism in Unity, including preparations for the 1996 Conference on World Mission and Evangelism in Salvador, Bahia, Brazil; Gospel and Cultures; CMC – Churches' Action for Health; Education for All God's People; Community and Justice/Urban Rural Mission, Theological Significance of Religions.

(iii) Justice, Peace and Creation – is concerned with Justice, Peace and the integrity of Creation (JPIC) as an educational and conciliar process; Economy, Ecology and Sustainable Society (ECOS); Programme to Combat Racism (PCR); Indigenous People and Land Rights; International Affairs, Peace and Human Rights (CCIA); Concerns and Perspectives of Women; Youth: Solidarity and Action.

(iv) Sharing and Service – is concerned with meeting urgent human need in situations of Emergencies, assistance to Refugees; Sharing of Ecumenical Resources; understanding *diakonia*; Advocacy and Action with the Poor; Equipping and linking Churches in Service; Biblical and theological analysis in partnership with those concerned with mission and *diakonia.*

The General Secretariat includes Offices for Church and Ecumenical Relations, Inter-religious Relations, Programme Co-ordination, the Department of Communication, the Office of Management and Finance and the Ecumenical Institute at Bossey.

Since 1975 the WCC has held several major world conferences on diverse themes.

Officers of the Central and Executive Committees: *Moderator:* His Holiness Aram I, Catholicos of Cilicia (Lebanon). *Vice-Moderators:* Ephorus Dr S. A. E. Nababan (Indonesia), Pastor Nélida Ritchie (Argentina). *General Secretary:* The Rev. Dr Konrad Raiser (Germany).

Office: PO Box 2100, 150 route de Ferney, 1211 Geneva 2, Switzerland.

Further Reading

Official Reports: The First [. . . *etc.*] *Assembly* (London, 1948, 1955, 1962, Geneva, 1968, 1975, 1983, 1991)
Dictionary of the Ecumenical Movement. Geneva, 1991
Directory of Christian Councils. 1985
Handbook of Member Churches of the WCC. Geneva, 1985
A History of the Ecumenical Movement. Geneva, 1993
The Ecumenical Review. Quarterly. *Ecumenical News International: ENI Bulletin.* Fortnightly. *International Review of Mission.* Quarterly
Baptism, Eucharist and Ministry. Genena, 1994. *Churches Respond to* Baptism, Eucharist and Ministry
Vancouver to Canberra, 1983–1990. Geneva, 1990
Official Reports of the Faith and Order Conferences at Lausanne 1927, Edinburgh 1937, Lund 1952, Montreal 1963, Santiago de Compostela; Meeting of Faith and Order Commission, Louvain 1972, Accra 1974, Bangalore 1978, Lima 1982, Stavanger 1985, Budapest, 1989
Reports of Conferences of WCC Commission on World Mission and Evangelism, Mexico City 1963, Bangkok 1973, Melbourne 1980, San Antonio 1990
Minutes of the WCC Central Committee. Geneva, 1949 to date
Castro, E., *A Passion for Unity.* Geneva, 1992
Potter, P., *Life in all its Fullness.* Geneva, 1981
Raiser, K., *Ecumenism in Transition.* Geneva, 1994
Van Elderen, M., *Introducing the World Council of Churches.* Geneva, 1990
Vermaat, J. A. A., *The World Council of Churches and Politics.* New York, 1989
Visser 't Hooft, W. A., *The Genesis and Formation of the World Council of Churches.* Geneva, 1982. *Memoirs.* Geneva, 1987

BANK FOR INTERNATIONAL SETTLEMENTS (BIS)

Founded in 1930, originally to settle the question of German First World War reparations, the BIS is the 'central banks' bank'. It aims to promote co-operation between central banks, to provide facilities for international financial operations and act as agent or trustee in international financial settlements. Its assets are owned by 32 central banks, and in 1991 it held US$70,000m. on behalf of 80 central banks.

Organization. The Board of Directors consists of the governor of the central bank and one other appointee from Belgium, France, Germany, Italy, the UK and the USA which took up its seat in Sept. 1994. Governors of not more than 9 more central banks are eligible for election. The Chairman of the Board may act as President.

In 1988 it defined standard minimum levels of capital adequacy for banks: in 1990 a capital-to-asset ratio of 7·25%, rising to 8% in 1992.

Chairman: Willem Duisenberg (Netherlands).
Headquarters: Centralbahnplatz 2, 4002 Basel, Switzerland.

Further Reading

Deane, M. and Pringe, R., *The Central Banks.* London and New York, 1995
Goodhart, C. A. E., *The Central Bank and the Financial System.* London, 1995

INTERNATIONAL TRADE UNIONISM

INTERNATIONAL CONFEDERATION OF FREE TRADE UNIONS (ICFTU). The founding congress of the ICFTU was held in London in Dec. 1949, following the withdrawal of some Western trade unions from WFTU which had come under Communist control. The constitution as amended provides for co-operation with the UN and the ILO and for regional organizations to promote free trade unionism, especially in developing countries.

Organization. The Congress meets every 4 years. It elects the Executive Board of 50 members nominated on an area basis for a 4-year period; 5 seats are reserved for women nominated by the Women's Committee; the Board meets at least once a year. Various committees cover economic and social policy, violation of trade union and other human rights, trade union co-operation projects and also the administration of the International Solidarity Fund. There are joint ICFTU–International Trade Secretariat committees for co-ordinating activities.

Headquarters: Bd. Emile Jacqmain 155, Brussels 1210, Belgium.
General Secretary: Bill Jordan (UK).

Regional organizations exist in America, office in Caracas; Asia, office in Singapore; and Africa, office in Nairobi.

Membership. The ICFTU had in Dec. 1994 188 affiliated organizations in 135 countries, which together represented about 123m. workers.

Publications (in 4 languages). *Free Labour World* (fortnightly).

WORLD CONFEDERATION OF LABOUR (WCL). The first congress of the International Federation of Christian Trade Unions, as the WCL was then called, met in 1920; but a large proportion of its 3·4m. members were in Italy and Germany, where affiliated unions were suppressed by the Fascist and Nazi régimes, and in 1940 it went out of existence. It was reconstituted in 1945, and declined to merge with the WFTU or the ICFTU. Its policy was based on the papal encyclicals *Rerum novarum* (1891) and *Quadragesimo anno* (1931), but in 1968, when the Federation became the WCL, it was broadened to include other concepts. The WCL now has Protestant, Buddhist and Moslem member confederations as well as its mainly Roman Catholic members. In its concern to defend trade union freedoms and assist trade union development the WCL differs little in policy from the ICFTU.

Organization. The WCL is organized on a federative basis which leaves wide discretion to its autonomous constituent unions. Its governing body is the Congress, which meets every 4 years. The Congress appoints (or re-appoints) the Secretary-General at each 4-yearly meeting. The General Council which meets at least once a year, is composed of the members of the Confederal Board (at least 22 members, elected by the Congress) and representatives of national confederations, international trade federations, and trade union organizations where there is no confederation affiliated to the WCL. The Confederal Board is responsible for the general leadership of the WCL, in accordance with the decisions and directives of the Council and Congress.

Secretary-General: Carlos Luís Custer.
Headquarters: 71 rue Joseph II, Brussels 1040, Belgium.

There are regional organizations in Latin America (office in Caracas), Africa (office in Banjul, Gambia) and Asia (office in Manila) There is also a liaison centre in Montreal.

Membership. A total membership of 11m. in about 90 countries is claimed. The biggest group is the Confederation of Christian Trade Unions (CSC) of Belgium (1·2m.).

Publication. Labour Press and Information (11 each year, in 5 languages).

WORLD FEDERATION OF TRADE UNIONS (WFTU). The WFTU came into existence on 3 Oct. 1945, representing trade union organizations in more than 50 countries, both Communist and non-Communist.

Organization. The Congress meets every 4 years. In between, the General Council is the governing body, meeting (in theory) at least once a year. The Bureau controls the activities of WFTU between meetings of the General Council; it consists of the President, the General Secretary and members from different continents, the total number being decided at each Congress. The Bureau is elected by the General Council. Regional bureaux were instituted in 1990 as a move towards decentralization.

General Secretary: Aleksandr Zharikov (Russia).
The headquarters is in Prague.

Membership. From the outset the American Federation of Labor declined to participate. In Jan. 1949 British, US and Netherlands trade union organizations withdrew from WFTU, which had come under complete Communist control, and went on to found the ICFTU; by June 1951 all non-Communist trade unions, and the Yugoslav federation, had withdrawn. With the collapse of the European Communist regimes membership became uncertain after 1990. Unions broke their links with the Communist parties and most were later accepted into the ICFTU. Most of the national trade union centres in Africa and Latin America also moved to the ICFTU after 1989. At the Nov. 1994 congress in Damascus most delegates were from developing countries (Cuba, India, South Korea, Vietnam). The French Confédération Générale du Travail has proposed withdrawal to its members.

Publications. Trade Union Press (in 3 languages).

EUROPEAN TRADE UNION CONFEDERATION (ETUC). In Feb. 1973 the ETUC was formed by trade unionists in 15 Western European countries to deal with questions of interest to European working people arising inside and outside the EC. All the founding organizations were ICFTU affiliates but subsequently they accepted into membership European WCL affiliates, the Irish Congress of Trade Unions and the Italian Communist and Socialist trade union centre (CGIL) and other national organizations. In 1992 and 1993 the ETUC accorded observer status to several national trade union organizations from Eastern Europe. The ETUC Congress meets every 3 years and the Executive Committee 4 times a year. The membership was (1994) about 45m. from national trade union centres in 21 countries.

General Secretary: Mathias Hinterscheid.
Headquarters: Rue Montagne aux Herbes Potagères 37, 1000 Brussels.

ORGANISATION FOR ECONOMIC CO-OPERATION AND DEVELOPMENT (OECD)

History and Membership. On 30 Sept. 1961 the Organisation for European Economic Co-operation (OEEC), after a history of 13 years (*see* THE STATESMAN'S YEAR-BOOK, 1961, p. 32), was replaced by the Organisation for Economic Co-operation and Development. The change of title marks the Organisation's altered status and functions: With the accession of Canada and USA as full members it ceased to be a purely European body; while at the same time it added development aid to the list of its other activities. The member countries are now Australia, Austria, Belgium, Canada, the Czech Republic, Denmark, Finland, France, Germany, Greece, Iceland, Ireland, Italy, Japan, Luxembourg, Mexico, the Netherlands, New Zealand, Norway, Portugal, Spain, Sweden, Switzerland, Turkey, UK and USA. The EU Commission generally takes part in OECD's work.

Objectives. To promote economic and social welfare throughout the OECD area by assisting its member governments in the formulation of policies designed to this end and by co-ordinating these policies; and to stimulate and harmonize its members' efforts in favour of developing countries.

Organs. The supreme body is the *Council* composed of 1 representative for each member country. It meets either at Heads of Permanent Delegations level (about twice a month) under the chairmanship of the Secretary-General, or at ministerial level (usually once a year) under the chairmanship of a minister of a country elected annually to this function. Decisions and Recommendations are adopted by mutual agreement of all members of the Council.

The Council is assisted by an Executive Committee composed of 14 members of the Council designated annually by the latter. The major part of the Organisation's work is, prepared and carried out in specialized committees, working parties and sub-groups, of which there exist over 200, including Committees for Economic Policy; Economic and Development Review; Development Assistance (DAC); Trade; Capital Movements and Invisible Transactions; Financial Markets; Fiscal Affairs; Competition Law and Policy; Consumer Policy; Tourism; Maritime Transport; International Investment and Multinational Enterprises; Energy Policy; Industry; Steel; Scientific and Technological Policy; Information, Computer and Communications Policy; Education; Employment; Labour; Social Affairs; Public Management; Environment; Agriculture; Fisheries; and Commodities.

In 1990 the Centre for Co-operation with European Economies in Transition (CCET) was established to act as OECD's point of contact for Central and East European countries seeking guidance in moving towards a market economy.

4 autonomous or semi-autonomous bodies also belong to the Organisation: The International Energy Agency (IEA); the Nuclear Energy Agency (NEA); the Development Centre and the Centre for Educational Research and Innovation (CERI). Each one of these bodies has its own governing committee.

Committees and other bodies are, as a rule, composed of civil servants coming either from capitals or from the Permanent Delegations to the OECD which are established as normal diplomatic missions and headed by ambassadors. They are serviced by an *International Secretariat* headed by the OECD Secretary General.

Relations with other international organisations. The EU Commission generally takes part in the work of OECD under a protocol signed at the same time as the OECD Convention. EFTA may also send representatives to attend all OECD meetings. There are official or working relations with a number of other international governmental organizations. Special arrangements establishing close links with Council of Europe were concluded in 1962. Non-governmental international organizations deemed to be widely representative in general economic matters or in a specific economy sector can be granted a consultative status enabling them to discuss subjects of common interest with a Liaison Committee chaired by the Secretary-General, and be consulted in a particular field by the relevant OECD Committee or its officers.

Finance. Funding is by contributions from member states.

Official languages. English and French.

Secretary-General: Jean-Claude Paye (France; until June 1996).
Headquarters: 2, rue André Pascal, 75775 Paris Cedex 16, France.

Further Reading

OECD publishes numerous reports and statistical papers. Regular features include:
OECD Letter. Monthly.—*Activities of OECD.* Annual.—*News from OECD.* Monthly.—*Main Economic Indicators.* Monthly.—*The OECD Observer.* Bi-monthly.—*The OECD Economic Outlook.* Semi-annual.—*OEEC/OECD Economic Surveys of Member Countries.*—*OECD Employment Outlook.* Annual.—*Geographical Distribution of Financial Flows to Developing Countries.* Annual.—*Development Co-operation Report.* Annual.—*Tourism Policy and International Tourism in OECD Member Countries.*—*Maritime Transport.* Annual.—*Energy Policies and Programmes of the IEA Member Countries.*
Blair, D. J., *Trade Negotiations in the OECD: Structures, Institutions and States.* London, 1993

NORTH ATLANTIC TREATY ORGANIZATION (NATO)

On 4 April 1949 the foreign ministers of Belgium, Canada, Denmark, France, Iceland, Italy, Luxembourg, the Netherlands, Norway, Portugal, the UK and the USA signed the North Atlantic Treaty. In 1952 Greece and Turkey acceded to the Treaty, in 1955 the Federal Republic of Germany and in 1982 Spain, so bringing the total to 16 member nations.

The Atlantic Alliance was established as a defensive political and military alliance of independent countries in accordance with the terms of the UN Charter. It provides common security for its members through co-operation and consultation in political, military and economic as well as scientific and other non-military fields. The Alliance also links the security of North America to that of Europe. NATO is the organization which enables the goals of the Alliance to be implemented.

With the demise of the Warsaw Pact in 1991 and the end of the Cold War, the Atlantic Alliance has undertaken a fundamental transformation of its structures and policies, following the London (July 1990), Rome (Nov. 1991) and Brussels (Jan. 1994) Summits, to meet the new security challenges in Europe. An essential component of this transformation has been the establishment of close security links with the states of Central and Eastern Europe and those of the former USSR through the *North Atlantic Cooperation Council (NACC)* and, later, the Partnership for Peace (PFP).

Other key changes and innovations undertaken since 1989 include the adoption of a new Strategic Concept; a reduced and more flexible force structure, development of increased co-ordination and co-operation with other international institutions, such as the UN, OSCE, WEU and EU; and agreement to make NATO's assets and experience available to support international peacekeeping operations. During 1992-95, NATO provided practical support for UN peacekeeping efforts in the former Yugoslavia. With the signing of the Bosnian peace agreement in Dec. 1995, the Alliance began implementation of the military aspects of the accord, through the NATO-led multi-national Implementation Force.

Partnership for Peace. The 1994 Brussels Summit launched Partnership for Peace (PFP), which is open to NACC states and other OSCE countries able and willing to participate. PFP is expanding and intensifying political and military co-operation throughout Europe. Depending on the capacity and desire of each participating state, Partners work towards transparency in defence budgeting, democratic control of defence ministries, joint planning, joint military exercises, and creating an ability to operate with NATO forces in such fields as peacekeeping, search and rescue, and humanitarian operations. NATO will consult with any active Partner which perceives a direct threat to its territorial integrity, political independence, or security.

Three PFP exercises were held in autumn 1994, 11 land and sea exercises in 1995, five of which were in Partner countries, and 130 PFP military exercises were planned for 1996. These exercises are designed to improve practical military co-operation and common capabilities in the areas on which PFP focuses, and help to develop inter-operability between the forces of NATO Allies and Partner countries. They also have an important political role. A large number of nationally-sponsored exercises in the spirit of PFP are also taking place.

There are now 27 PFP Partners: Albania, Armenia, Austria, Azerbaijan, Belarus, Bulgaria, the Czech Republic, Estonia, Finland, Georgia, Hungary, Kazakhstan, Kyrgyzstan, Latvia, Lithuania, Macedonia, Malta, Moldova, Poland, Romania, Russia, Slovakia, Slovenia, Sweden, Turkmenistan, the Ukraine and Uzbekistan. Many of these countries have accepted the Alliance's invitation to send liaison officers to permanent facilities at NATO Headquarters in Brussels and to the Partnership Co-ordination Cell in Mons (Belgium) where the Supreme Headquarters Allied Powers Europe (SHAPE) is also located.

The *North Atlantic Council (NAC)* is the highest decision-making body and forum for consultation within the Atlantic Alliance. It is composed of Permanent Representatives of all 16 member countries meeting together at least once a week. The NAC also meets at higher levels involving foreign ministers or heads of state or government, but it has the same authority and powers of decision-making, and its decisions have the same status and validity, at whatever level it meets. All decisions are taken on the basis of consensus, reflecting the collective will of all member governments. The NAC is the only body within the Atlantic Alliance which derives its authority explicitly from the North Atlantic Treaty. The NAC itself was given responsibility under the Treaty for setting up subsidiary bodies. Committees and planning groups have since been created to support the work of the NAC or to assume responsibility in specific fields such as defence planning, nuclear planning and military matters.

The *Defence Planning Committee* is composed of representatives of all member countries except France [1]. Like the Council, it meets both in permanent session at the level of Ambassadors and twice a year at Ministerial level. At Ministerial Meetings member nations are represented by Defence Ministers.

The Council and Defence Planning Committee are chaired by the Secretary General of NATO at whatever level they meet. Opening sessions of Ministerial Meetings of the Council are presided over by the President, an honorary position held annually by the Foreign Minister of one of the member nations.

Nuclear matters are discussed by the *Nuclear Planning Group* in which 15 countries participate. It meets regularly at the level of Permanent Representatives (ambassadors) and twice a year at the level of ministers of defence.

The Permanent Representatives of member countries are supported by the National Delegations located at NATO Headquarters. The Delegations are composed of advisors and officials qualified to represent their countries on the various committees created by the Council. The Committees are supported by the International Staff responsible to the Secretary General.

The *Military Committee* is responsible for making recommendations to the Council and the Defence Planning Committee on military matters and for supplying guidance to the Allied Commanders. Composed of the Chiefs-of-Staff of member countries (Iceland, which has no military forces may be represented by a civilian), the Committee is assisted by an International Military Staff. It meets at Chiefs-of-Staff level at least twice a year but remains in permanent session at the level of national military representatives. The chairman of the Military Committee is elected by the Chiefs-of-Staff for a period of 2–3 years.

The area covered by the North Atlantic Treaty is divided into 2 commands: the European and the Atlantic.

The *Canada–US Regional Planning Group*, which covers the North American area, develops and recommends to the Military Committee plans for the defence of this area. It meets alternately in Washington and Ottawa.

Enlargement. As part of the process of promoting stability and security across the whole of Europe, the Alliance is also addressing the issue of its eventual enlargement to take in additional member states. In Dec. 1994, foreign ministers initiated an internal Alliance study to determine how NATO will enlarge, the principles to guide this process and the implications of membership. They stated that enlargement, when it takes place, will be part of a broad European security architecture based on true co-operation throughout the whole of Europe. It will threaten no one, and will enhance security and stability for all of Europe. This study was completed in Sept. 1995, after which interested Central and Eastern European Partner states were given briefings on the results of the study. NATO foreign ministers, meeting in Brussels in Dec. 1995, decided that the next phase of the enlargement process in 1996 would include: intensified, individual dialogue with interested Partners; further enhancement of the Partnership for Peace to help those interested Partners to prepare to assume the responsibilities of membership and to strengthen long-term partnership between NATO and other Partner countries; and further consideration of what NATO must do internally to ensure that enlargement preserves the effectiveness of the Alliance.

Peacekeeping. NATO's long-standing role in supporting the UN peacekeeping operations in Bosnia-Hercegovina contributed to bringing an end to hostilities there and to the eventual peace accord. Following the signing of the Bosnian Peace Agreement in Paris on 14 Dec. 1995, and on the basis of the UN Security Council's Resolution 1031, NATO commenced implementation of the military aspects of the Peace Agreement. The NATO-led multi-national force is called the Implementation Force (IFOR) and the operation which began on 16 Dec. is code-named 'Joint Endeavour'. IFOR is in Bosnia to help the parties implement a peace accord to which they have freely agreed, and is doing so in an even-handed way. IFOR is to help create a secure environment for civil and economic reconstruction. Its mission is of a limited duration of approximately 12 months. The NATO-led IFOR is the largest military operation undertaken by the Alliance, which has adapted its forces and policies to the requirements of the post-Cold War world while continuing to provide collective security and defence for all Allies. NATO's own military capabilities and its adaptability to include forces of non-NATO countries are decisive factors in the Alliance's role in implementing the Bosnian Peace Agreement.

In Nov. 1995 Belgium, France, Germany, Luxembourg and Spain joined forces to form the 50,000-strong *Eurocorps*, which may be employed by NATO or the Western European Union, as well as humanitarian and peacekeeping missions under the aegis of the UN or OSCE.

Headquarters: NATO, 1110 Brussels, Belgium.
Secretary-General: Javier Solana Madariaga (b. 1942; Spain).
Flag: Dark blue with a white compass rose of 4 points in the centre.

[1] After 1966 France attended only foreign minister-level meetings of a political nature, but began to attend meetings with an agenda of French interest from Jan. 1994. In Dec. 1995 France announced that it would take its seat on the Military Committee.

Further Reading

The NATO Information Service publishes documentation, reference material and information brochures.

Cook, D., *The Forging of an Alliance.* London, 1989
Heller, F. H. and Gillingham, J. R. (eds.) *NATO: the Founding of the Atlantic Alliance and the Integration of Europe.* London, 1992
Smith, J. (ed.) *The Origins of NATO.* Exeter Univ. Press, 1990
Williams, P., *North Atlantic Treaty Organization.* [Bibliography]. Oxford and New Brunswick (NJ), 1994

WESTERN EUROPEAN UNION

On 17 March 1948 a 50-year treaty 'for collaboration in economic, social and cultural matters and for collective self-defence' was signed in Brussels by the foreign ministers of the UK, France, the Netherlands, Belgium and Luxembourg. (*See* THE STATESMAN'S YEAR-BOOK, 1954, pp. 32 f.)

On 20 Dec. 1950 the functions of the Western Union defence organization were transferred to the North Atlantic Treaty command, but it was decided that the reorganization should not affect the right of the Western Union defence ministers and the chiefs of staff to meet to consider matters of mutual concern to the Brussels Treaty powers.

At a Conference of Ministers held in Paris from 20 to 23 Oct. 1954 these decisions were embodied in 4 Protocols modifying the Brussels Treaty: the Federal Republic of Germany and Italy were to accede to the Brussels Treaty; the occupation of West Germany was to be ended; West Germany was to be invited to accede to the North Atlantic Treaty; and other provisions concerning armaments control and the UK's military presence in Europe. These came into force on 6 May 1955.

At a meeting of the foreign and defence ministers of WEU members held in Rome on 26–27 Oct. 1984, the Council adopted the 'Rome Declaration' and a document on institutional reform. Member Governments support the reactivation of the Organization as a means of strengthening the European contribution to the North Atlantic Alliance and improving defence co-operation among the countries of Western Europe.

At a meeting on 27 Oct. 1987 WEU foreign and defence ministers adopted the 'Hague Platform on European Security Interests' defining the conditions and criteria for European security and the responsibilities of WEU members.

At a meeting in June 1992 WEU foreign and defence ministers adopted the 'St Petersburg Declaration', agreeing that the WEU should have a military capability in order to take part in peacekeeping and humanitarian operations at the request of other international organizations.

Since the 1984 reforms, the WEU *Council of Ministers* (foreign and defence) meets twice a year in the capital of the presiding country. The presidency rotates annually. The *Permanent Council* meets weekly at the seat of the Secretariat-General. The WEU *Assembly* in Paris comprises 108 parliamentarians of the member states and meets twice a year. A *WEU Institute for Security Studies* was set up in Paris in 1989.

Spain and Portugal became members in 1988 and Greece in 1992.

Members in Feb. 1995: Belgium, France, Germany, Greece, Italy, Luxembourg, the Netherlands, Portugal, Spain and the UK. Austria, Denmark, Ireland, Finland and Sweden are observers, Iceland, Norway and Turkey are associated members and Bulgaria, the Czech Republic, Estonia, Hungary, Latvia, Lithuania, Poland, Romania and Slovakia are associate partners.

For the Eurocorps *see* NATO.

Secretariat-General: 4 rue de la Régence, B-1000 Brussels.
Secretary-General: José Cutileiro (b. 1935; Portugal).

COUNCIL OF EUROPE

In 1948 the 'Congress of Europe', bringing together at The Hague nearly 1,000 influential Europeans from 26 countries, called for the creation of a united Europe, including a European Assembly. This proposal, examined first by the Ministerial Council of the Brussels Treaty Organization, then by a conference of ambassadors, was at the origin of the Council of Europe, which is, with its 38 member States, the widest organization bringing together all European democracies. The Statute of the Council was signed at London on 5 May 1949 and came into force 2 months later. The founder members were Belgium, Denmark, France, Ireland, Italy, Luxembourg, the Netherlands, Norway, Sweden and the UK. Turkey and Greece joined in 1949, Iceland in 1950, the Federal Republic of Germany in 1951 (having been an associate since 1950), Austria in 1956, Cyprus in 1961, Switzerland in 1963, Malta in 1965, Portugal in 1976, Spain in 1977, Liechtenstein in 1978, San Marino in 1988, Finland in 1989, Hungary in 1990, Czechoslovakia (after partitioning the Czech Republic and Slovakia rejoined in 1993) and Poland in 1991, Bulgaria in 1992, Estonia, Lithuania, Romania and Slovenia in 1993, Andorra in 1994 and Albania, Latvia, Macedonia, Moldova and the Ukraine in 1995.

Membership is limited to European states which 'accept the principles of the rule of law and of the enjoyment by all persons within [their] jurisdiction of human rights and fundamental freedoms'. The Statute provides for both withdrawal (Art. 7) and suspension (Arts. 8 and 9). Greece withdrew during 1969–74.

Structure. Under the Statute two organs were set up: An inter-governmental *Committee of* [*Foreign*] *Ministers* with powers of decision and of recommendation to governments, and an inter-parliamentary deliberative body, the *Parliamentary Assembly* (referred to in the Statute as the *Consultative Assembly*)—both of which are served by the Secretariat. In addition, a number of committees of experts have been established. On municipal matters the Committee of Ministers receives recommendations from the Congress of Local and Regional Authorities of Europe.

The Committee of Ministers meets usually twice a year, their deputies for several days each month.

The Parliamentary Assembly consists of 263 parliamentarians elected or appointed by their national parliaments (Albania 4, Austria 6, Belgium 7, Bulgaria 6, Cyprus 3, the Czech Republic 7, Denmark 5, Estonia 3, Finland 5, France 18, Germany 18, Greece 7, Hungary 7, Iceland 3, Ireland 4, Italy 18, Liechtenstein 2, Lithuania 4, Luxembourg 3, Macedonia 5, Malta 3, Moldova 5, Netherlands 7, Norway 5, Poland 12, Portugal 7, Romania 10, San Marino 2, Slovakia 5, Slovenia 3, Spain 12, Sweden 6, Switzerland 6, Turkey 12, Ukraine 12, UK 18). It meets 3 times a year for approximately a week. The work of the Assembly is prepared by parliamentary committees. Since June 1989 representatives of a number of central and East European countries have been permitted to attend as non-voting members ('special guests'), namely Albania, Belarus, Bosnia-Hercegovina, Croatia, Latvia, Macedonia, Moldova, Russia and Ukraine.

The *Joint Committee* acts as an organ of co-ordination and liaison between representatives of the Committee of Ministers and members of the Parliamentary Assembly and gives members an opportunity to exchange views on matters of important European interest.

The European Convention on Human Rights, signed in 1950, set up special machinery to guarantee internationally fundamental rights and freedoms. The *European Commission of Human Rights* investigates alleged violations of the Convention submitted to it either by States or, in most cases, by individuals. Its findings can then be examined by the *European Court on Human Rights* (set up in 1959), whose obligatory jurisdiction has been recognized by 25 States, or by the Committee of Ministers, empowered to take binding decisions by two-thirds majority vote.

The Social Development Fund, formerly the Resettlement Fund was created in 1956. The main purpose of the Fund is to give financial aid, particularly in the spheres of housing, vocational training, regional planning and development. Since 1956 the Fund has granted loans totalling ecu 10,000m.

The European Youth Foundation provides money to subsidize activities by European youth organizations in their own countries.

Aims and Achievements. Art. 1 of the Statute states that the Council's aim is 'to achieve a greater unity between its members for the purpose of safeguarding and realising the ideals and principles which are their common heritage and facilitating their economic and social progress'; 'this aim shall be pursued. . . by discussion of questions of common concern and by agreements and common action'. The only limitation is provided by Art. 1 *(d)*, which excludes 'matters relating to national defence'.

Although without legislative powers, the Assembly acts as the power-house of the Council, initiating European action in key areas by making recommendations to the Committee of Ministers. As the widest parliamentary forum in Western Europe, the Assembly also acts as the conscience of the area by voicing its opinions on important current issues. These are embodied in resolutions. The Ministers' rôle is to translate the Assembly's recommendations into action, particularly as regards lowering the barriers between the European countries, harmonizing their legislation or introducing where possible common European laws, abolishing discrimination on grounds of nationality and undertaking certain tasks on a joint European basis.

The main areas of the Council's activity are: Human rights, the media, social and socio-economic questions, education, culture and sport, youth, public health, heritage and environment, local and regional government, and legal co-operation.

152 Conventions and Agreements have been concluded covering such matters as social security, cultural affairs, conservation of European wild life and natural habitats, protection of archaeological heritage, extradition, medical treatment, equivalence of degrees and diplomas, the protection of television broadcasts, adoption of children and transportation of animals. Treaties in the legal field include the adoption of the European Convention on the Suppression of Terrorism, the European Convention on the Legal Status of Migrant Workers and the Transfer of Sentenced Persons. The Committee of Ministers adopted a European Convention for the protection of individuals with regard to the automatic processing of personal data (1981), a Convention on the compensation of victims of violent crimes (1983), a Convention on spectator violence and misbehaviour at sport events and in particular at football matches (1985), the European Charter of Local Government (1985), and a Convention for the Prevention of Torture and Inhuman or Degrading Treatment or Punishment (1987). The European Social Charter of 1961 sets out the social and economic rights which all member governments agree to guarantee to their citizens.

The official languages are English and French.

Chairman of the Committee of Ministers: (held in rotation).

President of the Parliamentary Assembly: Miguel Angel Martínez (Spain).

President of the European Court on Human Rights: Rolv Ryssdal (Norway).

President of the European Commission of Human Rights: Carl Aage Nørgaard (Denmark).

Secretary-General: Daniel Tarschys (Sweden).
Headquarters: Council of Europe, F-67075, Strasbourg, Cedex, France.
Flag: Blue with a ring of 12 gold stars in the centre.

Further Reading

The Information Department, Council of Europe, BP 431, F-67075 Strasbourg-Cedex.
European Yearbook. The Hague, from 1955
Forum. Strasbourg, from 1978, 4 times a year
Yearbook on the Convention on Human Rights. Strasbourg, from 1958
Cook, C. and Paxton, J., *European Political Facts, 1918–90.* London, 1992

EUROPEAN UNION (EU)

Origins. In May 1950 Belgium, France, the Federal Republic of Germany, Italy, Luxembourg and the Netherlands started negotiations with the aim of ensuring continual peace by a merging of their essential interests. The negotiations culminated in the signing in 1951 of the Treaty of Paris creating the European Coal and Steel Community (ECSC). 2 more communities with the aims of gradually integrating the economies of the 6 nations and of moving towards closer political unity, the European Economic Community (EEC) and the European Atomic Energy Community (EAEC or Euratom) were created on 25 March 1957 by the signing of the Treaties of Rome.

Membership. There were 15 member countries in 1996: Austria, Belgium, Denmark, Finland, France, Germany, Greece, Ireland, Italy, Luxembourg, the Netherlands, Portugal, Spain, Sweden and the UK.

On 30 June 1970 membership negotiations began between the European Community (EC) and the UK, Denmark, Ireland and Norway. On 22 Jan. 1972 those 4 countries signed a Treaty of Accession, although this was rejected by Norway in a referendum in Nov. 1972. On 1 Jan. 1973 the UK, Denmark and Ireland became full members. Greece joined the Community on 1 Jan. 1981; Spain and Portugal on 1 Jan. 1986. In Dec. 1985 the Treaties were amended again by the Single European Act of Luxembourg. Further amendments were agreed at the Maastricht Summit of Dec. 1991, whereby moves to a common currency were agreed subject to specific conditions including an 'opt-out' clause for the UK, and the social dimension was recognized in a protocol not applicable to the UK allowing the other member states to use EC institutions for this purpose. Ratification by member states of the Maastricht Treaty, however, proved unexpectedly controversial (in June 1992 the Danish electorate in a referendum voted against ratifying it, but reversed this decision in a second referendum in May 1993), but was completed in 1993 (the UK ratifying on 2 Aug.), and the *European Union (EU)* came into being on 1 Nov. The EU exists alongside the EC and pertains to the foreign affairs and security, and judicial and police spheres. The EU gives EC citizens the right to vote and stand in local and European Parliament elections, and creates a *Committee of the Regions.*

The territory of the former German Democratic Republic entered into full membership on re-unification with Federal Germany in Oct. 1990. Following referendums in favour, Austria, Finland and Sweden became members of the EU on 1 Jan. 1995. At a referendum in Nov. 1994 Norway rejected membership. Turkey applied for membership in April 1987, Malta in July 1990, Cyprus in July 1991, Switzerland in May 1992 (though in a referendum of Dec. 1992 Switzerland rejected joining the European Economic Area), Poland in March 1994, Hungary in April 1994, Slovakia in June 1995, Latvia in Oct. 1995, Estonia in Nov. 1995, Lithuania in Dec. 1995 and the Czech Republic in Jan. 1996. The Prince of Liechtenstein has presented his government with the task of making an application for membership. Associate membership agreements ('Europe Agreements') have been signed with Bulgaria, the Czech Republic, Hungary, Poland, Romania and Slovakia.

Greenland exercised its autonomy under the Danish Crown to secede in 1985.

Official Languages: Danish, Dutch, English, Finnish, French, German, Greek, Italian, Portuguese, Spanish and Swedish.

Organization. The institutional arrangements of the EU provide for an independent executive with powers of proposal (the Commission), various consultative bodies, and a decision-making body drawn from the Governments (the Council). Until 1967 the ECSC, EEC and Euratom were distinct, though they shared some non-decision-making bodies. Then the executives were merged in the European Commission, and the decision-taking bodies in the Council. The institutions and organs of the Communities are:

The **European Commission** consists of 20 members appointed by the member states to serve for 5 years. The *President* of the Commission is selected by consensus of prime ministers and serves a 5-year term. The present Commission started its term of office on 23 Jan. 1995. In Jan. 1996 the members were, with their areas of responsibility, nationalities and political party affiliation (CD = Christian-Democrat; Cons = Conservative; Lab = Labour; Lib = Liberal; S = Socialist; SD = Social-Democrat):

President, responsible for Monetary and Institutional Affairs, Foreign Policy and Common Security: Jacques Santer (b. 1937; Luxembourg; CD; appointed 1994).

Relations with the Southern Mediterranean, Near East, Latin America and part of Asia: Manuel Marin[1] (Spain; S). *Industry, Information Technology and Telecommunications:* Martin Bangemann (Germany; Lib). *Trade Policy and Relations with the Industrialized Countries of America and the Pacific Zone:* Sir Leon Brittan [1] (UK; Cons). *Competition:* Karel van Miert (Belgium; S). *EU Enlargement, Foreign Policy and Common Security, Relations with East Europe and the CIS:* Hans van den Broek (Netherlands; CD). *Relations with South Africa and the ACP Countries:* João de Deus Pinheiro (Portugal; Lib). *Social Affairs and Employment:* Pádraig Flynn (Ireland; Cons). *Institutional Questions and Relations with the European Parliament:* Marcelino Oreja (Spain: CD). *Development, Research, Education and Training and Competitiveness:* Edith Cresson (France; S). *Environment:* Ritt Bjerregaard (Denmark; S). *Regional Policies and Funding:* Monika Wulf-Mathies (Germany; SD). *Transport:* Neil Kinnock (UK; Lab). *Domestic Market and Taxation:* Mario Monti (Italy; ind Lib). *Consumers, Fisheries and Humanitarian Aid:* Emma Bonino (Italy; Radical). *Economic, Financial and Monetary Affairs:* Yves Thibault de Silguy (France; Rightist). *Energy and Primary Materials:* Christos Papoutsis (Greece; S). *Immigration, Internal and Judicial Affairs:* Anita Gradin (Sweden; S). *Agriculture:* Franz Fischler (Austria; Cons). *Budget:* Erkki Liikanen (Finland; S).

The Commission acts independently of any country in the interests of the EU as a whole, with as its mandate the implementation and guardianship of the Treaties. In this it has the right of initiative (putting proposals to the Council of Ministers for action); and execution (once the Council has decided); and can take the other institutions or individual countries before the European Court of Justice should any of these renege upon its responsibilities. The Commission operates through 23 Directorates-General.

Flag: Blue with a ring of 12 gold stars.
Address: 200 rue de la Loi, B-1049, Brussels, Belgium.

The **Council of Ministers** consists of foreign ministers from the 15 national governments and represents the national as opposed to the Community interests. It is the body which takes decisions under the Treaties. Numbers of votes: France, 10; Germany, 10; Italy, 10; UK, 10; Spain, 8; Belgium, 5; Greece, 5; the Netherlands, 5; Portugal, 5; Austria, 4; Sweden, 4; Denmark, 3; Finland, 3; Ireland, 3; Luxembourg, 2. Since the adoption of the Single European Act, an increasing number of its decisions are taken by majority vote, though some areas (e.g. taxation) are still reserved to unanimity. 27 votes are needed to veto a decision. Specialist Councils (e.g. the *Agriculture Council*) meet to discuss matters related to individual policies. The Single European Act also formalized the meetings of heads of state and government in the *European Council*, which normally meets twice a year; and of foreign ministers in *Political Co-operation*, to discuss co-operation outside the framework of the pre-Maastricht Treaties. The presidency of the Council is held for a 6-month term in

[1] Vice-President.

the following order from the beginning of 1996: Italy, Ireland, the Netherlands, Luxembourg, UK, Austria, Germany, Finland, Portugal, France, Sweden, Belgium.

Address: 170 rue de la Loi, B-1048, Brussels.

The **European Parliament** consists of 626 members, 567 elected for 5-year terms from 12 member states on 9 and 12 June 1994. All EU citizens may stand or vote in their adoptive country of residence. Germany returned 99 members, France, Italy and the UK 87 members each, Spain 64, the Netherlands 31, Belgium, Greece and Portugal 25 each, Denmark 16, Ireland 15 and Luxembourg 6. Seats allocated to countries which joined in Jan. 1995: Sweden, 22; Austria, 21; Finland, 16.

Political groupings: European Socialist Party, 217 seats; Popular European Party, 173; Liberal, Democratic and Reformist Group, 52; Unified European Left, 33; Forza Europa, 29; European Democrats' Rally, 26; Greens, 28; Radical European Alliance, 19; Europe of Nations, 19. 31 members were unattached to any group. The Parliament has a right to be consulted on a wide range of legislative proposals, and forms one arm of the Community's Budgetary Authority. Since the Single European Act it has an increased role in legislation, through the 'concertation' procedure, under which it can reject certain Council drafts in a second reading procedure. With the ratification of the Maastricht Treaty it gained the right of 'co-decision' on legislation with the Council of Ministers on a restricted range of domestic matters.

President: Klaus Hänsch (Germany; Social Democrat).
Location: Brussels, but meets at least once a month in Strasbourg.

European Parliament. *Members of the European Parliament, 4th Electoral Period, 1994–99.* 1995
Westlake, M., *Modern Guide to the European Parliament.* London, 1994

The **Economic and Social Committee** has an advisory role and consists of 189 representatives of employers, trade unions, consumers, etc.

President: Susanne Tiemann.
Address: 2, rue Ravenstein, B-1000 Brussels.

The **Court of Auditors** was established by a Treaty of 22 July 1975 which took effect on 1 June 1977. It consists of 12 members and was raised to the status of a full EU institution by the 1993 Maastricht Treaty. It audits all income and current and past expenditure of the EU.

President: André J. Middelhoek.
Address: 12, rue Alcide de Gasperi, L-1615 Luxembourg.

Annual Report of the Court of Auditors, from 1977

The **European Investment Bank** (EIB) was created in 1958 by the EEC Treaty to which its statute is annexed. Its governing body is the Board of Governors consisting of ministers designated by member states. Its main task is to contribute to the balanced development of the common market in the interest of the Community by financing projects: For developing less-developed regions; modernizing or converting undertakings; or developing new activities.

President: Sir Brian Unwin.
Address: 100 boulevard Konrad Adenauer, L-2950 Luxembourg.

Annual Report of the European Investment Bank

The **European Monetary Institute** in Frankfurt was established by the Maastricht Treaty in 1993 as the precursor of a European central bank.

President: Alexandre Lamfalussy (b. 1929; Belgium).

Europol was founded in 1994 to exchange criminal intelligence between EU countries. Its precursor was the European Drug Unit, whose field of operations was extended in 1994 to include traffic in nuclear and radio-active substances, illegal immigration and stolen vehicles. All EU states are represented by liaison officers (ELOs) working for their national police, gendarme or customs services.

The 1995 budget was ecu 4·5m. (1994, ecu 2·5m.). Member countries subscribe in proportion to their GNP.

Co-ordinator: Jürgen Storbeck (Germany).

Law. Provisions of the Treaties and secondary legislation may be either directly applicable in Member States or only applicable after Member States have enacted their own implementing legislation. Secondary legislation consists of: Regulations, which are of general application and binding in their entirety and directly applicable in all member states; directives which are binding upon each Member State as to the result to be achieved within a given time, but leave the national authority the choice of form and method of achieving this result; decisions, which are binding in their entirety on their addressees. In addition the Council and Commission can issue recommendations and opinions, which have no binding force.

The Community's Legislative Process starts with a proposal from the Commission (either at the suggestion of its services or in pursuit of its declared political aims) to the Council. The Council generally seeks the views of the European Parliament on the proposal, and the Parliament adopts a formal Opinion, after consideration of the matter by its specialist Committees. The Council may also (and in some cases is obliged to) consult the Economic and Social Committee, which similarly delivers an opinion. When these opinions have been received, the Council will decide. Most decisions are taken on a majority basis, but will take account of reserves expressed by individual member states. The text eventually approved may differ substantially from the original Commission proposal.

The **Court of Justice of the European Communities** is composed of 13 judges and 6 advocates-general, is responsible for the adjudication of disputes arising out of the application of the treaties, and its findings are enforceable in all member countries. A Court of First Instance was created in 1989.

President: Gil Carlos Rodríguez Iglesias (Spain).
Address: Palais de la Cour de Justice, Kirchberg, Luxembourg.

The office of **EU Ombudsman** was inaugurated in 1995. The present incumbent is Jacob Söderman (Finland).

Finances. Revenue for financial years in ecu 1m.:

	1994	*1995*	*1996*
Own resources	68,082	70,245	81,320
Miscellaneous Community taxes, levies and dues	361	405	445
Administrative operation of the institutions	75	92	92
Contributions to EU programmes	349	9	9
Borrowing and lending	15	17	17
Miscellaneous	7	5	5
Total	68,889	75,438	81,888

Expenditure for 1995 was ecu 76,527m.

The resources of the Community (the levies and duties mentioned above, and up to a 1·4% VAT charge) have been surrendered to it by Treaty. The Budget is made by the Council and the Parliament acting jointly as the Budgetary Authority. The Parliament has control, within a certain margin, of non-obligatory expenditure (*i.e.*, expenditure where the amount to be spent is not set out in the legislation concerned), and can also reject the Budget. Otherwise, the Council decides.

An agreement of 1992 fixed the permissible ceiling of expenditure at 1·2% of EC GDP in 1993 and 1994, rising to 1·27% in 1999.

The *Schengen Accord* abolished border controls on persons and goods between those member states which have signed it. It came into effect on 26 March 1995. Signatories are Austria, Belgium, France, Germany, Greece, Italy, Luxembourg, Netherlands, Portugal and Spain, but Austria, Greece and Italy have not yet implemented it.

THE EUROPEAN COAL AND STEEL COMMUNITY. The ECSC

was the first of the 3 European Communities, coming into existence on 10 Aug. 1952 following the signature of the Treaty of Paris on 18 April 1951. Its aim was to contribute towards economic expansion, growth of employment and a rising standard of living in Member States, through common action in the coal and steel sector. Since 1957 it has had the same membership as the other Communities. Operations are partly funded by a turnover levy on the coal and steel industries of the EU, partly from the general budget. A *Consultative Committee* of 96 representatives of employers, trade unions, consumers etc. has an advisory role.

THE EUROPEAN ECONOMIC COMMUNITY (EEC; 'COMMON MARKET')

Based on the Treaty of Rome of 25 March 1957 the EEC came into being on 1 Jan. 1958 with the same original members as the ECSC. The Treaty guarantees certain rights to the citizens of all member states (*e.g.*, the outlawing of economic discrimination by nationality, and equal pay for equal work as between men and women) and sets out certain other areas where secondary legislation is to fill in the details. The most important policy areas are as follows:

Freedom of movement for persons, goods and capital. Under the Treaty individuals or companies from one Member State may establish themselves in another country (for the purposes of economic activity) or sell goods or services there on the same basis as nationals of that country. With a few exceptions, restrictions on the movement of capital have also been ended. Under the Single European Act the member states bound themselves to achieve the suppression of all barriers to free movement of persons, goods and services by 31 Dec. 1992.

Customs Union and External Trade Relations. Goods or Services originating in one Member State have free circulation within the EEC, which implies common arrangements for trade with the rest of the world. Member States can no longer make bilateral trade agreements with third countries: This power has been ceded to the Community. The Customs Union was achieved in July 1968.

In Oct. 1991 a treaty forming the European Economic Area (EEA) was approved by the member states of the EC and EFTA. (For details *see* EFTA). Association agreements which could lead to accession or customs union have been made with Cyprus, Estonia, Latvia, Lithuania, Israel, Malta, Morocco and Turkey. The customs union with Turkey came into force on 1 Jan. 1996. Commercial, industrial, technical and financial aid agreements have been made with Algeria, Egypt, Jordan, Lebanon, Morocco, Russia, Syria, Tunisia and the former Yugoslavia. In 1976 Canada signed a framework agreement for co-operation in industrial trade, science and natural resources, and a transatlantic pact was signed with the USA in Dec. 1995. Co-operation agreements also exist with a number of Latin American countries and groupings (e.g. the Andean Group) and with Arab and Asian countries; and an economic and commercial agreement has been signed with ASEAN. A co-operation agreement was signed with Slovenia in Nov. 1992 and partnership and co-operation agreements with the Ukraine in June 1994, Kazakhstan in Jan. 1995 and Kyrgyzstan in Feb. 1995. Free trade agreements were concluded with Estonia, Latvia and Lithuania in July 1994.

In the *Development Aid* sector, the EU has an agreement (the Lomé Convention, originally signed in 1975 but renewed and enlarged in 1979 and 1984) with some 60 African, Caribbean and Pacific (ACP) countries which removes customs duties without reciprocal arrangements for most of their imports to the Community, and under which ecu 8,760m. of aid was granted between 1986–90. An economic and commercial agreement has also been signed with ASEAN.

The Common Agricultural Policy (CAP). The objectives set out in the Treaty are to increase agricultural productivity, to ensure a fair standard of living for the agricultural community, to stabilise markets, to assure supplies, and to ensure reasonable consumer prices. In Dec. 1960 the Council laid down the fundamental principles on which the CAP is based: A single market, which calls for common prices, stable currency parities and the harmonising of health and veterinary legislation; Community preference, which protects the single Community market from imports; common financing, through the European Agricultural Guidance and

Guarantee Fund (EAGGF), which seeks to improve agriculture through its Guidance section, and to stabilise markets against world price fluctuations through market intervention, with levies and refunds on exports. At present common market organizations cover over 95% of EEC agricultural production.

Following the disappearance of stable currency parities, artificial currency levels have been applied in the CAP. This factor, together with over-production due to high producer prices, meant that the CAP consumed about two-thirds of the Communities' budget. It was agreed in May 1992 to reform CAP and lessen over-production by reducing the price supports to farmers by 29% for cereals, 15% for beef and 5% for dairy products. Compensatory grants are available to farmers who remove land from production or take early retirement.

The European Monetary System (EMS). Founded in March 1979 to control inflation, protect European trade from international disturbances and ultimately promote convergence between the European economies. The *Exchange Rate Mechanism (ERM)* is run by the finance ministries and central banks of the EU countries on a day-to-day basis; monthly reviews are carried out by the EU Monetary Committee (finance ministries) and the EU Committee of Central Bankers. All EU countries are members of EMS, but only Belgium, Denmark, France, Germany, Luxembourg, the Netherlands, Portugal and Spain are in the ERM; the UK suspended its membership on
17 Sept. 1992. Members are obliged to restrict the fluctuations in the value of their currencies to a variation 'band', of 15% (2·25% for Germany and the Netherlands) higher or lower than a central rate established by comparing all the currencies in the ERM and the European Currency Unit, the ecu (XEU). If a currency reaches its top or bottom limits, central banks are obliged to buy or sell currency on the foreign exchanges. Further stabilization measures would involve adjustment of national interest rates, central bank borrowing from other central banks or withdrawal of reserves from the European Monetary Co-operation Fund. The adjustment of last resort is re- or devaluation.

In March 1995, £1 = ecu 0·80; US$1 = ecu 1·29.

Dod's European Companion. Hurst Green, East Sussex, 1990

Competition. The Competition (anti-trust) law of the EU is based on 2 principles: That businesses should not seek to nullify the creation of the common market by the erection of artificial national (or other) barriers to the free movement of goods; and against the abuse of dominant positions in any market. These two principles have led among other things to the outlawing of prohibitions on exports to other Member States, of price-fixing agreements and of refusal to supply; and to the refusal by the Commission to allow mergers or take-overs by dominant undertakings in specific cases. Increasingly heavy fines are imposed on offenders.

THE EUROPEAN ATOMIC ENERGY COMMUNITY (EURATOM)

Like the EEC, Euratom came into being on 1 Jan. 1958 following a Treaty signed in Rome on 25 March 1957, and it had the same member states as the EEC. Its task is to promote common efforts between its members in the development of nuclear energy for peaceful purposes, and for this purpose it has monopoly powers of acquisition of fissile materials for civil purposes. It is in no way concerned with military uses of nuclear power.

The execution of the Treaty now rests with the European Commission, which is advised by the Scientific and Technical Committee (28 members). Major decisions rest with the Council. Euratom has 1 substantial research institute of its own, at Ispra, in Italy; it does other work in co-operation with research institutes in the member states, or in joint and international undertakings.

A common market for nuclear materials and equipment came into force, and external tariffs were suspended, in Jan. 1959.

European Community Delegation to the US: 2100 M Street NW (Suite 707), Washington DC 20037.
Head of Delegation: Andreas van Agt.

US Delegation to the European Community: 40 boulevard du Régent, 1000 Brussels.
Head of Delegation: James F. Dobbins.
European Community Delegation to the United Nations: 3 Dag Hammarskjöld Plaza, 305 East 47th Street, New York NY 10017.
Head of Delegation: Angel Viñas.

Further Reading

Official Journal of the European Communities.—General Report on the Activities of the European Communities (annual, from 1967).—*The Agricultural Situation in the Community.* (annual).—*The Social Situation in the Community.* (annual).—*Report on Competition Policy in the European Community.* (annual).—*Basic Statistics of the Community* (annual).— *Bulletin of the European Community* (monthly).—*Register of Current Community Legal Instruments.* 1983
Europe (monthly), obtainable from the Information Office of the European Commission, 8 Storey's Gate, London, SW1P 3AT
Brittan, L., *The Europe We Need.* London, 1994
Cox, A. and Furlong, P., *A Modern Companion to the European Community: a Guide to Key Facts, Institutions and Terms.* Aldershot, 1992
Delors, J., *Our Europe: the Community and National Development.* London, 1993
Dinan, D., *Ever Closer Union? An Introduction to the European Community.* London, 1994.
Hitiris, T., *European Community Economics: a Modern Introduction.* London, 1991
Hurwitz, L. and Lequesne, C. (eds.) *The State of the European Community: Policies, Institutions and Debates in the Transition Years.* Harlow, 1992
Kirschner, E. J., *Decision-Making in the European Community: the Council Presidency and European Integration.* Manchester Univ. Press, 1992
Leonardi, R., *Convergence, Cohesion and Integration in the European Union.* London, 1995
Lewis, D. W. P., *The Road to Europe: History, Institutions and Prospects of European Integration, 1945–1993.* Berne, 1994
Nugent, N., *The Government and Politics of the European Union.* 3rd ed. London, 1994
Nuttall, S. J., *European Political Co-operation.* Oxford, 1993
Paxton, J., *European Communities.* [Bibliography]. Oxford and New Brunswick (NJ), 1992
Weigall, D. and Stirk, P., *The Origins and Development of the European Community.* Leicester Univ. Press, 1992
Williams, A. M., *The European Community: the Contradictions of Integration.* 2nd ed. Oxford, 1994
Winters, L. and Venables, A. (eds.) *European Integration: Trade and Industry.* CUP, 1993

EUROPEAN FREE TRADE ASSOCIATION (EFTA)

The Stockholm Convention establishing the Association entered into force on 3 May 1960. Founder members were Austria, Denmark, Norway, Portugal, Sweden, Switzerland and the UK. With the accession of Austria, Denmark, Finland, Portugal, Sweden and the UK to the EU, EFTA was reduced to 4 member countries by 1996: Iceland, Liechtenstein, Norway and Switzerland.

Free trade in industrial goods among members was achieved by 1966. Co-operation with the EU began in 1972 with the signing of free trade agreements and culminated in the establishment of a European Economic Area (EEA), encompassing the free movement of goods, services, capital and labour throughout EFTA and EU countries. The EEA Agreement was signed by all members of the EU and EFTA on 2 May 1992, but was rejected by Switzerland in a referendum on 6 Dec. 1992. Entry into force took place on 1 Jan. 1994.

Its main provisions are: Free movement of products within the EEA from 1993 (special arrangements to cover food, energy, coal and steel); EFTA to assume EU rules on company law, consumer protection, education, the environment, research and development and social policy; EFTA to adopt EU competition rules on anti-trust matters, abuse of a dominant position, public procurement, mergers and state aid; EFTA to create an EFTA Surveillance Authority and an EFTA Court; individuals to be free to live, work and offer services throughout the EEA, with mutual recognition of professional qualifications; capital movements to be free with some restrictions on investments; EFTA countries to maintain their own domestic agricultural policies if they wish.

The EEA-EFTA states have established a *Surveillance Authority* and a *Court* to ensure implementation of the Agreement among the EFTA-EEA states. Political direction is given by the EEA Council which meets twice a year at ministerial level, while ongoing operation of the Agreement is overseen by the EEA Joint Committee. Legislative power remains with national governments and parliaments.

EFTA has formal relations with several other states. Declarations on co-operation were signed with Hungary, Czechoslovakia and Poland (June 1990), Bulgaria, Estonia, Latvia, Lithuania and Romania (Dec. 1991), Slovenia (May 1992), Albania (Dec. 1992), and Egypt, Morocco and Tunisia (Dec. 1995). Free trade agreements have followed with Czechoslovakia (March 1992 – with protocols on succession with the Czech Republic and Slovakia in April 1993), Poland and Romania (Dec. 1992), Bulgaria and Hungary (March 1993) and Slovenia (July 1995); free trade agreements with Turkey (Dec. 1991), Israel (Sept. 1992) and Estonia, Latvia and Lithuania (Dec. 1995) have also been signed, and contacts with the Gulf Co-operation Council established. Co-operation with Yugoslavia was suspended in Nov. 1991.

The operation of the free trade area among the EFTA states is the responsibility of the EFTA Council which meets regularly in Geneva at the level of ambassadors. The Council is assisted by a Secretariat and a number of standing committees. Each EFTA country holds the chairmanship of the Council for 6 months.

Flag: White with the letters EFTA in black in the centre, within a ring of the flags of the member countries.

Secretary-General: Kjartan Jóhansson (Iceland).
Headquarters: 9–11 rue de Varembé, 1211 Geneva 20, Switzerland.
Brussels Office: 74 rue de Trèves, B-1040, Brussels.

Convention Establishing the European Free Trade Association
EFTA Annual Report
EFTA Expert Papers: Information Papers on Aspects of the EEA
EFTA News/Bulletin. (approximately 10 a year)

ORGANIZATION FOR SECURITY AND CO-OPERATION IN EUROPE (OSCE)

Initiatives from both NATO and the Warsaw Pact culminated in the first summit Conference on Security and Co-operation in Europe (CSCE) attended by heads of state and government in Helsinki on 30 July–1 Aug. 1975, which adopted a 'Final Act' laying down 10 principles concerning human rights, self-determination and the inter-relations of the participant states. Conferences followed in Belgrade (1977–78), Madrid (1980–83), Stockholm (1984–86) and Vienna (1986–89). At the Paris summit of 19–21 Nov. 1990 the members of NATO and the Warsaw Pact signed a Treaty on the Reduction of Conventional Forces in Europe (CFE) and a declaration that they were 'no longer adversaries' and did not intend to 'use force against the territorial integrity or political independence of any state'. All the 34 participants adopted the Confidence and Security-Building Measures (CSBMs), which pertained to the exchange of military information, verification of military installations, objection to unusual military activities etc., and signed the Charter of Paris.

On 1 Jan. 1995 the CSCE changed its name to the Organization for Security and Co-operation in Europe (OSCE).

Members. In 1996 the 54 member nations were: Albania, Armenia, Austria [1], Azerbaijan, Belgium [1], Belarus, Bosnia-Hercegovina, Bulgaria [1], Canada [1], Croatia, Cyprus [1], the Czech Republic [2], Denmark [1], Estonia, Finland [1], France [1], Georgia, Germany [1], Greece [1], Hungary [1], Iceland [1], Ireland [1], Italy [1], Kazakhstan,

Kyrgyzstan, Latvia, Liechtenstein [1], Lithuania, Luxembourg [1], Macedonia, Malta [1], Moldova, Monaco [1], Netherlands [1], Norway [1], Poland [1], Portugal [1], Romania [1], Russia (succeeding USSR [1]), San Marino [1], Slovakia [2], Slovenia, Spain [1], Sweden [1], Switzerland [1], Tajikistan, Turkey [1], Turkmenistan, Ukraine, UK [1], USA [1], Uzbekistan, Vatican [1] and Yugoslavia [1].

The Charter sets out principles of human rights, democracy and the rule of law to which all the signatories undertake to adhere, lays down the bases for east-west co-operation and other future action, and institutionalizes the OSCE. The *Council of Foreign Ministers* is the highest decision-making body and meets at least once a year. The Council's agent is the *Committee of Senior Officials.* It meets 4 times a year at the *Secretariat* in Prague. There is also a *Conflict Prevention Centre* in Vienna and an *Office for Democratic Institutions and Human Rights* in Warsaw. The *Parliamentary Assembly* is formally independent, but maintains close links with the OSCE process. Meetings take place annually in OSCE capitals in rotation. It has a secretariat in Copenhagen. The *High Commissioner on National Minorities* has the duty of early and impartial evaluation of ethnic conflicts and recommendation of action. There is an office in The Hague.

In July 1992 the member nations unanimously agreed to set up an armed peacekeeping force.

Secretary–General: Wilhelm Hoynck (Germany).

[1] Founder member. [2] Founder member as part of the former Czechoslovakia.

Further Reading

Freeman, J., *Security and the CSCE Process: the Stockholm Conference and Beyond.* London, 1991

EUROPEAN BANK FOR RECONSTRUCTION AND DEVELOPMENT (EBRD, BERD)

History and Membership. A treaty to establish the EBRD was signed May 1990; it was inaugurated on 15 April 1991. It had 41 original members: the European Commission, the European Investment Bank, all the EEC countries and all the countries of East Europe except Albania. Albania became a member in Oct. 1991, and all the republics of the former USSR in March 1992, bringing membership to 59 in 1994.

Its founding capital was of ecu 10m., of which the USA contributed 10%, the UK, France, Germany, Italy, Japan 8·5% each, and the USSR 6%.

Objectives. It was set up to lend funds at market rates to Central and Eastern European companies and countries 'which are committed to, and applying, the principles of multi-party democracy and market economics'. Facilities were extended to the countries of thhe former USSR in 1992.

A policy statement of May 1991 says that initial emphasis will be placed on programmes to support the creation and strengthening of infrastructure; privatization, reform of the financial sector, including development of capital markets and privatization of commercial banks; development of productive competitive private sectors of small and medium-sized enterprises in industry, agriculture and services; restructuring industrial sectors to put them on a competitive basis; encouraging foreign investment and cleaning up the environment.

Organization. There is a Board of Governors with full management powers, and a 23-member Board of Directors which is involved in day-to-day operations.

Adminstration costs were frozen in 1993, and rose 3·5% in 1994.

President: Jacques de Larosière (b. 1930; France).
General Secretary: Bart le Blanc.
Headquarters: 122, Leadenhall St., London EC3V 4EB.

COLOMBO PLAN

History: Founded in 1950 to promote the development of newly independent Asian member countries, the Colombo Plan has grown from a group of 7 Commonwealth nations into an international organization of 24 countries. Originally the Plan was conceived for a period of 6 years. This was renewed from time to time until the Consultative Committee gave the Plan an indefinite span of life in 1980; its need and relevance will henceforth be examined only if considered necessary.

The Plan is multilateral in approach but bilateral in operation: Multilateral in that it takes cognizance of the problems of development of member countries in the Asia and Pacific region and endeavours to deal with them in a co-ordinated way; bilateral because negotiations for assistance are made direct between a donor and a recipient country.

Aims: The aims of the Colombo Plan are: *(a)* to promote interest in and support for the economic and social development in Asia and the Pacific; *(b)* to keep under review economic and social progress in the region and help accelerate development through co-operative effort; and *(c)* to facilitate development assistance to and within the region.

Member Countries: Afghanistan, Australia, Bangladesh, Bhutan, Burma, Cambodia, Fiji, India, Indonesia, Iran, Japan, South Korea, Laos, Malaysia, Maldives, Nepal, New Zealand, Pakistan, Papua New Guinea, Philippines, Singapore, Sri Lanka, Thailand and USA.

Structure: There are four organs which give focus to the Plan:

Consultative Committee: The Committee is the highest deliberative body of the Plan and consists of Ministers of member Governments who meet once in two years. The Ministerial meeting is preceded by a meeting of senior officials who are directly concerned with the operation of the Plan in various countries.

Colombo Plan Council: The Council is also a deliberative body which meets several times a year in Colombo, where most member countries have resident diplomatic missions, to review the economic and social development of the Asia-Pacific region and promote co-operation among member countries.

Colombo Plan Bureau: Its functions include servicing the meetings of the Colombo Plan Council and the Consultative Committee, carrying out research, and dissemination of statistical and other information relating to activities under the Plan. Since 1973 the Bureau has been operating a Drug Advisory Programme to assist national and regional efforts to eliminate the causes and ameliorate the effects of drug abuse.

Colombo Plan Staff College: The Colombo Plan Staff College for Technician Education, established in 1975, transferred from Singapore to the Philippines in 1987. The College helps member countries in developing their systems of technician education, mainly through training courses, seminars and consultancies. It is separately financed by most Colombo Plan member countries and functions under the guidance of its own Governing Board consisting of the heads of member countries' diplomatic missions resident in the Philippines.

Flag: Dark blue with a central white disc containing the Colombo Plan logo in black.

Headquarters: Colombo Plan Bureau, 12 Melbourne Avenue, PO Box 596, Colombo 4, Sri Lanka.

ASIA-PACIFIC ECONOMIC CO-OPERATION GROUP (APEC)

The APEC was founded in Nov. 1989 to devise programmes of co-operation between member nations and hold annual meetings of trade and foreign ministers. It was institutionalized in June 1992 after a meeting in Bangkok at which it was agreed to set up a *Secretariat* in Singapore. There are 18 member states: Australia, Brunei, Canada, Chile, China, Hong Kong, Indonesia, Japan, South Korea, Malaysia, Mexico, New Zealand, Papua New Guinea, the Philippines, Singapore, Taiwan, Thailand and the USA.

At the Bogor (Indonesia) summit of Nov. 1994 it was agreed to work towards the establishment of a free trade zone by 2020.

Executive Director: Rusli Noor.

ASSOCIATION OF SOUTH EAST ASIAN NATIONS (ASEAN)

History and Membership. ASEAN is a regional organization formed by the governments of Indonesia, Malaysia, the Philippines, Singapore and Thailand through the Bangkok Declaration which was signed by their foreign ministers on 8 Aug. 1967. Brunei joined in 1984 and Vietnam in 1995. Cambodia, Laos and Papua New Guinea have observer status.

Objectives. The main objectives are to accelerate economic growth, social progress and cultural development, to promote active collaboration and mutual assistance in matters of common interest, to ensure the stability of the South East Asian region and to maintain close co-operation with existing international and regional organizations with similar aims. Principal projects concern economic co-operation and development, with the intensification of intra-ASEAN trade and trade between the region and the rest of the world; joint research and technological programmes; co-operation in transportation and communications; promotion of tourism and South East Asian studies; including cultural, scientific, educational and administrative exchanges.

Organs. The highest authority in ASEAN are the Heads of Government of the Member Countries who meet as and when necessary to give directions to ASEAN. The highest policy-making body is the Meeting of Foreign Ministers, commonly known as the Annual Ministerial Meeting, which convenes in each of the ASEAN member countries on a rotational basis in alphabetical order. The Standing Committee, comprising the Foreign Minister of the country hosting the Ministerial Meeting in that particular year and the accredited ambassadors of the other member countries, carries out the work of the Association in between the Ministerial Meetings and handles the routine matters to ensure continuity and to make decisions based on the guidelines or policies set by the Ministerial Meetings and submit for the consideration of the Foreign Ministers all reports and recommendations of the various ASEAN committees. There are 5 economic committees under the ASEAN Economic Ministers and 5 non-economic committees that recommend and draw up programmes for ASEAN co-operation. These committees are responsible for the operation and implementation of ASEAN projects in their respective fields. Each ASEAN capital has an ASEAN National Secretariat. The central secretariat for ASEAN is located in Jakarta, Indonesia, and is headed by the Secretary General, a post that revolves among the member states in alphabetical order every 3 years. Bureau directors and other officers of the ASEAN Secretariat remain in office for 3 years.

The *Asean Free Trade Area (AFTA)* was set up by all the member states in Oct. 1991 with the aim of creating a common market in 15 years, with a common tariff regime for manufactured and processed agricultural goods (Common Effective Preferential Tariff, CEPT) as a first step. In Oct. 1992 it was agreed that CEPT would be put into effect on 1 Jan. 1993 with progressive tariff reductions.

The *ASEAN Regional Forum* was founded at a meeting of ASEAN foreign ministers at Bangkok in July 1994 to discuss security issues. It comprised initially: The ASEAN and EU countries, Australia, Canada, China, Japan, South Korea, Laos, New Zealand, Papua New Guinea, Russia and Vietnam.

Secretary-General: Roderick Yong (Brunei Darussalam).

Headquarters: POB 2072, Jakarta, Indonesia.

Further Reading

Broinowski, A., *Understanding ASEAN*. London, 1982;—(ed.) *ASEAN into the 1990s*. London, 1990
Wawn, B., *The Economies of the ASEAN Countries*. London, 1982

ORGANIZATION OF AMERICAN STATES (OAS)

On 14 April 1890 representatives of the American republics, meeting in Washington at the First International Conference of American States, established an 'International Union of American Republics' and, as its central office, a 'Commercial Bureau of American Republics', which later became the Pan American Union. This international organization's object was to foster mutual understanding and co-operation among the nations of the western hemisphere. Since that time, successive inter-American conferences have greatly broadened the scope of work of the organization.

This led to the adoption on 30 April 1948 by the Ninth International Conference of American States, at Bogotá, Colombia, of the Charter of the Organization of American States. This co-ordinated the work of all the former independent official entities in the inter-American system and defined their mutual relationships.

The Charter of 1948 subsequently was amended by the Protocol of Buenos Aires (1967) and the Protocol of Cartagena de Indias (1985). The purposes of the OAS are to strengthen the peace and security of the continent; promote and consolidate representative democracy, with due respect for the principle of non-intervention; prevent possible causes of difficulties and ensure the pacific settlement of disputes among member states; provide for common action in the event of aggression; seek the solution of political, juridical and economic problems; promote by co-operative action economic, social and cultural development; and achieve an effective limitation of conventional weapons in order to devote maximum resources to economic and social development. Within the framework of the UN, the OAS is a regional organization.

In Dec. 1992 the OAS General Assembly adopted the Protocol of Washington to amend the OAS Charter by incorporating certain provisions of a resolution (1080) on representative democracy adopted at the 21st Regular Session in 1991, and to deal with the issue of critical poverty. Specifically, the General Assembly approved a new article which provides that a member of OAS whose democratically-constituted government has been overthrown by force may be suspended from the exercise of the right to participate in the sessions of OAS organs, and spells out the way such suspension shall be applied. The Protocol of Washington also incorporates among the essential purposes of the OAS the eradication of extreme poverty which constitutes an obstacle to the full democratic development of the peoples of the hemisphere.

In June 1993 the General Assembly adopted the Protocol of Managua which introduces additional Charter amendments. The current Inter-American Councils on Economic and Social Affairs and on Education, Science and Culture are to be replaced with a new Inter-American Council for Integral Development. Other measures are designed to improve the delivery of technical co-operation to the member states, in an effort to help eradicate extreme poverty from the hemisphere.

Both the Protocol of Washington and the Protocol of Managua will enter into force when ratified by two-thirds of the OAS member states.

Membership is on a basis of absolute equality. Each country has one vote and there is no veto power. Member countries (1996): Antigua and Barbuda, Argentina, Bahamas, Barbados, Belize, Bolivia, Brazil, Canada, Chile, Colombia, Costa Rica, Cuba (not present government), Dominica, Dominican Republic, Ecuador, El Salvador, Grenada, Guatemala, Guyana, Haiti, Honduras, Jamaica, Mexico, Nicaragua, Panama, Paraguay, Peru, St Kitts and Nevis, St Lucia, St Vincent and the Grenadines, Suriname, Trinidad and Tobago, USA, Uruguay, Venezuela.

With the emergence of democratically-elected governments throughout the continent, the OAS has been increasingly concerned with the preservation, protection and promotion of democracy. At its 21st Regular Session (Santiago, Chile, June 1991) the OAS General Assembly adopted *The Santiago Commitment to Democracy and the Renewal of the Inter-American System,* as well as a resolution (1080) on representive democracy. The latter calls for collective action in the event of a 'sudden or irregular interruption of the democratic political institutional process or of the legitimate exercise of power by the democratically-elected government in any of the Organization's member states'.

At its 20th Special Session (Feb. 1994, Mexico City) the OAS General Assembly approved 2 resolutions, one containing a *General Policy Framework and Priorities: Partnership for Development* and the second agreeing on a *Commitment on a Partnership for Development annd Struggle to Overcome Extreme Poverty.* At its 24th Regular Session (June 1994l, Belém do Pará) the General Assembly adopted the *Declaration of Belém do Pará* in which the Ministers of Foreign Affairs and Heads of Delegation of Member States, declared: Their commitment to strengthening the OAS as the main hemispheric forum of political consensus so that it may support the realization of the aspirations of member states in promoting and consolidating peace, democracy, social justice, and development, in accordance with the purposes and principles of the Charter; Their decision to promote and deepen co-operative relations in the economic, social, educational, cultural, scientific, technological, and political fields; Their commitment to continue and further the dialogue on hemispheric security in order to consolidate and strengthen mutual confidence; Their determination to continue to contribute to the objective of general and complete disarmament, under effective international control; Their determination to strengthen regional co-operation to increase the effectiveness of efforts to combat the illicit use of narcotic drugs and traffic therein; Their decision to co-operate in a reciprocal effort towards preventing and punishing terrorist acts, methods and practices, and the development of international law in this matter; and, Their commitment to promote economic and social development for the indigenous populations of their countries.

The OAS also carries out programmes to promote the economic and social development of its member states. Specialized training is provided for Latin American and Caribbean citizens each year in development-related fields, and development projects are executed each year in response to requests from member governments.

Under its Charter the OAS accomplishes its purposes by means of:

(a) The *General Assembly*, which meets annually.

(b) The *Meeting of Consultation of Ministers of Foreign Affairs*, held to consider problems of an urgent nature and of common interest.

(c) The Councils: The *Permanent Council*, which meets on a permanent basis at OAS headquarters amd carries out decisions of the General Assembly, assists the member states in the peaceful settlement of disputes, acts as the Preparatory Committee of that Assembly, submits recommendations with regard to the functioning of the Organization, and considers the reports to the Assembly of the other organs; the *Inter-American Economic and Social Council* and the *Inter-American Council for Education, Science and Culture*, both of which promote and co-ordinate the Organization's activities in their respective spheres of competence and render the governments such specialized services as they may request. Each of the Councils is composed of a representative from each member state, appointed by the government of that state.

(d) The *Inter-American Juridical Committee* which acts as an advisory body to the OAS on juridical matters and promotes the development and codification of international law. Eleven jurists, elected for 4-year terms by the General Assembly, represent all the American States.

(e) The *Inter-American Commission on Human Rights* which oversees the observance and protection of human rights. 7 members elected for 4-year terms by the General Assembly represent all the OAS member states.

(f) The *General Secretariat*, which is the central and permanent organ of the OAS.

(g) The *Specialized Conferences*, meeting to deal with special technical matters or to develop specific aspects of inter-American co-operation.

(h) The *Specialized Organizations*, inter-governmental organizations established by multilateral agreements to discharge specific functions in their respective fields of action, such as women's affairs, agriculture, child welfare, Indian affairs, geography and history, and health.

Associated with the OAS as permanent observers are: Algeria, Angola, Austria, Belgium, Croatia, Cyprus, the Czech Republic, Egypt, Equatorial Guinea, Finland, France, Germany, Greece, Hungary, India, Israel, Italy, Japan, South Korea, Lebanon, Morocco, the Netherlands, Pakistan, Poland, Portugal, Romania, Russia, Saudi Arabia, Spain, Switzerland, Tunisia, the Ukraine, the Vatican and the EU.

Secretary General: César Gavíria Trujillo (Colombia).

The Secretary General is elected by the General Assembly for 5-year terms. The General Assembly approves the annual budget which is financed by quotas contributed by the member governments.

General Secretariat: Washington, D.C., 20006, USA.
Flag: Light blue with the OAS seal in colour in the centre.

Further Reading

Publications of the OAS General Secretariat include:

Charter of the Organization of American States. 1948.—*As Amended by the Protocol of Buenos Aires in 1967 and the Protocol of Cartagena de Indias in 1985*
The OAS and the Evolution of the Inter-American System. 1991
Annual Report of the Secretary-General
Status of Inter-American Treaties and Conventions. Annual

LATIN AMERICAN ECONOMIC GROUPINGS

Central American Common Market (CACM). In Dec. 1960 El Salvador, Guatemala, Honduras and Nicaragua concluded the General Treaty of Central American Economic Integration under the auspices of the Organization of Central American States (ODECA) in Managua. A protocol signed by all 6 members in Oct. 1993 reaffirmed an eventual commitment to regional integration with a common external tariff of 20%. It is to be introduced voluntarily and gradually. Members in 1995 were: Costa Rica, El Salvador, Guatemala, Honduras, Nicaragua and Panama.

Headquarters: 4a Avda 10–25, Zona 14, Apdo 1237, Guatemala City, Guatemala.

The **Andean Group**. On 26 May 1969 an agreement was signed by Bolivia, Chile, Colombia, Ecuador and Peru creating the Andean Group. Venezuela was initially actively involved but did not sign the agreement until 1973. Chile withdrew from the Group in 1977. Members: Bolivia, Colombia, Ecuador, Peru and Venezuela. The Act of Caracas signed at the Group's 5th meeting in May 1991 established a free trade zone between member states to come into effect on 1 Jan. 1992 as the first step towards the creation of a common market in 1995. There is a common external tariff in 4 bands from 5% to 20%. Tariffs between Bolivia, Colombia and Ecuador were abolished in Oct. 1992.

The Group's *Presidential Council* is composed of the presidents of the member states.

Headquarters: Avda Paseo de la Republica 3895, Casilla 18–1177, Lima 27, Peru.

Mercado Común del Sur (Mercosur)

Founded in March 1991 by the Treaty of Asunción between Argentina, Brazil, Paraguay and Uruguay the treaty committed the signatories to the progressive reduction of tariffs culminating in the formation of a common market of 1 Jan.

1995. This duly came into effect as a free trade zone affecting 90% of commodities. A common external tariff applies to trade with countries outside Mercosur. Details were agreed at foreign minister level by the Protocol of Ouro Preto signed on 17 Dec. 1994. The member states' foreign ministers form a council responsible for political questions, the chairmanship of which rotates every 6 months. The permanent executive body is the 'group' of member states, which takes decisions by consensus. There is an arbitration tribunal whose decisions are binding on member countries.

Group of Three. In June 1994 the presidents of Colombia, Mexico and Venezuela signed a free trade pact which came into effect on 1 Jan. 1995. The pact aims gradually to eliminate tariff and most non-tariff barriers between the signatories, and establish a dispute resolution body.

CARIBBEAN COMMUNITY (CARICOM)

Establishment and Functions. The Treaty establishing the Caribbean Community, including the Caribbean Common Market, and the Agreement establishing the Common External Tariff for the Caribbean Common Market, was signed by the Prime Ministers of Barbados, Guyana, Jamaica and Trinidad and Tobago at Chaguaramas, Trinidad, on 4 July 1973, and entered into force on 1 Aug. 1973. 6 further countries signed the Treaty of Chaguaramas on 17 April 1974: Belize, Dominica, Grenada, St Lucia, St Vincent and the Grenadines and Montserrat, and the Treaty came into effect for those countries on 1 May 1974. Antigua acceded to membership on 4 July and St Kitts–Nevis on 26 July 1974, Bahamas (not Common Market) on 4 July 1983 and Suriname on 4 July 1995.

The Caribbean Community has 3 areas of activity: *(i)* economic co-operation through the Caribbean Common Market; *(ii)* co-ordination of foreign policy; *(iii)* functional co-operation in areas such as health, education and culture, youth and sports, science and technology, and tax administration.

The Caribbean Common Market provides for the establishment of a Common External Tariff, a common protective policy and the progressive co-ordination of external trade policies; the adoption of a scheme for the harmonization of fiscal incentives to industry; double taxation arrangements among member countries; the co-ordination of economic policies and development planning; and a special regime for the less developed countries of the community.

In 1990 a target date of 1994 for the creation of a common market was agreed. A common tariff was applied by some members in 1991–92.

Membership: Antigua and Barbuda, Bahamas, Barbados, Belize, Dominica, Grenada, Guyana, Jamaica, Montserrat, St Kitts and Nevis, St Lucia, St Vincent and the Grenadines, Suriname and Trinidad and Tobago. The British Virgin Islands and Turks and Caicos Islands are associate members. The Dominican Republic and Haiti have observer status.

Structure: The *Conference of Heads of Government* is the principal organ of the Community, and its primary responsibility is to determine the policy of the Community. It is the final authority of the Community and the Common Market, and for the conclusion of treaties and relationships between the Community and international organizations and States. It is responsible for financial arrangements for meeting the expenses of the Community.

The *Common Market Council* is the second highest organ of the Community and consists of Ministers of Government designated by each member state. Decisions in both the Conference and the Council are in the main taken on the basis of unanimity.

The *Bureau of Heads of Government* was established on 1 Jan. 1993 with competence to initiate proposals, update consensus, mobilize action and secure the implementation of Community decisions. It comprises the current Chairman of the

Conference of Heads of Government, rotating on a 6-monthly basis, and the outgoing and incoming Chairmen, as well as the Secretary-General as chief executive officer.

The *Secretariat*, successor to the Commonwealth Caribbean Regional Secretariat, is the principal administrative organ of the Community and of the Common Market. The Secretary-General is appointed by the Conference on the recommendation of the Council for a term not exceeding 5 years and may be reappointed. The Secretary-General shall act in that capacity in all meetings of the Conference, the Council, and of the institutions of the Community.

Institutions of the Community, established by the Heads of Government Conference, are: Conference of Ministers responsible for Health; Standing Committees of Ministers responsible for Education, Tourism, Labour, Foreign Affairs, Finance, Agriculture, Energy, Mines and Natural Resources, Industry, Science and Technology, Transport and Legal Affairs, respectively.

Associate Institutions: Caribbean Development Bank; Caribbean Examinations Council; Council of Legal Education; University of the West Indies; University of Guyana; Caribbean Meteorological Organization.

Flag: Divided horizontally light blue over dark blue; in the centre a white disc bearing the linked letters CC in light blue and dark blue respectively.
Chairman: Owen Arthur (Barbados).
Secretary-General: Edwin Carrington.
Headquarters: Bank of Guyana Building, PO Box 10827, Georgetown, Guyana.

The language of the Community is English.

Further Reading

CARICOM Perspective. (twice a year). Georgetown, CARICOM Secretariat
CARICOM Secretary-General's Report. Georgetown, annual *Treaty Establishing the Caribbean Community.* Georgetown, CARICOM Secretariat, 1982
Parry, J. H., *et. al. A Short History of the West Indies.* Rev. ed. London, 1987

SOUTH PACIFIC FORUM

The South Pacific Forum held its first meeting of Heads of Government in New Zealand in 1971. Membership (and year of adhesion): Australia (1971), Cook Islands (1971), the Federated States of Micronesia (1987), Fiji (1971), Kiribati (1979), Nauru (1971), New Zealand (1971), Niue (1975), Papua New Guinea (1974), the Republic of the Marshall Islands (1987), Solomon Islands (1978), Tonga (1971), Tuvalu (1978), Vanuatu (1980) and Western Samoa (1971).

The South Pacific Bureau for Economic Co-operation was established by the Agreement of 17 April 1973; a Memorandum of Understanding of 16 June 1977 established the Pacific Forum Line. The South Pacific Regional Trade and Economic Co-operation Agreement was signed on 14 July 1980.

In 1985 the Forum adopted a treaty for a nuclear-free zone in the South Pacific, and in 1987 a treaty on fisheries with the USA; and in 1978, 1986 and 1989 conventions on fishery and protection of marine resources.
Secretary-General: Ieremia Tabai.
Headquarters: POB 856, Suva, Fiji.

THE LEAGUE OF ARAB STATES

Origin. An Arab conference met in Alexandria in the autumn of 1944; it formulated the 'Alexandria Protocol', which delineated the outlines of the Arab League. It was found that neither a unitary state nor a federation could be achieved, but only a league of sovereign states. A covenant, establishing such a league, was signed in

Cairo on 22 March 1945 by the representatives of Egypt, Iraq, Saudi Arabia, Syria, Lebanon, Jordan and Yemen. There were (1995) 22 members of the League: Algeria, Bahrain, Comoros, Djibouti, Egypt, Iraq, Jordan, Kuwait, Lebanon, Libya, Mauritania, Morocco, Oman, Palestine, Qatar, Saudi Arabia, Somalia, Sudan, Syria, Tunisia, United Arab Emirates and Yemen.

Organization. The machinery of the League consists of a Council, a number of Special Committees and a Permanent Secretariat. On the Council each state has one vote. The Council may meet in any of the Arab capitals. Its functions include mediation in any dispute between any of the League states or a League state and a country outside the League. The Council has a Political Committee consisting of the Foreign Ministers of the Arab states. There are also 22 specialized agencies.

The Permanent Secretariat of the League, under a Secretary-General (who enjoys, along with his senior colleagues, full diplomatic status), has its seat in Cairo.

The League considers itself a regional organization within the framework of the United Nations at which its secretary-general is an observer.

Secretary-General: Esmat Abdel Meguid (Egypt; b. 1923; elected for a 5-year term May 1991).

Flag: Dark green with the seal of the Arab League in white in the centre.

Arab Common Market. The Arab Common Market came into operation on 1 Jan. 1965. The agreement, reached on 13 Aug. 1964 and open to all the Arab League states, has been signed by Iraq, Jordan, Syria and Egypt. The agreement provides for the abolition of customs duties on agricultural products and natural resources within 5 years, by reducing tariffs at an annual rate of 20%. Customs duties on industrial products are to be reduced by 10% annually. The agreement also provides for the free movement of capital and labour between member countries, the establishment of common external tariffs, the co-ordination of economical development and the framing of a common foreign economic policy.

Further Reading

Clements, F. A., *Arab Regional Organizations.* [Bibliography]. Oxford and New Brunswick (NJ), 1992

Gomaa, A. M., *The Foundation of the League of Arab States.* London, 1977

CO-OPERATION COUNCIL FOR THE ARAB STATES OF THE GULF (GULF CO-OPERATION COUNCIL)

Aims. The Council was founded in 1982 by Bahrain, Kuwait, Oman, Qatar, Saudi Arabia and the United Arab Emirates to promote solidarity and political, economic and social co-operation between the Arab oil-producing states on the west coast of the Persian Gulf. A later declaration enjoins members to combine efforts to protect their mutual sovereignty, independence and territorial integrity.

Organization. Policy is decided by a Supreme Council of heads of state who meet annually. The Ministerial Council of foreign ministers ordinarily meets quarterly. The Secretary-General is appointed by the Supreme Council for a 3-year term.

Secretary-General: Abdullah Yacoub Bishara.

Headquarters: POB 7153, Riyadh 11462, Saudi Arabia.

In March 1991 the 6 member states together with Egypt and Syria established an armed regional peace-keeping force by the Damascus Declaration, which also envisaged political and economic co-operation. The Declaration was effectively superseded by the Security Pact signed on 13 Nov. 1995 by Bahrain, Oman, Saudi Arabia and UAE. A 6,000-strong Rapid Deployment Force is stationed in Saudi Arabia.

In April 1991 members created an aid fund to promote development in Arab countries which had helped liberate Kuwait in 1991.

Further Reading

Twinam, J. W., *The Gulf, Co-operation and the Council: an American Perspective.* Washington, 1992

ORGANIZATION OF THE PETROLEUM EXPORTING COUNTRIES (OPEC)

Aims. The Organization was founded in Baghdad in 1960 by Iran, Iraq, Kuwait, Saudi Arabia and Venezuela. The principal aims are unifying the petroleum policies of member countries and determining the best means for safeguarding their interests, individually and collectively; to devise ways and means of ensuring the stabilization of prices in international oil markets with a view to eliminating harmful and unnecessary fluctuations; and to secure a steady income for the producing countries, an efficient, economic and regular supply of petroleum to consuming nations, and a fair return on their capital to those investing in the petroleum industry.

Membership (1996). Algeria, Gabon, Indonesia, Iran, Iraq, Kuwait, Libya, Nigeria, Qatar, Saudi Arabia, United Arab Emirates and Venezuela. Membership applications may be made by any other country having substantial net exports of crude petroleum, which has fundamentally similar interests to those of member countries.

Organization. The main organs are the Conference, the Board of Governors and the Secretariat. The Conference, which is the supreme authority meeting at least twice a year, consists of delegations from each member country, normally headed by the respective minister of oil, mines or energy. All decisions, other than those concerning procedural matters, must be adopted unanimously.

OPEC Fund for International Development: The OPEC Special Fund was established in 1976 to provide financial aid to developing countries, other than OPEC members, on advantageous terms. In 1980 this was transformed into a permanent autonomous international agency, the OPEC Fund for International Development. *Director-General:* Dr Y. Seyyid Abdulai. *Headquarters:* POB 995, A–1011 Vienna, Austria.

Secretary-General: Dr Rilwanu Lukman.
Headquarters: Obere Donaustrasse 93, A–1020 Vienna, Austria.
Flag: Light blue with the OPEC logo in white in the centre.

Further Reading

Publications include: *Annual Statistical Bulletin. Annual Report. OPEC Bulletin* (monthly). *OPEC Review* (quarterly). *Facts and Figures* (annually). *OPEC General Information.*
Al-Chalabi, F., OPEC at the Crossroads. Oxford, 1989
Skeet, *OPEC: Twenty-five years of Prices and Policies.* CUP, 1988

ORGANIZATION OF AFRICAN UNITY

On 25 May 1963 the heads of state or government of 32 African countries, at a conference in Addis Ababa, signed a charter establishing an 'Organization of African Unity'. It had 53 members in 1996.

In June 1991 the heads of state of member countries signed a treaty to create an Africa-wide economic community by 2000. In 1993 heads of state adopted a mechanism for conflict prevention, management and resolution by the OAU.

Its chief objects are the furtherance of African unity and solidarity; the co-ordination of the political, economic, cultural, health, scientific and defence policies and the elimination of colonialism in Africa.

The organs of the Organization are: (1) the Assembly of the Heads of State and Government; (2) the Council of Ministers; (3) the General Secretariat; (4) a Commission of Mediation, Conciliation and Arbitration. Arabic, French, Portuguese and English are recognized as working languages.

In Nov. 1995, the following countries were suspended from voice and vote for failure to pay their dues: Central African Republic, Chad, Comoros, Equatorial Guinea, Guinea-Bissau, Niger, Sao Tome e Principe, Seychelles and Sierra Leone.

Chairman: Meles Zenawi (Ethiopia).
Secretary-General: Dr Salim Ahmed Salim (Tanzania).
Headquarters: POB 3243, Addis Ababa, Ethiopia.
Flag: Horizontally green, white, green, with the white fimbriated yellow, and the seal of the OAU in the centre.

Further Reading

El-Ayouty, Y. (ed.) *The Organization of African Unity after Thirty Years.* New York, 1994
Harris, G., *The Organization of African Unity.* [Bibliography]. Oxford and New Brunswick (NJ), 1994

SOUTHERN AFRICAN DEVELOPMENT COMMUNITY (SADC)

The SADC was founded by treaty on 17 Aug. 1992 to develop the activities of the former Southern African Development Co-ordination Council, which had been set up in 1980 to combat the effects of sanctions against South Africa. The 10 founder member countries were Angola, Botswana, Lesotho, Malawi, Mozambique, Namibia, Swaziland, Tanzania, Zambia and Zimbabwe. South Africa joined in Aug. 1994 and Mauritius became the 12th member in Aug. 1995.

The aim of the SADC is to promote economic integration. The founding treaty imposes binding obligations on members, and provides for the establishment of an arbitration tribunal. At the Johannesbourg summit in Aug. 1995 an agreement was reached committing members to the sharing of water resources. A treaty to eliminate internal trade barriers by 2000 is being drafted.

The *Frontline States Organisation* is the political and security arm of SADC, comprising all members except Malawi, Mauritius, Lesotho and Swaziland.

Secretary: Kaire Mbuende.

DANUBE COMMISSION

The Danube Commission was constituted in 1949 based on the Convention regarding the regime of navigation on the Danube, which was signed in Belgrade on 18 Aug. 1948. The Belgrade Convention reaffirmed that navigation on the Danube from Ulm to the Black Sea, with access to the sea through the Sulina arm and the Sulina Canal, is equally free and open to the nationals, merchant shipping and merchandise of all states as to harbour and navigation fees as well as conditions of merchant navigation.

The Danube Commission is composed of representatives from the countries on the Danube (1 for each of these countries), namely, Austria, Bulgaria, Hungary, Romania, Russia, Slovakia, the Ukraine and Yugoslavia. Croatia, Germany and Moldavia have observer status.

The functions of the Danube Commission are to check that the provisions of the Convention are carried out, to establish a uniform buoying system on all the Danube's navigable waterways and to establish the basic regulations for navigation on the river. The Commission co-ordinates the regulations for river, customs and sanitation control as well as the hydrometeorological service and collects statistical data concerning navigation on the Danube.

The Danube Commission enjoys legal status. It has its own seal and flag. The members of the Commission and elected officers enjoy diplomatic immunity. The Commission's official buildings, archives and documents are inviolable. French and Russian are the official languages of the Commission.

President: György Misur (Hungary).
Director-General: Hellmuth Strasser (Austria).
Headquarters: Benczúr utca 25, H-1068 Budapest, Hungary.

Flag: Blue, with a red strip fimbriated white along the bottom edge, and the initials of the Commission within a wreath in the canton—Latin letters on obverse Cyrillic on reverse.

Further Reading

The Danube Commission's publications include *Proceedings of Sessions, Compilation of Agreements on Danube Navigation, General Information on the Danube Commission* and a great many technical manuals and recommendations.

ANTARCTIC TREATY

Antarctica is an island continent some 15·5m. sq. km in area which lies almost entirely within the Antarctic Circle. Its surface is composed of an ice sheet over rock, and it is uninhabited except for research and other workers in the course of duty. It is in general ownerless; for countries with territorial claims, *see* Argentina (p. 93), Australian Antarctic Territory (p. 125), British Antarctic Territory (p. 238), Chile (p. 349), French Southern and Antarctic Territories (p. 582), the Ross dependency, New Zealand (p. 1019) and Queen Maud Land, Norway (p. 1050).

12 countries which had maintained research stations in Antarctica during International Geophysical Year, 1957–58, (Argentina, Australia, Belgium, Chile, France, Japan, New Zealand, Norway, South Africa, the USSR, the UK and the USA) signed the Antarctic Treaty (Washington Treaty) on 1 Dec. 1959. Austria, Brazil, Bulgaria, Canada, China, Colombia, Cuba, Czechoslovakia, Denmark, Ecuador, Finland, Germany, Greece, Hungary, India, Italy, South Korea, North Korea, the Netherlands, Papua New Guinea, Peru, Poland, Romania, Spain, Sweden, Switzerland and Uruguay have subsequently acceded to the Treaty. The Treaty reserves the Antarctic area south of 60° S. lat. for peaceful purposes, provides for international co-operation in scientific investigation and research, and preserves, for the duration of the Treaty, the *status quo* with regard to territorial sovereignty, rights and claims. The Treaty entered into force on 23 June 1961. The 39 nations party to the Treaty (26 full voting signatories and 13 adherents) meet biennially. Decisions taken by the signatories of the 1959 Washington Treaty must be unanimous.

An agreement reached in Madrid in April 1991 and signed by all 39 parties in Oct. imposes a ban on mineral exploitation in Antarctica for 50 years, at the end of which any one of the 26 voting parties may request a review conference. After this the ban may be lifted by agreement of three quarters of the nations then voting, which must include the present 26. The agreement demilitarizes the continent, establishes the right to scientific research for all countries and creates a procedure for monitoring the environment.

Further Reading

Elliott, L. M., *International Environmental Politics: Protecting the Antarctic*. London, 1994
Jørgensen-Dahl, A. and Østreng, W., *The Antarctic Treaty System in World Politics*. London, 1991
Meadows, J. *et al.*, *The Antarctic* [Bibliography]. Oxford and New Brunswick (NJ), 1994

PART II

COUNTRIES OF THE WORLD

A—Z

AFGHANISTAN

Jamhuria Afghanistan

(Republic of Afghanistan)

Capital: Kabul
Population: 20·5m. (1994)
HDI/world rank: 0·228/170 (1992)

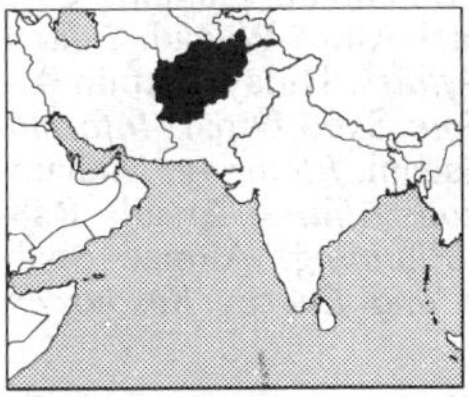

KEY HISTORICAL EVENTS. A military coup on 17 July 1973 led by Mohammad Daoud overthrew King Zahir Shah and set up a Republic. President Daoud was killed in a military coup in April 1978 which led to the establishment of a pro-Soviet government.

In Dec. 1979 Soviet troops invaded Afghanistan on the pretext of a 1978 Treaty of Friendship. Dr Sayid Mohammed Najibullah was elected President in Sept. 1987 by the Revolutionary Council. After talks in Nov. 1991 with Afghan opposition movements ('mujahideen') the Soviet government agreed to transfer its support from the Najibullah regime to an 'Islamic Interim Government'. As mujahideen insurgents closed in on Kabul President Najibullah stepped down on 16 April 1992. On 28 April an interim council received power from the outgoing government. Factional fighting between troops of the Minister of Defence, Ahmed Shah Massoud, and the Hezb-i-Islami, led by Gulbuddin Hekmatyar, continued until the signing of a peace agreement on 21 May providing for the withdrawal of armed forces from Kabul and the establishment of a neutral zone. On 11 Aug. 1992 fighting between government forces and the Hezb broke out again.

Late in 1994 a newly-formed militant Islamic movement, 'Taliban' (i.e. 'students of religion') took possession of Kandahar and routed Hekmatyar's Hezb-i-Islami at Kabul in Feb. 1995. They were in turn defeated by the troops of President Rabbani, who regained possession of Kabul by 11 March 1995, but had rallied by Sept. 1995 and captured Herat, carrying out air and rocket raids on Kabul in Nov. 1995.

TERRITORY AND POPULATION. Afghanistan is bounded in the north by Turkmenistan, Uzbekistan and Tajikistan, east by China, east and south by Pakistan and west by Iran.

The area is 251,773 sq. miles (652,090 sq. km). Population according to the last (1979) census was 15,551,358, of which some 2·5m. were nomadic tribes. Estimate (1994, excluding nomads) 20·5m. (21% urban). Population density, 25 per sq. km. In 1995 there remained 3·5m. refugees in Pakistan and Iran. Infant mortality, 1991, 296 per 1,000 live births; annual growth rate, 2·6%; expectation of life, 42·5 years in 1990.

The capital, Kabul, had an estimated population of 0·7m. in 1993. Other towns (with UN population estimates, 1988): Kandahar (225,500), Herat (177,300), Mazar i Sharif, (130,600), Jalalabad (55,000).

Main ethnic groups: Pashtun, 62%; Tajiks, 20%; Uzbeks, 9%; Hazaras, 9%. The official languages are Pashto and Dari.

CLIMATE. The climate is arid, with a big annual range of temperature and very little rain, apart from the period Jan. to April. Winters are very cold, with considerable snowfall, which may last the year round on mountain summits. Kabul. Jan. 27°F (–2·8°C), July 76°F (24·4°C). Annual rainfall 13" (338 mm).

CONSTITUTION AND GOVERNMENT. After the departure of President Najibullah power was exercised by a 10-member Ruling Council chaired by Burhanuddin Rabbani who became interim President of the Republic on 28 June 1992. In Dec. 1992 a Grand Council of 1,335 national delegates convened and re-elected Burhanuddin Rabbani President. The Grand Council was wound up after

205 of its members had been designated a constituent assembly. PresidentRabbani's mandate expired in June 1994 but he remained in office.

President and Minister of Defence: Burhanuddin Rabbani (b. 1942; Jamiat Party; sworn in 2 Jan. 1993).

In Aug. 1995 the government comprised: *Prime Minister and Minister of the Interior:* Gulbuddin Hekmatyar (Hezb-i-Islami). *Deputy Prime Minister:* Qutbuddin Hilal. *Agriculture:* Noorullah Emad. *Border Security:* Soleimam Gailani. *Civil Aviation:* Hashmattullah Mojadedi. *Communications:* Qazi Amin Waqad. *Education:* Jali Ullah. *Finance:* Abdul Karim Khalili. *Foreign Affairs:* Hidayat Amin Arsalla. *Health:* Mohammad Amin Fatimi. *Higher Education:* Syed Omar. *Information and Culture:* Din Mohammad. *Justice:* Jalaluddin Haqqani. *Planning:* Mohammad Ali Jawad. *Reconstruction:* Fas Mohammad. *Religious Affairs:* Arsalla Rahmani. *Repatriation of Refugees:* Farooq Azam. *Town Planning:* Ahmad Shah. *Trade:* Hayat Balajhi. *Transport:* Syed Anwari. *Water and Energy Resources:* Mohammad Ayub.

National flag: 3 horizontal stripes of green, white and black with the national emblem in gold, centred.

National anthem: 'Garam shah la garam shah' ('Become hot, become hotter'); words by S. Laeq, tune by U. S. Sarmad.

Local Government: There are 32 provinces each administered in theory by an appointed governor.

DEFENCE

Army. Army organization disintegrated into factional groups after the deposition of President Najibullah in April 1992. Equipment included 1,200 T-54/-55/-62 main battle tanks. Strength was (1993) about 40,000, mainly conscripts, but most units of the Army are well below strength, largely as a result of desertions.

Air Force. Prior to the overthrow of the regime of President Najibullah in 1992 the Air Force had about 180 combat aircraft and 5,000 officers and men. Nominal strength comprised 3 squadrons of Su-7 and Su-20 attack aircraft, 4 squadrons of MiG-21 interceptors (about 60 aircraft), 3 squadrons of MiG-17s and 2 squadrons of MiG-23s, a helicopter attack force of at least 50 Mi-24s, a transport wing with 12 An-12s, 25 twin-turboprop An-26s and An-32s, about 10 piston-engined An-2s, 50 Mi-8/17 and 10 Mi-4 helicopters and 2 turboprop Il-18s, and Yak-18, Aero L-29 and L-39 and MiG-15UTI trainers. The main fighter station was Bagram, with facilities for the largest jet transports and bombers. There was a fighter-bomber station at Shindand, a training station at Mazar-i-Sharif and an air academy at Sherpur.

INTERNATIONAL RELATIONS

Membership. Afghanistan is a member of the UN and Colombo Plan.

ECONOMY

Currency. The unit of currency is the *afghani* (AFA) of 100 *puls*. Notes are in denominations of 1, 2, 5, 10, 100, 500 and 1,000 afghanis. Rates of exchange in March 1996: Afs. 7,259·90 = £1; Afs. 4,750 = US$1; Afs. 3,218·38 = DM1.

Banking and Finance. The Afghan State Bank is the largest of the 3 main banks and also undertakes the functions of a central bank, holding the exclusive right of note issue. Foreign banks have been permitted to operate since 1990.

Weights and Measures. The metric system is in increasingly common use. Local units include: 1 *khurd* = 0·244 lb.; 1 *pao* = 0·974 lb.; 1 *charak* = 3·896 lb.; 1 *sere* = 16 lb.; 1 *kharwar* = 1,280 lb. or 16 maunds of 80 lb. each; 1 *gaz* = 40 inches; 1 *jarib* = 60 x 60 kabuli yd or ½ acre; 1 *kulba* = 40 jaribs (area in which 2½ kharwars of seed can be sown); 1 jarib yd = 29 inches.

ENERGY AND NATURAL RESOURCES

Electricity. Most generating plant is hydro-electric. Installed capacity was estimated at 408 MW in 1993. Total output (1989) 1,109m. kWh.

Oil and Gas. Oil reserves are estimated at 100m. tonnes; gas at 100,000m. cu. metres.

Minerals. Mineral resources are scattered and little developed: Coal, iron ore, beryllium, gold, silver, lapis lazuli, asbestos, mica, sulphur, chrome and copper.

Agriculture. The greater part of Afghanistan is mountainous but there are many fertile plains and valleys. In 1991 there were 7·91m. ha of arable land, 0·14m. ha of permanent cropland and 30m. ha of pasture. 9·07m. persons depended on agriculture in 1990. 2·76m. ha were irrigated in 1991.

Production, 1992, in 1,000 tonnes: Wheat, 1,650; barley, 150; maize, 300; rice, 300. Livestock (1992): Cattle, 1·65m.; horses, 0·4m.; camels, 265,000; sheep, 13·5m.; goats 2·15m.; chickens, 7m.

INDUSTRY. Industry is small-scale and largely based on the processing of local agricultural produce. Manufactures include cement, coalmining, cotton textiles, small vehicle assembly plants, fruit canning, carpet making, leather tanning, footwear manufacture, sugar manufacture, preparation of hides and skins, and building.

Labour. The economically active population was 4·91m. in 1990, of whom 54·8% worked in agriculture.

FOREIGN ECONOMIC RELATIONS.

Commerce. In 1991 imports totalled US$411m. and exports US$140m. Main export commodities in 1990 were karakul skins (US$3m.), raw cotton (US$3m.), dried fruit and nuts (US$93m.), carpets (US$44m.) and wool (US$10).

Total trade between Afghanistan and UK (in £1,000 sterling, British Department of Trade returns):

	1992	*1993*	*1994*	*1995*
Imports to UK	4,676	4,310	4,096	1,165
Exports and re-exports from UK	4,926	5,915	7,830	7,156

COMMUNICATIONS

Roads. There are some 18,000 km of roads, of which 2,800 km are surfaced. All roads, particularly outside the towns, are in a very poor state of repair as a result of military action.

Railways. There are no railways in the country, but the Oxus bridge opened in 1982, brought a short-section of 1,524mm gauge track into the country from Uzbekistan. A Trans-Afghan Railway is proposed in an Afghan-Pakistan-Turkmen agreement of 1994.

Civil Aviation. There are international airports at Kabul (Khwaja Rawash Airport) and Kandahar, and 18 domestic airports. The national carrier is Ariana Afghan Airlines. In 1995 it had 2 B-727-100s, 3 B-727-200 Advs and 8 ex-Soviet aircraft. Air India and Aeroflot Russian International Airlines also operate services. There are direct flights from Kabul to Amritsar, Bandar Abbas (Iran), Delhi, Dubai, Moscow, Prague and Tashkent.

Shipping. There are practically no navigable rivers. A port has been built at Qizil Qala on the Oxus and there are 3 river ports on the Amu Darya, linked by road to Kabul.

Telecommunications. Telephones, installed in most of the large towns, numbered 31,200 in 1978. There is telegraphic communication between all the larger towns and with other parts of the world. Radio and TV Afghanistan is government-controlled. In 1993 there were 1·5m. radio receivers and about 100,000 television receivers (colour by PAL and SECAM).

Press. In 1983 there were 3 daily newspapers with a circulation of 67,000.

SOCIAL INSTITUTIONS

Justice. A Supreme Court was established in June 1978. If no provision exists in the Constitution or in the general laws of the State, the courts follow the Hanafi jurisprudence of Islamic law.

Religion. The predominant religion is Islam. 84% of the population are Sunni Moslems and 15% Shiites.

Education. Some 25% of the population were estimated to be literate in 1990. There are elementary schools throughout the country, but secondary schools exist only in Kabul and provincial capitals. Both elementary and secondary education are free. In 1985 there were 580,000 pupils (16,000 teachers) in primary education and 105,000 pupils (5,700 teachers) in secondary education. In 1995-96 there were 5 universities, 1 university of Islamic studies, 1 state medical institute and 1 polytechnic. Kabul University had 9,500 students and 500 academic staff.

Health. In 1990 there were 2,233 doctors, 267 dentists, 1,451 nurses, 510 pharmacists and 338 midwives.

DIPLOMATIC REPRESENTATIVES

Of Afghanistan in Great Britain (31 Prince's Gate, London, SW7 1QQ)
Chargé d'Affaires: Ahmad Wali Masud.

Of Great Britain in Afghanistan (Karte Parwan, Kabul)
Ambassador: Sir Christopher MacRae, KCMG (resides at Islamabad).

Of Afghanistan in the USA (2341 Wyoming Ave., NW, Washington, D.C., 20008)
Chargé d'Affaires: Yar Mohammad Mohabbat.

Of the USA in Afghanistan (Wazir Akbar Khan Mina, Kabul)
Ambassador: Vacant.

Of Afghanistan to the United Nations
Ambassador: Dr Ravan A. G. Farhadi.

Further Reading

Amin, S. H., *Law, Reform and Revolution in Afghanistan.* London, 1991
Arney, G., *Afghanistan.* London, 1990
Hyman, A., *Afghanistan under Soviet Domination, 1964–1991.* 3rd ed. London, 1992
Jones, S., *Afghanistan.* [Bibliography]. Oxford and Santa Barbara, 1991
Roy, O., *Islam and Resistance in Afghanistan.* 2nd ed. CUP, 1990
Rubin, B.R., *The Fragmentation of Afghanistan: State Formation and Collapse in the International System.* Yale Univ. Press, 1995
Sykes, P. M., *A History of Afghanistan.* 2 vols. New York, 1975

ALBANIA

Republika e Shqipërisë

Capital: Tirana
Population: 3·41m. (1995)
GNP per capita: US$360 (1994)
HDI/world rank: 0·714/76 (1992)

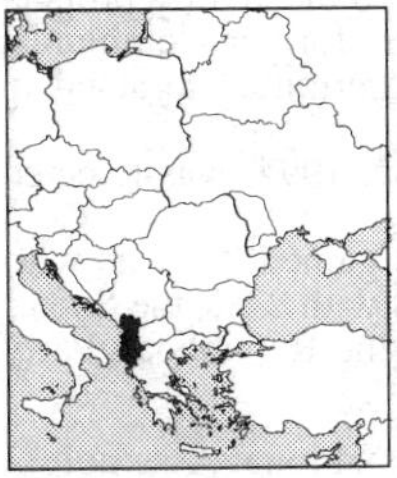

KEY HISTORICAL EVENTS. For the history of Albania up to the Second World War and the establishment of the Communist regime *see* THE STATESMAN'S YEAR-BOOK 1991–92, p. 68.

Beginning in July 1990 there were several demonstrations against the government often led by students. In Dec. 1990 the People's Assembly adopted a decree legalizing opposition parties. A Communist government was elected in March 1991, but following a general strike resigned in June. A successor government was itself replaced by a non-party interim government in Dec. 1991. A non-Communist government was elected in March 1992.

TERRITORY AND POPULATION. Albania is bounded in the north by Yugoslavia, east by Macedonia, south by Greece and west by the Adriatic. The area is 28,748 sq. km (11,101 sq. miles). At the census of 1989 the population was 3,184,417. Estimate, 1994, 3,412,000 (40% urban; density 118·7 per sq. km). The capital is Tirana (population in 1,000 in 1991, 251); other large towns are Durrës (86·9), Shkodër (83·7), Elbasan (83·2), Vlorë (76), Korçë (67·1), (populations in 1990) Fier (37), Berat (37), Lushnjë (24), Kavajë (23) and Gjirokastër (Argyrocastro) (21).

Vital statistics, 1988: Marriages, 28,174; births, 80,241; deaths, 17,027; divorces, 2,597. Rates (per 1,000, 1988): Births, 25·5; deaths, 5·4; marriages, 9; divorces, 0·8; natural increase, 20·1 per 1,000. Infant mortality was 27 per 1,000 live births in 1993. Life expectancy in 1993: Males, 71 years; females, 78. Growth rate, 1991, 1·8% per annum. Abortion was legalized in 1991.

The country is administratively divided into 26 districts, 66 towns, 306 town boroughs, 537 village unions and 2,844 villages.

Districts	*Area (sq. km)*	*Population (1990)*	*Districts*	*Area (sq. km)*	*Population (1990)*
Berat	1,027	180,489	Lushnjë	712	137,830
Dibrë	1,568	153,775	Mat	1,028	78,754
Durrës	848	251,029	Mirditë	867	51,701
Elbasan	1,481	248,676	Permet	929	40,419
Fier	1,175	251,115	Pogradec	725	73,333
Gjirokastër	1,137	67,392	Pukë	1,034	50,286
Gramsh	695	44,791	Sarandë	1,097	89,456
Kolonjë	805	25,291	Shkodër	2,528	241,549
Korçë	2,181	218,219	Skrapar	775	47,605
Krujë	607	109,876	Tepelenë	817	51,022
Kukës	1,330	104,731	Tirana	1,238	374,483
Lezhë	479	63,505	Tropojë	1,043	45,965
Librazhd	1,013	73,871	Vlorë	1,609	180,725

Districts are named after their capitals; exceptions: Tropojë, capital—Bajram Curri; Mat—Burrel; Mirditë—Rrëshen; Skrapar—Çorovodë; Dibrë—Peshkopi; Kolonjë—Ersekë.

At the 1989 census, members of ethnic minorities totalled 64,816, including 58,758 Greeks and 4,697 Macedonians. 2m. ethnic Albanians live in Yugoslavia, mainly in Kosovo.

The official language is Albanian.

CLIMATE. Mediterranean-type, with rainfall mainly in winter, but thunderstorms are frequent and severe in the great heat of the plains in summer. Winters in the highlands can be severe, with much snow. Tirana. Jan. 44°F (6·8°C), July 75°F

(23·9°C). Annual rainfall 54" (1,353 mm). Shkodër. Jan. 39°F (3·9°C), July 77°F (25°C). Annual rainfall 57" (1,425 mm).

CONSTITUTION AND GOVERNMENT. A new constitution was promulgated on 26 April 1991. The supreme legislative body is the single-chamber *National Assembly* of 140 deputies, 100 directly elected and 40 elected by proportional representation, for 4-year terms. Senior members of the former Communist Party, or members of parliament before May 1991, are not permitted to stand in national or local elections until 2002.

A draft new constitution, submitted to a referendum in Nov. 1994, was rejected by 53·8% of votes cast; turn-out was 75%.

At the elections of March 1992 the Democratic Party (DP) gained 92 seats with 68% of votes cast, the Socialist Party (former Communists) 38 with 22%, the Social Democratic Party (SDP) 7, Omonia (Greek minority) 2 and the Republican Party (RP) 1. Elections were scheduled for not later than May 1996.

President: Dr Sali Berisha (b. 1944; elected April 1992 by the National Assembly).

In Nov. 1995 the government comprised:

Prime Minister: Alexander Meksi (b. 1939; DP).

Deputy Prime Minister and Minister of Finance: Dylber Vrioni (DP). *Deputy Prime Minister and Minister of Construction and Tourism:* Dashamir Shehi (DP). *Minister of Agriculture and Food:* Hasan Halili (DP). *Culture, Youth and Sport:* Teodor Laco (SDP). *Defence:* Safet Zhulali (DP). *Education:* Xhazair Teliti (ind). *Foreign Affairs:* Alfred Serreqi (DP). *Health and the Environment:* Maksim Cikuli (DP). *Industry, Trade and Transport:* Suzana Panariti (DP). *Interior and Local Government:* Agron Musaraj (DP). *Justice:* Hektor Frasheri (DP). *Labour, Social Affairs, Emigration and Former Political Prisoners:* Engjell Dakli (ind). *Energy and Mineral Resources:* Abdyl Xhaja (DP). *Chairman, Commission for Science and Technology:* Maksim Konomi (DP). *Chairman, Control Commission:* Blerim Cela (DP).

The *Speaker* is Pjeter Arbnori.

Local government. There are 12 prefectures each under a prefect nominated by the Prime Minister, subdivided into 36 districts. Elected councils function at district, municipal and commune level. At the elections of 26 July 1992 the Socialist Party gained 23 mayoralties (the DP, 18) and 44% of votes cast for district (DP, 38%), 43% for municipal (DP, 41%) and 46% for commune, councils (DP, 35%).

National flag: Red, with a black double-headed eagle in the centre.

National anthem: 'Rreth Flamurit të për bashkuar' ('The flag that united us in the struggle'); words by A. S. Drenova, music by C. Porumbescu.

DEFENCE. Conscription is for 15 months.

Army. The Army consists of 9 infantry divisions. Equipment includes 138 T-34 and 721 T-59 main battle tanks. Strength (1996) 60,000 (including 20,000 conscripts). There is an internal security force of 5,000; frontier guards number 5,000. There is a People's Militia of 3,500.

Navy. The combatant navy includes 2 submarines, 2 offshore patrol craft, 24 hydrofoil torpedo boats, 11 inshore patrol craft and 4 inshore minesweepers. Auxiliaries include 2 tankers and about 10 service craft. Navy personnel in 1995 totalled 2,500 officers and ratings, including 250 coastal defence guards. There are naval bases at Durrës and Vlorë.

Air Force. The Air Force, controlled by the Army, had (1994) about 11,000 personnel (1,400 conscripts), and in 1994 operated 80 combat aircraft, mostly Chinese. There are 5 aviation regiments and an independent transport squadron. The force included 7 squadrons with Chinese-built F-6s, and 3 with F-2s, F-5s and F-7s respectively. 3 transport squadrons operated Mi-4 helicopters, and one, An-2s. There are also 3 Il-14s. Serviceability is reported to be low because of a shortage of funds.

INTERNATIONAL RELATIONS

Membership. Albania is a member of the UN, the Council of Europe and the NATO Partnership for Peace.

ECONOMY

Policy. Priority is given to the development of agriculture and the exploitation of tourism and natural resources. Privatization of land, small businesses and housing was effected in 1991–93. A privatization programme for large enterprises was initiated in 1995 under the aegis of the National Privatization Agency. Sales are at auction or through vouchers.

Budget. The fiscal year is the calendar year. Budget expenditure in 1994 (in 1m. leks) included: Social insurance, 10,926; unemployment benefit, 3,373; economic subsidies, 3,068; health, 1,921; education, 1,268; support for the politically persecuted, 1,113; culture, 145.

Currency. The monetary unit is the *lek* (ALL) notionally of 100 *qindars*. In Aug. 1965 a new *lek* was introduced: 10 old *leks* = 1 new *lek*. There are 5, 10, 20 and 50 *qindar* coins and a 1 lek coin; notes are for 1, 3, 5, 10, 50, 100, 500 and 1,000 leks. In Sept. 1991 the lek was pegged to the ecu at a rate of 30 leks = 1 ecu. In June 1992 it was devalued from 50 to 110 to US$1. Annualized inflation was 24·5% in 1994 (85% in 1993). In May 1992 the UK agreed to restore 1,574 kg of gold which had been held in compensation for the mining of 2 British warships in the 'Corfu incident' of 1946. Exchange rates, March 1996: £1 = 149·48 leks; US$1 = 97·80 leks; DM1 = 66·26 leks.

Banking and Finance. The central bank and bank of issue is the formally independent Bank of Albania, founded in 1925 with Italian aid as the Albanian State Bank and renamed in 1993. Its *governor* is Kristaq Luniku (b. 1962). In 1995 there were 3 state-owned commercial banks, 1 foreign bank and 2 joint ventures.

Weights and Measures. The metric system is in force.

ENERGY AND NATURAL RESOURCES

Electricity. Albania is rich in hydro-electric potential. Electric power production in 1990 was 3,198m. kWh.

Oil and Gas. Offshore exploration began in 1991. Oil has been produced onshore since 1920. Oil reserves are some 20m. tonnes. Output of crude in 1992, 0·99m. tonnes. Natural gas is extracted. Reserves, 8,000m. cu. metres. Output, 1993, 100m. cu. metres.

Minerals. Mineral wealth is considerable and includes lignite, chrome and ferronickel ores, but it is only recently being developed. Production, 1991 (in 1,000 tonnes): Lignite, 2,071; chromium ore (1994), 223; copper ore, 931; iron-nickel ore, 931.

Agriculture. In 1994 65% of the population depended upon agriculture, which contributed 56% of GDP. The country is rugged, wild and mountainous, except the Adriatic littoral and the Korçë (Koritza) Basin, which are fertile. In 1992 there were 0·57m. ha of arable land, 0·13m. ha of permanent cropland and 0·4m. ha of pasture. 0·43m. ha were irrigated.

A law of Aug. 1991 privatized co-operatives' land. Families received allocations according to their size made by village committees. In 1994 there were 0·42m. private farms; holdings averaged 1·4 ha. In 1988 there were 21,033 tractors (in 15HP units).

Production (in 1,000 tonnes), 1993: Wheat, 430; sugar-beet, 70; maize, 110; potatoes, 56; grapes, 67; oats, 15; sorghum, 20; seed cotton, 11; barley, 30; sunflower seeds, 14; wine, 15; olives, 8; tobacco, 12.

Livestock, 1993: Cattle, 0·5m.; sheep, 1·2m.; goats, 0·75m.; pigs, 0·14m.; horses, 0·11m.; mules, 0·23m.; asses, 0·53m.; chickens, 5m.

Forestry. Forests covered 1,046,150 ha in 1988, mainly oak, elm, pine and birch. In 1988 171,000 cu. metres of sawn timber were produced.

Fisheries. The catch in 1988 was 4,000 tonnes.

INDUSTRY. Output is small, and the principal industries are agricultural product processing, textiles, oil products and cement. Closures of loss-making plants in the chemical and engineering industries built up in the Communist era led to a 60% decline in production by 1993. Output, 1990 (in 1,000 tonnes): Copper cable, 9; carbonic ferrochrome, 24; rolled steel, 65; phosphate fertilizer, 142; ammonium nitrate, 93; urea, 90; sulphuric acid, 68; caustic soda, 33; soda ash, 23; cement, 645; machinery (in 1m. lek) 369; 18,000 TV sets; 26,000 radio sets; 6m. pairs of footwear.

Labour. In 1994 the workforce was 1·54m., including 0·6m. in the private sector. Estimated unemployed in June 1993, 0·44m. (0·24m. females). Non-agricultural unemployed: 281,929 in Jan. 1994.

Minimum wages may not fall below one-third of maximum. Hours of labour: 8-hour day, 6-day week and 12 days yearly paid holiday. Retirement age is 60 for men and 55 for women. Average monthly wage, 1990: 570 leks.

Trade Unions. Independent trade unions became legal in Feb. 1991.

FOREIGN ECONOMIC RELATIONS. Foreign investment was legalized in Nov. 1990. Foreign debt was some US$1,118m. in 1994. Remittances from Albanians working abroad totalled US$334m. in 1993.

In June 1992 the USA granted most-favoured-nation status.

Commerce. Exports in 1994 totalled US$210m.; imports, US$500m. In 1988 exports included 39·8% minerals, 16·1% plant and animal products, 8·7% processed foodstuffs, 7·3% electricity; imports: 28·5% machinery, 25·2% fuels and minerals, 14% plant and animal raw materials, 13·1% chemical products.

Main export markets, 1992 (in US$1m.): Italy, 28; Greece, 18; Yugoslavia, 16; Germany, 15. Main import suppliers: Italy, 145; France, 107; Greece, 41; Germany, 31; Yugoslavia, 29; Hungary, 12.

Total trade between Albania and UK (British Department of Trade returns, in £1,000 sterling):

	1992	*1993*	*1994*	*1995*
Imports to UK	290	465	220	1,017
Exports and re-exports from UK	2,763	5,406	5,607	7,555

Tourism. In 1994 there were some 60,000 foreign visitors, 63% on business trips. In 1995 there were 3,000 hotel beds.

COMMUNICATIONS

Roads. In 1995 there were 2,900 km of paved main roads, 5,000 km of unpaved secondary roads and 9,500 km of rural tracks. 0·15m. vehicles were registered in 1994.

Railways. Total length in 1993 was 670 km. They comprise the lines from Durrës to Tirana, Vlorë, Ballsh, Korcë, Shkodër and across the Yugoslav border to Podgorica. 4m. passengers and 0·5m. tonnes of freight were carried in 1994.

Civil Aviation. The national carrier is Albanian Airlines, a joint venture with a Kuwaiti firm. It began operations in Oct. 1995 with 1 Airbus 320. In 1996 it flew services to Athens, Bologna, Brussels, Istanbul, London, Munich, Paris, Rome and Skopje. Tirana (Rinas Airport) is also served by Adria Airways, Alitalia, Austrian Airlines, Balkan Bulgarian, Croatia Airlines, Lufthansa, Malév, Olympic, Swissair and Tarom. 0·2m. passengers used Rinas in 1995 (30,000 in 1990).

Shipping. In 1995 merchant shipping totalled 80,954 GRT. The main ports are Durrës, Vlorë, Sarandë and Shëngjin. 1·1m. tonnes of freight were carried in 1988 (769,000 tonnes overseas).

Telecommunications. Number of post and telegraph offices (1988), 635; telephones (1995), 50,000. A mobile telephone network was set up in 1996, initially serving 8,000 subscribers. The government-controlled Albanian Radio-Television broadcasts a national radio programme and a second radio programme from 14 stations. There are also regional programmes and an external service. In 1993 there were 210,000 radio and 0·3m. TV receivers (colour by PAL).

Cinemas. In 1988 there were 106 cinemas with an attendance of 3·03m.

Press. In 1995 there were 4 national dailies, 2 owned by political parties, and 45 other newspapers.

SOCIAL INSTITUTIONS

Justice. A new criminal code was introduced in June 1995. The administration of justice is presided over by the *Council of Justice*, chaired by the President of the Republic, which appoints judges to courts. A Ministry of Justice was re-established in 1990 and a Bar Council set up. In Nov. 1993 the number of capital offences was reduced from 13 to 6 and the death penalty abolished for women.

Religion. The population is 70% of Moslem origin, mainly Sunni with some Belaktashi, 20% Orthodox and 10% Roman Catholic. The Albanian Orthodox Church is autocephalous; it is headed by an Exarch and 3 metropolitans. In 1993 there were 47 priests. The Roman Catholic cathedral in Shkodër has been restored. In 1993 there were 4 Roman Catholic bishops.

Education. Primary education is free and compulsory in 8-year schools from 7 to 15 years. Secondary education lasts 4 years. There were, in 1988, 3,251 nursery schools with 121,000 pupils and 5,299 teachers, 1,691 primary schools with 547,000 pupils (5,000 part-time) and 27,862 teachers, 485 secondary schools with 194,000 pupils (63,000 part-time) and 9,004 teachers (including 442 vocational secondary schools with 135,000 pupils and 7,221 teachers), and 8 tertiary institutions, with 25,000 students (5,000 part-time) and 1,659 lecturers. In 1991–92 there were some 2,500 schools with 0·8m. pupils and 50,000 teachers. In 1995–96 there were 4 universities, 1 agricultural university, 1 technological university, 1 polytechnic, 1 academy of fine arts and 1 higher institute of physical education. There were 14,699 university students and 1,138 academic staff in 1994–95.

Health. Medical services are free, though medicines are charged for. In 1992 there were 130 hospitals, 6,308 doctors and 6,801 nurses. In 1995 there were about 10,000 hospital beds.

DIPLOMATIC REPRESENTATIVES

Of Albania in Great Britain (6 Wilton Ct., 59 Eccleston Sq., London SW1V 1PH)
Ambassador: Pavli Qesku.

Of Great Britain in Albania (Rruga Vaso Pasha 7/1, Tirana)
Ambassador: Andrew Tesoriere.

Of Albania in the USA (1150 18th St., NW, Washington DC 20036)
Ambassador: Lublin Dilja.

Of the USA in Albania
Ambassador: Joseph E. Lake.

Of Albania to the United Nations
Ambassador: Pellumb Kulla.

Further Reading

Bland, W. B., *Albania.* [Bibliography] Oxford and Santa Barbara, 1988
Sjoberg, O., *Rural Change and Development in Albania.* Boulder (CO.), 1992
Vickers, M., *The Albanians: a Modern History.* London, 1995
Winnifrith, T. (ed.) *Perspectives on Albania.* London, 1992

National statistical office: Statistical Institute of Albania, Tirana.

ALGERIA

Jumhuriya al-Jazairiya ad-Dimuqratiya ash-Shabiya

(People's Democratic Republic of Algeria)

Capital: Algiers
Population: 28·58m. (1995)
GNP per capita: US$1,690 (1994)
HDI/world rank: 0·732/85 (1992)

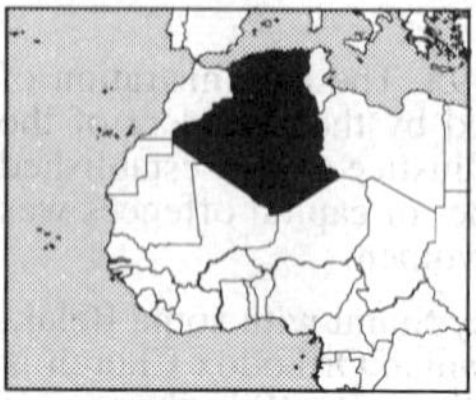

KEY HISTORICAL EVENTS. For post-colonial history *see* THE STATESMAN'S YEAR-BOOK, 1991–92, p. 76. France declared Algeria independent on 3 July 1962; the Republic was declared on 25 Sept. 1962.

The government was overthrown by a junta of army officers which, on 19 June 1965, established a Revolutionary Council under Col. Houari Boumédienne.

After the first round of elections was decisively won by the Islamic Salvation Front (FIS) on 26 Dec. 1991 the President resigned on 11 Jan. 1992 and his functions were assumed by a High Committee of State. The second round of elections was cancelled. In March 1992 the FIS was dissolved by court order. The head of state, Mohamed Boudiaf, was assassinated on 29 July 1992, and a campaign of terrorism was launched by Moslem fundamentalists.

TERRITORY AND POPULATION. Algeria is bounded in the west by Morocco and Western Sahara, south-west by Mauritania and Mali, south-east by Niger, east by Libya and Tunisia, and north by the Mediterranean Sea. It has an area of 2,381,741 sq. km (919,595 sq. miles). Population (census 1987) 22,971,558; estimate (1995) 28,575,000. (44·3% urban). Population density (1995), 12 per sq. km. Vital statistics, 1991: Births, 755,459; deaths, 116,120; marriages, 151,467; stillbirths, 17,520. Rates: Births, 30·1%; deaths, 6%; growth, 2·41%. Expectation of life (1992), 65·6 years. 2·5m. Algerians live in France.

83% of the population speak Arabic, 17% Berber; French is widely spoken. A law of Dec. 1990 made Arabic the sole official language, but in July 1992 its implementation was delayed for further discussion.

The populations (1987 Census) of the 48 *wilayat* were as follows:

Adrar	216,931	Mila	511,047
Ain Defla	536,205	Mostaganem	504,124
Ain Témouchent	271,454	M'Sila	605,578
Annaba (Bône)	453,951	Naâma	112,858
Batna	757,059	Ouahran (Oran)	916,578
al-Bayadh	155,494	Ouargla	286,696
Béchar	183,896	al-Oued	379,512
Béjaia (Bougie)	697,669	Oum al-Bouaghi	402,683
Biskra	429,217	Qacentina (Constantine)	662,330
Bordj Bou Arreridj	429,009	Relizane	545,061
Bouira	525,460	Saida	235,240
al-Boulaida (Blida)	704,462	Setif	997,482
Boumerdes	646,870	Sidi bel-Abbès	444,047
Cheliff (Orléansville)	679,717	Skikda	619,094
Djelfa	490,240	Souk Ahras	298,236
Guelma	353,329	Tamanrasset	94,219
Ghardaia	215,955	at-Tarf	276,836
Illizi	19,698	Tébessa	409,317
al-Jaza'ir (Algiers)	1,687,579	Tiaret	574,786
Jijel	471,319	Tindouf	16,339[1]
Khenchela	243,733	Tipaza	615,140
Laghouat	215,183	Tissemsilt	227,542
Mascara	562,806	Tizi-Ouzou	931,501
Médéa	650,623	Tlemcen	707,453

[1] Excluding Saharawi refugees (170,000 in 1988) in camps.

The capital is Algiers (1995 population, 2,168,000). Other major towns (with 1987 census populations): Oran, 609,823; Constantine, 440,842; Annaba, 222,518; Batna, 181,601; Sétif, 170,182; Sidi-Bel-Abbès, 152,778; Skikda, 128,747; Biskra, 128,280; Blida, 127,284; Bejaia, 114,534; Mostaganem, 114,037; Tlemcen, 107,632; Tebassa, 107,559; Bechar, 107,311.

CLIMATE. Coastal areas have a warm temperate climate, with most rain in winter, which is mild, while summers are hot and dry. Inland, conditions become more arid beyond the Atlas Mountains. Algiers. Jan. 54°F (12·2°C), July 76°F (24·4°C). Annual rainfall 30" (762 mm). Biskra. Jan. 52°F (11·1°C), July 93°F (33·9°C). Annual rainfall 6" (158 mm). Oran. Jan. 54°F (12·2°C), July 76°F (24·4°C). Annual rainfall 15" (376 mm).

CONSTITUTION AND GOVERNMENT. A Constitution was approved by referendum in Feb. 1989. There was a turnout of 83% and 92% of the voters approved of the constitutional reforms which included the separation of the National Liberation Front (FLN) from the State, the legalization of opposition parties and the omission of references to socialism.

The *President* is elected by universal suffrage for 5-year terms (renewable). A *Constitutional Council* functions as an electoral supervisory body. The President appoints a Prime Minister and other ministers, and heads meetings of the Council of Ministers. At the presidential elections on 16 Nov. 1995 the electorate was 15, 969,904; turn-out was 74·92%. Gen. Lamine Zeroual was elected for a second term with 61·34% of votes cast against 3 opponents.

Legislative power is held by the *National Assembly*, whose 430 members are elected for a 5-year term by proportional representation. Elections were held on 26 Dec. with a second round scheduled for 15 Jan. 1992. The electorate was 13·5m.; 5,712 candidates stood. At the first round 231 seats were decided. Turn-out was 58·5%. The Islamic Salvation Front (FIS) won 188 seats, the Socialist Forces Front (FFS – a Berber party) 25 and the FLN 15. The President resigned and his functions were assumed by a High Committee of State until Jan. 1994. The second round of elections was cancelled.

President and Minister of Defence: Gen. Lamine Zeroual (b. 1941; sworn in 27 Nov. 1995).

In Jan. 1996 the government comprised:

Prime Minister: Ahmed Ouyahia.

Interior, Local Communities and Environment: Mustafa Benmansour. *Education:* Slimane Chikh. *Foreign:* Ahmed Attaf. *Justice:* Mohamed Adami. *Finance:* Ahmed Benbitour. *Higher Education and Research:* Boubakour Benbouzid. *Trade:* Abdelkrim Harchaoui. *Agriculture and Fisheries:* Noureddine Bahbouh. *Communication and Culture:* Mihoub Mihoubi. *Youth and Sport:* Mouldi Aissaoui. *Energy and Mining:* Amar Makhloufi. *Posts and Telecommunications:* Mohand Said Youyou. *Transport:* Essaid Bendakir. *Labour, Social Protection and Professional Training:* Hacene Laskri. *Religious Affairs:* Ahmed Merani. *Housing:* Kamel Hakimi. *Health and Population:* Yahia Guidoum. *Industry and Restructuring:* Mourad Benachenou. *Tourism and Craft Industry:* Abdelaziz Benmhidi. *Small and Medium Business:* Abdelkader Hamiani. *War Veterans:* Said Abadou. *Equipment and National and Regional Development:* Smain Dine.

National flag: Vertically green and white, a red crescent and star over all in centre.

National anthem: 'Qassaman bin nazilat Il-mahiqat' ('We swear by the lightning that destroys'); words by M. Zakaria, tune by Mohamed Fawzi.

Local government: There are 48 provincial (*wilayat*) councils and 1,539 local authorities. At elections in June 1990 turn-out was 65%. FIS gained control of 32 provincial and 853 local councils, the FLN of 14 and 487. In March 1992 the government dissolved some 400 councils controlled by the FIS.

DEFENCE. Conscription is for 18 months (6 months basic training and 12 months civilian tasks) at the age of 19.

Army. There are 6 military regions. The Army had a strength of 105,000 (90,000 conscripts) in 1996, organized in 2 armoured and 2 mechanized divisons, 5 motorized infantry brigades, 1 airborne division, and 7 artillery and 5 air defence battalions. Equipment includes 330 T-54/-55, 330 T-62 and 300 T-72 main battle tanks. The Ministry of the Interior maintain a Gendarmerie of 24,000 personnel and National Security Forces of 16,000. The Republican Guard numbers 1,200.

Navy. The Naval combatant force, largely supplied from the former USSR, consists of 2 modern diesel-powered patrol submarines, 3 frigates, 3 missile-armed corvettes, 11 fast missile craft, 8 other patrol craft, 1 ocean minesweeper, 2 tank landing ships, and 1 tank landing craft. There are some 10 auxiliaries. An associated coastguard 600 strong operates 28 fast cutters. Naval personnel in 1995 totalled 6,700. There are naval bases at Algiers, Annaba, Mers el Kebir, and Jijel.

Air Force. Five MiG-15 jet-fighters were delivered in 1962 as the nucleus of an Algerian Air Force. Since then many more aircraft of Soviet design have followed, and the Air Force currently has about 250 combat aircraft and 12,000 personnel. Training and technical assistance have been given by Egypt and the Soviet Union. There are 8 squadrons of MiG-21s, 3 squadrons of MiG-23 variable-geometry interceptors and fighter-bombers, 3 squadrons of Su-20 variable-geometry attack aircraft, 1 squadron with MiG-25 fighter and reconnaissance aircraft, more than 30 Mi-24 assault helicopters and gunships, 17 C-130H Hercules, 3 F.27, 4 Il-76 and 5 An-12 transports and a variety of smaller transports, a wing of 4 Mi-6, 30 Mi-8, about 30 Mi-17, 5 Puma, 6 Alouette III and 6 Hughes 269 helicopters, and training units equipped with CM.170 Magister and L-39 Albatros armed jet counter-insurgency/trainers, Beech King Air 2000 twin-engine/instrument trainers, MiG-15UTIs and MiG-17s, and two-seat versions of operational types. Surface-to-air missile units have Soviet-built 'Guidelines', 'Goas', 'Gainfuls' and 'Gaskins'. Personnel numbered 10,000 in 1995.

INTERNATIONAL RELATIONS

Membership. Algeria is a member of UN, OAU, the Arab League and OPEC.

ECONOMY

Policy. A law on privatization of July 1995 envisages the creation of small and medium size businesses in commerce, tourism and transport. Strategic industries (gas and oil) and large industrial complexes are to remain state-owned. Some 1,200 small and 50 large businesses were offered for sale to Algerian citizens; 30% of the shares are reserved for employees (5% free of charge).

Budget. 1994 budget revenue (in DA 1m.): 474,100 (including 221,800 from oil and 184,300 from direct taxation); expenditure: 613,700 (including 74,100 on education; 46,800 on defence; 23,900 on home affairs; 19,800 on public health; 12,400 on veterans' affairs).

Currency. The unit of currency is the *Algerian dinar* (DZD) of 100 *centimes*. There are banknotes of DA 10, 20, 50, 100, 200 and 1,000 and coins of 1, 2, 5, 20 and 50 centimes and DA 1, 5 and 10. DA 211,410m. were in circulation in 1993. Foreign exchange reserves were US$1,500m. in Jan. 1994; gold reserves were US$1,565m. in Sept. 1993. Inflation was 32% in 1995. The dinar was devalued by 28·6% in April 1994. In March 1996, £1 = DA 81·94; US$1 = DA 53·61; DM1 = DA 36·32.

Banking and Finance. The central bank and bank of issue is the Banque d'Algérie. The *Governor* is Abdelwahab Keramane. Private banking recommenced in Sept. 1995.

Weights and Measures. The metric system is in use.

ENERGY AND NATURAL RESOURCES

Electricity. Production (1992) 17,636m. kWh. 7% is hydro-electric.

Oil and Gas. A law of Nov. 1991 permits foreign companies to acquire up to 49% of known oil and gas reserves. Oil production in 1995 was 1·21m. bbls. a day. Production of natural gas in 1992 was 109,300m. cu. metres. Proven reserves are 3,700,000m. cu. metres.

Minerals. Output in 1992 (in tonnes): Iron ore 2,565,300; lead, 1,507; phosphates, 1,173; zinc, 7,488. There are also deposits of mercury, silver, copper, antimony, kaolin, marble, onyx, salt and coal.

Agriculture. Much of the land is unsuitable for agriculture. The northern mountains provide grazing. There were an estimated 7·09m. ha of arable land in 1991, 0·57m. ha of permanent crops and 31m. ha of permanent pasture. 0·43m. ha were irrigated in 1992. In 1987 the government sold back to the private sector land which had been nationalized on the declaration of independence in 1962; a further 0·5m. ha, expropriated in 1973, were returned to some 30,000 small landowners in 1990. In 1992 6m. persons were dependent upon agriculture, the agricultural workforce being 1·44m. There were 91,500 tractors and 9,500 combine harvesters in 1991.

The chief crops in 1993 were (in 1,000 tonnes): Wheat, 1,350; barley, 600; dates, 210; potatoes, 900; oranges, 194; mandarins and tangerines, 95; watermelons, 397; wine, 50; tomatoes, 510; olives, 130; onions, 232; oats, 57.

Livestock (in 1,000), 1993: Horses, 84; mules, 107; asses, 340; cattle, 1,460; camels, 130; sheep, 18,800; goats, 2,500.

Forestry. Forests cover 4·7m. ha. The greater part of the state forests are brushwood, but there are large areas with cork-oak trees, Aleppo pine, evergreen oak and cedar. The dwarf-palm is grown on the plains, alfa on the table-land. Timber is cut for firewood and for industrial purposes and for bark for tanning.

Fisheries. There are extensive fisheries for sardines, anchovies, sprats, tunny fish, and shellfish.

INDUSTRY. 1992 output of state enterprises (in 1,000 tonnes): Pig iron, 930; crude steel, 768; rolled steel, 439; steel tubes, 106; concrete bars, 134; cement, 7,093; bricks, 1,776; ammonitrates, 193; phosphate fertilizers, 154; tobacco, 24; (in units) tractors, 3,009; lorries, 2,434; TV sets, 218,000.

Labour. In 1992 the economically active population was estimated at 6·19m. In 1991 the non-agricultural workforce numbered 3,511,000 of whom 1,307,000 were engaged in administration, 744,000 in trade and services, 615,000 in industry, 588,000 in building and public works and 257,000 in transport. In 1994, 27% of the workforce was unemployed. The minimum wage was raised by 40% in Nov. 1991, to reach DA 3,000 per month on 1 Jan. 1992 and DA 3,500 on 1 July 1992.

Trade Unions. The General Union of Algerian Workers had in 1982 1m. members in 8 affiliated groups; the National Union of Algerian Peasants had 0·7m. The Islamic Federation of Trade Unions was formed in 1990.

FOREIGN ECONOMIC RELATIONS. Foreign debt was US$26,000m. in April 1994. Foreign investors are permitted to hold 100% of the equity of companies, and to repatriate all profits.

Commerce. In 1994 exports were valued at US$9·67m. and imports at US$8·89m.

Main trade partners in 1994, with percentages of total trade: USA (exports, 16·4%; imports, 14·2%); Italy (15·9%; 11·1%); France (14·2%; 28·8%); Germany (10·2%; 5·5%).

1994 exports included (in US$1m.): Crude oil, 1,980; gas, 2,270; condensates, 2,190; refined products, 1,670.

Total trade between Algeria and UK (British Department of Trade returns, in £1,000 sterling):

	1992	*1993*	*1994*	*1995*
Imports to UK	162,560	187,081	182,853	244,279
Exports and re-exports from UK	38,130	56,162	47,257	64,277

Tourism. In 1989, there were 851,181 foreign visitors.

COMMUNICATIONS

Roads. There were in 1991, 26,179 km of national highways and 22,132 km of local roads. There were 1,104,000 vehicles registered in 1990. In 1991 55m. passengers were conveyed by public transport and 6·2m. tonnes of freight.

Railways. In 1992 there were 4,733 km of route (301 km electrified) of which 1,157 km were of 1,055mm gauge. In 1994 the railways carried 9·9m. tonnes of freight and 56m. passengers.

Civil Aviation. There is an international airport at Algiers (Houari Boumediene). The national carrier is the state-owned Air Algérie, which had 3 A310-200s, 2 B-767-200s, 9 B-727-200 Advs, 13 B-737-200 Advs, 2 B-737-200C Advs, 3 B-767-300s, 7 F-27-400Ms and 2 other aircraft in 1995. Algeria is also served by Air France, Alitalia, Balkan, Egyptair, Libyan Arab Airlines, Royal Air Maroc, Saudia and Tunis Air. In 1993 the airports handled 6m. passengers and 27,851 tonnes of freight.

Shipping. In 1991, 17·2m. tonnes of cargo were unloaded and 64·9m. tonnes loaded, and 382,880 passengers embarked or disembarked. The state shipping line, Compagnie Nationale Algérienne de Navigation, owned 70 vessels in 1994. The shipping fleet totalled 1·09m. GRT in 1994, including oil tankers, 52,547 GRT.

Telecommunications. There were, in 1991, 2,877 post offices; number of telephones (1991), 862,000; telex subscribers, 10,487. The state-controlled Radiodiffusion Algérienne and Entreprise Nationale de Télévision broadcast home services in Arabic, Kabyle (Berber) and French and an external service. There are 18 TV transmitting stations (colour by PAL). In 1993 there were 3·5m. radio and 2m. TV receivers.

Cinemas. In 1988 there were 249 cinemas. 21,000 attendances were recorded.

Press (1989). There were 6 daily newspapers, with a combined circulation of 1m.

SOCIAL INSTITUTIONS

Justice. The judiciary is constitutionally independent. Judges are appointed by the Supreme Council of Magistrature chaired by the President of the Republic. Criminal justice is organized as in France. The Supreme Court is at the same time Council of State and High Court of Appeal. The death penalty is in force for terrorism.

Religion. Virtually the whole population are Sunni Moslems. There are about 150,000 Christians, mainly Roman Catholic. In 1995, the latter had an archbishop, 130 priests and 250 nuns.

Education. Adult literacy was 60·6% in 1992. In 1991–92 there were 13,461 state primary schools with 154,685 teachers and 4,357,352 pupils, 3,343 secondary schools with 131,232 teachers and 2,232,780 pupils, of whom 43·9% were female. In higher education there were 223,300 university and 43,900 other students with 14,496 teachers.

In 1995-96, there were 6 universities, 2 universities of science and technology, 5 university centres, 1 agronomic institute, 1 telecommunications institute, 1 veterinary institute, 1 school of architecture and town planning and 1 *école normale supérieure*. In 1994-95 there were 107,121 university students and 7,947 academic staff.

Health. In 1991 there were 24,719 doctors, 7,563 dental surgeons and 2,575 pharmacists. In 1990 there were 284 hospitals (with 60,124 beds), 1,309 health centres, 510 poly clinics, 475 maternity clinics and 3,344 care centres.

Welfare. Welfare payments to 7·4m. beneficiaries on low incomes were introduced in March 1992.

DIPLOMATIC REPRESENTATIVES

Of Algeria in Great Britain (54 Holland Park, London, W11 3RS)
Ambassador: Vacant.

Of Great Britain in Algeria (Résidence Cassiopée, 7 Chemin des Glycines, Algiers)
Chargé d'affaires: P. J. Marshall, CMG.

Of Algeria in the USA (2118 Kalorama Rd., NW, Washington, D.C., 20008)
Ambassador: Hadj Osmane Bencherif.

Of the USA in Algeria (4 Chemin Cheich Bachir Ibrahimi, Algiers)
Ambassador: Ronald E. Neumann.

Of Algeria to the United Nations
Ambassador: Ramtane Lamamra.

Further Reading

Ageron, C.-R., *Modern Algeria: a History from 1830 to the Present.* London, 1991
Bennoune, M., *The Making of Contempory Algeria, 1830–1987.* CUP, 1988
Eveno, P., *L'Algérie.* Paris, 1994
Heggoy, A. A. and Crout, R. R. *Historical Dictionary of Algeria.* Metuchen (NJ), 1995
Lawless, R. I., *Algeria.* [Bibliography] Oxford and Santa Barbara, 1981
Ruedy, J., *Modern Algeria: the Origins and Development of a Nation.* Indiana Univ. Press, 1992
Stora, B., *Histoire de l'Algérie depuis l'Indépendance.* Paris, 1994

National statistical office: Office National des Statistiques, 8 rue des Moussebiline, Algiers.

ANDORRA

Capital: Andorra-la-Vella
Population: 62,500 (1994)

Principat d'Andorra

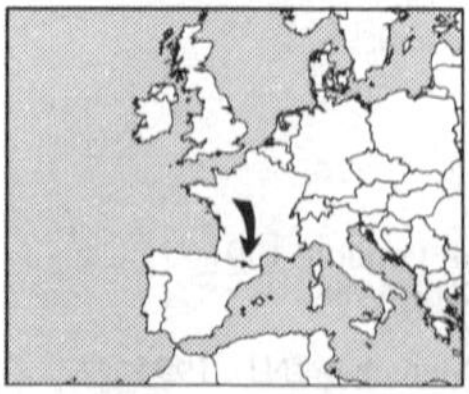

KEY HISTORICAL EVENTS. The political status of Andorra was regulated by the *Paréage* of 1278 which placed Andorra under the joint suzerainty of the Comte de Foix and of the Bishop of Urgel. The rights vested in the house of Foix passed by marriage to that of Bearn and, on the accession of Henri IV, to the French crown. A new democratic constitution was adopted in 1993.

TERRITORY AND POPULATION. The co-principality of Andorra is situated in the eastern Pyrenees on the French–Spanish border. The country is mountainous. Area, 453 sq. km (175 sq. miles). In lieu of a census, a register of population is kept. The registered population on 1 Jan. 1993 was 61,599; 1994 estimate, 62,500 (62·5% urban). The chief towns are Andorra-la-Vella, the capital (registered population, 1993, 22,387) and its suburb Escaldes-Engordany (13,177). 28% of the residential population are Andorran, 46% Spanish, 11% Portuguese and 8% French. Catalan is the official language; Spanish is widely spoken.

CLIMATE. Escaldes-Engordany. Jan. 36°F (2·3°C), July 67°F (19·3°C). Annual rainfall 32" (808 mm).

CONSTITUTION AND GOVERNMENT. The joint heads of state are the President of the French Republic and the Bishop of Urgel, the co-princes.

A new democratic constitution was approved by 74·2% of votes cast at a referendum on 14 March 1993. The electorate was 9,123; turn-out was 75·7%. The new Constitution, which came into force on 4 May 1993, makes the co-princes a single constitutional monarch and provides for a parliament, the *General Council of the Andorran Valleys*, elected by universal suffrage. The General Council has 28 members elected, 4 from each of the 7 parishes, for 4 years. In 1982 an *Executive Council* was appointed and legislative and executive powers were separated.

Elections to the General Council were held on 12 Dec. 1993. Electorate, 9,700. 5 political groups stood. The Andorran National Democrats (AND) gained 4 seats with 26·4% of votes cast, the Liberal Union 3 with 22%, New Democracy 3 with 19·1% and the Social Democrats 2. A new government was formed on 21 Dec. 1994.

President, Executive Council: Marc Forne (Liberal Union).

National flag: Three vertical strips of blue, yellow, red, with the national arms optionally in the centre.

National anthem. 'El Gran Carlemany, mon pare' ('Great Charlemagne, my father'); words by Enric Marfany, tune by D.J. Benlloch i Vivò).

INTERNATIONAL RELATIONS. The 1993 Constitution empowers Andorra to conduct its own Foreign affairs, with consultation on matters affecting France or Spain.

Membership. Andorra is a member of the UN and the Council of Europe.

ECONOMY

Currency. French and Spanish currency are both in use. *Diner* coins are minted for collectors.

ENERGY AND NATURAL RESOURCES

Agriculture. In 1992 there were some 1,000 ha of arable land, 10,000 ha of forests and 25,000 ha of pasture. Tobacco is a principal crop.

INDUSTRY

Labour. 20% of the workforce is employed in agriculture, the rest in tourism, commerce, services and light industry.

FOREIGN ECONOMIC RELATIONS. Andorra is a member of the EEC Customs Union for industrial goods, and a third country for agricultural produce. There is a free economic zone.

Commerce. Total trade between Andorra and UK (British Department of Trade returns, in £1,000 sterling):

	1992	*1993*	*1994*	*1995*
Imports to UK	19	89	298	8
Exports and re-exports from UK	13,071	18,680	12,070	13,043

Tourism. Tourism is the main industry, averaging 12m. visitors a year.

COMMUNICATIONS

Roads. There are 220 km of roads (120 km paved). Motor vehicles (1983) 24,789.

Civil Aviation. There is an airport for Andorran traffic at Seo de Urgel.

Telecommunications. Servei de Telecomunicacions d'Andorra relays French and Spanish programmes. Radio Andorra is the government station; Radio Valira is commercial. Number of receivers (1993), radio, 10,000; TV, 4,000.

SOCIAL INSTITUTIONS

Justice. Judicial power is exercised in civil matters in the first instance, according to the plaintiff's choice, by either the *Bayle Français* or the *Bayle Episcopal*, nominated by the respective co-princes. The judge of appeal is nominated alternately for 5 years by each co-prince; the third instance is the Supreme Court at Perpignan or the supreme court of the Bishop at Urgel.

Criminal justice is administered by the *Corts* consisting of the judge of appeal, 2 *rahonadors* elected by the General Council of the Valleys, a general attorney and an attorney nominated for 5 years alternately by each of the co-princes.

Religion. The Roman Catholic is the established church, but the 1993 Constitution guarantees religious liberty.

Education. Schooling is compulsory to age 16. In 1986–87 there were 1,866 pupils at infant schools, 3,458 at primary schools, 3,271 at secondary schools, 230 at technical schools and 46 at special schools.

DIPLOMATIC REPRESENTATIVES

Of Great Britain in Andorra
Ambassador: C. D. Brighty, CMG, CVO (resides in Madrid).

Of Andorra to the United National
Deputy Permanent Representative: Juli Minoves-Triquell.

Further Reading

Taylor, B., *Andorra.* [Bibliography]. Oxford and Santa Barbara (CA), 1993

ANGOLA

República de Angola

Capital: Luanda
Population: 11·5m. (1995)
GNP per capita: US$620 (1989)
HDI/world rank: 0·291/164 (1992)

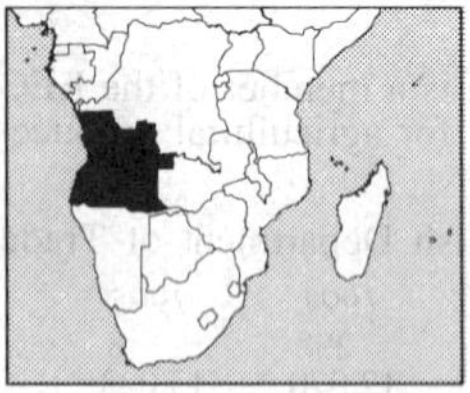

KEY HISTORICAL EVENTS. Angola was a Portuguese colony until 11 June 1951, when it became an Overseas Province of Portugal. On 11 Nov. 1975 Angola became fully independent as the People's Republic of Angola. The People's Liberation Movement of Angola (MPLA) and the National Union for the Total Independence of Angola (UNITA) committed themselves to putting their rival claims to power to a popular vote, but the agreement broke down in battles which left MPLA in control of the government and UNITA banished to the countryside. A peace agreement between the government and UNITA was signed on 31 May 1991. The agreement provided for a political-military mission backed by US, Soviet and Portuguese experts to supervise the ceasefire under UN monitoring. In Sept. 1992 José Eduardo dos Santos was re-elected President against the UNITA leader Jonas Savimbi, but the latter refused to accept the result, and fighting broke out again. On 15 Sept. 1993 the UN Security Council unanimously voted not to supply UNITA with war materiel. On 20 Nov. 1994 an agreement was signed in Lusaka between President Dos Santos and a representative of UNITA, but in the absence of Jonas Savimbi. The agreement envisages a ceasefire, the integration of UNITA's forces into the Angolan military, the formation of a coalition government and the holding of fresh elections. On 8 Feb. 1995 the UN Security Council unanimously resolved to send to Angola a force of 7,000 military and 1,000 civilian personnel.

On 15 April 1995 the government, UNITA and the UN Mission for Angola (UNAVEM II) signed an agreement for the installation of UN military observers. On 6 May 1995 Dos Santos and Savimbi met and agreed to apply the agreement of 20 Nov. 1994. However, on 4 Dec. 1995 UNITA declared it would no longer participate in the disarmament of its forces under the Lusaka agreement because of an offensive by government troops.

TERRITORY AND POPULATION. Angola is bounded in the north by Congo, north and north-east by Zaïre, east by Zambia, south by Namibia and west by the Atlantic Ocean. The area is 1,246,700 sq. km (481,354 sq. miles) including the province of Cabinda, an exclave of territory separated by 30 sq. km of Zaïrean territory. The population at census, 1970, was 5,646,166, of whom 14% were urban. Official estimate, 1995, 11·5m. (50% urban); density, 9 per sq. km. Expectation of life was 45·6 years in 1992. Infant mortality, 1992, 124 per 1,000 live births.

There were 0·3m. Angolan refugees in Zaïre, Zambia and the Congo in 1995.

Area, population and chief towns of the provinces:

Province	*Area (in sq. km)*	*Population estimate, 1992 (in 1,000)*	*Chief town*
Bengo	31,371	196·1	Caxito
Benguela	31,788	656·6	Benguela
Bié	70,314	1,119·8	Kuito
Cabinda	7,270	152·1	Cabinda
Cuando-Cubango	199,049	139·6	Menongue
Cuanza Norte	24,190	385·2	Ndalatando
Cuanza Sul	55,660	694·5	Sumbe
Cunene	89,342	241·2	Ondjiva
Huambo	34,274	1,521·0	Huambo
Huíla	75,002	885·1	Lubango
Luanda	2,418	1,588·6	Luanda

Province	*Area (in sq. km)*	*Population estimate, 1992 (in 1,000)*	*Chief town*
Lunda Norte	102,783	305·9	Lucapa
Lunda Sul	45,649	169·1	Saurimo
Malanje	97,602	906·0	Malanje
Moxico	223,023	319·3	Luena
Namibe	58,137	107·3	Namibe
Uíge	58,698	802·7	Uíge
Zaire	40,130	237·5	Mbanza Congo

The most important towns (populations) are Luanda, the capital (1995, 2·25m.), Huambo (1995, 0·4m.), Lobito (1970, 59,258), Benguela (1970, 40,996), Lubango (1984, 105,000), Malange (1970, 31,559) and Namibe (formerly Moçâmedes, 1981, 0·1m.).

The main ethnic groups are the Ovimbundu, the Mbundu and the Bakongo. Portuguese is the official language.

CLIMATE. The climate is tropical, with low rainfall in the west but increasing inland. Temperatures are constant over the year and most rain falls in March and April. Luanda. Jan. 78°F (25·6°C), July 69°F (20·6°C). Annual rainfall 13" (323 mm). Lobito. Jan. 77°F (25°C), July 68°F (20°C). Annual rainfall 14" (353 mm).

CONSTITUTION AND GOVERNMENT. Under the Constitution adopted at independence, the sole legal party was the MPLA. In Dec. 1990, however, the MPLA announced that the Constitution would be revised to permit opposition parties. The supreme organ of state is the 220-member *National Assembly*. There is an executive *President* elected for renewable terms of 5 years, who appoints a *Council of Ministers*. There are 2 *Vice-Presidencies*, one of which is reserved for the leader of UNITA.

At the presidential and parliamentary elections of 29–30 Sept. 1992 the electorate was 4,862,748. Turn-out was about 90%. Eduardo Dos Santos (MPLA) was re-elected as President with 49·5% of votes cast as against 40·7% for his single opponent, Jonas Savimbi (UNITA). The latter refused to accept the result.

The MPLA gained 129 seats in the National Assembly with 53·74% of votes cast, UNITA 70 with 34%.

The Council of Ministers in Oct. 1995 comprised:

President: José Eduardo dos Santos (b. 1943; re-elected 9 Dec. 1985 and 29–30 Sept. 1992).

Prime Minister: Marcolino Moco.

Defence: Agusto da Silva Tomas. *Interior:* Santana André Pitra. *Foreign Affairs:* Dr Venancio de Silva Moura. *Territorial Administration:* Anibal Lopes Rocha. *Finance:* Vacant. *Oil:* Albina Pereira Africano. *Industry:* Dr Idalino Manuel Mendes. *Agriculture and Rural Development:* Isaac Maria dos Anjos. *Fisheries:* Maria Monteiro Jardin. *Geology and Mines:* José António Dias. *Public Works and Urbanization:* Dr Mateus de Brito Junior. *Transport and Communications:* Dr André Luis Brandão. *Commerce and Tourism:* João Celestino Dias. *Health:* Dr Martinho Sanches Epalanga. *Education:* Dr João Manuel Bernardo. *Assistance and Social Reintegration:* Albino Malunga. *Youth and Sport:* José Rocha de Castro. *Justice:* Dr Paulo Chipilika. *Public Administration, Employment and Social Security:* Dr António Costa Neto. *Planning:* José Pedro de Morais. *Implementation of the Peace Process:* Faustina Muteka. *Information:* Pedro Hendrik Vaal Neto. *Governor of Luanda:* Justino Fernandes.

National flag: Horizontally red over black, with a star and an arc of cogwheel crossed by a machete, all yellow over all in the centre.

National anthem: 'O Pátria, nunca mais esqueceremos' ('Oh Fatherland, never shall we forget'); words by M. R. Alves Monteiro, tune by R. A. Dias Mingas.

Local government: The 18 provinces, each under a Provincial Commissioner appointed by the President and an elected legislative of from 55 to 85 members, are subdivided into 139 districts.

DEFENCE. Conscription is for 2 years.

Army. In 1995 the Army had 25 regiments. Total strength 75,000. Equipment includes Soviet 100 T-34, 100 T-54/55 and some T-62 and T-72 main battle tanks.

Navy. The Navy, almost all Soviet-built, includes 6 fast missile boats, 4 fast torpedo boats, 7 inshore patrol boats, 2 mine-hunters, 2 landing ships and 6 landing craft, together with 10 auxiliary vessels. Naval personnel in 1995 totalled about 1,500. Naval bases are at Luanda, Lobito and Namibe.

Air Force. The Angolan People's Air Force (FAPA) was formed in 1976. The combat force had been expanded since 1983 with Soviet assistance. It included (1993) 50 MiG-21, 30 MiG-23 and 40 Su-22 fighters, plus 25 Mi-24 and 12 Gazelle armed helicopters. (The MiG-17 is being withdrawn from service.) There are 10 An-2, 15 An-26, 12 Islander, 4 Turbo-Porter, 8 Aviocar and 2 F.27 transports, 2 Embraer EMB-111 and 5 Aviocar maritime surveillance aircraft, 4 PC-9, 15 PC-7 and 3 MiG-15UTI trainers, and 40 Mi-8/17, 12 Gazelle, 12 Dauphin, 2 Lama and 35 Alouette III helicopters. Personnel (1995) 5,500.

INTERNATIONAL RELATIONS

Membership. Angola is a member of the UN, OAU, SADC and is an ACP state of the EU.

ECONOMY

Policy. Reforms are in train to introduce a market economy and restore private property. An Economic and Social Programme covers 1995-96.

Budget. The 1995 budget envisaged recurrent revenue (in 1,000m. former kwanzas) of 3,765·3 (of which taxes, 2,257·6; royalties, 1,159); capital revenue of 15·8 (mainly from privatization); recurrent expenditure of 2,515·6 and capital expenditure of 2,177·2.

Currency. The unit of currency is the *readjusted kwanza* (AOK) of 100 *lwei*, which replaced the former new kwanza at Kzr1=Nkz1,000 in July 1995. There were notes of 100, 500, 1,000, 5,000, 10,000, 50,000 and 100,000 former kwanzas, which remained legal tender until 1996. In Jan. 1994 a 2-tier system was replaced by a single floating exchange rate. Foreign exchange reserves were US$202m. in 1994; gold reserves were 46,500 troy oz. in 1990. Inflation was an annualized 2,040% in Aug. 1995. In March 1996, £1 = 8,612·53; US$1 = 5,635; DM1 = 3,818 kwnazas.

Banking and Finance. Banking was nationalized in 1975 but re-opened to commercial competition in 1991. The Banco Nacional de Angola is the central bank and bank of issue (*Governor*, António Furtado). All banks remain state-owned, though the government is progressively reducing its stake in them. An agricultural bank and a commercial and industrial bank were founded in 1991. 3 Portuguese banks have branches.

Weights and Measures. The metric system is in force.

ENERGY AND NATURAL RESOURCES

Electricity. Production (1994) totalled 1,027·8m. kWh (772m. kWh hydro-electric in 1991).

Oil. Oil is produced mainly in the Cabinda exclave and contributed 49·9% of Angolan GDP in 1994. Total production (1992) 25·57m. tonnes.

Minerals. Production of diamonds in 1993 totalled 46,000 carats (1,235,000 carats in 1992); (1991) granite, 635,000 cu. metres; marble, 244,000 cu. metres; salt, 6,600 tonnes. Iron ore, phosphate, manganese and copper deposits exist.

Agriculture. Agriculture contributed 12% of GDP in 1994. In 1992 there were 3m.

ha of arable land, 0·5m. ha of permanent crops and 29m. ha of permanent pasture. In 1993 7m. persons depended upon agriculture, of whom 2·69m. were economically active. The principal cash crops (with 1993 production, in 1,000 tonnes): Sugar-cane (290), coffee (5), bananas (280), palm oil (40), palm kernels (12), seed cotton (12); others include tobacco, citrus fruit and sisal. Food crops comprise cassava (1,870), maize (274), sweet potatoes (170) and dry beans (36).

Livestock (1993): 3·2m. cattle, 250,000 sheep, 1,550,000 goats, 810,000 pigs.

Forestry. In 1990 there were 52·95m. ha of forests, including mahogany and other hardwoods. Production (1991) 25·6m. cu. metres (7·9m. cu. metres sawn wood).

Fisheries. In 1993 the fishing fleet had 73 vessels over 100 GRT totalling 17,332 GRT. Total catch (1993) was 122,000 tonnes.

INDUSTRY. The principal manufacturing branches are foodstuffs, textiles and oil refining. Output, 1991 (in tonnes): Maize flour, 21,200; wheat flour, 18,900; bread, 25,100; soap, 4,700; plate glass, 6,900; plastic bags, 1,600; pesticides, 46; zinc sheets, 6,012; cable, 112; 52,000 radio sets; 15,600 TV sets.

Labour. The economically active population was 4·08m. in 1990 (1·57m. females, 0·29m. aged 10–15), of whom 69·8% worked in agriculture.

FOREIGN ECONOMIC RELATIONS. In 1994 foreign debt was US$11,178m.

Commerce. Imports and exports for calendar years in US$1m.:

	1990	*1991*	*1992*	*1993*	*1994*
Imports	1,578	1,347	1,988	1,463	1,633
Exports	3,884	3,449	3,833	2,900	3,002

Main exports, 1994 (in US$1m.): Crude oil, 2,821; diamonds, 96; refined oil, 61; gas, 14. Chief import suppliers (1991 trade in US$1m.): Portugal, 587; USA, 207; France, 194; Japan, 153; Brazil, 144. Chief export markets: USA, 1,751; France, 328; Germany, 174; Brazil, 152; Netherlands, 131.

Total trade between Angola and UK (British Department of Trade returns, in £1,000 sterling):

	1992	*1993*	*1994*	*1995*
Imports to UK	144,324	21,202	12,173	22,408
Exports and re-exports from UK	64,371	27,512	23,681	29,387

COMMUNICATIONS

Roads. There were, in 1994, about 75,000 km of roads (7,955 km asphalted and 7,870 km gravelled), and in 1989, 125,000 passenger cars and 42,000 commercial vehicles. Many roads remain mined as a result of the civil war; a programme of demining and rehabilitation is in train.

Railways. The length of railways open for traffic in 1987 was 2,952 km comprising 2,798 km of 1,067 mm gauge and 154 km of 600 mm gauge. The Benguela Railway runs from Lobito to the Zaïre border at Dilolo where it connects with the National Railways of Zaïre. Other lines link Luanda with Malange; Gunza with Gabela; and Namibe with Menongue. In 1993 railways carried 4m. passengers and 2·8m. tonnes of freight.

Civil Aviation. There is an international airport at Luanda (Fourth of February). The national carrier is Linhas Aéreas de Angola (TAAG). In 1995 it operated 1 B-707-320B, 3 B-737-200 Advs, 1 B-737-200C, 1 F-27-200, 1 F-200-400M, 2 F-27-600s and 3 ex-Soviet aircraft. There are also services by Aeroflot, Air France, Air Gabon, Air Namibia, Ethiopian Airlines, Lina Congo, SABENA, SAA and TAP. 0·46m. passengers were carried in 1991 (0·11m. international).

Shipping. There are ports at Luanda, Lobito and Namibe, and oil terminals at Malongo and Soyo. 1·24m. tonnes of cargo were discharged in 1994. There are 3 state shipping companies. In 1995 the merchant fleet totalled 0·12m. GRT, including oil tankers, 2,665 GRT.

Telecommunications. There were 78,000 telephones in 1991.

The government-controlled Rádio Nacional de Angola broadcasts 3 programmes and an international service. There are also regional stations. Televisão Popular de Angola transmits from 7 stations (colour by PAL). In 1993 there were 0·45m. radio and 50,000 TV receivers.

Press. The press was nationalized in 1976. In 1991 there were 2 dailies and 8 journals. The government daily is *Diário da República.*

SOCIAL INSTITUTIONS

Justice. The Supreme Court and Court of Appeal are in Luanda. The death penalty was abolished in 1992.

Religion. In 1992 there were 9·39m. Christians, the remainder following traditional animist religion.

Education. In 1992, 58% of the population over 15 were illiterate. The education system provides 3 levels of general education totalling 8 years, followed by schools for technical training, teacher training or pre-university studies. Enrolment (in 1,000) in 1991–92: Pre-school, 188. General education first level, 923; second level, 141; third level, 42. Technical training, 12·7; teacher training, 109; pre-university studies (1990-91), 6·1. There is 1 university. Private schools have been permitted since 1991. The University of Luanda has campuses at Luanda, Huambo and Lubango. It had 8,954 students in 1991-92.

Health. In 1990 there were 662 doctors, 10 dentists, 9,334 nurses, 4,165 medical auxiliaries and 266 hospitals and health centres with 11,857 beds. There were 1,339 medical posts.

DIPLOMATIC REPRESENTATIVES

Of Angola in Great Britain (98 Park Lane, London, W1)
Ambassador: António da Costa Fernandes.

Of Great Britain in Angola (Rua Diogo Cão, 4, Luanda)
Ambassador: R. D. Hart.

Of Angola in the USA
Ambassador: António Franca.

Of the USA in Angola (32 rua Houari Boumedienne, Miramar, Luanda)
Ambassador: Donald K. Steinberg.

Of Angola to the United Nations
Ambassador: Afonso Van Dunem 'Mbinda'.

Further Reading

James, W. M., *Political History of the War in Angola.* New York, 1991
Roque, F., *Económia de Angola.* Lisbon, 1991
Somerville, K., *Angola: Politics, Economics and Society.* London and Boulder, 1986

National statistical office: Instituto Nacional de Estatística, Luanda.

ANGUILLA

Capital: The Valley
Population: 8,960 (1992)

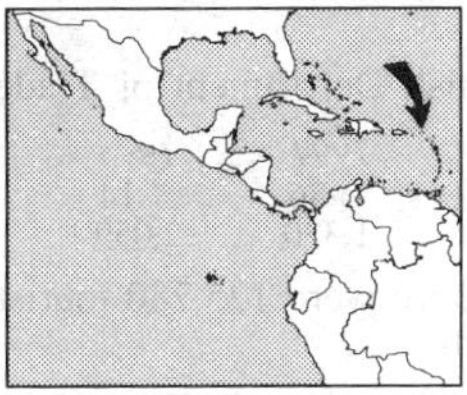

KEY HISTORICAL EVENTS. After British colonization in 1650, the territory was administered as part of the Leeward Islands. From 1825 it became more closely associated with St Kitts and ultimately incorporated in the colony of St Kitts-Nevis-Anguilla. Opposition to this association grew and in 1967 the island seceded unilaterally. Following direct intervention by the UK in 1969 Anguilla became a separate dependency of Britain on 19 Dec. 1980 under the Anguilla Act 1980. A new Constitution came into effect in April 1982.

TERRITORY AND POPULATION. Anguilla is the most northerly of the Leeward Islands, some 70 miles (112 km) to the north-west of St Kitts and 5 miles (8 km) to the north of St Martin/Sint Maarten. The territory also comprises the island of Sombrero and several other off-shore islets or cays. The total area of the territory is about 60 sq. miles (155 sq. km). Census population (1984) was 6,897. Population, 1992, 8,960. The capital is The Valley.

CONSTITUTION AND GOVERNMENT. A set of amendments to the constitution came into effect in 1990, providing for a Deputy Governor, a Parliamentary Secretary and an Opposition Leader. The *House of Assembly* consists of a Speaker, Deputy Speaker, 7 directly elected members for 5-year terms, 2 nominated members and 2 *ex-officio* members: the Deputy Governor and the Attorney-General.

Executive power is vested in the Governor who is appointed by HM The Queen. Apart from his special responsibilities (External Affairs, Defence, Internal Security, including the Police, and the Public Service) and his reserve powers in respect of legislation, the Governor discharges his executive powers on the advice of an Executive Council comprising a Chief Minister, 3 Ministers and 2 *ex-officio* members: the Deputy Governor, Attorney-General and the Secretary to the Executive Council.

Elections were held in March 1994 for the House of Assembly. The Anguilla National Alliance gained 2 seats, the Anguilla National Party (ANP), 2, the Anguillan Democratic Party, 2 and ind, 1.

Governor: Alan Hoole, OBE.

Deputy-Governor: Henry McCrory, LVO, OBE.

Chief Minister and Minister of Lands, Agriculture and Fisheries: Hubert Hughes (ANP).

National flag. British Blue Ensign with the shield of Anguilla in the fly.

ECONOMY

Budget. In 1994, current revenue was US$41·8m. and expenditure, US$38·6m. The main sources of revenue are custom duties and bank licence fees. There is little taxation. A 'Policy Plan' with the UK provides for £10·5m. of aid in 1994-97.

Currency. The *Eastern Caribbean dollar* (*see* ANTIGUA AND BARBUDA).

Banking and Finance. The East Caribbean Central Bank based in St Kitts-Nevis functions as a central bank. There is a small offshore banking sector. In 1995 there were 1 domestic and 3 foreign commercial banks.

ENERGY AND NATURAL RESOURCES

Electricity. Production (1992) 6·2m. kWh.

Agriculture. Because of low rainfall agriculture potential is limited. About 1,200 ha are cultivable. Main crops are pigeon peas, maize and sweet potatoes. Livestock consists of sheep, goats, cattle and poultry. The island relies on imports for food.

Fisheries. Fishing is a thriving industry (mainly lobster).

FOREIGN ECONOMIC RELATIONS

Commerce. Total trade between Anguilla and UK (British Department of Trade returns, in £1,000 sterling):

	1992	*1993*	*1994*	*1995*
Imports to UK	12	118	86	14
Exports and re-exports from UK	1,064	1,501	1,320	2,059

Tourism. Tourism accounts for 50% of GDP. In 1994 there were 125,780 tourist arrivals (66% from the USA), bringing revenue of US$51m.

COMMUNICATIONS

Roads. There are about 40 miles of tarred roads and 25 miles of secondary roads. In 1991 there were 2,450 passenger cars and 733 commercial vehicles.

Civil Aviation. Wallblake is the airport for The Valley. Anguilla is linked to neighbouring islands by services operated by Air Anguilla, LIAT, Tyden Air and WINAIR.

Shipping. The main seaports are Sandy Ground and Blowing Point, the latter serving passenger and cargo traffic to and from St Martin.

Telecommunications. There is a modern internal telephone service with (1992) 2,923 exchange lines; and international telegraph, telex, fax and telephone services. There is 1 government (Radio Anguilla) and 2 commercial radio broadcasters. TV is privately owned; there are 2 channels and a cable system.

Press. In 1995 there were 1 daily, 2 weeklies and a quarterly periodical.

SOCIAL INSTITUTIONS

Justice. Based on UK common law as exercised by the Eastern Caribbean Supreme Court on St Lucia. Final appeal lies to the UK privy council.

Religion. There were in 1992 Anglicans, Roman Catholics, Methodists, Seventh Day Adventists, Church of God and Baptists.

Education. Adult literacy was 80% in 1995. Education is free and compulsory between the ages of 5 and 16 years. There are 6 government primary schools with (1991) 1,360 pupils and 1 comprehensive school with (1991) 772 pupils. Higher education is provided at regional universities and similar institutions.

Health. In 1995 there were 2 hospitals with a total of 60 beds, 4 health centres and a government dental clinic. There were 5 government-employed and 4 private doctors.

Welfare. A social security system was instituted in 1982 to provide age and disability pensions and sickness and maternity benefits.

Further Reading

Petty, C. L., *Anguilla: Where there's a Will, there's a Way*. Anguilla, 1984.—*A Handbook History of Anguilla*. Anguilla, 1991.

ANTIGUA AND BARBUDA

Capital: St John's
Population: 65,962 (1991)
GNP per capita: US$6,970 (1994)
HDI/world rank: 0·840/55 (1992)

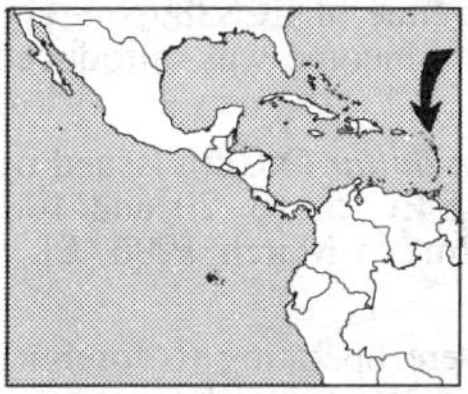

KEY HISTORICAL EVENTS. Antigua was discovered by Colombus in 1493. It was first colonized by English settlers in 1632; nearby Barbuda was colonized in 1661 from Antigua. Antigua and Barbuda formed part of the Leeward Islands Federation from 1871 until 30 June 1956, when Antigua became a separate Crown Colony, which was part of the West Indies Federation from 3 Jan. 1958 until 31 May 1962. It became an Associated State of the UK on 27 Feb. 1967 and obtained independence on 1 Nov. 1981.

TERRITORY AND POPULATION. Antigua and Barbuda comprises 3 islands of the Lesser Antilles situated in the Eastern Caribbean with a total land area of 442 sq. km (171 sq. miles); it consists of Antigua (280 sq. km), Barbuda, 40 km to the north (161 sq. km) and uninhabited Redonda, 40 km to the southwest (1 sq. km). The population at the census of 1991 was 65,962 (1,400 on Barbuda). 31% are urban. Expectation of life was 74 years in 1992. The chief towns are St John's, the capital on Antigua (30,000 inhabitants in 1982) and Codrington (1,200), the only settlement on Barbuda.

CLIMATE. A tropical climate, but drier than most West Indies islands. The hot season is from May to Nov., when rainfall is greater. Mean annual rainfall is 40" (1,000 mm).

CONSTITUTION AND GOVERNMENT. H.M. Queen Elizabeth, as Head of State, is represented by a Governor-General appointed by her on the advice of the Prime Minister. There is a bicameral legislature, comprising a 17-member Senate appointed by the Governor-General and a 17-member House of Representatives elected by universal suffrage for a 5-year term. The Governor-General appoints a Prime Minister and, on the latter's advice, other members of the Cabinet.

Barbuda is adminstered by a 9-member directly-elected council.

At the elections of March 1994 the Antigua Labour Party (ALP) gained 11 seats, the United Progressive Party, 5 and the Barbuda People's Movement, 1.

Governor-General: Sir James Carlisle, GCMG.

In Sept. 1995 the government comprised:

Prime Minister, Minister of Foreign Affairs, Minister of Social Affairs: Lester Bird (ALP).

Finance and Social Security: Molwyn Joseph. *Justice, Legal Affairs and Attorney-General:* Clare Roberts. *Public Utilities, Communications, Transportation and Energy:* Robin Yearwood. *Agriculture, Fisheries, Commerce, Industry and Consumer Affairs:* John St Luce. *Home Affairs and Health:* Hilroy Humphries. *Education, Youth, Sports and Community Development:* Dr Rodney Williams. *Labour, Civil Service and Co-operatives:* Adolphus Eleazer Freeland. *Tourism, Culture and Environment:* Bernard Percival. *Housing:* Henderson Simon.

National flag: Red, with a triangle based on the top edge, divided horizontally black, blue, white, with a rising sun in gold on the black portion.

National anthem: 'Fair Antigua, we salute thee'; words by N. H. Richards, tune by W. G. Chambers.

DEFENCE. The Antigua and Barbuda Defence Force numbers 150. A coastguard service has been formed.

INTERNATIONAL RELATIONS

Membership. Antigua and Barbuda is a member of the UN, the Commonwealth, CARICOM and is an ACP state of the EU.

ECONOMY

Budget. The budget for 1993–94 envisaged recurrent revenue of EC$289·9m. and recurrent expenditure of EC$288·9m. A graduated levy on income was introduced in 1994.

Currency. The unit of currency is the *Eastern Caribbean dollar* (XCD), issued by the Eastern Caribbean Central Bank. There are notes of EC$5, 10, 20 and 100. Foreign exchange reserves in Sept. 1993 were US$38·7m. In March 1996, £1 = EC$4·13; US$1 = EC$2·70; DM1 = EC$1·83.

Banking and Finance. In 1993, 9 commercial banks were operating (6 foreign). There is also the Antigua Co-operative Bank and a government savings bank.

Offshore exemptions have been established by legislation of 1983.

ENERGY AND NATURAL RESOURCES

Water. Water shortages are frequent, and agriculture is affected. There is a desalination plant with a capacity of 0·6m. gallons per day.

Agriculture. Diversification programmes have been introduced after the collapse of the sugar industry by 1970. Cotton and fruits are the main crops. Production (1993) of fruits, 9,000 tonnes.

Livestock (1993): Cattle, 16,000; pigs, 4,000; sheep, 13,000; goats, 12,000.

INDUSTRY. An oil refinery was opened in 1982. Manufactures include toilet tissue, stoves, refrigerators, blenders, fans, garments and rum (molasses imported from Guyana).

Labour. In 1985 the workforce numbered 32,254, and there was 21% unemployment.

FOREIGN ECONOMIC RELATIONS. Foreign debt was US$260m. in 1994.

Commerce. Imports in 1992 amounted to US$261m. and exports to US$55m. The main trading partners were the USA, the UK and Canada.

Total trade between Antigua and Barbuda and UK (British Department of Trade returns, in £1,000 sterling):

	1992	*1993*	*1994*	*1995*
Imports to UK	2,511	2,524	2,166	1,517
Exports and re-exports from UK	16,528	17,752	24,177	23,272

Tourism. Tourism is the main industry, contributing 25% of GDP and 60% of foreign exchange earnings. In 1994 there were 234,745 staying visitors and 222,936 cruise ship arrivals.

COMMUNICATIONS

Roads. In 1995 there were 384 km of main roads, 164 km of secondary roads, 320 km of rural roads and 293 km of other roads.

Civil Aviation. V. C. Bird International Airport is near St John's. Antigua is served by Air Canada, Air France, Air Micronesia, American Airlines, British Airways, BWIA, Caledonian Airlines, Carib Express, Condor Flugdienst, Continental Airlines, Key Airlines, LIAT, Lufthansa, Love Air and Virgin Islands Airways. There are flights to Barbados, Dominica, Frankfurt, Grenada, Guadeloupe, Jamaica, Martinique, Miami, Montserrat, the Netherlands Antilles, New York, Orlando,

Puerto Rico, St Kitts-Nevis, St Lucia, St Vincent, Toronto, Trinidad, the UK, the British and US Virgin Islands and Washington DC. A domestic flight links Antigua and Barbuda Airport.

Shipping. The main port is the St John's deep water harbour.

Telecommunications. Telephone supply, 1995: 40 lines per 100 inhabitants. There is a mobile phone system. The government-controlled Antigua and Barbuda Broadcasting Service broadcasts a radio and TV programme (colour by NTSC). There is a commercial radio and a commercial TV station, a religious radio station and relay stations. In 1993 there were estimated to be 75,000 radio and 28,000 TV receivers.

Press. In 1995 there was a government weekly, an independent daily with a circulation of 2,000 and 4 other newspapers.

SOCIAL INSTITUTIONS

Justice. Law is based on UK common law as exercised by the Eastern Caribbean Supreme Court (ECSC) on St Lucia. There are Magistrates' Courts and a Court of Summary Jurisdiction. Appeals lie to the Court of Appeal of ECSC, or ultimately to the UK Privy Council.

Religion. The majority of the population are Anglican.

Education. Adult literacy was 90% in 1995. There were 72 government primary and secondary schools in 1992–93. Other schools were run by religious organizations.

Health. In 1995 there were 3 hospitals.

Welfare. The state operates a Medical Benefits Scheme providing free medical attention, and a Social Security Scheme, providing age and disability pensions and sickness benefits.

DIPLOMATIC REPRESENTATIVES

Of Antigua and Barbuda in Great Britain (15 Thayer St., London, W1M 5LD)
High Commissioner: Ronald Sanders.

Of Great Britain in Antigua and Barbuda (11, Old Parham Rd., St John's)
High Commissioner: R. Thomas, CMG (resides in Bridgetown).

Of Antigua and Barbuda in the USA (3400 International Dr., NW, Washington, D.C., 20008)
Ambassador: Dr Patrick A. Lewis.

The US Embassy closed on 30 June 1994. US visas are issued in Barbados.

Of Antigua and Barbuda to the United Nations
Ambassador: Lionel Alexander Hurst.

Further Reading

Berleant-Schiller, R., *et al.*, *Antigua and Barbuda.* [Bibliography] Oxford and Santa Barbara (CA), 1995

ARGENTINA

República Argentina

Capital: Buenos Aires
Population: 34·59m. (1995)
GNP per capita: US$8,060 (1994)
HDI/world rank: 0·882/30 (1992)

KEY HISTORICAL EVENTS. In 1816 Argentina proclaimed its independence from Spain. A stable government was established and a constitution promulgated in 1853.

On 24 March 1976 a military junta deposed Isobel Perón and her Government elected in 1972. Return to civilian rule took place on 10 Dec. 1983. A new Constitution was adopted in Aug. 1994.

TERRITORY AND POPULATION. The Argentine Republic is bounded in the north by Bolivia, in the north-east by Paraguay, in the east by Brazil, Uruguay and the Atlantic Ocean and the west by Chile. The republic consists of 23 provinces and 1 federal district with the following areas and populations at the 1991 census:

Provinces	*Area Sq. km.*	*Population (1991 census)*	*Capital*	*Population (1991 census)*
Federal Capital	200	2,965,403	Buenos Aires	–
Buenos Aires	307,571	12,594,974	La Plata	542,567
Corrientes	88,199	795,594	Corrientes	258,103
Entre Ríos	78,781	1,020,257	Paraná	277,338
Chaco	99,633	839,677	Resistencia	292,350
Santa Fé	133,007	2,798,422	Santa Fé	406,388
Formosa	72,066	398,413	Formosa	148,074
Misiones	29,801	788,915	Posadas	210,755
Jujuy	53,219	512,329	San Salvador de Jujuy	180,102
Salta	155,488	866,153	Salta	370,904
Santiago del Estero	136,351	671,988	Santiago del Estero	263,471
Tucumán	22,524	1,142,105	San Miguel de Tucumán	622,324
Córdoba	165,321	2,766,683	Córdoba	1,208,713
La Pampa	143,440	259,996	Santa Rosa	80,592
San Luis	76,748	286,458	San Luis	110,136
Catamarca	102,602	264,234	Catamarca	132,626
La Rioja	89,680	220,729	La Rioja	103,727
Mendoza	148,827	1,412,481	Mendoza	121,696
San Juan	89,651	528,715	San Juan	352,691
Neuquén	94,078	388,833	Neuquén	243,803
Chubut	224,686	357,189	Rawson	19,161
Rio Negro	203,013	506,772	Viedma	57,473
Santa Cruz	243,943	159,839	Rio Gallegos	64,640
Tierra del Fuego	21,571	69,369	Ushuaia	29,166

Argentina also claims territory in Antarctica.

The area is 2,780,400 sq. km excluding the claimed Antarctic territory and the population at the 1991 census was 32,615,528 (16,677,548 females); 1995 estimate, 34,586,635. In 1993, 86·6% lived in urban areas. Vital statistics rates, 1993 (per 1,000 population): Birth, 19·8; death, 7·9; infantile mortality, 22·9 per 1,000 live births. Expectation of life in 1995 was 68·6 years for men and 75·7 for women.

The official census included the 'sovereign territories of Argentina in the Antarctic': Population 3,300.

In April 1990 the National Congress declared that the Falklands and other British-held islands in the South Atlantic were part of the new province of Tierra del Fuego formed from the former National Territory of the same name. 1991 census data for Tierra del Fuego above do not include these territories. The 1994 Constitution re-affirms Argentine sovereignty over the Falkland Islands.

The population of the principal metropolitan areas in 1992 (provisional) was: Buenos Aires, 11,662,050; Córdoba, 1,179,420; Rosario, 1,157,372; Mendoza, 801,920; La Plata, 676,128; Tucumán, 642,473.

In 1980, 95% spoke the national language, Spanish, while 3% spoke Italian, 1% Guaraní and 1% other languages.

CLIMATE. The climate is warm temperate over the pampas, where rainfall occurs at all seasons, but diminishes towards the west. In the north and west, the climate is more arid, with high summer temperatures, while in the extreme south conditions are also dry, but much cooler. Buenos Aires. Jan. 74°F (23·3°C), July 50°F (10°C). Annual rainfall 37" (950 mm). Bahía Blanca. Jan. 74°F (23·3°C), July 48°F (8·9°C). Annual rainfall 21" (523 mm). Mendoza. Jan. 75°F (23·9°C), July 47°F (8·3°C). Annual rainfall 8" (190 mm). Rosario. Jan. 76°F (24·4°C), July 51°F (10·6°C). Annual rainfall 35" (869 mm). San Juan. Jan. 78°F (25·6°C), July 50°F (10°C). Annual rainfall 4" (89 mm). San Miguel de Tucumán. Jan. 79°F (26·1°C), July 56°F (13·3°C). Annual rainfall 38" (970 mm). Ushuaia. Jan. 50°F (10°C), July 34°F (1·1°C). Annual rainfall 19" (475 mm).

CONSTITUTION AND GOVERNMENT. On 10 April 1994 elections were held for a 230-member constituent assembly to reform the 1853 constitution. The Justicialist National Movement (Peronist) gained 38·8% of votes cast and the Radical Union, 20%. On 22 Aug. 1994 this assembly unanimously adopted a new Constitution. This reduces the presidential term of office from 6 to 4 years, but permits the President to stand for 2 terms. The President is no longer elected by an electoral college, but directly by universal suffrage. A presidential candidate is elected who gains more than 45% of votes cast, or 40% if at least 10% ahead of an opponent; otherwise there is a second round. The Constitution attenuates the President's powers by instituting a *Chief of Cabinet.* The *National Congress* consists of a Senate and a Chamber of Deputies: The Senate comprises 72 members, 3 nominated by each provincial legislature and 3 from the Federal District for 9 years (one-third retiring every 3 years). The Chamber of Deputies comprises 259 members directly elected by universal suffrage (at age 18). Elections for half the seats were held on 3 Oct. 1993. The ruling Justicialist Party (JP; Peronist) gained 42% of votes cast, the Radical Civil Union 31%. Representation in the Chamber of Deputies following the 1993 elections was: JP, 126 seats; Radicals, 83; others, 50. Elections for the remaining seats were held on 14 May 1995. The JP gained 132 seats (and 38 in the Senate).

In the presidential elections held on 14 May 1995 Carlos Saúl Menem was re-elected in the first round by 49% of votes cast.

President: Carlos Saúl Menem (b. 1930; JP; sworn in 8 July 1995).

The Cabinet in Jan. 1996 was composed as follows:

Chief of Cabinet: Eduardo Bauzo. *Defence:* Oscar Camillón. *Economy and Public Works:* Dr Domingo Cavallo. *Education and Culture:* Jorge Rodríguez. *Foreign Relations:* Dr Guido José Maria di Tella. *Interior:* Dr Carlos Corach. *Labour and Social Security:* Armando Caro-Figueroa. *Health and Social Welfare:* Dr Alberto Mazza. *Justice:* Dr D. Rodolfo Carlos Barra.

National flag: Three horizontal stripes of light blue, white and light blue, with the gold Sun of May in the centre.

National anthem: Oid, mortales, el grito sagrado Libertad ('Hear, mortals, the sacred cry of Liberty'; words by V. López y Planes, 1813; tune by J. Blas Parera).

Provincial and Local Government: 23 provincial gubernatorial elections were held Aug.–Dec. 1991. Peronists won 14 governorships, the Radical Civil Union 4 and the Union of the Democratic Centre, 3.

DEFENCE. Conscription was abolished in 1995.

Army. There are 5 military regions. The Army is organized in 3 corps, 1 with 1 armoured, 1 mechanized and 1 training brigade; 1 with 1 infantry and 1 mountain brigade, and with 1 armoured, 1 mountain and 2 mechanized brigades. Equipment in 1996 included 96 M-4 Sherman and 200 TAM main battle tanks. In 1996 the Army was 40,400 strong, of whom 13,400 were conscripts. The trained reserve numbers about 250,000, of whom 200,000 belong to the National Guard and 50,000 to the Territorial Guard.

There is a paramilitary gendarmerie of 18,000 run by the Ministry of Defence.

Navy. The light aircraft carrier *Veinticinco de Mayo* has been formally withdrawn from service but remains in reserve. Combatant forces include 3 German-built diesel submarines with 1 more in major refit, 4 modern German-built destroyers, 2 British-built guided missile destroyers (Type 42), 4 German-designed and 3 French-built frigates, 2 old training frigates, 2 fast torpedo craft, 6 patrol ships, 4 coastal minesweepers, 2 minehunters and 1 tank landing ship. Auxiliaries include 1 survey ship, 2 training ships, 3 transports, 1 icebreaker and numerous harbour and service craft.

The new construction programme includes 2 diesel submarines (both building – but slowly) and 2 small frigates.

The Naval Aviation Service has some 45 combat aircraft and 13 helicopters with (1995) 3,000 personnel, in 5 wings. Aircraft include 12 Super-Etendard strike aircraft, 16 EMB-326 and 5 EMB-339A light jet armed trainers, 3 Lockheed Electra maritime surveillance aircraft and 6 S-2E carrier-adapted Tracker anti-submarine aircraft, as well as varied training, transport and general purpose aircraft. There is a squadron of 7 SH-3 anti-submarine helicopters, 6 Alouettes and 6 S-61 transport helicopters. A variable mix of Super-Etendards and Trackers as well as Sea King and Alouette helicopters could operate from the aircraft carrier if she is re-activated.

Main bases are at Buenos Aires, Puerto Belgrano (HQ and Dockyard), Mar del Plata, Ushuaia and Puerto Deseado.

The active personnel of the navy in 1995 comprised 18,000, 3,500 of whom were conscripts, and including 4,000 marines.

The Prefectura Naval Argentina (PNA) for Coast Guard and rescue duties was 13,000 strong in 1995 and operates 5 910-tonne corvettes with helicopter and hangar, an ex-whaler of 700 tonnes, and 23 patrol vessels.

Air Force. The Air Force is organized into Air Operations, Air Regions, Materiel and Personnel Commands. Air Operations Command, responsible for all operational flying, is made up of air brigades, each with 1 to 4 squadrons, usually operating from a single base. No. I Air Brigade is a military air transport service, with responsibility also for LADE (state airline) operations into areas of Argentina not served by civilian companies. Its equipment includes 6 C-130E/H Hercules and 10 F.27 Friendship/Troopship turboprop transports, 2 KC-130H Hercules tanker/transports, 4 twin-turbofan F.28 Fellowship freighters, 7 Twin Otters, 15 Guarani IIs, the Presidential Boeing 707-320B and 707-320C, 4 more 707s, 2 VIP Fellowships, and many older or smaller types. No. II Air Brigade has 4 Canberra twin-jet bombers and 2 Canberra trainers; a photographic squadron with Guarani IIs and Learjets. No. III Air Brigade has 2 squadrons of IA 58 Pucara twin-turboprop COIN aircraft. No. IV Air Brigade comprises 2 ground attack squadrons, one equipped with about 20 Paris light jet combat and liaison aircraft, and the other with 15 IA 63 Pampas, and one squadron with Mirage IIIs. No. V Air Brigade comprises 2 squadrons with a total of about 15 A-4P Skyhawk strike aircraft. No. VI Air Brigade has 30 Dagger (Israeli-built Mirage III) fighters, equipping 2 squadrons, and 1 squadron with 15 Mirage IIIE fighter-bombers and 4 Mirage IIID trainers. No. VII Air Brigade has 2 helicopter squadrons with 12 armed Hughes 500M, 6 Bell 212, 4 Bell UH-1 and 2 Chinook helicopters. No. X Air Brigade has 1 squadron of Mirage IIIC/5 fighters. There is a flying school at Córdoba, equipped with turboprop-powered Embraer Tucanos and Paris jets. There were (1995) 8,900 personnel (1,200 conscripts) and 237 combat aircraft.

INTERNATIONAL RELATIONS

Membership. Argentina is a member of the UN, OAS and Mercosur.

ECONOMY

Policy. In 1990, to reduce the public deficit (US$5,000m. in 1989), the government introduced a programme privatizing some 40 public enterprises. An economic plan entering into force 1 April 1991 guaranteed the convertibility of the currency, lowered interest rates and opened the economy to foreign imports. Agricultural export taxes were abolished in March 1991.

Budget. The financial year commences on 1 Jan. Estimated revenue in 1995 (in US$1m.) was 55,650·6 and expenditure, 55,650.6. Components of revenue included: Current, 53,905·2 (tax, 50,100·2). Expenditure: Current, 53,655·6 (personnel, 7,030·1; goods and services, 2,925·4; debt servicing, 3,665·9); capital, 1,745·4.

Currency. The monetary unit is the *peso* (ARP) which replaced the austral on 1 Jan. 1992 at a rate of 1 peso = 10,000 australs. There are notes of 1, 2, 5, 10, 20, 50 and 100 pesos. In 1994, 12,346m. pesos were in circulation. Inflation was 3·9% in 1994. In March 1996, £1 = 1·53 pesos; US$1 = 1 peso; DM1 = 0·68 pesos.

Banking and Finance. In 1994 there were 33 government banks, 135 private banks, 31 foreign banks and 37 other financial institutions. Bank and non-bank total monetary resources totalled 55,830·83m. pesos as at Dec. 1994. The *Governor* of the Central Bank is Roque Fernández. Convertibility regulations of April 1991 require the Central Bank to back the entire currency in circulation with its foreign currency reserves.

There is a stock exchange at Buenos Aires.

Weights and Measures. The metric system is legal.

ENERGY AND NATURAL RESOURCES

Electricity. Electric power production (1994) was 62,126m. kWh (8,290m. kWh nuclear). In 1995 there were 2 nuclear plants.

Oil and Gas. Crude oil production, 1995, 726,000 bbls a day. Reserves were estimated at some 358m. cu. metres in 1994. The oil industry was privatized in 1993. Natural gas production (1994) 27,697m. cu. metres. Reserves were about 535,528m. cu. metres in 1994.

Minerals. An estimated 215,000 tonnes of washed coal were produced in 1992. Other minerals (with estimated production in 1994) include iron ore (30,000 tonnes of metal), gold (899 kg), silver (38,000 kg), tungsten, beryllium, clays (5·5m. tonnes), marble, lead (10,000 tonnes of metal), zinc (27,000 tonnes of metal), borates (213,000 tonnes), bentonite (0·11m. tonnes) and granite.

Agriculture. In 1992 there were 25m. ha of arable land, 2·2m. ha of permanent crops and 142m. ha of permanent pasture. 3·24m. persons depended on agriculture in 1993, of whom 1,166,000 were economically active. 1·7m. ha were irrigated in 1992.

Livestock (1994): Cattle, 53,156,954; sheep, 16,920,159; pigs, 4,770,000; horses, 3·3m. Wool production, 1992, was 202,200 tonnes; butter, 42,000 tonnes; beef, 2·56m. tonnes.

Crop production (in 1,000 tonnes) in 1994/95: Wheat, 11,143; sugar-cane, 12,500; potatoes, 2,720; tobacco, 105; sunflower seed, 4,730. Cotton, vine, citrus fruit, olives, rice, soya, and yerba maté (Paraguayan tea) are also cultivated.

Forestry. The woodland area was 44,975,115 ha in 1994. Production in 1994 included 1·07m. cu. metres of sawn wood, 5,985,452 tonnes of logs and 73,000 tonnes of tannin.

Fisheries. Fish landings in 1994 amounted to 938,602 tonnes.

INDUSTRY. Production (1994 in tonnes): Paper, 966,000; primary iron, 2,659,000; crude steel, 3,274,000; primary aluminium, 173,371; sulfuric acid, 199,285; cement, 6,306,000; synthetic rubber, 48,830; polyethylene, 246,595; sugar, 1,110,000; vegetable oils, 3,027,000. Motor vehicles produced totalled 408,777; tractors, 3,667; tyres, 7,329,000.

Labour. The economically active population was 13·2m. in 1991, of whom 10·4% worked in agriculture.

FOREIGN ECONOMIC RELATIONS. External debt was US$72,279m. in 1994.

Commerce. Foreign trade (in US$1m.):

	1989	*1990*	*1991*	*1992*	*1993*	*1994*
Imports	4,203	4,077	8,275	14,872	16,784	21,590
Exports	9,579	12,353	11,978	12,235	13,118	15,839

Principal exports in 1994 (in US$1m.) were cereals (1,333), residues and waste from the food industry (1,349), oils and fats (1,534), fuels, mineral oils and distillates (1,348), oilseeds and fruits (952) and fish, shellfish and molluscs (672).

Principal imports in 1994 (in US$1m.) were boilers, machines and mechanical equipment (4,256), electrical machinery and equipment (3,190), land vehicles (3,389), organic chemical products (1,020), cast iron and steel (728) and plastic materials (833).

In 1994 imports (in US$1m.) were mainly from Brazil (4,286), USA (4,928), Germany (1,382), Italy (1,431), Japan (620), Chile (831) and France (1,072); exports went mainly to Brazil (3,655), USA (1,737), Netherlands (1,180), Germany (605), Chile (999), Italy (654) and Spain (584).

Total trade between Argentina and UK (British Department of Trade returns, in £1,000 sterling):

	1992	*1993*	*1994*	*1995*
Imports to UK	124,603	141,143	170,970	252,265
Exports and re-exports from UK	118,746	179,259	224,942	233,682

Tourism. In 1994, an estimated 3,866,474 tourists visited Argentina.

COMMUNICATIONS

Roads. In 1993 there were 36,837 km of national and provincial highways. The 4 main roads constituting Argentina's portion of the Pan-American Highway were opened in 1942.

Railways. Much of the 33,000 km state-owned network (on 1,000 mm, 1,435 mm and 1,676 mm gauges; 210 km electrified) was privatized in 1993–94. 30-year concessions were awarded to 5 freight operators; long-distance passenger services are run by contractors to the requirements of local authorities. Metro, light rail and suburban railway services are also operated by concessionaires.

In 1994 railways carried 13,174,000 tonnes of freight and 248,331,000 passengers. The metro and light rail network in Buenos Aires extends to 46 km.

Civil Aviation. There is an international airport at Buenos Aires (Ministro Pistarini). In 1995 the national carrier, Aerolíneas Argentinas, 15% state-owned, operated 3 A310-300s, 1 B-707-320B, 8 B-727-200 Advs, 4 B-737-200s, 6 B-737-200 Advs, 1 B-737-200C, 6 B-747-200Bs and 6 other aircraft. Services are also operated by Aeroflot Russian Airlines, Aeroperú, Air France, Alitalia, American Airlines, Avianca, British Airways, BWIA, Canadian Airlines, Cubana, Iberia, KLM, Ladeco, Lan-Chile, Lapsa, Lloyd Aéreo Boliviano, Lufthansa, Malaysia Airlines, Pluna, SAA, Swissair, United Airlines, VASP, Varig and Viasa.

In 1994 4,984,000 passengers and 114,651 tonnes of freight were carried on international flights and 4,538,000 passengers and 18,320 tonnes of freight on internal flights.

Shipping. The merchant fleet, 1993, consisted of 1,413 vessels totalling 1,799,633 GRT, of which 176 were tankers totalling 586,744 GRT.

Telecommunications. The telephone service Entel was privatized in 1990. There are state-owned, provincial, municipal and private radio stations overseen by the Secretaria de Comunicaciones, the Comité Federal de Radiodifusión, the Servicio Oficial de Radiodifusión (which also operates an external service and a station in

Antarctica) and the Asociación de Teleradiodifusoras Argentinas. In 1991 there were 21,582,456 radio and 7,165,000 TV (colour by PAL) receivers.

Cinemas. In 1993 there were 260 cinemas.

SOCIAL INSTITUTIONS

Justice. Justice is administered by federal and provincial courts. The former deal only with cases of a national character, or those in which different provinces or inhabitants of different provinces are parties. The chief federal court is the Supreme Court, with 5 judges whose appointment is approved by the Senate. Other federal courts are the appeal courts, at Buenos Aires, Bahía Blanca, La Plata, Córdoba, Mendoza, Tucumán and Resistencia. Each province has its own judicial system, with a Supreme Court (generally so designated) and several minor chambers. The death penalty was re-introduced in 1976 for the killing of government, military police and judicial officials, and for participation in terrorist activities.

The police force is centralized under the Federal Security Council.

Religion. The Roman Catholic religion is supported by the State and membership was 30·08m. in 1992. There are several Protestant denominations. The Jewish congregation numbered 0·35m. in 1992.

Education. Adult literacy was 95·5% in 1992. In 1991-92, 490,385 children attended pre-school institutions, 5,044,398 primary schools, 2,263,263 secondary schools and 344,862 tertiary colleges. Numbers of teachers in 1994-95: Pre-school, 62,521; primary, 286,885; secondary, 233,564; tertiary, 43,103.

In 1995-96, in the public sector, there were 31 universities; 1 technical university; and university institutes of aeronautics, military studies, naval and maritime studies and police studies. In the private sector, there were 15 universities; 7 Roman Catholic universities; 1 Adventist university; universities of business administration, business and social science, the cinema, notarial studies, social studies, and theology; and university institutes of biomedical science, health and the merchant navy. In 1994-95, there were 652,585 university students and 75,592 academic staff.

Health. Free medical attention is obtainable from public hospitals. In 1993 there were 76,969 beds available in health care institutions.

DIPLOMATIC REPRESENTATIVES

Of Argentina in Great Britain (53, Hans Place, London, SW1X 0LA)
Ambassador: Rogelio Pfirter.

Of Great Britain in Argentina (Dr Luis Agote 2412/52, 1425 Buenos Aires)
Ambassador: Sir Peter Hall, KBE, CMG.

Of Argentina in the USA (1600 New Hampshire Ave., NW, Washington, D.C., 20009)
Ambassador: Raúl Granillo Ocampo.

Of the USA in Argentina (4300 Colombia, 1425, Buenos Aires)
Ambassador: James R. Cheek.

Of Argentina to the United Nations
Ambassador: Dr Emilio J. Cárdenas.

Further Reading

INDEC. *Statistical Yearbook of Argentina*
Bethell, I (ed.) *Argentina since Independence.* CUP, 1994
Biggins, A., *Argentina.* [Bibliography]. Oxford and Santa Barbara, 1990
Lewis, P., *The Crisis of Argentine Capitalism.* North Carolina Univ. Press, 1990
Manzetti, L., *Institutions, Parties and Coalitions in Argentine Politics.* Univ. of Pittsburgh Press, 1994
Rock, D., *Argentina 1516–1982.* London, 1986
Shumway, N., *The Invention of Argentina.* California Univ. Press, 1991
Wynia, G. W., *Argentina: Illusions and Realities.* 2nd ed. Hoddesdon, 1993

National statistical office: Instituto Nacional de Estadística y Censos (INDEC). Av. Presidente Julio A. Roca 609, 1067 Buenos Aires. *Director:* Dr Hector E. Montero.

ARMENIA

Hayastani Hanrapetoutiun

(Republic of Armenia)

Capital: Yerevan
Population: 3·7m. (1994)
GNP per capita: US$670 (1994)
HDI/world rank: 0·715/90 (1992)

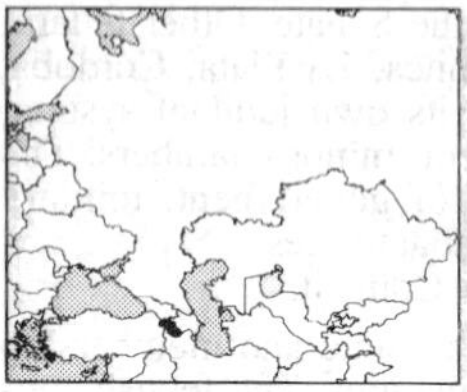

KEY HISTORICAL EVENTS. On 29 Nov. 1920 Armenia was proclaimed a Soviet Socialist Republic. The Soviet-Turkish Treaty of Kars (March 1921), confirmed the Turkish possession of the former Government of Kars and of the Surmali District of the Government of Yerevan. From 1922 to 1936, Armenia formed part of the Transcaucasian Soviet Federal Socialist Republic. In 1936 it was proclaimed a constituent republic of the USSR. In Dec. 1991 it became a member of the CIS.

TERRITORY AND POPULATION. Armenia covers an area of 29,800 sq. km (11,490 sq. miles). It is bounded in the north by Georgia, in the east by Azerbaijan and in the south and west by Turkey and Iran. The 1989 census population was 3,304,776, of whom Armenians accounted for 93·3%, Azerbaijanis 2·6%, Kurds 1·7% and Russians, 1·6%. Estimate, Jan. 1995, 3,742,000 (1·8m. male; 2·5m. urban). Vital statistics rates, 1994 (per 1,000 population): Births, 15·8; deaths, 7·4; growth, 8·4; infant mortality (per 1,000 live births), 17·1.

The capital is Yerevan (1·2m. population in 1994). Other large towns are Kumairi (formerly Leninakan) (0·12m.) and Kirovakan (159,000).

CONSTITUTION AND GOVERNMENT. The Supreme Soviet adopted a declaration of sovereignty in Aug. 1990 and voted to unite Armenia with Nagorno-Karabakh. A popular vote in Sept. 1991 resulted in a 99% majority support for a fully independent status.

A referendum was held on 5 July 1995 on the adoption of a new constitution; turn-out was 55·6%. 68% of votes cast were in favour. Parliament is a 190-member *National Assembly*, of which 150 members are directly elected on a first-past-the-post system, and 40 by proportional representation, distributed among those parties gaining more than 5% of votes cast. The government is nominated by the President.

On 16 Oct. 1991 Ter-Petrosyan was elected the republic's first President in a popular ballot by 83% of votes cast against 5 opponents. Turn-out was 73%.

Elections for the National Assembly were held in 2 rounds on 5 and 29 July 1995. 1,369 candidates representing 13 parties stood; turn-out was 54·9%. The Republican Bloc, in which the Pan-Armenian National Movement (PANM) was the major element, won 119 seats with 42·66% of votes cast; the Shamiram Women's Party, 8 with 16·88%; the Communist Party, 7 with 12·1%; the National Democratic Union, 5 with 7·51%; the National Self-Determination Union, 3 with 5·57%; the Armenian Liberal Democratic Party, 1 with 2·52%; the Armenian Revolutionary Federation Dashnaktsoutioun, 1 with 2%. 45 ind were also elected.

President: Levon Ter-Petrosyan (b. 1945; PANM).
Vice-President: Gagik Arutyunyan.
In Sept. 1995 the government comprised:
Prime Minister: Grant Bagratyan (b. 1958).
Foreign: Vagan Papazyan. *Interior:* Vano Siradegyan. *Defence:* Serzh Sarkisyan. *Justice:* Vage Stepanyan. *Education and Science:* Armenak Gazaryan. *Health:* Ara Babloyan. *Culture, Youth Affairs and Sport:* Akop Akopyan. *Nature and Environmental Protection:* Suren Avetisyan. *Industry:* Ashot Safaryan. *Communications:* Grigor Pokhpatyan. *Agriculture:* Ashot Voskanyan. *Commerce, Services and Tourism:* Vagan Melkonyan. *Transport:* Genrikh Kochinyan. *Finance:* Levon

Barhudaryan. *The Economy:* Andranik Andreasyan. *Energy and Fuel:* Gagik Martirosyan. *State National Security Agency:* Serzhik Sargisyan. *Relations with CIS and EU:* Gagik Shagbazyan. *Information:* Grach Tamrazyan. *Relations with the National Assembly:* Arsen Kamyalyan. *Local Government:* Rubik Barsegyan. *Social Security, Migration and Refugee Affairs:* Rafael Bagoyan. *Town Planning and Construction:* Feliks Pirumyan.

The *Speaker* is Babken Ararktsyan.

National flag: 3 horizontal stripes of red, blue and orange.
National anthem: 'Mer Hayrenik azat, ankakh' ('Land of our fathers, free and independent'); words by M. Nalbandyan, tune by B. Kanachyan.

DEFENCE. There is conscription for 18 months.

Army. The Army is organized in 4 motor rifle, 2 surface-to-air missile, and 1 artillery brigade; 9 independent motor rifle, 1 artillery, 2 surface-to-air missile and 1 anti-tank regiment; and 1 tank training and 1 independent helicopter squadron with 7 Mi-24s. Equipment includes 98 T-72 and 30 T-55 main battle tanks. Personnel, 1996, about 51,800.

INTERNATIONAL RELATIONS

Membership. Armenia is a member of the UN and the NATO Partnership for Peace.

ECONOMY

Policy. GDP was valued at 779,600m. rubles in current prices in 1993, 85·2% of the 1992 figure. A privatization scheme was launched on 1 March 1995 under the auspices of a Privatization Commission.

Budget. Budgetary income in 1994 was 293,800m. rubles; expenditure was 303,400m. rubles.

Currency. In Nov. 1993 a new currency unit, the *dram* (AMD) of 100 *humma*, was introduced to replace the ruble. There are coins of 1, 2, 3, 5, 10, 20 and 50 humma, notes of 1, 2, 5, 10, 25, 50, 100, 200 and 500 drams. Inflation averaged 3% per month in 1995. In March 1996, £1 = 615·76; US$1 = 402·88; DM1 = 272·97 drams.

Banking and Finance. The President of the Central Bank is Bagrat Asatryan.

ENERGY AND NATURAL RESOURCES

Electricity. Output of electricity in 1993 was 6,300m. kWh. A nuclear plant closed in 1989 was re-opened in 1995 because of the blockade of the electricity supply by Azerbaijan; it was anticipated that domestic supply would be raised from 4 to 12 hours daily.

Minerals. There are deposits of copper, zinc, aluminium, molybdenum, marble and granite.

Agriculture. The chief agricultural area is the valley of the Arax and the area round Yerevan. Here there are cotton plantations, orchards and vineyards. Almonds, olives and figs are also grown. In the mountainous areas the chief pursuit is livestock raising. Land under cultivation in 1993, 1·3m. ha, of which 0·4m. ha were accounted for by commercial farming, in 298,100 farms. Private and commercial agriculture accounted for 96% of the value of agricultural output; this was valued at 900m. rubles (in constant 1983 prices) in 1993, 95% of the 1992 figure.

Output of main agricultural products (in 1,000 tonnes) in 1993: Grain, 314; potatoes, 372; vegetables, 376; fruit and berries, 48; meat, 59; milk, 395; and 188m. eggs. Livestock in Jan. 1994 included 0·5m. cattle, 0·1m. pigs and 0·7m. sheep and goats.

INDUSTRY. Among the chief industries are the chemical, producing chiefly synthetic rubber and fertilizers, and the extraction and processing of building materials, ginning- and textile-mills, carpet weaving, and food processing, including wine-making. Machine-tool and electrical engineering works have also been established. Industrial production in 1993 was valued at 477,000m. rubles, 88·9% of the 1992 figure.

Output in 1993 (in tonnes): Paper, 0·8m.; cement, 0·2m.; milk products, 9,900; processed meats, 8,600; fabrics, 5·4m. sq. metres; footwear, 3·5m. pairs; 1,600 lathes; 1,200 lorries; 200 washing machines.

Labour. In 1993 the population of working age was 2·1m., of whom 1·53m. were employed, 817,800 in the state sector, 517,000 in the private sector and 160,500 in the co-operative sector. In July 1994 there were 112,800 registered unemployed, of whom 33,100 were receiving benefits. The average monthly income in 1995 was 3,000 drams.

FOREIGN ECONOMIC RELATIONS

Commerce. In 1993 imports were valued at US$84·5m. and exports at US$29·4m. The main trading partners in 1994 were Russia, Turkmanistan and Iran.

Total trade of Armenia with UK (British Department of Trade returns, in £1,000 sterling):

	1993	*1994*	*1995*
Imports to UK	18	27	173
Exports and re-exports from UK	5,346	4,371	918

COMMUNICATIONS

Roads. There were 10,200 km (9,500 km with hard surface) of motor roads in 1990. In 1993, 170·4m. passengers and 12·8m. tonnes of freight were carried.

Railways. Total length in 1992 was 830 km of 1,520 mm gauge (590 km electrified). In 1993, 1·1m. passengers and 1·1m. tonnes of freight were carried.

Civil Aviation. There is an international airport at Yerevan (Zvartnots). The state-owned Armenian Airlines was not yet operational in 1995. In 1993 air transport carried 0·8m. passengers and 59,500 tonnes of freight.

Telecommunications. The government-controlled Armenian Radio broadcasts 2 national programmes and relays of Radio Moscow and Voice of America, and a foreign service, Radio Yerevan (Armenian, English, French, Spanish, Arabic, Kurdish, Russian). Television broadcasting is by the state-controlled Armenian Television (colour by SECAM).

Press. In 1995 there were 2 government dailies and several sponsored by political parties. Total circulation was about 40,000 per day.

SOCIAL INSTITUTIONS

Religion. The Armenian Apostolic Church is headed by its Catholicos (Karekin II, b. 1932) whose seat is at Etchmiadzin, and who is head of all the Armenian (Gregorian) communities throughout the world. In 1995 it numbered 7m. adherents (4m. in diaspora). The Catholicos is elected by representatives of parishes. The Catholicos of the diaspora is Kachechyan of Cilicia, with seat at Antelias.

Education. In Jan. 1994, 0·1m. children 23% of those eligible attended pre-school institutions. In 1994–95 there were 590,000 pupils in 1,400 primary and secondary schools; 69 technical colleges with 25,200 students; 14 higher educational institutions with 46,500 students. Yerevan houses the Armenian Academy of Sciences, 43 scientific institutes, a medical institute and other technical colleges, and a state university. In Jan. 1989, 33 institutions with 3,330 scientific staff were under the Academy of Sciences; scientific workers in 101 institutions totalled 21,800.

In 1995-96 there were 2 universities (including the American University), an engineering university, 10 other institutes of higher education and a conservatory.

Health. In Jan. 1994 there were some 14,000 doctors, 36,200 junior medical personnel and 183 hospitals with 31,000 beds.

Welfare. In Jan. 1995 there were 437,000 age, and 202,000 other pensioners.

DIPLOMATIC REPRESENTATIVES

Of Armenia in Great Britain (25A Cheniston Gdns, London W8 6TG)
Ambassador: Dr Armen Sarkissian.

Of Great Britain in Armenia (1 Vramshapouh Arka St., Yerevan 375010)
Ambassador: David Miller, OBE.

Of Armenia in the USA (122 C St., NW, Washington DC 20001)
Ambassador: Rouben Shugarian.

Of the USA in Armenia (18 Gen. Bagramian, Yerevan)
Ambassador: Peter Tomsen.

Of Armenia to the United Nations
Ambassador: Alexander Arzoumanian.

Further Reading

Brook, S., *Claws of the Crab: Georgia and Armenia in Crisis.* London, 1992
Lang, D.M., *Armenia: Cradle of Civilization.* London, 1978.—*The Armenians: a People in Exile.* London, 1981
Nersessian, V. N., *Armenia.* [Bibliography]. Oxford and Santa Barbara, 1993
Walker, C. J., *Armenia.* 2nd ed. London, 1990

AUSTRALIA

Commonwealth of Australia

Capital: Canberra
Population: 17·9m. (1994)
GNP per capita: US$17,980 (1994)
HDI/world rank: 0·927/11 (1992)

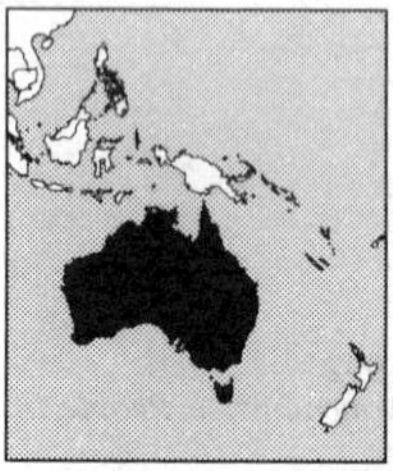

KEY HISTORICAL EVENTS. On 1 Jan. 1901 the former British colonies of New South Wales, Victoria, Queensland, South Australia, Western Australia and Tasmania were federated under the name of the 'Commonwealth of Australia', the designation of 'colonies' being at the same time changed into that of 'states', except in the case of Northern Territory, which was transferred from South Australia to the Commonwealth as a 'territory' on 1 Jan. 1911.

In 1911 the Commonwealth acquired from New South Wales the Canberra site for the Australian federal capital.

TERRITORY AND POPULATION. Australia, including Tasmania but excluding external territories, covers a land area of 7,682,300 sq. km, extending from Cape York (10° 41' S) in the north some 3,680 km to Tasmania (43° 39' S), and from Cape Byron (153° 39' E) in the east some 4,000 km west to Western Australia (113° 9' E). External territories under the administration of Australia comprise the Ashmore and Cartier Islands, Australian Antarctic Territory, Christmas Island, the Cocos (Keeling) Islands, the Coral Sea Islands, the Heard and McDonald Islands and Norfolk Island. For these *see below*.

Growth in Census population has been:

1901	3,774,310	1947	7,579,358	1976	13,915,500
1911	4,455,005	1961	10,508,186	1981	15,053,600
1921	5,435,734	1966	11,599,498	1986	15,763,000
1933	6,629,839	1971	12,755,638	1991	16,849,496

Area and resident population (estimate), 31 Dec. 1994, 17,935,800 (9,005,300 females). divided as follows:

States and Territories	*Area (sq. km)*	*Total*	*Per sq. km*
New South Wales (NSW)	801,600	6,081,200	7·6
Victoria (Vic.)	227,600	4,487,000	19·7
Queensland (Qld.)	1,727,200	3,233,900	1·9
South Australia (SA)	984,000	1,471,900	1·5
Western Australia (WA)	2,525,500	1,715,300	0·7
Tasmania (Tas.)	67,800	472,600	7·0
Northern Territory (NT)	1,346,200	172,200	0·1
Australian Capital Territory (ACT)	2,400	301,700	126·0
Total	7,682,300	17,935,800	2·3

Rate of population increase (per 1,000) in 1994: 7·7 (natural), 10·6 (with migration).

85·4% of the population was urban in 1986. Resident population (estimate) in Capitals and other major cities (statistical districts), 30 June 1994:

Capital	*State*	*Population*	*Capital*	*State*	*Population*
Canberra [1]	ACT	328,000	Darwin	NT	78,100
Sydney	NSW	3,738,500	*Statistical district*		
Melbourne	Vic.	3,198,200	Newcastle	NSW	460,200
Brisbane	Qld.	1,454,800	Wollongong	NSW	251,400
Adelaide	SA	1,076,400	Gold Coast [2]	Qld.	314,000
Perth	WA	1,239,400	Geelong	Vic.	152,200
Hobart	Tas.	194,200	Townsville	Qld.	122,500

[1] Includes Queanbeyan. [2] Includes part of Tweed Shire (in NSW).

At 30 June 1994 the age-group distribution was: Under 15, 3,844,899; 15–64, 11,889,260; 65 and over, 2,109,109. Life expectancy in 1993 was 75 (males), 80·9 (females).

Australians born overseas (30 June 1993), 4·03m., of whom 1·22m. came from the UK and Ireland; 1·16m. from continental Europe; 796,100 from Asia and 284,500 from New Zealand.

Aboriginals have been included in population statistics only since 1967. At the 1991 census they numbered 257,333. A 1992 High Court ruling that the Meriam people of the Murray Islands had land rights before the European settlement reversed the previous assumption that Australia was *terra nullius* before that settlement. The Native Title Act setting up a system for deciding land claims by Aborigines came into effect on 1 Jan. 1994.

Vital statistics for 1994:

States and Territories	*Marriages*	*Divorces*	*Births*	*Deaths*	*Infant deaths*
New South Wales	38,814	13,999	87,557	44,476	530
Victoria	26,972	11,320	64,422	32,313	338
Queensland	20,797	9,762	46,481	21,830	290
South Australia	8,909	4,192	19,475	11,725	96
Western Australia	10,366	5,024	25,114	10,297	138
Tasmania	2,889	1,544	6,781	3,950	37
Northern Territory	766	344	3,610	772	48
ACT	1,661	2,071	4,807	1,346	27
Total	111,174	48,256	258,247	126,709	1,504
Rate [1]	6·4	2·7	14·5	7·1	5·8 [2]

[1] Resident (estimate). [2] Per 1,000 live births registered.

Overseas arrivals and departures:

	1992	*1993*	*1994*
Arrivals	4,990,100	5,409,300	5,886,200
of whom long-term	220,450	197,930	221,910
(including settlers)	(94,250)	(65,680)	(77,940)
Departures	4,953,400	5,338,500	5,810,200
of whom long-term	143,660	140,430	141,680
(including former settlers and other residents)	(28,140)	(28,080)	(27,020)

The 1994–95 quota for settlers was 86,000. The Migration Act of Dec. 1989 sought to curb illegal entry and ensure that annual immigrant intakes were met but not exceeded. Provisions for temporary visitors to become permanent were restricted.

CLIMATE. Over most of the continent, four seasons may be recognised. Spring is from Sept. to Nov., Summer from Dec. to Feb., Autumn from March to May and Winter from June to Aug., but because of its great size there are climates that range from tropical monsoon to cool temperate, with large areas of desert as well. In Northern Australia there are only two seasons, the wet one lasting from Nov. to March, but rainfall amounts diminish markedly from the coast to the interior. Central and southern Queensland are subtropical, north and central New South Wales are warm temperate, as are parts of Victoria, Western Australia and Tasmania, where most rain falls in winter. Canberra. Jan. 68°F (20°C), July 42°F (5·6°C). Annual rainfall 23" (629 mm). Adelaide. Jan. 73°F (22·8°C), July 52°F (11·1°C). Annual rainfall 21" (528 mm). Brisbane. Jan. 77°F (25°C), July 58°F (14·4°C). Annual rainfall 45" (1,153 mm). Darwin. Jan. 83°F (28·3°C), July 77°F (25°C). Annual rainfall 59" (1,536 mm). Hobart. Jan. 62°F (16·7°C), July 46°F (7·8°C). Annual rainfall 24" (629 mm). Melbourne. Jan. 67°F (19·4°C), July 49°F (9·4°C). Annual rainfall 26" (659 mm). Perth. Jan. 74°F (23·3°C), July 55°F (12·8°C). Annual rainfall 35" (873 mm). Sydney. Jan. 71°F (21·7°C), July 53°F (11·7°C). Annual rainfall 47" (1,215 mm).

CONSTITUTION AND GOVERNMENT. *Federal Government:* Under the Constitution legislative power is vested in a Federal Parliament, consisting of the Queen, represented by a Governor-General, a Senate and a House of Representatives. Under the terms of the constitution there must be a session of parliament at least once a year.

The *Senate* comprises 76 Senators (12 for each State voting as one electorate and as from Aug. 1974, 2 Senators respectively for the Australian Capital Territory and the Northern Territory). Senators representing the States are chosen for 6 years. The terms of Senators representing the Territories expire at the close of the day next preceding the polling day for the general elections of the House of Representatives. In general, the Senate is renewed to the extent of one-half every 3 years, but in case of disagreement with the House of Representatives, it, together with the House of Representatives, may be dissolved, and an entirely new Senate elected. The *House of Representatives* consists, as nearly as practicable, of twice as many Members as there are Senators, the numbers chosen in the several States being in proportion to population as shown by the latest statistics, but not less than 5 for any original State. Elections to the Senate are on the single transferable vote system; voters list candidates in order of preference. A candidate must reach a quota to be elected, otherwise the lowest-placed candidate drops out and his or her votes are transferred to other candidates. Elections to the House of Representatives are on the alternative vote system; voters list candidates in order of preference, and if no one candidate wins an overall majority, the lowest-placed drops out and his or her votes are transferred. The numerical size of the House after the election in 1991 was 148, including the Members for Northern Territory and the Australian Capital Territory. The Northern Territory has been represented by 1 Member in the House of Representatives since 1922, and the Australian Capital Territory by 1 Member since 1949 and 2 Members since May 1974. The Member for the Australian Capital Territory was given full voting rights as from the Parliament elected in Nov. 1966. The Member for the Northern Territory was given full voting rights in 1968. The House of Representatives continues for 3 years from the date of its first meeting, unless sooner dissolved. The annual salary of both Senators and Representatives is $A69,693, with increments for holders of office.

Every Senator or Member of the House of Representatives must be a subject of the Queen, be of full age, possess electoral qualifications and have resided for 3 years within Australia. The franchise for both Houses is the same and is based on universal (males and females aged 18 years) suffrage. Compulsory voting was introduced in 1925. If a Member of a State Parliament wishes to be a candidate in a federal election, he must first resign his State seat.

Executive power is vested in the *Governor-General* advised by an Executive Council. The Governor-General presides over the Council, and its members hold office at his pleasure. All Ministers of State, who are members of the party or parties commanding a majority in the lower House, are members of the Executive Council under summons. A record of proceedings of meetings is kept by the Secretary to the Council. At Executive Council meetings the decisions of the Cabinet are (where necessary) given legal form, appointments made, resignations accepted, proclamations, regulations and the like made.

The policy of a ministry is, in practice, determined by the Ministers of State meeting without the Governor-General under the chairmanship of the Prime Minister. This group is known as the *Cabinet*. There are 11 Standing Committees of the Cabinet comprising varying numbers of Cabinet and non-Cabinet Ministers. In Labour Governments all Ministers have been members of Cabinet. In Liberal and National Country Party Governments, only the senior ministers. Cabinet meetings are private and deliberative and records of meetings are not made public. The Cabinet does not form part of the legal mechanisms of Government; the decisions it takes have, in themselves, no legal effect. The Cabinet substantially controls, in ordinary circumstances, not only the general legislative programme of Parliament but the whole course of Parliamentary proceedings. In effect, though not in form, the Cabinet, by reason of the fact that all Ministers are members of the Executive Council, is also the dominant element in the executive government of the country.

The legislative powers of the Federal Parliament embrace trade and commerce, shipping, etc.; taxation, finance, banking, currency, bills of exchange, bankruptcy, insurance; defence; external affairs, naturalization and aliens, quarantine, immigration and emigration; the people of any race for whom it is deemed necessary to make special laws; postal, telegraph and like services; census and statistics; weights and measures; astronomical and meteorological observations; copyrights; railways; conciliation and arbitration in disputes extending beyond the limits of any one State; social services; marriage, divorce etc.; service and execution of the civil and criminal process; recognition of the laws, Acts and records, and judicial proceedings of the States. The Senate may not originate or amend money bills; and disagreement with the House of Representatives may result in dissolution and, in the last resort, a joint sitting of the two Houses. No religion may be established by the Commonwealth. The Federal Parliament has limited and enumerated powers, the several State parliaments retaining the residuary power of government over their respective territories. If a State law is inconsistent with a Commonwealth law, the latter prevails.

The Constitution also provides for the admission or creation of new States. Proposed laws for the alteration of the Constitution must be submitted to the electors, and they can be enacted only if approved by a majority of the States and by a majority of all the electors voting.

The Australia Acts 1986 removed residual powers of the British government to intervene in the government of Australia or the individual states.

The 37th Parliament was elected on 13 March 1993.

House of Representatives (1994): Australian Labor Party, 80 seats; Liberal Party, 49; National Party, 16; independent, 2.

Senate (1994): Australian Labor Party, 30; Liberal Party, 30; Australian Democratic Party, 7; National Party, 6; Greens, 2; Country Liberal Party, 1.

Governor-General: Sir William Deane.

National flag: The British Blue Ensign with a large star of 7 points beneath the Union Flag, and in the fly 5 stars of the Southern Cross, all in white.

National anthem: Advance Australia Fair (adopted 19 April 1984; words and tune by P. D. McCormick). The 'Royal Anthem' (i.e. 'God Save the Queen') is used in the presence of the British Royal Family.

The Australian Labor Party formed a government on 25 March 1993 which in Nov. 1995 comprised the following (for the government formed in 1996 *see* ADDENDA:

Prime Minister: Paul Keating (b. 1945).

Cabinet: Deputy Prime Minister, Minister of Finance, Leader of the House: Kim Beazley. *Minister of Housing, Local Government and Human Services:* Brian Howe. *Human Services and Health, Minister assisting the Prime Minister for the Status of Women:* Carmen Lawrence. *Foreign Affairs, Government Leader in the Senate:* Gareth Evans. *Trade:* Bob McMullan. *Defence:* Robert Ray. *Treasurer:* Ralph Willis. *Environment, Sport and Territories:* John Faulkner. *Immigration and Ethnic Affairs and Minister assisting the Prime Minister for Multicultural Affairs:* Nick Bolkus. *Employment, Education and Training:* Simon Crean. *Industry, Technology and Regional Development:* Peter Cook. *Primary Industries and Energy:* Bob Collins. *Social Security:* Peter Baldwin. *Industrial Relations and Transport:* Laurie Brereton. *Attorney-General:* Michael Lavarch. *Communications, the Arts and Tourism:* Michael Lee.

Outer: Aboriginal and Torres Strait Islander Affairs: Robert Tickner. *Development Co-operation and Pacific Island Affairs:* Gordon Bilney. *Schools, Vocational Education and Training:* Ross Free. *Resources:* David Beddall. *Consumer Affairs:* Jeannette McHugh. *Justice:* Duncan Kerr. *Science and Small Business:* Chris Schacht. *Assistant Treasurer:* George Gear. *Defence, Veterans' Affairs, Science and Personnel:* John Faulkner. *Family Services:* Rosemary Crowley. *Special Minister of State:* Frank Walker. *Assistant Minister for Industrial Relations and Minister assisting the Prime Minister on the Public Service:* Gary Johns.

The leader of the Liberal Party is John Howard; of the National Party, Tim Fischer.

State Government: In each of the 6 States (New South Wales, Victoria, Queensland, South Australia, Western Australia, Tasmania) there is a State government whose constitution, powers and laws continue, subject to changes embodied in the Australian Constitution and subsequent alterations and agreements, as they were before federation. The system of government is basically the same as that described above for the Commonwealth—*i.e.*, the Sovereign, her representative (in this case a Governor), an upper and lower house of Parliament (except in Queensland, where the upper house was abolished in 1922), a cabinet led by the Premier and an Executive Council. Among the more important functions of the State governments are those relating to education, health, hospitals and charities, law, order and public safety, business undertakings such as railways and tramways, and public utilities such as water supply and sewerage. In the domains of education, hospitals, justice, the police, penal establishments, and railway and tramway operation, State government activity predominates. Care of the public health and recreative activities are shared with local government authorities and the Federal Government, social services other than those referred to above are now primarily the concern of the Federal Government, and the operation of public utilities is shared with local and semi-government authorities.

Administration of Territories. Since 1911, responsibility for administration and development of the Australian Capital Territory (ACT) has been vested in Federal Ministers and Departments. The ACT became self-governing on 11 May 1989.

The ACT House of Assembly has been accorded the forms of a legislature, but continues to perform an advisory function for the Minister for the Capital Territory.

On 1 July 1978 the Northern Territory of Australia became a self-governing Territory with expenditure responsibilities and revenue-raising powers broadly approximating those of a State.

Local Government. The system of municipal government is broadly the same throughout Australia, although local government legislation is a State matter.

Each State is sub-divided into areas known variously as municipalities, cities, boroughs, towns, shires or district councils, totalling about 900. Within these areas the management of road, street and bridge construction, health, sanitary and garbage services, water supply and sewerage, and electric light and gas undertakings, hospitals, fire brigades, tramways and omnibus services and harbours is generally part of the functions of elected aldermen and councillors. State governments may also be responsible for some services.

In some instances, *e.g.*, in New South Wales, a number of local government authorities combine to conduct a public undertaking such as the supply of water or electricity. State taxation revenue was $A26,757m. in 1993–94; local, $A5,266m.

Howard, C., *Australia's Constitution.* Melbourne, 1985
Lucy, R., *The Australian Form of Government.* Melbourne, 1985

DEFENCE. The Minister for Defence has responsibility under legislation for the control and administration of the Defence Force. The Chief of Defence Force Staff is vested with command of the Defence Force. He is the principal military adviser to the Minister. The Secretary, Department of Defence is the Permanent Head of the Department. He is the principal civilian adviser to the Minister and has statutory responsibility for financial administration of the Defence outlay. The Chief of Defence Force Staff and the Secretary are jointly responsible for the administration of the Defence Force except with respect to matters falling within the command of the Defence Force or any other matter specified by the Minister.

The Chief of Naval Staff, the Chief of the General Staff and the Chief of the Air Staff command the Navy, Army and Air Force respectively. They have delegated authority from the Chief of Defence Force Staff and the Secretary to administer matters relating to their particular Service.

The structure of Defence is characterized by 3 organizational types: *(i)* A Central Office comprising 5 groups of functional orientated Divisions: Strategic Policy and Force Development; Supply and Support; Manpower and Financial Services; Management and Infrastructure Services; and, Defence Science and Technology; *(ii)* the 3 Armed Services of the Defence Force, each having a Service Office element in addition to the command structure; and *(iii)* a small number of outrider organizations concerned with such specialist fields as intelligence and natural disasters.

Defence Support. The Department of Defence Support purchases goods and services for defence purposes; provides technical expertise and other assistance to the defence industry; involves Australian industry in defence equipment to the maximum practical extent; administers the Australian Offsets Program so as to stimulate technological advancement and broaden the capabilities of strategic industries; within overall defence policies helps the capacity, efficiency and capability of Australian industry to design and export defence materiel; manages the Government's munitions and aircraft factories, and dockyards; markets defence and allied products and services to help maintain strategic industries.

Army. Overall organization and financial control of the Army is vested in the Chief of General Staff. The Army is organized in a Land Headquarters and a Northern Command.

The strength of the Army was 23,700, including 2,600 women, in 1996. There was 1 infantry division, 1 armoured regiment, 1 armoured reconnaissance regiment, 1 armoured personnel carrier squadron, 4 infantry battalions, 2 artillery regiments, 1 air defence regiment, 2 combat engineer regiments, 1 special forces regiment and 2 aviation regiments. Equipment included 90 Leopard 1A3 main battle tanks. The Army Aviation Corps has 22 GAF N22-B Missionmaster transports, and 120 helicopters.

The effective strength of the Army Reserve in 1996 was 22,850.

Women have been eligible for combat duties since 1993.

Navy. The Chief of Naval Staff is assisted by the Deputy Chief of Naval Staff and Assistant Chiefs for Personnel and for Materiel. The command, operation and administration of the Fleet is vested in the Maritime Commander, Australia headquartered at Sydney.

The fleet includes 4 UK-built Oxley class diesel submarines, 3 US-built guided missile destroyers, 4 US- and 2 Australian-built guided missile frigates and 2 older frigates, 6 mine countermeasure vessels, 2 landing ships, 5 tank landing craft and 16 inshore patrol craft. Major auxiliaries include 2 fleet replenishment tankers and 2 survey ships, and there are some 80 minor auxiliaries and service craft.

The first of 6 new Collins class Swedish-designed diesel submarines, and the first of 8 German-designed Anzac class frigates are now on trials.

The Fleet Air Arm operates a shore-based anti-submarine helicopter squadron of 7 Sea Kings and 16 S-70B Seahawk helicopters for the guided missile frigates. There are additionally 2 transport and 1 survey aircraft and 9 transport and utility helicopters.

The fleet main base is at Sydney, with subsidiary bases at Cockburn Sound (Western Australia), Cairns and Darwin.

The all-volunteer Navy was (1995) 15,000 strong including 900 Fleet Air Arm.

Air Force. Command of the Royal Australian Air Force (RAAF) is vested in the Chief of the Air Staff (CAS) assisted by the Deputy Chief of the Air Staff, Chief of Air Force Operations and Plans, Chief of Air Force Materiel, Chief of Air Force Personnel, Chief of Air Force Technical Services, Director-General Supply—Air Force and Assistant Secretary Resources Planning.

The CAS administers and controls RAAF units through two commands: Operational Command and Support Command. Operational Command is responsible to the CAS for the command of operational units and the conduct of their operations within Australia and overseas. Support Command is responsible to the CAS for training of personnel, and the supply and maintenance of service equipment.

Flying establishment comprises 16 squadrons, of which 2 are equipped with 22 F-111 strike/reconnaissance aircraft. Of the others, 3 are equipped with missile-armed F-18 Hornet interceptors and 2 with Orion maritime reconnaissance aircraft. There are 5 transport squadrons, 2 with Hercules turboprop transports, 1 with Caribou STOL transports, 1 with Boeing 707 tanker and transport aircraft, and 1 with Falcon 900 VIP transports. All helicopters have either been transferred to the Army or retired. Primary training has been transferred to a civilian school. Training aircraft include Pilatus PC-9 turboprop-powered basic trainers, Aermacchi MB 326H jets for pilot training, and HS 748 aircraft for navigator training. A training unit has F-18 Hornets for crew conversion.

Training for commissioned rank is carried out at the RAAF Academy and Officers' Training School, both located at Point Cook, Victoria. Other major training activities which lead to commissioned rank include basic aircrew training and technical and commercial cadet schemes. Basic ground training to tradesman level is conducted at RAAF technical training schools. Higher command and staff training is, in the main, carried out at the RAAF Staff College, Fairbairn, ACT.

Personnel (1995) 17,425, including 2,700 women. There is also an Australian Air Force Reserve, 4,400 strong. There were 125 combat aircraft.

INTERNATIONAL RELATIONS

Membership. Australia is a member of the UN, the Commonwealth, OECD, Colombo Plan, the South Pacific Forum and the South Pacific Bureau for Economic Co-operation.

ECONOMY

Policy. Since 1942 the Federal Government alone has levied taxes on incomes. In return for vacating this field of taxation, the State Governments are reimbursed by grants from the Federal Government out of revenue received. Payments to the States represent about one-third of Federal Government outlays, and in turn the payments State Governments receive from the Federal Government account for nearly half of their revenues.

The Financial Agreement of 1927 established the Australian Loan Council which represents the Federal and six State Governments, and co-ordinates domestic and overseas borrowings by these governments, including annual borrowing programmes. The Federal Government acts as a central borrowing agency in raising loans to finance the major part of those programmes. The Loan Council in 1984 agreed upon arrangements for the co-ordination of borrowings by semi-government and local authorities and government-owned companies.

Reforms were initiated at a special Premiers' Conference in Oct. 1990 to form a partnership between the Commonwealth, States, Territories and local government with a view to improving national efficiency, international competitiveness and enhancing delivery and quality of government services. In July 1991 the premiers agreed a programme of inter-state standardization and integration in such areas as the railway system, electricity grid, product control and professional qualifications.

Budget. In 1929, under a financial agreement between the Federal Government and States, approved by a referendum, the Federal Government took over all State debts existing on 30 June 1927 and agreed to pay $A15·17m. a year for 58 years towards the interest charges thereon, and to make substantial contributions towards a sinking fund on State debt. The Sinking Fund arrangements were revised under an amendment to the agreement in 1976.

Outlays and revenues of the Commonwealth Government for years ending 30 June (in $A1m.):

	1993–94	*1994-95*
Total outlays	114,154	121,877
including		
Defence	9,746	9,795
Education	9,704	10,093
Health	16,083	17,134
Social security and welfare	41,805	43,302
Housing	1,124	1,116
Culture and recreation	1,120	1,263
Economic services	7,438	8,505
Public services	7,665	7,713
Payments to States, NT and local government	15,449	15,074

	1993–94	*1994-95*
Public debt interest	6,473	8,005
Other	–2,454	–124
Total revenue	100,480	110,247
including		
Customs duty	3,226	3,474
Excise duty	10,814	12,001
Sales tax	10,415	11,624
PAYE income tax	47,111	50,928
Other individual tax	8,444	9,178
Medicare levy	2,870	...
Prescribed payments	1,871	2,169
Company tax	12,700	15,588
Superannuation	1,191	1,913
Withholding	877	903
Fringe benefits tax	1,418	2,740
Bank accounts debit tax	...	...
Other	1,734	1,954

The Consumer Price Index rose by 3·2% over the year to June 1995.

Currency. On 14 Feb. 1966 Australia adopted a system of decimal currency. The currency unit, the *Australian dollar* (AUD) is divided into 100 *cents*. Notes are issued in denominations of $A1, 2, 5, 10, 20, 50 and 100. Coins are issued in denominations of 1, 2, 5, 10, 20 and 50 cents and $A1. Gold bullion legal tender coins weighing 1 kg (the 'Australian Nugget'), 10 oz. and 2 oz. with respective face values of $A10,000, $A2,500 and $A500 were introduced in March 1991, and a 1 kg platinum coin with a face value of $A3,000 was issued in Oct. 1992.

Foreign currency reserves were $A20,184m. in 1995.

The estimated inflation rate for the year ending June 1995 was 2·5%.

Money in circulation in June 1995, $A18,233m. In March 1996, £1 = $A2·01; US$1 = $A1·31; DM1 = $A0·89.

Banking and Finance. The banking system comprises:

(a) The Reserve Bank of Australia is the central bank and bank of issue. The *Governor* is Bernie Fraser. Its Rural Credits Department provides short-term credit for the marketing of primary produce. Its assets were $A36,624m. in June 1995 and its liabilities $A36,624m., of which notes on issue, $A18,452m.; deposits by trading banks, $A3,535m.; deposits by Commonwealth Government, $A2,415m.; of the assets are: Gold and foreign exchange (including IMF Special Drawing Rights), $A19,948m., treasury notes $A2,869m., other Commonwealth Government securities $A15,117m. Its functions and responsibilities derive from the Reserve Bank Act 1959, the Banking Act 1959, and the Financial Corporations Act 1974. For the history of the Reserve Bank *see* THE STATESMAN'S YEAR-BOOK 1986–87, p. 104.

(b) 4 major banks: (i) The Commonwealth Bank of Australia; (ii) The Australia and New Zealand Banking Group Ltd; (iii) Westpac Banking Corporation and (iv) National Australia Bank.

(c) Other banks: (i) 3 State Government banks—The State Bank of New South Wales, The State Bank of South Australia, and the Rural and Industries Bank of Western Australia; (ii) one joint stock bank—The Bank of Queensland Ltd, formerly The Brisbane Permanent Building and Banking Co. Ltd, which has specialized business in one district only; (iii) The Australian Bank Ltd; (iv) branches of 17 overseas banks—the restrictions on foreign banks operating in Australia, and on foreign investment in the merchant banks, were lifted in 1984–85.

(d) The Commonwealth Development Bank of Australia commenced operations on 14 Jan. 1960. Its function is to provide finance for primary production and small business.

(e) The Australian Resources Development Bank Ltd opened on 29 March 1968, to assist Australian enterprises in developing Australia's natural resources, through direct loans and equity investment or by re-financing loans made by trading banks. The bank is jointly owned by the 4 major Australian trading banks.

(f) The Primary Industry Bank of Australia Ltd commenced operations on

22 Sept. 1978. The equity capital of the bank consists of eight shares. Seven shares are held by the Australian Government and the major trading banks while the eighth share is held equally by the 4 State banks. The main objective of the bank is to facilitate the provision of loans to primary producers on longer terms than are otherwise generally available. The role of the bank is restricted to re-financing loans made by banks and other financial institutions.

(*g*) The Banking Legislation Amendment Act of 1989 removed the legislative differences between savings and trading banks. In June 1995 there were 49 authorized banks under 44 banking groups. In June 1994 there were 6,790 branches and 6,060 agencies.

Total deposits in June 1995 were $A255,641m. (including $A6,810m. of non-residents' deposits).

(*h*) In March 1992 there were 45 building societies. Assets were $A12,011m. in June 1994. Building societies are permitted to have up to 50% of their assets in non-home loans.

There is an Australian Stock Exchange (ASX).

Weights and Measures. The metric system is in use.

ENERGY AND NATURAL RESOURCES

Electricity. Electricity supply is the responsibility of the State governments. Production 1993–94, 161,813m. kWh (16,272m. hydro-electric).

Oil and gas. The main fields are Gippsland (Vic.) and Carnarvon (WA). Crude oil production was 31,700m. litres in 1994–95; natural gas, 29,245,000m. litres.

Minerals. Australia is a leading producer of bauxite and diamonds. Coal is Australia's major source of energy. Reserves are large (1995 estimate: 69,000m. tonnes) and easily worked. The main fields are in New South Wales and Queensland. Production in 1994-95 was 237·2m. tonnes. Brown coal (lignite) reserves are mainly in Victoria and were estimated at 41,700m. tonnes in 1990. Production, 1994-95 was 48·3m. tonnes.

Production of other major minerals in 1994-95 (1,000 tonnes): Bauxite, 41,900; copper, 360; iron ore and concentrate, 131,000; manganese ore, 2,020; nickel, 103; tin, 7; uranium, 2·65; gold, 256 tonnes.

Agriculture. In 1991 there were 125,615 farms. Farms in 1993 covered 459m. ha. 414m. ha were grazing or fallow, 17·1m. ha sown to crops. The most important are (1994) wheat (16·48m. tonnes from 8·4m. ha); sugar-cane (31·31m. tonnes from 0·34m. ha); barley (6·67m. tonnes from 3·4m. ha); oats (1·65m. tonnes from 0·95m. ha); rice (1·04m. tonnes from 0·13m. ha). Vineyards (62,048 ha) produced 531m. litres of wine from 777,373 tonnes of grapes in 1993–94.

Gross value of agricultural production in 1993-94, $A23,302m., including (in $A1m.): Crops, 11,937; livestock slaughtering, 6,415; wool, 2,459; other livestock products, 2,491.

In 1993, 71,803 farms had cattle and 56,026 sheep.

Livestock (in 1,000) at 31 March 1995:

	NSW	*Vic.*	*Qld*	*SA*	*WA*	*Tas.*	*NT*	*ACT*	*Australia*
Cattle	6,409	4,294	10,164	1,248	1,841	700	1,525	...	26,187
Sheep	39,780	20,961	12,193	13,367	30,373	3,961	...	...	120,651
Pigs	850	456	609	416	386	30	3	...	2,750
Poultry[1]	27,377	14,728	10,055	5,094	6,025	...	225	217	63,722

[1] 31 March 1993

Livestock products (in 1,000 tonnes) for the year ending 30 June 1995: Beef, 1,742; veal, 38; lamb and mutton, 589; pigmeat, 349; poultry meat, 462; wool (1994), 865; milk, 8,206m. litres.

Williams, D. B. (ed.), *Agriculture in the Australian Economy*. 3rd ed. Sydney Univ. Press and OUP, 1991

Forestry. The Federal Government is responsible for forestry at the national level. Each State is responsible for the management of publicly-owned forests. Total forest area was 41m. ha in 1991, of which 30m. ha were publicly-owned. The major part of wood supplies derives from coniferous plantations, of which there were 939,507 ha in 1991. Production was 3·5m. cu. metres of sawn timber and 996,162 tonnes of wood pulp in 1993–94.

INDUSTRY. Statistics of manufacturing industries, June 1994: Number of firms, 44,921; persons employed, 922,600; salaries paid, $A28,309m.; turnover, $A185,115m. (excludes small single-establishment enterprises employing fewer than 4 persons).

Manufacturing by sector as at June 1994:

	No. of firms	*Persons employed*	*Salaries in $A1m.*	*Turnover in $A1m.*
Food, beverages and tobacco	3,590	168,100	5,034	40,936
Textiles, clothing, footwear and leather products	4,503	77,000	1,825	9,602
Wood and paper products	3,985	62,000	1,790	10,740
Printing, publishing and recording media	5,274	89,600	2,831	11,920
Chemical, petroleum, coal and associated products	3,026	89,400	3,270	29,060
Non-metallic mineral products	1,936	39,400	1,315	8,909
Metal products	7,576	146,100	4,842	33,669
Machinery and equipment	9,011	196,000	6,181	34,661
Other manufacturing	6,020	55,000	1,220	5,617

Manufactured products in 1994–95 included: Bricks, 1,863m.; cement, 7·1m. tonnes; carpets, 47·3m. sq. metres; confectionery (1993-94), 180,210 tonnes; electric motors, 3·1m.; washing machines, 305,100; refrigerators, 408,000; TV sets (1993-94), 163,000; pig iron, 7·4m. tonnes; crude steel, 7·8m. tonnes; tobacco, 23,083 tonnes; woollen wove, 8·6m. sq. metres; woollen yarn, 23,083 tonnes; scoured wool (1993-94), 154,242 tonnes; motor cars, 301,100; caravans, 9,394; beer, 1,789m. litres; sulphuric acid (1993-94), 62,231 tonnes; superphosphates, 1·36m. tonnes.

Labour. In June 1995 the total workforce (persons aged 15 and over) numbered (in 1,000) 8,998, of whom there were employed: 8,274 (females, 1994, 3,358) (married, 2,223). In 1994 the labour force included 354,100 employers, 6,647,400 wage and salary earners and 802,200 self-employed. The majority of wage and salary earners have had their minimum wages and conditions of work prescribed in awards by the Industrial Relations Commission, which in April 1991 awarded a 2·5% rise, making the minimum weekly wage about $A442, but in Oct. 1991 the Commission decided to allow direct employer-employee wage bargaining, provided agreements reached are endorsed by the Commission. In some States, some conditions of work (*e.g.*, weekly hours of work, leave) are set down in State legislation. Average weekly wage, May 1995: men $A652·70, women, $A429·90. Average working week, 1994: 35·9 hours (males 40·9; females 29·3). 4 weeks annual leave is standard.

Employees in all States are covered by workers' compensation legislation and by certain industrial award provisions relating to work injuries.

During 1994 there were 558 industrial disputes in progress which accounted for 501,000 working days lost. In these disputes 264,500 workers were involved.

The following table shows the distribution of employed persons by industry in 1994, by sex and average weekly hours worked:

Industry	*Numbers (in 1,000)*		*Hours worked*	
	Persons	*(Females)*	*Per person*	*(Females)*
Agriculture, forestry, fishing and hunting	395·8	(126·5)	42·9	(29·9)
Mining	88·9	(10·6)	41·8	(38·2)
Manufacturing	1,107·3	(295·6)	38·3	(32·9)
Electricity, Gas and Water	83·9	(12·3)	37·1	(28·5)
Construction	605·8	(89·0)	37·5	(21·1)
Wholesale trade	518·1	(162·1)	39·5	(32·2)
Retail trade	1,199·5	(610·9)	32·2	(25·6)

Industry	*Numbers (in 1,000)* Persons	*(Females)*	*Hours worked* Per person	*(Females)*
Transport and storage	385·5	(82·4)	40·1	(33·0)
Property and business services	791·9	(363·6)	37·1	(30·9)
Education	578·6	(382·2)	34·4	(31·4)
Cultural and recreation services	193·7	(95·0)	32·4	(28·1)
Accommodation, cafés and restaurants	393·9	(217·0)	32·8	(28·5)
Communication	153·0	(44·7)	36·9	(30·0)
Finance and insurance	320·9	(187·0)	36·3	(32·6)
Government administration and defence	370·4	(156·4)	34·4	(31·4)
Health and community services	746·6	(569·1)	32·4	(28·1)
Personal and other services	297·0	(153·0)	33·3	(29·3)
Totals	8,230·8	(3,557·7)	35·9	(29·5)

In March 1994 1,588,500 wage and salary earners worked in the public sector and 4,160,200 in the private sector.

The following table shows the distribution of employed persons in 1994 according to the *Australian Standard Classification of Occupations*:

Occupation	*Employed persons (in 1,000)* Persons	*(Females)*
Managers and administrators	881·3	(216·7)
Professionals	1,149·1	(506·6)
Para-professionals	466·8	(223·1)
Tradespersons	1,192·4	(129·0)
Clerks	1,347·9	(1,062·9)
Salespersons and personnel service	1,389·2	(898·8)
Plant and machine operators, and drivers	581·7	(81·4)
Labourers and related workers	1,222·5	(439·2)
	8,230·8	(3,557·7)

In June 1995, 724,800 persons (8·1% of the labour force) were unemployed, (including 287,500 females of whom 84,700 persons were seeking part-time work. In June 1995, 243,100 persons had been unemployed for more than one year. In May 1995 there were 53,700 job vacancies. In June 1993, 913,800 unemployment beneficiaries received a total of $A7,500m. (year to June 1993); in June 1993 46,552 sickness beneficiaries received a total of $A370·2m. (year to June 1993) and 181,513 special beneficiaries received a total of $A304m. in the year ended June 1992.

Trade Unions. In June 1994 there were 157 trade unions with 2,890,200 members (1,135,600 females). About 44% of wage and salary earners (36% females) were estimated to be members of unions. In 1994 there were 26 unions with fewer than 100 members and 13 unions with 80,000 or more members. Many of the larger trade unions are affiliated with central labour organizations, the oldest and by far the largest being the Australian Council of Trade Unions formed in 1927. In July 1992 the Industrial Relations Legislation Amendment Act freed the way for employers and employees to negotiate enterprise-based awards and agreements. In 1995 wage accord trade unions committed themselves to the objective of keeping inflation at 2-3%, and the government agreed to create 0·6m. jobs by 1999 and raised the 'safety net' wage rates to a weekly $A12-14.

FOREIGN ECONOMIC RELATIONS. In 1990 Australia and New Zealand completed a Closer Economic Relations agreement (initiated in 1983) which establishes free trade in goods. Gross foreign debt was $A205,927m. in 1994.

Commerce. Merchandise imports and exports for years ending 30 June, in $A1m.:

	Imports	*Exports*
1992–93	59,436	60,037
1993–94	64,401	63,872
1994–95	74,638	67,036

The Australian customs tariff provides for preferences to goods produced in and shipped from certain countries as a result of reciprocal trade agreements. These include UK, New Zealand, Canada and Ireland.

Exports and imports, 1993–94 (in $A1m.):

	Exports	*Imports*
Live animals	323	77
Meat and preparations	4,044	46
Dairy goods and eggs	1,287	161
Fish, shellfish and their preparations	115	542
Cereals and preparations	3,206	143
Vegetables and fruit	932	515
Sugar and honey	1,316	67
Coffee, tea, cocoa, spices and their manufacturers	166	383
Animal feed (excl. unmilled cereal)	385	102
Miscellaneous edible products	194	441
Beverages	474	332
Tobacco and manufactures	32	135
Raw hides and skins	392	3
Oil seeds and fruit	121	81
Crude rubber (incl. synthetic and reclaimed)	10	117
Cork and wood	519	659
Pulp and waste paper	16	126
Textile fibres (not wool tops)	3,977	162
Crude fertilizers, minerals (not coal, petroleum, gems)	358	141
Metal ores and scrap	7,315	141
Crude animal and vegetable materials	208	165
Coal, coke and briquettes	7,259	27
Petroleum and products	2,676	3,392
Gas, natural and manufactured	1,185	23
Animal oils and fats	170	3
Fixed vegetable oils and fats	7	181
Processed oils and fats, waxes thereof	31	18
Organic chemicals	81	1,615
Inorganic chemicals	257	488
Dyeing, colouring and tanning materials	363	340
Medicinal and pharmaceutical products	701	1,427
Essential oils, perfume and cleansing preparations	208	527
Manufactured fertilizers	19	394
Plastics in primary forms	201	741
Plastics in non-primary forms	113	635
Chemical materials and products	408	878
Leather and manufactures, dressed furskins	368	146
Rubber manufactures	120	954
Cork and wood manufactures (not furniture)	92	288
Paper, board and pulp	258	1,518
Textile yarn, fabrics and products	385	2,246
Non-metallic mineral goods	666	1,080
Iron and steel	1,496	1,041
Non-ferrous metals	3,900	498
Metal manufactures	625	1,674
Power generators	586	1,690
Special machinery, industrial	822	3,061
Metalworking machinery	92	378
General machinery and parts, industrial	891	3,638
Office machines and data-processing equipment	1,371	4,828
Telecommunications and sound equipment	674	2,538
Electrical machinery and parts	968	4,051
Road vehicles (inc. air-cushion vehicles)	1,074	7,108
Other transport equipment	1,024	1,620
Sanitary, plumbing, heating and lighting fittings, pre-fabricated buildings	45	191

	Exports	Imports
Furniture and parts	72	396
Travel goods, handbags etc.	9	286
Clothing and accessories	247	1,480
Footwear	61	512
Professional, scientific and controlling instruments	416	1,707
Photographic and optical goods, watches and clocks	460	1,066
Miscellaneous manufactured articles	798	4,160
Other commodities and transactions	348	31
Gold and other coin	253	1
Non-monetary gold	5,295	981
Confidential items	1,095	72
Total trade	64,578	64,470

Trade by country in 1994–95:

	Exports		Imports	
	$A1m.	%	*$A1m.*	%
ASEAN	10,236	15	6,117	8
Indonesia	2,099	3	1,197	2
Malaysia	2,040	3	1,421	2
Singapore	3,649	5	2,247	3
Other	2,448	4	1,252	2
Canada	1,132	2	1,277	2
China	2,958	4	3,651	5
EEC	7,483	11	18,226	24
France	793	1	1,754	2
Germany	1,080	2	4,865	7
Italy	1,249	2	2,027	3
Netherlands	706	1	713	1
UK	2,267	3	4,439	6
Other	1,388	2	4,428	6
Hong Kong	2,626	4	924	1
Japan	16,286	24	12,779	17
Korea (Republic)	5,270	8	2,028	3
New Zealand	4,768	7	3,554	5
Papua New Guinea	929	1	1,124	2
Saudi Arabia	276	0·41	750	1
Switzerland	287	0·42	991	1
Taiwan	3,098	5	2,570	3
USA	4,633	7	16,048	22
Other countries	7,054	11	4,599	6
	67,036	100	74,638	100

Total trade between UK and Australia (British Department of Trade returns, in £1,000 sterling):

	1991	*1992*	*1993*	*1994*	*1995*
Imports to UK	870,823	1,013,680	996,153	1,063,253	1,110,448
Exports and re-exports from UK	1,356,127	1,376,737	1,598,359	1,914,442	2,121,352

Tourism. During 1994, 3,104,600 overseas visitors arrived in Australia intending to stay for less than 12 months; tourists spent $A5,885m. in 1994.

COMMUNICATIONS

Roads. In 1992 there were 810,000 km of roads (16,000 km of National Highways).

At 30 June 1993, 8,050,000 cars, 2,089,900 vans, trucks and buses and 291,700 motor cycles were registered. New registrations, 1994–95, included 528,499 cars, 110,410 vans, trucks and buses and 20,502 motor cycles.

472·77m. passenger journeys were made by bus in 1989-90.

In 1995, 2,014 persons were killed in road accidents (1,959 in 1994).

Railways. There are 6 government-owned railway systems. In 1991 the National Rail Corporation was set up to market inter-state freight service. Statistics for the year ended 30 June 1993:

System	*Route length in km* [4]	*Passenger journeys, 1,000*	*Goods carried, (1,000 tonnes)*	*Freight earnings, ($A1m.)*
State:				
New South Wales	9,810	231,354	61,597	815·3
Victoria	5,107	111,324	9,646	151·3
Queensland	9,797	40,392	90,303	1,192·5
South Australia [3]	120	7,540	...	...
Western Australia	5,583	10,584	2,654	248·3
Australian National [1, 2]	6,235	200	13,899	276·6
	36,652	401,394	178,099	2,684·0

[1] The Australian National Railways operates services of the former Commonwealth Railways, the non-metropolitan South Australian Railways and the Tasmanian Railways.
[2] Excludes Adelaide metropolitan rail passenger services and the Tasmanian Region.
[3] The South Australian State Transport Authority operates services in the Adelaide metropolitan area.
[4] Inter-system traffic is included in the total for each system over which it passes.

The State railway gauges are: New South Wales, 1,435 mm; Victoria, 1,600 mm (325 km 1,435 mm); Queensland, 1,067 mm (111 km 1,435 mm); South Australia, 1,600 mm for 2,533 km, 1,824 km 1,435 mm and the rest 1,067 mm; West Australia, 137 km, 1,435 mm and the rest 1,067 mm, and Tasmania, 1,067 mm. Australian National Railways comprises 3,530 km of 1,435 mm ('standard') gauge, 1,173 km of 1,600 mm ('broad') gauge and 1,532 km of 1,067 mm ('narrow') gauge routes. Under various Commonwealth–State standardization agreements, all the State capitals are now linked by standard gauge track (except Darwin; the Central Australia railway extends only as far north as Alice Springs).

The National Rail Corporation operating as 'National Rail' was incorporated in Sept. 1991; terminal operations commenced in 1993. It is scheduled to take over inter-state rail freight operations and the ownership of rail assets.

There are also private industrial and tourist railways.

Civil Aviation. Qantas Airways, Australia's international airline, in 1995 operated 4 A300B4-200s, 16 B-737-300s, 17 B-737-400s, 3 B-747-200Bs, 2 B-747-200B Combis, 6 B-747-300s, 18 B-747-400s, 7 B-767-200ERs and 14 B-767-300ERs. In 1992 Qantas merged with Australian Airlines and in 1993 25% of the company was purchased by British Airways. The remainer is government-owned. In 1993–94 10·6m. passengers and 475,962 tonnes of freight were flown on international flights. The major international airports are Adelaide, Brisbane, Darwin, Melbourne, Perth, Sydney and Townsville. Services are also provided by Aeroflot, Aerolíneas Argentinas, Air Calédonie, Air China, Air France, Air India, Air Mauritius, Air Nauru, Air New Zealand, Air Niugini, Air Pacific, Air Vanuatu, Air Zimbabwe, Alitalia, All Nippon, American Airlines, Ansett, AOM, Biritsh Airways, Canadian Airlines, Cathay Pacific, Continental Airlines and Air Micronesia, Egyptair, Garuda Indonesia, Gulf Air, Japan Airlines, JAT, KLM, Korean Air, Lauda Air, Lufthansa, Malaysia Airlines, Middle East Airlines, Olympic Airlines, Philippine Airlines, Polynesian Airlines, Royal Brunei Airlines, Royal Tongan Airlines, SAA, Singapore Airlines, Solomon Airlines, Thai Airways, United Airways, United Airlines, Vietnam Airlines, Virgin Atlantic, Western Airlines.

Internal airlines carried 18·59m. passengers in 1992–93 and 144,200 tonnes of freight. Domestic airlines were deregulated in Oct. 1990.

At 30 June 1992 there were 428 Commonwealth or licensed aerodromes in Australia and its Territories.

Shipping. The chief ports are Sydney, Newcastle, Port Kembla; Melbourne, Geelong, Westernport; Hay Point, Gladstone, Brisbane; Port Hedland, Dampier, Port Walcott, Fremantle. In 1995 the merchant fleet comprised 104 vessels totalling 3·45m. DWT. 21 vessels (7·99% of tonnage) were registered under foreign flags.

Total tonnage registered, 3·04m. GRT, including tankers, 0·8m. GRT and container ships, 0·12m. GRT.

Arrivals and departures of vessels engaged in overseas trade:

	Arrivals			Departures		
	No of port visits	DWT (1,000 tonnes)	Cargo discharged (1,000 tonnes gross)	No. of port visits	DWT (1,000 tonnes)	Cargo loaded (1,000 tonnes gross)
1990-91	13,325	329,196	32,126	14,737	544,708	304,202
1991–92	...	...	34,396	...	...	316,783

29·36m. tonnes of cargo were carried by inter-state shipping in 1991–92.

Telecommunications. Postal services are operated by Australia Post, established by the Postal Services Act, 1975. Revenue was $A2,165·8m. in 1992–93, expenditure $A2,171·3m. There were 4,233 post offices and other agencies in 1993. 4,166·2m. postal items were handled.

Telecommunications were operated by Telecom Australia under the Telecommunications Act, 1975. Revenue was $A12,656m. in 1992–93, expenditure $A10,299·8m. There were 8·5m. telephones. Services to other countries were operated by the Overseas Telecommunications Commission Australia (OTC), established by the Overseas Telecommmunications Act, 1946. In 1992 OTC merged with Telecom to form AOTC. Their monopoly in telecommunication was ended. Optus Communications, a consortium of American, Australian and British companies is the new national telecommunications carrier. The market is scheduled to be opened to full competition in 1997.

Australia's National Satellite System is operated by AUSSAT Pty Ltd under the Satellite Communications Act, 1984. In 1991 it was sold by the Commonwealth Government to Optus Communications; 3 satellites are in orbit covering the entire continent.

Broadcasting is regulated by the Broadcasting Act, 1942 and the Broadcasting Ownership and Control Acts, 1987. Foreign ownership of commercial radio and TV companies is restricted to 20%. The National Broadcasting Service is provided by the Australian Broadcasting Corporation (ABC), which at 30 June 1991 operated 108 MW, 288 FM and 14 high-frequency radio stations. In addition, 140 MW and 63 FM commercial stations and 12 MW and 106 FM public stations were operating. The short-wave international service Radio Australia broadcasts in English, Bahasa Malay, Cantonese, Chinese, French, Japanese, Thai, Tok Pisin and Vietnamese.

A National Television Service is provided by the ABC and by the Special Broadcasting Service (SBS). In addition, 43 commercial companies are operating. Pay television services began in 1995.

In 1991 there were estimated to be 29·1m. radios and in 1992 9·2m. TV sets in use.

Cinemas. In 1993 there were 515 cinemas (940 screens).

Press (1994). There were 4 national newspapers, 19 metropolitan daily newspapers and 121 suburban newspapers with a weekly combined circulation of some 5m.

SOCIAL INSTITUTIONS

Justice. The judicial power of the Commonwealth of Australia is vested in the High Court of Australia (the Federal Supreme Court), in the Federal courts created by the Federal Parliament (the Federal Court of Australia and the Family Court of Australia) and in the State courts invested by Parliament with Federal jurisdiction.

High Court. The High Court consists of a Chief Justice and 6 other Justices, appointed by the Governor-General in Council. The Constitution confers on the High Court original jurisdiction, *inter alia*, in all matters arising under treaties or affecting consuls or other foreign representatives, matters between the States of the Commonwealth, matters to which the Commonwealth is a party and matters between residents of different States. Federal Parliament may make laws conferring original jurisdiction on the High Court, *inter alia*, in matters arising under the Constitution or under any laws made by the Parliament. It has in fact conferred jurisdiction on the High Court in matters arising under the Constitution and in matters arising under certain laws made by Parliament.

The High Court may hear and determine appeals from its own Justices exercising original jurisdiction, from any other Federal Court, from a Court exercising Federal jurisdiction and from the Supreme Courts of the States. It also has jurisdiction to hear and determine appeals from the Supreme Courts of the Territories. The right of appeal from the High Court to the Privy Council was abolished in 1986.

Other Federal Courts. Since 1924, 4 other Federal courts have been created to exercise special Federal jurisdiction, *i.e.* the Federal Court of Australia, the Family Court of Australia, the Australian Industrial Court and the Federal Court of Bankruptcy. The Federal Court of Australia was created by the Federal Court of Australia Act 1976 and began to exercise jurisdiction on 1 Feb. 1977. It exercises such original jurisdiction as is invested in it by laws made by the Federal Parliament including jurisdiction formerly exercised by the Australian Industrial Court and the Federal Court of Bankruptcy, and in some matters previously invested in either the High Court or State and Territory Supreme Courts. The Federal Court also acts as a court of appeal from State and Territory courts in relation to Federal matters. Appeal from the Federal Court to the High Court will be by way of special leave only. The State Supreme Courts have also been invested with Federal jurisdiction in bankruptcy.

State Courts. The general Federal jurisdiction of the State courts extends, subject to certain restrictions and exceptions, to all matters in which the High Court has jurisdiction or in which jurisdiction may be conferred upon it.

Industrial Tribunals. The chief federal industrial tribunal is the Australian Conciliation and Arbitration Commission, constituted by presidential members (with the status of judges) and commissioners. The Commission's functions include settling industrial disputes, making awards, determining the standard hours of work and wage fixation. Questions of law, the judicial interpretation of awards and imposition of penalties in relation to industrial matters, are dealt with by the Industrial Division of the Federal Court.

Religion. Under the Constitution the Commonwealth cannot make any law to establish any religion, to impose any religious observance or to prohibit the free exercise of any religion. The following percentages refer to those religions with the largest number of adherents at the census of 1986. The census question on religious adherence was not obligatory, however.

Christian, 73% of population; Catholic, 26%; Anglican, 23·9%; Uniting, 7·6%; Presbyterian, 3·6%; Orthodox, 2·7%; Baptist, 1·3%; Lutheran, 1·3%; Church of Christ, 0·6%; Religion other than Christian 2·%, No religion 12·7%, No statement 12·3%.

The Anglican Synod voted for the ordination of 10 women in Nov. 1992.

Thompson, R. C., *Religion in Australia: a History*. OUP, 1995

Education. The Governments of the Australian States and the Northern Territory have the major responsibility for education, including the administration and substantial funding of primary, secondary, and technical and further education. In most States, a single Education Department is responsible for these three levels, but in New South Wales and South Australia there is a separate department responsible solely for technical and further education and in Victoria, a Technical and Further Education Board. Furthermore, in New South Wales an Education Commission advises the Minister on primary, secondary and post-secondary education.

The Australian Government is responsible for education in Norfolk Island, Christmas Island and the Cocos (Keeling) Islands. It also provides supplementary finance to the States and is responsible for the total funding of universities and colleges of advanced education. It has special responsibilities for student assistance, education programmes for Aboriginal people and children from non-English-speaking backgrounds, and for international relations in education.

The Australian Constitution empowers the Federal Government to make grants to the States and to place conditions upon such grants. The National Board of Employment, Education and Training was established in 1988 to advise the Federal Government on the financial needs of educational institutions. It is assisted by 4 councils: The Schools Council, the Higher Education Council, the Employment and Skills Formation Council and the Australian Research Council.

The Commonwealth has been working with the states to develop a national perspective for schools and a common curriculum. The Curriculum Corporation has been established under the auspices of the Australian Education Council.

School attendance is compulsory between the ages of 6 and 15 years (16 years in Tasmania), at either a government school or a recognized non-government educational institution. Many children attend pre-schools for a year before entering school (usually in sessions of 2-3 hours, for 2-5 days per week). Government schools are usually co-educational and comprehensive. Non-government schools have been traditionally single-sex, particularly in secondary schools, but there is a trend towards co-education. Tuition is free at government schools, but fees are normally charged at non-government schools.

Primary and secondary schools at July 1994:

	Schools		*Teachers* [1]		*Pupils* [2]	
States and Territories	*Government*	*Non-government*	*Government schools*	*Non-government schools*	*Government schools*	*Non-government schools*
New South Wales	2,187	862	47,371	19,142	755,771	296,078
Victoria	1,731	679	34,635	16,661	520,328	252,866
Queensland	1,323	406	25,718	8,933	403,234	145,297
South Australia	674	189	12,665	4,057	181,640	64,371
Western Australia	767	251	14,055	5,048	223,105	76,307
Tasmania	233	68	4,207	1,372	64,061	21,298
Northern Territory	147	26	1,991	471	26,934	7,212
ACT	97	39	2,738	1,281	39,865	21,013
Australia	7,159	2,520	143,379	56,965	2,214,938	884,442

[1] Full-time teachers plus the full-time equivalent of part-time teaching.
[2] Full-time pupils only.

In post-secondary education, tuition fees were abolished in 1974 and student allowances are provided for full-time students subject to a means test. Universities are autonomous institutions. From 1 Jan. 1989 the university and college of advanced education sectors were merged by the Federal Government. The resulting institutions are self-governing, though funded by the Federal Government. A private university sector is developing. The major part of technical and further education is provided in government-administered technical and further education institutions (TAFE). These had 1,743,943 students in 1992.

There were 38 universities in 1994. They were, with numbers of academic staff (and students): *NSW:* Sydney, 2,500 (30,995); New South Wales, 1,823 (26,295); New England, 544 (13,638); Newcastle, 858 (14,721); Macquarie, 754 (15,526); Wollongong, 833 (11,266); Southern Cross, 283 (6,374); Sydney University of Technology, 1,011 (20,986); Western Sydney, 1,073 (21,207); Charles Sturt, 572 (16,369); *Vic.:* Melbourne, 2,576 (29,930); Monash, 2,391 (37,316); La Trobe, 1,380 (21,180); Deakin, 1,039 (24,538); Ballarat, 256 (3,911); Victoria University of Technology, 630 (13,693); Swinburne University of Technology, 420 (8,831); Royal Melbourne Institute of Technology, 1,244 (24,343); *Qld.:* Queensland, 1,884 (24,590); James Cook, 598 (7,847); Griffith, 1,004 (17,415); Queensland University of Technology, 1,252 (25,874); Central Queensland, 347 (8,383); Southern Queensland, 386 (12,957); Bond (1993), 310 (1,643); *SA:* Adelaide, 1,041 (12,899); Flinders, 777 (10,243); South Australia, 1,209 (21,817); *WA:* Western Australia, 958 (12,370); Curtin University of Technology, 1,052 (19,326); Edith Cowan, 830 (16,845); Murdoch, 461 (7,860); Notre Dame (1993), 33 (200); *Tas.:* Tasmania, 877 (11,618); *NT:* Northern Territory, 275 (3,779); *ACT:* Canberra, 416 (8,553); Australian National, 1,494 (10,290); Australian Catholic University, 520 (8,439).

Teacher education usually takes place in colleges of advanced education, though a substantial number of secondary teachers and a few primary teachers receive their pre-service education in a university.

The Australian Government provides assistance for students. The Assistance for Isolated Children Scheme provides special support to families whose children are isolated from schooling or are handicapped. AUSTUDY is a means-tested scheme to assist students aged 16 years and over enrolled for full-time study in approved courses at secondary and post-secondary institutions. Allowances are also available for post-graduate study and overseas study. Aboriginal students are eligible for assistance under the ABSTUDY scheme. In addition, under the Higher Education Contribution Scheme students may be funded by a government loan repaid interest-free later through the tax system. The Federal Government introduced a supplementary loans scheme for eligible students in 1993. The States also offer various schemes of assistance, principally at the primary and secondary levels.

National bodies with a co-ordinating, planning or funding rôle include: the Australian Education Council, comprising the Federal and State Ministers of Education, the Conference of Directors-General of Education, the Australian Council for Educational Research and advisory bodies, the National Aboriginal Education Committee, and the Vocational Education Employment and Training Advisory Committee.

Commonwealth government expenditure on education (public and private sectors) in 1994–95 was estimated at $A10,056m.

Health. In 1992 there were an average 4·5 hospital beds per 1,000 population. There were 1,104 hospitals (general). The Royal Flying Doctor Service serves remote areas. Commonwealth government expenditure on health (1994–95) was estimated at $A17,276m.

Social Security and Welfare. All Commonwealth Government social security pensions, benefits and allowances are financed from the Commonwealth Government's general revenue. In addition, assistance is provided for welfare services.

Expenditure on main programmes, 1994–95, $A43,449m.

The following summarizes the conditions of the major benefits.

Age and disability pensions—age pensions are payable to men 65 years of age or more and women 60 years of age or more who have lived in Australia for a specified period and, unless permanently blind, also satisfy an income test. Persons over 16 years of age who are permanently blind or permanently incapacitated for work to the extent of at least 85% may receive an invalid pension. Invalid pension is paid subject to a residence qualification, income and assets test, unless the person is permanently blind. Additional amounts are paid to pensioners with dependent children. Supplementary assistance may be paid to a pensioner paying rent or private lodging subject to an income test. Remote area allowance is payable to pensioners living in certain remote areas, except for those aged 70 or more receiving the special rate of age pension. Supplementary assistance, additional pension for children, mother's/guardian's allowance and remote area allowance are not taxable.

In 1994–95, age pensioners received a total of $A11,734m., and disability support pensioners received $A4,556m.

Wife's pension—payable to the wife of an age or invalid pensioner if she is not eligible for a pension in her own right. The maximum rate and the income test are identical to those for age and invalid pensioners. The amount paid out in 1992–93 was $A222·4m.

Carer's pension—payable to a person who is providing constant care and attention at home for a severely disabled age or invalid pensioner living in the same house, where the carer is not eligible for pension in his own right. The maximum rate and the income test are identical to those for age and invalid pensions. The amount paid out in 1992–93 was $A100·8m.

Sole parent pensions—sole parents who have custody, care and control of any dependent children may, if they satisfy a residence requirement and an income test, receive sole parent pensions. Mother's/guardian's allowance, additional pension for each dependent child, supplementary assistance and remote area allowance are also payable.

In 1992-93 298,444 beneficiaries received a total of $A2,869·5m.

Sheltered employment allowance—is payable to disabled persons under age—pension age engaged in approved sheltered employment who are qualified to receive invalid pension. The rates of payment and allowances and income test are the same as invalid pension. The amount paid out in 1991–92 was $A36m.

Rehabilitation allowance—persons undertaking a rehabilitation programme with the Commonwealth Rehabilitation Service who are eligible for a social security pension or benefit are eligible to receive a non taxable rehabilitation allowance during treatment or training and for up to 6 months thereafter. The allowance is equivalent to the invalid pension and is subject to the same income test. The amount paid out in 1992–93 was $A14m.

Family Allowance—is paid subject to an income test to assist families with children under 16 years or dependent full-time students aged 16 years to under 25 years. It is not subject to income tax.

In 1991-92 1,929,508 families comprising 3,720,088 children received a total of $A2,329m.

Family allowance supplement—payable subject to an income test to families with one or more children eligible for family allowances so long as they are not in receipt of any Commonwealth pension, benefit or allowance which provides additional payment for dependent children; this is not taxable.

In 1991-92 241,241 families received a total $A723·9m.

From 1 Jan. 1993 a new system of family payments, Basic Family Payment and Additional Family Payment, was introduced. In 1993 1,933,696 families received $A2,074m. under the Basic Family Payment system.

Child disability allowance—payable to parents or guardians of severely physically or mentally handicapped children in the family home and needing constant care and attention. The allowance is free of an income test but is subject to a residence qualification similar to that for family allowance.

In 1992–93 allowances totalling $A33m. were paid.

Double orphan's pension—the guardian of a child under 16 years of age or of a full-time student under 25, both of whose parents are dead, or one of whose parents is dead and the whereabouts of the other parent unknown, and for refugee children where both parents are outside Australia or in prison, may receive double orphan's pension. The payment is not subject to an income test nor is it taxable. The amount paid out in 1992–93 was $A1·6m.

Unemployment and sickness benefits—are paid, subject to an income test, to persons between the ages of 18 and 16 respectively and age pensioners who are unemployed, able and willing to work and making efforts to obtain work, or temporarily unable to work because of sickness or injury. Unemployment benefit was replaced in July 1991 by a two-payment structure under the 'Newstart Strategy'. A 'Jobsearch Allowance' is payable to persons aged 18 and over who have been unemployed for less than 12 months, and to unemployed 16 and 17-year olds. A 'Newstart Allowance' is payable to those who have been unemployed for more than 1 year and are aged 18 and over. Income support under this structure is means-tested and linked to active labour market programmes. To be granted benefit a person must have resided in Australia for at least 12 months preceding his or her claim or intend to remain in Australia permanently. For unemployment benefit purposes unemployment must not be due to industrial action by that person or by members of a union to which that person is a member. Special benefits may be granted to persons not qualified above. For numbers of beneficiaries and amounts paid *see* LABOUR, *above*.

Service Pensions are paid by the Department of Veterans' Affairs, similar to the age and invalid pensions provided by the Department of Social Security. Male Veterans who have reached the age of 60 years or are permanently unemployable, and who served in a theatre of war, are eligible subject to an income test. Female Veterans who served abroad and who have reached the age of 55 or are permanently unemployable, are also eligible. Wives of service pensioners are also eligible provided that they do not receive a pension from the Department of Social Security. *Disability pension* is a compensatory payment in respect of incapacity attributable to war service. It is paid at a rate commensurate with the degree of incapacity and is free of any income test. A separate allowance may be paid to dependents. In 1993–94 $A2,382m. of service pensions and $A1,507m. of disability and dependents' pensions were paid out; in 1994 there were 325,800 eligible veterans.

In addition to cash benefits, welfare services are provided either directly or through State and Local government authorities and voluntary agencies, for people with special needs.

Medicare. On 1 Feb. 1984 the Commonwealth Government introduced a universal health scheme known as Medicare. This covers: Automatic entitlement under a single public health fund to medical and optometrical benefits of 85% of the Medical Benefits Schedule fee, with a maximum patient payment for any service where the Schedule fee is charged; access without direct charge to public hospital accommodation and to inpatient and outpatient treatment by doctors appointed by the hospital; the restoration of funds for community health to approximately the same real level as 1975; a reduction in charges for private treatment in shared wards of public hospitals, and increases in the daily bed subsidy payable to private hospitals.

The Medicare programme is financed in part by a 1·25% levy on taxable incomes, with low income cut-off points, which were $A12,689 p.a. for a single person in 1995 and $A21,366 p.a. for a family with an extra allowance of $A2,100 for each child. The Commonwealth Government subsidises registered health insurance organizations by contributing to the Health Benefits, and makes an annual contribution to the Reinsurance Trust Fund of $A20m. for payments of benefits to patients with hospital treatment in excess of 35 days.

Medicare benefits are available to all persons ordinarily resident in Australia. Visitors from UK, New Zealand, Italy, Sweden, the Netherlands and Malta have immediate access to necessary medical treatment, as do all visitors staying more than 6 months.

Medical Benefits. The Health Insurance Act provides for a Medical Benefits Schedule which lists medical services and the Schedule (standard) fee applicable in each State in respect of each medical service. Schedule fees are set and updated by an independent fees tribunal appointed by the Government. The fees so determined are to apply for Medicare benefits purposes.

Home and Community Care Program was introduced in 1985 to provide support services to enable aged and disabled persons to live at home. It is jointly funded by the Commonwealth and State or Territory Governments. Commonwealth funding was $A313·7m. in 1992–93.

DIPLOMATIC REPRESENTATIVES

Of Australia in Great Britain (Australia House, Strand, London, WC2B 4LA)
High Commissioner: Neal Blewett.

Of Great Britain in Australia (Commonwealth Ave., Canberra)
High Commissioner: R. J. Carrick, CMG, LVO.

Of Australia in the USA (1601 Massachusetts Ave., NW, Washington, D.C., 20036)
Ambassador: Don Russell.

Of the USA in Australia (Moonah Pl., Canberra)
Ambassador: Edward Perkins.

Of Australia to the United Nations
Ambassador: Richard Butler.

Further Reading

Australian Bureau of Statistics (ABS). *Year Book Australia.—Pocket Year Book Australia.—Monthly Summary of Statistics.* ABS also publish numerous specialized statistical digests.

Australian Encyclopædia. 12 vols. Sydney, 1983
Blainey, G., *The Tyranny of Distance: How Distance Shaped Australia's History.* Melbourne, 1982
The Cambridge Encyclopedia of Australia. CUP, 1994
Clark, M., *Manning Clark's History of Australia*; abridged by M. Cathcart. London, 1994
Concise Oxford Dictionary of Australian History. 2nd ed. OUP, 1995
Docherty, J. D., *Historical Dictionary of Australia.* Metuchen (NJ), 1993
Emy, H. and Hughes, O., *Australian Politics: Realities in Conflict.* Sydney, 1991
Gilbert, A. D. and Inglis, K. S. (eds.) *Australians: a Historical Library.* 5 vols. CUP, 1988
Hancock, K. (ed.) *Australian Society.* Cambridge Univ. Press, 1990
Hocking, B. (ed.) *Australia towards 2000.* London, 1990
Kepars, I., *Australia.* [Bibliography] 2nd ed. Oxford and Santa Barbara, 1994
Oxford History of Australia. vol 2: 1770–1860. OUP, 1992. vol 5: 1942–88. OUP, 1990
The Oxford Illustrated Dictionary of Australian History. OUP, 1993
Serle, P., *Dictionary of Australian Biography.* 2 vols. Sydney, 1949
Turnbull, M., *The Reluctant Republic.* London, 1994
Who's Who in Australia. Melbourne, 1906 to date

For other more specialized titles see under CONSTITUTION AND GOVERNMENT *and* AGRICULTURE, *above*

National library: The National Library, Canberra, ACT.
National statistical office: Australian Bureau of Statistics (ABS), Belconnen, ACT. The statistical services of the states are integrated with the Bureau.

AUSTRALIAN TERRITORIES

AUSTRALIAN CAPITAL TERRITORY

KEY HISTORICAL EVENTS. The area, now the Australian Capital Territory (ACT), was first visited by Europeans in 1820 and settlement commenced in 1824. It was surrendered by New South Wales on 1 Jan. 1911 (Jervis Bay port area was additionally transferred in 1915). Canberra became the seat of the Commonwealth government on 9 May 1927.

TERRITORY AND POPULATION. The area is 2,432 sq. km (including Jervis Bay area). Population (1991 census), 280,085 (140,922 females). 1993 estimate, 298,303. Vital statistics for 1993: Births, 4,414; deaths, 1,110; marriages, 1,783; divorces, 2,061; Infant mortality (per 1,000 live births), 4·3.

CONSTITUTION AND GOVERNMENT. The ACT became self-governing on 11 May 1989. It is represented by 2 members in the Commonwealth House of Representatives and 2 senators.

The parliament of the ACT, the *Legislative Assembly*, consists of 17 members elected for a 3-year term. Its responsibilities are at state and local government level. The Legislative Assembly elects a Chief Minister and a 3-member cabinet. At the elections of 19 Feb. 1995 the Liberal Party won 7 seats, Labor 6, Greens 2 and ind 2. The Liberals formed a coalition government with the minority parties.

Chief Minister: Kate Carnell.

FINANCE. In 1987–88 the ACT was given its own budget. It is treated equitably with the States regarding local revenue raising, expenditure and assistance by the Commonwealth government. In 1994–95 current outlays were $A1,086m., capital outlays $A187m. and revenue $A1,195m.

PRODUCTION. Outside Canberra the Territory is mainly reserved for forestry and nature conservation (Namadgi National Park is 105,000 ha). A considerable amount of reafforestation (mostly pine) has been undertaken, the total area of coniferous plantations at 30 June 1993 being 17,000 ha. Farming is mainly in grazing: Livestock (1994 preliminary), 10,921 cattle, 88,395 sheep, and 200,750 poultry. In 1993-94, 7,415 tonnes of beef and veal and 395 tonnes of greasy wool were produced.

EDUCATION. In July 1994 there were 96 government schools comprising 65 primary schools, 25 secondary schools and colleges, 1 combined primary/secondary school and 5 special schools. Non-government schools numbered 41 (38 in 1993 of which there were 24 primary schools, 6 secondary schools and 8 schools with both primary and secondary enrolments). Students enrolled full-time in government schools in 1994 numbered 22,211 and 17,513 in primary and secondary school levels respectively. Enrolments at non-government schools comprised 10,461 primary school students and 10,576 secondary school students. Pre-school education was provided at 79 centres with a total enrolment of 4,302. There is an Institute of Technical and Further Education. There are 3 higher education institutions: the Australian National University (10,290 students in 1994); the University of Canberra (8,553); the Australian Defence Force Academy (1,359).

Further Reading

Australian Capital Territory in Focus (formerly *Statistical Summary*). Australian Bureau of Statistics. Annual.
Wigmore, L., *Canberra: A History of Australia's National Capital*. 2nd ed. Canberra, 1971

NORTHERN TERRITORY

KEY HISTORICAL EVENTS. The Northern Territory, after forming part of New South Wales, was annexed on 6 July 1863 to South Australia and in 1901 entered the Commonwealth as a corporate part of South Australia. It passed under the control of the Commonwealth Government on 1 Jan. 1911. The Commonwealth Government retained responsibility until Self-Government was granted on 1 July 1978.

TERRITORY AND POPULATION. The Northern Territory is bounded by the 26th parallel of S. lat. and 129° and 138° E. long. Its total area is 1,346, 200 sq. km and includes adjacent islands. The greater part of the interior consists of a tableland rising gradually from the coast to a height of about 700 metres. On this tableland there are large areas of excellent pasturage. The southern part of the Territory is generally sandy and has a small rainfall, but water may be obtained by means of sub-artesian bores.

The population of the Territory in June 1994 was 171,134. The capital, seat of Government and principal port is Darwin, on the north coast; population 68,876 in June 1994. Other main centres include Katherine (8,732), 330 km south of Darwin; Alice Springs (24,852), in Central Australia; Tennant Creek (3,140), a rich mining centre 500 km north of Alice Springs; Nhulunbuy (3,847), a bauxite mining centre on the Gove Peninsula in eastern Arnhem Land; and Jabiru, a model town built to serve the rich Uranium Province in eastern Arnhem Land. Palmerston is a Darwin satellite town (11,209); Yulara (2,169 in 1991) is a resort village serving Uluru National Park and Ayers Rock. There also are a number of large self-contained Aboriginal communities. Aboriginals numbered 39,287 and Torres Strait Islanders 623 at the 1991 Census.

Vital statistics for 1992: Births, 3,742; deaths, 776; marriages, 860; divorces, 345. Infant mortality per 1,000 live births, 15·5.

CONSTITUTION AND GOVERNMENT. The Northern Territory (Self-Government) Act 1978 established the Northern Territory as a body politic as from 1 July 1978, with Ministers having control over and responsibility for Territory finances and the administration of the functions of government as specified by the Federal Government. Regulations have been made conferring executive authority for the bulk of administrative functions. At 31 Dec. 1979 the only important powers retained by the Commonwealth related to rights in respect of Aboriginal land, some significant National Parks and the mining of uranium and other substances prescribed in the Atomic Energy Act. Proposed laws passed by the Legislative Assembly require the assent of the Administrator. The Governor-General may disallow any law assented to by the Administrator within 6 months of the Administrator's assent.

The Northern Territory has federal representation, electing 1 member to the House of Representatives and 2 members to the Senate.

The Legislative Assembly has 25 members, directly elected for a period of 4 years. The Chief Minister, Deputy Chief Minister and Speaker are elected by, and from, the members. The *Administrator* (Austin Asche, QC) appoints Ministers on the advice of the Leader of the majority party.

The Legislative Assembly, elected in 1994, comprised in 1995: Country Liberal Party, 16; Australian Labor Party, 8; Independents, 1.

The Country Liberal Party Cabinet was as follows in Jan. 1996:

Chief Minister, Minister for Police, Fire and Emergency Services, Ethnic Affairs, Arts and Museums: Shane Stone.

Deputy Chief Minister, Treasurer, Mines and Energy, Lands, Planning and Environment: Mike Reed. *Asian Relations, Trade and Industry, Regional Development, Minister Assisting the Chief Minister for Central Australia:* Eric Poole. *Housing and Local Government, Aboriginal Development, Correctional Services:* Daryl Manzie. *Attorney General, Education and Training, Sport and Recreation, Constitutional Develoment:* Steve Hatton. *Transport and Works, Primary Industry and Fisheries:* Mick Palmer. *Tourism, Parks and Wildlife, Racing and Gaming, Railway, Leader of Government Business:* Barry Coulter. *Health Services, Public Employment, Liquor Commission:* Fred Finch. *Power and Water, Work Health, Territory Insurance:* Denis Burke.

Local Government: Local government was established in Darwin in 1957 and later in 3 regional centres. These are each managed by a mayor and a municipal council elected at intervals of not more than 4 years by universal adult franchise. Provision has been made for a limited form of local government for smaller communities. In 1995 there were 6 municipal and 31 community government councils and 29 other incorporated community associations responsible for local government.

FINANCE. Budgets in $A1m.:

	1990–91	*1991–92*	*1992–93*	*1993–94*	*1994–95*
Revenue	1,777·8	1,989·0	2,162·4	2,236·6	2,383·6
Expenditure	1,777·8	1,989·0	2,125·1	2,196·1	2,332·8

The revenue in 1994–95 comprised $A1,149·0m. in grants to the Northern Territory from the Commonwealth together with $A1,234m. raised by the Northern Territory which included $A215m. through state-like taxes.

Financing transactions in 1994–95 included Borrowings of $A122m. offset by a repayment of Commonwealth Advances of $A68m. and an increase in cash balances of $A51m.

Expenditure during 1994–95 included $A415m. for education; $A194m. for housing and community amenities; $A293m. for health; $A243m. for power and water services and $A240m. for transport and infrastructure.

ENERGY AND NATURAL RESOURCES

Oil and Gas. Significant oil and gas reserves have been discovered and developed offshore in the Joseph Bonaparte Gulf and Timor Sea areas and onshore in the Amadeus Basin. In 1995, 1,718 megalitres of oil (97% from offshore fields in the Timor Sea) and 383,746 megalitres of natural gas were produced. Total value of oil and gas production in 1994–95 was $A281·25m. Natural gas is piped from the Amadeus Basin to Darwin.

Minerals. The most important natural resources are minerals, and mining is one of the largest industries. Value of production, 1994–95 (in $A1m.): Gold bullion, 298; uranium concentrate, 27; bauxite, 143; manganese ore, 195; other metallic minerals, 335. In 1994–95 the Territory produced 90% of Australia's manganese, 14·5% of its bauxite and 6·5% of gold bullion. In terms of value it produced 29% of its uranium.

Agriculture. Cattle and buffalo production constitute the largest farming industry. Livestock, 1991–92 (in 1,000): Cattle, 1,334; domesticated buffalo, 13; pigs, 3. In 1992, 82,485 cattle and buffalo were exported overseas. Value of live cattle exports, 1990-91, $A18·5m.; total value of beef cattle industry, 1990-91, $A102·1m. Total value of the buffalo industry in 1990–91 was $A4·4m. The value of livestock slaughterings, other disposals and livestock products in 1992 was $A125m. Other animal industries contributed $A13·5m. in the financial year 1990–91. This sector consists of poultry, pig and milk production, as well as crocodile farming for hides and flesh. Value of crocodile flesh, skins and other products, 1991–92, £A864,700.

The horticultural industry was valued at $A33m. in 1994 for fruit and vegetable production and the main crops are mangoes, bananas, melons and grapes.

In 1993–94, 6,599 ha were used for crops, including cereal for grain, 1,705 ha, fruit and vegetables (1991–92), 1,132 ha and stockfeed, 471 ha; some 252,000 ha were under sown pasture.

Fisheries. The total value of fish products in 1994 was $A108·1m. Of this, prawns contributed $A48·2m., aquaculture. $A48·6m. and barramundi $A2·2m. Mud crabs, threadfin salmon, shark, mackerel, bay lobster and molluscs made up most of the remainder. The expanding aquaculture industry produces crayfish, prawns, giant clams and beta carotene extracts.

INDUSTRY. In 1994 there were 255 manufacturing establishments (with 4 or more persons employed). Turnover was $A673m. in 1991–92. 2,700 persons were employed in manufacturing in 1994. The labour force totalled 87,314 in June 1995. In 1993, 35 trade unions had 17,300 members.

Tourism. In 1994-95, 1,087,716 people travelled to the Territory and tourism generated approximately $A603m. in 1993–94.

National Parks and Reserves. There are 96 parks and reserves totalling some 4,781,621 ha, which includes Cobourg Marine Park.

COMMUNICATIONS

Roads. There were (in 1995) 6,159 km of sealed road. They include three major interstate links: The Stuart Highway from Darwin to the South Australian border (1,787 km), the Barkley Highway, Three Ways to the Queensland border (434 km), and the Victoria Highway, Katherine to the Western Australian border (470 km). In addition to this there were 6,338 km of gravel roads and 4,798 km of formed roads. Total roads, excluding township and municipal, 20,209 km. Registered motor vehicles (excluding tractors and trailers) at 30 June 1995 numbered 91,600, including 81,773 passenger vehicles and 3,820 motorcycles. There were 61 fatalities in road accidents in 1995.

Railways. In 1980 Alice Springs was linked to the Trans-continental network by a standard (1,435 mm) gauge railway to Tarcoola in South Australia (831 km).

Civil Aviation. There are daily flights by national carriers connecting Darwin, Alice Springs and Yulara to all state capitals and other major cities. Darwin has direct international passenger flights to Singapore, Kuala Lumpur, Bali, Brunei and East Timor. In 1994–95 Darwin airport handled 668,595 domestic and 160,390 international passengers, Alice Springs 971,462 domestic passengers and Yulara 255,245.

Shipping. Regular freight shipping services connect Darwin with Western Australia, the eastern States and overseas. Passenger vessels also call at Darwin at irregular intervals.

The Port of Darwin is equipped to handle bulk, container and roll-on-roll-off traffic. 1,524 vessels visited the port and it handled 922,797 tonnes of cargo in 1994–95. There is a cyclone shelter for fishing vessels.

The ports of Melville Bay (Gove) and Milner Bay (Groote Eylandt) are connected with Darwin, the eastern States and overseas by regular shipping freight services.

Telecommunications. Darwin's radio services include four ABC stations, 1 SBS station, 2 commercial stations and a community station.

Darwin has 2 commercial, 1 ABC and 1 SBS TV service.

Alice Springs radio services include 4 ABC stations, 2 commercial and 2 community stations. It has 2 commercial, 1 ABC and 1 SBS TV service.

Most other Northern Territory centres have 1 commercial and 1 national radio service, with 1 each of ABC, SBS and commercial television, many of these being provided by self-help projects.

SOCIAL INSTITUTIONS

Justice. Voluntary euthanasia for the terminally ill was legalized in 1995.

Education. In 1993 there were 3,265 children and 102 teachers in government and private pre-schools. Education is compulsory from the age of 6 to 15 years. There were (1993) 26,837 full-time students enrolled in 146 government primary, secondary and special schools with 1,950 full-time equivalent teaching staff, and 7,035 full-time students enrolled in 26 private primary and secondary schools with 463 full-time equivalent teaching staff. The proportion of migrant and of Aboriginal and Torres Strait Islander students in the Territory is high, with the 2 latter comprising 34·1% of all full-time enrolments in 1993 (8,856 primary and 2,724 secondary students). Schools range from single classrooms and transportable units catering for the needs of small Aboriginal communities and pastoral properties to urban high schools and secondary colleges (years 11–12) catering for about 7,500 students. Bilingual programmes operate in some Aboriginal communities where traditional Aboriginal culture prevails. Secondary education extends from school years 8 to 12 (7 to 12 in Alice Springs). The Northern Territory University (NTU) was founded in 1989 by amalgamating the existing University College of the Northern Territory and the Darwin Institute of Technology, with the technical and further education courses hitherto offered by the latter to be conducted by an Institute of Technical and Further Education within the new University. Approximately 6% of all Northern Territory residents were enrolled in a course at the NTU in 1992. Batchelor College, a multi-purpose institution of Aboriginal tertiary education, had 826 students enrolled in higher education or TAFE courses in 1993. There are 5 colleges of higher education, with a total of 3,943 full- and part-time students enrolled in 1993. The TAFE sector had 4,174 students enrolled in tertiary courses in 1992.

Health. In 1995 there were 5 public hospitals. Community health services are provided from urban and rural Health Centres including mobile units. Remote communities are served by the Aerial Medical Service and by resident Aboriginal health workers.

Further Reading

The Northern Territory: Annual Report. Dept. of Territories, Canberra, from 1911. Dept. of the Interior, Canberra, from 1966–67. Dept. of Northern Territory, from 1972

Australian Territories, Dept. of Territories, Canberra, 1960 to 1973. Dept. of Special Minister of State, Canberra, 1973–75. Department of Administrative Services, 1976

Northern Territory Statistical Summary. Australian Bureau of Statistics, Canberra, from 1960

Donovan, P. F., *A Land Full of Possibilities: A History of South Australia's Northern Territory 1863–1911.* 1981.—*At the Other End of Australia: The Commonwealth and the Northern Territory 1911–1978.* Univ. of Queensland Press, 1984

Heatley, A., *The Government of the Northern Territory.* Univ. of Queensland Press, 1979.—*Almost Australians: the Politics of Northern Territory Self-Government.* Australian National Univ. Press, 1990

Mills, C. M., *A Bibliography of the Northern Territory.* Canberra, 1977

Powell, A., *Far Country: A Short History of the Northern Territory.* Melbourne Univ. Press, 1982

AUSTRALIAN EXTERNAL TERRITORIES

AUSTRALIAN ANTARCTIC TERRITORY. An Imperial Order in Council of 7 Feb. 1933 placed under Australian authority all the islands and territories other than Adélie Land situated south of 60° S. lat. and lying between 160° E.

long. and 45° E. long. The Order came into force with a Proclamation issued by the Governor-General on 24 Aug. 1936 after the passage of the Australian Antarctic Territory Acceptance Act 1933. The boundaries of Adélie Land were definitively fixed by a French Decree of 1 April 1938 as the islands and territories south of 60° S. lat. lying between 136° E. long. and 142° E. long. The Australian Antarctic Territory Act 1954 declared that the laws in force in the Australian Capital Territory are, so far as they are applicable and are not inconsistent with any ordinance made under the Act, in force in the Australian Antarctic Territory.

The area of the territory is estimated at 6,119,818 sq. km (2,362,875 sq. miles).

There is a research station on MacRobertson Land at lat. 67° 37' S. and long. 62° 52' E. (Mawson), one on the coast of Princess Elizabeth Land at lat. 68° 34' S. and long. 77° 58' E. (Davis) and one at lat. 66° 17' S. and long. 110° 32' E. (Casey). The Antarctic Division also operates a station on Macquarie Island.

COCOS (KEELING) ISLANDS. The Cocos (Keeling) Islands are 2 separate atolls comprising some 27 small coral islands with a total area of about 14·2 sq. km, and are situated in the Indian Ocean at 12° 05' S. lat. and 96° 53' E. long. They lie 2,768 km north-west of Perth and 3,685 km west of Darwin.

The main islands are West Island (the largest, about 10 km from north to south) on which is an airport and an animal quarantine station, and most of the European community; Home Island, occupied by the Cocos Malay community; Direction, South and Horsburgh Islands, and North Keeling Island, 24 km to the north of the group.

The islands were discovered in 1609 by Capt. William Keeling but remained uninhabited until 1826. In 1857 the islands were annexed to the Crown; in 1878 responsibility was transferred from the Colonial Office to the Government of Ceylon, and in 1886 to the Government of the Straits Settlement. By indenture in 1886 Queen Victoria granted all land in the islands to George Clunies-Ross and his heirs in perpetuity (with certain rights reserved to the Crown). In 1903 the islands were incorporated in the Settlement of Singapore and in 1942–46 temporarily placed under the Governor of Ceylon. In 1946 a Resident Administrator, responsible to the Governor of Singapore, was appointed.

On 23 Nov. 1955 the Cocos Islands were placed under the authority of the Australian Government as the Territory of Cocos (Keeling) Islands. An Administrator, appointed by the Governor-General, is the Government's representative in the Territory and is responsible to the Minister for Territories and Local Government. The Cocos (Keeling) Islands Council, established as the elected body of the Cocos Malay community in July 1979, advises the Administrator on all issues affecting the Territory.

In 1978 the Australian Government purchased the Clunies-Ross family's entire interests in the islands, except for the family residence. A Cocos Malay co-operative was established to take over the running of the Clunies-Ross copra plantation and to engage in other business with the Commonwealth in the Territory, including construction projects. In 1993 the Australian Government took control of the Clunies-Ross family residence also.

The population of the Territory (1993) was 593, distributed between Home Island (75%) and West Island (25%).

The islands are low-lying, flat and thickly covered by coconut palms, and surround a lagoon in which ships drawing up to 7 metres may be anchored, but which is extremely difficult for navigation.

An equable and pleasant climate, affected for much of the year by the south-east trade winds. Temperatures range over the year from 68° F (20° C) to 88° F (31·1° C) and rainfall averages 80" (2,000 mm) a year.

The Cocos (Keeling) Islands Act 1955 is the basis of the Territory's administrative, legislative and judicial systems. Under section 8 of this Act, those laws which were in force in the Territory immediately before the transfer continued in force there.

Roads. There are 15 km of roads.

Civil Aviation. There are 5 flights a fortnight to Perth (Western Australia), 1 weekly to Singapore and 1 daily to Jakarta (Indonesia).

Telecommunications. In 1992 there were 190 radio receivers and 287 telephones.

Religion. About 85% are Moslems and 15% Christians.

Education. In 1992 there were 2 primary schools (on Home Island and West Island) with 98 pupils and 7 teachers and 1 teaching assistant and 2 secondary schools with 70 pupils and 9 teachers and 1 teaching assistant, and 29 students in a technical school.

Health. In 1992 there was 1 doctor and 7 nursing personnel, with 5 beds in clinics.

Administrator: Barry Cunningham.

CHRISTMAS ISLAND is an isolated peak in the Indian Ocean, lat. 10° 25' 22" S., long. 105° 39' 59" E. It lies 360 km S., 8° E. of Java Head, and 417 km N. 79° E. from Cocos Islands, 1,310 km from Singapore and 2,623 km from Fremantle. Area about 135 sq. km. The climate is tropical with temperatures varying little over the year at 27° C. The wet season lasts from Nov. to April with an annual total of about 2,673 mm. The island was formally annexed by the UK on 6 June 1888, placed under the administration of the Governor of the Straits Settlements in 1889, and incorporated with the Settlement of Singapore in 1900. Sovereignty was transferred to the Australian Government on 1 Oct. 1958. The population at the 1991 census was 1,275; 1994 estimate, 2,500 of whom 1,300 were of Chinese, 400 of Malay and 800 of Australian/European origin.

The legislative, judicial and administrative systems are regulated by the Christmas Island Act, 1958–73. They are the responsibility of the Commonwealth Government and operated by an Administrator. The Territory underwent major changes to its legal system when the Federal Parliament passed the Territories Law Reform Bill of 1992; Commonwealth and State laws applying in the state of Western Australia now apply in the Territory as a result, although some laws have been repealed to take into account the unique status of the Territory. The first Island Assembly was elected in Sept. 1985, and is now replaced by the elected members of the Christmas Island Shire Council.

Extraction and export of rock phosphate dust is the main industry. The Government is also encouraging the private sector development of tourism.

Electricity. Production (1994–95) 20m. kWh.

Roads. In 1993 there were 205 km of roads, 917 passenger cars and 362 commercial vehicles.

Civil Aviation. There are twice-weekly flights to Perth (Western Australia), fortnightly to Singapore, and weekly to Jakarta (Indonesia).

Shipping. In 1991, 40,000 tonnes of cargo were loaded and 45,600 tonnes discharged at the port. 2,000 cu. metres of general cargo were also discharged.

Telecommunications (1992). There is one post office and 1,500 radio receivers. A local radio and television station operate 24 hours per day.

Religion. About 50% are Buddhists or Taoists, 16% Moslems and 30% Christians.

Education. In 1995 there was a district high school with 50 pre-primary, 369 primary and 73 secondary level pupils.

Health. In 1994 there were 2 doctors, a visiting dentist, a pharmacist, and 1 hospital with 10 beds.

Administrator: M. J. Grimes.

NORFOLK ISLAND. 29° 02' S. lat. 167° 57' E. long., area 3,455 ha, population, (June 1986), 1,977. The island was formerly part of the colony of New South Wales and then of Van Diemen's Land. It was a penal colony 1788–1814 and 1825–55. In 1856 it received all 194 descendants of the *Bounty* mutineers from

Pitcairn Island. It has been a distinct settlement since 1856, under the jurisdiction of the state of New South Wales; and finally by the passage of the Norfolk Island Act 1913, it was accepted as a Territory of the Australian Government. The Norfolk Island Act 1957 is the basis of the Territory's legislative, administrative and judicial systems. An Administrator, appointed by the Governor-General and responsible to the Minister for Territories and Local Government, is the senior government representative in the Territory.

The Norfolk Island Act 1979 gives Norfolk Island responsible legislative and executive government to enable it to run its own affairs to the greatest practicable extent. Wide powers are exercised by the Norfolk Island Legislative Assembly of 9 elected members, and by an Executive Council, comprising the executive members of the Legislative Assembly who have ministerial-type responsibilities. The seat of administration is Kingston, the only major settlement. The Act preserves the Commonwealth's responsibility for Norfolk Island as a Territory under its authority, indicating Parliament's intention that consideration would be given to an extension of the powers of the Legislative Assembly and the political and administrative institutions of Norfolk Island within 5 years. Some powers were transferred in 1985 and further transfers are being considered.

The office of the Administrator's financed from Commonwealth expenditure which in 1991–92 was approximately $A493,000; local revenue for 1990–91 totalled $A6,411,000; expenditure, $A6,222,000.

Public revenue is derived mainly from tourism, the sale of postage stamps, customs duties, liquor sales and company registration and licence fees. Residents are not liable for income tax on earnings within the Territory, nor are death and personal stamp duties levied.

In 1991–92, 27,351 visitors travelled to Norfolk. Descendants of the *Bounty* mutineer families constitute the 'original' settlers and are known locally as 'Islanders', while later settlers, mostly from Australia, New Zealand and UK, are identified as 'mainlanders'. Over the years the Islanders have preserved their own lifestyle and customs, and their language remains a mixture of West Country English, Gaelic and Tahitian. The resident population in 1993 was 2,665.

Roads. There are 80 km of roads (53 km paved), 1,802 passenger cars and 90 commercial vehicles.

Telecommunications. There is one post office and (1984) 1,090 telephones, 400 television and (1987) 1,500 radio receivers.

Press. There is one weekly with a circulation of 1,200.

SOCIAL INSTITUTIONS

Justice. The island's Supreme Court sits as required and a Court of Petty Sessions exercises both civil and criminal juristiction.

Religion. 40% of the population are Anglicans.

Education. A school is run by the New South Wales Department of Education covering pre-school to 10th year. It had 322 pupils at 30 June 1990.

Health. In 1985 there were 2 doctors, a pharmacist and a hospital with 20 beds.

Administrator: Alan Gardner Kerr.

HEARD AND McDONALD ISLANDS. These islands, about 2,500 miles south-west of Fremantle, were transferred from UK to Australian control as from 26 Dec. 1947. Heard Island is about 43 km long and 21 km wide; Shag Island is about 8 km north of Heard. The total area is 412 sq. km (159 sq. miles). The McDonald Islands are 42 km to the west of Heard. In 1985–88 a major research programme was set up by the Australian National Antarctic Research Expeditions to investigate the wildlife as part of international studies of the Southern Ocean ecosystem. Subsequent expeditions followed from June 1990 throughout 1992.

TERRITORY OF ASHMORE AND CARTIER ISLANDS. By Imperial Order in Council of 23 July 1931, Ashmore Islands (known as Middle, East and West Islands) and Cartier Island, situated in the Indian Ocean, some 320 km off the north-west coast of Australia (area, 5 sq. km), were placed under the authority of the Commonwealth.

Under the Ashmore and Cartier Islands Acceptance Act, 1933, the islands were accepted by the Commonwealth under the name of the Territory of Ashmore and Cartier Islands, and the effective date was proclaimed by the Governor-General to be 10 May 1934. It was the intention that the Territory should be administered by the State of Western Australia, but owing to administrative difficulties the Territory was annexed to and deemed to form part of the Northern Territory of Australia (by amendment to the Act in 1938) with relevant laws of the Northern Territory, applying to the Territory of Ashmore and Cartier Islands. Responsibility for the administration of Ashmore and Cartier Islands rests with the Minister for the Arts, Sport, the Environment, Tourism and Territories.

On 16 Aug. 1983 a national nature reserve was declared over Ashmore Reef and the area so declared is now known as Ashmore Reef National Nature Reserve.

The islands are uninhabited but Indonesian fishing boats, which have traditionally plied the area, fish within the Territory and land to collect water in accordance with an agreement between the governments of Australia and Indonesia.

TERRITORY OF CORAL SEA ISLANDS. The Coral Sea Islands became a Territory of the Commonwealth of Australia under the Coral Sea Islands Act 1969. It comprises scattered reefs and islands over a sea area of about 1m. sq. km. The Territory is uninhabited apart from a meteorological station on Willis Island.

Further Reading

Australian Department of Arts, Sport, the Environment, Tourism and Territories. *Christmas Island: Annual Report.—Cocos (Keeling) Islands: Annual Report.—Norfolk Island: Annual Report.*

NEW SOUTH WALES

KEY HISTORICAL EVENTS. New South Wales became a British possession in 1770; the first settlement was established at Port Jackson in 1788; a partially elective Council was established in 1843, and an elective Parliament and responsible government in 1856. New South Wales federated with the other Australian states to form the Commonwealth of Australia in 1901.

TERRITORY AND POPULATION. New South Wales is situated between the 29th and 38th parallels of S. lat. and 141st and 154th meridians of E. long., and comprises 309,433 sq. miles (801,600 sq. km), inclusive of Lord Howe Island, 6 sq. miles (17 sq. km), but exclusive of the Australian Capital Territory (911 sq. miles, 2,359 sq. km) and 28 sq. miles (73 sq. km) at Jervis Bay.

Lord Howe Island, 31° 33' 4" S., 159° 4' 26" E., which is part of New South Wales, is situated about 702 km north-east of Sydney; area, 1,654 ha, of which only about 120 ha are arable; resident population, estimate (30 June 1989), 320. The Island, which was discovered in 1788, is of volcanic origin. Mount Gower, the highest point, reaches a height of 866 metres.

The Lord Howe Island Board manages the affairs of the Island and supervises the Kentia palm-seed industry.

Census population of New South Wales (including full-blood Aboriginals from 1966):

	Males	*Females*	*Persons*	*Population per sq. km*	*Average annual increase % since previous census*
1901	710,264	645,091	1,355,355	2	1·86

	Males	*Females*	*Persons*	*Population per sq. km*	*Average annual increase % since previous census*
1911	857,698	789,036	1,646,734	2	1·97
1921	1,071,501	1,028,870	2,100,371	3	2·46
1933	1,318,471	1,282,376	2,600,847	3	1·76
1947	1,492,211	1,492,627	2,984,838	4	0·99
1954	1,720,860	1,702,669	3,423,529	4	1·98
1961	1,972,909	1,944,104	3,917,013	5	1·94
1971	2,307,210	2,293,970	4,601,180	6	1·66
1981	2,548,984	2,577,233	5,126,217	6	1·42
1986	2,684,570	2,717,311	5,401,881	7	1·05
1991	2,844,532	2,886,415	5,730,947	7	6·10

At 30 June 1993 the estimated resident population was 5,997,400 (3,015,300 females); population density, 7·5 per sq.km.

The state is divided into 12 *Statistical Divisions*. The population of these (in 1,000) in 1993 was: Sydney, 3,713·2; Hunter, 544·4; Illawarra, 359·6; Richmond-Tweed, 189; Mid-North Coast, 251·8; Northern, 186·9; North Western, 117·9; Central West, 172·5; South Eastern, 174·8; Murrumbidgee, 149·4; Murray, 110; Far West, 27·9. Population of the Statistical Subdivisions Newcastle (within Hunter) and Wollongong (within Illawarra) was 454·8 and 249·5 respectively.

Vital statistics for calendar years:

	Live births	*Marriages*	*Divorces*	*Deaths*
1991	87,367	39,594	13,151	42,467
1992	92,585	40,734	13,949	44,801
1993	89,354	39,993	16,358	43,069

The annual rates per 1,000 of mean estimated resident population in 1992 were: Births, 15·5; deaths, 7·5; marriages, 6·8; natural increase (1991), 7·62; infant mortality, 6·2 per 1,000 live births. Expectation of life in 1993: Males, 74·84 years, females, 80·79.

CONSTITUTION AND GOVERNMENT. Within the State there are three levels of government: The Commonwealth Government, with authority derived from a written constitution; the State Government with residual powers; the local government authorities with powers based upon a State Act of Parliament, operating within incorporated areas extending over almost 90% of the State.

The Constitution of New South Wales is drawn from several diverse sources; certain Imperial statutes such as the Commonwealth of Australia Constitution Act (1900); the Australian States Constitution Act (1907); an element of inherited English law; amendments to the Commonwealth of Australia Constitution Act; the (State) Constitution Act; the Australia Acts of 1986; the Constitution (Amendment) Act 1987 and certain other State Statutes; numerous legal decisions; and a large amount of English and local convention.

The Parliament of New South Wales may legislate for the peace, welfare and good government of the State in all matters not specifically reserved to the Commonwealth Government.

The State Legislature consists of the Sovereign, represented by the Governor, and two Houses of Parliament, the Legislative Council (upper house) and the Legislative Assembly (lower house).

Australian citizens aged 18 and over, and other British subjects who were enrolled prior to 26 Jan. 1984, men and women aged 18 years and over, are entitled to the franchise. Voting is compulsory. The optional preferential method of voting is used for both houses.

The Legislative Council has 42 members elected for a term of office equivalent to three terms of the Legislative Assembly, with 21 members retiring at the same time as the Legislative Assembly elections. The whole State constitutes a single electoral district. In 1995, the Council consisted of the following parties: Australian Labor Party (ALP), 17; Liberal Party of Australia (Lib), 12; National Party (NP), 6; Call to Australia Group (CTA), 2; Australian Democrats (AD), 2; A Better Future for Our Children, 1; Shooters' Party, 1; The Greens, 1.

The Legislative Assembly has 99 members elected in single seat electoral districts for a maximum period of 4 years. The Legislative Assembly elected in 1995 consisted of the following parties: ALP, 50; Lib, 29; NP, 17; ind, 3.

Governor: Gordon Samuels.

The New South Wales ALP Ministry, in Nov. 1995, was as follows:

Premier, Minister for Arts and Ethnic Affairs: Bob Carr (b. 1948).

Deputy Premier, Minister for Health and Aboriginal Affairs: Andrew Refshauge. *Treasury, State Development, Energy:* Michael Egan. *Police, Leader of the Government in the Lower House:* Paul Whelan. *Transport and Tourism:* Brian Langton. *Education and Training:* John Aquilina. *Environment:* Pam Allan. *Olympic Games, Public Works and Services, Roads:* Michael Knight. *Community Services and Aged and Disability Services:* Ron Dyer. *Attorney-General, Industrial Relations:* Jeff Shaw. *Land and Water Conservation:* Kim Yeadon. *Urban Affairs, Planning and Housing:* Craig Knowles. *Agriculture:* Richard Amery. *Small Business and Regional Development:* Carl Scully. *Corrective Services:* Bob Debus. *Gaming and Racing:* Richard Face. *Consumer Affairs and Status of Women:* Faye Lo Po. *Mineral Resources and Fisheries:* Bob Martin. *Sport and Recreation:* Gabrielle Harrison. *Local Government:* Ernie Page.

The *Speaker* is John Murray.

Local Government. A system of local government extends over most of the State, including the whole of the Eastern and Central land divisions and almost three-quarters of the sparsely populated Western division. Since 1 July 1993, an area established for local government purposes is known as a council or city council, and the terms municipality or shire have been abandoned (except for Sutherland Shire). At 1 July 1993 there were 39 city councils and 138 councils. In addition there is one unincorporated area in the far west of the State. Local government councils most importantly provide the general services of administration, health, community amenities, recreation and culture, roads and debt servicing. County councils administer electricity or water supply or render other local services of common benefit in districts which comprise a number of councils.

ECONOMY

Budget. State Government outlays (in $A1m.) for financial years ending 30 June:

	1990–91	*1991–92*	*1992–93*
General public services	989	1,374	1,066
Public order and safety	1,658	1,673	1,692
Education	5,532	5,759	6,169
Health	3,458	3,426	3,567
Social security and welfare	1,305	1,495	1,507
Housing and community amenities	1,150	1,373	1,450
Recreation and culture	443	506	643
Fuel and energy	482	707	587
Agriculture, forestry and fishing	491	498	530
Mining, manufacturing and construction	60	16	14
Transport and communications	2,886	2,905	3,271
Other economic affairs	329	368	410
Other purposes	4,176	4,111	2,818
Total	*22,960*	*24,211*	*23,723*

State Government receipts (in $A1m.) for 1992–93 included taxes, fees and fines, 9,308 and Commonwealth Government grant, 9,724.

State Government taxes, fees and fines, by type:

	1990–91	*1991–92*	*1992–93*
Employers' payroll taxes	2,288	2,344	2,329
Taxes on property—			
Taxes on immovable property	859	935	669
Taxes on financial and capital transactions	1,580	1,823	1,941
Taxes on provision of goods and services—			
Excises and levies	17	16	21
Taxes on gambling	771	780	834

	1990–91	*1991–92*	*1992–93*
Taxes on insurance	536	570	643
Taxes on goods and performance of activities—			
Motor vehicle taxes	943	892	1,000
Franchise taxes	941	1,052	1,294
Other taxes on use of goods etc.	–	17	34
Fees and fines—			
Compulsory fees	313	358	350
Fines	155	182	194

Banking and Finance. Banking business is transacted chiefly by the Commonwealth Bank of Australia, the State Bank of New South Wales (government banks) and 3 private banks. In June 1993, 32 banking groups (15 domestic and 17 foreign) operated 2,439 branches and 1,530 agencies in New South Wales.

Lending activity of financial institutions in New South Wales in 1991–92 comprised (in $A1m.): Business loans, 3,602·3; personal, 617·5; house purchase, 1,015·1; lease financing, 248·5.

ENERGY AND NATURAL RESOURCES

Electricity. In 1994 the total nominal capacity of the Electricity Commission of New South Wales system was 11,520 MW. 57,794m. kWh were produced in 1992–93.

Minerals. New South Wales contains extensive mineral deposits. 16,833 were working in mining at 30 June 1993. The value of output in mining and quarrying in 1990–91 was $A4,372m. (including coal $A3,133m.). The value in 1992–93 was $A1,010·5m. (excluding coal), of which metallic minerals $A422·6m., construction materials $A437·6m. and industrial minerals $A150·3m. Output of principal products:

	1990–91	*1991–92*	*1992–93*
Antimony (tonnes)	1,558	1,839	2,114
Brick clay and shale (1,000 tonnes)	2,549	2,584	2,729
Coal (1,000 tonnes)	80,116	83,874	84,211
Copper (tonnes)	103,933	130,567	174,703
Gold (kg)	11,825	10,929	10,309
Lead (tonnes)	312,793	300,051	315,997
Limestone (1,000 tonnes)	3,318	3,410	3,554
Magnesite (tonne)	36,212	22,832	26,159
Magnetite (tonne)	46,263	56,682	45,670
Rutile (tonnes)	62,837	55,693	50,386
Sand (1,000 tonnes)	10,269	10,127	10,647
Silver concentrates (tonnes)	6,296	–	–
Zinc (tonnes)	665,070	580,080	586,300
Zircon (tonnes)	47,128	54,807	44,510

Agriculture. In 1992–93 GDP at factor cost for agriculture, forestry, hunting and fishing was $A2,802m. Farm income (including Australian Capital Territory) was $A73m. At 31 March 1993 there were 35,285 establishments with agricultural activity. Area under cultivation (in ha) during 3 years (ended 31 March) and the principal crops (in tonnes) produced were as follows (Data relates to farms whose estimated value of agricultural operations was $A20,000 or more at the census):

	1991	*1992*	*1993*
Area under cultivation (ha)	4,361,193	4,148,455	4,188,124

		1991		*1992*		*1993*	
Principal crops		*Sown area*	*Production*	*Sown area*	*Production*	*Sown area*	*Production*
Wheat	Grain	2,165,755	4,127,586	1,499,321	2,182,990	1,694,016	3,582,628
	Hay	19,327	51,513	30,000	64,000	21,000	60,000
Barley	Grain	463,250	822,453	517,464	748,749	559,711	1,043,772
Oats	Grain	374,283	538,350	456,662	578,830	447,638	761,376
	Hay	51,929	143,751	91,000	252,000	65,000	225,000
Grain Sorghum		83,649	...	146,957	...	117,684	...
Potatoes		6,023	119,542	6,297	122,521	6,487	134,444
Lucerne (hay)		77,753	340,116	83,600	385,000	88,000	447,000
Rice		85,102	719,000	109,186	929,000	104,598	846,000

Principal crops	1991 Sown area	1991 Production	1992 Sown area	1992 Production	1993 Sown area	1993 Production
Cotton (raw and seed)	202,036	1,167,035	225,100	1,318,646	204,053	962,734
Oilseeds	133,804	169,912	154,597	191,485	118,640	198,401

In 1993, 15,536 ha of sugar-cane were cut for crushing. The total area under grapes was 12,681 (including 689 not bearing) ha; the production of table grapes was 7,195 tonnes; of wine grapes, 139,336 tonnes; for drying, 28,082 tonnes (fresh weight).

In 1993, there were 3,966 ha of banana plantations; production, 45,409 tonnes. There were 4·39m. citrus fruit trees; production, 294,922 tonnes.

At 31 March 1993 there were 48·1m. sheep and lambs, 5·8m. cattle and 0·8m. pigs. The production of shorn and crutched wool in 1992–93 was 236,834 tonnes (greasy). In the year ended 30 June 1993 production of butter was 3,377 tonnes; cheese, 16,919 tonnes, and pig meat, 94,760 tonnes.

INDUSTRY AND TRADE

Industry. A wide range of manufacturing is undertaken in the Sydney area, and there are large iron and steel works near the coalfields at Newcastle and Port Kembla.

Manufacturing establishments' operations, 1991–92:

Industry	*No. of establishments* [1]	*No. of persons employed* [2]	*Wages and salaries* [3] *($A1m.)*	*Turnover ($A1m.)*
Food, beverages and tobacco	1,173	50,419	1,482·9	11,413·4
Textiles	278	6,424	194·7	1,270·6
Clothing and footwear	875	17,203	384·1	1,792·5
Wood, wood products and furniture	1,999	22,481	546·1	2,520·7
Paper, paper products, printing and publishing	1,950	37,782	1,256·2	5,617·6
Chemical, petroleum and coal products	455	21,809	860·8	8,763·2
Non-metallic mineral products	556	11,813	422·6	2,520·5
Basic metal products	319	27,819	1,182·1	8,007·7
Fabricated metal products	2,434	31,849	880·3	4,136·1
Transport equipment	592	16,559	595·2	2,195·6
Other machinery and equipment	2,156	46,571	1,443·9	6,788·8
Miscellaneous manufacturing	1,329	18,415	508·5	1,768·3
Total manufacturing	14,116	309,144	9,757·3	57,795·0

[1] Operating at 30 June 1992.
[2] Persons employed at 30 June 1992, including working proprietors.
[3] Excludes drawings of working proprietors.

Some of the principal articles manufactured in 1993–94 were:

Article	*Quantity*	*Article*	*Quantity*
Flour (1,000 tonnes)	649	Ready mixed concrete (1,000 cu. metres)	4,794
Footwear (1,000 pairs)	4,363	Clay bricks (1m.)	716
Aluminium products (tonnes)	193,218		

Value of building jobs, 1992–93:

Commenced	*Under construction*	*Completed*
$A7,925·8m.	$A8,214·7m.	$A9,136·6m.

Value of building work, 1992–93: Private sector, $A7,102·6m.; public sector, $A1,592·4m.

Labour. In May 1994, 2,645,400 persons were employed out of a total workforce of 2,921,600. 276,200 were unemployed. In May 1994, 469,100 persons were employed as clerks, 411,900 as salespersons and personal service workers, 402,500 as labourers and related workers, 376,200 as professionals, 352,000 as tradepersons, 293,800 as managers and administrators, 178,100 as plant and machine operators and drivers, and 161,700 as para-professionals.

Industrial tribunals are authorized to fix minimum rates of wages and other conditions of employment. Their awards may be enforced by law, as may be industrial agreements between employers and organizations of employees, when registered.

The principal State arbitration and conciliation tribunal is the Industrial Commission of New South Wales. The Commission is empowered to exercise all the powers conferred on subsidiary tribunals, and has in addition authority to determine any widely defined 'industrial matter', to adjudicate in case of illegal strikes and lockouts, to investigate union ballots when irregularities are alleged and to hear appeals from subsidiary tribunals. Subsidiary tribunals are Conciliation Committees for various industries, each having an equal number representing employers and employees and a Conciliation Commissioner as chairman.

Trade Unions. Registration of trade unions is effected under the New South Wales Trade Union Act 1881, which follows substantially the Trade Union Acts of 1871 and 1876 of England. Registration confers a quasi-corporate existence with power to hold property, to sue and be sued, etc., and the various classes of employees covered by the union are required to be prescribed by the constitution of the union. For the purpose of bringing an industry under the review of the State industrial tribunals, or participating in proceedings relating to disputes before Commonwealth tribunals, employees and employers must be registered as industrial unions, under State or Commonwealth industrial legislation respectively. At 30 June 1993, there were 93 trade unions with a total membership of 1,037,500. In Aug. 1993 38% of employees were members of trade unions.

Commerce. External commerce, exclusive of inter-state trade, is included in the statement of the commerce of Australia. Overseas commerce of New South Wales in $A1m. for years ending 30 June:

	Imports	*Exports*		*Imports*	*Exports*
1988–89	20,871	10,908	1991–92	23,317	11,700
1989–90	23,385	12,361	1992–93	26,435	13,196
1990–91	22,383	11,992	1993–94	28,495	14,694

The major commodities exported in 1993–94 (in $A1m.) were coal briquettes (3,035·1), alumiinium (867·1), iron and steel (855·2), wool and other animal hair (830·2), meat (757·4) and office machines and computers (723·7). Principal imports were computers (2,071·9), parts and accessories for computers (1,557·2), private cars (1,380·9) and medical and pharmaceutical products (1,114·2).

Principal destinations of exports in 1993–94 (in $A1m.) were Japan (3,759·1), New Zealand (1,242·9), South Korea (1,158·2), USA (1,062·3) and Taiwan (809·3). Major sources of supply were USA (6,833·8), Japan (4,593·2), UK (1,831·7), Germany (1,457) and New Zealand (1,370·1).

Tourism. In the year ended 30 June 1994, 1,396,800 overseas visitors arrived for short term visits. At 30 June 1994 there were 1,728 hotels and motels providing 57,012 rooms, and 794 caravan parks.

COMMUNICATIONS

Roads. In 1993 there were some 205,000 km of public roads of all sorts. The Roads and Traffic Authority of New South Wales is responsible for the administration and upkeep of major roads. In 1994 there were 39,300 km of roads under its control, including 2,900 km of national highways, 14,000 km of state roads and 22,400 km of regional and local roads.

The number of registered motor vehicles (excluding tractors and trailers) at 21 June 1994 was 3,262,600, including 2,498,800 passenger vehicles, 550,100 light commercial vehicles, 130,300 trucks, 11,000 buses and 72,300 motor cycles. There were 631 fatalities in road accidents in 1993–94.

Railways. At 30 June 1994, 9,000 km of government railway were open (618 km electrified). In 1993–94, 237m. passengers were carried and 65·6m. tonnes of freight. Also open for traffic are 325 km of Victorian Government railways which extend over the border; 68 km of private railways (mainly in mining districts) and 53 km of Commonwealth Government-owned track.

Civil Aviation. Sydney is the major airport in New South Wales and Australia's principal international air terminal.

Shipping. The main ports are at Sydney, Newcastle, Port Kembla and Botany Bay. Visits by vessels to the ports of New South Wales in 1992–93 totalled 4,245 (97·43m. GRT). The number of overseas vessels which entered in 1992–93 was 3,091.

SOCIAL INSTITUTIONS

Justice. Legal processes may be conducted in Local Courts presided over by magistrates or in higher courts (District Court or Supreme Court) presided over by judges. There is also an appellate jurisdiction. Persons charged with the more serious crimes must be tried before a higher court.

Children's Courts have been established with the object of removing children as far as possible from the atmosphere of a public court. There are also a number of tribunals exercising special jurisdiction, *e.g.*, the Industrial Commission and the Compensation Court.

At 6 June 1993 there were 6,301 persons in prison.

Religion. At the 1991 census of those who stated a religion, 29·5% were Roman Catholic and 27·3% Anglican. Non-Christian religions accounted for 3·5%.

Education. The State Government maintains a system of free primary and secondary education, and attendance at school is compulsory from 6 to 15 years of age. Non-government schools are subject to government inspection.

In 1993 there were 2,184 government schools with 757,975 pupils (446,911 primary and 311,064 secondary) and 47,197 teachers, and 851 non-government schools with 294,121 pupils (154,633 primary and 139,488 secondary) and 18,761 teachers.

There were 173,976 students in higher education in 1993.

The University of Sydney, founded in 1850, had 30,343 students in 1993. There are 7 colleges providing residential facilities at the university. The University of New England at Armidale, previously affiliated with the University of Sydney, was incorporated in 1954, and in 1993 had 20,231 students.

The University of New South Wales was established in 1949. Enrolments in 1993 numbered 26,073. There are 7 colleges providing residential facilities at the university. The University of Newcastle, previously affiliated with the University of New South Wales, was granted autonomy from 1965, and in 1993 had 14,221 students. The University of Wollongong, also previously associated with the University of New South Wales, became autonomous in 1975, and in 1993 had 11,056 students. Macquarie University in Sydney, established in 1964, had 15,549 students in 1993. In 1993 the University of Technology, Sydney, had 20,518 students, the University of Western Sydney, 19,697, and Charles Sturt University, 15,240.

Colleges of advanced education were merged with universities in 1990.

Post-school technical and further education is provided at State TAFE colleges. Enrolments in 1993 totalled 423,614 (86% being part-time).

Social Welfare. The Commonwealth Government makes provision for social benefits, such as age and disability pensions, widows' pensions, supporting parents' benefits, family allowances, and unemployment, sickness and special benefits.

The number of age and disability pensions (including wives' and carers' pensions) current in New South Wales on 30 June 1993 was: Age, 536,329 (carers, 13,111); disability, 179,004 (carers, 39,404). Expenditure for the year ended 30 June 1993 was $A3,730m. for age pensions and $A1,349m. for disability pensions.

In addition there were 24,466 widows' pensions current at 30 June 1993. Expenditure on widows' pensions totalled $A209m. Sole parents' benefits 101,931; expenditure was $A1,011m.

Under the Basic Family Payment scheme, which commenced in 1993, at 30 June 1993 1,225,066 children and students in 635,534 families were receiving payments totalling $A710m.

302,461 unemployment, 15,222 sickness and 12,247 special benefits were payable in June 1993 totalling $A2,809m. (monthly average).

Direct State Government social welfare services are limited, for the most part, to the assistance of persons not eligible for Commonwealth Government pensions or benefits and the provision of certain forms of assistance not available from the Commonwealth Government. The State also subsidizes many approved services for needy persons.

Health. At 30 June 1993 there were 20,779 medical practitioners, 3,715 dentists and 71,361 nurses. In 1993 there were 198 public hospitals with 19,293 beds and 90 private hospitals with 6,094 beds.

Further Reading

Statistical Information: The NSW Government Statistician's Office was established in 1886, and in 1957 was integrated with the Commonwealth Bureau of Census and Statistics (now called the Australian Bureau of Statistics). *Deputy Commonwealth Statistician:* Denis Farrell. Its principal publications are:

New South Wales Year Book (1886/87–1900/01 under the title *Wealth and Progress of New South Wales*). Annual.—*Regional Statistics.—New South Wales Pocket Year Book.—Monthly Summary of Statistics.—New South Wales in Brief.*

State Library: The State Library of NSW, Macquarie St., Sydney.

QUEENSLAND

TERRITORY AND POPULATION. Queensland comprises the whole northeastern portion of the Australian continent, including the adjacent islands in the Pacific Ocean and in the Gulf of Carpentaria. Estimated area 1,727,000 sq. km.

The increase in the population as shown by the censuses since 1901 has been as follows (including Aboriginals from 1966):

	Census counts			*Intercensal increase*	
Year	*Males*	*Females*	*Total*	*Numerical*	*Rate per annum %*
1901	277,003	221,126	498,129	—	—
1911	329,506	276,307	605,813	107,684	1·98
1921	398,969	357,003	755,972	150,159	2·24
1933	497,217	450,317	947,534	191,562	1·86
1947	567,471	538,944	1,106,415	158,881	1·11
1954	676,252	642,007	1,318,259	211,844	2·53
1961	774,579	744,249	1,518,828	200,569	2·04
1966	849,390	824,934	1,674,324	144,857	1·84
1971	921,665	905,400	1,827,065	152,741	1·76
1976	1,024,611	1,012,586	2,037,197	210,132	2·20
1981	1,153,404	1,141,719	2,295,123	257,926	2·41
1986	1,295,630	1,291,685	2,587,315	292,192	2·43
1991	1,482,406	1,495,404	2,977,810	390,495	2·60

At the 1991 census there were 70,070 Aboriginals.

Since the 1981 census, official population estimates are according to place of usual residence and are referred to as estimated resident population. Estimated resident population at 30 June 1993, 3,112,600.

Statistics on birthplaces from the 1991 census are as follows: Australia, 80·7% (83·6% in 1986); UK and Ireland, 6·2% (6·1%); other countries, 17·1% (14·4%); at sea and not stated, 2·3% (1·4%).

Vital statistics (including Aboriginals) for calendar years:

	Total births	*Marriages*	*Divorces*	*Deaths*
1990	44,868	19,671	8,509	19,321
1991	44,160	19,844	8,934	19,175
1992	46,240	20,316	8,984	20,496

The annual rates per 1,000 population in 1992 were: Marriages, 6·7; births, 15.2; deaths, 6·8. The infant death rate was 7·9 per 1,000 live births.

Brisbane, the capital, had at 30 June 1991 (estimate) a resident population of 1,358,000 (Statistical Division). The estimated resident populations of the other major centres (Statistical Districts) at 30 June 1993 were: Gold Coast-Tweed, (including that part in New South Wales) 299,870; Townsville, 121,581; Sunshine Coast, 133,306; Cairns, 92,830; Rockhampton, 65,868; Mackay, 55,772; Bundaberg, 52,267 and Gladstone, 35,055.

CONSTITUTION AND GOVERNMENT. Queensland, formerly a portion of New South Wales, was formed into a separate colony in 1859, and responsible government was conferred. The power of making laws and imposing taxes is vested in a parliament of one house—the *Legislative Assembly*, which comprises 89 members, returned from 4 electoral zones for 3 years, elected from single-member constituencies at compulsory ballot. Members are entitled to $A54,500 per annum, with individual electorate allowances for travelling, postage, etc., of from $A21,525 to $A43,884.

Queensland elects 25 members to the Commonwealth House of Representatives.

The Elections Act, 1983, provides franchise for all males and females, 18 years of age and over, qualified by 6 months' residence in Australia and 3 months in the electoral district.

At the elections to the Legislative Assembly of Sept. 1992 the Australian Labor Party won 55 seats, the National Party, 25 and the Liberal Party, 9. (Previous Assembly: Labor, 26; National, 54; Liberal, 9).

Governor of Queensland: Mrs Leneen Forde (assumed office 29 July 1992).

An 18-member *Executive Council* is elected from the party in power in the Legislative Assembly. In Dec. 1994 it consisted of:

Premier, Minister for Economic and Trade Development: Wayne Goss.

Deputy Premier, Minister for Tourism, Sport and Youth: Tom Burns. *Police and Corrective Services:* Paul Braddy. *Treasurer:* Keith De Lacy. *Primary Industries, Racing:* Bob Gibbs. *Transport and Minister Assisting the Premier on Economic and Trade Development:* Jim Elder. *Employment and Training, Minister Assisting the Premier on Public Service Matters:* Wendy Edmond. *Minerals and Energy:* Tony McGrady. *Health:* Peter Beattie. *Education:* David Hamill. *Environment and Heritage:* Thomas Barton. *Justice, Attorney-General, Industrial Relations, the Arts:* Matt Foley. *Family and Community Services, Minister Assisting the Premier on the Status of Women:* Margaret Woodgate. *Administrative Services:* Glen Milliner. *Business, Industry and Regional Development:* Ken Hayward. *Lands:* Kenneth McElligott. *Emergency Services, Consumer Affairs:* Kenneth Davies. *Housing, Local Government and Planning, Rural Communities, Provision of Infrastructure for Aboriginal and Torres Strait Islander Committees:* Terence Mackenroth.

Ministers have a salary of $A88,229, the Premier receives $A111,524, the Deputy Premier, $A95,941, and the Leader of the Opposition, $A79,666.

Local Government. At 1 July 1994, following a reorganization of local government boundaries, the state was subdivided into 18 cities, 3 towns and 107 shires. These are under the management of aldermen or councillors, who are elected by all persons 18 years and over. Elections were held on 26 March 1994. In addition to government grants and subsidies, local authority revenue is derived from general rates, paid by landowners on the unimproved capital value of land, and by charging for some specific services.

For the year ended 30 June 1993, the receipts and expenditure (including loans) for the 134 local authorities balanced at $A1,801·1m.

ECONOMY

Budget. In 1992–93 current outlays by the state totalled $A8,818·8m., of which $A6,095·9m. were general government final consumption expenditure, and capital outlays totalled $A2,644·2m. Revenue and grants received totalled $A12,313·4m.

Commonwealth payments for current purposes totalled $A4,915·7m. and for capital purposes, $A841·4m.

Banking and Finance. In June 1993 deposits at all banks in Queensland totalled $A27,846m., of which $A7,387m. were current, $A12,479m. were term deposits and $A4,194m. were investment savings. Other lending totalled $A30,677m. In 1992 there were 9 building societies with total assets of $A3,567·42m.

ENERGY AND NATURAL RESOURCES

Electricity. Installed capacity in 1991–92 was 5,285 MW. Output, 28·92m. MWh, of which 22·9m. MWh to 1·25m. consumers. Some 3% of production is hydro-electric.

Water. In the western portion of the State water is comparatively easily found by sinking artesian bores. At 30 June 1988, 3,700 such bores had been drilled, of which 2,595 were flowing.

Minerals. Principal minerals produced during 1992–93 (in tonnes): Copper, 229,281; coal, 85,301,000; lead, 233,415; zinc, 331,940; bauxite, 8·77m.; mineral sands concentrates, 269,253; silver, 603 (kg); gold, 33,827 (kg); crude oil, 1,085m. litres. Value of output, at the mine, was $A5,626·8m.

Agriculture. In 1992–93 there were 25,131 agricultural establishments farming 149·52m. ha. Livestock on farms and stations at 31 March 1993 numbered 9·87m. cattle, 13·4m. sheep and 617,000 pigs. Total wool production in the year ended 31 March 1993, 60,290 tonnes. The total area under crops during 1992–93 was 2·37m. ha.

	Area (ha)		*Production (tonnes)*	
Crop	*1991–92*	*1992–93*	*1991–92*	*1992–93*
Sugar-cane, crushed	314,048	312,123	19,225,000	26,292,000
Wheat	491,651	669,150	344,000	735,000
Maize	33,676	27,156	141,000	75,000
Sorghum	420,000	308,000	1,045,000	315,000
Barley	128,000	189,000	70,000	285,000
Potatoes	5,000	5,334	113,000	125,230
Pumpkins	3,000	3,250	33,000	35,627
Tomatoes	4,000	4,065	104,000	114,926
Peanuts	21,000	21,877	38,000	31,014
Tobacco	3,000	2,244	7,000	6,183
Apples [1]	2,000	2,000	25,000	29,000
Grapes [2]	943	908	3,612	4,736
Citrus [1]	502	...	58,641	58,280
Bananas [2]	5,441	4,972	113,554	147,787
Pineapples [2]	5,740	3,414	133,218	142,336
Green forage and hay [3]	492,000	435,000	352,000	253,000
Cotton (raw)	87,188	82,150	112,545	104,418

[1] Area of trees 6 years and over. [2] Bearing area only.
[3] Excluding lucerne and other pastures.

The gross value of agricultural commodity production (in $A1m.) during 1992–93, amounted to 4,760, which comprised crops (2,293), livestock disposals (1,961) and livestock products (506).

Forestry. A considerable area consists of natural forest, eucalyptus, pine and cabinet woods being the timbers mostly in evidence; a large quantity of ornamental woods is utilized by cabinet makers. The amount of sawn timber processed in 1992–93 was 640,927 cu. metres.

INDUSTRY AND TRADE

Industry. In 1991–92, there were 6,705 establishments with 4 or more workers, employing 122,893 persons, and producing goods and services worth $A23,147m. The manufacturing establishments contributing most to the overall production were those predominantly engaged in the processing of food, beverages and tobacco.

Labour. In 1994 the labour force numbered 1,570,200, of whom 1,423,200 (599,000 females) were employed. Unemployment was 9·4%.

Trade Unions. There were 94 trade unions in June 1992 with 455,200 members.

Commerce. Total value of direct overseas imports and exports (in $A1,000) f.o.b. port of shipment for both imports and exports:

	1987–88	*1988–89*	*1989–90*	*1990–91*	*1991–92*
Imports	2,844,208	3,788,296	4,394,340	4,903,223	5,626,691
Exports	8,289,659	9,083,994	10,901,410	10,801,738	10,857,561

In 1992–93 interstate exports totalled $A4,235,353 and imports $A9,768,709. Chief sources of imports in 1992–93 were Japan ($A1,499·2m.), USA ($A974·4m.), Papua New Guinea ($A958·4m.), EEC excluding UK ($A432·7m.), New Zealand ($A367m.). Exports went chiefly to Japan ($A4,267·9m.), EEC excluding UK ($A1,196·1m.), South Korea ($A909·6m.), USA ($A849m.), Taiwan ($A545·1m.).

The chief exports overseas in 1992–93 (in $A1m.) were: Coal (4,379·2); meat and meat preparations (1,779·4); sugar (986·5); non-ferrous metals (934·6); metalliferous ores and metal scrap (595·7); machinery and transport equipment (408·7). Principal overseas imports were: Road vehicles (1,181·2); machinery and equipment (914·1); non-monetary gold (783·6); petroleum and petroleum products (686·4).

Tourism. Overseas visitors to Australia who specified Queensland as their primary destination numbered 857,100 in 1993.

COMMUNICATIONS

Roads. At 30 June 1993 there were 175,020 km of roads. Of these, 61,538 km were surfaced with sealed pavement.

At 30 June 1993 motor vehicles registered (in 1,000) totalled 1,895, comprising 1,393·6 cars and station wagons, 348 utilities and panel vans, 74·6 trucks, 11·5 buses and 67·3 motor cycles. There were 395 fatalities in road accidents in 1993.

Railways. Queensland Rail is owned by the State government. Total length of line at 30 June 1993 was 9,375 km, of which 2,460 km were electrified. In 1993–94, 39·3m. passengers and 99·2m. tonnes of freight were carried.

Civil Aviation. Queensland is well served with a network of air services, with overseas and interstate connexions. Subsidiary companies provide planes for taxi and charter work, and the Flying Doctor Service operates throughout western Queensland. In 1993 there were 134 licensed airports. In 1992-93 (provisional) Brisbane handled 1,428,860 international passengers with 41,118 tonnes of freight, Cairns, 600,147 with 7,671 tonnes and Townsville, 2,874 with 151 tonnes. The number of aircraft registered at 30 June 1993 was 2,113.

Shipping. In 1992–93, cargo discharged was 22·19m. mass tonnes and cargo loaded was 97·65m. mass tonnes.

Telecommunications. There were 1·45m. telephones in 1993. In 1993 there were 225 post offices and 488 postal agencies. In addition to the national networks Queensland is served by 13 public radio stations (non-profit-making), 44 commercial radio stations and 3 commercial TV channels.

SOCIAL INSTITUTIONS

Justice. Justice is administered by Higher Courts (Supreme and District), Magistrates' Courts and Children's Courts. The Supreme Court comprises the Chief Justice, and 19 judges; the District Courts, 30 district court judges of whom 1 is chairman. Stipendiary magistrates preside over the Magistrates' and Children's Courts, except in the smaller centres, where justices of the peace officiate. A parole board may recommend prisoners for release.

The total number of appearances resulting in conviction as the most serious outcome in the Higher Courts in 1991–92 was 3,809; summary convictions in Magistrates' Courts totalled 139,189, and proven offences in Children's Courts (1992-93) totalled 4,294. At 30 June 1993 there were 11 correctional centres with 2,068 prisoners (79 women). The total police force was 6,504 at 30 June 1993.

Religion. Religious affiliation at the 1991 census: Roman Catholic, 25·4%; Anglican, 25·2%; Uniting Church, 10·4%; Presbyterian, 5·4%; Lutheran, 2·3%; Baptist, 1·9%; other Christian, 6·4%; non-Christian, 1%; no religion, 11·6%; not stated, 10%.

Education. Education is compulsory between the ages of 6 and 15 years and is provided free in government schools.

At July 1992, pre-school education and child care was provided at 742 government and 800 non-government centres with 6,448 teaching and other staff and 92,874 children.

Primary and secondary education comprises 12 years of full-time formal schooling and is provided by both the government and non-government sectors. At July 1993, the State administered 1,326 schools with 260,493 primary students and 143,770 secondary students. In 1992–93 there were 25,782 teachers in government schools. There were 403 private schools in July 1993 with 72,343 primary students and 67,125 secondary students. Educational programmes at private schools were provided by 8,477 teachers in 1992–93.

In 1992 there were 23,140 full-time students at TAFE institutes. The 6 universities and other higher education institutes had 93,955 full-time students in 1992–93. Teaching staff totalled 12,626.

Health. In 1991-92 there were 192 hospitals (146 public with over 10,000 beds), 8 psychiatric institutions and 200 nursing care homes. At 24 Dec. 1993 there were 6,455 doctors, 2,603 specialists, 1,660 dentists and 35,875 registered nurses.

Social Welfare. Welfare institutions providing shelter and social care for the aged, the handicapped, and children, are maintained or assisted by the State. A child health service is provided throughout the State. Age, invalid, widows', disability and war service pensions, family allowances, and unemployment and sickness benefits are paid by the Federal Government. At 30 June 1993 age pensioners in the State numbered 258,607 and invalid/disability support pensioners, 88,007 (including wife and carer pensioners); disability pensioners, 66,117; and service pensioners, 72,377 (including dependants).

There were 65,352 widows' and sole parent pensions current at 30 June 1993, and at the same date basic family payment was being paid for 688,742 children under 16 years and eligible students aged 16 to 24 years in 356,043 families.

Further Reading

Statistical Information: The Statistical Office (313 Adelaide St., Brisbane) was set up in 1859. *Deputy Commonwealth Statistician:* R. A. Crockett. *A Queensland Official Year Book* was issued in 1901, the annual *ABC of Queensland Statistics* from 1905 to 1936 with exception of 1918 and 1922. Present publications include: *Queensland Year Book.* Annual, from 1937 (omitting 1942, 1943, 1944, 1987, 1991).—*Queensland Pocket Year Book.* Annual from 1950.—*Monthly Summary of Statistics, Queensland.* From Jan. 1961

Australian Sugar Year Book. Brisbane, from 1941
Johnston, W. R., *A Bibliography of Queensland History.* Brisbane, 1981.—*The Call of the Land: A History of Queensland to the Present Day.* Brisbane, 1982
Johnston, W. R. and Zerner, M., *Guide to the History of Queensland.* Brisbane, 1985

State Library: The State Library of Queensland, Queensland Cultural Centre, South Bank, South Brisbane.

SOUTH AUSTRALIA

TERRITORY AND POPULATION. The total area of South Australia is 380,070 sq. miles (984,377 sq. km). The settled part is divided into counties and hundreds. There are 49 counties proclaimed, covering 23m. ha, of which 19m. ha are occupied. Outside this area there are extensive pastoral districts, covering 76m. ha, 49m. of which are under pastoral leases.

At the 1991 census the population was 1,446,299 (728,677 females; 16,249 Aboriginal and Torres Strait Islander people, of whom 8,323 were female).

Estimated mean resident population at 31 Dec. 1993 was 1,463,200.

Vital statistics:

	Live Births	Marriages	Divorces	Deaths
1991	19,640	9,392	4,215	11,176
1992	19,311	9,423	4,074	10,925
1993	20,078	. . .	4,063	11,528

The infant mortality rate in 1992 was 6·1 per 1,000 live births.

The Adelaide Statistical Division had 1,023,617 persons at the 1991 census in 22 cities and 8 municipalities and other districts. Cities outside this area (with 1991 census populations) are Whyalla (25,526), Mount Gambier (21,153), Port Augusta (14,595), Port Pirie (14,110) and Port Lincoln (11,345).

CONSTITUTION AND GOVERNMENT. South Australia was formed into a British province by letters patent of Feb. 1836, and a partially elective Legislative Council was established in 1851. The present Constitution dates from 24 Oct. 1856. It vests the legislative power in an elected Parliament, consisting of a Legislative Council and a House of Assembly. The former is composed of 22 members. Every 4 years half the members retire, and the resulting vacancies are filled at a general election on the basis of proportional representation with the State as one multi-member electorate. The qualifications of an elector are, to be an Australian citizen, or a British subject who on 25 Jan. 1984 was enrolled on a Commonwealth electoral roll and/or at some time between 26 Oct. 1983 and 25 Jan. 1984 inclusive was enrolled on an electoral roll for a South Australian Assembly district or a Commonwealth electoral roll in any State. The person must be of at least 18 years of age and have lived continuously in Australia for at least 6 months, in South Australia for at least 3 months and in the sub-division for which he is enrolled at least 1 month. War service may substitute for residential qualifications in some cases. By the Constitution Act Amendment Act, 1894, the franchise was extended to women, who voted for the first time at the general election of 25 April 1896. The qualifications for election as a member of both Houses are the same as for an elector. Certain persons are ineligible for election to either House.

The House of Assembly consists of 47 members elected for 4 years, representing single electorates. Election of members of both Houses takes place by preferential secret ballot. Voting is compulsory for those on the Electoral Roll.

The House of Assembly, elected on 11 Dec. 1993, consists of the following members: Liberal Party of Australia (LP), 36; Australian Labor Party (ALP), 11. The Legislative Council consists of 11 LP, 9 ALP and 2 Australian Democrat members.

Electors enrolled (11 Dec. 1993) numbered 1,006,035.

The executive power is vested in a Governor appointed by the Crown and an Executive Council, consisting of the Governor and the Ministers of the Crown. The Governor has the power to dissolve the House of Assembly but not the Legislative Council unless that Chamber has twice consecutively with an election intervening defeated the same or substantially the same Bill passed in the House of Assembly by an absolute majority.

Governor: Dame Hon. Roma Mitchell, AC, DBE.

In Dec. 1995 the Liberal Ministry was as follows:

Premier, Minister for Multicultural and Ethnic Affairs: The Hon. Dean Brown.

Deputy Premier, Treasurer: The Hon. Stephen John Baker. *Minister for Education and Children's Services:* The Hon. Robert Ivan Lucas. *Attorney-General, Minister for Consumer Affairs:* The Hon. Kenneth Trevor Griffin. *Minister for Tourism, Minister for Industrial Affairs:* The Hon. Graham Alexander Ingerson. *Minister for Industry, Manufacturing, Small Business and Regional Development, Minister for Infrastructure:* The Hon. John Wayne Olsen. *Minister for Health, Minister for Aboriginal Affairs:* The Hon. Michael Harry Armitage. *Minister for Transport, Minister for the Arts, Minister for the Status of Women:* The Hon. Diana Vivienne Laidlaw. *Minister for Housing, Urban Development and Local Governemnt Relations, Minister for Recreation, Sport and Racing:* The Hon. John Oswald. *Minister for Mines and Energy, Minister for Primary Industries:* The Hon. Dale Spehr Baker.

Minister for the Environment and Natural Resources, Minister for Family and Community Services, Minister for the Aging: The Hon. David Charles Wotton. *Minister for Emergency Services, Minister for Correctional Services:* The Hon. Wayne Anthony Matthew. *Minister for Employment, Training and Further Education, Minister for Youth Affairs:* The Hon. Robert Bruce Such.

Ministers are jointly and individually responsible to the legislature for all their official acts.

Local Government. The closely settled part of the State (mainly near the sea-coast and the River Murray) is incorporated into local government areas, and sub-divided into district councils (rural areas only), municipal corporations (mainly metropolitan, but including larger country towns) and cities (more densely populated areas with a qualification of 15,000 residents in the Adelaide metropolitan area, and 10,000 in the country). At 1 Jan. 1994 there were 118 local government authorities. The main functions of councils are the construction and maintenance of roads and bridges, sport and recreational facilities and garbage collection and disposal.

The number and area of the sub-divisions, together with expenditure (in $A1,000) for the year ended 30 June 1992, were:

	No.	*Area (1,000 ha)*	*Roads and bridges*	*Recreation and culture*	*All other*	*Total expenditure*
Adelaide statistical division	30	189·3	74,033	87,935	71,252	452,224
Other municipal corporations and district councils	89	15,225·9	58,093	25,756	26,702	213,158
Total	119	15,415·3	132,126	113,691	97,956	689,203

ECONOMY

Budget. Public sector revenue and outlays (in $A1m.) for years ended 30 June:

	1990	*1991*	*1992*	*1993*	*1994*
Revenue	4,787	5,154	5,324	6,139	6,433
Outlays	5,516	6,172	8,134	6,995	6,555

Banking and Finance. In March 1993 the average weekly balance of deposits held by all banks was $A14,651m. The average weekly balance of loans, advances and bills discounted was $A17,240m.

NATURAL RESOURCES

Minerals. The value of minerals produced in 1992–93 was $A1,312·2m. (metallic minerals, $A288·1m.; opals, $A39·2m.; natural gas, $A371m.; crude oil, $A175·7m.; condensates, $A135·1m.; liquefied petroleum gas, $A113·2m.; coal, $A54·7m.; construction materials, $A82·1m.). The principal metallic minerals produced are iron ore, copper, uranium oxide, gold and silver.

Agriculture. Total area of agricultural establishments, at 31 March 1993, was 56,554,511 ha.

Soil Conservation. A Department of Agriculture programme to deal with the problems of erosion and soil conservation includes the planting of cereal rye, perennial rye and other grasses to check sand drifts; contour-furrowing and contour banking; contour planting with vines and fruit trees; and several water-diversion schemes.

Gross value of agricultural production (in $A1,000), 1992–93: Crops, 1,355,133; livestock slaughtering, 387,657; livestock products, 474,649. Total gross value, 2,217,439.

Sown area (in ha) and output (in tonnes) of the chief crops in 1992-93: Wheat, 1,419,451 and 2,421,214; barley, 1,023,310 and 1,855,320; oats, 191,929 and 164,500; hay, 121,419 and 419,545; vines, 26,134 and 286,138.

Fruit culture is extensive, and in 1992–93, 253,522 tonnes of citrus and 62,092 tonnes of other orchard fruit were produced. Other products, in addition to root crops and vegetables, are grass seeds and oil seeds.

Livestock, 31 March 1993: 1,104,179 cattle, 15,701,756 sheep and 434,665 pigs.

In 1993, 102,333 tonnes of wool clip and (1992–93) 436m. litres of milk were produced.

Irrigation. For the year ended 31 March 1993, 117,117 ha were under irrigated culture, being used as follows: Vineyards, 20,564; fruit (excluding grapes), 15,604; vegetables, 9,164; other crops, 9,904 and pasture, 61,881.

INDUSTRY AND TRADE

Industry. The turnover for manufacturing industries for 1991–92 was $A15,443m.

Industry sub-division	*Establish-ments (No.)*	*Persons employed (1,000)*	*Wages and salaries ($A1m.)*	*Turnover ($A1m.)*
Food, beverages and tobacco	441	15·0	378	2,705
Textiles	69	2·2	70	436
Clothing and footwear	122	3·4	76	319
Wood, wood products and furniture	505	6·8	155	678
Paper, paper products, printing and publishing	321	6·8	213	930
Chemical, petroleum and coal products	83	2·6	93	1,260
Non-metallic mineral products	161	2·9	88	508
Basic metal products	62	6·1	248	1,486
Fabricated metal products	512	6·8	173	831
Transport equipment	179	14·4	444	3,918
Other machinery and equipment	482	12·9	360	1,578
Miscellaneous manufacturing	312	6·5	171	794
Total	3,249	86·2	2,410	15,443

Practically all forms of secondary industry are to be found, the most important being motor vehicle manufacture, saw-milling and the manufacture of household appliances, basic iron and steel, meat and meat products, and wine and brandy.

Labour. Two systems of industrial arbitration and conciliation for the adjustment of industrial relations between employers and employees are in operation—the State system, which operates when industrial disputes are confined to the territorial limits of the State, and the Federal system, which applies when disputes involve other parts of Australia as well as South Australia.

The industrial tribunals are authorized to fix minimum rates of wages and other conditions of employment, and their awards may be enforced by law. Industrial agreements between employers and organizations of employees, when registered, may be enforced in the same manner as awards.

Commerce. Overseas imports and exports in $A1m. (year ending 30 June):

	1989–90	*1990–91*	*1991–92*	*1992–93*	*1993–94*
Imports	2,050·0	2,193·7	2,396·9	3,068·1	2,803·4
Exports	2,841·3	3,005·4	3,505·1	3,756·3	3,873·1

Principal exports in 1993–94 were (in $A1m.): Cereals and cereal preparations, 435·2; road vehicles, parts and accessories, 350·8; meat and meat preparations, 323·9; textile fibres and their wastes, 280·6; non-ferrous metals, 279·6; petroleum and petroleum products, 273·5; beverages, 239·1; fish, seafood and their preparations, 186·6.

Principal imports in 1993–94 were (in $A1m.): Road vehicles, parts and accessories, 663·6; machinery, 505·6; petroleum and petroleum products, 404·6.

In 1993–94 the leading suppliers of imports were (in $A1m.): Japan (845·1), USA (362·2), UK (146·3), New Zealand (104·4). Main export markets were Japan (622·6), USA (392·3), New Zealand (312·4), UK (259·5), China (219·9), Hong Kong (165).

Tourism. In June 1993 there were 360 hotels and motels with 10,632 rooms; 211 caravan parks had a total of 24,434 sites.

COMMUNICATIONS

Roads. At 30 June 1994, of the roads customarily used by the public, there were 2,749 km of national highways, 9,557 km of arterial roads and 82,919 km of local roads, totalling 95,225 km. Lengths of road classified by surface were as follows: Sealed, 25,319 km; unsealed, 69,906 km. Costs of construction and maintenance are shared by the State and Commonwealth governments and by the councils of the local areas. Motor vehicles registered at 30 June 1994: Passenger and other motor vehicles, 893,200; motorcycles, 27,000. In 1993 there were 218 fatalities in road accidents.

Railways. At 30 June 1993, Australian National Railways operated 4,415 km of railway in country areas. TransAdelaide operated 120 km of railway in the metropolitan area of Adelaide, which carried 8·7m. passengers in 1993–94.

Civil Aviation. There is an international airport at Adelaide. During 1992-93, 56,872 aircraft movements, 3,022,204 passengers and 24,781 tonnes of freight were handled on domestic and international services. In July 1994 there were 27 licensed aerodromes.

Shipping. There are 7 state and 4 private deep sea ports. In 1993, 741 vessels conducting overseas trade entered South Australia with 3·62m. import tonnes of cargo and left with 6·51m. export tonnes. In 1993–94 the state-owned ports handled 13·6m. tonnes of cargo out of a total of 21·02m. tonnes.

Telecommunications. At 30 June 1991, there were 510 post offices. Telephone services in operation totalled 805,478 at 30 June 1994. Apart from the national services, there were in 1993, 13 commercial and 13 public radio stations and 4 commercial TV stations. There were 64 radio and 34 television stations at 30 June 1992.

SOCIAL INSTITUTIONS

Justice. There is a Supreme Court, which incorporates admiralty, civil, criminal, land and valuation, and testamentary jurisdiction; district criminal courts, which have jurisdiction in many indictable offences, and magistrates courts, which include the Youth Court. Circuit courts are held at several places. In the year ended 31 Dec. 1991, there were 1,943 appearances in the higher criminal courts. In 1,164 of those cases, the defendant was found guilty of the major charge. In 1994 the police force numbered 3,813. There were 5,685 prisoners received under sentence in 1992-93.

Religion. Religious affiliation at the 1991 census: Catholic, 236,252; Anglican, 191,060; Uniting Church, 123,864; Lutheran, 34,395; Orthodox, 36,599; Baptist, 22,151; Presbyterian, 17,275; other Christians, 19,923. Non-Christians, 16,464; indefinite, 2,734; no religion, 182,101; not stated, 108,620.

Education. Education is secular and is compulsory for children 6–15 years of age. Primary and secondary education at government schools is free. In 1993 there were 19,430 children in 321 pre-school centres. In 1993 there were 861 schools operating, of which 184 were non-government and 675 government schools, the latter comprising 473 primary, 2 primary-secondary, 88 secondary, 53 area, 22 special, 21 rural and 16 Aboriginal schools. There were 124,802 children in government and 36,481 in non-government primary schools, and 59,818 children in government and 26,126 in non-government secondary schools. 10 Institutes of Vocational Education were formed in 1993 by a merger of the former 19 TAFE colleges. There were 44,471 students at the 3 universities in 1993.

Social Welfare. The number of pensioners at 30 June 1993 was: Age, 150,583; disability support, 38,592; wife's/carer's pension, 15,434; widow's, 5,189; sole parent, 26,011; rehabilitation, 33.

Further Reading

Statistical Information: The State branch of the Australian Bureau of Statistics is at 55 Currie St., Adelaide (GPO Box 2272). *Deputy Commonwealth and Government Statistician:* P. M. Gardner. Although the first printed statistical publication was the *Statistics of South Australia, 1854* with the title altered to *Statistical Register* in 1859, there is a written volume for each year back to 1838. These contain simple records of trade, demography, production, etc. and were prepared only for the use of the Colonial Office; one copy was retained in the State.

The publications of the State branch include the *South Australian Year Book*, the *Pocket Year Book of South Australia* and a *Monthly Summary of Statistics, South Australia*, a quarterly bulletin of building activity, a quarterly bulletin of tourist accommodation and approximately 40 special bulletins issued each year as particulars of various sections of statistics become available.

Gibbs, R. M., *A History of South Australia: From Colonial Days to the Present.* Adelaide, 1984
Whitelock, D., *Adelaide, 1836–1976: A History of Difference.* Univ. of Queensland Press, 1977

State Library: The State Library of S.A., North Terrace, Adelaide. *State Librarian:* Frances H. Awcock.

TASMANIA

KEY HISTORICAL EVENTS. Abel Janszoon Tasman discovered Van Diemen's Land (Tasmania) on 24 Nov. 1642. The island became a British settlement in 1803 as a dependency of New South Wales; in 1825 its connection with New South Wales was terminated; in 1851 a partially elected Legislative Council was established, and in 1856 responsible government came into operation. On 1 Jan. 1901 Tasmania was federated with the other Australian states into the Commonwealth of Australia.

TERRITORY AND POPULATION. Tasmania is a group of islands separated from the mainland by Bass Strait with an area (including islands) of 68,331 sq. km, or 6·83m. ha, of which 6,441,000 ha form the area of the main island. The population at 10 consecutive censuses (including full-blood Aboriginals from 1966) was:

	Population		*Population*
1933	227,599	1971	390,413
1947	257,078	1976	402,868
1954	308,752	1981	418,957
1961	350,340	1986	436,353
1966	371,435	1991	452,837

At the census of 30 June 1991, 24,251 were born in the UK or Ireland, 11,779 in other European countries and 396,313 in Australia.

Vital statistics for calendar years:

	Marriages	*Divorces*	*Births*	*Deaths*
1990	3,026	1,170	7,043	3,713
1991	3,069	1,383	6,870	3,686
1992	3,074	...	6,869	3,694

The largest cities and towns (with populations at the 1991 Census) are Hobart (181,838), Launceston (93,347), Devonport (24,622) and Burnie (20,483).

CONSTITUTION AND GOVERNMENT. Parliament consists of the Governor, the Legislative Council and the House of Assembly. The Council has 19 members, elected by adults with 6 months' residence. Members sit for 6 years, 3 retiring annually and 4 every sixth year. There is no power to dissolve the Council. Vacancies are filled by by-elections. The House of Assembly has 35 members; the maximum term for the House of Assembly is 4 years. Members of both Houses are paid a basic salary of $A46,820 (Oct. 1993), plus an electorate allowance, according to the division represented. The annual allowance payable is calculated as a percentage of basic salary. The amounts vary from $A5,151 (11%) to $A16,390 (35%). Women received the right to vote in 1903. Proportional representation was adopted in 1907, the method now being the single transferable vote in 7-member constituencies. Casual vacancies in the House of Assembly are determined by a transfer of the preference of the vacating member's ballot papers to consenting candidates who were unsuccessful at the last general election.

A Minister must have a seat in one of the two Houses.

At the elections of Feb. 1992 the Liberal Party won 19 seats in the House of Assembly, the Labor Party 11 and the Tasmanian Greens 5.

The Legislative Council is predominantly independent without formal party allegiance; 1 member is Labor-endorsed and 1 Liberal.

Governor: Gen. Sir Phillip Bennett, AC, KBE, DSO.

The Liberal Party Ministry in Aug. 1994 was as follows:

Premier, Minister for State Development and Resources, Minister for Mines, Minister for Forests: Hon. R. J. Groom.

Deputy Premier, Minister for Education and the Arts, Minister for Employment, Industrial Relations and Training: Hon. R. J. Beswick. *Minister for Transport and Works:* Hon. I. M. Braid. *Minister for Environment and Land Management, Minister for National Parks and Wildlife, Minister for Inland Fisheries, Minister for Local Government:* Hon. T. J. Cleary. *Attorney-General, Minister for Justice, Minister assisting the Treasurer, Leader of the Government in the House:* Hon. R. Cornish. *Minister for Primary Industry and Fisheries, Minister for Energy, Minister for TT-Line:* Hon. R. T. Gray. *Minister for Community and Health Services:* Hon. F. R. Groom. *Minister for Tourism, Sport and Recreation, Minister for the Status of Women, Minister for Antarctic Affairs:* Hon. P. C. Hodgman. *Minister for Police and Emergency Services, Minister for Multicultural and Ethnic Affairs, Minister for Consumer Affairs, Minister assisting the Premier:* Hon. F. L. Madill. *Treasurer, Minister for Finance, Minister for Public Sector Management, Minister for Racing and Gaming:* Hon. A. M. Rundle.

Local Government. The State is divided into 29 municipal areas comprising the cities of Hobart, Launceston, Glenorchy, Clarence, Burnie and Devonport and 26 municipalities. The number of municipalities was reduced from 46 in 1993 because of the amalgamation of smaller into larger municipalities. The cities and municipalities are managed by elected aldermen and councillors, respectively, with reference to local matters such as sanitation and health services, domestic water supplies and roads and bridges within each particular area. The chief source of revenue is rates (based on assessed annual value) levied on owners of property.

Tasmanian Islands. 2 inhabited Tasmanian islands (King and Flinders) are organized as municipalities. Nearly 1,360 km south-east lies Macquarie Island (123 sq. km), part of the State, and used only as a research base and meteorological station.

ECONOMY

Budget. The revenue is derived chiefly from taxation (pay-roll, motor, lottery and land tax, business franchises and stamp duties), and from grants and reimbursements from the Commonwealth Government. Customs, excise, sales and income tax are levied by the Commonwealth Government, which makes grants to Tasmania for both revenue and capital purposes. Commonwealth payments to Tasmania in 1991–92 totalled $A1,074m.

Specific Purpose Grants are mainly used to provide essential services such as hospitals, housing, roads and educational services, while General Purpose Revenue Funds have been paid since 1942 to compensate the State for the loss of income tax to the federal government.

Consolidated Revenue Fund receipts and expenditure, in $A1,000, for financial years ending 30 June:

	1986–87	*1987–88*	*1988–89*	*1989–90*	*1990–91*	*1991–92*
Revenue	1,107,870	1,201,397	1,259,754	1,674,955	1,665,020	1,854,000
Expenditure	1,106,608	1,201,175	1,258,945	1,684,849	1,671,808	1,878,000

Net State and local government debt, 1991–92, $A3,306m.

In 1991–92 State taxation revenue amounted to $A558m., of which pay-roll tax provided $A135m.; motor tax, $A64m.; stamp duties, $A67m.; business franchises, $A97m. and lottery tax, $A22m.

Banking and Finance. Trading bank activity in Tasmania is divided between 3 private banks and the Commonwealth Trading Bank. For the month of Dec. 1988 liabilities represented by depositors' balances averaged $A749m. and assets represented by advances, $A929m. The 6 savings banks operating in Tasmania are the Commonwealth Savings Bank, 2 trustee savings banks and 3 private savings banks operated by trading banks. At 31 Dec. 1988 total savings bank deposits were $A1,761m.

ENERGY AND NATURAL RESOURCES

Electricity. Installed capacity was 2·46m. kW in 1992. Production, 1991–92, 8,968m. kWh. Tasmania has good supplies of hydro-electric power because of assured rainfall and high level water storages (natural and artificial). The Hydro-Electric Commission is the sole commercial supplier of electricity.

Minerals. Output of principal metallic minerals in 1992–93 was (in tonnes): Zinc, 233,837; iron ore pellets, 1,458,909; copper, 28,395; lead, 66,459; tin, 6,760; tungsten, 142; gold, 1·4; silver, 95·3. Coal production, 0·3m. tonnes. Value of output, 1992–93 (in $A1,000): Metallic minerals, 348,169; non-metallic and fuel minerals, 32,766; construction materials, 26,897.

Agriculture. The estimated gross value of recorded production from agriculture in 1991–92 was (in $A1m.): Livestock products, 180·4; livestock slaughterings and other disposals, 125·7; crops, 227·4; total gross value, 533·5. The agricultural census includes only establishments having an 'Estimated Value of Agricultural Operations' of $A20,000 or more. The area occupied by the 3,413 holdings in 1991–92 totalled 1,844,900 ha, of which 905,700 ha were devoted to crops and sown pasture. Area (in ha) and production (in tonnes) of the principal crops:

	1989–90		*1990–91*		*1991–92*	
	Area	*Production*	*Area*	*Production*	*Area*	*Production*
Wheat	792	2,687	599	2,448	1,167	3,249
Barley	7,983	19,320	9,766	25,979	11,344	31,793
Oats	7,568	12,824	9,257	18,825	9,146	18,576
Green peas	6,535	30,486	5,628	26,669	5,342	...
Potatoes	6,852	297,488	5,727	235,465	5,967	249,769
Hay	50,741	241,013	53,228	246,620	51,440	220,944
Hops (bearing) (dry)	690	1,489	713	2,001	799	2,118

Livestock at 31 March 1992: Sheep, 4,294,800; cattle, 446,700; pigs, 40,000.

Wool produced during 1992–93 was 23,270 tonnes, valued at $A116·8m. Butter production was 6,288 tonnes; cheese, 19,927 tonnes. In 1991–92, 50,400 tonnes of apples and 939 tonnes of grapes were produced.

Forestry. Indigenous forests cover a considerable part of the State, and the saw-milling and woodchipping industries are very important. Production of sawn timber in 1992–93 was 324,100 cu. metres. 883,200 cu. metres of logs were used for milling in 1992–93 and a further 3,350,600 cu. metres were used for chipping, grinding or flaking. Newsprint and paper are produced from native hardwoods, principally eucalypts.

Fisheries. Estimated gross value of fisheries production was $A160,385,000 in 1990–91.

INDUSTRY AND TRADE

Industry. The most important manufactures for export are refined metals, news-print and other paper manufactures, pigments, woollen goods, fruit pulp, confectionery, butter, cheese, preserved and dried vegetables, sawn timber, and processed fish products. The electrolytic-zinc works at Risdon near Hobart treat large quantities of local and imported ore, and produce zinc, sulphuric acid, superphosphate, sulphate of ammonia, cadmium and other by-products. At George Town, large-scale plants produce refined aluminium and manganese alloys. During 1992–93, 3,565,800 tonnes (green weight) of woodchips were produced. In 1991–92 employment in manufacturing establishments was 23,500; wages and salaries totalled $A714m.; turnover, $A3,873m. The number operating at 30 June 1992 was 873.

Labour. In March 1993, 215,000 persons (59·5% of the civilian population aged 15 and over) were in the workforce, of whom 189,300 were employed.

The Commonwealth Industrial Court (judicial powers) and Commonwealth Conciliation and Arbitration Commission (arbitral powers) have jurisdiction over federal unions, *i.e.*, with interstate membership. Most Tasmanian employees are covered by federal awards.

State Industrial Boards, established for the various trades by resolution of Parliament or proclamation of the Governor, cover most of the remaining employees. Each Board consists of a Chairman appointed by the Governor with equal representation of employers and employees. The Boards have authority over minimum rates for wages or piecework, number of working hours for which the wage is payable, conditions of apprenticeship, annual leave and adjustment of wage and piecework rates. Industrial Boards follow to a large extent the wage rates fixed by the Conciliation and Arbitration Commission.

Commerce. In 1991–92 exports totalled $A1,439,275,000 to overseas countries. The principal countries of destination (with values in $A1m.) for overseas exports were: Japan, 486·9; USA, 181; Taiwan, 104·7; UK, 90·7; Indonesia, 82·6; Malaysia, 66·2. In 1991–92 imports totalled $A287,155,000 from overseas countries. The principal countries of origin (with values in $A1m.) for overseas imports were: USA, 57·7; Japan, 48·4; Canada, 26·6; Germany, 26·2; New Zealand, 17·4.

The main commodities by value (in $A1m.) exported to overseas countries in 1991–92 were: Non-ferrous metals (mainly copper, lead, tin and tungsten), 381·8; metalliferous ores and metal scrap, 218·5; fish, crustaceans and molluscs, 123·8; textile fibres and waste, 60·4; iron and steel, 58·2; meat and meat preparations, 57·2. Other exports were woodchips, newsprint, printing and writing papers, refined aluminium, ferro-alloys and chocolate confectionery. The main imports from overseas countries in 1991–92 (in $A1m.) were: Industrial machinery and parts, 60·7; pulp and waste paper, 29·3; road vehicles, 21; coffee, tea, cocoa and spices, 11·3 and petroleum products, 11·9.

Tourism. In 1992, 771,500 passengers arrived in Tasmania by sea and air from other states or New Zealand of whom 437,200 were visitors.

COMMUNICATIONS

Roads. The total classified road length at 30 June 1992 was 3,796 km. Motor vehicles registered at 30 June 1992 comprised 227,900 cars and station wagons, 70,500 other vehicles and 6,300 motor cycles.

Railways. There is a 784-km network of 1,067-mm gauge lines linking Hobart and Launceston with coastal and country areas, part of Australian National Railways. A private railway of 142 km, operated by the Emu Bay Railway Co. Ltd, connects Burnie with the mining settlements on the west coast.

Civil Aviation. Regular daily passenger and freight services connect the south, north and north-west of the State with the mainland of Australia. For the year ended 30 June 1992 there was a total of 17,120 scheduled aircraft movements; 1·1m. passengers were carried.

Shipping. In 1991–92 there were 2,078 ship visits with 11,793,653 mass tonnes of cargo carried through Tasmanian ports.

Telecommunications. In 1993 there were 40 post offices and 165 post office agencies. There were 4 TV broadcasters and 27 radio stations.

SOCIAL INSTITUTIONS

Justice. The Supreme Court of Tasmania, with civil, criminal, ecclesiastical, admiralty and matrimonial jurisdiction, established by Royal Charter on 13 Oct. 1823, is a superior court of record, with both original and appellate jurisdiction, and consists of a Chief Justice and 6 puisne judges. There are also inferior civil courts with limited jurisdiction, licensing courts, mining courts, courts of petty sessions and coroners' courts.

During 1992, 26,886 offences were finalized in the lower courts, 1,262 in the higher courts and 3,082 in the children's courts. The total police force at June 1992 was 1,014. There is 1 prison, with 800 imprisonments in 1991-92.

Religion. At the census of 1991 the following numbers of adherents of the principal religions were recorded:

Anglican Church	166,492	Other Christian	27,895
Roman Catholic	89,496	Indefinite and not stated	49,077
Methodist / Uniting Church	38,612	No religion	55,372
		Non Christian	2,669
Presbyterian	13,300		
Baptist	9,924	Total	452,837

Education. Education is controlled by the State and is free, secular and compulsory between the ages of 6 and 16. In 1992 government schools had a total enrolment of 65,713 pupils, including 27,795 at secondary level; private schools had a total enrolment of 20,576 pupils, including 9,547 at secondary level.

Technical and further education is conducted at technical and community colleges in the major centres throughout the state. In 1992 there were 19,021 students enrolled in the Division of Technical and Further Education and 37,275 students in the Division of Adult Education.

Tertiary education is offered at the University of Tasmania in Hobart and Launceston and the Australian Maritime College in Launceston. The University (established 1890) had (1992) 7,853 full-time and 3,460 part-time students, and 769 academic staff. There were 2,619 full-time and 1,159 part-time students enrolled in advanced education courses in 1990. The Maritime College had 1,363 students in 1992.

Social Welfare. The number of pensioners in Tasmania on 30 June 1992 was: Age (including wife and carer pensioners), 44,993; invalid, 11,719; war (service), 16,407; widows, 1,703.

Further Reading

Statistical Information: The State Government Statistical Office (175 Collins St., Hobart), established in 1877, became in 1924 the Tasmanian Office of the Australian Bureau of Statistics, but continues to serve State statistical needs as required.

Deputy Commonwealth Statistician and Government Statistician of Tasmania: William P. McReynolds.

Main publications: *Annual Statistical Bulletins (e.g., Demography, Courts, Agricultural Industry, Finance, Manufacturing Establishments* etc.).—*Tasmanian Pocket Year Book.* Annual (from 1913).—*Tasmanian Year Book.* Annual (from 1967).—*Monthly Summary of Statistics* (from July 1945).

Robson, L., *A History of Tasmania. Vol. 1: Van Diemen's Land from the Earliest Times to 1855.* Melbourne, 1983

Townsley, W. A., *The Government of Tasmania.* Brisbane, 1976

State Library: The State Library of Tasmania, 91 Murray St., Hobart. *State Librarian:* Robyn Collins, BA, MLibSc.

VICTORIA

TERRITORY AND POPULATION. The State has an area of 228,113 sq. km, and a resident population (estimate) of 4,462,100 at 30 June 1993. Density, 19·6 per sq. km.

Estimated population at 30 June 1992, within 11 'Statistical Divisions': Melbourne, 3,177,900; Barwon, 229,770; Western District, 102,500; Central Highlands, 139,790; Wimmera, 53,100; Mallee, 82,500; Loddon-Campaspe, 178,950; Goulburn, 155,100; Ovens-Murray, 92,180; East Gippsland, 67,240; Gippsland, 169,760.

At the census of 6 Aug. 1991 the population was 4,244,304 (2,147,852 females).

Population of urban centres with over 10,000 inhabitants at the 1991 census: Melbourne, 2,761,995; Geelong, 126,306; Ballarat, 64,980; Bendigo, 57,427; Shepparton-Mooroopna, 30,511; Melton, 29,039; Warrnambool, 23,946; Albury-Wodonga (Wodonga Part), 23,639; Mildura, 23,176; Traralgon, 19,699; Cranbourne,

18,886; Sunbury, 18,533; Moe-Yallourn, 17,990; Wangaratta, 15,984; Morwell, 15,423; Sale, 13,858; Horsham, 12,552; Bairnsdale, 10,770; Colac, 10,241; Portland, 10,115; Craigieburn, 10,098; Ocean Grove-Barwon Heads, 10,069.

Vital statistics for calendar years:

	Births	*Marriages*	*Divorces*	*Deaths*
1990	66,970	30,120	10,406	30,986
1991	65,438	28,535	11,134	31,216
1992	65,766	28,429	10,533	31,951

The annual rates per 1,000 of the mean resident population (estimate) in 1992 were: Marriages, 6·4; births, 14·8; deaths, 7·2; divorces, 2·4. Expectation of life: Males, 74·8 years; females, 80·7.

CONSTITUTION AND GOVERNMENT. Victoria, formerly a portion of New South Wales, was, in 1851, proclaimed a separate colony, with a partially elective Legislative Council. In 1856 responsible government was conferred, the legislative power being vested in a parliament of two Houses, the Legislative Council and the Legislative Assembly. At present the Council consists of 44 members who are elected for 2 terms of the Assembly, one-half retiring at each election. The Assembly consists of 88 members, elected for 4 years from the date of its first meeting unless sooner dissolved by the Governor. Members and electors of both Houses must be aged 18 years and Australian citizens or those British subjects previously enrolled as electors, according to the Constitution Act 1975. No property qualification is required, but judges, members of the Commonwealth Parliament, undischarged bankrupts and persons convicted of an offence which is punishable by life imprisonment, may not be members of either House. Single voting (one elector one vote) and compulsory preferential voting apply to Council and Assembly elections. Enrolment for Council and Assembly electors is compulsory. The Council may not initiate or amend money bills, but may suggest amendments in such bills other than amendments which would increase any charge. A bill shall not become law unless passed by both Houses.

Governor: Richard E. McGarvie.

In the exercise of the executive power the Governor is advised by a Cabinet of responsible Ministers. Section 50 of the Constitution Act 1975 provides that the number of Ministers shall not at any one time exceed 22, of whom not more than 6 may sit in the Legislative Council and not more than 17 may sit in the Legislative Assembly.

At the elections of Oct. 1992 the Liberal and National Party coalition gained 61 seats. The Liberal-National coalition Cabinet was as follows in Nov. 1995:

Premier, Minister for Ethnic Affairs: Jeffrey Gibb Kennett.

Deputy Premier, Minister for Police and Emergency Services, Minister for Corrections, Minister for Tourism: Pat McNamara. *Minister for Roads and Ports:* Bill Baxter. *Deputy Leader of the National Party, Minister for Agriculture:* Bill McGrath. *Minister for Conservation and Environment, Minister for Major Projects:* Mark Birrell. *Minister for Public Transport:* Alan Brown. *Minister for Natural Resources:* Geoff Coleman. *Minister for Industry and Employment:* Phil Gude. *Minister for Local Government, Minister for Regional Development:* Roger Hallam. *Minister for Education:* Don Hayward. *Minister for Small Business, Minister for Youth Affairs:* Vin Heffernan. *Minister for Community Services, Minister responsible for Aboriginal Affairs:* Michael John. *Minister for Housing, Minister for Aged Care:* Rob Knowles. *Minister for Planning:* Rob Maclellan. *Minister for Industry Services:* Roger Pescott. *Minister for Energy and Minerals, Minister assisting the Treasurer on State-Owned Enterprises:* Jim Plowman. *Minister for Sport, Recreation and Racing:* Tom Reynolds. *Minister for Finance:* Ian Smith. *Treasurer:* Alan Stockdale. *Minister for Tertiary Education and Training, Minister for the Arts, Minister for Gaming:* Haddon Story. *Minister for Health:* Marie Tehan. *Attorney-General, Minister for Fair Training, Minister for Women's Affairs:* Jan Wade. *Parliamentary Secretary of the Cabinet:* Rosemary Varty.

Local Government. With the exception of Yallourn Works area (26·9 sq. km) and the unincorporated areas—French Island (154 sq. km), Lady Julia Percy Island (1·3 sq. km), the Bass Strait Islands (3·8 sq. km), part of Gippsland Lakes (309 sq. km) and Tower Hill Lake Reserve (5 sq. km), the State was divided at 30 June 1993 into 205 municipal districts (reducing to 78 through amalgamations), comprising 66 cities, 4 rural cities, 3 towns, 6 boroughs and 126 shires. The constitution of cities, towns, boroughs and shires is based on statutory requirements concerning population, rate revenue and net annual value of rateable property.

ECONOMY

Budget. State and local government outlays and receipts (excluding financial enterprises e.g. government savings banks, insurance offices, etc.) in $A1m.:

State 1993–94: Current outlays, 16,807·2; capital outlays, 691. Revenue, 17,648·9. State expenditure included (capital outlay): Education, 4,319·7 (197·2); health, 2,621·6 (133·7); general public services, 1,133·1 (–52·7); public order and safety, 974·7 (52·2). Revenue included: Property taxes, 2,207·2; payroll taxes, 1,702·4; taxes on uses of goods and performance of activities, 1,804·9; taxes on provision of goods and services, 1,518·8.

Local 1992–93: Outlays, 2,743, including roads, streets and bridges, 545·7; recreation and culture, 530·4; general public services, 476·2; community amenities, 449; social security and welfare, 328·8. Revenue, 2,967·8, including rates, 1,421·1; Commonwealth and State grants, 679·9.

Banking and Finance. The State Bank of Victoria, the largest bank in the State, provides domestic and international services for business and personal customers and is the largest supplier of housing finance in Victoria. In 1990 it ran into debt and was acquired by the Commonwealth from the Victorian government in Sept. 1990.

The 8 major trading banks in Victoria are the Commonwealth Bank of Australia, the Australia and New Zealand Banking Group, the Westpac Banking Corporation, the National Australia Bank, the Bank of Melbourne, the National Mutual Royal Bank, the Challenge Bank and Citibank. Banks had a total of 1,983 branches and 1,583 agencies between them at 30 June 1993.

In June 1993 bank deposits repayable in Australia totalled $A58,313m.; other lending, $A58,733m.

There were 10 building societies in 1993.

ENERGY AND NATURAL RESOURCES

Electricity. Electricity is supplied by the State Electricity Commission of Victoria either directly or through 11 metropolitan councils which buy in bulk and distribute electricity through their own systems.

Electricity production in 1992–93 was 39,084m. kWh.

About 85% of the power generated for the state system is supplied by 5 brown-coal fired generating stations. There are 2 other thermal stations and 3 hydro-electric stations in north east Victoria. Victoria is also entitled to approximately 30% of the output of the Snowy Mountains hydro-electric scheme and half the output of the Hume hydro-electric station, both of which are in New South Wales.

Oil and Natural Gas. Crude oil in commercially recoverable quantities was first discovered in 1967 in 2 large fields offshore in East Gippsland in Bass Strait between 65 and 80 km from land. These fields, with 10 other fields since discovered, have been assessed as containing initial recoverable reserves of more than 2,930m. bbls of treated crude oil. Estimated reserves of crude oil (1992) 120,000m. litres; gas, 151m. cu. metres.

In 1990-91 Gippsland Basin produced 51% of Australia's crude oil and 41% of its natural gas. Production of crude oil (1991), 110,617,000 bbls.

Natural gas was discovered offshore in East Gippsland in 1965. The initial recoverable reserves of treated gas are 220,400m. cu. metres. Reserves are sufficient for at least 30 years. Natural gas is distributed to residential and industrial consumers through a network of 23,400 km of mains.

Liquefied petroleum gas is produced after extraction of the propane and butane fractions from the untreated oil and gas.

Brown Coal. Major deposits of brown coal are located in the Central Gippsland region and comprise approximately 94% of the total resources in Victoria. In 1993 the resource was estimated to be 0·2m. megatonnes, of which about 52,000 megatonnes was economically recoverable. It is young and soft with a water content of 60% to 70%. In the La Trobe Valley section of the region, the thick brown coal seams underlie an area from 10 to 30 km wide extending over approximately 70 km from Yallourn in the west to the south of Sale in the east. It can be won continuously in large quantities and at low cost by specialized mechanical plant.

The primary use of these reserves is to fuel electricity generating stations. Production of brown coal in 1990-91 was 49,389,000 tonnes, value $A367·1m.

Minerals. Production (in tonnes) and value, 1990–91: Gold, 4·9, $A70·9m.; kaolin, 146,000; gypsum, 49,000; bauxite, 7,925, $A159,000; clays, 1,363,000, $A5,385,000; limestone, 2,346,000, $A19,409,000.

Land Settlement. Of the total area of Victoria (22·76m. ha), 13,973,915 ha on 30 June 1984 were either alienated or in process of alienation. The remainder (8,786,085) constituted Crown land as follows: Perpetual leases, grazing and other leases and licences, 2,160,352; reservations including forest and timber reserves, water, catchment and drainage purposes, national parks, wildlife reserves, water frontages and other reserves, plus unoccupied and unreserved including areas set aside for roads, 6,625,733.

Agriculture. In 1991-92 the total area of land utilized for agricultural activity was 12,374,000 ha, and the gross value of agricultural commodities produced was $A4,822m. There were 31,358 agricultural establishments. The following table shows the area under the principal crops and the produce of each for 3 seasons (in 1,000 units) [1]:

Season	*Total crop area* Ha	*Wheat* Ha	Tonnes	*Oats* Ha	Tonnes	*Barley* Ha	Tonnes	*Potatoes* Ha	Tonnes	*Hay* Ha	Tonnes
1989–90	1,989	952	1,961	189	330	389	696	13	368	492	1,966
1990–91	2,063	911	1,493	177	301	463	651	14	377	486	1,925
1991–92	2,039	664	1,150	183	300	534	898	14	369	551	2,030

[1] Excluding establishments with an estimated value of agricultural operations less than $A20,000.

In 1991–92 there were 19,471 ha of vineyards with 18,490 ha of bearing vines, yielding 104,398 tonnes of grapes for wine-making and 294,514 tonnes for drying or table use. Other produce (in tonnes), 1991-92: Nuts, 2,732; pears, 158,394; apples, 105,725; oranges, 68,507; kiwi fruit, 2,380; strawberries, 1,976; tobacco (dry), 4,219.

Livestock (in 1,000), 1991-92: Beef cattle, 2,152; dairy cattle, 1,422; sheep, 24,782; pigs, 431.

Animal products (in tonnes), 1991-92: Wool clip, 116,574; poultry, 112,036; mutton, 87,000; lamb, 111,000; milk, 4,118m. litres; eggs, 45·3m. dozens; honey, 3,579.

INDUSTRY AND TRADE

Industry. At 30 June 1992 there were 12,668 manufacturing establishments with 296,108 persons employed. Selected articles manufactured (in tonnes) 1992–93: Butter and butteroil, 106,887; cheese, 127,788; wheat flour, 271,883; wool yarn, 13,915; wool cloth, 5,053 sq. metres; 142,000 cars and station wagons; plastic and synthetic resins, 713,000 tonnes; 304m. clay bricks; ready mixed concrete, 2,927,000 cu. metres.

Labour. In Aug. 1993 there were 2,199,900 persons in the labour force (62·2% of the civilian population aged 15 years and over) of whom 1,930,900 were employed:

Agriculture, forestry, fishing and hunting, 89,200; mining, 3,400; manufacturing, 340,100; electricity, gas and water, 23,600; construction, 112,100; wholesale and retail trade, 430,800; transport and storage, 78,900; communication, 35,500; finance, property and business services, 226,500; public administration and defence, 100,400; community services, 352,200; recreation, personal and other services, 138,100. There were 269,000 unemployed persons in Aug. 1993 (12·2% of the labour force).

Trade Unions. There were 89 trade unions with a total membership of 770,600 in June 1993.

Commerce. The total value of the overseas imports and exports of Victoria, including bullion and specie, was as follows (in $A1m.):

	1987–88	*1988–89*	*1989–90*	*1990–91*	*1991–92*	*1992–93*
Imports	14,015	15,951	16,790	14,907	15,732	18,162
Exports [1]	9,051	8,576	8,581	8,846	9,531	11,037

[1] Includes re-exports.

The chief exports in 1992–93 (in $A1m.) were: Textile fibres and their wastes, 1,084; non-ferrous metals, 933; dairy products and birds' eggs, 929; petroleum, petroleum products and related materials, 779; meat and meat preparations, 550; vegetables and fruit, 440; road vehicles, 376; cereals and cereal preparations, 344; power generating machinery and equipment, 291; iron and steel, 249. Exports in 1992–93 went mainly to Japan ($A1,629m.), Singapore ($A1,188m.), New Zealand ($A951m.) and USA ($A934m.).

The chief imports in 1992–93 (in $A1m.) were: Road vehicles, 1,887; general industrial machinery and equipment and machine parts, 1,240; electrical machinery, apparatus and appliances and parts, 1,157; textile yarns, fabrics, made-up articles and related products, 1,074. Imports in 1992–93 came mainly from the USA ($A3,974m.), Japan ($A3,315m.), Germany ($A1,448m.), China ($A1,171m.) and the UK ($A1,050).

COMMUNICATIONS

Roads. In 1987–88 there were 160,398 km of roads open for general traffic, consisting of 7,537 km of state highways and freeways, 14,793 km of main roads, 1,848 km of tourist and forest roads and 136,220 km of other roads and streets. The number of registered motor vehicles (other than tractors) at 30 June 1993 was 2,718,400. There were 396 fatalities in road accidents in 1992.

Railways. All the railways are the property of the State and are under the management of the Public Transport Corporation, responsible to the Victorian Government.

At 30 June 1993, 4,790 km of government railway were open. In 1993–94, 7·6m. tonnes of freight and 4·6m. passengers (non-urban) were carried. Melbourne's suburban railways carried 101m. passengers. Melbourne's tramway and light rail network extends to 238 km.

Civil Aviation. In 1992–93, at Melbourne (Tullamarine) airport there were 8·13m. passengers who either embarked or disembarked from 82,835 domestic aircraft movements; 1·81m. passengers from 16,093 international aircraft movements. 64,279 tonnes of freight and 11,891 tonnes of mail was handled by domestic air services.

Telecommunications. In 1991 there were 3·1m. telephones. In 1989 there were 55 broadcasting stations and 18 television stations.

SOCIAL INSTITUTIONS

Justice. There is a Supreme Court with a Chief Justice and 21 puisne judges. There are a county court, magistrates' courts, a court of licensing, and a bankruptcy court, etc.

Major crime during 1991–92: 306,190 offences were reported to the police; 89,252 offences were cleared and 79,888 people were proceeded against.

At 30 June 1992 there were 14 prisons and 2,277 prisoners in custody.

Religion. There is no State Church, and no State assistance has been given to religion since 1875. At the 1986 census the following were the enumerated numbers of each of the principal religions: Catholic,[1] 1,104,044; Church of England, 715,414; Uniting, 280,262 (including Methodist); Orthodox, 177,565; Presbyterian, 138,000; Protestant (undefined), 87,557; other Christian, 90,756; Moslem, 37,965; Hebrew, 32,387; no religion, 557,939; no reply, 574,712; other groups, 222,877.

Education. In 1993 there were 1,934 government schools with 526,636 pupils and 37,551 full-time teaching staff plus full-time equivalents of part-time teaching staff: 303,985 pupils were in primary schools and 222,651 in secondary schools. As from 1990 students attending special schools have not been identified separately and have been allocated to either primary or secondary level of education. They are integrated where possible into mainstream education. There were in 1993, 683 non-government schools, excluding commercial colleges, with 16,227 teaching staff and 250,961 pupils: 127,529 pupils at primary schools and 123,432 pupils at secondary schools.

All higher education institutions, excluding continuing education and technical and further education (TAFE), now fall under the Unified National System, and can no longer be split into universities and colleges of advanced education. In addition, a number of institutional amalgamations and name changes occurred in the 12 months prior to the commencement of the 1992 academic year. In 1992 there were 12 higher education institutions with 156,055 students. There had been 4 universities: Deakin (founded 1974), La Trobe (1964), Melbourne (1853) and Monash (1958).

Health. In 1992–93 there were 148 public hospitals with 12,869 beds and in 1991–92 111 private hospitals.

Social Services. Victoria was the first State of Australia to make a statutory provision for the payment of Age Pensions. The Act providing for the payment of such pensions came into operation on 18 Jan. 1901, and continued until 1 July 1909, when the Australian Invalid and Old Age Pension Act came into force. The Social Services Consolidation Act, which came into operation on 1 July 1947, repealed the various legislative enactments relating to age (previously old-age) and invalid pensions, maternity allowances, child endowment, and unemployment, and sickness benefits and while following in general the Acts repealed, considerably liberalized many of their provisions: it has since been amended. On 30 June 1993 there were 387,931 age and 94,765 invalid pensioners. In 1992–93, the amount paid in pensions including payments to 10,077 wives and spouse carers of age pensioners was $A2,696,995,000 and to 27,088 of invalid pensioners was $A899,951,000.

Under the Australian Unemployment and Sickness Benefit Act 1944, amounts paid and beneficiaries, 1992–93: $A1,951,072,000 to 232,059 unemployment, $A85,483,000 to 9,538 sickness, $A624,246,000 to 65,262 supporting parents and $A78,819 to 8,515 special benefits.

At 30 June 1993, there were 16,585 widow pensioners receiving $A137,758,000.

In 1992–93 the total amount paid in family allowances was $A516,994,000 to 477,940 families with 918,677 children and students, and institutions, $A32,831,000 were paid to 16,677 recipients of child disability allowance and (1991–92) $A163,541,000 in family allowance supplement to 56,071 families with 131,404 children.

Further Reading

Australian Bureau of Statistics Victorian Office. *Victorian Year Book.—Summary of Statistics (annual).*

State library: The State Library of Victoria, 328 Swanston St., Melbourne, 3000.

State statistical office: Victorian Office, Australian Bureau of Statistics, 525 Collins Street, Melbourne 3000. *Deputy Commonwealth Statistician:* Stuart Jackson.

[1] So described on individual census schedules.

WESTERN AUSTRALIA

KEY HISTORICAL EVENTS. In 1791 Vancouver, in the *Discovery*, took formal possession of the country about King George Sound. In 1826 the Government of New South Wales sent 20 convicts and a detachment of soldiers to King George Sound and formed a settlement then called Frederickstown. In 1829 Charles Fremantle took possession of the territory. In 1829 Captain Stirling, newly appointed Lieut.-Governor, founded the colony now known as the State of Western Australia. On 1 Jan. 1901 Western Australia became one of the 6 federated States within the Commonwealth of Australia.

TERRITORY AND POPULATION. Western Australia lies between 113° 09' and 129° E. long. and 13° 44' and 35° 08' S. lat.; its area is 2,525,500 sq. km.

The population at each census from 1947 was as follows [1]:

	Males	*Females*	*Total*		*Males*	*Females*	*Total*
1947	258,076	244,404	502,480	1976	599,959	578,383	1,178,342
1954	330,358	309,413	639,771	1981	659,249	642,807	1,300,056
1961	375,452	361,177	736,629	1986	736,131	722,888	1,459,019
1966	432,569	415,531	848,100	1991	793,626	792,767	1,586,393
1971	539,332	514,502	1,053,834				

[1] 1961 and earlier exclude persons of predominantly Aboriginal descent; from 1966 figures refer to total population (*i.e.*, including Aborigines). Figures from 1971 are based on estimated resident population.

The population count at the 1991 census was 1,586,393. Of these 1,097,500 were born in Australia. Married persons numbered 683,554 (340,607 males and 342,947 females); widowers, 12,967; widows, 53,892; divorced, 29,854 males and 36,247 females; never married, 199,261 males and 156,450 females. Estimated resident population at 31 Dec. 1994 was 1,715,300 (853,900 females).

Perth, the capital, had an estimated resident population of 1,239,400 at June 1994. Of this, the area administered by the City of Perth had a population of 80,517 while the population in the area for which the City of Fremantle is responsible (which includes the chief port of the State) was 23,834.

Principal local government areas outside the metropolitan area, with population at 30 June 1991 (estimate): Bunbury, 25,657; Geraldton, 20,587; Mandurah, 26,838; Roebourne, 17,291; Port Hedland, 12,599; Albany, 11,186; Busselton, 13,528; Kalgoorlie-Boulder, 26,079.

Vital statistics for calendar years [1]:

	Births	*Marriages*	*Divorces*	*Deaths*
1992	25,052	10,118	4,540	9,902
1993	25,081	10,382	4,654	10,318
1994	25,114	10,366	5,024	10,297

[1] Figures are on state of usual residence basis.

CONSTITUTION AND GOVERNMENT. In 1870 partially representative government was instituted, and in 1890 the administration was vested in the Governor, a Legislative Council and a Legislative Assembly. The Legislative Council was, in the first instance, nominated by the Governor, but it was provided that in the event of the population of the colony reaching 60,000, it should be elective. In 1893 this limit of population being reached, the Colonial Parliament amended the Constitution accordingly.

The *Legislative Council* consists of 34 members elected for a term of 4 years. There are 6 electoral regions for Legislative Council elections. 4 return 5 members and 2, 7 members. Each member represents the entire region.

There are 57 members of the *Legislative Assembly*, each member representing one of the 57 electoral districts of the State. Members are elected for the duration of the Assembly which may be for a period of up to 4 years. The qualifications applying to candidates and electors are identical for the Legislative Council and the Legislative Assembly. A candidate must be at least 18 years of age and free from legal incapacity, be an Australian citizen, and be enrolled, or qualified for enrolment, as an elector. A member of the Commonwealth Parliament or of the legislature of a territory or another state, an undischarged bankrupt or a debtor against whose estate there is a subsisting receiving order in bankruptcy, or a person who has been attainted or convicted of treason or felony is disqualified from membership of the legislature. No person may hold office as a member of the Legislative Assembly and the Legislative Council at the same time. An elector must be at least 18 years of age, be an Australian citizen (or a British subject who was at some time within the 3 months preceding 26 Jan. 1984 an elector of the Assembly or the Commonwealth parliament), be free from legal incapacity, and must have resided in Western Australia for 3 months continuously and in the electoral district for which he or she claims enrolment for a continuous period of 1 month immediately preceding the date of his or her claim. Enrolment is compulsory for all qualified persons. Voting at elections is on the preferential system and is compulsory for all enrolled persons. A system of proportional representation is used to elect members of the Legislative Council.

Ordinary members of the legislature were paid (1995) a salary of $A73,910 a year with an additional electorate allowance, ranging from $A19,538 to $A33,478 a year according to location of the electorate. All members of Parliament also receive a basic postage and lettergram allowance of $A4,730.

In addition to the basic member's salary, electorate and postage allowances, the Premier receives a salary and expense of office allowances of $A96,172. On the same basis the Deputy Premier receives $A60,658; the Leader of the Government in the Legislative Council $A54,254; and other ministers $A44,660.

The Legislative Assembly representation as at Jan. 1996 was: Liberal Party, 26; Australian Labour Party, 23; National Party of Australia, 6; Independent, 2. Legislative Council: Liberal Party, 15; Australian Labour Party, 14; National Party of Australia, 3; Independent, 1; Greens (Western Australia), 1.

Governor: His Excellency Maj.-Gen. Michael Jeffery, AO, MC.

Lieut-Governor: The Hon. David Kingsley Malcolm.

In Jan. 1996 the Cabinet comprised:

Premier, Treasurer, Minister for Public Sector Management and Federal Affairs: Hon. Richard Court.

Deputy Premier, Minister for Commerce and Trade, Regional Development and Small Business: Hon. Hendy Cowan. *Resources Development and Energy, Leader of the Government in the Legislative Assembly:* Hon. Colin Barnett. *Primary Industry and Fisheries:* Hon. Monty House. *Mines and Lands, Minister assisting the Minister for Public Sector Management and Leader of the Government in the Legislative Council:* Hon. George Cash. *Water Resources:* Hon. Roger Nicholls. *Transport:* Hon. Eric Charlton. *Tourism, Employment and Training and Sports and Recreation, Parliamentary and Electoral Affairs:* Hon. Norman Moore. *Family and Children's Services, Youth, Seniors' and Women's Interests, Fair Trading:* Hon. Cheryl Edwardes. *Finance, Racing and Gaming, Minister assisting the Treasurer:* Hon. Max Evans. *Local Government, Multicultural and Ethnic Affairs:* Hon. Paul Omodei. *Aboriginal Affairs and Housing:* Hon. Kevin Prince. *Attorney-General, Justice, Environment, the Arts:* Hon. Peter Foss. *Water and Services, Disability Services, Minister assisting the Minister for Justice:* Hon. Kevin Minson. *Community Development, Family:* Hon. Roger Nicholls. *Housing, Labour Relations:* Hon. Graham Kierath. *Police and Emergency Services:* Hon. Robert Wiese. *Planning and Heritage, Minister assisting in Transport:* Hon. Richard Lewis. *Parliamentary Secretary of the Cabinet:* John Bradshaw.

The *Speaker* is Jim Clarko.

Local Government. The only unincorporated area in mainland Western Australia is King's Park, a public reserve of about 403 ha. in Perth. Including the lord-mayoralty of Perth there were 18 cities, 11 towns and 110 shires at 30 June 1993. The executive body in each of these districts is normally an elected council, presided over by a mayor (city and town) or a president (shire), but in certain circumstances it may be a commissioner appointed by the Governor. Their functions include road construction and repair, the provision of parks and recreation grounds, the administration of building controls and health and library services. Finance is derived largely from rates levied on property owners as well as charges for services and government grants.

ECONOMY

Budget. Revenue and expenditure (in $A), as reported in the Consolidated Revenue Fund, in years ended 30 June:

	1992	*1993*	*1994*	*1995*
Revenue	5,134,520,520	5,061,500,000	6,028,000,000	6,020,600,000
Expenditure	5,123,222,596	5,061,500,000	6,113,300,000	5,998,100,000

Main items of revenue in 1994–95: Departmental ($A590,410,983), taxation ($A2,340,253,929), timber and mining ($A426,731,764), from Federal funds ($A2,421,787,099). Western Australia had a gross debt of $A24,399m. on 30 June 1994 ($A6,707m. from Public Trading Enterprises, $A6,104m. General Government debt and $A11,588m. State Public sector debt).

Banking and Finance. There are 28 banks including the Commonwealth Trading Bank and the Rural and Industries Bank of Western Australia.

ENERGY AND NATURAL RESOURCES

Minerals. Mining is important. Until the mid-1960s the major mineral produced was gold. It was then replaced by iron ore in terms of value, and has at various times fallen behind nickel concentrates, bauxite, oil, mineral sands and salt. In the latter half of the 1980s gold enjoyed a resurgence and in 1987-88 exceeded iron ore in value terms.

The total ex-mine value of minerals from mining and quarrying in 1993–94 was $A12,924m. Principal minerals produced in 1993–94 were: Iron ore, 124·3m. tonnes, value $A2,630·6m.; gold bullion, 193 kg, value $A3,256·8m.; crude oil, 8,752·6 kilolitres, value $A1,299·8m.; natural gas, 4,915,300m. kilolitres, value $A441·9m.; salt, 6·8m. tonnes, value $A152·3m.; diamonds, 27·7m. carats, value $A470·2m.; heavy mineral sands concentrates valued at $A416·3m.; alumina, 7,933·3 tonnes, value $A1,702·1m.; nickel concentrates, 678,667 tonnes, value $A637m.; tin concentrates, 209 tonnes, value $A1·4m.; black coal, 5m. tonnes, value $A235·1m.

Agriculture.

	1993–94		*1994–95*	
	Area	*Production*	*Area*	*Production*
Crop	*1,000 ha*	*1,000 tonnes*	*1,000 ha*	*1,000 tonnes*
Wheat	3,859	6,702	3,974	5,652
Oats	275	514	261	435
Barley	776	1,356	590	945
Lupins	929	1,177	1,200	989

	1991–92		*1992–93*	
	No. Trees	*Production*	*No. Trees*	*Production*
Crop	*(1,000)*	*Tonnes*	*(1,000)*	*Tonnes*
Apples	842	...	878	36,551
Pears	164	...	194	8,311
Oranges	179	5,000	189	6,000

Irrigation has been established by the government along the south-western coastal plain and in the north. Reservoirs with an aggregate capacity of 6,207m. cu. metres provided irrigation water for 88,408 ha in 4 districts during 1991–92.

Livestock at 31 March 1994 (in 1,000): Cattle, 1,713; sheep, 32,693; pigs, 288.

The wool clip in 1993–94 was 179,606 tonnes.

Forestry. The area of State forests and timber reserves at 30 June 1990 was 1,894,756 ha; production of sawn timber was 781,440 cu. metres in 1993, principally Jarrah and Karri hardwoods.

Fisheries. The catch of fish, crustaceans and molluscs in 1991–92 totalled 55,484 tonnes for a gross value of $A374·2m. Of this, rock lobsters, with a total catch of 12,202 tonnes accounted for $A252·1m.

INDUSTRY AND TRADE

Industry. Heavy industry is concentrated in the south-west, and is largely tied to export-orientated mineral processing, especially alumina and nickel. Other significant manufacturing industries include meat and seafood processing, production of timber and wood products, metal fabrication and production of industrial and mining machinery. The North West Shelf development has stimulated recent growth in industries involved in providing materials and equipment during the construction phase, as well as in new and existing industries using gas in processing.

The following table shows manufacturing industry statistics for 1993–94 [1]:

Industry sub-division	*Number of establishments operating at 30 June*	*Persons employed [2] 1,000*	*Wages and salaries $A1m.*	*Turnover $A1m.*
Food, beverages and tobacco	355	11·1	314	2,680
Textiles, clothing, footwear and leather products	232	3·7	83	318
Wood and paper products	319	4·6	128	695
Printing and publishing and recorded media	405	6·1	171	649
Chemical, petroleum, coal and associated products	243	5·4	190	2,717
Non-metallic mineral products	216	4·9	158	1,017
Metal products	686	14·0	484	3,841
Machinery and equipment	878	10·5	286	1,474
Other manufacturing	627	5·8	125	564
Total	3,960	66·2	1,940	13,957

[1] Excludes single establishment enterprises with fewer than 4 persons employed.
[2] At 30 June. Includes working proprietors.

Labour. The labour force was 829,000 employed and 65,300 unemployed in June 1995. The average weekly wage in May 1995 was $A539·90 (males $A656·60, females $A403·90).

The Western Australian Industrial Appeal Court consists of 3 Judges, one of whom is the Presiding Judge. The members are nominated by the Chief Justice of Western Australia. An appeal lies to the Court from decisions of the President of the Western Australian Industrial Commission, the Full Bench or the Commission in Court Session. The Western Australian Industrial Commission consists of a President (who must be a judge), a Chief Industrial Commissioner, a Senior Commissioner, and 'such number of other Commissioners as may, from time to time, be necessary'. The President or a Commissioner sitting or acting alone constitutes the Commission and may exercise the appropriate powers of the Commission. The Commission can inquire into any industrial matter and make an award, order or declaration relating to such matter. The Commission may also make inquiries where industrial action has occurred or is likely to occur. The Commission in Court Session is constituted by not less than 3 Commissioners sitting or acting together, and may make General Orders, hear matters referred by the Commission, and hear appeals from decisions of Boards of Reference.

The Full Bench is constituted by not less than 3 members of the Commission, 1 of whom is the President, and may hear matters referred by the Commission on questions of law, and appeals from decisions of the Commission and Industrial Magistrates.

The following table shows details of the number of industrial awards, unions and members registered with the Western Australian Industrial Commission.

At 30 June	*1990*	*1991*	*1992*	*1993*	*1994*
Awards in force	610	587	447	431	376
Employee organizations:					
Number	72	83	62	64	65
Membership	174,312	231,569	212,061	216,524	205,650[1]

At 30 June	*1990*	*1991*	*1992*	*1993*	*1994*
Employer organizations:					
Number	15	21	18	17	
Membership	2,180	3,132	3,188	3,065	

[1] Excluding the Builders' Union.

During 1994 there were 82 industrial disputes involving 15,700 workers. A total of 27,400 working days were lost.

Commerce. Foreign commerce is comprised in the statement of the commerce of the Commonwealth of Australia.

Value of foreign imports and exports (i.e. excluding inter-state trade) for years ending 30 June (in $A1m.):

	1991–92	*1992–93*	*1993–94*
Imports	3,548·2	4,966·0	4,793·0
Exports [1]	14,039·5	14,993·0	15,690·0

[1] Including ships' stores.

Total value of trade (including inter-state trade), 1992–93: Imports, $A11,160·6m.; exports, $A18,117·1m.

Selected overseas exports (in $A1m.) for 1993–94: Iron ore and concentrates, 2,765·1 petroleum and products, 929·9m.; gold bullion, 3,285·7; meat and meat products, 163·2m.; fish, crustaceans, molluscs, etc., 413·3m.; cereals and other cereal preparations, 656·8m.; metalliferous ores and metal scrap, 2,999·4m.; textile fibres and other work, 656·8m; salt (1992-93), 179.

Selected overseas imports (in $A1m.) for 1993–94: Petroleum and products, 678·4m.; machinery, 875·9m.; road vehicles, 690m.; miscellaneous manufactured articles, 33·5 (1992-93).

The chief countries exporting to Western Australia in 1993–94 were (in $A1m.): USA, 934; Japan, 828·6; UAE, 388·4; South Korea, 255·7; Main export markets in 1993–94 (in $A1m.): Japan, 3,999; South Korea, 1,204; UK, 1,180; Singapore, 1,009; Hong Kong, 698; China, 665.

Tourism. In 1993–94 there were 447,000 overseas, and 366,000 interstate visitors.

COMMUNICATIONS

Roads. At 30 June 1992 there were 140,976 km of prepared and formed roads comprising 8,232 km of highways, 7,493 km of main roads, 8,397 km of secondary roads and 116,854 km unclassified. Of these, 43,031 km are sealed. In addition, there are 29,222 km of roads unprepared except for clearing which are used for forestry traffic.

New motor vehicles registered during the year ended 30 June 1994 were 63,178.

In 1995 there were 208 fatalities in road accidents.

Railways. At 30 June 1994 the State had 5,411 km of State government railway and 731 km of Federal line, the latter being the western portion of the Trans-Australian line (Kalgoorlie–Port Pirie), which links the State railway system to those of the other States of the Commonwealth. At 30 June 1989, mining companies operated 1,198 km of private railways for the transport of ore to ports on the north-west coast. In 1993–94 state railways carried 28m. tonnes and 461,000 passengers. Perth suburban lines (91·5 km electrified), controlled by a separate authority, carried 16·2m. passengers in 1993–94.

Civil Aviation. An extensive system of regular air services operates for passengers, freight and mail. During 1992–93, Perth Airport handled 32,346 aircraft movements and 2,036,461 passengers on domestic and international services.

Shipping. In 1990–91, the number of overseas direct vessels through the major ports was: Port of Fremantle, 1,231 entered, 1,035 cleared; Port Hedland, 327 entered, 418 cleared; other ports, 218 entered, 1,316 cleared. The gross weight (in tonnes) of overseas cargo through those ports was: Port of Fremantle, 29,140,000 discharged, 26,885,000 loaded; Port Hedland, 543,000 discharged, 37,980,000 loaded; other ports, 85,520,000 discharged, 95,665,000 loaded.

Telecommunications. Postal, telephone and telegraph facilities are afforded at 393 offices. Telephone services connected totalled 728,734 at 30 June 1990.

There were 186 radio broadcasting and 226 television stations, including translator stations, in operation at 30 June 1991.

SOCIAL INSTITUTIONS

Justice. Justice is administered by a Supreme Court, consisting of a Chief Justice, 12 other judges and 3 masters; a District Court comprising a chief judge and 14 other judges; a Magistrates Court, a Chief Stipendiary Magistrate, 36 Stipendiary Magistrates and Justices of the Peace, as at 30 June 1990. All courts exercise both civil and criminal jurisdiction except Justices of the Peace who deal with summary criminal matters only. Juvenile offenders are dealt with by the Children's Court. Overall responsibility for the Children's Court is vested in a President, who has the status of a District Court Judge. A children's court may be constituted by a judge, a magistrate or 2 lay members. Each has different sentencing powers. For certain offences involving first offenders under the age of 16 years who have pleaded guilty, such cases may be dealt with by the Children's (suspended Proceedings) Panel which comprises a representative from the Department for Community Services and one from the Police Department. The Family Court also forms part of the justice system and comprises a Chief Judge, 4 other judges, 7 magistrates/registrars and exercises both State and Federal jurisdictions.

In 1993–94 209,907 crimes were reported (57,638 cleared). 111,580 charges were laid in the courts (including children) in 1992–93; 35,581 persons were convicted.

Persons in prison at 31 Dec. 1994 numbered 2,078.

Religion. At the census, 30 June 1991, the principal denominations were: Anglican, 418,800; Catholic, 408,600; Uniting, 93,200; Presbyterian, 48,300; Baptist, 25,900; other Christian, 112,100; all other, including not stated and no religion, 480,200.

Education. School attendance is compulsory from the age of 6 until the end of the year in which the child attains 15 years. A non-compulsory year of education is available to children from the beginning of the year in which they reach 5 years of age, at pre-primary centres attached to most government primary schools or at community-based and privately owned pre-school centres, and at some non-government schools. Children may be enrolled during their fourth year where vacancies exist. In 1994 there were 705 government primary and secondary schools providing free education to 223,105 students and 249 non-government primary and secondary schools providing education, for which fees are charged, to 76,307 students.

Technical and Further Education (TAFE) is offered by the Department of TAFE, a sub-department of the Ministry of Education, and by three independent regional colleges. The latter also provide higher education facilities. Additionally, higher education is available through 5 universities.

Tertiary education (1994):

	Academic Staff [1]	*Students Enrolled*
University of Western Australia	958	12,370
Murdoch University	461	7,060
Curtin University of Technology	1,052	19,326
Edith Cowan University	830	16,845
University of Notre Dame, Australia	33[2]	200[2]

[1] Teaching and research.
[2] 1993.

State government expenditure from consolidated revenue on education during the year ended 30 June 1995 amounted to $A1,060,707,156.

Social Welfare. At 30 June 1992 there were 88 acute public hospitals, 22 acute private hospitals, and 4 day hospitals.

The Department for Community Development is responsible for the provision of welfare and community services throughout the State. Operations and planning are managed through a decentralized structure of 5 regions and 21 districts. There are 8 directorates (2 support, 1 special services and 5 regional).

Direct services provided to the community include emergency financial assistance, family and substitute care, and counselling and psychological services. The Department supervises children's Day Care Centres. There is a 24-hour emergency welfare service provided through the Crisis Care Unit. Specialist units work in the areas of child abuse, adoptions, youth activities and Family Court counselling.

The Department provides residential facilities for the temporary accommodation, care and training of children, is responsible for young offenders recommended for detention or remand by a Court and also supervises young offenders subject to non-custodial court orders.

Age, invalid, widows', disability and service pensions, and unemployment benefits are paid by the Federal Government. The number of pensioners in Western Australia at 30 June 1993 was: Age, 121,387; invalid, 36,817; widows, 5,545; disability, 36,817; service, 35,003 (1991); and sole parents, 24,558 (1990). There were 79,903 recipients of unemployment benefits at 30 June 1993, comprising 46,610 jobsearch allowance recipients and 33,294 newstart allowance recipients.

During 1992–93 the department provided emergency assistance in 59,345 cases. This assistance, valued at $A4,745,388, was in the form of cash, vouchers to purchase goods and services, and payment on behalf of individuals.

Further Reading

Statistical Information: The State Government Statistician's Office was established in 1897 and now functions as the Western Australian Office of the Australian Bureau of Statistics (Level 16 Exchange Plaza, 2 The Esplanade, Perth). *Deputy Commonwealth Statistician and Government Statistician:* Ian Castles. Its principal publications are: *Western Australian Year Book* (new series, from 1957). *Western Australia: Facts and Figures* (from 1989). *Monthly Summary of Statistics* (from 1958)

Broeze, F. J. A. (ed.) *Private Enterprise, Government and Society.* Univ. of Western Australia, 1993

Crowley, F. K., *Australia's Western Third: A History of Western Australia from the First Settlements to Modern Times.* (Rev. ed.). Melbourne, 1970

Stannage, C. T. (ed.) *A New History of Western Australia.* Perth, 1980

State Library: Alexander Library Building, Perth.

AUSTRIA

Republik Österreich

Capital: Vienna
Population: 8·03m. (1994)
GNP per capita: US$24,950 (1994)
HDI/world rank: 0·925/14 (1992)

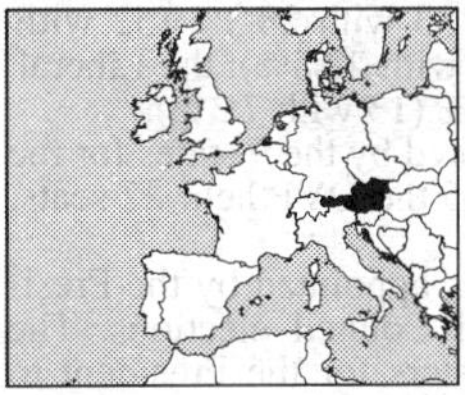

KEY HISTORICAL EVENTS. Following the break-up of the Austro–Hungarian Empire, the Republic of Austria was proclaimed on 12 Nov. 1918. On 12 March 1938 Austria was forcibly absorbed into Nazi Germany. On 27 April 1945 a provisional government was set up and recognized by the Allies on 20 Oct. 1945. Austria recovered its full independence by the Austrian State Treaty of 15 May 1955.

TERRITORY AND POPULATION. Austria is a land-locked country bounded in the north by Germany and the Czech Republic, east by Slovakia and Hungary, south by Slovenia and Italy, and west by Switzerland and Liechtenstein. It has an area of 83,858 sq. km (32,378 sq. miles) and its population at censuses has been:

1923	6,534,742	1951	6,933,905	1981	7,555,338
1934	6,760,233	1971	7,491,526	1991	7,795,786

In 1991, 93·4% of residents were of Austrian nationality and 94% were German-speaking, with linguistic minorities of Slovenes (29,000), Croats (60,000), Hungarians (33,000) and Czechs (19,000). 65% were urban. Population estimate, 1994, 8,029,717. The areas, populations and capitals of the 9 federal states:

Federal States	*Area sq. km*	*Population (1994)*	*State capitals*
Vienna (Wien)	415	1,595,768	Vienna
Lower Austria (Niederösterreich)	19,174	1,511,555	St Pölten
Burgenland	3,965	273,613	Eisenstadt
Upper Austria (Oberösterreich)	11,980	1,383,620	Linz
Salzburg	7,154	504,258	Salzburg
Styria (Steiermark)	16,388	1,203,993	Graz
Carinthia (Kärnten)	9,533	559,696	Klagenfurt
Tirol	12,648	654,753	Innsbruck
Vorarlberg	2,601	342,461	Bregenz

Vital statistics, 1994: Births, 92,415; stillbirths, 307; deaths, 80,684; marriages, 43,284; divorces, 16,928.

The populations of the principal towns at the census of 1991: Vienna, 1,539,848; Graz, 237,810; Linz, 203,044; Salzburg, 143,978; Innsbruck, 118,112; Klagenfurt, 89,415; Villach, 54,640; Wels, 52,594; St Pölten, 50,026.

The official language is German.

CLIMATE. Climate ranges from cool temperate to mountain type according to situation. Winters are cold, with considerable snowfall, but summers are very warm. The wettest months are May to August.

Vienna, Jan. 36°F (2·4°C), July 71°F (21°C). Annual rainfall 23·7" (602 mm). Graz, Jan. 31°F (–0·4°C), July 69°F (20·3°C). Annual rainfall 32" (812 mm). Innsbruck, Jan. 28°F (–2°C), July 68°F (20·1°C). Annual rainfall 35·5" (902 mm). Salzburg, Jan. 32°F (–0·2°C), July 69°F (20·3°C). Annual rainfall 44·7" (1,135 mm).

CONSTITUTION AND GOVERNMENT. The Constitution of 1 Oct. 1920 was restored on 27 April 1945. Austria is a democratic federal republic comprising 9 states *(Länder)*, with a federal *President (Bundespräsident)* directly elected for not more than 2 successive 6-year terms, and a bicameral National Assembly which comprises a National Council and a Federal Council.

In the second round of the presidential elections on 24 May 1992 Thomas Klestil was elected by 56·85% of votes cast against a single opponent.

The National Council *(Nationalrat)* comprises 183 members directly elected for a 4-year term by proportional representation in a 3-tier system by which seats are allocated at the level of 43 regional and 9 state constituencies and 1 federal constituency. Any party gaining 4% of votes cast nationally is represented in the National Council. Elections were held on 17 Dec. 1995. The electorate was 5·8m; turn-out was 85·98%. The Social Democratic Party (SPÖ) won 71 seats with 38·1% of votes cast (65 with 34·9% in 1994); the People's Party (ÖVP), 53 with 28·3% (52 with 27·7%); the Freedoms (formerly FPÖ), 40 with 21·9% (42 with 22·5%); the Liberal Forum, 10 with 5·5% (11 with 6%); the Greens, 9 with 4·8% (13 with 7·3%).

The Federal Council *(Bundesrat)* has 64 members appointed by the 9 states for the duration of the individual State Assemblies' terms; in 1995 the ÖVP held 27 seats, the SPÖ 25 and Freedoms, 12.

The head of government is a *Federal Chancellor*, who is appointed by the President from the party winning the most seats in National Council elections. The Chancellor nominates a Vice-Chancellor and other Ministers for the President to appoint to a Council of Ministers which the Chancellor leads.

Federal President: Dr Thomas Klestil (b. 1933; ÖVP) (elected 24 May 1992; sworn in 8 July).

In March 1996, a new government was still in process of formation following the Dec. 1995 elections (*see* ADDENDA).

National flag: 3 horizontal stripes of red, white, red.

National anthem: Land der Berge, Land am Strome ('Land of mountains, land on the river'; words by Paula Preradović; tune attributed to Mozart).

State and local government. Each state (*Land*) has its assembly. Seats gained by parties at the latest state elections:

Burgenland (June 1991): SPÖ, 17; ÖVP, 15; FPÖ, 4.
Carinthia (March 1994): SPÖ, 14; FPÖ, 13; ÖVP, 9.
Lower Austria (May 1993): ÖVP, 26; SPÖ, 20; FPÖ, 7; Left Bloc, 3.
Salzburg (March 1994): ÖVP, 14; SPÖ, 11; FPÖ, 8; Greens, 3.
Styria (Sept. 1995): ÖVP, 21; SPÖ, 21; FPÖ, 10; Greens, 2; LIF, 2.
Tyrol (March 1994): ÖVP, 19; SPÖ, 7; FPÖ, 6; Greens, 4.
Upper Austria (Oct. 1991): ÖVP, 26; SPÖ, 19; FPÖ, 11.
Vienna (Nov. 1991): SPÖ, 52; FPÖ, 23; ÖVP, 18; Greens, 7.
Vorarlberg (Sept. 1994): ÖVP, 20; FPÖ, 7; SPÖ, 6; Greens, 3.

Every community has a Council, which chooses one of its members to be head of the Community (burgomaster) and a committee for the administration and execution of its resolutions.

DEFENCE. The Federal President is C.-in-C. of the armed forces. The armed forces underwent a major re-organization in 1995. Conscription is for a 7-month period, with liability for 30 days reservist refresher training spread over 10 years.

Army. There are 3 corps, 1 comprises 3 mechanized infantry brigades, 1 engineer battalion, 1 reconnaissance battalion, 1 artillery regiment, 2 *Land* military commands and 7 infantry regiments. The other 2 each comprise: 1 engineer battalion, 1 reconnaissance regiment, 1 artillery regiment, 3 Land military commands and 5 infantry regiments. Equipment includes 169 M-60A3 main battle tanks. Personnel, 1996, 51,500 (22,000 conscripts). The army aviation division comprises 3 aviation and 3 air-defence regiments with about 6,000 personnel, more than 160 aircraft and a number of fixed and mobile radar stations. Some 24 Draken interceptors equip a surveillance wing responsible for the defence of Austrian air space and a fighter-bomber wing operates SAAB 105s. Helicopters equip 7 squadrons for transport/support, communication, observation, search and rescue duties. Fixed-wing aircraft such as PC-6s, PC-7s and Skyvans are operated as trainers and for transport. The procurement of a fourth generation fighter, armed helicopters and medium range air-defence missiles is planned for the end of the decade.

INTERNATIONAL RELATIONS

Membership. Austria is a member of the UN, EU, Council of Europe, OECD and NATO Partnership for Peace. Austria is a signatory to the Schengen Accord abolishing border controls between Belgium, France, Germany, Greece, Italy, Luxembourg, Netherlands, Portugal and Spain. Austria, Greece and Italy have not yet implemented it. With Croatia, the Czech Republic, Hungary, Italy, Poland, Slovakia and Slovenia Austria is a member of the Central European Initiative, which evolved from the Pentagonal/Hexagonal grouping of 1990–91.

At a referendum on 12 June 1994 on joining the EU the electorate was 5,790,578; turn-out was 82·3%. 66·58% of votes cast were in favour.

ECONOMY

Policy. In 1991 some 50% of production derived from the state-owned or state-protected sector, but a privatization programme in accordance with EU directives had largely been completed by 1995.

Budget. The federal budget for calendar years provided revenue and expenditure (ordinary and extraordinary) as follows (in 1m. schilling):

	1991	*1992*	*1993*	*1994*	*1995*
Revenue	557,154	591,563	601,445	626,629	650,547
Expenditure	619,857	657,960	699,685	731,447	752,820

VAT is 20% (10% reduced rate).

Currency. The unit of currency is the *schilling* (ATS) of 100 *groschen*. There are notes of 20, 50, 100, 500, 1,000 and 5,000 schillings. The schilling is linked to the German Mark at DM1 = 7 schillings. All restrictions on foreign currency transactions were abolished by Nov. 1991. In Dec. 1995 foreign exchange amounted to 179,304m. and note circulation to 161,413m. schilling. The rate of exchange in March 1996, £1 = 15·86 *schilling*, US$1 = 10·38 *schilling*.

Banking and Finance. The National Bank of Austria, opened on 2 Jan. 1923, was taken over by the German Reichsbank on 17 March 1938. It was re-established on 3 July 1945. Its *President* is Klaus Liebscher. Bank accounts up to 0·2m. schilling are anonymous for Austrians, but foreign depositors must declare their identity.

There were 1,051 banks in June 1995. The 10 principal banks with total assets (in 1m. schilling, 1994): Bank Austria, 630,600 (merger of Zentralsparkasse and Länderbank in Oct. 1991; the state retains a 21·7% stake); Creditanstalt-Bankverein, 575,400 (the state has a 49·4% stake in it); Girocredit Bank AG der Sparkassen, 313,300; Österreichische Kontrollbank AG, 248,100; Bank für Arbeit und Wirtschaft AG, 223,200; Bank der Österreichischen Postsparkasse, 248,100; Raiffeisen Zentralbank Österreich AG, 204,900; Die Erste Österreichische Spar-Casse-Bank, 205,300; Bank für Oberösterreich und Salzburg (Oberbank), 72,800; Österreichische Volksbanken AG, 65,700.

There is a stock exchange in Vienna (Börse).

Weights and Measures. The metric system is in force.

ENERGY AND NATURAL RESOURCES

Electricity. In 1992 there were 15 nationalized electricity supply companies. Electric energy produced (1m. kWh): 1994, 53,309.

Oil. The commercial production of petroleum began in the early 1930s. Production of crude oil (in tonnes): 1994, 1,099,994.

Gas. Production of natural gas (in 1,000 cu. metres): 1994, 1,354,892.

Minerals. The mineral production (in tonnes) was as follows:

	1993	*1994*		*1993*	*1994*
Lignite	1,691,175	1,368,317	Graphite	4,146	12,162
Iron ore	1,427,000	1,664,000	Talcum	136,640	135,371
Lead and zinc ore [1]	279,325	. . .	Kaolin	341,956	467,320
Raw magnesite [1]	648,864	654,127	Gypsum	876,341	1,011,807

[1] Including recovery from slag.

Agriculture. In 1994 the total area cultivated amounted to 3,483,073 ha (estimate). The chief products (area in 1,000 ha, yield in tonnes) were as follows:

	1992		*1993*		*1994*	
	Area	*Yield*	*Area*	*Yield*	*Area*	*Yield*
Wheat	245·7	1,325,401	241·0	1,018,013	241·0	1,255,122
Rye	69·1	277,838	73·7	291,635	77·0	318,790
Barley	275·0	1,342,141	265·3	1,099,646	252·7	1,184,350
Oats	54·7	185,053	52·9	190,896	49·4	171,716
Potatoes	33·0	738,256	31·1	885,833	29·7	593,720

Farmers are no longer subsidized through the price mechanism.

Livestock (1994): Cattle, 2,328,518; pigs, 3,728,991; sheep, 324,144; goats, 49,749; horses, 66,748; poultry, 13,265,572.

Forestry. Forested area in 1992, 3·9m. ha (46% of the land area) of which 78% coniferous. Felled timber, in 1,000 cu. metres: 1993, 12,255·9; 1994, 14,359·6.

INDUSTRY. Output (in tonnes if not stated otherwise):

	1993	*1994*		*1993*	*1994*
Raw steel	4,148,865	4,398,887	Glass (flat)		
Rolled steel	3,445,504	3,820,353	(1,000 sq. metres)	4,078	5,995
Cellulose	1,079,453	1,197,451	Cement	4,941,242	4,828,460
Cardboard	367,909	413,345	Salt (unrefined)	715,594	785,835
Paper	2,932,025	3,190,069	Sugar (refined)	518,214	458,262
Sawnwood			Margarine	50,486	47,195
(1,000 cu. metres)	6,779	7,538	Milk	580,000	597,000
Viscose staple yarn	34,378	36,479	Fertilizers	1,250,804	1,222,578

In 1994, 8,428 industrial establishments employed 480,466 persons, producing a value of 818,697·8m. schillings (excluding VAT).

Labour. In July 1994 there were 3,152,952 employed persons; the unemployment rate was 5·4%. There were 32,026 job vacancies. In Oct. 1995 there were 204,122 registered unemployed.

The number of foreigners who may be employed in Austria is limited to 9% of the potential workforce.

FOREIGN ECONOMIC RELATIONS. The budgetary external debt was 260,941m. schillings in 1994.

Commerce. Imports and exports are as follows (excluding coined gold):

	Imports			*Exports*		
	1992	*1993*	*1994*	*1992*	*1993*	*1994*
Quantity (1,000 tonnes)	46,730	45,692	49,217	22,222	22,638	25,283
Value (1m. sch.)	593,924	564,909	628,878	487,556	467,171	512,515

The total trade between Austria and UK (British Department of Trade returns, in £1,000 sterling):

	1990	*1991*	*1992*	*1993*	*1994*
Imports to UK	957,789	916,265	948,894	971,124	1,017,879
Exports and re-exports from UK	705,850	766,735	795,107	911,661	1,034,899

Tourism. Tourism is an important industry. In 1994, 18,402 hotels and boarding-houses had a total of 650,020 beds available; 17,893,824 foreigners visited Austria; of these 608,706 came from the UK and 575,629 from the USA. Revenue was 162,700m. schillings in 1992.

COMMUNICATIONS

Roads. On 31 Dec. 1994 federal roads had a total length of 10,207 km, 1,589 km autobahn; provincial roads, 23,472 km. On 31 Dec. 1994 there were registered 4,772,520 motor vehicles, including 3,479,595 passenger cars, 283,157 lorries, 9,598 buses, 405,462 tractors and 532,325 motorcycles.

Railways. The major railways are nationalized. Length of route in 1994, 5,813 km, of which 3,318 km were electrified. There are also 19 private railways with a total length of 562 km. In 1994 190·4m. passengers and 66·2m. tonnes of freight were carried by Federal Railways.

Civil Aviation. Austrian Airlines is 51·9% state-owned. In 1995 it operated 4 A310-300s, 2 A340-200s, 7 MD-81s, 7 MD-82s, 2 MD-83s, 5 MD-87s. There are international airports at Vienna (Schwechat), Linz, Salzburg, Graz, Klagenfurt and Innsbruck. In 1994, 193,123 commercial aircraft and 9,933,754 passengers arrived and departed; 90,811 tonnes of freight, 9,004 tonnes of transit freight and 6,472 tonnes of mail were handled.

Shipping. Austria has no sea frontiers, but the Danube is an important waterway. Goods traffic (in 1,000 tonnes): 6,542 in 1993; 7,706 in 1994 (including the Rhine-Main-Danube Canal).

Telecommunications. All postal, telegraph and telephone services are run by the State. In 1994 there were 3,681,370 telephone main connexions.

The 'Österreichische Rundfunk' (Austrian Broadcasting Corporation) is state-controlled. Private TV broadcasting is not permitted. It transmits 4 national and 9 regional radio programmes. An additional special service in English and French can be received all over the country; there is also a 24 hour foreign service (short wave). Broadcasting is financed by licence payments and advertisements. There were 2·79m. registered listeners in Dec. 1994. 2 TV programmes are transmitted (colour by PAL), with 2·63m. licences in 1994.

Cinemas (1995). There were 377 cinemas.

Press. There were 17 daily newspapers (6 of them in Vienna) in 1994 and a circulation of 3·11m. of all daily newspapers in 1992.

SOCIAL INSTITUTIONS

Justice. The Supreme Court of Justice *(Oberster Gerichtshof)* in Vienna is the highest court in the land. In addition, there were in 1995 4 higher provincial courts *(Oberlandesgerichte)*, 16 provincial courts *(Landesgerichte)* and 187 local courts *(Bezirksgerichte)*.

Religion. In 1991 there were 6,081,454 Roman Catholics (78%), 388,709 Protestants (5%), 158,776 (2%) Moslems, 223,631 others (2·9%), 672,251 without religious allegiance (8·6%) and 270,965 (3·5%) unknown. The Roman Catholic Church has 2 archbishoprics and 7 bishoprics.

Education (1994–95). There were 5,053 general compulsory schools (including special education) with 72,752 teachers and 688,092 pupils. Of all kinds of secondary schools there were 1,120 with 477,006 pupils in 1992–93.

There were also 119 commercial academies with 35,345 pupils and 5,038 teachers. In 1992-93 there were 300 schools of technical and industrial training (including schools of hotel management and catering) with 6,746 teachers and 65,367 pupils; 58 higher schools of women's professions (secondary level) with 15,111 pupils; 9 training colleges of social workers with 1,104 pupils; 114 trade schools with 12,863 pupils.

The dominant institutions of higher education are the 12 universities and 6 colleges of arts. These are (with students enrolled in winter term 1994-95): Universities at Vienna (75,043), Graz (38,416), Innsbruck (26,706), Salzburg (12,336) and Linz (14,400); technical universities at Vienna (23,206) and Graz (11,655); a mining university at Leoben (2,281); an agricultural university at Vienna (7,091); a veterinary university at Vienna (2,752); a university of economics and business administration at Vienna (22,138); a university for educational science at Klagenfurt (4,981); an academy of fine arts (659) and a college of applied arts (1,032) at Vienna; 3 colleges of music and dramatic art, at Vienna (2,953), Salzburg (1,568) and Graz (1,541); a college of art and industrial design at Linz (578). In 1993-94 there were 13,655 teachers at the universities and colleges of arts.

Health. In 1994 there were 30,449 doctors, 325 hospitals and 77,527 hospital beds.

Welfare. Maternity leave is for 2 years, and applies to mothers or fathers.

DIPLOMATIC REPRESENTATIVES

Of Austria in Great Britain (18 Belgrave Mews West, London, SW1X 8HU)
Ambassador: Dr Georg Hennig.

Of Great Britain in Austria (Jaurèsgasse 12, 1030 Vienna)
Ambassador: Terence C. Wood, CMG.

Of Austria in the USA (3524 International Court, NW, Washington, D.C., 20008)
Ambassador: Dr Helmut Türk.

Of the USA in Austria (Boltzmanngasse 14/3 and 16, A-1091 Vienna)
Ambassador: Swanee Hunt.

Of Austria to the United Nations
Ambassador: Dr Ernst Sucharipa.

Further Reading

Austrian Central Statistical Office. *Main publications: Statistisches Jahrbuch für die Republik Österreich.* New Series from 1950. Annual.—*Statistische Nachrichten.* Monthly.—*Beiträge zur österreichischen Statistik* (1,104 vols.).—*Statistik in Österreich 1918–1938.* [Bibliography] 1985.—*Veröffentlichungen des Österreichischen Statistischen Zentralamtes 1945-1985.* [Bibliography], 1990.—*Republik Österreich, 1945–1995.*

Salt, D., *Austria* [Bibliography]. Oxford and Santa Barbara (CA), 1986
Sully, M. A., *A Contemporary History of Austria.* London, 1990
Wolfram, H. (ed.) *Österreichische Geschichte.* 10 vols. Vienna, 1994–

National statistical office: Austrian Central Statistical Office, POB 9000, A-1033 Vienna.
National library: Österreichische Nationalbibliothek, Josefsplatz, 1015 Vienna.

AZERBAIJAN

Azarbaijchan Respublikasy

Capital: Baku
Population: 7·5m. (1994)
GNP per capita: US$500 (1994)
HDI/world rank: 0·696/99 (1992)

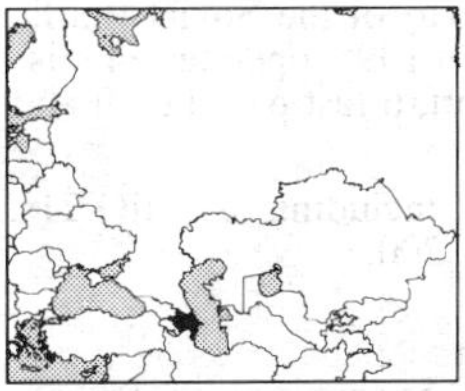

KEY HISTORICAL EVENTS. The 'Mussavat' (Nationalist) party declared the independence of Azerbaijan on 28 May 1918. On 28 April 1920 Azerbaijan was proclaimed a Soviet Socialist Republic. From 1922, with Georgia and Armenia it formed the Transcaucasian Soviet Federal Socialist Republic. In 1936 it assumed the status of one of the Union Republics of the USSR. In 1990 it adopted a declaration of republican sovereignty, and in Aug. 1991 declared itself formally independent; this was approved by 99·6% of votes at a referendum in Jan. 1992. Under the presidency of Gaidar Aliev, parliament ratified its adhesion to the CIS on 20 Sept. 1993.

Nagorno-Karabakh was largely occupied by Armenian forces in 1993. A ceasefire was signed on 18 Feb. 1994 under Russian auspices by representatives of Armenia, Azerbaijan and Nagorno-Karabakh.

TERRITORY AND POPULATION. Azerbaijan is bounded in the west by Armenia, in the north by Georgia and the Russian Federation (Dagestan), in the east by the Caspian sea and in the south by Iran. Its area is 86,600 sq. km (33,430 sq. miles), and it includes the Nakhichevan Autonomous Republic and the largely Armenian-inhabited Nagorno-Karabakh Autonomous Region.

The 1989 census population was 7,021,178, of whom 82·7% were Azerbaijanis, 5·6% Russians, 5·6% Armenians and 2·4% Lezgins. Estimate, Jan. 1995, 7,431,000 (3·6m. males; 4m. urban). Chief cities: Baku (1993 population, 1·7m.), Gyanda and Sumgait.

Vital statistics rates, 1994 (per 1,000 population): Births, 24·2; deaths, 7·3; growth, 16·9; infant mortality (per 1,000 live births), 28·2.

The official language is Azeri.

CONSTITUTION AND GOVERNMENT. At elections on 3 Oct. 1993 Gaidar Aliev was elected President against 2 opponents with 98·8% of votes cast.

Parliament is the 50-member *Melli-Majlis.* Elections and a constitutional referendum were held on 12 Nov. 1995. Representatives from 8 parties stood; turnout was 54·6%. The New Azerbaijan Party (NAP) gained 70% of votes cast. (The OSCE declared these elections 'not in accordance with international standards.')

President: Gaidar Aliev (b. 1924; NAP; sworn in 10 Oct. 1993).

In Oct. 1995 the government comprised:

Prime Minister: Fuad Kuliev.

Deputy Prime Ministers: Abbas Abbasov; Tofig Azizov; Asker Mamedov; Elchin Efendiev; Samed Sadyhov. *Foreign Affairs:* Hasan Hasanov. *Interior:* Ramil Usubov. *Housing and Communal Services:* Suddgedin Abdullaev. *Culture:* Byul-Byul Polad. *Material Resources:* Faruh Zeinalov. *Land Improvement and Water Conservancy:* Salekh Gadzhiev. *Local Industry:* Agabba Abdulaev. *Education:* Lidiya Rasulova. *National Security:* Namig Abbasov. *Defence:* Safar Abiev. *Information:* Vacant. *Communications:* Sirus Abbasbeily. *Agriculture and Food:* Ershad Aliev. *Commerce:* Miri Ganbarov. *The Economy:* Samed Sadyhov. *Justice:* Ilyas Ismailov. *Health:* Ali Insanov. *Finance:* Fikret Usifov.

National flag: 3 horizontal stripes of blue, red and green, with a white crescent and 8-pointed star in the centre of the red stripe.

National anthem: 'Azerbaijan! Azerbaijan!'; words by A. Javady, tune by U. Hajebaev.

DEFENCE. Conscription is for 17 months.

Army. The Army is organized in 1 tank, 12 motor rifle, 1 air assault, 2 motor rifle training and 2 artillery brigades; and 2 motor rifle, 2 mountain infantry and 1 anti-tank regiment. Equipment includes 325 T-55 and T-72 main battle tanks. Personnel, 1996, 73,300. There is also a paramilitary Ministry of the Interior militia of about 20,000.

Navy. The former Soviet Caspian Sea base at Baku and part of the Soviet flotilla have been taken over. The Azeri flotilla, numbering 2,200 in 1995, operates 34 miscellaneous vessels, including 2 small frigates, 2 missile craft, 6 fast patrol craft and 4 small amphibious vessels.

Air Force. In 1995 there were 46 combat aircraft, including 7 MiG-21s, 28 MiG-25s, 2 Su-17s, 9 Su-24s and 1 Su-25. Personnel, 11,200.

INTERNATIONAL RELATIONS

Membership. Azerbaijan is a member of the UN and the NATO Partnership for Peace.

ECONOMY

Budget. In 1993, revenue was 53,600m. manats, of which profits tax account for 13,000m. manats, and VAT 12,500m. manats. Expenditure was 64,800m. manats of which support for state-owned enterprises accounted for 18,800m. manats, and welfare 24,000m. manats.

Currency. The *manat* (AZM), of 100 *gyapiks* replaced the ruble in Jan. 1994. There are coins of 5, 10 and 50 gyapiks, notes of 1, 2, 5, 10, 50, 100, 250, 500, 1,000 and 10,000 manats. In March 1996, £1=6,793·74; US$1=4,445; DM1=3,011·72 manats.

ENERGY AND NATURAL RESOURCES

Electricity. Output was 19,000m. kWh in 1993.

Oil and Gas. The most important industry is crude oil extraction; production (including gas concentrate) was 11·1m. tonnes in 1992. Natural gas, 7,900m. cu. metres.

Minerals. The republic is rich in natural resources: Iron, aluminium, copper, lead, zinc, precious metals, sulphur pyrites, limestone and salt. In 1991, 1·6m. tonnes of iron ore were produced.

Agriculture. The chief agricultural products are grain, cotton, rice, grapes, fruit, vegetables, tobacco and silk. The Mexican rubber plant *grayule* has been acclimatized. A new kind of high-yielding winter wheat has been produced for use in mountainous parts of the republic. Agricultural production was valued at 2,200m. rubles (in constant 1983 prices) in 1993, 83% of its 1992 level.

Livestock on 1 Jan. 1994: Cattle, 1·6m.; pigs, 0·05m.; sheep and goats, 4·5m.

Output of main agricultural products (in 1m. tonnes) in 1993: Grain, 1·1; cotton, 0·3; potatoes, 0·2; vegetables, 0·5; fruit and berries, 0·3; meat, 0·09; milk, 0·8; and 660m. eggs.

Fisheries. About 10 tonnes of caviare are produced annually.

INDUSTRY. There are iron and steel, aluminium, copper, chemical, cement, building materials, food, timber, synthetic rubber, salt, textiles and fishing industries. Output was valued at 123,000m. manats in current prices in 1993, 93·2% of the 1992 figure. Output, 1993 (in tonnes): Rolled ferrous metals, 0·2m.; mineral fertilizers, 30,000; cement, 0·6m.; processed meat, 16,500; milk products, 48,000; fabrics, 116m. sq. metres; footwear, 4·1m. pairs; 200 lathes; 90 lorries; 8,700 TV sets; 229,000 refrigerators and freezers.

Labour. In 1993 the population of working age was 4·4m. of whom 2·7m. were employed, 67·5% in the state sector and 17·2% in co-operatives (in 1991). There were 22,700 registered unemployed in July 1994 (0·7% of the labour force), of whom 4,400 were receiving benefits. The average monthly salary in 1993 was 2,071 manats.

FOREIGN ECONOMIC RELATIONS

Commerce. In 1993 imports were valued at US$241m. and exports at US$350·9m.

Total trade between Azerbaijan and UK (British Department of Trade returns, in £1,000 sterling):

	1993	*1994*	*1995*
Imports to UK	823	1,517	6,080
Exports and re-exports from UK	2,965	5,803	13,906

COMMUNICATIONS

Roads. There were 30,400 km of motor roads (28,600 km hard-surfaced) in 1990. 533m. passengers and 21·9m. tonnes of freight were carried in 1993.

Railways. Total length was 2,125 km in 1993. In 1993, 8·9m. passengers and 18·4m. tonnes of freight were carried.

Shipping. In 1995, merchant shipping totalled 0·48m. GRT, including oil tankers, 0·23m. GRT.

Civil Aviation. There is an international airport at Baku. The national carrier is the state-owned Azerbaijan Airlines, which has routes to Istanbul and other Turkish cities and in 1995 operated 2 B-707-320Cs, 2 B-727-200s and 38 ex-Soviet aircraft. In 1993, 1·5m. passengers and 14,400 tonnes of freight were carried.

Telecommunications. The government-controlled Azerbaijan Radio broadcasts 2 national and 1 regional programme, a relay of Radio Moscow and a foreign service, Radio Baku (Azeri, Arabic, Iranian and Turkish).

Press. In 1995, 422 newspapers were registered with the Ministry of Justice, but only about 50 were actually appearing. There is 1 daily, published by parliament, with a circulation of 5,000, and 2 independent thrice-weeklies with a combined circulation of 30,000. 73 journals were registered in 1995, but only 12 were appearing. 80% of all newspapers circulate in the Baku area.

SOCIAL INSTITUTIONS

Religion. In 1993 the population was 62% Shia Moslem and 26% Sunni Moslem, the balance being mainly Orthodox Christian.

Education. In 1993–94 there were 1·4m. pupils in 4,332 primary and secondary schools and 2,200 children (16% of those eligible) attended pre-school institutions. There were 78 technical colleges with 33,900 students, and 23 higher educational institutions, including a state university at Baku, with 94,300 students (including correspondence students). The Azerbaijan Academy of Sciences, founded in 1945, has 30 research institutions.

Health. In 1994 there were 28,800 doctors, 70,100 junior medical personnel and 787 hospitals with 76,900 beds.

Welfare. In Jan. 1994 there were 797,000 age pensioners and 454,000 other pensioners.

NAKHICHEVAN

Area, 5,500 sq. km (2,120 sq. miles), population (Jan. 1994), 315,000. Capital, Nakhichevan (66,800). This territory, on the borders of Turkey and Iran, forms part of Azerbaijan although separated from it by the territory of Armenia. Its population, in 1989 was 95·9% Azerbaijani. It was annexed by Russia in 1828. In June 1923 it was constituted as an Autonomous Region within Azerbaijan. On 9 Feb. 1924 it was elevated to the status of Autonomous Republic. Its Supreme Soviet, elected 24 Feb. 1985, has 110 members including 52 women.

There are silk, clothing, cotton, canning, meat-packing and other factories. Nearly 70% of the people are engaged in agriculture, of which the main branches are cotton and tobacco growing. Fruit and grapes are also produced. There are 35 collective and 37 state farms. Crop area 37,400 ha.

In 1989–90 there were 219 primary and secondary schools with 60,200 pupils, and 2,200 students in higher educational institutions.

In Jan. 1990 there were 381 doctors and 2,445 junior medical personnel.

NAGORNO-KARABAKH

Area, 4,400 sq. km (1,700 sq. miles); population (Jan. 1990), 192,400. Capital, Stepanakert (33,000). Populated by Armenians (76·9% at the 1989 census) and Azerbaijanis (21·5%) and a separate khanate in the 18th century, it was established on 7 July 1923 as an Autonomous Region within Azerbaijan.

President: Robert Kocharyan (elected by parliament Dec. 1994).

Main industries are silk, wine, dairying and building materials. Crop area is 67,200 ha; cotton, grapes and winter wheat are grown. There are 33 collective and 38 state farms.

In 1989–90 34,200 pupils were studying in primary and secondary schools, 2,400 in colleges and 2,100 in higher educational institutions. In Jan. 1983 there were 523 doctors and 1,800 hospital beds.

In Feb. 1988 the republican Supreme Soviet voted to assume Armenian rather than Azerbaijani sovereignty, and the area was placed under a 'special form of administration' subordinate to the USSR government in 1989. In Sept. 1991 the regional Soviet and the Shaumyan district Soviet jointly declared a Nagorno-Karabakh republic, which declared itself independent with a 99·9% popular vote in Dec. 1991. The autonomous status of the region was meanwhile abolished by the Azerbaijan Supreme Soviet in Nov. 1991, and the capital renamed Khankendi. A presidential decree of Jan. 1992 placed the region under direct rule. Azeri-Armenian fighting for possession of the region culminated in its occupation by Armenia in 1993, despite attempts at international mediation.

DIPLOMATIC REPRESENTATIVES

Of Azerbaijan in Great Britain (Kensington Court, London, W8 5DL)
Ambassador: Mahmud Mamed-Kuliyev.

Of Great Britain in Azerbaijan (2 Izmir St., Baku 370065)
Ambassador: Thomas Young.

Of Azerbaijan in the USA
Chargé d'Affaires: Hafiz Pashayev.

Of the USA in Azerbaijan (83 Azadliq Prospekt, Baku)
Ambassador: Richard D. Kauzlarich.

Of Azerbaijan to the United Nations
Ambassador: Eldar Kouliev.

BAHAMAS

Commonwealth of The Bahamas

Capital: Nassau
Population: 275,700 (1995)
GNP per capita: US$11,790 (1994)
HDI/world rank: 0·894/26 (1992)

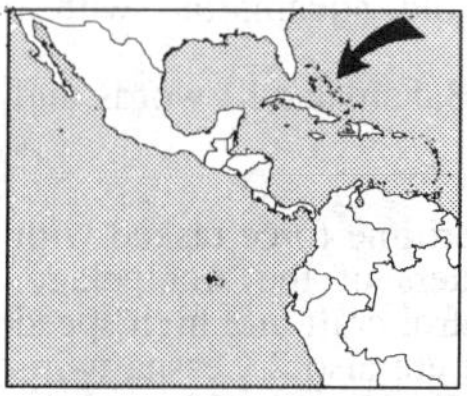

KEY HISTORICAL EVENTS. The Bahamas were discovered by Columbus in 1492 but the Spanish did not make a permanent settlement. British settlers arrived in the 17th century and it was occupied by Britain, except for a short period in the 18th century, until it gained independence. Internal self-government with cabinet responsibility was introduced on 7 Jan. 1964 and full independence achieved on 10 July 1973.

TERRITORY AND POPULATION. The Commonwealth of The Bahamas consists of 700 islands and more than 1,000 cays off the south-east coast of Florida extending for about 800 km. Only 22 islands are inhabited. Land area, 5,382 sq. miles (13,939 sq. km).

The areas and populations of the major islands in 1990 were as follows:

	Area (in sq. km)	*Population*		*Area (in sq. km)*	*Population*
Grand Bahama	1,373	40,898	Exuma Islands	290	3,556
Abaco	1,681	10,003	San Salvador	163	465
Bimini Islands	23	1,639	Rum Cay	78	53
Berry Islands	31	628	Long Island	448	2,949
New Providence	207	172,196	Ragged Island	23	89
Andros	5,957	8,177	Crooked Island	238	412
Eleuthera, Harbour Island			Acklins Island	389	405
and Spanish Wells	518	10,584	Mayaguana	285	312
Cat Island	388	1,698	Inagua Islands	1,671	985

1990 census population, 255,049 (130,091 females). 1995 estimate, 275,700; density, 20 per sq. km. The capital is Nassau on New Providence Island (172,000 in 1990); the other large town is Freeport (26,574) on Grand Bahama. Vital statistics rates, 1994 (per 1,000 populaton): Birth, 22·3; death, 5·6; marriage, 9·3; infant mortality (per 1,000 live births), 19·7. Expectation of life was 68 years for males and 75 for females in 1989–90.

CLIMATE. Winters are mild and summers pleasantly warm. Most rain falls in May, June, Sept. and Oct., and thunderstorms are frequent in summer. Rainfall amounts vary over the islands from 30" (750 mm) to 60" (1,500 mm). Nassau. Jan. 71°F (21·7°C), July 81°F (27·2°C). Annual rainfall 47" (1,179 mm).

CONSTITUTION AND GOVERNMENT. The Commonwealth of The Bahamas is a free and democratic sovereign state. Executive power rests with Her Majesty the Queen, who appoints a Governor-General to represent her, advised by a Cabinet whom he appoints. There is a bicameral legislature. The *Senate* comprises 16 members all appointed by the Governor-General, 9 on the advice of the Prime Minister, 4 on the advice of the Leader of the Opposition, and 3 after consultation with both of them. The *House of Assembly* consists of 49 members elected from single-member constituencies for a maximum term of 5 years. At the election of 19 Aug. 1992, the Free National Movement gained 32 seats and the Progressive Liberal Party, 17.

Governor-General: Sir Orville Turnquest, GCMG, QC.

The Cabinet in March 1996 was composed as follows:

Prime Minister: Hubert Alexander Ingraham.
Deputy Prime Minister and Minister of Tourism: Frank Watson. *Agriculture and*

Fisheries: Pierre Dupuch. *Foreign Affairs and Attorney-General:* Janet Gwenneth Bostwick. *Education and Training:* Dame Ivy Leona Dumont. *Finance and Planning:* William Allen. *Health and Environment:* Theresa Moxey-Ingraham. *Public Safety and Immigration:* Cornelius Alvin Smith. *Public Works:* Arlington Griffith Butler. *Social Development:* Maurice Elijah Moore. *Transport:* Tennyson Wells. *Youth and Culture:* Algernon Allen.

National flag: Three horizontal stripes of aquamarine, gold, aquamarine, with a black triangle on the hoist.

National anthem: 'Lift up your head to the rising sun, Bahamaland'; words and tune by T. Gibson.

DEFENCE. The Royal Defence Force is a primarily maritime force tasked with naval patrols and protection duties in the extensive waters of the archipelago. Equipment comprises 3 fast patrol craft and 12 smaller patrol craft and high speed craft for shallow water duty and 2 small transports. There are also 2 Cessna twin-engined light reconnaissance aircraft. Personnel in 1995 numbered 820, and the base is at Coral Harbour on New Providence Island.

INTERNATIONAL RELATIONS

Membership. The Commonwealth of The Bahamas is a member of the UN, OAS, the Commonwealth, CARICOM and is an ACP state of the EU.

ECONOMY

Budget (in B$1m.):

	1993-94	*1994-95*
Revenue	594·1	613·1
Expenditure	610·2	668·4

The main sources of revenue are customs duties and receipts from fees, post office and public utilities. There is no direct taxation.

Currency. The unit of currency is the *Bahamian dollar* (BSD) of 100 *cents.* Notes: B$0.50, 1, 3, 5, 10, 20, 50, 100; coins: 1, 5, 10, 15, 25, 50 cents, $1, 2, 5. American currency is generally accepted. Annual inflation was 2·2% in March 1995. Foreign exchange reserves were US$176·6m. in 1994. In March 1996, £1 = B$1.53; US$1 = B$1.00; DM1 = B$0·68.

Banking and Finance. The Central Bank of The Bahamas was established in 1974. Its Governor is James Smith. The Bahamas is an important centre for offshore banking. Financial business produces about 20% of GDP. In March 1995, 410 banks and trust companies were licensed, about half being branches of foreign companies.

Weights and Measures. The UK (Imperial) system is in force.

ENERGY AND NATURAL RESOURCES

Electricity. In 1995, installed capacity was 406 MW, all thermal. Output, 1994–95, 1,306 MWh.

Minerals. Aragonite is extracted from the seabed.

Agriculture. In 1995 there were some 8,000 ha of arable land, 2,000 ha of permanent crops and 2,000 ha of pasture. Production (in 1,000 tonnes), 1993: Sugar-cane, 200; vegetables and melons, 28; fruit, 12.

Livestock (1994): Cattle, 769; sheep, 6,292; goats, 13,580; pigs, 4,777; poultry, 1m.

Fisheries. In 1994 the total catch was valued at B$64·5m., mainly lobsters.

INDUSTRY. 2 industrial sites, one in New Providence and the other in Grand

Bahama, have been developed as part of an industrialization programme. The main products are pharmaceutical chemicals, salt and rum.

Labour. The workforce was estimated at 138,700 in 1994. Unemployment was 13·3%.

Trade Unions. In 1986 there were 36 unions, the largest being The Bahamas Hotel Catering and Allied Workers' Union (5,000 members).

FOREIGN ECONOMIC RELATIONS. Public-sector foreign debt was US$410·5m. in 1994. There is a freeport zone of Grand Bahama. Although a member of CARICOM, the Bahamas is not a signatory to its trade protocols.

Commerce. In 1993 imports (excluding bullion and specie) were valued at US$223·9m., and exports at US$1,149·9m.

The principal exports are oil products and transshipments, chemicals, fish, rum and salt.

In 1993, the main export markets were: USA, 41·5%; Sweden, 7%; Singapore, 7%. The main import suppliers were: USA, 25·7%; Italy, 20%; Japan, 16·9%; France, 10·5%.

Total trade in £1,000 sterling, between Bahamas and UK (British Department of Trade returns):

	1991	*1992*	*1993*	*1994*	*1995*
Imports to UK	37,142	38,178	25,163	25,628	33,029
Exports and re-exports from UK	19,631	24,532	41,662	30,580	30,912

Tourism. Tourism is the most important industry, accounting for about 70% of GDP. In 1994 there were 1,516,031 stop-over and 1,805,607 cruise-ship visitors. Tourist expenditure was US$1,332·6m. in 1994.

COMMUNICATIONS

Roads. There are about 1,350 km of paved roads and 2,000 km of gravel roads. In 1992, 55,887 motor vehicles were registered on New Providence.

Civil Aviation. There are international airports at Nassau and Freeport (Grand Bahama Island). The national carrier is the state-owned Bahamasair, which operated 6 aircraft in 1995, and flew to Miami, Newark, Orlando and Tampa. Scheduled flights are also operated by Air Canada; Air Jamaica; American Airlines; American TransAir; AOM; British Airways; Caledonian Airways; Canadian Airlines; Carnival Airlines; Condor Flugdienst; Delta Airlines; Gulfstream International Airlines; Turks and Caicos Airways; United Airlines; USAir.

Shipping. The Bahamas has an open shipping register. In 1995, registered shipping totalled 34·7m DWT, of which 8% was Bahamian-owned.

Telecommunications. In 1985 there were 127 post offices. New Providence and most of the other major islands have automatic telephone systems in operation, interconnected by a radio network, while local distribution within the islands is by overhead and underground cables. In 1995 there were 83,707 telephones in use. International telecommunications service is provided by a submarine cable system to Florida, USA, and an INTELSAT Standard 'A' Earth Station and a Standard 'F2' Earth Station. International operator assisted and direct dialling telephone services are available to all major countries. There is an automatic Telex system and a packet switching system for data transmission, and land mobile and marine telephone services. The Broadcasting Corporation of The Bahamas is a government-owned company which operates 5 radio broadcasting stations and a TV service with 3 channels. In 1995, 2 independent radio stations were operating. In 1993 there were 60,000 television and 0·2m. radio receivers. TV colour is by NTSC. There is cable TV on Grand Bahama and New Providence.

Cinemas (1990). There is 1 cinema.

Press (1995). There were 2 national dailies and 1 weekly.

SOCIAL INSTITUTIONS

Justice (1986). 32,878 cases (traffic, 11,334; criminal, 17,970; civil, 2,178; domestic, 1,396) were dealt with in the magistrates' court, and civil, 1,561; divorce, 516; criminal, 200 in the Supreme Court. The strength of the police force (1995) was 2,223 officers.

Religion. Religious adherents as enumerated at the 1990 census: Baptist, 79,453; Anglican/Episcopalian, 40,878; Roman Catholic, 40,875; Pentecostal, 14,094; Church of God, 12,843; Methodist, 12,242.

Education. Education is compulsory between 5 and 14 years. Adult literacy was 98% in 1994. In 1995 there were 215 schools (45 independent). Total school enrolment, Sept. 1994, 61,876. Courses lead to The Bahamas General Certificate of Secondary Education (BGCSE). Independent schools provide education at primary, secondary and high school levels.

The 4 institutions offering higher education are: The Government-sponsored College of The Bahamas, established in 1974; the University of the West Indies (regional), affiliated with The Bahamas since 1960; the Bahamas Hotel Training College, sponsored by the Ministry of Education and the hotel industry; and the Industrial Training Programme established to provide basic skills. Several schools of continuing education offer secretarial and academic courses.

Health. In 1993 there was a government general hospital (465 beds) and a psychiatric/geriatric care centre (485 beds) in Nassau, and a hospital in Freeport (82 beds). The Family Islands, comprising 20 health districts, had 13 health centres and 107 main clinics in 1991. There were 2 private hospitals (84 beds) in New Providence in 1993.

DIPLOMATIC REPRESENTATIVES

Of The Bahamas in Great Britain (10 Chesterfield St., London, W1X 8AH)
High Commissioner: Arthur Foulkes.

Of Great Britain in The Bahamas (Bitco Bldg., East St., Nassau)
High Commissioner: B. Attewell.

Of The Bahamas in the USA (2220 Massachusetts Ave., NW, Washington, D.C., 20008)
Ambassador: Timothy B. Donaldson.

Of the USA in The Bahamas (Mosmar Bldg., Queen St., Nassau)
Ambassador: Sidney Williams.

Of The Bahamas to the United Nations
Ambassador: Harcourt L. Turnquest.

Further Reading

Albury, P., *The Story of The Bahamas.* London, 1975.—*Paradise Island Story.* London, 1984
Boultbee, P. G., *Bahamas.* [Bibliography] Oxford and Santa Barbara, 1989
Cash, P., *et al., Sources of Bahamian History.* London, 1991
Craton, M. and Saunders, G., *Islanders in the Stream: a History of the Bahamian People.* vol. 1. Univ. of Georgia Press, 1992
Hughes, C. A., *Race and Politics in The Bahamas.* Univ. of Queensland Press, 1981
Hunte, G., *The Bahamas.* London, 1975

BAHRAIN

Dawlat al Bahrayn

(State of Bahrain)

Capital: Manama
Population: 568,000 (1995)
GNP per capita: US$7,500 (1994)
HDI/world rank: 0·862/44 (1992)

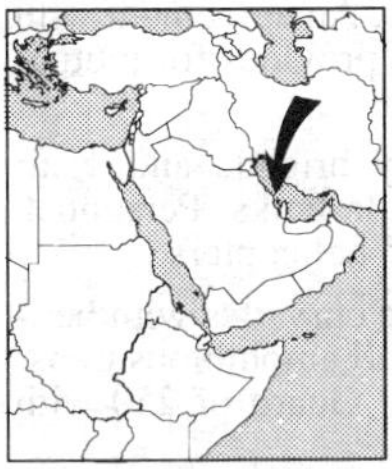

KEY HISTORICAL EVENTS. Treaties with Britain of 1882 and 1892 were replaced by a treaty of friendship which was signed on 15 Aug. 1971. Under the earlier treaties Britain had been responsible for Bahrain's defence and foreign relations. On the same day the State of Bahrain declared its independence.

TERRITORY AND POPULATION. The State of Bahrain forms an archipelago of 33 low-lying islands in the Arabian (Persian) Gulf, between the Qatar peninsula and the mainland of Saudi Arabia. The total area is about 265·5 sq. miles (687·75 sq. km). The island Bahrain (578 sq. km) is connected by a 1·5-mile causeway to the second largest island, Muharraq to the north-east, and by a causeway with the island of Sitra to the east. A causeway links Bahrain with Saudi Arabia. From Sitra oil pipelines and a causeway carrying a road extend out to sea for 3 miles to a deep-water anchorage.

Population at the 1991 census was 508,037 (36·4% resident foreigners). Estimate (1995) 568,000 (32% resident foreigners; 83% urban); density, 818 per sq. km. Expectation of life was 71 years in 1992. Infant mortality was 26 per 1,000 live births in 1991; annual growth rate, 1994, 3·1% (Bahraini's).

Manama, the capital and commercial centre, had a 1991 census population of 136,999. Other towns are Muharraq (74,254), Rifa'a (45,596), Jidhafs (44,769), Sitra (36,755) and Isa Town (34,509).

Arabic is the official language. English is widely used in business.

CLIMATE. The climate is pleasantly warm between Dec. and March but from June to Sept. the conditions are very hot and humid. The period June to Nov. is virtually rainless. Bahrain. Jan. 66°F (19°C), July 97°F (36°C). Annual rainfall 5·2" (130 mm).

RULING HOUSE: The ruling family is the Al-Khalifa who have been in power since 1782. The present Amir, HH Shaikh Isa bin Sulman Al-Khalifa (born 1933) succeeded on 2 Nov. 1961. *Crown Prince:* Shaikh Hamad bin Isa Al-Khalifa.

CONSTITUTION AND GOVERNMENT. A Constitution was ratified in June 1973 providing for a National Assembly of 30 members, popularly elected for a 4-year term, together with a Cabinet, appointed by the Amir. Elections took place in Dec. 1973, but in Aug. 1975 the Amir dissolved the Assembly and has since ruled through the Cabinet alone.

By decree of the Amir on 20 Dec. 1992 a *Consultative Council* was set up. It consists of 30 members nominated by the Amir for 4-year terms.

In Sept. 1995 the cabinet was composed as follows:

Prime Minister: Shaikh Khalifa bin Sulman Al-Khalifa (b. 1935).

Defence: Shaikh Khalifa bin Ahmed Al-Khalifa. *Transport and Communications:* Shaikh Ali bin Khalifa bin Sulman Al-Khalifa. *Housing, Municipalities and Environment:* Shaikh Khalid bin Abdulla Al-Khalifa. *Cabinet Affairs and Information:* Mohammed Ibrahim Al-Mutawa. *Education:* Abdul-Aziz Mohammed Al-Fadhil. *Health:* Faisal Radhi Al-Musawi. *Justice and Islamic Affairs:* Shaikh Abdullah bin Khalid Al-Khalifa. *Labour and Social Affairs:* Abdul-Nabi al-Shoala. *Power and Water:* Abdullah Mohammed Jumaa. *Interior:* Shaikh Mohammed bin

Khalifa Al-Khalifa. *Foreign Affairs:* Shaikh Mohammed bin Mubarak Al-Khalifa. *Finance and National Economy:* Ibrahim Abdul Karim. *Oil and Industry:* Shaikh Isa bin Ali Hamad Al-Khalifa. *Commerce:* Ali Saleh Abdullah Al-Saleh. *Works and Agriculture:* Majid Al-Jishi. *Adviser to the Amir:* Mahmoud Al-Alawi.

National flag: Red, with white serrated vertical strip on hoist.

National anthem: 'Bahrain ona, baladolaman' ('Our Bahrain, secure as a country'); words by M. S. Ayyash, tune anonymous.

DEFENCE. The Crown Prince is C.-in-C. of the armed forces. An agreement with the USA of Oct. 1991 gives port facilities to the US Navy and provides for mutual manoeuvres.

Army. The Army consists of 1 infantry brigade, 1 artillery brigade and 1 air defence battalion. Equipment includes 106 M-60A3 main battle tanks. Personnel, 1996, 8,500. There is a paramilitary police force of 9,000 with 5 helicopters.

Navy. The Naval force consists of 2 West German-built missile corvettes with helicopter facilities, 4 fast missile craft, 4 fast patrol craft and 4 small amphibious transports. Personnel in 1995 numbered 700. There is also a Coast Guard of 250 with 6 coastal patrol craft, 4 other vessels and 1 hovercraft.

Air Force. 1 fighter squadron operates 12 F-5E/F Tiger IIs, while a second unit has 12 F-16s. 3 MBB BO 105 helicopters are also in use as well as an S-70 VIP helicopter. Personnel (1995), 1,500.

INTERNATIONAL RELATIONS

Membership. Bahrain is a member of UN, the Arab League, the Gulf Co-operation Council and OAPEC.

ECONOMY

Budget. The 1996 budget envisaged revenue of BD530m. (of which BD285m. from oil) and expenditure of BD644m.

Currency. The unit of currency is the *Bahraini dinar* (BHD), divided into 1,000 *fils*. There are notes of 500 fils and 1, 5, 10, 20 dinars and coins of 100, 50, 25, 10, 5 and 1 fils. Annualized inflation was 0·9% in 1994. Foreign exchange reserves were US$1,170m. in 1994. BD101.21m. were in circulation in Nov. 1995. Gold reserves were 150,000 troy oz. in 1991. £1 = BD 0·58 in March 1996; US$1 = BD 0·38; DM1 = BD 0·26.

Banking and Finance. The Bahrain Monetary Agency (*Governor*, Abdullah Hassam Saif) has central banking powers. In 1994 there were 17 commercial banks, 2 Islamic banks, 2 specialized banks, 22 investment banks and 47 offshore banking units. 38 foreign banks had representative offices. Offshore banking units may not engage in local business; their assets totalled US$64,465m. in Dec. 1994.

There is a stock exchange linked with that of Oman.

Weights and Measures. The metric system is in use.

ENERGY AND NATURAL RESOURCES

Electricity. Production (1988) 2,996·1m. kWh.

Oil and Gas. In 1931 oil was discovered. Operations were at first conducted by the Bahrain Petroleum Co. (BAPCO) under concession. In 1975 the government assumed a 60% interest in the oilfield and related crude oil facilities of BAPCO. Production of crude oil in 1992 was 1·9m. tonnes. Oil reserves in 1988 were 150m. bbls.

There were known natural gas reserves of 7·1m. cu. ft. in 1987. Production, 1993, 7,670m. cu. metres. Gas reserves are government-owned.

Water. Water is obtained from artesian wells and desalination plants and there is a piped supply to Manama, Muharraq, Isa Town, Rifa'a and most villages. In 1987 total water production was about 60m. gallons per day; daily consumption 59·7m.

Agriculture. There are about 900 farms and small holdings (average 2·5 ha) operated by about 2,500 farmers who produce a wide variety of fruits (23,000 tonnes in 1993) and vegetables (10,000 tonnes). The major crop is alfalfa for animal fodder. 19,000 tonnes of dates were produced in 1993.

Livestock (1993): Cattle, 16,000; camels, 1,000; sheep, 9,000; goats, 17,000; poultry 1m.

Fisheries. In 1990 the government operated a fleet of 2 large and 5 smaller trawlers totalling 1,004 GRT. In 1988 total landings weighed 6,736 tonnes of which 5,339 tonnes were marine.

INDUSTRY. Industry is being developed with foreign participation: Aluminium smelting (and ancillary industries), ship-building and repair, petrochemicals, electronics assembly and light industry. Aluminium production was 447,514 tonnes in 1993.

Traditional crafts include boat-building, weaving and pottery.

Labour. Total work force in the private sector (estimate 1987) was 85,979, of which 25·2% were Bahraini. There were 3,383 persons registered unemployed in 1989.

FOREIGN ECONOMIC RELATIONS. Totally foreign-owned companies have been permitted to register since 1991. Foreign debt was US£3,106m. in 1993.

Commerce. In 1994 total imports were US$3,360m. and total exports were US$3,450m. In 1994, the principal exports were (in US£1m.): Petroleum products, 2,225; manufactures, 885. Principal imports: Mineral fuels, 1,248; machinery and transport equipment, 807; manufactures, 587; chemicals, 321.

In 1994 the main export markets were: India, 21·5%; Japan, 12·2%; Saudi Arabia, 5·8%; USA, 5·6%; UAE, 4·8%. Main import suppliers: Saudi Arabia, 40%; USA, 13·1%; UK, 6·8%; Japan, 5·2%; Switzerland, 4·6%.

Total trade between Bahrain and UK (British Department of Trade returns, in £1,000 sterling):

	1991	*1992*	*1993*	*1994*	*1995*
Imports to UK	39,120	49,702	51,712	25,380	26,379
Exports and re-exports from UK	147,494	167,104	151,093	150,378	150,757

COMMUNICATIONS

Roads. A 25-km causeway links Bahrain with Saudi Arabia. In 1986 there were 2,275 km of roads. In 1987 there were 112,520 registered vehicles.

Civil Aviation. Bahrain International Airport is at Muharraq. Bahrain has a 25% share (with Oman, Qatar and UAE) in Gulf Air, which in 1995 operated 12 A320-200s, 3 A340-300s, 1 B-757-200PF, 18 B-767-300ERs and 5 other aircraft. Services are also operated by Aeroflot Russian Airlines, Air India, Air Lanka, Air Malta, Alitalia, American Airlines, Balkan Bulgarian, Biman Bangladesh, British Airways, Cathay Pacific Airways, Cyprus Airways, CSA, Egyptair, Finnair, Gulf Air, Iran Air, KLM, Korean Air, Kuwait Airways, Lufthansa, Middle East Airlines, Northwest Airlines, Pakistan International Airlines, Royal Brunei Airlines, Royal Jordanian, Saudia, Syrian Arab Airlines, Turkish Airlines, Yemenia and Zas.

Shipping. In 1995, the merchant fleet totalled 0·24m. GRT, including oil tankers, 98,297 GRT. The port of Mina Sulman is a free transit and industrial area; about 800 vessels are handled annually.

Telecommunications. The government has a 37% stake in Bahrain Telecommunications (BATELCO). There were 0·12m. telephone lines in 1995. Radio Bahrain is government controlled, Bahrain Television part-commercial. In 1993 there were 0·32m. radio and 0·27m. TV receivers (colour by PAL).

Cinemas. There were 6 cinemas in 1987.

Press. In 1988 there were several Arabic and 1 English language daily newspaper.

SOCIAL INSTITUTIONS

Justice. Criminal law is codified, based on English jurisprudence.

Religion. Islam is the State religion. In 1981 85% of the population were Moslem (60% Shi'ite in 1990) and 7·3% Christian. There are also Jewish, Bahai, Hindu and Parsee minorities.

Education. Government schools provide free education from primary to technical college level. There were, in 1987, 143 schools for boys and girls with 4,967 teachers and 88,132 pupils. In addition there were 7 private schools. There is a teacher training college for men and one for women. In 1988, 405 Bahrainis were in higher education abroad. The Gulf Technical College opened in Bahrain in 1968 and Bahrain University in 1978. In 1987, 6,922 adult education centres were open. Literacy was 77·4% of the population over 15 in 1990.

Health. There is a free medical service for all residents. In 1985 there were 518 doctors and 23 dentists. In 1987, there were 5 government hospitals, 4 other hospitals and 19 health centres. There were 1,276 hospital beds.

Social Security. In 1976 a pensions, sickness benefits and unemployment, maternity and family allowances scheme was established. Employers contribute 11% of salaries and Bahraini employees, 11%.

DIPLOMATIC REPRESENTATIVES

Of Bahrain in Great Britain (98 Gloucester Rd., London, SW7 4AU)
Ambassador: Vacant.

Of Great Britain in Bahrain (21 Government Ave., P.O. Box 114, Manama, 306)
Ambassador: Ian Lewty.

Of Bahrain in the USA (3502 International Dr., NW, Washington D.C., 20008)
Ambassador: Muhammad Abdul Ghaffar.

Of the USA in Bahrain (Road No. 3119, P.O. Box 26431, Manama)
Ambassador: David M. Ransom.

Of Bahrain to the United Nations
Ambassador: Jassim Buallay.

Further Reading

Al-Khalifa, A. and Rice, M. (eds.) *Bahrain through the Ages.* London, 1993
Al-Khalifa, H. bin I., *First Light: Modern Bahrain and its Heritage.* London, 1995
Lawson, F. H., *Bahrain: The Modernization of Autocracy.* Boulder, 1989
Unwin, P. T. H., *Bahrain.* [Bibliography]. London and Santa Barbara, 1984

National statistical office: Central Statistics Organization, Council of Ministers, Manama.

BANGLADESH

Gana Prajatantri Bangladesh

(People's Republic of Bangladesh)

Capital: Dhaka
Population: 118·7m. (1993)
GNP per capita: US$230 (1994)
HDI/world rank: 0·364/146 (1992)

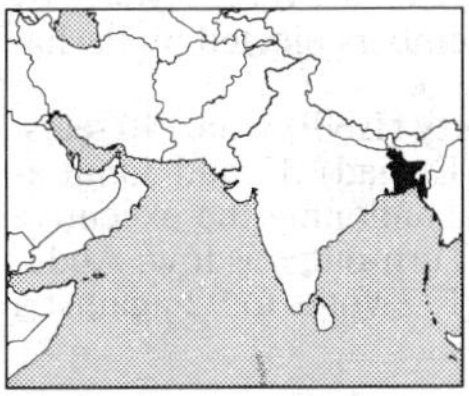

KEY HISTORICAL EVENTS. The state was formerly the Eastern Province of Pakistan. In 1970 the Awami League gained 167 seats out of 300 at the Pakistan general election and made known their wish for greater independence for the province. Following a civil war in 1971 Bangladesh was proclaimed independent. For developments between Jan. 1975 and March 1982, *see* THE STATESMAN'S YEAR-BOOK, 1986–87, pp. 186–187.

On 23 March 1982 there was a bloodless military coup, by which Lieut.-Gen. Hossain Mohammad Ershad became chief martial law administrator. Assanuddin Chowdhury was sworn in as civilian president on 27 March. Lieut-Gen. Ershad assumed the presidency on 11 Dec. 1983. He was re-elected on 15 Oct. 1986. Following popular unrest President Ershad declared a state of emergency on 27 Nov. 1990, but was forced to resign on 4 Dec. and arrested on 12 Dec.

Democratic parliamentary elections were held in Feb. 1991.

TERRITORY AND POPULATION. Bangladesh is bounded in the west and north by India, east by India and Burma and south by the Bay of Bengal. The area is 57,295 sq. miles (148,393 sq. km). In 1992 India granted a 999-year lease of the Tin Bigha corridor linking Bangladesh with its enclaves of Angarpota and Dahagram. At the 1991 census the population was 111,455,000 (54,141,000 females). Population density, 1991, 740 per sq. km. In 1994 the birth-rate was 27·8 per 1,000 population; death-rate, 9·0; marriage rate, 10·7; infant mortality, 77 per 1,000 live births. Growth rate was 2·4% in 1992. Life expectancy, 1994: Males, 58·2 years, females, 57·9. The country is administratively divided into 5 divisions, subdivided into 64 *zila*. Area (in sq. km) and population (in 1,000) in 1994 of the 5 divisions:

	Area	*Population*
Barisal division	13,297	7,757
Chittagong division	46,367	29,015
Dhaka division	31,119	33,940
Khulna division	22,274	13,243
Rajshahi division	34,513	27,500

The populations of the chief cities (1991 Census) were as follows:

Dhaka [1]	3,397,187	Mymensingh	185,517	Nawabganj	121,205
Chittagong [2]	1,363,998	Barisal	163,481	Pabna	104,479
Khulna [3]	545,849	Jessore	160,198	Tangail	104,387
Rajshahi [4]	299,671	Tongi	154,175	Saidpur	102,030
Narayanganj	268,952	Comilla	143,282	Jamalpur	101,242
Rangpur	203,931	Dinajpur	126,189	Naogaon	100,794

[1] Metropolitan area 6,105,160. [2] Metropolitan area 2,040,663. [3] Metropolitan area 877,388. [4] Metropolitan area 517,136.

The official language is Bengali. English is also in use for official, legal and commercial purposes.

CLIMATE. A tropical monsoon climate with heat, extreme humidity and heavy rainfall in the monsoon season, from June to Oct. The short winter season (Nov.–Feb.) is mild and dry. Rainfall varies between 50" (1,250 mm) in the west to 100" (2,500 mm) in the south-east and up to 200" (5,000 mm) in the north-east.

Dhaka.Jan. 66°F (19°C), July 84°F (28·9°C). Annual rainfall 81" (2,025 mm). Chittagong. Jan. 66°F (19°C), July 81°F (27·2°C). Annual rainfall 108" (2,831 mm).

CONSTITUTION AND GOVERNMENT. Bangladesh is a unitary republic. The Constitution came into force on 16 Dec. 1972 and provides for a parliamentary democracy. The head of state is the *President*, elected by parliament every 5 years. He or she appoints a *Vice-President*. There is a *Council of Ministers* to assist and advise the President. The President appoints the government ministers.

Parliament has one chamber of 300 members directly elected every 5 years by citizens over 18. There are 30 seats reserved for women members elected by Parliament.

At the elections of Feb. 1991 the Bangladesh National Party (BNP) won 140 seats, the Awami League 95, the Jatiya Party (led by Hossain Ershad) 35 and Jamit-e-Islami 18. A referendum of Sept. 1991 was in favour of abandoning the executive presidential system and opted for a parliamentary system. Turn-out was low. Abdur Rahman Biswas (b. 1926; BNP) was elected *President* by 172 votes to 92 against a single opponent.

In Nov. 1995 the government comprised:

Prime Minister with responsibility for Defence, Establishment and Cabinet Division: Khaleda Zia (b. 1944; BNP; sworn in 19 Sept. 1991).

Minister of Law, Justice and Parliamentary Affairs: Mirza Golam Hafiz. *Irrigation, Flood Control and Water Development:* Maj.-Gen. Majedul Haque. *Foreign Affairs:* Mostafizur Rahman. *Finance:* M. Saifur Rahman. *Local Government, Rural Development and Co-operatives:* Abdus Salam Talukdar. *Communications:* Col. Oli Ahmed. *Health and Family Welfare:* Chowdhury Kamal Ibne Yusuf. *Posts and Telecommunications:* Tariqul Islam. *Commerce and Information:* Shamsul Islam. *Food and Agriculture:* Abdul Mannan Bhuiyan. *Home Affairs:* Abdul Matin Chowdhury. *Energy and Mineral Resources:* Dr Khandakar Mosharraf Hossain. *Works:* Rafiqul Islam Miah. *Labour and Manpower:* Lieut.-Gen. Mir Shawkat Ali. *Education:* Zamiruddin Sircar. *Environment and Forests:* Col. Akbar Hossain. *Jute:* Hannan Shah. *Fisheries and Livestock:* Abdullah Al-Noman. *Shipping:* M. K. Anwar. *Religious Affairs:* Keramat Ali.

National flag: Bottle green with a red disc in the centre.

National anthem: 'Amar Sonar Bangla, ami tomay bhalobashi' ('My golden Bengal, I love you'); words and tune by Rabindranath Tagore.

Local Government. The country is divided into 5 divisions, each headed by a Divisional Commissioner, and subdivided into 64 districts administered by Deputy Commissioners and elected District Council. The districts are divided into 490 *thana*, of which 30 are urban. In Nov. 1991 the government dismissed all 460 elected mayors and dissolved opposition-controlled local councils. Municipal elections were held in Jan. 1993. The electorate was 60m.; turn-out was about 50%. Elections were held on 30 Jan. 1994 for 4 mayors and about 200 ward commissioners. The Awani League gained 2 mayoralties and 60% of the ward commissioner seats.

DEFENCE. The supreme command of defence services is vested in the President.

Army. There are 7 infantry divisional headquarters, with 16 infantry brigades, 1 armoured brigade, 2 artillery brigades, 1 engineer brigade and 2 armoured regiments. Strength (1996) 101,000. There are also an armed police reserve, 5,000 strong, 20,000 security guards (Ansars) and the Bangladesh Rifles (border guard) numbering 30,000. Equipment includes 60 Soviet T-54 and 80 Chinese Type-59 main battle tanks.

Navy. Naval bases are at Chittagong, Kaptai, Khulna and Dhaka. The fleet comprises 1 new Chinese-built missile-armed frigate, 3 old ex-British frigates, 8 Chinese-built fast missile craft, 8 Chinese-built fast torpedo boats, 1 ex-British offshore patrol vessel, 2 ex-Yugoslav 200-tonne patrol craft, 15 other patrol craft,

5 minesweepers, 5 locally-built 70-tonne river gunboats, 1 oiler, 1 repair vessel and 12 auxiliaries. Personnel, 1995, 8,000.

Air Force. Deliveries, from the USSR and China successively, comprised 6 MiG-21 and 16 F-17M interceptors and about 20 J-6 (MiG-19) fighter-bombers; 1 An-24 and 3 An-26 turboprop transports; over 30 Mi-8, Bell 212, Bell 206L and Alouette III helicopters; 20 Chinese CJ-6 piston-engined primary trainers, FT-2 (MiG-15UTI) jet advanced trainers, 15 Magister armed jet trainers and some light aircraft. Pakistan supplied about 40 surplus J-6s in 1990, but most were written off, along with other aircraft, during serious floods in the spring of 1991. Personnel strength, (1995) 6,500. There were 57 combat aircraft in 1995.

INTERNATIONAL RELATIONS

Membership. Bangladesh is a member of the UN, the Commonwealth and the Colombo Plan.

ECONOMY

Policy. The National Economic Council is responsible for policy. The fourth 5-year development plan, 1991–95, had its envisaged outlays reduced by 10% to 620,000m. taka in 1993. Alongside the 5-year plan are 3-year rolling plans and annual development plans. A perspective plan, in which localities set priorities for development in their area, was scheduled to follow the fourth 5-year plan.

Budget. The fiscal year ends on 30 June. Budget estimates, 1994–95: Revenue, Tk.136,370m. (including Tk.106,250m. tax); current expenditure, Tk.99,480m. In 1993–94 total Government receipts were Tk.98,230m., of which Tk.123,350m. were revenue receipts (Tk.99,650m. tax), and total expenditure was Tk.167,140m., divided into Tk.93,620m. revenue expenditure and Tk.73,520m. development expenditure. Estimated revenue expenditure (in Tk.1m.) in 1993–94: Administration, 24,035; education, 18,247; defence, 16,256; debt service, 10,250; justice (1992-93), 7,791; health, 6,018.

Currency. The unit of currency is the *taka* (BDT) of 100 *paisas,* which was floated in 1976. There are 1, 5, 10, 25 and 50 paisa and 1 taka coins and 1, 2, 5, 10, 20, 50, 100 and 500 taka notes. Money supply, 1992: Tk.82,572m. (of which Tk.45,344m. were in circulation). Foreign exchange reserves, 1994: US$2,800m. Inflation was 5% in 1992. In March 1996, Tk.61·90 = £1; Tk.40·50 = US$1; Tk.27·44 = DM1.

Banking and Finance. Bangladesh Bank is the central bank. There are 3 nationalized commercial banks, 11 private commercial banks, 4 specialized banks and 7 foreign commercial banks. In May 1992 the Bangladesh Bank had Tk.22,402m. deposits; Tk.33,612m. foreign liabilities, Tk.57,619m. assets. The scheduled banks had Tk.244,533m. deposits, Tk.53,442m. assets and Tk.36,289m. borrowings from the Bangladesh Bank. Post office savings deposits were Tk.6,265·7m. in 1994.

There is a stock exchange in Dhaka.

Weights and Measures. The metric system was introduced from July 1982, but some imperial and traditional measures are still in use. 1 *maund* = 37·32 kg = 40 *seers*; 1 *seer* = 0·93 kg..

ENERGY AND NATURAL RESOURCES

Electricity. Installed capacity, June 1992, 2,398 MW.; electricity generated, 1991–92, 8,378·49m. kWh.; consumption, 6,325·58m. kWh.

Gas. There are 17 natural gas fields with recoverable reserves of 10,438,700m. cu. ft. Production, 1992–93, 53,973m. cu. metres; consumption, 50,512m. cu. metres.

Water. India and Bangladesh are working towards agreement on sharing the water of the river Ganges.

Minerals. The principal minerals are lignite, limestone, china clay and glass sand. There are reserves of good-quality coal of 300m. tonnes. Production, 1992–93:

Limestone, 23,209m. tonnes (value Tk.13·93m.); china clay, 1,637m. tonnes (Tk.12·48m.).

Agriculture. In 1993 81·29m. persons depended upon agriculture, of whom 25·94m. were economically active. Agriculture contributed 33·5% of GDP in 1992–93. In 1992 there were 8·8m. ha of arable and 0·6m. ha of pasture. In 1993 10·90m. ha were sown to rice, 0·51m. ha to jute and 0·64m. ha to wheat. About 3·25m. ha (1993) is irrigated. 0·11m. tonnes of fertilizer were distributed in 1992-93.

Bangladesh is a major producer of jute: Production, 1993, 898,000 tonnes.

Rice is the most important food crop; production in 1993, 18m. tonnes. Other crops (1,000 tonnes): Sugar-cane, 7,507; millet, 63; wheat, 1,176; tobacco, 36; pulses, 502; tea, 49; potatoes, 1,384.

Livestock in 1993 (in 1,000): Cattle, 23,923; goats, 25,967; sheep, 940; buffalo, 866. Livestock products in 1993 (tonnes): Beef and veal, 144,000; cow milk, 767,000; buffalo milk, 24,000; goats' milk, 997,000; eggs, 98,670.

Forestry. The area under forests in 1991 was 4·69m. acres. Output of timber, 1992–93, was 8·12m. cu. ft.

Fisheries. Bangladesh is a major producer of fish and products. In 1988–89 there were 508,000 sea- and 769,000 inland-fishermen, with 1,249 mechanized boats, including 52 trawlers, and 3,317 motor boats. Inland catch, 1991–92, was 707,000 tonnes; sea, 245,000 tonnes.

INDUSTRY. Industry contributed 9·4% of GDP in 1992-93. The principal industries are jute and cotton textiles, tea, paper, newsprint, cement, chemical fertilizers and light engineering. In 1986-87 there were 4,386 factories (including 881 textile, 801 food and 564 chemical).

Production, 1993–94: Jute goods, 422,000 tonnes; cotton yarn, 57·59m. kg.; cotton cloth, 31·73m. metres; cement, 323,673 tonnes; sugar, 221,352 tonnes; vegetable oil, 15,009 tonnes; fertilizer, 2,257,745 tonnes; paper, 90,815 tonnes; bicycles (1992-93) 12,965; motor vehicles, 610; television sets, 22,916.

Labour. In 1990-91, the labour force was 51·2m. (20·1m. female), of whom 50·2m. (19·7m.) were employed (5·7m. children between 10 and 14 years were also employed). Employment (in 1,000) by industry: Agriculture, forestry and fishing, 33,303; manufacturing, 5,925; trade and catering, 4,285; services, 1,909; transport and communications, 1,611. Average daily industrial wages, 1992–93, by division: Dhaka, skilled Tk.80·61, unskilled Tk.51·68; Rajshani, skilled Tk.61·88, unskilled Tk.47·60; Khulna, skilled 80·61; unskilled 59·10; Chittagong, skilled 61·79, unskilled 49·95. In 1992, 763 industrial disputes arose.

FOREIGN ECONOMIC RELATIONS. Foreign companies are permitted wholly to own local subsidiaries. Tax concessions are available to foreign firms in the export zones of Dhaka and Chittagong. Foreign debt was US$13,051m. in 1991.

Commerce. The main exports are jute and jute goods, tea, hides and skins, newsprint, fish and garments, and the main imports are machinery, transport equipment, manufactured goods, minerals, fuels and lubricants. In 1992 exports were valued at US$2,118m., and imports at US$3,447m.

Main trading partners, 1992: USA (5·1% of imports, 26·6% of exports), Germany (3·6%, 10·4%) and Japan (8·9%, 3·2%).

Principal exports (in Tk.1m.), 1992–93: Raw jute, 2,795; jute goods, 10,195; tea, 1,555; leather and products, 5,393; ready-made clothes, 51,098; shrimps and prawns, 6,996. Imports: Wheat, 5,979; crude oil, 7,191; pharmaceuticals, 1,820; cement, 5,516; raw cotton, 3,737; machinery and electrical appliances, 20,322; vehicles, 4,731.

Total trade between Bangladesh and UK (British Department of Trade returns, in £1,000 sterling):

	1991	*1992*	*1993*	*1994*	*1995*
Imports to UK	80,568	94,952	140,114	156,004	231,644
Exports and re-exports from UK	39,086	39,355	54,274	55,678	89,145

Tourism. In 1993 there were 126,785 foreign visitors (42,285 from India, 15,633 from UK, 8,202 from USA). Foreign exchange earnings in 1993, Tk.594·4m.

COMMUNICATIONS

Roads. In 1992 there were 8,546 km of main roads and 6,507 km of paved secondary roads. In 1993 there were 25,194 buses, 31,757 lorries, 2,181 taxis, 32,879 motorized rickshaws and 35,372 private cars. There were 411,000 rickshaws and 714,000 bullock carts.

Railways. In 1993 there were 2,706 km of railways, comprising 884 km of 1,676 mm gauge and 1,822 km of metre gauge. In 1992-93 they carried 2·4m. tonnes of freight and 40m. passengers.

Civil Aviation. There are international airports at Dhaka (Zia), Chittagong and Sylhet, and 7 domestic airports. Bangladesh Biman Airlines is state-owned. In 1995 it operated 2 BAe ATPs, 5 DC-10-30s and 2 F-28-4000s and has domestic flights from Zia International Airport and services to Calcutta, Kathmandu, Bombay, Dubai, Abu Dhabi, Jeddah, Bangkok, Singapore, London, New York, Doha, Kuwait, Amsterdam, Rome, Karachi, Kuala Lumpur, Bahrain, Tripoli, Athens and Muscat. Services are also operated by Aeroflot, British Airways, Dragonair, Druk-Air, Emirates, Gulf Air, Indian Airlines, KLM, Kuwait Airways, Malaysia Airlines, Myanma Airways, Northwest Airlines, Pakistan International Airlines, Saudia, Singapore Airlines and Thai Airways. 2,127,000 passengers and 49,746 tonnes of freight passed through all airports in 1993.

Shipping. There are sea ports at Chittagong and Mongla, and inland ports at Dhaka, Chandpur, Barisal, Khulna and 5 other towns. There are 5,000 miles of navigable inland waterways. The Bangladesh Shipping Corporation owned 18 ships in 1993. Total tonnage registered, 1995, 0·53m. GRT, including oil tankers, 86,388 GRT. In 1992–93 the 2 sea ports handled 8·26m. tonnes of imports and 1·74m. tonnes of exports. Vessels entered (1992–93) 1,460 and cleared, 1,467. The Bangladesh Inland Water Transport Corporation had 323 vessels in 1993. 70·29m. passengers were carried in 1992–93.

Telecommunications. There were 8,312 post offices in 1993 and 249,800 telephones in 1994. International communications are by the Indian Ocean Intelsat IV satellite.

The government-controlled Radio Bangladesh and part-commercial Bangladesh Television transmit a home service and an external service radio programmes and a TV programme (colour by PAL). In 1993 there were 4·5m. radio and 0·51m. TV receivers.

Cinemas. In 1993 there were 905 cinemas with 411,193 seats. 75 full-length films were made.

Press. In 1993 there were 122 daily newspapers in Bengali with a circulation of 1·52m. and 15 in English with a circulation of 0·2m. There were 336 other periodicals (20 in English) with a circulation of 1·23m. In 1993, 1,041 book titles were published (92 in English).

SOCIAL INSTITUTIONS

Justice. The Supreme Court comprises an Appellate and a High Court Division, the latter having control over all subordinate courts. Judges are appointed by the President and retire at 65. There are benches at Comilla, Rangpur, Jessore, Barisal, Chittagong and Sylhet, and courts at District level.

Religion. Islam is the state religion. In 1992 the population was 86·7% Moslem and 12·1% Hindu.

Education. About 32·4% of the entire population was literate in 1993. In 1992–93 there were 50,898 primary schools, with 14·2m. pupils and 214,779 teachers; 11,382 secondary schools, with 4·7m. pupils and 129,655 teachers; 1,031 colleges of further education (797 private), with 912,895 students and 26,263 teachers; 78 professional colleges with 42,634 students and 2,429 teachers.

In 1995-96, there were 5 universities, an Islamic university, an open university and iniversities of agriculture, engineering and technology, and science and technology; there were 5 teacher training colleges, 5 medical, 3 law and 2 fine arts colleges, an institute of ophthalmology and a rehabilitation institute. In 1994-95, there were 92,654 university students and 2,217 academic staff.

Health. In 1993 there were 611 state and 292 private hospitals with a total of 35,280 beds. There were 22,400 doctors, 9,455 nurses, 10,104 midwives and 81,744 other medical personnel.

DIPLOMATIC REPRESENTATIVES

Of Bangladesh in Great Britain (28 Queen's Gate, London, SW7)
High Commissioner: Dr A. F. M. Yusuf.
(There are also Assistant High Commissioners in Birmingham and Manchester)

Of Great Britain in Bangladesh (Abu Bakr Hse., Gulshan, Dhaka 12)
High Commissioner: Peter Fowler, CMG.

Of Bangladesh in the USA (2201 Wisconsin Ave., NW, Washington, D.C., 20007)
Ambassador: Hamayun Kabir.

Of the USA in Bangladesh (Madani Ave., Baridhara, Dhaka 1212)
Ambassador: David N. Merrill.

Of Bangladesh to the United Nations
Ambassador: Reaz Rahman.

Further Reading

Bangladesh Bureau of Statistics. *Statistical Yearbook of Bangladesh.—Statistical Pocket Book of Bangladesh.*

Baxter, C., *Bangladesh: a New Nation in an Old Setting.* Boulder (CO), 1986
Chowdhury, R., *The Genesis of Bangladesh.* London, 1972
Hajnoczy, R., *Fire of Bengal.* Bangladesh Univ. Press, 1993
O'Donnell, C. P., *Bangladesh: Biography of a Muslim Nation.* Boulder (CO), 1986
Ziring, L., *Bangladesh from Mujib to Ershad: an Interpretive Study.* OUP, 1993

National statistical office: Bangladesh Bureau of Statistics, Ministry of Planning, Dhaka

BARBADOS

Capital: Bridgetown
Population: 264,300 (1994)
GNP per capita: US$6,530 (1994)
HDI/world rank: 0·900/25 (1992)

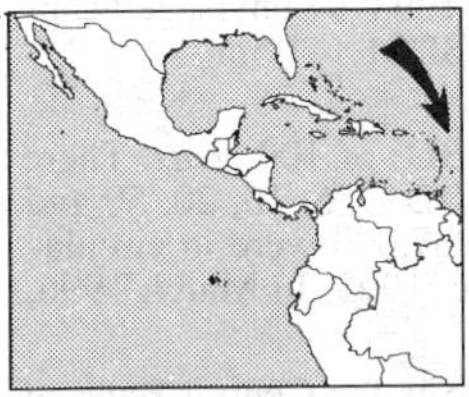

KEY HISTORICAL EVENTS. Barbados was occupied by the British in 1627. Full internal self-government was attained in 1961 and independence on 30 Nov. 1966.

TERRITORY AND POPULATION. Barbados lies to the east of the Windward Islands. Area 166 sq. miles (430 sq. km). In 1990 the census population was 260,491; 1994 estimate, 264,300. Bridgetown is the principal city: Population, 6,720 in 1990.

Growth rate (1994), 2 per 1,000 population; birth rate, 13·4; death rate, 8·7; infant mortality, 9·8 per 1,000 live births; expectation of life, 1991: Males, 72·9 years; females, 77·4.

CLIMATE. An equable climate in winter, but the wet season, from June to Nov., is more humid. Rainfall varies from 50" (1,250 mm) on the coast to 75" (1,875 mm) in the higher interior. Bridgetown. Jan. 76°F (24·4°C), July 80°F (26·7°C). Annual rainfall 51" (1,275 mm).

CONSTITUTION AND GOVERNMENT. The Legislature consists of the Governor-General, a Senate and a House of Assembly. The *Senate* comprises 21 members appointed by the Governor-General, 12 being appointed on the advice of the Prime Minister, 2 on the advice of the leader of the opposition and 7 in the Governor-General's discretion. The *House of Assembly* comprises 28 members elected every 5 years. In 1963 the voting age was reduced to 18.

The *Privy Council* is appointed by the Governor-General after consultation with the Prime Minister. It consists of 12 members and the Governor-General as chairman. It advises the Governor-General in the exercise of the royal prerogative of mercy and in the exercise of his disciplinary powers over members of the public and police services.

In the general election of Sept. 1994 turn-out was 60%; the Barbados Labour Party (BLP) gained 19 seats, the Democratic Labour Party, 8 and the National Democratic Party, 1.

Acting Governor-General: Sir Denys Williams.

In Dec. 1995, the government comprised:

Prime Minister, Minister of Finance and Economic Affairs, Civil Service: Owen Arthur (b. 1950; BLP).

Deputy Prime Minister, Minister of Foreign Affairs, Tourism and International Transport: Billie Miller. *Attorney-General, Minister of Home Affairs:* David Simmons, QC. *Agriculture and Rural Development:* Rawle Eastmond. *Education, Youth Affairs and Culture:* Mia Mottley. *Health and Environment:* Elizabeth Thompson. *Labour, Community Development and Sport:* Rudolph Greenidge. *Public Works, Transport and Housing:* George Payne. *Industry, Commerce and Business Development:* Reginald Farley. *International Trade:* Phillip Goddard.

National flag: Three vertical strips of blue, gold, blue, with a black trident in the centre.

National anthem. 'In plenty and in time of need'; words by Irvine Burgie, tune by V. R. Edwards.

DEFENCE. The Barbados Defence Force has a strength of about 1,000. A small maritime unit numbering 110 (1995) operates 5 lightly-armed coastal patrol vessels.

INTERNATIONAL RELATIONS

Membership. Barbados is a member of UN, OAS, CARICOM, the Commonwealth and is an ACP state of the EU.

ECONOMY

Budget. The financial year runs from April. The budget for 1993–94 envisaged capital expenditure of BD$138·7m. and current expenditure of BD$1,141·5m.

Various taxes were replaced by VAT in 1995.

Currency. The unit of currency is the *Barbados dollar* (BBD) of 100 *cents*. There are coins of 1, 5, 10 and 25 cents and BD$1, and notes of BD$2, 5, 10, 20, 50 and 100. Inflation was 3·7% in 1993. In Dec. 1993 BDS$176,987,000 were in circulation. Foreign exchange reserves were BDS$286·5m. in Dec. 1993. In March 1996, £1 = BDS$3·07; US$1 = BDS$2·01; DM1 = BDS$1·36.

Banking and Finance. The central bank and bank of issue is the Central Bank of Barbados, which had total assets of BD$753·74m. in Dec. 1994. The total assets of commercial banks were BD$2,650·06m.; savings banks' deposits, BD$1,231·57m. Barbados is of growing importance as an offshore banking centre. In 1993 there were 1,171 international business companies, 926 foreign sales corporations, 190 exempt insurance companies and 23 offshore banks.

There is a stock exchange which participates in the regional Caribbean exchange.

NATURAL RESOURCES

Electricity. Production (1994) 571m. kWh.

Oil and Gas. There is 1 oilfield. Crude oil production (1994) 453,427 bbls and reserves (1994), 3·2m. bbls. Output of gas (1994) 28·9m. cu. metres and reserves 200m. cu. metres.

Agriculture. The agricultural sector accounted for 5·1% (provisional) of GDP in 1994 (24% in 1967). In 1994, 5·1% of the total labour force were employed in agriculture. Of the total area of 42,995 ha, about 18,211 ha are arable land, which is intensively cultivated. In 1994, 7,800 ha were under sugar-cane cultivation and 1,280 ha were planted with vegetables and root crops, of which 34·9% were sweet potatoes, yams and carrots. Cotton was successfully replanted in 1983. Production, 1994 (in tonnes): Sugar-cane, 0.5m.; sweet potatoes, 1,254; yams, 1,173; carrots, 1,047; onions, 726; tomatoes, 565; cucumbers, 367; cabbages, 514; beets, 699; cotton 49·9. Meat and dairy products, 1994 (in tonnes): Pork, 1,688; mutton, 55; beef, 866; veal, 13; poultry, 10,152; milk, 7,297; eggs, 1,322.

Livestock (1994): Cattle, 33,000; sheep, 66,000; goats, 38,000; pigs, 45,000; poultry, 2m.

Fisheries. In 1994 there were 740 fishing vessels employed during the flying-fish season. Large numbers of these boats are laid up from July to Oct. The catch in 1994 was 4,338 tonnes.

INDUSTRY. Industrial establishments in 1994 numbered 442 and ranged from the manufacture of processed food to small specialized products such as garment manufacturing, furniture and household appliances, electrical components, plastic products and electronic parts. In 1994, 51,396 tonnes of sugar were produced.

Labour. In 1994 the workforce was 128,800 (60,800 females), of whom 96,900 were employed (46,500 females). Unemployment was 22% of the workforce in 1994.

Trade Unions. About one-third of employees are unionized. The Barbados Workers' Union was founded in 1938 and has the majority of members. There are also a National Union of Public Workers and 2 teachers' unions.

FOREIGN ECONOMIC RELATIONS

Commerce. Total trade for calendar years in BDS$1,000:

	1990	*1991*	*1992*	*1993*
Domestic Imports	1,407,918	1,397,719	1,048,457	1,153,881
Domestic Exports	253,916	241,420	269,139	272,242

In 1993 the main exports (in BDS$1,000) were: Electrical components, 50,329; sugar, 47,678; chemicals, 42,177; foodstuffs, 32,284; clothing, 9,293; other manufactures, 69,360. Imports: Foodstuffs, 189,130; motor cars, 27,893; other durables, 37,055; other manufactures, 81,782.

Total trade between Barbados and UK (British Department of Trade returns, in £1,000 sterling):

	1991	*1992*	*1993*	*1994*	*1995*
Imports from UK	13,316	22,306	25,079	15,906	25,639
Exports and re-exports to UK	33,454	21,027	28,229	30,992	101,144

Tourism. in 1994, tourism contributed 15·51% of GDP. In 1994 there were 425,632 visitors (395,979 in 1993). There were also 459,502 cruise ship passengers. Tourists spent BD$1,195·1m. in 1994.

COMMUNICATIONS

Roads. There are 2,333 km of paved roads. In 1994 there were 40,120 private cars, 2,442 hired cars and taxis, 865 buses including minibuses and 10,797 other vehicles including motorcycles.

Civil Aviation. The Grantley Adams International Airport is 11 km from Bridgetown, served in 1995 by Air Canada, Air Martinique, American Airlines, BWIA, British Airways, Canadian Airlines, Cardinal Airlines, Carib Express, Condor, Helenair, LIAT, LTU, Martinair Holland and Surinam Airways.

Shipping. There is a deep-water harbour at Bridgetown. 665,595 tonnes of cargo were handled in 1994. Shipping registered in 1995 totalled 0·11m. GRT, including oil-tankers, 76,219 GRT. The number of merchant vessels entering in 1994 was 1,956, of 17·3m. net tons.

Telecommunications. There is a general post office in Bridgetown and 16 branches on the island. In 1991 there were 87,343 telephones in service. The Caribbean Broadcasting Corporation is a part-government, part-commercial TV and radio service. There are 2 other commercial services (one for rediffusion). In 1993 there were 200,000 radios and 69,350 television sets (colour by NTSC).

Cinemas. There were (1992) 2 cinemas and 1 drive-in cinema for 600 cars.

Press. In 1995, there were 2 daily newspapers, 5 weeklies and a monthly.

SOCIAL INSTITUTIONS

Justice. Justice is administered by the Supreme Court and Justices' Appeal Court; and by magistrates' courts. All have both civil and criminal jurisdiction. There is a Chief Justice, 5 puisne judges of the Supreme Court and 9 magistrates. The death penalty is authorized. Final appeal lies to the Privy Council in London.

In 1995, the police force numbered 1,200.

Religion. At the 1990 census count, 32·9% of the population were Anglicans, 12·6% Pentecostalists, 5·9% Methodists, 4·4% Roman Catholics, 4·5% Seventh Day Adventists, 16·8% other religions and 22·9% no stated religion.

Education. Adult literacy is 99%. In 1991-92 there were 26,921 primary, 21,261 secondary and 202 vocational pupils in government schools and 2,573 pre-primary/primary and 3,818 secondary pupils in private schools. There were 22 secondary schools altogether in 1994-95. Education is free in all government-owned and maintained institutions from primary to university level.

In 1994–95 the University of the West Indies in Barbados (founded 1963) had

2,883 students and the Samuel Jackman Prescod Polytechnic 1,311.

Health. In 1995 there were 1 general hospital, 1 geriatric hospital, 1 psychiatric hospital, 1 leprosy hospital, 5 district hospitals and 8 health centres. In 1992 there were 1,966 hospital beds and 312 doctors.

Welfare. The National Insurance and Social Security Scheme provides contributory sickness, age, maternity, disability and survivors benefits. Sugar workers have their own scheme.

DIPLOMATIC REPRESENTATIVES

Of Barbados in Great Britain (1 Great Russell St., London, WC1B 3NH)
High Commissioner: Peter Simmons.

Of Great Britain in Barbados (Lower Collymore Rock, Bridgetown)
High Commissioner: Richard Thomas, CMG.

Of Barbados in the USA (2144 Wyoming Ave., NW, Washington, D.C. 20008)
Ambassador: Rudi Webster.

Of the USA in Barbados (PO Box 302, Bridgetown)
Ambassador: Jeanette Hyde.

Of Barbados to the United Nations
Ambassador: Carlston Boucher.

Further Reading

Beckles, H., *A History of Barbados: from Amerindian Settlement to Nation-State.* Cambridge Univ. Press, 1990

Hoyos, F. A., *Barbados: A History from the Amerindians to Independence.* 2nd ed. London, 1992.—*Tom Adams: a Biography.* London, 1988

Potter, R. B. and Dann, G. M. S., *Barbados* [Bibliography]. Oxford and Santa Barbara (CA), 1987

National statistical office: Barbados Statistical Service, Fairchild Street, Bridgetown.

BELARUS

Respublika Belarus

Capital: Minsk
Population: 10·4m. (1994)
GNP per capita: US$2,160 (1994)
HDI/world rank: 0·866/42 (1992)

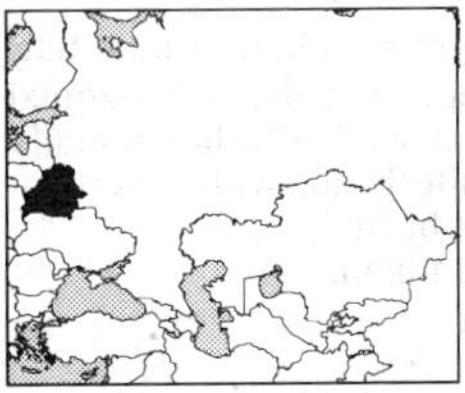

KEY HISTORICAL EVENTS. The Belorussian Soviet Socialist Republic was set up on 1 Jan. 1919.

On 25 Aug. 1991, following the unsuccessful coup, the Supreme Soviet adopted a declaration of independence, and the republic was renamed the 'Republic of Belarus' in Sept. In Dec. it became a founder member of the CIS.

TERRITORY AND POPULATION. Belarus is situated along the Western Dvina and Dnieper. It is bounded in the west by Poland, north by Latvia and Lithuania, east by Russia and south by the Ukraine. The area is 207,600 sq. km (80,134 sq. miles). The capital is Minsk (1·7m. population in 1994). Other important towns are Homel, Vitebsk, Mahilyoŭ, Bobruisk, Hrodno and Brest. On 2 Nov. 1939 western Belorussia was incorporated with an area of over 108,000 sq. km and a population of 4·8m. The 1989 census population was 10,151,806, of whom 77·9% were Belorussians, 13·2% Russians, 4·12% Poles, 2·9% Ukrainians and 1·1% Jews. Estimate, Jan. 1994, 10,367,000 (53% female; 68·2% urban).

Vital statistics rates, 1993 (per 1,000 population): Births, 11·3; deaths, 12·4; growth, –1·1; infant mortality (per 1,000 live births), 12·5.

Belarus comprises 6 provinces. Areas and populations, Jan. 1991:

Province	*Area sq. km*	*Population 1991*	*Capital*	*Population 1991*
Brest	32,300	1,483,700	Brest	277,000
Homel	40,400	1,628,400	Homel	503,300
Hrodno	25,000	1,188,700	Hrodno	284,800
Minsk	40,800	3,256,000	Minsk	1,633,600
Mahilyoŭ	29,000	1,269,400	Mahilyoŭ	363,000
Vitebsk	40,100	1,434,200	Vitebsk	369,200

CONSTITUTION AND GOVERNMENT. A new Constitution was adopted on 15 March 1994. It provides for a *President* who must be a citizen of at least 35 years of age, have resided for 10 years in Belarus and whose candidacy must be supported by the signatures of 70 deputies or 100,000 electors. Parliament is a 260-member *Assembly*, directly elected by a turn-out of a majority of the electorate. To be elected candidates must gain more than 50% of votes in their constituency. An election of two-thirds of Assembly members constitutes a quorum. The first 2 rounds of parliamentary elections were held on 14 and 28 May 1995, as a result of which 120 deputies were elected. At the third round on 29 Nov. 1995 for 141 constituencies not elected in May, turn-out was 61·8%; 20 candidates were elected. A fourth round was held on 10 Dec. 1995 and enough deputies were elected to form a quorum. Presidential elections were held on 23 June 1994. The electorate was 7·2m.; turn-out was 79%. Alyaksandr Lukashenka gained 45% of votes cast against 5 opponents, and was elected President at a run-off on 11 July 1994 by 80·1% of votes cast against 1 opponent. Turn-out was 69·9%.

At 4 referendums held on 14 May 1995 voters were in favour of giving the President powers to dissolve parliament, closer economic integration with Russia, the establishment of Russian as an official language of equal status with Belorussian and the introduction of a new flag.

President: Alyaksandr Lukashenka (b. 1955; sworn in 20 July 1994).

In Dec. 1995 the government comprised:

Prime Minister: Mikhail Chyrhir (b. 1949).

First Deputy Prime Minister: Mikhail Myasnikovych. *Deputy Prime Ministers:*

Uladzimir Harkun, Syarhei Ling, Uladzimir Rustakyavych. *Minister of Defence:* Anatol Kastenka. *Foreign Affairs:* Hryhori Navitsky. *Interior:* Yuri Zakharenka. *Justice:* Leanid Dushak. *Commerce:* Valentin Baidak. *Economy:* Badzei Pyatrovych. *Finance:* Stefan Yanchuk. *Health:* Vasili Kazakoŭ. *Information:* Anatol Butyavych. *Education:* Viktor Haisenok. *Culture:* Yevheni Voitavych. *Agriculture:* Fyodir Mirachinsky. *Transport and Communications:* Stefan Shkapych. *Social Welfare:* Tamara Krutivtsova. *Construction:* Mykalai Navitsky.

National flag: On 7 June 1995, following a favourable referendum, a new flag reminiscent of that of the Soviet era was introduced, replacing the 3 horizontal stripes of white, red and white introduced in 1991. The new flag is horizontally divided in the proportions 2:1 into a red field and a white band, with a vertical white band charged with the national ornament in red in the hoist.

National anthem: The music is that of the former Soviet anthem.

Local Government. Elections were held on 4 March 1990.

DEFENCE. Conscription is for 18 months. A treaty with Russia of April 1993 co-ordinates their military activities.

Army. In 1996 ground forces numbered 50,500 and were organized in Ministry of Defence troops comprising 2 motor rifle, 1 airborne, 1 artillery and 1 rear defence division, 1 independent airborne brigade and 2 artillery and 2 multiple rocket launcher regiments; 1 surface-to-surface missile, 1 anti-tank, 1 special forces and 2 surface-to-air missile brigades; and 3 corps (1 with 3 mechanized, 1 surface-to-surface missile and 1 surface-to-air missile brigade and 1 artillery and 1 multiple rocket launcher regiment; 1 with 1 mechanized, 1 surface-to-surface missile and 1 surface-to-air missile brigade and 1 artillery and 1 multiple rocket launcher regiment; and 1 non-combatant). Equipment includes 2,348 main battle tanks (381 T-55, 170 T-62 and 1,797 T-72), 419 medium-range launchers, 60 surface-to-surface and 350 surface-to-air missiles.

Air Force. The Air Force operates 2 interceptor regiments with MiG-23/25/29s, 3 strike regiments equipped with MiG-27, Su-17/24/25 aircraft and 1 reconnaissance regiment with MiG-25s and Su-24s. Helicopter assets are divided among 4 regiments with 300 machines, and 1 transport regiment has over 40 aircraft. Personnel, 1995, 13,700; 349 combat aircraft.

INTERNATIONAL RELATIONS. A treaty of friendship with Russia was signed on 21 Feb. 1995.

Membership. Belarus is a member of the UN and the NATO Partnership for Peace.

ECONOMY

Policy. Subsidies were removed in Jan. 1992 but under a reform programme of Jan. 1993 53% of retail prices were state-controlled. An economic programme for 1994 limited credit, linked the National Bank's base rate to inflation and abolished subsidies on dairy products and bread. Some 50% of state enterprises were scheduled for privatization under a scheme initiated in April 1994. GDP was valued at 12,619,000m. roubles in 1993, 91% of the 1992 figure.

Budget. Budget income in 1993 (in 1,000m. roubles), 3,624·9, including profits tax, 1,065·4; VAT, 998·3; excise duty, 437·7; income tax, 258·3. Expenditure in 1992 was 314·1, including subsidies to state enterprises, 131·5; welfare, 96·2.

Currency. The ruble was retained under an agreement of Sept. 1993 and a treaty with Russia on monetary union of April 1994. Foreign currencies ceased to be legal tender in Oct. 1994. In March 1996, £1 = 18,615; US$1 = 12,180; DM1 = 8,253 roubles.

Banking and Finance. The central bank is the National Bank.

ENERGY AND NATURAL RESOURCES

Electricity. Output was 33,400 kWh in 1993.

Oil and Gas. In 1993, 2m. tonnes of crude oil (including gas concentrate) and 300m. cu. metres of natural gas were produced.

Minerals. Particular attention has been paid to the development of the peat industry with a view to making Belarus as far as possible self-supporting in fuel. There are over 6,500 peat deposits. There are rich deposits of rock salt.

Agriculture. Belarus is hilly, with a general slope towards the south. It contains large tracts of marsh land, particularly to the south-west.

Agriculturally, it may be divided into 3 main sections—Northern: Growing flax, fodder, grasses and breeding cattle for meat and dairy produce; Central: Potato growing and pig breeding; Southern: Good natural pasture land, hemp cultivation and cattle breeding for meat and dairy produce. Agricultural output was valued at 10,500m. rubles (in constant 1983 prices) in 1993, 102% of its 1992 value.

Output of main agricultural products (in 1m. tonnes) in 1993: Grain, 7·5; meat and fats, 0·8; milk, 5·6; potatoes, 11·6; vegetables, 1; sugar-beet, 1·6; and 3,505m. eggs. In 1994, there were 5·8m. cattle, 4·2m. pigs and 0·3m. sheep and goats.

Since 1991 individuals may own land and pass it to their heirs, but not sell it. The area under cultivation was 11·9m. ha in 1993, of which the private subsidiary sector accounted for 1·4m. ha. There were 2,700 farms. The private and commercial sectors accounted for 38% of the value of agricultural output in 1993 (particularly potatoes and vegetables).

Forestry. There are valuable forests of oak, elm, maple and white beech. 5·8m. cu. metres of timber were produced in 1991.

INDUSTRY. Industrial production was valued at 16,868,000m. rubles in current prices in 1993, or 90% of the 1992 figure. There are food-processing, chemical, textile, artificial silk, flax-spinning, motor vehicle, leather, machine-tool and agricultural machinery industries. Output in 1993 (in tonnes): Rolled ferrous metals, 0·7m.; mineral fertilizers, 2·5m.; paper, 58,800; cement, 1·9m.; milk products, 1·4m.; artificial fabrics, 293,000; fabrics, 372m. cu. metres; footwear, 33·4m. pairs; 10,000 lathes; 30,800 lorries; 82,400 tractors; 609,000 TV sets; 738,000 refrigerators and freezers.

Labour. In 1993 the population of working age was 6m., of whom 4·76m. were employed, 69·2% in the state sector and 17·2% in co-operatives. In July 1994 there were 90,400 registered unemployed. The average monthly pay in 1993 was 60,859 rubles.

Trade Unions. Trade unions are grouped in the Federation of Trade Unions of Belarus.

FOREIGN ECONOMIC RELATIONS

Commerce. In 1993 imports were valued at US$747·2m. and exports at US$715·2m.

Total trade between Belarus and the UK (British Department of Trade returns, in £1,000 sterling):

	1993	*1994*	*1995*
Imports to UK	4,105	12,035	20,981
Exports and re-exports from UK	10,506	11,097	22,570

COMMUNICATIONS

Roads. In 1990 there were 92,200 km of motor roads (60,900 km hard-surfaced). In 1993, 1,702m. passengers and 209m. tonnes of freight were carried.

Railways. In 1993 there were 5,488 km of 1,520 mm gauge railways (873 km electrified). In 1993, 201m. passengers and 133m. tonnes of freight were carried.

Civil Aviation. The national carrier is Belavia, which flew 73 ex-Soviet aircraft in 1995. In 1993, 0·5m. passengers and 3,000 tonnes of freight were carried.

Inland Waterways. In 1993, 0·3m. passengers and 8·9m. tonnes of freight were carried.

Telecommunications. The government-controlled Belarus Radio broadcasts 2 national programmes and various regional programmes, a foreign service (Belorussian, German) and a shared relay with Radio Moscow. Belarus Television broadcasts on 1 channel (colour by SECAM).

Press (1989). Of 220 newspapers published 131 were in Belorussian. Daily circulation of Belorussian-language newspapers, 1·8m., other languages, 3·6m.

SOCIAL INSTITUTIONS

Religion. The Orthodox is the largest church. There is a Roman Catholic archdiocese of Minsk and Mahilyoŭ, and 5 dioceses embracing 455 parishes.

Education. The number of children in 5,187 primary and secondary schools was 1·5m. in 1993–94. 0·5m. children attended pre-school institutions in 1994.

In 1995-96, there were 4 universities; specialized universities of agriculture, culture, economics, informatics and radio-electronics, linguistics, teacher training and transport; academies of agriculture, arts, music, physical culture and sport and a polytechnical academy; 4 medical, 3 polytechnical and 3 teacher training institutes, and institutes of agriculture, co-operation, light industry technology, machine-building and veterinary science. In 1993-94, there were 304,600 students in higher education.

Health. In 1994 there were 43,900 doctors, 116,000 junior medical staff and 878 hospitals with 129,000 beds.

Welfare. In Jan. 1994 there were 1,987,000 age, and 0·6m. other pensioners.

DIPLOMATIC REPRESENTATIVES

Of Belarus in Great Britain (1 St. Stephens Cres., London W2 5QT)
Ambassador: Uladzimir Shchasny.

Of Great Britain in Belarus (37 Karl Marx St., Minsk 220030)
Ambassador: Jessica Pearce.

Of Belarus in the USA (1511 K Street NW, Washington, D.C., 20005)
Chargé d'Affaires: Syarhei Martynov.

Of the USA in Belarus (46 Starovilenskaya, Minsk)
Ambassador: Kenneth S. Yalowitz.

Of Belarus to the United Nations
Ambassador: Alyaksandr Sychoŭ.

Further Reading

Zaprudnik, J., *Belarus at the Crossroads in History*. Boulder (CO), 1993

BELGIUM

Royaume de Belgique—
Koninkrijk België

(Kingdom of Belgium)

Capital: Brussels
Population: 10·13m. (1995)
GNP per capita: US$22,920 (1994)
HDI/world rank: 0·926/12 (1992)

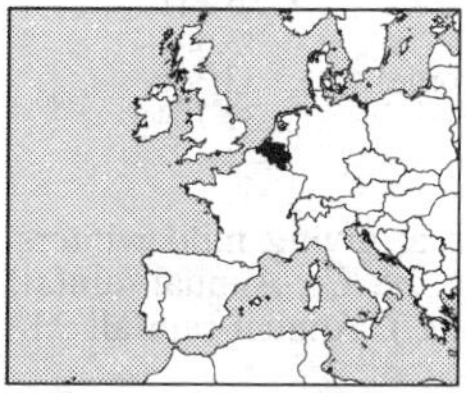

KEY HISTORICAL EVENTS. The kingdom of Belgium formed itself into an independent state in 1830, having from 1815 been part of the Netherlands. The secession was decreed on 4 Oct. 1830 by a provisional government, established in consequence of a revolution which broke out at Brussels, on 25 Aug. 1830. A National Congress elected Prince Leopold of Saxe-Coburg King of the Belgians on 4 June 1831; he ascended the throne 21 July 1831. The Treaty of London, 19 April 1839, established peace between King Leopold I and the King of the Netherlands.

Following constitutional reforms voted by parliament in May 1993, Belgium became a federal state.

TERRITORY AND POPULATION. Belgium is bounded in the north by the Netherlands, north-west by the North Sea, west and south by France, east by Germany and Luxembourg. Its area is 30,528 sq. km (11,778 sq. miles). The Belgian exclave of Baarle-Hertog in the Netherlands has an area of 7 sq. km, and a population (1995) of 2,073. Population (1991 census), 9,978,681; (1995 estimate), 10,130,574 (5,175,903 females); density, 331 per sq. km. There were 922,338 resident foreign nationals in 1995.

Dutch (Flemish) is spoken by the Flemish section of the population in the north, French by the Walloon south. The linguistic frontier passes south of the capital, Brussels, which is bilingual. Some German is spoken in the east. Each language has official status in its own community. (Bracketed names below contain French or Dutch alternatives).

Area, population and chief towns of the 10 provinces on 1 Jan. 1995:

Province	*Area (sq. km)*	*Population*	*Chief Town*
Flemish Region			
Antwerp	2,867	1,628,710	Antwerp
Flemish Brabant	2,106	995,266	Leuven (Louvain)
East Flanders	2,982	1,349,382	Ghent
West Flanders	3,134	1,121,135	Bruges (Brugge)
Limburg	2,422	771,613	Hasselt
Walloon Region			
Walloon Brabant	1,091	336,505	Wavre
Hainaut	3,787	1,286,649	Mons (Bergen)
Liège (Luik)	3,862	1,015,007	Liège
Luxembourg	4,441	240,281	Arlon
Namur (Namen)	3,665	434,446	Namur (Namen)

Population of the regions on 1 Jan. 1995: Brussels Capital Region, 951,580; Flemish Region, 5,866,106; Walloon Region, 3,312,888 (including the German-speaking Region, 68,961).

Vital statistics:

	Births	*Deaths*	*Marriages*	*Divorces*	*Immigration*[1]	*Emigration*[1]
1992	124,182	103,741	58,156	22,262	495,992	470,603
1993	119,828	106,601	54,112	21,602	502,530	483,592
1994	115,361	103,566	51,962	22,041	517,481	499,847

[1] Including internal.

The most populous towns, with estimated population on 1 Jan. 1995:

Brussels	951,580	St Niklaas (St Nicolas)	68,397
Antwerp	459,072	Tournai (Doornik)	68,086
Ghent	227,483	Hasselt	67,486
Charleroi	206,491	Genk	61,996
Liège (Luik)	192,393	Seraing	61,408
Brugge (Bruges)	116,273	Mouscron (Moeskroen)	52,987
Namur (Namen)	105,014	Verviers	53,940
Mons (Bergen)	92,666	Roeselare (Roulers)	53,617
Leuven (Louvain)	87,165	Turnhout	38,516
La Louvière	76,879	Herstal	36,841
Aalst (Alost)	76,256	Lokeren	35,602
Kortrijk (Courtrai)	76,040	Vilvoorde (Vilvorde)	33,346
Mechelen (Malines)	75,718	Lier (Lierre)	31,704
Ostend	68,858		

CLIMATE. Cool temperate climate, influenced by the sea, giving mild winters and cool summers. Brussels. Jan. 36°F (2·2°C), July 64°F (17·8°C). Annual rainfall 33" (825 mm). Ostend. Jan. 38°F (3·3°C), July 62°F (16·7°C). Annual rainfall 31" (775 mm).

ROYAL HOUSE. The reigning King is **Albert II,** born 6 June 1934, who succeeded his brother, Baudouin, on 9 Aug. 1993. Married on 2 July 1959 to Paola Ruffo di Calabria, daughter of Don Fuleo and Donna Luisa Gazelli des comtes de Rossena. *Offspring:* Prince Philippe, Duke of Brabant, b. 15 April 1960; Princess Astrid, b. 5 June 1962; married to Archduke Lorenz of Austria, 22 Sept. 1984. *Offspring:* Prince Amedeo, b. 21 Feb. 1986; Princess Maria Laura, b. 26 Aug. 1988; Prince Joachim, b. 9 Dec. 1991; Princess Luisa Maria, b. 11 Oct. 1995; Prince Laurent, b. 19 Oct. 1963.

The Dowager Queen. Queen Fabiola de Mora y Aragón, daughter of the Conde de Mora y Aragón and Marqués de Casa Riera; married to King Baudouin on 15 Dec. 1960. *Sister of the King.* Josephine Charlotte, Princess of Belgium, b. 11 Oct. 1927; married to Prince Jean of Luxembourg, 9 April 1953. *Half-brother and half-sisters of the King.* Prince Alexandre, b. 18 July 1942; Princess Marie Christine, b. 6 Feb. 1951; Princess Maria-Esmeralda, b. 30 Sept. 1956. *Aunt of the King.* Princess Marie-José, b. 4 Aug. 1906, married to Prince Umberto (King Umberto II of Italy in 1946) on 8 Jan. 1930.

A constitutional amendment of June 1991 permits women to accede to the throne.

The King receives an annual tax-free sum from the civil list of 244m. francs for the duration of his reign; Prince Philippe receives 13·5m. francs; Queen Fabiola, 45m. francs.

CONSTITUTION AND GOVERNMENT. According to the constitution of 1831, Belgium is a constitutional, representative and hereditary monarchy. The legislative power is vested in the King, the federal parliament and the community and regional councils. The King convokes parliament after an election or the resignation of a government, and has the power to dissolve it in accordance with Article 46 of the Constitution.

Constitutional reforms begun in Dec. 1970 culminated in May 1993 in the transformation of Belgium from a unitary into a 'federal state, composed of communities and regions'. The communities are 3 in number and based on language: Flemish, French and German. The regions also number 3, and are based territorially: Flemish; Walloon and the Capital Brussels.

Since 1995 the federal parliament has consisted of a 150-member *Chamber of Representatives*, directly elected by obligatory universal suffrage from 21 constituencies on a proportional representation system for 4-year terms; and a *Senate* of 71 members (excluding senators by right, i.e. certain members of the Royal Family). 25 senators are elected by a Flemish, and 15 by a French, electoral college; 21 are designated by community councils (10 Flemish, 10 French and 1 German). These senators co-opt a further 10 senators (6 Flemish and 4 French).

The federal parliament's powers relate to constitutional reform, federal finance, foreign affairs, defence, justice, internal security, social security and some areas of public health. The Senate is essentially a revising chamber, though it may initiate certain legislation, and is equally competent with the Chamber of Representatives in matters concerning constitutional reform and the assent to international treaties.

The number of ministries in the federal government is limited to 15. The Council of Ministers, apart from the Prime Minister, must comprise an equal number of Dutch- and French-speakers. Members of parliament, if appointed ministers, are replaced in parliament by the runner-up on the electoral list for the minister's period of office. Community and regional councillors may not be members of the Chamber of Representatives or Senate.

Elections were held on 21 May 1995. The electorate was 7,199,440; turn-out was 6,562,149. Flemish Christian Social Party (CVP) won 29 seats with 17·18% of votes cast, Flemish Liberal and Democratic Party (VLD) 21 with 13·15%, Francophone Socialist Party (PS) 21 with 11·87%, Flemish Socialist Party (SP) 20 with 12·56%, Francophone Liberal Reform Party-Democratic Front of Francophones (PRL-FDF) 18 with 10·26%, Francophone Christian Social Party 12 with 7·73%, Vlaams Blok (VB) 11 with 7·83%, Francophone Ecology Party (ECOLO) 6 with 4·01%, Volksunie (VU) 5 with 4·67%, Flemish Ecology Party (AGALEV) 5 with 4·43%, National Front (FN) 2 with 2·28%.

A 4-party coalition government was formed in June 1995 which in Dec. 1995 comprised:

Prime Minister: Jean-Luc Dehaene (CVP).

4 Deputy Prime Ministers: Elio di Rupa (PS) *(Communications and Economic Affairs)*; Johan Vande Lanotte (SP) *(Interior)*; Philippe Maystadt (PSC) *(Finance and Foreign Trade)*; Hermann Van Rompay (CVP) *(Budget)*. *Cabinet Ministers: Science Policy:* Yvan Ylieff (PS). *Health and Pensions:* Marcel Colla (SP). *Foreign Affairs:* Eric Derycke (SP). *Employment and Work, with responsibility for Equality of the Sexes:* Miet Smet (CVP). *Social Affairs:* Magda De Galan (PS). *Agriculture and Small Business:* Karel Pinxten (CVP). *Transport:* Michel Daerden (PS). *Justice:* Stefaan De Clerck (CVP). *Civil Service:* André Flahaut (PS). *Defence:* Jean-Paul Poncelet (PSC).

There are 2 *Secretaries of State* who are not members of the Council of Ministers: Reginald Moreels (CVP) (*Foreign Aid*); Jan Peeters (SP) (*Security, Social Integration and Environment*).

National flag: 3 vertical strips of black, yellow, red.

National anthem: La Brabançonne; words by C. Rogier, tune by F. van Campenhout). The Flemish version is 'O Vaderland, o edel land der Belgen' (Oh Fatherland, noble land of the Belgians).

European Parliament. Belgium has 25 representatives. At the June 1994 elections turn-out was 90·7%. The CVP won 4 seats with 17·1% of votes cast (group in European Parliament: Popular European Party); the Flemish Liberal and Democratic Party, 3 with 11·4% (Liberal, Democratic and Reformist Group); the PS, 3 with 11·3% (European Socialist Party); the SP, 3 with 11% (European Socialist Party); the PRL, 3 with 9% (Liberal, Democratic and Reformist Group); the Vlaams Blok, 2 with 7·8% (Radical European Alliance); the PSC, 2 with 7% (Popular European Party); Agalev, 1 with 6·7% (Greens); the Ecology Party, 1 with 4·8% (Greens); Volksunie, 1 with 4·4% (Europe of Nations); the National Front, 1 with 2·9% (Radical European Alliance); PSC, 1 with 0·2% (Popular European Party).

Community, Regional and Local Government. Communities and Regions elect parliaments ('councils') which in turn form governments. The Flemish Community and the Flemish Region are represented by a single council, whereas the French Community and the Walloon Region have a council each. There are also councils for the Brussels Capital Region and the German-speaking Region.

The areas of competence of Community Councils are culture, education, the media, medicine, protection of young people, the use of languages, some branches of scientific research and international relations affecting any of these areas.

Regional Councils have responsibility for land use, town-planning, the environment, conservation and rural renewal, housing, water resources, overseeing provincial and local authorities, labour, public works, transport, the economy, credit, foreign trade, agriculture, energy, some branches of scientific research and international relations affecting any of these areas. Regions raise their own revenues and also have a right to draw upon central government funds in some cases. Grants are available from the federal budget when the regional average product is lower than the national level.

Community and Regional Councils and Governments in 1995:

Community/Region	*Seat*	*No. of Council members*	*No. of Government members*	*Chief Minister*
Flemish Council	Ghent	124 [1]	11 [3]	Luc van den Brande
French Community	Brussels	94 [2]	4	Laurette Onkelinx
Walloon Region	Namur	75	7	Robert Collignon
Brussels Capital Region	Brussels	75	5	Charles Picqué
German-speaking Community	Eupen	25	3	Joseph Maraite

[1] Including 6 representatives of Flemings in Brussels.
[2] Includes 19 representatives of French-speakers in Brussels.
[3] 11 is the maximum number; the actual number in 1996 was 9.

There are 10[1] provinces and 589 communes with elected councils under a governor and burgomaster respectively. Governors and burgomasters are appointed by the King. Elections were held on 10 Oct. 1994.

[1] The 19 communes of the Brussels Capital Region stand outside the provincial administrative structure. They are administered by a governor appointed by the King.

DEFENCE. Conscription was abolished in 1995. It is aimed progressively to reduce the size of the armed forces, making more use of civilian personnel.

Army. The Army was restructured in 1995 into 3 divisions. The first, the Intervention Force, comprises 3 mechanized brigades, 1 paracommando brigade, 1 light aviation group (helicopter battalions) and support troops. The second, the Combat Support Division, comprises 5 branch training schools and 10 schools. The third, the Logistical Support Division, comprises 1 supply group, 1 maintenance group, 1 transport battalion and 1 logistical battalion. Total strength (1996) 30,600. The Gendarmerie ceased to be part of the Army in Jan. 1992.

Equipment includes 132 Leopard main battle tanks and 28 Epervier remotely-piloted vehicles. Aircraft operated: 10 Islander aircraft, 32 Alouette II helicopters and 46 Agusta A109 helicopters.

Navy. The naval forces, based at Ostend and Zeebrugge, include 3 frigates including 1 in reserve, 2 ocean minehunters/sweepers, 2 command and logistic support ships, 7 coastal tripartite minehunters, 1 research ship and 1 training sailing vessel. Naval personnel in 1995 totalled 2,800.

The naval air arm comprises 3 Alouette SA-318 general utility helicopters.

Air Force. The Belgian Royal Air Force has a strength of (1995) 12,500 personnel and comprises a Tactical Air Force and a Training and Support Command (schools and logistical units). The Tactical Air Force includes 2 tactical wings (each has 36 F-16s), an operational reserve of 18 F-16s, 1 transport wing (equipped with 12 C-130s, 2 Boeing 727s and 11 smaller passenger aircraft and 1 helicopter squadron of 5 Sea King helicopters for search and rescue missions.

INTERNATIONAL RELATIONS

Membership. Belgium is a member of the UN, EC, Council of Europe, NATO, OECD and WEU. The Schengen Accord abolishing border controls between Austria, Belgium, France, Germany, Greece, Italy, Luxembourg, the Netherlands, Portugal and Spain came into effect on 26 March 1995. Austria, Greece and Italy have not yet implemented it.

ECONOMY

Budget. In 1994, federal revenue (in 1,000m. francs) was 2,633·3 and expenditure,

2,702·8; regional and community revenue was 751·3 and expenditure, 795·1.

VAT is 20·5% (reduced rate, 6%).

On 30 Nov. 1995 the public debt consisted of (in 1,000m. francs): Internal debt consolidated, 6,644·6; short and middle terms, 1,912·2; at sight, 91·3.

Currency. The unit of currency is the *Belgian franc* (BEF) of 100 *centimes.* There are coins of 50 centimes and 1, 5, 20 and 50 francs and notes of 100, 200, 500, 1,000, 2,000 and 10,000 francs. In 1990 the Belgian franc was pegged to operate within a narrow band against the German Deutschmark within the EMS. Note circulation, Dec. 1995, 445,837m. francs. In March 1996, £1 = BFr46·38; US$1 = BFr30·34; Dm1 = BFr20·56.

Banking and Finance. The bank of issue is the National Bank (*Governor*, Alfons Verplaetse), instituted in 1850. The Governor is appointed for 5 years. It is the cashier of the State, and is authorized to conduct monetary and exchange rate policy. A law of 1993 guarantees its independence.

Savings banks: The Federal Participation Company (Société Fédérale de Participation), a state holding under the authority of the Minister of Finance, is part-owner of a unit (the Caisse d'Epargne) which performs the whole range of banking activities and a further unit which embodies the funds engaged in social security and insurance activities. In 1993 these units became 2 corporations. The savings deposits and savings bonds of the Caisse d'Epargne amounted to BFr1,295·5m. on 31 Dec. 1994. By a law of 1993 all credit institutions are permitted to exercise banking and financial services under the supervision of the Banking and Finance Commission. At 30 Sept. 1995 there were 127 credit institutions with total deposits of 24,747,000 francs.

There is a stock exchange in Brussels. Reforms of 1995 strengthened the exercise conditions for securities dealers.

Weights and Measures. The metric system is in force.

ENERGY AND NATURAL RESOURCES

Electricity. The production of electricity amounted to 68,379m. kWh. in 1992. 59% was nuclear-produced.

Gas. Production of gas, 1992, 548,804m. cu. metres.

Minerals. Output (in tonnes) for 4 calendar years:

	1991	*1992*	*1993*	*1994*
Coal	633,800	277,800	–	–
Coke	4,887,652	4,575,242	3,909,280	3,735,744
Cast iron	9,353,176	8,523,799	8,178,891	8,979,387
Wrought steel	11,334,883	10,334,352	10,118,116	11,265,234
Finished steel	8,980,361	9,385,031	9,750,433	10,979,804

Agriculture. 93,000 persons worked in agriculture in 1993. There were, in 1994, 1,365,034 ha under cultivation, of which 309,412 ha were under cereals, 30,312 ha vegetables, 119,417 ha industrial plants, 162,352 ha root crops and 620,112 ha pastures and meadows.

Chief	*Area in ha*		*Produce in tonnes*		
crops	*1993*	*1994*	*1992*	*1993*	*1994*
Wheat	196,656	195,218	1,328,915	1,427,672	1,385,098
Barley	66,189	57,753	449,635	390,569	346,239
Oats	11,452	9,646	35,735	54,167	42,442
Rye	2,310	2,568	9,072	10,350	11,737
Potatoes	48,120	51,591	2,428,681	2,175,189	1,661,592
Beet (sugar)	99,087	95,178	5,958,671	6,264,267	5,393,732
Beet (fodder)	10,469	9,952	1,001,424	995,072	855,766
Tobacco	418	390	1,552	1,563	1,459

In 1994 there were 23,362 horses, 3,251,968 cattle, 179,266 sheep, 9,026 goats and 7,089,214 pigs.

Forestry. In 1994 forest covered 608,364 ha.

Fisheries. In 1994 the fishing fleet had a total tonnage of 24,174 GRT. Total catch, 1994, 21,372 tonnes.

INDUSTRY. Output in 1992 of sugar factories and refineries, 959,445 tonnes; 10 distilleries, 27,140 hectolitres of alcohol; 126 breweries, 14,259,354 hectolitres of beer; margarine factories, 198,231 tonnes.

Labour. Retirement age is flexible for men and 60–65 for women. In 1993, 1,010,000 persons worked in industry and 2,596,000 in other sectors. There were 507,000 registered unemployed in June 1994.

FOREIGN ECONOMIC RELATIONS. In 1922 the customs frontier between Belgium and Luxembourg was abolished; their foreign trade figures are amalgamated. For Benelux *see* THE STATESMAN'S YEAR-BOOK, 1992–93, p. 197.

External debt was 1,271·4m. francs in 1993.

Commerce. Trade by selected countries (in 1,000 Belgian francs):

	Imports from			*Exports to*		
	1992	*1993*	*1994*	*1992*	*1993*	*1994*
France	662,581,453	606,289,148	677,516,010	764,017,881	789,956,781	871,528,777
USA	176,979,573	206,211,893	227,085,408	153,036,692	197,185,560	229,457,709
UK	309,693,062	350,674,516	395,330,004	311,429,951	351,301,405	388,526,570
Netherlands	704,661,363	608,291,314	745,683,436	544,160,544	543,707,993	604,089,508
Germany	961,638,971	807,902,404	849,270,502	906,902,219	871,496,634	962,775,920
Argentina	6,796,565	7,563,425	9,615,203	3,160,748	4,469,841	6,353,250
Italy	180,757,475	162,422,630	180,176,345	233,749,283	226,173,879	237,329,587
Switzerland	69,810,946	75,644,314	66,990,452	87,692,974	88,071,792	94,919,039
Zaïre	20,327,366	14,474,511	21,758,974	5,124,598	4,355,509	4,661,639
Denmark	27,000,022	23,102,103	26,573,667	36,014,167	38,562,751	42,665,898
Russia	15,411,641	39,229,708	47,648,290	7,127,529	20,019,298	25,084,590
India	20,282,838	27,222,410	31,370,837	45,344,344	63,493,376	62,143,924
South Africa	24,249,383	21,893,914	21,238,026	11,616,033	13,016,435	17,649,662
Canada	18,413,627	16,123,427	24,785,688	11,810,441	15,645,465	18,816,190
Brazil	21,634,085	16,897,966	20,786,479	5,171,672	7,703,439	12,722,239
Australia	13,543,099	10,304,248	10,416,036	10,912,597	13,203,903	15,897,395

Imports and exports for 6 calendar years (in 1,000 Belgian francs):

	Imports	*Exports*		*Imports*	*Exports*
1989	3,883,879,983	3,943,071,108	1992	4,023,293,094	3,969,810,672
1990	4,011,588,827	3,944,460,802	1993	3,791,873,785	4,154,142,399
1991	4,116,261,744	4,023,360,763	1994	4,206,413,923	4,588,184,485

The total trade between Belgium-Luxembourg and the UK was as follows (British Department of Trade returns, in £1,000 sterling):

	1991	*1992*	*1993*	*1994*
Imports to UK	5,472,663	5,741,401	6,123,700	6,742,800
Exports and re-exports from UK	5,870,876	5,714,150	6,429,700	6,971,700

Tourism. In 1994, 27,375,660 tourist nights were spent in 3,398 establishments in accommodation for 599,715 persons. In 1994 receipts totalled 171·2m. francs.

COMMUNICATIONS

Roads. Length of roads, 1995: Motorways, 1,665 km; other state roads, 12,737 km; provincial roads, 1,353 km; local roads, about 126,800 km. The number of motor vehicles registered on 1 Aug. 1995 was 5,136,342, including 4,273,451 passenger cars, 14,667 buses, 402,389 lorries, 40,074 non-agricultural tractors, 157,464 agricultural tractors, 200,258 motor cycles and 48,039 special vehicles. In 1991 there were 58,216 road accidents, with 2,535 fatalities.

Railways. The main Belgian lines were a State enterprise from their inception in 1834. In 1926 the *Société Nationale des Chemins de Fer Belges (SNCB)* was formed to take over the railways. The State is sole holder of the ordinary shares of SNCB, which carry the majority vote at General Meetings. The length of railway operated in 1994 was 3,396 km, (electrified, 2,293 km). Revenue (1994), 76,512m.

francs; expenditure, 80,445m. francs. In 1994, 63·41m. tonnes of freight and 142·6m. passengers were carried.

The regional transport undertakings Vlaamse Vervoermaatschappij and Société Régionale Wallonne de Transport operate electrified light railways around Charleroi (19 km) and from De Panne to Knokke (68 km). There is also a metro and tramway in Brussels (165 km), and tramways in Antwerp (180 km) and Ghent (29 km).

Civil Aviation. There are international airports at Brussels and Antwerp (Deurne). In 1994, 5·73m. passengers departed and 5·61m. arrived. The national airline SABENA (*Société anonyme belge d'exploitation de la navigation aérienne*) was set up in 1923. It was announced in Nov. 1990 that it was to be partially privatized, the state retaining a 25% stake. SABENA operates routes to Europe, North and South America, North, Central and South Africa and to the Near, Middle and Far East. In 1992 its fleet comprised 1 B-747-100, 2 B-747-300s, 5 DC-10s, 13 B-737-200s, 6 B-737-300s, 2 A310-200s and 1 A310-300. In 1994 SABENA flew 90m. km, carrying 4,261,561 passengers and 401 tonne/km of freight. 61 other airlines operate services.

Shipping. On 1 Jan. 1994 the merchant fleet was composed of 68 vessels of 1,625,401 tonnes. There were 37 shipping companies. In 1993, 55·55m. tonnes of cargo were loaded and 77·5m. tonnes discharged at Belgian ports. In 1994 14,730 vessels entered, and 14,576 cleared, the port of Antwerp.

The length of navigable inland waterways was 1,569·3 km in 1994. 89·53m. tonnes of freight were carried on inland waterways in 1992.

Telecommunications. On 31 Dec. 1992 there were 1,815 post offices. Gross revenue was 44,238m. francs in 1992.

In 1992 there were 5,691,000 telephones and in 1993 4,395,695 telephone subscribers. In 1994 there were 67,771 mobile telephone subscribers and 9,359 telex subscribers. There were 50,167 data transmission lines.

Broadcasting is organized according to the language communities. BRTN, RTBF and BRF are public institutions transmitting in Dutch, French and German respectively. BRTN has 7 radio and 2 TV services: Radio 1 (news), Radio 2 (news and entertainment), Radio 3 (cultural), Studio Brussels (youth emphasis), World Service, Night Radio, Radio Donna (entertainment), TV-1 and TV-2. It transmits from 10 radio and 6 TV stations. RTBF has 4 radio and 2 TV services: Radio 1 (documentary), Radio 2 (news and entertainment), Radio 3 (cultural), Radio 21 (youth emphasis), RTBF1 (TV) and Télé 21. It transmits from 12 radio and 7 TV stations. BRF transmits a radio programme from 3 stations. TV colour is by PAL. There are also 3 commercial networks: VTM (Dutch; cable only), RTL-TV1 (French; 1 station) and Canal Plus (French; 3 stations). Number of receivers (1994), radio, 2,568,398; TV, 3,384,091 (including 3,286,438 colour).

Cinemas (1994). There were 432 cinemas, with a seating capacity of 98,681.

Press. In 1993 there were 33 dailies in 94 regional editions (18 in French, 14 in Dutch and 1 in German). Total circulation in 1992, 2,057,169.

SOCIAL INSTITUTIONS

Justice. Judges are appointed for life. There is a court of cassation, 5 courts of appeal, and assize courts for political and criminal cases. There are 27 judicial districts, each with a court of first instance. In each of the 222 cantons is a justice and judge of the peace. There are, besides, various special tribunals. There is trial by jury in assize courts. The death penalty, which had been in abeyance for 45 years, was formally abolished in 1991.

The Gendarmerie ceased to be part of the army in Jan. 1992.

Religion. There is full religious liberty, and part of the income of the ministers of all denominations is paid by the State. In 1993 there were 9·06m. Roman Catholics. Numbers of clergy, 1991: Roman Catholic, 4,571; Protestant, 85; Anglican, 8; Jews, 25; Greek Orthodox, 30. There are 8 Roman Catholic dioceses subdivided into 260 deaneries. The Protestant (Evangelical) Church is under a synod. There is also a

Central Jewish Consistory, a Central Committee of the Anglican Church and a Free Protestant Church.

Education. Following the constitutional reform of 1988, education is the responsibility of the Flemish and Wallon communities. There were 4,453 (1993–94) primary schools, with 731,527 pupils and 4,119 infant schools, with 418,171 pupils. 1,950 (1993–94) middle schools had a total of 18,769 pupils in the general classes and 53,195 in the technical classes in the traditional system and 724,950 in the new system.

Under the French and German linguistic systems there were 22 (1993–94) schools for training secondary teachers (4,342 students); 23 for training elementary teachers (4,681 students); 13 technical normal schools with 502 students and 16 normal infant schools with 3,472 pupils.

Higher Education (1992–93). Higher education is given in state universities: Ghent (14,555 students), Liège (11,962), Mons (2,359), the Polytechnic Faculty in Mons (1,201), the Antwerp State University Centre (2,455), the Gembloux Faculty of Agronomical Sciences (948), the Royal Military School in Brussels (676) and in the private universities: Catholic University of Louvain (43,061), the Free University of Brussels (24,432), University Institution Antwerp (2,489), St Ignatius Antwerp (3,283), Our Lady of Peace in Namur (3,771), Catholic University Faculty in Mons (1,696), St Louis in Brussels (1,149), St Aloysius in Brussels (652), the Limburg University Centre (1,406) and the Protestant Faculty of Theology in Brussels (155). The total number of students in university colleges, faculties and institutes was 116,250.

There are 5 royal academies of fine arts and 5 royal conservatoires at Brussels, Liège, Ghent, Antwerp and Mons.

Health. On 1 Jan. 1995 there were 37,792 physicians, 7,070 dentists and 13,657 pharmacists. Hospital beds numbered 80,549 in 1991.

Social Security. Expenditure in 1993 (in 1m. francs): Sickness and injury benefit (wage-earners), 504,470; (self-employed), 36,773; unemployment benefit, 241,537; retirement and survivors' (wage-earners), 416,531; (self-employed), 66,787; family allowances, 173,638.

DIPLOMATIC REPRESENTATIVES

Of Belgium in Great Britain (103 Eaton Sq., London, SW1W 9AB)
Ambassador: Prosper Thuysbaert.

Of Great Britain in Belgium (Britannia Hse., rue Joseph II 28, 1040 Brussels)
Ambassador: Sir John Gray, KBE, CMG.

Of Belgium in the USA (3330 Garfield St., NW, Washington, D.C., 20008)
Ambassador: André Adam.

Of the USA in Belgium (Blvd. du Régent 27, 1000 Brussels)
Ambassador: Alan J. Blinken.

Of Belgium to the United Nations
Ambassador: Alex Reyn.

Further Reading

The Institut National de Statistique. *Statistiques du commerce extérieur* (monthly). *Bulletin de Statistique.* Bi-monthly. *Annuaire Statistique de la Belgique* (from 1870).—*Annuaire statistique de poche* (from 1965).

Annuaire administratif et judiciaire de Belgique. Annual. Brussels
Guide des Ministères: Revue de l'Administration Belge. Brussels, Annual
Hermans, T. J. *et al.* (eds.) *The Flemish Movement: a Documentary History.* London, 1992
Riley, R. C., *Belgium.* [Bibliography] Oxford and Santa Barbara, 1989

National statistical office: Institut National de Statistique, Rue de Louvain 44, 1000 Brussels.

BELIZE

Capital: Belmopan
Population: 209,500 (1994)
GNP per capita: US$2,550 (1994)
HDI/world rank: 0·883/29 (1992)

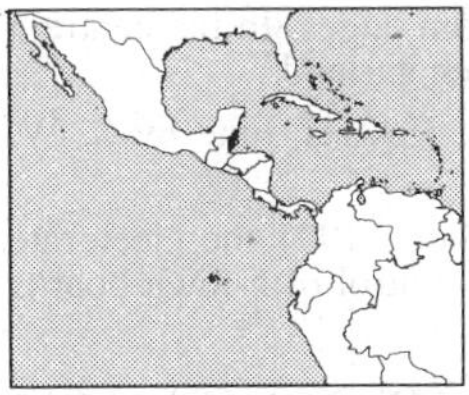

KEY HISTORICAL EVENTS. British settlers fended off Spanish occupation attempts from the 1630s. In 1780 the UK appointed a superintendent, and in 1862 the settlement was declared a colony, subordinate to Jamaica. It became a colony in 1884. Self-government was attained in 1964, independence on 21 Sept. 1981.

TERRITORY AND POPULATION. Belize is bounded in the north by Mexico, west and south by Guatemala and east by the Caribbean. Fringing the coast there are 3 atolls and some 400 islets (cays) in the world's second longest barrier reef (140 miles). Area, 22,963 sq. km.

There are 6 districts as follows, with area, population at the 1991 census and chief city:

District	*Area (in sq. km)*	*Population*	*Chief City*	*Population*
Corozal	1,860	28,217	Corozal	7,062
Belize	4,307	56,131	Belize City	44,087
Orange Walk	4,636	29,462	Orange Walk	10,966
Cayo	5,196	35,194	San Ignacio	8,962
Stann Creek	2,554	18,061	Dangriga	6,435
Toledo	4,413	17,275	Punta Gorda	3,458

Population (1991 census), 184,340 (47·3% urban); (1994 estimate), 209,500. In 1991 the birth rate per 1,000 was 38 and the death rate 5; infantile mortality in 1989 was 19·4 per 1,000 births and there were 1,138 marriages. Life expectancy was 67 years in 1989. In 1995, some 45,000 Belizeans were working abroad.

The capital Belmopan had a population of 3,852 in 1993. Other towns (with 1993 population) are: Belize City (47,724), Orange Walk Town (11,922), San Ignacio (9,701), Corozal Town (7,645), Dangriga (6,966).

English is the official language. Spanish is widely spoken. At the 1991 census the main ethnic groups were Mestizo (Spanish-Maya), 43·6%, Creole (African descent), 29·8%, Mayans, 14·6% and Garifuna (Caribs), 6·6%.

CLIMATE. A tropical climate with high rainfall and small annual range of temperature. The driest months are Feb. and March. Belize. Jan. 74°F (23·3°C), July 81°F (27·2°C). Annual rainfall 76" (1,890 mm).

CONSTITUTION AND GOVERNMENT. The Constitution, which came into force on 21 Sept. 1981, provided for a National Assembly, with a 5-year term, comprising a 29-member *House of Representatives* elected by universal suffrage, and a *Senate* consisting of 8 members, 5 appointed by the Governor-General on the advice of the Prime Minister, 2 on the advice of the Leader of the Opposition and 1 on the advice of the Belize Advisory Council.

At the general election of 30 June 1993 the United Democratic Party (UDP) won 16 seats and the People's United Party 13.

Governor-General: Sir Colville Young, GCMG.

The cabinet in Sept. 1995 was composed as follows:

Prime Minister and Minister of Finance and Economic Development: The Rt Hon. Manuel Esquivel (b. 1940; UDP).

Deputy Prime Minister, Attorney-General, Minister of Foreign Affairs and National Security: Dean Barrow. *Natural Resources:* Eduardo Juan. *Trade and*

Industry: Salvador Fernandez. *Works:* Melvin Hulse. *Health and Sports:* Ruben-Campos. *Tourism and the Environment:* Henry Young. *Agriculture and Fisheries:* Russell García. *Home Affairs and Labour:* Elito Urbino. *Science, Technology and Transportation:* Joseph Cayetano. *Education and Public Service:* Elodio Aragón. *Housing, Urban Development and Co-operatives:* Hubert Elrington. *Youth Development, Women's Affairs and Human Resources:* Philip Goldson.

The *Speaker* is B. Q. Pitts.

National flag: Blue with red band along the top and bottom edges. In the centre a white disc containing the coat of arms surrounded by a green garland.

National anthem: 'O, Land of the Free'; words by S. A. Haynes, tune by S. W. Young.

Local Government. At elections to 7 municipalities in March 1991 the electorate was 23,215 and 19,527 votes were cast. The PUP gained control of 5 town boards and the UDP of 2.

DEFENCE. The Belize Defence Force consists of 1 infantry battalion, with 5 active and 3 reserve companies. The Air Wing operates 2 Islander patrol aircraft. There is also a Maritime wing. In 1995 it numbered 50 and operated 1 fast patrol craft and 10 boats and support craft. Total personnel (1996) 1,050, with a reserve militia of 700.

INTERNATIONAL RELATIONS. While not giving up its territorial claims, Guatemala recognized Belize's independence in Sept. 1991. In return Guatemala may make use of Belizean ports, and Belize reduced its maritime zones to 3 miles.

Membership. Belize is a member of the UN, the Commonwealth, OAS, CARICOM and is an ACP state of the EU.

ECONOMY

Policy. The National Social and Economic Council was set up in 1993 to provide a forum for discussion between the public and private sectors. There are national economic plans.

Budget. The 1993-94 budget envisaged recurrent expenditure of $B205·7m., capital expenditure of $B163·4m., recurrent revenue of $B263·3m. and capital revenue of $B7·5m.

Currency. The unit of currency is the *Belize dollar* (BZD) of 100 *cents.* There are coins of 1-, 5-, 10-, 25- and 50-cent and $B1, and notes of $B1, 2, 5, 10, 20, 50 and 100. Money supply was $B380·2m. in 1991. Since 1976 $B2 has been fixed at US$1. In March 1996, £1 = $B3·06; DM1 = $B1·36.

Banking and Finance. A Central Bank was established in 1981 (*governor*, Keith Arnold). There were (1993) 4 commercial banks of which 2 are locally-owned, and a Government Savings Bank. The Development Finance Corporation provides long-term credit for development of agriculture and industry. Amendments to the Banking Ordinance permit offshore banking.

ENERGY AND NATURAL RESOURCES

Electricity. Production (1988) 90·5m. kWh. Supply 110 and 220 volts; 60 Hz. A rural electrification unit was set up in 1991.

Agriculture. 0·8m. ha are suitable for agriculture, but in 1994 only 121,400 ha were in use. In 1992 agriculture and produce-processing provided 25% of GDP and 40% of employment. The main crops are sugar-cane, citurs fruits and bananas. Maize, rice and kidney beans are grown for domestic consumption.

Livestock (1992): Cattle, 54,000; sheep, 4,000; pigs, 26,000; poultry, 1m.

Forestry. 1m. ha were under forests in 1988, which include mahogany, cedar, Santa Maria, pine and rosewood and many secondary hardwoods, as well as woods suitable for pulp.

Fisheries. There were (1995) 13 registered fishing co-operatives.

INDUSTRY. Manufacturing is mainly confined to processing agricultural products and timber. There is also a clothing industry. Sugar production was 105,397 tonnes in 1993-94 (100,200 tonnes in 1992-93).

Labour. The labour market alternates between full employment, often accompanied by local shortages in the citrus and sugar-cane harvesting (Jan.–July), and underemployment during the wet season (Aug.–Dec.), aggravated by the seasonal nature of the major industries.

Trade Unions. There are 14 accredited unions with an estimated membership of 8,200 (about 55% of the labour force).

FOREIGN ECONOMIC RELATIONS

Commerce. In 1993 imports amounted to $B562m., exports, $B263m. Main exports in 1993 were sugar ($B82·9m); clothes, ($B40·6); citrus products, ($B27·9); fish products, ($B26·4); bananas, ($B24·2).

Main export markets in 1991: USA, 39·5% of trade, UK, 29·5%, Mexico, 9·7%, Jamaica, 4·6%. Main import suppliers: USA, 53·8%, UK, 12·6%, Mexico, 8·8%.

Total trade between Belize and UK (British Department of Trade returns, in £1,000 sterling):

	1991	*1992*	*1993*	*1994*	*1995*
Imports to UK	20,849	32,157	37,405	42,504	47,010
Exports and re-exports from UK	14,574	11,072	16,642	12,767	14,261

Tourism. Tourists totalled 107,641 in 1993 spending US$72·5m.

COMMUNICATIONS

Roads. In 1995 there were 416 km of main roads and 1,834 km of other roads.

Civil Aviation. There is an international airport (Philip S. W. Goldson) at Belize City. The national carrier is Maya Airways, which operated 1 aircraft in 1995. American Airlines, Continental Airlines and Air Micronesia, Island Air and Taca International Airlines also operate services. Domestic air services provide connections to all main towns and 3 of the main offshore islands.

Shipping. The main port is Belize City, with a modern deep-water port able to handle containerized shipping. There are also ports at Commerce Bight and Big Creek. In 1995, the merchant marine totalled 0·43m. GRT, including oil tankers, 0·11m. GRT and container vessels, 17,641 GRT. 9 cargo shipping lines serve Belize, and there are coastal passenger services to the offshore islands and Guatemala.

Telecommunications. Number of telephones (1995), 28,250 (about half in Belize City). Belize Telecommunications Ltd has instituted a country-wide fully automatic telephone dialling facility. There were 1,200 mobile telephones in 1995, 1,000 paging users, 300 voice mail users and 200 Internet customers. There are 7 main post offices and 61 sub-post offices.

The Broadcasting Corporation of Belize operates a national broadcasting service. Proportion of programmes, 60% in English, the remainder in Spanish and the Amerindian languages. There is also a commercial radio station. There are 2 commercial TV channels (colour by NTSC). There are satellite links with Bermuda, the USA and the UK, and radio links with Central America. In 1993 there were some 100,000 radio and 27,048 TV sets in use.

Cinemas (1988). There were 5 cinemas with seating capacity of 5,000.

Press. There were 4 weekly newspapers and several monthly magazines in 1995.

SOCIAL INSTITUTIONS

Justice. Each of the 6 judicial districts has summary jurisdiction courts (criminal) and district courts (civil), both of which are presided over by magistrates. There is a

Supreme Court, a Court of Appeal and a Family Court. There is a Director of Public Prosecutions, a Chief Justice and 2 Puisne Judges.

In 1995, the police force was 450 strong.

Religion. In 1995 58% of the population was Roman Catholic and 34% Protestant, including Anglican, Methodist, Seventh Day Adventist, Mennonite, Nazarene, Jehovah's Witness, Pentecostal and Baptist. There was a small group of Bahai.

Education. 93% literacy was claimed in 1991. Education is in English. State education is managed jointly by the government and the Roman Catholic and Anglican Churches. It is compulsory for children between 6–14 years and primary education is free. In 1992, 241 primary schools had 48,612 pupils with 1,861 teachers (1989); 31 secondary schools, 9,457 pupils with, in 1988, 576 teachers; 8 other post secondary schools, with in 1987, 932 students and 69 teachers. There is a Technical College offering craft and technical courses, a vocational Training Centre providing courses for primary school leavers, a Youth Development Centre and a College of Agriculture. There is a teachers' training college. The University College of Belize opened in 1986. There are
2 government-maintained special schools for disabled children. The University of the West Indies maintains an extra-mural department in Belize City.

Health. In 1994 there were 7 government hospitals (1 in Belmopan, 1 in Belize City and 1 in each of the other 5 districts) and an infirmary for geriatric and chronically ill patients, with in 1990, 94 doctors and 525 hospital beds. Medical services in rural areas are provided by health care centres and mobile clinics.

DIPLOMATIC REPRESENTATIVES

Of Belize in Great Britain (200 Sutherland Ave., London, W9 1RX)
High Commissioner: Dr Ursula H. Barrow.

Of Great Britain in Belize (P.O. Box 91, Belmopan)
High Commissioner: Gordon Baker.

Of Belize in the USA (3400 International Dr., NW, Washington, D.C., 20008)
Ambassador: Dean R. Lindo.

Of the USA in Belize (Gabourel Lane and Hutson St., Belize City)
Ambassador: George C. Bruno.

Of Belize to the United Nations
Ambassador: Edward A. Laing.

Further Reading

Dobson, D., *A History of Belize.* Belize, 1973
Fernandez, J., *Belize: Case Study for Democracy in Central America.* Aldershot, 1989
Grant, C. H., *The Making of Modern Belize.* CUP, 1976
Wright, P. and Coutts, B. E., *Belize.* [Bibliography] 2nd ed. Oxford and Santa Barbara, 1993

National statistical office: Central Statistical Office, Belmopan.

BENIN

République du Bénin

Capital: Porto-Novo
Population: 5·23m. (1994)
GNP per capita: US$370 (1994)
HDI/world rank: 0·332/155 (1992)

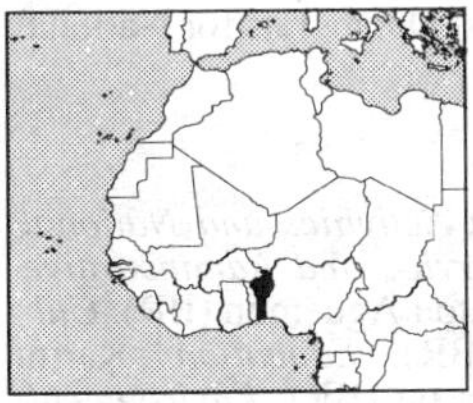

KEY HISTORICAL EVENTS. The territory of the present State was occupied by France in 1892 and was constituted a division of French West Africa in 1904 under the name of Dahomey. It became an independent republic within the French Community on 4 Dec. 1958, and acquired full independence on 1 Aug. 1960.

In the sixth coup since independence, Maj. Mathieu (now Ahmed) Kerekou came to power on 26 Oct. 1972 and proclaimed a Marxist–Leninist state, whose name was altered from Dahomey to Benin on 1 Dec. 1975. In Dec. 1989 the leadership abandoned Marxism-Leninism and called a national conference in Feb. 1990 to steer the country towards pluralist democracy.

TERRITORY AND POPULATION. Benin is bounded in the east by Nigeria, north by Niger and Burkina Faso, west by Togo and south by the Gulf of Guinea. The area is 112,622 sq. km, and the population, census 1992, 4,855,349. Estimate (1994) 5,234,000 (2,647,000 females); density, 46·5 per sq. km.

Vital statistics, 1985–90: Growth rate, 3·2%; infant mortality, 110 per 1,000; expectation of life, 1992, 46·1 years.

The areas, populations and capitals of the 6 provinces are as follows:

Province	*Sq. km*	*Census 1992*	*Capital*	*Census 1992*
Atakora	31,200	648,330	Natitingou	57,535
Borgou	51,000	816,278	Parakou	106,708
Zou	18,700	813,985	Abomey	65,725
Mono	3,800	646,954	Lokossa	52,909
Atlantique	3,200	1,060,310	Cotonou	533,212
Ouéme	4,700	869,492	Porto-Novo	177,660

Other large towns (with 1992 census population): Djougou (132,192), Bohicon (81,121), Kandi (74,169), Ouidah (64,068).

In 1992 the main ethnic groups numbered (in 1,000): Fon, 1,930; Yoruba, 590; Adja, 540; Baribo, 420; Aizo, 420; Somba, 320; Fulani, 270. The official language is French.

CLIMATE. In coastal parts there is an equatorial climate, with a long rainy season from March to July and a short rainy season in Oct. and Nov. The dry season increases in length from the coast, with inland areas having rain only between May and Sept. Porto Novo. Jan. 82°F (27·8°C), July 78°F (25·6°C). Annual rainfall 52" (1,300 mm). Cotonou. Jan. 81°F (27·2°C), July 77°F (25°C). Annual rainfall 53" (1,325 mm).

CONSTITUTION AND GOVERNMENT. The Benin Party of Popular Revolution (PRPB) held a monopoly of power from 1977 to 1989.

In Feb. 1990 a 'National Conference of the Vital Elements (*'Vives forces'*) of the Nation' proclaimed its sovereignty and appointed Nicéphore Soglo *Prime Minister* of a provisional government. At a referendum in Dec. 1990 93·2% of votes cast were in favour of the new constitution, which has introduced a presidential regime. The *President* is directly elected for renewable 5-year terms. Parliament is the 83-member *National Assembly*, elected by proportional representation for 4-year terms.

A 30-member advisory *Social and Economic Council* was set up in 1994. There is a *Constitutional Court*.

At the presidential elections of March 1991 Nicéphor Soglo defeated the incumbent president, Brig.-Gen. Ahmed Kerekou, by gaining 67·7% of votes cast. New presidential elections were scheduled for March 1996. Parliamentary elections were held on 28 March 1995. Some 2,600 candidates, representating 50 parties stood. The electorate was 2,531,122. Benin Renaissance (BR) gained 20 seats; the Presidential Movement alliance (PM), 12; the Democratic Renewal Party, 19; Action Front for Renewal and Development, 10; the Social Democratic Party, 8; Our Common Cause, 3; Push for Progress and Democracy, 3; Liberal Democrats for National Reconstruction, 3; others, 1 each.

President: Nicéphor Soglo (BR; sworn in 4 April 1991).

In Dec. 1995 the government comprised:

Minister of State for the Co-ordination of Government Activities and National Defence: Désiré Vieyra (BR). *Minister for the Civil Service and Adminstrative Reform:* Yarou Zimi Kora. *Commerce and Tourism:* Sikiratou Aguémon (BR). *Culture and Communications:* Félicienne Guinikoukou (BR). *Education:* Karim Dramane (PM). *Energy, Mines and Water:* Aurélien Hoéssou (BR). *Environment, Housing and Urban Planning:* Aziadomé Kogblévi (BR). *Finance:* Paul Dossou. *Foreign Affairs and Co-operation:* Yves Monnou (BR). *Health:* Véronique Lawson. *Industry:* Wallis Zoumarou (PM). *Interior, Security and Territorial Administration:* Alabi Gbégan (BR). *Justice and Law:* Grace Abamon. *Labour, Unemployment and Social Affairs:* Kodjo Atchode (BR). *Planning and Economic Restructure:* Robert Tagnon (PM). *Public Works and Transport:* Georges Kédou (BR). *Relations with Government and Government Spokesperson:* Théodore Holo. *Rural Development:* Mama N'Diaye (PM). *Youth and Sport:* Alassane Tigri.

The *Speaker* of the National Assembly is Bruno Amoussou (Social Democratic Party).

National flag: Horizontally yellow over red with a green vertical strip in the hoist.

National anthem: 'L'Aube Nouvelle' ('New Dawn'); words and tune by Gilbert Dagnon.

Local Government. The 6 provinces are divided into 84 districts. In Nov. 1990 elections were held for mayors and district chiefs.

DEFENCE. There is selective conscription for 18 months.

Army. The Army consists of 3 infantry, 1 para-commando and 1 engineer battalions, 1 armoured squadron and 1 artillery battery. Equipement includes 20 PT-76 light tanks. Strength (1996) 4,500, with an additional 2,500-strong paramilitary gendarmerie.

Navy. The flotilla comprises 1 French-built inshore craft and 4 Soviet-built inshore patrol craft reported in reserve. There is 1 tug. Personnel in 1995 numbered 150, and the force is based at Cotonou.

Air Force. The Air Force has suffered a shortage of funds and in 1995 operated only 1 Twin Otter and 2 Ecureuil helicopters. Personnel, 1995, 150.

INTERNATIONAL RELATIONS

Membership. Benin is a member of the UN, OAU and is an ACP state of the EU.

ECONOMY

Policy. The Second Structural Adjustment Programme began in 1991, which seeks to provide resources for priority social and economic goals by economies, reforms and rationalization. An action plan envisages some privatization. Price controls were imposed in 1994.

Budget. The fiscal year is the calendar year. In 1994 revenue was 127,100m. francs CFA and expenditure, 161,800m. francs CFA, of which 108,400m. francs CFA were current expenditure. The 1995 budget balanced at 204,000m. francs CFA.

Currency. The monetary unit is the *franc CFA* (XOF), with a parity value of 100 francs CFA to 1 French franc. There are coins of 5, 10, 25, 50 and 100 francs CFA, and banknotes of 500, 1,000, 5,000 and 10,000 francs CFA. 45,580m. francs CFA were in circulation in 1993. Foreign exchange reserves were US$258·2m. in 1994. Gold reserves were US$2·8m in 1993. Annualized inflation was 25% in 1995 (54% in 1994). In March 1996, £1 = 772·97 francs CFA; US$1 = 505·74 francs CFA; DM1 = 342·67 francs CFA.

Banking and Finance. The bank of issue and the central bank is the regional West African Central Bank (BCEAO). There are 5 private commercial banks. Total deposits were 182,000m. francs CFA in May 1995.

ENERGY AND NATURAL RESOURCES

Electricity. In 1993, 236·1m. kWh were produced or imported. A solar energy programme was initiated in 1993.

Oil. The Semé oilfield, located 10 miles offshore, was discovered in 1968. Production commenced in 1982 and was 195,000 tonnes in 1992.

Agriculture. In 1992, 2·93m. persons depended on agriculture, of whom 1·35m. were economically active. 36·8% of GDP was furnished by agriculture in 1993. Small independent farms produce about 90% of output. In 1991 1·42m. ha were arable, 0·45m. ha permanent crops and 0·44m. ha permanent pasture. The chief food products, 1994–95 (in 1,000 tonnes) were: Cassava, 1,145·8; yams, 1,250·5; maize, 491·5; sorghum and millet, 137·6; beans, 64; rice, 13·7, while cash crops were: Groundnuts, 77·6; cotton, 251·2; sugar-cane, 34·6.

Livestock 1992, (in 1,000): Cattle, 1,000; sheep, 920; goats, 1,120; pigs, 750; poultry, 25,000.

Forestry. There were (1989) 3·52m. ha of forest, mainly in the north. Timber production in 1991 was 5·2m. cu. metres, of which 4·9m. cu. metres were for fuel.

Fisheries. In 1991 there were 8 fishing boats totalling 1,078 GRT. Total catch, 41,000 tonnes, of which fresh fish, 21,076 tonnes, marine fish, 11,310 tonnes and shellfish, 7,704 tonnes.

INDUSTRY. Industries include palm-oil processing, brewing and the manufacture of cement, sugar and textiles. Firms by product in 1994: Printing, paper, publishing, 33; chemicals, 22; wood, 16; foodstuffs, 11.

Labour. The economically active population numbered 1·34m. in 1990.

Trade Unions. In 1973 all trade unions were amalgamated to form a single body, the *Union Nationale des Syndicats des Travailleurs du Bénin*. In 1990 some unions declared their independence from this Union, which itself broke its links with the PRPB. In 1992 there were 3 trade union federations.

FOREIGN ECONOMIC RELATIONS. Foreign debt was US$1,487m. in 1993.

Commerce. Imports in 1994, US$366m.; exports, US$301m. The main exports in 1994 were cotton (US$132m.) and crude oil (US$12m.). Other exports include palm oil, palm kernel cake and oil and cotton cake.

Principal export markets, 1994: Morocco, 37·6%; Portugal, 13·8%; Libya, 7·9%; Italy, 5·8%; USA, 5·3%. Principal import suppliers: France, 24·3%; Thailand, 11·9%; China, 6·4%; Hong Kong, 6%; USA, 5·6%.

Total trade between Benin and UK (British Department of Trade returns, in £1,000 sterling):

	1991	*1992*	*1993*	*1994*	*1990*
Imports to UK	589	1,564	1,436	3,820	1,012
Exports and re-exports from UK	10,716	16,788	31,014	30,352	43,115

Tourism. In 1990 some 50,000 foreign visitors brought in US$47m. in revenue.

COMMUNICATIONS

Roads. There were 7,500 km of classified roads in 1994. In 1992 there were 2,212 road accidents with 349 fatalities.

Railways. There are 438 km of metre-gauge railway. In 1994, 0·6m. passengers and 250m. tonne-km of freight were carried.

Civil Aviation. The international airport is at Cotonou. It handled 244,217 passengers in 1992. There are other airports at Abomey, Natitingou, Kandi and Parakou. Benin is a member of Air Afrique. Benin Interregional flies to Burkina Faso, Niger and Togo as well as domestic destinations. Services are also provided by Aeroflot, Air Burkina, Air France, Air Gabon, Cameroon Airlines, Ghana Airways, Nigeria Airways and Sabena.

Shipping. There is a port at Cotonou. In 1992 the merchant fleet numbered 12 ships totalling 1,666 GRT. 1·36m. tonnes of cargo were unloaded and 0·22m. tonnes loaded in 1992.

Telecommunications. There were, in 1994, about 10,000 telephones. The media are overseen by the 9-member Haute Autorité de l'Audiovisuel et de la Communication. The government-controlled Office de Radiodiffusion et Télévision du Bénin broadcasts a radio programme from Cotonou and a regional programme from Parakou, and a TV service (colour by SECAM) from Cotonou. In 1993 there were 0·35m. radio and some 20,000 TV sets.

Press. In 1995 there were 2 daily newspapers.

SOCIAL INSTITUTIONS

Justice. The Supreme Court is at Cotonou. There are Magistrates Courts, and a *tribunal de conciliation* in each district.

Religion. Some 60% of the population follow traditional animist beliefs. In 1994 there were 1·1m. Roman Catholics and 0·8m. Moslems.

Education. Adult illiteracy was 75% in 1992. There were, in 1990–91, 457,100 pupils in 2,808 primary schools with 13,200 teachers and 72,256 pupils in secondary and high schools with 2,493 teachers. The University of Benin (Cotonou) had 9,000 students and 240 academic staff in 1994–95.

DIPLOMATIC REPRESENTATIVES

Of Benin in Great Britain
Ambassador: Richard Adjaho (resides in Paris).

Of Great Britain in Benin
Ambassador: J. T. Masefield, CMG (resides in Abuja).

Of Benin in the USA (2737 Cathedral Ave., NW, Washington, D.C., 20008)
Ambassador: Lucien Tonoukouin.

Of the USA in Benin (Rue Caporal Anani Bernard, Cotonou)
Ambassador: Ruth A. Davis.

Of Benin to the United Nations
Ambassador: René Valéry Mongbe.

BERMUDA

Capital: Hamilton
Population: 60,500 (1994)
GNP per capita: US$27,720 (1993)

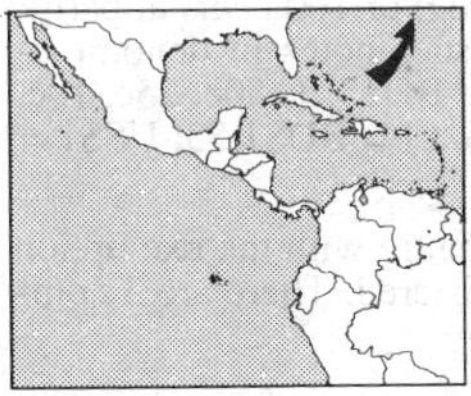

KEY HISTORICAL EVENTS. The islands were discovered by Juan Bermúdez, probably in 1503, but were uninhabited until colonists under Sir George Somers were wrecked there in 1609. A company was formed for the 'Plantation of the Somers' Islands', and in 1684 the Crown took over the government.

A referendum in Aug. 1995 rejected independence from the UK.

TERRITORY AND POPULATION. Bermuda consists of a group of 138 islands and islets (about 20 inhabited), situated in the western Atlantic (32° 18' N. lat., 64° 46' W. long.); the nearest point of the mainland, 940 km distant, is Cape Hatteras (NC). The area is 20·59 sq. miles (53·3 sq. km). In June 1995 the USA surrendered its lease on land used since 1941 for naval and air force bases. A permanent register of population is now kept instead of a census. In 1991 the population (excluding British military personnel) numbered 58,460. Estimate, 1994, 60,500.

Chief town, Hamilton; population, 1994, 1,100.

In 1991 there were 901 live births, 871 marriages and 452 deaths.

CLIMATE. A pleasantly warm and humid climate, with up to 60" (1,500 mm) of rain, spread evenly throughout the year. Hamilton. Jan. 63°F (17·2°C), July 79°F (26·1°C). Annual rainfall 58" (1,463 mm).

CONSTITUTION AND GOVERNMENT. Bermuda is a colony with representative government. At a referendum on 17 Aug. 1995, 16,369 votes were cast against the option of independence, and 5,714 were in favour. The electorate was 38,000; turn-out was 58%. Under the 1968 constitution the *Governor*, appointed by the Crown, is normally bound to accept the advice of the Cabinet in matters other than external affairs, defence, internal security and the police, for which he retains special responsibility. The legislature consists of a *Senate* of 11 members, 5 appointed by the Governor on the recommendation of the Premier, 3 by the Governor on the recommendation of the Opposition Leader and 3 by the Governor in his own discretion. The 40 members of the *House of Assembly* are elected, 2 from each of 20 constituencies by universal suffrage. A general election was held on 5 Oct. 1993; turn-out was 78%. The United Bermuda Party won 22 seats with 50% of votes cast, the Progressive Labour Party 18 with 46%.

Governor: The Rt Hon. The Lord Waddington, GCVO, PC, QC.

Premier and Minister of Finance: Dr David J. Saul.

Deputy Premier, Labour and Home Affairs: J. Irving Pearman. *Health, Social Services and Housing:* Quinton L. Edness, CBE. *Environment:* Gerald D. E. Simons. *Education:* Dr Clarence R. Terceira. *Tourism:* David Dodwell. *Works and Engineering:* Leonard O. Gibbons. *Youth, Sport and Recreation:* Pamela F. Gordon. *Transport:* Maxwell Burgess. *Human Affairs and Information:* C. Jerome Dill. *Community and Cultural Affairs:* Wayne L. Furbert. *Management and Technology:* Dr Edmund Graham 'Grant' Gibbons.

Flag: The British Red Ensign with the badge of the Colony in the fly.

Local Government. The City of Hamilton and the Town of St. George's.

DEFENCE. The Bermuda Regiment numbered about 700 in 1995.

ECONOMY

Budget. The fiscal year ends on 31 March. The 1995-96 budget envisaged revenue of BD$426m. and current expenditure of BD$390·4m.

The estimated chief sources of revenue in 1993–94 were: Customs duties, $126m.; employment tax, $26m.; land tax, $20m.; hospital levy, $47m.; vehicle licenses, $12m.; stamp duties, $15m.; passenger taxes, $14m.

Currency. The unit of currency is the *Bermuda dollar* (BMD) of 100 *cents* at parity with the US dollar. The Bermuda Monetary Authority issues notes in denominations of BD$100, 50, 20, 10, 5 and 2, and coins in values of BD$5, 1, 50c, 25c, 10c, 5c and 1c. Inflation averaged 2·3% in 1994. In March 1996, £1 = BD$1·53; US$1 = BD$1·00; DM1 = BD$0·68.

Banking and Finance. Bermuda is an offshore financial centre with tax exemption facilities. In 1994, 8,224 international companies were registered. There are 3 commercial banks.

There is a stock exchange.

Weights and Measures. Metric, except that US and Imperial (British) measures are used in certain fields.

ENERGY AND NATURAL RESOURCES

Electricity. Production (1991) 454m. kWh.

Agriculture. The chief products are fresh vegetables, bananas and citrus fruit. In 1990, 838 acres were being used for production of vegetables, fruit and flowers as well as for pasture, forage and fallow. In 1991, 6,542 persons were employed in agriculture, fishing and quarrying.

In 1991 the total value of agricultural products was BD$6,923,000.

Fisheries. In 1993 there were 195 fishing vessels and about 300 registered fishermen. Fishing is centred on reef-dwelling species such as groupers and lobsters.

INDUSTRY. At 31 Dec. 1992 7,271 international companies were registered in Bermuda, with insurers the most important category.

Labour. The labour force numbered 34,143 in 1994. Unemployment was 3%.

Trade Unions. There are 9 trade unions with a total membership (1990) of 8,791.

FOREIGN ECONOMIC RELATIONS. Foreign firms conducting business overseas only are not subject to a 60% Bermuda ownership requirement. In 1993, over 6,600 international companies had a physical presence in Bermuda.

Commerce. The visible adverse balance of trade is more than compensated for by invisible exports, including tourism and off-shore insurance business.

Merchandise imports and exports in BD$1m.:

	1992	*1993*	*1994*
Imports	483	519	551
Exports	84	35	51

Imports in 1992 from USA, BD$324m.; Canada, BD$18m.

In 1992 the principal imports (in BDA$1m.) were food, beverages and tobacco (106); machinery (68); chemicals (67); clothing (36); fuels (31); transport equipment (22). The bulk of exports comprise sales of fuel to aircraft and ships, and re-exports of pharmaceuticals.

Total trade between Bermuda and UK, in £1,000 sterling (British Department of Trade returns):

	1991	*1992*	*1993*	*1994*	*1995*
Imports to UK	3,559	5,773	1,687	6,309	3,085
Exports and re-exports from UK	16,205	27,040	23,344	23,512	17,316

Tourism. In 1994, 589,855 tourists visited, of whom 172,865 were cruise ship passengers.

COMMUNICATIONS

Roads. In 1994 there were 140 miles of public highway and 138 miles of private roads. In 1993, 20,148 private cars and 25,287 other vehicles were registered.

Civil Aviation. There is an international airport at Kindley Field, 19 km from Hamilton. Bermuda is served on a regularly scheduled basis by Air Canada, American Airlines, British Airways, Condor Flugdienst, Continental Airlines and Air Micronesia, Delta Airlines, Kiwi and US Air.

Shipping. There are 3 ports, Hamilton, St George's and Dockyard. There is an open shipping registry. In 1995, ships registered totalled 4·49m. DWT, all foreign-owned.

Telecommunications. There were 15 post offices in 1993 and 54,000 telephones in 1991. Radio and television broadcasting are commercial; there are 3 TV and 7 radio channels. In 1992 there were 0·1m. radio and 30,000 TV receivers.

Press (1995). There is 1 daily newspaper with a circulation of about 17,000 and 3 weeklies with a total circulation of about 33,300.

SOCIAL INSTITUTIONS

Justice. There are 4 magistrates' courts, 3 Supreme Courts and a court of appeal. The police had a strength of about 500 men and women in 1995.

Religion. Mainly Anglican.

Education. Education is compulsory between the ages of 5 and 16, and government assistance is given by the payment of grants, and, where necessary, of school fees. In 1992, a total of 7,254 students were enrolled in 18 primary schools, 14 secondary schools (of which 5 are private, including 2 denominational schools and one run by the US Armed Forces in Bermuda), 4 special schools at the primary and secondary levels for handicapped persons aged 14–21, and 11 pre-schools. There were about 600 full-time students attending the Bermuda College in 1992.

Health. In 1992 there were 2 hospitals, 59 doctors, 27 dentists, 548 nurses and 36 pharmacists.

Further Reading

Government Statistical Department. *Bermuda Facts and Figures.* Annual.
Ministry of Finance. *Bermuda Digest of Statistics.* Annual.
Zuill, W. S., *The Story of Bermuda and Her People.* 2nd ed. London, 1992

National library: The Bermuda Library, Hamilton.
National statistical office: Government Statistical Department, Hamilton.

BHUTAN

Druk-yul

(Kingdom of Bhutan)

Capital: Thimphu
Population: 0·6m. (1990)
GNP per capita: US$400 (1994)
HDI/world rank: 0·305/160 (1992)

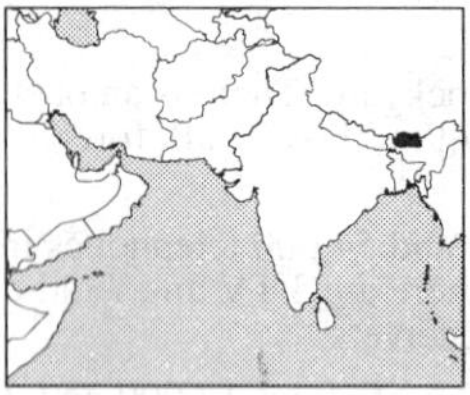

KEY HISTORICAL EVENTS. The East India Company concluded a treaty with the ruler of Bhutan in 1774. By a treaty of 1865 Bhutan was granted an annual subsidy and by an amending treaty of 1910 the UK undertook to exercise no interference in the internal affairs of Bhutan, and Bhutan agreed to be guided by the advice of the British government in its external relations.

India concluded a fresh treaty with Bhutan on 8 Aug. 1949 under which Bhutan continues to be guided by India in its external relations, and India undertakes not to interfere in the internal administration of Bhutan. The subsidy paid to Bhutan was increased to Rs 0·5m.

TERRITORY AND POPULATION. Bhutan is situated in the eastern Himalayas, bounded in the north by China and on all other sides by India. In 1949 India retroceded 32 sq. miles of Dewangiri, annexed in 1865. Area about 18,000 sq. miles (46,500 sq. km); Official population estimate, 1990, 0·6m. A Nepalese minority makes up 30–35% of the population, mainly in the south. Life expectancy (1985) was about 48 years. The capital is Thimphu (1993, 30,340 population).

The official language is Dzongkha.

CLIMATE. The climate is largely controlled by altitude. The mountainous north is cold, with perpetual snow on the summits, but the centre has a more moderate climate, though winters are cold, with rainfall under 40" (1,000 mm). In the south, the climate is humid sub-tropical and rainfall approaches 200" (5,000 mm).

ROYAL HOUSE. The reigning King is **Jigme Singye Wangchuck**, who succeeded his father Jigme Dorji Wangchuck (died 21 July 1972).

In 1907 the Trongsa Penlop (the governor of the province of Trongsa in central Bhutan), Sir Ugyen Wangchuk, GCIE, KCSI, was elected as the first hereditary Maharaja of Bhutan. The Bhutanese title is Druk Gyalpo, and his successor is now addressed as King of Bhutan.

CONSTITUTION AND GOVERNMENT. There is no formal constitution. There is an absolute monarchy which in practice acts in consultation with a National Assembly (*Tshogdu*), which was reinstituted in 1953. This has 150 members and meets at least once a year. Two-thirds are representatives of the people and are elected for a 3-year term. All Bhutanese over 30 years may be candidates. 12 monastic representatives are elected by the central and regional ecclesiastical bodies, while the remaining members are nominated by the King, and include members of the Council of Ministers (the Cabinet) and the Royal Advisory Council.

National flag: Diagonally yellow over orange, over all in the centre a white dragon.

National anthem: 'Druk tsendhen koipi gyelknap na' ('In the Thunder Dragon Kingdom'); words by Dasho Shinkar Lam, tune by A. Tongmi.

Local government: There are 20 districts, each under a district officer *(dzongda)* responsible to the Royal Civil Service Commission through the Home Ministry.

DEFENCE

Army. There was (1994) an Army of 5,500 men. 3 to 5 weeks militia training was introduced in 1989 for senior students and government officials, and 3 months training for some 10,000 volunteers from the general population in 1990 and 1991. Since 1992 only refresher training has been implemented.

INTERNATIONAL RELATIONS

Membership. Bhutan is a member of the UN.

ECONOMY

Policy. The 7th development plan (1992–97) allows for expenditure of Nu15,590m. Forest and mineral wealth is to be exploited and educational and medical facilities extended.

Budget. The budget for 1993–94 envisaged current expenditure of Nu1,427m. and internal domestic revenue of Nu1,500m.

Currency. The unit of currency is the *ngultrum* (BTN) of 100 *chetrum*, at parity with the Indian rupee. There are coins of 1, 5, 10, 25 and 50 chetrum and 1 ngultrum, and notes of 1, 2, 5, 10, 20, 50, 100 and 500 ngultrum. Indian currency is also legal tender. In March 1996, £1 = Nu52·81; US$ = Nu34·55; DM1 = Nu23·41.

Banking and Finance. The Bank of Bhutan was established in 1968. The headquarters are at Phuentsholing with 26 branches throughout the country. The Royal Monetary Authority (founded 1982) acts as the central bank. Deposits (Dec. 1993) Nu1,918m.

ENERGY AND NATURAL RESOURCES

Electricity. Installed capacity at June 1993 was 349 mW (of which 342 mW were hydro-electric). Production (1990) was 1,950m. kWh. In 1993, 35 towns and 255 villages had electricity.

Minerals. Large deposits of limestone, marble, dolomite, slate, graphite, lead, copper, coal, talc, gypsum, beryl, mica, pyrites and tufa have been found. Most mining activity (principally limestone, coal, slate and dolomite) is small-scale.

Agriculture. The area under cultivation in 1988 was 0·13m. ha. The chief products (1990 production in 1,000 tonnes) are rice (43), millet (7), wheat (5), barley (4), maize (40), potatoes (31), oranges (58), apples (5), handloom cloth, timber and cardamom.

Livestock (1990, in 1,000): Cattle, 422; pigs, 73; sheep, 54; goats, 37; horses, 27; yaks (1988), 36.

Forestry. In 1989, 2·61m. ha were forested.

INDUSTRY. In 1986 there were 349 manufacturing and mining firms (14 government-owned). 249 were in the food industry, mostly with fewer than 10 employees. There are a cement plant, a tea-chest ply veneer factory, a resin and turpentine factory, a salt iodization plant and 3 distilleries.

FOREIGN ECONOMIC RELATIONS. The cumulative outstanding convertible currency debt at 30 June 1993 was US$80·04m. To the same date, cumulative debt service payments totalled US$7m.

Financial support is received from India, the UN and other international aid organizations.

Commerce. Trade with India dominates but oranges and apples, timber, cardamom and liquor are also exported to the Middle East, Singapore and Europe.

Total trade between Bhutan and UK (British Department of Trade returns, in £1,000 sterling):

	1991	*1992*	*1993*	*1994*	*1995*
Imports to UK	231	237	1,642	857	492
Exports and re-exports from UK	565	15,505	2,263	1,631	2,428

Tourism. Tourism is the largest source of foreign exchange (1993, US$3·24m. gross). In 1993, 2,997 tourists visited Bhutan (2,854 in 1992).

COMMUNICATIONS

Roads. In 1993 there were about 2,336 km of roads and in 1989, 7,664 registered vehicles, including 5,660 private cars, jeeps or scooters, and 1,504 heavy vehicles.

Civil Aviation. In 1994 Druk-Air made 2 weekly flights to Delhi via Kathmandu and 3 weekly services to Bangkok alternately via Dhaka and Calcutta using 2 71-seater BAe-146s.

Telecommunications. In 1989 there were 2 general post offices, 55 post offices and 28 branch post offices. In 1989 there were 754 km of telephone lines, 13 automatic exchanges and 2,105 telephones.

An international microwave link connects Thimphu to the Calcutta and Delhi satellite connexions. A telecommunications link between Thimphu and London by Intelsat-satellite was inaugurated in 1990. Thimphu and Phuentsholing are connected by telex to Delhi.

In 1989 there were 44 radio stations for internal administrative communications, and 13 hydro-met stations, with an estimated 15,000 radio receivers. Bhutan Broadcasting Service (autonomous since 1992) broadcasts a daily programme in English, Sharchopkha, Dzongkha and Nepali.

Cinemas. There are 2 in Thimpu and 4 others.

Press. There is 1 weekly newspaper, published in English, Dzongkha and Nepali. Total circulation (1994) about 12,000.

SOCIAL INSTITUTIONS

Justice. The High Court consists of 8 judges appointed by the King. There is a Magistrate's Court in each district, under a *Thrimpon*, from which appeal is to the High Court at Thimphu.

Religion. Government estimates, 1995: 70% of the population are Mahayana Buddhists, 25% Hindu and 5% Moslem.

Education. In April 1994 there were 9,425 pupils and 223 teachers in community schools, 45,937 pupils and 1,388 teachers in primary schools, 13,055 pupils and 544 teachers in 18 junior high and 8 high schools and 1,753 pupils and 211 teachers in technical, vocational and tertiary-level schools. There were 716 students and 52 teachers in private schools. Many students receive higher technical training in India, as well as under the UN Development Programme and the Colombo Plan, in Australia, Germany, New Zealand, Japan, Singapore, the USA and the UK. In Oct. 1990, 140 students were receiving university education in India. Literacy was 35% in 1993.

Health. There were (1993) 27 hospitals, 43 dispensaries, 74 basic health units, 6 indigenous dispensaries, 350 outreach clinics, 17 malaria centres and 3 training institutes. In 1993 beds totalled 954; there were 157 doctors and 671 paramedics in 1989.

DIPLOMATIC REPRESENTATIVE

Of Bhutan to the United Nations
Ambassador: Ugyen Tshering.

Further Reading

Bhutan, Himalayan Kingdom. Bhutan Government, Thimphu, 1979
Aris, M., *Bhutan: The Early History of an Himalayan Kingdom.* Warminster, 1979.—*The Raven Crown: the Origins of Buddhist Monarchy in Bhutan.* London, 1994
Chakravarti, B., *A Cultural History of Bhutan.* 2nd rev. ed., 2 vols. Chitteranjan, 1981
Collister, P., *Bhutan and the British.* London, 1987
Dogra, R. C., *Bhutan:* [Bibliography]. Oxford and Santa Barbara, 1991
Edmunds, T. O., *Bhutan: Land of the Thunder Dragon.* London, 1988
Hickman, K., *Dreams of the Peaceful Dragon: a Journey through Bhutan.* London, 1987
Hutt, M., *Bhutan: Perspectives on Conflict and Dissent.* London, 1994

Mehra, G. N., *Bhutan: Land of the Peaceful Dragon.* Rev. ed. New Delhi, 1985
Misra, H. N., *Bhutan: Problems and Policies.* New Delhi, 1988
Parmanand, *The Politics of Bhutan: Retrospect and Prospect.* Delhi, 1992
Rahul, R., *Royal Bhutan.* New Delhi, 1983
Rose, L. E., *The Politics of Bhutan.* Cornell Univ. Press, 1977
Rustomji, N., *Bhutan: The Dragon Kingdom in Crisis.* OUP, 1978
Savada, A. M. (ed.) *Nepal and Bhutan: Country Studies.* Washington, DC, 1993
Sinha, A. C., *Bhutan: Ethnic Identity and National Dilemma.* Delhi, 1991
Strydonck, G. van, *et al., Bhutan: a Kingdom of the Eastern Himalayas.* Geneva and London, 1984
Verma, R., *India's Role in the Emergence of Contemporary Bhutan.* Delhi, 1988

National statistical office: Central Statistical Organization, Thimpu

BOLIVIA

República de Bolivia

Capital: Sucre
Seat of Government: La Paz
Population: 8·07m. (1995)
GNP per capita: US$770 (1994)
HDI/world rank: 0·588/113 (1992)

KEY HISTORICAL EVENTS. The Republic of Bolivia was proclaimed on 6 Aug. 1825.

TERRITORY AND POPULATION. Bolivia is a landlocked state bounded in the north and east by Brazil, south by Paraguay and Argentina and west by Chile and Peru, with an area of some 424,165 sq. miles (1,098,581 sq. km). A coastal strip of land on the Pacific passed to Chile after a war in 1884. In 1953 Chile declared Arica a free port and Bolivia has certain privileges there.

Population estimate, 1995: 8·07m. (55% urban); density, 7·3 per sq. km. There was a census in 1992, which gave a population figure of 6,420,792, but the actual population was estimated at 7·52m. In 1993 population growth rate was estimated at 2%; the birth rate was 36 per 1,000 population in 1991; death rate, 10 per 1,000; infant mortality was officially stated to be 92 per 1,000 live births. Expectation of life was 56 years in 1991. Area and population of the departments (capitals in brackets) at the 1982 census and in 1988:

Departments	*Area (sq. km)*	*Census 1992*	*Density (per sq. km) 1992*
La Paz (La Paz)	133,985	1,900,786	14·2
Cochabamba (Cochabamba)	55,631	1,110,205	20·0
Potosí (Potosí)	118,218	645,889	5·5
Santa Cruz (Santa Cruz)	370,621	1,364,389	3·7
Chuquisaca (Sucre)	51,524	453,756	8·8
Tarija (Tarija)	37,623	291,407	7·7
Oruro (Oruro)	53,588	340,114	6·3
Beni (Trinidad)	213,564	276,174	1·3
Pando (Cobija)	63,827	38,072	0·6
Total	1,098,581	6,420,792	6·9

Population (1992 census) of the principal towns: La Paz, 711,036; Santa Cruz, 694,616; Cochabamba, 404,102; El Alto, 404,367; Oruro, 183,194; Sucre, 130,952; Potosí, 112,291; Tarija, 90,000.

Spanish is the official and commercial language. The Amerindian languages Aymara and Quechua are spoken exclusively by 22% and 5·2% of the population respectively.

CLIMATE. The varied geography produces different climates. The low-lying areas in the Amazon Basin, are warm and damp throughout the year, with heavy rainfall from Nov. to March; the Altiplano is generally dry between May and Nov. with sunshine but cold nights in June and July, while the months from Dec. to March are the wettest. La Paz. Jan. 53°F (11·7°C), July 47°F (8·3°C). Annual rainfall 23" (574 mm). Sucre. Jan. 55°F (13°C), July 49°F (9·4°C). Annual rainfall 27" (675 mm).

CONSTITUTION AND GOVERNMENT. Bolivia's first constitution was adopted on 19 Nov. 1826. The *President* is elected by universal suffrage for a 4-year term. If 50% of the vote is not obtained, the result is determined by a secret ballot in Congress amongst the leading 3 candidates. The President appoints the members of his Cabinet. There is a bicameral legislature; the *Senate* comprises

27 members, 3 from each department, and the *Chamber of Deputies* 130 members, all elected for 4 years. Voting is compulsory.

At the presidential and parliamentary elections of 6 June 1993 the electorate was 2·4m. Gonzalo Sánchez de Lozada was elected President against 13 opponents by 36% of votes cast. The National Revolutionary Movement (NRM) won 52 seats; Patriotic Accord, 35; the Civic Solidarity Union (CSU), 20; the Conscience of the Fatherland, 13; the Free Bolivia Movement (FBM), 7 and others, 3.

President: Gonzalo Sánchez de Lozada (NRM; sworn in 6 Aug. 1993).

Vice-President: Victor Hugo Cardenas (Katarist).

The Cabinet was composed as follows in Nov. 1995:

Foreign Affairs and Worship: Dr Antonio Araníbar Quiroga (FBM). *Interior and Social Defence:* Carlos Sánchez Berzain (NRM). *Defence:* Jorge Otasevic Toledo (NRM). *Labour:* Dr Reynaldo Peters Arzabe (NRM). *Education and Culture:* Fernando Romero Moreno. *Presidency:* José Guillermo Sandóval (NRM). *Human Development:* Jaime Villalobos (NRM). *Information:* Ernesto Machicado. *Justice:* Rene Blattmann Bauer (ind). *Economic Development Finance:* Fernando Candía Castillo (NRM). *Privatization:* Alfonso Revollo Thenier (NRM). *Sustainable Development and the Environment:* Moisés Jarmusz Levy (CSU). *Social Communication:* Irving Alcaraz del Castillo (NRM).

National flag: 3 horizontal stripes of red, yellow, and green.

National anthem: 'Bolivianos, el hado propicio' ('Bolivians, the propitious fate'); words by I. de Sanjinés; tune by B. Vincenti.

Local Government: The republic is divided into 9 departments, with 108 provinces administered by sub-prefects, and 1,713 cantons administered by corregidores. The supreme authority in each department is vested in a prefect appointed by the President.

DEFENCE. There is selective conscription for 12 months at the age of 18 years.

Army. There are 6 military regions. The Army consists of 2 armoured battalions, 1 mechanized cavalry regiment and a Presidential Guard infantry regiment under direct Headquarters command, and 10 divisions comprising altogether 8 cavalry groups, 1 motorized infantry regiment, 22 infantry, 1 artillery, 1 armoured, 1 airborne and 6 engineer battalions. Equipment includes 36 Kuerassier SK-105 light tanks. There are 1 King Air 90, 1 Super King Air 200 and 2 C-212 Aviocar transports. Strength (1996) 25,000 (18,000 conscripts).

Navy. A small force exists for river and lake patrol duties, comprising 10 patrol craft operating on Lake Titicaca, and in the 6,000-mile Beni and Bolivia-Paraguay river systems, and also 1 Cessna 402 transport and 1 Cessna 206 for patrol duties. 1 ocean-going transport for use to and from Bolivian free zones in Argentina and Uruguay and 2 17-tonne hospital craft on Lake Titicaca complete the inventory.

Personnel in 1995 totalled 4,500, including 2,000 marines.

Air Force. The Air Force, established in 1923, has 6 combat-capable Groups, 2 equipped with T-33 armed jet trainers, 1 with armed PC-7s and 1 with Hughes 500 helicopters, for counter-insurgency operations. A search and rescue helicopter Group has 6 Brazilian-assembled Lamas and 20 UH-1 Iroquois. Other types in service include Brazilian T-23 Uirapuru and American T-41 primary trainers and Italian SF-260 basic trainers, 1 Electra 4-turbo-prop transport, 6 Fokker F.27 and 2 Israeli-built Arava twin-turboprop light transports, 5 Convair transports, 2 Learjet VIP aircraft, 11 C-130/L-100 Hercules, 3 C-47s, 15 Turbo-Porters and some single- and twin-engined light aircraft, some confiscated from drug smugglers. Personnel strength (1995) about 4,000 (2,000 conscripts).

INTERNATIONAL RELATIONS

Membership. Bolivia is a member of the UN, OAS, LAIA, the Andean Group and the Amazon Pact.

ECONOMY

Policy. Following the collapse of the international tin market in 1985 and severe inflation, a New Economic Policy was introduced derestricting foreign trade, ending price controls and subsidies and freezing public-sector wages. A privatization programme affecting some 60 state-owned enterprises was instituted in June 1992. A programme of capitalization aims to attract foreign investment into state enterprises in oil, telephones, electricity supply, railways, airlines and smelters, while distributing 50% of the shares to adult citizens to be held in retirement accounts.

Currency. The unit of currency is the *boliviano* (BOB) of 100 *centavos*, which replaced the *peso* on 1 Jan. 1987 at a rate of 1 boliviano = 1m. pesos. There are coins of 5, 10, 20 and 50 centavos and notes of 2, 5, 10, 20, 50, 100 and 200 bolivianos. Inflation was an annualized 9% in 1995. Foreign exchange reserves were US$197·2m. in 1993. In March 1996, £1 = $b.7·64; US$1 = $b.5; DM1 = $b.3·39.

Banking and Finance. The Central Bank is the bank of issue. In 1994 there were 18 commercial banks operating, including 5 foreign. There is also a State Bank and 8 specialized development banks.

There are stock exchanges in La Paz and Santa Cruz.

Weights and Measures. The metric system is legal, but the old Spanish system is also employed.

ENERGY AND NATURAL RESOURCES

Electricity. Installed capacity was estimated at 490,000 kW. in 1985. Estimated production from all sources (1986), 2,080m. kWh.

Oil and Gas. There are petroleum and natural gas deposits in the Santa Cruz-Camiri areas. Production of crude oil in 1993 was estimated at 21,000 barrels a day. National gas output was 109,000m. cu. feet.

Minerals. Mining accounts for (1992) 8·4% of GDP and about 70% of foreign-exchange earnings. Tin-mining had been the mainstay of the economy until the collapse of the international tin market in 1985. Production, 1993 (in tonnes): Zinc, 122,638; lead, 22,408; tin, 18,907; antimony, 4,564; tungsten, 408; gold, 6,560 kg; silver, 360.

Agriculture. In 1994 agriculture contributed 16·4% of GDP. The rural population was 3·4m. in 1993. Output in 1,000 tonnes in 1993 was: Sugar-cane, 3,102; rice, 223; coffee, 31; maize, 504; potatoes, 756; wheat, 146. In 1992, 77,000 tonnes of coca (the source of cocaine) were grown. Since 1987 Bolivia has received international (mainly US) aid to reduce the amount of coca grown, with compensation for farmers who co-operate.

Livestock, 1993 (in 1,000): Cattle, 5,800; horses, 322; asses and mules, 710; pigs, 2,273; sheep, 7,512; goats, 1,450; poultry, 33m.

Forestry. Forests cover 55·8m. ha. Tropical forests with woods ranging from the 'iron tree' to the light balsa are exploited. Roundwood production was 1·63m. cu. metres in 1991; wood cut for fuel totalled 1·13m. cu. metres.

INDUSTRY. At the 1992 census there were 14,389 factories employing a total of 76,718 persons. The principal manufactures are foodstuffs and tobacco, and textiles.

Labour. In 1994 the minimum wage was fixed at 160 bolivianos a month.

FOREIGN ECONOMIC RELATIONS. An agreement of Jan. 1992 with Peru gives Bolivia duty-free transit for imports and exports through a corridor leading to the Peruvian Pacific port of Ilo from the Bolivian frontier town of Desaguadero, in return for Peruvian access to the Atlantic via Bolivia's roads and railways. The mining code of 1991 gives tax incentives to foreign investors. Foreign debt was US$4,243m. in 1992.

Commerce. The value of imports and exports in US$1m.

	1988	*1989*	*1990*	*1991*	*1992*	*1993*
Imports	595	615	715	970	1,090	1,206
Exports	597	817	900	849	710	728

Mineral exports made up 44% of all exports in 1990, totalling US$401·25m. in value (including US$51·5m. for gold). Exports of sawn timber were worth US$46m. in 1992. Main exports, 1994 (in US$1m.): Gold, 158·5; jewellery, 150; tin, 99·5; natural gas, 95; zinc, 87·1.

Main export markets, 1992: Argentina, 21·5%; UK, 18·1%; USA, 16%; Belgium, 11·7%. Main import suppliers: USA, 23·3%; Brazil, 14·5%; Japan, 12·6%; Argentina, 10·4%.

Imports and exports pass chiefly through the ports of Arica and Antofagasta in Chile, Mollendo-Matarani in Peru, through La Quiaca on the Bolivian-Argentine border and through river-ports on the rivers flowing into the Amazon.

Total trade between Bolivia and UK (British Department of Trade returns in £1,000 sterling):

	1991	*1992*	*1993*	*1994*	*1995*
Imports to UK	9,303	10,404	13,144	16,780	14,732
Exports and re-exports from UK	5,787	17,640	7,997	10,147	17,042

Tourism. Revenue from tourism was estimated at US$168m. in 1992.

COMMUNICATIONS

Roads. The total length of the road system was 40,987 km in 1984, of which 1,538 km were hard-surfaced. Motor cars in use in 1989, 75,000; commercial vehicles, 135,000.

Railways. In 1994, the state railway ENFE network totalled 3,697 km of metre gauge, comprising unconnected Eastern (1,423 km) and Andina (2,274 km) systems, and carried 0·8m. passengers and 1·4m. tonnes of freight.

Civil Aviation. The 2 international airports are La Paz (El Alto) and Santa Cruz (Viru Viru). The national airlines are the state-owned Aerosur, which operated 8 aircraft in 1995, and Lloyd Aéreo Boliviano (97·5% state-owned), which in 1995 operated 2 A310-300s, 1 B-707-320C, 1 B-727, 1 B-727-100, 1 B-727-100C, 3 B-727-200 Advs and 1 F-27-200. The airline runs regular services between La Paz and Lima, São Paulo, Buenos Aires, Miami, Caracas, Salta and Arica as well as many internal services. Other airlines serving Bolivia are Aerolíneas Argentinas, Aeroperú, American Airlines, Lan Chile, Lufthansa and Varig.

Shipping. Lake Titicaca and about 12,000 miles of rivers are open to navigation.

Telecommunications. There were 191,000 telephones in 1988. The broadcasting authority is the Dirección General de Telecomunicaciones. There were (1987) about 85 radio stations, the majority of which are local and commercial. There is a commercial government television service. There are 4 private television stations and 1 University station (educational channel) in La Paz. In 1993 there were 4m. radio and 0·5m. TV (colour by NTSC) receivers.

Cinemas. In 1989 there were 30 cinemas in La Paz and 50 in other cities.

SOCIAL INSTITUTIONS

Justice. Justice is administered by the Supreme Court, superior district courts (of 5 or 7 judges) and courts of local justice. The Supreme Court, with headquarters at Sucre, is divided into two sections, civil and criminal, of 5 justices each, with the Chief Justice presiding over both. Members of the Supreme Court are chosen on a two-thirds vote of Congress.

Religion. The Roman Catholic church was disestablished in 1961. It is under a cardinal (in Sucre), an archbishop (in La Paz), 6 bishops and vicars apostolic. It had 7·16m. adherents in 1992.

Education. Literacy was 63% in 1994. Primary instruction is free and obligatory between the ages of 6 and 14 years. In 1986 there were 1·4m. pupils and 51,000 teachers in 9,093 primary and elementary schools, and 225,000 pupils, 10,400 teachers in 2,300 secondary schools.

In 1994-95 there were 7 universities, 2 technical universities, 1 Roman Catholic university, 1 musical conservatory, and colleges in the following fields: Business, 6; teacher training, 4; industry, 1; nursing, 1; technical teacher training, 1; fine arts, 1, rural education, 1; physical education, 1. There were 103,900 university students in 1995-96 and 4,920 academic staff.

DIPLOMATIC REPRESENTATIVES

Of Bolivia in Great Britain (106 Eaton Sq., London, SW1W 9AD)
Ambassador: Carlos Morales-Landivar.

Of Great Britain in Bolivia (Avenida Arce 2732–2754, La Paz)
Ambassador: David Ridgeway, OBE.

Of Bolivia in the USA (3014 Massachusetts Ave, NW, Washington, D.C., 20008)
Ambassador: Andrés Petricevic.

Of the USA in Bolivia (Banco Popular Del Peru Bldg, La Paz)
Ambassador: Curt W. Kamman.

Of Bolivia to the United Nations
Ambassador: Edgar Camacho Omiste.

Further Reading

Fifer, J. V., *Bolivia: Land, Location and Politics Since 1825.* CUP, 1972
Klein, H., *Bolivia: The Evolution of a Multi-Ethnic Society.* OUP, 1982
Yeager, G. M., *Bolivia.* [Bibliography] Oxford and Santa Barbara, 1988

BOSNIA-HERCEGOVINA

Capital: Sarajevo
Population: 4·37m. (1991)

Republika Bosna i Hercegovina

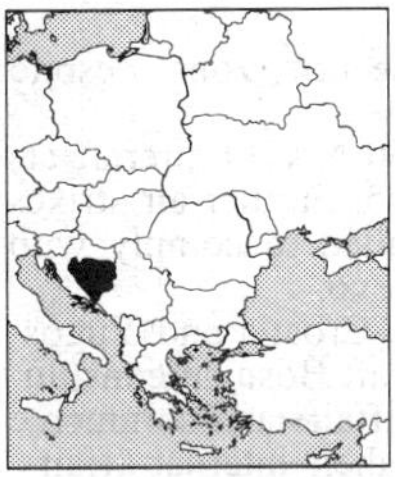

KEY HISTORICAL EVENTS. The country was settled by Slavs in the 7th century, the original clan system evolving between the 12th and 14th centuries into a principality under a *Ban,* during which time the Bogomil Christian heresy spread from Bulgaria in the Patarene form. Bosnia was conquered by the Turks in 1463, and many of the population were gradually converted to Islam. At the Congress of Berlin (1878) the territory was assigned to Austro-Hungarian administration under nominal Turkish suzerainty. Austria-Hungary's outright annexation in 1908 generated international tensions which contributed to the outbreak of the First World War.

On 15 Oct. 1991 the National Assembly adopted a 'Memorandum on Sovereignty', the Serbian deputies abstaining. This envisaged Bosnian autonomy within a Yugoslav federation. A referendum on independence was held on 29 Feb.–1 March 1992. Turn-out was 63·04%, the Serbian population largely boycotting it; 99·78% of votes cast were in favour. In March 1992 an agreement was reached under EC auspices by Moslems, Serbs and Croats to set up 3 autonomous ethnic communities under a central Bosnian authority.

Bosnia-Hercegovina declared itself independent on 5 April 1992, and was recognized by the EU and USA on 7 April. The 2 Serbian members of the Bosnian collective presidency resigned. Fighting broke out between the Serb, Croat and Moslem communities, with particularly heavy casualties and destruction in Sarajevo, leading to extensive Moslem territorial losses and an exodus of refugees. UN-sponsored ceasefires from June on were repeatedly violated. On 29 June the UN Security Council unanimously voted the deployment of UN forces to secure the functioning of Sarajevo Airport and protect humanitarian aid missions.

On 13 Aug. 1992 the UN Security Council voted by 12 to nil with 3 abstentions (China, India and Zimbabwe) to authorize the use of force if necessary to ensure the delivery of humanitarian aid to besieged civilians.

Internationally-sponsored peace talks were held in Geneva in Jan. and at the UN in Feb. 1993, but Serb-Moslem-Croat fighting continued.

A NATO ultimatum of 10 Feb. 1994 gave Bosnian Serbs 10 days to withdraw their artillery from around Sarajevo. A ceasefire was agreed and Serbs began handing over their weapons to UN peacekeeping forces. On 17 Feb. Russia also requested the Serbs to withdraw and announced the dispatch of more Russian troops to the UN peacekeeping force. 4 Bosnian Serb light attack aircraft violating the no-fly zone were shot down by US fighters of the NATO force on 28 Feb.

NATO forces used air strikes for the first time against Serb forces at Gorazde on 10 April 1994.

In Aug. 1994 Yugoslavia ceased supplying Bosnian Serbs and sealed the frontier.

A peace plan sponsored by France, Germany, Russia, the UK and the USA was rejected by 96·13% of votes cast by 1m. electors in a referendum held in the self-proclaimed 'Serbian Republic of Bosnia'.

An upsurge in fighting began in Oct. 1994 with Moslem-Croat attacks in the Bihać area. The Moslem advance was beaten back by Serb forces which bombed Bihać with napalm on 18 Nov. NATO air forces retaliated with a raid on the Serbian airfield, but Serb forces occupied Bihać.

On 12 Nov. 1994 the USA ceased to participate in enforcing the embargo on the supply of arms to Bosnian forces.

On 23 Dec. 1994 Bosnian Serbs and Moslems signed a country-wide interim ceasefire agreement under the good offices of former US President Carter. Bosnian-Croats also signed on 2 Jan. 1995. However, Croatian Serbs and the Moslem secessionist forces under Fikret Abdić did not sign the agreement, and fighting continued.

On 28 May 1995 Bosnian Serb forces took some 400 UN peacekeeping troops hostage. Under pressure from Serbian President Milošević all had been released by 18 June.

On 16 June 1995 Bosnian government forces launched an attack to break the Bosnian Serb siege of Sarajevo.

On 11 July 1995 Bosnian Serb forces began to occupy UN security zones despite retaliatory NATO air strikes, and on 28 Aug. shelled Sarajevo.

In order to stop the shelling of UN safe areas more than 60 NATO aircraft attacked Bosnian Serb military installations on 30-31 Aug. 1995. Further air strikes on military targets began on 5 Sept. after Bosnian Serbs failed to comply with demands that they withdraw heavy weapons from around Sarajevo.

On 26 Sept. in Washington the foreign ministers of Bosnia, Croatia and Yugoslavia (the latter negotiating for the Bosnian Serbs) agreed a draft Bosnian constitution under which a central government would handle foreign affairs and commerce and a Serb Zone and a Moslem-Croat Federation would run their internal affairs. The Bosnian Presidency and Parliament would be elected, one third from the Serb Republic (i.e. the Serb zones of Bosnia) and two thirds from the Moslem-Croat Federation. A ceasefire was negotiated which came into force on 12 Oct. 1995.

In Dayton (OH) on 21 Nov. 1995 the prime ministers of Bosnia, Croatia and Yugoslavia initialled a US-brokered agreement to end hostilities in Bosnia, and this was signed by the respective presidents on 14 Dec. in Paris. Under this the Bosnian state is to be divided into a Serb Republic containing 49% of Bosnian territory and a Moslem-Croat Federation; a central government authority representing all ethnic groups and responsible for foreign and monetary policy and citizenship issues is to be established and free elections held. On 20 Dec. 1995 a 63,000-strong NATO contingent (IFOR) took over from UN peacekeeping forces to enforce the Paris peace agreements and set up a 4-km separation zone between the Serb and Moslem-Croat territories. Some 1,500 advisers have been sent by the UN to help in the formation and training of local civil police units.

TERRITORY AND POPULATION. The republic is bounded in the north and west by Croatia and in the east and south-east by Yugoslavia. It has a coastline of only 20 km with no harbours. Its area is 51,129 sq. km. The capital is Sarajevo.

Population at the 1991 census: 4,366,000 (34·2% urban), of which the predominating ethnic groups were Moslems (1,905,000), Serbs (1,364,000) and Croats (752,000). Population density per sq. km, 1991: 85·4. Vital statistics rates, 1990 (per 1,000 population): Birth, 14·8; death, 6·4; growth, 8·4; infant mortality (per 1,000 live births), 15·3.

Population (1991 census) of the principal cities: Sarajevo, 415,631; Banja Luka, 142,634; Zenica, 96,238.

The official language is Serbo-Croat.

CONSTITUTION AND GOVERNMENT. There is a 240-member bicameral *National Assembly* and 7-member collective presidency. Elections were held to both in Nov. and Dec. 1990. Democratic Action (DA; Moslem-based) gained 86 National Assembly seats, the Serb Democratic Party, 72, the Croat Democratic Union, 44, the Democratic Party of Socialists (former Communists), 20 and others, 18. Alija Izetbegović (b. 1925; DA) was elected *President*. He assumed a third 1-year term of office in Dec. 1992, although only 2 terms are permitted by the constitution, by reason of the emergency.

On 18 March 1994 in Washington Bosnian Moslems and Croats reached an agreement for the creation of a federation of cantons with a central government responsible for foreign affairs, defence and commerce. It is envisaged that there will be a president elected by a 2-house legislature alternating annually between the nationalities.

On 30 March 1994 a 123-member constituent assembly adopted the constitution by 112 votes in favour. On 31 May 1994 the National Assembly approved the creation of the Moslem Croat federation and elected Kresimir Zubak (b. 1948; Croatian) and Ejup Ganić (Moslem) its President and Vice-President respectively, alongside Alija Izetbegović, who remains the unitary states's President.

An interim government with Hasan Muratović as *Prime Minister* was formed on 30 Jan. 1996. Elections were scheduled for late 1996.

National flag: A white field on which is a blue shield with a white bend and gold fleur de lys.

DEFENCE

Army. In 1996 the Army numbered 92,000 and was organized in 6 corps headquarters. There were 78 infantry, 13 mountain, 1 reconnaissance, 2 artillery, 9 motorized, 1 special forces and 5 territorial defence units and 2 air defence regiments. Equipment included 31 main battle tanks T-34 and T-35. The Croatian Defence Council also had a force of some 50,000 active in the country, with 100 main battle tanks, and the forces of the Serb Republic were estimated at up to 75,000, with 370 main battle tanks.

ECONOMY

Currency. Dinars are issued by the National Bank of Bosnia-Hercegovina in Sarajevo in denominations up to 100,000. The national bank of the self-proclaimed 'Serb Republic of Bosnia-Hercegonia' also issues dinars, at par with the Yugoslav dinar. In Hercegovina Croatian currency is used.

Banking and Finance. The governor of the National Bank is Obrad Piljak.

ENERGY AND NATURAL RESOURCES

Electricity. 1990 output, 14,632m. kWh.

Agriculture. In 1990 the cultivated area was 1·58m. ha. Yields (in 1,000 tonnes): Wheat, 457; maize, 728; potatoes, 343; plums, 76. Livestock in 1990 (1,000 head): Cattle, 853; sheep, 1,317; pigs, 617; poultry, 11,465. Timber cut in 1988: 7·05m. cu. metres.

INDUSTRY. In 1991 there were 7,823 enterprises (4,563 private, 1,882 social, 655 limited companies, 322 co-operatives and 157 public). Production (1990): Coal and lignite, 17·93m. tonnes; crude steel, 1·42m. tonnes; cement, 797,000 tonnes; cotton fabrics, 29m. sq. metres; cars, 38,000; sugar, 67,000 tonnes; TV sets, 21,000.

Labour. Population of working age, 1990, 3m. Non-agricultural workforce, 1·05m. (379,000 women). There were 283,000 unemployed in 1990.

FOREIGN ECONOMIC RELATIONS

Commerce. 1990 external trade (in US$1m.): Exports, 2,876; imports, 2,548.

Total trade between Bosnia-Hercegovina and UK (British Department of Trade returns, in £1,000 sterling):

	1993	*1994*	*1995*
Imports to UK	70	191	240
Exports and re-exports from UK	3,494	3,120	4,084

COMMUNICATIONS

Roads. In 1990 there were 21,168 km of roads altogether, 11,436 km classified as modern. In 1990 there were 437,000 passenger cars and 59,000 lorries.

Railways. There were 1,021 km of railways in 1991 (795 km electrified); they carried 554m. passenger-km and 1,946m. tonne-km of freight.

SOCIAL INSTITUTIONS

Religion. At the 1991 census 40% of the population were Moslem, 31% Orthodox and 15% Roman Catholic.

Education. In 1990–91 there were 543,500 pupils in primary schools, 173,100 in secondary schools and 2,400 in tertiary schools. In 1995 there were 4 universities.

Social Security. In 1990 there were 380,000 pensions (including 140,000 old age). There were 543,500 doctors and 18,627,000 hospital beds.

DIPLOMATIC REPRESENTATIVES

Of Bosnia-Hercegovina in Great Britain (40 Conduit St., London, W1R 9FB)
Ambassador: Muhamed Filipović.

Of Great Britain in Bosnia-Hercegovina (8 Mustafa Golubica, Sarajevo)
Ambassador: Bryan Hopkinson.

Of Bosnia-Hercegovina in the USA
Ambassador: Sven Alkalaj.

Of the USA in Bosnia-Hercegovina
Ambassador: Vacant.

Of Bosnia-Hercegovina to the United Nations
Ambassador: Muhamad Sačirbej.

Further Reading

Cigar, N., *Genocide in Bosnia: the Policy of Ethnic Cleansing*. Texas Univ. Press, 1995
Fine, J. V. A. and Donia, R. J., *Bosnia-Hercegovina: a Tradition Betrayed.* Farnborough, 1994
Garde, P., *Journal de Voyage en Bosnie-Herzégovine*. Paris, 1995
Malcolm, N., *Bosnia: a Short History.* London, 1994
O'Ballance, E., *Civil War in Bosnia, 1992–94.* London, 1995

BOTSWANA

Republic of Botswana

Capital: Gaborone
Population: 1·4m. (1994)
GNP per capita: US$2,800 (1994)
HDI/world rank: 0·763/74 (1992)

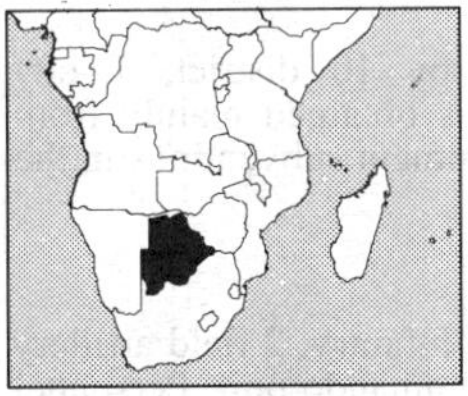

KEY HISTORICAL EVENTS. On 30 Sept. 1966 the former British Bechuanaland Protectorate became the independent Republic of Botswana. For previous history *see* THE STATESMAN'S YEAR-BOOK, 1992–93, p. 224.

TERRITORY AND POPULATION. Botswana is bounded in the west and north by Namibia, north-east by Zambia and Zimbabwe and east and south by South Africa. The area is 581,730 sq. km. Population (1991 census), 1,326,796 (45·7% urban). Life expectancy in 1991: Males, 63·3 years; females, 67·1. Population growth rate, 1991, was 3·5%.

The country is divided into 10 districts: Central, Chobe, Ghanzi, Kgalagadi, Kgatleng, Kweneng, North East, North West, Serowe-Palapye, South East and Southern,.

The chief towns (with population, 1991 census) are Gaborone (133,468), Francistown (65,244), Selebi-Phikwe (39,772) and Lobatse (26,052). The other large towns are Molepolole (36,931), Kanye (31,354), Serowe (30,260), Mahalapye (28,079), Maun (26,769) and Mochudi (25,542).

The official language is English; the national language is Setswana, spoken by 75% of the population. 12% speak Sishona, 3·4% San and 2·5% Hottentot.

CLIMATE. In winter, days are warm and nights cold, with occasional frosts. Summer heat is tempered by prevailing north-east winds. Rainfall comes mainly in summer, from Oct. to April, while the rest of the year is almost completely dry with very high sunshine amounts. Gaborone. Jan. 79°F (26·1°C), July 55°F (12·8°C). Annual rainfall varies from 650 mm in the north to 250 mm in the south-east. The country is prone to droughts.

CONSTITUTION AND GOVERNMENT. The Constitution adopted on 30 Sept. 1966 provides for a republican form of government headed by the President with 3 main organs: The Legislature, the Executive and the Judiciary. The executive rests with the President who is responsible to the National Assembly. The President is elected for 5-year terms by the National Assembly.

The *National Assembly* consists of 47 members, 40 elected by universal suffrage, and 7 elected by itself. Elections are held every 5 years. Voting is on the first-past-the-post system.

The President is an *ex-officio* member of the Assembly.

There is also a *House of Chiefs* to advise the Government. It consists of the Chiefs of the 8 tribes who were autonomous during the days of the British protectorate, 4 members elected by and from among the sub-chiefs in 4 districts; these 12 members elect a further 3 politically independent members.

At the elections of 15 Oct. 1994 the Botswana Democratic Party gained 26 seats and the Botswana National Front, 13.

President: Sir Ketumile Masire, GCMG (b. 1925; re-elected 1994, sworn in 19 Oct.).

In Jan. 1996 the Cabinet was as follows:

Vice-President and Minister of Finance and Development Planning: Festus G. Mogae. *Presidential Affairs and Public Administration:* Ponatshego Kedikilwe. *Foreign Affairs:* Lieut.-Gen. Mompati Merafhe. *Health:* Chapson Butale. *Works, Transport and Communications:* Daniel Kwelagobe. *Commerce and Industry:*

George Kgoroba. *Mineral Resources and Water Affairs:* David N. Magang. *Education:* Dr Gaositwe Chiepe. *Labour and Home Affairs:* Bahiti Temane. *Agriculture:* Roy Blackbeard. *Local Government, Lands and Housing:* Patrick Balopi.

National flag: Light blue with a horizontal black stripe, edged white, across the centre.

National anthem: 'Fatshe leno la rona' ('Blessed be this noble land'); words and tune by K. T. Motsete.

Local Government. Local government is carried out by 10 district, 1 city (Gaborone), 3 town, and 3 township councils. Revenue is obtained mainly from sales taxes, from rates in the towns and from central government subventions in the districts.

DEFENCE

Army. The Army is organized in 2 brigades comprising 4 infantry, 2 field artillery and 2 air defence battalions, 1 engineer regiment and 1 commando unit. Personnel (1996), 7,000.

Air Force. Equipment includes 6 BAC Strikemaster light strike aircraft, 5 Britten-Norman Defender armed light transports for border patrol, counter-insurgency and casualty evacuation duties, 7 PC-7 basic trainers, 2 CN-235 turboprop-powered medium transports, 2 C-212 turboprop passenger/cargo transports, 4 Islander, 5 Ecureuil and 6 Bell 412 helicopters and 2 Cessna 152 light aircraft. Personnel (1995), 500.

INTERNATIONAL RELATIONS

Membership. Botswana is a member of the UN, the Commonwealth, OAU, SADC and is an ACP state of the EU.

ECONOMY

Policy. The Seventh National Development Plan is running from 1991 to 1997. It is aimed to diversify the economy and create jobs.

Budget. The fiscal year begins in April. Budgets for recent years (in P1m.):

	1993–94	*1994–95*	*1995–96* [1]
Revenue	5,359	4,472	5,145
Expenditure	4,480	4,277	5,414

[1] Provisional.

Items of 1993–94 revenue (in P1m.) included: Mineral taxes, 2,456; customs pool, 830; other revenue, 1,858.

Expenditure: Recurrent, 3,470; development and capital transfer,1,735.

Currency. The unit of currency is the *pula* (BWP) of 100 *thebe*. There are coins of 1, 5, 10, 25, and 50 thebe and 1 and 2 pula, and notes of 2, 5, 10, 20, 50 and 100 pula. Inflation was 10·5% in Jan. 1996. Foreign exchange reserves were P13,263m. in Aug. 1995. In March 1996, £1 = 4·54; US$1 = P2·97; DM1 = P2·01.

Banking and Finance. There were 4 commercial banks at 1 Jan. 1996 with 46 branches. Total assets were P3,729m. at 30 Nov. 1995. The Bank of Botswana (*Governor*, H. C. L. Hermans), established in 1976, is the central bank. The National Development Bank, founded in 1964, has 6 regional offices and agricultural, industrial and commercial development divisions. The Botswana Co-operative Bank is banker to co-operatives and thrift and loan societies. The government-owned Post Office Savings Bank operates throughout the country.

There is a stock exchange.

Weights and Measures. The metric system is in use.

ENERGY AND NATURAL RESOURCES

Electricity. The coal-fired power station at Morupule supplies cities and major towns. Production (1994–95) 916·6m. kWh.

Water. Surface water resources are about 18,000m. cu. metres a year. Nearly all flows into northern districts from Angola through the Okavango and Kwando river systems. The Zambezi, also in the north, provides irrigation in the Chobe District. In the south-east, there are dams to exploit the ephemeral flow of the tributaries of the Limpopo. 80% of the land has no surface water, and must be served by some 6,000 boreholes.

Minerals. Coal reserves are estimated at 17,000m. tonnes. There is also salt and soda ash. Mineral production, 1994: Diamonds, 15,547,178 carats (value P1,807m.); copper–nickel ore, 3,462,823 tonnes; coal, approximately 0·94m. tonnes.

Agriculture. 70-80% of the total land area is desert. 80% of the population is rural, 71% of all land is 'tribal', protected and allocated to prevent over-grazing, maintain small farmers and foster commercial ranching. Cattle-rearing is the chief industry after diamond-mining, and the country is more a pastoral than an agricultural one, crops depending entirely upon the rainfall. 100,446 persons worked in agriculture in 1991. In 1990, 128,000 ha were sown to sorghum. In 1993 the number of cattle was 1,821,000. 80% were owned by traditional farmers, about half owning fewer than 20 head. In 1990 there were: Goats, 2·09m.; sheep, 301,000; poultry, 2m.; pigs, 16,000.

Production (1993, in 1,000 tonnes): Maize, 4·3; sorghum, 16·5; (1992) millet, 1; roots and tubers, 8; pulses, 12; seed cotton, 3; vegetables, 16; fruit, 11.

17% of the land is set aside for wildlife conservation and 20% for wildlife management areas, with 4 national parks and game reserves.

Forestry. There are forest nurseries and plantations. Concessions have been granted to harvest 7,500 cu. metres in Kasane and Chobe Forestry Reserves and up to 2,500 cu. metres in the Masame area.

INDUSTRY. Meat is processed and textiles, foodstuffs and soap manufactured. 565 companies were registered at the end of 1992. Rural technology is being developed and traditional crafts encouraged.

Labour. In March 1994, 321,200 persons were in formal employment. At the 1991 census there were 276,950 paid employees (including informal employment) and 28,764 self-employed. A further 76,101 persons worked on a non-cash basis, e.g. as family helpers. 60,757 were seeking work. In March 1994 there were 12,342 Botswana nationals employed in the mines of South Africa. In 1991 there were 57,001 building workers, 34,322 in trade and 29,325 in domestic service. Average earnings in 1994 in the formal sector were P807 per month.

FOREIGN ECONOMIC RELATIONS. Botswana is a member of the South African customs union with Lesotho, Namibia, South Africa and Swaziland. There are no foreign exchange restrictions.

Commerce. In 1994 imports totalled P4,392m. Of 1987 imports, 79·6% came from the South African customs area, 7·7% from other African countries and included (in P1,000) vehicles and transport equipment, 242,785; food, beverages and tobacco, 253,422; machinery and electrical equipment, 260,370.

In 1994 export earnings totalled P4,962m., including diamonds (P3,727m.), copper and nickel (P266m.) and beef (P215m.).

Total trade between Botswana and UK (British Department of Trade returns, in £1,000 sterling):

	1991	*1992*	*1993*	*1994*	*1995*
Imports to UK	22,552	27,446	26,051	19,618	23,647
Exports and re-exports from UK	35,233	19,999	20,555	22,461	25,837

Tourism. There were 961,844 foreign visitors in 1993. Tourist earnings were P60m. in 1988.

COMMUNICATIONS

Roads. In 1995 some 4,200 km of road were bitumen-surfaced out of a total of 18,327km. In 1994 there were 101,454 registered motor vehicles including 27,058 cars and 42,696 light duty vehicles.

Railways. The main line from Mafikeng in South Africa to Bulawayo in Zimbabwe traverses Botswana. With 3 branches the total was (1994) 971 km. In 1993–94 railways carried 0·3m. passengers and 1·7m. tonnes of freight.

Civil Aviation. There is an international airport at Gaborone (Sir Seretse Khama) and 6 domestic airports. The national carrier is the state-owned Air Botswana, which had 3 aircraft in 1995. Services are also operated by Air Zimbabwe, British Airways, Commercial Airways and, Kalahari Air Services. Direct services are operated to the UK, Namibia, Tanzania, Zambia and Zimbabwe.

Telecommunications. In 1994 there were 109 post offices and 65 agencies. There were some 50,000 working telephone lines by 1995. The government-controlled Radio Botswana broadcasts daily in English and Setswana. A commercial television company transmits on a 50 km-radius from Gaborone (colour by SECAM). There were 1·1m. radio and 13,800 TV sets in 1993.

Press. In 1994 there were 1 government newspaper (distributed free) and 5 independent newspapers, with a total circulation of about 100,500, and 6 other periodicals.

SOCIAL INSTITUTIONS

Justice. Law is based on the Roman-Dutch law of the former Cape Colony, but judges and magistrates are also qualified in English common law. The Court of Appeal has jurisdiction in respect of criminal and civil appeals emanating from the High Court and in all criminal and civil cases and proceedings. Magistrates' courts and traditional courts are in each administrative district. As well as a national police force there are local customary law enforcement officers.

Religion. Freedom of worship is guaranteed under the Constitution. About 50% of the population is Christian. Non-Christian religions include Bahais, Moslems and Hindus.

Education. Literacy was 67·3% in 1993. Basic free education, introduced in 1986, consists of 7 years of primary and 3 years of junior secondary schooling. 83% of eligible children were in schools in 1990. In 1993 enrolment in primary schools was 305,479, in community junior schools, 62,234 and in senior secondary schools 22,604. In 1993 there were 67 primary, 163 community junior and 23 senior secondary schools. In 1993 there were 1,261 students in teacher training colleges. 'Brigades' (community-managed private bodies) provide lower level vocational training. The Department of Non-Formal Education offers secondary level correspondence courses and is the executing agency for the National Literacy Programme. There is 1 university (4,466 students in 1993–94) and 1 polytechnic.

Health (1994). There were 16 general hospitals, a mental hospital, 13 health centres, 200 clinics and 310 health posts. There were also 701 stops for mobile health teams. In 1994 there were 339 doctors and 3,329 nurses. The health facilities are the concern of central and local government, medical missions, mining companies and voluntary organizations.

DIPLOMATIC REPRESENTATIVES

Of Botswana in Great Britain (6 Stratford Pl., London, W1N 9AE)
High Commissioner: Alfred Uyapo Dube.

Of Great Britain in Botswana (Private Bag 0023, Gaborone)
High Commissioner: David Beaumont.

Of Botswana in the USA (4301 Connecticut Ave., NW, Washington, D.C., 20008)
Ambassador: Archie Mogwe.

Of the USA in Botswana (PO Box 90, Gaborone)
Ambassador: Howard F. Jeter.

Of Botswana to the United Nations
Ambassador: Legwaila Joseph Legwaila.

Further Reading

Central Statistics Office. *Statistical Bulletin* (Quarterly).
Ministry of Information and Broadcasting. *Botswana Handbook*. – *Kutlwano* (monthly).
Colclough, C. and McCarthy, S., *The Political Economy of Botswana.* OUP, 1980
Harvey, C., (ed.) *Papers on the Economy of Botswana.* London and Nairobi, 1981
Molomo, M. G. and Mokopakgosi, B. (eds.) *Multi-Party Democracy in Botswana.* Harare, 1991
Parson, J., *Botswana: Liberal Democracy and Labour Reserve in Southern Africa.* Aldershot, 1984
Perrings, C., *Sustainable Development and Poverty Alleviation in Sub-Saharan Africa: the Case of Botswana*. London, 1995

National statistical office: Central Statistics Office, Private Bag 0024, Gaborone.

BRAZIL

República Federativa do Brasil

Capital: Brasília, (Federal District)
Population: 159·1m. (1994)
GNP per capita: US$3,370 (1994)
HDI/world rank: 0·804/63 (1992)

KEY HISTORICAL EVENTS. Brazil was discovered on 22 April 1500 by the Portuguese Admiral Pedro Alvares Cabral, and thus became a Portuguese settlement. In 1815 the colony was declared a kingdom, and it was proclaimed an independent Empire in 1822. The monarchy was overthrown in 1889 and a republic declared. Following a coup in 1964 the armed forces retained overall control until civilian government was restored on 15 March 1985.

TERRITORY AND POPULATION. Brazil is bounded in the east by the Atlantic and on its northern, western and southern borders by all the Latin American countries except Chile and Ecuador. The area is 8,547,404 sq. km including 55,457 sq. km of inland water. Population as at censuses 1 Sept. 1980 and 1 Sept. 1991:

Federal Unit and Capital	*Area (sq. km)*	*Census 1980*	*Census 1991*
North	3,869,638	6,619,152	10,030,556
Rondônia (Pôrto Velho)	238,513	491,069	1,132,692
Acre (Rio Branco)	153,150	301,303	417,718
Amazonas (Manaus)	1,577,820	1,430,089	2,103,243
Roraima (Boa Vista)	225,116	79,159	217,583
Pará (Belém)	1,253,165	3,403,391	4,950,060
Amapá (Macapá)	143,454	175,257	289,397
Tocantins (Palmas)	278,421	738,884	919,863
North-East	1,561,178 [1]	34,812,356	42,497,540
Maranhão (São Luís)	333,366	3,996,404	4,930,253
Piaui (Teresina)	252,378	2,139,021	2,582,137
Ceará (Fortaleza)	146,348	5,288,253	6,366,647
Rio Grande do Norte (Natal)	53,307	1,898,172	2,415,567
Paraíba (João Pessoa)	56,585	2,770,176	3,201,114
Pernambuco (Recife)	98,938	6,143,272	7,127,855
Alagoas (Maceió)	27,933	1,982,591	2,514,100
Sergipe (Aracajú)	22,050	1,140,121	1,491,876
Bahia (Salvador)	567,295	9,454,346	11,867,991
South-East:	927,286	51,734,125	62,740,401
Minas Gerais (Belo Horizonte)	588,384	13,378,553	15,743,152
Espírito Santo (Vitória)	46,184	2,023,340	2,600,618
Rio de Janeiro (Rio de Janeiro)	43,910	11,291,520	12,807,706
São Paulo (São Paulo)	248,809	25,040,712	31,588,925
South	577,214	19,031,162	22,129,377
Parana (Curitiba)	199,709	7,629,392	8,448,713
Santa Catarina (Florianópolis)	95,443	3,627,933	4,541,994
Rio Grande do Sul (Pôrto Alegre)	282,062	7,773,837	9,138,670
Central West	1,612,077	6,805,911	9,427,601
Mato Grosso (Cuiabá)	906,807	1,138,691	2,027,231
Mato Grosso do Sul (Campo Grande)	358,159	1,369,567	1,780,373
Goiás (Goiânia)	341,290	3,120,718	4,018,903
Distrito Federal (Brasília)	5,822	1,176,935	1,601,094
Total	8,547,404	119,002,706	146,825,475

[1] Including disputed areas between states of Piauí and Ceará (2,977 sq. km).

Density, 17 per sq. km. Population estimate, 1994, 159·1m. The 1991 census showed 72,485,122 males and 74,340,353 females. The urban population comprised 75·6% in 1989. Life expectancy was 66 years in 1989.

The official language is Portuguese.

Population of principal cities (1991 census):

São Paulo	9,646,185	São Luis	696,371	Niterói	436,155
Rio de Janeiro	5,480,768	Duque de Caxias	667,821	Santos	428,923
Salvador	2,075,273	Maceió	629,041	São João de Meriti	425,772
Belo Horizonte	2,020,161	Santo André	616,991	Feira de Santana	406,447
Fortaleza	1,768,637	Natal	606,887	Cuiabá	402,813
Brasília	1,601,094	Teresina	599,272	Aracaju	402,341
Curitíba	1,315,035	Osasco	568,225	Londrina	390,100
Recife	1,298,229	São Bernardo do Campo	566,893	Campos dos Goytacazes	389,109
Nova Iguaçu	1,297,704	Campo Grande	526,126	Juiz de Fora	385,996
Porto Alegre	1,263,403	João Pessoa	497,600	Sorocaba	379,006
Belém	1,244,689	Jaboatão	487,119	Uberlândia	367,061
Manaus	1,011,501	Contagem	449,588	Joynville	347,151
Goiânia	922,222	São José dos Campos	442,370	Olinda	341,394
Campinas	847,595	Ribeirão Preto	436,682	Diadema	305,287
Guarulhos	787,866			Jundiaí	289,269
São Gonçalo	779,832				

The principal metropolitan areas (census, 1991) were São Paulo (16,567,317), Rio de Janeiro (10,389,441), Belo Horizonte (4,620,624), Porto Alegre (3,757,500), Salvador (3,134,886), Recife (2,921,665), Fortaleza (2,357,100), Curitiba (2,319,526) and Belém (1,620,564).

CLIMATE. Because of its latitude, the climate is predominantly tropical, but factors such as altitude, prevailing winds and distance from the sea cause certain variations, though temperatures are not notably extreme. In tropical parts, winters are dry and summers wet, while in Amazonia conditions are constantly warm and humid. The N.E. sertão is hot and arid, with frequent droughts. In the south and east, spring and autumn are sunny and warm, summers are hot, but winters can be cold when polar air-masses impinge. Brasilia. Jan. 72°F (22·3°C), July 68°F (19·8°C). Annual rainfall 63" (1,603 mm). Belém. Jan. 78°F (25·8°C), July 80°F (26·4°C). Annual rainfall 102" (2,315 mm). Manaus. Jan. 79°F (26·1°C), July 80°F (26·7°C). Annual rainfall 110" (2,842 mm). Recife. Jan. 80°F (26·6°C), July 77°F (24·8°C). Annual rainfall 94" (2,474 mm). Rio de Janeiro. Jan. 83°F (28·5°C), July 67°F (19·6°C). Annual rainfall 67" (1,758 mm). São Paulo. Jan. 75°F (24°C), July 57°F (13·7°C). Annual rainfall 71" (1,800 mm). Salvador. Jan. 80°F (26·5°C), July 74°F (23·5°C). Annual rainfall 90" (2,315 mm). Porto Alegre. Jan. 75°F (23·9°C), July 62°F (16·7°C). Annual rainfall 67" (1,775 mm).

CONSTITUTION AND GOVERNMENT. The present Constitution came into force on 5 Oct. 1988, the eighth since independence. *President* and *Vice-President* are elected for a 4-year term and are not immediately re-eligible. To be elected candidates must secure 51% of the votes, otherwise a second round of voting is held to elect the President between the two most voted candidates. Voting is compulsory for men and women between the ages of 18 and 70 and optional for illiterates, persons from 16 to 18 years old and persons over 70. A referendum on constitutional change was held on 21 April 1993. Turn-out was 80%. 66·1% of votes cast were in favour of retaining a republican form of government, and 10·2% for re-establishing a monarchy. 56·4% favoured an executive presidency, 24·7% parlimentary supremacy.

At the elections of 3 Oct. 1994 Fernando Henrique Cardoso was elected President by 54·3% of votes cast against 6 opponents.

Congress consists of an 81-member *Senate* (3 Senators per federal unit) and a 513-member *Chamber of Deputies*. The Senate is two-thirds directly elected (50% of these elected for 8 years in rotation) and one-third indirectly elected. The Chamber of Deputies is elected by universal franchise for 4 years. There is a *Council of the Republic* which is convened only in national emergencies. Elections were held in Oct. 1990 for the governors of the 26 states and 1 federal district, 27 senators (one-third of the Senate), 503 federal deputies and 1,049 state deputies. Some 70,000 candidates from 22 parties stood. The electorate was 84m.

In Feb. 1995 the composition of Congress was:

Senate: Cardoso coalition, 33 seats; Democratic Movement, 23; right-wing parties, 7; Workers' Party and allies, 7; others, 11.

Chamber of Deputies: Cardoso coalition, 182 seats; Democratic Movement, 107; right-wing parties, 100; Workers' Party and allies, 80; others, 44.

President: Fernando Henrique Cardoso (b. 1931; Social Democrat; sworn in 1 Jan. 1995).

In Dec. 1995 the government comprised:

Justice: Nelson Jobim. *Navy:* Mauro Cesar Rodrigues Pereira. *Army:* Zenildo Zoroastro de Lucena. *External Relations:* Luiz Felipe Lampreia. *Finance:* Pedro Sampaio Malan. *Transport:* Odacir Klein. *Agriculture:* José Eduardo Andrade Vieira. *Education:* Paulo Renato de Souza. *Culture:* Francisco Correa Weffort. *Labour:* Paulo Paiva. *Social Security:* Reinholds Stephanes. *Air Force:* Lélio Viana Lobo. *Health:* Adib Jatene. *Industry, Trade and Tourism:* Dorothea Werneck. *Mining and Energy:* Raimundo Britto. *Communications:* Sergio Vieira da Motta. *Science and Technology:* José Israel Vargas. *Environment:* Gustavo Krause. *Planning:* José Serra. *Sports:* Edson Arantes do Nascimento ('Pele').

National flag: Green, with yellow lozenge on which is placed a blue sphere, containing 27 white stars and crossed with a band bearing the motto *Ordem e Progresso.*

National anthem: 'Ouviram do Ipiranga...' ('They hear the river Ipiranga'); words by J. O. Duque Estrada; tune by F. M. da Silva.

Local Government. Brazil consists of 27 federal units (26 states and 1 federal district). Each has its distinct administrative, legislative and judicial authorities and its own constitution and laws, which must, however, agree with federal constitutional principles. The governors and members of the legislatures are elected for 4-year terms. The country is sub-divided into 4,974 municipalities, each under an elected mayor and municipal council, and then further sub-divided into districts. The Federal District is the national capital, inaugurated in 1960; it is divided into 12 administrative Regions, the first Region being Brasília. Gubernatorial elections were held for all 27 federal units etc. in Oct.–Nov. 1994. Municipal elections were held in Oct.–Nov. 1992.

Constituição da Republica Federativa do Brasil. Brasília, 1988
Baaklini, A. I., *The Brazilian Legislature and Political System.* London, 1992

DEFENCE. Conscription is for 12 months, extendable by 6 months.

Army. There are 7 military commands and 11 military regions. The Army consists of 8 divisions, 1 armoured cavalry, 3 armoured infantry, 4 mechanized cavalry, 13 motor infantry, 1 mountain, 4 jungle, 1 frontier, 1 airborne and 2 coast and air defence brigades, 3 cavalry guard regiments, 28 artillery and 2 engineer groups. Equipment includes 546 light tanks. Strength (1996) 195,000 (125,000 conscripts). A helicopter brigade has 52 Dauphin and Ecureuil helicopters.

There are para-military state militias under Army control and considered an Army reserve, totalling about 385,000 personnel.

Navy. The principal ship of the Navy is the 20,200-tonne Light Aircraft Carrier *Minas Gerais*, formerly the British *Vengeance*, completed in 1945, purchased in 1956, and capable of operating an air group of 8 S-2E Tracker anti-submarine aircraft, and 8 ASH-3H anti-submarine Sea King helicopters.

There are also 5 diesel submarines (1 built in Germany, 1 in Brazil and 3 British Oberon-class) and 16 frigates including the first 2 of 4 Type 22 bought from the UK in 1995. The fleet still includes 1 old ex-US Gearing class destroyer and 4 Sumner class, but these are decommissioning. There are also 6 inshore minesweepers and a patrol force of 9 tug/trawler types, 6 ex-US inshore craft, 2 locally-built and a number for work on the rivers. Major auxiliaries include 1 oiler, 1 repair ship, 4 transports, 4 survey and rescue, 1 training frigate and 5 tugs. There are some 70 minor auxiliaries. Amphibious forces consist of 2 ex-US landing ships (dock) and 1 tank landing ship. A further diesel submarine is being built.

Fleet Air Arm personnel only fly helicopters, the 8 S-2E Tracker anti-submarine aircraft held for carrier operations and the 21 shore-based maritime patrol EMB-111 being operated by the Air Force. Naval aircraft include 7 ASH-3 Sea King for carrier service, 5 Lynx, and 17 Esquilo for embarkation in the smaller ships. Utility and search-and-rescue duties are performed by 16 Bell 206B Sea Ranger, and 6 Super Puma helicopters. Naval bases are at Rio de Janeiro, Aratu (Bahia), Belém, Natal, Rio Grande do Sul and Salvador, with river bases at Ladario and Manaus.

Active personnel, 1995, totalled 50,000, including 15,000 well-equipped Marines and 700 Naval Aviation.

Air Force. The Air Force is organized in 6 zones, centred on Belém, Recife, Rio de Janeiro, São Paulo, Porto Alegre and Brasília. The 1a GDA (Air Defence Group) has 12 Mirage IIIE fighters and 4 Mirage IIID trainers, integrated with Roland mobile short-range surface-to-air missile systems deployed by the Army, and a radar/communications/computer network. Two fighter groups have 3 squadrons of F-5E Tiger II supersonic fighter-bombers and two-seat F-5Bs; 3 others operate AT-26 (Aermacchi MB 326G) Xavante light jet attack/trainers, licence-built by Embraer in Brazil and 2 squadrons operate the AM-X fighter-bomber, jointly developed by Italy and Brazil, is now entering service; 79 AM-Xs are being delivered. Counter-insurgency squadrons are equipped with armed Ecureuil helicopters for liaison and observation. 2 air-sea rescue units are equipped with Bandeirantes. Equipment of transport units includes 1 squadron of C-130E/H Hercules transports; 1 squadron of Boeing 707 tanker/transports; 1 group made up of a squadron of HS 748 and a second squadron of Bandeirante turboprop transports; 2 troop-carrier groups with DHC-5 Buffaloes; 1 group with Bandeirantes; 1 group with UH-1 Iroquois and Super Puma helicopters; and 7 independent squadrons with Bandeirantes and Buffaloes. Light aircraft for liaison duties include 30 Embraer U-7s (licence-built Piper Senecas), 30 Neiva Regente lightplanes and 7 Cessna Caravans. The VIP transport group has 2 Boeing 737s, 11 HS 125 twin-jet light transports, 4 Embraer Brasilias, 6 Embraer Xingu (VU-9) twin-turboprop pressurized transports and Ecureuil and JetRanger helicopters. Training is performed primarily on locally-built T-25 Universal and turboprop T-27 Tucano (EMB-312) basic trainers, and AT-26 Xavante armed jet basic trainers. Personnel strength (1995) 50,000 (5,000 conscripts).

INTERNATIONAL RELATIONS

Membership. Brazil is a member of the UN, OAS and Mercosur.

ECONOMY

Policy. In 1991 a National Reconstruction Plan was introduced to promote growth and investment and reduce the role of the state. State monopolies in ports, communications and fuels were reduced and agricultural and industrial subsidies ended. A sixth economic plan was introduced in 1993 to cut spending and accelerate privatization. Phases of a new economic plan were introduced in 1994.

Budget. In 1993, current revenues were Cr$4,455,312m. and capital revenues, Cr$9,440,694m.; current expenditure was Cr$4,280,334m. and capital expenditure Cr$9,545,662m.

Internal federal debt, May 1995 was R$88,199m. Internal states and municipalities (main securities outstanding), R$30,147m.

Currency. The unit of currency is the *real* (BRC) of 100 centavos which was introduced on 1 July 1994 to replace the former cruzeiro real at a rate of 1 real (R$1) = 2,750 cruzeiros reais (CR$2,750). The real was devalued 6·54% in June 1995. There are coins of 1, 5, 10, 25 and 50 centavos and R$1, and notes of R$1, 5, 10, 50 and 100. The real was devalued in Sept. 1994 and March 1995. Inflation was 2% in Sept. 1995. Foreign exchange reserves were US$43,090m. in July 1994. The exchange rate in March 1996 was US$1 = R$0·98; £1 = R$1·50; DM1 = R$0·67.

Banking and Finance. On 31 Dec. 1964 the Banco Central do Brasil (*President*, Gustavo Loyola) was founded as the national bank of issue.

The Bank of Brazil (founded in 1853 and reorganized in 1906) is a state-owned commercial bank; it had 3,107 branches in 1993 throughout the republic. On

31 Dec. 1993 deposits were Cr$3,622,241,626,000. In 1994 there were 6 public-sector banks and 24 banks controlled by state governments.

There are 9 stock exchanges of which Rio de Janeiro and São Paulo are the most important. All except São Paulo are linked in the National Electronic Trading System (Senn).

Lees, F. A. *et al.* (eds.), *Banking and Financial Deepening in Brazil.* London, 1990

Weights and Measures. The metric system has been compulsory since 1872.

ENERGY AND NATURAL RESOURCES

Electricity. Hydro-electric potential capacity was estimated at 255,000 MW per year in Dec. 1990, of which 41% belongs to the Amazon hydro-electric basin. Installed capacity (1993) 52,741 MW of which 47,976 MW hydro-electric. There is 1 nuclear power plant, supplying some 0·2% of total output. Production (1993) 237,623m. kWh (231,389m. kWh hydro-electric).

Oil. There are 13 oil refineries, of which 11 are state-owned. Crude oil production (1995), 745,000 bbls. a day.

Gas. Production (1993) 7,352,435,000 cu. metres.

Minerals. Brazil is the only source of high-grade quartz crystal in commercial quantities; output, 1992, 38,148 tonnes raw, 27,275 tonnes processed. It is a major producer of chrome ore: Output, 1992, 948,788 tonnes; reserves, 1992, 14·2m tonnes. Other minerals, with 1992 output in tonnes, are mica, 14; zirconium, 15,017; beryllium 1,412; graphite, 685,850; and magnesite, 1,161,200. Along the coasts of the states of Rio de Janeiro, Espírito Santo and Bahia are found monazite sands containing thorium: Output, 1991, 560 tonnes; estimated reserves, 1991, 772,000 tonnes. Manganese ores of high content are important: Output, 1995, 3,395,078 tonnes; estimated reserves, 1992, 81·2m tonnes. Output, 1992 (in tonnes) of bauxite, 12,763,150; mineral salt, 1,230,608; tungsten ore, 28,767, unrough, 205; lead, 334,426; asbestos, 3,895,805; coal, 9,241,099. Primary aluminium production in 1989 was 888,000 tonnes. Deposits of coal exist in Rio Grande do Sul, Santa Catarina and Paraná. Total reserves were estimated at 5,190·2m. tonnes in 1988.

Iron is found chiefly in Minas Gerais, notably the Cauê Peak at Itabira. The Government is opening up iron-ore deposits in Carajás, in the northern state of Para, with estimated reserves of 35,000m. tonnes, representing a 66% concentration of high-grade iron ore. Total output of iron ore, 1992, mainly from the Cia. Vale do Rio Doce mine at Itabira, was 205,346,525 tonnes.

Production of tin ore (cassiterite, processed) was 33,749 tonnes in 1992; output of barytes, 72,171 tonnes, and of phosphate rock, 15·5m. tonnes.

Gold is chiefly from Pará (18,837 kg in 1992), Mato Grosso (18,009 kg) and Minas Gerais (23,120 kg); total production (1992), 80,543 kg processed. Silver output (processed in 1992) 20,042 tonnes. Diamond output in 1992 was 1,285,402 carats (157,805 carats from Minas Gerais, 1m. carats from Mato Grosso).

Agriculture. In 1992, 35·67m. people depended on agriculture, of whom 13·25m. were economically active. There were 5·83m. farms in 1985. Production (in tonnes):

	1993	*1994*		*1993*	*1994*
Bananas (1,000 bunches)	557,980	572,165	Grapes	787,363	806,609
Beans	2,478,325	3,368,430	Coconut (1,000 fruits)	837,495	902,217
Cassava	21,837,385	24,452,358	Coffee	2,557,518	2,612,538
Castor beans	43,188	53,497	Cotton	1,135,305	1,367,183
Oranges (1,000 fruits)	93,985,944	87,091,089	Maize	30,051,333	32,487,400
Potatoes	2,367,571	2,480,162	Soya	22,574,762	24,912,345
Rice	10,108,434	10,499,455	Sugar-cane	244,343,616	292,070,449
Sisal	126,076	131,421	Wheat	2,156,114	2,092,424
Tomatoes	2,348,201	2,678,147	Cocoa	340,885	330,398

Harvested coffee area, 1994, 2,095,620 ha, principally in the states of Minas Gerais, Espírito Santo, São Paulo and Paraná. Harvested cocoa area, 1994,

698,319 ha. Bahia furnished 82% of the output in 1994. 2 crops a year are grown. Harvested castor-bean area, 1994, 105,894 ha. Tobacco output was 518,980 tonnes in 1994, grown chiefly in Rio Grande do Sul and Santa Catarina.

Rubber is produced chiefly in the states of Acre, Amazonas, Rondônia and Pará. Output, 1993, 40,663 tonnes (natural). Brazilian consumption of rubber in 1993 was 131,717 tonnes. Plantations of tung trees were established in 1930; output, 1992, 1,536 tonnes. Soya bean production was estimated at 25·6m. tonnes (from 11·6m. ha) in 1995.

2·8m. ha were irrigated in 1992.

Livestock (in 1,000) 1993: Cattle, 155,134; pigs, 34,184; sheep, 18,008; goats, 10,619; horses, 6,314; asses, 1,302 and mules, 1,993. Livestock slaughtered for meat in 1993 (in 1,000): Cattle, 14,953; pigs, 13,307; sheep and lambs, 927; goats, 803; poultry, 1,229,025.

Forestry. Roundwood production (1989) 111,707,851 cu. metres.

Fisheries. The fishing industry had a 1989 catch of 798,638 tonnes.

INDUSTRY. The National Iron and Steel Co. at Volta Redonda, State of Rio de Janeiro, furnishes a substantial part of Brazil's steel. Total output, 1994: Pig-iron, 23,981,700 tonnes; crude steel, 25,169,600 tonnes.

Cement output, 1994, was 25,231,000 tonnes. Output of paper, 1994, was 5,301,040 tonnes. Production of rubber tyres for motor vehicles (1992), 30,306,000 units; motor vehicles (1993), 1,391,376.

Labour. The work force in 1990 numbered 62,100,499, of whom 14,180,519 were in agriculture and 13,233,866 (including the construction industry) worked in industry. In 1995, there was a minimum monthly wage of R$100.

Trade Unions. The main union is the United Workers' Centre (CUT).

FOREIGN ECONOMIC RELATIONS. In 1990 Brazil repealed most of its protectionist legislation. Import tariffs on some 13,000 items were reduced in 1995. Since 1991 direct foreign investment on equal terms with domestic has been permitted. In 1991 the government permitted an annual US$100m. of foreign debt to be converted into funds for environmental protection.

Foreign debt (including states and municipalities) on 31 March 1994 amounted to US$119,668m.

Commerce. Imports and exports for calendar years in US$1m.:

	1991	*1992*	*1993*	*1994*
Imports	21,041,459	20,554,091	25,480,350	32,900,000
Exports	31,620,459	35,792,966	38,596,848	43,600,000

Principal imports in 1994 were (in US$1m.): Machinery and electrical equipment, 6,271; chemical products, 3,844; transport equipment, 2,320; crude oil, 2,139; food-stuffs, 1,090; wheat, 726; coal, 656; fertilizers, 511; cast iron and steel, 368.

Principal exports in 1993 were (in US$1m.): Transport equipment, 4,226; soya, 3,074; machinery, 2,530; iron, manganese and other ores, 2,466; footwear and leather products, 2,002; paper and cellulose, 1,516; textiles, 1,364; meat, 1,333; coffee, 1,282; orange juice, 826; sugar, 773; tobacco, 697; cocoa beans, 254.

Main export markets, 1993 (in US$1m.): USA, 8,023; Argentina, 3,659; Netherlands, 2,488; Japan, 2,313; Germany, 1,824; Italy, 1,304; UK, 1,140; Chile, 1,110. Main import suppliers: USA, 5,958; Argentina, 2,623; Germany, 2,290; Japan, 1,542; Italy, 982.

Total trade between Brazil and UK (according to British Department of Trade returns, in £1,000 sterling):

	1991	*1992*	*1993*	*1994*	*1995*
Imports to UK	765,102	885,632	903,531	919,360	966,520
Exports and re-exports from UK	339,442	273,106	415,070	525,240	674,502

Tourism. In 1993, 1,448,540 tourists visited Brazil. 583,901 were Argentinian, 153,027 Uruguayan, 115,363 US citizens, 71,103 Paraguayan, 68,133 Italian,

62,752 German, 42,262 Spanish, 36,954 French, 29,621 Portuguese, 27,641 Chilean, 26,888 Bolivian, 24,274 UK citizens, 22,935 Swiss, 17,671 Japanese.

COMMUNICATIONS

Roads. There were (1993) 1,824,363 km of highways of which 1,660,352 km were in operation. In 1988 there were 12,682,199 motor vehicles, including 10,274,419 passenger cars, 2,283,384 commercial vehicles and an estimated 124,396 buses and minibuses.

Railways. Public railways are operated by two administrations, the Federal Railways (RFFSA) formed in 1957 and São Paulo Railways (Fepasa) formed in 1971, which is confined to the state of São Paulo. RFFSA had a route-length of 22,069 km (65 km electrified) in 1994 and Fepasa 4,344 km (1,044 km electrified). An RFFSA subsidiary CBTU (the Brazilian Urban Train Company) runs passenger services in some cities, while others are in the hands of the local authorities. Principal gauges are metre (24,720 km) and 1,600 mm (5,419 km). Traffic moved by RFFSA in 1994 amounted to 86m. tonnes of freight and (1993) 1,713m. passengers. Fepasa carried 19·1m. tonnes and 104·9m. passengers in 1993.

There are several important independent freight railways, including the Vitoria à Minas (898 km in 1993), the Carajas (opened 1985, 1,076 km in 1991) and the Amapa (194 km). There are metros in São Paulo (44 km), Rio de Janeiro (23 km), Belo Horizonte (14 km), Pôrto Alegre (28 km) and Brasília (38·5 km).

Civil Aviation. There are international airports at Rio de Janeiro and São Paulo (Guarulhos). The 4 national airlines are Viação Aérea Rio Grande do Sul (Varig), Cruzeiro do Sul, Transbrasil and Viação Aérea São Paulo (Vasp; 38% state-owned). In 1995, Transbrasil operated 1 B-707-320C, 8 B-737-300s, 4 B-737-400s, 3 B-767-200s, 4 B-767-200ERs and 2 B-767-300ERs; Varig 2 B-727 Fs, 2 B-727-100Cs, 1 B-727C, 17 B-737-200 Advs, 25 B-737-300s, 3 B-747-200B Combis, 3 B-747-300s, 2 B-747-300 Combis, 6 B-767-200ERs, 4 B-767-300ERs, 7 DC-10-30s, 2 DC-10-30Fs and 6 MD-11s; Vasp, 2 A300B2-200s, 1 B-707-320C, 6 B-737-200s, 11 B-737-200 Advs, 1 B-737-200F, 1 B-737-200C, 1 B-737-200C Adv, 2 B-737-300s and 4 MD-11s. Brazil is also served by Aeroflot, Aerolíneas Argentinas, Aeroperú, Air Aruba, Air France, Alitalia, American Airlines, Avianca, British Airways, Canadian Airlines, Cubana, Delta, Iberia, JAL, KLM, Korean Air, Lacsa, Ladeco, Lan-Chile, Lapsa, Lloyd Aéreo Boliviano, Lufthansa, Pluna, SAA, SAS, Swissair, TAAG, TAP, Tower Airlines, United Airlines and Viasa. Brazilian airlines carried 17,004,909 passengers (11,098,600 domestic) in 1993.

Shipping. Inland waterways, mostly rivers, are open to navigation over some 43,000 km. Santos and Rio de Janeiro are the 2 leading ports; there are 19 other large ports. During 1993, 37,360 vessels entered and cleared the Brazilian ports. 347m. tonnes of cargo were loaded and unloaded in 1993. In 1995 the merchant fleet comprised 249 vessels totalling 10·22m. DWT, representing 1·55% of the world's total fleet tonnage. 16 vessels (14·67% of tonnage) were registered under foreign flags. Total tonnage registered, 5·3m. GRT, including oil tankers, 2·12m. GRT, and container ships, 192,777 GRT.

Telecommunications. There were 12,766 post and telegraph offices in 1993. There were 14,426,673 telephones in 1991 (São Paulo, 4,762,311; Rio de Janeiro, 1,745,709; Federal District, 454,154). In 1988 there were 2,033 radio and (in 1991) 119 television stations (colour by PAL). In 1993 there were 60m. radio and 30m. television receivers.

Cinemas (1988). Cinemas numbered 3,737.

Press (1985). There were 322 daily newspapers with a total yearly circulation of 1,699m.

SOCIAL INSTITUTIONS

Justice. There is a Supreme Federal Court of Justice at Brasília composed of 11 judges, and a Supreme Court of Justice; all judges are appointed by the President with the approval of the Senate. There are also Regional Federal Courts, Labour Courts, Electoral Courts and Military Courts. Each state organizes its own courts and judicial system in accordance with the federal Constitution.

Religion. At the 1980 census Roman Catholics numbered 105,861,113 (89% of the total), Protestants, 7,885,846 (6·6%) and Spiritualists, 1,538,230. Roman Catholic estimates in 1991 suggest that 90% were baptized Roman Catholic but only 35% were regular attenders. In 1991 there were 338 bishops and some 14,000 priests.

In 1992 there were 0·2m. Jews. There are numerous sects, some evangelical and some African-derived (e.g. *Candomble*).

Education. Elementary education is compulsory. Adult literacy was 79·93% in 1991. There were 50,646 literacy classes in 1993 with 1,584,147 students and 75,413 teachers. In 1993 there were 83,267 pre-primary schools with 4,085,978 pupils and 192,333 teachers; 195,544 primary schools, with 30,520,748 pupils and 1,346,285 teachers; 12,603 secondary schools, with 4,208,766 pupils and 275,845 teachers; and 873 higher education institutions, with 1,594,668 students and 150,823 teachers.

The tertiary education sector includes 114 universities (53 private, 37 federal, 20 state and 4 municipal), 85 private and 3 municipal college-faculty federations and 671 other higher education institutions (514 private, 80 municipal, 57 state and 20 federal).

Health. In 1992 there were 49,676 hospitals and clinics (22,584 private) of which 7,430 were for in-patients (5,316 private). In 1987 there were 206,382 doctors, 28,772 dentists, 6,094 pharmacists and 29,082 nurses.

DIPLOMATIC REPRESENTATIVES

Of Brazil in Great Britain (32 Green St., London, W1Y 4AT)
Ambassador: Rubens Antonio Barbosa.

Of Great Britain in Brazil (Av. das Nações, CP 07-0586, 70.359, Brasília, D.F.)
Ambassador: Donald Keith Haskell, CMG, CVO.

Of Brazil in the USA (3006 Massachusetts Ave., NW, Washington, D.C., 20008)
Ambassador: Paulo Tarso Flecha de Lima.

Of the USA in Brazil (Av. das Nações, Lote 03, Quadra 801, CEP: 70403-900, Brasília, D.F.)
Ambassador: Melvyn Levitsky.

Of Brazil to the United Nations
Ambassador: Celso Luiz Nunes Amorim.

Further Reading

Instituto Brasileiro de Geografia e Estatística. *Anuário Estatístico do Brasil.—Censo Demográfico de 1991.—Indicadores IBGE.* Monthly

Boletim do Banco Central do Brasil. Banco Central do Brasil. Brasília. Monthly

Baer, W., *The Brazilian Economy: Growth and Development.* 4th ed. New York, 1995

Bryant, S. V., *Brazil* [Bibliography] Oxford and Santa Barbara, 1985

Burns, E. B., *A History of Brazil.* 2nd ed. Columbia Univ. Press, 1980

Falk, P. S. and Fleischer, D. V., *Brazil's Economic and Political Future.* Boulder (CO), 1988

Font, M. A., *Coffee, Contention and Change in the Making of Modern Brazil.* Oxford, 1990

Guirmaraes, R. P., *Politics and Environment in Brazil: Ecopolitics of Development in the Third World.* New York, 1991

Mainwaring, S., *The Catholic Church and Politics in Brazil, 1916–86.* Stanford Univ. Press, 1986

Stepan, A. (ed.) *Democratizing Brazil: Problems of Transition and Consolidation.* OUP, 1993

Welch, J. H., *Capital Markets in the Development Process: the Case of Brazil.* London, 1992

For other more specialized titles see under CONSTITUTION AND GOVERNMENT *and* BANKING AND FINANCE, *above.*

National library: Biblioteca Nacional Avenida Rio Branco 219–39, Rio de Janeiro, RJ.

National statistical office: Instituto Brasileiro de Geografia e Estatística (IBGE), Rua General Canabarro 666, 20.271-201 Maracanã, Rio de Janeiro, RJ.

BRITISH ANTARCTIC TERRITORY

KEY HISTORICAL EVENTS. The British Antarctic Territory was established on 3 March 1962, as a consequence of the entry into force of the Antarctic Treaty, to separate those areas of the then Falkland Islands Dependencies which lay within the Treaty area from those which did not (i.e. South Georgia and the South Sandwich Islands).

TERRITORY AND POPULATION. The territory encompasses the lands and islands within the area south of 60°S latitude lying between 20°W and 80°W longitude (approximately due south of the Falkland Islands and the Dependencies). It covers an area of some 660,000 sq. miles, and its principal components are the South Orkney and South Shetland Islands, the Antarctic Peninsula (Palmer Land and Graham Land) the Filchner and Ronne Ice Shelves and Coats Land.

There is no indigenous or permanently resident population. There is however an itinerant population of scientists and logistics staff of about 300, manning a number of research stations.

The territory was administered by a High Commissioner resident in Port Stanley, Falkland Islands until 1989 and thereafter by the Foreign and Commonwealth Office in London. Designated personnel of the scientific stations of the British Antarctic Survey are appointed to exercise certain legal and administrative functions.

Commissioner: P. M. Newton (non-resident).
Administrator: Dr. M. G. Richardson (non-resident).

Fox, R., *Antarctica and the South Atlantic.* London, 1985
Parsons, A., *Antarctica: the Next Decade.* CUP, 1987

BRITISH INDIAN OCEAN TERRITORY

KEY HISTORICAL EVENTS. This territory was established by an Order in Council on 8 Nov. 1965, consisting then of the Chagos Archipelago (formerly administered from Mauritius) and the islands of Aldabra, Desroches and Farquhar (all formerly administered from Seychelles). The latter islands became part of Seychelles when that country achieved independence on 29 June 1976.

TERRITORY AND POPULATION. The group, with a total land area of 23 sq. miles (60 sq. km) comprises 5 coral atolls (Diego Garcia, Peros Banhos, Salomon, Eagle and Egmont) of which the largest and southernmost, Diego Garcia, covers 17 sq. miles (44 sq. km) and lies 450 miles (724 km) south of the Maldives. The British Indian Ocean Territory was established to meet UK and US defence requirements in the Indian Ocean. In accordance with the terms of Exchanges of Notes between the UK and US governments in 1966 and 1976, a US Navy support facility has been established on Diego Garcia. There is no permanent population.

Commissioner: D. R. MacLennan (non-resident).
Administrator: H. D. H. Cairns (non-resident).
Commissioner's Representative: Cdr H. F. Hatton.
Flag: Blue and white wavy stripes with the Union Flag in the canton and a crowned palm-tree in the fly.

BRUNEI

Negara Brunei Darussalam–
State of Brunei Darussalam

Capital: Bandar Seri Begawan
Population: 276,300 (1993)
GNP per capita: US$14,240 (1994)
HDI/world rank: 0·868/41 (1992)

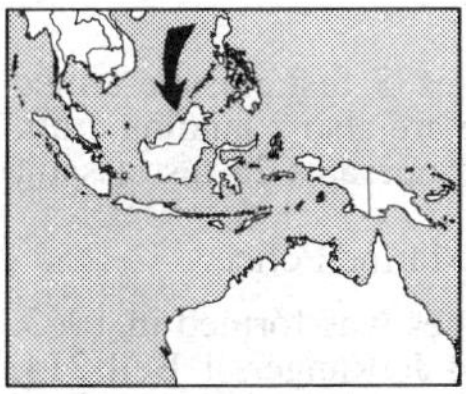

KEY HISTORICAL EVENTS. The Sultanate of Brunei once had authority over the whole of Borneo and parts of the Sulu Islands and the Philippines, but from the end of the 16th century cessions were made to Great Britain, the Rajah of Sarawak and the British North Borneo Company until by the middle of the 19th century the State had been reduced to its present limits. In 1847 the Sultan of Brunei entered into a treaty with the UK for the furtherance of commercial relations and the suppression of piracy; in 1888 Brunei was placed under British protection. On 7 Jan. 1979 the Sultan and the UK signed a treaty under which Brunei became a sovereign independent state on 31 Dec. 1983.

TERRITORY AND POPULATION. Brunei, on the coast of Borneo, is bounded in the north-west by the South China Sea and on all other sides by Sarawak (Malaysia), which splits it into two parts, the smaller portion forming Temburong district. Area, 2,226 sq. miles (5,765 sq. km). Population (1991 census) 260,482; (1993 estimate) 276,300. The 4 districts are Brunei/Muara (1993: 181,600), Belait (56,000), Tutong (30,700), Temburong (about 8,000). The capital is Bandar Seri Begawan (census 1991: 45,867); other large towns are Seria (1991: 21,082) and Kuala Belait (21,163). Ethnic groups include Malays, 67% and Chinese, 15%.

Vital statistics rates, 1992: Birth per 1,000, 27·2; death, 3·3; natural increase, 23·9 (annual rate 3·2%); infant mortality per 1,000 live births, 9·6. There were 1,874 marriages in 1993. Life expectancy in 1991: Males, 72 years; females, 76·6.

The official language is Malay but English is in use.

CLIMATE. The climate is tropical marine, hot and moist, but nights are cool. Humidity is high and rainfall heavy, varying from 100" (2,500 mm) on the coast to 200" (5,000 mm) inland. There is no dry season. Bandar Seri Begawan. Jan. 80°F (26·7°C), July 82°F (27·8°C). Annual rainfall 131" (3,275 mm).

RULER. The Sultan and Yang Di Pertuan of Brunei Darussalam is HM Paduka Seri Baginda Sultan Haji Hassanal Bolkiah Mu'izzadin Waddaulah. He succeeded on 5 Oct. 1967 at his father's abdication and was crowned on 1 Aug. 1968.

CONSTITUTION AND GOVERNMENT. On 29 Sept. 1959 the Sultan promulgated a Constitution, but parts of it have been in abeyance since Dec. 1962. There is no legislature and supreme power is vested in the Sultan.

The Council of Ministers was composed as follows in Jan. 1996:

Prime Minister, Minister of Defence: The Sultan.

Foreign Affairs: Prince Haji Mohammad Bolkiah. *Finance:* Prince Haji Jefri Bolkiah. *Special Adviser to the Sultan in the Prime Minister's Department, Minister of Home Affairs:* Pehin Dato Haji Isa. *Education:* Pehin Dato Haji Abdul Aziz. *Law:* Pengiran Haji Bahrin. *Industry and Primary Resources:* Pehin Dato Haji Abdul Rahman. *Religious Affairs:* Pehin Dato Dr Haji Mohammad Zain. *Development:* Pengiran Dato Dr Haji Ismail. *Culture, Youth and Sports:* Pehin Dato Haji Hussain. *Health:* Dato Dr Haji Johar. *Communications:* Dato Haji Zakaria.

National flag: Yellow, with 2 diagonal strips of white over black with the national arms in red placed over all in the centre.

National anthem: 'Ya Allah, lanjutkan lah usia' ('O God, long live His Majesty'); words by P. Rahim, tune by I. Sagap.

DEFENCE

Army. The armed forces are known as the Task Force and contain the naval and air elements. Only Malays are eligible for service. Strength (1996) 3,900. Military units include 3 infantry battalions, 1 armoured reconnaissance squadron, 1 engineer squadron, 1 special forces squadron and 1 surface-to-air missile battalion. Equipment includes 16 Scorpion light tanks.

There is a paramilitary Gurkha reserve unit 2,300 strong.

Navy. The Royal Brunei Armed Forces Flotilla comprises 3 fast missile-armed attack craft of 200 tonnes and 3 coastal patrol boats. There are also 2 landing craft, 2 utility craft and 3 small patrol boats. The River Division operates 24 fast assault boats. Personnel in 1995 numbered 700.

3 coastal patrol craft operate with 7 smaller boats for the Marine Police.

Air Wing. The Air Wing of the Royal Brunei Armed Forces was formed in 1965. Current equipment includes 6 MBB BO 105, 2 Bell 206B JetRanger, 1 Bell 214, 1 S-70 Black Hawk and 11 Bell 212 helicopters, and 2 SF.260M piston-engined trainers. Personnel (1995), 300.

Police. The Royal Brunei Police numbers 2,044 officers and men (1994). In addition, there are 500 additional police officers mostly employed on static guard duties.

INTERNATIONAL RELATIONS

Membership. Brunei is a member of the UN, the Commonwealth and ASEAN.

ECONOMY

Budget. The budget for 1993 envisaged expenditure of B$3,397m. and revenue of B$3,416m.

Currency. The unit of currency is the *Brunei dollar* or *ringgit* (BND) of 100 *cents*, which is at parity with the Singapore dollar (also legal tender). There are coins of 1, 5, 10, 20 and 50 cents and notes of B$1, 5, 10, 25, 50, 100, 1,000 and 10,000. B$459·7m. were in circulation in 1992. In March 1996, £1 = B$2·16; US$1 = B$1·41; DM1 = B$0·96.

Banking and Finance. The Brunei Currency Board is the note-issuing monetary authority. In 1993 there were 7 banks (1 incorporated in Brunei) with a total of 33 branches. Savings deposits totalled B$999·3m. in 1993, fixed time deposits B$1,935·4m. Total assets of banks in 1993 were B$6,567·7m.

ENERGY AND NATURAL RESOURCES

Electricity. Electric power production (1993) was 1,449m. kWh. Installed capacity was 402,500 kW, consumption, 1,250m. kWh.

Oil. The Seria oilfield, discovered in 1929, has passed its peak production. The high level of crude oil production is maintained through the increase of offshore oilfields production. There were 735 producing wells at 31 Dec. 1993. Production was 8·85m. tonnes in 1992. The crude oil is exported directly, and only a small amount is refined at Seria for domestic uses.

Gas. Natural gas is produced (9,789m. cu. metres in 1993) at one of the largest liquefied natural gas plants in the world and is exported to Japan.

Agriculture. The main crops produced in 1993 were, rice (1,000 tonnes), vegetables (4,500 tonnes), cereals (1,000 tonnes) and fruits (1,000 tonnes).

Livestock in 1993: Cattle, 1,450; buffaloes, 3,500; pigs (1992), 4,400; chickens, 4m.

Forestry. Most of the interior is under forest, containing large potential supplies of serviceable timber. In 1993 production of round timber was 119,200 cu. metres; sawn timber, 63,000 cu. metres.

Fisheries. The 1993 catch totalled 1,727 tonnes, including 1,340 tonnes of marine fish.

INDUSTRY. Brunei depends primarily on its oil industry. Other minor products are rubber, pepper, sawn timber, gravel and animal hides. Local industries include boat-building, cloth weaving and the manufacture of brass- and silverware.

FOREIGN ECONOMIC RELATIONS

Commerce. In 1993 imports c.i.f. totalled B$2,012·6m.; exports f.o.b. B$3,684·5m. In 1993 crude oil exports totalled B$1,785·6m., liquefied natural gas, B$1,591·4m. In 1991 Singapore supplied 22% of imports, the USA 14% and Japan 16%. Japan took 62% of all exports.

Total trade between Brunei and UK (British Department of Trade returns, in £1,000 sterling):

	1991	*1992*	*1993*	*1994*	*1995*
Imports to UK	147,665	126,365	307,552	294,186	125,918
Exports and re-exports from UK	215,222	211,384	324,432	417,540	254,282

Tourism. There were 411,876 visitor arrivals in 1992 (38,035 tourists). 1,353 males and 1,371 females made the pilgrimage to Mecca in 1993.

COMMUNICATIONS

Roads. There were (1993) 2,443 km of road, of which 1,296 km have a permanent surface. The main road connects Bandar Seri Begawan with Kuala Belait and Seria. In 1993 there were 129,772 private cars, 13,320 goods vehicles and 4,702 motor cycles. There were 79 fatalities in 3,864 road accidents in 1993.

Civil Aviation. Brunei International Airport serves 0·8m. passengers annually. The national carrier is the state-owned Royal Brunei Airlines (RBA), which in 1995 operated 3 B-757-200ERs, 7 B-767-300ERs and 2 other aircraft. RBA and Singapore Airlines provide daily services linking Brunei and Singapore. RBA also operates services to Bangkok, Manila, Kuala Lumpur, Kuching, Kota Kinabalu, Hong Kong, Darwin, Jakarta, Taipei, Bali, Perth, London, Frankfurt, Jeddah, Bahrain and Dubai (via Singapore). Cathay Pacific Airways also operates to Brunei and on to Western Australia from Hong Kong. British Airways provides a weekly service between Brunei and UK. Malaysian Airlines System has air connections from neighbouring regions. In 1993, 790,000 passengers and 24,425 tonnes of freight were carried.

Shipping. Regular shipping services operate from Singapore, Hong Kong, Sarawak and Sabah to Bandar Seri Begawan, and there is a daily passenger ferry between Bandar Seri Begawan and Labuan. 97 sea-going vessels were licensed in 1993.

Telecommunications. There were 17 post offices (1993) and a telephone network (67,293 telephones in 1992) linking the main centres. Radio Television Brunei operates on medium- and shortwaves in Malay, English, Chinese and Nepali. Number of receivers (1993): Radio 0·1m. and television 85,000 (colour by PAL).

Press. In 1993 there was a local newspaper with a circulation of 76,200.

SOCIAL INSTITUTIONS

Justice. The Supreme Court comprises a High Court and a Court of Appeal and the Magistrates' Courts. The High Court receives appeals from subordinate courts in the districts and is itself a court of first instance for criminal and civil cases. The Judicial Committee of the Privy Council in London is the final court of appeal. Shariah Courts deal with Islamic law. 25,310 crimes were reported in 1993.

Religion. The official religion is Islam. In 1991, 67% of the population were Moslem (mostly Malays), 13% Buddhists and 10% Christian.

Education. The government provides free education to all citizens from pre-school up to the highest level at local and overseas universities and institutions. In 1993 there were 201 kindergartens and schools, with 11,478 children in kindergartens, 40,194 in primary and 26,166 in secondary schools and 2,931 teachers in kindergarten and primary schools and 1,953 in secondary schools. There were 7 technical and vocational colleges with 1,593 students and 371 teachers and a teacher training college with 418 students and 28 teachers.

In 1993 the University of Brunei Darussalam (founded 1985) had 1,138 students and 207 teachers, and an institute of advanced education 310 students and 71 teachers.

Health. Medical and health services are free to citizens and those in government service and their dependants. Citizens are sent overseas at government expense for medical care not available in Brunei. Flying medical services are provided to remote areas. In 1993 there were 10 hospitals with 967 beds; there were 197 doctors, 27 dentists, 10 pharmacists, 254 midwives and 1,228 nursing personnel.

DIPLOMATIC REPRESENTATIVES

Of Brunei in Great Britain (19 Belgrave Sq., London, SW1X 8PG)
High Commissioner: Dato Kassim Daud.

Of Great Britain in Brunei (Hong Kong Bank Chambers, Bandar Seri Begawan 2085)
High Commissioner: I. R. Callan, CMG.

Of Brunei in the USA (2600 Virginia Ave., NW, Washington, D.C., 20037)
Ambassador: H. J. bin Abdul Latif.

Of the USA in Brunei (Teck Guan Plaza, Bandar Seri Begawan 2085)
Ambassador: Theresa A. Tull.

Of Brunei to the United Nations
Ambassador: Pengiran Haji Momin Abdul.

Further Reading

Ministry of Finance Statistics Department. *Brunei Darussalam Statistical Yearbook.*
Cleary, M. and Wong, S. Y., *Oil, Economic Development and Diversification in Brunei.* London, 1994
Krausse, S. C. E. and G. H., *Brunei.* [Bibliography] Oxford and Santa Barbara, 1988
Saunders, G., *History of Brunei.* OUP, 1996

National statistical office: Ministry of Finance Statistics Department.

BULGARIA

Republika Bulgaria

Capital: Sofia
Population: 8·46m. (1994)
GNP per capita: US$1,160 (1994)
HDI/world rank: 0·796/65 (1992)

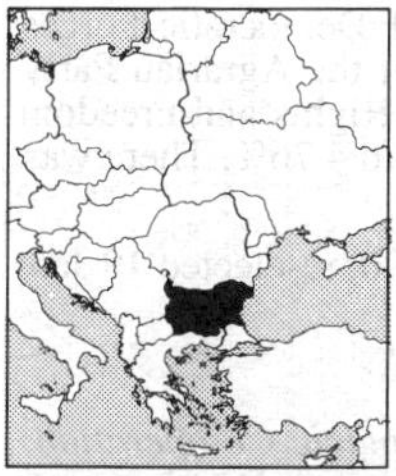

KEY HISTORICAL EVENTS. The Bulgarian state was founded in 681, but fell under Turkish rule in 1396. By the Treaty of Berlin (1878), the Principality of Bulgaria was constituted under Turkish suzerainty. On 5 Oct. 1908 Bulgaria declared her independence of Turkey.

For the establishment of the Communist régime *see* THE STATESMAN'S YEAR-BOOK, 1992–93, p. 243. Following demonstrations in Sofia in Nov. 1989 which were occasioned by the Helsinki Agreement ecological conference, but broadened into demands for political reform, Todor Zhivkov was replaced as Communist Party leader and head of state by the foreign minister Petŭr Mladenov. In Dec. the National Assembly approved 21 measures of constitutional reform, including the abolition of the Communist Party's sole right to govern. The government was succeeded in Feb. 1990 by the Communist government of Andrei Lukanov. Following demonstrations and a general strike Lukanov's government was replaced by a caretaker government in Nov. 1990. A non-Communist government was elected in Oct. 1991.

TERRITORY AND POPULATION. The area of Bulgaria is 110,994 sq. km (42,855 sq. miles). It is bounded in the north by Romania, east by the Black Sea, south by Turkey and Greece and west by Yugoslavia.

The country is divided into 9 regions (*oblast*) formed from amalgamations of 28 former provinces in 1987 (for these *see* THE STATESMAN'S YEAR-BOOK 1989-90, p. 243). Area and population in 1994:

Region	*Area (sq. km)*	*Pop. (1,000)*	*Region*	*Area (sq. km)*	*Pop. (1,000)*
Burgas	14,657	850	Ruse	10,842	766
Khaskovo	13,892	904	Sofia (city)	1,311	1,189
Lovech	15,150	1,009	Sofia (region)	18,979	981
Montana	10,607	626	Varna	11,929	914
Plovdiv	13,628	1,221			

The capital, Sofia, has regional status. The population at the census of 1992 was 8,472,724 (females, 4,515,936). Estimated population on 1 Jan. 1994 was 8,459,723 (females, 4,308,107; urban, 67·6%). Population density 80·9 per sq. km.

Population of principal towns (1990): Sofia, 1,141,142; Plovdiv, 379,083; Varna, 314,913; Burgas, 204,915; Ruse, 192,365; Stara Zagora, 164,553; Pleven, 138,323; Dobrich, 115,786; Sliven, 112,220; Shumen, 110,754; Pernik, 99,643; Yambol, 99,225; Khaskovo, 95,807; Pazardzhik, 87,277; Vratsa, 85,272; Gabrovo, 80,694.

Vital statistics, 1993: Live births, 84,987; deaths, 109,540. Rates per 1,000 population, 1993: Birth, 10; death, 12·9; marriage, 4·7; infant deaths, 15·5; growth per 1,000 live births, –2·9. Abortions, 1993, 106,863, of which 10,577 were spontaneous. Expectation of life in 1991 was 71·22 years (males, 68·02; females, 74·66).

Ethnic groups at the 1992 census: Bulgarians, 7,271,185; Turks, 800,052; Gypsies, 313,396.

CLIMATE. The southern parts have a Mediterranean climate, with winters mild and moist and summers hot and dry, but further north the conditions become more continental, with a larger range of temperature and greater amounts of rainfall in summer and early autumn. Sofia. Jan. 28°F (–2·2°C), July 69°F (20·6°C). Annual rainfall 25·4" (635 mm).

CONSTITUTION AND GOVERNMENT. A new constitution was adopted at Tŭrnovo in July 1991. The *President* is directly elected for not more than 2 5-year terms. Candidates for the presidency must be at least 40 years old and have lived for the last 5 years in Bulgaria. Presidential elections were held in Jan. 1992. There were 23 candidates at the first round; turn-out was 73%. 44% of votes cast were for Zhelyu Zhelev. At the second round against 1 opponent Zhelev was elected with 58·85% of votes cast. Turn-out was 76%.

The 240-member *National Assembly* is directly elected by proportional representation. At the elections of 18 Dec. 1994 the Socialist Party (BSP, former Communists) won 125 seats with 43·5% of votes cast, the Union of Democratic Forces (UDF) 69 with 24·23%, the Popular Union (PU; a coalition of the Agrarian Party and the Democratic Party) 18 with 6·25%, the Movement for Rights and Freedom (Turkish) 15 with 5·5% and the Bulgarian Business Bloc 13 with 4·76%. There was a 4% threshold.

President: Zhelyu Zhelev (b. 1935; UDF; elected 1 Aug. 1990, re-elected 19 Jan. 1992). *Vice-President:* Blaga Dimitrova.

In Nov. 1995 the government comprised:

Prime Minister: Zhan Videnov (b. 1959; BSP).

Deputy Prime Minister, Minister of Trade and Foreign Economic Co-operation: Kiril Tsochev (ind). *Deputy Prime Minister, Minister for Economic Development:* Rumen Gechev (BSP). *Deputy Prime Minister, Minister of Territorial Development and Construction:* Doncho Konakchiev (BSP). *Deputy Prime Minister:* Svetoslav Shivarov (PU). *Foreign:* Georgi Pirinski (BSP). *Transport:* Stamen Stamenov (ind). *Industry:* Klimen Vuchev (ind). *Finance:* Dimitŭr Kostov (ind). *Defence:* Dimitŭr Pavlov (ind). *Interior:* Lyubomir Nachev (BSP). *Justice:* Mladen Chervenyakov (BSP). *Environment:* Georgi D. Georgiev (Ekoglasnost). *Education, Science and Technology:* Ilcho Dimitrov (BSP). *Agriculture:* Vasil Chichibaba (PU). *Culture:* Georgi K. Georgiev (ind). *Health:* Mini Vitkova (ind). *Labour and Social Welfare:* Mincho Koralski.

The *Speaker* is Blagovest Sendov (BSP).

National flag: Three horizontal stripes of white, green and red.

National anthem: 'Gorda stara planina' ('Proud and ancient mountains'); words and tune by T. Radoslavov.

Local Government. Local authorities for the 9 regions and 278 districts within them are elected for 30 months. Elections were held for mayors and councillors on 29 Oct. and 12 Nov. 1995. Turn-out was 54·7% for the former and 53·1% for the latter. A large majority of mayorships were won by the BSP and its allies. In the elections for councillors the BSP and its allies won 41% of votes cast, the UDF 24·1%, the PU 12·3%, the Movement for Rights and Freedom 8·2% and the Bulgarian Business Bloc 5%.

DEFENCE. Conscription was reduced from 18 to 12 months in 1992.

Army. There are 3 military districts based on Sofia, Plovdiv and Sliven. In 1996 the Army had a strength of 51,600, including 33,300 conscripts, and is organized in 4 tank, 1 mechanized, 1 surface-to-air missile and 1 airborne brigade, 3 motor rifle divisions and 3 artillery, 3 anti-tank, 1 surface-to-air missile and 3 air defence brigades. Equipment includes 177 T-34, 1,276 T-55 and 333 T-72 main battle tanks. There are 12 regiments of border guards numbering 12,000.

Navy. The Navy, all ex-Soviet or Soviet-built, comprises 2 'Romeo' class diesel submarines, 1 Koni class small frigate, 4 'Poti', 1 'Tarantul' and 2 'Pauk' class corvettes, 6 'Osa' class missile craft, 7 patrol vessels, 4 coastal and 14 inshore minesweepers. There are 2 medium landing ships and 20 craft. Major auxiliaries include 2 oilers, 2 research ships, 1 electronic intelligence gatherer, 2 training ships and 1 tug. There are some 20 minor auxiliaries and service craft. There are 2 regiments of coastal artillery including some missile-armed, and some 10 shore-based Ka-25 and Mi-14 helicopters. The naval headquarters is at Varna, and there are bases at Atiya, Burgas and Sozopol. Personnel in 1995 totalled 3,000.

Air Force. The Air Force has (1995) 21,600 personnel (16,000 conscripts). There are 3 regiments of MiG-21/23/29 interceptors; 3 regiments of fighter/ground attack MiG-23s and Su-20/25s; 1 regiment of Mi-24 helicopter gunships; a total of about 20 Tu-134, L-410, An-2 and An-24/26 transport aircraft; a total of about 40 Mi-2 and Mi-8/17 helicopters; and Yak-18T, Zlin 142, L-29 Delfin and L-39 Albatros trainers. Soviet-built 'Guideline', 'Goa' and 'Ganef' surface-to-air missiles have also been supplied to Bulgaria.

INTERNATIONAL RELATIONS

Membership. Bulgaria is a member of the UN, the Council of Europe and the NATO Partnership for Peace, and is an Associate Partner of the WEU.

ECONOMY

Policy. At the beginning of 1992 95% of enterprises were still in state ownership. A plan to privatize a further 500 large and medium-sized firms was introduced in 1993: Each citizen was to receive a non-transferable option on shares worth 30,000 leva. Mining, energy, oil processing, railways and munitions production remain in state hands. A law of April 1992 allocates 10% of the proceeds of privatization to agricultural development, 20% to the compensation of former owners, 30% to social funds and 40% to local management councils to cover irrecoverable debts. A Centre for Mass Privatization was set up in 1994 to supervise a new stage of privatization by which citizens may buy for 500 leva bonds with a face value of 25,000 leva.

Budget. The fiscal year is the calendar year. In the 1993 budget revenue was 71,350m. leva and expenditure 98,933m. leva.

18% VAT was introduced in April 1994.

Currency. The unit of currency is the *lev* (BGL) of 100 *stotinki.* Notes are issued for 1, 2, 5, 10, 20, 50, 100, 200, 500 and 1,000 leva and coins for 1, 2, 5, 10, 20, 50 stotinki and 1, 2, 5, 10, 20 and 50 leva. 17,383,000m. leva were in circulation in Jan. 1993. Foreign exchange reserves were US$1,530m. in June 1995. Gold reserves were 36·5m. tonnes. In March 1996, £1 = 117·80; US$1 = 77·07; DM1 = 52·22 leva.

Banking and Finance. The National Bank (*Governor*, Lyubomir Filipov) is the central bank and bank of issue. There is a Foreign Trade Bank (founded 1964) and a State Savings Bank, the latter serving local enterprises as well as the public. In 1993, there were savings accounts totalling 28,049m. leva. 5 commercial banks serving various specific industrial sectors, and 3 more broadly-based (the Economic Bank, the Agricultural Bank and the Bank for Economic Initiative) have been set up.

There is a stock exchange in Sofia.

Weights and Measures. The metric system is in general use. On 1 April 1916 the Gregorian calendar came into force.

ENERGY AND NATURAL RESOURCES

Electricity. Bulgaria has little oil, gas or high-grade coal and energy policy is based on the exploitation of its low-grade coal and hydro-electric resources. There is 1 nuclear power station. Output, 1993, 37,903m. kWh (thermal, 22,066m. kWh; nuclear, 13,896m. kWh; hydro-electric, 1,941m. kWh).

Oil. Oil is extracted in the Balchik district on the Black Sea, in an area 100 km north of Varna and at Dolni Dubnik near Pleven. There are refineries at Burgas (annual capacity 5m. tonnes) and Dolni Dubnik (7m. tonnes). Crude oil production (1993) was 43,000 tonnes; gas, 6·61m. cu. metres.

Minerals. Production in 1993: Manganese ore, 4,000 tonnes; iron ore, 266,000 tonnes; lignite, 25·35m. tonnes; brown coal, 3·42m. tonnes; hard coal, 29·03m. tonnes.

Agriculture. In 1993 agricultural land covered 6,159,000 ha, of which 4,642,700 ha were arable. In 1991 sown area was 3,764,000 ha; there were 286,400 ha of meadows and 1,516,300 ha of commons and pastures.

Legislation of 1991 and 1992 provided for the redistribution of collectivized land to its former owners up to 30 ha. Landless peasants received state land or compensation in lieu. Bulgarians resident abroad may acquire such land, as may also legal bodies with up to 50% foreign ownership. It may be rented out, but not sold for 3 years. There were 2,073 agricultural collectives and firms in 1992. There were 1,364 private farms in 1993.

Production in 1993 (in 1,000 tonnes, with percentage from private holdings): Wheat, 3,681 (16·4%); maize, 1,087 (68·5%); barley, 948; sugar beet, 106; sunflower seed, 442; seed cotton, 5; tobacco, 37; tomatoes, 347 (83%); potatoes, 358 (97·2%); grapes, 488 (51·5%). Bulgaria is a leading producer of attar of roses. In 1993 an estimated 3,000 ha were under rose cultivation, with an annual output of over 1,500 kg. Other products (in 1,000 tonnes) in 1991: Meat, 758 (57·7%); wool, 26 (47·7%); honey, 6·81 (88·6%); (1992) 1,684m. (51·4%) eggs; 1,805m. (50·5%) litres of milk.

Livestock (1994, in 1,000): Cattle, 750 (milch cows, 419) (in private holdings, 507 and 321); sheep, 3,763 (3,293); pigs, 2,071 (747); poultry, 18,211 (12,497).

There were 51,171 tractors in use in 1991.

Forestry. Forest area, 1993, was 3,877,000 ha (1·32m. ha coniferous, 2·56m. ha broad-leaved). 46,000 ha were afforested in 1990 and 6·62m. cu. metres of timber were cut.

Fisheries. Catch, 1990: 66,800 tonnes.

INDUSTRY. In 1992 there were 30,660 registered firms (3,491 in 1991), of which 10,752 were manufacturers and 19,908 services. Firms by ownership: State, 3,356; municipal, 16,276; joint-stock companies, 376; co-operative; 1,676; social organizations, 4,403; associations, 559; foreign and joint ventures, 390; agricultural collectives, 1,158.

In 1993 there were produced (in 1,000 tonnes): Pig iron and ferro-alloys, 1,027; steel, 1,941; rolled steel, 1,555; artificial fertilizers, 386; sulphuric acid, 409; cement, 2,000; paper, 125; cotton fabric, 70·3m. metres; woollen yarn, 14·2m. metres. 19,800 TV sets (11,000 colour) and 81,300 refrigerators were made.

Labour. In 1993 24·2% of employed persons worked in the private sector. There is a 42½-hour 5-day working week. Retirement is at 55 for women and 60 for men, or 52 and 57 after 25 years in the last employment. The average wage (excluding peasantry) was 3,145 leva per month in 1993; minimum wage was 1,200 leva per month. Population of working age (males 16–59; females 16–54), 1994, 4,738,559 (47·4% females). At the 1992 census the economically-active population was 3,932,468 (1,902,275 females), of whom 3,286,655 were employed. There were 408,453 registered unemployed in July 1995; there were 7,625 job vacancies in March 1993.

Trade Unions. An independent white-collar trade union movement, Podkrepa, was formed in 1989. It claimed 100,000 members in July 1990. The former official Central Council of Trade Unions reconstituted itself in 1990 as the Confederation of Independent Trade Unions.

FOREIGN ECONOMIC RELATIONS. Legislation in force as of Feb. 1992 abolished restrictions imposed in 1990 on the repatriation of profits and allows foreign nationals to own and set up companies in Bulgaria. Joint Western-Bulgarian industrial ventures have been permitted since 1980. There were 837 in May 1993. Western share participation may exceed 50%. Total foreign debt was US$9,300m. in June 1994.

Commerce. Foreign trade (in 1m. leva):

	1989	*1990*	*1991*	*1992*	*1993*
Imports	12,796	10,160	45,132	80,596	119,288
Exports	13,673	10,496	57,368	81,645	99,043

Principal exports in 1992 (in tonnes): Meat, 258,979; tomatoes, 37,600; cheese, 19,500; wine, 72,300; tobacco, 28,500; soda ash, 337,300; carbamide, 508,000;

ammonium nitrate, 369,600; polyethylene, 33,300; footwear, 2·26m. pairs; rolled iron and steel products, 356,500; zinc, 40,900; electric motors, 539,900 items. Principal imports: Medicines, 1,004·4; pesticides, 5,300; newsprint, 48,300; cotton, 19,900; cotton fabrics, 12m. metres; iron and steel tubes, 33,700; buses, 1,000 items; motor cars, 44,900 items; lorries, 12,000 items; sugar, 198,800; coal, 1,381,100; anthracite, 1,017,700; crude oil, 3·2m.; petrol, 444,300; natural gas, 5,261·5m. cu. metres.

Main export markets in 1992 (trade in 1m. leva): CIS, 20,351; Germany, 8,143; Turkey, 4,659; Italy, 4,322; Greece, 3,478. Main import suppliers: CIS, 23,030; Germany, 10,297; Greece, 4,750; Italy, 4,251.

Total trade between Bulgaria and UK (British Department of Trade returns, in £1,000 sterling):

	1991	*1992*	*1993*	*1994*	*1995*
Imports to UK	36,786	49,780	76,218	69,927	118,550
Exports and re-exports from UK	35,547	59,932	84,229	86,138	104,224

Tourism. There were 8,302,472 foreign visitors in 1993, of whom 2,334,763 were tourists. 2,141,908 Bulgarians made visits abroad.

COMMUNICATIONS

Roads. In 1993 there were 33,900 km of hard-surfaced roads, including 266 km of motorways and 2,935 km of main roads. 1,095m. passengers and 67·77m. tonnes of freight were carried in 1993. There were 4,875 road accidents in 1991 with 1,114 fatalities.

Railways. In 1994 there were 4,294 km of 1,435 mm gauge railway (2,650 km electrified). 5,100m. passenger-km and 30·3m. tonnes of freight were carried.

Civil Aviation. There is an international airport at Sofia (Vrazhdebna). The state-owned Balkan Airlines is the national carrier. In 1995 it had 4 A320-200s, 3 B-737-500s, 2 B-767-200ERs and 41 ex-Soviet aircraft. In 1992 it carried 1·46m. passengers (1·32m. international) and 17,800 tonnes of freight. Services are also operated by Aeroflot, Air France, Air Koryo, Air Malta, Air Moldova, Air Ukraine, Alitalia, Armenian Airlines, Austrian Airlines, British Airways, CSA, El Al, Hemus Air, Libyan Airlines, LOT, Lufthansa, Malév, Olympic, Swissair, Syrian Arab Airlines and Tarom.

Shipping. In 1995, the merchant fleet totalled 1·84m. GRT, including oil tankers, 0·42m. GRT and container ships, 63,305 GRT. Burgas is a fishing and oil-port. Varna is the other important port. There is a rail ferry between Varna and Ilitchovsk (Ukraine). In 1991 115,000 passengers and 18·61m. tonnes of cargo were carried. There were 102,000 km of inland waterways in 1991. 13,000 passengers and 1·55m. tonnes of freight were carried.

Telecommunications. In 1993 there were 3,102 post and telecommunications offices and 2,773,293 telephones (1,856,378 private). Broadcasting is under the aegis of the state-controlled Bulgarian National Radio and Bulgarian Television. There are 4 national and 6 regional radio programmes. A service for tourists is broadcast from Varna. There are 2 TV programmes; Bulgaria also receives transmissions from the French satellite channel TV5. An independent TV channel started broadcasting in 1994. Colour programmes by SECAM system. Radio receiving sets in 1994, 1,651,300; television, 1,494,100.

Cinemas (1993). There were 271 cinemas (attendance, 11·08m.).

Press. In 1993 there were 910 newspapers with an annual circulation of 615,000 and 768 other periodicals. 5,500 book titles were published in 58·3m. copies in 1993.

SOCIAL INSTITUTIONS

Justice. A law of Nov. 1982 provides for the election (and recall) of all judges by the National Assembly. There are a Supreme Court, 28 provincial courts (including Sofia) and regional courts. Jurors are elected at the local government elections.

The maximum term of imprisonment is 20 years. 'Exceptionally dangerous crimes' carry the death penalty.

The Prosecutor General and judges are elected by the Supreme Judicial Council established in 1992.

In 1993 there were 5,949 crimes reported (180 murders) and 6,935 convictions (557 females, 515 juveniles under 17).

Religion. 'The traditional church of the Bulgarian people' (as it is officially described), is that of the Eastern Orthodox Church. It was disestablished under the 1947 Constitution. In 1953 the Bulgarian Patriarchate was revived. The Patriarch Maksim (enthroned 1971) was dismissed in 1992 for collaborating with the former Communist government. The seat of the Patriarch is at Sofia. There are 11 dioceses, each under a Metropolitan, 10 bishops, 2,600 parishes, 1,700 priests, 400 monks and nuns, 3,700 churches and chapels, one seminary and one theological college.

The Constitution provides for freedom of conscience and belief but forbids propaganda against the Government.

In 1992 there were some 70,000 Roman Catholics with 53 priests, in 3 bishoprics. In 1987 there were 10,000 Uniates with 20 priests. At the 1992 census 7,349,544 Christians were recorded and 1,110,295 Moslems (Pomaks). There is a Chief Mufti elected by regional muftis.

Education. Education is free, and compulsory for children between the ages of 7 and 16. Complete literacy is claimed.

In 1993–94 there were 3,856 kindergartens (247,000 children, 25,623 teachers); 3,360 primary schools with 70,131 teachers and 987,999 pupils; 136 special needs schools with 2,381 teachers and 14,193 pupils; 6 vocational technical schools with 155 teachers and 3,323 pupils; 220 secondary vocational technical schools with 6,580 teachers and 107,839 pupils; 268 technical colleges and schools of art with 12,256 teachers and 103,396 students; 47 post-secondary institutions with 2,990 teachers and 27,791 students; 40 institutes of higher education, with 18,158 teachers and 175,810 students. There are 4 state universities, an American university, and universities of mining and geology, and architecture, civil engineering and geodesy.

There were 22 private schools with 1,348 pupils in 1993–94.

The Academy of Sciences was founded in 1869.

Health. All medical services are free. Private medical services were authorized in Jan. 1991. In 1993 there were 286 hospitals and clinics with 90,372 beds. There were 28,457 doctors, 5,727 dentists, 2,376 pharmacists, 6,903 midwives, 6,928 medical auxiliaries and 52,038 nurses.

Welfare. Retirement and disablement pensions and temporary sick pay are calculated as a percentage of previous wages (respectively 55–80%, 35–100%, 69–90%) and according to the nature of the employment. Free medical treatment is available to all, but private practice also exists. Medicines are free to people with chronic conditions or on low incomes.

In 1992 there were 2,426,000 recipients of pensions; disbursements 32,596m. leva in 1993. The average annual pension was 5,157 leva in 1992.

DIPLOMATIC REPRESENTATIVES

Of Bulgaria in Great Britain (186 Queen's Gate, London, SW7 5HL)
Ambassador: Stefan Tafrov.

Of Great Britain in Bulgaria (Blvd. Vasil Levski 65–67, Sofia)
Ambassador: G. Short, MVO.

Of Bulgaria in the USA (1621 22nd St., NW, Washington, D.C., 20008)
Ambassador: Snejana Botoucharova.

Of the USA in Bulgaria (1 Stamboliski Blvd., Sofia)
Ambassador: William D. Montgomery.

Of Bulgaria to the United Nations
Ambassador: Slavi Pashovski.

Further Reading

Natsionalen Statisticheski Institut. *Statisticheski Godishnik.—Statisticheski Spravochnik* (annual).—*Statistical Reference Book of Republic of Bulgaria* (annual).
Kratka Bŭlgarska Entsiklopediia (Short Bulgarian Encyclopaedia), 5 vols. Sofia, 1963–69
Crampton, R. J., *A Short History of Modern Bulgaria.* CUP, 1987.—*Bulgaria.* [Bibliography] Oxford and Santa Barbara, 1989

National statistical office: Natsionalen Statisticheski Institut/Central Statistical Office, Sofia. *Chairman:* Zakhari Karamfilov.

BURKINA FASO

République Démocratique du Burkina Faso

Capital: Ouagadougou
Population: 10m. (1994)
GNP per capita: US$300 (1994)
HDI/world rank: 0·228/169 (1992)

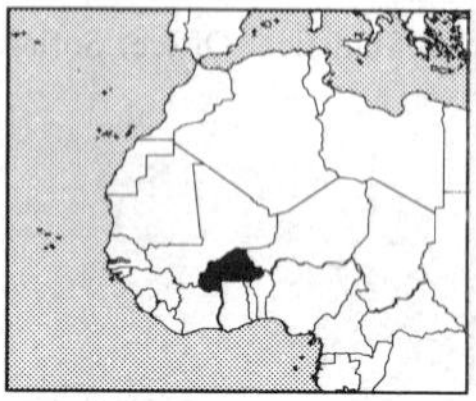

KEY HISTORICAL EVENTS. Having been a colony since 1919, Upper Volta became an autonomous republic within the French Community in 1958 and reached full independence in 1960. The name was changed to Burkina Faso in 1984.

TERRITORY AND POPULATION. Burkina Faso is bounded in the north and west by Mali, east by Niger and south by Benin, Togo, Ghana and the Côte d'Ivoire. Area: 274,122 sq. km; population (census, 1985) 7,967,019 (3,846,518 males). Estimate (1994), 10m. (17% urban); density, 35·5 per sq. km. Vital statistics (1992): Infant mortality, 132 per 1,000 live births; expectation of life, 48 years; growth rate (1993), 2·6%. The largest cities (1985 census) are Ouagadougou, the capital (442,223), Bobo-Dioulasso (231,162), Koudougou (51,670), Ouahigouya (38,604), Banfora (35,204), Kaya (25,799), Fada N'Gourma and Tenkodogo.

The areas and populations of the 30 provinces were:

Province	*Sq. km*	*Estimate 1991*
Bam	4,017	173,516
Bazéga	5,313	352,104
Bougouriba	7,087	242,986
Boulgou	9,033	465,845
Boulkiemdé	4,138	393,900
Comoé	18,393	296,083
Ganzourgou	4,087	223,555
Gnagnan	8,600	272,203
Gourma	26,613	350,336
Houet	16,672	724,803
Kadiogo	1,169	652,377
Kénédougou	8,307	162,010
Kossi	13,177	389,360
Kouritenga	1,627	227,060
Mouhoun	10,442	329,115

Province	*Sq. km*	*Estimate 1991*
Nahouri	3,843	119,114
Namentenga	7,755	214,564
Oubritenga	4,693	328,682
Oudalan	10,046	123,495
Passoré	4,078	232,278
Poni	10,361	258,647
Sanguié	5,165	234,079
Sanmatenga	9,213	404,563
Séno	13,473	269,892
Sissili	13,736	297,598
Soum	13,350	217,972
Sourou	9,487	313,355
Tapoa	14,780	187,785
Yatenga	12,292	558,318
Zoundwéogo	3,453	175,166

The principal ethnic groups are the Mossi (49%), Fulani (8%), Mandé (7%), Bobo (7%), Gourounsi (7%), Gourmantché (7%), Bissa (4%), Lobi-Dagari (4%), Sénoufo (2%). French is the official language.

CLIMATE. A tropical climate with a wet season from May to Nov. and a dry season from Dec. to April. Rainfall decreases from south to north. Ouagadougou. Jan. 76°F (24·4°C), July 83°F (28·3°C). Annual rainfall 36" (894 mm).

CONSTITUTION AND GOVERNMENT. At a referendum in June 1991 a new constitution was approved; there is an executive presidency. At the presidential elections of 1 Dec. 1991 Blaise Compaoré was the sole candidate, and was elected by 86·4% of votes cast. The electorate was 3·5m.; turn-out was 27·3%.

Parliament consists of the 107-member *Assembly of People's Deputies*, elected by universal suffrage, and the 120-member *Chamber of Representatives*, a consultative body representing social, religious, professional and political organizations. There is also a 90-member *Economic and Social Council. National Assizes* of about 2,000 representatives of a broad spectrum of government, public, social and professional bodies may be convened by the President *ad hoc* to discuss public issues.

At the elections of 24 May 1992 the electorate was 4m. Turn-out was 33·8%. The Organization for Popular Democracy-Labour Movement (ODP-MT) won 78 seats, the National Convention of Progressive Patriots-Social Democratic Party (CNPP-PSD), 12.

A coalition government of 10 parties dominated by the ODP-MT was formed by the President in Jan. 1994, which comprised in Dec. 1995:

President: Capt. Blaise Compaoré

Prime Minister: Roch Marc Christian Kaboré.

Ministers of State: Salif Diallo (*Environment and Water*); Hermann Yaméogo (*Integration and African Solidarity*).

Ministers: Agriculture and Livestock: Jean-Paul Sawadogo. *Civil Service and Modernization of the Administration:* Juliette Bonkoungou. *Culture and Communications:* Claude Somda. *Defence:* Badayé Fayama. *Economy, Finance and Planning:* Zéphirin Diabré. *Employment and Social Security:* Alphonse Ouédraogo. *Energy and Mines:* Elie Ouédraogo. *Foreign Affairs:* Alassé Ouédraogo. *Health:* Christophe Dabiré. *Industry, Trade and Handicrafts:* Talata Kafando. *Justice:* Yarga Larba. *Primary Education and Literacy:* Baworo Seydou Sanou. *Public Works, Housing and Town Planning:* Joseph Kaboré. *Relations with Parliament:* Thomas Sanon. *Science, Secondary and Higher Education:* Melégué Traoré. *Social Affairs and the Family:* Bana Ouandaogo.*Territorial Administration:* Yero Boly. *Transport:* Ouala Koutiébou. *Youth and Sport:* Joseph Tiendrébéogo.

National flag: Horizontally red over green with a yellow star over all in the centre.

National anthem: 'Contre la férule humiliante' ('Against the shameful fetters'); words by T. Sankara, tune anonymous.

Local government: The country is divided into 30 provinces and 250 districts.

DEFENCE. There are 6 military regions. All forces form part of the Army.

Army. The Army consists of 8 infantry companies, 1 airborne company and tank, artillery and engineer support units. Equipment includes 83 armoured cars. Strength (1996), 5,600 with a paramilitary Gendarmerie of 4,200.

Air Force. Equipment comprises 1 Super King Air 200, 1 Aero Commander 500 and 1 Reims/Cessna Super Skymaster for transport and liaison duties, 1 Cessna 172 trainer, and 1 Dauphin and 2 Alouette III helicopters. Personnel total (1995) 200.

INTERNATIONAL RELATIONS

Membership. Burkina Faso is a member of the UN, OAU and is an ACP state of the EU.

ECONOMY

Policy. The second 5-year plan (1991–96) was scaled down by 50% in 1991. A development programme for 1994–96, based mainly on agriculture and costing 62,000m. francs CFA, is being financed largely by foreign aid. It is proposed to privatize and restructure the banking and industrial sectors. 11 enterprises had been privatized by Nov. 1994. A second phase of privatization was then initiated.

Price controls were imposed on basic items following the devaluation of the franc CFA in Jan. 1994.

Budget. The 1994 budget envisaged expenditure of 373,000m. francs CFA and domestic revenue of 296,000m. francs CFA.

Currency. The unit of currency is the *franc CFA* (XOF) with a parity rate of 100 francs CFA to 1 French franc. In Sept. 1994, 91,030m. francs CFA were in circulation. In 1994 foreign exchange reserves were US$237·2m.; gold reserves were 11,000 troy oz in 1993. In March 1996, £1 = 772·97; US$1 = 505·74; DM1 = 342·67 francs.

Banking and Finance. The bank of issue which functions as the central bank is the regional West African Central Bank (BCEAO; *Governor*, Charles Konan Banny).

There are 3 commercial banks, 4 specialized development institutions, a savings bank, 5 non-bank credit institutions and an investment company.

Weights and Measures. The metric system is in use.

ENERGY AND NATURAL RESOURCES

Electricity. Production of electricity (1991) was 193m. kWh. There are 5 thermal power stations with a total capacity in 1995 of 38·9MW. Hydro-electric capacity in 1994 was 15 MW.

Minerals. There are deposits of manganese, zinc, limestone, phosphate and diamonds. Gold production was 1·8 tonnes in 1992.

Agriculture. In 1991 there were 3·55m. ha of arable land and 10m. ha of permanent pasture. 20,000 ha were irrigated. 7·98m. persons depended on agriculture, of whom 4·12m. were economically active. Production (1992, in 1,000 tonnes): Sorghum, 1,292; millet, 784; sugar-cane, 340; maize, 341; groundnuts, 143; rice, 47; cotton, 172; sesame, 8. Rice and groundnuts are of increasing importance.

Livestock (1992, in 1,000): Cattle, 4,096; sheep, 5,350; goats, 6,860; pigs, 530; asses, 427; horses, 22.

Forestry. In 1992, 6·66m. ha were forested.

Fisheries. River fishing produces about 5,500 tonnes annually. There is some fish farming.

INDUSTRY. In 1994 manufacturing contributed 14% of GDP, mainly food-processing and textiles. Plant is primitive, and employs only about 1% of the work-force. There are about 100 firms, most publicly-owned.

Labour. In 1990 the labour force was 4,744,000.

Trade Unions. There are 4 federations: the CGTB, USTB, CNTB and ONSL.

FOREIGN ECONOMIC RELATIONS. Foreign debt was US$1,311m. in 1994.

Commerce. In 1994 imports totalled US$361·5m. and exports US$225·9m. Value of main exports (in USS1m.), 1994: Cotton, 59; gold, 22. Principal export markets, 1994: France, 13·2%; Côte d'Ivoire, 10·8%; Thailand, 10·2%; Itlay, 7·8%; Taiwan, 7·2%. Principal import suppliers: Côte d'Ivoire, 25·6%; France, 15·6%; Niger, 3·5%; Nigeria, 3%; Japan, 2·3%.

Total trade between Burkina Faso and UK (British Department of Trade returns, in £1,000 sterling):

	1991	*1992*	*1993*	*1994*	*1995*
Imports to UK	235	423	477	851	398
Exports and re-exports from UK	6,472	5,612	5,077	6,107	8,881

COMMUNICATIONS

Roads. The road system comprises 13,134 km, of which 4,396 km are national, 1,744 km departmental, 2,364 km regional and 1,940 km unclassified roads. Only 1,500 km are asphalted.

Railways. An independent Burkina Faso railway organization was established in 1988 to run the portion in Burkina (622 km of metre-gauge) of the former Abidjan-Niger Railway, which was extended from Ouagadougou to Kaya in 1993 (107 km). The railways carried 0·6m. passengers and 0·2m. tonnes of freight in 1993.

Civil Aviation. The international airports are Ouagadougou and Bobo-Dioulasso. The national carrier is Air Burkina (66% state-owned) which had 2 aircraft in 1995, and operates flights to Abidjan, Brussels, Niamey and Paris.

Telecommunications. There were, in 1993, about 21,000 telephones. Radio and television services (colour by SECAM) are provided by the state-controlled Radiodiffusion-Télévision Burkina. Radio Bobo is a regional service and there is a commercial radio station. In 1993 there were estimated to be 0·2m. radio and 45,000 television receivers.

Press. There were 4 dailies (1 government-owned) and 2 weeklies in 1994.

SOCIAL INSTITUTIONS

Justice. Civilian courts replaced revolutionary tribunals in 1993. There is a Supreme Court in Ouagadougou and Courts of Appeal at Ouagadougou and Bobo-Dioulasso.

Religion. In 1991 there were 4·81m. Moslems and 1·9m. Christians (mainly Roman Catholic). Many of the remaining population follow traditional animist religions.

Education. In 1994 adult literacy was about 10%. The 1994–96 development programme has established an adult literacy campaign and centres for the education of 10–15-year-old non-school-attenders. In 1992 there were 0·53m. pupils in primary schools (6,560 teachers in 1987) and 97,171 pupils in secondary schools (2,727 teachers in 1987). In 1986 there were 4,808 students in 18 technical schools (421 teachers in 1987) and 347 students in a teacher-training establishment. The Université d'Ouagadougou had 7,837 students in 1992 and 289 teaching staff in 1987.

DIPLOMATIC REPRESENTATIVES

Of Burkina Faso in Great Britain
Ambassador: Youssouf Ouedraogo (resides in Brussels).

Of Great Britain in Burkina Faso
Ambassador: Margaret Rothwell, CMG (resides in Abidjan).

Of Burkina Faso in the USA (2340 Massachusetts Ave., NW, Washington, D.C., 20008)
Ambassador: Gaëten Rimwanguiya Ouedraogo.

Of the USA in Burkina Faso (PO Box 35, Ouagadougou)
Ambassador: Donald J. McConnell.

Of Burkina Faso to the United Nations
Ambassador: Gaëtan Rimwanguiya Ouedraogo.

Further Reading

Decalo, S., *Burkina Faso* [Bibliography]. Oxford and Santa Barbara (CA), 1994
Nnaji, B. O., *Blaise Compaore: Architect of the Burkina Faso Revolution.* Lagos, 1991

BURMA

Myanmar Naingngandaw

(Union of Myanmar)

Capital: Rangoon (Yangon)
Population: 43·13m. (1994)
GNP per capita: US$200 (1986)
HDI/world rank: 0·457/132 (1992)

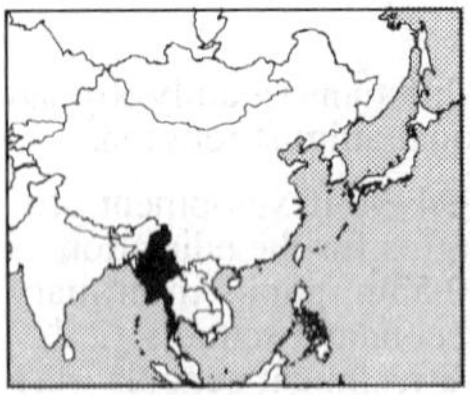

KEY HISTORICAL EVENTS. A treaty establishing Burma's independence from the UK was signed in London on 17 Oct. 1947. For the history of Burma's connexion with Great Britain *see* THE STATESMAN'S YEAR-BOOK, 1950, p. 836. The Union of Burma came formally into existence on 4 Jan. 1948 and became the Socialist Republic of the Union of Burma in 1974. On 18 Sept. 1988, the Armed Forces seized power and set up a State Law and Order Restoration Council (SLORC). On 19 June 1989 the government changed the official name of the country in English to the Union of Myanmar.

By Nov. 1995 the government had come to ceasefire agreements with 15 of the 16 insurgent groups.

Aung San Suu Kyi was released from house arrest on 10 July 1995.

TERRITORY AND POPULATION. Burma is bounded in the east by China, Laos and Thailand, and west by the Indian Ocean, Bangladesh and India. The total area of the Union is 261,228 sq. miles (676,577 sq. km). The population in 1983 (census) was 35,313,905. Estimate (1995) 43·92m. (22·09m. female). Growth rate in 1995, 1·87%. Birth rate (1994 estimate), 28·2 per 1,000 population; death rate, 8·7; infant deaths, 47·5 per 1,000 live births; still births, 10·3 per 1,000 live births. Expectation of life was 62 years in 1990.

The leading towns are: Rangoon (Yangon), the capital (1983), 2,458,712; other towns, Mandalay, 532,985; Moulmein, 219,991; Pegu, 150,447; Bassein, 144,092; Sittwe (Akyab), 107,907; Taunggye, 107,607; Monywa, 106,873.

The population of the 7 states and 7 administrative divisions at the 1983 census: Kachin State, 903,982; Kayah State, 168,355; Karen State, 1,057,505; Chin State, 368,985; Sagaing Division, 3,855,991; Tenasserim Division, 917,628; Pegu Division, 3,800,240; Magwe Division, 3,241,103; Mandalay Division, 4,580,923; Mon State, 1,682,041; Rakhine State, 2,045,891; Rangoon Division, 3,973,782; Shan State, 3,718,706; Irrawaddy Division, 4,991,057.

The official language is Burmese; English is also in use.

CLIMATE. The climate is equatorial in coastal areas, changing to tropical monsoon over most of the interior, but humid temperate in the extreme north, where there is a more significant range of temperature and a dry season lasting from Nov. to April. In coastal parts, the dry season is shorter. Very heavy rains occur in the monsoon months May to Sept. Rangoon. Jan. 77°F (25°C), July 80°F (26·7°C). Annual rainfall 104" (2,616 mm). Akyab. Jan. 70°F (21·1°C), July 81°F (27·2°C). Annual rainfall 206" (5,154 mm). Mandalay. Jan. 68°F (20°C), July 85°F (29·4°C). Annual rainfall 33" (828 mm).

CONSTITUTION AND GOVERNMENT. In Oct. 1995 the government comprised:

Prime Minister, Chairman of SLORC and Minister of Defence: Gen. Than Shwe.

Deputy Prime Ministers: Vice-Adm. Maung Maung Khin; Lieut.-Gen. Tin Tun. *Planning and Finance:* Brig.-Gen. D. O. Abel. *Energy:* Khin Maung Thein. *Transport:* Maj.-Gen. Thein Win. *Construction:* Maj. Gen. Saw Tun. *Home Affairs:* Maj.-Gen. Myo Thinn. *Health:* Rear-Adm. Than Nyunt. *Industry:* Lieut.-Gen. Sein Aung. *Commerce:* Maj.-Gen. Tun Kyi. *Social Affairs:* Brig.-Gen. Thaung Myint. *Religious Affairs:* Maj.-Gen. Myo Nyunt. *Railways:* Win Sein. *Agriculture:* Maj.-

Gen. Myint Aung. *Borders:* Maj.-Gen. Maung Thint. *Telecommunications:* Soe Tha. *Livestock:* Brig.-Gen. Maung Maung. *Co-operation:* Than Aung. *Culture:* Lieut.-Gen. Thaung Myint. *Education:* Pan Aung. *Finance:* Brig.-Gen. Win Tin. *Foreign:* Ohn Gyaw. *Forests:* Lieut.-Gen. Chit Swe. *Tourism:* Maj.-Gen. Kyaw Ba. *Information:* Maj.-Gen. Aye Kyaw. *Employment:* Maj.-Gen. Aye Thoung. *Minerals:* Maj.-Gen. Kyaw Min. *Immigration and Population:* Lieut.-Gen. Maung Hla. *Minister in the Prime Minister's Office:* Brig.-Gen. Lun Maung.

In elections in May 1990 the opposition National League for Democracy (NLD), led by Aung San Suu Kyi (b. 1945), won 392 of the 485 People's Assembly seats contested with some 60% of the valid vote. Turn-out was 72%, but 12·4% of ballots cast were declared invalid. SLORC said it would hand over power after the People's Assembly had agreed on a new constitution, but in July 1990 it stipulated that any such constitution must conform to guidelines which it would itself prescribe.

In May 1991 48 members of the NLD were given prison sentences on charges of treason. In July, opposition members of the People's Assembly were unseated for alleged offences ranging from treason to illicit foreign exchange dealing. Such members, and unsuccessful candidates in the May 1990 elections, are forbidden to stand in future elections. Aung San Suu Kyi was under house arrest from July 1989 to July 1995. She was awarded the Nobel Peace Prize in 1991.

On 28 Nov. 1995 the government re-opened a 706-member Constitutional Convention in which the NLD was given 107 places. The NLD withdrew on 29 Nov.

National flag: Red with a blue canton bearing 2 ears of rice within a cog-wheel and a ring of 14 stars, all in white.

National anthem: 'Gba majay Bma' ('We shall love Burma for ever'); words and tune by Saya Tin.

Local government: Burma is divided into 7 states and 7 administrative divisions; these are sub-divided into 314 townships and then into villages and wards.

DEFENCE

Army. The strength of the Army (1996) was 265,000. The Army is organized into 10 regional commands comprising 10 light infantry divisions. Combat units comprise 3 armoured, 245 infantry and 7 artillery battalions, and 1 anti-aircraft artillery battalion. Equipment includes 26 Comet and 36 Ch T-69II main battle tanks. There are 2 paramilitary units: People's Police Force (50,000) and People's Militia (35,000).

Navy. The fleet includes 2 old escort patrol vessels (ex-USA PCE and MSF types) and about 50 patrol craft, half sea-going and half riverine. Auxiliaries include 1 patrol craft support ship, 2 survey ships and 15 small landing craft. Personnel in 1995 totalled about 14,000 including 800 naval infantry.

The Fishery Protection Service (under the Pearl and Fishery Department) operates 3 coastal and 8 inshore patrol craft.

Air Force. The Air Force is intended primarily for internal security duties. Its combat force comprises 10 G-4 Super Galeb supplied by Yugoslavia, 30 F-7 fighters and 24 A-5 fighter-bombers received from China, 18 turboprop Pilatus PC-7s and PC-9s. Transport and second-line units are equipped with 4 FH-227, 1 Turbo-Porter, 1 Citation and 6 Cessna 180 aircraft, 10 Polish-built W-3 Sokol, 12 Bell UH-1, and 10 Alouette III helicopters. Personnel (1995) 9,000.

INTERNATIONAL RELATIONS

Membership. Burma is a member of the UN and Colombo Plan.

ECONOMY

Policy. A short-term plan ran from 1992–93 to 1995–96. There were within it annual plans with targets. Liberalization measures to promote a market economy were introduced in 1990. 1992–93 was designated 'Economic Year'.

Budget. The fiscal year ends 31 March. Estimates for 1992–93: Revenue, K.65,305m.; expenditure, K.69,066m.

State budget estimates are classified into 3 parts, *viz.* State Administrative Organizations, State Economic Enterprises and Town and City Development Committees.

Receipts included: Tax revenue, 6,427; receipts from state economic enterprises, 7,820.

Currency. The unit of currency is the *kyat* (MMK) of 100 *pyas*. There are notes of kyat 500, 200, 100, 90, 50, 45, 15, 10, 5 and 1 and pyas 50, and coins of kyat 1 and pyas 50, 25, 10, 5 and 1. In 1993 K.65,822m. were in circulation. Foreign exchange reserves were K.2,127m. in Sept. 1994; gold reserves were K.74·8m. Inflation was about 40% in 1994. In March 1996, £1 = K.8·89; US$1 = K.5·82; DM1 = K.3·94

Banking and Finance. The Central Bank of Myanmar was established in 1990. Its *Governor* is Kyi Aye. In 1995 there were 15 private domestic banks. Since 1996 foreign banks with representative offices (there were 31 in 1996) have been permitted to set up joint ventures with Burmese banks. The foreign partner must provide at least 35% of the capital. The state insurance company is the Myanmar Insurance Corporation. Deposits in savings banks were K.19,050m. in 1993.

Weights and Measures. The metric system is in use alongside traditional measures. A *viss* = 3·6lb.

ENERGY AND NATURAL RESOURCES

Electricity. In 1994–95 the installed capacity of Myanma Electric Power was 845 MW, of which 299 MW was hydro-electric, 62 MW thermal, 406 MW natural gas and 78 MW diesel. Capacity of other networks was 367 MW. Total generated, 3,500m. kWh.

Oil. Production (1994–95) of crude oil was 5·7m. bbls.; natural gas, 51,090m. cu. feet.

Minerals. Production in 1994–95 (in tonnes): Zinc concentrates, 5,644; nickel speiss, 57; antimonial lead, 192; refined lead, 3,951; tin concentrates, 413; tungsten concentrates, 53; tin, tungsten and scheelite mixed, 1,400; refined silver, 240,000 fine oz.; gold, 24,066 troy oz; refined tin metal, 295; copper concentrates, 39,500; coal, 74.

Agriculture. In 1994-95 4·5m. peasant families cultivated 24·9m. acres. Liberalization measures of 1990 permit farmers to grow crops of their choice. The total sown area in 1994-95 was 21·66m. acres. 4·07m. acres were irrigated. In 1994–95 376,601 tonnes of fertilizer were distributed. Production (1994–95, in 1,000 tonnes): Paddy, 18,813; sugar-cane, 2,271; maize, 255; jute, 35; cotton, 105; wheat, 114; butter beans, 32; soya beans, 52; rubber, 17; groundnuts, 636.

Livestock (1994–95): Cattle, 10m.; buffaloes, 2·2m.; pigs, 2·9m.; sheep and goats, 1·5m.; poultry, 29·4m. In 1994–95 there were 6·7m. draught cattle and about 12,000 tractors.

Net output of agriculture for 1993–94 was valued at K.23,595m.

Forestry. Forest area in 1994–95 was 80·04m. acres (25·52m. acres reserved). Teak extracted in 1994–95, 260,000 cu. tons; hardwood, 1,111,000 cu. tons.

Fisheries. In 1994–95 sea fishing produced 367·5m. *viss* and freshwater fisheries 137·4m. *viss*. Aquacultural fish production was 45·1m. *viss*. Cultured pearls and oyster shells are produced.

INDUSTRY. Of the 47,227 industrial enterprises in 1994-95, 1,675 were state-owned, 640 were co-operatives and 44,912 were private. Production (1994–95) in 1,000 tonnes: Cement, 485; fertilizers, 235; sugar, 71·4; paper, 14·0; cotton yarn, 16·8. 1,502 motor cars, 282 tractors and 35,042 bicycles were produced. In 1994–95 manufacturing output was valued at K.5,799m.

Labour. The population of working age (15 to 59) in 1995 was 25·81m. Economically active persons in 1994–95: 17·23m., of whom 11·12m. were employed in agriculture, 1·72m. in services, 1·41m. in manufacturing and 1·66m. in trade.

FOREIGN ECONOMIC RELATIONS.

In Aug. 1991 the USA imposed trade sanctions in response to alleged civil rights violations. Foreign debt was some US$4,200m. in 1990, of which US$2,000m. was owed to Japan. A law of 1989 permitted joint ventures, with foreign companies or individuals able to hold 100% of the shares.

Commerce. Since 1990 in line with market-oriented measures firms have been able to participate directly in trade.

Imports and exports (K.1m.) for 1994–95: Imports 9,117·0; exports 4,772.6. Main imports (in K.1m.), 1993–94: Raw materials, 2,127·8; transport equipment, 1,364; tools and spares, 308·3; machinery, 824·1; construction materials, 507·6. Main exports: Teak, 741·1; pulses and beans, 724·5; rubber, 300·1; hardwood, 499·9; rice, 267·6. Main export markets: India, 634·7; Singapore, 819·8; Thailand, 736·8; China, 209·8; Hong Kong, 453·0.

Total trade between Burma and UK (British Department of Trade returns, in £1,000 sterling):

	1991	*1992*	*1993*	*1994*	*1995*
Imports to UK	2,771	5,046	9,100	14,004	9,283
Exports and re-exports from UK	8,294	9,145	19,274	13,011	15,244

Tourism. There were 89,238 tourists in 1994 (13,523 in 1992), bringing a revenue of K.143,375m.

COMMUNICATIONS

Roads. There were 16,770 miles of road in 1993–94, of which 2,452 miles were union highway. In 1994–95 the state service ran 1,082 buses, 200 taxis and 2,044 lorries. There were also 147,729 buses and 31,836 lorries in private co-operative ownership. In 1994–95 101·48m. passengers and 1·02m. tonnes of freight were carried by road.

Railways. In 1992 there were 3,569 km of route on metre gauge. In 1994–95 Myanma Railways carried 3·35m. tonnes of freight and 60m. passengers.

Civil Aviation. Myanma Airways maintains international services to Bangkok, Hong Kong and Singapore. In 1995 it had 8 Fokker F-27 and 3 F-28 aircraft. There were, in 1995, 43 civil airfields. In 1994–95 0·59m. passengers were carried on domestic, and 130,000 on international, flights (78,000 in 1993–94). Services are also provided by Aeroflot Russian Airlines, Air China, Biman Bangladesh, Silk Air and Thai Airways.

Shipping. There are 60 miles of navigable canals. The Irrawaddy is navigable up to Myitkyina, 900 miles from the sea, and its tributary, the Chindwin, is navigable for 390 miles. The Irrawaddy delta has nearly 2,000 miles of navigable water. The Salween, the Attaran and the G'yne provide about 250 miles of navigable waters around Moulmein. In 1994–95 27m. passengers and 3·1m. tonnes of freight were carried on inland waterways. The ocean-going fleet of the state-owned Myanma Five Star Line in 1994 comprised 11 liners, 5 short-haul vessels and 3 coastal passenger/cargo vessels. In 1994–95 60,000 passengers and 857,000 tonnes of freight were transported coastally and overseas. The port is Rangoon.

Telecommunications. In 1994–95 there were 1,186 post offices, 141,246 telephones, 398 telegraph offices, 231 telexes and 773 fax machines. The government runs a TV and a radio station. In 1993 there were 3·2m. radio and 1m. television receivers (colour by NTSC).

Press. 1 newspaper is published, by the government, in Burmese and English versions.

SOCIAL INSTITUTIONS

Justice. The highest judicial authority is the Chief Judge, appointed by SLORC.

Religion. In 1990 there were 37·27m. Buddhists, 2·05m. Christians and 1·6m. Moslems (mainly in the west).

Education. Education is free in primary, middle and vocational schools; fees are charged in senior secondary schools and universities. In 1994–95 there were 36,499 primary schools with 198,899 teachers and 6,406,993 pupils; 1,124 monastic primary schools (permitted since 1992) with 53,200 pupils; 2,062 middle schools with 49,111 teachers and 1,392,117 pupils and 857 high schools with 18,366 teachers and 374,393 pupils.

In higher education in 1994–95 there were 13 teacher training schools with 248 teachers and 2,025 students, 5 teacher training institutes with 255 teachers and 2,400 students, 16 technical high schools with 477 teachers and 5,286 students, 11 technical institutes, with 640 teachers and 8,004 students, 10 agricultural high schools with 97 teachers and 1,144 students, 7 agricultural institutes with 173 teachers and 1,327 students, 41 vocational schools with 364 teachers and 7,347 students, 6 universities with 3,652 teachers and 67,345 students, 6 degree colleges with 704 teachers and 13,668 students and 10 colleges with 550 teachers and 9,286 students.

There was also a University for the Development of the National Races of the Union and institutes of medicine (3), dentistry, paramedical science, pharmacy, nursing, veterinary science, economics , technology (2), agriculture, education (2), foreign languages, computer science and forestry. An institute of remote education maintains a correspondence course at university level.

Health. In 1994–95 there were 12,464 doctors, 810 dentists, 9,704 nurses, 8,724 midwives and 720 hospitals with 28,202 beds.

Welfare. In 1994–95 contributions to social security totalled (K.1m.) 103·2 (from employers, 64·2; from employees, 38·6). Benefits paid totalled 74·5, and included: Sickness, 11·1m. maternity, 3·6; disability, 3·2; survivors' pensions, 1·2.

DIPLOMATIC REPRESENTATIVES

Of Burma in Great Britain (19A Charles St., London, W1X 8ER)
Ambassador: U Hla Maung.

Of Great Britain in Burma (80 Strand Rd., Rangoon)
Ambassador: R. A. Eagleson, OBE.

Of Burma in the USA (2300 S. St., NW, Washington, D.C., 20008)
Ambassador: U Daw Thaung.

Of the USA in Burma (581 Merchant St., Rangoon)
Ambassador: (Vacant).

Of Burma to the United Nations
Ambassador: Win Mra.

Further Reading

Union of Myanmar, Ministry of National Planning and Economic Development. *Review of the Financial, Economic and Social Conditions*. Annual. – *Statistical Yearbook*
Herbert, P., Burma [bibliography]. Santa Barbara and Oxford, 1991
Lintner, B., *Outrage: Burma's Struggle for Democracy*. 2nd ed. London, 1990
O'Brien, H., *Forgotten Land: a Rediscovery of Burma*. London, 1991
Smith, M., *Burma: Insurgency and the Politics of Ethnicity*. London, 1991
Suu Kyi, Aung San, *Freedom from Fear and Other Writings*. London, 1991
Taylor, R. H., *The State in Burma*. London, 1988

National statistical office: Ministry of National Planning and Economic Development, Rangoon.

BURUNDI

Republika y'Uburundi

Capital: Bujumbura
Population: 5·8m. (1994)
GNP per capita: US$150 (1994)
HDI/world rank: 0·286/165 (1992)

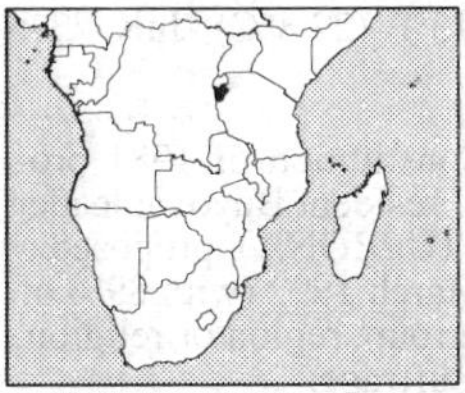

KEY HISTORICAL EVENTS. Tradition recounts the establishment of a Tutsi kingdom in the 16th century. German military occupation in 1890 incorporated the territory into German East Africa. From 1919 Burundi formed part of Ruanda-Urundi administered by the Belgians, first as a League of Nations mandate and then as a UN trust territory. Internal self-government was granted on 1 Jan. 1962, followed by independence on 1 July 1962.

On 8 July 1966 Prince Charles Ndizeye deposed his father Mwami Mwambutsa IV, suspended the constitution and made Capt. Michel Micombero Prime Minister. On 1 Sept. Prince Charles was enthroned as Mwami Ntare V. On 28 Nov., while the Mwami was attending a Head of States Conference in Kinshasa (Congo), Micombero declared Burundi a republic with himself as president.

On 31 March 1972 Prince Charles returned to Burundi from Uganda and was placed under house arrest. On 29 April 1972 President Micombero dissolved the Council of Ministers and took full power; that night heavy fighting broke out between rebels from both Burundi and neighbouring countries, and the ruling Tutsi, apparently with the intention of destroying the Tutsi hegemony. Prince Charles was killed during the fighting and it was estimated that up to 120,000 were killed. On 14 July 1972 President Micombero reinstated a Government with a Prime Minister. On 1 Nov. 1976 President Micombero was deposed by the Army, as was President Bagaza on 3 Sept. 1987. Pierre Buyoya assumed the presidency on 1 Oct. 1987.

On 21 Oct. 1993 President Ndadaye and 6 ministers were killed in an attempted military coup. A wave of Tutsi-Hutu massacres broke out. On 6 April 1994 President Ntaryamira was killed, possibly assassinated, together with the President of Rwanda.

TERRITORY AND POPULATION. Burundi is bounded in the north by Rwanda, east and south by Tanzania and west by Zaïre, and has an area of 27,834 sq. km (10,759 sq. miles). The population at the 1990 census was 5,292,793; estimate (1994) 5·4m.; population density, 208·5 per sq. km. 12% of the population was urban in 1990; life expectancy was 48·2 years in 1992.

There are 15 regions, all named after their chief towns. Area and population:

Region	*Area (in sq. km.)*	*Population (1990 census)*
Bubanza	1,093	222,953
Bujumbura	1,334	608,931
Bururi	2,515	385,490
Cankuzo	1,940	142,707
Cibitoke	1,639	279,843
Karuzi	1,459	287,905
Kayanza	1,229	443,116
Kirundo	1,711	401,103
Kitega	1,989	596,174
Makamba	1,972	223,799
Muhinga	1,825	373,382
Muramuya	1,530	441,653
Ngozi	1,468	482,246
Rutana	1,898	195,834
Ruyigi	2,365	238,567

The capital, Bujumbura, had an estimated population of 0·3m. in 1994.

There are 3 ethnic groups—Hutu (Bantu, forming over 83% of the total): Tutsi (Nilotic, less than 15%); Twa (pygmoids, less than 1%). The local language is Kirundi. French is also an official language. Kiswahili is spoken in the commercial centres.

CLIMATE. An equatorial climate, modified by altitude. The eastern plateau is generally cool, the easternmost savanna several degrees hotter. The wet seasons are from March to May and Sept. to Dec. Bujumbura. Jan. 73°F (22·8°C), July 73°F (22·8°C). Annual rainfall 33" (825 mm).

CONSTITUTION AND GOVERNMENT. The Constitution of 1981 provided for a one-party state. In Jan. 1991 the government of President Buyoya, leader of the sole party, the Party of Unity and National Progress (UPRONA), proposed a new constitution which was approved by a referendum in March 1992 (with 89% of votes cast in favour) legalizing parties not based on ethnic group, region or religion, and providing for presidential elections by direct universal suffrage.

There is a *National Assembly* with 81 members elected from 16 constituencies by proportional representation. There is a 5% threshold. Government activities are overseen by a 10-member *National Security Council*, of which the President and Prime Minister are members.

At the presidential elections of 1 June 1993 the electorate was 2·36m.; turn-out was 97·18%. Melchior Ndadaye was elected against former President Buyoya and one other opponent with 64·79% of votes cast, and sworn in on 10 July 1993. Following his assassination Cyprien Ntaryamira was elected President by the National Assembly on 13 Jan. 1994 to serve out President Ndadaye's 5-year term of office. After the latter's death and possible assassination Sylvestre Ntibantungaanya (b. 1956; FRODEBU) was elected *President* by the National Assembly on 5 Sept. 1994 against 5 opponents.

At the parliamentary elections of 29 June 1993, 740 candidates stood representing 6 parties. The Front for Democracy in Burundi (FRODEBU) gained 65 seats with 71·4% of votes cast and UPRONA, 16 with 21·4%.

In March 1995 a new government was formed which in Sept. 1995 comprised:

Prime Minister: Antoine Nduwayo (UPRONA).

Minster of State, Development Planning and Reconstruction: Gerard Niyibigira. *Minister of State, Foreign Affairs and Co-operation:* Jean-Marie Ngendahayo. *Minister of State, Interior and Public Security:* Gabriel Sinarinzi. *Finance:* Salvator Toyi. *Defence:* Lieut.-Col. Firmin Sinzoyiheba. *Justice:* Melchior Ntahobama. *Reintegration and Resettlement of Displaced Persons:* Claudine Matuturu. *Agriculture and Livestock:* Pierre-Claver Nahimana. *Primary Education and Adult Literacy:* Nicéphore Ndimurukundo. *Secondary and Higher Education:* Liboire Ngendahayo. *Labour and Professional Training:* Vénérand Bakevyumusaya. *Civil Service:* Vincent Ndikumasabo. *Communal Development:* Sévérin Mfatiye. *Commerce and Industry:* Astere Nzisibira. *Energy and Mines:* Vacant. *Ports and Telecommunications:* Innocent Nimpagaritse. *Public Works and Equipment:* Bernard Barandereka. *Lands:* Ignace Bankamwabo. *Communications:* Germain Nkhshimana. *Human Rights and Women's Development:* Marcienne Mujawaha. *Health:* Charles Batungwanayo. *Culture, Youth and Sport:* Alphonse Rugambarara. *Relations with the National Assembly:* Terence Sinunguruza.

Speaker: Léonce Ngendakumana (FRODEBU).

National flag: White diagonal cross dividing triangles of red and green, in the centre a white disc bearing 3 red green-bordered 6-pointed stars.

National anthem: 'Uburundi Bwacu' ('Dear Burundi'); words by a committee, tune by M. Barengayabo.

Local Government: The 15 regions are each under a military governor, and are sub-divided into 114 districts and then into communes.

DEFENCE. The Army had a strength (1996) of 12,500 (there are also about 2,000 in paramilitary units) and include a small naval flotilla and air force flight of

6 SF 260, 3 Cessna 150 and 1 DO27 liaison aircraft, 3 Alouette III and 1 armed Gazelle helicopter. There were 100 air force personnel in 1995. The Army comprises 5 infantry and 2 light-armed battalions.

INTERNATIONAL RELATIONS

Membership. Burundi is a member of the UN and OAU and is an ACP state of the EU.

ECONOMY

Budget. The 1991 budget envisaged receipts of 36,823m. Burundi francs and expenditure at 41,670m. Burundi francs.

Currency. The unit of currency is the *Burundi franc* (BIF) of 100 *centimes.* There are coins of 1, 5 and 10 francs and notes of 10, 20, 50, 100, 500, 1,000 and 5,000 francs. 10,766m. francs were in circulation in 1990. Gold reserves were valued at US$4·3m. in 1992; foreign exchange reserves, US$169·2m. In March 1996, £1 = 395·80 Burundi francs; US$1 = 258·96 Burundi francs; DM1 = 175·46 Burundi francs.

Banking and Finance. The Bank of the Republic of Burundi is the central bank and bank of issue and there are 3 commercial banks; a state development bank, a savings bank and a property investment bank. Bank deposits totalled 10,680m. francs in 1989; savings banks deposits, 9,474 francs.

Weights and Measures. The metric system operates.

ENERGY AND NATURAL RESOURCES

Electricity. Electricity production was (1991) 99·5m. kWh.

Minerals. Gold is mined on a small scale. Deposits of nickel (280m. tonnes) and vanadium remain to be exploited. There are proven reserves of phosphates of 17·6m. tonnes.

Agriculture. The main economic activity and 85% of employment is subsistence agriculture. Beans, cassava, maize, sweet potatoes, groundnuts, peas, sorghum and bananas are grown according to the climate and the region.

The main cash crop is coffee, of which about 95% is arabica. It accounts for 90% of exports and taxes and levies on coffee constitute a major source of revenue. A coffee board (OCIBU) manages the grading and export of the crop. Production (1992) 34,000 tonnes. The main food crops (production 1992, in 1,000 tonnes) are cassava (597), yams (8), bananas (1,645), dry beans (346), maize (178), sorghum (67), groundnuts (99) and peas (37). Other cash crops are cotton (8) and tea (6).

Cattle play an important traditional role, and there were about 440,000 head in 1992. There were (1992) some 932,000 goats, 370,000 sheep and 105,000 pigs.

Forestry. Forests covered an estimated 66,000 ha in 1989. Production (1987) was 3·85m. cu. metres (3·80m. cu. metres for fuel).

Fisheries. There is a small commercial fishing industry on Lake Tanganyika.

INDUSTRY. In 1991 manufacturing contributed 10·3% of GDP. Textile and leather industries constituted 20% of production, foodstuffs 13% and agricultural industries 9%. In 1992 17,302 tonnes of sugar were produced.

FOREIGN ECONOMIC RELATIONS. With Rwanda and Zaïre, Burundi forms part of the Economic Community of the Great Lakes. Foreign debt was US$961m. in 1991.

Commerce. The total value of exports in 1992 was (in 1m. Burundi francs) 15,361; imports, 46,106. Main exports: Coffee, 10,033; manufactures, 2,009; tea, 1,899. Main imports: Producer goods, 16,933; equipment, 16,217; consumer goods, 12,937. Main export markets, 1992: Belgium, 33·7%; Germany, 27·4%; USA,

7·8%; France, 4·9%. Main import suppliers: Belgium, 14·9%; France, 11·1%; Tanzania, 8·9%; Japan, 8·1%.

Total trade between Burundi and the UK (British Department of Trade returns, in £1,000 sterling):

	1991	*1992*	*1993*	*1994*	*1995*
Imports to UK	2,341	1,526	1,968	4,251	3,670
Exports and re-exports from UK	3,817	2,581	2,267	3,288	3,339

Tourism. In 1987 there were 79,745 foreign visitors of whom 19,380 were tourists.

COMMUNICATIONS

Roads. In 1993 there were 5,162 km of roads of which 310 km were paved. In 1987 there were 12,260 passenger cars and 7,672 commercial vehicles.

Civil Aviation. The national carrier is the state-owned Air Burundi, which had 2 aircraft in 1995. In 1988, about 9,000 international and 2,000 domestic passengers were carried by Air Burundi and 43,755 passengers and 4,868 tonnes of freight passed through Bujumbura International airport. There are local airports at Kitega, Nyanza-Lac, Kiofi and Nyakagunda. International services are also provided by Air France, Air Rwanda, Air Tanzania, Cameroon Airlines, Ethiopian Airlines, Kenya Airways and Sabena.

Shipping. There are lake services from Bujumbura to Kigoma (Tanzania) and Kalémie (Zaïre). The main route for exports and imports is via Kigoma, and thence by rail to Dar es Salaam.

Telecommunications. In 1983 there were 38 post offices and in 1987 7,200 telephones. Broadcasting is provided by the state-controlled Radiodiffusion et Télévision du Burundi. In 1993 there were estimated to be 0·05m. radio and 4,500 TV (colour by SECAM) receivers.

Cinemas. In 1980 there were 7 cinemas with 2,000 seats.

Press. There was (1984) one daily newspaper *(Le Renouveau)* with a circulation of 20,000.

SOCIAL INSTITUTIONS

Justice. There is a Supreme Court, an appeal court and a court of first instance at Bujumbura and provincial courts in each provincial capital.

Religion. In 1993 there were 3·69m. Roman Catholics with an archbishop and 3 bishops. About 3% of the population are Pentecostal, 1% Anglican and 1% Moslem, while the balance follow traditional tribal beliefs.

Education. In 1986–87 there were 452,400 pupils in 1,171 primary schools with 7,256 teachers, 16,792 in 97 secondary schools with 857 teachers, 12,229 in vocational schools with 1,101 teachers, 2,237 students in 8 higher education institutes with 514 teachers. In 1995-96 there were 3,750 students and 170 academic staff at the university.

Health. In 1987 there were 32 hospitals with 3,239 beds and 209 treatment centres. In 1987 there were 272 doctors, 10 dentists, 29 pharmacists, 1,060 nursing personnel and 80 midwives.

DIPLOMATIC REPRESENTATIVES

Of Burundi in Great Britain
Ambassador: Vacant (resides in Brussels).

Of Great Britain in Burundi
Ambassador: Kaye Oliver (resides in Kampala).

Of Burundi in the USA (2233 Wisconsin Ave., NW, Washington, D.C., 20007)
Ambassador: Severin Ntahomvukiye.

Of the USA in Burundi (PO Box 1720, Ave. du Zaïre, Bujumbura)
Ambassador: Robert C. Krueger.

Of Burundi to the United Nations
Ambassador: Tharcisse Ntakibirora.

Further Reading

Daniels, M., *Burundi:* [Bibliography]. Oxford and Santa Barbara (CA), 1992
Lemarchand, R., *Rwanda and Burundi.* London, 1970
Weinstein, W., *Historical Dictionary of Burundi.* Metuchen (NJ), 1976

National statistical office: Service des Etudes et Statistiques, Ministère du Plan, Bujumbura.

CAMBODIA

Roat Kampuchea

(State of Cambodia)

Capital: Phnom Penh
Population: 9·29m. (1993)
GNP per capita: US$200 (1991)

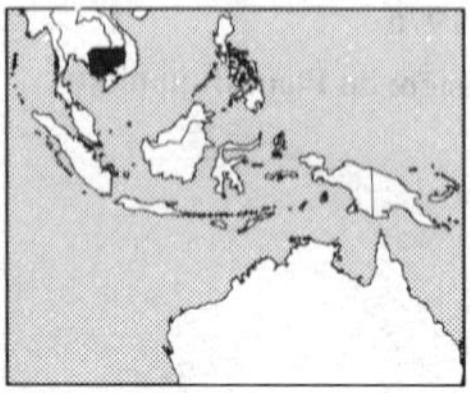

KEY HISTORICAL EVENTS. For history to 1969 *see* THE STATESMAN'S YEAR-BOOK, 1992–93, p. 263; to 1991, *see* THE STATESMAN'S YEAR-BOOK, 1994–95, p. 257. On 23 Oct. 1991 the warring factions and 19 countries signed an agreement in Paris instituting a ceasefire in Cambodia to be monitored by UN troops. On 31 Oct. the UN Security Council unanimously agreed to establish a UN Transitional Authority in Cambodia (UNTAC), and on 28 Feb. 1992 the Security Council voted to send a force of 22,000 soldiers, police and officials to disarm the factions and organize elections.

Following the election of a constituent assembly in May 1993, a new constitution was promulgated on 23 Sept. 1993 restoring parliamentary monarchy.

During 1993–94 the Khmer Rouge continued hostilities against the government in disregard of the 1991 Paris Agreement, refusing to take part in the 1993 elections. They were formally banned by the National Assembly in June 1994.

TERRITORY AND POPULATION. Cambodia is bounded in the north by Laos and Thailand, west by Thailand, east by Vietnam and south by the Gulf of Thailand. It has an area of about 181,035 sq. km (69,898 sq. miles).

Population, 5,756,141 (census, 1981) of whom 93% were Khmer, 4% Vietnamese and 3% Chinese. Estimate, based on the UN's electoral roll (1993), 9,287,000 (12% urban), including 0·6m. Vietnamese and 0·1m. Thais. Life expectancy in 1993 was 50 years; growth rate, 1993, 2·37% per annum; birth rate, 48 per 1,000 population; death, 16.

The capital, Phnom Penh, had an estimated population of 0·92m. in 1994. Other cities are Kompong Cham and Battambang. Khmer is the official language.

CLIMATE. A tropical climate, with high temperatures all the year. Phnom Penh. Jan. 78°F (25·6°C), July 84°F (28·9°C). Annual rainfall 52" (1,308 mm).

MONARCHY. A parliamentary monarchy was re-established by the 1993 constitution. Prince **Norodom Sihanouk** (b. 31 Oct. 1922) regained the throne (which had been abolished in 1955) as King on 23 Sept. 1993. He had previously reigned from 1941 to 1955. The protocol of succession is to be determined by a Throne Council consisting of the Speaker and 2 Deputy Speakers, the First and Second Prime Ministers and 2 Buddhist patriarchs. In Jan. 1996 King Sihanouk's wife, Queen Monineath, was dubbed 'First Lady'.

CONSTITUTION AND GOVERNMENT. Elections for a 120-member constituent assembly were held under UN auspices in May 1993. The electorate was 4·7m. 20 parties presented candidates (the Khmer Rouge did not take part). Turn-out was 90%. The royalist FUNCINPEC gained 58 seats with 45·47% of votes cast, the Cambodian People's Party (CPP) 51 with 38·22%, the Buddhist Democratic Liberal Party (BDLP) 10 and Molinaka 1.

On 14 June 1993 the constituent assembly elected Prince Sihanouk head of state, and on 21 Sept. adopted a constitution (promulgated on 23 Sept) by 113 votes to 5 with 2 abstentions making him monarch of a parliamentary democracy. The constitution converted the constituent assembly into a legislature sitting for a 5-year term.

An 18-member government was formed in Oct. 1993 which comprised in Oct. 1995:

First Prime Minister: Prince Ranariddh (b. 1944, son of King Sihanouk; FUNCINPEC).

Second Prime Minister: Hun Sen (CPP).

Vice-Prime Ministers: Ing Huot (*Foreign Affairs and International Co-operation*), Sar Kheng (*Interior*), Ing Kiet (*Public Works and Transport*).

State Minister, Finance and Economy, Rehabilitation and Development: Keat Chhon. *State Minister, Inspection:* Ung Phan. *State Minister, Cultural Affairs and Urbanization:* Van Molivan. *State Minister, Justice:* Chem Snguon. *State Minister, Finance and Economy:* Sam Rangsi. *Ministers in the Office of the Council of Ministers:* Sok An; Veng Sereivut. *Agriculture, Forestry, Wildlife and Fisheries:* Tau Senghuo. *Interior:* Yu Hokkri. *Education, Youth Affairs and Sport:* Tol Loah. *Tourism:* Veng Sereivut. *Defence:* Tie Banh. *Industry, Minerals and Energy:* Ith Prang. *Planning:* Chea Chanto. *Health:* Chhea Thang. *Culture:* Nut Narang. *Rural Development:* Hong Sun-huot. *Commerce:* Cham Prasit. *Environmental Management:* Mok Maret.

The *Speaker* is Chea Sim (CPP).

National flag: Divided red over blue with a depiction of the temple of Angkor Vat in yellow over all in the centre.

National anthem: 'Jham kraham cral' ('Bright red blood was spilt'); words and tune anonymous.

Local Government. There are 22 provinces administered by governors.

DEFENCE. The King is C.-in-C. of the armed forces.

Army. Conscription is for 5 years. Strength (1996) 36,000 including 7 infantry divisions, 3 independent infantry brigades and 9 independent infantry and 3 armoured regiments. Equipment includes 250 T-54/-55/-59 main battle tanks. There are also provincial (50,000) forces, and paramilitary local forces.

Navy. The navy is believed to include 2 ex-Soviet hydrofoil patrol craft, 10 inshore patrol craft and a miscellany of riverine and support craft. Naval personnel in 1995 totalled about 1,500.

Air Force. Aviation operations were resumed in 1988 under the aegis of the Army, equipment includes a squadron of 15 MiG-21 fighters, 15 Mil Mi-8/17 transport helicopters and Mi-24 gunships, and 2 Ecureuil helicopters. At least 4 An-24 and 2 Yak-40 transports are in use as well as 6 L-39 trainers. Personnel (1995), 500.

INTERNATIONAL RELATIONS

Membership. Cambodia is a member of the UN and an observer at ASEAN.

ECONOMY

Policy. Reforms of 1989 permit a much greater role for the private sector.

Currency. The unit of currency is the *riel* (KHR) of 100 *sen*. There are banknotes of 5, 50, 100, 200, 500 and 1,000 riels. In March 1996, £1 = 3,515·32 riels; US$1 = 2,300 riels; DM1 = 1,558·37 riels.

Banking and Finance. In 1964 all bank functions were taken over by the National Bank of Cambodia, which is the bank of issue.

ENERGY AND NATURAL RESOURCES

Electricity. Production (1986) 142m. kWh.

Minerals. There are phosphates and high-grade iron-ore deposits. Some small-scale gold panning and gem (mainly zircon) mining is carried out.

Agriculture. The majority of the population is engaged in agriculture, fishing or forestry. Some 8m. ha of the total land area are cultivable. In 1980, 1·5m. ha were cultivated. Before the spread of war the high productivity provided for a low, but well-fed standard of living for the peasant farmers, the majority of whom owned the land they worked before agriculture was collectivized. A relatively small proportion of the food production entered the cash economy. The war and unwise pricing policies led to a disastrous reduction in production to a stage in which the country became a net importer of rice. Private ownership of land was restored by the 1989 Constitution.

A crop of 2·25m. tonnes of rice was produced in 1992. Rubber production in 1992 amounted to 35,000 tonnes. Production of other crops, 1992 (in tonnes): Maize, 50,000; dry beans, 47,000; soya beans, 18,000.

Livestock (1992): Cattle, 2·27m.; buffaloes, 794,000; pigs, 1·73m.; horses, 19,000; poultry, 8m.

Forestry. Some 8m. ha of the land area are covered by forests, 3·8m. ha of which are reserved by the Government to be awarded to concessionaires, and are not at present worked to any extent. The remainder is available for exploitation by the local residents, and as a result some areas are over-exploited and conservation is not practised. There are substantial reserves of pitch pine.

Fisheries. There are large freshwater fish resources.

INDUSTRY. Some development of industry had taken place before the spread of open warfare in 1970, but little was in operation by the 1990s except rubber processing, sea-food processing, jute sack making and cigarette manufacture. In the private sector small family concerns produce a wide range of goods. Apart from rice-mills, about 70 factories were functioning in 1994.

FOREIGN ECONOMIC RELATIONS. Foreign investment has been encouraged since 1989. Legislation of 1994 exempts profits from taxation for 8 years, removes duties from various raw and semi-finished materials and offers tax incentives to investors in tourism, energy, the infrastructure and labour-intensive industries.

Commerce. Total trade between Cambodia and UK (British Department of Trade returns, in £1,000 sterling):

	1991	*1992*	*1993*	*1994*	*1995*
Imports to UK	29	4	711	1,672	7,531
Exports and re-exports from UK	409	1,238	3,113	2,327	2,989

COMMUNICATIONS

Roads. There were, in 1981, 2,670 km of asphalt roads, and 10,680 km of unsurfaced roads.

Railways. Main lines link Phnom Penh with Sisophon near the Thai border and the port of Kompong Som (total 603 km, metre-gauge). After a long period of disruption due to political unrest, limited services were restored on both lines in 1992, when 1·2m. passengers and 0·1m. tonnes of freight were carried.

Civil Aviation. Pochentong airport is 10 km from Phnom Penh. Royal Air Cambodia was reconstituted in Jan. 1995 with 60% of the equity government-owned. It had 1 B-737-400 in 1995. There are regular domestic services, and services to Bangkok, Ho Chi Minh-ville, Hong Kong, Kuala Lumpur and Singapore. There are also services by Aeroflot, Air Lao and Air Vietnam.

Shipping. There is an ocean port at Kompong Som; the port of Phnom Penh can be reached by the Mekong (through Vietnam) by ships of between 3,000 and 4,000 tonnes.

Telecommunications. There are telephone exchanges in all the main towns; number of telephones in 1981, 7,315. Broadcasting is provided by the state-owned Voice of the People of Cambodia and Cambodian Television (colour by PAL). In 1993 there were an estimated 70,000 TV and 0·8m. radio sets.

Press. In 1984 there were 16 daily newspapers. There is 1 daily in English.

SOCIAL INSTITUTIONS

Religion. The Constitution of 1989 reinstated Buddhism as the state religion; it had 8·2m. adherents in 1994. About 2,800 monasteries were active in 1994. There are small Roman Catholic and Moslem minorities.

Education. In 1984 there were 1,504,840 pupils in primary schools, 147,730 in secondary schools and 7,334 in vocational establishments. There is a university (with 8,400 students and 350 academic staff in 1995-96) and a fine arts university.

Health. In 1984 there were 200 doctors, 130 pharmacists and 146 hospitals and clinics with 16,200 beds.

DIPLOMATIC REPRESENTATIVES

Of Great Britain in Cambodia (29, St. 75, Phnom Penh)
Ambassador: P. Reddicliffe.

Of Cambodia in the USA
Ambassador: Var Huoth.

Of the USA in Cambodia (27, EO St. 240, Phnom Penh)
Chargé d'affaires: Charles Twining.

Of Cambodia to the United Nations
Ambassador: Sisowath Sirirath.

Further Reading

Ablin, D. A. and Hood, M., (eds.) *The Cambodian Agony*. London and New York, 1987
Chandler, D. P., *The Tragedy of Cambodian History: Power, War and Revolution since 1945.* Yale Univ. Press, 1992
Martin, M. A, *Cambodia: a Shattered Society*. California Univ. Press, 1994
Peschoux, C., *Le Cambodge dans la Tourmente: le Troisième Conflit Indochinois, 1978–1991.* Paris, 1992.—*Les 'Nouveaux' Khmers Rouges.* Paris, 1992

CAMEROON

République du Cameroun—
Republic of Cameroon

Capital: Yaoundé
Population: 12·2m. (1992)
GNP per capita: US$680 (1994)
HDI/world rank: 0·503/127 (1992)

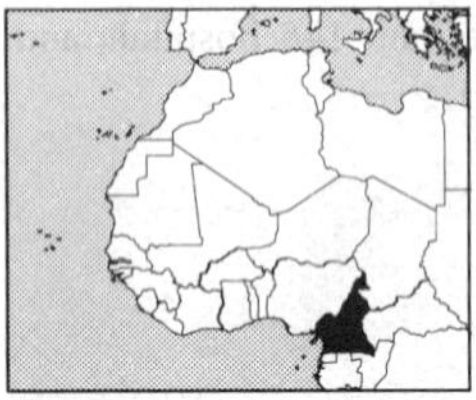

KEY HISTORICAL EVENTS. The former German colony of Kamerun was occupied by French and British troops in 1916. The greater portion of the territory (422,673 sq. km) was in 1919 placed under French administration, excluding the territory ceded to Germany in 1911, which reverted to French Equatorial Africa. The portion under French trusteeship was granted full internal autonomy on 1 Jan. 1959 and complete independence was proclaimed on 1 Jan. 1960.

The portion assigned to British trusteeship consisted of 2 parts where separate plebiscites were held in Feb. 1961. The northern part decided in favour of joining Nigeria, while the southern part decided to join the Cameroon Republic. This was implemented on 1 Oct. 1961 with the formation of a Federal Republic of Cameroon. As a result of a national referendum, Cameroon became a unitary republic on 2 June 1972. In Jan. 1984 the country was renamed the Republic of Cameroon.

TERRITORY AND POPULATION. Cameroon is bounded in the west by the Gulf of Guinea, north-west by Nigeria, east by Chad and the Central African Republic, and south by Congo, Gabon and Equatorial Guinea. The total area is 475,442 sq. km. On 29 March 1994 Cameroon asked the International Court of Justice to confirm its sovereignty over the Bakassi Peninsula, occupied by Nigerian troops. Population (1987 census) 10,494,000. Estimate (1992) 12,198,000 (6,089,000 females; 38% urban); density, 25·7 per sq. km. Population growth rate (1991): 3·4%; infant mortality, 86 per 1,000 live births; expectation of life: Males, 53·5 years; females, 56·5.

The areas, populations and chief towns of the 10 provinces were:

Province	*Sq. km*	*Census 1987*	*Chief town*	*Estimate 1981*
Adamaoua	63,691	495,185	Ngaoundéré	47,508
Centre	68,926	1,651,600	Yaoundé	649,000 [1]
Est	109,011	517,198	Bertoua	18,254
Extrême-Nord	34,246	1,855,695	Maroua	124,000 [1]
Littoral	20,239	1,354,833	Douala	810,000 [1]
Nord (Bénoué)	65,576	832,165	Garoua	142,000 [1]
Nord-Ouest	17,810	1,237,348	Bamenda	110,000 [1]
Ouest	13,872	1,339,791	Bafoussam	113,000 [1]
Sud	47,110	373,798	Ebolowa	22,222
Sud-Ouest	24,471	838,042	Buéa	29,953

[1] 1991

Other large towns (1981): Nkongsamba (86,870), Kumba (53,823), Foumban (41,358), Limbe (32,917), Edéa (31,016), Mbalmayo (26,934) and Dschang (21,705).

The population is composed of Sudanic-speaking people in the north (Fulani, Sao and others) and Bantu-speaking groups, mainly Bamileke, Beti, Bulu, Tikar, Bassa, Douala, in the rest of the country. The official languages are French and English.

CLIMATE. An equatorial climate, with high temperatures and plentiful rain, especially from March to June and Sept. to Nov. Further inland, rain occurs at all seasons. Yaoundé. Jan. 76°F (24·4°C), July 73°F (22·8°C). Annual rainfall 62" (1,555 mm). Douala. Jan. 79°F (26·1°C), July 75°F (23·9°C). Annual rainfall 160" (4,026 mm).

CONSTITUTION AND GOVERNMENT. The 1972 Constitution, subsequently amended, provides for a *President* as head of state and government. The President is directly elected for a 5-year term, and there is a Council of Ministers whose members must not be members of parliament.

Presidential elections were held on 11 Oct. 1992. The electorate was 4,195,687; turn-out was 71·87%. Paul Biya was elected against 4 opponents by 39·9% of votes cast.

The *National Assembly*, elected by universal adult suffrage for 5 years, consists of 180 representatives. After 1966 the sole legal party was the Cameroon People's Democratic Movement (RDPC), but in Dec. 1990 the National Assembly legalized opposition parties. At the elections of March 1992 751 candidates from 32 parties stood. Turn-out was 60·58%. The RDPC won 89 seats, the National Union for Democracy and Progress 65, the Cameroon People's Union 20, and the Democratic Movement for the Defence of the Republic 6.

The Council of Ministers in Oct. 1995 comprised:

President: Paul Biya (assumed office 6 Nov. 1982, elected 14 Jan. 1984, re-elected 24 April 1988, re-elected 10 Oct. 1992 and sworn in 3 Nov. 1992).

Prime Minister: Simon Achidi Achu.

Deputy Prime Minister and Minister of Housing and Town Planning: Hamadou Mustapha. *Deputy Prime Minister and Minister of Territorial Administration:* Gilbert André Tsoungui. *External Relations:* Ferdinand Oyono. *Defence:* Eduard Akame Mfoumou. *Justice, Keeper of the Seals:* Douala Moutome. *Posts and Telecommunications:* Dakole Daissala [1]. *Livestock, Fisheries and Animal Industries:* Titus Edzoa. *Higher Education:* Peter Agbortabi. *Health:* Joseph Owona. *Labour and Social Welfare:* Simon Mbila. *Industrial and Commercial Development:* Pierre Eloundou Mani. *Economy and Finance:* Justin Naioro. *Social and Women's Affairs:* Aissatou Yaou. *Public Service and State Controls:* Adjoudi Hamadjoda. *Plan and Regional Development:* Augustin Kodock [1]. *Communications:* Augustin Kontchou Kouomengi [1]. *Public Works:* Jean Baptiste Bokam. *Research:* Joseph Mbede. *Tourism:* Pierre Souman. *Environment and Forestry:* Dr Bava Djingoer. *Youth and Sport:* Joseph Woum. *Education:* Dr Robert Mbella Mbappe. *Mining, Water and Energy:* André Bello Mbelle. *Transport:* Issa Bakary Tchiroma. *Culture:* Toko Mangan.

[1] Minister of State.

National flag: 3 vertical strips of green, red, yellow, with a gold star in the centre.

National anthem: 'O Cameroon, Thou Cradle of our Fathers/O Cameroun, Berceau de nos Ancêtres'; music by S. M. Bamba, tune by M. Nkoro.

Local Government: The 10 provinces are each administered by a governor appointed by the President. They are sub-divided into 49 departments (each under a prefect) and then into 336 communes (each under an under-prefect). Elections for councillors were held on 21 Jan. 1996. The electorate was 4·5m. 38 parties presented candidates. The RDPC gained a majority overall.

DEFENCE. The President of the Republic is C.-in-C. of the armed forces.

Army. There are 8 military regions. The Army consists of a Presidential Guard, 5 infantry battalions, 1 para-commando, 1 engineer, 1 artillery and 1 anti-aircraft battalion. Total strength (1996) 13,000; there is a Gendarmerie 9,000 strong.

Navy. The Navy, all French-built, operates 1 missile craft and 1 inshore patrol vessel. There are 2 landing craft and about 30 boats and service craft. Personnel in 1995 numbered 1,300. The marine wing of the Gendarmerie operates 10 inshore patrol craft.

Air Force. The Air Force has 2 Hercules turboprop transports, 4 Buffalo short-take-off-and-landing transports, 1 Puma and 1 Super Puma transport helicopters, 5 Magister armed jet basic trainers, 4 Alpha Jet close support/trainers, and 5 Alouette and 2 Bell 206 helicopters. Some of 4 Gazelle light helicopters are armed with anti-tank missiles. A small VIP transport fleet, maintained in civil markings, comprises 1 Boeing 727 jet aircraft, 1 Gulfstream III and 4 Aerospatiale helicopters. Radar-equipped Dornier 128-6 twin-turboprop aircraft serve for offshore patrol. Aircraft availability is low because of funding problems. Personnel (1995), 300.

INTERNATIONAL RELATIONS

Membership. Cameroon is a member of the UN, the Commonwealth and the OAU and is an ACP state of the EU.

ECONOMY

Budget. The financial year ends on 30 June. Budget for 1993–94 (in 1,000m. francs CFA): Revenue, 546 (of which fiscal revenue, 389, including direct taxes, 185; customs dues, 176·5; and non-fiscal revenue, 111·5, including oil royalties, 90). Expenditure, 546 (of which current expenditure, 409·5, and capital expenditure, 136·5, including debt servicing, 85).

Currency. The unit of currency is the *franc CFA* (XAF), with a parity rate of 100 *francs CFA* to 1 French *franc*. Gold reserves were 30,000 troy oz. in 1992; foreign exchange reserves were US$20·4m. 155,560m. francs CFA were in circulation in 1992. In March 1996, £1 = 772·97; US$1 = 505·74; DM1 = 342·67 francs CFA.

Banking and Finance. The Banque des Etats de l'Afrique Centrale is the sole bank of issue. There are 10, including 3 foreign, commercial banks.

Weights and Measures. The metric system is in use.

ENERGY AND NATURAL RESOURCES

Electricity. Installed capacity, 1988, 754 MW. Total production (1991) 2,652m. kWh (95% hydro-electric).

Oil. Production (estimate, 1992) mainly from Kole oilfield was 7·46m. tonnes.

Minerals. Tin ore and limestone are extracted. There are deposits of bauxite, uranium, nickel, gold, cassiterite and kyanite.

Agriculture. In 1991 there were 5·95m. ha of arable land, 1·07m. ha of permanent crops and 8·3m. ha of permanent pasture. 30,000 ha were irrigated in 1991. The main food crops (with 1992 production in 1,000 tonnes): Cassava, 1,230; sorghum, 380; millet, 55; maize, 380; plantains, 860; yams, 80; groundnuts, 100; bananas, 520. Cash crops include: Palm oil, 107; palm kernels, 53; cocoa, 94; coffee, 85; rubber, 48; cotton lint, 48. Banana cultivation is being redeveloped.

Livestock (1991): 4·7m. cattle, 3·6m. sheep, 3·6m. goats, 1·4m. pigs.

Livestock products (in 1,000 tonnes), 1990: Beef, 78; pork, 16; mutton, 14; goat meat, 13; poultry meat, 14; cow's milk, 50; eggs, 12; honey, 2·7.

Forestry. Forests cover 24·65m. ha, ranging from tropical rain forests in the south (producing hardwoods such as mahogany, ebony and sapele) to semi-deciduous forests in the centre and wooded savannah in the north. Log production, 1991, 2·1m. cu. metres. 10·94m. cu. metres were used for fuel in 1990.

Fisheries. In 1991 the total catch was 91,750 tonnes, of which 20,000 tonnes were freshwater fish.

INDUSTRY. Manufacturing is largely small-scale, with some 30 firms employing more than 10 workers. Aluminium production in 1989 was 87,300 tonnes. Production of cement totalled 586,000 tonnes in 1988. There are also factories producing shoes, beer, soap, oil and food products, cigarettes. 1989 output included: Veneer, 32,000 cu. metres; plywood, 48,000 cu. metres; paper and board, 10,000 cu. metres; sugar (1992), 65,000 tonnes; palm oil, 102,000 tonnes; cigarettes, 4,300m.

Labour. In 1990 the work-force numbered 4,351,000 of whom 61% were occupied in agriculture.

Trade Unions. The principal trade union federation is the *Organisation des syndicats des travailleurs camerounais* (OSTC) established on 7 Dec. 1985 to replace the former body, the UNTC.

FOREIGN ECONOMIC RELATIONS.

Foreign debt was 1,503,400m. francs CFA in 1991.

Commerce. Imports and exports in US$1m.:

	1987	*1988*	*1989*	*1990*	*1991*
Imports	1,749	1,271	1,350	1,574	1,265
Exports	829	924	1,743	2,223	1,720

Principal exports (in 1,000m. francs CFA), 1991: Oil, 262·1; logs, 37·5; cocoa, 31·7; coffee, 31·5; aluminium, 24·1; timber products, 23·9; cotton, 17·4; bananas, 13·2.

Main export markets, 1992: France, 26·2%; Spain, 17·1%; Italy, 11·5%; Netherlands, 8·7%; Germany, 5·3%. Main import suppliers: France, 39·4%; Germany, 8·3%; Belgium, 5·3%; USA, 4·8%; Italy, 3·9%.

Total trade between Cameroon and UK (British Department of Trade returns, in £1,000 sterling):

	1991	*1992*	*1993*	*1994*	*1995*
Imports to UK	6,135	6,495	17,878	34,889	31,328
Exports and re-exports from UK	23,813	19,156	16,565	15,452	25,234

Tourism. There were an estimated 115,203 foreign visitors in 1987.

COMMUNICATIONS

Roads. In 1993 there were about 33,000 km of classified roads, of which 2,922 km were tarmac. In 1987 there were 78,272 passenger cars and 43,868 commercial vehicles.

Railways. Cameroon Railways, *Regifercam* (1,104 km in 1990) link Douala with Nkongsamba and Ngaoundéré, with branches M'Banga–Kumba and Makak–M'Balmayo. In 1992–93 railways carried 1·9m. passengers and 1·2m. tonnes of freight.

Civil Aviation. There are international airports at Douala, Garona and Yaoundé (Nsimalen). Cameroon Airlines (Camair), the national carrier, serves Dakar, Addis Ababa, destinations in Europe and 7 domestic airports. In 1992–93 it carried 388,469 passengers and 1,059 tonnes of freight. In 1995 it operated 1 B-737-200 Adv, 2 B-737-200C Advs, 1 B-747-200B Combi, and 1 BAe(HS)-748. Cameroon is also served by Aeroflot, Air Afrique, Air France, Air Gabon, Ecuato Guineana, Nigeria Airlines, Sabena and Swissair.

Shipping. In 1995 the merchant marine totalled 40,194 GRT. Ports handled (1991–92) 3·78m. tonnes of cargo. The main port is Douala; other ports are Bota, Campo, Garoua (only navigable in the rainy season), Kribi and Limbo-Tiko.

Telecommunications. There were 36,737 telephone and fax subscribers in 1991. The state-controlled Cameroon Radio Television provides home, national, provincial and urban radio programmes and a TV service (colour by PAL). In 1993 there were about 2m. radio and 15,000 TV receivers.

Cinemas. There were (1987) 69 cinemas and 163 mobile cinemas with a capacity of 41,000 seats.

Press. There was (1994) 1 national daily newspaper (daily in French, twice a week in English) with a circulation of 66,000.

SOCIAL INSTITUTIONS

Justice. The Supreme Court sits at Yaoundé, as does the High Court of Justice (consisting of 9 titular judges and 6 surrogates all appointed by the National Assembly). There are magistrates' courts situated in the provinces.

Religion. In 1992 there were 4·43m. Roman Catholics, 2·79m. Moslems and 2·23m. Protestants. Some of the population follow traditional animist religions.

Education. In 1987–88 there were 6,328 primary schools, 425 general secondary and tertiary schools, 321 technical schools, 33 teacher training colleges and 5 institutions of higher education. In 1989-90 there were 2,107,100 pupils and 39,968 teachers in primary schools, 397,200 pupils and 15,221 teachers in general secondary schools and 139,100 pupils and 7,671 teachers in technical secondary schools. In 1986–87 there were 19,600 students and 975 teaching staff at higher education institutions. In 1994-95 there were 6 universities and 1 Roman Catholic university, 4 specialized *Ecoles Nationales*, an *Ecole Supérieure* for posts and telecommunications, 6 specialized institutes, a national school of administration and magistracy and a faculty of Protestant theology. In 1995-96 there were 15,220 university students and 830 academic staff.

Health. In 1987 there were 251 hospitals and 809 health centres with 29,285 beds, 588 dispensaries, 177 pharmacies and 137 maternity clinics. In 1987 there were 888 doctors, 48 dentists, 201 pharmacists, 5,418 nurses and 6,520 auxiliary medical personnel.

DIPLOMATIC REPRESENTATIVES

Of Cameroon in Great Britain (84 Holland Pk., London, W11 3SB)
Ambassador: Samuel Libock.

Of Great Britain in Cameroon (Ave. Winston Churchill, BP 547, Yaoundé)
Ambassador: Nicholas McCarthy, OBE.

Of Cameroon in the USA (2349 Massachusetts Ave., NW, Washington, D.C., 20008)
Ambassador: Jerome Mendouga.

Of the USA in Cameroon (Rue Nachtigal, BP 817, Yaoundé)
Ambassador: Harriet W. Isom.

Of Cameroon to the United Nations
Ambassador: M. Pascal Biloa Tang.

Further Reading

DeLancey, M. W., *Cameroon: Dependence and Independence.* London, 1989
DeLancey, M. W. and Schraeder, P. J., *Cameroon.* [Bibliography] Oxford and Santa Barbara, 1986

National statistical office: Direction de la Statistique et de la Comptabilité Nationale, Ministère du Plan et de l'Aménagement du Territoire, Yaoundé

CANADA

Capital: Ottawa
Population: 28·5m. (1995)
GNP per capita: US$19,570 (1994)
HDI/world rank: 0·950/1 (1992)

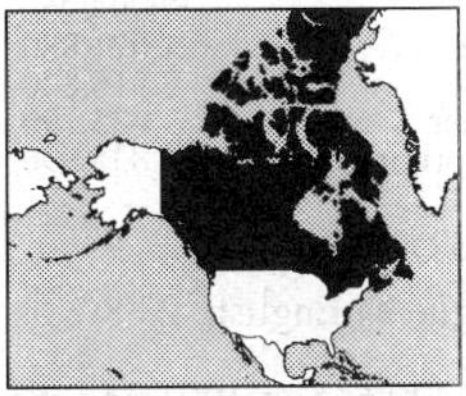

KEY HISTORICAL EVENTS. The first European discovery of Canada was made by John Cabot in 1497. France claimed possession in 1534. The territories which now constitute Canada came under British power at various times by settlement, conquest or cession. The Hudson's Bay Company's charter, conferring rights over all the territory draining into Hudson Bay, was granted in 1670; Canada, with all its dependencies, was ceded to Great Britain by France in 1763; Vancouver Island was acknowledged to be British by the Oregon Boundary Treaty of 1846, and British Columbia was established as a separate colony in 1858. As originally constituted, Canada was composed of Upper and Lower Canada (now Ontario and Quebec), Nova Scotia and New Brunswick. They were united under the British North America Act, 1867. Provision was made in the Act for the admission of British Columbia, Prince Edward Island, Newfoundland, Rupert's Land and the Northwest Territory into the Union. In 1870, Rupert's Land and the Northwest Territory were annexed and named the Northwest Territories, Canada compensating the Hudson's Bay Company in cash and land. By the same action the Province of Manitoba was created from a small portion of this territory and they were admitted into the Confederation in 1870. In 1871 British Columbia was admitted, and Prince Edward Island in 1873. Alberta and Saskatchewan, originally parts of the Northwest Territories, were admitted in 1905. Newfoundland joined in 1949.

In 1931 Norway recognized the Canadian title to the Sverdrup group of Arctic islands.

The Statute of Westminster, 1931, removed what legal limitations existed as regards Canada's legislative autonomy.

TERRITORY AND POPULATION. Canada is bounded in the north-west by the Beaufort Sea, north by the Arctic Ocean, north-east by Baffin Bay, east by the Davis Strait, Labrador Sea and Atlantic Ocean, south by the USA and west by the Pacific Ocean and USA (Alaska). The area is 9,970,610 sq. km, of which 755,180 sq. km are fresh water. Census population, 1991, 27,296,859[1] (13,842,300 females, 20,907,135 urban).

1851	2,436,297	1901	5,371,315	1951	14,009,429
1861	3,229,633	1911	7,206,643	1961	18,238,247
1871	3,689,257	1921	8,787,949	1971	21,568,311
1881	4,324,810	1931	10,376,786	1981	24,343,181
1891	4,833,239	1941	11,506,655	1991	27,296,859

[1] Excludes data from incompletely enumerated Indian reserves and Indian settlements.

Of the total population in 1991, 22,343,315 were Canadian born and 4,335,185 foreign born (249,075 of the latter being USA born and 2,364,700 European born).

The population (1991) born outside Canada in the provinces was in the following ratio (%): Newfoundland, 0·19; Prince Edward Island, 0·09; Nova Scotia, 0·89; New Brunswick, 0·55; Quebec, 13·6; Ontario, 54·6; Manitoba, 3·1; Saskatchewan, 1·3; Alberta, 8·8; British Columbia, 16·7; Yukon, 0·07; Northwest Territories, 0·06.

In 1991, figures for the population, according to ethnic origin, were [1]:

Single origins	19,199,790	Belgian	31,475
Austrian	27,130	British	5,611,050

[1] Data on ethnic origins for the 1991 Census excludes the population on incompletely enumerated Indian reserves and settlements. For Canada there were 78 such reserves and settlements and the total population was estimated to be about 38,000 in 1991.

Czech and Slovak	59,125	Russian	38,220
Chinese	586,645	Scandinavian	174,370
Dutch (Netherlands)	358,180	Spanish	82,675
Finnish	39,230	Swiss	23,610
French [2]	6,146,600	Ukrainian	406,645
German	911,560	Other single origins	3,104,400
Greek	151,150		
Hungarian	100,725	*Multiple origins*	7,794,250
Italian	750,055	British and French	1,071,880
Japanese	48,595	British and Other	2,516,840
Polish	272,810	French and Other	425,190
Portuguese	246,890	Other multiple origins	835,990
Romanian	28,650		

[2] Includes the single origins of French, Acadian and Québécois.

In 1991, 60·5% of the population gave their mother tongue as English, 23·8% as French.

The total aboriginal population single origins numbered 470,615 in 1991 and the Inuit population was 30,085 in 1991.

Populations of Census Metropolitan Areas (CMA) and Cities (proper), 1991 census:

	CMA	*City proper*		*CMA*	*City proper*
Toronto	3,893,046	635,395	Victoria	287,897	71,228
Montreal	3,127,242	1,017,666	Windsor	262,075	191,435
Vancouver	1,602,502	471,844	Oshawa	240,104	129,344
Ottawa-Hull	920,857	—	Saskatoon	210,023	186,058
Ottawa	—	313,987	Regina	191,692	179,178
Hull	—	60,707	St John's	171,859	95,770
Edmonton	839,924	616,741	Sudbury	157,613	92,884
Calgary	754,033	710,677	Chicoutimi-		
Winnipeg	652,354	616,790	Jonquière	160,928	—
Quebec	645,550	167,517	Chicoutimi	—	62,710
Hamilton	599,760	318,499	Jonquière	—	57,933
London	381,522	303,165	Sudbury	157,613	92,884
St Catharines-			Sherbrooke	139,194	76,429
Niagara	364,552	—	Trois Rivières	136,303	49,426
St Catharines	—	129,300	Thunder Bay	124,427	113,946
Niagara Falls	—	75,399	London	381,522	303,165
Kitchener	356,421	168,282	Kitchener	356,421	168,282
Halifax	320,501	114,455	Saint John	124,981	74,969

Population estimate, 1995, 28,537,000 (14,491,000 females; 22,298,000 urban); density, 3·1 per sq. km.

Vital statistics:

	Live births	*Deaths*	*Marriages*
1991	402,528	195,568	172,251
1992	398,642	196,545	164,573
1993	397,110	201,020	161,610

Growth rate, 1991-95, 1·12%.

In 1993 there were 251,800 immigrants, comprising (in 1,000) from Asia: 135·4 (including Hong Kong, 35·8); Europe, 48·1; America (including USA, 6·5); Africa, 19·5; elsewhere, 3·6.

CLIMATE. The climate ranges from polar conditions in the north to cool temperate in the south, but with considerable differences between east coast, west coast and the interior, affecting temperatures, rainfall amounts and seasonal distribution. Winters are very severe over much of the country, but summers can be very hot inland. *See* individual provinces for climatic details.

CONSTITUTION AND GOVERNMENT. In Nov. 1981 the Canadian government agreed on the provisions of an amended constitution, to the end that it should replace the British North America Act and that its future amendment should be the prerogative of Canada. These proposals were adopted by the Parliament of Canada and were enacted by the UK Parliament as the Canada Act of 1982. This was the final act of the UK Parliament in Canadian constitutional development. The

Act gave to Canada the power to amend the Constitution according to procedures determined by the Constitutional Act 1982. The latter added to the Canadian Constitution a charter of Rights and Freedoms, and provisions which recognize the nation's multi-cultural heritage, affirm the existing rights of native peoples, confirm the principle of equalization of benefits among the provinces, and strengthen provincial ownership of natural resources.

Parliament consists of the Senate and the House of Commons. The members of the *Senate* are appointed until age 75 by summons of the Governor-General under the Great Seal of Canada. Members appointed before 2 June 1965 may remain in office for life. The Senate consists of 104 senators, namely, 24 from Ontario, 24 from Quebec, 10 from Nova Scotia, 10 from New Brunswick, 4 from Prince Edward Island, 6 from Manitoba, 6 from British Columbia, 6 from Alberta, 6 from Saskatchewan, 6 from Newfoundland, 1 from the Yukon Territory and 1 from the Northwest Territories. Each senator must be at least 30 years of age and reside in the province for which he or she is appointed. The *House of Commons* is elected by universal secret suffrage, by a first-past-the-post system, for 5-year terms. Representation is based on the population of all the provinces taken as a whole with readjustments made after each census.

The Special Joint Committee of the Senate and the House of Commons on a Renewed Canada released a unanimous report on 28 Feb. 1992 (Beaudoin-Dobbie Report). Another constitutional document was released on 16 July 1992 by the provincial premiers which summarized the multilateral meetings on the Constitution. A final constitutional accord was arrived at by the provinces and the federal government in Aug. 1992. At a national referendum on 26 Oct. 1992 proposed constitutional reforms were rejected by 54·4% of votes cast.

Indians have representation in the *Assembly of First Nations* (Chief, Ovide Mercredi).

The thirty-fifth Parliament, elected on 25 Oct. 1993, comprises 295 members and the provincial and territorial representation are: Ontario, 99; Quebec, 75; Nova Scotia, 11; New Brunswick, 10; Manitoba, 14; British Columbia, 32; Prince Edward Island, 4; Saskatchewan 14; Alberta, 26; Newfoundland, 7; Yukon, 1; Northwest Territories, 2.

State of the parties in the Senate (1995): Progressive Conservatives, 51; Liberals, 42; Bloc Québécois, 8; Reform Party, 1; Independent Conservatives, 1; Vacant, 1.

At the elections of 25 Oct. 1993 turn-out was 80%. The Liberal Party gained 177 seats (82 in 1988) with 41·6% of votes cast, the Bloc Québécois 54 (nil) with 14%, the Reform Party 52 (nil) with 18%, the New Democratic Party 9 (43) with 6·6%, the Progressive Conservative Party 2 (170) with 16%, ind 1. By 1995 the Liberals had 178 seats and the New Democratic Party, 8.

The office and appointment of the Governor-General are regulated by letters patent of 1947. In 1977 the Queen approved the transfer to the Governor-General of functions discharged by the Sovereign. The Governor-General is assisted by a *Privy Council* composed of Cabinet Ministers.

Governor-General: Roméo Leblanc (b. 1928; term of office, 1994–99).

The following is the list of the Liberal Cabinet in Jan. 1996, in order of precedence based on date of nomination:

Prime Minister: The Rt. Hon. Jean Chrétien.

Solicitor General of Canada and Leader of the Government in the House of Commons: The Hon. Herbert Eser Gray. *Minister of Foreign Affairs:* The Hon. Lloyd Axworthy. *National Defence and Veterans Affairs:* The Hon. David Michael Collenette. *Transport:* The Hon. David Anderson. *Agriculture and Agri-Food:* The Hon. Ralph E. Goodale. *Health:* The Hon. David Charles Dingwall. *Indian Affairs and Northern Development:* The Hon. Ron Irwin. *Leader of the Government in the Senate and Minister with special responsibility for Literacy:* The Hon. Joyce Fairbairn. *Deputy Prime Minister and Minister of Canadian Heritage:* The Hon. Shella Copps. *Environment:* The Hon. Sergio Marchi. *Industry, Atlantic Canada Opportunities Agency, Western Economic Diversification and Minister responsible for the Federal Office of Regional Development – Quebec:* The Hon. John Manley.

Public Works and Government Services: The Hon. Diane Marleau. *Finance:* The Hon. Paul Martin. *Human Resources Development:* The Hon. Douglas Young. *International Trade:* The Hon. Arthur C. Eggleton. *President of the Treasury Board and Minister responsible for Infrastructure:* The Hon. Marcel Massé. *Natural Resources:* The Hon. Anne McLellan. *Minister of Justice and Attorney General of Canada:* The Hon. Allan Rock. *Labour and Deputy Leader of the Government in the House of Commons:* The Hon. Alfonso Gagliano. *Citizenship and Immigration:* The Hon. Lucienne Robillard. *Fisheries and Oceans:* The Hon. Fred Mifflin. *National Revenue:* The Hon. Jane Stewart. *President of the Queen's Privy Council for Canada and Minister for Inter-Governmental Affairs:* The Hon. Stéphane Dion. *International Co-operation and Minister responsible for Francophonie:* The Hon. Pierre S. Pettigrew.

National flag: Vertically red, white, red with the white of double width and bearing a stylized red maple leaf.

National anthem: 'O Canada, our home and native land'/'O Canada, terre de nos aïeux'; words by A. Routhier, tune by C. Lavallée.

Canadian Parliamentary Guide. Annual. Ottawa
Federalism and the Charter: Leading Constitutional Decisions. Edited and with an introduction by Peter H. Russell, 5th ed. Carleton Univ. Press, Ottawa, 1989
Laskin's Canadian Constitutional Law. 5th ed., Vol. 2, Neil Finkelstein. Toronto: Carswell, 1986
Bayefsky, A. F., *Canada's Constitution Act 1982 and Amendments: A Documentary History.* 2 vols. Toronto, 1989
Bejermi, J., *Canadian Parliamentary Handbook.* Ottawa, 1993
Cairns, A. C., *Charter versus Federalism: the Dilemmas of Constitutional Reform.* Montreal, 1992
Canada: The State of the Federation. Queen's Univ., annual
Cheffins, R. I. and Johnson, P. A., *The Revised Canadian Constitution: Politics as law.* Toronto, 1986
Forsey, E. A., *How Canadians Govern Themselves.* Ottawa, 1991
Fox, P. W. and White, G., *Politics Canada.* 7th ed. Toronto, 1991
Franks, C. E. S., *The Parliament of Canada.* Univ. of Toronto Press, 1987
Hogg, P. W., *Constitutional Law of Canada.* 3rd ed. Toronto, 1992
Kaplan, W. (ed.) *Belonging: the Meaning and Future of Canadian Citizenship.* McGill-Queen's Univ. Press, 1993
Kernaghan, K., *Public Administration in Canada: a Text.* Scarborough, 1991
Osbaldston, G. F., *Organizing to Govern.* Toronto, 1992
Reesor, B., *The Canadian Constitution in Historical Perspective.* Scarborough, 1992
Tardi, G., *The Legal Framework of Government: a Canadian Guide.* Aurora, 1992
White, W. L., *Introduction to Canadian Politics and Government.* 5th ed. Toronto, 1990

Source: Library of Parliament

DEFENCE. The armed forces are unified and organized in functional commands: Mobile Command (land forces), Air Command (air forces) and Maritime Command (naval and naval air forces). There is a Tactical Air Group under the control of Mobile Command. In 1995 the armed forces numbered 70,500 (8,700 women); reserves, 56,650.

Army. The Land Forces numbered 20,300 in 1996 and were organized in 1 Task Force Headquarters, 3 mechanized infantry brigade groups (each with 1 armoured regiment, 2 infantry battalions, 1 mechanized infantry battalion, 1 artillery regiment, 1 engineer regiment and 1 air defence battery), 1 independent air defence regiment and 1 independent engineer support regiment. Reserves comprise a Militia of 28,400 and the Canadian Rangers, 3,100. Equipment includes 114 Leopard C-1 main battle tanks and 130 surface-to-air missiles.

Navy. The naval combatant force, which, organizationally, forms part of the Maritime Command of the unified armed forces, is headquartered at Halifax (Nova Scotia), and comprises 3 diesel submarines, 4 guided-missile destroyers, 9 helicopter-carrying frigates and 3 other frigates. 2 offshore support vessels have been converted to offshore patrol craft, and there is a force of 11 coastal patrol craft all used for training, together with the first of a new class of maritime coastal defence vessel. Major auxiliaries include 3 helicopter-carrying replenishment tankers, 2 survey/research ships, 2 tugs and a diver support ship, and there are some 40 minor auxiliaries, tenders and service craft. The Maritime Air Group includes 28 Sea King for embarked service.

Naval personnel in 1995 numbered about 10,000, with 6,500 reserves. The main bases are Halifax, where about two-thirds of the fleet is based and Esquimault (British Columbia).

The Coast Guard, a branch of the Department of Fisheries, numbers 5,200, and operates 18 icebreakers, numerous search-and-rescue and support craft, together with 2 fixed-wing aircraft, 37 helicopters and 5 hovercraft.

Air Force. The air forces numbered 17,100 in 1995 (5,000 women) with 190 combat aircraft and 150 helicopters. They are organized in the Air Combat and Mobility Group, the Maritime Air Group and Air Command HQ. The first controls air defence, tactical transport and helicopter units; the second oversees patrol, search-and-rescue and electronic countermeasures units; the third is responsible for training and logistics transports.

INTERNATIONAL RELATIONS

Membership. Canada is a member of the UN, the Commonwealth, OAS, OECD, and NATO.

ECONOMY

Budget. Budgetary revenue and expenditure of the Government of Canada for years ended 31 March (in $1m.):

	1989–90	*1990–91*	*1991–92*	*1992–93*	*1993–94*
Revenue	113,707	119,353	121,073	120,440	126,900
Expenditure	142,703	152,629	155,191	159,500	164,800

In 1993-94, items of revenue included (in $1,000m.): Personal income tax, 58·1; corporate income tax, 9·7; GST, 18·1. Expenditure: Debt servicing, 41·8; defence 11·5; government enterprises, 4·6; Canada Assistance Plan and other funding, 26·4; family benefit, 1·6; unemployment benefit, 19·4; retirement pensions, 20.

On 31 March 1994 the net public debt was $409,100m.

On 1 Jan. 1991 a 7% Goods and Services Tax (GST) was introduced, superseding a 13·5% manufacturers' sales tax.

Sources: Finance Canada and Statistics Canada

Currency. The unit of currency is the *Canadian dollar* (CAD) of 100 *cents*. There are coins of 1, 5, 10, 25, 50 cents and $1, and notes of $2, $5, $10, $20, $50, $100 and $1,000. In June 1994, gold reserves were 5·03m. fine troy oz., and foreign exchange reserves totalled US$9,575m. $22,270m. were in circulation in April 1994. In March 1996, £1 = $2·09; US$1 = $1·37; DM1 = $0·93.

Banking and Finance. The Bank of Canada (established 1935) is the central bank and bank of issue. The *governor* (in 1995 Gordon G. Thiessen) is appointed by the Bank's directors for 7-year terms. The Minister of Finance owns the capital stock of the Bank on behalf of Canada. Banks in Canada are chartered under the terms of the Bank Act, which imposes strict conditions on capital reserves, returns to the federal government, types of lending operations, ownership and other matters. In July 1993 there were 61 chartered banks - 9 domestic and 52 foreign. The 6 biggest domestic banks had 7,101 branches serving over 1,600 communities in all provinces and both territories in Canada and 259 branches in 56 other countries. The foreign bank subsidiaries operate 269 offices in Canada. Bank charters expire every 10 years which gives the federal government an opportunity to a review and amend sections of the Bank Act. Extensive changes were brought into force in June 1992. As a result of the substantial revision, bank charters were only renewed for 5 years. It is expected that after the next review in 1997, the government will revert to decennial reviews. The chartered banks make regular detailed returns to and are subject to periodic inspection by the Superintendent of Financial Institutions, an official appointed by the Government.

The Bank Act of 1980 required chartered banks to maintain a statutory primary reserve of 10% on demand deposits, 3% on foreign-currency deposits and 2% on notice deposits, with an additional 1% on the portion of notice deposits exceeding $500m. This reserve is required to be maintained in the form of notes and deposits with the Bank of Canada. A secondary reserve of 4% in the form of treasury bills, government bonds, etc., is also required.

Source: Canadian Bankers' Association and Bank of Canada.

Weights and Measures. The legal weights and measures are in transition from the Imperial to the International system of units. The Metric Commission, established in June 1971, co-ordinates Canada's conversion to the metric system.

ENERGY AND NATURAL RESOURCES

Electricity. Net electricity generation in 1993 was 511,300,000 MWh. In 1992, 476,450,300 MWh was to meet domestic demand. Of this total, 62·2% was from hydro generation, 22·6% from thermal generation and 15·1% from nuclear generation.

Oil and Natural Gas. Production of marketable petroleum crude, 1995, 2,386,000 bbls. a day; natural gas, 1992, 116,663,500 cu. metres, and natural gas by-products 26,734,500 cu. metres. Canada's first off-shore field, 250 km off Nova Scotia, began producing in June 1992.

Minerals. Mineral production in 1993 (in tonnes): Coal, 35·3m.; lignite, 33·7; iron ore, 33·7; copper, 0·72m.; lead 0·18m.; zinc, 1m.; molybdenum, 9,800; antimony, 622; nickel, 0·19m.; uranium, 8,900; silver, 881; gold, 153; salt, 11·4m.; asbestos, 0·51m.; cobalt, 2,370; barytes, 37,000; lime, 2·45m.; gypsum, 7·84m.; peat, 0·82m.

Agriculture. According to the census of 1991 the total land area is 2,278·6m. acres of which 167·4m. acres are agricultural land.

Grain growing, dairy farming, fruit farming, ranching and fur farming are all carried on. Total farm cash receipts (1991) $21,285·8m.

The following table shows the value of farm cash receipts for 1992, for selected agricultural commodities, in $1,000:

Wheat	2,625,302	Tobacco	330,517
Oats and barley	549,773	Cattle and calves	4,579,959
Canola	968,414	Hogs	1,758,759
Potatoes	362,415	Sheep and lambs	43,302
Vegetables	767,983	Dairy products	3,043,520
Fruit	393,067	Poultry and eggs	1,645,414

Number of occupied farms (census of 1991) was 280,043; average farm size, 598 acres.

Output (in 1,000 tonnes) and sown area (in 1,000 ha) of crops:

	Output		*Sown Area*	
	1992	*1993*	*1992*	*1993*
Wheat	29,871	27,825	13,830	12,626
Barley	10,919	13,342	3,790	4,240
Maize	4,883	6,300	858	950
Rye	265	314	138	159
Oats	2,823	3,615	1,238	1,357
Potatoes	3,588	3,333	124	125
Beans	53	120	54	82
Peas	505	1,000	277	482
Lentils	349	300	267	332
Soya beans	1,455	1,900	623	725
Sunflowers	65[1]	79[1]	74	85
Rape	3,872[1]	5,400[1]	3,045	4,027
Tomatoes	474	475	11	12
Carrots	299	310	7	8
Sugar beet	776	1,050	23	22
Hops	480	490	300	305
Tobacco	65	76	30	30

[1] Seeds

Livestock. In parts of Saskatchewan and Alberta stockraising is still carried on as a primary industry, but the livestock industry of the country at large is mainly a subsidiary of mixed farming. The following table shows the numbers of livestock (in 1,000) by provinces in July 1992:

Provinces	*Milch cows*	*Total cattle and calves*	*Sheep and lambs*	*Pigs*
Newfoundland	4·9	8·6	8·9	15·0
Prince Edward Island	18·5	94·0	3·2	103·0
Nova Scotia	28·3	128·0	30·0	126·0
New Brunswick	22·8	104·0	8·5	83·0
Quebec	505·0	1,430·0	116·0	3,068·0
Ontario	433·0	2,175·0	250·0	3,092·0
Manitoba	55·0	1,176·0	35·0	1,452·0
Saskatchewan	45·0	2,442·0	92·0	879·0
Alberta	105·0	4,866·0	311·0	1,868·0
British Columbia	75·0	773·5	72·5	213·5
Total	1,292·5	13,197·1	927·1	10,900·0

Livestock products. Slaughterings in 1993: Cattle, 3·37m.; sheep, 0·53m.; pigs, 15·4m. Production, 1993 (in 1,000 tonnes): Beef, 930; pork, 1,200; mutton, 11; horsemeat, 22; poultry meat, 735; cow's milk, 7,045; hens' eggs, 315; honey, 31; greasy wool, 1·52; rinsed wool, 0·96; hides, 85·84.

Fruit production in 1993 (and 1992), in 1,000 tonnes: Apples, 482 (553); pears, 16 (21); peaches and nectarines, 43 (40); plums, 3 (3); strawberries, 28 (29); raspberries, 15 (15).

Forestry. Forestry is of great economic importance, and forestry products (pulp, newsprint, building timber) constitute Canada's most valuable exports. As of 1986, the total area of land covered by forests was estimated at 453·3m. ha, of which 243·7m. ha were classed as productive forest land.

In 1992, 186m. cu. metres of timber were felled, including 171·8m. cu metres of conifers. 6·8m. cu metres were cut for fuel.

Fur Trade. In 1991–92, 1,919,025 wild-life and ranch raised pelts valued at $45,372,131, were taken (1,745,369 pelts in 1990–91). In wild-life pelt production marten led in total value; in fur farm production, mink. In 1993, 788,200 mink pelts were produced from fur farms with a value of $31·3m. There were, in 1992, 571 fur farms reporting fox and 257 mink.

Source: Statistics Canada

Fisheries. In 1993, the fishing fleet comprised 432 vessels totalling 169,900 GRT.

In 1993, Atlantic landings totalled 827,695 tonnes, Pacific 279,984 tonnes. Freshwater landings totalled 22,514 tonnes.

Source: Department of Fisheries and Oceans

INDUSTRY. Principal manufactures in 1993 (in 1,000 tonnes): Cement, 9,396; crude iron and alloys, 9,391; crude steel, 14,387; aluminium, 2,309; copper, 562; lead, 220; nickel, 141; zinc, 662; cadmium, 2; synthetic rubber, 199; passenger cars, 1·17m. units; lorries, 0·84m. (1992): Petroleum products, 31,293; heating oil, 28,336; mechanical wood pulp, 22,830; paper and cardboard, 16,585; newsprint, 8,931; sugar, 114; sawn timber, 56·3m. cu. metres; plywood, 1·84m. cu. metres; chipboard, 3·26m. cu. metres.

Labour. In 1994 the workforce was (in 1,000) 13,838 (6,253 females), of whom 12,231 were in employment distributed as follows: Community, private and social services, 5,426; commerce and catering, 2,174; manufacturing, 1,781; transport and communications, 752; finance and real estate, 748; building, 593; agriculture, 381; mining, 143; energy and water supply, 137; forestry, 65; hunting and fishing, 32. Unemployed: 1,607 (females, 651).

Average weekly earnings in industry in April 1994 were $567·53.

Trade Unions. Union returns filed for 1990 in compliance with the Corporations and Returns Act 1983 showed 510 labour organizations reporting on 15,030 local union branches. Union membership in 1993 was 4·07m. 65·8% of the membership belonged to the 223 national unions, with 59·7% of the membership affiliated to the Canadian Labour Congress.

It is generally established by legislation, both federal and provincial, that a trade union to which the majority of employees in a unit suitable for collective bargaining belong, is given certain rights and duties. An employer is required to meet and negotiate with such a trade union to determine wage-rates and other working conditions of his employees. The employer, the trade union and the employees affected are bound by the resulting agreement. If an impasse is reached in negotiation conciliation services provided by the appropriate government board are available. Generally, work stoppages do not take place until an established conciliation or mediation procedure has been carried out and are prohibited while an agreement is in effect.

Source: Department of Labour

FOREIGN ECONOMIC RELATIONS. A North American Free Trade Agreement (NAFTA) between Canada, Mexico and the USA was signed on 7 Oct. 1992 and came into force on 1 Jan. 1994.

Commerce. In 1994 (and 1993), exports totalled $226,607m. ($186,682m.) including re-exports of $13,206m. ($9,925m.); imports totalled $202,020m. ($169,460).

Main export markets, 1994 (in $1m.): USA, 185,217; Japan, 9,652; UK, 3,269; China, 2,292; Germany, 2,278; South Korea, 2,191; France, 1,361; Belgium, 1,335; Italy, 1,309; Netherlands, 1,217; Taiwan, 1,215; Hong Kong, 1,163; Mexico, 1,048. Main import suppliers: USA, 136,624; Japan, 11,343; UK, 4,990; Germany, 4,385; China, 3,853; Taiwan, 2,780; Italy, 2,585; France, 2,579; South Korea, 2,504; Norway, 1,661; Malaysia, 1,214; Hong Kong, 1,191; Singapore, 1,152; Sweden, 1,128.

Main categories of exports, 1994 (in $1m.): Vehicles and transport equipment, 60,045; machinery and electronic equipment, 31,127; mineral products, 25,510; paper, wood-pulp, 18,889; metal articles, 16,935; wood and wooden articles, 14,419; chemicals, 9,385; vegetable products, 7,730; plastic and rubber goods, 7,029. Imports: Machinery and electronic equipment, 62,809; vehicles and transport equipment, 42,107; metal articles, 13,490; chemicals, 13,116; plastic and rubber goods, 9,158; mineral products, 8,628; textiles, 7,278.

Total trade of Canada with UK (British Department of Trade returns, in £1,000 sterling):

	1992	*1993*	*1994*	*1995*
Imports to UK	1,897,115	1,854,312	1,880,941	2,379,624
Exports and re-exports from UK	1,582,124	1,843,814	1,916,664	1,811,964

Tourism. The number of visitors to Canada in 1993 was 36,100,461 (1992, 35,730,803). In 1993, 32,622,740 came from the USA (1992, 32,427,324). Revenue from visitors was US$6,940m. in 1993.

COMMUNICATIONS

Roads. The total length of federal and provincial territorial roads and highways at the end of March 1991 was 290,194 km.

In general highways are controlled and maintained by the provinces who also have the responsiblity of providing assistance to their municipalities and townships. Federal expenditures are directed largely to the maintenance of national park highways, Indian Reserve roads and designated provincial/territorial highway construction in projects. The Alaska Highway is part of the Canadian highway system.

In 1991 intercity and rural bus services carried 15·3m. passengers 163·6m. vehicle-km, earning $408·2m.

Registered motor vehicles totalled 17,223,039 in 1991; they included 13,061,084 passenger cars and taxis, 3,679,804 trucks and truck tractors, 64,208 buses and 324,118 motor cycles.

There were 4,210 fatalities in road accidents in 1990.

Railways. Canada has 2 great trans-continental systems: The Canadian National Railway system (CN), a government-owned body which operated 32,500 km (1994) of routes, and the Canadian Pacific Railway (CP), a joint-stock corporation operating 30,039 km (1994). A government-funded organization, Via Rail, operates passenger services; 3·6m. passengers were carried in 1994. There are several provincial and private railways.

There are metros in Montreal, Toronto and Vancouver, and tram/light rail systems in Calgary, Edmonton and Toronto.

Civil Aviation. Civil aviation is under the jurisdiction of the federal government. The technical and administrative aspects are supervised by Transport Canada, while the economic functions are assigned to the National Transportation Agency.

In 1992 Canadian airports handled 40,405,937 revenue passengers on major scheduled services and 675,738,100 kg of cargo. Operating revenue for commercial air carriers (1992) was $7,459·7m.; operating expenditure, $7,698·8m.

The 2 major airlines are Air Canada (privatized in July 1989) and Canadian Airlines International. In 1995, Air Canada operated 34 A320-200s, 3 B-747-100s, 3 B-747-200B Combis, 3 B-747-400 Combis, 8 B-767-200s, 14 B-767-200ERs, 1 B-767-300ER, 8 Canadair RJs, 35 DC-9-30s, 1 L-1011-1 and 2 L-1011-100s; Canadian Airlines International, 12 A320-200s, 38 B-737-200 Advs, 1 B-737-200C, 7 B-737-200C Advs, 4 B-747-400s, 11 B-767-300ERs, 5 DC-10-30s and 5 DC-10-30ERs.

Shipping. In 1993 the merchant marine comprised 1,049 vessels over 100 GRT, including 31 oil tankers. Total tonnage, 1995, 0·66m. GRT, including oil tankers, 0·2m. GRT and container ships, 1,910 GRT. Total vessel arrivals and departures at Canadian ports in domestic shipping was 46,226 in 1991, totalling a cumulative GRT of 197,287,947. A total of 58,820 vessel movements in international shipping at Canadian ports in 1991 loaded and unloaded 234m. tonnes of cargo, totalling a GRT of 605,281,315.

The major canals are those of the St Lawrence–Great Lakes waterway. In 1992, traffic on the Montreal–Lake Ontario Section of the Seaway numbered 2,493 transits carrying 31·4m. cargo tonnes; on the Welland Canal Section, 3,140 transits with 33·2m. cargo tonnes.

Source: Statistics Canada and St. Lawrence Seaway Authority.

Telecommunications. At the end of the fiscal year 1992–93 Canada Post Corporation's retail network consisted of 19,000 retail locations. During fiscal year 1992–93, 10,410m. pieces of mail were processed. Total revenue (1992–93) was $3,921m.; total expenditure, $3,895m.

There were 15·9m. telephone access lines reported by major telephone companies in 1992, and an estimated 0·4m. fax machines in 1992.

The Canadian Radio-Television and Telecommunications Commission is an independent authority established by parliament in 1968 to regulate public and private radio and television. The Canadian Broadcasting Corporation operates 2 national TV networks, one in English and one in French, and there are 3 private TV networks. In 1994, 1,854 cable TV systems delivered programmes to 7·3m. households.

There were 930 originating stations operating in 1994, of which 361 were AM radio stations, 432 FM radio stations and 137 television stations.

Sources: Statistics Canada, Canada Post Corporation, Canadian Radio-Television Telecommunication Commission.

Cinemas. (1991–92). There were 620 cinemas and 103 drive-in theatres.

Press. In 1991 there were 95 dailies in English (total circulation, 4·8m.) and 11 in French (1m.).

SOCIAL INSTITUTIONS

Justice. There is a Supreme Court in Ottawa, having general appellate jurisdiction in civil and criminal cases throughout Canada. The Exchequer Court (established in 1875) was replaced by the Federal Court in 1971. This has a Trial Division, consisting of the Associate Chief Justice and 9 other judges, and an Appeal Division, consisting of the Chief Justice and 3 other judges. Its seat is in Ottawa, but each Division may sit in any place in Canada. Decisions of the Trial Division may be appealed to the Appeal Division, those of the latter to the Supreme Court. There is a Superior Court in each province and county courts, with limited jurisdiction, in most of the provinces, all the judges in these courts being appointed by the Governor-General. Police, magistrates and justices of the peace are appointed by the provincial governments.

For the year ended 31 Dec. 1992, 2,848,091 Criminal Code Offences (excluding traffic) were reported and 475,041 adults were charged.

Source: Statistics Canada

Royal Canadian Mounted Police (RCMP). The RCMP is a civil force maintained by the federal government. Established in 1873 as the North-West Mounted Police, it became 'Royal' in 1904. Its sphere of operations was expanded in 1918 to include all of Canada west of Thunder Bay. In 1920 the force absorbed the Dominion Police, its headquarters was transferred from Regina to Ottawa, and its title was changed to Royal Canadian Mounted Police. The force is responsible to the Solicitor-General of Canada and is controlled by a Commissioner who holds the rank of Deputy Minister. The Commissioner is empowered to appoint peace officers in all the provinces and territories of Canada.

The responsibilities of the RCMP are national in scope. The administration of justice within the provinces, including the enforcement of the Criminal Code of Canada, is the responsibility of provincial governments, but all the provinces except Ontario and Quebec have entered into contracts with the RCMP to enforce criminal and provincial laws under the direction of the respective Attorneys-General. In addition, in these 8 provinces the RCMP is under agreement to provide police services to municipalities. The RCMP is also responsible for all police work in the Yukon and Northwest Territories enforcing federal law and territorial ordinances. The 13 Divisions, alphabetically designated, make up the strength of the RCMP across Canada; they comprise 52 sub-divisions which include 723 detachments. Headquarters Division, as well as the Office of the Commissioner, is located in Ottawa.

Assisting the criminal investigation work of the RCMP is the Directorate of Identification Services; its services, together with those of divisional and sub-divisional units, and of 8 Crime Detection Laboratories, are available to police forces throughout Canada. The Canadian Police Information Centre at RCMP Headquarters, a national computer network, is staffed and operated by the RCMP. Law Enforcement agencies throughout Canada have access via remote terminals to information on stolen vehicles, licences and wanted persons.

In Feb. 1993, the Force had a total strength of 21,311 including regular members, special constables, civilian members and public service employees. It maintained 6,992 motor vehicles, 92 police service dogs and 156 horses.

The Force has 13 divisions actively engaged in law enforcement, 1 Headquarters Division and 1 training division. Marine services are divisional responsibilities and the Force currently has 402 boats at various points across Canada. The Air Directorate has stations throughout the country and maintains a fleet of 21 fixed-wing aircraft and 8 helicopters.

Source: Public Information Branch, RCMP Headquarters

Religion. The *Yearbook of American and Canadian Churches*, published by the National Council of the Churches of Christ in the USA, New York, presents the figures available from official statisticians of church bodies:

Religious body	*Inclusive membership*	*Number of churches*	*Number of clergy*
Anglican Church of Canada	848,256	1,767	3,463
Canadian Baptist Federation	129,720	1,165	1,292
Evangelical Lutheran Church (1991)	206,187	656	859
Pentecostal Assemblies of Canada	192,706	976	1,593
Presbyterian Church	156,513	1,023	1,218
Roman Catholic Church (1989)	11,852,350	11,268	44,669
Ukrainian Greek Orthodox (1988)	120,000	258	91
United Church of Canada	2,018,808	4,044	3,939

Membership of other denominations: Mormons (1993), 118,000; Jehovah's Witnesses (1993), 109,303; Lutheran Church – Canada (1991), 78,566; Salvation Army (1993), 102,018.

Education. Under the Constitution the provincial legislatures have powers over education. These are subject to certain qualifications respecting the rights of denominational and minority language schools. School board revenues derive from local taxation on real property and government grants from general provincial revenue.

Statistics for 1993–94 of all elementary and secondary schools, public, federal and private:

Province	*Schools*	*Teachers*	*Pupils*
Newfoundland	497	7,546	123,050
Prince Edward Island	68	1,355	24,410
Nova Scotia	519	10,180	169,820
New Brunswick	444	8,270	139,830
Quebec	3,335	63,150	1,148,950
Ontario	5,574	122,590	2,109,290
Manitoba	838	13,150	221,680
Saskatchewan	960	11,030	208,040
Alberta	1,830	28,610	547,860
British Columbia	2,050	33,300	646,780
Yukon	32	406	5,970
Northwest Territories	80	1,150	17,210
National Defence (overseas)	4	60	500
Total	16,231	300,797	5,360,900

Source: Statistics Canada

Enrolment for Indian and Inuit children, 1992-93: Federal schools, 5,096; band operated schools, 49,426; provincial schools, 44,418; private schools, 1,950.

In 1995-96 there were 48 universities, 1 technical university, 4 university colleges, 10 colleges, 1 Dominican college, 1 college of agriculture, 1 college of art and design, 2 open universities, 2 polytechnics, higher schools of business, public administration, and technology, and institutes of education, microbiology and virology, and scientific research.

In 1991–92, 553,931 full-time regular students (graduates and undergraduates) were enrolled in universities. In 1991-92, 114,861 received first degrees of which 19,949 were in education; 14,805 in humanities; 7,973 in engineering and applied sciences; 3,532 in fine and applied arts; 44,320 in social sciences; 7,283 in agriculture/biological sciences; 7,548 in health professions; 6,376 in mathematics/physical sciences; and 3,075 were unclassified.

Health. Constitutional responsibility for health care services rests with the provinces and territories. Accordingly, Canada's national health insurance system consists of an interlocking set of provincial and territorial hospital and medical insurance plans conforming to certain national standards rather than a single national programme. These national standards, which are set out in the Canada Health Act, include: Provision of a comprehensive range of hospital and medical benefits; universal population coverage; access to necessary services on uniform terms and conditions; portability of benefits; and public administration of provincial and territorial insurance plans.

Provinces and territories satisfying these national standards are eligible for federal financial transfer payments. The provinces and territories are entitled to receive equal-per-capita federal health contributions escalated annually by the 3-year average increase in nominal GNP. These federal contributions, estimated at $3,734m. in 1993–94, are paid in the form of a combination of tax point and cash transfers. Over and above these health transfers, the federal government also provides financial support for such provincial and territorial extended health care service programmes as nursing home care, certain home care services, ambulatory health care services and adult residential care services. These supplementary equal-per-capita cash payments are estimated at $1,475m. in 1993–94.

The national health insurance programmes were introduced in stages. The Hospital Insurance and Diagnostic Services Act was passed in 1957, providing prepaid coverage to all Canadians for in-patient and, at the option of each province and territory, out-patient hospital services. The Medical Care Act was introduced in 1968 to extend universal coverage to all medically-equipped services provided by medical practitioners. The Canada Health Act, which took effect 1 April 1984, consolidated the original federal health insurance legislation and clarified the national standards provinces and territories are required to meet in order to qualify for full federal health contributions.

The approach taken by Canada is one of state-sponsored health insurance. Accordingly, the advent of insurance programmes produced little change in the ownership of hospitals, almost all of which are owned by non-government non-profit corporations, or in the rights and privileges of private medical practice. Patients are free to choose their own general practitioner. Except for a small percent of the population whose care is provided for under other legislation (such as serving members of the Canadian Armed Forces and inmates of federal penitentiaries), all residents are eligible, regardless of whether they are in the work force. Benefits are available without upper limit so long as they are medically necessary, provided any registration obligations are met.

In addition to the benefits qualifying for federal contributions, provinces and territories provide additional benefits at their own discretion. Most fund their portion of health costs out of general provincial and territorial revenues. There are no co-charges for medically necessary short-term hospital care or medical care. Most provinces and territories have charges for long-term chronic hospital care geared, approximately, to the room and board portion of this OAS–GIS payment mentioned under Social Welfare. In 1991, total health expenditures were about $66·77m., representing 10·2% of GNP. Public sector spending accounts for about 72·2% of total national health expenditure.

Social Welfare. The social security system provides financial benefits and social services to individuals and their families through a variety of programmes administered by federal, provincial and municipal governments, and voluntary organizations. Federally, Human Resources and Labour is responsible for research into the areas of social issues, provision of grants and contributions for various social services, and the administration of several income security programmes. These services are: The Old Age Security programme, introduced in 1952 and to which were added the Guaranteed Income Supplement in 1967 and the Spouse's Allowance in 1975; and the Canada Pension Plan and Canada Assistance Plan which came into being in 1966.

The Old Age Security (OAS) pension is payable to persons 65 years of age and over who satisfy the residence requirements stipulated in the Old Age Security Act. The amount payable, whether full or partial, is also governed by stipulated conditions, as is the payment of an OAS pension to a recipient who absents himself from Canada. OAS pensioners with little or no income apart from OAS may, upon application, receive a full or partial supplement known as the Guaranteed Income Supplement (GIS). Entitlement is normally based on the pensioner's income in the preceding year, calculated in accordance with the Income Tax Act. The spouse of an OAS pensioner, aged 60 to 64, meeting the same residence requirements as those stipulated for OAS, may be eligible for a full or partial Spouse's Allowance (SPA). SPA is payable, on application, depending on the annual combined income of the couple (not including the pensioner spouse's basic OAS pension or GIS). In 1979, the SPA programme was expanded to include a spouse, who is eligible for SPA in the month the pensioner spouse dies, until the age of 65 or until remarriage (Extended Spouse's Allowance). Since Sept. 1985, SPA has also been available to low income widow(er)s aged 60–64 regardless of the age of their spouse at death. For the third quarter of 1993, the basic OAS pension was $383·51 monthly; the maximum Guaranteed Income Supplement was $455·76 monthly for a single pensioner or a married pensioner whose spouse was not receiving a pension or a Spouse's Allowance, and $296·87 monthly for each spouse of a married couple where both were pensioners. The maximum Spouse's Allowance for the same quarter was $680·38 monthly (equal to the basic pension plus the maximum GIS married rate), and $751·13 for widow(er)s. Total OAS/GIS/SPA benefit expenditures for 1991–92 were $18,921m.; in July 1992, over 3m. Canadians received benefits through these programmes.

The Canada Pension Plan (CPP) is designed to provide workers with a basic level of income protection in the event of retirement, disability or death. Benefits may be payable to a contributor, a surviving spouse or an eligible child. As of 1 Jan. 1992, payment of actuarially adjusted retirement benefits may begin as early as age 60 or as late as age 70. Benefits are determined by the contributor's earnings and contributions made to the Plan. Contribution is compulsory for most employed and self-employed Canadians 18 to 65 years of age. The CPP does not operate in Quebec, which has exercised its constitutional prerogative to establish a similar plan. In 1993, the maximum retirement pension payable under CPP was $667·36, the maximum disability pension was $812·85, and the maximum surviving spouse's pension was $400·42 (for survivors 65 years of age and over). For survivors under 65 years of age CPP pays a reduced flat rate. In 1993 CPP was funded by equal contributions of 2·5% of pensionable earnings from the employer and 2·5% from the employee (self-employed persons contribute the full 5%), in addition to the interest on the investment of excess funds. In 1993, the range of yearly pensionable earnings was from $3,300 to $33,400; a person who earned and contributed at less than the maximum level receives monthly benefits at rates lower than the maximum allowable under CPP. In July 1993, over 3·8m. Canadians received Canada or Quebec Pension Plan benefits. Total expenditures in 1992–93 for CPP were about $13,100m.

Social security agreements co-ordinate the operation of the Old Age Security and the CPP with the comparable social security programmes of certain other countries.

The Federal Government passed legislation in Nov. 1992, which replaced the Family Allowances programme with a new Child Tax Benefit, administered jointly by Human Resources and Labour and Revenue Canada. The programme delivered Canada its first payments in Jan. 1993.

Ismael, J. S., (ed.) *Canadian Welfare State: Evolution and Transition.* Univ. of Alberta Press, 1987

Source: Human Resources and Labour

DIPLOMATIC REPRESENTATIVES

Of Canada in Great Britain (Macdonald House., Grosvenor Sq., London, W1X 0AB)
High Commissioner: Royce Frith, QC.

Of Great Britain in Canada (80 Elgin St., Ottawa, K1P 5K7)
High Commissioner: Anthony Goodenough, CMG.

Of Canada in the USA (501 Pennsylvania Ave., NW, Washington, D.C., 20001)
Ambassador: Raymond A. Chretien.

Of the USA in Canada (100 Wellington St., Ottawa, K1P 5TI)
Ambassador: James J. Blanchard.

Of Canada to the United Nations
Ambassador: Robert R. Fowler.

Further Reading

Statistics Canada. *The Canada Year Book.*
Cambridge History of the British Empire. Vol. VI. Canada and Newfoundland. Cambridge, 1930
Canadian Annual Review. From 1960
Canadian Encyclopedia. 2nd ed. 4 vols. Edmonton, 1988
Brown, R. C., *An Illustrated History of Canada.* Toronto, 1991
Cook, C., *Canada after the Referendum of 1992.* McGill-Queens Univ. Press, 1994
Dawson, R. M. and Dawson, W. F. *Democratic Government in Canada.* 5th ed. Toronto Univ. Press, 1989
Granatstein, J. L., *Twentieth-Century Canada.* Toronto, 1983
Harris, R. C., (ed.) *Historical Atlas of Canada.* Vol 1. Univ. of Toronto, 1987
Ingles, E., *Canada.* [Bibliography] Oxford and Santa Barbara, 1990

Jackson, R. J., *Politics in Canada: Culture, Institutions, Behaviour and Public Policy.* 2nd ed. Scarborough (Ont.), 1990
Leacy, F. H., (ed.) *Historical Statistics of Canada.* Government Printer, Ottawa, 1983
Longille, P., *Changing the Guard: Canada's Defence in a World in Transition.* Toronto Univ. Press, 1991
McCann, L. D., (ed.) *Heartland and Hinterland: A Geography of Canada.* Scarborough, Ontario, 1982
Silver, A. I. (ed.) *Introduction to Canadian History.* London, 1994
Smith, D. L., (ed.) *History of Canada: an Annotated Bibliography.* Oxford and Santa Barbara, 1983

Other more specialized titles are listed under CONSTITUTION AND GOVERNMENT *and* SOCIAL WELFARE, *above.*
National library: The National Library of Canada, Ottawa, Ontario. *Librarian:* Marianne Scott.
National statistical office: Statistics Canada, Ottawa, K1A 0T6

CANADIAN PROVINCES

The 10 provinces have each a separate parliament and administration, with a Lieut.-Governor, appointed by the Governor-General in Council at the head of the executive. They have full powers to regulate their own local affairs and dispose of their revenues, provided only they do not interfere with the action and policy of the central administration. Among the subjects assigned exclusively to the provincial legislatures are: The amendment of the provincial constitution, except as regards the office of the Lieut.-Governor; property and civil rights; direct taxation for revenue purposes; borrowing; management and sale of Crown lands; provincial hospitals, reformatories, etc.; shop, saloon, tavern, auctioneer and other licences for local or provincial purposes; local works and undertakings, except lines of ships, railways, canals, telegraphs, etc., extending beyond the province or connecting with other provinces, and excepting also such works as the Canadian Parliament declares are for the general good; marriages, administration of justice within the province; education. On 18 July 1994 the federal and provincial governments signed an agreement easing inter-provincial barriers on government procurement, labour mobility, transport licences and product standards. Federal legislation of Dec. 1995 grants provinces a right of constitutional veto.

For the administration of the 2 territories *see* Northwest Territories, Yukon Territory *below.*

Areas of the 10 provinces and 2 territories (Yukon and Northwest Territory) (in sq. km) and population at recent censuses:

Province	*Land area*	*Total land and fresh water area*	*Population, 1981*	*Population, 1986*	*Population, 1991* [1,2]
Newfoundland (Nfld.)	371,634	405,720	567,681	568,349	568,474
Prince Edward Island (PEI)	5,660	5,660	122,506	126,646	129,765
Nova Scotia (NS)	52,840	55,490	847,442	873,199	899,942
New Brunswick (NB)	71,569	73,440	696,403	710,442	723,900
Quebec (Que.)	1,357,811	1,540,680	6,438,403	6,540,276	6,895,963
Ontario (Ont.)	916,733	1,068,580	8,625,107	9,113,515	10,084,885
Manitoba (Man.)	547,703	649,950	1,026,241	1,071,232	1,091,942
Saskatchewan (Sask.)	570,113	652,330	968,313	1,010,198	988,928
Alberta (Alta.)	638,232	661,190	2,237,724	2,375,278	2,545,553
British Columbia (BC)	892,677	947,800	2,744,467	2,889,207	3,282,061
Yukon Territory (YT)	531,843	483,450	23,153	23,504	27,797
Northwest Territories (NWT) [3]	3,246,389	3,426,320	45,471	52,238	57,649

[1] Excludes data from incompletely enumerated Indian reserves and Indian settlements.
[2] Comparison of the 1991 census data with data from earlier censuses is affected by a change in the definition of the 1991 census population. Persons in Canada on student authorizations, Minister's permits, and as refugee claimants were enumerated in the 1991 census but not in previous censuses. These persons are referred to as non-permanent residents.
[3] For data on the new territory of Nunavut in course of formation *see* NORTHWEST TERRITORIES: Constitution and Government.

Local Government. Under the terms of the British North America Act the provinces are given full powers over local government. All local government institutions are, therefore, supervised by the provinces, and are incorporated and function under provincial acts.

The acts under which municipalities operate vary from province to province. A municipal corporation is usually administered by an elected council headed by a mayor or reeve, whose powers to administer affairs and to raise funds by taxation and other methods are set forth in provincial laws, as is the scope of its obligations to, and on behalf of, the citizens. Similarly, the types of municipal corporations, their official designations and the requirements for their incorporation vary between provinces. The following table sets out the classifications as at the 1991 census:

	Federal electoral districts	*Sub-provincial regions*	*Census divisions*
Nfld.	7	4	10
PEI	4	1	3 [1]
NS	11	5	18 [1]
NB	10	5	15 [1]
Que.	88	16	99 [2]
Ont.	95	5	49 [3]
Man.	14	8	23
Sask.	14	6	18
Alta.	21	8	19
BC	28	8	30 [4]
YT	1	1	1 [5]
NWT	2	1	5 [5]

[1] Counties.
[2] 4 census divisions, 3 communautés urbaines, 92 municipalités régionales de comté.
[3] 24 counties, 10 districts, 1 district municipality, 1 metropolitan municipality, 10 regional municipalities, 3 united counties. [4] 1 region, 29 regional districts. [5] Regions.

Justice. The administration of justice within the provinces, including the enforcement of the Criminal Code of Canada, is the responsibility of provincial governments, but all the provinces except Ontario and Quebec have entered into contracts with the Royal Canadian Mounted Police (RCMP) to enforce criminal and provincial law. In addition, in these 8 provinces the RCMP is under agreement to provide police services to municipalities.

ALBERTA

KEY HISTORICAL EVENTS. The southern half of the province of Alberta was part of Rupert's land which was granted by royal charter in 1670 to the Hudson's Bay Company. The intervention by the North West Company in the fur trade after 1783 led to the establishment of trading posts. In 1869 Rupert's land was transferred from the Hudson's Bay Company (which had absorbed its rival in 1821) to the new Dominion, and in the following year this land was combined with the former Crown land of the North Western Territories to form the Northwest Territories.

In 1882 'Alberta' first appeared as a provisional 'district', consisting of the southern half of the present province. In 1905 the Athabasca district to the north was added when provincial status was granted to Alberta.

TERRITORY AND POPULATION. The area of the province is 661,185 sq. km; 644,389 sq. km being land area and 16,796 sq. km water area. The population (estimate 1 July 1992) was 2,565,200; the urban population (1991), centres of 1,000 or over, was 2,030,893 and the rural 514,660. Population (4 July 1991) of the 16 cities (*see below under* Local Government for definition): Calgary, 710,677; Edmonton, 616,741; Lethbridge, 60,974; Red Deer, 58,134; Medicine Hat, 43,265; St Albert, 42,146; Fort McMurray, 34,706; Grande Prairie, 28,271; Leduc, 13,970; Camrose, 13,420; Spruce Grove, 12,884; Fort Saskatchewan, 12,078; Airdrie, 12,456; Lloydminster (Alberta portion), 10,042; Wetaskiwin, 10,634; Drumheller, 6,277.

Vital statistics, *see* CANADA: Territory and Population.

CLIMATE. A continental climate: Long, cold winters and mild summers. Rainfall amounts are greatest between May and Sept. Edmonton. Jan. 5°F (–15°C), July 63°F (17°C). Annual rainfall 13·6" (345·6 mm).

CONSTITUTION AND GOVERNMENT. The constitution of Alberta is contained in the British North America Act of 1867, and amending Acts; also in the Alberta Act of 1905, passed by the Parliament of the Dominion of Canada, which created the province out of the then Northwest Territories. All the provisions of the British North America Act, except those with respect to school lands and the public domain, were made to apply to Alberta as they apply to the older provinces of Canada. On 1 Oct. 1930 the natural resources were transferred from the Dominion to provincial government control. The province is represented by 6 members in the Senate and 26 in the House of Commons of Canada.

The executive is vested nominally in the Lieut.-Governor, who is appointed by the federal government, but actually in the Executive Council or the Cabinet of the legislature. Legislative power is vested in the Assembly in the name of the Queen.

Members of the Legislative Assembly are elected by the universal vote of adults over the age of 18 years.

There are 83 members in the legislature (elected 15 June 1993): 51 Progressive Conservative, 32 Liberal.

Lieut.-Governor: Hon. Gordon Towers (sworn in 11 March 1991).

Flag: Blue with the shield of the province in the centre.

The members of the Ministry were as follows in Feb. 1994:

Premier, President of Executive Council, Minister of Federal and Intergovernmental Affairs: Hon. Ralph Klein (b. 1942; Progressive Conservative).

Deputy Premier and Minister of Economic Development and Tourism: Ken Kowalski. *Advanced Education and Career Development:* Jack Ady. *Energy:* Pat Black. *Family and Social Services:* Mike Cardinal. *Labour:* Stockwell Day. *Provincial Treasurer:* Jim Dinning. *Environmental Protection:* Brian Evans. *Education:* Halvar Jonson. *Community Development:* Gary Mar. *Health:* Shirley McClellan. *Without portfolio responsible for the Health Planning Secretariat:* Dianne Mirosh. *Agriculture, Food and Rural Development:* Walter Paszkowski. *Justice and Attorney-General:* Ken Rostad. *Public Works, Supply and Services:* Tom Thurber. *Transportation and Utilities:* Peter Trynchy. *Municipal Affairs:* Stephen West.

Local Government. The local government units are City, Town, New Town, Village, Summer Village, County, Municipal District and Improvement District.

There are 16 cities (*see* TERRITORY AND POPULATION, *above*). These cities operate under the Municipal Government Act. The governing body consists of a mayor and a council of from 6 to 20 members. A city can be incorporated by order of the Lieut.-Governor-in-Council. A population of 10,000 is required on incorporation.

There are no limits of area specified in the statutes for any of the different local government units. The population requirement for a Town as specified in the Municipal Government Act is 1,000 people, and the area at incorporation is that of the original village.

A Village must contain 75 separate and occupied dwellings. The Municipal Government Act requires each dwelling to have been occupied continuously for a period of at least 6 months. A Summer Village must contain 50 separate dwellings.

A rural county area is an area incorporated through an order of the Lieut.-Governor-in-Council under the provisions of the County Act. One board of councillors deal with both municipal and school affairs.

A rural Municipal District is an area which has been incorporated under the Municipal Government Act. In Municipal Districts separate boards control municipal and school affairs.

Areas not incorporated as counties or Municipal Districts are termed Improvement Districts or Special Areas. Sparsely populated, such districts are administered and taxed by the Department of Municipal Affairs of the provincial government. There are no requirements as to the minimum number of residents of a County or Municipal District.

FINANCE. The budgetary revenue and expenditure (in $1m.) for years ending 31 March were as follows:

	1988–89	*1989–90*	*1990–91*	*1991–92* [2]	*1992–93* [1]
Revenue	9,106	9,720	11,766	11,145	10,984
Expenditure	10,889	12,044	12,995	12,728	13,273

[1] Forecast. [2] Estimates.

Personal income *per capita* (1991), $22,568.

ENERGY AND NATURAL RESOURCES

Oil. In 1991, 72,178,000 cu. metres of crude oil were produced with gross sales value of $8,783·9m. Alberta produced 80% of Canada's crude petroleum output in 1988.

Oil sands underlie some 60,000 sq. km of Alberta, the 4 major deposits being: The Athabasca, Cold Lake, Peace River and Buffalo Head Hills deposits. Some 7% (3,250 sq. km) of the Athabasca deposit can be exploited through open-pit mining. The rest of the Athabasca, and all the deposits in the other areas, are deeper reserves which must be developed through in situ techniques. These reserves reach depths of 760 metres.

Two oil sands mining plants in the Fort McMurray area produced 13·2m. cu. metres of synthetic crude oil in 1991.

Gas. Natural gas is found in abundance in numerous localities. In 1991, 85,203m. cu. metres valued at $4,306·5m. were produced. Production of natural gas by-products was 22,486,000 cu. metres, valued at $2,120m.

Minerals. Coal reserves are estimated at 2,300,000m. tonnes, of which 720,000m. tonnes are recoverable. Production (1991) 32·35m. tonnes valued at $541·1m.

Value of total mineral production decreased from $19,110·4m. in 1990 to $16,147·7m. in 1991.

Agriculture. Total area of farms (1991) 51,425,111 acres; improved land, 34,933,052; (under crops, 22,961,142; improved pasture, 4,305,760; summer fallow, 4,377,212; other improved land, 3,288,938); unimproved land, 19,780,997; (unimproved pasture, 16,429,059; other unimproved land, 3,228,938). Number of farms (1991) 57,245.

For particulars of agricultural production and livestock *see* CANADA: Agriculture. Farm cash receipts in 1991 totalled $4,210·3m., of which crops contributed $1,526·1m., livestock and products, $2,245·2m., and direct payments, $439m.

Forestry. Forest land in 1991 covered some 203,000 sq. km. In 1990–91 9,326,603 cu. metres were cut from land managed by the Crown.

Fisheries. The largest catch in commercial fishing is whitefish. Perch, tullibee, walley, pike and lake trout are also caught in smaller quantities. In 1984 a provincial fish marketing policy was implemented and a new commercial fishery licensing system was implemented in 1987. Commercial fish production in 1990–91 was 2,210 tonnes, value $2·49m.

INDUSTRY. The leading manufacturing industries are food and beverages, petroleum refining, metal fabricating, wood industries, primary metal, chemical and chemical products and non-metallic mineral products industries. There were in 1987 2,590 manufacturing establishments, in which were employed 78,220 persons, who earned in salaries and wages $2,278,685,000.

Manufacturing shipments had a total value of $19,278,590m. in 1991. Chief among these shipments were: Food, $4,350·7m.; beverages, 348·6; chemicals and chemical products, $3,209·8m.; refined petroleum and coal products, $3,336·1m.; primary metals, $861·8m.; fabricated metal products, $1,052·1m.; wood, $840·8m.; printing, publishing and allied products, $760·7m.; machinery, $831·2m.; paper and allied products, $911·7m.; non-metal mineral products, $706·8m.; furniture and fixtures, $213·4m.; other, $258·7m.

Total retail sales (1991) $18,950m.

Tourism is important and in 1991 contributed an estimated $2,770m. to the economy.

COMMUNICATIONS

Roads. In 1992 there were 155,325 km of roads and highways, including 110,555 km gravelled and 21,208 km paved.

At 31 March 1992 there were 1,875,212 motor vehicles registered, including 1,467,732 passenger cars.

Railways. In 1992 the length of main railway lines was 10,234 km. There are rail local transit networks in Edmonton (12·4 km) and Calgary (29·2 km).

Telecommunications. The telephone system is owned and operated by the Telus Corporation (in which the Alberta Government holds 44% of the shares), except in the city of Edmonton (owned and operated by the City Council). There were 1,526,252 telephone subscriber lines in service in April 1992.

SOCIAL INSTITUTIONS

Justice. The Supreme Judicial authority of the province is the Court of Appeal. Judges of the Court of Appeal and Court of Queen's Bench are appointed by the Federal Government and hold office until retirement at the age of 75. There are courts of lesser jurisdiction in both civil and criminal matters. The Court of Queen's Bench has full jurisdiction over civil proceedings. A Provincial Court which has jurisdiction in civil matters up to $2,000 is presided over by provincially appointed judges. Youth Courts have power to try boys and girls 12–17 years old inclusive for offences against the Young Offenders Act.

The jurisdiction of all criminal courts in Alberta is enacted in the provisions of the Criminal Code. The system of procedure in civil and criminal cases conforms as nearly as possible to the English system.

Education. Schools of all grades are included under the term of public school (including those in the separate school system which are publicly supported). The same board of trustees controls the schools from kindergarten to university entrance. In 1991–92 there were 481,843 pupils enrolled in grades 1-12, including private schools and special education programmes. The University of Alberta (in Edmonton), organized in 1907, had, in 1991–92, 34,050 full-time students; the University of Calgary, formerly part of the University of Alberta and autonomous from April 1966, had 17,881 and the University of Lethbridge, organized in 1966, had 3,659. The Athabasca University had in 1991–92, 11,500 part-time students. Banff Centre for Continuing Education had in 1991–92, 1,130 part-time students. The full-time enrolment at Alberta's 11 public colleges totalled 21,238 students in 1988–89.

Further Reading

MacGregor, J. G., *A History of Alberta.* 2nd ed. Edmonton, 1981

Masson, J., *Alberta's Local Governments and their Politics.* Univ. of Alberta Press, 1985

Richards, J., *Prairie Capitalism: Power and Influence in the New West.* Toronto, 1979

Wiebe, R., *Alberta: a Celebration.* Edmonton, 1979

Statistical office: Alberta Bureau of Statistics, 10611-98 Avenue, Edmonton, T5K 2R7.

BRITISH COLUMBIA

KEY HISTORICAL EVENTS. Vancouver Island was organized as a colony in 1849; the mainland as far as the watershed of the Rocky Mountains was organized as a colony following a gold rush on the Fraser River in 1859. The two were united as the colony of British Columbia in 1866; this became a Canadian Province in 1871.

TERRITORY AND POPULATION. British Columbia has an area of 952,263 sq. km. The capital is Victoria. The province is bordered westerly by the Pacific Ocean and Alaska Panhandle, northerly by the Yukon and Northwest Territories, easterly by the Province of Alberta and southerly by the USA along the 49th parallel. A chain of islands, the largest of which are Vancouver Island and the Queen Charlotte Islands, affords protection to the mainland coast.

The 1991 census population was 3,282,061.

The principal cities and their 1991 census populations are as follows: Metropolitan Vancouver, 1,602,502; Metropolitan Victoria, 287,897; Kelowna, 75,950; Prince George, 69,653; Matsqui, 68,064; Kamloops, 67,057; Nanaimo, 60,129; Chilliwack, 50,228; Penticton, 27,258; Mission, 26,202; Vernon, 23,514; North Cowichan, 21,373; Campbell River, 21,175; Abbotsford, 18,864; Port Alberni, 18,403.

Vital statistics, *see* CANADA: Territory and Population.

CLIMATE. The climate is cool temperate, but mountain influences affect temperatures and rainfall very considerably. Driest months occur in summer. Vancouver. Jan. 36°F (2·2°C), July 64°F (17·8°C). Annual rainfall 58" (1,458 mm).

CONSTITUTION AND GOVERNMENT. British Columbia (then known as New Caledonia) originally formed part of the Hudson's Bay Company's concession. In 1849 Vancouver Island and in 1858 British Columbia were constituted Crown Colonies; in 1866 the two colonies amalgamated. The British North America Act of 1867 provided for eventual admission into Canadian Confederation, and on 20 July 1871 British Columbia became the sixth province of the Dominion.

British Columbia has a unicameral legislature of 75 elected members. Government policy is determined by the Executive Council responsible to the Legislature. The Lieut.-Governor is appointed by the Governor-General of Canada, usually for a term of 5 years, and is the head of the executive government of the province.

Lieut.-Governor: His Honour the Hon. Garde B. Gardom, QC.

The Legislative Assembly is elected for a maximum term of 5 years. There are 75 electoral districts. Every Canadian citizen 19 years and over, having resided a minimum of 6 months in the province, duly registered, is entitled to vote. The province is represented in the Federal Parliament by 32 members in the House of Commons, and 6 Senators.

At the Legislative Assembly elections of Oct. 1991 the New Democratic Party (NDP) gained 41% of votes cast and 51 seats, the Liberal Party gained 17 seats and Social Credit 7.

The 19-member NDP Executive Council comprised in Sept. 1995:

Premier and President of the Executive Council: Hon. Mike Harcourt.

Deputy Premier and Minister of Finance and Corporate Relations: Hon. Elizabeth Cull. *Aboriginal Affairs:* Hon. John Cashore. *Agriculture, Fisheries and Food:* Hon. David Zirnhelt. *Attorney General and Minister Responsible for Multiculturalism, Human Rights and Immigration:* Hon. Ujjal Dosanjh. *Education:* Hon. Art Charbonneau. *Employment and Investment:* Hon. Glen Clark. *Energy, Mines and Petroleum Resources:* Hon. Anne Edwards. *Environment, Lands and Parks:* Hon. Moe Sihota. *Forests:* Hon. Andrew Petter. *Government Services and Responsible for Sports:* Hon. Colin Gabelmann. *Health and Ministry Responsible for Seniors:* Hon. Paul Ramsey. *Housing, Recreation and Consumer Services:* Hon. Joan Smallwood. *Municipal Affairs:* Hon. Darlene Marzari. *Skills, Training and Labour:* Hon. Dan Miller. *Small Business, Tourism and Culture:* Hon. Bill Barlee. *Social Services:* Hon. Joy Macphail. *Transportation and Highways:* Hon. Jackie Pement. *Women's Equality:* Hon. Penny Priddy.

Local Government. Vancouver City was incorporated by statute and operates under the provisions of the Vancouver Charter of 1953 and amendments. This is the only incorporated area in British Columbia not operating under the provisions of the Municipal Act. Under this Act municipalities are divided into the following classes: *(a)* a village with a population between 500 and 2,500, governed by a council consisting of a mayor and 4 aldermen; *(b)* a town with a population between 2,500 and 5,000, governed by a council consisting of a mayor and 4 aldermen; *(c)* a city where the population exceeds 5,000 governed by a council consisting of a mayor and 6 or 8 aldermen depending on population; *(d)* a district where the area exceeds 810 hectares and the average density is less than 5 persons per hectare, governed by a council consisting of a mayor and 6 or 8 aldermen depending on population; *(e)* an Indian government district.

There are 2 other forms of local government: The Regional District covering a number of areas both incorporated and unincorporated, governed by a board of directors; and the improvement district governed by a board of 3 trustees.

Revenue for municipal services is derived mainly from real-property taxation, although additional revenue is derived from licence fees, business taxes, fines, public utility projects and grants-in-aid from the provincial government.

ECONOMY

Budget. Current provincial revenue and expenditure $1m. for fiscal years ending 31 March:

	1992–93	*1993–94*	*1994–95* [1]	*1995–96* [2]
Revenue	16,243·0	17,997·8	19,244·0	20,300·0
Expenditure	17,935·7	18,912·9	19,614·0	20,186·0

[1] Forecast. [2] Estimate.

The main sources of current revenue are the income taxes, contributions from the federal government, and privileges, licences and natural resources taxes and royalties.

The main items of expenditure in 1995–96 (estimate) are as follows: Health, $6,706·7m.; education, $5,597·7m.; social services, $2,897·7m.; transportation, $890·6m.; natural resources and economic development, $1,252·7m.; protection of persons and property, $1,023·7m.; general government, $232·8m.

Banking and Finance. On 31 Dec. 1994, Canadian chartered banks maintained 887 branches and had total assets of $99,027m. in British Columbia; credit unions at 101 locations had total assets of $16,398m. Several foreign banks have Canadian head offices in Vancouver and several others have branches.

ENERGY AND NATURAL RESOURCES

Electricity. Generation in 1994 totalled 61,015m. kWh of which 9,541m. kWh were exported. Available within the province was 68,851m. kWh (with imports 5,691m. kWh).

Minerals. Copper, coal, natural gas, crude oil, gold and silver are the most important minerals produced. The 1994 total of mineral production was estimated at $3,813m. Total value of mineral fuels produced in 1994 was estimated at: Coal, $904·8m.; oil and gas, $1,178·5m.

Agriculture. Only 2·4m. ha or 4% of the total land area is arable or potentially arable. Farm cash receipts, in 1994, were $1,500m. of which livestock and products $876·1m., crops, $595·9m.

Forestry. About 46% of British Columbia's land is productive forest land, with 43·3m. hectares bearing commercial forest. Over 94% of the forest area is owned or administered by the provincial government. The total timber harvest in 1994 was 75·7m. cu. metres. Output of forest-based products, 1994: Lumber, 33·7m. cu. metres; plywood, 1·57m. cu. metres; pulp, 7·63m. tonnes; newsprint, paper and paperboard, 2·96m. tonnes; newsprint, 1·7m. tonnes.

Fisheries. In 1994, the total landed value of the catch was $685m., wholesale value $1,172m.

INDUSTRY AND TRADE

Industry. The value of shipments from all manufacturing industries reached an estimated $30,727m. in 1994.

Labour. The labour force averaged 1,913,000 persons in 1994 with 1,713,000 employed, of whom 671,000 were in service industries, 303,000 in trade, 196,000 in manufacturing, 131,000 in transportation and communications, 111,000 in finance, insurance and real estate, 0·1m. in public administration, 141,000 in construction, 29,000 in agriculture, 32,000 in forestry, 12,000 in mining and 8,000 in fishing and trapping.

Commerce. Exports of British Columbia origin during 1994 totalled $22,834·5m. in value, while imports amounted to $18,193·9m. The USA is the largest market for products exported through British Columbia customs ports ($12,354·6m. in 1994) followed by Japan ($5,657·9m.) and South Korea ($738·5m.).

The leading exports in 1994 were: Lumber, $8,262m.; pulp, $3,524m.; metallic minerals, $1,474m.; coal, $1,328m.; paper and newsprint, $1,133m.

Tourism. In 1994, 25·6m. tourists spent $6,314m.

COMMUNICATIONS

Roads. In 1994 there were 42,600 km of provincial roads and rights of way in the province, of which 23,300 km were paved. At 31 Dec. 1994, 1·53m. passenger cars and 531,000 commercial vehicles were licensed.

Railways. The province is served by two transcontinental railways, the Canadian Pacific Railway and the Canadian National Railway. Passenger service is provided by VIA Rail, a Crown Corporation, the publicly owned British Columbia Railway, and Rocky Mountain Railtours. In 1995 the American company Amtrak began operating a high speed rail service between Seattle and Vancouver after a 14-year hiatus. British Columbia is also served by the Railway Freight Service of the B.C. Hydro and Power Authority, the Northern Alberta Railways Company and the Burlington Northern and Southern Railways Inc. The combined route-mileage of mainline track operated by the CPR, CNR and BCR totals 6,800 km. The system also includes CPR and CNR wagon ferry connections to Vancouver Island, between Prince Rupert and Alaska, and interchanges with American railways at southern border points. A metro line was opened in Vancouver in 1986 (29 km). A commuter rail service linking Vancouver and the Fraser Valley was established in 1995 (69 km).

Civil Aviation. International airports are located at Vancouver and Victoria. Daily interprovincial and intraprovincial flights serve all main population centres. Small public and private airstrips are located throughout the province. Total passenger arrivals and departures on scheduled services (1994) 10·8m.

Shipping. The major ports are Vancouver, Prince Rupert and the Fraser River. Other coastal harbours include Nanaimo, Port Alberni, Campbell River, Powell River, Kitimat, Stewart and Squamish. Total cargo shipped through the port of Vancouver during 1994 was 67·8m. tonnes; from the port of Prince Rupert, 12·9m. tonnes. 21 cruise ships with 591,000 passengers visited Vancouver in 1994.

The British Columbia Ferries connect Vancouver Island with the mainland and also provide service to other coastal points; in 1994, 22m. passengers and 8·4m. vehicles were carried. Service by other ferry systems is also provided between Vancouver Island and the USA. The Alaska State Ferries connect Prince Rupert with centres in Alaska.

Telecommunications. The British Columbia Telephone Company had (1994) approximately 2·3m. telephones in service. In March 1994 there were 95 radio and 11 television stations originating in British Columbia. In addition there were 248 rebroadcasting stations in the province.

SOCIAL INSTITUTIONS

Justice. The judicial system is composed of the Court of Appeal, the Supreme Court, County Courts, and various Provincial Courts, including Magistrates' Courts and Small Claims Courts. The federal courts include the Supreme Court of Canada and the Federal Court of Canada.

Education. Education, free up to Grade XII levels, is financed jointly from municipal and provincial government revenues. Attendance is compulsory from the age of 5 to 16. There were approximately 604,910 pupils enrolled in 1,673 public schools from kindergarten to Grade 12 in the 1994-95 school year.

The universities had a full-time enrolment of approximately 65,753 for 1994–95. As of Sept. 1995 they are the University of British Columbia, Vancouver; University of Victoria, Saanich; Simon Fraser University, Burnaby, and the University of Northern British Columbia, Prince George. The regional colleges are Camosun College, Victoria; Capilano College, North Vancouver; Cariboo College, Kamloops; College of New Caledonia, Prince George; Douglas College, New Westminister; East Kootenay Community College, Cranbrook; Fraser Valley College, Chilliwack/Abbotsford; Kwantlen College, Surrey; Malaspina College, Nanaimo; North Island College, Comox; Northern Lights College, Dawson Creek/Fort St John; Northwest Community College, Terrace/Prince Rupert; Okanagan College, Kelowna with branches at Salmon Arm and Vernon; Selkirk College, Castlegar; Vancouver Community College, Vancouver. The colleges had a total enrolment of approximately 66,032 for 1994-95.

There are also the British Columbia Institute of Technology, Burnaby; Emily Carr College of Art and Design, Vancouver; Justice Institute of British Columbia, Vancouver; Open Learning Institute, Richmond; Pacific Marine Training Institute, North Vancouver; Pacific Vocational Institute, Burnaby/Maple Ridge/Richmond. The institutes had 26,992 persons enrolled in 1994-95. A televised distance education and special programmes through KNOW, the Knowledge Network of the West is provided.

Health. The Government operates a hospital insurance scheme giving universal coverage after a qualifying period of 3 months' residence in the province. The province has come under a national medicare scheme which is partially subsidized by the provincial government and partially by the federal government.

Further Reading

Barman, J., *The West beyond the West: a History of British Columbia.* Toronto Univ. Press, 1991

Morley, J. T., *The Reins of Power: Governing British Columbia.* Vancouver, 1983

Statistical office: BC STATS, Ministry of Government Services, Parliament Buildings, Victoria, V8V 1X4.

MANITOBA

KEY HISTORICAL EVENTS. The Hudson's Bay Company formed a colony on the Red River in 1812, which was part of territory annexed to Canada in 1870. The Metis colonists (part-Indian, mostly French-speaking, Catholic) objected to the arrangements for the purchase of the Company territory by Canada and the province of Manitoba was created to accommodate them. It was extended northwards and westwards in 1881 and to Hudson Bay in 1912.

TERRITORY AND POPULATION. The area of the province is 250,946 sq. miles (649,947 sq. km), of which 211,721 sq. miles are land and 39,225 sq. miles water. From north to south it is 1,225 km and at the widest point it is 793 km.

In 1994 the estimated population was 1,131,100. Population (estimate 1991) of Winnipeg, the capital, 652,355; other principal cities: Brandon, 38,567; Thompson, 14,977; Portage la Prairie, 13,186; Flin Flon, 7,119.

Vital statistics *see* CANADA: Area and Population.

CLIMATE. The climate is cold continental, with very severe winters but pleasantly warm summers. Rainfall amounts are greatest in the months May to Sept. Winnipeg. Jan. –3°F (–19·3°C), July 67°F (19·6°C). Annual rainfall 21" (539 mm).

CONSTITUTION AND GOVERNMENT. Manitoba was known as the Red River Settlement before its entry into the Dominion in 1870. The provincial government is administered by a *Lieut.-Governor* assisted by an *Executive Council* (Cabinet) which is appointed from and responsible to a *Legislative Assembly* of 57 members elected for 5 years. Women were enfranchised in 1916. The Electoral Division Act, 1955, created 57 single-member constituencies and abolished the transferable vote. There are 28 rural electoral divisions, and 29 urban electoral divisions. The province is represented by 6 members in the Senate and 14 in the House of Commons of Canada.

Lieut.-Governor: Yvon Dumont (appointed 1993).
Flag: The British Red Ensign with the shield of the province in the fly.

Elections to the Legislative Assembly were held on 11 Sept. 1990: the Progressive Conservative Party gained 30 seats (with 42% of votes cast), the New Democratic Party, 20 (29%) and the Liberal Party, 7 (28%). As a result of by-elections in Sept. 1993 the state of the parties was: Progressive Conservative Party, 29 seats; New Democratic Party, 21; Liberal Party, 7.

The members of the Progressive Conservative Ministry (sworn in as of Sept. 1993) were:

Premier, President of the Executive Council, Minister of Federal-Provincial Relations: Gary Albert Filmon.

Deputy-Premier, Minister of Industry, Trade and Tourism: James Erwin Downey. *Energy and Mines:* Donald W. Orchard. *Natural Resources:* Albert Driedger. *Education and Training:* Clayton S. Manness. *Culture, Heritage and Citizenship:* Harold Gilleshammer. *Finance:* Eric Stefanson. *Highways and Transportation:* Glen Findlay. *Justice and Attorney General:* Rosemary Vodrey. *Consumer and Corporate Affairs:* James A. Ernst. *Agriculture:* Harry Enns. *Rural Development:* Leonard Derkach. *Health:* James McCrae. *Environment:* Glen Cummings. *Labour and Northern Affairs:* Darren Praznik. *Housing and Urban Affairs:* Linda McIntosh.

Local Government. Rural Manitoba is organized into rural municipalities which vary widely in size. Some have only 4 townships (a township is 6 sq. miles), while the largest has 22 townships. The province has 106 rural municipalities, as well as 36 incorporated towns, 38 incorporated villages and 5 incorporated cities.

On 1 Jan. 1972, the cities and towns comprising the metropolitan area of Winnipeg were amalgamated to form the City of Winnipeg. A mayor and council are elected to a central government, but councillors also sit on 'community committees' which represent the areas or wards they serve. These committees are advised by non-elected residents of the area on provision of municipal services within the community committee jurisdiction. Taxing powers and overall budgeting rest with the central council. The mayor is elected at the same time as the councillors in a city-wide vote. Revisions to the City of Winnipeg Act came into effect with the municipal elections held in Oct. 1977.

Since Jan. 1945, 17 Local Government Districts have been formed in the less densely populated areas of the province. They are administered by a provincially appointed person, who acts on the advice of locally elected councils.

In the extreme north, many communities have locally elected councils, while others are administered directly by the Department of Northern Affairs. This department provides most of the funding in all these northern settlements.

FINANCE. Provincial revenue and expenditure (current account) for fiscal years ending 31 March (in Canadian $1m.):

	1990–91	*1991–92*	*1992–93*	*1993–94*	*1994–95* [1]
Revenue	4,798	4,927	5,095	4,909	5,050
Expenditure	5,081	5,275	5,425	5,107	5,032

[1] Forecast.

ENERGY AND NATURAL RESOURCES

Electricity. The total generating capacity of Manitoba's power stations is 5·34 mw.

The Manitoba Hydro system, owned by the province, provides most of this power, while the city-owned Winnipeg Hydro provides about 190,000 kw. The systems have over 482,000 customers and hydro consumption was 18·1m. kwh. in 1993.

Oil. Crude oil production in 1993 was valued at $77·5m.

Minerals. Total value of mineral production in 1993 was about $912m. Principal minerals mined are nickel, zinc, copper, and small quantities of gold and silver.

Agriculture. Rich farmland is the main primary resource, although the area in farms is only about 14% of the total land area. In 1993 the total value of agricultural production was (estimated) $2,200m., with $1,000m. from crops, $855m. from livestock.

Forestry. About 51% of the land area is wooded, of which 334,460 sq. km is productive forest land. Total sales of wood-using industries (1993, estimate) $139m.

Fur Trade. Value of fur production to the trapper was $2·6m. in 1993.

Fisheries. From 57,000 sq. km of rivers and lakes fisheries production was about $20·5m. in 1992–93. Whitefish, sauger, pickeral and pike are the principal varieties of fish caught.

INDUSTRY AND TRADE

Industry. Manufacturing, the largest industry in the province, encompasses almost every major industrial activity in Canada. Estimated exports in 1993 totalled $6,438m. Manufacturing employed about 55,000 persons in 1992. Due to the agricultural base of the province, the food and beverage group of industries is by far the largest, valued at $1,560m. in 1993. The next largest segments are transportation equipment, $823m., electric, $489m. and primary metals, $505m.

Trade. Products grown and manufactured in Manitoba find ready markets in other parts of Canada, in the USA, particularly the upper midwest region, and in other countries. Export shipments to foreign countries from Manitoba in 1993 were valued at an estimated $3,454m. Of total exports, an estimated $1·8m. were processed and manufactured goods in 1992.

Tourism. In 1993, non-Manitoban tourists numbered an estimated 1·7m. All tourists including Manitobans contributed over $1,000m. to the economy.

COMMUNICATIONS

Roads. Highways and provincial roads totalled over 18,000 km on 1 Jan. 1994.

Railways. As of Sept. 1993 the province had over 4,470 km of track, not including industrial track, yards and sidings.

Civil Aviation. A total of 91 licensed commercial air services operate from bases in Manitoba, as well as 5 regularly scheduled major national and international airlines.

Telecommunications. The Manitoba Telephone System provided network access to over 735,000 customers at 31 Dec. 1993.

EDUCATION. Education is controlled through locally elected school divisions. There were an estimated 209,000 children enrolled in the province's elementary, secondary, private and home schools in the 1993–94 school year. Manitoba has 3 universities with an enrolment of about 35,500 for the 1994–95 year; the University of Manitoba, founded in 1877, in Winnipeg, the University of Winnipeg, and Brandon University. Expenditure (estimate) on education in the 1994–95 fiscal year was $990m.

Three community colleges, in Brandon, The Pas and Winnipeg, offer 2-year diploma courses in a number of fields, as well as specialized training in many trades. They also give a large number and variety of shorter courses, both at their campuses and in many communities throughout the province.

Further Reading

General Information: Inquiries may be addressed to the Information Services Branch, Room 29, Legislative Building, Winnipeg, R3C OV8.

The Department of Agriculture publishes: *Year Book of Manitoba Agriculture*
Manitoba Statistical Review. Manitoba Bureau of Statistics, Quarterly
Jackson, J. A., *The Centennial History of Manitoba.* Toronto, 1970
Morton, W. L., *Manitoba: A History.* Univ. of Toronto Press, 1967

NEW BRUNSWICK

KEY HISTORICAL EVENTS. Touched by Jacques Cartier in 1534, New Brunswick was first explored by Samuel de Champlain in 1604. It was ceded by the French in the Treaty of Utrecht in 1713 and became a permanent British possession in 1763. It was separated from Nova Scotia and became a province in June 1784, as a result of the great influx of United Empire Loyalists. Responsible government came into being in 1848, and consisted of an executive council, a legislative council (later abolished) and a House of Assembly.

TERRITORY AND POPULATION. The area of the province is 28,354 sq. miles (73,440 sq. km), of which 27,834 sq. miles (72.090 sq. km) are land area. The population (census 1991) was 723,900. Estimate (1995) 760,300. Of the individuals identifying a single ethnic origin (at the 1991 census), 33% were British and 32·8% French. Other significant ethnic groups were German, Dutch and Scandinavian. Among those who provided a multiple response 9·2% were of British and French descent and 5·4% British and other. In 1991 there were 11,835 Native People or Native People and other. Census 1991 population of urban centres: Saint John, 90,457; Moncton, 80,744; Fredericton (capital), 45,364; Bathurst, 15,890; Edmundston, 12,007; Campbellton, 10,173. The official languages are English and French.

Vital statistics *see* CANADA: Territory and Population.

CLIMATE. A cool temperate climate, with rain at all seasons but temperatures modified by the influence of the Gulf Stream. Saint John. Jan. 18°F (–7·8°C), July 62°F (16·7°C). Annual rainfall 57" (1,444·4 mm).

CONSTITUTION AND GOVERNMENT. The government is vested in a Lieut.-Governor and a Legislative Assembly of 55 members each of whom is individually elected to represent the voters in one constituency or riding. A simultaneous translation system is used in the Assembly. Any Canadian subject of full age and 6 months' residence is entitled to vote. The last provincial election was held on 11 Sept. 1995. As of Dec. 1995, the Legislative Assembly consists of 48 Liberals, 6 Progressive Conservatives, and 1 from the New Democratic Party. The province has 10 members in the Canadian Senate and 10 members in the federal House of Commons.

Lieut.-Governor: Hon. Margaret McCain (appointed June 1994).

Flag: A banner of the Arms, *i.e.*, yellow charged with a black heraldic ship on wavy lines of blue and white; across the top a red band with a gold lion.

The members of the Liberal government are as follows (Dec. 1995):

Premier: Hon. Francis J. McKenna.

Executive Council: Hon. Raymond Frenette. *Justice, Attorney General:* Hon. Paul Duffie. *Finance:* Hon. Edmond Blanchard. *Supply and Services:* Hon. Bruce Smith. *Transportation:* Hon. Sheldon Lee. *Natural Resources and Energy:* Hon. Alan Graham. *Agriculture:* Hon. Doug Tyler. *Health and Community Services:* Hon. Russell King, MD. *Human Resources Development:* Hon. Marcelle Mersereau. *Advanced Education and Labour:* Hon. Roland MacIntyre. *Education:* Hon. James Lockyer. *Municipalities, Culture and Housing:* Hon. Ann Breault. *Environment:*

Hon. Vaughn Blaney. *Economic Development and Tourism:* Hon. Camille Thériault. *Fisheries and Aquaculture:* Hon. Bernard Theriault. *Solicitor General:* Hon. Jane Barry. *Information Highway Secretariat:* Hon. Camille Thériault.

Local Government. Under the reforms introduced in 1967 the province has assumed complete administrative and financial responsibility for education, health, welfare and administration of justice. Local government is now restricted to provision of services of a strictly local nature. Under the new municipal structure, units include existing and new cities, towns and villages. Counties have disappeared as municipal units. Areas with limited populations have become local service districts. The former local improvement districts have become towns, villages or local service districts depending on their size.

FINANCE. The ordinary budget (in Canadian $1m.) is shown as follows (financial years ended 31 March):

	1991	*1992*	*1993*	*1994*
Gross revenue	3,701·9	3,762·3	3,994·3	3,982·4
Gross expenditure	3,723·8	3,947·6	4,266·0	4,273·1

Funded debt and capital loans outstanding (exclusive of Treasury Bills) as of 31 March 1994 was $5,887·6m. Sinking funds held by the province at 31 March 1994, $1,719m. The ordinary budget excludes capital spending.

ENERGY AND NATURAL RESOURCES

Electricity. Hydro-electric, thermal and nuclear generating stations of NB Power had an installed capacity of 4,116 MW at 31 March 1995, consisting of 15 generating stations. The Mactaquac hydroelectric development near Fredericton has a name plate capacity of 672 MW. The largest thermal generating station, Coleson Cove, near Saint John, has 1,006 MW of installed capacity. Atlantic Canada's first nuclear generating station, a 635 MW plant on a promontory in the Bay of Fundy, near Saint John, went into operation in 1983. New Brunswick is electrically interconnected with utilities in neighbouring provinces of Quebec, Nova Scotia and Prince Edward Island, as well as the New England States of the USA. The sale of out-of-province power accounted for 17·4% of revenue in 1994–95. Total revenue amounted to $942·3m.

Minerals. In 1994, approximately 18 different metals, minerals and commodities were produced. These included lead, zinc, copper, cadmium, bismuth, gold, silver, antimony, potash, salt, lime, stone, gas, coal, sand and gravel, clay, peat and marl. The total value of minerals produced in 1994 reached $813·7m. The top 3 contributors to mineral production are zinc, silver and lead, accounting for 57·7% of total value in 1994. In Canada in 1994, New Brunswick ranked first in the production of bismuth, zinc, lead and silver, second in antimony, and fifth in the production of copper. Brunswick Mining operates 2 zinc-lead-copper mines, Brunswick and Heath Steele, which together represent over one-half of total Provincial mining production. Potash production continues at 2 mines near Sussex. Not all of the province's minerals have been explored sufficiently and research continues. The Geological Survey of Canada and the New Brunswick Department of Natural Resources and Energy plan to commit $6·8m. over 5 years in exploration of the eastern part of the Province.

Agriculture. The total area under crops is estimated at 122,247 ha. Farms numbered 3,252 and averaged 116 ha each (census 1991). Potatoes account for 27·9% of total farm cash income. Mixed farming is common throughout the province. Dairy farming is centred around the larger urban areas, and is located mainly along the Saint John River Valley and in the south-eastern sections of the province. Income from dairy products provides 20·1% of farm cash income. New Brunswick is self-sufficient in fluid milk and supplies a processing industry. For particulars of agricultural production and livestock, *see* CANADA: Agriculture. Farm cash receipts in 1994 were $292·6m.

Forestry. New Brunswick contains some 61,000 sq. km of productive forest lands. The value of manufacturing shipments for the wood related industries in 1994 was \$2,381·5m., representing 34·3% of total shipments in the province. The paper and allied industry group is the largest component of the industry contributing 66·9% of forestry output. In 1994 wood industries employed about 14,713 people for all aspects of the forest industry, including harvesting, processing and transportation. Practically all forest products are exported from the province's numerous ports and harbours near which many of the mills are located or sent by road or rail to the USA.

Fisheries. Commercial fishing is one of the most important primary industries of the province, in 1994 employing 8,891. Nearly 50 commercial species of fish and shellfish are landed, including scallop, shrimp, crab, herring and cod. Landings in 1994 (125,651 tonnes) amounted to \$143·6m. In 1995 there were 137 fish processing plants employing an average of 7,200 people. In 1994 molluscs and crustaceans ranked first with a value of \$126·7m., 88·2% of the total landed value; pelagic fish second, 10·1%, and groundfish third, 1·2%. Exports (1994) \$392·7m., mainly to the USA and Japan.

INDUSTRY. In 1995 there were 1,472 manufacturing and processing establishments, employing on average 42,200 persons. New Brunswick's location, with deepwater harbours open throughout the year and container facilities at Saint John, makes it ideal for exporting. Industries include food and beverages, paper and allied industries, timber products. Nearly 20% of the industrial labour force work in Saint John.

TOURISM. Tourism is one of the leading contributors to the economy. In 1994, tourism revenues reached an all time high of \$676m.

COMMUNICATIONS

Roads. There are 1,541·9 km of arterial highways and 2,381·7 km of collector roads, all hard-surfaced, and 12,279·9 km of local roads provide access to most areas. The main highway system, including 596·4 km of the Trans-Canada Highway, links the province with the principal roads in Quebec, Nova Scotia, and Prince Edward Island, as well as the Interstate Highway System in the eastern seaboard states of the USA. Passenger vehicles, 31 March 1995, numbered 328,112; commercial vehicles, 181,506; motor cycles, 9,963.

Railways. New Brunswick is served by main lines of both Canadian Pacific and Canadian National railways.

Telecommunications. In 1993 the New Brunswick Telephone Co. Ltd had 480,314 access lines in service. The province is served by 32 radio stations. 18 are privately owned and 3 owned by the Canadian Broadcasting Corporation, 2 are university stations and 6 community stations. 11 stations broadcast in French, 3 are bilingual and the CBC International Service broadcasts in several languages from its station at Sackville. The province is served by 6 television stations, 2 of which broadcast in French.

Press. New Brunswick had (1995) 4 daily newspapers, 1 in French, and 17 weekly newspapers, 3 in French and 3 bilingual.

EDUCATION. Public education is free and non-sectarian. There are 4 universities. The University of New Brunswick at Fredericton (founded 13 Dec. 1785 by the Loyalists, elevated to university status in 1823, reorganized as the University of New Brunswick in 1859) had 7,787 full-time students at the Fredericton campus and 1,972 full-time students at the Saint John campus (1994–95); Mount Allison University at Sackville had 2,235 full-time students; the Université de Moncton at Moncton, 4,395 full-time students, with 481 and 594 full-time students respectively at its satellite campuses at Shippegan and Edmundston; St Thomas University at Fredericton, 1,968 full-time students.

There were, in Sept. 1994, 136,596 students (including kindergarten) and 8,198 full-time equivalent/professional educational staff in the province's 398 schools. There are 18 school boards.

Further Reading

Industrial Information: Dept. of Economic Development and Tourism, Fredericton. *Economic Information:* Dept. of Finance, New Brunswick Statistics Agency, Fredericton. *General Information:* Communications New Brunswick, Fredericton.

Thompson, C., *New Brunswick Inside Out*. Ottawa, 1977
Trueman, S., *The Fascinating World of New Brunswick*. Fredericton, 1973

NEWFOUNDLAND AND LABRADOR

KEY HISTORICAL EVENTS. Archaeological finds at L'Anse-au-Meadow in northern Newfoundland show that the Vikings had established a colony there at about A.D. 1000. This site is the only known Viking colony in North America. Newfoundland was discovered by John Cabot 24 June 1497, and was soon frequented in the summer months by the Portuguese, Spanish and French for its fisheries. It was formally occupied in Aug. 1583 by Sir Humphrey Gilbert on behalf of the English Crown, but various attempts to colonize the island remained unsuccessful. Although British sovereignty was recognized in 1713 by the Treaty of Utrecht, disputes over fishing rights with the French were not finally settled till 1904. By the Anglo-French Convention of 1904, France renounced her exclusive fishing rights along part of the coast, granted under the Treaty of Utrecht, but retained sovereignty of the offshore islands of St Pierre and Miquelon.

TERRITORY AND POPULATION. Area, 143,501 sq. miles (371,690 sq. km) of which freshwater, 13,139 sq. miles (34,030 sq. km). In March 1927 the Privy Council decided the boundary between Canada and Newfoundland in Labrador. This area, now part of the Province of Newfoundland and Labrador, is 102,699 sq. miles. The coastline is extremely irregular. Bays, fiords and inlets are numerous and there are many good harbours with deep water close to shore. The coast is rugged with bold rocky cliffs from 200 to 400 ft high; in the Bay of Islands some of the islands rise 500 ft, with the adjacent shore 1,000 ft above tide level. The interior is a plateau of moderate elevation and the chief relief features trend north-east and south-west. Long Range, the most notable of these, begins at Cape Ray and extends north-east for 200 miles, the highest peak reaching 2,673 ft. Approximately one-third of the area is covered by water. Grand Lake, the largest body of water, has an area of about 200 sq. miles. The principal rivers flow towards the north-east. On the borders of the lakes and water-courses good land is generally found, particularly in the valleys of the Terra Nova River, the Gander River, the Exploits River and the Humber River, which are also heavily timbered.

Census population, 1991, was 568,474.

The capital of Newfoundland is the City of St John's (1991 population, 171,859, metropolitan area). The other cities are Mt Pearl (23,689), Corner Brook (22,410); important towns are Conception Bay South (17,590), Grand Falls-Windsor (14,693), Gander (10,339), Labrador City (9,061), Happy Valley–Goose Bay (8,610), Stephenville (7,621), Marystown (6,739), Channel-Port aux Basques (5,644), Bay Roberts (5,474), Carbonear (5,259).

Vital statistics *see* CANADA: Territory and Population.

CLIMATE. The cool temperate climate is marked by heavy precipitation, distributed evenly over the year, a cool summer and frequent fogs in spring. St. John's. Jan. –4°C, July 15·8°C. Annual rainfall 1,240 mm.

CONSTITUTION AND GOVERNMENT. Until 1832 Newfoundland was ruled by the Governor under instructions of the Colonial Office. In that year a Legislature was brought into existence, but the Governor and his Executive Council were not responsible to it. Under the constitution of 1855, which lasted until its suspension in 1934, the government was administered by the Governor appointed by the Crown with an Executive Council responsible to the House of Assembly of 27 elected members and a Legislative Council of 24 members nominated for life by the Governor in Council. Women were enfranchised in 1925. At the Imperial Conference of 1917 Newfoundland was constituted as a Dominion.

In 1933 the financial situation had become so critical that the Government of Newfoundland asked the Government of the UK to appoint a Royal Commission to investigate conditions. On the strength of their recommendations, the parliamentary form of government was suspended and Government by Commission was inaugurated on 16 Feb. 1934.

A National Convention, elected in 1946, made, in 1948, recommendations to H.M. Government in Great Britain as to the possible forms of future government to be submitted to the people at a national referendum. Two referenda were held. In the first referendum (June 1948) the three forms of government submitted to the people were: Commission of government for 5 years, confederation with Canada and responsible government as it existed in 1933. No one form of government received a clear majority of the votes polled, and commission of government, receiving the fewest votes, was eliminated. In the second referendum (July 1948) confederation with Canada received 78,408 and responsible government 71,464 votes.

In the Canadian Senate on 18 Feb. 1949 Royal assent was given to the terms of union of Newfoundland and Labrador with Canada, and on 23 March 1949, in the House of Lords, London, Royal assent was given to an amendment to the British North America Act made necessary by the inclusion of Newfoundland and Labrador as the tenth Province of Canada.

Under the terms of union of Newfoundland and Labrador with Canada, which was signed at Ottawa on 11 Dec. 1948, the constitution of the Legislature of Newfoundland and Labrador as it existed immediately prior to 16 Feb. 1934 shall, subject to the terms of the British North America Acts, 1867 to 1946, continue as the constitution of the Legislature of the Province of Newfoundland and Labrador until altered under the authority of the said Acts.

The franchise was in 1965 extended to all male and female residents who have attained the age of 19 years and are otherwise qualified as electors.

The House of Assembly (Amendment) Act, 1979, established 52 electoral districts and 52 members of the Legislature.

Elections were held on 3 May 1993. In Nov. 1994 there were 35 Liberals, 16 Progressive-Conservatives and 1 New Democrat.

The province is represented by 6 members in the Senate and by 7 members in the House of Commons of Canada.

Lieut.-Governor: Hon. Frederick William Russell (assumed office 5 Nov. 1991).

Flag: White, in the hoist 4 solid blue triangles; in the fly 2 red triangles voided white, and between them a yellow tongue bordered in red.

The Liberal Executive Council was, in Nov. 1995, composed as follows:

Premier: Hon. Clyde Kirby Wells.

Education and Training: Hon. Christopher Decker. *Employment and Labour Relations:* Hon. Tom Murphy. *Environment:* Hon. Kevin Aylward. *Finance, President of Treasury Board:* Hon. Paul Dicks. *Fisheries, Food and Agriculture:* Hon. Dr Bud Hulan. *Health:* Hon. Lloyd Matthews. *Industry, Trade and Technology:* Hon. Charles Furey. *Justice:* Hon. Edward Roberts. *Municipal and Provincial Affairs:* Hon. Arthur Reid. *Natural Resources:* Hon. Dr Rex Gibbons. *Social Services:* Hon. Kay Young. *Tourism, Culture and Recreation:* Hon. Roger Grimes. *Works, Services and Transportation:* Hon. John Efford.

FINANCE. Budget in Canadian $1,000 for fiscal years ended 31 March:

Current account:

	1992–93	*1993–94*	*1994–95* [1]	*1995–96* [2]
Gross revenue	3,044,401	3,071,526	3,243,602	3,398,268
Gross expenditure	3,124,001	3,125,222	3,218,471	3,270,412

[1] Revised estimates. [2] Estimates.

Capital account:

	1992–93	*1993–94*	*1994–95* [1]	*1991–92* [2]
Gross revenue	149,215	86,920	149,841	146,892
Gross expenditure	330,664	238,474	311,275	272,804

[1] Revised estimates. [2] Estimates.

Public debenture debt as at 31 March 1995 (estimate) was $5,623m.; sinking fund, $1,538m.

ENERGY AND NATURAL RESOURCES

Electricity. The electrical energy requirements of the province are met mainly by hydro-electric power, with petroleum fuels being utilized to provide the balance. The total amount of energy generated in the province in 1993 was 40,849,949 MWh, of which 96% was derived from hydro-electric facilities. The greater part of the energy produced in 1993 came from Churchill Falls, of which 29,942,214 MWh was sold to Hydro-Quebec under the terms of a long-term contract. Energy consumed in the province during 1993 totalled 10,907,775 MWh, with 9,251,443 MWh, or 85%, coming from hydro-electric facilities.

At Dec. 1994 total electrical generating capacity in the province was 7,343 MW, with hydro-electric plants accounting for 6,601 MW, or 90%. It is estimated that potential additional hydro-electric generating capacity of up to 4·5m. kW can be developed at various sites in Labrador.

Oil. Since 1965, 140 wells have been drilled on the Continental Margin of the Province. Only the Hibernia discovery had commercial capability with production starting in the early 1990's. In Sept. 1990 the governments of Canada and Newfoundland and a development consortium signed an agreement to start developing the Hibernia discovery from Oct. 1990.

Minerals. The mineral resources are vast but only partially documented. Large deposits of iron ore, with an ore reserve of over 5,000m. tons at Labrador City, Wabush City and in the Knob Lake area are supplying approximately half of Canada's production. Other large deposits of iron ore are known to exist in the Julienne Lake area. There are a variety of other minerals being produced in more limited amounts. The Central Mineral Belt, which extends from the Smallwood Reservoir to the Atlantic coast near Makkovik, holds uranium, copper, beryllium and molybdenite potential.

There is a gold mine at Hope Brook on the south coast east of Port aux Basques.

In 1994, a rich nickel, copper and cobalt discovery was made at Voisey's Bay, Labrador, with defined reserves of 31·7m. tonnes. Production in 1994 (preliminary): Iron ore, 20·9m. tonnes ($747,038,000); gold, 2,799,360 grammes ($47,219,000); sand and gravel, 3,128,000 tonnes ($14,202,000); stone, ($5,939,000); cement, 56,882 tonnes ($7,395,000); dolomite, 267,145 tonnes ($2,885,000).

Agriculture. The estimated value of agricultural products sold, including livestock, 1994, was $62·2m.

Forestry. The forestry economy in the province is mainly dependent on the operation of 3 newsprint mills. In 1994 the gross value of newsprint exported from these 3 mills totalled $472m. Lumber mills and saw-log operations produced 57m. flat bd ft in 1994–95.

Fisheries. The principal fish landings are cod, flounder, redfish, Queen crabs, lobster, salmon and herring. In 1994 (preliminary) a yearly average of some 2,800 persons were employed by the fish-processing industry and there were 22,045 licensed full-, part-time and casual fishermen engaged in harvesting operations. 207 processing operations were licensed in 1994. The production of fresh and frozen fish products was $490m. in 1994.

The total catch in 1993 was 245,942 tonnes valued at $197,125,873, including (in tonnes): Cod, 37,177 ($24,771,725); flounders and soles, 22,128 ($8,863,274); herring, 21,355 ($3,012,684); redfish, 26,284 ($7,253,497); capelin, 48,469 ($19,298,947); crab, 23,160 ($32,058,472); other, 41,612 ($31,499,911).

INDUSTRY. The total value of manufacturing shipments in 1993 was $1,324m. This consists largely of first-stage processing of primary resource products with two of the largest components being paper and fish products.

TRADE UNIONS. There were 35 unions in 1993 representing 75,627 members of international and national unions and government employee associations.

COMMUNICATIONS

Roads. In 1993 there were 8,895 km, of which 6,356 were paved.

Railways. In 1993 the Quebec North Shore and Labrador Railway operated 576 km of standard-gauge main railway track. The route runs from Sept-Iles, Quebec, to Shefferville, Quebec, with a branch at Ross Bay Junction to Wabush, Labrador. In 1993, 18m. tonnes of freight were carried.

Civil Aviation. The province is linked to the rest of Canada by regular air services provided by Air Canada, Canadian International Airways, Quebecair and a number of smaller air carriers.

Shipping. At 21 Dec. 1995 there were 1,624 ships on register in Newfoundland. In 1993 Marine Atlantic provided a freight and passenger service all year round to the south of the island and during the ice-free season as far north as Nain. There is a year-round ferry from Port-aux-Basques to North Sydney, Nova Scotia, and seasonal ferries connect Argentia with North Sydney, and Lewisporte with Goosebay, Labrador.

Telecommunications. There were 430 post offices in 1995. Telephone access lines numbered 262,856 in 1993 (193,987 private). There were 3,384 public pay phones.

EDUCATION. The number of schools in 1994–95 was 479. The enrolment was 114,010; full-time teachers numbered 7,331. The Memorial University, offering courses in arts, science, engineering, education, nursing and medicine, had 17,226 full- and part-time students in 1994 (calendar year). Total expenditure for education by the Government in 1995–96 (estimate) was $716m.

Further Reading

Horwood, H., *Newfoundland.* Toronto, 1969
Perlin, A. B., *The Story of Newfoundland, 1497–1959.* St John's, 1959
Taylor, T. G., *Newfoundland: A Study of Settlement.* Toronto, 1946

Statistical office: Newfoundland Statistics Agency, POB 8700, St. John's, A1B 4J6.

NOVA SCOTIA

KEY HISTORICAL EVENTS. The first permanent settlement was made by the French early in the 17th century, and the province was called Acadia until finally ceded to the British by the Treaty of Utrecht in 1713.

TERRITORY AND POPULATION. The area of the province is 21,425 sq. miles (55,000 sq. km), of which 20,401 sq. miles are land area, 1,024 sq. miles water area. The population (census 1991) was 899,942. Estimate (1995) 938,205.

Population of the principal cities and towns (census 1991): Halifax, 114,455; Dartmouth, 67,798; Sydney, 26,063; Glace Bay, 19,501; Truro, 11,683; Bedford, 11,618; New Glasgow, 9,905; Amherst, 9,742; Yarmouth, 7,781; New Waterford, 7,695; Sydney Mines, 7,551; North Sydney, 7,260.

Vital statistics, *see* CANADA: Territory and Population.

CLIMATE. A cool temperate climate, with rainfall occurring evenly over the year. The Gulf Stream moderates the temperatures in winter so that ports remain ice-free. Halifax. Jan. 23·7°F (–4·6°C), July 63·5°F (17·5°C). Annual rainfall 54" (1,371 mm).

CONSTITUTION AND GOVERNMENT. Under the British North America Act of 1867 the legislature of Nova Scotia may exclusively make laws in relation to local matters, including direct taxation within the province, education and the administration of justice. The legislature of Nova Scotia consists of a Lieut.-Governor, appointed and paid by the federal government, and holding office for 5 years, and a House of Assembly of 52 members, chosen by popular vote at least every 5 years. The province is represented in the Canadian Senate by 11 members, and in the House of Commons by 11.

The franchise and eligibility to the legislature are granted to every person, male or female, if of age (19 years), a British subject or Canadian citizen, and a resident in the province for 1 year and 2 months before the date of the writ of election in the county or electoral district of which the polling district forms part, and if not by law otherwise disqualified. State of parties in Sept. 1995: 40 Liberals, 9 Progressive Conservatives, 3 New Democrats.

Lieut.-Governor: Hon. John James Kinley.

Flag: A banner of the Arms, *i.e.*, white with a blue diagonal cross, bearing in the centre the royal shield of Scotland.

The members of the Liberal Ministry were as follows in March 1995:

Premier, President of the Executive Council, Minister of Intergovernmental Affairs, Co-Chair Round Table on Environment and Economy, Minister responsible for Aboriginal Affairs: Hon. John P. Savage, MD.

Deputy Premier, Deputy President of the Executive Council, Attorney-General and Minister of Justice, Minister responsible for the Administration of the Human Rights Act, Minister in charge of the Regulations Act: Hon. J. William Gillis. *Minister of Finance, Chair of the Priorities and Planning Committee, Minister responsible for the Nova Scotia Gaming Corporation and for the Sydney Steel Corporation Act:* Hon. J. Bernard Boudreau, QC. *Minister of Education and Culture:* Hon. John MacEachern. *Minister of Health:* Hon. Ronald D. Stewart, QC, MD. *Minister of Community Services, Chairman of the Senior Citizens Secretariat, Minister responsible for the Disabled Persons Commission Act:* Hon. James A. Smith, MD. *Minister of Transportation and Communications:* Hon. Richard W. Mann. *Minister of Municipal Affairs, Minister in charge of the Administration of the Heritage Property Act, Minister responsible for Halifax Harbour Clean Up Incorporated:* Hon. Sandra L. Jolly. *Minister of Natural Resources, Minister responsible for the Tidal Power Corporation Act:* Hon. Donald R. Downe. *Minister of the Environment, Minister responsible for the Emergency Measures Act, Co-Chair of the Round Table on Environment and Economy:* Hon. F. Wayne Adams. *Minister of Agriculture and Marketing, Minister responsible for Acadian Affairs:* Hon. Wayne J. Gaudet. *Minister responsible for the Nova Scotia Economic Renewal Agency, including Tourism Nova Scotia and the Nova Scotia Marketing Agency, for the Administration of the Research Foundation Corporation Act, for the Voluntary Planning Act and for the Administration of the Maritime Economic Co-operation Act, Chair of the Trade Development Authority:* Hon. Robert S. Harrison. *Minister of Housing and Consumer Affairs, Minister in charge of the Residential Tenancies Act, Minister responsible for the Housing Development Corporation Act, for the Nova Scotia Gaming Control Commission, for the Adminstration of the Liquor Control Act, for the Administration of the Advisory Council on the Status of Women Act and for the Women's Directorate:* Hon. Eleanor E. Norrie. *Minister of Labour, Minister responsible for the Workers' Compensation Act:* Hon. Guy A. C. Brown. *Minister of Fisheries:* Hon. James A. Barkhouse. *Minister of Human Resources, Minister responsible for the Nova Scotia Sport and Recreation Commission, for the Nova Scotia Boxing Authority and for the Administration of the Youth Secretariat Act:* Hon. Jay F. Abbass. *Minister of Supply and Services, Minister responsible for the Communications and Information Act:* Hon. Gerald J. O'Malley.

Local Government. In 1995 the new Cape Breton Regional Municpality was formed to amalgamate the former City of Sydney, the rural municipality of Cape Breton and 6 towns within the county. On 1 April 1996 a new Regional Municipality of Halifax incorporated the cities of Halifax and Dartmouth, the town of Bedford and the rural municipality of Halifax County. The other main divisions of the province for governmental purposes are 32 towns and 22 rural municipalities, each governed by a council and a mayor or warden. The cities have independent charters, and the various towns take their powers from and are limited by The Towns Act, and the various municipalities take their powers from and are limited by The Municipal Act as revised in 1967. The majority of municipalities comprise 1 county, but 6 counties are divided into 2 municipalities each. In no case do the boundaries of any municipality overlap county lines. The 18 counties as such have no administrative function.

Any incorporated town (of which there are 32) that lies within the boundaries of a municipality is excluded from any jurisdiction by the municipal council and has its own government.

FINANCE. Revenue is derived from provincial sources, payments from the federal government under the Federal-Provincial Fiscal Arrangements and Established Programs Financing Act. Recoveries consist generally of amounts received under various federal cost-shared programmes. Main sources of provincial revenues include income and sales taxes.

Revenue, expenditure and debt (in Canadian $1m.) for fiscal years ending 31 March:

	1991	*1992*	*1993*	*1994*	*1995* [1]
Budgetary Transactions					
Current Expenditure	3,698·9	3,852·4	3,981·9	3,890·9	3,933·8
Current Revenues and Recoveries	3,553·1	3,530·5	3,510·5	3,547·7	3,636·3
Operating Deficit (Surplus)	145·8	321·9	471·4	343·2	297·5
Sinking Fund Instalments and Serial Retirements	99·9	108·1	109·2	182·3	182·2
Net Capital Expenditures	254·4	236·1	297·7	326·1	302·1
Net Budgetary Transactions	500·1	666·1	878·3	851·6	781·9
Non-Budgetary Transactions					
Capital Expenditures	1·0	1·9	2·8	2·0	2·8
Net Increase (Decrease) in Advances and Investments	38·8	(10·8)	(95·1)	(19·4)	30·1
Proceeds from Sale of NSPC [2]	0·0	0·0	(192·3)	0·0	0·0
Net Other Transactions	(22·5)	(29·3)	22·9	(42·9)	(11·1)
Non-Budgetary Transactions	17·3	38·2	(261·7)	(60·3)	21·7
	517·4	704·3	616·6	791·3	803·6

[1] Estimate. [2] Nova Scotia Power Corporation.

Banking and Finance. In the fourth quarter of 1995 total deposits with chartered banks totalled $7,525m.

NATURAL RESOURCES

Minerals. Principal minerals in 1994 were: Coal, 3·5m. tonnes, valued at $216m.; gypsum, 6·4m. tonnes, valued at $62·4m.; sand and gravel, 4·4m. tonnes, valued at $19·2m. Total value of mineral production in 1994 was about $610m.

Agriculture. Dairying, poultry and egg production, livestock and fruit growing are the most important branches. Farm cash receipts for 1994 were estimated at $317·3m., with an additional $4·3m. going to persons on farms as income in kind.

Cash receipts from sale of dairy products were $85·1m., with total milk and cream sales of 164,059,000 litres.

The production of poultry meat in 1994 was 26,426 tonnes, of which 23,013 tonnes were chickens and 3,413 tonnes were turkeys. Egg production was 17·9m. dozen.

The main 1994 fruit crops were apples, 56,700 tonnes; blueberries, 13,742 tonnes; strawberries, 1,701 tonnes.

Forestry. The estimated forest area of Nova Scotia is 15,830 sq. miles (40,990 sq.

km), of which about 28% is owned by the province. The principal trees are spruce, balsam fir, hemlock, pine, larch, birch, oak, maple, poplar and ash. 4,211,218 cu. metres of round forest products were produced in 1993.

Fisheries. The fisheries of the province in 1994 had a landed value of $478m. of sea fish including scallop fishery, $105·8m., and lobster fishery, $167·7m. In 1994 there were 7,900 employees in the fish processing industry; the value of shipment of goods was $735m. in 1994.

INDUSTRY. The number of manufacturing establishments was 708 in 1992; the number of employees was 37,168; wages and salaries, $1,103·7m. The value of shipments in 1994 was $5,695m., and the leading industries were food, paper and allied, and beverage industries.

TRADE UNIONS. Total union membership in 1993 was 102,852 belonging to 81 unions comprised of 644 individual locals. The largest union membership was in the service sector followed by public administration and defence.

COMMUNICATIONS

Roads. In 1993 there were 26,091 km of highways; paved included 167 km freeway, 2,802 km arterial and 5,769 km local. 12,186 km of highway are unpaved.

Railways. The province is covered with a network of 705 km of mainline track. In 1991 it carried 21·6m. tonnes of freight.

Civil Aviation. There is direct air service to all major Canadian points and international scheduled service to Boston, New York, Bermuda, London, Glasgow and Amsterdam. There are winter charter services to Florida and the Caribbean.

Shipping. Ferry services connect Nova Scotia with Newfoundland, Prince Edward Island, New Brunswick and Maine. Direct service by container vessels is provided from the Port of Halifax to ports in the USA (east and west coast), Europe, Asia, Australia/New Zealand and the Caribbean.

SOCIAL INSTITUTIONS

Justice. The Supreme Court (Trial Division and Appeal Division) is the superior court of Nova Scotia and has original and appellate jurisdiction in all civil and criminal matters unless they have been specifically assigned to another court by Statute. An appeal from the Supreme Court, Appeal Division, is to the Supreme Court of Canada. The other courts in the Province are the Provincial Court, which hears criminal matters only, the Small Claims Court, which has limited monetary jurisdiction, Probate Court, County Court, which has jurisdiction in criminal matters as well as original jurisdiction over actions not exceeding $50,000, and Family Court. Young offenders are tried in the Family Court or the Provincial Court.

For the year ending 31 March 1992 there were 4,021 adult admissions to provincial custody; of these, 2,542 were sentenced.

Education. Public education in Nova Scotia is free, compulsory and undenominational through elementary and high school. Attendance is compulsory to the age of 16. There are 472 public schools, plus the Atlantic Provinces Resource Centres for the Hearing Handicapped and for the Visually Impaired; the Nova Scotia Youth Centres for young offenders in Shelburne and in Waterville; and the Nova Scotia Youth Training Centre in Truro for mentally handicapped children. The province has 12 degree-granting institutions, of which the largest is Dalhousie University in Halifax. The Nova Scotia Agricultural College is located at Truro. The Technical University of Nova Scotia at Halifax grants degrees in engineering and architecture. Through the Nova Scotia Community College, the Department of Education administers 19 college campuses, including 2 adult vocational training centres, 2 institutes of technology, a nautical institute, plus College de l'Acadie, the French component of the Nova Scotia Community College. There are also 7 teaching hospitals.

The Nova Scotia government offers financial support and organizational assistance to local school boards for provision of weekend and evening courses in academic and vocational subjects, and citizenship for new Canadians. It also provides local authorities with specialist support services to assist them in providing community workshops and it operates a correspondence study service for children and adults.

Total estimated expenditure on all levels of education for the year 1995–96 was $1,597·3m., of which 61% was borne by the provincial government. In 1995–96 there were 500 elementary-secondary schools, with 9,813 full-time teachers and 168,560 pupils.

Further Reading

Nova Scotia Fact Book. N.S. Department of Economic Development, Halifax, 1991
Nova Scotia Resource Atlas. N.S. Department of Economic Development, Halifax, 1986
Nova Scotia Statistical Review. N. S. Department of Economic Development, Halifax, 1993
Nova Scotia Facts at a Glance. N. S. Department of Economic Development, Halifax, 1993

Atlantic Provinces Economic Council. *The Atlantic Vision, 1990.* Halifax, 1979
Beck, M., *The Evolution of Municipal Government in Nova Scotia, 1749–1973.* 1973
McCreath, P. and Leefe, J., *History of Early Nova Scotia.* Halifax, 1982
Vaison, R., *Nova Scotia Past and Present: A Bibliography and Guide.* Halifax, 1976

Statistical office: Statistics Branch, Department of Economic Development, POB 519, Halifax, Nova Scotia, B3J 2R7.

ONTARIO

KEY HISTORICAL EVENTS. The French explorer Samuel de Champlain explored the Ottawa River from 1613. The area was governed by the French, first under a joint stock company and then as a royal province, from 1627 and was ceded to Great Britain in 1763. A constitutional act of 1791 created there the province of Upper Canada, largely to accommodate loyalists of English descent who had immigrated after the United States war of independence. Upper Canada entered the Confederation as Ontario in 1867.

TERRITORY AND POPULATION. The area is 412,580 sq. miles (1,068,580 sq. km), of which some 344,100 sq. miles (891,190 sq. km) are land area and some 68,480 sq. miles (177,390 sq. km) are lakes and fresh water rivers. The province extends 1,050 miles (1,690 km) from east to west and 1,075 miles (1,730 km) from north to south. It is bounded on the north by the Hudson and James Bays, on the east by Quebec, on the west by Manitoba, and on the south by the USA.

Estimated population in 1995 was 11·1m. Population of the principal cities (1991 census):

Toronto [1]	635,395	Brampton	234,445	Oakville	114,670
North York [1]	562,564	Windsor	191,435	Thunder Bay	113,746
Scarborough [1]	524,598	Kitchener	168,282	East York [1]	102,696
Mississauga	463,388	Markham	153,811	Cambridge	92,884
Hamilton	318,499	York [1]	140,525	Sudbury	92,772
Ottawa	313,987	Burlington	129,575	Guelph	87,976
Etobicoke [1]	309,993	Oshawa	129,344	Brantford	81,997
London	303,165	Saint Catherines	129,300	Sault Sainte Marie	81,476

[1] Municipality of metropolitan Toronto.

There are over 1m. French-speaking people and 0·24m. native Indians. An agreement with the Ontario government of Aug. 1991 recognized Indians' right to self-government.

Vital statistics, *see* CANADA: Territory and Population.

CLIMATE. A temperate continental climate, but conditions can be quite severe in winter, though proximity to the Great Lakes has a moderating influence on temperatures. Ottawa. Jan. –10·8°C, July 20·8°C. Annual rainfall 910·5 mm. Toronto. Jan. –4·5°C, July 22·1°C. Annual rainfall 818 mm.

CONSTITUTION AND GOVERNMENT. The provincial government is administered by a *Lieut.-Governor*, a cabinet and a single-chamber 130-member *Legislative Assembly* elected by a general franchise for a period of no longer than 5 years. The minimum voting age is 18 years.

At the elections on 8 June 1995 to the *Legislative Assembly*, the Progressive Conservative Party won 82 seats (20 in 1990), the Liberal Party, 30 (36), the New Democratic Party (PCP), 17 (74) and independents, 2. The PCP formed an Executive Council with Michael Harris as *Premier.*

Lieut.-Governor: Right Hon. Henry Jackman (b. 1932; appointed Dec. 1991).

Flag: The British Red Ensign with the shield of Ontario in the fly.

Local Government. Local government is divided into 2 branches, one covering municipal institutions and the other education.

Local government was restructured in 1968. There are 2 levels of municipal government in the southern, settled part of Ontario. The upper level consists of 26 counties plus 12 restructured regional municipalities including metropolitan Toronto. The local level comprises more than 600 cities, towns and townships. Cities in the traditional county system function independently of the county in which they lie, as do 4 towns and 1 township which have been separated for municipal purposes. There are no separated municipal units in regional governments.

Ontario's local municipalities are governed by councils elected by popular vote.

Lower tier municipal councils are composed of a head of council (mayor or reeve) and councillors. In the case of regional municipalities, one or more regional councillors represent the area municipalities on the regional council. Three regions, Niagara, Metro and Ottawa-Carleton, have their own directly elected upper level councils.

County councils are federations. A county council consists of at least 1 representative of each local municipality, generally the head of the local council. The head of the county council is the warden, who is elected by the council from among its own members.

A regional council consists of the heads of council of the local municipalities, as well as a varying number of regional councillors, who are elected on the basis of representation, either directly or indirectly.

No municipality may incur long-term debts over a reasonable level without the sanction of the tribunal created by the Provincial Legislature and known as the Ontario Municipal Board. Debenture obligations incurred by municipalities for utility undertakings are discharged out of revenues derived from the sale of utility services and do not fall upon the ratepayers.

Municipal councils have no jurisdiction for education beyond the collection of taxes for school purposes. Responsibility for providing, operating and maintaining school facilities, and for the supply of teachers, rests with elected local education authorities known as Boards of Education or School Boards. These Boards are now generally organized on a large city, county or regional basis.

Municipal institutions come under the jurisdiction of the Provincial Ministry of Municipal Affairs and Housing. One of the principal functions of the Ministry is to ensure municipalities have the legislative authority to respond to local needs and offer management and administrative support along with financial assistance to Ontario's 816 municipalities. Educational support and guidance at the provincial level is the responsibility of the Ministry of Education and Training, which deals with the training of teachers and the formulation of curriculum.

There are areas in the north where there is little or no settlement of population. Administration of such areas remains in the hands of the Provincial Government. Where there are municipalities in the north they are single lower tier, with the exception of the regional municipality of Sudbury.

FINANCE. Provincial revenue and expenditure (in $1m.) for years ending 31 March:

	1991–92	*1992–93*	*1993–94*	*1994–95*
Gross revenue	40,753	41,807	44,077	46,039
Gross expenditure	51,683	54,235	53,355	56,168

Gross revenue and expenditure figures include all non-budgetary transactions, *i.e.*, the lending and investment activity of the Government to Crown corporations, agencies and municipalities as well as the repayment of these loans or recovery of investments. Transactions on behalf of Ontario Hydro are excluded.

Personal income per capita, 1994, was $23,600.

ENERGY AND NATURAL RESOURCES

Electricity (1994). Ontario Hydro recorded for the calendar year an installed generating capacity of 34,432m. kW and a net energy output generated and purchased of 134,874m. kWh.

Minerals (1994). The total value of mine production was $4,866m. The top 10 commodities (in $1m.) were: Gold, 1,154; nickel, 947; copper, 698; cement, 289; sand and gravel, 350; zinc, 213; stone, 216; salt, 167; platinum group (data confidential); lime, 114. Direct employment in the mining industry was 17,450 in 1994.

Agriculture. In 1994, 3,314,500 ha were under field crops with total farm receipts of $2,345,311,000.

Forestry. According to the most recent inventory (1994) the total area of productive forest is 34·5m. ha, comprising: Softwoods, 22·7m. ha; hardwoods, 11·8m. ha. The growing stock equals 5,078,871 cu. metres.

INDUSTRY AND TRADE

Industry. Ontario is Canada's most highly industrialized province, with Gross Domestic Product (GDP) in 1994 at $302,482m., or 40·3% of the Canadian total. Manufacturing accounts for about 24·3% of Ontario GDP.

In 1994, the labour force was 5,707,000. Total labour income was $166,119m.

Leading manufacturing industries include: Motor vehicles and parts; office and industrial electrical equipment; food processing; chemicals; and steel.

Trade. In 1994 Ontario was responsible for about 51·2% ($115,731m.) of Canada's merchandise exports. Motor vehicles and parts accounted for about 41·7% of exports.

COMMUNICATIONS

Roads. There were, in 1994, 157,547 km of roads. Motor licences (on the road) numbered (1994) 8,141,379, of which 5,069,383 were passenger cars, 1,097,588 commercial vehicles, 28,330 buses, 1,342,951 trailers, 105,835 motor cycles and 391,847 snow vehicles.

Railways. The provincially-owned Ontario Northland Railway has about 926 km of track and the Algoma Central Railway 518 km. The Canadian National and Canadian Pacific Railways operate a total of about 10,991 km in Ontario. There is a metro and tramway network in Toronto.

Telecommunications (1994). Telephone service is provided by 30 independent systems and Bell Canada.

EDUCATION. There is a provincial system of publicly-financed elementary and secondary schools as well as private schools. In 1993–94 publicly-financed elementary and secondary schools had a total enrolment of 2,042,710 pupils.

There are 18 universities (Brock, Carleton, Dominicain, Guelph, Lakehead, Laurentian, McMaster, Nipissing, Ottawa, Queen's, Ryerson, Toronto, Trent, Waterloo, Western Ontario, Wilfred Laurier, Windsor and York) and 1 institute of equivalent status (Ontario College of Art) with full-time enrolment in 1993 of 230,857. All receive operating grants from the Ontario government. There are also 25 publicly-financed Colleges of Applied Arts and Technology (CAAT),with a full-time enrolment of 127,256 in 1993.

Expenditure by the Ontario government on education for 1993-94 was $9,683m.

Further Reading

Statistical Information: Annual publications of the Ontario Ministry of Finance include: *Ontario Statistics; Ontario Budget; Public Accounts; Financial Report.*

McDonald, D. C. (ed.) *The Government and Politics of Ontario.* 2nd ed. Toronto, 1980
Schull, J., *Ontario since 1867.* Toronto, 1978

PRINCE EDWARD ISLAND

KEY HISTORICAL EVENTS. The first recorded European visit was by Jacques Cartier in 1534, who named it Isle St-Jean. In 1719 it was settled by the French, but was taken from them by the English in 1758, annexed to Nova Scotia in 1763, and constituted a separate colony in 1769. Named Prince Edward Island in honour of Prince Edward, Duke of Kent, in 1799, it joined the Canadian Confederation on 1 July 1873.

TERRITORY AND POPULATION. The province lies in the Gulf of St Lawrence, and is separated from the mainland of New Brunswick and Nova Scotia by Northumberland Strait. The area of the island is 2,185 sq. miles (5,660 sq. km). Total population (census, 1991), 129,765; (estimate, 1993), 131,600. Population of the principal cities: Charlottetown (capital), 15,396; Summerside, 7,474.

Vital statistics *see* CANADA: Territory and Population.

CLIMATE. The cool temperate climate is affected in winter by the freezing of the St. Lawrence, which reduces winter temperatures. Charlottetown. Jan. 3·4°C, July 23°C. Annual rainfall 869 mm.

CONSTITUTION AND GOVERNMENT. The provincial government is administered by a Lieut.-Governor-in-Council (Cabinet) and a Legislative Assembly of 32 members who are elected for up to 5 years. In Sept. 1995, parties in the Legislative Assembly were: Liberals, 29; Progressive Conservatives, 1; vacant 2.

Lieut.-Governor: Gilbert R. Clements (sworn in 30 Aug. 1995).

The Executive Council was composed as follows in June 1994:

Premier and President of the Executive Council: Hon. Catherine S. Callbeck.

Economic Development and Tourism: Hon. Robert J. Morrissey. *Provincial Treasurer:* Hon. Wayne D. Cheverie, QC. *Transportation and Public Works:* Hon. Keith Milligan. *Education:* Hon. Gordon MacInnis. *Environmental Resources:* Hon. Barry Hicken. *Agriculture, Fisheries and Forestry:* Hon. Walter Bradley. *Health and Social Services:* Hon. Walter McEwen, QC. *Provincial Affairs, and Attorney-General:* Hon. Alan Buchanan. *Without Portfolio:* Hon. Jeannie Lea.

Flag: A banner of the arms, *i.e.*, a white field bearing 3 small trees and a larger tree on a compartment, all green, and at the top a red band with a golden lion; on 3 sides a border of red and white rectangles.

Local Government. The Municipalities Act, 1983, provides for the incorporation of Towns and Communities. The City of Charlottetown and the town of Summerside are incorporated under private Acts of the Legislature.

FINANCE. Revenue and expenditure (in Canadian $1,000) for 5 financial years ending 31 March:

	1991–92	*1992–93*	*1993–94*	*1994–95*	*1995–96*
Revenue	714,744	710,840	737,481	809,265	793,576
Expenditure	764,673	793,329	809,974	817,045	790,922

Per capita personal income rose from $17,915 in 1992 to $18,159 in 1993.

ENERGY AND NATURAL RESOURCES

Electricity. In 1994, total supply of electric energy was about 815m. kWh; net generation, 40m. kWh. An undersea cable links Prince Edward Island with New Brunswick and the Maritime Power Grid. Electricity received from other provinces in 1994 totalled 775m. kWh. In 1994, 95% of power requirements were supplied through this system.

Agriculture. Total area of farmland occupies approximately half of the total land area of 566,177 ha. Farm cash receipts in 1994 were $308·5m. with cash receipts from potatoes accounting for about 40% of the total. Cash receipts from dairy products, cattle and hogs followed in importance. For particulars of agricultural production and livestock, *see* CANADA: Agriculture.

Forestry. Forested lands cover 0·28m. ha. During 1993, 104,000 cords of roundwood were burnt for heating, and 36m. bd ft of timber, worth some $14m., were sawn.

Fisheries. The total catch of 96·3m lbs in 1994 had a landed value of $93m. Lobsters accounted for $64m. or 70% of the total value; other shellfish, $18·6m.; pelagic and estuarial, $3·8m.; groundfish, $1·1m.; seaplants, $1·5m.

INDUSTRY AND TRADE

Industry. Value of manufacturing shipments for all industries in 1994 was $686·9m.

In 1994, provincial GDP in constant prices for manufacturing was $169·5m.; construction, $127·4m. In 1994 the total value of retail trade was $870·3m.

Labour. The average weekly wage (industrial aggregate) rose from $453·9 in 1993 to $454 in 1994. The labour force averaged 68,000 in 1994, while employment averaged 56,000.

Tourism. The value of the tourist industry was estimated at $127·8m. in 1994 with 258,458 tourist parties.

COMMUNICATIONS

Roads. At the end of 1994 there were 5,308 km of road, including 3,803 km of paved highway. A bus service operates twice daily to the mainland.

Civil Aviation (1995). Air Canada provides a daily service between Charlottetown and Toronto, Prince Edward Air a daily service to Halifax from Summerside and Charlottetown and Air Nova and Air Atlantic a service between Charlottetown and other centres, including Toronto, to connect with Air Canada and Canadian Airlines International flights at Halifax.

Shipping. Modern car ferries link the Island to New Brunswick and Nova Scotia. Service is provided year round to New Brunswick on schedules which vary from 14 to 20 return crossings daily, with ice-breaking ferries maintaining the service during the winter months. Ferry service is operated to Nova Scotia from late April to mid-Dec. on schedules ranging from 9 to 19 return crossings daily. A third ferry service, to the Magdalen Islands (Quebec), operates from 1 April to 31 Jan. There is also a substantial water movement of certain commodities, primarily through the ports of Summerside and Charlottetown.

Telecommunications. At 30 Sept. 1994 there were 76,814 telephone lines in service.

EDUCATION

EDUCATION (1994–95). Under the regional school boards there were 65 public schools, 1,418 teaching positions and 24,219 students. There is one undergraduate university (2,318 full-time and 7,504 part-time students), a veterinary college (200 students), and a Master of Science programme (25 students), all in Charlottetown. Holland College provides training for employment in business, applied arts and technology, with approximately 2,300 full-time students in post-secondary and vocational career programmes. The college offers extensive academic and career preparation programmes for adults.

Government expenditure on education, 1993–94, $179·4m.

Further Reading

Baldwin, D. O., *Abegweit: Land of the Red Soil.* Charlottetown, 1985
Bolger, F. W. P., *Canada's Smallest Province.* Charlottetown, 1973
Clark, A. H., *Three Centuries and the Island.* Toronto, 1959
Hocking, A., *Prince Edward Island.* Toronto, 1978
MacKinnon, F., *The Government of Prince Edward Island.* Toronto, 1951

QUEBEC—QUÉBEC

KEY HISTORICAL EVENTS. Quebec was formerly known as New France or Canada from 1534 to 1763; as the province of Quebec from 1763 to 1790; as Lower Canada from 1791 to 1846; as Canada East from 1846 to 1867, and when, by the union of the four original provinces, the Confederation of the Dominion of Canada was formed, it again became known as the province of Quebec (Québec).

The Quebec Act, passed by the British Parliament in 1774, guaranteed to the people of the newly conquered French territory in North America security in their religion and language, their customs and tenures, under their own civil laws.

In a referendum on 20 May 1980, 59·5% voted against 'separatism'. At a further referendum on 30 Oct. 1995, 50·6% of votes cast were against Quebec becoming 'sovereign in a new economic and political partnership' with Canada. The electorate was 5m.; turn-out was 93%.

TERRITORY AND POPULATION. The area of Quebec (as amended by the Labrador Boundary Award) is 1,667,926 sq. km (594,860 sq. miles), of which 1,315,134 sq. km is land area and 352,792 sq. km water. Of this extent, 911,106 sq. km represent the Territory of Ungava, annexed in 1912 under the Quebec Boundaries Extension Act. The population (census 1991) was 6,895,963; (official estimate, 1994), 7,275,785.

Principal cities: (1991 census populations): Quebec (capital), 167,517; Montreal, 1,017,666; Laval, 314,398; Longueuil, 129,874; Montreal North, 85,516; Sherbrooke, 76,429; Saint-Hubert, 74,027; LaSalle, 73,804; Sainte-Foy, 73,133; Saint-Laurent, 72,402, Charlesbourg, 70,788; Beauport, 69,158; Chicoutimi, 62,670; Verdun, 61,307; Hull, 60,707; Jonquière, 57,933.

Vital statistics, *see* CANADA: Territory and Population.

CLIMATE. Cool temperate in the south, but conditions are more extreme towards the north. Winters are severe and snowfall considerable, but summer temperatures are quite warm. Quebec. Jan. –12·8°C, July 19·1°C. Annual rainfall 1,174 mm. Montreal. Jan. –10·3°C, July 20·8°C. Annual rainfall 939·7 mm.

CONSTITUTION AND GOVERNMENT. There is a Legislative Assembly consisting of 125 members, elected in 125 electoral districts for 4 years. At the elections of 12 Sept 1994, the Parti Québécois won 77 seats with 44·7% of votes cast, the Liberal Party 47 with 44·3%. Action Démocratique won 1 seat.

Lieut.-Governor: The Hon. Martial Asselin.

Flag: The Fleurdelysé flag, blue with a white cross, and in each quarter a white fleur-de-lis.

Members of the Council of Ministers in Jan. 1996:

Premier: Lucien Bouchard.

Deputy Premier and Minister of State for the Economy and Finance: Bernard Landry. *Education:* Pauline Marois. *Culture and Communications, Minister responsible for the French Language Charter:* Louise Beaudoin. *Justice:* Paul Bégin.*Transport, and Minister responsible for Canadian Inter-Governmental Affairs:* Jacques Brassard. *Environment and Fauna:* David Cliche. *Agriculture, Fisheries and Food:* Guy Julien. *Public Safety:* Robert Perreault. *Labour:* Matthias Rioux. *Health and Social Services:* Jean Rochon. *International Relations, Minister responsible for Francophonie:* Sylvain Simard. *Municipal Affairs:* Rémy Trudel.

Ministers of State: Louise Harel (*Employment, Solidarity, Conditions of Women*); Guy Chevrette (*Natural Resources, Regional Development, Autochthonous Affairs, Electoral and Parliamentary Reform*); Serge Ménard (*Metropolitan Affairs*).

Ministers Delegate: Pierre Bélanger (*Electoral and Parliamentary Reform, Government Leader in Parliament*); Roger Bertrand (*Revenue*); André Boischir (*Relations with Citizens*); Denise Carrier-Perreault (*Mines, Land, Forestry*); Rita Dionne-Marsolais (*Industry and Commerce*); Jacques Léonard (*Administration, Civil Service, President of the Treasury Council*).

ECONOMY

Budget. Ordinary revenue and expenditure (in Canadian $1,000) for fiscal years ending 31 March:

	1988–89	*1989-90*	*1990-91*	*1991–92*	*1992–93*
Revenue	29,967,892	31,073,900	33,023,993	34,457,600	35,445,600
Expenditure	31,578,118	32,733,000	35,848,798	38,649,000	40,377,000

The total net debt at 31 March 1994 was $45,527m.

ENERGY AND NATURAL RESOURCES

Electricity. Water power is one of the most important natural resources of Quebec. Its turbine installation represents about 40% of the aggregate of Canada. At the end of 1992 the installed generating capacity was 35,209 mw. Production, 1992, was 147,077 gwh.

Minerals (1993). The estimated value of mineral production (metal only) was $1,620,845,000. Chief minerals: Iron ore, (confidential); copper, $199,158,000; gold, $623,172,000; zinc, $152,432,000.

Non-metallic minerals produced include: Asbestos ($218,798,000; about 97% of Canadian production), titane-dioxide (confidential), industrial lime, dolomite and brucite, quartz and pyrite. Among the building materials produced were: Stone, $202,287,000; cement, $138,047,000; sand and gravel, $87,041,000; lime, (confidential).

Agriculture. In 1993 the agricultural area was 2·27m. ha. The yield of the principal crops was (1991 in 1,000 tonnes):

Crops	*Yield*	*Crops*	*Yield*
Tame hay	4,800	Fodder corn	1,240
Oats for grain	200	Maize for grain	1,882
Potatoes	362	Barley	490
Mixed grains	71	Buckwheat	20

About 40,000 farms were operating in 1993. Cash receipts, 1993, $3,419·4m. (dairy products, 33·4%; livestock, 29·5%; crops, 23·2%; poultry and eggs, 12·9%).

Forestry. Forests cover an area of 757,900 sq. km. 516,603 sq. km are classified as productive forests, of which 447,515 sq. km are provincial forest land and 66,017 sq. km are privately owned. Quebec leads the Canadian provinces in pulp and paper production, having nearly half of the Canadian estimated total.

In 1993 production of lumber was: Softwood and hardwood, 12,066,000 cu. metres; pulp and paper, 8,032,000 tonnes.

Fisheries. The principal fish are cod, herring, red fish, lobster and salmon. Total catch of sea fish, 1993, 58,553 tonnes, valued at $91·56m.

INDUSTRY AND TRADE

Industry. In 1993 there were 11,793 industrial establishments in the province; employees, 468,782; salaries and wages, $14,944·68m.; cost of materials, $42,255·98m.; value of shipments, $76,745·3m. Among the leading industries are petroleum refining, pulp and paper mills, smelting and refining, dairy products, slaughtering and meat processing, motor vehicle manufacturing, women's clothing, saw-mills and planing mills, iron and steel mills, commercial printing.

Commerce. In 1993 the value of Canadian exports through Quebec custom ports was $30,837·84m.; value of imports, $28,035·48m.

COMMUNICATIONS

Roads. In 1993 there were 28,719 km of roads and 4,165,890 registered motor vehicles.

Railways. There were (1994) 6,338 km of railway. There is a metro system in Montreal (64 km).

Civil Aviation. There are 2 international airports, Dorval (Montreal) and Mirabel (Montreal).

Telecommunications. Telephones numbered 3,927,000 in 1992 and there were 28 television and 130 radio stations.

Newspapers (1993). There were 10 French- and 2 English-language daily newspapers.

EDUCATION. The province has 7 universities: 3 English-language universities, McGill (Montreal) founded in 1821, Bishop (Lennoxville) founded in 1845 and the Concordia University (Montreal) granted a charter in 1975; 4 French-language universities: Laval (Quebec) founded in 1852, Montreal University, opened in 1876 as a branch of Laval and became independent in 1920, Sherbrooke University founded in 1954 and University of Quebec founded in 1968.

In 1990–91 there were 129,669 full-time university students and 121,282 part-time students.

In 1991–92, in pre-kindergartens, there were 7,598 pupils; in kindergartens, 85,276; primary schools, 576,601; in secondary schools, 478,571; in colleges (post-secondary, non-university), 218,989; and in classes for children with special needs, 151,249. The school boards had a total of 58,394 teachers.

Expenditure of the Departments of Education for 1992–93, $9,223·05m. net. This included $1,716·03m. for universities, $5,428·37m. for public primary and secondary schools, $279·9m. for private primary and secondary schools and $1,301·9m. for colleges.

Further Reading

Dickinson, J. A. and Young, B., *A Short History of Quebec.* 2nd ed. Harlow, 1994
Hamelin, J., *Histoire du Québec.* St-Hyacinthe, 1978
Jacobs, J., *The Question of Separatism: Quebec and the Struggle for Sovereignty.* London, 1981
McWhinney, E., *Quebec and the Constitution.* Univ. of Toronto Press, 1979
Wade, F. M., *The French Canadians, 1760–1967.* Toronto, 1968

Statistical office: Bureau de la Statistique du Québec, 117 rue Saint-André, Québec, G1K 3Y3

SASKATCHEWAN

KEY HISTORICAL EVENTS. Saskatchewan derives its name from its major river system, which the Cree Indians called 'Kis-is-ska-tche-wan', meaning 'swift flowing'. It officially became a province when it joined the Confederation on 1 Sept. 1905.

In 1670 King Charles II granted to Prince Rupert and his friends a charter covering exclusive trading rights in 'all the land drained by streams finding their outlet in the Hudson Bay'. This included what is now Saskatchewan. The trading company was first known as The Governor and Company of Adventurers of England; later as the Hudson's Bay Company. In 1869 the Northwest Territories was formed, and this included Saskatchewan. In 1882 the District of Saskatchewan was formed. By 1885 the North-West Mounted Police had been inaugurated, with headquarters in Regina (now the capital), and the Canadian Pacific Railway's transcontinental line had been completed, bringing a stream of immigrants to southern Saskatchewan.

The Hudson's Bay Company surrendered its claim to territory in return for cash and land around the existing trading posts. Legislative government was introduced.

TERRITORY AND POPULATION. Saskatchewan is bounded on the west by Alberta, on the east by Manitoba, on the north by the Northwest Territories and on the south by the USA. The area of the province is 251,700 sq. miles (570,113 sq. km), of which 220,182 sq. miles is land area and 31,518 sq. miles is water. The population, 1991 census, was 988,928. Population of cities, 1991 census: Regina (capital), 179,178; Saskatoon, 186,058; Prince Albert, 34,181; Moose Jaw, 33,593; Yorkton, 15,315; Swift Current, 14,815; North Battleford, 14,350; Estevan, 10,240; Weyburn, 9,673; Lloydminster, 7,241; Melfort, 5,628; Melville, 4,905.

Vital statistics, *see* CANADA: Territory and Population.

CLIMATE. A cold continental climate, with severe winters and warm summers. Rainfall amounts are greatest from May to Aug. Regina. Jan. 0°F (–17·8°C), July 65°F (18·3°C). Annual rainfall 15" (373 mm).

CONSTITUTION AND GOVERNMENT. The provincial government is vested in a Lieut.-Governor, an Executive Council and a Legislative Assembly, elected for 5 years by universal suffrage. State of parties in Dec. 1995: New Democratic Party, 42; Progressive Conservative Party, 5; Liberal Party, 10; ind, 1.

Lieut.-Governor: Hon. Jack Wiebe.

Flag: Green over gold, with the shield of the province in the canton, and a green and red prairie lily in the fly.

The New Democratic Party Ministry in Dec. 1995 was composed as follows:

Premier: Roy Romanow (b. 1939).

Deputy Premier, Minister of Economic Development: Hon. Dwain Lingenfelter. *Health:* Hon. Eric Cline. *Education:* Hon. Pat Atkinson. *Agriculture and Food:* Hon. Eric Upshall. *Labour:* Hon. Doug Anguish. *Highways and Transportation:* Hon. A. Renaud. *Municipal Government:* Hon. Carol Teichrob. *Environment and Resource Management:* Hon. Lorne Scott. *Justice, Attorney General:* Hon. John Nilson. *Finance:* Hon. Janice MacKinnon. *Social Services:* Hon. Lorne Calvert. *Energy and Mines:* Hon. Eldon Lautermilch. *SPMC:* Hon. Clay Serby. *Post-Secondary Education and Skills Training:* Hon. Bob Mitchell. *Crown Investments Corporation:* Hon. Berry Weins. *Inter-Governmental Relations, Provincial Secretary:* Hon. Ned Shillington. *IMAS, Women's Secretariat:* Hon. Joanne Crofford.

Local Government. The organization of a city requires a minimum population of 5,000 persons; that of a town, 500; that of a village, 100 people. No requirements as to population exist for the rural municipality. Cities, towns, villages and rural municipalities are governed by elected councils, which consist of a mayor and 6–20 aldermen in a city; a mayor and 6 councillors in a town; a mayor and 2 other members in a village; a reeve and a councillor for each division in a rural municipality (usually 6).

FINANCE. Budget and net assets (years ending 31 March) in Canadian $1,000:

	1991–92	*1992–93*	*1993–94*	*1994–95*
Budgetary revenue	4,052,300	4,491,500	4,631,800	4,841,700
Budgetary expenditure	4,903,952	5,008,800	4,928,142	5,030,424

ENERGY AND NATURAL RESOURCES. Agriculture used to dominate the history and economics of Saskatchewan, but the 'prairie province' is now a rapidly developing mining and manufacturing area. It is a major supplier of oil, has the world's largest deposits of potash and the net value of its non-agricultural production accounted for (1994 estimate) 89·5% of the provincial economy.

Electricity. The Saskatchewan Power Corporation generated 14,994m. kWh. in 1994.

Minerals. 1994 mineral sales were valued at $4,143m., including (in $1m.): Petroleum, 1,884·8 natural gas, 522·8; coal and others, 126·5; potash, 1,108·7; salt, 20·2; uranium, 407·8; sodium sulphate, 26·1.

Agriculture. Saskatchewan produces normally about two-thirds of Canada's wheat. Wheat production in 1994 (in 1,000 tonnes), was 12,947 from 16·4m. acres; oats, 1,110 from 1·5m. acres; barley, 4,354 from 4·3m. acres; rye, 140 from 0·23m. acres; rapeseed, 2,653 from 6·2m. acres; flax, 640 from 1·3m. acres. Livestock (1 July 1995): Cattle and calves, 2·9m.; swine, 976,000; sheep and lambs, 83,000. Poultry in 1994: Chickens, 14·3m.; turkeys, 735,000. Cash income from the sale of farm products in 1994 was $5,010m. At the June 1991 census there were 60,840 farms in the province, each being a holding of 1 acre or more with sales of agricultural products during the previous 12 months of $250 or more.

The South Saskatchewan River irrigation project, whose main feature is the Gardiner Dam, was completed in 1967. It will ultimately provide for an area of 0·2m. to 0·5m. acres of irrigated cultivation in Central Saskatchewan. As of 1994, 226,155 acres were intensively irrigated. Total irrigated land in the province, 321,548 acres.

Forestry. Half of Saskatchewan's area is forested, but only 115,000 sq. km are of commercial value at present. Forest products valued at $559m. were produced in 1994.

Fur Production. In 1992–93 wild fur production was estimated at $952,349 ($1,671,651 in 1991-92). Ranch-raised fur production amounted to $97,177 in 1993 and $87,162 in 1994.

Fisheries. The lakeside value of the 1993–94 commercial fish catch of 2·4m. kg was $3·5m.

INDUSTRY. In 1993 there were 716 manufacturing establishments, employing 15,388 persons. Manufacturing contributed $1,175·5m. and construction $1,018·8m. to total GDP at factor cost of $18,067m. in 1994.

TOURISM. An estimated 2m. out-of-province tourists spent $273·3m. in 1994.

COMMUNICATIONS

Roads. In 1994 there were 25,380 km of provincial highways and 197,798 km of municipal roads (including prairie trails). Motor vehicles registered totalled (1994) 721,309. Bus services are provided by 2 major lines.

Railways. There were (1994) 10,553 km of railway track.

Civil Aviation. There were 2 major airports, 176 airports and landing strips in 1994.

Telecommunications. There were (1994) 460 post offices (excluding sub-post offices), 85 TV and re-broadcasting stations and 59 radio stations. There were 581,816 telephone network access services to the Saskatchewan Telecommunications system in 1994.

EDUCATION. The Saskatchewan education system in 1993–94 consisted of 110 school divisions and 5 comprehensive school boards, of which 22 are Roman Catholic separate school divisions, serving 135,256 elementary pupils, 58,543 high-school students and 2,137 students enrolled in special classes. In addition, the Saskatchewan Institute of Applied Science and Technology, established 1 Jan. 1988, had 13,510 full-time and 31,867 part-time students in 1993-94. There are also 10 regional colleges with an enrolment of approximately 30,000 students in 1993–94.

The University of Saskatchewan was established at Saskatoon in 1907. In 1994–95 it had 16,183 full-time students, 2,952 part-time students and 1,141 full-time academic staff. The University of Regina was established in 1974; in 1994–95 it had 8,145 full-time and 3,570 part-time students and 349 academic staff.

Further Reading

Archer, J. H., *Saskatchewan: A History*. Saskatoon, 1980
Arora, V., *The Saskatchewan Bibliography*. Regina, 1980

Statistical office: Bureau of Statistics, 2350 Albert St., Regina, S4P 4A6.

THE NORTHWEST TERRITORIES

KEY HISTORICAL EVENTS. The Territory was developed by the Hudson's Bay Company and the North West Company (of Montreal) from the 17th century. The Canadian Government bought out the Hudson's Bay Company in 1869 and the Territory was annexed to Canada in 1870. The Arctic Islands lying north of the Canadian mainland were annexed to Canada in 1880.

A plebiscite held in March 1992 approved the division of the Northwest Territories into 2 separate territories.(For the new territory of Nunavut *see* CONSTITUTION AND GOVERNMENT, *below*).

TERRITORY AND POPULATION. The total area of the Territories is 3,426,320 sq. km, divided into 5 administrative regions: Fort Smith, Inuvik, Kitikmeot, Keewatin and Baffin. The population in April 1992 was 57,649, 37% of whom were Inuit (Eskimo), 16% Dene (Indian) and 7% Metis. After the formation of Nunavut the population was reduced to about 36,000. The capital is Yellowknife, population (1991); 15,179. Other main centres (with population in 1991): Iqaluit (3,552), Hay River (3,206), Inuvik (3,206), Fort Smith (2,480), Rankin Inlet (1,706), Rae-Edzo (1,521) and Arviat (1,323).

CLIMATE. Conditions range from cold continental to polar, with long hard winters and short cool summers. Precipitation is low. Yellowknife. Jan. mean high –24·7°C, low –33°C; July mean high 20·7°C, low 11·8°C. Annual rainfall 26·7 cm.

CONSTITUTION AND GOVERNMENT. The Northwest Territories comprises all that portion of Canada lying north of the 60th parallel of N. lat. except those portions within the Yukon Territory and the Provinces of Quebec and Newfoundland: It also includes the islands in Hudson Bay, James Bay and Ungava Bay except those within the Provinces of Manitoba, Ontario and Quebec.

The Northwest Territories is governed by a Government Leader, with a 7-member cabinet and a Legislative Assembly. The Assembly is composed of 24 members elected for a 4-year term of office. A Commissioner of the Northwest Territories acts as a lieutenant-governor and is the federal government's senior representative in the Territorial government. The seat of government was transferred from Ottawa to Yellowknife when it was named Territorial capital on 18 Jan. 1967.

Government Leader: Nellie Cournoyea.
Commissioner: Daniel L. Norris.
Flag: Vertically, blue, white, blue, with the white of double width and bearing the shield of the Territory.

Legislative powers are exercised by the Executive Council on such matters as taxation within the Territories in order to raise revenue, maintenance of justice, licences, solemnization of marriages, education, public health, property, civil rights and generally all matters of a local nature.

The Territorial Government has assumed most of the responsibility for the administration of the Northwest Territories but political control of Crown lands and non-renewable resources still rests with the Federal Government. On 6 Sept. 1988, the Federal and Territorial Governments signed an agreement for the transfer of management responsibilities for oil and gas resources, located on- and off-shore, in the Northwest Territories to the Territorial Government. In a Territory-wide plebiscite in April 1982, a majority of residents voted in favour of dividing the Northwest Territories into two jurisdictions, east and west. In a plebiscite held in March 1992 residents voted in favour of an east-west boundary line. Constitutions for an eastern and western government have been under discussion since 1992. A referendum was held in Nov. 1992 among the Inuit on the formation of a third territory, **Nunavut** ('Our Land'), in the eastern Arctic, and comprising the present administrative regions of Kitikmeot, Keewatin and Baffin. The electorate was 9,648; turn-out was 80%. 69% of votes cast were in favour. An agreement was signed on 25 May 1993 by the federal Prime Minister beginning the process of establishing this territory. Its area of 2,201,400 sq. km is to be made over to the population of 22,000, of which some 80% are Inuit. The remainder will remain federal property. The capital is Iqaluit (formerly Frobisher Bay) with a 1991 population of 3,552. Rankin Inlet had 1,706 inhabitants in 1991.

ENERGY AND NATURAL RESOURCES

Oil and Gas. As of July 1993, 13 licences for oil and gas exploration were held for 1·4m. ha, 20 production licences were held for 64,578 ha and 108 significant discovery licences were retained on 695,473 ha.

Crude oil is produced at Norman Wells and piped to Alberta. Value of crude oil production in 1992 was $142·5m.; 1,850,379 cu. metres.

Minerals. Mineral production in 1992 was valued at $476·2m. 4·7% of Canada's total. The Northwest Territories yielded 12·3% of lead, 15·1% of zinc, 8·8% of gold, and 2% of silver produced in Canada in 1992.

Trapping and Game. The 39,629 pelts, furs and hides sold by 1,838 Northwest Territories hunters and trappers in the 1991–92 season were valued at $2,325,814. The pelts of highest value are those of the polar bear, black and brown bear, wolf, wolverine and lynx. There are some 1·3m. barren-ground caribou, 113,000 muskox and 12,700 polar bears. There are 2 protected herds of wood bison.

Forestry. Forest land area in the NWT consists of 61·4m. ha, about 18% of the total land area. The principal trees are white and black spruce, jack-pine, tamarack, balsam poplar, aspen and birch. In 1990–91, 56,000 cu. metres of timber, valued at $1·83m., was produced.

Fisheries. Commercial fishing, principally on Great Slave Lake, in 1991–92 produced 1,431,000 kg of fish valued at $912,000, principally trout, whitefish and pickerel.

CO-OPERATIVES. There are 39 active co-operatives, including 2 housing co-operatives and one central organization to service local co-operatives, in the Northwest Territories. They are active in handicrafts, furs, fisheries, retail stores, hotels and print shops. Total revenue in 1991 was about $41m.

COMMUNICATIONS

Roads. The Mackenzie Route connects Grimshaw, Alberta, with Hay River, Pine Point, Fort Smith, Fort Providence, Rae-Edzo and Yellowknife. The Mackenzie Highway extension to Fort Simpson and a road between Pine Point and Fort Resolution have both been opened.

Highway service to Inuvik in the Mackenzie Delta was opened in spring 1980, extending north from Dawson, Yukon as the Dempster Highway. The Liard Highway connecting the communities of the Liard River valley to British Columbia opened in 1984.

Railways. There is one small railway system in the north which runs from Hay River, on the south shore of Great Slave Lake, 435 miles south to Grimshaw, Alberta, where it connects with the Canadian National Railways, but it is not in use.

Civil Aviation (1993). 9 certified airports are operated by the federal Department of Transport and there are 33 certified and 9 uncertified airports operated by the Government of the Northwest Territories. Numerous certified and uncertified airports are operated privately in support of military operations, mining and resource exploration, and tourism. There are also privately-owned float plane bases. Major communities receive daily jet service to southern points. Most smaller communities are served by scheduled turbo-prop air service several times weekly.

Shipping. A direct inland-water transportation route for about 1,700 miles is provided by the Mackenzie River and its tributaries, the Athabasca and Slave rivers. Subsidiary routes on Lake Athabasca, Great Slave Lake and Great Bear Lake total more than 800 miles. Communities in the eastern Arctic are resupplied by ship each summer via the Atlantic and Arctic Oceans or Hudson Bay.

Telecommunications (1993). There is a postal service in all communities. The CBC northern service operates radio stations at Yellowknife, Inuvik, Iqaluit and Rankin Inlet. All communities receive television via satellite. Telephone service is provided to nearly all communities in the Northwest Territories. Those few communities without service have high frequency or very high frequency radios for emergency use.

SOCIAL INSTITUTIONS

Education. In 1993-94 there were 8 divisional boards of education, which provide for more local and regional control of education. There were also 3 boards of education operating in Yellowknife: A separate school board, a public school board and a board of secondary education.

In 1993-94 there were 80 schools operating, with 1,091 teachers for 16,089 enrolled students. Residences in regional larger communities provide accommodation for students from smaller communities that cannot provide all education services up to grade 12. There is a full range of courses available in the school system: Academic, French immersion, native language and culture, commercial, technical and occupational training, post-secondary programmes, along with a first-year general arts university programme. Financial assistance (from the territorial government) is available to qualifying students for post-secondary studies.

Health. In 1988 complete responsibility for health services was transferred to the Territorial Government by the Government of Canada. There are (1993) 8 Boards of Management established to operate, manage and control the health services and programmes in their respective service regions. The health system is comprised of: 6 hospitals, providing both acute and long term care; 6 public health clinics; 43 community health centres; 8 lay dispensaries; 6 boarding homes for patients and escorts travelling.

Welfare. Welfare services are provided by professional social workers. Facilities included (1993) for children: 7 group homes and 2 residential treatment centres.

Further Reading

Annual Report of the Government of the Northwest Territories
Government Activities in the North, 1983–84. Indian and Northern Affairs, Canada
NWT Data Book 90/91. Yellowknife, 1991
Dawson, C. A., *The New North-West.* Toronto, 1947
MacKay, D., *The Honorable Company.* Toronto, 1949
Zaslow, M., *The Opening of the Canadian North 1870–1914.* Toronto, 1971

YUKON TERRITORY

KEY HISTORICAL EVENTS. Formerly part of the Northwest Territories, the Yukon was joined to the Dominion as a separate territory on 13 June 1898.

TERRITORY AND POPULATION. The Yukon is situated in the extreme north-western section of Canada and comprises 483,450 sq. km. of which 4,480 fresh water. The census population in 1991 was 27,797; June 1995 (estimate), 31,569. Principal centres (with 1995 populations) are Whitehorse, the capital, 22,884; Watson Lake, 1,784; Dawson City, 1,988; Haines Junction, 800.

Vital statistics, *see* CANADA: Territory and Population.

CLIMATE. A cold climate in winter with moderate temperatures in summer provide a considerable annual range of temperature and moderate rainfall. Whitehorse. Jan. 5°F (–20°C), July 56°F (14·1°C). Annual rainfall 10" (261 mm). Dawson City. Jan. –22°F (–30°C), July 57°F (15·6°C). Annual rainfall 13" (306·1 mm).

CONSTITUTION AND GOVERNMENT. The Yukon was constituted a separate territory in June 1898. It is governed by a Cabinet (Executive Council) appointed from the majority party in the 17-member elected Legislative Assembly. The members are elected for terms not to exceed 4 years. In the territorial elections on 19 Oct. 1992 the Yukon Party gained 7 seats, the New Democratic Party 6, the Liberal Party 1 and independents 3.

The seat of government is at Whitehorse. A federally appointed Commissioner serves in a similar capacity to the provincial lieutenant governors.

Commissioner: Judy Gingell (appointed 12 June 1995)

Flag: Vertically green, white, blue, in the proportions 2 : 3 : 2, charged in the centre with the arms of the Territory.

The Yukon government consists of 12 departments, as well as a Women's Directorate and 4 Crown corporations, each taking direction from a responsible Cabinet Minister and generally from Cabinet. Government departments and agencies are responsible for a similar range of activities as found in Canadian provinces, including education, economic development, municipal affairs, housing, social services, transportation, tourism, justice, renewable resources, and finance. The administration of certain programmes, mostly in the the natural resources field, remains under federal control. The Yukon government is, however, involved in negotiations with the federal government on the transfer of further responsibilities to its jurisdiction.

ECONOMY

Activities. GDP at market prices decreased by 2·7% in 1994, to $913m. The key sectors of the economy are mining, tourism and government. Renewable resource industries' production was estimated at $10m. in 1992. Processing of renewable resources is an important source of economic diversification. In the manufacturing sector, manufacturers' shipments were valued at $15–20m. in 1992. Forestry is becoming an important source of economic diversification, with production increasing 220% in 1994-95.

Finance. The Territorial Government's revenue and expenditure (in $1,000) for years ended 31 March was:

	1992–93	*1993–94*	*1994–95*	*1995–96* [1]
Revenue	356,241	473,176	489,894	497,780
Expenditure	420,386	471,705	481,388	489,508

[1] Projected.

ENERGY AND NATURAL RESOURCES

Electricity. Hydro-generated power is supplied through plants at Whitehorse Rapids, Aishihik Lake, Fish Lake and Mayo. Diesel generated power is supplied from plants at several communities (including Whitehorse, Faro, Haines Junction, Ross River, Dawson City, Mayo and Watson Lake). Current capacity is 78 MW hydro and 52 MW diesel-generated power.

Oil and Gas. In 1993, the Canada-Yukon Northern Oil and Gas Accord was signed transferring management and legislative authority of onshore oil and gas resources to the Yukon government. Exploration has been active in the south-east Yukon and Eagle Plains areas. The Kotaneelee gas field in the south-east has 2 wells producing.

Minerals. Mining is the main industry. Lead, zinc and gold are the chief minerals. Production in tonnes (and value) in 1993: Gold, 4 ($52·8m.); zinc, 35,204 ($43·7m.); lead, 27,857 ($14·6m.); silver, 30 ($5·3m.).

Agriculture. Many areas have suitable soils and climate for the production of forages, cereal grains and vegetables, domestic livestock and game farming. In 1995 there were 150 farms operating full- and part-time. There were about 20,000 acres associated with farm operations, of which 14,000 acres were in production or under development. Farm receipts in 1995 were estimated at $2·6m. Total farm capital, 1995, was $25m.

Forestry. The forests are part of the great Boreal forest region of Canada which stretches from the east coast of Canada into Alaska and north well above the Arctic Circle. Vast areas are covered by coniferous stands in the southern portion of Yukon with white spruce and lodgepole pine forming pure stands on wet sites and in northern aspects. Deciduous species form pure stands or occur mixed with conifers throughout forest areas.

Production from forestry was 0·48m. cu. metres in 1994.

Fisheries. Commercial fishing concentrates on chinook salmon, chum salmon, lake trout and whitefish.

Game and Furs. The country abounds with big game, such as moose, goat, caribou, mountain sheep and bear (grizzly and black). The fur trapping industry is considered vital to rural and remote residents and especially First Nations people wishing to maintain a traditional lifestyle. Fur production in 1993 was valued at $208,641.

TOURISM. In 1994 tourists spent an estimated $59m. Some 254,721 tourists visited in 1994.

COMMUNICATIONS

Roads. The Alaska Highway and branch highway systems connect Yukon's main communities with Alaska and the provinces and with adjacent mining centres. Interior roads connect the mining communities of Elsa (silver–lead), Faro (lead–zinc–silver) and Dawson City (gold) and mineral exploration properties (lead–zinc and tungsten) north of Ross River. The 727 km Dempster Highway north of Dawson City connects with Inuvik, on the Arctic coast; this highway, the first public road to be built to the Arctic Ocean, was opened in Aug. 1979. The Carcross–Skagway road was opened in May 1979, providing a new access to the Pacific Ocean. There are 4,910 km of roads in the Territory, of which about 250 km are paved. The other major roads, including the Alaska Highway, have received a new surface treatment which resembles pavement and the rest are all-weather gravel of which 700 km are accessible during the summer months only.

Railways. The 176-km White Pass and Yukon Railway connected Whitehorse with year-round ocean shipping at Skagway, Alaska, but was closed in 1982. A modified passenger service was restarted in 1988 to take cruise ship tourists from Skagway to the White Pass summit and back.

Civil Aviation. In 1995, Canadian International Airlines provided regular daily service between Whitehorse and Vancouver. Regular air service also extended beyond the Yukon to Yellowknife and Inuvik, Northwest Territories, and Juneau and Fairbanks, Alaska, with connecting service to other points in Alaska and other states in the US. Regularly scheduled air services extend from Whitehorse to the Yukon communities of Dawson City, Old Crow and Watson Lake, with limited air service to Mayo. Commercial operations offering charter services are located throughout the Territory.

Shipping. The majority of goods are shipped into the Territory by truck over the Alaska and Stewart–Cassiar Highways. Some goods are shipped through the ports of Skagway and Haines, Alaska, and then trucked to Whitehorse for distribution throughout the Territory. The majority of goods are transported by road within the Territory, while a modest amount is shipped by air. Although navigable, the rivers are no longer used for shipping.

Telecommunications. There are 3 radio stations in Whitehorse and 15 low-power relay radio transmitters operated by CBC, and 6 operated by the Yukon Government. CHON-FM, operated by Northern Native Broadcasting, is broadcast to virtually all Yukon communities by satellite. Dawson City has its own community run radio station, CFYT-FM. There are also 19 basic and 11 extended pay-cable TV channels in Whitehorse, and private cable operations in Faro and Watson Lake. Live CBC national television and TVNC is provided by satellite and relayed to all communities. All telephone and telecommunications are provided by Northwestel, a subsidiary of Bell Canada Enterprises. Microwave stations, satellite ground stations and radio-telephone facilities provide most of the telephone transmission services to the communities.

Press. In 1995 there were 1 daily and 1 semi-weekly newspapers in Whitehorse, and a monthly paper in Dawson City and in Faro. There are also periodic specialized publications for francophones, women and the business and mining communities.

SOCIAL INSTITUTIONS

Education. The Yukon Department of Education operates (with the assistance of elected school councils) the Territory's 29 schools, both public and separate, from kindergarten to grade 12. There are also 3 private schools. In Sept. 1994 there were about 422 teachers and 5,800 pupils. A separate francophone school opened in Sept. 1988. French immersion is offered from kindergarten through grade 12. Yukon College provides adult education for young and mature students, 26% of whom are of First Nations ancestry; Ayandigut Campus in Whitehorse is the administrative and programme centre for 13 other campuses located throughout the Territory. In the 1993–94 academic year a total of 946 full-time and 2,400 part-time students enrolled in programmes and courses. The Yukon government provides financial assistance to students for post-secondary education whether they study at Yukon College or outside the Territory. Financial assistance is provided to First Nations students by the federal Department of Indian Affairs and Northern Development.

Health. The health care system provides all residents with the care demanded by illness or accident. One general hospital at Whitehorse is operated by the Yukon Hospital Corporation. The federal government operates 1 cottage hospital, 4 nursing stations, 8 health centres, 3 public health units and 2 health stations. The territorial government also operates a medical travel programme to send patients to Edmonton or Vancouver for specialized treatment not available in the Territory.

Further Reading

Annual Report of the Government of the Yukon.
Yukon Executive Council, *Statistical Review.*
Berton, P., *Klondike.* (Rev. ed.) Toronto, 1987
Coates, K. and Morrison, W., *Land of the Midnight Sun: A History of the Yukon.* Edmonton, 1988
McClelland, C., *Part of the Land, Part of the Water.* Vancouver, 1987
Minter, R., *White Pass: Gateway to the Klondike.* Toronto, 1987

There is a Yukon Archive at Yukon College, Whitehorse.

CAPE VERDE

República de Cabo Verde

Capital: Praia
Population: 0·36m. (1995)
GNP per capita: US$910 (1994)
HDI/world rank: 0·536/123 (1992)

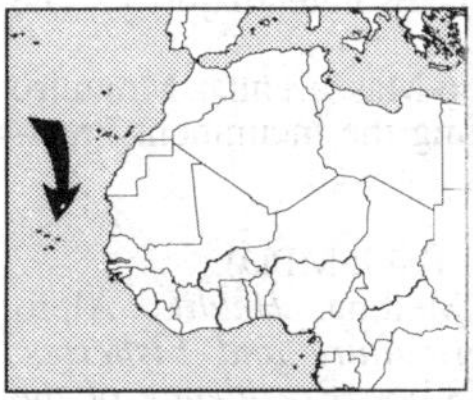

KEY HISTORICAL EVENTS. The Cape Verde Islands were discovered in 1460 by Diogo Gomes, the first settlers arriving in 1462. In 1587 its administration was unified under a Portuguese governor. The colony became an Overseas Province on 11 June 1951.

On 30 Dec. 1974 Portugal transferred power to a transitional government headed by the Portuguese High Commissioner. Full independence was granted on 5 July 1975.

TERRITORY AND POPULATION. Cape Verde is situated in the Atlantic Ocean 620 km off West Africa and consists of 10 islands (Boa Vista, Brava, Fogo, Maio, Sal, Santa Luzia, Santo Antão, São Tiago and São Vicente) and 5 islets. The islands are divided into 2 groups, named Barlavento (windward) and Sotavento (leeward). The total area is 4,033 sq. km (1,557 sq. miles). The population was 341,491 at the census of 1990 (29·7% urban). Estimate (1995) 359,500; density, 89·1 per sq. km. About 600,000 Cape Verdeans live abroad.

Areas, populations and chief towns of the islands and districts:

District/Island	*Area (sq. km)*	*Population Census 1980*	*Population Census 1990*	*Chief town*
Paul	54·3	7,983	8,121	Pombas
Porto Novo	558	13,236	14,873	Porto Novo
Ribeira Grande	166·7	22,102	20,851	Ponta do Sul
Santo Antão	779	43,321	43,845	
São Vicente [1]	227	41,594	51,277	Mindelo
São Nicolau	388	13,572	13,665	Ribeira Brava
Sal	216	5,826	7,715	Santa Maria
Boa Vista	620	3,372	3,452	Sal Rei
Barlovento	*2,230*	*107,685*	*119,954*	
Maio	269	4,098	4,969	Porto Inglês
Praia	395·7	57,748	82,802	Praia
Santa Catarina	242·9	41,012	41,584	Assomada
Santa Cruz	149·3	22,995	25,892	Pedra Badejo
Tarrafal	203·1	24,202	25,413	Tarrafal
São Tiago	991	145,957	175,691	
Fogo	476	30,978	33,902	São Felipe
Brava	67	6,985	6,975	Nova Sintra
Sotavento	*1,803*	*188,018*	*221,537*	

[1] Including Santa Luzia island, which is uninhabited.

The main towns (1990 census) are Praia, the capital, on São Tiago (61,644) and Mindelo on São Vicente, 47,109). Ethnic groups, 1986: Mixed, 71%; Black, 28%; White, 1%. The official language is Portuguese; a creole (Crioulo) is in ordinary use.

Vital statistics, 1993: Births, 16,500; deaths, 3,300. Natural increase, 3·76%. Emigration, 9,800. Net population increase, 0·98%. Life expectancy, 1993, 62·3 years.

CLIMATE. The climate is arid, with a cool dry season from Dec. to June and warm dry conditions for the rest of the year. Rainfall is sparse, rarely exceeding 5" (127 mm) in the northern islands or 12" (304 mm) in the southern ones. There are periodic severe droughts. Praia. Jan. 72°F (22·2°C), July 77°F (25°C). Annual rainfall 10" (250 mm).

CONSTITUTION AND GOVERNMENT. The Constitution of 1981 made the *Partido Africano da Independencia de Cabo Verde* (PAICV) the sole legal party.

In Sept. 1990 the People's National Assembly abolished the PAICV's sole right to rule. A constitutional referendum was held on 28 Dec. 1994; turn-out was 45%. 82·06% of votes cast favoured a reform extending the powers of the presidency and strengthening the autonomy of local authorities.

Elections for the *People's National Assembly* of 79 members elected domestically and 3 from Cape Verdeans living abroad were held on 17 Dec. 1995. 5 parties stood. The Movement for Democracy (MPD) gained an absolute majority. The National Assembly is elected for 5-year terms.

Presidential elections took place on 17 Feb. 1991. Antonio Mascarenhas Monteiro (b. 1943; MPD) was elected by 72% of votes cast, defeating the incumbent President Pereira.

In Oct. 1994 the government consisted of:

Prime Minister and Minister of Defence: Carlos Veiga (b. 1949; MPD).

Foreign Minister: Manuel Chantre. *Finance:* João Medina. *Health:* Alpio Fernandes. *Education and Sport:* Manuel Faustino. *Agriculture and Fisheries:* Helena Semedo. *Infrastructure and Transport:* Teofilo Silva. *Presidency of the Council of Ministers:* Mario Silva. *Culture and Communication:* Ondina Ferreira. *Tourism, Industry and Trade:* João Higino do Rosário. *Justice:* Carlos Veiga. *Employment, Youth and Social Advancement:* José António Mendes. *Economic Co-ordination:* José Veiga.

The *Speaker* is Amilcar Spencer Lopes.

National flag: A blue field, in the lower half of which are 3 horizontal stripes of white, red and white, on which are superimposed 10 yellow stars arranged in a circle.

National anthem: 'Sol, suor, o verde e mar' ('Sun, sweat, the green and the sea'); words and tune by A. Lopes Cabral.

Local Government. There are 14 districts (*conçelhos*).

DEFENCE. There is selective conscription.

Army. The Army is composed of 2 battalions and had a strength of 1,000 in 1996.

Navy. The small force numbered 50 in 1995 and has 2 US-built inshore patrol craft.

Air Force. The Air Force has 2 An-2b transport and 1 DO228 patrol aircraft and fewer than 100 personnel.

INTERNATIONAL RELATIONS

Membership. Cape Verde is a member of the UN, OAU and is an ACP state of the EU.

ECONOMY

Policy. The third National Development Plan (1992–95) emphasized rural development, balanced regional development and promotion of private enterprise.

Currency. The unit of currency is the *Cape Verde escudo* (CVE) of 100 *centavos*. There are coins of 20 and 50 centavos and of 1, 2½, 10, 20 and 50 escudos, and banknotes of 100, 200, 500, 1,000 and 2,500 escudos. In March 1996, £1 = 126·81 escudos; US$1 = 82·97 escudos; DM1 = 56·22 escudos.

Banking and Finance. The Banco de Cabo Verde is the central bank and bank of issue and was also a commercial bank. Its latter functions have been taken over by the new Banco Comercial do Atlântico, mainly financed by public funds.

Weights and Measures. The metric system is in use.

ENERGY AND NATURAL RESOURCES

Electricity. Production in 1986 amounted to 18m. kWh; capacity (1986), 14,000 kW.

Minerals. Salt is obtained on the islands of Sal, Boa Vista and Maio. Volcanic rock (pozzolana) is mined for export.

Agriculture. Some 34,000 ha are cultivated, mainly confined to inland valleys. About 2,000 ha are irrigated. The chief crops (production, 1993, in 1,000 tonnes) are: Coconuts, 10; sugar-cane, 19; bananas, 6; potatoes, 3; cassava, 2; sweet potatoes, 4; maize, 6; beans, groundnuts and coffee. Bananas and coffee are mainly for export.

Livestock (1993): 128,000 goats, 21,000 cattle, 105,000 pigs and 11,000 asses.

Fisheries. In 1993 there were 64 large and 1,400 small fishing vessels. Annual average catch, 9,000 tonnes, mainly tuna. About 200 tonnes of lobsters are caught annually.

INDUSTRY. In 1991 industry accounted for 17·6% of GDP, services 69·2%. In 1988 8,454 tonnes of wheat flour, 1,740 hectolitres of rum and 73 hectolitres of molasses were produced.

Labour. In 1990 the workforce was 141,000 (41,000 females), 10,000 aged 10–15.

FOREIGN ECONOMIC RELATIONS. Foreign debt was US$159·9m. in 1992.

Commerce. Imports in 1990 totalled US$99m., exports US$10m. Exports: Fish, salt and bananas.

Main export markets, 1992: Algeria, 39·8%; Portugal, 24·1%; Italy, 11·1%; Netherlands, 6·5%. Main import suppliers: Portugal, 35·3%; Netherlands, 9·5%; Côte d'Ivoire, 5·5%; Spain, 1·4%.

Total trade of Cape Verde with UK (British Department of Trade returns, in £1,000 sterling):

	1991	*1992*	*1993*	*1994*	*1995*
Imports to UK	193	409	123	484	584
Exports and re-exports from UK	1,908	2,990	3,539	3,763	4,465

Tourism. Tourism is in the initial stages of development, with some 2,000 visitors in 1993.

COMMUNICATIONS

Roads. There were 2,250 km of roads (653 km paved) in 1992 and there were 3,000 private cars and 750 commercial vehicles in 1984.

Civil Aviation. Amilcar Cabral International Airport, at Espargos on Sal, is a major refuelling point on flights to Africa and Latin America. Transportes Aéreos (TACV) de Cabo Verde, the national carrier, provides services to most of the other islands, and internationally to Amsterdam, Dakar, Lisbon, Nouakchott and Paris. In 1995 it operated 6 aircraft. Scheduled flights are also provided by Aeroflot, American Airlines, SAA, TAP and TAAG.

Shipping. The main ports are Mindelo and Praia. In 1995, the merchant marine totalled 32,320 GRT. There is a state-owned ferry service between the islands.

Telecommunications. There were 2,600 telephones in 1987. There are 4 radio stations and an experimental TV service. There were (1993) 50,000 radio receivers.

Press. In 1994 there were 2 weeklies and a Catholic monthly.

SOCIAL INSTITUTIONS

Justice. There is a network of People's Tribunals, with a Supreme Court in Praia.

Religion. At the 1990 census 93·2% of the population were Roman Catholic and 6·8% were mainly Protestant (Nazarence Church).

Education. In 1987 there were 49,703 pupils and 1,464 teachers at 347 primary schools, 10,304 pupils and 321 teachers at 16 preparatory schools, 5,026 pupils and 170 teachers at 4 secondary schools, and 531 students and 52 teachers at a technical school. There were 211 students and 53 teachers in 3 teacher-training colleges and about 500 students were at foreign universities.

In 1988, 64,500 adults (45,100 women) were illiterate.

Health. In 1987 there were 5 general hospitals with 394 beds, 70 health centres with 104 beds and 43 first aid posts; there were also 70 doctors, and 305 nursing personnel.

DIPLOMATIC REPRESENTATIVES

Of Cape Verde in Great Britain
Ambassador: (Vacant; resides in The Hague).

Of Great Britain in Cape Verde
Ambassador: A. E. Furness, CMG (resides in Dakar).

Of Cape Verde in the USA (3415 Massachusetts Ave., NW, Washington, D.C., 20007)
Ambassador: Corentino Virgilio Santos.

Of the USA in Cape Verde (Rua Hojl Ya Yenna 81, Praia)
Ambassador: Joseph M. Segars.

Of Cape Verde to the United Nations
Ambassador: José Luis Leão Monteiro.

Further Reading

Carreira, A., *The People of the Cape Verde Islands.* London, 1982
Foy, C., *Cape Verde: Politics, Economics and Society.* London, 1988
Shaw, C., *Cape Verde Islands:* [Bibliography]. Oxford and Santa Barbara (CA), 1990

National statistical office: Direcção Geral de Estatística, Praia.

CAYMAN ISLANDS

Capital: George Town
Population: 31,930 (1994)
GNP per capita: US$24,360 (1991)

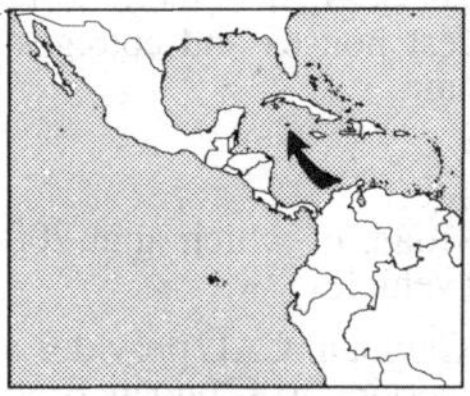

KEY HISTORICAL EVENTS. The islands were discovered by Columbus on 10 May 1503 and (with Jamaica) were recognized as British possessions by the Treaty of Madrid in 1670. Grand Cayman was settled in 1734 and the other islands in 1833. They became a separate Crown Colony on 4 July 1959.

TERRITORY AND POPULATION. Cayman Islands consist of Grand Cayman, Little Cayman and Cayman Brac. Situated in the Caribbean Sea, about 200 miles NW of Jamaica. Area, 100 sq. miles (260 sq. km). Census population of 1989, 25,355 (13,202 Caymanians by birth). Estimate, 1994, 31,930 of which 20,116 were Caymanians. The spoken language is English. The chief town is George Town, census (1989) 12,921. Vital statistics (1994): Births, 531; marriages, 237; deaths, 149.

The areas and populations of the islands are:

	Sq. km	*Census 1979*	*Census 1989*
Grand Cayman	197	15,000	23,881
Cayman Brac	36	1,607	1,441
Little Cayman	26	70	33

CLIMATE. The climate is tropical maritime, with a cool season from Nov. to March and temperatures some 10°F warmer for the remaining months. Rainfall averages 56" (1,400 mm) a year at George Town. Hurricanes may be experienced between July and Nov.

CONSTITUTION AND GOVERNMENT. The 1972 Constitution provides for a *Legislative Assembly* consisting of the Speaker, 3 official members, and 15 elected members. The *Executive Council* consists of the Governor (as Chairman), the 3 official members and 5 members elected by the elected members of the Legislative Assembly.

Governor: John W. Owen, MBE.

Flag: British Blue Ensign with the arms of the Colony on a white disc in the fly.

ECONOMY

Budget. Estimated revenue 1996, CI$184·57m.; expenditure, CI$199·7m. Public debt (Dec. 1994), CI$37m.; total reserves (Dec. 1994), CI$3·9m.

Currency. The unit of currency is the *Cayman Island dollar* (KYD) of 100 *cents.* There are coins of 1, 5, 10, 25 and 50 cents and CI$1, 2 and 5 and notes of CI$1, 5, 10, 25, 50 and 100. In March 1996, £1 = CI$1·27; US$1 = CI$0·83; DM1 = CI$0·56.

Banking and Finance. The note-issuing authority is the Cayman Islands Currency Board. 560 commercial banks and trust companies held licences at Dec. 1994, which permit the holders to offer services to the public, 30 domestically. Financial services are the Islands' chief industry.

INDUSTRY

Electricity. Production (1994) 281·05m. kWh.

Industry. At Dec. 1994, 31,612 companies were registered in the Islands.

FOREIGN ECONOMIC RELATIONS

Commerce. Exports, 1994 (f.o.b.), totalled CI$2m. Imports, (c.i.f.), CI$272·9m.

Total trade between Cayman Islands and UK (British Department of Trade returns, in £1,000 sterling):

	1991	*1992*	*1993*	*1994*	*1995*
Imports to UK	1,736	2,497	1,268	2,575	1,330
Exports and re-exports from UK	6,081	6,173	7,136	6,780	10,621

Tourism. Tourism is the chief industry after financial services, and there were (1994) 3,880 beds in hotels and 3,162 in apartments, guest houses and cottages. There were 940,578 visitors in 1994, including 341,491 by air.

COMMUNICATIONS

Roads. There were (1994) about 252 miles of motorable road, of which abut 200 miles were surfaced with tarmac, and (1992) 14,707 motor vehicles.

Civil Aviation. There is an international airport at Grand Cayman. CAL provides a regular inter-island service. Cayman Airways operates a service to Cayman Brac and also flies to Miami, Orlando, Houston, Tampa, Atlanta, Honduras and Jamaica. American Airlines and Northwest Airlines provide services to Miami; US Air to Baltimore and North Carolina; American Airlines to Raleigh/Durham; Air Jamaica to Jamaica; and British Airways to Gatwick, London.

Shipping. Motor vessels ply regularly between the Cayman Islands, Jamaica, Costa Rica and Florida. Shipping registered at George Town, 820 vessels (Dec. 1994).

Telecommunications. There were 23,515 telephones in 1994 and there are 3 radio broadcasting stations in the Islands, with (1993) an estimated 18,000 receivers. There is one local commercial TV company.

Press. The *Caymanian Compass* is published 5 days a week.

SOCIAL INSTITUTIONS

Justice. There is a Grand Court, sitting 6 times a year for criminal sessions at George Town under a Chief Justice and 2 puisne judges. There are 2 Magistrates presiding over the Summary Court.

Religion. There are Anglican, Roman Catholic, Presbyterian and other Christian communities represented in the islands.

Education. In 1994 there were 10 government primary schools with 1,683 pupils and 6 private schools (4 with secondary departments) with 1,516 pupils. Post-primary education at the 3 government high schools was attended by 1,409 pupils. There is also a private institution for tertiary education; a government school for special educational needs; a government-operated community college offering technical, vocational and business studies and a 2-year programme in arts and sciences, as well as adult, educational and recreational courses; and a centre for training of handicapped persons.

Health. In 1994 there was a general hospital in George Town with 23 doctors, a dental clinic, 4 district clinics and a hospital in Cayman Brac with specialist services (19 beds).

Further Reading

Cayman Islands Government, *Annual Report*
Compendium of Statistics of the Cayman Islands, 1994. Cayman Islands Government Statistics Office, 1995

CENTRAL AFRICAN REPUBLIC

République Centrafricaine

Capital: Bangui
Population: 3·07m. (1994)
GNP per capita: US$370 (1994)
HDI/world rank: 0·361/149 (1992)

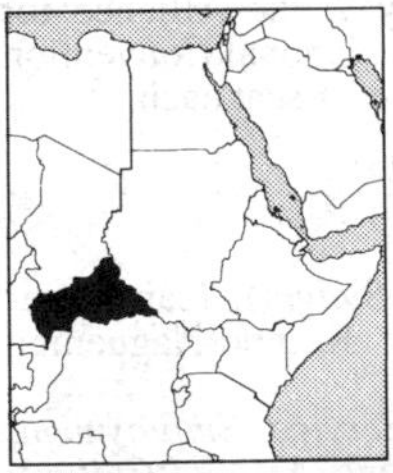

KEY HISTORICAL EVENTS. Central African Republic became independent on 13 Aug. 1960, after having been one of the 4 territories of French Equatorial Africa (under the name of Ubangi Shari) and from 1 Dec. 1958 a member state of the French Community. A Constitution of 1976 provided for the country to be a parliamentary democracy to be known as the Central African Empire. President Bokassa became Emperor Bokassa I. He was overthrown in a coup on 20–21 Sept. 1979 and the empire was abolished. On 15 March 1981 David Dacko was re-elected President but Army Chief General André Kolingba took power in a bloodless coup on 1 Sept. 1981 at the head of a Military Committee for National Recovery (CMRN), which held supreme power until 21 Sept. 1985 when President Kolingba dissolved it and initiated a return towards constitutional rule.

TERRITORY AND POPULATION. The republic is bounded in the north by Chad, east by Sudan, south by Zaïre and Congo, and west by Cameroon. The area covers 622,436 sq. km (240,324 sq. miles). The population at the 1988 census was 2,568,426; estimate, 1994, 3,068,000 (47% urban). Expectation of life in 1992 was 47·2 years.

The areas, populations and capitals of the prefectures are as follows:

Prefecture	*Sq. km*	*1988 census*	*Capital*
Bangui [1]	67	451,690	Bangui
Ombella-M'poko	31,835	180,857	Bimbo
Lobaye	19,235	169,554	M'baiki
Sangha M'baéré	19,412	65,961	Nola
Mambere Kadéi	30,203	230,364	Berbérati
Nana-Mambere	26,600	191,970	Bouar
Ouham-Pendé	32,100	287,653	Bozoum
Ouham	50,250	262,950	Bossangoa
Nana Gribizi	19,996	95,497	Kaga-Bandoro
Bamingui-Bangoran	58,200	28,643	Ndele
Vakaga	46,500	32,118	Birao
Kemo	17,204	82,884	Sibut
Ouaka	49,900	208,332	Bambari
Basse-Kotto	17,604	194,750	Mobaye
Haute-Kotto	86,650	58,838	Bria
M'bomou	61,150	119,252	Bangassou
Haut-M'bomou	55,530	27,113	Obo

[1] Autonomous commune.

There are about 30 ethnic groups, conventionally divided into river (M'Baka, Yakoma) and savannah (Mandjia, Sara, Gbaya) peoples.

French and Sango are the official languages.

CLIMATE. A tropical climate with little variation in temperature. The wet months are May, June, Oct. and Nov. Bangui. Jan. 31·9°C, July 20·7°C. Annual rainfall 1,289·3 mm. Ndele. Jan. 36·3°C, July 30·5°C. Annual rainfall 203·6 mm.

CONSTITUTION AND GOVERNMENT. Under the Constitution adopted by a referendum on 21 Nov. 1986, the sole legal political party was the *Rassemble-*

ment Démocratique Centrafricaine. In Aug. 1992 the Constitution was revised to permit multi-party democracy. The President is elected by popular vote for a term of 6 years, and appoints and leads a Council of Ministers. There is an 85-member *National Assembly*.

At the presidential and parliamentary elections held in 2 rounds on 22 Aug. and 19 Sept. 1993 there were 8 presidential and some 500 parliamentary candidates. Turn-out was 68·47%. Ange-Félix Patasse gained 37·8% of votes cast in the first round and 52·24% in the second. The Central African People's Liberation Movement (MLPC) gained 34 seats, the Democratic Central African Rally 13, the Patriotic Front for Progress 7, the Liberal Democratic Party 7, the Alliance for Democracy and Progress 6, the David Dacko Movement 6, the National Convention 3 and the Social Democratic Party 3, ind 2. 4 other parties gained 1 seat each.

President: Ange-Félix Patasse (MLPC; sworn in 22 Oct. 1993).

In Jan. 1996 the government comprised:

Prime Minister: Jean Koyambonou.

Ministers of State: Emmanuel Dokouna (*Finance and the Budget*); Jean Mete-Yapende (*Defence, Veterans and War Disabled*); Nestor Kombo-Naguemon (*Relations with Parliament*).

Agriculture and Livestock: Gabriel Dotte Badekara. *Civil Service, Employment, Social Security and Training:* Eloi Anguimate. *Communications, Art and Culture:* Maurice Saragba. *Education, Research and Technology:* Albert Mberio. *Energy and Mining:* Charles Massi. *Economy, Planning and International Co-operation:* Dogonendji Be. *Foreign:* Simon Bedaya Ngaro. *Decentralization and Regionalization:* Gérard Gaba. *Health and Population:* Dr Gabriel Fio-Ngaïndiro. *Industry, Trade and Handicrafts:* Joseph Agbo. *Justice, Law Reform and Keeper of the Seals:* Betty Marasse. *Transport and Civil Aviation:* Albert Yomba Eyamo. *Tourism and the Environment:* Daniel Emery Dede. *Women's Affairs and National Solidarity:* Marie Ande Koyara. *Youth and Sport:* Fidèle Ogbami. *Public Works and Territorial Management:* Dieudonne Becket. *Territorial Administration and National Security:* Thierry Kiandji. *Posts and Telecommunications:* Vincent Sakanga. *Water, Forests Hunting and Fishing:* Laurent Ngon Baba.

The *Speaker* is Hugues Dobozendi (MLPC).

National flag: Four horizontal stripes of blue, white, green, yellow; over all in the centre a vertical red strip, and in the canton a yellow star.

National anthem: La Renaissance (*Rebirth*); words by B. Boganda, tune by H. Pepper.

Local Government: The Republic is divided into 16 prefectures (subdivided into 67 sub-prefectures and 2 administrative control posts) comprising 65 urban and 102 rural communes and 7 cattle-grazing communes. The 8 arrondissements of Bangui, the capital, have the status of communes.

DEFENCE. Selective national service for a 2-year period is in force. Some 1,200 French military personnel were stationed in 1993.

Army. The Army consisted (1996) of about 2,500 personnel, comprising a Republican Guard, 1 territorial defence, 1 combined arms and 1 support HQ regiment. Equipment includes 4 T-55 tanks. There are some 2,300 personnel in the paramilitary Gendarmerie.

Navy. The naval wing of the army has 9 river patrol craft and (1995) about 80 personnel.

Air Force. The Air Force has 2 Rallye light aircraft, 2 C-47 transports, 1 Falcon 20 VIP aircraft and 1 Ecureuil helicopter. Personnel strength (1995) about 150.

INTERNATIONAL RELATIONS

Membership. The Central African Republic is a member of the UN and OAU and is an ACP state of the EU.

ECONOMY

Budget. The budget for 1994 provided for expenditure of 54,406m. francs CFA, and for revenue of 43,904m. francs CFA.

Currency. The unit of currency is the *franc CFA* with a parity of 100 francs CFA to 1 French franc. There are coins of 1, 5, 10, 25, 50, 100 and 500 francs CFA, and banknotes of 500, 1,000, 2,000, 5,000 and 10,000 francs CFA. In 1992 42,800m. francs CFA were in circulation. Foreign exchange reserves were US$99·9m.; gold reserves, US$2·8m. In March 1996, £1 = 772·97 francs CFA; US$1 = 505·74 francs CFA; DM1 = 342·67 francs CFA.

Banking and Finance. The Banque des Etats de l'Afrique Centrale (BEAC) acts as the central bank and bank of issue.

Weights and Measures. The metric system is in use.

ENERGY AND NATURAL RESOURCES

Electricity. Production in 1994 totalled 96,617 kWh (96,268 kWh hydro-electric).

Minerals. In 1994, 531,992 carats of gem diamonds, 95,957 carats of industrial diamonds and 138·18 kg of gold were mined. There are significant regions of uranium in the Bakouma area.

Agriculture. In 1993 1·9m. persons subsisted on agriculture, of whom 0·877m. were economically active. The main crops (production 1993, in 1,000 tonnes) are cassava, 610; groundnuts, 43; bananas, 96; plantains, 68; millet, 7; maize, 55; seed cotton, 20; coffee, 11; rice, 7.

Livestock, 1993, (in 1,000): Cattle, 2,781; goats, 1,334; sheep, 142; pigs, 474.

Forestry. There are 35·8m. ha of forest. The extensive hardwood forests, particularly in the south-west, provide mahogany, obeche and limba. Production (1994) 374,794 cu. metres.

Fisheries. Catch (1983) 13,000 tonnes.

INDUSTRY. The small industrial sector includes factories producing cotton fabrics, footwear, beer and radios. Output in 1994: Beer, 258,149 hectolitres; cotton fabrics (1992), 5·32m. metres; soap, 1,896 tonnes; leather, 19 tonnes.

FOREIGN ECONOMIC RELATIONS

Commerce. Imports and exports in 1m. francs CFA:

	1990	*1991*	*1992*	*1993*	*1994*
Imports	65,800	44,770	43,211	35,559	73,263
Exports	32,760	30,750	28,328	31,073	79,541

In 1992, France took 74·4% of exports and provided 11% of imports. Main exports are coffee, diamonds, timber and cotton.

Total trade of Central African Republic with UK (British Department of Trade returns, in £1,000 sterling):

	1991	*1992*	*1993*	*1994*	*1995*
Imports to UK	37	100	53	151	192
Exports and re-exports from UK	502	656	1,487	1,056	638

COMMUNICATIONS

Roads. In 1994 there were 24,307 km of roads, of which 520 km were bitumenized. In 1992 46,982 vehicles were in use.

Civil Aviation. There is an international airport at Mpoko, near Bangui. The country is a member of Air Afrique, the regional carrier, with services to Paris and African capitals. Air Gabon and Air France also operate services.

Shipping. Timber and barges are taken to Brazzaville (Congo).

Telecommunications. There were 16,867 telephones in 1992. Broadcasting is provided by the state-controlled Radiodiffusion-Télévision Centrafricaine. There were 0·55m. radio and 7,500 TV (colour by SECAM) sets in 1993.

Cinemas. In 1992 there were 5 cinemas.

Press. In 1993 there were 1 daily and several other newspapers.

SOCIAL INSTITUTIONS

Justice. The Criminal Court and Supreme Court are situated in Bangui. There are 16 high courts throughout the country.

Religion. In 1992 there were 1·44m. Protestants and 0·97m. Roman Catholics. Traditional animist beliefs are still current.

Education. A national education plan was initiated in 1994 to fund capital educational projects. Adult illiteracy was 62% in 1992. In 1990-91 there were 308,409 pupils at primary schools and 46,985 at secondary schools; technical schools had 1,862 students. There is a university at Bangui. It had 3,590 students and 140 academic staff in 1995-96.

Health. In 1990 there were 255 hospitals and health centres with 4,120 beds; there were also 170 doctors, 8 dentists, and 1,353 nursing personnel.

DIPLOMATIC REPRESENTATIVES

Of Central African Republic in Great Britain
Ambassador: Vacant (resides in Paris).

Of Great Britain in Central African Republic
Ambassador: Nicholas McCarthy, OBE (resides in Yaoundé).

Of Central African Republic in the USA (1618 22nd St., NW, Washington, D.C. 20008)
Ambassador: Henri Koba.

Of the USA in Central African Republic (Ave. David Dacko, Bangui)
Ambassador: Robert E. Gribbin.

Of Central African Republic to the United Nations
Ambassador: Henri Koba.

Further Reading

Kalck, P., *Central African Republic* [Bibliography]. Oxford and Santa Barbara (CA), 1993

CHAD

République du Tchad

Capital: N'Djaména
Population: 6·28m. (1993)
GNP per capita: US$190 (1994)
HDI/world rank: 0·296/162 (1992)

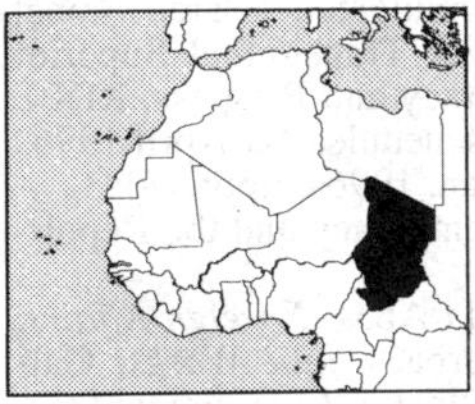

KEY HISTORICAL EVENTS. France proclaimed a protectorate over Chad on 5 Sept. 1900, and in July 1908 the territory was incorporated into French Equatorial Africa. It became a separate colony in 1920, and in 1946 one of the 4 constituent territories of French Equatorial Africa. On 28 Nov. 1958 it became an autonomous republic within the French Community and achieved full independence on 11 Aug. 1960.

Conflicts between the government and secessionist groups, particularly in the Moslem north and centre, began in 1965 and developed into civil war. In 1982 forces led by Hissène Habré gained control of the country. In June 1983 the Libyan-backed forces of former President Goukouni Oueddei re-occupied some territory, but by April 1987 they were forced back into the Aozou Strip in the north, occupied by Libyan forces since 1973. A ceasefire took effect in Sept. 1987. There was an attempted coup on 1 April 1989.

Rebel forces of the Popular Salvation Movement led by Idriss Deby entered Chad from Sudan in Nov. 1990 and, meeting little resistance, overcame the government forces of President Hissène Habré, who took refuge in Cameroon. On 4 Dec. 1990 Deby declared himself President.

TERRITORY AND POPULATION. Chad is bounded in the west by Cameroon, Nigeria and Niger, north by Libya, east by Sudan and south by the Central African Republic. In Feb. 1994 the International Court of Justice ruled that the Aouzou Strip along the Libyan border, occupied by Libya since 1973, was part of Chad. Area, 1,284,000 sq. km. At the 1993 census the population was 6,279,931 (5,929,192 settled, of whom 1,327,570 were urban and 359,069 nomadic). The capital is N'Djaména with 530,965 inhabitants (1993 census), other large towns being Moundou (282,103), Sarh (193,753), Bongor (196,713), Abéché (187,936) and Doba (185,461).

The areas, populations and chief towns of the 14 prefectures were:

Prefecture	*Area sq. km*	*Population (1993 census)*	*Capital*
Borkou-Ennedi-Tibesti	600,350	73,185	Faya (Largeau)
Biltine	46,850	184,807	Biltine
Ouaddaï	76,240	543,900	Abéché
Batha	88,800	288,458	Ati
Kanem	114,520	279,927	Mao
Lac	22,320	252,932	Bol
Chari-Baguirmi	82,910	1,251,906	N'Djaména
Guéra	58,950	306,253	Mongo
Salamat	63,000	184,403	Amtiman
Moyen-Chari	45,180	738,595	Sarh
Logone Oriental	28,035	441,064	Doba
Logone Occidental	8,695	455,489	Moundou
Tandjilé	18,045	453,854	Laï
Mayo-Kebbi	30,105	825,158	Bongor

The official languages are French and Arabic, but more than 100 different languages and dialects are spoken. The largest ethnic group is the Sara of southern Chad.

CLIMATE. A tropical climate, with adequate rainfall in the south, though Nov. to

April are virtually rainless months. Further north, desert conditions prevail. N'Djaména. Jan. 75°F (23·9°C), July 82°F (27·8°C). Annual rainfall 30" (744 mm).

CONSTITUTION AND GOVERNMENT. After overthrowing the regime of Hissène Habré (*see* THE STATESMAN'S YEAR-BOOK, 1991-92, pp. 345-46), Idriss Deby proclaimed himself *President* and was sworn in on 4 March 1991.

A law of Oct. 1991 permits the formation of political parties provided they are not based on regionalism, tribalism or intolerance. There were 59 parties in 1996.

In April 1993 the Sovereign National Conference promulgated a Transitional Charter to regulate the political regime for 12 months. A Transitional Superior Council was set up headed by Abas Ali (Rally for Democracy and Progress, RDP). Multi-party presidential and parliamentary elections were scheduled for April 1996.

A new government was formed in April 1995 which in Jan. 1996 comprised:

Prime Minister: Djimasta Koïbla (b. 1950; Union for Democracy and the Republic).

Security: Noudjalbaye N'gariena. *Justice:* Maldom Bada Abas. *Foreign Affairs:* Mahamat Abderamane Haggar. *Civil Service:* Salibou Garba. *Public Works:* Gali Gothé Gatta. *Finance and Information:* Mahamat Ahmat Alhabo. *Planning and Co-operation:* Mariam Mahamat Nour. *Public Health:* Aba Ngaré Mahamat. *Education:* Nassour Ouaïdou. *Livestock:* Mahamat Nour Mallaye. *Communications:* Youssouf Mbodou Mbami. *Economy and Industry:* Abas Mahamat Ambadi. *Mines and Energy:* Mbaïnodoum Paul. *Social Affairs:* Asta Selgué Aguidi. *Territorial Administration:* Mahamat Nourri. *Tourism and the Environment:* Ketté Nodji Moïse. *Defence:* Youssouf Togoïmi.

National flag: Three vertical strips of blue, yellow, red.

National anthem: 'Peuple tchadien, debout et à l'ouvrage' ('People of Chad, arise and to the task'); words by L. Gidrol, tune by P. Villard.

Local Government: The 14 prefectures are divided into 54 sub-prefectures and the Aouzou Strip.

DEFENCE. There are 8 military regions. Conscription is for 3 years.

Army. In 1996 the strength was 25,000 and there was a paramilitary Gendarmerie of 4,500 and a Republican Guard of 5,000. Equipment included 60 T-55 main battle tanks.

Air Force. The Air Force has 2 C-130 Hercules, 2 Turbo-Porters, 2 armed PC-7 aircraft and 2 Alouette helicopters.

Personnel (1995) about 350.

INTERNATIONAL RELATIONS

Membership. Chad is a member of the UN, OAU and is an ACP state of the EU.

ECONOMY

Budget. Budget revenue and expenditure (in 1m. francs CFA):

	1992	*1993*	*1994*	*1995*
Revenue:	31,422	42,694	39,042	42,704
Expenditure:	52,651	46,771	70,868	61,652

1993 revenue included: Income tax, 9,192; taxes on goods and services, 6,522; customs duties, 10,988; non-tax receipts, 6,383.

Currency. The unit of currency is the *franc CFA* with a parity value of 100 francs CFA to 1 French franc. For exchange rates *see* BENIN: Currency.

Banking and Finance. The Banque des Etats de l'Afrique Centrale is the bank of issue, and the principal commercial banks are the Banque de Développement du Tchad and the Banque Tchadienne de Crédit et de Dépôts.

ENERGY AND NATURAL RESOURCES

Electricity. Production (1994) amounted to 84·78m. kWh.

Oil. The oilfield in Kanem préfecture has been linked by pipeline to a new refinery at N'Djaména but production has remained minimal. There is a larger oilfield in the Doba Basin.

Minerals. Salt (about 4,000 tonnes per annum) is mined around Lake Chad, and there are deposits of uranium, gold, iron ore and bauxite. There are small-scale workings for gold and iron.

Agriculture. Cotton growing (in the south) and animal husbandry (in the central zone) are the most important branches. Production, 1994 (in 1,000 tonnes): Millet, 320; sugar-cane, 336; yams, 245; seed cotton, 160; groundnuts, 207; gum arabic, 7; dry beans, 24; sweet potatoes, 48; mangoes, 32; dates, 25; maize, 159; cotton lint, 39.

Livestock: Cattle (1995, in 1,000), 4,653; sheep and goats, 5,850; horses, 467; camels, 663.

Fisheries. Fish production, from Lake Chad and the Chari and Logone rivers, was estimated at 31,000 tonnes in 1993.

INDUSTRY. Output, 1994: Cotton fibre, 38,600 tonnes; edible oil, 5·41m. litres; sugar, 26,800 tonnes; beer, 1·1m. litres; cigarettes, 23·16m. packets; soap, 2,801 tonnes; bicycles, 1,827.

FOREIGN ECONOMIC RELATIONS

Commerce. Trade (in 1m. francs CFA):

	1992	*1993*	*1994*	*1995*
Imports	127,700	126,560	173,870	223,450
Exports	62,400	52,890	105,590	124,570

The main trading partners are France and Nigeria. Cotton exports in 1994, 28,857m. francs CFA; cattle, 15,401 francs CFA.

Total trade with UK (British Department of Trade returns, in £1,000 sterling):

	1991	*1992*	*1993*	*1994*	*1995*
Imports to UK	1,477	1,604	1,471	1,113	3,173
Exports and re-exports from UK	1,789	1,359	2,006	1,924	1,939

COMMUNICATIONS

Roads. In 1994 there were 32,000 km of roads, of which 0·82% were surfaced.

Civil Aviation. There is an international airport at N'Djaména, from which UTA and Air Afrique run 4 flights per week to Paris; there are also flights to Bangui and Kinshasa. There are also services by Camair, Ethiopian Airlines and Sudan Airlines. Air Tchad operates internal services to 12 secondary airports.

Telecommunications. In 1994 there were 4,733 telephones. The state-controlled Radiodiffusion Nationale Tchadienne broadcasts a national and 3 regional services in French, Arabic and Sara. There were estimated to be 1·26m. radio sets in 1993. Television is being developed (colour by SECAM) by the state-controlled Télé-Tchad.

SOCIAL INSTITUTIONS

Justice. There are criminal courts and magistrates courts in N'Djaména, Moundou, Sarh and Abéché, with a Court of Appeal situated in N'Djaména.

Religion. The northern and central parts of the country are predominantly Moslem. At the 1993 census there were 3,335,869 Moslems, 2,151,996 Christians and 456,064 animists.

Education. In 1994-95 there were 547,696 pupils in primary schools, 82,559 in secondary schools, 2,108 in technical schools and 2,000 at the university, with 120 academic staff.

Health. In 1994 there were 3,962 hospital beds, 217 doctors, 878 nurses, 130 midwives and 10 pharmacists.

DIPLOMATIC REPRESENTATIVES

Of Chad in Great Britain
Ambassador: Ramadane Barma (resides in Brussels).

Of Great Britain in Chad
Ambassador: J. T. Masefield, CMG (resides in Abuja).

Of Chad in the USA (2002 R. St., NW, Washington, D.C., 20009)
Ambassador: Ahmat Mahamat Saleh.

Of the USA in Chad (Ave. Felix Eboue, N'Djaména)
Ambassador: Laurence E. Pope.

Of Chad to the United Nations
Ambassador: Ahmat Mahamat Saleh.

Further Reading

Joffe, G. and Day-Viaud, C. (eds.) *Chad.* [Bibliography]. Oxford and Santa Barbara (CA), 1995

National statistical office: Direction de la Statistique des Etudes Economiques et Démographiques, Ministère du Plan et de la Cooperation, N'Djaména.

CHILE

República de Chile

Capital: Santiago
Population: 13·29m. (1995)
GNP per capita: US$3,560 (1994)
HDI/world rank: 0·880/33 (1992)

KEY HISTORICAL EVENTS. Chile freed itself from Spanish rule in 1818.

The Marxist coalition government of President Salvador Allende Gossens was ousted on 11 Sept. 1973 by a military junta, headed by Gen. Augusto Pinochet Ugarte, C.in-C. of the Army, who took over the presidency. President Allende committed suicide on the day of the coup.

The new government assumed wide-ranging powers. A constitution of 1981 provided for an eventual return to democracy and Gen. Pinochet was rejected as president in a plebiscite in 1988.

TERRITORY AND POPULATION. Chile is bounded in the north by Peru, east by Bolivia and Argentina, and south and west by the Pacific Ocean. The area is 736,905 sq. km (284,520 sq. miles) excluding the claimed Antarctic territory. Many islands to the west and south belong to Chile: The Islas Juan Fernández (179 sq. km with 516 inhabitants in 1982) lie about 600 km west of Valparaíso, and the volcanic Isla de Pascua (Easter Island or Rapa Nui, 118 sq. km with 1,867 inhabitants in 1982), lies about 3,000 km WNW of Valparaíso. Small uninhabited dependencies include Sala y Goméz (400 km east of Easter Is.), San Ambrosio and San Félix (1,000 km northwest of Valparaíso, and 20 km apart) and Islas Diego Ramírez (100 km SW of Cape Horn).

In 1940 Chile declared, and in each subsequent year has reaffirmed, its ownership of the sector of the Antarctic lying between 53° and 90° W. long.; and asserted that the British claim to the sector between the meridians 20° and 80° W. long. overlapped the Chilean by 27°. Seven Chilean bases exist in Antarctica. A law of 1955 put the governor of Magallanes in charge of the 'Chilean Antarctic Territory' which has an area of 1,269,723 sq. km. and a population (1982) of 1,368.

The population at the census of 1992 was 13,231,803 (6,730,478 females). Estimate, 1995, 13,292,200 (83·5% urban in 1993).

Vital statistics rates, 1991 (per 1,000 population): Birth, 22·4; death, 5·6; infant mortality (per 1,000 live births), 14·6. Life expectancy (1993), 72 years.

Area, population and capitals of the 13 regions:

Region	*Sq. km*	*Population (1992 census)*	*Capital*	*Population (1992 census)*
Tarapacá	58,786	341,112	Iquique	152,654
Antofagasta	125,253	407,409	Antofagasta	226,749
Atacama	74,705	230,786	Copiapó	100,946
Coquimbo	40,656	502,460	La Serena	120,336
Valparaíso	16,396	1,373,967	Valparaíso	276,736
Metropolitan	15,549	5,170,293	Santiago	5,180,757 [1]
Libertador	16,456	688,385	Rancagua	187,134
Maule	30,518	834,053	Talca	171,467
Bíobío	36,939	1,729,920	Concepción	330,448
Araucanía	31,946	774,959	Temuco	240,880
Los Lagos	67,247	953,330	Puerto Montt	130,737
Aysén	108,997	82,071	Coihaique	31,167 [2]
Magallanes	132,034	143,058	Punta Arenas	113,661

[1] Metropolitan area; city proper, 4,385,481. [2] 1982 census.

Other large towns (1992 census population) are: Viña del Mar (302,765), Puente Alto (254,534), Talcahuano (246,566), San Bernardo (188,850), Arica (169,217), Chillán (158,731), Los Angeles (142,136), Osorno (128,709), Coquimbo (122,872),

Valdívia (122,436), Calama (120,602), Curicó (103,919) and Quilpué (102,824).

79% of the population is mixed or *mestizo*, 20% are of European descent and 1% are indigenous Amerindians of the Araucanian, Fuegian and Chango groups. Language and culture remain of European origin, with the 675,000 Araucanian-speaking (mainly Mapuche) Indians the only sizeable minority.

The official language is Spanish.

CLIMATE. With its enormous range of latitude and the influence of the Andean Cordillera, the climate of Chile is very complex, ranging from extreme aridity in the north, through a Mediterranean climate in Central Chile, where winters are wet and summers dry, to a cool temperate zone in the south, with rain at all seasons. In the extreme south, conditions are very wet and stormy. Santiago. Jan. 67°F (19·5°C), July 46°F (8°C). Annual rainfall 15" (375 mm). Antofagasta. Jan. 69°F (20·6°C), July 57°F (14°C). Annual rainfall 0·5" (12·7 mm). Valparaíso. Jan. 64°F (17·8°C), July 53°F (11·7°C). Annual rainfall 20" (505 mm).

CONSTITUTION AND GOVERNMENT. A new Constitution was approved by 67·5% of the voters on 11 Sept. 1980 and came into force on 11 March 1981. It provided for a return to democracy after a minimum period of 8 years. Gen. Pinochet would remain in office during this period after which the Government would nominate a single candidate for President. At a plebiscite on 5 Oct. 1988 President Pinochet was rejected as a presidential candidate by 54·6% of votes cast.

The ***President*** is directly elected for a non-renewable 6-year term. Parliament consists of a 120-member *Chamber of Deputies* and a *High Assembly* of 39 senators.

Elections were held on 12 Dec. 1993 for the presidency, the Chamber of Deputies and 18 senators. Eduardo Frei was elected President by 58% of votes cast. The Christian Democratic Party (PDC) won 37 seats, the Socialist Party (PS) 33, National Renovation 31, the Independent Democratic Union 15 and ind 4.

A government was formed in Jan 1994 with the party composition: PDC, 10; PS, 4; Party for Democracy (PPD) and 4 ind.

In Nov. 1995 the government comprised:

President: Eduardo Frei (b. 1943; PDC; sworn in 11 March 1994).

Agriculture: Emiliano Ortega (ind). *Business:* Felipe Sandoval. *Defence:* Edmundo Péréz Yoma (PDC). *Economy:* Alvaro García (PPD). *Education:* Sergio Molina (PDC). *Energy:* Alejandro Jadresic (ind). *Finance:* Eduardo Aninat (PDC). *Foreign Affairs:* José Miguel Insulzá (PS). *Health:* Carlos Massad (PDC). *Housing and Urban Development:* Edmundo Hermosilla (PDC). *Interior:* Carlos Figueroa (PDC). *Justice:* Soledad Alvear (PDC). *Labour:* Jorge Arrate (PS). *Minerals:* Benjamín Teplisky (Radical Party). *National Resources:* Adriano del Piano (PPD). *Planning:* Luis Maira (PS). *Public Works:* Ricardo Lagos (PS). *Transport and Communications:* Narcisso Irureta (PDC). *Women's Affairs:* Josefina Bilbao (PDC).

National flag: 2 horizontal bands, white, red, with a white star on blue square in top sixth next to staff.

National anthem: 'Dulce patria, recibe los votos' ('Sweet Fatherland, receive the vows'); words by E. Lillo, tune by Ramón Carnicer.

Local Government. There are 334 municipalities. At the mayoral elections on 28 June 1992 the electorate was 8m.; turn-out was 89%. The Concertation coalition (of Christian Democrats, Party for Democracy, Socialists and Radicals) gained 53·4% of votes cast, National Renewal 17·9%, the Independent Democratic Union 12·1% and the Communist Party 6·8%. Local elections were scheduled for July 1996 under a new system whereby mayors and councillors are elected jointly and directly from the same list.

DEFENCE. Military service is for 1 year in the Army and 2 in the Navy and Air Force.

Army. A modernization plan of 1995 provides for the transformation of the 7 Army divisions into 3 garrisons: North, Centre-South and Austral, independent and adapted to the terrains in which they operate. Equipment includes 100 M4-A3 and

19 AMX-30 main battle tanks. The service operates 17 transport and 15 training aircraft and 60 helicopters. Strength (1996) 54,000 (27,000 conscripts) with 50,000 reserves. There is a 31,000-strong para-military force of Carabineros.

Navy. The principal ships of the Navy are the 4 ex-British 'County'-class guided missile armed destroyers of which 2 have had the missile launcher removed and replaced with an extended helicopter hangar and flight deck to operate 2 Super-Puma helicopters.

There are also 2 small modern West German-built diesel submarines, 2 British Oberon class submarines, 1 other British-built destroyer, 4 British Leander class frigates, 4 fast missile craft, 4 torpedo boats, 1 offshore patrol vessel and 8 coastal and 10 fast inshore patrol craft. There are 3 French-built medium landing ships. Major auxiliaries include 1 tanker, 1 submarine support vessel, 1 survey ship, 2 transports, and 1 Antarctic patrol ship. There are 11 service craft and numerous boats.

The Naval Air Service numbering 750 personnel operates 5 squadrons: 16 maritime patrol aircraft, 6 transport utility aircraft, 8 anti-submarine helicopters and 10 training aircraft.

Naval personnel in 1995 totalled 31,000 (3,000 conscripts) including 3,000 marines and 1,600 Coast Guard who operate 15 patrol craft and 1 helicopter.

Air Force. Strength (1995) is 14,000 personnel (1,000 conscripts), with over 100 first-line and 150 second-line aircraft, divided among 13 groups, each comprising 1 squadron, within 4 combat and support brigades. Groups 3 and 12 have twin-jet A-37Bs and Group 1 has C-101CC Aviojets, all strike/reconnaissance duties. Group 2 is equipped for photo-reconnaissance with 3 Canberras. Group 4 has 14 Mirage 50 fighters. Group 5 has 14 Twin Otters for light transport and survey duties. Group 7 has 12 F-5E Tiger II fighter-bombers and 2 F-5F trainers. Group 8 fighter-bomber unit has 25 Mirage 5s. Group 10 is a transport wing, with 4 C-130 Hercules, 4 Aviocars, 4 Boeing 707s, including 1 equipped for airborne early warning and various helicopters. An aerial survey unit has 2 Learjets and 3 Beech twin-engined aircraft. Training aircraft include piston-engined Piper Dakota and T-35 Pillan basic trainers and licence-built CASA C-101BB Aviojets.

INTERNATIONAL RELATIONS

Membership. Chile is a member of the UN, OAS and LAIA.

ECONOMY

Budget. In 1991 revenue was 2,273,790m. pesos. 1994 government expenditure (in 1m. pesos): 3,825,817, including on health, 256,902; housing, 217,081; social security, 1,089,454; education, 610,247. The 1996 budget balanced at 6,267,200m. pesos. Sources of revenue included (in 1,000m. pesos): Taxes, 4,894·4; pension contributions, 389·3; sales of assets, 160·3; loan recoveries, 125·6. Expenditure included: Pensions, 1,644·3; personnel, 1.023·7; national investment, 760·1; consumer goods and services, 424·7; public debt service, 192·2. VAT is 18%.

Currency. The unit of currency is the *Chilean peso* (CLP) of 100 *centavos*. There are coins of 1, 5, 10, 50 and 100 pesos and notes of 10, 50, 100, 500, 1,000, 5,000 and 10,000 pesos. Annualized inflation was 8·3% in 1994. In Dec. 1994, 667,532m. pesos were in circulation. Gold reserves were US$700m. in 1993. Foreign exchange reserves were US$9,640m. in 1993. The peso was revalued 3·5% against the US dollar in Nov. 1994. In March 1996, £1=628·86; US$1=411·45; DM1=278·78 pesos.

Banking and Finance. Banking is regulated by legislation of 1995. There is a Central Bank and a State Bank. The Central Bank (*President*, Roberto Zahler) was made independent of government control in March 1990. There were 12 domestic and 24 foreign banks in 1995. In May 1995, deposits in domestic banks totalled 8,623,323m. pesos; in foreign banks, 1,771,057m. pesos, and in other finance companies, 347,415m. pesos.

There are stock exchanges in Santiago and Valparaíso.

Weights and Measures. The metric system has been legally established since 1865, but the old Spanish weights and measures are still in use to some extent.

ENERGY AND NATURAL RESOURCES

Electricity. In 1994, production of electricity was 25,267m. kWh, of which 17,302m. kWh were hydro-electric.

Oil and Gas. Production of crude oil, 1992, was 732,000 tonnes. Gas production, 1994, was 4,423·9m. cu. metres.

Minerals. The wealth of the country consists chiefly in its minerals. Copper is the most important source of foreign exchange and government revenues. Production, 1994, 2,219,900 tonnes. Coal is low-grade and difficult to mine, and mining is made possible by state subsidies. Production, 1994, 1,524,235 tonnes.

Output of other minerals, 1993 (in tonnes): Iron, 7,409,000; iron pellets, 3,494,350; limestone, 4,460,369; molybdenum, 14,900; zinc, 29,619; manganese, 63,400; gold, 34,000 kg; silver, 985,000 kg.Lithium, nitrate, iodine and sodium sulphate are also produced.

Agriculture. In 1991 4·13m. ha of land was arable, 0·25m. ha permanent crops and 13·6m. ha pasture. 1·3m. ha were irrigated in 1992. Some 35,000 tractors were in use in 1991.

Some principal crops were as follows:

Crop	*Area harvested, 1,000 ha 1995*	*Production, 1,000 tonnes 1994*	*Crop*	*Area harvested, 1,000 ha 1994*	*Production, 1,000 tonnes 1992*
Wheat	390	1,322	Potatoes	58	1,023
Oats	65	202	Dry beans	44	91
Barley	25	84	Lentils	10	16
Maize	104	899	Sugar-beet	52	2,978
Rice	30	131			

Fruit production, 1993 (in 1,000 tonnes): Apples, 870; grapes, 880; pears, 230; peaches and nectarines, 160; plums, 130; oranges, 112; lemons and limes, 100. 0·32m. tonnes of wine were produced in 1992.

Livestock, 1992 (in 1,000): Cattle, 3,461; horses, 530; sheep, 6,600; goats, 600; pigs, 1,330; poultry, 35,000. Products, 1994 (in 1,000 tonnes): Beef, 247; mutton, 13; pork, 158; poultry, 310; milk, 1,222; eggs, 1,856m.

Forestry. In 1995 there were 9m. ha of natural forest and woodland (eucalyptus, pine and poplar are important species) and 1·3m. ha of planted forest. 16·86 cu. metres of timber were cut in 1989 (6,540 cu. metres for fuel).

Fisheries. Chile has 4,200 km of coastline and exclusive fishing rights to 1·6 m. sq. km. There are 220 species of edible fish. In 1990 the fishing fleet comprised 250 vessels over 100 GRT totalling 111,140 GRT. Catch in 1993 was 6·19m. tonnes. Fish farms produced 60,728 tonnes of salmon in 1992.

INDUSTRY. Manufacturing contributed 17·3% of GDP in 1993. Output in 1994 (in 1,000 tonnes): Fishmeal, 1,008·1; cellulose, 1,150·8; newsprint, 183·1; paper and cardboard, 108·2; motor tyres, 2,285,400 items; cement, 2,617·9; iron or steel plates, 333·6; copper wire, 5·9; beer, 304·9m. litres; steel, 997·2; motor vehicles, 19,428 items.

Labour. In 1995 the workforce numbered 4,994,600, of whom 448,500 were unemployed. In 1995 1,291,600 persons were employed in social or personal services, 714,100 in agriculture, forestry and fisheries, 908,700 in trade, 823,100 in manufacturing, 363,300 in transport and communications and 360,600 in building. In 1992 there was a monthly minimum wage of 38,600 pesos.

Trade Unions. Trade unions were established in the middle 1880s.

FOREIGN ECONOMIC RELATIONS. In Sept. 1991 Chile and Mexico signed the free trade Treaty of Santiago envisaging annual tariff reductions of 10% from Jan. 1992. Foreign debt was US$21,448m. in Sept. 1995.

Commerce. Imports and exports in US$1m.:

	1989	*1990*	*1991*	*1992*	*1993*	*1994*
Imports	6,535	7,272	7,686	9,670	10,869	11,501
Exports	6,954	8,580	9,048	10,126	9,416	11,645

In 1994 the principal exports were (in US$1m.): Agricultural products, 1,272; chemicals, 1,345; (1993) minerals, 3,976 (of which copper, 3,248). Major export markets (in US$1m.), 1994: USA, 2,012; Japan, 1,976; Argentina, 637; Brazil, 605; South Korea, 584; Germany, 582. Major import suppliers: USA, 2,638; Japan, 1,007; Brazil, 1,000; Argentina, 955.

Total trade between Chile and UK (British Department of Trade returns, in £1,000 sterling):

	1992	*1993*	*1994*	*1995*
Imports to UK	205,737	246,826	194,555	299,959
Exports and re-exports from UK	125,832	141,773	152,839	170,949

Tourism. There were 1·6m. foreign visitors in 1994. Tourist receipts were US$800m in 1993.

COMMUNICATIONS

Roads. In 1987 there were 78,025 km of roads, including 10,299 km hard-surfaced. There were 65 km of motorways and 10,255 km of main roads. In 1991 there were 705,100 private cars, 60,500 taxis, 86,900 lorries, 281,700 vans, 30,400 buses and 52,500 motor cycles.

Railways. The total length of state railway (EFE) lines was (1992) 4,229 km, including 1,653 km electrified, of broad- and metre-gauge. In 1992 the EFE carried 5·6m. tonnes of freight and 9·5m. passengers, including freight traffic on the Northern Railway (1,429 km of metre-gauge) which was taken over by a mixed corporation in 1989. The Antofagasta (Chili) and Bolivia Railway (728 km, metre-gauge) links the port of Antofagasta with Bolivia and Argentina and carried 1·6m. tonnes in 1990. Pacific Railways, formed in 1993, runs freight services over the southern portion of EFE.

There is a metro in Santiago (27·3 km).

Civil Aviation. There is an international airport at Santiago (Comodoro Arturo Merino Benítez). The 2 major airlines merged in 1995: Línea Aérea Nacional Chile (Lan-Chile) operating (1995) 3 B-767-200ERs; 3 B-767-300ERs; 7 B-737-200s and 4 other aircraft; and Línea Aérea de Colore (Ladeco) operating (1995) 2 B-757-200ERs, 2 B-737-100s, 10 B-737-200s, 1 B-737-300 and 1 A300. Services are also provided by Aeroflot, Aerolíneas Argentinas, Aeroperú, Air France, Alitalia, American Airlines, Avianca, British Airways, Canadian Airlines, Cubana, Iberia, KLM, LACSA, LAPSA, Lloyd Aéreo Boliviano, Lufthansa, National Airlines, Pluna, Swissair, United Airlines, Varig and Viasa. There are 3 domestic airlines operating internal flights.

Shipping. The mercantile marine in 1995 totalled 0·98m. GRT, including oil tankers, 71,150 GRT, but most of the fleet operates under flags of convenience. The 6 major ports, the largest being Valparaíso, San Antonio, Antofagusta, Arica and Iquique are state-owned; there are 11 smaller private ports. In 1990 28·56m. tonnes of cargo were loaded, and 19·19m. unloaded.

Telecommunications. In 1988 there were 1,486 post offices and agencies and in 1994 1·5m. telephones.

In 1993 there were 168 radio stations grouped in the Asociación de Radiodifusores de Chile. The state-controlled Televisión Nacional de Chile transmits from 23 stations (colour by NTSC). 4 universities also transmit programmes. In 1993 there were 4·25m. radio and 2m. TV sets.

Cinemas (1993). Cinemas numbered 110; 48 were in Santiago. Total attendance, 1993, 7,733,407.

Press (1994). There were 8 national daily newspapers, a large number of regional newspapers and 100 magazines.

SOCIAL INSTITUTIONS

Justice. There are a High Court of Justice in the capital, 12 courts of appeal distributed over the republic, courts of first instance in the departmental capitals and second-class judges in the sub-delegations.

Religion. In 1990 there were 10·63m. Roman Catholics with 1 cardinal-archbishop, 5 archbishops, 22 bishops and 2 vicars apostolic. 15% of the population defined themselves as evangelical. There were 0·13m. Jews in 1991.

Education. In 1993 7·7% of the population over 15 were illiterate. Education is in 3 stages: Basic (6–14 years), Middle (15–18) and University (19–23). In 1988-89 there were 2,005,000 pupils and 69,000 teachers in the basic schools, 736,000 pupils and 42,000 teachers in the middle schools and 224,000 students and 15,000 teachers in higher education, including universities.

In 1995-96 in the public sector there were 12 universities, 5 Roman Catholic universities, 2 universities of educational science and 1 technological university. In the private sector there were 33 universities, 2 Roman Catholic universities, 1 Adventist university, 2 technical universities, 2 maritime universities, 1 IndoAmerican university, 1 international university and 1 university for each of the following: arts, science and communications; arts and social science; Christian humanism; computer science; science and arts; teaching. There were also 83 other institutes of higher education.

Health. In 1988 there were 354 hospitals with (in 1991) 44,404 beds. In 1987 there were 5,744 doctors, 1,834 dentists, 232 pharmacists, 1,825 midwives and 2,461 other medical personnel.

Social Security. The Pension Fund Administration was founded in 1981. Employees are required to save 13% of their pay. In 1995 it had 5,152,395 members and assets of 9,906,012m. pesos. In 1995 about 25% of adults had private health insurance.

DIPLOMATIC REPRESENTATIVES

Of Chile in Great Britain (12 Devonshire St., London, W1N 2DS)
Ambassador: Vacant.

Of Great Britain in Chile (La Concepción 177, Casilla 72-D, Santiago 9)
Ambassador: Frank Wheeler, CMG.

Of Chile in the USA (1732 Massachusetts Ave., NW, Washington, D.C., 20036)
Ambassador: John Biehl.

Of the USA in Chile (Agustinas 1343, Santiago)
Ambassador: Gabriel Guerra-Mondragon.

Of Chile to the United Nations
Ambassador: Juan Somavía.

Further Reading

Banco Central de Chile. *Boletín Mensual.*

Bethell, L. (ed.) *Chile since Independence.* CUP, 1993
Blakemore, H., *Chile.* [Bibliography] Oxford and Santa Barbara, 1988
Garretón, M. A., *The Chilean Political Process.* London and Boston, 1989
Hojman, D. E., *Chile: the Political Economy of Development and Democracy in the 1990s.* London, 1993.—(ed.) *Change in the Chilean Countryside: from Pinochet to Aylwin and Beyond.* London, 1993
Oppenheim, L. H., *Politics in Chile: Democracy, Authoritarianism and the Search for Development.* Boulder (CO), 1993

National statistical office: Instituto Nacional de Estadísticas (INE), Santiago.

CHINA

Zhonghua Renmin Gonghe Guo

(People's Republic of China)

Capital: Beijing (Peking)
Population: 1,185m. (1994)
GNP per capita: US$530 (1994)
HDI/world rank: 0·594/111 (1992)

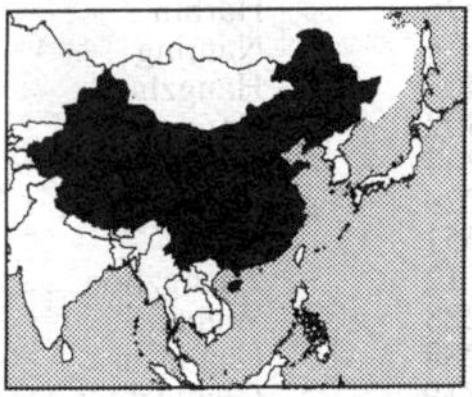

KEY HISTORICAL EVENTS. In the course of 1949 the Communists obtained full control of the mainland of China, and in 1950 also over most islands off the coast (but not Taiwan *see below*). On 1 Oct. 1949 Mao Zedong (Tse-tung) proclaimed the establishment of the People's Republic of China. For the early history of the Communist régime *see* THE STATESMAN'S YEAR-BOOK, 1992– 93, p. 355. For the Tiananmen Square demonstration (1989) *see* THE STATESMAN'S YEAR-BOOK, 1994–95, p. 346. Most prominent leader during this period was sometime Party Leader Deng Xiaoping, who resigned from the Politburo in Nov. 1987 and from the chairmanship of the Military Commissions in Nov. 1989.

TERRITORY AND POPULATION. China is bounded in the north by Russia and Mongolia, east by North Korea, the Yellow Sea and the East China Sea, with Hong Kong and Macao as enclaves on the south-east coast; south by Vietnam, Laos, Burma, India, Bhutan and Nepal; west by India, Pakistan, Afghanistan, Tajikistan, Kyrgyzstan and Kazakhstan. The total area (including Taiwan) is estimated at 9,572,900 sq. km (3,696,100 sq. miles). A law of Feb. 1992 claimed the Spratly, Paracel and Diaoyutasi Islands. An agreement of 7 Sept. 1993 at prime ministerial level settled Sino-Indian border disputes which had first emerged in the war of 1962.

At the 1991 census the population was 1,130,510,638 (548,690,231 females). Population estimate, 1994: 1,185·17m. (580·45m. female; 333·51m. urban).

1979 regulations restricting married couples to a single child, a policy enforced by compulsory abortions and economic sanctions, have been widely ignored, and it was admitted in 1988 that the population target of 1,200m. by 2000 would have to be revised to 1,270m. Since 1988 peasant couples have been permitted a second child after 4 years if the first born is a girl, a measure to combat infanticide.

Vital statistics, 1993: Birth rate (per 1,000), 18·09; death rate, 6·64; growth rate, 11·45. There were 9,121,622 marriages and 909,195 divorces in 1993. Expectation of life was 70 in 1989.

43·2m. persons of Chinese origin lived abroad in 1993.

A number of widely divergent varieties of Chinese are spoken. The official 'Modern Standard Chinese' is based on the dialect of North China. The ideographic writing system of 'characters' is uniform throughout the country, and has undergone systematic simplification. In 1958 a phonetic alphabet (*Pinyin*) was devised to transcribe the characters, and in 1979 this was officially adopted for use in all texts in the Roman alphabet. The previous transcription scheme (Wade) is still used in Taiwan.

China is administratively divided into 22 provinces, 5 autonomous regions (originally entirely or largely inhabited by ethnic minorities, though in some regions now outnumbered by Han immigrants) and 3 government-controlled municipalities. These are in turn divided into 335 prefectures, 570 cities (of which 196 are at prefecture level and 371 at county level), 2,166 counties and 669 urban districts.

Government-controlled municipalities	*Area (in 1,000 sq. km)*	*Population (1990 census, in 1,000)*	*Density per sq. km (in 1987)*	*Capital*
Beijing	17·8	10,870	644	—
Tianjin	4·0	8,830	777	—
Shanghai	5·8	13,510	2,152	—

Government-controlled municipalities	*Area (in 1,000 sq. km)*	*Population (1990 census, in 1,000)*	*Density per sq. km (in 1987)*	*Capital*
Provinces				
Hebei [2]	202·7	60,280	301	Shijiazhuang
Shanxi	157·1	28,180	183	Taiyuan
Liaoning [2]	151·0	39,980	261	Shenyang
Jilin [2]	187·0	25,150	132	Changchun
Heilongjiang [2]	463·6	34,770	76	Harbin
Jiangsu	102·2	68,170	654	Nanjing
Zhejiang [2]	101·8	40,840	407	Hangzhou
Anhui	139·9	52,290	402	Hefei
Fujian	123·1	30,610	244	Fuzhou
Jiangxi	164·8	38,280	229	Nanchang
Shandong	153·3	83,430	551	Jinan
Henan	167·0	86,140	512	Zhengzhou
Hubei [2]	187·5	54,760	288	Wuhan
Hunan [2]	210·5	60,600	288	Changsha
Guangdong [2]	197·1	63,210	319	Guangzhou
Hainan [2]	34·3	6,420	191	Haikou
Sichuan [2]	569·0	106,370	188	Chengdu
Guizhou [2]	174·0	32,730	186	Guiyang
Yunnan [2]	436·2	36,750	85	Kunming
Shaanxi	195·8	32,470	168	Xian
Gansu [2]	366·5	22,930	61	Lanzhou
Qinghai [2]	721·0	4,430	6	Xining
Autonomous regions				
Inner Mongolia	1,177·5	21,110	18	Hohhot
Guangxi Zhuang	220·4	42,530	192	Nanning
Tibet [1]	1,221·6	2,220	2	Lhasa
Ningxia Hui	170.0	4,660	70	Yinchuan
Xinjiang Uighur	1,646·8	15,370	9	Urumqi

[1] See also paragraph on Tibet below.
[2] Also designated minority nationality autonomous area.

Population of largest cities in 1993: Shanghai, 8·76m.; Beijing (Peking), 6·56m.; Tianjin, 4·97m.; Shenyang, 3·86m.; Wuhan, 3·86m.; Guangzhou (Canton), 3·56m.; Chongqing, 3·78m.; Harbin, 3·1m.; Chengdu, 2·67m.; Zibo (1991), 2·46m.; Nanjing, 2·43m.; Xian, 2·36m.; Changchun, 2·4m.; Dalian, 2·33.; Qingdao, 2·24m.; Jinan, 2·05m.; Hangzhou, 1·74m.; Taiyuan, 1·68m.; Zhengzhou, 1·53m.; Kunming, 1·45m.; Tangshan (1990), 1·5m.; Changsha, 1·48m.; Nanchang, 1·42m.; Anshan (1991), 1·39m.; Qiqihar (1991), 1·38m.; Fushun (1991), 1·35m.; Lanzhou, 1·32m.; Fuzhou, 1·29m.; Jilin (1991), 1·27m.; Shijiazhuang, 1·21m.; Baotou (1991), 1·2m.; Huainan (1991), 1·2m.; Luoyang (1991), 1·19m.; Urumqi, 1·11m.; Datong (1991), 1·11m.; Handan (1991), 1·11m.; Guiyang, 1·07m.; Ningbo, 1·07m.

The autonomous regions and 14 provinces (*see table above*) have non-Han components in their populations ranging from 96·3% (in 1992) in Tibet to 10% in Zhejiang. Total minority population, 1993, 70,252,000. 55 ethnic minorities are identified. At the 1990 census the largest were: Zhuang, 15,555,820; Manchu, 9,846,776; Hui, 8,612,001; Miao, 7,383,622; Uighur, 7,207,024; Yi, 6,578,524; Tujia, 5,725,049; Mongolian, 4,802,407; Tibetan, 4,593,072.

Li Chengrui, *The Population of China.* Beijing, 1992
The Population Atlas of China. OUP, 1988
Song, J. *et al.*, *Population Control in China.* New York, 1985

Tibet. For events before and after the revolt of 1959 *see* THE STATESMAN'S YEAR-BOOK, 1964–65 (under TIBET), and 1988–89. On 9 Sept. 1965 Tibet became an Autonomous Region. 301 delegates were elected to the first People's Congress, of whom 226 were Tibetans. The Chief of Government is Gyaincain Norbu. The senior spiritual leader, the Dalai Lama, is in exile. He was awarded the Nobel Peace Prize in 1989. The Banqen Lama died in Jan. 1989. In 1993 the population was 2·29m. (Tibetan, 2·22m.). Birth rate (per 1,000), 1993, 26·68; death rate, 7·6; growth rate, 19·08. Population of the capital, Lhasa, in 1992 was 124,000. Expectation of life was 65 years in 1990. 2m. Tibetans live outside Tibet, in China, and in India and Nepal. Chinese efforts to modernize Tibet include irrigation, road-building and the establishment of light industry: in 1991 there were 328 township and 123 village enterprises employing 21,168 persons; 12,000 persons worked in heavy industry, 16,000 in state-owned enterprises, 1990 output included 136,300 metres of woollen fabrics, 1,000 tonnes of salt, 1,900 tonnes of vegetable oil, 208,200 cu. metres of timber and 132,300 tonnes of cement. Electricity production in 1990 was 330m. kWh, of which 323m. kWh were hydro-electric.

In 1991, 859,000 persons were engaged in agriculture. The total sown area was 213,500 ha, including 41,600 ha sown to wheat, 24,900 ha to soya beans and 10,700 ha to oil-bearing crops. Output (in 1,000 tonnes), 1990: Wheat, 164; soya beans, 60; oil-bearing crops, 17. There were 5·06m. cattle (0·23m. milch cows), 1·26m. draught animals, 0·33m. horses, 0·16m. pigs, 5·66m. sheep and 11·11m. goats in 1991.

In 1991 there were 21,842 km of roads, of which 6,240 km were paved. Air routes link Lhasa with Chengdu, Xian and Kathmandu. Six more were opened in 1987. 30,000 tourists visited Tibet in 1986.

The borders were opened for trade with neighbouring countries in 1980. In July 1988 Tibetan was reinstated as a 'major official language', competence in which is required of all administrative officials.

Monasteries and shrines have been renovated and reopened. There were some 15,000 monks and nuns in 1987. In 1984 a Buddhist seminary in Lhasa opened with 200 students. On 8 Dec. 1995, the Chinese government designated Gyaincain Norbu (b. 1989) the tenth reincarnation of the Panchen Lama; this was repudiated by the Tibetan government-in-exile. In 1988 there were 2,437 primary schools, 67 secondary schools, 14 technical schools and 3 higher education institutes. The total number of primary school pupils in 1990–91 was 101,000. A university was established in 1985. In 1990 there were some 9,000 medical personnel and 1,006 medical institutions, with a total of about 5,000 beds.

Since 1987 there have been several anti-Chinese demonstrations in which a number of people have been killed.

Barnett, R. and Akiner, S. (eds.) *Resistance and Reform in Tibet.* Farnborough, 1994
Batchelor, S., *The Tibet Guide.* London, 1987
The Dalai Lama, *My Land and My People* (ed. D. Howarth). London, 1962:—*Freedom in Exile.* London, 1990.
Grunfeld, A. T., *The Making of Modern Tibet.* London, 1987
Levenson, C. B., *The Dalai Lama: A Biography.* London, 1988
Pinfold, J., *Tibet:* [Bibliography]. Oxford and Santa Barbara, 1991
Schwartz, R. D., *Circle of Protest: Political Ritual in the Tibetan Uprising.* Farnborough, 1994
Shakabpa, T. W. D., *Tibet: A Political History.* New York, 1984
Sharabati, D., *Tibet and its History.* London, 1986

CLIMATE. Most of China has a temperate climate but, with such a large country, extending far inland and embracing a wide range of latitude as well as containing large areas at high altitude, many parts experience extremes of climate, especially in winter. Most rain falls during the summer, from May to Sept., though amounts decrease inland. Peking (Beijing). Jan. 24°F (–4·4°C), July 79°F (26°C). Annual rainfall 24·9" (623 mm). Chongqing. Jan. 45°F (7·2°C), July 84°F (28·9°C). Annual rainfall 43·7" (1,092 mm). Shanghai. Jan. 39°F (3·9°C), July 82°F (27·8°C). Annual rainfall 45·4" (1,135 mm). Tianjin. Jan. 24°F (–4·4°C), July 81°F (27·2°C). Annual rainfall 21·5" (533·4 mm).

CONSTITUTION AND GOVERNMENT. On 21 Sept. 1949 the *Chinese People's Political Consultative Conference* met in Beijing, convened by the Chinese Communist Party. The Conference adopted a 'Common Programme' of 60 articles and the 'Organic Law of the Central People's Government' (31 articles). Both became the basis of the Constitution adopted on 20 Sept. 1954 by the 1st National People's Congress, the supreme legislative body. The Consultative Conference continued to exist after 1954 as an advisory body. Its 8th session was convened in 1993. It has 2,093 members.

New Constitutions were adopted in 1975, 1978, 1982 (for details *see* THE STATESMAN'S YEAR-BOOK 1993-94, p. 358) and 1993, the latter embodying the principles of a 'Socialist market economy'.

The *National People's Congress* can amend the Constitution and nominally elects and has power to remove from office the highest officers of state. The Congress elects a *Standing Committee* (which supervises the State Council) and the *President* and *Vice-President* for a 5-year term. Congress has 2,978 deputies and is elected for a 5-year term and meets once a year for 2 or 3 weeks. When not in session, its business is carried on by its *Standing Committee.* It is composed of deputies elected on a constituency basis by direct secret ballot. Any voter, and certain organizations, may nominate candidates. Nominations may exceed seats by 50–100%. The 8th Congress was elected in March 1993.

The *State Council* is the supreme executive organ and comprises the Prime Minister, Deputy Prime Ministers and State Councillors (in Oct. 1995: Li Tieying, Chi Haotian, Song Jian, Li Guixian, Ismail Amat, Peng Peiyun, Luo Gan, Chen Junsheng.)

President: Jiang Zemin (b. 1926; sworn in April 1993).
Deputy President: Rong Yiren.

In Oct. 1995 the government comprised:
Prime Minister: Li Peng.
Deputy Prime Ministers: Li Lanqing, Qian Qichen (*Foreign Minister*), Zhu Rongji (*Director, People's Bank*), Zou Jiahua, Wu Bangguo, Jiang Chunyun.

Minister of Agriculture: Liu Jang. *Chemical Industries:* Gu Xiulian. *Civil Affairs:* Doje Cering. *Coal:* Wang Senhao. *Communications:* Huang Zhendong. *Construction:* Hou Jie. *Culture:* Liu Zhongde. *Defence:* Chi Haotian. *Domestic Trade:* Chen Bangzhu. *Electronics Industry:* Hu Qili. *Finance:* Liu Zhongli. *Foreign Trade and Economic Co-operation:* Wu Yi. *Forests:* Xu Youfang. *Geology and Mineral Resources:* Song Ruixiang. *Health:* Chen Minzhang. *Justice:* Xiao Yang. *Labour:* Li Boyong. *Machine Building:* He Guangyuan. *Metallurgy:* Liu Qi. *Personnel:* Song Defu. *Posts and Telecommunications:* Wu Jichuan. *Public Security:* Tao Siju. *Radio, Cinema and Television:* Sun Jiazheng. *Railways:* Han Zhubin. *State Security:* Jia Chunwang. *Supervision:* Cao Qingze. *Water:* Niu Maosheng.

Ministers heading State Commissions: *Economics and Commerce*, Wang Zhongyu. *Education*, Zhu Kaixuan. *Family Planning*, Peng Peiyun. *Minorities*, Ismail Amat. *Planning*, Chen Jinhua. *Restructuring the Economy*, Li Tieying. *Science and Technology*, Song Jian. *Science and Technology in Defence*, Ding Henggao. *Sport*, Wu Shaozhu.

National flag: Red with a large star and 4 smaller stars all in yellow in the canton.
National anthem: March of the Volunteers; words by Tien Han, tune by Nieh Erh.

De facto power is in the hands of the Communist Party of China, which had 40m. members in 1995. There are 8 other parties, all members of the Chinese People's Political Consultative Conference. The members of the Politburo in Oct. 1995 (the first 7 constituting its Standing Committee) were Jiang Zemin (*General Secretary*), Li Peng, Qiao Shi, Zhu Rongji, Liu Huaqing, Hu Jintao, Li Ruihuan, Tian Jiyun, Li Tieying, Ding Guangen, Huang Ju, Jiang Chunyun, Li Lanqing, Qian Qichen, Wei Jianxing, Wu Bangguo, Xie Fei, Yang Baibing, Zou Jiahua; candidate members, Wen Jibao, Wang Hanbin. Deng Xiaoping (b. 1904) has no formal post but is officially still a member of the 'second-generation leadership.'

Local Government. There are 4 administrative levels: (1) Provinces, Autonomous Regions and the municipalities directly administered by the Government; (2) prefectures and autonomous prefectures (*zhou*); (3) counties, autonomous counties and municipalities; (4) towns. Local government organs ('congresses') exist at provincial, county and township levels and in national minority autonomous prefectures, but not in ordinary prefectures which are just agencies of the provincial government. Up to county level congresses are elected directly. Elections take place every 3 years. Any person proposed by 10 electors may stand after political vetting. There are quotas for Party members and women. Multiple candidacies are permitted at local elections.

DEFENCE. President Jiang Zemin is chairman of the State and Party's Military Commissions. China is divided into 7 military regions. The military commander also commands the air, naval and civilian militia forces assigned to each region.

Conscription is compulsory but for organizational reasons selective: Only some 10% of potential recruits are called up. Service is 3 years with the Army and 4 years with the Air Force and Navy.

A military academy to train senior officers in modern warfare was established in 1985.

Army. The Army (PLA: 'People's Liberation Army') is divided into main and local forces. Main forces, administered by the 7 military regions in which they are stationed but commanded by the Ministry of Defence, are available for operation anywhere and are better equipped. Local forces concentrate on the defence of their own regions. There are 24 Integrated Group Armies comprising 78 infantry, 10 armoured and 5 artillery divisions; and 15 engineer regiments. Equipment includes some 700 T-34/85 and T-54, 6,000 T-59 and 200 T-69 main battle tanks. Land-based missile forces consisted of (1995 estimate): 17 intercontinental and 70 intermediate range. Military aviation has 8 Gazelle armed helicopters, 20 S-70 Black Hawk and 24 Mi-17 transport helicopters. Total strength in 1994 was 2·93m. including 1·28m. conscripts and 136,000 women.

There is a para-military force of 0·6m. People's Armed Police under PLA command.

Navy. The naval arm of the PLA comprises 1 nuclear-powered ballistic missile armed submarine, 5 nuclear-propelled fleet submarines, 1 diesel-powered cruise missile submarine and some 40 patrol submarines. Surface combatant forces include 18 missile-armed destroyers, 32 frigates, some 215 missile craft and 160 torpedo craft. There is a mixed coastal and inshore patrol force of some 500 vessels and 50 riverine craft. The mine warfare force consists of 40 ex-Soviet offshore minesweepers, some 12 inshore, and about 60 unmanned drones. There are 54 landing ships of various types and some 400 craft. Major auxiliaries number over 100, including 3 underway replenishment oilers and 1 fleet stores ship, and there are several hundred minor auxiliaries, yard craft and service vessels.

The land-based naval air force of about 860 combat aircraft, primarily for defensive and anti-submarine service, is organized into 3 bomber and 6 fighter divisions. The force includes some 120 H-5 torpedo bombers, about 100 Q-5 fighter/ground attack aircraft and 600 fighters, including J-5 (MiG-17), J-6 (MiG-19), and J-7 (MiG-21) types. Maritime patrol tasks are performed by 10 Be-6 and a small number of PS-5 flying boats, and anti-submarine operations by 40 Z-5 and 15 Super Frelon helicopters from shore and about 10 Z-9 afloat. There are also about 60 communications, training and transport aircraft.

Main naval bases are at Qingdao (North Sea Fleet), Shanghai (East Sea Fleet), and Zhanjiang (South Sea Fleet).

In 1995 personnel numbered some 260,000, including 25,000 in the naval air force, 27,000 coastal defence troops and 5,000 naval infantry.

Air Force. The Air Force has an estimated 4,000 front-line aircraft, organized in over 100 regiments of jet-fighters and about 12 regiments of tactical bombers, plus reconnaissance, transport and helicopter units. Each regiment is made up of 3 or 4 squadrons (each 12 aircraft), and 3 regiments form a division.

Equipment includes about 500 J-7 (MiG-21), 2,000 J-6 (MiG-19) and 500 J-5 (MiG-17) interceptors and fighter-bombers, with about 500 H-5 (Il-28) jetbombers, about 120 H-6 Chinese-built copies of the Soviet Tu-16 twin-jet strategic bomber, plus 500 Q-5 twin-jet fighter-bombers, evolved from the MiG-19, while 24 Su-27 fighters have been supplied by Russia. About 100 of a locally-developed fighter designated J-8 (known in the west as 'Finback') are in service. Transport aircraft include about 500 Y-5 (An-2), Y-8 (An-12), Y-12, An-24/26, Il-76, Challenger, Li-2 and Il-14 fixed-wing types, plus 300 Z-5 (Mi-4) and Z-6 (Mi-8) helicopters, as well as 6 Super Puma VIP transport helicopters. The MiG fighters and Antonov transports have been manufactured in China, initially under licence, and other types have been assembled there, including several hundred JJ-5 (2-seat MiG-17) and JJ-6

(2-seat MiG-19) trainers. Total strength (1995) 470,000 (160,000 conscripts), including 220,000 in air defence organization.

Joffe, E., *The Chinese Army after Mao.* London, 1987

INTERNATIONAL RELATIONS

Membership. The People's Republic of China is a member of UN (and its Security Council).

ECONOMY

Policy. A ninth 5-year plan covers 1996–2000; there is also a 15-year strategic plan 'Long-Term Target for 2010'. These plans envisage a contined opening to the outside world, an enhanced development of agriculture, the reduction of tariff barriers and the development of the poorer regions.

A Communist Party statement of Nov. 1993 declared that public ownership should remain the mainstay of the economy, but alongside a modern enterprise system suited to the demands of a market economy in which government control is separated from management.

Budget. 1993 revenue was 508,820m. yuan; expenditure, 528,740m. yuan. Of this, local government revenue accounted for 339,150m. yuan and expenditure, 333,020m. yuan.

Sources of revenue, 1993 (in million yuan): Tax receipts, 425,530; revenue from enterprises, 4,949; debt revenues, 69,022; funds levied for industrial development, 11,772; others, 38,673. Expenditure: Capital construction, 90,083; culture, education, science and health, 95,777; price subsidies, 29,930; defence, 42,580; administration, 63,426; agriculture, 32,342; technical renovation of enterprises, 42,138; circulating funds, 1,848; geological prospecting, 4,906; industry and trade, 7,662; welfare, 7,527; debt service, 33,622.

Currency. The currency is called Renminbi (*i.e.,* People's Currency). The unit of currency is the *yuan* (CNY) which is divided into 10 *jiao*, the *jiao,* into 10 *fen.* Notes are issued for 1, 2 and 5 *jiao* and 1, 2, 5, 10, 50 and 100 *yuan* and coins for 1, 2 and 5 *fen.* Foreign exchange reserves in Sept. 1994 were US$39,830m. Gold reserves in 1993 were 12·67m. troy oz. of gold. Annualized inflation was 21·7% in 1994. The yuan was floated to reflect market forces on 1 Jan. 1994 though remaining state-controlled, and the official rate of exchange was abolished. In March 1996, £1 = 12·72 yuan; US$1 = 8·32 yuan; DM1 = 5·64 yuan.

Banking and Finance. The People's Bank is the central bank and bank of issue (*Director:* Dai Xianglong, b. 1945). There are 5 other banks: The Industrial and Commercial Bank, the Agricultural Bank, the Bank of China, the People's Construction Bank and the Communications Bank. Legislation of 1995 permitted the establishment of commercial banks; credit co-operatives may be transformed into banks, mainly to provide credit to small businesses. Insurance is handled by the People's Insurance Company. There were also (1993) 339,942 credit co-operatives. The Bank of China is responsible for foreign banking operations.

Savings bank deposits were 1,520,350m. yuan in 1993.

There are stock exchanges in the Shenzhen Special Economic Zone and in Shanghai. A securities trading system linking 6 cities (Securities Automated Quotations System) was inaugurated in 1990 for trading in government bonds.

Weights and Measures. The metric system is in general use alongside traditional units of measurement, for which *see* THE STATESMAN'S YEAR-BOOK, 1975–76, p. 826 and 1954, pp. 877–88.

ENERGY AND NATURAL RESOURCES

Electricity. Sources of energy (excluding nuclear) in 1992: Coal 74·3%; oil, 18·9%; hydroelectric power, 4·8%; gas, 2%. Generating is not centralized; local units range between 30 and 60 MW of output. Output in 1993: 839,500m. kWh.

There is a nuclear energy plant at Shanghai which produced 0·3% of national output in 1993.

Oil. There are on-shore fields at Daqing, Shengli, Dagang and Karamai, and 10 provinces south of the Yangtze River have been opened for exploration in co-operation with foreign companies. Crude oil production was 2,994,000 bbls. a day in 1995.

Gas. Natural gas is available from fields near Canton and Shanghai and in Sichuan province. Production was 16,765m. cu. metres in 1993, but it is only used locally.

Minerals. *Coal.* Most provinces contain coal, and there are 70 major production centres, of which the largest are in Hebei, Shanxi, Shandong, Jilin and Anhui. Coal reserves were estimated at 1,001,865m. tonnes in 1993. Coal production was 1,150m. tonnes in 1993.

Iron. Iron ore deposits are estimated at 49,790m. tonnes and are abundant in the anthracite field of Shanxi, in Hebei and in Shandong and are found in conjunction with coal and worked in the north-east.

Tin. Tin ore is plentiful in Yunnan, where the tin-mining industry has long existed. Tin production was 40,000 tonnes in 1989.

Tungsten. China is a major producer of wolfram (tungsten ore). Mining of wolfram is carried on in Hunan, Guangdong and Yunnan.

Salt production was 29·43m. tonnes in 1993; gold production was 110 tonnes in 1992; output of other minerals in 1989 (in 1,000 tonnes): Aluminium, 770; copper, 540; nickel, 30; lead, 270; zinc, 430. Other minerals produced: Barite, bismuth, graphite, gypsum, mercury, molybdenum, silver. Reserves (in tonnes) of phosphate ore 15,766m.; sylvite, 458m.; salt, 402,400m.

Agriculture. In 1993 the sown area was 147·74m. ha (comprising in 1m. ha, rice, 30·36; wheat, 30·2; maize, 20·69; beans, 12·38; tubers, 9·22; industrial crops, 24·28m.). Intensive agriculture and horticulture have been practised for millennia. Present-day policy aims to avert the traditional threats from floods and droughts by soil conservancy, afforestation, irrigation and drainage projects, and to increase the 'high stable yields' areas by introducing fertilizers, pesticides and improved crops. 487·3m. ha were irrigated in 1993.

'Township and village enterprises' in agriculture comprise enterprises previously run by the communes of the Maoist era, co-operatives run by rural labourers and individual firms of a certain size. There were 279,000 such enterprises in 1993, employing 28·5m. persons. There were 2,159 state farms in 1993 with 5·32m. employees, and 229·80m. rural households. The rural workforce was 442·56m., of whom 339·66m. were employed in agriculture, fishing or land management. Net *per capita* annual peasant income, 1993: 922 yuan.

In 1992 there were 25,023 agricultural technical stations. There were 721,216 large and medium-sized tractors and 51,075 combine harvesters in 1993.

Agricultural production (in 1m. tonnes), 1993: Rice, 177·70; wheat, 106·39; maize, 102·7; beans, 19·5; tubers, 31·81; tea, 0·6; cotton, 3·74; oilseed crops, 8·04; sugar-cane, 64·19; fruit, 30·1. The gross value of agricultural output in 1992 was 1,099,553m. yuan.

Livestock, 1993 (in 1,000): Draught animals, 80,600; cattle, 113,157 (including 3,421 milch cows); goats, 105,696; pigs, 393,001; sheep, 111,618. Meat production in 1993 was 32·25m. tonnes; milk, 5·64m. tonnes; eggs, 11·8m. tonnes.

Powell, S. G., *Agricultural Reform in China: from Communes to Commodity Economy, 1978–1990.* Manchester Univ. Press, 1992

Forestry. Forest area in 1993 was 128·63m. ha, including 2·6m. ha of timber forest. Timber output in 1993 was 63·90m. cu. metres.

Fisheries. Total catch, 1993: 18·23m. tonnes, of which 7·47m. tonnes were freshwater produce.

INDUSTRY. 'Cottage' industries persist into the late 20th century. Modern industrial development began with the manufacture of cotton textiles, and the establishment of silk filatures, steel plants, flour-mills and match factories. In 1993 there were 9,911,600 industrial enterprises, (459,011 with independent accounting, of which 18,749 were classified as 'large or medium'). 104,700 were state-owned, 1,803,600 were collectives and 7,971,200 were individually owned. A law of 1988 ended direct state control of firms and provided for the possibility of bankruptcy.

Output of major products, 1993 (in tonnes): Cotton yarn, 5·01m.; paper, 19·14m.; sugar, 7·71m.; salt, 29·43m.; plastics, 3·60m.; aluminium ware, 99,200; steel, 89·56m.; rolled steel, 77·16m.; cement, 367·88m.; sulphuric acid, 13·36m.; chemical fertilizers, 19·56m.; pig-iron, 87·39m., cotton cloth, 20·30m. metres; silk, 94·00; woollen fabrics, 353·83m. metres; bicycles, 41·50m.; TV sets, 30·33m.; tape recorders, 36·48m.; cameras, 11·36m.; washing machines, 8·96m.; refrigerators, 5·97m.; motor vehicles, 1,298,500; large tractors, 37,700; locomotives, 922.

The gross value of industrial output in 1993 was 5,269,199m. yuan.

Labour. In 1991 the population of working age was 704·2m. The employed population at the 1990 census was 647·2m. (291·1m. female). The social labour force in 1993 was 602·20m. 339·66m. worked in agriculture, 92·95m. in manufacturing, 34·59m. in commerce, 30·50m. in building and 16·88m. in transport and communications. 109·20m. worked in state-owned enterprises, 33·93m. in urban collectives, and 442·56m. as individual rural labourers or in rural collectives. There were 11·16m. individual urban labourers. At the 1990 census there was a floating population of 21m. internal migrants who tour the country seeking seasonal employment. There were 4·2m. urban unemployed in 1993. Average annual non-agricultural wage in 1993: 3,371 yuan. There is a 6-day 48-hour working week. Minimum working age was fixed at 16 in 1991. There were 12,368 labour disputes in 1993.

Trade Unions. The All-China Federation of Trade Unions is headed by Wei Jiangxing. In 1991 there were 614,000 union branches with a total membership of 103·89m. (39·92m. female).

FOREIGN ECONOMIC RELATIONS. Foreign debt was US$83,573m. in 1993. Actual foreign investment totalled US$33,800m. by 1994.

There are 6 Special Economic Zones at Shanghai and in the provinces of Guangdong and Fujian, in which concessions are made to foreign businessmen. The Pudong New Area in Shanghai is designated a special development area. Since 1979 joint ventures with foreign firms have been permitted. About 80% of the investment is from Hong Kong. A law of April 1991 reduced taxation on joint ventures to 33%. There is no maximum limit on the foreign share of the holdings; the minimum limit is 25%. Contracts between Chinese and foreign firms are only legally valid if in writing and approved by the appropriate higher authority.

In May 1994 the US president extended most-favoured-nation status to China for a further year.

Commerce. Trade in 1993: Imports, US$103,950m.; exports, US$91,763m.

Major exports in 1993 (in 1,000 tonnes): Crude oil, 19,430; fishery products, 460; cereals, 15,350; canned food, 799·78; tea, 201·44; raw silk, 8·7; tungsten ore, 6·99; coal, 19,810; cotton cloth, 3,786,110m. metres. Imports: Wheat, 6,420; rolled steel, 29,990; motor vehicles, 310,461 units; chemical fertilizers, 10,210.

Exports to (and imports from) major trade partners in 1993 (in US$1m.): Hong Kong, 22,064 (10,473); Japan, 15,779 (23,253); USA, 16,964 (10,688); Germany, 3,968 (6,040); South Korea, 2,860 (5,360); Russia, 2,692 (4,987); Singapore, 2,245 (2,646). Customs duties with Taiwan were abolished in 1980.

Total trade between China and UK (British Department of Trade returns, in £1,000 sterling):

	1991	*1992*	*1993*	*1994*	*1995*
Imports to UK	706,585	953,583	1,327,128	1,641,798	1,937,869
Exports and re-exports from UK	321,935	429,865	739,484	844,865	824,403

Tourism. 41,526,900 tourists visited in 1993, including 36,704,800 Hong Kong, Taiwan and Macao Chinese, and 166,200 other overseas Chinese. Income from tourists in 1993 was US$4,683m. There were 43·68m. visitors in 1994.

Lardy, N. R., *Foreign Trade and Economic Reform in China, 1978–1990.* CUP, 1992
Pearson, M. M., *Joint Ventures in the People's Republic of China: the Control of Foreign Direct Investment under Socialism.* Princeton Univ. Press, 1991
Wong, K. and Chu, D. (eds.) *Modernization in China: the Case of the Shenzhen Special Economic Zone.* OUP, 1986

COMMUNICATIONS

Roads. The total road length was 1,083,476 km in 1993, of which 960,236 km were hard-surfaced. In 1992 there were 4·41m. lorries and 2·26m. passenger vehicles. 1,182,009 vehicles were privately owned. The use of bicycles is very widespread. In 1993, 8,402·56m. tonnes of freight and 8,607·19m. persons were transported by road.

There were 240,623 traffic accidents in 1993, with 63,551 fatalities.

Railways. In 1993 there were 53,802 km of railway including 8,935 km electrified. Gauge is standard except for some 600 mm track in Yunnan.

The Beijing–Lanzhou line connects through a branch with the Trans–Siberian Railway in Russia.

In 1994 the railways carried 1,571m. tonnes of freight and 1,008m. passengers.

Civil Aviation. There are international airports at Beijing and Shanghai (Hongqiao). The national and major arilines are state-owned, except Shanghai Airlines (75% municipality-owned, 25% private) and Shenzhen Airlines (private). In 1995 they operated the following numbers of aircraft:

Air China, 58 (including 2 B-707-320Cs, 18 B-737-300s, 3 B-747-200B Combis, 1 B-747-200F, 5 B-747-400s, 3 B-747-400 Combis, 4 B-747SPs, 6 B-767-200ERs, 4 B-767-300s); Air Great Wall, 8 (including 3 B-737-200 Advs); China Eastern Airlines, 46; China General Aviation, 25; China Northern Airlines, 46 (including 6 A300B4-600Rs); China Northwest Airlines, 33 (including 4 A300B4-600Rs, 4 A310-200s); China Southern Airlines, 78 (including 20 B-737-300s, 11 B-737-500s, 20 B-757-200s, 6 B-767-300ERs); China Southwest Airlines, 42 (including 1 B-707-320C, 20 B-737-300s, 13 B-757-200s); China United Airlines , 31 (including 4 B-737-300s); China Yunnan Airlines, 8 B-737-300s; Shanghai Airlines, 6 B-757-200s, 1 B-767-300; Shenzhen Airlines, 4 B-737-300s.

In 1993 airlines carried 33·83m. passengers (2·34m. international) and 0·69m. tonnes of freight.

Services are also provided by Aeroflot, Air Koryo, Air Macau, Air Ukraine, Alitalia, All Nippon Airways, Asiana, Austrian Airlines, British Airways, Canadian Airlines, Dragonair, El Al, Ethiopian Airlines, Finnair, Garuda Indonesia, Iran Air, JAL, Kazakhstan Airlines, Korean Air, LOT, Lufthansa, Malaysia Airlines, Mongolian Airlines, Pakistan International Airlines, Qantas, Royal Brunei Airlines, Royal Nepal Airlines, SAS, Singapore Airlines, Swan, Swissair, Tarom, Thai Airways, United Airlines and Uzbekistan Airways.

Shipping. In 1995 the ocean-going fleet consisted of 1,826 vessels totalling 34·27m. DWT, representing 5·18% of the world's total fleet tonnage. 308 vessels (35·22% of tonnage) were registered under foreign flags. Total tonnage registered, 15·83m. GRT, including oil-tankers, 2·28m. GRT, and container ships, 1·35m. GRT.

Cargo handled by the major ports in 1993 (in tonnes): Shanghai, 176m.; Qinhuangdao, 78m.; Dalian, 60m.; Guangzhou (Canton), 66m.; Ningbo, 53m.; Qingdao, 31m. In 1993 125·08m. tonnes of freight were carried.

Inland waterways totalled 110,174 km in 1993. 854·30m. tonnes of freight and 270·74m. passengers were carried.

Telecommunications. There were 57,005 post offices in 1993. There were 26,129,383 telephones, 23,393 telex and 12,276 fax machines in 1993. The use of *Pinyin* transcription of place names has been requested for mail to addresses in China (*e.g.*, 'Beijing' *not* 'Peking').

In 1993 there were 987 radio and 684 TV stations. The Central People's Broadcasting Station provides 2 central programmes, regional services, special services, a Taiwan service and external services. China Central Television (colour by PAL) transmits 3 programmes from Beijing, a programme from Shanghai, and an English-language programme. There are 29 regional programmes transmitted from 361 local stations. By 1995 about 600 cable TV systems had been licensed. In 1993 there were 20m. radio and 26m. TV receivers. In urban areas 96%, and in rural areas 48·5% of households possessed a TV set in 1994. The use of satellite receiving dishes was prohibited in 1993.

Cinemas. There were 14,639 cinemas in 1991. 154 feature films were made in 1993, of which 70 were co-productions. In 1992 there were some 10,600m. cinema attendances.

Press. In 1993 there were 1,635 newspapers with a combined circulation of 125,200m. and 7,011 periodicals with 2,350m. The Party newspaper is *Renmin Ribao* (People's Daily), which had a daily circulation of 3m. in 1993. 96,761 book titles were produced in 5,933·7m. copies in 1993. There were 2,579 public libraries in 1993.

SOCIAL INSTITUTIONS

Justice. Six new codes of law (including criminal and electoral) came into force in 1980, to regularize the legal unorthodoxy of previous years. There is no provision for *habeas corpus*. The death penalty has been extended from treason and murder to include rape, embezzlement, smuggling, drug-dealing, bribery and robbery with violence. There were 1,791 executions in 1994 (1,419 in 1993). 'People's courts are divided into some 30 higher, 200 intermediate and 2,000 basic-level courts, and headed by the Supreme People's Court. The latter tries cases, hears appeals and supervises the people's courts.

People's courts are composed of a president, vice-presidents, judges and 'people's assessors' who are the equivalent of jurors. 'People's conciliation committees' are charged with settling minor disputes.

There are also special military courts.

Procuratorial powers and functions are exercised by the Supreme People's Procuracy and local procuracies.

Religion. The government accords legality to 5 religions only: Buddhism, Islam, Protestantism, Roman Catholicism and Taoism. Confucianism, Buddhism and Taoism have long been practised. Confucianism has no ecclesiastical organization and appears rather as a philosophy of ethics and government. Taoism—of Chinese origin—copied Buddhist ceremonial soon after the arrival of Buddhism two millennia ago. Buddhism in return adopted many Taoist beliefs and practices. It is no longer possible to estimate the number of adherents to these faiths. A more tolerant attitude towards religion had emerged by 1979, and the Government's Bureau of Religious Affairs was reactivated.

Ceremonies of reverence to ancestors have been observed by the whole population regardless of philosophical or religious beliefs.

Moslems are found in every province of China, being most numerous in the Ningxia–Hui Autonomous Region, Yunnan, Shaanxi, Gansu, Hebei, Honan, Shandong, Sichuan, Xinjiang and Shanxi. They totalled 28m. in 1992.

Roman Catholicism has had a footing in China for more than 3 centuries. In 1992 there were about 3·5m. Catholics who are members of the Patriotic Catholic Association, which declared its independence of Rome in 1958. In 1979 there were about 1,000 priests. In 1977 there were 78 bishops and 4 apostolic administrators, not all of whom were permitted to undertake religious activity. This figure included 46 'democratically elected' bishops not recognized by the Vatican. A bishop of Beijing was consecrated in 1979 without the consent of the Vatican and 2 auxiliary bishops of Shanghai in 1984. Archbishop Gong Pinmei, arrested in 1955, was freed in 1988. Protestants are members of the All-China Conference of Protestant Churches. 2 Protestant bishops were installed in 1988, the first for 30 years.

Legislation of 1994 prohibits foreign nationals from setting up religious organizations.

Education. In 1990 182m. persons over 15 (128m. female) were illiterate. In 1993

97·7% of school-age children attended school. In 1993 maximum school fees were 10 yuan a term, to which other charges might be added. In 1993 there were 165,197 kindergartens with 25·53m. children and 0·84m. teachers. An educational reform of 1985 is phasing in compulsory 9-year education consisting of 6 years of primary schooling and 3 years of secondary schooling, to replace a previous 5-year system. In 1993 there were 165,197 primary schools with 5·55m. teachers and 124·21m. pupils, 96,744 secondary schools, with 3·69m. teachers and 53·83m. pupils and 9,985 vocational schools with 0·26m. teachers and 3·33m. students. There were 1,065 institutes of higher education, including 59 universities, with 387,808 teachers and 2,535,517 students.

There is an Academy of Sciences with provincial branches. An Academy of Social Sciences was established in 1977.

In 1995-96 in the private sector there were 3 general universities and 9 specialized universities (aeronautics and astronautics; agricultural engineering; agriculture; chemical technology; foreign studies; labour; medicine; traditional Chinese medicine; polytechnic). In the public sector there were 60 general universities, 2 for ethnic minorities and the following specialized universities: Agriculture, 12; agriculture and land reclamation, 1; land reclamation, 1; architecture, 2; architecture and technology, 1; chemical technology, 1; coal and chemical technology, 1; electronic science and technology, 1; engineering,1; fisheries, 1; foreign languages, 1; forestry, 1; hydraulic and electrical engineering, 1; international business and economics, 1; international studies, 1; iron and steel technology, 1; maritime studies, 1; medicine, 11; traditional Chinese medicine, 2; mining and technology, 1; petroleum, 1; pharmacology, 1; political science and law, 1; polytechnic, 8; radio and television, 1; science and technology, 5; surveying and mapping, 1; teaching, 4; technology, 6; textiles, 1.

In 1994-95 there were also 167 teacher training and 449 other specialized colleges. In 1993 10,742 students were studying abroad. Fees were introduced for university students in 1996-97.

Adult education comprises literacy courses, primary and secondary schools, and colleges and remote courses in higher education. In 1993 there were 89,500 full-time teachers and 1·86m. students in 1,183 higher adult education institutions, 235,000 and 44·47m. in 308,957 secondary schools and 40,500 and 7·88m. in 159,435 primary schools.

Health. Medical treatment is free only for certain groups of employees, but where costs are incurred they are partly borne by the patient's employing organization. In 1993 there were 1·83m. doctors, of whom 0·36m. practised Chinese medicine, and 1·06m. nurses. About 10% of doctors are in private practice.

In 1993 there were 60,784 hospitals (with 2·80m. beds), 600 sanatoria (with 119,000 beds) and 115,161 clinics.

Welfare. In 1993 there were 43,680 social welfare institutions with 723,645 inmates. Numbers (in 1,000) of beneficiaries of relief funds: Persons in poor rural households, 28,869; in poor urban households, 2,004; persons in rural households entitled to 'the 5 guarantees' (food, clothing, medical care, housing, education for chldren or funeral expenses), 2,447; retired, laid-off or disabled workers, 546. The major relief funds (in 1,000 yuan) in 1993 were: Families of deceased or disabled servicemen, 3,017,280; poor households, 532,220; orphaned, disabled, old and young persons, 1,105,870; welfare institutions, 1,070,520.

DIPLOMATIC REPRESENTATIVES

Of China in Great Britain (49 Portland Pl., London, W1N 3AH)
Ambassador: Jiang Enzhu.

Of Great Britain in China (Guang Hua Lu 11, Jian Guo Men Wai, Beijing)
Ambassador: Sir Len Appleyard, KCMG.

Of China in the USA (2300 Connecticut Ave., NW, Washington, D.C., 20008)
Ambassador: Zi Daoyu.

Of the USA in China (Xiu Shui Bei Jie 3, Beijing)
Ambassador: Vacant.

Of China to the United Nations
Ambassador: Qin Huasun.

Further Reading

State Statistical Bureau. *China Statistical Yearbook*
China Directory [in Pinyin and Chinese]. Tokyo, annual
Baum, R., *Burying Mao: Chinese Politics in the Age of Deng Xiaoping*. Princeton Univ. Press, 1994
Boorman, H. L. and Howard, R. C., (eds.) *Biographical Dictionary of Republican China*. 5 vols. Columbia Univ. Press, 1967–79
Brugger, B. and Reglar, S., *Politics, Economics and Society in Contemporary China*. London, 1994
The Cambridge Encyclopaedia of China. 2nd ed. CUP, 1991
The Cambridge History of China. 14 vols. CUP, 1978 ff.
Cheng, P., *China*. [Bibliography] Oxford and Santa Barbara, 1983
De Crespigny, R., *China this Century*. 2nd ed. OUP, 1993
Deng Xiaoping, *Speeches and Writings*. 2nd ed. Oxford, 1987
Dreyer, J. T., *China's Political System: Modernization and Tradition*. London, 1993
Dietrich, C., *People's China: a Brief History*. OUP, 1986
Evans, R., *Deng Xiaoping and the Making of Modern China*. London, 1993
Fairbank, J. K., *The Great Chinese Revolution 1800–1985*. London, 1987.—*China: a New History*. Harvard Univ. Press,1992
Fathers, M. and Higgins, A., *Tiananmen: the Rape of Peking*. London and New York, 1989
Glassman, R. M., *China in Transition: Communism, Capitalism and Democracy*. New York, 1991
Goldman, M., *Sowing the Seeds of Democracy in China: Political Reform in the Deng Xiaoping Era*. Harvard Univ. Press, 1994
Goodman, D., *Deng Xiaoping and the Chinese Revolution: a Political Biography*. 2nd ed. London, 1994.—and Segal, G., (eds.) *China in the 90s: Crisis Management and Beyond*. Oxford, 1991
Gray, J., *Rebellions and Revolutions: China from the 1800s to the 1980s*. CUP, 1990
Hinton, H. C. (ed.) *The People's Republic of China 1949–1979*. 5 vols. Wilmington, 1980
Jenner, W. J. F., *The Tyranny of History: the Roots of China's Crisis*. London, 1992
Lichtenstein, P. M., *China at the Brink: the Political Economy of Reform and Retrenchment in the Post-Mao Era*. New York, 1991
Lieberthal, K. G., *From Revolution through Reform*. New York, 1995. – and Lampton, D. M. (eds.) *Bureaucracy, Politics and Decision-Making in Post-Mao China*. California Univ. Press, 1992
Lippit, V. D., *The Economic Development of China*. Armonk, 1987
Loewe, M. *The Pride that was China*. London, 1990
McCormick, B. L., *Political Reform in Post-Mao China: Democracy and Bureaucracy in a Leninist State*. California Univ. Press, 1990
Mackerras, C. *et al.*, *China since 1978: Reform, Modernization and Socialism with Chinese Characteristics*. New York, 1994.—and Yorke, A., *The Cambridge Handbook of Contemporary China*. CUP, 1991
Moise, E. E., *Modern China: A History*. London, 1986
Nathan, A. J., *Chinese Democracy*. London, 1986:-*China's Crisis: Dilemmas of Reform and Prospects for Democracy*. Columbia Univ. Press, 1990
Nolan, P., *State and Market in the Chinese Economy: Essays on Controversial Issues*. London, 1993
Riskin, C., *China's Political Economy: The Quest for Development since 1949*. OUP, 1987
Rodzinski, W., *A History of China*. Oxford, 1981–84
Sheng Hua, *et al.*, *China: from Revolution to Reform*. London, 1992
Shirk, S. L., *The Political Logic of Economic Reform in China*. Univ. of California Press, 1993
Spence, J. D., *The Search for Modern China*. London, 1990
White, G., (ed.) *The Chinese State in the Era of Economic Reform: the Road to Crisis*. London, 1991.—*Riding the Tiger: the Politics of Economic Reform in Post-Mao China*. London, 1993
Womack, B. (ed.) *Contemporary Chinese Politics in Historical Perspective*. CUP, 1992

Other more specialized titles are listed under TERRITORY AND POPULATION; TIBET; DEFENCE; AGRICULTURE; FOREIGN ECONOMIC RELATIONS.

National statistical office: State Statistical Bureau, 38 Yuetan Nanjie, Beijing.

TAIWAN [1]

'Republic of China'

Capital: Taipei
Population: 21m. (1994)
GNP per capita: US$11,296 (1994)

KEY HISTORICAL EVENTS. The island of Taiwan was ceded to Japan by China in 1895. It was returned to Chinese Nationalist administration on 25 Oct. 1945. USA broke off diplomatic relations with Taiwan on 1 Jan. 1979 on establishing diplomatic relations with the Beijing Government.

TERRITORY AND POPULATION. Taiwan lies between the East and South China Seas about 100 miles from the coast of Fujian. The total area of Taiwan Island, the Penghu Archipelago and the Kinmen area (including the fortified offshore islands of Quemoy and Matsu) is 13,970 sq. miles (36,182 sq. km). Population (1995), 21m. The indigenous Han population are of Fujian origin. 15% of the population are Hakka, and 15% mainland Chinese who came with the Nationalist forces. There are also 365,007 aboriginals of Malay origin. Population density: 585 per sq. km.

In 1994, the birth rate was 1·53%; death rate, 0·54%; rate of growth, 0·87% per annum (2000 target: 0·72% per annum). Life expectancy, 1994: Males, 71·81 years; females, 77·76 years.

Taiwan's adminstrative units comprise (with 1995 populations): 2 special municipalities: Taipei, the capital (2,639,283) and Kaohsiung (1,423,821); 5 cities outside the county structure: Chiayi (261,749), Hsinchu (340,149), Keelung (368,173), Taichung (849,549), Tainan (705,940); 16 counties (*hsien*): Changhwa (1,286,998), Chiayi (565,172), Hsinchu (340,149), Hualien (358,835), Ilan (465,054), Kaohsiung (1,191,258), Miaoli (559,327), Nantou (545,823), Penghu (91,263), Pingtung (911,149), Taichung (849,549), Tainan (705,940), Taipei (3,297,579), Taitung (254,208), Taoyuan (1,517,835), Yunlin (754,021).

CLIMATE. The climate is subtropical in the north and tropical in the south. The typhoon season extends from July to Sept. The average monthly temperatures of Jan. and July in Taipei are 59·5°F (15·3°C) and 80·6°F (27·0°C) respectively and average annual rainfall is 85·6" (2,160 mm). Kaohsiung's average monthly temperatures of Jan. and July are 65·1°F (18·4°C) and 82·6°F (28·1°C) respectively and average annual rainfall is 63·7" (1,618 mm).

CONSTITUTION AND GOVERNMENT. A National Assembly was elected on the Mainland in 1947. A dwindling number of mainland delegates retained their seats until a new 325-member National Assembly was elected in Dec. 1991. The electorate was 13m.; turn-out was 70%. The Kuomintang (KMT) gained 71% of votes cast and 254 seats; the Democratic Progressive Party (DPP) gained 23% of votes cast. This Assembly's powers comprise amendment of the Constitution, approval of the President's nominees to the Judicial, Examination and Control Yuans, voting in the exercise of its rights of referendum on constitutional amendments proposed by the Legislative Yuan, and impeachment of the President. 5 extraordinary sessions have been held by this Assembly and 10 constitutional amendments promulgated in 1994.

Before 1996 the *President* was elected by the pre-1991 National Assembly; thereafter the President and Vice-President have been directly elected. Elections were scheduled for March 1996.

Elections were held on 19 Dec. 1992 for a new parliament on a purely Taiwanese basis, the 164-member *Legislative Yuan*, to which 128 members are directly elected, including 6 representatives of the aboriginal community, and the remainder appointed on a proportional basis according to the parties' share of the popular vote, 6 seats being reserved for overseas Chinese. 332 candidates stood; turn-out was

[1] See note on transcription of names in CHINA: Territory and Population.

67·65%. The KMT gained 85 seats with 52% of votes cast, the DPP 54 with 33%, the New Party 21 with 13% and independents 4 with 2%.

President: Lee Teng-hui (re-elected 21 March 1990). *Vice-President:* Li Yuan-zu.

The cabinet comprised the following in Dec. 1995:

Prime Minister: Lien Chan (b. 1936).

Deputy Prime Minister: Hsu Li-teh. *Foreign Affairs:* Fredrick F. Chien. *Defence:* Gen. Chiang Chung-ling. *Interior:* Huang Kun-huei. *Finance:* Lin Chen-kuo. *Education:* Kuo Wei-fan. *Economic Affairs:* P. K. Chiang. *Justice:* Ma Ying-jeou. *Transportation and Communications:* Liu Chao-shiuan. *Chairman, Council of Planning and Development:* Wang Jen-huong. *Chairman, Overseas Chinese Affairs Commission:* John Chang. *Acting Chairman, Mainland Affairs Council:* Kao Koong-lian. *Chairman, Labour Affairs Council:* Hsieh Shan-san. *Chairman, Health Council:* Chang Po-Ya. *Governor of Taiwan Province:* James Soong. *Mayor of Taipei:* Chen Shui-ban. *Secretary-General of the Presidency:* Wu Poh-hsiung.

National flag: Red with a blue first quarter bearing the state emblem, a 12-pointed white sun in a blue sky, in white.

National anthem: 'San Min Chu I'; words by Dr Sun Yat-sen, tune by Cheng Mao-yun.

Local Government. Councillors for Taiwan province have been elected since 1951. Councillors for the special municipalities of Taipeh and Kaohsiung have been elected by universal suffrage since 1969 and 1981 respectively. Elections were held on 29 Jan. 1994 for 309 town and village mayors. The KMT won 215 posts, the DPP 21. The KMT won all 23 of the city and county speakerships elected on 1 March 1994. On 18 June 1994 901 community headships were contested: The KMT won 665, ind 209, DPP 27. On 3 Dec. 1994 elections were held for 2 city mayors and the Governor of Taiwan Province.

DEFENCE. Conscription is for 2 years.

Army. The Army numbered about 240,000 in 1996, including 21,000 military police. In 1995 it consisted of 10 infantry divisions, 2 mechanized infantry divisions, 2 airborne brigades, 6 independent armoured brigades, 1 tank group and 2 surface-to-air missile battalions. The aviation element comprises 6 squadrons with about 100 transport and 68 armed helicopters. Equipment includes 100 M-48A5, 450 M-48H and 20 M-60A3 main battle tanks.

Navy. The navy consists principally of former US Navy ships over 40 years old. A major programme of new ships have commenced entering service, including new submarines, frigates and support ships. Current fleet strength is 2 new Netherlands-built diesel submarines, 20 ex-US 1940s destroyers, 4 new guided-missile frigates, 6 ex-US Knox class and 2 other older frigates, 52 fast missile craft, 45 other patrol craft and 16 coastal minesweepers. The amphibious force includes 1 amphibious flagship, 2 dock landing ships, 20 landing ships and about 280 amphibious craft. Auxiliary craft include 1 combat support ship, 4 support tankers, 2 repair and salvage ships, 7 tugs and 3 survey ships. Main bases are at Tsoying, Makung and Keelung.

Active personnel in 1995 totalled 38,000 in the Navy and 30,000 in the Marine Corps. There are over 67,500 naval and marine reservists.

The Naval Air Command operates 32 S-2 Tracker aircraft, 12 small anti-submarine helicopters from the destroyers and 12 SH-2F and 10 S-70 Seahawk helicopters based ashore.

The Customs service operates 12 cutters.

Air Force. The Air Force is equipped mainly with aircraft of US design, including F-5E fighters built in Taiwan. It has 12 front-line squadrons of F-5E/F Tiger IIs, 2 of locally-produced Ching-kuo interceptors, 1 of locally-built AT-3 twin-jet light strike aircraft and 1 tactical reconnaissance squadron of RF-104G Starfighters. The 6 transport squadrons are equipped with a VIP Boeing 720, 4 Boeing 727s, 11 Beech 1900s, 3 Fokker 50s, a few remaining C-119Gs and 25 C-130H Hercules.

4 E-2 Hawkeye airborne early warning aircraft have been delivered. Search and rescue units operate S-70 and Iroquois helicopters, and there are other helicopter and large training elements, some equipped with AT-3 twin-jet trainers designed and built in Taiwan and others with US-supplied T-34Cs and T-38s. Total strength in 1995: 68,000 personnel.

INTERNATIONAL RELATIONS. By a treaty of 1 Dec. 1954 the USA was pledged to protect Taiwan, but this treaty lapsed 1 year after the USA established diplomatic relations with the People's Republic of China on 1 Jan. 1979. In April 1979 the Taiwan Relations Act was passed by the US Congress to maintain commercial, cultural and other relations between USA and Taiwan through the American Institute on Taiwan and its Taiwan counterpart, the Taipei Economic and Cultural Representative Office in the USA, which were accorded quasi-diplomatic status in 1980.

The People's Republic took over the China seat in the UN from Taiwan on 25 Oct. 1971.

In May 1991 Taiwan ended its formal state of war with the People's Republic.

ECONOMY

Policy. The 6-year National Development Plan (1991–96) aims to provide the infrastructure to increase productivity and improve the quality of life, with emphasis on culture, education and the environment, at an estimated cost of US$224,000m. The Economic Revitalization Programme introduced in June 1993 has the goals of accelerating industrial upgrading and transforming Taiwan into an Asia-Pacific regional operations centre.

Budget. There are 2 budgets, the central government's general budget together with some special defence and infrastructure appropriations and the provincial budget for Taiwan proper. For the fiscal year July 1994–June 1995 the central government's general budget was NT$1,029,217m. Expenditure planned: 23·3% on defence; 13·6% on economic development; 20·55% on social security; 15·45% on education, science and culture. Foreign exchange reserves were US$90,608m. in Sep. 1995.

Currency. The unit of currency is the *New Taiwan dollar* (TWD), of 100 *cents*. There are coins of 50 cents and NT$ 1, 5, 10 and 50 and notes of NT$ 50, 100, 500 and 1,000. Mainland currency has been legal tender since 1992. Gold reserves were 13,565,000 oz. in Nov. 1995. Exchange rates in March 1996, £1 = NT$42·03; US$1 = NT$27·50; DM1 = NT$18·63.

Banking and Finance. The Central Bank of China (reactivated in 1961) regulates the money supply, manages foreign exchange and issues currency. *Governor:* Sheu Yuan-dong.

The Bank of Taiwan is the largest commercial bank and the fiscal agent of the Government. In June 1995 there were 42 domestic banks and 58 local branches of 38 foreign banks. Most banks had been state-controlled until June 1991, when 15 new private-sector commercial banks were licensed.

There were also 74 credit co-operatives, 312 agricultural credit unions, 5 trust and investment companies and 52 assurance companies.

There is a stock exchange in Taipei.

ENERGY AND NATURAL RESOURCES

Electricity. Output of electricity in 1994 was 124,635m. kWh; total installed capacity was 22,833,040 kW, comprising 61% thermal, 23% nuclear and 16% hydroelectric. There are 3 nuclear power-stations (capacities 1·27m., 1·97m. and 1·9m. kW) and a fourth is envisaged.

Minerals. There are reserves of coal (175·0m. tonnes), gold (2·6m. tonnes), copper (4·5m. tonnes), oil (0·7m. kl.) and natural gas (14,648 cu. metres). In 1994, coal production was 0·3m. tonnes; refined oil, 29·0m. kl.; natural gas, 908m. cu. metres. Crude oil production (1994), 68,578 kl.

Agriculture. The cultivated area was 872,308 ha in 1994, of which 461,227 ha were paddy fields. Production in 1,000 tonnes, in 1994: Rice, 1,679; tea, 24; bananas, 184; pineapples, 252; sugar-cane, 5,275; sweet potatoes, 181; soybeans, 12; peanuts, 81.

Livestock (1994): Cattle, 164,270; pigs, 10,065,582; goats, 310,283.

Forestry. Forest area, 1994: 1,866,208 ha; forest reserves, trees, 326,490,203 cu. metres, bamboo, 1,153m. poles; timber production, 56,128 cu. metres.

Fisheries. The fleet comprised 5,422 vessels over 20 GRT in 1994; the catch was 1,255,273 tonnes in 1994.

INDUSTRY. Output (in tonnes) in 1994 (and 1993): Steel bars, 18·8m. (17·9m.); pig-iron, 27,039 (21,261); shipbuilding, 1,036,215 DWT (1,015,766); sugar, 0·47m. (0·40m.); cement, 22·7m. (24·0m.); fertilizers, 1·9m. (1·8m.); paper, 1,114,481 (1,025,025); cotton fabrics, 970m. metres (957m.).

Labour. In 1994 the labour force was 9·08m., of whom 1m. worked in agriculture, forestry and fisheries, 3·51m. in industry (including 2·49m. in manufacturing and 967,000 in construction), 1·88m. in commerce, 473,000 in transport and communications, and 2·11m. in other services. 0·14m. were registered unemployed in 1994.

FOREIGN ECONOMIC RELATIONS. Restrictions on the repatriation of investment earnings by foreign nationals were removed in 1994.

Commerce. Total trade, in US$1m.:

	1990	*1991*	*1992*	*1993*	*1994*
Imports	54,716	62,861	72,007	77,061	85,359
Exports	67,214	76,178	81,470	84,917	93,056

The USA, Japan and Hong Kong are Taiwan's major trade partners followed by Singapore, Germany, Thailand and Malaysia.

Principal exports in 1993, in US$1,000m. (and percentage of total exports): Textiles, 12·03 (14·2%); electronic products, 10·21 (12%); base metals and articles, 7·13 (8·4%); machinery, 7·04 (8·3%); information and communication products, 6·41 (7·5%); plastic and rubber products, 5·69 (6·7%); vehicles and transport equipment, 4·68 (5·5%); footwear, headwear and umbrellas, 3·33 (3·9%); toys, games, sports equipment, 2·81 (3·3%).

Principal imports in 1993, in US$1,000m. (and percentage of total imports): Electronic products, 10·34 (13·4%); base metals and articles, 9·86 (12·8%); chemicals, 7·56 (9·8%); machinery, 7·46 (9·7%); minerals, 6·68 (8·7%); vehicles and transport equipment, 6·31 (8·2%); textile products, 2·76 (3·6%); precision instruments, clocks and watches, musical instruments, 2·63 (3·4%).

Total trade between Taiwan and UK (British Department of Trade returns, in £1,000 sterling):

	1991	*1992*	*1993*	*1994*	*1995*
Imports to UK	1,271,990	1,393,718	1,617,418	1,580,880	1,726,761
Exports and re-exports from UK	519,821	545,422	667,765	735,287	961,933

Tourism. In 1994, 2,127,249 tourists visited Taiwan, and 4,744,434 Taiwanese made visits abroad.

COMMUNICATIONS

Roads. In 1994 there were 20,180·9 km of roads. 12,377,083 motor vehicles were registered including 3,570,501 passenger cars, 21,252 buses, 711,810 lorries and 8,034,500 motor cycles. 1,413m. passengers and 313·4m. tonnes of freight were transported (including urban buses).

Railways. Total route length in 1994 was 2,378·1 km (1,067 mm and 762 mm gauges), of which a large proportion is owned by the Taiwan Railway Administration and other concerns. The state network consisted of 1,191·6 km. Freight traffic amounted to 31·2m. tonnes and passenger traffic to 160·3m.

Civil Aviation. There are 2 international airports: Chiang Kai-shek at Taoyuan near Taipei, and Kaohsiung in the south. In Dec. 1995 there were 17 domestic airlines, of which 4 are international carriers: China Airlines (CAL), EVA Airways Corp (EVA Air), Mandarin Airlines (MDA; CAL's subsidiary) and TNA operate international services to 42 destinations in 27 countries. CAL and MDA had a fleet of 3 B-737-209s, 5 A-300B4-600Rs, 2 A-300B4-220s, 2 B-747SP-09s, 1 B-747-209SF, 3 B-747-209Bs, 1 B-747-209F and 2 MD-11s. EVA Air had a fleet of 3-B-767-300ERs, 4 B-767-200s, 2 B-747-400s, 4 B-747-400-COMBIs and 2 MD-11s. 34 foreign airlines also operate services. In 1994, 36·97m. passengers and 880,273 tonnes of freight were flown.

Services are also provided by Air France, Air New Zealand, Air Nippon, Ansett Australia, British Airways, Canadian Airlines, Cathay Pacific, China Airlines, Continental Airlines and Air Micronesia, Delta, Eva Airways, Foshing Airlines, Garuda Indonesia, JAL, KLM, Lufthansa, Malaysia Airlines, Mandarin Airlines, Northwest Airlines, Pacific Airlines, Philippine Airlines, Qantas, Royal Brunei Airlines, Sempati Air, Singapore Airlines, SAA, Swissair, Thai Airways, United Airlines and Vietnam Airlines.

Shipping. The merchant marine in 1994 comprised 91 container ships, 102 bulk carriers, 20 tankers and 32 other service ships, with a total DWT of 9·2m.

There are 4 international ports: Kaohsiung, Keelung, Hwalien and Taichung. The first 2 are container centres. Suao port is an auxiliary port to Keelung.

Telecommunications. In 1994 there were 14,079 post offices. In 1994 there were 8,503,201 telephone subscribers and, in 1993, 11,230,526 stations for telephone service. The Broadcasting Corporation of China is a private enterprise. It broadcasts news and popular music on 8 networks. The Central Broadcasting System broadcasts to mainland China. There are 2 external services, 3 commercial TV services and an educational service (colour by NTSC). In 1994 there were 14·1m. radio and 7·2m. TV sets.

Cinemas (1994). Cinemas numbered 166, and 29 full-length films were made.

Press. There were 380 daily papers and 5,365 periodicals in 1995. 14,743 book titles were published in 1994.

SOCIAL INSTITUTIONS

Religion. There were 3·85m. Taoists in 1994 with 8,292 temples and 31,950 priests, 4·86m. Buddhists with 4,020 temples and 9,130 priests, 0·42m. Protestants and 0·3m. Catholics.

Education. Since 1968 there has been compulsory education for 9 years (6–15) with free tuition. In that year the curriculum was modernized to give more emphasis to science while retaining the traditional basis of Confucian ethics. Since 1983 school-leavers aged 15-18 receive part-time vocational education. There were, in 1994–95, 2,528 primary schools with 84,150 teachers and 2,032,361 pupils; 1,126 secondary schools with 93,617 teachers and 1,947,022 students; 130 schools of higher education, including 58 universities and colleges, with 35,163 teachers and 720,180 students.

Health. In 1994 there were 114,076 medical personnel, including 24,455 doctors, 6,973 dentists and 2,833 doctors of Chinese medicine. There were 98 public hospitals with 37,586 beds and 730 private hospitals with 58,684 beds.

Social Security. A universal health insurance scheme came into force in Jan. 1995, state-run and financed 60% by employers and 30% by employees.

Further Reading

Statistical Yearbook of the Republic of China. Taipei, annual
The Republic of China Yearbook. Taipei, annual
Taiwan Statistical Data Book. Taipei, annual
Annual Review of Government Administration, Republic of China. Taipei, annual

Arrigo, L. G. *et al. The Other Taiwan: 1945 to the Present Day*. New York, 1994
Cooper, J. F., *Historical Dictionary of Taiwan*. Metuchen (NJ), 1993
Gälli, A., *Taiwan ROC: A Chinese Challenge to the World*. London, 1987
Gold, T. B., *State and Society in the Taiwan Miracle*. Armonk, 1986
Lee, S.-Y., *Money and Finance in the Economic Development of Taiwan*. London, 1990
Lee, W.-C., *Taiwan:* [Bibliography]. Oxford and Santa Barbara, 1990
Liu, A. P. L., *Phoenix and the Lame Lion: Modernization in Taiwan and Mainland China, 1950–1980*. Stanford, 1987
Long, S., *Taiwan: China's Last Frontier*. London, 1991
Moody, P. R., *Political Change in Taiwan: a Study of Ruling Party Adaptability*. New York, 1992
Tsang, S. (ed.) *In the Shadow of China: Political Developments in Taiwan since 1949*. Farnborough, 1994

National library: National Central Library, Taipei (established 1986).

COLOMBIA

República de Colombia

Capital: Bogotá
Population: 34·5m. (1994)
GNP per capita: US$1,620 (1994)
HDI/world rank: 0·836/57 (1992)

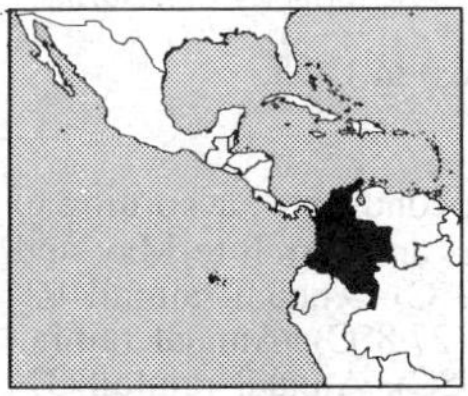

KEY HISTORICAL EVENTS. The Vice-Royalty of New Granada gained independence from Spain in 1819, and was officially constituted on 17 Dec. 1819, together with the present territories of Panama, Venezuela and Ecuador, as 'Greater Colombia'. This split into Venezuela, Ecuador and the Republic of New Granada in 1830. The constitution of 1858 changed New Granada into a confederation of 8 states, the Confederación Granadina. Under the constitution of 1863 the country was renamed 'Estados Unidos de Colombia', which were 9 in number. After the revolution of 1885 the unitary Republic of Colombia was formed and the states were converted into departments.

TERRITORY AND POPULATION. Colombia is bounded in the north by the Caribbean Sea, north-west by Panama, west by the Pacific Ocean, south-west by Ecuador and Peru, north-east by Venezuela and south-east by Brazil. The estimated area is 1,141,748 sq. km (440,829 sq. miles). Population census, (1985) 29,481,852; estimate (1994) 34,479,000; density, 40·2 per sq. km. Bogotá, the capital, (census, 1985) 4,236,490; estimate (1990) 4,819,696.

The following table gives population estimates for departments and their capitals for 1992.

Departments	*Area (sq. km)*	*Population*	*Capital*	*Population*
Antioquia	63,612	4,467,914	Medellín	1,581,364
Atlántico	3,388	1,703,968	Barranquilla	1,018,763
Bolívar	25,978	1,451,726	Cartagena	688,306
Boyacá	23,189	1,274,393	Tunja	112,360
Caldas	7,888	909,848	Manizales	327,115
Caquetá	88,965	309,506	Florencia	108,313
Cauca	29,308	933,643	Popayán	203,772
César	22,905	799,875	Valledupar	251,594
Chocó	46,530	350,934	Quibdó	119,027
Córdoba	25,020	1,115,142	Montería	265,754
Cundinamarca [1]	22,478	1,658,751	Bogotá [2]	4,921,264
La Guajira	20,848	347,538	Riohacha	126,293
Huila	19,890	777,876	Neiva	232,610
Magdalena	23,188	979,747	Santa Marta	286,471
Meta	85,635	564,276	Villavicencio	233,026
Nariño	33,268	1,163,436	Pasto	303,401
Norte de Santander	21,658	1,006,919	Cúcuta	450,318
Quindío	1,845	414,524	Armenia	212,310
Risaralda	4,140	735,700	Pereira	335,960
Santander	30,537	1,642,579	Bucaramanga	349,403
Sucre	10,917	611,421	Sincelejo	167,588
Tolima	23,562	1,193,450	Ibagué	334,078
Valle del Cauca	22,140	3,335,827	Cali	1,624,401

[1] Excluding Bogotá. [2] Capital District of Santafé de Bogotá; 1994 estimate, 4,921,264.

New Departments [1]	*Area (sq. km)*	*Population*	*Capital*	*Population*
Arauca	23,818	96,972	Arauca	29,624
Casanare	44,460	176,826	Yopal	41,606
Putumayo	24,885	221,872	Mocoa	29,145
San Andrés y Providencia	44	41,581	San Andrés	37,724

[1] Created 5 July 1991; formerly *Intendencias.*

New Departments [1]	Area (sq. km)	Population	Capital	Population
Amazonas [2]	109,665	52,874	Leticia	32,694
Guainía [2]	72,238	13,092	Puerto Inírida	11,921
Guaviare [2]	42,327	63,886	San José del Guaviare	56,557
Vaupés [2]	54,135	34,428	Mitú	20,926
Vichada [2]	100,242	19,370	La Primavera	9,676

[1] Created 5 July 1991; formerly *Intendencias*. [2] Created 5 July 1991; formerly *Comisarías*.

The Amerindian population was 268,359 (131,192 females) in 1985.

The official language is Spanish.

CLIMATE. The climate includes equatorial and tropical conditions, according to situation and altitude. In tropical areas, the wettest months are March to May and Oct. to Nov. Bogotá. Jan. 58°F (14·4°C), July 57°F (13·9°C). Annual rainfall 42" (1,052 mm). Baranquilla. Jan. 80°F (26·7°C), July 82°F (27·8°C). Annual rainfall 32" (799 mm). Cali. Jan. 75°F (23·9°C), July 75°F (23·9°C). Annual rainfall 37" (915 mm). Medellin. Jan. 71°F (21·7°C), July 72°F (22·2°C). Annual rainfall 64" (1,606 mm).

CONSTITUTION AND GOVERNMENT. Simultaneously with the presidential elections of May 1990, a referendum was held in which 7m. votes were cast for the establishment of a special assembly to draft a new constitution. Elections were held on 9 Dec. 1990 for this 74-member 'Constitutional Assembly' which operated from Feb. to July 1991. The electorate was 14·2m.; turn-out was 3·7m. The Liberals gained 24 seats, M-19 (a former guerilla organization), 19. The Assembly produced a new constitution which came into force on 5 July 1991. It stresses the state's obligation to protect human rights, and establishes constitutional rights to health care, social security and leisure. Indians are allotted 2 Senate seats. Congress may dismiss ministers, and representatives may be recalled by their electors.

The *President* is elected by direct vote for a term of 4 years, and is not eligible for re-election until 4 years afterwards. A vice-presidency was instituted in July 1991. The first round of presidential elections was held on 29 May 1994; turn-out was 35%. Ernesto Samper gained 45·2% of votes cast against 16 opponents. At the second round on 19 June Samper elected by 50·3% of votes cast against 1 opponent. Turn-out was 45%.

The legislative power rests with a *Congress* of 2 houses, the *Senate*, of 102 members, and the *House of Representatives*, of 163 members, both elected for 4 years. Congress meets annually at Bogotá on 20 July. Congressional elections were held on 13 March 1994. The electorate was 17·1m.; turn-out was 31%. 5,333 candidates stood. In the House of Representatives the Liberals gained 89 seats, the Social Conservatives, 56, and M19, 2; in the Senate the Liberals gained 52 seats, the Social Conservatives, 21, and M19, 1.

National Flag: Three horizontal stripes of yellow, blue, red with the yellow of double width.

National anthem: 'O! Gloria inmarcesible' ('Oh Glory unfading!'); words by R. Núñez, tune by O. Síndici.

President: Ernesto Samper (b. 1951; sworn in 7 Aug. 1994).

In Jan. 1996 the government comprised:

Interior: Horacio Serpa Uribe. *Defence:* Juan Carlos Esquerra. *Finance:* Guillermo Perry Rubio. *Agriculture:* Antonio Hernández Gamarra. *Development:* Rodrigo Marin Bernal. *Labour and Social Security:* Mariá Sol Calderón. *Health:* Alonzo Gómez Duque. *Mines and Energy:* Jorge Eduardo Londoño. *Education:* Arturo Sarravia Better. *Communications:* Armando Benedetti Jimeno. *Foreign Trade:* Daniel Mazuera Gómez. *Foreign Affairs:* Rodrigo Pardo García-Peña. *Justice:* Nestor Martínez. *Planning:* Jesús Antonio Ocampo. *Environment:* Cecília López Montaño.

Local government: The country is divided into 32 departments and the Capital

District of Bogotá (properly, Santafé de Bogotá), and subdivided into 1,011 municipalities. The governor of each department is elected by universal suffrage, and each has also a directly-elected legislature. The departments are subdivided into municipalities. The mayors of these, and the Special District of Bogotá, are elected by direct vote for a 2-year term. Mayoral elections were held on 30 Oct. 1994.

Elections were held in March 1992. The largest number of seats was gained by the Liberal Party, followed by the Conservative Party and M–19.

DEFENCE. Selective conscription at 18 years varies from 1 to 2 years of service.

Army. The Army consists of 16 infantry brigades, 2 counter-insurgency brigades, 1 Presidential Guard battalion and 1 air defence artillery battalion. Equipment includes 12 M-3A1 light tanks and 6 light transports. Personnel (1996) 121,000 (conscripts, 63,800); reserves 54,700. Number of national police (1996) 87,000.

Navy. The Navy has 2 German-built 1,200-tonne diesel powered submarines completed in 1975, 2 Italian-built midget submarines, 4 small German-built missile-armed frigates with helicopter decks, 4 offshore patrol vessels and 11 fast patrol craft. There are 3 river gunboats and 11 riverine patrol craft. Auxiliaries include 2 surveying vessels, 1 small transport and 1 training ship. Personnel in 1995 totalled 6,000. There are also 2 brigades of marines numbering 8,000. An air arm operates 7 light reconnaissance aircraft and 4 BO-105 helicopters for ship-borne anti-submarine and rescue duties. There is a shore-based Coastguard integrated with the Navy numbering 4,000.

Air Force. Formed in 1922, the Air Force has been independent of the Army and Navy since 1943, when its reorganization began with US assistance. In 1994 it had about 90 combat aircraft, including 2 fighter-bomber squadrons, one with Mirage 5s and one with Kfirs. 2 squadrons of AC-47 armed transports and 1 with A-37B jets for counter-insurgency duties; a transport group equipped with 7 C-130, 8 C-47s, and a small number of Arava and Turbo-Porter light transports; a presidential F-28 Fellowship jet transport; 1 Boeing 707, 2 Bandeirante, UH-1B/H and UH-60A Black Hawk utility helicopters; and a reconnaissance unit with Iroquois, Lama, Hughes OH-6A, 300C and TH-55 helicopters. 10 Aviocars, 1 F-28 and 2 HS.748 transports are flown by the Air Force operated airline SATENA. There are several dozen light transports, confiscated from drug-smugglers, in use. Cessna T-41D primary trainers, Tucanos, T-34s and 10 T-37C jet advanced trainers are in service. Total strength (1995) 7,300 personnel (3,500 conscripts).

INTERNATIONAL RELATIONS

Membership. Colombia is a member of the UN, OAS, the Andean Group and LAIA.

ECONOMY

Budget. Revenue and expenditure of central government in 1991: Revenue, 2,847,237m. pesos; expenditure, 2,821,756m. pesos.

Currency. The unit of currency is the *Colombian peso* (COP) of 100 *centavos*. There are coins of 50 centavos and 1, 2, 5, 10, 20 and 50 pesos, and notes of 100, 200, 500, 1,000, 2,000, 5,000, 10,000 and 20,000 pesos. Money in circulation, May 1991: 773,691m. pesos. Inflation was 32·4% in 1990. The government target for 1991 was 22%. Exchange rates, March 1996: 1,590·61 pesos = £1 sterling; 1,040·70 pesos = US$1; 705·13 pesos = DM1.

Banking and Finance. In 1923 the Bank of the Republic was inaugurated as a semi-official central bank, with the exclusive privilege of issuing bank-notes. Its note issues must be covered by a reserve in gold of foreign exchange of 25% of their value. Its international reserves in May 1992 were US$7,315·2m. Total assets (Jan. 1991) 3,351,570m.

There are 24 commercial banks, of which 18 are private or mixed, and 6 official. There is also an Agricultural, Industrial and Mining Credit Institute, a Central Mortgage Bank and a Social Savings Bank. Bank deposits totalled 1,446,686 pesos in May 1991.

There are stock exchanges in Bogotá, Medellín and Cali.

Weights and Measures. The metric system was introduced in 1857, but Spanish weights and measures are generally used, *e.g.*, *botella* (750 grammes), *galón* (5 *botellas*), *vara* (70 cm), *arroba* (25 lb., of 500 grammes; 4 *arrobas* = 1 quintal).

ENERGY AND NATURAL RESOURCES

Electricity. Capacity of electric power (1989) was 8·85m. kW. Electric power produced in 1987, 29,650m. kWh.

Oil. Production in 1992 was 22·33m. tonnes.

Minerals. Output of gold, 1991, 1,016,625 troy oz. Other minerals found are silver (258,386 troy oz. in 1991), copper, lead, mercury, manganese, emeralds (of which Colombia accounts for about half of world production) and platinum; production of platinum, 1991, 51,522 troy oz.

Salt production in 1991 was 89,494 tonnes of land salt and 172,442 tonnes of sea salt. Coal reserves were estimated at 20,963m. tonnes in 1986; production (1990, provisional) 20·5m. tonnes. Iron ore production was 595,952 tonnes in 1991.

Agriculture. There is a wide range of climate and, consequently, crops. In 1992 there were 3·9m. ha of arable land, 1·54m. ha of permanent crops and 40·6m. ha of pasture.

Production, 1993 (in 1,000 tonnes): Coffee, 1,080; potatoes, 2,860; rice, 1,650; maize, 1,164; sorghum, 631.

Livestock (1993): 25,324,000 cattle, 2,635,000 pigs, 2,540,000 sheep, 62m. poultry. Meat production, 1991: Beef and veal, 651,000 tonnes; pork, 134,000 tonnes.

Fisheries. Total catch (1987) 83,569 tonnes.

INDUSTRY. Production (1991): Steel ingots, 332,485 tonnes; cement, 6,389,250 tonnes; motor cars, 35,286; industrial vehicles, 8,877; sugar, 1,633,353 tonnes. In 1987 there were 6,927 manufacturing establishments.

Labour. In 1987 477,170 persons were employed in manufacturing (145,644 women).

FOREIGN ECONOMIC RELATIONS. Foreign companies are liable for basic income tax of 30% and surtax of 7·5%. Since 1993 tax on profit remittance has started at 12%, reducing (except for oil companies) to 7% after 3 years. Foreign debt was US$20,000m. in Dec. 1994.

The Group of Three (G-3) free trade pact with Mexico and Venezuela came into effect on 1 Jan. 1995.

Commerce. Exports in 1994 were valued at US$8,600m.; imports at US$10,900m.

The principal exports in 1991 were coffee (734,021 tonnes valued at US$1,336·4m. f.o.b.) and petroleum and other mineral products (29,480,329 tonnes). Main export markets, 1994: USA, 36·7%; EU, 27·7%; Andean Group, 13·1%; Japan, 4·3%. Main import suppliers: USA, 38·4%; EU, 16·9%; Andean Group, 13·1%; Japan, 8·3%.

Total trade between Colombia and UK (British Department of Trade returns, in £1,000 sterling):

	1991	*1992*	*1993*	*1994*	*1995*
Imports to UK	110,122	126,097	176,094	191,449	174,109
Exports and re-exports from UK	56,426	75,340	104,592	231,445	145,244

Tourism. Foreign visitors totalled 828,903 in 1988.

COMMUNICATIONS

Roads. Total length of highways, about 75,000 km in 1983. Of the 2,300-mile Simón Bolívar highway, which runs from Caracas in Venezuela to Guayaquil in

Ecuador, the Colombian portion is complete. Motor vehicles in 1990 numbered 1,461,476, of which 757,114 were passenger cars and 121,221 lorries. In 1988 4,917m. passengers were carried by road transport.

Railways. The National Railways (2,532 km of route, 914 mm gauge) went into liquidation in 1990 prior to takeover of services and obligations by 3 new public companies in 1992. In 1994 railways carried 0·7m. tonnes of freight.

Civil Aviation. There is an international airport at Bogotá (Eldorado). The national carriers are Avianca, which operated 2 B-727-200 Advs, 4 B-757-200s, 2 B-767-200ERs, 1 B-767-300ER and 21 other aircraft in 1992; and ACES with 4 B-727s, 4 B-727-200Advs and 15 other aircraft. In 1991 1,297,000 passengers and 294,041 tonnes of freight were carried on international flights, and 5,601,000 passengers and 83,816 tonnes of freight on domestic flights. Services are also provided by Aerolíneas Argentinas, Aeroperu, Aerorepublica, Air Aruba, Air France, Aires, Alitalia, American Airlines, British Airways, Copa, Compania Mexicana, Continental Airlines and Air Micronesia, Cubana, Iberia, Intercontinental de Aviación, Ladeco, Lufthansa, Saeta, Varig and Viasa.

Shipping. Vessels entering Colombian ports in 1991 unloaded 6,107,000 tonnes of imports and loaded 21,630,000 tonnes of exports. The merchant marine totalled 0·18m. GRT in 1995, including oil tankers, 9,681 GRT.

The Magdelena River is subject to drought, and navigation is always impeded during the dry season, but it is an important artery of passenger and goods traffic. The river is navigable for 900 miles; steamers ascend to La Dorada, 592 miles from Barranquilla.

Telecommunications. The length of telephone lines in service in 1989 was 943,076 km (Bogotá), nationally, 1,976,618 km.; instruments in use, 1 Jan. 1984, 2,547,222. The cable company is government owned. There are 5 radio companies overseen by the Dirección General de Radiocomunicaciones. Instituto Nacional de Radio y Televisión transmits on 3 networks (colour by NTSC) and rents air time to 26 commercial companies. In 1993 there were 34,487,000 radio and 5·5m. TV sets.

Cinemas (1987). There were 657 cinemas, of which 64 were in Bogotá.

Press (1984). There were 31 daily newspapers, with daily circulation totalling 1·5m.

SOCIAL INSTITUTIONS

Justice. The July 1991 constitution introduced the offices of public prosecutor and public defence. There is no extradition of Colombians for trial in other countries. The Supreme Court, at Bogotá, of 20 members, is divided into 3 chambers—civil cassation (6), criminal cassation (8), labour cassation (6). Each of the 61 judicial districts has a superior court with various sub-dependent tribunals of lower juridical grade. 257,511 crimes were reported in 1988.

The police force numbered 73,176 in 1989.

Religion. The religion is Roman Catholic (33·92m. adherents in 1992), with the Cardinal Archbishop of Bogotá as Primate of Colombia and 9 other archbishoprics. There are also 44 bishops, 8 apostolic vicars, 5 apostolic prefects and 2 prelates. In 1990 there were 1,546 parishes and 4,020 priests. Other forms of religion are permitted so long as their exercise is 'not contrary to Christian morals or the law.'

Education. Primary education is free but not compulsory, and facilities are limited. Schools are both state and privately controlled. In 1988 there were 7,759 pre-primary schools with 14,918 teachers and 340,244 pupils, 37,948 primary schools with 136,549 teachers and 4,044,220 pupils and 6,134 secondary schools with 99,392 teachers and 2,076,455 pupils. There were 235 higher education establishments with 457,680 students.

In 1995-96 in the public sector there were 20 universities, 1 open university, 3 technological universities and universities of education, educational technology and industry. There were also 2 colleges of public administration, 1 school of police studies, 1 institute of fine art, 1 polytechnic and 1 conservatory. In the private sector there were 25 universities, 4 Roman Catholic universities, 1 college of education and 1 school of administration. There were 8 public, and 44 private, other institutions of higher education. In 1994-95, there were 208,394 university students.

Health. In 1988 there were 926 hospitals and clinics. There were also 861 health centres.

DIPLOMATIC REPRESENTATIVES

Of Colombia in Great Britain (3 Hans Cres., London, SW1X 0LR)
Ambassador: Carlos Lemos-Simmonds.

Of Great Britain in Colombia (Calle 98, No. 9–03 Piso 4, Bogotá)
Ambassador: Leycester Coltman, CMG.

Of Colombia in the USA (2118 Leroy Pl., NW, Washington, D.C., 20008)
Ambassador: Carlos Lleras.

Of the USA in Colombia (Calle 38, 8-61, Bogotá)
Ambassador: Myles R. Frechette.

Of Colombia to the United Nations
Ambassador: Julio Londoño-Paredes.

Further Reading

Departamento Administrativo Nacional de Estadística. *Boletín de Estadística.* Monthly.
Davis, R. H., *Historical Dictionary of Colombia.* 2nd ed. Metuchen (NJ), 1994
Thorp, R., *Economic Management and Economic Development in Peru and Colombia.* London, 1991

National statistical office: Departamento Administrativo Nacional de Estadística (DANE), Avenida Eldorado, Bogotá.

COMOROS

République Fédérale
Islamique des Comores

Capital: Moroni
Population: 535,600 (1994)
GNP per capita: US$510 (1994)
HDI/world rank: 0·415/139 (1992)

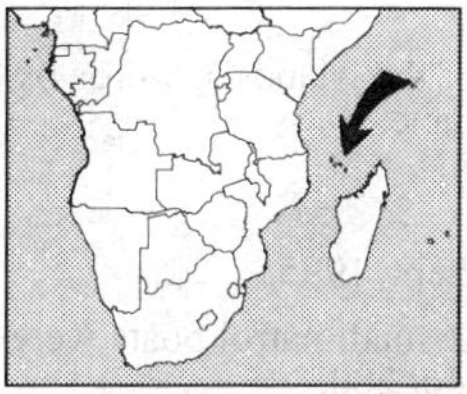

KEY HISTORICAL EVENTS. The 3 islands forming the present state became French protectorates at the end of the 19th century, and were proclaimed colonies in 1912. With neighbouring Mayotte they were administratively attached to Madagascar from 1914 until 1947, when the 4 islands became a French Overseas Territory, achieving internal self-government in Dec. 1961.

In referendums held on each island on 22 Dec. 1974, the 3 western islands voted overwhelmingly for independence, while Mayotte voted to remain French. The Comorian Chamber of Deputies unilaterally declared the islands' independence on 6 July 1975, but Mayotte remained a French dependency.

During a coup by the French mercenary Bob Denard in Sept. 1995, President Djohar was held prisoner by the insurrectionists. The coup was suppressed by French forces, and the President was released but not reinstated.

TERRITORY AND POPULATION. The Comoros consist of 3 islands in the Indian Ocean between the African mainland and Madagascar with a total area of 1,862 sq. km (719 sq. miles). The population at the 1991 census was 446,817; estimate, 1995, 544,000 (28% urban); density, 292·3 per sq. km.

	Area (sq. km)	*Population (1980 census)*	*Population (1994 estimate)*	*Chief town*
Njazídja (Grande Comore)	1,148	192,177	286,100	Moroni
Mwali (Mohéli)	290	17,194	28,200	Fomboni
Nzwani (Anjouan)	424	137,621	221,300	Mutsamudu

Annual growth rate, 1991, 3·6%; infantile mortality (per 1,000 live births), 89. Expectation of life was 56 years in 1991. Estimated population of the chief towns in 1988: Moroni, 22,000; Fomboni, 7,000; Mutsamudu, 14,000.

The indigenous population are a mixture of Malagasy, African, Malay and Arab peoples; the vast majority speak Comorian, an Arabised dialect of Swahili, but a small proportion speak Makua (a Bantu language), French or Arabic. In 1990, 27·1% of the population were urban.

CLIMATE. There is a tropical climate, affected by Indian monsoon winds from the north, which gives a wet season from Nov. to April. Moroni. Jan. 81°F (27·2°C), July 75°F (23·9°C). Annual rainfall, 113" (2,825 mm).

CONSTITUTION AND GOVERNMENT. Under the Constitution approved by referendum on 1 Oct. 1978 (amended 1983), the Comoros were a Federal Islamic Republic. Mayotte had the right to join when it so chose. At a referendum on 7 June 1992 74·25% of votes cast were in favour of a new constitution. The electorate was 213,000; turn-out was 63·51%.

Under the 1992 constitution the *President* is Head of State, directly elected for a 5-year term (renewable once). He appoints Ministers to form the Council of Government, on which each island's Governor has a non-voting seat. The 42-member *Legislative Council* is directly elected for 4 years in 2 rounds. There is a 15-member *Senate* (5 members for each island) which is nominated for 6 years by an electoral college.

At the presidential elections of March 1990 Said Mohamed Djohar gained 55% of votes cast, against one opponent.

Elections for the Legislative Council were held in Dec. 1993. The Rally for Democracy and Renewal won 24 seats and the Forum for National Recovery, 18.

President: Said Mohamed Djohar (b. 1915; sworn in 20 March 1990). After the failed coup in Sept. 1995, the Prime Minister, Mohamed Caambi El Yachourtou, proclaimed himself president ad interim and formed a new government in Nov. 1995. The *Speaker* is Mohamed M'Changama.

National flag: Green with a crescent and 4 stars all in white in the centre, tilted towards the lower fly.

National anthem: 'Udzima wa ya Masiwa' ('The union of the islands'); words by S. H. Abderamane, tune by K. Abdallah and S. H. Abderamane.

DEFENCE

Army. The Army was reorganized after the failed coup of Sept. 1995.

Navy. 1 landing craft with ramps was purchased in 1981. 2 small patrol boats were supplied by Japan in 1982. Personnel in 1995 numbered about 200.

Air Arm. 1 Cessna 402B communications aircraft and 1 Ecureuil helicopter were reported to be in operation.

INTERNATIONAL RELATIONS

Membership. Comoros is a member of the UN and Arab League and an ACP state of the EU.

ECONOMY

Budget. In 1992 current expenditure amounted to 14,628m. Comorian francs, revenue to 15,222m. Comorian francs

Currency. The unit of currency is the *Comorian franc* (KMF) of 100 *centimes.* It is within France's Franc Zone (*see* FRANCE: Currency) and was devalued 25% in Jan. 1994. There are banknotes of 50, 100, 500, 1,000, and 5,000 Comorian francs. Foreign exchange reserves were US$29·02m. In March 1996, £1 = CF580·68; US$1 = CF379·93; DM1 = CF257·42.

Banking and Finance. The Central Bank is the bank of issue. The chief commercial banks are the Banque Internationale des Comores and the Banque de Développement des Comores.

Weights and Measures. The metric system is in force.

ENERGY AND NATURAL RESOURCES

Electricity. In 1991 installed capacity was 9,180 kW. Output was 23,957,000 kWh in 1991.

Agriculture. 80% of the economically-active population depend upon agriculture. The chief product was formerly sugar-cane, but now vanilla, copra, maize and other food crops, cloves and essential oils (citronella, ylang, lemon-grass) are the most important products. Production (1991 in 1,000 tonnes): Cassava, 46; coconuts, 50; bananas, 52; sweet potatoes, 18; rice, 15; maize, 4 and copra, 4.

Livestock (1991): Cattle, 47,000; sheep, 14,000; goats, 125,000; asses, 5,000.

Forestry. The forested area has been severely reduced because of the shortage of cultivable land and ylang-ylang production.

Fisheries. Fishing is on an individual basis, without modern equipment. The catch was 8,000 tonnes in 1991.

INDUSTRY. Branches include saw milling, printing, soft drinks, plastics and the processing of vanilla and copra.

Labour. The workforce in 1991 was 238,000.

FOREIGN ECONOMIC RELATIONS. Total foreign debt was US$210m. in 1991.

Commerce. In 1991 imports amounted to US$60m.; exports to US$18m. France provided 56% of imports and took 56% of exports. The main exports are vanilla, cloves, ylang-ylang, essences, copra and coffee.

Trade between Comoros and UK (British Department of Trade returns, in £1,000 sterling):

	1991	*1992*	*1993*	*1994*	*1995*
Imports to UK	228	194	8	52	13
Exports and re-exports from UK	796	279	440	1,272	2,021

Tourism. In 1992 there were about 19,000 foreign visitors (8,500 from France).

COMMUNICATIONS

Roads. In 1983 there were 750 km of classified roads, of which 262 km were tarmac. There were 3,600 passenger cars and about 2,000 commercial vehicles.

Civil Aviation. There is an international airport at Hahaya (on Njazídja). The state-owned Air Comores had no aircraft in 1995. Services are provided by Air Austral, Air France, Air Madagascar, Air Mauritius, Emirates and Sudan Airways.

Shipping. In 1995 the merchant marine totalled 2,959 GRT.

Telecommunications. There were 3,770 telephones in 1991. The state-controlled Radio Comoro broadcasts in French and Comorian. Number of radios (1993), 50,000.

Press. There is 1 weekly newspaper.

SOCIAL INSTITUTIONS

Justice. French and Moslem law is in a new consolidated code.The Supreme Court comprises 7 members, 2 each appointed by the President and the Federal Assembly, and 1 by each island's Legislative Council.

Religion. Islam is the official religion, and over 99% of the population are Sunni Moslems; there are about 1,300 Christians.

Education. After 2 pre-primary years at Koran school, which 50% of children attend, there are 6 years of primary schooling for 7- to 13-year-olds followed by a 4-year secondary stage attended by 25% of children. Some 5% of 17- to 20-year-olds conclude schooling at *lycées.* In 1989–90 there were 257 primary schools with 64,737 pupils and 1,777 teachers. 14,383 pupils attended secondary schools and *lycées* in 1991–92. There is a teacher training college.

Health. In 1978 there were 20 doctors, 1 dentist, 2 pharmacists, 35 midwives and 124 nursing personnel. In 1980 there were 17 hospitals and clinics with 763 beds.

DIPLOMATIC REPRESENTATIVES

Of Great Britain in the Comoros
Ambassador: Peter J. Smith (resides in Antananarivo).

Of the Comoros in the USA
Ambassador: Amini Moumin.

Of the USA in the Comoros
The post closed in Sept. 1993.

Of the Comoros to the United Nations
Ambassador: Mohamed Djimbanaou.

Further Reading

Newitt, N., *The Comoro Islands.* London, 1985
Ottenheimer, M. and Ottenheimer, H. J., *Historical Dictionary of the Comoro Islands.* Metuchen (NJ), 1994

CONGO

République du Congo

Capital: Brazzaville
Population: 2·94m. (1995)
GNP per capita: US$640 (1994)
HDI/world rank: 0·538/122 (1992)

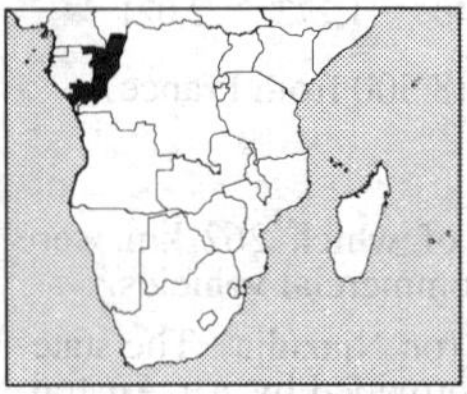

KEY HISTORICAL EVENTS. First occupied by France in 1882, the Congo became a territory of French Equatorial Africa from 1910–58, and then a member state of the French Community. It became an independent Republic on 15 Aug. 1960.

The first President, Fulbert Youlou, was deposed on 15 Aug. 1963 by a coup led by Alphonse Massemba-Débat, who became President on 19 Dec. Following a second coup in Aug. 1968, the Army took power under the leadership of Major Marien Ngouabi, whose colleague, Major Alfred Raoul, was appointed President from 3 Sept. until 1 Jan. 1969, when Ngouabi himself became President. A Marxist-Leninist state was introduced in 1970. Ngouabi was assassinated on 18 March 1977, and succeeded by Col. Joachim Yhombi-Opango, who in turn was replaced on 5 Feb. 1979 by Col. Denis Sassou-Nguesso. Multi-party democracy was restored in 1992.

TERRITORY AND POPULATION. The Congo is bounded by Cameroon and the Central African Republic in the north, Zaïre to the east and south, Angola and the Atlantic Ocean to the south-west and Gabon to the west, and covers 341,821 sq. km. At the census of 1984 the population was 1,909,248.

Estimated population in 1995, 2,936,000 (40% urban); density, 8·6 per sq. km. Brazzaville, the capital, 937,579; Pointe-Noire, 576,206; Loubomo, 83,605; N'Kayi, 42,465; Mossendjo, 16,405; Ouesso, 16,171).

Area, estimated population and capitals of the regions in 1992 were:

Region	*Sq. km*	*Population*	*Capital*	*Region*	*Sq. km*	*Population*	*Capital*
Kouilou	13,694	665,502	Pointe-Noire	Capital District	100	937,579	Brazzaville
Niari	25,940	220,087	Loubomo	Plateaux	38,400	119,722	Djambala
Lékoumou	20,950	74,420	Sibiti	Cuvette	74,850	151,839	Owando
Bouenza	12,266	219,822	Madingou	Sangha	55,800	52,132	Ouesso
Pool	33,955	182,671	Kinkala	Likouala	66,044	70,675	Impfondo

Life expectancy was 52 years in 1991.

French is the official language. Kongo languages are widely spoken. Monokutuba and Lingala serve as lingua francas.

CLIMATE. An equatorial climate, with moderate rainfall and a small range of temperature. There is a long dry season from May to Oct. in the S.W. plateaux, but the Congo Basin in the N.E. is more humid, with rainfall approaching 100" (2,500 mm). Brazzaville. Jan. 78°F (25·6°C), July 73°F (22·8°C). Annual rainfall 59" (1,473 mm).

CONSTITUTION AND GOVERNMENT. From Feb. to June 1991 a national conference was held consisting of representatives of 67 political parties, 134 associations and 30 specialists. This abolished the constitution of July 1979 (for details *see* THE STATESMAN'S YEAR-BOOK, 1991–92, pp, 381–82), dissolved the National Assembly, Constitutional Council and Economic Council, and adopted a basic law to regulate a period of transition. It established a presidency of the republic with newly-defined powers, a 153-member Supreme Council of the Republic and a prime ministership. At a referendum in March 1992 proposing multi-party democracy 96·32% of votes were in favour. Turn-out was 70·93%.

At the second round of the presidential elections in Aug. 1992 Pascal Lissouba was elected President with 61·32% of votes cast against a single opponent.

At the elections of 24 June and 19 July 1992 for the new 125-member *National Assembly*, the Pan-African Union for Social Democracy (UPADS) had gained 39 seats, the Congolese Movement for Democracy and Integral Development (MCDDI) 29, the Congolese Labour Party 19, the Democratic Rally for Social Progress 9 and the Rally for Democracy and Development 5.

In the 60-member *Senate*, UPADS gained 23 seats, MCDDI 13.

In Nov. 1992 the President dismissed the government of Stéphane Bongho-Nouarra and dissolved the National Assembly. At the first round of elections in May–June 1993 for 114 seats in the National Assembly, the Presidential Movement (PM; a coalition of some 60 parties) gained 62 seats, the Congolese Labour Party – Union for Democratic Renewal Coalition 49 and minor parties 3. At the second round in Oct. for the remaining 11 seats the PM gained 4 and CLP-UDR 7.

President: Pascal Lissouba (b. 1931; sworn in 31 Aug. 1992).

In Jan. 1995 a new government was formed which in Aug. 1995 comprised:

Prime Minister: Jacques-Joachim Yhombi-Opango. *Ministers of State:* Martin M'Beri (*Development*), Col. Philippe Bikinkita (*Interior, Security and Regional Development*), Maurice-Stéphane Bongho-Nouarra (*National Defence*). *Foreign and Francophone Affairs and Co-operation:* Arsène Tsaty-Bongou. *Economy and Finance:* N'Guila Moungounga Nkombo. *Communications, Government Spokesman:* Albertine Lipou Massala. *Justice and Adminstration:* Joseph Ouabari. *Industrial Development, Mines and Energy, Posts and Telecommunications:* Jean Esau Etachi. *Equipment and Public Works:* Lambert Galibali. *Education, Research and Technology:* Martial de Paul Ikounga. *Agriculture, Fisheries and Animal Husbandry:* Jean-Prosper Koyo. *Transport and Civil Aviation:* Seraphin Dieken. *Commerce, Consumer Affairs, Small and Medium-sized Enterprises:* Marius Mouambenga. *Health and Social Welfare:* Jean Mouyabi. *Civil Service, Labour and Social Security:* Anachet Tsomambet. *Hydrocarbon Resources:* Benoit Koukebene. *Culture, Arts, Human Rights, Tourism and Environment:* Gabriel Matsiola. *Women's Development:* Maria Thérèse Avemeka. *Youth and Sports:* Gen. Claude-Emmanuel Eta-Onka.

Speaker: André Milongo.

National flag: Diagonal stripes of green, yellow and red.

National anthem: La Congolaise; words and tune by Jean Royer and others.

Local Government: The country is administratively divided into 9 prefectures, subdivided into 47 sub-prefectures, 30 administrative control posts and 6 communes: Brazzaville, Dolisie, Mossendjo, Nkayi, Ouesso and Pointe-Noire. Elections were held on 3 May 1992.

DEFENCE

Army. The Army consists of 2 infantry battalion groups, 2 armoured and 1 infantry battalion, 1 artillery group, 1 engineer and 1 paracommando battalion. Equipment includes 25 T-54/-55 and 15 T-59 main battle tanks. Total personnel (1996) 8,000. There is a Gendarmerie of 2,000. The 'People's Militia' is being absorbed into the Army.

Navy. The combatant flotilla includes 3 modern Spanish-built and 3 ex-Soviet inshore patrol craft. There is also 1 French-built tug and some river patrol boats. Personnel in 1995 totalled about 600.

Air Force. The Air Force had (1995) about 1,200 personnel, 5 Antonov An-24/26 turboprop transports and 2 Noratlas piston-engined transports. Most of these aircraft are in store.

INTERNATIONAL RELATIONS

Membership. Congo is a member of the UN, OAU and is an ACP state of the EU.

ECONOMY

Policy. An economic and social recovery plan (Paséco) was launched in 1994.

Budget. Provisional figures for 1992 (in 1,000m. francs CFA): Revenue, 175; expenditure, 314·2 (267·4 current).

Currency. The unit of currency is the *franc CFA* (BEAC) with a parity of 100 francs CFA to 1 French franc. There are coins of 1, 2, 5, 10, 25, 50, 100 and 500 francs CFA, and banknotes of 500, 1,000, 5,000 and 10,000 francs CFA. Currency in circulation, June 1993, 60,700m. francs CFA. Foreign exchange reserves, US$15,900m. Gold reserves, 11,000 troy oz. For exchange rates *see* BENIN: Currency.

Banking and Finance. The *Banque des États de l'Afrique Centrale* (BEAC) is the bank of issue. There are 3 commercial banks and a development bank in all of which the government has majority stakes.

Weights and Measures. The metric system is in use.

ENERGY AND NATURAL RESOURCES

Electricity. Total production in 1990 was 503·99m. kWh (500·73m. kWh. hydro-electric).

Oil and Gas. Oil reserves are estimated at 500–1,000m. tonnes. Output in 1992 was 8,303,000 tonnes from the 26 offshore oil platforms operated by Elf Congo and Agip Congo. There is a refinery at Pointe-Noire. Gas reserves are estimated at 71,000m. cu. metres.

Minerals. A government mine produces several metals; gold and diamonds are extracted by individuals. There are reserves of potash (4·5m. tonnes), and iron ore (1,000m. tonnes),and also clay, bituminous sand, phosphates, zinc and lead.

Agriculture. In 1991 agriculture produced 12·2% of GDP. Only 1,680 sq. km are cultivated. Production (1991, in thousand tonnes): Cassava, 780; bananas, 40; plantains, 80; yams, 12; maize, 25; groundnuts, 27; coffee, 1; cocoa, 2; rice, 1.

Livestock (1991, in 1,000): Cattle, 68; pigs, 52; sheep, 108; goats, 272; poultry, 2m. There were some 700 tractors in use in 1991.

Forestry. Equatorial forests cover 21m. ha from which (in 1991) 302,175 cu. metres of timber were produced, mainly okoumé from the south and sapele from the north. Timber companies are required to replant, and to process at least 60% of their production locally.

Fisheries. Annual catch by large companies is about 10,000 tonnes, by independent fishermen, 8,000 tonnes. Freshwater catch averages 12,000 tonnes annually. There are fish farms.

INDUSTRY. There is a growing manufacturing sector, located mainly in the 4 major towns, producing processed foods, textiles, cement, metal goods and chemicals. Industry produced 37·4% of GDP in 1991, including 7·6% from manufacturing. Production: Printed cloth (1990), 8·79m. metres; cement (1989), 121,000 tonnes; shoes (1989), 14,670 pairs; corrugated iron sheets (1990), 1·68m. tonnes; household goods (1990), 186 tonnes; nails (1990), 377 tonnes.

Trade Unions. In 1964 the existing unions merged into one national body, the Confédération Syndicale Congolaise. The 40,000-strong Confédération Syndicale des Travailleurs Congolais split off from the latter in 1993.

FOREIGN ECONOMIC RELATIONS. Foreign debt was US$4,751m. in 1992.

Commerce. Imports in 1992 totalled 141,800m. francs CFA and exports 296,100m. francs CFA (crude oil and products, 228,800m. francs CFA, timber and processed wood, 27,300m. francs CFA).

Main export markets, 1992: USA, 37%; Belgium, 22%; Italy, 13%; Spain, 10%; France, 5%. Main import suppliers: France, 37%; Italy, 10%; USA, 8%; Hong Kong, 8%.

Total trade between the Congo and UK (British Department of Trade returns, in £1,000 sterling):

	1991	*1992*	*1993*	*1994*	*1990*
Imports to UK	2,407	2,813	4,807	4,061	5,229
Exports and re-exports from UK	9,190	8,680	12,408	14,649	18,426

COMMUNICATIONS

Roads. In 1992 there were 12,745 km of all-weather roads, of which 1,236 km were bitumenized. In 1991 there were 27,000 cars, 3,000 buses, 2,610 motorcycles and 9,618 commercial vehicles.

Railways. A railway (610 km, 1,067 mm gauge) connects Brazzaville with Pointe-Noire via Loubomo and Bilinga and a 285 km branch links Mont-Belo with Mbinda on the Gabon border. In 1994 railways carried 285m. passenger-km and 223m. tonne-km of freight.

Civil Aviation. The principal airports are at Brazzaville (Maya Maya) and Pointe-Noire. Congo is a member of the multinational Air Afrique, which absorbed the former national carrier Lina-Congo in 1992. Services are also provided by Aeroflot, Air France, Cameroon Airlines, Ethiopian Airlines, Guinea Airlines, Sabena, Swissair, TAAG and TAP.

Shipping. The only seaport is Pointe-Noire, which handled 2·59m. tonnes of freight in 1990. The merchant marine totalled 11,010 GRT in 1995. There are some 5,000 km of navigable rivers, and river transport is an important service for timber and other freight as well as passengers. There are hydrofoil connexions from Brazzaville to Kinshasa.

Telecommunications. Telephones (1990) numbered 15,900. Broadcasting is under the aegis of the government-controlled Radiodiffusion-Télévision Congolaise, which transmits a national and a regional radio programme and a programme in French. In 1993 there were 6 hours of TV broadcasting daily (colour by SECAM). There were 0·25m. radio and about 8,500 TV receivers in 1993.

Press. In 1986 there were 3 daily newspapers with a combined circulation of 24,000.

SOCIAL INSTITUTIONS

Justice. The Supreme Court, Court of Appeal and a criminal court are situated in Brazzaville, with a network of *tribunaux de grande instance* and *tribunaux d'instance* in the regions.

Religion. In 1990 there were 1·25m. Roman Catholics and 0·5m. Protestants. There are some Moslems and traditional animist beliefs are still practised.

Education. In 1990 there were 502,900 pupils and 7,626 teachers in 1,655 primary schools, 172,600 pupils and 4,774 teachers in secondary schools, 11,100 students with 1,813 teachers in technical schools and 19,000 students and 115 teachers in teacher-training establishments. There is 1 university, with 12,045 students and 670 academic staff in 1995-96. Adult literacy (1990) 57% (women 44%).

Health. There were (1988) 567 doctors, 2 dentists and 246 midwives.

DIPLOMATIC REPRESENTATIVES

Of the Congo in Great Britain
Ambassador: Alphonse Niangoula (resides in Paris).

Of Great Britain in the Congo
Chargé d'Affaires: Marcus L. Hope (resides in Kinshasa).

Of the Congo in the USA (4891 Colorado Ave., NW, Washington D.C., 20011)
Ambassador: Pierre Boussoukou-Boumba.

Of the USA in the Congo (PO Box 1015, Brazzaville)
Ambassador: William C. Ramsay.

Of the Congo to the United Nations
Ambassador: Daniel Abibi.

Further Reading

Thompson, V. and Adloff, R., *Historical Dictionary of the People's Republic of the Congo*. 2nd ed. Metuchen (NJ), 1984

COSTA RICA

República de Costa Rica

Capital: San José
Population: 3·39m. (1995)
GNP per capita: US$2,380 (1994)
HDI/world rank: 0·883/28 (1992)

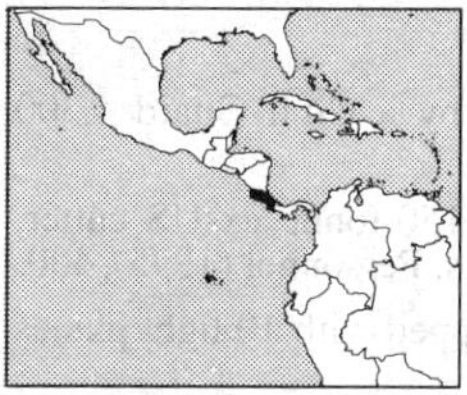

KEY HISTORICAL EVENTS. Part of the Spanish Viceroyalty of New Spain from 1540, Costa Rica formed part of the United Provinces of Central America on its formation in 1823. Costa Rica left the Confederation and achieved full independence in 1838. The first Constitution was promulgated on 7 Dec. 1871.

TERRITORY AND POPULATION. Costa Rica is bounded in the north by Nicaragua, east by the Caribbean, south-east by Panama, and south and west by the Pacific. The area is estimated at 51,100 sq. km (19,730 sq. miles). The population at the census of 1 June 1984 was 2,416,809. Estimate (1995) 3,385,000 (44% urban); density, 66·2 per sq. km. There are 7 provinces (with 1993 population): Alajuela (562,781); Cartago (375,356); Guanacaste (216,688); Heredia (296,342); Limón (253,724); Puntarenas (344,063); San José (1,183,572).

Vital statistics for calendar years:

	Marriages	*Births*	*Deaths*
1989	22,984	83,460	11,272
1990	22,703	81,939	11,366

The population is mainly of Spanish (85%) and mixed (8%) descent. About 3% are Afro-Caribbean (including some 70,000 speakers of an English creole along the Caribbean coast). There is a residual Amerindian population of about 10,000.

Spanish is the official language.

CLIMATE. The climate is tropical, with a small range of temperature and abundant rains. The dry season is from Dec. to April. San José. Jan. 66°F (18·9°C), July 69°F (20·6°C). Annual rainfall 72" (1,793 mm).

CONSTITUTION AND GOVERNMENT. The Constitution was promulgated in Nov. 1949. The legislative power is vested in a single-chamber *Legislative Assembly* of 57 deputies elected for 4 years. The *President* and 2 Vice-Presidents are elected for 4 years; the candidate receiving the largest vote, provided it is over 40% of the total, is declared elected, but a second ballot is required if no candidate gets 40% of the total. Elections are normally held on the first Sunday in February.

The President may appoint and remove members of the cabinet.

Presidential elections took place on 6 Feb. 1994. José-María Figueres was elected by 49·7% of votes cast.

At the simultaneous parliamentary elections the National Liberation Party (NLP) won 28 seats, the Social Christian Unity Party 25 and ind 4.

President: José-María Figueres (b. 1955; NLP; sworn in 8 May 1994).
Vice-Presidents: Rodrigo Oreamuno; Sandra Piszk.

In Oct. 1995 the government also comprised:
Minister for the Presidency: Elias Soley. *Agriculture:* Marío Carvajal. *Culture, Youth and Sport:* Arnoldo Mora. *The Economy, Industry and Commerce:* Marcos Varga. *Education:* Marvin Herrera. *Environment:* René Castro. *Finance:* Fernando Herrera. *Foreign Affairs:* Dr Fernando Naranjo. *Foreign Trade:* José Rossi. *Health:* Dr Germán Weinstoke. *Housing:* Edgar Arroyo. *Information:* Florisabel Rodríguez. *Interior:* Maureen Clarke. *Justice:* Enrique Castillo. *Labour:* Farid Ayales. *National Co-ordination:* Sergio Quiros. *Planning:* Leonardo Garnier. *Public Works and Transport:* Bernardo Arce. *Rural Development:* Roberto Solozano. *Science and*

Technology: Roberto Dobles. *Security:* Juan Diego Castro. *Special Projects:* Dr Longino Soto. *Tourism:* Carlos Roesch.

National flag: Five unequal stripes of blue, white, red, white, blue, with the national arms on a white disc near the hoist.

National anthem: 'Noble patria, tu hermosa bandera' ('Noble fatherland, thy beautiful banner'); words by J. M. Zeledón Brenes, tune by M. M. Gutiérrez).

DEFENCE

Army. The Army was abolished in 1948, and replaced by a Civil Guard 4,300 strong in 1996.

Navy. The para-military Civil Guard flotilla includes 1 150-tonne ex-US cutter, 1 fast patrol craft, 5 small coastguard cutters and some boats. Personnel (1995), 400.

Air Wing. The Civil Guard operates a small air wing equipped with 10 light planes and helicopters and 2 Caribou transports.

INTERNATIONAL RELATIONS

Membership. Costa Rica is a member of the UN, CACM and OAS.

ECONOMY

Currency. The unit of currency is the *Costa Rican colón* (CRC) of 100 *céntimos.* There are coins of 25 and 50 céntimos and ₡5, 10 and 20, and notes of ₡50, 100, 500, 1,000 and 5,000. The official rate is used for all imports on an essential list and by the Government and autonomous institutions and a free rate is used for all other transactions. 43,500m. colons were in circulation in 1993. Inflation was 9% in 1994. Official rate, March 1995: £1 = ₡304·87; US$1 = ₡199·47; DM1 = ₡135·15.

Banking and Finance. The bank of issue is the Central Bank (founded 1950) which supervises the national monetary system, foreign exchange dealings and banking operations. The bank has a board of 7 directors appointed by the Government, including *ex officio* the Minister of Finance and the Planning Office Director. The *Governor* is Carlos Manuel Castillo.

Weights and Measures. The metric system is legally established, but in country districts the following old Spanish weights and measures may be found: *Libra* = 1·014 lb. avoirdupois; *arroba* = 25·35 lb. avoirdupois; *quintal* = 101·40 lb. avoirdupois, and *fanega* = 11 Imperial bushels.

ENERGY AND NATURAL RESOURCES

Electricity. Electricity, derived from water power in the highlands, is increasingly used as motive power. Output, 1991, was 3,872m. kWh.

Minerals. Gold output is about 3,000 troy oz. per year. Salt production was 50,000 tonnes in 1991.

Agriculture. Agriculture is the principal industry; 734,000 persons depended upon it in 1993, of whom 247,900 were economically active. The arable area is about 285,000 ha. The principal agricultural products are coffee, bananas, sugar and cattle.

Coffee production in 1992 (in tonnes) was 168,000; sugar-cane, 2·84m.; bananas, 1·63m.; maize, 40,000; tobacco, 2,000; rice, 209,000; potatoes, 50,000.

In 1992 cattle numbered 1·71m. and pigs 225,000.

Forestry. The forest area (1·6m. ha. in 1988) is being depleted. 4·2m. cu. metres of timber were cut in 1991.

Fisheries. Total catch (1991) 18,000 tonnes.

INDUSTRY. The main manufactured goods are foodstuffs, textiles, fertilizers, pharmaceuticals, furniture, cement, tyres, canning, clothing, plastic goods, plywood and electrical equipment.

Trade Unions. There are two main trade unions, *Rerum Novarum* (anti-Communist) and *Confederación General de Trabajadores Costarricenses* (Communist).

FOREIGN ECONOMIC RELATIONS.

A free trade agreement was signed with Mexico in March 1994. Some 2,300 products were freed from tariffs, with others to follow over 10 years.

Commerce. The value of imports and exports in US$1m.:

	1991	*1992*	*1993*
Imports	1,853	2,449	2,907
Exports	1,543	1,741	2,085

Chief exports: Manufactured goods and other products, coffee (mostly to Germany, USA, UK and Italy), bananas (to USA), sugar, cocoa.

Total trade between Costa Rica and UK (British Department of Trade returns in £1,000 sterling):

	1991	*1992*	*1993*	*1994*	*1995*
Imports to UK	21,823	17,559	41,286	76,795	78,515
Exports and re-exports from UK	11,312	28,774	18,473	20,930	23,271

Tourism. There was a total of 504,600 tourists in 1991.

COMMUNICATIONS

Roads. In 1992 there were about 35,560 km of all-weather motor roads open. On the Costa Rica section of the Inter-American Highway it is possible to motor to Panama during the dry season. The Pan-American Highway into Nicaragua is metalled for most of the way and there is now a good highway open almost to Puntarenas. Motor vehicles, 1992, numbered 339,206.

Railways. The nationalized railway system *(Incofer)* was closed in 1995.

Civil Aviation. The national carrier is Líneas Aéreas Costarriquenses (LACSA), which in 1995 operated 4 A320-200s and 2 B-737-200 Advs.

Shipping. The chief ports are Limón on the Atlantic and Caldera on the Pacific. The merchant marine totalled 2,895 GRT in 1995.

Telecommunications. There were 305,000 telephones in 1991. The Government has 202 telegraph offices and 88 official telephone stations. In 1993 there were 255,000 radio and 340,000 television receivers (colour by NTSC).

Cinemas (1979). Cinemas numbered 106, with seating capacity of 105,000.

Press (1984). There were 4 daily newspapers all published in San José.

SOCIAL INSTITUTIONS

Justice. Justice is administered by the Supreme Court, 5 appeal courts divided into 5 chambers; the Court of Cassation, the Higher and Lower Criminal Courts, and the Higher and Lower Civil Courts. There are also subordinate courts in the separate provinces and local justices throughout the republic. Capital punishment may not be inflicted.

Religion. Roman Catholicism is the state religion; it had 2·55m. adherents in 1991. There is entire religious liberty under the constitution. The Archbishop of Costa Rica has 4 bishops at Alajuela, Limón, San Isidro el General and Tilarán. Protestants number about 40,000.

Education. Adult literacy was 92·8% in 1991. Primary instruction is compulsory and free from 6 to 15 years; secondary education (since 1949) is also free. Primary schools are provided and maintained by local school councils, while the national government pays the teachers, besides making subventions in aid of local funds. In

1991-92 there were 3,317 public primary schools with 14,100 teachers and administrative staff and 453,300 enrolled pupils; there were 179 public and private secondary schools with 4,671 teachers and 101,500 pupils in 1990–91. In 1995-96 there was 1 university and 1 technological institute in the public sector, and 8 universities, 1 Adventist university and 1 university of science and technology in the private sector. There were also 4 other institutions of higher education. In 1994-95 there were 48,354 university students and 3,687 academic staff.

Health. In 1990 there were 2,518 doctors, 206 dentists and 6,536 hospital beds.

DIPLOMATIC REPRESENTATIVES

Of Costa Rica in Great Britain (19A Cavendish Sq., London, W1M 9AI)
Ambassador: Jorge Borbón Zeller.

Of Great Britain in Costa Rica (Edificio Centro Colón, Apartado 815, San José)
Ambassador and Consul-General: Richard M. Jackson, CVO.

Of Costa Rica in the USA (1825 Connecticut Ave., NW Washington D.C., 20009)
Ambassador: José Muñoz.

Of the USA in Costa Rica (Pavas, San José)
Ambassador: Peter J. De Vos.

Of Costa Rica to the United Nations
Ambassador: Fernando Berrocal Soto.

Further Reading

Ameringer, C. D., *Democracy in Costa Rica*. New York, 1982
Biesanz, R., *(et al), The Costa Ricans*. Hemel Hempstead, 1982
Bird, L., *Costa Rica: Unarmed Democracy*. London, 1984
Creedman, T. S. *Historical Dictionary of Costa Rica*. 2nd ed. Metuchen (N.J.), 1991
Stansifer, C., *Costa Rica*. 2nd ed. [Bibliography] Oxford and Santa Barbara (CA), 1991

National statistical office: Dirección General de Estadística y Censos, San José.

CÔTE D'IVOIRE

République de la
Côte d'Ivoire
(Republic of the Ivory Coast)

Capital: Yamoussoukro
Seat of Government: Abidjan
Population: 13·72m. (1994)
GNP per capita: US$510 (1994)
HDI/world rank: 0·369/145 (1992)

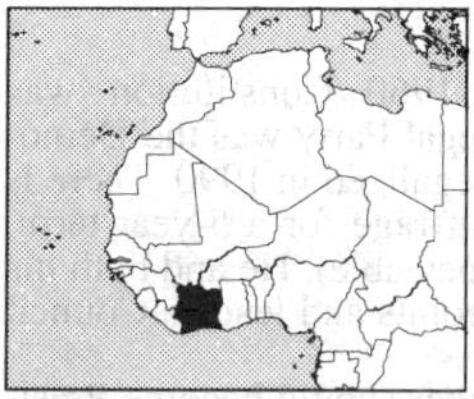

KEY HISTORICAL EVENTS. France obtained rights on the coast in 1842, but did not actively and continuously occupy the territory till 1882. On 10 Jan. 1889 Ivory Coast was declared a French protectorate, and it became a colony on 10 March 1893; in 1904 it became a territory of French West Africa. The Ivory Coast became an autonomous republic within the French Community on 4 Dec. 1958 and achieved full independence on 7 Aug. 1960.

TERRITORY AND POPULATION. Côte d'Ivoire is bounded in the west by Liberia and Guinea, north by Mali and Burkina Faso, east by Ghana, and south by the Gulf of Guinea. It has an area of 320,783 sq. km and a population at the 1988 census of 10,812,782 (40% urban). Estimate (1994) 13·72m.; density, 42·8 per sq. km.

Since 1991, the country has been divided into 10 regions (North-West, North, North-East, West, Centre-West, Centre-North, Centre, Centre-East, South-West, South) comprising 50 departments. Departments are named after their chief towns.

The areas and populations (1988 census) of the departments:

	Area (in sq. km)	*Population*		*Area (in sq. km)*	*Population*
Abengourou	5,200	214,162	Guiglo	11,220	169,660
Abidjan	8,550	2,492,513	Issia	3,590	194,974
Aboisso	6,250	225,882	Katiola	9,420	131,221
Adzopé	5,230	237,265	Korhogo	12,500	387,947
Agboville	3,850	203,730	Lakota	2,730	115,948
Agnibilekrou [1]	1,700	84,404	Man	4,990	286,860
Bangolo [2]	2,060	80,374	Mankono	10,660	123,723
Béoumi [3]	2,860	91,062	M'bahiakro [3]	5,460	102,774
Biankouma	4,950	99,431	Odiénné	20,600	169,433
Bondoukou	10,040	175,632	Oumé	2,400	140,166
Bongouanou	5,570	225,432	Sakassou [3]	1,880	59,494
Bouaflé	3,980	163,917	San-Pédro [7]	6,900	168,174
Bouaké	4,700	453,074	Sassandra	5,190	107,616
Bouna	21,470	134,459	Séguéla	11,240	121,120
Boundiali	7,895	127,231	Sinfra [8]	1,690	120,301
Dabakala	9,670	82,094	Soubré	8,270	309,307
Daloa	5,450	361,472	Tabou [7]	5,440	59,708
Danané	4,600	222,045	Tanda [9]	6,490	203,129
Daoukro [4]	3,610	86,425	Tiassalé [6]	3,370	132,626
Dimbokro	4,920	141,934	Tingréla	2,200	55,251
Divo	7,920	389,530	Touba	8,720	109,155
Duékoué [5]	2,930	101,451	Toumodi [3]	2,780	80,909
Ferkessedougou	17,728	172,850	Vavoua [10]	6,160	169,454
Gagnoa	4,500	275,765	Yamoussoukro [3]	6,160	284,613
Grand-Lahou [6]	2,280	52,645	Zuénoula	2,830	114,440

[1] Formerly part of Abengourou. [2] Formerly part of Man. [3] Formerly parts of Bouaké.
[4] Formerly part of Dimbokro. [5] Formerly part of Guiglo. [6] Formerly parts of Abidjan.
[7] Formerly parts of Sassandra. [8] Formerly part of Bouaflé.
[9] Formerly part of Bondougou. [10] Formerly part of Daloa.

Major towns (with 1988 census population): Abidjan, 1,929,079; Boaké, 329,850; Daloa, 121,842; Korhogo, 109,445; Yamoussoukro, 106,786.

There are about 60 ethnic goups, the principal being the Baule, (23%), the Bete (18%) and the Senufo (15%).

French is the official language.

CLIMATE. A tropical climate, affected by distance from the sea. In coastal areas, there are wet seasons from May to July and in Oct. and Nov., but in central areas the periods are March to May and July to Nov. In the north, there is one wet season from June to Oct. Abidjan. Jan. 81°F (27·2°C), July 75°F (23·9°C). Annual rainfall 84" (2,100 mm). Bouaké. Jan. 81°F (27·2°C), July 77°F (25°C). Annual rainfall 48" (1,200 mm).

CONSTITUTION AND GOVERNMENT. The 1960 Constitution was amended in 1971, 1975, 1980, 1985 and 1986. The sole legal Party was the Democratic Party of Côte d'Ivoire, but opposition parties were legalized in 1990. There is a 175-member *National Assembly* elected by universal suffrage for a 5-year term. The President is also directly elected for a 5-year term (renewable). He and both his parents must be citizens born in the Côte d'Ivoire. He appoints and leads a Council of Ministers.

In Nov. 1990 the National Assembly voted that its Speaker should become President in the event of the latter's incapacity, and created the post of Prime Minister to be appointed by the President. Following the death of President Houphouët-Boigny on 7 Dec. 1993 the speaker, Henri Konan Bedie, proclaimed himself head of state till the end of the presidential term in Sept. 1995. Presidential elections were held on 22 Oct. 1995; turn-out was 56·03%. President Konan Bedie was re-elected by 96·44% of votes cast against 1 opponent.

At the National Assembly elections of 25 Nov. 1995 the electorate was 3·8m. The Democratic Party won 149 seats; the Republican Rally, 16; the Ivorian Popular Front, 11.

In Aug. 1995 the government comprised:

Prime Minister and Minister for the Economy, Finances and Planning: Daniel Kablan Duncan.

Relations with Parliament: Ahoua N'Guetta Timothee. *National Integration:* Laurent Dona-Fologo. *Defence:* Leon Konan Koffi. *Foreign Affairs:* Amara Essy. *Interior:* Emile Constant Bombet. *Justice:* Faustin Kouame. *Higher Education and Scientific Research:* Saliou Touré. *Agriculture and Livestock:* Lambert Kouassi Konan. *Raw Materials:* Alain Gauze. *Education:* Pierre Kipre. *Environment and Tourism:* Lancine Gon Coulibaly. *Industry and Commerce:* Ferdinand Kacou Angora. *Mines and Energy:* Mohamed Lamine Fadika. *Health and Social Affairs:* Maurice Kakou Guikahue. *Communication:* Daniele Boni-Claverie. *Equipment, Transport and Telecommunications:* Ezan Akele. *Construction and Town Planning:* Albert Kakou Tiapani. *Employment and Civil Service:* Achi Atsain. *Security:* Gaston Ouassenan Kone. *Culture:* Bernard Zadi Zaourou. *Women and the Family:* Albertine Gnanazan Hipie. *Youth and Sport:* Komenan Zakpa.

The *Speaker* is Charles Donwahi.

National flag: Three vertical strips of orange, white, green.

National anthem: L'Abidjanaise (words by M. Ekra and others, tune by P. M Pango).

Local government: There are 50 departments, each under an appointed Prefect and an elected General Council, sub-divided into 183 sub-prefectures. At the elections of Dec. 1990 turn-out was low. The Democratic Party won 123 out of the 132 councils contested; the Ivoirian Popular Front, 6; independents, 3.

DEFENCE. There is selective conscription for 6 months.

Army. There are 4 military regions. The Army consists of 1 armoured battalion, 3 infantry battalions, 1 artillery group and 1 airborne, 1 anti-aircraft and 1 engineer company. Equipment includes 5 AMX-13 light tanks. Total strength (1996), 6,800. Paramilitary forces, 7,800.

Navy. Offshore, riverine and coastal patrol squadrons include 2 fast missile craft, 2 patrol vessels, 1 riverine defence craft, 1 light amphibious transport and 2 minor landing craft. Personnel in 1995 totalled 900 and the force is based at Locodjo (Abidjan).

Air Force. There are 5 Alpha Jet light strike combat aircraft. Transport aircraft include 5 fixed-wing and 4 rotary-wing aircraft. 4 Bonanzas are used for training and patrol. Personnel (1995) 700.

INTERNATIONAL RELATIONS

Membership. Côte d'Ivoire is a member of the UN, OAU and is an ACP state of the EU.

ECONOMY

Policy. Austerity measures were introduced in May 1990. A privatization programme has been announced.

Budget. 1993 budget (in 1,000m. francs CFA): Revenue, 621 (of which fiscal receipts, 533); expenditure, 996 (of which capital expenditure, 99).

Currency. The currency is the *franc CFA* with a parity rate of 100 francs CFA to 1 French franc. In 1993 gold reserves were 45,000 troy oz; foreign exchange reserves were US$4m. In 1992 252,100m. francs CFA were in circulation. Inflation was 0·5% per month in 1995.

For exchange rates *see* BENIN: Currency.

Banking and Finance. The regional *Banque Centrale des Etats de l'Afrique de l'Ouest* is the central bank and bank of issue. In 1994 there were 12 commercial banks; 3 other banks maintained representative offices. The African Development Bank is based in Abidjan. There is a stock exchange in Abidjan.

ENERGY AND NATURAL RESOURCES

Electricity. The electricity industry was privatized in 1990. Production in 1992 amounted to 1,845m. kWh (1,025m. kWh from hydroelectric projects).

Oil. Petroleum has been produced (offshore) since Oct. 1977. Production (1992) 63,000 tonnes.

Minerals. Diamond extraction was 20,000 carats in 1987. There are iron ore deposits at Bangolo and gold-mining began in Jan. 1990, reserves being estimated at 4,500 kg.

Agriculture. In 1992 some 8m. persons subsisted on agriculture in 0·56m. family smallholdings averaging 2 ha. In 1991 there were 2·4m. ha of arable land, 1·26m. ha of permanent crop land and 13m. ha of meadow and pasture. The main crops (production, 1991, in 1,000 tonnes) are coffee (240), cocoa (710), bananas (116), pineapples (189), palm oil (217), palm kernels (43), seed cotton (302), rubber (74), yams (269), cassava (1,435), plantains (1,110), rice (690), maize (510), millet (52), sugar-cane (1,600) and groundnuts (140).

Livestock, 1992: 1·18m. cattle, 1·2m. sheep, 0·92m. goats and 0·38m. pigs.

Forestry. In 1987 the forest area was 6·38m. ha. Products include teak, mahogany and ebony. Production in 1988 was 12·75. cu. metres (9·43 cu. metres for fuel).

Fisheries. In 1989 the fishing fleet comprised 32 vessels over 100 GRT totalling 9,386 GRT. The catch in 1988 amounted to 107,600.

INDUSTRY. Industrialization has developed rapidly since independence, particularly food processing, textiles and sawmills. Output in 1988 (in 1,000 tonnes): Petrol, 311; paraffin, 237; fuel oil, 1,089; cement, 144; sawn timber, 775; veneer wood, 266; centrifugal sugar, 140; palm-oil (1989), 190; copra (1989), 75.

Labour. In 1988 the workforce was 4·4m.

Trade Unions. The main trade union is the *Union Générale des Travailleurs de Côte d'Ivoire*, with over 100,000 members.

FOREIGN ECONOMIC RELATIONS. External debt was US$17,500m. in 1993.

Commerce. Trade for calendar years in US1m.:

	1988	*1989*	*1990*	*1991*
Imports	1,696	1,738	1,701	1,600
Exports	2,774	2,806	3,118	2,900

Principal exports, 1992 (in 1,000m. francs CFA): Cocoa, 256; petroleum products, 85; timber, 62; coffee, 56; cotton, 29; tinned tuna, 25. Principal imports: Crude oil, 116; machinery and vehicles, 96; pharmaceuticals, 34; fish, 27; plastics, 20. Main export markets, 1992: France, 15·1%; Germany, 9·9%; Italy, 7·6%; Netherlands, 7·4%; USA, 5·9%. Main import suppliers: France, 36%; Nigeria, 20·2%; Netherlands, 4·4%; USA, 3·9%; Italy, 3·8%.

Total trade between the Côte d'Ivoire and UK (British Department of Trade returns, in £1,000 sterling):

	1991	*1992*	*1993*	*1994*	*1995*
Imports to UK	45,630	53,022	67,424	65,958	101,737
Exports and re-exports from UK	24,131	29,480	33,411	27,057	49,428

COMMUNICATIONS

Roads. In 1988 roads totalled 55,000 km (including 128 km of motorway) and there were (1994) about 311,000 motor vehicles.

Railways. From Abidjan a metre-gauge railway runs to Léraba on the border with Burkina Faso (655 km), and thence through Burkina Faso to Ouagadougou and Kaya. In 1991–92 the railways carried 0·9m. passengers and 0·5m. tonnes of freight. Route length in 1986, 1,177 km.

Civil Aviation. There are international airports at Abidjan-Port-Bouet and Yamoussoukro. The national carrier is the state-owned Air Ivoire, which provides domestic services to 10 regional airports and flights to Burkina Faso, Ghana, Guinea, Liberia and Mali. Air Ivoire had 3 aircraft in 1995. Services are also provided by Air Afrique, Air Burkina, Air France, Air Gabon, Air Guinée, Air Liberté, Cameroon Airlines, Egyptair, Ethiopian Airlines, Ghana Airways, Middle East Airlines, Nigeria Airways, Royal Air Maroc, Sabena, Swissair and TAP.

Shipping. The main ports are Abidjan and San Pedro. In 1992 Abidjan loaded 3·98m. tonnes of cargo and unloaded 6·18m. tonnes. In 1995 the merchant marine totalled 76,399 GRT, including oil-tankers, 1,170 GRT.

Telecommunications. There were 87,700 telephones in 1984 and 1,800 telex machines. The government-controlled Radiodiffusion Télévision Ivoirienne is responsible for broadcasting. In 1993 there were 810,000 television (colour by SECAM) and 1·5m. radio receivers.

Press. In 1984 there was 1 daily newspaper.

SOCIAL INSTITUTIONS

Justice. There are 28 courts of first instance and 3 assize courts in Abidjan, Bouaké and Daloa, 2 courts of appeal in Abidjan and Bouaké, and a supreme court in Abidjan. The death penalty is authorized, but has not been applied since independence in 1960.

Religion. In 1994 there were 5·2m. Moslems (mainly in the north) and 3·8m. Christians (chiefly Roman Catholics in the south). Traditional animist beliefs are also practised.

Education. In 1990 54% of the population over 15 were literate. There were, in 1992, 1,447,785 pupils in 6,844 primary schools, 289,510 pupils in 147 secondary schools and 3,094 students at 15 technical or teacher training institutes and 14,200 students in higher education. In 1986 there were 33,500 primary school teachers. In 1995-96 there was 1 university with 21,000 students and 730 academic staff, and 3 university centres. There were 6 other institutions of higher education.

Health. There were 93 hospitals and 669 health centres in 1984. In 1982 there were 10,062 hospital beds. In 1980 there were 591 doctors. In 1985 there were 60 dentists and 85 pharmacists.

DIPLOMATIC REPRESENTATIVES

Of the Côte d'Ivoire in Great Britain (2 Upper Belgrave St., London, SW1X 8BJ)
Ambassador: Gervais Attoungbré.

Of Great Britain in the Côte d'Ivoire (Immeuble 'Les Harmonies', angle Blvd. Carde et Ave. Dr Jamot, Plateau, Abidjan)
Ambassador: Margaret Rothwell, CMG.

Of the Côte d'Ivoire in the USA (2424 Massachusetts Ave., NW, Washington, D.C., 20008)
Ambassador: Koffi Moïse Koumoue.

Of the USA in the Côte d'Ivoire (5 Rue Jesse Owens, Abidjan)
Ambassador: Lannon Walker.

Of the Côte d'Ivoire to the United Nations
Ambassador: Jean-Marie K. Gervais.

Further Reading

Direction de la Statistique. *Bulletin Mensuel de Statistique.*

Sugar, H., *Ivory Coast.* [Bibliography] Oxford and Santa Barbara (CA), 1990
Zartman, I. W. and Delgado, C., *The Political Economy of Ivory Coast.* New York, 1984

National statistical office: Direction de la Statistique, Ministère du Plan, Abidjan.

CROATIA

Republika Hrvatska

Capital: Zagreb
Population: 4·84m. (1994)
GNP per capita: US$2,530 (1994)

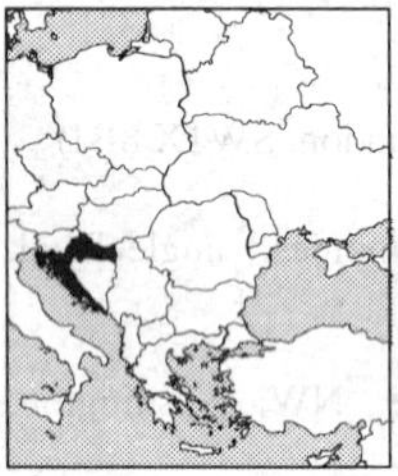

KEY HISTORICAL EVENTS. The original Croats migrated to their present territory in the 6th century and were converted to Roman Catholicism. Croatia was united with Hungary by a personal union of thrones in 1091 and remained under Hungarian administration until the end of the first world war. On 1 Dec. 1918 Croatia became a part of the new Kingdom of Serbs, Croats and Slovenes, which was renamed Yugoslavia in 1929.

During the second world war an independent fascist (Ustaša) state was set up under the aegis of the German occupiers. During the Communist period Croatia became one of the 6 'Socialist Republics' constituting the Yugoslav federation. (*See* THE STATESMAN'S YEAR-BOOK, 1991–92, p. 1607).

At a referendum on 19 May 1991 turn-out was 82·97% of the electorate of 3·6m. 94·17% of votes cast were in favour of Croatia becoming an independent sovereign state with the option of joining a future Yugoslav confederation as opposed to remaining in the existing Yugoslav federation. The Krajina, and other predominantly Serbian areas of Croatia, proclaimed the desire for union with Serbia and seized power by force of arms. Croatian forces and Serb insurgents backed by federal forces ostensibly of law and order became embroiled in a conflict throughout 1991 until the arrival of a UN peace-keeping mission at the beginning of 1992 and the establishment of 4 UN ('pink zones') peace-keeping zones. Croatia obtained a reduction in the UN peace-keeping forces after 1 April 1995.

In early May 1995 Croatian forces retook Western Slavonia from the Serbs and opened the Zagreb-Belgrade highway. Serb rockets fell on Zagreb during the campaign, and civilians were killed. In a 60-hour operation mounted on 4 Aug. 1995 the former self-declared Serb Republic of Krajina was occupied, provoking an exodus of 0.18m. Serb refugees. Croats who had left the area in 1991 began to return. On 12 Nov. 1995 the Croatian government and Bosnian Serbs reached an agreement to place Eastern Slavonia, the last Croatian territory still under Bosnian Serb control, under UN administration for at least a year.

TERRITORY AND POPULATION. Croatia is bounded in the north by Slovenia and Hungary and in the east by Yugoslavia and Bosnia-Hercegovina. It includes the areas of Dalmatia, Istria and Slavonia which no longer have administrative status. Its area is 56,538 sq. km. Population at the 1991 census was 4,784,265 (50·8% urban), of whom the predominating ethnic groups were Croats (3,736,356) and Serbs (581,663). Estimate, 1994, 4,837,000; density, 85·5 per sq. km. Principal towns (with 1991 census population): Zagreb (726,770), Split (189,388), Rijeka (167,964), Osijek (104,761).

At the beginning of 1991 there were some 0·6m. resident Serbs. A law of Dec. 1991 guaranteed the autonomy of Serbs in areas where they are in a majority after the establishment of a permanent peace.

Vital statistics:

	Live births	*Marriages*	*Deaths*	*Growth rate per 1,000*
1990	55,651	28,938	52,569	0·7
1991	51,829	21,583	54,832	–0·63
1992	46,970	22,169	51,800	–1·01

Rates, 1990: Birth, 11·8 per 1,000 population; death, 11·1; infant mortality, 10·6 per 1,000 live births.

The official language is the western variant of Serbo-Croat (in Croatia called Croato-Serb or, familiarly, Croatian).

CLIMATE. Inland Croatia has a Central European type of climate, with cold winters and hot summers, but the Adriatic coastal region experiences a Mediterranean climate with mild, moist winters and hot, brilliantly sunny summers with less than average rainfall. Jan./July temperature/annual rainfall: Dubrovnik, 9·2°C/24·7°C/1,006 mm. Zadar, 7·2°C/23·5°C/688 mm. Rijeka, 6·2°C/23°C/1,251 mm. Zagreb, 0°C/23·5°C/652 mm. Osijek, 0·6°C/20·8°C/541 mm.

CONSTITUTION AND GOVERNMENT. A new constitution was adopted on 21 Dec. 1990. The *President* is elected by parliament for 5-year terms. Franjo Tudjman was elected President in May 1990, and re-elected on 3 Aug. 1992 against 7 opponents by 56·7% of votes cast. Parliament consists of the 127-member *Sabor*, in which 12 seats are reserved for the Croat diaspora and 3 for the Serb minority. It is elected by a combination of proportional representation and first-past-the-post methods. There is also an upper house, the 68-member *Chamber of Counties*, composed of representatives of counties elected by proportional representation, and 5 members nominated by the President. The role of the Chamber of Counties is primarily consultative.

At elections to the Sabor on 29 Aug. 1995 the electorate was 3·6m.; turn-out was 66%. The Croatian Democratic Union (CDU) won 75 seats with 44·82% of votes cast, the Peasant Party coalition 16 with 18·44%, the Croatian Social Liberal Party (CSLP) 12 with 11·62%, the Social Democratic Party 10, the Croat Right-Wing Party 4, the Istrian Democratic Diet 2, and the Independent Democrats 1. At elections to the Chamber of Counties in Feb. 1993 the CDU gained 37 seats, the CSLP 16 and others 15.

President: Franjo Tudjman (b. 1922; CDU; sworn in 12 Aug. 1992).

In Aug. 1995 the government comprised:

Prime Minister: Nikica Valentić (b. 1950; CDU).

Deputy Prime Ministers: Mate Granić (*also Foreign Minister*), Jure Radić (*also Minister for Reconstruction and Development*), Ivica Kostović, Borislav Skegro. *Defence:* Gojko Šušak. *Interior:* Ivan Jarnjak. *Commerce and Tourism:* Niko Bulić. *Agriculture and Forestry:* Ivica Gaži. *Construction, Town Planning and Housing:* Marina Dropulić-Matulović. *Finance:* Božo Prka. *Education and Sport:* Ljilja Vokić. *Health:* Andrija Hebrang. *Justice:* Ivica Crnić. *Administration:* Davorin Mlakar. *Labour and Social Welfare:* Joso Škara. *Science and Technology:* Branko Jeren. *Maritime Affairs, Transport and Communications:* Ivica Mudrinić. *Economy:* Nadan Vidošević. *Privatization and Property Management:* Ivan Benić. *Culture:* Zlatko Vitez. *Without portfolio:* Adalbert Rebić, Zlatko Mateša, Juraj Njavro, Cedomir Pavlović, Ivan Majdak.

The *Speaker* is Nedjeljko Mihanović.

National flag: 3 horizontal stripes of red, white and blue with the arms over all in the centre.

National anthem: 'Lijepa naša domovino' ('Beautiful our homeland'); words by A. Mihanović, tune by J. Runjanin.

Local Government. The country is divided into 21 counties (*županija*), 2 districts (Knin and Glina, at present under local Serbian control), 68 towns and 383 municipalities, all administered by elected councils. County councils elect as leader a prefect approved by the President. County councils have broad responsibilities in the spheres of economic development, health and education; town and municipal councils (the latter for areas with fewer than 10,00 population) are concerned with detailed administration. Elections were held in Feb. 1993.

DEFENCE. Conscription is for 10 months.

Army. The country is divided into 6 operations zones. The Army consists of 29 infantry, 1 air defence, 1 special forces, 1 artillery-multiple rocket launcher, 1 anti-tank, 1 engineer and 6 mechanized brigades. Equipment includes 9 T-34, 140 T-55 and 27 M-84 main battle tanks. Personnel, 1996, 99,600 (65,000 conscripts). Paramilitary forces include an armed police of 40,000. There are also 10,000 reserves in Home Defence regiments and 180,000 regular Army reservists.

Navy. In 1995 the fleet comprised 1 submarine for special operations, 1 corvette, 3 missile craft, 1 torpedo craft, 3 patrol craft, 2 minelayers and 3 small mine countermeasures vessels. There are 12 small amphibious craft and some 5 support vessels. A Marine service fields 7 independent infantry companies, and the coast defence force mans artillery batteries. Total personnel in 1995 numbered about 3,000 including marines.

Air Force. The Air Force has 5 squadrons, 1 with MiG-21 fighters, 1 with Mi-24 armed helicopters, 1 with Mi-8/17 transport helicopters, 1 with An-2 fixed-wing transports and 1 with trainer aircraft. Personnel, 1995, 4,000 (including Air Defence).

INTERNATIONAL RELATIONS. In Jan. 1994 relations with Yugoslavia were established with the opening of mutual representative offices.

Membership. Croatia is a member of the UN and the Central European Initiative, which evolved from the Pentagonal/Hexagonal grouping of 1990–91.

ECONOMY

Budget. Revenue and expenditure in 1993 balanced at 10,002m. kuna. 1995 estimate, 28,600m. kuna.

Currency. On 30 May 1994 the *kuna* (HRK; a name used in 1941–45) of 100 *lipa*, replaced the Croatian dinar at 1 kuna = 1,000 dinars. There are coins of 1, 2, 5, 10, 20 and 50 lipa and 1, 2 and 5 kuna, and notes of 5, 10, 20, 50, 100, 200, 500 and 1,000 kuna. In March 1996, £1 = 8·29 kuna; US$1 = 5·42 kuna; DM1 = 3·67 kuna.

Banking and Finance. The National Bank is the bank of issue. Total savings deposits on 31 Dec. 1994 were 8,915m. kuna.

There are stock exchanges in Zagreb and Varaždin.

Weights and Measures. The metric system is in use.

ENERGY AND NATURAL RESOURCES

Electricity. Output was 9,437m. kWh in 1993.

Oil and Gas. 1·73m. tonnes of crude oil were produced in 1993, and 1,835m. cu. metres of natural gas in 1991.

Minerals. Production, 1993 (in 1,000 tonnes): Coal, 104; brown coal and lignite, 37 (1991); bauxite, 1·7; iron ore (1989), 653; salt, 30.

Agriculture. At the 1993 census 409,647 persons subsisted on agriculture. In 1993 agricultural land totalled 2·3m. ha (1·06m. ha arable, 0·78m. ha pasture, 60,000 ha vineyards). The cultivated area was 1·48m. ha. Yields (in 1,000 tonnes, 1993): Wheat, 882; maize, 1,671; potatoes, 508; plums, 60.

Livestock, 1994 (in 1,000): Cattle, 519 (milch cows, 347); sheep, 444; pigs, 1,347; poultry, 12,503. Animal products, 1993: Meat, 346,000 tonnes; honey, 782 tonnes; milk, 618m. litres; eggs, 0·84m.

Forestry. Forests covered 2,074,207 ha in 1993. 3·14m. cu. metres of timber were cut in 1993.

Fisheries. The total catch was 25,862 tonnes in 1993, of which 5,339 tonnes were freshwater fish.

INDUSTRY. Production, 1993 (in 1,000 tonnes): Crude steel, 74; cement, 1,682; cellulose, 110; cotton fabric, 29m. sq. metres; cotton cloth, 10m. sq. metres; woollen yarn, 4m. sq. metres; wine, 2·08m. hectolitres; beer, 2·5m. hectolitres.

Labour. The population of working age (15–59) in 1991 was 2,951,091. The non-agricultural workforce was 1,108,400 in 1993, of whom 872,300 worked in industry (45% female). There were 250,779 registered unemployed in 1993.

FOREIGN ECONOMIC RELATIONS

Commerce. Exports in 1993 were worth US$3,903·82m.; imports, US$4,666·37m.

The main exports are machinery and transport equipment, chemicals and food-stuffs.

Total trade between Croatia and UK (British Department of Trade returns, in £1,000 sterling):

	1993	*1994*	*1995*
Imports to UK	30,627	41,238	36,725
Exports and re-exports from UK	42,645	142,332	231,512

Tourism. 12·9m. tourist nights were spent in 1993 (61·85m. in 1989).

COMMUNICATIONS

Roads. In 1993 there were 21,736 km of roads, including 302 km of motorways. In 1993 there were 646,210 passenger cars (619,513 private), 3,895 buses and 35,308 goods vehicles. 79m. passengers and 6·1m. tonnes of freight were carried by public transport in 1993.

There were 13,888 traffic accidents in 1989; 869 persons were killed in 1992.

Railways. In 1993 there were 2,699 km of 1,435 mm gauge (983 km electrified). In 1994 railways carried 29m. passengers and 10·9m. tonnes of freight.

Civil Aviation. There are international airports at Zagreb (Pleso) and Dubrovnik. The national carrier is Croatia Airlines, which operated 5 B-737-200 Advs and 2 other aircraft in 1995. Services are also provided by Aeroflot, Air France, Austrian Airlines, CSA, LOT, Lufthansa, SAS and Swissair. 498,000 passengers were flown in 1991.

Shipping. In 1995 there were 168 ocean-going vessels, totalling 3·29m. DWT. 132 of the vessels (94·09% of tonnage) were registered under foreign flags. Total GRT, 0·27m., including oil-tankers 30,549 GRT and container ships, 46,131 GRT. 5·8m. passengers and 22·39m. tonnes of cargo were transported.

Telecommunications. In 1993 there were 1,216,000 telephones. Broadcasting is controlled by the state Croatian Radio-Television (colour by PAL). In 1993 there were 902,908 radio sets.

Cinemas. There were 132 cinemas with a total of 45,002 seats in 1993. 3 feature films were made in 1993.

Press. In 1992 there were 9 dailies with an annual circulation of 342m. and 603 other newspapers. There were 64 weeklies and 401 periodicals. In 1990 2,413 book titles were published.

SOCIAL INSTITUTIONS

Religion. At the 1991 census there were 76·5% Roman Catholics, 11·1% Orthodox, and 12·4% others (mainly Old Catholics and Moslems).

Education. In 1992–93 there were 814 pre-school institutions with 68,252 children and 482 childcare workers; 1,930 primary schools with 446,621 pupils and 23,873 teachers; 522 secondary schools with 190,269 pupils and 13,451 teachers. In 1993–94 there were 63 institutes of higher education with 80,410 students and 6,146 academic staff. In 1994-95 there were 3 universities with 74,721 students and 7,632 academic staff.

Health. In 1993 there were 9,280 doctors and 1,940 dentists. There were 95 hospitals with 29,012 beds.

Social security. The health insurance scheme covered 4,571,955 persons in 1993, of whom 1,410,638 were contributing and 731,982 were receiving retirement pensions.

DIPLOMATIC REPRESENTATIVES

Of Croatia in Great Britain (19 Conway St., London W1)
Ambassador: Dr Ante Čičin-Šain.

Of Great Britain in Croatia (Vlaška 121/III, POB 454, 10000 Zagreb)
Ambassador: G. W. Hewitt, CMG.

Of Croatia in the USA
Ambassador: Petar Sarčević.

Of the USA in Croatia (2 Andrije Hebranga, Zagreb)
Ambassador: Peter W. Galbraith.

Of Croatia to the United Nations
Ambassador: Mario Nobilo.

Further Reading

Stallaerts, R. and Laurens, J., *Historical Dictionary of the Republic of Croatia*. Metuchen (NJ), 1995

National statistical office: Republički Zavod za Statistiku, 3 Ilica, Zagreb. *Director:* Dr Jakov Gelo.

CUBA

República de Cuba

Capital: Havana
Population: 10·98m. (1994)
HDI/world rank: 0·769/72 (1992)

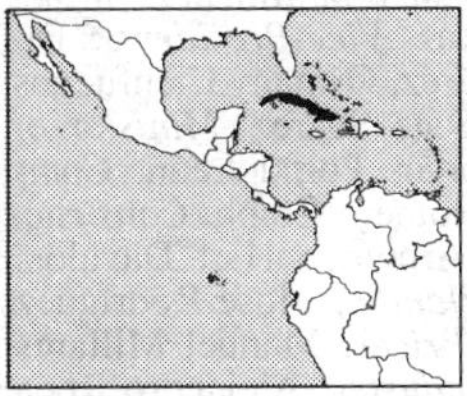

KEY HISTORICAL EVENTS. Cuba, except for the brief British occupancy in 1762–63, remained a Spanish possession from its discovery by Columbus in 1492 until 10 Dec. 1898, when the sovereignty was relinquished under the terms of the Treaty of Paris, which ended the struggle of the Cubans against Spanish rule. Cuba became independent as a republic.

The revolutionary movement against the Batista dictatorship, led by Dr Fidel Castro Ruíz, started on 26 July 1953. It achieved power on 1 Jan. 1959, when Batista fled the country. Emigrés made an unsuccessful invasion at the Bay of Pigs on 17 April 1961.

TERRITORY AND POPULATION. The island of Cuba forms the largest and most westerly of the Greater Antilles group and lies 135 miles south of the tip of Florida, USA. The area is 110,860 sq. km, and comprises the island of Cuba, (104,945 sq. km.); the Isle of Youth (Isla de la Juventud, formerly the Isle of Pines; 2,200 sq. km.), and some 1,600 small isles ('cays'; 3,715 sq. km.). Population, census (1981) 9,723,605; estimate, 1994, 10,977,000; density, 99 per sq. km.

The area, population and density of population of the 14 provinces and the special Municipality of the Isle of Youth were as follows (1989 estimate):

	Area sq. km	*Population*		*Area sq. km.*	*Population*
Pinar del Río	10,860	681,500	Camagüey	14,134	727,700
La Habana	5,671	633,400	Las Tunas	6,373	481,500
Ciudad de La Habana	727	2,068,600	Holguín	9,105	927,700
Matanzas	11,669	599,500	Granma	8,452	777,300
Cienfuegos	4,149	356,700	Santiago de Cuba	6,343	974,100
Villa Clara	8,069	788,800	Guantánamo	6,366	487,900
Sancti Spíritus	6,737	422,300			
Ciego de Avila	6,485	355,500	Isla de la Juventud	2,199	70,900

Chief cities (1991 population estimate in 1,000): Havana, the capital (2,124), Santiago de Cuba (418), Camagüey (289), Holguín (206), Guantánamo (206), Santa Clara (200); 1990, Bayamo (125,021), Cienfuegos (123,600), Pinar del Río (121,774), Las Tunas (119,400), Matanzas (113,724) and Manzanillo (107,650).

CLIMATE. Situated in the sub-tropical zone, Cuba has a generally rainy climate, affected by the Gulf Stream and the N.E. Trades, though winters are comparatively dry after the heaviest rains in Sept. and Oct. Hurricanes are liable to occur between June and Nov. Havana. Jan. 72°F (22·2°C), July 82°F (27·8°C). Annual rainfall 48" (1,224 mm).

CONSTITUTION AND GOVERNMENT. A Communist Constitution came into force on 24 Feb. 1976. It was amended in July 1992 to permit direct parliamentary elections.

Legislative power is vested in the *National Assembly of People's Power*, consisting of 589 deputies elected for a 5-year term by universal suffrage. Lists of candidates are drawn up by mass organizations (trade unions, etc.). The National Assembly elects a 31-member *Council of State* as its permanent organ. The Council of State's President, who is head of state and of government, nominates and leads a Council of Ministers approved by the National Assembly.

President: Dr Fidel Castro Ruz (b. 1927) became *President* of the Council of State on 3 Dec. 1976; re-elected for 5 years on 15 March 1993. He is also First Secretary of the Cuban Communist Party and C.-in-C. of the National Defence Council.

Elections to the National Assembly were held on 24 Feb. 1993. The electorate was 7·5m.; turn-out was 98·75%. All 589 candidates received the requisite 50% of votes for election.

In Dec. 1995 the government comprised:

First Vice-President of the Council of State and of the Council of Ministers, Minister of the Revolutionary Armed Forces: Raúl Castro Ruz. *Vice-Presidents:* Dr Carlos Rodríguez, Pedro Miret Prieto, José Fernández Alvárez, Osmany Cienfuegos Gorriarán, Jaime Crombet Hernández-Baquero, Adolfo Díaz Suárez. *Minister of Agriculture:* Alfredo Jordán Morales. *Base Industry:* Marcos Portal León. *Communications:* Gen. Silvano Colás Sánchez. *Construction:* Homero Crabb. *Construction Materials Industry:* José Cañete Alvárez. *Culture:* Armando Hart Davalos. *Domestic Trade:* Barbara Castillo Cuesta. *Economy and Planning:* José Rodríguez Garciá. *Education:* Luís Gómez Gutiérrez. *Finance and Prices:* Manuel Millares Rodríguez. *Fisheries:* Orlando Rodríguez Romay. *Food Industry:* Alejandro Roca Iglesias. *Foreign Investment and Economic Co-operation:* Ibrahim Ferradaz García. *Foreign Relations:* Roberto Robaina. *Foreign Trade:* Ricardo Cabrisas Ruíz. *Higher Education:* Fernando Vecino Alegret. *Interior:* Gen. Abelardo Colomé Ibarra. *Iron, Steel, Machinery and Electronics Industries:* Ignacio González Planas. *Justice:* Carlos Amat Fores. *Labour and Social Security:* Salvador Valdes Mesa. *Light Industry:* Jesús Pérez Oton. *Public Health:* Carlos Dotres Martínez. *Science, Technology and Environment:* Rosa Simeón Negrín. *Sugar:* Nelson Torres Pérez. *Tourism:* Osmany Cienfuegos Gorriarán. *Transport:* Gen. Senén Casas Regueiro. *Without portfolio:* Vilfredo López Rodríguez.

The *Speaker* of the National Assembly is Ricardo Alarcón de Quesada.

Various left-wing parties and movements amalgamated as the Communist Party of Cuba (PCC).

The Congress of the PCC elects a Central Committee of 225 members, which in turn appoints a Political Bureau comprising 26 members.

National flag: 3 blue, 2 white stripes (horizontal); a white 5-pointed star in a red triangle at the hoist.

National anthem: 'Al combate corred bayameses' ('Run, Bayamans, to the combat'); words and tune by P. Figueredo).

Local Government. The country is divided into 14 provinces, a special municipality (the Isle of Youth) and 169 municipalities. Elections are held for delegates to the Municipal Assemblies by universal suffrage for $2\frac{1}{2}$ year terms; the municipal assemblies then elect the provincial assemblies for similar terms. Elections were held on 9 July 1995.

DEFENCE. The National Defence Council is headed by the President of the republic. Conscription is for 2 years.

Army. The strength was 85,000 (including conscripts and Ready Reservists) in 1996. There are 3 regional commands. The Army is organized in 5 armoured, 9 mechanized infantry, 1 airborne, 1 frontier guard, 1 surface-to-air missile and 14 reserve brigades; and 1 air defence regiment. Equipment includes 75 T-34, 1,100 T-54/55 and 400 T-62 main battle tanks. Border Guard and State Security forces total 19,000 and the Territorial Militia, 1·3m. (reservists), all armed.

Navy. Naval combatants, all ex-Soviet, include 2 'Foxtrot' class diesel submarines, 3 'Koni' class frigates, 1 'Pauk' class corvette, 17 fast missile craft, 6 patrol hydrofoils, 3 coastal minehunters and 12 inshore minesweepers. There are 2 medium landing ships and 6 craft. The major auxiliaries include 1 tanker, 1 electronic intelligence gatherer. Some 24 minor auxiliaries and service craft complete the total.

Personnel in 1995 totalled about 5,000 conscripts including about 550 marines. Main bases are at Cienfuegos, Havana and Mariel. The USA still occupies the Guantánamo naval base.

There is a coastal defence force equipped with artillery and some anti-ship missiles. A separate coast guard division of the Frontier Guards numbering 4,000 operates about 30 inshore patrol craft.

Air Force. The Air Force has been extensively re-equipped with aircraft supplied by USSR and in 1995 had a strength of some 15,000 (6,000 conscripts) and about 130 combat aircraft. About 10 interceptor and 3 ground-attack squadrons fly MiG-29, MiG-23 and MiG-21 jet fighters. There is a squadron of An-26 twin-turboprop transports, some An-24 twin-turboprop transports, and about 20 Mi-24 armed helicopters, Mi-8 (some armed), Mi-17 and Mi-2 helicopters, Zlin 326 piston-engined trainers and L-39, MiG-15UTI, MiG-21U, MiG-23U and MiG-29U jet trainers. 10 An-2M biplanes are operated by the Air Force, mainly on agricultural and liaison duties. Soviet-built surface-to-air ('Guideline', 'Goa' and 'Gainful') and coastal defence ('Samlet') missiles are in service.

INTERNATIONAL RELATIONS

Membership. Cuba is a member of the UN and SELA.

ECONOMY

Policy. Prices were increased by at least 50% on 1 June 1994. The Central Planning Board was abolished in Jan. 1995. In 1995 income tax and property tax were levied on self-employed persons and recipients of foreign exchange.

Budget. The 1995 budget envisaged revenue of 11,680m. pesos and expenditure of 12,680m. pesos. Hard-currency earners and the self-employed became liable to a 10-50% income tax in Nov. 1995.

Currency. The unit of currency is the *Cuban peso* (CUP) of 100 *centavos*, which is not convertible although an official exchange rate is announced daily reflecting any changes in the strength of the US dollar. The US dollar has been legal tender since 1993. There are coins of 1, 5, 20 and 40 centavos and 1 peso, and notes of 3, 5, 10, 20 and 50 pesos. 11,750m. pesos were in circulation in 1994. In March 1996, £1 = 1·53 pesos; US$1 = 1 peso; DM1 = 0·68 pesos.

Banking and Finance. The central bank was created in 1948 (with capital of US$10m.) and began operating on 27 April 1950 (*Governor*, Francisco Soberón Valdes). On 14 Oct. 1960 all banks were nationalized. All banking is now carried out by the National Bank of Cuba through its 250 agencies, or via the Banco Financiero Internacional, which deals in foreign currency. 11 foreign banks had representative offices in 1995.

All insurance business was nationalized in Jan. 1964. A National Savings Bank was established in 1983.

Weights and Measures. The metric system is legally compulsory, but the American and old Spanish systems are much used. The sugar industry uses the Spanish long ton (1·03 tonnes) and short ton (0·92 tonne). Cuba sugar sack = 329·59 lb. or 149·49 kg. Land is measured in *caballerías* (of 13·4 ha or 33 acres).

ENERGY AND NATURAL RESOURCES

Electricity. Production in 1991 was 16,300m. kWh.

Oil. Crude oil production (1992) 771,000 tonnes.

Minerals. Iron ore abounds, with deposits estimated at 3,500m. tonnes. Output of copper concentrate (1989) was 2,800 tonnes; refractory chrome (1987), 52,400 tonnes. Other minerals are nickel (1994, 26,772 tonnes) and cobalt (1989, 46,500 tonnes), silica and barytes. Gold and silver are also worked. Salt output from the solar evaporation of sea water was 114,900 tonnes in 1989.

Agriculture. In 1959 all land over 30 *caballerías* was nationalized and eventually turned into state farms. Under legislation of 1993, state farms are being reorganized as 'units of basic co-operative production'. These units have the use of the land in perpetuity from the state. Unit workers select their own managers, and are paid an advance on earnings. In 1963 private holdings were reduced to a maximum of 5 *caballerías*. In Sept. 1984 there were 1,472 co-operatives comprising 70,000 *caballerías* of land. In 1994 farmers were permitted to trade on free market principles after state delivery quotas had been met.

The most important product is sugar and its by-products. 1994–95 production was 3·3m. tonnes (6·9 tonnes in 1991-92). Production of other important crops in 1992 was (in 1,000 tonnes): Tobacco, 44; rice, 308; coffee, 25; maize, 95.

1992 fruit and vegetable production (in 1,000 tonnes): Pineapples, 21; oranges, 570; mangoes, 83; bananas, 200; grapefruit and pomelos, 315 and potatoes, 245.

In 1992 the livestock included 1·85m. pigs; 625,000 horses; 0·37m. sheep; 0·1m. goats; 4·7m. cattle.

Forestry. Cuba has 2·7m ha of forests representing 25% of the land area. These forests contain valuable cabinet woods, such as mahogany and cedar, besides dye-woods, fibres, gums, resins and oils. Cedar is used locally for cigar-boxes, and mahogany is exported.

Fisheries. Fishing is the third most important export industry, after sugar and nickel. Catch (1989) 191,889 tonnes.

INDUSTRY. In 1994, manufacturing accounted for 26% of GDP. All industrial enterprises are state-controlled. Production in 1989 was: Textiles, 218·6m. sq. metres (cotton fabrics 182·6m. sq. metres); cement (1989), 3,800m. tonnes; wheat flour, 398,000 tonnes; fuel oil (1989), 4,152,800 tonnes; diesel oil (1989), 1,178,500 tonnes; processed crude oil, 7,916,000 tonnes; steel, 314,200 tonnes; steel bars, 367,100 tonnes; nickel and cobalt, 46,500 tonnes; copper, 2,759,100 tonnes; 314,700 tyres; 231,200 inner tubes; leather shoes, 11·00m. pairs; paint (1989), 121,000 hectolitres; soft drinks (1989), 2,396,500 hectolitres; 308,500m. cigars; 16,519,700m. cigarettes; fertilizers, 898,600 tonnes; 2,345 buses; 172,700 radios; 70,500 TVs; 9,100 refrigerators; sulphuric acid, 381,500 tonnes; fine salt, 114,900 tonnes.

Labour. In 1989 the monthly average salary was 188 pesos. Self-employment was legalized in 1993. Under legislation of Sept. 1994 employees made redundant must be assigned to other jobs or to strategic social or economic tasks; failing this, they are paid 60% of former salary.

Trade Unions. The Workers' Central Union of Cuba groups 23 unions.

FOREIGN ECONOMIC RELATIONS. Foreign debt was US$14,803m. in 1990. Since July 1992 foreign investment has been permitted in selected state enterprises, and Cuban companies have been able to import and export without seeking government permission. Foreign ownership is recognized in joint ventures. A free-trade zone opened at Havana 1993. In 1994, the productive, real estate and service sectors were opened to foreign investment. Legislation of 1995 opened all sectors of the economy to foreign investment except defence, education and health services. 100% foreign-owned investments, and investments in property, are now permitted.

Commerce. In 1994, exports totalled US$1,530m., and imports US$2,200m. The principal exports are sugar, minerals, tobacco, citrus fruit and fish. In 1992 exports included (in 1m. pesos): Sugar, 1,162; minerals, 210; fruit and vegetables, 150; fish, 130; tobacco, 95.

In 1990 the USSR provided 66% of imports (by value) and took 81% of exports. The loss of this covertly subsidized market has caused economic hardship since 1990.

Total trade between Cuba and UK (British Department of Trade returns, in £1,000 sterling):

	1991	*1992*	*1993*	*1994*	*1995*
Imports to UK	17,860	12,979	8,000	10,634	8,184
Exports and re-exports from UK	28,413	28,345	14,009	26,456	19,160

Tourism. Tourism is Cuba's largest foreign exchange earner. In 1994 there were 617,000 visitors, bringing US$850m. in net foreign exchange earnings. The age at which Cubans may obtain exit visas was lowered to 20 years in Aug. 1991.

COMMUNICATIONS

Roads. In 1990 there were some 30,000 km of roads, half of which were paved.

Railways. There were (1992) 4,807 km of public railway (1,435 mm gauge) of which 147 km is electrified. In 1994 it carried 30·5m. passengers and 4·4m. tonnes of freight. In addition, the large sugar estates have 7,773 km of lines on 1,435, 914 and 760 mm gauges.

Civil Aviation. There is an international airport at Havana (Jose Martí). The state airline Cubana operates all services internally, and internationally from Havana to London, Madrid, Berlin, Prague, Paris, Zürich and Brussels, and also to Jamaica, Barbados, Trinidad and Tobago, Bahamas, Guyana, Canada, Argentina, Chile, Nicaragua and the Dominican Republic. It had 66 ex-Soviet aircraft in 1995. The other regular foreign services are Aeroflot, Aerorepublica, ALM, AOM, Bahamasair, Compania Mexicana, COPA, Iberia, KLM, LTU, LACSA, Ladeco, SAM, TAAG-Angola and Viasa.

Shipping. There are 11 ports, the largest being Havana, Cienfuegos and Mariel. The merchant marine in 1995 totalled 0·54m. GRT of which 0·1m. GRT were oil-tankers.

Telecommunications. The national telephone system (1989) had 311,100 lines in use.

Broadcasting is the responsibility of the state-controlled Instituto Cubano de Radio y Televisión. There are 5 national radio networks, provincial and local stations and an external service, Radio Habana (Spanish, Arabic, Creole, English, Esperanto, French, Guaraní, Portuguese, Quechua). There are 2 TV channels (colour by NTSC). In 1993 there were 2·14m. radio and 2·5m. TV sets (colour by NTSC).

Cinemas and Theatres. In 1987 there were 535 (35mm) and 905 (16mm) cinemas. In 1989, 99 films were made, there were 44·8m. cinema attendances; there were 49 theatres and 1,387,700 attendances.

Press. Since Oct. 1990 *Granma* has been the only national daily newspaper due, it was stated, to shortage of paper.

SOCIAL INSTITUTIONS

Justice. There is a Supreme Court in Havana and 7 regional courts of appeal. The provinces are divided into judicial districts, with courts for civil and criminal actions, with municipal courts for minor offences. The civil code guarantees aliens the same property and personal rights as are enjoyed by nationals.

The 1959 Agrarian Reform Law and the Urban Reform Law passed on 14 Oct. 1960 have placed certain restrictions on both. Revolutionary Summary Tribunals have wide powers.

Religion. Religious liberty was constitutionally guaranteed in July 1992. There were 4·3m. Roman Catholics in 1992. In 1994 Cardinal Jaime Ortega was nominated Primate by the Pope. There is a bishop of the American Episcopal Church in Havana; there are congregations of Methodists in Havana and in the provinces as well as Baptists and other denominations.

Education. Education is compulsory (between the ages of 6 and 14), free and universal. In 1964 illiteracy was declared eliminated. In 1989 there were 899,900 pupils and 73,200 teachers at 9,522 primary schools, 800,300 pupils and 77,800 teachers at 1,540 intermediate schools and in 1988 there were 164,891 students at adult primary schools.

In 1995-96 there were 4 universities with 33,190 internal and 11,620 external students and 4,165 academic staff. In 1994-95 there were also the following higher educational institutions: 10 teacher training, 2 agricultural, 4 medical and 10 other.

Health. There were (1989) 34,752 doctors, 6,482 dentists, 58,589 nursing personnel and 264 hospitals with 74,407 beds. The 1989 health and education budget was 2,906·2m. pesos.

Free medical services are provided by the state polyclinics, though a few doctors still have private practices.

DIPLOMATIC REPRESENTATIVES

Of Cuba in Great Britain (167 High Holborn, London, WC1 6PA)
Ambassador: Rodney López Clemente.

Of Great Britain in Cuba (Calle 34, No. 702/4, entre 7ma Avenida y 17 Miramar, Havana)
Ambassador: P. A. McLean, CMG.

Of Cuba to the United Nations
Ambassador: Bruno Rodríguez Parrilla.

The USA broke off diplomatic relations with Cuba on 3 Jan. 1961 but in 1977 Interest Sections were opened, officially attached to the Swiss Embassy in Havana and to the Czech Embassy in Washington respectively.

Further Reading

Bethell, L. (ed.) *Cuba: a Short History.* CUP, 1993
Bunck, J. M., *Fidel Castro and the Quest for a Revolutionary Culture in Cuba.* Pennsylvania State Univ. Press, 1994
Cabrera Infantye, G., *Mea Cuba*; translated into English from Spanish. London, 1994
Eckstein, S. E., *Back from the Future: Cuba under Castro.* Princeton Univ. Press, 1994
Cardoso, E. and Helwege, A., *Cuba after Communism.* Boston (Mass.), 1992
Mesa-Lago, C. (ed.) *Cuba: After the Cold War.* Pittsburgh Univ. Press, 1993
Ruttin, P., *Capitalism and Socialism in Cuba: a Study of Dependency, Development and Underdevelopment.* London, 1990
Zimbalist, A. and Brundenius, C., *The Cuban Economy: Measurement and Analysis of Socialist Performance.* Johns Hopkins Univ. Press, 1990

CYPRUS

Kypriaki Dimokratia—
Kibris Çumhuriyeti
(Republic of Cyprus)

Capital: Nicosia
Population: 725,000 (1994)
GNP per capita government controlled area: US$11,121 (1993)
HDI/world rank: 0·906/23 (1992)

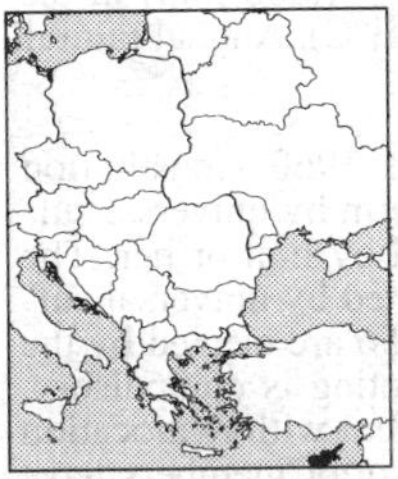

KEY HISTORICAL EVENTS. For the history of Cyprus to 1974 *see* THE STATESMAN'S YEAR-BOOK, 1990–91, p. 400.

On 15 July 1974 a coup was staged by supporters of the military junta then ruling Greece and President Makarios left until 7 Dec. 1974.

Turkey invaded the island on 20 July 1974, eventually occupying the northern part. 0·2m. Greek Cypriots fled to live as refugees in the south. The UN General Assembly unanimously adopted resolutions calling for the withdrawal of all foreign troops from Cyprus and the return of refugees to their homes, but without result.

On 13 Feb. 1975 a Turkish Cypriot Federated State was proclaimed. Rauf Denktaş was appointed President. On 15 Nov. 1983 the Turkish state unilaterally proclaimed itself the 'Turkish Republic of Northern Cyprus' (TRNC). In Nov. 1983 and May 1984 the UN Security Council declared all secessionist actions illegal. Several UN-inspired talks were held 1985–91 without success.

In March 1991 the UN Security Council adopted unanimously a resolution rejecting new TRNC demands. In Sept. discussions were held between the UN Secretary-General's representatives, the Cypriot president and Rauf Denktaş. In Oct. the UN Secretary-General rejected Rauf Denktaş's demands for the recognition of separate sovereignty for the TRNC including a right to secession.

Further talks were held without results in May–Aug. 1992. On 26 Aug. the UN Security Council adopted a resolution endorsing the Secretary-General's ideas and territorial adjustments as the basis for reaching an agreement. Talks were held in Oct. 1992 and in 1993 after the election of President Clerides without result. Cyprus has accepted confidence-building measures suggested by the UN but these were opposed by the TRNC. In July 1994 the UN Security Council adopted a resolution reaffirming its position that a settlement must be based on a single sovereignty and exclude any form of partition or succession. In Oct. 1994 informal talks were held between President Clerides and Rauf Denktaş, but no progress was made.

TERRITORY AND POPULATION. The island lies in the Mediterranean, about 60 km off the south coast of Turkey and 90 km off the coast of Syria. Area, 3,572 sq. miles (9,251 sq. km). The Turkish-occupied area is 3,335 sq. km. Population by ethnic group:

Ethnic group	*1946*	*1960*	*1973*	*1992*
Greek Cypriot	361,199	447,901	498,511	599,000
Turkish Cypriot	80,548	103,822	116,000	95,000 [1]
Others	8,367	20,984	17,267	20,000
Total	450,114	572,707	631,778	714,000

[1] Revised to take into account Turkish Cypriots who have emigrated from the Turkish-occupied area since 1974 (estimated at over 41,000).

Principal towns with populations (1992 estimate): Nicosia (the capital), 177,451; Limassol, 136,741; Larnaca, 60,557; Paphos, 32,575.

As a result of the Turkish occupation of the northern part of Cyprus, 0·2m. Greek Cypriots were displaced and forced to find refuge in the south. The urban centres of Famagusta, Kyrenia and Morphou were completely evacuated. *See below* for details of the 'Turkish Republic of Northern Cyprus'.

Vital statistics rates, 1993 (per 1,000 population): Births, 16·8; deaths, 7·7; infantile mortality (per 1,000 live births), 9.

Greek and Turkish are official languages. English is widely spoken.

CLIMATE. The climate is Mediterranean, with very hot, dry summers and variable winters. Maximum temperatures may reach 112°F (44·5°C) in July and Aug., but minimum figures may fall to 22°F (–5·5°C) in the mountains in winter when snow is experienced. Rainfall is generally between 10" and 27" (250 and 675 mm) and occurs mainly in the winter months, but it may reach 48" (1,200 mm) in the Troodos mountains. Nicosia. Jan. 50°F (10·0°C), July 83°F (28·3°C). Annual rainfall 15" (371 mm).

CONSTITUTION AND GOVERNMENT. Under the 1960 Constitution executive power is vested in a *President* elected for a 5-year term by universal suffrage and exercised through a Council of Ministers appointed by him or her. The *House of Representatives* exercises legislative power. It is elected by universal suffrage for 5-year terms, and consists of 80 members, of whom 56 are elected by the Greek Cypriot and 24 by the Turkish Cypriot community. Voting is compulsory, and is by preferential vote in a proportional representation system with reallocation of votes at national level. As from Dec. 1963 the Turkish Cypriot members have ceased to attend.

At the second round of presidential elections on 14 Feb. 1993 the electorate was 393,993; turn-out was 93·27%. Glafcos Clerides was elected by 50·31% of votes cast against President Vassiliou.

National flag: White with a copper-coloured outline of the island with 2 green olive-branches beneath.

National anthem: 'Segnoriso apo tin kopsi' ('Always shall I know you'); words by D. Solomos, tune by N. Mantzaros.

At the elections of May 1991 the electorate was 0·4m. The Democratic Rally Liberal Party coalition won 20 seats with 35·8% of votes cast, the Akel Party (Communists) 18 with 30·6%, the Democratic Party 11 with 19·5% and the EDEK Party (Socialists) 7 with 10·9%.

President: Glafcos Clerides (b. 1919; Democratic Rally).

The Council of Ministers in Nov. 1995 was as follows:

Foreign Affairs: Alecos P. Michaelides. *Interior:* Dinos Michaelides. *Defence:* Costas Eliades. *Agriculture, Natural Resources and Environment:* Costas Petrides. *Commerce and Industry:* Kyriacos Christophy. *Health:* Manolis Christophides. *Communications and Works:* Adamos Adamides. *Finance:* Christodoulos Christodoulou. *Education and Culture:* Claire Angelidou. *Labour and Social Insurance:* Andreas Moushouttas. *Justice and Public Order:* Alecos Evangelou.

The Speaker is Alexis Galanos.

DEFENCE. Conscription is for 26 months.

National Guard. Total strength (1996) 10,000 (8,700 conscripts) organized in 2 brigade HQ, 2 light infantry divisions, 2 light infantry and 1 armoured brigade, 2 light infantry regiments, 1 coastal defence surface-to-surface missile battery, and 1 special forces, 1 anti-tank and 7 artillery battalions. Equipment includes 52 AMX-30B-2 main battle tanks, 2 Islander transport/surveillance aircraft, 2 PC-9 trainers, and 3 Jet Ranger, 1 Bell 412, 2 Mi-2 and 4 armed Gazelle helicopters. There is also a para-military force of 3,700 armed police.

There are 2 British bases (Army and Royal Air Force) and some 3,900 personnel. Greek (950) and UN peacekeeping (1,138; UNFICYP) forces are also stationed on the island.

INTERNATIONAL RELATIONS

Membership. Cyprus is a member of the UN, Commonwealth and Council of Europe. An application to join the EU was made in July 1990.

ECONOMY

Policy. There is a Central Planning Commission, headed by the President of the Republic and including the Council of Ministers. Its administrative arm is the Planning Bureau.

Budget. Total public revenue and expenditure for calendar years (in £C1m.):

	1988	*1989*	*1990*	*1991*	*1992*	*1993*
Expenditure	631	699	847	907	1,023	1,070
Revenue	536	633	710	725	875	992

Main sources of ordinary revenue in 1993 (in £C1m.) were: Import duties, 102 (including 19 temporary refugee levy on imports); excise duties, 89; income tax, 167; rents, royalties and interest, 30; sales of goods and services, 34; other duties and taxes, 186; social security contributions, 154.

Main divisions of ordinary expenditure in 1993 (in £C1m.): Wages and salaries, 298; pensions and gratuities, 43; commodity subsidies, 39; expenditures on goods and services, 70; public debt charges, 142; social insurance benefits, 159.

Development expenditure for 1993 (in £C1m.) included 15 for water development, 9 for agriculture, forests and fisheries, 8 for rural development, 33 for roads and 4 for airports.

The outstanding long-term public debt as at 31 Dec. 1993 was £C520m.

Currency. The *Cyprus pound* (CYP) is divided into 100 *cents*. Notes of the following denominations are in circulation: £C20, £C10, £C5 and £C1. Coins in circulation: 20, 5, 2 and 1 cent. Inflation was 4% in 1994. Rate of exchange, March 1996: £1 = £C0·71; US$1 = £C0·47; DM1 = £C0·32.

Banking and Finance. The Central Bank of Cyprus, established in 1963, is the bank of issue, regulates money supply, credit and foreign exchange and supervises the banking system.

In 1993 there were 7 commercial banks (3 foreign) and 4 specialized banks (co-operative, development, mortgage and savings). At 31 Dec. 1993 total deposits in banks were £C2,912m. The country's foreign exchange reserves at 31 Dec. 1993 were £C1,342m.

Weights and Measures. The metric (SI) system was introduced in 1986 and is now widely applied.

ENERGY AND NATURAL RESOURCES

Electricity. Production (1993) 2,581m. kWh.

Water Resources. In 1993, £C15m. was spent on water dams, water supplies, hydrological research and geophysical surveys. Existing dams had (1993) a capacity of 297m. cu. metres.

Minerals. The principal minerals extracted in 1993 were (in tonnes): Copper precipitates, 278; bentonite, 94,270; umber and other ochres, 7,125.

Agriculture. Chief agricultural products in 1993 (1,000 tonnes): Grapes, 135·5; potatoes, 199; milk, 157; cereals (wheat and barley), 105; citrus fruit, 166; meat, 77; carobs, 17; fresh fruit, 32; olives, 120; other vegetables, 126; eggs, 12m. dozen.

28% of the government-controlled area is cultivated. About 13% (1993) of the economically active population are engaged in agriculture.

Livestock in 1991 (in 1,000): Cattle, 59; sheep, 295; goats, 205; pigs, 282; poultry, 2,800.

Forestry. Total forest area, 1,754 sq. km. In 1993 the chief forest products were timber, 38,800 cu. metres valued at £C0·92m.; charcoal, £C1·4m.

Fisheries. Catch (1993) 2,978 tonnes.

INDUSTRY. The most important industries in 1993 were: Food, beverages and tobacco, textiles, wearing apparel and leather, chemicals and chemical petroleum, rubber and plastic products, metal products, machinery and equipment, wood and wood products including furniture. Manufacturing industry in 1993 contributed about £C407m. at current market prices to the GDP and gave employment to 45,500 of the economically active population.

Labour. Unemployment was 2·6% at the end of 1993.

Trade Unions. About 80% of the workforce is organized and the majority of workers belong either to the Pancyprian Federation of Labour or the Cyprus Workers Confederation.

FOREIGN ECONOMIC RELATIONS. Equity capital for foreign investors must come from abroad, and the terms of foreign loans need approval by the Central Bank. Profits may be freely repatriated. Foreign debt was £C926m. in 1993.

Commerce. Trade figures for calendar years were (in £C1,000):

	1989	*1990*	*1991*	*1992*	*1993*
Imports	1,130,298	1,174,538	1,215,827	1,490,800	1,261,078
Exports [1]	393,049	435,599	441,789	443,045	431,462

[1] Including re-exports and ships' stores.

Chief civil imports, 1993 (in £C1m.):

Live animals and animal products	27·2
Vegetable products	47·4
Prepared foodstuffs, beverages and tobacco	148·8
Mineral products	132·5
Products of chemical or allied industries	89·6
Plastics and rubber and articles thereof	52·0
Pulp, waste paper and paperboard and articles thereof	45·4
Textiles and textile articles	110·5
Footwear, headgear, umbrellas, prepared leathers, etc.	10·5
Articles of stone, plaster, cement, etc., ceramic and glass products	31·9
Machinery, electrical equipment, sound and television recorders	231·7
Vehicles, aircraft, vessels and equipment	119·8
Optical, photographic, medical, musical and other instruments, clocks and watches	30·7
Base metal and articles of base metal	100·8
Wood and articles, charcoal, cork and articles, basketware, etc.	21·8
Pearls, precious stones and metals, semi-precious stones and articles	60·4

Chief domestic exports, 1993 (in £C1,000):

Grapes	3,106
Citrus fruit	13,483
Potatoes	20,149
Wine	4,628
Fruit, preserved and juices	5,723
Cigarettes	6,969
Paper products	3,671
Cement	5,834
Clothing	51,217
Footwear	8,977
Medicinal and pharmaceutical products	13,001

In 1993 the EU countries supplied 54·2% of the imports; Arab countries, 3·4%; others, 47·6%. Of the exports (1993), 37·4% went to EU countries and 30·4% to Arab countries.

Total trade between Cyprus and UK (British Department of Trade returns, in £1,000 sterling):

	1991	*1992*	*1993*	*1994*	*1995*
Imports to UK	141,138	144,746	136,217	120,857	156,451
Exports and re-exports from UK	209,877	221,910	235,930	245,192	307,438

Tourism. Foreign visitors (1993), 1,841,000 (long-stay). Tourist revenue amounted to some £C696m. in 1993.

COMMUNICATIONS

Roads. In 1993 the total length of roads in the government-controlled area was 10,857 km, of which 5,806 km were bituminous and 5,051 km were earth or gravel roads. The asphalted roads maintained by the Ministry of Communications and Works (Public Works Department) by the end of 1993 totalled 2,203 km, of which 287 km were within the municipal areas. Roads improved or constructed and asphalted in 1993 totalled 95 km. On 31 Dec. 1993, there were 412,944 motor vehicles including 2,856 buses, 99,130 goods vehicles, 71,127 motorcycles, and 10,385 tractors etc.

The area controlled by the Government of the Republic and that occupied by the TRNC are now served by separate transport systems, and there are no services linking the two areas.

Civil Aviation. Nicosia airport has been closed since Aug. 1974. During 1993, 3,932,114 persons travelled and 24,605 tonnes of commercial air-freight was handled through Larnaca and Paphos international airports. The national carrier is Cyprus Airways, which is 80·46% state-owned, and which in 1993 operated 2 A310-300s, 5 A320-200s and 2 BAC1-11-500s. Its subsidiary, Eurocypria, operated 3 A320-200s in 1993. Services are also provided by Aeroflot, Air Malta, Air Moldova, Air Ukraine, Air Zimbabwe, Alitalia, American Airlines, Austrian Airlines, Balkan, Belavia, British Airways, CSA, Donavia, Egyptair, El Al, Emirates, Finnair, Gulf Air, Hapag Lloyd, Iran Air, JAT, KLM, Kuwait Airways, Latvian Airlines, Libyan Airlines, Lithuanian Airlines, LOT, LTU, Lufthansa, Luxair, Malév, Middle East Airlines, Olympic, Royal Jordanian, Swissair, Syrian Airlines and Tarom.

Shipping. The 2 main ports are Limassol and Larnaca. In 1993, 5,005 ships of 14,676,000 net tonnes entered Cyprus ports carrying 8,694,000 tonnes of cargo from, to, and via Cyprus. Ships on the Cyprus open registry in 1995 totalled 35·79m. DWT (8% Cypriot-owned). Famagusta has been closed to international traffic since Aug. 1974.

Telecommunications. In 1993 there were 56 post offices and 722 postal agencies. In 1993 there were 310,990 telephone lines (51·6% per 100 population). The Cyprus Telecommunications Authority provides telephone and data transmission services nationally and to 190 countries.

Cyprus Broadcasting Corporation has 3 radio channels and broadcasts mainly in Greek, but also in Turkish, English and Armenian. The Corporation also broadcasts on 2 TV channels (colour by PAL). A law of June 1990 permits the operation of commercial radio and TV stations. In 1994 there were 2 independent radio stations broadcasting nationwide and numerous radio stations broadcasting locally. There were also 2 private TV stations operating and 1 private PAY-TV. There are also 2 foreign broadcasting stations. In 1993 there were 0·27m. radio and 234,000 TV sets.

Cinemas (1993). In the government-controlled area there were 16 cinemas and 17 screens.

Press (1994). There were 9 Greek, 7 Turkish and 1 English daily newspapers and 3 Greek, 3 Turkish weeklies and 2 English weeklies.

SOCIAL INSTITUTIONS

Justice. The administration of justice is exercised by a separate and independent judiciary. There is a Supreme Court, Assize Courts and District Courts.

The Supreme Court is composed of 13 judges one of whom is the President of the Court (in 1994, Demetrios Stylianides). There is a continuing Assize Court that holds sessions in every district according to the cases committed for trial before it. The Assize Courts have unlimited criminal jurisdiction and may order the payment of compensation up to £C3,000. The District Courts exercise original civil and criminal jurisdiction, the extent of which varies with the composition of the Bench.

There is a Supreme Council of Judicature, consisting of the President and Judges of the Supreme Court, entrusted with the appointment, promotion, transfers, termination of appointment and disciplinary control over all judicial officers, other than the Judges of the Supreme Court.

The Attorney-General (in 1994, Michalakis Triantafyllides) is head of the independent Law Office and legal advisor to the President and his Ministers.

Religion. The Greek Cypriots are Greek Orthodox Christians and the Turkish Cypriots are Moslems (mostly Sunnis of the Hanafi sect). There are also small groups of the Armenian Apostolic Church, Roman Catholics (Maronites and Latin Rite) and Protestants (mainly Anglicans). *See also* CYPRUS: Territory and Population.

Education. *Greek-Cypriot Education.* Elementary education is compulsory and is provided free in 6 grades to children between 5½ and 11½ years of age. There are also schools for the deaf and blind, and 10 schools for handicapped children. In 1992–93 the Ministry ran 218 kindergartens for children in the age group 2½–5; there were 390 privately run pre-primary schools. There were 391 primary schools with 64,313 pupils and 3,365 teachers in 1992–93.

Secondary education is also free and attendance for the first cycle is compulsory. The secondary school is 6 years, 3 years at the gymnasium followed by 3 years at the *lykeion* (lyceum) or 3 years at one of the technical schools which provide technical and vocational education for industry. In 1990–91 there were 108 secondary schools with 3,605 teachers and 44,614 pupils.

Post-secondary education is provided at 6 public institutions: The Higher Technical Institute, which provides 3–4-year courses for technicians in civil, electrical, mechanical and marine engineering; a 2-year Forestry College (administered by the Ministry of Agriculture, Natural Resources and Environment); a Hotel and Catering Institute; the Mediterranean Institute of Management (Ministry of Labour and Social Insurance); the School of Nursing (Ministry of Health) which runs 2–3 year courses; the Cyprus Academy of Public Administration set up to help civil servants improve their management skills. There are also a number of private institutions that offer a variety of 1–4-year courses. Adult education is conducted through youth centres in rural areas, foreign language institutes in the towns and private institutions offering courses in business administration and secretarial work.

There is 1 university with 1,492 students and 128 academic staff in 1995-96.

Social Security. The administration of the social-security services is in the hands of the Ministry of Labour and Social Insurance, with the Ministry of Health providing medical services through public clinics and hospitals on a means test, except medical treatment for employment accidents, which is given free to all insured employees and financed by the Social Insurance Scheme.

DIPLOMATIC REPRESENTATIVES

Of Cyprus in Great Britain (93 Park St., London, W1Y 4ET)
High Commissioner: Vanias Markides.

Of Great Britain in Cyprus (Alexander Pallis St., Nicosia)
High Commissioner: David C. A. Madden, CMG.

Of Cyprus in the USA (2211 R. St., NW, Washington, D.C., 20008)
Ambassador: Andreas Jacovides.

Of the USA in Cyprus (Metochiou and Ploutarchou Streets, Engomi, Nicosia)
Ambassador: Richard A. Boucher.

Of Cyprus to the United Nations
Ambassador: Alecos H. Shambos.

'TURKISH REPUBLIC OF NORTHERN CYPRUS (TRNC)'

KEY HISTORICAL EVENTS. *See* CYPRUS: Key Historical Events.

TERRITORY AND POPULATION. The Turkish Republic of Northern Cyprus occupies 3,355 sq. km (about 33% of the island of Cyprus) and its population in 1994 was estimated to be 177,120. Distribution of population by districts (1994): Nicosia, 82,424; Famagusta, 67,167; Kyrenia, 27,529.

CONSTITUTION AND GOVERNMENT. The Turkish Republic of Northern Cyprus was proclaimed on 15 Nov. 1983. Presidential elections were held in 2 rounds on 15 and 22 April 1995. Rauf Denktaş (b. 1924) failed to gain an outright majority against 6 opponents in the first round but, was re-elected at the second round against 1 opponent by 62·48% of the vote. Presidential elections were scheduled for 16 April 1995.

A 50-seat Legislative Assembly was elected in Dec. 1993. The position of the parties in Dec. 1995 was: Democratic Party (DP) 16, National Unity Party 15, Republican Turkish Party (RTP) 13, Communal Liberation Party 5, National Birth Party 1. The Council of Ministers consisted in Dec. 1995 of:

Prime Minister: Hakkı Atun (DP).

Minister of State and Deputy Prime Minister: Mehmet Ali Talat (RTP). *Foreign and Defence:* Atay Raşit (DP). *Interior:* Mustafa Adaoğlu (DP). *Economy and Finance:* Salih Coşar (DP). *Education and Culture:* Ahmet Derya (RTP). *Agriculture, Natural Resources and Energy:* Özkan Murat (RTP). *Communications and Works:* Süha Türköz (DP). *Health:* Hüseyin Celal (RTP). *Labour and Social Security:* Ömer Kalyoncu (RTP). *Youth, Sport and Environment:* Mustafa Gökmen (DP).

The Speaker of the Legislative Assembly is Ayhan Acarkan.

Flag: White with horizontal bars of red set near the top and bottom; between these a crescent and star in red.

Defence. In 1994, 30,000 members of Turkey's armed forces were stationed in the TRNC with 200 main battle tanks. TRNC forces comprise 7 infantry battalions and 3 patrol boats with a total personnel strength of 4,000. Conscription is for 2 years.

Budget. Revenue (in 1,000m. Turkish lira) in 1994 was 4,748·5; expenditure, 6,260·5.

Currency. The Turkish lira is used.

Banking and Finance. 50 banks, including offshore banks, were operating in 1995. Control is exercised by the Central Bank of the TRNC.

Agriculture. Agriculture accounted for 10·9% of GDP in 1994.

Foreign Economic Relations. Exports earned US$53·4m. in 1994. Imports cost US$286·6m. Customs tariffs with Turkey were reduced in July 1990. There is a free port at Famagusta.

Tourism. There were over 0·35m. tourists in 1994, including 95,098 from Europe. Tourist earnings totalled US$172·9m.

Civil Aviation. There are international airports at Ercan and Geçitkale. Flights operate to Europe, the Middle East and the Gulf via Istanbul and Ankara.

Telecommunications. The local radio, Radio Bayrak (BRTK) broadcasts in several languages including Greek, Arabic and English. BRT Television broadcasts for an average of 10 hours a day (colour by PAL). In 1994 there were 108,800 TV and radio sets.

Press. In 1995 there were 7 daily and 4 weekly newspapers.

Education. In 1994-95 there were 15,914 pupils and 1,097 teachers in primary schools, and 14,943 pupils and 1,027 teachers in secondary and general high schools, 2,498 students and 341 teachers in technical and vocational schools, and 5,710 students in higher education. There are 6 universities and a teacher training college.

Health. In 1994 there were 270 doctors, and 1,152 beds in state hospitals and private clinics.

Further Reading

Statistical Information: Statistics and Research Department, Nicosia.

North Cyprus Almanack, London, 1987

Christodolou, D., *Inside the Cyprus Miracle: the Labours of an Embattled Mini-Economy.* Univ. of Minnesota Press, 1992

Dodd, C. H. (ed.) *The Political, Social and Economic Development of Northern Cyprus.* Huntingdon, 1993

Hanworth, R., *The Heritage of Northern Cyprus.* Nicosia, 1993
Ioannides, C. P., *In Turkey's Image: the Transformation of Occupied Cyprus into a Turkish Province.* New Rochelle (N.Y.), 1991
Kitromilides, P. M. and Evriviades, M. L., *Cyprus,* [Bibliography]. 2nd ed. Oxford and Santa Barbara (CA), 1995
Salem N. (ed.) *Cyprus: a Regional Conflict and its Resolution.* London, 1992
Tamkoç, M., *The Turkish Cypriot State.* London, 1988

CZECH REPUBLIC

Česká Republika

Capital: Prague
Population: 10·36m. (1995)
GNP per capita: US$3,210 (1994)
HDI/world rank: 0·872/38 (1992)

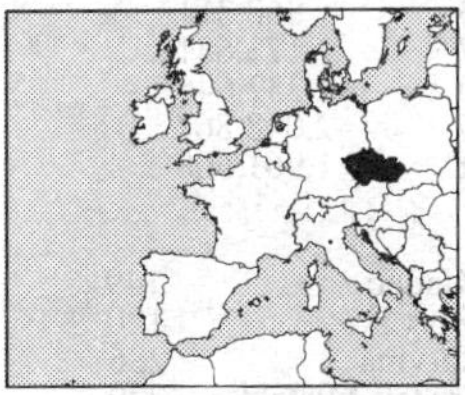

KEY HISTORICAL EVENTS. Czechoslovakia came into existence on 28 Oct. 1918, when the Czech (National Committee) took over the government of the Czech lands upon the dissolution of Austria–Hungary. Two days later the Slovak National Council manifested its desire to unite politically with the Czechs. On 14 Nov. 1918 the first Czechoslovak National Assembly declared the Czechoslovak State to be a republic with T. G. Masaryk as President (1918–35). For terrritorial changes up to and during the Second World War *see* THE STATESMAN'S YEAR-BOOK, 1995-96, p. 464. Liberation by the Soviet Army and US Forces was completed by May 1945 and territories taken by Germans, Poles and Hungarians were restored to Czechoslovak sovereignty. Subcarpathian Ruthenia was transferred to the USSR.

Elections were held in May 1946, at which the Communist Party obtained about 38% of the votes.

A coalition government under a Communist Prime Minister, Klement Gottwald, remained in power until 20 Feb. 1948, when 12 of the non-Communist ministers resigned in protest against infiltration of Communists into the police.

In Feb. a predominantly Communist government was formed by Gottwald. In May elections resulted in an 89% majority for the government and President Beneš resigned.

In 1968 pressure for liberalization culminated in the overthrow of the Stalinist leader, Antonín Novotný, and his associates. The Communist Party introduced an 'Action Programme' of far-reaching reforms.

Soviet pressure to abandon this programme was exerted between May and Aug. 1968, and finally, Warsaw Pact forces occupied Czechoslovakia on 21 Aug. The Czechoslovak government was compelled to accept a policy of 'normalization' (*i.e.*, abandonment of most reforms) and the stationing of Soviet forces.

Mass demonstrations demanding political reform began in Nov. 1989. After the authorities' use of violence to break up a demonstration on 17 Nov., the Communist leader resigned. On 30 Nov. the Federal Assembly abolished the Communist Party's sole right to govern, and a new Government was formed on 3 Dec. The protest movement continued to grow, and on 10 Dec. another government was formed. Gustáv Husák resigned as President, and was replaced by Václav Havel on the unanimous vote of 323 members of the Federal Assembly on 29 Dec.

On 25 Nov. 1992 the Federal Assembly voted the dissolution of the Czech and Slovak Federal Republic. This came into effect at midnight on 31 Dec. 1992. Economic property was divided in accordance with a federal law of 13 Nov. 1992. Real estate became the property of the republic in which it was located. Other property was divided by specially-constituted commissions in the proportion of 2 (Czech Republic) to 1 (Slovakia) on the basis of population size. Military materiel was divided on the 2:1 principle. Regular military personnel were invited to choose which armed force they would serve in.

TERRITORY AND POPULATION. The Czech Republic is bounded in the west by Germany, north by Poland, east by Slovakia and south by Austria. Minor exchanges of territory to straighten their mutual border were agreed between the Czech Republic and Slovakia on 4 Jan. 1996. Its area is 78,864 sq. km. At the 1991 census the population was 10,302,215. 1995 estimate, 10,362,400; density, 131 per sq. km. Vital statistics, 1992: Births, 122,142 (rate per 1,000 population, 11·8); deaths, 120,337 (11·7); marriages, 74,060 (7·2); divorces, 29,572 (2·77); infant deaths, 1,989 (per 1,000 live births, 6·2).

There are 8 administrative regions *(Kraj)*, one of which is the capital, Prague (Praha).

Region	*Chief city*	*Area in sq. km*	*Population 1991 census*
Prague	—	496	1,212,010
Středočeský	Prague (Praha)	11,038	1,112,374
Jihočeský	Ceské Budějovice	11,345	697,334
Západočeský	Plzeň (Pilsen)	10,873	860,311
Severočeský	Ustí nad Labem	7,777	1,173,681
Východočeský	Hradec Králove	11,240	1,232,646
Jihomoravský	Brno	15,027	2,048,867
Severomoravský	Ostrava	11,068	1,961,508

The population of the principal towns in 1993 (in 1,000):

Prague (Praha)	1,217	Liberec	159	Kladno	149
Brno	390	Hradec Králové	162	Most	120
Ostrava	327	České Budějovice	175	Karviná	286
Plzeň	172	Pardubice	163	Frýdek-Místek	229
Olomouc	225	Havířov	92		
Ustí nad Labem	118	Zlín	198		

At the 1991 census 81·2% of the population was Czech, 13·2% Moravian and 3·1% Slovak. There were also (in 1,000): Poles, 59; Germans, 48; Silesians, 44; Roma (Gypsies), 34; Hungarians, 21.

The official language is Czech.

CLIMATE. A humid continental climate, with warm summers and cold winters. Precipitation is generally greater in summer, with thunderstorms. Autumn, with dry, clear weather and spring, which is damp, are each of short duration. Prague. Jan. 29·5°F (–1·5°C), July 67°F (19·4°C). Annual rainfall 19·3" (483mm). Brno. Jan. 31°F (–0·6°C), July 67°F (19·4°C). Annual rainfall 21" (525mm).

CONSTITUTION AND GOVERNMENT. At the elections of June 1992 to the Czech National Council (then responsible for Czech affairs within Czechoslovakia) the Civic Democratic Party-Christian Democratic Party coalition gained 76 seats with 29·73% of votes cast, the Left Bloc 35 with 14·05%, the Czechoslovak Social Democratic Party 16 with 6·53%, the Liberal Social Union 16 with 6·52%, the Christian Democratic Union-Czechoslovak People's Party coalition 15 with 6·28%, the Republican Party 14 with 5·98%, the Civic Democratic Alliance 14 with 5·93% and the Movement for the Self-Government of Moravia and Silesia 14 with 5·87%. There was a 5% threshold.

The Constitution of 1 Jan. 1993 provides for a parliament comprising a 200-member *House of Representatives*, elected for 4-year terms by proportional representation, and an 81-member *Senate* elected for 6-year terms in single-member districts 27 senators being elected every 2 years. The first elections for the Senate were scheduled for mid-1996.

There is a *Constitutional Court* at Brno whose 15 members are nominated by the President and approved by the Senate for 10-year terms.

The *President* of the Republic is elected for a 5-year term by both chambers of parliament. He or she must be at least 40 years of age. The President names the Prime Minister at the suggestion of the Speaker.

The *President* of the Republic is Václav Havel, elected by parliament on 26 Jan. 1993 against 2 opponents and sworn in on 2 Feb.

The Civic Democratic Party (ODS)-Christian Democratic Union/Czech People's Party (KDU-ČSL)-Civic Democratic Alliance (ODA)-Christian Democratic Party (KDS) coalition government formed after the Czech National Council elections in July 1992 became the government of the Czech Republic on 1 Jan. 1993 and in Nov. 1995 comprised:

Prime Minister: Václav Klaus (ODS).

Deputy Prime Minister: Jan Kalvoda (ODA). *Deputy Prime Minister and Minister of Finance:* Ivan Kočárník (ODS). *Deputy Prime Minister and Minister of Agriculture:* Josef Lux (KDU-ČSL). *Minister for Administration of National Property and Privatization:* Jiří Skalický (ODA). *Defence:* Vilém Holáň (KDU-ČSL). *Economic*

Policy and Development: Karel Dyba (ODS). *Industry and Commerce:* Vladimír Dlouhý (ODA). *Foreign:* Josef Zieleniec (ODS). *Labour and Social Affairs:* Jindřich Vodička (ODS). *Health:* Jan Stráský (ODS). *Environment:* František Benda (KDS). *Culture:* Pavel Tigrid (KDU-ČSL). *Education, Youth and Sport:* Ivan Pilip (KDS). *Justice:* Jiří Novák (ODS). *Interior:* Jan Ruml (ODS). *Transport:* Vacant. *Economic Competition:* Stanislav Bělehrádek (KDU-ČSL). *State Control:* Igor Němec (ODS).

National flag: White and red (horizontal), with a blue triangle of full depth at the hoist, point to the fly (the same flag as the former Czechoslovakia).

National anthem: 'Kde domov můj' ('Where is my homeland'); words by J. K. Tyl, tune by F. J. Škroup.

Local Government. At elections on 18–19 Nov. 1994 turn-out was 60%. The Civic Democratic Party gained 25·4% of votes cast, ind, 17%, the Party of Democratic Left 16·6%, the Christian Democratic Party 10·6% and the Social Democratic Party 8·1%. The former National Committees have been replaced by district bureaux with the power to raise local taxes and with responsibility for roads, schools, utilities and public health.

DEFENCE. The President is C.-in-C. of the armed forces. Conscription is for 12 months.

Army. The Army comprises 2 Corps HQ, 1 rapid-reaction, 1 special forces, 6 mechanized, 1 reconnaissance, 2 artillery and 2 engineer brigades, 1 operations, 1 air defence and 5 civil defence regiments and 2 air defence and 1 operations battalion. Equipment includes 469 T-54/-55 and 542 T-72M main battle tanks. Strength (1996), 37,400 (21,400 conscripts). There are also paramilitary Border Guards (4,000 strong) and Internal Security Forces (1,600).

Air Force. The Air Force was recently reorganized; it now has a strength of some 25,000 (including air defence troops) and operates 120 combat aircraft. The Air Defence Corps operates a regiment of MiG-21s and MiG-23s. The Tactical Air Corps has a regiment of L-39, Su-22 and Su-25 strike aircraft, a helicopter regiment with Mi-24 armed helicopters and Mi-2/8/17s for transport, and a training regiment with Zlin 142s, L-29s, L-39s and some transport aircraft. A transport regiment reporting to Air Force HQ has An-24/26 and Tu-134/154 aircraft and Mi-2/8/17 helicopters.

INTERNATIONAL RELATIONS. In 1974 the German Federal Republic and the then Czechoslovakia annulled the Munich agreement of 1938.

Membership. The Czech Republic is a member of the UN, the OECD, CEFTA, and the NATO Partnership for Peace, and is an Associate Partner of the WEU. Together with Austria, Croatia, Hungary, Italy, Poland, Slovakia and Slovenia, it is also a member of the Central European Initiative which evolved from the Pentagonal/Hexagonal grouping of 1990–91. An application to join the EU was made in Jan. 1996.

ECONOMY

Policy. By the end of 1992 assets valued at Kč. 470,000m. had been privatized. 21,400 small businesses were auctioned off in 1992, and some 900 enterprises privatized through the sale of vouchers. A second stage of privatization, affecting 770 enterprises, took place by vouchers on sale to all citizens in Oct.–Nov. 1993. This stage came to an end in Dec. 1994, by which time 80% of the Czech Republic's assets were in private hands. The privatization of shares in 53 large companies was announced in 1995, the state to retain some of these shares. The privatization of the remaining minor state companies is scheduled for 1997.

Budget. At the 1993 budget, revenue was Kč. 289,163m. and expenditure Kč. 420,085. Items of expenditure in the 1994 budget (in Kč. 1,000): Welfare, 139; education, 42; defence, 27.

Currency. The unit of currency is the *koruna* (CEK) or crown of 100 *haler*, introduced on 8 Feb. 1993 at parity with the former Czechoslovakian koruna. Notes in circulation: Kč. 20, 50, 100, 500, 1,000, 2,000 and 5,000. Coin: 5, 10, 20, 50 *halers*, and Kč. 1, 2, 5. Gold reserves were 105 tonnes in 1992. Exchange reserves were US$5,723m. in Dec. 1994. Inflation was 11·1% in 1992. The koruna became convertible on 1 Oct. 1995. In March 1996, £1 = Kč. 41·74; US$1 = Kč. 27·31; DM1 = Kč. 18·51.

Banking and Finance. The central bank and bank of issue is the Czech National Bank (*Governor*, Josef Tošovský), which also acts as banking supervisor and regulator. Decentralization of the banking system began in 1991, and private banks began to operate. The Commercial Bank and Investment Bank are privatized nationwide networks with a significant government holding. Specialized banks include the Czech Savings Bank and the Czech Commercial Bank (for foreign trade payments). Private banks tend to be on a regional basis, many of them agricultural banks. There are also subsidiaries of foreign banks, joint ventures with foreign participation and branches and representative offices of foreign banks. There were 59 banks in 1995.

Savings deposits were Kč. 289,163m. in 1993.

A stock exchange was founded in Prague in 1992.

Weights and Measures. The metric system is in force.

ENERGY AND NATURAL RESOURCES

Electricity. Output, 1993, 58,882 MWh. In 1993 76% of electricity was produced by thermal power stations using brown coal, 21% was nuclear (1 station) and the rest was hydro-electric. 29·2% of output was nuclear-generated in 1993.

Minerals. There are hard coal and lignite reserves (chief fields: Most, Chomutov, Kladno, Ostrava and Sokolov). Gold deposits were found near Prague in 1985.

Agriculture. In 1993 there were 4,282,000 ha of agricultural land (3,173,000 ha arable). 31·1% of agricultural land was state-owned, 61% co-operative, 4·4% private and 2·2% public.

A law of May 1991 returned land seized by the Communist regime to its original owners, to a maximum of 150 ha of arable to a single owner.

Livestock, 1994: Cattle, 2·16m. (including 0·83m. milch cows); pigs, 4·07m.; sheep, 196,000; poultry, 24·97m. In 1993 production of meat was 1,140,711 tonnes (live weight); milk, 3,350m. litres; 3,100m. eggs.

Forestry. In 1994 forests covered 2,628,628 ha. 10,405,639 cu. metres of timber were cut in 1993.

INDUSTRY. In 1993 there were 45,138 trading companies, 4,420 joint stock companies, 45,138 other registered businesses, 4,385 co-operatives and 3,081 government enterprises. Output, 1993, included: Steel, 6·76m. tonnes; cement, 5·4m. tonnes; motor cars, 173,000.

Labour. In 1993, 1·71m. persons were employed in mining, manufacture, electricity, gas and water; 609,000 in wholesale and retail trade and repairs; 453,000 in construction; 331,000 in agriculture; 263,000 in health and social work, and 65,000 in financial services. Unemployment was 2·63% in June 1993. The average monthly wage was Kčs. 5,816 in 1993. In December 1993 93,380 persons were registered unemployed. Pay increases are regulated in firms where wages grow faster than production. Fines are levied if wages rise by more than 15% over 4 years.

FOREIGN ECONOMIC RELATIONS. A memorandum envisaging a customs union and close economic co-operation was signed with Slovakia in Oct. 1992. An agreement of Dec. 1992 with Hungary, Poland and Slovakia abolishes tariffs on raw materials and goods where exports do not compete directly with locally-produced items, and envisages tariff reductions on agricultural and industrial goods in 1995–97.

Foreign debt was US$3,400m. at the beginning of 1993. There were 10,599 joint ventures in June 1993.

Commerce. Trade, 1993 (in Kč. 1m.): Imports, 308,911; exports, 297,752. Main export markets: Germany, 98,358; Austria, 22,874; Italy, 18,760; Poland, 10,217; Russia, 16,406. Main import suppliers: Germany, 95,193; Austria, 29,181; France, 11,471; Russia, 35,908; USA, 11,242.

Total trade between the Czech Republic and UK (British Department of Trade returns, £1,000 sterling):

	1993	*1994*	*1995*
Imports to UK	245,265	278,301	321,497
Exports and re-exports from UK	287,568	374,453	567,923

COMMUNICATIONS

Roads. In 1993 0·99m. passengers and 37·1m. tonnes of freight were transported.

Railways. In 1994 Czech State Railways had a route length of 9,316 km (1,435 mm gauge), of which 2,640 km were electrified. In 1994, 228·7m. passengers and 110·6m. tonnes of freight were carried. There is a metro (44 km) and tram/light rail system (496 km) in Prague, and tram/light rail networks in Brno, Liberec, Most, Olomouc, Ostrava, Plzeň and Teplice-Trečianské.

Civil Aviation. The main airports are: Prague (Ruzyně), Brno (Cernovice) and Olomouc (Holice). The national carrier is Czech Airlines, 68·1% state-owned, which in 1995 operated 2 A310-300s, 2 B-737-400s, 5 B-737-500s and 13 ex-Soviet aircraft. Services are also provided by Adria, Aefoflot, Air Algérie, Air France, Air Ukraine, Alitalia, Austrian Airlines, Balkan, British Airways, British Midland, Croatia Airlines, Crossair, Delta, El Al, Eurowings, Finnair, KLM, Libyan Airlines, Lithuanian Airlines, LOT, Lufthansa, Luxair, Malév, Orbi, Sabena, SAS, Swissair, Syrian Airlines and Tunis Air. 1·36m. passengers were transported by air in 1993.

Shipping. 4·9m. tonnes of freight were carried by inland waterways in 1993.

Telecommunications. The national telecommunications operator is SPT Telecom, scheduled in 1995 for a 27% privatization. Telephone supply in 1995 was 20 per 100 inhabitants. Broadcasting is the responsibility of the independent Board for Radio and Television. Czech Television (ČTV; colour by SECAM) and Czech Radio are public corporations. The former federal Czechoslovakian broadcasting stations in the Czech Republic have become a second service. There is also a nationwide private TV company and 2 radio companies as well as local private stations.

Cinemas. In 1993, there were 1,900 screens. Attendance was 21,898,000 in 1993. 12 full-length films were made in 1994.

SOCIAL INSTITUTIONS

Justice. The post-Communist judicial system was established by a law of July 1991. This provides for a unified system of 4 types of court: civil, criminal, commercial and administrative. Commercial courts arbitrate in disputes arising from business activities. Administrative courts examine the legality of the decisions of state institutions when appealed by citizens. In addition, there are military courts which operate under the jurisdiction of the Ministry of Defence. There is a Supreme Court, and a hierarchy of courts under the Ministry of Justice at republic, region and district level. District courts are courts of first instance. Cases are usually decided by senates comprising a judge and 2 associate judges, though occasionally by a single judge. (Associate judges are citizens in good standing over the age of 25 who are elected for 4-year terms). Regional courts are courts of first instance in more serious cases and also courts of appeal for district courts. Cases are usually decided by a senate of 2 judges and 3 associate judges, although again occasionally by a single judge. There is also a Supreme Administrative Court. The Supreme Court interprets law as a guide to other courts and functions also as a court of appeal.

Decisions are made by senates of 3 judges. Judges are appointed for life by the National Council.

There is no death penalty. In 1993, 398,505 crimes were reported, of which 31·7% were solved.

Religion. In 1991 18 churches were registered. At a census in March 1991, church membership was: Roman Catholic, 1,038,720; Evangelical Church of the Czech Brethren, 182,693; Hussites, 173,232.

Miloslav Vlk (b. 1932) was installed as archbishop of Prague and primate of Czechoslovakia in 1991. The national Czech church, created in 1918, took the name 'Hussite' in 1972. In 1991 it had a patriarch, 5 bishops, 300 pastors (40% women) and some 0·8m. adherents. In 1991 there were also some 0·5m. adherents of a dozen Protestant churches the largest being the Evangelical, which unites Calvinists and Lutherans and numbered about 0·2m.

Education. In 1995–96 there were 9 universities, 4 technical universities, 2 universities for agriculture, 1 for economics and 1 for veternary science. There were also 7 other higher education institutions.

DIPLOMATIC REPRESENTATIVES

Of the Czech Republic in Great Britain (26 Kensington Palace Gdns., London, W8 4QY)
Ambassador: Karel Kühnl.

Of Great Britain in the Czech Republic (Thunovská 14, 11800 Prague 1)
Ambassador: Sir Michael Burton, KCVO, KCMG.

Of the Czech Republic in the USA (3900 Linnean Ave., NW, Washington, D.C., 20008)
Ambassador: Michael Zantovský.

Of the USA in the Czech Republic (Tržiste 15 12548, Prague)
Ambassador: Jennone Walker.

Of the Czech Republic to the United Nations
Ambassador: Karel Kovanda.

Further Reading

Czech Statistical Office. *Statistical Yearbook of the Czech Republic.*
Havel, V., *Disturbing the Peace.* London, 1990.—*Living in Truth: Twenty-Two Essays.* London, 1990. —*Summer Meditations.* London, 1992
Hermann, A. H., *A History of the Czechs.* London, 1975
Kalvoda, J., *The Genesis of Czechoslovakia.* New York, 1986
Leff, C. S., *National Conflict in Czechoslovakia: The Making and Remaking of a State, 1918–1987.* Princeton, 1988
Short, D., *Czechoslovakia.* [Bibliography] Oxford and Santa Barbara, 1986
Simmons, M., *The Reluctant President: a Political Life of Vaclav Havel.* London, 1992

National statistical office: Czech Statistical Office, Sokolovská 142, 186 04 Prague 8.

DENMARK

Kongeriget Danmark
(Kingdom of Denmark)

Capital: Copenhagen
Population: 5·2m. (1995)
GNP per capita: US$28,110 (1994)
HDI/world rank: 0·920/16 (1992)

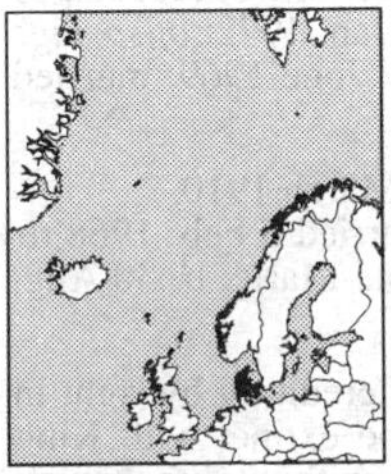

KEY HISTORICAL EVENTS. First organized as a unified state in the 10th century, Denmark acquired approximately its present boundaries in 1815, having ceded Norway to Sweden and its north German territory to Prussia. Denmark became a constitutional monarchy in 1849.

TERRITORY AND POPULATION. Denmark is bounded in the west by the North Sea, north-west and north by the Skagerrak and Kattegat straits (separating it from Norway and Sweden) and south by Germany. At the census of Nov. 1970 the area was 43,075 sq. km (16,631 sq. miles) and the population 4,937,579.

Administrative divisions		*Area (sq. km) 1994*	*Population 1970*	*Population 1995*	*Population per sq. km*
København (Copenhagen)	(city)	88	622,773	471,300	5,340·5
Frederiksberg	(borough)	9	101,874	88,002	10,034·4
Københavns	(county)	526	615,343	605,868	1,151·9
Frederiksborg	,,	1,347	259,442	350,236	259·9
Roskilde	,,	891	153,199	224,052	251·3
Vestsjælland	,,	2,984	259,057	288,221	96·6
Storstrøm	,,	3,398	252,363	256,562	75·5
Bornholm	,,	588	47,239	44,936	76·4
Fyn	,,	3,486	432,699	467,695	134·2
Sønderjylland	,,	3,938	238,062	251,992	64·0
Ribe	,,	3,131	197,843	221,750	70·8
Vejle	,,	2,997	306,263	336,663	112·3
Ringkøbing	,,	4,853	241,327	270,128	58·7
Århus	,,	4,561	533,190	619,232	135·8
Viborg	,,	4,122	220,734	230,778	56·0
Nordjylland	,,	6,173	456,171	488,303	79·1
Total		43,094	4,937,579	5,215,718	121·0

In 1992, 95·3% of the inhabitants were born in Denmark, including the Faroe Islands and Greenland.

On 1 Jan. 1995 the population of the capital, Copenhagen (comprising Copenhagen, Frederiksberg and Gentofte municipalities), was 625,810 (including suburbs, 1,353,333); Århus, 277,477; Odense, 182,617; Aalborg, 159,056; Esbjerg, 82,579; Randers, 61,435; Kolding, 59,558; Herning, 57,751; Helsingør, 56,855; Horsens, 55,252.

Vital statistics for calendar years:

	Living births	*Still births*	*Marriages*	*Divorces*	*Deaths*	*Emigration*	*Immigration*
1992	67,726	339	32,188	12,981	60,821	31,915	43,377
1993	67,369	308	31,638	12,971	62,809	32,344	43,400
1994[1]	69,684	...	35,321	13,709	61,173	34,710	49,961

[1] Preliminary.

Single-parent births: 1990, 46·4%; 1992, 46·4%; 1993, 46·8%.

CLIMATE. The climate is much modified by marine influences, and the effect of the Gulf Stream, to give winters that may be both cold or mild and often cloudy.Summers may be warm and sunny or chilly and rainy. In general, the east is drier than the west. Long periods of calm weather are exceptional and windy conditionsare common. Copenhagen. Jan. 33°F (0·5°C), July 63°F (17°C). Annual rainfall 650 mm. Esbjerg. Jan. 33°F (0·5°C), July 61°F (16°C). Annual rainfall 800 mm. 10% of rainfall precipitates as snow.

ROYAL HOUSE. The reigning Queen is **Margrethe II,** b. 16 April 1940; married 10 June 1967 to Prince Henrik, b. Count de Monpezat. She succeeded to the throne on the death of her father, King Frederik IX, on 14 Jan. 1972; *offspring:* Crown Prince Frederik, b. 26 May 1968; Prince Joachim, b. 7 June 1969, married 18 Nov. 1995 Alexandra Manley (b. 30 June 1964).

Mother of the Queen: Queen Ingrid, b. Princess of Sweden, 28 March 1910.
Sisters of the Queen: Princess Benedikte, b. 29 April 1944 (married 3 Feb. 1968 to Prince Richard of Sayn-Wittgenstein-Berleburg); Princess Anne-Marie, b. 30 Aug. 1946 (married 18 Sept. 1964 to King Constantine of Greece).

The crown was elective from the earliest times but became hereditary by right in 1660. The direct male line of the house of Oldenburg became extinct with King Frederik VII on 15 Nov. 1863. In view of the death of the king, without direct heirs, the Great Powers signed a treaty at London on 8 May 1852, by the terms of which the succession to the crown was made over to Prince Christian of Schleswig-Holstein-Sonderburg-Glücksburg, and to the direct male descendants of his union with the Princess Louise of Hesse-Cassel. This became law on 31 July 1853. Linked to the constitution of 5 June 1953, a new law of succession, dated 27 March 1953, has come into force, which restricts the right of succession to the descendants of King Christian X and Queen Alexandrine, and admits the sovereign's daughters to the line of succession, ranking after the sovereign's sons.

The Queen receives a tax-free annual sum of 41·5m. kroner from the state.

CONSTITUTION AND GOVERNMENT. The present constitution is founded upon the Basic Law of 5 June 1953. The legislative power lies with the Queen and the *Folketing* (parliament) jointly. The executive power is vested in the monarch, who exercises authority through the ministers. The judicial power is with the courts. The monarch must be a member of the Evangelical-Lutheran Church, the official Church of the State and may not assume major international obligations without the consent of the Folketing. The Folketing consists of one chamber. All men and women of Danish nationality of more than 18 years of age and permanently resident in Denmark possess the franchise and are eligible for election to the Folketing, which is at present composed of 179 members; 135 members are elected by the method of proportional representation in 17 constituencies. In order to attain an equal representation of the different parties, 40 additional seats are divided among such parties which have not obtained sufficient returns at the constituency elections. 2 members are elected for the Faroe Islands and 2 for Greenland. The term of the legislature is 4 years, but a general election may be called at any time. The Folketing convenes every year on the first Tuesday in October. Besides its legislative functions, it appoints every 6 years judges who, together with the ordinary members of the Supreme Court, form the *Rigsret*, a tribunal which can alone try parliamentary impeachments.

At the elections on 21 Sept. 1994 the electorate was 3,233,422; turn-out was 84%. The Social Democratic Party (SD) won 62 seats with 34·6% of votes cast (69 with 37·4% in 1990); the Liberal Party, 42 with 23·3% (29 with 15·8%); the Conservative Party, 27 with 15% (30 with 16%); the Socialist Party, 13 with 7·3% (15 with 8·3%); the Progress Party, 11 with 6·4% (12 with 6·4%); the Social Liberal Party (SL; formerly Radical Liberal Party), 8 with 4·6% (7 with 3·5%); the Red-Green Alliance, 6 with 3·2%; the Centre Democrats (CD), 5 with 2·8% (9 with 5·1%); ind, 1 with 1%.

Following the 1994 elections a coalition government of the Social Democratic

(SD), Social Liberal (SL) and Centre Democratic (CD) Parties took office on 21 Sept. 1994 consisting in Feb. 1996 of:

Prime Minister: Poul Nyrup Rasmussen (b. 1943; SD).

Minister of Economic Affairs and Minister for Nordic Co-operation: Marianne Jelved (SL). *Business and Industry:* Mimi Jakobsen (CD). *Finance:* Mogens Lykketoft (SD). *Foreign Affairs:* Niels Helvig Petersen (SL). *Justice:* Bjørn Westh (SD). *Environment and Energy:* Svend Auken (SD). *Education:* Ole Vig Jensen (SL). *Development Co-operation:* Poul Nielson (SD). *Interior and Ecclesiastical Affairs:* Birthe Weiss (SD). *Labour:* Jytte Andersen (SD). *Taxation:* Carsten Koch (SD). *Defence:* Hans Haekkerup (SD). *Culture:* Jytte Hilden (SD). *Transport:* Jan Trøjborg (SD). *Social Affairs:* Karen Jespersen (SD). *Health:* Yvonne Herløv Andersen (CD). *Housing and Building:* Ole Løvig Simonsen (SD). *Research:* Frank Jensen (SD). *Agriculture and Fisheries:* H. E. Henrik Dam Kristensen (SD).

National flag: Red with white Scandinavian cross (Dannebrog).

National anthem: 'Kong Kristian stod ved højen mast' ('King Christian stood by the lofty mast'); words by J. Ewald, tune by J. E. Hartmann.

European Parliament. Denmark has 16 representatives. At the June 1994 elections turn-out was 52·5%. The Liberal Party won 4 seats with 18·9% of votes cast (group in European Parliament: Liberal, Democratic and Reformist Group); the Conservative Party, 3 with 17·7% (Popular European Party); the SD, 3 with 15·8% (European Socialist Party); the June Movement, 2 with 15·2% (Europe of Nations); the People's Anti-EU Movement, 2 with 10·3% (Europe of Nations); the Socialist People's Party, 1 with 8·6% (Greens); the Radical Liberal Party, 1 with 8·5% (Liberal, Democratic and Reformist Group).

Local Government. For administrative purposes Denmark is divided into 275 communes; each of them has a district council of between 7 and 31 members, headed by an elected mayor. The city of Copenhagen forms a district by itself and is governed by a city council of 55 members, elected every 4 years, and an executive, consisting of the chief burgomaster and 6 burgomasters, appointed by the city council for 4 years. There are 14 counties, each of which is administered by a county council of between 13 and 31 members, headed by an elected mayor. All councils are elected directly by universal suffrage and proportional representation for 4-year terms. There are also about 2,100 parishes. Government at this level is administered by parish councils elected for 4 years.

The counties and Copenhagen are superintended by the Ministry of Interior Affairs. The municipalities are superintended by 14 local supervision committees, headed by a state county prefect who is a civil servant appointed by the Queen.

County and municipal elections were held on 16 Nov. 1993. The Social Democrats won 34% of votes cast, the Liberals 27%.

DEFENCE. Military defence is organized in accordance with the Defence Act of Dec. 1993. The overall organization of the Danish Armed Forces comprises the Defence Command, the Army, the Navy, the Air Force and interservice authorities and institutions. To this should be added the Home Guard, which is an indispensable part of Danish military defence. The Home Guard is based on the Home Guard Act of May 1982 as amended in Dec. 1993.

In accordance with the Defence Act the Chief of Defence has full command of the three services: The Army, the Navy and the Air Force. The Chief of Defence, and the Defence Staff constitute the Defence Command.

The Constitution of 1849 declared it the duty of every fit man to contribute to the national defence, and this provision is still in force. According to the Personnel Act of May 1982 as amended in June 1986 and Dec. 1993, the military personnel comprises officers, n.c.o.s and privates. Private personnel are provided by enlistment and by recruiting of volunteers. Selection of conscripts takes place at the age of 18–19 years, and the conscripts are normally called up for service ½–1½ years later. Afterwards conscripts may be recalled for refresher training or musters. The initial training period for conscripts is between 4 and 12 months.

Army. The Army in 1995 comprised field army formations and the local defence forces. The peacetime strength of the army numbers 19,100 (including about 3,900 civilians and about 7,100 conscripts). The wartime strength is about 64,500. The army is organized in brigades and some brigade size structures, headquarters units and support units. The brigade units are organized in 5 mechanized infantry brigades including the Danish Reaction Brigade. The field army is equipped with 353 battle tanks, about 533 armoured personnel carriers and 161 light armoured fighting vehicles as well as artillery including 76 self-propelled howitzers. The Army has 12 Fennec anti-armour and 14 Hughes 500 helicopters for observation and liaison. The local defence units are organized in infantry battalions and some artillery battalions as well as a number of support units. The men of the latest annual service groups form the troops of the line, while those of the previous years form the local defence, the reserve and the reserve for the Home Guard.

Navy. The Navy, some 6,300 strong (including 1,800 civilians and 700 conscripts) in 1995, is supported by 5,000 reservists. The wartime strength is 9,600. The fleet includes 5 coastal submarines, 3 corvettes, 5 offshore patrol ships with Lynx helicopters, 3 inshore patrol cutters, 14 Standard Flex 300 multirole ships, 9 inshore patrol craft, 10 fast missile craft, 4 large minelayers, 2 coastal minelayers and 1 coastal minesweeper. Major auxiliaries include 2 tankers, and the Royal Yacht; and there are a number of auxiliaries. The naval Air Arm comprises 8 Lynx helicopters, and the Home Guard operates 35 inshore patrol craft.

Coastal Defence forces comprise 1 permanent fortress armed with 150mm guns and 2 coastal batteries with Harpoon missiles.

Additional forces of a paramilitary nature include 4 icebreakers maintained by the Navy. The main base is at Frederikshavn.

Air Force. The Air Force, in 1995, comprised some 8,000 (including 2,300 civilians and 500 conscripts). The wartime strength force is about 18,600.

The flying squadrons comprise 4 all-weather air-defence squadrons with a total of 65 F-16s. All squadrons have an air-defence and a fighter-bomber rôle. One squadron has an additional photo-reconnaissance rôle. The operational units also comprise 8 Hawk surface-to-air missile squadrons.

In addition the Air Force has a number of supplementary units, including 1 transport squadron (C-130 Hercules and Gulfstream III), 1 helicopter survey and rescue squadron (S-61As), and a control and warning system. T-17 Supporter aircraft are used for initial training; pilots then go to the USA for further training.

Home Guard. The overall Home Guard organization comprises the Home Guard Command, the Army Home Guard, the Naval Home Guard, the Air Force Home Guard and the Service Corps.

The personnel of the Home Guard is recruited on a voluntary basis. The personnel establishment of the Home Guard was in 1995 about 68,000 persons (53,900 in the Army Home Guard, 4,000 in the Navy Home Guard, 8,200 in the Air Force Home Guard and 1,800 in the Service Corps.).

INTERNATIONAL RELATIONS. In a referendum in June 1992 the electorate voted against ratifying the Maastricht Treaty for closer political union within the EU. Turn-out was 82%. 50·7% of votes were against ratification, 49·3% in favour. However, a second referendum on 18 May 1993 reversed this result, with 56·8% of votes cast in favour of ratification and 43·2% against. Turn-out was 86·2%.

Membership. Denmark is a member of the UN, NATO, OECD, the EU, Council of Europe and the Nordic Council.

ECONOMY

Budget. The following shows the actual revenue and expenditure as shown in central government accounts for the calendar years 1993 and 1994, the approved budget figures for 1995 and the budget for 1996 (in 1,000 kroner):

	1993	*1994*	*1995*	*1996*
Revenue	310,875,000	342,510,700	350,213,600	352,685,600
Expenditure	359,322,900	382,237,400	390,217,600	386,219,100

Receipts and expenditures of special government funds and expenditures on public works are included.

The 1996 budget envisaged revenue of 125,303m. kroner from income and property taxes and 164,286m. from consumer taxes.

The central government debt on 31 Dec. 1994 amounted to 690,653m. kroner.

VAT is 25%.

Currency. The monetary unit is the *Danish krone* (DKK) of 100 *øre*. There are notes of 1,000, 500, 100 and 50 kroner, and coins of 20, 10, 5 and 1 krone and 50 and 25 øre. In March 1996, £1 = 8·72 kroner; US$1 = 5·70 kroner; DM1 = 3·86 kroner.

Banking and Finance. On 31 Dec. 1994 the accounts of the National Bank (*Governor*, Bodil Nyboe) balanced at 166,045m. kroner. The assets included official net foreign reserves of 54,094m. kroner. The liabilities included notes and coin of 32,688m. kroner. On 31 Dec. 1994 there were 113 commercial banks and savings banks, with deposits of 537,310m. kroner. On 31 Dec. 1994 the money supply was 393,900m. kroner.

There is a stock exchange in Copenhagen.

Weights and Measures. The metric system has been obligatory since 1912.

ENERGY AND NATURAL RESOURCES

Electricity. Production (1994), 35,277m. kWh.

Oil and Gas. Oil production was (1994) 9·1m. tonnes. Production of natural gas was (1994) 4·3m. cu. metres.

Agriculture. Land ownership is widely distributed. In June 1994 there were 69,346 holdings with at least 5 ha of agricultural area (or at least a production equivalent to that from 5 ha of barley). There were 12,377 small holdings (with less than 10 ha), 40,543 medium-sized holdings (10–50 ha) and 16,426 holdings with more than 50 ha.

There were 25,991 agricultural workers in 1994.

In 1994 the cultivated area was (in 1,000 ha): Grain, 1,403; pulses, 101; root crops, 165; other crops, 208; green fodder and grass, 555; set aside, 259; total cultivated area, 2,691.

	Area (1,000 ha)			*Production (in 1,000 tonnes)*		
Chief crops	*1992*	*1993*	*1994*	*1992*	*1993*	*1994*
Wheat	581	619	572	3,583	4,334	3,725
Rye	88	78	88	308	356	423
Barley	892	709	700	2,924	3,369	3,446
Oats [1]	30	31	40	89	138	206
Potatoes	55	47	39	1,735	1,741	1,359
Other root crops	146	137	126	7,760	8,490	7,005

[1] Including mixed grain.

Livestock, 1994: Horses, 0·02m.; cattle, 2,105,000; pigs, 10,923,000; poultry, 18,954,000.

Production (in 1,000 tonnes) in 1994: Milk, 4,642; butter, 59; cheese, 288; beef, 210; pork and bacon, 1,604; eggs, 90.

In 1994 tractors numbered 146,573 and combine harvesters, 29,775.

Fisheries. The total value of the fish caught was (in 1m. kroner): 1950, 156; 1955, 252; 1960, 376; 1965, 650; 1970, 854; 1975, 1,442; 1980, 2,888; 1985, 3,542; 1986, 3,576; 1987, 3,510; 1988, 3,476; 1989, 3,625; 1990, 3,439; 1991, 3,681; 1992, 3,398; 1993, 2,560; 1994, 2,834 (preliminary).

INDUSTRY. The following table sets forth the gross factor income (in 1m. kroner) by industrial origin in 3 calendar years:

	1992 Current Prices	1992 1980 Prices	1993 Current Prices	1993 1980 Prices	1994 Current Prices	1994 1980 Prices
Agriculture, fur-farming, forestry, etc.	25,186	22,505	25,131	26,350	27,385	26,554
Fishing	1,954	1,099	1,361	801	1,596	864
Total	27,140	23,604	26,492	27,151	28,981	27,418
Mining and quarrying	7,437	16,232	7,683	17,993	7,334	19,401
Manufacturing	141,816	71,745	142,592	69,512	155,259	75,406
Electricity, gas and water	12783	7,638	15,224	8,808	15,331	8,895
Construction	39,838	18,634	39,589	18,376	43,703	19,271
Total	281,874	114,249	205,088	114,689	221,627	122,973
Wholesale and retail trade	94,460	55,054	92,972	54,387	99,717	57,837
Restaurants and hotels	10,015	4,822	10,602	4,071	11,183	4,314
Transport and storage	52,419	33,485	55,864	38,979	59,517	35,506
Communication	14,859	7,356	14,728	7,056	17,651	8,983
Financing and insurance	13,006	8,191	19,512	9,123	20,657	9,044
Dwellings	76,026	32,832	78,056	31,866	79,288	31,028
Business services	50,517	24,197	51,861	24,046	55,121	25,180
Market services of education, health	10,028	5,166	9,964	5,043	10,143	5,036
Recreational and cultural services	8,453	4,867	8,746	4,615	10,121	5,082
Household services, incl. auto repair	21,393	8,347	20,373	7,886	22,468	8,294
Total	351,175	184,318	362,678	187,072	385,866	190,304
Other producers, excl. government	5,648	2,979	6,260	3,274	6,600	3,333
Producers of government services	166,512	84,851	172,920	86,144	176,052	86,630
Total	172,160	87,830	179,181	89,418	182,652	89,963
Imputed bank service charges	−15,463	−7,868	−18,678	−10,922	−19,185	−10,923
Gross domestic product at factor cost	736,887	402,131	754,761	407,407	799,941	419,733
Plus indirect taxes	148,593	64,701	153,351	66,402	168,428	75,073
Less subsidies	34,227		34,875		35,187	
Gross domestic product at market prices	851,253	466,832	873,237	473,808	933,182	494,806

In the following table 'number of employees' refers to 25,477 local activity units including one-man units (Nov. 1993), while 'gross-output' and 'value-added' cover 2,844 enterprises with 20 employees or more (1994).

Branch of industry	*Number of employees*	*Gross output at factor cost (1m. kroner)*	*Value added at factor cost (1m. kroner)*
Food, beverages and tobacco	93,933	116,137	38,813
Textiles, wearing apparel, leather	26,040	12,901	5,833
Wood and wood products	14,399	8,124	3,967
Paper products	60,996	22,399	13,812
Refined petroleum products	903	9,790	1,124
Chemicals and man-made fibres	25,335	31,363	18,362
Rubber and plastic products	20,872	12,791	7,254

Branch of industry	*Number of employees*	*Gross output at factor cost (1m. kroner)*	*Value added at factor cost (1m. kroner)*
Non-metallic mineral products	19,190	12,948	7,831
Basic metals	53,524	25,872	13,239
Machinery and equipment	68,026	43,205	23,298
Electrical and optical equipment	42,933	27,747	14,541
Transport equipment	20,053	14,537	6,248
Furniture, other manufactures	34,602	19,731	10,601
Total manufacturing	480,866	357,545	164,923

Labour. In 1994, 5% of the working population lived on agriculture, forestry and fishery, 20% on industries and handicrafts, 6% on construction, 16% on commerce, etc., 7% on transport and communication, and 46% on administration, professional services, etc. In 1994, 512,139 persons were employed in manufacturing. Retirement age is 67.

FOREIGN ECONOMIC RELATIONS

Commerce. The following table shows the value, in 1,000 kroner, of imports and exports (including trade with the Faroe Islands and Greenland) for calendar years:

	1990	*1991*	*1992*	*1993*	*1994* [1]
Imports	195,780,682	206,797,874	212,086,678	191,325,238	215,008,724
Exports	216,443,861	229,764,807	247,254,759	232,884,236	252,287,150

[1] Excluding trade not distributed.

Imports and exports (in 1m. kroner) for calendar years:

Leading commodities	*1993* [1] *(Imports)*	*1993* [1] *(Exports)*	*1994* [1] *Imports*	*1994* [1] *Exports*
Live animals, meat and meat preparations	1,965	22,358	2,159	25,031
Dairy products, eggs	969	9,230	1,064	9,168
Fish, crustaceans, etc. and preparations	6,208	13,363	6,815	14,311
Cereals and cereal preparations	2,043	4,678	1,807	4,284
Sugar, sugar preparations and honey	1,018	1,620	872	1,768
Coffee, tea, cocoa, spices, etc.	1,742	698	2,184	733
Feeding stuff for animals	4,462	2,438	4,241	2,829
Wood and cork	2,761	606	4,019	715
Textile fibres, yarns, fabrics and articles of	5,296	4,549	5,741	4,880
Mineral fuels, lubricants, etc.	11,648	7,755	11,426	6,821
Medicine and pharmaceutical products	3,926	9,501	4,601	10,822
Fertilizers, etc.	1,655	1,012	1,888	1,007
Metals, manufactures of metals	15,267	10,326	18,498	11,489
Machinery, electrical, equipment, etc.	42,186	47,567	48,330	53,892
Transport equipment	15,762	11,935	21,507	12,544

[1] Excluding trade not distributed.

Distribution of foreign trade (in 1,000 kroner) according to countries of origin and destination, for calendar years:

Countries	Imports *1992*	Imports *1993* [1]	Imports *1994* [1]	Exports *1992*	Exports *1993* [1]	Exports *1994* [1]
Belgium	7,172,722	6,881,182	7,595,280	5,094,323	4,445,810	4,567,040
Finland	5,572,423	5,483,690	6,643,312	5,135,955	4,448,012	6,041,679
France	11,222,396	10,071,030	11,580,333	13,973,983	12,491,352	13,821,782
Germany	50,717,701	43,350,413	46,695,725	57,901,327	55,354,266	56,484,279
Norway	11,316,404	9,888,817	10,865,769	14,907,720	16,156,506	16,308,605
Sweden	23,424,105	20,819,619	24,874,708	26,513,577	23,392,170	26,277,889
Switzerland	4,369,121	4,282,556	4,069,228	4,636,845	4,245,412	4,827,470
UK	16,923,991	14,291,274	14,042,521	24,436,610	20,377,402	20,591,479
USA	10,796,335	9,188,698	11,075,596	10,418,673	12,300,623	13,889,430

[1] Excluding trade not distributed.

Total trade between Denmark (without the Faroe Islands) and UK (British Department of Trade returns, in £1,000 sterling):

	1991	*1992*	*1993*	*1994*
Imports to UK	2,226,706	2,384,964	1,954,100	2,024,400
Exports and re-exports from UK	1,408,549	1,560,607	1,476,200	1,685,000

Tourism. In 1994, foreigners visiting Denmark spent some 20,191m. kroner. In 1994 foreigners spent 5,932,000m. nights in hotels and 4,234,000 nights at camping sites.

COMMUNICATIONS

Roads. Denmark proper had (1 Jan. 1995), 786 km of motorways, 3,764 km of other state roads, 7,063 km of provincial roads and 59,642 km of commercial roads. Motor vehicles registered at 1 Jan. 1995 comprised 1,610,955 passenger cars, 288,433 lorries, 10,348 taxicabs (including 5,243 for private hire), 13,564 buses and 49,194 cycles.

Railways. In 1994 there were 2,349 km of State railways of 1,435 mm gauge (326 km electrified), which carried 141·1m. passengers and 9·7m. tonnes of freight. There were also 494 km of private railways.

Civil Aviation. There is an international airport at Copenhagen. The Scandinavian Airlines System (SAS) resulted from the 1950 merger of the 3 former Scandinavian airlines. Services are also provided by Adria, Aer Lingus, Aeroflot, Air China, Air France, Air India, Air Malta, Air UK, Alitalia, Atlantic Airways, Austrian Airlines, Balkan, British Airways, British Midland, Cimber Air, Continental Airlines and Air Micronesia, Croatia Airlines, Crossair, Czech Airlines, Delta, Egyptair, El Al, Estonian Air, Finnair, Iberia, Icelandair, JAT, KLM, Kenya Airways, Kuwait Airways, LOT, Lithuanian Airlines, Lufthansa, Luxair, Malév, Middle East Airlines, Northwest Airlines, Olympic, Pakistan International Airlines, Palair Macedonian, Royal Air Maroc, Sabena, Singapore Airlines, Swissair, TAP, Tarom, Thai Airways, Tunis Air, Turkish Airlines, United Airlines and Varig. In 1993 SAS flew 225·5m. km and carried 18,584,391 passengers.

On 1 Jan. 1994 Denmark had 1,063 aircraft with a capacity of 17,443 seats. In 1993 there were 191,400 take-offs and landings to and from abroad and 197,900 to and from Danish airports, excluding local flights.

Shipping. On 1 Jan. 1994 the merchant fleet consisted of 941 vessels (above 20 GRT) of 5,098,449 GRT.

In 1994, 45m. tonnes of cargo were unloaded and 29m. tonnes were loaded in Danish ports; traffic by passenger ships and ferries is not included.

Telecommunications. There were, in 1994, 1,291 post offices. On 31 Dec. 1994 there were 3·12m. telephone subscribers. 503,500 mobile telephones were in use in 1994.

Danmarks Radio is the government broadcasting station and is financed by licence fees. Television is broadcast by *Danmarks Radio* and *TV2* with colour programmes by PAL system. Number of receivers (1 Jan. 1994): TV, 2·05m., including 2m. colour sets; radio, 2·1m.

Cinemas. In 1994 there were 309 auditoria.

Press. In 1994 there were 37 daily newspapers with a combined circulation of 1·62m. on weekdays.

SOCIAL INSTITUTIONS

Justice. The lowest courts of justice are organized in 82 tribunals *(byretter)*, where minor cases are dealt with by a single judge. The tribunals at Copenhagen have 40 judges and Århus 15; the other tribunals have 1 to 10. Cases of greater consequence are dealt with by the 2 superior courts *(Landsretterne)*; these courts are also courts of appeal for the above-named minor cases. The Eastern superior court in Copenhagen has 48 judges and the Western in Viborg, 32. From these an appeal lies to the Supreme Court in Copenhagen, composed of 17 judges. Judges under 65 years of age can be removed only by judicial sentence.

In 1993, 15,835 men and 1,892 women were convicted of violations of the criminal code, fines not included. In 1994, the daily average population in penal institutions was 3,454 men and 173 women, of whom 789 men and 48 women were on remand.

Religion. There is complete religious liberty. The state church is the Evangelica-Lutheran. About 90% of the population belong to it. It is divided into 10 dioceses each with a Bishop. The Bishop together with the Chief Administrative Officer of the county make up the diocesan governing body, responsible for all matters of ecclesiastical local finance and general administration. Bishops are appointed by the Crown after an election by the clergy and parish council members. Each diocese is divided into a number of deaneries (107 in the whole country) each with its Dean and Deanery Committee, who have certain financial powers.

Education. Education has been compulsory since 1814. The *folkeskole* (public primary and lower secondary school) comprises a pre-school class *(børnehaveklasse)*, a 9-year basic school corresponding to the period of compulsory education and a 1-year voluntary tenth form. Compulsory education may be fulfilled either through attending the *folkeskole* or private schools or through home-instruction, on the condition that the instruction given is comparable to that given in the *folkeskole*. The *folkeskole* is mainly a municipal school and no fees are paid. In the year 1993–94, 2,654 primary and lower secondary schools had 587,629 pupils; they employed 56,323 teachers in 1992–93. 16·6% of the total number of schools were private schools and they were attended by 11·3% of the total number of pupils. The 9-year basic school is in practice not streamed. However, a certain differentiation may take place in the eighth and ninth forms.

On completion of the eighth and ninth forms the pupils may sit for the leaving examination of the *folkeskole (folkeskolens afgangsprøve)*. On completion of the tenth form the pupils may sit for either the leaving examination of the *folkeskole (folkeskolens afgangsprøve)* or the advanced leaving examination of the *folkeskole (folkeskolens udvidede afgangsprøve)*.

For 14–18 year olds there is an alternative of completing compulsory education at continuation schools, with the same leaving examinations as in the *folkeskole*. In the year 1993–94 there were 225 continuation schools with 18,639 pupils.

Under certain conditions the pupils may continue school either in the 3-year gymnasium (upper secondary school) or 2-year *studenterkursus* (adult upper secondary school) ending with *studentereksamen* (upper secondary school leaving examination) or in the 2-year higher preparatory examination course ending with the *højere forberedelseseksamen*. There were (1993–94) 153 of these upper secondary schools with 75,299 pupils.

Vocational education and training consists of vocational education, consisting of a 1-year basic course, followed by a second part.

Vocational education and training cover courses in commerce and trade, iron and metal industry, chemical industry, construction industry, graphic industry, service trades, food industry, agriculture, horticulture, forestry and fishery, transport and communication, and health related auxiliary programmes.

In 1993–94, 46,200 students were enrolled within trade and commerce, of whom 89 were in apprenticeship training and 46,083 in vocational education. 73,762 students were enrolled within technical education, of whom 4,620 were in apprenticeship training and 68,621 in vocational education.

Tertiary education comprises all education after the 12th year of education, no matter whether the 3 years after the 9th form of the *folkeskole* have been spent on a course preparing for continued studies *(studentereksamen, højere forberedelseseksamen* or *HHX/HTX*), or a course preparing for a vocation (*EUD*). Tertiary education can be divided into 2 main groups, short courses of further education and long courses of higher education. There was a total of 20,425 students at short courses of further education.

There were 18 teacher-training colleges with 8,739 students and 33 colleges for training of personnel for kindergartens, leisure-time and social care institutions with 10,292 students.

Degree-courses in engineering: The Technical University of Denmark had 7,566 students. 9 engineering colleges had 7,692 students.

Universities: The University of Copenhagen (founded 1479) 27,990 students. The University of Århus (founded in 1928) 17,023 students. The University of Odense (founded in 1964) 8,945 students. Roskilde University Centre (founded in 1972) 4,594 students. Aalborg University Centre (founded in 1974) 8,641 students.

Other types of post-secondary education: The Royal Veterinary and Agricultural University had 3,162 students. The Danish School of Pharmacy had 950 students. The 10 colleges of economics, business administration and modern languages had 28,312 students. The 2 schools of architecture had 1,771 students. 7 academies of music had 1,040 students. The 2 schools of librarianship had 794 students. The Royal Danish School of Educational Studies had 2,536 students. The 5 schools of social work had 1,168 students. The Danish School of Journalism had 862 students. The 10 colleges of physical therapy had 1,782 students. The 2 schools of Midwifery Education had 147 students. The 2 colleges of home economics had 524 students. The School of Visual Arts had 166 students. The 28 schools of nursing had 8,189 students. The 3 military academies had 495 students.

Among adult education the most well-known are *Folkeskolehøjskoler*, folk high schools (with 54,524 students). Adult education in general programmes, single subjects (since 1978, with 95,388 students) and courses for semi-skilled workers and for skilled workers (with 158,146 students).

Social Security. The main body of Danish social welfare legislation is consolidated in 7 acts concerning (1) public health security, (2) sick-day benefits, (3) social pensions (for early retirement and old age), (4) employment injuries insurance, (5) employment services, unemployment insurance and activation measures, (6) social assistance including assistance to handicapped, rehabilitation, child and juvenile guidance, day-care institutions, care of the aged and sick, and (7) family allowances.

Public health security, covering the entire population, provides free medical care, substantial subsidies for certain essential medicines together with some dental care and a funeral allowance. Hospitals are primarily municipal and the hospital treatment is normally free. All employed workers are granted daily sickness allowances, others can have limited daily sickness allowances. Daily cash benefits are granted in the case of temporary incapacity for work because of illness, injury or child-birth to all persons who earn an income derived from personal work. The benefit is paid up to the rate of 100% of the average weekly earnings. There was however a maximum rate of 2,556 kroner a week in 1995.

Social pensions cover the entire population. Entitlement to old-age pensions at the full rates is subject to the condition that the beneficiary has been ordinarily resident in Denmark for a number of years (40). For a shorter period of residence, the benefits are reduced proportionally. The basic amount of the old-age pension in July 1995 was 128,112 kroner a year to married couples and 86,616 to single persons. Various supplementary allowances, depending on age and income, may be payable with the basic amount. Persons aged 60–66 may, depending on health and income, apply for an early retirement pension. Persons over 67 years of age are entitled to the basic amount. The pensions to a married couple are calculated and paid to the husband and the wife separately. Early retirement pension to a disabled person is payable at ages 18–66 years, having regard to the degree of disability (physical as well as otherwise), at a rate of up to 138,168 kroner to a single person. Early retirement pensions may be subject to income regulation. The same applies to the basic amount of the old age pension to persons aged 67–69. Members of the unemployment funds have a right to early retirement pay at ages 60–66 years.

Employment injuries insurance provides for disablement or survivors' pensions and compensations. The scheme covers practically all employees.

Employment services are provided by regional public employment agencies. The insurance against unemployment provides daily allowances and the coverage is about 85% of the unemployed. The unemployment insurance system is based on state subsidized insurance funds linked to the trade unions. The unemployment insurance funds had in Oct. 1995 a membership of 2,212,686.

The *Social Assistance Act* applies to the field of social legislation which rules the individually granted benefits in contrast to the other fields of social legislation which apply to fixed benefits.

Total social expenditure, including hospital and health services, statutory pensions, etc, amounted in the financial year 1993 to 279,787m. kroner.

DIPLOMATIC REPRESENTATIVES

Of Denmark in Great Britain (55 Sloane St., London, SW1X 9SR)
Ambassador: Vacant.

Of Great Britain in Denmark (Kastelsvej 36–40, DK-2100, Copenhagen Ø)
Ambassador: Hugh Arbuthnott, CMG.

Of Denmark in the USA (3200 Whitehaven St., NW, Washington, D.C., 20008-3683)
Ambassador: K.-E. Tygesen.

Of the USA in Denmark (Dag Hammarskjölds Allé 24, DK-2100, Copenhagen Ø)
Ambassador: Edward E. Elson.

Of Denmark to the United Nations
Ambassador: Benny Kimberg.

Further Reading

Statistical Information: Danmarks Statistik (Sejrøgade 11, 2100 Copenhagen Ø.) was founded in 1849 and reorganized in 1966 as an independent institution; it is administratively placed under the Minister of Economic Affairs. Its main publications are: *Statistisk Årbog* (Statistical Yearbook). From 1896; *Statistiske Efterretninger* (Statistical News). *Statistiske Månedsoversigt* Monthly Review of Statistics), *Statistisk tiårsoversigt* (Statistical Ten-Year Review).

Dania polyglotta. Annual Bibliography of Books . . . in Foreign Languages Printed in Denmark. State Library, Copenhagen. Annual
Kongelig Dansk Hof og Statskalender. Copenhagen. Annual
Johansen, H. C., *The Danish Economy in the Twentieth Century.* London, 1987
Miller, K. E., *Denmark.* [Bibliography] Oxford and Santa Barbara, 1987.—*Denmark: a Troubled Welfare State.* Boulder (Colo.), 1991
Petersson, O., *The Government and Politics of the Nordic Countries.* Stockholm, 1994

National library: Det kongelige Bibliotek, P.O.B. 2149, DK-1016 Copenhagen K. *Director:* Erland Kolding Nielsen.

THE FAROE ISLANDS

Føroyar/Færøerne

KEY HISTORICAL EVENTS. A Norwegian province till the peace treaty of 14 January 1814, the islands have been represented by 2 members in the Danish parliament since 1851, and in 1852 they obtained an elected parliament of their own which in 1948 secured a certain degree of home-rule. The islands are not included in the EU, but left EFTA together with Denmark on 31 Dec. 1972.

TERRITORY AND POPULATION. The archipelago is situated due north of Scotland, 300 km from the Shetland Islands, 675 km from Norway and 450 km from Iceland, with a total land area of 1,399 sq. km (540 sq. miles). There are 17 inhabited islands (the main ones being Stremoy, Eysturoy, Vágoy, Suðuroy, Sandoy and Borðoy) and numerous islets, all mountainous and of volcanic origin. The census population in 1977 was 41,969; registered population (31 Dec. 1994) 43,719. The capital is Tórshavn (13,687) on Stremoy. The official languages are Faroese and Danish.

CONSTITUTION AND GOVERNMENT. The parliament comprises 32 members elected by proportional representation by universal suffrage at age 18. Parliament elects a government of at least 3 members which administers home rule. Denmark is represented in parliament by the chief administrator.

At the general elections held on 7 July 1994, 8 seats were won by the Union Party, 6 by the People's Party, 5 by the Social Democratic Party, 4 by the Republican Party, 3 by the Workers' Front, 2 by the Home Rule Party, 2 by the Christian People's Progressive and Fishing Industry Party, and 2 by the Centre Party. A 4-party coalition of the Union, Social Democratic, Workers' and Home Rule Parties was formed on 15 Sept. 1994.

Chief Minister (Lømaður): Edmund Joensen (Unionist).

Local government is vested in the 50 *kommunur*, which have 29 or more inhabitants and income taxes of their own.

Flag: White with a red blue-edged Scandinavian cross.

ECONOMY

Budget. The 1994 Budget balanced at 2,600m. kr.

Currency. Since 1940 the currency has been the Faroese *króna* (kr.) which remains freely interchangeable with the Danish krone.

Banking and Finance. The largest bank is the state-owned Føroya Banki.

ENERGY AND NATURAL RESOURCES

Electricity. There are 5 hydro-electric stations at Vestmanna on Stremoy and one at Eiði on Eysturoy. Total production (1993) 179·8m. kWh, of which hydro-electric 74m. kWh.

Agriculture. Only 2% of the surface is cultivated. The chief use is for grazing. A small amount of potatoes is grown for home consumption. Livestock: Sheep (1988), 55,503; cattle (1993), 2,341.

Fisheries. Deep sea fishing now forms the most important sector of the economy, primarily in the 200-mile exclusive zone but also off Greenland, Iceland, Svalbard and Newfoundland and in the Barents Sea. Total catch (1995) 275,741 tonnes, primarily cod, coalfish, redfish, mackerel, blue whiting, capelin, prawns and herring.

COMMERCE. Exports, mainly fresh, frozen, filleted and salted fish, amounted to 2,076m. kr. in 1994; imports to 1,570m. kr. In 1994 Denmark supplied 35% of imports, Norway 17% and UK 11%; exports were mainly to Denmark (27%), UK (20%), Germany (11%), France (11%) and Spain (5%).

Total trade with UK (British Department of Trade returns, in £1,000 sterling):

	1991	*1992*	*1993*	*1994*	*1995*
Imports to UK	32,515	44,303	52,601	67,936	79,435
Exports and re-exports from UK	7,330	7,755	7,767	10,747	8,334

COMMUNICATIONS

Roads. In 1994 there were 458 km of highways, 11,339 passenger cars and 2,701 commercial vehicles.

Civil Aviation. The airport is on Vágoy, from which there are regular services to Copenhagen, Reykjavík and Glasgow (in summer).

Shipping. The chief port is Tórshavn, with smaller ports at Klaksvik, Vestmanna, Skálafjørður, Tvøroyri, Vágur and Fuglafjørður.

Telecommunications. Radio and TV broadcasting (colour by PAL) are provided by Utvarp Føroya and Sjónvarp Føroya respectively. In 1991 there were 20,000 radio and 13,000 TV receivers.

SOCIAL INSTITUTIONS

Religion. About 80% are Evangelical Lutherans and 20% are Plymouth Brethren or belong to small communities of Roman Catholics, Pentecostal, Adventists, Jehovah Witnesses and Bahai.

Education. In 1993–94 there were 4,873 primary and 3,095 secondary school pupils with 563 teachers.

Health. In 1991 there were 89 doctors, 43 dentists, 10 pharmacists, 17 midwives and 356 nursing personnel. In 1991 there were 3 hospitals with 306 beds.

Further Reading

Årbog for Færøerne. Annual.
Rutherford, G. K., (ed.) *The Physical Environment of the Færoe Islands.* The Hague, 1982
West, J. F., *Faroe.* London, 1973
Wylie, J., *The Faroe Islands: Interpretations of History.* Lexington, 1987

GREENLAND

Grønland/Kalaallit Nunaat

KEY HISTORICAL EVENTS. A Danish possession since 1380, Greenland became on 5 June 1953 an integral part of the Danish kingdom. Following a referendum in Jan. 1979, home rule was introduced from 1 May 1979.

TERRITORY AND POPULATION. Area 2,175,600 sq. km (840,000 sq. miles), made up of 1,833,900 sq. km of ice cap and 341,700 sq. km of ice-free land. The population, 1 Jan. 1993, numbered 55,117, of whom 7,560 were born outside Greenland. In 1993, 44,289 persons were urban; 37,730 were Greenlanders and 6,559 Danes. 1993 population of West Greenland, 52,217; East Greenland, 2,644; North Greenland (Thule), 607, and 564 not belonging to any specific municipality. The capital is Nuuk (Godthåb), with a population in 1993 of 12,181.

CONSTITUTION AND GOVERNMENT. There is a 31-member Home Rule Parliament, which is elected for 4-year terms and meets 2 or 3 times a year. At the elections of 4 March 1995 a Social Democratic Party (SDP)–Liberal Party (LP) coalition gained 22 seats, the Socialist Party, 6, the Centre Party 2 and the Union of Independents 1. The 7-member cabinet is elected by parliament. Ministers need not be members of parliament. In Dec. 1995 the cabinet comprised 5 SDP and 2LP ministers. Greenland elects 2 representatives to the Danish parliament (Folketing). Denmark is represented by an appointed High Commissioner. The *Prime Minister* is Lars Emil Johansen.

Local Government. Administratively Greenland is divided into 3 regions (North, East and West Greenland) and subdivided into 18 municipalities (1 in North, 2 in East and 15 in West Greenland). Town councils are elected for 4-year terms. There were elections in April 1993.

ECONOMY

Budget. Revenue, 1991: 5,985m. kroner; expenditure, 5,928m. kroner.

Currency. The Danish krone remains the legal currency.

Banking and Finance. There are 2 private banks, Grønlandsbanken and Nuna Bank.

ENERGY AND NATURAL RESOURCES

Electricity. Production (1991) 160·5m. kWh.

Agriculture. Livestock, 1992: Sheep, 17,900; domesticated reindeer, 5,600.

Fisheries. Fishing and product-processing are the principal industry. In 1992 the catch totalled 101,100 tonnes (shrimps, 71,300 tonnes; cod, 10,300 tonnes). In 1992 120 whales were caught (subject to the International Whaling Commission's regulations) and 69,000 sealskins sold.

INDUSTRY. Production of lead and zinc concentrates was in 1989 about 35,500 tonnes and 130,500 tonnes respectively. The mine closed down in 1990. 6 shipyards repair and maintain ships and produce industrial tanks, containers and steel constructions for building.

COMMERCE. Imports (c.i.f. Greenland) (in 1m. kroner): 1990, 2,756; 1991, 2,576; 1992, 2,737. Exports (f.o.b. Greenland) (in 1m. kroner): 1990, 2,795; 1991, 2,178; 1992, 2,000. Trade is mainly with Denmark. In 1992 shrimps and products made up 76% of exports.

Total trade with UK (British Department of Trade returns, in £1,000 sterling):

	1991	*1992*	*1993*	*1994*	*1990*
Imports to UK	5,039	3,098	5,904	11,295	9,549
Exports and re-exports from UK	635	1,034	2,209	927	1,884

COMMUNICATIONS

Civil Aviation. Greenlandair operates services to Iceland and Frobisher Bay (Canada) and domestic services. Icelandair and SAS also serve Greenland. There are international airports at Søndre Srømfjord and Narsarsuaq, and 18 local airports/heliports with scheduled services. There were 64,246 international passengers in 1992.

Shipping. There are no overseas passenger services. In 1991, 67,900 passengers were carried on coastal services. There are cargo services to Denmark, Iceland and St John's (Canada).

Telecommunications. In 1992 there were 16,800 telephones. The government Kalaallit Nunaata Radioa provides broadcasting services, and there are also local services. In 1991 there were estimated to be 25,000 radio and 12,000 TV sets (colour by PAL). Several towns have local television stations. In 1984 there were 10,000 television sets and 13,500 radio sets.

SOCIAL INSTITUTIONS

Justice. The High Court in Nuuk comprises one professional judge and 2 lay magistrates, while there are 18 district courts under lay assessors.

Religion. About 98% of the population are Evangelical Lutherans. In 1991 there were 17 parishes with 83 churches and chapels and 26 ministers.

Education. Education is compulsory from 6 to 15 years. A further 3 years of schooling are optional. There were (1990–91) 9,249 pupils in 86 primary comprehensive schools. On 1 Sept. 1988, 2,297 students were enrolled in vocational training.

Health. The medical service is free to all inhabitants. There is a central hospital in Nuuk and 18 smaller district hospitals. In 1990 there were 64 doctors and 513 hospital beds.

Further Reading

The Greenland Home Rule Authority has published since 1989 *Greenland/Kalaallit Nunaat: Statistical Yearbook.*
Gad, F., *A History of Greenland.* 2 vols. London, 1970–1973
Miller, K. E., *Greenland* [Bibliography]. Oxford and Santa Barbara (CA), 1991

Greenland National Library, P.O. Box 1011, DK-3900, Nuuk
Greenland Statistical Office, Nuuk.

DJIBOUTI

Jumhouriyya Djibouti

(Republic of Djibouti)

Capital: Djibouti
Population: 586,000 (1995)
HDI/world rank: 0·336/154 (1992)

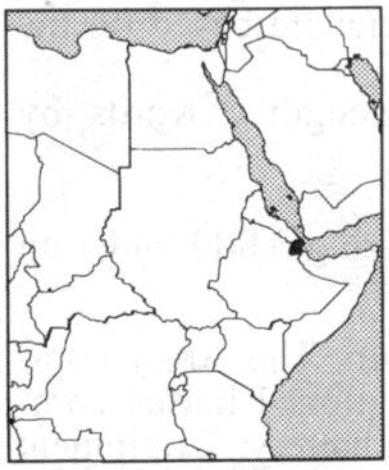

KEY HISTORICAL EVENTS. At a referendum held on 19 March 1967, 60% of the electorate voted for continued association with France rather than independence and the new statute for the territory came into being on 5 July 1967. France affirmed that the Territory of the Afars and the Issas was destined for independence but no date was fixed. Legislative elections were held on 8 May and independence as the Republic of Djibouti was achieved on 27 June 1977.

Afar rebels in the north belonging to the Front for the Restoration of Unity and Democracy (FRUD) signed a 'Peace and National Reconciliation Agreement' with the government on 26 Dec. 1994 envisaging the formation of a national coalition government, the redrafting of the electoral roll and the integration of FRUD militants into the armed forces and civil service.

TERRITORY AND POPULATION. Djibouti is in effect a city-state surrounded by a semi-desert hinterland bounded in the north-west by Eritrea, north-east by the Gulf of Aden, south-east by Somalia and south-west by Ethiopia. The area is 23,200 sq. km (8,958 sq. miles). The population was estimated in 1995 at 586,000 (81% urban), of whom about half were Somali (Issa, Gadaboursi and Issaq), 35% Afar and some Europeans (mainly French) and Arabs. Births in 1989, 9,920; infant mortality, 114 per 1,000 live births. Growth rate, 1992. 3·1%. Expectation of life, 1990, 48 years. There are 5 administrative districts (areas in sq. km): Ali-Sabieh (2,600); Dikhil (7,800); Djibouti (600); Obock (5,700); Tadjoura (7,300). The capital is Djibouti (1995 population, 383,000).

CLIMATE. Conditions are hot throughout the year, with very little rain. Djibouti. Jan. 78°F (25·6°C), July 96°F (35·6°C). Annual rainfall 5" (130 mm).

CONSTITUTION AND GOVERNMENT. After a referendum at which turn-out was 70% a new constitution was approved on 4 Sept. 1992 by 96·63% of votes cast which permits the existence of up to 4 political parties. Parties are required to maintain an ethnic balance in their membership. The *President* is directly-elected for a renewable 6-year term. Parliament is a 65-member *Chamber of Deputies* elected for 5-year terms.

At the presidential elections of 7 May 1993 the electorate was 150,487; turn-out was 50·26%. Hassan Gouled Aptidou was elected against 3 opponents by 60·71% of votes cast.

At the parliamentary elections of 18 Dec. 1992 turn-out was 48·5%. The RPP won 65 seats with 74·6% of votes cast, the Party of Democratic Renewal nil with 25·4%.

President: Hassan Gouled Aptidon (elected 1977, re-elected 1981, 1987 and 1993).

The Council of Ministers in Nov. 1995 was composed as follows:

Prime Minister, Planning and Territorial Administration: Barkat Gourad Hamadou.

Interior and Decentralization: Idriss Harbi Farah. *Justice and Islamic Affairs:* Moumin Bahdou Farah. *Foreign Affairs and International Co-operation:* Mohammed Moussa Chehem. *Defence:* Ahmed Boulaleh Barreh. *Finance and Economy:* Mohammed Ali Mohammed. *Industry, Energy and Mines:* Abdi Farah.

Labour and Professional Organizations: Osman Robleh Daach. *Education:* Ahmed Guire Waberi. *Public Works, Construction and Housing:* Attayeh Ismail Waiss. *Health and Social Affairs:* Ali Mohammed Daoud. *Ports, Transport and Telecommunications:* Saleh Omar Hildid. *Agriculture and Water Resources:* Ougoure Kifleh Ahmed. *Youth, Sport and Culture:* Abdou Balad Abdou. *Civil Service and Administrative Reform:* Mohammed Dini Farah. *Commerce and Tourism:* Rifki Abdoulkader.

National flag: Horizontally blue over green, with a white triangle based on the hoist charged with a red star.

National anthem: 'Hinjinne u sara kaca' ('Arise with strength'); words by A. Elmi, tune by A. Robleh.

DEFENCE. France maintains a naval base and forces numbering 3,900 under an agreement renewed in Feb. 1991.

Army. There are 3 Army commands: North, Central and South. The Army comprises 1 infantry battalion, 1 armoured squadron, 1 support battalion, 1 border commando battalion and 1 parachute company, and 1 artillery battery. Equipment includes 31 armoured cars. The strength of the Army was (1996) 8,000. There is also a paramilitary Gendarmerie of some 1,200 and an Interior Ministry National Security Force of 3,000.

Navy. A coastal patrol is maintained consisting of 8 small inshore patrol craft and some boats. Personnel (1995), 100.

Air Force. There is a small air force. There are no combat aircraft. Fixed-wing aircraft comprise 1 An-28 transport and 2 Cessna 206s for liaison. There are also 3 Ecureuil, 3 Mi-8 and 2 Mi-2 helicopters. Personnel (1995), 200.

INTERNATIONAL RELATIONS

Membership. Djibouti is a member of the UN, OAU, the Arab League and is an ACP state of the EU.

ECONOMY

Budget. Revenue for 1989 was 22,393m. Djibouti francs and expenditure 22,480m. Djibouti francs.

Currency. The currency is the *Djibouti franc* (DJF) notionally of 100 *centimes.* There are coins of 10, 20, 50, 100, 500 and notes of 1,000, 5,000 and 10,000 Djibouti francs. 10,402m. Djibouti francs were in circulation in 1993. In March 1996, £1 = 244·54; US$1 = 160; DM1 = 108·41 Djibouti francs.

Banking and Finance. The Banque Nationale de Djibouti is the bank of issue (*Governor*, Luc Aden). There are 6 commercial banks.

Weights and Measures. The metric system is in use.

ENERGY AND NATURAL RESOURCES

Electricity. Production (1989) 187·85m. kWh. Installed capacity, 80,100 kW.

Agriculture. Agricultural land was 674 ha in 1989, of which 407 ha were exploited, mainly by market gardening. Tomato production (1992) 1,000 tonnes. Livestock (1992): 180,000 cattle, 450,000 sheep, 506,000 goats, 61,000 camels.

Fisheries. The catch in 1989 was 389·28 tonnes.

INDUSTRY. Services provided 79% of GDP in 1990.

Labour. In 1986 there were 2,134 persons employed in construction and 1,235 in manufacturing. A 40-hour working week is standard. In 1989 there was a minimum monthly wage of 15,850 Djibouti francs.

FOREIGN ECONOMIC RELATIONS. Foreign debt totalled US$189·5m. in 1992.

Commerce. The main economic activity is the operation of the port; in 1990 only 36% of imports were destined for Djibouti. Exports are largely re-exports. The chief imports are cotton goods, sugar, cement, flour, fuel oil and vehicles; the chief exports are hides, cattle and coffee (transit from Ethiopia). In 1989 France supplied 27·9% of imports; Ethiopia, 12·6%.

	1985	*1986*	*1987*	*1988*	*1989*
Imports	35,670	33,106	36,487	35,640	35,054
Exports	2,488	3,628	4,976	4,111	4,459

Total trade between Djibouti and UK (British Department of Trade returns, in £1,000 sterling):

	1991	*1992*	*1993*	*1994*	*1995*
Imports to UK	119	58	1,146	373	62
Exports and re-exports from UK	21,889	25,472	21,601	13,701	13,699

Tourism. 40,762 visitors spent 76,189 nights in 1989.

COMMUNICATIONS

Roads. There were (1993) 2,905 km of roads, of which 281 km were hard-surfaced. In 1987 there were 11,799 passenger cars and 1,501 commercial vehicles.

Railways. For the line from Djibouti to Addis Ababa, of which 106 km lie within Djibouti, *see* ETHIOPIA: Communications. Traffic carried is mainly in transit to and from Ethiopia.

Civil Aviation. There is an international airport at Djibouti (Ambouli). The national airlines are Daallo Airlines, which had 6 aircraft in 1995, and Puntavia Airlines, which operated 3 B-727-200s and 5 other aircraft. Services are also provided by Aeroflot, Air France, Air Tanzania, Ethiopian Airlines and Yemenia. In 1993 Djibouti airport handled 305,155 passengers and 15,000 tonnes of freight.

Shipping. Djibouti is a free port and container terminal. 950 ships berthed in 1989, (including 177 warships) totalling 3·87m. NRT. 3,211 passengers embarked or disembarked, and 0·87m. tonnes of cargo were handled (1·48m. tonnes in 1992). In 1995 the merchant marine totalled 4,800 GRT.

Telecommunications. Number of telephones (1989), 5,100. The state-run *Radiodiffusion-Télévision de Djibouti* broadcasts in French, Somali, Afar and Arabic. There is a television transmitter in Djibouti, broadcasting for 35 hours a week. Number of receivers (1993): Radio, 30,000; TV, 17,000 (colour by SECAM).

SOCIAL INSTITUTIONS

Justice. There is a Court of First Instance and a Court of Appeal in the capital. The judicial system is based on Islamic law.

Religion. In 1995, 96% of the population were Moslem, with about 12,000 Roman Catholics and 10,000 Protestant and Orthodox.

Education. In 1989–90 there were 57 state primary schools (and 9 private) with 27,884 (2,895) pupils and 641 (66) teachers, 10 (6) secondary schools, with 6,892 (946) pupils and 307 teachers. There was an *école normale* with 112 pupils and 12 teachers. Professional education is all in private hands. In 1989–90 there were 11 institutions and 1,074 students.

Health. In 1993 there were 2 hospitals, 6 medical centres and 21 dispensaries. There were 91 doctors, 10 dentists and 14 pharmacists in 1989.

DIPLOMATIC REPRESENTATIVES

Of Djibouti in Great Britain
Ambassador: Ahmd Omar Farah (resides in Paris).

Of Great Britain in Djibouti
Ambassador: D. R. C. Christopher (resides in Addis Ababa).

Of the USA in Djibouti (Plateau du Serpent Blvd., Djibouti)
Ambassador: Martin L. Cheshes.

Of Djibouti to the United Nations and in the USA
Ambassador: Roble Olhaye.

Further Reading

Direction Nationale de la Statistique. *Annuaire Statistique de Djibouti*
Schraeder, P. J., *Djibouti*. [Bibliography] Oxford and Santa Barbara, 1990

National statistical office: Direction Nationale de la Statistique, Ministère du Commerce, des Transports et du Tourisme, BP 1846, Djibouti

DOMINICA

Commonwealth of Dominica

Capital: Roseau
Population: 74,200 (1994)
GNP per capita: US$2,830 (1994)
HDI/world rank: 0·776/69 (1992)

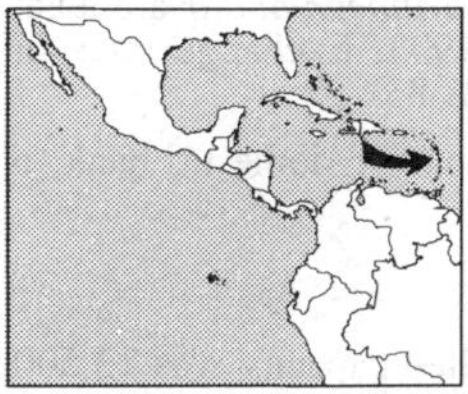

KEY HISTORICAL EVENTS. Dominica was discovered by Columbus. It was a British possession from 1805, a member of the Federation of the West Indies 1958–62, an Associated State of the UK, 1967–78 and became an independent republic as the Commonwealth of Dominica on 3 Nov. 1978.

TERRITORY AND POPULATION. Dominica is an island in the Windward group of the West Indies situated between Martinique and Guadeloupe. It has an area of 748·5 sq. km (289·5 sq. miles) and a population at the 1991 census of 71,794. 1994 estimate, 74,200. The chief town, Roseau, had 15,853 inhabitants in 1991.

The population is mainly of African and mixed origins, with small white and Asian minorities. There is a Carib settlement of about 500, almost entirely of mixed blood.

The official language is English, though 95% of the population speak a French Creole.

CLIMATE. A tropical climate, with pleasant conditions between Dec. and March, but there is a rainy season from June to Oct., when hurricanes may occur. Rainfall is heavy, with coastal areas having 70" (1,750 mm) but the mountains may have up to 2250" (6,250 mm). Roseau. Jan. 76°F (24·2°C), July 81°F (27·2°C). Annual rainfall 78" (1,956 mm).

CONSTITUTION AND GOVERNMENT. The head of state is the *President*, nominated by the Prime Minister and the Leader of the Opposition, and elected for a 5-year term (renewable once) by the House of Assembly. The *House of Assembly* has 21 elected and 9 members nominated by the President. Elections were held on 6 June 1995. The United Workers Party (UWP) won 11 seats (6 in 1990), the Dominica Labour Party (DLP), 5 (4) and the Dominica Freedom Party 5 (11).

President: Crispin Sorhaindo, OBE (elected 4 Oct. 1993, sworn in 25 Oct.).

The Cabinet in Nov. 1995 was composed as follows:

Prime Minister and Minister of External Affairs, Legal Affairs and Labour: Edison James (b. 1944; UWP).

Finance, Industry and Planning: Julius Timothy. *Tourism, Ports and Employment:* Norris Prevost. *Health and Social Security:* Doreen Paul. *Trade and Marketing:* Norris Charles. *Community Development and Women's Affairs:* Gertrude Roberts. *Communications, Works and Housing:* Earl Williams. *Agriculture and the Environment:* Peter Carbon. *Education, Sports and Youth Affairs:* Ronald Green.

National flag: Green with a cross over all of yellow, black, and white pieces, and in the centre a red disc charged with a Sisserou parrot in natural colours facing the hoist within a ring of 10 green yellow-bordered stars.

National anthem: 'Isle of beauty, isle of splendour'; words by W. Pond, tune by L. M. Christian.

Local Government. Roseau and Portsmouth have town councils with powers to raise property taxes. There are 25 rural districts administered by partially-elected village councils.

INTERNATIONAL RELATIONS

Membership. Dominica is a member of the UN, OAS, CARICOM, the Commonwealth and is an ACP state of the EU.

ECONOMY

Budget. The 1994–95 budget allocated US$106·1m. to current expenditure and US$41m. to capital expenditure. Revenue was expected to be US$220·8m.

Currency. The French *franc,* the £ sterling and the *East Caribbean dollar* are legal tender. Foreign exchange reserves were US$19·9m. in 1993. Exchange rates in March 1996: £1 = EC$4·13; US$1 = EC$2·70; DM1 = EC$1·83.

Banking and Finance. In 1995 there were 3 foreign banks, 1 domestic bank, a development bank and a credit union.

ENERGY AND NATURAL RESOURCES

Electricity. There is a hydro-electric power station. Installed capacity was 13,500 kWh in 1995. Production (1987) 16m. kWh.

Agriculture. In 1994, agriculture provided 30% of GDP and employed 26% of the labour force. Production (1992): Bananas, 70,000 tonnes; coconuts, 12,000 tonnes. Livestock (1992): Cattle, 9,000; pigs, 5,000; sheep, 8,000; goats, 10,000.

INDUSTRY. Manufactures include clothing, footwear, fruit juice, rum, electronic assemblies, candles and paint.

Labour. In 1994 the minimum wage was US$0·75 an hour.

FOREIGN ECONOMIC RELATIONS. Total external debt in 1994 was US$93·1.

Commerce. In 1993 imports were worth US$98·8m. and exports US$48·3m. Chief products: Bananas, soap, fruit juices, essential oils, coconuts, vegetables, fruit and fruit preparations, and alcoholic drinks.

Total trade between Dominica and UK (British Department of Trade returns, in £1,000 sterling):

	1991	*1992*	*1993*	*1994*	*1995*
Imports to UK	25,221	21,870	23,534	18,892	15,324
Exports and re-exports from UK	11,573	8,559	10,226	8,055	9,038

Tourism. In 1993, there were 87,836 cruise ship visitors and 52,200 staying visitors.

COMMUNICATIONS

Roads. In 1994 there were 750 km of road of which 500 km were paved.

Civil Aviation. There are international airports at Melville Hall and Canefield. There are direct flights from Antigua, Barbados, Grenada, Guadeloupe, Puerto Rico, St Lucia, St Maarten, St Thomas, St Vincent, Trinidad and the US Virgin Islands. Services are provided by Air Anguilla, Air Caraïbes, Cardinal Airlines, Helenair, Air Guadeloupe, LIAT and Windward Island Airways.

Shipping. There are deep-water harbours at Roseau and Woodbridge Bay. Roseau has a cruise ship berth.

Telecommunications. Number of telephones, 1993, 14,613. Radio and television broadcasting is provided by the part government-controlled, part-commercial Dominica Broadcasting Corporation. There are also 2 religious radio networks, 2 commercial TV channels (colour by NTSC) and a commercial cable service. In 1993 there were 45,000 radio and 5,200 TV sets.

Cinemas. In 1987 there was 1 cinema with a seating capacity of 1,000.

Press. In 1994 there were 3 newspapers, including 1 government and 1 independent weekly.

SOCIAL INSTITUTIONS

Justice. There is a supreme court and 12 magistrates' courts. Law is based on UK common law as exercised by the Eastern Caribbean Supreme Court on St Lucia. Final appeal lies to the UK Privy Council.

In 1995 the police force numbered 439; it has a residual responsibility for defence.

Religion. 77% of the population was Roman Catholic in 1995.

Education. In 1994 adult literacy was 90%. In 1993–94 there were 54 private kindergartens. Education is free and compulsory between the ages of 5 and 15 years. In 1993–94 there were 65 primary and 13 secondary schools, a teachers' training college and a Community College with academic and technical divisions.

Health. In 1994 there were 54 hospitals and health centres with 312 beds, 23 doctors, 6 dentists, 27 pharmacists and 265 nursing personnel.

DIPLOMATIC REPRESENTATIVES

Of Dominica in Great Britain (1 Collingham Gdns, London SW5 0HW)
High Commissioner: Ashworth Elwin.

Of Great Britain in Dominica
High Commissioner: R. Thomas, CMG (resides in Bridgetown).

Of Dominica in the USA
Ambassador: Vacant.

Of the USA in Dominica
Ambassador: Jeanette W. Hyde.

Of Dominica to the United Nations
Ambassador: Vacant.

Further Reading

Baker, P. L., *Centring the Periphery: Chaos, Order and the Ethnohistory of Dominica:* McGill-Queen's Univ. Press, 1994
Myers, R. A., *Dominica.* [Bibliography] Oxford and Santa Barbara (CA), 1987

DOMINICAN REPUBLIC

República Dominicana

Capital: Santo Domingo
Population: 7·77m. (1994)
GNP per capita: US$1,320 (1994)
HDI/world rank: 0·705/96 (1992)

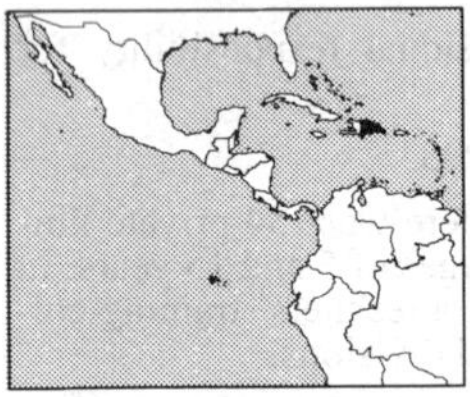

KEY HISTORICAL EVENTS. On 5 Dec. 1492 Columbus discovered the island of Hispaniola (at times also known as Santo Domingo and Quisqueya). The city of Santo Domingo, founded by his brother, Bartholomew, in 1496, is the oldest city in the Americas. The western third of the island—now the Republic of Haiti—was later occupied and colonized by the French. The Spanish colony declared its independence in 1821. It was occupied by Haiti from 1822 to 1844, when the Dominican Republic was founded and a constitution adopted. The country was occupied by the USA from 1916 until 1924. In 1930 Rafael Trujillo established a dictatorship which lasted until his assassination in May 1961. The deposition of the president in 1965 led to civil war and a second US intervention. Joaquín Balaguer was elected president in 1966 and a new constitution was promulgated.

TERRITORY AND POPULATION. The Dominican Republic occupies the eastern portion (about two-thirds) of the island of Hispaniola, the western division forming the Republic of Haiti. The frontier with Haiti is closed. The area is 48,442 sq. km (18,700 sq. miles). The 1990 area and population of the 29 provinces and National District (Santo Domingo area):

	Area (in sq. km)	*Population*		*Area (in sq. km)*	*Population*
La Altagracia	3,084	111,241	Pedernales	967	18,896
Azua	2,430	195,420	Peravia	1,622	186,810
Bahoruco	1,376	87,376	Puerto Plata	1,881	229,738
Barahona	2,528	152,405	La Romana	541	169,223
Dajabón	890	64,123	Salcedo	533	110,216
Distrito Nacional	1,477	2,411,895	Samaná	989	73,002
Duarte	1,292	261,725	Sánchez Ramírez	1,174	140,635
Espaillat	1,000	182,248	San Cristóbal	1,564	320,921
La Estrelleta	1,788	72,651	San Juan	3,561	266,628
Hato Mayor	1,330	77,823	San Pedro de Macorís	1,166	197,862
Independencia	1,861	43,077	Santiago	3,122	704,835
María Trinidad Sánchez	1,310	125,148	Santiago Rodríguez	1,020	61,570
Monseñor Nouel	1,004	124,794	El Seíbo	1,659	97,590
Monte Cristi	1,989	92,678	Valverde	570	111,470
Monte Plata	2,179	174,799	La Vega	2,373	303,047

Census (1981) 5,647,977. Estimate (1994) 7·77m. (58% urban). Vital statistics rates, 1990: Birth, 30 (per 1,000 population); death, 6·5. Life expectancy, 1992, 67 years.

Population of the main towns (1991 estimate, in 1,000): Santo Domingo, the capital, 2,055; Santiago de los Caballeros, 375; La Vega, 189; San Francisco de Macorís, 162; San Pedro de Macorís, 137; La Romana, 136.

The population is mainly composed of a mixed race of European (Spanish) and African blood. The official language is Spanish; about 150,000 persons speak a Haitian-French creole.

CLIMATE. A tropical maritime climate with most rain falling in the summer months. The rainy season extends from May to Nov. and amounts are greatest in the north and east. Hurricanes may occur from June to Nov. Santo Domingo. Jan. 75°F (23·9°C), July 81°F (27·2°C). Annual rainfall 56" (1,400 mm).

CONSTITUTION AND GOVERNMENT. The constitution dates from 28 Nov. 1966.

The *President* is elected for 4 years, by direct vote, and has executive power. A constitional amendment of Aug. 1994 prohibits the President from serving consecutive terms. There is a bicameral legislature, the *Congress*, comprising a 30-member Senate (one member for each province and one for the National District of Santo Domingo) and a 120-member Chamber of Deputies, both elected for 4-year terms at the same date as the President. Citizens are entitled to vote at the age of 18, or less when married.

Presidential and parlimentary elections were held on 16 May 1994. The electorate was 3·3m. President Balaguer was re-elected for a 7th term (restricted to May 1996) by 42·4% of votes cast against 1 opponent.

Presidential elections were scheduled for May 1996.

President: Dr Joaquín Balaguer (b. 1907; Social Christian Reform Party; sworn in, 16 Aug. 1994).

Vice-President: Jacinto Peynado.

In Sept. 1995 the government comprised:

Finance: Florencio Lorenzo Silva. *Foreign:* Carlos Morales Troncoso. *Education and Culture:* Jacqueline Malagón. *Labour:* Rafael Albuquerque. *Health and Social Welfare:* Dr Miguel Strepán. *Agriculture:* Luis Toral Córdoba. *Industry and Commerce:* Juan González Pérez. *Sport and Recreation:* Crístobal Marte. *Interior and Police:* Dr Atilio Guzmán Fernández. *Armed Forces and Defence:* Maj.-Gen. Constantino Matos Villanueva. *Tourism:* Jorge Elías. *Without Portfolio:* Domingo Gutiérrez.

National flag: Blue, red; quartered by a white cross.

National anthem: 'Quisqueyanos valientes, alcemos' ('Valient Quisqueyans, Let us raise our voices'); words by E. Prud'homme, tune by J. Reyes.

Local Government: The 29 provinces have a governor appointed by the President. They and the National District are divided into 18 municipal districts and 72 municipalities run by elected councils. Elections for mayors took place simultaneously with the presidential and parliamentary elections of May 1994.

DEFENCE

Army. There are 3 defence zones. The Army has a strength (1996) of about 15,000. It is organized in 4 infantry brigades, 1 artillery, 1 engineer, 1 special forces and 1 armoured battalion and a Presidential Guard. Equipment includes 15 light tanks. There is a paramilitary National Police 15,000 strong.

Navy. The Navy is equipped with former US vessels. The combatant force consists of 1 frigate (built 1944) acting as the flagship, 6 offshore, 2 coastal and 8 inshore patrol craft. There is 1 utility landing craft and support is provided by 1 small oiler, 1 ocean tug and some 12 harbour and service craft. Personnel in 1995 totalled 4,000, based at Santo Domingo and Calderas.

Air Force. The Air Force, with HQ at San Isidoro, has 1 combat squadron with 8 Cessna A-37s; 1 squadron with 6 Bell 205A-1, 1 Dauphin and 1 OH-6a helicopters; 1 transport squadron with 3 C-47s, 5 Cessna 337s and some smaller communications aircraft, and 10 T-34B Mentor and 5 Cessna T-41 trainers. Personnel strength was (1995) 5,500.

INTERNATIONAL RELATIONS

Membership. The Dominican Republic is a member of the UN and OAS and an ACP member of the EU.

ECONOMY

Policy. In Jan. 1995 subsidies to the 33 state companies were discontinued. 20 state companies were put up for sale in Nov. 1995.

Budget. In 1993 government revenue was RD$19,415·9m. and expenditure RD$20,256·7m. Tax revenue was RD$18,029·5m. (including customs duties, RD$6,696·4m.); non-tax revenue, RD$1,386·4m.; extraordinary items, RD$1,299·3m.

Currency. The unit of currency is the *peso oro* (DOP) of 100 *centavos.* There are coins of 1, 5, 10, 25 and 50 centavos and RD$1 peso oro, and notes of RD$1, 5, 10, 20, 50, 100, 500 and 1,000. RD$52,699m. were in circulation in 1993. Inflation was 2·7% in 1993 (4·6% in 1992). Gold reserves were US$6·8m. in 1993; foreign exchange reserves, US$564·5m.

In March 1996, £1 = RD$21·24; US$1 = RD$13·90; DM1 = RD$9·42.

Banking and Finance. In 1947 the Central Bank was established (*Governor*, Mario Read Vittini). Its total assets were RD$34,958·7m. in 1993. In 1993 there were 20 commercial banks (2 foreign); total assets, RD$30,765·5m.

The Santo Domingo Securities Exchange is a member of the Association of Central American Stock Exchanges (Bolcen).

Weights and Measures. The metric system was adopted on 1 Aug. 1913, but English and Spanish units have remained in common use.

ENERGY AND NATURAL RESOURCES

Electricity. Installed capacity, 1993, 1,500 MW, of which 356 MW was hydro-electric. Output, 1992, 4,626,147 MWh (660,907 MWh hydro-electric).

Minerals. Bauxite output in 1988 was 167,800 tonnes, but had declined to nil by 1992. Output, 1992: Ferro-nickel, 58,313 tonnes; gold, 76,349 troy oz.; silver, 478,320 troy oz.

Agriculture. Agriculture and processing are the chief source of income, sugar cultivation being the principal industry. In 1990 there were 1m. ha of arable land, 0·45m. ha of permanent cropland and 2·09m. ha of pasture.

Production, 1992 (in tonnes): Sugar-cane, 6,915,786 (8·37m. in 1988); cocoa, 47,050; coffee, 82,056; bananas, 1·22m. items; rice, 565,653; tobacco, 19,895 (27,976 in 1988); beans, 37,086; maize, 46,154; tomatoes, 89,486.

Livestock in 1991: 2·25m. cattle, 435,000 pigs, 0·12m. sheep. Livestock products, 1992: Poultry meat, 122,011 tonnes; other meat, 83,029 tonnes; 839·36m. eggs; milk, 18·89m. litres.

Forestry. Forests and woodlands covered 0·61m. ha in 1990. In 1991 1,611,780 tonnes of timber were cut.

Fisheries. The total catch (1991) was 21,815 tonnes.

INDUSTRY. Manufacturing contributed 17% of GDP in 1991. Production, 1992 (in tonnes): Raw sugar, 427,950; refined sugar, 90,021; cement, 1,364,877; paint, 16,328; beer, 195·64m. litres; rum, 43·41m. litres; cigarettes, 220,203 packets (of 20).

Labour. Average monthly wage, 1992, RD$2,136·98.

FOREIGN ECONOMIC RELATIONS. In 1994 there were 38 industrial free zones (employing 164,296 persons), which enjoy duty-free imports of raw materials and various tax exemptions. Legislation of 1995 allows foreign investments of 100% in all sectors except industries affecting the environment and arms production. Profits may be repatriated. Foreign debt was US$4,500m. in 1994.

Commerce. Total imports and exports in US$1m.:

	1989	*1990*	*1991*	*1992*	*1993*
Imports	1,964	1,793	1,729	2,174	2,118
Exports	924	735	658	562	530

Main exports, 1993 (in tonnes): Raw sugar, 342,197 (513,920 in 1988); molasses, 176,234; coffee, 18,079; cocoa, 42,077; tobacco, 11,410; ferro-nickel, 67,405; gold,

11,718 troy oz. (139,969 troy oz. in 1990); silver, 53,496 troy oz. (734,987 troy oz. in 1990). Main imports (in US$1m.): Oil and products, 453; coal, 10·3; foodstuffs, 11·6; wheat, 38·1.

Main export markets (trade in US$1m.), 1992: USA, 343·33; Netherlands, 74·73; South Korea, 25·29; Belgium, 17·42; Japan, 16·85.

Total trade between the Dominican Republic and UK (British Department of Trade returns, in £1,000 sterling):

	1991	*1992*	*1993*	*1994*	*1995*
Imports to UK	22,076	19,792	21,645	20,687	24,343
Exports and re-exports from UK	19,773	16,668	24,316	24,708	27,946

Tourism. 2·04m. tourists visited in 1993, bringing foreign exchange earnings of US$1,233m.

COMMUNICATIONS

Roads. In 1991 there were 4,325 km of first- and second-class roads. In 1991 there were 242,038 motor vehicles.

Railways. Some 142 km of the Dominican Government Railway remains in use between Guayubin and the port of Pepillo. 12 lines exist to serve the sugar industry, totalling 1,600 km.

Civil Aviation. There are international airports at Santo Domingo (Punta Caucedo), Puerto Plata, La Romana and Punta Cana. Dominican Airlines ceased operations in 1995 and was put up for privatization. Bavaro Sunlight operates scheduled domestic services.

Shipping. The main ports are Santo Domingo, Puerto Plata, La Romana and Haina. In 1995 the merchant marine totalled 2,833 GRT.

Telecommunications. There were 0·43m. telephone lines in 1994.

There were (1994) more than 170 broadcasting stations in Santo Domingo and other towns; this includes the 2 government stations. There were 7 television stations (colour by NTSC). In 1993 there were 1·15m. radio and 728,000 television receivers.

Press (1995). There were 9 dailies and 1 weekly.

SOCIAL INSTITUTIONS

Justice. The judicial power resides in the Supreme Court of Justice, the courts of appeal, the courts of first instance, the communal courts and other tribunals created by special laws, such as the land courts. The Supreme Court consists of a president and 8 judges chosen by the Senate, and the procurator-general, appointed by the executive; it supervises the lower courts. Each province forms a judicial district, as does the National District, and each has its own procurator fiscal and court of first instance; these districts are subdivided, in all, into 97 municipalities, each with one or more local justices. The death penalty was abolished in 1924.

Religion. The religion of the state is Roman Catholic; there were 6·78m. adherents in 1992.

Education. Adult illiteracy was 25% in 1992. Primary instruction (5,956 schools) is free and compulsory for children between 7 and 14 years of age; there are also secondary, normal, vocational and special schools, all of which are either wholly maintained by the State or state-aided. In 1994–95, there were 4 universities, 3 Roman Catholic universities, 1 Adventist university, 3 technological universities and 1 Roman Catholic university college, and 5 other higher education institutions.

Health. There were, in 1980, 2,142 doctors and 8,953 hospital beds.

DIPLOMATIC REPRESENTATIVES

Of the Dominican Republic in Great Britain
Ambassador: Dr Alfonso Canto Dinzey (resides in Paris).

Of Great Britain in the Dominican Republic
Ambassador: R. Thomson (resides in Caracas).

Of the Dominican Republic in the USA (1715 22nd St., NW, Washington, D.C., 20008)
Ambassador: José del Carmen Ariza.

Of the USA in the Dominican Republic (Calle Cesar Nicolas Penson, Santo Domingo)
Ambassador: Donna J. Hrinak.

Of the Dominican Republic to the United Nations
Ambassador: Vacant.

Further Reading

Atkins, G. P., *Arms and Politics in the Dominican Republic.* London, 1981
Bell, I., *The Dominican Republic.* London, 1980
Black, J. K., *The Dominican Republic: Politics and Development in an Unsovereign State.* London, 1986
Schoenhals, K., *Dominican Republic:* [Bibliography]. London and Santa Barbara (CA), 1990
Wiarda, H. J. and Kryzanek, M. J., *The Dominican Republic: A Caribbean Crucible.* Boulder, 1982

ECUADOR

República del Ecuador

Capital: Quito
Population: 11·7m. (1996)
GNP per capita: US$1,310 (1994)
HDI/world rank: 0·784/68 (1992)

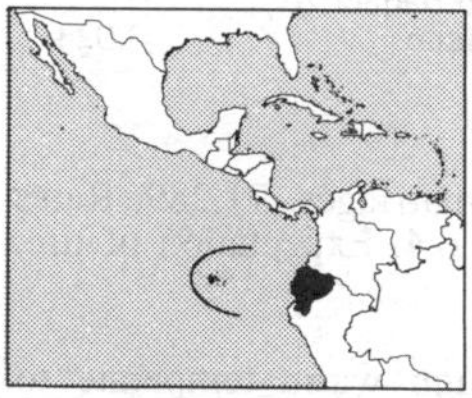

KEY HISTORICAL EVENTS. Being a Spanish colony since 1532, Ecuador became independent in 1822 as part of the federation of Gran Colombia. It seceded in 1830.

TERRITORY AND POPULATION. Ecuador is bounded on the north by Colombia, on the east and south by Peru and on the west by the Pacific ocean. The frontier with Peru has long been a source of dispute. The latest delimitation of it was in the treaty of Rio, 29 Jan. 1942, when, after being invaded by Peru, Ecuador lost over half her Amazonian territories. Ecuador unilaterally denounced this treaty in Sept. 1961. Fighting between Peru and Ecuador began again in Jan. 1981 over this border issue but a ceasefire was agreed in early Feb. Following a confrontation of soldiers in Aug. 1991 the foreign ministers of both countries signed a pact creating a security zone, and took their cases to the UN in Oct. 1991. Armed clashes with Peruvian forces broke out again in Jan. 1995. On 26 Jan. further armed clashes broke out with Peruvian forces in the undemarcated mututal border area ('Condor Cordillera'). On Feb. 2 talks were held under the auspices of the guarantor nations of the 1942 Protocol of Rio de Janeiro (Argentina, Brazil, Chile and the USA) but fighting continued. Ceasefires were agreed on 17 Feb., which was broken, and on 28 Feb. On 25 July 1995 an agreement between Ecuador and Peru established a demilitarized zone along their joint frontier. The frontier was re-opened on 4 Sept. 1995.

No definite figure of the area of the country can yet be given, as this part of the frontier has not been delimited (2,289 sq. km). One estimate of the area of Ecuador is 275,830·0 sq. km, excluding the litigation zone between Peru and Ecuador, which is 190,807 sq. km, but including the **Galápagos** Archipelago (8,010 sq. km), situated in the Pacific ocean about 960 km west of Ecuador and comprising 13 islands and 19 islets. These were discovered in 1535 by Fray Tomás de Berlanga and had a population of 10,207 in 1996. They are a national park, and had about 80,000 visitors in 1995.

The population is an amalgam of European, Amerindian and African origins. Some 40% of the population is Amerindian: Quechua, Swiwiar, Achuar and Zaparo. In May 1992 they were granted title to the 1m. ha of land they occupy in Pastaza.

The official language is Spanish. Quechua and other languages are also spoken.

Census population in 1990, 9,648,189. Estimate, 1996, 11,698,496.

The population was distributed by provinces as follows:

Province	*Sq. km*	*Population*	*Capital*	*Population* [1]
Azuay	8,124·7	506,090	Cuenca	194,981
Bolívar	3,939·9	155,088	Guaranda	15,730
Cañar	3,122·1	189,347	Azogues	21,060
Carchi	3,605·1	141,482	Tulcán	37,069
Chimborazo	6,569·3	364,682	Riobamba	94,505
Cotopaxi	6,071·9	276,324	Latacunga	39,882
El Oro	5,850·1	412,572	Machala	144,197
Esmeraldas	15,239·1	306,628	Esmeraldas	98,558
Guayas	20,502·5	2,515,146	Guayaquil	1,508,444
Imbabura	4,559·3	265,499	Ibarra	80,991
Loja	11,026·5	384,698	Loja	94,305
Los Ríos	7,175·0	527,559	Babahoyo	50,285
Manabi	18,878·8	1,031,927	Portoviejo	132,937
Pichincha	12,914·7	1,756,228	Quito	1,100,847

[1] Corresponding to city limits.

Province	*Sq. km*	*Population*	*Capital*	*Population* [1]
Sucumbíos	18,327·5	76,952	Nueva Loja	13,165
Tungurahua	3,334·8	361,980	Ambato	124,166
Napo	33,930·9	103,387	Tena	7,873
Pastaza	29,773·7	41,811	Puyo	14,438
Morona-Santiago	25,690·0	84,216	Macas	8,246
Zamora-Chinchipe	23,110·8	66,167	Zamora	8,048
Galápagos	8,010·0	9,785	Puerto Baquerizo Moreno	3,023
Non-delimited zones	2,288·8	70,621		

[1] Corresponding to city limits.

Vital statistics, 1994: Births, 350,838; deaths, 51,165; marriages, 71,289. Rates (per 1,000 population): Birth, 31·3; death, 4·6; marriage, 6·4. Expectation of life, 1990-95: 66·4 years for males, 71·4 for females.

CLIMATE. The climate varies from equatorial, through warm temperate to mountain conditions, according to altitude which affects temperatures and rainfall. In coastal areas, the dry season is from May to Dec., but only from June to Sept. in mountainous parts, where temperatures may be 20°F colder than on the coast. Quito Jan. 59°F (15°C), July 58°F (14·4°C). Annual rainfall 44" (1,115 mm). Guayaquil. Jan. 79°F (26·1°C), July 75°F (23·9°C). Annual rainfall 39" (986 mm).

CONSTITUTION AND GOVERNMENT. A new Constitution came into force on 10 Aug. 1979. It provides for an executive President and a Vice-President to be directly elected for a non-renewable 4-year term by universal suffrage, with a further 'run-off' ballot being held between the two leading candidates where no-one has secured an absolute majority of the votes cast. The President appoints and leads a Council of Ministers. A referendum on constitutional reform was held in Nov. 1995.

Legislative power is vested in a unicameral 77-member *National Congress*, also directly elected, 12 members on a national basis for a 4-year term and 65 on a provincial basis for a 2-year term. Voting is obligatory for all literate citizens of 18–65 years. Mid-term Congressional elections were held on 1 May 1994. The Social Christian Party won 28 seats; the United Republican Party, 10.

Presidential elections took place in 2 rounds in May and July 1992. 12 candidates stood in May and 2 in July. The electorate was 5·5m. Sixto Durán Ballén was elected by 57% of votes cast in the second electoral round.

Presidential, parliamentary and local elections were scheduled for 19 May 1996.

President: Sixto Durán Ballén (b. 1922; United Republican Party; elected 5 July 1992; installed 10 Aug. 1992).

Vice-President: Eduardo Peña Trivino.

The Cabinet in Nov. 1995 was composed as follows:

Government and Police: Marcelo Santos Vera. *Defence:* Gen. José Gallardo. *Education and Culture:* Fausto Segovia Baus. *Agriculture and Livestock:* Mariano González. *Public Works and Communications:* Pedro López Torres. *Finance and Public Credit:* Mauricio Pinto. *Foreign Affairs:* Galo Leoro Franco. *Industry, Commerce, Integration and Fishing:* José Vicente Maldonado. *Public Health:* Alfredo Palacios. *Social Welfare:* Alberto Cárdenas. *Information and Tourism:* Armando Espinel. *Housing and Development:* Francisco Albornoz. *Secretary General for Public Administration:* Carlos Larreátegui. *Energy and Mines:* Vacant. *Labour and Human Resources:* Alfredo Corral Borrero. *Interior:* Abraham Romero.

National flag: Three horizontal stripes of yellow, blue, red, with the yellow of double width, and in the centre over all the national arms.

National anthem: 'Oh Patria, mil veces, Oh Patria' ('Hail, Oh Fatherland, a thousand times, Oh Fatherland'); words by J. L. Mera, music by A. Neuman.

Local Government. The country is divided administratively into 21 provinces. The provinces are administered by governors, appointed by the Government; their subdivisions, or cantons, by political chiefs and elected cantonal councillors; and the parishes by political lieutenants. The 21 provinces are made up of 193 cantons, 322 urban parishes and 757 rural parishes. Elections for 54 provincial and 608 municipal councillors were held in June 1994.

DEFENCE. Military service is selective, with a 1-year period of conscription. The country is divided into 4 military zones, with headquarters at Quito, Guayaquil, Cuenca and Pastaza.

Army. The Army consists of 1 infantry division, 1 armoured, 2 infantry, 1 special forces and 3 'jungle' brigades, 1 aviation group, 1 air defence artillery group and 3 engineer battalions. Equipment includes 45 American M-3 and 108 French AMX-13 light tanks. The aviation element has about 35 transport and communications aircraft, including 16 helicopters. Strength (1996) 50,000, with about 100,000 reservists.

Navy. Navy combatant forces include 2 German-built diesel submarines, 2 ex-UK missile-armed Leander class frigates, 6 Italian-built missile corvettes (with helicopter deck) and 6 fast missile craft. Amphibious capability is 1 landing ship and 6 small craft. Auxiliaries consist of 1 ex-German depot ship, 1 small tanker, 1 survey ship, 1 armament carrier, 2 tugs and 1 training ship as well as some 8 harbour and service vessels. The Maritime Air Force has 11 aircraft, including 1 CN-235 transport, 3 Cessna light aircraft, 3 T-34C trainers, and 4 Jet Ranger helicopters. Naval personnel in 1995 totalled 4,100 including some 1,500 marines.

There are 6 inshore Coast Guard cutters and some 20 boats.

Air Force. The Air Force had a 1995 strength of about 3,000 personnel and 70 combat aircraft and includes a strike squadron equipped with 8 single-seat and 2 two-seat Jaguars; an interceptor squadron of 12 single-seat and 1 two-seat Mirage F.1; an interceptor squadron with 9 Kfirs; 3 counter-insurgency units equipped with 10 Cessna A-37B, 20 T-33 and 10 Strikemaster light jet attack and training aircraft, 1 squadron with 2 C-130, 1 Buffalo, 1 Twin Otter and 3 HS 748 turboprop transports; Alouette III, AS 332 Super Puma, SA 330 Puma, Bell 212, UH-1 Iroquois and SA 315B Lama helicopters; and Cessna 150, T-34C-1 and T-41A/D trainers. 1 F.28, 1 Boeing 737 and 3 Boeing 727 transports are operated by the military airline TAME.

INTERNATIONAL RELATIONS

Membership. Ecuador is a member of the UN, OAS, the Andean Group and LAIA.

ECONOMY

Policy. A reform programme was announced in 1992, including the privatization of 20 state-owned enterprises. Further privatization legislation followed in 1993 and the opening to private investment of the oil, mining, telecommunications, electricity and water sectors.

Budget. Revenue in 1994 was 5,647,643m. sucres and expenditure, 5,532,433m. sucres.

Currency. The monetary unit is the *sucre* (ECS), of 100 *centavos*. There are coins of 10, 20, 50, 100 and 500 sucres, and notes of 100, 500, 1,000, 5,000, 10,000 and 20,000 sucres. Inflation was 22·9% in 1995. Foreign exchange reserves were US$1,710m. in April 1995. In March 1996, £1 = 4,550·05 sucres; US$1 = 2,977 sucres; DM1 = 2,017·07 sucres.

Banking and Finance. The Central Bank of Ecuador (*Governor*, Augusto de la Torre), the bank of issue, with a capital and reserves of US$1,557m. at 31 Dec. 1995, is modelled after the Federal Reserve Banks of the USA: through branches opened in 16 towns it now deals in mortgage bonds. All commercial banks must be affiliated to the Central Bank. Legislation of May 1994 liberalized the financial sector.

There are stock exchanges in Quito and Guayaquil.

Weights and Measures. The metric system is the legal standard but English and old Spanish measures are still in use. A case (*caja*) of bananas = 18·14 kg.

ENERGY AND NATURAL RESOURCES

Electricity. In 1992, total capacity of hydro-electric and thermal plants was 2,228·9 MW. Output was 7,164·6 MWh.

Oil and Gas. Production of crude oil in 1995 was 138,414,000 bbls. Estimated reserves, 1995, 3,500m. bbls. In 1993, natural gas production was 6,485,400 bbls.

Minerals. Production (1983): Silver, 3,137·6 troy oz; gold, 607·6 troy oz; copper, 7,900 kg; zinc, 14,820 kg. The country also has some iron, uranium, lead, coal, cobalt, manganese and titanium.

Agriculture. In 1991 3·23m. persons subsisted on agriculture, of whom 999,000 were economically active.

50,000 ha of rich virgin land in the Santo Domingo de los Colorados area has been set aside for settlement by medium and large landowners. A law of 1994 restricts the redistribution of land to small farmers to land which has lain fallow for more than 3 years.

The staple export products are bananas, cacao and coffee. Main crops, in 1,000 tonnes, in 1994: Rice, 1,420; potatoes, 531; maize, 498; barley, 32; cocoa beans, 81; bananas, 5,086; coffee, 187; sugar-cane, 3,635.

Livestock, 1994 (in 1,000): Cattle, 4,937; sheep, 1,690; pigs, 2,546; goats, 369; poultry, 60,900.

Forestry. Excepting the agricultural zones and a few arid spots on the Pacific coast, Ecuador is a vast forest. In 1988 11·8m. ha, 43% of the land area, was forested, but much of the forest is not commercially accessible.

Fisheries. In 1993 primary sea export products were valued at US$498·9m.

INDUSTRY. Production in 1991: Cement, 1·58m. tonnes.

Trades Unions. The main trade union federation is the United Workers' Front.

FOREIGN ECONOMIC RELATIONS. Most restrictions on foreign investment were removed in 1992 and the repatriation of profits was permitted. Foreign debt was US$7,800m. in 1994.

Commerce. Imports and exports for calendar years, in US$1m.:

	1991	*1992*	*1993*	*1994*	*1995*
Imports (f.o.b.)	2,116	1,976	2,223	3,209	3,724
Exports (f.o.b.)	2,851	3,008	3,062	3,843	4,322

Ecuador is a major exporter of shrimps (US$491m. in 1991). Other major exports (1994, in US$1m.): Bananas, 650; coffee beans, 350; cocoa beans and products, 94; cut flowers, 54. Main export markets, 1994: USA, 42·4%; Colombia, 5·9%; Germany, 4·8%; Chile, 4·4%; Peru, 4·2%. Main import suppliers: USA, 25·3%; Colombia, 7·8%; Germany, 5·6%.

Total trade between Ecuador and UK (British Department of Trade returns, in £1,000 sterling):

	1991	*1992*	*1993*	*1994*	*1995*
Imports to UK	16,264	15,657	19,855	22,891	20,390
Exports and re-exports from UK	45,213	33,064	48,269	65,290	52,825

Tourism. There were 403,242 visitors in 1993 (37·7% from Colombia, 11% from Peru, 12·7% from other Latin American countries; 19·5% from the USA, 17% from Europe). Income from tourism, 1994, US$252m. (US$192m. in 1993).

COMMUNICATIONS

Roads. In 1985, there were 36,187 km of roads. A trunk highway through the coastal plain will link Machala in the extreme south-west with Esmeraldas in the north-west and with Quito and the northern section of the Pan-American Highway; in

1994, 1,214 km had been built and 273 km were under construction. In 1992, there were 353,393 cars and 52,586 commercial vehicles.

Railways. The railway was closed in 1995.

Civil Aviation. There is an international airport at Quito (Mariscal Sucre). The national carriers are SAETA, SAN and TAME. In 1995, SAETA operated 2 A310-300s, 3 A320-200s, 1 B-727, 1 B-727-200 Adv, 1 B-737-200 Adv and 1 B-737-300. Services are also provided by Aeroperú, Air France, American Airlines, AOM, Avianca, Continental Airlines and Air Micronesia, COPA, Cubana, Iberia, KLM, LACSA, LAPSA, Lloyd Aereo Boliviano, Lufthansa, Servivensa, Varig and Viasa.

Shipping. Ecuador has 3 major seaports, of which Guayaquil is the chief, and 6 minor ones. In 1995, the merchant navy totalled 0·36m. GRT of ocean-going vessels, including oil-tankers, 0·13m. GRT.

Telecommunications. In 1994 there were 586,300 telephones. In 1993 there were 3m. radios and 0·9m. TV receivers (colour by NTSC).

Press (1994). There were 75 daily, weekly and fortnightly newspapers.

SOCIAL INSTITUTIONS

Justice. The Supreme Court in Quito, consisting of a President and 30 Justices, comprises 6 chambers each of 5 Justices. It is also a Court of Appeal. There is a Superior Court in each province, comprising chambers (as appointed by the Supreme Court) of 3 magistrates each. The Superior Courts are at the apex of a hierarchy of various tribunals. There is no death penalty.

Religion. The state recognizes no religion and grants freedom of worship to all. In 1993 there were 10·21m. Roman Catholics.

Education. In 1993–94, there were 127,355 pre-primary pupils with 7,020 teachers. Primary education is free and compulsory. Private schools, both primary and secondary, are under some state supervision. In 1993 there were 16,825 primary schools and 2,868 secondary schools. In 1993–94 there were 1,742,984 pupils and 63,708 teachers in primary schools. In 1995–96, there were in the public sector: 9 universities, 3 Roman Catholic, 12 technical, 1 agricultural and 2 polytechnical universities, 2 institutes of technology and 1 military polytechnic; and in the private sector: 2 universities, 1 Roman Catholic and 1 technological university.

Health. In 1993 there were 12,149 doctors and 433 hospitals, 1,542 dentists and 906 pharmacists.

DIPLOMATIC REPRESENTATIVES

Of Ecuador in Great Britain (3 Hans Cres., London, SW1X 0LS)
Ambassador: Patricio Maldonado.

Of Great Britain in Ecuador (Calle González Suárez 111, Quito)
Ambassador: Richard Lavers.

Of Ecuador in the USA (2535 15th St., NW, Washington, D.C., 20009)
Ambassador: Edgar Terán.

Of the USA in Ecuador (Avenida 12 de Octubre y Avenida Patria, Quito)
Ambassador: Peter Romero.

Of Ecuador to the United Nations
Ambassador: Luis Valencia Rodríguez.

Further Reading

Corkill, D., *Ecuador.* [Bibliography] Oxford and Santa Barbara (CA), 1989
Hidrobo, J. A., *Power and Industrialization in Ecuador.* Boulder (CO), 1993
Martz, J. D., *Ecuador: Conflicting Political Culture and the Quest for Progress.* Boston, 1972.—*Politics and Petroleum in Ecuador.* New Brunswick, 1987

EGYPT

Jumhuriyat Misr al-Arabiya

(Arab Republic of Egypt)

Capital: Cairo
Population: 58·82m. (1995)
GNP per capita: US$710 (1994)
HDI/world rank: 0·613/107 (1992)

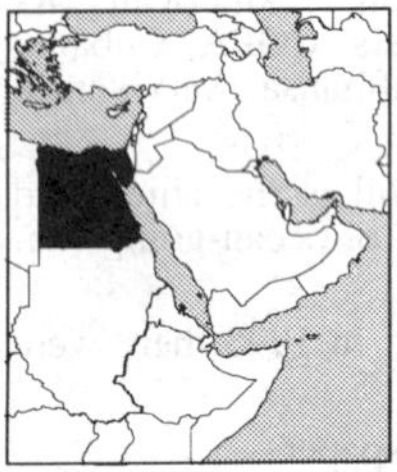

KEY HISTORICAL EVENTS. Part of the Ottoman Empire from 1517 until Dec. 1914 when it became a British protectorate, Egypt became an independent monarchy on 28 Feb. 1922. Following a revolution on 23 July 1952, a republic was proclaimed on 18 June 1953. Egypt was merged with Syria from 22 Feb. 1958 to 28 Sept. 1961 as the United Arab Republic.

TERRITORY AND POPULATION. Egypt is bounded in the east by Israel, the Gulf of Aqaba and the Red Sea, south by Sudan, west by Libya and north by the Mediterranean. The total area is 1,001,449 sq. km (386,659 sq. miles), but the cultivated and settled area, that is, the Nile Valley, Delta and oases, covers only 35,189 sq. km. Population density in this latter, 1992, 1,557·9 per sq. km. At the 1986 census the population was 48,205,049 (23,549,752 female; 46·7% urban). Population estimate, 1995, 58,819,000 (of whom 98% live in the Nile Valley and Delta).

Vital statistics: Marriages, 1994, 0·53m. (rate per 1,000, 9·1); divorces, 90,000 (1.5); births (1994), 1·75m. (28·6); deaths, 0·42m. (6·8). Growth rate, 1994, 22 per 1,000. (It is government policy to reduce this to 21 per 1,000). Fertility rate, 1993, 3·9 births per woman. In 1991 the average family size was 4·3. 40% of the population was under 40 years. Expectation of life was 60·9 years in 1992.

Area, population and capitals of the governorates (1986 census and 1995 estimate):

Governorate	*Area (in sq. km)*	*Population (1986 census)*	*1995 estimate (in 1,000)*	*Capital*
Alexandria	2,679·36	2,917,327	3,431	Alexandria
Aswan	678·50	801,408	1,042	Aswan
Asyut	1,553·00	2,223,034	2,843	Asyut
Behera	10,129·49	3,257,168	3,973	Damanhur
Beni Suef	1,321·65	1,442,981	1,836	Beni Suef
Cairo	214·20	6,052,836	6,955	Cairo
Dakahlia	3,470·90	3,500,470	4,226	Mansura
Damietta	589·17	741,264	898	Damietta
Fayum	1,827·15	1,544,047	1,995	Fayum
Gharbia	1,942·21	2,870,960	3,437	Tanta
Giza	1,058·20	3,700,054	4,525	Giza
Ismailia	1,441·59	544,427	681	Ismailia
Kafr El Shaikh	3,437·12	1,800,129	2,266	Kafr El Shaikh
Kalyubia	1,001·09	2,514,244	3,045	Benha
Matruh	212,112·00	160,567	186	Matruh
Menia	2,261·72	2,648,043	3,372	Menia
Menufia	1,532·13	2,227,087	2,672	Shibin Al Kom
New Valley	376,505·00	113,838	136	Al Kharija
Port Said	72·01	399,793	467	Port Said
Qena	1,850·70	2,252,315	2,766	Qena
Red Sea	203,685·00	90,491	115	El Gurdakah
Sharkia	4,179·55	3,420,119	4,220	Zagazig
North Sinai	27,574·00	171,505	219	At Tur
South Sinai	33,140·00	28,988	35	Al Arish
Suez	17,840·42	326,820	411	Suez
Suhag	1,547·21	2,455,134	3,067	Suhag

Principal cities, with estimated 1990 populations (in 1,000): Cairo, 6,452; Alexandria, 3,170; Giza, 2,156; Shubra Al Khayma, 811; Port Said, 461; Suez, 392.

Smaller cities, with 1986 census populations: Mahalla Al Kubra, 358,844; Tanta,

334,505; Hulwan, 328,000; Mansura, 316,870; Asyut, 273,191; Zagazig, 255,000; Kafr Ad Dawwar, 223,000; Ismailia, 212,567; Fayum, 212,523; Aswan, 191,461; Damanhur, 190,840; Menia, 179,136; Beni Suef, 151,813; Uqsur (Luxor), 138,000; Suhag, 132,965; Shibin Al Kom, 132,751; Qena, 119,794; Benha, 115,571; Damietta, 113,000; Kafr Ash Shaikh, 102,910.

The official language is Arabic, although French and English are widely spoken.

CLIMATE. The climate is mainly dry, but there are winter rains along the Mediterranean coast. Elsewhere, rainfall is very low and erratic in its distribution. Winter temperatures are everywhere comfortable, but summer temperatures are very high, especially in the south. Cairo. Jan. 56°F (13·3°C), July 83°F (28·3°C). Annual rainfall 1·2" (28 mm). Alexandria. Jan. 58°F (14·4°C), July 79°F (26·1°C). Annual rainfall 7" (178 mm). Aswân. Jan. 62°F (16·7°C), July 92°F (33·3°C). Annual rainfall trace. Giza. Jan. 55°F (12·8°C), July 78°F (25·6°C). Annual rainfall 16" (389 mm). Ismailia. Jan. 56°F (13·3°C), July 84°F (28·9°C). Annual rainfall 1·5" (37 mm). Luxor. Jan. 59°F (15°C), July 86°F (30°C). Annual rainfall trace. Port Said. Jan. 58°F (14·4°C), July 78°F (27·2°C). Annual rainfall 3" (76 mm).

CONSTITUTION AND GOVERNMENT. The Constitution was approved by referendum on 11 Sept. 1971. It defines Egypt as 'an Arab Republic with a democratic, socialist system' and the Egyptian people as 'part of the Arab nation'. The *President* is nominated by the People's Assembly and confirmed by plebiscite for a 6-year term. The President may appoint 1 or more *Vice-Presidents.* The *People's Assembly* is a unicameral legislature consisting of 444 members directly elected from 222 constituencies for a 5-year term, and 10 members appointed by the President. There is a *Constitutional Court.*

The President appoints the Prime Minister and a Council of Ministers. It is traditional for 2 ministers to be Christian Copts.

A 210-member consultative body, the *Shura Council,* was established in 1980. Two-thirds of its members are elected and one-third appointed by the President.

Elections for the People's Assembly were held in 2 rounds on 29 Nov. and 6 Dec. 1995. The electorate was 21m.; turn-out was 50%. 3,980 candidates representing 14 parties stood. The National Democratic Party (NDP) gained 317 seats; ind (mainly NDP sympathizers), 113; Wafd, 6; Progressive Rally (former Communists), 5; Nasserites, 1; Liberal Socialists, 1, Islamic Workers, 1. 109 results were challenged by the Constitutional Court.

President: Hosni Mubarak (NDP; sworn in for a third term Oct. 1993).

A new government was formed on 4 Jan. 1996 which comprised:

Prime Minister and Minister of Planning: Dr Kamal El Ganzouri (b. 1934).

Deputy Prime Minister and Minister of Agriculture and Land Reclamation: Dr Youssouf Amin Wali. *Insurance and Social Affairs:* Dr Amel Abdel Othman. *Transport and Communication:* Suliman Metwalli Suliman. *Electricity and Energy:* Maher Abaza. *Defence and Military Production:* Field-Marshal Mohammed Hussein Tantawi. *Information:* Mohammed Safat El Sharif. *Foreign Affairs:* Amr Moussa. *Public Enterprises:* Dr Atef Mohammed Ebeid. *Justice:* Farouq Sayef El Nasser. *Culture:* Farouq Hosni. *Local Administration:* Dr Mahmoud Sharif. *Manpower and Emigration:* Ahmed El Amawi. *Trade and Supply:* Ahmed Geili. *Finance:* Dr Mohieddin Abu Bakr El Gharib. *Cabinet Affairs and Follow-up:* Tala'at Sayed Hammad. *Religious Affairs (Waqfs):* Mahmoud Hamdi Zakzouk. *Industry and Mineral Wealth:* Suliman Reda Suliman. *Health and Population:* Dr Ismail Awadallah Sallam. *Economy and International Co-operation:* Dr Nawal Monein El Tatawi. *Education:* Dr Hussein Kamal El Din. *Oil:* Dr Hamdi El Banbi. *Interior:* Maj.-Gen. Hassan El Alfi. *Tourism:* Mamdouh El Beltagi. *Public Works and Water Resources:* Abdel Hamid Radi. *Housing, Utilities and New Communities:* Dr Mohammed Ibrahim Suliman.

National flag: Three horizontal stripes of red, white, black, with the national emblem in the centre in gold.

National anthem: 'Biladi' ('My homeland'); words and tune by S. Darwish.

Local Government: The 26 governorates are divided into districts (*mudiriya*) and communes. Provincial governors are nominated by the President. Municipal elections were held on 3 Nov. 1992.

DEFENCE. Conscription is selective, for 3 years.

Army. There are 4 military districts and 2 Army headquarters. The Army comprises 1 infantry, 4 armoured and 7 mechanized infantry divisions; 1 Republican Guard, 4 independent armoured, 2 independent infantry, 4 independent mechanized, 1 air mobile, 1 parachute, 15 independent artillery and 2 surface-to-surface missile brigades and 6 commando groups. Equipment includes 840 T-54/-55, 500 T-62, 1,700 M-60 and 260 Ramses II (modified T-54/55) main battle tanks. Strength (1996) 310,000 (200,000 conscripts) and about 150,000 reservists.

Navy. 2 of the current submarine force of 6 old ex-Soviet and ex-Chinese 'Romeo' class submarines are being modernized in the USA. Major surface combatants include 1 very old destroyer, 2 Spanish-built, 2 Chinese-built missile-armed frigates and 2 ex-US Knox class. There are also 25 missile craft of mixed British, Soviet and Chinese origin and 18 coastal and inshore patrol craft. A small shore-based naval aviation branch operates 5 Sea King and 9 Gazelle helicopters. Mine warfare forces include 7 coastal minesweepers. 3 ex-Soviet medium landing ships provide amphibious lift supported by 11 minor landing craft. There are 6 major auxiliaries and some 14 minor service vessels. There are naval bases at Alexandria, Port Said, Mersa Matruh, Port Tewfik, Hurghada and Safaqa. Naval personnel in 1995 totalled 16,000 with reserves of 14,000. An associated para-military coastguard about 2,000 strong operates 33 inshore cutters and numerous boats.

Air Force. Until 1979, the Air Force was equipped largely with aircraft of USSR design, but subsequent re-equipment involves aircraft bought in the West, as well as some supplied by China. Strength (1995) is about 30,000 personnel (10,000 conscripts), 94 attack helicopters and 420 combat aircraft, of which the interceptors are operated by an independent Air Defence Command, in conjunction with many 'Guideline', 'Goa', 'Gainful', Hawk and Crotale missile batteries. The interceptor/ground attack fighter divisions are equipped with 150 F-16 Fighting Falcons, 60 Mirage 5s, 32 F-4E Phantoms, 19 Mirage 2000s, 70 F-6s (Chinese-built MiG-19s), 14 Alpha Jets and 60 F-7s (Chinese-built MiG-21s). Airborne early warning capability is provided by 5 E-2C Hawkeyes. Transport units have 22 C-130H Hercules turboprop heavy freighters, 5 An-12s, 9 twin-turboprop Buffaloes, 4 Beech 1900s, and up to 175 Gazelle, AH-64 Apache, Mi-8, Commando and Agusta-built CH-47C helicopters; some Commando helicopters, Beech 1900s and 2 EC-130H Hercules are equipped for electronic warfare duties. Training units are equipped with Embraer Tucanos, Czech-built L-39 Albatros and French-designed Alpha Jet jet trainers, two-seat FT-6s, Mirage 5s and UH-12E helicopters. Main aircrew training centre is the Air Force Academy at Bilbeis.

INTERNATIONAL RELATIONS

Membership. Egypt is a member of the UN, OAU, Arab League and OAPEC.

ECONOMY

Policy. A privatization programme which began in 1993 envisages the sale of 85 out of the 314 public sector companies by 1997.

Budget. The financial year runs from 1 July. The 1993–94 budget envisaged revenue of £E51,711m. and expenditure of £E55,325m. Sources of revenue (in £E1m.) included: Tax, 31,164; customs duties, 6,070; oil industry, 4,610; Suez Canal, 2,610. Items of expenditure included: Salaries, 11,026; pensions, 3,864; subsidies, 3,170; debt service, 16,426; defence, 5,892; public health (1992-93), 6,620.

Currency. The monetary unit is the *Egyptian pound* (EGP) of 100 *piastres*. There are coins of 5, 10 and 50 piastres, notes of 25 and 50 piastres and notes of £E1, 5, 10, 20, 50 and 100. Currency in circulation in 1994 was £E20,981m. In Feb. 1991 the official exchange rate was abolished, leaving a free rate, and a rate set by a panel of bankers. Annualized inflation was 9·1% in 1992. Foreign exchange reserves were US$10,200m. Gold reserves were 2·43m. troy oz. In March 1996, £1 sterling = £E5·22; US$1 = £E3·41; DM1 = £E2·31.

Banking and Finance. The Central Bank of Egypt (founded 1960) is the central bank and bank of issue. The *Governor* is Ismail Hassan.

In 1994, 4 major public sector commercial banks accounted for some 70% of all banking assets: the National Bank of Egypt, the Banque Misr, the Bank of Alexandria and the Banque du Caïre. There were 40 other domestic commercial banks, 15 investment banks and 30 regional development banks, as well as foreign banks, branches and joint ventures.

Savings and term deposits in 1992 totalled £E83,034m.

There are stock exchanges in Cairo and Alexandria.

Weights and Measures. In 1951 the metric system was made official with the exception of the feddan and its subdivisions. However, other traditional measures are still in use:

Kadah = 1/96th ardeb = 3·36 pints. *Rob* = 4 kadahs = 1·815 gallons. *Keila* = 8 kadahs = 3·63 gallons. *Ardeb* = 96 kadahs = 43·555 gallons, or 5·44439 bu., or 198 cu. decimetres. *Rotl* = 144 dirhems = 0·9905 lb. *Oke* = 400 dirhems = 2·75137 lb. *Qantar* or 100 rotls or 36 okes = 99·0493 lb. 1 *Qantar* of unginned cotton = 315 lb. 1 *Qantar* of ginned cotton = 99·05 lb. The approximate weight of the ardeb is as follows: Wheat, 150 kg; beans, 155 kg; barley, 120 kg; maize, 140 kg; cotton seed, 121 kg. *Feddan,* the unit of measure for land = 4,200·8 sq. metres = 7,468·148 sq. pics = 1·03805 acres. 1 sq. pic = 6·0547 sq. ft = 0·5625 sq. metre.

ENERGY AND NATURAL RESOURCES

Electricity. Electricity generated in 1993–94 was 48,600m. kWh. Installed capacity was 10,838mw in 1991. By 1995, 75% of power was gas-generated.

Oil and Gas. Oil was discovered in 1909. Oil policy is controlled by the state-owned Egyptian General Petroleum Corporation, whole or part-owner of the production and refining companies. Production of crude (1994), 44·8m. tonnes. Gas reserves were 21,000,000m. cu. ft in 1995. Output was 9·1m. tonnes in 1993–94.

Minerals. Production (1993–94, in tonnes): Phosphate, 0·86m.; iron ore, 2·7m.; salt, 1·12m.; kaolin, 0·2m.; quartz, 84,000; asbestos and fermacolite, 916. Mining for uranium ore began near Aswan in May 1991.

Water. The Aswan High Dam, completed in 1970, allows for a perennial irrigation system.

Agriculture. The cultivated area in 1993 was 11·25m. feddans. 5·81m. feddans were under winter crops, 5·43m. under summer crops, 0·65m. under Nile crops and 0·9m. under orchards.

Irrigation is vital to agriculture and is being developed by government programmes; it now reaches most cultivated areas. 6·5% of the land area is arable. Between 1952 and 1993–4 2,410,400 feddan of land had been reclaimed.

In 1994 there were 5,214 agricultural co-operatives. 0·71m. feddan of land had been distributed by 1991 to 0·35m. families under an agrarian reform programme. In 1992 32·7% of the workforce worked in agriculture. Cotton, sugar-cane and rice are subject to government price controls and procurement quotas.

Output (in 1,000 tonnes), 1994: Barley, 130; broad beans, 357; chickpeas, 11; cotton seed (1993), 652; seed cotton (1993), 1,114; garlic, 150; lentils, 9; flax fibre and tow (1992), 11; maize, 5,550; dry onions, 481; peanuts, 194; potatoes, 1,032; rice, 4,583; sesame, 29; soya beans, 68; sugar-cane, 12,412; sugar-beet, 825; strawberries, 28; wheat, 4,437; sorghum (1992), 736.

Livestock (in 1,000), 1994: Cattle, 3,764; buffaloes, 2,592; sheep, 4,666; goats, 5,492; camels, 245; pigs, 134. There were 36·6m. chickens (egg production 2,214m.). 9,000 tonnes of honey were produced.

Forestry. In 1990 total removal of roundwood was 2·25m. cu. metres of which 2m. was fuel wood.

Fisheries. The catch in 1994 was 307,516 tonnes, of which 219,404 tonnes were freshwater fish.

INDUSTRY. Almost all large-scale enterprises are in the public sector and these account for about two-thirds of total output. The private sector, dominated by food processing and textiles, consists of about 150,000 small and medium businesses, most employing less than 50 workers. Industry produced 25% of GDP in 1991.

Production in 1993–94 (in 1,000 tonnes) included: White sugar crystal, 629; refined sugar, 481; tobacco, 50; cotton yarn, 299; jute yarn, 21; sulphuric acid, 112; paper, 200; fertilizers, 6,697; steel billets and sections, 368. 6,557 cars, 1,379 lorries, 100 tractors, 247,000 refrigerators, 209,000 washing machines, 24,000 bicycles, 13,000 radio (1992-93) and 281,000 TV sets were produced. Production of cotton textiles and synthetic textiles in 1990-91 was 1·38m. tonnes and 0·11m. tonnes respectively.

Labour. In 1990 the workforce was 14,574,000 (1,467,000 females; 388,000 between 6 and 15). According to official figures, 1·4m. Egyptians worked abroad. In 1992 32·7% of the workforce were employed in agriculture, forestry and fisheries, 29·7% in services, 21·4% in manufacturing, 15·5% in mining, 10·6% in business, 4·5% in transport and communications and 1·1% in tourism. 2,220 working days were lost through strikes in 1990.

FOREIGN ECONOMIC RELATIONS

Commerce. Imports and exports, 1991: US$9,831m., US$3,856m.; 1992: US$9,045m.; US$4,743m.

Export of principal commodities (in £E1m.) in 1994: Crude oil, 2,684·98; raw cotton, 791·08; cotton yarn, 1,279·54; cotton fabrics, 409·03; clothing, 780; refined petroleum, 742·08; aluminium bars, etc., 405; oranges, 278·4; potatoes, 98·2. Imports: Wheat, 2,501·17; maize, 892·46; dairy products, 509·4; chemicals, 1,107·3; iron bars, 90·78; motor car parts, 762·05; motor cars, 746·46.

Main trading partners, 1991 (percentage share of total trade): USA, exports 7·6%, imports 16·1%; Italy, 14·8%, 6·8%; Germany, 3·7%, 10·4%; France, 5·9%, 6·9%.

Total trade between Egypt and UK (British Department of Trade returns, in £1,000 sterling):

	1991	*1992*	*1993*	*1994*	*1995*
Imports to UK	186,408	137,008	188,355	252,203	246,619
Exports and re-exports from UK	282,928	252,271	337,105	368,000	383,541

Tourism. In 1993 terrorist attacks on tourists reduced visitor numbers and revenue: 2·5m, US$1,300m. (1992: 3·2m., US$2,100m.). In 1994 there were 2·6m. visitors.

COMMUNICATIONS

Roads. In 1990 there were 30,105 km of highways and 22,690 km of desert roads. Vehicles (in 1,000), 1994: Motor cars, 968; lorries, 399; motor cycles, 371; buses, 37.

Railways. In 1990 there were 4,751 km of state railways (1,435 mm gauge), of which 42 km were electrified. In 1992 828m. passengers and 11·2m. tonnes of freight were carried.

Civil Aviation. There are international airports at Cairo and Luxor. The national carrier is Egyptair, which in 1995 operated 4 A300B4-200s, 9 A300B4-600Rs, 7 A320-200s, 1 B-707-320C, 2 B-737-200 Advs, 4 B-737-500s, 2 B-747-300 Combis, 3 B-767-200ERs and 2 B-767-300ERs.

Services were also provided by Aeroflot, Air Algérie, Air France, Air Malta, Air Ukraine, Alitalia, Austrian Airlines, Balkan, British Airways, Cyprus Airways, Czech Airlines, El Al, Emirates, Ethiopian Airlines, Gulf Air, Iberia, JAT, KLM, Kenya Airways, Korean Air, Kuwait Airways, Libyan Airlines, LOT, Lufthansa,

Malév, Middle East Airlines, Northwest Airlines, Olympic Airways, Pakistan International Airlines, Qatar Airways, Royal Air Maroc, Royal Jordanian, Saudia, Singapore Airlines, SAA, Sudan Airways, Swissair, Syrian Airlines, Tarom, TransWorld, Tunis Air, Turkish Airlines, United Airlines and Yemenia. 8·96m. passengers arrived or departed in 1993–94 (11·44m. in 1989–90) and 107,207 tons of freight were carried (102,144 tons in 1989–90).

Shipping. In 1995 the merchant marine totalled 1·9m. GRT, including oil-tankers, 0·45m. GRT. Vessels arriving and leaving at major ports in 1994: Alexandria, 3,930; Port Said, 1,416; Suez, 985.

Suez Canal. The Suez Canal was opened for navigation on 17 Nov. 1869 and nationalized in June 1956. By the convention of Constantinople of 29 Oct. 1888 the canal is open to vessels of all nations and is free from blockade, except in time of war. It is 173 km long (excluding 11 km of approach channels to the harbours), connecting the Mediterranean with the Red Sea. It is being deepened from 16 to 17 metres and widened from 365 to 415 metres to permit the passage of vessels of 180,000 DWT.

In 1994 16,370 vessels (net tonnage, 364m. tonnes; cargo, 290m. tons; passengers, 15,800) went through the canal. Toll revenue in 1994 was US$1,897m. Tolls for tankers were reduced by 20% after Jan. 1996.

Telecommunications. There were, in 1993–94, 2,035 postal agencies, 1,972 mobile offices, 2,655 government and 2,472 private post offices. Number of telephones in 1994, 2,474,225. The internal telecommunications system is owned and operated by the Telecommunications Organization.

Broadcasting is conducted by the government-controlled Egyptian Radio and TV Union. Number of radio sets in 1993, 14m.; TV sets, 5m. Colour is by SECAM.

Cinemas. In 1994 there were 202 cinemas. 57 full-length films were made in 1994.

Press. In 1984 there were 11 dailies published in Cairo and 6 in Alexandria.

SOCIAL INSTITUTIONS

Justice. The court system comprises: A Court of Cassation with a bench of 5 judges which constitutes the highest court of appeal in both criminal and civil cases; 5 Courts of Appeal with 3 judges; Assize Courts with 3 judges which deal with all cases of serious crime; Central Tribunals with 3 judges which deal with ordinary civil and commercial cases; Summary Tribunals presided over by a single judge which hear minor civil disputes and criminal offences.

The death penalty is in force.

Religion. Islam is constitutionally the state religion. In 1992 there were 50·4m. Moslems, mostly of the Sunni sect. Some 7% of the population are Coptic Christians, the remainder being Roman Catholics, Protestants or Greek Orthodox, with a small number of Jews. A Patriarch heads the Coptic Church, and there are 25 metropolitans and bishops in Egypt; 4 metropolitans for Ethiopia, Jerusalem, Khartoum and Omdurman, and 12 bishops in Ethiopia. The Copts use the Diocletian (or Martyrs') calendar, which begins in A.D. 284.

Education. Adult literacy was 50% in 1992. Free compulsory education is provided in primary schools (6 years). Secondary and technical education is also free. In 1993–94 there were 15,861 primary schools with 7,049,549 pupils and 241,000 teachers, 6,202 preparatory schools with 3,353,358 pupils, 2,753 secondary schools with 2,466,609 pupils and 124 training colleges with 46,109 students.

Al Azhar institutes educate students who intend enrolling at Al Azhar University. In 1993–94 in the Al Azhar system there were 1,912 primary schools with 704,446 pupils, 1,030 preparatory schools with 147,762 pupils and 587 secondary schools with 165,829 pupils.

In 1993–94 there were 49,703 students in commerce institutes (24,906 women) and 31,259 in technical institutes (9,401 women). In 1995–96 there were 13 universities, 1 American university and 1 academy of science and technology. There were 612,844 students (231,065 women) and 33,100 academic staff in 1993–94.

Health. In 1992 there were 101,500 doctors, 15,150 dentists, 34,700 pharmacists and 98,500 other medical personnel. In 1994 there were 6,332 treatment units (including 330 general hospitals) with 113,020 beds.

DIPLOMATIC REPRESENTATIVES

Of Egypt in Great Britain (26 South St., London, W1Y 8EL)
Ambassador: Mohamed I. Shaker.

Of Great Britain in Egypt (Ahmed Ragheb St., Garden City, Cairo)
Ambassador: David Blatherwick, CMG.

Of Egypt in the USA (2310 Decatur Pl., NW, Washington, D.C., 20008)
Ambassador: Ahmed Maher El Sayed.

Of the USA in Egypt (Lazougi St., Garden City, Cairo)
Ambassador: Edward S. Walker.

Of Egypt to the United Nations
Ambassador: Nabil A. Elaraby.

Further Reading

CAPMAS, *Statistical Year Book, Arab Republic of Egypt*
Hopwood, D., *Egypt: Politics and Society 1945–1990.* 3rd ed. London, 1992
King, J. W., *Historical Dictionary of Egypt.* 2nd ed. Revised by A. Goldschmidt. Metuchen (NJ), 1995
McDermott, A., *Egypt: From Nasser to Mubarak.* London, 1988
Makar, R. N., *Egypt.* [Bibliography] Oxford and Santa Barbara (CA), 1988
Malek, J. (ed.) *Egypt.* Univ. of Oklahoma Press, 1993
Vatikiotis, P. J., *History of Modern Egypt: from Muhammad Ali to Mubarak.* London, 1991

National statistical office: Central Agency for Public Mobilization and Statistics (CAPMAS), Nasr City, Cairo.

EL SALVADOR

República de El Salvador

Capital: San Salvador
Population: 5·05m. (1992)
GNP per capita: US$1,480 (1994)
HDI/world rank: 0·579/115 (1992)

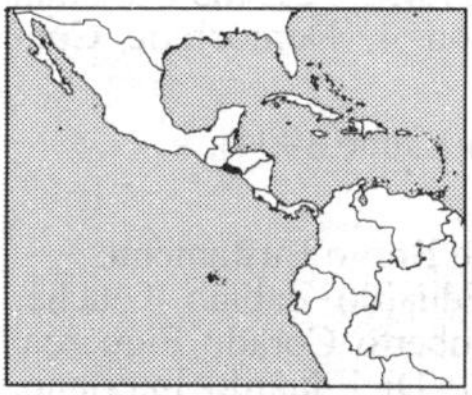

KEY HISTORICAL EVENTS. In 1839 the Central American Federation, which had comprised the states of Guatemala, El Salvador, Honduras, Nicaragua and Costa Rica, was dissolved, and El Salvador declared itself formally an independent republic in 1841.

Throughout the 1980s the Farabundo Marti National Liberation Front (FMLN) waged guerilla war against the government.

Talks between the government and the FMLN in April 1991 led to constitutional reforms in May envisaging the establishment of civilian control over the armed forces and a reduction in their size. In May the UN Security Council decided to send a mission to observe the government-FMLN negotiations, in the first place for one year. An agreement reached in Sept. 1991 permits the FMLN to participate in a newly-created police force under civilian authority. On 16 Jan. 1992 the government and the FMLN signed a peace agreement. A permanent ceasefire began on 1 Feb., and the FMLN agreed to demobilize by 15 Dec.

TERRITORY AND POPULATION. El Salvador is bounded in the north-east by Guatemala, north-east and east by Honduras and south by the Pacific Ocean. The area (including 247 sq. km of inland lakes) is 21,041 sq. km. Population (1992 census), 5,047,925 (female 52%). Population density, 255·5 per sq. km. 1m. Salvadoreans were living abroad in 1995, mainly in the USA. Vital statistics 1990, (rates per 1,000 population): Birth, 36·3; death, 8·5; infant mortality (1992, per 1,000 births), 46. Expectation of life was 65 years in 1992.

The republic is divided into 14 departments. Areas (in sq. km) and 1992 census populations:

Department	*Area*	*Population*	*Chief town*	*Population*
Ahuachapán	1,240	260,563	Ahuachapán	83,885
Cabañas	1,140	136,293	Sensuntepeque	38,073
Chalatenango	2,017	180,627	Chalatenango	27,600
Cuscatlán	756	167,290	Cojutepeque	43,564
La Libertad	1,653	522,071	Nueva San Salvador	116,575
La Paz	1,224	246,147	Zacatecoluca	57,032
La Unión	2,074	251,143	La Unión	36,927
Morazán	1,447	166,772	San Francisco	20,497
San Miguel	2,077	380,442	San Miguel	182,817
San Salvador	886	1,477,766	San Salvador	422,570 [1]
San Vicente	1,184	135,471	San Vicente	45,842
Santa Ana	2,023	451,620	Santa Ana	202,337
Sonsonate	1,226	354,641	Sonsonate	76,200
Usulatán	2,130	317,079	Usulután	62,967

[1] Greater San Salvador conurbation, 1,522,126.

The official language is Spanish.

CLIMATE. Despite its proximity to the equator, the climate is warm rather than hot and nights are cool inland. Light rains occur in the dry season from Nov. to April while the rest of the year has heavy rains, especially on the coastal plain. San Salvador. Jan. 71°F (21·7°C), July 75°F (23·9°C). Annual rainfall 71" (1,775 mm). San Miguel. Jan. 77°F (25°C), July 83°F (28·3°C). Annual rainfall 68" (1,700 mm).

CONSTITUTION AND GOVERNMENT. A new Constitution was enacted in Dec. 1983. Executive power is vested in a *President* and *Vice-President* elected for a non-renewable term of 5 years. There is a *Legislative Assembly* of 84 members elected by universal suffrage and proportional representation, 64 locally and 20 nationally for a term of 3 years.

Presidential and parliamentary elections were held on 20 March 1994 with a run-off for President on 24 April. The electorate was 2·7m. Armando Calderón Sol (Alianza Republicana Nacionalista, ARENA) was elected President.

ARENA gained 39 seats in the Legislative Assembly, the FMLN 21, the Christian Democratic Party 18, the Party of National Conciliation 4, Democratic Convergence 1 and the Unity Movement 1.

President: Dr Armando Calderón Sol (ARENA; sworn in 1 June 1994).

In Nov. 1995 the Cabinet comprised:

Vice-President and Minister of the Presidency: Dr Enrique Borgo Bustamente.

Minister of Agriculture: Oscar Gutiérrez. *Economy:* Eduardo Zablah Touché. *Education:* Cecilia Gallardo de Cano. *Defence:* Col. Humberto Corado Figueroa. *Finance:* Manuel Hinds. *Foreign Affairs:* Vacant. *Health:* Dr Eduardo Interiano. *Interior:* Mario Acosta Oertel. *Justice:* Dr Rubén Mejía Peña. *Labour and Social Security:* Dr Juan Sifontes. *Public Works:* Jorge Sansivirini. *Planning:* Ramón Gonzáles Giner. *Public Safety:* Hugo Cesar Barrero.

National flag: Blue, white, blue (horizontal): the white stripe charged with the arms of the republic.

National anthem: 'Saludemos la patria orgullosos' ('We proudly salute the Fatherland'); words by J. J. Cañas, tune by J. Aberle.

Local Government. Each of the 14 departments is under an appointed governor. There are 262 municipalities. At the elections of March 1994 ARENA gained control of 211.

DEFENCE. There is selective conscription for 2 years.

Army. There are 3 military zones. The Army comprises 1 special security and 6 infantry brigades, 8 infantry detachments, 1 mechanized cavalry regiment, 1 artillery brigade, 1 engineer command, 2 independent battalions including the Presidential Guard and 1 special operations group. Equipment includes 68 armoured personnel carriers. Strength was (1996) 28,000. The National Civilian Police numbers 8,000.

Navy. A small coastguard force based largely at Acajutla, with 500 (1995) personnel, operates 5 inshore patrol craft, 2 landing craft and numerous boats. There was also (1995) 1 company of Naval Infantry numbering 150.

Air Force. The Air Force equipment includes 10 A-37B and 5 Magister attack aircraft, 2 Rallye armed trainers, 6 armed C-47 transports and 6 Hughes 500MD helicopters for counter-insurgency operations. Other aircraft are 2 C-47, 3 Arava, 1 DC-6 and 1 C-123 transports, 6 Cessna O-2 patrol aircraft, as well as 60 UH-1H helicopters. Training types include piston-engined Cessna light aircraft and 4 A-37s. Strength totalled about 2,000 personnel (500 conscripts) in 1995.

INTERNATIONAL RELATIONS

Membership. El Salvador is a member of the UN, CACM, SELA and OAS.

ECONOMY

Policy. An economic liberalization programme aims at raising exports, foreign investment and domestic savings.

Budget. In 1993 current revenue was ₡8,311m., current expenditure ₡7,761m., capital revenue, ₡5m. and capital expenditure ₡2,767m.

Currency. The monetary unit is the *colón* (SVC) of 100 *centavos*. There are coins of 1, 5, 10, 25, 50 and 100 centavos and ₡1, and notes of ₡1, 2, 5, 10, 25, 50 and 100. Inflation was 8·9% in 1994. Foreign exchange reserves were US$536·2m. in

1993; gold reserves, 469,000 troy oz. In March 1996, £1 = ₡13·39; US$1 = ₡8·76; DM1 = ₡5·94.

Banking and Finance. The bank of issue is the Central Reserve Bank (*Governor*, José Roberto Orellana Milla), formed in 1934 and nationalized in 1961. There are 12 commercial banks (2 foreign). Individual private holdings may not exceed 5% of the total equity.

There is a stock exchange in San Salvador, founded in 1992.

Weights and Measures. On 1 Jan. 1886 the metric system was made obligatory. But other units are still commonly in use, of which the principal are as follows: *Libra* = 1·014 lbs; *quintal* = 100 lbs; *arroba* = 25·35 lbs; *fanega* = 1·5745 bushels.

ENERGY AND NATURAL RESOURCES

Electricity. Installed capacity in 1992 was 740 MW (50% hydro-electric, 37% thermal, 13% geothermal). Production in 1993, 2,685m. kWh.

Minerals. Production (in tonnes), 1987: Salt, 3,100; limestone, 1·45m.; gypsum, 4,500.

Agriculture. In 1988 0·61m. ha was pasture, 0·57m. ha arable and 0·17m. ha permanent cropland. In 1993, 36% of the working population was engaged in farming.

Large landholdings have been progressively expropriated and redistributed in accordance with legislation initiated in 1980. By 1994 some 12,000 individuals had received plots of 4–5 ha.

Production (1993, in 1,000 quintals): Coffee, 3,820; seed cotton, 207; maize, 15,339; beans, 1,354; rice, 1,564; sorghum, 4,656; sugar-cane, 7,994 tonnes.

Livestock (1992, in 1,000): 1,276 cattle, 310 pigs, 15 goats. Animal products, 1992 (in 1,000 tonnes): Beef, 26; pork, 9; poultry, 44; milk, 350; eggs, 47.

Forestry. Forest area was 104,000 ha in 1988. In the national forests are found dye woods, mahogany, cedar and walnut. Balsam trees also abound: El Salvador is a major source of this medicinal gum. 4·32m. cu. metres of timber were cut in 1989, mainly for fuel.

Fisheries. In 1989 there were 24 fishing vessels with a tonnage of 3,514 GRD. Total catch 1987, 18,000 tonnes.

INDUSTRY. 1988 production (in 1,000 tonnes) included: Petroleum, 136; fuel oil, 208; paper and products, 16.

Labour. In 1992 the economically active population was 1,745,000.

FOREIGN ECONOMIC RELATIONS. In May 1992 El Salvador, Guatemala and Honduras agreed to create a free trade zone for almost all goods and capital. Import duties are to be standardized. Foreign debt was US$2,131m. in 1992.

Commerce. Imports (including parcels post) and exports in calendar years in ₡1,000:

	1987	*1988*	*1989*	*1990*	*1991*
Imports	4,970,335	5,034,860	6,448,700	9,594,800	11,276,120
Exports	2,954,705	2,982,095	2,784,100	4,410,700	4,715,760

139,000 quintals of coffee were exported in 1991.

In 1990 the USA took ₡1,464,277,000 of exports and furnished ₡4,082,766,000 of imports. In 1992 the main export markets were the USA, Guatemala, Germany, Costa Rica, Nicaragua and Honduras; main import suppliers were the USA, Guatemala, Mexico, Germany, Japan and Venezuela.

Total trade between El Salvador and UK (British Department of Trade returns, in £1.000 sterling):

	1991	*1992*	*1993*	*1994*	*1995*
Imports to UK	4,063	7,890	8,895	7,200	3,419
Exports and re-exports from UK	14,545	15,002	15,160	19,217	22,737

Tourism. There were 181,332 tourists in 1994.

COMMUNICATIONS

Roads. In 1989 there were 15,120 km of national roads, including 1,770 km of main paved roads, 3,507 km of main asphalted roads and 9,843 km of other roads. Vehicles registered, 1992: Cars, 221,900; commercial vehicles, 33,200.

Railways. Railways are run by National Railways of El Salvador. Route length, 1994, 602 km. There is a link to the Guatemalan system. Total railway traffic in 1992 was 326,000 tonnes of freight and 408,000 passengers.

Civil Aviation. The international airport is at Comalapa, 40 km from San Salvador. The national carrier is TACA, which was operating 1 B-737-200, 2 B-737-200 Advs, 1 B-737-200C Adv, 4 B-737-300s, 1 B-767-200ER, 1 B-767-300ER and 1 other aircraft in 1995. It flies services to various destinations in the USA, Mexico and all Central American countries.

Shipping. The main ports are Cutuco and Acajutla. The merchant fleet numbered 14 vessels in 1989 with a total tonnage of 3,819 GRT.

Telecommunications. The telephone and telegraph systems are government-owned; the radio-telephone systems are partly private, partly government-owned. In 1989 there were 94,691 telephones. Broadcasting is under the control of the Administración Nacional de Telecomunicaciones. There are 6 commercial television channels, a government-owned channel and 2 educational channels sponsored by the Ministry of Education. In 1993 there were 1,935,000 radio receivers and 500,700 television sets (colour by NTSC).

Cinemas (1976). Cinemas numbered 65.

Press (1995). There are 5 daily newspapers.

SOCIAL INSTITUTIONS

Justice. Justice is administered by the Supreme Court (6 members appointed for 3-year terms by the Legislative Assembly and 6 by bar associations), courts of first and second instance, and minor tribunals.

Following the disbanding of security forces in Jan. 1992 a new National Civilian Police Force was created which is planned to number 10,500 by 1997.

Religion. About 90% of the population is Roman Catholic. Under the 1962 Constitution churches are exempted from the property tax; the Catholic Church is recognized as a legal person, and other churches are entitled to secure similar recognition. There is an archbishop in San Salvador and bishops at Santa Ana, San Miguel, San Vicente, Santiago de María, Usulután, Sonsonate and Zacatecoluca. There are about 200,000 Protestants.

Education. Adult literacy was 75% in 1992. Education is run by the state and is free and compulsory. In 1986 there were 72,500 pupils in nursery schools and 1,140,000 in primary and secondary schools. In 1995–96 in the public sector there were 3 universities; in the private sector there were 21 universities and 14 specialized universities (1 American, 3 Evangelical, 1 Roman Catholic, 1 Open and 1 each for business, integrated education, polytechnic, science and development, teaching, science and technology, technical studies and technology). In 1994–95, there were 63,413 university students and 3,983 academic staff.

Health. In 1986 there were 5,548 hospital beds. In 1985 there were 1,649 doctors.

Welfare. The Social Security Institute now administers the sickness, old age and death insurance, covering industrial workers and employees earning up to ₡700 a month. Employees in other private institutions with salaries over this amount are included but are excluded from the medical and hospital benefits.

DIPLOMATIC REPRESENTATIVES

Of El Salvador in Great Britain (159 Great Portland St., London, W1N)
Ambassador: Vacant.

Of Great Britain in El Salvador (Paseo General Escalón 4828, POB 1591, San Salvador)
Ambassador and Consul General: Ian Gerken, LVO.

Of El Salvador in the USA (2308 California St., NW, Washington, DC., 20008)
Ambassador: Ana C. Sol.

Of the USA in El Salvador (25 Ave. Norte, Colonia Dueñas, San Salvador)
Ambassador: Alan H. Flanigan.

Of El Salvador to the United Nations
Ambassador: Dr Ricardo G. Castaneda-Cornejo.

Further Reading

Armstrong, R. and Shenk, J., *El Salvador: the Face of Revolution.* London, 1982
Baloyra, E. A., *El Salvador in Transition.* Univ. of North Carolina Press, 1982
Didion, J., *Salvador.* London, 1983
Kufeld, A., *El Salvador.* NY, 1991
Montgomery, T.S., *Revolution in El Salvador: Origins and Evolution.* Boulder (CO), 1982
North, L., *Bitter Grounds: Roots of Revolt in El Salvador.* London, 1981
Woodward, R. L., *El Salvador.* [Bibliography] Oxford and Santa Barbara (CA), 1988

National statistical office: Dirección General de Estadística y Censos, Calle Arce, San Salvador.

EQUATORIAL GUINEA

República de Guinea Ecuatorial

Capital: Malabo
Population: 420,000 (1992)
GNP per capita: US$430 (1994)
HDI/world rank: 0·399/142 (1992)

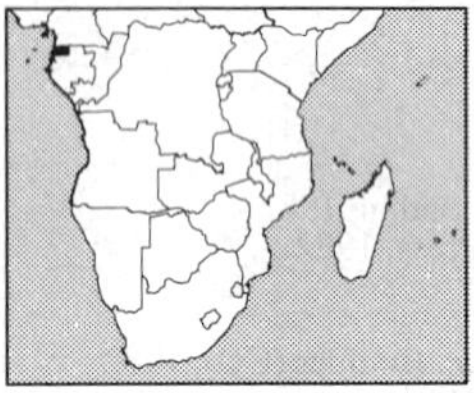

KEY HISTORICAL EVENTS. Equatorial Guinea was a Spanish colony (Territorios Españoles del Golfo de Guinea) until 1 April 1960. The territory was then divided into two Spanish provinces with a status comparable to the metropolitan provinces until 20 Dec. 1963, when they were re-joined as an autonomous Equatorial Region. It became an independent Republic on 12 Oct. 1968 as a federation of the two provinces, and a unitary state was established on 4 Aug. 1973. The first President, Francisco Macías Nguema, was declared President-for-Life on 14 July 1972, but was overthrown by a military coup on 3 Aug. 1979. A Supreme Military Council then created was the sole political body until constitutional rule was resumed on 12 Oct. 1982.

TERRITORY AND POPULATION. The mainland part of Equatorial Guinea is bounded north by Cameroon, east and south by Gabon, and west by the Gulf of Guinea in which lie the islands of Bioko (formerly Macías Nguema, formerly Fernando Póo) and Annobón (called Pagalu from 1973 to 1979). The total area is 28,051 sq. km (10,831 sq. miles) and the population at the last (1983) census was 304,000. Estimate (1992) 420,000. Another 110,000 are estimated to remain in exile abroad.

The 7 provinces are grouped into 2 regions, Continental (C), chief town Bata and Insular (I), chief town Malabo, with areas and populations as follows:

	Sq. km	*Census 1983*	*Chief town*
Annobón (I)	17	2,006	San Antonio de Palea
Bioko Norte (I)	776	46,221	Malabo
Bioko Sur (I)	1,241	10,969	Luba
Centro Sur (C)	9,931	52,393	Evinayong
Kié-Ntem (C)	3,943	70,202	Ebebiyin
Litoral (C)	6,665 [1]	66,370	Bata
Wele-Nzas (C)	5,478	51,839	Mongomo

[1] Including the adjacent islets of Corisco, Elobey Grande and Elobey Chico (17 sq. km).

In 1986 the largest towns were Bata (17,000) and the capital Malabo (10,000).

The main ethnic group on the mainland is the Fang, which comprises 85% of the total population; there are several minority groups along the coast and adjacent islets. On Bioko the indigenous inhabitants (Bubis) constitute 60% of the population there, the balance being mainly Fang and coast people. On Annobón the indigenous inhabitants are the descendants of Portuguese slaves and still speak a Portuguese patois. The official language is Spanish.

CLIMATE. The climate is equatorial, with alternate wet and dry seasons. In Río Muni, the wet season lasts from Dec. to Feb.

CONSTITUTION AND GOVERNMENT. A Constitution was approved in Aug. 1982 by 95% of the votes cast in a plebiscite. It provided for an 11-member Council of State, and for a 41-member House of Representatives of the People, the latter being directly elected on 28 Aug. 1983 for a 5-year term and re-elected on 10 July 1988. The President appointed and leads a Council of Ministers.

On 12 Oct. 1987 a single new political party was formed as the *Partido Democrático de Guinea Ecuatorial.*

A referendum on 17 Nov. 1991 approved the institution of multi-party democracy, and a law to this effect was passed in Jan. 1992. The electorate is restricted to citizens who have resided in Equatorial Guinea for at least 10 years. A new parliament, the *National Assembly*, has 80 seats. At the elections on 21 Nov. 1993 candidates from 8 parties stood. The main opposition parties called for a boycott. Turn-out was 30%. The Democratic Party gained 68 seats, the Social Democratic and Popular Convergence Party 6, the Social and Democratic Union 5 and the Liberal Party 1.

President of the Supreme Military Council, Minister of Defence: Brig.-Gen. Teodoro Obiang Nguema Mbasogo.

A government was formed in Dec. 1993 which in Sept. 1995 comprised:

Prime Minister: Silvestre Siale Bileka.

Deputy Prime Minister, Minister of the Economy and Finance: Anatólio Ndong Mba. *Agriculture, Fisheries and Food:* Alfredo Mokudi Nanga. *Culture, Tourism and French Community Affairs:* Agustín Nse Nfumu. *Education and Science:* Ricardo Obama Nfube. *Foreign Affairs and Co-operation:* Miguel Oyono Ndong. *Health and the Environment:* Bemabe Ngore. *Industry, Energy and Small Business:* Severino Obiang Bengono. *Justice and Religion:* Francisco Mbengono. *Labour and Social Welfare:* Ernesto Cayetano Toherida. *Mines and Hydrocarbons:* Juan Olo Nseng. *Social Affairs and Women:* Balbina Nchama Nvo. *Works, Housing and Town Planning:* Alejandro Nvoro Ovono.

National flag: Three horizontal stripes of green, white, red; a blue triangle based on the hoist; in the centre the national arms.

National anthem: 'Caminemos pisando las sendas' ('Let us journey treading the pathways'); words by A. N. Miyongo, tune anonymous.

Local Government. There are some 600 rural councils.

DEFENCE

Army. The Army consists of 3 infantry battalions with (1996) 1,100 personnel. There is also a paramilitary Guardia Civil.

Navy. A small force, numbering 120 in 1995, and based at Malabo, operates 4 inshore patrol craft.

Air Force. There is no formal air service but the National Guard Air Wing has 1 Yak-40 and 2 An-32 transports.

INTERNATIONAL RELATIONS

Membership. Equatorial Guinea is a member of the UN and OAU and is an ACP state of the EEC.

ECONOMY

Budget. In 1991 revenue was 7,700m. francs CFA and expenditure 13,100m. francs CFA, of which 7,600m. francs CFA were current expenditure.

Currency. On 2 Jan. 1985 the country joined the Franc Zone and the *epkwele* was replaced by the *franc CFA* which now has a parity value of 50 francs CFA to 1 French franc. There are coins of 1, 2, 5, 10, 25, 50, 100 and 500 francs CFA, and banknotes of 100, 500, 1,000, 5,000 and 10,000 francs CFA. Foreign exchange reserves were US$10·31m. at the end of 1992. For exchange rates *see* BENIN: Currency.

Banking and Finance. The *Banque des Etats de l'Afrique Centrale* became the bank of issue in Jan. 1985. There is 1 commercial bank.

ENERGY AND NATURAL RESOURCES

Electricity. Production (1986) 17m. kWh. There are 2 hydroelectric plants.

Minerals. There is some small-scale alluvial gold production.

Oil. Production started in 1992.

Agriculture. In 1990 agriculture accounted for 55·9% of GDP. The chief products are cocoa (60,000 ha in 1992) and coffee (19,000 ha). Production (in 1,000 tonnes in 1992): Cocoa, 5; coffee 7; palm oil, 5; palm kernels, 3; bananas, 17; cassava, 47; sweet potatoes, 35. Plantations in the hinterland have been abandoned by their Spanish former owners and except for cocoa, commercial agriculture is under serious difficulties.

Livestock (1992): Cattle, 5,000; sheep, 36,000; goats, 8,000; pigs, 5,000.

Forestry. 2·2m. ha are forested, of which 0·8m. ha are suitable for commercial forestry. Output (1992) was estimated at 0·15m. cu. metres.

Fisheries. Tuna and shellfish are caught. The freshwater catch in 1990 was 150 tonnes.

INDUSTRY. The once-flourishing light industry collapsed under the Macías regime. Processing timber for export is now the major activity. Food processing is also being developed.

Labour. The wage-earning non-agricultural workforce is small. The average monthly wage was 14,000 francs CFA in 1992.

FOREIGN ECONOMIC RELATIONS. Foreign debt was US$249·3m. in 1991.

Commerce. In 1991 imports amounted to 19,800m. francs CFA and exports to 10,100m. francs CFA. Main exports (in US$1m.), 1991: Timber, 14; cocoa, 6; coffee, 1. Main export markets, 1991: Spain, 47%; Italy, 14·6%; Netherlands, 12·9%; Germany, 8·4%. Main import suppliers: Cameroon, 34%.

Total trade between Equatorial Guinea and UK (British Department of Trade returns, in £1,000 sterling):

	1991	*1992*	*1993*	*1994*	*1995*
Imports to UK	33	40	6	nil	94
Exports and re-exports from UK	1,967	1,357	1,237	387	347

COMMUNICATIONS

Roads. Length (1993) 1,326 km of which 508 km were paved and 818 km laterite. There were also 1,356 km of dirt roads. Most roads are in a state of disrepair. There were about 3,000 cars and 4,000 commercial vehicles in 1987.

Civil Aviation. There are international airports at Malabo and Bata. The national carrier, Ecuato Guineana, was dissolved in 1990. Services are provided by Iberia.

Shipping. Bata is the main port, handling mainly timber. The other ports are Luba, formerly San Carlos (bananas, cocoa) in Bioko and Malabo, Evinayong and Mbini on the mainland. Ocean-going shipping totalled 3,279 GRT in 1995.

Telecommunications. Telephone services are rudimentary. 2 radio programmes are broadcast by the state-controlled Radio Nacional de Guinea Ecuatorial and Televisión Nacional. There is also a commercial radio network, and a cultural programme produced with Spanish collaboration. In 1993 there were 100,000 radio and 2,500 TV receivers (colour by SECAM).

Press. There are no daily newspapers. There is a government gazette and 2 periodicals.

SOCIAL INSTITUTIONS

Justice. The Constitution guarantees an independent judiciary. The Supreme Tribunal is the highest court of appeal and is located at Malabo. There are Courts of First Instance and Courts of Appeal at Malabo and Bata.

Religion. Christianity was proscribed under President Macías but reinstated in 1979. In 1994 there were 0·3m. Roman Catholics and 8,000 Protestants.

Education. In 1990 adult literacy was 50%. In 1987–88 there were 63,850 primary school pupils (85% of eligible children) and 1,180 teachers, and 9,204 secondary school pupils with 301 teachers. In 1993 there were 2 teacher training colleges, 2 post-secondary vocational schools and 1 agricultural institute.

Health. In 1989 there were 929 health workers including 100 doctors.

DIPLOMATIC REPRESENTATIVES

Of Equatorial Guinea in Great Britain
Ambassador: (Vacant; resides in Paris).

Of Great Britain in Equatorial Guinea
Ambassador and Consul-General: Nicholas McCarthy, OBE (resides in Yaoundé).

Of the USA in Equatorial Guinea (Calle de Los Ministros, Malabo)
Ambassador: Joseph O'Neill.

Of Equatorial Guinea in the USA (57 Magnolia Ave, Mt. Vernon, NY 10553)
Ambassador: Micha Ondo Bile.

Of Equatorial Guinea to the United Nations
Ambassador: Vacant.

Further Reading

Fegley, R., *Equatorial Guinea, an African Tragedy.* New York, 1989.—*Equatorial Guinea:* [Bibliography]. Oxford and Santa Barbara (CA), 1991

Liniger-Goumaz, M., *Guinea Ecuatorial: Bibliografía General.* Geneva, 1974-91.—*Historical Dictionary of Equatorial Guinea.* 2nd ed. Metuchen (NJ), 1988.—*Small Is Not Always Beautiful: the Story of Equatorial Guinea.* London, 1988

Molino, A. M. del, *La Ciudad de Clarence.* Madrid, 1994

ERITREA

Capital: Asmara
Population: 3·53m. (1994)
GNP per capita: US$77 (1993)

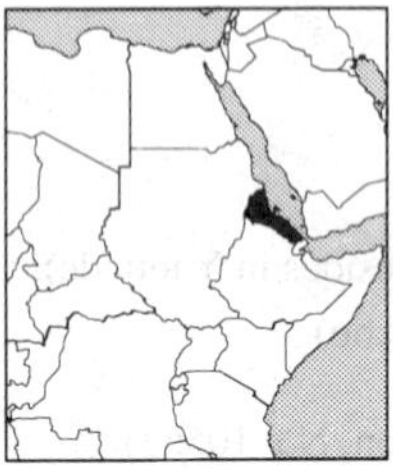

KEY HISTORICAL EVENTS. Italy was the colonial ruler of Eritrea from 1890 until 1941, when it fell to British forces in the Second World War and a British protectorate was set up. This ended in 1952 when the UN sanctioned its federation with Ethiopia. In 1962 Ethiopia became a unitary state and Eritrea was incorporated as a province. Eritreans began an armed struggle for independence, from 1972 under the leadership of the Eritrean People's Liberation Front (EPLF) which culminated successfully in the capture of Asmara on 24 May 1991. From then on the EPLF maintained a *de facto* independent administration which was recognized by the Ethiopian government succeeding the deposed President Mengistu.

At a referendum on 23–25 April 1993 there was a 99·8% majority in favour of independence. Sovereignty was proclaimed on 24 May 1993.

TERRITORY AND POPULATION. Eritrea is bounded in the north-east by the Red Sea, south-east by Djibouti, south by Ethiopia and west by Sudan. Some 300 islands form the Dahlak Archipelago, most of them uninhabited. For the dispute with Yemen over the island of Greater Hanish *see* YEMEN: Territory and Population. Its area is 93,679 sq. km (36,171 sq. miles). Population, 1994 estimate, 3,525,000 (20% urban). 1m. Eritreans lived abroad in 1995, 0·5m. as refugees in Sudan. A UN Programme for Refugee Reintegration and Rehabilitation of Resettlement Areas in Eritrea (PROFERI) is running from 1993 to 1997.

In 1993 infant mortality was 135 per 1,000 live births. Expectation of life was 46 years.

There are 10 provinces: Akele Guzai, Asmara, Barka, Denkel, Gash-Setir, Hamasien, Sahel, Semhar, Senhit and Seraye. The capital is Asmara (1991 population, 367,300). Other large towns (with 1989 populations) are Assab (39,569), Keren (32,110) and Massawa (19,404). An agreement of July 1993 gives Ethiopia rights to use the ports of Assab and Massawa.

48% of the population speak Tigrinya and 31% Tigré, and there are 7 other indigenous languages. Arabic is spoken on the coast and along the Sudanese border, and English is used in secondary schools. Arabic and Tigrinya are the official languages.

CLIMATE. Massawa. Jan. 78°F (25·6°C), July 94°F (34·4C). Annual rainfall 8" (193 mm).

CONSTITUTION AND GOVERNMENT. A referendum to approve independence was held on 23–25 April 1993. The electorate was 1,173,506. 99·8% of votes cast were in favour.

The transitional government has a 4-year term and consists of the *President* and a 130-member *National Assembly.* The latter consists of the members of the People's Front for Democracy and Justice (PFDJ; until Feb. 1994 EPLF) Central Committee and 60 other deputies (including 11 seats reserved for women). It elects the President who in turn appoints the *State Council* made up of 14 ministers and the governors of the 10 provinces. The President chairs both the State Council and the National Assembly.

Presidential and legislative elections are scheduled for May 1997.

President: Issaias Afewerki (b. 1945; elected 22 May 1993).

In Oct. 1993 the ministers in the State Council were:

Agriculture: Tesfai Ghermasien. *Commerce, Industry and Tourism:* Ogbeh Abraha.

Construction: Abraha Asfaha. *Culture and Information:* Alamin Mohammed Said. *Defence:* Petros Solomon. *Education:* Osman Saleh. *Energy, Mining and Water Resources:* Tesfai Gebereselassie. *Finance and Development:* Haile Weldeteasae. *Foreign:* Mohammed Ahmed Sherifo. *Health:* Haile Mihtsan. *Interior:* Ali Said Abdella. *Justice:* Fozia Hashim. *Marine Resources:* Saleh Meky. *Provincial Administration:* Ramadan Mohammed Nar.

National flag: The flag is divided into segments by a red triangle based on the hoist on which is a green olive wreath and branch. The upper segment is green and the lower light blue.

Local Government. There are 10 provinces, each under a governor.

DEFENCE. Conscription for 18 months was introduced in 1994. The total strength of all forces was estimated at 35,000 in 1996.

Navy. The former Ethiopian Navy is now in Eritrean hands. Strength is esimated as 1 small frigate, 1 fast missile craft and 5 patrol craft. There are also 2 mine countermeasure vessels, 2 medium landing ships and 6 craft, 1 transport and 1 training ship. The main base and training establishments are at Massawa and Assab.

Air Force. There are 15 aircraft, including 4 Y-12 transports, 2 Mi-8 helicopters, 8 L-90TP Redigo liaison/training machines and 1 Astra VIP transport.

INTERNATIONAL RELATIONS

Membership. Eritrea is a member of the UN and OAU.

ECONOMY

Budget. Government finance (in 1m. Ethiopian birr), 1991–92: Revenue, 154·5 (including sales taxes, 46·3; customs dues, 27·4; direct taxes, 21·4; sales, 8·3); expenditure, 128·6.

Currency. Ethiopian currency is in use.

Banking and Finance. The central bank is the National Bank of Eritrea (*Governor*, Tequie Beyene). All banks and financial institutions are state-run. There is a Commercial Bank of Eritrea with 12 branches, an Agricultural and Industrial Bank, a Housing and Savings Bank and an Insurance Corporation.

ENERGY AND NATURAL RESOURCES

Electricity. Installed capacity was 40 MW in 1993.

Minerals. There are deposits of gold, silver, copper, zinc, sulphur, nickel, chrome and potash. Basalt, limestone, marble, sand and silicates are extracted.

Agriculture. Several systems of land ownership (state, colonial, traditional) co-exist. In 1994 the PFDJ proclaimed the sole right of the state to own land. Sorghum is cultivated. Livestock includes goats and camels.

INDUSTRY. Light industry was well developed in the colonial period but capability has declined. Processed food, textiles, leatherware, building materials, glassware and oil products are produced.

FOREIGN ECONOMIC RELATIONS. Eritrea is dependent on foreign aid for most of its capital expenditure, but there is no external debt.

Commerce. In 1992 exports were valued at 16m. birr and imports at 367m. birr. The main exports are drinks, leather and products, textiles and oil products. Most exports go to Ethiopia; principal import suppliers: Saudi Arabia, Ethiopia, UAE.

British Department of Trade returns, 1995: Imports to UK, £41,000; exports from UK, £768,000.

COMMUNICATIONS

Roads. There is a tarmac road from Asmara to Massawa and about 600 km of unsurfaced other roads. About 500 buses operate regular services.

Railways. The 117 km Asmara–Massawa line is being rebuilt. A short section in Massawa was reopened in 1994.

Civil Aviation. There is an international airport at Asmara. Services are provided by Egyptair, Ethiopian Airlines, Lufthansa, Saudia, Sudan Airways, United Airlines and Yemenia.

Shipping. Massawa is the main port; Assab is used mainly for imports to Ethiopia, both are free ports for Ethiopia. Ethiopian Shipping Lines provide services.

Telecommunications. There is daily radio and TV broadcasting. International telephone links were restored in 1992.

Press. There is a government daily in Arabic and Tigrinya.

SOCIAL INSTITUTIONS

Justice. The legal system derives from a decree of May 1993.

Religion. Half the population are Sunni Moslems (along the coast and in the north), and half Coptic Christians (in the south).

Education. Adult literacy was about 20% in 1994. In 1993 there were 261 state primary schools and 52 secondary schools as well as some private schools. There were 0·25m. pupils and 6,965 teachers in 1994. There is 1 university, with 3,200 students and 250 academic staff in 1994–95.

Health. In 1993 there were 10 small regional hospitals, 32 health centres, 65 medical posts, 68 doctors, 488 nurses, 33 midwives and 850 auxiliary medical personnel.

DIPLOMATIC REPRESENTATIVES

Of Eritrea in Great Britain
Ambassador: Vacant (resides in Brussels).

Of Great Britain in Eritrea
Ambassador: D. R. C. Christopher (resides in Addis Ababa).

Of Eritrea in the USA
Ambassador: Amdemichael Kahsai.

Of the USA in Eritrea (34 Zera Yacob St., POB 211, Asmara)
Ambassador: Robert G. Houdek.

Of Eritrea to the United Nations
Ambassador: Amdemichael Kahsai.

Further Reading

Connel, D., *Against All Odds: a Chronicle of the Eritrean Revolution.* Trenton (NJ), 1993
Fegley, R., *Eritrea.* [Bibliography]. Oxford and Santa Barbara (CA), 1995
Lewis, R., *Eritrea: Africa's Newest Country.* London, 1993

ESTONIA

Eesti Vabariik

(Republic of Estonia)

Capital: Tallinn
Population: 1·6m. (1992)
GNP per capita: US$2,820 (1994)
HDI/world rank: 0·862/43 (1992)

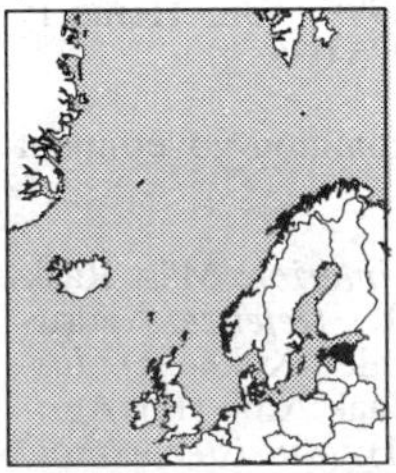

KEY HISTORICAL EVENTS. The early Estonians did not create state units and were subjected to Viking incursions. In 1346 the Danes relinquished Estonia to German rule, and it became part of the Holy Roman Empire and then a Swedish possession in the middle of the 17th century. On Sweden's defeat by Peter the Great, Estonia passed to the Russian Empire in 1721. For events during the 1917 Russian Revolution *see* THE STATESMAN'S YEAR-BOOK, 1995–96, p. 521.

An independent republic was proclaimed in May 1919.

The secret protocol of the Soviet-German agreement of 23 Aug. 1939 assigned Estonia to the Soviet sphere of interest. An ultimatum (16 June 1940) led to the formation of a government acceptable to the USSR. On 21 July the Estonian parliament proclaimed the establishment of an Estonian Soviet Socialist Republic and applied to join the USSR; on 6 Aug. the Supreme Soviet of the USSR accepted the application.

On 30 March 1990 the Estonian Supreme Soviet proclaimed that the Soviet occupation of Estonia on 17 June 1940 had not disrupted the continuity of the former republic, and adopted, by 73 votes to nil with 3 abstentions, a declaration calling for the eventual re-establishment of full sovereignty. At a referendum in March 1991 77·8% of votes cast were in favour of independence. While an attempted coup was taking place in the USSR parliament declared independence on 20 Aug. 1991. A fully independent status was conceded by the USSR State Council on 6 Sept. 1991.

TERRITORY AND POPULATION. Estonia is bounded in the west and north by the Baltic Sea, east by Russia and south by Latvia. There are numerous offshore islands, of which the largest are Saaremaa and Hiiumaa. Area, 45,100 sq. km (17,413 sq. miles); population, 1,595,000 (1992 estimate). The 1989 census population was 1,565,662, of whom Estonians accounted for 61·5%, Russians 30·3%, Ukrainians 3·1%, Belorussians 1·8% and Finns 1·1%. Vital statistics rates (1991, per 1,000 population): Birth, 14, death, 12; infant mortality (per 1,000 live births), 12. There were 25,587 induced abortions in 1993 (29,406 in 1991). Expectation of life was 70 years in 1991.

The capital is Tallinn (1994 population, 490,000). Other large towns are Tartu (110,100), Kohtla-Järve (75,000), Narva (85,000) and Pärnu (60,000). There are 15 districts, 33 towns and 26 urban settlements.

The official language is Estonian.

CLIMATE. Because of its maritime location Estonia has a moderate climate, with cool summers and mild winters. Rainfall is heavy, 500–700 mm per year, and evaporation low.

CONSTITUTION AND GOVERNMENT. A draft constitution drawn up by a constitutional assembly was approved by 91·1% of votes cast at a referendum on 28 June 1992. Turn-out was 66·6%. The constitution came into effect on 4 July 1992. It defines Estonia as a 'democratic state guided by the rule of law, where universally recognized norms of international law are an inseparable part of the legal system.' It provides for a 101-member national assembly (*Riigikogu*) elected for 4-year terms. There are 11 electoral districts with 8 to 11 mandates each. Candidates may be elected a) by gaining more than 'quota', i.e. the number of votes cast in a district divided by the number of its mandates; b) by standing for a party which attracts for all of its candidates more than the quota, in order of listing; c) by being listed nationally for parties which clear a 5% threshold and eligible for the seats remaining according to position on the lists. The *President* is elected by the Riigikogu.

Elections were held on 5 March 1995. There were 1,265 candidates representing 16 parties. The electorate was 792,119; turn-out was 69%. The Coalition Party-Rural Union won 41 seats with 32·23% of votes cast; the Estonian Reform Party-Liberals, 19 with 16·19%; the Estonian Centre Party, 16 with 14·17%; the Fatherland Alliance, 8 with 7·86%; the Moderate Party, 6 with 5·99%; Our Home is Estonia (ethnic Russians), 6 with 5·87%; the Right Wing, 5 with 5·03%.

President: Lennart Meri (b. 1929; FA; sworn in 6 Oct. 1992).

A Coalition Party (K)-Reform Party (R)-Rural Union (M) coalition government was formed in Oct. 1995, comprising:

Prime Minister: Tiit Vähi.

Deputy Prime Minister and Foreign Minister: Siim Kallas. *Interior:* Märt Rask (R). *Economics:* Andres Lipstok (R). *Finance:* Mart Opmann (K). *Defence:* Andrus Öövel (K). *Social Affairs:* Toomas Vilosius (R). *Transport:* Kalev Kukk (R). *Justice:* Paul Varul (K). *Education:* Jaak Aaviksoo (R). *Culture:* Jaak Allik (K). *Agriculture:* Ilmar Mändmets (M). *Environment:* Villu Reiljan (M). *Minsister without portfolio for European Affairs:* Endel Lippmaa (K). *Minister without portfolio for Regional Affairs:* Tiit Kulori (M).

The *Speaker* is Toomas Savi (R).

Citizenship requirements are 2 years residence and competence in Estonian for existing residents. For residents immigrating after 1 April 1995 5 years qualifying residence is required.

National flag: 3 horizontal stripes of blue, black and white.

National anthem: 'Mu isamaa, mu õnn ja rõõm' ('My native land, my pride and joy'); words by J. V. Jannsen, tune by F. Pacius (same as Finland).

Local Government. There are 12 city and 241 district councils. The electorate consists of citizens and residents of 5 years' standing. Only citizens may stand for office. Elections were held on 17 Oct. 1993. The electorate was 870,041; turn-out was 60%. 8,738 candidates contended for 3,427 seats.

DEFENCE. Conscription is 12 months for men and women. Conscientious objectors may opt for 15 months civilian service instead.

Army. The Army comprises 3 infantry and 1 guard and 1 air defence battalion. Personnel (1996) 3,300. There is a reserve Militia and a para-military Border Guard (2,000 strong). The Army has 1 Mi-2 and 8 Mi-8 transport helicopters and 1 L-410 transport.

Navy. The Navy numbered 150 in 1995 and operates 8 patrol craft. A Maritime element of the Border Guard numbering about 800 in 1995 operates 4 ex-Norwegian fast coastal patrol craft and 8 others.

INTERNATIONAL RELATIONS

Membership. Estonia is a member of the UN, the Council of Europe and the NATO Partnership for Peace, and is an Associate Partner of the WEU. Estonia applied to join the EU in Nov. 1995.

ECONOMY

Policy. Privatization is being managed by the Estonian Privatization Agency under the jurisdiction of the Ministry of Finance. It is mainly achieved by direct sales, though there is some distribution by vouchers. In 1994, 183 sales worth 1,150m. kroons took place (353m. kroons in 1993).

Budget. Budget estimates for 1995 balanced at 8,793m. kroons.

Sources of revenue included sales tax, 2,260m. kroons; personal and corporate income tax, 2,000m. kroons. Items of expenditure: Education, culture, health and sport, 1,450m. kroons; economic reforms, 1,300m. kroons; justice and law enforcement, 713m. kroons; local government, 528m. kroons; social welfare, 385m. kroons.

Currency. The unit of currency is the *kroon* (EKR) of 100 *sents*. The kroon is pegged to the German mark within 3% of DM1 = 8 kroons. There are coins of 1, 5, 10, 20 and 50 sents and 1 kroon, and notes of 1, 2, 5, 10, 25, 50, 100 and 500 kroons. There were 2,810·2m. kroons in circulation in May 1994. Gold reserves were US$110m. in 1992. Foreign exchange reserves were 4,876m. kroons in May 1995. Inflation was an annualized 36% in 1993. In March 1996, £1 = 18·06 kroons; US$1 = 11·82 kroons; DM1 = 8 kroons.

Banking and Finance. A central bank, the Bank of Estonia, was re-established in 1990 (*Governor:* Vahur Kraft). In 1996 there were 15 commercial banks. Since 1 Jan. 1996 banks have been required to have an equity of at least 50m. kroons. Assets (in 1,000m. kroons) of the largest banks in 1995: Hansapank, 3·3; North Estonian Bank, 1·4; Bank of Tallinn, 1·1; the state-owned Savings Bank, 2·9; Union Bank, 2·6. The Estonian Investment Bank was established in 1992 to provide financing for privatized and private companies.

A stock exchange was scheduled to open in 1996.

Weights and Measures. The metric system is in use.

ENERGY AND NATURAL RESOURCES

Electricity. Output, 1989, was 17,600m. kWh. Some power stations are fuelled by peat.

Oil and Gas. There are rich oil-shale deposits estimated at 3,700m. tonnes. A factory for the production of gas from shale and a 208 km-pipeline from Kohtla-Järve supplies shale gas to Tallinn and exports to St Petersburg.

Minerals. There are extensive peat deposits. Phosphorites and super-phosphates are found and refined.

Agriculture. Farming is concentrated on milk and meat production. Large state and collective farms are being converted into shareholding enterprises. The remainder are being divided into small private holdings for collective farm workers or former owners. In 1993 there were some 8,400 private farms averaging 25·4 ha, and 600 co-operatives ranging between 1,000–2,000 ha.

In 1993 there were 614,500 cattle (253,400 milch cows), 143,000 sheep and goats, and 541,100 pigs.

Output of main agricultural products (in 1,000 tonnes) in 1992: Wheat, 92; rye, 150; barley, 302; potatoes, 648; other vegetables, 115; meat, 176; milk, 900; eggs, 24·1m. Livestock products, 1992: Meat, 131,600 tonnes; milk, 919,300 tonnes; eggs, 456m.

Forestry. Some 22% of the land is covered by forests which provide material for sawmills, furniture, match and pulp industries, as well as wood fuel.

INDUSTRY. Manufactures were valued at 14,610m. kroons before tax in 1993. Private firms employed 6% of the industrial workforce and produced 26·5% of total output. Output in 1989 included steel, 11,100 tonnes; timber, 2m. cu. metres; paper, 92,000 tonnes; cement, 1·1m. tonnes; fabrics, 235m. sq. metres; hosiery, 17m. pairs; footwear, 7·1m. pairs; knitwear, 23·6m. items; butter, 31,000 tonnes; preserves, 355m. standard jars. In 1990 there were some 5,600 enterprises of which 51% were state-owned, 32% co-operatives, 5% joint stock companies and 1·4% joint ventures.

Labour. In 1996 there was a monthly minimum wage of 680 kroons. Retirement age was 55 years for women and 60 for men in 1993, but is being extended to 60 and 65 respectively in 6-month stages by 2005. The official measure of unemployment is based on the number of job-seekers. There were 36,183 in May 1995.

FOREIGN ECONOMIC RELATIONS. On 12 April 1990 Estonia, Latvia and Lithuania concluded a Baltic Economic Co-operation Agreement. A free trade agreement came into force on 1 April 1994.

Joint ventures are permitted, but non-Estonians may not own more than 50% of the equity without government permission. New ventures enjoy a 2-year tax exemption.

Commerce. Exports (in 1m. kroons) in 1993 (and 1994) were valued at 10,641·7 (16,727); imports, 11,847·8 (20,793). Main export markets, 1993: Russia, 2,406·6; Finland, 2,202·6; Sweden, 1,011·4; Latvia, 914; Germany, 851·4; Netherlands, 431·5; Lithuania, 395·8; UK, 378; Denmark, 253·1; USA, 197·6. Main import suppliers: Finland, 3,304·4; Russia, 2,033·3; Germany, 1,272·3; Sweden, 1,055; Japan, 497·7; Netherlands, 429·1; Lithuania, 391; USA, 322·4; Denmark, 307·3; Latvia, 267·4. Total trade between Estonia and UK (British Department of Trade returns, in £1,000 sterling):

	1993	*1994*	*1995*
Imports to UK	20,039	58,830	111,840
Exports and re-exports from UK	8,043	15,285	29,665

Tourism. There were 1·6m. foreign tourists in 1993.

COMMUNICATIONS

Roads. In 1990 there were 30,200 km of motor roads (29,100 km hard-surfaced).

Railways. Length of railways in 1994 was 1,024 km (1,520 mm gauge), of which 132 km was electrified. In 1994, 11·5m. passengers and 22·6m. tonnes of freight were carried.

Civil Aviation. There is an international airport at Tallinn (Ulemiste). The national carrier is the state-owned Estonian Air. It carried 164,000 passengers in 1994. It had 15 ex-Soviet aircraft in 1995, and operated services to Amsterdam, Copenhagen, Frankfurt, Helsinki, Kiev, London, Minsk, Moscow, Riga, St Petersburg, Sochi, Stockholm, Tampere and Vilnius. Services are also provided by Aeroflot, Drakk Air Lines, Finnair, Hamburg Airlines, Lithuanian Airlines, LOT, Lufthansa, SAS and United Airlines, and by Estonian Aviation (ELK) with flights to Helsinki, Kuressaare, Riga, Tartu and Turku.

Shipping. There are 2 major shipping companies, of which the Estonian Shipping Company is state-owned. It had 73 vessels totalling 517,000 DWT in 1994. There are ice-free, deep-water ports at Tallinn and Muuga which handled 10·93m. tonnes of cargo in 1994. The ex-Soviet naval base at Paldiski is now vacant.

Telecommunications. There were 0·38m. telephone subscribers in 1994. Postal services are run by the state-owned Eesti Post. Estonian Radio operates under the aegis of the Broadcasting Council. There are also 3 commercial radio networks and the government's foreign service, Radio Estonia (Estonian, English, Esperanto, Finnish, German, Spanish). In 1993 there were 4 TV networks (colour by SECAM): Estonian State Television, 2 commercial channels and a Russian service. On the Estonian channels programming ventures must be at least 51% Estonian-owned, and foreign programmes must not exceed 30% of output. In 1993 there were 0·6m. TV receivers.

Cinemas. Attendances were 2·1m. in 1993.

Press. In 1995 there were 4 national dailies in Estonian, 2 in Russian and 2 evening papers and 6 weeklies.

SOCIAL INSTITUTIONS

Justice. A post-Soviet criminal code was introduced in 1992. The death penalty is retained for murder and terrorism. There is a 3-tier court system with the State Court at its apex, and there are both city and district courts. The latter act as courts of appeal. The State Court is the final court of appeal, and also functions as a constitutional court. There are also administrative courts for petty offences. Judges are appointed for life. City and district judges are appointed by the President; State Court judges are elected by Parliament.

There are 11 prisons; at 1 Aug. 1993, 4,516 persons were in custody.

Religion. There are about 0·35m. Lutherans and a Methodist Church. The Estonian Orthodox Church owed allegiance to Constantinople until it was forcibly brought under Moscow's control in 1940; a synod of the free Estonian Orthodox Church was established in Stockholm. In 1996 there were some 35,000 Orthodox in 84 congregations.

Education. There are 9 years of comprehensive school starting at age 6, followed by 2 years secondary school. In 1989–90 pupils in 600 primary, secondary and special schools numbered 200,000. In Jan. 1990 60% of eligible children attended pre-school institutions. There are 6 universities, 1 teacher training college, 1 polytechnical university and 1 agricultural university. There were 26,300 students in higher educational establishments in 1994–95, and 19,900 students in 36 technical colleges.

Health. There were 111 state hospitals in 1994. In 1992 there were 34 doctors and 94 hospital beds per 10,000 population.

Welfare. In 1994 there were 0·32m. pensioners. The average monthly pension was 918 kroons in 1996. An official poverty line was introduced in 1993 (then 280 kroons per month). Persons receiving less are entitled to state benefit. Unemployment benefit was 240 kroons a month in 1996

DIPLOMATIC REPRESENTATIVES

Of Estonia in Great Britain (16 Hyde Park Gate, London SW7 5DG)
Ambassador: Vacant.

Of Great Britain in Estonia (Kentmanni 20, Tallinn EE 0100)
Ambassador: C. R. L. De Chassiron.

Of Estonia in the USA (1030 15th Street NW, Washington DC 20005)
Ambassador: Toomas Hendrik Ilves.

Of the USA in Estonia (Kentmanni 20, Tallinn EE 0001)
Ambassador: Lawrence P. Taylor.

Of Estonia to the United Nations
Ambassador: Trivimi Velliste.

Further Reading

Statistical Office of Estonia. *Statistical Yearbook.*
Ministry of the Economy. *Estonian Economy.* Annual
Lieven, A., *The Baltic Revolution: Estonia, Latvia, Lithuania and the Path to Independence.* 2nd ed. Yale Univ. Press, 1994
Misiunas, R.-J. and Taagepera, R., *The Baltic States: Years of Dependence 1940–1991.* 2nd ed, Farnborough, 1993
Raun, T. U., *Estonia and the Estonians.* Stanford, 1987
Smith, I. A. and Grunts, M. V. *The Baltic States.* [Bibliography]. Oxford and Santa Barbara, 1993
Taagepera, R., *Estonia: Return to Independence.* Boulder (CO), 1993

National library: The Estonian National Library was opened in 1993.
National statistical office: Statistical Office of Estonia, Tallinn.

ETHIOPIA

Federal Democratic Republic of Ethiopia

Capital: Addis Ababa
Population: 55m. (1994)
GNP per capita: US$130 (1994)
HDI/world rank: 0·227/171 (1992)

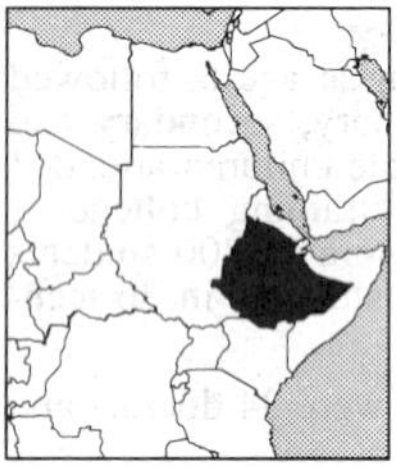

KEY HISTORICAL EVENTS. Modern Ethiopia dates from the reign of the Emperor Theodore (1855–68). Menelik II (1889–1913) defeated would-be Italian colonists in 1896 and united the country. In 1936 Ethiopia was eventually conquered by the Italians, who were in turn defeated by the Allied forces in 1941 when the Emperor returned.

A provisional military government deposed the Emperor and assumed power on 12 Sept. 1974. In Feb. 1977 Lieut.-Col. Mengistu Haile Mariam became Chairman of the Provisional Military Administrative Council, and in Sept. 1987 he was elected President of the newly-inaugurated People's Democratic Republic.

Following ever-increasing territorial gains by the insurgent Ethiopian People's Revolutionary Democratic Front (EPRDF) and the Eritrean People's Liberation Front (EPLF), Mengistu stepped down as president and fled the country. An interim EPRDF government led by Meles Zenawi took over after the flight of President Mengistu. In July 1991 a conference of 24 political groups called to appoint a transitional government agreed a democratic charter guaranteeing freedom of expression and association and the right to self-determination for ethnic groups. An 87-member Council of Representatives was formed which unanimously elected Meles President.

Eritrea seceded, and became independent on 24 May 1993.

TERRITORY AND POPULATION. Ethiopia is bounded in the north-east by Eritrea, east by Djibouti and Somalia, south by Kenya and west by Sudan. It has a total area of 1,098,000 sq. km. The secession of Eritrea in 1993 left Ethiopia without a coastline. An Eritrean-Ethiopian agreement of July 1993 gives Ethiopia rights to use the Eritrean ports of Assab and Massawa.

The first census was carried out in 1984: Population, 42,019,418 (without Eritrea, 39,570,266). Estimate (1994), 55m. (15% urban). Growth rate was 2·9% in 1989; expectation of life, (1991): Males, 47 years; females, 50.

The 1994 Constitution provides for a federation of 9 regions: Afar, Amhara, Benshangi, Gambella, Harar, Oromia, The Peoples of the South, Somalia and Tigre.

The population of the capital, Addis Ababa, was estimated at 1·7m. in 1990. Other large towns (population, May 1984): Dire Dawa, in Hararge, 98,104; Nazret, in Shoa, 76,284; Bahr Dar, 54,800; Debre Zeit, 51,143.

There are 8 major and some 60 minor ethnic groups and 286 languages spoken. The *de facto* official language is Amharic, though Oromo-speakers form the largest group.

CLIMATE. The wide range of latitude produces many climatic variations between the high, temperate plateaus and the hot, humid lowlands. The main rainy season lasts from June to Aug., with light rains from Feb. to April, but the country is very vulnerable to drought. Addis Ababa. Jan. 59°F (15°C), July 59°F (15°C). Annual rainfall 50" (1,237 mm). Harar. Jan. 65°F (18·3°C), July 64°F (17·8°C). Annual rainfall 35" (897 mm). Massawa. Jan. 78°F (25·6°C), July 94°F (34·4°C). Annual rainfall 8" (193 mm).

CONSTITUTION AND GOVERNMENT. A 547-member constituent assembly was elected on 5 June 1994; turn-out was 55%. The EPRDF gained 484 seats. On 8 Dec. 1994 it unanimously adopted a new federal Constitution which provides for the creation of a federation of 9 regions based (except the capital and the southern region) on a predominant ethnic group. These regions have the right of secession after a referendum. The *President*, a largely ceremonial post, is elected by the 548-member *Federal Assembly*.

Parliamentary and regional elections were held on 18 June 1995. The electorate was 24m. Candidates from 47 parties stood. The EPRDF won 540 seats.

President: Negasso Guidada (b. 1950; EPRDF; elected 22 Aug. 1995).

A new government was formed on 24 Aug. 1995 which comprised:

Prime Minister: Meles Zenawi (b. 1955; EPRDF).

Deputy Prime Minister, Minister of Defence: Tamrat Layne. *Deputy Prime Minister for Economic Affairs:* Kassu Illala. *Agriculture:* Teketel Forsido. *Education:* Guenet Zewde. *Finance:* Sufyan Ahmed. *Foreign Affairs:* Seyoum Mesfin. *Health:* Adam Ibrahim. *Information and Tourism:* Wolde-Mikael Chamo. *Justice:* Mehetema Solomon. *Labour and Social Affairs:* Hassan Abdullah. *Mines and Energy:* Azedin Ali. *Planning and Economic Co-operation:* Girma Biru. *Public Works and Urban Development:* Haile Aseged. *Trade and Industry:* Kassahun Ayele. *Transport and Communications:* Abdul Meyid Hussein. *Water Resources:* Shiferaw Yarso.

National flag: Three horizontal stripes of green, yellow and red.

National anthem: 'Yazegennat keber ba-Ityop yachchen santo' ('In our Ethiopia our civic pride is strong'); words anonymous, tune by S. Lulu.

Local Government. Local authority elections were held on 21 June 1992. The electorate was about 33m.

DEFENCE

Army. Following the overthrow of President Mengistu's government organized armed forces ceased to exist. The strength of the armed forces is estimated at 120,000. Equipment includes some 350 T-54/-55 main battle tanks.

Air Force. Most of the Air Force is grounded and in the process of reorganization. Surviving aircraft are reported to include 20 MiG-21 and some MiG-23 fighters, 18 Mi-24 armed helicopters and 25 Mi-28 transport helicopters. There were airfields at Debre Zeyit, Asmara, Gode, Dire Dawa and Deke.

INTERNATIONAL RELATIONS

Membership. Ethiopia is a member of the UN, OAU and is an ACP state of the EU.

ECONOMY

Policy. An Economic Reform Programme was instituted in 1992.

Budget. The fiscal year ends 6 July. Revenue, 1993–94 (in 1,000m. birr), 3·9 (of which tax revenue, 3·31); expenditure, 8·45 (of which capital expenditure, 3·85; education, 1·1; defence, 0·66).

Currency. The *birr* (ETB), of 100 *cents*, is the unit of currency. There are coins of 1, 5, 10, 25 and 50 cents, and notes of 1, 5, 10, 50 and 100 birr. The birr was devalued in Oct. 1992. Currency in circulation, 1992, 4,709m. birr. Foreign exchange reserves, 1993, US$414·3m. In March 1996, £1 sterling = 8·86 birr; US$1 = 5·80 birr; DM1 = 3·93 birr.

Banking and Finance. The central bank and bank of issue is the National Bank of Ethiopia (founded 1964; *Governor*, Dubale Yale). There is an Agricultural and Industrial Development Bank, and a Housing and Savings Bank. On 1 Jan. 1975 the Government nationalized all banks, mortgage and insurance companies.

Weights and Measures. The metric system is officially in use. Traditional units include the *frasilla* = approximately 37½ lb., and the *gasha*, which can vary between 80 and 300 acres.

ENERGY AND NATURAL RESOURCES

Electricity. 98% of generation is hydro-electric. Output, 1992, 1·13m. kWh. Supply 220 volts; 50 Hz.

Minerals. Gold, cement and salt are produced.

Agriculture. In 1992 agriculture contributed 50·3% of GDP. About 80% of the workforce are employed in agriculture. There are 85m. ha of arable land, of which 16m. ha were cultivated in 1994. In 1990 farmers were permitted to vote on the dissolution of co-operatives, and by 1993 96% of agricultural land was worked by smallholdings averaging 0·5–1·5 ha. Land remains the property of the state, but individuals are granted rights of usage which can be passed to their children, and produce may be sold on the open market instead of compulsorily to the state at low fixed prices.

Coffee is by far the most important source of rural income. Teff (*Eragrastis abyssinica*) is the principal food grain, followed by barley, wheat, maize and durra. Cane sugar is an important crop.

Production (1991 in 1,000 tonnes): Maize, 1,590; sorghum, 805; barley, 965; pulses, 763.

Livestock (1991): 30m. cattle, 23m. sheep, 18m. goats, 5·1m. asses, 2·7m. horses, 0·61m. mules and 1·06m. camels. Hides and skins and butter (ghee) are important for home consumption and export.

Forestry. In 1994 forests covered 2·7% of the land area.

INDUSTRY. Most public industrial enterprises are controlled by the state. Industrial activity is centred around Addis Ababa. Processed food, textiles and drinks are the main commodities produced.

Labour. The labour force in 1993 was 22m.; it was estimated by the UN that 30% were unemployed.

FOREIGN ECONOMIC RELATIONS. Foreign debt was US$4,354m. in 1992.

Commerce. Exports, 1992 (in 1m. birr), 448; imports, 2,604. Principal exports: Coffee, 168; hides and skins, 59; oil products, 19; fruit and vegetables, 6. Principal imports: Machinery and aircraft, 314; other vehicles, 179; oil products, 101; crude oil, 92; textiles, 74. The main export markets in 1991 were: Germany, 27·9%; Japan, 22·9%; Saudi Arabia, 8·4%; Italy, 6·8%. Main import suppliers: USA, 13·1%; Germany, 11·4%; Italy, 10·2%; Saudi Arabia, 9·9%. Coffee exports were worth US$250m. in 1994 (US$100m. in 1993).

Total trade between Ethiopia and UK (British Department of Trade returns, in £1,000 sterling):

	1991	*1992*	*1993*	*1994*	*1995*
Imports to UK	14,660	13,216	13,011	13,128	15,928
Exports and re-exports from UK	29,773	53,312	57,660	48,236	53,337

Tourism. There were 81,000 foreign visitors in 1993.

COMMUNICATIONS

Roads. There were (1989) 3,508 km of ashphalt roads and 9,687 km of rural and gravel roads.

Railways. The Ethiopian-Djibouti Railway Corp. (782 km, metre-gauge) in 1993 carried 0·24m. tonnes of freight and 0·71m. passengers.

Civil Aviation. There are international airports at Addis Ababa (Bole) and Dire Dawa. The national carrier is the state-owned Ethiopian Airlines, which in 1995 had a fleet of 1 B-707-320C, 1 B-737-200 Adv, 4 B-757-200s, 1 B-757-200PF, 3 B-767-200ERs and 10 other aircraft.

Telecommunications. The postal system serves 301 offices, mainly by air-mail. All the main centres are connected with Addis Ababa by telephone or radio telegraph.

The government-run Voice of Ethiopia broadcasts a national programme and an external service in English. Ethiopian Television (colour by PAL) transmits about 28 hours a week. In 1993 there were 3·3m. radio and 0·1m. TV receivers.

Press. There were (1991) 4 government-controlled daily newspapers with a combined circulation of about 60,000 and (1993) about 50 independent periodicals.

SOCIAL INSTITUTIONS

Justice. The legal system is said to be based on the Justinian Code. A new penal code came into force in 1958 and Special Penal Law in 1974. Codes of criminal procedure, civil, commercial and maritime codes have since been promulgated.

Provincial and district courts have been established, and High Court judges visit the provincial courts on circuit. The Supreme Court at Addis Ababa is presided over by the Chief Justice.

Religion. About 45% of the population are Moslem and 40% Christian, mainly belonging to the Ethiopian Orthodox Church. Amhara, Tigreans and some Oromos are Christian. Somalis, Afars and some Oromos are Moslems. About 12% of the population follow traditional animist beliefs, and some Oromos are Protestant.

Education. Adult literacy was 62·5% in 1990. Primary education commences at 7 years and continues with optional secondary education at 13 years. Up to the age of 12 education is in the local language of the federal region. In 1994–95 there was 1 university with 19,200 students and 900 academic staff, and 1 agricultural university with 1,551 students and 324 academic staff. There were also 2 institutes of health sciences and water technology; and 2 colleges, of teacher training and town planning.

DIPLOMATIC REPRESENTATIVES

Of Ethiopia in Great Britain (17 Prince's Gate, London, SW7 1PZ)
Ambassador: Dr Solomon Gidada.

Of Great Britain in Ethiopia (Fikre Mariam Abatechan St., Addis Ababa)
Ambassador: D. R. C. Christopher.

Of Ethiopia in the USA (2134 Kalorama Rd., NW, Washington D.C., 20008)
Ambassador: Berhane Gebre-Chirstos.

Of the USA in Ethiopia (Entoto St., Addis Ababa)
Ambassador: Irvin Hicks.

Of Ethiopia to the United Nations
Ambassador: Mulugeta Eteffa.

Further Reading

Alemneh Dejene. *Environment, Famine and Politics in Ethiopia: a View from the Village.* Boulder (Colo.), 1991

Araia, G., *Ethiopia: the Political Economy of Transition.* Univ. Press of America, 1995

Griffin, K. (ed.) *The Economy of Ethiopia.* London, 1992

Keller, E. J. *Revolutionary Ethiopia: From Empire to People's Republic.* Indiana Univ. Press, 1989

Marcus, H.G., *A History of Ethiopia.* California Univ. Press, 1994

Mekonnen, T. (ed.) *The Ethiopian Economy: Structure, Problems and Policy Issues.* Addis Ababa, 1992

Munro-Hay, S. and Pankhurst, R., *Ethiopia:* [Bibliography]. Oxford and Santa Barbara (CA), 1991

Tiruneh, A., *The Ethiopian Revolution: a Transformation from an Aristocratic to a Totalitarian Autocracy.* CUP, 1993

National statistical office: Central Statistical Office, Addis Ababa.

FALKLAND ISLANDS

Capital: Stanley
Population: 2,121 (1991)

KEY HISTORICAL EVENTS. France established a settlement in 1764 and Britain a second settlement in 1765. In 1770 Spain bought out the French and drove off the British. This action on the part of Spain brought that country and Britain to the verge of war. The Spanish restored the settlement to the British in 1771, but the settlement was withdrawn on economic grounds in 1774. In 1806 Spanish rule was overthrown in Argentina, and the Argentine claimed to succeed Spain in the French and British settlements in 1820. The British objected and reclaimed their settlement in 1832 as a Crown Colony.

On 2 April 1982 Argentine forces invaded the Falkland Islands and the Governor was expelled. At a meeting of the UN Security Council, held on 3 April, the voting was 10 to 1 in favour of the resolution calling for Argentina to withdraw. Britain regained possession on 14–15 June after Argentina surrendered.

In April 1990 Argentina's Congress declared the Falkland and other British-held South Atlantic islands part of the new Argentine province of Tierra del Fuego.

TERRITORY AND POPULATION. The Crown Colony is situated in the South Atlantic Ocean about 480 miles north-east of Cape Horn. The numerous islands cover 4,700 sq. miles. The main East Falkland Island, 2,610 sq. miles; the West Falkland, 2,090 sq. miles, including the adjacent small islands. The population at the census of 1991 was 2,121. The only town is Stanley, in East Falkland, with a population of 1,557. The population is nearly all of British descent, with about 67% born in the islands. A British garrison of servicemen, stationed in East Falkland in 1991, is not included in the population figures.

CLIMATE. A cool temperate climate, much affected by strong winds, particularly in spring. Stanley. Jan. 49°F (9·4°C), July 35°F (1·7°C). Annual rainfall 27" (681 mm).

CONSTITUTION AND GOVERNMENT. A new Constitution came into force on 3 Oct. 1985. This incorporated a chapter protecting fundamental human rights and in the preamble recalled the provisions on the right of self-determination contained in international covenants.

Executive power is vested in the Governor who must consult the Executive Council except on urgent or trivial matters. He must consult the Commander British Forces on matters relating to defence and internal security (except police).

There is a *Legislative Council* consisting of 8 elected members and 2 *ex officio* members, the Chief Executive and Financial Secretary. Only elected members have a vote. The Commander British Forces has a right to attend and take part in its proceedings but has no vote. The Attorney General also has a similar right to take part in proceedings with the consent of the person presiding. The Governor presides over sittings. He also presides over sittings of the Executive Council which consists of 3 elected members (elected by and from the elected members of Legislative Council) and the Chief Executive and Financial Secretary (*ex officio*). The Commander British Forces and Attorney General have a right to attend but may not vote.

Offices in the Public Service are constituted by the Governor and he makes appointments and is responsible for discipline. The Constitution allows for the establishment of a public service commission.

Governor: Richard Ralph, CVO.

Chief Executive: R. Sampson. *Financial Secretary:* D. F. Howatt. *Attorney General:* David Lang, QC, CBE. *Government Secretary:* P. T. King. *Senior Assistant Secretary:* K. G. Clarke.

Flag: British Blue Ensign with arms of Colony on a white disc in the fly.

DEFENCE. Since 1982 the Islands have been defended by a large garrison of British servicemen. In addition there is a local volunteer defence force.

ECONOMY

Policy. The Falkland Islands Development Corporation began operations in 1984. Projects assisted include a spinning mill dairy, hydroponic market garden, tourist lodges, agricultural supply co-operatives, and research into seabird populations and their diets.

Budget. Revenue and expenditure (in £ sterling) for fiscal years ending 30 June:

	1989–90	*1990–91*	*1991–92*	*1992–93*	*1993–94* [1]	*1994–95* [1]
Revenue	44,060,260	41,940,000	40,270,000	40,452,000	32,690,000	33,812,000
Expenditure	35,911,730	45,967,000	39,145,000	30,452,000	24,535,000	33,614,000

[1] Estimate.

Currency. The unit of currency is the *Falkland Islands pound* (FKP) of 100 *pence*, at parity with £1 sterling.

Banking. The Standard Chartered Bank provides a full range of banking facilities.

Oil. The UK government authorized exploration for oil in Nov. 1991 in the 200-mile economic exclusion zone except where it overlapped Argentina's zone in the west. An Anglo-Argentine agreement of 27 Sept. 1995 establishes 2 legal frameworks for marine oil exploration areas without prejudice to either country's claim to sovereignty over the Falkland Islands. The first, close to the Islands, is to have licensing terms which give companies 22 years to explore and complete drilling. The second extends between the Islands and Argentina wherein licensing will be overseen by a joint Anglo-Argentine commission. Argentina may bid for licences in the first area, and draws revenue directly from the second.

Agriculture. The economy was formerly based solely on agriculture, principally sheep farming. Following a programme of sub-division, much of the land is divided into family size units. There were 90 farms in 1992, 79 of which were family units. During 1991 the Falklands Islands Co. sold its agricultural holdings to the Falkland Island government. Less than 5% of the total land area is owned outside the islands. Wool is the principal product; output was 2,521 tonnes in 1991. In 1991 there were 729,349 sheep, 5,054 cattle and 1,640 horses in the islands.

Fisheries. Since the establishment of a 150-mile interim conservation and management zone around the Islands in 1986 and the consequent introduction, on 1 Feb. 1987, of a licensing regime for vessels fishing within the zone, income from the associated fishing activities is now the largest source of revenue. Licences raised £25m. in 1992. Some 0·2m. tonnes of illex squid are caught annually. In 1994 Argentina's quota was raised to 0·22m. tonnes; that of the Falkland Islands remained at 0·15m. tonnes.

On 26 Dec. 1990 the Falklands outer conservation zone was introduced which extends beyond the 150 mile zone out to 200 miles from baselines. In Nov. 1992 commercial fishing in the outer zone was banned, the zone was reopened to fishing in 1994. A UK-Argentine South Atlantic Fisheries Commission was set up in 1990; it meets at least twice a year.

TRADE. Total trade between the Falkland Islands and UK (British Department of Trade returns, in £1,000 sterling):

	1991	*1992*	*1993*	*1994*	*1995*
Imports to UK	3,379	3,091	4,317	4,516	4,721
Exports and re-exports from UK	16,039	13,100	10,380	9,360	15,665

COMMUNICATIONS

Roads. There are 27 km of made-up roads in and around Stanley and another 54 km of all-weather road between Stanley and Mount Pleasant Airport. Other settlements outside Stanley are linked by tracks. A rural all-weather road to Port Louis was completed in early 1991 and construction of a further one to the Northern areas of East Falkland was continuing. A similar project on West Falkland commenced in 1993.

Civil Aviation. Air communication is currently via Ascension Island. An airport, completed in 1986, is sited at Mount Pleasant on East Falkland. RAF Tristar aircraft operate a twice-weekly service between the Falklands and the UK. Internal air links are provided by the government-operated air service, which carries passengers, mail, freight and medical patients between the settlements and Stanley on non-scheduled flights in Islander aircraft. A Chilean airline runs a weekly service to Punta Arenas.

Shipping. A charter vessel calls 4 or 5 times a year to/from the UK. Vessels of the Royal Fleet Auxiliary run regularly to South Georgia. Sea links with Chile and Uruguay began in 1989.

Telecommunications. Number of telephones (Sept. 1991) 1,180. International direct dialling is available, as are international telex and facsimile links. There is a government-operated radio and TV station at Stanley.

SOCIAL INSTITUTIONS

Justice. There is a Supreme Court, and a Court of Appeal sits in the UK; appeals may go from that court to the judicial committee of the Privy Council. Judges may only be removed for inability or misbehaviour on the advice of the judicial committee of the Privy Council. The senior resident judicial officer is the Senior Magistrate. There is an Attorney General and a Senior Crown Counsel.

Education. Education is compulsory between the ages of 5 and 15 years. In 1992 there were 350 children receiving education in the Islands. 60 of these were of primary school age living on isolated farms and receiving teacher visits and radio lessons. There is a primary school in Stanley, and a community school opened in 1992 with secondary study and sport facilities. Estimated recurrent expenditure on education and training from own funds in 1994–95 £2,041,440.

Health. The Government Medical Department is responsible for all medical services to civilians. Estimated expenditure (1994–95) £2,092,490. A new hospital and some sheltered accommodation was completed in March 1987. Services include all primary care for Stanley and the flying doctor service for outlying farm settlements.

WILD LIFE. The Falkland Islands are noted for their outstanding wild life, including penguin and seal. Four Nature Reserves have been declared and 18 Wild Animal and Bird Sanctuaries gazetted. The brown trout introduced between 1947 and 1952 can now be found in nearly all the rivers and there are good runs of sea-trout during spring and autumn.

Further Reading

Day, A., *The Falkland Islands.* [Bibliography]. Oxford and Santa Barbara (CA), 1995

Gough, B., *The Falkland Islands/Malvinas: the Contest for Empire in the South Atlantic.* London, 1992

Hoffmann, F. L. and Hoffmann, O. M., *Sovereignty in Dispute.* London, 1984

Smith, W. S. (ed.) *Towards Resolution? The Falklands/Malvinas Dispute.* London, 1991

Strange, I. J., *The Falkland Islands.* 3rd ed. Newton Abbot, 1983.—*The Falkland Islands and their Natural History.* Newton Abbot, 1987

FIJI

Republic of Fiji

Capital: Suva
Population: 783,800 (1995)
GNP per capita: US$2,320 (1994)
HDI/world rank: 0·860/46 (1992)

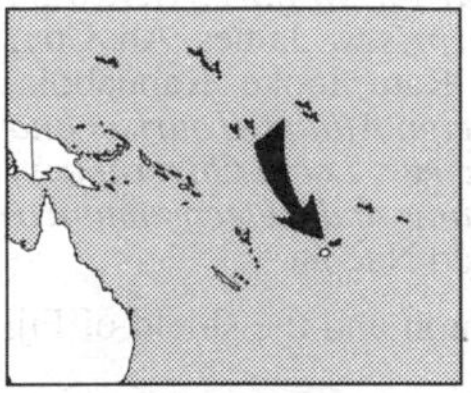

KEY HISTORICAL EVENTS. The first European discovery of the Fiji Islands was by the Dutch navigator Abel Tasman in 1643, and they were recorded in detail by Capt. Bligh after the mutiny of the *Bounty* (1789). In the 19th century the search for sandalwood, in which enormous profits were made, brought many ships. The influence of the deserters, shipwrecked sailors and missionaries who settled on the islands disrupted the pattern of life of the indigenous Fijians and gave rise to inter-tribal wars until Fiji was ceded to Britain on 10 Oct. 1874. Fiji became an independent state within the Commonwealth on 10 Oct. 1970. Following the electoral defeat of the Fijian-dominated National Alliance Party by an Indian-supported coalition in April 1987, Brig. Sitiveni Rabuka seized power after two coups, and declared Fiji a republic in Oct.; membership of the Commonwealth lapsed.

TERRITORY AND POPULATION. Fiji comprises 332 islands and islets (about one-third are inhabited) lying between 15° and 22° S. lat. and 174° E. and 177° W. long. The largest is Viti Levu, area 10,429 sq. km (4,027 sq. miles), next is Vanua Levu, area 5,556 sq. km (2,145 sq. miles). The island of Rotuma (47 sq. km, 18 sq. miles), about 12° 30' S. lat., 178° E. long., was added to the colony in 1881. Total area, 7,078 sq. miles (18,333 sq. km).

Total population (census, 1986), 715,375 (38·7% urban). The 1989 estimated total population of 727,104 consisted of the following: 351,966 (48·4%) Fijians; 337,557 (46·4%) Indians (whose ancestors had been introduced as field workers by the British); 37,581 (5·2%) were of other races. 1995 estimate, 783,800 (40% urban).

Suva, the capital, is on the south coast of Viti Levu; population (census, 1986), 71,608. Lautoka had 28,728 inhabitants in 1986.

Vital statistics, 1987: Crude birth rate per 1,000 population, Fijian, 30·7, Indian, 25·6; crude death rate per 1,000 population, Fijian, 5·4, Indian, 5·2. Growth rate, 1989–90, 1·3%. Average life expectancy (1993), 61·4 years for males and 65·2 for females.

CLIMATE. A tropical climate, but oceanic influences prevent undue extremes of heat or humidity. The S.E. Trades blow from May to Nov., during which time nights are cool and rainfall amounts least. Suva. Jan. 80°F (26·7°C), July 73°F (22·8°C). Annual rainfall 117" (2,974 mm).

CONSTITUTION AND GOVERNMENT. On 25 July 1990 a new constitution was promulgated giving 'indigenous Fijians' the right to hold the prime ministership and a guaranteed 37 seats in the 70-seat *House of Representatives.* Fijian citizens of Indian descent have 27 seats, other races 5, and the Polynesian island of Rotuma, 1. The Upper House has 24 seats for Fijians, 9 for other races and 1 for Rotuma.

The *President* must be an indigenous Fijian, and is chosen by the Great Council of Chiefs.

At the elections of 18–25 Feb. 1994 the Soqosoqo ni Vakavulewa ni Taukei (SVT) won 31 of the 'indigenous' seats and the Fijian Nationalist United Front 1. The National Federation Party won 20 of the Indian seats, the Fiji Labour Party 13 and the General Voters' Party (non-Fijian, non-Indian) 5.

In Oct. 1995 the government comprised:

President: Ratu Sir Kamisese Mara, GCMG, KBE (sworn in 18 Jan. 1994).

Prime Minister, Minister for Constitutional Review: Maj.-Gen. Sitiveni Rabuka, OBE (b. 1948; SVT).

Deputy Prime Minister, Minister for Agriculture, Fisheries and Forests: Ratu Timoci Vesikula. *Attorney-General and Minister for Justice:* Kelemedi Bulewa. - *Education, Women, Culture, Science and Technology:* Taufa Vakatale. *Finance and Economic Development:* Berenado Vunibobo. *Infrastructure and Public Works, Transport:* Leo Smith. *Fijian Affairs:* Vacant. *Health, Social Welfare:* Seruwaia Hong Tiy. *Commerce, Industry, Trade and Public Enterprises:* James Ah Coy, CBE. *Regional Development and Multi-Ethnic Affairs:* Ratu Inoke Kabuabola. *Home Affairs, Immigration:* Col. Paul Manueli, OBE. *Foreign Affairs, Tourism and Civil Aviation:* Filipe Bole. *Lands, Mineral Resources, Energy, Local Government, Environment:* Ratu Ovini Bokini. *Information, Broadcasting and Telecommunications:* Isimeli Bose. *Labour and Industrial Relations:* Ratu Jo Nacola.

National flag: Light blue with the Union Flag in the canton and the shield of Fiji in the fly.

National anthem: 'Blessing grant, oh God of Nations, on the isles of Fiji'; words by M. Prescott, tune anonymous.

Local Government. Fiji is divided into 14 provinces subdivided into 188 *tikinas*, each with its own council. Tikinas are composed of village units headed by a locally-elected or appointed chief. The number of tikina councils within a province varies from 4 to 22. Tikina councils have wide powers to make by-laws and levy rates to raise revenue. 50% of the rates collected is credited to the provincial council treasury for the running of the council and 50% is used for the financing of the tikina and village projects.

DEFENCE.

Army. The Army consists of 7 infantry battalions and 1 engineer battalion. Personnel (1996), 3,600.

Navy. A naval division of the armed forces consists of 4 Israeli-built fast inshore patrol craft, 5 other patrol craft, 1 small naval-manned survey ship and the presidential yacht. There are 2 naval-manned helicopters. Naval personnel in 1995 numbered 300. The naval base is in Suva.

Air Force. The Fiji Air Wing operates 1 Dauphin and 1 Ecureuil helicopter, both supplied by France.

INTERNATIONAL RELATIONS

Membership. Fiji is a member of the UN, the Colombo Plan, the South Pacific Forum and is an ACP state of the EU.

ECONOMY

Budget. The financial year corresponds with the calendar year. Government revenue (including grants) and expenditure (in $F1m.):

	1991	*1992*	*1993*	*1994*	*1995*
Revenue	576·43	600·29	654·00	694·40	693·8
Expenditure	679·79	714·17	818·90	832·10	827·8

VAT of 10% was introduced in 1992.

Currency. The unit of currency is the *Fiji dollar* (FJD) of 100 *cents*. There are coins of 1, 2, 5, 10, 20 and 50 cents and $F1, and notes of $F2, 5, 10 and 20. $F85·8m. were in circulation in 1991. Inflation was 7·1% in June 1993. Foreign exchange reserves were $F480·64m. in 1992. In March 1996, £1 = $F2·16; US$1 = $F1·42; DM1 = $F0·96.

Banking and Finance. The central bank and bank of issue is the Reserve Bank of Fiji, which superseded the Central Monetary Authority in 1984. Its assets were $F496·89m. in Sept. 1992. The National Bank of Fiji is a government-owned commercial bank, and there is a Development Bank. 5 foreign banks are operating. Total assets of commercial banks were $F1,452·73m. in Sept. 1992.

Savings deposits were $F242·11m. in 1991.

ENERGY AND NATURAL RESOURCES

Electricity. In 1994 there were 7 thermal and 1 hydro-electric power stations. Production (1991) 474m. kWh.

Minerals. In 1991 2,743 kg of gold and 477 kg of silver were produced.

Agriculture. 16% of the land is suitable for agriculture. Agriculture provides about 25% of GDP. Sugar-cane is the principal cash crop; one quarter of the population depend on it directly for their livelihood. Copra, Fiji's second major cash crop, provides coconut oil and other products for export. Ginger is the third major export crop. Tobacco and cocoa are also cultivated. 1991 output (in tonnes): Sugar-cane, 3·38m.; copra, 15,193; rice, 29,038; tobacco, 252; cocoa, 465; ginger, 6,500. There were 5,045 tractors in 1991.

Livestock (1992, in 1,000): Cattle, 160; horses, 43; goats, 124; pigs, 15; poultry, 3,000. Products, 1991 (in tonnes): Beef, 2,847; pork, 715; goat meat, 660; chicken meat, 5,888; eggs, 2,191.

Forestry. In 1994 the forest cover was 935,000 ha, mainly on communally-owned land. A comprehensive pine scheme has been implemented. About 415,000 ha are available for timber. 248,000 cu. metres of saw logs were produced in 1991.

Fisheries. The catch in 1991 was 13,796 tonnes. Aquaculture is carried on.

INDUSTRY. The Tax Free Factory scheme was instituted in 1987 as an encouragement to industry. Output, 1994 (in tonnes): Sugar, 475,000; (1991) coconut oil, 8,775; flour, 26,933; butter, 1,477; cigarettes, 585; animal feed, 25,377; cement, 78,800; soap, 7,068; beer, 18·31m. litres. There is a garment industry.

Labour. In 1992 the workforce was 265,337. 94,812 persons were in paid employment in March 1993.

Trade Unions. In 1987 there were 46 trade unions operating with about 45,000 members.

FOREIGN ECONOMIC RELATIONS. The Tax-Free Factory/Tax-Free Zone Scheme was introduced in 1987 to stimulate investment and encourage export-oriented businesses.

Foreign debt was $F433·3m. in 1992.

Commerce. In 1993 exports and re-exports totalled $F692·4m. and imports $F1,109·8m. Chief exports in 1992 (in $F1m.): Sugar, 221·28; gold, 60·72; prepared and preserved fish, 28·73; fresh, dried and smoked fish, 10·37; clothing, 105·54; timber, 30·19; ginger, 2·53; molasses, 2·27. Major import suppliers, 1993 (in $F1m.): Australia, 363·8; New Zealand, 213·3; Japan, 122·5; USA, 84·5; Singapore, 62; China, 37·9; Hong Kong, 36·1; UK, 33·9. Major export markets (in $F1m.): Australia, 150·8; UK, 142·5; USA, 71·7; Japan, 50·9; Canada, 42·1; Malaysia, 37·7; New Zealand, 32·1.

Total trade between Fiji and UK (British Department of Trade returns, in £1,000 sterling):

	1991	*1992*	*1993*	*1994*	*1995*
Imports to UK	81,540	79,189	86,688	80,642	82,020
Exports and re-exports from UK	6,258	7,656	8,299	6,179	6,770

Tourism. Tourism is the main source of foreign exchange earnings, which totalled $F419·6m. in 1994. In 1993, there were 287,462 visitors; tourism earnings were $F363·3m.

COMMUNICATIONS

Roads. Total road length in 1995 was about 5,100 km, of which 1,000 km were sealed. In 1992, there were 35,955 private cars, 27,858 goods vehicles, 1,367 buses, 2,441 taxis and 3,616 rental and hire cars.

Railways. Fiji Sugar Cane Corporation runs 600 mm gauge railways at four of its mills on Viti Levu and Vanua Levu, totalling 595 km.

Civil Aviation. There are international airports at Nadi and Nausori. In 1991 they handled 603,535 passengers. 18 other airports are in use for domestic services. The national carrier is Air Pacific (79·54% government-owned), which was operating 1 B-737-300, 1 B-737-500, 1 B-747-200B and 1 B-767-300ER and 2 other aircraft in 1995, and provides services to Australia, Japan, New Zealand, USA and several Pacific islands. Services are also provided by Air Calédonie, Air Marshall Islands, Air Nauru, Air New Zealand, Air Vanuatu, Canadian Airlines, Island Air, Korean Air, Polynesian Airlines, Qantas, Royal Tongan Airlines, Solomon Airlines, Sunflower Airlines and Turtle Airways.

Shipping. The 3 ports of entry are Suva, Lautoka and Levuka. Ocean-going shipping totalled 27,385 GRT in 1995, including oil tankers, 4,705 GRT.

Telecommunications. There were (1988) 50 post offices and 185 postal agencies. There are cable and satellite telephone links to the international network. The automatic telex network operates through New Zealand into the international telex system. There were 60,017 telephones in 1987. The Fiji Broadcasting Commission is an independent statutory body, half commercial and half cultural. It broadcasts 3 programmes. There is another commercial network. The Fiji Television Co. runs 3 channels (including 2 pay channels). In 1993 there were 450,000 radio receivers. 2 TV stations are under construction (colour by NTSC).

Press. In 1995 there were 2 daily newspapers in English (circulation 54,000). There are 2 weeklies in Fijian and 1 in Hindi, and 3 monthly periodicals in English.

SOCIAL INSTITUTIONS

Justice. An independent Judiciary is guaranteed under the Constitution of Fiji. The Constitution allows for a High Court of Fiji which has unlimited original jurisdiction to hear and determine any civil or criminal proceedings under any law.

The High Court also has jurisdiction to hear and determine constitutional and electoral questions including the membership of members of the House of Representatives.

The Chief Justice of Fiji is appointed by the President acting after consultation with the Prime Minister.

The Fiji Court of Appeal of which the Chief Justice is *ex officio* President is formed by three specially appointed Justices of Appeal. The Justices of Appeal are appointed by the President acting after consultation with the Judicial and Legal Services Commission. Generally any person convicted of any offence has a right of appeal from the High Court to the Fiji Court of Appeal. The final appellant court is the Supreme Court. Most matters coming before the Superior Courts originate in Magistrates' Courts.

Police. The Royal Fiji Police Force had (1994) a total strength of 1,913.

Religion. The 1986 census showed: Christians, 378,452; Hindus, 273,088; Sikhs, 4,674; Moslems, 56,001; Confucians, 82.

Education. Adult literacy was 87% in 1992. School attendance is not compulsory but in 1994 98% of children between 6 and 14 were attending school. In 1987 there were 815 schools scattered over 56 islands, staffed by 7,082 teachers, of whom about 99·3% were trained. There were also 236 pre-schools. The 674 primary and 141 secondary schools had 180,514 pupils.

The University of the South Pacific is in Suva. The University has an operating budget of $F12·13m. a year provided by the 12 countries it serves. There are also schools of agriculture, medicine and nursing, an institute of technology and 2 teacher training colleges.

Health. In 1987 there were 25 hospitals with 1,721 beds, 271 doctors and 48 dentists. There were 2,472 registered nurses in 1992.

DIPLOMATIC REPRESENTATIVES

Of Fiji in Great Britain (34 Hyde Park Gate, London, SW7 5DN)
Ambassador: Brig.-Gen. Ratu Epeli Nailatikau, LVO, OBE.

Of Great Britain in Fiji (47 Gladstone Rd., Suva)
Ambassador: Michael Peart, CMG, LVO.

Of Fiji in the USA (2233 Wisconsin Ave., NW, Washington, D.C., 20007)
Ambassador: Pita Kewa Nacuva.

Of the USA in Fiji (31 Loftus St., Suva)
Ambassador: Don Gevirtz.

Of Fiji to the United Nations
Ambassador: Posesi Bune.

Further Reading

Bureau of Statistics. *Current Economic Statistics.* Quarterly
Reserve Bank of Fiji. *Quarterly Review*
Bain, K., *Fiji at the Crossroads.* London, 1989
Gorman, G. E. and Mills, J. J., *Fiji* [Bibliography]. Oxford and Santa Barbara (CA), 1994
Howard, M. C., *Fiji: Race and Politics in an Island State.* Univ. of British Columbia Press, 1991
Lal, B. J., *Broken Waves: a History of the Fiji Islands in the Twentieth Century.* Univ. of Hawaii Press, 1992
Lal, V., *Fiji: Coups in Paradise.* London, 1991
Ravuvu, A., *The Façade of Democracy: Fijian Struggles for Political Control.* Suva, 1991
Scarr, D., *Fiji: a Short History.* Sydney, 1984
Sutherland, W., *Beyond the Politics of Race: an Alternative History of Fiji to 1992.* Australian National Univ. Press, 1992
Wright, R., *On Fiji Islands.* London, 1987

National statistical office: Bureau of Statistics, POB 2221, Government Buildings, Suva.

FINLAND

Suomen Tasavalta—
Republiken Finland

Capital: Helsinki
Population: 5·1m. (1994)
GNP per capita: US$19,174 (1994)
HDI/world rank: 0·934/5 (1992)

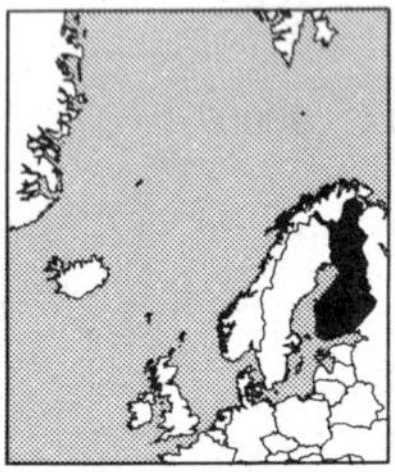

KEY HISTORICAL EVENTS. Since the Middle Ages Finland had been a part of the realm of Sweden. In the 18th century parts of south-eastern Finland were conquered by Russia, and the rest of the country was ceded to Russia by the peace treaty of Hamina in 1809. Finland became an autonomous Grand Duchy which retained its previous laws and institutions under its Grand Duke, the Emperor of Russia. After the Russian revolution Finland declared itself independent on 6 Dec. 1917. The Civil War, in which 'Whites' supported by Germans fought 'Reds' supported by revolutionary Russians, was won by the 'Whites'. After the war relations between Finland and Soviet Russia were normalized in the Dorpat (Tartu) peace treaty of 14 Oct. 1920.

On 30 Nov. 1939 Soviet troops invaded Finland, after Finland had rejected territorial concessions demanded by the USSR. These, however, had to be made in the peace treaty of 12 March 1940, amounting to 32,806 sq. km and including the Carelian Isthmus, Viipuri and the shores of Lake Ladoga. When the German attack on the USSR was launched in June 1941 Finland again became involved in the war against the USSR. On 19 Sept. 1944 an armistice was signed in Moscow. Finland agreed to cede to Russia the Petsamo area in addition to cessions made in 1940 (total 42,934 sq. km). The peace treaty was signed in Paris on 10 Feb. 1947.

TERRITORY AND POPULATION. Finland is bounded in the north-west and north by Norway, east by Russia, south by the Baltic Sea and west by the Gulf of Bothnia and Sweden. The area and the population of Finland on 31 Dec. 1994 (Swedish names in brackets):

Province	*Area (sq. km)* [1]	*Population* [2]	*Population per sq. km* [2]
Uusimaa (Nyland)	9,898	1,309,549	132·3
Turku-Pori (Åbo-Björneborg)	19,954	700,703	35·1
Ahvenanmaa (Åland)	1,527	25,158	16·5
Häme (Tavastehus)	19,226	727,418	37·8
Kymi (Kymmene)	10,783	333,411	30·9
Mikkeli (St Michel)	16,323	206,682	12·7
Pohjois-Karjala (Norra Karelen)	17,782	177,917	10·0
Kuopio	16,510	258,800	15·7
Keski-Suomi (Mellersta Finland)	16,249	257,716	15·9
Vaasa (Vasa)	26,418	449,366	17·0
Oulu (Uleåborg)	56,868	449,709	7·9
Lappi (Lappland)	93,057	202,325	2·2
Total	304,595	5,098,754	16·7

[1] Excluding inland water area which totals 33,522 sq. km. [2] Resident population.

The growth of the population, which was 421,500 in 1750, has been:

End of year	*Urban*	*Rural*	*Total*	*Percentage urban*
1800	46,600	786,100	832,700	5·6
1900	333,300	2,322,600	2,655,900	12·5
1950	1,302,400	2,727,400	4,029,800	32·3
1970	2,340,300	2,258,000	4,598,300	50·9
1980	2,865,100	1,922,700	4,787,800	59·8
1990	3,079,800	1,918,700	4,998,500	61·6
1993	3,253,038	1,824,874	5,077,912	64·1
1994	3,279,195	1,819,559	5,098,754	64·3

The population on 31 Dec. 1994 by language primarily spoken: Finnish, 4,742,387; Swedish, 295,182; other languages, 59,459; Lappish, 1,726.

The principal towns with resident population, 31 Dec. 1994, are (Swedish names in brackets):

Helsinki (Helsingfors)—capital	515,765	Kokkola (Karleby)	35,592
Espoo (Esbo)	186,507	Rovaniemi	34,895
Tampere (Tammerfors)	179,251	Järvenpää	34,282
Vantaa (Vanda)	164,379	Mikkeli (St Michel)	32,581
Turku (Åbo)	162,370	Imatra	32,302
Oulu (Uleåborg)	106,419	Kouvola	32,233
Lahti	94,706	Kerava	29,298
Kuopio	83,955	Seinäjoki	28,972
Pori (Björneborg)	76,561	Savonlinna (Nyslott)	28,710
Jyväskylä	73,083	Nokia	26,318
Lappeenranta (Villmanstrand)	56,412	Riihimäki	25,754
Kotka	56,087	Kemi	24,936
Vaasa (Vasa)	55,089	Varkaus	24,209
Joensuu	50,110	Iisalmi	24,117
Hämeenlinna (Tavastehus)	44,564	Tornio	23,274
Hyvinkää (Hyvinge)	41,089	Salo	22,545
Rauma (Raumo)	38,217	Raisio	22,088
Kajaani	36,859	Kuusankoski	21,580

Vital statistics in calendar years:

	Living births	*Of which outside marriage*	*Still-born*	*Marriages*	*Deaths (exclusive of still-born)*	*Emigration*
1990	65,549	16,543	303	24,998	50,058	6,477
1991	65,395	17,896	306	24,732	49,294	5,984
1992	66,731	19,257	288	23,560	49,844	6,055
1993	64,826	19,665	271	24,660	50,988	6,405
1994	65,231	20,439	249	24,898	48,000	8,672

In 1994 the rate per 1,000 was: Births, 13; marriages, 5; deaths, 9; infantile deaths (per 1,000 live births), 4·6.

CLIMATE. The climate is severe in winter, which lasts about 6 months, but mean temperatures in south and south-west are less harsh, 21°F (–6°C). In the north, mean temperatures may fall to 8·5°F (–13°C). Snow covers the ground for three months in the south and for over six months in the far north. Summers are short but quite warm, with occasional very hot days. Precipitation is light throughout the country, with one third falling as snow, the remainder mainly as convectional rain in summer and autumn. Helsinki (Helsingfors). Jan. 21°F (–6°C), July 62°F (16·5°C). Annual rainfall 24·7" (618 mm).

CONSTITUTION AND GOVERNMENT. Finland is a republic according to the Constitution of 17 July 1919.

Parliament consists of one chamber of 200 members chosen by direct and proportional election by all citizens of 18 or over. The country is divided into 15 electoral districts with a representation proportional to their population. Every citizen over the age of 18 is eligible for Parliament, which is elected for 4 years, but can be dissolved sooner by the President.

The *President* is elected for 6 years by direct popular vote. In case no candidate wins an absolute majority, a second round is held between the 2 most successful candidates. Presidential elections were held in 2 rounds on 16 Jan. and 6 Feb. 1994. Martti Ahtisaari won the first round against 10 opponents with 25·9% of votes cast, and the second against 1 opponent with 53·9%. Turn-out at the second round was 82·3%.

President of Finland: Martti Ahtisaari (b. 1937; Social Democrat; sworn in 1 March 1994).

At the 19 March 1995 elections for the 200-member parliament, the electorate was 3·9m.; turn-out was 71·9%; 18 parties contested. The Social Democratic Party (SDP) won 63 seats with 28·3% of votes cast (48 seats in 1991); Centre Party

(Cen), 44 with 19·8% (55); National Coalition Party (NCP; Conservative), 39 with 17·9% (40); Left Wing Alliance (LWA), 22 with 11·2% (19); Swedish People's Party (SPP), 12 (including 1 for coalition of Åland) with 5·1% (12); Greens, 9 with 6·5% (10); Finnish Christian League (FCL), 7 with 3% (8); Progressive Finnish Party, 2 with 2·8%; Rural Party, 1 with 1·3% (7); Ecological Party 1 with 0·3%.

The Council of State (Cabinet) was composed as follows in Feb. 1996:

Prime Minister: Paavo Lipponen (b. 1941; SDP).

Foreign Affairs: Tarja Halonen (SDP). *Finance:* Sauli Niinistö (NCP); Arja Alho (SDP). *Justice:* Karl Häkämies (NCP). *Education:* Olli-Pekka Heinonen (NCP). *Culture:* Claes Andersson (LWA). *European Affairs:* Ole Norrback (SPP). *Interior:* Jan-Erik Enestam (SPP). *Trade and Industry:* Antti Kalliomäki (SDP). *Transport and Communication:* Tula Linnainmaa (NCP). *Social Affairs and Health:* Sinikka Mönkäre (SDP); Terrtu Huttu-Juntunen (LWA). *Labour:* Liisa Jaakonsaari (SDP). *Defence:* Anneli Taina (NCP). *Environment:* Pekka Haavisto (Greens). *Administration:* Jouni Backman (SDP). *Agriculture and Forestry:* Kalevi Hemllä (ind).

The *Speaker* is Riitta Uosukainen.

National flag: White with a blue Scandinavian cross.

National anthem: 'Oi Maamme Suomi, synyinmaa'/'Vårt land, vårt land, vårt fosterland' ('Our land, Finland/our land, our native land'); words by J. L. Runeberg, tune by F. Pacius (same as Estonia).

Finnish and Swedish are the official languages.

Local Government. For administrative purposes Finland is divided into 12 provinces (*lääni*, Sw.: *län*). The administration of each province is entrusted to a governor (*maaherra*, Sw.: *landshövding*) appointed by the President. The governor directs the activities of the provincial office (*lääninhallitus*, Sw.: *länsstyrelse*) and of local sheriffs (*nimismies*, Sw.: *länsman*). In 1995 the number of sheriff districts was 209.

The unit of local government is the commune. Main fields of communal activities are local planning, roads and harbours, sanitary services, education, health services and social aid. The communes raise taxes independent from state taxation. Two different kinds of communes are distinguished: Urban communes (*kaupunki*, Sw.: *stad*) and rural communes. In 1996 there were altogether 455 communes of which 104 were urban and 351 rural. In all communes communal councils are elected for terms of 4 years; all inhabitants (men and women) of the commune who have reached their 18th year are entitled to vote and eligible. The executive power is in each commune vested in a board which consists of members elected by the council and one or a few chief officials of the commune. Several communes often form an association for the administration of some common institution, *e.g.*, a hospital or a vocational school. Elections were held on 18 Oct. 1992. The SDP gained 27·1% of votes cast, the Centre Party, 19·2%.

The autonomous province of **Åland** has considerable self-government rights. It elects a 30-member Parliament with executive power under an appointed governor. The capital is Mariehamn (Maarianhamina). It is 95% Swedish-speaking. At a referendum on 20 Nov. 1994 Åland voted to join the EU along with the rest of Finland.

DEFENCE. The period of military training is 240, 285 or 330 days and refresher training obligation 40 to 100 days between conscript service and age 50 (officers and non-commissioned officers age 60). Total strength of trained and equipped reserves is about 700,000.

Army. The country is divided into 3 military commands and 12 military provinces. The Army consisted in 1995 of 1 armoured training brigade, 8 infantry training brigades, 1 infantry training regiment, 1 artillery brigade, 2 special regiments, 2 coastal artillery regiments, 3 independent coastal artillery battalions, 3 anti-aircraft regiments and Reserve Officer School, making a total strength, of 36,880 (30,000 conscripts).

Frontier Guard. This is responsible for the control of immigration and guarding the borders under the command of the Ministry of the Interior. It is militarily-organized and participates in the defence of the country should the situation require it. The Frontier Guard is divided into 4 frontier and 3 coast guard districts. The latter operate 11 patrol craft. The frontier guard districts operate an air patrol squadron of 3 Super Puma, 3 AB 412 and 4 AB 206 helicopters and 2 Dornier 228 surveillance aircraft. Personnel, 1995, 3,500.

Navy. The Navy is divided into 2 commands, Archipelago Sea Naval Command and Gulf of Finland Naval Command. About 50% of the combatant units are kept manned, with the others in short-notice reserve and re-activated on a regular basis. The inventory comprises 2 corvettes, 8 missile craft, 4 patrol craft, 8 minelayers and 6 inshore minesweepers. There are 4 landing craft and some 30 auxiliaries and tenders.

Naval bases exist at Upinniemi (near Helsinki) and Turku. Total personnel strength (1995) was 3,000 of whom 1,500 are conscripts, and there are about 12,000 reserves.

The Coastal Artillery also operates numerous vessels, many with minelaying capability.

The National Board of Navigation has 9 civil-manned icebreakers.

Air Force. The Air Force has 3 fighter squadrons, 1 transport squadron, an air academy, a technical school, a signal school, 2 depots, and a signal equipment testing centre. The fighter squadrons have 60 MiG-21bis and Saab J35 Draken S and F aircraft, including two-seat trainer models. 7 double-seater and 57 single-seater F-18 Hornets are to replace these; the first were delivered in 1995. Other equipment includes 28 Valmet Vinka piston-engined primary trainers of Finnish design and 54 Hawk Mk51 advanced jet trainers, 3 Fokker F.27 Friendship transport aircraft, 3 Gates Learjet 35 transport aircraft, Piper Arrow and locally-built Redigo liaison aircraft, Piper Chieftain utility transports, and 7 Mi-8 and 2 Hughes 500 D helicopters. Personnel (1995), 3,000 (1,300 conscripts).

INTERNATIONAL RELATIONS

Membership. Finland is a member of the UN, EU, Nordic Council, OECD, the NATO Partnership for Peace and the Council of Europe.

At a referendum on 16 Oct. 1994 on joining the EU turn-out was 74%; 53% of votes cast were in favour.

ECONOMY

Budget. Actual revenue and expenditure for the calendar years 1989–94, the ordinary budget for 1995 and the proposed budget for 1996 in 1m. marks:

	1989	*1990*	*1991*	*1992*	*1993*	*1994*	*1995*	*1996*
Revenue	134,828	138,739	163,462	182,660	207,567	193,612	195,835	192,989
Expenditure	129,459	140,893	167,959	186,107	202,184	196,755	195,833	192,985

Of the total revenue, 1994, 18% derived from sales tax, 15% from income and property tax, 10% from excise duties, 7% from other taxes and similar revenue, 35% from loans and 15% from miscellaneous sources. Of the total expenditure, 1994, 14% went to education and culture, 5% to transport, 3% to communities and housing, 9% to promotion of industry, 27% to social security, 6% to agriculture and forestry, 8% to general administration, public order and safety, 5% to defence and 23% to other expenditure.

VAT is 22% (reduced rate, 12%).

At the end of Dec. 1995 the central government debt totalled 366,000m. marks. Domestic debt amounted to 193,700m. marks; foreign debt, 172,300m. marks.

Currency. The unit of currency is the *markka* (FIM) or mark of 100 *pennis*. There are coins of 10 and 50 pennis and 1, 5 and 10 marks, and notes of 10, 20, 50, 100, 500 and 1,000 marks. The mark was pegged to the ecu in June 1991 with a 3% margin of fluctuation. It was devalued by 12·3% in Nov. 1991, and unpegged from the ecu in Sept. 1992. In March 1996, £1 = 6·97 marks; US$1 = 4·56 marks; DM1 = 3·09 marks.

Banking and Finance. The central bank is the Bank of Finland (founded in 1811), owned by the State and under the guarantee and supervision of Parliament. Its *Governor* is Sirkka Hämäläinen. It is the only bank of issue, and the limit of its right to issue notes is fixed equal to the value of its assets of gold and foreign holdings plus 1,500m. marks. Notes in circulation at the end of 1995 amounted to 15,611m. marks.

At the end of 1994 the deposits in banking institutions totalled 288,514m. marks and the loans granted by them 311,255m. marks. The most important groups of banking institutions in 1994 were:

	Number of institutions	*Number of offices*	*Deposits (1m. marks)*	*Loans (1m. marks)*
Commercial banks	10	919	181,097	208,664
Savings banks	41	274	16,173	18,049
Co-operative banks	302	988	91,244	84,542

The 5 largest banks are Kansallis-Osake-Pankki, Union Bank of Finland, SKOP-Bank, Okobank and the state-owned Postipankki.

There is a stock exchange in Helsinki.

Weights and Measures. The metric system is legal.

ENERGY AND NATURAL RESOURCES

Electricity. Electricity production was (in 1m. kWh) 58,007 in 1993; 62,180 in 1994, of which 18·8% was hydro-electric. In 1995 there were 4 nuclear power stations, which contributed 29·5% of production in 1994. Parliament has rejected the construction of a fifth.

Minerals. Notable of the mines are Pyhäsalmi (zinc, copper), Enonkoski (nickel) and Keminmaa (chromium); the zinc-copper mine at Vihanti closed in 1993. In 1994 (preliminary) the metal content (in tonnes) of the output of copper concentrates was 9,257, of zinc concentrates 19,122, of nickel concentrates 3,126, of nickel-copper concentrates 6,378 and of chromium 230,566.

Agriculture. The cultivated area covers only 8% of the land and of the economically active population 8% were employed in agriculture and forestry in 1994. The arable area was divided in 1994 into 189,925 farms, and the distribution of this area by the size of the farms was: Less than 5 ha cultivated, 64,867 farms; 5–20 ha, 82,775 farms; 20–50 ha, 36,638 farms; 50–100 ha, 4,935 farms; over 100 ha, 710 farms.

The principal crops (area in 1,000 ha, yield in 1,000 tonnes) were in 1995:

Crop	*Area*	*Yield*	*Crop*	*Area*	*Yield*
Rye	20·8	57·7	Oats	329·3	1,097·2
Barley	516·2	1,763·5	Potatoes	36·1	798·0
Wheat	100.7	379·5	Hay	287·1	1,086·1

The total area under cultivation in 1995 was 2,001,500 ha. Production of dairy butter in 1994 was 45,304 tonnes, and of cheese, 87,416 tonnes.

Livestock (1995): Horses, 25,700; cattle, 1,148,100; pigs, 1,400,300; poultry, 5,657,400; reindeer, 333,000.

Forestry. The total forest land (1995) amounts to 26·4m. ha. The productive forest land covers 20·1m. ha.

INDUSTRY. The following data cover establishments with a total personnel of 5 or more in 1993:

Industry	*Establishments*	*Personnel* [1]	*Value of production (in 1m. marks)* Gross	*Value added*
Mining and quarrying	121	3,069	2,553	1,353
Metal ore mining	6	780	581	297
Other mining	115	2,289	1,953	1,057
Manufacturing	5,595	342,843	281,370	100,424
Manufacture of food, beverages and tobacco	718	43,886	49,501	13,435

[1] Working proprietors, salaried employees and wage earners.

Industry	*Establish-ments*	*Person-nel* [1]	*Value of production (in 1m. marks)*	
			Gross	*Value added*
Textile, wearing apparel and leather industries	433	17,575	6,155	2,850
Manufacture of textiles	171	7,362	3,229	1,383
Manufacture of wearing apparel, except footwear	172	7,283	1,945	1,026
Manufacture of wood and wood products, incl. furniture	749	30,908	18,002	6,883
Manufacture of paper and paper prod., printing, publishing	799	69,264	63,763	23,276
Manufacture of paper and paper products	162	38,969	48,746	16,616
Printing, publishing, etc.	637	30,295	15,016	6,661
Manufacture of chemicals and chemical, petroleum, coal, rubber and plastic products	455	33,147	36,686	12,438
Manufacture of industrial chemicals	147	11,871	13,160	5,042
Manufacture of other chemical products	107	9,319	6,682	3,105
Petroleum refineries	3	2,989	11,083	1,825
Manufacture of non-metallic mineral products	350	12,253	6,527	3,074
Basic metal industries	73	15,486	24,465	6,659
Iron and steel basic industries	54	11,244	15,971	4,948
Non-ferrous metal basic industries	19	4,242	8,494	1,711
Manufacture of fabricated metal products, machinery, etc.	1,931	117,013	74,853	31,069
Manufacture of fabricated metal products, excl. machinery	698	23,002	13,278	5,544
Manufacture of machinery, except electrical	657	40,606	25,718	10,339
Manufacture of electrical machinery, apparatus, etc.	266	24,308	19,018	8,159
Manufacture of transport equipment	198	23,697	13,544	5,292
Other manufacturing industries	87	3,311	1,416	739
Electricity, gas and water	514	22,755	37,460	12,792
All industry	6,230	368,667	321,363	114,569

[1] Working proprietors, salaried employees and wage earners.

GDP (at market prices) *per capita* (1994) 100,052 marks.

Trade Unions. According to an incomes policy agreement reached by the central labour market organizations in Sept. 1995, which is in force until Jan. 1998, wages and salaries were raised by 1·8% in Nov. 1995 and were to be raised by 1·3% in Oct. 1996. The Government undertook to cut taxes on wages and salaries in 1997 in order to support moderate pay developments.

FOREIGN ECONOMIC RELATIONS

Commerce. Imports and exports for calendar years, in 1m. marks:

	1990	*1991*	*1992*	*1993*	*1994*
Imports	105,519	87,744	94,974	103,167	120,547
Exports	101,327	92,842	107,463	134,112	154,163

The trade with some principal import and export countries was (in 1,000 marks):

Country	*Imports*		*Exports*	
	1993	*1994*	*1993*	*1994*
Australia	413,606	693,798	1,665,502	2,173,539
Austria	1,180,200	1,349,405	1,426,951	1,600,477
Belgium–Luxembourg	3,023,075	3,291,017	2,956,730	3,460,683
Brazil	590,466	907,325	425,220	568,788
Canada	724,484	838,855	1,073,327	1,034,594
China	1,467,377	1,829,540	1,467,800	2,260,717
Colombia	481,653	614,904	166,163	219,849
Czech Republic	334,240	438,154	446,847	855,342
Denmark	3,233,395	3,667,750	4,480,450	5,287,359
Estonia	761,476	1,127,025	1,883,418	3,381,488
France	4,718,071	4,911,252	7,115,125	7,783,502
Germany	16,923,852	17,735,872	17,633,177	20,678,161

Country	Imports 1993	Imports 1994	Exports 1993	Exports 1994
Greece	277,336	327,648	745,693	892,568
Hungary	322,486	410,417	772,026	1,163,306
Iran	10,301	21,881	396,637	524,787
Ireland	689,035	896,288	691,987	708,141
Israel	155,797	196,506	504,437	537,228
Italy	3,813,408	4,685,088	4,350,820	4,605,243
Japan	5,966,445	7,837,686	2,193,894	3,185,762
Netherlands	3,849,298	4,352,478	6,733,874	7,874,202
Norway	5,005,844	5,760,908	4,280,215	4,881,445
Poland	1,382,872	1,548,944	2,043,484	2,550,944
Portugal	1,090,487	1,091,783	875,602	804,654
Russia	7,835,829	10,697,472	6,059,135	8,028,996
Saudi Arabia	45,262	62,830	702,666	591,276
Spain	1,246,562	1,586,843	3,263,051	3,549,949
Sweden	10,544,739	12,576,112	14,860,524	16,845,561
Switzerland	2,043,988	2,108,683	2,111,432	2,325,220
UK	9,113,075	10,021,036	14,033,470	15,917,134
USA	7,502,598	9,137,287	10,504,480	11,036,533

Principal imports in 1994 (in 1m. marks): Machinery, apparatus and appliances, 43,318; mineral fuels, lubricants, etc., 13,918; chemicals, 15,414; food and live animals, 7,249; road vehicles, 7,358; crude materials, inedible, except fuels, 7,995; textile yarn, fabrics, etc., 2,965; iron and steel, 4,503.

Principal exports in 1994 (in 1m. marks): Paper and paper-board, 36,108; machinery and transport equipment, 49,148; wood shaped or simply worked, 8,109; wood pulp, 3,749; ships, 2,691; clothing, 1,303; veneers, plywood, etc., and other wood manufactures, 2,871; food and live animals, 4,634; road vehicles, 4,668.

Timber exports in 1994 (in 1,000 cu. metres): Round timber, 1,087; sawn wood, 7,181; plywood and veneers, 694.

Total trade between Finland and UK (British Department of Trade returns, in £1,000 sterling):

	1990	1991	1992	1993	1994
Imports to UK	1,775,766	1,522,337	1,676,575	1,904,694	2,253,250
Exports and re-exports from UK	1,041,739	847,671	994,656	1,129,722	1,297,265

Tourism. In 1994 the total revenue from tourism was 6,812m. marks and the total expenditure 8,189m. marks.

COMMUNICATIONS

Roads. In Jan. 1995 there were 79,166 km of public roads, of which 48,841 km were paved. At the end of 1994 there were 1,872,588 registered cars, 45,786 lorries, 202,614 vans and pick-ups, 8,054 buses and coaches and 20,908 special automobiles.

Railways. On 31 Dec. 1994 the total length of the line operated was 5,859 km (1,950 km electrified), of which all was owned by the State. The gauge is 1,524 mm. In 1994, 44m. passengers and 40·2m. tonnes of freight were carried. The total revenue in 1994 was 3,393m. marks and the total expenditure 3,064m. marks. There is a metro (17 km) and tram/light rail network (70 km) in Helsinki.

Civil Aviation. There is an international airport at Helsinki (Vantaa). The national carrier is Finnair, which in 1995 operated 2 A300B4-200s, 1 DC-10-30, 1 DC-10-30ER, 5 DC-9-40s, 12 DC-9-50s and 21 other aircraft. Its scheduled traffic covered 67m. km in 1994. The number of passengers was 4·5m. and the number of passenger-km 6,719,000 in 1994; the air transport of freight and mail amounted to 205m. tonne-km. Services are also provided by Aeroflot, Air Botnia, Air China, Air France, Austrian Airlines, Balkan, Baltic Airlines, British Airways, Czech Airlines, Delta, El Al, Estonian Air, KLM, Karair, Lithuanian Airlines, LOT, Lufthansa, Malév, Northwest Airlines, Sabena, SAS, Swissair and United Airlines.

Shipping. The total registered mercantile marine on 31 Dec. 1994 was 589 vessels of 1,557,501 gross tons. In 1994 the total number of vessels arriving in Finland from abroad was 22,432 and the goods discharged amounted to 38·6m. tonnes. The goods loaded for export from Finland ports amounted to 35·6m. tonnes.

The lakes, rivers and canals are navigable for about 6,300 km. Timber floating has some importance, and there are about 9,650 km of floatable inland waterways. In 1994 bundle floating was about 1·3m. tonnes.

Telecommunications. In 1994 there were 1,879 post offices. The number of telephone subscriber lines (1994), 2·79m.; 675,565 mobile telephones were in use. The net sales of Post Finland in 1994 were 4,874m. marks and of Telecom Finland, 4,927m.marks.

On 31 Dec. 1994 the number of television licences was 1,881,753 (colour by PAL). *Oy Yleisradio AB* broadcasts 4 programmes (1 in Swedish), covering the whole country. 4 TV programmes (1 commercial) are broadcast. In Jan. 1994 there were 59 local radio stations in operation and 186 private cable networks.

Cinemas. In Dec. 1994 there were 326 cinema halls with a seating capacity of 58,600.

Press. In 1994 the number of newspapers published more often than 3 times a week was 56, of which 8 were in Swedish.

SOCIAL INSTITUTIONS

Justice. The lowest court of justice is the District Court. In most civil cases a District Court has a quorum with 3 legally-qualified members present. In criminal cases as well as in some cases related to family law the District Court has a quorum with a chair and 3 lay judges present. In the preliminary preparation of a civil case and in a criminal case concerning a minor offence a District Court is composed of the chair only. From the District Court an appeal lies to the courts of appeal in Turku, Vaasa, Kuopio, Helsinki, Kouvola and Rovaniemi. The Supreme Court sits in Helsinki. Appeals from the decisions of administrative authorities are in the final instance decided by the Supreme Administrative Court, also in Helsinki. Judges can be removed only by judicial sentence.

Two functionaries, the Chancellor of Justice, and the Ombudsman or Solicitor-General, exercise control over the administration of justice. The former acts also as counsel and public prosecutor for the Government; the latter is appointed by Parliament.

At the end of 1994 the prison population numbered 2,967 men and 125 women; the number of convictions in 1993 was 386,863, of which 362,228 were for minor offences with a maximum penalty of fines and 24,376 with penalty of imprisonment. 10,126 of the prison sentences were unconditional.

Religion. Liberty of conscience is guaranteed to members of all religions. National churches are the Lutheran National Church and the Greek Orthodox Church of Finland. The Lutheran Church is divided into 8 bishoprics (Turku being the archiepiscopal see), 80 provostships and 600 parishes. The Greek Orthodox Church is divided into 3 bishoprics (Kuopio being the archiepiscopal see) and 27 parishes, in addition to which there are a monastery and a convent.

Percentage of the total population at the end of 1994: Lutherans, 85·9; Greek Orthodox, 1·1; others, 1; not members of any religion, 12.

Education (1994). *Primary and Secondary Education:*

	Number of institutions	*Teachers*	*Students*
First-level Education			
(Lower sections of the comprehensive schools, grades I–VI)			390,432
Second-level Education			
General education (Upper sections of the comprehensive schools, grades VII–IX, and senior secondary schools)	5,001	...	321,699
Vocational education	495	21,245 [1]	125,666

[1] Second and third level at vocational and professional institutions.

Higher Education. Education at the third level (including universities and third level education at vocational and professional institutions) was provided for 197,367 students. Education at universities was provided at 21 institutions with 7,709 teachers and 127,846 students.

University Education. Universities and university-type institutions with the number of teachers and students in 1994:

			Students	
	Founded	*Teachers*	*Total*	*Women*
Universities				
Helsinki	1640	1,755	29,967	18,164
Turku (Swedish)	1919	317	5,083	2,963
Turku (Finnish)	1922	789	12,182	7,596
Jyväskylä	1958	576	9,419	5,959
Oulu	1958	795	11,032	5,376
Tampere	1966	612	12,191	7,683
Joensuu	1969	388	5,675	3,516
Kuopio	1972	300	3,638	2,444
Lapland	1979	137	2,238	1,355
Vaasa	1968	135	2,956	1,610
Universities of Technology				
Helsinki	1849	534	12,232	2,278
Lappeenranta	1969	188	3,171	653
Tampere	1972	297	6,957	1,171
College of Veterinary Medicine, Helsinki	1946	48	382	300
Schools of Economics and Business Administration				
Helsinki (Finnish)	1911	146	3,838	1,763
Helsinki (Swedish)	1927	105	1,988	791
Turku (Finnish)	1950	87	1,926	965
Universities of Art				
Academy of Fine Arts	1848	19	168	106
Sibelius Academy	1939	273	1,412	798
University of Industrial Arts	1949	143	1,369	836
Theatre Academy	1979	65	292	162

General adult education (at folk high schools, music schools and colleges, sports institutes and study centres) had 113,000 students in 1994.

Health. In 1993 there were 13,763 physicians, 4,745 dentists and (1994) 51,272 hospital beds.

Welfare. The Social Insurance Institution administers general systems of old age pensions (to all persons over 65 years of age and disabled younger persons) and of health insurance. An additional system of compulsory old age pensions paid for by the employers is in force and works through the Central Pension Security Institute. Systems for other public aid are administered by the communes and supervised by the National Social Board and the Ministry of Social Affairs and Health.

The total cost of social security amounted to 182,189m. marks in 1993. Out of this 42,493m. (23·3%) was spent for health, 27,962m. (15·3%) for unemployment, 80,603m. (44·2%) for old age and disability, 23,371m. (12·8%) for family allowances and child welfare, 7,761m. (4·4%) for general welfare purposes and administration. Out of the total expenditure, 32% was financed by the State, 16% by local authorities, 35% by employers, 13% by the beneficiaries and 4% by users.

DIPLOMATIC REPRESENTATIVES

Of Finland in Great Britain (38 Chesham Pl., London, SW1X 8HW)
Ambassador: Leif Blomqvist.

Of Great Britain in Finland (Itäinen Puistotie, 17, Helsinki 00140)
Ambassador: David Burns, CMG.

Of Finland in the USA (3301 Massachusetts Ave., NW, Washington, D.C., 20008)
Ambassador: Jaakko Laajava.

Of the USA in Finland (Itäinen Puistotie 14A, Helsinki 00140)
Ambassador: Derek N. Shearer.

Of Finland to the United Nations
Ambassador: Wilhelm Breitenstein.

Further Reading

Statistics Finland. *Statistical Yearbook of Finland* (from 1879).—*Bulletin of Statistics* (monthly, from 1924).
Constitution Act and Parliament Act of Finland. Helsinki, 1984
Suomen valtiokalenteri–Finlands statskalender (State Calendar of Finland). Helsinki. Annual
Facts About Finland. Helsinki. Annual (Union Bank of Finland)
Finland in Figures. Helsinki, Annual
Arter, D., *Politics and Policy-Making in Finland.* Brighton, 1987
Jakobson, M. *Myth and Reality.* Helsinki, 1987
Jutikkala, E. and Pirinen, K., *A History of Finland.* 3rd ed. New York, 1979
Kekkonen, U., *President's View.* London, 1982
Kirby, D. G., *Finland in the Twentieth Century.* 2nd ed. London, 1984
Klinge, M., *A Brief History of Finland.* Helsinki, 1987
Mead, W. R., *Experience of Finland.* Farnborough, 1993
Petersson, O., *The Government and Politics of the Nordic Countries.* Stockholm, 1994
Screen, J. E. O., *Finland.* [Bibliography] Oxford and Santa Barbara (CA), 1981
Singleton, F., *The Economy of Finland in the Twentieth Century.* Univ. of Bradford Press, 1987
Tillotson, H. M., *Finland at Peace and War, 1918–1993.* London, 1993

National statistical office: Statistics Finland, Tilastokeskus, FIN-00022.

FRANCE

République Française

Capital: Paris
Population: 57·8m. (1994)
GNP per capita: US$23,470 (1994)
HDI/world rank: 0·930/8 (1992)

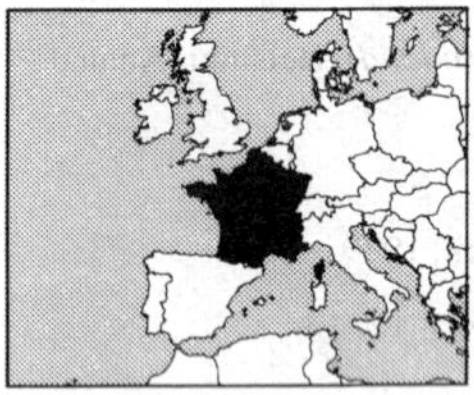

KEY HISTORICAL EVENTS. The republic proclaimed on the fall of the Bourbon monarchy in 1792 lasted until the First Empire, under Napoleon I, was established in 1804. The Bourbon monarchy was restored in 1814 and (with an interval during 1815) lasted until the abdication of Louis Philippe in 1848. The Second Republic was established on 12 March 1848, the Second Empire (under Louis Napoleon) on 2 Dec. 1852. The Third Republic was established on 4 Sept. 1870 following the capture and imprisonment of Louis Napoleon in the Franco-Prussian war, and lasted until the German occupation of 1940. Power during the occupation was nominally exercised by the Vichy regime of Marshal Pétain. Following the liberation of 1944, the Fourth Republic was established on 24 Dec. 1946 but was dogged throughout by weak governments with unstable parliamentary support. It collapsed on 4 Oct. 1958 under the impetus of military revolt in Algeria, following which General de Gaulle assumed power. He subsequently inspired the constitution of the Fifth Republic, now in force.

TERRITORY AND POPULATION. France is bounded in the north by the English Channel *(La Manche)*, north-east by Belgium and Luxembourg, east by Germany, Switzerland and Italy, south by the Mediterranean (with Monaco as a coastal enclave), south-west by Spain and Andorra, and west by the Atlantic Ocean. The total area is 543,965 sq. km (210,033 sq. miles).

The population (present in actual boundaries) at successive censuses has been:

1801	27,349,003	1891	38,342,948	1954	42,777,174
1821	30,461,875	1901	38,961,945	1962	46,519,997
1841	34,230,178	1911	39,604,992	1968	49,778,540
1861	37,386,313	1921	39,209,518	1975	52,655,802
1866	38,067,064	1931	41,834,923	1982	54,334,871
1872	36,102,921	1946	40,506,639	1990	56,615,100
1881	37,672,048				

Estimated population, 1 Jan. 1994, 57·8m.

The largest groups of foreign residents (1992) are Portuguese (649,714), Algerians (614,207) and Moroccans (572,652).

Controls on illegal immigration were tightened as from July 1991.

Vital statistics for calendar years:

	Marriages	*Live births*	*Deaths*
1985	269,300	768,431	552,500
1988	271,124	771,300	524,600
1991	280,200	759,100	524,700
1992	271,400	743,700	521,400
1993	254,000	712,000	528,000

Live birth rate in 1993 (estimated) was 12·3 per 1,000 inhabitants; death rate, 9·2; marriage rate, 4·4; divorce rate, 1·9; infant mortality, 6·5 per 1,000 live births.

Abortions were legalized in 1975; there were 162,620 in 1990. Expectation of life (1993); men, 73·3 years; women, 81·5. Population growth rate (1993, estimated), 3·2 per 1,000. Average density (1990), 104 persons per sq. km.

The areas, populations and chief towns of the 22 Metropolitan regions were as follows:

Regions	*Area (sq. km)*	*Census 1982*	*Census 1990*	*Chief town*
Alsace	8,280	1,566,048	1,624,400	Strasbourg
Aquitaine	41,308	2,656,544	2,795,800	Bordeaux
Auvergne	26,013	1,332,678	1,321,200	Clermont-Ferrand

Regions	*Area (sq. km)*	*Census 1982*	*Census 1990*	*Chief town*
Basse-Normandie	17,589	1,350,979	1,391,300	Caen
Bourgogne (Burgundy)	31,582	1,596,054	1,609,700	Dijon
Bretagne (Brittany)	27,208	2,707,886	2,795,600	Rennes
Centre	39,151	2,264,164	2,371,000	Orléans
Champagne-Ardenne	25,606	1,345,935	1,347,800	Reims
Corse (Corsica)	8,680	240,178	250,400	Ajaccio
Franche-Comté	16,202	1,084,049	1,097,300	Besançon
Haute-Normandie	12,317	1,655,362	1,737,200	Rouen
Île-de-France	12,012	10,073,059	10,660,600	Paris
Languedoc-Roussillon	27,376	1,926,514	2,115,000	Montpellier
Limousin	16,942	737,153	722,900	Limoges
Lorraine	23,547	2,319,905	2,305,700	Nancy
Midi-Pyrénées	41,348	2,325,319	2,430,700	Toulouse
Nord-Pas-de-Calais	12,414	3,932,939	3,965,100	Lille
Pays de la Loire	32,082	2,930,398	3,059,100	Nantes
Picardie	19,399	1,740,321	1,810,700	Amiens
Poitou-Charentes	25,810	1,568,230	1,595,100	Poitiers
Provence-Alpes-Côte d'Azur	31,400	3,965,209	4,257,900	Marseille
Rhône-Alpes	43,698	5,015,947	5,350,700	Lyon

Populations of the principal conurbations and towns at the 1990 census:

	Conurbation	*Town*		*Conurbation*	*Town*
Paris	9,318,821 [1]	2,152,423	Bayonne	164,378	41,846
Lyon	1,262,223 [2]	415,487	Perpignan	157,873	105,983
Marseille-Aix-en-Provence	1,230,936 [3]	800,550	Amiens	156,120	131,872
Lille	959,234 [4]	172,142	Pau	144,674	82,157
Bordeaux	696,364	210,336	Nîmes	138,527	128,471
Toulouse	650,336	358,688	Thionville	132,413	40,835
Nice	516,740	342,439	Saint-Nazaire	131,511	64,812
Nantes	496,078	244,995	Annecy	126,729	51,143
Toulon	437,553	167,619	Troyes	122,763	59,271
Grenoble	404,733	150,758	Besançon	122,623	113,828
Strasbourg	388,483	252,338	Montbéliard	117,510	30,639
Rouen	380,161	102,723	Lorient	115,488	59,437
Valenciennes	338,392	39,276	Hagondange-Briey	112,061	9,091 [5]
Cannes	335,647	68,676	Valence	107,965	63,437
Nancy	329,447	99,351	Melun	107,705	36,489
Lens	323,174	35,278	Poitiers	107,625	78,894
Saint-Étienne	313,338	197,536	Chambéry	103,283	54,120
Tours	282,152	129,509	Angoulême	102,908	46,194
Béthune	261,535	25,261	Maubeuge	102,772	35,225
Clermont-Ferrand	254,416	136,181	Calais	101,768	75,309
Le Havre	253,627	195,854	La Rochelle	100,264	71,094
Montpellier	248,303	207,996	Forbach	98,758	27,357
Rennes	245,065	199,396	Creil	97,119	32,501
Orléans	243,153	105,111	Bourges	94,731	75,609
Dijon	230,451	146,703	Cherbourg	92,045	28,773
Mulhouse	223,856	108,357	Boulogne-sur-Mer	91,249	44,244
Angers	208,282	141,404	Chartres	85,933	41,850
Reims	206,437	180,620	Saint-Brieuc	83,861	47,370
Brest	201,480	147,956	Colmar	83,816	63,498
Douai	199,562	44,195	Saint-Chamond	81,795	39,262
Metz	193,117	119,594	Tarbes	80,680	50,228
Caen	191,490	112,846	Arras	79,607	42,715
Dunkerque	190,879	70,331	Belfort	78,215	50,125
Le Mans	189,107	145,502	Chalon-sur-Saône	77,764	54,575
Mantes-la-Jolie	189,103	45,254	Roanne	77,160	42,848
Avignon	181,136	86,939	Alès	76,856	–
Limoges	170,065	133,464	Béziers	76,304	70,996

[1] Including towns of Boulogne-Billancourt (101,743), Montreuil (94,754), Argenteuil (93,096), Versailles (87,789), Saint-Denis (89,988), Nanterre (84,565), Vitry-sur-Seine (82,400), Aulnay-sous-Bois (82,314) and Créteil (82,088).

[2] Including towns of Villeurbanne (116,872) and Vénissieux (60,644).

[3] Including town of Aix-en-Provence (123,842).

[4] Including towns of Roubaix (97,746) and Tourcoing (93,765). [5] Census 1982.

The official language is French. Regional languages are also spoken. In 1990 the Conseil Supérieur de la Langue Française (established 1989) recommended minor orthographic changes, to be introduced in schools in 1991. Legislation of 1994 (*loi Toubon*) seeks to restrict the use of foreign words in official communications, broadcasting and advertisements. (A previous such decree dated from 1975). The Constitutional Court has ruled that imposing such restrictions on private citizens would infringe their freedom of expression.

Monnier, A., *La Population de la France*. Paris, 1990

CLIMATE. The north-west has a moderate maritime climate, with small temperature range and abundant rainfall, but inland, rainfall becomes more seasonal, with a summer maximum, and the annual range of temperature increases. Southern France has a Mediterranean climate, with mild moist winters and hot dry summers. Eastern France has a continental climate and a rainfall maximum in summer, with thunderstorms prevalent.

Paris. Jan. 37°F (3°C), July 64°F (18°C). Annual rainfall 22·9" (573 mm). Bordeaux. Jan. 41°F (5°C), July 68°F (20°C). Annual rainfall 31·4" (786 mm). Lyon. Jan. 37°F (3°C), July 68°F (20°C). Annual rainfall 31·8" (794 mm).

CONSTITUTION AND GOVERNMENT. The Constitution of the Fifth Republic, superseding that of 1946, came into force on 4 Oct. 1958. It consists of a preamble, dealing with the Rights of Man, and 92 articles.

France is a republic, indivisible, secular, democratic and social; all citizens are equal before the law (Art. 2). National sovereignty resides with the people, who exercise it through their representatives and by referendums (Art. 3). Constitutional reforms of July 1995 widened the range of issues on which referendums may be called. Political parties carry out their activities freely, but must respect the principles of national sovereignty and democracy (Art. 4).

The head of state is the *President*, who sees that the Constitution is respected; ensures the regular functioning of the public authorities, as well as the continuity of the state; is the protector of national independence and territorial integrity (Art. 5). The President is elected for 7 years by direct universal suffrage (Art. 6). The President appoints a Prime Minister and, on the latter's advice, appoints and dismisses the other members of the Government (Art. 8); presides over the Council of Ministers (Art. 9); may dissolve the National Assembly, after consultation with the Prime Minister and the Presidents of the two Houses (Art. 12); appoints to the civil and military offices of the state (Art. 13). In times of crisis, the President may take such emergency powers as the circumstances demand; the National Assembly cannot be dissolved during such a period (Art. 16).

At the first round of presidential elections on 23 April 1995, Lionel Jospin gained the largest number of votes (23·31% of those cast) against 8 opponents. At the second round on 7 May 1995, the electorate was 39,976,944; turn-out was 79·77%. Jacques Chirac was elected President against Jospin by 52·64% of votes cast.

President: Jacques Chirac (RPR; sworn in 17 May 1995).

Parliament consists of the *National Assembly* and the *Senate*. The National Assembly is elected by direct suffrage by the second ballot system (by which candidates winning 50% or more of the vote in their constituencies are elected, candidates winning less than 12·5% are eliminated and other candidates go on to a second round of voting) and the Senate by indirect suffrage (Art. 24). Since 1996 it has convened for an annual 9-month session. It comprises 577 Deputies, elected for a 5-year term from single-member constituencies (555 in Metropolitan France and 22 in the various overseas departments and dependencies).

The Senate comprises 321 Senators elected for 9-year terms (one-third every 3 years) by an electoral college in each Department or overseas dependency, made up of all members of the Departmental Council or its equivalent in overseas dependencies, together with all members of Municipal Councils within that area; there are 296 Senators for Metropolitan France, 13 for the Overseas Departments and dependencies, and 12 for French citizens residing outside France and its dependencies.

The *Speaker* of the Senate deputizes for the President of the Republic in the event of the latter's incapacity. Following the partial election held on 24 Sept. 1995, the Senate was composed of (by group, including 'affiliates'): UDF, 129; RPR, 94; Socialist group, 75; Communist group, 15; ind, 8. In Oct. 1995 René Monory was elected *Speaker* of the Senate for a second 3-year term.

The *Constitutional Council* is composed of 9 members whose term of office is 9 years (non-renewable), one-third every 3 years; 3 are appointed by the President of the Republic, 3 by the President of the National Assembly, and 3 by the President of the Senate; in addition, former Presidents of the Republic are, by right, life members of the Constitutional Council (Art. 56). It oversees the fairness of the elections of the President (Art. 58) and Parliament (Art. 59) and of referendums (Art. 60), and acts as a guardian of the Constitution (Art. 61). Its President is Roland Dumas (appointed 1995).

The *Economic and Social Council* advises on Government and Private Members' Bills (Art. 69). It comprises representatives of employers', workers' and farmers' organizations in each Department and Overseas Territory.

At the elections of 21 and 28 March 1993 to the National Assembly the electorate was 38,968,660. In the first round, turn-out was 68·93%. The Rassemblement pour la République (Republican Rally, RPR; Gaullists) won 42 seats with 20·39% of votes cast; its coalition partner, the Union for French Democracy (UDF), 36 with 19·08%; right-wing parties, 2 with 4·71%. Vote for parties gaining no seats: Socialist Party (PS), 17·59%; National Front, 12·41%; Communist Party (PCF), 9·18%; Greens, 4·01%; Ecology, 3·62%. In the second round, turn-out was 67·52%. The RPR gained 28·27% of votes cast, the PS 28·25%, the UDF 25·84%, the National Front 5·66%, the PCF 4·61%. Seats in the National Assembly: RPR, 247 (126 in 1988); UDF, 213 (131); PS and allies, 70 (282); various right-wing parties, 24 (11); PCF, 23 (26); National Front, nil (1).

A new government was formed in Nov. 1995 consisting of:

Prime Minister: Alain Juppé (b. 1945; RPR).

Ministers:

Justice, Keeper of the Seals: Jacques Toubon (RPR). *Education:* François Bayrou (UDF-CDS). *Defence:* Charles Millon (UDF). *Public Works, Housing, Transport and Tourism:* Bernard Pons (RPR). *Foreign Affairs:* Hervé de Charette (UDF-PPDF). *Labour and Social Affairs:* Jacques Barrot (UDF-CDS). *Interior:* Jean-Louis Debré (RPR). *Economy and Finance:* Jean Arthuis (UDF-CDS). *Relations with the Parliament:* Roger Romani (RPR). *Environment:* Corinne Lepage (ind). *Culture:* Philippe Douste-Blazy (UDF-CDS). *Industry, Posts and Telecommunications:* Franck Borotra (RPR). *Agriculture, Fisheries and Food:* Philippe Vasseur (UDF-PR). *Planning:* Jean-Claude Gaudin (UDF-PR). *Small and Medium Enterprises, Commerce and Crafts:* Jean-Pierre Raffarin (UDF-PPDF). *Civil Service, State Reform and Decentralization:* Dominique Perben (RPR).

Ministers-Delegate:

Veterans and War Victims: Pierre Pasquini (RPR). *Overseas:* Jean-Jacques de Peretti (RPR). *Youth and Sport:* Guy Drut (RPR). *Housing:* Pierre-André Périssol (RPR). *Co-operation:* Jacques Godfrain (RPR). *European Affairs:* Michel Barnier (RPR). *Employment:* Anne-Marie Couderc (RPR). *Budget and Government Spokesman:* Alain Lamassoure (UDF-PR). *Finance and Foreign Trade:* Yves Galland (UDF). *Post, Telecommunications and Space:* Francois Fillon (RPR). *Town and Integration:* Eric Raoult (RPR).

(CDS = Social Democratic Centre group; PR = Republican group; PPDF = People's Party for French Democracy).

The *Speaker* is Philippe Séguin.

National flag: The Tricolour of three vertical stripes of blue, white and red.
National anthem: La Marseillaise; words and tune by C. Rouget de Lisle.

European Parliament. France has 87 representatives. At the June 1994 elections turn-out was 53·5%. The RPR-UDF won 29 seats with 25·5% of votes cast (group in European Parliament: Liberal, Democratic and Reformist Group; Popular European Party); the PS, 16 with 14·5% (European Socialist Party); the Other Europe group, 13 with 12·3%; the Radical Energy group, 13 with 12%; the National Front, 10 with 10·5% (Europe of Nations); the Communist Party, 6 with 6·9%.

Local and Regional Government. France is divided into 22 regions for national development, planning and budgetary policy. Many of these regions are broadly comparable with the provinces of pre-revolutionary France, and give a measure of recognition to the distinctive personalities of peripheral areas such as Alsace and Brittany. In March 1982 state-appointed Regional Prefects were abolished and their executive powers transferred to the Presidents of the Regional Councils, which are directly elected.

By a law of 13 May 1991 **Corsica** became a territorial collectivity. After the regional elections of March 1992 it had an assembly which elects an executive council. Since Feb. 1995 the **Pays Basque**, which formed part of the department Pyrénées-Atlantique, has had an elected 65-member council bringing together parliamentary deputies, regional and general councillors and representatives of mayors.

There are 96 departments within the 22 regions each governed by a directly-elected *General Council.* From 1982 the powers of the councils' presidents were extended to take over local administration and expenditure from the departmental prefects with responsibility for public order. Legislation of 1993 provides for the election every 3 years of half the members of these councils. Councillors elected in 1992 will serve for 6 years. Those elected in March 1994 will serve for 7 years. Elections for 2,009 seats in the *General Councils* were held in 2 rounds on 20 and 27 March 1994. The electorate was 18,563,056; turn-out was 60·39% at the first round and 58·78% at the second. The PS gained 532 seats, the UDF 446, the RPR 382, various right-wing groups 309, various left-wing groups 171, the Communist Party 145, Greens 7, the National Front 3, others 12.

The unit of local government is the *commune*, the size and population of which vary very much. There were, in 1995, in the 96 metropolitan departments, 36,763 communes. Most of them (30,919) had fewer than 1,500 inhabitants. The local affairs of the commune are under a Municipal Council, composed of from 9 to 36 members, elected by universal suffrage for 6 years. In 1995, there were 512,850 municipal councillors. Each Municipal Council elects a mayor, who is both the representative of the commune and the agent of the central government. Communes are associated in the Assemblée des Districts et des Communantés de France, and also co-operate in inter-commune public enterprise projects, of which there were some 1,200 in 1995.

Municipal elections were held in June 1995.

In Paris the *Conseil de Paris* is composed of 109 members elected from the 20 *arrondissements*. It combines the functions of departmental General and Municipal Council.

Ameller, M., *L'Assemblée Nationale.* Paris, 1994
Duhamel, O. and Mény, Y., *Dictionnaire Constitutionnel.* Paris, 1992

DEFENCE. The President of the Republic exercises command over the Armed Forces. He is assisted by the Supreme Council of Defence, which studies defence problems, and by two Committees *(Comité de Défense* and *Comité de Défense restreint)* which formulate directives. The Prime Minister is responsible for national defence, exercising his military responsibilities and co-ordinating inter-ministry defence activities through the General Secretariat of National Defence (SGDN). Under the Prime Minister's authority, the Minister of Defence is responsible for the execution of military policy, in particular the organization and administration of the Armed Forces.

The Ministry of Defence has overall responsibility for defence. The preparation and control of the Armed Forces is exercised by the Chief of Staff of the Armed Forces, the Chiefs of Staff of the 3 services—Army, Navy and Air—and the head of the *Gendarmerie.*

French forces are not formally under the NATO command structure, although

France signed the NATO strategic document on Eastern Europe in Nov. 1991. The Minister of Defence attends informal NATO meetings which have an agenda of French interest, but not the formal twice-yearly meetings. In 1994 21,600 service personnel were stationed in Germany, 20,480 in the overseas departments and territories, 6,281 on UN peacekeeping missions and 2,240 constituted the 'French Maritime Presence' abroad.

The General Directorate for Armament (DGA) is responsible for all aspects of the procurement of defence equipment. It employs about 50,000 personnel, and co-ordinates another 200,000 others employed in the defence industry.

Conscription was reduced from 12 to 10 months on 1 Jan. 1992. Conscripts may not be compelled to serve abroad unless war is declared.

Army. The Army consisted in 1995 of 239,400 personnel, of whom 8,600 were women and 136,800 were conscripts.

The Army comprises 1 corps with 3 armoured and 1 infantry divisions, 1 armoured division in Eurocorps, 1 Franco-German brigade, 7 armoured, 6 mechanized infantry, 8 artillery, 3 mountain infantry and 4 motorized infantry regiments and 3 anti-tank and 3 reconnaissance squadrons, and corps units including 1 armoured reconnaissance, 1 parachute special forces, 1 motorized infantry, 1 missile-launching, 5 surface-to-air missile, 2 combat helicopter and 4 engineer regiments.

The Rapid Action Force (FAR) comprises 42,500 personnel organized, equipped and trained for rapid engagement either in Europe or over large distances elsewhere; it includes 1 parachute division, 1 air-portable marine division, a light armoured division, 1 mountain division and 1 air-mobile division, together with various specialized units.

Equipment includes 974 AMX-30/30B2 and 40 Leclerc main battle tanks, 325 AMX-10RC armoured vehicles, 1,364 other armoured vehicles, 1,435 pieces of artillery, 180 *Roland* surface-to-air missile systems and 1,455 *Milan* anti-tank weapons.

The *Aviation Légère de l'Armée de Terre* (ALAT) with about 7,000 personnel is an integral part of the Army, equipped with over 700 helicopters of various types for observation, reconnaissance, combat area transport, liaison and supply duties.

The *Foreign Legion* was formed in 1831 for duty in North Africa. It is officered by French nationals and based at Aubagne, near Marseilles. About half the other ranks are French. It numbered 8,500 in 1996.

Gendarmerie. The para-military police force exists to ensure public security and maintain law and order, as well as participate in the operational defence of French territory as part of the armed forces. It consisted in 1995 of 93,000 personnel including 12,000 conscripts, 2,600 women and 1,000 civilians. It comprises a territorial force of 57,000 personnel in 3,640 brigades throughout the country, a mobile force of 17,000 personnel in 128 squadrons and specialized formations including the Republican Guard, the Air Force and Naval Gendarmeries and an anti-terrorist unit. It is equipped with 28 VBC-90 armoured gun-carriers, 121 light armoured cars, 155 armoured vehicles and 33 troop transport vehicles, as well as 40 helicopters.

Navy. The missions of the Navy are to provide the prime element of the French independent nuclear deterrent through its force of strategic submarines, to assure the security of the French offshore zones, to contribute to NATO's missions and to provide on-station and deployment forces overseas in support of French territorial interests and UN commitments.

French territorial seas and economic zones are organized into 3 maritime regions, each under the authority of a Maritime Prefect (with headquarters in Cherbourg, Brest and Toulon). Offshore, the seas and oceans are divided into 5 zones: Atlantic, Mediterranean, Indian Ocean, Pacific and Antilles-Guiana. Home-based forces are commanded by Commanders-in-Chief based in Brest and Toulon, those in the Indian Ocean and Pacific by Flag Officers based afloat in the Indian Ocean, and at Nouméa (in New Caledonia). Naval forces in the Caribbean come under a joint force commander based at Cayenne.

The following is a summary of the strength of the fleet at the end of the years shown:

	1990	*1991*	*1992*	*1993*	*1994*	*1995*
Aircraft carriers	2	2	1	1	1	1
Strategic-missile submarines	6	5	4	5	5	5
Other submarines	13	13	14	14	13	13
Cruisers	2	1	1	1	1	1
Destroyers	5	4	4	4	4	4
Frigates	35	34	34	35	36	35

The strategic deterrent force comprises 5 nuclear-powered strategic-missile submarines. The most modern of these is *L'Inflexible*, 9,100 tonnes, completed in 1985, together with 4 vessels, *Foudroyant*, *Terrible*, *Indomptable* and *Tonnant*, completed between 1973 and 1980, now converted to the same standard, and all deploying 16 M-4 missiles. A new, much larger class, (14,200 tonnes) is being built, of which the first, *Le Triomphant*, has commenced trials, and is scheduled to become operational in 1995. She will deploy 16 M-45 missiles.

There are also 6 small (2,700 tonne) nuclear-powered submarines and 7 operational diesel submarines.

The principal surface ships are the aircraft carriers *Clemenceau* and *Foch* of 33,300 tonnes each, completed in 1961 and 1963, one of which is always operational, and 1 cruiser. The operational carrier embarks an air group typically comprising 16 Super-Etendard strike aircraft, 7 F-8E Crusader, 6 Alize anti-submarine and warning and a flight of 4 utility helicopters. Both are due to be withdrawn from service in 1998 and 2004, when nuclear-powered replacements are planned. The first of these, *Charles de Gaulle*, was launched at Brest in 1994. The helicopter cruiser *Jeanne d'Arc*, of 12,600 tonnes completed in 1963 is used in peacetime as a training vessel, but could perform amphibious or anti-submarine tasks in war. In these roles she could accommodate up to 8 Lynx helicopters, and 700 personnel. Her armament comprises 6 Exocet and 4 100mm guns.

Other surface combatants include 4 guided-missile destroyers and 35 frigates of which 16 carry helicopters. A modern mine countermeasure force consists of 9 tripartite coastal minehunters and 5 others and 4 diver support vessels. The amphibious force includes 4 dock landing ships of which one is assigned to the Pacific nuclear test centre, 5 medium landing ships, and some 30 craft. Patrol forces include 1 ship (usually deployed in the South Indian Ocean), 20 coastal and 2 inshore patrol vessels. The Navy deploys a substantial support force which includes 5 large and 2 small tankers, 15 other maintenance and logistic ships, 5 weapon system trials ships and 6 survey and research ships. There are several hundred minor auxiliaries.

All warships, and a proportion of naval weapons, are produced by the government armaments service, of which the naval element, *Direction des Constructions Navales* (DCN), operates the shipbuilding yards as well as dockyards. Building takes place at Cherbourg, Brest and Lorient. In addition to units already mentioned, 4 frigates are being built.

The naval air arm, *Aéronavale*, numbers some 8,000 personnel. Operational aircraft include 53 Super-Etendard nuclear-capable strike aircraft, 10 Etendard reconnaissance aircraft, 16 US-built Crusader F-8E all-weather fighters, 25 Alize turboprop anti-submarine aircraft, 8 Atlantic and 20 Atlantique and 5 Gardian maritime reconnaissance aircraft. The Crusaders' fatigue safe life is being extended to keep the type operational until 1999, when the maritime Rafale combat aircraft will enter service. Rotary wing strength includes 16 commando Super Frelon, and 35 anti-submarine and search-and-rescue Lynx helicopters. Numerous training, utility and transport aircraft bring the total strength to about 300 comprising 200 fixed-wing aircraft and 100 helicopters.

A small Marine force of 3,500 'Fusiliers Marins' provides 4 assault groups, an attack swimmer section as well as numerous naval base protection units.

Personnel in 1995 numbered 63,500, including 18,250 conscripts.

Air Force. Created in 1934, the Air Force was reorganized in June 1994. France is divided into 3 air regions corresponding to the 3 military defence regions and 2 air defence zones. There are 2 operational commands (Strategic Air Forces Command—FAS; Air Defence and Air Operations Command—CDAOA) and 5 organizational commands (Combat Air Force Command—CFAC; Projection Air Force Command—CFAP; Air Observation System, Information and Communication Command—CASSIC; Training Command—CEAA; Air Base Protection Infantry Command—CFCA). The FAS is responsible for nuclear weapons; all other combat aircraft are operated by the CFAC under the authority of the CDAOA.

The Conventional Forces in Europe (CFE) agreement imposes a ceiling of 450 combat aircraft. Equipment summary (main types only) Combat: 140 Mirage 2000 B/C, 70 Mirage 2000 N, 30 Mirage 2000 D, 16 Mirage IV P, 30 Mirage F1 B/C, 37 Mirage F1 CT, 42 Mirage F1 Cr, 80 Jaguar. Airborne Early Warning: 4 E3F Awacs. Transport: 12 Hercules C 130, 4 DC8, 2 Airbus A 310, 68 C160 Transall, 24 N 262. Training: 105 Alphajet. Helicopters: 17 Alouette, 39 Fennec, 27 Puma, 4 Super Puma.

Organization and equipment of the Commands (bases in parentheses):

Strategic Air Forces Command (FAS): ICBM Squadrons 18 S-3D silos. Bomber squadron 1/91 (Mont de Marsan) with 8 Mirages IV P/ASMP, Bomber squadron 2/91 (Cazaux) with 7 Mirage IV ASMP. Two additional aircraft in storage (Chateaudun). All but 5 Mirage IV P to be retired by 1996. Fighter squadrons 1/4 and 2/4 with 30 Mirage 2000 N (Luxeuil), fighter squadrons 3/4 with 15 Mirage 2000 N (Istres). Flight refuelling squadrons 1/93 and 3/93 with 11 C 135FR (Istres). 59 Airbone strategic communication squadron (Evreux): 4 C 160 Transall Astarte V/UHF airborne relay posts (flown and maintained by COTAM). Tactical training centre: 3 Falcon 20, 6 Jaguar E (Luxeuil).

Combat Air Forces Command (CFAC): (Nancy): 3 squadrons with 30 Mirage 2000 D and 15 Mirage 2000 Nk 2. (Saint Dizier): 3 squadrons with 48 Jaguar A and 12 Jaguar E (two-seater). Fighter squadrons 2/11 and 3/11 (Toul) with 36 Jaguar A and 3 Jaguar E. (Colmar), 2 squadrons: with 40 Mirage F1 CT. Recce squadrons 1/33, 2/33 with 40 Mirage F1 CR and fighter squadron 4/33 (Djibouti) 10 Mirage F1 C. (Dijon): 1/2 Fighter squadron: 20 Mirage 2000 C and 2/2 Fighter squadron: 17 Mirage 2000 B and 8 Mirage 2000 C. (Orange) 3 squadrons with 45 Mirage 2000 C and B. (Cambrai): 2 squadrons with 30 Mirage 2000 C and B. 54 electronic warfare squadrons (Metz): 2 Transall Gabriel for SIGINT operations (flown and maintained by COTAM).

Projection Air Forces Command (CFAP): 3/60 Transport squadron (Creil): 4 DC8, 2 A 310. (Orléans): transport squadrons 1/61 and 3/61 with 29 C 160F Transall and 2/61 with 9 C130H-30 and 3 C 130H. Transport squadron 1/64: 10 C160 NG and Transport squadron 2/64: 11 C160 NG (Evreux). Transport squadron 1/65 (Villacoublay): 5 N 262, 8 Mystere 20, 4 TBM 700, 2 Falcon 900, 4 Falcon 50, 3 Twin Otters. 1/62 Transport squadron (Creil): 6 CASA 235, 3 Fennec, 3 Twin Otters. 56 special transport squadron (GAM 56) (Evreux): 3 C160, 3 Cougar. CIET 340 (Toulouse): 8 C160, 4 N 262. CIEH 341 (Toulouse): 6 Alouette II, 2 Alouette III, 9 Fennec, 4 Puma. ETE 41 (Metz): 2 N 262, 1 MS 760 Paris and 2 TBM 700. ETE 43 (Bordeaux): 3 N 262, 2 TBM 700. ETE 44 (Aix): 4 N 262 and 1 TBM 700. EH 1/67 (Cazaux): 5 Fennec, 4 Puma. EH 2/67 (Metz): 3 Alouette III, 5 Fennec. EH 3/67 (Villacoublay): 3 Alouette III, 3 Super Puma, 6 Ecureuil, 3 Fennec. EH 4/67 (Apt): 2 Fennec, 2 Puma. EH 5/67 (Aix): 5 Fennec, 4 Puma and 1 Super Puma. EH 6/67 (Solenzara): 2 Puma. Overseas transport squadron (ETOM 50) (Saint Denis la Réunion): 2 C 160, 2 Fennec. ETOM 52 (Noumea): 2 C 160, 2 Fennec, 6 Puma. ETOM 55 (Dakar): 1 C 160, 1 Alouette III. ETOM 58 (Martinique): 2 C 160, 1 Alouette III, 2 Puma. ETOM 82 (Papeete): 2 CN 235, 3 Super Puma. ETOM 88 (Djibouti): 3 Alouette III, 1 C 160.

Air Observation System, Information and Communication Command (CASSIC): 36 AEW squadron (Avord: 2 flights with 4 E3F Awacs).

Air Training Command (CEAA): EC 1/8 and EC 2/8: 36 Alphajet (Cazaux). ERACLES: 1 Mystere 20 SP (Cazaux). GE 312: Training group (Salon de Provence): 2 Paris MS 760, 30 Fouga, 12 Tucano. GE 314 (Tours): 55 Alphajet. GE 315 (Cognac): 98 Epsilon. GE 316 (Avord): 25 Xingu.

Personnel (1995) 94,965 (33,730 conscripts; 4,905 civilians).

INTERNATIONAL RELATIONS

Membership. France is a member of the UN, the Council of Europe, NATO, WEU and the EU. At a referendum in Sept. 1992 to approve the ratification of the Maastricht treaty on European union of 7 Feb. 1992, 12,967,498 votes (50·81%) were cast for and 12,550,651 (49·18%) against.

The Schengen Accord of June 1990 which abolishes border controls between Austria, Belgium, France, Germany, Greece, Italy, Luxembourg, the Netherlands, Portugal and Spain came into effect on 26 March 1995. Austria, Greece and Italy have not yet implemented it and France suspended it in 1995.

France is the focus of the *French Community* which formally links France with many of its former colonies in Africa. A wide range of agreements both with members of the Community and with other French-speaking countries extend to economic and technical matters and in particular to the disbursement of overseas aid.

ECONOMY

Policy. For planning in France from 1947 to 1993, *see* THE STATESMAN'S YEAR-BOOK, 1993–94, p. 567.

A second phase of privatization (the first was in 1986–87) involving some 20 state enterprises was initiated by legislation of May 1993. The state retains the right to acquire a 'golden share' to give itself veto powers in the national interest.

Budget. Receipts and expenditure in 1m. francs:

Receipts	*1993*	*1994*	*1995*
Income tax	309,776	296,328	303,525
Corporation tax	127,229	127,857	145,748
Other direct taxes	109,753	111,148	116,820
Stamp duty	78,544	77,758	83,400
Customs duties	138,122	155,080	158,801
VAT	622,254	648,393	673,216
Other indirect taxes	43,960	41,040	44,707
Non-fiscal receipts	166,158	161,661	150,365
Total	*1,142,698*	*1,154,165*	*1,211,036*
Expenditure			
Public debt	183,931	199,834	198,983
Administration	475,656	506,410	524,275
Subsidies	407,734	406,420	417,531
Civil investments	99,589	89,111	86,172
Defence	239,440	242,558	243,456
Total	*1,410,129*	*1,436,333*	*1,486,143*

The rate of VAT is 18·6% (reduced rate, 5·5%).

Ministère de l'Economie, des Finances et du Plan. *Le Budget de l'Etat: de la Préparation à l'Exécution.* Paris, 1995

Currency. The unit of currency is the *franc* (FRF) of 100 *centimes.* Coins are issued for 5, 10 and 20 centimes and 1, 2, 5 and 10 francs, and notes for 20, 50, 100, 200 and 500 francs. Currency in circulation in Dec. 1994 was 1,676,000m. francs. Annualized rate of inflation was 2·1% in 1993. In March 1996, £1 sterling = 7·73 francs; US$1 = 5·06 francs; DM1 = 3·43 francs.

13 former French colonies (Benin, Burkina Faso, Cameroon, Central African Republic, Chad, Comoros, Congo, Côte d'Ivoire, Gabon, Mali, Niger, Senegal and Togo) and the former Spanish colony of Equatorial Guinea are members of a *Franc Zone*, the CFA (Communauté Financière Africaine). Comoros uses the Comorian franc. From 1948 to 1994 1 French franc = 50 francs CFA. The franc CFA was devalued by 50% on 11 Jan. 1994, the Comorian franc by 25%.

The *franc CFP (Comptoirs Français du Pacifique)* is the common currency of the French dependencies of French Polynesia, New Caledonia and Wallis and Futuna.

Banking and Finance. The central bank and bank of issue is the Banque de France, founded in 1800, and nationalized on 2 Dec. 1945. In 1993 it received greater autonomy in line with EU conditions. Its governor is appointed for a 6-year term (renewable once) and heads the 9-member Council of Monetary Policy (*Governor*: Jean-Claude Trichet, b.1943, appointed Sept. 1993).

The National Credit Council, formed in 1945 to regulate banking activity and consulted in all political decisions on monetary policy, comprises 45 members nominated by the Government; its president is the Minister for the Economy, its vice-president is the Governor of the Banque de France. Four principal deposit banks were nationalized in 1945 and the remainder in 1982 but the latter were privatized in 1987. The 9 chief banks in 1992 in order of their capital assets were: Crédit Agricole; Crédit Lyonnais (state-owned); Banque Nationale de Paris; Société Générale; Banques Populaires; Crédit-Mutuel; Indosuez (investment); Paribas (investment); Crédit Commercial de France.

The state savings organization Caisse Nationale d'Epargne is administered by the post office on a giro system. There are also commercial savings banks (*Caisses d'epargne et de prévoyance*). Deposited funds are centralized by a non-banking body, the *Caisse de Dépôts et Consignations*, which finances a large number of local authorities and state aided housing projects, and carries an important portfolio of transferable securities.

There is a stock exchange (Bourse) in Paris.

Weights and Measures. The metric system is in general use.

ENERGY AND NATURAL RESOURCES

Electricity. The state-owned monopoly Electricité de France is reponsible for power generation and supply under the Ministry of Industry. France is not rich in natural energy resources. In 1993 there were 56 nuclear reactors in operation, and some 77% of the electricity output was nuclear-produced, providing 38% of total energy consumption. In 1993 a further 40·4% came from oil, 13·3% from gas, 6·4% from coal and 1·9% from renewable resources. Production (in 1m. kWh): 1993, 454,100, of which 67,600 was hydroelectric and 350,200 nuclear.

Oil and Gas. In 1992, 2·9m. tonnes of crude oil were produced. The greater part came from the Parentis oilfield in the Landes. The importation and distribution of natural gas is the responsibility of the government monopoly Gaz de France. Production of natural gas was 36,200m. cu. metres in 1992.

Minerals. Principal minerals and metals produced in 1993, in 1,000 tonnes: Coal, 10,250; crude steel, 17,106; iron ore, 3,549; pig iron, 12,396; aluminium, 1,264; potash salts (1992), 1,233.

Agriculture. Of the total area of France (54·9m. ha), the utilized agricultural area comprised 30·22m. ha in 1993. 18·26m. ha were arable, 10·8m. ha were pasture, and 1·2m. ha were under permanent crops including vines (0·94m. ha). In 1993 there were 801,000 holdings and 1·6m. persons were employed in agriculture, hunting, fishing and forestry.

The following table shows the area under the leading crops and the production for 3 years:

	Area (1,000 ha)				*Produce (1,000 tonnes)*			
	1990	*1991*	*1992*	*1993*	*1990*	*1991*	*1992*	*1993*
Wheat	5,148	5,147	5,080	4,515	33,312	34,397	32,507	29,252
Rye	65	59	55	45	236	217	208	177
Barley	1,756	1,751	1,800	1,623	10,020	10,647	10,476	8,981
Oats	218	179	168	174	848	733	694	726
Potatoes	164	170	134	116	5,800	3,902	4,310	4,046
Sugar-beet	475	459	461	441	31,735	29,280	31,675	31,805
Maize	1,561	1,764	1,869	1,848	9,291	12,797	14,886	14,843

Production (1992, in 1,000 tonnes): Centrifugal raw sugar (1991), 4,675; beef and veal, 2,079; pork, 1,950; lamb and mutton, 156; poultry, 1,496; milk, 24,334; eggs, 10·93m.; wine, 6,504.

The production of fruits (other than for cider making) for 3 years was (in 1,000 tonnes) as follows:

	1991	1992	1993		1991	1992	1993
Apples	1,198	2,398	2,079	Melons	342	298	305
Pears	215	393	251	Nuts	17	24	19
Plums	110	314	186	Grapes	5,451	...	...
Peaches	401	529	528	Strawberries	76	82	82
Apricots	107	167	78	Oranges	4	...	...

Livestock (in 1,000) in 1993 (and 1992): Horses, 345 (341); cattle, 20,517 (20,687); sheep, 10,731 (10,891); goats, 1,160 (1,180); pigs, 13,378 (13,000); poultry, 217m. (210m.).

Forestry. In 1993 forest (36% coniferous, 31% oak) covered some 15m. ha, about 27% of the land area. 1·8m. ha are state property. Timber cut (1992), 35·36m. cu. metres, of which 11·1m. cu. metres were for industry. 0·55m. persons were employed in forestry in 1990.

Fisheries. In 1993 there were 181 fishing vessels of over 25 metres in length totalling 82,972 GRT. Catch (in tonnes) in 1993: Marine fish, total, 467,000; crustaceans, 23,000; shell fish, 95,000.

INDUSTRY. Industrial production (in 1,000 tonnes) for 4 years was as follows:

	1989	1990	1991	1993
Sulphuric acid	4,187	3,771	3,487	2,357
Caustic soda	1,537	1,496	1,333	1,473
Sulphur	907	919	1,167	1,106
Polystyrene	542	542	530	481
Polyvinyl	1,068	1,033	1,051	1,176
Polyethylene	1,159	1,116	1,200	1,308
Wool	66	56	64	56
Cotton	185	170	153	152
Linen	6·5	5·3	5·3	6·2
Silk	78	81	73	71
Jute	4.7	...	...	...
Cheese	1,342	1,369	1,400	1,413
Chocolate	436	451	491	496
Biscuits	444	460	477	478
Sugar	4,350	4,059	4,602	4,320
Fish preparations	110	106	111	104
Jams and jellies	159	159	170	163
Cement and lime	25,884	26,388	25,022	21,599

Engineering production (in 1,000 units) for 4 years:

	1989	1990	1991	1993
Motor vehicles	3,415	3,294	3,190	2,836
Television sets	2,429	2,758	2,549	2,523
Radio sets	2,039	1,845	...	...
Tyres (cars only)	63,580	51,662	54,740	50,475

Labour (1992). Out of an economically active population of 22,302,600 persons, 1,171,800 were engaged in agriculture, forestry and fishing, 1,599,500 in building, 1,436,500 in transport and telecommunications, 1,539,500 in manufacturing industries, 620,700 in banking and insurance, 4,442,500 in services, 2,668,700 in commerce. In May 1995, there were 3,250,200 persons registered unemployed. A new definition of 'unemployed' was adopted in Aug. 1995, omitting persons who had worked at least 78 hours in the previous month. By this classification there were 2,936,300 unemployed in July 1995.

Conciliation boards (*conseils de prud'hommes*) mediate in labour disputes. They are elected for 5-year terms by 2 colleges of employers and employees. 14,453,277 voters were registered at the Dec. 1992 elections.

On 1 July 1994 the minimum wage (SMIC) was raised to 35.56 francs an hour or 6,010 francs a month. SMIC affects about 1·48m. wage-earners. Retirement age is 60. A 5-week annual holiday is statutory.

The average monthly wage was 10,650 francs in April 1992.

Trade Unions. There were 5 confederations in 1995: the CGT (Confédération

Générale du Travail), founded in 1895; the CGT-FO (Confédération Générale du Travail–Force Ouvrière) which broke away from the CGT in 1948 as a protest against Communist influence therein; the CFTC (Confédération Française des Travailleurs Chrétiens), which was founded in 1919 and divided in 1964, with a breakaway group retaining the old name and the main body continuing under the new name of CFDT (Confédération Française Démocratique du Travail); and the CGC (Confédération Générale des Cadres) formed in 1944 which only represents managerial and supervisory staff.

Unions are not required to publish membership figures, but in 1993 the CGT had an estimated 0·63m. members and the CFDT, 0·65m.

FOREIGN ECONOMIC RELATIONS. Privatization legislation of May 1993 permits foreign nationals to acquire more than 20% of a firm's capital (the previous limit).

Commerce. Imports (c.i.f.) and exports (f.o.b.) in 1m. francs for 5 calendar years were (including gold):

	1989	*1990*	*1991*	*1992*	*1993*
Imports	1,216,650	1,266,789	1,297,344	1,263,934	1,135,291
Exports	1,102,411	1,142,183	1,200,540	1,227,505	1,166,648

In 1993 the chief export markets were (in 1m. francs f.o.b.): Germany, 202,148; Italy, 109,552; UK, 109,550; Belgium-Luxembourg, 99,956; USA, 83,564; Spain, 76,997; Netherlands, 55,909; Switzerland, 44,449; Japan, 23,046; Portugal, 17,863. In 1992 the chief suppliers of imports (in 1m. francs c.i.f.) were: Germany, 200,033; USA, 129,423; Italy, 112,109; Belgium-Luxembourg, 100,899; UK, 91,329; Spain, 61,706; Netherlands, 58,034; Japan, 46,781; Switzerland, 28,173; Sweden, 16,311.

Foreign trade by sector, 1992, in 1m. francs:

	Imports (c.i.f)	*Exports (f.o.b.)*
Agriculture and agri-food industry	147,294	200,955
Energy	108,449	27,993
Raw materials and semi-products	315,413	290,607
Capital goods	306,213	338,832
Surface transport equipment	139,219	170,783
Consumer goods	214,482	187,405

Total trade between France and UK (British Department of Trade returns, in £1,000 sterling):

	1991	*1992*	*1993*	*1994*
Imports to UK	11,066,081	12,215,890	12,555,700	14,343,000
Exports and re-exports from UK	11,591,139	11,486,695	11,100,000	12,779,100

Tourism. In 1993 there were some 60m. foreign visitors, bringing foreign exchange earnings of 132,000m. francs. Countries of origin of visitors (in 1,000): Germany, 12,900; UK, 8,000; Netherlands, 7,100; Italy, 6,300; Spain, 3,000; Belgium, 2,000; USA, 1,900; Switzerland, 1,900; Portugal, 1,700; Sweden, 878; Canada, 694; Denmark, 687; Ireland, 475; Greece, 348; Austria, 329; Japan, 320; Norway, 320. 589,216 classified hotel rooms were available in 1992.

COMMUNICATIONS

Roads. In 1992 there were 354,000 km of departmental roads and 28,000 km of national road network of which 7,000 km were motorway. In 1992 there were 24·02m. private cars, 3·68m. lorries, 42,942 buses and 0·76m. motorcycles and scooters. In 1992 there were 9,083 road deaths (9,617 in 1991).

Railways. As from 1 Jan. 1938 all the independent railway companies were merged with the existing state railway system in a Société Nationale des Chemins de Fer Français (SNCF), which became a public industrial and commercial establishment in 1983.

In 1994, SNCF totalled 32,275 km (13,742 km electrified) and carried 129·3m. tonnes of freight and 806m. passengers. A new railway for high-speed trains (TGV) was completed in 1983 between Paris and Lyon and was extended to Valence in

1994. 2 further routes opened in 1989 to Le Mans to serve Britanny and in 1990 to Tours to serve the south-west. Services from London through the Channel tunnel started in 1994. A network (TGV Nord) links Paris, Lille and Brussels to the tunnel.

The Paris transport network consisted in 1993 of 201 km of metro, 352 km of regional express railways, 9·1 km of light rail and 7 km of peoplemover. There are also metros in Lille (29 km), Lyon (20·8 km), Toulouse (10 km) and Marseille (19·5 km), and tram/light railway networks in Grenoble (14·6 km), Lille (23 km), Marseille (3 km), Nantes (16·5 km), Rouen (17 km), St Étienne (7 km) and Strasbourg (11·4 km).

Civil Aviation. There are 9 international airports: Paris (Orly), Paris (Charles de Gaulle), Bordeaux (Mérignac), Lille (Lesquin), Lyon (Satolas), Marseille-Provence, Nice-Côte d'Azur, Strasbourg (Entzheim) and Toulouse (Blagnac). Air France, UTA and Air Inter, the national airlines, merged in 1990 to control 97% of French air traffic. In 1992 they operated 4 A300B2-100s, 4 A300B4-200s, 6 A310-200s, 4 A310-300s, 7 A320-100s, 13 A320-200s, 5 A340-200s, 6 A340-300s, 19 B-737-200 Advs, 6 B-737-300s, 16 B-737-500s, 6 B-747-100s, 2 B-747-200Bs, 8 B-747-200B Combis, 2 B-747-200B Sud/Combis, 1 B-747-200B(F), 10 B-747-200Fs 2 B-747-300 Combis, 8 B-747-400s, 5 B-747-400 Combis, 5 B-767-300ERs, 6 Concordes and 11 F-27-500s. In 1994 Air France and Air Inter flew 8,652m. tonne-km (excluding mail) and 52,435m. passenger-km.

Shipping. Merchant ships, in 1992, numbered 221 vessels of 3,833,000 GRT (241 in 1988). During 1992, 218m. tonnes of cargo were unloaded, of which 128m. tonnes were crude and refined petroleum products, and 83m. tonnes were loaded; total passenger traffic, 27·3m.

Canals are administered by the public authority France Navigable Waterways (FVN). In 1992 there were 8,500 km of navigable rivers, waterways and canals (of which 1,647 km accessible to vessels over 3,000 tons), with a total traffic of 59·8m. tonnes.

Telecommunications. There were 16,855 post offices in 1992. France Télécom is now a public enterprise under autonomous management. La Poste is a similar body responsible for mail delivery and financial services. In 1993 the telephone system had 30·9m. subscribers. 655,000 mobile telephones were in use in 1994. In 1995, there were 1·7m. fax machines in use, including 0·4m. domestically.

6·5m. Minitel videotext terminals were rented out by France Télécom to the public in 1995.

Radio and television broadcasting was reorganized under the Act of 7 Aug. 1974 which replaced the Office de Radiodiffusion Télévision Française with 4 broadcasting companies, a production company and an audio-visual institute. The broadcasting authority is the *Conseil Supérieur de l'Audiovisuel.* Radio programmes are broadcast from 874 VHF transmitters of which 418 belong to 4 stations: *France Info, France Inter, France Musique* and *France Culture.* An external service, Radio-France Internationale, was founded in 1931 as 'Poste Coloniale', and broadcasts in 20 languages. There are 2 state-owned TV channels, Antenne-2 and FR3, which are partly financed by advertising, and 5 commercial channels (colour by SECAM). TV broadcasts must contain at least 60% EC-generated programmes and 50% of these must be French. There were about 49m. radio and 29·3m. TV sets in use in 1993.

Cinemas. There were 4,441 screens in 1993; attendances totalled 123m. in 1994 (133m. in 1993). 110 full-length films were made in 1994.

Press (1994). There were 68 daily papers published in the provinces and 9 in Paris. In 1993, total national daily press circulation was 1·6m. copies.

SOCIAL INSTITUTIONS

Justice. The system of justice is divided into 2 jurisdictions: the judicial, and the administrative.

Within the judicial jurisdiction are common law courts including 473 lower courts (*tribunaux d'instance*, including 11 in overseas departments), 186 higher courts (*tri-*

bunaux de grande instance, including 5 *tribunaux de première instance* in the overseas territories), and 454 police courts (*tribunaux de police*, including 11 in overseas departments).

The *tribunaux d'instance* are presided over by a single judge. The *tribunaux de grande instance* usually have a collegiate composition, although may be presided over by a single judge in some civil cases. The police courts, presided over by a judge on duty in the *tribunal d'instance*, deal with petty offences (*contraventions*); correctional chambers (*chambres correctionelles*, of which there is at least one in each *tribunal de grande instance*) deal with graver offences (*délits*), including cases involving imprisonment up to 5 years. Correctional chambers consist of 3 judges of a *tribunal de grande instance* (a single judge in some cases). Sometimes in cases of *délit*, and in all cases of more serious *crimes*, a preliminary inquiry is made in secrecy by one of 569 examining magistrates (*juges d'instruction*), who either dismisses the case or sends it for trial before a public prosecutor.

Still within the judicial jurisdiction are various specialised courts, including 227 commercial courts (*tribunaux de commerce*), composed of tradesmen and manufacturers elected for 2 years initially and then for 4 years; 271 conciliation boards (*conseils de prud'hommes*), composed of an equal number of employers and employees elected for 5 years to deal with labour disputes; 437 courts for settling rural landholding disputes (*tribunaux paritaires des baux ruraux*, including 11 in overseas departments); and 113 social security courts (*tribunaux des affaires de sécurité sociale*).

When the decisions of any of these courts are susceptible of appeal, the case goes to one of the 35 courts of appeal (*cours d'appel*) composed each of a president and a variable number of members. There are 102 courts of assize (*cours d'assises*), each composed of a president who is a member of the court of appeal, and 2 other magistrates, and assisted by a lay jury of 9 members. These try crimes involving imprisonment of over 5 years. The decisions of the courts of appeal and the courts of assize are final, However, the Court of Cassation (*Cour de cassation*) has discretion to verify if the law has been correctly interpreted and if the rules of procedure have been followed exactly. The Court of Cassation may annul any judgment, following which the cases must be retried by a court of appeal or a court of assizes.

The administrative jurisdiction exists to resolve conflicts arising between citizens and central and local government authorities. It consists of 34 administrative courts (*tribunaux administratifs*, including 7 in overseas departments and territories) and 7 administrative courts of appeal (*cours administratives d'appel*). The Council of State is the final court of appeal in administrative cases, though it may also act as a court of first instance.

Cases of doubt as to whether the judicial or administrative jurisdiction is competent in any case are resolved by a *Tribunal de conflits* composed in equal measure of members of the Court of Cassation and the Council of State.

Capital punishment was abolished in Aug. 1981.

On 24 Jan. 1973 the first Ombudsman (*médiateur*) was appointed for a 6-year period.

A revised penal code came into force on 1 March 1994, replacing the *Code Napoléon* of 1810.

Penal institutions consist of: (1) *maisons d'arrêt*, where persons awaiting trial as well as those condemned to short periods of imprisonment are kept; (2) punishment institutions – (a) central prisons (*maisons centrales*) for those sentenced to long imprisonment, and (b) detention centres for offenders showing promise of rehabilitation; (3) hospitals for the sick. Special attention is being paid to classified treatment and the rehabilitation and vocational re-education of prisoners including work in open-air and semi-free establishments. There are 3 penal institutions for women.

Juvenile delinquents go before special judges in 137 (11 in overseas departments and territories) juvenile courts (*tribunaux pour enfants*); they are sent to public or private institutions of supervision and re-education.

The population at 1 Jan. 1996 of the 183 penal establishments was 52,810 men and 2,217 women.

Weston, M., *English Reader's Guide to the French Legal System*. Oxford, 1991

Religion. A law of 1905 separated church and state. In 1992 there were 43·77m. Roman Catholics, 0·8m. Protestants and 1·72m. Moslems.

Education. The primary, secondary and higher state schools constitute the 'Université de France'. The Supreme Council of 84 members has deliberative, administrative and judiciary functions, and as a consultative committee advises respecting the working of the school system, the inspectors-general are in direct communication with the Minister. For local education administration France is divided into 25 academic areas, each of which has an Academic Council whose members include a certain number elected by the professors or teachers. The Academic Council deals with all grades of education. Each is under a Rector, and each is provided with academy inspectors, 1 for each department.

Compulsory education is provided for children of 6–16. The educational stages are as follows:

1. Non-compulsory pre-school instruction for children aged 2–5, to be given in infant schools or infant classes attached to primary schools.

2. Compulsory elementary instruction for children aged 6–11, to be given in primary schools and certain classes of the *lycées*. It consists of 3 courses: Preparatory (1 year), elementary (2 years), intermediary (2 years). Physically or mentally handicapped children are cared for in special institutions or special classes of primary schools.

3. Lower secondary education (*Enseignement du premier cycle du Second Degré*) for pupils aged 11–15, consists of 4 years of study in the *lycées* (grammar schools), *Collèges d'Enseignement Technique* or *Collèges d'Enseignement Général*.

4. Upper secondary education (*Enseignement du second cycle du Second Degré*) for pupils aged 15–18:

Long, général or *professionel* provided by the *lycées* and leading to the *baccalauréat* or to the *baccalauréat de technicien* after 3 years.

Court, professional courses of 3, 2 and 1 year are taught in the *lycées d'enseignement professionel*, or the specialized sections of the *lycées*, CES or CEG.

The following table shows the number of schools in 1993–94 and the numbers of pupils in full-time education:

	State		*Private*	
	Schools	*Pupils*	*Schools*	*Pupils*
Nursery	18,660	5,605,417	368	903,988
Primary	35,974		5,682	
Secondary	7,477	4,341,700	3,758	1,154,800

Higher education is provided by the state free of charge in the universities and in special schools, and by private individuals in the free faculties and schools.

Legislation of 1968 redefined the activities and working of universities. Bringing several disciplines together, 780 units for teaching and research (UER–Unités d'Enseignement et de Recherche) were formed which decided their own teaching activities, research programmes and procedures for checking the level of knowledge gained. They and the other parts of each university must respect the rules designed to maintain the national standard of qualifications. The UERs form the basic units of 69 Universities and 3 National Polytechnic Institutes (with university status), grouped into 25 *académies* with 1,280,242 students in 1991–92.

There are also Catholic university facilities in Paris, Angers, Lille, Lyon and Toulouse and private universities with (1991–92) 21,355 students. The following universities have been established since 1991: Artois (Arras, Béthune, Lens, Donai); Cergy-Pontoise; La Rochelle; the Littoral (Boulogne, Calais, Dunkirk, Saint-Omer); Evry; Marne-la-Vallée; Saint-Quentin-Versailles.

Outside the university system, higher education (academic, professional and technical) is provided by over 400 schools and institutes, including the 177 Grandes Écoles, highly-selective public or private institutions offering mainly technological or commercial curricula, with an annual output of about 17,000 graduates. In 1993–94 there were also 70,278 students in preparatory classes leading to the

Grandes Écoles, 205,485 in the Sections de Techniciens Supérieurs and 67,072 in the Écoles d'ingénieurs.

Health. On 1 Jan. 1992 there were 155,896 doctors, 51,613 chemists, 38,451 dentists, 313,474 nurses and 11,205 midwives. There were 3,834 hospitals with 689,020 beds.

Welfare. An order of 4 Oct. 1945 laid down the framework of a comprehensive plan of Social Security and created a single organization which superseded the various laws relating to social insurance, workmen's compensation, health insurance, family allowances, etc. All previous matters relating to Social Security are dealt with in the Social Security Code, 1956; this has been revised several times. The Chamber of Deputies and Senate, meeting as Congress on 19 Feb. 1996, adopted a revision of the constitution giving parliament powers to review annually the funding of social security and to fix targets for expenditure in the light of anticipated receipts.

Contributions. All wage-earning workers or those of equivalent status are insured regardless of the amount or the nature of the salary or earnings. The funds for the general scheme are raised mainly from professional contributions, these being fixed within the limits of a ceiling and calculated as a percentage of the salaries. The calculation of contributions payable for family allowances, old age and industrial injuries relates only to this amount; on the other hand, the amount payable for sickness, maternity expenses, disability and death is calculated partly within the limit of the 'ceiling' and partly on the whole salary. These contributions are the responsibility of both employer and employee, except in the case of family allowances or industrial injuries, where they are the sole responsibility of the employer.

Self-employed Workers. From 17 Jan. 1948 allowances and old-age pensions were paid to self-employed workers by independent insurance funds set up within their own profession, trade or business. Schemes of compulsory insurance for sickness were instituted in 1961 for farmers and in 1966, with modifications in 1970, for other non-wage-earning workers.

Social Insurance. The orders laid down in Aug. 1967 ensure that the whole population can benefit from the Social Security Scheme; at present all elderly persons who have been engaged in the professions, as well as the surviving spouse, are entitled to claim an old-age benefit.

Sickness Insurance refunds the costs of treatment required by the insured and the needs of dependants.

Maternity Insurance covers the costs of medical treatment relating to the pregnancy, confinement and lying-in period; the beneficiaries being the insured person or the spouse.

Insurance for Invalids is divided into 3 categories: (1) those who are capable of working; (2) those who cannot work; (3) those who, in addition, are in need of the help of another person. According to the category, the pension rate varies from 30 to 50% of the average salary for the last 10 years, with additional allowance for home help for the third category.

Old-age Pensions for workers were introduced in 1910 and are now fixed by the Social Security Code of 28 Jan. 1972. Since 1983 people who have paid insurance for at least 37½ years (150 quarters) receive at 60 a pension equal to 60% of basic salary. People who have paid insurance for less than 37½ years but no less than 15 years can expect a pension equal to as many 1/150ths of the full pension as their quarterly payments justify. In the event of death of the insured person, the husband or wife of the deceased person receives half the pension received by the latter. Compulsory supplementary schemes ensure benefits equal to 70% of previous earnings.

Family Allowances. The system comprises: (*a*) Family allowances proper, equivalent to 25·5% of the basic monthly salary for 2 dependent children, 46% for the third child, 41% for the fourth child, and 39% for the fifth and each subsequent child; a supplement equivalent to 9% of the basic monthly salary for the second and each subsequent dependent child more than 10 years old and 16% for each dependent child over 15 years. (*b*) Family supplement for persons with at least 3 children or one child aged less than 3 years. (*c*) Antenatal grants. (*d*) Maternity grant equal to 260% of basic salary; increase for multiple births or adoptions, 198%; increase for birth or adoption of third or subsequent child, 457%. (*e*) Allowance for specialized education of handicapped children. (*f*) Allowance for orphans. (*g*) Single parent allowance. (*h*) Allowance for opening of school term. (*i*) Allowance for accommodation, under certain circumstances. (*j*) Minimum family income for those with at least 3 children. Allowances (*b*), (*g*), (*h*) and (*j*) only apply to those whose annual income falls below a specified level.

Workmen's Compensation. The law passed by the National Assembly on 30 Oct. 1946 forms part of the Social Security Code and is administered by the Social Security Organization. Employers are invited to take preventive measures. The application of these measures is supervised by consulting engineers (assessors) of the local funds dealing with sickness insurance, who may compel employers who do not respect these measures to make additional contributions; they may, in like manner, grant rebates to employers who have in operation suitable preventive measures. The injured person receives free treatment, the insurance fund reimburses the practitioners, hospitals and suppliers chosen freely by the injured. In cases of temporary disablement the daily payments are equal to half the total daily wage received by the injured. In case of permanent disablement the injured person receives a pension, the amount of which varies according to the degree of disablement and the salary received during the past 12 months.

Unemployment Benefits vary according to circumstances (full or partial unemployment) which are means-tested.

Ambler, J. S. (ed.) *The French Welfare State: Surviving Social and Ideological Change.* New York Univ. Press, 1992

DIPLOMATIC REPRESENTATIVES

Of France in Great Britain (58 Knightsbridge, London, SW1X 7JT)
Ambassador: Jean Gueguinou.

Of Great Britain in France (35 rue du Faubourg St Honoré, 75383 Paris Cedex 08)
Ambassador: Michael Jay.

Of France in the USA (4101 Reservoir Rd., NW, Washington, D.C., 20007)
Ambassador: Vacant.

Of the USA in France (2 Ave. Gabriel, Paris)
Ambassador: Pamela Harriman.

Of France to the United Nations
Ambassador: Jean-Bernard Mérimée.

Further Reading

Institut National de la Statistique et des Études Économiques. *Annuaire statistique de la France* (from 1878).—*Bulletin mensuel de statistique* (monthly).—*Documentation économique* (bimonthly).—*Economie et Statistique* (monthly).—*Tableaux de l'Economie Française* (biennially, from 1956).—*Tendances de la Conjoncture* (monthly)

Agulhon, M., *The French Republic, 1879–1992.* Oxford, 1993
Ardant, P., *Les Institutions de la Ve République.* Paris, 1992
Balladur, E., *Deux Ans à Matignon.* Paris, 1995
Braudel, F., *The Identity of France.* 2 vols. London, 1988-90
Caron, F., *An Economic History of Modern France.* London, 1979
Chambers, F. J., *France.* [Bibliography] Oxford and Santa Barbara (CA), (rev. ed.) 1990
Chazal, C., *Balladur.* [in French] Paris, 1993
Cubertafond, A., *Le Pouvoir, la Politique et l'État en France.* Paris, 1993
L'État de la France. Paris, annual
Gouze, R., *Mitterand par Mitterand.* Paris, 1994
Hollifield, J. F. and Ross, G., *Searching for the New France.* London, 1991
Jones, C., *The Cambridge Illustrated History of France.* CUP, 1994

McMillan, J. F., *Twentieth-Century France: Politics and Society in France, 1898–1991*. 2nd ed. [of *Dreyfus to De Gaulle*]. London, 1992
Mendras, H. and Cole, A., *Social Change in Modern France: towards a Cultural Anthopology of the Fifth Republic*. CUP, 1991
Morris, P., *French Politics Today*. Manchester Univ. Press, 1994
Pinchemel, P., *France: A Geographical, Social and Economic Survey*. CUP, 1987
Popkin, J. D., *A History of Modern France*. New York, 1994
Price, R., *Concise History of France*. CUP, 1993
Schmidt, V. A., *Democratizing France: the Political and Administrative History of Decentralization*. CUP, 1991
Stevens, A., *The Government and Politics of France*. London, 1992
Todd, E., *The Making of Modern France: Politics, Ideology and Culture*. Oxford, 1991
Verdié, M. (ed.) *L'État de la France et de ses Habitants*. Paris, 1992
Vesperini, J.-P., *L'Économie de la France sous la Ve République*. Paris, 1993
Who's Who in France [in French]. Paris, annual

Other more specialized titles are listed under TERRITORY AND POPULATION, CONSTITUTION AND GOVERNMENT, BUDGET, JUSTICE *and* WELFARE, *above*.

National statistical office: Institut National de la Statistique et des Etudes Economiques (INSEE), 75582 Paris CEDEX 12.

DEPARTMENTS AND TERRITORIES OVERSEAS

Départements et Territoires d'Outre-Mer (DOM-TOM)

These fall into 3 categories: *Overseas Departments* (French Guiana, Guadeloupe, Martinique, Réunion), *Territorial Collectivities* (Mayotte, St Pierre and Miquelon) and *Overseas Territories* (French Polynesia, New Caledonia, Southern and Antarctic Territories, Wallis and Futuna).

Further Reading

Aldrich, R. and Connell, J., *France's Overseas Frontier: Départements et Territoires d'Outre-Mer*. CUP, 1992

OVERSEAS DEPARTMENTS

GUADELOUPE

KEY HISTORICAL EVENTS. The islands were discovered by Columbus in 1493. The Carib inhabitants resisted Spanish attempts to colonize. A French colony was established on 28 June 1635, and apart from short periods of occupancy by British forces, Guadeloupe has since remained a French possession. On 19 March 1946 Guadeloupe became an Overseas Department.

TERRITORY AND POPULATION. Guadeloupe consists of a group of islands in the Lesser Antilles. The two main islands, Basse-Terre to the west and Grande-Terre to the east, are joined by a bridge over a narrow channel. Adjacent to these are the islands of Marie Galante to the south-east, La Désirade to the east, and the Îles des Saintes to the south. The islands of St Martin and St Barthélemy lie 250 km to the north-west.

	Area in sq. km	*Census 1982*	*Census 1990* [3]	*Chief town*
St Martin [1]	54 [2]	8,072	28,518	Marigot
St Barthélemy	21	3,059	5,038	Gustavia
Basse-Terre	848	135,341	149,943	Basse-Terre
Grande-Terre	590	163,668	177,570	Pointe-à-Pitre
Îles des Saintes	13	2,901	2,036	Terre-de-Bas
La Désirade	20	1,602	1,610	Grande Anse
Marie-Galante	158	13,757	13,463	Grand-Bourg
	1,705	328,400	378,178	

[1] Northern part only; the southern third is Dutch. [2] Includes uninhabited Tintamarre.
[3] Preliminary results.

Population at the 1990 census, 386,987; 1994 estimate, 425,400. French is the official language, but a Creole is spoken by the vast majority except on St Martin.

The seat of government is Basse-Terre (13,796 inhabitants in 1988) at the south-west end of that island but the largest towns are Pointe-à-Pitre (25,312 inhabitants), the economic centre and main port, and its suburb, Les Abymes (62,605 inhabitants in 1992).

Vital statistics (1987): Live births, 6,855; deaths, 2,244; marriages, 1,880.

CLIMATE. Warm and humid. Pointe-à-Pitre. Jan. 74°F (23·4°C), July 80°F (26·7°C). Annual rainfall 71" (1,814 mm).

CONSTITUTION AND GOVERNMENT. Guadeloupe is administered by a *General Council* of 42 members directly elected for 6-year terms (assisted by an Economic and Social Committee of 40 members) and a Regional Council of 41 members. It is represented in the National Assembly by 4 deputies, in the Senate by 2 senators and on the Economic and Social Council by 2 councillors. There are 4 *arrondissements,* sub-divided into 34 communes, each administered by an elected municipal council. The French government is represented by an appointed Prefect.

Prefect: Michel Diefenbacher.

President of the General Council: Dominique Larifla.

President of the Regional Council: Lucette Michaux-Chevry (b. 1929; RPR).

ECONOMY

Banking and Finance. In 1995 the main commercial banks were the Banque des Antilles Françaises (with 6 branches), the Banque Regionale d'Escompte et de Depôts (with 5 branches), the Banque Nationale de Paris (8 branches), the Crédit Agricole (18), the Banque Française Commerciale (8), the Société Generale de Banque aux Antilles (5), the Credit Lyonnais (6), the Credit Martiniquais (3) and the Banque Inschauspé et Cie (1). The Caisse Française de Développement is the official bank of the department and issues its bank-notes.

ENERGY AND NATURAL RESOURCES

Electricity. Production in 1993 totalled 1,024m. kWh.

Agriculture. Chief products (1993) are bananas (105,400 tonnes) and sugar-cane (748,000 tonnes). Other fruits and vegetables are grown for domestic consumption. 8·9m. flowers were grown in 1992.

Livestock (1992): Cattle, 56,100; goats, 39,500; sheep, 3,500; pigs, 47,500.

Fisheries. The catch in 1993 was 7,950 tonnes; crustacea and shell fish, 650 tonnes.

INDUSTRY. The main industries are sugar refining, food processing and rum distilling carried out by small and medium-sized businesses.

Labour. Economically active population in 1990 was 117,516. 40,100 persons were registered unemployed in 1993. Of the estimated 17,600 jobs in the industrial sector in 1989, 9,152 persons were employed in the food processing business; about 69,000 persons (31,200 men, 38,700 women) were employed in the commercial sector. In 1993 there were 15,020 persons in trade, 6,950 in transport and communications and 34,223 in services. The minimum wage (SMIC) was raised to 1,214.07 francs a week in Dec. 1993.

COMMERCE. Trade for 1993 (in 1m. francs) was imports 8,044 and exports 735·3; 68% of imports were from France, while 78% of exports went to France and 14% to Martinique. In 1993 bananas made up 26% of the exports, sugar 26% and rum 7%. St Martin and St Barthélemy are free ports.

Total trade between Guadeloupe and UK (British Department of Trade returns, £1,000 sterling):

	1992	*1993*	*1994*	*1995*
Imports to UK	57	62	63	211
Exports and re-exports from UK	6,358	7,693	5,772	6,896

Tourism. Tourism is the chief economic activity; 458,181 tourists visited in 1994, including 313,613 cruise visitors.

COMMUNICATIONS

Roads. In 1996 there were 3,200 km of roads.

Civil Aviation. Air France and 12 other airlines call at Guadeloupe. In 1993 there were 37,065 arrivals and departures of aircraft and 1,461,699 passengers at Raizet (Pointe-à-Pitre) airport. There are also airports at Marie-Galante, La Désirade, St Barthélemy and St Martin.

Shipping. In 1993, 2,812 vessels arrived to disembark 105,217 passengers and 1,933,000 tonnes of freight and to embark 95,882 passengers and 431,000 tonnes of freight.

Telecommunications. In 1984 there were 47 post offices and 64,916 telephones. Radiodiffusion Française d'Outre-Mer broadcasts for 17 hours a day in French and television (2 channels: 1 regional and 1 by satellite) broadcasts for 6 hours a day. There were (1993) 0·1m. radio and 0·15m. TV receivers.

Press. There was (1995) 1 daily newspaper with a circulation of 20,000.

SOCIAL INSTITUTIONS

Justice. There are 4 *tribunaux d'instance,* and 2 *tribunaux de grande instance* at Basse-Terre and Pointe-à-Pitre; there is also a court of appeal and a court of assizes.

Religion. The majority of the population are Roman Catholic.

Education. Education is free and compulsory from 6 to 16 years. In 1993 there were 60,181 pupils at primary schools and 50,778 at secondary schools. In 1988 there were 2,217 students at the University of Antilles-Guyana.

Health. The medical services in 1989 included 17 public hospitals and 13 private clinics.

FRENCH GUIANA

Guyane Française

KEY HISTORICAL EVENTS. A French settlement on the island of Cayenne was established in 1604 and the territory between the Maroni and Oyapock rivers finally became a French possession in 1817. Convict settlements were established from 1852, that on off-shore Devil's Island being most notorious; all were closed by 1945. On 19 March 1946 the status of French Guiana was changed to that of Overseas Department.

TERRITORY AND POPULATION. French Guiana is situated on the north-east coast of Latin America, and is bounded in the north-east by the Atlantic Ocean, west by Suriname and south and east by Brazil. It includes the offshore islands of Devil's Island, Royal Island and St Joseph, and has an area of 90,909 sq. km (35,135 sq. miles). Population at the 1990 census: 114,808 (including 34,087 of foreign origin). Estimate, 1994, 132,500. Vital statistics (1988): Live births, 2,700; deaths, 562; marriages (1987), 365. The chief towns (1990 populations) are Cayenne, the capital (41,600), Kourou (11,208) and Saint-Laurent-du-Maroni (13,900).

About 66% of the inhabitants are of African descent.

CONSTITUTION AND GOVERNMENT. French Guiana is administered by a *General Council* of 19 members directly elected for 5-year terms and a Regional Council of 31 members. It is represented in the National Assembly by 2 deputies and in the Senate by 1 senator. The French government is represented by a Prefect. There are 2 *arrondissements* (Cayenne and Saint Laurent-du-Maroni) subdivided into 19 communes.

Prefect: Jean-François Cordet (also of Martinique).
President of the General Council: Stéphan Phinera.
President of the Regional Council: Vacant.

ECONOMY

Banking and Finance. The Caisse Centrale de Coopération Economique is the bank of issue. In 1995 commercial banks comprised the Banque Nationale de Paris-Guyane, Crédit Populaire Guyanais and Banque Française Commerciale.

ENERGY AND NATURAL RESOURCES

Electricity. Production in 1993 totalled 445m. kWh.

Minerals. In 1993, 2,235 kg of gold were produced.

Agriculture. Only 21,670 ha are under cultivation. The crops (1993, in tonnes) consist of rice (26,962), manioc (23,350) and sugar-cane (3,200).

Livestock (1993): 0·01m. cattle, 10,700 swine, 6,000 sheep and goats and 0·22m. poultry.

Forestry. The country has immense forests (about 83,000 sq. km in 1993) rich in many kinds of timber. Roundwood production (1993) 0·05m. cu. metres. The trees yield oils, essences and gum products.

Fisheries. The fishing fleet for shrimps comprises 70 French boats. The catch in 1993 totalled 3,431 tonnes of shrimps and 4,300 tonnes of fish.

INDUSTRY. Products include rum, rosewood essence, beer and there is a sugar factory and sawmills.

Labour. Economically active population in 1989 was 31,183. 8,115 persons were registered unemployed in 1993. In Dec. 1993 the minimum wage (SMIC) was raised to 1,214.07 francs a week.

COMMERCE. In 1992 exports totalled 542m. francs and imports, 3,811m. francs.

Total trade between French Guiana and UK (British Department of Trade returns, in £1,000 sterling):

	1991	*1992*	*1993*	*1994*	*1995*
Imports to UK	2,367	4,052	259	927	591
Exports and re-exports from UK	6,032	3,410	4,807	6,483	3,734

COMMUNICATIONS

Roads. There were (1996) 356 km of national and 366 km of departmental roads. In 1989 there were 23,520 passenger cars, 1,568 trucks and 121 buses.

Civil Aviation. In 1993, 145,115 passengers and 3,656 tonnes of freight arrived and 154,927 passengers and 1,533 tonnes of freight departed by air at Rochambeau International Airport (Cayenne). Services are provided by Air France, Cruzeiro do Sol and Suriname Airways. There are regular internal flights to 7 other airports.

The base of the European Space Agency (ESA) is located near Kourou and has been operational since 1979.

Shipping. The chief ports are: Cayenne, St-Laurent-du-Maroni and Kourou. In 1993, 359 vessels arrived and departed; 249,160 tonnes of petroleum products and 230,179 tonnes of other products were discharged, and 69,185 tonnes of products were loaded.

There are inland waterways navigable by small craft.

Telecommunications. Number of telephones (1989), 26,146.

Radiodiffusion Française d'Outre-Mer-Guyane broadcasts for 133 hours each week on medium- and short-waves and FM in French. Television is broadcast for

60 hours each week on 2 channels. In 1993 there were 44,000 radio and 6,500 TV receivers (colour by SECAM).

Press. There was (1996) 1 daily newspaper with a circulation of 1,000 and a paper published 4 times a week with a circulation of 5,500.

SOCIAL INSTITUTIONS

Justice. At Cayenne there is a *tribunal d'instance* and a *tribunal de grande instance*, from which appeal is to the regional *cour d'appel* in Martinique.

Religion. In 1984, 77·6% of the population was Roman Catholic and 4% Protestant.

Education. Primary education is free and compulsory. In 1993 public primary schools had 24,000 pupils and secondary schools 12,000. Private schools had 152 teachers and 2,224 pupils in 1988. The Henri Visioz Institute, with 644 students in 1993, forms part of the University of Antilles-Guyana (with 8,290 students in 1993).

Health. There were (1986) 160 physicians, 44 dentists, 33 pharmacists, 29 midwives and 496 nursing personnel. In 1995 there were 2 hospitals with a total of 567 beds, 3 private clinics and a care centre.

MARTINIQUE

KEY HISTORICAL EVENTS. Discovered by Columbus in 1502, Martinique became a French colony in 1635 and apart from brief periods of British occupation the island has since remained under French control. On 19 March 1946 its status was altered to that of Overseas Department.

TERRITORY AND POPULATION. The island, situated in the Lesser Antilles between Dominica and St Lucia, occupies an area of 1,079 sq. km (417 sq. miles). Population at the 1990 Census: 359,579: 1994 estimate, 382,200. Vital statistics (1992): Live births 6,305; deaths 2,180; marriages 1,646. Fort-de-France (1990 population, 101,540) is the capital and port. Other towns are Le Lamentin (30,026), Schoelcher (19,825), Sainte-Marie (19,683), Rivière-Pilote (11,261) and La Trinité (10,330).

French is the official language, but the majority of the population speak Creole.

CLIMATE. Fort-de-France. Jan. 74°F (23·5°C), July 78°F (25·6°C). Annual rainfall 72" (1,840 mm).

CONSTITUTION AND GOVERNMENT. The island is administered by a *General Council* of 45 members, directly elected for 6-year terms and a Regional Council of 42 members. The French government is represented by an appointed Prefect. There are 4 *arrondissements*, sub-divided into 34 communes, each administered by an elected municipal council. Martinique is represented in the National Assembly by 4 deputies, in the Senate by 2 senators and on the Economic and Social Council by 1 councillor.

At the Regional Council elections of March 1992, the electorate was 227,877. 131,930 votes were cast. The UPF (RPR-UDF coalition) won 16 seats with 30,776 votes, the Martinique Independence Movement 9 with 19,029, the Progressive Martinique Party (PPM) 9 with 18,790, the Communist Party (PCM) 4 with 8,120 and the PS 3 with 7,368.

Prefect: Jean-François Cordet (also of French Guiana).
President of the General Council: Claude Lise (PPM).
President of the Regional Council: Emile Capgras (b. 1926; PCM).

ECONOMY

Banking and Finance. The Institut d'Émission des Départements d'Outre-Mer is the official bank of the department. The Caisse Centrale de Développement is used by the Government to promote economic development.

In 1995 there were 4 commercial banks, 6 credit societies and 1 savings bank.

ENERGY AND NATURAL RESOURCES

Electricity. Production in 1993 totalled 818m. kWh.

Agriculture. Bananas and rum are the chief products, followed by sugar, pineapples, food and vegetables. In 1993 there were 3,223 ha under sugar-cane, 8,500 ha under bananas and 600 ha under pineapples. Production (1993): Sugar, 6,626 tonnes; sugar-cane, 227,076 tonnes; (1992): Bananas, 228,000 tonnes; pineapples, 28,500 tonnes.

Livestock (1993): 36,000 cattle, 36,200 sheep, 21,200 pigs, 16,500 goats and 263,000 poultry.

Forestry. Production (1993) 5,000 cu. metres. Forests comprise 42% of the land area.

Fisheries. The catch in 1992 was 4,553 tonnes.

INDUSTRY. Some food processing and chemical engineering is carried out by small and medium-size businesses. There is an oil refinery with a treatment capacity of 0·55m. tonnes annually. There are 5 industrial zones.

Labour. The economically active population in 1994 was 164,870 (75% in trade and commerce and 10% in agriculture). 52,945 persons were registered unemployed in 1990. On 1 July 1995 the minimum wage (SMIC) was raised to 5,854.16 francs a month.

COMMERCE. In 1993 exports were valued at 1,449m. francs and imports at 8,836m. francs.

In 1987 the main imports were crude petroleum and foodstuffs; main exports were petroleum products (14%), bananas (46%) and rum (13%). In 1991, 62·1% of imports came from France and 57% of exports went to France and 31·5% to Guadeloupe.

Total trade between Martinique and UK (British Department of Trade returns, in £1,000 sterling):

	1990	*1991*	*1992*	*1993*	*1995*
Imports to UK	1,071	752	87	133	14
Exports and re-exports from UK	26,315	6,127	6,920	26,078	13,839

Tourism. In 1993 there were 819,276 tourists, including 428,695 cruise visitors.

COMMUNICATIONS

Roads. In 1995 there were 1,606 km of roads, of which 1,200 km were surfaced. 252 km were classified as national routes and 862 km as first-class roads. In 1992 there were 12,591 passenger cars and 2,443 commercial vehicles registered.

Civil Aviation. There is an international airport at Fort-de-France (Lamentin). In 1993, 1,488,834 passengers arrived. Services are provided by Air Canada, Air France, Air Guadeloupe, Air Liberté, Air Martinique, American Airlines, AOM and LIAT.

Shipping. The island is visited regularly by French, American and other lines. In 1993, 2,856 vessels called at Martinique and discharged 80,605 passengers and 1,612,000 tonnes of freight and embarked 82,119 passengers and 789,000 tonnes of freight.

Telecommunications. There were, in 1985, 46 post offices and, 81,985 telephones. Radio Diffusion Française d'Outre-Mer broadcasts on FM wave, and operates 2 channels (1 satellite). There are also 2 private TV stations. In 1993 there were 60,000 radio and 65,000 TV receivers (colour by SECAM).

Press. In 1996 there was 1 daily newspaper with a circulation of 30,000.

SOCIAL INSTITUTIONS

Justice. Justice is administered by 2 lower courts (*tribunaux d'instance*), a higher court (*tribunal de grande instance*), a regional court of appeal, a commercial court and an administrative court.

Religion. In 1982, 94% of the population was Roman Catholic.

Education. Education is compulsory between the ages of 6 and 16 years. In 1993, there were 54,455 pupils in primary schools, and 47,295 pupils in 79 secondary schools. There were 29 institutes of higher education. The University of Antilles-Guyana had (1993) 8,290 students of whom 3,670 were from Martinique.

Health. In 1989 there were 17 hospitals, including 1 central, 10 general, 5 maternity, 1 psychiatric and 1 sanatorium. There were (1991) 3,747 hospital beds, 625 doctors, 199 pharmacists, 121 dentists and 130 midwives.

Further Reading

Crane, J., *Martinique.* [Bibliography]. Oxford and Santa Barbara (CA), 1995

RÉUNION

KEY HISTORICAL EVENTS. Réunion (formerly Île Bourbon) became a French possession in 1638 and remained so until 19 March 1946, when its status was altered to that of an Overseas Department.

TERRITORY AND POPULATION. The island of Réunion lies in the Indian Ocean, about 880 km east of Madagascar and 210 km south-west of Mauritius. It has an area of 2,512 sq. km. Population at the 1990 census: 597,828. 1995 estimate, 653,400. The capital is Saint-Denis (population, 1995: 207,158); other towns are Saint-Pierre (192,462) and Saint-Paul (113,071).

Vital statistics (1994): Live births, 13,330; deaths, 3,410; marriages, 3,284.

The islands of Juan de Nova, Europa, Bassas da India, Îles Glorieuses and Tromelin, with a combined area of 32 sq. km, are uninhabited and lie at various points in the Indian Ocean adjacent to Madagascar. They remained French after Madagascar's independence in 1960, and are now administered by the Commissioner of Réunion. Both Mauritius and the Seychelles claim Tromelin and Madagascar claims all 5 islands.

CLIMATE. A sub-tropical maritime climate, free from extremes of weather, though the island lies in the cyclone belt of the Indian Ocean. Conditions are generally humid and there is no well-defined dry season. Saint-Denis. Jan. 80°F (26·7°C), July 70°F (21·1°C). Annual rainfall 56" (1,400 mm).

CONSTITUTION AND GOVERNMENT. Réunion is administered by a *General Council* of 44 members, directly elected for 6-year terms and a Regional Council of 45 members. Réunion is represented in the National Assembly in Paris by 5 deputies, in the Senate by 3 senators, and in the Economic and Social Council by 1 councillor. There are 4 *arrondissements*, sub-divided into 24 communes each administered by an elected municipal council. The French government is represented by an appointed Commissioner.

At the Regional Council elections of June 1993 the electorate was 339,929; turnout was 45·43%. Free-DOM won 13 seats with 24% of votes cast, the Thien Ah Koon list 10 with 20%, the Communist Party 9 with 18% and the RPR 7 with 15%.

Commissioner: Robert Pommies.
President of the General Council: Christophe Payet.
President of the Regional Council: Margie Sudre (Free-DOM).

ECONOMY

Banking and Finance. The Institut d'Émission des Départements d'Outre-mer has the right to issue bank-notes. Banks operating in Réunion are the Banque de la Réunion (Crédit Lyonnais), the Banque Nationale de Paris Intercontinentale, the Caisse Régionale de Crédit Agricole Mutuel de la Réunion, the Banque Française Commerciale (BFC) CCP, Trésorerie Générale, and the Banque de la Réunion pour l'Economie et la Développement (BRED).

ENERGY AND NATURAL RESOURCES

Electricity. Production (1994) 1,206·2m. kWh.

Agriculture. Production (in tonnes), 1994: Sugar, 177,400; vanilla (1993), 114·8; tobacco, 37; maize (1992), 13,270; potatoes, 335; rum, 70,005 hectolitres of pure alcohol; geranium oil, 5·3; onions, 2,415; pineapples, 6,781.

Livestock (1992): 18,600 cattle, 94,480 pigs, 31,200 sheep and 366,700 poultry. Meat production, 1993 (in tonnes): Cattle 1,000, pigs 8,000, goats (1989, 13,000) and poultry 14,080. Milk production (1993), 5,000 tonnes.

Forestry. There were (1994) 101,000 ha. of forest.

Fisheries. In 1994 the catch was 4,487 tonnes.

INDUSTRY. The major industries are electricity and sugar. Food processing, chemical engineering, printing and the production of textiles, tobacco, wood and construction materials are carried out by small and medium-sized businesses.

Labour. The workforce was 264,200 in 1993. 164,100 persons were registered unemployed. The sugar industry employed 3,844 in 1989. In Dec. 1993 the minimum wage (SMIC) was raised to 1,214.07 francs a week.

COMMERCE. Trade in 1m. French francs:

	1990	*1991*	*1992*	*1993*
Imports	11,322	12,028	12,676	11,756
Exports	999	825	1,100	992

The chief export is sugar, making up (1994) 57% by value. In 1994 (by value) 67% of imports were from, and 74% of exports to, France.

Total trade between Réunion and UK (British Department of Trade returns, in £1,000 sterling):

	1991	*1992*	*1993*	*1994*	*1995*
Imports to UK	1,668	1,707	5,453	1,410	2,278
Exports and re-exports from UK	11,878	15,726	13,283	14,096	15,345

Tourism. There were 262,200 visitors in 1994, including 195,400 from France.

COMMUNICATIONS

Roads. There were, in 1994, 2,724 km of roads. There were some 185,700 registered vehicles in Jan. 1995.

Civil Aviation. Réunion is served by Air France, AOM French Airlines, Air Liberté, Corsair, Air Austral, Air Mauritius and Air Madagascar. In 1994, 528,940 passengers and 12,960 tonnes of freight arrived at, and 525,605 passengers and 4,397 tonnes of freight departed from, Roland Garros Saint-Denis airport.

Shipping. In 1994, 586 vessels visited the island, unloading 1,961,000 tonnes of freight and loading 388,200 tonnes at Port-Réunion.

Telecommunications. There were (1994) 720 post offices and a central telephone office; number of telephones (1994), 209,672.

Radiodiffusion Française d'Outre-Mer broadcasts in French on medium- and short-waves for more than 18 hours a day. There are 4 television channels and 1 independent channel.

Cinemas. In 1995 there were 17 cinemas.

Press. There were (1994) 4 daily newspapers, 1 weekly, 1 monthly and 3 periodicals.

SOCIAL INSTITUTIONS

Justice. There are 3 lower courts (*tribunaux d'instance*), 2 higher courts (*tribunaux de grande instance*), 1 appeal, 1 administrative court and 1 conciliation board.

Religion. In 1990, 95% of the population was Roman Catholic.

Education. In 1994-95 there were 343 primary schools with 117,562 pupils. Secondary education was provided in 21 *lycées,* 64 colleges, and 16 technical *lycées,* with, together, 92,281 pupils. The *Université Française de l'Océan Indien* (founded 1971) had 11,291 students in 1994–95.

Health. In 1994 there were 19 hospitals with 2,902 beds, 1,119 physicians, 292 dentists, 250 pharmacists, 155 midwives and 2,684 nursing personnel.

Further Reading

Institut National de la Statistique et des Etudes Economiques. *Tableau Economique de la Réunion.* Paris, Annual.
Bertile, W., *Atlas Thématique et Régional.* Réunion, 1990

TERRITORIAL COLLECTIVITIES

MAYOTTE

KEY HISTORICAL EVENTS. Mayotte was a French colony from 1843 until 1914, when it was attached, with the other Comoro islands, to the government-general of Madagascar. The Comoro group was granted administrative autonomy within the French Republic and became an Overseas Territory.

When the other 3 islands voted to become independent (as the Comoro state) in 1974, Mayotte voted against this and remained a French dependency. In Dec. 1976, it became (following a further referendum) a Territorial Collectivity.

TERRITORY AND POPULATION. Mayotte, east of the Comoro Islands, consists of a main island (362 sq. km) with 94,410 inhabitants at the 1991 Census (estimate in 1994, 109,600) containing the chief town, Mamoudzou (1985 population, 12,119); and the smaller island of Pamanzi (11 sq. km) lying 2 km to the east, with 9,775 inhabitants in 1985, containing the old capital of Dzaoudzi (5,675). The whole territory covers 373 sq. km (144 sq. miles). The spoken language is Mahorian (akin to Comorian, an Arabized dialect of Swahili), but French remains the official and commercial language.

CONSTITUTION AND GOVERNMENT. The island is administered by a *General Council* of 17 members, directly elected for a 6-year term. The French government is represented by an appointed Prefect. Mayotte is represented by 1 deputy in the National Assembly and by 1 member in the Senate. There are 17 communes, including 2 on Pamanzi.

Prefect: Alain Weil.
President of the General Council: Younoussa Bamana.

ECONOMY

Currency. Since Feb. 1976 the currency has been the (metropolitan) *French franc.*

Banking and Finance. The Institut d'Emission d'Outre-mer and the Banque Française Commerciale both have branches in Dzaoudzi and Mamoudzou.

ENERGY AND NATURAL RESOURCES

Electricity. Production (1993) 9·64m. kWh.

Agriculture. The area under cultivation in 1990 was some 8,000 ha. The main food crops (1985 production in tonnes) were mangoes (1,500), bananas (1,300), breadfruit (700), cassava (500) and pineapples (200). The chief cash crops (1993 output in tonnes) were: Essence of ylang-ylang (20·2), vanilla (5·9), coffee (9·2, 1985), copra, cinnamon and cloves.

Livestock (1991): Cattle, 12,000; goats, 15,000; sheep, 3,000; poultry, 30,000.

Forestry. There are some 20,000 ha of forests.

Fisheries. A lobster and shrimp industry has been created. Catch in 1989 was 1,700 tonnes.

COMMERCE. In 1993 exports totalled 15·13m. francs (mainly to France) and imports 573·6m. francs.

Total trade between Mayotte and UK (British Department of Trade returns, in £1,000 sterling):

	1991	*1992*	*1993*	*1994*	*1995*
Imports to UK	138	132	209	72	312
Exports and re-exports from UK	3,255	3,278	10,646	11,086	5,064

Tourism. In 1993 there were 21,260 visitors.

COMMUNICATIONS

Roads. In 1984 there were 93 km of main roads and 137 km of local roads, with 1,528 motor vehicles.

Civil Aviation. There are regular services by Air Australe to Réunion and Madagascar and by Air Comores.

Telecommunications. Broadcasting is conducted by Radio-Télévision Française d'Outre-Mer (RFO-Mayotte). In 1994 there were 30,000 radio and 3,500 TV receivers (colour by SECAM).

Press. There is 1 weekly newspaper.

SOCIAL INSTITUTIONS

Justice. There is a *tribunal de première instance* and a *tribunal supérieur d'appel*.

Religion. The population is 97% Sunni Moslem, with a small Christian (mainly Roman Catholic) minority.

Education. In 1993 there were 22,351 pupils in primary and 4,835 pupils in secondary schools. There is a teacher training college.

Health. In 1985 there were 9 doctors, 1 dentist, 1 pharmacist, 2 midwives and 51 nursing personnel. There were 2 hospitals with 100 beds in 1991.

ST PIERRE AND MIQUELON

Îles Saint-Pierre et Miquelon

KEY HISTORICAL EVENTS. The only remaining fragment of the once-extensive French possessions in North America, the archipelago was settled from France in the 17th century. It was a French colony from 1816 until 1976, an overseas department until 1985, and is now a Territorial Collectivity.

TERRITORY AND POPULATION. The archipelago consists of 2 islands off the south coast of Newfoundland, with a total area of 242 sq. km, comprising the Saint-Pierre group (26 sq. km) and the Miquelon-Langlade group (216 sq. km). The population (census, 1990) was 6,392 of whom 5,683 were on Saint-Pierre and 709 on Miquelon. The chief town is St Pierre.

Vital statistics (1994): Births, 81; marriages, 24; deaths, 48.

CONSTITUTION AND GOVERNMENT. The territorial collectivity is administered by a *General Council* of 19 members, directly elected for a 6-year term. It is represented in the National Assembly in Paris by 1 deputy, in the Senate by 1 senator and in the Economic and Social Council by 1 councillor. The French government is represented by a Prefect.

Prefect: René Maurice.
President of the General Council: Gérard Grignon.
Local Government: There are 2 municipal councils.

ECONOMY

Budget. The ordinary budget for 1992 balanced at 149m. francs.

Currency. The French franc is in use.

Banking and Finance. Banks include the Banque des Îles Saint-Pierre et Miquelon, the Crédit Saint-Pierrais and the Caisse d'Epargne.

ENERGY AND NATURAL RESOURCES

Electricity. Production (1994) 43·9m. kWh.

Agriculture. The islands, being mostly barren rock, are unsuited for agriculture, but some vegetables are grown and livestock kept for local consumption.

Fisheries. In June 1992 an international tribunal awarded France a 24-mile fishery and economic zone around the islands and a 10·5-mile-wide corridor extending for 200 miles to the high seas. The catch amounted in 1994 to 14,800 tonnes, chiefly cod, lumpfish and scallops. A Franco-Canadian agreement regulating fishing in the area was signed in Dec. 1994.

INDUSTRY. The main industry, fish processing, resumed in 1994 after a temporary cessation due to lack of supplies in 1992.

Labour. Economically active population in 1990 was 2,980.

COMMERCE. Trade in 1m. francs:

	1991	*1992*	*1993*	*1994*
Imports	459·0	404·2	344·0	413·6
Exports	248·1	199·6	28·8	68·6

In 1994, 43% of imports came from Canada, while 96·76% of exports were to France.

Total trade between St Pierre and Miquelon and UK (British Department of Trade returns in £1,000 sterling):

	1991	*1992*	*1993*	*1994*	*1990*
Imports to UK	444	1,414	–	–	25
Exports and re-exports from UK	966	1,439	1,075	584	561

Tourism. There were (1994) 14,470 visitors.

COMMUNICATIONS

Roads. In 1995 there were 114 km of roads, of which 69 km were surfaced. In 1994 there were 2,076 passenger cars and 1,104 commercial vehicles.

Civil Aviation. Air Saint-Pierre connects St Pierre with Montreal, with Halifax and Sydney (Nova Scotia), and there are regular flights to and from St John's (Newfoundland) with Provincial Airlines.

Shipping. St Pierre has regular services to Fortune and Halifax in Canada. In 1994 32,421 tonnes of freight were unloaded and 3,092 tonnes loaded. 868 vessels called in 1994.

Telecommunications. There were 3,650 telephones in 1994. Radio Télévision Française d'Outre-mer (RFO) broadcasts in French on medium-waves and on 2 television channels (1 satellite). There are 24 cable TV channels from Canada and the USA. In 1992 there were about 3,000 radio and 2,000 TV sets in use.

SOCIAL INSTITUTIONS

Justice. There is a court of first instance and a higher court of appeal at St Pierre.

Religion. The population is chiefly Roman Catholic.

Education. Primary instruction is free. There were, in 1994, 3 nursery and 5 primary schools with 794 pupils, 3 secondary schools with 693 pupils and 2 technical schools with 177 pupils.

Health. There was (1994) 1 hospital with 44 beds, 1 convalescent home with 20 beds and 1 retirement home with 40 beds; there were 17 doctors and 4 dentists.

Further Reading

De La Rüe, E. A., *Saint-Pierre et Miquelon.* Paris, 1963
Ribault, J. Y., *Histoire de Saint-Pierre et Miquelon: des Origines à 1814.* St Pierre, 1962

OVERSEAS TERRITORIES

SOUTHERN AND ANTARCTIC TERRITORIES

Terres Australes et Antarctiques Françaises (TAAF)

The Territory of the TAAF was created on 6 Aug. 1955. It comprises the Kerguelen and Crozet archipelagoes, the islands of Saint Paul and Amsterdam (formerly Nouvelle Amsterdam), all in the southern Indian ocean, and Terre Adélie.

The administration has its seat in Paris. The Administrator is assisted by a 7-member consultative council which meets twice yearly in Paris; its members are nominated by the Government for 5 years. The 12 members of the Scientific Council are appointed by the Senior Administrator after approval by the Minister in charge of scientific research. The 15-member Polar Environment Committee, which in 1995 replaced the former Consultative Committee on the Environment, created in Nov. 1982, meets at least once a year to discuss all problems relating to the preservation of the environment.

In Jan. 1992 the French Institute for Polar Research and Technology was set up to organize scientific research and expeditions.

Administrateur supérieur: Vacant.

The staff of the permanent scientific stations of the TAAF (159 in 1994) is renewed every 6 or 12 months and forms the only population.

Kerguelen islands, situated 48–50° S. lat., 68–70° E. long., consists of 1 large and 85 smaller islands and over 200 islets and rocks with a total area of 7,215 sq. km (2,786 sq. miles), of which Grande Terre occupies 6,675 sq. km (2,577 sq. miles). It was discovered in 1772 by Yves de Kerguelen, but was effectively occupied by France only in 1949. Port-aux-Français has several scientific research stations (60 members). Reindeer, trout and sheep have been acclimatized.

Crozet islands, situated 46° S. lat., 50–52° E. long., consists of 5 larger and 15 tiny islands, with a total area of 505 sq. km (195 sq. miles); the western group includes Apostles, Pigs and Penguins islands; the eastern group, Possession and Eastern islands. The archipelago was discovered in 1772 by Marion Dufresne, whose mate, Crozet, annexed it for Louis XV. A meteorological and scientific station (20 members) at Base Alfred-Faure on Possession Island was built in 1964.

Amsterdam Island and **Saint-Paul Island,** situated 38–39° S. lat., 77° E. long. Amsterdam, with an area of 54 sq. km (21 sq. miles) was discovered in 1522 by Magellan's companions; Saint-Paul, lying about 100 km to the south, with an area of 7 sq. km (2·7 sq. miles), was probably discovered in 1559 by Portuguese sailors. Both were first visited in 1633 by the Dutch explorer, Van Diemen, and were annexed by France in 1843. They are both extinct volcanoes. The only inhabitants are at Base Martin de Vivies, established in 1949 on Amsterdam Island, with several scientific research stations, hospital, communication and other facilities (20 members). Crayfish are caught commercially on Amsterdam.

Terre Adélie comprises that section of the Antarctic continent between 136° and 142° E. long., south of 60° S. lat. The ice-covered plateau has an area of about 432,000 sq. km (166,800 sq. miles), and was discovered in 1840 by Dumont d'Urville. A research station (30 members) is situated at Base Dumont d'Urville, which is maintained by the French Institute for Polar Research and Technology.

NEW CALEDONIA

Nouvelle Calédonie et Dépendances

KEY HISTORICAL EVENTS. New Caledonia was annexed by France in 1853 and, together with most of its former dependencies, became an Overseas Territory in 1958.

TERRITORY AND POPULATION. The territory comprises the island of New Caledonia and various outlying islands, all situated in the south-west Pacific with a total land area of 18,576 sq. km (7,172 sq. miles). In 1989 the population (census) was 164,173, including 55,085 Europeans (majority French), 73,598 Melanesians (Kanaks), 7,652 Vietnamese and Indonesians, 4,750 Polynesians, 14,186 Wallisians, 8,902 others. Population estimate, 1994, 183,200. The capital, Nouméa had (1989) 65,110 inhabitants. Vital statistics (1993): Live births, 4,337; marriages, 896; divorces, 220; deaths, 954; growth rate, 18·8 (per 1,000 population).

The main islands are:

1. The island of New Caledonia with an area of 16,372 sq. km, has a total length of about 400 km, and an average breadth of 50 km, and a population (census, 1989) of 144,051. The east coast is predominantly Melanesian, the Nouméa region predominantly European, and the rest of the west coast of mixed population.
2. The Loyalty Islands, 100 km (60 miles) east of New Caledonia, consisting of 3 large islands, Maré, Lifou and Uvéa, and many small islands with a total area of 1,981 sq. km and a population (census, 1989) of 17,912, nearly all Melanesians except on Uvéa, which is partly Polynesian. The chief culture in the islands is that of coconuts and the chief export, copra.
3. The Isle of Pines, 50 km (30 miles) to the south-east of Nouméa, with an area of 152 sq. km and a population of 1,465 (census 1989), is a tourist and fishing centre.
4. The Bélep Archipelago, about 50 km north-west of New Caledonia, with an area of 70 sq. km and a population of 745 (census 1989).

The remaining islands are all very small and none have permanent inhabitants. The largest are the Chesterfield Islands, a group of 11 well-wooded coral islets with a combined area of 10 sq. km, about 550 km west of the Bélep Archipelago. The Huon Islands, a group of 4 barren coral islets with a combined area of just 65 ha, are 225 km north of the Bélep Archipelago. Walpole, a limestone coral island of 1 sq. km, lies 150 km east of the Isle of Pines; Matthew Island (20 ha.) and Hunter Island (2 sq. km), respectively 250 km and 330 km east of Walpole, are spasmodically active volcanic islands also claimed by Vanuatu.

At the 1989 census there were 337 tribes (which have legal status under a high chief) living in 184 reserves.

CLIMATE. Nouméa. Jan. 26·8°C, July 21°C. Annual rainfall 832·3 mm.

CONSTITUTION AND GOVERNMENT. Following constitutional changes introduced by the French government in 1985 and 1988, the Territory is administered by a High Commissioner assisted by a 4-member Consultative Committee, consisting of the President of the Territorial Congress (as President) and the

Presidents of the 3 Provincial Assemblies. The French government is represented by the appointed High Commissioner.

There is a 54-member Territorial Congress consisting of the complete membership of the 3 Provincial Assemblies. Elections were held on 9 July 1995. The electorate was 102,487; turn-out was 70·23%. The Rally for Caledonia in the Republic (RPCR) won 22 seats with 36·41% of votes cast; the Kanak Socialist Front for National Liberation, 12 with 19·21%; New Caledonia for All, 9 with 15·27%, the National Union for Independence, 5 with 9·87%; the National Front, 2 with 3·29%; the Rally for New Caledonia within France, 2 with 3·2%; Socialist Kanak Liberation, 1 with 3·26% and the Front for the Development of the Loyalty Isles, 1 with 2·12%.

President of the Territorial Congress: Pierre Frogier (RPCR).

New Caledonia is represented in the French National Assembly by 2 deputies, in the Senate by 1 senator and in the Economic and Social Council by 1 councillor.

The Territory is divided into 3 provinces, Nord, Sud and Îles Loyauté, each under a directly-elected Regional Council. They are sub-divided into 32 communes administered by locally-elected councils and mayors.

In Sept. 1987 the electorate voted in favour of remaining a French possession. Agreement was reached in June 1988 between the French government and representatives of both the European and Melanesian communities on New Caledonia, and confirmed in Nov. 1988 by plebiscites in both France and New Caledonia, under which the territory has been divided into 3 autonomous provinces, and a further referendum on full independence is scheduled for 1998.

High Commissioner: Henri-Michel Comet.

ECONOMY

Budget. The budget for 1995 balanced at 68,750m. francs CFP.

Currency. The unit of currency is the *franc CFP* (XPF), with a parity of 18·18 to the French franc. 8,254m. francs CFP were in circulation in Dec. 1993.

Banking and Finance. There is a Banque Calédonienne d'Investissement, and branches of the Westpac Banking Corporation, the Banque Nationale de Paris, the Banque Paribas Pacifique, the Société Générale, Calédonienne de Banque, the Credit Agricole Mutuel and the Banque de la Nouvelle-Calédonie (Crédit Lyonnais).

ENERGY AND NATURAL RESOURCES

Electricity. In 1994, production totalled 1,416m. kWh.

Minerals. The mineral resources are very great; nickel, chrome and iron abound; silver, gold, cobalt, lead, manganese, iron and copper have been mined at different times. The nickel deposits are of special value, being without arsenic. Production of nickel ore in 1994, 5·7m. tonnes. In 1994 the furnaces produced 10,641 tonnes of matte nickel and 39,488 tonnes of ferro-nickel.

Agriculture. In 1993, 48,715 persons worked in agriculture. In 1993, 228,969 ha were pasture land. The chief products are beef, pork, poultry, coffee, copra, maize, fruit and vegetables. Produce, 1993 (in tonnes): Cereals, 450; coffee, 78; copra, 225.

Livestock (1991): Cattle, 125,461; pigs, 38,252; goats, 16,498.

Forestry. There are 0·98m. ha of forest. Roundwood production (1993), 2,747 cu. metres.

Fisheries. The catch in 1993 totalled 5,667 tonnes. Aquaculture is practised.

INDUSTRY. Local industries include chlorine and oxygen plants, cement, soft drinks, barbed wire, nails, pleasure and fishing boats, clothing, pasta, household cleaners, confectionery, beer and biscuits.

Labour. The working population (1989 census) was 54,230. The guaranteed monthly minimum wage was 72,725 francs CFP in Dec. 1994. There were 8,737 job seekers in Dec. 1993. In 1993 there were 52 industrial disputes and 25,010 working days were lost.

COMMERCE. Imports and exports in 1m. francs CFP:

	1990	*1991*	*1992*	*1993*	*1994*
Imports	86,929	88,798	89,160	87,951	87,305
Exports	43,931	45,917	39,448	38,747	36,209

In 1994, 43·7% of the imports came from France and 11·8% from Australia, while 27·7% of the exports went to France. Refined minerals (mainly ferro-nickel and nickel) made up 59% of exports by value and nickel ore 19%.

Total trade between New Caledonia and UK (British Department of Trade returns, in £1,000 sterling):

	1992	*1993*	*1994*	*1995*
Imports to UK	13	2,413	12,910	9,534
Exports and re-exports from UK	5,450	7,744	7,012	9,006

Tourism. Tourists, 1994, 85,103 (28% Japanese, 25% French).

COMMUNICATIONS

Roads. There were, in 1993, 5,562 km of roads, of which 975 km were paved. There were almost 67,000 vehicles. In 1993 there were 689 road accidents with 61 fatalities.

Civil Aviation. New Caledonia is connected by air routes with France and Tahiti (by Air France, AOM and Corsair), Australia (Air France, Air Caledonie International and Qantas), New Zealand (Air France, Air Caledonie International and Air New Zealand), Fiji and Wallis and Futuna (by Air Caledonie International), Vanuatu (by Air France), and Nauru (by Air Nauru). In 1994, 150,071 passengers arrived and 148,102 departed via La Tontouta international airport, near Nouméa. Internal services connect Nouméa with 21 domestic air fields. In 1994, 307,636 passengers and 5,343 tonnes of freight were carried on international routes.

Shipping. In 1994, 660 vessels entered Nouméa unloading 1,089,000 tonnes of cargo and loading 3,534,000 tonnes.

Telecommunications. There were (1993) 42 post offices and 38,748 telephones. Radio Télévision Française d'Outre-Mer broadcasts in French on medium- and short-wave radio (there are also 3 private stations) and on 2 television channels (colour by SECAM). There were about 0·09m. radios in 1991 and 35,000 TV sets.

Cinemas. In 1994 there were 12 cinemas and 1 mobile cinema.

Press. In 1994 there was 1 daily newspaper with a circulation of 0·02m.

SOCIAL INSTITUTIONS

Justice. There are courts at Nouméa, Koné and Wé, a court of appeal, a labour court and a joint commerce tribunal.

Religion. There were about 0·1m. Roman Catholics in 1994.

Education. In 1995, there were 35,914 pupils in 279 primary schools, 25,481 pupils in 54 secondary schools, 5,109 students (in 1993) in 28 technical and vocational schools, and 436 students and 66 (in 1993) teaching staff in 5 higher education establishments. The University of the Pacific had 983 students and 43 academic staff in 1994.

Welfare. There are 3 forms of social security cover: Free Medical Aid provides total sickness cover for non-waged persons and low-income earners, the Family Benefit, Workplace Injury and Contingency Fund for Workers (CAFAT) and mutual benefit societies. In 1993 Free Medical Aid paid 54,559 beneficiaries a total of 5,109m. francs CFP; CAFAT paid 122,000 beneficiaries 27,701m. francs CFP.

Health. In 1993 there were 370 physicians, 98 dentists, 58 pharmacists, 63 midwives and 1,126 paramedical personnel; 6 hospitals, 27 medical centres, 10 infirmaries and 24 dispensaries had a total of 1,259 beds.

Further Reading

Journal Officiel de la Nouvelle Calédonie
Institut Territorial de la Statistique et des Etudes Economiques. *Tableaux de l'Economie Calédonienne.*—Every 3 years. English version, *New Caledonia: Facts & Figures (TEC 94)*, 1994
Informations Statistiques Rapides de Nouvelle-Calédonie. (monthly)
Dommel, D., *La Crise Calédonienne: Démission ou Guérison?* Paris, 1993

Local statistical office: Institut Territorial de la Statistique et des Études Économiques, BP 823, 98845 Nouméa.

FRENCH POLYNESIA

Territoire de la Polynésie Française

KEY HISTORICAL EVENTS. French protectorates since 1843, these islands were annexed to France 1880–82 to form 'French Settlements in Oceania', which opted in Nov. 1958 for the status of an overseas territory within the French Community.

TERRITORY AND POPULATION. The total land area of these 5 archipelagoes, scattered over a wide area in the Eastern Pacific is 3,265 sq. km (1,260 sq. miles). The population (1988 census) was 188,814; 1994 estimate, 216,600.

The official languages are French and Tahitian.

Vital statistics (1987): Births, 5,384; marriages, 1,251; deaths, 980.

The islands are administratively divided into 5 *circonscriptions:*

1. The **Windward Islands** (Îles du Vent) (140,341 inhabitants in 1988) comprise Tahiti with an area of 1,042 sq. km and 115,820 inhabitants; Moorea with an area of 132 sq. km and 7,059 inhabitants; Maio (Tubuai Manu) with an area of 9 sq. km and 190 inhabitants, and the smaller Mehetia and Tetiaroa. The capital is Papeete (78,814 inhabitants including suburbs).

2. The **Leeward Islands** (Îles sous le Vent), comprise the volcanic islands of Raiatéa, Tahaa, Huahine, Bora-Bora and Maupiti, together with 4 small atolls, the group having a total land area of 404 sq. km and 22,232 inhabitants in 1988. The chief town is Uturoa on Raiatéa.

The Windward and Leeward Islands together are called the Society Archipelago (Archipel de la Société). Tahitian, a Polynesian language, is spoken throughout the archipelago and used as a *lingua franca* in the rest of the territory.

3. The **Tuamotu Archipelago**, consisting of two parallel ranges of 78 atolls lying north and east of the Society Archipelago, have a total area of 690 sq. km; the most populous atolls are Rangiroa, Hao and Turéia. Mururoa and Fangataufa atolls in the south-east of the group have been used by France for nuclear tests since 1966, having been ceded to France in 1964 by the Territorial Assembly.

The *circonscription* (12,374 inhabitants in 1988) also includes the **Gambier Islands** further east (of which Mangareva is the principal), with an area of 36 sq. km and a population of 582; the chief centre is Rikitea on Mangareva.

4. The **Austral or Tubuai Islands**, lying south of the Society Archipelago, comprise a 1,300 km chain of volcanic islands and reefs. They include Rimatara, Rurutu, Tubuai, Raivaevae and, 500 km to the south, Rapa-Iti, with a combined area of 148 sq. km and 6,509 (1988) inhabitants; the chief centre is Mataura on Tubuai.

5. The **Marquesas Islands**, lying north of the Tuamotu Archipelago, with a total area of 1,049 sq. km and 7,538 (1988) inhabitants, comprise Nukuhiva, Uapu, Uahuka, Hivaoa, Tahuata, Fatuhiva and 4 smaller (uninhabited) islands; the chief centre is Taiohae on Nukuhiva.

CLIMATE. Papeete. Jan. 81°F (27·1°C), July 75°F (24°C). Annual rainfall 83" (2,106 mm).

CONSTITUTION AND GOVERNMENT. Under the 1984 Constitution, the Territory is administered by a Council of Ministers, whose President is elected by the Territorial Assembly from among its own members; the President appoints a Vice-President and 9 other ministers. There is an advisory Economic and Social Committee. French Polynesia is represented in the French Assembly by 2 deputies, in the Senate by 1 senator, and in the Economic and Social Council by 1 councillor. The French government is represented by a High Commissioner. The *Territorial Assembly* comprises 41 members elected every 5 years by universal suffrage using the same proportional representation system as in metropolitan French regional elections. To be elected a party must gain at least 5% of votes cast. The Assembly elects a head of local government.

A statute drafted at the end of 1995 proposes to create French Polynesia an 'Autonomous Overseas Territory' in which the President of the Council of Ministers will become the President of the territory.

Elections were held in March 1991. The electorate was 109,462; turn-out was 84,798 (78·35%). Elections were scheduled for May 1996.

Rassemblement pour le Peuple (RPP; affiliated to the French Rassemblement pour la République) won 18 seats with 31·41% of votes cast; Polynesian Union 14 with 23·27%; New Fatherland (NF) 5 with 12·28%; Independent Liberation Front of Polynesia 4 with 11·43%. An RPR-NF coalition was formed under Gaston Flosse (RPR).

High Commissioner: Paul Roncière.
President of the Council of Ministers: Gaston Flosse (RPR).

Flag: Three horizontal stripes of red, white, red, with the white of double width containing the emblem of French Polynesia in yellow.

ECONOMY

Currency. The unit of currency is the *franc CFP* (XPF), with a parity of *CFP francs* 18·18 to the French *franc*.

Banking and Finance. There are 6 commercial banks, Indosuez, the Bank of Tahiti, the Banque de Polynésie, Paribas Polynésie, Société de Crédit et de Développement de l'Océanie and Westpac Banking Corp.

ENERGY AND NATURAL RESOURCES

Electricity. Production in 1993 amounted to 323·4m. kWh (18% hydro-electric).

Agriculture. An important product is copra (coconut trees covering the coastal plains of the mountainous islands and the greater part of the low-lying islands), production (1993) 10,055 tonnes. Tropical fruits, such as bananas, pineapples, oranges, etc., are grown only for local consumption.

Livestock (1993): Cattle, 7,000; pigs, 16,800; goats, 12,000; (1990): sheep, 2,000; poultry, 1m.

Fisheries. There are some 400 traditional fishermen. The estimated catch in 1993 was 3,240 tonnes. Industrial fishing is carried out by foreign fleets.

COMMERCE. In 1993 exports were worth 15,252m. francs CFA and imports, 86,905m. francs CFA.

Total trade between French Polynesia and UK (British Department of Trade returns, in £1,000 sterling):

	1991	*1992*	*1993*	*1994*	*1995*
Imports to UK	58	27	46	52	235
Exports and re-exports from UK	4,362	2,892	3,873	4,028	6,078

Chief exports are coconut oil and cultured pearls (599,436 grammes of pearls were exported in 1990). In 1987, France provided 52% of imports and USA 13%, while (1985) 44% of exports went to France and 21% to USA.

Tourism. Tourism is very important, earning almost half as much as the visible exports. There were 147,800 visitors in 1993 (including 49,200 from North America, 58,200 from Europe and 16,100 from Japan).

COMMUNICATIONS

Roads. In 1985 there were 797 km of roads and 44,000 vehicles.

Civil Aviation. Air France and 8 other international airlines connect Tahiti International Airport with Paris, Los Angeles, San Francisco and many Pacific locations. Local companies connect the islands with services from secondary airports at Bora-Bora, Rangiroa and Raiatea. In 1993, 473,903 international passengers arrived and departed via the airports at Faaa and on Mooréa and Bora-Bora. Thirty other airfields have regular domestic services.

Shipping. Several shipping companies connect France, San Francisco, New Zealand, Japan, Australia, South East Asia and most Pacific locations with Papeete.

Telecommunications. Number of telephones (1985), 28,192. Radio Télévision Française d'Outre-mer (RFO) broadcasts in French, Tahitian and English. There are also 9 private radio stations. Number of receivers (1991): Radio, 90,000; TV, 26,500.

Cinemas. In 1986 there were 8 cinemas in Papeete.

Press. In 1991 there were 2 daily newspapers.

SOCIAL INSTITUTIONS

Justice. There is a *tribunal de première instance* and a *cour d'appel* at Papeete.

Religion. In 1980 it was estimated that 46·5% of the inhabitants were Protestants, 39·4% Roman Catholic and 5·1% Mormon.

Education. There were, in 1991-92, 32,544 pupils in 235 primary schools, 12,933 pupils in 23 secondary schools. The French University of the South Pacific was founded in 1987.

Health. There were (1987) 273 physicians, 88 dentists, 35 pharmacists, 24 midwives and 464 nursing personnel. There were (1991) 1 territorial hospital centre, 6 general hospitals, 1 psychiatric hospital and 22 medical centres and dispensaries.

DEPENDENCY. The uninhabited Clipperton Island, 1,000 km off the west coast of Mexico, is administered by the High Commissioner for French Polynesia but does not form part of the Territory; it is an atoll with an area of 5 sq. km.

Further Reading

Bounds, J. H., *Tahiti.* Bend, Oregon, 1978
Luke, Sir Harry, *The Islands of the South Pacific.* London, 1961
O'Reilly, P. and Reitman, E., *Bibliographie de Tahiti et de la Polynésie française.* Paris, 1967
O'Reilly, P. and Teissier, R., *Tahitiens. Répertoire bio-bibliographique de la Polynésie française.* Paris, 1963

Local statistical office: Institut Territorial de la Statistique, Papeete.

WALLIS AND FUTUNA

KEY HISTORICAL EVENTS. French dependencies since 1842, the inhabitants of these islands voted on 22 Dec. 1959 by 4,307 votes out of 4,576 in favour of exchanging their status to that of an overseas territory, which took effect from 29 July 1961.

TERRITORY AND POPULATION. The territory comprises two groups of islands (total area 240 sq. km) in the central Pacific. The Iles de Hoorn lie 240 km north-east of Fiji and consist of 2 main islands–Futuna (64 sq. km) and uninhabited

Alofi (51 sq. km). The Wallis Archipelago lies another 160 km further north-east, and has an area of 159 sq. km. It comprises the main island of Uvea (60 sq. km) and neighbouring uninhabited islands, with a surrounding coral reef. The capital is Mata-Utu (815 inhabitants, 1983) on Uvea.

The resident population, census March 1990, was 13,705 (Wallis, 8,973; Futuna, 4,732); estimate, 1993, 14,400. In 1991 14,186 Wallisians and Futunians lived in New Caledonia. Wallisian and Futunian are distinct Polynesian languages.

CONSTITUTION AND GOVERNMENT. A Prefect represents the French government and carries out the duties of head of the territory, assisted by a 20-member Territorial Assembly, directly elected for a 5-year term, and a 6-member Territorial Council, comprising the 3 traditional chiefs and 3 nominees of the Prefect agreed by the Territorial Assembly. The territory is represented by 1 deputy in the French National Assembly, by 1 senator in the Senate, and by 1 member on the Economic and Social Council. There are 3 districts: Singave and Alo (both on Futuna) and Wallis. In each tribal kings exercise customary powers assisted by ministers and district and village chiefs. Territorial Assembly elections were held in March 1992. The electorate was 6,972; 5,657 votes were cast.

Prefect: Léon Legrand.
President of the Territorial Assembly: Soane Muni Uhila (b.1960; ind).

ECONOMY

Currency. The unit of currency is the *franc CFP* (XPF), with a parity of 100 to 5·50 French francs.

Banking and Finance. There is a branch of Indosuez at Mata-Utu.

ENERGY AND NATURAL RESOURCES

Electricity. There is a thermal power station at Mata-Utu.

Agriculture. The chief products are copra, cassava, yams, taro roots and bananas.
Livestock (1993): Pigs, 25,000; goats, 7,000.

COMMERCE. Imports (1984) amounted to 1,302m. CFP francs. Exports from the UK (British Department of Trade returns, 1995), £17,000; (1994), £4,000.

COMMUNICATIONS

Roads. There are about 100 km of roads on Uvea.

Civil Aviation. There is an airport on Wallis, at Hihifo, and another near Alo on Futuna. 3 flights a week link Wallis and Futuna. Air Calédonie International operates 2 flights a week to Nouméa.

Shipping. A regular cargo service links Mata-Utu (Wallis) and Singave (Futuna) with Nouméa (New Caledonia).

Telecommunications. In 1986 there were 2 radio stations and 6 post offices. In 1985 there were 340 telephones.

SOCIAL INSTITUTIONS

Justice. There is a court of first instance, from which appeals can be made to the court of appeal in New Caledonia.

Religion. The majority of the population is Roman Catholic.

Education. In 1993, there were 3,624 pupils in primary schools and 1,777 in secondary schools. Further education is available in New Caledonia.

Health. In 1991 there was 1 hospital with 60 beds and 4 dispensaries.

GABON

République Gabonaise

Capital: Libreville
Population: 1·01m. (1993)
GNP per capita: US$3,550 (1994)
HDI/world rank: 0·579/114 (1992)

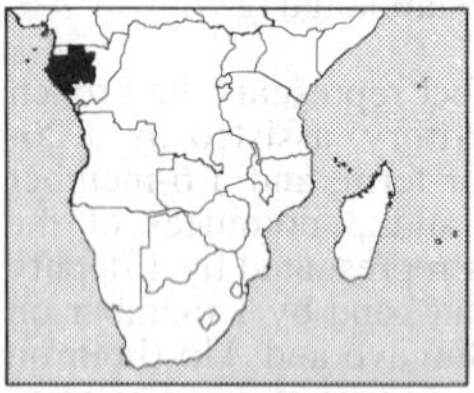

KEY HISTORICAL EVENTS. First colonized by France in the mid-19th century, Gabon was annexed to French Congo in 1888 and became a separate colony in 1910 as one of the 4 territories of French Equatorial Africa. It became an autonomous republic within the French Community on 28 Nov. 1958 and achieved independence on 17 Aug. 1960.

TERRITORY AND POPULATION. Gabon is bounded in the west by the Atlantic Ocean, north by Equatorial Guinea and Cameroon and east and south by the Congo. The area covers 267,667 sq. km; its population at the 1993 census was 1,011,710 (48% urban); density, 4·5 per sq. km. The capital is Libreville (352,000 inhabitants, 1992), other large towns being Port-Gentil (75,800), Masuku (formerly Franceville, 40,450), Lambaréné (26,257 in 1978) and Mouanda (22,909 in 1978).

Growth rate (1993): 3·4%; birth rate (per 1,000 population), 1993: 45·3; death, 16·1; infant mortality, 94 per 1,000 live births. Expectation of life was 52 years for men and 55 for women in 1990.

Provincial areas, populations (1990, in 1,000) and capitals:

Province	*Sq. km*	*1990*	*Capital*	*Province*	*Sq. km*	*1990*	*Capital*
Estuaire	20,740	404·7	Libreville	Nyanga	21,285	81·4	Tchibanga
Woleu-Ntem	38,465	216·2	Oyem	Ngounié	37,750	166·8	Mouila
Ogooué-Ivindo	46,075	92·5	Makokou	Ogooué-Lolo	25,380	76·4	Koulamoutou
Moyen-Ogooué	18,535	80·4	Lambaréné	Haut-Ogooué	36,547	136·8	Masuku
Ogooué-Maritime	22,890	110·3	Port-Gentil				

The largest ethnic groups are the Fang (30%) and Eshira (25%) in the north. There are some 40 smaller groups. French is the official language.

CLIMATE. The climate is equatorial, with high temperatures and considerable rainfall. Mid-May to mid-Sept. is the long dry season, followed by a short rainy season, then a dry season again from mid-Dec. to mid-Feb., and finally a long rainy season once more. Libreville. Jan. 80°F (26·7°C), July 75°F (23·9°C). Annual rainfall 99" (2,510 mm).

CONSTITUTION AND GOVERNMENT. At a referendum on electoral reform on 23 July 1995, 96·48% of votes cast were in favour; turn-out was 63·45%. The 1991 Constitution provides for an Executive President directly elected for a 5-year term (renewable once only). The head of government is the Prime Minister who appoints a Council of Ministers. The unicameral *National Assembly* consists of 120 members, directly elected for a 5-year term. There is constitutional provision for the formation of an upper house. Elections were held in Sept. 1990, but because of irregularities the results were partially annulled and a second round of voting took place in Oct. In the final result the Gabonese Democratic Party (the former sole party permitted) won 63 seats. There are 7 opposition parties, including Morena-Bûcheron, with 20 seats, and the Gabonese Progress party, with 18.

Presidential elections were held on 5 Dec. 1993. The electorate was 484,319. President Bongo was re-elected against 12 opponents with 51·18% of votes cast.

President: Omar Bongo (succeeded 2 Dec. 1967, re-elected in 1973, 1979, 1986 and 1993; sworn in 22 Jan. 1994).

The Council of Ministers in Sept. 1995 comprised:
Prime Minister: Dr Paulin Obame-Nguema.
Minister of State for Justice, Keeper of the Seals: Pierre-Louis Agondjo-Okawe.

Minister of State for Foreign Affairs and Co-operation: Casimir Oye Mba. *Minister of State for Equipment and Construction:* Zacharie Myboto. *Minister of State for Habitat, Lands and Urban Planning and Welfare:* Jean-François Ntoutoume-Emane. *Minister of State for Labour, Human Resources and Training:* Jean-Remy Pendy Bouyiki. *Minister of State for Planning and Territorial Administration:* Pierre-Claver Maganga Moussavou. *Minister of State for Agriculture, Livestock and Rural Economy:* Emmanuel Ondo Methogo. *Public Health and Population:* Dr Serge Mba Bekale. *National Defence, Security and Immigration:* Gen. Idriss Ngari. *Communication, Culture, Art, Mass Education and Human Rights:* Alexandre Sambat. *Transport, Merchant Marine, Fishing, in charge of Tourism and National Parks:* Antoine Mboumbou Miyakou. *Finance, Economy and Participation:* Marcel Doupambi Matoka. *Civil Service and Administrative Reform:* Simon Oyono Aba'a. *Commerce, Industry, Small and Medium Size Enterprises, Handicrafts, Reform of the Parastatal Sector and Privatization:* Andre-Dieudonne Berre. *Mining, Energy and Oil:* Paul Toungui. *Higher Education and Scientific Research:* Gaston Mozogo Ovono. *Forestry, Posts and Telecomunnications and Environment:* Martin Fidele-Magnaga. *National Education, Youth and Sports, in charge of Women's Affairs, Spokesperson for the Government:* Paulette Missambo. *Social Affairs and National Solidarity:* Sebastien Mamboundou Mouyama.

National flag: Three horizontal stripes of green, yellow, blue.

National anthem: 'Uni dans la concorde' ('United in concord'); words and tune by G. Damas.

Local government: The 9 provinces, each administered by a governor appointed by the President, are divided into 37 *départements*, each under a prefect.

DEFENCE

Army. The Army consists of 1 all-arms Presidential Guard battalion group with support units and 8 infantry, 1 airborne commando and 1 engineer company, totalling (1996) 3,200. A referendum of 23 July 1995 favoured the transformation of the Presidential Guard into a republican guard. There is also a paramilitary Gendarmerie of 2,000. France maintains a 600-strong marine infantry battalion.

Navy. The small naval flotilla consists of 1 French-built fast missile craft and 2 coastal patrol craft. The flagship is a French-built medium landing ship, and there are about 3 minor service tenders. A separate Coast Guard operates some 10 small launches. Personnel in 1995 totalled 500.

Air Force. The Air Force has 6 single-seat, 2 two-seat Mirage 5 and 2 Magister ground-attack aircraft, and 1 EMB-111 maritime patrol aircraft. Transport duties are performed primarily by 3 Hercules and 1 EMB-110 Bandeirante turboprop aircraft and 1 CN-235. Single Falcon 900, Gulfstream III and DC-8 aircraft are used for VIP duties. Three T-34C-1 armed turboprop aircraft and a Super Puma are operated for the Presidential Guard. Also in service are 2 Puma, 3 Gazelle, 1 Bell 212, 1 Bell 412 and 2 Alouette III helicopters. Personnel (1995) 1,000.

INTERNATIONAL RELATIONS

Membership. Gabon is a member of the UN, OAU and OPEC and is an ACP state of the EU.

ECONOMY

Policy. The *Economic and Social Council* was established in 1993 to advise the Council of Ministers. It comprises representatives of central government, local government, employers' groups, trade unions and other interest groups. 5-year development plans, of which there were 5 after 1966, have been replaced by 3-year rolling investment plans.

Budget. The 1994 budget provided for expenditure of 415,000m. francs CFA and revenue of 372,000m. francs CFA. Expenditure (in 1,000m. francs CFA): Current, 315 (administration, 246; debt servicing, 68); capital, 100.

Currency. The unit of currency is the *franc CFA*, with a parity value of 100 francs CFA to 1 French franc. There are coins of 1, 2, 5, 10, 25, 50, 100 and 500 *francs* CFA, and banknotes of 100, 500, 1,000, 5,000 and 10,000 *francs* CFA. 59,690m. francs CFA were in circulation in 1992. Foreign exchange reserves were US$293m. in 1992. Gold reserves were 13,000 troy oz. in March 1992. For exchange rates *see* BENIN: Currency.

Banking and Finance. The *Banque des États de l'Afrique Centrale* is the bank of issue. There are 9 commercial banks. The *Banque Gabonaise de Développement* and the *Union Gabonaise de Banque* are Gabonese-controlled.

ENERGY AND NATURAL RESOURCES

Electricity. The semi-public *Société d'energie et d'eau du Gabon* produced 918m. kWh. in 1990, 80% hydro-electric.

Oil and Gas. Proven oil reserves (1984) 490m. bbls. Crude oil production, 1995, 344,000 bbls. a day. Natural gas production (1985) was 201m. cu. metres.

Minerals. There are an estimated 200m. tonnes of manganese ore and 850m. tonnes of iron ore deposits; proven reserves of uranium, 35,000 tonnes. Gold, zinc and phosphates also occur. Output, 1992: Manganese ore, 0·81m. tonnes; uranium, 270 tonnes.

Agriculture. Agriculture contributed 4·1% of GDP in 1991. There were 0·46m. ha of cultivable land in 1990. The major crops (production, 1991, in 1,000 tonnes) are: Sugar-cane, 210; cassava, 250; plantains, 240; maize, 20; groundnuts, 16; bananas, 9; palm oil, 4·9; cocoa, 2; coffee, 4 and rice, 1.

Livestock (1991): 28,000 cattle, 165,000 sheep, 81,000 goats, 162,000 pigs.

Forestry. Equatorial forests cover 20·4m. ha. 1·27m. cu. metres of timber were produced in 1991, 70% okoumé.

Fisheries. In 1992 there were 14 fishing vessels over 100 GRT, totalling 2,141 GRT. Industrial fleets account for about 25% of the catch. About 80,000 tonnes of tuna are caught annually.

INDUSTRY. Most manufacturing (5·2% of GDP in 1991) is based on the processing of food (particularly sugar), timber and mineral resources.

Labour. The workforce in 1990 numbered 536,000 (0·2m. female) of whom 66·8% were agricultural. In 1993 the legal minimum monthly wage was 1,200 francs CFA. There is a 40-hour working week.

FOREIGN ECONOMIC RELATIONS. Foreign debt was US$3,842m. in 1992. The government retains the right to participate in foreign investment in oil and mineral extraction.

Commerce. In 1991 imports totalled US$826·2m. and exports US$2,255·3m. In 1991 the main exports were worth (in US$1m.): Oil, 1,740; manganese, 191; timber and wood products, 39·9; uranium, 17·8 (52·4 in 1990). Imports are mainly industrial goods. In 1991 the main export markets were: France, 31·1%; USA, 27·1%; Netherlands, 6·9%; Chile, 6%; Japan, 5·4%. Main import suppliers: France, 45·7%; USA, 9·7%; Japan, 6·9%; UK, 6·2%.

Total trade between Gabon and the UK (British Department of Trade returns, in £1,000 sterling):

	1991	*1992*	*1993*	*1994*	*1995*
Imports to UK	3,221	3,456	6,065	3,851	5,948
Exports and re-exports from UK	30,597	19,703	21,887	26,900	25,358

Tourism. There were 108,000 foreign visitors in 1990. There were 5,598 tourist beds.

COMMUNICATIONS

Roads. There were (1992) 7,200 km of roads (614 km asphalted) and in 1990 there were some 22,000 passenger cars and in 1985 9,960 commercial vehicles. There were 896 road accidents in 1990 with 121 fatalities.

Railways. The 657-km standard gauge Transgabonais railway runs from the port of Owendo to Franceville. Total length of railways, 1994, 639 km. In 1994, 180,000 passengers and 2·5m. tonnes of freight were transported.

Civil Aviation. There are 3 international airports at Port-Gentil, Masuku, and Libreville; internal services link these to 65 domestic airfields. The national carrier is Air Gabon (80% state-owned), which in 1995 operated 1 B-727-200 Adv, 1 B-737-200C Adv, 1 B-747-200B Coombi, 2 F-28-2000s and 2 other aircraft. 435,962 passengers and 9·95m. tonnes of freight were carried in 1991. Services are also provided by Air Afrique, Air France, Air São Tomé e Príncipe, Cameroon Airlines, Nigeria Airways, Royal Air Maroc, Sabena and Swissair. 398,000 passengers were carried in 1991, including 120,000 on international routes.

Shipping. In 1995 vessels over 100 GRT totalled 37,000 GRT, including 2 tankers totalling 742 GRT. Owendo (near Libreville), Mayumba and Port-Gentil are the main ports. In 1990, 15·3m. tonnes of cargo were handled at the ports. Rivers are an important means of inland transport.

Telecommunications. In 1991 there were 22,000 telephones. Broadcasting is the responsibility of the state-controlled Radiodiffusion Télévision Gabonaise which transmits 2 national radio programmes and provincial services. There is also a commercial radio station and 2 TV channels. In 1993 there were 0·25m. radio and 40,000 TV sets (colour by SECAM).

Press. There was (1993) a government-run daily, *L'Union*, and 4 independent periodicals.

SOCIAL INSTITUTIONS

Justice. There are *tribunaux de grande instance* at Libreville, Port-Gentil, Lambaréné, Mouila, Oyem, Masuku and Koulamoutou, from which cases move progressively to a central Criminal Court, Court of Appeal and Supreme Court, all 3 located in Libreville. Civil police number about 900.

Religion. In 1992 there were 0·82m. Roman Catholics, the majority of the remaining population following animist beliefs. There are about 10,000 Moslems.

Education. Adult literacy was 60·7% in 1990. Education is compulsory between 6–16 years. In 1989–90 there were 209,700 pupils and 5,242 teachers in primary schools; 36,600 pupils with 1,686 teachers in 73 secondary schools; 8,414 students with 421 teachers in 12 technical schools and 780 students with 43 teachers in 8 teacher-training establishments.

In 1994–95 there was 1 university and 1 university of science and technology, with a total of 2,950 students and 410 academic staff.

Health. In 1985 there were 565 doctors, and in 1977, 20 dentists, 28 pharmacists, 99 midwives and 823 nursing personnel. In 1988 there were 27 hospitals and 633 medical centres, with a total of 5,329 beds.

DIPLOMATIC REPRESENTATIVES

Of Gabon in Great Britain (27 Elvaston Place, London, SW7 5NL)
Ambassador: Honorine Dossou-Naki.

Of Great Britain in Gabon
Ambassador: Nicholas McCarthy, OBE (resides in Yaoundé).

Of Gabon in the USA (2034 20th St., NW, Washington, D.C., 20009)
Ambassador: Paul Boundoukou-Latha.

Of the USA in Gabon (Blvd de la Mer, Libreville)
Ambassador: Joseph C. Wilson.

Of Gabon to the United Nations
Ambassador: Denis Dangue Rewaka.

Further Reading

Barnes, J. F. G., *Gabon: beyond the Colonial Legacy.* Boulder (Colo.), 1992
Gardiner, D. E. (ed.) *Historical Dictionary of Gabon.* 2nd ed. Metuchen (NJ), 1994
Saint Paul, M. A., *Gabon: the Development of a Nation.* London, 1989

National statistical office: Direction Générale de la Statistique et des Etudes Economiques, Ministère de la Planification, de l'Economie et de l'Aménagement du Territoire, Libreville.

THE GAMBIA

Republic of The Gambia

Capital: Banjul
Population: 1·03m. (1993)
GNP per capita: US$360 (1994)
HDI/world rank: 0·299/161 (1992)

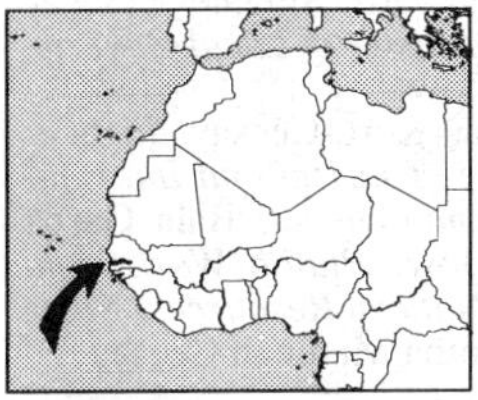

KEY HISTORICAL EVENTS. The Gambia was discovered by the early Portuguese navigators, but they made no settlement. During the 17th century various companies of merchants obtained trading charters and established a settlement on the river, which, from 1807, was controlled from Sierra Leone; in 1843 it was made an independent Crown Colony; in 1866 it formed part of the West African Settlements, but in Dec. 1888 it again became a separate Crown Colony. The boundaries were delimited only after 1890. The Gambia achieved full internal self-government on 4 Oct. 1963 and became an independent member of the Commonwealth on 18 Feb. 1965. The Gambia became a republic within the Commonwealth on 24 April 1970. The Gambia with Senegal formed the Confederation of Senegambia on 1 Feb. 1982; this was officially dissolved on 21 Sept. 1989.

In a bloodless coup on 22–23 July 1994 a military junta seized power under the leadership of Lt. Yayah Jammeh; President Jawara left the country. An attempted counter-coup by Vice-President Sana Sabally was foiled in Jan. 1995.

TERRITORY AND POPULATION. The Gambia takes its name from the River Gambia, and consists of a strip of territory never wider than 10 km on both banks. It is bounded in the west by the Atlantic Ocean and on all other sides by Senegal. The land area is 11,295 sq. km. Population (census, 1993), 1,025,867; density, 90 per sq. km.

Growth rate (1993) 4·1%; infant mortality (1991), 134 per 1,000 live births. Expectation of life, 1991, 45 years.

The largest ethnic group is the Mandingo, followed by the Wolofs, Fulas, Jolas and Sarahulis. The country is administratively divided into the capital, Banjul (1983 census 44,188), and the surrounding urban area, Kombo St Mary (101,504), and 5 divisions (with chief town): Lower River (Mansa Konko); MacCarthy Island (Georgetown); North Bank (Kerewan); Upper River (Basse Santa Su); Western (Brikama; population, 19,584 in 1983). Other principal towns are Serekunda (68,433), Bakau (19,309), Sukuta (7,227), Gunjur (7,115) and Farafenni (10,168).

The official language is English.

CLIMATE. The climate is characterized by two very different seasons. The dry season lasts from Nov. to May, when precipitation is very light and humidity moderate. Days are warm but nights quite cool. The SW monsoon is likely to set in with spectacular storms and produces considerable rainfall from July to Oct., with increased humidity. Banjul. Jan. 73°F (22·8°C), July 80°F (26·7°C). Annual rainfall 52" (1,295 mm).

CONSTITUTION AND GOVERNMENT. The 1970 constitution provides for an executive *President* elected directly for renewable 5-year terms. The President appoints a *Vice-President* who is the government's chief minister. There is a single-chamber *House of Assembly* of 50 members: 36 directly-elected, 8 non-voting appointed, 5 chiefs elected by the Chiefs in Assembly and the Attorney-General.

A general election was held on 29 April 1992. The electorate was 338,739; turnout was 55·8%. Sir Dawda Jawara was re-elected President by 58·4% of votes cast against 3 opponents. The People's Progressive Party won 25 seats, the National Convention Party 6, The Gambia People's Party 2 and independents 3.

Presidential and parliamentary elections were scheduled for June 1996.

Following his deposal of the government of Sir Dawda Jawara, Lt. Yayah Jammeh announced a new government on 26 July 1994 headed by a Ruling Military Council.

In Oct. 1995 the government comprised:

President, Chairman of the Ruling Military Council: Captain Yayah Jammeh.

Members of the Ruling Military Council: Captain Edward Singatey (*Vice-President, Minister of Defence*), Captain Yakuba Touray (*Minister of Local Government and Lands*), Captain Monofou Bajo, Captain Ebou Jallow.

Ministers: Interior, Captain Kaba Barjo. *Finance:* Ousman Koro-Ceesay. *Justice:* Mustapha Marong. *Foreign Affairs:* Baboucar Blaise Jagne. *Tourism and Information:* Captain Mamat Omar Cham. *Trade, Industry and Employment:* Bala Garba Jhumpa. *Education, Youth, Sport and Culture:* Satang Jow. *Public Works and Telecommunications:* Mbemba Tambedu. *Agriculture and Natural Resources:* Musa Mbenga. *Health, Social Welfare and Women's Affairs:* Coumba Marenah Ceesay.

National flag: Three wide horizontal stripes of red, blue, green, with narrower stripes of white between them.

National anthem: 'For The Gambia, our homeland'; words by V. J. Howe, tune traditional.

Local Administration. The Gambia is divided into 35 districts, each traditionally under a Chief, assisted by Village Heads and advisers. These districts are grouped into 6 Area Councils containing a majority of elected members, with the Chiefs of the district as *ex-officio* members. The city of Banjul is administered by a City Council. Local elections were scheduled for May 1996.

DEFENCE. The Gambia National Army, 800 strong, has 2 infantry battalions and 1 engineer squadron.

The marine unit of the Army consisted in 1995 of 70 personnel operating 2 ex-Chinese and 1 British-built inshore patrol craft and some boats, based at Banjul.

INTERNATIONAL RELATIONS

Membership. The Gambia is a member of the UN, OAU, Commonwealth, ECOWAS and is an ACP state of the EU.

ECONOMY

Budget. Revenue and expenditure for years ending 30 June are (in 1m. dalasis):

	1988–89	*1989–90*	*1990–91*	*1991–92*
Revenue	565·3	659·6	678·5	807·8
Expenditure	504·8	700·6	644·8	780·6

Currency. The unit of currency is the *dalasi* (GMD), of 100 *bututs.* There are coins of 1, 5, 10, 25 and 50 bututs and 1 dalasi, and notes of 1, 5, 10, 25 and 50 dalasis. Inflation was 5% in 1993. Currency in circulation, 1993, 207·1m. dalasis. Foreign exchange reserves were US$94·03m. in 1992. In March 1996, £1 = 15·05 dalasis; US$1 = 9·85 dalasis; DM1 = 6·67 dalasis.

Banking and Finance. The Central Bank of The Gambia (founded 1971) is the bank of issue. There are 3 commercial banks.

Weights and Measures. The UK imperial system is in common use, but the metric system is being introduced.

ENERGY AND NATURAL RESOURCES

Electricity. Production (1990) 59·5m. kWh.

Minerals. Heavy minerals, including ilmenite, zircon and rutile, have been discovered (1m. tons up to 31 Dec. 1980) in Sanyang, Batokunku and Kartong areas.

Agriculture. About 80% of the population depend upon agriculture, which in 1992 contributed 23·3% of GDP. Almost all commercial activity centres upon the marketing of groundnuts, which is the only export crop of financial significance; in 1991, 85,000 tonnes were produced. Cotton is also exported on a limited scale. Rice is of increasing importance for local consumption; production (1992) 22,000 tonnes.

Livestock (1992, in 1,000): 400 cattle, 150 goats, 121 sheep, 11 pigs and 100 poultry.

Forestry. Forests cover 200,000 ha, 17% of the land area.

Fisheries. Total catch (1986) 10,700 tonnes, of which 2,700 tonnes were from inland waters.

FOREIGN ECONOMIC RELATIONS. Foreign debt was US$379·4m. in 1992.

Commerce. Exports and imports (in 1m. dalasis):

	1987–88	*1988–89*	*1989–90*	*1990–91*
Exports	218·5	316·2	248·2	291·0
Imports	861·6	1,054·2	1,447·3	1,932·7

Chief items of export: Groundnuts, groundnut oil, groundnut cake, cotton lint, fish and fish preparations, hides and skins.

Main export markets, 1992: Belgium, 51·5%; Italy, 19·7%; Japan, 14·3%. Main import suppliers: Hong Kong, 16%; China, 14·8%; UK, 10·1%.

Total trade between the Gambia and UK (British Department of Trade returns, in £1,000 sterling):

	1991	*1992*	*1993*	*1994*	*1995*
Imports to UK	2,865	3,118	5,617	4,638	3,119
Exports and re-exports from UK	19,141	20,092	23,714	16,521	13,591

Tourism. Tourism is The Gambia's biggest foreign exchange earner. In 1990–91, 101,419 tourists visited.

COMMUNICATIONS

Roads. There are 2,990 km of motorable roads, of which 1,718 km rank as all-weather roads including 306 km of bituminous surface and 531 km of laterite gravel. Number of licensed motor vehicles (1985): 5,200 private cars, 700 buses, lorries and coaches, 2,000 motorcycles, scooters and mopeds.

Civil Aviation. There is an international airport at Banjul (Yundum). The national carrier is Gambia Airways. Services are also provided by Air Guinée, Air Mauritanie, Air Sénégal, Ghana Airways, Nigeria Airways, Sabena, Swissair and Transportes Aéreos da Guiné-Bissau.

Shipping. The chief port is Banjul. Ocean-going vessels can travel up the Gambia River as far as Kuntaur. The merchant marine totalled 2,745 GRT in 1995.

Telecommunications. There are several post offices and agencies; postal facilities are also afforded to all river towns. Telephones numbered about 11,000 in 1991.

Radio Gambia, a government station, broadcasts a national programme. There is 1 commercial station. Number of radio receivers (1993, estimate), 180,000.

Cinemas. In 1992 there were 15 cinemas.

Press. There is a government-owned daily; an independent newspaper appears 3 times a week, there is a weekly and several news-sheets.

SOCIAL INSTITUTIONS

Justice. Justice is administered by a Supreme Court consisting of a chief justice and puisne judges. It has unlimited jurisdiction but there is a Court of Appeal. Two magistrates' courts and divisional courts are supplemented by a system of resident divisional magistrates. There are also Moslem courts, group tribunals dealing with cases concerned with customs and traditions, and one juvenile court.

The death penalty was abolished in 1993.

Religion. About 90% of the population is Moslem. Banjul is the seat of an Anglican and a Roman Catholic bishop. There are some Methodist missions. A few sections of the population retain their original animist beliefs.

Education. Adult literacy was 27·2% in 1991. In 1991–92 there were about 600 primary schools, 16 secondary technical schools and 8 high schools. Higher education institutes comprise The Gambia College, a technical training institute, a management institute, a hotel training school, and centres for self-development training, telecommunications training and continuing education.

Health. In 1994 there were 2 hospitals, 1 clinic, 10 health centres and some 60 dispensaries.

DIPLOMATIC REPRESENTATIVES

Of The Gambia in Great Britain (57 Kensington Ct., London, W8 5DG)
High Commissioner: Vacant.

Of Great Britain in The Gambia (48 Atlantic Rd., Fajara, Banjul)
High Commissioner: John Wilde.

Of The Gambia in USA (1030, 15th St, NW, Washington, D.C. 2005)
Ambassador: Vacant.

Of the USA in The Gambia (Fajara (East), Kairaba Ave., Banjul)
Ambassador: Andrew J. Winter.

Of The Gambia to the United Nations
Ambassador: Momodou Jallow.

Further Reading

The Gambia since Independence 1965–1980. Banjul, 1980
Gamble, D. P., *The Gambia.* [Bibliography] Oxford and Santa Barbara (CA), 1988
Hughes, A. and Perfect, D., *Political History of The Gambia, 1816–1992.* Farnborough, 1993

GEORGIA

Sakartvelos Respublika

(Republic of Georgia)

Capital: Tbilisi
Population: 5·43m. (1994)
GNP per capita: US$580 (1993)
HDI/world rank: 0·709/92 (1992)

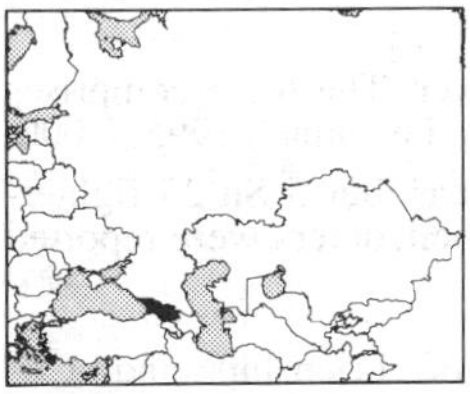

KEY HISTORICAL EVENTS. The independent Georgian Social Democratic Republic was declared on 26 May 1918 by the National Council, elected by the National Assembly of Georgia on 22 Nov. 1917, and was recognized by the RSFSR on 7 May 1920. On 12 Feb. 1921 a rising broke out in Mingrelia, Abkhazia and Adjaria, and Soviet troops invaded the country, which, on 25 Feb. 1921, was proclaimed the Georgian Soviet Socialist Republic. On 15 Dec. 1922 Georgia was merged with Armenia and Azerbaijan to form the Trancaucasian Soviet Federal Socialist Republic. In 1936 the Georgian Soviet Socialist Republic became one of the constituent republics of the USSR. Following nationalist successes at elections in Oct. 1990, the Supreme Soviet resolved in Nov. 1990 to begin a transition to full independence and on 9 April 1991, following a 98·9% popular vote in favour, unanimously declared the republic an independent state based on the treaty of independence of May 1918.

Following an armed insurrection the president elected in May 1991, Zviad Gamsakhurdia, was deposed on 6 Jan. 1992 and a military council took control. After elections in which he gained 95% of votes cast, Eduard Shevardnadze became *de facto* head of state in Oct. 1992.

On 22 Oct. 1993 Georgia joined the CIS by decree of the head of state, Eduard Shevardnadze; parliament ratified this on 1 March 1994.

Supporters of the deposed president Gamsakhurdia were also in intermittent armed conflict with the government, mainly in Mingrelia, but these suffered heavy defeats once Russian support became available after Georgia joined the CIS.

TERRITORY AND POPULATION. Georgia is bounded in the west by the Black Sea and south by Turkey, Armenia and Azerbaijan. Area, 69,700 sq. km (26,900 sq. miles). Its population on 1 Jan. 1994 was 5,429,000 (2·6m. male; 3m. urban). The capital is Tbilisi (1994 population estimate, 1·3m.). Other important towns (with 1991 population estimates) are Kutaisi (235,000), Rustavi (159,000), Batumi (136,000), Sukhumi (121,000), Poti (54,000), Gori (59,000). Vital statistics rates, 1993: Birth, 12·6 per 1,000; death, 10·1 per 1,000; natural increase, 2·5%; infant mortality, 18·3 per 1,000 live births.

Georgians accounted for 70·1% of the 1989 census population of 5,400,841; others included 8·1% Armenians, 6·3% Russians, 5·7% Azerbaijanis, 3% Ossetians, 1·9% Greeks, 1·8% Abkhazians and 1% Ukrainians. Georgia includes the Autonomous Republics of Abkhazia and Adjaria and the former Autonomous Region of South Ossetia.

CONSTITUTION AND GOVERNMENT. A new Constitution of 24 Aug. 1995 defines Georgia as a presidential republic with federal elements. The 225-member parliament is elected by a system combining 75 single-member districts with proportional representation based on party lists. Presidential and parliamentary elections were held on 5 Nov. 1995. Eduard Shevardnadze (b. 1928; Citizens' Union) was re-elected *President* with 74·3% of votes cast against 5 opponents.

National flag: Dark red, with a canton divided black over white.
National anthem: 'Dideba zetsit kurtheuls' ('Praise be to the Heavenly Bestower of Blessings'); words anonymous, tune by K. Potskhverashvili.

Local Government. Local administration was reorganized in Jan. 1991 into prefectures headed by prefects who report to the central government. Prefects may serve a maximum of two 4-year terms. Villages are administered by councils.

DEFENCE. Conscription is for 2 years. An 8-member *Defence Council* headed by the President was set up in Oct. 1992. In 1996 some 22,000 Russian troops were stationed in 3 military bases.

Army. Forces of 20,000 are planned. Equipment includes 40 T-55 and 8 T-72 main battle tanks.

Navy. Former Soviet facilities at Poti have been taken over. The force comprises 2 small frigates, 4 torpedo boats and some 12 patrol vessels. Personnel, 1995, 2,000.

Air Force. In 1995 the status of aviation units was unclear, but 5 Su-25 fighter-bombers, Mi-24 armed helicopters and Mi-8/17 transport helicopters were reported in use. Personnel, 1995, 1,000.

INTERNATIONAL RELATIONS. A Treaty of Frienship and Co-operation was signed with Russia in Feb. 1994.

Membership. Georgia is a member of the UN, CIS and the NATO Partnership for Peace.

ECONOMY

Policy. A privatization programme was inaugurated in 1995.

Currency. In April 1993 coupons were introduced alongside the *ruble*, pending the introduction of a Georgian unit, the *lari*. This latter was introduced on 25 Sept. 1995. No meaningful exchange rates were available in March 1996.

Banking and Finance. The *Governor* of the Central Bank is Nodar Javakhishvili.

ENERGY AND NATURAL RESOURCES

Electricity. The many fast-flowing rivers provide an important hydro-electric resource. Power output in 1993 was 9,700m. kWh.

Oil and Gas. Output (1993) of oil and gas concentrates, 0·1m. tonnes; natural gas, 100m. cu. metres.

Minerals. Manganese deposits are calculated at 250m. tonnes. Other important minerals are coal, barytes, clays, gold, diatomite shale, agate, marble, alabaster, iron and other ores, building stone, arsenic, molybdenum, tungsten and mercury. Output of coal in 1990 was 1m. tonnes.

Agriculture. Land under cultivation was 4·6m. ha in 1986.

Output of main agricultural products (in 1,000 tonnes) in 1993: Grain, 440; tea (1989), 496; potatoes, 190; vegetables, 270; fruit and berries, 184; grapes (1989), 514; meat, 82; milk, 394; eggs, 138m.; wool, 2·9.

Livestock on 1 Jan. 1994: Cattle, 0·9m.; pigs, 0·4m.; sheep and goats, 1m.

Forestry. Forest area, 2·4m. ha.

INDUSTRY. There is a metallurgical plant and a motor works. There are factories for processing tea, creameries and breweries. There are also textile and silk industries.

Production in 1993 (in tonnes): Rolled steel, 0·1m.; fertilizer, 0·06m.; cement, 0·3m.; processed meat, 0·7m.; textiles, 16·6m. cu. metres; footwear, 1·4m. pairs. Total output was valued at 129,000m. rubles in 1993.

Labour. There were 1,959,000 employees in 1993. The average monthly wage in 1993 was 21,720 coupons.

FOREIGN ECONOMIC RELATIONS

Commerce. Total trade between Georgia and UK (British Department of Trade returns, in £1,000 sterling):

	1993	*1994*	*1995*
Imports to UK	283	143	1,185
Exports and re-exports from UK	9,166	6,392	2,842

COMMUNICATIONS

Roads. There were 35,100 km of motor roads in 1990 (31,200 km hard-surfaced).

Railways. Total length was 1,583 km of 1,520 mm gauge in 1993. In 1993, railways carried 5·4m. tonnes of freight and ran 1,000 passenger-km.

Civil Aviation. The national carrier is Orbi.

Shipping. In 1995, sea-going shipping totalled 0·65m. GRT, of which oil tankers accounted for 0·34m. GRT.

Telecommunications. The government-controlled Georgian Radio broadcasts 2 national and 3 regional programmes, and a foreign service, Radio Georgia (English, Russian). There are local independent TV stations in 10 towns.

Press. In 1995 there were 25 dailies and weeklies.

SOCIAL INSTITUTIONS

Religion. The Georgian Orthodox Church has its own organization under Catholicos (patriarch) Ilya II who is resident in Tbilisi.

Education. In 1994, 0·1m. children (28·5% of those eligible) were attending pre-school institutions. In 1993–94 there were 727,000 pupils in 3,200 primary and secondary schools, 30,200 in 76 technical colleges and 91,100 students in 23 higher educational institutions. There is 1 university and 1 technical university, with a total of 34,590 students and 6,464 academic staff in 1994-95.

Health. There were 29,900 doctors and 57,100 hospital beds in 1994.

Welfare. There were 804,000 age, and 355,000 other, pensioners in 1994.

ABKHAZIA

Area, 8,600 sq. km (3,320 sq. miles); population (Jan. 1990), 537,500. Capital Sukhumi (1990 population, 121,700). This area, the ancient Colchis, saw the establishment of a West Georgian kingdom in the 4th century and a Russian protectorate in 1810. In March 1921 a congress of local Soviets proclaimed it a Soviet Republic, and its status as an Autonomous Republic, within Georgia, was confirmed on 17 April 1930 and again by the Georgian Constitution of 1995.

Ethnic groups (1989 census) Georgians, 45·7%, Abkhazians, 17·8%, Armenians, 14·6% and Russians, 14·3%.

In July 1992 the Abkhazian parliament declared sovereignty under the presidency of Vladislav Ardzinba and the restoration of its 1925 constitution. Fighting broke out as Georgian forces moved into Abkhazia. On 3 Sept. and on 19 Nov. ceasefires were agreed, but fighting continued into 1993 and by Sept. Georgian forces were driven out. On 15 May 1994 Georgian and Abkhazian delegates under Russian auspices signed an agreement on a ceasefire and deployment of 2,500 Russian troops as a peacekeeping force.

On 26 Nov. 1994 parliament adopted a new Constitution proclaiming Abkhazian sovereignty.

President: Vladislav Ardzinba (elected by parliament 26 Nov. 1994).

The republic has coal, electric power, building materials and light industries. In 1985 there were 89 collective farms and 56 state farms; main crops are tobacco, tea, grapes, oranges, tangerines and lemons. Crop area 43,900 ha.

Livestock, 1 Jan. 1987: 147,300 cattle, 127,900 pigs, 28,800 sheep and goats.

In 1990–91 16,700 children were attending pre-school institutions. There is a university at Sukhumi with 3,000 students and 270 academic staff in 1995-96. In 1990 there were 2,100 students at colleges and 7,700 students at other institutions of higher education.

In Jan. 1990 there were 2,500 doctors and 6,600 junior medical personnel.

ADJARIA

Area, 3,000 sq. km (1,160 sq. miles); population (Jan. 1990), 382,000. Capital, Batumi (1990 population, 137,300). Adjaria fell under Turkish rule in the 17th century, and was annexed to Russia (rejoining Georgia) after the Berlin Treaty of 1878. On 16 July 1921 the territory was constituted as an Autonomous Republic within the Georgian SSR, a status confirmed by the Georgian Constitution of 1995.

Ethnic groups (1989 census): Georgians, 82·8%, Russians, 7·7% and Armenians 4%.

Acting President: Aslan Abashidze.

Adjaria specializes in sub-tropical agricultural products. These include tea, mandarines and lemons, grapes, bamboo, eucalyptus, etc. Livestock (Jan. 1990): 112,300 cattle, 6,200 pigs, 7,000 sheep and goats. In 1980 there were 69 collective farms and 21 state farms.

There are shipyards at Batumi, modern oil-refining plant (the pipeline from the Baku oilfields ends at Batumi), food-processing and canning factories, clothing, building materials, drug factories, etc.

The population is almost exclusively Sunni Moslem.

In 1990–91 77,239 pupils were engaged in study at all levels.

In Jan. 1990 there were 1,700 doctors and 4,400 junior medical personnel.

SOUTH OSSETIA

Area, 3,900 sq. km (1,505 sq. miles); population (Jan. 1990), 99,800 (ethnic groups at the 1989 census, Ossetians, 66·2% and Georgians, 29%). Capital, Tskhinvali (34,000). This area was populated by Ossetians from across the Caucasus (North Ossetia), driven out by the Mongols in the 13th century. The region was set up within the Georgian SSR on 20 April 1922. Formerly an Autonomous Region, its administrative autonomy was abolished by the Georgian Supreme Soviet on 11 Dec. 1990, and it has been named the Tskhinvali Region.

Fighting broke out in 1990 between insurgents wishing to unite with North Ossetia (in the Russian Federation) and Georgian forces. By a Russo-Georgian agreement of July 1992 Russian peacekeeping forces moved into a 7-km buffer zone between South Ossetia and Georgia pending negotiations.

Main industries are mining, timber, electrical engineering and building materials. Crop area, chiefly grains, was 21,600 ha in 1985; other pursuits are sheepfarming (128,500 sheep and goats on 1 Jan. 1987) and vine-growing. There were 14 collective farms and 18 state farms.

In 1989–90 there were 21,200 pupils in elementary and secondary schools. There were 6,525 children in pre-school insitutions.

In Jan. 1987 there were 511 doctors and 1,400 hospital beds.

DIPLOMATIC REPRESENTATIVES

Of Georgia in Great Britain (45 Avonmore Rd., London W14 8RT)
Ambassador: Teimuraz Mamatsashvili.

Of Great Britain in Georgia (Metechi Palace Hotel, Tbilisi 380003)
Ambassador: Stephen Nash.

Of Georgia in the USA
Ambassador: Tedo Djaparidze.

Of the USA in Georgia (25, Antoneli Street, 380026 Tbilisi)
Ambassador: Kent N. Brown.

Of Georgia to the United Nations
Ambassador: Peter Chkheidze.

Further Reading

Brook, S., *Claws of the Crab: Georgia and Armenia in Crisis.* London, 1992
Lang, D. M., *A Modern History of Georgia.* London, 1962. — *The Georgians.* London, 1966
Nasmyth, P., *Georgia: a Rebel in the Caucasus.* London, 1992
Suny, R. G., *The Making of the Georgian Nation.* 2nd ed. Indiana Univ. Press, 1994

GERMANY

Bundesrepublik Deutschland

(Federal Republic of Germany)

Capital: Berlin
Seat of Government: Bonn/Berlin
Population: 81·34m. (1994)
GNP per capita: US$25,580 (1994)
HDI/world rank: 0·921/15 (1992)

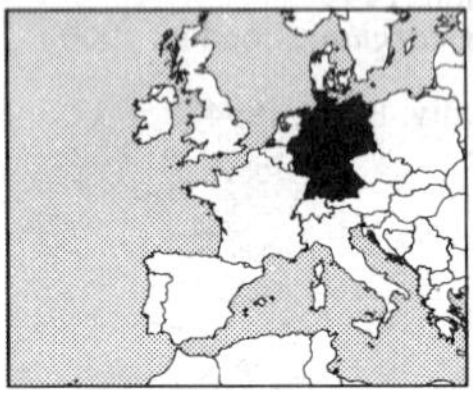

KEY HISTORICAL EVENTS. Following the unconditional surrender of the German armed forces on 8 May 1945 there was no central authority whose writ ran in the whole of Germany, and consequently no peace treaty was signed. France, the USSR, the UK and the USA assumed supreme authority over Germany by the Berlin Declaration of 5 June 1945. Each was allotted an occupation zone, in which the supreme power was to be exercised by the commander-in-chief in that zone (*see* map in THE STATESMAN'S YEAR-BOOK, 1947). Jointly these 4 commanders-in-chief constituted the Allied Control Council in Berlin, which was to be competent in all 'matters affecting Germany as a whole'. The territory of Greater Berlin, divided into 4 sectors, was to be governed as an entity by the 4 occupying powers.

At the Potsdam Conference (July–Aug. 1945) the northern part of the province of East Prussia, including its capital Königsberg (renamed Kaliningrad), was transferred to the USSR, and it was agreed that Poland should administer those parts of Germany east of a line running from the Baltic Sea west of Swinemünde along the river Oder to its confluence with the Western Neisse and thence along the Western Neisse to the Czechoslovak frontier (the 'Oder-Neisse line').

In June 1948 USA, UK and France agreed on a central government for the 3 western zones. An Occupation Statute, which came into force on 30 Sept. 1949, reduced the responsibilities of the occupation authorities. Formally, the Federal Republic of Germany came into existence on 21 Sept. 1949. The Petersberg Agreement of 22 Nov. 1949 freed the Federal Republic of numerous restrictions of the Occupation Statute. In 1951 the USA, the UK and France as well as other states terminated the state of war with Germany; the USSR followed on 25 Jan. 1955. On 5 May 1955 the Paris and London treaties, signed in Oct. 1954, came into force making the Federal Republic of Germany a sovereign independent country.

The eastern zone was administered by the USSR through a military government. A 'People's Chamber' (Volkskammer) was set up which promulgated a Soviet-type constitution in Oct. 1949 and proclaimed the German Democratic Republic. The GDR attained sovereignty in 1954 and obtained *de facto* diplomatic recognition from most countries. In 1961 the GDR built the mined and guarded 'Berlin Wall' to separate East from West Berlin.

In the autumn of 1989 movements for political liberalization and re-unification with Federal Germany gathered strength. Erich Honecker and other long-serving Communist leaders were replaced in Oct.–Nov. The Berlin Wall was opened on 9 Nov.

Following the reforms in the GDR in Nov. 1989 the Federal Chancellor Helmut Kohl issued a plan for German confederation. The ambassadors of the 4 war-time allies met in Berlin in Dec. After talks with Chancellor Kohl on 11 Feb. 1990, President Gorbachev said the USSR had no objection to German re-unification. Allies agreed a formula ('two-plus-four') for re-unification talks to begin after the GDR elections on 18 March. 'Two-plus-four' talks began on 5 May 1990. On 18 May Federal Germany and the GDR signed a treaty transferring Federal Germany's currency, and its economic, monetary and social legislation, to the GDR as of 1 July. On 23 Aug. the Volkskammer by 294 votes to 62 'declared its accession to the jurisdiction of the Federal Republic as from 3 Oct. according to article

23 of the Basic Law', which provided for the Länder of pre-war Germany to accede to the Federal Republic.

On 12 Sept. the Treaty on the Final Settlement with Respect to Germany was signed by Federal Germany, the GDR and the 4 war-time allies: France, the USSR, the UK and the USA. For details *see* THE STATESMAN'S YEAR-BOOK, 1993–94, p. 605.

TERRITORY AND POPULATION. Germany is bounded in the north by Denmark and the North and Baltic Seas, east by Poland, east and south-east by the Czech Republic, south-east and south by Austria, south by Switzerland and west by France, Luxembourg, Belgium and the Netherlands. Area: 356,974 sq. km. Population estimate, 1994: 81,338,093 (41,819,700 females); density, 228 per sq. km. There were 36·23m. households in 1993; 12·38m. were single-person, and 10·96m. had a female principal breadwinner. There were 1·58m. unmarried couple households.

There were some 110,000 Sorbs, a Slav minority, in 1985.

On 14 Nov. 1990 Germany and Poland signed a treaty confirming Poland's existing western frontier and renouncing German claims to territory lost as a result of the Second World War.

The capital is Berlin; after re-unification government offices began to move in phases to Berlin from Bonn.

The Federation comprises 16 Länder (states). Area and population:

Länder	*Area in sq. km*	*Population (in 1,000) 1987 census*	*1994 estimate*	*Density per sq. km*
Baden-Württemberg (BW)	35,751	9,286	10,234	286
Bavaria (BY)	70,554	10,903	11,863	168
Berlin (BE) [1]	889	...	3,475	3,909
Brandenburg (BB) [2]	29,481	...	2,538	86
Bremen (HB)	404	660	683	1,690
Hamburg (HH)	755	1,593	1,703	2,254
Hessen (HE)	21,114	5,508	5,967	283
Lower Saxony (NI)	47,606	7,162	7,648	161
Mecklenburg-West Pomerania (MV) [2]	23,169	...	1,843	80
North Rhine-Westphalia (NW)	34,071	16,712	17,759	521
Rhineland-Palatinate (RP)	19,845	3,631	3,926	198
Saarland (SL)	2,570	1,056	1,085	422
Saxony (SN) [2]	18,409	...	4,608	250
Saxony-Anhalt (ST) [2]	20,446	...	2,778	136
Schleswig-Holstein (SH)	15,739	2,554	2,695	171
Thuringia (TH) [2]	16,175	...	2,533	157

[1] 1987 census population of West Berlin: 2,013,000.
[2] Reconstituted in 1990 in the GDR.

Vital statistics:

	Marriages	*Live births*	*Of these to single parents*	*Deaths*	*Divorces*
1991	454,291	830,019	125,187	911,245	136,484
1992	453,428	809,114	120,448	885,443	135,179
1993	442,605	798,447	118,284	897,270	156,646

Rates (per 1,000 population), 1993: Birth, 9·8; marriage, 5·5; death, 11·1; infant mortality (per 1,000 live births): Stillborn rate, 3·1 per 1,000 births. Expectation of life, 1993: Men, 72·47; women, 79·1.

Legislation of 1995 categorizes abortions as illegal, but stipulates that prosecutions will not be brought if they are performed in the first 3 months of pregnancy after consultation with a doctor.

On 31 Dec. 1993 there were 6,878,100 resident foreigners, including 1,918,400 Turks, 1,239,000 Yugoslavs, 563,000 Italians and 352,000 Greeks. In 1994, 127,210 foreigners sought asylum (322,599 in 1993; 438,191 in 1992). Tighter controls on entry from abroad were applied as from 1993. 199,443 persons were naturalized in 1993. In 1993 there were 796,859 emigrants and 1,268,004 immigrants.

Populations of the 84 towns of over 100,000 inhabitants in 1993 (in 1,000):

Town (and Land)	Population (in 1,000)	Ranking by population	Town (and Land)	Population (in 1,000)	Ranking by population
Aachen (NW)	246·1	33	Kiel (SH)	249·1	32
Augsburg (BY)	265·0	29	Koblenz (RP)	109·9	73
Bergisch Gladbach (NW)	104·6	81	Krefeld (NW)	249·2	31
Berlin (BE)	3,471·5	1	Leipzig (SN)	494·2	13
Bielefeld (NW)	324·4	18	Leverkusen (NW)	161·9	49
Bochum (NW)	400·7	16	Lübeck (SH)	217·1	36
Bonn (NW)	297·9	21	Ludwigshafen am Rhein (RP)	168·2	46
Bottrop (NW)	119·4	67	Magdeburg (ST)	272·4	25
Braunschweig (NI)	257·8	30	Mainz (RP)	185·2	42
Bremen (HB)	552·7	10	Mannheim (BW)	318·8	19
Bremerhaven (HB)	131·7	55	Moers (NW)	106·4	79
Chemnitz (SN)	282·0	23	Mönchengladbach (NW)	265·1	28
Cologne (NW)	961·6	4	Mülheim (NW)	177·4	45
Cottbus (BB)	129·1	56	Munich (BY)	1,256·3	3
Darmstadt (HE)	140·9	52	Münster (NW)	267·0	27
Dortmund (NW)	602·4	7	Neuss (NW)	148·6	50
Dresden (SN)	480·5	15	Nuremberg (BY)	499·8	14
Duisburg (NW)	538·1	11	Oberhausen (NW)	226·3	35
Düsseldorf (NW)	577·6	9	Offenbach am Main (HE)	117·1	69
Erfurt (TH)	202·1	38	Oldenburg (NI)	147·3	51
Erlangen (BY)	102·7	82	Osnabrück (NI)	167·5	47
Essen (NW)	624·6	6	Paderborn (NW)	129·5	56
Frankfurt am Main (HE)	663·6	5	Pforzheim (BW)	117·5	68
Freiburg im Breisgau (BW)	196·7	40	Potsdam (BB)	139·5	54
Fürth (BY)	107·8	76	Recklingshausen (NW)	127·1	61
Gelsenkirchen (NW)	294·8	22	Regensburg (BY)	125·0	62
Gera (TH)	124·1	63	Remscheid (NW)	124·0	64
Göttingen (NI)	128·4	60	Reutlingen (BW)	107·6	77
Hagen (NW)	215·0	37	Rostock (MV)	239·7	34
Halle (ST)	398·1	20	Saarbrücken (SL)	191·3	41
Hamburg (HH)	1,701·6	2	Salzgitter (NI)	117·1	69
Hamm (NW)	183·2	43	Schwerin (MV)	123·5	65
Hanover (NI)	525·3	12	Siegen (NW)	111·8	72
Heidelberg (BW)	139·9	53	Solingen (NW)	166·2	48
Heilbronn (BW)	122·6	66	Stuttgart (BW)	598·0	8
Herne (NW)	180·5	44	Ulm (BW)	114·7	71
Hildesheim (NI)	106·5	78	Wiesbaden (HE)	269·6	26
Ingolstadt (BY)	109·2	75	Witten (NW)	105·7	80
Jena (TH)	100·4	84	Wolfsburg (NI)	128·5	59
Kaiserslautern (RP)	102·1	83	Wuppertal (NW)	387·7	17
Karlsruhe (BW)	278·5	24	Würzburg (BY)	129·2	57
Kassel (HE)	201·2	39	Zwickau (SN)	109·4	74

The official language is German. Minor orthographical amendments were agreed in 1995.

CLIMATE. Oceanic influences are only found in the north-west where winters are quite mild but stormy. Elsewhere a continental climate is general. To the east and south, winter temperatures are lower, with bright frosty weather and considerable snowfall. Summer temperatures are fairly uniform throughout. Berlin. Jan. 31°F (–0·5°C), July 66°F (19°C). Annual rainfall 22·5" (563 mm). Dresden. Jan. 30°F (–0·1°C), July 65°F (18·5°C). Annual rainfall 27·2" (680 mm). Frankfurt. Jan. 33°F (0·6°C), July 66°F (18·9°C). Annual rainfall 24" (601 mm). Hamburg. Jan. 31°F (–0·6°C), July 63°F (17·2°C). Annual rainfall 29" (726 mm). Hanover. Jan. 33°F (0·6°C), July 64°F (17·8°C). Annual rainfall 24" (604 mm). Köln. Jan. 36°F (2·2°C), July 66°F (18·9°C). Annual rainfall 27" (676 mm). Munich. Jan. 28°F (–2·2°C), July 63°F (17·2°C). Annual rainfall 34" (855 mm). Stuttgart. Jan. 33°F (0·6°C), July 66°F (18·9°C). Annual rainfall 27" (677 mm).

CONSTITUTION AND GOVERNMENT. The Basic Law (*Grundgesetz*) was approved by the parliaments of the participating Länder and came into force on

23 May 1949. It is to remain in force until 'a constitution adopted by a free decision of the German people comes into being'.

The Federal Republic is a democratic and social constitutional state on a parliamentary basis. The federation is constituted by the 16 Länder (states). The Basic Law decrees that the general rules of international law form part of the federal law. The constitutions of the Länder must conform to the principles of a republican, democratic and social state based on the rule of law. Executive power is vested in the Länder, unless the Basic Law prescribes or permits otherwise. Federal law takes precedence over state law.

Legislative power is vested in the *Bundestag* (Federal Assembly) and the *Bundesrat* (Federal Council). The Bundestag is composed of 672 members and is elected in universal, free, equal and secret elections for a term of 4 years. A party must gain 5% of total votes cast in order to gain representation in the Bundestag. The electoral system combines relative-majority and proportional voting; each voter has 2 votes, the first for the direct constituency representative, the second for the competing party lists in the Länder. If a party wins more seats on the first vote than its share on the second vote the number of seats is increased by the difference ('overhang votes'). The Bundesrat consists of 79 members appointed by the governments of the Länder in proportions determined by the number of inhabitants. Each Land has at least 3 votes.

The Head of State is the Federal *President* who is elected for a 5-year term by a *Federal Convention* specially convened for this purpose. This Convention consists of all the members of the Bundestag and an equal number of members elected by the Länder parliaments in accordance with party strengths, but who need not themselves be members of the parliaments. No president may serve more than 2 terms.

Executive power is vested in the Federal Government, which consists of the Federal *Chancellor*, elected by the Bundestag on the proposal of the Federal President, and the Federal Ministers, who are appointed and dismissed by the Federal President upon the proposal of the Federal Chancellor.

The Federal Republic has exclusive legislation on: (1) foreign affairs (2) federal citizenship; (3) freedom of movement, passports, immigration and emigration, and extradition; (4) currency, money and coinage, weights and measures, and regulation of time and calendar; (5) customs, commercial and navigation agreements, traffic in goods and payments with foreign countries, including customs and frontier protection; (6) federal railways and air traffic; (7) post and telecommunications; (8) the legal status of persons in the employment of the Federation and of public law corporations under direct supervision of the Federal Government; (9) trade marks, copyright and publishing rights; (10) co-operation of the Federal Republic and the Länder in the criminal police and in matters concerning the protection of the constitution, the establishment of a Federal Office of Criminal Police, as well as the combating of international crime; (11) federal statistics.

In the field of finance the Federal Republic has exclusive legislation on customs and financial monopolies and concurrent legislation on: (1) excise taxes and taxes on transactions, in particular, taxes on real-estate acquisition, incremented value and on fire protection; (2) taxes on income, property, inheritance and donations; (3) real estate, industrial and trade taxes, with the exception of the determining of the tax rates. The Federal Republic can claim part of the income and corporation taxes to cover its expenditures not covered by other revenues. Financial jurisdiction is uniformly regulated by federal legislation.

Federal laws are passed by the Bundestag and after their adoption submitted to the Bundesrat, which has a limited veto. The Basic Law may be amended only upon the approval of two-thirds of the members of the Bundestag and two-thirds of the votes of the Bundesrat.

On 23 May 1994 Roman Herzog was elected President by the Federal Convention against 4 opponents.

Bundestag elections were held on 16 Oct. 1994; turn-out was 79·1%. The Christian Democratic Union/Christian Social Union (CDU/CSU; the CSU is a Bavarian party where the CDU does not stand) won 294 seats with 41·5% of votes cast (319 with 43·8% in 1990); the Social Democratic Party (SPD), 252 with 36·4% (239 with 33·5%); the Greens, 49 with 7·3% (8 with 5·1%); the Free Democratic Party (FDP), 47 seats with 6·9% (79 with 11%); the Party for Democratic Socialism (PDS; former Communists), 30 with 4·4% (17 with 2·4%).

Federal President: Roman Herzog (b. 1934; sworn in 1 July 1994).
Speaker of the Bundestag: Rita Süssmuth (elected Nov. 1988; re-elected Nov. 1994).

In Feb. 1996 the government comprised:

Chancellor: Dr Helmut Kohl (b. 1930; CDU).
Deputy Chancellor and Foreign Minister: Dr Klaus Kinkel (FDP). *Special Tasks and Head of the Federal Chancellery:* Friedrich Bohl (CDU). *Interior:* Manfred Kanther (CDU). *Justice:* Eduard Schmidt-Jortzig (FDP). *Finance:* Dr Theo Waigel (CSU). *Economy:* Dr Günter Rexrodt (FDP). *Food, Agriculture and Forestry:* Jochen Borchert (CDU). *Labour and Social Affairs:* Dr Norbert Blüm (CDU). *Defence:* Volker Rühe (CDU). *Family, Youth, Women and Senior Citizens:* Claudia Nolte (CDU). *Health:* Horst Seehofer (CSU). *Transport:* Matthias Wissman (CDU). *Environment, Nature Conservation and Reactor Safety:* Dr Angela Merkel (CDU). *Posts and Telecommunications:* Wolfgang Bötsch (CSU). *Regional Planning, Housing and Urban Development:* Dr Klaus Töpfer (CDU). *Education and Science, Research and Technology:* Dr Jürgen Rüttgers (CDU). *Economic Cooperation and Development:* Carl-Dieter Spranger (CSU).

National flag: 3 horizontal stripes of black, red, gold.
National anthem: 'Einigkeit und Recht und Freiheit' ('Unity and right and freedom'); words by H. Hoffmann, tune by J. Haydn.

European Parliament. Germany has 99 representatives. At the June 1994 elections turn-out was 58%. The SPD won 40 seats with 32·2% of votes cast (group in European Parliament: European Socialist Party); the CDU, 39 with 32% (Popular European Party); the Greens, 12 with 10·1% (Greens); the CSU, 8 with 6·8% (Popular European Party).

Local Government. The 16 Länder are divided into a total of 29 administrative regions (*Regierungsbezirke*). Below *Land* level local government is carried on by elected councils to 426 rural districts *(Landkreise)* and 117 urban districts *(Kreisfreie Städte)*, which form the electoral districts for the *Land* governments, and are subdivided into 16,043 communes *(Gemeinden)*.

Die Bundesrepublik Deutschland: Staatshandbuch. Cologne, annual
Hucko, E. M. (ed.) *The Democratic Tradition* [Texts of German constitutions]. Leamington Spa, 1987
Koch, J. W., *A Constitutional History of Germany in the Nineteenth and Twentieth Centuries.* London, 1984
König, K. *et al.* (eds.) *Public Administration in the Federal Republic of Germany.* Boston (MA), 1983

DEFENCE. Russian (ex-Soviet) forces had withdrawn from the territory of the former GDR by 1994.

Conscription is for 10 months. In July 1994, the Constitutional Court ruled that German armed forces might be sent on peacekeeping missions abroad.

Army. The Army is organized in the Army Forces Command, comprising 1 airmobile division with 3 airborne brigades, 3 army aviation brigades, 1 signals/electronic intelligence brigade and 1 support brigade; and 8 military district commands grouped in 3 corps—2 with armoured divisions and 1 with an armed infantry division (I Corps: German-Netherlands), 2 with armoured divisions and 1 with a mountain division (II Corps), and 2 with armoured infantry divisions (IV Corps). The 8 military district commands control 6 armoured, 12 armoured infantry and 1 mountain brigade, and the German element of the German-French brigade. 1 armoured division is earmarked for Eurocorps. Corps units comprise 2 armoured reconnaissance battalions, 3 air defence regiments and 3 helicopter regiments.

Equipment includes 731 Leopard 1A5 and 1,964 Leopard 2 main battle tanks and 1,511 surface-to-air missiles. The equipment of the former East German army is in store. An air component operates 205 BO 105P anti-armour helicopters, 107 CH-53G and 175 UH-1D Iroquois transport helicopters, as well as 40 Alouette II and 95 BO 105M liaison/observation helicopters. The Territorial Army is organized into 5 Military Districts, under 3 Territorial Commands. Its main task is to defend rear areas and remains under national control even in wartime. Total strength was (1996) 254,300 (conscripts 122,800).

Navy. The Fleet Commander operates from a modern Maritime Headquarters at Glücksburg, close to the Danish border.

The fleet includes 20 diesel coastal submarines, 3 US-built guided-missile destroyers, 10 frigates including 2 new guided-missile ships and 36 fast missile craft. There is a mine-warfare force of 42 vessels, comprising 32 coastal minesweepers and hunters, of which 10 are new combined minelayer/hunters and 6 control ships for TROIKA minesweeping drones, 5 inshore minesweepers and 1 diver support ship. Major auxiliaries include 4 repair ships, 4 transport oilers, 4 minesweeper/patrol craft support and HQ ships, 3 logistic transports, 8 large tugs, 3 intelligence collectors and 2 trial ships. There are several dozen minor auxiliaries and service craft.

The main naval bases are at Wilhelmshaven, Bremerhaven, Kiel, Eckenförde and Warnemünde.

The Naval Air Arm, 4,500 strong, is organized into 3 wings and comprises 55 missile-armed Tornado strike aircraft. 16 Atlantic long range, 17 shore-based Sea King helicopters, 17 Lynx (12 frigate-based) and 1 Do-228 anti-pollution patrol aircraft are also in use.

Procurement of 2 further new frigates and 4 further replacement mine warfare craft is in hand. Personnel in 1995 numbered 28,500.

Air Force. Since 1970, the *Luftwaffe* has comprised the following commands: German Air Force Tactical Command, German Air Force Support Command (including two German Air Force Regional Support Commands—North and South) and General Air Force Office. Personnel in 1995 was 75,300 (18,700 conscripts). Combat units, including 12 heavy fighter-bomber squadrons with Tornados and F-4Fs, 8 surface-to-surface missile squadrons, and an air defence force of 6 interceptor squadrons with F-4Fs and MiG-29s, 24 batteries of *Nike-Hercules* and 36 batteries of *Improved Hawk* surface-to-air missiles, are assigned to NATO. 3 wings operating both Transall C-160 aircraft and UH-1D Iroquois helicopters add to the air mobility of the *Bundeswehr*. There are also VIP, support and light transport aircraft. About 12 L-410 and Tu-154 transports and Mi-8 helicopters from the GDR air force are still in use, the Tu-154s being assigned to arms control surveillance duties. Guided weapons in service include 8 squadrons of *Pershing* surface-to-surface missiles and 6 battalions of *Nike-Hercules* and 9 battalions of *Improved Hawk* surface-to-air missiles.

INTERNATIONAL RELATIONS. A treaty of friendship with Poland signed on 17 June 1991 recognized the Oder-Neisse border and guaranteed minorities' rights in both countries.

Membership. Germany is a member of the UN, OECD, EU, WEU, NATO and the Council of Europe. The Schengen Accord, which abolishes border controls between Germany, Austria, Belgium, France, Greece, Italy, Luxembourg, the Netherlands, Portugal and Spain, came into effect on 26 March 1995. Austria, Italy and Greece are to implement it later.

ECONOMY

Budget. Since 1 Jan. 1979 tax revenues have been distributed as follows: Federal Government. Income tax, 42·5%; capital yield and corporation tax, 50%; turnover tax, 67·5%; trade tax, 15%; capital gains, insurance and accounts taxes, 100%; excise duties (other than on beer), 100%. Länder. Income tax, 42·5%; capital yield and corporation tax, 50%; turnover tax, 32·5%; trade tax, 15%; other taxes, 100%. Local authorities. Income tax, 15%; trade tax, 70%; local taxes, 100%.

VAT is 15% (reduced rate, 7%).

Budgets for 1994 and 1995 (in DM1m.):

	All public authorities		*Federal portion*	
Revenue	*1994*	*1995*	*1994*	*1995*
		Current		
Taxes	700,763	1,313,656	382,286	360,338
Economic activities	24,404	36,486	17,427	16,413
Interest	6,086	19,419	2,119	2,610
Current allocations and subsidies	139,861	414,066	3,163	3,585
Other receipts	19,323	120,642	6,663	7,778
minus equalising payments	117,382	385,937	...	...
	773,055	1,518,332	411,658	390,454
		Capital		
Sale of assets	3,197	13,025	2,036	953
Allocations for investment	22,067	60,184	6	4
Repayment of loans	11,282	14,744	3,726	3,367
Public sector borrowing	817	1,807	...	...
minus equalising payments	20,635	55,007	...	...
	16,728	34,753	5,768	4,324
Totals	*789,820*	*1,553,085*	*417,426*	*394,778*
Expenditure		*Current*		
Staff	221,399	355,739	52,234	52,713
Materials	85,114	378,945	41,141	41,749
Interest	106,877	102,921	52,769	45,800
Allocations and subsidies	497,596	1,033,465	280,405	255,148
minus equalising payments	117,382	385,937	...	...
	793,602	1,485,133	426,549	395,409
		Capital		
Construction	23,409	77,993	10,887	9,992
Acquisition of property	7,566	24,832	2,263	2,476
Allocations and subsidies	88,260	112,089	32,686	39,702
Loans	39,784	32,550	18,201	12,859
Acquisition of shares	2,780	5,581	1,640	1,319
Repayments in the public sector	663	1,911	...	...
minus equalising payments	20,635	55,007	...	...
	141,827	199,748	65,677	66,347
Totals	*927,156*	*1,684,881*	*487,076*	*461,756*

Currency. The unit of currency is the *deutsche Mark* (DEM) of 100 *pfennig* (pf.). There are coins of 1, 2, 5, 10 and 50 pf. and DM 1, 2, 5 and 10, and notes of DM 5, 10, 20, 50, 100, 200, 500 and 1,000. Money in circulation in 1993, DM 236,165m.

Foreign exchange reserves in 1994 were DM 60,208m.; gold reserves were DM 13,688m. Inflation was an annualized 4·2% in 1993 (4% in 1992). In March 1996, £1 = DM 2·26; US$1 = DM 1·48.

Banking and Finance. The Deutsche Bundesbank (German Federal Bank) is the central bank and bank of issue. Its duty is to protect the stability of the currency. It is independent of the government but obliged to support the government's general policy. Its Governor is appointed by the government for 8 years. The *Governor* is Hans Tietmayer (b.1931). Its assets were DM 356,483m. in 1994. The largest private banks are the Deutsche Bank, Dresdner Bank and Commerzbank. The former GDR central bank Staatsbank has become a public commercial bank. In 1994 there were 3,727 credit institutes, including 336 banks, 657 savings banks, 33 mortgage banks and 2,666 credit societies. They are represented in the wholesale market by the Länder banks. Total assets, 1994, DM 6,952,822m. Savings deposits were DM 959,360m. in 1994.

A single stock exchange, the Deutsche Börse, was created in 1992, based on the former Frankfurt stock exchange in a union with the smaller exchanges in Berlin, Bremen, Düsseldorf, Hamburg, Hanover, Munich and Stuttgart.

Gull, L. *et al.*, *The Deutsche Bank, 1870-1995*. London, 1996
Marsh, D., *The Bundesbank: the Bank that Rules Europe*. London, 1992

Weights and Measures. The metric system is in force.

ENERGY AND NATURAL RESOURCES

Electricity. In 1993 there were 21 nuclear reactors producing 34% of electricity output. In 1993 output was 452,728,000 mWh, of which 153,476,000 mWh were nuclear and 19,779,000 mWh hydro-electric. There is a moratorium on further nuclear plant construction.

Oil and Gas. The chief oilfields are in Emsland (Lower Saxony). In 1994, 2·93m. tonnes of crude oil were produced. Gas production was 836,194,000 mWh in 1993, of which 765,305,000 mWh were natural gas.

Minerals. The main production areas are: North Rhine-Westphalia (for coal, iron and metal smelting-works), Central Germany (for lignite), and Lower Saxony (Salzgitter for iron ore; the Harz for metal ore).

Production (in tonnes), 1994: Coal, 52,402,762; lignite, 207,180,513.

Agriculture. Land in agricultural use, 1994 (in 1,000 ha): 17,307·7, including arable, 11,805·3; pasture, 5,270·7. Sown areas included: Wheat, 2,434·9; rye, 722·5; barley, 2,069·5; oats, 391·9; maize, 345·4; potatoes, 293·4; sugar-beet, 500·0; rape, 1,057·6; fodder, 1,721·4. Crop production, 1994 (and 1993) (in 1,000 tonnes): Wheat, 16,480·5 (15,766·6); rye, 3,450·6 (2,983·6); barley, 10,902·5 (11,005·7); oats, 1,663·0 (1,730·6); maize, 2,446·0 (2,656·5); potatoes, 9,668·6 (12,260·3); sugar-beet, 24,211·3 (28,605·8); rape, 2,895·5 (2,847·7); fodder, 52,187·9 (64,443·5).

In 1994 there were 578,033 farms, of which 72,887 were under 2 ha and 18,278 over 100 ha. In 1993 there were 600,400 farmers assisted by 669,300 household members and 306,700 hired labourers (98,000 seasonal). *In the former GDR* in 1990 state farms have been leased to farmers until 2004 and will then be sold. Collective farms have continued operating as co-operatives or been turned over to their former members.

In 1994 wine production was 10,303,000 hectolitres.

Livestock, 1994 (in 1,000): Cattle, 16,022·9 (including milch cows, 5,191·6); sheep, 2,881·5; pigs, 25,435·7; horses, 598·8; poultry, 101,139. Livestock products, 1994 (in 1,000 tonnes): Milk, 27,866; meat, 4,968·5. 1992: Eggs, 15,525m. units.

Forestry. Forest area in 1992 was 8,033,600 ha, of which 4,419,200 ha were owned by the State. Timber production was 28·3m. cu. metres in 1993 and 27·8m. cu. metres in 1992.

In recent years depredation has occurred through pollution with acid rain.

Fisheries. In 1994 the yield of sea fishing was 143,527 tonnes live weight. The fishing fleet consisted of 54 ocean-going vessels and 2,367 coastal cutters.

INDUSTRY. Public limited companies are managed on the 'co-determination' principle, and have 3 statutory bodies: a board of directors, a works council elected by employees, and a supervisory council which includes employee representatives but has an in-built management majority.

In 1993 there were 67,014 firms (with 20 and more employees) employing 9·4m. persons, made up of 371,000 in energy and water services, 195,000 in mining, 1·4m. in raw materials processing, 4·01m. in the manufacture of producers' goods, 1·35m. in the manufacture of consumer goods, 587,000 in food and tobacco production and 1·44m. in building.

Output of major industrial products, 1994 (in 1,000 tonnes): Cement, 40,217; pig-iron, 29,923; crude steel, 40,837; rolled steel, 26,691; aluminium, 2,042; copper, 1,926; nitrogenous fertilizers, 1,199; plastics, 11,307; glassware, 4,882; cotton yarn,

108; synthetic fibre, 85; flour, 3,651; paper, 12,015; passenger cars, 3,497,000 (units); refrigerators, 3,794,000; beer, 116·27m. hectolitres.

Labour. Retirement age is 63 years. In 1993 the workforce was 40·18m. (17·09m. females), of whom 3·8m. (2·01m. females) were unemployed and 36·38m. (15·08m. females) working. In 1994 there were 3·06m. self-employed, 2·32m. officials and 22·91m. employees. 2·99m. foreign workers and 0·85m. females were employed in 1993. Major categories (1994): Manufacturing industries, 10·37m.; services, 6·12m.; commerce and transport, 5·51m.; agriculture, forestry and fishing, 0·83m. In 1994 there were 284,753 unfilled vacancies and 372,288 workers on short time. There were 5·46m. part-time workers in 1993.

Trade Unions. The majority of trade unions belong to the *Deutscher Gewerkschaftsbund* (DGB, German Trade Union Federation), which had 9·8m. (3·02m. women) members in 1994, including 6·02m. (1·2m.) manual workers, 2·78m. (1·53m.) white-collar workers and 762,695 (178,461) officials. DGB unions are organized in industrial branches such that only one union operates within each enterprise. Outside the DGB are several smaller unions: The *Deutscher Beamtenbund* (DBB) or public servants' union with 1,089,213 (322,411) members, the *Deutsche Angestellten-Gewerkschaft* (DAG) or union of salaried staff with 520,709 (277,917) members and the *Christlicher Gewerkschaftsbund Deutschlands* (CGD, Christian Trade Union Federation of Germany) with 306,481 (74,566) members. The official GDR trade union organization (FDGB) was merged in the Deutscher Gewerkschaftsbund.

Strikes are not legal unless called by a union with the backing of 75% of members. Certain public service employees are contractually not permitted to strike. 229,436 working days were lost through strikes in 1994, 592,995 in 1993.

FOREIGN ECONOMIC RELATIONS

Commerce. Imports and exports in DM 1m.:

Imports				*Exports*			
1991	*1992*	*1993*	*1994*	*1991*	*1992*	*1993*	*1994*
643,914	637,546	566,495	611,138	665,813	671,203	628,387	685,267

Most important trading partners in 1994 (trade figures in DM 1m.) Imports: France, 67,653; Netherlands, 50,090; Italy, 51,592; Belgium with Luxembourg, 37,459; UK, 38,134; USA, 44,442; Japan, 33,999. Exports: France, 82,192; Italy, 51,891; Netherlands, 51,447; UK, 54,753; Belgium with Luxembourg, 45,868; USA, 54,159; Austria, 39,739; Switzerland, 37,067.

Distribution by commodities in 1994 (in DM 1m.) Imports and exports: Live animals, 621 and 942; foodstuffs, 53,769 and 29,489; drinks and tobacco, 10,149 and 7,206; raw materials, 33,124 and 6,957; semi-finished goods, 55,931 and 34,857; finished goods, 440,759 and 603,576.

Total trade between Germany and UK (British Department of Trade returns, in £1,000 sterling):

	1991	*1992*	*1993*	*1994*
Imports to UK	17,741,093	19,034,628	18,349,100	20,862,400
Exports and re-exports from UK	14,653,972	15,060,073	14,641,300	16,389,100

Tourism. In 1994 there were 50,095 places of accommodation with 2,128,352 beds (including 12,170 hotels with 762,400 beds). In 1994 there were 13,364,000 foreign visitors.

COMMUNICATIONS

Roads. In 1994 the total length of classified roads was 227,200 km, including 11,080 km of motorway *(Autobahn)*, 41,995 km of federal highways, 88,054 km of first-class and 88,054 km of second-class country roads. On 1 Jan. 1995 there were 46·8m. motor vehicles, including (in 1,000): Passenger cars, 39,918; lorries, 2,168; buses, 87·4; motorcycles, 2,121. In 1993 7,919m. passengers were transported by long-distance road traffic, and 3,629·6m. tonnes of freight.

Road casualties in 1994 (and 1993) totalled 516,019 injured (505,591) and 9,805 killed (9,949).

Railways. Legislation of 1993 provides for the eventual privatization of the railways. On 1 Jan. 1994 West German Bundesbahn and the former GDR Reichsbahn were amalgamated as the Deutsche Bahn, a joint-stock company in which track, long-distance passenger traffic, regional passenger traffic and goods traffic are run as 4 separate administrative entities. These are intended after 3–5 years to become themselves companies, at first under a holding company, and ultimately independent. Initially the government will hold all the shares. Length of railway in 1994 was 40,355 km (1,435 mm gauge) of which 17,015 km were electrified, and 148 km of narrow gauge. 1,508m. passengers and 309m. tonnes of freight were carried in 1994.

There are metros in Berlin (136 km), Hamburg (95 km), Frankfurt am Main (51 km), Munich (63 km) and Nuremberg (23 km), and tram/light rail networks in 55 cities.

Civil Aviation. Lufthansa, the national carrier, was set up in 1953 and is 36% state-owned. In 1995 it operated 11 A300B4-600s, 12 A312-300s, 33 A320-200s, 10 A321-100s, 6 A340-200s, 8 A340-300s, 19 B-737-200 Advs, 39 B-737-300s, 7 B-737-300QCs, 6 B-737-400s, 30 B-737-500s, 4 B-747-200Bs, 3 B-747-200B Combis, 10 B-747-400s, 7 B-747-400 Combis, 1 A310-200, 3 B-737-300s, 17 B-757-200s, 1 B-757-200ER, 8 B-767-300ERs and 5 DC-10-30s. Other airlines include Condor, Deutsche-British Airways and LTU International.

In 1994 civil aviation had 440 aircraft over 20 tonnes (388 jets). In 1993 there were 47·08m. passenger arrivals and 47·4m. departures. 30·58m. passengers were carried to destinations abroad. International airports: Cologne-Bonn, Düsseldorf, Frankfurt am Main, Hamburg (Fuhlsbuttel), Hanover, Leipzig, Munich, Nuremberg, Stuttgart and 3 at Berlin (Tegel, Tempelhof and Schönefeld).

Shipping. In 1993 the mercantile marine comprised 872 ocean-going vessels of 4,918,000 GRT. Sea-going ships in 1993 carried 184m. tonnes of cargo.

Navigable rivers have a total length of 4,842 km; canals, 2,087 km. The inland-waterways fleet on 31 Dec. 1993 included 1,676 motor freight vessels totalling 1·68m. tonnes and 387 tankers of 530,673 tonnes. 218·33m. tonnes of freight were transported in 1993.

Telecommunications. Telecommunications were deregulated in 1989. On 1 Jan. 1995, 3 state-owned joint-stock companies were set up: Deutsche Telekom, Postdienst and Postbank.

In 1993 there were 20,000 post offices, 37m. telephones and 1·28m. fax transmitters. 2,202,000 mobile telephones were in use in 1994.

The national public broadcasters Deutschlandfunk, RIAS Berlin and Deutschlandsender Kultur form part of the *Nationaler Hörfunk.* The foreign service, Deutsche Welle, broadcasts in 30 languages, and there is a commercial European service. There are 12 regional radio and TV networks (colour by PAL). The *Arbeitsgemeinschaft der öffentlich-rechtlichen Rundfunkanstalten der Bundesrepublik Deutschland* (ARD) represents public-right broadcasters and organizes co-operation between them and also broadcasts a federal-wide TV programme of its own. There is another public TV channel, ZDF, and 4 commercial TV networks, as well as a sport channel, a pay-TV film channel and Deutsche Telekom's cable network. In 1993 there were 40m. radio and 30·5m. TV sets in use.

Cinemas. In 1993 there were 3,709 cinemas with a total seating capacity of 745,704. 67 feature films were made in 1993.

Press. 67,206 book titles were published in 1993, of which 49,096 were new works. In 1992, 392 newspapers and 9,010 periodicals were published with respective circulations of 31·3m. and 395m. In 1993 there were 1,325 academic and special libraries, and 13,474 public libraries, the latter with 9·12m. users.

SOCIAL INSTITUTIONS

Justice. Justice is administered by the federal courts and by the courts of the Länder. In criminal procedures, civil cases and procedures of non-contentious jurisdiction the courts on the Land level are the local courts *(Amtsgerichte)*, the regional courts *(Landgerichte)* and the courts of appeal *(Oberlandesgerichte)*. Constitutional federal disputes are dealt with by the Federal Constitutional Court *(Bundesverfassungsgericht)* elected by the Bundestag and Bundesrat. The Länder also have constitutional courts. In labour law disputes the courts of the first and second instance are the labour courts and the Land labour courts and in the third instance, the Federal Labour Court *(Bundesarbeitsgericht)*. Disputes about public law in matters of social security, unemployment insurance, maintenance of war victims and similar cases are dealt with in the first and second instances by the social courts and the Land social courts and in the third instance by the Federal Social Court *(Bundessozialgericht)*. In most tax matters the finance courts of the Länder are competent and in the second instance, the Federal Finance Court *(Bundesfinanzhof)*. Other controversies of public law in non-constitutional matters are decided in the first and second instance by the administrative and the higher administrative courts *(Oberverwaltungsgerichte)* of the Länder, and in the third instance by the Federal Administrative Court *(Bundesverwaltungsgericht)*.

For the inquiry into maritime accidents the admiralty courts *(Seeämter)* are competent on the Land level and in the second instance the Federal Admiralty Court *(Bundesoberseeamt)* in Hamburg.

The death sentence has been abolished.

Religion. In 1993 there were 28,460,000 Protestants in (in 1992) 18,216 parishes, 27,552,000 Roman Catholics in 13,329 parishes, and in 1994 47,172 Jews with 12 rabbis and 53 synagogues.

There are 5 Roman Catholic archbishoprics (Bamberg, Cologne, Freiburg, Munich and Freising, Paderborn) and 23 bishoprics. Chairman of the German Bishops' Conference is Cardinal Joseph Höffner, Archbishop of Cologne. A concordat between Germany and the Holy See dates from 10 Sept. 1933.

The Evangelical (Protestant) Church (EKD) consists of 24 member-churches including 7 Lutheran Churches, 8 United-Lutheran-Reformed, 2 Reformed Churches and 1 Confederation of United member Churches: 'Church of the Union'. Its organs are the Synod, the Church Conference and the Council under the chairmanship of Bishop Dr Eduard Lohse (Hanover). There are also some 12 Evangelical Free Churches.

Education. Education is compulsory for children aged 6 to 15. After the first 4 (or 6) years at primary school *(Grundschulen)* children attend post-primary *(Hauptschulen)*, secondary modern *(Realschulen)*, grammar *(Gymnasien)*, or comprehensive schools *(Integrierte Gesamtschulen)*. Secondary modern school comprises 6, grammar school 9, years. Entry to higher education is by the final Grammar School Certificate (Abitur-Higher School Certificate). There are special schools *(Sonderschulen)* for handicapped or maladjusted children.

In 1993–94 there were 4,044 kindergartens with 84,757 pupils and 5,357 teachers, 17,911 primary schools with 3,475,055 pupils and 210,834 teachers and 8,585 post-primary schools with 1,478,228 pupils and 99,899 teachers. There were also 3,389 special schools with 371,880 pupils and 59,129 teachers, 3,527 secondary modern schools with 1,106,182 pupils and 59,453 teachers; 3,143 grammar schools with 2,115,847 pupils and 146,659 teachers; 956 comprehensive schools with 523,804 pupils and 49,583 teachers.

Vocational education is provided in part-time, full-time and advanced vocational schools (*Berufs-, Berufsaufbau-, Berufsfach-* and *Fachschulen*, including *Fachschulen für Technik* and *Schulen des Gesundheitswesens*). Occupation-related, part-time vocational training of 6 to 12 hours per week is compulsory for all (including unemployed) up to the age of 18 years or until the completion of the practical vocational training. Full-time vocational schools comprise courses of at least one year. They prepare for commercial and domestic occupations as well as specialized occupations in the field of handicrafts. Advanced full-time vocational schools are attended by pupils over 18. Courses vary from 6 months to 3 or more years.

In 1993–94 there were 9,069 full- and part-time vocational schools with 2,449,083 students and 105,363 teachers.

Higher Education. In 1994–95 there were 325 institutes of higher education (*Hochschulen*) with 1,856,542 students including 82 universities (1,222,158 students), 7 polytechnics (*Gesamtschulen*; 142,480), 6 teacher training colleges (14,787), 17 theological seminaries (2,770), 46 schools of art (29,660), 136 technical institutes (392,392) and 31 colleges of management (52,295).

Health. In 1994 there were 267,186 doctors, 59,211 dentists, and 43,822 pharmacists. In 1993 there were 2,354 hospitals (including 162 psychiatric) with 628,658 beds.

Welfare. *Social Health Insurance* (introduced in 1883). Wage-earners and apprentices, salaried employees with an income below a certain limit and social insurance pensioners are compulsorily insured. Voluntary insurance is also possible.

Benefits: Medical treatment, medicines, hospital and nursing care, maternity benefits, death benefits for the insured and their families, sickness payments and out-patients' allowances. Economy measures of Dec. 1992 introduced prescription charges related to recipients' income.

50·6m. persons were insured in 1994 (30·4m. compulsorily) and 14·66m. persons (including 9·1m. women) were drawing pensions. Number of cases of incapacity for work (1993) totalled 36·86m., and the number of working days lost were 316·7m. (men) and 246·13m. (women). Total disbursements, DM 211,781m.

Accident Insurance (introduced in 1884). Those insured are all persons in employment or service, apprentices and the majority of the self-employed and the unpaid family workers.

Benefits in the case of industrial injuries and occupational diseases: Medical treatment and nursing care, sickness payments, pensions and other payments in cash and in kind, surviving dependants' pensions.

Number of insured in 1993, 51·84m.; number of current pensions, 1,187,999; total disbursements, DM 23,349m.

Workers' and Employees' Old-Age Insurance Scheme (introduced in 1889). All wage-earners and salaried employees, the members of certain liberal professions and—subject to certain conditions—self-employed craftsmen are compulsorily insured. The insured may voluntarily continue to insure when no longer liable to do so or increase the insurance.

Benefits: Measures designed to maintain, improve and restore the earning capacity; pensions paid to persons incapable of work, old age and surviving dependants' pensions.

Number of insured in 1993, 44·55m. (21·29m. women); number of current pensions, 19·18m.; pensions to widows and widowers, 5m. Total disbursements, DM 342,741m.

There are also special retirement and unemployment pension schemes for miners and farmers, assistance for war victims and compensation payments to members of German minorities in East European countries expelled after the Second World War and persons who suffered damage because of the war or in connexion with the currency reform.

Family Allowances. DM 16,580m. were dispensed to 7·87m. recipients (0·78m. foreigners) in 1994 on behalf of 12·88m. children. Paid child care leave is available for 3 years to mothers or fathers.

Unemployment Allowances. In 1994 1·91m. persons (0·91m. women) were receiving unemployment benefit and 0·95m. (0·42m. women) earnings-related benefit. Total expenditure on these and similar benefits (e.g. short-working supplement, job creation schemes) was DM 99,864m. in 1994.

Public Welfare (introduced in 1962). In 1993 DM 48·02m. were distributed to 4·72m. recipients (2·52m. women).

Public Youth Welfare. For supervision of foster children, official guardianship, assistance with adoptions and affiliations, social assistance in juvenile courts, educational assistance and correctional education under a court order. Total expenditure in 1993, DM 24,480m.

DIPLOMATIC REPRESENTATIVES

Of Germany in Great Britain (23 Belgrave Sq., London, SW1X 8PZ)
Ambassador: Jürgen Oesterhelt.

Of Great Britain in Germany (Friedrich-Ebert-Allee 77, 5300 Bonn 1)
Ambassador: Vacant.

Of Germany in the USA (4645 Reservoir Rd, NW, Washington, D.C., 20007)
Ambassador: Jürgen Chrobog.

Of the USA in Germany (Deichmanns Ave., 5300, Bonn)
Ambassador: Charles E. Redman.

Of Germany to the United Nations
Ambassador: Tono Eitel.

Further Reading

Statistisches Bundesamt. *Statistisches Jahrbuch für die Bundesrepublik Deutschland; Wirtschaft und Statistik* (monthly, from 1949); *Das Arbeitsgebiet der Bundesstatistik* (latest issue 1988; Abridged English version: *Survey of German Federal Statistics*).

Ardagh, J., *Germany and the Germans.* 2nd ed. London, 1991
Balfour, M., *Germany: the Tides of Power.* London, 1992
Bark, D. L. and Gress, D. R., *A History of West Germany, 1945–1991.* 2nd ed. 2 vols. Oxford, 1993
Betz, H. G., *Postmodern Politics in Germany.* London, 1991
Carr, W., *A History of Germany, 1815-1990.* 4th ed. London, 1991
Childs, D., *Germany in the 20th Century.* London, 1991
Dennis, M., *German Democratic Republic.* London, 1987
Detwiler, D. S. and Detwiler, I. E., *West Germany.* [Bibliography] Oxford and Santa Barbara, 1988
Edinger, L. J., *West German Politics.* New York, 1986
Eley, G., *From Unification to Nazism: Reinterpreting the German Past.* London, 1986
Fulbrook, M., *A Concise History of Germany.* CUP, 1991.—*The Divided Nation: a History of Germany, 1918–1990.* CUP, 1992
Huelshoff, M. G. *et al.* (eds.) *From Bundesrepublik to Deutschland: German Politics after Reunification.* Michigan Univ. Press, 1993
Marsh, D., *The New Germany: at the Crossroads.* London, 1990
Marshall, B., *The Origins of Post-War German Politics.* London, 1988
Orlow, D., *The History of Modern Germany, 1871 to the Present.* 3rd ed. New York, 1994
Pulzer, P., *German Politics, 1945-1995.* OUP, 1995
Schmidt, H., *Handeln für Deutschland.* Berlin, 1993
Schweitzer, D.-C., (ed.) *Politics and Government in the Federal Republic of Germany: Basic Documents.* 2nd ed. Oxford, 1994
Sinn, G. and Sinn, H.-W., *Jumpstart: the Economic Reunification of Germany.* Boston (MA), 1993
Smyser, W. R., *The Economy of United Germany: Colossus at the Crossroads.* New York, 1992
Stürmer, M., *Die Grenzen der Macht.* Berlin, 1992
Thompson, W. C. *et al., Historical Dictionary of Germany.* Metuchen (NJ), 1995
Turner, H. A., *Germany from Partition to Reunification.* 2nd ed. [of *Two Germanies since 1945*]. Yale Univ. Press, 1993
Wallace, I., *East Germany: the German Democratic Republic.* [Bibliography]. Oxford and Santa Barbara (CA), 1987
Watson, A., *The Germans: Who Are They Now?* 2nd ed. London, 1994

Other more specialized titles are listed under CONSTITUTION AND GOVERNMENT *and* BANKING AND FINANCE, *above.*

National statistical office: Statistiches Bundesamt, 62 Wiesbaden 1, Gustav Stresemann Ring 11. *President:* Hans Günther Merk.

National libraries: Deutsche Bibliothek, Zeppelinallee 4–8; Frankfurt-am-Main. *Director:* K.-D. Lehmann; (Berliner) Staatsbibliothek Preussischer Kulturbesitz, Potsdamer Str., Postfach 1407 D-1000 Berlin 30. *Director:* Dr. Richard Landwehrmeyer.

THE LÄNDER

BADEN–WÜRTTEMBERG

TERRITORY AND POPULATION. Baden-Württemberg comprises 35,752 sq. km, with a population (at 31 Dec. 1994) of 10,272,069 (5,022,585 males, 5,249,484 females).

The Land is divided into 4 administrative regions, 9 urban and 35 rural districts, and numbers 1,111 communes. The capital is Stuttgart.

Vital statistics for calendar years:

	Live births	*Marriages*	*Divorces*	*Deaths*
1992	117,559	60,724	17,289	95,977
1993	117,982	59,885	19,108	98,572
1994	113,398	59,591	19,910	96,638

CONSTITUTION. The Land Baden-Württemberg is a merger of the 3 Länder, Baden, Württemberg-Baden and Württemberg-Hohenzollern, which were formed in 1952. The merger was approved by a plebiscite held on 9 Dec. 1951, when 70% of the population voted in its favour. It has 6 seats in the Bundesrat.

At the elections to the 136-member Diet of April 1992, turn-out was 70·2%. The Christian Democrats won 64 seats with 39·6% of the vote, the Social Democrats 46 with 29·4%, the Republicans 15 with 10·9%, the Greens 13 with 9·5% and the Free Democrats 8 with 5·9%.

Erwin Teufel (CDU) is *Prime Minister* (Minister President).

AGRICULTURE. Area and yield of the most important crops:

	Area (in 1,000 ha)			*Yield (in 1,000 tonnes)*		
	1992	*1993*	*1994*	*1992*	*1993*	*1994*
Rye	13·1	14·0	14·0	65·5	71·4	67·2
Wheat	206·1	199·1	204·7	1,273·9	1,290·5	1,226·4
Barley	195·6	193·5	194·6	1,033·4	1,044·0	926·8
Oats	58·2	58·2	63·4	258·1	316·1	294·1
Potatoes	10·9	9·7	9·7	365·0	370·4	294·1
Sugar-beet	24·5	24·1	22·5	1,359·6	1,495·6	1,252·0

Livestock in 1,000 (3 Dec. 1994): Cattle, 1,410·6 (including 503·3 milch cows); pigs, 2,250·5; sheep, 281·1; poultry, 5,570.

INDUSTRY. In 1994, 9,280 establishments (with 20 and more employees) employed 1,293,178 persons; of these, 243,295 were employed in machine construction (excluding office machines, data processing equipment and facilities); 44,446 in the textile industry; 255,407 in electrical engineering; 189,716 in car manufacture.

LABOUR. Economically active persons totalled 4,744,200 at the 1%-EC-sample survey of April 1994. Of the total 517,700 were self-employed (including familyworkers), 4·23m. employees; 139,100 were engaged in agriculture and forestry; 2,080,300 in power supply, mining, manufacturing and building, 743,400 in commerce and transport, 1,781,400 in other industries and services.

ROADS. On 1 Jan. 1995 there were 28,068 km of 'classified' roads, including 1,020 km of autobahn, 5,004 km of federal roads, 10,011 km of first-class and 12,033 km of second-class highways. Motor vehicles, at 1 Jan. 1995, numbered 6,312,715, including, 5,331,131 passenger cars, 9,706 buses, 238,716 lorries, 324,087 tractors and 320,942 motor cycles.

JUSTICE. There are a constitutional court *(Staatsgerichtshof)*, 2 courts of appeal, 17 regional courts, 108 local courts, a Land labour court, 9 labour courts, a Land social court, 8 social courts, a finance court, a higher administrative court *(Verwaltungsgerichtshof)*, 4 administrative courts.

RELIGION. On 1 Jan. 1995, 39·4% of the population were Protestants and 44% were Roman Catholics.

EDUCATION. In 1994–95 there were 2,658 primary schools *(Grund- und Hauptschulen)* with 34,025 teachers and 646,120 pupils; 544 special schools with 8,969 teachers and 48,025 pupils; 447 intermediate schools with 11,273 teachers and 193,921 pupils; 409 high schools with 18,639 teachers and 251,767 pupils; 35 *Freie Waldorf* schools with 1,287 teachers and 17,771 pupils. Other general schools together had 640 teachers and 8,785 pupils; there were also 724 vocational schools with 359,806 pupils. There were 39 *Fachhochschulen* (colleges of engineering and others) with 58,439 students in winter term 1993–94.

In the winter term 1993–94 there were 9 universities (Freiburg, 23,282 students; Heidelberg, 27,981; Konstanz, 9,582; Tübingen, 25,473; Karlsruhe, 20,665; Stuttgart, 20,969; Hohenheim, 5,269; Mannheim, 12,921; Ulm, 6,081); 6 teacher-training colleges with 16,153 students; 5 colleges of music with 2,895 students and 3 colleges of fine arts with 1,129 students.

Statistical Information: Statistisches Landesamt Baden-Württemberg (P.O.B. 10 60 33, 70049 Stuttgart) (*President:* Dr Eberhard Leibing), publishes: '*Baden-Württemberg in Wort und Zahl*' (monthly); *Jahrbücher für Statistik und Landeskunde von Baden-Württemberg; Statistik von Baden-Württemberg* (series); *Statistisch-prognostischer Bericht* (latest issue 1995); *Statistisches Taschenbuch* (latest issue 1995).

State libraries: Württembergische Landesbibliothek, Konrad-Adenauer-Str. 8, 70173 Stuttgart. Badische Landesbibliothek Karlsruhe, Lamm-Str. 16, 76133 Karlsruhe 1.

BAVARIA

Bayern

TERRITORY AND POPULATION. Bavaria has an area of 70,546 sq. km. The capital is Munich. There are 7 administrative regions, 25 urban districts, 71 rural districts, 266 unadopted areas and 2,056 communes, 1,021 of which are members of 325 administrative associations. The population (31 Dec. 1994) numbered 11,921,944 (5,815,965 males, 6,105,979 females).

Vital statistics for calendar years:

	Live births	*Marriages*	*Divorces*	*Deaths*
1992	133,946	72,247	20,686	120,753
1993	133,897	70,475	23,011	122,649
1994	127,828	69,401	23,087	121,581

CONSTITUTION. The Constituent Assembly, elected on 30 June 1946, passed a constitution on the lines of the democratic constitution of 1919, but with greater emphasis on state rights; this was agreed upon by the Christian Social Union (CSU) and the Social Democrats (SPD). Bavaria has 6 seats in the Bundesrat. The CSU replaces the Christian Democratic Party in Bavaria.

At the Diet elections on 25 Sept. 1994 the CSU won 120 seats with 52·8% of votes cast; the SPD, 70 with 30·1%, and Alliance 90/The Greens, 14 with 6·1%. The *Prime Minister* is Dr Edmund Stoiber (CSU).

AGRICULTURE. Area and yield of the most important products:

	Area (in 1,000 ha)			*Yield (in 1,000 tonnes)*		
	1992	*1993*	*1994*	*1992*	*1993*	*1994*
Wheat	478·3	453·0	446·1	3,014·5	2,715·0	2,873·0
Rye	50·4	59·8	67·3	255·2	302·1	332·2
Barley	465·0	454·5	457·0	2,442·5	2,259·4	2,339·5
Oats	89·0	88·3	92·5	374·4	433·1	386·9
Potatoes	69·0	61·5	58·7	2,380·2	2,415·4	1,932·7
Sugar-beet	81·0	80·4	78·2	4,816·6	5,018·1	4,494·5

Livestock (3 Dec. 1994): 4,296,512 cattle (including 1,594,176 milch cows); 98,922 horses; 370,063 sheep; 3,722,308 pigs; 10,518,366 poultry.

INDUSTRY. In 1994, 8,802 establishments (with 20 or more employees) employed 1,260,512 persons; of these, 233,905 were employed in electrical engineering; 164,351 in mechanical engineering; 73,190 in clothing and textile industries.

LABOUR. The economically active persons totalled 5,771,400 at the 1% sample survey of the microcensus of 1994. Of the total, 622,500 were self-employed, 187,300 unpaid family workers, 4,961,700 employees; 2,260,300 in power supply, mining, manufacturing and building; 1,000,400 in commerce and transport; 2,201,100 in other industries and services.

ROADS. There were, on 1 Jan. 1995, 41,591 km of 'classified' roads, including 2,162 km of autobahn, 7,029 km of federal roads, 13,822 km of first-class and 18,578 km of second-class highways. Number of motor vehicles, at 1 July 1995, was 7,755,074, including 6,281,948 passenger cars, 301,611 lorries, 14,144 buses, 589,733 tractors, 458,306 motor cycles.

JUSTICE. There are a constitutional court *(Verfassungsgerichtshof)*, a supreme Land court *(Oberstes Landesgericht)*, 3 courts of appeal, 22 regional courts, 72 local courts, 2 Land labour courts, 11 labour courts, a Land social court, 7 social courts, 2 finance courts, a higher administrative court *(Verwaltungsgerichtshof)*, 6 administrative courts.

RELIGION. At the census of 25 May 1987 there were 67·2% Roman Catholics and 23·9% Protestants.

EDUCATION. In 1994–95 there were 2,833 primary schools with 45,671 teachers and 810,066 pupils; 378 special schools with 6,841 teachers and 52,161 pupils; 332 intermediate schools with 9,089 teachers and 133,600 pupils; 396 high schools with 20,736 teachers and 293,378 pupils; 244 part-time vocational schools with 7,954 teachers and 281,631 pupils, including 49 special part-time vocational schools with 737 teachers and 10,012 pupils; 574 full-time vocational schools with 4,105 teachers and 52,349 pupils including 252 schools for public health occupations with 1,241 teachers and 15,943 pupils; 361 advanced full-time vocational schools with 2,552 teachers and 26,993 pupils; 84 vocational high schools *(Berufsoberschulen, Fachoberschulen)* with 2,010 teachers and 27,275 pupils.

In the winter term 1994–95 there were 11 universities with 188,695 students (Augsburg, 14,809, Bamberg, 8,248; Bayreuth, 8,438; Eichstätt, 3,669; Erlangen–Nürnberg, 25,952; München, 59,739; Passau, 8,641; Regensburg, 16,324; Würzburg, 20,270; the Technical University of München, 19,983; München University of the Federal Armed Forces (Universität der Bundeswehr), 2,622); the college of politics, München, 759; the college of philosophy, München, 353, and 2 philosophical-theological colleges with together 404 students (Benediktbeuern, 130; Neuendettelsau, 274). There were also 2 colleges of music, 2 colleges of fine arts and 1 college of television and film, with together 2,379 students; 16 vocational colleges *(Fachhochschulen)* with 62,757 students including one for the civil service *(Bayerische Beamtenfachhochschule)* with 6,727 students.

Statistical Information: Bayerisches Landesamt für Statistik und Datenverarbeitung, Neuhauser Str. 8, 80331 Munich, was founded in 1833. *President:* Rudolf Giehl. It publishes: *Statistisches Jahrbuch für Bayern.* 1894 ff.—*Bayern in Zahlen.* Monthly (from Jan. 1947).—*Zeitschrift des Bayerischen Statistischen Landesamts.* July 1869–1943; 1948 ff.—*Beiträge zur Statistik Bayerns.* 1850 ff.—*Statistische Berichte.* 1951 ff.— *Schaubilderhefte.* 1951 ff.—*Kreisdaten.* 1972 ff.—*Gemeindedaten.* 1973 ff.

Nawiasky, H. and Luesser, C., *Die Verfassung des Freistaates Bayern vom 2. Dez. 1946.* Munich, 1948; supplement, by H. Nawiasky and H. Lechner, Munich, 1953

State Library: Bayerische Staatsbibliothek, Munich. *Director:* Dr Hermann Leskin.

BERLIN

KEY HISTORICAL EVENTS. Greater Berlin was under 4-power (France,

USSR, UK and USA) Allied government (the *Kommandatura*) from 5 June 1945 until 1 July 1948, when the Soviet element withdrew. On 30 Nov. 1948 a separate municipal government was set up in the Soviet sector. The French, UK and US sectors coalesced to form the administrative unit of 'West Berlin', covering 480 sq. km. With the establishment of the German Democratic Republic, the Soviet sector ('East Berlin', 403 sq. km) was designated its capital.

East and West Berlin were amalgamated on the re-unification of Germany in Oct. 1990, and Berlin was declared the national capital. All except 6 federal ministries are scheduled to move to Berlin from Bonn in phases by 2000.

TERRITORY AND POPULATION. The area is 889 sq. km. Population, 1994, 3,461,724 (52·1% female), including 413,604 foreign nationals; density, 3,898 per sq. km.

Vital statistics for calendar years:

	Live births	*Marriages*	*Divorces*	*Deaths*
1991	30,562	18,130	6,113	43,654
1992	29,667	17,895	6,644	42,004
1993	28,724	17,111	6,557	41,273

In April 1994 the Land governments of Berlin and Brandenburg agreed to merge the 2 Länder in 1999 or 2002, subject to the approval of their respective parliaments, and of their electorates in referendums scheduled for May 1996

CONSTITUTION AND GOVERNMENT. According to the constitutions of Sept. 1950 and Oct. 1995, Berlin is simultaneously a Land of the Federal Republic and a city. It is governed by a House of Representatives (of at least 150 members); executive power is vested in a Senate, consisting of the Governing Mayor, the Mayor and not more than 16 senators.

Berlin has 5 seats in the Bundesrat.

At the elections of 22 Oct. 1995 the Christian Democrats (CDU) won 87 seats in the House of Representatives with 37·4% of votes cast; the Social Democrats (SPD), 55, with 23·6%; the Party of Democratic Socialism (former Communists), 34, with 14·6%; and the Alliance '90/Greens, 30, with 13·2%.

In Jan. 1996 a CPU-SPD coalition government was formed.

Governing Mayor: Eberhard Diepgen (CDU).

INDUSTRY. In 1995 the main industries in terms of percentage of the labour force employed were: Electronics, 31·3%; food and tobacco, 13%; machine-building, 10·4%; chemicals, 8·5%; vehicle production, 6·6%; metallurgy, 6·3%; printing, 3·8%. There were some 25,000 business enterprises.

LABOUR. In 1995 the workforce was 1·6m., including 0·26m. craft workers. There were 203,924 persons registered unemployed in 1993 and 15,198 on short time. 11,454 jobs were available.

ROADS. In 1993 there were 5,169 km of roads, including 64 km of autobahn and 191 km of federal roads. At Dec. 1994, 1,535,924 motor vehicles were registered, including 1,238,897 passenger cars, 94,688 lorries and buses, and 73,697 motor cycles. There were 26,089 road accidents in 1993.

JUSTICE. There are a court of appeal *(Kammergericht)*, a regional court, 9 local courts, a Land Labour court, a labour court, a Land social court, a social court, a higher administrative court, an administrative court and a finance court.

EDUCATION. In 1993–94 there were 477,655 pupils attending schools. There were 476 schools providing general education with 212,771 pupils, 122 vocational schools with 76,575 pupils and 94 special schools with 13,650 pupils. In 1994–95, there were 2 universities and 1 technical university, 4 art colleges and 9 technical colleges. There was a total of some 147,000 students in higher education.

Statistical Information: The Statistisches Landesamt Berlin was founded in 1862 (Alt-Friedrichsfelde 60, 10315 Berlin (Lichtenberg)). *Director:* Prof. Günther Appel. It publishes: *Statistisches Jahrbuch* (from 1867): *Berliner Statistik* (monthly, from 1947).—*100 Jahre Berliner Statistik* (1962).

State Library: Amerika-Gedenkbibliothek-Berliner Zentralbibliothek-, Blücherplatz 1, D1000 Berlin 61. *Director:* Dr Klaus Bock.

BRANDENBURG

TERRITORY AND POPULATION. The area is 29,480 sq. km. Population on 31 Dec. 1994 was 2,536,747 (1,293,943 females). There are 4 urban districts, 14 rural districts and 1,696 communes. The capital is Potsdam.

Vital statistics for calendar years:

	Live births	*Marriages*	*Divorces*	*Deaths*
1992	29,238	7,901	1,687	29,352
1993	12,238	7,901	3,341	29,024
1994	12,443	8,502	3,851	28,490

For the proposed merger with Berlin *see* BERLIN: Territory and Population.

CONSTITUTION AND GOVERNMENT. The Land was reconstituted on former GDR territory on 14 Oct. 1990. Brandenburg has 4 seats in the Bundesrat.

At the Diet elections on 11 Sept. 1994 the Social Democrats (SPD) won 52 seats with 54·1% of the vote; the Christian Democrats (CDU), 18, with 18·7%; the Party of Democratic Socialism (PDS, former Communists), 18, with 18·7%. At a referendum on 14 June 1992, 93·5% of votes cast were in favour of a new constitution guaranteeing direct democracy and the right to work and housing.

At the *local government* elections of Dec. 1993 the SPD won 34·53% of votes cast, the PDS 21·23%, the CDU 20·4%, the FDP 7·1% and the Greens, 4·2%.

The *Prime Minister* is Dr Manfred Stolpe (SPD).

AGRICULTURE. Livestock at 3 Dec. 1994: Cattle, 698,294 (including 226,367 milch cows); horses, 17,605; pigs, 761,594; sheep, 122,291; poultry, 5,842,016.

Area and yield of the most important crops:

	Area (in 1,000 ha)			*Yield (in 1,000 tonnes)*		
	1992	*1993*	*1994*	*1992*	*1993*	*1994*
Rye	153·6	163·4	173·2	364·0	528·4	665·2
Wheat	114·7	102·8	94·9	410·6	513·2	507·5
Barley	143·2	119·0	93·5	458·3	395·0	459·5
Oats	15·5	15·2	17·4	22·9	64·7	53·7
Potatoes	31·4	19·6	15·8	488·0	583·0	304·0
Sugar-beet	16·0	16·5	13·5	546·3	826·2	453·0

INDUSTRY. In 1994, 963 establishments (20 and more employees) employed 106,196 persons; of these, 20,326 were employed in mining; 5,413 in machine construction; 9,572 in electrical engineering; 6,155 in chemical industries.

LABOUR. In April 1994 at the 1%-sample of the microcensus, 1,097,800 persons were economically active, including 76,800 self-employed and family assistants, 473,100 manual and 522,600 white-collar workers, and 25,400 civil servants. In Dec. 1994 there were 161,222 unemployed persons.

ROADS. In Jan. 1995 there were 1,181,980 passenger cars, 91,595 lorries, 2,971 buses and 29,690 motorcycles.

EDUCATION. In 1994–95 there were 1,167 schools providing general education (including special schools) with 400,854 pupils, and (1991–92) 49 vocational schools with 48,340 pupils.

In the winter term 1994–95 there were 3 universities and 8 colleges with 17,121 students.

BREMEN

Freie Hansestadt Bremen

TERRITORY AND POPULATION. The area of the Land, consisting of the 2 urban districts and ports of Bremen and Bremerhaven, is 404 sq. km. Population, 31 Dec. 1993, 683,096 (328,906 males, 354,190 females).

Vital statistics for calendar years:

	Live births	*Marriages*	*Divorces*	*Deaths*
1991	6,789	4,264	1,636	8,601
1992	6,757	4,005	1,437	8,275
1993	6,656	3,969	1,736	8,643

CONSTITUTION. Political power is vested in the 100-member House of Burgesses *(Bürgerschaft)* which appoints the executive, called the Senate. Bremen has 3 seats in the Bundesrat.

At the elections of 14 May 1995 the Social Democratic Party won 37 seats with 33·4% of votes cast (41 with 38·8% in 1991); the Christian Democrats, 37 with 32·6% (32 with 30·7%); the Alliance '90/Greens, 14 with 13·1% (11 with 11·4%) and the AFB, 12 with 10·7%. The Free Democrats gained no seats with 3·4% (10 with 9·5%). The Senate president is Klaus Wedemeier (Social Democrat).

AGRICULTURE. Agricultural area comprised (1992) 9,900 ha. Livestock (3 Dec. 1992): 14,041 cattle (including 3,928 milch cows); 3,095 pigs; 467 sheep; 1,059 horses; 19,318 poultry.

INDUSTRY. In 1993, 354 establishments (20 and more employees) employed 77,828 persons; of these, 6,575 were employed in shipbuilding (except naval engineering); 6,467 in machine construction; 10,027 in electrical engineering; 2,065 in coffee and tea processing.

LABOUR. The economically active persons totalled 295,100 at the microcensus of April 1993. Of the total, 23,900 were self-employed, 271,200 employees; 68,600 in commerce and transport, 131,200 in other industries and services; 92,900 in power supply, mining, manufacturing and building, and 2,000 in agriculture and fishing.

ROADS. On 1 Jan. 1992 there were 108 km of 'classified' roads, including 46 km of autobahn and 62 km of federal roads. Registered motor vehicles on 1 Jan. 1994 numbered 323,566, including 287,987 passenger cars, 15,373 trucks, 2,692 tractors, 692 buses and 11,909 motor cycles.

SHIPPING. Vessels entered in 1993, 7,841 of 37·02m. net tons; cleared, 7,861 of 37,013,000 net tons. Sea traffic, 1993, incoming 17·17m. tonnes; outgoing, 11·19m. tonnes.

JUSTICE. There are a constitutional court *(Staatsgerichtshof)*, a court of appeal, a regional court, 3 local courts, a Land labour court, 2 labour courts, a Land social court, a social court, a finance court, a higher administrative court, an administrative court.

RELIGION. On 25 May 1987 (census) there were 61% Protestants and 10% Roman Catholics.

EDUCATION. In 1993 there were 393 new system schools with 5,327 teachers and 66,920 pupils; 30 special schools with 582 teachers and 2,848 pupils; 26 part-time vocational schools with 20,043 pupils; 27 full-time vocational schools with 4,102 pupils; 8 advanced vocational schools (including institutions for the training of technicians) with 897 pupils; 10 schools for public health occupations with 870 pupils.

In the winter term 1993–94, 17,627 students were enrolled at the university. In addition to the university there were 4 other colleges in 1993–94 with 9,412 students.

Statistical Information: Statistisches Landesamt Bremen (An der Weide 14–16 (P.B. 101309), D28195 Bremen), founded in 1850. *Director:* Reg. Dir. Jürgen Dinse. Its current publications include: Statistisches Jahrbuch.—*Statistische Mitteilungen Freie Hansestadt Bremen* (from 1948).—*Monatliche Zwischenberichte* (1949–53); *Statistische Monatsberichte* (from 1954).—*Statistische Berichte* (from 1956).—*Statistisches Handbuch für das Land Freie Hansestadt Bremen (1950–60,* 1961; *1960–64,* 1967; *1965–69,* 1971; *1970–74,* 1975; *1975–80,* 1982; *1981–85,* 1987).—*Bremen im statistischen Zeitvergleich 1950–1976.* 1977.—*Bremen in Zahlen.* 1994.

State and University Library: Bibliotheks Str., D28359 Bremen. *Director:* Annette Rath-Beckmann.

HAMBURG

Freie und Hansestadt Hamburg

TERRITORY AND POPULATION. Total area, 755·3 sq. km (1993), including the islands Neuwerk and Scharhörn (7·6 sq. km). Population (31 Dec. 1993), 1,702,900 (818,300 males, 884,600 females). The Land forms a single urban district (*kreisfreie Stadt*) with 7 administrative subdivisions.

Vital statistics for calendar years:

	Live births	*Marriages*	*Divorces*	*Deaths*
1991	16,503	9,241	4,361	21,434
1992	16,497	9,006	4,028	20,444
1993	16,257	8,575	4,303	20,703

CONSTITUTION. The constitution of 6 June 1952 vests the supreme power in the House of Burgesses *(Bürgerschaft)* of 121 members. The executive is in the hands of the Senate, whose members are elected by the Bürgerschaft. Hamburg has 3 seats in the Bundesrat.

The elections of 19 Sept. 1993 had the following results: Social Democrats, 58 seats with 40·4% of votes cast; Christian Democrats, 36 with 25·1%; Green Alternatives 19, with 13·5%; Statt Partei, 8 with 5·6%. The First Burgomaster is Dr Henning Voscherau (Social Democrat).

AGRICULTURE. The agricultural area comprised 14,723 ha in 1993. Yield, 1993, in tonnes, of cereals, 18,121; potatoes, 699.

Livestock (3 Dec. 1992): Cattle, 9,926 (including 1,814 milch cows); pigs, 4,335; horses, 2,754; sheep, 2,233; poultry, 13,330.

INDUSTRY. In June 1994, 712 establishments (with 20 and more employees) employed 119,071 persons; of these, 16,964 were employed in electrical engineering; 16,288 in machine construction; 13,886 in aeronautics; 13,003 in chemical industry; 7,528 in mineral oil industry; 6,029 in shipbuilding (except naval engineering).

LABOUR. The economically active persons totalled 788,700 at the 1%-sample survey of the microcensus of April 1992. Of the total, 86,900 were self-employed or unpaid family workers, 701,700 were employees; 7,400 were engaged in agriculture and forestry, 188,900 in power supply, mining, manufacturing and building, 219,900 in commerce and transport, 372,500 in other industries and services.

ROADS. On 31 Dec. 1993 there were 3,894 km of roads, including 81 km of autobahn, 150 km of federal roads. Number of motor vehicles (1 July 1994), 803,430, including 713,919 passenger cars, 41,492 lorries, 1,673 buses, 5,442 tractors, 27,790 motor cycles and 13,114 other motor vehicles.

SHIPPING. Hamburg is the largest sea port in Germany.

Vessels		*1990*	*1991*	*1992*
Entered:	Number	12,893	12,917	12,767
	Tonnage	57,170,182	57,943,559	59,665,418
Cleared:	Number	12,828	12,982	12,893
	Tonnage	56,785,708	58,131,608	59,681,929

JUSTICE. There is a constitutional court *(Verfassungsgericht)*, a court of appeal *(Oberlandesgericht)*, a regional court *(Landgericht)*, 6 local courts *(Amtsgerichte)*, a Land labour court, a labour court, a Land social court, a social court, a finance court, a higher administrative court, an administrative court.

RELIGION. On 25 May 1987 (census) Evangelical Church and Free Churches 50·2%, Roman Catholic Church 8·6%.

EDUCATION. In 1992 there were about 357 schools of general education (not including *Internationale Schule*) with 11,710 teachers and 158,512 pupils; 58 special schools with 1,264 teachers and 7,399 pupils; 46 part-time vocational schools with 39,262 pupils; 5 schools with 544 pupils in their vocational preparatory year; 23 schools with 2,161 pupils in manual instruction classes; 41 full-time vocational schools with 7,591 pupils; 10 economic secondary schools with 2,353 pupils; 2 technical *Gymnasien* with 441 pupils; 21 advanced vocational schools with 4,322 pupils; 39 schools for public health occupations with 2,588 pupils; 5 vocational introducing schools with 130 pupils and 28 technical superior schools with 1,901 pupils; all these vocational and technical schools have a total number of 3,319 teachers.

In the summer term 1993 there was 1 university with 43,490 students; 1 technical university with 2,026 students; 1 college of music and 1 college of fine arts with together 1,593 students; 1 university of the *Bundeswehr* with 2,040 students; 1 university of economics and political sciences with 2,369 students; 3 professional colleges with a total of 16,462 students.

Statistical Information: The Statistisches Landesamt der Freien und Hansestadt Hamburg (Steckelhörn 12, D20457 Hamburg 11) publishes: *Hamburg in Zahlen, Statistische Berichte, Statistisches Taschenbuch, Statistik des Hamburgischen Staates.*

Hamburgische Gesellschaft für Wirtschaftsförderung. *Hamburg.* Oldenburg, 1993
Klessmann, E., *Geschichte der Stadt Hamburg.* Hamburg, 1981
Möller, I., *Hamburg-Länderprofile.* Hamburg, 1985
Schubert, D. and Harms, H., *Wohnen am Hafen.* Hamburg, 1993
Schütt, E. C., *Die Chronik Hamburgs.* Hamburg, 1991

State Library: Staats- und Universitätsbibliothek, Carl von Ossietzky, Von-Melle-Park 3, D20146 Hamburg 13. *Director:* Prof. Dr Horst Gronemeyer.

HESSEN

TERRITORY AND POPULATION. Area, 21,114 sq. km. Its capital is Wiesbaden. There are 3 administrative regions with 5 urban and 21 rural districts and 426 communes. Population, 31 Dec 1994, was 5,980,693 (2,927,269 males, 3,053,424 females).

Vital statistics for calendar years:

	Live births	*Marriages*	*Divorces*	*Deaths*
1992	61,146	36,601	11,609	63,308
1993	61,610	35,070	12,852	64,028
1994	60,565	35,215	13,697	63,385

CONSTITUTION. The constitution was put into force by popular referendum on 1 Dec. 1946. Hessen has 4 seats in the Bundesrat. At the Diet elections on 19 Feb. 1995 the Christian Democrats gained 39·2% of votes cast, the Social Democrats 38%, the Alliance 90/The Greens 11·2% and the Free Democrats 7·4%.

The Social Democrat/Green cabinet is headed by *Prime Minister* Hans Eichel (SPD).

AGRICULTURE. Area and yield of the most important crops:

	Area (in 1,000 ha)			*Yield (in 1,000 tonnes)*		
	1992	*1993*	*1994*	*1992*	*1993*	*1994*
Wheat	142·0	133·8	130·2	945·5	865·3	880·7
Rye	21·9	23·7	26·6	119·9	131·3	143·9
Barley	119·3	112·8	109·9	675·7	588·2	576·2
Oats	28·8	28·8	30·0	122·6	138·6	130·7
Potatoes	7·1	6·3	5·9	246·3	240·2	205·1
Sugar-beet	22·4	22·4	21·0	1,201·2	1,301·5	1,098·4
Rape	58·4	46·3	48·3	150·9	137·6	137·4

Livestock, Dec. 1994: Cattle, 599,977 (including 192,784 milch cows); pigs, 916,765; sheep, 154,416; horses, 42,695; poultry, 2·23m.

INDUSTRY. In June 1995, 3,423 establishments (with 20 and more employees) employed 525,191 persons; of these, 82,299 were employed in chemical industry; 76,742 in car building; 74,831 in electrical engineering; 67,551 in machine construction; 34,030 in food industry.

LABOUR. The economically active persons totalled 2·7m. at the 1% sample survey of the microcensus of April 1994. Of the total, 260,200 were self-employed, 41,500 unpaid family workers, 2,394,300 employees; 63,100 were engaged in agriculture and forestry, 958,600 in power supply, mining, manufacturing and building, 508,000 in commerce and transport, 1,166,300 in other services.

ROADS. On 1 Jan. 1995 there were 16,686 km of 'classified' roads, comprising 955 km of autobahn, 3,459 km of federal highways, 7,201 km of first-class highways and 5,070 km of second-class highways. Motor vehicles licensed on 1 July 1995 totalled 3,709,857, including 3,208,575 passenger cars, 6,147 buses, 142,506 trucks, 136,731 tractors and 168,990 motor cycles.

JUSTICE. There are a constitutional court *(Staatsgerichtshof)*, a court of appeal, 9 regional courts, 58 local courts, a Land labour court, 12 labour courts, a Land social court, 7 social courts, a finance court, a higher administrative court *(Verwaltungsgerichtshof)*, 5 administrative courts.

RELIGION. In 1987 (census) there were 52·7% Protestants and 30·4% Roman Catholics.

EDUCATION. In 1994 there were 1,236 primary schools with 282,133 pupils (including *Förderstufen*); 154 intermediate schools with 47,230 pupils; 18,511 teachers in primary and intermediate schools together; 230 special schools with 3,194 teachers and 18,484 pupils; 158 high schools with 9,036 teachers and 128,455 pupils; 207 *Gesamtschulen* (comprehensive schools) with 11,445 teachers and 169,882 pupils; 120 part-time vocational schools with 126,629 pupils; 260 full-time vocational schools with 34,371 pupils; 107 advanced vocational schools with 11,379 pupils; 7,663 teachers in the vocational schools.

In the winter term 1994–95 there were 3 universities (Frankfurt/Main, 36,464 students; Giessen, 21,782; Marburg/Lahn, 17,816); 1 technical university in Darmstadt (17,122); 1 private *Wissenschaftliche Hochschule,* (779); 1 *Gesamthochschule* (17,821); 16 *Fachhochschulen* (46,710); 2 Roman Catholic theological colleges and 1 Protestant theological college with together 386 students; 1 college of music and 2 colleges of fine arts with together 1,270 students.

Statistical Information: The Hessisches Statistisches Landesamt (Rheinstr. 35–37, D65175 Wiesbaden). *President:* Eckart Hohmann. Main publications: *Statistisches Handbuch für das Land Hessen* (zweijährlich).—*Staat und Wirtschaft in Hessen* (monthly).— *Beiträge zur Statistik Hessens.*—*Statistische Berichte.*—*Hessische Gemeindestatistik* (annual, 1980 ff.).

State Library: Hessische Landesbibliothek, Rheinstr. 55–57, D65185 Wiesbaden.

LOWER SAXONY

Niedersachsen

TERRITORY AND POPULATION. Lower Saxony has an area of 47,609 sq. km, and is divided into 4 administrative regions, 9 urban districts, 38 rural districts and 1,030 communes; capital, Hanover.

Estimated population, on 31 Dec. 1994, was 7,715,363 (3,761,843 males, 3,953,520 females).

Vital statistics for calendar years:

	Live births	*Marriages*	*Divorces*	*Deaths*
1992	83,669	48,796	12,832	83,186
1993	84,579	48,247	14,674	85,397
1994	81,520	47,349	15,342	85,700

GOVERNMENT. The Land Niedersachsen was formed on 1 Nov. 1946 by merging the former Prussian province of Hanover and the *Länder* Brunswick, Oldenburg and Schaumburg-Lippe. Lower Saxony has 7 seats in the Bundesrat. At the Diet elections on 13 March 1994 the electorate was 5·8m.; turn-out was 73·8%. The Social Democratic Party (SPD) won 81 seats with 44·3% of votes cast; the Christian Democratic Union, 67 with 36·4%; and the Greens, 13 with 7·5%.

The cabinet of the Social Democratic Party is headed by *Prime Minister* Gerhard Schröder (SPD).

AGRICULTURE. Area and yield of the most important crops:

	Area (in 1,000 ha)			*Yield (in 1,000 tonnes)*		
	1992	*1993*	*1994*	*1992*	*1993*	*1994*
Wheat	334	292	303	2,337	2,270	2,325
Rye	128	134	138	596	673	699
Barley	327	299	299	1,741	1,480	1,583
Oats	47	45	52	149	201	228
Potatoes	120	118	117	3,930	4,945	4,257
Sugar-beet	137	132	131	6,710	7,115	6,291

Livestock, 3 Dec. 1994: Cattle, 3,008,945 (including 863,260 milch cows); pigs, 6,900,588; sheep, 233,023; horses, 105,885; poultry, 45,551,289.

FISHERIES. In 1993 the yield of sea and coastal fishing was 58,161 tonnes valued at DM 86m.

INDUSTRY. In Sept. 1994, 4,223 establishments (with 20 and more employees) employed 597,103 persons; of these 56,484 were employed in machine construction; 55,269 in electrical engineering.

LABOUR. The economically active persons totalled 3,341,400 in April 1994. Of the total, 294,500 were self-employed, 53,400 unpaid family workers, 2,993,400 employees; 141,500 were engaged in agriculture and forestry, 1,200,800 in power supply, mining, manufacturing and building, 631,500 in commerce and transport, 1,367,500 in other industries and services.

ROADS. At 1 Jan. 1994 there were 28,224 km of 'classified' roads, including 1,271 km of autobahn, 4,863 km of federal roads, 8,346 km of first-class and 13,744 km of second-class highways.

Number of motor vehicles, 1 Jan. 1995, was 4,605,634 including 3,901,440 passenger cars, 187,485 lorries, 8,696 buses, 238,549 tractors, 208,148 motor cycles.

JUSTICE. There are a constitutional court *(Staatsgerichtshof)*, 3 courts of appeal, 11 regional courts, 79 local courts, a Land labour court, 15 labour courts, a Land social court, 8 social courts, a finance court, a higher administrative court and 4 administrative courts.

RELIGION. On 25 May 1987 (census) there were 66·12% Protestants and 19·6% Roman Catholics.

EDUCATION. In 1994 there were 1,849 primary schools with 328,023 pupils; 246 special schools with 27,436 pupils; 304 stages of orientation with 129,138 pupils; 379 intermediate schools with 77,269 pupils; 257 secondary schools with 97,658 pupils; 206 grammar schools with 124,960 pupils; 5 evening high schools with 804 pupils; 22 integrated comprehensive schools with 19,183 pupils; 25 co-operative comprehensive schools with 22,770 pupils. In 1993 there were 1,801 vocational training institutes (full and part-time) with 256,917 pupils and 213 public health schools with 11,952 pupils.

In the winter term 1994–95 there were 6 universities (Göttingen, 29,612 students; Hanover, 31,571; Oldenburg, 12,866; Osnabrück, 14,323; Hildesheim, 3,800; Lüneburg, 6,218); 2 technical universities (Braunschweig, 16,238; Clausthal, 3,515); the medical college of Hanover (3,418), the veterinary college in Hanover (1,906).

Statistical Information: The Niedersächsisches Landesamt für—Statistik' Postfach 4460, D30044 Hanover. *Head of Division:* President Hans Wolfgang Günther. Main publications are: *Statistisches Jahrbuch Niedersachsen* (from 1950).—*Statistische Monatshefte Niedersachsen* (from 1947).—*Statistik Niedersachsen.—Statistiches Taschenbuch Niedersachsen 1994* Biennial.

State Libraries: Niedersächsische Staats- und Universitätsbibliothek, Prinzenstr. 1, 37073, Göttingen. *Director:* Helmut Vogt; Niedersächsische Landesbibliothek, Waterloostr. 8, 30169 Hannover. *Director:* Dr W. Dittrich.

MECKLENBURG-WEST POMERANIA

Mecklenburg-Vorpommern

TERRITORY AND POPULATION. The area is 23,170 sq. km. It is divided into 6 urban districts, 12 rural districts and 1,080 communes. Population on 31 Dec. 1994 was 1,832,298 (932,862 females). The capital is Schwerin.

Vital statistics for calendar years:

	Live births	*Marriages*	*Divorces*	*Deaths*
1992	10,875	5,386	1,256	20,352
1993	9,432	5,458	2,126	19,563
1994	8,934	5,626	2,540	19,835

CONSTITUTION AND GOVERNMENT. The Land was reconstituted on former GDR territory in 1990. It has 3 seats in the Bundesrat.

At the Diet elections of Oct. 1994, the Christian Democrats (CDU) won 30 seats with 37·7% of the vote; the Social Democrats, 23, with 29·5%; and the Party of Democratic Socialism (former Communists), 18, with 22·7%. The *Prime Minister* is Berndt Seite (CDU).

AGRICULTURE. Area and yield of the most important crops:

	Area (in 1,000 ha)			*Yield (in 1,000 tonnes)*		
	1992	*1993*	*1994*	*1992*	*1993*	*1994*
Wheat	234·0	211·0	210·2	1,144·4	1,319·5	1,235·2
Rye	62·9	64·7	74·1	213·8	278·4	351·1
Barley	203·0	171·3	129·5	919·8	880·7	693·1
Oats	20·8	22·4	20·7	50·4	117·5	78·0
Potatoes	29·1	23·1	17·0	541·6	853·2	378·5
Sugar-beet	34·8	34·1	31·7	1,287·1	1,693·3	1,029·4

Livestock in 1994: Cattle, 629,478 (including 226,202 milch cows); pigs, 609,074; sheep, 73,162; horses, 17,964; poultry, 7,190,416.

FISHERIES. Sea catch, 1994: 21,500 tonnes. Freshwater catch, 1993: 1,140 tonnes (mainly carp, trout and eels).

INDUSTRY. At the end of 1994 there were 530 enterprises (with 20 or more employees) employing 50,176 persons.

LABOUR. 795,900 persons (349,300 females) were employed at the 1%-sample survey of the microcensus of April 1994, including 53,900 self-employed and family assistants, 343,600 manual and 372,600 white-collar workers. Employment by sector: Manufacturing, 119,000; agriculture, forestry and fisheries, 58,300; trade, 92,700; transport and communications, 56,800; construction, 125,900; energy, water resources and mining, 12,300.

ROADS. There were (1 Jan. 1994) 9,900 km of 'classified' roads, including 237 km of autobahn, 2,077 km of federal roads, 4,199 km of first-class and 3,837 km of second-class highways. Number of motor vehicles, 1 Jan. 1995, 893,345, including 782,996 passenger cars, 58,386 lorries, 2,122 buses and 17,060 motorcycles.

SHIPPING. There is a lake district of some 660 lakes. The ports of Rostock, Stralsund and Wismar are important for ship-building and repairs. In 1994 the cargo fleet consisted of 108 vessels (including 5 tankers) of 862,000 DWT. Sea traffic, 1994, incoming 13·08m. tonnes; outgoing 9·16m. tonnes.

JUSTICE. There is a court of appeal (*Oberlandesgericht*), 4 regional courts, 31 local courts (*Amtsgerichte*), a Land labour court, 4 labour courts, a Land social court, 4 social courts, a finance court and a higher administrative court.

RELIGION. In 1994 the Evangelical Lutheran Church of Mecklenburg had 254,800 adherents, 318 pastors and 383 parishes. Roman Catholics numbered 71,900, with 67 priests and 80 parishes. The Pomeranian Evangelical Church had (1994) 141,000 adherents, 192 pastors and 250 parishes.

EDUCATION. In 1994-95 there were 348 primary schools, 19 comprehensives, 500 secondary schools and 98 special needs schools. There are universities at Rostock and Greifswald with (in 1994-95) 13,114 students and 3,796 academic staff, and 5 institutions of equivalent status with 4,480 students and 712 academic staff.

Statistical Office: Statistisches Landesamt Mecklenburg-Vorpommern, Postfach 020135, D-19016, Schwerin. Main publications are *Statistische Monatshefte Mecklenburg-Vorpommern* (since 1991).—*Statistische Berichte* (since 1991; various).—*Statistisches Jahrbuch Mecklenburg-Vorpommern* (since 1991).—*Statistische Sonderhefte* (since 1992; various).

NORTH RHINE-WESTPHALIA

Nordrhein-Westfalen

TERRITORY AND POPULATION. The Land comprises 34,077 sq. km. It is divided into 5 administrative regions, 23 urban districts, 31 rural districts and 396 communes. Capital Düsseldorf. Population, 31 Dec. 1994, 17,816,079 (8,639,741 males, 9,176,338 females).

Vital statistics for calendar years:

	Live births	*Marriages*	*Divorces*	*Deaths*
1992	196,899	110,904	35,727	188,805
1993	194,156	106,315	39,230	194,667
1994	186,079	104,200	40,523	192,669

GOVERNMENT. Since Oct. 1990 the North Rhine-Westphalia has had 6 seats in the Bundesrat. It is governed by Social Democrats (SPD); *Prime Minister*, Johannes Rau (SPD). The Diet, elected on 14 May 1995, consists of 108 Social Democrats (46% of votes cast), 89 Christian Democrats (37·7%) and 24 Greens (10%).

AGRICULTURE. Area and yield of the most important crops:

	Area (in 1,000 ha)			*Yield (in 1,000 tonnes)*		
	1992	*1993*	*1994*	*1992*	*1993*	*1994*
Wheat	249·1	233·3	244·8	1,837·4	1,828·9	1,877·1
Rye	36·6	40·4	39·4	232·9	253·3	223·0
Barley	237·4	210·2	190·8	1,405·2	1,108·5	1,022·7
Oats	36·3	35·2	40·0	108·6	155·9	181·5
Potatoes	27·1	26·7	26·3	1,083·8	1,144·6	999·0
Sugar-beet	76·6	77·0	76·4	4,226·8	4,608·1	3,942·6

Livestock, 3 Dec. 1994: Cattle, 1,779,604 (including 477,961 milch cows); pigs, 5,762,336; sheep, 245,783; horses, 107,094; poultry, 10,756,943.

INDUSTRY. In Sept. 1994, 11,226 establishments (with 20 and more employees) employed 1,716,963 persons; of these, 101,163 were employed in mining; 239,796 in machine construction; 83,856 in iron and steel production; 170,123 in chemical industry; 174,633 in electrical engineering; 44,414 in textile industry.

Output and/or production in 1,000 tonnes, 1994: Hard coal, 43,729; lignite, 101,362; pig-iron, 17,216; raw steel ingots, 19,739; rolled steel, 14,998; castings (iron and steel castings), 965; cement, 12,617; fireproof products, 651; sulphuric acid (including production of cokeries), 1,290; staple fibres and rayon, 298; metal-working machines, 86; equipment for smelting works and rolling mills, 108; machines for mining industry, 93; cranes and hoisting machinery, 64; installation implements, 2,419,025 (1,000 pieces); cables and electric lines, 241; springs of all kinds, 176; chains of all kinds, 75; locks and fittings, 510 spun yarns, 167. Of the total population, 9·6% were engaged in industry.

LABOUR. The economically active persons totalled 7,412,700 at the 1%-sample survey of the microcensus of April 1994. Of the total, 651,100 were self-employed, 73,700 unpaid family workers, 6·69m. employees; 141,400 were engaged in agriculture and forestry, 2,942,900 in power supply, mining, manufacturing and building, 1,377,600 in commerce and transport, 2,950,800 in other industries and services.

ROADS. There were (1 Jan. 1995) 29,861 km of 'classified' roads, including 2,149 km of autobahn, 5,097 km of federal roads, 12,653 km of first-class and 9,962 km of second-class highways. Number of motor vehicles, 1 July 1995, 10,036,150, including 7,482,458 passenger cars, 1,303,765 lorries, 403,944 motor lorries/trucks, 17,420 buses, 211,713 tractors and 499,303 motor cycles.

JUSTICE. There are a constitutional court *(Verfassungsgerichtshof)*, 3 courts of appeal, 19 regional courts, 130 local courts, 1 Land labour court, 30 labour courts, 1 Land social court, 8 social courts, 3 finance courts, a higher administrative court, 7 administrative courts.

RELIGION. On 25 May 1987 (census) there were 35·2% Protestants and 49·4% Roman Catholics.

EDUCATION. In 1994 there were 4,223 primary schools with 61,309 teachers and 1,061,868 pupils; 708 special schools with 13,873 teachers and 87,216 pupils; 516 intermediate schools with 14,767 teachers and 267,973 pupils; 233 *Gesamtschulen* (comprehensive schools) with 14,767 teachers and 185,644 pupils; 623 high schools with 34,926 teachers and 494,327 pupils; in 1994 there were 260 part-time vocational schools with 301,974 pupils; vocational preparatory year 143 schools with 7,717 pupils; 242 full-time vocational schools with 64,131 pupils; 184 full-time vocational schools leading up to vocational colleges with 13,666 pupils; 237 advanced full-time vocational schools with 41,254 pupils; 650 schools for public health occupations with 15,003 teachers and 41,302 pupils; 40 schools within the scope of a pilot system of courses with 79,491 pupils and 3,483 teachers.

In the winter term 1994–95 there were 8 universities (Bielefeld, 18,772 students; Bochum, 35,879; Bonn, 35,552; Cologne, 52,772; Dortmund, 24,664; Düsseldorf,

19,174; Münster, 43,652; Witten, 604); the Technical University of Aachen (35,197); 4 Roman Catholic and 2 Protestant theological colleges with together 846 students. There were also 4 colleges of music, 3 colleges of fine arts and the college for physical education in Cologne with together 10,720 students; 20 *Fachhochschulen* (vocational colleges) with 106,489 students, and 6 *Universitäten-Gesamthochschulen* with together 124,727 students.

Statistical Information: The Landesamt für Datenverarbeitung und Statistik Nordrhein-Westfalen (Mauerstr. 51, D-40476 Düsseldorf) was founded in 1946, by amalgamating the provincial statistical offices of Rhineland and Westphalia. The Landesamt publishes: *Statistisches Jahrbuch Nordrhein-Westfalen.* From 1949. More than 550 other publications yearly.

Först, W., *Kleine Geschichte Nordrhein-Westfalens.* Münster, 1986.

Land Library: Universitätsbibliothek, Universitätsstr. 1, D-40225 Düsseldorf. *Director:* Dr Niggemann.

RHINELAND-PALATINATE
Rheinland-Pfalz

TERRITORY AND POPULATION. Rhineland-Palatinate has an area of 19,852 sq. km. It comprises 3 administrative regions, 12 urban districts, 24 rural districts and 2,305 communes. The capital is Mainz. Population (at 31 Dec. 1994), 3,951,573 (2,021,249 females).

Vital statistics for calendar years:

	Live births	*Marriages*	*Divorces*	*Deaths*
1992	42,722	24,626	7,589	42,635
1993	42,291	24,006	8,555	43,871
1994	40,539	23,182	9,003	42,857

CONSTITUTION. The constitution of the Land Rheinland-Pfalz was approved by the Consultative Assembly on 25 April 1947 and by referendum on 18 May 1947, when 579,002 voted for and 514,338 against its acceptance. It has 4 seats in the Bundesrat.

At the elections of 21 April 1991 the Social Democratic Party won 47 seats of the 101 in the state parliament with 44·8% of votes cast; the Christian Democrats 40 with 38·7%; the Free Democrats 7 with 6·9%; and the Greens, 7 with 6·5%.

The coalition cabinet is headed by Kurt Beck (b. 1949; Social Democrat).

AGRICULTURE. Area and yield of the most important products:

	Area (1,000 ha)			*Yield (1,000 tonnes)*		
	1992	*1993*	*1994*	*1992*	*1993*	*1994*
Wheat	88·9	81·0	77·7	540·8	453·1	484·0
Rye	15·5	17·6	19·0	78·0	86·2	94·3
Barley	133·4	126·7	118·8	663·3	589·5	541·0
Oats	23·2	23·4	22·8	96·5	100·7	87·1
Potatoes	11·8	10·3	10·6	384·6	341·6	329·1
Sugar-beet	22·9	22·4	22·9	1,247·5	1,196·3	1,228·1
Wine (1,000 hectolitres)	63·3	65·6	66·2	9,190·8	6,674·1	6,902·2

Livestock (1994, in 1,000): Cattle, 488 (including milch cows, 150·9); horses, 27·7; sheep, 137; pigs, 435·3; poultry, 2,165·2.

INDUSTRY. In 1994, 2,478 establishments (with 20 and more employees) employed 335,795 persons; of these 71,476 were employed in the chemical industry; 18,113 in electrical equipment manufacture; 8,344 in leather goods and footwear; 41,243 in machine construction; 12,184 in processing stones and earthenware.

LABOUR. The economically active persons totalled 1,708,000 in 1994. Of the total, 159,600 were self-employed, 24,200 were unpaid family workers, 1,524,200 employees; 62,500 were engaged in agriculture and forestry, 663,700 in power supply, mining, manufacturing and building, 283,700 in commerce and transport, 698,100 in other industries and services.

ROADS. In 1994 there were 18,397 km of 'classified' roads, including 816 km of motorway (*Autobahn*), 3,062 km of federal roads, 7,132 km of first-class and 7,387 km of second-class highways. Number of motor vehicles, 1 July 1995, was 2,504,408, including 2,102,581 passenger cars, 97,390 lorries, 5,324 buses, 139,826 tractors and 129,846 motor cycles.

JUSTICE. There are a constitutional court *(Verfassungsgerichtshof)*, 2 courts of appeal, 8 regional courts, 47 local courts, a Land labour court, 5 labour courts, a Land social court, 4 social courts, a finance court, a higher administrative court, 4 administrative courts.

RELIGION. On 25 May 1987 (census) there were 37·7% Protestants and 54·5% Roman Catholics.

EDUCATION. In 1994 there were 1,183 primary schools with 15,112 teachers and 253,528 pupils; 147 special schools with 1,980 teachers and 13,356 pupils; 110 intermediate schools with 3,416 teachers and 58,609 pupils; 136 high schools with 7,271 teachers and 102,772 pupils; 73 vocational schools with 79,002 pupils; 76 advanced vocational schools and institutions for the training of technicians (full- and part-time) with 14,717 pupils.

In the winter term 1993–94 there were the University of Mainz (29,025 students), the University of Kaiserslautern (9,622 students), the University of Trier (10,966 students), the University of Koblenz-Landau (6,232 students), the *Hochschule für Verwaltungswissenschaften* in Speyer (450 students), the Koblenz School of Corporate Management *(Wissenschaftliche Hochschule für Unternehmensführung Koblenz in Vallendar)* with 216 students, the Roman Catholic Theological College in Trier (192 students) and the Roman Catholic Theological College in Vallendar (78 students). There were also the *Fachhochschule des Landes Rheinland-Pfalz* with 20,457 students and 4 *Verwaltungsfachhochschulen* with 3,250 students.

Statistical Information: The Statistisches Landesamt Rheinland-Pfalz (Mainzer Str., 14–16, D-56130 Bad Ems) was established in 1948. *Adminstration Commissioner:* Klaus Maxeiner. Its publications include: *Statistisches Jahrbuch für Rheinland-Pfalz* (from 1948); *Statistische Monatshefte Rheinland-Pfalz* (from 1958); *Statistik von Rheinland-Pfalz* (from 1949) 361 vols. to date; *Rheinland-Pfalz im Spiegel der Statistik* (from 1968); *Rheinland-Pfalz-seine kreisfreien Städte und Landkreise* (1992); *Rheinland-Pfalz heute* (from 1973); *Benutzerhandbuch des Landesinformationssystems* (1995); *Raumordnungsbericht 1993 der Landesregierung Rheinland-Pfalz* (Mainz, 1993).

SAARLAND

KEY HISTORICAL EVENTS. In 1919 the Saar territory was placed under the control of the League of Nations. Following a plebiscite, the territory reverted to Germany in 1935. In 1945 the territory became part of the French Zone of occupation, and was in 1947 accorded an international status inside an economic union with France. In pursuance of the German–French agreement signed in Luxembourg on 27 Oct. 1956 the territory returned to Germany on 1 Jan. 1957. Its reintegration was completed by 5 July 1959.

TERRITORY AND POPULATION. Saarland has an area of 2,570 sq. km. Population, 31 Dec. 1994, 1,084,201 (525,432 males, 558,769 females). It comprises 6 rural districts and 52 communes. The capital is Saarbrücken.

Vital statistics for calendar years:

	Live births	*Marriages*	*Divorces*	*Deaths*
1992	10,954	6,943	2,648	12,579
1993	10,653	6,528	2,907	13,053
1994	10,028	6,427	3,035	12,711

CONSTITUTION. Saarland has 3 seats in the Bundesrat.

The Saar Diet, elected on 16 Oct. 1994, is composed as follows: 27 Social Democrats, 21 Christian Democrats, 3 Greens.

Saarland is governed by Social Democrats in Parliament. *Prime Minister*: Oskar Lafontaine (Social Democrat).

AGRICULTURE AND FORESTRY. The cultivated area (1993) occupied 116,848 ha or 45·5% of the total area; the forest area comprises nearly 33·4% of the total (257,026 ha).

Area and yield of the most important crops:

	Area (in 1,000 ha)			*Yield (in 1,000 tonnes)*		
	1992	*1993*	*1994*	*1992*	*1993*	*1994*
Wheat	6·6	6·6	6·3	37·9	37·7	32·5
Rye	5·4	5·3	4·9	26·3	28·2	23·1
Barley	9·4	8·5	8·1	43·6	39·3	33·1
Oats	4·6	5·0	4·9	18·4	21·7	18·7
Potatoes	0·4	0·3	0·4	8·7	9·5	9·0

Livestock, Dec. 1994: Cattle, 62,551 (including 17,720 milch cows); pigs, 26,675; sheep, 18,049; horses, 5,058; poultry, 202,481.

INDUSTRY. In June 1995, 535 establishments (with 20 and more employees) employed 113,195 persons; of these 16,459 were engaged in coalmining, 17,423 in manufacturing motor vehicles, parts, accessories, 10,676 in iron and steel production, 13,780 in machine construction, 5,039 in electrical engineering, 4,135 in steel construction. In 1994 the coalmines produced 8·3m. tonnes of coal. 5 blast furnaces and 7 steel furnaces produced 4m. tonnes of pig-iron and 4·5m. tonnes of crude steel.

LABOUR. The economically active persons totalled 424,000 at the 1%-sample survey of the microcensus of April 1994. Of the total, 37,300 were self-employed, 383,300 employees; 4,600 were engaged in agriculture and forestry, 168,700 in power supply, mining, manufacturing and building, 85,600 in commerce and transport, 165,100 in other industries and services.

ROADS. At 1 Jan. 1995 there were 2,035 km of classified roads, including 226 km of autobahn, 352 km of federal roads, 825 km of first-class and 632 km of second-class highways. Number of motor vehicles, 31 Dec. 1994, 649,273, including 569,333 passenger cars, 25,280 lorries, 1,496 buses, 13,737 tractors and 32,426 motor cycles.

JUSTICE. There are a constitutional court *(Verfassungsgerichtshof)*, a court of appeal, a regional court, 11 local courts, a Land labour court, 3 labour courts, a Land social court, a social court, a finance court, a higher administrative court, an administrative court.

RELIGION. In 1993, 71·7% of the population were Roman Catholics and 20·6% were Protestants.

EDUCATION. In 1995–96 there were 309 primary schools with 2,885 teachers and 53,319 pupils; 41 special schools with 575 teachers and 3,126 pupils; 59 intermediate and secondary schools with 1,422 teachers and 22,847 pupils; 37 high schools with 1,795 teachers and 26,201 pupils; 15 comprehensive high schools with 643 teachers and 9,846 pupils; 3 *Freie Waldorfschulen* with 96 teachers and 962 pupils; 2 evening intermediate schools with 204 pupils; 2 evening high schools and 1 Saarland College with 272 pupils; 39 part-time vocational schools with 20,196 pupils; year of commercial basic training: 50 institutions with 2,117 pupils; 21 advanced full-time vocational schools and schools for technicians with 2,776 pupils; 52 full-time vocational schools with 4,772 pupils; 2 *Berufsaufbauschulen* (vocational extension schools) with 57 pupils; 29 *Fachoberschulen* (full-time vocational schools leading up to vocational colleges) with 3,280 pupils; 43 schools for public health occupations with 2,029 pupils. The number of pupils visiting the vocational schools amounts to 35,402. They are instructed by 1,559 teachers.

In the winter term 1995–96 there was the University of the Saarland with 19,262 students; 1 academy of fine art with 234 students; 1 academy of music and drama with 336 students; 1 vocational college (economics and technics) with 2,969 students; 1 vocational college for social affairs with 265 students; 1 vocational college for public administration with 177 students; and 1 private vocational college for mining with 53 students.

Statistical Information: The Statistisches Landesamt Saarland (Virchowstrasse 7, D–66119 Saarbrücken) was established on 1 April 1938. As from 1 June 1935, it was an independent agency; its predecessor, 1920–35, was the Statistical Office of the Government Commission of the Saar. *Chief:* Direktor Josef Mailänder. The most important publications are: *Statistisches Handbuch für das Saarland,* from 1950.—*Statistisches Taschenbuch für das Saarland,* from 1959.—*Saarland in Zahlen* (special issues).—*Einzelschriften zur Statistik des Saarlandes,* from 1950—*Statistische Nachrichten,* from 1981.

SAXONY

Freistaat Sachsen

TERRITORY AND POPULATION. The area is 18,412 sq. km. It is divided into 3 administrative regions, 6 urban districts, 28 rural districts and 929 communes. Population on 31 Dec. 1994 was 4,584,345 (2,392,046 females). The capital is Dresden.

Vital statistics for calendar years:

	Live births	*Marriages*	*Divorces*	*Deaths*
1992	25,298	13,405	2,010	61,565
1993	23,423	13,808	5,116	59,900
1994	22,734	14,795	6,519	58,234

CONSTITUTION AND GOVERNMENT. The Land was reconstituted as the Free State of Saxony on former GDR territory in 1990. It has 4 seats in the Bundesrat.

At the Diet elections of Sept. 1994 the Christian Democrats won 77 seats, with 58·1% of the vote; the Social Democrats, 22, with 16·6%; the Party of Democratic Socialism (former Communists), 21, with 16·5%.

The *Prime Minister* is Kurt Biedenkopf (b. 1930; Christian Democrat).

AGRICULTURE. Area and yield of the most important crops:

	Area (in 1,000 ha)			*Yield (in 1,000 tonnes)*		
	1992	*1993*	*1994*	*1992*	*1993*	*1994*
Wheat	135·7	132·5	142·3	651·3	787·0	884·5
Rye	27·5	31·7	41·0	94·1	146·0	212·9
Barley	160·7	140·8	144·2	751·5	713·9	789·9
Maize	67·5	73·7	57·1	2,435·5	3,354·2	2,237·9
Potatoes	15·4	10·9	8.4	449·8	431·0	238·5
Fodder	172·8	199·8	195·9	1,525·0	1,998·0	1,661·7
Hops	0·5	0·5	0·5	0·6	0·7	0·4

Livestock in 1994 (in 1,000): Cattle, 652 (including milch cows, 251); pigs, 614; sheep, 123.

INDUSTRY. In Sept. 1995, 2,292 establishments (with 20 and more employees) employed 208,325 persons.

ROADS. In 1994 there were 421 km of motorways and 2,448 km of main roads. There were, 1 July 1995, 2,381,456 registered motor vehicles, including 2,090,154 motor cars, 206,491 lorries and tractors, 4,555 buses and 61,225 motorcycles.

EDUCATION. In 1994–95 there were 1,247 primary schools with 228,654 pupils and 12,805 teachers; 663 secondary schools with 217,299 pupils and 14,993 teachers, 191 grammar schools with 158,945 pupils and 9,137 teachers and 208 high schools (*Förderschulen*) with 26,217 students and 3,772 teachers. There were 5 universities with 44,438 students, 9 technical colleges with 14,906 students, 6 colleges for the arts with 1,888 students and 1 management college with 2,317 students.

Statistical office: Statistisches Landesamt des Freistaates Sachsen, Postfach 105, 01911 Kamenz. It publishes *Statistisches Jahrbuch des Freistaates Sachsen* (since 1990).

SAXONY-ANHALT

Sachsen-Anhalt

TERRITORY AND POPULATION. The area is 20,444 sq. km. It is divided into 3 administrative regions, 3 urban districts, 21 rural districts and 1,301 communes. Population in 1994 was 2,759,213 (1,427,086 females). The capital is Magdeburg.

Vital statistics for calendar years:

	Live births	*Marriages*	*Divorces*	*Deaths*
1992	16,284	8,329	1,917	35,754
1993	14,610	8,854	4,042	34,838
1994	14,280	9,415	4,287	33,816

CONSTITUTION AND GOVERNMENT. The Land was reconstituted on former GDR territory in 1990. It has 4 seats in the Bundesrat.

At the Diet elections on 26 June 1994 turn-out was 54·9%. The Christian Democrats won 37 seats, with 34·4% votes cast; the Social Democratic Party (SPD), 36, with 34%; the Party of Democratic Socialism (former Communists), 21 with 19·9%; Alliance '90/Greens, 5, with 5·1%.

The *Prime Minister* is Dr Manfred Höppner (SPD).

AGRICULTURE. Area and yield of the most important crops:

	Area (in 1,000 ha)			*Yield (in 1,000 tonnes)*		
	1992	*1993*	*1994*	*1992*	*1993*	*1994*
Cereals	499·3	474·1	494·0	41·7	53·2	63·4
Potatoes	23·8	15·8	14·9	233·9	345·6	288·9
Sugar-beet	62·4	61·1	56·0	378·9	517·4	418·7
Maize	71·3	71·7	60·2	293·3	460·6	315·1

Livestock in 1994 (in 1,000): Cattle, 444·2 (including milch cows, 168·9); pigs, 711·9; sheep, 132·4; poultry, 2,623.

INDUSTRY. In 1994, 1,317 establishments (with 20 or more employees) employed 139,945 persons; of these, 38,364 were employed in basic industry, 65,921 in capital goods industry and 15,746 in food and kindred industry. Major sectors are machine and transport equipment, electrical engineering, chemicals and energy and fuel.

LABOUR. In 1993 there were 1,098,655 economically-active persons. Of these, 449,763 worked in local authorities, social security and services, 237,521 in mining and manufacturing, 162,328 in building, 120,212 in trade, 87,422 in transport and communications and 41,409 in agriculture, forestry and fisheries.

ROADS. In 1994 there were 202 km of motorways, 2,323 km of main and 7,376 km of local roads. In 1994 there were 1,520,048 registered motor vehicles, including 1,194,515 passenger cars, 89,131 lorries, 2,958 buses and 29,935 motorcycles.

RELIGION. There are Saxon and Anhalt branches of the Evangelical Church. There were some 0·2m. Roman Catholics in 1990.

EDUCATION. In 1994–95 there were 1,555 schools with 391,335 pupils. There were 10 universities and institutes of equivalent status with 25,572 students.

Statistical office: Statistisches Landesamt Sachsen-Anhalt, Postfach 20 11 56, D-06012 Halle. It publishes *Statistisches Jahrbuch des Landes Sachsen-Anhalt* (since 1991).

SCHLESWIG-HOLSTEIN

TERRITORY AND POPULATION. The area of Schleswig-Holstein in 1994 was 15,738 sq. km. It is divided into 4 urban and 11 rural districts and 1,131 communes. The capital is Kiel. The population (estimate, 31 Dec. 1994) numbered 2,708,392 (1,320,784 males, 1,387,608 females).

Vital statistics for calendar years:

	Live births	*Marriages*	*Divorces*	*Deaths*
1992	28,757	18,897	5,446	30,299
1993	28,632	18,451	6,250	31,223
1994	27,542	18,295	6,196	30,766

GOVERNMENT. The Land has 4 seats in the Bundesrat. At the elections of 5 April 1992 the Social Democrats won 45 seats with 46·2% of votes cast, the Christian Democrats 32 with 33·8%, the German People's Union 6 with 6·3%, the Free Democrats 5 with 5·6% and the (Danish) South Schleswig Association 1 with 1·9%. The latter has a guaranteed seat.

Prime Minister: Heide Simonis (b. 1943; SPD).

AGRICULTURE. Area and yield of the most important crops:

	Area (in 1,000 ha)			*Yield (in 1,000 tonnes)*		
	1992	*1993*	*1994*	*1992*	*1993*	*1994*
Wheat	175·3	146·6	157·2	1,312·7	1,178·7	1,223·3
Rye	35·9	29·9	32·6	168·9	164·8	188·0
Barley	84·4	73·3	67·5	560·2	465·7	430·3
Oats	13·0	13·1	16·9	41·5	68·1	76·4
Potatoes	5·5	5·3	4·8	154·0	183·7	146·3
Sugar-beet	16·0	15·4	15·0	768·2	779·5	699·5

Livestock, 3 Dec. 1994: 1,396,237 cattle (including 425,733 milch cows), 1,308,643 pigs, 225,305 sheep; 49,349 horses, 2,934,807 poultry.

FISHERIES. In 1994 the yield of small-scale deep-sea and inshore fisheries was 28,726 tonnes valued at DM74·8m.

INDUSTRY. In 1994 (average), 1,644 establishments (with 20 and more employees) employed 163,027 persons; of these, 7,433 were employed in ship-building (except naval engineering); 26,032 in machine construction; 22,639 in food and kindred industry; 16,375 in electrical engineering.

LABOUR. The economically active persons totalled 1,244,900 in 1994. Of the total, 126,100 were self-employed, 13,000 unpaid family workers, 1,105,900 employees; 52,900 were engaged in agriculture and forestry, 363,100 in power supply, mining, manufacturing and building, 261,900 in commerce and transport and 567,000 in other industries and services.

ROADS. There were (1 Jan. 1995) 9,881·7 km of 'classified' roads, including 447·9 km of autobahn, 1,758·5 km of federal roads, 3,624·3 km of first-class and 4,050·9 km of second-class highways. Number of motor vehicles, 1 Jan. 1995, was 1,615,056, including 1,372,561 passenger cars, 70,239 lorries, 3,045 buses, 70,967 tractors, 72,282 motor cycles.

SHIPPING. The Kiel Canal is 98·7 km (51 miles) long; in 1994, 43,727 vessels of 38·3m. NRT passed through it.

JUSTICE. There are a court of appeal, 4 regional courts, 28 local courts, a Land labour court, 6 labour courts, a Land social court, 4 social courts, a finance court, an upper administrative court and an administrative court.

RELIGION. On 25 May 1987 (census) there were 73·3% Protestants and 6·2% Roman Catholics.

EDUCATION. In 1994–95 there were 680 primary schools with 9,004 teachers and 148,081 pupils; 153 special schools with 1,808 teachers and 12,270 pupils; 166 intermediate schools with 3,631 teachers and 50,280 pupils; 99 high schools with 5,002 teachers and 63,549 pupils; 27 integrated comprehensive schools with 1,064 teachers and 12,627 pupils; 42 part-time vocational schools with 1,938 teachers and 63,009 pupils; 143 full-time vocational schools with 682 teachers and 9,868 pupils; 57 advanced vocational schools for foreigners with 377 teachers and 5,643 pupils; 66 schools for public health occupations with 3,981 pupils; 66 vocational grammar schools with 553 teachers and 7,294 pupils; 6 vocational colleges with 18,571 pupils in the summer term of 1993.

In the summer term of 1993 the University of Kiel had 19,095 students, 2 teacher-training colleges had 4,069 students; 1 music college had 349 students, 1 Medical University in Lübeck had 1,404 students.

Statistical Information: Statistisches Landesamt Schleswig-Holstein (Fröbel Str. 15–17, D24113 Kiel). *Director:* Dr Kirschner. Publications: *Statistisches Taschenbuch Schleswig-Holstein,* since 1954.—*Statistisches Jahrbuch Schleswig-Holstein,* since 1951.—*Statistische Monatshefte Schleswig-Holstein,* since 1949.—*Statistische Berichte,* since 1947.—*Beitrage zur historischen Statistik Schleswig-Holstein,* from 1967.—*Lange Reihen,* from 1977.

Baxter, R. R., *The Law of International Waterways.* Harvard Univ. Press, 1964
Brandt, O., *Grundriss der Geschichte Schleswig-Holsteins.* 5th ed. Kiel, 1957
Handbuch für Schleswig-Holstein. 27th ed. Kiel, 1994

State Library: Schleswig-Holsteinische Landesbibliothek, Kiel, Schloss. *Director:* Prof. Dr Dieter Lohmeier.

THURINGIA

Thüringen

TERRITORY AND POPULATION. The area is 16,171 sq. km. Population on 31 Dec. 1994 was 2,517,776 (1,299,842 females); density, 156 per sq. km. It is divided into 5 urban districts, 17 rural districts and 1,241 communes. The capital is Erfurt.

Vital statistics for calendar years:

	Live births	*Marriages*	*Divorces*	*Deaths*
1992	14,615	7,763	2,233	30,155
1993	13,307	7,955	2,643	29,866
1994	12,721	8,581	3,795	28,877

CONSTITUTION AND GOVERNMENT. The Land was reconstituted on former GDR territory in 1990. It has 4 seats in the Bundesrat.

At the Diet elections of Oct. 1994 the Christian Democrats (CDU) won 42 seats, with 42·6% of the vote; the Social Democrats (SPD), 29 with 29·6%; the Party of Democratic Socialism (PDS), 17, with 16·6%.

The *Prime Minister* is Dr Bernhard Vogel (CDU).

AGRICULTURE. Area and yield of the most important crops:

	Area (in 1,000 ha)			*Yield (in 1,000 tonnes)*		
	1992	*1993*	*1994*	*1992*	*1993*	*1994*
Wheat	174·0	168·2	162·4	886·2	1,076·4	1,110·3
Rye	9·4	13·5	18·6	47·1	77·4	114·1
Barley	159·4	137·3	122·4	778·5	716·8	695·0
Oats	6·3	8·0	10·7	24·6	42·3	46·6
Potatoes	9·4	5·0	4·2	306·2	193·8	144·0
Sugar-beet	17·2	16·1	13·4	703·2	796·1	578·3

Livestock, 3 Dec. 1994: 471,702 cattle (including 168,712 milch cows), 671,082 pigs, 230,589 sheep; 12,585 horses, 3,466,775 poultry.

INDUSTRY. In 1994, 1,517 establishments (with 20 and more employees) employed 0·12m. persons; of these, 1,684 were employed in mining, 16,457 in the production of raw materials, 59,587 in the manufacture of producers' goods, 28,930 in consumer goods industries and 13,342 in foodstuffs.

LABOUR. The economically active persons totalled 1,082,000 in April 1994, including 0·51m. professional workers, 468,900 manual workers and 77,800 self-employed. 35,200 persons were engaged in agriculture and forestry, 431,300 in production industries, 191,000 in commerce, transport and communications and 424,600 in other sectors. There were 169,321 persons registered unemployed in Dec. 1994 (111,721 females), and 10,286 on short time; unemployment rate was 14·7%.

ROADS. In 1994 there were 7,899·3 km of 'classified' roads (309 km of autobahn, 1,942·1 km of federal roads, 5,648·2 km of first- and second-class highways). Number of motor vehicles, Jan. 1995, 1,316,065, including 1,148,917 private cars, 88,929 lorries, 3,087 buses, 32,123 tractors and 32,132 motorcycles.

EDUCATION. In 1994–95 there were 702 primary schools with 132,666 pupils, 397 core curriculum schools with 123,415 pupils, 116 grammar schools with 86,797 pupils and 102 special schools with 17,088 pupils; there were 73,485 pupils in technical and professional education, and 4,126 in professional training for the disabled.

In the winter term 1994–95 there were 11 universities and colleges with 25,912 students enrolled.

Statistical information: Thüringer Landesamt für Statistik (Postfach 863, D-99017 Erfurt, Leipziger Str. 71, D-99085 Erfurt). *President:* Gerhard Scheuerer. Publications: *Statistisches Jahrbuch Thüringen,* since 1993. *Kreiszahlen für Thüringen,* since 1995. *Statistische Monatshefte Thüringen,* since 1994. *Statistische Berichte,* since 1991.

State library: Thüringer Universitäts- und Landesbibliothek, Jena.

GHANA

Republic of Ghana

Capital: Accra
Population: 16·47m. (1995)
GNP per capita: US$430 (1994)
HDI/world rank: 0·482/129 (1992)

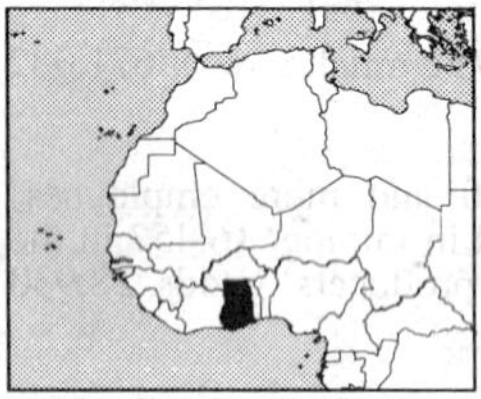

KEY HISTORICAL EVENTS. The State of Ghana came into existence on 6 March 1957 when the former Colony of the Gold Coast and the Trusteeship Territory of Togoland attained Dominion status.

The Ghana Independence Act received the royal assent on 7 Feb. 1957. The UN in Dec. 1956 approved the termination of British administration in Togoland and the union of Togoland with the Gold Coast on the latter's attainment of independence.

The country was declared a Republic within the Commonwealth on 1 July 1960 with Dr Kwame Nkrumah as the first President. On 24 Feb. 1966 the Nkrumah regime was overthrown in a military coup and ruled by the National Liberation Council until 1 Oct. 1969 when the military regime handed over power to a civilian regime under a new constitution. On 13 Jan. 1972 the armed forces and police took over power again.

In Oct. 1975 the National Redemption Council was subordinated to a Supreme Military Council (SMC). In 1979 the SMC was toppled in a coup led by Flight-Lieut. J. J. Rawlings. The new government permitted elections already scheduled and these resulted in a victory for Dr Hilla Limann and his People's National Party. However on 31 Dec. 1981 another coup led by Flight-Lieut. Rawlings dismissed the government and Parliament, suspended the constitution and established a Provisional National Defence Council to exercise all government powers.

A new pluralist democratic constitution was approved by referendum in April 1992. The Fourth Republic was proclaimed on 7 Jan. 1993.

TERRITORY AND POPULATION. Ghana is bounded west by the Côte d'Ivoire, north by Burkina Faso, east by Togo and south by the Gulf of Guinea. The area is 92,099 sq. miles (238,537 sq. km). Census population, 1984, 12,296,081. Estimate (1995) 16,470,000 (35% urban); density, 69 per sq. km.

Growth rate, 3·2%; infant mortality, 81 per 1,000 live births. Expectation of life was 53 years for males and 57 for females in 1991. 1m. Ghanaians lived abroad in 1995.

Ghana is divided into 10 regions:

Regions	*Area (sq. km)*	*Population census 1984*	*Capital*	*Population census 1984*
Eastern	19,977	1,680,890	Koforidua	58,731
Western	23,921	1,157,807	Sekondi-Takoradi	93,400
Central	9,826	1,142,335	Cape Coast	57,224
Ashanti	24,390	2,090,100	Kumasi	376,246
Brong-Ahafo	39,557	1,206,608	Sunyani	38,834
Northern	70,383	1,164,583	Tamale	135,952
Volta	20,572	1,211,907	Ho	37,777
Upper East	8,842	772,744	Bolgatanga	32,495
Upper West	18,477	438,008	Wa	. . .
Greater Accra	2,593	1,431,099	Accra	867,459

Chief cities with 1988 estimated populations: Accra, the capital, 949,113; Kumaisi, 385,192; Tamale, 151,069; Tema, 109,975; Sekondi-Takoradi, 103,653.

About 40% of the population are Akan. Other ethnic groups include Ashanti, Ewe, Fante, Ga and Gur. About 75 languages are spoken; the official language is English.

CLIMATE. The climate ranges from the equatorial type on the coast to savannah in the north and is typified by the existence of well-marked dry and wet seasons. Temperatures are relatively high throughout the year. The amount, duration and seasonal distribution of rain is very marked, from the south, with over 80" (2,000 mm) to the north, with under 50" (1,250 mm). In the extreme north, the wet season is from March to Aug., but further south it lasts until Oct. Near Kumasi, two wet seasons occur, in May and June and again in Oct. and this is repeated, with greater amounts, along the coast of Ghana. Accra. Jan. 80°F (26·7°C), July 77°F (25°C). Annual rainfall 29" (724 mm). Kumasi. Jan. 77°F (25°C), July 76°F (24·4°C). Annual rainfall 58" (1,402 mm). Sekondi-Takoradi. Jan. 79°F (25°C), July 76°F (24·4°C). Annual rainfall 47" (1,181 mm). Tamale. Jan. 82°F (27·8°C), July 78°F (25·6°C). Annual rainfall 41" (1,026 mm).

CONSTITUTION AND GOVERNMENT. After the coup of 31 Dec. 1981, supreme power was vested in the Provisional National Defence Council (PNDC), chaired by Flight-Lieut. Jerry John Rawlings.

A new constitution was approved by 92·6% of votes cast at a referendum on 28 April 1992. The electorate was 8,255,690; turn-out was 43·8%. The constitution sets up a presidential system on the US model, with a multi-party parliament and an independent judiciary.

At the presidential elections of 3 Nov. 1992 the electorate was 8·2m.; turn-out was 3·9m. Jerry John Rawlings was elected *President* by 58% of votes cast against 4 opponents.

At the elections for the 200-member parliament on 29 Dec. 1992 turn-out was 30%. The National Democratic Congress (NDC) won 198 seats, independents 2.

In Sept. 1995 the government comprised:

President: Jerry John Rawlings (b. 1947; NDC).

Vice-President: Kow Arkaah.

Minister of Foreign Affairs, Justice and Attorney-General: Dr Obed Y. Asamoah. *Interior:* Col. M. Osei-Owusu. *Defence:* Mahama Iddrisu. *Finance and Economic Planning:* Dr Kwesi Botchwey. *Trade and Industries:* Emma Mitchell. *Information:* Kofi Totobi Quakyi. *Food and Agriculture:* Ibrahim Adam. *Education:* Harry Sawyerr. *Health:* Commodore Steven G. Obimpeh. *Transport and Communications:* Edward Salia. *Local Government and Rural Development:* Kwamena Ahwoi. *Employment and Social Welfare:* David S. Boateng. *Lands and Forestry:* Dr Kwabena Adjei. *Mines and Energy:* Kwame Peprah. *Environment, Science and Technology:* Dr Christine Amoaka-Nuamah. *Parliamentary Affairs:* J. H. Owusu-Acheampong.

The *Speaker* is Daniel Annan.

National flag: Red, gold, green (horizontal); a black star in the centre.

National anthem: 'God bless our Homeland, Ghana'; words by the government, tune by P. Gbeho.

Local government: The 10 Regions, each under a Regional Secretary appointed by the PNDC, are divided into 110 districts.

DEFENCE

Army. The Army consists of 2 brigades, 1 reconnaissance regiment, 1 airborne force, 1 field engineer battalion, and 1 mortar battalion, with armoured cars and ancillary units. Total strength, (1996) 5,000. There is a paramilitary People's Militia of 5,000, a part-time force with police duties, and a Presidential Guard comprising 1 infantry battalion.

Navy. The Navy, based at Sekondi and Tema, comprises 2 German-built coastal patrol, 2 inshore patrol craft and 2 small service craft. 2 unarmed F-27 aircraft are available for maritime patrol. Naval strength in 1995 was 1,060 including support personnel.

Air Force. The Ghana Air Force has 4 Italian-built Aermacchi M.B.326K light ground attack jets. It also operates, for training, transport, search and rescue, and air survey operations, 4 Fokker Friendship twin-turboprop transports and a twin-turbofan Fokker Fellowship for Presidential use, 12 Islander piston-engined light transports and 4 Shorts Skyvan twin-turboprop short-take-off-and-landing transports; 2 Bell 212 helicopters; 4 Alouette III helicopters, and 8 L-29 Delfin and 2 M.B.339 jet trainers. There are air bases at Takoradi and Tamale. Personnel strength (1995) about 1,000.

INTERNATIONAL RELATIONS

Membership. Ghana is a member of the UN, the Commonwealth, OAU, ECOWAS and is an ACP state of the EU.

ECONOMY

Policy. A privatization programme was inaugurated in 1988. By 1995, 74 of the 260 enterprises in which the government had a majority stake had been sold.

Budget. The 1994 budget provided for (in ₵ 1,000m.): Revenue, 1,078 (of which petroleum tax, 157); expenditure, 1,016 (of which capital expenditure, 177).

VAT was abolished in 1995.

Currency. The monetary unit is the *cedi* (GHC) of 100 *pesewas* (P). There are coins of 0·5, 1, 5, 10, 20 and 50 pesewas and notes of ₵ 10, 20, 50, 100, 200, 500 and 1,000. Inflation was 50% in 1995. In March 1996, £1 = ₵2,346·09; US$1 = ₵1,535; DM1 = ₵1,040.

Banking and Finance. The Bank of Ghana was established in 1957 as the central bank and bank of issue. There are 3 large commercial banks, 7 secondary banks, 3 merchant banks and 100 rural banks. There are 2 discount houses. Banks are required to have a capital base of at least 6% of net assets.

There is a stock exchange in Accra.

ENERGY AND NATURAL RESOURCES

Electricity. Production (1990) 5,801m. kWh, mainly from 2 hydro-electric stations operated by the Volta River Authority, Akosombo (6 units) and Kpong (4 units), with a total capacity of 1,072 mW.

Minerals. In 1991 diamond production was 146,000 carats; manganese (1992), 284,000 tonnes; bauxite; 310,000 tonnes; gold (1994), 44·5 tonnes; (1993), 41·5 tonnes.

Agriculture. In 1992 agriculture contributed 41% of GDP. In southern and central Ghana main food crops are maize, rice, cassava, plantain, groundnuts, yam and cocoyam, and in northern Ghana groundnuts, rice, maize, sorghum, millet and yams.

Production of main food crops, 1993 (in 1,000 tonnes): Maize, 961; rice, 157; millet, 198; sorghum, 328; cassava, 4,200; cocoyam, 1,236; yam, 1,000; plantains, 1,322.

Cocoa is the main cash crop. Production (1994–5), 0·3m. tonnes. Among other cash crops, tobacco and coffee are important, and improved types of palm oil and coconuts are being planted.

Livestock, 1993: Cattle, 1·2m.; sheep, 2·2m.; goats, 2·2m.; pigs, 450,000; poultry, 12m.

Forestry. In 1988 the closed forest zone covered 8,225,900 hectares (36% of the land area), of which 2,559,400 hectares were reserves and 46,600 hectares unreserved forest lands. In 1990, 1,290,000 cu. metres of logs were produced.

Fisheries. Catch (1987) 324,630 tonnes (54,630 tonnes from inland waters).

INDUSTRY. Production of aluminium (1986) 120,000 tonnes.

FOREIGN ECONOMIC RELATIONS. Foreign debt was US$4,895m. in 1994.

Commerce. In 1992 exports were US$986·3m.; imports, US$1,456·6m. Principal exports, 1993 (in US$1m.): Gold, 416; cocoa and products, 280; timber, 140.

Imports were raw materials, capital equipment, petroleum and food. Main export markets, 1993: USA, 19·3%; Germany, 17·3%; UK, 9·5%. Main import suppliers: UK, 18·1%; USA, 12%; Germany, 6%.

Total trade between Ghana and UK (British Department of Trade returns, in £1,000 sterling):

	1991	*1992*	*1993*	*1994*	*1995*
Imports to UK	77,345	81,881	71,814	138,814	163,812
Exports and re-exports from UK	169,296	174,098	214,081	190,625	240,081

Tourism. In 1995 there were 335,000 tourists, bringing in foreign exchange earnings of US$273m.

COMMUNICATIONS

Roads. In 1988 agencies of the Ministry of Roads and Highways maintained about 14,514 km of trunk roads, 14,000 km of feeder and 10,000 km of other rural roads, and 1,700 km of city and municipal roads.

Railways. Total length of railways in 1993 was 954 km of 1,067 mm gauge. In 1993 railways carried 0·8m. tonnes of freight and 1·5m. passengers.

Civil Aviation. There is an international airport at Accra (Kotoka). The national carrier is the state-owned Ghana Airways, which in 1995 operated 1 DC-10-30, 1 DC-9-50, 1 F-28-2000 and 1 F-28-4000. Services were also provided by Aeroflot, Air Afrique, Air Ivoire, Alitalia, British Airways, Egyptair, Ethiopian Airlines, KLM, Libyan Airlines, Lufthansa, Middle East Airlines, Nigeria Airways, Northwest Airlines, Sierra National and Swissair.

Shipping. The chief ports are Takoradi and Tema. In 1995, sea-going shipping totalled 92,510 GRT, including oil tankers, 1,167 GRT.

Telecommunications. In 1987 there were 74,935 telephones. The Ghana Broadcasting Corporation is an autonomous statutory body. There are 2 national radio programmes (1 in English) and an external service (English, French, Hausa). In 1994 there was 1 public national and 1 independent local TV network. In 1993 there were 3,593,920 radio and 0·25m. TV receivers (colour by PAL).

Cinemas. In 1987 there were 83 cinemas with an average seating capacity of 1,200.

Press. There were (1994) 2 daily newspapers and several weeklies.

SOCIAL INSTITUTIONS

Justice. The Courts were constituted as follows:

Supreme Court. The Supreme Court consists of the Chief Justice who is also the President and not less than 4 other Justices of the Supreme Court. The Supreme Court is the final court of appeal in Ghana. The final interpretation of the provisions of the constitution has been entrusted to the Supreme Court.

Court of Appeal. The Court of Appeal consists of the Chief Justice together with not less than 5 other Justices of the Appeal court and such other Justices of Superior Courts as the Chief Justice may nominate. The Court of Appeal is duly constituted by 3 Justices. The Court of Appeal is bound by its own previous decisions and all courts inferior to the Court of Appeal are bound to follow the decisions of the Court of Appeal on questions of law. Divisions of the Appeal Court may be created, subject to the discretion of the Chief Justice.

High Court of Justice. The Court has jurisdiction in civil and criminal matters as well as those relating to industrial and labour disputes including administrative complaints. The High Court of Justice has supervisory jurisdiction over all inferior Courts and any adjudicating authority and in exercise of its supervisory jurisdiction has power to issue such directions, orders or writs including writs or orders in the nature of habeas corpus, certiorari, mandamus, prohibition and quo qarrantto. The High Court of Justice has no jurisdiction in cases of treason. The High Court consists of the Chief Justice and not less than 12 other judges and such other Justices of the Superior Court as the Chief Justice may appoint.

The PNDC has established Public Tribunals in addition to the traditional courts of justice.

There is a Public Tribunal Board consisting of not less than 5 members and not more than 15 members of the public appointed by the PNDC, at least one of whom shall be a lawyer of not less than 5 years' standing as a lawyer. The Board is responsible for the administration of all tribunals.

A tribunal consists of at least three persons and not more than five persons, selected by the Board from among persons appointed by the Council as members of public tribunals.

Religion. In 1990 9·4m. Christians represented 62·5% of the population and 2·36m. Moslems, 15·7%.

Education. Schooling is free and compulsory, and consists of 6 years of primary, 3 years of junior secondary and 3 years of senior secondary education. In 1989–90 75% of eligible children attended primary, and 39% secondary, school. In 1988–89 there were 1·7m. pupils in primary and 793,388 in secondary schools. University education is free. There are 2 universities, 1 university each for development studies, and science and technology. In 1994–95 there were 11,225 university students and 779 academic staff. There was also an institute of of management and a teacher training college.

Health. In 1988 medical facilities included 46 government hospitals, 252 health centres and posts, 3 university hospitals, 3 mental hospitals, 35 mission hospitals, 34 mission clinics and 40 private hospitals. In addition, there are 26 nurses and midwives training schools. There were 600 doctors, 5,190 nurses and 2,830 midwives in 1986.

DIPLOMATIC REPRESENTATIVES

Of Ghana in Great Britain (104 Highgate Hill, London N6 5HE)
High Commissioner: Vacant.

Of Great Britain in Ghana (Osu Link, off Gamel Abdul Nasser Ave., Accra)
High Commissioner: D. C. Walker, CMG, CVO.

Of Ghana in the USA (3512 International Dr., NW, Washington, D.C., 20008)
Ambassador: Ekwo Spio-Garbrah.

Of the USA in Ghana (Ring Rd. East, Accra)
Ambassador: Edward Bryun.

Of Ghana to the United Nations
Ambassador: George O. Lamptey.

Further Reading

Carmichael, J., *Profile of Ghana.* London, 1992.—*African Eldorado: Ghana from Gold Coast to Independence.* London, 1993
Davidson, B., *Black Star.* London, 1973
Herbst, J., *The Politics of Reform in Ghana, 1982–1991.* California Univ. Press, 1993
Myers, R. A., *Ghana:* [Bibliography]. Oxford and Santa Barbara, 1991
Petchenkine, Y., *Ghana in Search of Stability, 1957–1992.* New York, 1992
Ray, D. I., *Ghana: Politics, Economics and Society.* London, 1986
Rimmer, D., *Staying Poor: Ghana's Political Economy, 1950–1990.* Oxford, 1993
Rothchild., D. (ed.): *Ghana: the Political Economy of Recovery.* Boulder, (Colo.), 1991

National statistical office: Statistical Service, Accra.

GIBRALTAR

Population: 28,051 (1993)
GNP per capita: US$14,711 (1991)

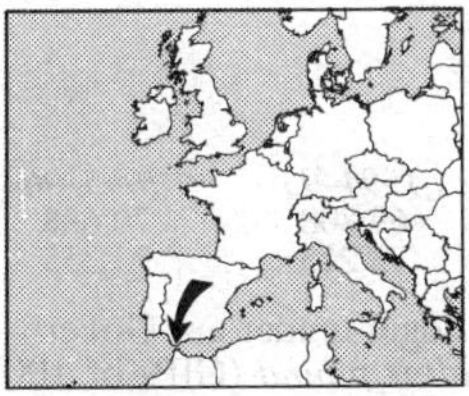

KEY HISTORICAL EVENTS. The Rock of Gibraltar was settled by Moors in 711. In 1462 it was taken by the Spaniards, from Granada. It was captured by Admiral Sir George Rooke on 24 July 1704, and ceded to Great Britain by the Treaty of Utrecht, 1713. The cession was confirmed by the treaties of Paris (1763) and Versailles (1783).

On 10 Sept. 1967, in pursuance of a UN resolution on the decolonization of Gibraltar, a referendum was held to ascertain whether the people of Gibraltar wished to retain their link with the UK or pass under Spanish sovereignty. Out of an electorate of 12,762, 12,138 voted to retain the British connexion.

The border was closed by Spain in 1969, opened to pedestrians in 1982 and fully opened in 1985.

TERRITORY AND POPULATION. Area, 2½ sq. miles (6·5 sq. km). Total population, including port and harbour (census, 1991), 28,074. Estimate (31 Dec. 1994) 27,107 (of whom 20,313 were British Gibraltarian, 4,150 Other British and 2,644 Non-British). The population is mostly of Genoese, Portuguese and Maltese as well as Spanish descent.

Vital statistics (1994): Births, 509; marriages, 697; deaths, 261.

CLIMATE. The climate is warm temperate, with westerly winds in winter bringing rain. Summers are pleasantly warm and rainfall is low. Jan. 56°F (13·4°C), July 75°F (23·7°C). Annual rainfall 30" (768 mm).

CONSTITUTION AND GOVERNMENT. A new Constitution was introduced in 1969. The Legislative and City Councils were merged to produce an enlarged legislature known as the *Gibraltar House of Assembly*. Executive authority is exercised by the Governor, who is also Commander-in-Chief. The Governor, while retaining certain reserved powers, is normally required to act in accordance with the advice of the Gibraltar Council, which consists of 4 *ex-officio* members (the Deputy Governor, the Deputy Fortress Commander, the Attorney-General and the Financial and Development Secretary) together with 5 elected members of the House of Assembly appointed by the Governor after consultation with the Chief Minister. Matters of primarily domestic concern are devolved to elected Ministers, with Britain responsible for other matters, including external affairs, defence and internal security. There is a Council of Ministers presided over by the Chief Minister.

The House of Assembly consists of a Speaker appointed by the Governor, 15 elected and 2 *ex-officio* members (the Attorney-General and the Financial and Development Secretary). No more than 8 of the elected seats may go to the winning party at elections.

A Mayor of Gibraltar is elected by the elected members of the Assembly.

At the elections of Jan. 1992 the electorate was 17,800; turn-out was 72%. The Gibraltar Socialist and Labour Party (GSLP) gained 8 seats with 73% of votes cast (58% in 1988). The Gibraltar Social Democratic Party gained 7 with 20%.

Governor and C.-in-C.: Adm. Sir Hugo White.
Chief Minister: Joseph John Bossano (b.1940; GSLP).

Flag: White with a red strip along the bottom, a red triple-towered castle with a gold key depending from the gateway.

DEFENCE. The Ministry of Defence presence consists of a tri-service garrison numbering approximately 780 uniformed personnel with an additional 220 part-time Gibraltar Regiment volunteer soldiers. Supporting the garrison are approximately 1,100 locally-employed civilian personnel. In addition to the defence of the Rock the garrison supports a NATO Headquarters, provides and operates communications and surveillance facilities, operates the airfield and provides berthing facilities for naval vessels in the harbour.

ECONOMY

Budget. Revenue and expenditure (in £1,000 sterling):

	1991–92	*1992–93*	*1993–94*	*1994–95*	*1995–96*
Revenue	92,810	72,735	73,443	69,808	70,688
Expenditure	97,239	77,915	74,697	73,215	73,255

Currency. The legal tender currency is UK sterling. Also legal tender are Government of Gibraltar Currency Notes and coins for the *Gibraltar pound* (GIP) of 100 *pence*, at parity with the UK £1 sterling. There are Gibraltar Government coins of 1, 2, 5, 10, 20 and 50 pence and Gib£1, 2 and 5, and notes of Gib£1, 5, 10, 20 and 50. The amount in notes in circulation at 31 March 1995 was £11·42m.

Banking and Finance. In Dec. 1995 domestic and offshore banking services were provided by 27 banks. There are 4 building societies.

INDUSTRY. There is a bottling plant and a floppy diskette manufacturer.

Labour. The total insured labour force at 31 Dec. 1994 was 11,972. 32·5% of the local labour force is employed by the UK departments and the Gibraltar Government. In the private sector the main sources of employment are the construction industry, wholesale and retail distribution, and banking, finance and insurance.

Trade Unions. In 1991 there were 8 registered trade unions.

FOREIGN ECONOMIC RELATIONS. Gibraltar has a special status within the EU which exempts it from the latter's fiscal policy.

Commerce. Imports and exports (in £1,000 sterling):

	1988	*1989*	*1990*	*1991*	*1992*
Imports	144,787	200,493	266,348	278,900	...
Exports	46,093	76,138	101,679	70,600	82,238

Britain and the Commonwealth provide the bulk of imports, but fresh vegetables and fruit come mainly from the Netherlands and Spain. Foodstuffs accounted for 10% of total imports (about £27m.) in 1991; about 30% of non-fuel imports originated from the UK. Other sources include Japan, Spain and the Netherlands. Value of non-fuel imports, 1991, £219·1m. Exports are mainly re-exports of petroleum and petroleum products supplied to shipping. Gibraltar depends largely on tourism, offshore banking and other financial sector activity, the entrepôt trade and the provision of supplies to visiting ships. Exports of local produce are negligible.

Total trade between Gibraltar and UK (British Department of Trade returns, in £1,000 sterling):

	1991	*1992*	*1993*	*1994*	*1995*
Imports to UK	4,289	4,059	3,693	4,819	10,598
Exports and re-exports from UK	80,105	82,238	103,402	74,866	79,579

Tourism. The number of tourists in 1993 was 4,279,995.

COMMUNICATIONS

Roads. There are 33 miles of roads including 4·25 miles of pedestrian way.

Civil Aviation. There is an international airport, Gibraltar North Front. Scheduled flights are operated by GB Airways to London (Heathrow and Gatwick), Manchester, Tangiers, Marrakesh, Casablanca and Agadir. 0·09m. passengers arrived by air in 1994.

Shipping. A total of 3,528 merchant ships of 57·9m. GRT entered port during 1995, including 2,566 deep-sea ships of 57·3m. GRT. In addition, 256 ships of 11·3m. GRT called off limits. In 1995, 4,415 calls were made by yachts of 198,401 GRT. 130 cruise liners called during 1995 involving 85,681 passengers.

Telecommunications. The national Telephone Service is operated by Gibraltar Nynex Communications, in which the Government has a stake. The number of telephones (1994) was 19,356. A new Digital System X Exchange became operational in 1990 with capacity for 25,800 lines by 1994. A Fibre Optic Network became operational in 1991. International direct dialling is available to over 150 countries via the Gibraltar Telecommunications Ltd (Gibtel) Earth Satellite Station and other international circuits. Gibtel began operating a mobile system in 1994. A direct airmail service to Morocco, servicing Casablanca, and to London (Heathrow and Gatwick), is run by GB Airways. Radio Gibraltar broadcasts for 24 hours daily, in English and Spanish, and GBC Television operates for 24 hours daily on weekdays in English. Estimated number of TV licenses as at 31 Dec. 1994, 5,763.

Press. There were (1992) 1 daily and 4 weeklies.

SOCIAL INSTITUTIONS

Justice. The judicial system is based on the English system. There is a Court of Appeal, a Supreme Court, presided over by the Chief Justice, a court of first instance, a magistrates' court, a coroner's court and a juvenile court.

Religion. Religion of civil population mostly Roman Catholic; 1 Anglican and 1 Roman Catholic cathedral and 2 Anglican and 6 Roman Catholic churches; 1 Presbyterian and 1 Methodist church and 4 synagogues; annual subsidy to each communion, £500.

Education. Free compulsory education is provided between ages 5 and 15 years. The medium of instruction is English. The comprehensive system was introduced in Sept. 1972. There were (1995) 12 primary and 2 comprehensive schools. Primary schools are mixed and divided into first schools for children aged 4-8 years and middle schools for children aged 8-12 years. The comprehensives are single-sex. In addition, there is 1 Services primary school and 1 private primary school. A new purpose-built Special School for severely handicapped children aged 2-16 years was opened in 1977, and there are 3 Special Units for children with special educational needs (1 attached to a first school, 1 to a middle school and 1 at secondary level), 2 nurseries for children aged 3-4 years and an occupational therapy centre for handicapped adults. Technical education is available at the Gibraltar College of Further Education managed by the Gibraltar Government. In Sept. 1995, there were 2,748 pupils at government primary schools, 189 at private and 304 at the Services school; 19 at the special school; 936 at the boys' comprehensive school and 882 at the girls' comprehensive. There were 196 full-time and 498 part-time students in the Gibraltar College of Further Education in Sept. 1995. Scholarships are made available for universities, teacher-training and other higher education in the UK. Government expenditure on education in the year ended 31 March 1995 was £11·1m.

Health. In 1994 there were 2 hospitals with 244 beds and 29 doctors. Total expenditure on medical and health services during year ended 31 March 1994 was £17,933,599.

Further Reading

Gibraltar Year Book. Gibraltar, (Annual)
Ellicott, D., *Our Gibraltar.* Gibraltar, 1975
Green, M. M., *A Gibraltar Bibliography.* London, 1980.—*Supplement.* London, 1982
Hills, G., *Rock of Contention: a History of Gibraltar.* London, 1974
Jackson, W. G. F., *The Rock of the Gibraltarians.* Farleigh Dickinson Univ. Press, 1987
Magauran, H. C., *Rock Siege: the Difficulties with Spain 1964–85.* Gibraltar, 1986
Morris, D. S. and Haigh, R. H., *Britain, Spain and Gibraltar, 1945-90: the Eternal Triangle.* London, 1992
Shields, G. J., *Gibraltar.* [Bibliography] Oxford and Santa Barbara (CA), 1988

GREECE

Elliniki Dimokratia

(Hellenic Republic)

Capital: Athens
Population: 10·4m. (1993)
GNP per capita: US$7,710 (1994)
HDI/world rank: 0·907/22 (1992)

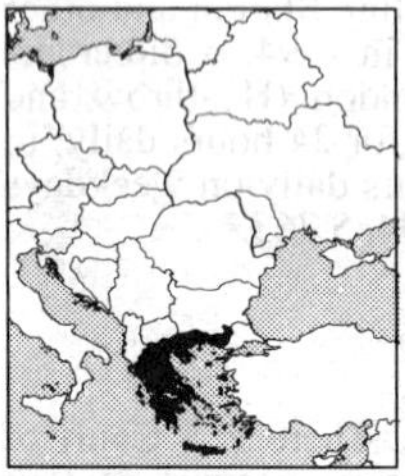

KEY HISTORICAL EVENTS. Greece gained her independence from Turkey in 1821–29, and by the Protocol of London, of 3 Feb. 1830, was declared a kingdom, under the guarantee of Great Britain, France and Russia. For details of the subsequent history to 1947 *see* THE STATESMAN'S YEAR-BOOK, 1957, pp. 1069–70. A coup took place on 21 April 1967, and a military government was formed which suspended the 1952 constitution. King Constantine went abroad in 1967, and a republic was established after referendums in 1973 and 1974. The military government collapsed on 23 July 1974 and a new constitution was introduced in June 1975.

TERRITORY AND POPULATION. Greece is bounded in the north by Albania, the Former Yugoslav Republic of Macedonia (FYROM) and Bulgaria, east by Turkey and the Aegean Sea, south by the Mediterranean and west by the Ionian Sea. The total area is 131,957 sq. km (50,949 sq. miles), of which the inhabited islands account for 25,042 sq. km (9,669 sq. miles).

The population was 10,259,900 (5,204,492 females) according to the census of March 1991. Therre were 166,031 resident foreign nationals. 1993 estimate, 10·4m.

In 1987 the territory of Greece was administratively reorganized into 13 *regions* comprising in all 51 *departments.* Areas and populations according to the 1991 census:

Region/Department	*Area in sq. km*	*Population*	*Chief town*
Attica [1]	*3,808*	*3,523,407*	*Athens*
Aegean North	*3,836*	*199,231*	*Mytilene*
Chios	904	52,184	Chios
Lesbos	2,154	105,082	Mytilene
Samos	778	41,965	Samos
Aegean South	*5,286*	*257,481*	*Hermoupolis*
Cyclades	2,572	94,005	Hermoupolis
Dodecanese	2,714	163,476	Rhodes
Crete	*8,336*	*540,054*	*Heraklion*
Canea	2,376	133,774	Canea
Heraklion	2,641	264,906	Heraklion
Lassithi	1,823	71,279	Aghios Nikolaos
Rethymnon	1,496	70,095	Rethymnon
Epirus	*9,203*	*339,728*	*Ioannina*
Arta	1,662	78,719	Arta
Ioannina	4,990	158,193	Ioannina
Preveza	1,036	58,628	Preveza
Thesprotia	1,515	44,188	Hegoumenitsa
Greece Central [2]	*15,549*	*582,280*	*Lamia*
Boeotia	2,952	134,108	Levadeia
Euboea	4,167	208,408	Chalcis
Evrytania	1,869	24,307	Karpenissi
Phocis	2,120	44,183	Amphissa
Phthiotis	4,441	171,274	Lamia
Greece West	*11,350*	*707,687*	*Patras*
Achaia	3,271	300,078	Patras
Elia	2,618	179,429	Pyrgos
Aetolia and Acarnania	5,461	228,180	Missolonghi

[1] Attica is both region and department. [2] Without Attica.

Region/Department	Area in sq. km	Population	Chief town
Ionian Islands	*2,307*	*193,734*	*Corfu*
Cephalonia	904	32,474	Argostoli
Corfu	641	107,592	Corfu
Leucas	356	21,111	Leucas
Zante	406	32,557	Zante
Macedonia Central	*19,147*	*1,710,513*	*Thessaloniki*
Chalcidice	2,918	92,117	Polygyros
Imathia	1,701	138,934	Veroia
Kilkis	2,519	81,710	Kilkis
Mount Athos	336	1,536	–
Pella	2,506	138,761	Edessa
Pieria	1,516	116,763	Katerini
Serres	3,968	192,828	Serres
Thessaloniki	3,683	946,864	Thessaloniki
Macedonia East and Thrace	*14,157*	*570,496*	*Comotini*
Cavalla	2,111	135,937	Cavalla
Drama	3,468	96,554	Drama
Evros	4,242	143,752	Alexandroupolis
Rhodope	2,543	103,190	Comotini
Xanthi	1,793	91,063	Xanthi
Macedonia West	*9,451*	*293,015*	*Kozani*
Florina	1,924	53,147	Florina
Grevena	2,291	36,797	Grevena
Kastoria	1,720	52,685	Kastoria
Kozani	3,516	150,386	Kozani
Peloponnese	*15,490*	*607,428*	*Tripolis*
Arcadia	4,419	105,309	Tripolis
Argolis	2,154	97,636	Nauplion
Corinth	2,290	141,823	Corinth
Laconia	3,636	95,696	Sparta
Messenia	2,991	166,964	Calamata
Thessaly	*14,037*	*734,846*	*Larissa*
Karditsa	2,636	126,854	Karditsa
Larissa	5,381	270,612	Larissa
Magnesia	2,636	198,434	Volo
Trikala	3,384	138,946	Trikala

The largest cities (1991 census populations) are Athens (the capital), 772,072 (total conurbation of Greater Athens, 3,072,922); Thessaloniki, 383,967; Piraeus, 182,671; Patras, 152,570; Peristerion, 137,288; Heraklion, 115,124; Larissa, 112,777; Kallithea, 114,233.

The Monastic Republic of Mount Athos (or Agion Oros, i.e. 'Holy Mountain'), the easternmost of the three prongs of the peninsula of Chalcidice, is a self-governing community composed of 20 monasteries. The peninsula is administered by a Council of 4 members and an Assembly of 20 members, 1 deputy from each monastery. The Constitution of 1927 gives legal sanction to the Charter of Mount Athos, drawn up by representatives of the 20 monasteries on 20 May 1924, and its status is confirmed by the 1952 and 1975 Constitutions.

Vital statistics (1992): 104,081 live births; 629 still births; 2,745 births to unmarried mothers; 48,631 marriages; 98,231 deaths.

There are small Slav- and Turkish-speaking minorities. The 1991 census did not enumerate such groups.

The modern Greek language had 2 contesting literary standard forms, the archaizing *Katharevousa* ('purist'), and a version based on the spoken vernacular, 'Demotic'. In 1976 Standard Modern Greek was adopted as the official language, with Demotic as its core.

CLIMATE. Coastal regions and the islands have typical Mediterranean conditions, with mild, rainy winters and hot, dry, sunny summers. Rainfall comes almost entirely in the winter months, though amounts vary widely according to position and relief. Continental conditions affect the northern mountainous areas, with severe winters, deep snow cover and heavy precipitation, but summers are hot. Athens. Jan. 48°F (8·6°C), July 82·5°F (28·2°C). Annual rainfall 16·6" (414·3 mm).

CONSTITUTION AND GOVERNMENT. A new Constitution was introduced in June 1975. The 300-member *Chamber of Deputies* is elected for 4-year terms by proportional representation. Extra seats are awarded to the party which leads in an election. The Chamber of Deputies elects the head of state, the *President*, for a 5-year term.

President: Costis Stefanopoulos (elected 8 March 1995).

Parliamentary elections were held on 10 Oct. 1993. The electorate was 8,792,082; turn-out was 78·18%. Seats gained (and % of vote): Pasok (i.e. Panhellenic Socialist Movement), 170 (46·9%); New Democracy, 111 (39·33%); Political Spring, 10 (4·86%); Communist Party, 9 (4·52%).

A new government was formed on 22 Jan. 1996, comprising:

Prime Minister: Costas Simitis (b. 1937).

Interior, Public Administration and Decentralization: Akis Tsohatzopoulos. *Defence:* Gerasimos Arsenis. *Foreign Affairs:* Theodoros Pangalos. *Economy:* Yiannos Papantoniou. *Finance:* Alekos Papadopoulos. *Agriculture:* Stephanos Tzoumakas. *Labour and Social Security:* Evangelos Yannopoulos. *Health and Welfare:* Anastasios Peponis. *Justice:* Evangelos Venizelos. *Education and Religious Affairs:* George Papandreou. *Culture:* Stavros Benos. *Merchant Marine:* Kosmas Sfiriou. *Public Order:* Kostas Geitonas. *Macedonia and Thrace:* Phillipos Petsalnikos. *The Aegean:* Antonis Kotsakas. *Environment, Town Planning and Public Works:* Kostas Laliotis. *Industry, Energy and Technology and Commerce and Tourism:* Vasso Papandreou. *Transport and Communications:* Haris Kastanidis. *Press and Media Government Spokesman:* Dimitris Reppas.

National flag: Nine horizontal stripes of blue and white, with a canton of blue with a white cross.

National anthem: Imnos eis tin Eleftherian (*Hymn to Freedom*); words by Dionysios Solomos, tune by N. Mantzaros.

European Parliament. Greece has 25 representatives. At the June 1994 elections turn-out was 71·9%. Pasok won 10 seats with 37·6% of votes cast (group in European Parliament: European Socialist Party); New Democracy, 9 with 32·7% (Popular European Party); left-wing coalition, 4 with 12·5%; others, 2 with 8·7%.

Local government: Departments are headed by prefects, elected for the first time in Oct. 1994. Mayoral elections were also held in 434 municipalities. Pasok and other socialists gained 213 municipalities and 37 departments with 45% of votes cast; New Democracy, 160 and 13 with 39%.

DEFENCE. Conscription is (Army) 19 months, (Navy) 23 months, (Air Force) 21 months.

Army. The Field Army is organized in 3 military regions, with 1 Army, 4 corps and 2 divisional headquarters. There are 9 infantry divisions, 5 independent armoured, 2 independent mechanized, 2 infantry and 1 marine brigade, 1 commando and 1 raider regiment, 4 reconnaissance, 10 field artillery, 8 air defence artillery, 2 surface-to-air missile and 2 army aviation battalions and 1 independent aviation company. There is also a Territorial Defence Force of 36,000, with 4 military command headquarters, comprising 1 infantry division, 1 parachute regiment and 8 field artillery, 4 air defence artillery and 1 army aviation battalion. Reserves of 35,000 form a National Guard whose role is internal security. Equipment includes 89 M-47, 998 M-48, 154 AMX-30 and 356 Leopard 1A3 main battle tanks. Hellenic Army Aviation has over 150 helicopters, including 12 armed AH-64 Apaches, 40 AB-205 and 50 UH-1H Iroquois, 15 JetRangers, 9 Chinooks, 15 Nardi-Hughes 300s, and 20 Cessna U-17A observation aircraft and 1 Super King Air transport. Total Army strength (1996) 125,000 (98,000 conscripts, 2,900 women). There is also a paramilitary gendarmerie of 26,500.

Navy. The current strength of the Hellenic Navy includes 8 diesel submarines,

4 ex-US guided-missile destroyers, 9 frigates, 5 corvettes and 18 fast missile craft. Smaller units include 10 fast torpedo craft, 4 coastal and 5 inshore patrol craft and 16 mine countermeasure vessels. Substantial amphibious lift is provided by 1 dock landing ship, 7 tank landing ships and 4 medium landing ships as well as about 65 landing craft. Major auxiliaries include 2 small replenishment tankers, 2 oilers, 1 logistic support, 1 ammunition transport, 5 survey ships and 1 training ship. There are about 40 minor auxiliaries and service craft. Main bases are at Salamis, Patras, and Soudha Bay (Crete).

The Air Force operates 2 HU-16 Albatross maritime patrol amphibians on naval tasks; and the Navy 11 AB-212 and 6 S-70B Seahawk anti-submarine helicopters and 2 Alouettes for search-and-rescue operations and liaison.

Personnel in 1995 totalled 19,500.

The Coastguard and Customs service, 4,000 strong, operate about 100 small patrol craft and 4 reconnaissance aircraft.

Air Force. The Hellenic Air Force (HAF) had a strength (1995) of 26,800 (14,400 conscripts, 1,100 women). There are 3 squadrons of F-4E Phantom and 2 squadrons of Mirage 2000 air-superiority fighters, 2 squadrons of F-16 fighter-bombers, 2 squadrons of Mirage F.1 fighters, 5 squadrons of A-7H Corsair II attack aircraft, 1 squadron of F-5 fighters, 1 squadron of RF-4E reconnaissance fighters and 1 squadron of PC–Orions replacing HU-16B Albatross ASW amphibians (under Navy control). There are also transport squadrons equipped with C-130 Hercules (17), NAMC YS-11, 12 Canadair CL-215 twin-engined amphibians, 32 T-2E Buckeye training/attack aircraft, other training and helicopter equipment, and anti-aircraft units equipped with Nike-Hercules and Hawk surface-to-air missiles.

The HAF is organized into Tactical and Air Support Commands.

INTERNATIONAL RELATIONS. On 13 Sept. 1995 under UN auspices an agreement was reached with the former Yugoslav Republic of Macedonia to normalize relations following the latter's modification of its national flag.

Membership. Greece is a member of the UN, EU, WEU, Council of Europe and NATO. The Schengen Accord of 1990 abolishes border controls between Greece and Austria, Belgium, France, Germany, Italy, Luxembourg, the Netherlands, Portugal and Spain. On 26 March 1995 it came into effect, but has not yet been implemented by Austria, Greece and Italy.

ECONOMY

Policy. In 1990 the Government embarked on a large-scale privatization of state industries.

Budget. Estimated revenue for 1993, Dr 9,156,719m.; expenditure, Dr 8,181,719m.

VAT is 18% (reduced rate, 8%).

Currency. The unit of currency is the *drachma* (GRD), notionally divided into 100 *lepta*. There are coins of 1, 2, 5, 10, 20, 50 and 100 and notes of 500, 1,000, 5,000 and 10,000 drachmai. Inflation was 11·8% in Dec. 1994. In March 1996, £1 = 369·81 drachmai; US$1 = 241·96 drachmai; DM1 = 163·94 drachmai.

Banking and Finance. The central bank and bank of issue is the Bank of Greece. Its *Governor* is Loukas Papademos. There were 25 domestic banks in 1994, 8 private and the remainder in 4 state groupings. In 1993 the major banks (with assets in US$1,000m.) were: The state-owned National Bank (6,487), Agricultural Bank (2,531), Commercial Bank (1,792) and Ionian and Popular Bank (893); and the private Credit Bank (1,054). Total assets of all banks were US$21,302,000m.

There is a stock exchange in Athens.

Weights and Measures. The metric system was made obligatory in 1959; the use of other systems is prohibited. The Gregorian calendar was adopted in Feb. 1923.

ENERGY AND NATURAL RESOURCES

Electricity. Total installed capacity was 9,228,730 kW as at 31 Dec. 1991. 75% of power is supplied by lignite-fired power stations. A national grid supplies the mainland, and islands near its coast. Power is produced in remoter islands by local generators. Total net production in 1992 was 33,454m. kWh.

Oil. Output, 1992, 5,008,368 bbls.

Minerals. Greece produces a variety of ores and minerals, including (with production, 1991, in tonnes) iron-pyrites (35,332), bauxite (2,132,716), nickel (2,023,678), magnesite (590,188), asbestos (285,950), chromite (113,378), barytes (546), marble (white and coloured) and various other earths. There is little coal, and the lignite is of indifferent quality (51·9m. tonnes, 1989). Salt production (1992) 143,184 tonnes.

Agriculture. Of the total area (131,957 sq. km) 39,300 sq. km is arable and fallow. Another 52,550 sq. km is grazing land.

Production (1992 provisional, in 1,000 tonnes):

Wheat	2,344	Grapes	234
Rye	36	Wine must	439
Tobacco	187	Citrus fruit	1,198
Seed cotton	790	Other fruit	1,694
Sugar-beet	3,191	Milk	1,731
Raisins	97	Meat	470
Olive oil	197		

Olive production in 1989 was about 1·5m. tonnes. Rice, 1993, 145,000 tonnes. The main kinds of cheese produced are *fetta* (white cheese in brine, 111,000 tonnes in 1993), and hard cheese, 38,000.

Livestock (1990, in 1,000): 624 cattle, 1 buffaloes, 996 pigs, 8,660 sheep, 5,334 goats, 45 horses, 60 mules, 127 asses, 26,767 poultry.

Forestry. Forest covered 29,511 sq. km in 1991.

Fisheries. In 1993, 20,149 fishermen were active and landed 169,958 tonnes of fish. 2,000 kg of sponges were produced in 1993.

INDUSTRY. Manufacturing contributed an estimated 2,219,730m. drachmai to GDP in 1993. The main products are canned vegetables and fruit, fruit juice, beer, wine, alcoholic beverages, cigarettes, textiles, yarn, leather, shoes, synthetic timber, paper, plastics, rubber products, chemical acids, pigments, pharmaceutical products, cosmetics, soap, disinfectants, fertilizers, glassware, porcelain sanitary items, wire and power coils and household instruments.

Production, 1992 (1,000 tonnes): Textile yarns, 144; cement, 12,761; fertilizers, 1,234; ammonia, 168; iron (concrete-reinforcing bars), 761; alumina, 626; aluminium, 175; beer, 403; bottled wine, 110; chemical acids, 1,276; iron wire, 113; glass products, 98; packing materials, 538; cigarettes (1,000 pieces), 33,948; petroleum, 8,498; detergents, 145.

Labour. Of the employed people in 1992, 806,661 were engaged in agriculture, 698,780 in manufacturing and 2,178,987 in other employment. Automatic index-linking of wages was abolished at the end of 1990. Wage increases of 8% were made in the public sector in 1991. In the private sector trade unions agreed to a 12% increase in 1991 and one of 9% in 1992. Since 1989 a statutory minimum of wage-bills must be spent on training. Retirement age is 65 years for men and 60 for women.

Trade Unions. The status of trade unions is regulated by the Associations Act 1914. Trade-union liberties are guaranteed under the Constitution, and a law of June 1982 altered the unions' right to strike.

The national body of trade unions is the Greek General Confederation of Labour.

FOREIGN ECONOMIC RELATIONS. Following the normalization of their relations, Greece lifted its trade embargo (imposed in Feb. 1994) on Macedonia on 13 Oct. 1995.

Commerce. In 1993 exports totalled (in 1m. drachmai) 1,933,432 including: Miscellaneous manufactured articles, 472,172; clothing and accessories (excluding footwear), 406,347; basic manufactures, 387,578; food and live animals, 382,714; vegetables and fruit, 230,408; mineral fuels, lubricants, etc., 151,653; petroleum and petroleum products, 148,423; refined petroleum products, 134,502; beverages and tobacco, 121,235; crude materials (inedible) except fuels, 111,558. Imports totalled 5,050,531 including: Machinery and transport equipment, 1,775,985; road vehicles and parts and other transport equipment (excluding tyres, engines and electrical parts), 931,044; basic manufactures, 834,445; food and live animals, 567,058; chemicals and related products, 557,661; mineral fuels, lubricants, etc., 535,679; petroleum and petroleum products, 516,688; miscellaneous manufactured articles, 495,764; crude petroleum, 383,910; ships, boats and floating structures, 329,188.

Exports in 1993 (in 1m. drachmai) were mainly to Germany (458,984), Italy (255,982), France (119,616), UK (110,301) and USA (86,467). Imports were mainly from Germany (854,475), Italy (707,466), France (398,504), Japan (343,756), the Netherlands (334,920) and UK (307,081).

Total trade between Greece and UK (British Department of Trade returns, in £1,000 sterling):

	1990	*1991*	*1992*	*1993*	*1994*
Imports to UK	400,476	378,146	372,191	296,900	331,900
Exports and re-exports from UK	682,887	667,741	770,742	830,700	871,700

Tourism. Tourists in 1993 numbered 9,913,267. Tourist spending, US$3,335m. in 1993. In 1993 there were 499,606 hotel beds.

COMMUNICATIONS

Roads. There were, in 1992, 38,606 km of roads, of which 9,255 were national and 29,351 provincial roads. Number of motor vehicles in 1993: 2,807,447, of which 1,958,544 were passenger cars, 825,697 goods vehicles and 23,206 buses.

Railways. In 1992 the state network, Hellenic Railways (OSE), totalled 2,484 km including 1,565 km of 1,435 mm gauge, 874 km of 1,000 mm gauge, and 22 km of 750 mm gauge. Railways carried 3·4m. tonnes of freight and 11·7m. passengers in 1993.

Civil Aviation. There are international airports at Athens (Hellinikon) and Thessaloniki-Macedonia. In 1995 the state-owned Olympic Airways operated 4 A300B4-100s, 2 A300B4-200s, 2 A300B4-600Rs, 2 B-727-200s, 1 B-727-200 Adv, 11 B-737-200 Advs, 7 B-737-400s and 4 B-747-200Bs. 6·7m. passengers were carried in 1989. It operates routes from Athens to all important cities of the country, Europe, the Middle East and USA. Services are also provided by Aeroflot, Air France, Air Malta, Air Moldova, Air Ukraine, Alitalia, Armenian Airlines, Austrian Airlines, Azerbaijan Hava Yollary, Balkan, British Airways, Condor, Cyprus Airways, Czech Airlines, Delta, Egyptair, El Al, Ethiopian Airlines, Finnair, Gulf Air, Hamburg Airlines, Hapag Lloyd, Iberia, Iran Air, JAT, KLM, Kuwait Airways, Libyan Airlines, LOT, LTU, Lufthansa, Luxair, Malév, Middle East Airlines, Pakistan Airlines, Royal Air Maroc, Royal Jordanian, Sabena, SAS, Singapore Airlines, Swissair, Syrian Airlines, TAP, Tarom, Thai Airways, Trans World, Tunis Air, Turkish Airlines, Uzbekistan Airways and Virgin Atlantic.

Shipping. In 1995 the merchant navy comprised 2,937 vessels of 118·4m. DWT, representing 17·89% of the world's total fleet tonnage. 1,889 vessels (55·69% of tonnage) were registered under foreign flags. Totalled registered tonnage, 30·25m. GRT, including 13·45m. GRT of oil tankers and 0·64m. GRT of container ships.

There is a canal (opened 9 Nov. 1893) across the Isthmus of Corinth (about 4 miles).

Telecommunications. In 1993 there were 5,161 telephone exchanges and 5,571,293 telephones.

Elliniki Radiophonia Tileorasis (ERT), the Hellenic National Radio and Television Institute, is the government broadcasting station. There are 4 national and regional programmes, and an external service, Voice of Greece (16 languages). ERT broadcasts 2 TV programmes (colour by SECAM). Number of receivers in 1993: Radio, 4,085,000; television, 2·3m.

Cinemas. There were 236 screens in 1994. There were 6·2m. admissions in 1992. 11 full-length films were made in 1994.

Press (1988). There were 35 daily newspapers published in Athens, 6 in Piraeus and 76 elsewhere.

SOCIAL INSTITUTIONS

Justice. Judges are appointed for life by the President after consultation with the judicial council. Judges enjoy personal and functional independence. There are 3 divisions of the courts: Administrative, civil and criminal and they must not give decisions which are contrary to the Constitution. Final jurisdiction lies with a Special Supreme Tribunal.

Religion. The Christian Eastern (Greek) Orthodox Church is the established religion to which 98% of the population belong. It is under an archbishop and 67 metropolitans, 1 archbishop and 7 metropolitans in Crete, and 4 metropolitans in the Dodecanese. Roman Catholics have 3 archbishops (in Naxos and Corfu and, not recognized by the State, in Athens) and 1 bishop (for Syra and Santorin). The Exarchs of the Greek Catholics and the Armenians are not recognized by the State. There were 0·15m. Moslems in 1995.

Complete religious freedom is recognized by the Constitution of 1968, but proselytizing from, and interference with, the Greek Orthodox Church is forbidden.

Education. Public education is provided in nursery, primary and secondary schools, starting at 5½–6½ years of age and free at all levels.

In 1990–91 there were 5,518 nursery schools with 8,400 teachers and 136,536 pupils; 7,653 primary schools with 43,599 teachers and 813,353 pupils; 1,808 high schools with 29,571 teachers and 442,815 pupils; 1,158 lycea with 20,231 teachers and 273,589 pupils; 48 ecclesiastical and technical secondary schools of the first cycle with 291 teachers and 3,554 pupils, and 524 ecclesiastical and technical secondary schools of the second cycle with 10,210 teachers and 131,395 pupils. There was also 1 teacher training school with 5 teachers and 151 students; 12 technical education institutions (TEI) with 5,180 teachers and 75,679 students; 22 vocational and ecclesiastical schools with 496 teachers and 2,477 students and 1 technical teacher training school with 41 teachers (and 102 teachers shared with other institutions) and 2,477 students. In 1994–95 there were 11 universities, 2 technical universities and 3 specialized universities (agriculture; economics and business; economics and political science), 1 institute of home economics and 1 school of fine art. There were 184,516 students and 6,466 academic staff.

Health (1989). There were 402 hospitals and sanatoria with a total of 51,448 beds. There were 33,151 doctors and 9,628 dentists.

DIPLOMATIC REPRESENTATIVES

Of Greece in Great Britain (1A Holland Park, London, W11 3TP)
Ambassador: Elias Gounaris.

Of Great Britain in Greece (1 Ploutarchou St., 106 75 Athens)
Ambassador: Oliver Miles, CMG.

Of Greece in the USA (2221 Massachusetts Ave., NW, Washington, D.C., 20008)
Ambassador: Loukas Tsilas.

Of the USA in Greece (91 Vasilissis Sophias Blvd., 10160 Athens)
Ambassador: Thomas M. Niles.

Of Greece to the United Nations
Ambassador: Christos Zacharakis.

Further Reading

Clogg, R., *Greece in the 1980s.* London, 1983.—*A Concise History of Greece.* CUP, 1992
Clogg, M. J. and R., *Greece.* [Bibliography] Oxford and Santa Barbara (CA), 1980

Freris, A. F., *The Greek Economy in the Twentieth Century*. London, 1986
Jougnatos, G. A., *Development of the Greek Economy, 1950–91: an Historical, Empirical and Econometric Analysis.* London, 1992
Pettifer, J., *The Greeks: the Land and the People since the War.* London, 1994
Sarafis, M. and Eve, M. (eds.) *Background to Contemporary Greece.* London, 1990
Tsakalotos, E., *Alternative Economic Strategies: the Case of Greece.* Aldershot, 1991
Woodhouse, C. M., *Modern Greece: a Short History.* rev. ed. London, 1991

National statistical office: National Statistical Service; 14–16 Lycourgou St., Athens.

GRENADA

Capital: St George's
Population: 96,000 (1995)
GNP per capita: US$2,304 (1994)
HDI/world rank: 0·786/67 (1992)

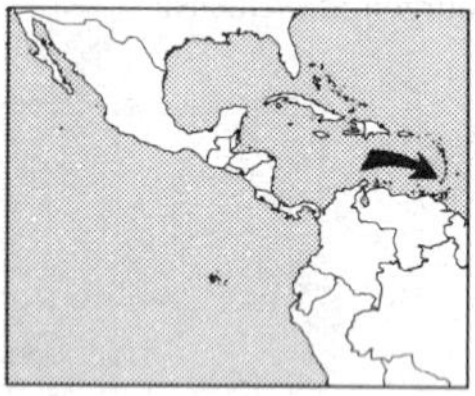

KEY HISTORICAL EVENTS. Grenada became an independent nation within the Commonwealth on 7 Feb. 1974. Grenada was formerly an Associated State under the West Indies Act, 1967. The 1973 Constitution was suspended in 1979 following a revolution.

On 19 Oct. 1983 the army took control after a power struggle led to the killing of Maurice Bishop, the Prime Minister. At the request of a group of Caribbean countries, Grenada was invaded by US-led forces on 25–28 Oct. On 1 Nov. a State of Emergency was imposed which ended on 15 Nov. when an interim government was installed. The 1973 Constitution was restored.

TERRITORY AND POPULATION. Grenada is the most southerly island of the Windward Islands with an area of 120 sq. miles (311 sq. km); the state also includes the Southern Grenadine Islands to the north, chiefly Carriacou and Petit Martinique, with an area of 13 sq. miles (34 sq. km). The total population (Census, 1991) was 95,343 (48,169 females); density, 263 per sq. km. Estimated population (1995) 96,000; density, 276 per sq. km. The Borough of St George's, the capital, had 35,742 inhabitants in 1989. In 1991, 84·9% of the population were of African descent, 11% of mixed origins and 3% Indian.

Vital statistics (1987): Births, 3,102; deaths, 781.

The official language is English. A French-African patois is also spoken.

CLIMATE. The tropical climate is very agreeable in the dry season, from Jan. to May, when days are warm and nights quite cool, but in the wet season there is very little difference between day and night temperatures. On the coast, annual rainfall is about 60" (1,500 mm) but it is as high as 150–200" (3,750–5,000 mm) in the mountains. Average temperature, 24°C.

CONSTITUTION AND GOVERNMENT. The British sovereign is represented by an appointed Governor-General. There is a bicameral legislature, consisting of a 13-member *Senate,* appointed by the Governor-General, and a 15-member *House of Representatives,* elected by universal suffrage. At the elections of 20 June 1995 for the House of Representatives, the New National Party (NNP) won 8 seats, the National Democratic Congress, 5 and the Grenada United Labour Party, 2.

Governor-General: Sir Reginald Oswald Palmer, GCMG.

In Jan. 1996 the government comprised:

Prime Minister: Dr Keith Mitchell (NNP).

Agriculture: Joslyn Whiteman. *Tourism:* Grace Duncan. *Education:* Laurina Waldron. *Legal Affairs:* Lawrence Joseph. *Works and Communication:* Gregory Bowen. *Sports:* Adrian Mitchell. *Culture:* William Dewsbury. *Health:* Mark Isaac. *Without Portfolio:* Dr Raphael Fletcher.

National flag: Divided into 4 triangles of yellow, top and bottom, and green, hoist and fly; in the centre a red disc bearing a gold star; along the top and bottom edgedred stripes each bearing 3 gold stars; on the green triangle near the hoist a pod of nutmeg.

National anthem: 'Hail Grenada, land of ours'; words by I. M. Baptiste, tune by L. A. Masanto.

Local government: Not yet implemented.

DEFENCE

Royal Grenadian Police Force. Modelled on the British system, the 730-strong police force includes an 80-member paramilitary unit and a 30-member coastguard.

INTERNATIONAL RELATIONS

Membership. Grenada is a member of the UN, OAS, Caricom, the Commonwealth and is an ACP state of the EU.

ECONOMY

Budget. Current revenue in 1992 was US$59·17m.; recurrent expenditure, US$63·5m. Capital expenditure was US$7·87m. Provisional estimates for 1993: Current revenue, EC$172·4m.; recurrent expenditure, EC$172·1m. Income tax has been abolished. VAT is 25% (reduced rate, 5%).

Currency. The unit of currency is the *Eastern Caribbean dollar* (XCD). In March 1996, £1 = EC$4·13; US$ = EC$2·70; DM1 = EC$1·83.

Banking and Finance. Grenada is a member of the Eastern Caribbean Central Bank. In 1995 there were 5 commercial banks (2 foreign). The Grenada Agricultural Bank was established in 1965 to encourage agricultural development; in 1975 it became the Grenada Agricultural and Industrial Development Corporation. In 1991, bank deposits were EC$393·8m.

ENERGY AND NATURAL RESOURCES

Electricity. Production (1991) 59·9m. kWh. 68·9% of households had an electricity supply in 1991.

Agriculture. Agriculture contributed 10·82% of GDP in 1994. Principal crop production (1993): Cocoa, 2,000 tonnes; bananas, 10,000 tonnes and in 1991: nutmegs, 5,800·3 lbs; mace, 451·1 lbs. Corn and pigeon peas, citrus, sugar-cane, root-crops and vegetables are also grown, in addition to small scattered cultivations of cotton, cloves, cinnamon, pimento, coffee and fruit trees.

Livestock (1993): Cattle, 4,000; sheep, 12,000; goats, 11,000; pigs, 3,000.

Fisheries. The catch (1993) was 4·47m. lbs.

INDUSTRY

Labour. In 1993 the labour force was estimated at 27,820. Unemployment was 16·7%.

FOREIGN ECONOMIC RELATIONS

Commerce. 1993 exports (including re-exports) were valued at EC$55·1m., of which domestic imports, EC$45·3m. Imports, EC$309·4m. The principal exports are nutmeg, cocoa, bananas, mace and textiles. Exports were mainly to the UK, Trinidad and Tobago, the Netherlands and Germany.

Total trade between Grenada and UK (British Department of Trade returns, in £1,000 sterling):

	1991	*1992*	*1993*	*1994*	*1995*
Imports to UK	4,236	3,519	3,919	2,707	3,311
Exports and re-exports to UK	7,730	5,546	6,628	7,335	7,582

Tourism. In 1995, there were 357,886 visitors, including 249,879 cruise ship passengers. Foreign exchange earnings from the sector were estimated at US$60m. in 1995.

COMMUNICATIONS

Roads. In 1995 there were 1,127 km of roads, of which 580 km were hard-surfaced. Vehicles registered (1988) 12,198.

Civil Aviation. Point Salines international airport is served by American Airlines,

BWIA, British Airways and LIAT. 82,319 passengers landed in 1993. Lauriston Airport is on Carriacou.

Shipping. The main port is at St George's; there are 8 minor ports. Total number of containers handled in 1991 was 5,161; cargo landed, 187,039 tonnes; cargo loaded, 24,786 tonnes. Sea-going shipping totalled 555 GRT in 1995.

Telecommunications. At 30 Sept. 1993 there were 20,269 telephone lines. The government-owned Grenada Broadcasting Corporation operates Radio Grenada and Grenada Television. There are also 2 independent radio stations. Grenada Television transmits on 2 channels (colour by NTSC). A private cable TV company provides services on 15 channels, and there is a religious TV service. In 1993 there were 80,000 radio and 30,000 TV sets.

Press. In 1993 there were 5 weekly, 1 monthly and 2 bi-monthly newspapers.

SOCIAL INSTITUTIONS

Justice. The Grenada Supreme Court, situated in St George's, comprises a High Court of Justice, a Court of Magisterial Appeal (which hears appeals from the lower Magistrates' Courts exercising summary jurisdiction) and an Itinerant Court of Appeal (to hear appeals from the High Court). For police *see* DEFENCE, *above*.

Religion. At the 1991 census 53% of the population were Roman Catholic, 14% Anglican, 8·5% Seventh Day Adventists and 7·2% Pentecostal.

Education. Adult literacy was 95% in 1995. In 1992 there were 75 pre-primary schools with 3,916 pupils, 57 primary schools with 22,330 pupils and 18 secondary schools with 6,970 pupils. In 1991 there were 10 schools for special education and 12 day care centres caring for 249 children. The Grenada National College was established in 1988. There is also a branch of the University of the West Indies.

Health. In 1990 there was 1 main hospital with 2 subsidiaries. In 1990 there were 36 clinics, 52 doctors, 7 dentists, 28 pharmacists, 36 midwives, 296 nursing personnel and 28 medical technologists (laboratory, radiography and biomedical).

DIPLOMATIC REPRESENTATIVES

Of Grenada in Great Britain (1 Collingham Gdns., London, SW5)
High Commissioner (Acting): June Lendore.

Of Great Britain in Grenada (14 Church St., St George's)
High Commissioner: R. Thomas, CMG.

Of Grenada in the USA (1701 New Hampshire Ave., NW, Washington, D.C., 20009)
Ambassador: Denneth Modeste.

Of the USA in Grenada
Ambassador: Jeannette W. Hyde (resides in Bridgetown).

Of Grenada to the United Nations
Ambassador: Vacant.

Further Reading

Davidson, J. S., *Grenada: a Study in Politics and the Limits of International Law.* London, 1987
Ferguson, J., *Grenada: Revolution in Reverse.* London, 1991
Gilmore, W. G., *The Grenada Intervention: Analysis and Documentation.* London, 1984
Heine, J. (ed) *A Revolution Aborted: the Lessons of Grenada.* Pittsburgh Univ. Press, 1990
O'Shaughnessy, H., *Grenada: Revolution, Invasion and Aftermath.* London, 1984
Page, A., Sutton, P. and Thorndike, T., *Grenada and Invasion.* London, 1984
Sandford, G. and Vigilante, R., *Grenada: the Untold Story.* London, 1988
Schoenhals, K., *Grenada*: [Bibliography]. Oxford and Santa Barbara (CA), 1990
Sinclair, N., *Grenada: Isle of Spice.* London, 1987
Thorndike, T., *Grenada: Politics, Economics and Society.* London, 1985

GUATEMALA

República de Guatemala

Capital: Guatemala City
Population: 9·74m. (1992)
GNP per capita: US$1,190 (1994)
HDI/world rank: 0·591/112 (1992)

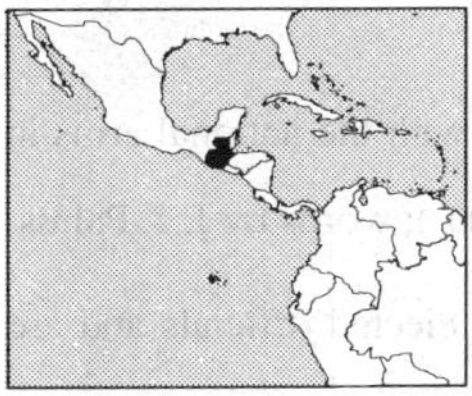

KEY HISTORICAL EVENTS. From 1524 to 1821 Guatemala was a Spanish captaincy-general, comprising the whole of Central America. It became independent from Spain in 1821 and formed part of the Confederation of Central America from 1823 to 1839, when Rafael Carrera dissolved the Confederation and Guatemala became independent.

Following a failed presidential coup on 25 May 1993, President Serrano went into exile.

TERRITORY AND POPULATION. Guatemala is bounded on the north and west by Mexico, south by the Pacific ocean and east by El Salvador, Honduras and Belize, and the area is 108,889 sq. km (42,042 sq. miles). In March 1936 Guatemala, El Salvador and Honduras agreed to accept the peak of Mount Montecristo as the common boundary point.

The census population was 6,054,227 in 1981. Estimate (1992) 9,742,000 (39% urban); density, 86·9 per sq. km. In 1983, 53% were Amerindian, of 21 different groups descended from the Maya; most of the remainder are mixed Amerindian and Spanish. 45% of the population in 1990 spoke Mayan languages. Density of population, 1989, 82 per sq. km.

Growth rate, 1991, 2·9%; infant mortality, 48 per 1,000 live births. Expectation of life in 1990 was 65 years.

Guatemala is administratively divided into 22 departments, each with a governor appointed by the President. Population, 1991:

Departments	*Area (sq. km)*	*Population*	*Departments*	*Area (sq. km)*	*Population*
Alta Verapaz	8,686	591,911	Petén	35,854	253,326
Baja Verapaz	3,124	184,462	Quezaltenango	1,951	557,831
Chimaltenango	1,979	343,818	Quiché	8,378	574,746
Chiquimula	2,376	252,052	Retalhuleu	1,858	238,857
El Progreso	1,922	108,399	Sacatepéquez	465	180,155
Escuintla	4,384	542,091	San Marcos	3,791	702,288
Guatemala	2,126	2,018,179	Santa Rosa	2,955	267,790
Huehuetenango	7,403	716,666	Sololá	1,061	242,067
Izabal	9,038	326,402	Suchitepéquez	2,510	361,678
Jalapa	2,063	190,847	Totonicapán	1,061	297,483
Jutiapa	3,219	354,337	Zacapa	2,690	161,644

The capital is Guatemala City with about 2m. inhabitants (1989). Other towns are Quezaltenango (246,000), Puerto Barrios (338,000), Mazatenango (38,319), Antigua (26,631), Zacapa (35,769) and Cobán (120,000).

CLIMATE. A tropical climate, with little variation in temperature and a well marked wet season from May to Oct. Guatemala City. Jan. 63°F (17·2°C), July 69°F (20·6°C). Annual rainfall 53" (1,316 mm).

CONSTITUTION AND GOVERNMENT. A new Constitution, drawn up by the Constituent Assembly elected on 1 July 1984, was promulgated in June 1985 and came into force on 14 Jan. 1986. In 1993, 43 amendments were adopted, reducing *inter alia* the President's term of office from 5 to 4 years. The President and Vice-President are elected by direct election (with a second round of voting if no candidate secures 50% of the first-round votes). The unicameral *Congress* comprises 80 members, 64 elected locally and 16 from a national list.

A referendum on constitutional reform was held on 30 Jan. 1994. The electorate was 3·4m.; turn-out was 17·5%. The reforms were approved by 83% of votes cast.

At the first round of the presidential elections on 12 Nov. 1995 the electorate was 3·7m.; turn-out was 40%, Alvaro Arzú gained 36·56% of votes cast against 18 opponents. At the second round on 7 Jan. 1996 Arzú was elected President against 1 opponent by 51·22% of votes cast.

Congressional elections were held on 12 Nov. 1995. The Party of National Advancement (PNA) won 42 seats, the Guatemalan Republic Front, 21 and the Guatemala New Democratic Front, 5.

President: Alvaro Arzú (PNA; sworn in 14 Jan. 1996).

National flag: Three vertical strips of blue, white, blue, with the national arms in the centre.

National anthem: '¡Guatemala! Feliz' ('Happy Guatemala'); words by J. J. Palma, tune by R. Alvarez.

Local Government. Municipalities are autonomous under elected officials and are funded by 8% of the central government budget.

DEFENCE. There is selective conscription for 30 months.

Army. The Army numbered (1996) 42,000 (30,000 conscripts) and is organized in 19 military zones. There are 2 strategic reserve brigades, 1 special forces group, 39 infantry, 1 engineer and 2 airborne battalions, 6 armoured squadrons and a Presidential Guard battalion. Equipment includes 10 light tanks and armoured cars. There is a paramilitary national police of 9,800, Treasury police of 2,500 and a territorial militia of about 300,000.

Navy. A naval element of the combined armed forces operates 9 inshore patrol craft, as well as 20 river patrol boats. The force was (1995) 1,500 strong of whom 650 are marines for maintenance of riverine security. Main bases are Puerto Barrios (on the Atlantic Coast), Puerto Quetzal and Puerto San José (Pacific).

Air Force. There is a small Air Force with 8 A-37B light attack aircraft, 1 DC-6, 6 C-47, 3 F.27 and 6 Israeli-built Arava transports, 6 Pilatus PC-7 turboprop trainers, and a number of light aircraft and helicopters, including a few armed UH-1 Iroquois. Strength was (1995) about 700.

INTERNATIONAL RELATIONS

Membership. Guatemala is a member of the UN and OAS.

ECONOMY

Policy. The 1988 National Economic Development Plan, called 'Guatemala 2000', calls for sustained GDP growth of at least 6% per annum until 2000.

Budget. In 1992 revenue was Q.5,752·4m. and expenditure Q.5,753·4m.

Currency. The unit of currency is the *quetzal* (CTQ) of 100 *centavos*, established 7 May 1925. There are coins of 1, 5, 10 and 25 centavos and notes of 50 centavos and 1, 5, 10, 20, 50 and 100 quetzals. Foreign exchange reserves were US$749·6m. in 1992; gold reserves, US$30·9m. Inflation was an annualized 14% in 1994. In March 1996, £1 = Q.9·45; US$1 = Q.6·18; DM1 = Q.4·19.

Banking and Finance. The Banco de Guatemala is the central bank and bank of issue (*Governor*, Willy Zapata). Constitutional amendments of 1993 placed limits on its financing of government spending. In 1994 there were 22 private banks, 3 state banks and 18 foreign banks.

Weights and Measures. The metric system has been officially adopted, but traditional measures are still used locally.

ENERGY AND NATURAL RESOURCES

Electricity. There is a large hydro-electric potential. Output, 1989, 2,800m. kWh.

Oil. There are proven reserves of 36·2m. bbls. Production (1992), 0·29m. tonnes.

Minerals. There are deposits of gold, silver and nickel.

Agriculture. Agriculture contributes 25% of GDP. Production, 1993 (in 1,000 tonnes): Coffee, 177; bananas, 500; cotton lint, 23. Rubber development schemes are under way, assisted by US funds. Guatemala is one of the largest sources of essential oils (citronella and lemon grass).

Livestock (1993): Cattle, 2·1m.; pigs, 850,000; sheep, 430,000; horses, 116,000; poultry, 16m.

Forestry. Forests cover 36% of the land area. Mahogany and cedar are grown, and chick, a chewing gum base, is produced.

INDUSTRY. The principal industries are food and beverages, tobacco, chemicals, hides and skins, textiles, garments and non-metallic minerals. Raw sugar production in 1992 was 943,000 tonnes. New industries include electrical goods, plastic sheet and metal furniture.

Trade Unions. There are 3 federations for private sector workers.

FOREIGN ECONOMIC RELATIONS. In May 1992 Guatemala, El Salvador and Honduras agreed to create a free trade zone and standardize import duties. External debt was US$2,703m. in 1994.

Commerce. Values in US$1,000 were:

	1988	*1989*	*1990*	*1991*	*1992*
Imports (c.i.f.)	1,250	1,695	1,762	1,626	2,328
Exports (f.o.b.)	875	1,155	1,196	1,210	1,284

In 1992 the principal exports were (in US$1m.): Coffee, 252·9; bananas, 110·4; sugar, 136·5; cardamom, 32·8. Main export markets, 1990: USA, 35%; El Salvador, 14·1%; Costa Rica, 6·9%; Nicaragua, 4·8%; Honduras, 4·7%. Main import suppliers: USA, 43·8%; Japan, 5·9%: Mexico, 5·8%; El Salvador, 5·6%.

Total trade between Guatemala and UK (British Department of Trade returns, in £1,000 sterling):

	1991	*1992*	*1993*	*1994*	*1995*
Imports to UK	10,458	10,611	16,708	14,683	14,898
Exports and re-exports from UK	16,224	20,779	25,966	22,686	31,103

Tourism. Tourism is an important source of foreign exchange (US$265m. in 1993). There were 0·56m. visitors in 1993.

COMMUNICATIONS

Roads. In 1994 there were 26,429 km of roads, of which 2,850 are paved. There is a highway from coast to coast via Guatemala City. There are 2 highways from the Mexican to the Salvadorean frontier: the Pacific Highway serving the fertile coastal plain and the Pan-American Highway running through the highlands and Guatemala City. Motor cars numbered about 160,000 in 1990; commercial vehicles, 135,000.

Railways. The railway system has closed.

Civil Aviation. The part-government-owned airline, Aviateca, and 2 private airlines furnish both domestic and international services. Aviateca had 3 B-737-200 Advs and 1 B-737-300 in 1995. Services are also provided from La Aurora international airport in Guatemala City by American Airlines, Compania Mexicana, Continental Airlines and Air Micronesia, COPA, Iberia, KLM, LACSA, Sociedad Aeronáutica de Medellín, Taca International Airlines and United Airlines.

Shipping. The chief ports on the Atlantic coast are Puerto Barrios and Santo Tomás de Castilla: on the Pacific coast, Puerto Quetzal and Champerico. Total tonnage handled was, 1987, 7m. tonnes.

Telecommunications. The Government own and operate the telecommunications services; there were 210,000 telephones in 1993. There are 5 government and 6 educational broadcasting services. Radio receiving sets in use, 1993, numbered about 0·4m. There are 4 commercial TV stations, 1 government station and about 475,000 TV receivers (colour by NTSC). There is also reception by US television satellite.

Cinemas (1989). Cinemas numbered approximately 100.

Press (1994). There were 3 independent dailies and 1 evening newspaper, and 1 government daily.

SOCIAL INSTITUTIONS

Justice. Justice is administered in a Constitution Court, a Supreme Court, 6 appeal courts and 28 courts of first instance. Supreme Court and appeal court judges are elected by Congress. Judges of first instance are appointed by the Supreme Court.

The death penalty for kidnapping was introduced in 1995.

Religion. Roman Catholicism is the prevailing faith (7·1m. adherents in 1992) and there is a Roman Catholic archbishopric. Membership of the approximately 100 evangelical Protestant churches was estimated at 30% of the population in 1991 (75% Pentecostalist), with about 14,000 places of worship.

Education. Adult literacy was 55·1% in 1990. In 1988 there were 11,587 schools with 45,611 teachers and an attendance of 1,331,294 pupils; these figures include private schools. There are 1,237 secondary and other schools having 13,891 teachers and an attendance of 194,484 pupils. In 1994–95 there were 5 universities with 70,233 students and 4,450 academic staff.

Health. In 1990 there were some 1,250 doctors, 275 dentists, 60 state hospitals and 100 dispensaries.

Welfare. A comprehensive system of social security was outlined in a law of 30 Oct. 1946.

DIPLOMATIC REPRESENTATIVES

Of Guatemala in Great Britain (13 Fawcett St., London, SW10 9HN)
Ambassador: Edmundo Nanne.

Of Great Britain in Guatemala (7a Avenida 5-10, Zona 4, Guatemala City)
Ambassador: Peter Newton.

Of Guatemala in the USA (2220 R. St., NW, Washington, D.C., 20008)
Ambassador: Edmund A. Mulet.

Of the USA in Guatemala (7–01 Avenida de la Reforma, Zone 10, Guatemala City)
Ambassador: Marilyn McAfee.

Of Guatemala to the United Nations
Ambassador: Julio Armando Martini Herrara.

Further Reading

Woodward, R. L., *Guatemala.* [Bibliography] Oxford and Santa Barbara (CA), 1992

National library: Biblioteca Nacional, 5a Avenida y 8a Calle, Zona 1, Guatemala City.

GUINEA

République de Guinée

Capital: Conakry
Population: 6·5m. (1994)
GNP per capita: US$510 (1994)
HDI/world rank: 0·237/168 (1992)

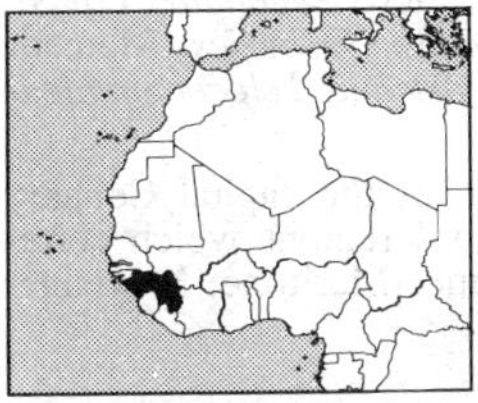

KEY HISTORICAL EVENTS. Guinea was proclaimed a French protectorate in 1888 and a colony in 1893. It became a constituent territory of French West Africa in 1904. The independent republic of Guinea was proclaimed on 2 Oct. 1958, after the territory of French Guinea had decided at the referendum of 28 Sept. to leave the French Community. Following the death of the first President, Ahmed Sekou Touré on 27 March 1984, the armed forces staged a coup on 3 April and a Military Committee of National Rectification (CMRN) held power till Jan. 1991, when a Transitional Committee for National Rectification (CTRN) took over. Following popular disturbances a multiparty system was introduced in April 1992.

TERRITORY AND POPULATION. Guinea is bounded in the north-west by Guinea-Bissau and Senegal, north-east by Mali, south-east by the Côte d'Ivoire, south by Liberia and Sierra Leone, and west by the Atlantic Ocean.

The area is 245,857 sq. km (94,926 sq. miles). Population estimate, 1994, 6·5m. A census of 1992 gave a figure of 5·04m.; it is officially acknowledged that this may be an under-count. Population growth, 1994, was 3%. The capital is Conakry. In 1995, 29·6% were urban. Expectation of life, 1990, 43 years for males and females.

The areas, populations and chief towns of the major divisions are:

	Sq. km	*1991 population*	*Chief town*	*Population (in year)*
Conakry (city)	308	1,320,000	Conakry	950,000 (1992)
Guinée-Maritime	43,980	975,000	Kindia	80,000 (1986)
Moyenne-Guinée	51,710	1,262,000	Labé	110,000 (1986)
Haute-Guinée	92,535	1,147,000	Kankan	70,000 (1992)
Guinée-Forestière	57,324	1,033,000	Nzérékoré	55,356 (1983)

The ethnic composition is Fulani (40·3%, predominant in Moyenne-Guinée), Malinké (or Mandingo, 25·8%, prominent in Haute-Guinée), Susu (11%, prominent in Guinée-Maritime), Kissi (6·5%) and Kpelle (4·8%) in Guinée-Forestière, and Dialonka, Loma and others (11·6%).

The official language is French.

CLIMATE. A tropical climate, with high rainfall near the coast and constant heat, but conditions are a little cooler on the plateau. The wet season on the coast lasts from May to Nov., but only to Oct. inland. Conakry. Jan. 80°F (26·7°C), July 77°F (25°C). Annual rainfall 172" (4,293 mm).

CONSTITUTION AND GOVERNMENT. Presidential elections were held on 19 Dec. 1993. President Conté was re-elected against 7 opponents by 51·7% of votes cast. There is a 114-member *National Assembly*, 38 of whose members are elected on a first-past-the-post system, and the remainder from national lists by proportional representation. Elections were held on 11 June 1995. 21 parties or groups stood. The Party of Unity and Progress Party (PUP) gained 71 seats; the Guinean People's Rally, 19; the Renewal and Progress Party, 9; the Union for a New Republic, 9.

In Oct. 1995 the government comprised:

President and Minister of Defence: Brig-Gen. Lansana Conté (PUP; seized power 3 April 1984, re-elected 19 Dec. 1993).

Foreign Affairs and Co-operation: Kozo Zomanigui. *Minister at the Presidency in charge of Defence:* Lt.-Col. Abdourahmane Diallo. *Interior and Security:* Alseny René Gómez. *Planning and Co-operation:* Michel Kamano. *Justice:* Salifou Sylla. *Finance:* El Hadj Camara. *Agriculture and Livestock:* Makale Kamara. *Energy and Environment:* Assifat Dorank. *Higher Education and Research:* Alioune Banire Diallo. *Health:* Kandjoura Drame. *Youth, Arts and Sport:* Toumani Dakoum Sako. *Administrative Reform:* Germaine Dualamu. *Commerce and Industry:* Seku Konate. *Transport:* Maj. Ibrahim Sylla. *The Economy:* Kazaliou Balde. *Mines and Geology:* Facinet Fofana. *Urban Affairs and Housing:* Lt.-Col. Jean Traore. *Secondary Education:* Aicha Bah Diallo. *Public Works:* Cellon Dalen Diallo. *Fisheries:* Mamadi Diare. *Labour and Social Affairs:* Josephine Guilavo. *Post and Telecommunications:* Emmanuel Gnan. *Children's Affairs:* Yvonne Conde.

Local Government: The administrative division comprises the capital Conakry and 33 provinces divided into 175 districts, grouped into 4 regions which correspond to the 4 major geographical and ethnic areas: Guinée-Maritime; Moyenne-Guinée; Haute-Guinée and Guinée-Forestière.

National flag: Three vertical strips of red, gold, green.

National anthem: 'Peuple d'Afrique, le passé historique' ('People of Africa, the historic past'); words anonymous, tune by K. Fodeba.

Besides French, there are 8 official languages taught in schools: Fulani, Malinké, Susu, Kissi, Kpelle, Loma, Basari and Koniagi.

DEFENCE. Conscription is for 2 years.

Army. The Army of 8,500 (1996), comprises 1 armoured, 5 infantry, 1 commando and 1 engineer, 1 artillery, 1 air defence and 1 special forces battalion. Equipment includes 30 T-34 and 8 T-54 main battle tanks. There are also 3 paramilitary forces: People's Militia (7,000), Gendarmerie (1,000) and Republican Guard (1,600).

Navy. A small force of 400 (1995) operate 2 French-built, 1 US-built and 5 Soviet-built inshore patrol craft, and a number of riverine boats from bases at Conakry and Kakanda.

Air Force. The Air Force, formed with Soviet assistance, is reported to be equipped with a few MiG-21 jet fighters and 2 MiG-15UTI trainers, 2 An-2 piston-engined transports and a Yak-40 jet aircraft for VIP duties, all Russian built, and a few French-supplied helicopters are in service. Personnel (1995) 800.

INTERNATIONAL RELATIONS

Membership. Guinea is a member of the UN, OAU and is an ACP state of the EU.

ECONOMY

Budget. Government revenue, 1994 (in 1,000m. Guinean francs): 608, of which taxes, 441·9; grants, 146·6. Expenditure: 730·3, of which current, 342.

Currency. The monetary unit is the *Guinean franc* (GNF). There are coins of 1, 5, 10 and 25 and notes of 25, 50, 100, 500, 1,000 and 5,000 Guinean francs. Inflation was 7·1% in 1995. In March 1996, £1 = 1,523·81 Guinean francs; US$1 = 997·00 Guinean francs; DM1 = 675·52 Guinean francs.

Banking and Finance. In 1986 the Central Bank and commercial banking were restructured, and commercial banks returned to the private sector. There were 6 commercial banks in 1993.

ENERGY AND NATURAL RESOURCES

Electricity. Production was 521m. kWh. in 1991.

Minerals. 1992 output: Bauxite, 16,000,000 tonnes (17,054,000 tonnes in 1991); alumina, 603,000 tonnes (651,000 tonnes in 1991); diamonds, 100,000 carats; gold, 2,100 kg. There are also deposits of granite, iron ore, chrome, copper, lead, manganese, molybdenum, nickel, platinum, uranium and zinc.

Agriculture. Subsistence agriculture supports about 80% of the population. Some 25% of potential arable land is cultivated. The chief crops (production, 1993, in 1,000 tonnes) are: Cassava, 781; millet, 10; rice, 733; plantains, 429; sugar-cane, 225; bananas, 115; groundnuts, 105; sweet potatoes, 104; yams, 73; maize, 95; palm-oil, 40; palm kernels, 40; pineapples, 87; pulses, 60; coffee, 29; coconuts, 18.

Livestock (1993): Cattle, 1·65m.; sheep, 435,000; goats, 580,000; pigs, 33,000; poultry, 14m.

Forestry: In 1988, 41% of the country was forested (10m. ha).

Fisheries: Annual catch, 0·1m. tonnes.

INDUSTRY. Manufacturing accounted for 3·9% of GDP in 1991. Cement, beer, soft drinks and cigarettes are produced.

FOREIGN ECONOMIC RELATIONS. Foreign debt was US$2,652m. in 1992. Imports require authorization and there are restrictions on the export of capital.

Commerce. In 1993 imports totalled US$730m. and exports US$607m. Alumina forms about 15% and bauxite 44% of the exports. Major imports are foodstuffs, fuel, textiles, clothing, machinery, transport equipment and building materials. Main export markets, 1992: USA, 15·6%; Belgium, 12·3%; Spain, 8·8%; Ireland, 9%; France, 6·4%. Main import suppliers: France, 36·7%; USA, 11%; Belgium, 7·7%; Hong Kong, 10·5%; Germany, 4·8%.

Total trade between Guinea and the UK (British Department of Trade returns, in £1,000 sterling):

	1991	*1992*	*1993*	*1994*	*1995*
Imports to UK	5,854	239	593	1,675	2,983
Exports and re-exports from UK	7,800	7,965	11,059	22,307	16,643

COMMUNICATIONS

Roads. In 1992 there were 6,351 km of main and national roads and about 9,200 km of other roads. In 1992 there were 23,155 cars and 13,000 commercial vehicles.

Railways. A railway connects Conakry with Kankan (662 km) and is to be extended to Bougouni in Mali. A line 134 km long linking bauxite deposits at Sangaredi with Port Kamsar was opened in 1973 (carried 12·5m. tonnes in 1993), a third line links Conakry and Fria (144 km; carried 1m. tonnes in 1993) and a fourth, the Kindia Bauxite Railway (102 km) linking Débéle with Conakry, carried 3m. tonnes in 1994.

Civil Aviation. There is an international airport at Conakry (Gbessia). The national carrier is the state-owned Air Guinée, which operated 1 B-737-200C, 1 DHC-7-102 and 2 ex-Soviet aircraft in 1995.

Shipping. There are ports at Conakry and for bauxite exports at Kamsar (opened 1973). There were (1993) 24 vessels of 5,600 GRT.

Telecommunications. Telephones, 1994, numbered about 18,000. Broadcasting is the responsibility of the state-controlled Radiodiffusion Télévision Guinéenne. There were 0·13m. radio and 65,000 television receivers in 1993 (colour by PAL).

Press. In 1979 there was 1 daily newspaper (circulation 20,000).

SOCIAL INSTITUTIONS

Justice. There are *tribunaux du premier degré* at Conakry and Kankan, and a *juge de paix* at Nzérékoré. The High Court, Court of Appeal and Superior Tribunal of Cassation are at Conakry.

Religion. 85% of the population are Moslem, 1·5% Christian. Traditional animist beliefs are still found.

Education. Adult literacy was 24% in 1991. In 1990–91, there were 346,800 pupils and 8,700 teachers in primary schools, 75,700 pupils and 4,800 teachers in secondary schools, 8,202 students in technical schools and 2,066 in teacher-training colleges and 5,366 in higher education. In 1995–96 there were 2 universities with 5,735 students and 525 academic staff.

Health. In 1991 there were 375 hospitals and dispensaries. In 1988 there were 3,382 beds; there were also 920 doctors (1991), 22 dentists (1988), 197 pharmacists (1991), 371 midwives (1991) and 1,243 trained nursing personnel (1988).

DIPLOMATIC REPRESENTATIVES

Of Guinea in Great Britain (resides in Paris)
Ambassador: Lamine Kamara.

Of Great Britain in Guinea
Ambassador: Alan Furness, CMG (resides in Dakar).

Of Guinea in the USA (2112 Leroy Pl., NW, Washington, D.C., 20008)
Ambassador: Elhadj Boubarcar Barry.

Of the USA in Guinea (2nd Blvd. and 9th Ave., Conakry)
Ambassador: Joseph A. Saloom.

Of Guinea to the United Nations
Ambassador: Mahawa Camara.

Further Reading

Bulletin Statistique et Economique de la Guinée. Monthly. Conakry

GUINEA-BISSAU

Republica da Guiné-Bissau

Capital: Bissau
Population: 1·06m. (1994)
GNP per capita: US$240 (1994)
HDI/world rank: 0·293/163 (1992)

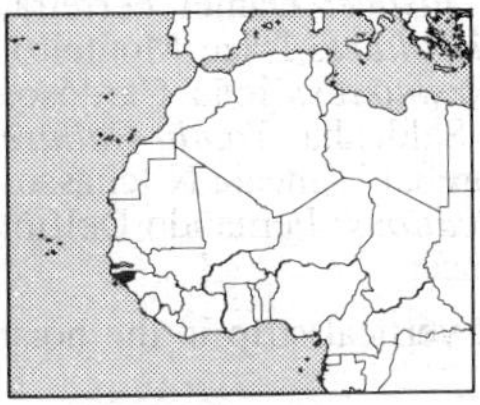

KEY HISTORICAL EVENTS. Guinea-Bissau, formerly Portuguese Guinea, was discovered in 1446 by Nuno Tristão. It became a separate colony in 1879. It is bounded by the limits fixed by the convention of 12 May 1886 with France. In 1951 Guinea-Bissau became an overseas province of Portugal. The struggle against colonial rule began in 1963. Independence was declared on 24 Sept. 1973. On 14 Nov. 1980 the then president Luiz Cabral was deposed and replaced by the prime minister, João Bernardo Vieira.

TERRITORY AND POPULATION. Guinea-Bissau is bounded by Senegal in the north, the Atlantic Ocean in the west and by Guinea in the east and south. It includes the adjacent archipelago of Bijagós. Area, 36,125 sq. km (13,948 sq. miles); population (last census, 1979), 777,214, of whom 125,000 (estimate, 1988) resided in the capital, Bissau; (estimate, 1994) 1,058,000. Density, 27·8 per sq. km; 30% urban. Annual growth rate (1985–90), 2·1%; infant mortality, 149 per 1,000 live births in 1993; expectation of life, 1990, 45 years.

The area population, and chief town of the capital and the 8 regions:

Region	*Area in sq. km*	*Population (1979 census)*	*Population (1985 estimate)*	*Chief town*
Bissau City	78	109,214	126,900	–
Bafatá	5,981	116,032	134,100	Bafatá
Biombo	838	56,463	65,000	Bissau
Bolama	2,624	25,473	29,700	Bolama
Cacheu	5,175	130,227	150,500	Cacheu
Gabú	9,150	104,315	120,800	Gabú
Oio	5,403	135,114	156,600	Farim
Quinara	3,138	35,532	41,000	Fulacunda
Tombali	3,736	55,099	64,500	Catió

The main ethnic groups were (1979) the Balante (33%), Manjaco (17%), Mandingo (12%), Fulani (12%) and Papeis (6%). Portuguese remains the official language, but Crioulo is spoken throughout the country.

CLIMATE. The tropical climate has a wet season from June to Nov., when rains are abundant, but the hot, dry Harmattan wind blows from Dec. to May. Bissau. Jan. 76°F (24·4°C), July 80°F (26·7°C). Annual rainfall 78" (1,950 mm).

CONSTITUTION AND GOVERNMENT. A new Constitution was promulgated on 16 May 1984. The Revolutionary Council, established following the 1980 coup, was replaced by a 15-member Council of State, while in April 1984 a new National People's Assembly was elected comprising 150 Representatives elected by and from the directly-elected regional councils for 5-year terms. The sole political movement was the *Partido Africano da Independencia da Guiné e Cabo Verde* (PAIGC), but in Dec. 1990 a policy of 'integral multi-partyism' was announced, and in May 1991 the National Assembly voted unanimously to abolish the law making the PAIGC the sole party. The *President* is Head of State and Government and is elected for a 5-year term. The *National Assembly* has 100 members.

Presidential elections were held in 2 rounds on 3 July and 7 Aug. 1994. At the first round President Vieira gained 46·18% of votes cast against 7 opponents. At the second round turn-out was 70%. President Vieira was re-elected by 52·02% of votes cast against 1 opponent.

At the parliamentary elections on 3 July 1994 there were 1,136 candidates. The PAIGC gained 64 seats.

President: Brig-Gen. João Bernardo Vieira (b. 1939; seized power 1980; elected 1989; re-elected 1994).

In Nov. 1995 the government comprised:

Prime Minister: Manuel Saturnino da Costa (PAICG; sworn in 25 Oct. 1994).

Foreign Affairs and Co-operation: Ansumane Mane. *Justice:* Daniel Ferreira. *Finance:* Rui Dia de Sousa. *Rural Development and Agriculture:* Isaac Monteiro. *Fisheries:* Artur Silva. *Energy and Industry, Natural Resources:* Joãa Cardoso. *Commerce and Industry:* Zeca Martins. *Health:* Eugenia Saldanha. *Youth, Culture and Sport:* Paulo Silva. *Social and Women's Affairs:* N'harebat N'incaia N'tchasso. *Public Works:* Abubacar Balde. *Transport and Communications:* Fernando Delfim da Silva. *Defence:* Arafan Mane. *Interior:* Luis Olivier Sanca.

National flag: Horizontally yellow over green with red vertical strip in the hoist bearing a black star.

National anthem: Same as Cape Verde.

Local government: The administrative division is in 8 regions (each under a regional council elected for 5 years), in turn subdivided into 37 sectors; and the city of Bissau, an autonomous sector treated as a separate region.

DEFENCE. There is selective conscription.

Army. The Army consisted in 1996 of 1 armoured, 1 artillery and 5 infantry battalions and 1 engineer and 1 reconnaissance company. Equipment includes 10 T-34 main battle tanks. Personnel, 6,800. There is a paramilitary Gendarmerie 2,000 strong.

Navy. The naval flotilla, based at Bissau, is equipped with 8 inshore patrol craft of diverse origins and 1 utility landing craft. Personnel in 1995 totalled 350.

Air Force. Formation of a small Air Force began in 1978 with the delivery of a French-built Cessna FTB-337 twin-engined counter-insurgency and general-purpose light transport. It has been followed by 2 Alouette III helicopters and 1 Falcon 20 VIP transport. Personnel (1995) 100.

INTERNATIONAL RELATIONS

Membership. Guinea-Bissau is a member of the UN, OAU and is an ACP state of the EU.

ECONOMY

Budget. Estimated revenue in 1990 (in 1m. pesos) was 81,900, of which 40,600 were non-tax revenue; tax revenue included taxes on commerce (25,100), income tax (7,400) and indirect taxes (6,200). Current expenditure totalled 63,900, and included goods and services (31,900), salaries (21,700) and interest payments (3,000).

Currency. The monetary unit is the *peso* (GWP) of 100 *centavos*. There are coins of 50 centavos and 1, 2·5, 5, 10 and 20 pesos, and banknotes of 50, 100, 500, 1,000, 5,000 and 10,000 pesos. In March 1996, £1 = 27,566 pesos; US$1 = 18,036 pesos; DM1 = 12,200 pesos.

Banking and Finance. The Banco da Guiné-Bissau, which replaced the Banco Nacional in 1989, is the central bank and bank of issue (*Governor* Dr Pedro A. Godinho Gomes). A commercial bank was set up in 1990, with 51% of the capital held by the state and local companies and 49% by Portuguese banks. There is also a commercial bank.

ENERGY AND NATURAL RESOURCES

Electricity. Production (1986) 28m. kWh.

Minerals. Mineral resources are not exploited. There are estimated to be 200m. tonnes of bauxite and 112m. tonnes of phosphate.

Agriculture. Agriculture accounts for 45% of GDP and employs 80% of the labour force. Chief crops (production, 1993, in 1,000 tonnes) are: Groundnuts, 18; sugar-cane, 6; plantains, 34; coconuts, 25; rice, 126; palm kernels, 8; millet, 26; palm-oil, 5; sorghum, 14; maize, 13; cashew nuts, 30; timber, hides, seeds and wax.

Livestock (1993): Cattle, 475,000; sheep, 255,000; goats, 270,000; pigs, 310,000; poultry, 1m.

Forestry. The forest area was 2·35m. ha in 1993. Timber output averages an annual 40,000 cu. metres of logs and 16,000 cu. metres of saw wood.

Fisheries. Total catch is about 20,000 tonnes annually. The EU pays for fishing permits.

INDUSTRY

Labour. The workforce in 1988 was 279,100 (9,300 females).

FOREIGN ECONOMIC RELATIONS.

Foreign debt totalled US$634m. in 1992.

Commerce. Imports in 1992, US$60m. of which a third were from Portugal; exports, US$16m. Main exports in 1991 (in US$1m.) were: Cashew nuts, 11·8; frozen shrimps, 1·2; frozen fish, 1; logs, 0·9; saw timber, 0·3. Imports: Food, 27·8; transport equipment, 17·5; fuel, 7·7; machines, 5·5; construction materials, 3·7.

Main export markets, 1992: India, 67%; Portugal, 14%; Côte d'Ivoire, 7%; Spain, 3%. Main import suppliers: Portugal, 22%; Thailand, 16%; Netherlands, 6%; Japan, 5%.

Total trade between Guinea-Bissau and UK (British Department of Trade returns, in £1,000 sterling):

	1991	*1992*	*1993*	*1994*	*1995*
Imports to UK	36	4	9	4	60
Exports and re-exports from UK	1,201	1,117	1,260	4,016	1,889

COMMUNICATIONS

Roads. There are about 2,500 km of roads of which 1,400 km are paved and (1985) 2,700 passenger cars and 2,100 lorries.

Civil Aviation. There is an international airport serving Bissau at Bissalanca. The national carrier is the state-owned Air Bissau, which had 4 aircraft in 1995. There are services to Abidjan, Dakar, London, Luanda and São Tomé.

Shipping. The main port is Bissau; minor ports are Boloma, Cacheu and Catió. In 1995 the merchant marine totalled 1,846 GRT.

Telecommunications. In 1991 there were about 40,000 telephones and (in 1987) 26,000 radio receivers. An experimental TV service started in 1989.

Cinemas. There were 4 cinemas (1988) with a seating capacity of 950.

Press (1984). There was 1 weekly newspaper, with a circulation of 3,000.

SOCIAL INSTITUTIONS

Religion. In 1987 about 30% of the population were Moslem and about 5% Christian (mainly Roman Catholic). The remainder held traditional animist beliefs.

Education. Illiteracy was estimated at 64% in 1990. Some 60% of children of primary school age attend school.

Health. In 1993 there were 10 private, 2 national and 4 regional hospitals with a total of 1,300 beds. There were 125 dispensaries.

DIPLOMATIC REPRESENTATIVES

Of Guinea-Bissau in Great Britain (resides in Brussels)
Chargé d'affaires: Maria Araujo Vieira.

Of Great Britain in Guinea-Bissau
Ambassador: Alan Furness, CMG (resides in Dakar).

Of Guinea-Bissau in the USA
Ambassador: Alfredo Lopes Cabral.

Of the USA in Guinea-Bissau (Ave. Domingos Ramos, 1067 Bissau)
Ambassador: Peggy Blackford.

Of Guinea-Bissau to the United Nations
Ambassador: Boubacar Toure.

Further Reading

Forrest, J. A., *Guinea-Bissau: Power, Conflict and Renewal in a West African Nation.* Boulder (CO), 1992

Galli, R., *Guinea-Bissau:* [Bibliography]. Oxford and Santa Barbara (CA), 1991

GUYANA

Co-operative Republic of Guyana

Capital: Georgetown
Population: 730,000 (1994)
GNP per capita: US$530 (1994)
HDI/world rank: 0·622/105 (1992)

KEY HISTORICAL EVENTS. First settled by the Dutch West Indian Company about 1620 the territory was captured by Great Britain to whom it was ceded in 1814 and named British Guiana. On 26 May 1966 British Guiana became independent under the name of Guyana and a Co-operative Republic on 23 Feb. 1970.

TERRITORY AND POPULATION. Guyana is situated on the north-east coast of Latin America on the Atlantic Ocean, with Suriname on the east, Venezuela on the west and Brazil on the south and west. Area, 83,000 sq. miles (214,969 sq. km). Estimated population (1994), 730,000. Ethnic groups by origin: 49% Indian, 36% African, 7% mixed race, 7% Amerindian and 1% others. The capital is Georgetown; other towns are New Amsterdam, Linden, Rose Hall and Corriverton.

Venezuela demanded the return of the Essequibo region in 1963. It was finally agreed in March 1983 that the UN Secretary-General should mediate. There was also an unresolved claim (1984) by Suriname for the return of an area between the New river and the Corentyne river.

Vital statistics (1988): Birth rate 26·1%; death rate 8%. Expectation of life was 65 years in 1991.

The official language is English.

CLIMATE. A tropical climate, with rainy seasons from April to July and Nov. to Jan. Humidity is high all the year but temperatures are moderated by sea-breezes. Rainfall increases from 90" (2,280 mm) on the coast to 140" (3,560 mm) in the forest zone. Georgetown. Jan. 79°F (26·1°C), July 81°F (27·2°C). Annual rainfall 87" (2,175 mm).

CONSTITUTION AND GOVERNMENT. A new Constitution was promulgated in Oct. 1980. There is an *Executive Presidency*, and a *National Assembly* which consists of 53 elected members and 12 members appointed by the regional authorities. Elections for 5-year terms are held under the single-list system of proportional representation, with the whole of the country forming one electoral area and each voter casting a vote for a party list of candidates.

At the elections of 5 Oct. 1992 turn-out was 81%. The People's Progressive Party/Civic (PPP/Civic) gained 35 seats with 53·5% of votes cast, the People's National Congress, 27 with 44%; other parties gained 3 seats. At the concurrent presidential elections Dr Cheddi Jagan was elected by 129,848 votes against 98,918 for President Hoyte.

President: Dr Cheddi Jagan (b. 1918; PPP/Civic; sworn in, 9 Oct. 1992).

In Oct. 1995 the government comprised:

Vice-President, Prime Minister and Senior Minister of Public Works, Communications and Regional Development: Samuel Hinds.

Attorney-General and Minister of Legal Affairs: Bernard De Santos. *(Senior Ministers) Agriculture:* Reepu Baman Persaud. *Finance:* Asgar Ally. *Foreign:* Clement Rohee. *Health:* Gail Teixeira. *Education and Cultural Development:* Dale Bisnauth. *Labour, Human Services and Social Security:* Henry Jeffrey. *Home Affairs:* Feroze Mohamed. *Trade, Industry and Tourism:* Shree Chand. *(Ministers) Public Works, Communications and Regional Development:* Harripersaud Nokta. *Agriculture:* Clinton Collymore. *Labour, Human Services and Social Security:* Indra

Chandarpaul. *Amerindian Affairs:* Vibert D'Souza. *President's Office:* George Fung-On.

National flag: Green with a yellow triangle based on the hoist, edged in white, charged with a red triangle edged in black.

National anthem: 'Dear land of Guyana'; words by A. L. Luker, tune by R. Potter.

Local Government: There are 10 administrative regions: Barima/Waini, Pomeroon/Supernaam, Essequibo Islands/West Demerara, Demerara/Mahaica, Mahaica/Berbice, East Berbice/Corentyne, Cuyuni/Mazaruni, Potaro/Siparuni, Upper Takutu/Upper Essequibo, Upper Demerara/Berbice.

DEFENCE

Army. The Guyana Army had (1996) a strength of 1,400. It comprises 1 infantry battalion and 1 special forces, 1 support weapons and 1 engineer company. There is a paramilitary Guyana People's Militia 1,500 strong.

Navy. The Maritime Corps is an integral part of the Guyana Defence Force. In 1995 it had 30 personnel and 2 armed boats.

Air Force. The Air Command has no combat aircraft. It is equipped with light aircraft and helicopters, including 1 Islander twin-engined short take-off and landing transport, and 1 Bell 206, 1 Bell 212 and 2 Mi-8 helicopters. Personnel (1995) 100.

INTERNATIONAL RELATIONS

Membership. Guyana is a member of the UN, Commonwealth, CARICOM, OAS and is an ACP state of the EU.

ECONOMY

Policy. State control is being reduced, and some 30 enterprises were scheduled for privatization in 1991.

Budget. Revenue and expenditure for calendar years (in G$1,000):

	1984	*1985*	*1986*	*1987*	*1988*	*1989*
Revenue	1,537,928	1,200,208	1,667,708	2,004,391	2,296,587	7,012,345
Expenditure	1,585,840	1,562,858	2,551,380	2,976,517	3,528,120	8,796,129

Currency. The unit of currency is the *Guyana dollar* (GYD) of 100 *cents*. There are notes of $1, 5, 10, 20, 100, 500 and 1,000, and coins of 1, 5, 10, 25 and 50 cents. In March 1996, £1 = G$212·30; US$1 = G$138·90; DM1 = G$94·11.

Banking and Finance. The bank of issue is the Bank of Guyana. Of the 6 commercial banks operating 2 are foreign-owned.

ENERGY AND NATURAL RESOURCES

Electricity. Production (1986) 500m. kWh.

Minerals. Placer gold mining commenced in 1884, and was followed by diamond mining in 1887. Output of gold was 0·11m. oz. in 1993. Production of diamonds was 36,717 stones in 1988. Bauxite production was 1·5m. tonnes in 1991. Other minerals include copper, tungsten, iron, nickel, quartz and molybdenum.

Agriculture. Production, 1993: Sugar, 243,000 tonnes; rice, 204,511 tonnes. Other products include coffee, cocoa, coconut and edible oils, copra, fruit, vegetables and tobacco.

Livestock estimate (1992): Cattle, 225,000; pigs, 60,000; sheep, 130,000; goats, 77,000; poultry, 13m.

Forestry. In 1988, 16·4m. ha of the land area (83%) was forested. Production (1988) 4·4m. cu. ft of timber.

Fisheries. Production (1989) of fish, 40,300 tons and shrimp, 1,872 tons.

INDUSTRY. The main industries are agro-processing (sugar, rice, timber and coconut) and mining (gold and diamonds). There is a light manufacturing sector, and textiles and pharmaceuticals are produced by state and private companies.

FOREIGN ECONOMIC RELATIONS

Commerce. In 1990 imports were worth US$511m. and exports US$251m. Chief domestic exports are sugar, rice, gold, bauxite, rum, timber, molasses and shrimps. Exports in 1993 (in US$1m.): Sugar, 110·8; rice, 33; gold, 99·8; bauxite, 89·9.

Total trade between Guyana and UK (British Department of Trade returns, in £1,000 sterling):

	1991	*1992*	*1993*	*1994*	*1995*
Imports to UK	50,479	78,742	75,001	71,717	72,821
Exports and re-exports from UK	19,275	20,242	34,218	26,922	33,946

COMMUNICATIONS

Roads. There are some 5,697 km of roads, of which 644 km are paved and 547 km are along the coastal plain.

Railways. There is a government-owned railway in the North West District, while the Guyana Mining Enterprise operates a standard gauge railway of 133 km from Linden on the Demerara River to Ituni and Coomacka.

Civil Aviation. There is an international airport at Timehri. The national carrier is the state-owned Guyana Airways, which in 1995 operated 1 B-757-200 and 1 DHC-6-300. Services are also provided by BWIA, Carib Express, LIAT, Surinam Airways and TABA.

Shipping. The major port is Georgetown; there are 3 other ports. In 1995 sea-going shipping totalled 13,925 GRT. There are 217 nautical miles of river navigation. There are ferry services across the mouths of the Demerara, Berbice and Essequibo rivers.

Telecommunications. The inland public telegraph and radio communication services are operated by the Telecommunication Corporation. In 1988 there were 57 post offices and 28 agencies. In 1988 telephone exchanges had 28,450 direct exchange lines with 20,000 telephones.

The Guyana Broadcasting Corporation has 2 radio programmes. In 1993 there were 0·31m. radio and about 50,000 TV receivers (colour by NTSC). Guyana Television is government-controlled and there are 2 private stations relaying US satellite services.

Cinemas (1989). There were 51 cinemas.

Press (1995). There is 1 daily newspaper with a circulation of 19,500 weekdays and 29,000 Sundays, 1 paper published every day except Monday with a circulation of 20-30,000 weekdays and 40,000 Sundays, and 3 weekly papers with a combined circulation of 41,500.

SOCIAL INSTITUTIONS

Justice. The law, both civil and criminal, is based on the common and statute law of England, save that the principles of the Roman–Dutch law have been retained in respect of the registration, conveyance and mortgaging of land.

The Supreme Court of Judicature consists of a Court of Appeal, a High Court and a number of courts of summary jurisdiction.

Religion. In 1980, 34% of the population were Hindu, 34% Protestant, 18% Roman Catholic and 9% Moslem.

Education. In 1976 the government assumed responsibility for education from nursery school to university and took over all private and church schools. In 1989 there were 364 nursery, 423 primary and 93 secondary schools.

There is 1 university, which in 1994–95 had 3,357 students and 204 academic staff.

Health. In 1994 there were 30 hospitals (5 private), 162 health centres and 14 health posts. There were (1989) 111 doctors, 15 dentists, 29 pharmacists, 172 midwives and 854 nursing personnel.

DIPLOMATIC REPRESENTATIVES

Of Guyana in Great Britain (3 Palace Ct., London, W2 4LP)
High Commissioner: Laleshwar K. N. Singh.

Of Great Britain in Guyana (44 Main St., Georgetown)
High Commissioner: Richard Thomas, CMG.

Of Guyana in the USA (2490 Tracy Pl., NW, Washington, D.C., 20008)
Ambassador: Mohammed Ali Odeen Ishmael.

Of the USA in Guyana (31 Main St., Georgetown)
Ambassador: David L. Hobbs.

Of Guyana to the United Nations
Ambassador: Samuel R. Insanally.

Further Reading

Baber, C. and Jeffrey, H. B., *Guyana: Politics, Economics and Society.* London, 1986
Braveboy-Wagner, J. A., *The Venezuela-Guyana Border Dispute: Britain's Colonial Legacy in Latin America.* London, 1984
Chambers, F., *Guyana.* [Bibliography] Oxford and Santa Barbara (CA), 1989
Daly, P. H., *From Revolution to Republic.* Georgetown, 1970
Daly, V. T., *A Short History of the Guyanese People.* 3rd. ed. London, 1992
Sanders, A., *The Powerless People.* London, 1987
Spinner, T. J., *A Political and Social History of Guyana, 1945–83.* Epping, 1985
Williams, B. F., *Stains on My Name, War in My Veins: Guyana and the Politics of Cultural Struggle.* Duke Univ. Press, 1992

HAITI

République d'Haïti

Capital: Port-au-Prince
Population: 6·76m. (1992)
GNP per capita: US$220 (1994)
HDI/world rank: 0·362/148 (1992)

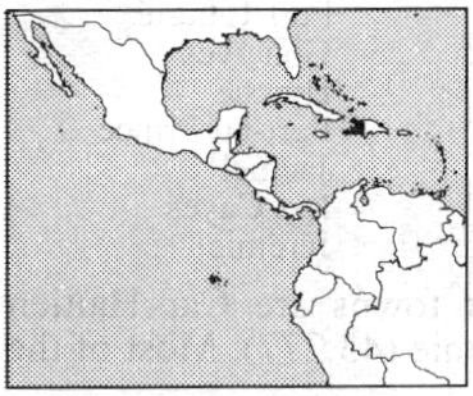

KEY HISTORICAL EVENTS. The island of Hispaniola was discovered by Christopher Columbus in 1492. Haiti occupies the western third. The Spanish colony was ceded to France in 1697. After the extirpation of the Indians by the Spaniards (by 1533) large numbers of African slaves were imported whose descendants now populate the country. The slaves obtained their liberation following the French Revolution, but Napoleon restored French authority and imprisoned Toussaint Louverture, the leader of the slaves who had been appointed a French general and governor. Subsequently the French surrendered to a blockading British squadron.

The country declared its independence on 1 Jan. 1804, and Gen. Jean-Jacques Dessalines proclaimed himself Emperor of the newly-named Haiti. After the assassination of Dessalines (1806) a separate régime was set up in the north under Gen. Henri Christophe who in 1811 had himself proclaimed King. In the south and west a republic was constituted, with Alexander Pétion as its first President. Pétion died in 1818 and was succeeded by Jean-Pierre Boyer, under whom the country became re-united after Henri Christophe had committed suicide in 1820. From 1822 to 1844 Haiti and the eastern part of the island (later the Dominican Republic) were united. After one more monarchical interlude, under the Emperor Faustin (1847–59), Haiti has been a republic. From 1915 to 1934 Haiti was under United States occupation.

Dr François Duvalier was elected President on 22 Sept. 1957 and became president for life in 1964. He died on 21 April 1971 and was succeeded as president for life by his son, Jean-Claude Duvalier who fled the country on 7 Feb. 1986. Gen. Henry Namphy formed a Council of Government. In Jan. 1988 Leslie Manigat was elected president, but Namphy again seized power in June 1988. In Sept. 1988 he was deposed and replaced by the military government of Lieut.-Gen. Prosper Avril. In March 1990 Ertha Pascal-Trouillot became head of an interim government. Father Jean-Bertrand Aristide was elected president in Dec. 1990

On 30 Sept. 1991 President Aristide was deposed by a military junta and went into exile abroad. Under international diplomatic pressure parliament again recognized Aristide as president in June 1993. After 2 agreements brokered by the UN and OAS a new government was formed in Aug. President Aristide was scheduled to return on 30 Oct. However, the military régime prevented UN forces from landing on 11 Oct., and on 13 Oct. the UN Security Council voted to apply new sanctions if the agreements were not adhered to. On 14 Oct. the Minister of Justice was assassinated, and the USA and other UN members mounted a naval blockade.

The UN and OAS civil missions were expelled by the junta on 11 July 1994. On 15 Sept. US President Clinton demanded that the junta step down. Former US President Carter flew to Haiti on 17 Sept. to negotiate their removal. 20,000 US troops moved into Haiti on 19 Sept. in an uncontested occupation. President Aristide returned to office on 15 Oct. 1994. On 1 April 1995 a UN peacekeepng force took over from the US military mission. All UN contingents were scheduled to leave by 30 April 1996.

TERRITORY AND POPULATION. Haiti is bounded in the east by the Dominican Republic and elsewhere by the Caribbean Sea. The area is 27,750 sq. km (10,714 sq. miles). The Île de la Gonave, some 40 miles long, lies in the gulf of the same name. Among other islands is La Tortue, off the north peninsula. The population at the census in 1982 was 5,053,792 of which 21% were urban and 48·5% male. Estimate (1992) 6,763,746, of which 30% were urban. Population density,

244 per sq. km. Infant mortality, 1992, 94 per 1,000 live births. Expectation of life, 1992, 54 years.

Areas, populations and chief towns in 1992 of the 9 departments:

Department	*Area (in sq. km)*	*Population*	*Chief town*
Nord-Ouest	2,094	395,442	Port-de-Paix
Nord	2,175	724,084	Cap Haïtien
Nord-Est	1,698	239,734	Fort-Liberté
L'Artibonite	4,895	961,447	Gonaïves
Centre	3,597	467,514	Hinche
Ouest	4,595	2,285,044	Port-au-Prince
Sud-Est	2,077	444,323	Jacmel
Sud	2,602	630,007	Les Cayes
Grande Anse	3,100	616,151	Jérémie

The capital is Port-au-Prince (1992, 1,255,078); other towns are Cap-Haïtien (92,122); Gonaives (63,291), Les Cayes (45,904) and Jérémie (43,277). Most of the population is of African or mixed origin.

The official languages are French and Créole. Créole is spoken by all Haitians; French by only a small minority.

CLIMATE. A tropical climate, but the central mountains can cause semi-arid conditions in their lee. There are rainy seasons from April to June and Aug. to Nov. Hurricanes and severe thunderstorms can occur. The annual temperature range is small. Port-au-Prince. Jan. 77°F (25°C), July 84°F (28·9°C). Annual rainfall 53" (1,321 mm).

CONSTITUTION AND GOVERNMENT. The 1987 Constitution, ratified by a referendum, provides for a bicameral legislature (an 83-member *Chamber of Deputies* and a 27-member *Senate*), and an executive *President*, directly elected for a non-renewable 5-year term.

At the presidential, parliamentary and local elections of Dec. 1990 the electorate was some 3m.; turn-out was estimated at 55% by international observers. Father Jean-Bertrand Aristide (b. 1957) was elected President by about 66% of votes cast. He was sworn in on 7 Feb. 1991 but deposed on 30 Sept. 1991 by a military junta.

Following the ouster of the junta, elections were held in 3 rounds on 25 June, 13 Aug. and 17 Sept. 1995. The electorate was 3·5m. Lavalas gained 17 Senate and 66 Chamber of Deputies seats. Presidential elections were held on 17 Dec. 1995. There were 14 candidates; turn-out was 28%. Rene Préval was elected with 88% of votes cast.

President: René Préval (b. 1943; Lavalas; sworn in 7 Feb. 1996).

A new government was formed in Feb. 1996 with Rony Smarth (b. 1941; Lavalas) as *Prime Minister*.

The *Speaker* of the Senate is Edgard Leblanc, and of the Chamber of Deputies, Fritz Robert Saint-Paul.

National flag: Horizontally blue over red with the national arms on a white panel in the centre.

National anthem: La Dessalinienne; words by J. Lhérisson, tune by N. Geffrard.

Local Government. Elections for 133 mayors and 565 3-member local councils were held on 17 Dec. 1995. Lavalas was the overall winner.

DEFENCE. After the restoration of civilian rule in 1994 the armed forces and police were disbanded and a 3,000-strong Interim Public Security Force formed. For Police, *see* JUSTICE, *below*.

INTERNATIONAL RELATIONS

Membership. Haiti is a member of the UN and OAS and is an ACP state of the EU.

ECONOMY

Budget. The budget for the fiscal year ending 30 Sept. 1991 was 1,350m. gourdes.

Currency. The unit of currency is the *gourde* (HTG) of 100 *centimes*. There are coins of 50, 20, 10 and 5 centimes and notes of 1, 2, 5, 10, 25, 50, 100, 250 and 500 gourdes. Money in circulation in 1989, 1,459m. gourdes. In March 1996, £1 = 24·72 gourdes; US$1 = 16·18 gourdes; DM1 = 10·96 gourdes.

Banking and Finance. The Banque Nationale de la République d'Haïti is the central bank and bank of issue (*Governor:* Bonivert Claude). In 1995 there were 8 commercial banks, of which 4 were foreign.

Weights and Measures. The metric system and British imperial and US measures are in use.

ENERGY AND NATURAL RESOURCES

Electricity. Production (1990–91) 491m. kWh.

Agriculture. The agricultural area is 1·4m. ha, of which 0·91m. ha are cultivated and 0·49m. ha pasture. 65% of the workforce, mainly smallholders, make a living by agriculture carried on in 7 large plains, from 0·2m. to 25,000 acres, and in 15 smaller plains down to 2,000 acres. Irrigation is used in some areas. The main crops are coffee, sugar, rice, maize, sorghum, millet, beans, cocoa, sweet potatoes, sisal, cotton, bananas and citrus fruits. Output in 1992 (in 1,000 tonnes): Coffee, 30; sugar-cane, 2,700; sorghum, 50; rice, 90; dry beans, 45; cocoa, 3; mangoes, 230; maize, 100; bananas, 180; sisal, 8; cotton, 2; sweet potatoes, 300.

Livestock (1992); Cattle, 1·3m.; sheep, 0·09m.; goats, 1·15m.; horses, 0·4m.; pigs, 0·88m.; poultry, 13m.

Forestry. The forest area was less than 2% of the total area in 1993.

Fisheries. Production (1986) 8,000 tonnes.

INDUSTRY. Manufacturing is largely based on the assembly of imported components: Toys, sports equipment, clothing, electronic and electrical equipment. Textiles, steel, soap, chemicals, paint, shoes and cement were also produced, but much of industry had to close down during the international embargo following President Aristide's deposal in 1991.

FOREIGN ECONOMIC RELATIONS. Foreign debt was US$820m. in 1995.

Commerce. In 1991 exports were US$103m. and imports, US$374m. The leading imports are petroleum products, foodstuffs, textiles, machinery, animal and vegetable oils, chemicals, pharmaceuticals, raw materials for transformation industries and vehicles.

Total trade between Haiti and UK (British Department of Trade returns, in £1,000 sterling):

	1991	*1992*	*1993*	*1994*	*1995*
Imports to UK	1,253	762	932	539	1,254
Exports and re-exports from UK	7,280	7,212	10,199	7,754	13,466

Tourism. In 1991, 51,000 tourists visited Haiti.

COMMUNICATIONS

Roads. Total length of roads is some 3,200 km, of which 600 km are surfaced. There were (1984) about 50,000 vehicles.

Civil Aviation. There is an international airport at Port-au-Prince. The national carrier is Air Haiti. Services are also provided by Air France, Carnival Airlines and Trans-Jamaican Airlines. Air services connecting Port-au-Prince with other Haitian towns are operated by Caraïbes Inter.

Shipping. Port-au-Prince, Jacmel and Cap Haïtien are the principal ports, and there are 12 minor ports.

Telecommunications. There were about 60,000 telephones in 1995. The state telecommunications agency is Teleco.

The aegis of the Conseil National des Télécommunications, Radio Nationale and Télévision Nationale broadcast radio and TV programmes (colour by NTSC). There is a privately-owned cable TV company, and several privately-owned radio stations. There were 3m. radio and 25,000 TV sets in 1993.

Cinemas (1984). There were 10 cinemas in Port-au-Prince.

Press (1995). There were 4 daily and 3 weekly newspapers.

SOCIAL INSTITUTIONS

Justice. The Court of Cassation is the highest court in the judicial system. There are 4 Courts of Appeal and 4 Civil Courts. Judges are appointed by the President. The legal system is basically French. A 4,000-strong police force has been re-recruited from former military personnel and others not implicated in human rights violations.

Religion. Since the Concordat of 1860 Roman Catholicism has been given special recognition, under an archbishop with 9 bishops. The Episcopal Church now has its first Haitian bishop who was consecrated in 1971. 90% of the population are nominally Roman Catholic, while other Christian churches number perhaps 10%, but probably two-thirds of these to some extent adhere to African-derived traditional beliefs ('Voodoo'). A national Voodoo temple began construction in 1995.

Education. Education is divided into primary (6 years, compulsory), secondary (7 years) and university/higher education. The school system is based on the French system and instruction is in French.

In 1994–95, there were 360 primary schools (221 state, 139 religious), 21 public lycées, 123 private secondary schools, 18 vocational training centres and 42 domestic science centres.

There are 2 universities with 11,497 students and 1,136 academic staff in 1994–95, and an Institute of Administration and Management.

Health. There were, in 1989, 944 doctors and 98 dentists in practice, and 87 hospitals and health centres with 4,566 beds.

DIPLOMATIC REPRESENTATIVES

Of Haiti in Great Britain. The Embassy closed on 30 March 1987.

Of Great Britain in Haiti
Ambassador: D. F. Milton, CMG (resides in Kingston).

Of Haiti in the USA (2311 Massachusetts Ave., NW, Washington, D.C., 20008)
Ambassador: Jean Casimir.

Of the USA in Haiti (Harry Truman Blvd., Port-au-Prince)
Ambassador: William Lacy Swing.

Of Haiti to the United Nations
Ambassador: Fritz Longchamp.

Further Reading

Chambers, F. J., *Haiti.* [Bibliography] 2nd ed. Oxford and Santa Barbara (CA), 1994
Ferguson, J., *Papa Doc, Baby Doc: Haiti and the Duvaliers.* Oxford, 1987
Laguerre, M. S., *The Complete Haitiana.* [Bibliography] London and New York, 1982.—*Voodoo and Politics in Haiti.* London, 1989
Lawless, R., *Haiti: a Research Guide.* New York, 1990
Lundahl, M., *The Haitian Economy: Man, Land and Markets.* London, 1983
Nicholls, D., *From Dessalines to Duvalier: Race, Colour and National Independence in Haiti.* 2nd ed. CUP, 1992.—*Haiti in Caribbean Context: Ethnicity, Economy and Revolt.* London, 1985
Thomson, I., *Bonjour Blanc: a Journey through Haiti.* London, 1992
Weinstein, B. and Segal, A., *Haiti: the Failure of Politics.* New York, 1992
Wilentz, A., *The Rainy Season: Haiti since Duvalier.* New York, 1989

National library: Bibliothèque Nationale, Rue du Centre, Port-au-Prince.

HONDURAS

República de Honduras

Capital: Tegucigalpa
Population: 5·29m. (1994)
GNP per capita: US$580 (1994)
HDI/world rank: 0·578/116 (1992)

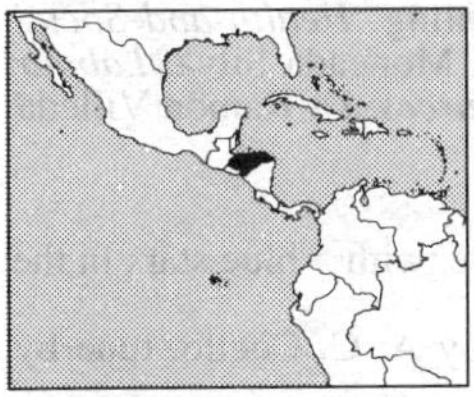

KEY HISTORICAL EVENTS. Honduras gained independence from Spain on 15 Sept. 1821. Until 5 Nov. 1838 Honduras was part of the Federation of Central America.

TERRITORY AND POPULATION. Honduras is bounded in the north by the Caribbean, east and south-east by Nicaragua, west by Guatemala, south-west by El Salvador and south by the Pacific Ocean. The area is 112,088 sq. km (43,277 sq. miles). At the 1988 census the population was 4,443,721 (2,237,498 female; 1·68m. urban). Population (1994 estimate), 5,294,000 (2,674,100 females, 44% urban); density, 47·2 per sq. km.

The chief cities (populations in 1,000, 1991) were Tegucigalpa, the capital (670·1), San Pedro Sula (325·9), El Progreso (68·5), Choluteca (63·2), Danlí (20·2) and the Atlantic coast ports of La Ceiba (77·1), Puerto Cortés (32·5) and Tela (24); other towns include Olanchito (14·1), Juticalpa (14·3), Comayagua (32·9), Siguatepeque (27·7) and Santa Rosa de Copán (21·2).

Areas and 1988 census populations of the 18 departments and the Central District (Tegucigalpa):

Department	*Area (in sq. km)*	*Population*	*Department*	*Area (in sq. km)*	*Population*
Atlántida	4,251	238,742	Islas de la Bahía	261	22,062
Choluteca	4,211	295,484	La Paz	2,331	105,927
Colón	8,875	149,677	Lempira	4,290	177,055
Comayagua	5,196	239,859	Ocotepeque	1,680	74,276
Copán	3,203	219,455	Olancho	24,350	283,852
Cortés	3,954	662,772	Santa Bárbara	5,115	278,868
El Paraíso	7,218	254,295	Valle	1,565	119,645
Francisco Morazán	6,298	251,613	Yoro	7,939	333,508
Gracias a Dios	16,630	34,970	Central District	1,648	576,661
Intibucá	3,072	124,681			

Over the period 1990–93, population growth has averaged 2·91%: Infant mortality rate in 1991 was 57 per 1,000 live births; life expectancy in 1992, 66·7 years.

The official language is Spanish. The Spanish-speaking population is of mixed Spanish and Amerindian descent. There are some 350,000 Amerindians.

CLIMATE. The climate is tropical, with a small annual range of temperature but with high rainfall. Upland areas have two wet seasons, from May to July and in Sept. and Oct. The Caribbean Coast has most rain in Dec. and Jan. and temperatures are generally higher than inland. Tegucigalpa. Jan. 66°F (19°C), July 74°F (23·3°C). Annual rainfall 64" (1,621 mm).

CONSTITUTION AND GOVERNMENT. The present Constitution came into force in 1982. The *President* is elected for a 4-year term. Members of the *National Congress* and municipal mayors are elected simultaneously on a proportional basis, according to combined votes cast for the Presidential candidate of their party.

Presidential, parliamentary and municipal elections were held on 28 Nov. 1993. The electorate was 2·7m. Turn-out was 62%. Carlos Roberto Meina was elected President against 3 opponents by 51% of votes cast.

The Liberal Party (Lib) gained 71 seats in Congress and 171 mayoralties with 51% of votes cast, the National Party 55 and 120 with 41%. The National Innovation and Unity Party gained 2 seats in Congress with 2·4% of votes cast.

President: Carlos Roberto Meina (b. 1926; Lib; sworn in 27 Jan. 1994).

In Sept. 1995 the government consisted of:

Communications, Public Works and Transport: Germán Aparicio. *Culture, Tourism and Information:* Rodolfo Pastor Fasquelle. *Defence and National Security:* Gen. Reynaldo Andino Flores. *Economic Planning:* Guillermo Molina Chocano. *Economy and Commerce:* Gustavo Adolfo Aguilar. *Environment:* Carlos Medina. *Finance:* Juan Ferrera. *Foreign:* José Delmer Urbizo Panting. *Health and Social Affairs:* Dr Enrique Samayoa. *Interior and Justice:* Efraín Moncada Silva. *Labour and Social Security:* Cecilio de Jesús Zavala. *Natural Resources:* Dr Ramón Villeda Bermúdez. *Public Education:* Xenobia de León Gómez.

The *Speaker* is Carlos Flores Facussé.

National flag: Three horizontal stripes of blue, white, blue, with 5 blue stars in the centre.

National anthem: 'Tu bandera' ('Thy Banner'); words by A. C. Coello, tune by C. Hartling.

Local Government: Honduras comprises a Central District (containing the cities of Tegucigalpa and Comayaguela) and 18 departments; (each administered by an appointed Governor), sub-divided into 293 municipalities. Mayors are elected simultaneously with Congressional deputies.

DEFENCE. Conscription was abolished in 1995.

Army. The Army consists of 3 infantry brigades, 1 special tactics group, 1 territorial force, 1 armed cavalry regiment and 1 artillery and 1 engineer battalion. Equipment includes 12 Scorpion light tanks. Strength (1996) 14,000 (12,000 conscripts). There is also a paramilitary Public Security Force of 5,500.

Navy. A small flotilla operates 5 US-built fast inshore patrol craft, some 6 other inshore craft, 4 landing craft and a number of boats. Personnel (1995), 1,000 including 400 marines. Bases are at Puerto Cortés and Amapala.

Air Force. Equipment includes 12 F-5E/F Tiger II fighters, 12 A-37B jet light attack aircraft, 4 Spanish-built CASA C-101BB armed jet trainers, 3 four-engined Lockheed transports, 3 C-47, 1 Israeli-built Arava transport, about 20 helicopters and Tucano and T-41D trainers. Total strength was (1995) about 1,800 personnel (700 conscripts).

INTERNATIONAL RELATIONS

Membership. Honduras is a member of the UN and OAS.

ECONOMY

Budget. Expenditure approved for 1992 was 4,338m. lempiras.

Currency. The unit of currency is the *lempira* (HNL) of 100 *centavos*. There are coins of 1, 2, 5, 10, 20 and 50 centavos and notes of 1, 2, 5, 10, 20, 50 and 100 lempiras. Cash in circulation 1993, 1,099m. lempiras. Foreign exchange reserves were US$200·2m. in 1992; gold reserves were US$5·4m. Year-end annual inflation was 13·7% in 1993. In March 1996, £1 = 15·96 lempiras; US$1 = 10·44 lempiras; DM1 = 7·07 lempiras.

Banking and Finance. The central bank of issue is the Banco Central de Honduras (*Governor:* Hugo Noé Pino). There is an agricultural development bank, Banadesa, for small grain producers, a state land bank and a network of rural credit agencies managed by peasant organizations. The Central American Bank for Economic Integration (BCIE) has its head office in Tegucigalpa. In 1993 there were 13 private banks, including 2 foreign.

There are stock exchanges in Tegucigalpa and San Pedro Sula.

Weights and Measures. The metric system has been legal since 1 April 1897, although there are still some minor traces of the Imperial and old Spanish systems.

ENERGY AND NATURAL RESOURCES

Electricity. Production (1991) 2,318m. kWh (mainly hydro-electric).

Minerals. Output in 1992 (in 1,000 tonnes): Lead, 10·4; zinc, 32·1; silver, 0·04. Small quantities of gold are mined, and there are also deposits of tin, iron, copper, coal, antimony and pitchblende.

Agriculture. In 1994 1·79m. ha were devoted to arable farming and permanent crop land, and 2·5m. ha to permanent pasture. Legislation of 1975 provided for the compulsory redistribution of land, but in 1992 the grounds for this were much reduced, and a 5-ha minimum area for land titles abolished. Members of the 2,800 co-operatives set up in 1975 received individual shareholdings which can be broken up into personal units. Since 1992 women may have tenure in their own right. The state monopoly of the foreign grain trade was abolished in 1992.

Crop production in 1993 (in 1,000 tonnes): Bananas, 931; coffee, 121; maize, 638; dry beans, 54; sorghum, 91.

Livestock (1993): Cattle, 2,315,000; sheep, 8,000; pigs, 596,000; goats, 28,000; horses, 172,000; poultry, 14m.

Forestry. Forests cover 4·1m. ha; another 2·5m. ha are suitable for re-afforestation.

Fisheries. Shrimps and lobsters are important catches.

INDUSTRY. Industry is small-scale and local. 1992 output: Cement, 760 tonnes; fabrics, 19,544 yards. 171,196 bottles of beer and 5,308 litres of rum were produced in 1991.

Labour. The workforce was (in 1,000) 1,728·6 in 1992. In 1991 (in 1,000) 702·9 worked in agriculture, hunting and fishery; 282·7 in manufacturing; 156·5 in trade; 88·7 in building; 42·8 in transport and communications and 27·9 in finance.

Trade Unions. About 346,000 workers were unionized in 1994.

FOREIGN ECONOMIC RELATIONS. In May 1992 Honduras, El Salvador and Guatemala agreed to create a free trade zone. Import duties are to be standardized. Foreign debt was US$3,712m. in 1994.

Commerce. Imports in 1991 were valued at US$1,095m. and exports at US$925m..

Main exports are bananas, coffee, timber, refrigerated meats and shrimps and lobsters. Major trading partners are: USA, Japan, Germany, Italy, Netherlands, Belgium, Spain and UK.

Total trade between Honduras and UK (British Department of Trade returns, in £1,000 sterling):

	1991	*1992*	*1993*	*1994*	*1995*
Imports to UK	9,065	13,255	12,313	19,157	18,130
Exports and re-exports from UK	6,784	6,101	14,124	13,861	15,537

Tourism. There were 226,500 foreign visitors in 1991; 175,700 Hondurans went abroad.

COMMUNICATIONS

Roads. Honduras is connected with Guatemala, El Salvador and Nicaragua by the Pan-American Highway. Out of a total of 18,819 km of road (1991), 2,401 km were asphalted and 9,215 km were unpaved but of all-weather construction. In 1991 there were 136,560 motor vehicles.

Railways. The small government-run railway was built to serve the banana industry and is confined to the northern coastal region and does not reach Tegucigalpa. The total railways operating in 1986 were 955 km of 1,067 mm and 914 mm gauge, which carried 1m. passengers and 1·2m. tonnes of freight.

Civil Aviation. There are 4 international airports: Tegucigalpa (Toncontín), San Pedro Sula, Roatún and La Ceiba, with over 30 smaller airstrips in various parts of the country. The national carrier is Servicio Aéreo de Honduras (Sahsa), which in 1995 operated 1 B-737-200 and 1 B-737-200 Adv. Services are also provided by

American Airlines, Continental Airlines and Air Micronesia, Islena Airlines, LACSA and TACA.

Shipping. The largest port is Puerto Cortés on the Atlantic coast. There are also ports at Henecán (on the Pacific) and Puerto Castilla and Tela (northern coast). Sea-going shipping totalled 1·75m. GRT in 1995, including oil tankers, 0·16m. GRT and container ships 8,643 GRT.

Telecommunications. Hondutel, a government agency run by the military and scheduled in 1994 for privatization, had operated 87,311 telephones in 1990. Some 66,000 telephones were in operation. The telegraph remains important and there were 364 offices in the country in 1988.

In 1993, there were 6 commercial TV channels (colour by NTSC) and various radio stations (mostly local) operating. In 1993 there were 1·8m. radio and 0·16m. TV sets.

Press (1993). There are 4 national daily papers. Several local papers exist.

SOCIAL INSTITUTIONS

Justice. Judicial power is vested in the Supreme Court, with 9 judges elected by the National Congress for 4 years; it appoints the judges of the courts of appeal, and justices of the peace.

Religion. Roman Catholicism is the prevailing religion, but the constitution guarantees freedom to all creeds, and the State does not contribute to the support of any. Evangelical movements from North America are spreading their influence.

Education. Adult literacy was 72·1% in 1991. Education is free, compulsory (from 7 to 12 years) and secular. There is a high drop out rate after the first years in primary education. In 1991–92 the 7,487 primary schools had 923,902 children (25,854 teachers); the 540 secondary, normal and technical schools had 132,953 pupils (8,517 teachers). In 1991–92 there were 5 universities and 3 specialized colleges, with a total of 49,504 students and 3,654 academic staff.

Health. In 1990 there were about 2,900 doctors. In 1991 there were 24 public hospitals and 16 private, with 5,303 beds, and 729 health centres.

DIPLOMATIC REPRESENTATIVES

Of Honduras in Great Britain (115 Gloucester Pl., London, W1H 3PJ)
Ambassador: Vacant.

Of Great Britain in Honduras (Edificio Palmira, 3er Piso, Colonia Palmira, Tegucigalpa)
Ambassador: Peter Holmes.

Of Honduras in the USA (3007 Tilden St., NW, Washington, D.C., 20008)
Ambassador: Roberto Flores Bermúdez.

Of the USA in Honduras (Av. La Paz, Tegucigalpa)
Ambassador: William T. Pryce.

Of Honduras to the United Nations
Ambassador: Gerardo Martínez Blanco.

Further Reading

Banco Central de Honduras. *Honduras en Cifras 1990–92.* Tegucigalpa, 1993
Howard-Reguindin, P., *Honduras.* [Bibliography]. Oxford and Santa Barbara (CA), 1991
Meyer, H. K. and Meyer, J. H., *Historical Dictionary of Honduras.* 2nd ed. Metuchen (NJ), 1994
Sheehan, E. R. F., *Agony in the garden: a Stranger in Central America.* New York, 1989

HONG KONG

Population: 6·19m. (1995)
GNP per capita: US$21,650 (1994)
HDI/world rank: 0·905/24 (1992)

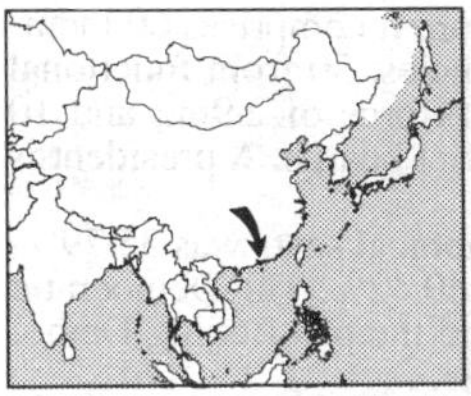

KEY HISTORICAL EVENTS. Hong Kong island and the southern tip of the Kowloon peninsula were ceded by China to Britain after the first and second Anglo-Chinese Wars by the Treaty of Nanking 1842 and the Convention of Peking 1860. The New Territories were leased to Britain for 99 years by China in 1898. Talks began in Sept. 1982 between Britain and China over the future of Hong Kong after the lease expiry in 1997. On 19 Dec. 1984, the two countries signed the Joint Declaration of the British and Chinese Governments on the Question of Hong Kong which entered into force on 27 May 1985. By the terms of this Hong Kong is to become, with effect from 1 July 1997, a Special Administrative Region of the People's Republic of China enjoying a high degree of autonomy, and vested with executive, legislative and independent judicial power, including that of final adjudication. The laws currently in force in Hong Kong are to remain basically unchanged. The existing social and economic systems, and the present life-style, are to remain unchanged for another 50 years. This 'one country, two systems' principle, embodied in the Basic Law, which was enacted by the National People's Congress of the People's Republic of China in 1990, is to become the constitution for the Hong Kong Special Administrative Region. In June 1991 the Legislative Council approved a Bill of Rights. China (People's Republic) objected to it.

In Dec. 1995 the Standing Committee of China's National People's Congress set up a 150-member body (including 94 members from Hong Kong) to oversee the retrocession of Hong Kong on 30 June 1997.

TERRITORY AND POPULATION. Hong Kong island is situated off the southern coast of the Chinese mainland 32 km east of the mouth of the Pearl River. The area of the island is 79·99 sq. km. It is separated from the mainland by a fine natural harbour. On the opposite side is the peninsula of Kowloon (46·27 sq. km). Total area of the Territory is 1,091 sq. km, a large part of it being steep and unproductive hillside. Country parks and special areas cover over 40% of the land area. Since 1945, the Government has reclaimed over 5,400 ha from the sea, principally from the seafronts of Hong Kong and Kowloon, facing the harbour. The 'New Territories' are on the mainland, north of Kowloon.

The population was 5,674,100 at the 1991 census. Estimate (30 June 1995) 6,189,800. Annual growth rate, 1994, 2·4%. Vital statistics, 1994: Known births, 71,646 (34,368 females); known deaths, 29,950; registered marriages, 38,264. Rates (per 1,000): Birth, 11·9; death, 5; infant mortality, 4·5; natural increase, 6·9. Life expectancy, 1994: Males, 75·8 years; females, 81·2. Some 60,000 persons emigrated in 1994. The British Nationality Scheme enables persons to acquire citizenship without leaving Hong Kong. There were 38,200 legal immigrants from China in 1994. 60% of the population was born in Hong Kong, 34% in China (1991 census). The population of Vietnamese migrants ('boat people') in Oct. 1995 was 22,176. All remaining 'boat people' were scheduled for repatriation in 1996.

The official languages are Chinese and English.

CLIMATE. The climate is sub-tropical, tending towards temperate for nearly half the year, the winter being cool and dry and the summer hot and humid, May to Sept. being the wettest months. Jan. 60°F (15·8°C), July 84°F (28·8°C). Annual rainfall 87" (2,214·3 mm).

CONSTITUTION AND GOVERNMENT. Hong Kong is administered by the Hong Kong Government. The Governor is the head of Government and presides over the *Executive Council*, which advises the Governor on all important matters. In Oct. 1995, the Executive Council consisted of 3 ex-officio members and 10 appointed members, of whom 1 is an official member. The chief functions of the *Legislative Council* are to enact laws, control public expenditure and put questions to the administration on matters of public interest. The Legislative Council elected in Sept. 1995 is, for the first time, constituted solely by election. It comprises 60 members, of whom 20 are elected from geographical constituencies, 30 from functional constituencies encompassing all eligible persons in a workforce of 2·9m., and 10 from an election committee formed by members of 18 district boards. A president is electred from and by the members.

At the elections on 17 Sept. 1995, turn-out for the geographical seats was 35·79%, and for the functional seats (21 of which were contested), 40·42%. The Democratic Party and its allies gained 29 seats, the Liberal Party 10 and the pro-Beijing Democratic Alliance, 6. The remaining seats went to independents.

Local Government. There are 2 municipal councils, the Urban Council and the Regional Council. With all appointed seats abolished in 1995, 59 of 80 seats were open to direct election in the March 1995 elections. Turn-out was 25·8%. Elections to the 18 Consultative District Boards set up in 1982 were held in Sept. 1994; turn-out was 33·1%.

At local council elections on 18 Sept. 1994 for 346 council seats turn-out was 33·1%. The United Democratic Party gained 77 seats; the Alliance for Democracy, 28; the Democratic Alliance for a Better Hong Kong (pro-Beijing), 37; the Liberal Party, 30, the United Democrats of Hong Kong won 11 out of 27 seats, independents 11, the Liberal Democratic Federation 3 and Communists 2.

Governor and C.-in-C.: Chris Patten.
Chief Secretary: Anson Chan, CBE, JP.
Financial Secretary: Donald Tsang, OBE, JP.
Attorney General: J. F. Mathews, CMG, JP.
Flag: British Blue Ensign with the arms of the Territory on a white disc in the fly.

DEFENCE. The Hong Kong Garrison, under the Commander British Forces, comprises units of all three services. Its principal role is to demonstrate British sovereignty, maintain the integrity of the Territory's boundaries and contribute towards the overall security, stability and prosperity of Hong Kong. During 1994-95 the Garrison was reduced from a strength of about 9,000 to 3,250 as part of the run-down towards transfer of sovereignty in 1997.

Army. The Army constitutes the bulk of the Garrison. The sole UK battalion left in mid-1994, leaving 1 Gurkha battalion and supporting units in the Territory. The Gurkha battalion was to be replaced by a roulement battalion from the UK in Nov. 1996.

Navy. The Royal Naval Hong Kong Squadron comprises 3 Peacock class patrol craft and is based at the shore establishment HMS *Tamar* on Stonecutters Island. The Royal Hong Kong Police force also operates some 40 lightly-armed inshore patrol craft.

Air Force. In 1993 the Government Flying Service assumed principal responsibility for civilian medical evacuation and search and rescue duties. A Royal Air Force army co-operation squadron provides medium-lift short-range helicopter support for the Garrison and support for the Government Flying Service when required in emergencies. It has a strength of about 200, operating a fleet of 6 Wessex helicopters.

ECONOMY

Budget. The total Government revenue and expenditure for financial years ending 31 March were as follows (in HK$1m.):

	1991–92	*1992-93*	*1993-94*	*1994–95*
Revenue	114,699	135,311	166,602	173,561
Expenditure	92,191	113,332	147,438	165,826

Estimated operating revenue (in HK$1m.) for 1995-96, 156,995; capital revenue, 32,605. Estimated operating expenditure, 124,540; capital expenditure, 45,200.

Currency. The unit of currency is the *Hong Kong dollar* (HKD) of 100 *cents*. Banknotes are issued by the Hongkong and Shanghai Banking Corporation and the Standard Chartered Bank, and, from May 1994, the Bank of China. At 31 Dec. 1994, the total value of notes in circulation was HK$74,395m. There are coins of HK$10, HK$2, HK$1, 50 cents, 20 cents and 10 cents. Total vaule of coins in circulation as at 31 Dec. 1994 was HK$3,372m.

Since Oct. 1983 the HK$ has been linked to the US$ at a fixed exchange rate of US$1 = HK$7·80. In March 1996, £1 = HK$11·82; DM1 = HK$5·24.

Banking and Finance. As at Dec. 1995 there were 185 banks licensed under the Banking Ordinance, of which 31 were locally incorporated, 63 restricted licence banks and 157 representative offices of foreign banks. Licensed bank deposits were HK$2,117,121m. in Nov. 1995; restricted licence bank deposits were HK$37,497m. There were 132 deposit-taking companies registered under the Banking Ordinance with total deposits of HK$18,419m. as at Nov. 1995.

There is a stock exchange.

Weights and Measures. Metric, British Imperial, Chinese and US units are all in current use in Hong Kong. However, Government departments have now effectively adopted metric units; all new legislation uses metric terminology and existing legislation is being progressively metricated. Metrication is also proceeding in the private sector.

ENERGY AND NATURAL RESOURCES

Electricity. Production (1992) 34,914m. kWh.

Water. Reservoirs are needed to store the summer rainfall in order to meet supply requirements. There are 17 impounding reservoirs with a total capacity of 586m. cu. metres. Water is also purchased (720m. cu. metres in 1996).

Agriculture. Agriculture supplies about a quarter of domestic demand. Only 3·4% of the total land area is suitable for crop farming and most produce derives from intensive market gardening: 1,350 ha were under cultivation in 1995. In 1995, 88,000 tonnes of vegetables and 4,820 tonnes of fruit and nuts were produced. Poultry production was 24,921 tonnes; milk, 407 tonnes; eggs, 1,112 tonnes. There were 0·21m. pigs in 1995.

Fisheries. The fishing fleet of 4,800 vessels supplies about 62% of fresh marine fish consumed locally. In 1995 the marine fish catch was 203,300 tonnes. Inland freshwater farming and coastal marine farming provided 8,200 tonnes of fish.

INDUSTRY

INDUSTRY. An economic policy based on free enterprise and free trade; a skilled work force; an efficient commercial infrastructure; the modern and efficient seaport (including container shipping terminals) and airport facilities; a geographical position relative to markets in North America; and traditional trading links with the UK have all contributed to Hong Kong's success as a modern industrial territory.

In 1995 there were 31,114 manufacturing firms employing 386,106 persons. Firms by product type (and persons employed): Textiles and clothing, 7,046 (139,931); plastics, 2,250 (15,997); electronics, 1,109 (44,078); watches and clocks, 1,006 (12,119); electrical appliances, 136 (2,589); ship-building, 374 (4,510).

Labour. In the third quarter of 1995 the labour force (economically active population aged 15 and over) totalled 3·09m. (1·18m. female). The employed population included 0·81m. administrative and managerial workers, professional and associate professionals, 0·55m. clerks, 0·51m. in elementary occupations, 0·42m. service and shop sales workers, 0·36m craft and related workers and 0·32m. plant and machine operators and assemblers. The seasonally adusted unemployment rate was 3·5%.

FOREIGN ECONOMIC RELATIONS

Commerce. Industry is mainly export-oriented. The total value of domestic exports in 1994 was HK$222,092m.; re-exports, HK$947,921m. The major markets for domestic exports were USA (27·7%), People's Republic of China (27·5%), Germany (5·8%), Singapore (5·5%) and Japan (4·7%). The total value of imports in 1994 was HK$1,250,709m., mainly from the People's Republic of China (37·6%), Japan (15·6%), Taiwan (8·6%), USA (7·1%), Singapore (5%) and South Korea (4·6%).

In 1994, 78% of domestic exports were made up by (in HK$1m.): Textiles and clothing, 88,124; electronic products, 58,091; clocks and watches, 13,196; jewellery, 5.229; plastic products, 5,152; metal goods, 4,594; printed matter, 4,520; toys and dolls, 2,478; electrical appliances, 1,401. The chief import items were manufactured goods (597,084), machinery and transport equipment (443,633), chemicals (84,122) and foodstuffs (50,776).

Visible trade normally carries an adverse balance which is offset by a favourable balance of invisible trade, in particular transactions in connexion with air transportation, shipping, tourism and banking services.

Hong Kong has a free exchange market. Foreign merchants may remit profits or repatriate capital. Import and export controls are kept to the minimum, consistent with strategic requirements.

Total trade between Hong Kong and UK (British Department of Trade returns, in £1,000 sterling) is given as follows:

	1991	*1992*	*1993*	*1994*	*1995*
Imports to UK	2,147,611	2,397,362	2,997,774	3,079,611	3,538,821
Exports and re-exports from UK	1,385,892	1,612,934	2,170,115	2,297,561	2,656,583

Tourism. There were about 9·3m. visitor arrivals in 1994 (1,441,000 from Japan, 776,000 from the USA) who spent HK$64,000m.

COMMUNICATIONS

Roads. At 31 Dec. 1995 there were 1,717 km of roads, distributed as follows: Hong Kong Island, 420; Kowloon, 397, and New Territories, 900. There are 8 major road tunnels, including 2 under Victoria Harbour. At 31 Dec. 1995 there were 458,785 licensed motor vehicles, including 285,467 private cars and 118,205 goods vehicles. There were 14,790 road accidents in 1995, 259 fatal.

Railways. There is an electric tramway with a total track length of 33 km, and a cable tramway connecting the Peak district with the lower levels in Victoria. The electrified Kowloon-Canton Railway runs for 34 km from the terminus at Hung Hom in Kowloon to the border point at Lo Wu. It carried 232m. passengers and 2·7m. tonnes of freight in 1995. A light rail system (32 km) is operated by the Kowloon-Canton Railway Corporation in Tuen Mun, Yuen Long and Tin Shui Wai; it carried 123m. passengers in 1995.

A metro, the Mass Transit Railway system comprises 43·2 km with 38 stations. It carried 812m. passengers in 1995.

Civil Aviation. Hong Kong International Airport (Kai Tak) is situated on the north shore of Kowloon Bay. 61 airlines operate services. British Airways operates 14 flights per week to the UK. Cathay Pacific Airways, one of the 3 Hong Kong-based airlines, operates more than 365 passenger and cargo services weekly to Europe (including 16 passenger and 5 cargo services per week to the UK), the Far and Middle East, South Africa, Australasia and North America. In 1995, Cathay Pacific had a fleet of 2 A330-300s, 4 A340-200s, 7 B-747-200Bs, 1 B-747-200B(F), 3 B-747-200Fs, 6 B-747-300s, 19 B-747-400s, 1 B-747-400F and 14 other aircraft. Hong Kong Dragon Airlines Ltd operates A330 and A320 scheduled and non-scheduled services to a number of cities in Asia and the People's Republic of China. Air Hong Kong, an all-cargo operator, provides a scheduled service 5 times a week to Manchester, UK, and operates non-scheduled services around the region. In 1994–95, 145,085 aircraft arrived and departed carrying 25·5m. passengers and 1·33m. tonnes of freight.

Shipping. The port of Hong Kong handled 12·6m. 20-ft equivalent units in 1995. The Kwai Chung Container Port has 31 berths with 6,059 metres of quay backed by 228 ha of cargo handling area. In 1995, more than 41,000 ocean-going vessels, 108,000 river trading vessels and 64,000 international passenger vessels called at Hong Kong. Over 173m. tonnes of cargo was handled, 50% in containers.

Telecommunications. There were 126 post offices in 1995. In Nov. 1995 there were 4,216,800 telephones and 268,678 fax lines. Basic local telephone services are provided by Hong Kong Telecom, which also offers fax services and value-added telephone services. The company also provides international voice, data and video transmission services, telex and telegram services, international private leased circuits, and shore-to-ship and ground-to-air communications. International facilities are provided through submarine cables, microwave and satellite radio systems.

Broadcasting is regulated by the Broadcasting Authority, a statutory body comprising 3 government officers and 9 non-official members. There is a government broadcasting station, Radio Television Hong Kong, which broadcasts on 7 channels (4 Chinese, 1 English and 1 bi-lingual service and 1 dedicated to BBC World Service), 6 of which provide a 24-hour service. Hong Kong Commercial Broadcasting Co. Ltd and Metro Broadcast Co. Ltd transmit commercial sound programmes on 6 channels. Television Broadcasts Ltd and Asia Television Ltd transmit commercial television in English and Chinese on 4 channels, in colour (by PAL). Hutchvision Hong Kong broadcasts by satellite to the entire Asian region on 14 TV and 2 radio channels and also carries the BBC World Service. There is also a cable TV network. In 1992 there were some 3m. radio; in 1995 there were over 2·3m. TV receivers.

Cinemas. In 1995 there were 181 cinemas; attendance was 27·4m. (57m. in 1990). 154 films were made in 1995.

Press. In 1995 there were 59 registered newspapers, including 36 dailies in Chinese and 5 in English, and 675 periodicals. A number of news agency bulletins are registered as newspapers.

SOCIAL INSTITUTIONS

Justice. The common law of England and the rules of equity are in force so far as they are applicable to the circumstances of Hong Kong. UK Acts of Parliament, however, are only binding if expressly applied to Hong Kong. By 1997 Hong Kong will possess a comprehensive body of law which owes its authority to its own legislature. The Hong Kong Act of 1985 provides for Hong Kong ordinances to replace English laws in specified fields.

The courts of justice comprise the Supreme Court (which includes the Court of Appeal and the High Court), the District Court (which includes the Family Court), the Magistracies, the Coroner's Court, the Juvenile Court and 4 tribunals. The Court of Appeal hears appeals on all matters, civil and criminal, from the lower courts. Further appeal lies at present from the Court of Appeal to the Juidicial Committee of the Privy Council in London. But pursuant to the Joint Declaration, the powers of final judgement shall be vested in the Court of Final Appeal to be set up in the territory in July 1997. While the High Court has unlimited jurisdiction in both civil and criminal matters, the District Court has limited jurisdiction. The maximum term of imprisonment it may impose is 7 years. Magistracies exercise criminal jurisdiction over a wide range of indictable and summary offences, and the powers of punishment are generally restricted to a maximum of 2 years' imprisonment. The Lands Tribunal determines on statutory claims for compensation over land and certain landlord and tenant matters. The Labour Tribunal provides a quick and inexpensive method of settling disputes between employers and employees. The Small Claims Tribunal deals with monetary claims involving amounts not exceeding HK$15,000. The Obscene Articles Tribunal has jurisdiction to determine whether an article referred to it by a court is obscene or indecent and whether matter publicly displayed is indecent.

After being in abeyance for 25 years, the death penalty was abolished in 1992.

91,886 crimes were reported in 1995. The prison population was 13,117 in 1995.

Police. In July 1995, the establishment of the Royal Hong Kong Police Force was 27,324.

Education. Free and compulsory education is available to all children aged from 6 to 15 years. In 1995–96 there were 180,317 pupils in 731 kindergartens (all private), 467,718 in 860 primary schools (some 10·3% in private schools) and 459,845 in 38 government, 337 aided and 91 private secondary schools.

There are 7 technical institutes with (in 1994–95) 9,900 full-time and 40,100 part-time students; 2 technical colleges with 9,300 students, and 5 teacher training colleges of education with 2,863 full-time students.

The University of Hong Kong (founded 1911) had 10,325 full-time and 2,618 part-time students in the academic year of 1995-96, the Chinese University of Hong Kong (founded 1963), 10,388 full-time and 2,536 part-time students, the Hong Kong University of Science and Technology (founded 1991), 5,792 full-time and 503 part-time students, the Hong Kong Polytechnic University (founded 1972 as the Hong Kong Polytechnic), 11,157 full-time and 9,289 part-time students, the City University of Hong Kong (founded 1984 as the City Polytechnic of Hong Kong), 10,061 full-time and 6,881 part-time students, the Hong Kong Baptist University (founded 1956 as the Hong Kong Baptist College), 4,146 full-time and 600 part-time students and the Lingnan College (founded 1967), 2,059 full-time and 2 part-time students.

Social Welfare. The Government co-ordinates and implements expanding programmes in social welfare, which include social security, family services, child care, services for the elderly, youth and community work, probation and corrections and rehabilitation. 170 non-governmental organizations are subsidized by public funds.

The Government gives non-contributory cash assistance to needy families, unemployed able-bodied adults, the severely disabled and the elderly. Caseload as at 31 Dec. 1995 totalled 623,029. Victims of natural disasters, crimes of violence and traffic accidents are financially assisted.

Health. In 1992 there were 6,818 doctors, 1,565 dentists and 26,385 hospital beds.

Further Reading

Statistical Information: The Census and Statistics Department is responsible for the preparation and collation of Government statistics. These statistics are published mainly in the *Hong Kong Monthly Digest of Statistics.* The Department also publishes monthly trade statistics, economic indicators and an annual review of overseas trade, etc.

Hong Kong [various years] Hong Kong Government Press
Bonavia, D., *Hong Kong 1997.* London, 1984
Cameron, N., *An Illustrated History of Hong Kong.* OUP, 1991
Chill, H., *et al* (eds.) *The Future of Hong Kong: Toward 1997 and Beyond.* Westport, 1987
Cottrell, R., *The End of Hong Kong: the Secret Diplomacy of Imperial Retreat.* London, 1993
Endacott, G. B., *A History of Hong Kong.* 2nd ed. OUP, 1973.–*Government and People in Hong Kong, 1841–1962: a Constitutional History.* OUP, 1965
Lo, C. P., *Hong Kong.* London, 1992
Morris, J., *Hong Kong: Epilogue to an Empire.* 2nd ed. [of *Hong Kong: Xianggang*]. London, 1993
Patrikeeff, F., *Mouldering Pearl: Hong Kong at the Crossroads.* London, 1989
Roberts, E. V. *et al. Historical Dictionary of Hong Kong and Macau.* Metuchen (NJ), 1993
Scott, I., *Hong Kong:* [Bibliography]. Oxford and Santa Barbara (CA), 1990
Segal, G., *The Fate of Hong Kong.* London, 1993
Welsh, F., *A History of Hong Kong.* 2nd ed. London, 1994
Wilson, D., *Hong Kong, Hong Kong.* London, 1991

HUNGARY

Magyar Köztársaság

(Hungarian Republic)

Capital: Budapest
Population: 10·25m. (1995)
GNP per capita: US$3,840 (1994)
HDI/world rank: 0·856/50 (1992)

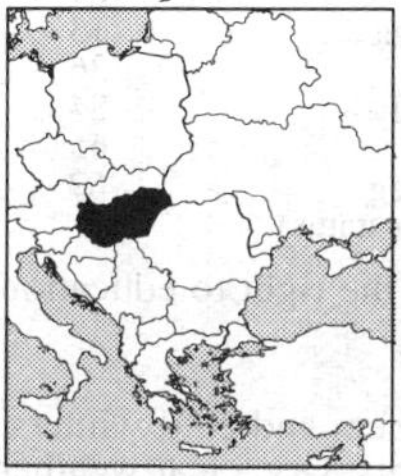

KEY HISTORICAL EVENTS. Hungary first became an independent kingdom in 1001. On 1 Feb. 1946 the National Assembly proclaimed a republic. The Communist People's Republic was established in Aug. 1949 (for details *see* THE STATESMAN'S YEAR-BOOK, 1989–90, p. 615).

On 23 Oct. 1956 an anti-Stalinist revolution broke out, and the newly-formed coalition government of Imre Nagy on 1 Nov. withdrew from the Warsaw Pact and asked the UN for protection. János Kádár formed a counter-government on 3 Nov. and asked the USSR for support. Soviet troops suppressed the revolution and abducted Nagy and his ministers; Nagy was secretly executed in 1958.

A gathering reformist tendency within the Hungarian Socialist Workers' (i.e. Communist) Party led by Imre Pozsgay culminated in its self-dissolution in Oct. 1989 and reconstitution as the Hungarian Socialist Party. The People's Republic was abolished on 23 Oct. 1989.

Nagy had been reburied with state honours on 16 Aug. 1989.

TERRITORY AND POPULATION. Hungary is bounded in the north by Slovakia, north-east by the Ukraine, east by Romania, south by Croatia and Yugoslavia and west by Austria. The peace treaty of 10 Feb. 1947 restored the frontiers as of 1 Jan. 1938. The area of Hungary is 93,032 sq. km (35,911 sq. miles).

At the census of 1 Jan. 1990 the population was 10,374,823 (5,389,919 females); estimate, 1995, 10,245,677 (5,341,973 females). 62·8% of the population was urban (18·8% in Budapest) in 1995; population density, 1995, 110 per sq. km. Ethnic minorities, 1990: Germans, 30,824; Croats, 13,570; Romanians, 10,740; Slovaks, 10,459; Serbs, 2,905; Slovenes, 1,930; others, 19,460. There were about 142,683 Gypsies in 1990 with a Gypsy Council. A law of 1993 permits ethnic minorities to set up self-governing councils. It specifies the following as having ethnic minority status: Armenians, Bulgarians, Croats, Germans, Greeks, Gypsies, Poles, Romanians, Ruthenians, Serbs, Slovaks, Slovenes and Ukrainians. There is a worldwide Hungarian diaspora, of 1·5m. in 1988 (730,000 in US; 220,000 in Israel; 140,000 in Canada), and Hungarian minorities (3·5m. in 1992) in Romania (2m.), Slovakia (0·6m.), Yugoslavia (Vojvodina, 0·4m.) and the Ukraine (0·16m.).

Vital statistics, 1994: Births, 115,598; marriages, 54,114 (14,798 remarriages); divorces, 23,417; deaths, 146,899; abortions, 74,491. There were 3,625 suicides. Rates (per 1,000), 1994: Birth, 11·3; death, 14·3; marriage, 5·3; divorce, 2·3; infant mortality, 11·5 (per 1,000 live births). Since 1981 the population has been decreasing, by 3 per 1,000 in 1994; expectation of life (1994): males, 64·8 years; females, 74·2.

Hungary is divided into 19 counties (*megyék*) and the capital, Budapest, which has county status.

Area (in sq. km) and population (in 1,000) of counties and county towns (estimate, 1 Jan. 1995):

Counties	*Area*	*Population*	*Chief town*	*Population*
Baranya	4,487	412	Pécs	163
Bács-Kiskun	8,362	541	Kecskemét	105
Békés	5,631	405	Békéscsaba	65
Borsod-Abaúj-Zemplén	7,247	750	Miskolc	182
Csongrád	4,263	429	Szeged	169

Counties	*Area*	*Population*	*Chief town*	*Population*
Fejér	4,373	426	Székesfehérvár	108
Győr-Moson-Sopron	4,062	426	Győr	127
Hajdú-Bihar	6,211	550	Debrecen	211
Heves	3,637	330	Eger	60
Jász-Nagykún-Szolnok	5,607	423	Szolnok	79
Komárom-Esztergom	2,251	313	Tatabánya	73
Nógrád	2,544	224	Salgótarján	46
Pest	6,394	973	Budapest	1,930
Somogy	6,036	338	Kaposvár	69
Szabolcs-Szatmár-Bereg	5,937	573	Nyíregyháza	113
Tolna	3,704	250	Szekszárd	36
Vas	3,336	273	Szombathely	84
Veszprém	4,639	379	Veszprém	65
Zala	3,784	302	Zalaegerszeg	62
Budapest	525	4,487	(has county status)	

The official language is Hungarian. Ethnic minorities have the right to education in their own language.

CLIMATE. A humid continental climate, with warm summers and cold winters. Precipitation is generally greater in summer, with thunderstorms. Dry, clear weather is likely in autumn, but spring is damp and both seasons are of short duration. Budapest. Jan. 32°F (0°C), July 71°F (21·5°C). Annual rainfall 25" (625 mm). Pécs. Jan. 30°F (–0·7°C), July 71°F (21·5°C). Annual rainfall 26·4" (661 mm).

CONSTITUTION AND GOVERNMENT. On 18 Oct. 1989 the National Assembly approved by an 88% majority a constitution which abolished the People's Republic, and established Hungary as an independent, democratic, law-based state.

The head of state is the *President*, who is elected for 5-year terms by the National Assembly. On 19 June 1995 Árpád Göncz was re-elected President.

The single-chamber *National Assembly* has 386 members, made up of 176 individual constituency winners, 152 allotted by proportional representation from county party lists and 58 from a national list. It is elected for 4-year terms. A *Constitutional Court* was established in Jan. 1990 to review laws under consideration.

Parliamentary elections were held in 2 rounds on 8 and 29 May 1994. Turn-out was 68·9% in the first round and 55·1% in the second. The Hungarian Socialist Party (HSP; former Communists) won 209 seats with 54·1% of votes cast (33 seats in 1990); the Alliance of Free Democrats (AFD), 70 with 18·13% (92); the Hungarian Democratic Forum (HDF), 37 with 9·58% (165); the Independent Smallholders (IS), 26 with 6·73% (43); the Christian Democratic People's Party (CDPP), 22 with 5·69% (21); the Federation of Young Democrats (FYD), 20 with 5·18% (21); the Agrarian Alliance, 1 with 0·26%; the Liberal Bloc, 1 with 0·26%.

President: Árpád Göncz (b. 1922; AFD; elected 3 Aug. 1990, re-elected 19 June 1995).

An HSP-AFD coalition government was formed, which in Feb. 1996 consisted of:
Prime Minister: Gyula Horn (b. 1932; HSP).

Deputy Prime Minister, Minister of the Interior: Gábor Kuncze (AFD). *Environment and Regional Development:* Ferenc Baja (HSP). *Finance:* Vacant. *Culture and Education:* Balint Magyar (AFD). *Defence:* György Keleti (HSP). *Foreign Affairs:* László Kovács (HSP). *Health and Welfare:* György Szábó (HSP). *Labour:* Vacant. *Transport, Telecommunications and Water Resources:* Károly Lotz (AFD). *Agriculture:* László Lakos (HSP). *Industry and Commerce:* Imre Dunai (HSP). *Justice:* Pál Vastagh (HSP). *Without portfolio:* István Nikolits (HSP), Támás Suchman (HSP; *responsible for Privatization*).

National flag: 3 horizontal stripes of red, white and green.

National anthem: 'Isten áldd meg a magyart' ('God bless the Hungarians'); words by Ferenc Kölcsey, tune by Ferenc Erkel.

Local Government. Elections were held on 11 Dec. 1994 for mayors and local councils. 3,150 seats were contested. The HSP gained 32·3% of votes cast; the AFD, 15·67%; the FYD, 9·66%; the IS, 7·99%; the CDPP, 5·77%; the HDF, 4·33%

DEFENCE. The President of the Republic is C.-in-C. of the armed forces.

Men between the ages of 18 and 23 are liable for 12 months' conscription.

Army. Hungary is divided into 4 army districts: Budapest, Debrecen, Kiskunfélegyháza, Pécs. The strength of the Army was (1996) 53,700 (including 36,300 conscripts). It is organized in 3 tank, 7 mechanized, 3 artillery, 1 engineer, 1 air defence artillery, 1 (Budapest) rivercraft and 1 anti-tank brigade, and 1 multiple rocket launcher, 2 anti-tank, 4 engineer and 2 air defence artillery regiments. Equipment includes 857 T-55, 16 T-54, 138 T-72 and 5 T-34 main battle tanks.

There are also 730 border guards.

Navy. The Danube Flotilla, the maritime wing of the Army, in 1995 consisted of some 300 personnel operating 6 river minesweepers and numerous boats and special-purpose vessels.

Air Force. The Air Force is under the control of the Army General Staff, with a strength (1995) of 16,800 (11,200 conscripts). The combat aircraft strength comprises 1 regiment of MiG-23 fighters and 1 of MiG-29 interceptors, 1 squadron of Su-22 fighter-bombers and a regiment of Mi-8 and Mi-24 armed helicopters. Transport units are equipped with An-26 and L-410 aircraft. Other types in service include Mi-8/17 helicopters and L-39 Albatros and Yak-52 trainers.

In addition, 'Guideline' and 'Goa' surface-to-air missiles are operational.

INTERNATIONAL RELATIONS

Membership. Hungary is a member of the UN, Council of Europe and the NATO Partnership for Peace, and is an Associate Partner of the WEU. In April 1994 Hungary applied to join the EU.

ECONOMY

Policy. In 1995 the State Property Agency and the State Holding Company were merged in a new body charged with extending the private sector's share of former state assets to 80%. Legislation of June 1991 provides for compensating former owners or their descendants for property nationalized after May 1939. Land is being restored whether or not it is intended to cultivate it, or bonds are issued for buying into privatization. A Small Shareholder Programme of Privatization was launched in April 1994.

Budget. The budget for calendar years was as follows (in 1,000 forints):

	1988	*1989*	*1990*	*1991*	*1992*	*1993*	*1994*
Revenue	898,200	1,063,700	1,279,000	1,588,700	1,894,400	2,449,000	3,060,200
Expenditure	908,400	1,112,400	1,279,700	1,641,800	2,070,900	2,597,500	3,330,300

1994 revenue included (1,000m. forints): Payments by companies, 798; consumer taxes, 500·6; personal taxes, 495·9. Expenditure included: Support of enterprises, 132·6; social security, 737; consumer price subsidies, 27; capital expenditure, 343·9.

Currency. A decree of 26 July 1946 instituted a new monetary unit, the *forint* (HUF) of 100 *fillér*. There are coins of 10, 20 and 50 fillér and 1, 2, 5, 10, 20 forints, and notes of 50, 100, 500, 1,000, 5,000 and 10,000 forints. The forint was made fully convertible in Jan. 1991. It was devalued by 8% in Aug. 1994, 1·1% in Oct. 1994 and 9% in March 1995. Annualized inflation was 22·3% in 1993. In March 1996, £1 = 217·81 forints; US$1 = 142·51 forints; DM1 = 96·55 forints.

Banking and Finance. In 1987 a two-tier system was established. The National Bank (*Director,* György Surányi) remained the central state financial institution, responsible for the circulation of money and foreign currency exchange, but also became a central clearing bank, with general (but not operational) control over commercial banks and development banks. There were 31 commercial banks in 1992. A law of June 1991 sets capital and reserve requirements, and provides for foreign investment in Hungarian banks. Permission is needed for investments of more than 10%.

The Hungarian International Trade Bank opened in London in 1973. In 1980 the Central European International Bank was set up in Budapest with 7 Western banks holding 66% of the shares. The National Savings Bank handles local government as well as personal accounts. Total savings deposits in 1994, 951,900m. forints.

A stock exchange was opened in Budapest in Jan. 1989.

Weights and Measures. The metric system is in use.

ENERGY AND NATURAL RESOURCES

Electricity. Installed capacity in 1991 was 6,403 mW (1,655 mW nuclear; 46 mW hydro-electric). There is an 880-mW nuclear power station at Paks which produced 42% of total output in 1994. 33,486m. kWh were produced in 1994 (14,049m. kWh by nuclear power), and 2,954m. kWh imported.

Oil and Gas. Oil and natural gas are found in the Szeged basin and Zala county. Production in 1994: Oil, 1,631,000 tonnes; gas, 5,564m. cu. metres.

Minerals. Production in 1994 (in 1,000 tonnes): Hardcoal, 940; lignite, 6,727; brown coal, 6,158; bauxite, 836.

Agriculture. Agriculture contributed 11% of GDP in 1992. Agricultural land was collectivized in 1950. It was announced in 1990 that land would be restored to its pre-collectivization owners if they wished to cultivate it. A law of April 1994 restricts the area of land that may be bought by individuals to 300 ha, and prohibits the sale of arable land and land in conservation zones to companies and foreign nationals.

In 1995 the agricultural area was (in 1,000 ha) 6,179, of which 4,716 were arable, 1,148 meadows and pastures, 90 market gardens, and 225 orchards and vineyards.

In 1993 there were 122 agricultural companies with 1,082,600 ha of land, 1,194 co-operatives with 3,602,400 ha of land and 1·45m. farms and smallholdings with 2,204.600 ha. The irrigated area was 210,000 ha in 1994; 36,200 tractors were in use.

Sown area, 1994 (in 1,000 ha): 4,479 (wheat, 1,059; barley, 423; maize, 1,204; sunflowers, 416; sugar-beet, 105). Crop production (in 1,000 tonnes) in 1994: Wheat, 4,874; rye, 193; barley, 1,558; oats, 131; maize, 4,761; sugar-beet, 3,370; sunflower seed, 667; potatoes, 946.

Livestock as at 30 Sept. 1995 (in 1,000): Cattle, 944; pigs, 5,572; and at 31 Dec. 1994, chickens, 33,665; sheep, 947.

Livestock products (1994): Eggs, 3,877m.; milk, 1,878m. litres; wool, 3,875 tonnes; and, in 1993, meat, 979,300 tonnes.

The north shore of Lake Balaton and the Tokaj area are important wine-producing districts. Wine production in 1994 was 369m. litres.

Forestry. The forest area was 1,763,900 ha in 1993. 32,000 ha were afforested and 8·33m. cu. metres of timber were cut in 1989.

Fisheries. There are fisheries in the rivers Danube and Tisza and Lake Balaton. In 1993 there were 27,100 ha of commercial fishponds. Fish production was 20,293 tonnes in 1992.

INDUSTRY. In 1993 there were 429 state enterprises, 14,293 limited liability companies, 1,523 co-operative societies, 4,186 working teams and 79,970 individual businesses.

Production (in 1,000 tonnes) in 1994: Crude steel, 1,937; rolled steel, 2,083; alumina, 184; cement, 2,793; sulphuric acid, 80; petrol, 2,314; plastics, 720; chemical fertilizers, 236; synthetic fibres, 27; antibiotics (tonnes), 186; buses (units), 1,625; TV receivers, 272,000; refrigerators, 550,362.

Labour. In 1994 the workforce (in 1,000) was 6,271·7, of whom 6,071·6 (2,912·3 females) were of working age. The economically active population was 4,768·5 (2,296·6 females) of whom 3,700·7 were active earners. Persons employed, 4,136·4.

Employed persons by sector, 1994 (in 1,000, women in parentheses): Mining, manufacturing, electricity, 1,036·3 (414·1); building, 201 (22·2); agriculture and forestry, 327·6 (92·6); transport and telecommunications, 314·5 (85·3); (1993) commerce, 654·1 (428·9); water supply, 56·3 (14·4); personal and business services, 244·9 (122·7); health, social and cultural services, 768·3 (586·1); public administration, 274 (120·9). Average monthly wages in 1993: 33,309 forints. Minimum monthly wage, 1996, 14,500 forints. There were 519,592 unemployed in Dec. 1994, of whom 191,593 were receiving unemployment benefit (payable for 12 months; monthly average, 7,310 forints). Retirement age: Men, 60; women, 55.

Trade Unions. The former official Communist organization (National Council of Trade Unions), renamed the Confederation of Hungarian Trade Unions (MSZOSZ), groups 70 organizations and claimed 1m. members in 1993. A law of 1991 abolished its obligatory levy on pay packets; its assets derived from this period are to be distributed to other unions. Other unions are grouped in 6 federations (with 1993 membership): the Association of Autonomous Trade Unions (ASZOK, 0·3m.); Coalition of Christian Trade Unions (KESZOSZ, 0·15m.); Co-operation Forum of Trade Unions (SZEF, 0·5m.); Council of Intellectual Trade Unions (ÉSZT, 0·1m.); League of Independent Trade Unions (Liga, 0·25m.); Works Councils (60,000).

Social security benefits are administered jointly by elected representatives of trade unions and employers' organizations.

FOREIGN ECONOMIC RELATIONS. Hungary is a member of CEFTA, along with the Czech Republic, Poland, Slovakia and Slovenia. Foreign debt was US$23,600m. in 1993. At the end of 1995, foreign investments totalled US$12,000m.

Commerce. The economy is heavily dependent on foreign trade. Trade for calendar years (in 1m. forints):

	1989	*1990*	*1991*	*1992*	*1993*	*1994*
Imports	523,507	544,921	855,643	878,503	1,162,500	1,537,002
Exports	571,323	603,636	764,274	843,566	819,900	1,128,695

Principal export markets (trade in 1,000m. forints), 1994: Germany, 318·5; CIS, 125·2; Austria, 122·8; Italy, 95·4; USA, 45·4; France, 40·0. Principal import suppliers: CIS, 257·9; Germany, 359·1; Austria, 184·3; Italy, 107·2; USA, 47·7.

Commodity structure of foreign trade (in 1,000m. forints), 1994:

	Imports	*Exports*
Fuels and electricity	168·7	37·0
Raw materials and semi-finished products	566·2	411·5
Machinery and capital goods	359·2	147·0
Industrial consumer goods	338·3	301·3
Agricultural and food industry products	104·7	232·0

Total trade between Hungary and UK (British Department of Trade returns, in £1,000 sterling):

	1991	*1992*	*1993*	*1994*	*1995*
Imports to UK	103,869	117,636	152,209	240,075	371,571
Exports and re-exports from UK	132,448	161,510	205,692	259,189	295,859

Tourism. In 1994, 39·9m. foreigners visited Hungary, of whom 21·4m. were tourists, and 14·4m. Hungarians travelled abroad. Revenue from foreign tourists in 1993 was 41,351m. forints.

COMMUNICATIONS

Roads. In 1994 there were 30,031 km of roads, including motorways, 293 km; highways, 85 km and other first class main roads, 2,041 km. Passenger cars numbered (1994) 2,176,922, trucks, vans and special-purpose vehicles, 258,081; buses, 21,472 and motorcycles, 157,327. 40·9m. tonnes of freight and 483·1m. passengers were transported by road in 1994 (excluding intra-urban passengers). In 1994 there were 20,722 road accidents with 1,706 fatalities.

Railways. Route length of public lines in 1994, 7,715 km, of which 2,283 km were electrified. 48·2m. tonnes of freight and 160·5m. passengers were carried. There is a metro in Budapest (30·1 km), and tram/light rail networks in Budapest (161·2 km), Debrecen, Miskolc and Szeged.

Civil Aviation. Budapest airport (Ferihegy) handled 2·87m. passengers in 1994. The national carrier is Malév, 65% state-owned, which carried 1·53m. passengers in 1994. Malév had 6 B-737-200 Advs, 4 B-737-300s, 2 B-737-400s, 2 B-767-200ERs and 11 ex-Soviet aircraft in 1995. Services are also provided by Aeroflot, Air France, Air Malta, Air Moldova, Air Ukraine, Alitalia, Austrian Airlines, Balkan, British Airways, Czech Airlines, Delta, Egyptair, El Al, Finnair, Kazakhstan Airlines, KLM, Libyan Airlines, Lithuanian Airlines, LOT, Lufthansa, Northwest Airlines, Sabena, SAS, Swissair, Syrian Airlines, Tarom, Tunis Air and United Airlines.

Shipping. Navigable waterways had (1993) a length of 1,622 km. In 1994 there were 3 sea-going ships. River craft included: Passenger ships, 63; tugs, 35; self-propelled barges and other ships, 21; barges, 170. In 1994, 1·74m. tonnes of cargo and 2·71m. passengers were carried. The Hungarian Shipping Company (MAHART) has agencies at Amsterdam, Alexandria, Algiers, Beirut, Rijeka and Trieste. It has 3 sea-going ships.

Telecommunications. In 1994 there were 2,601 post offices, 1,785,441 telephones, (1,399,066 private), and 9,275 telex subscribers. The government network *Magyar Rádio* broadcasts 4 programmes on medium-waves and FM and also regional programmes, including transmissions in German, Romanian and Serbo-Croat. There are 2 other networks, one of them commercial. *Magyar Televizió* operates 2 TV channels (colour by PAL). *Duna Televizió* broadcasts to Hungarians abroad. There were 6m. radios and 4,261,600 TV sets in use in 1993.

Cinemas (1994). There were 592 cinemas; attendance, 16m. 17 full-length feature films were made.

Press. In 1993 there were 11 national dailies with a combined circulation of 1,018m. copies, and 20 regional dailies (990m.). There were 25 weeklies. 9,383 book titles were published in 1994 in 70·3m. copies. There were 4,727 public and workplace libraries.

SOCIAL INSTITUTIONS

Justice. The administration of justice is the responsibility of the Procurator-General, elected by Parliament for 6 years. There are 105 local courts, 20 labour law courts, 20 county courts, 6 district courts and a Supreme Court. Criminal proceedings are dealt with by the regional courts through 3-member councils and by the county courts and the Supreme Court in 5-member councils. A new Civil Code was adopted in 1978 and a new Criminal Code in 1979.

Regional courts act as courts of first instance; county courts as either courts of first instance or of appeal. The Supreme Court acts normally as an appeal court, but may act as a court of first instance in cases submitted to it by the Public Prosecutor. All courts, when acting as courts of first instance, consist of 1 professional judge and 2 lay assessors, and, as courts of appeal, of 3 professional judges. Local government Executive Committees may try petty offences.

Regional and county judges and assessors are elected by the appropriate local councils; members of the Supreme Court by Parliament.

The Office of Ombudsman was instituted in 1993. He or she is elected by parliament for a 6-year term, renewable once.

There are also military courts of the first instance. Military cases of the second instance go before the Supreme Court.

The death penalty was abolished in Oct. 1990.

70,787 sentences were imposed on adults in 1994, including 21,404 of imprisonment. There were 14,479 juvenile offenders. 12,697 persons were in prison in 1994.

Religion. Church-state affairs are regulated by a law of Feb. 1990 which guarantees freedom of conscience and religion and separates church and state by prohibiting state interference in church affairs. Religious matters are the concern of the Department for Church Relations, under the auspices of the Prime Minister's Office. State aid to all churches was 2,800m. forints in 1993.

In 1992 67·8% of the population aged 14 and over were Roman Catholic, 20·9% Calvinist and 4·2% Lutheran.

The Primate of Hungary is Archbishop László Paskai, appointed Aug. 1986. There are 11 dioceses, all with bishops or archbishops. There is one Uniate bishopric.

In 1993 there were estimated to be 7m. Roman Catholics, 1·9m. Calvinists and 0·43m. Lutherans. 47 other sects had registered as churches. There were 4 Orthodox denominations with 40,000 members in 1979. The Unitarian Church had 10,000 members, 11 ministers and 6 churches. In 1991 there were 100,000 Jews (825,000 in 1939) with 136 synagogues, 26 rabbis and a rabbinical college which enrols 10 students a year.

Education. Education is free and compulsory from 6 to 14. Primary schooling ends at 14; thereafter education may be continued at secondary, secondary technical or secondary vocational schools, which offer diplomas entitling students to apply for higher education, or at vocational training schools which offer tradesmen's diplomas. Students at the latter may also take the secondary school diploma examinations after 2 years of evening or correspondence study. Optional religious education was introduced in schools in 1990.

In 1994–95 there were 4,719 kindergartens with 33,007 teachers and 396,184 pupils; 3,814 primary schools with 89,939 teachers and 985,291 pupils; 867 secondary schools with 27,396 teachers and 337,317 pupils; 196 schools for special needs with 41,696 pupils and 6,824 teachers, 317 vocational training schools with 1,305 teachers and 22,421 students, and 335 trade training schools, with 163,330 apprentices and 10,961 teachers and instructors. In 1994–95 there were 91 higher education institutions, including 6 universities (Budapest, Pécs, Szeged, Debrecen, Miskolc and Veszprém). At these there were 19,103 teachers and 116,370 full-time students.

Schools for ethnic minorities, 1994–95: Kindergartens, 355, with 19,070 pupils and 882 teachers; primary schools, 397, with 49,679 pupils and 1,210 teachers; secondary schools, 18, with 4,348 pupils and 430 teachers.

Health. In 1994 there were 41,562 doctors and dentists, 98,453 hospital beds and 1,479 pharmacies.

Social Security. Since 1993 social security and retirement pensions have been administered by the Social Security Administration, composed of members elected from the employers' organizations and trade unions (*which see*). Medical treatment is free. Patients bear 15% of the cost of medicines. Sickness benefit is 75% of wages, old age pensions (at 60 for men, 55 for women) 60–70%. In 1994, 384,436m. forints were paid out in pensions to 2·93m. pensioners (including old age, 1·6m.; disabled, 0·72m.; widows, 0·22m.) In 1994, 102,970m. forints in family allowances were paid to 1·4m. families on behalf of 2·35m. children. Monthly allowances (in forints) are: One child, 2,750; two, 3,250; three and more, 3,750 (more for single parents).

DIPLOMATIC REPRESENTATIVES

Of Hungary in Great Britain (35 Eaton Pl., London, SW1X 8BY)
Ambassador: Tádé Alfödy.

Of Great Britain in Hungary (Harmincad Utca 6, Budapest V)
Ambassador: Christopher Long, CMG.

Of Hungary in the USA (3910 Shoemaker St., NW, Washington, D.C., 20008)
Ambassador: György Bánlaki.

Of the USA in Hungary (Szabadság Tér 12, Budapest V)
Ambassador: Donald M. Blinken.

Of Hungary to the United Nations
Ambassador: István Náthon.

Further Reading

Central Statisitical Office. *Statisztikai Évkönyv.* Annual since 1871.—*Magyar Statisztikai Zsebkönyv.* Annual.—*Statistical Yearbook.—Statistical Handbook of Hungary.—Monthly Bulletin of Statistics.*

Bako, E., *Guide to Hungarian Studies.* 2 vols. Stanford Univ. Press, 1973
Batt, J., *Economic Reform and Political Change in Eastern Europe: a Comparison of the Czechoslovak and Hungarian Experiences.* Basingstoke, 1988
Bölöny, J., *Magyarország Kormányai, 1848–1975.* Budapest, 1978. [Lists governments and politicians]
Bozóki, A., *et al.* (eds.) *Post-Communist Transition: Emerging Pluralism in Hungary.* London, 1992
Brown, D. M., *Towards a Radical Democracy: the Political Economy of the Budapest School.* Cambridge, 1988
Burawoy, M. and Lukács, J., *The Radiant Past: Ideology and Reality in Hungary's Road to Capitalism.* Chicago Univ. Press, 1992
Cox, T. and Furlong, A. (eds.) *Hungary: the Politics of Transition.* London, 1995
Gerő, A., *Modern Hungarian Society in the Making: the Unfinished Experience*; translated from Hungarian. Budapest, 1995
Hann, C. M. (ed.), *Market Economy and Civil Society in Hungary.* London, 1990
Kabdebó, T., *Hungary.* [Bibliography] Oxford and Santa Barbara (CA), 1980
Kornai, J., *The Road to a Free Economy: Shifting from a Socialist System—the Example of Hungary.* New York and London, 1990
Lendvai, P., *Hungary: the Art of Survival.* London, 1989
Macartney, C. A., *Hungary: A Short History.* London, 1962
Mitchell, K. D. (ed.) *Political Pluralism in Hungary and Poland: Perspectives on the Reforms.* New York, 1992
Sugar, P. F. (ed.) *A History of Hungary.* London, 1991
Szekely, I. P., *Hungary: an Economy in Transition.* CUP, 1993

National statistical office: Központi Statisztikai Hivatal/Central Statistical Office, Keleti Károly u. 5/7, H-1024 Budapest. *Director:* Dr György Vukovich.
National library: Széchenyi Library, Budapest.

ICELAND

Lýðveldið Ísland

(Republic of Iceland)

Capital: Reykjavík
Population: 266,783 (1994)
GNP per capita: US$22,580 (1994)
HDI/world rank: 0·933/6 (1992)

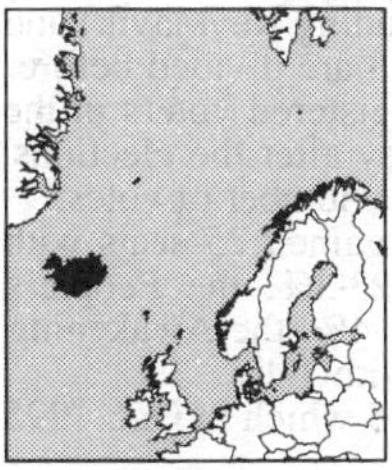

KEY HISTORICAL EVENTS. The first settlers came to Iceland in 874. Between 930 and 1262 Iceland was an independent republic, but by the 'Old Treaty' of 1262 the country recognized the rule of the King of Norway. In 1380 Iceland, together with Norway, came under the rule of the Danish kings, but when Norway was separated from Denmark in 1814, Iceland remained under the rule of Denmark. Since 1 Dec. 1918 it has been acknowledged as a sovereign state. It was united with Denmark only through the common sovereign until it was proclaimed an independent republic on 17 June 1944 following a referendum favouring severance from the Danish crown.

TERRITORY AND POPULATION. Iceland is an island in the North Atlantic, close to the Arctic Circle. Area, 103,000 sq. km (39,758 sq. miles).

There are 8 regions:

Region	*Inhabited land (sq. km)*	*Mountain pasture (sq. km)*	*Waste-land (sq. km)*	*Total area (sq. km)*	*Population (1 Dec. 1994)*
Capital area	1,266	716	—	1,982	156,513
Southwest Peninsula					15,656
West	5,011	3,415	275	8,711	14,292
Western Peninsula	4,130	3,698	1,652	9,470	9,453
Northland West	4,867	5,278	2,948	13,093	10,293
Northland East	9,890	6,727	5,751	22,368	26,785
East	16,921	17,929	12,555	21,991	12,911
South				25,214	20,880
Iceland	42,085	37,553	23,181	102,819	266,783

The census population (1980) was 229,187. In 1994, 22,644 were domiciled in rural districts and 244,139 in towns and villages (of over 200 inhabitants). Population density (1993), 2·6 per sq. km.

The population is almost entirely Icelandic. In 1994 foreigners numbered 4,715 (1,027 Danish, 595 US, 340 British, 299 Norwegian, 285 German).

The capital, Reykjavík, had on 1 Dec. 1994 a population of 103,020; other towns were Akranes, 5,156; Akureyri, 14,913; Bolungarvík, 1,139; Dalvík, 1,509; Eskifjörður, 1,064; Garðabær, 7,688; Grindavík, 2,144; Hafnarfjörður, 17,231; Húsavík, 2,513; Ísafjörður, 3,098; Keflavík, 7,627; Kópavogur, 17,427; Neskaupstaður, 1,562; Njarðvík, 2,583; Ólafsfjörður, 1,189; Sauðárkrókur, 2,726; Selfoss, 4,136; Seltjarnarnes, 4,502; Seyðisfjörður, 866; Siglufjörður, 1,734; Vestmannaeyjar, 4,888.

Vital statistics for calendar years:

	Living births	*Still-born*	*Marriages*	*Divorces*	*Deaths*	*Infant deaths*	*Net immigration*
1992	4,609	16	1,241	531	1,719	22	–254
1993	4,623	9	1,219	537	1,752	22	–203
1994	4,442	15	1,310	489	1,718	15	–760

Life expectancy (1993–94): Males, 77·1 years; females, 81·0.

The official language is Icelandic.

CLIMATE. The climate is cool temperate oceanic and rather changeable, but mild for its latitude because of the Gulf Stream and prevailing S.W. winds. Precipitation is high in upland areas, mainly in the form of snow. Reykjavik. Jan. 34°F (1°C), July 52°F (11°C). Annual rainfall 34" (860 mm).

CONSTITUTION AND GOVERNMENT. The President is elected by direct, popular vote for a period of 4 years.

President: Vigdís Finnbogadóttir (elected 29 June 1980; re-elected unopposed in 1984 and 1992; re-elected with 94% of valid votes in 1988).

An electoral law of 1984 provides for an *Alþingi* (parliament) of 63 members. Of these, 54 seats are distributed among the 8 constituencies as follows: 14 seats are allotted to Reykjavík, 8 to Reykjanes (i.e. the South-west excluding Reykjavík) and 5 or 6 to each of the remaining 6. From the 9 seats then left, 8 are divided beforehand among the constituencies according to the number of registered voters in the preceding elections. Finally, one seat is given to a constituency after the elections, to compensate the party with the fewest seats as compared to its number of votes.

At the elections on 8–9 April the Independence Party (IP) gained 25 seats with 37·1% of votes cast, the Progressive Party (PP) 15 with 23·3%, the People's Alliance 9 with 14·3%, the Social Democratic Party 7 with 11·4%, the Awakening of the Nation Party 4 with 7·2% and the Women's Alliance 3 with 4·9%.

An IP-PP coalition government was formed on 22 April 1995 which in Oct. 1995 comprised:

Prime Minister, Minister for the Statistical Bureau: Davíð Oddsson (IP).

Foreign Affairs and Foreign Trade: Halldór Ásgrímsson (PP). *Finance:* Friðrik Sophusson (IP). *Social Affairs:* Páll Pétursson (PP). *Fisheries, Justice and Church:* Þorsteinn Pálsson (IP). *Agriculture and Environment:* Guðmundur Bjarnason (PP). *Health and Social Security:* Ingibjörg Pálmádottir (PP). *Education and Culture:* Björn Bjarnason (PP). *Trade and Industry:* Finnur Ingólfsson (PP). *Communications:* Halldór Blöndal (IP).

National flag: Blue with a red white-bordered Scandinavian cross.

National anthem: 'Ó Guð vors lands' ('Oh God of Our Country'); words by M. Jochumsson, tune by S. Sveinbjörnsson.

Local Government. Iceland was on 1 Dec. 1994 divided into 171 communes, of which 31 had the status of a town. The commune councils are elected by universal suffrage, in towns and other urban communes by proportional representation, in rural communes by simple majority. For general co-operation the communes are free to form district councils. All the communes except 10 towns are members in 20 district councils. The communes appoint one or more representatives to the district councils according to their population size. The commune councils are supervised by the Ministry of Social Affairs. In 1992 the government administration and the jurisdictional system at local level were fundamentally reformed, so that the jurisdictional power was totally separated from the executive power, resulting in a new division of responsibilities and functions between the magistrates and the district courts. For national government there are 27 divisions exercised by the magistrates.

Municipal elections were held on 28 May 1994.

DEFENCE. Iceland possesses no army or navy. Under the North Atlantic Treaty, US and Netherlands forces are stationed in Iceland as the Iceland Defence Force. 3 armed offshore patrol craft and 1 smaller vessel for fishery protection are maintained by the National Coastguard, with 1 patrol aircraft and 1 helicopter. Coastguard Service personnel (1995), 130.

INTERNATIONAL RELATIONS

Membership. Iceland is a member of the UN, EFTA, OECD, the Council of Europe, NATO and the Nordic Council, and is an Associate Member of the WEU.

ECONOMY

Budget. Total revenue and expenditure for calendar years (in 1m. kr.):

	1989	*1990*	*1991*	*1992*	*1993*	*1994*
Revenue	80,098	92,453	99,953	103,447	103,220	109,602
Expenditure	86,056	96,899	112,487	110,607	112,863	116,986

Central government debt was on 31 Dec. 1994, 197,106m. kr, of which the foreign debt amounted to 113,633m. kr.

Currency. The unit of currency is the *króna* (ISK) of 100 *aurar*, (singular: *eyrir*). There are coins of 1, 5, 10 and 50 kr. and notes of 100, 500, 1,000 and 5,000 kr. Foreign exchange markets were deregulated on 1 Jan. 1992. Note and coin circulation, 31 Dec. 1994, was 4,695m. kr. The krona was devalued 7·5% in June 1993. In March 1996, £1 = kr. 101·56; US$1 = kr. 66·45; DM1 = kr. 45·02.

Banking and Finance. The Central Bank of Iceland (founded 1961; *Governor:* Birgir Ísleifur Gunnarsson) is responsible for note issue and carries out the central banking functions which before 1961 were carried out by The National Bank of Iceland (owned entirely by the State), currently the largest commercial bank. There are 2 other commercial banks, 1 state-owned. Banking is being deregulated in stages.

On 31 Dec. 1994 the accounts of the Central Bank balanced at 64,232m. kr. On 31 Dec. 1994 commercial bank deposits were 129,050m. kr.; deposits in the 30 savings banks, 31,624m. kr.

There is a stock exchange.

Weights and Measures. The metric system is obligatory.

ENERGY AND NATURAL RESOURCES

Electricity. The installed capacity of public electrical power plants at the end of 1994 totalled 1,050,313 kW. In 1993, installed capacity of hydro-electric plants was 874,534. Total electricity production in public-owned plants in 1994 amounted to 4,774m. kWh; in privately-owned plants, 5m. kWh.

Agriculture. Of the total area, about six-sevenths is unproductive, but only about 1·3% is under cultivation, which is largely confined to hay, potatoes and turnips. In 1994 the total hay crop was 3,061,055 cu. metres; the crop of potatoes, 11,145 tonnes, and of turnips, 1,010 tonnes. Livestock (1994): Horses, 78,517; cattle (1993), 73,912; sheep, 499,110; pigs, 3,752; poultry (1993), 173,933. Livestock products (1994, in tonnes): Milk, 105,114; butter and dairy margarines, 1,717; cheese, 3,351; lamb, 8,798.

Fisheries. Fishing is of vital importance to the economy. Fishing vessels at the end of 1994 numbered 869 with a GT of 177,311 and GRT of 4,292 (23 ships). Total catch in 1991, 1,043,400 tonnes; 1992, 1,567,700 tonnes; 1993, 1,699,300 tonnes; 1994, 1,510,900 tonnes.

Fishery limits were extended from 12 to 50 nautical miles in 1972 and to 200 nautical miles in 1975.

INDUSTRY.

Production, 1994, in 1,000 tonnes: Aluminium, 99·3; diatomite, 25·2; fertilizer, 51·7; ferro-silicon, 65·1; cement, 80·9.

Labour. In 1994 the economically active population was 145,700, of which 5·5% were unemployed. In April 1995 the unemployment rate among the working population was 5·8%.

Trade Unions. In 1989 trade union membership was 76% of the workforce. Only union members receive unemployment benefit.

FOREIGN ECONOMIC RELATIONS.

The economy is heavily trade-dependent.

Commerce. Total value of imports (c.i.f.) and exports (f.o.b.) in 1,000 kr.:

	1990	*1991*	*1992*	*1993*	*1994*
Imports	96,620,900	104,129,200	96,895,400	91,306,600	102,571,300
Exports	92,625,100	91,560,400	87,832,900	94,657,600	112,653.800

Main exports, 1994 (in 1m. kr.): Fish, crustaceans, molluscs and preparations thereof, 79,911; non-ferrous metals, 10,836; feeding stuff for animals (excluding unmilled cereals), 5,559; iron and steel, 2,691. Main imports: Road vehicles, 5,799; petroleum and products, 7,832; other transport equipment, 4,725.

Value of trade with principal countries for 3 years (in 1,000 kr.):

	1992		*1993*		*1994*	
	Imports (c.i.f.)	*Exports (f.o.b.)*	*Imports (c.i.f.)*	*Exports (f.o.b.)*	*Imports (c.i.f.)*	*Exports (f.o.b.)*
Austria	649,900	40,400	747,700	94,500	692,300	153,300
Belgium	1,754,300	1,288,200	1,747,600	1,415,400	2,037,200	1,993,300
Brazil	235,700	131,000	280,700	184,000	248,900	190,800
Canada	985,300	301,800	567,300	499,500	1,069,300	1,507,200
Czechoslovakia	292,500	34,000	299,100 [1]	18,800 [1]	...	...
Denmark	8,550,600	4,943,100	8,563,600	5,325,600	9,232,800	7,255,000
Faroe Islands	1,031,000	441,800	97,000	247,700	65,200	306,100
Finland	1,642,900	843,900	1,801,400	672,800	1,946,200	1,065,900
France	3,155,900	8,666,500	3,108,300	7,795,600	3,543,900	8,074,200
Germany	11,998,700	10,940,400	10,880,600	10,450,200	11,508,700	14,403,200
Greece	118,900	1,012,000	131,400	780,500	107,600	935,800
Hungary	56,400	13,500	51,600	3,700	85,000	1,800
India	103,200	3,700	184,800	13,100	281,200	32,500
Ireland	577,800	79,700	693,800	97,200	991,600	191,200
Israel	361,400	64,500	60,600	127,700	78,900	43,200
Italy	3,424,000	2,456,300	3,188,400	1,934,600	3,302,400	2,621,400
Japan	5,579,100	6,628,000	5,059,800	8,777,100	4,123,900	15,737,200
Netherlands	7,218,700	1,774,500	5,476,400	2,082,900	6,431,200	1,843,700
Nigeria	—	685,900	—	853,400	—	687,200
Norway	14,113,800	1,956,600	11,298,700	3,187,300	14,672,300	3,168,900
Poland	378,500	25,500	437,600	38,600	375,900	89,900
Portugal	1,149,700	2,531,100	928,300	1,549,100	1,229,700	1,420,900
Russia	1,526,200	267,900	2,309,600	370,700	2,283,200	686,800
Spain	841,600	4,502,800	1,267,500	4,617,600	1,423,400	5,272,800
Sweden	6,614,500	1,377,300	6,186,600	1,103,800	7,195,000	1,179,500
Switzerland	1,234,100	2,217,100	1,569,200	3,464,500	1,267,600	1,979,900
UK	8,244,400	22,078,100	8,186,800	20,467,600	10,121,600	23,085,400
USA	8,012,100	9,982,200	8,510,800	15,030,500	9,132,800	16,183,600

[1] 1993 Czech Republic.

Total trade between Iceland and UK (British Department of Trade returns, in £1,000 sterling):

	1991	*1992*	*1993*	*1994*	*1995*
Imports to UK	238,428	239,510	249,705	239,275	251,887
Exports and re-exports from UK	95,615	92,127	146,891	109,693	138,103

Tourism. There were 179,241 visitors in 1994.

COMMUNICATIONS

Roads. On 31 Dec. 1994 the length of the public roads (including roads in towns) was 12,340 km. Of these 8,181 km were national main roads and 4,159 km were provincial roads. Total length of surfaced roads was 2,838 km. A ring road of 1,400 km runs just inland from much of the coast; about 80% of it is smooth-surfaced. Motor vehicles registered at the end of 1994 numbered 131,840, of which 117,492 were passenger cars and 14,348 trucks; there were also 1,342 motor cycles. There were 12 fatal road accidents in 1994 with 12 persons killed.

Civil Aviation. Icelandair is the national carrier. It serves 20 destinations in west Europe and 4 in the USA. In 1995 it operated 5 B-737-400s, 3 B-757-200s and 2 other aircraft. In 1994 it carried in scheduled foreign flights 774,079 passengers. There are international airports at Reykjavík and Keflavík (Leifsstöd). Services are also provided by Greenlandair, Lufthansa and SAS.

Shipping. Total registered vessels, 1,020 (237,172 GT and 5,496 GRT) on 1 Jan. 1995, of these 869 were sea-going fishing vessels.

Telecommunications. At the end of 1994 the number of post offices was 120 and telephone and telegraph offices 126; number of telephone subscribers, 148,300. The government-controlled Icelandic National Broadcasting Service broadcasts

2 national and 3 regional radio programmes and 1 TV channel. 7 privately-owned radio stations and 1 TV station were in operation in 1994. In 1994, 93,600 TV sets were licensed (colour by PAL).

Cinemas There were 31 screens in 1993; attendences totalled 1,304,587 in 1993.

Press (1993). There are 5 daily newspapers, 4 in Reykjavík and one in Akureyri, with a combined circulation of about 100,000.

SOCIAL INSTITUTIONS

Justice. In 1992 jurisdiction in civil and criminal cases was transferred from the provincial magistrates to 8 new district courts, separating the judiciary from the prosecution. From the district courts, there is an appeal to the Supreme Court in Reykjavík, which has 8 judges.

Religion. The national church, the Evangelical Lutheran, is endowed by the state. There is complete religious liberty. The affairs of the national church are under the superintendence of a bishop. In 1994, 91·8% of the population were members of it (93·2% in 1980). 9,583 persons (3·6%) were Dissenters and 3,788 persons (1·4%) did not belong to any religious community.

Education. Primary education is compulsory and free from 6–15 years of age. Optional secondary education from 16 to 19 is also free. In 1994–95 there were about 4,600 pupils in pre-schooling, 37,600 in primary schools, 17,000 in secondary schools and 7,200 tertiary-level students in Iceland. Some 25% of tertiary-level students study abroad.

There are 2 universities, Reykjavík (founded 1911) and Akureyri (1987). Total enrolment was 5,400 students in 1994–95. There are in Reykjavík a teachers' training and a technical college, and various other specialized institutions.

Health. On 31 Dec. 1991 there were 54 hospitals with 3,960 beds, 734 doctors, 241 dentists, 1,816 nurses, and 139 pharmacists.

Social Welfare. The main body of social welfare legislation is consolidated in 6 acts:

(i) The social security legislation (a) health insurance, including sickness benefits; *(b)* social security pensions, mainly consisting of old age pension, disablement pension and widows' pension, and also children's pension; *(c)* employment injuries insurance.

(ii) The unemployment insurance legislation, where daily allowances are paid to those who have met certain conditions.

(iii) The subsistence legislation. This is controlled by municipal government, and social assistance is granted under special circumstances, when payments from other sources are not sufficient.

(iv) The tax legislation. Prior to 1988 children's support was included in the tax legislation, according to which a certain amount for each child in a family was subtracted from income taxes or paid out to the family. Since 1988 family allowances are paid directly to all children age 0-15 years. The amount is increased with the second child in the family, and children under the age of 7 get additional benefits. Single parents receive additional allowances.

(v) The rehabilitation legislation.

(vi) Child and juvenile guidance.

Health insurance covers the entire population. Citizenship is not demanded and there is no waiting period. Most hospitals are both municipally and state run, a few solely state run and all offer free medical help. Medical treatment out of hospitals is partly paid by the patient, the same applies to medicines, except medicines of life-long necessary use, which are paid in full by the health insurance. Dental care is partly paid by the state for children under 17 years old and also for old age and disabled pensioners. Sickness benefits are paid to those who lose income because of periodical illness. The daily amount is fixed and paid from the 11th day of illness.

The pension system is composed of the public social security system and some 90 private pension funds. The social security system pays basic old age and disablement pensions of a fixed amount regardless of past or present income, as well as supplementary pensions to individuals with low present income. The pensions are index-linked, i.e. are changed in line with changes in wage and salary rates in the labour market. The private pension funds pay pensions that depend on past payments of premiums that are a fixed proportion of earnings. The payment of pension fund premiums is compulsory for all wage and salary earners. The pensions paid by the funds differ considerably between the individual funds, but are generally index-linked. In the public social security system, entitlement to old age and disablement pensions at the full rates is subject to the condition that the beneficiary has been resident in Iceland for 40 years at the age period of 16–67. For shorter period of residence, the benefits are reduced proportionally. Entitled to old age pension are all those who are 67 years old, and have been residents in Iceland for 3 years of the age period of 16–67. Entitled to disablement pension are those who have lost 75% of their working capacity and have been residents in Iceland for 3 years before application or have had full working capacity at the time when they became residents. Old age and disablement pension are of equally high amount, in the year 1994 the total sum was 147,948 kr. for an individual. Married pensioners are paid 90% of two individuals' pensions. In addition to the basic amount, supplementary allowances are paid according to social circumstances and income possibilities. Widows' pensions are the same amount as old age and disablement pension, provided the applicant is over 60 when she becomes widowed. Women at the age 50–60 get reduced pension. Women under 50 are not entitled to widows' pensions.

The employment injuries insurance covers medical care, daily allowances, disablement pension and survivors' pension and is applicable to practically all employees.

Social assistance is primarily municipal and granted in cases outside the social security legislation. Domestic assistance to old people and disabled is granted within this legislation, besides other services.

Child and juvenile guidance is performed by chosen committees according to special laws, such as home guidance and family assistance. In cases of parents' disablement the committees take over the guidance of the children involved.

DIPLOMATIC REPRESENTATIVES

Of Iceland in Great Britain (1 Eaton Terrace, London, SW1W 8EY)
Ambassador: Benedikt Ásgeirsson.

Of Great Britain in Iceland (Laufásvegur 49, 101 Reykjavík)
Ambassador and Consul-General: Michael Hone, OBE.

Of Iceland in the USA (2022 Connecticut Ave., NW, Washington, D.C., 20008)
Ambassador: Einar Benediktsson.

Of the USA in Iceland (Laufásvegur 21, 101 Reykjavík)
Ambassador: Parker Borg.

Of Iceland to the United Nations
Ambassador: Gunnar Palsson.

Further Reading

Statistics Iceland, *Landshagir* (Statistical Yearbook of Iceland).—*Hagtíðindi* (Monthly Statistics)

Central Bank of Iceland. *Economic Statistics Quarterly.—The Economy of Iceland.* May 1994

Horton, J. J., *Iceland.* [Bibliography] Oxford and Santa Barbara, 1983

National statistical office: Statistics Iceland, Skuggasund 3, IS-150 Reykjavík.

National library: Landsbókasafn Islands.—Háskólabókasafn, Reykjavík, *Librarian:* Einar Sigurðsson.

INDIA

Bharat

(Republic of India)

Capital: New Delhi
Population: 913·07m. (1994)
GNP per capita: US$310 (1994)
HDI/world rank: 0·439/134 (1992)

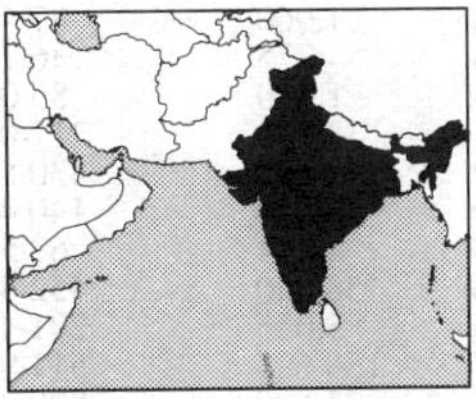

KEY HISTORICAL EVENTS. Moslem, Hindu and Buddhist states developed together with frequent conflict until the establishment of the Mogul dynasty in 1526. The first settlements by the East India Company were made after 1600 and the Company established a formal system of government for Bengal in 1700. During the decline of the Moguls frequent wars between the Company, the French and the native princes led to the Company's being brought under British Government control in 1784; the first Governor-General of India was appointed in 1786. The powers of the Company were abolished by the India Act, 1858, and its functions and forces transferred to the British Crown. Representative government was introduced in 1909, and the first parliament in 1919. The separate dominions of India and Pakistan became independent within the Commonwealth in 1947 and India became a republic in 1950.

The leader of the Congress (I) Party, Rajiv Gandhi, was assassinated on 21 May 1991.

TERRITORY AND POPULATION. India is bounded in the north-west by Pakistan, north by China, Tibet, Nepal and Bhutan, east by Burma, and south-east, south and south-west by the Indian Ocean. The far eastern states and territories are almost separated from the rest by Bangladesh as it extends northwards from the Bay of Bengal. The area (excluding the Pakistan and China-occupied parts of Jammu and Kashmir) is 3,165,596 sq. km. An agreement of 7 Sept. 1993 between the Indian and Chinese prime ministers settled frontier disputes which had first emerged in the Sino-Indian war of 1962.

Its population (excluding occupied Jammu and Kashmir) according to the 1991 census was 846,302,688 (407,072,230 females; 217m. urban); density of population, 274 per sq. km. About 24·7% of the population was urban in 1991 (in Maharashtra, 35%; in Arunachal Pradesh, 6·6%). 1994 estimate: 913·07m.

Many births and deaths go unregistered. Data from the office of the Registrar General of India suggest that the birth rate for 1990–91 was about 29·9 per 1,000 population, the death rate 9·6 per 1,000. In 1991 expectation of life was 60 years.

Marriages and divorces are not registered. The minimum age for a civil marriage is 18 for women and 21 for men; for a sacramental marriage, 14 for girls and 18 for youths.

Area and population of states and union territories:

	Area in sq. km	*1991 census*	*Population 1994 estimate (in 1,000)*	*Density per sq. km*
States				
Andhra Pradesh (And P)	275,045	66,508,008	71,800	261·0
Arunachal Pradesh (Arun P)	83,743	864,558	965	11·5
Assam (Ass)	78,438	22,414,322	24,200	308·5
Bihar (Bih)	173,877	86,374,465	93,080	535·3
Goa	3,702	1,169,793	1,235	333·5
Gujarat (Guj)	196,024	41,309,582	44,235	225·7
Haryana (Har)	44,212	16,463,648	17,925	405·4
Himachal Pradesh (Him P)	55,673	5,170,877	5,530	99·3
Jammu and Kashmir (J and K) [1]	100,569	7,718,700 [2]	8,435	83·9
Karnataka (Kar)	191,791	44,977,201	48,150	251·1

[1] Excludes the area occupied by Pakistan and China. [2] Projection.

States—*cont.*	*Area in sq. km*	*1991 census*	*Population 1994 estimate (in 1,000)*	*Density per sq. km*
Kerala (Ker)	38,863	29,098,518	30,555	786·3
Madhya Pradesh (MP)	443,446	66,181,170	71,950	162·2
Maharashtra (Mah)	307,713	78,937,187	85,565	278·1
Manipur (Man)	22,327	1,837,149	2,010	90·0
Meghalaya (Meg)	22,429	1,774,778	1,960	87·4
Mizoram (Miz)	21,081	689,756	775	36·7
Nagaland (Nag)	16,579	1,209,546	1,410	85·0
Orissa (Or)	155,707	31,659,736	33,795	217·0
Punjab (Pun)	50,362	20,281,969	21,695	430·8
Rajasthan (Raj)	342,239	44,005,990	48,040	140·4
Sikkim (Sik)	7,096	406,457	444	62·5
Tamil Nadu (TM)	130,058	55,858,946	58,840	452·4
Tripura (Tri)	10,486	2,757,205	3,055	291·4
Uttar Pradesh (UP)	294,411	139,112,287	150,695	511·9
West Bengal (WB)	88,752	68,077,965	73,600	829·3
Union Territories				
Andaman and Nicobar Islands (ANI)	8,249	280,661	322	39·0
Chandigarh (Chan)	114	642,015	725	6,359·7
Dadra and Nagar Haveli (DNH)	491	138,477	153	311·9
Daman and Diu (D and D)	112	101,586	111	990·7
Delhi (Del)	1,483	9,420,644	10,865	7,326·5
Lakshadweep (Lak)	32	51,707	56	1,764·2
Pondicherry (Pon)	492	807,785	894	1,816·3

In 1991, 25·72% were urban.

Urban Agglomerations with populations over 1·6m., together with their core cities at the 1991 census:

	Urban Agglomeration	*Core City*		*Urban Agglomeration*	*Core City*
Bombay	12,596,243	9,925,891	Ahmedabad	3,312,216	2,954,526
Calcutta	11,021,915	4,309,819	Pune (Poona)	2,493,987	1,566,651
Delhi	8,419,084	7,206,704	Kanpur	2,029,889	1,879,420
Madras	5,421,985	3,841,396	Lucknow	1,669,204	1,619,115
Hyderabad	4,253,759	3,145,939	Nagpur	1,664,006	1,624,752
Bangalore	4,130,288	3,302,296			

Smaller Urban Agglomerations and cities with populations over 250,000 (with 1991 census populations, in 1,000):

Agra (UP)	892	Davangere (Kar)	266	Kakinada (And P)	280
Ajmer (Raj)	403	Dehra Dun (UP)	368	Kharagpur (WB)	265
Akola (Mah)	328	Dhanbad (Bih) [1]	815	Kochi (Ker)	565
Aligarh (UP)	481	Dhule (Mah)	278	Kolhapur (Mah)	406
Allahabad (UP)	806	Durgapur (WB)	426	Kota (Raj)	537
Amravati (Mah)	422	Faridabad Complex (Har)	618	Kozhikode (Ker)	420
Amritsar (Pun)	709			Ludhiana (Pun)	1,043
Asansol (WB)	262	Gaya (Bih)	292	Madurai (TN)	941
Aurangabad (Mah)	573	Ghaziabad (UP)	454	Malegaon (Mah)	342
Bareilly (UP)	591	Gorakhpur (UP)	506	Mangalore (Kar)	273
Belgaum (Mah)	326	Gulbarga (Kar)	304	Meerut (UP)	850
Bhagalpur (Bih)	253	Guntur (And P)	273	Moradabad (UP)	444
Bhavnagar (Guj)	402	Guwahati (Ass)	584	Mysore (Kar)	481
Bhilainagar (MP)	386	Gwalior (MP)	691	Nanded (Mah)	275
Bhiwandi (Mah)	379	Hubli-Dharwad (Kar)	648	Nashik (Mah)	657
Bhopal (MP)	1,063	Indore (MP)	1,092	Nellore (And P)	316
Bhubaneswar (Or)	412	Jabalpur (MP)	742	New Bombay (Mah)	308
Bikaner (Raj)	416	Jaipur (Raj)	1,458	New Delhi (Del)	301
Bokaro Steel City (Bih)	334	Jalandhar (Pun)	510	Panihati (WB)	276
		Jamnagar (Guj)	342	Patna (Bih)	917
Chandigarh (Chan)	511	Jamshedpur (Bih)	461	Raipur (MP)	439
Coimbatore (TN)	816	Jhansi (UP)	313	Rajamundry (And P)	325
Cuttack (Or)	403	Jodhpur (Raj)	668	Rajkot (Raj)	559

[1] Urban Agglomeration.

Ranchi (Bih)	599	Thiruvananthapuram (Ker)	524	Varanasi (UP)	932
Saharanpur (UP)	375	Tiruchirapalli (TN)	387	Vijayawada (And P)	702
Salem (TN)	367	Udaipur (Raj)	309	Visakhapatnam (And P)	752
Sholapur (Mah)	604	Ujjain (MP)	362	Warangal (And P)	448
Srinagar (J and K)	595	Vadodara (Guj)	1,031		
Surat (Guj)	1,499				

CLIMATE. India has a variety of climatic sub-divisions. In general, there are four seasons. The cool one lasts from Dec. to March, the hot season is in April and May, the rainy season is June to Sept., followed by a further dry season till Nov. Rainfall, however, varies considerably, from 4" (100 mm) in the N.W. desert to over 400" (10,000 mm) in parts of Assam.

Range of temperature and rainfall: New Delhi. Jan. 57°F (13·9°C), July 88°F (31·1°C). Annual rainfall 26" (640 mm). Bombay. Jan. 75°F (23·9°C), July 81°F (27·2°C). Annual rainfall 72" (1,809 mm). Calcutta. Jan. 67°F (19·4°C), July 84°F (28·9°C). Annual rainfall 64" (1,600 mm). Cherrapunji. Jan. 53°F (11·7°C), July 68°F (20°C). Annual rainfall 432" (10,798 mm). Darjeeling. Jan. 41°F (5°C), July 62°F (16·7°C). Annual rainfall 121" (3,035 mm). Hyderabad. Jan. 72°F (22·2°C), July 80°F (26·7°C). Annual rainfall 30" (752 mm). Kochi. Jan. 80°F (26·7°C), July 79°F (26·1°C). Annual rainfall 117" (2,929 mm). Madras. Jan. 76°F (24·4°C), July 87°F (30·6°C). Annual rainfall 51" (1,270 mm). Patna. Jan. 63°F (17·2°C), July 90°F (32·2°C). Annual rainfall 46" (1,150 mm).

CONSTITUTION AND GOVERNMENT. The Constitution was passed by the Constituent Assembly on 26 Nov. 1949 and came into force on 26 Jan. 1950. It has since been amended 85 times.

India is a republic and comprises a Union of 25 States and 7 Union Territories. Each State is administered by a Governor appointed by the President for a term of 5 years while each Union Territory is administered by the President through a Lieut.-Governor or an administrator appointed by him. The head of the Union is the *President* in whom all executive power is vested, to be exercised on the advice of ministers responsible to Parliament. The President, who must be an Indian citizen at least 35 years old and eligible for election to the House of the People, is elected by an electoral college of all the elected members of Parliament and of the state legislative assemblies, holds office for 5 years and is eligible for re-election. There is also a *Vice-President* who is *ex-officio* chairman of the Council of States.

Parliament consists of the President, the *Council of States* (*Rajya Sabha*) and the *House of the People* (Lok Sabha). The Council of States, or the Upper House, consists of not more than 250 members; in Dec. 1995 there were 233 elected members and 12 members nominated by the President. The election to this house is indirect; the representatives of each State are elected by the elected members of the Legislative Assembly of that State. The Council of States is a permanent body not liable to dissolution, but one-third of the members retire every second year. The House of the People, or the Lower House, consists of 545 members, 543 directly elected on the basis of adult suffrage from territorial constituencies in the States, and the Union territories; in April 1995 there were 529 elected members, 2 members nominated by the President to represent the Anglo-Indian community and 16 vacancies. The House of the People unless sooner dissolved continues for a period of 5 years from the date appointed for its first meeting; in emergency, Parliament can extend the term by 1 year.

State Legislatures. For every State there is a legislature which consists of the Governor, and *(a)* 2 Houses, a Legislative Assembly and a Legislative Council, in the States of Bihar, Jammu and Kashmir, Karnataka, Madhya Pradesh (where it is provided for but not in operation), Maharashtra and Uttar Pradesh, and *(b)* 1 House, a Legislative Assembly, in the other States. Every Legislative Assembly, unless sooner dissolved, continues for 5 years from the date appointed for its first meeting. In emergency the term can be extended by 1 year. Every State Legislative Council is a permanent body and is not subject to dissolution, but one-third of the members retire every second year. Parliament can, however, abolish an existing Legislative

Council or create a new one, if the proposal is supported by a resolution of the Legislative Assembly concerned.

Legislation. The various subjects of legislation are enumerated in three lists in the seventh schedule to the constitution. List I, the Union List, consists of 97 subjects (including defence, foreign affairs, communications, currency and coinage, banking and customs) with respect to which the Union Parliament has exclusive power to make laws. The State legislature has exclusive power to make laws with respect to the 66 subjects in list II, the State List; these include police and public order, agriculture and irrigation, education, public health and local government. The powers to make laws with respect to the 47 subjects (including economic and social planning, legal questions and labour and price control) in list III, the Concurrent List, are held by both Union and State governments, though the former prevails. But Parliament may legislate with respect to any subject in the State List in circumstances when the subject assumes national importance or during emergencies.

Other provisions deal with the administrative relations between the Union and the States, interstate trade and commerce, distribution of revenues between the States and the Union, official language, etc.

Fundamental Rights. Two chapters of the constitution deal with fundamental rights and 'Directive Principles of State Policy'. 'Untouchability' is abolished, and its practice in any form is punishable. The fundamental rights can be enforced through the ordinary courts of law and through the Supreme Court of the Union. The directive principles cannot be enforced through the courts of law; they are nevertheless fundamental in the governance of the country.

Citizenship. Under the Constitution, every person who was on the 26 Jan. 1950, domiciled in India and *(a)* was born in India or *(b)* either of whose parents was born in India or *(c)* who has been ordinarily resident in the territory of India for not less than 5 years immediately preceding that date became a citizen of India. Special provision is made for migrants from Pakistan and for Indians resident abroad. Under the Citizenship Act, 1955, which supplemented the provisions of the Constitution, Indian citizenship is acquired by birth, by descent, by registration and by naturalization. The Act also provides for loss of citizenship by renunciation, termination and deprivation. The right to vote is granted to every person who is a citizen of India and who is not less than 18 years of age on a fixed date and is not otherwise disqualified.

Parliament. Parliament and the state legislatures are organized according to the following schedule (figures show distribution of seats in Dec. 1994):

	Parliament		*State Legislatures*	
	House of the People (Lok Sabha)	*Council of States (Rajya Sabha)*	*Legislative Assemblies (Vidhan Sabhas)*	*Legislative Councils (Vidhan Parishads)*
States:				
Andhra Pradesh	42	18	294	–
Arunachal Pradesh	2	1	60	–
Assam	14	7	126	–
Bihar	54	22	324	96
Goa	2	1	40	–
Gujarat	26	11	182	–
Haryana	10	5	90	–
Himachal Pradesh	4	3	68	–
Jammu and Kashmir	6	4	87 [2]	36 [3]
Karnataka	28	12	224	75
Kerala	20	9	140	–
Madhya Pradesh	40	16	320	–
Maharashtra	48	19	288	63
Manipur	2	1	60	–
Meghalaya	2	1	60	–

[2] Excludes 24 seats for Pakistan-occupied areas of the State which are in abeyance.
[3] Excludes seats for the Pakistan-occupied areas.

	Parliament		State Legislatures	
	House of the People (Lok Sabha)	*Council of States (Rajya Sabha)*	*Legislative Assemblies (Vidhan Sabhas)*	*Legislative Councils (Vidhan Parishads)*
States (continued):				
Mizoram	1	1	40	–
Nagaland	1	1	60	–
Orissa	21	10	147	–
Punjab	13	7	117	–
Rajasthan	25	10	200	–
Sikkim	1	1	32	–
Tamil Nadu	39	18	234	–
Tripura	2	1	60	–
Uttar Pradesh	85	34	425	108
West Bengal	42	16	294	–
Union Territories:				
Andaman and Nicobar Islands	1	–	–	–
Chandigarh	1	–	–	–
Dadra and Nagar Haveli	1	–	–	–
Delhi	7	3	70	–
Daman and Diu	1	–	–	–
Lakshadweep	1	–	–	–
Pondicherry	1	1	30	–
Nominated by the President under Article 80 (1) (a) of the Constitution	–	12	–	–
Total	545 [1]	245	4,072	378

[1] Includes 2 nominated members to represent Anglo-Indians.

The number of seats allotted to scheduled castes and scheduled tribes in the House of the People is 79 and 41 respectively. Out of the 4,072 seats allotted to the Legislative Assemblies, 557 are reserved for scheduled castes and 527 for scheduled tribes.

Composition of the House of the People in April 1995: Congress (I) 260; Janata Dal, 23; Bharatiya Janata Party, 117; CPI (Marxist), 36; CPI, 14; AIADMK (All India Anna Dravida Munnetra Kazagam), 12; Shiv Sena, 2; Janata Dal (A), 10; Samajwadi Party, 3; Revolutionary Socialist Party, 4; Bahujan Samaj Party, 3; Forward Bloc, 3; Jharkhand Mukti Morcha, 6; Moslem League, 2; Telugu Desam, 7; Independent and others, 11; nominated, 2; vacant, 16.

Composition of the Council of States in July 1995: Congress (I) 89; Communist Party of India (Marxist), 13; All-India Anna DMK, 11; Janata Dal, 28; Bharatiya Janata Party, 45; Telugu Desam, 3; Dravida Munnetra Kazagam, 4; Janata Dal (S), 5; Samajwadi Party, 5; Communist Party, 5; Ind, 7; Rashtriya Janata Dal, 3; Moslem League, 2; Forward Bloc, 2; Asom Gana Parishad, 2; others, 7; nominated, 4; vacant, 9.

National flag: Three horizontal stripes of saffron (orange), white and green, with the wheel of Asoka in the centre in blue.

National anthem: 'Jana-gana-mana' ('Thou art the ruler of the minds of all people'); words and tune by Rabindranath Tagore.

Language. The Constitution provides that the official language of the Union shall be Hindi in the Devanagari script. It was originally provided that English should continue to be used for all official purposes until 1965. But the Official Languages Act 1963 provides that, after the expiry of this period of 15 years from the coming into force of the Constitution, English might continue to be used, in addition to Hindi, for all official purposes of the Union for which it was being used immediately before that day, and for the transaction of business in Parliament. According to the Official Languages (Use for official purposes of the Union) Rules 1976, an employee may record in Hindi or in English without being required to furnish a translation thereof in the other language and no employee possessing a working knowledge of Hindi may ask for an English translation of any document in Hindi except in the case of legal or technical documents.

The 58th amendment to the Constitution (26 Nov. 1987) authorised the preparation of a Constitution text in Hindi.

The following 18 languages are included in the Eighth Schedule to the Constitution (with 1994 estimate of speakers where over 5m.): Assamese (14·8m.), Bengali (68·3m.), Gujarati (44m.), Hindi (350·3m.), Kannada (35·7m.), Kashmiri, Konkani, Malayalam (34·4m.), Manipuri, Marathi (65·8m.), Nepali, Oriya (30·3m.), Punjabi (24·7m.), Sanskrit, Sindhi, Tamil (59·3m.), Telugu (71·9m.), Urdu (46·8m.).

The head of state is the *President*. There is a *Council of Ministers* to aid and advise the President; this comprises Ministers who are members of the Cabinet and Ministers of State and deputy ministers who are not. A Minister who for any period of 6 consecutive months is not a member of either House of Parliament ceases to be a Minister at the expiration of that period. The Prime Minister is appointed by the President; other Ministers are appointed by the President on the Prime Minister's advice. The salary of each Minister is Rs 27,000 per annum.

Presidential elections were held on 18 July 1992. Dr Shankar Dayal Sharma was elected by 64·8% of votes cast against 1 opponent.

Parliamentary elections were held in May-June 1991. No party obtained an absolute majority in the House of the People. As the leader of the largest party, P. V. Narasimha Rao formed a Congress (I) Government at the Centre.

President: Dr Shankal Dayal Sharma (b. 1918; sworn in 25 July 1992).
Vice-President: Dr Kocheril Raman Narayan (elected 19 Aug. 1992).

The Cabinet was composed as follows in Dec. 1995:

Prime Minister, Minister of Defence: P. V. Narasimha Rao (b. 1921).

Portfolios held by the Prime Minister assisted by Ministers of State: *Personnel and Public Grievances, Science and Technology, Space, Ocean Development, Electronics, Atomic Energy, Rural Development and Railways.*

External Affairs: Pranab Kumar Mukherjee. *Human Resource Development:* Madhab Rao Scindia. *Agriculture:* Balram Jakhar. *Home Affairs:* S. B. Chavan. *Rural Employment and Rural Areas:* Dr Jagannath Mishra. *Industry:* K. Karunakaran. *Health and Family Welfare:* A. R. Antulay. *Welfare:* Sitaram Kesri. *Civil Aviation and Tourism:* Ghulam Nabi Azad. *Water Resources and Parliamentary Affairs:* Vidya Charan Shukla. *Finance:* Dr Manmohan Singh. *Information and Broadcasting:* Purno A. Sangma. *Labour:* G. Venkataswamy. *Civil Supplies and Public Distribution:* Buta Singh. *Power:* N. K. P. Salve. *Chemicals and Fertilizers:* Ram Lal Yadav. *Food:* Ajit Singh.

There were also 12 Ministers of State with independent responsibilities and 38 Ministers of State.

Singh, V. B., *Elections in India: Data Handbook on Lok Sabha Elections, 1986–91.* Delhi, 1994
Thakur, R., *The Government and Politics of India.* London, 1995

Local Government. There were in 1989-90, 72 municipal corporations, 1,770 municipal committees/boards/councils, 663 town area committees and 337 notified area committees. The municipal bodies have the care of the roads, water supply, drainage, sanitation, medical relief, vaccination, education, street lighting, etc. Their main sources of revenue are taxes on the annual rental value of land and buildings, octroi and terminal, vehicle and other taxes. The municipal councils enact their own bye-laws and frame their budgets, which in the case of municipal bodies other than corporations generally require the sanction of the State government. All municipal councils are elected on the principle of adult franchise.

For rural areas there is a 3-tier system of *panchayati raj* at village, block and district level, although the 3-tier structure may undergo some changes in State legislation to suit local conditions. All *panchayati raj* bodies are organically linked, and representation is given to special interests. Elected directly by and from among villagers, the *panchayats* are responsible for agricultural production, rural industries, medical relief, maternity and child welfare, common grazing grounds, village roads, tanks and wells, and maintenance of sanitation. In some places they also look after primary education, maintenance of village records and collection of land revenue. They have their own powers of taxation. There are some judicial *panchayats* or village courts.

Panchayati raj now cover almost all the States and Union Territories with variations in structural pattern. *Panchayati raj* involves a 3-tier arrangement: Village level, block level and district level. Tenure of *Panchayati raj* institutions range from 3–5 years.

The powers and responsibilities of *Panchayati raj* institutions are derived from State Legislatures, and from the executive orders of State governments.

DEFENCE. The Supreme Command of the Armed Forces vests in the President. Policy is decided at different levels by a number of committees, including the Political Affairs Committee presided over by the Prime Minister and the Defence Minister's Committee. Administrative and operational control rests in the respective Service Headquarters, under the control of the Ministry of Defence.

Army. The Army Headquarters functioning directly under the Chief of the Army Staff is divided into the following main branches: General Staff Branch; Adjutant General's Branch; Quartermaster-General's Branch; Master-General of Ordnance Branch; Engineer-in-Chief's Branch; Military Secretary's Branch.

The Army is organized into 5 commands each divided into areas, which in turn are subdivided into sub-areas.

The strength of the Army was (1996) 0·98m.; there is a Territorial Army 160,000 strong. There are 3 armoured, 17 infantry and 10 mountain divisions and 5 independent armoured, 7 independent infantry, 3 independent artillery, 1 parachute, 1 mountain, 16 air defence and 3 engineer brigades, and 1 surface-to-surface missile regiment. An Aviation Corps was formed in 1986 and operates 150 locally-built Alouette and Lama helicopters.

Equipment includes some 500 T-55, 1,100 T-72/-M1 and 800 Vijayanta main battle tanks.

Navy. The Navy has 3 commands; Eastern, Western and Southern, the latter a training and support command. The fleet is divided into 2 elements, Eastern and Western; and well-trained, all-volunteer personnel operate a mix of Soviet and Western vessels.

The principal ships are the 2 light aircraft carriers, *Viraat* and *Vikrant*. The *Viraat*, formerly HMS *Hermes*, is of 29,000 tonnes and was completed in 1959 and transferred to the Indian Navy in 1987. *Vikrant*, 19,800 tonnes, (the former HMS *Hercules*), was transferred to India in 1961, and completed conversion to the vertical/short take-off and landing role in 1990. Both embark an air group of 8 Sea Harrier fighters and 6 Sea King anti-submarine helicopters.

The fleet now includes 8 'Kilo' and 3 'Foxtrot' Soviet-built diesel submarines and 4 smaller German-designed boats. 5 Soviet-built missile armed destroyers, 3 heavily modified and 6 rather less modified 'Leander' class frigates, all built in India, together with 1 ex-British Batch 3 Leander class and 9 other Soviet-type frigates form the main surface force. Coastal forces include 14 Soviet-designed missile and 4 anti-submarine corvettes, 6 fast missile craft, 7 offshore and 10 inshore patrol craft. There are 12 Soviet-built offshore minesweepers, and 8 much smaller inshore vessels. Amphibious lift for the 1,000 strong marine force is provided by 1 tank landing ship and 8 medium landing ships, as well as about 8 craft. Support forces include 2 tankers, 1 submarine depot ship, 1 transport, 10 survey and research ships, 2 tugs and 1 training ship.

The Naval Air force, 5,000 strong, operates 22 Sea Harriers, 5 Il-38 'May', 8 Tu-142M 'Bear-F', 20 Dornier 228 and 13 Britten-Norman Islander maritime patrol aircraft. Armed helicopters include 26 Chetak, 7 Ka-25, 10 Ka-27 and 32 Sea King, and the inventory is completed with some 30 training and communications aircraft.

Main bases are at Bombay (HQ Western Fleet, and main dockyard), Goa, Visakhapatnam (HQ Eastern Fleet) and Calcutta on the sub-continent, Port Blair in the Andaman Islands and Lakhshadweep on the Laccadive Islands. HQ Southern Command is at Kochi.

Naval personnel in 1995 numbered 55,000 including 5,000 Naval Air Arm and 1,000 marines.

The Coast Guard is an independent para-military service 5,000 strong in 1995, which functions under Defence Ministry control, but is funded by the Revenue Department. The force comprises 10 offshore patrol vessels and 40 inshore patrol craft. Its 20 aircraft include Dornier-228, Fokker F-27 and Britten-Norman Islanders, and 13 Chetak helicopters.

Air Force. The Air Headquarters, under the Chief of Air Staff, consists of 4 main branches, viz., Air Staff, Administration, Policy and Plans, and Maintenance. Units of the IAF are organized into 5 operational commands–Western at Delhi, Central at Allahabad, Eastern at Shillong, Southern at Thiruvananthapuram and South-Western at Jodhpur. Training Command HQ is at Bangalore, Maintenance Command at Nagpur. Nominal strength in 1995 was 110,000 personnel, 844 combat aircraft of all types, in over 50 squadrons of aircraft, 36 armed helicopters and about 30 squadrons of 'Guideline' and 'Goa' surface-to-air missiles, and close-range missiles such as 'Gainful' and Tigercat.

Air defence units include 2 squadrons of MiG-23 variable-geometry interceptors, 3 squadrons of MiG-29s, 17 squadrons of MiG-21s and 2 of Mirage 2000s. Other combat units include 8 squadrons of MiG-27s, 2 of Canberras, 4 of Jaguars, 4 of MiG-23 supersonic fighter-bombers and one of MiG-25 reconnaissance aircraft plus a MiG-25U two seat trainer.

The large transport force includes An-32s, Il-76s, Do 228s, HS 748s, 2 Boeing 737s, and smaller aircraft and helicopters for VIP and other duties. Helicopter units have Mi-8s and Mi-17s (10 squadrons), Mi-26s, and Mi-25 gunships, but the bulk of the Air Force's Chetaks (Alouette IIIs) and Cheetahs (Lamas) have been transferred to Army control, main training types are the Hindustan HPT-32 and Kiran, Polish-built TS-11 Iskra, Hunter T.66, MiG-21UT1 and MiG-23U.

INTERNATIONAL RELATIONS

Membership. India is a member of the UN, the Commonwealth and the Colombo Plan.

ECONOMY

Policy. The highest economic decision-making body is the *National Development Council*, of which all state chief ministers are members. There is also a *Planning Commission.*

The eighth 5-year plan (1992–97) emphasizes job creation and increases rural investment, and aims at an annual growth of 5·6% of GDP, 3% in employment and a domestic savings rate of 21·6% of GDP. Indicative planning, however, is tending to take the place of centralized planning.

As a first step towards partial privatization of the 248 state-owned corporations, selected public sector enterprises are being allowed to raise funds through equity issues.

Requirements for government approval of investment decisions were reduced in 1990. The eighth plan (1992–97) envisages an outlay of Rs 7,920,000m., with public sector investment of Rs 3,420,000m. Central plan outlay (1995–96), Rs 788,490m.

Budget. Revenue and expenditure (on revenue account) of the central government for years ending 31 March, in Rs 1m.:

	1993–94	*1994–95* [1]	*1995–96* [2]
Revenue	1,196,016	1,445,674	1,605,857
Expenditure	1,523,172	1,786,988	1,961,276

[1] Revised. [2] Budget estimates.

Important items of revenue and expenditure on the revenue account of the central government for 1995–96 (estimates), in Rs 1m.:

Revenue		*Expenditure*	
Net tax revenue	743,740	General Services	846,476
Non-tax revenue	665,576	Defence	192,145
		Major subsidies	109,650

Total capital account receipts (1995–96 budget), Rs 2,368,095m.; capital account disbursements, Rs 2,234,065m. Total (revenue and capital) receipts, Rs 3,973,952m.; disbursements, Rs 4,195,340m.

Under the Constitution (Part XII and 7th Schedule), the power to raise funds has been divided between the central government and the states. Generally, the sources of revenue are mutually exclusive. Certain taxes are levied by the Union for the sake of uniformity and distributed to the states. The Finance Commission (Art. 280 of the Constitution) advises the President on the distribution of the taxes which are distributable between the centre and the states, and on the principles on which grants should be made out of Union revenues to the states. The main sources of central revenue are: customs duties; those excise duties levied by the central government; corporation, income and wealth taxes; estate and succession duties on non-agricultural assets and property, and revenues from the railways and posts and telegraphs. The main heads of revenue in the states are: taxes and duties levied by the state governments (including land revenues and agricultural income tax); civil administration and civil works; state undertakings; taxes shared with the centre; and grants received from the centre.

Currency. A decimal system of coinage was introduced in 1957. The Indian *rupee* (INR) is divided into 100 *paise*. There are coins of 1, 2, 3, 5, 10, 20, 25 and 50 *paise* and Rs 1, 2 and 5. The paper currency consists of: (1) Reserve Bank notes in denominations of Rs 2, 5, 10, 20, 50, 100 and 500; and (2) Government of India currency notes of denominations of Re 1 deemed to be included in the expression 'rupee coin' for the purposes of the Reserve Bank of India Act, 1934.

According to the Reserve Bank of India, the total money supply with the public on the last Friday of Sept. 1995 was Rs 5,497,850m. Foreign exchange reserves, Oct. 1995, US$17,757m. (Rs 614,740m.).

The official exchange rate was abolished on 1 March 1993; the rupee now has a single market exchange rate and is convertible. It was devalued by 18·74% against the dollar in July 1991. The pound sterling is the currency of intervention. In March 1996, Rs 52·81 = £1; Rs 34·55 = US$1; Rs 23·41 = DM1.

Banking and Finance. The Reserve Bank, the central bank for India, was established in 1934 and started functioning on 1 April 1935 as a shareholder's bank; it became a nationalized institution on 1 Jan. 1949. It has the sole right of issuing currency notes. Its *Governor* is Chakravarty Rangarajan (b.1932). The Bank acts as adviser to the Government on financial problems and is the banker for central and state governments, commercial banks and some other financial institutions. It manages the rupee public debt of central and state governments and is the custodian of the country's exchange reserve. The Bank has extensive powers of regulation of the banking system, directly under the Banking Regulation Act, 1949, and indirectly by the use of variations in Bank rate, variation in reserve ratios, selective credit controls and open market operations.

The commercial banking system consisted of 300 scheduled banks (*i.e.*, banks which are included in the 2nd schedule to the Reserve Bank Act) and 4 non-scheduled banks in Jan. 1993; scheduled banks included 196 Regional Rural Banks. Total deposits in commercial banks, Dec. 1994, stood at Rs 3,584,750m. The business of non-scheduled banks forms less than 0·1% of commercial bank business. Of the 300 scheduled banks, 26 are foreign banks which specialize in financing foreign trade but also compete for domestic business. The State Bank of India acts as the agent of the Reserve Bank for transacting government business as well as undertaking commercial functions. The 28 public sector banks (which comprise the State Bank of India and its 7 associate banks and 20 nationalized banks) account for about 83% of deposits and bank credit of all scheduled commercial banks.

There are stock exchanges in Ahmedabad, Bombay, Calcutta, Delhi, Madras and 17 other centres.

Weights and Measures. Uniform standards of weights and measures, based on the metric system, were established for the first time by the Standards of Weights and Measures Act, 1956.

A second Standards of Weights and Measures Act, 1976, recognizes the International System of Units and is in line with the recommendations of the International Organisation of Legal Metrology. This Act also protects consumers through proper indication of weight, quantity, identity, source, date and price on packaged goods.

While the Standards of Weights and Measures are laid down in the Central Act, enforcement of weights and measures laws is entrusted to the state governments; the central Directorate of Weights and Measures is responsible for co-ordinating activities so as to ensure national uniformity.

Calendar. The dates of the Saka era (named after the north Indian dynasty of the first century A.D.) are used alongside Gregorian dates in issues of the *Gazette of India*, news broadcasts by All-India Radio and government-issued calendars, from 22 March 1957, a date which corresponds with the first day of the year 1879 in the Saka era.

ENERGY AND NATURAL RESOURCES

Electricity. In Nov. 1994, 495,281 villages out of 579,132 had electricity. Production of electricity in 1994–95 was 350,505m. kWh, of which 262,076m. kWh came from thermal and nuclear stations and 88,429m. kWh from hydro-electric stations. 9 nuclear stations supplied 3% of output in 1993.

Oil and Gas. The Oil and Natural Gas Corporation Ltd and Oil India Ltd are the only producers of crude oil. Production 1994–95, 32·2m. tonnes, about 60% of consumption. The main fields are in Assam and Gujarat and offshore in the Gulf of Cambay (the Bombay High field). Natural gas production, 1994–95, 19,388m. cu. metres.

Water. 82·7m. ha (1992-93) are under irrigation, which equals about 45% of the total area under cultivation. Irrigation projects have formed an important part of all the Five-Year Plans. The possibilities of diverting rivers into canals being nearly exhausted, the emphasis is now on damming the monsoon surplus flow and diverting that. Ultimate potential of irrigation is assessed at 107m. ha, total cultivated land being 185m. ha.

Minerals. The coal industry was nationalized in 1973. Production (including lignite), 1994–95, 262·6m. tonnes; reserves (including lignite) are estimated at (1994) 197,000m. tonnes. Production of other minerals, 1993–94 (in 1,000 tonnes): Iron ore, 56,380; bauxite, 5,029; chromite, 1,094; copper ore, 5,224; manganese ore, 1,781; gold, 1,938 kg. Other important minerals are lead, zinc, limestone, apatite and phosphorite, dolomite, magnesite and silver. Value of mineral production, 1994–95, Rs 270,971m. of which mineral fuels produced Rs 230,480m., metallic minerals Rs 18,510m. and non-metallic Rs 21,980m.

Agriculture. About 70% of the people are dependent on the land for their living. In 1990-91 agriculture provided about 35% of GDP. The farming year runs from July to June through three crop seasons: Kharif (monsoon); rabi (winter) and summer.

Agricultural production, 1994-95 (in 1,000 tonnes): Rice, 81,250; wheat, 65,240; total foodgrains, 191,100; maize, 9,300; pulses, 14,460; sugar-cane, 259,950; oilseeds, 22,370; cotton, 11·76m. bales (of 170 kg); jute is grown in West Bengal (70% of total yield), Bihar and Assam, total yield, 8·3m. bales (of 170 kg). The coffee industry is growing: The main cash varieties are Arabica and Robusta (main growing areas Karnataka, Kerala and Tamil Nadu).

The tea industry is important, with production concentrated in Assam, West Bengal, Tamil Nadu and Kerala. Total crop in 1993–94, 753,500 tonnes from 414,232 ha; exports in 1993–94 valued at Rs 10,801m.

Livestock (1993): Cattle, 193m.; sheep, 45m.; pigs, 10·3m.; horses, 953,000; asses, 1,328,000m.; goats, 118m.; buffaloes, 79m.

Fertilizer consumption in 1993–94 was 12·4m. tonnes.

Land Tenure. There are three main traditional systems of land tenure: *Ryotwari* tenure, where the individual holders, usually peasant proprietors, are responsible for the payment of land revenues; *zamindari* tenure, where one or more persons own large estates and are responsible for payment (in this system there may be a number of intermediary holders); and *mahalwari* tenure, where village communities jointly hold an estate and are jointly and severally responsible for payment.

Agrarian reform, initiated in the first Five-Year Plan, being undertaken by the state governments includes: (1) The abolition of intermediaries under *zamindari* tenure. (2) Tenancy legislation designed to scale down rents to 1/4-1/5 of the value of the produce, to give permanent rights to tenants (subject to the landlord's right to resume a minimum holding for his personal cultivation), and to enable tenants to acquire ownership of their holdings (subject to the landlord's right of resumption for personal cultivation) on payment of compensation over a number of years. (3) Fixing of ceilings on existing holdings and on future acquisition; the holding of a family is between 4·05 and 7·28 ha if it has assured irrigation to produce two crops a year; 10·93 ha for land with irrigation facilities for only one crop a year; and 21·85 ha for all other categories of land. Tea, coffee, cocoa and cardamom plantations have been exempted. (4) The consolidation of holdings in community project areas and the prevention of fragmentation of holdings by reform of inheritance laws. (5) Promotion of farming by co-operative village management.

The average size of holding for the whole of India is 2·63 ha. Andhra Pradesh, 2·87; Assam, 1·46; Bihar, 1·53; Gujarat, 4·49; Jammu and Kashmir, 1·43; Karnataka, 4·11; Kerala, 0·75; Madhya Pradesh, 3·99; Maharashtra, 4·65; Orissa, 1·98; Punjab, 3·85; Rajasthan, 5·5; Tamil Nadu, 1·49; Uttar Pradesh, 1·78; West Bengal, 1·56.

Of the total 71m. rural households possessing operational holdings, 34% hold on the average less than 0·2 ha of land each.

Opium. By international agreement the poppy is cultivated under licence, and all raw opium is sold to the central government. Opium, other than for wholly medical use, is available only to registered addicts.

Fisheries. Total catch (1993–94) was 4·57m. tons, of which Kerala, Tamil Nadu, and Maharashtra produced about half. Of the total catch, 2·69m. tonnes were marine fish. There were 225 deep-sea (20 metres and above) fishing boats in Oct. 1990. There were 34,348 mechanized boats (1992–93). There were 8,450 fishermen's co-operatives with 1,157,000 members in June 1989; total sales, Rs 584·6m.

Forestry. The lands under the control of the state forest departments are classified as 'reserved forests' (forests intended to be permanently maintained for the supply of timber, etc., or for the protection of water supply, etc.), 'protected forests' and 'unclassed' forest land.

In 1990-91 the total forest area was 75·2m. ha. Main types are teak and sal. About 16% of the area is inaccessible, of which about 45% is potentially productive. Most states have encouraged planting small areas around villages.

INDUSTRY. In a number of industries (including the manufacture of iron and steel and mineral oils, shipbuilding and the mining of coal, iron and manganese ores, gypsum, gold and diamonds) new units are set up only by the state. In a further group of industries (road transport, manufacture of chemicals such as drugs, dyestuffs, plastics and fertilizers) the state established new undertakings, but private enterprise may develop either on its own or with state backing.

Oil refinery installed capacity, April 1995, was 56·4m. tonnes; production of petroleum refinery products (1994–95), 56·45m. tonnes. The Indian Oil Corporation was established in 1964 and had (1994) most of the market.

There is expansion in petrochemicals, based on the oil and associated gas of the Bombay High field, and gas from Krishna-Godavari Basin, Rajasthan, Tripura, Assam and Bassein field. Small industries numbering 2·38m., (initial outlay on capital equipment of less than Rs 7.5m.) are important; they employ about 13·94m. and produced (1994–95) goods worth Rs 1,811,330m.

Industrial production, 1993-94 (in 1,000 tonnes): Steel ingots, 13,900; aluminium, 465; 1,794,000 motor cycles, mopeds and scooters; 140,700 commercial vehicles; petroleum products, 55,310; cement, 57,800; board and paper, 2,731; nitrogen fertilizer, 7,393; phosphate fertilizer, 1,881; jute goods, 1,451; man-made fibre and yarn, 262; diesel engines, 146,400 (stationary) engines; electric motors, 6m. h.p.; 257,800 passenger cars and jeeps; 19,200 railway wagons; pig-iron, 15,700; finished steel, 15,100.

Labour. At the 1991 census there were 285·9m. workers, of whom 110·7m. were cultivators, 74·6m. agricultural labourers; 28·7m. in manufacturing, processing, servicing and repairs, 5·5m. in construction and 8·02m. in transport, communications and storage. Workdays lost by industrial disputes, 1993, 20·3m., through strikes and lockouts. An ordinance of 1981 gave the government power to ban strikes in essential services; the ordinance was to remain in force for 6 months and would then be renewable.

Companies. The total number of companies limited by shares at work as on 31 Dec. 1994 was 336,478; aggregate paid-up capital was Rs 1,177,540m. At 31 Dec. 1994 there were 42,399 public limited companies with an aggregate paid-up capital of Rs 791,460m., and 294,089 private limited companies (Rs 386,077m.). There were also 364 companies with unlimited liability and 2,395 companies limited by guarantee and association not for profit.

During 1993–94, 30,291 new limited companies were registered in the Indian Union under the Companies Act 1956 with a total authorized capital of Rs 86,080m.; 18 were government companies (Rs 25,538m.) and 30,273 were non-government companies (Rs 60,545m.). There were 13 private companies with unlimited liability and 89 companies with liability limited by guarantee and association not for profit also registered in 1993–94. During 1993–94, 263 non-government companies with an aggregate paid-up capital of Rs 319·4m. went into liquidation or were struck off the register.

On 31 Dec. 1994 there were 1,207 government companies at work with a total paid-up capital of Rs 676,230m.; 591 were public limited companies and 616 were private limited companies.

On 31 Dec. 1994, 605 companies incorporated elsewhere were reported to have a place of business in India; 137 were of UK and 113 of US origin in 1992–93.

Co-operative Movement. In 1993–94 there were 353,000 co-operative societies with a total membership of 175m. These included Primary Cooperative Marketing Societies, State Co-operative Marketing Federations and the National Agricultural Co-operative Marketing Federation of India. There were also State Co-operative Commodity Marketing Federations, and 29 general purpose and 16 Special Commodites Marketing Federations.

There were, in Dec. 1993, 28 State Co-operative Banks, 351 Central Co-operative Banks, 89,000 Primary Agricultural Credit Societies, 20 Central Land Development Banks, and 717 Primary Land Development Banks which provide long-term credits.

Agricultural credit is provided (31 Dec. 1993) through 32,641 rural and semi-rural branches of commercial banks and 14,543 branches of Regional Rural Banks, and (June 1993) 82,560 Primary Agricultural credit societies affiliated to 10,775 branches of District Central Co-operative Banks and 2,959 Primary units of Land Development Banks. Total agricultural credit disbursed by Co-operatives in 1993–94 was Rs 85,000m.

Value of agricultural produce marketed by Co-operatives in 1992–93 was about Rs 65,000m.

In 1992–93 there were 2,601 agro-processing units; 237 (224 in operation) sugar factories produced 7·84m. tons; 120 spinning mills (capacity 3·02m. spindles) produced 179m. kg. of yarn; there were 129 oilseed processing units; total storage capacity was 13m. tons.

In 1992–93 there were 76,500 retail depots distributing 4·13m. tons of fertilizers.

FOREIGN ECONOMIC RELATIONS. Foreign investment is encouraged by a tax holiday on income up to 6% of capital employed for 5 years. There are special depreciation allowances, and customs and excise concessions, for export industries. Proposals for investment ventures involving up to 51% foreign equity require only the Reserve Bank's approval under new liberalized policy. In Feb. 1991 India resumed trans-frontier trade with China, which had ceased in 1962.

Foreign debt was estimated at US$95,320m. in March 1995.

Commerce. The external trade of India (excluding land-borne trade with Tibet and Bhutan) was as follows (in Rs 100,000):

	Imports	*Exports and Re-exports*
1992–93	6,337,451	5,368,826
1993–94	7,310,101	6,975,139
1994–95 [1]	8,997,066	8,267,411

[1]Provisional.

The distribution of commerce by countries was as follows in the year ended 31 March 1995 (in Rs 100,000):

Countries	*Exports to*	*Imports from*	*Countries*	*Exports to*	*Imports from*
Argentina	15,520	14,368	Malaysia	89,948	78,376
Australia	108,771	206,802	Mexico	24,574	17,548
Austria	29,949	15,687	Morocco	4,026	49,558
Bahrain	18,543	170,295	Nepal	37,702	9,068
Bangladesh	202,413	5,607	Netherlands	183,815	120,532
Belgium	310,355	588,080	New Zealand	17,215	23,228
Burma	7,110	38,041	Nigeria	34,265	219,516
Canada	83,779	73,569	Pakistan	17,971	13,668
China	79,799	238,890	Philippines	31,218	3,698
CIS	279,881	119,302	Poland	21,099	14,242
Czech Republic	9,954	10,768	Qatar	9,399	41,447
Denmark	41,634	31,255	Romania	5,081	7,860
Egypt	37,619	21,487	Saudi Arabia	136,789	483,554
Finland	9,300	20,966	Singapore	241,109	196,644
France	182,784	186,026	Spain	84,547	38,182
Germany	548,748	561,537	Sri Lanka	115,093	6,282
Hong Kong	476,378	59,176	Sweden	46,129	50,686
Hungary	5,992	9,685	Switzerland	77,642	158,797
Indonesia	87,191	37,530	Taiwan	78,735	19,051
Iran	49,218	119,046	Thailand	127,641	17,944
Israel	47,180	81,109	Tunisia	1,799	53,885
Italy	259,380	168,594	UAE	397,299	314,617
Japan	636,051	477,428	UK	530,324	481,821
Jordan	16,932	34,790	USA	1,573,436	858,370
South Korea	104,383	177,075	Vietnam	18,379	13,837
Kuwait	42,048	353,244			

The value (in 100,000 rupees) of the leading articles of merchandise was as follows in the year ended 31 March 1995:

Exports	*Value*
Meat and meat preparations	34,594
Marine products	342,605
Processed foods (miscellaneous)	9,339
Rice	108,660
Wheat (1994)	128,700
Vegetables and fruits	61,631
Nuts and seeds (1994)	129,300
Coffee	85,154
Tea	62,504
Spices	53,054
Oil meals	170,539
Tobacco unmanufactured and tobacco refuse	20,575
Raw cotton	13,954
Iron ore	126,002
Ores and minerals (excluding iron, mica and coal)	82,811
Cotton yarn, fabrics and made-up articles	617,792

Exports	*Value*
Ready-made garments	694,122
Jute manufactures including twist and yarn	37,738
Leather and leather manufactures	459,060
Natural silk textiles	39,905
Man-made textiles	160,143
Carpets, mill-made	31,717
Plastics and linoleum	124,186
Rubber, glass and other products (1994)	164,200
Sports goods	18,450
Gems and jewellery	1,407,330
Handicrafts	115,742
Handmade carpets	134,382
Electronic goods (1994)	95,400
Engineering goods	928,436
Petroleum products	130,898
Basic chemicals, pharmaceuticals and cosmetics, chemicals including residual	504,271

Imports	*Value*
Rice	855
Raw wool	35,078
Pulp and waste paper	63,535
Crude rubber including synthetic and reclaimed	37,077
Synthetic and regenerated fibre	44,396
Fertilizers, crude	47,919
Sulphur and unroasted iron pyrites	42,651
Metalliferous ores and metal scrap	234,897
Petroleum, petroleum products and related materials	1,861,255
Edible oil	62,424
Cashew nuts (1994)	48,270
Organic and inorganic chemicals	671,043
Medical and pharmaceutical products	93,714
Fertilizers, manufactured	239,859
Artificial resins, plastic materials etc	190,350
Chemical materials and products	63,374
Paper, paper board and manufactures thereof	28,641
Textile yarn, fabrics and made-up articles	103,513
Pearls, precious and semi-precious stones	511,643
Non-metallic mineral manufactures exclg. pearls	41,285
Iron and steel	339,778
Non-ferrous metal	225,409
Manufactures of metal	64,757
Machinery other than electric	856,504
Electrical machinery	78,928
Transport equipment	349,668
Professional, scientific, controlling instruments, photographic, optical goods, watches and clocks	154,408

Total trade between India and UK (British Department of Trade returns, in £1,000 sterling):

	1991	*1992*	*1993*	*1994*	*1995*
Imports to UK	776,976	862,131	1,088,837	1,288,939	1,435,481
Exports and re-exports from UK	1,017,398	945,541	1,129,988	1,311,495	1,682,709

Tourism. There were 1·56m. visitors (excluding nationals of Pakistan and Bangladesh) in 1994 bringing about Rs 74,486m. in foreign exchange; 300,696 from UK, 176,482 from USA, 89,009 from Sri Lanka.

COMMUNICATIONS

Roads. In 1991–92 there were 2·16m. km of roads, of which 1m. km were surfaced. Roads are divided into 5 main administrative classes, namely, national highways, state highways, major district roads, other district roads and village roads. The national highways (33,500 km in 1992) connect capitals of states, major ports and foreign highways. The national highway system is linked with the UN Economic and Social Commission for Asia and the Pacific international highway system. The state highways are the main trunk roads of the states, while the major district roads connect subsidiary areas of production and markets with distribution centres, and form the main link between headquarters and neighbouring districts.

There were (31 March 1993) 25,299,024 motor vehicles in India, comprising 3·33m. private cars, taxis and jeeps, 17·03m. motor cycles and scooters, 381,003 buses, 1,599,382 goods vehicles and 2,963,000 others.

Railways. The Indian railway system is government-owned (under the control of the Railway Board) and is divided into 9 zones; route-km 1993–94:

Zone	*Headquarters*	*Route-km*
Central	Bombay	7,158 km (2,892 km elec.)
Eastern	Calcutta	4,034 km (1,281 km)
Northern	Delhi	10,995 km (909 km)
North Eastern	Gorakhpur	5,144 km
North East Frontier	Guwahati	3,727 km
Southern	Madras	7,019 km (959 km)
South Central	Secunderabad	7,226 km (1,058 km)
South Eastern	Calcutta	7,160 km (2,384 km)
Western	Bombay	9,728 km (1,755 km)

Principal gauges are 1,676 mm. and metre, with networks also of 762 and 610 mm. gauge.

Passengers carried in 1993–94 were 3,708m.; freight, 377·5m. tonnes. Revenue (1993–94) from passengers, Rs 48,912m.; from goods, Rs 122,755m.

Indian Railways pay to the central government a dividend on capital-at-charge at a rate fixed by the Convention Committee of Parliament. Railway finance in Rs 1m.:

Financial years	*Gross traffic receipts*	*Gross expenditure*	*Net revenues (receipts)*	*Net surplus or deficit (after dividend)*
1993–94	179,460	151,350	31,020	+18,060
1994–95	199,200	169,400	32,500	+18,700
1995–96 budget	219,550	187,600	34,260	+20,550

There is a metro (16·4 km) and tramway network (50 km) in Calcutta.

Civil Aviation. There are international airports at Bombay, Calcutta, Delhi (Indira Gandhi), Thiruvananthapuram and Madras. Air transport was nationalized in 1953 with the formation of 2 Air Corporations: Air India for long-distance international air services, and Indian Airlines for air services within India and to adjacent countries. A third airline, Vayudoot, formed in 1981 as an internal feeder, has been merged into Indian Airlines. Domestic air transport has been opened to private companies and by 1995 6 private airlines had been given scheduled status.

In Jan. 1995 Air India had 26 aircraft including B-747-200s, B-747-300 (Combi), B-747-400s, A-300-B4s and A-310-300s, and operated routes from Bombay, Delhi, Madras, Thiruvananthapuram, Hyderabad, Goa, Ahmedabed, Bangalore, Calicut, Amritsar and Calcutta to Africa (Nairobi, Dar-es-Salaam, Durban and Johannesburg); to Mauritius; to Europe (London, Paris, Frankfurt, Geneva, Moscow, Rome, Copenhagen and Manchester); to western Asia (Doha, Abu Dhabi, Dharan, Dubai, Bahrain, Kuwait, Muscat, Jeddah and Riyadh); to east Asia (Bangkok, Hong Kong, Tokyo, Osaka, Kuala Lumpur, Jakarta and Singapore); to North America (New York and Toronto) and to Australia (Perth). In addition, freight services are operated to Zurich, Brussels, Dubai, Singapore and Luxembourg. Air India carried 2·2m. passengers and made a profit of Rs 408m. in 1994–95.

Indian Airlines has a fleet of 54 aircraft including 10 A-300s, 30 A-320s and 14 B-737s. In 1995 it operated services to Bangkok, Chittagong, Colombo, Dhaka, Fujairah, Karachi, Khatmandu, Kuala Lumpur, Kuwait, Male, Muscat, Ras-al-Khaimah, Sharjah and Singapore. During 1994–95 the airline carried 7·66m. passengers.

Services are also provided by Aeroflot, Air Canada, Air France, Air Lanka, Air Maldives, Air Mauritius, Air Ukraine, Alitalia, Alyemda, Ariana Afghan Airlines, Biman Bangladesh, British Airways, Cathay Pacific, Druk-Air, Egyptair, El Al, Emirates Air, Ethiopian Airlines, Gulf Air, Iran Air, JAL, Kazakhstan Airways, Kenya Airways, KLM, Korean Air, Kuwait Airways, Lufthansa, Malaysia Airlines,

Oman Air, Pakistan International Airlines, Qatar Airways, Royal Brunei Airlines, Royal Jordanian, Royal Nepal Airlines, SAA, SAS, Saudia, Singapore Airlines, Swissair, Syrian Airlines, Tajikistan Airlines, Tarom, Thai Airways, Tower Air, Turkmenistan Airlines, United Airlines, Uzbekistan Airways and Yemenia Yemen Airways.

The Airports Authority of India maintains and operates 87 civil aerodromes, 28 civil enclaves and the 5 international airports at Bombay, Calcutta, Delhi, Madras and Thiruvananthapuram.

Shipping. In Dec. 1994, 437 ships totalling 6·35m. GRT were on the Indian Register; of these, 206 ships of 0·68m. GRT were engaged in coastal trade, and 231 ships of 5·67m. GRT in overseas trade. Traffic of major ports, 1994–95 (provisional), was as follows:

Port	*Cargo ships cleared*	*Imports (1m. tonnes)*	*Exports (1m. tonnes)*
Kandla	1,370	18·21	3·06
Bombay	2,485	17·20	5·79
Mormugao	625	1·98	15·46
New Mangalore	515	0·96	6·00
Cochin	650	1·78	0·80
Tuticorin	876	1·85	0·90
Madras	1,425	11·38	7·82
Visakhapatnam	1,200	12·62	7·10
Paradip	467	3·33	2·52
Haldia	779	11·59	1·48
Calcutta	718		
Jawaharlal Nehru	440	3·11	1·75

There are about 3,700 km of major rivers navigable by motorized craft, of which 2,000 km are used. Canals, 4,300 km, of which 900 km are navigable by motorized craft.

Telecommunications. On 31 March 1994 there were 152,786 post offices and 45,979 telegraph offices.

The telephone system is in the hands of the Telecommunications Department, except in Delhi and Bombay, served by public corporation. In April 1994 the Department had 8·03m. telephones, 412 telex exchanges and 47,200 subscribers.

There were 175 radio stations in Dec. 1994, and 289 transmitters in Dec. 1995. In Dec. 1995 television reached 86% of the population, through a network of 692 transmitters (colour by PAL). In 1991 there were estimated to be 55m. radio and 20m. TV sets.

Cinemas. In 1993–94 there were 12,908 cinemas and 754 feature films were produced in 1994. Attendances totalled 85m. in 1994.

Press. There were 35,595 newspapers in March 1993. In 1994 there were 369 dailies in 18 languages with a total circulation of 20m. In 1991 the total number of newspapers and periodicals was 30,214; about 30% were published in Delhi, Bombay, Calcutta and Madras. There were 3,229 daily and 9,621 weekly papers. Circulation of newspapers and periodicals (1992), 63·67m. Hindi papers have the highest number and circulation, followed by English, then Urdu, Bengali and Marathi.

SOCIAL INSTITUTIONS

Justice. All courts form a single hierarchy, with the Supreme Court at the head, which constitutes the highest court of appeal. Immediately below it are the High Courts and subordinate courts in each state. Every court in this chain administers the whole law of the country, whether made by Parliament or by the state legislatures.

The states of Andhra Pradesh, Assam (in common with Nagaland, Meghalaya, Manipur, Mizoram, Tripura and Arunachal Pradesh), Bihar, Gujarat, Himachal Pradesh, Jammu and Kashmir, Karnataka, Kerala, Madhya Pradesh, Maharashtra (in common with Goa and the Union Territories of Daman and Diu and Dadra and Nagar Haveli), Orissa, Punjab (in common with the state of Haryana and the Union

Territory of Chandigarh), Rajasthan, Tamil Nadu, Uttar Pradesh, West Bengal and Sikkim have each a High Court. There is a separate High Court for Delhi. For the Andaman and Nicobar Islands the Calcutta High Court, for Pondicherry the High Court of Madras and for Lakshadweep the High Court of Kerala are the highest judicial authorities. The Allahabad High Court has a Bench at Lucknow, the Bombay High Court has Benches at Nagpur, Aurangabad and Panaji, the Gauhati High Court has Benches at Kohima, Aizwal, Imphal and Agartala, the Madhya Pradesh High Court has Benches at Gwalior and Indore, the Patna High Court has a Bench at Ranchi and the Rajasthan High Court has a Bench at Jaipur. Judges and Division Courts of the Guwahati High Court also sit in Meghalaya. Similarly, judges and Division Courts of the Calcutta High Court also sit in the Andaman and Nicobar Islands. Below the High Court each state is divided into a number of districts under the jurisdiction of district judges who preside over civil courts and courts of sessions. There are a number of judicial authorities subordinate to the district civil courts. On the criminal side magistrates of various classes act under the overall supervision of the High Court.

The Code of Criminal Procedure came into force with effect from 1 April 1974. It provides for complete separation of the Judiciary from the Executive throughout India.

In Oct. 1991 the Supreme Court upheld capital punishment by hanging.

Police. The states control their own police forces. The Home Affairs Minister of the central government co-ordinates the work of the states. The Indian Police Service provides senior officers for the state police forces. The Central Bureau of Investigation functions under the control of the Cabinet Secretariat.

The cities of Pune, Ahmedabad, Nagpur, Bangalore, Calcutta, Madras, Bombay, Delhi and Hyderabad have separate police commissionerates.

Religion. India is a secular state; any worship is permitted, but the state itself has no religion. The principal religions in 1991 (census) were: Hindus, 687·6m. (82%); Moslems, 101·6m. (12·1%); Christians, 19·6m. (2·34%); Sikhs, 16·3m. (1·94%); Buddhists, 6·4m. (0·76%); Jains, 3·4m. (0·4%).

Education. Literacy. According to the 1991 census the literacy percentage in the country (excluding age-group, 0-6 years) was 52·19% (43·67% in 1981): 64·2% among males, 39·19% among females. Of the states and territories, Kerala and Chandigarh have the highest rates.

Educational Organization. Education is the concurrent responsibility of state and Union governments. In the Union Territories it is the responsibility of the central government. The Union Government is also directly responsible for the central universities and all institutions declared by parliament to be of national importance; the promotion of Hindi as the federal language and co-ordinating and maintaining standards in higher education, research, science and technology. Professional education rests with the Ministry or Department concerned. There is a Central Advisory Board of Education to advise the Union and the State Governments on any educational question which may be referred to it.

School Education. The school system has 4 stages: Primary, middle, secondary and senior secondary.

Primary education is imparted either at independent primary (or junior basic) schools or primary classes attached to middle or secondary schools. The period of instruction varies from 4 to 5 years and the medium of instruction is in most cases the mother tongue of the child or the regional language. Free primary education is available for all children.

Legislation for compulsory education has been passed by some state governments and Union Territories but it is not practicable to enforce compulsion when the reasons for non-attendance are socio-economic. There are residential schools for country children.

The period for the middle stage varies from 2 to 3 years.

Higher Education. Higher education is given in arts, science or professional colleges, universities and all-India educational or research institutions. In

1994–95 there were 172 universities, 11 institutions of national importance and 36 institutions deemed as universities. Of the universities, 10 are central: Aligarh Muslim University; Banaras Hindu University; University of Delhi; University of Hyderabad; Jamia Millia Islamia, New Delhi; Jawaharlal Nehru University; North Eastern Hill University; Visva Bharati; Pondicherry; Indira Gandhi National Open. The rest are state universities. Total enrolment at universities, 1993–94, 5,006,575, of which 4,410,791 were undergraduates. Women students, 1,664,121.

Grants are paid through the University Grants Commission to the central universities and institutions deemed to be universities for their maintenance and development and to state universities for their development projects only; their maintenance is the concern of state governments. During 1993–94 the University Grants Commission sanctioned grants of Rs 4,995·2m.

Technical Education. The number of institutions awarding degrees in engineering and technology in 1994-95 was 341, and those awarding diplomas, 1,107; the former admitted 290,853, the latter 351,283 students including 53,044 girl students.

Adult Education. The Directorate of Adult Education, established in 1971, is the national resource centre.

There is also a National Literacy Mission.

Educational statistics for 1994–95:

Type of recognized institution	*No. of institutions*	*No. of students on rolls*	*No. of teachers*
Primary/junior basic schools	581,302	109,043,663	1,714,395
Middle/senior basic schools	163,605	40,287,840	1,122,436
High/higher secondary schools [1]	92,252	24,137,835	1,446,000
Training schools and colleges	1,765	231,136 [2]	–
Arts, Science and Commerce colleges	8,210	5,006,575 [3]	220,830

[1] Including Junior Colleges.
[2] Enrolment by stages of teachers' training courses at school and college level.
[3] Enrolment by stages of all post-graduate and graduate courses in 1992–93.

Expenditure. Total budgeted expenditure of education and other departments 1994–95 is estimated at Rs 286,905·5m. Total public expenditure on education, sport, arts and youth welfare during the Eighth (1992–97) Plan, Rs 212,170·2m.; Seventh Plan spending on adult education, Rs 3,007m. in the central and Rs 6,098m. in the state sectors.

Health. Medical services are primarily the responsibility of the states. The Union Government has sponsored major schemes for disease prevention and control which are implemented nationally.

Total central expenditure on health and family welfare in 1995-96 was Rs 8,961·7m. on revenue account.

DIPLOMATIC REPRESENTATIVES

Of India in Great Britain (India House, Aldwych, London, WC2B 4NA)
High Commissioner: Dr L. M. Singhvi.

Of Great Britain in India (Chanakyapuri, New Delhi 110021)
High Commissioner: The Hon. David Gore-Booth, CMG.

Of India in the USA (2107 Massachusetts Ave., NW, Washington, D.C., 20008)
Ambassador: Siddhartha S. Ray.

Of the USA in India (Shanti Path, Chanakyapuri, New Delhi 110021)
Ambassador: Frank G. Wisner.

Of India to the United Nations
Ambassador: Prakash Shah.

Further Reading

Balasubramanyam, V. N., *The Economy of India.* London, 1985
Bardham, P., *The Political Economy of Development in India.* Oxford, 1984

Bhambhri, C. P., *The Political Process in India, 1947–91*. Delhi, 1991
Brown, J., *Modern India: The Origins of an Asian Democracy*. 2nd ed. OUP, 1994
Derbyshire, I. D., *India*. [Bibliography]. 2nd ed. Oxford and Santa Barbara (CA), 1995
Gupta, B. K. and Kharbas, D. S., *India*. [Bibliography] Oxford and Santa Barbara, 1984
Gupta, D. C., *Indian Government and Politics*. 3rd ed. London, 1992
Hall, A., *The Emergence of Modern India*. Columbia Univ. Press, 1981
The Indian Annual Register. Calcutta, from 1953
Jalan, B., *India's Economic Crisis: the Way Ahead*. OUP, 1991
Kulke, H. and Rothermund, D., *A History of India*. rev. ed. London, 1990
Mehra, P., *A Dictionary of Modern Indian History, 1707–1947*. Delhi, 1987
Moon, P., *The British Conquest and Dominion of India*. London and Indiana Univ. Press, 1989
New Cambridge History of India. 5 vols. CUP, 1988–93. 2nd ed. 1994–95
Ray, R. K., *Industrialisation of India*. OUP, 1983
Smith, V. E., *Oxford History of India*. 3rd ed. OUP, 1958
Spear, P., *India: A Modern History*. 2nd ed. Univ. of Michigan Press, 1972

Other more specialized titles are listed under CONSTITUTION AND GOVERNMENT, *above*.

STATES AND TERRITORIES

The Republic of India is composed of the following 25 States and 7 centrally administered Union Territories:

States	*Capital*	*States*	*Capital*
Andhra Pradesh	Hyderabad	Manipur	Imphal
Arunachal Pradesh	Itanagar	Meghalaya	Shillong
Assam	Dispur	Mizoram	Aizawl
Bihar	Patna	Nagaland	Kohima
Goa	Panaji	Orissa	Bhubaneswar
Gujarat	Gandhinagar	Punjab	Chandigarh
Haryana	Chandigarh	Rajasthan	Jaipur
Himachal Pradesh	Shimla	Sikkim	Gangtok
Jammu and Kashmir	Srinagar	Tamil Nadu	Madras
Karnataka	Bangalore	Tripura	Agartala
Kerala	Thiruvananthapuram	Uttar Pradesh	Lucknow
Madhya Pradesh	Bhopal	West Bengal	Calcutta
Maharashtra	Bombay		

Union Territories

Andaman and Nicobar Islands; Chandigarh; Dadra and Nagar Haveli; Daman and Diu; Delhi; Lakshadweep; Pondicherry.

For the constitutional history of the States and Territories, 1950–87, *see* THE STATESMAN'S YEAR-BOOK, 1992–93, p. 722.

ANDHRA PRADESH

KEY HISTORICAL EVENTS. Andhra was constituted a separate state on 1 Oct. 1953, on its partition from Madras, and consisted of the undisputed Telugu-speaking area of that state. To this region was added, on 1 Nov. 1956, the Telangana area of the former Hyderabad State, comprising the districts of Hyderabad, Medak, Nizamabad, Karimnagar, Warangal, Khammam, Nalgonda and Mahbubnagar, parts of the Adilabad district and some taluks of the Raichur, Gulbarga and Bidar districts, and some revenue circles of the Nanded district. On 1 April 1960, 221·4 sq. miles in the Chingleput and Salem districts of Madras were transferred to Andhra Pradesh in exchange for 410 sq. miles from Chittoor district. The district of Prakasam was formed on 2 Feb. 1970. Hyderabad was split into 2 districts on 15 Aug. 1978, (Ranga Reddy and Hyderabad). A new district, Vizianagaram, was formed in 1979.

TERRITORY AND POPULATION. Andhra Pradesh is in south India and is bounded in the south by Tamil Nadu, west by Karnataka, north and north-west by Maharashtra, north-east by Madhya Pradesh and Orissa and east by the Bay of Bengal. The state has an area of 275,045 sq. km and a population (1991 census) of

66·5m. Density, 242 per sq. km. Growth rate 1981–91, 24·2%. The principal language is Telugu. Cities with over 250,000 population (1991 census), *see* INDIA: Territory and Population. Other large cities (1991): Nizamabad (241,034); Kurnool (236,800); Ramagundam (214,384); Eluru (212,866); Anantapur (174,924); Tirupati (174,369); Vizianagaram (160,359); Machilipatnam (159,110); Karimnagar (148,583); Tenali (143,726); Adoni (136,182); Proddutur (133,914); Chittoor (133,462); Khammam (127,992); Cuddapah (121,463); Bheemavaram (121,314).

CONSTITUTION AND GOVERNMENT. Andhra Pradesh has a unicameral legislature; the Legislative Council was abolished in June 1985. There are 292 seats in the Legislative Assembly. At the election of 1 and 5 Dec. 1994, the Telugu Desam Party gained 224 seats, Congress I 25.

For administrative purposes there are 23 districts in the state. The capital is Hyderabad.

Governor: Krishna Kant.
Chief Minister: N. Chandrababu Naidu.

BUDGET. Budget estimate, 1994–95: receipts on revenue account, Rs 82,605·2m.; expenditure, Rs 89,641·8m. Annual plan, 1995-96: Rs 31,590m.

ENERGY AND NATURAL RESOURCES

Electricity. There are 6 hydro-electric plants, 5 thermal stations and 2 gas-based units. Several new thermal and gas-based power plants will be set up during the eighth 5-year plan period (1992–97). Installed capacity, 1994–95, 4,724·44 MW, power generated 27,865m. kWh. In 1994–95 all 27,379 villages were electrified and 1·6m. electric pump sets energized.

Oil and Gas. Oil/gas structures have been discovered at Lingala in the Krishna–Godavari basin. One gas-powered station has been commissioned and 2 gas-powered generating stations are proposed. 6m. cu. metres of natural gas were produced in 1994–95.

Water. In 1993–94, 15 major and 36 medium irrigation projects were in hand. The Telugu Ganga joint project with Tamil Nadu, now in execution, will irrigate about 233,000 ha, besides supplying drinking water to Madras city (Tamil Nadu).

Minerals The state is an important producer of asbestos and barytes. Other important minerals are copper ore, coal, iron and limestone, steatite, mica and manganese.

Agriculture. There were (1993–94) about 14·1m. ha of cropped land, of which 7m. ha were under food-grains. Irrigated area, 1993–94, 4·31m. ha. Production in 1993–94 (in tonnes): Foodgrains, 12·04m. (rice, 9·48m., wheat, 6,700); pulses, 0·61m.; sugar-cane (1992–93), 1·24m.; oil seeds, 3·23m.

Livestock (1993): Cattle, 10·95m.; buffaloes, 9·13m.; goats, 4·32m.; sheep, 7·77m.

Forestry. In 1993–94 it was estimated that forests occupy 23·2% of the total area of the state or 63,775 sq. km; main forest products are teak, eucalyuptus, cashew, casuarina, softwoods and bamboo.

Fisheries. Production 1992–93, 141,859 tonnes of marine fish and 151,475 tonnes of inland water fish. The state has a coastline of 974 km.

INDUSTRY. The main industries are textile manufacture, sugar-milling machine tools, pharmaceuticals, cement, chemicals, glass, fertilizers, electronic equipment, heavy electrical machinery, aircraft parts and paper-making. There is an oil refinery at Vishakhapatnam, where India's major shipbuilding yards are situated. In 1994 a major steel plant at Visakhapatnam and a railway repair shop at Tirupathi were functioning.

At 31 March 1994 there were 1,142 large and medium industries employing

600,187 persons, and 110,681 small businesses employing 0·96m.

There are cottage industries and sericulture. District Industries Centres have been set up to promote small-scale industry.

Tourism is growing; the main centres are Hyderabad, Nagarjunasagar, Warangal, Araku Valley, Horsley Hills and Tirupathi.

COMMUNICATIONS

Roads. In 1992–93 there were 2,587 km of national highways, 41,395 km of state highways and 137,476 km of major district roads. Number of vehicles during 1992–93 was 1,766,448, including 1,428,314 motor cycles and scooters, 123,251 cars and jeeps and 88,388 goods vehicles.

Railways. In 1994–95 there were 5,063 route-km of railway.

Civil Aviation. There are airports at Hyderabad, Tirupathi, Vijayawada and Visakhapatnam, with regular scheduled services to Bombay, Delhi, Calcutta, Bangalore and Madras. A feeder airline serves Rajahmundry and Cuddapah.

Shipping. The chief port is Vishakhapatnam. There are minor ports at Kakinada, Machilipatnam, Bheemunipatnam, Narsapur, Krishnapatnam, Nizampatnam, Vadarevu and Kalingapatnam.

SOCIAL INSTITUTIONS

Justice. The high court of Judicature at Hyderabad has a Chief Justice and 28 puisne judges.

Religion. At the 1991 census Hindus numbered 59,281,950; Moslems, 5,923,954; Christians, 1,216,348; Jains, 26,564; Sikhs, 21,910; Buddhists, 22,153.

Education. In 1991, 44·09% of the population were literate (55·13% of men and 32·72% of women). There were, in 1994–95, 49,153 primary schools (7,408,913 students); 6,851 upper primary (2·15m.); 7,518 high schools (2,956,576). Education is free for children up to 14.

In 1994–95 there were 1,465 junior colleges (650,762 students). In 1994–95 there were 582 degree colleges (341,057 students in 1993–94); 52 oriental colleges (14,081 students in 1992–93) and 13 universities: Osmania University, Hyderabad; Andhra University, Waltair; Sri Venkateswara University, Tirupathi; Kakatiya University, Warangal; Nagarjuna University, Guntur; Sri Jawaharlal Nehru Technological University, Hyderabad; Hyderabad University, Hyderabad; A.P. Agricultural University, Hyderabad; Sri Krishnadevaraya University, Anantapur; Smt. Padmavathi Mahila Vishwavidyalayam (University for Women), Tirupathi; Dr B. R. Ambedkar Open University, Hyderabad; Telugu University, Hyderabad and A. P. University of Health Science, Vijayawada.

Health. There were (1991-92) 1,915 allopathic hospitals and dispensaries, 1,498 Ayurvedic hospitals and dispensaries, 212 Unani and 321 homeopathy hospitals and dispensaries. There were also 181 nature cure hospitals and 1,243 primary health centres. Number of beds in hospitals was 32,116.

ARUNACHAL PRADESH

KEY HISTORICAL EVENTS. In Jan. 1972 the former North East Frontier Agency of Assam was created a Union Territory. In Dec. 1986, by the Constitution (55th Amendment) and State of Arunachal Pradesh Acts, the Territory became the 24th state of India.

TERRITORY AND POPULATION. The state is in the extreme north-east of India and is bounded in the north by China, east by Burma, west by Bhutan and south by Assam and Nagaland. It has 13 districts and comprises the former frontier divisions of Kameng, Tirap, Subansiri, Siang and Lohit; it has an area of 83,743 sq.

km and a population (1991 census) of 864,558; growth, 1981–91, 36·83%; density, 10 per sq. km.

The state is mainly tribal; there are 106 tribes using about 50 tribal dialects.

CONSTITUTION AND GOVERNMENT. There is a Legislative Assembly of 60 members. The capital is Itanagar (population, 1991, 16,545).

Governor: Mata Prasad.
Chief Minister: Gegong Apang.

BUDGET. Revenue receipts, 1993–94, Rs 5,266·1m.; revenue expenditure, Rs 3,970·7m. Plan outlay, 1995–96, Rs 4,700m.

ENERGY AND NATURAL RESOURCES

Electricity. Total installed capacity (1993–94), 39·4 MW. Power generated (1993–94): 60·08m. units. 1,535 out of 3,649 villages have electricity.

Oil and Minerals. Production, 1994–95, 35,000 tonnes of crude oil. Crude oil reserves are estimated at 30m. tonnes, coal, 84·23m. tonnes, dolomite, 154·13m. tonnes, limestone, 409·35m. tonnes.

Agriculture. Production of foodgrains, 1993–94, 220,700 tonnes.

Forestry. Area under forest, 51,540 sq. km; revenue from forestry (1993–94) Rs 396·5m.

INDUSTRY. There are 17 medium and 2,660 small industries, 155 craft or weaving centres and 28 sericulture centres. Most of the medium industries are forest-based.

COMMUNICATIONS. Total length of roads in the state, 11,158 km of which 2,050 km are surfaced. There were 9,359 vehicles in 1992–93. The state has 330 km of national highway. 4 towns are linked by air services.

SOCIAL INSTITUTIONS

Religion. At the 1991 census Hindus numbered 320,212; Moslems, 11,922; Christians, 89,013; Buddhists, 111,372.

Education. In 1991, 41·59% of the population were literate (51·45% of men and 29·69% of women). There were (1994–95) 1,195 primary schools with 135,417 students, 293 middle schools with 36,263 students, 136 high and higher secondary schools with 20,457 students, 4 colleges and 2 polytechnic institutes. Arunachal University was established in 1985.

Health. There are (1993) 13 hospitals, 10 community health centres, 36 primary health centres and 260 sub-centres. There are also 2 TB hospitals and 11 leprosy and other hospitals. Total number of beds, 2,359.

ASSAM

KEY HISTORICAL EVENTS. Assam first became a British Protectorate at the close of the first Burmese War in 1826. In 1832 Cachar was annexed; in 1835 the Jaintia Hills were included in the East India Company's dominions, and in 1839 Assam was annexed to Bengal. In 1874 Assam was detached from Bengal and made a separate chief commissionership. On the partition of Bengal in 1905, it was united to the Eastern Districts of Bengal under a Lieut.-Governor. From 1912 the chief commissionership of Assam was revived, and in 1921 a governorship was created. On the partition of India almost the whole of the predominantly Moslem district of Sylhet was merged with East Bengal (Pakistan). Dewangiri in North Kamrup was ceded to Bhutan in 1951. The Naga Hill district, administered by the

Union Government since 1957, became part of Nagaland in 1962. The autonomous state of Meghalaya within Assam, comprising the districts of Garo Hills and Khasi and Jaintia Hills, came into existence on 2 April 1970, and achieved full independent statehood in Jan. 1972, when it was also decided to form a Union Territory, Mizoram (now a state), from the Mizo Hills district.

TERRITORY AND POPULATION. Assam is in north-east India, almost separated from central India by Bangladesh. It is bounded in the west by West Bengal, north by Bhutan and Arunachal Pradesh, east by Nagaland, Manipur and Burma, south by Meghalaya, Bangladesh, Mizoram and Tripura. The area of the state is now 78,438 sq. km. Population (census 1991) 22·4m. Density, 286 per sq. km. Growth rate 1981–91, 24·24%. Principal towns with population (1991) are; Guwahati, 584,342; Dibrugarh, 125,667; Silchar, 115,483; Nagaon, 93,350; Tinsukia, 73,918; Dhubri, 66,216; Jorhat, 58,358; Tezpur, 55,084. The principal language is Assamese.

The central government is surveying the line of a proposed boundary fence to prevent illegal entry from Bangladesh.

CONSTITUTION AND GOVERNMENT. Assam has a unicameral legislature of 126 members. In the 1991 elections a Congress (I) government was returned. The temporary capital is Dispur. The state has 23 districts.

Governor: Lok Nath Mishra.

Chief Minister: Hiteswar Saikia.

BUDGET. The budget estimates for 1995–96 showed receipts of Rs 69,620·6m. and expenditure of Rs 70,845·2m. Plan allocation, 1995-96, Rs 14,180m.

ENERGY AND NATURAL RESOURCES

Electricity. In 1994–95 there was an installed capacity of 577 MW. In Nov. 1994, 21,495 villages (out of 21,995) had electricity. New power stations are under construction at Lakwa, and Karbi-Langpi hydro-electricity project.

Oil and Gas. Assam contains important oilfields and produces about 15% of India's crude oil. Production (1994–95): Crude oil, 5·04m. tonnes (including Nagaland); gas, 1,908m. cu. metres.

Water. In 1989–90, 232,744 ha were irrigated; 2 major and 11 medium projects were in hand.

Minerals. Coal production (1991), 982,000 tonnes. The state also has limestone, refractory clay, dolomite, and corundum.

Agriculture. There are 848 tea plantations, and growing tea is the principal industry. Production in 1990-91, 380m. kg, over 50% of Indian tea. Over 72% of the cultivated area is under food crops, of which the most important is rice. Total foodgrains, 1992–93, 3·45m. tonnes. Main cash crops: Jute, tea, cotton, oilseeds, sugarcane, fruit and potatoes. Wheat production 0·1m. tonnes in 1993–94; rice, 3·36m. tonnes; pulses, 57,000 tonnes. Cattle are important.

Forestry. There are 17,581 sq. km of reserved forests under the administration of the Forest Department and 10,064 sq. km of unclassed forests, altogether about 30% of the total area of the state. Revenue from forests, 1988–89, Rs 148·8m.

INDUSTRY. Sericulture and hand-loom weaving, both silk and cotton, are important home industries together with the manufacture of brass, cane and bamboo articles. The main heavy industry is petro-chemicals; there are 3 oil refineries with 1 under construction in 1994. Other industries include manufacturing paper, nylon, cement, fertilizers, sugar, jute and plywood products, rice and oil milling.

There were 15,392 small businesses in 1990. The state in 1991 ran 480,622 enterprises employing 1·3m. persons.

COMMUNICATIONS

Roads. In March 1992 there were 65,605 km of road maintained by the Public Works Department. There were 2,033 km of national highway in 1990. There were 325,264 motor vehicles in the state in 1992–93.

Railways. The route km of railways in 1993–94 was 2,336 km.

Civil Aviation. Daily scheduled flights connect the principal towns with the rest of India. There are airports at Guwahati, Tezpur, Jorhat, North Lakhimpur, Silchar and Dibrugarh.

Shipping. Water transport is important in Lower Assam; the main waterway is the Brahmaputra River. Cargo carried in 1988–89 was 109,051 tonnes.

SOCIAL INSTITUTIONS

Justice. The seat of the High Court is Guwahati. It has a Chief Justice and 6 puisne judges.

Religion. At the 1991 census Hindus numbered 15,047,293; Moslems, 6,373,204; Christians, 744,367; Buddhists, 64,008; Jains, 20,645; Sikhs, 21,910.

Education. In 1991, 52·89% of the population were literate (61·87% of men and 43·03% of women). In 1994–95 there were 29,173 primary/junior basic schools with 3,777,979 students; 6,729 middle/senior basic schools with 1,291,303 students; 3,793 high/higher secondary schools with 611,890 students. There were 233 colleges for general education, 5 medical colleges, 3 engineering and 1 agricultural, 13 teacher-training colleges, and a fisheries college at Raha. There were 5 universities: Assam Agricultural University, Jorhat; Dibrugarh University, Dibrugarh with 86 colleges and 55,982 students (1992–93); Guwahati University, Guwahati with 128 colleges and 80,363 students (1992–93); and 2 central universities, at Silchar and Tezpur.

Health. In 1994–95 there were 147 hospitals (13,103 beds), 656 primary health centres and 335 dispensaries.

BIHAR

The state contains the ethnic areas of North Bihar, Santhal Pargana and Chota Nagpur. In 1956 certain areas of Purnea and Manbhum districts were transferred to West Bengal.

TERRITORY AND POPULATION. Bihar is in north India and is bounded north by Nepal, east by West Bengal, south by Orissa, south-west by Madhya Pradesh and west by Uttar Pradesh. The area of Bihar is 173,877 sq. km and its population (1991 census), 86,374,465, a density of 497 per sq. km. Growth rate since 1981, 23·54%. Population of principal towns, *see* INDIA: Territory and Population. Other large towns (1991): Muzaffarpur, 241,107; Darbhanga, 218,391; Biharsharif, 201,323; Arrah, 157,082; Dhanbad, 151,789; Munger, 150,112; Chapra, 136,877; Katihar, 154,367; Purnea, 114,912.

The state is divided into 14 divisions covering 55 districts. The capital is Patna.

The official language is Hindi (55·8m. speakers at the 1981 census), the second, Urdu (6·9m.), the third, Bengali (2m.).

CONSTITUTION AND GOVERNMENT. Bihar has a bicameral legislature. The Legislative Assembly consists of 324 elected members and the Council, 96. After the elections in Feb. 1990 the party composition of the Legislative Assembly was: Janata Dal, 128; Congress-I, 72; Bharatiya Janata Party, 30; Communist Party of India, 23; Jharkhand Mukti Morcha, 19; Communist-Marxist, 6; Indian People's Front, 5; Samajwadi Janata Party, 6; Independent and others, 32; vacant, 3. Because of public disturbances the 1995 elections were postponed and direct rule imposed in March 1995.

Governor: A. R. Kidwai.
Chief Minister: Laloo Prasad Yadav.

BUDGET. The budget estimates for 1990–91 show total receipts of Rs 56,256·9m and expenditure of Rs 59,875·9m. Plan allocation, 1995–96, Rs 25,000m.

ENERGY AND NATURAL RESOURCES

Electricity. Installed capacity (1994–95) 1,765 MW. Power generated (1989–90), 3,924m. kWh; there were (Nov. 1994) 47,715 villages with electricity. Hydro-electric projects in hand will add about 149·2MW. capacity.

Minerals. Bihar is very rich in minerals, with about 40% of national production. There are huge deposits of copper, kyanite, coal, mica and china clay. Bihar is a principal producer of iron ore. Other important minerals: Manganese, limestone, graphite, chromite, asbestos, barytes, dolomite, bauxite, uranium ore, feldspar, columbite, pyrites, saltpetre, glass sands, slate, lead, silver, building stones and radio-active minerals. Revenue received from minerals (1994–95) Rs 7,039·3m.

Agriculture. The irrigated area was 4·13m. ha in 1993–94. Cultivable land, 11·6m. ha, of a total area of 17·4m. ha. Total cropped area, 1991–92, 9·79m. ha. Production (1993–94): Rice, 6·06m. tonnes; wheat, 4·32m.; total foodgrains, 12·73m. Other food crops are maize, rabi and pulses. Main cash crops are jute, sugar-cane, oil-seeds, tobacco and potato.

Forests in 1993–94 covered 2·92m. ha. There are 12 protected forests.

INDUSTRY. There are 28 industrial areas and 33 industrial estates. Iron and steel and aluminium are produced and there is an oil refinery. Other important industries are zinc and copper smelting, machine tools, fertilizers, electrical engineering, sugar-milling, paper-milling, silk-spinning, manufacturing explosives, chemicals and cement. There were 85,000 small industries in 1993–94.

TOURISM. The main tourist centres are Bodh Gaya, Patna, Nalanda, Jamshedpur, Sasaram, Hazaribagh, Rajgir, Ranchi and Vaishali.

COMMUNICATIONS

Roads. In March 1992 the state had 85,500 km of roads, including 2,118 km of national highway and 4,192 km of state highway, and 15,520 km of district roads. Passenger transport has been nationalized. There were 1,167,625 motor vehicles registered in March 1993.

Railways. The North Eastern, South Eastern and Eastern railways traverse the state; route-km, 1993–94, 5,288.

Civil Aviation. There are airports at Patna, Jamshedpur, Gaya and Ranchi with regular scheduled services to Calcutta and Delhi.

Shipping. The length of waterways open for navigation is 900 miles.

SOCIAL INSTITUTIONS

Justice. There is a High Court (constituted in 1916) at Patna, and a bench at Ranchi, with a Chief Justice, 25 puisne judges and 4 additional judges.

Police. The police force is under a Director General of Police; in 1990 there were 1,097 police stations.

Religion. At the 1991 census Hindus numbered 71,193,417; Moslems, 12,787,985; Christians, 843,717; Sikhs, 78,212; Jains, 23,049; Buddhists, 3,518.

Education. At the census of 1991 the number of literates was 26·85m. (38·48%: males, 52·49%; females, 22·89%). There were, 1994–95, 4,084 high and higher secondary schools with 940,409 pupils, 13,506 middle schools with 2·25m. pupils and 53,053 primary schools with 9,123,469 pupils. Education is free for children aged 6–11.

There were 10 universities in 1991–92: Patna University (founded 1917) with 18,895 students (1984–85); Bihar University, Muzaffarpur (1952) with 95 colleges, and 84,873 students (1989–90); Bhagalpur University (1960) with 140,718 students (1990–91); Ranchi University (1960) with 106 colleges, 94,683 students (1990–91); Kameswar Singh Darbhanga Sanskrit University (1961); Magadh University, Gaya (1962) with 186 colleges and 161,223 students (1992–93) and Lalit Narayan Mithila University (1972), Darbhanga; Bisra Agricultural University, Ranchi (1980); Rajendra Agricultural University, Samastipur (1970); Nalanda Open University, Nalanda. There were, in 1994–95, 742 degree colleges, 6 engineering colleges, 52 medical colleges and 15 teacher training colleges.

Health. In 1986 there were 1,289 hospitals and dispensaries with 28,997 beds in 1992.

GOA

KEY HISTORICAL EVENTS. The coastal area was captured by the Portuguese in 1510 and the inland area was added in the 18th century. In Dec. 1961 Portuguese rule was ended and Goa incorporated into the Indian Union as a Territory together with Daman and Diu. Goa was granted statehood as a separate unit on 30 May 1987. Daman and Diu remained Union Territories.

TERRITORY AND POPULATION. Goa, bounded on the north by Maharashtra and on the east and south by Karnataka, has a coastline of 105 km. The area is 3,702 sq. km. Population, 1991 census, 1,169,793. Density, 316 per sq. km. Mormugao is the largest town; population (urban agglomeration, 1991) 90,429. The capital is Panaji; population (urban agglomeration 1991) 85,515. The state has 2 districts. There are 183 village Panchayats.The languages spoken are Konkani (official language), Marathi, Hindi and English.

CONSTITUTION AND GOVERNMENT. The Indian Parliament passed legislation in March 1962 by which Goa became a Union Territory with retrospective effect from 20 Dec. 1961. On 30 May 1987 Goa attained statehood. It is represented by 3 elected representatives in Parliament. There is a Legislative Assembly of 40 members. Elections were held in Nov. 1994.

Governor: Romesh Bhandari.
Chief Minister: Pratap Singh Rane.

BUDGET. The total budget for 1992–93 was Rs 5,634·1m. Annual plan 1994–95, Rs 1,820m.

ENERGY AND NATURAL RESOURCES

Electricity. In 1994 installed capacity was 0·16m. MW, but Goa receives most of its power supply from the states of Maharashtra and Karnataka. In Nov. 1994, 377 out of 386 villages were electrified.

Minerals. Resources include bauxite, ferro-manganese ore and iron ore, all of which are exported. Iron ore production (1992–93) 12,435,334 tonnes. There are also reserves of lime stone and clay.

Agriculture. Agriculture is the main occupation, important crops are rice, pulses, ragi, mango, cashew and coconuts. Area under high yielding variety paddy (1992–93) 45,415 ha; production, 210,658 tonnes. Area under pulses 6,440 ha, sugar-cane 1,897 ha, groundnut 952 ha. Total production of foodgrains, 1992–93, 1·5m. tonnes.

Government poultry and dairy farming schemes produced 94m. eggs and 29,000m. litres of milk in 1992–93.

Fisheries. Fish is the state's staple food. In 1992–93 the catch of seafish was 97,017 tonnes (value Rs 354,566,000). There is a coastline of about 104 km and about 3,750 active fishing vessels.

INDUSTRY. In 1992–93 there were 52 large and medium industrial projects and 5,242 small units registered. Production included: Nylon fishing nets, ready made clothing, electronic goods, pesticides, pharmaceuticals, tyres, footwear, fertilizers, automotive components and shipbuilding.

In 1992-93, the 5,242 small-scale industry units employed 32,597 persons.

COMMUNICATIONS

Roads. In 1993-94 there were 7,419 km of roads (National Highway, 224 km). There were 159,414 motor vehicles in March 1993.

Railways. In 1993–94 there were 79 km. of route.

Civil Aviation. An airport at Dabolim is connected with Bombay, Delhi and Bangalore.

Shipping. There are seaports at Panaji, Marmugao and Margao.

SOCIAL INSTITUTIONS

Justice. There is a bench of the Bombay High Court at Panaji.

Religion. At the 1991 census Hindus numbered 756,651; Christians, 349,225; Moslems, 61,455; Sikhs, 1,087.

Education. In 1991, 75·51% of the population were literate (83·64% of men and 67·09% of women). In 1994-95 there were 1,021 primary schools (128,465 students), 113 middle schools (41,029 students) and 422 high and higher secondary schools (66,112 students). There were also 2 engineering colleges, 3 medical colleges, 2 teacher-training colleges, 20 other colleges and 4 polytechnic institutes. Goa University, Taleigao (1985) had 30 colleges and 15,454 students in 1992–93.

Health. There were (1992-93) 129 hospitals (4,232 beds), 256 rural medical dispensaries, health and sub-health centres and 268 family planning units.

Hutt, A., *Goa: A Traveller's Historical and Architectural Guide*. Buckhurst Hill, 1988

GUJARAT

KEY HISTORICAL EVENTS. On 1 May 1960, as a result of the Bombay Reorganization Act, 1960, the state of Gujarat was formed from the north and west (predominantly Gujarati-speaking) portion of Bombay State, the remainder being renamed the state of Maharashtra. Gujarat consists of the following districts of the former state of Bombay: Banas Kantha, Mehsana, Sabar Kantha, Ahmedabad, Kaira, Panch Mahals, Vadodara, Bharuch, Surat, Dang, Amreli, Surendranagar, Rajkot, Jamnagar, Junagadh, Bhavnagar, Kutch, Gandhinagar and Bulsar.

TERRITORY AND POPULATION. Gujarat is in western India and is bounded in the north by Pakistan and Rajasthan, east by Madhya Pradesh, south-east by Maharashtra, south and west by the Indian ocean and Arabian sea. The area of the state is 196,024 sq. km and the population at the 1991 census was 41,309,582; a density of 211 per sq. km. Growth rate 1981–91, 21·19%. The chief cities, *see* INDIA: Territory and Population. Other important towns (1991) are: Nadiad (167,051), Bharuch (133,102), Junagadh (130,484), Navsari (126,089), Gandhinagar (123,359), Porbandar (116,671), Anand (110,266), Gandhidham (104,585), Bhuj (102,376). Gujarati and Hindi in the Devanagari script are the official languages.

CONSTITUTION AND GOVERNMENT. Gujarat has a unicameral legislature, the *Legislative Assembly*, which has 182 elected members. After the elections in Feb. 1995 the Bharatiya Janata Party came to power. Party composition of the Legislative Assembly: Bharatiya Janata Party, 121 seats; Congress (I), 45; independents and others, 16.

The capital is Gandhinagar. There are 19 districts.
Governor: Naresh Chandra.
Chief Minister: Suresh Mehta.

BUDGET. The budget estimates for 1995–96 showed revenue receipts of Rs 80,699·4m. and revenue expenditure of Rs 81,955·3m. Plan outlay for 1995–96, Rs 26,100m.

ENERGY AND NATURAL RESOURCES

Electricity. In March 1995 the total capacity was 6,241 MW of electricity. In March 1992, 17,985 villages out of 18,114 were electrified.

Oil and Gas. There are large crude oil and gas reserves. Production, 1993–94: Crude oil, 5·91m. tonnes; gas, 1,693m. cu. metres.

Water. Water resources are limited. In 1995 irrigation potential was 6·49m. ha.

Minerals. Chief minerals produced in 1993–94 (in tonnes) included lime stone (9·16m.), agate stone (700), calcite (555), quartz and silica (98,000), bauxite (618,800), crude china clay (32,689), refined china clays (10,038), dolomite (311,100), crude fluorite (120,524), calcareous and sea sand (153,000) and lignite (3·88m.). Value of production (1993–94) Rs 22,236m. Reserves of coal lie under the Kalol and Mehsana oil and gas fields. The deposit, mixed with crude petroleum, is estimated at 100,000m. tonnes.

Agriculture. 3·42m. ha of the cropped area was irrigated in June 1994.

Production of principal crops, 1993–94: Rice, 0·84m. tonnes from 598,000 ha; foodgrains, 3·8m. tonnes (wheat, 0·93m. tonnes); pulses, 538,000 tonnes; cotton, 1·62m. bales of 170 kg. Tobacco and groundnuts are important cash crops.

Livestock (1992): Buffaloes, 5·27m.; other cattle, 6·8m.; sheep and goats, 6·25m.; horses and ponies (1988), 16,015.

Fisheries. There were (1993) 115,265 people engaged in fisheries. There were 18,935 fishing vessels (10,488 motor vessels). The catch for 1994–95 was 0·7m. tonnes.

INDUSTRY. Gujarat is one of the 4 most industrialized states. In 1994 there were 163,592 small-scale units and (1993) 16,000 factories including 1,185 cotton textile factories, 1,915 chemical and chemical products factories, 1,760 non-metallic mineral products factories, 1,480 machinery, machine tools and parts factories and 905 rubber, plastic, petroleum and coal products factories. There were 167 industrial estates in 1992–93. Principal industries are textiles, general and electrical engineering, oil-refining, fertilizers, petrochemicals, machine tools, heavy chemicals, pharmaceuticals, dyes, sugar, soda ash, cement, man-made fibres, salt, sulphuric acid, paper and paperboard.

State production of soda-ash is 90·4% of national output, and of salt, about 60%. Salt production (1993) 8·9m. tonnes; cement, 4·19m. tonnes.

COMMUNICATIONS

Roads. In 1994-95 there were 70,609 km of roads. Gujarat State Transport Corporation operated 18,185 routes. Number of vehicles, 3,021,166.

Railways. In 1993–94 the state had 5,281 route km of railway line.

Civil Aviation. Ahmedabad is the main airport. There are regular services between Ahmedabad and Bombay, Jaipur and Delhi. There are 9 other airports: Bhavnagar, Bhuj, Jamnagar, Kandla, Keshod, Porbandar, Rajkot, Surat and Vadodara.

Shipping. The largest port is Kandla. There are 40 other ports, 11 intermediate, 29 minor.

Telecommunications. There were (1993–94) 8,948 post offices, 1,770 telegraph offices. There were 658,224 telephone connexions in the state.

SOCIAL INSTITUTIONS

Justice. The High Court of Judicature at Ahmedabad has a Chief Justice and 29 puisne judges.

Religion. At the 1991 census Hindus numbered 36,964,228; Moslems, 3,606,920; Jains, 491,331, Christians, 181,753; Sikhs, 33,044; Buddhists, 11,615.

Education. In 1991 the number of literates was 21·28m. (60·91%; male, 72·45%, female 48·5%). Primary and secondary education up to Standard XI are free. Education above Standard XII is free for girls. In 1994–95 there were 14,338 primary schools with 6·27m. students, 18,943 middle schools with 1,878,539 students and 5,639 secondary schools (including 1,961 higher secondary schools) with 1,410,700 students.

There are 10 universities in the state. Gujarat University, Ahmedabad, founded in 1950, is teaching and affiliating; it has 119 affiliated colleges. The Maharaja Sayajirao University of Vadodara (1949) is residential and teaching; it has 3 colleges and 32,498 students (1992–93). The Sardar Patel University, Vallabh-Vidyanagar, (1955) has 20 constituent and affiliated colleges; Saurashtra University at Rajkot (1968) has 87 affiliated colleges and 70,044 students (1992–93); South Gujarat University at Surat (1967) has 53 colleges. Bhavnagar University (1978) is residential and teaching with 12 affiliated colleges. North Gujarat University was established at Patan in 1986 and has 20 colleges. Gujarat Vidyapith at Ahmedabad is deemed a university under the University Grants Commission Act. There are also Gujarat Agricultural University, Banaskantha and Gujarat Ayurved University, Jamnagar.

There are 3 engineering colleges, 29 polytechnics, 20 medical colleges and 6 agricultural colleges. There are also 285 arts, science and commerce colleges, 42 teacher-training colleges and 32 law colleges. There were 0·4m. students enrolled in 1993–94 in all colleges.

Health. In 1993 there were 2,388 hospitals (59,777 beds), 993 primary health centres and 7,284 sub-centres. In 1991, 10,626 medical institutions treated 36·35m. patients.

Desai, I. F., *Untouchability in Rural Gujarat.* Bombay, 1977

HARYANA

KEY HISTORICAL EVENTS. The state of Haryana, created on 1 Nov. 1966 under the Punjab Reorganization Act, 1966, was formed from the Hindi-speaking parts of the state of Punjab (India). It comprises the districts of Hissar, Mahendragarh, Gurgaon, Rohtak, Yamunanagar, Rewari, Kaithal, Karnal; Bhiwani, Faridabad, Jind, Kurukshetra, Sirsa, Sonipat, Ambala.

TERRITORY AND POPULATION. Haryana is in north India and is bounded north by Himachal Pradesh, east by Uttar Pradesh, south and west by Rajasthan and north-west by Punjab. Delhi forms an enclave on its eastern boundary. The state has an area of 44,212 sq. km and a population (1991) of 16,463,648; density, 372 per sq. km. Growth rate, 1981–91, 27·41%. Principal cities, *see* INDIA: Territory and Population. Other large towns (1991) are: Rohtak (216,096), Panipat (191,212), Hisar (181,255), Karnal (173,751), Yamunanagar (144,346), Sonipat (143,922), Ambala (139,889), Gurgaon (135,884), Bhiwani (121,629), Sirsa (112,841). The principal language is Hindi.

CONSTITUTION AND GOVERNMENT. The state has a unicameral legislature with 90 members. In Nov. 1991 Congress (I) held 51 seats; Janata Dal (S), 16; Haryana Vikas Party, 12; Janata Dal, 3; Bharatiya Janata, 2; others, 6. The state shares with Punjab (India) a High Court, a university and certain public services. The capital (shared with Punjab) is Chandigarh. Its transfer to Punjab, intended for 1986, has been postponed. There are 17 districts.

Governor: Mahabir Prasad.
Chief Minister: Bhajan Lal.

BUDGET. Budget estimates for 1994–95 show revenue income of Rs 43,058m. and revenue expenditure of Rs 48,181m. Annual plan 1995–96, Rs 12,500m.

ENERGY AND NATURAL RESOURCES

Electricity. Approximately 1,000 MW are supplied to Haryana, mainly from the Bhakra Nangal system. In 1994–95 installed capacity was 2,347 MW and all the villages had electric power.

Minerals. Minerals include placer gold, barytes and rare earths. Value of production, 1987–88, Rs 40m.

Agriculture. Haryana has sandy soil and erratic rainfall, but the state shares the benefit of the Sutlej-Beas scheme. Agriculture employs over 82% of the working population; in 1981 there were about 0·9m. holdings (average 3·7 ha), and the gross irrigated area was 2·05m. ha in 1993–94. Area under high yielding varieties of foodgrains, 1994–95, 2·8m. ha. Foodgrain production was 10·25m. tonnes (rice 2·06m. tonnes, wheat 7·23m. tonnes) in 1993–94; pulses, 469,400 tonnes; cotton, 1·37m. bales of 170 kg; sugar (gur) and oilseeds are important.

Forests cover 3·3% of the state.

INDUSTRY. Haryana has a large market for consumer goods in neighbouring Delhi. In 1994–95 there were 756 large and medium scale industries and 125,975 small units providing employment to 0·93m. persons, and 51,566 rural industrial units. The main industries are cotton textiles, agricultural machinery and tractors, woollen textiles, scientific instruments, glass, cement, paper and sugar milling, cars, tyres and tubes, motor cycles, bicycles, steel tubes, engineering goods, electrical and electronic goods. An oil refinery is being set up at Panipat.

COMMUNICATIONS

Roads. There were (1994–95) 23,168 km of metalled roads, linking all villages. Road transport is nationalized. There were 748,720 motor vehicles in 1992–93. In 1993–94 road transport carried 2·1m. passengers daily with a fleet of 3,716 buses.

Railways. The state is crossed by lines from Delhi to Agra, Ajmer, Ferozepur and Chandigarh. Route km, 1993–94, 1,499. The main stations are at Ambala and Kurukshetra.

Civil Aviation. There is no airport within the state but Delhi is on its eastern boundary.

SOCIAL INSTITUTIONS

Justice. Haryana shares the High Court of Punjab and Haryana at Chandigarh.

Religion. At the 1991 census Hindus numbered 14,686,512; Moslems, 763,775; Sikhs, 956,836; Christians, 15,699; Jains, 35,296.

Education. In 1991 the number of literates was 7·43m. (55·85%); 69·1% of men and 40·47% of women. In 1994–95 there were 5,659 primary schools with 2,283,000 students, 2,639 high and higher secondary schools with 353,385 students, 1,425 middle schools with 516,000 students and 128 colleges of arts, science and commerce, 4 engineering colleges and 5 medical colleges. There are 3 universities: Haryana Agricultural University, Hisar; Kurukshetra University, Kurukshetra with 72 colleges and 52,939 students (1992–93), and Maharshi Dayanand University, Rohtak.

Health. There were (1994–95) 78 hospitals (11,061 beds), 59 community health centres and dispensaries, 398 primary health centres and 2,299 sub-centres, and 445 Ayurvedic and Unani institutions.

HIMACHAL PRADESH

KEY HISTORICAL EVENTS. The territory came into being on 15 April 1948 and comprised 30 former Hill States. The state of Bilaspur was merged with Himachal Pradesh in 1954. The 6 districts were: Mahasu, Sirmour, Mandi, Chamba, Bilaspur and Kinnaur. On 1 Nov. 1966, under the Punjab Reorganization Act, 1966, certain parts of the State of Punjab (India) were transferred to Himachal Pradesh. These comprise the districts of Shimla, Kullu, Kangra, and Lahaul and Spiti; and parts of Hoshiarpur, Ambala and Gurdaspur districts.

TERRITORY AND POPULATION. Himachal Pradesh is in north India and is bounded north by Kashmir, east by Tibet, south-east by Uttar Pradesh, south by Haryana, south-west and west by Punjab. The area of the state is 55,673 sq. km and it had a population at the 1991 census of 5,170,877. Density, 93 per sq. km. Growth rate, 1981–91, 20·79%. Principal languages are Hindi and Pahari. The capital is Shimla, population (1991 census) of the urban agglomeration, 110,360.

CONSTITUTION AND GOVERNMENT. Full statehood was attained, as the 18th State of the Union, on 25 Jan. 1971. On 1 Sept. 1972 districts were reorganized and 3 new districts created, Solan, Hamirpur and Una, making a total of 12.

There is a unicameral *Legislative Assembly.* After the elections in Nov. 1993 a Congress-I government came to power. Total seats, 68: Congress-I, 52; Bharatiya Janata Party, 8; others, 8.

Governor: Sheila Kaul.

Chief Minister: Virbhadra Singh.

BUDGET. Budget estimates for 1994–95 showed receipts of Rs 15,201·1m. and expenditure of Rs 19,909·8m. Annual plan, 1995–96, Rs 7,500m.

ENERGY AND NATURAL RESOURCES

Electricity. In 1991, all the 16,807 villages had electricity. Installed capacity (1994–95), 272·34 MW. Electricity generated (1993–94), 1,087m. kWh.

Water. An artificial confluence of the Sutlej and Beas rivers has been made, directing their united flow into Govind Sagar Lake. Other major rivers are Ravi, Chenab and Yamuna.

Minerals. The state has rock salt, slate, gypsum, limestone, barytes, dolomite and pyrites.

Agriculture. Farming employs 71% of the people. Irrigated area is 17% of the area sown. There are 1,660 tea planters cultivating 2,000 ha. Main crops are seed potatoes, wheat, maize, rice and fruits such as apples, peaches, apricots, nuts, pomegranates; 0·56m. tonnes of fruits were produced in 1993–94.

Production (1993–94): Rice, 101,900 tonnes; wheat, 414,900 tonnes; pulses, 10,800 tonnes. Total foodgrains, 1·24m. tonnes.

Livestock (1992 census): Buffaloes, 701,000; other cattle, 2,152,000; goats and sheep, 2·19m.

Forestry. (1992) Himachal Pradesh forests cover 39·5% of the state and supply the largest quantities of coniferous timber in northern India. The forests also ensure the safety of the catchment areas of the Yamuna, Sutlej, Beas, Ravi and Chenab rivers. Commercial felling of green trees has been totally halted and forest working nationalized. Area under forests in 1991–92, 37,591 sq. km, of which 1,896 sq. km are reserved and 33,350 sq. km are protected.

INDUSTRY. The main sources of employment are the forests and their related industries; there are factories making turpentine and rosin. The state also makes fertilizers, cement, electronic items and TV sets. There is a foundry and a brewery. Other industries include salt production and handicrafts, including weaving. The state has 142 large and medium units, 23,265 small scale units, 5 industrial estates, 10 industrial areas and 7 electronic complexes.

COMMUNICATIONS

Roads. The national highway from Chandigarh runs through Shimla; other main highways from Shimla serve Kullu, Manali, Kangra, Chamba and Pathankot. The rest are minor roads. Pathankot is also on national highways from Punjab to Kashmir. Length of roads (March 1993), 23,353 km; number of vehicles (1992–93), 82,684; number of transport buses (1993–94), 1,598.

Railways. There is a line from Chandigarh to Shimla, and the Jammu-Delhi line runs through Pathankot. A Nangal-Talwara rail link has been approved by the central government. There are 2 narrow gauge lines, from Shimla to Kalka (96 km) and Jogindernagar to Pathankot (113 km), and a broad gauge line from Una to Nangal (16 km). Route-km in 1993–94, 267 km.

Civil Aviation. The state has airports at Bhuntar near Kullu, at Jubbarhatti near Shimla and at Gaggal in Kangra district.

SOCIAL INSTITUTIONS

Justice. The state has its own High Court at Shimla.

Religion. At the 1991 census Hindus numbered 4,958,560; Moslems, 89,134; Sikhs, 52,050; Buddhists, 64,081; Christians, 4,435.

Education. In 1991, 63·86% of the population were literate (75·36% of men and 52·32% of women). There were (1994–95) 7,611 primary schools with 720,980 students, 1,015 middle schools with 222,340 students, 1,059 high and higher secondary schools with 156,540 students, 51 (including 18 private) arts, science and commerce colleges, 1 engineering college, 2 medical colleges, 1 teacher training college and 3 universities. The universities are Himachal Pradesh University, Shimla (1970) with 48 affiliated colleges and 32,773 students (1992–93), Himachal Pradesh Agricultural University, Palampur (1978) and Dr Y. S. Parmar University of Horticulture and Forestry, Solan (1985).

Health. There were (1993–94) 69 hospitals (8,663 beds), 263 primary health centres and 1,831 sub-health centres, and 704 allopathic and Ayurvedic dispensaries.

JAMMU AND KASHMIR

KEY HISTORICAL EVENTS. The state of Jammu and Kashmir, which had earlier been under Hindu rulers and Moslem sultans, became part of the Mogul Empire under Akbar from 1586. After a period of Afghan rule from 1756, it was annexed by the Sikh rulers of the Punjab in 1819. In 1820 Ranjit Singh made over the territory of Jammu to Gulab Singh. After the decisive battle of Sobraon in 1846 Kashmir also was made over to Gulab Singh under the Treaty of Amritsar. British supremacy was recognized until the Indian Independence Act, 1947, when all states decided on accession to India or Pakistan. Kashmir asked for standstill agreements with both. Pakistan agreed, but India desired further discussion with the Government of Jammu and Kashmir State. In the meantime the state became subject to armed attack from the territory of Pakistan and the Maharajah acceded to India on 26 Oct. 1947, by signing the Instrument of Accession. India approached the UN in Jan. 1948; India-Pakistan conflict ended by ceasefire in Jan. 1949. Further conflict in 1965 was followed by the Tashkent Declaration of Jan. 1966. Following further hostilities between India and Pakistan a ceasefire came into effect on 17 Dec. 1971, followed by the Simla Agreement in July 1972, whereby a new line of control was delineated bilaterally through negotiations between India and Pakistan and came into force on 17 Dec. 1972.

TERRITORY AND POPULATION. The state is in the extreme north and is bounded north by China, east by Tibet, south by Himachal Pradesh and Punjab and west by Pakistan. The area is 222,236 sq. km, of which about 78,932 sq. km is occupied by Pakistan and 42,735 sq. km by China; the population of the territory on the Indian side of the line, 1991 projection, was 7,718,700. Growth rate, 1981–91, 28·92%. Srinagar (population, 1991, 892,506) is the summer and Jammu (1,207,996) the winter capital. The official language is Urdu; other commonly spoken languages are Kashmiri (3·1m. speakers at 1981 census), Hindi (1m.), Dogri, Gujri, Pahari, Ladakhi and Punjabi.

CONSTITUTION AND GOVERNMENT. The Maharajah's son, Yuvraj Karan Singh, took over as Regent in 1950 and, on the ending of hereditary rule (17 Oct. 1952), was sworn in as Sadar-i-Riyasat. On his father's death (26 April 1961) Yuvraj Karan Singh was recognized as Maharajah by the Indian Government.

The permanent Constitution of the state came into force in part on 17 Nov. 1956 and fully on 26 Jan. 1957. There is a bicameral legislature; the Legislative Council has 36 members and the Legislative Assembly has 87. Since the 1967 elections the 6 representatives of Jammu and Kashmir in the central House of the People are directly elected; there are 4 representatives in the Council of States. After a period of President's rule, a National Conference–Indira Congress coalition government was formed in March 1987. The government was dismissed and the state was brought under President's rule on 18 July 1990.

The state has 14 districts.

Governor: Gen. K. V. Krishna Rao.

Chief Minister: (Vacant).

BUDGET. Budget estimates for 1994-95 show revenue receipts of Rs 30,268·7m. and revenue expenditure of Rs 23,244m. Annual Plan (1995–96) Rs 10,500m.

ENERGY AND NATURAL RESOURCES

Electricity. Installed capacity (1994–95) 387·3 MW; 6,149 villages had electricity in 1994–95.

Minerals. Minerals include coal, bauxite and gypsum.

Agriculture. About 80% of the population are supported by agriculture. Rice, wheat and maize are the major cereals. The total area under foodgrains (1992–93) was estimated at 878,400 ha. Total foodgrains produced, 1994–95, 1·97m. tonnes (rice, 0·78m. tonnes; wheat, 0·4m. tonnes); pulses, 78,000 tonnes. Fruit is important: Production, 1993–94, 934,000 tonnes; exports, 0·76m. tonnes.

Irrigated area, 1993–94, 442,000 ha.

Livestock (1982): Cattle, 2,325,200; buffaloes, 5,631,000; goats, 1,003,900; sheep, 1,908,700; horses, 973,000, and poultry, 2,406,760.

Forestry. Forests cover about 20,182 sq. km., forming an important source of revenue, besides providing employment to a large section of the population. About 20,174 sq. km of forests yield valuable timber; state income in 1985–86 was Rs 477m.

INDUSTRY. There are 2 central public sector industries and 30 medium-scale. There are 35,576 small units (1994–95) employing over 125,000. There are industries based on horticulture, traditional handicrafts are silk spinning, wood-carving, papier-maché and carpet-weaving. 750 tonnes of silk cocoons were produced in 1994–95.

The handicraft sector employed 0·26m. persons and had a production turnover of Rs 2,450m. in 1994–95.

COMMUNICATIONS

Roads. Kashmir is linked with the rest of India by the motorable Jammu-Pathankot road. The Jawahar Tunnel, through the Banihal mountain, connects Srinagar and Jammu, and maintains road communication with the Kashmir Valley during the winter months. In 1994–95 there were 12,252 km of roads.

There were 149,882 motor vehicles in 1992–93.

Railways. Kashmir is linked with the Indian railway system by the line between Jammu and Pathankot; route km of railways in the state, 1993–94, 88 km.

Civil Aviation. Major airports, with daily service from Delhi, are at Srinagar and Jammu. There is a third airport at Leh.

Telecommunications. There were 1,583 post offices in 1994, 197 telephone exchanges and 48,962 telephones.

SOCIAL INSTITUTIONS

Justice. The High Court, at Srinagar and Jammu, has a Chief Justice and 4 puisne judges.

Religion. The majority of the population, except in Jammu, are Moslems. At the 1981 census Moslems numbered 3,843,451; Hindus, 1,930,448; Sikhs, 133,675; Buddhists, 69,706; Christians, 8,481; Jains, 1,576.

Education. The proportion of literates was 32·68% in 1991 (44·18% of men and 19·55% of women). Education is free. There were (1994–95) 1,278 high and higher secondary schools with 188,960 students, 2,668 middle schools with 338,815 students and 9,784 primary schools with 823,253 students. Jammu University (1969) has 5 constituent and 13 affiliated colleges, with 15,278 students (1992-93); Kashmir University (1948) has 18 colleges (17,000 students, 1992–93); the third university is Sher-E-Kashmir University of Agricultural Sciences and Technology. There are 3 medical colleges, 2 engineering and technology colleges, 4 polytechnics, 8 oriental colleges and an Ayurvedic college, 35 arts, science and commerce colleges and 4 teacher training colleges.

Health. In 1993-94 there were 43 hospitals with 9,256 beds, 264 primary health centres and 1,740 sub-centres, and 35 community health centres. There is a National Institute of Medical Sciences.

Lamb, A., *Kashmir: a Disputed Legacy, 1846–1990.* Hertingfordbury, 1991.

Wirsing, R. G., *India, Pakistan and the Kashmir Dispute: on Regional Conflict and its Resolution.* London, 1995

KARNATAKA

KEY HISTORICAL EVENTS. The state of Karnataka, constituted as Mysore under the States Reorganization Act, 1956, brought together the Kannada-speaking people distributed in 5 states, and consisted of the territories of the old states of Mysore and Coorg, the Bijapur, Kanara and Dharwar districts and the Belgaum district (except one taluk) in former Bombay, the major portions of the Gulbarga, Raichur and Bidar districts in former Hyderabad, the South Kanara district (apart from the Kasaragod taluk) and the Kollegal taluk of the Coimbatore district in Madras. The state was renamed Karnataka in 1973.

TERRITORY AND POPULATION. The state is in south India and is bounded north by Maharashtra, east by Andhra Pradesh, south by Tamil Nadu and Kerala, west by the Indian ocean and north-east by Goa. The area of the state is 191,791 sq. km, and its population (1991 census), 44,977,201, an increase of 21·82% since 1981. Density, 235 per sq. km. The state has 21 districts grouped in 4 divisions: Bangalore, Belgaum, Gulbarga and Mysore. The capital is Bangalore. Principal cities, *see* India: Territory and Population. Other large towns (1991) are: Bellary (245,391), Bijapur (186,939), Shimoga (178,882), Raichur (157,551), Timkur (138,903), Gadag-Betigeri (134,051), Mandya (120,265), Hospet (114,154), Bidar (108,016).

Kannada is the language of administration and is spoken by about 66% of the people. Other languages include Telugu (8·17%), Urdu (9%), Marathi (4·5%), Tamil (3·6%), Tulu and Konkani.

CONSTITUTION AND GOVERNMENT. Karnataka has a bicameral legislature. The Legislative Council has 75 members. The Legislative Assembly consists of 224 elected members. At the elections in Nov. 1994 the Janata Dal gained 116 seats; the Bharatiya Janata Party, 40; Congress I, 35; the Karnataka Congress Party, 10; independents and others, 23. Janata Dal formed a government.

The state has 21 districts (of which Bangalore Rural is one) in 4 divisions: Bangalore, Mysore, Belgaum and Gulbarga. The capital is Bangalore.

Governor: Khurshid Alam Khan.
Chief Minister: Haradanahalli Doddegowda Deve Gowda.

BUDGET. Budget estimates, 1995–96: Revenue receipts, Rs 88,799·7m.; revenue expenditure, Rs 90,936·3m. Plan allocation 1995–96, Rs 35,750m.

ENERGY AND NATURAL RESOURCES

Electricity. In 1994-95 the state's installed capacity was 3,376 MW. Electricity generated, 1992–93, 12,431m. kWh. 26,483 villages had electricity in Nov. 1994.

Water. About 2,113,100 ha were irrigated in 1991–92.

Minerals. Karnataka is an important source of gold and silver. The estimated reserves of high grade iron ore are 8,798m. tonnes. These reserves are found mainly in the Chitradurga belt. The National Mineral Development Corporation of India has indicated total reserves of nearly 332m. tonnes of magnesite and iron ore (with an iron content ranging from 25 to 40) which have been found in Kudremukh Ganga-Mula region in Chickmagalur District. Value of production (1992–93) Rs 2,590m. The estimated reserves of manganese are over 320m. tonnes.

Limestone is found in many regions; deposits (1992-93) are about 5,892m. tonnes.

Karnataka is the largest producer of chromite. It is one of the only two states of India producing magnesite. The other minerals of industrial importance are corundum and garnet.

Agriculture. Agriculture forms the main occupation of more than three-quarters of the population. Physically, Karnataka divides into 4 regions—the coastal region, the southern and northern plains, comprising roughly the districts of Bangalore, Tumkur, Chitradurga, Kolar, Bellary, Mandya and Mysore, and the hill country, comprising the districts of Chickmagalur, Hassan and Shimoga. Rainfall is heavy in the hill country, and there is dense forest. The greater part of the plains are cultivated. Coorg district is essentially agricultural.

The main food crops are rice paddy and jowar, and ragi which is also about 30% of the national crop. Total foodgrains production (1993–94), 8·46m. tonnes (rice 3·14m. tonnes, wheat 178,600 tonnes); pulses 0·6m. tonnes. Sugar, groundnut, castor-seed, safflower, mulberry silk and cotton are important cash crops. The state grows about 70% of the national coffee crop.

Production, 1992–93: Sugar-cane, 21,598 tonnes; cotton, 975,100 bales (each 170 kg).

Livestock (1992–93): Buffaloes, 4·07m.; other cattle, 10·18m.; sheep, 4·73m.; goats, 3·89m.

Forestry. Total forest in the state (1992–93) is 3,075,000 ha, producing sandalwood, bamboo and other timbers.

Fisheries. Production, 1992–93, 239,900 tonnes.

INDUSTRY. There were 7,089 factories, 105 industrial estates and 4,585 industrial sheds employing 760,200 in March 1992. In 1994–95, 163,524 small industries employed 1,076,312 persons. The Vishveshwaraiah Iron and Steel Works is situated at Bhadravati, while at Bangalore are national undertakings for the manufacture of aircraft, machine tools, telephones, light engineering and electronics goods. The Kudremukh iron ore project is of national importance. An oil refinery was under construction at Mangalore in 1995. Other industries include textiles, vehicle manufacture, cement, chemicals, sugar, paper, porcelain and soap. In addition, much of the world's sandalwood is processed, the oil being one of the most valuable productions of the state. Sericulture is a more important cottage industry giving employment, directly or indirectly, to about 2·7m. persons; production of raw silk, 1992–93, 7,147 tonnes, over two-thirds of national production.

COMMUNICATIONS

Roads. In 1991–92 the state had 129,849 km of roads, including 2,000 km of national highway. There were (31 March 1993) 1,718,494 motor vehicles.

Railways. In 1993–94 there were 3,078 km of railway (including 148 km of narrow gauge) in the state.

Civil Aviation. There are airports at Bangalore, Hubli, Mysore, Mangalore, Bellary and Belgaum, with regular scheduled services to Bombay, Calcutta, Delhi and Madras.

Shipping. Mangalore is a deep-water port for the export of mineral ores. Karwar is being developed as an intermediate port.

SOCIAL INSTITUTIONS

Justice. The seat of the High Court is at Bangalore. It has a Chief Justice and 21 puisne judges.

Religion. At the 1991 census there were 38,432,027 Hindus; 5,234,023 Moslems; 859,478 Christians; 326,114 Jains; 73,012 Buddhists; 10,101 Sikhs.

Education. The number of literates, according to the 1991 census, was 21·08m. (56·04%; 67·26% of men and 44·34% of women). In 1994–95 the state had 22,768 primary schools with 6,302,041 students, 18,916 middle schools with 2,137,925 students, 6,853 high and higher secondary schools with 1,127,058 students, 186 polytechnic and 18 medical colleges, 52 engineering and technology colleges, 617 arts, science and commerce colleges and 10 universities. Education is free up to pre-university level.

Universities: Mysore (1916); Karnataka (1949) at Dharwar; University of Agricultural Sciences (1964) at Hebbal, Bangalore; Gulbarga; Mangalore; University of Agricultural Sciences, Dharwad; Kuvempu University, Shimoga. Mysore has 6 university and 117 affiliated colleges; Karnataka, 5 and 115; Bangalore, 126 affiliated; Hebbal, 8 constituent colleges.

The Indian Institute of Science, Bangalore, has the status of a university.

Health. There were in 1992–93, 293 hospitals, 208 dispensaries, 1,297 primary health centres and 474 family welfare centres. Total number of beds in 1991–92, 49,929.

KERALA

KEY HISTORICAL EVENTS. The state of Kerala, created under the States Reorganization Act, 1956, consists of the previous state of Travancore-Cochin, except for 4 regions of the Thiruvananthapuram district and a part of the Shencottah region of Kollam (Quilon) district. It took over the Malabar district (apart from the Laccadive and Minicoy Islands) and the Kasaragod region of South Kanara (apart from the Amindivi Islands) from Madras State.

TERRITORY AND POPULATION. Kerala is in south India and is bounded north by Karnataka, east and south-east by Tamil Nadu, south-west and west by the Indian ocean. The state has an area of 38,863 sq. km. The 1991 census showed a population of 29,098,518; density of population was 749 per sq. km. Growth rate, 1981–91, 14·32%. Chief cities, *see* INDIA: Territory and Population. Other principal towns (1991): Alappuzha (174,666), Kollam (139,852), Palakkad (123,289), Thalassery (103,577).

Languages spoken in the state are Malayalam, Tamil and Kannada.

CONSTITUTION AND GOVERNMENT. The state has a unicameral legislature of 140 elected (and one nominated) members including the Speaker. After the elections of June 1991 the Indian National Congress (I) Party and allies held 90 seats, the Left Front (CPI, CPI (M) and allies), 50.

The state has 14 districts. The capital is Thiruvananthapuram.

Governor: P. Shiv Shanker.
Chief Minister: A. K. Anthony.

BUDGET. Budget estimates for 1995–96 showed total receipts of Rs 49,287m. expenditure Rs 57,772m. Annual Plan expenditure, 1995–96, Rs 15,500m.

ENERGY AND NATURAL RESOURCES

Electricity. Installed capacity (1994), 1,491·5 MW; energy generated in 1993–94 was 5,882m. kWh. The Idukki hydro-electric plant produced 2,580m. kWh, the Sabarigiri scheme 1,433m. kWh in 1993–94. All villages are electrified.

Minerals. The beach sands of Kerala contain monazite, ilmenite, rutile, zircon, sillimanite, etc. There are extensive whiteclay deposits; other minerals of commercial importance include magnesite, china clay, limestone, quartz sand and lignite. Iron ore has been found at Kozhikode (Calicut).

Agriculture. Area under irrigation in 1993–94 was 611,000 ha; 15 irrigation projects were under execution in 1993–94. The chief agricultural products are rice, tapioca, coconut, arecanut, cashewnut, oilseeds, pepper, sugar-cane, rubber, tea, coffee and cardamom. About 98% of Indian black pepper and about 95% of Indian rubber is produced in Kerala. Production of principal crops, 1993–94: Total foodgrains, 1·1m. tonnes (of which rice 1,072,509 tonnes from 530,332 ha); pulses, 15,898 tonnes; sugar-cane (1992–93), 42,578 tonnes; rubber, 408,311 tonnes.

Livestock (1987); Buffaloes, 329,000; other cattle, 3·4m.; goats, 1·6m. In 1993–94 milk production was 2m. tonnes; egg production, 1,844m.

Forestry. Forest occupied 11,241·97 sq. km in 1993–94, including teak, sandal wood, ebony and blackwood and varieties of softwood. Net forest revenue, 1993–94, Rs 1,029·5m.

Fisheries. Fishing is a flourishing industry; the catch (marine) in 1993 was 574,739 tonnes. Fish exports, 63,809 tonnes in 1993–94.

INDUSTRY. There are numerous cashew and coir factories. Important industries are rubber, tea, tiles, automotive tyres, watches, electronics, oil, textiles, ceramics, fertilizers and chemicals, pharmaceuticals, zinc-smelting, sugar, cement, rayon, glass, matches, pencils, monazite, ilmenite, titanium oxide, rare earths, aluminium, electrical goods, paper, shark-liver oil, etc. The state has a refinery and a shipyard at Kochi (Cochin).

The number of factories registered under the Factories Act 1948 on 31 Dec. 1993 was 14,399, with daily average employment of 413,000. There were 95,851 small-scale units employing 568,598 persons on 31 March 1993.

COMMUNICATIONS

Roads. In 1993–94 there were 141,010 km of roads in the state; national highways, 839 km. There were 887,672 motor vehicles at 31 March 1994.

Railways. There is a coastal line from Mangalore in Karnataka which connects with Tamil Nadu. In 1993–94 there were 1,053 route-km of track.

Civil Aviation. There are airports at Kozhikode, Kochi and Thiruvananthapuram with regular scheduled services to Delhi, Bombay and Madras; international flights leave from Thiruvananthapuram.

Shipping. Port Kochi, administered by the central government, is one of India's major ports; in 1983 it became the out-port for the Inland Container Depot at Coimbatore in Tamil Nadu. There are 13 other ports and harbours.

SOCIAL INSTITUTIONS

Justice. The High Court at Ernakulam has a Chief Justice and 21 puisne judges.

Religion. At the 1991 census there were 16,668,587 Hindus; 6,788,364 Moslems; 5,621,510 Christians; 3,641 Jains; 2,224 Sikhs.

Education. Kerala is the most literate Indian State with 22·66m. literates at the 1991 census (89·81%); 93·62% of men and 86·13% of women). Education is free up to the age of 14.

In 1993–94 there were 6,702 primary schools with 3·02m. students, 2,919 middle schools with 1·91m. students and 2,522 high and higher secondary schools with 1·02m. students. There were also 84 junior colleges with 169,967 pupils.

Kerala University (established 1937) at Thiruvananthapuram, is affiliating and teaching; in 1993–94 it had 45 affiliated colleges with 48,721 students. The University of Kochi is federal, and for post-graduate studies only. The University of Kozhikode (established 1968) is teaching and affiliating and has 72 affiliated colleges with 52,781 students (1993–94). Kerala Agricultural University (established 1971) has 7 constituent colleges. Mahatma Gandhi University at Kottayam was established in 1983 and has 57 affiliated colleges with 54,488 students (1993–94). There were also (1994) 5 medical colleges, 12 engineering and technology colleges, 12 teacher training colleges and 174 arts and science colleges.

Health. There were 148 allopathic hospitals, 924 primary health centres, 51 community health centres, 53 dispensaries, 22 TB centres/clinics and 15 leprosy control units, with 37,511 beds, in 1994. There were also 107 Ayurvedic hospitals with 2,309 beds and 31 homeopathy hospitals with 950 beds.

Further Reading

Jeffrey, R., *Politics, Women and Well-Being: How Kerala became a Model.* London, 1992

MADHYA PRADESH

KEY HISTORICAL EVENTS. Under the provisions of the States Reorganization Act, 1956, the State of Madhya Pradesh was formed on 1 Nov. 1956. It consists of the 17 Hindi districts of the former state of Madhya Pradesh, the former state of Madhya Bharat (except the Sunel enclave of Mandsaur district), the former states of Bhopal and Vindhya Pradesh and the Sironj subdivision of Kotah district, which was an enclave of Rajasthan in Madhya Pradesh.

For information on the former states, *see* THE STATESMAN'S YEAR-BOOK , 1958, pp. 180–84.

TERRITORY AND POPULATION. The state is in central India and is bounded north by Uttar Pradesh, east by Bihar and Orissa, south by Andhra Pradesh and Maharashtra, west by Gujarat and Rajasthan. Madhya Pradesh is the largest Indian state in size, with an area of 443,446 sq. km. In respect of population it ranks fifth. Population (1991 census), 66,181,170, an increase of 26·84% since 1981. Density, 149 per sq. km.

Cities with over 250,000 population, *see* INDIA: Territory and Population. Other large cities (1991): Ratlam, 195,776; Sagar, 195,346; Bilaspur, 192,396; Burhanpur, 172,710; Dewas, 164,364; Murwara, 163,431; Satna, 160,500; Durg, 150,645; Morena, 147,124; Khandwa, 145,133; Rewa, 128,981; Rajnandgaon, 125,371; Korba, 124,501; Bhind, 109,755; Shivpuri, 108,271; Guna, 100,490.

The number of persons speaking each of the more prevalent languages (1981 census) were: Hindi, 43,870,242; Urdu, 1,131,288; Marathi, 1,184,128; Gujarati, 581,084. In April 1990 Hindi became the sole official language.

CONSTITUTION AND GOVERNMENT. Madhya Pradesh is one of the 9 states for which the Constitution provides a bicameral legislature, but the Vidhan Parishad or Upper House (to consist of 90 members) has yet to be formed. The

Vidhan Sabha or Lower House has 320 elected members. Following the election in Nov. 1993, Congress-I came to power. Congress-I, 174; Bharatiya Janata Party, 116; Bahujan Samaj Party, 11; independents and others, 14; vacant, 1.

For administrative purposes the state has been split into 12 divisions with a Commissioner at the head of each; the headquarters of these are located at Bhopal, Bilaspur, Gwalior, Hoshangabad, Indore, Jabalpur, Jagdalpur, Morena, Raipur, Rewa, Sagar and Ujjain. There are 45 districts.

The seat of government is at Bhopal.

Governor: Mohammad Shafi Qureshi.

Chief Minister: Digvijay Singh.

BUDGET. Budget estimates for 1993–94 showed revenue receipts of Rs 71,416·2m. Annual plan, 1995–96, Rs 29,000m.

ENERGY AND NATURAL RESOURCES

Electricity. Madhya Pradesh is rich in low-grade coal suitable for power generation, and also has immense potential hydro-electric energy. Total installed capacity, 1994–95, 3,822·6 MW. Power generated, 16,597m. kWh in 1993–94. There is 1 hydro-electric power station. 67,238 out of 70,883 villages were electrified by 1994–95.

Water. Major irrigation projects include the Chambal Valley scheme (started in 1952 with Rajasthan), the Tawa project in Hoshangabad district, the Barna and Hasdeo schemes, the Mahanadi canal system and schemes in the Narmada valley at Bargi and Narmadasagar.

Minerals. The state has extensive mineral deposits, including 8,001m. tonnes of limestone, 126·8m. tonnes of bauxite, 26,853m. tonnes of coal and 2,186·2m. tonnes of iron ore.

In 1990 the output of major minerals was (in tonnes): Limestone, 17·7m.; diamonds, 18,081 carats; iron ore, 11·5m.; manganese ore, 255,000. Revenue from minerals, 1993–94, Rs 4,760·8m. Coal output was 67·52m. tonnes in 1990.

Agriculture. Agriculture is the mainstay of the state's economy and 80% of the people are rural. 43·7% of the land area is cultivable, of which 16·6% is irrigated. Production of principal crops, 1993–94 (in tonnes): Foodgrains, 18·6m. (rice, 5·8m., wheat, 6.2m.); pulses, 3.4m.; cotton (1993–94), 0·4m. bales of 170 kg.

Livestock (1989–90): Buffaloes, 7,262,022; other cattle, 27,612,636; sheep, 912,147; goats, 7,398,406; horses and ponies, 96,556.

Forestry. In 1991, 155,411 sq. km, or about 35% of the state's area was covered by forests. The forests are chiefly of sal, saja and teak species. They are the chief source in India of best-quality teak; they also provide firewood for about 60% of domestic fuel needs, and form valuable watershed protection. Forest revenue, 1989–90, Rs 4,230m.

INDUSTRY. The major industries are steel, aluminium, paper, cement, motor vehicles, ordnance, textiles and heavy electrical equipment. Other industries include sugar, fertilizers, straw board, vegetable oil, refractories, potteries, textile machinery, steel casting and rerolling, industrial gases, synthetic fibres, drugs, biscuit manufacturing, engineering, electronics, optical fibres, plastics, tools, rayon and art silk. The number of heavy and medium industries in the state is 614, with 181 ancillary industries; the number of small-scale establishments in production is 275,000. 39 out of 45 districts in the state are categorized as industrially backward.

There are 23 'growth centres' in operation, and 5 under development.

COMMUNICATIONS

Roads. Total length of roads in 1992–93 was 142,193 km. In 1993–94 there were 1,762,352 motor vehicles.

Railways. Bhopal, Bilaspur, Katni, Khandwa and Ratlam are junctions for the central, south, eastern and western networks. Route length (1993–94), 5,987 km.

Civil Aviation. There are airports at Bhopal, Gwalior, Indore, Khajuraho and Raipur with regular scheduled services to Bombay and Delhi, Varanasi, Nagpur, Raipur and Bhubaneswar.

SOCIAL INSTITUTIONS

Justice. The High Court of Judicature at Jabalpur has a Chief Justice and 21 puisne judges. Its benches are located at Gwalior and Indore.

Religion. At the 1991 census Hindus numbered 61,412,898; Moslems, 3,282,800; Christians, 426,598; Buddhists, 216,667; Sikhs, 161,111; Jains, 490,324.

Education. The 1991 census showed 23·49m. people to be literate (44·28%; 58·42% of men; 28·86% of women). Education is free for children aged up to 14.

In 1994–95 there were 72,478 primary schools with 9·04m. students, 16,301 middle schools with 3,203,000 students, 2,380 high schools with 975,626 students and 2,657 higher secondary schools with 531,147 students.

There are 15 universities in Madhya Pradesh: Dr. Hari Singh Gour University (established 1946), at Sagar, had 97 affiliated colleges and 74,386 students in 1992–93; Rani Durgavati University at Jabalpur (1957) had 46 affiliated colleges and 45,315 students; Vikram University (1957), at Ujjain, had 83 affiliated colleges and 39,723 students; Indira Kala Sangeet Vishwavidyalaya (1956), at Khairagarh, had 33 affiliated colleges and (1991–92) 6,720 students on roll (this university teaches music and fine arts); Devi Ahilya University at Indore (1964) had 32 affiliated colleges and 28,196 students; Jiwaji University (1963), at Gwalior, had 60 affiliated colleges and (1991–92) 58,825 students; Jawaharlal Nehru Krishi University (1964), at Jabalpur, had 10 constituent colleges and 2,053 students; Ravishankar University (1964), at Raipur, had 89 affiliated colleges; Indira Gandhi Krishi Vishwavidyalaya, Raipur; A. P. Singh University, Rewa had 81 colleges and 24,960 students; Barkatullah Vishwavidyalaya, Bhopal had 44 colleges and 18,817 students; Guru Ghasidas University, Bilaspur had 58 colleges and 34,717 students; Makhanlal Chaturvedi Rashtriya Patrakarita Vishwavidhyalaya Bhopal; Chitrakoot Gramodoya Vishwavidhayalaya Chitrakoot. In 1994-95 there were 448 colleges of arts, science and commerce, 20 teacher-training colleges, and 14 engineering and technology colleges, 6 medical colleges, 41 polytechnics and 69 technical-industrial arts and craft schools.

Health. In March 1993 there were 807 hospitals and dispensaries with 29,000 beds, and 1,841 primary health centres.

MAHARASHTRA

KEY HISTORICAL EVENTS. Under the States Reorganization Act, 1956, Bombay State was formed by merging the states of Kutch and Saurashtra and the Marathi-speaking areas of Hyderabad (commonly known as Marathwada) and Madhya Pradesh (also called Vidarbha) in the old state of Bombay, after the transfer from that state of the Kannada-speaking areas of the Belgaum, Bijapur, Kanara and Dharwar districts which were added to the state of Mysore, and the Abu Road taluka of Banaskantha district, which went to the state of Rajasthan.

By the Bombay Reorganization Act, 1960, which came into force 1 May 1960, 17 districts (predominantly Gujarati-speaking) in the north and west of Bombay State became the new state of Gujarat, and the remainder was renamed Maharashtra.

The state of Maharashtra consists of the following districts of the former Bombay State: Ahmednagar, Akola, Amravati, Aurangabad, Bhandara, Bhir, Buldana, Chanda, Dhulia (West Khandesh), Greater Bombay, Jalgaon (East Khandesh), Kolaba, Kolhapur, Nagpur, Nanded, Nasik, Osmanabad, Parbhani, Pune, Ratnagiri, Sangli, Satara, Sholapur, Thane, Wardha, Yeotmal; certain portions of Thane and Dhulia districts have become part of Gujarat.

TERRITORY AND POPULATION. Maharashtra is in central India and is bounded north and east by Madhya Pradesh, south by Andhra Pradesh, Karnataka and Goa, west by the Indian ocean and north-west by Daman and Gujarat. The state has an area of 307,713 sq. km. The population at the 1991 census was 78,937,187 (an increase of 25·73% since 1981), of whom about 30m. were Marathi-speaking. Density, 257 per sq. km. The area of Greater Bombay was 603 sq. km. and its population 9·93m. For other principal cities, *see* INDIA: Territory and Population. Other large towns (1991): Jalgaon (242,193), Chandrapur (226,105), Ichalkaranji (214,950), Latur (197,408), Sangli (193,197), Parbhani (190,255), Ahmadnagar (181,339), Jalna (174,958), Bhusawal (145,143), Miraj (125,407), Bid (112,434), Gondiya (109,470), Yavatmul (108,578), Wardha (102,985).

CONSTITUTION AND GOVERNMENT. Maharashtra has a bicameral legislature. The Legislative Council has 78 members. The Legislative Assembly has 288 elected members and 1 member nominated by the Governor to represent the Anglo-Indian community. Following the election of Feb. 1995 Shiv Sena and Bharatiya Janata formed a coalition government. The party composition of the Legislative Council was: Congress (I), 81; Shiv Sena, 73; Bharatiya Janata Party, 65; Janata Dal, 11; People's and Workers' Party, 6; independents and others, 52.

The Council of Ministers consists of the Chief Minister, 16 other Ministers, and 19 Ministers of State.

The capital is Bombay. The state has 30 districts.

Governor: P. C. Alexander.
Chief Minister: Manohar Joshi.

BUDGET. Budget estimates, 1994–95: Revenue receipts, Rs 135,795m.; revenue expenditure, Rs 145,784m. Plan outlay, 1995-96, Rs 57,070m.

ENERGY AND NATURAL RESOURCES

Electricity. Installed capacity, 1993–94, 9,414 MW (6,842 MW thermal, 1,590 MW hydro-electric, 792 MW gas and 190 MW nuclear). All villages are electrified. Electricity generated, 1993–94, 42,236m. kWh.

Oil and Gas. Bombay High (offshore) produced 20·2m. tonnes of crude oil and 14·2m. cu. metres of natural gas in 1994–95.

Minerals. The state has coal, silica sand, dolomite, kyanite, chromite, limestone, iron ore, manganese, bauxite. Value of mineral production, 1994, Rs 7,220m.

Agriculture. 3·3m. ha of the cropped area of 21·4m. ha are irrigated. In normal seasons the main food crops are rice, wheat, jowar, bajra and pulses. Main cash crops: Cotton, sugar-cane, groundnuts. Production, 1993-94 (in tonnes): Foodgrains, 13·6m. (rice, 2·48m., wheat, 1·06m.); pulses, 2·2m.; cotton, 446,300; sugar-cane, 27·89m.; groundnuts, 0·77m.

Livestock (1992 census, in 1,000): Buffaloes, 5,400; other cattle, 17,300; sheep and goats, 13,000; horses and ponies, 49; poultry, 30,500.

Forestry. Forests occupied 64,005 sq. km. in 1993–94. Value of forest products in 1994–95, Rs 2,090·8m.

Fisheries. In 1993-94 the marine fish catch was estimated at 354,000 tonnes and the inland fish catch at 84,000 tonnes; 17,918 boats, including 7,930 mechanized, were used for marine fishing.

INDUSTRY. Industry is concentrated mainly in Bombay, Pune and Thane. The main groups are chemicals and products, textiles, electrical and non-electrical machinery, petroleum and products, aircraft, rubber and plastic products, transport equipment, automobiles, paper, electronic items, engineering goods, pharmaceuticals and food products. The state industrial development corporation invested Rs 75,520m. in 20,100 industrial units in 1993–94. In June 1994 there were 26,102 working factories employing 1·2m. people. In 1993–94 there were 153,016 small scale industries employing 0·99m. people.

COMMUNICATIONS

Roads. On 31 March 1994 there were 180,241 km of roads, of which 145,995 km were surfaced. There were 3,449,071 motor vehicles on 1 Jan. 1995, of which 22% were in Greater Bombay. Passenger and freight transport has been nationalized.

Railways. The total length of railway on 31 March 1994 was 5,459 km; 66% was broad gauge, 14% metre gauge and 20% narrow gauge. The main junctions and termini are Bombay, Dadar, Manmad, Akola, Nagpur, Pune and Sholapur.

Civil Aviation. The main airport is Bombay, which has national and international flights. Nagpur airport is on the route from Bombay to Calcutta and there are also airports at Pune and Aurangabad.

Shipping. Maharashtra has a coastline of 720 km. Bombay is the major port, and there are 48 minor ports.

SOCIAL INSTITUTIONS

Justice. The High Court has a Chief Justice and 45 judges. The seat of the High Court is Bombay, but it has benches at Nagpur, Aurangabad and Panaji (Goa).

Religion. At the 1991 census Hindus numbered 64,033,213; Moslems, 7,628,755; Buddhists, 5,040,785; Christians, 885,030; Jains, 965,840; Sikhs, 161,184. Other religions, 99,768; religion not stated, 106,560.

Education. The number of literates, according to the 1991 census, was 42.8m. (64·87%; men, 76·56%, women, 52·32%). In 1994–95, there were 12,562 high and higher secondary schools with 6,875,000 pupils and 61,303 primary schools, with 11,512,000 pupils. There are 116 engineering and technology colleges, 82 medical colleges (including dental and Ayurvedic colleges), 183 teacher training colleges, 341 polytechnics and 739 arts, science and commerce colleges.

Bombay University, founded in 1857, is mainly an affiliating university. It has 208 colleges with a total (1992–93) of 220,134 students. Colleges in Goa can affiliate to Bombay University. Nagpur University (1923) is both teaching and affiliating. It has 172 colleges with 95,664 students. Poona University, founded in 1948, is teaching and affiliating; it has 167 colleges and 151,990 students. The SNDT Women's University had 32 colleges with a total of 20,501 students. Marathwada University, Aurangabad, was founded in 1958 as a teaching and affiliating body to control colleges in the Marathwada or Marathi-speaking area, previously under Osmania University; it has 189 colleges and 109,095 students. Shivaji University, Kolhapur, was established in 1963 to control affiliated colleges previously under Poona University. It has 196 colleges and 112,518 students. Amravati University has 130 colleges and 73,881 students. Other universities are: Marathwada Krishi Vidyapeeth, Parbhani; Y. Chavan Maharashtra Open University, Nashik; North Maharashtra University, Jalgaon, with 101 colleges and 66,092 students; Tilak Vidyapeeth, Pune; Mahatma Phule Krishi University, Rahuri; Punjabrao Krishi University, Akola; Konkan Krishi University, Dapoli; Dr Babasaheb Ambedkar Technological University.

Health. In 1993 there were 830 hospitals (116,075 beds), 1,702 dispensaries and 1,680 primary health centres, 151 primary health units and 1,977 TB hospitals and clinics.

MANIPUR

KEY HISTORICAL EVENTS. Formerly a state under the political control of the Government of India, Manipur, on 15 Aug. 1947, entered into interim arrangements with the Indian Union and the political agency was abolished. The administration was taken over by the Government of India on 15 Oct. 1949 under a merger agreement, and it was centrally administered by the Government of India through a Chief Commissioner. In 1950–51 an Advisory form of Government was introduced. In 1957 this was replaced by a Territorial Council of 30 elected and 2 nominated members. Later in 1963 a Legislative Assembly of 30 elected and 3 nominated members was established under the Government of Union Territories Act 1963. Because of the unstable party position in the Assembly, it had to be dissolved on 16 Oct. 1969 and President's Rule introduced. The status of the administrator was raised from Chief Commissioner to Lieut.-Governor with effect from 19 Dec. 1969. On the 21 Jan. 1972 Manipur became a state and the status of the administrator was changed from Lieut.-Governor to Governor.

TERRITORY AND POPULATION. The state is in north-east India and is bounded north by Nagaland, east by Burma, south by Burma and Mizoram, and west by Assam. Manipur has an area of 22,327 sq. km and a population (1991) of 1,837,149. Density, 82 per sq. km. Growth rate, 1981–91, 29·29%. The valley, which is about 1,813 sq. km, is 2,600 ft above sea-level. The hills rise in places to nearly 10,000 ft, but are mostly about 5,000–6,000 ft. The average annual rainfall is 65 in. The hill areas are inhabited by various hill tribes who constitute about one-third of the total population of the state. There are about 30 tribes and sub-tribes falling into two main groups of Nagas and Kukis. Manipuri and English are the official languages. A large number of dialects are spoken.

CONSTITUTION AND GOVERNMENT. With the attainment of statehood, Manipur has a Legislative Assembly of 60 members, of which 19 are from reserved tribal constituencies. There are 8 districts. Capital, Imphal. Following the elections in Feb. 1995, Congress (I) formed a government with the support of other parties. The party composition of the Legislative Assembly was: Congress (I), 22; Manipur People's Party, 18; Janata Dal, 7; independents, 3; others, 10.

Governor: O. N. Srivastava.
Chief Minister: Rishang Keishing.

BUDGET. Budget estimates for 1995–96 show revenue of Rs 6,437·6m. and expenditure of Rs 7,542·4m. Plan allocation 1995–96, Rs 3,000m.

ENERGY AND NATURAL RESOURCES

Electricity. Installed capacity (1994-95) is 12 MW from diesel and hydro-electric generators. This has been augmented since 1981 by the North Eastern Regional Grid. In March 1995 there were 1,591 villages with electricity.

Water. The main power, irrigation and flood-control schemes are the Loktak Lift Irrigation scheme (irrigation potential, 40,000 ha); the Singda scheme (potential 4,000 ha, and improved water supply for Imphal); the Thoubal scheme (potential 34,000 ha, and 4 other large projects. By 1994–95 59,100 ha had been irrigated.

Agriculture. Rice is the principal crop; with wheat, maize and pulses. Total foodgrains, 1993–94, 0·36m. tonnes (rice, 348,800 tonnes).

Agricultural work force, 453,040. Only 0·21m. ha are cultivable, of which 157,140 ha are under paddy. Fruit and vegetables are important in the valley, including pineapple, oranges, bananas, mangoes, pears, peaches and plums. Soil erosion, produced by shifting cultivation, is being halted by terracing. Fruit production in 1993–94, 0·11m. tonnes.

Forestry. Forests occupy about 17,685 sq km. The main products are teak, jurjan, pine; there are also large areas of bamboo and cane, especially in the Jiri and Barak river drainage areas, yielding about 300,000 tonnes annually. Total revenue from forests, 1990–91, Rs 9·95m.

Fisheries. Landings in 1993–94, 11,500 tonnes.

INDUSTRY. Handloom weaving is a cottage industry. Larger-scale industries include the manufacture of bicycles and TV sets, sugar, cement, starch, vegetable oil and glucose. Sericulture produces about 45 tonnes of raw silk annually. Estimated non-agricultural work force, 229,408.

COMMUNICATIONS. A national highway from Kaziranga (Assam) runs through Imphal to the Burmese frontier. A railway link was opened in 1990. There is an airport at Imphal with regular scheduled services to Delhi and Calcutta. Length of road (1993), 5,816 km; number of vehicles (1992–93) 54,388.

SOCIAL INSTITUTIONS

Religion. At the 1991 census Hindus numbered 1,059,470; Christians, 626,669; Moslems, 133,535.

Education. The 1991 census gave the number of literates as 895,223 (59·89%; men 71·63%, women 47·6%). In 1994–95 there were 3,027 primary schools with 275,400 students, 702 middle schools with 58,420 students, 504 high and higher secondary schools with 65,960 students, 29 colleges, 1 medical college, 2 teacher training colleges, 1 polytechnic, Manipur University with 50 colleges and 27,713 students (1992–93), and an agricultural university.

Health. In 1990–91 there were 11 hospitals, 52 dispensaries, 8 community health centres, 49 primary health centres and 389 sub-centres and 58 other facilities.

MEGHALAYA

KEY HISTORICAL EVENTS. The state was created under the Assam Reorganization (Meghalaya) Act 1969 and inaugurated on 2 April 1970. Its status was that of a state within the State of Assam until 21 Jan. 1972 when it became a fully-fledged state of the Union. It consists of the former Garo Hills district and United Khasi and Jaintia Hills district of Assam.

TERRITORY AND POPULATION. Meghalaya is bounded in the north and east by Assam, south and west by Bangladesh. In 1991 (census figure) the area was 22,429 sq. km and the population 1,774,778. Density, 79 per sq. km. Growth rate, 1981–91, 32·86%. The people are mainly of the Khasi, Jaintia and Garo tribes.

CONSTITUTION AND GOVERNMENT. Meghalaya has a unicameral legislature. The Legislative Assembly has 60 seats. Party position in Feb. 1993: Congress (I), 24; Hill People's Union, 11; Independents, 10; others, 15.

There are 7 districts. The capital is Shillong (population, 1991, 131,719).

Governor: Madhukar Dighe.
Chief Minister: Salseng C. Marak.

BUDGET. Budget estimates for 1990–91 showed revenue receipts of Rs 3,723m. and expenditure of Rs 3,340m. Annual Plan outlay, 1995–96, Rs 3,065m.

ENERGY AND NATURAL RESOURCES

Electricity. Total installed capacity (1994–95) was 193·76 MW. 2,407 villages out of 4,902 had electricity in Nov. 1994.

Minerals. The Khasi Hills, Jaintia Hills and Garo Hills districts produce coal, sillimanite (95% of India's total output), limestone, fire clay, dolomite, feldspar, quartz and glass sand. The state also has deposits of coal (estimated reserves 600m. tonnes), limestone (3,000m.), fire clay (6m.) and sandstone which are so far virtually untapped.

Agriculture. About 83% of the people depend on agriculture. Principal crops are rice, maize, potatoes, cotton, oranges, ginger, tezpata, areca nuts, jute, mesta, bananas and pineapples. Production 1991–92 (in tonnes) of principal crops: Rice,

121,067; potatoes, 153,159; maize, 23,788; jute, 43,444; wheat, 5,553; cotton, 5,432; rape and mustard, 3,961; pulses, 2,383.

Forest products are the state's chief resources.

INDUSTRY. Apart from agriculture the main source of employment is the extraction and processing of minerals; there are also important timber processing mills and cement factories. Other industries include electronics, tantalum capacitors, beverages and watches. The state has 5 industrial estates, 2 industrial areas and 1 growth centre. In 1993–94 there were 58 registered factories and 2,820 small-scale industries.

COMMUNICATIONS. Three national highways run through the state for a distance of 460 km. The state has no railways. Umroi airport (25 km from Shillong) connects the state with main air services. In 1992–93 there were 6,523 km of surfaced and unsurfaced roads. Total number of motor vehicles, 1993–94, 37,883.

SOCIAL INSTITUTIONS

Justice. The Guwahati High Court is common to Assam, Meghalaya, Nagaland, Manipur, Mizoram, Tripura and Arunachal Pradesh. There is a bench of the Guwahati High Court at Shillong.

Religion. At the 1991 census Hindus numbered 260,306; Moslems, 61,462; Christians, 1,146,092; Buddhists, 2,934; Sikhs, 2,612.

Education. In 1991, 38·2% of the population were literate (55·58% of men and 44·42% of women). In 1994–95 the state had 4,177 primary schools with 295,002 students, 827 middle schools with 74,482 students, 403 secondary schools with 28,546 students, 10 teacher training schools and 1 college, 1 polytechnic and 26 colleges. The North-eastern Hill University started functioning at Shillong in 1973; in 1992–93 it had 43 colleges and 18,920 students.

Health. In 1992–93 there were 5 government hospitals, 61 primary health centres, 23 government dispensaries and 272 sub-centres. Total beds (hospitals and health centres), 1,771.

MIZORAM

KEY HISTORICAL EVENTS. On 21 Jan. 1972 the former Mizo Hills District of Assam was created a Union Territory. A long dispute between the Mizo National Front (originally Seperatist) and the central government was resolved in 1986. Mizoram became a state by the Constitution (53rd Amendment) and the State of Mizoram Acts, July 1986.

TERRITORY AND POPULATION. Mizoram is one of the eastern-most Indian states, lying between Bangladesh and Burma, and having on its northern boundaries Tripura, Assam and Manipur. The area is 21,081 sq. km and the population (1991 census) 689,756. Density, 33 per sq. km; growth rate 1981–91, 39·7%.

CONSTITUTION AND GOVERNMENT. Mizoram has a unicameral Legislative Assembly with 40 seats: Congress I, 16; Mizo National Front, 14; Mizo Janata Dal, 8; Independents, 2. The capital is Aizawl (population, 1991, 155,240).

Governor: P. R. Kyndiah.
Chief Minister: Lal Thanhawla.

BUDGET. Budget estimates for 1993-94 show revenue receipts of Rs 4,239·1m. and revenue expenditure of Rs 3,648·8m. Annual plan outlay, 1995–96, Rs 2,270m.

ENERGY AND NATURAL RESOURCES

Electricity. Installed capacity (1993–94), 24·45 MW. 574 out of 721 villages had electricity in Nov. 1993.

Agriculture. About 60% of the people are engaged in agriculture, either on terraced holdings or in shifting cultivation. Total production of foodgrains, 1993–94, 146,700 tonnes (rice, 119,400 tonnes).

Total forest area, 15,935 sq. km.

INDUSTRY. Handloom weaving and other cottage industries are important. The state has (1992) 2,300 small scale industrial units, including furniture industries, steel fabrication, TV manufacturing, truck and bus body building.

COMMUNICATIONS. Aizawl is connected by road and air with Silchar in Assam and by air with Calcutta. Total length of roads, 31 March 1992, 5,095 km. There were 15,170 motor vehicles in 1993–94.

SOCIAL INSTITUTIONS

Religion. At the 1991 census Christians numbered 591,342; Buddhists, 54,024; Hindus, 34,788; Moslems, 4,538.

Education. The number of literates in 1991 was 462,246 (82·27%; 85·61% of men and 78·68% of women). In 1994–95 there were 1,149 primary schools with 114,386 students, 683 middle schools with 41,738 students and 289 high schools with 18,896 students; there were 29 colleges, 1 teacher training college, 3 teacher training schools, 1 polytechnic and 13 junior colleges.

Health. In 1993–94 there were 11 hospitals, 38 primary and 22 subsidiary health centres, and 314 health sub-centres. Total beds, 1,444.

NAGALAND

KEY HISTORICAL EVENTS. The territory was constituted by the Union Government in Sept. 1962. It comprises the former Naga Hills district of Assam and the former Tuensang Frontier division of the North-East Frontier Agency; these had been made a Centrally Administered Area in 1957, administered by the President through the Governor of Assam. In Jan. 1961 the area was renamed and given the status of a state of the Indian Union, which was officially inaugurated on 1 Dec. 1963.

For some years a section of the Naga leaders sought independence. Talks with the Naga underground movement resulted in the Shillong Peace Agreement of Nov. 1975, but insurgent movements have revived in 1995.

TERRITORY AND POPULATION. The state is in the north-east of India and is bounded in the north by Arunachal Pradesh, west by Assam, east by Burma and south by Manipur. Nagaland has an area of 16,579 sq. km and a population (1991 census) of 1,209,546. Density, 73 per sq. km. Growth rate, 1981–91, 56·08%. The major towns are the capital, Kohima (1991 population, 51,418) and Dimapur (57,182). Other towns include Wokha, Mon, Zunheboto, Mokokchung and Tuensang. The chief tribes in numerical order are: Angami, Ao, Sumi, Konyak, Chakhesang, Lotha, Phom, Khiamngan, Chang, Yimchunger, Zeliang-Kuki, Rengma, Sangtam and Pochury.

CONSTITUTION AND GOVERNMENT. An Interim Body (Legislative Assembly) of 42 members elected by the Naga people and an Executive Council (Council of Ministers) of 5 members were formed in 1961, and continued until the State Assembly was elected in Jan. 1964. The Assembly has 60 members, and after the elections of Feb. 1993 includes: Congress I, 35; Nagaland People's Council, 16; independents, 7; others, 1; vacant, 1. The Governor has extraordinary powers, which include special responsibility for law and order.

The state has 7 districts (Kohima, Mon, Zunheboto, Wokha, Phek, Mokokchung and Tuensang). The capital is Kohima.

Governor: O. N. Srivastava.
Chief Minister: S. C. Jamir.

BUDGET. Budget estimates for 1994–95 showed revenue receipts of Rs 5,850·24m. and expenditure of Rs 6,497·04m. Annual Plan, 1995–96, Rs 2,400m.

ENERGY AND NATURAL RESOURCES

Electricity. Installed capacity (1994–95) 6·82 MW; all towns and villages are electrified. In 1993–94, 7 electricity generation schemes were under implementation.

Minerals. Oil has been located in 3 districts. Other minerals include: Coal, limestone, chromite, iron ore, copper ore, clay, glass sand and slate.

Agriculture. 90% of the people derive their livelihood from agriculture. The Angamis, in Kohima district, practise a fixed agriculture in the shape of terraced slopes, and wet paddy cultivation in the lowlands. In the other two districts a traditional form of shifting cultivation (*jhumming*) still predominates, but some farmers have begun tea and coffee plantations and horticulture. About 61,000 ha were under terrace cultivation and 73,000 ha under *jhumming* in 1993–94. Production of rice (1993–94) was 0·18m. tonnes, total foodgrains 228,000 tonnes, pulses 11,500 tonnes.

Forests covered 862,930 ha in 1994–95.

INDUSTRY. There is a forest products factory at Tijit; a paper-mill (100 tonnes daily capacity) at Tuli, a distillery unit and a sugar-mill (1,000 tonnes daily capacity) at Dimapur, and a cement factory (50 tonnes daily capacity) at Wazeho. Bricks and TV sets are also made, and there are 1,850 small units. Sericulture is important.

COMMUNICATIONS. There is a national highway from Kaziranga (Assam) to Kohima and on to Manipur. There are state highways connecting Kohima with the district headquarters. Total length of roads in 1992, 14,933 km. Dimapur has a rail-head and a daily air service to Calcutta. Railway route-km in 1992–93, 9 km. There were 71,917 motor vehicles registered in 1992–93.

SOCIAL INSTITUTIONS

Justice. A permanent bench of the Guwahati High Court has been established in Kohima.

Religion. At the 1991 census there were 1,057,940 Christians; 122,473 Hindus; 20,642 Moslems; 1,202 Jains; 732 Sikhs.

Education. The 1991 census records 621,048 literates, or 61·65%: 67·62% of men and 54·75% of women. In 1994–95 there were 1,399 primary schools with 159,686 students, 418 middle schools with 56,594 students, 240 high and higher secondary schools with 22,503 students, 16 colleges, 2 teacher training colleges and 2 polytechnics. The North Eastern Hill University opened at Kohima in 1978. Nagaland University was established in 1994.

Health. In 1990–91 there were 31 hospitals (1,440 beds), 30 primary and 3 community health centres, 65 dispensaries, 243 sub-centres.

Aram, M., *Peace in Nagaland.* New Delhi, 1974

ORISSA

KEY HISTORICAL EVENTS. Orissa was conquered by the British in 1803 and in 1936 was constituted a separate province, some portions of the Central Provinces and Madras being transferred to the old Orissa division.

The rulers of 25 Orissa states surrendered all jurisdiction and authority to the Government of India on 1 Jan. 1948, on which date the Provincial Government took over the administration. The administration of 2 states, viz., Seraikella and Kharswan, was transferred to the Government of Bihar in May 1948. By an agreement with the Government of India, Mayurbhanj State was finally merged with the province on 1 Jan. 1949. By the States Merger (Governors' Provinces) Order, 1949, the states were completely merged with the state of Orissa on 19 Aug. 1949.

TERRITORY AND POPULATION. Orissa is in eastern India and is bounded north by Bihar, north-east by West Bengal, east by the Bay of Bengal, south by Andhra Pradesh and west by Madhya Pradesh. The area of the state is 155,707 sq. km, and its population (1991 census), 31,659,736, density 203 per sq. km. Growth rate, 1981–91, 20·06%. Cities with over 250,000 population at 1991 census, *see* INDIA: Territory and Population. Other large cities (1991): Rourkela (urban agglomeration), 398,864; Brahmapur, 210,418; Sambalpur, 131,138; Puri, 125,199. The principal and official language is Oriya.

CONSTITUTION AND GOVERNMENT. The Legislative Assembly has 147 members. After the elections in Feb. 1995 Congress (I) formed a government. Parties in the Legislative Assembly: Congress (I), 80 seats; Janata Dal, 46; Bharatiya Janata Party, 9; Jarkhand Mukti Morcha, 4; independents and others, 8.

The state consists of 30 districts.

The capital is Bhubaneswar (18 miles south of Cuttack).

Governor: G. Ramanujan.
Chief Minister: Janaki Ballav Patnaik.

BUDGET. Budget estimates, 1994–95, showed revenue receipts of Rs 39,943·3m. and revenue expenditure of Rs 44,162·8m. Annual plan outlay, 1995–96, Rs 16,500m.

ENERGY AND NATURAL RESOURCES

Electricity. The Hirakud Dam Project on the river Mahanadi irrigates 628,000 acres and has an installed capacity of 307·5 MW. There are other projects under construction; hydro-electric power is now serving a large part of the state. Other hydro-power projects are Balimela (360 MW), Upper Kolab (320 MW) and Rengali (250 MW). Total installed capacity (1993–94) 1,732 MW. In 1993–94 the state generated 5,455m. units. There were 32,908 electrified villages in March 1995.

Minerals. Orissa is India's leading producer of chromite (95% of national output), dolomite (50%), manganese ore (25%), graphite (80%), iron ore (16%), fire-clay (34%), limestone (20%), and quartz-quartzite (18%). Production in 1993 (1,000 tonnes): Iron ore, 7,990; manganese ore, 670; chromite, 1,020; coal, 24,120; limestone, 2,010; dolomite, 1,650; bauxite, 2,450. Value of production in 1993 was Rs 11,668m.

Agriculture. The cultivation of rice is the principal occupation of about 80% of the workforce, and only a very small amount of other cereals is grown. Production of foodgrains (1993–94) totalled 7·2m. tonnes from 5·71m. ha (rice 6·6m. tonnes, wheat 50,000 tonnes); pulses, 0·38m. tonnes; oilseeds, 0·27m. tonnes; sugar-cane, 781,000 tonnes. Turmeric is cultivated in the uplands of the districts of Ganjam, Phulbani and Koraput, and is exported.

Livestock (1991): Buffaloes, 1·51m.; other cattle, 13·6m.; sheep, 1·84m.; goats, 4·8m.; 12·44m. poultry including ducks.

Forestry. Forests occupy about 36·7% of the area of the state, the most important species being sal, teak, kendu, sandal, sisu, bija, kusum, kongada and bamboo.

Fisheries. There were, in March 1994, 635 fishery co-operative societies. Fish production in 1993–94 was 232,281 tonnes. The state has 4 fishing harbours.

INDUSTRY. 276 large and medium industries are in operation (1993–94), mostly based on minerals: steel, pig-iron, ferrochrome, ferromanganese, ferrosilicon, aluminium, cement, automotive tyres and synthetic fibres.

Other industries of importance are sugar, glass, paper, fertilizers, caustic soda, salt, industrial explosives, heavy machine tools, a coach-repair factory, a re-rolling mill, textile mills and electronics. Also, there were 44,777 small-scale industries employing 323,685 persons. There were 1,256,329 artisan units providing employment to 2·16m. persons; handloom weaving and the manufacture of baskets, wooden articles, hats and nets; silver filigree work and hand-woven fabrics are specially well known.

TOURISM. Tourist traffic is concentrated mainly on the 'Golden Triangle', Konark, Puri and Bhubaneswar, and its temples. Tourists also visit Gopalpur, the Similipal National Park, Nandankanan and Chilka Lake, Bhitar-Kanika and Ushakothi Wildlife Sanctuary.

COMMUNICATIONS

Roads. On 31 March 1994 length of roads was: State highway, 4,014 km; national highway, 1,625 km; other roads, 201,994 km. There were 386,877 motor vehicles in 1993–94. A 144-km expressway, part national highway, connects the Daitari mining area with Paradip Port.

Railways. The route-km of railway in 1992–93 was 2,002 km, of which 143 km was narrow gauge.

Civil Aviation. There is an airport at Bhubaneswar with regular scheduled services to New Delhi, Calcutta, Visakhapatnam and Hyderabad.

Shipping. Paradip was declared a 'major' port in 1966; it handled 8·3m. tonnes of traffic in 1993–94. There are minor ports at Bahabalpur and Gopalpur.

SOCIAL INSTITUTIONS

Justice. The High Court of Judicature at Cuttack has a Chief Justice and 13 puisne judges.

Religion. At the 1991 census Hindus numbered 29,971,257; Christians, 666,220; Moslems, 577,775; Sikhs, 17,296; Buddhists, 9,153; Jains, 6,302.

Education. The percentage of literates in the population in 1991 was 49·09% (males, 63·09%, females, 34·68%).

In 1994–95 there were 42,104 primary schools with 3·88m. students, 12,096 middle schools with 1·57m. students and 5,412 high and higher secondary schools with 830,500 students. There are 6 engineering and technology colleges, 3 medical colleges, 13 teacher training colleges, 15 engineering schools/polytechnics and 677 colleges.

Utkal University was established in 1943 at Cuttack and moved to Bhubaneswar in 1962; it is both teaching and affiliating. It has 132 affiliated colleges and 134,046 students (1992-93). Berhampur University has 61 affiliated colleges with 33,154 students, and Orissa University of Agriculture and Technology 8 constituent colleges with 641 students. Sambalpur University has 97 affiliated colleges. Sri Jagannath Sanskrit Viswavidyalaya at Puri was established in 1981 for oriental studies.

Health. There were (1993–94) 177 hospitals, 142 dispensaries, 875 primary health centres and 349 health centres/units.

PUNJAB (INDIA)

KEY HISTORICAL EVENTS. The Punjab was constituted an autonomous province of India in 1937. In 1947, the province was partitioned between India and Pakistan into East and West Punjab respectively, under the Indian Independence Act, 1947, the boundaries being determined under the Radcliffe Award. The name of East Punjab was changed to Punjab (India) under the Constitution of India. On 1 Nov. 1956 the erstwhile states of Punjab and Patiala and East Punjab States Union (PEPSU) were integrated to form the state of Punjab. On 1 Nov. 1966, under the Punjab Reorganization Act, 1966, the state was reconstituted as a Punjabi-speaking state comprising the districts of Gurdaspur (excluding Dalhousie), Amritsar, Kapurthala, Jullundur, Ferozepore, Bhatinda, Patiala and Ludhiana; parts of Sangrur, Hoshiarpur and Ambala districts; and part of Kharar tehsil. The remaining area comprising an area of 18,000 sq. miles and an estimated (1967) population of 8·5m. was shared between the new state of Haryana and the Union Territory of Himachal Pradesh. The existing capital of Chandigarh was made joint capital of Punjab and Haryana; its transfer to Punjab alone (due in 1986) has been delayed while the two states seek agreement as to which Hindi-speaking districts shall be transfered to Haryana in exchange.

TERRITORY AND POPULATION. The Punjab is in north India and is bounded at its northernmost point by Kashmir, north-east by Himachal Pradesh, south-east by Haryana, south by Rajasthan, west and north-west by Pakistan. The area of the state is 50,362 sq. km, with census (1991) population of 20,281,969. Density, 403 per sq. km. Growth rate, 1981-91, 20·81%. Cities with over 250,000 population at 1991 census, *see* INDIA: Territory and Population. Other principal towns (1991): Bathinda (159,042), Pathankot (123,930), Moga (108,304), Abohar (107,163). The official language is Punjabi.

CONSTITUTION AND GOVERNMENT. Punjab (India) has a unicameral legislature, the Legislative Assembly, of 117 members. Presidential rule was imposed in May 1987 after outbreaks of communal violence. In March 1988 the Assembly was officially dissolved. Elections were held in Feb. 1992. Turn-out was 28%. Congress (I) gained 87 seats in the Legislative Assembly, and 11 of Punjab's 13 seats in the Indian federal parliament.

There are 16 districts. The capital is Chandigarh. There are 106 municipalities, 118 community development blocks and 9,331 elected village councils (*panchayats*). Elections took place for 95 municipalities on 6 Sept. 1992, and for the 11,500 village councils in Jan. 1993.

Governor: Lieut.-Gen. Bakshi K. N. Chibber.
Chief Minister: Harcharan Singh Brar.

BUDGET. Budget estimates, 1995–96, showed revenue receipts of Rs 72,634·7m. and revenue expenditure of Rs 75,076·4m. Plan outlay, 1995-96, Rs 16,750m.

ENERGY AND NATURAL RESOURCES

Electricity. Installed capacity, 1994–95, was 3,499 MW; all villages had electricity.

Agriculture. About 75% of the population depends on agriculture which is technically advanced. The irrigated area rose from 2·21m. ha in 1950–51 to 3·95m. ha in 1992–93. In 1993–94, wheat production was 13·3m. tonnes; rice, 7·6m.; 1992–93: maize, 333,000; oilseeds, 90,000; cotton, 2·3m. bales of 170 kg.

Livestock (1977 census): Buffaloes, 4,110,000; other cattle, 3·31m.; sheep and goats, 1,219,600; horses and ponies, 75,900; poultry, 5·5m.

Forestry. In 1990–91 there were 284,450 ha of forest land, of which 134,844 ha belonged to the Forest Department.

INDUSTRY. In March 1995 the number of registered industrial units was 188,716, employing about 0·98m. people. In 1993–94 there were 475 large and medium industries. On 31 March 1995 there were 0·18m. small industrial units, investment Rs 19,730m. The chief manufactures are textiles (especially hosiery), sewing machines, sports goods, sugar, bicycles, electronic goods, machine tools, hand tools, vehicle parts, surgical goods, vegetable oils, tractors, chemicals and pharmaceuticals, fertilizers, food processing, electronics, railway coaches, paper and newsprint, cement, engineering goods and telecommunications items.

COMMUNICATIONS

Roads. The total length of roads on 31 March 1992 was 54,305 km. State transport services cover 1·9m. effective km daily with a fleet of 2,326 buses carrying a daily average of over 1m. passengers. Coverage by private operators is estimated as 40%. There were 1,537,220 vehicles in 1992–93.

Railways. The Punjab possesses an extensive system of railway communications, served by the Northern Railway. Route-km (1993-94) 2,121 km.

Civil Aviation. There is an airport at Amritsar, and Chandigarh airport is on the north-eastern boundary; both have regular scheduled services to Delhi, Jammu, Srinagar and Leh. There are also Vayudoot services to Ludhiana.

SOCIAL INSTITUTIONS

Justice. The Punjab and Haryana High Court exercises jurisdiction over the states of Punjab and Haryana and the territory of Chandigarh. It is located in Chandigarh. It consists (1988) of a Chief Justice and 21 puisne judges.

Religion. At the 1991 census Hindus numbered 6,989,226; Sikhs, 12,767,697; Moslems, 239,401; Christians, 225,163; Jains, 20,763.

Education. Compulsory education was introduced in April 1961; at the same time free education was introduced up to 8th class for boys and 9th class for girls as well as fee concessions. The aim is education for all children of 6-11. In 1991, 58·51% of the population were literate (65·66% of men and 50·41% of women).

In 1994–95 there were 12,509 primary schools with 2,076,657 students, 1,516 middle schools with 932,902 students, 2,126 high schools with 447,161 students and 847 higher secondary schools with 234,265 students.

Punjab University was established in 1947 at Chandigarh as an examining, teaching and affiliating body (in 1992–93 it had 96 colleges and 48,673 students). In 1962 Punjabi University was established at Patiala (it had 60 colleges with 24,304 students) and Punjab Agricultural University at Ludhiana. Guru Nanak Dev University has been established at Amritsar to mark the 500th anniversary celebrations for Guru Nanak Dev, first Guru of the Sikhs (it had 79 colleges and 54,989 students). Altogether there are 210 affiliated colleges, 177 for arts, science and commerce, 18 for teacher training, 11 medical and 4 engineering, and 12 polytechnic institutes.

Health. There were (1992–93) 219 hospitals, 2,151 allopathic, homeopathic, Ayurvedic and Unani dispensaries, 446 primary health centres and 38 community health centres. Total number of beds (1991–92), 24,742.

Singh, Khushwant, *A History of the Sikhs*. 2 vols. Princeton and OUP, 1964–67
Singh Tatla, D. and Talbot, I., *Punjab*. [Bibliography]. Oxford and Santa Barbara (CA), 1995

RAJASTHAN

KEY HISTORICAL EVENTS. As a result of the implementation of the States Reorganization Act, 1956, the erstwhile state of Ajmer, Abu Taluka of Bombay State and the Sunel Tappa enclave of the former state of Madhya Bharat were transferred to the state of Rajasthan on 1 Nov. 1956, whereas the Sironj subdivision of Rajasthan was transferred to the state of Madhya Pradesh.

TERRITORY AND POPULATION. Rajasthan is in north-west India and is bounded north by Punjab, north-east by Haryana and Uttar Pradesh, east by Madhya Pradesh, south by Gujarat and west by Pakistan. The area of the state is 342,239 sq. km and its population (census 1991), 44,005,990, density 129 per sq. km. Growth rate, 1981–91, 28·44%. For chief cities, *see* INDIA: Territory and Population. Other major towns (1991): Alwar (205,086), Bhilwara (183,965), Ganganagar (161,482), Bharatpur (148,519), Sikar (148,272), Pali (136,842), Beawar (105,363).

CONSTITUTION AND GOVERNMENT. There is a unicameral legislature, the Legislative Assembly, having 200 members. After the election in Nov. 1993 the Bharatiya Janata Party came to power. Bharatiya Janata Party, 95; Congress (I), 76; Janata Dal, 6; Independents and others, 22; vacant, 1.

The capital is Jaipur. There are 30 districts.

Governor: Bali Ram Bhagat.
Chief Minister: Bhairon Singh Shekhawat.

BUDGET. Estimates for 1995–96 show total revenue receipts of Rs 71,632·6m., and expenditure of Rs 79,881·9m. Annual plan, 1995–96, Rs 32,000m.

ENERGY AND NATURAL RESOURCES

Electricity. Installed capacity in 1994–95, 1,944·9 MW; 29,317 villages (Nov. 1994) and 479,665 wells had electric power.

Water. In 1994 the Bhakra Canal irrigated 0·3m. ha, the Chambal Canal, 0·2m. ha and the Rajasthan Canal, 0·94m. ha. The Indira Gandhi canal is the main canal system, of which (1994) 189 km. of main canal, 204 km of feeder and 3,400 km of distributors had been built, creating an irrigation potential of 582,000 ha. There were 36,397 villages with full or partial drinking water facilities in Dec. 1993, out of 37,124.

Minerals. The state is rich in minerals, including silver, tungsten, granite, marble, dolomite, lignite, lead, zinc, emeralds, soapstone, asbestos, feldspar, copper, limestone and salt. Total revenue from minerals in 1993–94, Rs 1,611·8m. 4 blocs are being explored for mineral oils and gas.

Agriculture. The state has suffered drought and encroaching desert for several years. The cultivable area is (1993–94) about 25·6m. ha, of which 5·33m. ha is irrigated. Production of principal crops (in tonnes), 1992–93: Pulses, 1·46m.; total foodgrains, 11·39m. (rice, 174,800; wheat, 5·1m.); cotton, 1m. bales of 170 kg.

Livestock (1992): Buffaloes, 7·75m.; other cattle, 11·6m.; sheep, 12·17m.; goats, 15·06m.; horses and ponies, 28,000; camels, 731,000.

INDUSTRY. In 1993–94 there were 167,400 small industrial units with an investment of Rs 13,163·1m. and employment of 0·64m. There were 171 industrial estates. Total capital investment (1993–94) Rs 13,160m. Chief manufactures are textiles, cement, glass, sugar, sodium, oxygen and acetylene units, pesticides, insecticides, dyes, caustic soda, calcium, carbide, synthetic fibres, fertilizers, shaving equipment, automobile components, tyres, watches, nylon tyre cords and refined copper. In 1993–94 there were 583 large and medium industries.

COMMUNICATIONS

Roads. In 1993–94 there were 124,133 km of roads including 47,451 km of good and surfaced roads in Rajasthan; there were 2,846 km of national highway. Motor vehicles numbered 1,217,705 in Dec. 1994.

Railways. Jodhpur, Marwar, Udaipur, Ajmer, Jaipur, Kota, Bikaner and Sawai Madhopur are important junctions of the north-western network. Route km (1993–94) 5,808.

Civil Aviation. There are airports at Jaipur, Jodhpur, Kota and Udaipur with regular scheduled services by Indian Airlines.

SOCIAL INSTITUTIONS

Justice. The seat of the High Court is at Jodhpur. There is a Chief Justice and 11 puisne judges. There is also a bench of High Court judges at Jaipur.

Religion. At the 1991 census Hindus numbered 39,201,099; Moslems, 3,525,339; Jains, 562,806; Sikhs, 649,174; Christians, 47,989; Buddhists, 4,467.

Education. The proportion of literates to the total population was 38·55% at the 1991 census; men 54·99% and women 20·44%.

In 1994–95 there were 34,569 primary schools with 5,818,000 students, 11,008 middle schools with 1,891,000 students, 3,237 high schools with 565,000 students and 1,275 higher secondary schools with 489,000 students. Elementary education is free but not compulsory.

In 1994–95 there were 173 colleges. Rajasthan University, established at Jaipur in 1947, is teaching and affiliating; in 1992–93 it had 121 colleges and 137,779 students. There are 5 other universities: Rajasthan Agricultural University, Bikaner; Mohanlal Sukhadia University, Udaipur; Maharishi Dayanand Saraswati University, Ajmer; Jai Narayan Vyas University, Jodhpur; Kota Open University, Kota. There are also 5 medical colleges, 6 engineering colleges, 21,436 adult and other education centres, 32 sanskrit institutions, 39 teacher-training colleges and 24 polytechnics.

Health. In 1993–94 there were 218 hospitals, 283 dispensaries, 1,453 primary health centres, 384 family welfare centres, 1,104 upgraded sub-centres and 118 maternity centres. There were 34,066 beds in hospitals.

SIKKIM

KEY HISTORICAL EVENTS. The Namgyal dynasty had been ruling Sikkim since the 14th century; the first consecrated ruler was Phuntsog Namgya I who was consecrated in 1642 and given the title of 'Chogyal', meaning 'King ruling in accordance with religious laws'. Sikkim was joined to the British Empire by a treaty in 1886 until 1947, but that relationship ceased when Britain withdrew from India in 1947. Thereafter there was a standstill agreement between India and Sikkim until a treaty was signed on 5 Dec. 1950 between India and Sikkim by which Sikkim became a protectorate of India and India undertook to be responsible for Sikkim's defence, external relations and strategic communications. By the Government of Sikkim Act, June 1974, the Chogyal became a constitutional monarch with power of assent to the Assembly's legislation. By the Constitution (Thirty-Sixth Amendment) Act 1974 Sikkim became a state associated with the Indian Union. The office of Chogyal was abolished in April 1975. By the Constitution (Thirty-Eighth Amendment) Act 1975 Sikkim became the twenty-second state of the Indian Union.

TERRITORY AND POPULATION. Sikkim is in the Eastern Himalayas and is bounded north by Tibet, east by Tibet and Bhutan, south by West Bengal and west Nepal. Area, 7,096 sq. km. It is inhabited chiefly by the Lepchas, a tribe indigenous to Sikkim, the Bhutias, who originally came from Tibet, and the Nepalis, who entered from Nepal in large numbers in the late 19th and early 20th century. Census population (1991), 406,457, of whom 25,024 lived in the capital, Gangtok. Density, 57 per sq km. Growth rate, 1981–91, 28·47%.

CONSTITUTION AND GOVERNMENT. The Assembly has 32 members. After the election of Nov. 1994 the Bikkim Democratic Front formed a government.

Governor: K. V. Raghunath Reddy.
Chief Minister: Pawan Kumar Changling.

The official language of the Government is English. Lepcha, Bhutia, Nepali and Limboo have also been declared official languages.

Sikkim is divided into 4 districts for administration purposes, Gangtok, Mangan, Namchi and Gyalshing being the headquarters for the Eastern, Northern, Southern and Western districts respectively. Each district is administered by a District Collector. Within this framework are the Panchayats or Village Councils.

ECONOMY

Budget. Budget estimates for 1991-92 show revenue receipt of Rs 2,168·5m. and total disbursements of Rs 2,299·3m. Annual plan outlay for 1995-96 is Rs 1,900m.

ENERGY AND NATURAL RESOURCES

Electricity. Installed capacity (1994–95) 33·6 MW. There are 4 hydro-electric power stations. All villages had electricity in 1991.

Minerals. Copper, zinc and lead are mined.

Agriculture. The economy is mainly agricultural; main food crops are rice, maize, millet, wheat and barley; cash crops are cardamom (a spice), mandarin oranges, apples, potatoes, and buckwheat. Foodgrain production, 1993-94, 101,200 tonnes (rice, 20,700 tonnes, wheat, 14,100 tonnes); pulses, 5,500 tonnes. Tea is grown. Forests occupy about 1,000 sq. km. and the potential for a timber and wood-pulp industry is being explored. Medicinal herbs are exported.

INDUSTRY AND TRADE

Industry. Small-scale industries include cigarettes, distilling, tanning, fruit preservation, carpets and watchmaking. Local crafts include carpet weaving, making handmade paper, wood carving and silverwork. The State Trading Corporation of Sikkim stimulates trade in indigenous products.

Tourism. There is great potential for the tourist industry, which has been stimulated by the opening of new roads.

COMMUNICATIONS

Roads. There are 1,615 km. of roads, all on mountainous terrain, and 18 major bridges under the Public Works Department. Public transport and road haulage is nationalized. There were 33,559 motor vehicles in 1992–93.

Railways. The nearest railhead is at Siliguri (115 km from Gangtok).

Civil Aviation. The nearest airport is at Bagdogra (128 km from Gangtok), linked to Gangtok by helicopter service.

Telecommunications. There are 1,445 telephones (1987) and 37 wireless stations. A radio broadcasting station, Akashvani Gangtok, was built in 1982, and a permanent station in 1983. Gangtok also has a low-power TV transmitter.

SOCIAL INSTITUTIONS

Religion. At the 1991 census there were 277,881 Hindus; 3,849 Moslems; 13,413 Christians; 110,371 Buddhists; 375 Sikhs; 40 Jains.

Education. At the 1991 census there were 186,789 literates (56·94%; men 65·74% and women 46·69%). Sikkim had (1994–95) 760 pre-primary schools with 15,775 students, 529 primary schools with 78,737 students, 118 middle schools with 24,239 students, 66 high schools with 6,568 students and 22 higher secondary schools with 3,456 students. Education is free up to class XII; text books are free up to class V. There are 500 adult education centres. There is also a training institute for primary teachers and a degree college.

TAMIL NADU

KEY HISTORICAL EVENTS. The first trading establishment made by the British in the Madras State was at Peddapali (now Nizampatnam) in 1611 and then at Masulipatnam. In 1639 the English were permitted to make a settlement at the place which is now Madras, and Fort St George was founded. By 1801 the whole of the country from the Northern Circars to Cape Comorin (with the exception of certain French and Danish settlements) had been brought under British rule.

Under the provisions of the States Reorganization Act, 1956, the Malabar district (excluding the islands of Laccadive and Minicoy) and the Kasaragod district taluk of South Kanara were transferred to the new state of Kerala; the South Kanara district (excluding Kasaragod taluk and the Amindivi Islands) and the Kollegal taluk of the Coimbatore district were transferred to the new state of Mysore; and the Laccadive, Amindivi and Minicoy Islands were constituted a separate Territory. Four taluks of the Trivandrum district and the Shencottah taluk of Quilon district were transferred from Travancore-Cochin to the new Madras State. On 1 April 1960, 405 sq. miles from the Chittoor district of Andhra Pradesh were transferred to Madras in exchange for 326 sq. miles from the Chingleput and Salem districts. In Aug. 1968 the state was renamed Tamil Nadu.

TERRITORY AND POPULATION. Tamil Nadu is in south India and is bounded north by Karnataka and Andhra Pradesh, east and south by the Indian Ocean and west by Kerala. Area, 130,058 sq. km. Population (1991 census), 55,858,946, density of 429 per sq. km. Growth rate, 1981–91, 15·39%. Tamil is the principal language and has been adopted as the state language with effect from 14 Jan. 1958. For the principal towns, *see* INDIA: Territory and Population. Other large towns (1991): Ambattur (215,424), Thanjavur City (202,013), Tuticorin (199,854), Nagercoil City (190,084), Avadi (183,215), Dindigul City (182,477), Vellore (175,061), Thiruvottir (168,642), Erode (159,232), Kanchipuram (144,955), Cuddalore City (144,561), Tirunelveli (135,825), Alandur (125,244), Neyveli (118,080), Rajapalaiyam City (114,202), Pallavaram (111,866), Tambaran (107,187). There are 21 districts. The capital is Madras.

CONSTITUTION AND GOVERNMENT. The Governor is aided by a Council of 18 ministers. There is a unicameral legislature; the Legislative Assembly has 235 members: AIADMK, 164 Congress I, 61; others, 10.

Governor: Dr M. Channa Reddy.
Chief Minister: J. Jayalalitha.

BUDGET. Budget estimates for 1995-96, revenue receipts, Rs 89,855·5m., revenue expenditure, Rs 99,106·2m. Annual plan, 1995–96, Rs 32,000m.

ENERGY AND NATURAL RESOURCES

Electricity. Installed capacity in 1994–95 was 4,520 MW, of which 1,945 MW was hydro-electricity and 2,550 MW thermal. All villages were supplied with electricity. The Kalpakkam nuclear power plant became operational in 1983; capacity, 330 MW.

Water. A joint project with Andhra Pradesh was agreed in 1983, to supply Madras with water from the Krishna river, also providing irrigation, *en route,* for Andhra Pradesh. In 1991–92, 3·26m. ha were irrigated.

Minerals. Value of mineral production, 1987, Rs 1,760m. The state has magnesite, salt, coal, lignite, chromite, bauxite, limestone, manganese, mica, quartz, gypsum and feldspar.

Agriculture. The land is a fertile plain watered by rivers flowing east from the Western Ghats, particularly the Cauvery and the Tambaraparani. Temperature ranges between 6°C. and 39°C., rainfall between 442 mm. and 1,307 mm. Of the total land area (13m. ha), 6,508,349 ha were cropped and 298,659 ha of waste were cultivable. The staple food crops grown are paddy, maize, jawar, bajra, pulses and millets. Important commercial crops are sugar-cane, oilseeds, cashew-nuts, cotton, tobacco, coffee, tea, rubber and pepper. Production, 1993–94 (in tonnes): Total foodgrains, 8,567,500 (rice, 6,602,000); pulses, 397,000.

Livestock (1993): Buffaloes, 3,116,647; other cattle, 9,318,666; sheep, 5,865,989; goats, 5,938,475; poultry, 21,454,890.

Forestry. Forest area, 1990–91, 2·24m. ha, of which 1,929,000 ha were reserved forest. Forests cover about 17·21% of land area. Main products are teak, soft wood, wattle, sandalwood, pulp wood, cashew and cinchona bark.

Fisheries. In 1991–92, 384,000 tonnes of fish were produced; marine, 299,900 tonnes.

INDUSTRY AND TRADE

Industry. The number of working factories was 14,202 in 1990, employing 840,086 workers. In 1991–92 there were 138,404 small industries employing

1,494,763 persons. The biggest central sector project is Salem steel plant. Cotton textiles is one of the major industries. There were 449 cotton textile mills in 1991–92 and many spinning mills supplying yarn to the decentralized handloom industry. Other important industries are cement, sugar, manufacture of textile machinery, power-driven pumps, bicycles, electrical machinery, tractors, motor-cars, rubber tyres and tubes, bricks and tiles and silk.

Main exports: Cotton goods, tea, coffee, spices, engineering goods, motor-car ancillaries, leather and granite.

In 1988 there were 4,468 registered trade unions. Work-days lost by strikes and lockouts in 1991, 2,084,920.

Tourism. In 1992, 203,985 foreign tourists visited the state.

COMMUNICATIONS

Roads. On 31 March 1992 the state had 198,104 km of national and state highways, major and other district roads. In 1992–93 there were 1,921,440 registered motor vehicles.

Railways. On 31 March 1994 there were 4,021 route km. Madras and Madurai are the main centres.

Civil Aviation. There are airports at Madras, Tiruchirapalli and Madurai, with regular scheduled services to Bombay, Calcutta and Delhi. Madras is the main centre of airline routes in South India.

Shipping. Madras and Tuticorin are the chief ports. Important minor ports are Cuddalore and Nagapattinam. Madras handled 26·5m. tonnes of cargo in 1993–94, Tuticorin, 6·7m. The Inland Container Depot at Coimbatore has a capacity of 50,000 tonnes of export traffic; it is linked to Cochin (Kerala).

SOCIAL INSTITUTIONS

Justice. There is a High Court at Madras with a Chief Justice and 26 judges. *Police:* Strength of police force, 1 Jan. 1990, 67,094.

Religion. At the 1991 census Hindus numbered 49,532,052 (88·67%), Christians, 3,179,410 (5·69%); Moslems, 3,052,717 (5·47%).

Education. At the 1991 census 30·38m. people were literate (62·66%; men 73·75% and women 51·33%).

Education is free up to pre-university level. In 1994–95 there were 30,351 primary schools with 8·11m. students, 5,578 middle schools with 3·66m. students, 3,348 high schools with 1·36m. students and 2,318 higher secondary schools with 0·61m. students. There are also 13 medical colleges, 45 engineering and technology colleges, 21 teacher training colleges and 234 general education colleges.

There are 13 universities. Madras University (founded in 1857) is affiliating and teaching (it had 119 colleges and 132,371 students in 1992-93); Annamalai University, Annamalainagar (founded 1929) is residential; Madurai Kamaraj University (founded 1966) is an affiliating and teaching university; 10 others include one agricultural university, Mother Theresa Women's University, and Tamil University, Tanjavur. There are 4 institutions which are deemed to be universities.

Health. There were (1989-90) 262 hospitals, 884 dispensaries (of which 701 were Indian medicine and homeopathy), 1,385 primary health centres and 8,681 health sub-centres.

Statistical Information: The Department of Statistics (Fort St George, Madras) was established in 1948 and reorganized in 1953. *Director:* C. Sethu. Main publications:
Annual Statistical Abstract; Decennial Statistical Atlas; Season and Crop Report; Quinquennial Wages Census; Quarterly Abstract of Statistics.

TRIPURA

KEY HISTORICAL EVENTS. A Hindu state of great antiquity having been ruled by the Maharajahs for 1,300 years before its accession to the Indian Union on

15 Oct. 1949. With the reorganization of states on 1 Sept. 1956 Tripura became a Union Territory, and was so declared on 1 Nov. 1957. The Territory was made a State on 21 Jan. 1972.

TERRITORY AND POPULATION. Tripura is bounded by Bangladesh, except in the north-east where it joins Assam and Mizoram. The major portion of the state is hilly and mainly jungle. It has an area of 10,486 sq. km and a population of 2,757,205 (1991 census); Density, 263 per sq. km. Growth rate, 1981–91, 34·3%.

The official languages are Bengali and Kokbarak. Manipuri is also spoken.

CONSTITUTION AND GOVERNMENT. The territory has 4 districts, divided into 14 administrative subdivisions, namely, Sadar, Khowai, Kailasahar, Dharmanagar, Sonamura, Udaipur, Gandachhara, Belonia, Kamalpur, Sabroom, Bishalgarh, Longthorai Velly, Kanchanpur and Amarpur. The capital is Agartala (population, 1991, 157,358).

The Communist Party won the elections of 6 April 1993.

Governor: Siddheshwar Prasad.
Chief Minister: Dasaratha Deb.

BUDGET. Budget estimates, 1994-95, show an expenditure of Rs 3,605m. Annual plan outlay for 1995-96 is Rs 3,500m.

ENERGY AND NATURAL RESOURCES

Electricity. Installed capacity (1994–95), 53·4 MW; there were (Nov. 1994) 3,471 electrified villages out of a total of 4,727.

Agriculture. About 24% of the land area is cultivable. The tribes practise shifting cultivation, but this is being replaced by modern methods. The main crops are rice, wheat, jute, mesta, potatoes, oilseeds and sugar-cane. Foodgrain production (1993–94), 455,400 tonnes. There are 54 registered tea gardens producing 5,741,000 kg per year, and employing 12,232 in 1992–93.

Forestry. Forests cover about 55% of the land area. They have been much depleted by clearance for shifting cultivation and, recently, for refugee settlements of Bangladeshis. About 8% of the forest area still consists of dense natural forest; losses elsewhere are being replaced by plantation. Commercial rubber plantation has also been encouraged. In 1992–93, 34,330 ha were under new rubber plantations.

INDUSTRY. Tea is the main industry. There is also a jute mill producing about 15 tonnes per day and employing about 2,000. The main small industries: Aluminium utensils, rubber, saw-milling, soap, piping, fruit canning, handloom weaving and sericulture. There were 1,092 registered factories which employed 36,358 persons, and 1,200 notified factories with 10,000 workers in 1992–93.

COMMUNICATIONS

Roads. Total length of motorable roads (1992–93) 14,069 km, of which 2,158 km were surfaced. Vehicles registered, 31 March 1993, 25,251 of which 4,235 were lorries.

Railways. There is a railway between Kumarghat and Kalkalighat (Assam). Route-km in 1992–93, 45 km.

Civil Aviation. There is 1 airport and 3 airstrips. The airport (Agartala) has regular scheduled services to Calcutta.

SOCIAL INSTITUTIONS

Religion. At the 1991 census Hindus numbered 2,384,934; Moslems, 196,495; Christians, 46,472; Buddhists, 128,260; Sikhs, 740; Jains, 301.

Education. In 1991, 60·44% of the population were literate (70·58% of men and 49·65% of women). In 1994–95 there were 2,055 primary schools (419,410 pupils); 435 middle schools (122,197); 498 high and higher secondary schools (79,832). There were 14 colleges of general education, 1 engineering college, 1 teacher training college and 1 polytechnic. Tripura University, established in 1987, has 19 affiliated colleges.

Health. There were (1993–94) 23 hospitals, with 2,087 beds, 536 dispensaries, 792 doctors and 761 nurses. There were 52 primary health centres and 67 family planning centres.

UTTAR PRADESH

KEY HISTORICAL EVENTS. In 1833 the then Bengal Presidency was divided into two parts, one of which became the Presidency of Agra. In 1836 the Agra area was styled the NorthWest Province and placed under a Lieut.-Governor. The two provinces of Agra and Oudh were placed, in 1877, under one administrator, styled Lieut.-Governor of the North-West Province and Chief Commissioner of Oudh. In 1902 the name was changed to 'United Provinces of Agra and Oudh', under a Lieut.-Governor, and the Lieut.-Governorship was altered to a Governorship in 1921. In 1935 the name was shortened to 'United Provinces'. On Independence, the states of Rampur, Banaras and Tehri-Garwhal were merged with United Provinces. In 1950 the name of the United Provinces was changed to Uttar Pradesh.

TERRITORY AND POPULATION. Uttar Pradesh is in north India and is bounded north by Himachal Pradesh, Tibet and Nepal, east by Bihar, south by Madhya Pradesh and west by Rajasthan, Haryana and Delhi. The area of the state is 294,411 sq. km. Population (1991 census), 139,112,287, a density of 473 per sq. km. Growth rate, 1981–91, 25·48%. Cities with more than 250,000 population, *see* INDIA: Territory and Population. Other important towns (1991): Rampur (243,742), Muzaffarnagar (240,609), Shahjahanpur (237,717), Mathura (226,691), Firozabad (215,128), Farrukhabad-Cum-Fatehgarh (194,567), Mirzapur-Cum-Vindhyachal (169,336), Sambhal (150,819), Hardwar (147,305), Noida (146,514), Hapur (146,262), Amroha (137,061), Maunath Bhanjan (136,697), Jaunpur (136,062), Bahraich (135,400), Rae Bareli (129,904), Bulandshahr (127,201), Faizabad (124,437), Etawah (124,072), Sitapur (121,842), Fatehpur (117,675), Budaun (116,695), Hathras (113,285), Unnao (107,425), Pilibhit (106,605), Haldwani-Cum-Kathgodam (104,195), Modinagar (101,660). The sole official language has been Hindi since April 1990.

CONSTITUTION AND GOVERNMENT. Uttar Pradesh has had an autonomous system of government since 1937. There is a bicameral legislature. The Legislative Council has 108 members; the Legislative Assembly has 426, of which 425 are elected. The state was brought under President's rule on 18 Oct. 1995 and the Legislative Assembly dissolved on 27 Oct. 1995.

There are 14 administrative divisions, each under a Commissioner, and 66 districts.

The capital is Lucknow.

Governor: Moti Lal Vora.
Chief Minister: Vacant.

BUDGET. Budget estimates 1995–96 show total receipts of Rs 209,538·7m.; total expenditure, Rs 229,516·2m. Annual plan outlay, 1995–96, Rs 57,020m.

ENERGY AND NATURAL RESOURCES

Electricity. The state had, 1994–95, an installed capacity of 6,075 MW. There were 85,008 villages with electricity in Nov. 1994, out of a total 112,566.

Minerals. The state has magnesite, fire-clay, coal, copper, dolomite, limestone, soapstone, gypsum, bauxite, diaspore, ochre, phosphorite, pyrophyllite, silica sand and steatite among others.

Agriculture. Agriculture occupies 78% of the work force. 10·13m. ha are irrigated. The state is India's largest producer of foodgrains; production (1993–94), 36·97m. tonnes (rice 10·1m. tonnes, wheat 20·8m. tonnes); pulses, 2·49m. tonnes. The state is one of India's main producers of sugar; production of sugar-cane (1989–90), 97·4m. tonnes. There were (1990–91) 1,735 veterinary centres for cattle.

Forests cover (1992–93) about 51,618 sq. km.

INDUSTRY. Sugar production is important; other industries include oil refining, aluminium smelting edible oils, textiles, distilleries, brewing, leather working, agricultural engineering, paper, automobile tyres, fertilizers, cement, jute, glass, heavy electricals, chemicals, automobiles and synthetic fibres. Large public-sector enterprises have been set up in electrical engineering, pharmaceuticals, locomotive building, general engineering, electronics and aeronautics. Village and small-scale industries are important; there were 0·31m. small units in 1992–93 providing employment to 1·85m. people. The state had 1,419 large and medium industries with an investment of Rs 116,730m. and employing 0·51m. persons in 1993–94.

COMMUNICATIONS

Roads. There were, 31 March 1992, 203,646 km of roads. In 1992–93 there were 2,289,019 motor vehicles of which 1,572,884 were two-wheelers.

Railways. Lucknow is the main junction of the northern network; other important junctions are Agra, Kanpur, Allahabad, Mughal Sarai, Dehra Dun and Varanasi. Route-km in 1993–94, 8,944 km.

Civil Aviation. There are airports at Lucknow, Kanpur, Varanasi, Allahabad, Agra and Gorakhpur.

SOCIAL INSTITUTIONS

Justice. The High Court of Judicature at Allahabad (with a bench at Lucknow) has a Chief Justice and 49 puisne judges including additional judges. There are 56 sessions divisions in the state.

Religion. At the 1991 census Hindus numbered 113,712,829; Moslems, 24,109,684; Sikhs, 675,775; Christians, 383,477; Jains, 176,259; Buddhists, 221,443.

Education. At the 1991 census 46·87m. people were literate (41·6%; 55·73% of men and 25·31% of women). In 1994–95 there were 82,023 primary schools with 16·26m. students, 15,976 middle schools with 5·63m. students, 2,735 high schools with 2,329,904 students and 3,902 higher secondary schools with 1,167,552 students.

Uttar Pradesh has 22 universities: Allahabad University (founded 1887); Agra University (1927); the Banaras Hindu University, Varanasi (1916); Lucknow University (1921); Aligarh Muslim University (1920) with 4 colleges and 12,016 students in 1992–93; Roorkee University (1949), formerly Thomason College of Civil Engineering (established in 1847); Gorakhpur University (1957) with 33 colleges and 72,373 students; Sampurnanand Sanskrit Vishwavidyalaya, Varanasi (1958); Kanpur University (1966); Meerut University (1966), with 61 colleges and 125,320 students in 1992–93; Govind Ballabh Pant University of Agriculture and Technology, Pantnagar (1960); H. N. Bahuguna Garhwal University, Srinagar, (1973). C. S. Azad University of Agriculture and Technology, Kanpur, Narendra Deva University of Agriculture and Technology, Faizabad, and Avadh (32 colleges and 64,142 students), Kumaon, Rohilkhand (32 colleges and 86,996 students) and Bundelkhand Universities were founded in 1975. Jaunpur University (Purvanchal Vishwavidyalaya) was founded in 1987.

There are also 6 institutions with university status: Gurukul Kangri

Vishwavidyalaya, Hardwar, Indian Veterinary Research Institute, Central Institute of Higher Tibetan Studies, Forest Research Institute, Sanjay Gandhi Post-Graduate Institute of Medical Sciences and Dayal Bagh Educational Institute. There are 9 medical colleges, 12 engineering colleges, 13 teacher-training colleges and 486 arts, science and commerce colleges.

Health. In 1992–93 there were 4,894 allopathic, 2,690 Ayurvedic and Unani and 1,125 homoepathic hospitals and dispensaries. There were also 3,737 primary health centres and 20,153 sub-centres, and TB hospitals and clinics.

WEST BENGAL

KEY HISTORICAL EVENTS. For the history of Bengal under British rule, from 1633 to 1947, *see* THE STATESMAN'S YEAR-BOOK , 1952, p. 183.

Under the terms of the Indian Independence Act, 1947, the Province of Bengal ceased to exist. The Moslem majority districts of East Bengal, consisting of the Chittagong and Dacca Divisions and portions of the Presidency and Rajshahi Divisions, became what was then East Pakistan (now Bangladesh).

TERRITORY AND POPULATION. West Bengal is in north-east India and is bounded north by Sikkim and Bhutan, east by Assam and Bangladesh, south by the Bay of Bengal, south-west by Orissa, west by Bihar and north-west by Nepal. The total area of West Bengal is 88,752 sq. km. At the 1991 census its population was 68,077,965, an increase of 24·73% since 1981, the density of population 767 per sq. km. Population of chief cities, *see* INDIA: Territory and Population. Other major towns (1991): Barddhaman (245,079), South Dum Dum (232,811), Baranagar (224,821), Siliguri (216,950), Bally (181,978), Burnpur (174,933), Uluberia (155,172), Hugli-Chinsura (151,806), Raiganj (151,045), North Dum Dum (149,965), Dabgram (147,217), English Bazar (139,204), Serampur (137,028), Barrackpur (133,265), Naihati (132,701), Medinipur (125,498), Nabadwip (125,037), Krishnanagar (121,110), Chandannagar (120,378), Balurghat (119,796), Baharampur (115,144), Bankura (114,876), Titagarh (114,085), Halisahar (114,028), Santipur (109,956), Kulti-Barakar (108,518), Basirhat (101,409), Haldia (100,347), Habra (100,223), Kanchrapara (100,194). The principal language is Bengali.

CONSTITUTION AND GOVERNMENT. The state of West Bengal came into existence as a result of the Indian Independence Act, 1947. The territory of Cooch-Behar State was merged with West Bengal on 1 Jan. 1950, and the former French possession of Chandernagore became part of the state on 2 Oct. 1954. Under the States Reorganization Act, 1956, certain portions of Bihar State (an area of 3,157 sq. miles with a population of 1,446,385) were transferred to West Bengal.

The Legislative Assembly has 295 seats (294 elected and 1 nominated). Distribution, Sept. 1993: Communist Party of India (Marxist), 191; All India Forward Bloc, 28; Revolutionary Socialist Party, 18; Communist Party of India, 6; Indian National Congress, 42; Independents and others, 9.

The capital is Calcutta.

For administrative purposes there are 3 divisions (Jalpaiguri, Burdwan and Presidency), under which there are 18 districts, including Calcutta. The Calcutta Metropolitan Development Authority has been set up to co-ordinate development in the metropolitan area (1,350 sq. km). For the purposes of local self-government there are 16 *zila parishads* (district boards) excluding Darjeeling, 328 *panchayat samities* (regional boards), and 3,222 *gram* (village) *panchayats*. There are 113 municipalities, 3 Corporations and 11 Notified Areas. The Calcutta Municipal Corporation is headed by a mayor in-Council.

Governor: K. V. Raghunatha Reddy.
Chief Minister: Jyoti Basu.

BUDGET. Budget estimates for 1995–96, revenue receipts Rs 78,558·2m. and expenditure Rs 92,083m. Plan outlay for 1995-96 was Rs 22,070m.

ENERGY AND NATURAL RESOURCES

Electricity. Installed capacity, 1994–95, 4,981·5 MW; 29,116 villages had electricity in March 1995.

Water. The largest irrigation and power scheme under construction is the Teesta Barrage (9,000 ha). Other major irrigation schemes are the Mayurakshi Reservoir, Kangsabati Reservoir, Mahananda Barrage and Aqueduct and Damodar Valley. In 1993–94 there were 8,997 tubewells, 6,681 open dugwells and 3,297 riverlift irrigation schemes.

Minerals. Value of production, 1993–94, Rs 9,286m. The state has coal (the Raniganj field is one of the 3 biggest in India) including coking coal. Coal production (1993, provisional) 17·73m. tonnes.

Agriculture. About 5·9m. ha were under rice-paddy in 1993–94. Total foodgrain production, 1993–94, 13·1m. tonnes (rice 12·11m. tonnes, wheat 632,100 tonnes); pulses, 170,800 tonnes; oilseeds, 415,800 tonnes; jute, 5·5m. bales of 180 kg; tea (1992–93), 150·69m. kg. The state produces 66·5% of the national output of jute and *mesta* (1993–94).

Livestock (1989 census): 16,509,487 cattle; 965,517 buffaloes; 1,459,771 sheep; 11,890,278 goats and 35,542,444 poultry.

The recorded forest area (1994–95) was 11,879 sq. km.

Fisheries. Landings, 1993–94, 0·8m. tonnes, of which inland 653,000 tonnes. During 1994–95 Rs 145·3m. was invested in fishery schemes. The state is the largest inland fish producer in the country.

INDUSTRY. The total number of registered factories, 1993, was 9,787 (excluding defence factories); average daily employment, 1993, 904,000. The coalmining industry, 1990, had 119 units with average daily employment of 108,000.

There is a large automobile factory at Uttarpara, and an aluminium rolling-mill at Belur. There is a steel plant at Burnpur (Asansol) and a spun pipe factory at Kulti. Durgapur has a large steel plant and other industries under the state sector—a thermal power plant, coke oven plant, fertilizer factory, alloy steel plant and ophthalmic glass plant. There is a locomotive factory at Chittaranjan and a cable factory at Rupnarayanpur. A refinery and fertilizer factory are operating at Haldia. Other industries include chemicals, engineering goods, electronics, textiles, automobile tyres, paper, cigarettes, distillery, aluminium foil, tea, pharmaceuticals, carbon black, graphite, iron foundry, silk and explosives.

Small industries, including the silk industry, are important; 400,184 units were registered at 31 March 1993, (estimated employment, 1992, 2,340,941).

COMMUNICATIONS

Roads. In 1989 the total length of roads was 61,494 km. On 31 March 1993 the state had 1,010,823 motor vehicles.

Railways. The route-km of railways within the state (1993–94) is 3,835 km. The main centres are Asansol, New Jalpaiguri and Kharagpur. There is a metro at Calcutta (16·4 km).

Civil Aviation. The main airport is Calcutta which has national and international flights. The second airport is at Bagdogra in the extreme north, which has regular scheduled services to Calcutta and Delhi. Vayudoot domestic airline also operates in the state.

Shipping. Calcutta is the chief port: A barrage has been built at Farakka to control the flow of the Ganges and to provide a rail and road link between North and South Bengal. A second port is being developed at Haldia, between the present port and the sea, which is intended mainly for bulk cargoes. West Bengal possesses 779 km of navigable canals.

SOCIAL INSTITUTIONS

Justice. The High Court of Judicature at Calcutta has a Chief Justice and 45 puisne judges. The Andaman and Nicobar Islands come under its jurisdiction.

Police. In March 1995 the police force numbered about 56,550, under a director-general and an inspector-general. Calcutta has a separate force under a commissioner directly responsible to the Government; its strength was about 22,000 in March 1995.

Religion. At the 1991 census Hindus numbered 50,866,624; Moslems, 16,075,836; Christians, 383,477; Buddhists, 203,578; Sikhs, 55,392; Jains, 34,355.

Education. At the 1991 census 32·72m. people were literate (57·7%; 67·81% of men and 46·56% of women). In 1994–95 there were 51,021 primary schools with 8,415,215 students, 2,804 junior high schools with 2,336,401 students and 6,363 high and higher secondary schools with 1,470,885 students. Education is free up to higher secondary stage. There are 9 universities.

The University of Calcutta (founded 1857) is affiliating and teaching; in 1992–93 it had 208 colleges and 139,679 students. Visva Bharati, Santiniketan, was established in 1951 and is residential and teaching; it had 3,115 students in 1992–93. The University of Jadavpur, Calcutta (1955), had 7,144 students in 1992–93. Burdwan University was established in 1960; in 1992–93 there were 91,433 students. Kalyani University was established in 1960 (8,571 students in 1992–93). The University of North Bengal (1962) had 36,521 students in 1992–93. Rabindra Bharati University had 8,309 students in 1992–93. Bidhan Chandra Krishi Viswavidyalaya (1974) had 389 students in 1992–93. There is also Vidyasagar University, Medinipur. Bengal Engineering College has university status. There are 11 engineering and technology colleges, 10 medical colleges, 43 teacher training colleges, 46 polytechnics and 303 arts, science and commerce colleges.

Health. There were (1994–95) 392 hospitals, 1,177 clinics, 1,258 health centres and 8,126 sub-centres with a total of 67,078 beds, and 551 dispensaries.

UNION TERRITORIES

ANDAMAN AND NICOBAR ISLANDS. The Andaman and Nicobar Islands are administered by the President of the Republic of India acting through a Lieut.-Governor. There is a 30-member Pradesh Council, 5 members of which are selected by the Administrator as advisory counsellors. The seat of administration is at Port Blair, which is connected with Calcutta (1,255 km away) and Madras (1,190 km) by steamer service which calls about every 10 days; there are air services from Calcutta and Madras. Roads in the islands, 733 km black-topped and 48 km others. There are 2 districts.

The population (1991 census) was 280,661; Area, 8,249 sq. km; density 34 per sq. km. Growth rate 1981–91, 48·7%. Port Blair (1991), 74,955.

The climate is tropical, with little variation in temperature. Heavy rain (125" annually) is mainly brought by the south-west monsoon. Humidity is high.

Budget figures for 1995–96 show total revenue receipts of Rs 650m., and total expenditure on revenue account of Rs 4,090m. Plan outlay, 1995–96, Rs 2,150m.

In 1994–95 there were 184 primary schools with 44,625 students, 45 middle schools with 20,150 students, 31 high schools with 8,868 students and 41 higher secondary schools with 4,482 students. There is a teachers' training college, 2 polytechnics and 2 colleges. Literacy (1991 census), 73·02% (78·99% of men and 65·46% of women).

Lieut.-Governor: V. Purushothaman.

The **Andaman Islands** lie in the Bay of Bengal, 193 km from Cape Negrais in Burma, 1,255 from Calcutta and 1,190 from Madras. Five large islands grouped together are called the Great Andamans, and to the south is the island of Little

Andaman. There are some 204 islets, the two principal groups being the Ritchie Archipelago and the Labyrinth Islands. The Great Andaman group is about 467 km long and, at the widest, 51 km broad.

The original inhabitants live in the forests by hunting and fishing. The total population of the Andaman Islands (including about 430 aboriginals) was 240,089 in 1991. Main aboriginal tribes: Andamanese, Onges, Jarawas and Sentinelese.

The Great Andaman group, densely wooded, contains hardwood and softwood and supplies the match and plywood industries. Annually the Forest Department export about 25,000 tons of timber to the mainland. Coconut, coffee and rubber are cultivated. The islands are slowly being made self-sufficient in paddy and rice, and now grow approximately half their annual requirements. Livestock (1982): 27,400 cattle, 9,720 buffaloes, 17,600 goats and 21,220 pigs. Fishing is important. There is a sawmill at Port Blair and a coconut-oil mill. Little Andaman has a palm-oil mill.

The islands possess a number of harbours and safe anchorages, notably Port Blair in the south, Port Cornwallis in the north and Elphinstone and Mayabandar in the middle.

The **Nicobar Islands** are situated to the south of the Andamans, 121 km from Little Andaman. The British were in possession 1869–1947. There are 19 islands, 7 uninhabited; total area, 1,841 sq. km. The islands are usually divided into 3 sub-groups (southern, central and northern), the chief islands in each being respectively, Great Nicobar, Camotra with Nancowrie and Car Nicobar. There is a harbour between the islands of Camotra and Nancowrie, Nancowrie Harbour.

The population numbered, in 1991, 39,208, including about 22,200 of Nicobarese and Shompen tribes. The coconut and areca nut are the main items of trade, and coconuts are a major item in the people's diet.

CHANDIGARH. On 1 Nov. 1966 the city of Chandigarh and the area surrounding it was constituted a Union Territory. Population (1991), 642,015; density, 5,632 per sq. km.; growth rate, 1981–91, 42·16%. Area, 114 sq. km. It serves as the joint capital of both Punjab (India) and the state of Haryana, and is the seat of a High Court. The city will ultimately be the capital of just the Punjab; joint status is to last while a new capital is built for Haryana.

Budget for 1995–96 shows revenue of Rs 2,711m. and expenditure of Rs 3,473m.

There is some cultivated land and some forest (27·5% of the territory).

In 1992 there were 15 large and medium scale industries and about 2,800 small scale industries.

In 1994–95 there were 29 primary schools (42,350 students), 12 middle schools (12,073 students), 37 high schools (10,193 students) and 27 higher secondary schools (9,705 students). There were also 4 engineering and technology colleges, 12 arts, science and commerce colleges, 2 polytechnic institutes and a university.

In 1991, 77·81% of the population were literate (82·04% of men and 72·34% of women).

Administrator: Lieut.-Gen. Bakshi K. N. Chibber.

DADRA AND NAGAR HAVELI. Formerly Portuguese, the territories of Dadra and Nagar Haveli were occupied in July 1954 by nationalists, and a pro-India administration was formed; this body made a request for incorporation into the Union, 1 June 1961. By the 10th amendment to the constitution the territories became a centrally administered Union Territory with effect from 11 Aug. 1961, forming an enclave at the southernmost point of the border between Gujarat and Maharashtra. Area 491 sq. km.; population (census 1991), 138,477; density 282 per sq. km; growth rate, 1981–91, 33·57%. There is an Administrator appointed by the Government of India. The day-to-day business is done by various departments, coordinated by the Resident Deputy Collector, Collector or Assistant Secretary. Headquarters are at Silvassa. 78·82% of the population is tribal and organized in 72 villages. Languages used are Bhilli, Gujarati, Bhilodi (91·1%), Marathi and Hindi.

Administrator: S. P. Aggarwal.
Collector: G. D. Badgaiyan.

Budget. Budget for 1995–96 shows revenue receipts of Rs 222m. and revenue expenditure of Rs 445·8m.

Electricity. Electricity is supplied by Gujarat, and all villages have been electrified.

Water. As the result of a joint project with the governments of Gujarat, Goa and Daman and Diu there is a reservoir at Damanganga with irrigation potential of 7,044 ha.

Agriculture. Farming is the chief occupation, and 27,855 ha were under crops in 1993–94. Much of the land is terraced and there is a 100% subsidy for soil conservation. The major food crops are rice and ragi; wheat, small millets and pulses are also grown. There is little irrigation (4,445 ha). There are 9 veterinary aid centres, a veterinary hospital, an agricultural research centre and breeding centres to improve strains of cattle and poultry. During 1994–95 the Administration distributed 167 tonnes of high yielding paddy and wheat seed, and 1,705 tonnes of fertilizer.

Forestry. 19,967 ha or 40·8% of the total area is forest, mainly of teak, sadad and khair. There was (1985) a moratorium on commercial felling, to preserve the environmental function of the forests and ensure local supplies of firewood, timber and fodder. The moratorium still continued in 1995.

Industry. There is no heavy industry, and the Territory is a 'No Industry District'. Industrial estates for small and medium units have been set up at Piparia, Masat and Khadoli. There were (1995) 349 small units, and 170 medium scale, employing about 13,000. Concessions (15 years' sales tax holiday) are available for small industries.

Tourism. The territory is a rural area between the industrial centres of Bombay and Surat-Vapi. The Tourism Department is developing areas of natural beauty to promote acceptable tourism.

Communications. There are (1995) 412 km of motorable road. The railway line from Bombay to Ahmedabad runs through Vapi near Silvassa. The nearest airport is Bombay. There were 9,160 motor vehicles in 1994–95.

Justice. The territory is under the jurisdiction of the Bombay (Maharashtra) High Court. There is a District and Sessions Court and one Junior Division Civil Court at Silvassa.

Education. Literacy was 40·71% of the population at the 1991 census (53·56% of men and 26·98% of women). In 1994–95 there were 150 adult education centres (4,500 students); there were 182 primary and middle schools and 15 high and higher secondary schools. Total primary and middle school enrolment was 25,689; high-school and higher secondary, 3,030.

Health. The territory had (1994) 1 cottage hospital, 6 primary health centres and 4 dispensaries; there is also a mobile dispensary.

DAMAN AND DIU. Daman (Damão) on the Gujarat coast, 100 miles (160 km) north of Bombay, was seized by the Portuguese in 1531 and ceded to them (1539) by the Shar of Gujarat. The island of Diu, captured in 1534, lies off the south-east coast of Kathiawar (Gujarat); there is a small coastal area. Former Portuguese forts on either side of the entrance to the Gulf of Cambay, in Dec. 1961 the territories were occupied by India and incorporated into the Indian Union; they were administered as one unit together with Goa, to which they were attached until 30 May 1987, when Goa was separated from them and became a state.

Territory and Population. Daman, 72 sq. km, population (1991) 62,101; Diu, 40 sq. km, population 39,485. Density, 907 per sq. km. Growth rate 1981–91, 28·62%. The main language spoken is Gujarati.

The chief towns are Daman (population, 1991, 26,905) and Diu (20,643).

Daman and Diu have been governed as parts of a Union Territory since Dec. 1961, becoming the whole of that Territory on 30 May 1987.

The main activities are tourism, fishing and tapping the toddy palm. In Daman there is rice-growing, some wheat and dairying. Diu has fine tourist beaches, grows coconuts and pearl millet, and processes salt.

Administrator: S. P. Aggarwal.

Budget. Budget for 1995–96 shows revenue receipts of Rs 340·4m. and revenue expenditure of Rs 397·6m. Plan outlay, 1995–96, Rs 230m.

Education. In 1991, 71·2% of the population were literate (82·66% of men and 59·4% of women). In 1993–94 there were 49 primary schools with 12,892 students, 16 middle schools with 6,679 students, 17 high schools with 3,278 students and 3 higher secondary schools with 1,469 students. There is a degree college and a polytechnic.

DELHI. Delhi became a Union Territory on 1 Nov. 1956 and was designated the National Capital Territory in 1995.

Territory and Population. The territory forms an enclave near the eastern frontier of Haryana and the western frontier of Uttar Pradesh in north India. Delhi has an area of 1,483 sq. km. At the 1991 census its population was 9,420,644 (density per sq. km, 6,352). Growth rate, 1981–91, 51·45%. In the rural area of Delhi there are 231 villages and 27 census towns. They are distributed in 5 community development blocks.

Government. The Lieut-Governor is the Administrator. Under the New Delhi Municipal Act 1994 New Delhi Municipal Council is nominated by central government and replaces the former New Delhi Municipal Committee.

Elections for the 70-member Legislative Assembly were held in Nov. 1993 and Bharatiya Janata Party formed the government. Bharatiya Janata Party, 49; Congress-I, 14; Janata Dal, 4; Independent and others, 3.

Lieut.-Governor: Prasannabhai Karunashankar Dave.
Chief Minister: Madan Lal Khurana.

Budget. Estimates 1995–96 show revenue receipts of Rs 22,966·9m. and expenditure of Rs 32,713·9m. Plan outlay (1995-96) Rs 17,200m.

Agriculture. The contribution to the economy is not significant. In 1992–93 about 52,100 ha were cropped (of which 36,000 ha were irrigated). Animal husbandry is increasing and mixed farms are common. Chief crops are wheat, bajra, paddy, sugar-cane and vegetables.

Industry. The modern city is the largest commercial centre in northern India and an important industrial centre. Since 1947 a large number of industrial units have been established; these include factories for the manufacture of razor blades, sports goods, electronic goods, bicycles and parts, plastic and PVC goods including footwear, textiles, chemicals, fertilizers, medicines, hosiery, leather goods, soft drinks, hand tools. There are also metal forging, casting, galvanising, electro-plating and printing enterprises. The number of industrial units functioning was about 89,000 in 1991–92; average number of workers employed was 0·8m. Production was worth Rs 50,000m. and investment was about Rs 15,000m in 1990–91.

Some traditional handicrafts, for which Delhi was formerly famous, still flourish; among them are ivory carving, miniature painting, gold and silver jewellery and papier mâché work. The handwoven textiles of Delhi are particularly fine; this craft is being successfully revived.

Delhi publishes major daily newspapers, including the *Times of India, Hindustan Times, The Hindu*, *Indian Express*, *National Herald*, *Patriot*, *Economic Times*, *The Pioneer*, *The Observer of Business and Politics*, *Financial Express* and *Statesman* (all in English); *Nav Bharat Times, Rashtriya Sahara, Jansatta* and *Hindustan* (in Hindi), and 3 Urdu dailies.

Roads. 5 national highways pass through the city. There were (1992–93) 2,097,155 registered motor vehicles. The Transport Corporation had 3,502 buses in 1992–93.

Railways. Delhi is an important rail junction with 3 main stations. There is an electric ring railway for commuters (route-km in 1993–94, 168).

Civil Aviation. Indira Gandhi International Airport operates international flights; Palam airport operates internal flights.

Religion. At the 1991 census Hindus numbered 7,882,164; Sikhs, 455,657; Moslems, 889,641; Jains, 94,672; Christians, 83,152; Buddhists, 13,906; others, 1,452.

Education. The proportion of literates to the total population was 75·29% at the 1991 census (82·01% of males and 66·99% of females). In 1993–94 there were 2,072 primary schools with 957,092 students, 531 middle schools with 525,413 students, 311 high schools with 255,660 students and 952 higher secondary schools with 147,796 students. There are 3 engineering and technology colleges, 6 medical colleges and 5 polytechnics.

The University of Delhi was founded in 1922; it had 71 affiliated colleges and 110,285 students in 1992–93. There are also Jawahar Lal Nehru University, Indira Gandhi National Open University and the Jamia Millia Islamia University; the Indian Institute of Technology at Hauz Khas; the Indian Agricultural Research Institute at Pusa; the All India Institute of Medical Science at Ansari Nagar and the Indian Institute of Public Administration are the other important institutions.

Health. In 1992 there were 82 hospitals including 46 general, 27 special, 6 Ayurvedic, 1 Unani, 2 Homeopathic. There were 656 dispensaries.

LAKSHADWEEP. The territory consists of an archipelago of 36 islands (10 inhabited), about 300 km off the west coast of Kerala. It was constituted a Union Territory in 1956 as the Laccadive, Minicoy and Amindivi Islands, and renamed in Nov. 1973. The total area of the islands is 32 sq. km. The northern portion is called the Amindivis. The remaining islands are called the Laccadives (except Minicoy Island). The inhabited islands are: Androth (the largest), Amini, Agatti, Bitra, Chetlat, Kadmat, Kalpeni, Kavaratti, Kiltan and Minicoy. Androth is 4·8 sq. km, and is nearest to Kerala. An Advisory Committee associated with the Union Home Minister and an Advisory Council to the Administrator assist in the administration of the islands; these are constituted annually. Population (1991 census), 51,707, nearly all Moslems. Density, 1,616 per sq. km.; growth rate, 1981–91, 28·4%. The language is Malayalam, but the language in Minicoy is Mahl. Budget for 1995–96 shows revenue of Rs 49·5m. and expenditure of Rs 1,135·7m. Plan outlay, 1990–91, Rs 211·3m. In 1991, 81·78% of the population were literate (90·18% of men and 72·89% of women). There were, in 1992-93, 9 high schools (1,427 students) and 9 nursery schools (1,056 students), 19 junior basic schools (8,773 students), 4 senior basic schools (3,673 students) and 2 junior colleges. There are 2 hospitals and 7 primary health centres. The staple products are copra and fish; coconut is the only major crop. There is a tourist resort at Bangarem, an uninhabited island with an extensive lagoon. Headquarters of administration, Kavaratti Island. An airport, with Vayudoot services, opened on Agatti island in April 1988. The islands are also served by ship from the mainland and have helicopter inter-island services.

Administrator: S. P. Aggarwal.

PONDICHERRY. Formerly the chief French settlement in India, Pondicherry was founded by the French in 1673, taken by the Dutch in 1693 and restored to the French in 1699. The English took it in 1761, restored it in 1765, re-took it in 1778, restored it a second time in 1785, retook it a third time in 1793 and finally restored it to the French in 1816. Administration was transferred to India on 1 Nov. 1954. A Treaty of Cession (together with Karaikal, Mahé and Yanam) was signed on 28 May 1956; instruments of ratification were signed on 16 Aug. 1962 from which date (by the 14th amendment to the Indian Constitution) Pondicherry, comprising the 4 territories, became a Union Territory.

Territory and Population. The territory is composed of enclaves on the Coromandel Coast of Tamil Nadu and Andhra Pradesh, with Mahé forming an enclave on the coast of Kerala. The total area of Pondicherry is 492 sq. km, divided into 4 Districts. On Tamil Nadu coast: Pondicherry (293 sq. km; population, 1991 census (provisional), 607,600), Karaikal (160; 145,723). On Kerala coast: Mahé (9;

33,425). On Andhra Pradesh coast: Yanam (30; 20,297). Total population (1991 census), 807,785; density, 1,642 per sq. km.; growth rate, 1981–91, 33·64%. Pondicherry Municipality had (1991) 203,065 inhabitants. The principal languages spoken are Tamil, Telugu, Malayalam, French and English.

Government. By the Government of Union Territories Act 1963 Pondicherry is governed by a Lieut.-Governor, appointed by the President, and a Council of Ministers responsible to a Legislative Assembly. A Congress (I) government was formed after the election in June 1991. Total seats, 30: Congress (I), 15; DMK, 4; Janata Dal, 1; All India Anna DMK, 6; CPI, 1; Independents, 3.

Governor: Rajendra Kumari Bajpai.
Chief Minister: V. Vaithilingam.

Budget. Budget estimates for 1992–93 show revenue receipts of Rs 2,572·8m. and expenditure of Rs 2,572·8m. Plan outlay, 1994–95, Rs 1,350m.

Electricity. Power is bought from neighbouring states. All 292 villages have electricity. Consumption, 1991–92, 747 units per head. Peak demand, 130 MW; total consumption, 607·73m. units.

Agriculture. Nearly 45% of the population is engaged in agriculture and allied pursuits; 90% of the cultivated area is irrigated. The main food crop is rice. Foodgrain production, 107,365 tonnes in 1991–92, of which 94,300 tonnes from 23,855 ha was rice; principal cash crops are cotton (10,934 bales of 180 kg), sugar-cane (240,557 tonnes) and groundnuts; minor food crops include ragi, bajra and pulses.

Industry. There were, 1994–95, 23 large and 73 medium-scale enterprises manufacturing items such as textiles, sugar, cotton yarn, spirits and beer, potassium chlorate, rice bran oil, vehicle parts, soap, amino acids, paper, plastics, steel ingots, washing machines, glass and tin containers and bio polymers. There were also 5,197 small industrial units engaged in varied manufacturing.

Roads. There were (1992–93) 3,282 km of roads of which 1,248 km were surfaced. Motor vehicles (March 1993) 96,464.

Railways. Pondicherry is connected to Villupuram Junction. Route-km in 1992–93, 27.

Civil Aviation. The nearest main airport is Madras. Vayudoot domestic airline connects Pondicherry with Madras.

Education. In 1991, 74·74% of the population were literate (83·68% of men and 65·63% of women). There were, in 1994–95, 172 pre-primary schools (12,060 pupils), 345 primary schools (103,851), 111 middle schools (62,091), 87 high schools (27,506) and 47 higher secondary schools (11,367). There were (1994–95) 7 general education colleges, 2 medical colleges, a law college, an engineering college, an agricultural college and a dental college, and 3 polytechnics. Pondicherry University had, in 1992–93, 16 colleges and 8,975 students.

Health. In 1992 there were 8 hospitals, 57 health centres and dispensaries and 79 sub-centres. In 1990 family schemes had reduced the birth rate to 19·9 per 1,000 and the infant mortality rate to 34·79 per 1,000 live births.

INDONESIA
Republik Indonesia

Capital: Jakarta
Population: 191·36m. (1994)
GNP per capita: US$880 (1994)
HDI/world rank: 0·637/104 (1992)

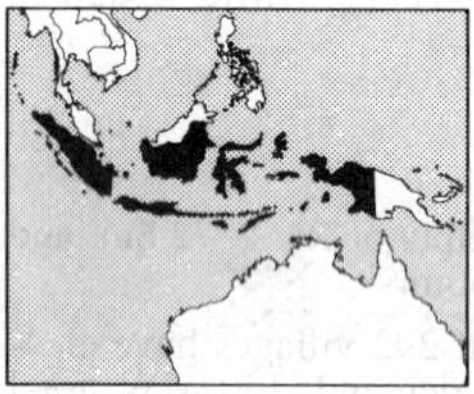

KEY HISTORICAL EVENTS. In the 16th century Portuguese traders in quest of spices settled in some of the islands, but were ejected by the British, who in turn were ousted by the Dutch (1595). The Netherlands East India Company ran the Netherlands East Indies from 1602 to 1798. Thereafter the Netherlands Government ruled the colony from 1816 to 1941, when it was occupied by the Japanese until 1945. An independent republic was proclaimed on 17 Aug. 1945.

For history 1949–66 *see* THE STATESMAN'S YEAR-BOOK, 1992–93, p. 772.

In March 1966 the military took power under the leadership of Lieut.-Gen. Suharto, who became President in Feb. 1967.

TERRITORY AND POPULATION. Indonesia, with a land area of 741,098 sq. miles (1,919,443 sq. km), consists of 13,677 islands (6,000 of which are inhabited) extending about 3,200 miles east to west through three time-zones (East, Central and West Indonesian Standard time) and 1,250 miles north to south. The largest islands are Sumatra, Java, Kalimantan (Indonesian Borneo), Sulawesi (Celebes) and Irian Jaya (the western part of New Guinea). Most of the smaller islands except Madura and Bali are grouped together. The two largest groups of islands are Maluku (the Moluccas) and Nusa Tenggara (the Lesser Sundas).

Population at the 1990 census was 179,378,946. Estimate, 1995, 195·28m. (42% urban).

Area, population and chief towns of the provinces, autonomous districts and major islands at the 1990 census:

	Area (in sq. km)	Population	Chief town	Population
Aceh [1]	55,392	3,416,156	Banda Aceh	143,409
Sumatera Utara	70,787	10,256,027	Medan	1,685,972
Sumatera Barat	49,778	4,000,207	Padang	477,344
Riau	94,561	3,303,976	Pakanbaru	341,328
Jambi	44,800	2,020,568	Jambi [2]	301,359
Sumatera Selatan	103,688	6,313,074	Palembang	1,084,483
Bengkulu	21,168	1,179,122	Bengkulu	146,439
Lampung	33,307	6,016,573	Tanjungkarang	284,275 [3]
Sumatra	473,481	36,505,703		
Jakarta Raya [1]	590	8,259,266	Jakarta	8,259,266
Jawa Barat	46,300	35,384,352	Bandung	2,026,893
Jawa Tengah	34,206	28,520,643	Semarang	1,005,316
Yogyakarta [1]	3,169	2,913,054	Yogyakarta	412,392
Jawa Timur	47,921	32,503,991	Surabaya	2,421,016
Java and Madura	132,186	107,581,306		
Kalimantan Barat	146,760	3,229,153	Pontianak	387,112
Kalimantan Tengah	152,600	1,396,486	Palangkaraya	60,447 [3]
Kalimantan Selatan	37,660	2,597,572	Banjarmasin	443,738
Kalimantan Timur	202,440	1,876,663	Samarinda	335,016
Kalimantan	539,460	9,099,874		

	Area (in sq. km)	*Population*	*Chief town*	*Population*
Sulawesi Utara	19,023	2,478,119	Menado	275,374
Sulawesi Tengah	69,726	1,711,327	Palu	298,584 [3]
Sulawesi Selatan	72,781	6,981,646	Ujung Padang	913,196
Sulawesi Tenggara	27,686	1,349,619	Kendari	41,021 [3]
Sulawesi	189,216	12,520,711		
Bali	5,561	2,777,811	Denpasar	261,263 [3]
Nusa Tenggara Barat	20,177	3,369,649	Mataram	141,387 [3]
Nusa Tenggara Timur	47,876	3,268,644	Kupang	403,110 [3]
Timor Timur [4]	14,874	747,750	Dili	60,150 [4]
Maluku	74,505	1,857,790	Amboina	206,260
Irian Jaya	421,981	1,648,708	Jayapura	149,618 [3]
Pulau–Pulau Lain	584,974	13,670,352		

[1] Autonomous District. [2] Formerly Telanaipura.
[3] 1980 census. [4] See section below.

The capital, Jakarta, had a population of 9m. in 1993. Other major cities (census 1990 in 1m.): Surabaya, 2·5; Bandung, 2; Medan, 1·7; Semarang, 1·3; Palembang, 1·1.

Vital statistics, 1988: Birth rate, 28·7 per 1,000; death rate, 7·9. Growth rate, 1992, 1·7%. Life expectancy in 1992 was 62 years.

The principal ethnic groups are the Acehnese, Bataks and Minangkabaus in Sumatra, the Javanese and Sundanese in Java, the Madurese in Madura, the Balinese in Bali, the Sasaks in Lombok, the Menadonese, Minahasans, Torajas and Buginese in Sulawesi, the Dayaks in Kalimantan, Irianese in Irian Jaya, the Ambonese in the Moluccas and Timorese in Timor Timur. There were some 6m. Chinese resident in 1991.

Bahasa Indonesia is the official language; Dutch is spoken as a colonial inheritance.

East Timor. Portugal abandoned its former colony, whose population is largely Roman Catholic, in 1975, when it was occupied by Indonesia and claimed as the province of Timor Timur. The UN does not recognize Indonesian sovereignty over the territory. An independence movement, FRETILIN, has maintained a guerilla resistance to the Indonesian government which has resulted in large-scale casualties and alleged atrocities.

Carey, P. and Bentley, G. C. (eds.) *East Timor at the Crossroads: the Forging of a Nation.* London, 1995

CLIMATE. Conditions vary greatly over this spread of islands, but generally the climate is tropical monsoon, with a dry season from June to Sept. and a wet one from Oct. to April. Temperatures are high all the year and rainfall varies according to situation on lee or windward shores. Jakarta. Jan. 78°F (25·6°C), July 78°F (25·6°C). Annual rainfall 71" (1,775 mm). Padang. Jan. 79°F (26·7°C), July 79°F (26·7°C). Annual rainfall 177" (4,427 mm). Surabaya. Jan. 79°F (27·2°C), July 78°F (25·6°C). Annual rainfall 51" (1,285 mm).

CONSTITUTION AND GOVERNMENT. The political system is based on *pancasila*, in which deliberations lead to a consensus. 400 members of the *House of People's Representatives* are elected every 5 years, and the remaining 100 are appointed from the armed forces. Together with 500 government appointees they make up the *People's Consultative Assembly* which meets every 5 years to choose a president. The military perform a dual function enshrined in law, combining conventional defence duties with participation in all areas of political and social life. Golkar is a 'functional group'. There are 2 officially-sanctioned parties also in the House of People's Representatives: the United Development Party (UDP, largely Moslem), and the Indonesian Democratic Party (IDP nationalist Christian).

General elections to the 400 elected seats in the House of Representatives were held on 9 June 1992. The electorate was 107m.; turn-out was 90%. Golkar won 282 seats with 68% of votes cast (73% in 1987), UDP 62 with 17·5% (16% in 1987) and IDP 56 with 15% (11% in 1987).

The Cabinet was as follows in Jan. 1996:

President and Prime Minister: Gen. Suharto (b. 1921; elected in 1968, 1973, 1978, 1983, 1988 and 1993). *Vice-President:* Gen. Try Sutrisno (elected 1993).

Co-ordinating Ministers: (*Political and Security*) Gen. Susilo Sudarman; (*Economy, Finance, Industry and Supervision of Development*) Saleh Afiff; (*Welfare*) Maj.-Gen. Azwar Anas; (*Production and Distribution*) Ir Hartarto.

Internal Affairs: Lieut.-Gen. Yogi Memet. *Foreign Affairs:* Ali Alatas. *Defence and Security:* Gen. Edi Sudrajat. *Justice:* Utoyo Osman. *Information:* Harmoko. *Finance:* Mar'ie Muhammed. *Industry and Trade:* Tinglei Arimibowo. *Agriculture:* Sjarifuddin Baharsyah. *Mines and Energy:* Idu Bagus Sujana. *Public Works:* Radinal Mochtar. *Communications:* Haryanto Danudirto. *Co-operatives and Small Business:* Subiakto Cakrawerdaya. *Manpower:* Abdul Latief. *Transmigration:* Siswono Yudohudoso. *Tourism, Post and Telecommunications:* Joop Ave. *Education and Culture:* Wardiman Joyonegoro. *Health:* Dr Suyudi. *Religious Affairs:* Tarmizi Taher. *Social Affairs:* Endang Suweno. *Forestry:* Jamaluddin Suryohadikasumo. *Research and Technology:* Habibie. *Secretary of State:* Dr Murdiono.

National flag: Horizontally red over white.

National anthem: 'Indonesia, tanah jang mulia' ('Indonesia, our native land'); words and tune by W. R. Supratman.

Local government: There are 27 provinces, 3 of which are special territories (the capital city of Jakarta, Yogyakarta and Aceh), each administered by a Governor appointed by the President; they are divided into 246 districts (*kabupatens*), each under a district head (*bupati*), and 55 municipalities (*kotamadya*), each under a mayor (*wali kota*). The districts are divided into 3,592 sub-districts (*kecamtans*), each headed by a *camat*. There were 66,594 villages (1988).

DEFENCE. There is selective conscription for 2 years.

Army. The Army is organized in a strategic reserve, with 2 infantry divisional headquarters, 3 infantry and 3 airborne brigades, 2 field artillery and 1 air defence artillery regiment and 2 engineer battalions; and 10 military area commands, with 62 infantry, 8 cavalry, 11 field artillery, 10 air defence and 8 engineer battalions, and 1 composite aviation and 1 helicopter squadron. Equipment includes 275 AMX-13, 30 PT-76 and 26 Scorpion light tanks. The Army has over 50 aircraft, including 1 Islander, 4 Aviocars and 12 other fixed-wing types, 15 Bell 205, 12 BO 105, 9 Hughes 300, 4 locally-built Bell 412 helicopters. Total strength in 1996 was 214,000. There is a paramilitary police some 174,000 strong, and 2 part-time local auxiliary forces: KAMRA (People's Security) and WANRA (People's Resistance).

Navy. The Navy in 1995 numbered about 40,500, including 12,000 in the Commando Corps, and 1,000 in the Naval Air Arm. Combatant strength includes 2 German-built diesel submarines (1 in long refit) and 13 frigates of which 6 are former Dutch Van Speijk class, and 3 former British Ashanti class each equipped with 1 helicopter. Delivery of 16 ex-East German Parchim class anti-submarine corvettes completed in 1996. There are also 4 fast missile craft, 2 torpedo-armed craft and 36 miscellaneous patrol craft as well as 2 Dutch-built tripartite coastal minehunters and 11 other minesweepers. Amphibious lift is provided by 14 tank landing ships (4 with helicopter facilities) and 50 craft. The auxiliary force includes 2 replenishment tankers, 2 transport tankers, 6 surveying vessels, 1 command and submarine support ship, 1 repair ship, 3 training ships and some dozens of minor auxiliaries and service craft.

The Naval Air Arm operates 60 aircraft, including 15 Searchmaster maritime reconnaissance and 8 NC-212 Aviocar transport aircraft, and 10 anti-submarine helicopters as well as miscellaneous communications and utility aircraft.

A separate Military Sealift Command operates about 25 inter-island transport ships (which number includes 3 of the tank landing ships in the navy listing) totalling approximately 30,000 tonnes. The Maritime Security Agency operates 10 cutters, the Customs about 70 and the armed Marine Police 60 craft.

Air Force. Operational combat units comprise two squadrons of A-4E Skyhawk attack aircraft, and single squadrons of F-5E Tiger II and of F-16 fighters and OV-10F Bronco twin-turboprop counter-insurgency aircraft. There are 5 transport squadrons, equipped with turboprop C-130 Hercules, Nurtanio/CASA NC-212 Avi-ocar and CN-235 and F27 Friendship aircraft, as well as 3 specially-equipped Boeing 737 dual-purpose maritime surveillance/transports; and an assortment of other aircraft in transport, helicopter and training units including 15 Hawk attack/trainers, 15 T-34C-1 armed turboprop trainers, and 36 Swiss-built AS 202 Bravo piston-engined primary trainers.

Personnel (1995) approximately 20,000.

INTERNATIONAL RELATIONS

Membership. Indonesia is a member of the UN, OPEC and ASEAN.

ECONOMY

Policy. The fifth Five-Year Development Plan (1990-94) constituted the final 5 years of the Government's first 25-Year Long Term Development Plan. The sixth Plan covers 1995-99.

Budget. By law the budget must balance. The fiscal year starts 1 April. Revenue and expenditure for 1995–96 were 78,000,000m. rupiahs.

Currency. The monetary unit is the *rupiah* (IDR) notionally of 100 *sen*. There are coins of 5, 10, 25, 50, 100 and 500, and notes of 100, 500, 1,000, 5,000, 10,000, 20,000 and 50,000 rupiahs. Inflation was 8·64% in 1995 (9·24% in 1994). Foreign exchange reserves were US$10,500m. In March 1996, 3,536·72 rupiahs = £1 sterling; 2,314 rupiahs = US$1; 1,567·86 rupiahs = DM1.

Banking and Finance. The Bank Indonesia, successor to De Javasche Bank established by the Dutch in 1828, was made the central bank of Indonesia on 1 July 1953. Its *Governor* is Sudradjat Djiwandono. It had an original capital of Rp. 25m.; a reserve fund of Rp. 18m. and a special reserve of Rp. 84m. Total assets and liabilities as at Dec. 1992, Rp. 123,689,000m.

There are 117 commercial banks, 28 development banks and other financial institutions, 8 development finance companies and 9 joint venture merchant banks. Commercial banking is dominated by 7 state-owned banks: Bank Rakyat Indonesia provides services to smallholder agriculture and rural development; Bank Bumi Daya, estate agriculture and forestry; Bank Negara Indonesia 1946, industry; Bank Dagang Negara, mining; and Bank Expor-Impor Indonesia, export commodity sector. All state banks are authorized to deal in foreign exchange.

There are 70 private commercial banks owned and operated by Indonesians. The 11 foreign banks specialize in foreign exchange transactions and direct lending operations to foreign joint ventures. The government owns 1 Savings Bank, Bank Tabungan Negara, and 1,000 Post Office Savings Banks. There are also over 3,500 rural and village savings bank and credit co-operatives.

There is a stock exchange in Jakarta.

Weights and Measures. The metric system is is use.

The following are the old weights and measures: *Pikol* = 136·16 lb. avoirdupois; *Katti* = 1·36 lb. avoirdupois; *Bau* = 1·7536 acres; *Square Pal* = 227 hectares = 561·16 acres; *Jengkal* = 4 yd; *Pal* (Java) = 1,506 metres; *Pal* (Sumatra) = 1,852 metres.

ENERGY AND NATURAL RESOURCES

Electricity. There were 7 hydro-electric plants in 1989; 19,044 out of 66,594 villages are supplied with electricity in Java and Sumatra. Installed capacity was 9m. MW in 1993. Electricity produced (1991) 37,700m. kWh.

Oil. The importance of oil in the economy is declining. The 1995 output of crude oil was 1,476,000 bbls. a day.

Gas. Natural gas production, 1993, was 2,823,228m. cu. ft.

Water. In 1988–89, 23,677 ha of new irrigation networks were constructed and 377,461 ha rehabilitated and maintained.

Minerals. The high cost of extraction means that little of the large mineral resources outside Java is exploited; however, there is copper mining in Irian Jaya, nickel mining and processing on Sulawesi, aluminium smelting in northern Sumatra. Open-cast coal mining has been conducted since the 1890s, but since the 1970s coal production has been developed as an alternative to oil. Reserves are estimated at 28,000m. tonnes. Coal production (1993) 27·9m. tonnes; bauxite (1993), 1,728,631 tonnes. Output (in 1,000 tonnes, 1993) of iron ore was 363·7; copper, 1,276·8; silver, 116,876 kg; gold, 73,522 kg; nickel ore, 2,696·1; tin, 30·1.

Agriculture. Agriculture contributed 19·5% of GDP in 1990. Production (1993, in 1,000 tonnes): Rice, 47,885; cassava, 16,356; maize, 6,513; sweet potatoes, 2,277; sugar-cane, 32,400; coconuts, 14m.; copra, 1,100; palm oil, 3,500; palm kernels, 748; soybeans, 1,630; rubber, 1,370; coffee, 441; groundnuts, 1,052; vegetables, 4,912; fruits, 7,341; tea, 169; tobacco, 85. In 1991 6,750 tonnes of nutmeg were produced, about 75% of world production.

Livestock (1993): Cattle, 11·0m.; buffaloes, 3·5m.; horses, 705,000; sheep, 6·3m.; goats, 11·8m.; pigs, 8·2m.; poultry, 620m.

Forestry. The forest area was (1993) 144m. ha, 75% of the land area. Of this, 66m. ha is scheduled for selective logging, 48m. ha for preservation for national parks and watersheds and 30m. ha for removal for agriculture, industry and settlement. Production (1991–92): Sawn timber, 3m. cu. metres; plywood, 9·1m. cu. metres.

Fisheries. In 1991 the catch of sea fish was 2,537,612 tonnes; inland fish was 811,989 tonnes. In 1991 there were 130,712 motorized and 373,086 other fishing vessels.

INDUSTRY. Manufacturing contributed 14·9% of GDP in 1990. There are shipyards at Jakarta Raya, Surabaya, Semarang and Amboina. There were (1985) more than 2,000 textile factories (total production in 1987–88, 2,925·6m. metres), large paper factories (817,200 tonnes, 1986–87), match factories, automobile and bicycle assembly works, large construction works, tyre factories, glass factories, a caustic soda and other chemical factories. Production (1987–88): Cement, 22,419,000 tonnes; fertilizers, 5,811,000 tonnes; 160,372 motor vehicles and 249,573 motorcycles; 2·36m. boxes of matches; glasses and bottles, 126,060 tonnes; steel ingots, 1,337,000 tonnes; 640 TV sets and 159,020 refrigerators.

Labour. Reforms announced in Nov. 1994 included an annual review of regional minimum wages, enhanced enforcement of salary, safety and health regulations, and an improved dispute resolution process. National daily average wage, 1996, 4,073 rupiahs.

Trade Unions. Workers have a constitutional right to organize. Unions are expected to affiliate to the Indonesian Welfare Labour Union (SBSI) which enjoys government approval, but in Nov. 1990 an independent union, Setia Kawan (Solidarity) was set up. About 40% of the labour force belong to unions. In 1993 (and 1992) there were 169 (197) strikes involving 97,807 (98,764) workers and resulting in the loss of 857,845 (1,044,519) working hours. Strikes are forbidden by law.

FOREIGN ECONOMIC RELATIONS. Since 1992 foreigners have been permitted to hold 100% of the equity of new companies in Indonesia with more than US$50m. part capital, or situated in remote provinces. Foreign debt was US$85,000m. in Dec. 1992.

Commerce. In June 1994 import duties were cut on 739 commodities, surcharges on 108 imports were removed and non-tariff barriers on 27 items abolished. Imports and exports (including oil and gas) in US$1m. for year ending March:

	1989–90	*1990–91*	*1991–92*	*1992–93*
Imports f.o.b.	21,837	25,200	28,300	27,956
Exports f.o.b.	25,675	26,800	33,000	39,005

Main export items: Gas and oil, forestry products, manufactured goods, rubber, coffee, fishery products, coal, copper, tin, pepper, palm products and tea. In 1993 main trade partners were Japan (21·3% of imports, 30·4% of exports), USA (11·7%, 13%), Singapore (6·5%, 9·9%) and South Korea (5·6%, 6·6%).

Total trade between Indonesia and UK (British Department of Trade returns, in £1,000 sterling):

	1991	*1992*	*1993*	*1994*	*1995*
Imports to UK	415,340	536,057	700,535	782,546	903,867
Exports and re-exports from UK	197,991	312,756	331,094	366,035	525,499

Tourism. In 1993 3,255,411 tourists visited Indonesia.

COMMUNICATIONS

Roads. In 1991 there were 137,060 km of asphalted, of which 103,622 km were in good condition. Motor vehicles, 1992, numbered 10,482,307.

Railways. In 1992 the national railways totalled 6,458 km of 1,067 mm gauge, comprising 4,967 km on Java (of which 125 km electrified) and 1,491 km on Sumatra. In 1992 they carried 66m. passengers and 13·4m. tonnes of freight.

Civil Aviation. Garuda Indonesia is the state-owned national flag carrier, in 1995 operating 1 A300B4-200, 10 A300B4-600Rs, 8 B-737-300s, 7 B-737-400s, 6 B-747-200Bs, 3 B-747-400s 6 DC-10-30s, 6 DC-9-30s, 12 F-28-4000s and 6 other aircraft. Merpati Nusantara Airways is their domestic subsidiary. There are international airports at Jakarta (Sukarno-Hatta), Denpasar (on Bali), Medan (Sumatra), Pekanbaru (Sumatra), Ujung Pandang (Sulawesi), Solo (Java), Manado, Ambon (Maluku), Biak (Irian Jaya) and Batu Ampar (Batam). The number of passengers carried in 1992 was 9,403,308; freight, 164,241 tonnes. Services are also provided by Aeroflot Russian Airlines, Air China, Air Lanka, Balkan Bulgarian, British Airways, Cathay Pacific, China Airlines, China Southern Airlines, CSA, Emirates, Eva Airways, JAL, KLM, Korean Air, Lufthansa, Malaysia Airlines, Myanma Airways, Philippine Airlines, Qantas, Royal Brunei Airlines, Royal Jordanian, Saudia, Silk Air, Singapore Airlines, Thai Airways and UTA.

Shipping. There are 16 ports for oceangoing ships, the largest of which is Tanjung Priok, which serves the Jakarta area and has a container terminal. The national shipping company Pelajaran Nasional Indonesia (PELNI) maintains inter-island communications. The Jakarta Lloyd maintains regular services between Jakarta, Amsterdam, Hamburg and London. In 1995, the merchant marine comprised 535 ocean-going ships totalling 4·13m. DWT. 95 vessels (36·22% of total tonnage) were registered under foreign flags. Total tonnage registered, 2·69m. GRT, including oil tanker, 0·65m. GRT, and container ships, 154,518 GRT. In 1992, 216,924,300 tonnes of freight were loaded and 150,117,400 tonnes discharged.

Telecommunications. Number of telephones (1993), 1,276,600.

Radio Republik Indonesia, under the Department of Information, operates 49 stations. In 1988–89 there were 8,948,195 TV receivers, and 54,318 public TV sets had been placed in villages within reach of the state-owned Televisi Republik Indonesia telecast.

Cinemas. There were 2,173 cinemas in 1990.

Press. (In 1987). There were 252 newspaper publishers with estimated circulation (1988-89) of 10,783,009, of which 3,716,056 were dailies. There were 270 publishers of weekly papers and magazines with a circulation (1988–89) of 3,444,802 and 1,721,130 respectively. 1,396 book titles were published in 1989.

SOCIAL INSTITUTIONS

Justice. There are courts of first instance, high courts of appeal in every provincial capital and a Supreme Court of Justice for the whole of Indonesia in Jakarta.

In civil law the population is divided into three main groups: Indonesians, Europeans and foreign Orientals, to whom different law systems are applicable. When, however, people from different groups are involved, a system of so-called 'inter-gentile' law is applied.

The present criminal law, which has been in force since 1918, is codified and is based on European penal law. This law is equally applicable to all groups of the population.

Religion. Religious liberty is granted to all denominations. In 1992 there were 160·62m. Moslems, 11·94m. Protestants and 5·78m. Roman Catholics. There were also 1·81m. Buddhists, probably for the greater part Chinese, and 3·59m. Hindus, of whom 2·5m. were on Bali.

Education. Adult literacy was 84·4% in 1992. In 1991–92 there were 26,325,701 pupils in primary schools, 5,510,287 students in junior high schools and, in 1990-91, 3,910,115 students in senior high schools, vocational schools, higher training and sports teachers' training colleges. Number of students in higher education (1991–92) 1,773,459. In 1994–95 in the state sector there were 31 universities and 1 open university, and 13 institutes of higher education, including 10 teacher training colleges. In the private sector there were 66 universities and the following specialized universities: Adventist, 1; Christian, 7; Islamic, 10; Methodist, 1; Roman Catholic, 5; Veterans', 1. There were 19 institutes of of higher education in the private sector, including 12 teacher training colleges. In 1994–95 there were 694,152 university students and 44,014 academic staff.

Health. In 1990 there were 25,752 doctors, 98,842 nurses and in 1991, 5,976 public health centres, 12,944 sub-public health centres and 3,521 mobile units.

DIPLOMATIC REPRESENTATIVES

Of Indonesia in Great Britain (38 Grosvenor Sq., London W1X 9AD)
Ambassador: Junus Effendy Habibie.

Of Great Britain in Indonesia (Jalan M.H. Thamrin 75, Jakarta 10310)
Ambassador: G. S. Burton.

Of Indonesia in the USA (2020 Massachusetts Ave., NW, Washington, D.C., 20036)
Ambassador: Arifin Mohamad Siregar.

Of the USA in Indonesia (Medan Merdeka Selatan 5, Jakarta)
Ambassador: Vacant.

Of Indonesia to the United Nations
Ambassador: Nugroho Wisnumurti.

Further Reading

Central Bureau of Statistics. *Statistical Yearbook of Indonesia.*
Bee, O. J., *The Petroleum Resources of Indonesia.* OUP, 1982
Cribb, R., *Historical Dictionary of Indonesia.* Metuchen (NJ), 1993.—and Brown, C., *Modern Indonesia: a History since 1945.* Harlow, 1995
International Commission of Jurists, *Indonesia and the Rule of Law.* London, 1987
Kim, T. J. *et al., Spatial Development in Indonesia.* Aldershot, 1992
Krausse, G. H. and Krausse, S. C. E., *Indonesia* [Bibliography]. Oxford and Santa Barbara (CA), 1994
Palmier, L., *Understanding Indonesia.* London, 1986
Rickefs, M. C., *A History of Modern Indonesia since 1300.* London, 1993
Schwartz, A., *A Nation in Waiting: Indonesia in the 1990s.* London, 1994
Thoolen, H., *Indonesia and the Rule of Law.* London, 1987
Vatikiotis, M.R.J., *Indonesian Politics under Suharto: Order, Development and Pressure for Change.* 2nd ed. London, 1994

See also EAST TIMOR, *above.*

National statisitcal office: Central Bureau of Statistics, POB1003, Jakarta, 10010.

IRAN

Jomhoori-e-Islami-e-Iran

(Islamic Republic of Iran)

Capital: Tehran
Population: 63·2m. (1994)
GNP per capita: US$2,190 (1992)
HDI/world rank: 0·770/70 (1992)

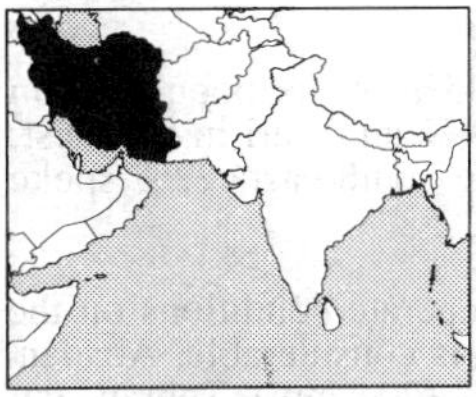

KEY HISTORICAL EVENTS. Following widespread civil unrest, the Shah left Iran on 17 Jan. 1979. The Ayatollah Ruhollah Khomeini, spiritual leader of the Shi'a Moslem community, returned from 15 years' exile on 1 Feb. 1979 and appointed a provisional government on 5 Feb. An Islamic Republic was proclaimed on 1 April 1979. For the 1980–90 war with Iraq *see* THE STATESMAN'S YEAR-BOOK, 1994–95, p. 771.

TERRITORY AND POPULATION. Iran is bounded in the north by Armenia, Azerbaijan, the Caspian Sea and Turkmenistan, east by Afghanistan and Pakistan, south by the Gulf of Oman and the Persian (Arabian) Gulf, and west by Iraq and Turkey. It has an area of 1,648,000 sq. km (634,293 sq. miles), but a vast portion is desert, and the average density is only (1993) 37 per sq. km.

Population, 1991 census, 55,837,163. Estimate in 1994, 63·2m. (58% urban). Abortion is illegal, but a family planning scheme was inaugurated in 1988.

By 1992 there were 2m. refugees from Afghanistan; repatriation started in 1993.

The areas, populations and capitals of the 25 provinces *(ostan)* were:

Province	*Area (sq. km)*	*Census 1986*	*Census 1991*	*Capital*
Ardebil	18,451	1,036,202	1,141,625	Ardebil
Azarbaijan, East	44,767	3,077,882	3,278,718	Tabriz
Azarbaijan, West	37,599	1,971,677	2,284,208	Orumiyeh
Bushehr	25,360	612,183	694,252	Bushehr
Chahar Mahal and Bakhtiari	14,820	631,179	747,297	Shahr-e-Kord
Esfahan	105,805	3,294,916	3,682,444	Esfahan
Fars	120,006	3,193,769	3,543,828	Shiraz
Gilan	14,820	2,081,037	2,204,047	Rasht
Hamadan	19,445	1,505,826	1,651,320	Hamadan
Hormozgan	65,379	762,206	924,433	Bandar-e-Abbas
Ilam	19,086	382,091	440,693	Ilam
Kerman	185,675	1,622,958	1,862,542	Kerman
Kermanshah	23,622	1,462,965	1,622,159	Kermanshah
Khorasan	315,687	5,280,605	6,013,200	Mashhad
Khuzestan	66,532	2,681,978	3,175,852	Ahvaz
Kohgiluyeh and Boyer Ahmad	13,699	411,828	496,739	Yasuj
Kordestan	27,858	1,078,415	1,233,480	Sanandaj
Lorestan	28,560	1,367,029	1,501,778	Khorramabad
Markazi	29,530	1,082,109	1,182,611	Arak
Mazandaran	46,645	3,419,346	3,793,149	Sari
Semnan	91,544	417,035	458,125	Semnan
Sistan and Baluchestan	181,471	1,197,059	1,455,102	Zahedan
Tehran	40,836	9,371,699	10,737,746	Tehran
Yazd	69,605	574,028	691,119	Yazd
Zanjan	23,767	928,988	1,020,696	Zanjan

At the 1991 census the populations of the principal cities were:

	Population		*Population*
Tehran	6,475,527	Abadan	84,774
Mashhad	1,759,155	Kermanshah	624,084
Esfahan	1,127,030	Qom	681,253
Tabriz	1,088,985	Orumiyeh	357,399
Shiraz	965,117	Rasht	340,637
Ahvaz	724,653	Ardebil	311,022

	Population		Population
Zahedan	361,623	Zanjan	254,100
Karaj	442,387	Islam Shahr	230,183
Hamadan	349,653	Khorramabad	249,258
Khorramshahr	34,750	Sanandaj	244,039
Arak	331,354	Bandar-e-Abbas	249,504
Kerman	311,643	Borujerd	201,016
Qazvin	278,826	Desful	181,309
Yazd	275,298		

The national language is Farsi or Persian, spoken by 45% of the population in 1986. 28% spoke related languages, including Kurdish (9%) and Luri in the west, Gilaki and Mazandarami in the north and Baluchi in the south-east; 22% spoke Turkic languages, primarily the north-west.

CLIMATE. Mainly a desert climate, but with more temperate conditions on the shores of the Caspian Sea. Seasonal range of temperature is considerable. Abadan. Jan. 54°F (12·2°C), July 97°F (36·1°C). Annual rainfall 8" (204 mm). Tehran. Jan. 36°F (2·2°C), July 85°F (29·4°C). Annual rainfall 10" (246 mm).

CONSTITUTION AND GOVERNMENT. The Constitution of the Islamic Republic was approved by a national referendum in Dec. 1979. It gives supreme authority to the *Spiritual Leader* (*wali faqih*), which position was held by Ayatollah Khomeini until his death on 3 June 1989. Ayatollah Seyed Ali Khamenei was elected to succeed him on 4 June 1989. Following the death of the previous incumbent, Ayatollah Ali Khamenei was proclaimed the *Source of Knowledge (Marja e Taghlid)* at the head of all Shi'ite Moslems in Dec. 1994.

The 83-member *Assembly of Experts* was established in 1982. It is popularly elected every 8 years. Its mandate is to interpret the constitution and select the Spiritual Leader. Candidates for election are examined by the Council of Guardians. At the elections of Oct. 1990 turn-out was 46%.

The *President* of the Republic is popularly-elected for a 4-year term and is head of the executive; he appoints Ministers, subject to approval by the *Majlis*.

Presidential elections were held on for 11 June 1993. The electorate was 29m.; turn-out was 57·6%. President Rafsanjani was re-elected by 63·2% of votes cast against 3 opponents.

President: Hojatolislam Ali Akbar Hashemi Rafsanjani (b. 1935; re-elected 11 June, 1993, sworn in on 3 Aug. 1993).

Vice President (Economic Affairs): Mohammad Hashemi.

The Cabinet was composed as follows in Aug. 1995:

Foreign Affairs: Ali Akbar Velayati. *Oil:* Gholamreza Aghazadeh. *Interior:* Ali Mohammad Besharati. *Economic Affairs and Finance:* Mohammad Khan. *Agriculture and Rural Affairs:* Isa Kalantari. *Commerce:* Yahya Al-Ishagh. *Energy:* Namdar Zanganeh. *Roads and Transport:* Akbar Torkan. *Construction Jihad:* Gholamreza Foruzesh. *Industry:* Mohammad Reza Nematzadeh. *Housing and Urban Development:* Abbas Ahmad Akhundi. *Labour and Social Affairs:* Hossein Kamali. *Posts, Telephones and Telegraphs:* Mohammed Gharazi. *Health, Treatment and Medical Education:* Ali Reza Marandi. *Education and Training:* Mohammad Ali Najafi. *Higher Education and Culture:* Dr Hashemi Golpeygani. *Justice:* Hojatolislam Ismail Shostari. *Defence and Armed Forces Logistics:* Mohammad Forouzandeh. *Intelligence and Security:* Hojatolislam Ali Fallahiyan. *Islamic Culture and Guidance:* Mostafa Mir-Salim. *Mines and Metals:* Mohammad Hossein Mahloji. *Co-operatives:* Gholem Reza Shafei.

The *Speaker* is Ali Akbar Nategh Nuri.

Legislative power is held by the 270-member Islamic Consultative Assembly *(Majlis)*, directly elected on a non-party basis for a 4-year term in April-May 1992. The electorate was 30m. citizens aged 15 or over. There were 2,060 candidates in 196 constituencies. 9 women were elected. The *Speaker* is Hojatoleslam Karrubi. All legislation is subject to approval by a 12-member *Council of Guardians* who ensure it is in accordance with the Islamic code and with the Constitution. Six members are appointed by the *Spiritual Leader* and 6 by the judiciary.

National flag: Three horizontal stripes of green, white and red; on the borders of the green and red stripes the legend *Allah Akbar* in white Kufi script repeated 22 times in all; in the centre of the white stripe the national emblem in red.

National anthem: 'Shod Jomhoori-e-Islami bepah' ('The Islamic Republic has been founded'); words and tune by M. Beglari-Pour.

Local Government. The country is divided into 25 provinces *(ostan)*. These are sub-divided into 195 counties, each under a governor, and thence into 500 districts, each under a district head. The districts are subdivided into *dehistan* (groups of villages) each under a *dehdar*, each village having its elected headman.

DEFENCE. Two years' military service is compulsory.

Army. The Army consisted (1996) of 345,000 men (about 250,000 conscripts). It is organized in 4 armoured, 2 special force and 7 infantry divisions, 1 airborne brigade, some independent armoured, infantry and commando brigades and 5 artillery groups. Equipment includes some 110 T-54/-55, 220 Chinese T-59, 150 T-62, 200 T-72, 250 Chieftain Mk 3/5, 150 M-47/-48, 160 M-60A1 and 200 Chinese T-69 main battle tanks and 664 multiple rocket launchers. The Army is estimated to have an inventory of 50 fixed-wing aircraft and over 200 helicopters but the effective strength is not known.

There is also a paramilitary gendarmerie of 45,000, including border guards.

Revolutionary Guard. This in 1995 numbered some 100,000 ground forces and 20,000 naval. The ground forces are loosely organized in battalions of no fixed size and grouped into 13 infantry and 2 armoured divisions and other independent units. It controls the Basij, a volunteer 'popular mobilization army' of about 0·2m., which may reach 1m. strong in war-time.

Navy. The Navy received the first 2 Soviet-built 'Kilo' class submarines before the end of 1993, but these have suffered operating problems and the third has been deferred to 1996. The remainder of the fleet comprises 2 ex-US 'Sumner' class destroyers, 3 UK-built frigates, 2 very old ex-US patrol frigates and about 10 missile craft. Other units include 35 inshore patrol craft (some of them hovercraft), 3 small minesweepers, 8 tank landing ships and 3 tank landing craft. Auxiliaries include 3 replenishment tankers, 1 repair ship, 4 water tankers and 2 accommodation ships.

Naval Aviation comprises 1 anti-submarine helicopter squadron with 9 Sea King and AB-212 helicopters, a mine counter-measures squadron with 2 RH-53D helicopters, a transport squadron with about a dozen various aircraft and about 20 AB-205 and AB-206 transport and liaison helicopters. Main naval bases are at Bandar-e-Abbas, Bushehr and Chah Bahar.

Naval strength in 1995 was 18,000 including naval air and 3 battalions of Marines.

Air Force. Strength (1995) 30,000 personnel (including 12,000 air defence). Combat aircraft include some Chinese-built F-6 fighter-bombers and F-7 interceptors, supplied via North Korea, surviving US fighters that include F-14 Tomcat, F-5E Tiger II and F-4D/E Phantom II fighter-bombers, as well as a few RF-4E reconnaissance-fighters, and a number of MiG-29 interceptors and Su-24 strike aircraft purchased from Russia. Transport aircraft include F27s, C-130 Hercules, PC-6 Turbo-Porters, Boeing 707s and 747s, some equipped as flight refuelling tankers. The status of the large fleet of CH-47C Chinook, Bell Model 214 and other helicopters is not known; but two P-3F Orion maritime patrol aircraft remain operational. Training aircraft include Pakistanti-built Mushshak and Bonanza basic trainers, 30 PC-7 Turbo-Trainers and 15 Tucanos for advanced training.

INTERNATIONAL RELATIONS

Membership. Iran is a member of the UN, OPEC and the Colombo Plan.

ECONOMY

Policy. A 5-year plan is running from March 1995. At the beginning of 1991 about 70% of industry was state-owned, much of it nationalized after the 1979 revolution, but the government is now committed to partial privatization. Strategic heavy industry will remain in the public sector.

Budget. The budget for 1991 (public funds) balanced at 9,008,105m. rials.

Currency. The unit of currency is the *rial* (IRR) of which 10 = 1 *toman*. There are notes of 100, 200, 500, 1,000, 2,000, 5,000, 10,000 and 50,000 rials and coins of 1, 2, 5, 10, 20, 50 and 100 rials. Annualized inflation was 40% in 1995. In March 1996, £1 = 4,585 rials; US$1 = 3,000 rials; DM1 = 2,033 rials.

Banking and Finance. The Central Bank is the note-issuing authority and government bank. Its *Governor* is Mohammad Adeli. All other banks and insurance companies were nationalized in 1979, and re-organized into new state banking corporations, of which there were 5 in 1994. Private banks were permitted to operate from 1994; their initial capital must be at least 5,000m. rials. The 'Law for Usury-Free Banking' dates from 1983. In 1985 interest on accounts was abolished.

A stock exchange re-opened in Tehran in 1992.

Weights and Measures. The metric system is in force.

The Iranian year is a solar year running from 21 March to 20 March; the Islamic *hegira* (622 Ad, when Mohammed left Mecca for Medina) year 1414 corresponds to 21 June 1993–9 June 1994; 1415 to 10 June 1994–20 May 1995.

ENERGY AND NATURAL RESOURCES

Electricity. Total installed capacity, 1992, was 19,784,000 kW; 68,419m. kWh were generated.

Oil. Oil companies were nationalized in 1979 and operations are now run by the National Petrochemical Company. Refining capacity, 1990, was 766·9 bbls per day. Crude oil production, 3,625,000 bbls. a day in 1995.

Gas. Natural gas production (1990) was 46,500m. cu. metres.

Minerals. 1992 output (in tonnes): Iron ore, 4,193,650; coal, 971,108; zinc concentrate, 107,358; lead concentrate, 32,625; copper, 314,738; manganese, 38,475; chromite, 143,008; salt, 1,017,627; bauxite, 122,120; decorative stone, 5,186,582.

Agriculture. In 1993 cultivable land totalled 18,215,000 ha: 12,580,000 ha were under annual crops (of which 5,649,000 ha were irrigated) and 5,636,000 ha were fallow (1,871,000 ha irrigated). In 1991 there were 1,095,700 ha of orchards and nurseries (929,110 ha irrigated).

Crop production for 1992 (in tonnes): Wheat, 7,695,800; barley, 2,817,100; rice (1991), 1,750,600; sugar-beet, 4,734,700; tobacco (1991), 21,220. Wool production, 1991, 32,000 tonnes greasy, 17,600 tonnes scoured.

Livestock (1991): 40,707,000 sheep, 22,244,000 goats, 6,126,000 cattle, 155,172 horses, 86,000 camels, 289,000 buffaloes, and 1,422,672 donkeys.

Fisheries. Total catch (1986) 152,000 tonnes.

INDUSTRY. Production of selected commodites in large-scale manufacturing establishments with 50 workers and more, 1992: Vegetable oils, 0·64m. tonnes; sugar, 866,000 tonnes; stockings, 12·1m. pairs; machine-made bricks, 2,459m.; cement, 14,906,000 tonnes; passenger cars, 27,086; vans, 25,170; lorries and trucks, 9,377; buses, 2,271; mini-buses, 6,154; jeeps, station wagons and ambulances, 11,681; motorcycles, 82,546. In 1992 there were 1,253 large-scale manufacturing establishments and the number of workers was 484,497.

FOREIGN ECONOMIC RELATIONS. There had been a limit on foreign investment, but legislation of 1995 permits foreign nationals to hold more than 50% of the equity of joint ventures with the consent of the Foreign Investment Board. Foreign debt was US$13,250m. in 1993.

Commerce. Imports and exports for calendar years (in 1m. rials):

	1988	*1989*	*1990*	*1991*
Imports	567,917	927,253	1,261,657	2,026,021
Exports	71,474	74,736	87,245	177,978

Total trade between Iran and UK (British Department of Trade returns, in £1,000 sterling):

	1991	*1992*	*1993*	*1994*	*1995*
Imports to UK	158,354	164,512	244,851	132,650	125,834
Exports and re-exports from UK	511,532	568,113	496,555	289,062	332,614

US imports were worth US$166m. in 1990. Germany is Iran's main trading partner: Imports were worth US$2,500m. in 1990.

Tourism. Total number of visitors (1989) 153,783.

COMMUNICATIONS

Roads. In 1986 the total length of roads was 151,485 km, of which 459 km were freeways, 21,577 km main roads, 36,343 km by-roads, 37,793 km rural roads and 55,316 km other roads.

In 1990 registered motor vehicles numbered 2,894,430, including 1,969,540 passenger cars, 47,776 taxis, 265,511 heavy vehicles, 106,374 buses and minibuses and 505,229 vans. There were also 1,000,280 motorcycles.

Railways. The State Railways totalled 5,093 km of main lines in 1994, of which 146 km were electrified. In 1994 the railways carried 9·4m. passengers and 21·4m. tonnes of freight. An isolated 1,676 mm gauge line in the south-east links with Pakistan Railways.

Civil Aviation. There is an international airport at Tehran (Mehrabad). In 1993 there were 0·76m. international and 6·9m. domestic passenger arrivals, and 0·68m. international and 6·9m. domestic departures. The state-owned airline, Iran Air, carried 5·6m. passengers and 34,600 tonnes of cargo in 1993. In 1995 it operated 5 A300B2-200s, 2 A300B4-600Rs, 4 B-707-320Cs, 2 B-727s, 5 B-727-200 Advs, 1 B-737-200 Adv, 2 B-737-200C Advs, 1 B-747-100B, 2 B-747-200B Combis, 2 B-747SPs and 6 others.

Services are also provided by Aeroflot, Air France, Air Ukraine, Alitalia, Ariana, Armenian Airlines, Austrian Airlines, Azerbaijan Hava Yollary, British Airways, Emirates, Gulf Air, KLM, Kuwait Airways, Lufthansa, Malaysia Airlines, Pakistan Airlines, Swissair, Syrian Airlines and Turkish Airlines.

Shipping. In 1995, the merchant fleet comprised 146 vessels totalling 6·71m. DWT, representing 1·01% of the world's total fleet tonnage. Total tonnage registered, 3·8m. GRT, including oil tankers, 2·14m. GRT and container ships, 1,593 GRT. In 1993, 1,922 ships, capacity 11·2m. tonnes, entered commercial ports, loading 4·5m. tonnes of goods (excluding oil products).

Telecommunications. In 1993 the number of telephones was 3·67m. Broadcasting is controlled by the government agency Islamic Republic of Iran Broadcasting. There are 2 national and about 40 regional radio programmes, a Koran programme and an external service, Voice of the Islamic Republic of Iran (20 languages). There are 4 television networks (colour by SECAM). Radio stations numbered 72 in 1993, and television stations, 993. A 3-year ban on TV satellite receiver dishes was imposed in Jan. 1995.

Cinemas (1993). There were 280 cinemas with 171,723 seats.

Press. There were in 1990 25 newspapers issued nationwide.

SOCIAL INSTITUTIONS

Justice. A legal system based on Islamic law (*Sharia*) was introduced by the 1979 constitution. A new criminal code on similar principles was introduced in Nov. 1995. The President of the Supreme Court and the public Prosecutor-General are appointed by the Spiritual Leader. The Supreme Court has 16 branches and

109 offences carry the death penalty. To these were added economic crimes in 1990.

Religion. The official religion is the Shi'a branch of Islam. Adherents numbered 93·8% of the population in 1990; 8% were Sunni Moslems.

Education. In 1991 adult literacy was 80·6% for men and 67·1% for women. Most primary and secondary schools are state schools. Elementary education in state schools and university education is free; small fees are charged for state-run secondary schools. In 1988–89 there were 8,262,441 pupils in primary schools, 2,724,606 in orientation schools and 1,363,130 in high schools; there were 209,887 students in technical and vocational schools, 41,884 in teacher-training schools, 29,127 gifted children, and 921,152 in adult education courses. In 1994–95 there were 30 universities and 30 medical universities, 13 specialized universities (agriculture, 1; art, 1; oil engineering, 1; teacher training, 4; technology, 5) and 2 open (distance) universities. There were 289,392 students and 10,745 academic staff.

Health. In 1988, 77,804 hospital beds were available in 609 hospitals. Medical personnel included 13,898 physicians and 954 dentists in 1988.

DIPLOMATIC REPRESENTATIVES

Of Iran in Great Britain (27 Prince's Gate, London, SW7 1PX)
Chargé d'Affaires: Gholamreza Ansari.

Of Great Britain in Iran (Ave. Ferdowsi Tehran)
Chargé d'Affaires: J. R. James, CMG.

Of Iran to the United Nations
Ambassador: Dr Kamal Kharrazi.

Further Reading

Abrahamian, E., *Khomeinism: Essays on the Islamic Republic.* Univ. of California Press, 1993
Amuzegar, J., *Iran's Economy under the Islamic Republic.* London, 1992
Bina, C. and Zanganeh, H. (eds.), *Modern Capitalism and Islamic Ideology in Iran.* London, 1991
The Cambridge History of Iran. 7 vols. CUP, 1968–91
Ehtesami, A., *After Khomeini: the Iranian Second Republic.* London, 1994
Foran, J., *Fragile Resistance: Social Transformation in Iran from 1500 to the Revolution.* Boulder (Colo.), 1993
Fuller, G. E., *Centre of the Universe: Geopolitics of Iran.* Boulder (Colo.), 1992
Hunter, S. T., *Iran after Khomeini.* New York, 1992
Hussain, A., *Islamic Iran: Revolution and Counter-Revolution.* London, 1985
Kamrava, M., *Political History of Modern Iran: from Tribalism to Theocracy.* London, 1993
Karshenas, M., *Oil, State and Industry in Iran.* CUP, 1990
Katouzian, H., *The Political Economy of Iran.* London, 1981
Lahsaelzadeh, A., *Contemporary Rural Iran.* London, 1993
Modaddel, M., *Class, Politics and Ideology in the Iranian Revolution.* Columbia Univ. Press, 1992
Navabpour, A. R., *Iran.* [Bibliography] Oxford and Santa Barbara (CA), 1988
Omid, H., *Islam and the Post-Revolutionary State in Iran.* London, 1994
Rahnema, A. and Nomani, F., *The Secular Miracle: Religion, Politics and Economic Activity.* London, 1990.—and Behdad, S. (eds.) *Iran after the Revolution: the crisis of an Islamic State.* London, 1995

National statistical office. Statistical Centre of Iran, Dr Fatemi Avenue, Tehran, Iran, 14144.

IRAQ

Jumhouriya al 'Iraqia

(Republic of Iraq)

Capital: Baghdad
Population: 19·41m. (1993)
GNP per capita: US$2,140 (1986)
HDI/world rank: 0·617/106 (1992)

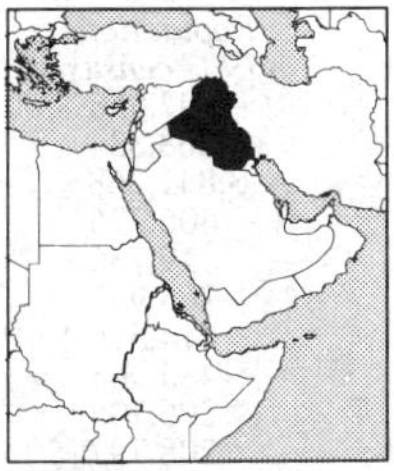

KEY HISTORICAL EVENTS. Part of the Ottoman Empire from the 16th century, Iraq was occupied by British forces in 1916 and became in 1921 a Kingdom under a League of Nations mandate, administered by Britain. It became independent on 3 Oct. 1932 under the Hashemite Dynasty, which was overthrown on 14 July 1958 by a military coup which established a Republic. In 1968 the Ba'ath Party seized power and established the Revolutionary Command Council as government.

For Iraq's 1980–90 war with Iran, and its occupation of and forcible expulsion from Kuwait, 1990–91, *see* THE STATESMAN'S YEAR-BOOK, 1994–95, p. 777.

On 3 April 1991 the UN Security Council adopted a permanant ceasefire resolution by 12 votes to 1 (Cuba) with 2 abstentions (Ecuador, Yemen). This provided for Iraq and Kuwait to respect the disputed border, the UN to demarcate it, and the Security Council to guarantee it. A UN observer force was to monitor a demilitarized zone extending 10 km into Iraq and 5 km into Kuwait. Iraq accepted the destruction of all chemical and biological weapons and nuclear weapons-usable material, under international supervision, and is liable for damages arising from its invasion of Kuwait.

Insurrections amongst Shi'ites in the south and Kurds in the north were put down by government forces. A massive exodus of Kurdish refugees to the borders of Iran and Turkey followed. International relief operations were succeeded in April by the establishment of 'safe havens' for refugees within Iraqi borders policed by US and other coalition troops. Kurdish opposition leaders began talks with the Iraqi government at the end of April, and refugees began to move from the border areas into camps in north Iraq under the supervision of US, UK and other coalition forces. In May 1991 a UN Security Council resolution adopted by 14 votes to 1 (Cuba) provided for a fund to compensate victims for damage caused during the Iraqi invasion of Kuwait. The fund is based at Geneva, administered by a council of representatives of all the Security Council members, and supplied from not more than 30% of Iraqi oil-export earnings. Iraq denounced the resolution as illegal, but said it would comply with it as it had no choice. Following a UN-Iraqi agreement, about 500 UN security guards were brought in in June 1991 to protect Kurds in the north. Coalition forces in Iraq withdrew in 1991, leaving only air forces based in Turkey.

In Sept. a UN Security Council resolution adopted by 13 votes to 1 (Cuba) with 1 abstention (Yemen) permitted Iraq to sell oil worth US1,600m. to pay for food and medical supplies and start a reparations fund. In Oct. the Security Council voted unanimously to prohibit Iraq from all nuclear activities except medical. Imports of materials used in the manufacture of nuclear, biological or chemical weapons are banned, and UN inspectors have received wide powers to examine and retain data throughout Iraq.

In Aug. 1992 the USA, UK and France began to enforce an air exclusion zone over southern Iraq in response to the government's persecution of Shi'ite Moslems. Following Iraqi violations of this zone, and incursions over the Kuwaiti border, US, British and French forces made air and missile attacks on Iraqi military targets in Jan. 1993. On 27 June 1993 US forces made a missile attack on an intelligence centre in Baghdad in retaliation for an attempt on former US President Bush's life while he was visiting Kuwait in April.

On 10 Nov. 1994 Iraq recognized the independence and boundaries of Kuwait.

TERRITORY AND POPULATION. Iraq is bounded in the north by

Turkey, east by Iran, south-east by the Persian (Arabian) Gulf, south by Kuwait and Saudi Arabia, and west by Jordan and Syria. In April 1992 the UN Boundary Commission redefined Iraq's border with Kuwait, moving it slightly northwards in line with an agreement of 1932. Area, 438,317 sq. km. Population, 1987 census, 16,335,198; 1993 estimate, 19·41m.; density, 44·7 per sq. km. Life expectancy was 65·7 years in 1992.

The areas, populations and capitals of the governorates:

Governorate	*sq. km*	*Population (1987 census)*	*Capital*	*Population (1987 census)*
Al-Anbar	138,501	820,690	Ar-Ramadi	192,556
Babil (Babylon)	6,468	1,109,574	Al-Hillah	268,834
Baghdad	734	3,841,268	Baghdad	3,841,268
Al-Basrah	19,070	872,176	Al-Basrah	406,296
Dahuk	6,553	293,304	Dahuk	19,736 [2]
Dhi Qar	12,900	921,066	An-Nasiriyah	265,937
Diyala	19,076	961,073	Ba'qubah	114,516 [3]
Irbil	14,471	770,439	Irbil	485,968
Karbala	5,034	469,282	Karbala	296,705
Maysan	16,072	487,448	Al-Amarah	208,797
Al-Muthanna	51,740	315,815	As-Samawah	33,473 [1]
An-Najaf	28,824	590,078	An-Najaf	309,010
Ninawa (Nineveh)	37,323	1,479,430	Mosul	664,221
Al-Qadisiyah	8,153	559,805	Ad-Diwaniyah	196,519
Salah ad-Din	24,751	726,138	Samarra	62,008 [2]
As-Sulaymaniyah	17,023	951,723	As-Sulaymaniyah	364,096
Ta'mim	10,282	601,219	Kirkuk	418,624
Wasit	17,153	564,670	Al-Kut	183,183

[1] Census 1965. [2] Estimate 1970. [3] Estimate 1985.

There were in 1993 3,688,000 Kurds, 270,000 Turkmens. The national language is Arabic.

CLIMATE. The climate is mainly arid, with small and unreliable rainfall and a large annual range of temperature. Summers are very hot and winters cold. al-Basrah. Jan. 55°F (12·8°C), July 92°F (33·3°C). Annual rainfall 7" (175 mm). Baghdad. Jan. 50°F (10°C), July 95°F (35°C). Annual rainfall 6" (140 mm). Mosul. Jan. 44°F (6·7°C), July 90°F (32·2°C). Annual rainfall 15" (384 mm).

CONSTITUTION AND GOVERNMENT. The Provisional Constitution was promulgated on 16 July 1970. The highest state authority is the Revolutionary Command Council (RCC) but some legislative power has now been given to the 250-member National Assembly, elected in April 1989.

The only legal political grouping was the National Progressive Front (founded 1973) comprising the Arab Socialist Renaissance (Ba'ath) Party and various Kurdish groups, but a law of Aug. 1991 legalized political parties provided they are not based on religion, racism or ethnicity.

The President and Vice-President are elected by the RCC; the President appoints and leads a Council of Ministers responsible for administration.

On 15 Sept. 1995 a referendum was held to determine whether President Saddam should remain in office for a further 7 years. The electorate was 8·4m. It was announced that turn-out was 99·47% and 99·96% of votes cast were in favour.

President: Saddam Hussein at-Takriti (b. 1937; assumed office 17 July 1979; re-investiture, 17 Oct. 1995).

Vice-Presidents: Taha Yassin Ramadhan; Taha Mohieddin Masarouf.

In Nov. 1995 the RCC comprised: President Saddam (*Chairman*); Ezzat Ibrahim (*Vice-Chairman*); Ahmed Hussein Al Khodair (*Head of the President's Office*); Mohieddin Masarouf; Tarek Aziz; Yassin Ramadhan; Mohammed Hamza Al Zubaidi; Gen. Ali Hassan Al Majid; Mizban Khider Hadi.

The Cabinet comprised:

Prime Minister: President Saddam.

Deputy Prime Ministers: Tarek Aziz; Taha Yassin Ramadhan; Mohammed Hamza Al Zubaidi.

Trade: Mohamed Mehdi Saleh. *Oil:* Lieut.-Gen. Amir Mohammed Rashid. *Information:* Hamad Youssef Hammadi. *Defence:* Lieut.-Gen. Sultan Hashim Ahmed. *Higher Education:* Humam Abdul Khaliq. *Minerals:* Vacant. *Justice:* Shabib Al Malki. *Education:* Vacant. *Labour and Social Affairs:* Latif Nasif Jassem. *Religious Affairs:* Abdul-Muneim Ahmed Saleh. *Finance:* Aikmef Mezban Ibrahim. *Interior:* Mohammed Zammam Abdel-Razzak. *Foreign Affairs:* Mohammed Said Al Sahhaf. *Health:* Umeed Madhat Mubarak. *Planning:* Samal Majid Faraj. *Housing and Building:* Mahmoud Diyab Al Ahmed. *Transport and Communications:* Ahmed Murtada Khalil.

National flag: Three horizontal stripes of red, white, black, with 3 green stars on the white stripe.

National anthem: 'Watanum Mede, al alufqi janalia' ('A homeland which extended its wings over the horizon'); words by S. Jabar Al Kamali, tune by W. G. Gholmieh.

Local Government. Iraq is divided into 18 governorates *(liwa),* each administered by an appointed Governor; three of the governorates form a (Kurdish) Autonomous Region, with an elected 57-member Kurdish Legislative Council. Each governorate is divided into *qadhas* (under Qaimaqams) and *nahiyahs* (under Mudirs).

DEFENCE. Conscription is 18-24 months. Military service is waived on payment of the equivalent of US$800.

Army. The Army is organized into 19 armoured/mechanized/infantry divisions, 7 Republican Guard divisions and 10 special forces brigades. Equipment includes 2,700 main battle tanks, including T-54/-55/M-77, Chinese T-59/-69, T-62, T-72 and Chieftain. Strength (1996 estimate) 350,000, including 100,000 active reserves.

Navy. The Iraqi Navy continues to lack operational capability. Current strength is believed to comprise 1 training frigate, 1 missile craft, 7 small patrol craft and 4 inshore minesweepers.

In 1995 naval personnel were estimated at about 2,500. Bases exist at Basra (unusable, except by small units, due to mines and obstructions in the Shatt al 'Arab), and Az Zubayr (exit controlled by Kuwait).

Air Force. The Iraqi Air Force suffered heavy losses during the Gulf War; over 60 aircraft were destroyed by the opposing Allied forces, many more were damaged beyond repair on the ground in Iraq and at least 100 aircraft are impounded in Iran. Reliable data on the status of the service are not available and the following are estimates. The combat aircraft are mostly of Soviet manufacture (MiG-21/23/29, Su-22/25), although there are French-supplied Mirage F1-E/B fighters, Alouette, Super Frelon and Super Puma helicopters, F-6 and F-7 fighters from China, Bell 214ST helicopters from the USA, Czech-built L-39 light attack/trainer aircraft, and BO 105 and BK-117 helicopters from Germany.

The combat helicopter inventory comprises anti-armour Gazelles, Mi-24s and BO 105s, and Super Pumas equipped for anti-shipping duties. Transports include fixed-wing An-12s, An-26s and Il-76s, and Puma, Bell 214ST, BO 105, BK-117, Mil, Mi-6, Mi-8/17, AB.212 and AS-61 transport and liaison helicopters. Training aircraft comprise AS.202 Bravo primary trainers, Tucano, PC-7 and PC-9 basic trainers and two-seat models of most combat types. Personnel (1995), about 30,000 (including 15,000 air defence).

INTERNATIONAL RELATIONS

Membership. Iraq is a member of the UN and Arab League.

ECONOMY

Budget. Revenue and expenditure for 1989 balanced at I.D. 19,434m.

Before UN sanctions were applied, oil revenues accounted for nearly 50% and customs and excise for about 26%, of the total revenue.

Currency. The monetary unit is the *Iraqi dinar* (IQD) of 1,000 *fils.* Silver alloy coins for 100 and 50 fils (*dirham*) and 25 fils are in circulation, and other coins for 10, 5 and 1 fils. Notes are for $^1/_4$, $^1/_2$ and 1 dinar, and for 5, 10, 25, 50, 100 and 250 dinars. In March 1996, £1 = 0·46; US$1 = 0·31; DM1 == 0·21 dinars.

Banking and Finance. All banks were nationalized on 14 July 1964. The Central Bank of Iraq is the sole bank of issue. In 1941 the Rafidain Bank, financed by the Iraqi Government, was instituted to carry out normal banking transactions. Its head office is in Baghdad and it has 239 branches, 11 abroad, including London. Its assets were US$47,000m. in Sept. 1990. In addition, there are 4 government banks which are authorized to issue loans to companies and individuals: the Industrial Bank, the Agricultural Bank, the Estate Bank, and the Mortgage Bank.

Weights and Measures. The metric system is in general use.

ENERGY AND NATURAL RESOURCES

Oil. Crude oil production was 650,000 bbls. a day in 1995.

Agriculture. In 1990 there were 5·45m. ha of arable land and 4m. ha of permanent cropland. The chief winter crops (1991) are wheat, 525,000 tonnes and barley, 520,000 tonnes. The chief summer crop is rice, 125,000 tonnes. The date crop is important (370,000 tonnes).

Livestock (1991): Cattle, 1·4m.; buffaloes, 110,000; sheep, 7·8m.; goats, 1·35m.; horses, 48,000; camels, 40,000; chickens, 50m.

Fisheries. Catch (1986) 20,600 tonnes.

INDUSTRY.

Iraq is still relatively under-developed industrially but work has begun on new industrial plants.

FOREIGN ECONOMIC RELATIONS

Commerce. Imports and exports for 4 calendar years were (in US$1m.):

	1988	*1989*	*1990*	*1991* [1]
Imports	9,311	10,170	6,605	...
Exports	9,613	12,408	10,353	...

[1] International embargo.

Total trade between Iraq and UK (British Department of Trade returns, in £1,000 sterling):

	1991	*1992*	*1993*	*1994*	*1995*
Imports to UK	2,548	311	39	122	164
Exports and re-exports from UK	4,399	34,023	11,956	9,581	5,044

COMMUNICATIONS

Roads. There were 25,500 km of main roads in 1985. Vehicles registered in 1986 totalled 492,000 passenger cars and 246,000 commercial vehicles.

Railways. Railways comprised in 1993 2,032 km of 1,435 mm gauge route. In 1993 it carried 1,566m. passenger-km and 1,649m. tonne-km of freight.

Civil Aviation. The national carrier is Iraqi Airways, which in 1992 operated 3 B-707-320Cs, 2 B-737-200s, 6 B-727s, 3 B-747s and 1 B-747SP.

Shipping. The merchant fleet in 1995 had a total tonnage of 1·55m. GRT, including oil tankers, 1·35m. GRT. 1980. A 565-km canal was opened in 1992 between Baghdad and the Persian (Arabian) Gulf for shipping, irrigation, the drainage of saline water and the reclamation of marsh land.

Telecommunications. Telephones, 1983, 624,685. Broadcasting is controlled by the government Broadcasting Service, and Baghdad Television. In 1992 there were 3·5m. radio and 1m. TV receivers (colour by SECAM).

Press (1989). In Baghdad there are 4 main daily newspapers (one of which is in English with a circulation of 550,000).

SOCIAL INSTITUTIONS

Justice. The courts are established throughout the country as follows: For civil matters: The court of cassation in Baghdad; 6 courts of appeal at Baghdad (2), Basra, Babylon, Mosul and Kirkuk; 18 courts of first instance with unlimited powers and 150 courts of first instance with limited powers, all being courts of single judges. In addition, 6 peace courts have peace court jurisdiction only. 'Revolutionary courts' deal with cases affecting state security.

For religious matters: The Sharia courts at all places where there are civil courts, constituted in some places of specially appointed Qadhis (religious judges) and in other places of the judges of the civil courts. For criminal matters: The court of cassation; 6 sessions courts (2 being presided over by the judge of the local court of first instance and 4 being identical with the courts of appeal). Magistrates' courts at all places where there are civil courts, constituted of civil judges exercising magisterial powers of the first and second class. There are also a number of third-class magistrates' courts, powers for this purpose being granted to municipal councils and a number of administrative officials.

The death penalty was introduced for serious theft in 1992; amputation of a hand for theft in 1994.

Religion. The constitution proclaims Islam the state religion, but also stipulates freedom of religious belief and expression. In 1993 there were 11·9m. Shi'ite Moslems and 6·6m. Sunni Moslems (including 3·5m. Kurds). There were 0·72m. Christians in 14 sects, including: 0·48m. Chaldean (Eastern rite Roman Catholic) Church, with some 100 priests in 9 dioceses; 0·15m. Apostolic Assyrian (Nestorian) Church, with 29 priests in 3 dioceses and 80,000 Syriac Orthodox in 2 dioceses. There were some 10,000 in various Protestant sects.

Education. Adult literacy was 62·5% in 1992. Primary and secondary education is free and primary education became compulsory in 1976. Primary school age is 6–12. Secondary education is for 6 years, of which the first 3 are termed intermediate. The medium of instruction is Arabic; Kurdish is used in primary schools in northern districts.

There were, in 1992, 8,875 primary schools with 3,316,036 pupils, and 2,746 secondary schools with 1,087,715 pupils. 296 vocational schools and teacher-training schools had 152,903 students. In 1994-95 there were 10 universities and 1 technological university, 1 institute of administration, 1 institute of applied arts, 1 technical teacher training institute and 22 technical institutes.

Health. In 1991 there were 9,366 doctors, 1,577 dentists, 1,552 pharmacists and 177 hospitals with 31,227 beds.

DIPLOMATIC REPRESENTATIVES

On 6 Feb. 1991 Iraq broke off diplomatic relations with Great Britain and the USA.

Of Iraq to the United Nations
Ambassador: Nizar Hamdoon.

Further Reading

Abdulrahman, A. J., *Iraq* [Bibliography]. Oxford and Santa Barbara, 1984
Al-Khalil, S., *Republic of Fear: the Politics of Modern Iraq.* Univ. of California Press, 1989
Baram, A., *Cultural History and Ideology in the Formation of Ba'athist Iraq, 1968–89.* London, 1991
Bleaney, C. H., *Iraq.* [Bibliography]. 2nd ed. Oxford and Santa Barbara (CA), 1995
Bulloch, J. and Morris, H., *Saddam's War: the Origins of the Kuwait Conflict and the International Response.* London, 1991
Chubin, S. and Tripp, C., *Iran and Iraq at War.* London, 1988
Farouk-Sluglett, M., and Sluglett, P., *Iraq since 1958: from Revolution to Dictatorship.* London, 1991

National statistical office: Central Statistical Organization, Ministry of Planning, Baghdad.

IRELAND

Republic of Ireland—
Poblacht na hÉireann

Capital: Dublin
Population: 3·56m. (1993)
GNP per capita: US$13,630 (1994)
HDI/world rank: 0·915/19 (1992)

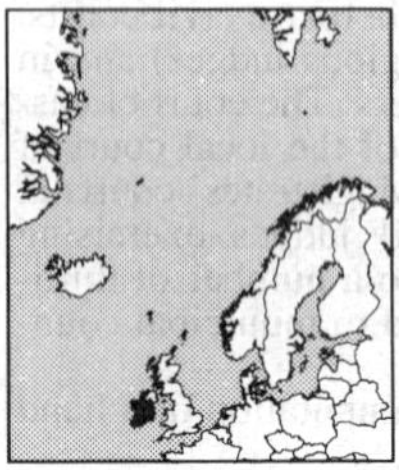

KEY HISTORICAL EVENTS. In April 1916 an insurrection against British rule took place and a republic was proclaimed. The armed struggle was renewed in 1919 and continued until 1921. The independence of Ireland was reaffirmed in Jan. 1919 by the Irish Parliament (*Dáil Éireann*), elected in Dec. 1918.

In 1920 an Act was passed by the British Parliament, under which separate Parliaments were set up for 'Southern Ireland' (26 counties) and 'Northern Ireland' (6 counties). The Unionists of the 6 counties accepted this scheme, and a Northern Parliament was duly elected on 24 May 1921. The rest of Ireland, however, ignored the Act.

On 6 Dec. 1921 a treaty was signed between Great Britain and Ireland by which Ireland accepted dominion status subject to the right of Northern Ireland to opt out. This right was exercised, and the border between the Irish Free State (26 counties) and Northern Ireland (6 counties) was fixed in Dec. 1925 as the outcome of an agreement between Great Britain, Ireland and Northern Ireland.

Subsequently the constitutional links between Ireland and the UK were gradually removed by the *Dáil*. The remaining formal association with the British Commonwealth by virtue of the External Relations Act, 1936, was severed when the Republic of Ireland Act, 1948, came into operation on 18 April 1949.

TERRITORY AND POPULATION. The Republic of Ireland lies in the Atlantic Ocean, separated from Great Britain by the Irish Sea to the east, and bounded in the north-east by Northern Ireland (UK). The population at the 1991 census was 3,525,719 (1,772,301 females).

Estimated population, 1993, 3·56m. The capital is Dublin (Baile Átha Cliath). Town populations, 1991: Greater Dublin including Dún Laoghaire, 915,516; Cork, 174,400; Limerick, 75,436; Galway, 50,853; Waterford, 41,853.

Vital statistics for 6 calendar years:

	Births	*Marriages*	*Deaths*		*Births*	*Marriages*	*Deaths*
1989	52,018	18,174	32,111	1992	51,557	16,109	31,002
1990	53,044	17,838	31,370	1993	49,456	15,728	31,896
1991	52,718	17,441	31,305	1994	47,929	16,297	30,744

At a referendum on 24 Nov. 1995 on the legalization of civil divorce the electorate was 1,628,580; 818,852 votes were in favour, 809,728 against.

Counties and county boroughs	*Area in ha* [1]	*Population, 1991* *Males*	*Females*	*Total*
Province of Leinster				
Carlow	89,635	20,785	20,157	40,942
Dublin County Borough		225,818	252,571	478,389
Dublin-Belgard	92,156	102,804	105,935	208,739
Dublin-Fingal		75,306	77,460	152,766
Dun Laoghaire-Rathdown		88,504	96,906	185,410
Kildare	169,425	62,207	60,449	122,656
Kilkenny	206,167	37,447	36,188	73,635
Laois	171,954	26,904	25,410	52,314
Longford	104,387	15,542	14,754	30,296
Louth	82,334	44,823	45,901	90,724
Meath	233,587	53,291	52,079	105,370
Offaly	199,774	29,892	28,602	58,494

[1] Exclusive of certain rivers, lakes and tideways.

Counties and county boroughs	*Area in ha* [1]	*Males*	*Population, 1991* *Females*	*Total*
Province of Leinster—contd.				
Westmeath	176,290	31,006	30,874	61,880
Wexford	235,143	51,444	50,625	102,069
Wicklow	202,483	48,076	49,189	97,265
Total of Leinster	1,963,335	913,849	947,100	1,860,949
Province of Munster				
Clare	318,784	46,367	44,551	90,918
Cork County Borough	3,731	61,346	65,907	127,253
Cork	742,257	143,196	139,920	283,116
Kerry	470,142	61,932	59,962	121,894
Limerick County Borough	1,904	25,318	26,765	52,083
Limerick	266,676	55,776	54,097	109,873
Tipperary, N. R.	199,622	29,355	28,499	57,854
Tipperary, S. R.	225,836	38,067	36,851	74,918
Waterford County Borough	3,809	19,717	20,611	40,328
Waterford	179,977	26,021	25,275	51,296
Total of Munster	2,412,738	507,095	502,438	1,009,533
Province of Connacht				
Galway County Borough	…	24,281	26,572	50,853
Galway	593,966	66,724	62,787	129,511
Leitrim	152,476	13,203	12,098	25,301
Mayo	539,846	55,981	54,732	110,713
Roscommon	246,276	26,694	25,203	51,897
Sligo	179,608	27,248	27,508	54,756
Total of Connacht	1,712,172	214,131	208,900	423,031
Province of Ulster (part of)				
Cavan	189,060	27,314	25,482	52,796
Donegal	483,058	64,817	63,300	128,117
Monaghan	129,093	26,212	25,081	51,293
Total of Ulster (part of)	801,211	118,343	113,863	232,206
Total	6,889,456	1,753,418	1,772,301	3,525,719

[1] Exclusive of certain rivers, lakes and tideways.

The official languages are Irish (the national language) and English; Irish is spoken as a mother tongue only residually, in certain western areas (Gaeltacht), and is no longer a compulsory subject at school.

CLIMATE. Influenced by the Gulf Stream, there is an equable climate with mild south-west winds, making temperatures almost uniform over the whole country. The coldest months are Jan. and Feb. (39–45°F, 4–7°C) and the warmest July and Aug. (57–61°F, 14–16°C). May and June are the sunniest months, averaging 5·5 to 6·5 hours each day, but over 7 hours in the extreme S.E. Rainfall is lowest along the eastern coastal strip. The central parts vary between 30–44" (750–1,125 mm), and up to 60" (1,500 mm) may be experienced in low-lying areas in the west. Dublin. Jan. 40°F (4·7°C), July 59°F (15°C). Annual rainfall 30" (750 mm). Cork. Jan. 42°F (5·6°C), July 61°F (16°C). Annual rainfall 41" (1,025 mm).

CONSTITUTION AND GOVERNMENT. Ireland is a sovereign independent, democratic republic. Its parliament exercises jurisdiction in 26 of the 32 counties of the island of Ireland.

The first Constitution of the Irish Free State came into operation on 6 Dec. 1922. Certain provisions which were regarded as contrary to the national sentiments were gradually removed by successive amendments, with the result that at the end of 1936 the text differed considerably from the original document. On 14 June 1937 a new Constitution was approved by Parliament and enacted by a plebiscite on 1 July

1937. This Constitution came into operation on 29 Dec. 1937. Under it the name Ireland (Éire) was restored. It states that the whole island of Ireland is the national territory, but that, pending its reintegration, laws enacted by Parliament have the same area and extent of application as those of the former Irish Free State.

The head of state is the *President*, whose role is largely ceremonial, but who has the power to refer proposed legislation which might infringe the Constitution to the Supreme Court.

The *Oireachtas* or National Parliament consists of the President, a House of Representatives, (*Dáil Éireann*) and a Senate (*Seanad Éireann*). The *Dáil*, consisting of 166 members, is elected by adult suffrage on the Single Transferable Vote system in constituencies of 3, 4 or 5 members. Of the 60 members of the Senate, 11 are nominated by the *Taoiseach* (Prime Minister), 6 are elected by the universities and the remaining 43 are elected from 5 panels of candidates established on a vocational basis, representing the following public services and interests: (1) national language and culture, literature, art, education and such professional interests as may be defined by law for the purpose of this panel; (2) agricultural and allied interests, and fisheries; (3) labour, whether organized or unorganized; (4) industry and commerce, including banking, finance, accountancy, engineering and architecture; (5) public administration and social services, including voluntary social activities. The electing body comprises members of the *Dáil*, Senate, county boroughs and county councils.

A maximum period of 90 days is afforded to the Senate for the consideration or amendment of Bills sent to that House by the *Dáil*, but the Senate has no power to veto legislative proposals.

No amendment of the Constitution can be effected except with the approval of the people given at a referendum.

President: Mary Robinson (b. 1944), elected out of 3 candidates by 817,000 votes to 731,000 on 7 Nov. 1990, inaugurated 3 Dec. 1990.

A general election was held on 25 Nov. 1992: Fianna Fáil (FF) gained 68 seats with 39·1% of votes cast (in 1989, 81 seats); Fine Gael (FG), 45 with 24·5% (55); Labour Party (L), 33 with 19·3% (15); Progressive Democrats, 10 with 4·7% (6); Democratic Left (DL), 4 with 2·8%; others, 6 with 9·6%.

In Feb. 1996 the government comprised:

Taoiseach (Prime Minister): John Bruton (b. 1947; FG).

Tánaiste (Deputy Prime Minister), Minister for Foreign Affairs: Dick Spring (b. 1950; L). *Finance:* Ruairi Quinn (b. 1946; L). *Social Welfare:* Proinsias De Rossa (b. 1940; DL). *Justice:* Nora Owen (b. 1945; FG). *Enterprise and Employment:* Richard Bruton (b. 1953; FG). *Environment:* Brendan Howlin (b. 1956; L). *Defence, and the Marine:* Seán Barrett (FG). *Agriculture, Food and Forestry:* Ivan Yates (b. 1959; FG). *Tourism and Trade:* Enda Kenny (b. 1951; FG). *Transport, Energy and Communications:* Michael Lowry (b. 1954; FG). *Equality and Law Reform:* Mervyn Taylor (b. 1931; L). *Arts, Culture and the Gaeltacht:* Michael D. Higgins (b. 1941; L). *Health:* Michael Noonan (b. 1943; FG). *Education:* Niamh Bhreathnach (b. 1945; L).

There were 17 Ministers of State.

Attorney-General: Dermot Gleeson, SC.

National flag: Three vertical strips of green, white, orange.

National anthem: Amhrán na bhFiann (*The Soldier's Song*); words by P. Kearney, tune by P. Heeney.

European Parliament. Ireland has 15 representatives. At the June 1994 election turn-out was 44%. Fianna Fáil gained 7 seats (group in European Parliament: European Democratic Alliance); Fine Gael, 4 (European People's Party); Greens, 2 (Green Group); Labour, 1 (European Socialist Party).

Local Government. The elected local authorities comprise 29 county councils, 5 county borough corporations, 5 borough corporations, 49 urban district councils and 26 Boards of Town Commissioners. All the members of these authorities are elected under a system of proportional representation, normally every 5 years. All residents of an area who have reached the age of 18 and whose names appear on the register of electors are entitled to vote in the local election for their area. Elected members are not paid, but provision is made for the payment of travelling expenses and subsistence allowances.

The range of services for which local authorities are responsible is broken down into 8 main programme groups as follows: Housing and Building; Road Transportation and Safety; Water Supply and Sewerage; Development Incentives and Controls; Environmental Protection; Recreation and Amenity; Agriculture, Education, Health and Welfare; Miscellaneous Services. Because of the small size of their administrative areas the functions carried out by town commissioners and some of the smaller urban district councils have tended to become increasingly limited, and the more important tasks of local government have tended to become the responsibility of the county councils.

The local authorities have a system of government which combines an elected council and a whole-time manager. The elected members have specific functions reserved to them which include the striking of rates (local tax), the borrowing of money, the adoption of development plans, the making, amending or revoking of bye-laws and the nomination of persons to other bodies. The managers, who are paid officers of their authorities, are responsible for the performance of all functions which are not reserved to the elected members, including the employment of staff, making of contracts, management of local authority property, collection of rates and rents and the day-to-day administration of local authority affairs. The manager for a county council is manager also for every borough corporation, urban district council and board of town commissioners whose functional area is wholly within the county.

At the elections of June 1991, at city and council level, 883 seats were contested. Fianna Fáil won 357 seats with 38% of votes cast. Fine Gael 270 with 26%. Labour 90 with 11%, the Progressive Democrats 37 with 5%, the Workers' Party 24 with 4%, the Greens 13 with 2%, and Sinn Fein 7 with 2%. Independents gained 85 seats.

DEFENCE. The supreme command of the Defence Forces is vested in the President. Military command is exercised by the government through the Minister for Defence, who is advised by the *Council of Defence* (the Minister of State at the Department of Defence, the Secretary of the Department of Defence, the Chief of Staff, the Adjutant-General, and the Quartermaster-General.

The Defence Forces comprise the Permanent Defence Force (the regular Army, the Air Corps and the Naval Service, with a total personnel of 12,900 in 1995) and the Reserve Defence Force (comprising a First Line Reserve of members who have served in the Permanent Defence Force, a second-line Territorial Army reserve and a second-line Naval reserve, totalling about 16,270).

Army. The Army is organized in 4 territorial commands and has 4 infantry brigades and an infantry force of 2 battalions. 3 of the brigades have 2 battalions and 1 brigade has 3 battalions. Each brigade has a field artillery regiment and a squadron/company-size unit for each of the support corps (cavalry, engineer, signals, supply and transport, military police, medical). Equipment includes 14 Scorpion light tanks. The 1996 strength of the Army was 10,900.

Navy. The Naval Service comprises 6 offshore patrol vessels and 1 helicopter patrol vessel. The Air Corps operates 2 Dauphin helicopters for use from the helicopter patrol vessel and 3 maritime reconnaissance aircraft. The Naval Base is at Haulbowline in Cork. The 1995 strength of the Naval Service was 1,000.

Air Corps. The Air Corps has its headquarters in Dublin and has 2 other bases. Most of the Corps' technical and administrative services are located at Casement Aerodrome which is also the main centre for flying and technical training. Fixed-wing aircraft types in service include 6 Fouga Magister armed jet trainers, 11 SIAI Marchetti SF 260W armed piston-engined trainers, 7 Cessna F 172 reconnaissance aircraft, 2 CASA CN 235 maritime patrol aircraft and 1 Beech Super Kingair and

1 Gulfstream G IV aircraft for VIP transport. 7 Alouette III, 5 Dauphin and 2 Gazelle helicopters are also used. The Air Corps had a strength of 1,000 personnel in 1995.

INTERNATIONAL RELATIONS

Membership. Ireland is a member of the UN, OECD, the Council of Europe and the EU.

ECONOMY

Budget. Current revenue and expenditure (in IR£1m.):

Current revenue	*1993* [1]	*1994* [2]
Customs duties	159	176
Excise duties	1,757	1,894
Capital taxes	87	97
Stamp duties	227	241
Income tax	3,712	3,797
Income levy	79	44
Corporation tax	952	1,019
Value-added tax	2,332	2,547
Agricultural levies (EU)	10	12
Motor vehicle duties	238	241
Employment and training levy	151	148
Tax Amnesty proceeds	–	242
Non-Tax Revenue	436	388
Total	10,140	10,846
Current expenditure		
Debt service	2,390	2,229
Industry and Labour	321	388
Agriculture	577	612
Fisheries, Forestry, Tourism	65	76
Health	1,907	2,069
Education	1,727	1,868
Social Welfare	3,742	3,900
Less: Receipts, e.g. social security	(–)2,534	(–)2,619
Total (including other items)	10,501	11,159

[1] Provisional. [2] Estimate.

VAT is 21% (reduced rate 12·5%).

Capital expenditure amounted to IR£2,216m. in 1994, with provision for IR£2,456m. in 1995.

On 31 Dec. 1993 the National Debt amounted to IR£28,358m. of which IR£16,972m. was denominated in Irish pounds and IR£11,386m. in foreign currencies. The official external reserves of the Central Bank of Ireland amounted to IR£4,278m. in 1994.

Currency. The unit of currency is the *Irish pound* (IEP) or *punt Éireannach* of 100 *pence.* From 10 Sept. 1928 when the first Irish legal-tender notes were issued, the Irish currency was linked to Sterling on a one-for-one basis. This relationship was discontinued on 30 March 1979 when, following Ireland's adherence to the EMS (which it had joined on its inception on 13 March 1979), it became inconsistent with Ireland's obligations. The Central Bank has the sole right of issuing legal tender notes; token coinage is issued by the Minister for Finance through the Bank. Notes are currently issued in denominations of IR£5, 10, 20 and 50. There are 1, 2, 5, 10, 20, 50 pence and IR£1 coins. The volume of legal-tender notes outstanding on 25 June 1993 was IR£1,339m. The Irish pound was realigned within the ERM on 30 Jan. 1993 with bilateral central rates of the IR£ against other ERM currencies being reduced by 10% effective 1 Feb. Inflation was an annualized 1·5% in 1993. In March 1996, £1 = IR£0·97; US$1 = IR£0·64; DM1 = IR£0·43.

Banking and Finance. The Central Bank (founded in 1943), replaced the Currency

Commission as the note-issuing authority. The Central Bank has the power of receiving deposits from banks and public authorities, of rediscounting Exchequer bills and bills of exchange, of making advances to banks against such bills or against Government securities, of fixing and publishing rates of interest for rediscounting bills, or buying and selling certain Government securities and securities of any international bank or financial institution formed wholly or mainly by governments. The Bank also collects and publishes information relating to monetary and credit matters. The Central Bank Acts, 1971 and 1989, give further powers to the Central Bank in the regulation of banking including licensing of banks, the supervision of their operations and control of liquidity and reserve ratios. The capital of the Bank is IR£40,000, of which IR£24,000 has been paid up and is held by the Minister for Finance.

The Board of Directors of the Central Bank consists of a Governor, appointed for a 7-year term by the President on the advice of the Government, and 9 directors, all appointed by the Minister for Finance. The Governor is Maurice O'Connell (b. 1937; appointed 1994).

The 4 Associated banks are Allied Irish Banks PLC., Bank of Ireland and two smaller banks, Ulster Bank and National Irish Bank. They operate the branch banking system; on 30 June 1993 their total deposit and current accounts within Ireland amounted to IR£10,618·9m. and their total gross assets amounted to IR£22,581·6m.

There are 30 Non-Associated Banks, 7 of which are subsidiaries of the Associated Banks. Of the remaining 23, 4 are Irish-owned, 12 are from other EU countries and 7 from outside the EU (mainly USA). On 30 June 1993 their total current and deposit accounts and interbank borrowings within Ireland amounted to IR£18,731·8m. and their total lending to IR£20,155·8m.; total gross assets in Ireland, IR£20,673·6m.

There are 2 state-owned credit corporations, one industrial and one agricultural, and 8 building societies. There is one Trustee Savings Bank and the Post Office Savings Bank.

The Dublin stock exchange has been affiliated to the London exchange since 1973.

Weights and Measures. Conversion to the metric system is in progress; with some exceptions which are confined to the domestic market, all imperial units of measurement ceased to be legal, for general use, after 31 Dec. 1994.

ENERGY AND NATURAL RESOURCES

Electricity. The total generating capacity was (1993) 4,037 mW. In 1993 the total sales of electricity amounted to 13,439m. units supplied to 1,348,196 customers. Electricity generated by fuel source 1993: Coal, 23%; oil, 18%; gas, 34%; peat, 12%; hydro, 13%.

Oil. Over 0·6m. sq. km of the Irish continental shelf has been designated an exploration area for oil and gas; at the furthest point the limit of jurisdiction is 520 nautical miles from the coast. Since 1970, 118 exploratory offshore wells have been drilled. A number of encouraging oil and gas flows have been recorded. In Nov. 1992 revised licensing terms were issued which allowed for a range of generous allowances against tax. In 1994, 172 blocks and 1 part-block in the Porcupine Basin off the west coast were the subject of a Frontier Licensing Round, the closing date of which was 15 Dec. 1994. In 1994, exploration was continuing.

Gas. (1994) All of Ireland's natural gas requirements are met by the Kinsale Head gas field, 50 km off the south coast, and the smaller Ballycotton field about 16 km north-west of Kinsale Head field, which was discovered in 1989 and which went into production in July 1991. These gas reserves should be depleted around the year 2000. Gas transmission and distribution is carried on by the Irish Gas Board (BGE). A gas pipeline from County Dublin to south-west Scotland was completed in 1994.

Peat. The country has very little indigenous coal, but possesses large reserves of peat, the development of which is handled largely by Bord na Mona (Peat Board). To date, the Board has acquired and developed 88,000 ha of bog and has 15 locations around the country. In the year ending 31 March 1994, the Board sold 106,000 tonnes of sod peat and 2,994,000 tonnes of milled peat for use in 6 milled peat electricity generating stations. 391,000 tonnes of briquettes were produced for sale to the domestic heating market. The Board also sold 1·2m. cu. metres of horticultural peat.

Minerals. Lead and zinc concentrates are important. By 1995, work at the existing mine and on 2 new discoveries increased reserves to 6·21m. tonnes of zinc and 1·46m. tonnes of lead. Metal content of production, 1993: Zinc, 194,100 tonnes; lead, 48,300 tonnes. Gypsum, limestone and aggregates are important, and there is some production of coal, silver (contained in lead), dolomite and silica sand. Barytes production has ceased. Exploration is centred on base metals, but with interest also in gold, industrial minerals and coal, and about 50 companies are prospecting.

Agriculture. Although in 1993 12·6% of the employed workforce made a living from agriculture, population is tending to migrate from rural areas, and in 1992 50% of farmers were over 50 years old. General distribution of surface (in ha) in 1992: Crops and pasture, 3,817,300; other land, including grazed mountain, 595,900; total, 4,413,200.

Estimated area (ha) under certain crops calculated from sample returns:

			Area		
Crops	*1989*	*1990*	*1991*	*1992*	*1993*
Wheat	60,700	70,100	85,700	90,600	76,600
Oats	22,400	21,800	20,600	20,100	20,200
Barley	236,500	206,600	193,400	184,400	176,900
Potatoes	24,700	24,300	20,500	22,100	22,100
Sugar-beet	32,100	32,300	33,300	31,300	...

Cereal production (in 1,000 tonnes) in 1993 (and 1992): Barley, 951 (1,167); wheat, 520 (713); oats, 134 (136). Sugar-beet production was 1,117 (1,377).

Gross agricultural output (including value of changes in stocks) for the year 1993 was valued at £3,456·8m.

Livestock (1993): Cattle, 7,022,700; sheep, 8,677,200; pigs, 1,512,800; horses and ponies (1992), 65,100; poultry, 12,039,200.

Forestry. The total area under forest at 31 Dec. 1993 was 0·5m. ha, of which some 80% was owned by the Coillte Teoranta (state forestry company). Timber production, 1993, 1·9m. cu. metres.

Fisheries. In 1992 approximately 16,000 people were engaged full- or part-time in the sea fishing industry. The quantities and values of fish landed during 1992 were: Demersal fish, 31,100 tonnes, value IR£43,385,000; pelagic fish, 194,757 tonnes, value IR£25,135,000; shellfish, 28,409 tonnes, value IR£29,497,000. Total quantity: 254,266 tonnes; total value, IR£98,017,000.

INDUSTRY. The census of industrial production for 1990 gives the following details of the values (in IR£1m.) of gross and net output for the principal manufacturing industries. The figures for net output are those of gross output minus cost of materials, including fuel, light and power, repairs to plant and machinery and amounts paid to others in connexion with products made.

	Gross output	*Net output*
Slaughtering, preparing and preserving meat	2,004·1	282·7
Manufacture of dairy products	2,068·2	368·8
Bread, biscuit and flour confectionery	215·3	94·7
Cocoa, chocolate and sugar confectionery	301·9	109·5
Animal and poultry foods	449·0	90·3
Brewing and malting	399·7	285·1
Spirit distilling and compounding	233·0	124·9
Paper and paper products	287·7	114·8
Printing and publishing	529·1	338·1
Manufacture of metal articles	662·0	283·3
Manufacture of non-metallic mineral products	884·9	441·4
Chemicals, including manmade fibres	531·2	1,492·6
Mechanical engineering	494·0	230·6
Office machinery and data-processing machinery	2,076·0	995·7

	Gross output	*Net output*
Electrical engineering	1,911·7	1,111·2
Manufacture and assembly of motor vehicles, parts and accessories	140·9	54·5
Manufacture of other means of transport	235·1	132·2
Instrument engineering	544·7	368·6
Textiles	495·1	192·4
Manufacture of footwear and clothing	399·5	153·5
Timber and wooden furniture	378·8	154·6
Processing rubber and plastics	584·1	271·2
Mineral oil refining	244·3	18·6
Gas, water and electricity	1,047·9	662·4
All other industries	4,263·5	1,484·4
Total (all industries)	21,381·7	9,856·2

Labour. The total labour force for 1993 was estimated to be 1,375,000, of which about 0·23m. persons were out of work. Of those at work, 144,000 were in the agricultural sector, 312,000 in industry and 0·69m. in services. Retirement age is 66 years.

Trade Unions. The number of trade unions in Dec. 1993 was 59; total membership, 488,000. Over 0·22m. were organized in 2 general unions catering both for white collar and manual workers. There were 11 employers' associations holding negotiation licences, with membership of 9,400. Centralized pay deals between the Government, trade unions and employers' organizations have been a feature since 1987. An agreement of Feb. 1994 provided for an 8% overall pay increase in the private sector for 1994–96, and an 8% increase, also, in the public sector up to June 1997 with a possible additional 3% arising from the preceding agreement.

FOREIGN ECONOMIC RELATIONS

Commerce. Value of imports and exports of merchandise for calendar years (in IR£1,000):

	1990	*1991*	*1992*	*1993*
Imports	12,468,819	12,850,806	13,194,772	14,798,000
Exports	14,336,715	15,018,918	16,628,836	19,655,800

The values of the chief imports and total exports are shown in the following table (in IR£1m.):

	Imports		*Exports*	
	1992	*1993*	*1992*	*1993*
Live animals and food	1,280·0	1,223·0	3,667·6	3,865·0
Raw materials	291·5	330·6	468·4	459·7
Mineral fuels and lubricants	684·2	706·3	96·6	115·8
Chemicals	1,713·0	1,822·5	3,198·8	3,780·9
Manufactured goods	1,935·8	1,724·1	1,255·5	1,140·4
Machinery and transport equipment	4,702·8	5,457·3	4,482·7	5,681·2
Manufactured articles	1,965·6	1,965·9	2,561·1	2,751·8
Beverages and tobacco	206·5	189·4	377·0	436·3

Exports, in IR£1m., for 1993 (and 1992): UK, 5,589 (5,232); Germany, 2,605 (2,122); France, 1,790 (1,603); USA, 1,790 (1,368); Netherlands, 1,126 (1,161); Belgium and Luxembourg, 796 (810); Japan, 727 (480); Italy, 714 (680); Spain, 413 (384); Switzerland, 352 (273); Sweden, 342 (292); Canada, 208 (174); Denmark, 180 (169); Norway, 178 (126). Imports: UK, 5,361 (5,602); USA, 2,530 (1,869); Germany, 1,072 (1,104); Japan, 967 (660); France, 578 (587); Netherlands, 466 (581); Singapore, 325 (111); Italy, 301 (314); Norway, 224 (214); Belgium and Luxembourg, 223 (273); China, 209 (87); Sweden, 205 (196); Taiwan, 155 (98).

Total trade between Ireland and UK (British Department of Trade returns, in £1,000 sterling):

	1990	*1991*	*1992*	*1993*	*1994*
Imports to UK	4,498,571	4,416,151	5,070,124	4,951,900	5,529,200
Exports and re-exports from UK	5,311,539	5,295,949	5,739,613	5,803,100	6,447,000

Tourism. Total number of overseas tourists in 1993 was 3,333,000. These, together with cross-border visitors, spent IR£1,367m.

COMMUNICATIONS

Roads. At 31 Dec. 1994 there were 92,394 km of public roads, consisting of 69 km of motorway, 2,656 km of national primary roads, 2,678 km of national secondary roads, 11,216 km of regional roads and 75,675 km of local roads.

Number of licensed motor vehicles at 31 Dec. 1993: Private cars, 891,027; public-service vehicles, 10,979; goods vehicles, 135,225; agricultural vehicles, 73,770; motor cycles, 23,921; other vehicles, 16,316.

Total travel by buses in 1993 was 299m. vehicle km.

Railways. The total length of railway open for traffic at 31 Dec. 1993 was 2,812 km (38 km electrified), all 1,600 mm gauge.

Railway statistics for years ending 31 Dec.	*1992*	*1993*
Passengers (journeys)	25,837,000	26,143,000
Km run by passenger trains	9,717,000	9,735,000
Freight (tonne-km)	633,267,000	574,568,000
Km run by freight trains	4,144,000	4,032,000
Receipts (IR£)	82,396,000	81,917,000
Expenditure (IR£)	174,988,000	170,046,000

Civil Aviation. The state-owned Aer Lingus Group plc comprises Aer Lingus plc, which operates services within Ireland and between Ireland and Britain and Europe, and Aer Lingus Shannon plc, which operates services to the USA. During the year ended 31 March 1994 Aer Lingus carried approximately 3·5m. passengers and 30,000 tonnes of cargo/mail on its European services and 0·43m. passengers and 16,100 tonnes of cargo/mail on its trans-Atlantic services. In 1995 Aer Lingus operated 3 A330-300s, 1 B-737-300, 6 B-737-400s, 9 B-737-500s and 1 B-747-100.

In addition to Aer Lingus, there were in 1994 13 independent air transport operators including Cityjet, Ryanair and Translift Airways which operate schedule and/or charter services to and from Ireland. Services are also provided by Aeroflot, Air Inter, Air Malta, Air Moldova, Air Ukraine, Alitalia, Belavia, British Airways, British Midland, Croatia Airlines, Delta, Hamburg Airlines, Iberia, KLM, Lauda Air, Lufthansa, Malaysia Airlines, Manx Airlines, Sabena, SAS, Saudia, TAP, Tarom, Tower Air, Uzbekistan Airways, Virgin Atlantic and Viva Air.

The principal airports are at Dublin, Shannon and Cork; there are also 6 privately-owned airports.

Shipping. The merchant fleet totalled 187,105 GRT in 1995, including oil tankers, 14,218 GRT and container ships, 10,167 GRT. Total cargo traffic passing through the country's ports amounted to 27,079,000 tonnes in 1992.

Inland Waterways. The principal inland waterways open to navigation are the Shannon Navigation (270 km), which includes the Shannon-Erne Waterway (Ballinamore/Ballyconnell Canal), and the Grand Canal and Barrow Navigation (249 km). The Office of Public Works is responsible for the waterways system as a public amenity. Merchandise traffic has now ceased and navigation is confined to pleasure craft operated either privately or commercially. The Royal Canal (146 km) from Dublin to Mullingar (53 km) was reopened for navigation in 1995.

Telecommunications. Telecommunication services are provided by Telecom Eireann, a statutory body set up under the Postal and Telecommunications Services Act, 1983. 35% of the state's holding was sold off in 1995. Number of working lines (March 1994), 1·17m.; telex lines, 2,400; data lines, 12,500; Eirpac (public packet-switched network), 2,942 customers; Eircell (mobile telephone network), 70,000 customers; Eirpage (radio paging network), 15,250 customers in Sept. 1994.

Postal services are provided by An Post, a statutory body established under the Postal and Telecommunications Services Act, 1983. Number of Post Offices as of Dec. 1993, 2,009; delivery points, 1,178,000. Number of items delivered in the year ended 31 Dec. 1993, 518·1m. An Post also offers a range of services throughout its Post Office network including National Savings services and payment of Social Welfare benefits/pensions on an agency basis for the State.

Public service broadcasting is provided by Radio Telefis Eireann (RTE), a statutory body established under the Broadcasting Authority Acts 1960–93. RTE is financed principally by advertising and TV licence. In 1993 a total of 930,270 TV licences were issued. Legislation enacted in 1988 provided for the establishment of the Independent Radio and Television Commission to arrange provision of independent commercial radio services and an independent TV service. There were (1994) 21 local commercial radio stations, 1 community radio station and 1 special interest Irish language radio station in operation; there is at present no independent TV or national radio service.

Cinemas. There were 203 screens in 1993.

Press (1986). There were 7 daily newspapers (all in English) with a combined circulation of 647,912; 5 of them are published in Dublin (circulation, 555,282).

SOCIAL INSTITUTIONS

Justice. The Constitution provides that justice shall be administered in public in Courts established by law by Judges appointed by the President on the advice of the Government. The jurisdiction and organization of the Courts are dealt with in the Courts (Establishment and Constitution) Act, 1961 and the Courts (Supplemental Provisions) Acts, 1961–91. These Courts consist of Courts of First Instance and a Court of Final Appeal, called the Supreme Court. The Courts of First Instance are the High Court with full original jurisdiction and the Circuit and the District Courts with local and limited jurisdictions. A judge may not be removed from office except for stated misbehaviour or incapacity and then only on resolutions passed by both Houses of the *Oireachtas*. Judges of the Supreme, High and Circuit Courts are appointed from among practising barristers. Judges of the District Court may be appointed from among practising barristers or practising solicitors.

The Supreme Court, which consists of the Chief Justice (who is *ex officio* an additional judge of the High Court) and 4 ordinary judges, has appellate jurisdiction from all decisions of the High Court. The President may, after consultation with the Council of State, refer a Bill, which has been passed by both Houses of the *Oireachtas* (other than a money bill and certain other bills), to the Supreme Court for a decision on the question as to whether such Bill or any provision thereof is repugnant to the Constitution.

The High Court, which consists of a President (who is *ex officio* an additional Judge of the Supreme Court) and 16 ordinary judges, has full original jurisdiction in and power to determine all matters and questions, whether of law or fact, civil or criminal. In all cases in which questions arise concerning the validity of any law having regard to the provisions of the Constitution, the High Court alone exercises original jurisdiction. The High Court on Circuit acts as an appeal court from the Circuit Court.

The Court of Criminal Appeal consists of the Chief Justice or an ordinary Judge of the Supreme Court, together with either 2 ordinary judges of the High Court or the President and one ordinary judge of the High Court. It deals with appeals by persons convicted on indictment where the appellant obtains a certificate from the trial judge that the case is a fit one for appeal, or, in case such certificate is refused, where the court itself, on appeal from such refusal, grants leave to appeal. The decision of the Court of Criminal Appeal is final, unless that court, the Attorney-General or the Director of Public Prosecutions certifies that the decision involves a point of law of exceptional public importance, in which case an appeal is taken to the Supreme Court.

The Offences against the State Act, 1939 provides in Part V for the establishment of Special Criminal Courts. A Special Criminal Court sits without a jury. The rules of evidence that apply in proceedings before a Special Criminal Court are the same as those applicable in trials in the Central Criminal Court. A Special Criminal Court is authorised by the 1939 Act to make rules governing its own practice and procedure. An appeal against conviction or sentence by a Special Criminal Court may be taken to the Court of Criminal Appeal. On 30 May 1972 Orders were made establishing a Special Criminal Court and declaring that offences of a particular class or kind (as set out) were to be scheduled offences for the purposes of Part V of the

Act, the effect of which was to give the Special Criminal Court jurisdiction to try persons charged with those offences.

The High Court exercising criminal jurisdiction is known as the Central Criminal Court. It consists of a judge or judges of the High Court, nominated by the President of the High Court. The Court sits in Dublin and tries criminal cases which are outside the jurisdiction of the Circuit Court.

The Circuit Court consists of a President (who is *ex officio* an additional judge of the High Court) and 17 ordinary judges. The country is divided into 8 circuits for the purposes of the Circuit Court. The jurisdiction of the court in civil proceedings is limited to IR£30,000 in contract and tort, IR£30,000 in actions founded on hire-purchase and credit-sale agreements, IR£15,000 in equity and IR£15,000 in probate and administration, save by consent of the parties, in which event the jurisdiction is unlimited. In criminal matters it has jurisdiction in all cases except murder, treason, piracy and allied offences. The Circuit Court acts as an appeal court from the District Court.

The District Court, which consists of a President and 45 ordinary judges, has summary jurisdiction in a large number of criminal cases where the offence is not of a serious nature. In civil matters the Court has jurisdiction in contract and tort (except slander, libel, seduction, slander of title and false imprisonment) where the claim does not exceed IR£5,000; in proceedings founded on hire-purchase and credit-sale agreements, the jurisdiction is IR£5,000.

All criminal cases, except those of a minor nature, and those tried in the Special Criminal Court, are tried by a judge and a jury of 12. A majority vote of the jury (10 must agree) is necessary to determine a verdict.

Bartholomew, P. C., *The Irish Judiciary.* Dublin, 1974

Religion. According to the census of population taken in 1991 the principal religious professions were as follows:

	Leinster	*Munster*	*Connacht*	*Ulster (part of)*	*Total*
Roman Catholics	1,685,334	941,675	397,848	203,470	3,228,327
Church of Ireland (Anglican)	50,912	15,758	5,321	10,849	82,840
Protestants	3,391	1,385	516	1,055	6,347
Presbyterians	3,799	548	333	8,519	13,199
Methodists	2,815	1,185	286	751	5,037
Jewish	1,439	111	21	10	1,581
Other religious denominations	24,829	9,192	3,208	1,514	38,743
Not stated or no religion	88,430	39,679	15,498	6,038	149,645

Cahal Daly (b. 1917) is the Roman Catholic Cardinal of Armagh and Primate of All Ireland. In Dec. 1994 Mgr Sean Brady (b. 1939) was appointed next Primate of Ireland to follow Cardinal Daly with the title of Coadjutor Archbishop of Armagh.

In May 1990 the General Synod of the Church of Ireland voted to ordain women.

Education. *Elementary.* Elementary education is free and was given in about 3,325 national schools (including 117 special schools) in 1992–93. The total number of pupils on rolls in 1992–93 was 521,250, including pupils in special schools and classes; the number of teachers of all classes was about 20,758 in 1992–93, including remedial teachers and teachers of special classes. The net non-capital state expenditure on elementary education for 1993 was IR£541,175,000m., excluding the cost of administration.

Special. Special provision is made for handicapped and deprived children in special schools which are recognized on the same basis as primary schools, in special classes attached to ordinary schools and in certain voluntary centres where educational services appropriate to the needs of the children are provided. Integration of handicapped children in ordinary schools and classes is encouraged wherever possible, if necessary with special additional supports. There are also part-time teaching facilities in hospitals, child guidance clinics, rehabilitation workshops, special 'Saturday-morning' centres and home teaching schemes. Special schools (1992–93) numbered 117 with approximately 8,084 pupils. There were also some 3,380 pupils enrolled in about 337 special classes, and 1,032 remedial teachers were employed for backward pupils in ordinary national schools. There is a National Education Officer for travelling children (e.g. Gypsies).

Secondary. Voluntary secondary schools are under private control and are conducted in most cases by religious orders. These schools receive grants from the State and are open to inspection by the Department of Education. The number of recognized secondary schools during the school year 1992–93 was 467, and the number of pupils in attendance was 221,180.

Vocational Education Committee schools provide courses of general and technical education. The number of vocational schools during the school year 1993–94 was 248, and the number of full-time students in attendance was 92,005. These schools are controlled by the local Vocational Education Committees; they are financed mainly by state grants and also by contributions from local rating authorities and Vocational Education Committee receipts.

Comprehensive. Comprehensive schools which are financed by the State combine academic and technical subjects in one broad curriculum so that each pupil may be offered educational options suited to his needs, abilities and interests. Pupils are prepared for State examinations and for entrance to universities and institutes of further education. The number of comprehensive schools during the school year 1993–94 was 16 and the number of students in attendance was 9,218.

Community. Community schools continue to be established through the amalgamation of existing voluntary secondary and Vocational Education Committee schools, where this is found feasible and desirable, and in new areas where a single larger school is considered preferable to 2 smaller schools under separate managements. These schools provide second-level education and also provide adult education facilities for their own areas. They also make facilities available to voluntary organizations and to the adult community generally. The number of community schools during the school year 1993–94 was 54 and the number of students in attendance was 35,959.

The net non capital State expenditure for second level and further education for 1994 was IR£613,951,000.

Education Third-Level. University education is provided by the National University of Ireland, founded in Dublin in 1908, by the University of Dublin (Trinity College), founded in 1592, and by the Dublin City University and the University of Limerick established in 1989. The National University comprises 3 constituent colleges–University College, Dublin, University College, Cork, and University College, Galway.

St Patrick's College, Maynooth, Co. Kildare, is a national seminary for Catholic priests and a pontifical university with the power to confer degrees up to doctoral level in philosophy, theology and canon law. It also admits lay students (men and women) to the courses in arts, science and education which it provides as a recognized college of the National University.

Besides the University medical schools, the Royal College of Surgeons in Ireland (a long-established independent medical school) provides medical qualifications which are internationally recognized. Courses to degree level are available at the National College of Art and Design, Dublin.

Regional Technical Colleges in 11 centres (Athlone, Carlow, Cork, Dundalk, Limerick, Tallaght, Galway, Letterkenny, Sligo, Tralee and Waterford) provide vocational and technical education and training for trade and industry from craft to professional level through certificate, diploma and some degree courses. These colleges were established on a statutory basis on 1 Jan. 1993. Prior to this they operated under the aegis of the Vocational Education Committees (VECs) for their areas. The Dublin Institute of Technology (DIT) was also established on a statutory basis on 1 Jan. 1993. Prior to this it operated under the aegis of City of Dublin VEC. The DIT provides certificate, degree and diploma level courses in engineering, architecture, business studies, catering, music, etc. The School of Art in Dunlaoghaire and the Hotel and Catering College in Killybegs continue to operate under the aegis of Dunlaoghaire and Co. Donegal VECs respectively. Total full-time enrolments in 1992–93 were approximately 31,500.

There are 5 Colleges of Education for training primary school teachers. For degree awarding purposes, 3 of these colleges are associated with Trinity College, 1 with the University of Ireland and 1 with The National University of Ireland. There are also 2 Home Economics Colleges for teacher training, 1 associated with Trinity College and the other with University College, Galway.

The total full-time enrolment at third-level for 1991–92 was approximately 75,000. The net non capital State expenditure on third-level education for 1992 was IR£427,392,000. The National Council for Educational Awards, established on a statutory basis in 1979, is the validating and awarding authority for courses in the third-level sector outside the universities.

Agricultural. Teagasc, the Agriculture and Food Development Authority, is the state agency responsible for providing advisory, training, research and development services for the agriculture and food industries. Full-time instruction in agriculture is provided for all sections of the farming community. There are 4 agricultural colleges, administered by Teagasc, and 7 private Teagasc-aided agricultural colleges. Courses in commercial horticulture are also offered, and short courses for adults already farming.

Coolahan, J., *Irish Education: its History and Structure.* Dublin, 1981

Health Services. Everybody ordinarily resident in Ireland has either full or limited eligibility for the public health services.

(i) A person who satisfies the criteria of a means test receives a medical card which confers Category 1 or full eligibility on them and their dependents. This entitles the holder to the full range of public health and hospital services, free of charge, i.e. family doctor, drugs and medicines, hospital and specialist services as well as dental, aural and optical services. Maternity care and infant welfare services are also provided.

(ii) The remainder of the population have Category 2 or limited eligibility. Category 2 patients receive consultants and hospital services but are not entitled to general practitioner, dental or aural services. They are not entitled to free drugs or medicines but receive reimbursement if their drug expenditure exceeds IR£90 in any quarter commencing Jan., April, July and Oct.

Persons in Category 2 are liable for a hospital in-patient charge of IR£20 per night up to a maximum of IR£200 in any 12 consecutive months. There is no charge for out-patient services. However persons in Category 2 are liable for a charge of IR£12 if they attend the Accident and Emergency Department of a hospital without a letter of referral from a General Practioner.

Drugs and medicines are made available free of charge to all persons suffering from specified long-term ailments such as diabetes, multiple sclerosis, epilepsy, etc. Hospital in-patient services are free of charge to all children under 16 years of age, suffering from specified long-term conditions such as cystic fibrosis, spina bifida, cerebral palsy, etc. Immunization and diagnostic services as well as hospital services are free of charge to everyone suffering from an infectious disease. A maintenance allowance is also payable in necessitous cases.

Services for Children: Health Boards are involved, with the co-operation of a wide network of voluntary organizations, in the provision of a range of child care services including adoption, fostering, residential care, day care and social work services for families in need of support.

Welfare Services: There are various services provided for the elderly, the chronic sick, the disabled and families in stress, such as social support service, day care services for children, home helps, home nursing, meals-on-wheels, day centres, cheap fuel, etc. Health Boards also provide disabled persons, without charge, with training for employment and place them in jobs.

Grants and Allowances: Disabled Persons' Maintenance Allowance is payable to persons with a disability between the ages of 16 and 66 years who are not in long term care. Recipients are entitled to free travel and, subject to certain conditions, to electricity allowance, free TV licence, telephone rental and fuel vouchers. Mobility allowance is payable to severely disabled persons between 16 and 66 years who are unable to walk. Domiciliary Care is payable to the mother of a severely handicapped child, maintained at home, but needing constant care and supervision. Blind welfare allowance: This allowance is in addition to the benefits for the blind operated by the Department of Social Welfare. A grant of up to IR£2,575 is payable, subject to a means test, to disabled persons towards the purchase of a car, in order that they might obtain or retain employment.

Health contributions: A health contribution of 1·25% of income is payable by those with Category 2 eligibility. Employers meet the levy in respect of those employees who have a medical card.

Hensey, B., *The Health Services of Ireland.* 4th ed. Dublin, 1988

Social Welfare Services. The Department of Social Welfare provides a range of payments and benefits in kind. The payments can be divided into two categories, social insurance and social assistance. The Department also administers a scheme of grants for voluntary organizations working in the social services area.

Social Insurance Payments. Payments under social insurance are funded by employers, their employees and the self-employed. Any deficit in the fund is met by Exchequer subvention. Employees and self-employed people between the ages of 16 and 66 are liable for pay-related social insurance contributions. The majority of employees must pay a contribution which gives cover for the full range of social insurance benefits while self-employed people must pay a contribution which gives cover for widows and orphans pensions and old age contributory pension. Entitlement to social insurance benefits depends on the claimant having a number of contributions paid or credited in a specific time period. The contribution conditions vary according to the different schemes. The social insurance schemes are: Old Age Contributory Pension; Widow's Contributory Pension; Orphan's Contributory Allowance; Disability Benefit; Pay-related Benefit, Dental and Optical Benefit; Retirement Pension; Deserted Wife's Benefit; Invalidity Pension, Unemployment Benefit; Maternity Benefit; Death Grant. There is also a scheme of occupational injuries benefits which is not strictly a social insurance scheme as there are no contribution conditions for entitlement. Expenditure on this scheme is paid from a fund which is financed by employers' contributions and income from investments.

Social Assistance Payments. Social assistance schemes are financed entirely by the Exchequer. One of the basic qualifying conditions for payment is that the applicant satisfies a means test. The social assistance payments are: Old Age Non-Contributory Pension; Blind Person's Pension; Lone Parent's Allowance; Widow's Non-Contributory Pension [1]; Deserted Wife's Allowance [1]; Prisoner's Wife's Allowance [1]; Unemployment Assistance; Supplementary Welfare Allowance; Orphan's Non-Contributory Pension; Pre-Retirement Allowance; Single Woman's Allowance [2]; Rent Allowance; Family Income Supplement; Carer's Allowance. Child benefit is payable without a means test in respect of each child under age 16 and children between 16 and 18 who are at school or incapacitated for a prolonged period. It is funded from the Exchequer.

Other Schemes. The Department also provides a range of benefits in kind, principally for the elderly and disabled. These are: Free travel; electricity allowance; natural gas allowance; free telephone rental; free TV licence; fuel allowance.

[1] For certain women who do not qualify for the lone parent's allowance.
[2] For women between ages 58 and 66.

DIPLOMATIC REPRESENTATIVES

Of Ireland in Great Britain (17 Grosvenor Pl., London, SW1X 7HR)
Ambassador: Edward Barrington.

Of Great Britain in Ireland (31/33 Merrion Rd., Dublin, 4)
Ambassador: James McCulloch.

Of Ireland in the USA (2234 Massachusetts Ave., NW, Washington, D.C., 20008)
Ambassador: Dermot Gallagher.

Of the USA in Ireland (42 Elgin Rd., Ballsbridge, Dublin)
Ambassador: Jean Kennedy Smith.

Of Ireland to the United Nations
Ambassador: John H. Campbell.

Further Reading

Central Statistics Office. *National Income and Expenditure* (annual), *Statistical Abstract* (annual), *Census of Population Reports* (quinquennial), *Census of Industrial Production Reports* (annual), *Trade and Shipping Statistics* (annual and monthly), *Trend of Employment and Unemployment*, *Reports on Vital Statistics* (annual and quarterly), *Statistical Bulletin* (quarterly), *Labour Force Surveys* (annual), *Trade Statistics* (monthly), *Economic Series* (monthly).

Ardagh, J., *Ireland and the Irish: a Portrait of a Changing Society*. London, 1994
Chubb, B., *Government and Politics in Ireland*. 3rd ed. London, 1992
Collins, N. (ed.), *Political Issues in Ireland Today*. Manchester, Univ. Press, 1994
Eager, A. R., *A Guide to Irish Bibliographical Material*. 2nd ed. London, 1980
Encyclopaedia of Ireland. Dublin, 1968
Fitzgerald, G., *All in a Life: an Autobiography*. London, 1991
Foster, R. F., *Modern Ireland 1600–1972*. London, 1988.—(ed.) *The Oxford Illustrated History of Ireland*. OUP, 1991
Harkness, D., *Ireland in the Twentieth Century: a Divided Island*. London, 1995
Hickey, D. J. and Doherty, J. E., *A Dictionary of Irish History since 1800*. Dublin, 1980
Hussey, G., *Ireland Today: Anatomy of a Changing State*. Dublin, 1993
Institute of Public Administration, *Ireland: a Directory*. Dublin, annual
Lee, J. J., *Ireland 1912-1985: Politics and Society*. CUP, 1989
Munck, R., *The Irish Economy: Results and Prospects*. London, 1993
O'Beirne Ranelagh, J., *A Short History of Ireland*. 2nd ed. CUP, 1994
O'Hagan, J. W. (ed.) *The Economy of Ireland: Policy and Performance of a Small European Country*. London, 1995
Shannon, M. O., *Irish Republic*. [Bibliography] Oxford and Santa Barbara (CA), 1986
Wiles, J. L. and Finnegan, R. B., *Aspirations and Realities: a Documentary History of Economic Development Policy in Ireland since 1922*. London, 1992.

Other more specialized titles are listed under JUSTICE, EDUCATION *and* HEALTH SERVICES, *above.*

National statistical office: Central Statistics Office, Earlsfort Terrace, Dublin 2. *Director:* Donal Murphy, M.Sc., M.Econ.Sc., M.Sc.(Mgt).

ISRAEL

Medinat Israel

(State of Israel)

Capital: Jerusalem
Population: 5·47m. (1994)
GNP per capita: US$14,410 (1994)
HDI/world rank: 0·907/21 (1992)

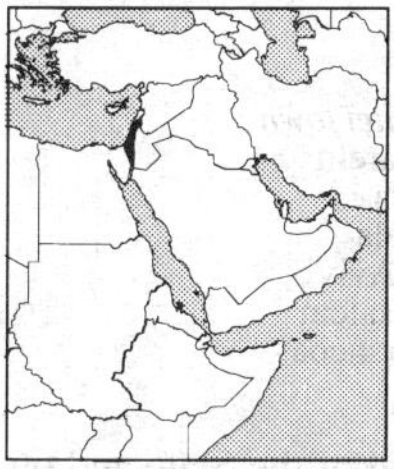

KEY HISTORICAL EVENTS. During the First World War the then Turkish province of Palestine, populated mainly by Arabs, was occupied by the British, who in 1917 issued the Balfour Declaration, viewing 'with favour the establishment in Palestine of a national home for the Jewish people'. This position was endorsed by the League of Nations. In Nov. 1947 the UN called for the establishment of both a Jewish and an Arab state. Jewish settlement had been taking place throughout the British mandate.

The State of Israel was proclaimed on 14 May 1948. No Arab state was established. Neighbouring Arab states invaded Israel on 15 May without success. At the ceasefire in Jan. 1949 Israel had increased its territory by one-third.

There have been conflicts with Egypt (sometimes with the involvement of other Arab states) in the 1956 Suez crisis; the 1967 'Six-Day War', which left Israel in possession of the Gaza Strip, the West Bank (of the River Jordan) and the Sinai Peninsula; and in 1973. (For details *see* THE STATESMAN'S YEAR-BOOK, 1990–91, p. 734).

Following declarations signed by the Prime Minister, Yitzhak Rabin, recognizing the Palestine Liberation Organization (PLO) as representative of the Palestinian people, and Yasser Arafat, leader of the PLO, renouncing terrorism and recognizing the State of Israel, an agreement was signed by representatives of Israel and the PLO on 13 Sept. 1993 in Washington providing for limited Palestinian self-rule in the Gaza Strip and Jericho. A further agreement, signed by the Foreign Minister, Shimon Peres, and Yasser Arafat on 9 Feb. 1994 dealt with control over the Egypt-Gaza Strip and Jericho-Jordan border crossings, and security arrangements for Jewish settlers in Gaza which would divide the strip into 3 zones. On 4 May 1994 in Cairo an Israeli-Palestinian agreement on the first phase of Palestinian self-rule in the Gaza Strip and Jericho was signed by the Israeli Prime Minister Itzhak Rabin and Yasser Arafat. An Israeli-Palestinian agreement was signed in Washington on 28 Sept. 1995. (For details *see* PALESTINIAN-ADMINISTERED TERRITORIES: Key Historical Events, *below*). Negotiations on the permanent status of the West Bank and Gaza were scheduled to begin in May 1996.

On 4 Nov. 1995 the Prime Minister, Yitzhak Rabin, was assassinated by a Jewish religious extremist.

TERRITORY AND POPULATION. The area of Israel, including the Golan Heights (1,150 sq. km) and East Jerusalem (70 sq. km) is 21,946 sq. km (8,473 sq. miles), with a population (1983 census) of 4,037,600 (estimate, 1994, 5·47m.), including East Jerusalem, the Golan Heights and Israeli settlers in the occupied territories; 81·1% were Jewish, 19·9% Arab and others.

Crude birth rate per 1,000 population of Jewish population (1994), 18·4; non-Jewish: Moslems, 37·1; Christians, 18·7; Druzes, 29·2. Crude death rate, Jewish, 6·9; non-Jewish: Moslems, 3; Christians, 4·3; Druzes, 3·2. Infant mortality rate per 1,000 live births, Jewish, 5·7; non-Jewish: Moslems, 12·1; Christians, 10·4; Druzes, 8·7. Life expectancy (1993): Males, 75·3 years; females, 79·1. Average population growth rate, 1983–93, 2·6%. Growth rate in 1994 was 2·7%, partly due to increased immigration from the former USSR.

Immigration. The following table shows the numbers of Jewish immigrants entering Palestine/Israel.

1989	24,050	1991	176,100	1993	76,805
1990	199,516	1992	77,057	1994	79,844

Population by place of origin as of 1994: Europe and America, 1·75m.; CIS, 0·66m.; Morocco, 0·5m.; Poland, 0·25m.; Romania, 0·25m.; Iraq, 0·25m.; Yemen, 0·15m.; Iran, 0·13m.; Tunisia, 0·13m.; Algeria, 0·12m.

The Jewish Agency, which, in accordance with Article IV of the Palestine Mandate played a leading role in establishing the State of Israel, continues to organize immigration.

Israel is administratively divided into 6 districts:

District	*Area (sq. km)*	*Population* [1]	*Chief town*
Northern	4,501	914,200	Nazareth
Haifa	854	713,600	Haifa
Central	1,242	1,155,700	Ramla
Tel Aviv	170	1,140,800	Tel Aviv
Jerusalem [2]	627	638,200	Jerusalem
Southern	14,107	715,000	Beersheba

[1] 1994 average. [2] Includes East Jerusalem.

On 23 Jan. 1950 the Knesset proclaimed Jerusalem the capital of the State and on 14 Dec. 1981 extended Israeli law into the Golan Heights. Population of the main towns (1994): Jerusalem, 578,800; Tel-Aviv/Jaffa, 355,200; Haifa, 246,700; Holon, 163,700; Petach Tikva, 152,000; Bat Yam, 142,300; Rishon le-Ziyyon, 162,200; Netanya, 144,900; Beersheba, 147,900; Ramat Gan, 122,200; Bene Berak, 127,100.

The official languages are Hebrew and Arabic.

CLIMATE. From April to Oct., the summers are long and hot, and almost rainless. From Nov. to March, the weather is generally mild, though colder in hilly areas, and this is the wet season. Jerusalem. Jan. 48°F (9°C), July 73°F (23°C). Annual rainfall, 495 mm. Tel Aviv. Jan. 57°F (14°C), July 81°F (27°C). Annual rainfall, 361 mm.

CONSTITUTION AND GOVERNMENT. Israel is an independent sovereign republic, established by proclamation on 14 May 1948.

In 1950 the Knesset (*Parliament*), which in 1949 had passed the Transition Law dealing in general terms with the powers of the Knesset, President and Cabinet, resolved to enact from time to time fundamental laws, which eventually, taken together, would form the Constitution. Some fundamental laws that have been passed: The Knesset (1958), Israel Lands (1960), the President (1964), the Government (1968), the State Economy (1975), the Army (1976), Jerusalem, capital of Israel (1980), and the Judicature (1984).

The Knesset, a one-chamber Parliament, consists of 120 members. It is elected for a 4-year term by secret ballot and universal direct suffrage. The system of election is by proportional representation. Voters choose between party lists of candidates in multi-member constituencies. Parties must gain 1·5% of the vote to qualify for a seat.

At the elections of 23 June 1992 the electorate was 3·4m. The Labour Party (Lab) won 44 seats with 34·8% of votes cast (39 seats in 1988); Likud, 32 with 24·9% (40); Meretz (Ratz-Shinui-Mapam coalition), 12 with 9·2%; Tsomet, 8 with 5·8% (2); Shas (Oriental Religious Jews), 6 with 5% (6); National Religious Party, 6 with 5% (5); United Torah Jewry (Agudat Israel-Degel Hatora coalition), 4 with 3·4% (7); Moledet, 3 with 2·3% (2); Hadash, 2 with 2·4%; Arab Democratic Party, 2 with 1·6% (1).

The *President* (head of state) is elected by the Knesset by secret ballot by a simple majority; his term of office is 5 years. He may be re-elected once.

President: Ezer Weizman (b. 1924; elected 24 March 1993, sworn in 13 May 1993).

Following the elections of June 1992 a Lab-Meretz-Shas coalition government was formed in July 1994. Shas left the coalition in Feb. 1995. In Feb. 1996 the government comprised:

Prime Minister and Minister of Defence: Shimon Peres (b. 1924; Lab).

Deputy Prime Minister, Foreign Affairs: Ehud Barak (Lab). *Transport:* Yisrael Kessar (b. 1931). *Finance:* Avraham Shohat (Lab). *Communications, Science and Technology:* Shulamit Aloni (Meretz). *Health:* Ephraim Sneh (Lab). *Industry and Trade:* Micha Harish (Lab). *Religious Affairs:* Shimon Shitreet (Lab). *Agriculture:* Yaacov Tsur (Lab). *Education and Culture:* Amnon Rubinstein (Meretz). *Immigration Absorption:* Yair Tsaban (Meretz). *Justice:* David Libai (Lab). *Internal Security and Police:* Moshe Shahal (Lab). *Tourism and Interior:* Uzi Baram (Lab). *Housing:* Binyamin Ben-Eliezer (Lab). *Environment:* Yossi Sarid (Lab). *Labour and Social Affairs:* Ora Namir (Lab). *Energy and Infrastructure:* Yossi Beiliu.

National flag: White with 2 horizontal blue stripes, the blue Shield of David in the centre.

National anthem: Hatikvah (*The Hope*); words by N. H. Imber.

Local Government. In 1992 there were 50 municipalities (5 Arab), 143 local councils (66 Arab or Druze) and 54 regional councils. Regional councils are local authorities set up in agricultural areas and include all the agricultural settlements in the area under their jurisdiction. All local authorities exercise their authority mainly by means of bye-laws approved by the Minister of the Interior. Their revenue is derived from rates and a surcharge on income tax. Local authorities are elected for a 4-year term. Elections were held for 158 municipal councils in Nov. 1993. The electorate was 3·3m.; turn-out was 36%.

Sayer, S., *The Parliamentary System of Israel.* Syracuse Univ. Press, 1986

DEFENCE. Conscription (for Jews and Druze only) is 3 years (usually 4 years for officers; 2 years for women).

The Israel Defence Force is a unified force, in which army, navy and air force are subordinate to a single chief-of-staff. The Minister of Defence is *de facto* C.-in-C. The cabinet usually forms a defence committee with authority to make decisions on military operations.

Army. The Army is organized in 3 territorial and 1 home front command, and has 3 corps headquarters, 2 divisional headquarters, 3 armoured divisions, 3 regional infantry divisions, 4 mechanized infantry brigades and 3 artillery battalions. The Reserves are organized in 9 armoured divisions, 1 mechanized (air mobile) division, 10 regional infantry and 4 artillery brigades. Equipment includes 1,080 Centurion, 325 M-48A5, 400 M-60, 600 M-60A1, 200 M-60A3, 150 Magach 7, 300 T-54/-55, 110 T-62 and 930 Merkava main battle tanks. Strength (1996) 134,000 (conscripts 114,700). There are also 430,000 reservists available on mobilization.

Navy. The Navy, tasked primarily for coastal protection and based at Haifa, Ashdod and Eilat, includes 3 small diesel submarines, 3 well-armed Sa'aR-5 corvettes of 1,200 tonnes, 23 missile craft of the smaller evolving Sa'aR types, from 250 to 500 tonnes, 40 fast inshore patrol craft, 1 tank landing ship, 4 amphibious craft and a few minor auxiliaries.

Naval personnel in 1995 totalled 6,500 including a Naval Commando of 300, of whom 2,500 are conscripts. There are also 10,000 naval reservists available on mobilization.

Air Force. The Air Force (including air defence) has a personnel strength (1995) of 32,000 (21,800 conscripts), with about 600 first-line aircraft, all jets, of Israeli and US manufacture. There are 4 squadrons with about 65 F-15s, and 8 squadrons with 240 F-16s in an interceptor role; 3 squadrons with 80 F-4E Phantoms, supported by 4 E-2C Hawkeye airborne early warning and control aircraft, RC-12 electronic intelligence aircraft. There are transport squadrons of turboprop C-130/KC-130 Hercules, C-47, Arava, Islander, and Boeing 707 (some equipped for tanker duties) aircraft, helicopter squadrons of UH-60 Black Hawk, CH-53, AH-64A Apache, AH-1 Huey-Cobra, Hughes 500MD/TOW Defender, JetRanger, Agusta-Bell 205, 206 and 212 aircraft, SOCATA Trinidad and DO-28 communications aircraft and training units with locally-built Magister jet trainers, which can be used also in a light ground attack role. Missiles in service include surface-to-air Hawks and surface-to-surface Lances.

INTERNATIONAL RELATIONS. A 46-year old formal state of hostilities with Jordan was brought to an end by a peace agreement on 26 Oct. 1994.

Membership. Israel is a member of UN.

ECONOMY

Policy. 30 to 40 of some 150 state-owned companies are scheduled for privatization under a scaled-down programme of 1991. Efforts to generate some 0·5m. jobs are being made to cope with the influx of Soviet immigrants.

Budget. The budget year runs from 1 Jan to 31 Dec. beginning with 1992. Previously it ran from 1 April to 31 March. Government revenue in 1991–92 amounted to 66,147m. shekels; expenditure, 66,147m. shekels.

Currency. The unit of currency is the *shekel* (ILS) of 100 *agorot.* There are coins of 5 and 50 agorot and 1 and 10 shekels, and notes of 10, 20, 50, 100 and 200 shekels. In March 1996, £1 = 4·74; US$1 = 3·10; DM1 = 2·10 shekels.

Banking and Finance. The Bank of Israel was established by law in 1954 as Israel's central bank. Its *Governor* is appointed by the President on the recommendation of the Cabinet for a 5-year term. He acts as economic adviser to the Government and has ministerial status. The *Governor* is Jacob Frenkel, appointed till 1996. There are 26 commercial banks headed by Bank Leumi Le Israel, Bank Hapoalim and Israel Discount Bank, 2 merchant banks, 1 foreign bank, 15 mortgage banks and 9 lending institutions specifically set up to aid industry and agriculture. The government holds a majority stake in the 4 largest banks, but these are now (1993) in process of privatization.

There is a stock exchange in Tel Aviv.

Weights and Measures. The metric system is in general use. The (metrical) *dunam* = 1,000 sq. metres (about 0·25 acre).

Jewish Year. The Jewish year 5755 corresponds to 6 Sept. 1994–24 Sept. 1995; 5756 to 25 Sept. 1995–13 Sept. 1996; 5757 to 14 Sept. 1996–1 Oct. 1997.

ENERGY AND NATURAL RESOURCES

Electricity. Electric-power production amounted during 1990 to 20,277m. kWh.

Oil and Gas. The only significant hydrocarbon is oil shale.

Water. In the northern Negev farming has been aided by the Yarkon–Negev water pipeline. This has become part of the overall project of the 'National Water Carrier', which is to take water from the Sea of Galilee (Lake Kinnereth) to the south. The plan includes a number of regional projects such as the Lake Kinnereth–Negev pipeline which came into operation in 1964; it has an annual capacity of 320m. cu. metres.

Minerals. The most valuable natural resources are the potash, bromine and other salt deposits of the Dead Sea. Potash production in 1990 was 2,124,000 tons.

Agriculture. In the coastal plain mixed farming, poultry raising, citriculture and vineyards are the main agricultural activities. The Emek (the Valley of Jezreel) is the main agricultural centre of Israel. Mixed farming is to be found throughout the valleys; the sub-tropical Beisan and Jordan plainlands are also centres of banana plantations and fish breeding. In Galilee mixed farming, olive and tobacco plantations prevail. The Hills of Ephraim are a vineyard centre; many parts of the hill country are under afforestation.

The area under cultivation (in 1,000 dunams) in 1993 was 4,360, of which 1,911 were under irrigation. Of the total cultivated area (1993) 2,190 dunams were under field crops, 545 under vegetables, potatoes, pumpkins and melons, 846 under citrus and plantations, 31 under fish ponds and the rest under miscellaneous crops. Production, 1993 (in 1,000 tonnes): Wheat, 217; barley, 8·2; maize grain, 4; potatoes, 219·5; melons, 90·3; tomatoes, 367; citrus fruit, 4,000; grapefruit, 412·6; cotton, 73·5.

Livestock (1993) included 357,000 cattle, 0·33m. sheep, 1m. goats, 27·0m. poultry.

Types of rural settlement: (1) The *Kibbutz* and *Kvutza* (communal collective settlement), where all property and earnings are collectively owned and work is collectively organized. (122,400 people lived in 263 *Kibbutzim* in 1994). (2) The *Moshav* (workers' co-operative smallholders' settlement) which is founded on the principles of mutual aid and equality of opportunity between the members, all farms being equal in size. (159,200 in 411). (3) The *Moshav Shitufi* (co-operative settlement), which is based on collective ownership and economy as in the *Kibbutz*, but with each family having its own house and being responsible for its own domestic services. (12,500 in 43). (4) Other rural settlements in which land and property are privately owned and every resident is responsible for his own well-being. In 1994 there were 239 villages with a population of 146,000.

INDUSTRY. Products include chemicals, metal products, textiles, tyres, diamonds, paper, plastics, leather goods, glass and ceramics, building materials, precision instruments, tobacco, foodstuffs, electrical and electronic equipment.

Labour. The workforce was 2·02m. in 1994. A 'social-economic pact' between government, employers and trade unions in May 1991 aimed to create some 32,000 new jobs to lessen the impact of increased immigration.

Trade Unions. The General Federation of Labour (Histadrut) founded in 1920, had, in 1987, 1·6m. members (including 0·17m. Arab and Druze members); including workers' families, this membership represents 71·5% of the population covering 87% of all wage-earners. Several trades unions also exist representing other political and religious groups.

FOREIGN ECONOMIC RELATIONS

Commerce. External trade, in US$1m., for calendar years:

	1990	*1991*	*1992*	*1993*	*1994*
Imports	15,104	16,688	18,007	20,209	23,369
Exports	11,576	11,219	12,444	14,083	16,051

The main exportable commodities are citrus fruit and by-products, fruit-juices, flowers, wines and liquor, sweets, polished diamonds, chemicals, tyres, textiles, metal products, machinery, electronic and transportation equipment. The main exports were, in 1994 (US$1m.): Diamonds, 3,553·5; chemical and oil products, 2,096·2; agricultural products including citrus fruit, 591·6; machinery and transport equipment, 1,695·5. Of exports in 1994, US$5,342·3m. went to EC and EFTA countries and US$5,276·9m. to USA.

Total trade between Israel and UK (British Department of Trade returns, in £1,000 sterling):

	1991	*1992*	*1993*	*1994*	*1995*
Imports to UK	455,765	485,078	550,200	572,375	692,156
Exports and re-exports from UK	529,484	586,236	876,330	1,031,644	1,108,455

Tourism. In 1994 there were about 1·8m. tourists.

COMMUNICATIONS

Roads. There were 14,169 km of paved roads in 1994. Registered motor vehicles in 1994 totalled 1,373,098, including 10,429 buses, 165,165 trucks and 1,047,848 private cars.

Railways. There were 596 km of standard gauge line in 1994. In 1994, 4·2m. passengers and 8·9m. tonnes of freight were carried.

Civil Aviation. There are international airports at Tel Aviv (Ben Gurion) and Eilat. In 1994, 21,980 planes landed at Israeli airports on international flights; 3,143,000 passengers arrived, 3,072,000 departed. In 1994, 126,794 tons of freight were loaded and 110,163 tons unloaded. In 1995 the state-owned airline El Al operated 1 B-747-100, 4 B-747-200Bs, 3 B-747-200Cs, 2 B-747-200Fs, 3 B-747-400s, 2 B-757-200s, 4 b-757-200ERs, 2 B-767-200s and 3 B-767-200ERs. Services are also provided by the Israeli airline Arkia, which flew 16 aircraft in 1995, and by Aeroflot, Air Canada, Air France, Air Malta, Air Moldova, Air Ukraine, Alitalia, Austrian Airlines, Azerbaijan Hava Yollary, Balkan, Belavia, British Airways, Cyprus Airways, Czech Airlines, Iberia, JAT, Kazakhstan Airlines, KLM, Korean Air, LOT, Lufthansa, Malév, Olympic Airways, Orbi Airways, SAA, SAS, Sabena, Swissair, TAP, Tarom, Tower Air, Trans World, Turkish Airlines, Uzbekistan Airways and World Airways.

Shipping. Israel has 3 commercial ports, Haifa, Ashdod and Eilat. In 1994, 5,678 ships departed from Israeli ports; 33m. tons of freight were handled. The merchant fleet consisted in 1994 of 65 vessels, totalling 1·5m. GRT.

Telecommunications. The Ministry of Communications supervises the postal service, and a public company responsible to the Ministry administers the telecommunications service. In 1994 there were 651 post offices and postal agencies, 50 mobile post offices and 2·1m. direct telephone lines.

Television and the state radio station, Kol Israel (Voice of Israel), are controlled by the Israel Broadcasting Authority. There is a national programme, 2 commercial programmes, a music programme and a service in Arabic. In 1993 there were 2·25m. radio and 1·5m. TV sets (colour by PAL).

Cinemas. There were 256 screens in 1993; attendances totalled 9·5m.

Press (1990). There were 22 daily newspapers.

SOCIAL INSTITUTIONS

Justice. *Law.* Under the Law and Administration Ordinance, 5708/1948, the first law passed by the Provisional Council of State, the law of Israel is the law which was obtaining in Palestine on 14 May 1948 in so far as it is not in conflict with that Ordinance or any other law passed by the Israel legislature and with such modifications as result from the establishment of the State and its authorities.

Capital punishment was abolished in 1954, except for support given to the Nazis and for high treason.

The law of Palestine was derived from Ottoman law, English law (Common Law and Equity) and the law enacted by the Palestine legislature, which to a great extent was modelled on English law.

Civil Courts. Municipal courts, established in certain municipal areas, have criminal jurisdiction over offences against municipal regulations and bye-laws and certain specified offences committed within a municipal area. Magistrates courts, established in each district and sub-district, have limited jurisdiction in both civil and criminal matters. District courts, sitting at Jerusalem, Tel-Aviv and Haifa, have jurisdiction, as courts of first instance, in all civil matters not within the jurisdiction of magistrates courts, and in all criminal matters, and as appellate courts from magistrates courts and municipal courts. The Supreme Court has jurisdiction as a court of first instance (sitting as a High Court of Justice dealing mainly with administrative matters) and as an appellate court from the district courts (sitting as a Court of Civil or of Criminal Appeal).

In addition, there are various tribunals for special classes of cases. Settlement Officers deal with disputes with regard to the ownership or possession of land in settlement areas constituted under the Land (Settlement of Title) Ordinance.

Religious Courts. The rabbinical courts of the Jewish community have exclusive jurisdiction in matters of marriage and divorce, alimony and confirmation of wills of members of their community and concurrent jurisdiction with the civil courts in all other matters of personal status of all members of their community with the consent of all parties to the action.

The courts of the several recognized Christian communities have a similar jurisdiction over members of their respective communities.

The Moslem religious courts have exclusive jurisdiction in all matters of personal status over Moslems who are not foreigners, and over Moslems who are foreigners, if under the law of their nationality they are subject in such matters to the jurisdiction of Moslem religious courts.

Where any action of personal status involves persons of different religious communities, the President of the Supreme Court will decide which court shall have jurisdiction, and whenever a question arises as to whether or not a case is one of personal status within the exclusive jurisdiction of a religious court, the matter must be referred to a special tribunal composed of 2 judges of the Supreme Court and the president of the highest court of the religious community concerned in Israel.

Religion. Religious affairs are under the supervision of a special Ministry, with departments for the Christian and Moslem communities. The religious affairs of each community remain under the full control of the ecclesiastical authorities concerned: in the case of the Jews, the Sephardi and Ashkenazi Chief Rabbis, in the case of the Christians, the heads of the various communities, and in the case of the Moslems, the Qadis. The Druze were officially recognized in 1957 as an autonomous religious community.

In 1994 there were: Jews, 4,441,100; Moslems, 781,500; Christians, 157,300; Druze, 91,700.

The Chief Rabbi is Israel Meir Lau.

Education. There is free and compulsory education from 5 to 16 years and optional free education until 18. There is a unified state-controlled elementary school system with a provision for special religious schools. The standard curriculum for all elementary schools is issued by the Ministry with a possibility of adding supplementary subjects comprising not more than 25% of the total syllabus. Most schools in towns are maintained by municipalities, a number are private and some are administered by teachers' co-operatives or trustees.

Statistics relating to schools under government supervision, 1994–95:

Type of School [1]	*Schools*	*Teachers*	*Pupils*
Hebrew Education			
Primary schools	1,323	41,104	526,324
Schools for handicapped children	209	4,028	12,946
Schools of intermediate division	354	17,829	142,664
Secondary schools	603	32,041	242,363
Vocational schools	304		105,226
Agricultural schools	23		6,840
Arab Education			
Primary schools	324	8,155	144,329
Schools for handicapped children	40	484	2,228
Schools of intermediate division	95	2,840	39,653
Secondary schools	98	3,468	42,032
Vocational schools	51		9,835
Agricultural schools	2		615

[1] Schools providing more than one type of education are included more than once.

There are also a number of private schools maintained by religious foundations—Jewish, Christian and Moslem—and also by private societies.

The Hebrew University of Jerusalem, founded in 1925, comprises faculties of the humanities, social sciences, law, science, medicine and agriculture. In 1994–95 it had 20,300 students. The Technion in Haifa had 10,480 students. The Weizmann Institute of Science in Rehovoth, founded in 1949, had 770 students.

Tel Aviv University had 26,030 students. The religious Bar-Ilan University at Ramat Gan, opened in 1965, had 16,890 students. The Haifa University had 12,440 students. The Ben Gurion University had 9,690 students.

Health. In 1994 there were 242 hospitals with 32,942 beds and (1990) 9,500 doctors.

Social Welfare. The National Insurance Law of 1954 provides for old-age pensions, survivors' insurance, work-injury insurance, maternity insurance, family allowances and unemployment benefits.

DIPLOMATIC REPRESENTATIVES

Of Israel in Great Britain (2 Palace Green, London, W8 4QB)
Ambassador: Moshe Raviv.

Of Great Britain in Israel (192 Hayarkon St., Tel Aviv 63405)
Ambassador: David Manning, CMG.

Of Israel in the USA (3514 International Dr., NW, Washington, D.C., 20008)
Ambassador: Itamar Rabinovich.

Of the USA in Israel (71 Hayarkon St., Tel Aviv)
Ambassador: Martin Indyk.

Of Israel to the United Nations
Ambassador: Gad Ya'acobi.

Further Reading

Central Bureau of Statistics. *Statistical Abstract of Israel.* (Annual).—*Statistical Bulletin of Israel.* (Monthly, with specialized supplements).
Atlas of Israel. 3rd ed. 1985
Aharoni, Y., *The Israeli Economy: the Dreams and Realities.* London, 1991
Ben-Gurion, D., *Ben-Gurion Looks Back.* London, 1965.—*The Jews in Their Land.* London, 1966.—*Israel: A Personal History.* New York, 1971
Beitlin, Y., *Israel: a Concise History.* London, 1992
Bleaney, C. H., *Israel* [Bibliography]. 2nd ed. Oxford and Santa Barbara (CA), 1994
Freedman, R. (ed.) *Israel under Rabin.* Boulder (CO), 1995
Harkabi, Y., *Israel's Fateful Decisions.* London, 1989
Louis, W. R. and Stookey, R. W., *The End of the Palestine Mandate.* London, 1986
Peres, S., *Battling for Peace: Memoirs.* London and New York, 1995
Reich, B., *Israel: Land of Tradition and Conflict.* London, 1986.— and Kieval (eds.) *Israeli Politics in the 1990s: Key Domestic and Foreign Policy Factors.* London, 1991
Sachar, H. M., *A History of Israel.* 2 vols. OUP, 1976–87
Segev, T., *1949: The First Israelis.* New York, 1986
Sharkansky, I., *The Political Economy of Israel.* Oxford and Santa Barbara (CA), 1986

Other more specialized titles are entered under PALESTINIAN-ADMINISTERED TERRITORIES *and* CONSTITUTION AND GOVERNMENT, *above.*

National statistical office: Central Bureau of Statistics, Prime Minister's Office, POB 13015, Jerusalem 91130.
National library: The Jewish National and University Library, Jerusalem.

PALESTINIAN-ADMINISTERED TERRITORIES

Key Historical Events. Under the Israeli-Palestinian agreement of 28 Sept. 1995 the Israeli army is to redeploy from 6 of the 7 of the largest Palestinian towns in the West Bank and frm 460 smaller towns and villages. Following this in April 1996 an 82-member *Palestinian Council* is to be elected and also a head (*Rais*) of the executive authority of the Council. The rest of the West Bank will stay under Israeli army control with some progressive redeployments at 6-month intervals, although Palestinian civil affairs here too will be administered by the Palestinian Council. Negotiations on the permanent status of the West Bank and Gaza were scheduled to begin in May 1996. Issues reserved for these included the position of 0·14m. Israelis in 144 settlements, the status of Jerusalem, military locations and water supplies.

Constitution and Government. The *President* is directly elected and heads the executive organ, the Palestinian National Authority, one fifth of whose members he appoints, while four fifths are elected by the *Legislative Council.* The latter comprises 88 members and is directly elected by the first-past-the-post system from 16 electoral districts.

Elections for *President* and *Legislative Council* were held on 20 Jan. 1996. The electorate was 1,013,200; turn-out was 84%. 672 candidates stood for the Council. Yasser Arafat was elected *President* against 1 opponent by 88·1% of votes cast, and was sworn in on 12 Feb. 1996.

Following an Israeli-Palestinian agreement on customs duties and VAT in Aug. 1994 the Palestinians set up their own customs and immigration points into Gaza and Jericho. Israel collects customs dues on Palestinian imports through Israeli entry points and transfers these to the Palestinian treasury.

Israeli currency is in use. The Central Bank of Jordan is responsible for regulating banking until such time as a Palestinian Monetary Authority is established.

Total trade between the Palestinian-administered territories and UK (British Department of Trade returns), 1995: Imports to UK, £3,000; exports and re-exports from UK, £162,000.

There is a Palestinian *Council for Reconstruction and Development.*

There is a Palestinian police of some 15,000; they are not empowered to arrest Israelis, but may detain them and hand them over to the Israeli authorities.

The **West Bank** has an area of 5,879 sq. km (2,270 sq. miles) and a population (1994) of 1,122,900. 97% of the population in 1988 were Palestinian Arabs of whom some 85% were Moslems, 7·4% Jewish and 8% Christian. In 1995 there was a Palestinian diaspora of 3·3m. In 1994, there were 77,604 private cars and 21,714 commercial vehicles and trucks registered. There were (1988) 183,041 pupils in primary schools and 105,007 in secondary schools, while (1983) there were 7,066 students in higher education. In 1993 there were 17 hospitals and clinics with 1,418 beds.

The **Gaza Strip** has an area of 363 sq. km (140 sq. miles) and a population (1993) of 748,400. The chief town is Gaza itself, with (1979) 0·12m. inhabitants. In 1984, over 98% of the population were Arabic-speaking Moslems; the birth rate was 4·8% and the death rate 0·8%. Citrus fruits, wheat and olives are grown, with farm land covering 193 sq. km (1980) and occupying most of the active workforce. In 1993 there were 20,434 private cars and 4,518 commercial vehicles and trucks registered. There were (1988) 112,959 pupils in primary schools and 64,699 in secondary schools, with (1983) 2,387 students in higher education. In 1993 there were 6 hospitals and clinics with 957 beds.

Kimmerling, B. and Migdal J. S., *Palestinians: the Making of a People.* Harvard Univ. Press, 1994

Rubin, B., *Revolution until Victory? The Politics and History of the PLO.* Harvard Univ. Press, 1994

Tessler, M., *A History of the Israeli-Palestinian Conflict.* Indiana Univ. Press, 1994

ITALY

Repubblica Italiana

Capital: Rome
Population: 56·96m. (1992)
GNP per capita: US$19,270 (1994)
HDI/world rank: 0·912/20 (1992)

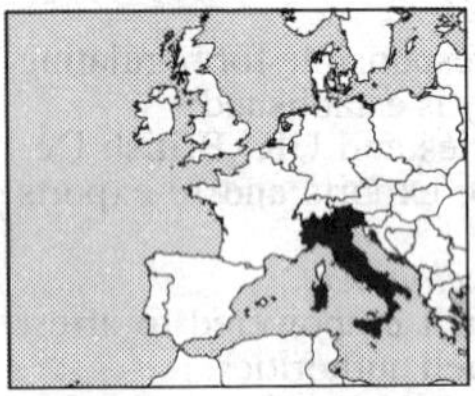

KEY HISTORICAL EVENTS. On 10 June 1946 Italy became a republic following a referendum held on 2 June at which votes for a republic numbered 12,718,641; for the retention of the monarchy, 10,718,502; invalid or contested, 1,509,735. The electorate was 28,005,449; turn-out was 24,946,878 (89·1%).

This ended the reign of the House of Savoy, whose kings had ruled over Piedmont for 9 centuries and as Kings of Italy since 18 Feb. 1861.

TERRITORY AND POPULATION. Italy is bounded in the north by Switzerland and Austria, east by Slovenia and the Adriatic Sea, south-east by the Ionian Sea, south by the Mediterranean Sea, south-west by the Tyrrhenian Sea and Ligurian Sea and west by France. Populations at successive censuses were as follows:

10 Feb. 1901	33,370,138	4 Nov. 1951	47,158,738
10 June 1911	35,694,582	15 Oct. 1961	49,903,878
1 Dec. 1921	37,403,956	24 Oct. 1971	53,744,737
21 April 1931	40,582,043	25 Oct. 1981	56,243,935
21 April 1936	42,302,680	20 Oct. 1991	56,778,031

The following table gives area and population of the Autonomous Regions (census 1991 and estimate 1992):

Regions	*Area in sq. km (1992)*	*Resident pop. census, 1991*	*Resident pop. 31 Dec. 1992*	*Density per sq. km (1992)*
Piedmont	25,399	4,302,565	4,303,830	169
Valle d'Aosta [1]	3,262	115,938	117,204	36
Lombardy	23,859	8,856,074	8,882,408	372
Trentino-Alto Adige [1]	13,607	890,360	896,722	66
Bolzano-Bozen	*7,400*	*440,508*	*444,243*	*60*
Trento	*6,207*	*449,852*	*452,479*	*73*
Veneto	18,365	4,380,797	4,395,263	239
Friuli-Venezia Giulia [1]	7,844	1,197,666	1,195,055	152
Liguria	5,418	1,676,282	1,668,896	308
Emilia Romagna	22,124	3,909,512	3,920,223	177
Tuscany	22,992	3,529,946	3,528,735	154
Umbria	8,456	811,831	814,796	96
Marche	9,693	1,429,205	1,433,994	148
Lazio	17,227	5,140,371	5,162,073	300
Abruzzi	10,794	1,249,054	1,255,549	116
Molise	4,438	330,900	331,494	75
Campania	13,595	5,630,280	5,668,895	417
Puglia	19,357	4,031,885	4,049,972	209
Basilicata	9,992	610,528	610,821	61
Calabria	15,080	2,070,203	2,074,763	138
Sicily [1]	25,707	4,966,386	4,997,705	194
Sardinia [1]	24,090	1,648,248	1,651,902	69
Total	301,302	56,778,031	56,960,300	189

[1] With special statute.

Vital statistics for calendar years:

	Marriages	*Living births Married parent*	*Living births Single parent*	*Total*	*Still-born*	*Deaths excl. of still-born*
1991	312,061	522,690	36,700	559,390	3,103	553,833
1992 [1]	303,785	523,003	37,765	560,768	2,778	541,488

[1] Provisional.

There were 538,168 births and 543,433 deaths in 1993. 1993 birth rate, 9·4 per 1,000 population.

In 1989 there were 65,647 emigrants (26,098 to Germany, 6,347 to Switzerland, 5,277 to France, 4,076 to USA) and 81,201 immigrants (13,198 from Germany, 7,531 from Argentina, 6,296 from Switzerland, 4,930 from France).

Communes of more than 100,000 inhabitants, with population resident at the census of 20 Oct. 1991 and on 31 Dec. 1992:

	1991	*1992*		*1991*	*1992*
Rome	2,775,250	2,723,327	Foggia	156,268	155,674
Milan	1,369,231	1,358,627	Salerno	148,932	147,564
Naples	1,067,365	1,071,744	Perugia	144,732	146,160
Turin	962,507	952,736	Ferrara	138,015	137,099
Palermo	698,556	696,735	Ravenna	135,834	136,099
Genoa	678,771	667,563	Reggio nell'Emilia	132,030	133,191
Bologna	404,378	401,308	Rimini	127,960	129,876
Florence	403,294	397,434	Syracuse	125,941	126,800
Bari	342,309	342,129	Sassari	122,339	121,961
Catania	333,075	329,898	Pescara	122,336	121,424
Venice	309,422	305,617	Monza	120,651	120,054
Verona	255,824	255,492	Bergamo	114,930	115,053
Taranto	232,334	230,207	Forlì	109,541	109,080
Messina	231,693	232,911	Terni	108,248	108,150
Trieste	231,100	228,398	Vicenza	107,454	107,481
Padua	215,137	213,656	Piacenza	102,268	102,161
Cagliari	204,237	180,309	Trento	101,545	101,538
Brescia	194,502	192,883	La Spezia	101,442	100,458
Reggio di C.	177,580	178,312	Torre del Greco	101,361	100,688
Modena	176,990	176,972	Ancona	101,285	100,701
Parma	170,520	170,555	Novara	101,112	102,029
Livorno	167,512	166,394	Lecce	100,884	100,508
Prato	165,707	166,108			

The official language is Italian, spoken by 94·1% of the population in 1991. There are 0·3m. German-speakers in Bolzano and 0·3m. French-speakers in Valle d'Aosta.

CLIMATE. The climate varies considerably with latitude. In the south, it is warm temperate, with little rain in the summer months, but the north is cool temperate with rainfall more evenly distributed over the year.

Florence, Jan. 44°F (6·8°C), July 74°F (23·3°C). Annual rainfall 32" (807 mm). Milan, Jan. 35°F (1·9°C), July 69°F (20·8°C). Annual rainfall 23" (573 mm). Naples, Jan. 48°F (8·9°C), July 77°F (25·6°C). Annual rainfall 34" (850 mm). Palermo, Jan. 54°F (12·3°C), July 79°F (26·1°C). Annual rainfall 14" (352 mm). Rome, Jan. 45°F (7·5°C), July 77°F (24·9°C). Annual rainfall 26" (657 mm). Venice, Jan. 38°F (3·2°C), July 75°F (23·9°C). Annual rainfall 8" (207 mm).

CONSTITUTION AND GOVERNMENT. The Constitution dates from 1948. Italy is 'a democratic republic founded on work'. Parliament consists of the *Chamber of Deputies* and the *Senate.* The Chamber is elected for 5 years by universal and direct suffrage and consists of 630 deputies. The Senate is elected for 5 years on a regional basis; each Region having at least 7 senators, consisting of 315 elected senators; the Valle d'Aosta is represented by 1 senator only, the Molise by 2. The President of the Republic can nominate 11 senators for life from eminent persons in the social, scientific, artistic and literary spheres. The President may become a senator for life. The *President* is elected in a joint session of Chamber and Senate, to which are added 3 delegates from each Regional Council (1 from the Valle d'Aosta). A two-thirds majority is required for the election, but after a third indecisive scrutiny the absolute majority of votes is sufficient. The President must be 50 years or over; term of office, 7 years. The Speaker of the Senate acts as the deputy President. The President can dissolve the chambers of parliament, except during the last 6 months of the presidential term.

A *Constitutional Court,* consisting of 15 judges who are appointed, 5 each, by the President, Parliament (in joint session) and the highest law and administrative courts, can decide on the constitutionality of laws and decrees, define the powers of the State and Regions, judge conflicts between the State and Regions and between the Regions, and try the President and Ministers.

The reorganization of the Fascist Party is forbidden. Direct male descendants of King Victor Emmanuel are excluded from all public offices, have no right to vote or to be elected, and are banned from Italian territory; their estates are forfeit to the State. Titles of nobility are no longer recognized, but those existing before 28 Oct. 1922 are retained as part of the name.

A referendum was held in June 1991 to decide whether the system of preferential voting by indicating 4 candidates by their listed number should be changed to a simpler system, less open to abuse, of indicating a single candidate by name. The electorate was 46m. Turn-out was 62·5% (there was a 50% quorum). 95·6% of votes cast were in favour of the change. As a result, an electoral reform of 1993 provides for the replacement of proportional representation by a system in which 475 seats in the Chamber of Deputies are elected by a first-past-the-post single-round vote and 155 seats by proportional representation in a separate single-round vote on the same day. There are 27 electoral regions. There is a 4% threshold for entry to the Chamber of Deputies.

At a further referendum in April 1993, turn-out was 77%. Votes favoured the 8 reforms proposed, including a new system of election to the Senate and the abolition of some ministries. 75% of the Senate is now elected by a first-past-the-post system, the remainder by proportional representation; no party may present more than 1 candidate in each constituency.

President: Oscar Luigi Scalfaro (b. 1919; DC; sworn in 28 May 1992).

The President dissolved parliament in Feb. 1996 and called for elections on 21 April 1996 (*see* ADDENDA).

National flag: Three vertical strips of green, white, red.

National anthem: Fratelli d'Italia ('Brothers of Italy'; words by G. Mameli; tune by M. Novaro, 1847).

European Parliament. Italy has 87 representatives. At the June 1994 elections turn-out was 74·8%. Forza Italia gained 27 seats with 30·6% of votes cast; the Party of the Democratic Left (former Communists), 16 with 19·1% (group in European Parliament: European Socialist Party); the National Alliance, 11 with 12·5%; the Popular Party (former Christian Democrats), 8 with 10% (Popular European Party); the Northern League, 6 with 6·6%; the Reformed Communists, 5 with 6·1%; the Greens, 3 with 3·2% (Greens); Segni, 3 with 3·2%; the Pannella Reformers, 2 with 2·1%; the Socialist Party, 2 with 1·8% (European Socialist Party); Rete, 1 with 1·1%; the Republican Party, 1 with 0·7% (Liberals, Democrats, Reformers); the Social Democratic Party, 1 with 0·7% (European Socialist Party); the South Tyrol People's Party, 1 with 0·6% (Popular European Party).

Regional and Local Government. Italy is administratively divided into 15 autonomous regions and 5 autonomous regions with special statute; these are subdivided into 94 provinces and 1,230 municipalities. The regions have their own councils and governments with certain legislative and administrative functions adapted to the circumstances of each region. A government commissioner co-ordinates regional and national activities. Since 1993 mayors have been directly elected for 4-year terms in towns of more than 15,000 inhabitants and allot 60% of seats on municipal councils, the remainder being apportioned according to party vote.

Measures for the autonomy of the largely German-speaking **Alto Adige** (South Tyrol) were granted in Jan. 1992 and accepted by Austria in June 1992.

On 7 and 20 June 1993 municipal elections were held for councils in 1,230 municipalities, 6 provinces and Friuli-Venezia-Giulia; the electorate was 10·5m. Further elections were held in 446 municipalities on 21 Nov. and 5 Dec. 1993 (electorate 8m.). At both elections the Northern League, La Rete, the Democratic Party of the Left (former communists) and MSI gained majorities at the expense of the parties forming the coalition government.

Elections were held for all 15 mainland regional, 76 provincial and 5,130 municipal councils in 2 rounds on 23 April and 7 May 1995, for the first time on the first-past-the-post system. The electorate was 43m.; turn-out was 80·5% at the first round and 63% at the second.

DEFENCE. Head of the armed forces is the Defence Chief of Staff. There is conscription for 12 months.

Army. The Field Army is organized into 3 corps headquarters (1 mountain), consisting of 3 mechanized, 2 armoured and 4 mountain brigades, 2 armoured cavalry, 2 heavy artillery and 2 amphibious battalions, 3 aviation groups, 3 artillery regiments and 2 anti-aircraft regiments; an air defence command with surface-to-air missiles; and an aviation group. There is a territorial defence force of 8 independent mechanized brigades deployed in 7 military regions, and a rapid intervention force and a support brigade with missiles. Equipment includes 167 M-60A1, 910 Leopard and 242 Centauro main battle tanks. The Army air corps operates 8 DO228 transports, over 40 light aircraft and 360 helicopters. Strength (1996) 175,000 (131,000 conscripts), with 520,000 reserves. The paramilitary Carabinieri number 111,800.

Navy. The principal ships of the Navy are the light aircraft carrier *Giuseppe Garibaldi* and the helicopter-carrying cruiser *Vittorio Veneto*. The *Giuseppe Garibaldi*, 13,450 tonnes, was completed in 1985 and operates an air group of 10 SH-3D Sea King anti-submarine helicopters and 5 AV8-B Harrier aircraft. She is also armed with 4 Teseo anti-ship missiles. The *Vittorio Veneto*, completed in 1969, is of 9,650 tonnes, and operates a squadron of 6 AB-212 anti-submarine helicopters as well as a twin launcher for ASROC and US Standard SM-1 surface-to-air missiles, and Teseo.

The combatant forces also include 9 diesel submarines, 4 guided-missile destroyers armed with Standard SM-I, 26 frigates, of which 18 carry one or more AB-212 helicopters and 6 missile-armed patrol hydrofoils. Mine countermeasure forces comprise 11 coastal minehunters. There are 4 new helicopter-carrying offshore patrol vessels for the protection of economic resources. Amphibious lift for the San Marco commando group (800 men) is provided by 3 dock landing ships and 40 craft. Auxiliaries include 2 replenishment oilers, 4 water carriers, 3 survey ships, 4 trial vessels, 2 training ships and 8 large tugs.

The Naval Air Arm, 1,500 strong, operates 75 anti-submarine and training helicopters and has acquired the first 5 operational and 2 training Harrier-type TAV-8B short take off/vertical landing aircraft for the carrier squadron.

There is a Special Forces commando of some 600 assault swimmers.

Main naval bases are at Spezia, Naples, Taranto and Ancona, with minor bases at Brindisi and Venice. The personnel of the Navy in 1995 numbered 44,000, including the naval air arm and the marine battalion.

Paramilitary maritime tasks are carried out by the Financial Guards fleet of some 70 patrol craft and a harbour control force with 12 inshore patrol craft and numerous boats.

Air Force. Control is exercised through 2 regional headquarters near Taranto and Milan. Units assigned to NATO comprise the 1st air brigade of Nike-Hercules surface-to-air missiles, 9 fighter-bomber, 7 interceptor and 1 tactical reconnaissance squadron, with supporting transport, search and rescue, and training units. 4 of the fighter-bomber squadrons have Tornados, and 5 squadrons operate AM-X Centauros. F-104S Starfighters have been standardized throughout the interceptor squadrons.

One transport squadron has turboprop C-130H Hercules aircraft; 2 others have turboprop Aeritalia G222s. There is a VIP and personnel transport squadron, equipped with AS-61, DC-9, Gulfstream III and Falcon 50 aircraft.

Electronic warfare duties are performed by specially equipped G222s, PD-808s and MB 339s. Two land-based anti-submarine squadrons operate Breguet Atlantics. Search and rescue are performed by 30 Agusta-Sikorsky HH-3F helicopters and smaller types. There are also strong support and training elements; some MB 339 jet trainers have armament provisions for secondary close air support and anti-helicopter roles.

Air Force strength in 1995 was about 67,800 (25,500 conscripts).

INTERNATIONAL RELATIONS

Membership. Italy is a member of the UN, NATO, EC and WEU. In Nov. 1990 Italy acceded to the Schengen Accord of June 1990 which abolished border controls between Italy and Austria, Belgium, France, Germany, Greece, Luxembourg, the Netherlands, Portugal and Spain. It came into effect on 26 March 1994 but has not yet been implemented by Austria, Greece or Italy.

ECONOMY

Policy. A programme of privatization began in 1993, starting with institutions in banking and financial services.

Budget. Total revenue and expenditure for fiscal years, in 1m. lire:

	Revenue	*Expenditure*		*Revenue*	*Expenditure*
1986	266,301,009	384,344,429	1989	346,389,962	464,648,999
1987	283,875,850	442,965,463	1990	410,227,544	535,253,636
1988	312,790,760	474,587,541	1991	441,050,659	575,328,563

In 1992 tax revenue totalled 409,321,000m. lire, including: Direct taxes, 238,628,000m. lire; taxes on goods and services, 119,270,000m. lire; consumer taxes, 17,789,000m. lire; business taxes, 29,063,000m. lire.

VAT is 19% (reduced rate, 10%).

The public debt at 31 Dec. 1991 totalled 1,313,506,600m. lire, including consolidated debt of 40,436m. lire and the floating debt of 501,072,300m. lire.

Currency. The unit of currency is the *lira* (ITL). There are coins of 10, 20, 50, 100, 200, 500 and 1,000 lire, and notes of 2,000, 5,000, 10,000, 50,000 and 100,000 lire. The lira left the EMS in Sept. 1993. Circulation of money at 31 Dec. 1992: State coins and notes, 1,642,621m. lire; bank-notes, 89,222,000m. lire. Annualized inflation was 6% in 1995. In March 1996, £1 = 2,386 lire; US$1 = 1,562 lire; DM1 = 1,058 lire.

Banking and Finance. The bank of issue is the Bank of Italy (founded 1893). It is owned by public-sector banks. Its *governor* (Antonio Fazio, b. 1936) is selected without fixed term by the 13 directors of the Bank's non-executive board. In 1991 it received increased responsibility for the supervision of banking and stock exchange affairs, and in 1993 greater independence from the government. Its gold reserve amounted to 29,944,000m. lire in Dec. 1992; the foreign credit reserves of the Exchange Bureau (*Ufficio Italiano Cambi*) amounted to 19,561,000m. lire.

Credit institutions are under the control of the state's 'Inspectorate of Credit'. Other credit institutions, totalling 1,024, are classified as: (1) 217 commercial banks including 126 private and 40 branches of foreign banks; (2) 102 co-operative banks; (3) 700 rural and artisans' banks; (4) 5 Istituti di Categoria.

The 'Amato' law of July 1990 gave public sector banks the right to become joint stock companies and permitted the placing of up to 49% of their equity with private shareholders.

On 31 Dec. 1992 the post office savings banks had deposits and current accounts of 173,288,000m. lire; credit institutions, 787,220,000m. lire.

Legislation reforming stock markets came into effect in Dec. 1990. There are stock exchanges in Milan, Rome, Turin and Genoa.

Weights and Measures. The metric system is in use. 1 quintal = 100 kg.

ENERGY AND NATURAL RESOURCES

Electricity. In 1992 the total power generated was 226,243m. kWh., of which 45,787m. kWh. were generated by hydro-electric plants.

Oil and Gas. Production, 1992, 4,468,191 tonnes, of which 856,077 tonnes came from Sicily. Natural gas production (1992) 639,019m. cu. ft.

Minerals. Fuel and mineral resources are inadequate to needs. Only sulphur and mercury yield a substantial surplus for exports.

Production of metals and minerals (in tonnes) was as follows:

	1987	*1988*	*1989*	*1990*	*1991*	*1992*
Iron pyrites	784,924	720,132	835,713	805,825	550,083	440,651
Manganese	3,802	9,701	5,899	6,654	8,350	8,198
Zinc	67,798	71,979	80,960	83,077	70,046	61,558
Bauxite	15,057	17,864	14,864	–	–	–
Lead	58,515	68,946	71,240	64,591	111,696	109,253
Aluminium	258,051	257,995	233,046	246,346	257,603	202,871

Agriculture. In 1993, 1,984,100 persons were dependent on agriculture, of whom 1,329,900 were economically active. In 1989 there were 261,632 sq. km of agricultural and forest land distributed as follows (in 1,000 ha): Forage and pasture, 7,274; woods, 6,750; cereals, 4,517; vines, 1,065; olive trees, 1,154; garden produce, 615; leguminous plants, 223; unproductive, 39.

At the 1990 census agricultural holdings numbered 3,023,344 and covered 22,702,356 ha. 2,893,145 owners (95·7%) farmed directly 15,961,093 ha (70·3%); 118,020 owners (3·9%) worked with hired labour on 6,603,522 ha (29·1%); 95,045 share-croppers (3·1%) tilled 1,208,337 ha (5·3%); the remaining 12,179 holdings (0·4%) of 137,740 ha (0·6%) were operated in other ways. In 1990 persons engaged in agriculture numbered 1·9m. (0·68m. females).

In 1989, 1,399,375 farm tractors were being used.

The production of the principal crops (in 1,000 metric quintals) in 1992: Sugar beet, 147,619; wheat, 89,384; maize, 74,127; tomatoes, 54,724; potatoes, 25,066; oranges, 20,989; rice, 13,143; barley, 17,413; lemons, 7,456; oats, 3,331; olive oil, 4,353; tangerines, mandarines and clementines, 5,017; other citrus fruit, 433; rye, 225; wine, 68,686,100 hectolitres; tobacco (1991), 193,296 tonnes.

Livestock, 1992: Cattle, 8,087,300; pigs, 8,548,000; sheep, 10,434,600; goats, 1,314,200; horses, 316,000; donkeys, 39,000; mules, 18,000.

Fisheries. The fishing fleet comprised, in 1989, 18,433 motor boats of 263,164 gross tonnes and 5,629 sailing vessels of 7,008 GRT. The catch in 1991 was 3,682,828 metric quintals.

INDUSTRY. The main branches of industry are: (% of industrial value added at factor cost in 1992) Textiles, clothing, leather and footwear (14·2%), food, beverages and tobacco (8·3%), energy products (10·7%), agricultural and industrial machines (8·6%), metal products except machines and means of transport (8·9%), mineral and non-metallic mineral products (7%), timber and wooden furniture (5·2%), electric plants and equipment (6·7%), chemicals and pharmaceuticals (7·9%), means of transport (6·2%).

Production, 1992: Steel, 24,791,866 tonnes; motor vehicles, 1,684,555; cement, 41,034,027 tonnes; artificial and synthetic fibres (including staple fibre and waste), 728,428 tonnes; polyethylene resins, 926,610 tonnes.

Labour. In 1993 the workforce was 22,787,000 of whom 2·36m. were unemployed. Unemployment was 11% in 1992. Pensionable retirement age was 60 for men and 55 for women in 1991, but this is being progressively raised to 65 for both sexes. Agreements between the government, employers and trade unions in 1992 and 1993 ended automatic wage indexation and regulated labour relations and wage increases.

Trade Unions. There are 3 main groups: the Confederazione Generale Italiana del Lavoro (CGIL; no longer Communist-dominated), the Confederazione Italiana Sindacati Lavoratori (CISL; Catholic), and the Unione Italiana del Lavoro (UIL). Membership in 1994: CGIL, 5·2m. (2·7m. retired); CISL, 3·7m. (1·5m. retired); UIL, 1·7m. (0·5m. retired). In referendums held in June 1995 the electorate voted to remove some restrictions on trade union representation, end government involvement in public sector trade unions and end the automatic deduction of trade union dues from wage packets.

FOREIGN ECONOMIC RELATIONS. Foreign debt was US$74,000m. in Nov. 1990.

Commerce. The territory covered by foreign trade statistics includes Italy and San Marino, but excludes the municipalities of Livigno and Campione.

The following table shows the value of Italy's foreign trade (in 1m. lire):

	1989	*1990*	*1991*	*1992*	*1993*
Imports	209,910,067	217,703,398	225,745,720	232,110,601	234,033,000
Exports	192,797,157	203,515,285	209,728,316	219,436,211	265,236,000

Main export markets in 1993 (in 1,000m. lire): Germany, 51,630; France, 34,822; USA and Canada, 22,683; UK, 16,957; Spain, 11,465; Switzerland, 10,417; Belgium, 7,897; Netherlands, 7,458; Austria, 6,609; Japan, 5,038; Greece, 4,702; Portugal, 3,548. Main import suppliers: Germany, 44,967; France, 31,639; USA and Canada, 14,264; UK, 13,535; Netherlands, 13,221; Switzerland, 11,925; Spain, 7,763; Japan, 5,987; Libya, 5,245; Austria, 5,140; China, 4,074.

Principal exports, 1993 (in 1,000m. lire): Metal products and machinery, 92,117; textiles and leather goods, 45,735; wood, paper and rubber goods, 34,024; transport equipment, 23,918; chemical products, 20,858; foodstuffs, beverages and tobacco, 12,228; metallic minerals, 11,996; non-metallic minerals and products, 10,951; agricultural, forestry and fishery products, 6,738; energy, 5,715. Principal imports: Metal products and machinery, 51,322; chemical products, 31,288; energy, 28,177; transport equipment, 23,528; foodstuffs, beverages and tobacco, 20,039; metallic minerals, 19,755; wood, paper and rubber goods, 19,616; textile and leather goods, 16,344; agriculture, forestry and fishery products, 15,060; non-metallic minerals and products, 4,611.

Total trade between Italy and UK (British Department of Trade returns, in £1,000 sterling):

	1990	*1991*	*1992*	*1993*	*1994*
Imports to UK	6,735,496	6,378,908	6,769,218	6,152,800	6,843,000
Exports and re-exports from UK	5,612,751	6,145,014	6,146,719	5,572,100	6,461,600

Tourism. In 1991, 51·3m. foreigners visited Italy; they included 9·2m. German, 10·2m. Swiss, 9·1m. French, 5·5m. Austrian, 4·4m. Yugoslav, 1·7m. British, 1·5m. Dutch and 1·1m. US citizens. They spent about 22,853,073m. lire.

COMMUNICATIONS

Roads. Roads totalled (1991) 303,518 km, of which 51,377 km were state roads and highways, 110,475 km provincial roads and 141,666 km communal roads. Motor vehicles, Dec. 1990: Cars, 27,415,828; buses, 77,731; lorries, 2,349,992; motor cycles, light vans, etc., 6,003,558. There were 7,434 fatalities in traffic accidents in 1992 (7,498 in 1991).

Railways. Length of railways (1991), 19,595 km, including 16,066 km of national railways (9,799 km electrified). In 1994 the national railways carried 48,900m. passenger-km and 22,900m. tonne-km of goods. There are metros in Milan (68 km) and Rome (33·5 km), and tram/light rail networks in Genoa (2·3 km), Milan (240 km), Naples (23 km) and Turin (119 km).

Civil Aviation. There are international airports at Bologna (G. Marconi), Genoa (Cristoforo Colombo), Milan (Linate and Malpensa), Naples (Capodichino), Pisa (Galileo Galilei), Rome (Leonardo da Vinci), Turin and Venice (Marco Polo). The national carrier Alitalia is 89·3% owned by the state, and in 1993 operated 2 A300B2-200s, 4 A300B4-100s, 8 A300B4-200s, 7 A321-100s, 7 B-747-200Bs, 4 B-747-200B Combis, 1 B-747-200F, 2 B-767-300ERs and 114 other aircraft. Domestic and international traffic in 1992 registered 25,170,486 passengers arrived and 25,104,018 departed, while freight and mail (excluding luggage) amounted to 261,729 tonnes unloaded and 270,391 tonnes loaded.

Shipping. The mercantile marine in 1995 consisted of 614 vessels of 11·88m.

DWT, representing 1·79% of the world's tonnage. 112 vessels (26·42% of tonnage) were registered under foreign flags. Total tonnage registered was 6·82m. GRT, including oil tankers, 2·18m. GRT and container ships, 0·14m. GRT. In 1992, 228·4m. tonnes of cargo were unloaded, and 47·04m. tonnes of international cargo were loaded.

Telecommunications. In 1991 there were 14,412 post offices and 13,918 telegraph offices. On 1 Jan. 1991 there were 32,945,122 telephones. In 1994, 1,782,000 mobile telephones were in use. Broadcasting is regulated by the Public Radio-Television Administration Council. This consists of 8 members elected by parliament who choose a ninth member as chair for 3-year terms. *Radiotelevisione Italiana* broadcasts 3 radio programmes and additional regional programmes. It also broadcasts 2 TV programmes. There are 12 national and about 820 local independent TV networks. In 1993 there were 15m. radio and 17m. TV sets (colour by PAL).

Cinemas. In 1991 there were 3,249 screens (1,200 full-time) and 590·2m. admissions).

Press. There were (1988) 73 dailies with a combined circulation of 6m.

SOCIAL INSTITUTIONS

Justice. Italy has 1 court of cassation, in Rome, and is divided for the administration of justice into 26 appeal court districts, subdivided into 161 tribunal *circondari* (districts), and these again into *mandamenti* each with its own magistracy (*Pretura*), 628 in all. There are also 90 first degree assize courts and 26 assize courts of appeal. For civil business, besides the magistracy above mentioned, *Conciliatori* have jurisdiction in petty plaints (those to a maximum amount of 1m. lire).

On 31 Dec. 1992 there were 35,902 male and 2,246 female prisoners in establishments for preventive custody, 7,795 males and 330 females in penal establishments and 1,238 males and 77 females in establishments for the execution of safety measures.

Religion. The treaty between the Holy See and Italy, of 11 Feb. 1929, confirmed by article 7 of the Constitution of the republic, lays down that the Catholic Apostolic Roman Religion is the only religion of the State. Other creeds are permitted, provided they do not profess principles, or follow rites, contrary to public order or moral behaviour.

The appointment of archbishops and of bishops is made by the Holy See; but the Holy See submits to the Italian Government the name of the person to be appointed in order to obtain an assurance that the latter will not raise objections of a political nature.

Catholic religious teaching is given in elementary and intermediate schools. Marriages celebrated before a Catholic priest are automatically transferred to the civil register. Marriages celebrated by clergy of other denominations must be made valid before a registrar.

There were 47·56m. Catholics in 1993.

Education. 5 years of primary and 3 years of secondary education are compulsory from the age of 6.

Senior secondary education is subdivided into classical (*ginnasio* and classical *liceo*), scientific (scientific *liceo*), language lyceum, professional institutes and technical education: agricultural, industrial, commercial, technical, nautical institutes, institutes for surveyors, institutes for girls (5-year course) and teacher-training institutes (4-year course).

University education is given in Universities and in University Higher Institutes (4, 5, 6 years, according to degree course).

Statistics for the academic year 1992–93:

Elementary schools	*No.*	*Pupils*
Kindergarten	27,274	1,569,811
Public elementary schools	20,510	2,716,439

Elementary schools	*No.*	*Pupils*
Private elementary schools Private elementary recognized schools (*parificate*)	2,200	243,125
Government secondary schools		*Total students*
Junior secondary schools	9,858	2,059,430
Classical lyceum	753	231,064
Lyceum for science	1,038	472,950
Language lyceum	369	42,100
Teachers' schools	165	21,522
Teachers' institutes	641	159,518
Professional institutes	1,702	534,044
Technical institutes, of which:		
Industrial institutes	624	321,172
Commercial institutes	1,357	653,978
Surveyors' institutes	563	173,955
Agricultural institutes	95	26,720
Nautical institutes	51	12,184
Technical institutes for tourism	47	17,599
Managerial institutes	155	45,015
Girls technical schools	70	23,109
Artistic studies	300	98,270

In 1994–95 there were 47 universities, 2 universities of Italian studies for foreigners and 3 specialized universities (commerce; education; Roman Catholic), 3 polytechnical university institutes and 7 other specialized university institutes: (architecture; bio-medicine; modern languages; naval studies; oriental studies; social studies; teacher training). In 1994–95 there were 946,704 university students and 36,787 academic staff.

Health. The provision of health services is a regional responsibility, but they are funded by central government. Medical consultations are free, but a portion of prescription costs have been payable since April 1989. In 1992 there were 296,385 doctors and (1991) 306,664 hospital beds.

Social Security. Social expenditure is made up of transfers which the central public departments, local departments and social security departments, make to families. Payment is principally for pensions, family allowances and health services. Expenditure on subsidies, public assistance to various classes of people and people injured by political events or national disasters are also included.

State pensions are indexed to prices; 19m. pensions were paid in 1990.

DIPLOMATIC REPRESENTATIVES

Of Italy in Great Britain (14 Three Kings Yard, London, W1Y 2EH)
Ambassador: Paolo Galli.

Of Great Britain in Italy (Via XX Settembre 80A, 00187, Rome)
Ambassador: Tom Richardson.

Of Italy in the USA (1601 Fuller St., NW, Washington, D.C., 20009)
Ambassador: Boris Biancheri.

Of the USA in Italy (Via Veneto 119/A, Rome)
Ambassador: Reginald Bartholomew.

Of Italy to the United Nations
Ambassador: Francesco Fulci.

Further Reading

Istituto Nazionale di Statistica. *Annuario Statistico Italiano.—Compendio Statistico Italiano.* (Annual).—*Italian Statistical Abstract* (Annual).—*Bollettino Mensile di Statistica* (Monthly).

Absalom, R., *Italy since 1880: a Nation in the Balance?* Harlow, 1995
Baldassarri, M. (ed.) *The Italian Economy: Heaven or Hell?* London, 1993
Clark, M., *Modern Italy 1871–1982.* London, 1984
Di Scala, S. M., *Italy from Revolution to Republic: 1700 to the Present.* Boulder (CO), 1995

Duggan, C., *A Concise History of Italy.* CUP, 1994
Frei, M., *Italy: the Unfinished Revolution*. London, 1996
Furlong, P., *Modern Italy: Representation and Reform.* London, 1994
Gilbert, M. *Italian Revolution: the Ignominious End of Politics, Italian Style.* Boulder (CO), 1995
Ginsborg, P., *A History of Contemporary Italy: Society and Politics, 1943–1988.* London, 1990
Gundie, S. and Parker, S. (eds.) *The New Italian Republic: from the Fall of the Berlin Wall to Berlusconi*. London, 1995
Hearder, H., *Italy: a Short History.* CUP, 1991
Putnam, R. *et al., Making Democracy Work: Civic Traditions in Modern Italy.* Princeton Univ. Press, 1993
Richards, C., *The New Italians.* London, 1994
Sponza, L. and Zancani, D., *Italy*. [Bibliography]. Oxford and Santa Barbara (CA), 1995

National statistical office: Istituto Nazionale di Statistica (ISTAT), 16 Via Cesare Balbo, 00100 Rome.

National library: Biblioteca Nazionale Centrale, Vittorio Emanuele II, Viale Castro Pretorio, Rome.

JAMAICA

Capital: Kingston
Population: 2·47m. (1993)
GNP per capita: US$1,420 (1994)
HDI/world rank: 0·721/88 (1992)

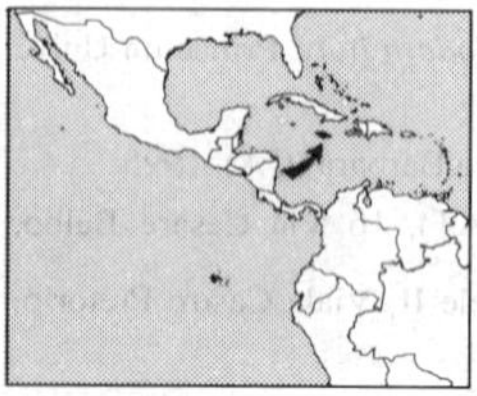

KEY HISTORICAL EVENTS. Jamaica was discovered by Columbus in 1494, and was occupied by the Spaniards between 1509 and 1655, when the island was captured by the English; their possession was confirmed by the Treaty of Madrid, 1670. Self-government was introduced in 1944 and gradually extended until Jamaica achieved complete independence within the Commonwealth on 6 Aug. 1962.

TERRITORY AND POPULATION. Jamaica is an island which lies in the Caribbean Sea about 150 km south of Cuba. The area is 4,411 sq. miles (11,425 sq. km). The population at the census of 7 April 1991 was 2,374,193. Estimated population in 1993 was 2,471,600, distributed on the basis of the 13 parishes of the island as follows: Kingston and St Andrew, 692,700; St Thomas, 88,500; Portland, 78,300; St Mary, 113,600; St Ann, 153,800; Trelawny, 74,100; St James, 168,400; Hanover, 66,400; Westmoreland, 130,200; St Elizabeth, 146,300; Manchester, 191,800; St Catherine, 369,200; Clarendon, 221,900.

Chief towns (population, 1991): Kingston and St Andrew, 587,798, metropolitan area; Spanish Town, 92,383; Portmore, 90,138; Montego Bay, 83,446; May Pen, 46,785; Mandeville, 36,430.

The population is about 75% of African ethnic origin.

Vital statistics (1993): Births, 57,400 (23·2 per 1,000 population); deaths, 13,900 (5·6); marriages, 14,352 (5·8%); divorces, 1,439 (0·6%). There were 21,300 emigrants in 1993, mainly to the USA.

CLIMATE. A tropical climate but with considerable variation. High temperatures on the coast are usually mitigated by sea breezes, while upland areas enjoy cooler and less humid conditions. Rainfall is plentiful over most of Jamaica, being heaviest in May and from Aug. to Nov. The island lies in the hurricane zone. Kingston. Jan. 76°F (24·4°C), July 81°F (27·2°C). Annual rainfall 32" (800 mm).

CONSTITUTION AND GOVERNMENT. Under the Constitution of Aug. 1962 the Crown is represented by a Governor-General appointed by the Crown on the advice of the Prime Minister. The Governor-General is assisted by a Privy Council of 6 appointed members. The Legislature comprises the *House of Representatives* and the *Senate*. The Senate consists of 21 senators appointed by the Governor-General, 13 on the advice of the Prime Minister, 8 on the advice of the Leader of the Opposition. The House of Representatives (60 members) is elected by universal adult suffrage for a period not exceeding 5 years. Electors and elected must be Jamaican or Commonwealth citizens resident in Jamaica for at least 12 months before registration.

At the elections of March 1993 the People's National Party (PNP) gained 52 seats and the Jamaica Labour Party, 8.

Governor-General: Sir Howard Felix Cooke.

The Cabinet in Sept. 1995 comprised:

Prime Minister and Minister of Defence: Percival Patterson, QC (b. 1935; PNP).

Deputy Prime Minister and Minister of Foreign Affairs and Trade: Seymour Mullings. *National Security and Justice:* K. D. Knight. *Education, Youth and Culture:* Burchell Whiteman. *Health:* Peter Phillips. *Labour, Social Security and Sports:* Portia Simpson. *Public Utilities, Transport and Energy:* Robert Pickersgill.

Local Government and Works: Roger Clarke. *Industry, Investments and Commerce:* Dr Paul Robertson. *Housing and the Environment:* Easton Douglas. *Agriculture and Mining:* Horace Clarke. *Legal Affairs:* David Coore. *Finance and Planning:* Omar Davies. *Tourism:* John Junor. *Without portfolio:* Maxine Henry-Wilson.

National flag: A yellow diagonal cross dividing triangles of green, top and bottom, and black, hoist and fly.

National anthem: Eternal Father, bless our land (words by H. Sherlock, tune by R. Lightbourne).

DEFENCE

Army. The Jamaica Defence Force consists of a Regular and a Reserve Force. The Regular Force is comprised of the 1st battalion, Jamaica Regiment and Support Services which include the Air Wing and Coast Guard. The Coast Guard, numbering 150 in 1995, operates 5 inshore patrol craft based at Port Royal. The Reserve Force consists of the 3rd battalion, Jamaica Regiment. Total strength (army, 1996), 3,000. Reserves, 800.

Air Force. The Air Wing of the Jamaica Defence Force was formed in July 1963 and has since been expanded and trained successively by the British Army Air Corps and Canadian air force personnel. There are no combat aircraft. Equipment for army liaison, search and rescue, police co-operation, survey and transport duties includes 2 Defender armed STOL transports; 1 Beech King Air and 1 Cessna 210 light transports; 4 JetRanger, 4 Bell 205 and 2 Bell 212 helicopters. Personnel (1995) 170.

INTERNATIONAL RELATIONS

Membership. Jamaica is a member of the UN, the Commonwealth, OAS, CARICOM and is an ACP state of the EU.

ECONOMY

Budget. Revenue and expenditure for fiscal years ending 31 March (in J$1m.):

	1990–91	*1991–92*	*1992–93*	*1993–94*
Revenue	10,139	14,550	21,029	34,243
Expenditure	9,308	17,511	26,871	41,256

The chief items of current revenue are income tax; consumption, customs and stamp duties. The other major share of current resources is generated by the Bauxite Production Levy. The chief items of current expenditure are public debt, education and health.

Currency. The unit of currency is the *Jamaican dollar* (JMD) of 100 *cents*. The Jamaican dollar was floated in Sept. 1990. There are coins of 1, 5, 10, 20, 25 and 50 cents and J$1, and notes of J$1, 2, 5, 10, 20, 50, 100 and 500. Currency in circulation in 1993 was J$5,118·6m. Inflation was 30·1% in 1993. In March 1996, £1 = J$57·32; US$1 = J$37·50; DM1 = J$25·41.

Banking and Finance. The central bank and bank of issue is the Bank of Jamaica.

There are 10 commercial banks with 171 branches and agencies in operation. 5 of these banks are subsidiaries of major British and North American banks, of which 4 are incorporated locally. Total assets of commercial banks in 1993 were J$62,291·8m.; deposits were J$45,676·8m.

There is a stock exchange in Kingston, which participates in the regional Caribbean exchange.

ENERGY AND NATURAL RESOURCES

Electricity. The Jamaica Public Service Co. is the public supplier. Total installed capacity, 1993, 568·4 MW. Production (1993) 2,215m. kWh.

Minerals. Jamaica is a major producer of bauxite. Ceramic clays, marble, silica sand and gypsum are also commercially viable. In 1993, 11·3m. tonnes of bauxite ore were mined; gypsum, 152,200 tonnes; marble, 5,800 tonnes; sand and gravel, 1·5m. cu. metres; industrial lime, 3·3m. cu. metres.

Agriculture (1993). Production (in tonnes): Sugar-cane, 2,661,000; bananas for export, 76,777; citrus fruit, 27,693; cocoa, 6,304; coconuts, 17,907.

Livestock (1991): Cattle, 0·3m.; goats, 0·44m.; pigs, 0·25m.; poultry, 8m. Slaughtered livestock in 1993: Cattle, 84,248 head; goats, 49,121; pigs, 112,422; poultry, 44,000 tonnes.

INDUSTRY. Alumina production, 1993, 3m. tonnes. Output of other products, 1993: Sugar, 219,046 tonnes; molasses, 102,486 tonnes; cornmeal, 15·13m. kg; flour, 147·8m. kg; edible oils, 72·2m. litres; condensed milk, 19·4m. kg; fertilizer, 62,892 tonnes; petrol, 918m. litres; glass, 27,247 tonnes; cement, 451,000 tonnes; steel, 2,894 tonnes; cigarettes, 1,298·5m. There is an oil refinery in Kingston. In 1993, manufacturing contributed J$17,667m. to the total GDP at current prices.

Labour. Average total labour force (1993), 1,083,000, of whom 906,300 were employed. 507,900 were employed in services (including 191,100 in trade and catering, 43,300 in business), 220,800 in agriculture, forestry and fisheries, 97,800 in manufacturing, 62,100 in building and 7,800 in mining.

FOREIGN ECONOMIC RELATIONS. Foreign debt was US$3,678m. in 1993.

Commerce. Value of imports and domestic exports for calendar years (in US$1m.):

	1989	*1990*	*1991*	*1992*	*1993*
Imports	1,873	1,942	1,809	1,693	2,165
Domestic exports	1,004	1,157	1,151	1,053	1,045

Principal imports in 1993 (in US$1m.): Consumer goods, 427 (19·7%), of which food including beverages, 145 (6·7%); raw materials/intermediate goods, 1,297 (60%); capital goods, 442 (20·4%), of which construction materials, 95 (4·4%) and machinery and equipment excluding transport, 155 (7%).

Principal domestic exports in 1993 (in US$1m.): Traditional exports, 714 (68·3%), of which bauxite, 84 (8·1%), alumina, 440 (42·1%), gypsum, 1 (0·1%), sugar, 97 (9·3%) and bananas, 36 (3·4%); non-traditional exports, 314 (30%), of which food, 60 (5·7%), beverages and tobacco, 19 (1·8%), mineral fuels, lubricants and related materials, 7 (0·6%), crude materials, 6 (0·6%), chemicals, 24 (7·7%), manufactured goods, 14 (1·3%), machinery and transport equipment, 3 (0·2%) and miscellaneous manufactures, 180 (17·2%).

Total trade between Jamaica and UK (British Department of Trade returns, in £1,000 sterling):

	1991	*1992*	*1993*	*1994*	*1995*
Imports to UK	123,773	127,051	121,623	133,963	149,076
Exports and re-exports from UK	54,669	43,521	56,257	56,354	69,771

Tourism. In 1993, 1,616,340 visitors (including 629,587 cruise ship arrivals) arrived, spending about US$850m.

COMMUNICATIONS

Roads (1993). The island has 3,000 miles of main roads, and over 7,000 miles of secondary and tertiary roads. In 1992 there were 117,388 licensed vehicles (including 77,840 passenger cars). There were 8,247 traffic accidents in 1993 with 434 fatalities.

Civil Aviation. International airlines operate through the Norman Manley and Sangster airports at Palisadoes and Montego Bay. In 1993 Norman Manley airport had 12,961 aircraft movements, handled 1·06m. passengers and 23,582 tonnes of freight. Sangster had 47,160 aircraft movements, with 3·34m. passengers. Trans-Jamaica Airlines Ltd operates internal flights. Air Jamaica, originally set up in conjunction with BOAC and BWIA in 1966, became a new company, Air Jamaica (1968) Ltd, and is affiliated to Air Canada. In 1969 it began operations as Jamaica's national airline. In 1993 Air Jamaica carried 1m. passengers. In 1995 it operated 5 A300B4-200s and 4 B-727-200 Advs.

Services are also provided by Air Canada, ALM, American Airlines, British Airways, BWIA, Cayman Airways, COPA, Cubana and KLM.

Shipping. In 1995 the merchant marine totalled 10,545 GRT, including oil tankers, 3,292 GRT. In 1993 there were 2,921 visits to all ports; 12·6m. tonnes of cargo were handled. Kingston had 1,750 visits and handled 2·9m. tonnes.

Telecommunications. In 1993 there were 316 post offices and 509 postal agencies. In 1993 there were 328,528 telephones.

There were (1993) 4 commercial and 1 publicly owned broadcasting stations; the latter also operates a television service (colour by NTSC), and there was 1 commercial television station. In 1991 there were 1,481,000 radio and 484,000 TV sets.

Cinemas. In 1993 there were 35 cinemas and 2 drive-in cinemas.

SOCIAL INSTITUTIONS

Justice. The Judicature comprises a Supreme Court, a court of appeal, resident magistrates' courts, petty sessional courts, coroners' courts, a traffic court and a family court which was instituted in 1975. The Chief Justice is head of the judiciary. 53,282 crimes were reported in 1993, of which 34,337 were cleared up. The daily average prison population, 1993, was 3,284.

Police. The Constabulary Force in 1993 stood at approximately 5,832 officers, sub-officers and constables (men and women).

Religion. Freedom of worship is guaranteed under the Constitution. The main Christian denominations are Anglican, Baptist, Roman Catholic, Methodist, Church of God, United Church of Jamaica and Grand Cayman (Presbyterian–Congregational), Moravian, Seventh-Day Adventist, Pentecostal, Salvation Army, Quaker, and Disciples of Christ. Pocomania is a mixture of Christianity and African survivals. Non-Christians include Hindus, Jews, Moslems, Bahai followers and Rastafarians.

Education. Education is free in government-operated schools. Schools and colleges in 1992–93 (government-operated and grant-aided): Basic, 1,627; infant, 29; primary, 306; primary with infant department, 486; all-age, 37; new secondary, 58; comprehensive, 12; technical, 12; vocational, 6; community college, 5; secondary high, 56; special, 11; (independent): Primary/all-age, 12; preparatory, 123; high/vocational, 6; business education, 19; (tertiary): Teacher-training, 8; other, 5.

Numbers of pupils and students, 1992–93: Basic schools, 108,278; infant, 10,077; infant departments in primary schools, 6,500; infant departments in all-age schools, 1,870; primary, 163,893; all-age (1 to 6 years), 141,658; all-age (7 to 11 years), 53,584; new secondary, 62,261; secondary high, 72,029; technical high, 14,425; comprehensive high, 17,714. Numbers of teachers, 1992–93: Infant schools, 298; primary, 4,414; all-age, 5,733; new secondary, 3,340; secondary high, 3,702; technical high, 779; comprehensive high, 885; vocational, 197.

The University of the West Indies is at Kingston. In 1994–95 it had 12,630 students, 800 external students and about 900 academic staff.

Health. In 1993 the public health service had 3,130 staff in medicine, nursing and pharmacology; 328 in dentistry; 283 public health inspectors; 59 in nutrition. In 1993 there were 360 primary health centres, 5,186 public hospital beds and 305 private beds.

DIPLOMATIC REPRESENTATIVES

Of Jamaica in Great Britain (1-2 Prince Consort Rd., London, SW7 2BZ)
High Commissioner: Derrick Heaven, CD.

Of Great Britain in Jamaica (Trafalgar Rd., Kingston 10)
High Commissioner: Richard Thomas, CMG.

Of Jamaica in the USA (1850 K. St., NW, Washington, D.C., 20006)
Ambassador: Richard L. Bernal.

Of the USA in Jamaica (2 Oxford Rd., Kingston 5)
Ambassador: Jerome Gary Cooper.

Of Jamaica to the United Nations
Ambassador: M. Patricia Durrant, CD.

Further Reading

Planning Institute of Jamaica. *Economic and Social Survey, Jamaica.* Annual
Statistical Institute of Jamaica. *Statistical Abstract.* Annual.—*Demographic Statistics.* Annual.—*Production Statistics.* Annual.

Bakan, A. B. *Ideology and Class Conflict in Jamaica: the Politics of Rebellion.* Montreal, 1990
Goulbourne, H., *Teachers, Education and Politics in Jamaica, 1892–1972.* London, 1988
Ingram, K. E., *Jamaica.* [Bibliography] Oxford and Santa Barbara (CA), 1984
Manley, M., *A Voice at the Work Place.* London, 1975.—*Jamaica: Struggle in the Periphery.* London, 1983
Payne, A. J., *Politics in Jamaica.* London and New York, 1988

National library: National Library of Jamaica, Kingston.
National statistical office: Statistical Institute of Jamaica (STATIN), POB 643, Kingston 5. *Director General*, Vernon James.

JAPAN

Nihon (*or* Nippon [1]) Koku

(Land of the Rising Sun)

Capital: Tokyo
Population: 125·57m. (1995)
GNP per capita: US$34,630 (1994)
HDI/world rank: 0·937/3 (1992)

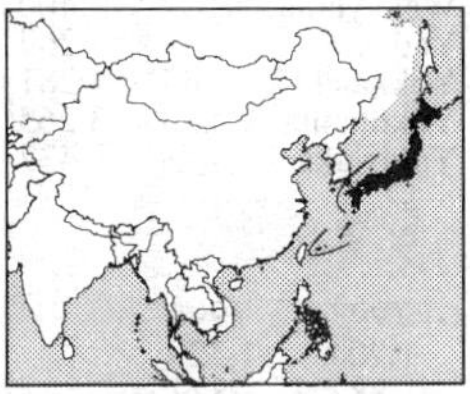

KEY HISTORICAL EVENTS. The house of Yamato, from about 500 B.C. the rulers of one of several kingdoms, in about A.D. 200 united the nation; the present imperial family are their direct descendants. From 1186 until 1867 successive families of Shoguns exercised the temporal power. In 1867 the Emperor Meiji recovered the imperial power after the abdication on 14 Oct. 1867 of the fifteenth and last Tokugawa Shogun. In 1871 the feudal system was abolished; this was the beginning of the rapid westernization.

Following the Second World War a peace treaty, signed in Sept. 1951, came into force in April 1952, when Japan regained its sovereignty. A security treaty of 1951 provided for the stationing of American forces in Japan.

TERRITORY AND POPULATION. Japan consists of 4 major islands, Honshu, Hokkaido, Kyushu and Shikoku, and many small islands, with an area of 377,812 sq. km. Census population (1 Oct. 1995) 125,568,504 (males 61,575,570, females 63,992,934); density, 332 per sq. km. Foreigners registered 31 Dec. 1994 were 1,354,011 of whom 676,793 were Koreans, 218,585 Chinese, 159,619 Brazilians, 85,968 Filipinos, 43,320 Americans, 35,382 Peruvians, 13,997 Thais, 12,453 British, 8,229 Vietnamese, 8,207 Iranians, 6,883 Canadians, 6,282 Indonesians, 6,219 Australians, 5,356 Malaysians and 1,664 stateless persons.

Japanese overseas, Oct. 1994, 689,895; of these 256,157 lived in the USA, 92,615 in Brazil, 45,617 in the UK, 23,756 in Canada, 22,908 in Germany, 21,452 in Australia, 21,296 in Singapore, 20,804 in Thailand, 18,528 in Hong Kong, 16,889 in France, 13,675 in China.

The areas, populations and chief cities of the principal islands (and regions) are:

Island/Region	*Sq. km*	*Census 1995*	*Chief cities*
Hokkaido	83,451	5,692,000	Sapporo
Honshu/Tohoku	66,883	9,834,000	Sendai
/Kanto	32,418	39,518,000	Tokyo
/Chubu	66,776	21,400,000	Nagoya
/Kinki	33,094	22,468,000	Osaka
/Chugoku	31,908	7,775,000	Hiroshima
Shikoku	18,798	4,183,000	Matsuyama
Kyushu	42,154	13,424,000	Fukuoka
Okinawa	2,265	1,274,000	Naha

The leading cities, with population, 31 March 1994 (in 1,000), are:

Akashi	281	Hakodate	301	Kasugai	271
Akita	304	Hamamatsu	550	Kawagoe	311
Amagasaki	487	Higashiosaka	495	Kawaguchi	445
Aomori	293	Himeji	462	Kawasaki	1,171
Asahikawa	360	Hirakata	394	Kitakyushu	1,015
Chiba	839	Hiroshima	1,077	Kobe	1,479
Fujisawa	358	Ibaraki	251	Kochi	317
Fukui	251	Ichihara	273	Koriyama	318
Fukuoka	1,221	Ichinomiya	267	Koshigaya	292
Fukushima	281	Ichikawa	432	Kumamoto	628
Fukuyama	373	Iwaki	363	Kurashiki	422
Funabashi	531	Kagoshima	534	Kyoto	1,391
Gifu	404	Kanazawa	433	Machida	356
Hachioji	476	Kashiwa	315	Maebashi	285

[1] Both forms are valid, and derive from different pronunciations of a Chinese character.

Matsudo	455	Omiya	421	Tokushima	261
Matsuyama	456	Osaka	2,481	Tokyo	7,874
Miyazaki	293	Otsu	268	Toyama	320
Nagano	351	Sagamihara	552	Toyohashi	343
Nagasaki	438	Sakai	797	Toyonaka	396
Nagoya	2,091	Sapporo	1,719	Toyota	332
Naha	304	Sasebo	247	Urawa	438
Nara	355	Sendai	928	Utsunomiya	429
Neyagawa	255	Shimonoseki	255	Wakayama	400
Niigata	479	Shizuoka	471	Yao	269
Nishinomiya	412	Suita	330	Yokkaichi	281
Oita	416	Takamatsu	329	Yokohama	3,265
Okayama	598	Takatsuki	359	Yokosuka	437
Okazaki	315	Tokorozawa	312		

Vital statistics (in 1,000) for calendar years:

	1988	*1989*	*1990*	*1991*	*1992*	*1993*	*1994*
Births	1,314	1,247	1,222	1,224	1,228	1,204	1,229
Deaths	793	789	820	830	854	882	877

Crude birth rate of Japanese nationals in present area, 1993, was 9·6 per 1,000 population (1947: 34·3); crude death rate, 7·1; crude marriage rate, 6·4; infant mortality rate per 1,000 live births, 4·3. Population growth rate was 2·5 per 1,000 in 1993. Expectation of life was 76·25 years for men, 82·51 years for women in 1993.

CLIMATE. The islands of Japan lie in the temperate zone, north-east of the main monsoon region of South-East Asia. The climate is temperate with warm, humid summers and relatively mild winters except in the island of Hokkaido and northern parts of Honshu facing the Japan Sea. There is a month's rainy season in June-July, but the best seasons are spring and autumn, though Sept. may bring typhoons. There is a summer rainfall maximum. Tokyo. Jan. 5·2°C, July 25·2°C. Annual rainfall 1,405 mm. Hiroshima. Jan. 4°C, July 25·7°C. Annual rainfall 1,555 mm. Nagasaki. Jan. 6·4°C, July 26·6°C. Annual rainfall 1,945 mm. Osaka. Jan. 5·5°C, July 27°C. Annual rainfall 1,318 mm. Sapporo. Jan. –4·6°C, July 20·2°C. Annual rainfall 1,130 mm.

IMPERIAL HOUSE. The Emperor is **Akihito** (b. 23 Dec. 1933), who succeeded his father, Hirohito on 7 Jan. 1989 (enthroned, 12 Nov. 1990); married 10 April 1959, to Michiko Shoda (b. 20 Oct. 1934). *Offspring:* Crown Prince Naruhito (Hironomiya; b. 23 Feb. 1960), married Masako Owada (b. 9 Dec. 1963) 9 June 1993; Prince Fumihito (Akishinomiya; b. 30 Nov. 1965); Princess Sayako (Norinomiya; b. 18 April 1969).

The succession to the throne is fixed upon the male descendants.

CONSTITUTION AND GOVERNMENT. The 1947 constitution supersedes the Meiji constitution of 1889. In it the Japanese people pledge themselves to uphold the ideas of democracy and peace. The Emperor is the symbol of the States and of the unity of the people. Sovereign power rests with the people. The Emperor has no powers related to government. Fundamental human rights are guaranteed.

Legislative power rests with the *Diet*, which consists of the *House of Representatives*, elected by men and women over 20 years of age for a 4-year term, and an upper house, the *House of Councillors* of 252 members (100 elected by party list system with proportional representation according to the d'Hondt method and 152 from prefectural districts), one-half of its members being elected every 3 years.

Elections to 126 seats of the House of Councillors were held on 23 July 1995; turn-out was 44%. The LDP gained 49 seats, Shinshinto 40, the SDP 16, the Communists 8, the NHP 3 and others 13.

In Nov. 1994 the Diet adopted electoral reforms changing the number of members in the House of Representatives from 511 to 500, of whom 300 are to be elected from single-seat constituencies, and 200 by proportional representation on a base of 11 regions. There is a 2% threshold to gain one of the latter seats. Donations to individual politicians are to be supplanted over 5 years by state subsidies to parties.

In 1995 the Prime Minister's salary was 2,234,000 yen per month.

Elections to the House of Representatives were held on 18 July 1993. There were 955 candidates; turn-out was 67·26%. The Liberal Democratic Party (LDP) gained 223 seats; the Socialist Party (SP), 70; Japan Renewal Party (Shinseito) [1], 55; Komeito (Buddhist) [1], 51; Japan New Party [1] (Nihonshinto), 35; Communist Party, 15; Social Democratic Party [1], 15; New Harbinger Party (Sakigake, NHP), 13; United Social Democratic Party (USDP), 4; ind, 30.

[1] Amalgamated as the Frontier Party (Shinshinto) in Dec. 1994.

In Feb. 1996 the House of Representatives consisted of LDP, 207; Shinshinto, 170; SDP, 63; NHP, 23; Communists, 15; others, 19.

An LDP-SDP-NHP coalition government was formed on 11 Jan. 1996:

Prime Minister: Ryutaro Hashimoto (b. 1912; LDP).

Deputy Prime Minister and Finance: Wataru Kubo (SDP). *Foreign Affairs:* Yukihiko Ikeda (LDP). *Justice:* Ritsuko Nagao. *Education:* Mikio Okuda (LDP). *Health and Welfare:* Naoto Kan (NHP). *Agriculture, Forestry and Fisheries:* Ichizo Ohara (LDP). *International Trade and Industry:* Shumpei Tsukahara (LDP). *Transport:* Yoshiyuki Kamei (LDP). *Posts and Telecommunications:* Ichiro Hino (SDP). *Labour:* Takanobu Nagai (SDP). *Construction:* Eiichi Nakao (LDP). *Home Affairs:* Hiroyuki Kurata (LDP). *Chief Cabinet Secretary:* Seiroku Kajiyama (LDP). *Management and Co-ordination:* Sekisuke Nakanishi (SDP). *National Land Agency:* Kazumi Suzuki (SDP). *Defence Agency:* Hideo Usui (LDP). *Economic Planning Agency:* Shusei Tanaka (NHP). *Science and Technology Agency:* Hidenao Nakagawa (LDP). *Environment Agency:* Sukio Iwatare (SDP).

The *Speakers* are Takako Doi (the House of Representatives, SDP) and Juro Saito (the House of Councillors, LDP).

National flag: White, with a red disc.

National anthem: 'Kimi ga yo wa'('May your peaceful reign long last'); words 9th century, tune by Hiromori Hayashi.

Local Government. The country is divided into 47 prefectures, each with an elected governor. Each prefecture, city, town and village has a representative elected assembly. There were 3,236 local authorities at 31 March 1994. Elections were held on 9 and 22 April 1995 for 13 prefectural governorships, 43 prefectural assemblies and 86 mayorships. Turn-out was 60%. 60% of prefectural assembly seats were won by independents.

DEFENCE. Japan has renounced war as a sovereign right and the threat or the use of force as a means of settling disputes with other nations. Its troops had not been able to serve abroad, but in 1992 the House of Representatives voted to allow up to 2,000 troops to take part in UN peacekeeping missions. A law of Nov. 1994 authorizes the Self-Defence Force to send aircraft abroad in rescue operations where Japanese citizens are involved.

In Jan. 1991 Japan and the USA signed a renewal agreement under which Japan pays 40% of the costs of stationing US forces and 100% of the associated labour costs. US forces in Japan totalled 45,500 in 1996.

Army. The 'Ground Self-Defence Force' is organized in 5 regional commands and had in 1996 an authorized strength of 151,200 (5,200 women) and a reserve of 46,000 men. The Army is organized in 12 infantry divisions, 1 armoured division, 1 airborne brigade, 2 air defence brigades, 1 artillery, 2 combined, 5 engineer and 1 helicopter brigade in addition to 4 training brigades. Equipment includes 190 T-61, 870 T-74 and 100 T-90 main battle tanks, approximately 90 AH-1S attack helicopters, as well as 190 transport helicopters and 16 MU-2H fixed-wing aircraft.

Navy. The 'Maritime Self-Defence Force' is tasked with coastal protection and defence of the sea lanes to 1,000 nautical miles range from Japan. The modern and well-equipped combatant forces are mainly fitted with American weapon systems, which in many cases have been re-engineered and improved in Japan.

The combatant fleet, all home-built, includes 15 diesel submarines and 2 trials and training boats. There are 2 Aegis-equipped guided-missile destroyers, 6 other guided-missile destroyers armed with US Standard SM-1 surface-to-air missiles, 24 helicopter-carrying frigates and 31 other frigates of which 2 are employed on non-military tasks. Light forces comprise 3 missile hydrofoils and 3 small inshore patrol craft. There are 39 mine warfare vessels: 1 minelayer, 1 layer/command ship, 3 1,200-tonne offshore mine countermeasure vessels, 29 coastal minesweepers and 4 smaller vessels. A substantial amphibious capability is provided by 6 tank landing ships supported by some 40 smaller craft. 12 major auxiliaries include 4 combined oiler/ammunition ships, 7 survey vessels and 3 training support vessels, and there are several hundred minor auxiliaries and service craft.

The Air Arm, organized into 7 operational Air Groups, includes 88 Orion anti-submarine patrol aircraft, 7 US-1A rescue flying boats, 60 Sea King anti-submarine helicopters, 10 mine countermeasures helicopters as well as about 100 transport, training and utility aircraft.

The main elements of the fleet are organized into 4 escort flotillas based at Yokosuka (2), Sasebo and Maizuru. The submarines are based at Sasebo and Kure.

Personnel in 1995 numbered 44,000 including about 12,000 in the Naval Air Arm.

Coastguard. This is administered by the Ministry of Transport. For details *see under* COMMUNICATIONS *below*.

Air Force. An 'Air Self-Defence Force' was inaugurated on 1 July 1954. Its equipment includes 7 interceptor squadrons of F-15J/DJ Eagles (total of 220 aircraft to be acquired by 1997) and 3 of F-4EJ Phantoms; 3 squadrons of Mitsubishi F-1 close-support fighters; 1 squadron of RF-4E reconnaissance fighters; 13 E-2C Hawkeye AWACS aircraft; ECM flight with 2 YS-11Es; 2 squadrons of turbofan Kawasaki C-1 and 1 with turboprop C-130H Hercules and NAMC YS-11 transports. About 70 CH-47 Chinooks and Black Hawk helicopters, and MU-2 twin-turboprop aircraft perform search, rescue and general duties. Training units use piston-engined Fuji T-3 basic trainers, Fuji T-1 jet intermediate trainers, Kawasaki T-4 jet trainers and supersonic Mitsubishi T-2 jet advanced trainers. 6 surface-to-air missile groups (19 squadrons) are in service. Strength (1995) 44,600.

INTERNATIONAL RELATIONS

Membership. Japan is a member of the UN, Colombo Plan, APEC and OECD.

ECONOMY

Policy. The head of the Economic Planning Agency (Shusei Tanaka) has cabinet rank. The 1992–96 Plan envisaged an onward real growth rate of 3·5% and a nominal 5%. The real growth rate for 1996 was envisaged at 2·5% and the nominal at 2·7%.

Budget. Ordinary revenue and expenditure for fiscal year ending 31 March 1996 balanced at 70,987,100m. yen.

Of the proposed revenue (in yen) in 1995, 53,731,000m. was to come from taxes and stamps, 12,598,000m. from public bonds. Main items of expenditure: Social security, 13,924,400m.; public works, 9,239,800m.; local government, 13,215,400m.; education, 6,076,500m.; defence, 4,723,600m.

The outstanding national debt incurred by public bonds was estimated in March 1994 to be 195,135,000m. yen.

The estimated 1995 budgets of the prefectures and other local authorities forecast a total revenue of 82,509,000m. yen, to be made up partly by local taxes and partly by government grants and local loans.

Currency. The unit of currency is the *yen* (JPY). There are coins of 1, 5, 10, 50, 100 and 500 yen and notes of 1,000, 5,000 and 10,000 yen.

In Dec. 1994 the currency in circulation consisted of 42,880,000m. yen Bank of Japan notes and 3,745,000m. yen subsidiary coins. In March 1996, £1 = 161·18 yen; US$1 = 105·46 yen; DM1 = 71·45 yen.

Banking and Finance. The Nippon Ginko (Bank of Japan), founded 1882 finances the government and the banks, its function being similar to that of a central bank in other countries. The Bank undertakes the management of Treasury funds and foreign exchange control. Its *Governor* is Yasuo Matsushita (b. 1926; appointed Jan. 1995 for a 5-year term). Its gold bullion and cash holdings at 31 Dec. 1994 stood at 439,000m. yen.

There were on 31 Dec. 1994, 11 city banks, 64 regional banks, 7 trust banks, 3 long-term credit banks, 65 member banks of the second association of regional banks, 422 Shinkin banks (credit associations), 376 credit co-operatives, and 91 foreign banks. There are also various governmental financial institutions, including postal savings which amounted to 204,847,400m. yen in Sept. 1995. Total savings by individuals, including insurance and securities, stood at 946,576,300m. yen on 30 Sept. 1995, and about 63% of these savings were deposited in banks and the post-office.

There are 8 stock exchanges, the largest being in Tokyo, Osaka and Nagoya.

Weights and Measures. The metric system is obligatory.

ENERGY AND NATURAL RESOURCES

Electricity. Japan is poor in energy resources, and nuclear power generation is important in reducing dependence on foreign supplies. In 1993 generating facilities were capable of an output of 212·91m. kW; electricity produced was 906,705m. kWh. There were 46 nuclear reactors in 19 power plants, producing 27·5% of electricity, and 8 more were under construction in 1993. 10 regional publicly-held supply companies produce 74·4% of output.

Oil and Gas. Output of crude petroleum, 1993, was 911,000 kl, almost entirely from oilfields on the island of Honshu, but 255·1m. kl crude oil had to be imported. Output of natural gas, 1993, 2,204m. cu. metres.

Minerals. Ore production in tonnes, 1993, of coal, 7,206,000; iron, 11,000; zinc, 118,599; copper, 10,277; lead, 16,470; tungsten, 109; silver, 136,886 kg; gold, 9,352 kg.

Agriculture. Agricultural workers in 1994 on farms with 0·3 ha or more of cultivated land or 0·5m. yen annual sales were 4·3m., including 0·4m. subsidiary and seasonal workers; 5·5% (1992) of the labour force as opposed to 24·7% in 1962. The arable land area in 1994 was 5,083,000 ha. Rice is the staple food, but its consumption is declining. Rice cultivation accounted for 2,212,000 ha in 1994. The area planted with industrial crops such as rapeseed, tobacco, tea, rush, etc., was 211,000 ha in 1993.

Average farm size was 1·4 ha in 1994. Farmers are represented by the co-operative organization in Nokyo.

In 1994 there were 3,729,000 power cultivators and tractors and 1,835,000 rice power planters. (1990): 1,871,000 power sprayers and dusters.

Output of rice (in 1,000 tonnes), was 9,604 in 1991, 10,573 in 1992, 7,834 in 1993 and 11,981 in 1994.

Production in 1994 (in 1,000 tonnes) of barley was 225; wheat, 565; soybeans, 99. Sweet potatoes, which in the past mitigated the effects of rice famines, have, in view of rice over-production, decreased from 4,955,000 tonnes in 1965 to 1,264,000 tonnes in 1994. Domestic sugar-beet and sugar-cane production accounted for only 33% of requirement in 1992. In 1993, 1·75m. tonnes were imported, 48·8% of this being imported from Australia, 36% from Thailand, 6·2% from the Philippines and 4·8% from Cuba.

Fruit production, 1993 (in 1,000 tonnes): Mandarins, 1,490; apples, 1,001; pears, 396; grapes, 260; peaches, 173 and persimmons, 241.

Livestock (1994): 4·99m. cattle (including about 2·02m. milch cows), 28,000 horses, 10·62m. pigs, 25,000 sheep, 31,000 goats, 324m. chickens. Milk (1993), 8·63m. tonnes.

Forestry. Forests and grasslands covered about 25m. ha (nearly 70% of the whole land area), in 1993, with an estimated timber stand of 2,956m. cu. metres in 1990. In 1992, 34,445,000 cu. metres were felled.

Fisheries. The catch in 1993 was 8·71m. tonnes, excluding whaling.

INDUSTRY. The industrial structure is dominated by corporate groups (*keiretsu*) either linking companies in different branches or linking individual companies with their suppliers and distributors.

Japan's industrial equipment, 1992, numbered 698,356 plants of all sizes, employing 11·76m. production workers.

Output includes: Television sets (1994: 11·19m.), radio sets (1994: 7·3m.), cameras (1994: 11·94m.), computing machines and automation equipment. The chemical industry ranks fourth in shipment value after machinery, metals and food products. Production, 1994, included (in tonnes): Sulphuric acid, 6·6m.; caustic soda, 3,672,000; ammonium sulphate, 1·71m.; calcium superphosphate, 395,000.

Output (1994), in 1,000 tonnes, of pig iron was 73,776; crude steel, 98,295; ordinary rolled steel, 76,631.

In 1994 paper production was 16,603,000 tonnes; paperboard, 11·92m. tonnes.

Output of cotton yarn, 1994, 235,000 tonnes, and of cotton cloth, 1,180m. sq. metres.

Output, 1994, 90,000 tonnes of woollen yarns and 286m. sq. metres of woollen fabrics.

Output, 1994, of rayon woven fabrics, 396m. sq. metres; synthetic woven fabrics, 2,143m. sq. metres; silk fabrics, 65m. sq. metres.

Shipbuilding has been decreasing and in 1993, 8,895,000 GRT were launched, of which 5,918,000 GRT were tankers.

Labour. Total labour force, 1994, was 64·5m., of which 3·5m. were in agriculture and forestry, 0·28m. in fishing, 60,000 in mining, 6·6m. in construction, 15m. in manufacturing, 17·05m. in commerce and finance, 4·31m. in transport and other public utilities, 15·42m. in services (including the professions) and 2·15m. in government work. Retirement age is being raised progressively from 60 years to reach 65 by 2013.

In 1994, 1·92m. (2·9%) were unemployed. In 1994, 85,000 working days were lost in industrial stoppages. In 1994 the average working week was 39·3 hours.

Trade Unions. In 1994 there were 12,699,000 workers organized in 71,674 unions. In Nov. 1989, the 'Japanese Private Sector Trade Union Confederation' (Rengo), which was organized in 1987, was reorganized into the 'Japan Trade Union Confederation' (Rengo) with the former 'General Council of Japanese Trade Unions' (Sohyo) and other unions, and was the largest federation with 7,823,000 members in 1994. The 'National Confederation of Trade Unions' (Zenroren) had 857,000 members and the 'National Trade Union Council' (Zenrokyo) 298,000 members in 1994.

FOREIGN ECONOMIC RELATIONS

Commerce. Trade (in US$1m.):

	1989	*1990*	*1991*	*1992*	*1993*	*1994*
Imports	210,847	234,799	236,737	233,021	240,670	274,742
Exports	275,175	286,948	314,525	339,650	360,911	395,600

Distribution of trade by countries (customs clearance basis) (US$1m.):

	Exports		*Imports*	
	1993	*1994*	*1993*	*1994*
Africa	4,439	3,968	1,817	1,773
Australia	7,694	8,718	12,218	13,627
Canada	6,297	5,906	8,096	8,929
China	17,273	18,681	20,565	27,566
Germany	18,021	17,787	9,786	11,133
Hong Kong	22,686	25,739	1,989	2,145
Latin America	16,915	18,742	8,359	9,542
South-east Asia	117,415	138,399	60,592	67,863
Korea, Republic of	19,115	24,359	11,678	13,508
Taiwan	22,081	23,792	9,678	10,753

	Exports 1993	Exports 1994	Imports 1993	Imports 1994
Russia	1,501	1,167	2,769	3,490
UK	12,047	12,734	4,951	5,914
USA	105,405	117,560	55,236	62,659

Principal items in 1994, with value in 1m. yen were:

Imports, c.i.f.		*Exports, f.o.b.*	
Mineral fuels	4,890,000	Machinery and transport equipment	30,801,000
Foodstuffs	4,771,000	Metals and metal products	2,481,000
Metal ores and scrap	764,000	Textile products	857,000
Machinery and transport equipment	6,098,000	Chemicals	2,422,000

The importation of rice was prohibited, but in 1993–94 there was an emergency importation of 1m. tonnes from Australia, China, Thailand and the USA to offset a poor domestic harvest. The prohibition was lifted in line with WTO agreements. Till 2000 rice imports will have limited access; thereafter the market will be fully open.

Total trade between Japan and UK (British Department of Trade returns, in £1,000 sterling):

	1991	1992	1993	1994	1995
Imports to UK	6,753,642	7,443,723	8,536,146	8,841,577	9,613,810
Exports and re-exports from UK	2,257,552	2,226,986	2,653,575	2,991,159	3,782,955

Tourism. In 1994, 3,831,367 foreigners visited Japan, 548,265 of whom came from USA, 233,140 from UK. Japanese travelling abroad totalled 13,578,934 in 1994.

COMMUNICATIONS

Roads. The total length of roads (including urban and other local roads) was 1,130,892 km at 1 April 1993. There were 53,304 km of national roads, of which 52,400 km were paved. Motor vehicles, at 31 Dec. 1994, numbered 63,591,000, including 42,679,000 passenger cars and 20,667,000 commercial vehicles.

Railways. The first railway was completed in 1872, between Tokyo and Yokohama (29 km). Most railways are of 1,069 mm., but the high-speed 'Shinkansen' lines are standard 1,435 mm gauge. In April 1987 the Japanese National Railways was reorganized into 7 private companies, the Japanese Railways (JR) Group – 6 passenger companies and 1 freight company. Total length of railways, in March 1994, was 27,152 km, of which the JR had 20,129 km and other private railways, 7,023 km. In 1993 the JR carried 8,906m. passengers (other private, 13,853m.) and 53m. tons of freight (other private, 26m.). An undersea tunnel linking Honshu with Hokkaido was opened to rail services in 1988.

There are metros in Tokyo (2 systems, total 230 km in 1994), Fukuoka (18 km), Kobe (2 systems total 30 km), Kyoto (11 km), Nagoya (77 km), Osaka (106 km), Sapporo (45 km), Sendai (15 km) and Yokohama (33 km), and tram/light rail networks in 19 cities.

Civil Aviation. There are international airports at Tokyo (Narita), Fukuoka, Kagoshima, Kansai, Nagoya Komaki and Osaka. The principal airlines are Japan Airlines (JAL), Japan Air System and All Nippon Airways. In 1995 their fleets were as follows: JAL: 1 B-737-400, 2 B-747-100s, 3 B–747-100Bs, 2 B-747-100B Suds, 21 B-747-200Bs, 1 B-747-200B(F), 6 B-747-200Fs, 9 B-747-300s, 24 B-747-400s, 8 B-747-400Ds, 4 B-747SR-300s, 3 B-767-200s, 17 B-767-300s and 20 other aircraft; Japan Air System: 9 A300B2-200s, 8 A300B4-200s, 14 A300B4-600Rs and 51 other aircraft; All Nippon Airways: 14 A320-200s, 6 B-747-200Bs, 7 B-747-400s, 10 B-747-400Ds, 14 B-747SRs, 25 B-767-200s, 32 B-767-300s, 5 B-767-300ERs and 3 other aircraft. In the financial year 1992 Japanese companies carried 69,687,000 passengers in domestic services and 11·03m. passengers in international services.

Shipping. On 1 July 1994 the merchant fleet consisted of 7,165 vessels of 100 GRT and over; total tonnage 22m. GRT; there were 694 ships for passenger transport

(1,598,000 GRT), 2,207 cargo ships (1,159,000 GRT) and 1,120 oil tankers (6·77m. GRT).

Coastguard. The 'Maritime Safety Agency' (Coastguard) consists of 1 headquarters, 11 regional headquarters, 66 offices, 1 maritime guard and rescue office, 51 stations, 14 air stations, 1 special rescue station, 10 district communications centres, 5 traffic advisory service centres, 4 hydrographic observatories, 1 Loran navigation system centre, and 97 navigation aids offices (with 5,362 navigation aids facilities) and controls 48 large patrol vessels, 47 medium patrol vessels, 19 small patrol vessels, 225 patrol craft, 13 hydrographic service vessels, 5 large firefighting boats, 10 medium firefighting boats, 66 guard and rescue boats and 72 navigation aids service supply vessels (as of May 1995). Personnel in 1995 numbered 12,192 officers and men.

The Coastguard aviation service includes 26 fixed-wing aircraft and 44 helicopters.

Telecommunications. Telephone services have been operated by private companies (NTT and others) since 1985. In 1993 there were 59m. subscribers.

Broadcasting is under the aegis of the public Japan Broadcasting Corporation (Nippon Hoso Kyokai) and the National Association of Commercial Broadcasters (Minporen). The former transmits 2 national networks and an external service, Radio Japan (22 languages). There is also a university station and a religious broadcasting station. Nippon Hoso Kyokai transmits a general and an educational TV programme, and there are 5 commercial networks. In 1993 there were 97m. radio and 100m. TV sets (colour by NTSC).

Cinemas (1994). Cinemas numbered 1,747 with an annual attendance of 123m. (1960: 1,014m.).

Press (1993). Daily newspapers numbered 122 with aggregate circulation of 72·04m., including 4 major English-language newspapers.

SOCIAL INSTITUTIONS

Justice. The Supreme Court is composed of the Chief Justice and 14 other judges. The Chief Justice is appointed by the Emperor, the other judges by the Cabinet. Every 10 years a justice must submit himself to the electorate. All justices and judges of the lower courts serve until they are 70 years of age.

Below the Supreme Court are 8 regional higher courts, district courts in each prefecture (4 in Hokkaido) and the local courts.

The Supreme Court is authorized to declare unconstitutional any act of the Legislature or the Executive which violates the Constitution.

The police are under central government control.

Religion. State subsidies have ceased for all religions, and all religious teachings are forbidden in public schools. In Dec. 1993 Shintoism claimed 117m. adherents, Buddhism 89·94m.; these figures obviously overlap. Christians numbered 1·54m.

Education. Education is compulsory and free between the ages of 6 and 15. Almost all national and municipal institutions are co-educational. On 1 May 1994 there were 14,832 kindergartens with 103,014 teachers and 1,852,183 pupils; 23,941 elementary schools with 434,945 teachers and 8,582,871 pupils; 11,203 junior high schools with 273,527 teachers and 4,681,166 pupils; 5,345 senior high schools with 282,085 teachers and 4,862,725 pupils; 593 junior colleges with 20,964 teachers and 520,638 pupils.

There were also 880 special schools for handicapped children (51,117 teachers, 87,219 pupils).

Japan has 7 main state universities: Tokyo University (1877); Kyoto University (1897); Tohoku University, Sendai (1907); Kyushu University, Fukuoka (1910); Hokkaido University, Sapporo (1918); Osaka University (1931), and Nagoya University (1939). In addition, there are various other state and municipal as well as private universities. There are 552 colleges and universities altogether with (1 May 1994) 2,481,805 students and 134,849 teachers.

Health. Hospitals on 1 Oct. 1993 numbered 9,844 with 1,680,952 beds. Physicians at the end of 1992 numbered 219,704; dentists, 77,416.

Social Welfare. There are in force various types of social security schemes, such as health insurance, unemployment insurance and age pensions. Citizens over 60 receive pensions of 70% of the average wage. In 1995 the basic retirement pension was 214,300 yen per month, funded by contributions of 17·35% of salary. There was a total of 27m. pensioners in 1994.

In 1992, 10,781,987 persons and 7,031,662 households received some form of regular public assistance, the total of which came to 1,353,310m. yen.

14 weeks maternity leave is statutory.

DIPLOMATIC REPRESENTATIVES

Of Japan in Great Britain (101 Piccadilly, London, W1V 9FN)
Ambassador: Hiroaki Fujii.

Of Great Britain in Japan (1 Ichiban-cho, Chiyoda-ku, Tokyo 102)
Ambassador: David Wright, CMG, LVO.

Of Japan in the USA (2520 Massachusetts Ave., NW, Washington, D.C., 20008)
Ambassador: Takakazu Kuriyama.

Of the USA in Japan (10–5, Akasaka 1-chome, Minato-ku, Tokyo)
Ambassador: Walter F. Mondale.

Of Japan to the United Nations
Ambassadors: Hisashi Owada.

Further Reading

Statistics Bureau of the Prime Minister's Office: *Statistical Year-Book* (from 1949).— *Statistical Abstract* (from 1950).—*Monthly Bulletin* (from April 1950)
Economic Planning Agency: *Economic Survey* (annual), *Economic Statistics* (monthly), *Economic Indicators* (monthly)
Ministry of International Trade: *Foreign Trade of Japan* (annual)
Allen, G. C., *The Japanese Economy.* London, 1981
Beasley, W. G., *The Rise of Modern Japan: Political, Economic and Social Change since 1850.* 2nd ed. London, 1995
The Cambridge Encyclopedia of Japan. CUP, 1993
Cambridge History of Japan. vols. 1-5. CUP, 1990–93
Campbell, A. (ed.) *Japan: an Illustrated Encyclopedia.* Tokyo, 1994
Cortazzi, H., *The Japanese Achievement.* London, 1990
Francks, P., *Japanese Economic Development: Theory and Practice.* London, 1991
Goodhart, C. A. E. and Sutija, G. (eds.) *Japanese Financial Growth.* London, 1990
Gordon, A., *Postwar Japan as History.* Univ. of California Press, 1993
Horsley, W. and Buckky, R., *Nippon, New Superpower: Japan since 1945.* London, 1990
Ito, T., *The Japanese Economy.* Boston (Mass.), 1992
Japan: an Illustrated Encyclopedia. London, 1993
Japan Times Year Book. Tokyo, first issue 1933
Johnson, C., *Japan: Who Governs? The Rise of the Developmental State.* New York, 1995
Martineau, L., *Caught in a Mirror: Reflections on Japan.* London, 1993
Nester, W. R., *The Foundation of Japanese Power: Continuities, Changes, Challenges.* London, 1990
Newland, K., (ed.) *The International Relations of Japan.* London, 1990
Okabe, M., (ed.) *The Structure of the Japanese Economy: Changes on the Domestic and International Fronts.* London, 1994
Perren, R., *Japanese Studies From Pre-History to 1990.* Manchester Univ. Press, 1992
Reischauer, E. O., *The Japanese Today: Change and Continuity.* Harvard Univ. Press, 1991
Schirokauer, C., *Brief History of Japanese Civilization.* New York, 1993
Shulman, F. J., *Japan.* [Bibliography] Oxford and Santa Barbara (CA), 1990
Steven, R., *Japan's New Imperialism.* London, 1990

National statistical office: Statistics Bureau, Prime Minister's Office, Tokyo

JORDAN

Mamlaka al Urduniya al Hashemiyah

(Hashemite [1] Kingdom of Jordan)

Capital: Amman
Population: 4·95m. (1994)
GNP per capita: US$1,390 (1994)
HDI/world rank: 0·758/80 (1992)

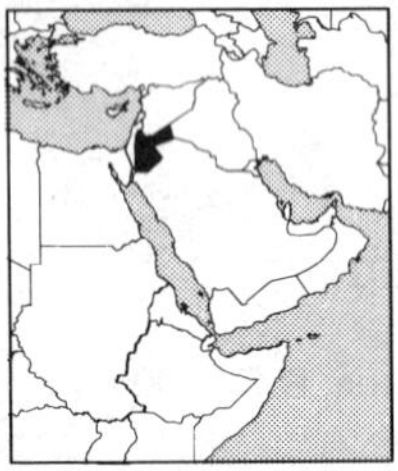

KEY HISTORICAL EVENTS. By a Treaty, signed in London on 22 March 1946, Britain recognized Transjordan as a sovereign independent state. On 25 May 1946 the Amir Abdullah assumed the title of King, and when the treaty was ratified on 17 June 1946 the name of the territory was changed to that of 'The Hashemite Kingdom of Jordan'. A new Anglo-Transjordan treaty was signed in Amman on 15 March 1948, by mutual consent terminated on 13 March 1957.

The part of Palestine remaining to the Arabs under the armistice with Israel on 3 April 1949, with the exception of the Gaza Strip on the Mediterranean coast, was in Dec. 1949 placed under Jordanian rule and formally incorporated in Jordan on 24 April 1950. In June 1967 this territory ('the West Bank') was occupied by Israel. On 31 July 1988 King Hussein announced the dissolution of Jordan's legal and administrative ties with the West Bank.

TERRITORY AND POPULATION. Jordan is bounded in the north by Syria, east by Iraq, south-east and south by Saudi Arabia and west by Israel. It has an outlet to an arm of the Red Sea at Aqaba. Its area is 97,740 sq. km (37,738 sq. miles) following an exchange of territory with Saudi Arabia on 10 Aug. 1965. Its population at the 1979 Census was 2,132,997; estimate (1994) 4,950,000 (1·99m. female; 3·2m. urban). Population of the 8 governorates:

Governorate	*1994*	*Governorate*	*1994*
Amman	1,567,908	Ma'an	79,401
Balqa	273,489	Mafraq	170,903
Irbid	745,774	Tafilah	61,156
Karak	169,552	Zarqa	623,943

The largest towns with suburbs, with estimated population, 1994: Amman, the capital, 1,300,042; Irbid, 379,844; Zarqa, 608,626.

Vital statistics, 1994: Births, 140,444; deaths, 12,290; marriages, 36,132; divorces, 6,251. Life expectancy was 64 years for males and 68 years for females in 1992.

The official language is Arabic.

CLIMATE. Predominantly a Mediterranean climate, with hot dry summers and cool wet winters, but in hilly parts summers are cooler and winters colder. Those areas below sea-level are very hot in summer and warm in winter. Eastern parts have a desert climate. Amman. Jan. 46°F (7·5°C), July 77°F (24·9°C). Annual rainfall 12" (290 mm). Aqaba. Jan. 61°F (16°C), July 89°F (31·5°C). Annual rainfall 1·5" (35 mm).

ROYAL HOUSE. The Kingdom is a constitutional monarchy headed by HM King **Hussein**, GCVO, born 14 Nov. 1935, and married Princess Dina Abdul Hamid on 19 April 1955 (divorced 1957), Toni Avril Gardiner (Muna al Hussein) on 25 May 1961 (divorced 1972), Alia Toukan on 26 Dec. 1972 (died in air crash 1977) and Elizabeth Halaby on 15 June 1978. *Offspring:* Princess Alia, born 13 Feb. 1956; Prince Abdulla, born 30 Jan. 1962; Prince Faisal, born 11 Oct. 1963; Prin-

[1] 'Hashemite' denotes a descendant of the prophet Mohammed.

cesses Zein and Aisha, born 23 April 1968; Princess Haya, born 3 May 1974; Prince Ali, born 23 Dec. 1975; Prince Hamzah, born 1 April 1980; Prince Hashem, born 10 June 1981; Princess Iman, born 4 April 1983; Princess Raya, born 9 Feb. 1986. *Crown Prince* (appointed 1 April 1965): Prince Hassan (b. 1947), younger brother of the King.

CONSTITUTION AND GOVERNMENT. The Constitution passed on 7 Nov. 1951 provides that the Cabinet is responsible to Parliament.

The legislature consists of a *Senate* of 40 members appointed by the King and a *Chamber of Deputies* of 80 members elected by universal suffrage. 9 seats are reserved for Christians, 6 for Bedouin and 3 for Circassians. A law of 1993 restricts each elector to a single vote, replacing a system in which electors had several votes depending on the number of seats in the constituency.

The lower house was dissolved in 1976 and elections postponed because no elections could be held in the West Bank under Israeli occupation. Parliament was reconvened on 9 Jan. 1984. By-elections were held in March 1984 and 6 members were nominated for the West Bank bringing Parliament to 60 members. Women voted for the first time in 1984. Elections were held on 8 Nov. 1993. There were 534 candidates (3 women). The electorate was 1·2m.; turn-out was 68%. Most members were elected for tribal constituencies without political affiliation. 1 woman was elected. The Islamic Action Front gained 16 seats.

On 9 June 1991 the King and the main political movements endorsed a national charter which legalized political parties in return for the acceptance of the constitution and monarchy. Movements linked to, or financed by, non-Jordanian bodies are not allowed.

On 4 Feb. 1996 King Hussein formed a new government which comprised:

Prime Minister, Minister of Defence and Minister for Foreign Affairs: Abdul Karim Kabariti.

Minister of Higher Education: Abdullah Ensour. *Interior:* Awad Khleifat. *Public Works and Housing:* Abdul Hadi Al-Majali. *Justice:* Abdul Karim Al-Dughmi. *Post and Communications:* Jamal Saraireh. *Water and Irrigation:* Samir Kawar. *Industry and Trade:* Ali Abul Ragheb. *Tourism and Antiquities:* Salah Irsheidat. *Municipal and Rural Affairs and the Environment:* Abdul Razzaq Tbeishat. *Health:* Aref Bataineh. *Awqaf (Religious Endowments) and Islamic Affairs:* Abdul Salam Al-Abbadi. *Planning:* Rima Khalaf-Ilncidi. *Energy and Mineral Resources:* Hashem Dabbas. *Minister of State for Parliamentary Affairs:* Mohammad Thweib. *Minister of State for Prime Ministry Affairs:* Hisham Al-Tal. *Minister of Social Development:* Hammad Abu Jamous. *Supply:* Munir Sobar. *Labour:* Abdul Hafez Shakhanbeh. *Minister of State:* Mufleh Rheimi. *Minister of Culture:* Ahmad Qudah. *Agriculture:* Mustafa Shneikat. *Minister of State:* Mahmoud Abdul Latif Hweimel. *Minister of Youth:* Mohammad Daoudieh. *Minister of State:* Mohammad Odeh Njadat. *Minister of Education:* Munther Al-Masri. *Finance:* Marwan Awad. *Minister of State for Foreign Affairs:* Khalid Madadha. *Minister of Information:* Marwan Muasher. *Administrative Development:* Kamal Nasser. *Transport:* Naser Al-Lawzi.

The *Speaker* is Sa'd Hayel Srour.

National flag: Three horizontal stripes of black, white, green, with a red triangle based on the hoist, bearing a white 7-pointed star.

National anthem: 'Asha al Malik' ('Long Live the King'); words by A. Al Rifai, tune by A. Al Tanir.

Local Government. The 8 governorates are divided into cities, towns, districts and sub-districts. Municipal elections were held in July 1995; turn-out was low.

DEFENCE

Army. The Army is organized in 2 armoured and 2 mechanized infantry divisions, 1 Royal Guard, 1 special force, and 1 field artillery brigade. Equipment includes 270 M-47/-48A5, 218 M-60A1/3, 360 Khalid Chieftain and 293 Tariq (Centurion) main battle tanks. Total strength (1996) 90,000.

Navy. The Royal Jordanian Naval Force numbered 600 in 1995 and operates 3 fast inshore patrol boats, 2 ex-East German patrol craft and some boats all based at Aqaba.

Air Force. The Air Force has 1 interceptor and 4 ground attack squadrons equipped with Mirage F1 and F-5E Tiger II fighters, and 2-seat F-5Fs. Two anti-armour squadrons have Bell AH-1S Huey Cobra helicopters. There are 4 C-130H Hercules and 2 CASA Aviocar turboprop transports, S-70 Blackhawk, Gazelle, and Hughes 500D helicopters, piston-engined Bulldog basic trainers and CASA Aviojet jet trainers. Hawk surface-to-air missiles equip 14 batteries. Strength (1995) 8,000 personnel, 75 combat aircraft and 24 armed helicopters, with 16 F-16s to be delivered in 1996-97.

INTERNATIONAL RELATIONS. A 46-year-old formal state of hostilities with Israel was brought to an end by a peace agreement on 26 Oct. 1994.

Membership. Jordan is a member of the UN and the Arab League.

ECONOMY

Policy. An economic adjustment programme has been adopted for 1992-98.

Budget. Revenue, 1994, JD.1,492·3m.; expenditure, JD.1,437·1m. Defence expenditure, JD.272·0m.; social services, culture and information services, JD.240·3m.

Currency. The unit of currency is the *Jordan dinar,* (JOD) of 1,000 *fils.* There are coins of 1, 5, 10, 20, 25, 50, 100, 250, 500 and 10,000 fls, and notes of 500 fils and JD.1, 5, 10 and 20. Foreign currency reserves were JD.1,001·1m. in 1992. The annual inflation rate was 1% in 1992 (8·2% in 1991). In March 1996, £1 = JD.1·08; US$1 = JD.0·71; DM1 = JD.0·48.

Banking and Finance. The Central Bank of Jordan was established in 1964 (*Governor,* Mohammed Nabulsi). In 1993 there were 28 licensed banks with a total of 410 branches and 95 offices. Assets and liabilities of the banking system (including the Central Bank, commercial banks, the Housing Bank and investment banks) totalled JD.10,641·5m. in 1994.

There is a stock exchange in Amman.

Weights and Measures. The metric system is in force. Land area is measured in *dunums* (1 dunum = 0·1 ha).

ENERGY AND NATURAL RESOURCES

Electricity. Production (1994) 5,076m. kWh. In 1992, 98·9% of the population were supplied with electricity.

Minerals. Phosphates production in 1994 was 4·22m. tonnes; potash, 1,550,000 tonnes.

Agriculture. In 1994 agriculture produced 8% of GDP. The country east of the Hejaz Railway line is largely desert; northwestern Jordan is potentially of agricultural value and an integrated Jordan Valley project began in 1973. Arable land was 315,000 ha in 1992; permanent crops, 90,000 ha; permanent pasture, 791,000 ha. The agricultural cropping pattern for irrigated vegetable cultivation was introduced in 1984 to regulate production and diversify the crops being cultivated. In 1986 the government began to lease state-owned land in the semi-arid southern regions for agricultural development by private investors, mostly for wheat and barley.

Production in 1994 (in tonnes): Wheat, 47,000; barley, 28,000; maize, 6·0m.; tobacco, 3,059; tomatoes, 40·0m.; potatoes, 264,000; olives, 94,000; fruits, 253,000 (1993); grapes, 27,000.

Livestock (1993): 1·9m. sheep; 0·5m. goats; 40,000 cattle; 18,000 camels. Total meat production was 102,000 tonnes in 1993; milk, 96,000 tonnes.

There were 5,850 tractors in 1992.

Forestry. There were 70,000 ha of forest and woodland in 1992.

INDUSTRY. In 1993 service industries accounted for 68% of GDP and manufacturing 15%. There were 18,592 firms in 1993, of which 6,883 were in the services and maintenance sectors. The industrial sector employs more than 0·1m. persons. Production (1993, in 1,000 tonnes): Alcoholic drinks, 6,292; phosphate, 4,215; petroleum products, 2,815; cement, 3,437; potash, 1,370; chemical acids, 846; fertilizers, 470.

Labour. The workforce in 1993 was 859,130, of whom 434,806 worked in social and public administration, 91,087 in mining and manufacturing, 129,754 in commerce, 57,573 in transport and communications and 54,995 in agriculture. In 1987 277,200 Jordanians worked abroad. Unemployment was 18.8% in 1993.

FOREIGN ECONOMIC RELATIONS. Foreign debt was US$6,870m. in 1992. Legislation of 1995 eases restrictions on foreign investment and makes some reductions in taxes and customs duties.

Commerce. Imports in 1994 were valued at JD.2,362m. and exports at JD.995m. Major exports are phosphate, potash, fertilizers, foodstuffs, pharmaceuticals, fruit and vegetables, textiles, cement, plastics, detergent and soap.

Exports in 1994 (in JD.1m.) were mainly to India, 88; Saudi Arabia, 72; Iraq, 78; Indonesia, 28; United Arab Emirates, 39. Imports were mainly from USA, 232; Germany, 184; Japan, 94; Italy, 139; UK, 120; Turkey, 62.

Total trade between Jordan and UK (British Department of Trade returns, in £1,000 sterling):

	1991	*1992*	*1993*	*1994*	*1995*
Imports to UK	10,984	20,743	21,520	24,034	20,894
Exports and re-exports from UK	89,411	110,859	140,083	114,716	119,597

Tourism. In 1993 there were 5·42m. foreign visitors.

COMMUNICATIONS

Roads. Total length of roads, 1994, 6,856 km, of which 2,820 km were main roads. Motor vehicles in 1993 included 175,325 motor cars (154,294 private), 901 motorcycles, 1,235 buses, 7,521 lorries and 38,595 vans. There were 26,837 road accidents in 1994.

Railways. The 1,050 mm gauge Hejaz Jordan and Aqaba Railway runs from the Syrian border at Nassib to Ma'an and Naqb Ishtar and Aqaba Port (total, 618 km). In 1994 it carried 2·5m. tonnes of freight. The state railway is only minimally operational.

Civil Aviation. The Queen Alia International airport is at Zizya, 30 km south of Amman. There are also international airports at Amman and Aqaba. The national carrier is the state-owned Royal Jordanian, which carried 1·2m. passengers and 54,062 tonnes of freight in 1994, and operated 1 A310-200, 4 A310-300s, 2 A320-200s, 3 B-707-320Cs, 2 B-727-200 Advs and 5 other aircraft in 1995.

Services are also provided by Aeroflot, Air Algérie, Air Canada, Air France, Air Lanka, Alitalia, Alyemda, Austrian Airlines, British Airways, British Mediterranean Airways, Cyprus Airways, Egyptair, Emirates, Gulf Air, JAT, KLM, Libyan Airlines, Malaysia Airlines, Middle East Airlines, Northwest Airlines, Olympic Airways, Pakistan International Airlines, Qatar Airways, Saudia, Sudan Airways, Tarom, Tunis Air, Turkish Airlines and Yemenia.

Shipping. In 1995 sea-going shipping totalled 0·11m. GRT, including oil tankers, 97,286 GRT. 11m. tonnes of cargo were handled by the port of Aqaba in 1994.

Telecommunications. In 1994 there were 116,778 post offices and agencies, 317,330 telephones and 2,094 telexes. Broadcasting is the responsibility of the Jordan Radio and Television Corporation, which transmits 2 national radio programmes (1 in English), a Koran programme and an external service, Radio Jordan. There are 2 television programmes (colour by PAL). In 1993 0·7m. radio and 0·25m. TV sets were in use.

Press (1994). There were 6 daily (including 1 in English) and 19 weekly papers, with a total circulation (1987) of 188,000. Newspapers were denationalized in 1990, though government institutions still hold majority ownership.

SOCIAL INSTITUTIONS

Religion. There were 3·38m. Sunni Moslems in 1992.

Education. In 1994 there were 664 kindergartens (662 private) with 2,422 teachers and 55,996 pupils; 2,482 basic schools (322 private) with 48,158 teachers and 1,036,079 pupils; 741 secondary schools (77 private) with 4,572 teachers and 93,773 pupils and 54 vocational schools with 2,519 teachers and 30,052 pupils. In 1994 there were 4 universities with 48,457 students (26,485 women) and 2,152 academic staff (258 women). The University of Jordan, (founded in 1962) had 22,058 students, Yarmouk University (1976), 15,278; Mu'tah University (1981), 6,314 and Jordan University of Science and Technology (1987), 4,797. 22,500 Jordanians were studying abroad.

Health In 1994 there were 6,183 doctors, 2,718 dentists and 6,801 hospital beds.

DIPLOMATIC REPRESENTATIVES

Of Jordan in Great Britain (6 Upper Phillimore Gdns., London, W8 7HB)
Ambassador: Fouad Ayoub.

Of Great Britain in Jordan (Abdoun, Amman)
Ambassador: Peter Hinchcliffe, CMG, CVO.

Of Jordan in the USA (3504 International Dr., NW, Washington, D.C., 20008)
Ambassador: Dr Fayez Tarawneh.

Of the USA in Jordan (Abdoun, Amman)
Ambassador: Wesley W. Egan.

Of Jordan to the United Nations
Ambassador: Hassan Abu Nam'eh.

Further Reading

Department of Statistics. *Statistical Yearbook*
Central Bank of Jordan. *Monthly Statistical Bulletin*
Gubser, *P., Jordan.* Boulder (CO), 1982
Rogan, E. and Tell, T. (eds.) *Village, Steppe and State: the Social Origins of Modern Jordan.* London, 1994
Salibi, K., *A Modern History of Jordan.* London, 1992
Satloff, R. B., *From Abdullah to Hussein: Jordan in Transition.* OUP, 1994
Seccombe, I., *Jordan.* [Bibliography] Oxford and Santa Barbara, 1984
Wilson, M. C., *King Abdullah, Britain and the making of Jordan.* CUP, 1987

National statistical office: Department of Statistics, Amman

KAZAKHSTAN

Kazak Respublikasy

Capital: Akmola
Population: 16·94m. (1994)
GNP per capita: US$1,110 (1994)
HDI/world rank: 0·798/64 (1992)

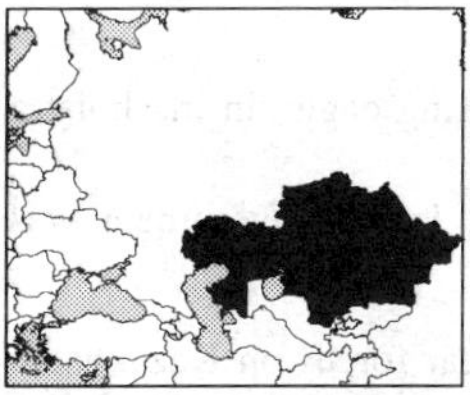

KEY HISTORICAL EVENTS. On 26 Aug. 1920 Uralsk, Turgai, Akmolinsk and Semipalatinsk provinces formed the Kyrgyz (in 1925 renamed Kazakh) Autonomous Soviet Socialist Republic within the RSFSR. It was made a constituent republic of the USSR on 5 Dec. 1936. To this republic were added the parts of the former Governorship of Turkestan inhabited by a majority of Kazakhs.

Independence was declared on 16 Dec. 1991, and Kazakhstan joined the CIS.

TERRITORY AND POPULATION. Kazakhstan is bounded in the west by the Caspian Sea and Russia, in the north by Russia, in the east by China and in the south by Uzbekistan and Kyrgyzstan. The area is 2,717,300 sq. km (1,049,155 sq. miles). The 1989 census population was 16,464,464, of whom Kazakhs accounted for 39·7%, Russians 37·8%, Germans 5·8%, Ukrainians 5·4%, Uzbeks and Tatars 2% each. Estimate, Jan. 1994, 16,942,000 (51·4% female; 57·2% urban). Vital statistics rates, 1993 (per 1,000 population): Births, 18·6; deaths, 9·2; natural increase, 9·4; infant mortality (per 1,000 live births), 28·4.

It consists of 19 provinces as follows, with area and population:

	Area (sq. km)	*Population (1991)*		*Area (sq. km)*	*Population (1991)*
Akmola [1]	92,100	885,400	Kzyl-Orda	228,100	664,900
Aktyubinsk	298,700	752,900	Mangyshlak	165,100	331,700
Almaty [2]	105,100	2,153,700	North Kazakhstan	44,300	610,400
Ateransk [3]	113,500	447,100	Pavlodar	127,500	956,900
Aulie-Ata [4]	144,200	1,056,400	Semipalatinsk	179,600	841,900
Dzhezkazgan	313,400	496,200	South Kazakhstan	116,300	1,879,200
East Kazakhstan	97,300	949,000	Taldy-Kurgan	118,500	731,000
Karaganda	117,900	1,339,900	Turgay	111,900	304,600
Kokchetav	78,100	669,400	West Kazakhstan	151,200	648,000
Kustanai	114,500	1,074,400			

[1] formerly Tselinograd. [2] formerly Alma-Ata. [3] formerly Gurev. [4] formerly Dzhambul.

The capital is Akmola (moved from Almaty in 1995). In all there are 82 towns, 197 urban settlements and 221 rural districts.

The official language is Kazakh.

CONSTITUTION AND GOVERNMENT. Relying on a judgement of the Constitutional Court that the 1994 parliamentary elections were invalid, President Nazarbaev dissolved parliament on 11 March 1995 and began to rule by decree. A referendum on the adoption of a new constitution was held on 30 Aug. 1995. The electorate was 8·8m.; turn-out was 80%. 89% of votes cast were in favour. The Constitution thus adopted allows the President to rule by decree and to dissolve parliament if it holds a no-confidence vote or twice rejects his nominee for Prime Minister. It establishes a parliament consisting of a 47-member Senate, 40 senators being elected by some 4,000 representatives of local authorities and 7 appointed by the President; and a lower house of 67, directly elected, though heads of families may cast votes for all of their family members. Candidates must gain an absolute majority of votes to be elected, and are not permitted to disclose their political affiliation.

At the elections of 9 Dec. 1995 turn-out was 78%. 43 candidates were elected. A second round of voting was held in Jan. 1996. A new Constitution was adopted on 28 Jan. 1993. A Constitutional Court was set up in Dec. 1991.

At the presidential elections of 2 Dec. 1991 Nursultan Nazarbaev (the sole candidate) was elected with 99% of votes cast. Turn-out was 88%. At a referendum in April 1995, 95.4% of votes cast favoured extending his term of office until 2000. Turn-out was 90%.

President: Nursultan Nazarbaev (b. 1940).
The *Speaker* is Abish Kekilbaev.

National flag: Light blue, in the centre a sun and a soaring eagle, in the hoist a vertical ornamentation, all in yellow.

Local Government. Elections were held in Dec. 1989. Local government was directly subordinated to the President in Jan. 1992.

DEFENCE. There are Russian-controlled strategic nuclear forces on Kazakhstan territory, comprising 48 inter-continental ballistic missiles. An agreement of Jan. 1995 provides for the eventual integration of Kazakhstan with Russian forces.

Army. The Army is organized in 1 tank and 2 motor rifle divisions; 1 independent motor rifle, 1 artillery, 1 multiple rocket launcher and 1 surface-to-surface missile regiment; and 1 artillery and 1 airborne brigade. Equipment includes 624 T-62 and T-72 main battle tanks. Personnel, 1996, 25,000. Paramilitary units: Republican Guard (2,500), Ministry of the Interior Security Troops (20,000), Frontier Guards (12,000).

Navy. That part of the former Soviet Caspian Sea Flotilla (some 75%) not ceded to Azerbaijan and amounting to some 30 small warships has been relocated to Astrakhan and operates under joint Russian, Kazakhstan and Turkmenistan command.

Air Force. In 1995 there was an Air Force division with about 15,000 personnel with 133 combat aircraft.

INTERNATIONAL RELATIONS. In Jan. 1995 agreements were reached for closer integration with Russia, including the combining of military forces, currency convertibility and a customs union.

Membership. Kazakhstan is a member of the UN and the NATO Partnership for Peace.

ECONOMY

Policy. A National Council for Economic Reform was instituted in Jan. 1993. A privatization programme for 1993–95 envisaged the sale of most state enterprises with more than 200 employees by a combination of cash and vouchers. Enterprises of national importance remain controlled by the government through holding companies. A privatization programme started in April 1994 involving the auctioning of 3,500 medium-size enterprises. Coupons are issued to citizens to be exchanged for shares in investment funds. Foreign nationals may participate in trading after the auctions. Large (i.e. with over 2,000 employees) and small (i.e. with fewer than 500) enterprises are being sold for cash.

Budget. Budgetary income in 1994 (and 1995) was 67,500m. tenge (111,050m. tenge); expenditure was 87,700 tenge (150,430m. tenge). The budget for 1996 envisaged revenue of 149,600m. tenge, and expenditure of 193,500m. tenge.

Currency. The unit of currency is the *tenge* of 100 *tiyn*, which was introduced on 15 Nov. 1993 at 1 tenge = 500 rubles. It became the sole legal tender on 25 Nov. 1993. There are notes of 50 tiyn, and 1, 3, 5, 10, 20, 50 and 100 tenge. In March 1996, £1=99·94 tenge; US$1=65·39 tenge; DM1 = 44·31 tenge.

Banking and Finance. The central bank and bank of issue is the National Bank (*Governor,* Daulet Sembaev). In 1995 there were 180 commercial banks, 60 privately owned.

ENERGY AND NATURAL RESOURCES

Electricity. Output in 1995 was 66,700m. kWh. There is 1 nuclear power station.

Minerals. Kazakhstan is extremely rich in mineral resources, including coal, bauxite, chromium, copper, Iceland spar, lead, manganese, molybdenum, nickel, tungsten and zinc. Coal production, 1993, 112m. tonnes; iron ore (1991), 42·5m. tonnes; gold (1994), 14 tonnes.

Oil and Gas. The Tengiz field has estimated oil reserves between 6,000m. and 9,000m. bbls; the Karachaganak field has oil reserves of 2,000m. bbls, and gas reserves of 20,000,000m. cu. feet. Output of crude oil (including gas concentrates), 1993, 23m. tonnes; natural gas, 6,700m. cu. metres.

Agriculture. Kazakh agriculture has changed from primarily nomad cattle breeding to production of grain, cotton and other industrial crops. In 1993, 181·3m. ha were under cultivation, of which private subsidiary agriculture accounted for 0·3m. ha and commercial farming 6·3m. ha in 16,300 farms. Private and commercial agriculture accounted for 35% of output by value in 1992; agricultural output was valued at 13,700m. rubles (in constant 1983 prices) in 1993, 97% of the 1992 figure.

Tobacco, rubber plants and mustard are also cultivated. Kazakhstan has rich orchards and vineyards, which accounted for 95,000 ha of cultivated land in 1985. Kazakhstan is noted for its livestock, particularly its sheep, from which excellent quality wool is obtained. Livestock on 1 Jan. 1994 included 9·3m. cattle, 34·2m. sheep and goats and 2·4m. pigs.

Output of main agricultural products (in 1m. tonnes) in 1993: Grain, 21·6; sugar-beet, 0·9; potatoes, 2·3; vegetables, 0·8; meat and fats, 1·3; milk, 5·5; cotton, 0·2; and 3,376m. eggs.

Forestry. In 1991 1·5m. cu. metres of timber were cut.

INDUSTRY. Kazakhstan was heavily industrialized in the Soviet period, with non-ferrous metallurgy, heavy engineering and the chemical industries prominent. Output was valued at 23,000m. tenge in current prices in 1993, 83·9% of the 1992 figure. Production (in tonnes) in 1993 included rolled ferrous metals, 3·5m.; mineral fertilizer, 0·3m.; chemical fibre, 1,900; paper, 2,100; cement, 4m.; fabrics, 188m. sq. metres; footwear, 13·5m. pairs; 1,200 lathes; 5,600 tractors; 20,100 TV sets; 12,900 refrigerators and freezers; 255,000 washing machines.

Labour. In 1993 the population of working age was 9·4m., of whom 6·9m. were employed, 64·8% in the state sector, 17.8% in the private sector and 6·3% in co-operatives. In Jan. 1994 there were 40,500 registered unemployed (0·6% of the labour force), of whom 15,400 were receiving benefits. Average monthly salaries in 1993 were 134·9 tenge.

FOREIGN ECONOMIC RELATIONS. In Jan. 1994 an agreement to create a single economic zone was signed with Kirghizia and Uzbekistan. Since Jan. 1992 individuals and enterprises have been able to engage in foreign trade without government permission, except for goods 'of national interest' (fuel, minerals, mineral fertilizers, grain, cotton, wool, caviare and pharmaceutical products) which may be exported only by state organizations. Foreign nationals may be licensed to purchase Kazakh assets for privatization.

Commerce. In 1993 imports were valued at US$358·3m. and exports at US$1,270·6m. Total trade between Kazakhstan and UK (British Department of Trade returns, in £1,000 sterling):

	1993	*1994*	*1995*
Imports to UK	57,915	70,576	48,902
Exports and re-exports from UK	14,943	40,699	26,561

COMMUNICATIONS

Roads. In Jan. 1990 there were 164,900 km of motor roads (99,000 km hard surface). In 1993, 2,225m. passengers and 296·4m. tonnes of freight were carried.

Railways. In 1992 there were 13,841 km of 1,520 mm gauge railways (3,050 km electrified). In 1993, 47·3m. passengers and 261m. tonnes of freight were carried.

Civil Aviation. The national carrier is Kazakhstan Airways, which operated 11 ex-Soviet aircraft in 1995. In 1993, 3·6m. passengers and 36·4m. tonnes of freight were carried. Services are also provided by Aeroflot, Aerosweet, Arax, Austrian Airlines, Belavia, Iran Air, KLM, Lufthansa, Mongolian Airlines, Pakistan Airlines, Siberia Airlines, Swissair, Transaero, Turkish Airlines, United Airlines, Uzbekistan Airways and Xinjiang Airlines.

Inland Waterways. In 1993, 1·2m. passengers and 4m. tonnes of freight were carried.

Telecommunications. Broadcasting is the responsibility of the Kazakh State Radio and Television Co. There are 3 national and 13 regional radio programmes, a Radio Moscow relay and a foreign service, Radio Alma-Ata (Kazakh, English). There is 1 TV channel (colour by SECAM).

Press. In 1995 there were 472 periodicals in Kazakh, 511 in Russian and 60 in both languages.

SOCIAL INSTITUTIONS.

Religion. There were some 4,000 mosques in 1996 (63 in 1990). An Islamic Institute opened in 1991 to train imams. A Roman Catholic diocese was established in 1991. In 1995, the Union of Evangelical Baptist Churches had 140 communities, the Russian Orthodox Church, 177, and the Evangelical Lutheran Church, 112.

Education. In Jan. 1994, 0·7m. children (39% of those eligible) were attending pre-school institutions. In 1993–94 there were 3,114,000 pupils at 8,700 elementary and secondary schools, 247 technical colleges with 222,100 students, 68 higher educational institutions with 272,100 students, and 207 research institutes.

Health. In Jan. 1994 there were 66,900 doctors, 187,000 junior medical personnel and 1,899 hospitals with 225,000 beds.

Welfare. In Jan. 1994 there were 2·1m. age, and 0·9m. other pensioners.

DIPLOMATIC REPRESENTATIVES

Of Kazakhstan in Great Britain
Ambassador: Nurtai Abykaev.

Of Great Britain in Kazakhstan (173 ul. Furmanova, Almaty)
Ambassador: Douglas McAdam.

Of Kazakhstan in the USA
Ambassador: Touleoutai Souleimenov.

Of the USA in Kazakhstan (99 Furmanova St., Alma-Ata, 480012)
Ambassador: A. Elizabeth Jones.

Of Kazakhstan to the United Nations
Ambassador: Akmaral Arystanbekova.

Further Reading

Olcott, M. B., *The Kazakhs*. Stanford, 1987

KENYA

Jamhuri ya Kenya
(Republic of Kenya)

Capital: Nairobi
Population: 26·44m. (1995)
GNP per capita: US$260 (1994)
HDI/world rank: 0·481/130 (1992)

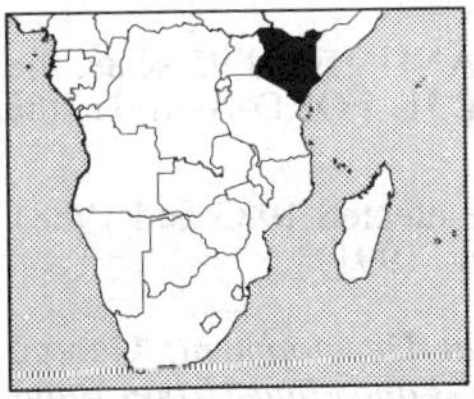

KEY HISTORICAL EVENTS. Until Kenya became independent it consisted of a colony and a protectorate. The protectorate comprised the mainland dominions of the Sultan of Zanzibar, a coastal strip of territory 10 miles wide to the northern branch of the Tana River, Mau, Kipini and the Island of Lamu, and all adjacent islands between the rivers Umba and Tana. The Sultan ceded the coastal strip to Kenya with effect from 12 Dec. 1963. The colony and protectorate (except the Sultan of Zanzibar's dominions) became a Crown Colony in 1920 under the name of the Colony of Kenya. The territories on the coast became the Kenya Protectorate. In 1925 the UK ceded the Juba River and a strip from 50 to 100 miles wide on its west bank to Italian Somaliland (now Somalia). The northern boundary is defined by an agreement with Ethiopia in 1947.

A Constitution conferring internal self-government was brought into force on 1 June 1963, and full independence was achieved on 12 Dec. 1963. On 12 Dec. 1964 Kenya became a republic.

TERRITORY AND POPULATION. Kenya is bounded by Sudan and Ethiopia in the north, Uganda in the west, Tanzania in the south and Somalia and the Indian Ocean in the east. The total area is 582,646 sq. km, of which 571,416 sq. km is land area. In the 1989 census, the population was 21,443,636, (19% urban). Estimate (1995), 26·44m. (20% urban); density, 50·3 per sq. km. Growth rate, 1993, 4·2%. Expectation of life, 1992, 58·6 years.

The land areas, populations and capitals of the provinces are:

Province	*Sq. km*	*Census 1979*	*Estimate 1993*	*Capital*	*Census 1989*
Rift Valley	171,108	3,240,402	6,107,900	Nakuru	162,800
Eastern	155,760	2,719,851	4,940,900	Embu	15,986 [1]
Nyanza	12,526	2,643,956	4,804,500	Kisumu	185,100
Central	13,173	2,345,833	4,152,600	Nyeri	88,600
Coast	83,040	1,342,794	2,430,700	Mombasa	465,000
Western	8,223	1,832,663	3,176,000	Kakamega	47,300
Nairobi Municipality	684	827,775	1,758,900	Nairobi	1,346,000
North-Eastern	126,902	373,787	741,400	Garissa	14,076 [1]

[1] 1979 census.

Other towns (1979): Machakos (84,320), Meru (70,439), Eldoret (59,503), Thika (41,324).

Swahili is the official language, but 21% speak Kikuyu as their mother tongue, 14% Luhya, 13% Luo, 11% Kamba, 11% Kalenjin, 6% Gusii, 5% Meru and 5% Mijikenda. English is spoken in commercial centres.

CLIMATE. The climate is tropical, with wet and dry seasons, but considerable differences in altitude make for varied conditions between the hot, coastal lowlands and the plateau, where temperatures are very much cooler. Heaviest rains occur in April and May, but in some parts there is a second wet season in Nov. and Dec. Nairobi. Jan. 65°F (18·3°C), July 60°F (15·6°C). Annual rainfall 39" (958 mm). Mombasa. Jan. 81°F (27·2°C), July 76°F (24·4°C). Annual rainfall 47" (1,201 mm).

CONSTITUTION AND GOVERNMENT. There is a unicameral *National Assembly* of 200 members, comprising 188 elected by universal suffrage for a 5-year term, 10 members appointed by the President, and the Speaker and Attorney-General ex-officio. The President is also directly elected for 5 years; he appoints a

Vice-President and other Ministers to a Cabinet over which he presides. A constitional amendment of Aug. 1992 stipulates that the winning presidential candidate must receive a nation-wide majority and also the vote of 25% of electors in at least 5 of the 8 provinces. The sole legal political party had been the Kenya African National Union (KANU), but in Dec. 1991 KANU agreed to legalize opposition parties.

At the presidential elections of 29 Dec. 1992 Daniel T. arap Moi was elected against 3 opponents with 36% of votes cast.

At the National Assembly elections of 29 Dec. 1992, KANU gained 95 seats, the Forum for the Restoration of Democracy (FORD)-Kenya 31, FORD-Asili 31, the Democratic Party 26 and independents 5.

President: Daniel T. arap Moi (b. 1924, elected 1978, re-elected 1983 and 1988). Ministers proclaimed him president for life at a rally in Sept. 1991.

In Nov. 1995 the government comprised:

Vice-President and Minister for Planning and National Development: George Saitoti. *Environment and Natural Resources:* John Sambu. *Lands and Urban Planning:* Jackson Mulinge. *Land Reclamation, Regional and Water Development:* Hussein Maalim Mohamed. *Home Affairs and National Heritage:* Francis Lotodo. *Transport and Communications:* Dalmos Otieno. *Local Government:* William Ntimama. *Foreign Affairs:* Stephen Musyoka. *Commerce and Industry:* Kirugi M'Mukindia. *Tourism and Wildlife:* Katana Ngala. *Culture and Social Services:* Winifred Nyiva Mwendwa. *Agriculture, Livestock Development and Marketing:* Simon Nyachae. *Health:* Joshua Angatia. *Public Works and Housing:* Jonathan N'Geno. *Co-operative Development:* Kamwithi Munyi. *Labour:* Philip Masinde. *Education:* Joseph J. Kamotho. *Information and Broadcasting:* Johnstone Makau. *Research and Technical Training:* Zachary Onyonka. *Finance:* Wycliffe Mudavadi. *Energy:* Darius Mbela. *Attorney-General:* Amos Wako.

National flag: Three horizontal stripes of black, red, green, with the red edged in white; bearing in the centre an African shield in black and white with 2 crossed spears behind.

National anthem: 'Ee Mungu nguvu yetu' ('Oh God of all creation'); words by a collective, tune traditional.

Local government. The country is divided into the Nairobi Municipality and 7 provinces and there are 40 districts.

DEFENCE

Army. The Army consists of 1 armoured, 1 engineer, 1 artillery and 2 infantry brigades and 1 air defence, 1 airborne, 1 independent air cavalry and 2 engineer battalions. Equipment includes 80 Vickers Mk3 main battle tanks. Total strength (1996) 20,500.

Navy. The Navy, based in Mombasa, in 1995 consisted of 2 56-metre fast missile craft, 4 smaller missile craft, and 1 inshore patrol craft, all built in Britain, and 1 tug. Personnel in 1995 totalled 1,200.

The Marine police and Customs operate an additional 15 patrol boats.

Air Force. An air force, formed 1 June 1964, was built up with RAF assistance and is under Army command. Equipment includes 8 F-5E/F-5F supersonic combat aircraft/trainers, 12 Hawk light jet attack/trainers, 11 twin-turboprop Buffaloes and Dash-8s for transport, air ambulance, anti-locust spraying and security duties, 6 Skyservant light twins, 10 Bulldog piston-engined primary trainers, 12 Tucano turbo-prop basic trainers and Puma, Gazelle and Hughes 500 helicopters. Personnel (1995) 2,500, with 20 combat aircraft and 24 armed helicopters.

INTERNATIONAL RELATIONS

Membership. Kenya is a member of the UN, Commonwealth, OAU and is an ACP state of the EU.

ECONOMY

Policy. In 1994, 207 commercial enterprises with direct or indirect public ownership were scheduled for liquidation or privatization.

Budget. The fiscal year ends on 30 June. Government revenue, 1994–95, 126,333m. shillings; expenditure, 132,305m. shillings.

Currency. The monetary unit is the *Kenya shilling* (KES) of 100 *cents*. There are notes of KSh.5, 10, 20, 50, 100, 200 and 500 and coins of 5, 10 and 50 cents and KSh.1 and 5. Inflation was 28·8% in 1994. Foreign exchange reserves were 58,400m. shillings in 1993. The currency became convertible in May 1994. The shilling was devalued by 23% in April 1993. In March 1996, £1 = 89·34 shillings; US$1 = 58·45 shillings; DM1 = 39·60 shillings.

Banking and Finance. The central bank and bank of issue is the Central Bank of Kenya. (*Governor*, Micah Cheserem). There were 28 banks and 50 other financial institutions operating in 1991. In March 1990 their combined assets totalled KSh.£3,545m. The Kenya Commercial Bank is 70% state-owned. Savings deposits totalled KSh.£724m. in March 1990.

There is a stock exchange in Nairobi.

ENERGY AND NATURAL RESOURCES

Electricity. Installed generating capacity was 807 MW in 1994; 75% was provided by hydropower from power stations on the Tana river, 20% by oil-fired power stations and the rest by geothermal power. Production (1994) 3,538m. kWh.

Minerals. In 1989 there were 49 mines and quarries. Production, 1994 (in 1,000 tonnes): Soda ash, 224; fluorspar, 89; salt, 75·8. Other minerals included gold, raw soda, lime and limestone, diatomite, garnets and vermiculite.

Agriculture. As agriculture is possible from sea-level to altitudes of over 9,000 ft, tropical, sub-tropical and temperate crops can be grown and mixed farming is pursued. Agriculture produces 30% of GDP. In 1992 there were 1·93m. ha of arable land, 520,000 ha of permanent crop land and 38·1m. ha of pasture. Four-fifths of the country is range-land which produces mainly livestock products and the wild game which is a major tourist attraction.

In 1989 there were 2,572 enterprises engaged in agriculture and forestry, including 772 mixed farms, 448 ranches, 400 coffee plantations and 105 tea plantations. 619 enterprises employed more than 50 persons. Coffee, tea, sisal, pyrethrum, maize and wheat are crops of major importance in the Highlands, while coconuts, cashew nuts, cotton, sugar, sisal and maize are the principal crops grown at the lower altitudes. Production, 1993 (in 1,000 tonnes): Maize, 1,748; wheat, 150; rice, 25; barley, 37; millet, 58; sorghum, 90; potatoes, 250; sweet potatoes, 630; cassava, 790; sugar-cane, 4,210; tobacco, 10; coffee, 76; tea, 211; vegetables, 655; fruit excluding melons, 974; seed cotton, 16; sisal, 34.

Livestock (1993): Cattle, 11m.; sheep, 5·5m.; goats, 7·3m.; pigs, 105,000; poultry, 25m.

52,000 ha were irrigated in 1992.

Forestry. Forest reserves are 16,800 sq. km, mainly between 6,000 and 11,000 ft above sea-level. There are coniferous, broad-leaved, hardwood and bamboo forests. The forest area in 1989 was (in 1,000 ha) 1,750, of which 1,691 were gazetted, 1,338 in state ownership, 412 in local authority ownership and 124 in private ownership. 630,000 cu. metres of timber were cut in 1994.

Fisheries. Landings in 1994 were 179,000 tonnes of fresh water fish, 5,194 tonnes of marine fish, 403 tonnes of crustaceans and 127 tonnes of other marine products; total value K£212,145,000.

INDUSTRY. In 1989 there were 1,971 manufacturing firms, 586 of which employed more than 50 persons. The main products are textiles, chemicals, vehicle assembly and transport equipment, leather and footwear, printing and publishing, food and tobacco processing and oil refining. Production in 1994 included (in tonnes): Sugar, 303,000; maize meal, 233,200; wheat flour, 191,400; animal feed (1988), 184,266; cotton yarn, 4,767; cotton fabrics, 45·69m. sq. metres.

FOREIGN ECONOMIC RELATIONS. Foreign debt was US$7·1m. in 1993. Foreign investment on the stock exchange has been permitted since 1 Jan. 1995. Export Processing Zones were introduced in 1990, offering foreign companies exemption from taxes and duties for 10 years.

Commerce. Exports were valued at 85,643m. shillings in 1994; imports, 115,080m. shillings.

Principal exports (in 1,000m. shillings) 1994: Tea, 16·9; coffee, 13; horticultural produce, 8·3. Imports: Petroleum, 18·6; machinery and transport equipment, 31·8; chemicals (1993), 19·9; manufactures, 14·7.

Main export markets in 1994 (in KSh.1m.): UK, 496·6; Germany, 332·7; Uganda, 544·3. Main import suppliers: UK, 757·6; United Arab Emirates, 643·6; Japan, 496·8; Germany, 357·6; France, 232·2.

Total trade between Kenya and UK (British Department of Trade returns, in £1,000 sterling):

	1991	*1992*	*1993*	*1994*	*1995*
Imports to UK	141,996	138,397	172,680	167,152	162,198
Exports and re-exports from UK	206,927	139,865	152,208	195,880	244,347

Tourism. In 1994 there were 0·68m. holiday visitors. Receipts from tourism were K£1,220m. in 1993.

COMMUNICATIONS

Roads. In 1994 there were 8,800 km of bitumen-surfaced roads and 54,900 km of gravel-surfaced roads. There were, in 1989, 150,681 motor cars, 22,368 motor cycles, 83,348 vans, 31,528 lorries and 12,340 buses. There were 10,106 road accidents in 1989 (2,014 fatal).

Railways. In 1992 route length was 2,650 km of metre-gauge. In 1994 2·2m. passengers and 1·9m. tonnes of freight were carried.

Civil Aviation. There are international airports at Mombasa (Moi) and Nairobi (Jomo Kenyatta). The national carrier is the state-owned Kenya Airways, which in 1995 operated 3 A310-300s, 2 B-737-200 Advs and 3 other aircraft. Services are also provided by Aero Zambia, Aeroflot, Air Afrique, Air Austral, Air Botswana, Air Burundi, Air France, Air India, Air Madagascar, Air Malaŵi, Air Mauritius, Air Seychelles, Air Tanzania, Air Zimbabwe, Alitalia, Alyemda, Balkan, British Airways, Cameroon Airlines, Egyptair, El Al, Emirates, Ethiopian Airlines, Gulf Air, KLM, LTU, Lufthansa, Northwest Airlines, Olympic Airways, Pakistan Airlines, Royal Swazi, SAA, Sabena, Saudia, Sudan Airways, Swissair and Uganda Airways. In 1994, 2,768, 200 passengers and 65,500 tonnes of freight were carried.

Shipping. The main port is Mombasa, which handled 8·27m. tonnes of cargo in 1994. The merchant marine totalled 15,579 GRT in 1995, including oil tankers, 6,412 GRT.

Telecommunications. In 1989 there were 357,251 telephones. Broadcasting is the responsibility of the Kenya Broadcasting Corporation, which transmits the following services: National (in Swahili), General (English), Central (4 languages), Western (6 languages), North-Eastern and Coastal (4 languages). Voice of Kenya Television (part-government, part-commercial; colour by PAL) provides programmes mainly in English and Swahili, and there is an independent commercial network. In 1993 4·2m. radio and 0·26m. TV sets were in use.

Press. In 1994 English-language dailies had an average circulation of 299,500, and Swahili, 66,800.

SOCIAL INSTITUTIONS

Justice. The courts of Justice comprises the court of Appeal, the High Court and a large number of subsidiary courts. The court of Appeal is the final Apellant court in the country and is based in Nairobi. It comprises of 7 Judges of Appeal. In the course of its Appellate duties the court of Appeal visits Mombasa, Kisumu, Nakuru and Nyeri. The High court with full jurisdiction in both civil and criminal matters comprises of a total of 28 puisne Judges. Puisne Judges sit in Nairobi (16), Mombasa (2), Nakuru, Kisumu, Nyeri, Eldoret Meru and Kisii (1 each).

The Magistracy consists of approximately 300 magistrates of various cadres based in all provincial, district and some divisional centres. In addition to the above there are the Kadhi courts established in areas of concentrated Moslem populations: Mombasa, Nairobi, Malindi, Lamu, Garissa, Kisumu and Marsabit. They exercise limited jurisdiction in matters governed by Islamic Law.

There were 20,961 criminal convictions in 1989; the prison population was 106,107.

Religion. In 1992 there were 7·12m. Roman Catholics, 1·94m. Protestants and 1·62m. Moslems. Traditional beliefs persist.

Education. Adult literacy was 70·5% in 1992. In 1994 there were 15,906 primary schools with 5,556,800 pupils and 178,097 teachers; 2,834 secondary schools with 619,839 pupils and 38,307 teachers; 20 teacher training schools with 16,461 students; 20 technical training institutes with 8,148 students. There were 3 polytechnics with 10,836 students, and 5 universities (Nairobi, Moi, Kenyatta, Egerton and Jomo Kenyatta University College of Agriculture and Technology) with 39,340 students.

Health. In 1994 there were 4,558 doctors and 630 dentists. There were 324 hospitals (with 37,271 beds), 522 health centres and 2,868 sub-centres and dispensaries. Free medical service for all children and adult out-patients was launched in 1965.

DIPLOMATIC REPRESENTATIVES

Of Kenya in Great Britain (45 Portland Pl., London, W1)
High Commissioner: Mwanyengela Ngali.

Of Great Britain in Kenya (Bruce Hse., Standard St., Nairobi)
High Commissioner: Simon Hemans, CVO, CMG.

Of Kenya in the USA (2249 R. St., NW, Washington, D.C., 20008)
Ambassador: Benjamin E. Kipkorir.

Of the USA in Kenya (Moi/Haile Selassie Ave., Nairobi)
Ambassador: Aurelia Brazeal.

Of Kenya to the United Nations
Ambassador: Francis Muthaura.

Further Reading

Collison, R. L., *Kenya.* [Bibliography] London and Santa Barbara (CA), 1982
Haugerud, A., *The Culture of Politics in Modern Kenya.* CUP, 1995
Miller, N. N., *Kenya: the Quest for Prosperity.* 2nd ed. Boulder (CO), 1994
Ochieng, W. R., (ed.) *Themes in Kenyan History.* Nairobi and Ohio Univ. Press, 1990
Widner, J. A., *The Rise of a Party State in Kenya: from 'Harambee' to 'Nayayo'.* Univ. of California Press, 1993

National statistical office: Central Bureau of Statistics, Ministry of Planning and National Development, POB 30266, Nairobi

KIRIBATI

Ribaberikin Kiribati

(Republic of Kiribati)

Capital: Tarawa
Population: 80,000 (1995)
GNP per capita: US$730 (1994)

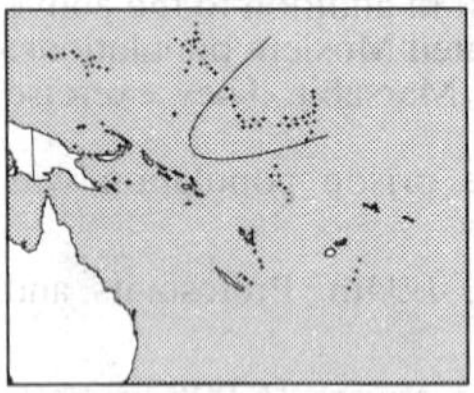

KEY HISTORICAL EVENTS. The Gilbert and Ellice Islands were proclaimed a protectorate in 1892 and annexed (at the request of the native governments) as the Gilbert and Ellice Islands Colony on 10 Nov. 1915 (effective on 12 Jan. 1916). On 1 Oct. 1975 the former Ellice Islands severed its constitutional links with the Gilbert Islands and took a new name Tuvalu.

Internal self-government was obtained on 1 Nov. 1976 and independence achieved on 12 July 1979 as the Republic of Kiribati.

TERRITORY AND POPULATION. Kiribati (pronounced Kiribass) consists of 3 groups of coral atolls and one isolated volcanic island, spread over a large expanse of the Central Pacific with a total land area of 717·1 sq. km (276·9 sq. miles). It comprises Banaba or Ocean Island (5 sq. km), the 16 Gilbert Islands (295 sq. km), the 8 Phœnix Islands (55 sq. km), and 8 of the 11 Line Islands (329 sq. km), the other 3 Line Islands (Jarvis, Palmyra and Kingman Reef) being uninhabited dependencies of the USA. Population, 1990 census, 72,298. 1995 estimate, 80,000. Between 1988 and 1993 4,700 people were resettled on Teraina and Tabuaeran atolls because the main island group was overcrowded. Banaba, all 16 Gilbert Islands, Kanton (or Abariringa) in the Phoenix Islands and 3 atolls in the Line Islands (Teraina, Tabuaeran and Kiritimati—formerly Washington, Fanning and Christmas Islands respectively) are inhabited; their populations in 1990 (census) were as follows:

Banaba (Ocean Is.)	284	Abemama	3,218	Onotoa	2,112
Makin	1,762	Kuria	985	Tamana	1,396
Butaritari	3,786	Aranuka	1,002	Arorae	1,440
Marakei	2,863	Nonouti	2,766	Kanton	45
Abaiang	5,314	North Tabiteuea	3,275	Teraina	936
North Tarawa	3,648	South Tabiteuea	1,325	Tabuaeran	1,309
South Tarawa	25,154	Beru	2,909	Kiritimati	2,537
Maiana	2,184	Nikunau	2,048		

The remaining 11 atolls have no permanent population; the 7 Phoenix Islands comprise Birnie, Rawaki (formerly Phoenix), Enderbury, Manra (formerly Sydney), Orona (formerly Hull), McKean and Nikumaroro (formerly Gardner), while the others are Malden and Starbuck in the Central Line Islands and Caroline, Flint and Vostok in the Southern Line Islands. The population is almost entirely Micronesian.

CLIMATE. The Line Islands, Phoenix Islands and Banaba have a maritime equatorial climate, but the islands further north and south are tropical. Annual and daily ranges of temperature are small and mean annual rainfall ranges from 50" (1,250 mm) near the equator to 120" (3,000 mm) in the north. Tarawa. Jan. 83°F (28·3°C), July 82°F (27·8°C). Annual rainfall 79" (1,977 mm).

CONSTITUTION AND GOVERNMENT. Under the independence Constitution the republic has a unicameral legislature, the *House of Assembly*, comprising 41 members, 39 of whom are elected and 2 (the Attorney-General *ex-officio*, and a representative from the Banaban community) appointed for a 4-year term. The *President* is directly elected, and is both Head of State and of Government.

The general election of July 1994 was won by the Maneaban te Mauri and its allies, with the National Progressive Party becoming the opposition.

In Aug. 1995 the government comprised:

President, Minister of Foreign Affairs and Trade: Teburoro Tito (elected 30 Sept. 1994; sworn in 1 Oct. 1994).

Vice-President, Minister of Home Affairs and Rural Development: Tewareka Tentoa. *Minister of Education, Science and Technology:* Willie Tokataake. *Finance and Economic Planning:* Benjamina Tinga. *Environment and Natural Resource Development:* Anote Tong. *Health, Family Planning and Social Welfare:* Tatoike Tekee. *Transport, Communications and Tourism:* Manroai Kaiea. *Commerce, Industry and Employment:* Tanieru Awerika. *Works and Energy:* Emile Schutz. *Line and Phoenix Islands Development:* Teiraoi Tetabea.

National flag: Red, with blue and white wavy lines in base, and in the centre a gold rising sun and a flying frigate bird.

National anthem: 'Teirake kain Kiribati' ('Stand up, Kiribatians'); words and tune by U. Ioteba.

INTERNATIONAL RELATIONS

Membership. Kiribati is a member of the UN, Commonwealth, South Pacific Forum and is an ACP state of the EU.

ECONOMY

Budget. Budget estimates for 1991 showed revenue, $A22·8m.; principal items: Fishing licences, $A2·9m.; customs duties, $A6·3m.; direct taxation, $A3·5m. Expenditure amounted to $A22·8m.

Currency. The currency in use is the Australian *dollar.*

ENERGY AND NATURAL RESOURCES

Electricity. Electric power production (1990) was 7,872,000 kWh.

Agriculture. The land is basically coral reefs upon which coral sand has built up, and then been enriched by humus from rotting vegetation and flotsam which has drifted ashore. About half the total land area is cultivated. The principal tree is the coconut, which grows on most of the islands. Other food-bearing trees are the pandanus palm and the breadfruit. The only vegetable which grows in any quantity is a coarse calladium (alocasia) with the local name 'bwabwai', which is cultivated in pits. Pigs and fowls are kept. Copra production (1993), 8,000 tonnes; coconuts, 65,000 tonnes.

Livestock (1993): Pigs, 9,000.

Fisheries. Tuna fishing is an important industry and licenses have been granted to the USA, Japan and South Korea.

FOREIGN ECONOMIC RELATIONS

Commerce. The principal imports (1990, in A$1m.) are: Food, 9·1; machinery and transport equipment, 6·6; manufactured goods, 4·1; fuels, 3·7. The value of exports for 1990 amounted to $A3·7m. Exports are almost exclusively copra.

Total trade between Kiribati and UK (British Department of Trade returns, in £1,000 sterling):

	1991	*1992*	*1993*	*1994*	*1995*
Imports to UK	9	2	2	13	3
Exports and re-exports from UK	253	571	327	300	431

Tourism. Tourism is in the early stages of development.

COMMUNICATIONS

Roads. There were (1988) 640 km of roads, of which 483 km suitable for vehicles.

Civil Aviation. Air Tungaru is the national carrier, which had 1 aircraft in 1995. It operates services from Tarawa to the other 15 outer Islands in the Gilbertese Group, services varying between one and four flights each week. A fortnightly service operates to Funafuti and weekly to Majuro and Nandi. Air Nauru has a weekly flight between Nauru and Tarawa.

Shipping. The main port is at Betio (Tarawa). Other ports of entry are Christmas Island and Banaba. In 1989, 58 vessels were handled at Betio.

Telecommunications. In 1991 there were 12,000 telephones on South Tarawa and Betio, and a direct link service for 7 other islands. Radio Kiribati, a division of the Broadcasting and Publications Authority, transmits daily in English and I-Kiribati from Tarawa. A satellite link to Australia was established in 1985. There were (1993 estimate) 10,000 radio receivers.

Cinemas. In 1990 there were 4 cinemas.

Press. There was (1991) 1 bi-lingual fortnightly newspaper.

SOCIAL INSTITUTIONS

Justice. In 1989 Kiribati had a police force of 232 under the command of a Commissioner of Police. The Commissioner of Police is also responsible for prisons, immigration, fire service (both domestic and airport) and firearms licensing.

Religion. At the 1990 census, 53% of the population were Roman Catholic and 39% Protestant (Congregational); there are small numbers of Seventh-day Adventist, Mormons, Baha'i and Church of God.

Education. In 1990 the government maintained boarding school had an enrolment of 593 pupils and there were 104 primary schools, with a total of 14,709 pupils, 8 secondary schools with 2,713 pupils, and 1 community high school with 117 pupils. The Government also maintains a teachers' training college with 39 students in 1990 and a marine training centre which offers training for about 100 merchant seamen each year. The Tarawa Technical Institute at Betio offers a variety of part-time and evening technical and commercial courses and had 389 students in 1986.

In 1990, 54 islanders were in overseas countries for secondary and further education or training.

Welfare. Government maintains free medical and other services. There were 16 doctors in 1990. There is a general hospital on Tarawa and dispensaries on other islands, with 283 beds.

DIPLOMATIC REPRESENTATIVES

Of Kiribati in Great Britain
High Commissioner: Vacant.

Of Great Britain in Kiribati
High Commissioner: Michael Peart, CMG, LVO (resides at Suva).

Of Kiribati in the USA
Ambassador: Vacant.

Further Reading

Bailey, E., *The Christmas Island Story.* London, 1977
Kiribati: Aspects of History. Univ. of South Pacific, 1979
Sabatier, E., *Astride the Equator.* Melbourne, 1978
Tearo, T., *Coming of Age.* Tarawa, 1989
Whincup, T., *Nareau's Nation.* London, 1979

KOREA

Daehan Min-kuk

(Republic of Korea)

Capital: Seoul
Population: 44·85m. (1995)
GNP per capita: US$8,483 (1994)
HDI/world rank: 0·882/31 (1992)

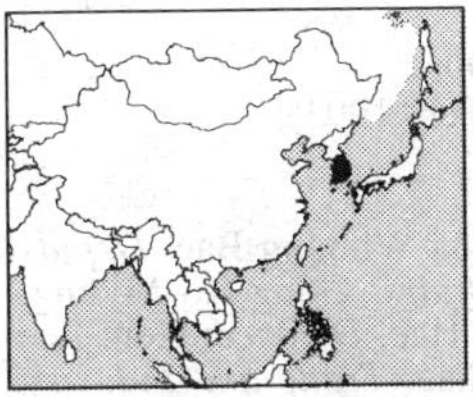

KEY HISTORICAL EVENTS. Korea was united in a single kingdom under the Silla dynasty from 668. China relinquished its tributary rights over Korea in 1895. Korea had already concluded trade agreements with the USA (1882), the UK and Germany (1883). After the Russo-Japanese war of 1904–5 Korea was virtually a Japanese protectorate until it was formally annexed by Japan on 29 Aug. 1910.

For the partition of Korea after the Second World War and the Korean War of 1950–53, *see* THE STATESMAN'S YEAR-BOOK, 1991–92, p. 781. A North Korean–UN agreement of 6 Sept. 1976 established a joint security area 850 metres wide, divided into 2 equal parts to ensure the separation of the two sides.

On 13 Dec. 1991 the prime ministers of North and South Korea signed a declaration of non-aggression and reconciliation, agreeing to respect each other's political systems, not to interfere in each other's internal affairs or slander each other.

TERRITORY AND POPULATION. South Korea is bounded in the north by the demilitarized zone (separating it from North Korea), east by the Sea of Japan (East Sea), south by the Korea Strait (separating it from Japan) and west by the Yellow Sea. The area is 99,263 sq. km. The population (census, 1 Nov. 1990) was 43,412,000 (urban, 74·4%). Estimate (1995), 44,851,000 (22,275,000 females) (84% urban); density, 451·3 per sq. km. Vital statistics rates per 1,000 in 1990: Birth, 15·6; death, 5·8; divorce, 20·8; infant mortality, 12·82; growth, 9·8%. Expectation of life, 1991: Males, 67·7; females, 75·7.

There are 9 provinces (*do*) and 6 cities with provincial status. Area and population in 1994:

Province	*Area (in sq. km)*	*Population (in 1,000)*	*Province*	*Area (in sq. km)*	*Population (in 1,000)*
Seoul (city)	605	10,799	North Chungchong	7,437	1,427
Pusan (city)	526	3,847	South Chungchong	8,317	1,845
Taegu (city)	456	2,347	North Cholla	8,052	2,005
Inchon (city)	313	2,208	South Cholla	11,812	2,198
Kwangju (city)	501	1,274	North Kyongsang	19,443	2,876
Taejon (city)	537	1,235	South Kyongsang	11,771	3,968
Kyonggi	10,769	7,438	Cheju	1,825	514
Kangwon	16,898	1,531			

Cities with over 400,000 inhabitants (census 1990):

Seoul	10,627,790	Taejon	1,062,084	Chonchu	517,104
Pusan	3,797,566	Ulsan	682,978	Chongchu	497,429
Taegu	2,228,834	Puchon	667,777	Masan	496,639
Inchon	1,818,293	Suweon	644,968	Anyang	480,668
Kwangchu	1,144,695	Seongnam	540,764		

CLIMATE. The extreme south has a humid warm temperate climate while the rest of the country experiences continental temperate conditions. Rainfall is concentrated in the period April to Sept. and ranges from 40" (1,020 mm) to 60" (1,520 mm). Pusan. Jan. 36°F (2·2°C), July 76°F (24·4°C). Annual rainfall 56" (1,407 mm). Seoul. Jan. 23°F (–5°C), July 77°F (25°C). Annual rainfall 50" (1,250 mm).

CONSTITUTION AND GOVERNMENT. The 1988 Constitution provides for a *President*, directly elected for a single 5-year term, who appoints and heads a *State Council*, and a *National Assembly* (299 members) directly elected for 4 years (237 from constituencies and 62 from party lists in proportion to the overall vote).

Presidential elections were held on 18 Dec. 1992. The electorate was 29,422,658; turn-out was 81·9%. Kim Young Sam was elected by 42% of votes cast.

Elections to the National Assembly were held in March 1992. The Democratic Liberal Party (DLP) gained 149 seats, the Democratic Party (DP) 97, the Party for National Unification (UPP) 32 and independents 22. In July 1992 the seats in the National Assembly were held as follows: DLP, 159; DP, 96; UPP, 32; independents, 11; Party for New Political Reform, 1.

National Assembly elections were scheduled for April 1996.

President: Kim Young Sam (b. 1927; DLP; sworn in 25 Feb. 1993).

A new government was formed in Dec. 1995 comprising:

Prime Minister: Lee Soo Song (b. 1940).

Deputy Prime Minister for Finance and the Economy: Rha Whoong Bae. *Deputy Prime Minister for Unification:* Kwon O Kie. *Foreign Affairs:* Gong Ro Myung. *Head of the National Security Agency:* Gen. Kwon Young Hae. *Defence*: Gen. Lee Yang Ho. *Information and Communications:* Lee Suk Chae. *Trade and Industry:* Park Jae Yoon. *Home Affairs:* Kim Woo Suk. *Environment:* Chung Chong Tek. *Justice:* Ahn Woo Mahn. *Culture and Sport:* Kim Young Soo. *Construction and Transport:* Choo Kyung Suk. *Labour:* Jin Nyum. *Government Administration:* Kim Ki Jae. *Science and Technology:* Chung Kun Mo. *Education:* Ahn Byung Young. *Agriculture:* Chang Wun Tae. *Health and Welfare:* Kim Yang Bae.

Speaker: Hwang Nak Joo.

National flag: White charged in the centre with the *yang-um* in red and blue and with 4 black *p'algwae* trigrams.

National anthem: 'Tong hae mulgwa' ('Until the East Sea is drained'); words anonymous, tune by An Ik Tae.

Local Government. The 15 provinces are divided into 136 districts *(Gun)* and 68 cities *(Shi)*. Elections were held on 27 June 1995 for the 9 provinces and 6 cities of provincial status and 5,700 other local government posts. The DLP gained 5 governorships, the DP 4, the UPP 4 and ind 2.

DEFENCE. Peacetime operational control, which had been transferred to the Combined Forces Command (CFC) under a US general in July 1950 on the outbreak of the Korean War, was restored to South Korea in Dec. 1994. In the event of a new crisis, operational control over the Korean armed forces will revert to CFC. Conscription is 26 months in the Army and 30 months in the Navy and Air Force. Conscripts may choose or be required to exchange military service for civilian work.

Army. The Army is organized in 19 infantry and 3 mechanized infantry divisions, 2 independent infantry brigades, 7 special forces brigades, 3 air defence artillery brigades, 3 counter-infiltration brigades, 1 army aviation command, 5 surface-to-air and 3 surface-to-surface missile battalions. Equipment includes 800 Type 88, 400 M-47 and 850 M-48A5 main battle tanks. Army aviation equipment includes 50 Hughes 500, 50 McDonnell Douglas 530 and 60 AH-1F helicopters for anti-armour operations, observation and liaison, and 18 CH-47D transport helicopters and over 100 utility helicopters. Delivery of 81 UH-60 Black Hawk transport helicopters began in 1991 and is scheduled to continue until 1995. Strength (1996) 520,000 (140,000 conscripts). Paramilitary Civilian Defence Corps, 3·5m.

Navy. A substantial force of 60,000 (19,000 conscripts), including 25,000 marines (1995), continues its steady modernization programme. Current strength includes the first 3 of a class of German-designed ocean-going diesel submarines, 3 midget submarines (175 tonnes), 7 aged (1943–46) ex-US destroyers, and 33 locally-built frigates with new US and European weapons, 4 corvettes, 11 fast missile craft, together with a patrol force of 100 inshore craft. There are 14 coastal minesweepers and an amphibious force of 8 tank landing ships, 7 medium landing ships, together with 35 amphibious craft. Major auxiliaries include 4 tankers, 2 large tugs, 4 survey vessels and 35 service craft. The Navy aviation element operates 8 P-3-C Orion, 15 shore-based S-2E Tracker anti-submarine aircraft and 25 Hughes 500MD, 12 Super-Lynx and 10 Alouette helicopters, some of which embark in frigates and destroyers.

Main bases are at Chinhae, Inchon and Pusan.

The Coastguard numbering some 6,000 (mostly shore-based) operates 10 off-shore, 26 coastal and 40 inshore patrol craft as well as 9 light helicopters.

Air Force. In 1995 the Air Force had a strength of 53,000 men and 461 combat aircraft. Its combat aircraft include F-16C/D Fighting Falcons, about 180 F-4D/E Phantoms, 40 F-5A/B tactical fighters, 200 F-5E/F tactical fighters, 15 RF-4E Phantom reconnaissance fighters, 10 O-2A and 10 OV-1 forward air control aircraft and 10 Hughes 500 Defender helicopters. There are also 12 CN-235, 10 C-130 Hercules turboprop-engined transports, 2 HS.748s, 1 Boeing 737 for VIP transport; UH-1, Bell 212 and Bell 412 transport helicopters, and Hawk T-41, T-33 and T-37C trainers.

INTERNATIONAL RELATIONS

Membership. The Republic of Korea is a member of the UN.

ECONOMY

Policy. The seventh 5-year social and economic plan, which began in 1992, has been replaced by a new plan for 1993–97. An annual plan for 1995 aimed at controlling growth and strengthening national competitiveness. Part of the plan ('the core industrial sector system') was to make conglomerates (*chaebol*) more competitive by restricting the industrial areas in which they may engage. The major conglomerates had selected their core industries and companies early in 1994. Restrictions on chaebols were relaxed in 1995 where family owners reduced their holdings to less than 20%.

40 state-owned or state-invested companies are scheduled for privatization between 1995 and 1998.

Budget. Revenue and expenditure (in 1,000m. won) at the 1995 budget (and estimates for 1996): 49,998 (58,003) and 54,824 (63,004). Sources of revenue: National tax, 48,098 (56,098); non-tax, 1,890·2 (1,905·3). Expenditure: Supports to provincial governments, 10,415 (12,095); personnel, 7,080 (7,885); defence, 11,507 (12,736); reserve fund, 687 (809); economic and social projects, 20,300 (24,478).

Currency. The unit of currency is the *won* (KRW) of 100 *chon*. Notes are in denominations of 10,000, 5,000 and 1,000 won and coins in denominations of 500, 100, 50, 10, 5 and 1 won. Notes and coins to the value of 9,234,600m. won were in circulation in 1993. In June 1995 foreign exchange reserves were US$28,380m.; gold reserves were US$34m. Inflation was 4·7% in 1993. In March 1996, £1 = 1,196·05 won; US$1 = 782·55 won; DM1 = 530·22 won.

Banking and Finance. The central bank and bank of issue is the Bank of Korea (*Governor*, Lee Kyung Shik). In Sept. 1995 bank deposits totalled 279,590,000m. won, of which 126,900,000m. won were savings deposits.

There are 23 national and provincial commercial banks, the 6 largest being Cho Hung, Commercial Bank, Korea First, Hanil, Bank of Seoul and Korea Exchange. There were 52 foreign banks in 1994, granted parity of treatment with domestic banks in July 1991, when the ceiling on their funds was lifted.

In addition, there are non-bank financial institutions consisting of 20 insurance companies, the Land Bank of Korea, the Credit Guarantee Fund, 32 short-term financial companies, 237 mutual credit companies, and the Merchant Banking Corporation.

The use of real names in financial dealings has been required since 1994.

There is a stock exchange in Seoul.

Weights and Measures. The metric system is in use alongside traditional measures. 1 *sok* = 144 kg. 1 *pyong* = 3·3 sq. metres.

ENERGY AND NATURAL RESOURCES

Electricity. Electricity generated (1994) was 188,348m. kWh; installed capacity (1993) was 27·65 kW. Sources of power in 1993: Nuclear, 40%; oil, 28·5%; coal, 15%; liquefied natural gas, 12·3%; hydro-electric, 4·2%.

Minerals. In 1991, 1,788 mining companies employed 60,983 people. Mineral deposits are small except tungsten. Output, 1993, included (in tonnes): Anthracite coal, 9·44m.; iron ore, 0·2m.; tungsten ore (1990), 2,451; limestone, 77m.; graphite, 59,100; lead ore, 14,818; zinc ore, 27,616.

Agriculture. Cultivated land was 2·07m. ha in 1992, of which 1·31m. ha were rice paddies. In 1995, the farming population was 5·16m. and there were 1·55m. farms. There were some 65,000 farms over 10 ha. The agricultural workforce was 2·8m. in 1994.

In 1995, 1·06m. ha were sown to rice. Production (1993, in tonnes): Rice, 5,315,000; barley, 354,389; wheat, 552,000; potatoes, 243,000; beans, 212,000. There were 64,159 tractors in 1992.

Livestock in 1992 (in 1,000): Draught cattle, 2,019; milch cows, 508; pigs, 5,463; sheep, 505; chickens, 73,324; ducks, 1,000.

Forestry. Forest area was 6·47m. ha in 1992. Total stock (1995) was 257·3m. cu. metres. In 1995, 71% of the national forest was privately owned. Timber output was 1·7m. cu. metres in 1992.

Fisheries. In 1992, there was a total of 94,135 boats (959,056 gross tonnes). 783 deep-sea fishing vessels were operating overseas in 1991. The fish catch (inland and marine) was 3·34m. tonnes in 1993.

INDUSTRY. Manufacturing industry is concentrated primarily on oil, petrochemicals, chemical fibres, construction, iron and steel, cement, machinery, shipbuilding, automobiles and electronics. Tobacco manufacture is a government monopoly. Industry is dominated by giant conglomerates (*chaebol*). There were 2,118,247 businesses in 1992.

Production in 1992 (in 1,000 tonnes): Paper and products, 2,568; artificial fertilizers, 3,077; plastic products, 727; pig-iron, 19,238; steel bars, 1,055; steel angles, 1,999; (in 1,000 sq. metres): Cotton fabrics, 469; silk fabrics, 18; synthetic fabrics, 3,434; petrol, 5,476,000 kilolitres; shoes, 19·4m. pairs; 1·6m. cars; 0·3m. lorries; 7·17m. microwave ovens; 1·3m. electronic calculators.

Labour. In 1995 the population of working age (15 to 59 years) was 33·56m. The economically-active population was 21·14m., of whom 0·39m. were unemployed. 4·77m. persons were employed in manufacturing, 11·22m. in services, 1·93m. in building, 27,000 in mining and 1·74m. in agriculture, fisheries and forestry. 5·84m. persons were self-employed in 1995. An annual legal minimum wage is set by the *Minimum Wage Council* each Sept. applicable to firms with more than 10 employees. In 1995-96 it was 288,250 won per month. There were 235 labour disputes in 1992; 1,520,364 working days were lost.

Trade Unions. In 1993 there were 7,531 unions with a total membership of 1,735,000. The government-recognized Federation of Korean Trade Unions groups 1·4m. of these.

FOREIGN ECONOMIC RELATIONS. Foreign debt was US$57,100m. in 1994. Since 1991 foreign partners in joint ventures holding less than 50% of the capital have needed only to report, instead of seek approval for, their projects. Tax concessions for foreign investments have been reduced. Since 1994 foreign investors have been able to buy 15% of the equity of most Korean companies. Since June 1995 South Korean businesses and individuals have been permitted to make investments and set up branch offices in North Korea. South Korea donated 0·15m. tonnes of rice to North Korea in 1995.

Commerce. In 1994 exports were US$96,263m., imports US$102,318m. Trade in

1994 with major partners (in US$1m.): Imports: Japan, 25,390; USA, 21,578; China, 5,463; Germany, 5,159. Exports: USA, 20,553; Japan, 13,523; Hong Kong, 8,015; China, 6,203.

Major exports in 1994 included (in US$1m.): Transistors and chips, 11,848; textiles, 7,838; clothing, 5,653; ships, 4,945; motor cars, 4,470; iron and steel, 4,456; telecommunications equipment, 3,687; office machines, 3,607; chemicals, 2,116. Major imports included: Machinery and transport equipment, 37,408; mineral fuels, 15,415; chemicals, 9,763; inedible raw materials, 9,405; food, 4,761. Rice imports were prohibited until 1994, but following the GATT Uruguay Round the rice market opened to foreign imports in 1995.

Total trade between Korea and UK (British Department of Trade returns, in £1,000 sterling):

	1991	*1992*	*1993*	*1994*	*1995*
Imports to UK	924,615	933,946	1,077,735	1,069,209	1,561,755
Exports and re-exports from UK	786,162	654,060	796,380	970,978	1,153,116

Tourism. In 1994, 3·17m. Koreans travelled abroad, spending an estimated US$4,063m. (in 1993, 2·42m. spending US$3,259m.). In 1994 there were 3·6m. foreign visitors spending US$3,836m. (not including direct spending in US dollars; in 1993, 3·33m. spending US$3,475m.).

COMMUNICATIONS

Roads. In 1993 there were 61,295 km of roads. 11·6m. passengers and 345·8m. tonnes of freight were carried in 1994. In 1995 motor vehicles totalled 8,022,652 (7,540,888 private) including 1,756,347 lorries, 601,571 buses and 5,632,838 passenger cars. There were 11,585 road deaths in 1992 (13,429 in 1991).

Railways. In 1994 the National Railroad totalled 3,081 km of 1,435 mm gauge (560 km electrified) and 20 km of 762 mm gauge. In 1994 railways carried 729m. passengers and 57·87m. tonnes of freight.

There are metros in Seoul (132 km) and Pusan (26·1 km).

Civil Aviation. There are international airports at Seoul (Kimpo), Kimhae and Chaeju. The national carrier is Korean Air which in 1995 operated 6 A300B4-200s, 5 A300B4-600s, 16 A300B4-600Rs, 2 A300F4-200s, 3 B-727-200 Advs, 4 B-747-200Bs, 2 B-747-200B(F)s, 1 B-747-200C, 8 B-747-200Fs, 2 B-747-300s, 1 B-747-300 Combi, 16 B-747-400s, 1 B-747-400 Combi, 2 B-7475Ps and 34 other aircraft. Asiana Airlines also provides services, and the foreign airlines Aeroflot, Air Canada, Air China, Air France, Air New Zealand, Alitalia, All Nippon Airways, British Airways, Cathay Pacific, China Eastern Airlines, China Northern Airlines, Continental Airlines and Air Micronesia, Delta, Garuda Indonesia, JAL, Japan Air System, KLM, Lufthansa, Malaysia Airlines, Northwest Airlines, Philippine Airlines, Qantas, Singapore Airlines, Swissair, Thai Airways, United Airlines, Uzbekistan Airways, VASP and Vietnam Airlines. In 1994, 18·4m. passengers and 0·31m. tonnes of cargo were carried on domestic routes and 13·08m. passengers and 1·11m. tonnes of cargo on international routes.

Shipping. In 1992 there were 48 ports, including 27 for international trade. In 1995 the merchant marine comprised 684 vessels totalling 19·49m. DWT, representing 2·95% of the world's tonnage. 234 vessels (49·56% of tonnage) were registered under foreign flags. Total GRT, 7·01m., including oil tankers, 0·52m. GRT and container ships, 1·15m. GRT. 7·87m. passengers and 234m. tonnes of freight were carried on domestic routes in 1994, and 0·41m. passengers and 353·42m. tonnes of cargo on international routes.

Telecommunications. Post offices totalled 3,390 in 1995; public telephones, 310,451; telephone subscribers, 18·08m.; telex subscribers, 4,006. The Korean Broadcasting System (KBS) is a public corporation which broadcasts 4 national radio programmes (1 commercial), regional programmes and a service for Koreans living abroad. An external service, Radio Korea, broadcasts in 8 languages. There is also a commercial network, an educational service and 4 religious networks. KBS transmits 3 TV channels (1 educational); colour by NTSC) and there is a commercial channel. Local commercial TV based on major cities began in 1994. Cable TV was inaugurated in March 1995. There were 42m. radio and 8·7m. television receivers in 1993.

Cinemas. In 1988 there were 696 with a seating capacity of 240,000. 96 full-length films were produced in 1992.

Press. In 1992 there were 77 dailies and 4,994 periodicals. 29,56? book titles were published 1994.

SOCIAL INSTITUTIONS

Justice. Judicial power is vested in the Supreme Court, High Courts, District Courts and Family Court. The 14 Justices of the Supreme Court are appointed by the President for renewable 6-year terms; the Chief Justice appoints other judges. The President appoints the Prosecutor-General.

Religion. The main religions have been Shamanism, Buddhism (introduced A.D. 372) and Confucianism, which was the official faith from 1392 to 1910. Catholic converts from China introduced Christianity in the 18th century, but a ban on Roman Catholicism was not lifted until 1882. The Anglican Church was introduced in 1890 and became an independent jurisdiction in 1993 under the Archbishop of Korea. In 1995 it had 84 churches, 110 priests and some 52,000 faithful. Religious affiliations of the population in 1991 (and 1985): Buddhism, 23·7% (27·7%); Protestantism, 16·3% (18·6%); Roman Catholicism, 4·8% (5·7%); Confucianism, 1·5% (1%); others, 0·9% (1%); no religion, 52·9% (46%).

Education. After 1 or 2 years of kindergarten, education is compulsory from 6 to 12, followed by the options of middle school till 15 and general or vocational high school to 18.

In 1992–93 there were 8,526 kindergartens with 263,562 pupils and 21,117 teachers; 6,122 elementary schools with 4,561,078 pupils and 137,819 teachers; 2,539 middle schools with 2,336,206 pupils and 93,439 teachers; 1,735 high schools with 2,123,621 pupils and 95,208 teachers; 126 junior colleges with 294,412 students and 10,146 teachers; 11 teacher training colleges with 14,347 students and 603 teachers; 121 colleges and universities with 814,426 students and 37,031 teachers; 9 open colleges with 231,197 students and 1,179 teachers; and 287 other institutions with 185,370 students and 8,199 teachers.

106,458 South Koreans were studying abroad in 1994.

Health. In 1992 there were 236 general hospitals (with 76,619 beds), 337 other hospitals (36,425), 4,901 oriental medical hospitals and clinics (2,096) and 6,639 dental hospitals and clinics. There were 48,390 physicians, 6,839 oriental medical doctors, 11,285 dentists, 8,012 midwives, 101,140 nurses, and 39,564 pharmacists.

Social Security. In 1992 5·02m. persons were covered by the National Pension System introduced in 1988. Employers and employees make equal contributions; persons joining by choice or in rural areas pay their own contributions. The System covers age pensions, disability payments and survivors' pensions. Recipients of benefit in 1992 included: Public livelihood aid, 2·42m.; veterans, 174,100.

DIPLOMATIC REPRESENTATIVES

Of Korea in Great Britain (4 Palace Gate, London, W8 5NF)
Ambassador: Choi Dong Jin.

Of Great Britain in Korea (4 Chung-Dong, Chung-Ku, Seoul)
Ambassador: Thomas George Harris, CMG.

Of Korea in the USA (2370 Massachusetts Ave., NW, Washington, D.C., 20008)
Ambassador: Kun Woo Park.

Of the USA in Korea (Sejong-Ro, Seoul)
Ambassador: James T. Laney.

Of Korea at the United Nations:
Ambassador: Park Soo Gil.

Further Reading

National Bureau of Statistics. *Korea Statistical Yearbook*
Bank of Korea. *Economic Statistics Yearbook*
Das, D. K., *Korean Economic Dynamism.* London, 1991
Eckert, C. J. *et al., Korea Old and New: a History.* Harvard Univ. Press, 1991
Gibney, F., *Korea's Quiet Revolution: from Garrison State to Democracy.* New York, 1992
Simons, G., *Korea: the Search for Sovereignty.* London, 1995
Song, P.-N., *The Rise of the Korean Economy.* 2nd ed. OUP, 1994

National statistical office: National Bureau of Statistics, Economic Planning Board, Seoul

NORTH KOREA

Chosun Minchu-chui
Inmin Konghwa-guk

(People's Democratic Republic of Korea)

Capital: Pyongyang
Population: 23·03m. (1994)
GNP per capita: US$923 (1994)
HDI/world rank: 0·733/83 (1992)

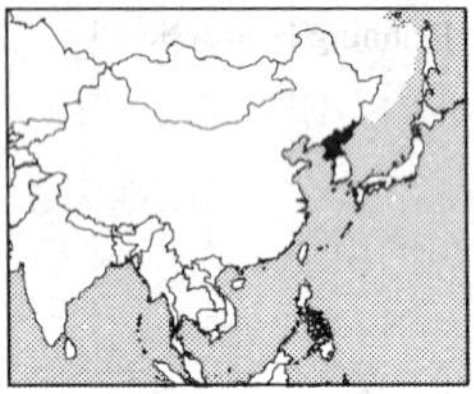

KEY HISTORICAL EVENTS. Following the Second World War Soviet forces occupied northern Korea in Aug. 1945 and established a Communist-led Provisional Government. In 1946 the Korean Workers' Party was formed from Communist groups. On 25 Aug. 1948 the Communists organized elections for a Supreme People's Assembly, both in Soviet-occupied North Korea and in US-occupied South Korea. A People's Democratic Republic was proclaimed on 9 Sept. 1948.

On 13 Dec. 1991 the prime ministers of North and South Korea signed a declaration of non-aggression, agreeing not to interfere in each other's internal affairs. 3 agreements were reached between the North and South Korean prime ministers in 1992 on proposals for military, economic, political and social co-operation.

Kim Il Sung, head of state, Communist Party and the military since 1948, died on 8 July 1994, and was apparently succeeded by his son, Kim Jong Il.

In June 1993, after negotiations with the USA, North Korea reversed its decision to withdraw from the Nuclear Non-Proliferation Treaty. On 21 Oct. 1994 an agreement to restrict nuclear power to peaceful purposes in Korea was signed by North Korea and the USA.

TERRITORY AND POPULATION. North Korea is bounded in the north by China, east by the sea of Japan, west by the Yellow Sea and south by South Korea, from which it is separated by a demilitarized zone of 1,262 sq. km. Its area is 122,762 sq. km. Population estimate in 1994, 23·03m. (64% urban); density, 187·6 per sq. km. Growth rate, 1994, 1·7%; birth rate, 1985, 3%; death rate, 0·6%. Marriage is discouraged before the age of 32 for men and 29 for women. Expectation of life in 1991 was: Males, 61·8 years; females, 66·8 years.

The area, 1987 population (in 1,000) and chief towns of the provinces and cities with provincial status:

	Area in sq. km	*Population*	*Chief Town*
North Hamgyong	17,570	2,003	Chongjin
South Hamgyong	18,970	2,547	Hamhung
Yanggang	14,317	628	Hyesan
Chagang	16,968	1,156	Kanggye
North Pyongan	12,191	2,408	Sinuiju
South Pyongan	11,577	2,653	Pyongsan
Pyongyang (city)	2,000	2,355	
Nampo (city)	753	715	
Kangwon	11,152	1,227	Wonsan
North Hwanghae	8,007	1,409	Sariwon
Kaesong (city)	1,255	331	
South Hwanghae	8,002	1,914	Haeju

Large towns (estimate, 1984): Pyongyang, the capital (2,639,448); Chongjin (754,128); Nampo (691,284); Sinuiju (500,000); Wonsan (350,000); Kaesong (345,642); Kimchaek (281,000); Haeju (131,000); Sariwon (130,000); Hamhung (775,000 in 1981).

CLIMATE. There is a warm temperate climate, though winters can be very cold in the north. Rainfall is concentrated in the summer months. Pyongyang. Jan. 18°F (–7·8°C), July 75°F (23·9°C). Annual rainfall 37" (916 mm).

CONSTITUTION AND GOVERNMENT. The political structure is based upon the Constitution of 27 Dec. 1972. Constitutional amendments of April 1992 delete references to Marxism-Leninism but retain the Communist Party's monopoly of rule. The Constitution provides for a *Supreme People's Assembly* of 687 delegates elected every 5 years by universal suffrage. Citizens of 17 years and over can vote and be elected. Elections were held in April 1990. It was claimed that 99·78% of the electorate voted for the list of single candidates presented. There are 687 deputies. The government consists of the *Administration Council* directed by the Central People's Committee (*Secretary,* Chi Chang Ik).

The head of state is the *President*, elected for 4-year terms. On 24 May 1990 the National Assembly unanimously elected Kim Il Sung for a fifth term. On his death on 8 July 1994 his son and designated successor, Kim Jong Il (b. 1942) is assumed to have informally assumed all his father's posts. The *Vice Presidents* are Kim Yong Ju, Pak Song Chol, Li Jong Ok and Kim Pyong Sik.

In Nov. 1995 the government included:

Prime Minister: Kang Song San (b. 1931).

Deputy Prime Ministers: Chang Choi, Choe Yong Nim, Hong Song Nam, Kang Hui Won, Kim Bok Sin, Kim Chang Chu, Kim Hwan, Kim Yong Nam, Kim Yun Hyok, Kong Chin Tae. *Chemicals Industry:* Kim Hwan. *Defence:* Choe Kwang. *Electronics and Automation Industries:* Kim Chang Ho. *Finance:* Yun Ki Chong. *Foreign Affairs:* Kim Yong Nam. *Machine Industry:* Kwak Bong I. *Metallurgy:* Choe Yong Nim. *Railways:* Pak Yong Sok. *Security:* Paek Hak Nim. *Trade:* Li Song Dae. *Chairman, State Planning Commission:* Hong Sok Hyong.

In practice the country is ruled by the Korean Workers' (*i.e.*, Communist) Party which elects a Central Committee which in turn appoints a Politburo.

By Nov. 1995 the Presidium of the Politburo was headed by Kim Jong Il, *(General Secretary of the Party, President of the Republic, Chairman of the Central People's Committee, Supreme Commander of the Armed Forces)*.

Party membership was 2m. in 1995. There are also the puppet religious Chongu and Korean Social Democratic Parties and various organizations combined in a Fatherland Front.

National flag: Blue, red and blue horizontal stripes separated by narrow white bands. The red stripe bears a white circle within which is a red 5-pointed star.

National anthem: 'A chi mun bin na ra i gang san' ('Shine bright, o dawn, on this land so fair'); words by Pak Se Yong, tune by Kim Won Gyun.

Local Government. The country is divided into 12 administrative units: 3 cities (Pyongyang, Nampo and Kaesong) and 9 provinces. These are sub-divided into 152 counties. There are 26,539 deputies in People's Assemblies at city/province, county and commune level. Elections were held in Nov. 1991. Turn-out was said to be 99·5%.

DEFENCE. The Supreme Commander of the Armed Forces is Kim Jong Il. Military service is compulsory at the age of 16 for periods of 5–8 years in the Army, 5–10 years in the Navy and 3–4 years in the Air Force, followed by obligatory part-time service in the Pacification Corps to age 40.

Army. The Army is organized in 26 infantry divisions (some motorized); 14 armoured, 23 motorized infantry and 5 independent infantry brigades; 1 special purpose corps numbering 88,000; 6 heavy artillery brigades with multiple rocket launchers, 1 independent surface-to-surface missile brigade and 1 regiment. Equipment includes some 3,400 T-34, T-54/55, T-62 and Type-59 main battle tanks. Strength (1996) 1m., with 0·75m. reserves. There is also a paramilitary worker-peasant Red Guard of some 3·8m. and a Ministry of Public Security force of 115,000 including border guards.

Navy. The Navy, principally tasked to coastal patrol and defence, comprises 24 diesel submarines (20 of Chinese design and 4 ex-Soviet). Surface forces include 3 small missile-armed frigates, 3 corvettes, 42 missile craft, 170 fast torpedo craft, 18 anti-submarine patrol craft and some 200 inshore patrol craft. Amphibious forces consist of some 130 small craft. Support is provided by 2 ex-Soviet ocean tugs and 100 service craft. There is a coastal defence element equipped with 6 missile batteries and old 122 mm, 130 mm and 152 mm guns. Personnel in 1995 totalled about 46,000 officers with 40,000 reserves.

Air Force. The Air Force had a total of 700 combat aircraft and 80 armed helicopters and 82,000 personnel in 1995. Since 1985 the Air Force has received 60 MiG-23 supersonic and 30 MiG-29 interceptors, 40 Su-25 fighter-bombers and 30 SA3 surface-to-air missiles. Other equipment is believed to include about 120 supersonic MiG-21 interceptors, more than 100 F-6s (Chinese-built MiG-19s), 150 MiG-17s for ground attack and reconnaissance, 40 Chinese-built A5 fighter-bombers, 200 An-2 light transport aircraft, 50 Mi-8 transport helicopters and 80 US Hughes 300 and 500 helicopters.

INTERNATIONAL RELATIONS

Membership. North Korea is a member of the UN.

ECONOMY

Policy. In Dec. 1993 it was officially admitted that the third 7-year plan had failed to achieve its industrial targets owing to the disappearance of Communist country markets and aid. Policy now concentrates on the development of agriculture, light industry and foreign trade.

Budget. Revenue, 1991, US$17,300m.; expenditure, US$17,170m. The 1992 budget balanced at US$18,550m.

Currency. The monetary unit is the *won* (KPW) of 100 *chon*. There are coins of 1, 5, 10 and 50 chon and 1, 5, 10, 50 and 100 won. Banknotes were replaced by a new issue in July 1992. Exchanges of new for old notes were limited to 500 won. In March 1996, £1 = 3·29 won; US$1 = 2·15 won; DM1 = 1·46 won.

Banking and Finance. The bank of issue is the Central Bank of Korea (*governor*, Chong Song Taek).

Weights and Measures. While the metric system is in force traditional measures are in frequent use. The *jungbo* = 1 ha; the *ri* = 3,927 metres.

ENERGY AND NATURAL RESOURCES

Electricity. There are 3 thermal power stations and 4 hydro-electric plants. A nuclear power plant is being built. Output in 1993 was 21,100m. kWh. Installed capacity was 7·1m. kW in 1993. Hydro-electric potential exceeds 8m. kW. A hydro-electric plant and dam under construction on the Pukhan near Mount Kumgang has been denounced as a flood threat by the South Koreans, who constructed a defensive 'Peace Dam' in retaliation.

Oil. Oilwells went into production in 1957. An oil pipeline from China came on stream in 1976. Crude oil refining capacity was 70,000 bbls. a day in 1990.

Minerals. North Korea is rich in minerals. Estimated reserves in tonnes: Iron ore, 3,300m.; copper, 2·15m.; lead, 6m.; zinc, 12m.; coal, 11,990m.; uranium, 26m.; manganese, 6,500m. 27·1m. tonnes of coal were mined in 1993, 8m. tonnes of iron ore and 15,000 tonnes of copper ore in 1986. 1986 production of gold was 160,000 fine troy oz; silver, 1·6m. fine troy oz; salt, 570,000 tonnes.

Agriculture. In 1992 there were 1·71m. ha. of arable land, 305,000 ha of permanent crop land and 50,000 ha of pasture. In 1991 there were 0.68m. ha of paddy fields. In 1992, 7·14m. persons subsisted on agriculture.

Collectivization took place between 1954 and 1958. 90% of the cultivated land is farmed by co-operatives. Land belongs either to the State or to co-operatives, and it is intended gradually to transform the latter into the former, but small individually-tended plots producing for 'farmers' markets' are tolerated as a 'transition measure'. Livestock farming is mainly carried on by large state farms.

There is a large-scale tideland reclamation project. In 1992 1·46m. ha were under irrigation, making possible 2 rice harvests a year. In 1992 there were 75,000 tractors. The technical revolution in agriculture (nearly 95% of ploughing, etc., is mechanized) has considerably increased the yield of wheat (sown on 90,000 ha). Production (1993, in 1,000 tonnes): Wheat, 100; rice, 2,940; maize, 1,960; potatoes, 1,750; soya beans, 380.

Livestock, 1993: Cattle, 1·3m.; pigs, 3·3m.; sheep, 0·39m.; goats, 0·3m.; 22m. poultry.

Forestry. Forest area in 1991 was 6,468,000 ha. 4·6m. cu metres of timber were cut in 1986.

Fisheries. Catch in 1993, 1·09m. tonnes. There is a fishing fleet of 30,600 vessels including 20,000 motor vessels.

INDUSTRY. Industries were intensively developed by the Japanese occupiers, notably cotton spinning, hydro-electric power, cotton, silk and rayon weaving, and chemical fertilizers. Production in 1986: Cement, 9m. tonnes; textiles, 600m. metres; motor-cars (1993), 10,000; TV sets, 240,000; ships, 50,000 GRT. Annual steel production capacity was 4·3m. tonnes in 1987.

Labour. The economically-active population was 10·08m. in 1991. Industrial workers make up some 60% of the work force.

FOREIGN ECONOMIC RELATIONS. Joint ventures with foreign firms have been permitted since 1984. A law of Oct. 1992 revised the 1984 rules: Foreign investors may now set up wholly-owned facilities in special economic zones, repatriate part of profits and enjoy tax concessions. Economic zones have been set up at the ports of Sonbong and Najin. In 1990 foreign debt was estimated at US$4,500m. (of which US$3,800m. were to the USSR). The USA imposed sanctions in Jan. 1988 for alleged terrorist activities. Since June 1995 South Korean businesses and individuals have been permitted to make investments and set up branch offices in North Korea. South Korea donated 0·15m. tonnes of rice to North Korea in 1995.

Commerce. Exports in 1994 were US$840m.; imports, US$1,270m. In 1992 China was the biggest trade partner (total trade US$620m.), followed by Japan, CIS and Iran. The chief exports are metal ores and products, the chief imports machinery and petroleum products.

Total trade between North Korea and UK (British Department of Trade returns, in £1,000 sterling):

	1991	*1992*	*1993*	*1994*	*1995*
Imports to UK	349	334	249	158	173
Exports and re-exports from UK	5,503	7,426	5,928	23,134	22,266

Tourism. A 40-year ban on non-Communist tourists was lifted in 1986.

COMMUNICATIONS

Roads. There were 23,219 km of road in 1993, including 240 km of motorways. There were 248,000 motor cars in 1990.

Railways. In 1990 the railway network totalled 8,533 km of which 3,250 km were electrified. In 1990 38·5m. tonnes of freight and 35m. passengers were carried.

There is a metro in Pyongyang.

Civil Aviation. The national carrier is Air Koryo which had 25 ex-Soviet aircraft in 1995 and flew services to Moscow, Khabarovsk, Beijing, Tokyo and Hong Kong. There are domestic flights from Pyongyang to Hamhung and Chongjin.

Shipping. The leading ports are Chongjin, Wonsan and Hungnam. Pyongyang is connected to the port of Nampo by railway and river. In 1995 the ocean-going merchant fleet totalled 1·08m. GRT, including oil tankers, 0·23m. GRT.

The biggest navigable river is the Yalu, 698 km up to the Hyesan district.

Telecommunications. In 1993 the provision of telephones was 3.5 per 100 inhabitants. An agreement to share in Japan's telecommunications satellites was reached in Sept. 1990. The government-controlled Korean Central Broadcasting Station and Korean Central Television Station are responsible for radio and TV broadcasting. In 1991 there were 34 radio and 11 TV stations (colour by PAL). There were 4·7m. radio and 2m. TV sets in 1993.

Cinemas. There were 1,778 cinemas in 1985 and 3,515 mobile cinemas.

Press. There were 3 national and 12 local newspapers in 1994. The party newspaper is *Nodong* (or *Rodong*) *Sinmun* (Workers' Daily News). Circulation about 600,000.

SOCIAL INSTITUTIONS

Justice. The judiciary consists of the Supreme Court, whose judges are elected by the Assembly for 3 years; provincial courts; and city or county people's courts. The procurator-general, appointed by the Assembly, has supervisory powers over the judiciary and the administration; the Supreme Court controls the judicial administration.

Religion. The Constitution provides for 'freedom of religion as well as the freedom of anti-religious propaganda'. In 1986 there were 3m. Chondoists, 400,000 Buddhists and 200,000 Christians. Another 3m. followed traditional beliefs.

Education. Free compulsory universal technical education lasts 11 years: 1 preschool year, 4 years primary education starting at the age of 6, followed by 6 years secondary. In 1994-95 there were 37 universities, 32 specialized universities (agriculture, 2; chemical industry; cinema; coal mining; construction; economics, 2; education, 5; fine arts; foreign studies; geology; hydraulics and dynamics; light industry; mechanical engineering; medicine; mining and metallurgy; music and dance; pharmacy; physical education; printing; railways; science; sea transport; technology, 2; veterinary science) and 108 specialized colleges.

Health. Medical treatment is free. In 1982 there were 1,531 general hospitals, 979 specialized hospitals and 5,414 clinics. The doctor/inhabitant ratio was 1:370 in 1993.

DIPLOMATIC REPRESENTATIVE

Of North Korea to the United Nations
Ambassador: Pak Gil Yon.

Further Reading

North Korea Directory. Tokyo, annual since 1988
Kihl, Y. W., *Politics and Policies in Divided Korea.* Boulder, 1984
Park, J. K. and Kim, J.-G., *The Politics of North Korea.* Boulder (CO), 1979
Scalapino, R. A. and Lee, C.-S., *Communism in Korea.* Univ. of California Press, 1972—and Kim, J-Y. (eds.), *North Korea Today: Strategic and Domestic Issues.* Univ. of California Press, 1983
Suh, D.-S., *Korean Communism, 1945–1980: A Reference Guide to the Political System.* Honolulu, 1981

National statistical office: Central Statistics Bureau, Pyongyang.

KUWAIT

Dowlat al Kuwait

(State of Kuwait)

Capital: Kuwait
Population: 1·59m. (1995)
GNP per capita: US$19,040 (1994)
HDI/world rank: 0·821/61 (1992)

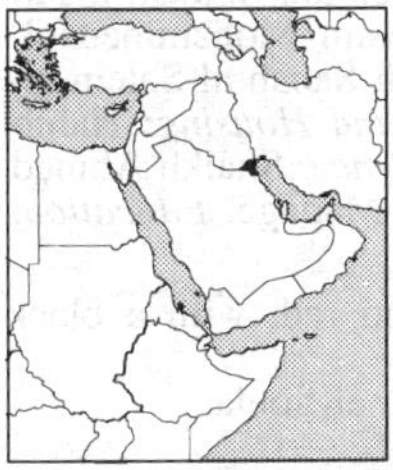

KEY HISTORICAL EVENTS. Agreements of 1899 and 1914 placed Kuwait under British protection, but the UK recognized its independence in 1961.

Early on 2 Aug. 1990 Iraqi forces without warning invaded and rapidly overran the country, meeting little resistance, and President Saddam of Iraq declared the annexation of Kuwait on 8 Aug. Following the expiry of the date required by the UN for the withdrawal of Iraqi forces on 15 Jan. 1991, an air offensive was launched by coalition forces against targets in Kuwait, followed by a land attack on 24 Feb. Iraqi forces were routed, and Kuwait City was liberated on 26 Feb. Iraq withdrew all its forces from Kuwait.

On 10 Nov. 1994 Iraq recognized the independence and boundaries of Kuwait.

TERRITORY AND POPULATION. Kuwait is bounded in the east by the Arabian (Persian) Gulf, north and west by Iraq and south and south-west by Saudi Arabia, with an area of 17,818 sq. km. In 1992-93 the UN Boundary Commission redefined Kuwait's border with Iraq, moving it slightly northwards in conformity with an agreement of 1932. The population at the census of 1995 was 1,590,013 (96% urban), of whom about 56% were non-Kuwaitis. Population density, 80 per sq. km. Life expectancy was 74·6 years in 1992.

Following the Iraqi occupation of 1990-91, the government announced plans to reduce its population to about 1m. to ensure that Kuwaitis formed a majority at about 0·55m. Many foreign workers who fled during the occupation would not be permitted to return.

The country is divided into 5 governorates: The capital (comprising Kuwait City, Kuwait's 9 islands and territorial and shared territorial waters) (population 237,892, 1993 estimate); Hawalli (386,953); Ahmadi (266,433); Jahra (178,688) and Farwaniya (363,255).

The chief cities are (1993 population estimate) Kuwait, the capital (31,241), and its suburbs Hawalli (84,478), as-Salimiya (116,104), Jahra (139,476) and Farwaniya (47,106).

The Neutral Zone (Kuwait's share, 2,590 sq. km), jointly owned and administered by Kuwait and Saudi Arabia from 1922 to 1966, was partitioned between the two countries in May 1966, but the exploitation of the oil and other natural resources continues to be shared.

Over 78% speak Arabic, the official language. English is also used as a second language.

CLIMATE. Kuwait has a dry, desert climate which is cool in winter but very hot and humid in summer. Rainfall is extremely light. Kuwait. Jan. 56°F (13·5°C), July 99°F (36·6°C). Annual rainfall 5" (125 mm).

RULER. HH Shaikh Jaber al-Ahmed al-Jaber al-Sabah the 13th Amir of Kuwait, succeeded on 31 Dec. 1977.

CONSTITUTION AND GOVERNMENT. In 1990 the *National Council* was established, consisting of 50 elected members and 25 appointed by the Amir. The franchise, limited to men over 21 whose families have been of Kuwaiti nationality since before 1920, produced an electorate of 62,000. Executive authority is vested in the Council of Ministers. At the elections of 5 Oct. 1992 the electorate was 81,440. There were 278 candidates. Turn-out was 86%.

A 16-member cabinet was formed in Oct. 1992 of whom 6 were elected National Council deputies. In Nov. 1995 the Cabinet comprised:

Prime Minister: HRH Crown Prince Shaikh Saad al-Abdullah al-Salim al-Sabah.

Deputy Prime Minister, Foreign Affairs: Shaikh Sabah al-Ahmed al-Jaber al-Sabah. *Second Deputy Prime Minister, Finance:* Nassar al-Rhodan. *Minister of Cabinet Affairs and Planning:* Abdulaziz al-Dekeel. *Commerce and Industry:* Ali Hilal al-Mutairi. *Communications, Electricity and Water:* Jasim Mohammed al-Aoun. *Health:* Abdel-Rahman Saleh al-Muheilan. *Interior:* Ali Sabah al-Salem al-Sabah. *Islamic Affairs:* Ali Fahd al-Zumeih. *Public Works and Housing:* Habib Jawhar al-Hayat. *Social Affairs:* Ahmed Khalid al-Kulard. *Defence:* Shaikh Ahmed al-Hamoud. *Justice:* Meshari al-Anjeri. *Oil:* Abdulmohsen al-Madage. *Education:* Ahmed al-Rubai. *Information:* Shaikh Soud Nassar al-Sabah.

National flag: Three horizontal stripes of green, white and red, with a black trapezium based on the hoist.

National anthem: There are no words, tune by Ibrahim Nassar al-Soula.

DEFENCE. In Sept. 1991 the USA signed a 10-year agreement with Kuwait to store equipment, use ports and carry out joint training exercises. In Feb. 1992 the UK signed an agreement with Kuwait to provide advisers and equipment. Conscription is for 2 years.

Army. The army consists of 2 mechanized, 2 armoured, 1 reserve; 1 engineer and 1 artillery brigade, 1 commando battalion and the Amiri Guard brigade . Equipment includes 150 M-84, 50 M-1A2 and 20 Chieftain main battle tanks. Strength (1996) about 10,000.

Navy. 2 German-built fast missile craft survived the 1991 war, together with 1 logistic support craft, and have now been supplemented by 4 Australian-built in-shore patrol craft and some 50 boats operated by the Coast Guard. Personnel in 1995 numbered 2,500.

Air Force. From a small initial combat force the Air Force has grown rapidly, although it suffered heavy losses after the Iraqi invasion of 1990–91. It has 2 squadrons with 40 F/A-18 Hornet strike aircraft and 1 squadron of Mirage F-1 interceptors. Other equipment includes 1 DC-9 and 1 MD-83 jet transport, 3 L-100-30 Hercules turboprop transports and 12 Hawk jet trainers, 9 Puma, 3 Exocet missile-armed Super Puma and 16 missile-armed Gazelle helicopters. 16 Tucano aircraft are in use. Hawk surface-to-air missiles are in service. Personnel strength (1995) 2,500, with 76 combat aircraft and 16 armed helicopters.

INTERNATIONAL RELATIONS

Membership. Kuwait is a member of the UN, Arab League, Gulf Co-operation Council and OPEC.

ECONOMY

Policy. The 4-year reconstruction and development plan covers 1995-2000.

Budget. The fiscal year begins on 1 July. At the 1995-96 budget revenue was KD 2,637·2m. (of which KD 2,234·9m. were oil revenue) and expenditure KD 4,327·7m.

Currency. The unit of currency is the *Kuwaiti dinar* (KWD) of 1,000 *fils*. There are coins of 1, 5, 10, 20, 50 and 100 fils and notes of KD 20, 10, 5, 1, ½ and ¼. In 1994 KD 365·3m. were in circulation. Foreign exchange reserves were US$3,892m. in June 1995; gold reserves were US$730·1m. In March 1996, £1 = KD 0·457; US$1 = KD 0·299; DM1 = KD 0·203.

Banking and Finance. The *Governor* of the Central Bank is Shaikh Salem Abdel-Aziz al-Sabah. There is also the Kuwait Finance House. In 1995 there were 8 local banks. Total assets of commercial banks as at 31 Dec. 1994 were KD 8,671·9m.; private deposits were KD 5,562m., of which KD 582m. were in savings accounts.

There is a stock exchange.

Weights and Measures. The metric system is in force.

ENERGY AND NATURAL RESOURCES

Electricity. There are 4 power stations with a total installed capacity of 6,898 MW in 1994. 20,173m. kWh were produced in 1993.

Oil and Gas. Estimated crude oil production in 1995, 2,029,000 bbls. a day. Gas production was 5,170m. cu. metres in 1993.

Water. The country depends upon desalination plants. In 1993 there were 4 plants with a daily total capacity of 216m. gallons. Fresh mineral water is pumped and bottled at Rawdhatain. Underground brackish water is used for irrigation, street cleaning and livestock. Production, 1993, 68,379m. gallons (46,409m. gallons fresh, 21,970m. gallons brackish).

Agriculture. In 1992 there were 5,000 ha of arable land, and 137,000 ha of permanent pasture. Production of main crops, 1993 (in tonnes): Melons, 4.000; tomatoes, 35,000; onions, 16,000; dates, 1,000.

Livestock (1993): Cattle, 12,000; sheep, 150,000; goats, 15,000; camels, 1,000; poultry, 10m. Milk production (1993) 15,000 tonnes.

Fisheries. Shrimp fishing was important, but has declined since the 1990-91 war through oil pollution of coastal waters. Pearl fishing is now on a small scale.

INDUSTRY. Industries, apart from oil, include boat building, fishing, food production, petrochemicals, gases and construction.

Labour. In 1994 the labour force totalled 990,518 (including 824,658 non-Kuwaitis) distributed by sector as follows: Social services, 469,645 (non-Kuwaitis, 333,743); commerce and catering, 184,284 (181,371); building, 128,813 (128,171); industry, 70,659 (64,979); transport and communications, 38,706 (33,939); finance and business, 35,341 (30,297); agriculture and fishing, 15,985 (15,939); mining, 7,017 (3,615); public utilities, 7,017 (3,383); others, 33,051 (29,221). There were 6,473 registered unemployed in 1994.

Trade Unions. In 1986 there were 16 trade unions and 17 labour federations.

FOREIGN ECONOMIC RELATIONS

Commerce. Imports were valued at KD 1,988·2m. in 1994 and exports at KD 3,341·6m. (including oil exports, KD 3,112m.). The main non-oil export is chemical fertilizer.

Main export markets, 1994 (in KD 1m.): France, 36; Saudi Arabia, 33·31;UAE,31·64; India, 30·93. Main import suppliers: USA, 289·1; Japan, 233·1; Germany, 163·5; UK, 138; France, 126·2.

Total trade between Kuwait and UK (British Department of Trade returns, in £1,000 sterling):

	1991	*1992*	*1993*	*1994*	*1995*
Imports to UK	29,386	127,226	236,480	239,359	151,377
Exports and re-exports from UK	178,248	262,288	311,669	312,037	550,870

COMMUNICATIONS

Roads. In 1989 there were 4,741 km of roads. Number of vehicles (1994) was 747,000. There were 15,921 road accidents in 1993 with 290 fatalities.

Civil Aviation. There is an international airport. The national carrier is the state-owned Kuwait Airways, which operated 5 A300B4-600Rs, 1 A300C4-600, 3 A310-300s, 3 A320-200s, 2 A340-300s, 2 B-707-320Cs, 4 B-747-200B Combis, and 1 B-747-400 combi in 1995. Services are also provided by Aeroflot, Air China, Air France, Air India, Air Lanka, Alitalia, Balkan, Biman Bangladesh, British Airways, Czech Airlines, Egyptair, Emirates, Gulf Air, Indian Airlines, Iran Air, KLM, Lufthansa, Middle East Airlines, Northwest Airlines, Olympic Airways, Oman Air, Pakistan Airlines, Qatar Airways, Saudia, Syrian Airlines, Tarom, Turkish Airlines, United Airlines and Zas.

Shipping. The port of Kuwait formerly served mainly as an entrepôt, but this function is declining in importance with the development of the oil industry. The largest oil terminal is at Mina Ahmade. 3 small oil ports lie to the south of Mina Ahmadi: Mina Shuaiba, Mina Abdullah and Mina Al-Zor. The main ports for other traffic are at Shuwaikh, Shuiaba and Doha. The merchant fleet totalled 7,783,000 GRT in 1990, of which 593,000 GRT were tankers.

Telecommunications. There were (1991), 548,000 telephones. The government-controlled Radio Kuwait and Kuwait Television broadcast a main and a second radio programme, a Koran programme and a service in English and 2 TV programmes (colour by PAL). In 1993 there were 0·8m. TV receivers and 1m. radios.

Cinemas. In 1989 there were 14 cinemas, including 2 drive-ins.

Press. In 1993 there were 5 daily newspapers in Arabic and 2 in English, with a combined circulation of about 418,000. Formal press censorship was lifted in Jan. 1992.

SOCIAL INSTITUTIONS

Justice. In 1960 Kuwait adopted a unified judicial system covering all levels of courts. These are: Courts of Summary Justice, Courts of the First Instance, Supreme Court of Appeal, Court of Cassation, Constitutional Court and State Security Court. Islamic Sharia is a major source of legislation. The death penalty was imposed for drug smuggling in April 1995.

Religion. In 1995 about 80% of the population were Sunni Moslems, 15% Shia Moslems, 6% Christians and 3% others.

Education. Education is free and compulsory from 6 to 14 years. In 1992–93 there were 46,601 pupils in kindergartens, 121,597 in primary schools, 125,891 in intermediate schools and 73,631 in secondary schools. In 1992 there were 1,103 students in the Religious Institute and 1,516 in special training institutes. The University of Kuwait had 12,500 students and 960 academic staff in 1994–95.

Health. Medical services are free to all residents. There were (1989) 16 hospitals and sanatoria with 6,104 beds, 88 clinics and 25 health centres. In 1989 there were 2,641 doctors, 320 dentists and 7,977 nursing staff.

DIPLOMATIC REPRESENTATIVES

Of Kuwait in Great Britain (45–46 Queen's Gate, London, SW7)
Ambassador: Khaled al-Duwaisan.

Of Great Britain in Kuwait (Arabian Gulf St., Kuwait)
Ambassador: W. H. Fullerton, CMG.

Of Kuwait in the USA (2940 Tilden St., NW, Washington, D.C., 20008)
Ambassador: Dr M. Sabah al-Salem al-Sabah.

Of the USA in Kuwait (PO Box 77, Safat, Kuwait)
Ambassador: Ryan C. Crocker.

Of Kuwait to the United Nations
Ambassador: Mohammad A. Abulhasan.

Further Reading

Al-Yahya, M.A., *Kuwait: Fall and Rebirth.* London, 1993
Clements, F. A., *Kuwait.* [Bibliography] Oxford and Santa Barbara, 1985
Crystal, J., *Kuwait: the Transformation of an Oil State.* Boulder (Colo.), 1992
Finnie, D. H., *Shifting Lines in the Sand: Kuwait's Elusive Frontier with Iraq.* London, 1992

KYRGYZSTAN

Kyrgyz Respublikasy

Capital: Bishkek
Population: 4·46m. (1994)
GNP per capita: US$610 (1994)
HDI/world rank: 0·717/89 (1992)

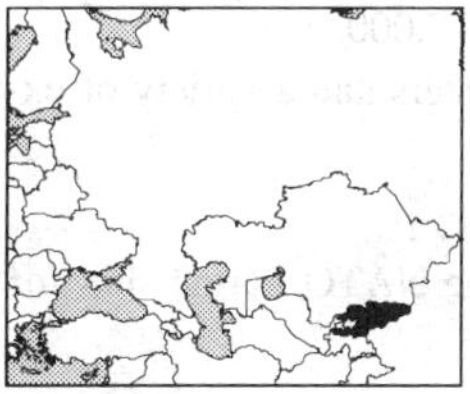

KEY HISTORICAL EVENTS. After the establishment of the Soviet regime in Russia, Kyrgyzstan became part of Soviet Turkestan, which itself became an Autonomous Soviet Socialist Republic within the RSFSR in April 1921. In 1924, when Central Asia was reorganized territorially on a national basis, Kyrgyzstan was separated from Turkestan and formed into an autonomous region within the RSFSR. On 1 Feb. 1926 the Government of the RSFSR transformed Kyrgyzstan into an Autonomous Soviet Socialist Republic within the RSFSR, and finally in Dec. 1936 Kyrgyzstan was proclaimed one of the constituent Soviet Socialist Republics of the USSR. The republic adopted a declaration of sovereignty in 1990 and then in Sept. 1991 it declared itself an independent, sovereign and democratic state.

It became a member of the CIS in Dec. 1991.

TERRITORY AND POPULATION. Kyrgyzstan is situated on the Tien-Shan mountains and bordered in the east by China, west by Kazakhstan and Uzbekistan, north by Kazakhstan and south by Tajikistan. Area, 199,900 sq. km (77,180 sq. miles). Population (estimate, Jan. 1994), 4,463,000 (50·7% female; 35·6% urban). Vital statistics rates, 1993 (per 1,000 population): Births, 26·1; deaths, 7·7; natural increase, 18·4; infant mortality (per 1,000 live births), 31·9 in 1992.

The republic comprises 6 provinces: Djalal-Abad, Issyk-Kul, Naryn, Osh, Talas and Chu. There are 18 towns, 31 urban settlements and 40 rural districts. Its capital is Bishkek (formerly Frunze; 1991 population estimate, 641,400). Other large towns are Osh (238,200), Djalal-Abad (74,200), Tokmak (71,200), Przhevalsk (64,300) and Kyzyl-Kiya.

The Kyrgyz are of Turkic origin and form 52·4% of the 1989 census population of 4,257,755; the rest include Russians (21·5%), Uzbeks (12·9%), Ukrainians (2·5%), Germans, (2·4%) and Tatars (1·6%).

The official language is Kyrgyz, and also Russian in provinces where Russians are in a majority. The Roman alphabet (in use 1928–40) was re-introduced in 1992.

CONSTITUTION AND GOVERNMENT. A new Constitution was adopted on 5 May 1993. The Presidency is executive, and directly elected for renewable 5-year terms. At a referendum on 30 Jan. 1994, 96% of votes cast favoured President Akaev's serving out the rest of his term of office; turn-out was 95%. At a referendum on 22–23 Oct. 1994 turn-out was 87%. 75% of votes cast were in favour of instituting referendums as a constitutional mechanism, and 73% were in favour of establishing a new bicameral parliament, with a 35-member directly-elected legislature, and a 70-member upper house elected on a regional basis and meeting twice a year. Elections were held in 2 rounds on 5 and 19 Feb. 1995. 94·5% of votes cast at a referendum on 10 Feb. 1996 were in favour of giving the President the right to appoint all ministers except the Prime Minister without reference to parliament.

Presidential elections were held on 24 Dec. 1995. President Akaev was re-elected by 71·6% of votes cast against 2 opponents. Turn-out was 82%.

President: Askar Akaev (b. 1945).

The government resigned on 26 Feb. 1996.

National flag: A red field in the proportions 3:5 charged with a gold sun of 40 wavy rays, in the centre of which is a yurt (tent) crossed by 2 sets of curved lines.

Local Government. Elections were held on 25 Feb. 1990. The appointment of leaders of local councils is approved or vetoed by the President of the Republic.

DEFENCE. Conscription is for 18 months.

Army. The Army consists of 1 motor rifle division and 1 mountain brigade. Equipment includes 204 T-72 main battle tanks. Personnel, 1996, 7,000.

Air Force. There is an aviation element with Mig-21 fighters and a variety of ex-Soviet equipment, including L-29 and L-39 trainers.

INTERNATIONAL RELATIONS

Membership. Kyrgyzstan is a member of the UN and the NATO Partnership for Peace.

ECONOMY

Budget. Budgetary income in 1993 was 1,288,100m. som; expenditure was 1,255,600m. som.

Currency. On 10 May 1993 Kyrgyzstan introduced its own currency unit, the *som* (KGS), of 100 *tyiyn*, at a rate of 1 som = 200 rubles. There are notes of 50 tyiyn, and 1, 5, 10 and 20 som. Inflation was 0·7% in Sept. 1994.

Banking and Finance. The *Governor* of the central bank is Kemil Nanaev.

ENERGY AND NATURAL RESOURCES

Electricity. Output was 11,100m. kWh in 1993.

Minerals. In 1993, 1·7m. tonnes of coal were produced.

Oil and Gas. Output of oil (including gas concentrate), 1993, 0·1m. tonnes; natural gas, 40m. cu. metres.

Agriculture. Kyrgyzstan is famed for its livestock breeding. On 1 Jan. 1994 there were 1·1m. cattle, 0·2m. pigs and 7·3m. sheep and goats. Yaks are bred as meat and dairy cattle, and graze on high altitudes unsuitable for other cattle. Crossed with domestic cattle, hybrids give twice the yield of milk. The small Kyrgyz horse is famed.

Area under cultivation (1993), 16m. ha, of which private subsidiary agriculture accounted for 0·15m. ha and commercial farming 3·3m. ha in 12,800 farms. Private and commercial agriculture accounted for 46% of output by value in 1993. Total output was valued at 2,400m. rubles (in constant 1983 prices) in 1993, 92% of the 1992 figure.

Kyrgyzstan raises wheat sufficient for its own use and other grains and fodder, particularly lucerne; also sugar-beet, hemp, kenaf, kendyr, tobacco, medicinal plants and rice. Sericulture, fruit, grapes and vegetables and bee-keeping are major branches.

Output of main agricultural products (in 1,000 tonnes) in 1993: Grain, 1,606; cotton, 42; sugar-beet, 207; potatoes, 291; vegetables, 249; fruit and berries, 45; meat, 237; milk, 920; and 400m. eggs.

INDUSTRY. Industrial enterprises include sugar refineries, tanneries, cotton and wool-cleansing works, flour-mills, a tobacco factory, food, timber, textile, engineering, metallurgical, oil and mining enterprises. Output was valued at 3,300m. som in current prices in 1993, 75·8% of the 1992 figure.

Production, 1993: Cement, 0·7m. tonnes; fabrics, 89·1m. sq. metres; footwear, 3·5m. pairs; 300 lathes; 5,000 lorries; 1,700 TV sets; 76,800 washing machines.

Labour. In 1993 the population of working age was 2·3m., of whom 1·7m. were employed, 54·1% in the state sector, 28·5% in the private sector and 14·6% in co-operatives. In Jan. 1994 there were 2,900 registered unemployed (0·2% of the labour force), of whom 1,700 were receiving benefits. Average monthly salaries in 1993 were 85·90 som.

FOREIGN ECONOMIC RELATIONS. In Jan. 1994 an agreement to create a single economic zone was signed with Kazakhstan and Uzbekistan.

Commerce. In 1993 imports were valued at US$112m. and exports at US$112·1m. Total trade between Kyrgyzstan and UK (British Department of Trade returns, in £1,000 sterling):

	1993	*1994*	*1995*
Imports to UK	331	2,600	846
Exports and re-exports from UK	7,629	6,729	4,086

COMMUNICATIONS

Roads. There were 28,400 km of motor roads (22,400 km hard surface) in 1990. In 1993, 219·5m. passengers and 14·6m. tonnes of freight were carried.

Railways. In the north a railway runs from Lugovaya through Bishkek to Rybachi on Lake Issyk-Kul. Towns in the southern valleys are linked by short lines with the Ursatyevskaya–Andizhan railway in Uzbekistan. Total length of railway (Jan. 1990) is 370 km. In 1993, 2·3m. passengers and 3·3m. tonnes of freight were carried.

Civil Aviation. There is an international airport at Bishkek Manas. The national carrier is Kyrgyzstan Airlines. Services are also provided by Azerbaijan Hava Yollery, Siberia Airlines and Uzbekistan Airways. In 1993, 0·3m. passengers and 800 tonnes of freight were carried.

Inland Waterways. Total length was 600 km in 1990. In 1993, 0·1m. tonnes of freight were carried.

Telecommunications. Kyrgyz Radio and Kyrgyz Television are state-controlled. There are 2 national radio programmes, with some broadcasting in English and German. There is 1 commercial radio station. In 1993 there were 3 hours of TV broadcasting a day (colour by SECAM).

Press (1989). Of 122 newspapers with a daily 1·6m. circulation, 41 with 819,000 circulation were in the Kyrgyz language.

SOCIAL INSTITUTIONS

Religion. In 1996, 70% of the population was Sunni Moslem. There were some 1,000 mosques, 30 Russian Orthodox , 17 Evangelical, 9 Seventh Day Adventist and 8 Lutheran, churches.

Education. In 1993–94 there were 1,900 primary and secondary schools with 938,000 pupils; 13% of eligible children were attending pre-school institutions. There were also 21 higher educational institutions with 52,300 students, 51 technical and teachers' training colleges with 38,700 students, as well as music and art schools. Kyrgyz University had 7,300 students in 1994–95.

Health. In Jan. 1994 there were 14,800 doctors, 42,600 junior medical personnel and 348 hospitals with 48,900 beds.

Welfare. In Jan. 1994 there were 443,000 age and 196,000 other pensioners.

DIPLOMATIC REPRESENTATIVES

Of Great Britain in Kyrgyzstan
Ambassador: Douglas McAdam (resides in Almaty).

Of Kyrgyzstan in the USA
Ambassador: Almas Chukin.

Of the USA in Kyrgyzstan (66 Erkindik Prospekt, Bishkek 720002)
Ambassador: Eileen A. Molloy.

Of Kyrgyzstan to the United Nations
Ambassador: Vacant.

LAOS

Saathiaranarath Prachhathipatay Prachhachhon Lao

(Lao People's Democratic Republic)

Capital: Vientiane
Population: 4·6m. (1993)
GNP per capita: US$320 (1994)
HDI/world rank: 0·420/138 (1992)

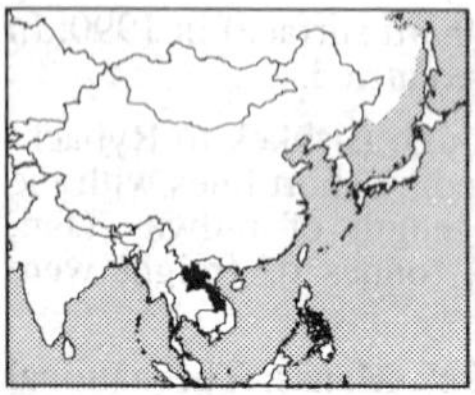

KEY HISTORICAL EVENTS. In 1893 Laos became a French protectorate and in 1907 acquired its present frontiers. On 9 March 1945 Vichy French authority was suppressed by the Japanese. When the Japanese withdrew later in 1945 an independence movement known as Lao Issara (Free Laos) established a government under Prince Phetsarath, the Viceroy of Luang Prabang. This government collapsed with the return of the French in 1946 and the leaders of the movement fled to Thailand.

Under a new Constitution of 1947 Laos became a constitutional monarchy under the Luang Prabang dynasty, and in 1949 became an independent sovereign state within the French Union. Most of the Lao Issara leaders returned to Laos but a few remained in dissidence under Prince Souphanouvong, who allied himself with the Vietminh and subsequently formed the 'Pathet Lao' (Lao State) rebel movement.

The war in Laos which began in 1953 between the Royal Lao Government (supported by the USA) and the Pathet Lao (supported by North Vietnam) ended in 1973 when an agreement was signed. A provisional coalition government was formed by the two sides in 1974. However, after the communist victories in Vietnam and Cambodia in April 1975, the Pathet Lao took over the running of the whole country, although maintaining the façade of a coalition. On 29 Nov. 1975 King Savang Vatthana abdicated and a 264-member People's Congress proclaimed a People's Democratic Republic of Laos on 2 Dec. For the history of *Pathet Lao* and the military intervention of the Vietminh, *see* THE STATESMAN'S YEAR-BOOK, 1971–72, pp. 1126–28 and 1975–76, pp. 1115–16.

TERRITORY AND POPULATION. Laos is a landlocked country of about 91,400 sq. miles (236,800 sq. km) bordered on the north by China, the east by Vietnam, the south by Cambodia and the west by Thailand and Burma. Apart from the Mekong River plains along the border of Thailand, the country is mountainous, particularly in the north, and in places densely forested.

The population (census, 1985) was 3,722,000 (1,824,000 male); estimate (1993) 4,598,000 (18·6% urban). Growth rate (1993), 3·16%. Population density, 19·4 per sq. km. Infant mortality was 97 per 1,000 live births in 1993. Expectation of life was 49·5 years for males and 52·5 years for females.

There are 17 provinces. Area, population and administrative centres in 1988:

Province	*Sq. km*	*Population (in 1,000)*	*Administrative centre*
Vientiane (town)	3,920	416	
Vientiane	19,990	293	–
Phongsaly	16,270	134	Phongsaly
Luang Nam Tha	9,325	107	Luang Nam Tha
Oudomsai	21,190	275	Ban Nahin
Bokeo	4,970	60	Ban Honei Sai
Luang Prabang	16,875	323	Luang Prabang
Houaphan	16,500	230	Sam Neua
Sayaboury	11,795	174	Sayaboury
Xiang Khouang	17,315	178	Xiang Khouang
Bolikhamsai	16,470	135	Paksane
Khammouane	16,315	235	Thakhek

Province	*Sq. km*	*Population (in 1,000)*	*Administrative centre*
Savannakhet	22,080	603	Savannakhet
Saravane	10,385	202	Saravane
Sekong	7,665	56	Sekong
Champassak	15,415	443	Pakse
Attopei	10,320	76	Attopei

The capital and largest town is Vientiane, with a population of (census 1985) 377,409. Other important towns are Savannakhet, 96,652; Luang Prabang, 68,399; Pakse, 47,323.

The population is divided into 3 groups: about 67% Lao-Lum (Valley-Lao), 17% Lao-Theung (Lao of the mountain sides); and 5% Lao-Soung (Lao of the mountain tops), who comprise the Meo and Yao. Lao is the official language. French and English are spoken.

CLIMATE. A tropical monsoon climate, with high temperatures throughout the year and very heavy rains from May to Oct. Vientiane. Jan. 70°F (21·1°C), July 81°F (27·2°C). Annual rainfall 69" (1,715 mm).

CONSTITUTION AND GOVERNMENT. On 14 Aug. 1991 the National Assembly adopted a new constitution.

Under the constitution the Lao People's Revolutionary Party (LPRP) remains the 'central nucleus ' of the 'people's democracy'; other parties are not permitted. The LPRP's Politburo comprises 11 members, including Gen. Khamtay Siphandon (*LPRP President*), Kamphoui Keobouaplapha, Thongsing Thamavong.

President: Nouhak Phoumsavan (elected by the National Assembly, 22 Feb. 1993).

In Dec. 1995 the government consisted of:

Prime Minister: Gen. Khamtay Siphandon (b. 1923).

Deputy Prime Minister: Khamphoui Keoboualapha *(President of the State Committee for Planning and Co-operation). Deputy Prime Minister:* Phoun Sipaseut. *Defence and Supreme Commander of the Army:* Lieut.-Gen. Choummali Saignason. *Head of the Office of the Council of Ministers:* Khamsai Souphanouvong. *Foreign:* Somsavat Lengsavath. *Interior:* Asang Laoli. *Finance:* Saysomphone Phonvihane. *Justice:* Khamyon Boupha. *Health:* Vannareth Rasaphe. *Agriculture:* Sisavat Keobounphan. *Industry and Handicraft:* Soulivong Daravong. *Communications, Transport, Posts and Building:* Phao Bounnaphon. *Education and Sport:* Phimmasone. *Foreign Economic Relations:* Sompadith Vorasane. *Information and Culture:* Osakan Thammatheva. *Labour and Social Affairs:* Thongloun Sisoulit. *Governor of the State Bank:* Butxabong Souvannavong. *Head of the President's Office:* Thongdam Chanthapon.

The *Speaker* is Samane Vignaket.

National flag: Three horizontal stripes of red, blue, red, with blue of double width with in the centre a large white disc.

National anthem: 'Xatlao tangtae dayma lao thookthuana nentxoo sootchay' ('For the whole of time the Lao people have glorified their Fatherland'); words by Sisana Sisane, tune by Thongdy Sounthonevichit.

Provincial Administration: All provincial administration is in the hands of the Lao People's Revolutionary Party. Orders come from the Central Committee through a series of 'People's Revolutionary Committees' at the province, town and village level.

DEFENCE. Military service is compulsory for a minimum of 18 months.

Army. There are 4 military regions. The Army is organized in 5 infantry divisions; 3 engineering regiments, 7 independent infantry regiments and 65 independent infantry companies; and 5 artillery and 9 anti-aircraft battalions. Equipment includes 30 T-54/-55 main battle tanks. Strength (1996) about 33,000.

Navy. There is a riverine force of about 500 personnel (1995) organized into 4 squadrons running some 12 patrol craft, 4 landing craft and 40 smaller river patrol for operations on the Mekong.

Air Force. Since 1975, the Air Force had received aircraft from the USSR, including 40 MiG-21 fighters, 6 An-24 and 3 An-26 turboprop transports and 10 Mi-8 helicopters. They have been supplemented by Chinese-built Y-12 transports. Personnel strength, about 3,500 in 1995.

INTERNATIONAL RELATIONS

Membership. Laos is a member of the UN and an observer at ASEAN.

ECONOMY

Policy. The priorities of the second Five Year Plan, 1986–90, continued to be infrastructure projects (telecommunications and transport), agriculture (crop diversification and improving paddy production), and agro-industrial processing. In 1989, in an attempt to stimulate the economy, the Government introduced a 'New Economic Management Mechanism' introducing managerial autonomy into state enterprises and a limited increase of private sector activities. Further moves towards a free market were announced in Dec. 1990.

The third Five-Year Plan ran from 1991 to 1995. The state played a smaller role, though retaining control of water supplies, energy and communications. The constitution of Aug. 1991 affirms the right to a market economy, private property and private investment, including foreign.

Budget. In 1992 revenue was 136,167m. kip and expenditure 172,828m. kip. Revenue included 69,663m. kip raised from taxation. Current expenditure was 93,420m. kip.

Currency. The unit of currency is the *kip* (LAK). There are notes of 10, 20, 50, 100, 500 and 1,000 kip. Inflation was 6–7% in 1993. In 1991, 20,233m. kip were in circulation. Foreign exchange reserves were US$55·1m., gold US$0·6m. In March 1996, £1 = 1,406 kip; US$1 = 920 kip; DM1 = 623 kip.

Banking and Finance. The central bank and bank of issue is the State Bank (*Governor*, Butxabong Souvannavong). There were 12 commercial banks in 1993 (6 foreign). Total savings and time deposits in 1991 amounted to 4,075m. kip.

ENERGY AND NATURAL RESOURCES

Electricity. Hydro-electric resources are important. Total installed capacity (1985) was 168,000 kW. Production (1990) 870m. kWh (825m. kWh hydro-electric).

Minerals. 1991 output (in tonnes): Coal, 1,250; tin, 344; gypsum, 70,000; baryte, 4,500.

Agriculture. Agriculture accounts for 60% of GDP. In 1992 there were 78,000 ha of arable land, 25,000 ha, permanent crop land and 800,000 ha, pasture. The chief products (1993 output in 1,000 tonnes) are rice (1,251), maize (48), tobacco (3), seed-cotton (12), coffee (8) and sugar-cane (90). Opium is produced but its manufacture is controlled by the state.

Livestock (1993): Cattle, 1,010,000; buffaloes, 1,167,000; horses, 29,000; pigs, 1,559,000; goats, 144,000; poultry, 9m.

Forestry. The forests, which covered 12·7m. ha in 1990, produce valuable woods such as teak. Logging was suspended in Sept. 1991 to conserve the forest area.

INDUSTRY. Industry accounts for 14% of GDP. Industry is limited to wood-processing, textiles and light industry. Production in 1991: Corrugated iron, 1,375 sheets; barbed wire, 1,481 bundles; nails, 52 tonnes; batteries, 241,000; oxygen, 7,800 cylinders; soap powder, 600 tonnes; rubber shoes, 13,000 pairs; cigarettes, 30m. packets; cement (1990), 6,500 tonnes.

Labour. The workforce was 1,955,800 in 1990, of whom 1,545,000 worked in agriculture, forestry and fishery, 293,400 in public administration, 48,900 in trade and 37,300 in manufacturing. Unemployment was 21%.

FOREIGN ECONOMIC RELATIONS. Since 1988 foreign companies have been permitted to participate in Lao enterprises. In 1990 foreign investments amounted to US$189m., mainly in hotels and textiles. Total foreign debt was US$1,922m. in 1992.

Commerce. In 1993 imports amounted to US$275m. and exports to US$81m. The main imports in 1991 (in tonnes): Rice, 26,100; sugar, 11,000; fuel, 147,000; cotton yarn, 400; cement, 56,000; textiles, 2m. metres; 276 cars. Main exports: Coffee, 6,111; gypsum, 84; tin, 354; timber, 65,000 sq. metres; plywood boards, 650,000. Main import suppliers, 1991 (in US$1,000): Thailand, 76,622; Japan, 21,360; China, 11,154; Italy, 6,093. Main export markets: Thailand, 47,039; Germany, 9,484; France, 9,082; Japan, 4,463.

Total trade between Laos and UK (British Department of Trade returns, in £1,000 sterling):

	1991	*1992*	*1993*	*1994*	*1995*
Imports to UK	39	201	87	1,804	13,993
Exports and re-exports from UK	1,173	656	1,486	1,308	3,472

Tourism. There were 102,700 foreign visitors in 1993.

COMMUNICATIONS

Roads. In 1992 there were 14,130 km of roads (2,261 km hard-surfaced) classified as: National highways, 4,065 km; regional class 2 roads, 5,990 km; other roads, 4,074 km. In 1992 there were 20,233 cars, 11,551 lorries, 1,435 buses and 105,921 motorcycles. There were 1,820 traffic accidents with 600 fatalities. A bridge over the River Mekong, providing an important north-south link, was opened in 1994.

Railways. The Thai railway system extends to Nongkhai, on the Thai bank of the Mekong River. A 20 km-spur to Vientiane across the bridge here is proposed.

Civil Aviation. There is an international airport at Vientiane (Wattay). Air Lao provides services to Bangkok, Phnom Penh and Hanoi. It had 9 Chinese aircraft in 1995. Services are also provided by Aeroflot, Air Vietnam and Thai Airways. 115,000 passengers were carried in 1991 (28,000 on international flights) and 0·8m. tonnes of freight.

Shipping. The River Mekong and its tributaries are an important means of transport.

Telecommunications. In 1991 there were 6,600 telephones. The government-controlled National Radio of Laos broadcasts a national and 6 regional programmes and an external service (6 languages). Lao National TV transmits for 3 hours daily. There were (1993) about 425,000 radio and 32,000 television receivers.

SOCIAL INSTITUTIONS

Justice. Criminal legislation of 1990 established a system of courts and a prosecutor's office. Polygamy became an offence.

Religion. In 1992 some 2·55m. were Buddhists (Hinayana), but about a third of the population follow tribal religions.

Education. 65% literacy was claimed in 1990. In 1989–90 there were 6,435 primary schools with 563,700 pupils and 20,000 teachers, 750 secondary schools with 125,600 pupils and 10,048 teachers, 567,000 students with 8,100 teachers at vocational colleges, 7,699 students and 1,105 teachers at teacher training colleges and 3,425 students and 476 teachers at institutions of higher education; 420 secondary schools (97,000 pupils); 60 senior high schools (4,900 pupils); and 55 vocational schools (6,800 students). There is 1 teachers' training college, 1 college of education, 1 school of medicine, 1 agricultural college and an advanced school of Pali.

In 1994-95 there was 1 university of medical science, 1 institute of pedagogy and

1 national polytechnic institute, and 8 other institutes of higher education. There were 4,507 university students and 494 academic staff.

Health. In 1985 there were 551 doctors, 15 dentists and 11,650 hospital beds.

DIPLOMATIC REPRESENTATIVES

Of Laos in Great Britain (resides in Paris)
Ambassador: Vacant.

Of Great Britain in Laos
Ambassador: C. C. W. Adams, CMG (resides in Bangkok).

Of Laos in USA (2222 S. St., NW, Washington, D.C., 20008)
Ambassador: Hiem Phommachanh.

Of USA in Laos (Rue Bartholonie, Vientiane)
Ambassador: Victor L. Tomseth.

Of Laos to the United Nations
Ambassador: Alounkeo Kittikhoun.

Further Reading

Cordell, H., *Laos*. [Bibliography] Oxford and Santa Barbara, 1990
Stuart-Fox, M., *Laos: Politics, Economics and Society*. London, 1986
Zasloff, J. J., and Unger, L. (eds.) *Laos: Beyond the Revolution*. London, 1991

LATVIA

Latvijas Republika

Capital: Riga
Population: 2·51m. (1995)
GNP per capita: US$2,290 (1994)
HDI/world rank: 0·857/48 (1992)

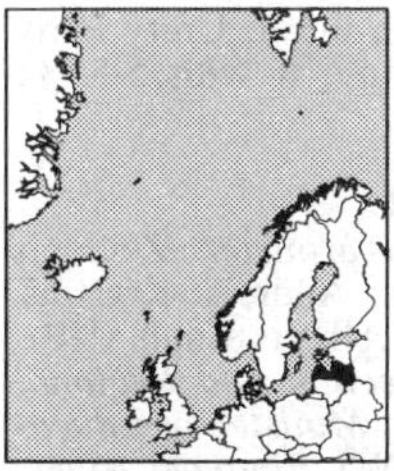

KEY HISTORICAL EVENTS. Latvian tribes were under the hegemony of the German Order of Livonian Knights until 1561, when Latvia fell into Polish and Swedish hands. Between 1721 and 1795 Latvia was absorbed into the Russian empire. In the part of Latvia unoccupied by the Germans during the First World War, the Bolsheviks won 72% of the votes in the Constituent Assembly elections (Nov. 1917). Soviet power was proclaimed in Dec. 1917, but was overthrown when the Germans occupied all Latvia (Feb. 1918). Restored when they withdrew (Dec. 1918), it was overthrown once more by combined British naval and German military forces (May–Dec. 1919), and a democratic government set up. This régime was in turn replaced when a coup took place in May 1934.

The secret protocol of the Soviet–German agreement of 23 Aug. 1939 assigned Latvia to the Soviet sphere of interest. An ultimatum (16 June 1940) led to the formation of a government acceptable to the USSR. On 21 July a People's Diet proclaimed the establishment of the Latvian Soviet Socialist Republic and applied to join the USSR, whose Supreme Soviet accepted the application on 5 Aug.

On 4 May 1990 the Latvian Supreme Soviet declared, by 138 votes to nil with 58 abstentions, that the Soviet occupation of Latvia on 17 June 1940 was illegal, and resolved to re-establish the authority of the Constitution of 1922. A transition period was set for the restoration of independence. In a referendum in March 1991 the principle of independence was supported by 73·6% of votes cast. A fully independent status was conceded by the USSR State Council in Sept. 1991.

TERRITORY AND POPULATION. Latvia is bounded in the north by Estonia and the Baltic Sea, west by the Baltic Sea, south by Lithuania and Belarus and east by Russia. Area, 64,600 sq. km. Population, Sept. 1995, 2,505,900 (53·7% female; 69·1% urban). The 1989 census population was 2,666,567, of whom Latvians accounted for 52%, Russians 34%, Belorussians, 45%, Ukrainians 3·5%, Poles 2·3%, Lithuanians 1·3% and Jews 0·9%. Main ethnic groups in Jan. 1995: Latvians, 1,385,200; Russians, 829,600; Belorussians, 102,500; Ukrainians, 75,300; Poles, 56,200; Lithuanians, 32,600; Jews, 12,200; Gypsies, 7,400.

Vital statistics, 1994: Births, 24,256; deaths, 41,757; marriages, 11,600; infantile deaths, 376. In 1994 life expectancy was: Males, 61 years; females, 74. There were 32,500 induced abortions in 1994. Birth rate, 1994 (per 1,000 population), 9·5; marriage, 11·6; divorce, 8·6. In 1994 there were 3,046 immigrants and 21,856 emigrants. The population is declining; natural increase (per 1,000 population) was –6·8 in 1994.

Citizenship is conferred upon all residents of pre-1940 Latvia and their descendants, and is open to immigrants of at least 16 years residence. Further legislation of July 1994 provides for the naturalization of non-citizens born in Latvia over the following 6 years and of those born outside Latvia from 2000. There were 1,715,930 citizens registered as of Oct. 1993.

There are 26 districts, 56 towns and 37 urban settlements. The capital is Riga (840,000 in 1995); other principal towns are Daugavpils (120,200), Liepāja (100,200), Jelgava (71,100), Jurmala (59,300) and Ventspils (47,000).

The official language is Latvian.

CONSTITUTION AND GOVERNMENT. The declaration of independence of 21 Aug. 1991 states that Latvia is an independent democratic republic whose status is defined by the constitution of 1922, which was unanimously re-adopted by parliament on 6 July 1993. The head of state is the *President*, elected by parliament. Parliament is the 100-member *Saeima*, which is elected from 5 electoral districts by proportional representation. There is a 5% threshold needed to be elected. At the elections of 30 Sept.-1 Oct. 1995, Saimnieks (S) won 18 seats with 15·1% of votes cast; Latvian Way (LW), 17 with 14·6%; For Latvia (Zigerists), 16 with 14·9%; Fatherland and Freedom (FF), 14 with 11.9%; Farmers' Union (FU)-Christian Democratic Union-Latgale Democratic Party, 8 with 6·3%; Unity Party (UP), 8 with 7·1%; Greens, 8 with 6·3%; National Harmony, 6 with 5·55%; Socialist Party, 5 with 5·58%.

President: Guntis Ulmanis (b. 1939; FU; elected July 1993).

A government was formed on 21 Dec. 1995 which comprised:

Prime Minister: Andris Škele (b. 1958; ind). *Deputy Prime Minister:* Zeidonis Cevers (S). *Deputy Prime Minister and Minister of Defence:* Andrejs Krastiņš (LNNK). *Deputy Prime Minister and Minister of Agriculture:* Alberts Kauls (UP). *Deputy Prime Minister and Minister of Environmental Protection and Regional Development:* Maris Geilis (LW). *Deputy Prime Minister and Minister of Education:* Maris Grinblats (FF). *Foreign Affairs:* Valdis Birkāvs (LW). *Finance:* Aivars Kreituss (S). *Economy:* Guntars Krasts (FF). *Interior:* Dainis Turlais (S). *Transport:* Vilis Krištopans (LW). *Justice:* Dintars Rasnacs (FF). *Welfare:* Vladimirs Makarovs (FF). *Culture:* Ojars Sparitis (FU). *European Affairs:* Aleksandrs Kiršteins (LNNK). *Local Government:* Ernests Jurkans (S).

National flag: Dark red, with a narrow horizontal white stripe across the centre.

National anthem: 'Dievs, svēti Latviju' ('God bless Latvia'); words and tune by Karlis Baumanis.

Local Government. Local councils are elected for 3-year terms. Citizens of 21 years or over who have resided in a locality for 12 months may stand for election. Elections took place on 29 May 1994 to elect 3,646 representatives to 492 rural communes, 807 representatives to 76 towns and cities and 318 representatives to 26 regions. Turn-out was 58·5%. There were some 12,000 candidates.

DEFENCE. There is conscription for 12 months.

Army. The Army is organized in 1 infantry, 1 reconnaissance and 1 engineer battalion, and was 1,500 strong in 1996. There is a Home Guard reserve of 5 brigades, and a paramilitary Frontier Guard of 4,300.

Navy. A small coastal protection force numbered 1,000 in 1995 and operates 14 patrol vessels of Swedish, German and Soviet origins based at Riga and Liepāja. There is a coastal defence battalion numbering 350.

Air Force. Personnel numbered 150 in 1995. There are 1 L-410 transport and 6 Mi-2 helicopters.

INTERNATIONAL RELATIONS

Membership. Latvia is a member of the UN, the Council of Europe and the NATO Partnership for Peace, and is an Associate Partner in WEU. In Oct. 1995 Latvia applied to join the EU.

ECONOMY

Policy. By 1994 70% of industrial capacity was still in state ownership, and a Privatization Agency was set up to accelerate the transfer to private hands. By Jan. 1995 86·9% of residents had taken out privatization vouchers. 230 state enterprises were privatized in 1995, realizing 37·3m. lats, of which 21·8m. lats were provided by vouchers.

Budget. The financial year runs from 1 Jan. The 1995 budget envisaged revenue of 476m. lats and expenditure of 516m. lats. There was also a special budget for social welfare of 269m. lats, mainly financed from social taxes specifically allocated.

Main items of expenditure (in 1m. lats): Social and cultural, 226; economic development, 47; administration, 36; defence, 23.

Currency. The unit of currency is the *lats* (LVL) of 100 *santims*. There are coins of 1, 2, 5, 10, 20 and 50 santims and 1 and 2 lats, and notes of 5, 10, 20, 50 and 100 lats. 216·6m. lats were in circulation in Sept. 1995. Inflation was an annualized 23·1% in 1995. In March 1996, £1 = 0·84 lats; US$1 = 0·55 lats; DM1 = 0·37 lats.

Banking and Finance. The central bank and bank of issue is the Bank of Latvia whose governor is appointed by Parliament for a 6-year term (*Governor*, Eiñars Repše). The Bank of Latvia also participates in commercial banking and has 48 semi-autonomous branches. There are 3 state banks (the Agricultural Bank, the Industry and Construction Bank and the Social and Housing Bank), and in 1995 there were 56 commercial banks with total assets of 1,019m. lats. The minimum share capital requirement is 3m. lats. The Latvian Investment Bank was set up in 1993 with state and private participation. There is also a Savings bank, whose foreign exchange department functions as a commercial bank. In 1994 1 foreign bank had a full licence and one a representative office.

There is a stock exchange in Riga.

ENERGY AND NATURAL RESOURCES

Electricity. Output in 1994 was 4,441m. kWh, of which 3,305 kWh were hydroelectric.

Minerals. Peat deposits extend over 645,000 ha or about 10% of the total area, and it is estimated that total deposits are 3,000–4,000m. tons; output, 1994, 430,000 tonnes. There are also gypsum deposits; amber is frequently found in the coastal districts.

Agriculture. Area under cultivation was 3·9m. ha in 1990. Cattle and dairy farming are the chief agricultural occupations. Oats, barley, rye, potatoes and flax are the main crops.

On 1 Jan. 1989 there were 248 state farms and 331 (including 11 fishery) collective farms. There were 38,100 tractors and 7,400 grain combine harvesters. Large state and collective farms are being converted into shareholding enterprises; the remainder are being divided into small private holdings for collective farm workers or former owners. There were 52,000 such farms in 1993 averaging 16 ha and 99,000 smallholdings averaging 4·4 ha.

Livestock (1993, in 1,000): Cattle, 1,144 (of which milch cows, 481); sheep, 165; pigs, 866; poultry, 5,432.

Output of crops (in 1,000 tonnes), 1992: Wheat, 338; sugar-beet, 380; potatoes, 1,000; rye, 317; vegetables, 236. Livestock products (1994): Meat, 0·2m. tonnes; milk, 1m. tonnes; eggs, 359·9m.

Forestry. In 1995, forest covered 2·7m. ha, with wood resources of 426m. cu. metres. 6·5m. cu. metres are cut annually.

Fisheries. There are fishing ports at Riga and Leipāja. The fishing fleet comprised 55 ships in 1994. In 1994, the total catch was 132,000 tonnes (124,200 tonnes marine).

INDUSTRY. Latvia is a major producer of electric railway passenger cars and long-distance telephone exchanges, paper and woollen goods, sawn timber, and mineral fertilizers.

Industrial output in 1994 (in 1,000 tonnes) included: Steel, 332; rolled steel, 317; cement, 244; chemical fibres, 18·1; paper, 2; meat, 98; sugar, 55; beer, 65m. litres.

Labour. In June 1995, 1,191,000 persons were employed. In 1995 there was a monthly minimum wage of 50-60 lats. Average monthly salary was 120 lats in 1995. Retirement age is 60 years for men and 55 for women, but flexible retirement ages will be possible under a new contributory pension scheme introduced in 1995. There were 76,559 registered unemployed in Sept. 1995.

Trade Unions. The Latvian Free Trade Union has Andris Siliņš as chairman.

FOREIGN ECONOMIC RELATIONS. Foreign debt was US$94·26m. in Jan. 1995. On 20 April 1990 Latvia, Estonia and Lithuania concluded a Baltic Economic Co-operation Agreement. A free trade agreement with Estonia and Lithuania came into force on 1 April 1994. A law on foreign investment of Nov. 1991 exempts from profit tax companies which are 30% foreign-owned. Foreign investors may own up to 100% of companies, but the defence industry, narcotics, mass media and education are not open to foreign investment.

Commerce. In 1994, exports were valued at 553,437,000 lats and imports at 694,588,000 lats. The main exports are wood and products, textiles and foodstuffs. In 1995 the main export markets were: Russia, 25%; Germany, 14·5%; Sweden, 9·3%. Main import suppliers: Russia, Lithuania, Finland, Estonia. Total trade between Latvia and the UK (British Department of Trade returns, in £1,000 sterling):

	1993	*1994*	*1995*
Imports to UK	69,254	222,378	170,411
Exports and re-exports from UK	15,823	30,696	40,058

COMMUNICATIONS

Roads. In 1990 there were 58,600 km of roads (32,500 km hard-surfaced). In 1994, 5,164,600 tonnes of freight were carried by road. In 1994 there were 3,814 traffic accidents with 717 fatalities.

Railways. In 1993 there were 2,413 km of 1,520 mm gauge route (271 km electrified). 55·67m. passengers and 27·8m. tonnes of freight were carried in 1994

Civil Aviation. There is an international airport at Riga. A new national carrier, Baltic Airlines, assumed control of Latavio and Baltic International Airlines in 1995 and began flying in Oct. to Amsterdam, Copenhagen, Frankfurt, Helsinki, London and Stockholm. It is 51% state-owned, and in 1995 operated 2 B-727s and 2 ex-Soviet aircraft. Services are also provided by Aeroflot, Aerosweet, Air Express, Austrian Airlines, Czech Airlines, Delta, Estonian Air, Finnair, Hamburg Airlines, LOT, Lufthansa, SAS, Transaero and Transeast Airlines.

Shipping. There are 3 large ports (with 1m. tonnes of cargo handled, 1994): Riga (5·95), Ventspils (27·72) and Leipāja (1·1). 4,600 ships in all docked at Riga and Ventspils in 1994. In 1994, 13·05m. tonnes of cargo were transported. In 1995 the merchant marine totalled 1·18m. GRT, including oil tankers, 0·73m. GRT.

Telecommunications. In 1994 there were 1,037 post offices. Telecommunications are conducted by companies in which the government has a 51% stake, under the aegis of the state-controlled Lattelecom. In 1994 there were 0·7m. telephones and 8,364 mobile telephones.

Broadcasting is overseen by the 9-member National Radio and Television Council appointed by parliament for 4-year terms. Latvijas Radio broadcasts 3 programmes and an external service (English, German, Swedish). There are also 1 municipal and 3 commercial broadcasters. The government-controlled Latvijas Televizija transmits on 2 networks (colour by SECAM; 1 commercial channel uses PAL) and relays Russian programmes. In 1993 there were over 100 regional, commercial and municipal TV stations. There were 1·2m. TV sets in use.

Cinema. In 1994 there were 261 cinemas; attendances totalled 1·6m.

Press. In 1994 there were 257 newspapers and 213 periodicals. 1,677 book titles were published.

SOCIAL INSTITUTIONS

Justice. The criminal code is inherited from the former USSR. Judges are appointed for life. There are a Supreme Court, regional and district courts and administrative courts. The death penalty is retained. 40,983 crimes were reported in 1994 (52,835 in 1993).

Religion. Church-state affairs are the concern of the Department of Religious Affairs attached to the Council of Ministers. New sects are required to demonstrate loyalty to the state and its traditional religions over a 3-year period. Traditionally, Lutherans constituted the largest church, but their numbers have declined from some 0·6m. in 1956 to 0·1m. in 1991. Estimates of Roman Catholics in 1991 varied from 0·3m. to 0·5m. Congregations in March 1991: Lutherans, 256; Roman Catholics, 186; Russian Orthodox, 90; Old Believers, 65; Baptists, 61; and in Oct. 1990: Adventists, 28; Pentecostalists, 6; Jews, 4.

Education. The Soviet education system has been restructured on the UNESCO model. Education may begin in kindergarten. From the age of 6 or 7 education is compulsory for 9 years in comprehensive schools. This may be followed by 3 years in special secondary school or 1 to 6 years in art, technical or vocational schools. In 1994-95 there were 695 comprehensive schools with 0·34m. pupils, 381 special secondary schools with 18,600 pupils, both together with 33,300 teachers. 166,000 pupils were attending Latvian-language schools, 117,300 Russian and 39,500 mixed. 27,000 pupils were attending vocational schools.

In 1994-95 there were 1 university and 4 specialized universities (agriculture; aviation; pedagogy; technical) and academies of arts, medicine and music, and 7 other institutions of higher education, with 28,300 full-time students in all.

Health. In 1994 there were 8,700 doctors, 19,400 paramedics and 170 hospitals with 30,400 beds.

Social Security. In 1994 there were 662,600 pensioners, including retirement, 496,000; disability, 104,300; survivors, 36,800; social, 19,000. Age pensions range from 15 to 23·5 lats per month according to years of employment. Legislation of 1995 provides for the phasing in of a new retirement pension scheme which links benefits to contributions made during working years and average life expectancy.

DIPLOMATIC REPRESENTATIVES

Of Latvia in Great Britain (45 Nottingham Place, London, W1M 3FE)
Ambassador: Janis Lusis.

Of Great Britain in Latvia (2 Elizabetes Iela, Riga 226010)
Ambassador: Nicholas Jarrold.

Of Latvia in the USA (4325 17th St., NW, Washington DC 20011)
Ambassador: Ojars Kalnins.

Of the USA in Latvia (7 Raina Bulevard, Riga, 226050)
Ambassador: Larry C. Napper.

Of Latvia to the United Nations
Ambassador: Aivars Baumanis.

Further Reading

Central Statistical Bureau. *Statistical Yearbook of Latvia. – Latvia in Figures.* Annual, – *Demographic Yearbook of Latvia.*
Bilmanis, A., *A History of Latvia.* Princeton Univ. Press, 1951
Lieven, A., *The Baltic Revolution: Estonia, Latvia, Lithuania and the Path to Independence.* 2nd ed. Yale UP, 1994
Misiunas, R. J. and Taagepera, R., *The Baltic States: the Years of Dependence, 1940–91.* 2nd ed. Farnborough, 1993
Spekke, A., *History of Latvia.* Stockholm, 1951
Smith, I. A. and Grunts, M. V., *The Baltic States.* [Bibliography]. Oxford and Santa Barbara, 1993

National statistical office: Central Statistical Bureau, Lāčplēša ielā 1, 1301 Riga.

LEBANON

Capital: Beirut
Population: 2·84m. (1992)
HDI/world rank: 0·675/101 (1992)

Jumhouriya al-Lubnaniya

(Republic of Lebanon)

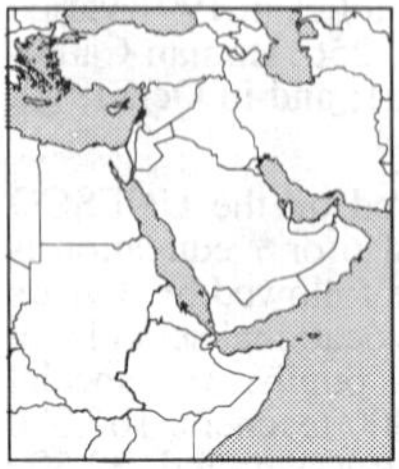

KEY HISTORICAL EVENTS. After 20 years as a mandate of France, Lebanon was proclaimed independent on 26 Nov. 1941.

For events between the insurrection of 1958 and the intervention of the Syrian-dominated Arab Deterrent Force in 1976, the civil wars and Israeli and Syrian interventions, 1976–90 *see* THE STATESMAN'S YEAR-BOOK, 1990–91, p. 799 and 1994–95, p. 868.

At the end of 1990 the various militias which had held sway in Beirut withdrew. A new Government of National Reconciliation was announced on 24 Dec. 1990. The dissolution of all militias was decreed by the National Assembly in April 1991, but the Shi'ite Moslem militia Hizbollah was allowed to remain active and deploy heavy weapons. In July the army defeated the Palestine Liberation Organization at Sidon, depriving the latter of their territorial base in South Lebanon, and bringing the army up to the Israeli-occupied southern strip ('security zone').

TERRITORY AND POPULATION. Lebanon is mountainous, bounded on the north and east by Syria, on the west by the Mediterranean and on the south by Israel. The area is 10,452 sq. km (4,036 sq. miles). Population estimate (1991), 2·84m. (84% urban); density, 265 per sq. km. The principal towns, with estimated population (1991), are: Beirut (the capital), 1·5m.; Tripoli, 0·2m.; Saida (Sidon), 0·1m.; Tyre, 70,000. Infant mortality was 44 per 1,000 live births in 1990; expectation of life, 66·1 years.

The official language is Arabic. French and, increasingly, English are widely spoken in official and commercial circles.

CLIMATE. A Mediterranean climate with short, warm winters and long, hot and rainless summers, with high humidity in coastal areas. Rainfall is largely confined to the winter months and can be torrential, with snow on high ground. Beirut. Jan. 55°F (13°C), July 81°F (27°C). Annual rainfall 35·7" (893 mm).

CONSTITUTION AND GOVERNMENT. The first Constitution was established under the French Mandate on 23 May 1926. It has since been amended in 1927, 1929, 1943 (twice), 1947 and 1990. It is based on a separation of powers, with a President, a single-chamber *National Assembly* elected by universal suffrage at age 21 in 12 electoral constituencies, and an independent judiciary. In Oct. 1995 the National Assembly extended the President's term of office from 6 to 9 years. The executive consists of the President and a Prime Minister and Cabinet appointed after consultation between the President and the National Assembly. The system is adapted to the communal balance on which Lebanese political life depends by an electoral law which allocates deputies according to the religious distribution of the population, and by a series of constitutional conventions whereby, *e.g.*, the President is always a Maronite Christian, the Prime Minister a Sunni Moslem and the Speaker of the Assembly a Shia Moslem. There is no party system. In Aug. 1990, and again in July 1992, the National Assembly voted to increase its membership, and now has 128 deputies with equal numbers of Christians and Moslems.

On 21 Sept. President Hrawi established the Second Republic by signing constitutional amendments which had been negotiated at Taif (Saudi Arabia) in Oct. 1989. These institute an executive collegium between the President, Prime Minister and Speaker, and remove from the President the right to recall the Prime Minister, dissolve the Assembly and vote in the Council of Ministers.

3-stage elections were held in Aug.–Sept. 1992. The electorate was 2·2m. Elections are scheduled for mid-1996.

President: Elias Hrawi (Maronite; elected 24 Nov. 1989).

In Nov. 1995 the cabinet comprised:

Prime Minister and Minister of Finance: Rafik Hariri (b. 1944).

Deputy Prime Minister and Minister of the Interior: Michel Murr. *Foreign and Emigration Affairs*, Farez Bouez. *Defence*, Mohsen Dalloul. *Justice:* Bahij Tabbara. *Health:* Marwan Hamadeh. *Labour:* Asad Hardan. *Posts and Telecommunications:* Alfadl Shalak. *Education and the Arts:* Mikhail Daher. *Economy and Commerce:* Yassin Jaber. *Information:* Farid Makkari. *Agriculture:* Shawqi Fakhouri. *Industry and Oil:* Shah Barsoumian. *Housing and Co-operatives:* Muhammad Abu Hamdan. *Tourism:* Nicolas Fattoush. *Water and Electricity:* Elie Hobeika. *Refugees:* Walid Jumblatt. *Municipal and Rural Affairs:* Suleiman Franjieh. *Finance (Minister of State):* Fouad Sanioura. *Works:* Ali Harajleh. *Social Affairs:* Estfan Doweihi. *Transport:* Omar Miskawi.

The *Speaker* is Nabih Berri.

National flag: Three horizontal stripes of red, white, red, with the white of double width and bearing in the centre a green cedar of Lebanon.

National anthem: 'Kulluna lil watan lil 'ula lil 'alam' ('All of us for our country, flag and glory'); words by Rashid Nachleh, tune by W. Sabra.

Local Government: The 6 governorates (including the city of Beirut) are subdivided into 26 districts.

DEFENCE. There were 30,000 Syrian troops in the country in 1995. In the Israeli-occupied southern strip the pro-Israeli South Lebanese Army is estimated to number 2,500 and has 30 main battle tanks.

Conscription is for 12 months.

Army. The strength of the Army was 43,000 in 1996. It is organized into a Presidential Guard, 11 infantry brigades, 2 artillery and 3 special forces regiments, and 1 ranger and 1 air assault regiment. Its equipment includes 100 M48A1/A5 and 200 T-54/-55 main battle tanks. There is an internal security force, run by the Ministry of the Interior, some 13,000 strong.

Navy. The flotilla consists of 9 inshore patrol craft, 2 tank landing craft and some armed boats, manned and supported by some 500 personnel (1995).

Air Force. The Air Force had (1995) about 800 personnel. About 30 Alouette, Gazelle, Puma and AB.212 helicopters survived the civil war, while the US government supplied 16 UH-1H Iroquois helicopters in 1994. A few Hunter fighters and Magister trainers also survived.

INTERNATIONAL RELATIONS. A Treaty of Brotherhood, Co-operation and Co-ordination with Syria of May 1991 provides for close relations in the fields of foreign policy, the economy, military affairs and security. The treaty stipulates that Lebanese government decisions are subject to review by 6 joint Syrian-Lebanese bodies.

Membership. Lebanon is a member of the UN and Arab League.

ECONOMY

Policy. The semi-autonomous Council of Development and Reconstruction, originally set up in 1977, was revived in 1991 to oversee a post-civil war rehabilitation programme, 'Horizon 2000'.

Budget. The fiscal year is the calendar year. Budget for 1992: Revenue, £Leb.1,200m.; expenditure, £Leb.1,930m.

Currency. The unit of currency is the *Lebanese pound* (LBP) of 100 *piastres*. There are coins of 1, 2·5, 5, 10, 25 and 50 piastres and £Leb.1, and notes of £Leb.50, 100, 250, 500, 1,000, 5,000, 10,000, 25,000, 50,000 and 100,000. Inflation was an annualized 15% in 1995. Foreign exchange reserves were US$3,800m. in June 1994; gold reserves were US$3,541·2m. Currency in circulation, 1994, £LEB.938,800m. There is a fluctuating official rate of exchange, fixed monthly (March 1996: £Leb.2,425·19 = £1; £Leb.1,586·75 = US$1; £Leb.1,075·11 = DM1); it in practice is used only for the calculation of *ad-valorem* customs duties on Lebanese imports and for import statistics. For other purposes the free market is used.

Banking and Finance. The Bank of Lebanon (*Governor,* Riad Salameh) is the bank of issue. In 1994 there were 52 domestic banks, 14 subsidiaries and 12 foreign banks, with 590 branches in all. There is a stock exchange in Beirut (closed 1983-95).

Weights and Measures. The use of the metric system is legal. For former traditional units *see* THE STATESMAN'S YEAR-BOOK, 1995-96, p. 867.

ENERGY AND NATURAL RESOURCES

Electricity. Generating capacity was 1,000 MW in 1993.

Minerals. There are no commercially viable deposits.

Agriculture. In 1992 there were 216,000 ha of arable land, 90,000 ha of permanent crop land and 10,000 ha of pasture. Crop production (in 1,000 tonnes), 1993: Total fruits excluding melons, 1,332; apples, 160; grapes, 365; potatoes, 280; sugar-beet, 190; wheat, 55; bananas, 62; olives, 103.

Livestock (1993): Goats, 450,000; sheep, 250,000; cattle, 77,000; pigs, 40,000; asses, 23,000; mules, 8,000.

Forestry. The forests of the past have been denuded by exploitation and in 1991 covered 80,000 ha.

Fisheries. Total catch (1990) was 2,200 tonnes (90% from seafishing).

INDUSTRY. In 1994 there were 23,518 factories operating.

Labour. The workforce was some 823,000 in 1990, of whom 72,000 worked in agriculture. Following considerable labour unrest, an agreement on wage increases and social benefits was concluded between the government and the GCLW in Dec. 1993.

Trade Unions. The main unions are the General Confederation of Lebanese Workers (GCLW) and the General Confederation of Sectoral Unions.

FOREIGN ECONOMIC RELATIONS. Foreign and domestic trade is the principal source of income. Foreign debt was US$1,300m. in 1995.

Commerce. Imports, 1994: US$10,159m.; exports, US$1,170m.

Total trade between Lebanon and UK (British Department of Trade returns, in £1,000 sterling):

	1991	*1992*	*1993*	*1994*	*1995*
Imports to UK	8,465	10,405	11,436	7,282	14,198
Exports and re-exports from UK	87,760	91,868	136,372	138,616	175,132

In 1994 the main export markets (in % of total trade) were: UAE, 18·1; Saudi Arabia, 15·3; Syria, 10·6; Kuwait, 5·7; France, 4·6; Jordan, 4. Main import suppliers: Italy, 13·4; Germany, 10·1; USA, 9·3; France, 9; Syria, 4·4.

COMMUNICATIONS

Roads. There were (1995) 7,100 km of roads of which 80% are asphalted.

Railways. Railways are state-owned. The only line functioning in 1994 was a 40-km stretch from Beirut to Jbeil.

Civil Aviation. Beirut International Airport is served by Aeroflot, Air Algérie, Air France, Alitalia, Armenian Airlines, Austrian Airlines, Balkan, British Airways, British Mediterranean Airways, Cyprus Airways, Czech Airlines, Egyptair,

Emirates, Gulf Air, Iberia, JAT, KLM, Kuwait Airways, LOT, Malaysia Airlines, Malév, Olympic Airways, Qatar Airways, Royal Jordanian, Saudia, Swissair, Syrian Airlines, Tarom, Turkish Airlines and Yemenia. It handled 1·43m. passengers in 1994. There are 2 national airlines, the state-owned Middle East Airlines, which in 1995 operated 2 A310-200s, 2 A310-300s, 1 B-707-320B, 7 B-707-320Cs, 2 B-720Bs, and 3 B-747-200B Combis, and Trans-Mediterranean Airways, which had 7 aircraft in 1995.

Shipping. Beirut is the largest port, followed by Tripoli, Jounieh and Sidon. Total GRT, 1995, 0·41m., including oil tankers 2,431 GRT and container ships, 1,162 GRT.

Telecommunications. In 1993 there were 0·35m. local and 700 international telephone lines. 2 companies are operating a mobile telephone network.

The government-controlled Radio Lebanon transmits in Arabic, French, English and Armenian. Tele-Liban, which is government-owned, transmits 3 programmes from 6 stations. Colour is by SECAM. There were 1·1m. TV sets in 1993 and 2·15m. radios.

Press (1994). There were about 30 daily newspapers in Arabic, 2 in French, 1 in English and 4 in Armenian, and 60 weekly periodicals.

SOCIAL INSTITUTIONS

Religion. In 1994 it was estimated that the population was 55·3% Moslem (34% Shi'ite and 21·3% Sunni), 37·6% Christian (mainly Maronite) and 7·1% Druze. In 1996 there were 119 Roman Catholic bishops.

Education. There are state and private primary and secondary schools. In 1994-95 there were 8 universities, including 2 American and 1 French, and 6 other institutions of higher education. In 1994-95 there were 64,055 university students and 4,449 academic staff.

There is an Academy of Fine Arts.

Health. There were 24 government-run hospitals in 1993.

DIPLOMATIC REPRESENTATIVES

Of Lebanon in Great Britain (21 Kensington Palace Gdns., London, W8 4QM)
Ambassador: Mahmoud Hammoud.

Of Great Britain in Lebanon (Shamma Bldg., Raouché, Ras Beirut)
Ambassador: Maeve Fort, CMG.

Of Lebanon in the USA (2560 28th St., NW, Washington, D.C., 20008)
Ambassador: Raid Tabbarah.

Of the USA in Lebanon (POB 70-840, Antelias, Beirut)
Ambassador: Vacant.

Of Lebanon to the United Nations
Ambassador: Samir Moubarak.

Further Reading

Bleaney, C. H., *Lebanon.* [Bibliography]. 2nd ed. Oxford and Santa Barbara, 1991
Choueiri, Y. M., *State and Society in Syria and Lebanon.* Exeter Univ. Press, 1994
Cobban, H., *The Making of Modern Lebanon.* London, 1985
Fisk, R., *Pity the Nation: Lebanon at War.* 2nd ed. OUP, 1992
Gemayel, A., *Rebuilding Lebanon.* New York, 1992
Hiro, D., *Lebanon Fire and Embers: a History of the Lebanese Civil War.* New York, 1993
Shehadi, N. and Mills, D.H., *Lebanon: A History of Conflict and Consensus.* London, 1988
Weinberger, N. J., *Syrian Intervention in Lebanon.* New York, 1986

National library: Dar el Kutub, Parliament Sq., Beirut.
National statistical office: Service de Statistique Générale, Beirut.

LESOTHO

Kingdom of Lesotho

Capital: Maseru
Population: 1·89m. (1992)
GNP per capita: US$700 (1994)
HDI/world rank: 0·473/131 (1992)

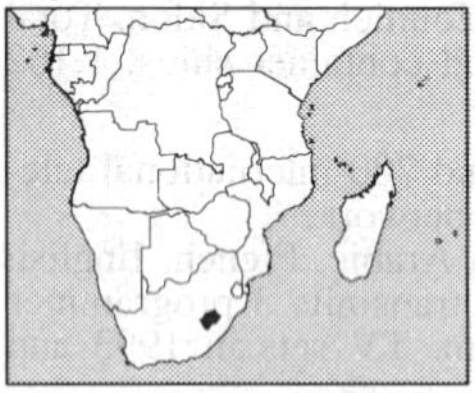

KEY HISTORICAL EVENTS. Basutoland first received the protection of Britain in 1868 at the request of Moshoeshoe I, the first paramount chief. In 1871 the territory was annexed to the Cape Colony, but in 1884 it was restored to the direct control of the British Government through the High Commissioner for South Africa.

On 4 Oct. 1966 Basutoland became an independent and sovereign member of the Commonwealth under the name of the Kingdom of Lesotho.

King Moeshoeshoe II was deposed by the Military Council in Nov. 1990 and replaced by King Letsie III. Maj.-Gen. Lekhanya was deposed from the chairmanship of the Military Council in a bloodless coup on 30 April 1991. The Military Council was dissolved and a democratic constitution promulgated in April 1993.

TERRITORY AND POPULATION. Lesotho is an enclave within South Africa. The area is 11,720 sq. miles (30,355 sq. km). Vital statistics rates, 1990: Birth (per 1,000 population), 41; death, 12; growth, 2·5%.

The census in 1986 showed a total population of 1,577,536 persons. Estimate (1992) 1,889,000 (20·3% urban); population density, 60·1 per sq. km.

There are 10 districts, all named after their chief towns, except Berea (chief town, Teyateyaneng). Area and population:

Region	*Area (in sq. km.)*	*Population (1986 census, in 1,000)*	*Population (1991 estimate, in 1,000)*
Berea	2,222	194·6	177·6
Butha-Buthe	1,767	100·6	121·0
Leribe	2,828	258·0	312·2
Mafeteng	2,119	195·6	232·8
Maseru	4,279	311·1	356·5
Mohale's Hoek	3,530	164·4	207·8
Mokhotlong	4,075	74·7	90·2
Qada's Nek	2,349	64·0	77·7
Quthing	2,916	110·4	136·1
Thaba-Tseka	4,270	104·1	122·5

The chief towns (with 1986 census population) are: Maseru, 367,000 (1992 estimate); Qacha's Nek, 80,000 (1992 estimate); Teyateyaneng, 14,251; Mafeteng, 12,667; Hlotse, 9,595.

The official languages are Sesotho and English.

The population is homogenous, some 99% Basotho.

CLIMATE. A healthy and pleasant climate, with variable rainfall, but averaging 29" (725 mm) a year over most of the country. The rain falls mainly in the summer months of Oct. to April, while the winters are dry and may produce heavy frosts in lowland areas and frequent snow in the highlands. Temperatures in the lowlands range from a maximum of 90°F (32·2°C) in summer to a minimum of 20°F (–6·7°C) in winter.

ROYAL HOUSE. Following the death of his father, Moeshoeshoe II, **Letsie III**, succeeded to the throne in Jan. 1996.

CONSTITUTION AND GOVERNMENT. Lesotho is a constitutional monarchy with the King as Head of State. The 1993 constitution provides for a *National Assembly* comprising an elected 65-member lower house and a *Senate* of 22 principal chiefs and 11 members nominated by the King.

Parliamentary elections were held on 28 March 1993 for the *National Assembly.* The Basotho Congress Party won 65 seats, the Basotho National Party, nil.

Following the elections the King swore allegiance to a new constitution and the Military Council was dissolved.

In Oct. 1995 the Council of Ministers comprised:

Prime Minister, Minister of Public Service: Ntsu Mokhele (sworn in 2 April 1993).

Deputy Prime Minister, Minister for Education and Training, Manpower Development and Youth Affairs: Pakalitha Mosisili. *Foreign Affairs:* Mpho Malie. *Trade, Industry, Tourism, Sport and Culture:* Shaklane Robong Mokhele. *Agriculture, Co-operatives and Marketing:* Ntsakunyane Mphanya. *Home Affairs:* Lesao Lehola. *Health and Social Welfare:* Dr Khauhelo Ralitapole. *Natural Resources:* Tseliso Makhakhe. *Transport, Post and Telecommunications:* David Mochochoko. *Information and Broadcasting:* Lira Motete. *Justice, Human Rights, Law and Constitutional Affairs:* Kelebone Maope. *Employment and Labour:* Not'si Molopo. *Works:* Molapo Qhobela. *Defence:* Sephiri Motanyane.

The *College of Chiefs* settles the recognition and succession of Chiefs and adjudicates cases of inefficiency, criminality and absenteeism among them.

National flag: Diagonally white over blue over green with the white of double width charged with a brown Basotho shield in the upper hoist.

National anthem: 'Lesotho fatsela bontat'a rona' ('Lesotho, land of our fathers'); words by F. Coillard, tune by L. Laur.

Local Government. The country is divided into 11 districts, subdivided into 22 wards. Most of the wards are presided over by hereditary chiefs.

DEFENCE. The Royal Lesotho Defence Force has 2,000 personnel and is organized in 7 infantry and 1 support company and 1 air squadron with 2 Aviocar transports, 1 Bell 47, 1 Bell 412 and 2 BO-105 helicopters and 1 Cessna 182 light aircraft.

INTERNATIONAL RELATIONS

Membership. Lesotho is a member of the UN, OAU, the Commonwealth, the SADC and is an ACP state of the EU.

ECONOMY

Policy. The Lesotho National Development Corporation promotes industrial and tourist trade development.

Budget. Expenditure (1992–93) 474·8m. maloti; revenue, 537·1m. maloti.

Currency. The unit of currency is the *loti* (plural *maloti*) (LSL) of 100 *lisente* at par with the South African rand, which is legal tender. There are coins of 1, 2, 5, 10, 25 and 50 lisente and 2 maloti, and notes of 5, 10, 20 and 50 maloti. Currency in circulation, 1993, was M43·80m. Annualized inflation was 8·4% in July 1994. Foreign exchange reserves were US$94·8m. in 1991. In March 1996, £1 = 5·95 maloti; US$1 = 3·90 maloti; DM1 = 2·64 maloti.

Banking and Finance. The Central Bank of Lesotho is the bank of issue, founded in 1982 to succeed the Lesotho Monetary Authority. There are 3 commercial banks and an Agricultural Development Bank. Savings deposits totalled 342·8m. maloti in 1993.

Weights and Measures. The metric system is in use.

ENERGY AND NATURAL RESOURCES

Electricity. Production (1985) 1m. kWh.

Minerals. Diamonds are the main product. 1990 output was 11,400 carats.

Agriculture. Agriculture contributes about 15% of GDP and employs two-thirds of the workforce. The chief crops were (1993 production in 1,000 tonnes): Wheat, 9; maize, 92; sorghum, 52; beans, 2; peas and other vegetables are also grown. Soil conservation and the improvement of crops and pasture are matters of vital importance. Area sown to crops, 1993, 264,000 ha.

Livestock (1993): Cattle, 658,000; horses, 107,000; pigs, 60,000; sheep, 1·18m.; goats, 811,000; poultry, 1m.

INDUSTRY. Manufacturing contributed 15·1% of GDP in 1991.

Labour. In 1991 the workforce numbered 826,000 (351,000 females). In 1993 117,600 were working in mines in South Africa.

FOREIGN ECONOMIC RELATIONS. Lesotho, Botswana and Swaziland are members of the South African customs union, by agreement dated 29 June 1910. Foreign debt was US$427·7m. in 1991.

Commerce. In 1992 imports were valued at US$933m. and exports at US$109m. In 1993 exports were valued at 410,725,000 maloti.

Principal exports in 1993 (in 1,000 maloti): Cattle, 8,409; wheat flour, 1,717; canned vegetables, 2,275; wool, 16,853; mohair, 5,131; manufactures, 13,426; machinery and transport equipment, 25,540.

The bulk of international trade is with South Africa.

Total trade between Lesotho and UK (British Department of Trade returns, in £1,000 sterling):

	1991	*1992*	*1993*	*1994*	*1995*
Imports to UK	2,799	4,159	2,343	1,605	399
Exports and re-exports from UK	3,258	2,725	908	665	1,324

Tourism. In 1993 there were 349,185 foreign visitors.

COMMUNICATIONS

Roads. In 1992 there were 1,005 km of tarred, and 4,319 km of untarred roads, 2,337 km gravelled and 1,806 earth. In 1983 there were 10,200 commercial vehicles and 4,359 passenger cars. In 1993 there were 1,650 traffic accidents with 286 fatalities.

Railways. A branch line built by the South African Railways, 1 mile long, connects Maseru with the Bloemfontein–Natal line at Marseilles. It was not open in 1993.

Civil Aviation. The national carrier is Lesotho Airways, which had 3 aircraft in 1995 and operates services to Botswana, Johannesburg, Mozambique and Swaziland. Moeshoeshoe International airport at Maseru is also served by Royal Swazi Airways. 21,657 passengers were carried on international, and 57,256 on domestic flights in 1993.

Telecommunications. There were 11,456 telephones in 1988. Radio Lesotho transmits daily in English and Sesotho. The broadcasting authority is the Lesotho National Broadcasting Service. In 1992 there were 420,000 radio and 50,000 TV sets (colour by PAL).

Press. In 1985, 3 daily newspapers had a combined circulation of 44,000.

SOCIAL INSTITUTIONS

Justice. The legal system is based on Roman-Dutch law. The Lesotho High Court and the Court of Appeal are situated in Maseru, and there are Magistrates' Courts in the districts. 5,888 criminal offences were reported in 1993.

Religion. About 93% of the population are Christians; in 1992 there were 0·81m. Roman Catholics and 0·55m. Protestants.

Education. 26·4% of persons over 15 were illiterate in 1985. Education levels: Pre-school, 3 to 5 years; first level (elementary), 6 to 12; second level (secondary or teacher training or technical training), 7 to 13; third level (university or teacher training college). In 1993–94 there were 354,275 pupils in 1,201 primary schools with 7,292 teachers; 55,312 pupils in 187 secondary schools with 2,526 teachers; 751 students in the National Teacher-Training College with 117 teachers; and 1,575 students in 8 technical schools with 108 teachers. The National University of Lesotho was established in 1975 at Roma; enrolment in 1992–93, 1,612 students and 190 teaching staff.

Health. Provision of doctors, 1993, 1 per 14,306 population.

DIPLOMATIC REPRESENTATIVES

Of Lesotho in Great Britain (10 Collingham Rd., London, SW5 0NR)
High Commissioner: Vacant.

Of Great Britain in Lesotho (PO Box Ms 521, Maseru 100)
High Commissioner: Peter Smith.

Of Lesotho in the USA (2511 Massachusetts Ave., NW, Washington, D.C., 20008)
Ambassador: Eunice Bulane.

Of the USA in Lesotho (PO Box 333, Maseru, 100)
Ambassador: Bismarck Myrick.

Of Lesotho to the United Nations
Ambassador: Percy Mangoaela.

Further Reading

Bureau of Statistics. *Statistical Reports.* Occasional
Bardill, J. E. and Cobbe, J. H., *Lesotho: Dilemmas of Dependence in South Africa.* London, 1986
Murray, C., *Families Divided: The Impact of Migrant Labour in Lesotho.* OUP, 1981
Willet, S. M. and Ambrose, D. P., *Lesotho.* [Bibliography] Oxford and Santa Barbara, 1981

National statistical office: Bureau of Statistics, PO Box 455, Maseru.

LIBERIA

Republic of Liberia

Capital: Monrovia
Population: 2·83m. (1992)
GNP per capita: US$440 (1987)
HDI/world rank: 0·325/159 (1992)

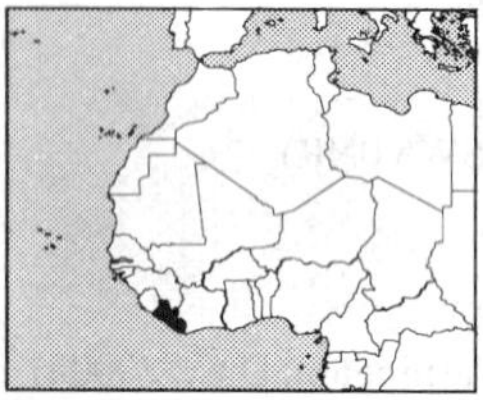

KEY HISTORICAL EVENTS. The Republic of Liberia had its origin in the efforts of several American philanthropic societies to establish freed American slaves in a colony on the West African coast. In 1822 a settlement was formed near the spot where Monrovia now stands. On 26 July 1847 the State was constituted as the Free and Independent Republic of Liberia.

On 12 April 1980, President Tolbert was assassinated and his government overthrown in a coup led by Master-Sergeant Samuel Doe, who was later installed as Head of State and Commander-in-Chief of the army.

At the beginning of 1990 rebel forces entered Liberia from the north and fought their way successfully southwards to confront President Doe's forces in Monrovia. The rebels comprised the National Patriotic Front of Liberia (NPFL) led by Charles Taylor, and the hostile breakaway Independent National Patriotic Front led by Prince Johnson. A peacekeeping force dispatched by the Economic Community of West African States (ECOWAS) disembarked at Monrovia on 25 Aug. 1990, and attempts to form a new provisional government were made.

On 9 Sept. President Doe was assassinated by Prince Johnson's rebels. At an ECOWAS summit at Bamako (Mali) on 28 Nov. government forces and the two rebel factions signed a ceasefire. ECOWAS installed a provisional government led by Amos Sawyer. Charles Taylor also declared himself president, as did the former vice-president, Harry Moniba.

On 13 Feb. 1991 Taylor, Johnson and the commander of the Liberian armed forces signed a second ceasefire. After a West African 12-nation summit meeting from July to Oct. 1991 Taylor signed an agreement to allow ECOWAS to disarm his troops and organize elections. However, fighting continued. A UN Security Council resolution in Nov. 1992 imposed an arms embargo and expressed support for ECOWAS's action.

Peace negotiations opened in Geneva in July 1993 between the interim government, the armed forces, the NPFL and the United Liberation Movement (ULIMO) under OAU auspices. A peace agreement was signed on 25 July.

On 12 Sept. 1994 the leaders of the 3 military factions, Charles Taylor (NPFL), Alhaji Kromah (ULIMO) and Gen. Hezekiah Bowen, commander of the Armed Forces, met in Ghana and agreed to form a new Council of State, but other warring factions and civilian forces in Monrovia repudiated this.

On 21 Dec. 1994 at Accra under Ghanaian auspices the factions concluded an agreement providing for a ceasefire on 28 Dec. 1994, the establishment of safe zones and buffer zones under ECOWAS control, elections on 14 Nov. 1995 and a new 5-member transitional executive. However, factional fighting continued into 1995.

On 19 Aug. 1995 an eleventh peace agreement was signed in Abuja by Taylor, Kromah and George Boley (Council for Peace in Liberia). On 14 Dec. 1995 ECOWAS forces began to deploy from Monrovia into the rest of the country.

TERRITORY AND POPULATION. Liberia is bounded in the north-west by Sierra Leone, north by Guinea, east by Côte d'Ivoire and south-west by the Atlantic ocean. The total area is 99,067 sq. km. At the census (1984) the population was 2,101,628. Estimate (1993) 2,825,000, of whom some 25% were refugees abroad. English is the official language spoken by 15% of the population. The rest belong in the main to 3 linguistic groups: Mande, West Atlantic, and the Kwa.

These are in turn subdivided into 16 ethnic groups: Bassa, Bella, Gbandi, Mende, Gio, Dey, Mano, Gola, Kpelle, Kissi, Krahn, Kru, Lorma, Mandingo, Vai and Grebo.

Monrovia, the capital, had (1984) a population of 425,000; other towns include Buchanan (24,000).

There are 13 counties, whose areas, populations (1984 census) and capitals were as follows:

County	*Sq. km*	*1984*	*Chief town*
Bomi	1,955	66,420	Tubmanburg
Bong	8,099	255,813	Gbarnga
Grand Bassa	8,759	159,648	Buchanan
Grand Cape Mount	5,827	79,322	Robertsport
Grand Gedeh	17,029	102,810	Zwedru
Lofa	19,360	247,641	Voinjama
Margibi	3,263	97,992	Kakata
Maryland	5,351	132,058	Harper
Montserrado	2,740	544,878	Bensonville
Nimba	12,043	313,050	Saniquillie
Rivercess	4,385	37,849	Rivercess
Sinoe	10,254	64,147	Greenville

The county of Grand Kru (chief town, Barclayville) was created in 1985 from the former territories of Kru Coast and Sasstown.

CLIMATE. An equatorial climate, with constant high temperatures and plentiful rainfall, though Jan. to May is drier than the rest of the year. Monrovia. Jan. 79°F (26·1°C), July 76°F (24·4°C). Annual rainfall 206" (5,138 mm).

CONSTITUTION AND GOVERNMENT. A Constitution was approved by referendum in July 1984 and came into force on 6 Jan. 1986. Under it the National Assembly consisted of a 26-member Senate and a 64-member House of Representatives.

A National Conference re-elected Amos Sawyer interim president in April 1991.

The peace agreement of 19 Aug. 1995 provided for the establishment of a state council comprising Charles Taylor (NPFL), Alhaji Kromah (ULIMO), George Boky (Council for Peace in Liberia), a traditional chief, a representative of the National Liberation Conference and Wilton Sankawulo as chair. The council is to govern until elections are held within a year.

A transitional government was announced on 2 Sept. 1995 which included:

Foreign Affairs: Momolu Sirleaf (NPFL). *Defence:* Hezekiah Bowen. *Finance:* Lansana Kromah (ULIMO-Mandingo). *Justice:* Francis Garlawolo (NPFL). *Information:* Victoria Reffell (NPFL).

National flag: Six red and five white horizontal stripes alternating. In the upper corner, nearest the staff, is a square of blue covering a depth of 5 stripes. In the centre of this blue field is a 5-pointed white star.

National anthem: 'All hail, Liberia, hail!'; words by President Daniel Warner, tune by O. Lucas.

DEFENCE. The Armed Forces of Liberia are confined to the capital, Monrovia, and number about 2,000. ULIMO and NPFL forces control most of the country with combat strengths of 7,000 and 12,000 respectively.

An ECOWAS peacekeeping force (ECOMOG, with forces from Ghana, Guinea, Nigeria and Sierra Leone) of some 8,600 is deployed. There is also a 70-strong UN Observer Mission (UNOMIL).

INTERNATIONAL RELATIONS

Membership. Liberia is a member of the UN, OAU, ECOWAS and is an ACP state of the EU.

ECONOMY

Budget. Revenue and expenditure was as follows (in US$1,000):

	1984–85	1985–86	1986–87	1987–88
Revenue	315,000	237,600	366,400	202,800
Expenditure	371,000	366,700	366,400	248,900

Currency. US currency is legal tender. There is a *Liberian dollar* (LRD), in theory at parity with the US dollar. There are coins of 1, 5, 10, 25 and 50 cents and $1, and notes of $5. Since 1993 different notes have been in use in government-held Monrovia and the rebel-held country areas.

Banking and Finance. The National Bank of Liberia opened on 22 July 1974 to act as a central bank.

Weights and Measures. Weights and measures are the same as in UK and USA.

ENERGY AND NATURAL RESOURCES

Electricity. Installed capacity, 1991, 325 MW. Production, 1986, 655m. kWh.

Minerals. Iron ore production was 8·9m. tonnes in 1985. Gold production (1986) 21,125 oz valued at US$7·3m. and diamond production (1985) 66,000 carats.

Agriculture. Over 65% of the labour force was engaged in agriculture. The soil is productive, but due to excessive rainfall there are large swamp areas. Rice, cassava, coffee, citrus and sugar-cane are cultivated. Coffee, cocoa and palm-kernels are produced mainly by the traditional agricultural sector.

Production (1988, in 1,000 tonnes): Rice, 279; cassava, 310; coffee, 5; oranges, 7; sugar-cane, 225; cocoa, 5; palm-kernels, 8.

Livestock (1988): Cattle, 42,000; pigs, 140,000; sheep, 240,000; poultry, 4m.

Forestry. There are about 165,000 acres of rubber plantations. Timber production in 1986 was 4·75m. cu. metres.

Fisheries. Catch (1986) 16,100 tonnes.

INDUSTRY. There are a number of small factories (brick and tile, soap, nails, mattresses, shoes, plastics, paint, oxygen, acetylene, tyre retreading, a brewery, soft drinks, cement, matches, candy and biscuits).

FOREIGN ECONOMIC RELATIONS. Foreign debt was US$1,989m. in 1991.

Commerce. Imports in 1991 totalled L$4,081·2m. (1990, L$4,186·8m.) and exports L$556·5m. (1990, L$1,940·6m.). Liberia's main trading partners in 1991 were Norway, South Korea, Spain and Belgium.

In 1987, iron ore accounted for about 70% of total export earnings, rubber 15% and sawn timber over 5%. Other exports were coffee, cocoa, palm-kernel oil, diamonds and gold.

Total trade between Liberia and UK (British Department of Trade returns, in £1,000 sterling):

	1991	1992	1993	1994	1995
Imports to UK	972	4,654	56	254	544
Exports and re-exports from UK	8,865	8,766	9,549	8,510	8,456

The figures for exports from the UK include the value of shipping transferred to the Liberian flag; the genuine exports are considerably lower.

COMMUNICATIONS

Roads. In 1981, there were 4,794 miles of public roads (1,165 primary, 366 paved, 799 all-weather, 3,629 secondary and feeder) and 1,474 miles of private roads (93 paved, 1,381 laterite and earth).

Railways. A railway (for freight only) was built in 1951, connecting Monrovia with the Bomi Hills iron-ore mines about 69 km distant; this has been extended to the National Iron Ore Co. area by 79 km. There is a line from Bong to Monrovia (78 km). All railways were out of use in 1996 because of the civil war.

Civil Aviation. There is an international airport (Roberts) at Monrovia. The national carrier is Air Liberia. Air services are also maintained by Air Afrique, Air Guinée, Ethiopian Airways and Nigerian Airways.

Shipping. Over 2,000 vessels enter Monrovia each year. The Liberian Government requires only a modest registration fee and an almost nominal annual charge and maintains no control over the operation of ships flying the Liberian flag. In 1995, shipping registered totalled 91·76m. DWT, all foreign-owned.

Telecommunications. There is a telephone service (8,510 telephones, 1983), in Monrovia, which was gradually being extended over the whole country. There were (1988) 570,000 radio and 43,000 television receivers.

Press. The 4 independent and 1 government newspaper ceased publication in the civil war, but 2 new independent titles appeared in 1992.

SOCIAL INSTITUTIONS

Justice. Justice is administered by a Supreme Court of 5 judges, 14 circuit courts and lower courts.

Religion. There were (1993) about 0·85m. Sunni Moslems, and some 125,000 Roman Catholics, 50,000 Methodists, 40,000 Baptists, 32,000 Lutherans and 25,000 Anglicans.

Education. Schools are classified as: (1) Public schools, maintained and run by the Government; (2) Mission schools, supported by foreign Missions and subsidized by the Government, and operated by qualified Missionaries and Liberian teachers; (3) Private schools, maintained by endowments and sometimes subsidized by the Government.

In 1986 there were estimated to be 1,830 schools with 8,744 teachers and 443,786 pupils. There is a university.

Health. There were 236 doctors in 1981 and about 3,000 hospital beds.

DIPLOMATIC REPRESENTATIVES

Of Liberia in Great Britain (2 Pembridge Pl., London, W2 4XB)
Ambassador: (Vacant).

Of Great Britain in Liberia (PO Box 10-0120, 1000, Monrovia)
The embassy closed on 8 March 1991.

Of Liberia in the USA (5201 16th St., NW, Washington, D.C., 20011)
Ambassador: Vacant.

Of the USA in Liberia (United Nations Drive, Monrovia)
Ambassador: Vacant.

Of Liberia to the United Nations
Ambassador: William Bull.

Further Reading

Daniels, A., *Monrovia Mon Amour: a Visit to Liberia.* London, 1992
Elwood Dunn, D., *Liberia.* [Bibliography]. Oxford and Santa Barbara (CA), 1995
Sawyer, A., *The Emergence of Autocracy in Liberia: Tragedy and Challenge.* San Francisco, 1992

LIBYA

Capital: Tripoli
Population: 4m. (1990)
GNP per capita: US$5,410 (1988)
HDI/world rank: 0·768/73 (1992)

Jamahiriya Al-Arabiya Al-Libiya Al-Shabiya Al-Ishtirakiya Al-Uzma
(Great Socialist People's Libyan Arab Republic)

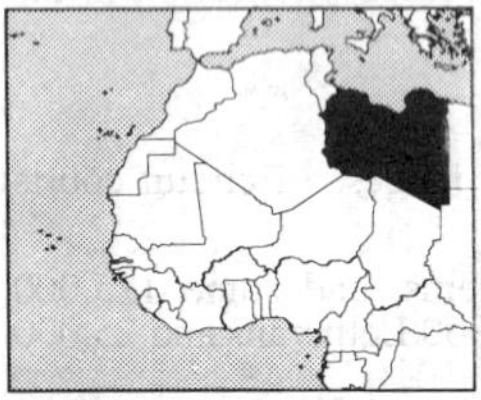

KEY HISTORICAL EVENTS. Tripoli fell under Turkish domination in the 16th century, and though in 1711 the Arab population secured some measure of independence, the country was in 1835 proclaimed a Turkish vilayet. In Sept. 1911 Italy occupied Tripoli and on 17 Oct. 1912, Turkey recognized the sovereignty of Italy in Tripoli.

After the expulsion of the Germans and Italians in 1942 and 1943, Tripolitania and Cyrenaica were placed under British, and the Fezzan under French, military administration. Britain recognized the Amir Mohammed Idris Al-Senussi as Amir of Cyrenaica in June 1949. Libya became an independent, sovereign, federal kingdom under the latter, as King of the United Kingdom of Libya, on 24 Dec. 1951.

On 1 Sept. 1969 King Idris was deposed by a group of army officers. Twelve of the group of officers formed the Revolutionary Command Council chaired by Col. Muammar Qadhafi and proclaimed a republic.

TERRITORY AND POPULATION. Libya is bounded in the north by the Mediterranean Sea, east by Egypt and Sudan, south by Chad and Niger and west by Algeria and Tunisia. The area is estimated at 1,759,540 sq. km (679,358 sq. miles). The population, at the census on 31 July 1984, was 3,637,488; estimate (1990), 4m.

In 1985, 65% of the population was urban. The chief cities (1981) were: Tripoli, the capital (858,000), Benghazi (368,000) and Misurata (117,000).

The populations (1984) of the municipalities were as follows:

Ajdabiya	100,547	Jabal al-Akhdar	120,662	Shati	46,749
Awbari	48,701	Khums	149,642	Surt	110,996
Aziziyah	85,068	Kufrah	25,139	Tarhunah	84,640
Benghazi	485,386	Marzuq	42,294	Tobruk	94,006
Derna	105,031	Misurata	178,295	Tripoli	990,697
Fatah	102,763	Niqat al-Khums	181,584	Yafran	73,420
Ghadames	52,247	Sabha	76,171	Zawia	220,075
Gharyan	117,073	Sawfajjin	45,195	Zlitan	101,107

The official language is Arabic.

CLIMATE. The coastal region has a warm temperate climate, with mild wet winters and hot dry summers, though most of the country suffers from aridity. Tripoli. Jan. 52°F (11·1°C), July 81°F (27·2°C). Annual rainfall 16" (400 mm). Benghazi. Jan. 56°F (13·3°C), July 77°F (25°C). Annual rainfall 11" (267 mm).

CONSTITUTION AND GOVERNMENT. In 1977 a new form of direct democracy, the state of the masses, was promulgated and the name of the country was changed to Great Socialist People's Libyan Arab Republic. Under this system, every adult is supposed to be able to share in policy making through the Basic People's Congresses of which there are some 2,000. These Congresses appoint People's Committees to execute policy. Provincial and urban affairs are handled by People's Committees responsible to Municipality People's Congresses, of which there are 13. Officials of these Congresses and Committees form at national level the 3,000-member General People's Congress which normally meets for about a week early each year (usually in March). This is the highest policy-making body in the country. The General People's Congress appoints its own General Secretariat and the General People's Committee, whose members (the equivalents of ministers elsewhere) head the government departments which execute policy at national level.

Until 1977 Libya was ruled by a Revolutionary Command Council (RCC) headed by Col. Muammar Qadhafi. Upon its abolition in that year the 5 surviving members of the RCC became the General Secretariat of the General People's Congress, still under Qadhafi's direction. In 1979 they stood down to be replaced by officials elected by the Congress. Since then, Col. Qadhafi has retained his position as Leader of the Revolution. But neither he nor his former RCC colleagues have any formal posts in the present administration, although they continue to wield considerable authority.

In Oct. 1995 the Secretariat of the Congress comprised:

Secretary: Zanati Mohammed Al-Zanati. *Deputy Secretary:* Abu Zaid Omar Durda. *Secretary for Congress Affairs:* Ali Al-Shairi. *Secretary for People's Committees' Affairs:* Mahmoud Al-Hitki. *Secretary for Trade Unions:* Ali Al-Shamikh. *Secretary for Women's Affairs:* Salma Rashid. *Secretary for Foreign Affairs:* Saad Mujbir.

The General People's Committee in Oct. 1995 comprised:

Secretary-General (Prime Minister): Abd Al-Majid Al-Qaud.

Foreign Affairs: Omar Mustapha Al-Muntasir. *Information and Culture:* Fauzia Shallabi. *Energy:* Abdullah Salem Al-Badri. *Transport and Communications:* Izz Al-Din Al-Hinshin. *Health and Social Security:* Dr Baghdadi Al-Mahmoudi. *Education, Youth and Sport, Training and Research:* Matug Mohammed Matug. *Marine Resources:* Miftah Mohammed Kuaybah. *Justice and Public Safety:* Mohammed Mahmoud Al-Hijazi. *Industry and Mining:* Mufta Azzouz. *Union with Maghreb, Egypt and the Sudan:* Juma Al-Mahdi Al-Fazzani. *State Inspection:* Mahmoud Badji. *Planning and Finance:* Dr Mohammed Bait-Al-Mal. *Economy and Commerce:* Tahir Al-Jihimi. *Utilities and Housing:* Mubarak Al-Shamikh. *'Great Man-Made River' Project:* Jadallah Azzouz Al-Talhi. *Livestock:* Messaoud Abusoud. *Tourism:* Boukhari Hawda.

The *Speaker* of the Congress is Abd Al-Raziq Sawsa.

National flag: Plain green.

National anthem: 'Allah Akbar' ('God is Great'); words by Abdullah Al-Din, tune by Mahmoud Al-Sharif.

Local Government. An administrative decentralizing reform of Oct. 1992 divided the country into some 1,500 self-managing communes, each with an elected 13-member People's Committee.

DEFENCE. There is selective conscription for 2 years.

Army. There are 7 military districts. The Army is organized into 5 elite and 5 surface-to-surface missile brigades and 21 infantry, 8 mechanized infantry, 22 artillery, 8 air defence, 10 tank and 15 parachute commando battalions. Equipment includes 1,600 T-54/-55, 350 T-62 and 260 T-72 main battle tanks. Strength (1996) 50,000 (25,000 conscripts).

Navy. The fleet, a mixture of Soviet and West European-built ships, comprises 4 old Soviet-built diesel submarines, 2 missile-armed frigates, 4 missile-armed corvettes, 24 fast missile craft, 8 inshore patrol craft and 8 offshore minesweepers. There are 2 tank landing ships and 3 medium landing ships as well as 3 landing craft. Auxiliaries include 1 logistic support ship, 1 salvage ship, 6 transports and 1 diving support ship.

There is a small Naval Aviation wing operating 25 Mi-14 Haze and 5 Super-Frelon helicopters from shore bases.

Personnel in 1995 totalled 8,000, including coastguard. The forces are based at Tripoli, Benghazi, Derna, Tobruk, Sidi Bilal and Al Khums.

Air Force. The creation of an Air Force began in 1959. In 1974, delivery was completed of a total of 110 Mirage 5 combat aircraft and trainers. They have been followed by 10 Tu-22 supersonic reconnaissance bombers, 70 MiG-25 interceptors and reconnaissance aircraft, 100 Su-22 ground attack fighters, 94 MiG-21s, and about 140 MiG-23 variable-geometry fighters and fighter-bombers from the USSR. In 1989 the first of 15 Su-24D supersonic bombers were delivered. Other equipment includes 50 Mirage F1 fighters from France, 6 Mirage F1-B two-seat trainers, 20 Mi-24 gunship helicopters, 10 C-130/L-100 Hercules, 10 An-26, 12 Il-76 and 20 Aeritalia G222T transports, 8 Super Frelon and 6 Agusta-built CH-47C Chinook heavy-lift helicopters, and a total of 16 Bell 212, Bell 47, Alouette III and Mi-8 helicopters. Training is performed on piston-engined SF.260Ms (some of which are armed for light attack duties) from Italy; L-39 Albatros, Galeb and Magister jet aircraft; and twin-engined L-410s built in Czechoslovakia. Personnel total (1995) about 22,000, with some of the combat aircraft operated by Syrian aircrew, with 417 combat aircraft and 52 armed helicopters, of which many are probably in store.

INTERNATIONAL RELATIONS

Membership. Libya is a member of the UN, OAU, OPEC and the Arab League.

ECONOMY

Policy. An enactment of the People's General Congress in Sept. 1992 authorizes the privatization of enterprises. A Plan covered 1994–96.

Budget. A budget of LD3,240m. was announced for 1991.

Currency. The unit of currency is the *Libyan dinar* (LYD) of 1,000 *millemes*. There are notes of LD 0·25, 0·50, 1, 5 and 10. The dinar was devalued 15% in Nov. 1994, and alongside the official exchange rate a new rate was applied to private sector imports. In March 1996, LD 0·543 = £1; LD 0·356 = US$1; LD 0·241 = DM1.

Banking and Finance. A National Bank of Libya was established in 1955; it was renamed the Central Bank of Libya in 1972. The *Governor* is Said Al-Zilitny. All foreign banks were nationalized by Dec. 1970. In 1972 the government set up the Libyan Arab Foreign Bank whose function is overseas investment and to participate in multinational banking corporations. The National Agricultural Bank has been set up to give loans and subsidies to farmers to develop their land and to assist them in marketing their crops.

Weights and Measures. Although the metric system has been officially adopted and is obligatory for all contracts, the following weights and measures are still used: *oke* = 1·282 kg; *kantar* = 51·28 kg; *draa* = 46 cm; *handaza* = 68 cm.

ENERGY AND NATURAL RESOURCES

Electricity. Electricity capacity (1985) 5,615 MW. Production (1986) 2,126m. kWh.

Oil. Oil revenues provided 28·2% of GDP in 1990. Crude oil production (1995) 1,426,000 bbls. a day. Reserves (1988) 23,000m. bbls. The Libyan National Oil Corporation (NOC) was established in March 1970 to be the state's organization for the exploitation of oil resources. NOC does not participate in the production of oil but has a majority share in nearly all operating companies.

Gas. Reserves (1988) 620,000m. cu. metres.

Water. Since 1984 a major project has been under way to bring water from wells in southern Libya to the coast. This scheme, called the 'Great Man-Made River', is planned, on completion, to irrigate some 185,000 acres of land with water brought along some 4,000 km of pipes. Phase I was completed in Aug. 1991 at a cost of US$3,300m; Phase II of the project (covering the west of Libya) was announced in Sept. 1989.

Minerals. Cement production (1987) 2·7m. tonnes. Gypsum output (1982) 172,400 tonnes. Iron ore deposits have been found in the south.

Agriculture. Only the coastal zone, which covers an area of about 17,000 sq. miles, is really suitable for agriculture. Of some 25m. acres of productive land, nearly 20m. are used for grazing and about 1m. for static farming. The sub-desert zone produces the alfa plant. The desert zone and the Fezzan contain some fertile oases.

Cyrenaica has about 10m. acres of potentially productive land and is suitable for grazing. Certain areas are suitable for dry farming; in addition, grapes, olives and dates are grown. About 143,000 acres are used for settled farming; about 272,000 acres are covered by natural forests. The Agricultural Development Authority plans to reclaim 6,000 ha each year for agriculture. In the Fezzan there are about 6,700 acres of irrigated gardens and about 297,000 acres are planted with date palms.

Production (1993, in tonnes): Wheat, 150,000; barley, 150,000; olives, 72,000; dates, 77,000; milk, 172,000; meat, 137,000.

Livestock (1993): 5·7m. sheep, 1·26m. goats, 135,000 cattle, camels, 160,000, 26m. poultry.

Fisheries. The catch in 1986 was 7,800 tonnes.

INDUSTRY. Industry is nationalized. Since the revolution there has been an ambitious programme of industrial development aimed at the local manufacture of building materials (steel and aluminium pipes and fittings, electric cables, cement, bricks, glass, etc.), foodstuffs (dairy products, flour, tinned fruits and vegetables, dates, fish processing and canning, etc.), textiles and footwear (ready-made clothing, woollen and cotton cloth, blankets, leather footwear, etc.) and development of mineral deposits (iron ore, phosphates, mineral salts). Small scale private sector industrialization in the form of partnerships is permitted.

FOREIGN ECONOMIC RELATIONS. Since 1986 the USA has applied a trade embargo on the grounds of Libya's alleged complicity in terrorism. In Dec. 1993 UN sanctions were imposed for Libya's refusal to deliver suspected terrorists for trial in the UK or USA. In Feb. 1989 Libya signed a treaty of economic co-operation with the 4 other Maghreb countries, Algeria, Mauritania, Morocco and Tunisia.

Commerce. Some 80% of GDP derives from trade. Oil accounts for over 95% of exports worth annually about US$10,000m. Total imports in 1991 were valued at US$8,690 and exports at US$10,200. Main trading partners in 1990 (values in US$1m.): Exports, Italy (5,023), Federal Germany (2,216), Spain (1,163), France (761); imports, Italy (1,153), Federal Germany (751), UK (434), France (378).

Total trade between Libya and UK (British Department of Trade returns, in £1,000 sterling):

	1991	*1992*	*1993*	*1994*	*1995*
Imports to UK	121,220	162,900	156,542	148,151	131,787
Exports and re-exports from UK	255,719	228,274	274,051	194,905	227,369

COMMUNICATIONS

Roads. In 1986 there were 25,675 km of roads.

Civil Aviation. A national airline, the Jamahiriya Libyan Arab Airlines, links Benghazi and Tripoli to Athens, Rome, Madrid, Malta, Moscow, Frankfurt, Paris, Amsterdam, Vienna and Zurich. In 1995 it operated 2 B-707-320Cs, 1 B-727-200, 8 B-727-200 Advs and 48 other aircraft (including 21 ex-Soviet).

Shipping. Sea-going vessels totalled 1·22m. GRT in 1995, including oil tankers, 1·09m. GRT.

Telecommunications. In 1982 some 102,000 telephones were in use. Broadcasting is controlled by the government Libyan Jamihiriya Broadcasting and People's Revolution Broadcasting-Television. Radio has a home service, external services in English, French and Arabic and a Holy Koran programme. In 1993 there were estimated to be 1m. radio and 0·5m. TV receivers (colour by PAL).

Press. There was (1990) 1 daily in Tripoli with a circulation of about 40,000 and a number of weeklies.

SOCIAL INSTITUTIONS

Justice. The Civil, Commercial and Criminal codes are based mainly on the Egyptian model. Matters of personal status of family or succession matters affecting Moslems are dealt with in special courts according to the Moslem law. All other matters, civil, commercial and criminal, are tried in the ordinary courts, which have jurisdiction over everyone.

There are civil and penal courts in Tripoli and Benghazi, with subsidiary courts at Misurata and Derna; courts of assize in Tripoli and Benghazi, and courts of appeal in Tripoli and Benghazi.

Religion. Islam is declared the State religion, but the right of others to practise their religions is provided for. In 1990, 97% were Sunni Moslems.

Education. There were (1981–82) 718,124 pupils in primary schools, 286,414 in preparatory and secondary schools, 44,789 pupils in technical schools and 25,700 students in higher education. In 1994–95 there were 3 universities and 1 medical and 1 technological university. There were 3 other institutes of higher education. In 1994–95 there were 31,140 university students and 1,710 academic staff.

Health. In 1981 there were 74 hospitals with 15,375 beds, 4,690 physicians, 314 dentists, 420 pharmacists, 1,080 midwives and 5,346 nursing personnel.

DIPLOMATIC REPRESENTATIVES

UK broke off diplomatic relations with Libya on 22 April 1984. Saudi Arabia looks after Libyan interests in UK and Italy looks after UK's interests in Libya.

USA suspended all embassy activities in Tripoli on 2 May 1980.

Of Libya to the United Nations
Ambassador: Mohamed A. Azwai.

Further Reading

Bearman, J., *Qadhafi's Libya.* London, 1986
Blundy, D. and Lycett, A., *Qadhafi and the Libyan Revolution.* London, 1987
Davis, J., *Libyan Politics: Tribe and Revolution.* London, 1988
Harris, L. C., *Libya: Qadhafi's Revolution and the Modern State.* Boulder (CO) and London, 1986
Lawless, R. I., *Libya.* [Bibliography] Oxford and Santa Barbara (CA), 1987
Simons, G., *Libya: the Struggle for Survival.* London, 1993
Vandewalle, D. (ed.) *Qadhafi's Libya, 1969–1994.* London, 1995
Wright, J., *Libya: A Modern History.* London, 1982

LIECHTENSTEIN

Capital: Vaduz
Population: 30,629 (1994)

Fürstentum Liechtenstein

(Principality of Liechtenstein)

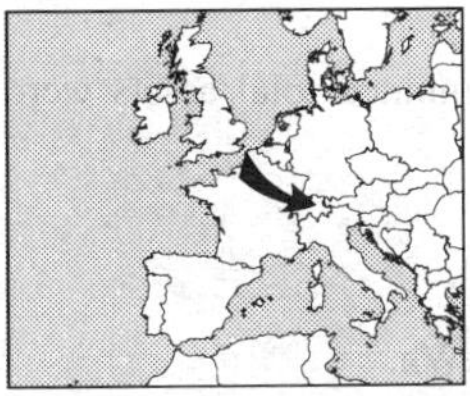

KEY HISTORICAL EVENTS. Liechtenstein is a sovereign state whose history dates back to 3 May 1342, when Count Hartmann III became ruler of the county of Vaduz. Additions were later made to the count's domains, and by 1434 the territory reached its present boundaries. It consists of the two former counties of Schellenberg and Vaduz (until 1806 immediate fiefs of the Holy Roman Empire). The former in 1699 and the latter in 1712 came into the possession of the house of Liechtenstein. On 23 Jan. 1719 the Emperor Charles VI constituted the two counties as the Principality of Liechtenstein.

TERRITORY AND POPULATION. Liechtenstein is bounded on the east by Austria and the west by Switzerland. Area, 160 sq. km (61·8 sq. miles); population (census 1990), 28,777; estimate, 1994, 30,629 (15,731 females), including 11,774 resident foreigners. In 1994 there were 358 births and 206 deaths. Population of Vaduz (census 1990), 4,870; estimate, 1994, 5,067. The language is German.

PRINCELY HOUSE. The reigning Prince is **Hans-Adam II,** b. 14 Feb. 1945; succeeded his father Prince Francis-Joseph, 13 Nov. 1989 (he exercised the prerogatives to which the Sovereign is entitled from 26 Aug. 1984); married on 30 July 1967 to Countess Marie Kinsky; there are 3 sons, Hereditary Prince Alois (b. 11 June 1968), married Duchess Sophie of Bavaria on 3 July 1993 and have 1 son, Prince Joseph Wenzel (b. 16 May 1995); Prince Maximilian (b. 16 May 1969) and Prince Constantin (b. 15 March 1972), and one daughter, Princess Tatjana (b. 10 April 1973). The monarchy is hereditary in the male line.

CONSTITUTION AND GOVERNMENT. Liechtenstein is a constitutional monarchy ruled by the princes of the House of Liechtenstein. The present constitution of 5 Oct. 1921 provided for a unicameral parliament (*Landtag*) of 15 members elected for 4 years, but this was amended to 25 members in 1988. Election is on the basis of proportional representation. The prince can call and dismiss the parliament. On parliamentary recommendation, he appoints the prime minister and the 4 councillors for a 4-year term. Any group of 1,000 persons or any 3 communes may propose legislation (initiative). Bills passed by the parliament may be submitted to popular referendum. A law is valid when it receives a majority approval by the parliament and the prince's signed concurrence. The capital is Vaduz.

At the elections for the Landtag, on 24 Oct. 1993, the Fatherland Union (FU) obtained 13 seats.

Head of Government and Foreign Minister: Dr Mario Frick (b. 1965; FU).
Speaker: Otmar Hasler.

National flag: Horizontally blue over red, with a gold coronet in the first quarter.
National anthem: 'Oben am jungen Rhein' ('Up above the young Rhine'); words by H. H. Jauch; tune, 'God save the Queen'.

Local government. There are 11 communes, fully independent administrative bodies within the laws of the principality. They levy additional taxes to the state taxes.

INTERNATIONAL RELATIONS

Membership. Liechtenstein is a member of the UN, EFTA and the Council of

Europe. At a referendum on 9 April 1995 55·9% of votes cast were in favour of joining the European Economic Area.

ECONOMY

Budget. Budget (in Swiss francs), 1996: Revenue, 562,485,000; expenditure, 537,878,000. There is no public debt.

Currency. Swiss currency has been in use since 1921.

Banking and Finance. There were (1995) 5 banks. Combined total assets were 23,477·9m. Swiss francs in 1995.

Weights and Measures. The metric system is in force.

ENERGY AND NATURAL RESOURCES

Electricity. Electricity produced in 1994 was 61,339,000 kWh.

Agriculture. In 1990 there were 3,890 ha of cultivated land and 2,510 ha of Alpine pasture. The rearing of cattle on the Alpine pastures is highly developed. In 1994 there were 5,844 cattle (including 2,677 milk cows), 273 horses, 2,627 sheep, 136 goats, 2,787 pigs. Total production of dairy produce, 1994, 12,685,464 kg.

Forestry. In 1990 there were 5,560 ha of forest. 26,315 cu. metres of timber were cut in 1994.

INDUSTRY. The country is highly industrialized, and has a great variety of light industries (textiles, ceramics, steel screws, precision instruments, canned food, pharmaceutical products, heating appliances, etc.).

Labour. The farming population has gone down from 70% in 1930 to 1·7% in 1994. The rapid change-over has led to the immigration of foreign workers (Austrians, Germans, Italians, Spaniards). The workforce was 14,759 in 1994, excluding employees commuting from abroad (7,334 in 1994). Industrial undertakings affiliated to the Liechtenstein Chamber of Commerce in 1994 employed 6,423 workers earning 420m. Swiss francs.

FOREIGN ECONOMIC RELATIONS. Liechtenstein has been in a customs union with Switzerland since 1923.

Commerce. Exports of home produce in 1994 (in Swiss francs), for member companies affiliated to the Chamber of Industry and Commerce, amounted to 2,644·6m.: 527·3m. (19·9%) went to EFTA countries, of which Switzerland took 369·8m. (14%), and 1,046·2m. (39·6%) went to EEC countries. Imports in 1994 amounted to 1,053·5m. Swiss francs.

Total trade with UK is included with Switzerland from 1968.

Tourism. In 1994, 62,080 overnight visitors arrived in Liechtenstein.

COMMUNICATIONS

Roads. There are 250 km of roads. Postal buses are the chief means of public transportation within the country and to Austria and Switzerland. There were 18,256 cars in 1994. There were 458 road accidents in 1994 (3 fatal).

Railways. The 18·5 km of main railway passing through the country is operated by Austrian Federal Railways.

Telecommunications. In 1994 there were 18,554 telephones and 148 telex, 11,203 radios and 10,819 TV sets. Post and telegraphs are administered by Switzerland.

Cinemas. There were 2 cinemas in 1994.

Press. In 1994 there were 2 daily newspapers with a total circulation of 17,400, and 1 weekly with a circulation of 13,900.

SOCIAL INSTITUTIONS

Justice. The principality has its own civil and penal codes. The lowest court is the county court, *Landgericht*, presided over by one judge, which decides minor civil cases and summary criminal offences. The criminal court, *Kriminalgericht*, with a bench of 5 judges is for major crimes. Another court of mixed jurisdiction is the court of assizes (with 3 judges) for misdemeanours. Juvenile cases are treated in the Juvenile Court (with a bench of 3 judges). The superior court, *Obergericht*, and Supreme Court, *Oberster Gerichtshof*, are courts of appeal for civil and criminal cases (both with benches of 5 judges). An administrative court of appeal from government actions and the State Court determines the constitutionality of laws.

The death penalty was abolished in 1989.

Police. The principality has no army. Police force, 1995: 59, auxiliary police, 19.

Religion. In 1994 there were 24,614 Roman Catholics and 2,175 Protestants.

Education (1994–95). In 14 primary, 3 upper, 5 secondary and 1 grammar schools there were 3,778 pupils and 258 teachers. There is also an evening technical school, a music school and a children's pedagogic-welfare day school.

Health. There is an obligatory sickness insurance scheme. In 1989 there was 1 hospital, but Liechtenstein has an agreement with the Swiss cantons of St Gallen and Graubünden and the Austrian Federal State of Vorarlberg that her citizens may use certain hospitals.

DIPLOMATIC REPRESENTATIVES

In 1919, Switzerland agreed to represent the interests of Liechtenstein in countries where it has diplomatic missions and where Liechtenstein is not represented in its own right. In so doing Switzerland always acts only on the basis of mandates of a general or specific nature, which it may either accept or refuse, while Liechtenstein is free to enter into direct relations with foreign states or to set up its own additional diplomatic missions.

Of Great Britain in Liechtenstein
Ambassador: D. Beattie, CMG (resides in Berne).

USA Consul-General: Sheldon I. Krebs (resident in Zürich).

Of Liechtenstein to the United Nations
Ambassador: Claudia Fritsche.

Further Reading

Amt für Volkswirtschaft. *Statistisches Jahrbuch.* Vaduz

Rechenschaftsbericht der Fürstlichen Regierung. Vaduz. Annual, from 1922
Jahrbuch des Historischen Vereins. Vaduz. Annual since 1901
Larke, T. A. T., *Index and Thesaurus of Liechtenstein.* 2nd ed. Berkeley (CA), 1984
Raton, P., *Liechtenstein: History and Institutions of the Principality.* Vaduz, 1970
Seger, O., *A Survey of Liechtenstein History.* 4th English ed. Vaduz, 1984

National library: Landesbibliothek, Vaduz
National statistical office: Amt für Volkswirtschaft, Vaduz

LITHUANIA

Lietuvos Respublika

Capital: Vilnius
Population: 3·74m. (1994)
GNP per capita: US$1,350 (1994)
HDI/world rank: 0·769/71 (1992)

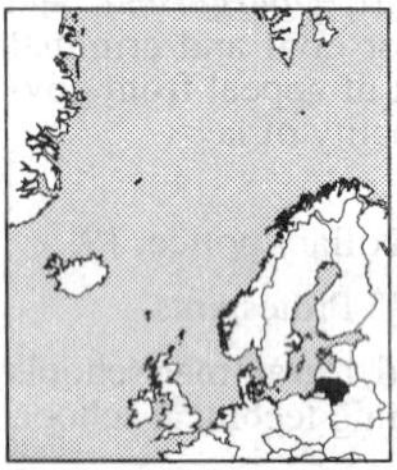

KEY HISTORICAL EVENTS. Lithuanian tribes, organized into state units in the 9th century, unified in the face of encroachment by the German order of Teutonic Knights. At the time of Tatar-Mongol domination of Russia, Lithuania annexed Russian lands until by the middle of the 15th century Belorussia, parts of Russia and the Ukraine as far as the Black Sea were under its rule. Lithuania united with Poland dynastically in 1385 and politically in 1569. During the Russian partitions of Poland in the 18th century Lithuania yielded its Russian territories and was itself absorbed into the Russian empire in 1795.

Germany occupied Lithuania during the First World War. Following the Russian revolution a Lithuanian government was formed on 7 Feb. 1918, but Soviet troops reoccupied Lithuania in Jan. 1919. These were expelled (having ceded Vilnius to Lithuania) by Polish forces in April 1919; the Lithuanian government re-formed and a democratic republic was established. In Oct. 1919 Poland occupied Vilnius and incorporated it into Poland in 1923. (This was acknowledged by Lithuania only in 1938). In Dec. 1926 the democratic regime was overthrown by a coup.

The secret protocol of the Soviet–German frontier treaty of 28 Sept. 1939 assigned the greater part of Lithuania to the Soviet sphere of influence. In Oct. 1939 the province and city of Vilnius (in Polish occupation 1920–39) were ceded by the USSR. An ultimatum (16 June 1940) led to the formation of a government acceptable to the USSR. Lithuania became a Soviet Socialist Republic of the USSR on 3 Aug.

On 11 March 1990 the newly-elected Lithuanian Supreme Soviet, by 120 votes to nil, proclaimed independence based on the continuing validity of the act of independence of 16 Feb. 1918. This decision was not accepted by the USSR government.

Massive price rises in Jan. 1991 triggered demonstrations from ethnic Russians and led the Prime Minister, Kazimiera Prunskiene, to resign. Initially dispatched to Vilnius to enforce conscription, Soviet army units occupied key buildings in the face of mounting popular unrest. On 13 Jan. the army fired on demonstrators and there were fatal casualties. A referendum on independence was held in Feb. 1991 at which 90·5% voted in favour. A fully independent status was conceded by the USSR State Council on 6 Sept. 1991.

CLIMATE. Vilnius. Jan. –2°C, July 15·6°C. Annual rainfall 826 mm. Klaipėda. Jan. 0·9°C, July 16·5°C. Annual rainfall 685 mm.

TERRITORY AND POPULATION. Lithuania is bounded in the north by Latvia, east and south by Belarus, and west by Poland, the Russian exclave of Kaliningrad and the Baltic Sea. The total area is 65,200 sq. km (25,170 sq. miles) and the population (Jan. 1994) 3,724,000 (1,962,800 females; 2,533,400 urban). The 1989 census population was 3,674,802, of whom Lithuanians accounted for 79·6%, Russians 9·4%, Poles 7%, Belorussians 1·7% and Ukrainians 1·2%. In 1994 there were the following ethnic groups (in 1,000): Russians, 316·6; Poles, 261·5; Belorussians, 57; Ukrainians, 38·5; Jews, 6·5; others, 25. Vital statistics, 1993: Births, 46,727; deaths, 46,107; marriages, 23,709; divorces, 13,884; infant deaths, 746. Rates (per 1,000 population): Growth, 0·2; birth, 12·5; death, 12·3; marriage, 6·3; divorce, 3·7; infant mortality (per 1,000 live births), 15·6. Expectation of life, 1994: Males, 62·8 years; females, 74·9. In 1993 there were 84,987 emigrants and 71,847 immigrants.

The capital is Vilnius (1994 population, 578,700). Other large towns are

Kaunas (419,000), Klaipėda (203,400), Šiauliai (147,300) and Panėvežys (131,600). The official language is Lithuanian, but ethnic minorities have the right to official use of their language where they form a substantial part of the population.

Residents who applied by 3 Nov. 1991 received Lithuanian citizenship, requirements for which are 10 years residence and competence in Lithuanian.

CONSTITUTION AND GOVERNMENT. Parliament is the 141-member *Seimas.* It is elected by a system partly proportional and partly constituency-based. 70 seats are allocated to parties according to their share of the vote (with a 4% threshold except for ethnic parties). The 71 constituency seats require candidates to poll more than 50% of the vote, otherwise there are run-offs.

The *Constitutional Court* is empowered to rule on whether proposed laws conflict with the constitution or existing legislation. It comprises 9 judges who serve 9-year terms, one third rotating every 3 years.

General elections and a referendum to approve a new constitution were held on 25 Oct. 1992 (with run-offs in 51 constituencies on 10 Nov.). The Lithuanian Democratic Labour Party (LDDP; former Communists) won 73 seats, Sajudis 30, the Christian Democrats 16, the Social Democrats 8, the Union of Poles 4, independents 1, others 9.

A the presidential elections of Feb. 1993 the electorate was 2,586,016; turn-out was 78·1%. Algirdas Brazauskas gained 60% of votes cast against a single opponent.

President: Algirdas Brazauskas (b. 1932; LDDP; sworn in 25 Feb. 1993).

A government was formed in Feb. 1993 which comprised in Feb. 1996:

Prime Minister: Mindaugas Stankevičius (b. 1928; LDDP).

Foreign: Povilas Gylys. *Economics:* Gytas Navickas. *Finance:* Reinoldijus Sarkinas. *Trade and Industry:* Kazimieras Klimasauskas. *Justice:* Jonas Prapiestis. *Interior:* Vacant. *Defence:* Linas Linkevičius. *Science and Education:* Vladislovas Domarkas. *Agriculture:* Vytautas Einoris. *Energy:* Arvydas Kostas Lescinskas. *Social Security and Labour:* Mindaugas Mikaila. *Transport:* Jonas Biržiškis. *Building and Town Planning:* Julius Laitsonas. *Communications and Information:* Gintautas Zintelis. *Forestry:* Albertas Vasiliauskas. *Health:* Jurgis Bredikis. *Environmental Protection:* Bronius Bradauskas. *Culture:* Juozas Nekrošius. *Government Reform and Local Government:* Laurynas Mindaugas Stankevičius. *Housing and Urban Development:* Algirdas Vapsys.

The *Speaker* is Ceslovas Jursenas.

National flag: 3 horizontal strips of yellow, green and red.

National anthem: 'Lietuva tėvynė mūsu' ('Lithuania land of heroes'); words and tune by V. Kurdirka.

Local Government: There are 12 regions subdivided into 12 municipalites and 44 districts, each with an appropriate authority. Elections were held in March 1995 for 1,488 city and regional council seats. There were 7,328 candidates representing 17 parties. Turn-out was 43%. The Homeland Union won 426 seats with 29·1% of votes cast, the LDDP 297 with 19·9%, the Christian Democrats 247 with 16·9%.

DEFENCE. Conscription is for 12 months.

Army. The Army consists of 1 motor rifle brigade and 1 peacekeeping company, and in 1996 numbered 4,300. There is a paramilitary Frontier Guard of 4,000, and a 12,000-strong volunteer Home Guard reserve.

Navy. A small coastal defence flotilla numbering some 350 in 1995 has been formed manning 2 small ex-Soviet frigates, 1 ex-Swedish and 2 ex-Soviet patrol-craft and some 7 miscellaneous converted civilian vessels. It is based at Klaipeda.

Air Force. A combat squadron has L-39 armed trainers, while 2 transport squadrons operate Antonov aircraft, Mi-8 helicopters and a few L-410s. Personnel (1995), 250.

INTERNATIONAL RELATIONS

Membership. Lithuania is a member of the UN, Council of Europe, and the NATO

Partnership for Peace, and is an Associate Partner of the WEU. In Dec. 1995 Lithuania applied to join the EU.

ECONOMY

Policy. There is a privatization programme. The Lithuanian Privatization Agency was set up in 1995 to take over functions previously discharged by the Economics Ministry. By Aug. 1995 5,700 former state enteprises had been sold. Privatization has proceeded by sales, sales of shares or auctions.

Budget. The 1995 budget envisaged revenue of 3,400m. litas and expenditure of 3,800m. litas. Revenue included (in 1m. litas): VAT, 1,200; income tax, 782; capital gains tax, 289.

Currency. The unit of currency is the *litas* of 100 *centas*, which was introduced on 25 June 1993 and became the sole legal tender on 1 Aug., replacing the talonas at 1 litas = 100 talonas. There are coins of 1, 2, 5, 10, 20 and 50 centas and 1, 2 and 5 litas, and notes of 1, 2, 5, 10, 20, 50 and 100 litas. The litas was pegged to the US dollar on 1 April 1994 at US$1 = 4 litas. Inflation was 189% in 1994. 792·2m. litas were in circulation in 1993. In March 1996, £1 = 6·11 litas; DM1 = 2·71 litas.

Banking and Finance. The central bank and bank of issue is the Bank of Lithuania (*Governor*, Reinoldijas Šarkinas), which also has commercial functions. The Savings Bank, Agricultural Bank and Investment Bank are state-owned. There were 26 commercial banks and a private investment bank in 1994. A Development Bank jointly owned by the government and the EBRD in the proportions 2:1 was founded in 1994. Total liabilities of commercial banks at the end of 1993 were 4,679·9m. litas.

A stock exchange opened in Vilnius in 1993.

ENERGY AND NATURAL RESOURCES

Electricity. Output was 14,138m. kWh in 1993. There is a nuclear power station responsible for 80% of total output, 2 hydro-electric and 5 thermal plants.

Oil. Production started from a small field at Kretinga in 1990. In 1993 recoverable reserves were estimated at 40m. tonnes on-shore and 38m. tonnes off-shore.

Minerals. Peat reserves total 4,000m. cu. metres. Output, 1993, 144,000 tonnes.

Agriculture. In 1994 the agricultural land area was 3,519,300 ha, of which 2,979,900 ha were arable, 473,600 ha pasture and 65,800 ha, orchards. Agriculture accounted for 21·3% of GDP in 1992. 399,300 persons were employed in agriculture in 1993.

Area under cultivation in Nov. 1990, 4·6m. ha. Output of main agricultural products (in 1,000 tonnes) in 1993: Wheat, 884·2; potatoes, 1,772·6; rye, 434·1; sugar-beet, 855·3; vegetables, 376; meat, 275·9; milk, 2,066·7; eggs, 610·2m. units. Estimated crop yields (tonnes per ha) in 1993: Wheat, 4·98; barley, 2·12; oats, 2; potatoes, 14.

Livestock, 1994 (in 1,000): Cattle, 1,384·3 (of which milch cows, 678·1); pigs, 1,196·2; sheep and goats, 55·4; horses, 81·3; poultry, 8,728·2.

The collective farms of the Communist regime were divided into smallholdings for former collective farm workers or owners. There were about 104,000 such farms in 1993. Average farm size was 9 ha, but a law of 1993 prohibits further division of farmland below 20 ha. Land could not at first be sold to foreign nationals, but the ban was lifted for citizens of OECD countries in 1996.

Forestry. Forests cover 1·55m. ha; 70% of the forests consist of conifers, mostly pines. Output of sawn timber, 1993, 14,800m. cu. metres.

Fisheries. In 1994 the fishing fleet comprised 167 vessels totalling 248,900 GRT.

INDUSTRY. Industry accounted for 36·9% of GDP in 1992. Industrial output included, in 1993 (in 1,000 tonnes): Steel, 2,100; cast iron, 23,200; sulphuric acid,

129; mineral fertilizers, 225; paper, 14; cotton fabrics, 47·8; woollen, 12·4; silk, 17·4; linen, 13·6; (units) fur coats, 100,200; refrigerators, 276,300; TV sets, 423,100; bicycles, 116,000.

Labour. In 1993, 1,778,200 persons were in employment. In 1989 there were 1,552,500 employees in the state sector; in 1992 there were 1,188,000. In 1996 there was a legal minimum monthly wage of 210 litas. In 1994 retirement age was 55 years for women and 60 for men. This is being progressively increased to reach 65 for both sexes by 2024. There were 0·11m. registered unemployed in Oct. 1995.

FOREIGN ECONOMIC RELATIONS. On 20 April 1990 Lithuania, Estonia and Latvia concluded a Baltic Economic Co-operation Agreement. A free trade agreement with Estonia and Latvia came into force on 1 April 1994. A 10-year treaty signed with Russia in July 1991 guarantees the future of the Russian exclave of Kaliningrad. Lithuania has undertaken to supply Kaliningrad with gas and electricity with the help of Russian energy imports, and promised a free flow of goods through its territory.

Foreign investors may purchase up to 100% of the equity of companies in Lithuania. By Jan. 1995 US$125m. of foreign capital had been invested (including pledges), and 4,400 joint ventures set up.

Total foreign debt was US$486m. in Jan. 1995. Lithuania does not accept liability for the former USSR's debt.

Commerce. In 1993 exports were valued at 5,335,800 litas and imports at 5,608,600 litas, 75% of trade was with Russia. Total trade between Lithuania and UK (British Department of Trade returns, in £1,000 sterling):

	1993	*1994*	*1995*
Imports to UK	143,377	155,387	173,228
Exports and re-exports from UK	13,746	24,080	49,435

COMMUNICATIONS

Roads. In 1993 there were 42,209 km of surfaced roads, including 21,111 km of main and 16,659 km of local roads. In 1993 there were 597,735 motor cars, 16,878 buses and trolley buses, 98,771 goods vehicles and 180,450 motor cycles. There were 4,319 traffic accidents in 1993, with 892 fatalities. In 1993 road transport carried 789·9m. passengers and 170·2m. tonnes of freight.

Railways. Length of railways in 1994 was 2,010 km. on 1,520mm gauge, of which 122 km was electrified. In 1993 24·8m. passengers and 38·4m. tonnes of freight were carried.

Civil Aviation. There is an international airport at Vilnius. The national carrier is the state-owned Lithuanian Airlines which operates flights to Abu Dhabi, Amsterdam, London, Paris, Copenhagen, Berlin, Frankfurt, Istanbul, Kiev, Larnaca, Moscow, Riga, St Petersburg, Stockholm and Warsaw. It had 1 B-737-200 Adv and 20 Soviet aircraft in 1995. Services are also provided by Aeroflot, Austrian Airlines, Delta, Estonian Air, Finnair, Hamburg Airlines, LOT, Lufthansa, SAS and United Airlines.

Shipping. In 1994 the merchant fleet numbered 70 ships totalling 372,500 GRT and 7 tankers totalling 11,700 GRT. The only large port is Klaipėda, which handled 27·72m tonnes of cargo in 1994. In 1994 there were 788 km of navigable inland waterways. The inland fleet comprised 101 vessels.

Telecommunications. In 1995, telephone provision was 26·1 per 100 inhabitants (28·3 urban, 15·4 rural). The state-owned Leituvos Radijas ir Televizija broadcasts 2 national radio programmes and an external service, Radio Vilnius (Lithuanian and English) and a regional programme from Kaunas, and national, regional and minority language TV programmes (colour by SECAM). There are 5 commercial radio and 2 TV companies. In 1993 1·42m. radio and 1·4m. TV sets were in use.

Press In 1993 there were 393 newspapers (including 336 in Lithuanian, 38 in Russian, 8 in Polish and 6 in English) and 138 periodicals. 2,224 book titles were published.

SOCIAL INSTITUTIONS

Justice. Trial by jury has been introduced for capital offences. The death penalty is retained for premeditated murder. 60,378 crimes were reported in 1993, including 465 murders. 16,299 persons were convicted.

Religion. Under the Constitution, the state supports religious groups which have been active in Lithuania for 400 years, i.e., the Roman Catholic, Lutheran, Reformed and Orthodox Churches. 90% of the population are Roman Catholic. There is an archbishopric of Vilnius and 10 bishops. In 1995, the Lutheran Church had 44 churches, 54 parishes, 12 pastors headed by a bishop and some 30,000 faithful.

Education. In 1993-94, there were 927 pre-school establishments with 78,596 pupils and 2,482 schools (including 17 private) with 48,700 teachers and 633,000 pupils, in the following categories

Type of School	*No. of Schools*	*No. of Pupils*
Nursery	109	9,700
Primary	841	33,600
Junior	4	300
Elementary	574	50,900
Special	56	7,800
Secondary	692	401,900
Specialized Secondary	57	24,000
Vocational	105	45,000
Adult	30	6,000

52,840 students (29,169 females) attended 14 institutions of higher education in 1993-94, including 5 universities.

Health. In 1993 there were 16,622 doctors, 2,000 dentists, 3,200 pharmacists, 39,896 paramedics and 198 hospitals with 43,600 beds.

Social Security. At 31 Dec. 1993, 892,000 persons were eligible for pensions, including (in 1,000): Retirement, 655; disability, 127; loss of breadwinner, 48; social benefits, 41. Average monthly pensions (in litas in 1993): Retirement, 84·06; disability, 79·77; loss of breadwinner, 69·26; social benefits, 74·78.

DIPLOMATIC REPRESENTATIVES

Of Lithuania in Great Britain (17 Essex Villas, London, W8 7BP)
Ambassador: Vacant.

Of Great Britain in Lithuania (2 Anta Kalnio., 2055 Vilnius)
Ambassador: Thomas Macan.

Of Lithuania in the USA (2622 16th St., NW, Washington, D.C., 20009)
Ambassador: Alfonsas Eidinotas.

Of the USA in Lithuania (Ak Menu 6, Vilnius)
Ambassador: James W. Swihart.

Of Lithuania to the United Nations
Ambassador: Oskaras Jusys.

Further Reading

Lithuanian Department of Statistics. *Lithuania's Statistics Yearbook – Demographic Yearbook – Lithuania in Figures.* Annual.
Jurgėla, C. R., *History of the Lithuanian Nation.* New York, 1948
Kantantas, A. and F., *A Lithuanian Bibliography.* Univ. of Alberta Press, 1975
Lieven, A., *The Baltic Revolution: Estonia, Latvia, Lithuania and the Path to Independence.* 2nd ed. Yale UP, 1994
Misiunas, R. J. and Taagepera, R., *The Baltic States: the Years of Dependence, 1940–91.* 2nd ed. Farnborough, 1993
Smith, I. A. and Grunts, M. V., *The Baltic States.* [Bibliography], Oxford and Santa Barbara, 1993

National statistical office: Lithuanian Department of Statistics, Gedimino Pr. 29, 2746 Vilnius. *Director:* Kestutis Zaborskas.

LUXEMBOURG

Grand-Duché de Luxembourg

Capital: Luxembourg
Population: 406,600 (1995)
GNP per capita: US$39,850 (1994)
HDI/world rank: 0·893/27 (1992)

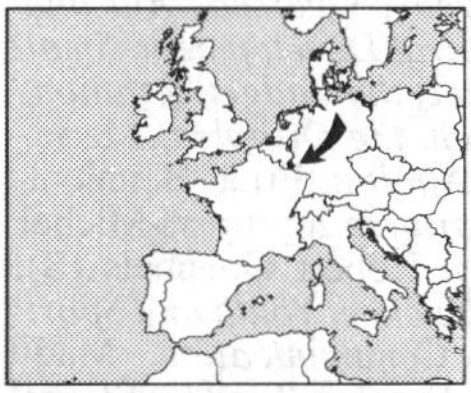

KEY HISTORICAL EVENTS. The country formed part of the Holy Roman Empire until it was conquered by the French in 1795. In 1815 the Grand Duchy of Luxembourg was formed under the house of Orange-Nassau, also sovereigns of the Netherlands. In 1839 the Walloon-speaking area was joined to Belgium. In 1890 the personal union with the Netherlands ended with the accession of a member of another branch of the house of Nassau, Grand Duke Adolphe of Weilburg.

TERRITORY AND POPULATION. Luxembourg has an area of 2,586 sq. km (999 sq. miles) and is bounded on the west by Belgium, south by France, east by Germany. The population (1995) was 406,600. The capital, Luxembourg, had (1995) 76,446 inhabitants; Esch-Alzette, the centre of the mining district, 24,255; Differdange, 16,196; Dudelange, 15,833, and Petange, 13,066. In 1995 the foreign population was about 132,500.

Vital statistics (1994): 5,451 births, 3,800 deaths, 2,352 marriages.

Letzebuergesch is spoken by most of the population, and since 1985 has been an official language with French and German.

CLIMATE. Cold, raw winters with snow covering the ground for up to a month are features of the upland areas. The remainder resembles Belgium in its climate, with rain evenly distributed throughout the year. Jan. 0·8°C, July 17·5°C. Annual rainfall 782·2 mm.

DUCAL HOUSE. The reigning Grand Duke is **Jean**, b. 5 Jan. 1921, son of the late Grand Duchess Charlotte and the late Prince Felix of Bourbon-Parma; succeeded 12 Nov. 1964 on the abdication of his mother; married to Princess Joséphine-Charlotte of Belgium, 9 April 1953. *Offspring:* Princess Marie-Astrid, b. 17 Feb. 1954, married Christian of Habsbourg-Lorraine 6 Feb. 1982 (*Offspring:* Marie Christine, b. 31 July 1983; Imre, b. 8 Dec. 1985; Christophe, b. 2 Feb. 1988; Alexander, b. 26 Sept. 1990); Prince Henri, *heir apparent*, b. 16 April 1955, married Maria Teresa Mestre 14 Feb. 1981; (*Offspring:* Prince Guillaume, b. 11 Nov. 1981, Prince Felix, b. 3 June 1984, Prince Louis, b. 3 Aug. 1986, Princess Alexandra, b. 16 Feb. 1991, Prince Sebastian, b. 16 April 1992). Prince Jean, b. 15 May 1957, married Hélène Vestur; Princess Margaretha, b. 15 May 1957, married Prince Nikolaus of Liechtenstein 20 March 1982; Prince Guillaume, b. 1 May 1963, married Sibilla Weiller 24 Sept. 1994.

CONSTITUTION AND GOVERNMENT. The Grand Duchy of Luxembourg is a constitutional monarchy. The constitution of 17 Oct. 1868 was revised in 1919, 1948, 1956, 1972, 1979, 1983, 1988 and 1989.

The country forms 4 electoral districts. Voters choose between party lists of candidates in multi-member constituencies. The parliament is the *Chamber of Deputies*, which consists of a maximum of 60 members elected for 5 years. There is a *Council of State* of 21 members appointed by the Sovereign for life. It advises on proposed laws and any other question referred to it.

The head of state takes part in the legislative power, exercises executive power and has a part in the judicial power. The constitution leaves to the sovereign the right to organize the Government, which consists of a Minister of State, who is Prime Minister, and of at least 3 Ministers.

At the elections of June 1994 the electorate was 217,131; turn-out was 82·5%.

The Christian Social Party (CS) gained 21 seats, the Socialist Workers' Party (S) 17, the Democratic Party 12, the Action Committee for Democracy 5 and Déi Gréng GLEI-GAP 5. A Christian Social-Socialist coalition was formed which in Dec. 1995 comprised:

Prime Minister, Minister of State, Employment, Finance and the Exchequer: Jean-Claude Juncker (b. 1945; CS; sworn in 20 Jan. 1995).

Deputy Prime Minister, Minister of Foreign Affairs, Trade, Overseas Aid and Development: Jacques Poos (S). *Agriculture, Viticulture, Rural Development, Small Business, Housing and Tourism:* Fernand Boden (CS). *Justice, the Budget, Relations with Parliament:* Marc Fischbach (CS). *The Family, Women, the Disabled:* Marie-Josée Jacobs (CS). *Education, Cultural and Religious Affairs:* Erna Hennicot-Schoepges (CS). *Home Affairs, Civil Service and Administrative Reforms:* Michel Wolter (CS). *Economy and Trade, Public Works, Energy:* Robert Goebbels (S). *Environment, Health:* Johnny Lahure (S). *Land Planning, Defence, Youth and Sport:* Alex Bodry (S). *Social Security, Transport, Post and Communication:* Mady Delvaux-Stehres (S). *Secretary of State (Foreign Affairs, Foreign Trade and Art, Public Works):* George Wohlfahrt (S).

The *Speaker* is Jean Spautz.

National flag: Three horizontal stripes of red, white and light blue.

National anthem: Ons Hemecht (*Our Homeland*); words by M. Lentz, tune by J. A. Zinnen.

European Parliament. Luxembourg has 6 representatives. At the June 1994 elections turn-out was 90%. CS won 2 seats with 31·4% of votes cast (group in European Parliament: Popular European Party); S, 2 with 24·8% (European Socialist Party); the Democratic Party, 1 with 18·8% (Liberal, Democratic and Reformist Group); the Greens, 1 with 10·9% (Greens).

DEFENCE. There is a volunteer light infantry battalion of (1996) 800, and a Gendarmerie of 560.

INTERNATIONAL RELATIONS

Membership. Luxembourg is a member of the UN, Benelux, the EU, OECD, the Council of Europe, NATO and WEU. The Schengen Accord of June 1990 abolished border controls between Luxembourg, Belgium, France, Germany, Greece, Italy, the Netherlands, Portugal and Spain. It came into force (except for Greece and Italy) on 26 March 1995.

ECONOMY

Budget. Revenue and expenditure (including extraordinary) for years ending 30 April (in 1m. francs):

	1990	*1991*	*1992*	*1993*	*1994*	*1995*
Revenue	110,236·5	113,675·6	121,360·9	133,087·7	136,023·2	145,150·8
Expenditure	109,814·1	114,877·5	124,739·2	132,952·4	137,729·5	146,433·0

VAT is 15%, with a reduced rate of 6%.

Consolidated debt at 31 Dec. 1994 amounted to 11,201·3m. francs (long-term) and 5,967·3m. francs (short-term).

Currency. The unit of currency is the *Luxembourg franc* (LUF) notionally of 100 *centimes*, at parity with the Belgian franc. There are coins of 1, 5, 20 and 50 francs and notes of 100, 500, 1,000, 2,000, 5,000 and 10,000 francs. Belgian francs are legal tender.

Banking and Finance. Luxembourg's equivalent of a central bank is its Monetary Institute (*Director-General*, Pierre Jaans). On 31 Dec. 1992 depositors in the State Savings Bank had a total of 58,512m. francs to their credit. In 1994 there were 222 banks and 74 other credit institutions established in Luxembourg, which has become an international financial centre. There is a stock exchange. The financial sector accounted for 14·4% of GDP in 1994.

Weights and Measures. The metric system is in force.

ENERGY AND NATURAL RESOURCES

Electricity. Power production was 1,166m. kWh in 1994.

Minerals. In 1994 production (in tonnes) of pig-iron, 1,926,890; of steel, 3,073,268.

Agriculture. There were 6,848 workers engaged in agricultural work in 1994 (628 wage-earners), and 3,314 farms with an average area of 44·65 ha; 126,765 ha were under cultivation in 1994. Production, 1994 (in tonnes) of main crops: Maize, 418,460; roots and tubers, 29,459; bread crops, 46,762; forage crops, 94,962; pulses, 1,836; grassland, 140,478. Production, 1994 (in 1,000 tonnes) of meat, 23·9; milk, 262·1; butter, 3·2; cheese, 3·5. In 1994, 174,998 hectolitres of wine were produced from 1,341 ha. In 1994 there were 8,177 tractors, 1,074 harvester-threshers, 2,036 manure spreaders and 2,241 gatherer-presses.

Livestock (1994): 2,123 horses, 208,744 cattle, 68,854 pigs, 7,744 sheep.

Forestry. In 1992 there were 88,620 ha of forests, which produced 218,800 cu. metres of broadleaved and 153,294 cu. metres of coniferous wood.

INDUSTRY. Production, 1994 (in 1,000 tonnes); Steel, 3,073; rolled steel products, 4,195. In 1994 there were 2,501 industrial enterprises, of which 1,487 building industry.

Labour. The government fixes a legal minimum wage. Retirement is at 65.

FOREIGN ECONOMIC RELATIONS. For Benelux *see* THE STATESMAN'S YEAR-BOOK, 1992–93, p.197.

Commerce. Trade between Luxembourg and the UK is included with Belgium.

Tourism. In 1994 there were 799,549 tourists.

COMMUNICATIONS

Roads. In 1995 there were 5,136 km of roads of which 123 km were motorways. Motor vehicles registered in 1995 included 229,037 passenger cars, 15,398 trucks, 846 buses, 8,375 motorcycles, 23,449 tractors and special vehicles.

Railways. In 1994 there were 275 km of railway (standard gauge) of which 262 km were electrified. Railways carried (1992) 13·6m. passengers and (1994) 19·2m. tonnes of freight.

Civil Aviation. Findel is the airport for Luxembourg. 1,164,729 passengers and 241,627 tonnes of freight were handled in 1994. The national carrier is Luxair, 23·1% state-owned, which in 1995 operated 2 B-737-400s, 2 B-737-500s and 7 other aircraft. Services are also provided by Aeroflot, British Airways, Hapag Lloyd, Icelandair, KLM, Lufthansa, Northwest Airlines, Sabena, SAS, TAP, and Tunis Air.

Shipping. A shipping register was set up in 1990. 59 vessels were registered at Sept. 1995.

Telecommunications. In 1994 there were 221,898 telephones and 106 post offices. The commercial Radio-Télé-Luxembourg broadcasts 1 programme in Letzebuergesch on FM. There are commercial and religious programmes in French, German, English and Italian. Ten TV programmes are broadcast. Colour transmission is by the SECAM system. In 1993 there were 0·23m. radio and 100,500 TV sets in use.

Cinemas (1995). There were 17 cinemas.

Press (1994). There were 5 daily newspapers with a circulation of 154,000.

SOCIAL INSTITUTIONS

Religion. The population is 95% Roman Catholic.

Education. Education is compulsory for all children between the ages of 6 and 15. In 1993-94 nursery schools had 9,408 pupils; primary schools, 27,595 pupils; technical secondary schools, 14,153 pupils; secondary schools, 8,985 pupils. In higher education (1993–94) the Higher Institute of Technology had 320 students and 973 students pursued university studies. In 1993–94 there were 217 students in teacher training. In 1994-95 the University Centre of Luxembourg had 1,100 students and 200 academic staff.

Health. In 1994 there were 848 doctors and 4,560 hospital beds.

DIPLOMATIC REPRESENTATIVES

Of Luxembourg in Great Britain (27 Wilton Crescent, London, SWIX 8SD)
Ambassador: Joseph Weyland.

Of Great Britain in Luxembourg (14 Blvd Roosevelt, Luxembourg)
Ambassador and Consul-General: J. N. Elam, CMG.

Of Luxembourg in the USA (2200 Massachusetts Ave., NW, Washington, D.C., 20008)
Ambassador: Alphonse Berns.

Of the USA in Luxembourg (22 Blvd. Emmanuel Servais, Luxembourg)
Ambassador: Clay Constantinou.

Of Luxembourg to the United Nations
Ambassador: Jean-Louis Wolzfeld.

Further Reading

STATEC. *Annuaire Statistique.*

The Institutions of the Grand Duchy of Luxembourg. Information and Press Service, Luxembourg, 1989

Calmes, C., *The Making of a Nation from 1815 up to our Days.* Luxembourg, 1989

Hury, C. and Christophory, J., *Luxembourg.* [Bibliography] Oxford and Santa Barbara, 1981

Newcomer, J., *The Grand Duchy of Luxembourg: the Evolution of Nationhood, 963 A.D. to 1983.* Washington, 1983

Trausch, G., *The Significance of the Historical Date of 1839.* Luxembourg, 1989

National Library: 37 Boulevard Roosevelt, Luxembourg City. *Director:* Jules Christophory.

National statistical office: Service Central de la Statistique et des Etudes Economiques (STATEC), CP 304, Luxembourg City

MACEDONIA

Republika Makedonija
(Former Yugoslav Republic of Macedonia)

Capital: Skopje
Population: 1·94m. (1994)
GNP per capita: US$790 (1994)

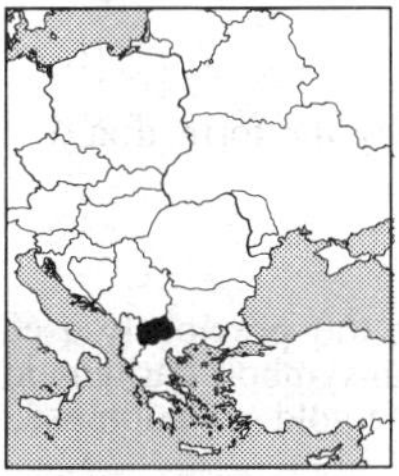

Source for statistics (*except* Defence *and* UK-Macedonian trade): Statistical Office of Macedonia.

KEY HISTORICAL EVENTS. The Slavs settled in Macedonia since the 6th century, who had been Christianized by Byzantium, were conquered by the non-Slav Bulgars in the 7th century and in the 9th century formed a Macedo-Bulgarian empire, the western part of which survived until Byzantine conquest in 1014. In the 14th century it fell to Serbia, and in 1355 to the Turks. After the Balkan Wars of 1912–13 Turkey was ousted, and Serbia received part of the territory, the rest going to Bulgaria and Greece. In 1918 Yugoslav Macedonia was incorporated into Serbia as 'South Serbia', becoming a republic in the Socialist Federal Republic of Yugoslavia. Claims to the historical Macedonian territory have long been a source of contention with Bulgaria and Greece.

Macedonia declared its independence on 20 Nov. 1992, and was admitted to the UN on 8 April 1993 under the name of 'Former Yugoslav Republic of Macedonia', a decision acceptable to Greece.

On 11 Dec. 1992 the UN Security Council authorized the expedition of a small peacekeeping force (UNPREDEP) to prevent hostilities spreading to Macedonia. In 1995 its mandate was extended for 6 months.

President Gligorov was wounded in an assassination attempt on 3 Oct. 1995

TERRITORY AND POPULATION. Macedonia is bounded in the north by Yugoslavia, in the east by Bulgaria, in the south by Greece and in the west by Albania. Its area is 25,713 sq. km. Population at the 1994 census was 1,936,877. The ethnic groups were Macedonians (1,288,330), Albanians (442,914), Turks (77,252), Gypsies (43,732), Serbs (39,260), Vlachs (8,467). There were 34,960 others and 1,962 not stated. Minorities are represented in the Council for Inter-Ethnic Relations.

The major cities (with 1994 census population) are: Skopje, the capital, 440,577; Bitola, 75,386; Prilep, 67,371; Kumanovo, 66,237; Tetovo, 50,376.

Vital statistics, 1994 (preliminary): Births, 33,817; deaths, 15,771; marriages, 15,736; divorces, 612; infant deaths, 752. Rates (per 1,000 population): Birth, 17·5; death, 8·1; marriage, 8·1; divorce, 0·3; natural increase, 9·1; infant mortality (per 1,000 live births), 22·5. In 1994 3,484 persons immigrated and 498 emigrated. Expectation of life, 1992: Men, 70·1 years, women, 74·4.

The official language is Macedonian, which uses the Cyrillic alphabet.

CLIMATE. Macedonia has a mixed Mediterranean-continental type climate, with cold moist winters and hot dry summers. Skopje, Jan. –0·4°C, July 23·1°C.

CONSTITUTION AND GOVERNMENT. At a referendum held on 8 Sept. 1991 turn-out was 74%; 99% of votes cast were in favour of a sovereign Macedonia with the option to rejoin a future reformed Yugoslav federation. Parliament confirmed the results on 18 Sept. On 20 Nov. 1991 parliament promulgated a new constitution which proclaimed Macedonia's independence.

The *President* is directly elected for 5-year terms. Candidates must be citizens aged at least 40 years. The parliament is a 120-member single-chamber *Assembly* (*Sobranie*), elected by universal suffrage for 4-year terms.

There is *a Constitutional Court* whose members are elected by the Assembly for non-renewable 8-year terms, and a *National Security Council* chaired by the President. Laws passed by the Assembly must be countersigned by the President, who may return them for reconsideration, but cannot veto them if they gain a two-thirds majority.

Presidential and parliamentary elections were held on 16 Oct. 1994. The electorate was 1·3m. President Gligorov was re-elected against 1 opponent by 52·4% of votes cast. Parliamentary run-off elections were held on 30 Oct. 1994. The Alliance for Macedonia (AM) won 58 seats; the Liberal Party, 29; the Democratic Prosperity Party (Albanian), 10; the Socialist Party, 7.

President: Kiro Gligorov (b. 1917; AM).

The Liberal Party left the coalition in Feb. 1996, necessitating the formation of a new government.

Prime Minister: Branko Crvenkovski (b. 1962; AM).

The *Speaker* is Stojan Andov.

National flag: To meet objections from Greece (i.e. that the previously-used Igrayed-sum, the 'Star of Vergina', was a Hellenic Macedonian symbol) parliament voted a new design on 5th Oct. 1995, namely: A red field with a gold sun composed of a disc with 8 rays expanding to the corners and sides.

National anthem: 'Denes nad Makedonija se radja novo sonce na slobodata' ('Today a new sun of liberty appears over Macedonia').

Local Government: Macedonia is administratively divided into 34 communes.

DEFENCE. The President is the C.-in-C. of the armed forces. There is conscription for 9 months. The Army numbered 10,400 (8,000 conscripts) in 1996. There is a paramilitary police force of 7,500. A UN peacekeeping force (UNPREDEP) numbered 1,150 in 1995.

INTERNATIONAL RELATIONS. On 13 Sept. 1995 under the auspices of the UN Macedonia and Greece agreed to normalize their relations following the formers modification of the national flag.

Membership. Macedonia is a member of the UN and the Council of Europe.

ECONOMY

Policy. Under legislation of 1993 115 large, 325 medium and 1,077 small businesses were scheduled for privatization at a total value of US$1,400m.

Budget. In 1993 revenue and expenditure balanced at 13,693m. (old) denars.

Currency. The unit of currency is the *denar* (MKD) of 100 *deni.* On 15 May 1993 the denar was renominated at 100 old denars = 1 new denar. There are notes of 10, 20, 50, 100, and 500 denars. National Bank foreign exchange reserves were US$258·3m. at 30 Nov. 1995; gold reserves were US$5m. in 1992. Inflation was 15·5% in 1995. In March 1996, £1 = 58·23 denars; US$1 = 38·10 denars; DM1 = 25·81 denars.

Banking and Finance. The central bank and bank of issue is the National Bank of Macedonia. Its *Governor* is Borko Stanoevski. At 30 Oct. 1995 commercial banks had total deposits of 17,328m. denars, and savings deposits totalled 10,296m. denars.

Weights and Measures. The metric system is in use.

ENERGY AND NATURAL RESOURCES

Electricity. Output in 1994, 5,923,666 MWh, of which 683,279 MWh were hydro-electric.

Minerals. Macedonia is relatively rich in minerals, including lead, zinc, copper, iron, chromium, nickel, antimony, manganese, silver and gold. Output, 1994 (in tonnes):Lead-zinc ore, 955,253; lead-zinc concentrates, 53,252; copper ore, 3,458,440; copper concentrate, 38,690; chromium concentrate, 4,158; refined silver, 13.

Agriculture. At the 1991 census the active agricultural population was 174,875. In 1994 there were 660,797 ha of arable land and 634,691 ha of pasture. 147,000 ha of arable land were owned by agricultural organizations and 460,741 ha by individual farmers.

Crop production, 1994 (in 1,000 tonnes): Wheat, 336; barley, 149; maize, 133; rice, 8·7; sugar-beet, 54·1; sunflower, 17·9; tobacco, 18·9; potatoes, 131·4; beans, 11·8; tomatoes, 120·8; pepper, 87·3; apples, 70; pears, 11·6; plums, 25·2; lucerne, 7·3; grapes, 205·5.

Livestock, 1994 (in 1,000): Cattle, 281; horses, 61·8; sheep, 2,466; pigs, 171·6. Livestock products, 1994 (in 1,000 tonnes): Beef, 7·5; pork, 9·7; mutton, 13; poultry, 22; cow's milk, 116m. litres; sheep milk, 61·3m. litres; wool, 3·1; honey, 0·9; 510m. eggs.

There were 52,036 tractors in use in 1994.

Forestry. In 1994 the forest area was 1,218,397 ha, chiefly oaks and beech. 1,074,138 cu. metres of timber were cut in 1994.

INDUSTRY. In 1994 there were 73,158 enterprises (69,561 private, 1,288 public, 973 co-operative, 1,312 mixed and 24 state-owned). Production (in tonnes): Ferro-alloys, 62,937; steel ingots, 2,477; buses, 2,792 (units); refrigerators, 105,865 (units); sulphuric acid, 72,106; medicines, 353, detergents, 39,709; wood pulp, 2,020; cotton yarn, 7,741.

Labour. In 1992 the population of working age was 1,332,000. In 1994, 395,686 persons were employed, including 37,440 self-employed. 185,906 persons (90,130 women) were seeking employment; unemployment rate, 30%.

FOREIGN ECONOMIC RELATIONS. The foreign debt of Macedonia, including debt taken over from the former Yugoslavia, was US$1,100m. in 1994. Following the normalization of relations in Sept. 1995 Greece lifted its trade embargo, imposed in Feb. 1994.

Commerce. Imports and exports (in US$1,000):

	1991	*1992*	*1993*	*1994*
Imports	1,095,450	1,198,626	1,055,298	1,086,343
Exports	1,274,166	1,206,106	1,199,351	1,484,092

Main export markets, 1994: Germany, CIS, Italy, Slovenia, USA, Yugoslavia (until sanctions were applied), Bulgaria, Netherlands. Total trade between Macedonia and the UK (British Department of Trade returns, in £1,000 sterling):

	1993	*1994*	*1995*
Imports to UK	41,005	5,897	5,323
Exports and re-exports from UK	47,612	14,166	18,079

Tourism. In 1994, 613,154 tourists spent 2·5m. nights.

COMMUNICATIONS

Roads. In 1994 there were 909 km of main roads, 2,916 km of regional roads and 5,439 km of local roads; 1,125 km of roads were macadamized and 5,197 km asphalted. 22·5m. passengers and 3·7m. tonnes of freight were transported. There were 263,181 cars and 17,436 lorries.

Railways. In 1994 there were 922 km of railways (233 km electrified). 1·25m. passengers and 1·92m. tonnes of freight were transported.

Civil Aviation. There are international airports at Skopje and Ohrid. The national carrier is Macedonia Airlines. Services are also provided by Adria, Aeroflot, Albanian Airlines, Balkan, Croatia Airlines, Hamburg Airlines, Hemus and JAT. In 1994 625,000 passengers and 6,852 tonnes of freight were carried.

Telecommunications. In 1994 there were 267 post offices and 454,507 telephones. The national Macedonian Radio and Television is government-funded. There were 31 local radio stations in 1994, and 312,901 TV sets were in use (colour by PAL).

Cinemas. There were 39 cinemas and 300,283 admissions in 1994.

Press. There were 3 national dailies in 1995, 2 in Macedonian and 1 in Albanian and 192 other newspapers and periodicals.

SOCIAL INSTITUTIONS

Justice. Courts are autonomous and independent. Judges are tenured and elected for life on the proposal of the *Judicial Council*, whose members are themselves elected for renewable 6-year terms. The highest court is the Supreme Court. There are 28 courts of first instance and 3 higher courts.

Religion. Macedonia is traditionally Orthodox but the church is not established and there is freedom of religion. At the 1991 census 66·66% of the population were Orthodox and 30·06% Moslem. In 1967 an autocephalous Orthodox church split off from the Serbian. Its head is the Archbishop of Ohrid and Macedonia whose seat is at Skopje. It has 5 bishoprics in Macedonia and 1 abroad (American-Canadian-Australian). It has some 300 priests.

The Moslem Religious Union has a superiorate at Skopje. The Roman Catholic Church has a seat at Skopje.

Education. Education is free and compulsory for 8 years. In 1994, 36,896 children attended 49 pre-school institutions and 337 pre-school groups in primary schools. In 1994 there were 261,105 pupils enrolled in 1,042 primary, 77,804 in 91 secondary and (in 1994–95) 2,098 in higher schools, and 26,959 students in higher education. There are universities at Skopje 34,430 students and 1,770 academic staff in 1994–95) and Bitola (9,140 students and 100 academic staff in 1994-95).

Health. In 1994 there were 4,505 doctors and 77 hospitals with 10,800 beds.

Welfare. In 1994 there were 216,838 pensioners (116,617 old age). 75,227 adults and 66,522 children received social benefits in 1993.

DIPLOMATIC REPRESENTATIVES

Of Macedonia in Great Britain (19A, Cavendish Sq., London, W1M 9AD)
Ambassador: Risto Nikovski.

Of Great Britain in Macedonia (26 Ulica Veljko Vlaković, 91000 Skopje)
Ambassador: Tony Millson.

Of USA in Macedonia (5 Ulica 27 Marta, 91000 Skopje)
Ambassador: Victor D. Comras.

MADAGASCAR

Repoblikan'i Madagasikara

Capital: Antananarivo
Population: 13·5m. (1994)
GNP per capita: US$230 (1994)
HDI/world rank: 0·432/135 (1992)

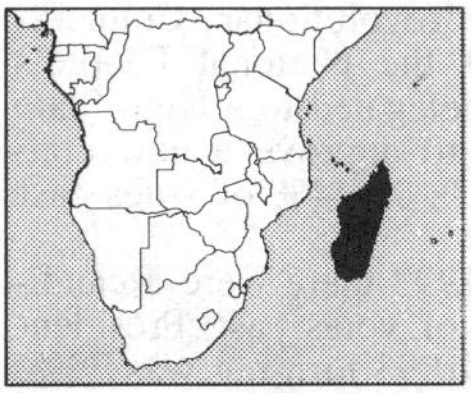

KEY HISTORICAL EVENTS. Madagascar was unified under a monarchy between 1797 and 1861, but French claims led to hostilities culminating in the establishment of a protectorate in 1895 and a colony in 1896; the monarchy was abolished in 1897.

Madagascar became an Overseas Territory in 1946, and on 14 Oct. 1958, following a referendum, was proclaimed the autonomous Malagasy Republic within the French Community, achieving full independence on 26 June 1960.

The government of Philibert Tsiranana, President from independence, resigned on 18 May 1972 and executive powers were given to Maj.-Gen. Gabriel Ramanantsoa, who replaced Tsiranana as President on 11 Oct. 1972. On 5 Feb. 1975, Col. Richard Ratsimandrava became Head of State, but was assassinated 6 days later. A National Military Directorate under Brig.-Gen. Gilles Andriamahazo was established on 12 Feb. On 15 June it handed over power to a Supreme Revolutionary Council (SRC) under Didier Ratsiraka.

After 6 months of anti-government unrest, during which the opposition formed an alternative 'government', in Oct. 1991 the government and the Committee of Living Forces, a coalition of 16 opposition parties led by Albert Zafy, agreed to form an 18-month transitional administration. However, Zafy refused to join a government formed on 13 Nov., and was instead appointed chairman of the High State Authority for a Provisional Government formed on 23 Nov.

The Third Republic was instituted in 1993.

TERRITORY AND POPULATION. Madagascar is situated off the south-east coast of Africa, from which it is separated by the Mozambique channel, the least distance between island and continent being 250 miles (400 km); its length is 980 miles (1,600 km); greatest breadth, 360 miles (570 km). Its area is 587,041 sq. km (226,658 sq. miles). At the 1975 census the population was 7,603,790. Estimate (1994), 13,469,000 (25% urban). Population density, 22·9 per sq. km.

Province	*Area in Sq. km*	*Population 1990*	*Chief town*	*Population 1990*
Antsiranana	43,046	715,000	Antsiranana	54,418
Mahajanga	150,023	1,253,000	Mahajanga	121,967
Toamasina	71,911	1,585,000	Toamasina	145,431
Antananarivo	58,283	3,811,000	Antananarivo	803,390
Fianarantsoa	102,373	2,420,000	Fianarantsoa	124,489
Toliary	161,405	1,659,000	Toliary	61,460

Growth rate, 1991: 3·2 per 1,000 population; infant mortality, 110 per 1,000 live births. Expectation of life, 56 years.

The indigenous population is of Malayo-Polynesian stock, divided into 18 ethnic groups of which the principal are Merina (26%) of the central plateau, the Betsimisaraka (15%) of the east coast, and the Betsileo (12%) of the southern plateau. Foreign communities include Europeans, mainly French (30,000), Indians (15,000), Chinese (9,000), Comorians and Arabs.

The official language is Malagasy. French is the language of international communication.

CLIMATE. A tropical climate, but the mountains cause big variations in rainfall, which is very heavy in the east and very light in the west. Antananarivo. Jan. 70°F

(21·1°C), July 59°F (15°C). Annual rainfall 54" (1,350 mm). Toamasina. Jan. 80°F (26·7°C), July 70°F (21·1°C). Annual rainfall 128" (3,256 mm).

CONSTITUTION AND GOVERNMENT. The new Constitution of the Democratic Republic of Madagascar was approved by referendum on 21 Dec. 1975 and came into force on 30 Dec. It provided for a National People's Assembly elected by universal suffrage for a 5-year term from the single list of the *Front National pour la Défense de la Révolution Socialiste Malgache.* Executive power was vested in the President with the guidance of a Supreme Revolutionary Council.

Under a convention of 31 Oct. 1991 the powers of the National People's Assembly and the Supreme Revolutionary Council were delegated to a High State Authority for a Provisional Government. A referendum to approve a new constitution was held on 19 Aug. 1992. Turn-out was 77·68%; 75·44% of votes cast were in favour.

At the first round of presidential elections on 25 Nov. 1992 there were 8 candidates; turn-out was 73·94%. Albert Zafy gained 45·16% of votes cast, President Didier Ratsiraka, 29·22%. At the second round on 9 Feb. 1993 turn-out was 79%. Zafy was elected by 66·74% of votes cast against President Ratsiraka.

The Third Republic was established in 1993. Under this the National Assembly has 138 seats. Elections were held on 16 June 1993; the electorate was 6m.

President: Albert Zafy (sworn in 12 March 1993).

A referendum on 17 Sept. 1995 was in favour of the President appointing and dismissing the Prime Minister, hitherto elected by parliament. The electorate was 6m.; turn-out was 50%.

On 13 Oct. 1995 Francisque Ravony was replaced as *Prime Minister* by Emmanuel Rakotovahiny.

The *Speaker* is Richard Andriamanjato.

National flag: Horizontally red over green, in the hoist a vertical white strip.

National anthem: 'Ry tanindrazanay malala ô!' ('O our beloved Fatherland'); words by Pastor Rahajason, tune by N. Raharisoa.

Local Government: The 6 provinces (*faritany*) are sub-divided into 111 *fivondronana*, which in turn are divided into 13,476 *fokontany* (the traditional communal divisions). Each level is governed by an elected council.

DEFENCE. There is conscription (including civilian labour service) for 18 months.

Army. The Army is organized in 2 battalion groups, and 1 engineer regiment. Equipment includes 12 PT-76 light tanks. Strength (1996) 20,000 and gendarmerie, 7,500.

Navy. In 1995 the small maritime force had a strength of 500 (including 100 marines), and was equipped with 1 250-tonne patrol craft, 1 medium landing ship, 4 landing craft, together with a 1,200-tonne former trawler used for transport and training.

Air Force. Equipment includes 1 Britten-Norman Defender armed transport, 2 C-47s, and 1 Yak-40 for VIP use, 1 Aztec, 2 Cessna Skymasters, 4 Cessna 172Ms and 4 Mi-8 helicopters. Personnel (1995), 500, with 12 combat aircraft.

INTERNATIONAL RELATIONS

Membership. Madagascar is a member of the UN, OAU and is an ACP state of the EU.

ECONOMY

Policy. A programme of privatization was launched in 1989.

Budget. The 1994 budget envisaged expenditure and revenue of MGFr2,462,800m.

Currency. The unit of currency is the *Malagasy franc* (MGF). 1 *ariary* = MGFr.5.

There are coins of MGFr1, 2, 5, 10, 20, 25, 50, 100 and 250 banknotes of MGFr500, 1,000, 2,500, 5,000, 10,000 and 25,000. MGFr317,230m. were in circulation in 1992. In 1990 foreign exchange reserves were US$131·5m. In March 1996, £1 = MGFr5,960·76; US$1 = MGFr3,900; DM1 = MGFr2,642.

Banking and Finance. A Central Bank was formed in 1973, replacing the former *Institut d'Emission Malgache* as the central bank of issue. All commercial banking and insurance was nationalized in 1975 and privatized in 1988. Industrial development is financed through the *Bankin'ny Indostria.* Other commercial banking is undertaken by the *Bankin'ny Tantsaha Mpamokatra,* the *Banky Fampandrosoana ny Varotra.* The Malagasy Bank of the Indian Ocean was set up in Sept. 1990 as part of a bank privatization programme.

Weights and Measures. The metric system is in use.

ENERGY AND NATURAL RESOURCES

Electricity. Production (1992) 484m. kWh (303m. kWh hydro-electric).

Oil. The oil refinery at Toamasina has a capacity of 12,000 bbls a day.

Minerals. Mining production in 1992 included: Graphite, 10,000 tonnes; chromite, 0·15m. tonnes; mica, 50 kg.

Agriculture. 80–85% of the workforce is employed in agriculture. The principal agricultural products in 1993 were (in 1,000 tonnes): Rice, 2,400; cassava, 2,200; mangoes, 170; bananas, 220; potatoes, 278; sugar-cane, 1,950; maize, 155; coffee, 87; seed cotton, 26; sisal, 17; tobacco, 5.

Cattle breeding and agriculture are the chief occupations. There were, in 1993, 10,287,000 cattle, 155,000 camels, 1·5m. pigs, 2·1m. sheep and goats.

Forestry. The forests covered (1989) 14·7m. hectares (about 25% of the land surface) and contain many valuable woods, while gum, resins and plants for tanning, dyeing and medicinal purposes abound. Production (1988) 7,634,000 cu. metres (6,827,000 cu. metres for fuel).

Fisheries. In 1989 the fishing fleet numbered 44 vessels over 100 GRT totalling 6,852 GRT. The catch of sea fish in 1993 was 57,500 tonnes; crustaceans, 11,300 tonnes; fresh-water fish, 60,000 tonnes.

INDUSTRY. Industry, hitherto confined mainly to the processing of agricultural products, is now extending to cover other fields.

Labour. In 1990 the workforce was 5,004,000 (1,964,000 females; 417,000 10–15 years old).

FOREIGN ECONOMIC RELATIONS

Commerce. Trade in MGFr1m.:

	1987	*1988*	*1989*	*1990*	*1991*	*1992*
Imports (c.i.f)	376,792	512,063	545,399	881,328	785,689	844,936
Exports (f.o.b)	348,025	385,080	506,193	460,343	559,073	499,806

Chief exports, in tonnes (and value) in 1992: Coffee, 49,448 (MGFr58,844m.); cloves, 10,585 (MGFr16,710m.); vanilla, 700 (MGFr95,541m.). In 1992 France took 27% of exports, the USA, 16% and Japan, 9%, while France supplied 30% of imports, Germany, 6% and the USA, 6%.

Total trade between Madagascar and UK (British Department of Trade returns, in £1,000 sterling):

	1991	*1992*	*1993*	*1994*	*1995*
Imports to UK	7,707	6,000	10,747	18,785	15,236
Exports and re-exports from UK	6,945	8,690	5,418	7,881	7,203

Tourism. There were 38,954 tourists in 1989.

COMMUNICATIONS

Roads. In 1989 there were 49,555 km of roads (5,401 km bitumenized). In 1988 there were 27,739 passenger cars, 13,426 vans, 5,103 lorries, 2,015 buses and 3,128 motor cycles.

Railways. In 1992 there were 883 km of railways, all metre gauge. In 1994, 0·6m. passengers and 0·3m. tonnes of freight were transported.

Civil Aviation. There are international airports at Antananarivo (Ivato) and Mahajanga (Amborovy). The national carrier is Air Madagascar, which is 89·5% state-owned, and in 1995 operated 1 B-737-200, 1 B-737-200 Adv, 1 B-737-300, 1 B-747-200B Combi and 7 other aircraft. There are also services by Aeroflot and Air France. In 1988, 452,000 passengers and 9,169 tonnes of cargo arrived and departed.

Shipping. In 1989, 760,100 tonnes were loaded and 1,062,900 tonnes unloaded at Toamasina, Mahajanga, Antsiranana and Nosy-Be. In 1995, registered merchant marine totalled 37,721 GRT, including oil tankers, 13,859 GRT.

Telecommunications. There were in 1986, 724 post offices and agencies. There were (1988) about 25,000 main telephones. The government-controlled Radio-Television Malagasy is responsible for broadcasting. There are radio programmes in Malagasy and French, and 3-4 hours TV transmission a day (colour by SECAM). In 1993 there were 1·5m. radio and 0·13m. TV sets.

Press. In 1985 there were 7 daily newspapers with a total circulation of 68,000.

SOCIAL INSTITUTIONS

Justice. The Supreme Court and the Court of Appeal are in Antananarivo. In most towns there are Courts of First Instance for civil and commercial cases. For criminal cases there are ordinary criminal courts in most towns.

Religion. In 1989 47% of the population practised the traditional religion; 26% were Roman Catholic, 22% Protestant (mainly belonging to the Fiangonan'i Jesosy Kristy eto Madagasikara) and 1·7% Moslem.

Education. Education is compulsory from 6 to 14 years of age in the primary schools. In 1988-89 there were 1,534,142 pupils and 37,894 teachers in 13,672 primary schools, 257,377 pupils and 11,200 teachers in 1,142 secondary schools and 87,925 students and 4,976 teachers in 366 *lycées*. In 1994-95 there were 6 universities.

Health. In 1985 there were 249 state hospitals and 1,904 health centres. There were (1985) 1,189 doctors, 100 dentists, 37 pharmacists, 1,638 midwives and 3,323 nursing personnel.

DIPLOMATIC REPRESENTATIVES

Of Madagascar in Great Britain
Ambassador: Vacant (resides in Paris)

Of Great Britain in Madagascar (Immeuble Ny Havana, Cite de 67 Ha, Antananarivo)
Ambassador: Robert Dewar.

Of Madagascar in the USA (2374 Massachusetts Ave., NW, Washington, D.C., 20008)
Ambassador: Pierrot J. Rajaonarivelo.

Of the USA in Madagascar (14 rue Rainitovo, Antsahavola, Antananarivo)
Ambassador: Dennis P. Barrett.

Of Madagascar to the United Nations
Ambassador: Jean Ravelomanantsoa Ratsimihah.

Further Reading

Banque des Données de l'Etat. *Bulletin Mensuel de Statistique*
Allen, P. M., *Madagascar.* Boulder (CO), 1995
Brandt, H., *Guide to Madagascar.* Chalfont St Peter, 1988
Bradt, H. and Brown, M., *Madagascar.* [Bibliography]. Oxford and Santa Barbara, 1993
Deschamps, H., *Histoire de Madagascar.* Paris, 4th ed. 1972
Rabetafika, R., *Réforme Fiscal et Révolution Socialiste à Madagascar.* Paris, 1990
Rajoelina, P. and Ramelet, A., *Madagascar, la Grande Ile.* Paris, 1989
Ramahatra, O., *Madagascar: une Economie en Phase d'Ajustement.* Paris, 1989

National statistical office: Banque des Données de l'Etat, Antananarivo.

MALAŴI

Dziko la Malaŵi—
Republic of Malaŵi

Capital: Lilongwe
Population: 9·7m. (1994)
GNP per capita: US$140 (1994)
HDI/world rank: 0·330/157 (1992)

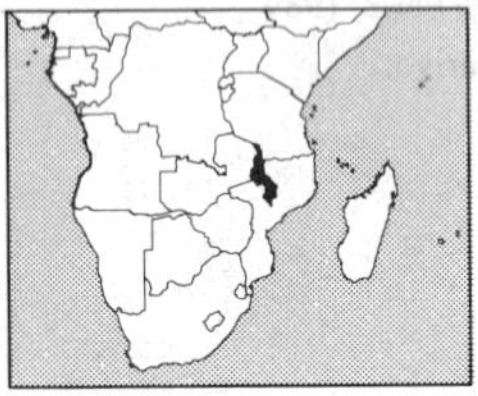

KEY HISTORICAL EVENTS. Nyasaland (a former British protectorate) became self-governing on 1 Feb. 1963, and on 6 July 1964 an independent member of the Commonwealth under the name of Malaŵi. It became a republic on 6 July 1966.

TERRITORY AND POPULATION. Malaŵi lies along the southern and western shores of Lake Malaŵi (the third largest lake in Africa), and is otherwise bounded in the north by Tanzania, south by Mozambique and west by Zambia. Area (including the inland water areas of Lake Malombe, Chilwa, Chiuta and the Malaŵi portion of Lake Malaŵi, which total 24,208 sq. km), 118,484 sq. km (45,747 sq. miles).

Population at census 1987, 7,982,607. Estimate (1994), 9·7m. (12% urban). Population of main towns (census 1987): Blantyre, 331,588; Lilongwe, 233,973; Mzuzu, 44,238; Zomba, 42,878. Population of the regions, census 1987 (and census 1977): Northern, 907,121 (648,853); Central, 3,116,038 (2,143,716); Southern, 3,959,448 (2,754,891).

In 1992 infantile mortality was 143 per 1,000 live births. Expectation of life was 44·6 years.

The official languages are Chichewa, spoken by over 50% of the population, and English.

CLIMATE. The tropical climate is marked by a dry season from May to Oct. and a wet season for the remaining months. Rainfall amounts are variable, within the range of 29–100" (725–2,500 mm), and maximum temperatures average 75–89°F (24–32°C), and minimum temperatures 58–67°F (14·4–19·4°C). Lilongwe. Jan. 73°F (22·8°C), July 60°F (15·6°C). Annual rainfall 36" (900 mm). Blantyre. Jan. 75°F (23·9°C), July 63°F (17·2°C). Annual rainfall 45" (1,125 mm). Zomba. Jan. 73°F (22·8°C), July 63°F (17·2°C). Annual rainfall 54" (1,344 mm).

CONSTITUTION AND GOVERNMENT. The *President* is also head of Government. Malaŵi was a one-party state, but following a referendum on 14 June 1993, in which 63% of votes cast were in favour of reform, a new Constitution was adopted on 17 May 1994 which ended Hastings Banda's life presidency and provided for the holding of multi-party elections. At these Bakili Muluzi was elected President by 47·16% of votes cast against President Banda and 2 other opponents.

Parliament is composed of 177 members. At the elections of 17 May 1994 the United Democratic Front (UDF) won 84 seats; the Malaŵi Congress Party (the former single party), 55; and the Alliance for Democracy (AFORD), 36. Results in the remaining 2 seats were nullified.

In Oct. 1995 the government comprised:

President: Bakili Muluzi (b. 1943; UDF; sworn in 21 May 1994).

First Vice-President and Minister of Defence: Justin Malewezi; *Second Vice-President and Minister for Irrigation:* Chakufwa Chihana.

Minister of Finance, Economic Planning and Development: Aleka Banda. *Tourism:* Patrick Mbewe. *External Affairs:* Edward Bwanali. *Information and Broadcasting, Posts and Telecommunications:* Brown James Mpinganjira. *Home Affairs:* Wenham Nakanga. *Education:* Cassim Chilumpha. *Justice and Attorney-General:* Collins Chizumira. *Transport and Civil Aviation:* Dr George Ntafu. *Agriculture and Livestock Development:* Mapopa Chipeta. *Health and Population:* Sam

Mpasu. *Local Government and Rural Development:* Dr Nasembo Mzunda. *Lands and Valuation:* Alhaji Shaiba Itimu. *Energy and Mining:* Dr Jombo Lemani. *Youth, Sports and Culture:* Kamangadadzi Chambalao. *Labour and Manpower Development:* Richard Sembenuka. *Physical Planning and Surveys:* Peter Fachi. *Women, Children's Affairs, Community Development and Social Welfare:* Edda Chitalo. *Relief and Rehabilitation Affairs:* Rolph Patel. *Natural Resources:* Zililo Chibambo. *Housing:* Timothy Mangwazu. *Works and Supplies:* Dr Mponda Mkandawire. *Research and Environment:* Bethwell Kaonga. *Commerce and Industry:* Peter Kalilombe. *Without portfolio:* Harry Thompson.

National flag: Three equal horizontal stripes of black, red, green, with a red rising sun on the centre of the black stripe.

National anthem: 'O God Bless our Land of Malaŵi'; words and tune by M.-F. Sauka.

Local Government. There are 3 regions and 24 districts, each administered by a district commissioner.

DEFENCE. All services form part of the Army and have a strength of (1996) 8,000.

Army. The army is organized into 3 infantry battalions and 1 support battalion.

Navy. 1 patrol craft, 2 landing craft and some boats operated by about (1995) 200 personnel based at Chilumba on Lake Nyasa.

Air Wing. To support the infantry battalion, the Air Wing has 2 C-47 and 4 Do 228 light transports, and 2 Ecureuil helicopters. An HS 125 jet is used for VIP transport. Personnel (1995), 200.

INTERNATIONAL RELATIONS

Membership. Malaŵi is a member of the UN, the Commonwealth, the Non-Aligned States, OAU, SADC and is an ACP state of the EU.

ECONOMY

Policy. The government operates a 3-year 'rolling' public-sector investment programme, revised annually to take into account changing needs and the expected level of resources available. The greatest part of the development programme is annually financed from external aid, and priority in the use of resources has always been given to providing the counterpart contributions to funds received from external sources. The balance of these local resources is used for financing projects commanding high national priority for which no external funds can be secured.

Budget. Revenue Account receipts and expenditure (in K.1,000) for years ending 31 March:

	1987–88	*1988–89*	*1989–90*	*1990–91*
Revenue	583,382	681,800	941,733	1,066,360
Expenditure	728,834	784,300	1,056,606	1,168,738

Currency. The unit of currency is the *kwacha* (MWK) of 100 *tambala*. There are coins of 1, 2, 5, 10, 20 and 50 tambalas, and notes of 1, 5, 10, 20, 50 and 100 kwachas. In 1991 currency in circulation totalled K.240.88m. Foreign exchange reserves were K.390·7m. in 1991. Foreign exchange controls were abolished in Feb. 1994. In March 1996, £1 = K.23·39, US$1 = K.15·31; DM1 = K.10·37.

Banking and Finance. The central bank and bank of issue is the Reserve Bank of Malaŵi (founded 1964). There are 2 commercial banks and an Investment Development Bank. The Post Office Savings Bank had (1985) 257 offices and (1990) total deposits of K.121·93m. The New Building Society had savings deposits of K.21·15m. in 1990 and investment deposits of K.57·49m.

Weights and Measures. The metric system is in use.

ENERGY AND NATURAL RESOURCES

Electricity. The Electricity Supply Commission of Malaŵi is the sole supplier. Production (1991), 747·9m. kWh.

Minerals. The main product in 1976 was marble (149,254 tonnes) for the manufacture of cement. Coal mining began in 1985.

Agriculture. Malaŵi is predominantly an agricultural country. In 1983 agriculture contributed about 43% to the GDP, and agricultural produce accounted for 90% of total exports. Maize is the main subsistence crop and is grown by over 95% of all smallholders; production, 1993, 2,034 tonnes. Almost all the surplus crops produced by smallholders are sold to the Agricultural Development and Marketing Corporation. Production (1993): Tobacco, 136,000 tonnes; sugar-cane, 1,980,000 tonnes; tea, 40,000 tonnes.

Livestock in 1993: Cattle, 0·97m.; sheep, 0·2m.; goats, 0·89m.; pigs, 0·24m.; chickens, 9m.

Forestry. There were (1989) 4·3m. ha of forests; 46% of the land area.

Fisheries. Landings in 1987 were 88,400 tonnes.

INDUSTRY. Index of manufacturing output in 1987 (1984 = 100): manufacturing for domestic consumption, excluding mining and quarrying, 290·8; of this consumer goods were at 109 and intermediate goods for building and construction were at 99·9. Manufacturing for export, 97·4.

FOREIGN ECONOMIC RELATIONS

Commerce. Major exports 1991 (in K.1m.): Tobacco, 982·1; tea, 103·8; sugar, 79·7; cotton, 33·3; groundnuts, 1·7. Major imports: Petroleum products, 152·6; fertilizers, 244·2; coal, 2·6.

Trade statistics for calendar years are (in K.1m.):

	1987	*1988*	*1989*	*1990*	*1991*
Imports	653·9	1,080·2	1,398·8	1,587·4	1,975·8
Exports	615·1	751·7	741·7	1,123·1	1,333·0

Total trade between Malaŵi and UK (British Department of Trade returns, in £1,000 sterling):

	1991	*1992*	*1993*	*1994*	*1995*
Imports to UK	25,381	22,107	21,714	25,816	16,188
Exports and re-exports from UK	31,462	23,880	18,021	19,594	13,449

Tourism. There were 129,912 visitors in 1990, of whom 31,691 were tourists.

COMMUNICATIONS

Roads. In 1988 there were 2,701 km of main road, of which 1,857 km were bitumen surfaced and 410 km gravel; 2,782 km of secondary roads, of which 285 km were surfaced and 239 km gravel; 5,354 km of district roads, of which 24 km were surfaced and 16 km gravel, and 8,008 km of earth roads. In 1987 there were 14,911 cars and 15,643 commercial vehicles. In 1991 there were 1,209 fatalities in road accidents.

Railways. Malaŵi Railways and its subsidiary the Central Africa Railway operate 797 km on 1,067 mm gauge, providing links to the Mozambican ports of Beira and Nacala. In 1993–94 railways carried 0·6m. passengers and 0·3m. tonnes of freight.

Civil Aviation. The national carrier is the state-owned Air Malaŵi, which flew 1 B-737-300 and 2 other aircraft in 1995. There are airports at Lilongwe (Kamuzu International Airport) and Chileka. In 1991 360,739 passengers and 10,578 tonnes of freight were handled. Services are also provided by Air Zimbabwe, British Airways, Ethiopian Airways, Kenya Airways, KLM, Northwest Airlines and SAA.

Shipping. In 1991 lake ships carried 170,000 passengers and 6,810 tonne-kilometres of freight.

Telecommunications. Number of telephones (1987) 25,000. The Malawi Broadcasting Corporation, a statutory body, broadcasts in English and Chichewa. There were 1·06m. radio sets in 1993.

Press (1989). *The Daily Times* (English, Monday to Friday); 17,000 copies daily. *Malawi News* (English and Chichewa, Saturdays); 23,000 copies weekly. *Odini* (English and Chichewa); 8,500 copies fortnightly. *Boma Lathu* (Chichewa); 80,000 copies monthly. *Za Alimi* (English and Chichewa); 10,000 copies monthly.

SOCIAL INSTITUTIONS

Justice. Justice is administered in the High Court, the magistrates' courts and traditional courts. There are 23 magistrates' courts, 176 traditional courts and 23 local appeal courts.

Appeals from traditional courts are dealt with in the traditional appeal courts and in the national traditional appeal court. Appeals from magistrates' courts lie to the High Court, and appeals from the High Court to Malawi's Supreme Court of Appeal.

Religion. In 1992 there 6·12m. Christians and 1·54m. Moslems. In 1988 the Roman Catholic Church claimed 1·5m. members.

Education. Adult literacy was 41·2% in 1993. Fees for primary education were abolished in 1994. In 1995–96 the number of pupils in primary schools was 3m. The primary school course is of 8 years' duration, followed by a 4-year secondary course. English is taught from the 1st year and becomes the general medium of instruction from the 4th year.

The University of Malawi had 3,657 students and 366 academic staff in 1994–95. There were also 4 colleges and 1 polytechnic.

Health. In 1989 there were two central hospitals, one general hospital, one mental hospital, two leprosaria and 45 hospitals of which 21 were government district hospitals. In 1986 there were 7,081 hospital beds of which 1,612 were for maternity.

DIPLOMATIC REPRESENTATIVES

Of Malawi in Great Britain (33 Grosvenor St., London, W1X 0DE)
High Commissioner: Jake Muwamba.

Of Great Britain in Malawi (Lingadzi Hse., Lilongwe, 3)
High Commissioner: J. F. R. Martin, CMG.

Of Malawi in the USA (2408 Massachusetts Ave., NW, Washington, D.C., 20008)
Ambassador: W. Chokani.

Of the USA in Malawi (PO Box 30016, Lilongwe, 3)
Ambassador: Peter Chaveas.

Of Malawi to the United Nations
Ambassador: David Rubadiri.

Further Reading

National Statistical Office. *Monthly Statistical Bulletin*
Ministry of Economic Planning and Development. *Economic Report*. Annual
Decalo, S., *Malawi.* [Bibliography]. 2nd ed. Oxford and Santa Barbara (CA), 1995

National statistical office: National Statistical Office, POB 333, Zomba.

MALAYSIA

Persekutuan Tanah Malaysia

(Federation of Malaysia)

Capital: Kuala Lumpur
Population: 19·5m. (1994)
GNP per capita: US$3,520 (1994)
HDI/world rank: 0·822/59 (1992)

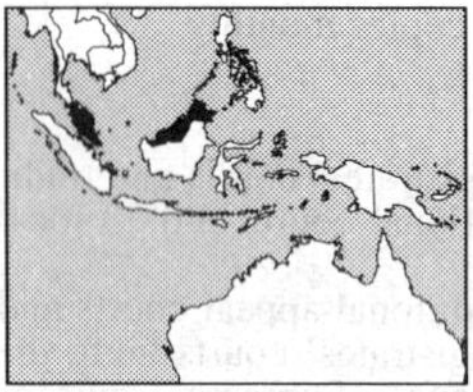

KEY HISTORICAL EVENTS. On 16 Sept. 1963 Malaysia came into being, consisting of the Federation of Malaya, the State of Singapore and the colonies of North Borneo (renamed Sabah) and Sarawak. The UK relinquished sovereignty over Singapore, North Borneo and Sarawak from independence day and extended the 1957 defence agreement with Malaya to apply to Malaysia. Malaysia became a member of the Commonwealth.

On 9 Aug. 1965, by a mutual agreement dated 7 Aug. 1965, Singapore seceded from Malaysia.

TERRITORY AND POPULATION. The federal state of Malaysia comprises the 11 states and 1 federal territory of peninsular Malaysia on the Malay peninsula, bounded in the north by Thailand, and with the island of Singapore as an enclave on its southern tip; and, on the island of Borneo to the east, the state of Sabah (which includes the federal territory of the island of Labuan), and the state of Sarawak, with Brunei as an enclave, both bounded in the south by Indonesia and in the north-west and north-east by the South China and Sulu Seas.

The area of Malaysia is 329,758 sq. km (127,317 sq. miles) and the population (1994 estimate) is 19·5m.; density, 59 per sq.km. The growth of census population has been:

Year	*Peninsular Malaysia*	*Sarawak*	*Sabah/Labuan*	*Total Malaysia*
1980	11,426,613	1,307,582	1,011,046	13,745,241
1990	14,127,556	1,648,217	1,791,209	17,566,982

The areas, populations and chief towns of the states and federal territories are:

Peninsular States	*Area (in sq. km)*	*Population (1993 estimate)*	*Chief Town*	*Population (1980 census)*
Johor	18,986	2,106,700	Johor Baharu	249,880
Kedah	9,426	1,412,000	Alor Setar	71,682
Kelantan	14,943	1,221,700	Kota Baharu	170,559
Kuala Lumpur [1]	243	1,231,500	Kuala Lumpur	937,875
Malacca	1,650	583,400	Malacca	88,073
Negeri Sembilan	6,643	723,900	Seremban	136,252
Pahang	35,965	1,056,100	Kuantan	136,625
Penang	1,031	1,141,500	Penang (Georgetown)	250,578
Perak	21,005	2,222,400	Ipoh	300,727
Perlis	795	187,600	Kangar	12,956
Selangor	7,956	1,981,200	Shah Alam	24,138
Terengganu	12,955	752,000	Kuala Terengganu	186,608
Other states		*Population (1990 census)*		
Labuan [1]	91	54,307	Victoria	…
Sabah	73,711	1,736,902	Kota Kinabalu	55,997
Sarawak	124,449	1,648,217	Kuching	74,229

[1] Federal territory.

Other large cities (1980 Census): Petaling Jaya (207,805), Kelang (192,080), Taiping (146,002), Sibu (85,231), Sandakan (70,420) and Miri (52,125).

Vital statistics rates, 1992 (per 1,000 population): Birth, 27·8; death, 4·6; infant mortality rate 12·1 per 1,000 live births; natural increase, 24 per 1,000. Life expectancy in 1992: Males, 69 years; females, 73·7.

Of the total population in 1980, 47% were Malay, 32% Chinese, 8% Indian and 13% others.

Over 58% speak Bahasa Malaysia, the official language, 9% Chinese, 4% Tamil and 3% Iban.

CLIMATE. Malaysia is affected by the monsoon climate. The N.E. monsoon prevails from Oct. to Feb., bringing rain to the east coast of the peninsula. The S.W. monsoon lasts from mid-May to Sept. and affects the opposite coastline the most. Temperatures are uniform throughout the year. Kuala Lumpur. Jan. 81°F (27·2°C), July 81°F (27·2°C). Annual rainfall 97·6" (2,441 mm). Penang. Jan. 82°F (27·8°C), July 82°F (27·8°C). Annual rainfall 109·4" (2,736 mm).

CONSTITUTION AND GOVERNMENT. The Constitution of Malaysia is based on the Constitution of the former Federation of Malaya, but includes safeguards for the special interests of Sabah and Sarawak. It was amended in 1983.

The Constitution provides for one of the Rulers of the Malay States to be elected from among themselves to be the *Yang di-Pertuan Agong* (Supreme Head of the Federation). He holds office for a period of 5 years. The Rulers also elect from among themselves a Deputy Supreme Head of State, also for a period of 5 years.

In Feb. 1993 the Rulers accepted constitutional amendments abolishing their legal immunity.

Supreme Head of State (Yang di-Pertuan Agong): HM Tuanku Ja'afar ibni Al-Marhum Tuanku Abdul Rahman, DMN, DK, elected as 10th *Yang di-Pertuan Agong* on 4 Feb. 1994, crowned 26 April 1994.

Raja of Perlis: HRH Tuanku Syed Putra ibni Al-Marhum Syed Hassan Jamalullail, DK, DKM, DMN, SMN, SPMP, SPDK, acceded 12 March 1949.

Sultan of Kedah: HRH Tuanku Haji Abdul Halim Mu'adzam Shah ibni Al-Marhum Sultan Badlishah, DK, DKH, DKM, DMN, DUK, SPMK, SSDK, acceded 20 Feb. 1959.

Sultan of Johor: HRH Sultan Mahmood Iskandar ibni Al-Marhum Sultan Ismail, DK, SPMJ, SPDK, DK (Brunei), SSIJ, PIS, BSI, acceded 11 May 1981 (Supreme Head of State from 26 April 1984 to 25 April 1989), returned as Sultan of Johor 26 April 1989.

Sultan of Selangor: HRH Sultan Salahuddin Abdul Aziz Shah ibni Al-Marhum Sultan Hisamuddin 'Alam Shah Al-Haj, DK, DMN, SPMS, SPDK, acceded 3 Sept. 1960 (Deputy Supreme Head of State from 4 Feb. 1994).

Sultan of Perak: HRH Sultan Azlan Shah Muhibbuddin Shah ibni Almarhum Sultan Yussuf Izzuddin Ghafarullahu-lahu Shah, DK, DMN, PMN, SPCM, SPMP.

Regent of Negeri Sembilan: HRH Tengku Naquiyuddin, appointed 26 April 1994.

Sultan of Kelantan: HRH Sultan Ismail Petra ibni Al-Marhum Sultan Yahya Petra, DK, SPMK, SJMK, SPSM, appointed 29 March 1979.

Sultan of Trengganu: HRH Sultan Mahmud Al-Marhum ibni Al-Marhum Tuanku Al-Sultan Ismail Nasiruddin Shah, DK, SPMT, SPCM, appointed 2 Sept. 1979.

Sultan of Pahang: Sultan Haji Ahmad Shah Al-Musta'in Billah ibni Al-Marhum Sultan Abu Bakar Ri'Ayatuddin Al-Mu'Adzam Shah, DKM, DKP, DK, SSAP, SPCM, SPMJ.

Yang di-Pertua Negeri Pulau Pinang: HE Tun Haji Hamdan Sheikh Tahir, appointed 2 May 1989.

Yang di Pertua Negeri Melaka: HE Tun Datuk Seri Utama Syed Ahmad Al-Haj bin Syed Mahmud Shahabudin, SSM, PSM, DUNM, SPMK, SSDK, PGDK, PNBS, JMN, JP, appointed 4 Dec. 1984.

Yang di-Pertua Negeri Sarawak: HE Datuk Patinggi Haji Ahmad Zaidi Adruce bin Muhammed Noor, SSM, DP, DUNM, PNBS, BM Adipradana (Indonesia) appointed 2 April 1985.

Yang di-Pertua Negeri Sabah: HE Tan Sri Sakaran Dandi, PMN, SPDK, appointed 31 Dec. 1994.

The federal parliament consists of the *Yang di-Pertuan Agong* and two *Majlis* (Houses of Parliament) known as the *Dewan Negara* (Senate) of 69 members (26 elected, 2 by each state legislature; and 43 appointed by the Yang di-Pertuan Agong) and *Dewan Rakyat* (House of Representatives) of 192 members. Appointment to the Senate is for 3 years. The maximum life of the House of Representatives is 5 years, subject to its dissolution at any time by the *Yang di-Pertuan Agong* on the advice of his Ministers.

Parliamentary and 11 state assembly elections were held on 24–25 April 1995. The 14-party National Front Coalition, in which the United Malays National Organization was the predominant partner, gained 162 seats with 63% of votes cast. The Democratic Action Party gained 9 seats. The National Front Coalition also gained a majority in every state assembly except Kelantan, which was won by the Islamic Party of Malaysia.

In Sept. 1995 the government comprised:

Prime Minister and Minister for Home Affairs: Dato Seri Dr Mahathir Mohamad (b. 1926).

Deputy Prime Minister and Minister of Finance: Datuk Seri Anwar Ibrahim. *Transport:* Dato Seri Dr Ling Liong Sik. *Energy, Telecommunications and Posts:* Datuk Seri Leo Moggie Anak Irok. *Primary Industries:* Dato Seri Dr Lim Keng Yaik. *Works:* Datuk Seri S. Samy Vellu. *International Trade and Industry:* Dato Seri Rafidah Aziz. *Education:* Datuk Seri Najib Tun Razak. *Rural Development:* Datuk Annuar Musa. *Agriculture:* Datuk Amar Dr Sulaiman Daud. *Domestic Trade and Consumer Affairs:* Dato Haji Abu Hassan bin Haji Omar. *Health:* Chua Jui Meng. *Foreign Affairs:* Dato Abdullah bin Haji Ahmad Badawi. *Defence:* Datuk Syed Hamid Albar. *Information:* Dato Mohamed bin Rahmat. *Culture, Arts and Tourism:* Dato Sabbaruddin bin Chik. *National Unity and Community Development:* Datin Paduka Zaleha Ismail. *Entrepreneur Development:* Datuk Mustapa Mohamed. *Human Resources:* Dato Lim Ah Lek. *Science, Technology and Environment:* Datuk Law Hieng Ding. *Housing and Local Government:* Dato Dr Ting Chew Peh. *Land and Co-operative Development:* Osu bin Haji Sukam. *Youth and Sports:* Muhyiddin Yassin. *Ministers in the Prime Minister's Department:* Datuk Abang Abu Bakar bin Datu Bandar Abang Haji Mustapha, Datuk Chong Kah Kiat, Dr Abdul Hamid Othman.

National flag: 14 horizontal stripes of red and white, with a blue quarter bearing a crescent and a star of 14 points, all in gold.

National anthem: Negara-Ku (My Country); words collective, tune by Pierre de Béranger.

Regional and Local Government. States have elected single-chamber legislative assemblies. The ruler appoints an executive council on the advice of the chief minister. In Peninsular Malaysia each state is divided into districts under a district officer. Each district is divided into *mukims* under a chief, and each village in the *mukim* has a headman.

DEFENCE. The Constitution provides for the Head of State to be the Supreme Commander of the Armed Forces who exercises his powers in accordance with the advice of the Cabinet. Under their authority the Armed Forces Council is responsible for all matters relating to the Armed Forces, other than those relating to their operational use. The Council is chaired by the Minister of Defence and its membership consists of the chief of the Defence Forces, the 3 Service Chiefs and 2 other senior military officers, the Secretary-General of the Ministry of Defence, a representative of State Rulers and an appointed member.

The chief of the Armed Forces Staff is the professional head of the Armed Forces and the senior military member in the Armed Forces Council. He chairs the Armed Forces Staff's committee, the highest level at which joint planning and co-ordination with the Armed Forces are carried out.

Malaysia is a member of the Five Powers Defence Arrangement with Australia, New Zealand, Singapore and the UK.

Army. The Army is organized into 2 military regions, 1 corps and 5 divisional headquarters. There are 10 infantry brigades made up of 35 infantry battalions, 4 armoured, 5 field artillery, 1 air defence artillery, 1 special forces and 5 engineer regiments, and 1 Rapid Deployment Force. Equipment includes 26 Scorpion light tanks. Strength (1996) about 85,000. There is a paramilitary Police Field Force of 18,000.

Navy. The Royal Malaysian Navy is commanded by the Chief of the Navy from the integrated Ministry of Defence in Kuala Lumpur. Main bases are at Lumut, and on Labuan Island which are also the headquarters for the Malay Peninsula and Borneo operational areas respectively. The peace-time tasks include fishery protection and anti-piracy patrols.

The combatants include 2 German-built and 2 British-built frigates all with helicopter platforms, 8 fast missile craft and 2 offshore and 27 inshore patrol craft. There are also 4 Italian-type offshore mine countermeasure vessels and 4 tank landing ships normally employed in support of patrol and missile craft. Auxiliaries include 2 multi-purpose support ships, 1 survey ship, 1 diving support ship and 33 amphibious craft. The first of 2 new well-equipped British-built frigates were expected to be delivered in 1996.

A Naval aviation squadron operates 12 ex-British Wasp helicopters. Navy personnel in 1995 totalled 12,000 and 2,700 reserves.

Paramilitary maritime forces include 50 armed patrol launches, 48 operated by the Royal Malaysian Police and 2 by the Government of Sabah which also operates 4 other patrol boats, 1 landing craft and a yacht.

Air Force. Formed on 1 June 1958, the Royal Malaysian Air Force is equipped primarily to provide air defence and air support for the Army, Navy and Police. Its secondary rôle is to render assistance to Government departments and civilian organizations. There are 15 squadrons, of which 9 operate transport aircraft and helicopters. Some 18 MiG-29s equip 2 squadrons. Other equipment includes 28 Hawk strike/trainer aircraft, 14 F-5E Tiger II jet fighterbombers, 2 RF-5E reconnaissance-fighters, and 3 F-5F trainers, 1 F.28 Fellowship and 1 Falcon 900 VIP transports, 14 C-130 Hercules four-engined transport and patrol aircraft, 12 Caribou twin-engined short-take-off-and-landing transports, 2 HU-16 amphibians, 33 Sikorsky S-61A-4 Nuri heavy troop and cargo transport helicopters, 20 Alouette III, and 6 Bell 47 helicopters, 9 Cessna 402Bs for twin-engine training and liaison, 39 PC-7 Turbo-Trainers, 11 MB.339 jet trainers, 2 H.S. 125 Merpati twin-jet executive transports, 1 A-109 and 1 Super Puma VIP transport helicopter. Personnel (1995) totalled about 12,500, with 120 combat aircraft.

INTERNATIONAL RELATIONS

Membership. Malaysia is a member of the UN, the Commonwealth, Non-Aligned movement, the Colombo Plan, Organization of Islamic Conference and ASEAN.

ECONOMY

Policy. The Second Outline Perspective Plan of 1991 set targets for the coming decade to be implemented by the New Development Policy. The sixth Malaysia Plan covers 1991–95 and is the first of two 5-year programmes under the Policy. It envisages public spending of RM104,000m.: RM55,000m. on federal improvements to communications, education, health and defence, and RM49,000m. by state and local authorities. There are privatization programmes involving telecommunications, railways, airports, electricity and shipping.

Budget. Revenue and expenditure for calendar years, in RM1m.:

	1990	*1991*	*1992*	*1993*	*1994* [1]
Revenue	29,521	34,053	39,250	41,231	44,730
Operating expenditure	27,105	28,296	32,075	32,315	32,285

[1] Estimate.

Sources of revenue in 1994: Direct taxes, 19,250; indirect taxes, 15,808; non-tax revenue, 9,672.

Federal government development (in addition to operating) expenditure in 1994 (RM1m.): Defence, 2,211; internal security, 356; education, 1,587; health, 342; housing, 504; agriculture and rural development, 1,528; public amenities, 940; commerce and industry, 1,106; transport, 3,425; administration, 528.

Currency. The unit of currency is the Malaysian *ringgit* (MYR) of 100 *sen*. Currency notes are of denominations of RM1, 5, 10, 20, 50, 100, 500 and 1,000. Coins are of denominations of 1 sen, 5, 10, 20, 50 sen and RM1, 5 and 100. Total amount of currency in circulation in 1993, RM30,395m. Inflation was 3·5% in Oct. 1993. In March 1996, £1 = RM3·89; US$1 = RM2·54; DM1 = RM1·72.

Banking and Finance. The central bank and bank of issue is the Bank Negara Malaysia (*Governor*, Jaffar Hussein). 37 commercial banks were operating at 31 Dec. 1993 (including 16 foreign) with a total of 1,050 branches. Total deposits with commercial banks at 31 July 1993 were RM92,657m. There were 12 merchant banks at 31 Dec. 1993. Their total assets were RM15,000m. The Islamic Bank of Malaysia began operations in July 1983. There were 43 finance companies in 1993 with 699 offices.

There is a stock exchange at Kuala Lumpur.

Weights and Measures. The metric system is standard, but British imperial units are still in residual use.

ENERGY AND NATURAL RESOURCES

Electricity. Installed capacity in 1992, 6,620 MW. In 1991, 28,374m. kWh were generated.

Oil and Gas. Estimated oil production (1994) 30·03m. tonnes. Natural gas reserves, 1987, 1,400,000m. cu. metres. Production of liquefied natural gas in 1994 was an estimated 9·33 tonnes.

Minerals. In 1992 mining contributed 8·6% of GDP. Production (1986, in 1,000 tonnes): Bauxite, 566; iron ore, 208; copper, 115; tin, 29. Tin production was an estimated 10,600 tonnes in 1994.

Agriculture. In 1994 agriculture contributed 14·5% of GDP. Production (1992): Rice, 2·07m. tonnes; fruit, 722,485 tonnes (of which pineapples, 167,900 tonnes); tobacco, 12,000 tonnes; cocoa, 270,000 tonnes; (1994 estimates) rubber, 1,210,000 tonnes; palm oil, 7,350,000 tonnes.

Livestock (1988): Cattle, 625,000, buffaloes, 220,000; sheep, 99,000; pigs, 2,258,000; goats, 347,000.

Forestry. In 1990 there were 19·6m. ha of forests. The total output of saw logs was 40·2m. cu. metres.

Fisheries. Total landings of marine fish, 1990, 907,300 tonnes.

INDUSTRY. In 1994 manufacturing contributed 32% of GDP.

Labour. In 1994 the workforce was 7,859,000 (47·4% female), of whom 7,607,000 were employed (20·2% in agriculture, 24·9% in manufacturing and 7·8% in building). Unemployment was 2·8%.

Trade Unions. Membership was 617,000 in 1988, of which the Malaysian Trades Union Congress, an umbrella organization of 138 unions, accounted for 0·5m.

FOREIGN ECONOMIC RELATIONS. Privatization policy permits foreign investment of 25–30% generally; total foreign ownership is permitted of export-oriented projects.

Commerce. In 1994 exports totalled US$56,700m. and imports US$55,300m.

In 1993 imports of consumer goods totalled RM17,744m.; intermediate goods, RM46,918m.; capital goods, RM47,841m.

Chief exports, 1993 (in RM1m.): Rubber, 2,138; palm oil, 5,841; saw logs, 3,441; crude oil, 8,002; tin (1991), 674; manufactures, 85,350.

In 1994 imports came chiefly from Japan (26·7%), USA (16·7%) and Singapore (14·1%). Exports went chiefly to USA (21·2%), Singapore (20·7%) and Japan (11·9%).

Total trade of Malaysia with UK (British Department of Trade returns, in £1,000 sterling):

	1991	*1992*	*1993*	*1994*	*1995*
Imports to UK	930,036	1,103,782	1,396,413	1,204,026	1,487,884
Exports and re-exports from UK	582,239	635,857	964,985	1,305,201	1,189,582

Tourism. 6m. tourists visited Malaysia in 1992 (65% from Singapore).

COMMUNICATIONS

Roads. Total road length in 1992 was 57,486 km, of which 42,135 km were surfaced. In 1990, there were 5·2m. motor vehicles.

Railways. In 1994 there were 1,672 km (metre gauge; 160 km electrified) which carried 5·5m. passengers and 5·1m. tonnes of freight.

Civil Aviation. There are 4 international airports and 15 other aerodromes at which regular public air transport is operated. 33 international airlines operate through Kuala Lumpur (Subang). Malaysia Airlines, the national airline, is 39% state-owned, and operates domestic flights within Peninsular Malaysia as well as between Kuala Lumpur and Sabah and Sarawak, and flies to Australia, Austria, Belgium, Burma, Cambodia, China, France, Germany, Hong Kong, India, Indonesia, Iran, Japan, Jordan, South Korea, Mauritius, Mexico, Netherlands, New Zealand, Pakistan, Philippines, Singapore, Spain, Sri Lanka, Switzerland, Taiwan, Thailand, Turkey, UAE, UK, USA and Vietnam. In 1995 its fleet comprised 2 A300B4-200s, 5 A330-300s, 2 B-737-300(F)s, 35 B-737-400s, 9 B-737-500s, 2 B-747-200Bs, 1 B-747-300 Combi, 10 B-747-400s, 2 B-747-400 Combis, and 22 other aircraft. Services are also provided by Aeroflot, Air India, Air Lanka, Air Maldives, Air Mauritius, All Nippon Airways, Ansett Australia, Berjaya Air, Biman Bangaldesh, British Airways, Canadian Airlines, Cathay Pacific, China Airlines, China Southern Airlines, Eva Airways, Garuda Indonesia, Gulf Air, Indian Airlines, Iran Air, JAL, KLM, Korean Air, Kuwait Airways, Lufthansa, Myanma Airways, Pakistan Airlines, Philippine Air, Qantas, Royal Air Cambodge, Royal Brunei Airlines, Royal Jordanian, Saudia, Singapore Airlines, Thai Airways, Uzbekistan Airways, Vietnam Airlines and Virgin Atlantic. In 1991, 3,358,600 international and 6,675,400 domestic passengers took off and 3,229,700 international and 6,694,800 domestic passengers landed.

Shipping. The major ports are Port Kelang, Labuan, Pulau Pinang, Pasir Gudang, Kuantan, Kota Kinabalu, Sandakan, Kuching, Sibu and Bintulu. In 1995 the merchant marine comprised 167 vessels totalling 3·11m. DWT. 17 vessels (12·87% of total tonnage) were registered under foreign flags. Total GRT was 2·82m., including oil tankers, 0·38m. GRT, and container ships, 0·29m. GRT. In 1992, 19,608 tonnes of cargo were loaded and 33,188 tonnes unloaded.

Telecommunications. Postal services are the responsibility of the Ministry of Energy, Telecommunications and Post. There were 2,550,957 telephones, 227,240 mobile telephones and 7,576 telex and 46,404 fax subscribers in 1992.

The government-controlled Radio Television Malaysia broadcasts radio and TV programmes in Peninsular Malaysia, Sabah and Sarawak. There is an external service, Voice of Malaysia (8 languages). System TV Malaysia Berhad transmits from Kuala Lumpur, TV Malaysia Sabah and Sarawak to east Malaysia. (Colour by PAL). In 1993 there were 3·5m. radio and 2m. TV sets.

Press. In 1993 there were 62 newspapers, including 17 in Bahasa Malaysia, 14 in English and 24 in Chinese.

SOCIAL INSTITUTIONS

Justice. The judicial power is vested in the Supreme Court, the High Court of Malaya, the High Court of Borneo and subordinate courts: Sessions Courts, Magistrates' Courts and *Mukim* chiefs' Courts.

The head of the Judiciary is the Lord President of the Supreme Court which consists of himself, the Chief Justices of the High Courts and Judges of the Supreme Court. The Supreme Court has jurisdiction to determine the validity of any law made by Parliament or by a State legislature and disputes between States or between the Federation and any State. It also has jurisdiction to hear and determine appeals from the High Courts.

Religion. Islam is the official religion but there is freedom of worship. In 1992 there were 9·86m. Moslems, 3·22m. Buddhists, 2·16m. adherents of Chinese traditional religions and 1·3m. Hindus.

Education. School education is free; tertiary education is provided at a nominal fee. There are 6 years of primary schooling starting at age 6, 3 years of universal lower secondary, 2 years of selective upper secondary and 2 years of pre-university education. In 1989 there were 2,390,000 pupils enrolled in primary schools with 111,729 teachers and 1,353,000 in lower and 53,476 in upper secondary schools with 66,937 teachers. In 1994–95 there were 4 universities, 3 specialized universities (agricultture; Islamic; technology), 1 college and 1 institute of technology. There were 53,180 university students and 5,296 academic staff.

Health. In 1990 there were 6,577 private and government doctors, (1986) 1,130 dentists, 12,721 government nurses, 102 hospitals and 2,681 government clinics. In 1994 there were 33,261 hospital beds.

Social Security. The Employment Injury Insurance Scheme provides medical and cash benefits and the Invalidity Pension Scheme provides protection to employees against invalidity due to disease or injury from any cause. Other supplementary measures are the Employees' Provident Fund, the pension scheme for government employees, free medical benefits for all who are unable to pay and the provision of medical benefits particularly for workers under the Labour Code.

DIPLOMATIC REPRESENTATIVES

Of Malaysia in Great Britain (45 Belgrave Sq., London, SW1X 8QT)
High Commissioner: Vacant.

Of Great Britain in Malaysia (185, Jalan Semantan, Ampang 50450, Kuala Lumpur)
High Commissioner: J. Moss, CMG.

Of Malaysia in the USA (2401 Massachusetts Ave., NW, Washington, D.C., 20008)
Ambassador: Dato Abdul Majid.

Of the USA in Malaysia (376 Jalan Tun Razak, Kuala Lumpur)
Ambassador: Vacant.

Of Malaysia to the United Nations
Ambassador: Razali Ismail.

Further Reading

Department of Statistics.
Yearbook of Statistics.

Brown, I. and Ampalavanar, R., *Malaysia.* [Bibliography] Oxford and Santa Barbara, 1986
Gullick, J., *Malaysia: Economic Expansion and National Unity.* Boulder and London, 1982
Information Malaysia Yearbook. Kuala Lumpur
Jomo, K. S., *Growth and Structural Change in the Malaysian Economy.* London, 1990
Kahn, J. S. and Wah, F. L. K., *Fragmented Vision: Culture and Politics in Contemporary Malaysia.* Sydney, 1992
King, V. T. and Parnwell, M. J. (eds), *Margins and Minorities: the Peripheral Areas and People of Malaysia.* Hull Univ. Press, 1990
Means, G. P., *Malaysian Politics: the Second Generation.* OUP, 1991
Zakaria, A., *Government and Politics in Malaysia.* OUP, 1987

National statistical office: Department of Statistics, Kuala Lumpur.

SABAH

KEY HISTORICAL EVENTS. The territory now named Sabah, but until Sept. 1963 known as North Borneo, was in 1877-78 ceded by the Sultans of Brunei and Sulu and various other rulers to a British syndicate, which in 1881 was chartered as the British North Borneo (Chartered) Company. The Company's sovereign rights and assets were transferred to the Crown with effect from 15 July 1946. On that date, the island of Labuan (ceded to Britain in 1846 by the Sultan of Brunei) became part of the new Colony of North Borneo. On 16 Sept. 1963 North Borneo joined the new Federation of Malaysia and became the State of Sabah.

TERRITORY AND POPULATION. Area, 29,388 sq. miles (73,711 sq. km), with a coastline of 973 miles (1,577 km). The interior is mountainous, Mount Kinabalu being 13,455 ft (4,175 metres) high. Population, 1990 census 1,736,902; 1993 estimate, 1,472,700.

The island of **Labuan** became Federal territory on 16 April 1984. It is 35 sq. miles (75 sq. km) in area, lying 6 miles (9·66 km) off the north-west coast of Borneo. It is a free port. Population (1991 census, preliminary), 54,307.

The principal towns are situated on or near the coast. They include Kota Kinabalu, the capital (formerly Jesselton), 1990 census population (preliminary), 208,484, Tawau (244,765), Sandakan (223,432), Keningau in the hinterland (89,517), and Kudat (55,932).

The official language is Bahasa Malaysia. English is widely used, especially in business.

CLIMATE. The climate is tropical monsoon, but on the whole is equable, with temperatures around 80°F (26·5°C) throughout the year. Annual rainfall varies, according to locality, from 10" (250 mm) to 148" (3,700 mm). The north-east monsoon lasts from Dec. to April and chiefly affects the east coast, while the south-west monsoon from May to Aug. gives the west coast its wet season.

CONSTITUTION AND GOVERNMENT. The Constitution of the State of Sabah provides for a Head of State, called the *Yang Dipertua Negeri Sabah.* Executive authority is vested in the State Cabinet headed by the Chief Minister. The *Legislative Assembly* consists of the Speaker, 48 elected members and not more than 6 nominated members.

At the elections on 18 Feb. 1994 the Parti Bersatu Sabah (PBS; Christian) won 25 of the 48 electable seats, and Datuk Joseph Pairin Kitingan was sworn in for a further 5-year term as Chief Minister, but lost his majority when 9 members of his party changed their allegiance. A 32-member anti-PBS Moslem/Christian/Chinese coalition took office, agreeing to rotate the Chief Ministership by ethnic group every 2 years.

Head of State: Tan Seri Mohamad Said Keruak.
Chief Minister: Sakaran Dandai.

Flag: Three horizontal stripes of blue, white and red with a large light blue canton bearing an outline of Mount Kinabalu in dark blue.

Local Government. The state is divided into residencies, each under a Resident, and these are subdivided into districts.

ECONOMY

Budget. Budgets (not including the Federal Territory of Labuan) for calendar years, in RM1,000:

Ordinary Budget	*1989*	*1990*	*1991*	*1992*	*1993*
Revenue	1,743,998	1,691,924	1,479,960	2,004,693	1,332,284
Expenditure	1,740,731	1,998,174	1,848,392	1,960,314	1,670,018
Development Budget					
Revenue	426,665	672,445	893,595	559,452	533,152
Expenditure	409,202	793,318	753,407	581,042	512,850

Banking and Finance. 12 banks were operating in 1990.

The National Savings Bank had (1993) RM56·8m. due to depositors. It also provides additional services to depositors including the granting of loans for housing.

Labuan is being developed as an international offshore financial centre.

COMMERCE. The main imports are machinery and transport equipment, manufactured goods and food. The main exports are crude petroleum, sawn timber and saw logs. Statistics for calendar years, in RM1,000:

	1989	*1990*	*1991*	*1992*	*1993*
Imports	5,344,688	6,614,232	7,771,534	7,209,931	6,842,468
Exports	7,640,191	8,822,601	9,311,688	9,176,293	9,061,274

Tourism. In 1993, 98,502 tourists visited Sabah, excluding foreign visitors arriving via Peninsular Malaysia, Sarawak and Labuan.

COMMUNICATIONS

Roads (1993). There were 9,782 km of roads, of which 2,958 km were bitumen surfaced, 5,986 km gravel surfaced and 838 km of earth.

Railways. A metre-gauge railway, 134 km, runs from Kota Kinabalu to Tenom in the interior. It carried 545,500 passengers and 45,400 tonnes of freight in 1993.

Civil Aviation. External communications are provided from the international airport at Kota Kinabalu by Cathay Pacific Airways to Hong Kong; Malaysian Airways to Hong Kong, Manila, Brunei, Kuching, Singapore, Tokyo, Seoul and Kuala Lumpur; Royal Brunei Airlines to Brunei and Kuching, Philippine Airlines to Manila and Thai Airways to Bangkok. The airport on Labuan can handle only small aircraft.

The total air traffic handled at Sabah airports during 1993 was 2,538,284 passengers, 27,638 tonnes of freight and 4,659 tonnes of mail.

Shipping (1993). Merchant shipping totalling 42,565,510 NRT used the ports, handling 20,821,224 tonnes of cargo.

Telecommunications. As at 31 Dec. 1993 there were 41 post offices. There were 152,529 telephones on 31 Dec. 1993, and 98,906 television licences were issued.

SOCIAL INSTITUTIONS

Justice. Pursuant to the Subordinate Courts Ordinance (Cap. 20) (1951) Courts of a Magistrate of the First Class, Second Class and Third Class were established to adjudicate upon the administration of civil and criminal law. The civil jurisdiction of a First Class Magistrate is limited to cases where the amount in dispute does not exceed RM1,000. but provision is made for the Chief Justice to enlarge that jurisdiction to RM3,000. This has been established so as to confer this jurisdiction on all stipendiary magistrates. A Second Class Magistrate can only try suits where the amount involved does not exceed RM500 and a Third Class Magistrate where it does not exceed RM100.

The criminal jurisdiction of these Magistrates' Courts is limited to offences of a less serious nature although stipendiary magistrates have enhanced jurisdiction.

There are also Native Courts with jurisdiction to try cases arising from breach of native law and custom (including Moslem Law and custom) where all parties are natives or one of the party is a native (if the matter is a religious, matrimonial or sexual one). Appeals from Native Courts lie to a District Judge or a Native Court of Appeal presided over by a Judge.

In 1992, 3,201 convictions were obtained in 4,590 cases taken to court.

Education. In 1993, there were 270,626 primary and 119,014 secondary pupils. There were 980 primary schools (823 government, 157 grant-aided), and 138 general secondary schools (101 government, 37 grant-aided) throughout the State. There were 4 teacher-training colleges, with (1992) 2,478 students. The Government also runs 7 vocational schools and further education classes in most towns and districts.

Health. As at 31 Dec. 1993 there were 16 hospitals (2,812 beds) and 265 clinics. 70 fixed dispensaries in outlying districts providing in-patient and out-patient care are staffed by hospital assistants under the supervision of district medical officers. There is 1 mental hospital at Kota Kinabalu. There are 19 maternity and child health centres.

Further Reading

Statistical Information: Director, Federal Department of Information, Kota Kinabalu.

SARAWAK

KEY HISTORICAL EVENTS. The Government of part of the present territory was obtained on 24 Sept. 1841 by Sir James Brooke from the Sultan of Brunei. Various accessions were made between 1861 and 1905. In 1888 Sarawak was placed under British protection. On 16 Dec. 1941 Sarawak was occupied by the Japanese. After the liberation the Rajah took over his administration from the British military authorities on 15 April 1946. The Council Negeri, on 17 May 1946, authorized the Act of Cession to the British Crown by 19 to 16 votes, and the Rajah ceded Sarawak to the British Crown on 1 July 1946.

On 16 Sept. 1963 Sarawak joined the Federation of Malaysia.

TERRITORY AND POPULATION. Area, 48,050 sq. miles (124,449 sq. km), with a coastline of 450 miles and many navigable rivers.

The population at the 1990 census was 1,648,217. Ethnic groups (1989 estimate): 481,960 Ibans; 474,176 Chinese; 339,368 Malays; 136,741 Bidayuhs; 93,946 Melanaus; 88,260 other indigenous; 18,618 others).

The capital, Kuching City, is about 34 km inland, on the Sarawak River (1989 population: 157,000). The other major towns (with 1989 population) are Sibu, 128 km up the Rejang River, which is navigable by large steamers (114,000) and Miri (91,000).

The official language is Bahasa Malaysia.

CONSTITUTION AND GOVERNMENT. On 24 Sept. 1941 the Rajah began to rule through a constitution. Since 1855 two bodies, known as Majlis Mesyuarat Kerajaan Negeri (Supreme Council) and the Dewan Undangan Negeri (State Legislature), had been in existence. By the constitution of 1941 they were given, by the Rajah, powers roughly corresponding to those of a colonial executive council and legislative council respectively. Sarawak has retained a considerable measure of local autonomy in state affairs. The State Legislature consists of 56 elected members and sits for 5 years unless sooner dissolved.

A ministerial system of government was introduced in 1963. The Chief Minister presides over the Supreme Council, which contains no more than 8 other members, all of whom are Ministers.

Elections to the State Legislature were held in Oct. 1991. The electorate was 0·7m. The National Front Coalition Three won 49 seats, the tribal nationalist Bangsa Dayak Sarawak Party, 7.

Sarawak has 27 seats in the Malaysia House of Representatives and 5 seats in the Senate.

Head of State: Tun Datuk Patinggi Haji Ahmad Zaidi Adruce bin Muhammed Noor, SMN, SSM, DP, PNBS, Bintang Mahaputera Adipradana (Indonesia), PSLJ (Brunei).

Chief Minister: Datuk Patinggi Tan Sri Haji Abdul Taib Mahmud, DP, PSM, SPMJ, DGSM, PGDK, Kt. WE (Thailand), KOU (Korea), KPPN (Indonesia).

Flag: Yellow with a diagonal stripe divided black over red charged with a yellow star of nine points.

Local Government. There are 9 administrative divisions each under an Administrator.

ECONOMY

Policy. The sixth Malaysia 5-year development plan (1991–95) provided for Sarawak an expenditure of RM8,100m.; of this amount, 78% was allocated to the economic sector (of which 53% to transport and communication and public utilities, 14% to the agricultural sector and 10% to commerce and industry), 15% to the social sector, 6% to administration and 1% to security and defence.

Budget. In 1992 State revenue was estimated at RM1,624·3m.; expenditure, M$1,399·1m. The revenue is mainly derived from royalties on oil, timber and gas.

Banking and Finance. The National savings bank had 166,714 depositors in July 1988; the amount to their credit was RM75m. 9 local banks have branches.

INDUSTRY AND TRADE

Industry. Industry includes petroleum and petroleum products, natural gas, timber and timber products and rubber. Emphasis is being given to the development of petro-chemical, timber-based and agriculture-based industries.

Commerce. Exports in 1990 totalled RM10,876·6m.; imports, RM6,479m. The main exports in 1989 were: Saw logs, which accounted for 29·7% of the total, with 14·96m. cu. metres, value RM2·67m.; liquefied natural gas, 22·9%, with 6,629,000 cu. metres, value, RM2·1m.; crude petroleum, 22·5%, with 5,792,000 tonnes, value RM2·03m.; petroleum products, 6·1%, with 1,302,000 tonnes, value RM549,018; sawn timber, 2·2%, with 27,900 cu. metres, value RM197,060. The major agricultural exports, which together accounted for RM355·9m. or 3·9% of the total in 1989, were pepper, cocoa beans, palm oil and rubber.

Tourism. In 1991 there were 509,597 tourists.

COMMUNICATIONS

Roads. In 1988 there were 6,902 km of roads, consisting of 2,878 km of bitumen surfaced, 3,062 km of gravel or stone surfaced and 962 km of earth roads.

Civil Aviation. There are daily Malaysian Airline System (MAS) B737 and Airbus flights between Kuching and Kuala Lumpur via Singapore, and also scheduled flights between Pontianak, Kuching, Brunei, Hong Kong and Singapore. Major towns in Sarawak are linked up by internal air routes.

Shipping. In 1989 Sarawak ports handled a total of 27m. tonnes of cargo. Kuching Port, operational since 1974, can accommodate vessels up to 15,000 tonnes. The Bintulu Port, the largest in the State, handled more than 11m. tonnes in 1989.

Telecommunications. There are 55 post offices, 18 mobile offices, 7 mini post offices and 213 postal agencies. The Telecommunications department was privatized in 1986 and renamed Telekom Malaysia Berhad. A telephone system with 65 automatic exchanges (118,000 telephone lines) covers the country. There are International Subscribers Dialling (ISD) links with 75 countries and Atur system was introduced in 1985. The government radio and television service had, in 1989, 37,286 electric radio sets and, in 1990, 92,189 TV receivers registered.

Press (1991). There are 2 Malay newspapers (1 weekly and 1 monthly), 3 English and 8 Chinese dailies. 1 Malay and 1 Iban monthly newspaper are published by the Government.

SOCIAL INSTITUTIONS

Justice (1992). In Sarawak there are the High Court and the Subordinate Court. High Court cases go on appeal to the Supreme Court which sits in Sarawak and Sabah twice a year. The Subordinate Courts (Amendment) Act 1987 was extended to Sarawak on 2 Sept. 1987 in which the jurisdiction of the Sessions Court judges and magistrates of the First Class and Second Class was enhanced.

In 1986 a Syariah (Islamic) Court was established, and the Juvenile Court was extended to Sarawak.

Police. There is a Royal Malaysia Police, Sarawak Component, with a total establishment of about 9,000 regular officers and men.

Religion. There is a large Moslem population and many Buddhists. Islam is the national religion.

Education (1991). There were 1,264 government and government-aided primary schools with 230,843 pupils and 13,523 teachers, and 137 secondary schools with 131,143 pupils and 6,276 teachers. There were 3 teacher-training colleges with (1989) 2,945 students and an agricultural university campus conducting pre-university courses. The MARA Institute of Technology campus, established in 1973, had 960 students in 1987 and offers 3-year courses leading to diploma in accountancy, stenography and business studies and a 6-month pre-commerce course.

The Kuching Polytechnic campus, established in 1989, offers 2 and 3-year courses leading to a diploma in accountancy and certificates in book-keeping, general mechanical, civil works, electronic and computer engineering.

Health. In 1990 there were 17 government hospitals, 4 polyclinics, 12 health centres, 115 rural clinics, 3 dispensaries and 38 sub-dispensaries, 180 maternity and child clinics and 120 mobile clinics. There were 358 doctors and 51 dentists. There is a flying doctor service for the interior.

Further Reading

Runciman, S., *The White Rajahs.* CUP, 1960

State library: The Sarawak Central Library, Kuching.

MALDIVES

Divehi Raajjeyge Jumhooriyyaa

(Republic of the Maldives)

Capital: Malé
Population: 238,363 (1993)
GNP per capita: US$900 (1994)
HDI/world rank: 0·554/118 (1992)

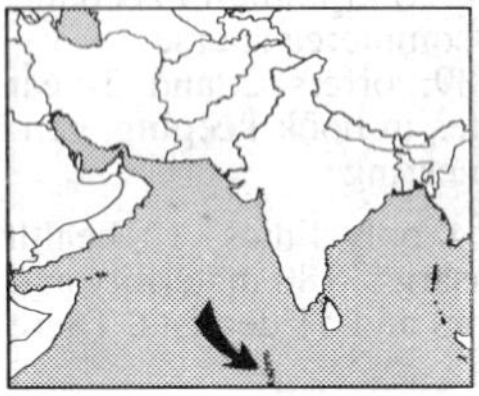

KEY HISTORICAL EVENTS. The islands were under British protection from 1887 until complete independence was achieved on 26 July 1965. The Maldives became a republic on 11 Nov. 1968.

TERRITORY AND POPULATION. The republic, some 400 miles to the south-west of Sri Lanka, consists of 1,200 low-lying (the highest point is 6 feet above sea-level) coral islands, grouped into 26 atolls. 199 are inhabited. Area 115 sq. miles (298 sq. km). At the 1990 census, the population was 213,215 (103,879 females). Estimate (1993), 238,363. Expectation of life was 60 years in 1989. Capital, Malé (1990 population, 55,130).

The official language is Divehi.

CLIMATE. The islands are hot and humid, and affected by monsoons. Malé: Average temperature 81°F (27°C), annual rainfall 59" (1,500 mm).

CONSTITUTION AND GOVERNMENT. There is a Citizens' *Majlis* (Parliament) which consists of 48 members, 8 of whom are nominated by the President and 40 directly elected (2 each from Malé and the 19 administrative districts) for a term of 5 years. There are no political parties. The President of the Republic is elected by the Citizens' Majlis.

In Nov. 1995 the Government consisted of:

President, Minister of Defence and National Security, Minister of Finance: Maumoon Abdul Gayoom (b. 1937; re-elected unopposed for a fourth 5-year term on 23 Aug. 1993; sworn in, 1 Oct. 1993).

Minister of Home Affairs and Sports: Abdulla Jameel. *Education:* Dr Mohamed sa Lateef. *Health and Welfare:* Ahmed Abdulla. *Fisheries and Agriculture:* Hassan Sabir. *Tourism:* Ibrahim Hussain Zaki. *Foreign Affairs:* Fathulla Jameel. *Atolls Administration:* Abdul Rasheed Hussain. *Justice and Islamic Affairs:* Mohamed Rasheed Ibrahim. *Transport and Shipping:* Ahmed Zahir. *Planning, Human Resources and Environment:* Ismail Shafeen. *Trade and Industries:* Abdulla Yameen. *Minister at the President's Office:* Mohamed Zahir Hussain.

Speaker of Citizens' Majlis: Abdulla Hameed.

The official and spoken language is Divehi.

National flag: Red with a green panel bearing a white crescent.

National anthem: 'Gavmii mi ekuverikan matii tibegen kuriime salaam' ('In national unity we salute our nation'); words by M. J. Didi, tune by W. Amaradeva.

Local government: The Maldives is divided into the capital and 19 other administrative districts, each under an appointed governor assisted by appointed local chiefs.

INTERNATIONAL RELATIONS

Membership. The Maldives is a member of the UN, the Commonwealth and the Colombo Plan.

ECONOMY

Budget. 1993 estimates: Revenue, 870·7m. rufiyaas; expenditure 1,495·3m. rufiyaas.

Currency. The unit of currency is the *rufiyaa* (MVR) of 100 *laari*. There are coins of 1, 2, 5, 10, 25 and 50 laari and 1 rufiyaa, and notes of 2, 5, 10, 20, 50, 100 and 500 rufiyaa. In March 1996, £1 = 17·99; US$1 = 11·77; DM1 = 7·97 rufiyaa.

ENERGY AND NATURAL RESOURCES

Electricity. Production, 1992, 34·62m. kWh.

Minerals. Inshore coral mining has been banned as a measure against the encroachment of the sea.

Agriculture. Principal crops in 1993 (in 1,000 tonnes): Coconuts (number of nuts), 15,324,732; maize, 9; cassava, 8; sweet potatoes, 44; onions, 0·1; chillies, 40·3.

Fisheries. Catch, 1992, 82,000 tonnes.

INDUSTRY. The main industries are fishing, tourism, shipping, lacquerwork and garment manufacturing.

FOREIGN ECONOMIC RELATIONS

Commerce. In 1992 imports amounted to 2,001,525,000 rufiyaas and exports to 416,682,000 rufiyaas. Bonito ('Maldive fish') is the main export commodity. It is exported principally to Thailand, Singapore, Sri Lanka, Japan, and some European markets.

Total trade between the Republic of the Maldives and UK (British Department of Trade returns, in £1,000 sterling):

	1991	*1992*	*1993*	*1994*	*1995*
Imports to UK	7,909	8,174	8,996	7,404	8,879
Exports and re-exports from UK	2,862	4,261	4,968	2,580	3,850

Tourism. Tourism is the major foreign currency earner. There were 235,852 visitors in 1992.

COMMUNICATIONS

Roads. In 1992 there were 804 cars, 4,126 motorbikes, 1,019 handcarts, 38,252 bicycles and 1,114 other vehicles.

Civil Aviation. There are direct flights from Colombo, Thiruvananthapuram, Dubai, Karachi, Singapore, Frankfurt, Munich, Dusseldorf, Zurich and Bucharest. In 1992, 4,295 aircraft, 273,982 passengers and 11,541,755 kg of freight were handled at Malé International Airport. There are 4 domestic airports. Air Maldives operates domestic flights only.

Shipping. The Maldives Shipping Line operated (1992) 10 vessels.

Telecommunications. There were (1992) 8,523 telephones. Voice of Maldives and Television Maldives are government-controlled. There were (1992) 28,284 radio receivers and 7,309 television sets (colour by PAL).

Press. There were (1991) 2 daily newspapers, 2 weekly, 2 fortnightly and a number of monthly periodicals.

SOCIAL INSTITUTIONS

Justice. Justice is based on the Islamic Shari'ah.

Religion. The State religion is Islam.

Education. Education is not compulsory. In 1992, there were 57 government schools (32,475 pupils) and 211 private schools (41,167 pupils) with a total of 1,925 teachers.

Health. In 1992 there was a 110-bed hospital in Malé, 4 regional hospitals (64 beds) and 225 health centres. In 1992 there were 35 doctors and 152 nurses.

DIPLOMATIC REPRESENTATIVES

Of the Maldives in Great Britain
High Commissioner: Ahmad Zaki.

Of Great Britain in the Maldives
High Commissioner: David Tatham (resides in Colombo).

Of the Maldives to the United Nations
Ambassador: Vacant.

Further Reading

Reynolds, C. H. B., *Maldives.* [Bibliography] Oxford and Santa Barbara (CA), 1993

MALI

République du Mali

Capital: Bamako
Population: 9·82m. (1992)
GNP per capita: US$250 (1994)
HDI/world rank: 0·222/172 (1992)

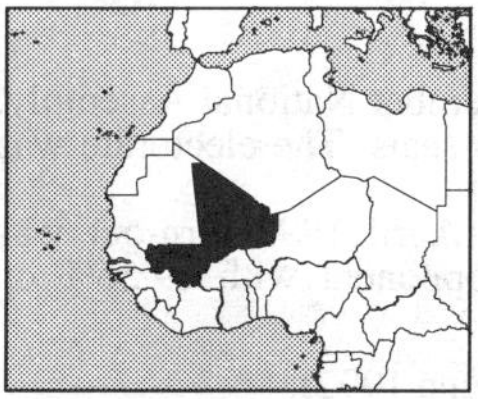

KEY HISTORICAL EVENTS. Annexed by France between 1881 and 1895, the region became the territory of French Sudan as a part of French West Africa. It became an autonomous state within the French Community on 24 Nov. 1958, and on 4 April 1959 joined with Senegal to form the Federation of Mali. The Federation achieved independence on 20 June 1960, but Senegal seceded on 22 Aug. and Mali proclaimed itself an independent republic on 22 Sept. The National Assembly was dissolved on 17 Jan. 1968 by President Modibo Keita, whose government was then overthrown by an Army coup on 19 Nov. 1968; power was assumed by a Military Committee for National Liberation led by Moussa Traoré, who became President on 19 Sept. 1969. He was deposed on 26 March 1991 in a military coup. Lieut.-Col. Amadou Touré was named head of a Transitional Committee of Public Safety.

In Jan. 1991 a ceasefire was signed with Tuareg insurgents in the north, but sporadic skirmishing continued. A further agreement was reached at a Special Conference on the North held in Dec. 1991, and in April 1992 a national pact was concluded providing for a special administration for the Tuareg north. A further accord with Tuareg insurgents under which their northern bases would be dismantled was signed in May 1994.

TERRITORY AND POPULATION. Mali is a landlocked state, consisting of the Middle and Upper Niger basin in the south, the Upper Senegal basin in the southwest, and the Sahara in the north. It is bounded west by Senegal, north-west by Mauritania, north-east by Algeria, east by Niger and south by Burkina Faso, Côte d'Ivoire and Guinea. The republic covers an area of 1,240,192 sq. km (478,841 sq. miles) and had a population of 7,620,225 at the 1987 census; UN estimate (1992) 9·82m.; population density, 8 per sq. km. In 1987, 20·3% lived in urban areas. Population growth (1989–90) was 3%. Vital statistics rates (1985–90): Birth, 50·1 per 1,000 population; death, 20·8; infant mortality (1992), 225 per 1,000 live births. Expectation of life in 1991, 48 years.

The areas, populations and chief towns of the regions are:

Region	*Sq. km*	*Census 1987*	*Chief town*	*1990 estimate*
Kayes	197,760	1,058,575	Kayes	35,000
Koulikoro	89,833	1,180,260	Koulikoro	–
Capital District	267	646,153	Bamako	646,000
Sikasso	76,480	1,308,828	Sikasso	27,000
Ségou	56,127	1,328,250	Ségou	35,000
Mopti	88,752	1,261,383	Mopti	40,000
Timbuktu	408,977	453,032	Timbuktu	...
Gao	321,996	383,734	Gao	–

An 8th region, Kidal (chief town, Kidal), was instituted in the north in 1991.

In 1983 the principal ethnic groups numbered (in 1,000): Bamara, 2,469; Fulani, 1,076; Senufo, 929; Soninke, 681; Tuareg, 565; Songhai, 557; Malinke, 511; Dogon, 310. The official language is French; Bambara is spoken by about 80% of the population.

CLIMATE. A tropical climate, with adequate rain in the south and west, but conditions become increasingly arid towards the north and east. Bamako. Jan. 76°F (24·4°C), July 80°F (26·7°C). Annual rainfall 45" (1,120 mm). Kayes. Jan. 76°F

(24·4°C), July 93°F (33·9°C). Annual rainfall 29" (725 mm). Tombouctou. Jan. 71°F (21·7°C), July 90°F (32·2°C). Annual rainfall 9" (231 mm).

CONSTITUTION AND GOVERNMENT. A constitution was approved by a national referendum in 1974; it was amended by the National Assembly on 2 Sept. 1981. The sole legal party was the *Union démocratique du peuple malien* (UDPM).

A national conference of 1,800 delegates agreed a draft constitution enshrining multi-party democracy in Aug. 1991, and this was approved by 99·76% of votes cast at a referendum in Jan. 1992. Turn-out was 43%.

A Constitutional Court was established in 1994.

Elections were held in Feb.–March 1992 for the 129-member National Assembly. The Alliance for Democracy in Mali (ADEMA) won 76 seats. The electorate was 5m.

At the second round of presidential elections on 29 April 1992 turn-out was 20·87%. Alpha Oumar Konaré was elected against 1 opponent with 69·56% of votes cast.

President: Alpha Oumar Konaré (b. 1946; sworn in, 8 June 1992).

In Nov. 1995 the government comprised:

Prime Minister: Boubacar Keita (b. 1945; ADEMA).

Foreign, Malians Abroad and African Integration: Dioucouda Traore. *Culture and Communications and Government Spokesman:* Bakiba Koniba Traore. *Finance and Commerce:* Soumeyla Cissé. *Youth and Sport:* Boubacar Karamoko Coulibaly. *Tourism and Handicraft:* Fatou Haidara. *Health, Solidarity and Pensioners:* Modibo Sidibe. *Mines, Energy and Water:* Cheikna Seydou Diawara. *Rural Development and Environment:* Modibo Traore. *Civil Service, Labour and Employment:* Boubacar Diarra. *Primary Education:* Adama Sammassekou. *Secondary and Higher Education and Research:* Moustapha Dicko. *Justice:* Cheikna Kamissoko. *Territorial Administration and Security:* Lieut.-Col. Sada Samake. *Public Works and Transport:* Mohammed Ag Erlaf. *Armed Forces and Veterans:* Momedou Ba. *Town Planning and Housing:* Sy Kadiatou Sow.

National flag: Three vertical stripes of green, yellow, red.

National anthem: 'A ton appel, Mali' ('At your call, Mali'); words by S. Kouyate, tune by B. Sissoko.

Local Government: Mali is divided into the Capital District of Bamako and 8 regions, sub-divided into 46 *cercles* and then into 279 *arrondissements*.

At the elections of Jan. 1992 turn-out was 35%. The Alliance for Democracy in Mali (ADEMA) gained 214 of the 751 seats contested, the Sudanese Union-RDA (US-RDA), 130, and the National Committee for Democratic Initiative (CNID), 96.

DEFENCE. There is a selective system of 2 years' conscription, for civilian or military service.

Army. The Army consists of 4 infantry 2 tank, 1 engineer, 1 parachute, 1 special force, 2 artillery battalions and 2 air defence and 1 surface-to-air missile battery. Equipment includes 21 T-34 main battle tanks. Strength (1996) 6,900. There are also paramilitary forces of 7,800.

Air Force. The Air Force MiG fighters are withdrawn from use. Threre are 2 An-24, 2 An-26 and 1 Mi-8 helicopter. A twin-turbofan Corvette is used for VIP transport. Personnel (1995) total about 400.

INTERNATIONAL RELATIONS

Membership. Mali is a member of the UN, OAU and is an ACP state of the EU.

ECONOMY

Budget. The budget for 1993 provided for revenue of 153,200m. francs CFA and expenditure of 184,500m. francs CFA.

Currency. The unit of currency is the *franc CFA*, which replaced the Mali franc in

1984. There are coins of 1, 2, 5, 10, 25, 50 and 100 francs CFA, and notes of 50, 100, 500, 1,000, 5,000 and 10,000 francs CFA. There were 60,800m. francs CFA in circulation in 1992. Foreign exchange reserves were US$323·7m. in 1993; gold reserves were US$4·8m. in 1992. For exchange rate *see* BENIN: Currency.

Banking and Finance. There are 4 domestic and 2 French-owned banks.

ENERGY AND NATURAL RESOURCES

Electricity. Production (1992) totalled 262m. kWh (210m. kWh hydro-electric).

Minerals. There are deposits of iron ore, uranium, diamonds, bauxite, manganese, copper and lithium. 6·2 tonnes of gold were extracted in 1994.

Agriculture. About 80% of the population depends on agriculture, mainly carried on by small peasant holdings. It contributes 44% of GDP. In 1992 there were 2·2m. ha of arable land, 3,000 ha, permanent cropland and 30m. ha, pasture. Production in 1993 included (in 1,000 tonnes): Millet, 691; sugar-cane, 311; groundnuts, 135; sorghum, 694; rice, 388; maize, 275; seed cotton, 317; cotton lint, 135; cassava, 73; sweet potatoes, 55.

Livestock, 1993: Cattle, 5,544,000; horses, 87,000; asses, 2,000; sheep, 6,658,000; goats, 6,658,000; camels, 250,000; chickens, 22m.

0.21m. ha were irrigated in 1992.

Forestry. The forest area was 8·52m. ha in 1987. Production (1987), 5·2m. cu. metres.

Fisheries. In 1992, 100,000 tonnes of fish were caught in the rivers.

INDUSTRY. Manufacturing accounted for 11% of GDP in 1991. The main branch is food processing, followed by cotton processing, textiles and clothes. Cement and pharmaceuticals are also produced.

Labour. In 1990 the workforce comprised 2,959,000 persons (479,000 females). Large numbers of Malians emigrate temporarily to work abroad, principally in Côte d'Ivoire.

FOREIGN ECONOMIC RELATIONS. Foreign debt was US$2,595m. in 1992.

Commerce. Exports in 1992 totalled 87,000m. francs CFA; imports, 126,300m. francs CFA. Principal exports (in 1,000m. francs CFA), 1992: Cotton, 35·8; livestock (1991), 27·3; gold, 15·2. The main export markets were: CIS countries, 14·2%; Algeria, 13·2%; Belgium, 11·4%; China, 10·6%; Ireland, 7·2%. Main import suppliers: Côte d'Ivoire, 25·3%; France, 23·1%; Senegal, 6·1%; CIS countries, 5·1%.

Total trade between Mali and UK (British Department of Trade returns, in £1,000 sterling):

	1991	*1992*	*1993*	*1994*	*1995*
Imports to UK	1,631	2,061	1,561	477	225
Exports and re-exports from UK	9,589	11,101	9,455	10,841	24,074

Tourism. There were 54,000 foreign tourists in 1986.

COMMUNICATIONS

Roads. There were (1992) 18,000 km of classified roads (of which 2,000 km were asphalted), 23,209 passenger cars and 6,802 commercial vehicles.

Railways. Mali has a railway from Kayes to Koulikoro by way of Bamako, a continuation of the Dakar–Kayes line in Senegal. Total length 642 km (metre-gauge) and in 1987 carried 196m. passenger-km and 199m. tonne-km of freight.

Civil Aviation. Air services connect the republic with Paris, Dakar and Abidjan.

There are international airports at Bamako (Senou) and Mopti, and Air Mali operates domestic services to 10 other airports. It had 2 aircraft in 1995.

Shipping. For about 7 months in the year small steamboats operate a service from Koulikoro to Timbuktu and Gao, and from Bamako to Kouroussa.

Telecommunications. There were, in 1984, 9,537 telephones. Broadcasting is the responsibility of the autonomous Radiodiffusion Télévision du Mali. In 1993 there were 7 independent radio networks, 6 private and 1 public. In 1991 there were estimated to be 0·15m. radio and 10,000 TV sets (colour by SECAM).

Press. In 1993 there were about 60 newspapers and periodicals.

SOCIAL INSTITUTIONS

Justice. The Supreme Court was established at Bamako in 1969 with both judicial and administrative powers. The Court of Appeal is also at Bamako, at the apex of a system of regional tribunals and local *juges de paix*.

Religion. The state is secular, but predominantly Sunni Moslem. 30% of the population follow traditional animist beliefs and there is a small Christian minority.

Education. Adult literacy was 32% in 1990. In 1987–88 there were 1,418 primary schools with 307,600 pupils (114,400 girls) and 8,124 teachers. 56,600 pupils (16,700 girls) were in intermediate and high schools with 4,601 teachers. Private Islamic schools (*medersas*) enrol more pupils than the state primary schools. There were 7,636 students (2,059 females) in trade-training schools, 2,177 (454) in teacher training schools with 317 teachers, and (in 1986–87) 5,536 (728) with 715 teachers in higher education. 1,489 students were studying abroad in 1987.

Health. In 1984 there were 12 hospitals, 333 health centres, 592 maternity homes and 590 dispensaries, with a total of 3,430 beds. In 1987 there were 114 doctors, 2 dentists, 23 pharmacists, 238 midwives and 1,219 nursing personnel.

DIPLOMATIC REPRESENTATIVES

Of Mali in Great Britain (resides in Brussels)
Ambassador: N'Tji Laico Traore.

Of Great Britain in Mali (resides in Dakar)
Ambassador: A. E. Furness, CMG.

Of Mali in the USA (2130 R. St., NW, Washington, D.C., 20008)
Ambassador: Siragatou Cisse.

Of the USA in Mali (Rue Rochester and Rue Mohamed V, Bamako)
Ambassador: Vacant.

Of Mali to the United Nations
Ambassador: Moctar Ouane.

MALTA

Repubblika ta' Malta

Capital: Valletta
Population: 370,402 (1995)
GNP per capita: US$7,395 (1994)
HDI/world rank: 0·880/34 (1992)

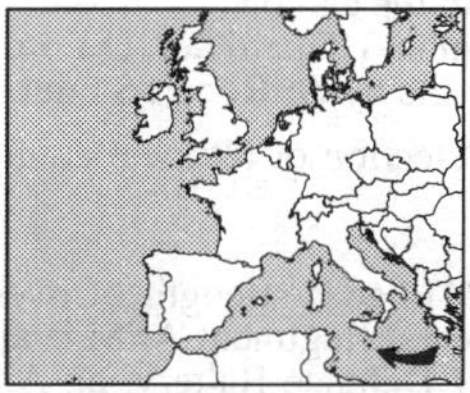

KEY HISTORICAL EVENTS. Malta was held in turn by Phoenicians, Carthaginians and Romans, and was conquered by Arabs in 870. From 1090 it was subject to the same rulers as Sicily until 1530, when it was handed over to the Knights of St John, who ruled until dispersed by Napoleon in 1798. The Maltese rose in rebellion against the French and the island was subsequently blockaded by the British aided by the Maltese from 1798 to 1800. The Maltese people freely requested the protection of the British Crown in 1802 on condition that their rights and privileges be preserved. The islands were finally annexed to the British Crown by the Treaty of Paris in 1814. On 15 April 1942, in recognition of the steadfastness and fortitude of the people of Malta during the Second World War, King George VI awarded the George Cross to the island. Malta became independent on 21 Sept. 1964 and became a republic within the Commonwealth on 13 Dec. 1974.

TERRITORY AND POPULATION. The 3 Maltese islands and minor islets lie in the Mediterranean 93 km (at the nearest point) south of Sicily and 288 km east of Tunisia. The area of Malta is 246 sq. km (94·9 sq. miles); Gozo, 67 sq. km (25·9 sq. miles); Comino, 3 sq. km (1·1 sq. miles); total area, 316 sq. km (121·9 sq. miles). Population, census 16 Nov. 1985, 345,418; estimate (June 1995) 370,402. Malta island (1994), 341,906; Gozo and Comino, 27,545. Chief town and port, Valletta, population (1995) 9,129 but the inner harbour area, 102,571. Vital statistics, 1994: Births, 4,826; deaths, 2,698; marriages, 2,483; emigrants, 104; returned emigrants, 761.

The constitution provides that the national language and language of the courts is Maltese, but both Maltese and English are official languages.

CLIMATE. The climate is Mediterranean, with hot, dry and sunny conditions in summer and very little rain from May to Aug. Rainfall is not excessive and falls mainly between Oct. and March. Average daily sunshine in winter is 6 hours and in summer over 10 hours. Valletta. Jan. 12·8°C (55°F), July 25·6°C (78°F). Annual rainfall 578 mm (23").

CONSTITUTION AND GOVERNMENT. Malta is a parliamentary democracy. The Constitution of 1964 provides for a *President*, a *House of Representatives* of members elected by universal suffrage and a Cabinet consisting of the Prime Minister and such number of Ministers as may be appointed. The Constitution makes provision for the protection of fundamental rights and freedom of the individual, and for freedom of conscience and religious worship, and guarantees the separation of executive, judicial and legislative powers. In 1996 the House of Representatives had 65 seats. At the elections of 22 Feb. 1992 the electorate was 0·26m. Turn-out was 96·08%. The Nationalist Party (NP) gained 34 seats with 51·77% of votes cast, the Labour Party 31 seats with 46·5%. In Jan. 1996 the party composition of the House of Representatives was: NP, 34; Labour, 29; ind, 2.

President: Dr Ugo Mifsud Bonnici (b. 1932; sworn in April 1994).

The NP Cabinet was in Jan. 1996:

Prime Minister: Dr Edward Fenech Adami.

Deputy Prime Minister, Minister of Foreign Affairs: Dr Guido de Marco. *Education and Human Resources:* Michael Falzon. *Social Development:* Dr Louis Galea.

Economic Services: Dr Josef Bonnici. *Environment:* Dr Francis Zammit Dimech. *Food, Agriculture and Fisheries:* Censu Galea. *Gozo:* Anton Tabone. *Finance:* John Dalli. *Justice and the Arts:* Dr Michael Refalo. *Transport, Communications and Technology:* Dr Michael Frendo. *Home Affairs:* Dr Tonio Borg.

Speaker: Dr Lawrence Gonzi.

National flag: 2 equal vertical stripes, white in the hoist and red in the fly, with a representation of the George Cross medal edged with red in the canton.

National anthem: 'Lil din l'art helwa, l'Omm li tatna isimha' ('Guard her, O Lord, as ever Thou hast guarded'); words by Dun Karm Psaila, tune by Dr Robert Samut.

Local Government: Legislation of 1993 provides for the election of 67 local councils on Malta and Gozo.

DEFENCE. In 1995 the Armed Forces of Malta (AFM) had a strength of over 1,900 and consisted of the Headquarters and 3 Regiments. 1st Regiment AFM is an Infantry Battalion, 2nd Regiment AFM comprises an Air Defence Battery, an Air Squadron and the Maritime Squadron. 3rd Regiment AFM consists of the logistics and support element and a Revenue Security Corps.

In addition to the usual infantry and artillery weapons, AFM are equipped with 10 helicopters (varying in size), 5 fixed-wing aircraft (single engine), and 15 patrol craft, the largest being 56 metres.

Apart from normal military duties, AFM are also responsible for airport security, air traffic control, sea traffic control, fishery protection and anti-pollution duties.

The Maritime Squadron numbering 200 in 1995 operated 2 ex-East German coastal and 4 inshore patrol craft and a number of boats.

INTERNATIONAL RELATIONS

Membership. Malta is a member of the UN, the Commonwealth, the OSCE, the Council of Europe and the NATO Partnership for Peace. An application to join the EU was made in July 1990.

ECONOMY

Policy. Overall policy is to deregulate the economy, the role of the state being limited to areas of strategic importance. National economic strategy aims especially at the attraction of new investment and the creation of new employment in the directly productive and market services (tertiary) sectors. Objectives are to bring in investment in advanced technology, develop a high quality of tourism and evolve into an international trade and business centre.

Budget. Revenue and expenditure (in Lm):

	1991	*1992*	*1993*	*1994*
Revenue	411,793,000	395,035,563	428,310,011	468,925,904
Expenditure	417,403,000	388,032,029	428,299,422	472,703,695

The most important sources of revenue are customs and excise duties, income tax, social security and receipts from the Central Bank of Malta.

Currency. The unit of currency is the *Maltese lira* (formerly *pound*) (MTL) of 100 *cents* of 10 *mils*. Central Bank of Malta notes of Lm2, Lm5, Lm10 and Lm20 are in circulation, and there are coins of Lm1, 50, 25, 10, 5, 2 and 1 cents and 5, 3 and 2 mils. Total notes and coins in circulation on 30 June 1995, Lm355m. In March 1996, £1 = Lm 0·55; US$1 = Lm 0·36; DM1 = Lm 0·24.

Banking and Finance. The Central Bank of Malta (*Governor*, Francis Vassallo) was founded in 1968. In 1995 there were 6 domestic commercial banks. Malta has been establishing itself as a financial international business centre since 1989, and there were 7 offshore banking institutions in 1995. The Malta Financial Services Centre is the autonomous government authority set up in 1994 as the primary regulator of financial sevices. The financial services framework available provides the necessary legal structure for the setting up of international business operations including banking, unit trusts, mutual funds, captive insurance and international trading and holding companies.

ENERGY AND NATURAL RESOURCES

Electricity. Electricity is generated at 2 interconnected power stations located at Marsa (265 MW) and Delimara (195 MW). Electricity generated, 1994–95, 1,630m. kWh.

Oil. The government launched exploration campaigns in 1988, 1991, 1992 and 1994. 2 wells have been drilled, but no commercial oil found.

Agriculture. Despite the dry-climate and the lack of fertile land, a wide-range of fruits and vegetables are cultivated. The two main crops are potatoes and tomatoes. The former is the country's primary export crop whilst the latter are the main input for the local canning industry. Peaches, plums, nectarines and apricots are Malta's main fruits produced during the summer. Sugar-melons, water-melons and strawberries are grown intensively and have significant export potential. Cereals and sulla are mainly grown for hay and straw for livestock feeding.

The livestock sector is very important. Malta is self-sufficient in chicken, eggs, pork and fresh milk. In Sept. 1995 livestock numbers were estimated at: Cattle, 17,870; swine, 87,765; sheep, 7,237; goats, 4,864; rabbits, 124,270; poultry, 596,000 layers and 3,840,000 broilers.

During 1995 the contribution of agriculture to the GDP was estimated at Lm30m. or 3%, and full-time eomployment in agriculture accounted for 2·3% of the gainfully occupied.

Fisheries. In Dec. 1995 the fishing industry employed 1,618 power-propelled and 9 other fishing boats, engaging some 321 full-time and 1,386 part-time fishermen. The catch for 1995 was 926 tonnes valued at Lm1,231,652. A National Aquaculture Centre was set up in 1988; the harvest in 1995 was almost 1,200 tonnes.

INDUSTRY. Besides manufacturing (food, clothing, chemicals and electrical and electronic parts), ship repair and shipbuilding and tourism are the mainstays of the economy. Over 500 state-aided manufacturing enterprises are in operation, the majority foreign-owned or with foreign interests. The Malta Development Corporation is the Government agency responsible for promoting and implementing new industrial projects.

Labour. The labour supply in June 1995 was 142,102 (females, 38,235), including 39,637 in private direct production (agriculture and fisheries, 3,227; manufacturing, 30,497; oil drilling, construction and quarrying, 5,913), 45,211 in private market services, 48,854 in the public sector (including government departments, armed forces, independent statutory bodies and market services), and 3,742 in temporary employment. Registered unemployed were 4,658 in June 1995 (3·3% of labour supply).

Trade Unions. There were 38 trade unions registered as at 1 Dec. 1995, with a total membership of 77,998, and 27 employers' associations with a total membership of 9,321.

FOREIGN ECONOMIC RELATIONS. Imports are being liberalized. Marsaxlokk is an all-weather freeport zone for transhipment activities. The Malta Export Trade Corporation promotes local exports.

Commerce. Imports and exports including bullion and specie (in Lm1,000):

	1989	*1990*	*1991*	*1992*	*1993*	*1994*
Imports	515,805	620,511	684,000	747,770	830,920	918,766
Exports	294,406	357,890	405,453	490,903	518,325	587,003

In 1994 the principal items of imports were: Semi-manufactures, Lm132m.; machinery and transport, Lm482m.; food, Lm64·7m.; fuels, Lm40·8m.; manufactures, Lm93·9m.; chemicals, Lm63·6m.; others, Lm43·2m. Of domestic exports:

Manufactures, Lm130·6m.; machinery and transport, Lm356·6m.; semi-manufactures, Lm33·4m.; beverages and tobacco, Lm1·3m.; food, Lm8·2m.; chemicals, Lm10·3m.

In 1994, Lm243·2m. of the imports came from Italy, Lm140·7m. from UK, Lm161·5m. from Germany, Lm46·8m. from USA; of domestic exports, Lm216·5m. to Italy, Lm80m. to Germany, Lm31·9m. to UK, Lm42·7m. to USA.

Total trade between Malta and UK (British Department of Trade returns, in £1,000 sterling):

	1991	*1992*	*1993*	*1994*	*1995*
Imports to UK	40,771	51,332	62,961	75,096	79,790
Exports and re-exports from UK	162,454	164,489	206,113	205,463	284,346

Tourism. Tourism is the major foreign currency earner. In 1994, 1,176,223 tourists (45% from the UK) generated earnings of Lm241·6m.

COMMUNICATIONS

Roads. There is a car ferry between Malta and Gozo. In 1994 there were 1,604 km of roads, including 1,422 km of main roads. About 94% of roads are paved. Motor vehicles registered at the end of 1994: Private cars, 163,310; commercial vehicles, 37,601; cars for hire, 7,325; buses and minibuses, 964; motor cycles, 17,179.

Civil Aviation. The national carrier is Air Malta, which is 96·4% state-owned, and in 1995 operated 1 A310-200, 2 A320-200s, 2 B-737-200 Advs, 5 B-737-300s and 4 other aircraft. Services are also provided by Aeroflot, Alitalia, Austrian Airlines, Balkan, British Airways, Condor, Corsair, Czech Airlines, Egyptair, Gulf Air, JAT, Libyan Airlines, LTU, Lufthansa, Sudan Airways, Swissair, Transavia, Tuninter and United Airlines. In 1994 there were 27,634 civil aircraft movements at Malta International Airport. 2,564,661 passengers and 10,134 tonnes of freight were handled.

Shipping. The number of vessels registered on 31 Dec. 1994 was 2,319 totalling 16,850,423 GRT. Ships entering harbour, excluding yachts and fishing vessels, during 1994, 4,362. 1,463 foreign yachts put in at Malta during 1994. In 1994 3,572,297 GRT (452 vessels) were registered in Malta.

Telecommunications. Telecommunications are operated by Telemalta Corporation. There are 14 telephone exchanges and 5 remote switching exchanges with a total installed capacity of 186,000 lines. There is a digital data transmission network. Radio and TV services are under the control of the Broadcasting Authority, an independent statutory body. The government-owned Public Broadcasting Services Ltd. was set up in 1991 to operate the national radio and TV services (colour by PAL). There are 11 radio stations and a cable TV operation. 2 private commercial TV stations are also licensed. On 31 Dec. 1995 there were some 160,000 licensed television sets and on 31 Dec. 1988 27,226 radio sets.

Cinemas (1993). There were 15 cinemas with a seating capacity of 8,000.

Press. There were (1995) 1 English and 2 Maltese dailies, 5 Maltese and 2 English weeklies, 1 financial weekly in English and 1 fortnightly in Maltese.

SOCIAL INSTITUTIONS

Justice. The number of persons convicted of crimes in 1994 was 1,686; those convicted for contraventions against various laws and regulations numbered 6,127. 125 were committed to prison and 7,688 were awarded fines.

Police. In Nov. 1995 police numbered 1,753 (196 women).

Religion. 98% of the population belong to the Roman Catholic Church, which is established by law as the religion of the country, though full liberty of conscience and freedom of worship are guaranteed.

Education. Education is compulsory between the ages of 5 and 16 and free in government schools from kindergarten to university. Kindergarten education is provided for 3- and 4-year old children. The primary school course lasts 6 years. In

Oct. 1995, there were 6,210 children in state kindergartens and 23,368 in 80 primary schools. Secondary schools, trade schools and junior lyceums provide secondary education. To the latter entry is by examination. In 1995, 10 junior lyceums had a total of 8,859 students. There were 18 secondary schools with a total of 9,133 students. 5 centres cater for 1,522 low achievers at secondary level. Secondary schools and junior lyceums offer a 5-year course leading to the Secondary Education Certificate and the General Certificate of Education, Ordinary Level. At the end of the third year of secondary education, students may opt for a course with a technology bias in a Trade School, where the full course lasts 6 years. Trade School students generally come from the Secondary Schools. Courses run by Trade Schools lead to a Journeyman's Certificate and/or a City and Guilds of London certificate. In Oct. 1995, there were 3,139 students enrolled in Trade Schools. At the end of the 5-year secondary course, students having the necessary qualifications may opt to follow a higher academic or technical or vocational course of from 1 to 4 years. The academic courses generally lead to Intermediate and Advanced Level Matriculation examinations set by the University of Malta or to Advanced Level examinations set by British universities. The Junior College, administered by the University, prepares students specifically for a university course. About 2,920 students attend state higher secondary educational institutions; 1,703 students attend the Junior College. Students following higher secondary courses who qualify for the Extended Skill Training Scheme or Technical Apprenticeship Scheme or the Sixth From Students' Scheme receive an allowance.

In 1995–96, 25,343 pupils attended private schools, 18,033 of whom were in schools run by the Roman Catholic Church which receive a government subsidy and provide free education.

In Oct. 1995 about 6,000 students were attending adult and evening courses, many of which lead to a recognized qualification.

The University of Malta consists of 10 faculties: Law; Medicine and Surgery; Arts; Architecture and Civil Engineering; Dental Surgery; Education; Economics; Management and Accountancy; Mechanical and Electrical Engineering; Theology; Science. There were 8,200 students in 1995–96. The Foundation for International Studies, the Mediterranean Academy of Diplomatic Studies, an International Ocean Institute and an International Maritime Law Institute are associated with the University.

Health. In 1995 there were 910 doctors, 110 dentists, 580 pharmacists, 290 midwives and 4,100 nursing personnel. There were 6 hospitals (1 private) with 2,152 beds and 8 health centres.

Welfare. Legislation provides a national contributory insurance scheme and also for the payment of non-contributory allowances, assistances and pensions. It covers the payment of marriage grants, maternity benefits, child allowances, parental allowances, handicapped child allowance, family bonus, sickness benefit, injury benefits, disablement benefits, unemployment benefit, contributory pensions in respect of retirement, invalidity and widowhood, and non-contributory medical assistance, free medical aids, social assistance, a carer's pension and pensions for the handicapped, blind and the aged.

DIPLOMATIC REPRESENTATIVES

Of Malta in Great Britain (36-38 Piccadilly, London, W1V 0PQ)
High Commissioner: Salv J. Stellini.

Of Great Britain in Malta (7 St Anne St., Floriana)
High Commissioner: Graham Archer.

Of Malta in the USA (2017 Connecticut Ave., NW, Washington, D.C., 20008)
Ambassador: Dr Albert Borg Olivier de Puget.

Of the USA in Malta (Development Hse., St Anne St., Floriana)
Ambassador: Joseph R. Paolino, Jr.

Of Malta to the United Nations
Ambassador: Dr Joseph Cassar.

Further Reading

Central Office of Statistics. *Statistical Abstracts of the Maltese Islands*, a quarterly digest of statistics, quarterly and annual trade returns, annual vital statistics and annual publications on shipping and aviation, education, agriculture, industry, National Accounts and Balance of Payments, *Economic Trends* (a monthly statistical bulletin).

Department of Information. *The Malta Government Gazette, Malta Information, Economic Survey 1995, Reports on the Working of Government Departments, The Maltese Economy in Figures, 1985–1994, Business Opportunities on Malta, Acts of Parliament and Subsidiary Legislation, Laws of Malta, Budget Estimates 1995, Constitution of Malta 1992.*

Central Bank of Malta. *Annual Reports.*

Chamber of Commerce (annual). *Trade Directory.*

Blouet, B., *The Story of Malta.* London, Rev. ed. 1981

Cremona, J. J., *The Constitutional Developments of Malta under British Rule.* Malta Univ. Press, 1963.—*Human Rights Documentation in Malta.* Malta Univ. Press, 1966

Gerada, E. and Zuber, C., *Malta: an Island Republic.* Paris, 1979

The Malta Yearbook. Valletta

Thackrah, J. R., *Malta* [Bibliography]. Oxford and Santa Barbara (CA), 1985

National statistical office: Central Office of Statistics, Auberge d'Italie, Valletta.

MARSHALL ISLANDS

Republic of the Marshall Islands

Capital: Dalap-Uliga-Darrit
Population: 54,000 (1994)
GNPper capita: US$1,680 (1994)

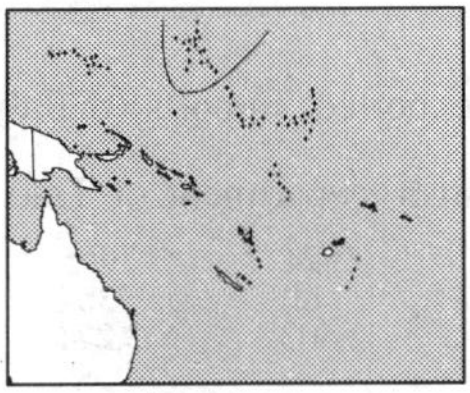

KEY HISTORICAL EVENTS. A German protectorate was formed in 1886 which was occupied at the beginning of the First World War by Japan. Japan was awarded a mandate by the League of Nations in 1919. During the Second World War the Islands were occupied by Allied forces in 1944, and became part of the UN Trust Territory of the Pacific Islands created on 18 July 1947 and administered by the USA. On 21 Oct. 1986 a Compact of Free Association with the USA came into force. The UN recognized the termination of the US Trusteeship on 22 Dec. 1990, and the Islands became a full UN member state on 17 Sept. 1991.

TERRITORY AND POPULATION. The Marshall Islands lie in the Pacific Ocean north of Kiribati and east of Micronesia, and consist of an archipelago of 31 coral atolls, 5 single islands and 1,152 islets strung out in 2 chains, eastern and western. The land area is 181 sq. km (70 sq. miles). The capital is Dalap-Uliga-Darrit on Majuro Atoll in the eastern chain (population, 1990, 20,000). The principal atoll in the western chain is Kwajalein containing the only other town, Ebeye (population, 1992, 10,000).

At the census of 1988 the population was 43,380 (48% urban); 1994 estimate, 54,000. About 97% of the population are Marshallese, a Micronesian people. Marshallese and English are both official languages.

CLIMATE. Jaluit, Jan. 81°F (27·2°C), July 82°F (27·8°C). Annual rainfall 161" (4,034 mm).

CONSTITUTION AND GOVERNMENT. For the US Trusteeship arrangements *see* THE STATESMAN'S YEAR-BOOK, 1991–92, p. 1556. Under the constitution which came into force on 1 May 1979 the Marshall Islands form a republic with a *President* as head of state and executive, who is elected for 4-year terms by the parliament. The parliament consists of a 33-member *House of Assembly* (Nitijela), directly elected for 4-year terms, and a 12-member appointed *Council of Chiefs* (Iroij) which has a consultative and advisory capacity.

The government elected in Nov. 1991 in Nov. 1995 comprised:

President: Amata Kabua (re-elected Jan. 1993).

Finance: Ruben Zackras. *Foreign:* Philip Muller. *Transport and Communications:* Kunio Lemari. *Resources and Development:* Lomes Mckay. *Education:* Evelyn Konou. *Social Services:* Christopher Loeak. *Public Works:* Hiroshi Yamamura. *Health and Environment:* Thomas Kijner. *Justice:* Luckner Abner. *Internal Affairs:* Brenson Wase.

National flag: Blue with a diagonal strip divided orange over white, and a white sun of 25 rays in the canton.

DEFENCE. The compact of free association gave the USA responsibility for defence in return for US assistance.

INTERNATIONAL RELATIONS

Membership. The Marshall Islands is a member of the UN and the South Pacific Forum.

ECONOMY

Currency. US currency is used.

ENERGY AND NATURAL RESOURCES

Minerals. High-grade phosphate deposits are mined on Ailinglaplap Atoll.

Agriculture. Coconuts, tomatoes, melons and breadfruit are grown for export.

FOREIGN ECONOMIC RELATIONS

Commerce. A small amount of agricultural produce is exported. Imports (mainly oil) totalled US$33·5m. in 1987.

Total trade between the Marshall Islands and UK (British Department of Trade returns, in £1,000 sterling):

	1992	*1993*	*1994*	*1995*
Imports to UK	nil	nil	nil	364
Exports and re-exports from UK	553	1,666	2,403	3,271

COMMUNICATIONS

Civil Aviation. Air Marshall Islands operates flights to Fiji, Kiribati, Micronesia and Tuvalu as well as domestic services. It had 4 aircraft in 1992.

Telecommunications. In 1988 there were 800 telephones on Majuro and Ebeye. There is a US communications satellite earth station on Kwajalein. There is a TV and 3 radio stations.

SOCIAL INSTITUTIONS

Justice. The Supreme Court is situated on Majuro. There is a Traditional Rights Court for customary disputes.

Religion. The population is mainly Protestant, but there are Roman Catholic and Baha'i communties.

Education. In 1985 there were 9,777 pupils in 86 primary schools, and 1,727 pupils in 7 secondary schools.

Health. In 1985 there were 17 doctors, 2 dentists, 51 nurses and 2 hospitals with a total of 54 beds.

DIPLOMATIC REPRESENTATIVES

Of Great Britain in the Marshall Islands (resides at Tarawa)
Ambassador: Michael Peart, CMG, CVO.

Of the Marshall Islands in the USA (2433 Massachusetts Ave., NW, Washington, D.C., 20008)
Ambassador: Wilfred I. Kendall.

Of the USA in the Marshall Islands (POB 1379, Majuro)
Ambassador: David C. Fields.

Of the Marshall Islands to the United Nations
Ambassador: Laurence N. Edwards.

MAURITANIA

République Islamique Arabe
et Africaine de Mauritanie

Capital: Nouakchott
Population: 2·4m. (1994)
GNP per capita: US$480 (1994)
HDI/world rank: 0·359/150 (1992)

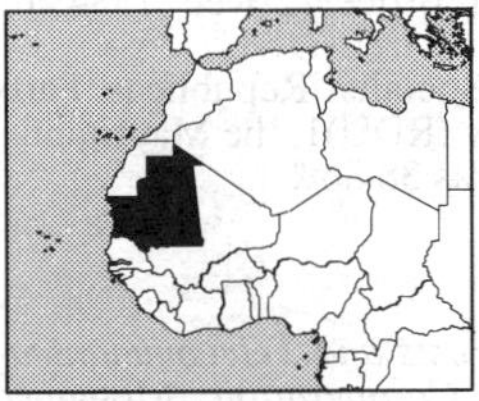

KEY HISTORICAL EVENTS. Mauritania became a French protectorate in 1903 and a colony in 1920. It became an autonomous republic within the French Community on 28 Nov. 1958 and achieved full independence on 28 Nov. 1960. Under its first President, Moktar Ould Daddah, Mauritania became a one-party state in 1964.

Following a coup on 10 July 1978, power was placed in the hands of a Military Committee for National Recovery (CMRN); the constitution was suspended and the 70-member National Assembly dissolved. On 6 April 1979 the CMRN was renamed the Military Committee for National Salvation (CMSN).

TERRITORY AND POPULATION. Mauritania is bounded west by the Atlantic Ocean, north by Western Sahara, north-east by Algeria, east and south-east by Mali, and south by Senegal. The total area is 1,030,700 sq. km (398,000 sq. miles) of which 47% is desert, and the population at the census of 1988 was 1,864,236; estimate (1992) 2·4m. (47% urban). Population density, 2·04 per sq. km. Vital statistics rates, 1985–90: Birth, 46·2 per 1,000 population; death, 19; infant mortality, 121 per 1,000 live births in 1990. Life expectancy, 44 years for males, 48 for females.

Area, population and chief towns of the Nouakchott Capital District and 12 Regions at the 1988 census:

Region	*Area (sq. km)*	*Population*	*Chief town*
Nouakchott District	1,000	393,325	Nouakchott
Hodh ech-Chargui	182,700	212,203	Néma
Hodh el-Gharbi	53,400	159,296	Aioun el Atrouss
Açâba	36,600	167,123	Kiffa
Gorgol	13,600	184,359	Kaédi
Brakna	37,100	192,157	Aleg
Trarza	67,800	202,596	Rosso
Adrar	215,300	61,043	Atâr
Dakhlet Nouâdhibou	22,300	63,030	Nouâdhibou
Tagant	95,200	64,908	Tidjikdja
Guidimaka	10,300	116,436	Sélibaby
Tiris Zemmour	252,900	33,147	Fdérik
Inchiri	46,800	14,613	Akjoujt

Principal towns (1988 census population): Nouâdhibou, 59,198; Kaédi, 30,155; Kiffa, 29,292; Rosso, 27,783.

In 1987 there were also 0·43m. nomads.

The major ethnic groups are (with numbers in 1983): Moors (of mixed Arab, Berber and African origin), 1,449,900; Wolof, 121,000; Tukulor, 94,300; Soninke, 49,800.

Arabic is the official language. French no longer has official status. Pulaar, Soninke and Wolof are national languages.

CLIMATE. A tropical climate, but conditions are generally arid, even near the coast, where the only appreciable rains come in July to Sept. Nouakchott. Jan. 71°F (21·7°C), July 82°F (27·8°C). Annual rainfall 6" (158 mm).

CONSTITUTION AND GOVERNMENT. A referendum was held in July

1991 to approve a new constitution instituting multi-party politics. Turn-out was 85·34%; 97·94% of votes cast were in favour.

The new constitution envisages that the President is elected by universal suffrage for renewable 6-year terms. There is a *Senate* and a *National Assembly*. Parties specifically Islamic are not permitted.

Presidential elections were held 24 Jan. 1992. There were 4 candidates. Col. Maaouiya Ould Sidi Ahmed Taya was elected with 62·8% of votes cast.

President: Maaouiya Ould Sidi Ahmed Taya (assumed office 12 Dec. 1984; re-elected 1992, sworn in 18 April).

At the elections of March 1992 the Democratic and Socialist Republican Party (PRDS) won 67 seats, the Rally for Democracy and Unity (RDU)1, the Mauritanian Renewal Party (PMR) 1 and independents 10. Turn-out was 38·86%.

Elections were scheduled for Oct. 1996.

In Jan. 1996 the government comprised:

Prime Minister: El Avia Ould Mohamed Khouna.

Minister of Defence: Abdallahi Ould Abdi. *Interior, Posts and Telecommunications:* Lemrabet Sheikh Ahmed. *Foreign Affairs and Co-operation:* Mohamed Salem Ould Lekhel. *Justice:* Sow Adema Samba. *Planning:* Sheikh Melainine Ould Shbih. *Finance:* Sidi Mohamed Ould Biya. *Fisheries and Marine Resources:* Vacant. *Trade, Crafts and Industry:* Diagana Moussa. *Mines and Industry:* N'Gaide Lamine. *Health and Social Affairs:* Mohamed Ould Lamar. *Culture and Islamic Affairs:* Limam Ould Tagaddi. *Civil Service, Labour, Youth and Sport:* Sidi Mohamed Ould Mohamed Fall. *Equipment and Transport:* Sow Mohamed Deina. *Education and Literacy:* Louleid Ould Weddad.

National flag: Green, with a crescent beneath a star in yellow in the centre.
National anthem: No words, tune by T. Nikiprowetzky.

Local Government: Mauritania is divided into a capital district and 12 regions. These are sub-divided into 49 departments and 208 communes. At the municipal elections of Jan.–Feb. 1994 the PRDS won a majority in 172 communes.

DEFENCE. Conscription is authorized for 2 years.

Army. There are 6 military regions. The Army consists of 7 motorized infantry, 1 parachute, 1 Presidential security, 3 artillery, 8 infantry and 2 Camel Corps battalions, 1 armoured car squadron, 4 air defence artillery batteries and 1 engineer company. Equipment includes 35 T-54/-55 main battle tanks. Strength 15,000 in 1996.

Navy. The Navy, some 500 strong in 1995, is based at Nouâdhibou and consists of 2 offshore patrol craft for fishery protection, 5 fast patrol craft and a few boats.

Air Force. The Air Force has 5 Britten-Norman Defender armed light transports, 2 Maritime Surveillance Cheyennes for coastal patrol, 1 Buffalo transport, 1 Y-12 transport, 4 Reims-Cessna 337 Milirole twin-engined counter-insurgency, forward air control and training aircraft and 2 Hughes 500 helicopters for communications. Personnel (1995), 150 with 7 combat aircraft.

INTERNATIONAL RELATIONS

Membership. Mauritania is a member of the UN, OAU, the Arab League and is an ACP state of the EU.

ECONOMY

Budget. 1992 revenue (in 1,000m. ougiya), 21·89 (including tax receipts, 17·18); expenditure, 23·17.

Currency. The monetary unit is the *ouguiya* (MRO) which is divided into 5 *khoums*. There are notes of 1,000, 500, 200 and 100 ouguiya and coins of 20, 10, 5 and 1 ouguiya and 1 and 0·2 khoum. 7,898m. ouguiya were in circulation in 1992. Foreign exchange reserves were US$61·1m. in 1993. Gold reserves were 12,000 troy oz. in 1989. In Oct. 1992 the ouguiya was devalued 28%. Inflation was 14·5% in 1994. In March 1996, £1 = 209·85; US$1 = 137·30; DM1 = 92·03 ouguiya.

Banking and Finance. The Central Bank (created 1973) is the bank of issue, and there are 4 commercial banks. Bank deposits totalled 12,304m. ouguiya in 1992.

Weights and Measures. The metric system is in use.

ENERGY AND NATURAL RESOURCES

Electricity. Installed public-sector capacity was 129 MW in 1990. Production (1990) was 129m. kWh.

Minerals. There are reserves of copper, gold, phosphate and gypsum. Iron ore production (1992) was 8·26m. tonnes.

Agriculture. Only 1% of the country receives enough rain to grow crops, so agriculture is mainly confined to the south, in the Senegal river valley. Production in tonnes (1993) of millet, 11,000; sorghum, 107,000; dates, 10,000; maize, 5,000; sweet potatoes, 2,000; rice, 40,000; groundnuts, 2,000.

Herding is the main occupation of the rural population and accounted for 16% of GDP in 1992. In 1993 there were 950,000 camels, 1·0m. cattle, 155,000 asses, 18,000 horses, 7m. sheep, 7m. goats.

Forestry. There were 15m. ha of forests in 1988, chiefly in the southern regions, where wild acacias yield the main product, gum arabic.

Fisheries. In 1989 there were 114 fishing vessels over 100 GRT totalling 35,800 GRT. Total catch (1987) was 99,300 tonnes.

INDUSTRY. Output, 1988 (in tonnes): Fish products, 352,200; cheese, 1,754; butter, 647.

Labour. In 1990 the workforce was 678,000 (150,000 females), of whom 39,000 were aged 10–15 and 17,000 were over 65. In 1985 66% worked in agriculture, forestry and fishing, 24% in services and 10% in industry.

FOREIGN ECONOMIC RELATIONS. Total foreign debt was US$2,298m. in 1991. In Feb. 1989 Mauritania signed a treaty of economic co-operation with the 4 other Maghreb countries, Algeria, Libya, Morocco and Tunisia.

Commerce. In 1992 imports (in 1m. ouguiya) totalled 38,696 and exports, 37,869. Main exports, 1991: Fish and products, 18,293; iron ore, 17,534. Imports: Machinery and transport equipment, 14,069; foodstuffs, 9,242; consumer goods, 5,395. Main export markets, 1991: Japan, 22·2%; Italy, 20·1%; Belgium, 10·1%; Spain, 9·6%. Main import suppliers: France, 30·2%; Spain, 12%; Belgium, 9·3%; Germany, 8·4%.

Total trade between Mauritania and UK (British Department of Trade returns, in £1,000 sterling):

	1991	*1992*	*1993*	*1994*	*1995*
Imports to UK	15,313	12,757	244,851	10,978	14,579
Exports and re-exports from UK	2,336	3,407	496,555	9,949	6,026

Tourism. In 1986 there were 13,000 tourists.

COMMUNICATIONS

Roads. There were 8,150 km of roads in 1988, of which 1,710 km were asphalted. In 1985 there were 15,017 passenger cars and 2,188 commercial vehicles.

Railways. A 652-km railway links Zouérate with the port of Point-Central, 10 km south of Nouâdhibou, and is used primarily for iron ore exports. In 1992 it carried 8·2m. tonnes of freight.

Civil Aviation. There are international airports at Nouakchott and Nouâdhibou. Air Mauritanie had 3 aircraft in 1995. 124,000 domestic and 92,000 international passengers were carried in 1988.

Shipping. In 1995 the merchant fleet totalled 20,311 GRT. The major ports are at Point-Central (for mineral exports), Nouakchott and Nouâdhibou.

Telecommunications. There were, in 1985, 3,161 telephones. The government-controlled Office de Radiodiffusion-Télévision de Mauritanie is responsible for broadcasting. There are 2 radio and 1 TV networks. In 1993 there were estimated to be 0·3m. radio and 1,100 TV sets (colour by SECAM).

SOCIAL INSTITUTIONS

Justice. There are courts of first instance at Nouakchott, Atâr, Kaédi, Aïoun el Atrouss and Kiffa. The Appeal Court and Supreme Court are situated in Nouakchott. Islamic jurisprudence was adopted in 1980.

Religion. Over 99% of Mauritanians are Sunni Moslem, mainly of the Qadiriyah sect.

Education. Education is compulsory but attendance is estimated at about 40%. In 1988–89 there were 165,000 primary and 38,000 secondary school pupils. There were 6,600 students in higher education (1,500 abroad). 1,218 students were studying abroad. The University of Nouakchott had 2,850 students and 70 academic staff in 1994-95.

Health. There were about 200 doctors in 1994.

DIPLOMATIC REPRESENTATIVES

Of Mauritania in Great Britain
Ambassador: Mohamed El Hanchi Ould Mohamed Saleh (resides in Paris).

Of Great Britain in Mauritania
Ambassador: Sir Allan Ramsay, KBE, CMG (resides in Rabat).

Of Mauritania in the USA (2129 Leroy Pl., NW, Washington, D.C., 20008)
Ambassador: Ismail Ould Iyahi.

Of the USA in Mauritania (PO Box 222, Nouakchott)
Ambassador: Dorothy Myers Sampas.

Of Mauritania to the United Nations
Ambassador: Hamad Ould Ely.

Further Reading

Belvaud, C., *La Mauritanie.* Paris, 1992
Calderini, S. *et al., Mauritania.* [Bibliography]. Oxford and Santa Barbara (CA), 1992

MAURITIUS

Republic of Mauritius

Capital: Port Louis
Population: 1·11m. (1993)
GNP per capita: US$3,130 (1994)
HDI/world rank: 0·821/60 (1992)

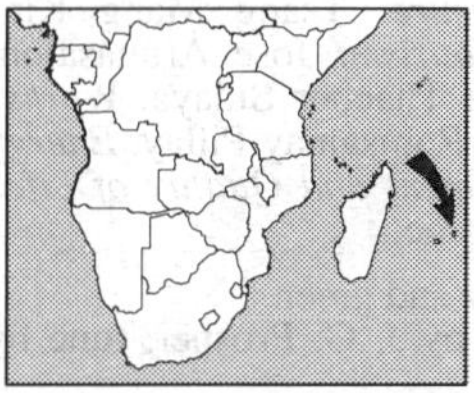

KEY HISTORICAL EVENTS. The Dutch were the first settlers (1598). In 1710 they abandoned the island, which was occupied by the French under the name of Ile de France (1715). The British occupied the island in 1810, and it was formally ceded to the UK in 1814. Mauritius became independent and a member of the Commonwealth in 1968, and a republic on 12 March 1992.

TERRITORY AND POPULATION. Mauritius, the main island, lies 500 miles (800 km) east of Madagascar. Rodrigues is 350 miles (560 km) east. The outer islands are Agalega and the St Brandon Group. Area and population:

Island	*Area in sq. km*	*Census 1990*	*1993*
Mauritius	1,865	1,024,571	1,071,033
Rodrigues	104	34,204	34,536
Outer Islands	71	167	170
Total	2,040	1,058,942	1,105,739

Port Louis is the capital (144,250, 1993). Other towns, Beau Bassin-Rose Hill, 95,966; Curepipe, 76,133; Quatre Bornes, 72,999; Vacoas-Phoenix, 94,086.

Vital statistics, 1993: Births, 22,329 (20·3 per 1,000); marriages, 11,576 (21·1); deaths, 7,433 (6·8).

Ethnic composition, 1996: Hindus, 52% 'General Population' (i.e. European, African, Creole), 33%; Moslems, 10%; Chinese, 5%.

The official language is English.

CLIMATE. The sub-tropical climate is humid. Most rain falls in the summer. Rainfall varies between 40" (1,000 mm) on the coast to 200" (5,000 mm) on the central plateau, though the west coast only has 35" (875 mm). Mauritius lies in the cyclone belt, whose season runs from Nov. to April, but is seldom affected by intense storms. Port Louis. Jan. 73°F (22·8°C), July 81°F (27·2°C). Annual rainfall 40" (1,000 mm).

CONSTITUTION AND GOVERNMENT. The head of state is the *President* elected by a simple majority of members of the National Assembly.

The *National Assembly* consists of 62 elected members (3 each for the 20 constituencies of Mauritius and 2 for Rodrigues) and 8 additional seats in order to ensure a fair and adequate representation of each community within the Assembly. Elections are held every 5 years on the basis of universal adult suffrage.

Parliamentary elections were held on 20 Dec. 1995. 481 candidates representing 42 parties stood. The electorate was 715,198; turn-out was 77·79%. All 62 elected seats were won by a coalition of the Partides Travailleurs Mauricien (PTM) and the Militant Mauritian Movement with 65·2% of votes cast.

President: Cassam Uteem.

The Cabinet was composed as follows in Jan. 1996:

Prime Minister, Minister of Defence and Internal Security, External Communications, Civil Service Affairs, Rodrigues and the Outer Islands, Reform Institutions, Housing, Lands and Town and Country Planning: Dr Navinchandra Ramgoolam (b. 1947; PTM). *Deputy Prime Minister, Minister of Foreign Affairs, International and Regional Co-operation:* Paul Berenger. *Minister of Economic Planning, Information and Telecommunications:* Rajkeswur Purryag. *Industry, Industrial Technology, Scientific Research and Handicraft:* Jayakrishna Cuttaree. *Employment, Manpower Resources and Training:* Ahmed Beebeejaun. *Finance:* Rundheersing Bheenick. *Attorney-General, Minister of Justice and Industrial Relations:* Abdool Peeroo. *Local Government:* James David. *Education, Science and Technology:* Marie-Thérèese Minerve. *Trade and Shipping:* Dhurma Nath. *Agriculture and Natural Resources:* Arvin Boolek. *Arts, Culture and Leisure:* Tsang Mang Kin. *Fisheries and Marine Resources:* Louis Obeegadoo. *Tourism:* José Arunasalon. *Women, Family Welfare and Child Development:* Indira Thacoor Sidaya. *Works:* Siddick Chady. *Co-operatives:* Motee Ramdass. *Health:* Ramsamay Pillay. *Energy and Water Resources:* Devanand Virahswamy. *Environment and Quality of Life:* Samioullah Lauthan. *Youth and Sports:* Sachindev Soonarane.

National flag: Horizontally 4 stripes of red, blue, yellow and green.

National anthem: 'Glory to thee, Motherland'; words by J. G. Prosper, tune by P. Gentille.

Local government: The Island of Mauritius (only) is divided into 5 municipalities and 4 district councils.

DEFENCE. The Police Department, which is responsible for defence, is equipped with arms, 4 inshore patrol craft and 22 boats; its strength was (1996) 1,800. 1 DO 228 and 1 Islander aircraft are used for maritime patrol.

INTERNATIONAL RELATIONS

Membership. Mauritius is a member of the UN, Commonwealth, OAU, SADC and is an ACP state of the EU.

ECONOMY

Budget. Revenue and expenditure (in Rs1m.) for years ending 30 June:

	1991–92	*1992–93*	*1993–94*	*1994–95* [1]
Revenue	10,548	11,565	12,937	13,800
Expenditure	10,880	10,880	13,250	14,290

[1] Estimate.

Principal sources of revenue, 1994–95 (estimate): Direct taxes, Rs 2,717m.; indirect taxes, Rs 9,574m.; receipts from public utilities, Rs 315m.; receipts from public services, Rs 395m.; rental of government property, Rs 35m.; interest and royalties, Rs 582m.; reimbursement, Rs 178m. On 30 June 1993 the public debt of Mauritius was Rs 2,760m.

Currency. The unit of currency is the *Mauritius rupee* (MUR) of 100 *cents*. There are: (i) Bank of Mauritius notes of Rs 1,000, 500, 200, 100, 50, 20, 10 and 5; (ii) cupro-nickel coins of 5 rupees and 1 rupee; (iii) nickel-plated steel coins of 50 cents, 25 cents, 20 cents and 10 cents; (iv) copper-plated steel coins of 5 cents and 1 cent. In March 1996, £1 = 28·69 rupees; US$1 = 18·77; DM1 = 12·72.

Banking and Finance. The Bank of Mauritius (founded 1966) is the central bank. The *Governor* is Sir Indurduth Ramphul. There are 12 commercial banks. Other financial institutions include the Mauritius Housing Company Ltd, the Development Bank of Mauritius, the Post Office Savings Bank and the State Investment Corporation. On 30 June 1994 the Post Office Savings Bank held 199,021 deposits amounting to Rs 392·8m.

There is a stock exchange.

ENERGY AND NATURAL RESOURCES

Electricity. Electric power production (1993) was 869m. kWh.

Agriculture. In 1993, 79,452 ha were planted with sugar-cane. There were 19 factories and sugar production (1993, in tonnes) was 565,026, molasses, 164,801. Main secondary crops (1993): Tea (3,151 ha from which 5,931 tonnes were produced), tobacco (1,015 tonnes), potatoes (13,780), maize (1,816) and onions (3,637).

Livestock (1993): Cattle, 10,867; goats, 17,088; pigs, 15,649; poultry, 2·7m.

Livestock products, 1993 (in tonnes): Beef, 2,523; pork, 1,054; goat meat, 124.

Forestry. The total forest area was estimated (1993) at 57,000 ha including some 12,400 ha of plantations. In 1993 production totalled 30,000 cu. metres of timber, poles and fuel wood.

Fisheries. Production (1993) 18,486 tonnes.

INDUSTRY. Manufactures include: Textile products, footwear and other leather products, diamond cutting, jewellery, furniture, watches and watchstraps, sunglasses, plastic ware, chemical products, electronic products, pharmaceutical products, electrical appliances, ship models and canned food.

Labour. In 1993 the labour force was estimated at 489,000. Manufacturing, with 29% of total employment, employed the most persons; community, social and personal services, 25%; agriculture and fishing, 15%; trade, restaurants and hotels, 14%. The unemployment rate was estimated at 1·8%.

Trade Unions. In 1993 there were 303 registered trade unions and 11 federations with a total membership of about 103,765.

FOREIGN ECONOMIC RELATIONS

Commerce. Total trade (in Rs1m.) for calendar years:

	1990	*1991*	*1992*	*1993* [1]
Imports c.i.f.	24,019	24,650	25,280	30,319
Exports f.o.b.	17,677	18,672	20,744	23,522

[1] Provisional.

In 1993, Rs 4,311m. of the imports came from the Republic of South Africa, Rs 3,830m. from France, Rs 2,144m. from the UK, Rs 898m. from Australia. In 1993, Rs 7,440m. of the exports went to the UK, Rs 4,709m. to France, Rs 4,117m. to USA and Rs 1,633m. to Germany.

Sugar exports in 1993 were 0·54m. tonnes, Rs 5,770m. Other major exports (1993) included clothing, Rs 13,944m.; tea, Rs 103m. and toys, games and sporting goods, sunglasses, watches and articles of jewellery, Rs 1,172m. Major imports included (1993) textiles and manufactured goods, Rs 9,141m. and machinery and transport equipment, Rs 6,787m.

Total trade between Mauritius and UK (British Department of Trade returns, in £1,000 sterling):

	1991	*1992*	*1993*	*1994*	*1995*
Imports to UK	250,218	272,610	281,362	292,504	345,149
Exports and re-exports from UK	52,360	59,892	73,335	75,182	71,018

Tourism. In 1994, there were 400,526 tourists bringing foreign exchange earnings of Rs 6,025m..

COMMUNICATIONS

Roads. In 1993 there were 29 km of motorway, 886 km of main roads, 966 km of secondary and other roads. At 31 Dec. 1993 there were 39,511 cars, 2,217 buses, 18,829 motor cycles, 66,711 auto cycles and 17,829 lorries and vans.

Civil Aviation. In 1993, 531,498 passengers arrived at Sir Seewoosagur Ramgoolam international airport and 11,068,263 kg of freight mail were unloaded. The national carrier is Air Mauritius, which is 42·29% state-owned and in 1995 operated 3 A340-300s, 1 B-747SP, 2 B-767-200ERs and 4 other aircraft. Services are also provided by Air Austral, Air France, Air Zimbabwe, Austrian Airlines, British Airways, Cathay Pacific, Condor, SAA and Singapore Airlines.

Shipping. A free port was established at Port Louis in 1991. In 1993, 1,264 vessels entered Port Louis with a total gross tonnage of approximately 10·7m. tonnes. The merchant fleet totalled 0·3m. GRT in 1995.

Telecommunications. Mauritius Telecom, formed in 1992, provides telephone services to 0·13m. customers through 40 exchanges and runs a data communication service. Communication with other parts of the world is by satellite and microwave links. Broadcasting is run by the commercial Mauritius Broadcasting Corporation. At 31 Dec. 1991 there were 151,096 television sets (colour by SECAM) and 0·25m. radio sets.

Cinemas (1994). There were 15 cinemas, with a seating capacity of about 20,000.

Press. There were (1994) 4 French daily papers (with occasional articles in English) and 2 Chinese daily papers with a combined circulation of about 80,000.

SOCIAL INSTITUTIONS

Justice. There is an Ombudsman. The death penalty was abolished in 1995.

Religion. At the 1990 Census (excluding Rodrigues) there were 287,726 Roman Catholics, 4,399 Protestants, 530,456 Hindus and 172,047 Moslems.

Education. Primary and secondary education is free, primary education being compulsory. About 90·5% of children aged 5 to 11 years attend schools. In 1993 there were 120,002 pupils in 269 primary schools and 85,522 pupils in 120 secondary schools in Mauritius and 5,541 pupils in 12 primary schools and 2,139 pupils in 3 secondary schools in Rodrigues. In 1992 there were 563 students in 3 technical schools, 182 students in handicraft training centres, 1,325 students in 9 pre-vocational training centres, and 1,870 students enrolled for industrial and vocational training courses. In 1993, 2,645 teachers were enrolled for training at the Mauritius Institute of Education.

In 1994–95, there were 2,186 students and 210 academic staff at the University of Mauritius.

Health. In 1993 there were 926 doctors, 12 hospitals with 3,142 beds, 132 health centres and 9 private clinics with 253 beds.

DIPLOMATIC REPRESENTATIVES

Of Mauritius in Great Britain (32–33 Elvaston Pl., London, SW7)
High Commissioner: Vacant.

Of Great Britain in Mauritius (King George V Ave., Floreal, Port Louis)
High Commissioner: J. C. Harrison, CVO.

Of Mauritius in the USA (4301 Connecticut Ave., NW, Washington, D.C., 20008)
Ambassador: Anand Priye Neewor.

Of the USA in Mauritius (Rogers Bldg., John Kennedy St., Port Louis)
Ambassador: Leslie Alexander.

Of Mauritius to the United Nations
Ambassador: Vacant.

Further Reading

Central Statistical Information Office. *Bi-annual Digest of Statistics.*
Bennett, P. R., *Mauritius.* [Bibliography] Oxford and Santa Barbara (CA), 1992
Bowman, L. W., *Mauritius: Democracy and Development in the Indian Ocean.* Aldershot, 1991
Mathur, H., *Parliament in Mauritius.* Rose Hill, 1991

National statistical office: Central Statistical Information Office, Rose Hill.

MEXICO

Estados Unidos Mexicanos
(United States of Mexico)

Capital: Mexico City
Population: 84·44m. (1992)
GNP per capita: US$4,010 (1994)
HDI/world rank: 0·842/53 (1992)

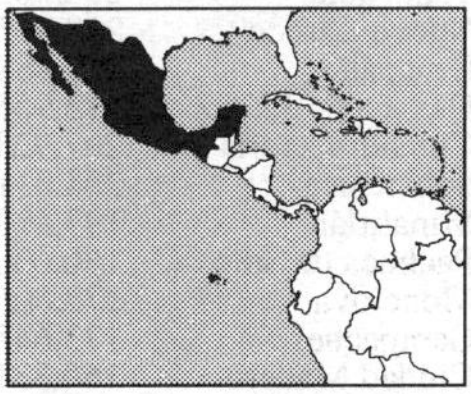

KEY HISTORICAL EVENTS. Mexico's history falls into four epochs: the era of the Indian empires (before 1521), the Spanish colonial phase (1521–1810), the period of national formation (1810–1910), which includes the war of independence (1810–21) and the long presidency of Porfirio Díaz (1876–80, 1884–1911), and the present period which began with the social revolution of 1910–21.

TERRITORY AND POPULATION. Mexico is bounded in the north by the USA, west and south by the Pacific Ocean, southeast by Guatemala, Belize and the Caribbean Sea, and north-east by the Gulf of Mexico. It comprises 1,967,183 sq. km (759,529 sq. miles), including uninhabited islands (5,073 sq. km) offshore. Population density, 41·3 per sq. km.

Population at recent censuses: 1970, 48,225,288; 1980, 66,846,833; 1990, 81,249,645. Estimate, 1992, 84,439,000.

Area, population and capitals of the Federal District and 31 states:

	Area (Sq. km)	*Population (1990 census)*	*Capital*
Federal District	1,499	8,235,744	Mexico City
Aguascalientes	5,589	719,659	Aguascalientes
Baja California	70,113	1,660,855	Mexicali
Baja California Sur	73,677	317,764	La Paz
Campeche	51,833	535,185	Campeche
Coahuila	151,571	1,972,340	Saltillo
Colima	5,455	428,510	Colima
Chiapas	73,887	3,210,496	Tuxtla Gutiérrez
Chihuahua	247,087	2,441,873	Chihuahua
Durango	119,648	1,349,378	Victoria de Durango
Guanajuato	30,589	3,982,593	Guanajuato
Guerrero	63,794	2,620,637	Chilpancingo
Hidalgo	20,987	1,888,366	Pachuca de Soto
Jalisco	80,137	5,302,689	Guadalajara
México	21,461	9,815,795	Toluca de Lerdo
Michoacán	59,864	3,548,199	Morelia
Morelos	4,941	1,195,059	Cuernavaca
Nayarit	27,621	824,643	Tepic
Nuevo Léon	64,555	3,098,736	Monterrey
Oaxaca	95,364	3,019,560	Oaxaca de Juárez
Puebla	33,919	4,126,101	Puebla de Zaragoza
Querétaro	11,769	1,051,235	Querétaro
Quintana Roo	50,350	493,277	Chetumal
San Luis Potosí	62,848	2,003,187	San Luis Potosí
Sinaloa	58,092	2,204,054	Culiacán Rosales
Sonora	184,934	1,823,606	Hermosillo
Tabasco	24,661	1,501,744	Villahermosa
Tamaulipas	79,829	2,249,581	Ciudad Victoria
Tlaxcala	3,914	761,277	Tlaxcala
Veracruz	72,815	6,228,239	Jalapa Enríquez
Yucatán	39,340	1,362,940	Mérida
Zacatecas	75,040	1,276,323	Zacatecas

At the 1980 census 33,039,307 were males, 33,807,526 females. Urban population was 72·6% in 1991. The official language is Spanish, the mother tongue of over 92% of the population, but there are some indigenous language groups (of which Náhuatl, Maya, Zapotec, Otomi and Mixtec are the most important) spoken by 5,282,347 persons over 5 years (1990 census).

The populations (1990 Census) of the largest cities were:

México [1]	15,047,685	Hermosillo	448,966	Ensenada	259,979
Guadalajara [1]	1,650,205	Saltillo	440,920	Guasave	258,130
Monterrey [1]	1,069,238	Victoria de Durango	413,835	Tepic	241,463
Puebla de Zaragoza	1,057,454	Villa Hermosa	261,231	Gómez Palacio	232,742
Léon de los Aldama	867,920	Irapuato	362,915	Coatzacoalcos	233,115
Ciudad Juárez	798,499	Veracruz Llave	328,607	Tapachula	222,405
Tijuana	747,381	Celaya	310,569	Nuevo Laredo	218,413
Mexicali	601,938	Atizapán de Zaragoza	315,192	Uruapán	219,468
Culiacán Rosales	415,046			Oaxaca de Juárez	213,985
Acapulco de Juárez	593,212	Mazatlán	314,345	Ciudad Victoria	207,923
Mérida	556,819	Ciudad Obregón	311,443	Salamanca	204,311
Chihuahua	530,783	Los Mochis	162,659	Minatitlán	195,523
San Luis Potosí	525,733	Matamoros	303,293	Pachuca de Soto	180,630
Aguascalientes	479,659	Tuxtla Gutiérrez	295,608	Monclova	178,606
Morelia	492,901	Jalapa Enríquez	288,454	Campeche	173,645
Toluca de Lerdo	487,612	Cuernavaca	281,294	Ciudad Madero	160,331
Torreón	464,825	Reynosa	282,667	Poza Rica de Hidalgo	151,739
Querétaro	456,458	Tampico	272,690	Córdoba	150,454

[1] Metropolitan Area.

Vital statistics for calendar years:

	Births	*Deaths*	*Marriages*	*Divorces*
1993	2,765,680	416,335	679,911	38,352
1994	2,904,389	419,074	671,640	34,691

Infant mortality was 52,502 in 1992.

CLIMATE. Latitude and relief produce a variety of climates. Arid and semi-arid conditions are found in the north, with extreme temperatures, whereas in the south there is a humid tropical climate, with temperatures varying with altitude. Conditions on the shores of the Gulf of Mexico are very warm and humid. In general, the rainy season lasts from May to Nov. Mexico City. Jan. 55°F (12·6°C), July 61°F (16·1°C). Annual rainfall 30" (747 mm). Guadalajara. Jan. 59°F (15·2°C), July 69°F (20·5°C). Annual rainfall 36" (902 mm). La Paz. Jan. 64°F (17·8°C), July 85°F (29·4°C). Annual rainfall 6" (145 mm). Mazatlan Jan. 66°F (18·9°C), July 82°F (27·8°C). Annual rainfall 33" (828 mm). Merida. Jan. 72°F (22·2°C), July 83°F (28·3°C). Annual rainfall 38" (957 mm). Monterrey. Jan. 58°F (14·4°C), July 81°F (27·2°C). Annual rainfall 23" (588 mm). Puebla de Zaragoza. Jan. 54°F (12·2°C), July 63°F (17·2°C). Annual rainfall 34" (850 mm).

CONSTITUTION AND GOVERNMENT. A new Constitution was promulgated on 5 Feb. 1917 and has been amended from time to time. Mexico is a representative, democratic and federal republic, comprising 31 states and a federal district, each state being free and sovereign in all internal affairs, but united in a federation established according to the principals of the Fundamental Law. The head of state and supreme executive authority is the *President*, directly elected for a non-renewable 6-year term.

There is complete separation of legislative, executive and judicial powers (Art. 49). Legislative power is vested in a General Congress of 2 chambers, a *Chamber of Deputies* and a *Senate*. The Chamber of Deputies consists of 500 members directly elected for 3 years, 300 of them from single-member constituencies and 200 chosen under a system of proportional representation. In 1990 Congress voted a new Electoral Code. This establishes a body to organize elections (IFE), an electoral court (TFE) to resolve disputes, new electoral rolls and introduces a voter's registration card. Priests were enfranchised in 1991.

The Senate comprises 128 members, 4 from each state and 4 from the federal district, directly elected for 6 years. After the elections of Aug. 1994, the party composition of the Senate was: PRI, 95; PAN, 25; PRD, 8. The PRI won 60 seats and the FDN 4 seats. Members of both chambers are not immediately re-eligible for election. Congress sits from 1 Sept. to 31 Dec. each year; during the recess there is a permanent committee of 15 deputies and 14 senators appointed by the respective chambers.

At the presidential and parliamentary elections of Aug. 1994 the electorate was 45·7m. Ernesto Zedillo was elected President by 48·77% of votes cast against 2 opponents. In the Chamber of Deputies 277 of the single-member seats were won by the Institutional Revolutionary Party (PRI) and 27 by proportional representation (PR); 18 by the Party of National Action (PAN) and 101 by PR; 5 by the Revolutionary Democratic Party (PRD) and 66 by PR; and 10 by the Workers' Party (PT), all by PR. At the mid-term elections of Aug. 1991 for 300 electoral districts, 32 Senate seats and 6 governorships, the PRI gained 61·4% of votes cast and won 290 Congress seats, 31 Senate seats and all 6 governorships. PAN gained 17·7% of votes cast, and the Party of Democratic Revolution, 8·3%.

In Jan. 1996 the government comprised:

President: Ernesto Zedillo (b. 1952; PRI; sworn in 1 Dec. 1994).

Minister of the Interior: Emilio Chauyffet Chemor. *Foreign Affairs:* José Angel Gurría Treviño. *Defence:* Gen. Enrique Cervantes Aguirre. *Naval Affairs:* Adm. José Ramón Lorenzo Franco. *Finance and Public Credit:* Guillermo Ortiz Martínez. *Social Development:* Carlos Rojas Guitiérrez. *Comptroller-General:* Arsenio Farell. *Energy:* Jesús Reyes Heroles. *Trade and Industry:* Herminio Blanco. *Agriculture, Rural Development and Livestock:* Francisco Labastida Ochoa. *Communication and Transport:* Carlos Ruiz Sacristán. *Education:* Miguel Limón Rojas. *Health:* Juan Ramón de la Fuente Ramírez. *Labour and Social Welfare:* Santiago Oñate Laborde. *Agrarian Reform:* Arturo Warman Gryj. *Tourism:* Silvia Hernández Enríquez. *Fishing, Environment and Natural Resources:* Julia Caravias. *Attorney-General:* Antonio Lozano. *Attorney of Justice for Mexico City:* José Antonio González. *Mexico City Mayor:* Oscar Espinoza Villareal. *Private Secretary to the President:* Liébano Sáenz. *Head of the Co-ordination Office of the Presidency:* Luis Téllez. *Social Communication of the Presidency:* Carlos Salomon. *Presidential Chief of Staff:* Gen. Roberto Miranda. *Director of PEMEX:* Adrian Lajous. *Director of Federal Electricity Commission:* Rogelio Gasca Neri. *Director of Mexican Social Security Institute:* Genaro Borrego Estrada. *Director of the Institute of Security and Social Services for the State Workers:* Manuel Aguilera Gómez.

National flag: Three vertical strips of green, white, red, with the national arms in the centre.

National anthem: 'Mexicanos, al grito de guerra' ('Mexicans, at the war-cry'); words by F. González Bocanegra, tune by Jaime Nunó.

Local Government. Mexico is divided into 31 states and a Federal District. The latter is co-extensive with Mexico City and is administered by a Governor appointed by the President. Each state has its own constitution, with the right to legislate and to levy taxes (but not inter-state customs duties); its Governor is directly elected for 6 years and its unicameral legislature for 3 years; judicial officers are appointed by the state governments. Mexico City is sub-divided into 16 municipalities and the 31 states into 2,378 municipalities.

DEFENCE

Army. Enlistment into the regular army is voluntary, but there is also one year of conscription (4 hours per week) by lottery. The army consists of 36 zonal garrisons, 1 armoured, 1 motorized infantry, 2 infantry, 2 airborne and 1 Presidential Guard brigade, and air defence, engineer and support units. Equipment includes 50 M-8 light tanks and 110 armoured cars. Strength of the regular army (1996) 130,000 (60,000 conscripts).

Navy. The Navy is primarily equipped and organized for offshore and coastal patrol duties. It comprises 3 old ex-US destroyers, 2 ex-US frigates, 10 modern offshore patrol vessels with small helicopter decks and hangars, and 31 older offshore ships, mostly ex-US. There are also 44 inshore patrol vessels and 20 small riverine patrol craft. There are 2 ex-US landing ships, and auxiliaries include 3 survey ships, 1 repair ship, 2 training ships, 6 tugs and 24 service craft.

The naval air force, 1,100 strong, operates 9 Aviocars for maritime patrol, 12 Bo-105 helicopters for service afloat, and 20 fixed wing and 3 helicopters for transport, training and liaison duties.

Naval personnel in 1995 totalled 37,000, including the naval air force and 8,500 marines.

Air Force. The Air Force had (1995) a strength of about 8,000 with 131 combat aircraft and 25 armed helicopters, and has 9 operational groups, each with 1 or 2 squadrons. No. 1 Group comprises No. 208 Squadron with 8 IAI Aravas for transport, search and rescue and counter-insurgency duties; and No. 209 Squadron with Bell 205A, 206B JetRanger, 212 and Puma helicopters. No. 2 Group has 2 Squadrons (Nos. 206 and 207) of Swiss-built Pilatus PC-7 Turbo-Trainers for light attack duty. No. 3 Group (203 and 204 Squadrons) also operates PC-7s; No. 4 Group (201 and 205 Squadrons) is equipped with PC-7s and AT-33As. No. 5 Group consists of No. 101 communications Squadron and a photo-reconnaissance unit, both equipped with Aero Commander 500S piston-engined light twins. Nos. 301 and 302 Squadrons, in No. 6 Group, operate a total of 9 turboprop-powered Lockheed C-130 Hercules and 6 C-118A piston-engined transports. The main combat Group, No. 7, comprises No. 401 Squadron with 11 F-5E Tiger II and F-5F 2-seat fighters; and No. 202 Squadron with AT-33A jet trainer/fighter-bombers. No. 8 Group has 7 C-47s in a VIP transport squadron. No. 9 Group operates the Air Force's remaining 10 C-47s in Nos. 311 and 312 transport Squadrons. There is a Presidential Squadron with 2 Boeing 727s, 1 757, 2 737s, 1 HS.125, 1 JetStar, 1 Islander, 3 Super Pumas, 3 Pumas and 1 Bell 212. Other training aircraft include 20 Maule MX-7s, 20 Beech Musketeers and 40 Bonanzas. There are 10 MD-530 helicopters for search and rescue.

INTERNATIONAL RELATIONS

Membership. Mexico is a member of the UN, OAS and OECD.

ECONOMY

Policy. An economic programme for 1995 aimed to reduce inflation and provided tax concessions to stimulate investment. Following the devaluation of the peso in Dec. 1994 an emergency economic plan was introduced to include an agreement between labour and employers to contain inflation, a fiscal adjustment to reduce the current account deficit, further privatization of infrastructural enterprises and the establishment of an international assistance fund.

Budget. In 1993 revenue was 192,826·8m. new pesos; expenditure, 188,670·7m. new pesos.

Currency. The unit of currency is the *Mexican peso* (MXP) of 100 *centavos.* A new peso was introduced on 1 Jan. 1993: 1 new peso = 1,000 old pesos. There are coins of 50, 100, 200, 500, 1,000 and 5,000 old pesos; and banknotes of 2,000, 5,000, 10,000, 20,000 and 50,000 old pesos. Notes for new and old pesos circulate jointly. There are coins for 1, 2, 5, 10 and 20 new pesos and notes for 5, 10, 20, 50 and 100 new pesos. The peso was devalued by 29% in Dec. 1994. International exchange reserves were US$13,543m. in Aug. 1995. Gold reserves were 947,000 troy oz. in 1991. Total currency in circulation (1993) was 43,197m. new pesos. Inflation was 7·2% in Feb. 1994. Rate of exchange (controlled rate), March 1996: £1 = 11·60 pesos; US$1 = 7·59 pesos; DM1 = 5·14 pesos. There is a higher rate, for 'essential imports'.

Banking and Finance. The Bank of Mexico, established 1 Sept. 1925, is the central bank of issue (*Governor*, Miguel Mancera, b. 1933). It gained autonomy over monetary policy in 1993. Exchange rate policy is determined jointly by the bank and the Finance Ministry. Banks were nationalized in 1982, but in May 1990 the government approved their reprivatization. The state continues to have a majority holding in foreign trade and rural development banks. Foreign holdings are limited to 30%. There were 23 banks in 1993; deposits were 4,500,000m. old pesos in 1992.

There is a stock exchange in Mexico City.

Weights and Measures. The metric system is legal.

ENERGY AND NATURAL RESOURCES

Electricity. Output in 1994 was 137,522m. kWh. Installed capacity, 1995, 32,737 MW.

Oil and Gas. Crude petroleum output was 3,075,000 bbls. a day in 1995. Natural gas, 1994, 3,624·7m. cu. ft.

Minerals. Output, (in 1,000 tonnes) 1994: Lead, 163·7; copper, 303·7; zinc, 361·2; fluorite, 326·2; iron, 5,601·7; sulphur, 876·9; manganese, 95·6; barite, 87; graphite, 30·6; silver (tonnes), 2,336·6; gold, 14,700 kg; coal, 6,392; feldspar, 122·8.

Agriculture. In 1988 Mexico had 20·3m. ha of arable land and 52·2m. ha of meadows and pastures. Agriculture provided 7% of GDP in 1992. Some 60% of agricultural land belongs to about 30,000 *ejidos* (with 15m. members), communal lands with each member farming his plot independently. *Ejidos* can be inherited but not sold or rented. A land-titling programme (PROCEDE) is establishing the boundaries of 4·6m. plots of land totalling 102m. ha. Other private farmers may not own more than 100 ha of irrigated land or an equivalent in unirrigated land. There is a theoretical legal minimum of 10 ha for holdings, but some 60% of private farms were less than 5 ha in 1990. Laws abolishing the *ejido* system were passed in 1992. Grains occupy most of the cultivated land, with about 43% given to maize, 10% to sorghum and 5% to wheat.

Livestock (1994): Cattle, 23·2m.; sheep, 3·9m.; pigs, 10m.; goats, 6m.; (1992) horses, 6·17m.; mules, 3·18m.; donkeys, 3·18; poultry, 315m. Meat production, 1994 (in 1,000 tonnes): Beef, 1,364·7; pork, 807·5; goat meat, 40·1; sheep meat, 31·4.

Production in 1994 (in 1,000 tonnes): Wheat, 4,171; rice, 380; beans, 1,353; soya, 525; barley, 572; maize, 18,499; sorghum, 3,169; cotton-seed, 102; grapes, 488; apples, 674; oranges, 2,988; lemons and limes, 778; mangoes, 1,286; pineapples, 241; bananas, 2,237; melons, 438; watermelons, 357; avocado pears, 773.

Forestry. Forests extended over 44m. ha in 1984, representing 23% of the land area, containing pine, spruce, cedar, mahogany, logwood and rosewood. There are 14 forest reserves (nearly 0·8m. ha) and 47 national park forests of 0·75m. ha. In 1992 total roundwood production amounted to 7,682,000 cu. metres.

Fisheries. Total catch, 1993, 1,246,438 tonnes (freshwater, 1,133,665 tonnes).

INDUSTRY. In 1992 manufacturing industry provided 21·2% of GDP. Output in 1991 (in 1,000 tonnes): Petrol, 10,034; cement, 18,400; crude iron, 2,475; crude steel, 5,867; aluminium, 95·8; copper, 90·4; lead, 124·8; zinc, 65·7; wheat flour, 1,835; butter, 34; passenger cars (units), 429,069; lorries, 252,030.

Labour. In 1993 the workforce was 24,063,283 (5,644,588 female). The daily minimum wage in 1994 was 14 new pesos.

Trade Unions. The Mexican Labour Congress (CTM) is incorporated into the Institutional Revolutionary Party, and is an umbrella organization numbering some 5m. An agreement, 'Alliance for Economic Recovery', was reached in Nov. 1995 between the government, trade unions and business, providing for an increase in the minimum wage of 21%, increased unemployment benefits, tax incentives, the staggering of price increases, and a commitment to reduce public spending.

FOREIGN ECONOMIC RELATIONS. In Sept. 1991 Mexico signed the free trade Treaty of Santiago with Chile, envisaging an annual 10% tariffs reduction from Jan. 1992. The North American Free Trade Agreement (NAFTA), between Canada, Mexico and the USA was signed on 7 Oct. 1992. A free trade agreement was signed with Costa Rica in March 1994. Some 8,300 products were freed from tariffs, with others to follow over 10 years. The Group of Three (G3) free trade pact with Colombia and Venezuela came into effect 1 Jan. 1995. Nominal foreign debt was US$105,000m. in 1992.

Commerce. Trade for calendar years in US$1m.:

	1990	*1991*	*1992*	*1993*	*1994*
Imports	31,272	49,967	62,129	65,368	79,346
Exports	26,838	42,688	46,196	51,833	60,882

Of total imports in 1992, 71·4% came from USA, 4·9% from Japan, 4% from Germany and 1% from UK.

Of total exports in 1992, 81·3% went to USA, 2·6% to Spain, 1·9% to Japan and 0·5% to UK.

The in-bond (*maquiladora*) assembly plants along the US border generate the largest flow of foreign exchange with oil (14·3% of exports in 1993) and tourism.

Total trade between Mexico and UK (British Department of Trade returns, in £1,000 sterling):

	1991	*1992*	*1993*	*1994*	*1995*
Imports to UK	147,214	152,205	165,743	239,740	298,124
Exports and re-exports from UK	276,557	291,334	355,872	389,299	276,753

Tourism. In 1992, there were 6·35m. tourists; gross revenue, including border visitors, amounted to US$3,868m.

COMMUNICATIONS

Roads. Total length, (1994) 307,142 km, of which 48,960 km were main roads, 57,364 km were secondary roads and 200,818 km by-roads. In 1992, 7,497,128 motor vehicles (7,150,531 private), 3,501,043 lorries, 106,239 buses and 263,568 motorcycles were registered.

Railways. The sole common carrier is National Railways, *Ferrocarriles Nacionales de Mexico*. It comprises 20,477 km of 1,435 mm gauge (246 km electrified). In 1994 it carried 52·1m. tonnes of freight and 7·2m. passengers. There is a 178 km metro in Mexico City. There are light rail lines in Guadalajara (31 km) and Monterrey (35 km).

Civil Aviation. There is an international airport at Mexico City (Benito Juárez) and 43 other international and 39 national airports. Each of the larger states has a local airline which links it with main airports. The national carriers are Aeromexico and Mexicana Airlines. In 1995, Aeromexico operated 6 B-757-200s, 2 B-767-300ERs and 47 other aircraft; and Mexicana, 12 A320-200s, 25 B-727-200 Advs and 12 other aircraft. Services are also provided by Aeroflot, Aerolineas Internacionales, Aeroperu, Air France, Alitalia, American West, American Airlines, Avensa, Aviacsa, Avianca, Aviateca, British Airways, Canadian Airlines, Continental Airlines and Air Micronesia, COPA, Cubana, Delta, Iberia, JAL, KLM, LACSA, Ladeco, Lan-Chile, Lloyd Aereo Boliviano, LTU, Lufthansa, Malaysia Airlines, Northwest Airlines, Taca, Taesa, Transworld, United Airlines and Varig. In 1992, 19,891,351 passengers arrived by air (5,855,492 international) and 19,814,565 departed (6,082,278 international).

Shipping. Mexico has 49 ocean ports, of which, on the Gulf coast, the most important include Coatzacoalcos, Carmen (Campeche), Tampico, Veracruz and Tuxpan. On the Pacific Coast are Salina Cruz, Isla de Cedros, Guaymas, Santa Rosalia, Manzanillo, Lázaro Cárdenas and Mazatlán. It was announced in 1992 that ports would be privatized.

Merchant shipping loaded 125·45m. tonnes and unloaded 52·09m. tonnes of cargo in 1992. In 1995, the merchant marine had a total tonnage of 1·55m. GRT, including oil tankers, 0·71m. GRT, and container ships, 0·14m. GRT.

Telecommunications. Telmex, previously a state-controlled company, was privatized in 1991. It controls about 98% of all the telephone service. There were 11,890,868 telephones in 1993.

There are over 1,500 stations licensed by the Dirección General de Concesiones y Permisos de Telecomunicaciones. Most carry the 'National Hour' programme. Television services are provided by the recently privatized Televisión Azteca and Azteca Televisa. In 1991 there were 16,325,000 radio and 12·35m. TV sets (colour by NTSC).

Cinemas. In 1993 there were 1,777 screens and 113m. admissions.

Press (1986). There were 308 dailies with a combined circulation of 10·36m., 25 newspapers of lesser frequency (0·72m.) and 98 journals (16·94m.).

SOCIAL INSTITUTIONS

Justice. Magistrates of the Supreme Court are appointed for 6 years by the President and confirmed by the Senate; they can be removed only on impeachment. The courts include the Supreme Court with 21 magistrates, 12 collegiate circuit courts with 3 judges each and 9 unitary circuit courts with 1 judge each, and 68 district courts with 1 judge each.

The penal code of 1 Jan. 1930 abolished the death penalty, except for the armed forces.

Religion. 93·5% of the population was Roman Catholic in 1992, with (1983) 3 cardinals, 12 archbishops and 87 bishops. The Church is separated from the State, and the constitution of 1917 provided strict regulation of this and all other religions. In Nov. 1991 Congress approved an amendment to the 1917 constitution permitting the recognition of churches by the state, the possession of property by churches and the enfranchisement of priests. Church buildings remain state property. Diplomatic relations with the Vatican were established in Sept. 1992. At the 1990 census there were also 4·9% Protestants, and 5·4% members of other religions. There were 711,000 Mormons in 1994.

Education. In 1990 12·7% of the population over 15 were illiterate. Primary and secondary education is free and compulsory, and secular, although religious instruction is permitted in private schools.

In 1995–96 there were:

	Establishments	*Teachers*	*Students (in 1,000)*
Pre-school	61,854	135,594	3,235·4
Primary	93,236	510,230	14,634·8
Secondary	23,619	268,155	4,701·4
Vocational training	4,085	25,576	464·9
Professional	2,026	38,697	408·6
Higher education	1,542	135,128	1,234·6
Postgraduate education	1,781	13,387	76·9

In 1994–95 in the public sector there were 36 universities, 1 technical institute and 3 specialized universities (1 agricultural; 2 pedagogical). In the private sector there were 48 universities, 1 institute of technical and higher educational studies, 1 women's university and 1 technical university.

Health. In 1992 there were 833 general hospitals with 71,500 beds. There were 39,578 general practitioners, 29,796 specialist doctors and 4,730 dentists.

Welfare. In 1993 there were 11·32m. workers insured as permanent beneficiaries with the Social Security Institute.

DIPLOMATIC REPRESENTATIVES

Of Mexico in Great Britain (42 Hertford Street, London, W1Y 7TF)
Ambassador: Andrés Rozental.

Of Great Britain in Mexico (Lerma 71, Col. Cuauhtémoc, Mexico City 06500, D.F.)
Ambassador: A. J. Beamish, CMG.

Of Mexico in the USA (1911 Pennsylvania Ave., NW, Washington, D.C., 20006)
Ambassador: Jesús Silva Herzog.

Of the USA in Mexico (Paseo de la Reforma 305, México City 5, D.F.)
Ambassador: James R. Jones.

Of Mexico to the United Nations
Ambassador: Manuel Tello.

Further Reading

Instituto Nacional de Estadística, Geografía e Informática. *Anuario Estadístico de los Estados Unidos Mexicanos. Mexican Bulletin of Statistical Information.* Quarterly.

Aspe, P., *Economic Transformation: the Mexican Way.* Cambridge (MA), 1993

Bailey, J. J., *Governing Mexico: The Statecraft of Crisis Management.* London and New York, 1988

Bartra, R., *Agrarian Structure and Political Power in Mexico.* Johns Hopkins Univ. Press, 1993

Bazant, J., *A Concise History of Mexico.* CUP, 1977

Bethell, L. (ed.) *Mexico since Independence.* CUP, 1992

Grayson, G. W., *Oil and Mexican Foreign Policy.* Univ. of Pittsburgh Press, 1988

Hamilton, N. and Harding, T. F., (eds.) *Mexico: State, Economy and Social Conflict.* London, 1986

Philip, G., (ed.) *Politics in Mexico.* London, 1985.—*The Presidency in Mexican Politics.* London, 1991.—*Mexico* [Bibliography]. 2nd ed. Oxford and Santa Barbara, 1993

Riding, A., *Distant Neighbours.* London, 1985.—*Mexico: Inside the Volcano.* London, 1987

Rodríguez, J. E., *The Evolution of the Mexican Political System.* New York, 1993

Robbins, N. C., *Mexico.* [Bibliography] Oxford and Santa Barbara, 1984

Ruíz, R. E., *Triumphs and Tragedy: a History of the Mexican People.* New York, 1992

Whiting, V. R., *The Political Economy of Foreign Investment in Mexico: Nationalism, Liberalism, Constraints on Choice.* Johns Hopkins Univ. Press, 1992

National statistical office: Instituto Nacional de Estadística, Geografía e Informática (INEGI), Aguascalientes.

MICRONESIA

Federated States of Micronesia

Capital: Palikir
Population: 107,900 (1990)
GNP per capita: US$1,890 (1994)

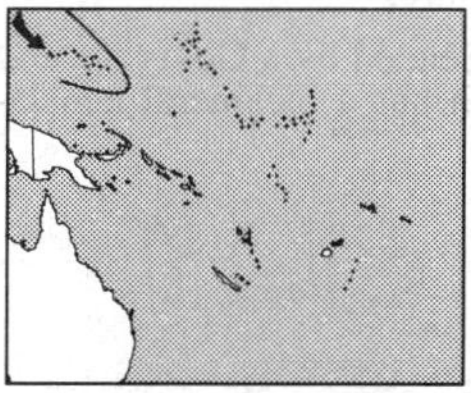

KEY HISTORICAL EVENTS. Spain acquired sovereignty over the Caroline Islands in 1886, but sold the archipelago to Germany in 1899. Japan occupied the Islands at the beginning of the First World War, and in 1921 they were mandated to Japan by the League of Nations. Captured by Allied Forces in the Second World War in 1944, the Islands became part of the UN Trust Territory of the Pacific Islands created on 18 July 1947 and administered by the USA. The Federated States of Micronesia came into being on 10 May 1979 comprising all of the Caroline Islands except the Belau (Palau) group. Its trusteeship was terminated on 3 Nov. 1986 when it entered into a 15-year Free Association with the USA. The UN recognized the termination of the Trusteeship Agreement on 22 Dec. 1990, and Micronesia became a full UN member state on 17 Sept. 1991.

TERRITORY AND POPULATION. The Federated States lie in the Western Pacific between 137° and 163° E, comprising 607 islands with a total land area of 701 sq. km (271 sq. miles) and a sea area of 2·5m. sq. km including the EEZ. The population (Census 1980) was 73,160; estimate (1990) 107,900. There are 8 indigenous languages spoken in the archipelago; English is used in the schools and is the official language.

The areas and populations of the 4 states (east to west) are as follows:

State	*Sq. km*	*1980 Census*	*1990 Estimate*	*Headquarters*
Kosrae	109	5,491	7,200	Tofol
Pohnpei	344	22,081	33,100	Kolonia
Chuuk	127	37,488	53,700	Weno
Yap	119	8,100	13,900	Colonia

Kosrae consists of a single island. **Pohnpei** comprises a single island, Pohnpei (covering 334 sq. km with 30,000 inhabitants in 1990), and 8 scattered coral atolls. **Chuuk** consists of a group of 14 islands within a large reef-fringed lagoon, with 45,000 inhabitants in 1990; the state also includes 12 coral atolls, the most important being the Mortlock Islands. **Yap** comprises a main group of 4 islands (covering 101 sq. km with 9,200 inhabitants in 1990), and 13 coral atolls, the main ones being Ulithi and Woleai.

The chief towns (1989) are Weno (15,253) in Chuuk State, Kolonia (6,169) in Pohnpei State, Colonia (3,456) in Yap State, and Lelu (2,422) in Kostae State. The federal capital Palikir is located in Pohnpei State.

CLIMATE. Palikir, Pohnpei, Jan. 80°F (26·7°C), July 79°F (26·1°C). Annual rainfall 194" (4,859 mm).

CONSTITUTION AND GOVERNMENT. Under the Constitution adopted on 18 July 1978, there is an executive presidency and a 14-member National Congress, comprising 10 members elected for 2-year terms from single-member constituencies of similar electorates, and 4 members elected one from each State for a 4-year term. The Federal President and Vice-President first run for the Congress before they are elected by it for 4-year terms:

In Oct. 1995 the government comprised:
President: Bailey Olter (b. 1932)
Vice-President: Jacob Nena.
Secretary for External Affairs: Resio Moses. *Finance:* Aloysius Tuuth. *Resources*

and Development: Asterio Takesy. *Transportation and Communication:* Robert Weilbacher. *Education:* Catalino Cantero. *Human Resources:* Eliuel Pretrick. *Attorney-General:* Camillo Noket. *Administrative Services:* Kohne Ramon. *Budget:* Patrick MacKenzie. *Planning and Statistics:* Marcelino Actouka. *Postmaster-General:* Henry Bethwell.

National flag: Blue, with a ring of 4 white stars in the centre.

State Government: Each State has an executive branch headed by a Governor and a unicameral State Legislature (except Chuuk State which has a bicameral legislature), all directly elected for terms of 4 years.

INTERNATIONAL RELATIONS

Membership. Micronesia is a member of the UN.

ECONOMY

Policy. The modern sector of the economy consists of a small private sector supported by public service incomes and demand. The traditional sector is based on subsistence farming.

Budget. US Compact funds are an annual US$100m.

Currency. US currency is used.

ENERGY AND NATURAL RESOURCES

Agriculture. Agriculture consists mainly of subsistence farming of coconuts, breadfruit, bananas, sweet potatoes and cassava. A small amount of cash crops are produced for export: Copra, bananas, citrus fruits, peppers and taro.

Fisheries. In 1989 the catch amounted to 155,000 tonnes. Fishing licence fees were US$20m. in 1993 and are a primary revenue source.

FOREIGN ECONOMIC RELATIONS

Commerce. The main export is copra. Major trading partners are the USA and Japan.

Total trade between Micronesia and UK (British Department of Trade returns, in £1,000 sterling):

	1993	*1994*	*1995*
Imports to UK	27	28	30
Exports and re-exports from UK	116	106	105

Tourism. Tourism is an important industry. In 1990 there were 23,171 visitors.

COMMUNICATIONS

Roads. In 1990 there were 226 km of roads (39 km paved).

Civil Aviation. There are international airports on Pohnpei, Chuuk, Yap and Kosrae. Services are provided by Air Nauru and Continental Airlines and Air Micronesia.

Shipping. The main ports are at Teketik (Pohnpei), Lepukos (Chuuk), Okat (Kosrae) and Colonia (Yap).

Telecommunications. In 1993 there were 6,015 telephone connexions. There are 4 earth stations linked to the INTELSAT satellite system. There are 5 radio and 2 TV stations, and 17,000 radio and 1,290 TV sets.

SOCIAL INSTITUTIONS

Justice. There is a National Supreme Court headed by the Chief Justice with 2 other judges in Palikir, and a State Court in each of the 4 states with 13 judges in all.

Religion. Yap is mainly Roman Catholic, while Protestantism is prevalent elsewhere.

Education. In 1983–84 there were 23,345 pupils in 151 primary schools, 4,159 pupils in 14 high schools and 920 students in the 2-year College of Micronesia in Pohnpei.

Health. In 1993 there were 50 doctors, 7 dentists, 7 pharmacists and 230 nurses. There were 4 hospitals with 325 beds.

DIPLOMATIC REPRESENTATIVES

Of Great Britain in Micronesia (resides at Tarawa)
Ambassador: Michael Peart, CMG, CVO.

Of Micronesia in the USA (1725 N St., NW, Washington, D.C., 20036)
Ambassador: Jesse B. Marehalau.

Of the USA in Micronesia (POB 1286, Kolonia, Pohnpei)
Ambassador: March Fong Eu.

Of Micronesia to the United Nations
Ambassador: Vacant.

Further Reading

Kluge, P. F., *The Edge of Paradise: America in Micronesia.* New York, 1991
Wuerch, W. L. and Ballendorf, D. A., *Historical Dictionary of Guam and Micronesia.* Metuchen (NJ), 1995

MOLDOVA

Republica Moldovenească

Capital: Chişinau
Population: 4·35m. (1994)
GNP per capita: US$870 (1994)

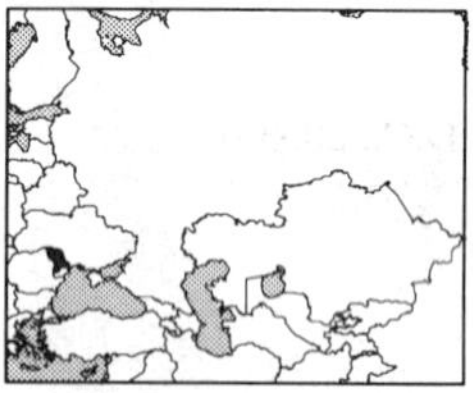

KEY HISTORICAL EVENTS. The Moldavian SSR (in 1990 renamed Moldova) was formed by the union of part of the former Moldavian ASSR (organized 12 Oct. 1924), formerly included in the Ukrainian SSR, and the areas of Bessarabia (ceded by Romania to the USSR, 28 June 1940) with a mainly Moldovan population. As from 2 Aug. 1940 the Moldavian SSR included the following regions of the former Moldavian ASSR: Grigoriopol, Dubossarsk, Kamensk, Rybnits, Slobodzeisk and Tiraspol, and the following districts of Bessarabia: Beltsk, Bendery, Chişinau (*then* Kishinev), Kagulsk, Orgeev and Sorok.

In Dec. 1991 Moldova became a member of the CIS, a decision ratified by parliament in April 1994.

Fighting took place in 1992 between government forces and separatists in the (largely Russian and Ukrainian) area east of the River Dniester (Transdniestria). A joint declaration by the Russian and Moldovan presidents on 3 July 1992 envisaged a demarcation line held by neutral forces and the withdrawal of the Russian army from Transdniestria until a suitable constitutional provision had been made.

TERRITORY AND POPULATION. Moldova is bounded in the east and south by the Ukraine and on the west by Romania. The area is 33,700 sq. km (13,000 sq. miles). In Jan. 1994 the population was 4,353,000 (52·3% female; 46·9% urban). The 1989 census population was 4,335,360, of whom Moldovans accounted for 64·5%, Ukrainians 13·9%, Russians 13%, Gagauzi 3·5%, Bulgarians 2% and Jews 1·5%. Vital statistics rates, 1993 (per 1,000 population): Births, 15·2; deaths, 10·7; natural increase, 4·5; infant mortality (per 1,000 live births), 21·5.

Apart from Chişinau, the capital (0·7m. population in 1994), larger towns are Tiraspol (182,000), Beltsy (159,000) and Bendery (0·13m.). The official Moldovan language (i.e., Romanian) was written in Cyrillic prior to the restoration of the Roman alphabet in 1989. It is spoken by 75% of the population; the use of other languages (Russian, Gagauz) is safeguarded by the Constitution.

CONSTITUTION AND GOVERNMENT. A declaration of republican sovereignty was adopted in June 1990 and in Aug. 1991 the republic declared itself independent. A new Constitution came into effect on 27 Aug. 1994, which defines Moldova as an 'independent, democratic and unitary state'. At a referendum on 6 March 1994 turn-out was 75·1%; 95·4% of votes cast favoured 'an independent Moldova within its 1990 borders'. The referendum (and the Feb. parliamentary elections) were not held by the authorities in Transdniestria.

Parliament has 104 seats and is elected for 4-year terms. There is a 4% threshold for election; votes falling below this are re-distributed to successful parties. The *President* is elected for 4-year terms.

At the elections on 27 Feb. 1994 turn-out was 74%. The Agrarian Democratic Party won 56 seats with 43·2% of votes cast, the Socialist/Unity Bloc 28 with 22%, the Bloc of Peasants and Intellectuals 11 with 9·2% and the Popular Front Alliance 9 with 7·5%.

In Dec. 1991 Mircea Snegur (the only candidate) was elected president with 98·2% of votes cast.

President: Mircea Snegur.

In Oct. 1995 the government comprised:

Prime Minister: Andre Sangheli.

Deputy Prime Ministers: Valentin Kunev, Ion Guţu, Grigorie Ojugu, Valeriu Bulgar. *Minister of Agriculture and Food:* Vitalie Gorincioi. *Information, Science and Communications:* Ion Cassian. *Culture:* Mihail Cetotari. *Defence:* Maj.-Gen. Pavel Creanga. *Economy:* Valerian Bobutac. *Education:* Pavel Ganges. *Finance:* Valeriu Chiţan. *Foreign Affairs:* Mihai Popov. *Foreign Economic Relations:* Andrei Cheptine. *Health:* Timofei Moşneaga. *Industry:* Grigore Trifoi. *Internal Affairs:* Maj.-Gen. Constantin Antoci. *Justice:* Vasile Sturza. *Social Welfare:* Dumitru Nidelcu. *National Security:* Col. Vasile Calmoi. *Privatization:* Çeslav Ciobănu. *State:* Gheorghe Gusac. *Transport:* Vasile Iov. *Relations with Parliament:* Victor Pascas. *Utilities:* Mihai Severovan. *Energy:* Valentin Ciumac.

Speaker: Petru Lucinschi.

National flag: 3 vertical stripes of blue, yellow and red, with the national arms in the centre.

National anthem: The Romanian anthem was replaced in Aug. 1994 by a traditional tune, *Lîmbă Noastră* (*Our Language*).

Local and Regional Government. There are local authorities at district, municipality and town/village level. Prefects and mayors of districts and municipalities are appointed by the President on the nomination of the local councils; mayors of towns and villages are elected. Local elections were held on 16 April 1995. The Agrarian Democratic Party gained most seats.

The 1994 Constitution makes provision for the autonomy of Transdniestria and the Gagauz (Gagauzi Yeri) region.

Transdniestria. In the predominantly Russian-speaking areas of Transdniestria a self-styled republic was established in Sept. 1991, and approved by a local referendum in Dec. 1991. A Russo-Moldovan agreement of 21 July 1992 provided for a special statute for Transdniestria and a guarantee of self-determination should Moldova unite with Romania. The population in 1995 was 0·72m. Romanian here is still written in the Cyrillic alphabet. At a referendum on 24 Dec. 1995, 81% of votes cast were in favour of adopting a new constitution proclaiming independence.

Gagauzi Yeri. This was created an autonomous territorial unit by Moldovan legislation of 13 Jan. 1995. In 1995 the population was 153,000. There is a 35-member *Popular Assembly* directly elected for 4-year terms and headed by a *Governor*, who is a member of the Moldovan cabinet. At the elections of 28 May and 11 June 1995 turn-out was 68%.

Governor: Georgi Tabunshchik (b. 1939).

DEFENCE. Conscription is up to 18 months.

Army. The Army is organized in 3 motor rifle and 1 artillery brigade and 1 reconnaissance battalion. Personnel, 1996, 10,550. There is also a paramilitary Interior Ministry force of 2,500 and riot police numbering 900.

Air Force. The Air Force has a small number of MiG-29 fighters, Antonov transport and Ilyushin aircraft and Mi-8 transport helicopters. Personnel (including air defence), 1995, 1,300.

INTERNATIONAL RELATIONS

Membership. Moldova is a member of the UN, the Council of Europe and the NATO Partnership for Peace.

ECONOMY

Policy. Starting in April 1993, 33% of state property, mainly small and medium-sized firms in construction, light industry, commerce and services, were being privatized through the distribution of vouchers to citizens. This phase was completed in Nov. 1995 with the sale of 1,132 large enterprises and 613 shops at voucher auctions. The second phase aims to attract foreign investment.

Budget. 1993 revenue, 372·4m. lei, including 102·5m. lei from profits tax; expenditure, 509m. lei, of which 299·5m. lei were allocated to welfare and 70·8m. lei to subsidizing state enterprises.

Currency. A new unit of currency, the *leu* (MLD), replaced the rouble in Nov. 1993. There are notes of 1, 10 and 20 lei. In March 1996, £1 = 6·98 lei; US$1 = 4·57 lei; DM1 = 3·10 lei.

Banking and Finance. The *Governor* of the National Bank is Leonid Talmaci.

ENERGY AND NATURAL RESOURCES

Electricity. Output was 10·2m. kWh in 1993.

Minerals. There are deposits of lignite, phosphorites, gypsum and building materials.

Agriculture. Agricultural output was valued in 1993 at 3,400m. rubles (in constant 1983 prices), 103% of its 1992 value. Land under cultivation in 1992 was 2·9m. ha, of which 0·3m. ha was accounted for by private subsidiary agriculture and 6,700 ha (in 1993) by commercial agriculture in 3,100 farms. Private and commercial agriculture accounted for 31% of the value of all output in 1993. The free sale of land is not permitted.

Output of main agricultural products (in 1,000 tonnes) in 1993: Grain, 3,200; sugar-beet, 1,900; potatoes, 300; vegetables, 900; fruit and berries (1992), 511; processed meat, 178; milk, 896; and 540m. eggs. Livestock included (1 Jan. 1994) 0·9m. cattle, 1·2m. pigs and 1·4m. sheep and goats.

Fisheries. The south is rich in sturgeon, mackerel and brill.

INDUSTRY. There are canning plants, wine-making plants, woodworking and metallurgical factories, a factory of ferro-concrete building materials, footwear, dairy products and textile plants. Output was valued at 1,200m. lei in 1993. Production, 1993 (in tonnes): Rolled ferrous metals (1992), 0·5m.; cement, 0·6m.; processed meat, 56,100; fabrics, 31·1m. sq. metres; footwear, 11·9m. pairs; 4,200 tractors; 167,000 TV sets; 57,600 refrigerators and freezers; 123,000 washing machines.

Labour. In 1993 there were 2·45m. persons of working age, of whom 2·03m. were employed, 57·6% in the state sector, 16·4% in the private sector and 21·9% in co-operatives. In Jan. 1994 there were 14,100 registered unemployed (0·7% of the labour force), of whom 4,100 were receiving benefits. Average monthly salaries in 1993 were 21,582 rubles.

FOREIGN ECONOMIC RELATIONS

Commerce. In 1993 imports were valued at US$181·2m. and exports at US$174·3m. Total trade between Moldova and UK (British Department of Trade returns, in £1,000 sterling):

	1993	*1994*	*1995*
Imports to UK	325	793	301
Exports and re-exports from UK	2,243	1,686	2,248

COMMUNICATIONS

Roads. There were 20,100 km of motor roads (14,000 km with hard surface) in 1990. In 1993, 71m. passengers and 7·8m. tonnes of freight were carried.

Railways. Total length in 1992 was 1,328 km. of 1,520 mm gauge. In 1993, 12·7m. passengers and 4·9m. tonnes of freight were carried.

Civil Aviation. The national carrier is Air Moldova, which operated 15 ex-Soviet aircraft in 1995. In 1993, 0·2m. passengers and 1,500 tonnes of freight were carried.

Inland Waterways. In 1993, 0·3m. passengers and 0·3m. tonnes of freight were carried.

Telecommunications. The government authority Radioteleviziunea Naţională is responsible for broadcasting. There are 2 national radio programmes, a Radio Moscow relay and a foreign service, Radio Moldova International (English, in abeyance in 1994 owing to separatists' seizure of the transmitting station).

Press (1989). There were 200 newspapers, 85 in Romanian. Daily circulation of Romanian-language newspapers, 1,143,000; other languages, 1,261,000.

SOCIAL INSTITUTIONS

Education. In 1993–94 there were 736,000 pupils in 1,654 primary, secondary and special schools, 43,000 students in 53 technical colleges and 47,000 students in 9 higher educational institutions including the state university. In Jan. 1994, 0·2m. children (52% of those eligible) attended pre-school institutions.

Health. In Jan. 1994 there were 17,400 doctors, 48,400 junior medical personnel and 339 hospitals with 54,300 beds.

Welfare. In Jan. 1994 there were 649,000 age pensioners and 267,000 other pensioners.

DIPLOMATIC REPRESENTATIVES

Of Moldova in Great Britain
Ambassador: Tudor Botnaru.

Of Great Britain in Moldova (resides in Moscow)
Ambassador: Andrew Wood, CMG

Of Moldova in the USA
Ambassador: Nicolae Tau

Of the USA in Moldova (103 strada Alexei Matveevici, Chişinau)
Ambassador: John T. Stewart.

Of Moldova to the United Nations
Ambassador: Tudor Pantiru.

MONACO

Principauté de Monaco

Capital: Monaco
Population: 29,972 (1990)

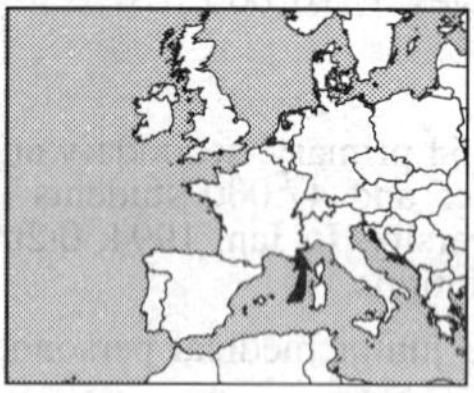

KEY HISTORICAL EVENTS. From 1297 Monaco belonged to the house of Grimaldi. In 1731 it passed into the female line, Louise Hippolyte, daughter of Antoine I, heiress of Monaco, marrying Jacques de Goyon Matignon, Count of Torigni, who took the name and arms of Grimaldi. The Principality was placed under the protection of the Kingdom of Sardinia by the Treaty of Vienna, 1815, and under that of France in 1861. Prince Albert I (reigned 1889–1922) acquired fame as an oceanographer; and his son Louis II (1922–49) was instrumental in establishing the International Hydrographic Bureau.

TERRITORY AND POPULATION. Monaco is bounded in the south by the Mediterranean and elsewhere by France (Department of Alpes Maritimes). The area is 195 ha. The Principality is divided into 4 districts: Monaco-Ville, la Condamine, Monte-Carlo and Fontvieille. Population (1990), 29,972, of whom 5,070 were Monegasques. A census is scheduled for 1997. Vital statistics, 1994: Births, 831; deaths, 599; marriages, 207; divorces, 58.

The official language is French.

CLIMATE. A Mediterranean climate, with mild moist winters and hot dry summers. Monaco. Jan. 50°F (10°C), July 74°F (23·3°C). Annual rainfall 30" (758 mm).

PRINCELY HOUSE. The reigning Prince is **Rainier III**, b. 31 May 1923, son of Princess Charlotte, Duchess of Valentinois, daughter of Prince Louis II, 1898–1977 (married 19 March 1920 to Prince Pierre, Comte de Polignac, who had taken the name Grimaldi, from whom she was divorced 18 Feb. 1933). Prince Rainier succeeded his grandfather Louis II, who died on 9 May 1949. He married on 19 April 1956 Miss Grace Kelly, a citizen of the USA (died 14 Sept. 1982). *Issue:* Princess Caroline Louise Marguerite, b. 23 Jan. 1957; married Philippe Junot on 28 June 1978, divorced, 9 Oct. 1980, married Stefano Casiraghi on 29 Dec. 1983 (died, 3 Oct. 1990), offspring: Andrea, b. 8 June 1984, Charlotte, b. 3 Aug. 1986, Pierre, b. 7 Sept. 1987. Prince Albert Alexandre Louis Pierre, b. 14 March 1958 *(heir apparent)*. Princess Stéphanie Marie Elisabeth, b. 1 Feb. 1965, married Daniel Ducruet on 1 July 1995; offspring Louis, b. 27 Nov. 1992, Pauline, b. 4 May 1994.

CONSTITUTION AND GOVERNMENT. On 17 Dec. 1962 a new constitution was promulgated. It maintains the hereditary monarchy, though Prince Rainier renounces the principle of divine right. Executive power is exercised jointly by the Prince and a 4-member *Council of Government*, headed by a Minister of State (in 1995, Jacques Dupont). An 18-member *National Council* is elected for 5-year terms. Elections are scheduled for Jan. 1998.

The constitution can be modified only with the approval of the National Council. A law of 1992 permits Monegasque women to give their nationality to their children.

National flag: Horizontally red over white.

National anthem: 'Principauté Monaco ma patrie' ('Principality of Monaco my fatherland'); words by T. Bellando de Castro, tune by C. Albrecht.

INTERNATIONAL RELATIONS. Monegasque relations with France are based on conventions of 1963. French citizens are treated as if in France.

Membership. Monaco is a member of the UN.

ECONOMY

Policy. A 22-ha site reclaimed from the sea at Fontvieille has been earmarked for office and residential development. The present industrial zone is to be reorganized and developed with a view to attracting new light industry.

Budget. The budget (in 1,000 francs) was as follows:

	1990	*1991*	*1992*	*1993*	*1994*
Revenue	2,666,568	2,844,940	2,989,540	3,298,079	3,166,743
Expenditure	2,657,565	2,840,040	2,754,064	3,327,130	3,165,190

Currency. Monaco is a member of the French Franc Zone.

Banking and Finance. There were 40 banks in 1994. Financial services represented 32% of economic activity in 1993.

Weights and Measures. The metric system is in use.

INDUSTRY. Light industry made up 11·6% of economic activity in 1993. There are some 700 small businesses, including chemicals, plastics, electronics, engineering and paper.

Labour. There were 30,540 persons employed on 1 Jan. 1994.

Trade Unions. Membership of trade unions was estimated at 2,000 out of a work force of 25,600 (1989).

FOREIGN ECONOMIC RELATIONS

Commerce. There is a customs union with France, and international trade is included with France.

Tourism. In 1994, 216,889 tourists and 40,334 business visitors spent a total of 602,059 and 113,080 nights respectively.

COMMUNICATIONS

Roads. There were 50 km of roads in 1991. In 1994 there were 28,501 motor vehicles.

Railways. The 1·6 km of main line passing through the country is operated by the French National Railways (SNCF).

Civil Aviation. The nearest airport is at Nice, France. At the Heliport of Monaco (Fontvieille) there were 104,345 passengers in the year ending Sept. 1994 (104,524 in the year ending Sept. 1993).

Shipping. In 1994 there were 1,054 vessels registered, of which 8 were over 100 tonnes. 1,331 yachts put in to the port in 1994.

Telecommunications. In 1994 there were 53,180 telephones.

Radio Monte Carlo broadcasts FM commercial programmes in French (long- and medium-waves). Radio Monte Carlo owns 55% of Radio Monte Carlo Relay Station on Cyprus. The foreign service is dedicated exclusively to religious broadcasts and is maintained by voluntary contributions. It operates in 36 languages under the name 'Trans World Radio' and has relay facilities on Bonaire, West Indies, and is planning to build relay facilities in the southern parts of Africa. *Télé Monté-Carlo* broadcasts TV programmes in French, Italian and English. There is a 30-channel cable service.

Cinemas. In 1996 there were 2 cinemas.

SOCIAL INSTITUTIONS

Justice. There are the following courts, *Juge de Paix*, Tribunal of the First Instance, a Court of Appeal, Criminal Tribunal, *Cour de Révision Judiciaire* and a Supreme Tribunal. There is no death penalty.

Police: There is an independent police force *(Sûreté Publique)* which comprised (1993) 500 personnel.

Religion. 90% of the resident population are Roman Catholic. There is a Roman Catholic archbishop.

Education. In 1993 there were 5,771 pupils and in 1994, 374 teachers.

Health. In 1994 there were 517 hospital beds and 124 doctors.

DIPLOMATIC REPRESENTATIVES

British Consul-General (resident in Marseilles): P. Yarnold.
British Honorary Consul Eric G. Blair.
Consul-General for Monaco in London: I. B. Ivanovic.

Of Monaco to the United Nations
Ambassador: Jacques Louis Boisson.

Further Reading

Journal de Monaco. Bulletin Officiel. 1858 ff.
Hudson, G. L. *Monaco.* [Bibliography]. Oxford and Santa Barbara (CA), 1990

MONGOLIA

Mongol Uls

Capital: Ulan Bator
Population: 2·2m. (1995)
GNP per capita: US$340 (1994)
HDI/world rank: 0·604/110 (1992)

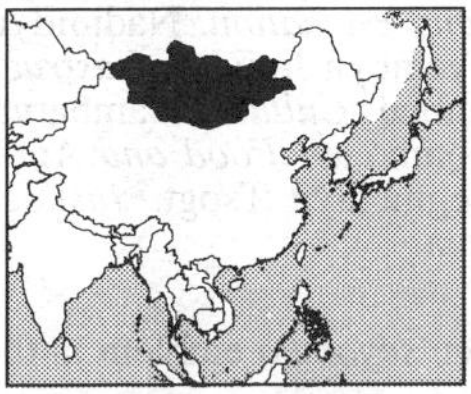

KEY HISTORICAL EVENTS. Outer Mongolia was a Chinese province from 1691 to 1911, an autonomous state under Russian protection from 1912 to 1919 and again a Chinese province from 1919 to 1921. On 13 March 1921 a Provisional People's Government was established which declared the independence of Mongolia and on 5 Nov. 1921 signed a treaty with Soviet Russia annulling all previous unequal treaties and establishing friendly relations. On 26 Nov. 1924 the Government proclaimed the country the Mongolian People's Republic.

On 5 Jan. 1946 China recognized the independence of Outer Mongolia after a plebiscite in Mongolia (20 Oct. 1945) had resulted in an overwhelming vote for independence. A Sino-Soviet treaty of 14 Feb. 1950 guaranteed this independence. In Aug. 1986 a consular agreement, in June 1987 a boundary agreement, and in Nov. 1988 a border treaty, were signed with China.

Until 1990 sole power was in the hands of the Mongolian People's Revolutionary (*i.e.*, Communist) Party (MPRP), but an opposition Mongolian Democratic Party, founded in Dec. 1989, achieved tacit recognition and held its first congress in Feb. 1990. Following demonstrations and hunger-strikes, on 12 March the entire MPRP Politburo resigned and political opposition was legalized.

TERRITORY AND POPULATION. Mongolia is bounded in the north by the Russian Federation, and in the east and south and west by China. Area, 1,566,500 sq. km (604,250 sq. miles). Population (1989 census), 2,095,600; 1995 estimate, 2·2m. (57% urban; 49·9% male). Density, 1·4 per sq. km. Birth rate (1990), 35·3 per 1,000; death rate, 8·5 per 1,000; marriage rate, 8·6 per 1,000; divorce rate, 0·5 per 1,000. Rate of increase, 26·8 per 1,000. The population is predominantly made up of Mongolian peoples (78·8% Halh). There is a Turkic Kazakh minority (5·9% of the population) and 20 Mongol minorities. The official language is Halh Mongol. Expectation of life in 1990 was 65 years.

The republic is administratively divided into 3 cities: Ulan Bator, the capital, (1990 population, 575,000), Darhan, (88,600) and Erdenet (58,200), and 18 provinces *(aimag)*. The provinces are sub-divided into 306 districts *(suums)*.

CLIMATE. A very extreme climate, with six months of mean temperatures below freezing, but much higher temperatures occur for a month or two in summer. Rainfall is very low and limited to the months mid-May to mid-Sept. Ulan Bator. Jan. –14°F (–25·6°C), July 61°F (16·1°C). Annual rainfall 8" (208 mm).

CONSTITUTION AND GOVERNMENT. For the constitution before 1992 *see* THE STATESMAN'S YEAR-BOOK 1992–93, p. 962. The Constitution of 12 Feb. 1992 abolished the 'People's Democracy', introduced democratic institutions and a market economy and guarantees freedom of speech.

The *President* is directly elected for renewable 4-year terms. At the presidential elections of 6 June 1993 the electorate was 1,183,000. Punsalmagiyn Ochirbat was re-elected by 60% of votes cast against 1 opponent.

Since June 1992, the legislature has consisted of a single-chamber 76-seat parliament. At the election of 28 June 1992 the electorate was 1·1m.; turn-out was 56·9%. There were 293 candidates. The Mongolian People's Revolutionary Party (MPRP, former Communists) won 70 seats.

President: Punsalmagiyn Ochirbat (b. 1942; elected Sept. 1990; re-elected 6 June 1993).

An MPRP government was formed in Aug. 1992 which in Oct. 1995 comprised:

Prime Minister: Puntsagiyn Jasray.

Deputy Prime Minister and Minister of Administration: Lhamsurengiyn Enebish. *Deputy Prime Minister:* Choijilsurengiyn Purevdorj. *Minister of State and Head of the Agency for National Development:* Chultemiyn Ulaan. *Minister of Natural Resources and the Environment:* Zambyn Batjargal. *Defence:* Mag.-Gen. Shagalyn Jadambaa. *Foreign:* Tserenpiliyn Gombosuren. *Science and Education:* Nadmidyn Olziykhutag. *Energy, Geology and Mineral Resources:* Byambyn Jigjid. *Infrastructure:* Razdakiyn Sandalhaan. *Finance:* Dalrain Davaasambuu. *Culture:* Nambaryn Enkhbayar. *Demography and Employment:* Erdeniyn Gombojav. *Food and Agriculture:* Tserenjaviyn Oold. *Trade and Industry:* Tsevegmediyn Tsogt. *Justice:* Namsraijaviyn Luvsanjav. *Health:* Pagvajaviyn Nyamdavaa.

The *Speaker* is Natsagiyn Bagaband.

National flag: Red–sky-blue–red (vertical), with a golden *soyombo* emblem in the hoist.

National anthem: 'Darkhan manai khuvsgalt uls' ('Our sacred revolutionary republic'); words by Tsendiyn Damdinsüren, tune by Bilegin Damdinsüren and Luvsanjamts Murjorj.

Local government is carried out by 380 local authorities. Some 13,000 deputies were elected in July 1990.

DEFENCE.

DEFENCE. Conscription is for 1 year.

Army. The Army comprises 4 motorized infantry divisions (3 under strength), 1 artillery and 1 air defence brigade and 1 airborne and 2 independent infantry battalions. Equipment includes 650 T-54/-55/-62 main battle tanks. Strength (1996) 20,000 (12,000 conscripts). There is a paramilitary militia of 10,000, including border guards.

Air Force. The Air Force had a strength of 1,100 in 1995 (350 conscripts), 15 combat aircraft and 12 armed helicopters. Aircraft included 15 MiG-21 fighters; a total of about 30 An-2, An-24 and An-26 transports used mainly on civil air services; 3 Wilga utility aircraft; 10 Mi-8 helicopters; and 12 Yakovlev trainers.

INTERNATIONAL RELATIONS

Membership. Mongolia is a member of the UN.

ECONOMY

Policy. Mongolia has had for centuries a traditional nomadic pastoral economy, which the Government aims to transform into a market economy. An Agency for National Development, whose head has cabinet rank, co-ordinates economic policy. A law of May 1991 envisages privatization by the issue of vouchers worth 10,000 tugriks to all citizens to acquire holdings in large privatizations or to buy small business or livestock.

Budget (in 1m. tugriks):

	1982	*1983*	*1985*	*1987*	*1989*	*1990*
Revenue	4,830	5,156	5,741	6,442	6,902	6,494
Expenditure	3,131	5,126	5,701	6,409	7,062	6,812

Sources of revenue, 1990: Turnover tax, 54%; profits tax, 31%; social insurance, 3·7%. Expenditure: Economy, 46%; social and cultural, 45%.

Currency. The unit of currency is the *tugrik* (MNT) of 100 *möngö*. Notes are issued for 1, 2, 5, 10, 20, 50, 100, 500 and 1,000 *tugriks*; and coins for 1, 2, 5, 10, 15, 20, 50 *möngö* and 1 *tugrik*. The tugrik was made convertible in 1993. Foreign exchange reserves were nil in July 1993. Inflation was 55% in 1994 (160% in 1993). In March 1996, £1 = 713·26; US$1 = 466·67; DM1 = 316·19 tugriks.

Banking and Finance. The Mongolian Bank (established 1924) is the bank of issue, being also a commercial, savings and development bank. It has 21 main branches. There are also a Trade and Industry Bank, an Insurance Bank and a Co-operative Bank.

A stock exchange opened in Ulan Bator in 1992.

Weights and Measures. The metric system is in use.

ENERGY AND NATURAL RESOURCES

Electricity. There are 6 thermal electric power stations. Production of electricity, 1990, 3,348m. kWh.

Minerals. There are large deposits of copper, nickel, zinc, molybdenum, phosphorites, tin, wolfram and fluorspar; production of the latter in 1990, 512,100 tonnes. There are major coalmines near Ulan Bator and Darhan. Coal (mainly lignite) production in 1990 was 7m. tonnes. Copper production (1992), 0·25m. tonnes.

Agriculture. 73% of agricultural production derives from cattle-raising. In 1993 there were 2·2m. horses, 2·8m. cattle, 14,657,000 sheep, 415,000 camels, 5,603,000 goats and 49,000 pigs. In 1990 there were 326,200 poultry.

Ownership of livestock (in 1m.) in 1990:

	Collective farms	*State farms*	*Private*
Cattle	1·09	0·30	1·46
Camels	0·44	0·01	0·09
Horses	1·00	0·15	1·11
Sheep	9·69	1·71	3·68
Goats	3·04	0·18	1·90

Production 1992 (in 1,000 tonnes): Meat, 212 (249 in 1990); cow's milk, 180; fermented mare's milk, 25m. litres. In 1990 there were 255 collective farms, 36 inter-farm associations, 20 fodder supply farms and 53 state farms.

The total agricultural area in 1990 was 125·7m. ha, 83% was sown to cereals, 18% to fodder and 2% to vegetables. In 1992 there was 1·4m. ha of arable land, 1,000 ha of permanent crop land and 124·8m. ha of pasture. The 1993 crop was 480,000 tonnes of wheat; 10,000 tonnes of oats; 18,000 tonnes of barley and 74,000 tonnes of potatoes. In 1992 there were 11,700 tractors (15 h.p. units) and 2,600 combine harvesters.

Forestry. Forests, chiefly larch, cedar, fir and birch, occupy 15·1m. ha. Production, 1990: 471,600 cu. metres of sawn wood.

INDUSTRY. Industry is still small in scale and local in character. The food industry accounts for 25% of industrial production. The main industrial centre is Ulan Bator; others are at Erdenet and Baga-Nur, and a northern territorial industrial complex is being developed based on Darhan and Erdenet to produce copper and molybdenum concentrates, lime, cement, machinery and wood- and metal-worked products. Production figures (1990): Scoured wool, 9,700 tonnes; cement, 440,800 tonnes; leather footwear, 4·8m. pairs; meat, 59,000 tonnes; soap, 2,600 tonnes.

Labour. The labour force was 648,700 in 1990 (49% female), including 123,400 in industry, 189,400 in agriculture, 44,600 in building, 48,000 in transport and communications and 49,200 in trade. Average wage was 16,000 tugriks per month in 1995. Unemployment was 8·5% in 1994.

Trade Unions. Membership was 0·53m. in 1988.

FOREIGN ECONOMIC RELATIONS. Mongolia is dependent on foreign aid. The largest donor in 1992 was Japan. Foreign debt was US$12,000m. in 1993.

Joint ventures with foreign firms are permitted. Foreign investors may acquire up to 49% of the equity in Mongolian companies. Foreign companies (except in precious metal mining) have a 5-year tax holiday and a further 5 years at 50% of the tax rate.

Commerce. Trade figures for 1990 (in 1m. tugriks): Exports, 1,967; imports, 2,751. Exports in 1990 included 48% minerals and fuels, 27% food and consumer goods and 15% non-food raw materials. Most foreign trade used to be with Communist countries. Main imports are machinery and fuel. The main non-Communist trading partner was Japan.

1993 trade was mostly in copper barter deals.

Total trade between Mongolia and UK (British Department of Trade returns, in £1,000 sterling):

	1991	*1992*	*1993*	*1994*	*1995*
Imports to UK	1,430	2,166	2,284	1,680	1,960
Exports and re-exports from UK	1,148	1,698	1,659	2,637	3,023

Tourism. 147,200 tourists visited Mongolia in 1990.

COMMUNICATIONS

Roads. There are 1,185 km of surfaced roads running around Ulan Bator, from Ulan Bator to Darhan, at points on the frontier with the Russian Federation and towards the south. Truck services run where there are no surfaced roads. 36·8m. tonnes of freight were carried in 1990, and 228·3m. passengers.

Railways. The Trans-Mongolian Railway (1,928 km of 1,524 mm gauge in 1992) connects Ulan Bator with the Russian Federation and China. There are spur lines to Erdenet and to the coalmines at Nalayh and Sharyn Gol. A separate line connects Choybalsan in the east with Borzaya on the Trans-Siberian Railway. 2·9m. passengers and 7·1m. tonnes of freight were carried in 1994.

Civil Aviation. Mongolian Airlines (MIAT) had 47 Soviet aircraft in 1992. It operates internal services, a flight to Irkutsk which links with a stopping service to Moscow, and a daily non-stop service to Moscow from Ulan Bator. There are weekly flights to Beijing. 10,000 tons of freight were carried in 1990 and 0·8m. passengers. Ulan Bator airport (Buyant Uhaa) was modernized and expanded in 1985.

Shipping. There is a steamer service on the Selenge River and a tug and barge service on Hövsgöl Lake. 70,000 tonnes of freight were carried in 1990.

Telecommunications. There were, in 1990, 428 post offices and 341 telephone exchanges. Number of telephones (1990), 66,400.

The government-controlled Ulaanbaatar Radio broadcasts 2 national programmes and an external service (English, Chinese, Japanese, Russian). Mongol Televiz transmits a daily programme and a Moscow relay (colour by SECAM). In 1993 186,000 radio and 120,000 TV sets were in use.

Cinemas. In 1990 there were 30 cinemas, 522 mobile cinemas and 30 theatres.

Press. In 1995 there was 1 government daily with a circulation of 50,000, and a police-run weekly. About 300 other titles were registered, but few were actually publishing. 717 book titles were published in 1990 in 6·4m. copies.

SOCIAL INSTITUTIONS

Justice. The Procurator-General is appointed, and the Supreme Court elected, by parliament for 5 years. There are also courts at province, town and district level. Lay assessors sit with professional judges.

Religion. Tibetan Buddhist Lamaism is the prevalent religion; the Dalai Lama is its spiritual head. In 1995 there were about 100 monasteries and 2,500 monks.

Education. In 1990 there were 872 nurseries with 97,200 children. Schooling begins at the age of 7. In 1990 there were 634 general education schools with 440,900 pupils and 20,600 teachers, 31 specialized secondary schools with 18,500 students and 1,300 teachers and 44 vocational technical schools with 29,100 pupils.

In 1994-95 there were 1 university and 4 specialized universities (agricultural; medical; pedagogical; technical). There were also colleges of commerce and business, economics, and railway engineering, and an institute of culture and art.

Health and Welfare. In 1990, 82·5m. tugriks were spent on maternity benefits.

Annual average per capita consumption (in kilogrammes) of foodstuffs in 1990: Meat, 97; milk and products, 118; sugar, 23; flour, 97; potatoes, 23; fresh vegetables, 20. In 1990 there were 29 doctors and 126 hospital beds per 10,000 population.

DIPLOMATIC REPRESENTATIVES

Of Mongolia in Great Britain (7 Kensington Ct., London, W8 5DL)
Ambassador: Gendengiin Nyamdoo.

Of Great Britain in Mongolia (30 Enkh Taivny Gudamzh, Ulan Bator 13)
Ambassador: I. C. Sloane.

Of Mongolia in the USA
Ambassador: Vacant.

Of the USA in Mongolia
Ambassador: Donald C. Johnson.

Of Mongolia to the United Nations
Ambassador: Luvsangiin Erdenechuluun.

Further Reading

The Central Statistical Office: *National Economy of the MPR, 1924–1984: Anniversary Statistical Collection*. Ulan Bator, 1984

Akiner. S. (ed.) *Mongolia Today*. London, 1992
Bawden, C. R., *The Modern History of Mongolia*. London, 1968
Becker, J., *The Lost Country*. London, 1992
Griffin, K. (ed.) *Poverty and the Transition to a Market Economy in Mongolia*. London, 1995
Jagchid, S. and Hyer, P., *Mongolia's Culture and Society*. Folkestone, 1979
Lattimore, O., *Nationalism and Revolution in Mongolia*. Leiden, 1955.—*Nomads and Commissars*. OUP, 1963
Nordby, J., *Mongolia in the Twentieth Century*. Farnborough, 1993
Sanders, A. J. K., *Mongolia: Politics, Economics and Society*. London, 1987
Shirendev, B. and Sanjdorj, M. (eds.) *History of the Mongolian People's Republic*. Vol. 3 (vols. 1 and 2 not translated). Harvard Univ. Press, 1976

MONTSERRAT

Capital: Plymouth
Population: 11,957 (1991)
GNP per capita: US$3,127 (1985)

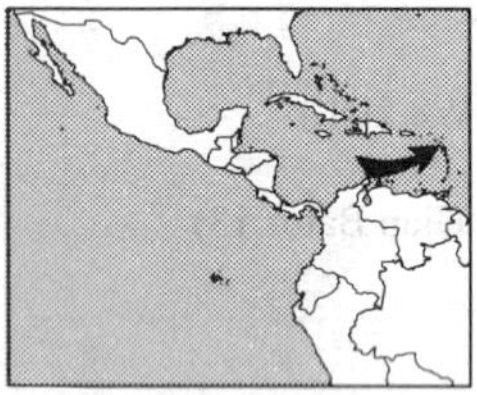

KEY HISTORICAL EVENTS. Montserrat was discovered by Columbus in 1493 and colonized by Britain in 1632 who brought Irish settlers to the island. Montserrat formed part of the federal colony of the Leeward Islands from 1871 until 1956, when it became a separate colony following the dissolution of the Federation.

TERRITORY AND POPULATION. Montserrat is situated in the Caribbean Sea 27 miles south-west of Antigua. The area is 39·5 sq. miles (102 sq. km). Population, 1991, 11,957. Chief town, Plymouth, 3,500 inhabitants.

CLIMATE. A tropical climate but with no well-defined rainy season, though July to Dec. shows slightly more rainfall, with the average for the year being about 60" (1,500 mm). Dec. to March is the cooler season while June to Nov. is the hotter season, when hurricanes may occur. Plymouth. Jan. 76°F (24·4°C), July 81°F (27·2°C). Annual rainfall 65" (1,628 mm).

CONSTITUTION AND GOVERNMENT. Montserrat is a crown colony. The Constitution dates from 1960. The head of state is Queen Elizabeth II, represented by a *Governor* who heads an Executive Council comprising also the Chief Minister, the Financial Secretary, the Attorney-General and 3 other ministers. The *Legislative Council* consists of 7 elected, 2 civil service officials (the Attorney-General and Financial Secretary) and 2 nominated members; it sits for 5-year terms. In elections to the Legislative Council in Oct. 1991, 4 seats were won by the National Progressive Party, 1 by the People's Liberation Movement, 1 by the National Democratic Party and 1 ind.

Governor: F. J. Savage, LVO, OBE.
Chief Minister: Reuben Meade.
Flag: The British Blue Ensign with the shield of Montserrat in the fly.

INTERNATIONAL RELATIONS

Membership. Montserrat is a member of CARICOM and the Organization of East Caribbean States.

ECONOMY

Budget. In 1994 current expenditure was EC$39·7m.; current revenue, EC$47·2m.

Currency. 100 cents = 1 Eastern Caribbean dollar (XCD). Coins: 1, 2, 5, 25, 50 cents. Notes: 1, 5, 10, 20 and 100 dollars.

Banking and Finance. In 1994 there were 3 commercial and 21 offshore banks. Responsibility for overseeing offshore banking rests with the Governor.

ENERGY AND NATURAL RESOURCES

Electricity. Production (1987) 16·3m. kWh.

Agriculture. 3,700 ha are suitable for agriculture, of which about half were in use in 1995. Potatoes, tomatoes, mangos and limes are produced. Sea island cotton is grown to supply local industries. Meat production began in 1995.

Livestock (1992,in 1,000); Cattle, 10; pigs, 1; sheep, 5; goats, 7; asses, 3.

Fisheries. Catch (1988) 100 tonnes. Aquaculture is pursued.

INDUSTRY. Manufacturing contributes about 6% to GDP and accounts for 10% of employment, but is responsible for up to 85% of exports. It is limited to small scale industries producing light consumer goods such as electronic components, plastic bags, leather goods and various items made from locally grown cotton.

FOREIGN ECONOMIC RELATIONS

Commerce. Imports in 1992 totalled US$80·6m.; exports, US$2·8m. The USA is the main trading partner. Chief exports were cotton clothing, electronic parts and lighting fittings.

Total trade between Montserrat and UK (British Department of Trade returns, in £1,000 sterling):

	1991	*1992*	*1993*	*1994*	*1995*
Imports to UK	39	143	65	15	4,720
Exports and re-exports from UK	2,720	1,854	2,141	2,651	2,554

Tourism. Tourism contributes about 30% of GDP; earnings in 1993 were EC$40m. There were 36,077 visitors including 11,636 cruise ship arrivals in 1994.

COMMUNICATIONS

Roads. In 1994 there were 203 km of surfaced roads, 24 km of unsurfaced roads and 42 km of tracks. In 1987 there were 1,368 passenger cars and 270 commercial vehicles.

Civil Aviation. At Blackburne airport LIAT provides services to Antigua, St Kitts-Nevis and St Martin and WINAIR to St Martin.

Shipping. Plymouth is the port of entry.

Telecommunications. Number of telephones, 1995, 4,783. Radio Montserrat is the government broadcaster and there are 3 commercial radio stations. There is a commercial TV cable company.

Press. In 1995 there were 2 weeklies.

SOCIAL INSTITUTIONS

Justice. Law is based on UK common law as exercised by the Eastern Caribbean Supreme Court. Final appeal lies to the UK Privy Council. Law is administered by the West Indies Associated States Court, a Court of Summary Jurisdiction and Magistrate's Courts.

Religion. In 1980 (census) there were 1,368 Roman Catholics, 3,676 Anglicans, 2,742 Methodists, 1,041 Seventh Day Adventists, 1,503 Pentecostals and 285 members of the Church of God. There is also a Christian Council of Churches.

Education. In 1995–96 there were 11 primary schools, a comprehensive secondary school with 3 campuses, and a technical college. Schools are run by the Government, the churches and the private sector. There is a medical school, the American University of the Caribbean.

Health. In 1995 there were 2 medical officers, 1 surgeon, 1 dentist and 68 hospital beds.

Further Reading

Fergus, H.A., *Montserrat: Emerald Isle of the Caribbean.* London, 1983

MOROCCO

Mamlaka al-Maghrebia

(Kingdom of Morocco)

Capital: Rabat
Population: 25·9m. (1993)
GNP per capita: US$1,150 (1994)
HDI/world rank: 0·554/117 (1992)

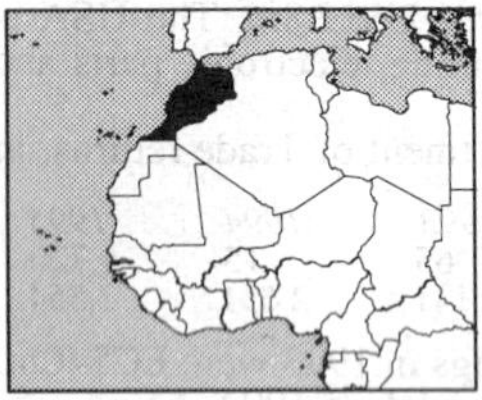

KEY HISTORICAL EVENTS. From 1912 to 1956 Morocco was divided into a French protectorate, a Spanish protectorate and the international zone of Tangiers (set up by France, Spain and Great Britain in 1923). These arrangements were terminated in 1956.

The northern strip of Spanish Sahara was ceded by Spain in 1958, and in 1969 the former Spanish province of Ifni was returned to Morocco.

A tripartite agreement of 1975 provided for the transfer of power from Spanish Sahara (Western Sahara) to the Moroccan and Mauritanian governments in 1976 but in 1979 Mauritania renounced its claim. For Western Sahara *see below.*

TERRITORY AND POPULATION. Morocco is bounded by Algeria to the east and south-east, Western Sahara to the south-west, the Atlantic Ocean to the north-west and the Mediterranean to the north. Excluding the Western Saharan territory claimed and occupied since 1976 by Morocco, the area is 458,730 sq. km and population at the 1982 census was 20,255,687. Western Sahara had an area of 252,120 sq. km and 163,868 population. Population in 1993: Morocco without Western Sahara, 25·9m. (50% urban); Western Sahara (1993), 208,000. Density, 36·7 per sq. km. There was a census in Sept. 1994. Vital statistics rates, 1993 (per 1,000 population): Birth, 27·3; death, 7·0; growth, 20·3.

The 49 provinces and 22 prefectures are grouped into 7 economic regions (in parentheses). Area and population in 1993 (WS indicates in Western Sahara):

Province	*Area in sq. km*	*Population in 1,000*
(South)		
Agadir	5,910	831
Boujdour (WS)	100,120	10
Es-Semara (WS)	61,760	26
Guelmim	28,750	171
El-Aaiún (WS)	39,360	144
Ouarzazate	41,550	661
Oued Eddahab (WS)	50,880	28
Tan-Tan	17,295	56
Taroudannt	16,460	668
Tata	25,925	107
Tiznit	6,960	387
(Tensift)		
El Kelâa Srahna	10,070	694
Essaouira	6,335	431
Marrakesh	14,755	1,549
Safi	7,285	862
(Centre)		
Azilal	10,050	421
Béni Mellal	7,075	966
Ben Slimane	2,760	206
Aïn Chok-Hay Hassani		470
Aïn Sebaâ-Hay Mohammadi		606
Ben Msik-Sidi Othmane	1,615	1,023
Casablanca-Anfa		1,081
Mohammadia-Znata		226
El Jadida	6,000	944
Khouribga	4,250	558
Settat	9,750	799
(North-West)		
Chefchaouen	4,350	369
Kénitra	4,745	940
Khémisset	8,305	480
Rabat		707
Salé	1,275	692
Skhirate-Témara		209
Sidi Kacem	4,060	610
Tangiers	1,195	579
Tétouan	6,025	878
Larache	...	...
(Centre-North)		
Al Hoceima	3,550	377
Boulemane	14,395	158
Fes	5,400	1,051
Taounate	5,585	609
Taza	15,020	724
(Eastern)		
Figuig	55,990	108
Nador	6,130	817
Oujda	20,700	992
(Centre-South)		
Errachidia	59,585	511
Ifrane	3,310	118
Khenifra	12,320	450
Meknes	3,995	765

The chief cities (with Census populations, 1982) are as follows:

Casablanca	2,139,204	Tangiers	266,346	Agadir	110,479
Rabat	518,616	Oujda	260,082	Mohammedia	105,120
Fez	448,823	Tétouan	199,615	Beni Mellal	95,003
Marrakesh	439,728	Safi	197,616	Al Jadida	81,455
Meknès	319,783	Kénitra	188,194	Taza	77,216
Salé	289,391	Khouribga	127,181	Ksar al Kabir	73,541

The official language is Arabic, spoken by 75% of the population; the remainder speak Berber. French and Spanish are considered subsidiary languages.

CLIMATE. The climate ranges from semi-arid in the south to warm temperate Mediterranean conditions in the north, but cooler temperatures occur in the mountains. Rabat. Jan. 55°F (12·9°C), July 72°F (22·2°C). Annual rainfall 23" (564 mm). Agadir. Jan. 57°F (13·9°C), July 72°F (22·2°C). Annual rainfall 9" (224 mm). Casablanca. Jan. 54°F (12·2°C), July 72°F (22·2°C). Annual rainfall 16" (404 mm). Marrakesh. Jan. 52°F (11·1°C), July 84°F (28·9°C). Annual rainfall 10" (239 mm). Tangier. Jan. 53°F (11·7°C), July 72°F (22·2°C). Annual rainfall 36" (897 mm).

ROYAL HOUSE. The ruling King is **Hassan II,** born on 9 July 1929, succeeded on 3 March 1961, on the death of his father Mohammed V, who reigned 1927–61. The royal style was changed from 'His Sherifian Majesty the Sultan' to 'His Majesty the King' on 18 Aug. 1957. *Heir apparent:* Crown Prince Sidi Mohammed, born 21 Aug. 1963.

The King holds supreme civil and religious authority, the latter in his capacity of Emir-el-Muminin or Commander of the Faithful. He resides usually at Rabat, but occasionally in one of the other traditional capitals, Fez (founded in 808), Marrakesh (founded in 1062), or at Skhirat.

CONSTITUTION AND GOVERNMENT. A new Constitution was approved by referendum in March 1972 and amendments were approved by referendum in May 1980. The Kingdom of Morocco is a constitutional monarchy with a legislature of a single chamber composed of 333 deputies. Deputies for 111 seats are elected by indirect vote through an electoral college representing the town councils, the regional assemblies, the chambers of commerce, industry and agriculture, and the trade unions. Deputies for the remaining 222 seats are by general election, on the first-past-the-post system. The King, as sovereign head of State, appoints the Prime Minister and other Ministers, has the right to dissolve Parliament and approves legislation.

At a referendum of 4 Sept. 1992 to approve a revision of the constitution, turn-out was 97·4%. 99·98% of votes cast were in favour.

Elections were held in 2 rounds on 25 June and 17 Sept. 1993. There were some 2,000 candidates representing 11 parties and independents. The electorate was 11·5m.; turn-out was 62·75%. Polling also took place in Western Sahara.

The King announced a new government on 11 Jan. 1995 but dissolved it on 31 Jan. Another government was formed on 27 Feb. 1995, which in Jan. 1996 comprised:

Prime Minister, Minister of Foreign Affairs and Co-operation: Abdellatif Filali. *Minister of State:* Moulay Ahmed Alaoui. *Minster of State, Interior:* Driss Basri. *Justice:* Abderrahmane Amalou. *Education:* Rachid Ben Mokhtar. *Health:* Ahmed Alami. *Religious Endowments and Islamic Affairs:* Abdelkebir Alaoui M'Daghri. *Public Works:* Abdelaziz Meziane Belfkih. *Finance and Foreign Investments:* Mohammad Kabbaj. *Transport:* Said Ameskane. *Energy and Mines:* Abdellatif Guerraoui. *Youth and Sport:* Ahmed Meziane. *Sea Fisheries and the Merchant Marine:* Mustapha Sahel. *Secretary-General of the Government:* Abdessadek Rabiah. *Culture:* Abdellah Azmani. *Housing:* Driss Toulali. *Posts and Telecommunications:* Hamza Kettani. *Agriculture and Agricultural Investment:* Hassan Abou Ayoub. *Trade, Industry and Handicrafts:* Driss Jettou. *Labour and Social Affairs:* Amine Demnati. *Foreign Trade:* Mohammad Alami. *Tourism:* Mohammad Alaoui M'Hamedi. *Communications, Government Spokesman:* Driss Alaoui

M'Daghri. *Privatization:* Abderrahmane Saaidi. *Higher Education and Research:* Driss Khalil. *Environment:* Dr Noureddine Benomar Alami. *Vocational Training:* Abdessalam Beroual.

National flag: Red, with a green pentacle star in the centre.

National anthem: 'Manbit al Ahrah, masriq al anwar' ('Fountain of freedom, source of light'); words by Ali Squalli Houssaini, tune by Leo Morgan.

*Local Government.*The country is administratively divided into 49 provinces and 22 prefectures divided into 159 circles, which are subdivided into 248 urban and 1,297 rural communes. At elections on 16 Oct. 1992 for the commune authorities, the Rassemblement National des Indépendants gained 18·05% of votes cast and 21·69% of seats.

DEFENCE. Conscription is authorized for 18 months.

Army. The Army is deployed in 2 commands: Northern Zone and Southern Zone. It comprises 3 mechanized infantry, 1 light security and 2 parachute brigades; 8 mechanized infantry regiments; 1 air defence group; 37 infantry, 3 camel corps, 2 cavalry, 1 mountain, 10 armoured, 12 artillery, 7 engineer and 2 airborne battalions and 4 commando units. There is also a Royal guard of 1,500. Equipment includes 224 M-48A5 and 300 M-60 main battle tanks. Strength (1996), 175,000 (100,000 conscripts). There is also a Royal Gendarmerie of 12,000 and an Auxiliary Force of 30,000.

Navy. The Navy includes 1 missile-armed Spanish-built frigate, 2 Italian-built missile-armed corvettes, 4 fast missile craft, 13 coastal patrol craft and 10 inshore patrol craft. There are additionally 1 ex-US tank landing ship, 3 medium landing ships of French origin, 2 transports and 1 Ro-Ro ferry in naval use. Personnel in 1995 numbered 7,000, including a 1,500 strong brigade of Naval Infantry. Bases are located at Casablanca, Agadir, Al-Hoceima and Dakhla.

The Coast Guard wing of the Royal Gendarmerie operates 12 patrol craft.

Air Force. The Air Force was formed in Nov. 1956. Equipment in current use is mainly of US and West European origin. It includes 32 Mirage F1s, a total of 32 F-5A/B/E/F fighter-bombers and RF-5A reconnaissance-fighters, 3 OV-10 Bronco counter-insurgency aircraft, 2 Falcon 20s for electronic warfare, and 18 Gazelle armed helicopters, 20 Alpha Jet advanced trainers, 20 Magister armed jet basic trainers, 10 T-34C-1 turboprop basic trainers, 10 Swiss-built Bravo primary trainers, 2 Mudry CAP 10B and 4 CAP 230 aerobatic trainers, 70 Agusta-Bell 205 and 212, Puma and JetRanger helicopters, 2 Do 28D Skyservants for coastal patrol, 9 CH-47C heavy-lift helicopters, 15 C-130H turboprop transport aircraft, 2 KC-130H tanker/transports, 2 Citation V, a Falcon 50 and a Gulfstream III VIP transport, 2 Boeing 707s, 7 CN-235s and 10 turboprop King Air light transports. Personnel strength (1995) about 13,500, with 99 combat aircraft and 24 armed helicopters.

INTERNATIONAL RELATIONS

Membership. Morocco is a member of the UN and the Arab League.

ECONOMY

Policy. There is a programme of privatization involving 112 companies. 30 had been privatized by mid-1995.

Budget. 1991 revenue was DH57,562m.; expenditure, DH46,451m. VAT is 20%.

Currency. The unit of currency is the *dirham* (MAD) of 100 *centimes*, introduced in 1959. There are coins of 5, 10, 20 and 50 centimes and 1 and 5 dirhams, and notes of 5, 10, 50, 100 and 200 dirhams. Foreign exchange reserves were US$3,400m. in 1993. DH38,713m. were in circulation at the end of 1993. Since 1993 the dirham has been convertible for current account operations. Inflation was 7% in 1995. In March 1996, £1 = 13·15; US$1 = 8·60; DM1 = 5·83 dirhams.

Banking and Finance. The central bank is the Bank Al Maghrib, which had assets of DH59,426m. on 31 Dec. 1993. There are 14 commercial banks (11 foreign). There are also 3 development banks, specializing respectively in industry, housing and agriculture.

There is a stock exchange at Casablanca.

Weights and Measures. The metric system is legal.

ENERGY AND NATURAL RESOURCES

Electricity. Installed capacity was 2,646,100 kW. in 1993. Production was 9,719·9m. kWh. (963·8m. hydro-electric) in 1992.

Minerals. The principal mineral exploited is phosphate, the output of which was 15·83m. tonnes in 1993. Other minerals (in tonnes, 1993) are: Lead (111,896), zinc (125,737), silver (236·25), copper (35,703), iron ore (66,318), manganese (42,585), barytine (349,613), salt (146,961).

Agriculture. In 1994, agriculture contributed 16·4% of GDP. Agricultural production is subject to drought; about 1m. ha are irrigated. 85% of farmland is individually owned, the rest belonging to tribes and religious orders. Only 1% of farms are over 50 ha; most are under 3 ha. Land suitable for cultivation, 1993, 9·26m. ha, of which (in 1,000 ha): Cereals, 5,020; leguminous vegetables, 322; market gardening, 204; oil-producing, 251, industrial crops, 146; fodder, 168; dense fruit plantations, 664; fallow, 2,687.

Production in 1993 (in 1,000 tonnes): Wheat, 1,573; barley, 1,027; maize, 92; fruit, 2,890 (of which citrus fruits, 1,230); pulses, 77·4; sunflower seeds, 44·6; groundnuts, 34; sugar beets, 3,162; sugar-cane, 946; cotton, 30·7.

Dairy production in 1991 included: Milk, 990,000 tonnes; butter, 15,570 tonnes; cheese, 7,346 tonnes. Meat production (1993) 426,430 tonnes.

Livestock (in 1,000 head), 1993: Cattle, 2,348; sheep, 11,868; goats, 3,867; camels (1991), 43,000; horses, 156.

Forestry. Natural forests covered (1993) 8·97m. ha. 520,364 ha were reafforested in 1992–93. Produce includes firewood, building and industrial timber and some cork and charcoal.

Fisheries. The fishing fleet numbered 2,564 coastal vessels in 1993 and 462 deep-sea vessels, the latter totalling 152,417 GRT. Total catch in 1993 was 619,602 tonnes, (deep-sea, 144,805 tonnes). Total catch value was DH4,646m.

INDUSTRY. In 1992 there were 5,855 industrial firms employing 351,149 persons. 1,785 of these employed fewer than 10 persons; 80, more than 500. 1,434 firms were engaged in food production, 789 in clothing, 723 in textiles and 397 in paper- and board-making and printing. Production, 1993 (in tonnes): Sugar, 497,767; olive oil, 38,000; cement, 6,175,000.

Labour. Amongst the total urban population in 1993 of 13,149,000, 3,659,319 persons were employed (784,963 females; 68,193 under 15 years) and 680,801 registered unemployed. The monthly non-agricultural minimum wage was DH1,510. The agricultural minimum was DH37·60 per day in 1994.

Trade Unions. In 1984 there were 8 trade unions.

FOREIGN ECONOMIC RELATIONS. In 1989 Morocco signed a treaty of economic co-operation with the 4 other Maghreb countries: Algeria, Libya, Mauritania and Tunisia. In 1995, Morocco signed an association agreement with the EU to create a free trade zone in 12 years

Foreign debt was US$22,000m. in 1995.

Commerce. In 1994 imports were US$6,600m. and exports, US$4,000m.

Imports in 1993 included (in 1,000 tonnes): Crude oil, 6,123; grain, 2,695; sulphur, 2,588; chemicals, 743; sawn wood, 528. Exports included: Foodstuffs and tobacco, 1,169; phosphates, 8,398; other mineral products, 2,063; natural and artificial fertilizers, 2,409.

Main export markets in 1993 (in DH1m.): France, 11,414; Spain, 3,037; India, 1,336; Italy, 1,797; Japan, 2,021. Main import suppliers: France, 14,210; Spain, 6,500; Italy, 3,886; Germany, 3,674; USA, 6,250.

Total trade between Morocco and UK (British Department of Trade returns, in £1,000 sterling):

	1991	*1992*	*1993*	*1994*	*1995*
Imports to UK	95,522	123,232	182,378	200,583	253,752
Exports and re-exports from UK	152,245	123,301	168,303	193,665	271,114

Tourism. In 1993, 2,945,700 foreign visitors stayed 9·31m. nights. Tourist revenue, DH11,222m.

COMMUNICATIONS

Roads. In 1993 there were 59,790 km of classified roads, of which 29,626 km were surfaced and including 9,584 km of surfaced main roads. A motorway links Rabat to Casablanca. 3·4m. passengers and 16·1m. tonnes of freight were carried in 1993. In 1993 there were 316,722 commercial vehicles, 849,344 private cars and 19,689 motor cycles. There were 41,821 road accidents in 1993 (3,359 fatalities).

Railways. In 1993 there were 1,893 km of railways, of which 1,003 km were electrified. In 1993 the railways carried 1,881m. passenger-km and 4,679m. tonne-km of freight.

Civil Aviation. The national carrier is Royal Air Maroc, which in 1995 operated 6 B-727-200 Advs, 4 B-737-200 Advs, 2 B-737-200C Advs, 6 B-737-400s, 5 B-737-500s, 1 B-747-200B Combi, 1 B-747-400, 2 B-757-200s and 2 other aircraft. Services are also provided by Aeroflot, Air Algérie, Air France, Air Inter, Air Malta, Air Mauritanie, Alitalia, Balkan, British Airways, Gulf Air, Iberia, KLM, Kuwait Airways, Libyan Airlines, Lufthansa, Royal Jordanian, Sabena, Saudia, Swissair, Tunis Air and Zas. The major international airport is Mohammed V at Casablanca; there are 8 other airports. 4,793,487 passengers and 47,482 tonnes of freight were carried in 1993.

Shipping. There are 12 ports, the largest being Casablanca, Tangiers and Jorf Lasfar. 11·428m. passengers and 40·4m. tonnes of freight were handled in 1993. In 1995 sea-going shipping totalled 0·39m. GRT, including oil tankers, 25,092 GRT, and container ships, 10,071 GRT.

Telecommunications. In 1993 there were 592 main post offices. Telephone subscribers totalled 1m. in 1995.

The government-controlled Radiodiffusion Télévision Marocaine broadcasts 3 national (1 in French, English and Spanish) and 8 regional radio programmes and 1 TV channel (colour by SECAM). Broadcasting in Berber languages commenced in 1994. There is also a government commercial radio service and an independent TV channel. In 1993 there were 4·5m. radio and 1·21m. TV sets in use.

Cinemas. There were 199 cinemas in 1993 and 20·43m. attendances. 2 full-length films were made.

Press. In 1984 there were 12 daily newspapers (7 Arabic, 5 French) and 18 main weeklies and monthlies (10 Arabic, 8 French).

SOCIAL INSTITUTIONS

Justice. The legal system is based on French and Islamic law codes. There are a Supreme Court, 21 courts of appeal, 65 courts of first instance, 196 centres with resident judges and 706 communal jurisdictions for petty offences.

Religion. Islam is the established state religion. 98% of the population are Sunni Moslems of the Malekite school and 2% are Christians, mainly Roman Catholic.

Education. Adult literacy was 49·5% in 1990. Education in Berber languages has been permitted since 1994. Education is compulsory from the age of 7 to 13. In

1993–94 there were 28,335 Koranic schools (33,721 in 1990) with 30,367 teachers and 611,729 pupils; 3,563 modern pre-primary schools (343 in 1990) with 5,836 teachers and 171,727 pupils; 4,349 primary schools (392 private) with 91,487 teachers and 2,769,323 pupils; 1,168 secondary schools with (in the public sector) 75,407 teachers and 1,226,194 pupils (38,692 private). There were 13 universities with 7,566 teachers and 218,516 students (89,223 women), 8,390 students (1,761 women) in teacher training and (1992-93) 8,967 students and 1,145 teachers in other higher education institutions. An English-language university was opened at Ifrane in Jan. 1995, initially with a staff of 35 and 300 students (scheduled to rise to 3,500).

Health. In the public sector in 1994 there were 4,371 doctors, and 72 dentists. In the private sector in 1993 there were 3,324 doctors and 1,132 dentists. In 1993 there were 2,214 pharmacists. In 1993 in the public sector there were 98 hospitals with 24,725 beds, 103 health centres with 1,548 beds and 1,220 dispensaries.

DIPLOMATIC REPRESENTATIVES

Of Morocco in Great Britain (49 Queen's Gate Gdns., London, SW7 5NE)
Ambassador: Khalil Haddaoui.

Of Great Britain in Morocco (17 Blvd de la Tour Hassan, Rabat)
Ambassador: William Fullerton, CMG.

Of Morocco in the USA (1601 21st St., NW, Washington, D.C., 20009)
Ambassador: Mohammed Beneissar.

Of the USA in Morocco (2 Ave. de Marrakech, Rabat)
Ambassador: Marc C. Ginsberg.

Of Morocco to the United Nations
Ambassador: Ahmed Snoussi.

Further Reading

Direction de la Statistique. *Annuaire Statistique du Maroc.—Conjoncture Économique.* Quarterly *Bulletin Official.* Rabat. Weekly
Findlay, A. M., *Morocco.* [Bibliography]. 2nd ed. Oxford and Santa Barbara (CA), 1995

National library: Bibliothèque Générale et Archives, Rabat.
National statistical office: Direction de la Statistique, BP178, Rabat.

WESTERN SAHARA

The colony of Spanish Sahara became a Spanish province in July 1958. On 14 Nov. 1975 Spain, Morocco and Mauritania reached agreement on the transfer of Western Sahara to Morocco and Mauritania on 28 Feb. 1976. Morocco occupied El-Aaiún in late Nov. and on 12 Jan. 1976 the Spanish army withdrew from Western Sahara which had ceased to be a Spanish province on 31 Dec. 1975. The country was partitioned by Morocco and Mauritania on 28 Feb. 1976; Morocco reorganized its sector into 3 provinces. In Aug. 1979 Mauritania withdrew from the territory it took over in 1976. The area was taken over by Morocco and reorganized into a fourth province.

A liberation movement, *Frente Polisario,* had launched an armed struggle against Spanish rule on 20 May 1973 and, in spite of occupation of all western centres by Moroccan troops, Saharawi guerrillas based in Algeria continue to attempt to take over the territory. They have renamed it the Saharawi Arab Democratic Republic and hold most of the desert beyond a defensive line built by Moroccan troops encompassing Es-Semara, Bu Craa and El-Aaiún.

In 1982 the Saharawi Arab Democratic Republic became a member of the Organization of African Unity.

In May 1991 the UN approved a Security Council decision to fund a Mission for the Organization of a Referendum in Western Sahara (MINURSO). Its mandate was extended to 31 May 1996. Some 65,000 are considered Saharawis and qualified to vote. A UN peacekeeping force proclaimed a ceasefire on 6 Sept. After a first proposal to establish an electorate on the basis of the approximately 74,000 persons registered at the Spanish census of 1974, the UN agreed to a widening of qualifications to include residents who had not been registered by the census, persons whose father was born in the territory, and those who had lived 6 years consecutively or 12 years intermittently in the territory, adding some 30,000-40,000 to the list.

President: Mohammed Abdelaziz.

Area 266,769 sq. km (102,680 sq. miles). The population at the census held by Morocco in Sept. 1982 was 163,868; estimate (1993) 214,000. Another estimated 196,000 Saharawis live in refugee camps around Tindouf in south-west Algeria. The main towns (1982 census) are El-Aaiún, the capital (96,784), Dakhla (17,822) and Es-Semara (17,753). The population is Arabic-speaking, and virtually entirely Sunni Moslem.

Rich phosphate deposits were discovered in 1963 at Bu Craa. Morocco holds 65% of the shares of the former Spanish state-controlled company. While production reached 5·6m. tonnes in 1975, exploitation has been severely reduced by guerrilla activity but in 1984 produced 1m. tonnes. After a nearly complete collapse, production and transportation of phosphate resumed in 1978, ceased again, and then resumed in 1982. There are about 6,100 km of motorable tracks, but only about 500 km of paved roads. There are airports at El-Aaiún and Dakhla. As most of the land is desert, less than 19% is in agricultural use, with about 2,000 tonnes of grain produced annually. There were (1983) about 22,000 sheep, as well as goats and camels raised. In 1989 there were 27 primary schools with 14,794 pupils and 18 secondary schools with 9,218 pupils.

Further Reading

Damis, J., *Conflict in Northwest Africa: The Western Sahara Dispute.* Stanford, 1983
Hodges, T., *Western Sahara: The Roots of a Desert War.* London and Westport, 1984
Sipe, L. F., *Western Sahara: A Comprehensive Bibliography.* New York, 1984
Thompson, V. and Adloff, R., *The Western Saharans: Background to Conflict.* London, 1980
Zoubir, Y. H. and Volman, D. (eds.) *The International Dimensions of the Western Sahara Conflict.* New York, 1993

MOZAMBIQUE

República de Moçambique

Capital: Maputo
Population: 16·11m. (1991)
GNP per capita: US$80 (1994)
HDI/world rank: 0·246/167 (1992)

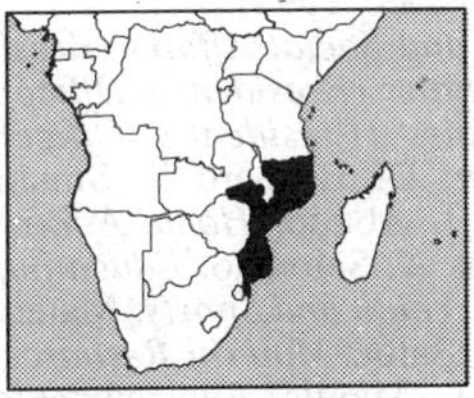

KEY HISTORICAL EVENTS. In 1506 Sofala was occupied by the Portuguese. Mozambique was at first ruled as part of Portuguese India, but a separate administration was created in 1752. In 1951 Mozambique became an Overseas Province of Portugal. Following a decade of guerrilla activity, Portugal and the nationalists jointly established a transitional government on 20 Sept. 1974. Independence was achieved on 25 June 1975. A one-party state dominated by the Mozambique Liberation Front (FRELIMO) was set up, but armed insurgency led by the Mozambique National Resistance (RENAMO) continued until on 4 Oct. 1992 President Chissano and Afonso Dhlakama, leader of RENAMO, signed a treaty in Rome ending the civil war. The treaty provided for all weapons to be handed over to the UN, and all armed groups to be disbanded within 6 months. The UN presence ended in Jan. 1995.

TERRITORY AND POPULATION. Mozambique is bounded east by the Indian ocean, south by South Africa, south-west by Swaziland, west by South Africa and Zimbabwe and north by Zambia, Malaŵi and Tanzania. It has an area of 799,380 sq. km (308,642 sq. miles) and a population, according to the census of 1980, of 11,673,725. Up to 1·5m. refugees abroad and 5m. internally displaced persons during the Civil War have begun to return home. Estimate (1991), 16,110,000. Infant mortality per 1,000 live births, 1991, 149. Life expectancy was 47·5 years in 1991.The areas, populations and capitals of the provinces are:

Province	*Sq. km*	*Census 1980*	*Estimate 1987*	*Capital*
Cabo Delgado	82,625	940,000	1,109,921	Pemba
Niassa	129,056	514,100	607,670	Lichinga
Nampula	81,606	2,402,700	2,837,856	Nampula
Zambézia	105,008	2,500,200	2,952,251	Quelimane
Tete	100,724	831,000	981,319	Tete
Manica	61,661	641,200	756,886	Chimoio
Sofala	68,018	1,065,200	1,257,710	Beira
Inhambane	68,615	997,600	1,167,022	Inhambane
Gaza	75,709	990,900	1,138,724	Xaixai
Province of Maputo	25,756	491,800	544,692	Maputo
City of Maputo	602	755,300	1,006,765	

The capital is Maputo (estimated population, 1993, 2m.). Other large cities are Beira (1990 population, 299,300), Nampula (202,600) and Nacala (104,300).

The main ethnolinguistic groups are the Makua/Lomwe (52% of the population), the Malaŵi (12%), Shona (6%) and Thonga (24%). Portuguese remains the official language, but vernaculars are widely spoken throughout the country.

CLIMATE. A humid tropical climate, with a dry season from June to Sept. In general, temperatures and rainfall decrease from north to south. Maputo. Jan. 78°F (25·6°C), July 65°F (18·3°C). Annual rainfall 30" (760 mm). Beira. Jan. 82°F (27·8°C), July 69°F (20·6°C). Annual rainfall 60" (1,522 mm).

CONSTITUTION AND GOVERNMENT. On 2 Nov. 1990 the People's Assembly unanimously voted a new Constitution, which came into force on 30 Nov. This changed the name of the state to 'Republic of Mozambique', legalized opposition parties, provided for universal secret elections and introduced a bill of rights including the right to strike, press freedoms and habeas corpus. The head of state is the *President*, directly elected for a 5-year term. Parliament is a 250-member *National Assembly*.

Presidential and parliamentary elections were held on 27-29 Oct. 1994. The electorate was 6·5m.; turn-out was 90%. President Chissano was re-elected by 53·3% of votes cast against 1 opponent. FRELIMO gained 44·3% of votes cast for the National Assembly, and RENAMO 37·7%.

A new government was formed on 16 Dec. 1994 which in Nov. 1995 comprised:
President: Joaquim A. Chissano (FRELIMO; sworn in 9 Dec. 1994).
Prime Minister: Dr Pascoal M. Mocumbi. *Economic and Social Affairs (President's Office):* Dr Eneas C. Comiche. *Parliamentary Affairs (President's Office):* Francisco C. J. Madeira. *Defence and Security Affairs (President's Office);* Almerindo Manheje. *Foreign Affairs and Co-operation:* Dr Leonard S. Simão. *National Defence:* Aguiar J. R. Mazula. *Justice:* Jose I. Abudo. *Home Affairs:* Manuel J. A. Mucananda. *Planning and Finance:* Tomas A. Salomão. *Education:* Arnaldo V. Nhavoto. *Health:* Aurelio A. Zilhao. *Culture, Youth and Sports:* Mateus M. Kathupa. *Industry, Trade and Tourism:* Oldemiro J. Baloi. *Mineral Resources and Energy:* John W. Katchamila. *Labour:* Guilherme L. Mavila. *Environmental Action Co-ordinator:* Bernardo P. Ferraz. *Social Action Co-ordinator:* Alcinda A. De Abreu. *State Administration:* Alfredo M. S. C. Gamito. *Agriculture and Fisheries:* Carlos A. Rosario. *Public Construction and Housing:* Roberto C. White. *Transport and Communication:* Paulo Muxanga.

National flag: Horizontally green, black, yellow with the black fimbriated in white; a red triangle based on the hoist, charged with a yellow star surmounted by an open white book and a crossed rifle and hoe in black.
National anthem: 'Viva, viva a Frelimo' ('Long live Frelimo'); words and tune by J. Sigaulane Chemane.

Local Government. The capital of Maputo and 10 provinces, each under a Governor, are sub-divided into 112 districts.

DEFENCE. The President of the Republic is C.-in-C. of the armed forces. Following the end of the civil war the government and RENAMO agreed to merge their forces to form a new 30,000-strong National Army.

Army. Equipment includes about 80 T-54/-55 main battle tanks.

Navy. The small flotilla based principally at Maputo, with subsidiary bases at Beira, Nacala, Pemba and Inhambane comprises 3 ex-Soviet inshore patrol craft, 2 ex-Soviet inshore minesweepers and 2 landing craft, but none is believed operational. Some boats are based at Metangula on Lake Nyasa. Naval personnel in 1995 were believed to total 750.

Air Force. The Air Force was reported to have about 40 MiG-21 fighters and 5 An-26 turboprop transports. About 5 Mi-24 armed helicopters and 5 Mi-8 transport helicopters, a small number of Cherokee primary trainers and a few ex-Portuguese Air Force Alouette liaison helicopters are also in use. Personnel (1995) 4,000 (including air defence units), with 40 combat aircraft and 4 armed helicopters.

INTERNATIONAL RELATIONS

Membership. Mozambique is a member of UN, the Commonwealth, OAU, SADC and is an ACP state of the EU.

ECONOMY

Policy. In 1990 the government abandoned economic planning in favour of a market economy. In Dec. 1993 the National Reconstruction Plan was launched to repair the rural economic and social infrastructure. Its implementation is dependent upon foreign aid.

Budget. Government income and expenditure in 1992 (in 1,000m. meticais): Total revenue, 644·5 (including income tax, 98; indirect taxes, 249; trade taxes, 213; non-fiscal receipts, 61). Expenditure, 1,541 (of which capital expenditure, 705). Budget estimates for 1994: Domestic revenue, 1,100; current expenditure, 1,300; capital expenditure, 1,200.

Currency. The unit of currency is the *metical* (MZM) of 100 *centavos*. There are coins of 1, 2·5, 5, 10 and 20 and notes of 50, 100, 500, 1,000, 5,000 and 10,000 meticais. Inflation was 30% in 1993. In March 1996, £1 = 15,131·2 meticais; US$1 = 9,900 meticais; DM1 = 6,707·77 meticais.

Banking and Finance. Most banks had been nationalized by 1979. The central bank and bank of issue is the Bank of Mozambique, which hived off its commercial functions in 1992 to the newly-founded Commercial Bank of Mozambique. There is a state Development Bank.

Weights and Measures. The metric system is in force.

ENERGY AND NATURAL RESOURCES

Electricity. Production (1986) 1,640m. kWh. Capacity (1986) 2,225,000 kW.

Minerals. There are deposits of pegamite, tantalite, graphite, apatite, tin, iron ore and bauxite. Output (in 1,000 tonnes), 1991: Coking coal, 584; lignite, 167; charcoal, 572; salt, 3,839; marble, 118; gold, 5,773 kg.

Agriculture. Production in tonnes (1992): Cereals, 239,000; maize, 133,000; bananas, 80,000; rice, 33,000; groundnuts, 80,000; copra, 72,000; vegetables, 115,000; potatoes, 72,000; cashews, 40,000; sunflower seed, 20,000; cotton (lint), 13,000.

Livestock 1992: 1·25m. cattle, 385,000 goats, 118,000 sheep, 170,000 pigs, 20,000 asses.

Forestry. There are 19m. ha of productive woodland, including eucalyptus, pine and rare hardwoods. Production of logs (1991) 50,280 cu. metres of cut timber.

Fisheries. 1991 catch (in tonnes): Shrimps, 7,675; prawns, 2,351; fish, 14,996; lobster, 208.

INDUSTRY. Although the country is overwhelmingly rural, there is some substantial industry in and around Maputo (steel, engineering, textiles, processing, docks and railways).

Trade Unions. The main trade union confederation is the Organização dos Trabalhadores de Moçambique, but several unions have broken away.

FOREIGN ECONOMIC RELATIONS. Foreign debt was US$4,928m. in 1992.

Commerce. Imports in 1992 totalled US$890m. and exports US$139m. Principal exports, 1992 (in US$1m.): Shrimps, 65; cashew nuts, 18; cotton, 11; sugar, 7. Principal imports: Foodstuffs, 234; equipment, 201; crude oil and products, 96; spares, 84. Main export markets, 1991: Spain, 19·2%; USA, 13·2%; Japan, 12·1%; Portugal, 6%. Main import suppliers: USA, 12·4%; Italy, 7·5%; Zimbabwe, 7·1%; France, 5·2%.

Total trade between Mozambique and UK (British Department of Trade returns, in £1,000 sterling):

	1991	*1992*	*1993*	*1994*	*1995*
Imports to UK	2,393	2,593	1,568	2,903	1,922
Exports and re-exports from UK	18,351	17,008	21,717	35,489	13,274

COMMUNICATIONS

Roads. In 1994 there were 5,000 km of paved and 23,000 km of unpaved roads, but most were in bad condition or mined.

Railways. The Mozambique State Railways consist of 5 networks: The Maputo, Mozambique, Sofala (Beira), Inhambane and Gaza, and Quelimane systems. Total route-km (1994), 2,988 km (1,067 mm gauge), and 143 km (762 mm gauge). In 1994, 0·9m. passengers and 2·6m. tonnes of freight were carried.

Civil Aviation. There are international airports at Maputo, Beira and Nampula. The national carrier is the state-owned Linhas Aéreas de Moçambique (LAM), which in 1995 operated 1 B-767-200ER, 1 B-737-200, 1 B-737-200C Adv, 1 B-767-200ER and 6 other aircraft. Services are also provided by Air France, Air Zimbabwe, Metavia Airlines, Royal Swazi, SAA and TAP.

Shipping. The principal ports are Maputo, Beira, Nacala and Quelimane. In 1995 sea-going shipping totalled 26,080 GRT.

Telecommunications. Number of telephones (1983), 59,000. Radio Moçambique is part state-owned and part commercial. There are 3 national programmes in Tsonga and Portuguese and an external service in English. Television is at a trial stage (colour by PAL). In 1991 there were about 0·5m. radio and 35,000 TV receivers.

Cinemas. There were 60 in 1987.

Press. There are 2 daily newspapers.

SOCIAL INSTITUTIONS

Justice. The 1990 Constitution provides for an independent judiciary, habeas corpus, and an entitlement to legal advice on arrest. The death penalty was abolished in Nov. 1990.

Religion. About 40% of the population follow traditional animist religions. In 1992 there were 4·72m. Christians (mainly Roman Catholic) and 1·95m. Moslems.

Education. Adult literacy was 33·5% in 1992. In 1987 there were 1,370,528 pupils in 4,105 primary schools and (1986) 144,015 in 171 secondary schools. Private schools were permitted to function in 1990. Eduardo Mondlane University had 3,470 students and 390 academic staff in 1995–96.

Health. There were (1990) 10 hospitals, 226 health centres and 996 medical posts. There were 2 psychiatric hospitals. In 1987 there were 327 doctors, 1,112 midwives, 2,871 nursing personnel, 138 dentists and 301 pharmacists. Private health care was introduced alongside the national health service in 1992.

DIPLOMATIC REPRESENTATIVES

Of Mozambique in Great Britain (21 Fitzroy Sq., London W1P 5HJ)
Ambassador: Lieut.-Gen. Armando Alexandre Panguene.

Of Great Britain in Mozambique (Ave. Vladimir I. Lenine 310, Maputo)
Ambassador: R. J. Edis, CMG.

Of Mozambique in the USA (1990 M. St., NW, Washington, D.C., 20036)
Ambassador: Hipolito Patrício.

Of the USA in Mozambique (Ave Kaunda 193, Maputo)
Ambassador: Dennis C. Jett.

Of Mozambique to the United Nations
Ambassador: Pedro Comissario Afonso.

Further Reading

Andersson, H., *Mozambique: a War against the People.* London, 1993
Darch, C., *Mozambique.* [Bibliography] Oxford and Santa Barbara, 1987
Finnegan, W., *A Complicated War: the Harrowing of Mozambique.* California Univ. Press, 1992

NAMIBIA

Republic of Namibia

Capital: Windhoek
Population: 1·51m. (1992)
GNP per capita: US$2,030 (1994)
HDI/world rank: 0·611/108 (1992)

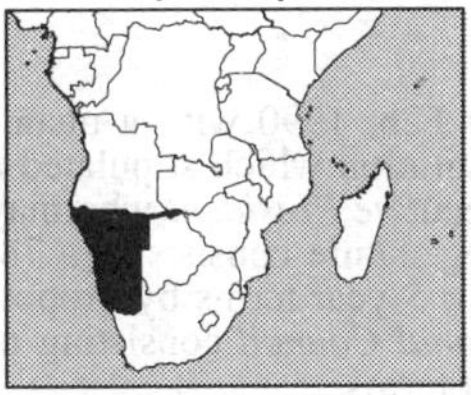

KEY HISTORICAL EVENTS. Independence was achieved on 21 March 1990. For events before independence *see* THE STATESMAN'S YEAR-BOOK, 1994–95, p. 977.

TERRITORY AND POPULATION. Namibia is bounded in the north by Angola and Zambia, west by the Atlantic Ocean, south and south-east by South Africa and east by Botswana. The Caprivi Strip (Liambezi Region), about 300 km long, extends eastwards up to the Zambezi river, projecting into Zambia and Botswana and touching Zimbabwe. The area, including the Caprivi Strip and Walvis Bay, is 824,268 sq. km. South Africa retained control of the enclave of Walvis Bay (1,124 sq. km.) until Aug. 1992, when it was agreed to place it under a joint transitional South African-Namibian administration. In Sept. 1993 South Africa agreed to transfer it to Namibian jurisdiction on 1 March 1994. Census population, 1991, 1,401,711 (720,784 females), an increase of 368,515 persons (35·7%) since the 1981 census. Population density, 1·7 per sq. km.; urban, 32·76%. Estimate, 1992, 1,511,600.

Population by ethnic group at the censuses of 1970 and 1981 and estimates for 1991:

	1970	*1981*	*1991*
Ovambos	342,455	506,114	665,000
Whites	90,658	76,430	85,000
Damaras	64,973	76,179	100,000
Hereros	55,670	76,296	100,000
Namas	32,853	48,541	64,000
Kavangos	49,577	95,055	124,000
Caprivians	25,009	38,594	50,000
Coloureds	28,275	42,254	...
Basters	16,474	25,181	...
Bushmen	21,909	29,443	...
Tswanas	4,407	6,706	...
Other	...	12,403	...
	732,260	1,033,196	1,401,711

Namibia is administratively divided into 13 regions. Area, estimated population and chief towns in 1992:

Region	*Area (in sq. km)*	*Population*	*Chief town*
Liambezi	19,532	92,000	Katima Mulilo
Okavango	43,417	136,000	Rundu
Otjozondjupa	105,327	85,000	Grootfontein
Oshikoto	26,607	176,000	Tsumeb
Omusati	13,637	158,000	Ongandjera
Oshana	5,290	159,000	Oshakati
Ohangwena	10,582	178,000	Oshikango
Kunene	144,254	58,500	Opuwo
Erongo	63,719	98,500	Omaruru
Khomas	36,804	161,000	Windhoek
Omaheke	84,731	55,600	Gobabis
Hardap	109,888	80,000	Mariental
Karas	161,324	73,000	Keetmanshoop

Towns with populations over 5,000 (1990): Windhoek, 125,000; Swakopmund, 15,500; Rehoboth, 15,000; Rundu, 15,000; Keetmanshoop, 14,000; Tsumeb, 13,500; Otjiwarongo, 11,000; Grootfontein, 9,000; Okahandja, 8,000; Mariental, 6,500; Gobabis, 6,500; Khorixas, 6,500; Lüderitz, 6,000.

For the 26 former administrative districts *see* THE STATESMAN'S YEAR-BOOK, 1993–94, p. 979.

English is the official language. Afrikaans and German are also spoken.

CLIMATE. The rainfall increases steadily from less than 50 mm. in the west and south-west up to 600 mm. in the Caprivi Strip. The main rainy season is from Jan. to March, with lesser showers from Sept. to Dec.

CONSTITUTION AND GOVERNMENT. On 9 Feb. 1990 with a unanimous vote the Constituent Assembly approved the Constitution which stipulated a multi-party republic, an independent judiciary and an executive *President* who may serve a maximum of two 5-year terms. The bicameral legislature consists of a 78-seat *National Assembly*, 72 members of which elected for 5-year terms by proportional representation and up to 6 appointed, and a *National Council* consisting of 2 members from each Regional Council elected for 6-year terms.

Presidential and parliamentary elections were held on 7-8 Dec. 1994. The electorate was 0·65m.; turn-out was 76%. Sam Nujoma was re-elected President by 76·3% of votes cast against 1 opponent. The South West Africa People's Organization (SWAPO) won 53 of the electable National Assembly seats; the Democratic Turnhalle Alliance, 15; the United Democratic Front, 2; others, 2.

President and Minister of Home Affairs: Sam Nujoma (b. 1928; SWAPO, elected Feb. 1990; re-elected Dec. 1994; sworn in 21 March 1995).

In Aug. 1995 the government comprised:

Prime Minister: Hage Geingob.

Deputy Prime Minister: Hendrik Witbooi. *Foreign Affairs:* Theo-Ben Gurirab. *Defence:* Phillemon Malima. *Finance:* Helmut Angula. *Tertiary Education and Vocational Training:* Nahas Angula. *Information and Broadcasting:* Ben Amathila. *Health and Social Services:* Dr Nicky Iyambo. *Labour and Manpower Development:* Moses Garoeb. *Mines and Energy:* Andimba Toivo Ya Toivo. *Justice:* Ngarikutuke Tjiriange. *Regional and Local Government and Housing:* Libertine Amathila. *Agriculture, Water and Rural Development:* Nangolo Mbumba. *Trade and Industry:* Hidipo Hamutenya. *Environment and Tourism:* Gert Hanekom. *Works, Transport and Communication:* Hampie Plichta. *Lands, Resettlement and Rehabilitation:* Richard Kapelwa-Kabajani. *Youth and Sport:* Pendukeni Iithana. *Fisheries and Marine Resources:* Hifikepunye Pohamba. *Prisons and Correctional Services:* Marco Hausiku. *Basic Education and Culture:* John Mutorwa.

National flag: Divided diagonally blue over green by a red white-edged stripe; in the canton a yellow sun of 12 rays.

National anthem: 'Namibia, land of the brave, freedom's fight we have won'; words and tune by Axali Doeseb.

Local Government. There are 13 elected regional and 93 local authority councils. Elections to regional councils and local authorities took place in Nov.–Dec. 1992. SWAPO gained 70 regional seats with 67·3% of votes cast; DTA, 20 with 27·1%.

A *Council of Traditional Chiefs* advises the President on the utilization and control of communal land.

DEFENCE

Army. The army consists of 1 Presidential Guard, 4 motorized infantry, 1 artillery, 1 air defence artillery and 1 anti-tank battalion. An Air Wing has 6 Cessa 337 patrol aircraft given by the USA in 1994, along with 4 Alouette helicopters from India. Personnel (1996), 8,000.

Coastguard. A force of 100 operates 3 offshore patrol craft based at Walvis Bay.

INTERNATIONAL RELATIONS

Membership. Namibia is a member of the UN, Commonwealth, SADC and OAU.

ECONOMY

Budget. The financial year runs from 1 April. In 1992-93 revenue was R2,821·4m. and expenditure, R3,544·7m. Tax revenue totalled R1,354m.; current expenditure was R2,831·5m.

Currency. The unit of currency is the *Namibia dollar* (NAD) of 100 *cents*, introduced on 14 Sept. 1993 at parity with the South African rand. There are coins of 1, 5, 10 and 50 cents and N$1 and 5, and notes of N$1, 2, 5, 10, 50, 100 and 200.

Banking and Finance. The Bank of Namibia is the central bank. Its *Governor* is Dr D. Carlsson. Commercial banks include First National Bank of Namibia, Namibia Banking Corporation, Standard Bank Namibia, Commercial Bank of Namibia and Bank Windhoek (the only locally-owned bank). There is an Agricultural Bank in Windhoek. Total assets of commercial banks were R2,383·2m. at 31 Dec. 1991.

There are 2 building societies with total assets (31 March 1990) R424.9m. A Post Office Savings Bank was established in 1916. In March 1991 its total assets were R21·8m. A stock exchange (NSE) is planned.

ENERGY AND NATURAL RESOURCES

Electricity. Installed capacity was 606,000 kW in 1990. In 1992 output was 1,714m. kWh.

Water. The 12 most important dams have a total capacity of 589·2m. cu. metres. Rainfall increases steadily from less than 50 mm. in the west and south-west up to 600 mm. in the Caprivi Strip.

The Kunene River and the Okavango, which form portions of the northern border of the country, the Zambezi, which forms the eastern boundary of the Caprivi Strip, the Kwando or Mashi, which flows through the Caprivi Strip from the north etween the Okavango and the Zambezi, and the Orange River in the south, are the only permanently running streams. But there is a system of great, sandy, dry river-beds throughout the country, in which water can generally be obtained by sinking shallow wells. In the Grootfontein area there are large supplies of underground water, but except for a few springs, mostly hot, there is no surface water in the country.

Minerals. 1991 output (in tonnes): Uranium oxide (1990), 2,849; copper, 31,928; lead, 33,367; zinc, 68,099; silver, 91,293 kg; tin, 17; gold, 1,851,150 grammes; diamonds, 1,186,870 carats.

Agriculture. Namibia is essentially a stock-raising country, the scarcity of water and poor rainfall rendering crop-farming, except in the northern and north-eastern parts, almost impossible. Generally speaking, the southern half is suited for the raising of small stock, while the central and northern parts are more suited for cattle. In 1989 there were 4,460 farms and 6,327 other agricultural enterprises raising stock on 34,887,659 ha. Guano is harvested from the coast, converted into fertilizer in South Africa and most of it exported to Europe. In 1991, 15% of the active labour force worked in the agricultural sector, while 70% of the population was directly or indirectly dependent on agriculture for their living.

Livestock (1991): 2·2m. cattle, 3·3m. sheep, 2m. goats.

In 1991, 13m. litres of milk and (in 1988) 70,000 tonnes of cheese were produced. Principal crops (1991 in tonnes): Wheat, 6,400; maize, 35,065; sunflower seed, 108; sorghum (1990), 8,000; vegetables (1990), 32,000.

Forestry. Forests cover 18m. ha (20% of the land area).

Fisheries. After independence a 200-mile exclusive economic zone was declared. The allowable hake catch for 1991 was set at 60,000 tonnes, 15% of this being open to foreign fleets. Total catch, 1991, 589,844 tonnes (hake, 53,164 tonnes, rock lobster and crab, 1,180 tonnes).

INDUSTRY. Of the estimated total of 400 undertakings, the most important branches are food production (accounting for 29·3% of total output), metals (12·7%) and wooden products (7%). The supply of specialized equipment to the mining industry, the assembly of goods from predominantly imported materials and the manufacture of metal products and construction material play an important part. Small industries, including home industries, textile mills, leather and steel goods, have expanded. Products manufactured locally include chocolates, beer, cement, leather shoes and delicatessen meats and game meat products.

Labour. In 1991 there were 0·75m. economically active persons. The estimated unemployment rate was 46·4%. The main employers were government services, agriculture and mining.

FOREIGN ECONOMIC RELATIONS

Commerce. Trade in 1991 (in R1m.): Imports, 3,410·6; exports, 3,236·2, including cattle (112·4), karakul pelts (15), small stock (104·9), unprocessed fish (324·2), diamonds (1,216·5), uranium (340·8), fish products (368) and meat products (189). The most important markets are UK, South Africa, Japan, Germany, France and USA.

Total trade between Namibia and UK (British Department of Trade returns, in £1,000 sterling):

	1991	*1992*	*1993*	*1994*	*1995*
Imports to UK	19,606	16,766	23,641	26,723	26,635
Exports and re-exports from UK	3,981	6,730	6,214	4,530	5,983

Tourism. In 1991 there were 318,028 visitors who spent R21,059,590.

COMMUNICATIONS

Roads. In 1991 the total national road network was 41,815 km, including 4,572 km of tarred roads. In 1991 there were 132,331 registered motor vehicles.

Railways. The Namibia system connects with the main system of the South African railways at Ariamsvlei. The total length of the line inside Namibia was 2,382 km of 1,065 mm gauge in 1991. In 1993-94 railways carried 91,000 passengers and 1·7m. tonnes of freight.

Civil Aviation. The national carrier is the state-owned Air Namibia, which in 1995 operated 1 B-737-200 Adv, 1 B-747SP and 3 other aircraft. In 1990–91 the 2 major airports, Windhoek (international) and Eros (domestic), handled about 215,175 passengers and 2·8m. kg of freight on international flights and 7,117 passengers and 211,218 kg of freight on internal flights. Windhoek is also served by Air Botswana, Air Zimbabwe, Commercial Airways, LTU, Lufthansa, SAA and TAAG.

Shipping. The main port is Walvis Bay. During 1991-92 820 ships called and 1m. tonnes of cargo were unloaded. There is a harbour at Lüderitz which handles mainly fishing vessels.

Telecommunications. Namibia Post and Telecom Namibia are the responsible corporations. In 1992 there were 72 post offices and 15 postal agencies which served 46,328 private box renters and 961 private bag services distributed by rail or road transport.

There were (1992) 89,722 telephones. There were 466 telex users.

The Namibian Broadcasting Corporation operates a national radio service from 3 stations and vernacular services. It also operates 10 TV stations (colour by PAL). In 1993 there were 27,000 TV sets in use.

Press (1993). There were 5 daily and 6 weekly newspapers.

SOCIAL INSTITUTIONS

Justice. There is a Supreme Court, a High Court and a number of magistrates' and lower courts. An Ombudsman is appointed. Judges are appointed by the president on the recommendation of the Judicial Service Commission.

Religion. About 90% of the population is Christian.

Education (1988). There were 1,153 schools for all races, 374,269 pupils and 12,525 teachers. This included 1,118 primary and senior secondary schools,

3 centres for the handicapped, 1 technical school and 2 agricultural schools, 3 technical institutes and 3 agricultural colleges. There were 4 teachers' training colleges and an academy. The University of Namibia had 2,240 students and 160 academic staff in 1994–95.

Health In 1992 there were 47 hospitals (4 private) and 238 clinics and health centres. There were 324 doctors, 51 dentists and 4,471 nursing staff.

DIPLOMATIC REPRESENTATIVES

Of Namibia in Great Britain (34 South Molton St., London W1Y 2BP)
High Commissioner: Veiccoh K. Nghiwete.

Of Great Britain in Namibia (116 Robert Mugabe Ave., 9000 Windhoek)
High Commissioner: Glyn Davis.

Of Namibia in the USA (1413 K St., NW, Washington DC 20005)
Ambassador: Tuliameni Kalomoh.

Of the USA in Namibia (14 Lossen St., Private Bag 12029, Windhoek)
Ambassador: Marshall F. McCallie.

Of Namibia to the United Nations
Ambassador: Dr Tunguru Huaraka.

Further Reading

Gupta, V., *Independent Namibia: Problems and Prospects.* Delhi, 1990
Herbstein, D. and Evenston, J., *The Devils are Among Us: the War for Namibia.* London, 1989
Katjavivi, P.H., *A History of Resistance in Namibia.* London, 1988
Schoeman, E. R. and H. S., *Namibia.* [Bibliography] Oxford and Santa Barbara (CA), 1984
Sparks, D.L. and Green, D., *Namibia: the Nation after Independence.* Boulder, (CO), 1992

National statistical office: Central Statistics Office, Windhoek.

NAURU

Republic of Nauru

Population: 8,100 (1990)
GNP per capita: US$9,091 (1985)

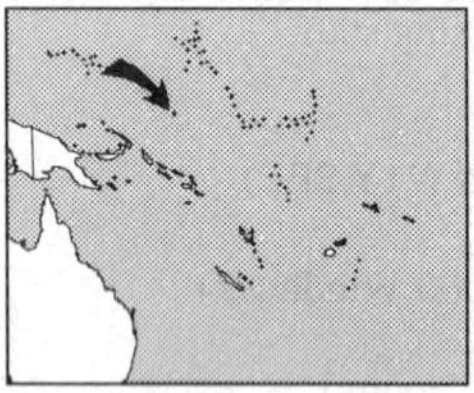

KEY HISTORICAL EVENTS. The island was discovered by Capt. Fearn in 1798, annexed by Germany in Oct. 1888, and surrendered to Australian forces in 1914. It was administered by the UK under a League of Nations mandate from 1920 until 1947, when the UN approved a trusteeship agreement with Australia, New Zealand and the UK as joint administering authorities. Independence was gained on 31 Jan. 1968.

TERRITORY AND POPULATION. Nauru is a coral island surrounded by a reef situated 0° 32' S. lat. and 166° 56' E. long. Area, 21·3 sq. km. At the 1983 census the population totalled 8,100, of whom 5,285 were Nauruans. Vital statistics rates, 1989: Births, 21 (per 1,000 population); deaths, 5; infant mortality, 41 (per 1,000 live births).

CLIMATE. A tropical climate, tempered by sea breezes, but with a high and irregular rainfall, averaging 82" (2,060 mm). Jan. 81°F (27·2°C), July 82°F (27·8°C). Annual rainfall 75" (1,862 mm).

CONSTITUTION AND GOVERNMENT. A Legislative Council was inaugurated on 31 Jan. 1966. An 18-member Parliament is elected on a 3-yearly basis.

The government in Nov. 1995 comprised:
President and Minister for External Affairs, Island Development and Industry, Civil Aviation and the Public Service: Bernard Dowiyogo (b. 1947).

Finance: Vinci Clodumar. *Internal Affairs, Works and Community Services:* Vinson Detenamo. *Education:* Nimes Ekwona. *Health:* Ludwig Scotti. *Justice:* Derog Gioura.

National flag: Blue with a narrow horizontal gold stripe across the centre, beneath this near the hoist a white star of 12 points.
National anthem: 'Nauru bwiema, ngabena ma auwe' ('Nauru our homeland, the country we love'); words by a collective, tune by L. H. Hicks.

INTERNATIONAL RELATIONS

Membership. Nauru is a member of the South Pacific Forum and has a special relation with the Commonwealth.

ECONOMY

Currency. The Australian dollar is in use.

ENERGY AND NATURAL RESOURCES

Minerals. A central plateau contained high-grade phosphate deposits. The interests in the phosphate deposits were purchased in 1919 from the Pacific Phosphate Company by the UK, Australia and New Zealand. In 1967 the British Phosphate Corporation agreed to hand over the phosphate industry to Nauru for approximately $A20m. over 3 years. Nauru took over the industry in July 1969. It is estimated that the deposits will be exhausted by 1995–97. In May 1989 Nauru filed a claim against Australia for environmental damage caused by the mining. In Aug. 1993 Australia agreed to pay compensation of $A73m. In March 1994 New Zealand and the UK each agreed to pay compensation of $A12m.

FOREIGN ECONOMIC RELATIONS

Commerce. The export trade consists almost entirely of phosphate shipped to Australia, New Zealand, the Philippines and Japan. The imports: food, building construction materials, machinery for the phosphate industry and medical supplies.

Total trade between Nauru and UK (British Department of Trade returns, in £1,000 sterling):

	1991	*1992*	*1993*	*1994*	*1995*
Imports to UK	718	1	35	nil	134
Exports from UK	1,189	904	185	837	1,195

COMMUNICATIONS

Civil Aviation. There is an airfield on the island capable of accepting medium size jet aircraft. Air Nauru, a wholly owned government subsidiary, in 1995 operated 2 B-737-400s to Melbourne, Sydney, Honiara, Guam, Tarawa, Port Vila, Suva, Nadi, Manila, Truk, Palau and Auckland.

Shipping. Deep offshore moorings can accommodate medium-size vessels. The Nauru Local Government Council, through its agency the Nauru Pacific Shipping Line, owns 3 ships and 1 fishing boat. These ships ply between Australia, the Pacific Islands, the USA, New Zealand, Japan and Singapore. Other shipping coming to the island consists of vessels under charter to the phosphate industry.

Telecommunications. There were 2,000 telephones in 1989. International telephone, telex and fax communications are maintained by satellite. A satellite earth station was commissioned in 1990. The government-controlled Nauru Broadcasting Service broadcasts a home service in Nauruan and English for 3 hours daily. There were 4,000 radio sets in use in 1993. New Zealand television programmes are received.

Cinemas. In 1989 there were 3 cinemas with seating capacity of 500.

SOCIAL INSTITUTIONS

Justice. The highest Court is the Supreme Court of Nauru. It is the Superior Court of record and has the jurisdiction to deal with constitutional matters in addition to its other jurisdiction. There is also a District Court which is presided over by the Resident Magistrate who is also the Chairman of the Family Court and the Registrar of Supreme Court. The laws applicable in Nauru are its own Acts of Parliament. A large number of British statutes and much common law has been adopted insofar as is compatible with Nauruan custom.

Religion. The population is mainly Roman Catholic or Protestant.

Education. Attendance at school is compulsory between the ages of 6 and 17. In 1989 there were 10 infant and primary schools and 2 secondary schools with a total of 165 teachers and 2,707 pupils. There is also a trade school with 4 instructors and an enrolment of 88 trainees. Scholarships are available for Nauruan children to receive secondary and higher education and vocational training in Australia and New Zealand.

DIPLOMATIC REPRESENTATIVES

Of Great Britain in Nauru
High Commissioner: Michael Peart, CMG (resides in Suva).

Of the USA in Nauru
Chargé d'affaires: Marilyn A. Meyers.

Further Reading

Macdonald, B., *Trusteeship and Independence in Nauru.* Wellington, 1988
Weeremantry, C., *Nauru: Environmental Damage under International Trusteeship.* OUP, 1992
Williams, M. and Macdonald, B., *The Phosphateers.* Melbourne Univ. Press, 1985

NEPAL

Nepal Adhirajya
(Kingdom of Nepal)

Capital: Kathmandu
Population: 19·36m. (1992)
GNP per capita: US$200 (1994)
HDI/world rank: 0·343/151 (1992)

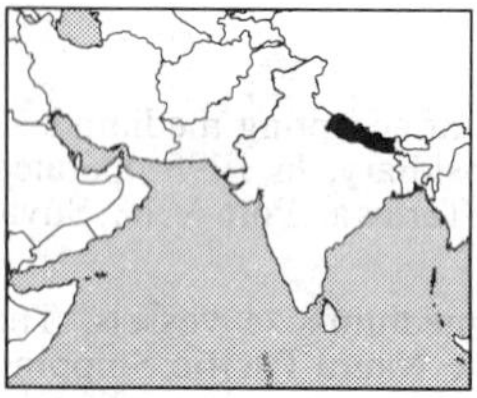

KEY HISTORICAL EVENTS. From 1846 to 1951 Nepal was virtually ruled by the Rana family, a member of which always held the office of prime minister. The 15 feudal chieftainships were integrated into the kingdom on 10 April 1961.

Following pro-democracy demonstrations, on 16 April 1990 King Birendra dismissed the government and proclaimed the abolition of the *panchayat* system of nominated councils. On 9 Nov. 1990 the King pro-claimed a constitution which relinquished his absolute powers.

TERRITORY AND POPULATION. Nepal is bounded in the north by China (Tibet) and the east, south and west by India. Area 147,181 sq. km; population (estimate, 1992), 19·36m.; (census, 1991) 18,462,081 (9,241,167 females; 9·6% urban). Density (1992), 125·4 per sq. km. Growth rate, 1991, 2·3%; infant mortality, 118 per 1,000 live births. Expectation of life was 51·5 years for males and 50·3 years for females in 1990.

The country is divided into 5 regions and subdivided into 14 zones. Area, population and administrative centres in 1990:

Zone/Region	*Sq. km*	*Population (in 1,000)*	*Administrative centre*
Mechi	8,196	1,268	Ilam
Koshi	9,669	1,885	Biratnagar (Morang)
Sagarmatha	10,591	1,597	Rajbiraj
East Region	28,456	4,750	Dhankuta
Janakpur	9,669	2,052	Jaleswar
Narayani	8,313	1,923	Birganj
Bagmati	9,428	2,093	Kathmandu
Central Region	27,410	6,068	Kathmandu
Gandaki	12,275	1,320	Pokhara
Lumbini	8,975	2,056	Butwal
Dhanlagiri	8,148	508	Baglung
West Region	29,398	3,884	Pokhara
Rapti	10,482	1,035	Tulsipur
Bheri	10,545	1,153	Nepalganj
Karuali	21,351	281	Jumla
Mid-West Region	42,378	2,469	Surkhet
Seti	12,550	724	Dhangarhi
Mahakali	6,989	1,022	Mahendra Nagar
Far West Region	19,539	1,746	Dipayal

Capital, Kathmandu; population (census 1991) 419,073. Other towns include Patan (Lalitpur), 117,203; Biratnagar (Morang), 130,129; Bhadgaon (Bhaktapur), 61,122.

The indigenous people are of Tibetan origin with a considerable Hindu admixture. The Gurkha clan became predominant in 1559 and has given its name to men from all parts of Nepal. There are 18 ethnic groups, the largest at the 1981 census being: Nepali, 58·4%; Maithili, 11·1%; Bhojpuri, 7·6%; Tamang, 3·5%. The official language is Nepalese.

CLIMATE. The rainfall is high, with maximum amounts from June to Sept., but conditions are very dry from Nov. to Jan. The range of temperature is moderate. Kathmandu. Jan. 50°F (10°C), July 76°F (24·4°C). Annual rainfall 57" (1,428 mm).

ROYAL HOUSE. The sovereign is HM Maharajadhiraja **Birendra Bir Bikram Shah Dev** (b. 1946), who succeeded his father Mahendra Bir Bikram Shah Dev on 31 Jan. 1972.

CONSTITUTION AND GOVERNMENT. Under the constitution of 9 Nov. 1990 Nepal became a constitutional monarchy based on multi-party democracy. *Parliament* has 2 chambers: a 205-member House of Representatives (*Pratinidhi Sabha*) elected for 5-year terms, and a 60-member House of Estates (*Rastriya Sabha*), of which 10 members are nominated by the king.

Elections were held on 15 Nov. 1994. The electorate was 12·3m.; turn-out was 58%. 24 parties stood. The Communist Party of Nepal-United Marxist-Leninist Party (CPN-UML) won 88 seats, the Nepali Congress, 75, and the National Democratic Party, 20. A Nepali Congress-Rastriya Prajatantra-Nepal Sadhavana coalition government was formed on 11 Sept. 1995, which in Feb. 1996 comprised:

Prime Minister: Sher Bahadur Deuba (b. 1946; Nepali Congress).

Minister of Labour: Bal Bahadur Rai. *Forest and Soil Conservation:* Shekh Idris. *Agriculture:* Padma Sundar Lawaiti. *Industry:* Dhundi Raj Shastri. *Information and Communications:* Chiranjibi Wagle. *Housing and Physical Planning:* Balaram Ghartimagar. *Home Affairs:* Khum Bahadur Khadka. *Education:* Govinda Raj Joshi. *Water:* Pashupati Rana. *Tourism and Civil Aviation:* Chakra Brasad Bastola. *Finance:* Ram Sharan Mahat. *Foreign Affairs:* Prakas Chandra Lohani. *Works and Transport:* Bijaya Gachhedar. *Health:* Arjun Narsingh. *Commerce:* Phatteh Sing Tharu. *Law and Justice:* Bhim Bahadur Tamang. *Local Development:* Kamal Thapa. *Supply:* Gajendra Narayan Singh. *Land Reform and Management:* Buddhi Ram Tamang. *Women and Social Welfare:* Lila Koirala. *Youth, Sport and Culture:* Bal Bahadur. *General Administration:* Bimalendra Nidhi. *Population and Environment:* Prakash Man Singh. *Parliamentary Affairs:* Narahari Acharya.

National flag: Two triangular parts of red, with a blue border all round, bearing symbols of the moon and the sun in white.

National anthem: 'Sri man gumbhira nepali prachanda pratapi bhupati' ('May glory crown our illustrious sovereign, the gallant Nepalese'); words by C. Chalise, tune by B. Budhapirthi.

Local Government. The country is administratively divided into 14 zones, subdivided into 75 districts and over 3,500 villages. Elections were held in May 1992. The Nepali Congress gained a majority of seats.

DEFENCE. The King is commander-in-chief of the armed forces, but shares supreme military authority with the National Defence Council, of which the Prime Minister is chairman.

Army. The Army consists of 1 Royal Guard brigade and 5 infantry and 1 support brigade. Strength (1996) 34,800, and there is also a 28,000-strong paramilitary police force.

Air Force. Independent of the army since 1979, the Air Force has 1 Twin Otter and 2 Skyvan transport aircraft, 1 Puma helicopter and 3 Chetak helicopters. An H.S. 748 turboprop transport and 1 Super Puma and 1 Puma helicopter are operated by the Royal Flight. There are no combat aircraft. Personnel, 1995, 200.

INTERNATIONAL RELATIONS

Membership. Nepal is a member of the UN and the Colombo Plan.

ECONOMY

Policy. The Eighth Plan is running from 1992 to 1997.

Budget. The budget for the fiscal year 1992–93 envisaged expenditure of NRs 33,595·2m. (35·7% current) and receipts of NRs 21,621·8m.

Currency. The unit of currency is the *Nepalese rupee* (NPR) of 100 *paisas.*

50 *paisas* = 1 *mohur*. There are coins of 1, 2, 5, 10, 25 and 50 paisas and 1 rupee, and notes of 1, 2, 5, 10, 20, 50, 100, 500 and 1,000 rupees. Currency in circulation, 1992, NRs 13,325m. Inflation was 30% in mid-1993. In 1993 foreign exchange reserves totalled US$496·3m. and gold reserves 153,000 troy oz. In March 1996, £1 = NRs 70·50; US$1 = NRs 57·25; DM1 = NRs 38·79.

Banking and Finance. The Central Bank is the bank of issue. There were 442 commercial bank branches in 1991 with total deposits of NRs 23,844·5m.

ENERGY AND NATURAL RESOURCES

Electricity. Installed capacity, 1991, was 293 mw, (of which 238 mw hydro-electric). Production, 1991, was 869m. kwh, almost entirely hydro-electric.

Minerals. Production (in tonnes), 1990: Lignite, 7,808; talcum, 1,798; magnesite, 25,000; limestone, 295,000.

Agriculture. In 1992 agriculture accounted for about 50% of GDP. Crop production (1993 in 1,000 tonnes): Rice, 3,100; maize, 1,200; wheat, 765; sugar-cane, 1,366; potatoes, 733; millet, 232.

Livestock (1993); Cattle, 6,237,000; buffaloes, 3,073,000; sheep, 911,000; goats, 5,452,000; pigs, 630,000; poultry, 7m.

Forestry. Forest area was 2·48m. ha. in 1992. There are 8 national parks, covering 1m. ha, 5 wildlife reserves (170,490 ha) and 2 conservation areas (349,000 ha). 18·22m. cu. metres of wood were cut in 1990, 17,657m. cu. metres for fuel.

Fisheries. 14,546 tonnes of fish were caught in 1990.

INDUSTRY. In 1990 there were 2,382 firms employing 10 or more persons in which 140,150 persons were working. Production, 1992: Cement, 214,800 tonnes; electrical cable, 18·3m. metres; soap, 18,600 tonnes; paper, 5,900 tonnes; leather, 958,000 sq. metres; shoes, 1·2m. pairs; jute goods, 17,300 tonnes; cotton fabrics, 8·2m. metres; synthetic textiles, 18·7m. metres; sugar, 52,000 tonnes; tea, 1,400 tonnes; beer, 17,240 litres; animal feed, 16,500 tonnes.

Labour. In 1992 the workforce (persons over 10 years old) was 8·66m., of whom 7·25m. worked in agriculture, forestry or fisheries, 0·69m. in services, 0·23m. in mining, 0·18m. in commerce, 0·18m. in communications and 0·1m. in building.

FOREIGN ECONOMIC RELATIONS. Foreign debt was US$1,705m. in 1991.

Commerce. Principal exports are food grains, jute, timber, oilseeds, ghee (clarified butter), potatoes, medicinal herbs, hides and skins, cattle.

Imports in 1991 were US$742m., exports, US$231m. Main import suppliers were (1992, in NRs 1m.): India, 7,772·4; Singapore, 3,372·1; Japan, 3,128·5; New Zealand, 1,215·3; China, 1,102·4. Main export markets: Germany, 2,728; India, 1,701·2; USA, 1,400·5; Switzerland, 497·1.

Total trade between Nepal and UK (British Department of Trade returns, in £1,000 sterling):

	1991	*1992*	*1993*	*1994*	*1995*
Imports to UK	4,531	5,888	6,440	6,877	4,562
Exports and re-exports from UK	4,938	6,300	11,920	9,419	7,618

Tourism. There were 293,000 tourists in 1991, bringing revenue of NRs 3,423m.

COMMUNICATIONS

Roads. In 1992 there were 7,615 km of roads, of which 3,072 km were macadamized. 368 persons were killed in road accidents in 1990.

Railways. Railways (762 mm gauge) connect Jayanagar on the North Eastern Indian Railway with Janakpur and thence with Bizalpura (54 km). 577,000 passengers and 8,200 tonnes of freight were carried in 1992.

Civil Aviation. There is an international airport (Tribhuvan) at Kathmandu. The national carrier is the state-owned Royal Nepal Airlines, which in 1995 operated 1 A310-300, 1 B-757-200, 1 B-757-200 Combi and 11 other aircraft. In 1991 672,000 passengers (357,000 on international flights) and 4·85m. tonnes of freight were flown. Services are also provided by Aeroflot, Biman Bangladesh, China Southwest Airlines, Druk-Air, Everest Air, Indian Airlines, Lufthansa, Necon Air, Pakistan Airlines, Singapore Airlines and Thai Airways.

Telecommunications. In 1991 there were 2,322 post offices. There were 67,100 telephones in 1992. Radio Nepal is part government-owned and part commercial. It broadcasts in Nepali and English from 3 stations. The government-owned Nepal Television Corporate transmits from 1 station (colour by PAL). In 1993 there were 0·6m. radio and 0·25m. TV sets.

Press. In 1991 there were 82 daily newspapers, including the official English-language *Rising Nepal*, 3 bi-weeklies, 454 weeklies and 48 fortnightlies. Press censorship was relaxed in June 1991.

SOCIAL INSTITUTIONS

Justice. The Supreme Court Act, established a uniform judicial system, culminating in a supreme court of a Chief Justice and no more than 6 judges. Special courts to deal with minor offences may be established at the discretion of the Government.

Religion. Nepal is a Hindu state. Hinduism was the religion of 89% of the people in 1992. Buddhists comprise 5% and Moslems 3%. Christian missions are permitted, but conversion is forbidden.

Education. In 1991, 25·6% of the population were literate. In 1990–91 there were 17,842 primary schools with 2,788,644 pupils (1,003,810 girls) and 71,213 teachers (26,775 trained); 3,964 lower secondary schools, with 344,138 pupils (103,282 girls) and 12,399 teachers (4,298 trained); and 1,953 secondary schools, with 364,525 pupils (102,006 girls) and 10,421 teachers (4,771 trained). The Tribhuvan University had 93,800 students and 4,300 academic staff in 1995–96. There is also a Sanskrit University.

Health. There were 1,182 doctors and 2,986 nurses in 1992. There were 111 hospitals with 4,341 beds, 18 health centres and 816 medical posts.

DIPLOMATIC REPRESENTATIVES

Of Nepal in Great Britain (12a Kensington Palace Gdns., London, W8 4QU)
Ambassador: Surya Prasad Shreshta.

Of Great Britain in Nepal (Lainchaur, Kathmandu, POB 106)
Ambassador: Lloyd Smith.

Of Nepal in the USA (2131 Leroy Pl., NW, Washington, D.C., 20008)
Ambassador: Basudev Prasad Dungana.

Of the USA in Nepal (Pani Pokhari, Kathmandu)
Ambassador: Sandra L. Vogelgesang.

Of Nepal to the United Nations
Ambassador: Narendra Bikram Shah.

Further Reading

Central Bureau of Statistics. *Statistical Pocket Book.* [Various years]

Borre, O. *et al.*, *Nepalese Political Behaviour.* Aarhus Univ. Press, 1994
Ghimire, K., *Forest or Farm?: The Politics of Poverty and Land Hunger in Nepal.* OUP, 1993
Pant, Y. P., *Trade and Co-operation in South Asia: a Nepalese Perspective.* Delhi, 1991
Sanwal, D. B. *Social and Political History of Nepal.* London, 1993
Whelpton, J., *Nepal.* [Bibliography]. Oxford and Santa Barbara (CA), 1990

National statistical office: Central Bureau of Statistics, National Planning Commission Secretariat, Kathmandu

THE NETHERLANDS

Koninkrijk der Nederlanden

(Kingdom of the Netherlands)

Capital: Amsterdam
Seat of Government: The Hague
Population: 15·42m. (1995)
GNP per capita: US$21,970 (1994)
HDI/world rank: 0·936/4 (1992)

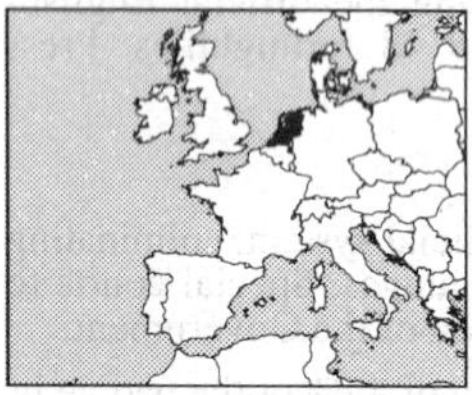

Source for statistics (*except* Climate, Defence *and* UK-Netherlands Trade): Netherlands Central Bureau of Statistics.

KEY HISTORICAL EVENTS. William of Orange (1533–84), as the German count of Nassau, inherited vast possessions in the Netherlands and the Princedom of Orange in France. He was the initiator of the struggle for independence from Spain (1568–1648); in the Republic of the United Netherlands he and his successors became the 'first servants of the Republic' with the title of 'Stadhouder' (governor). In 1689 William III acceded to the throne of England, becoming joint sovereign with Mary II, his wife. William III died in 1702 without issue, and after a stadhouderless period a member of the Frisian branch of Orange–Nassau was nominated hereditary stadhouder in 1747; but his successor, Willem V, had to take refuge in England, in 1795, at the invasion of the French Army. In Nov. 1813 the United Provinces were freed from French domination.

The son of the former stadhouder Willem V was proclaimed King of the Netherlands at The Hague on 16 March 1815 as Willem I. Belgium was united with the Netherlands from 1815 until 1839.

TERRITORY AND POPULATION. The Netherlands is bounded in the north and west by the North Sea, south by Belgium and east by Germany. The area is 41,447 sq. km, of which 33,811 sq. km is land. Projects of sea-flood control and land reclamation (polders) by the construction of dams and drainage schemes have continued since 1920.

The population was 13,060,115 at the census of 1971. On-going 'rolling' censuses have replaced the former decennial counts.

Area, density, estimated population and chief towns of the 12 provinces on 1 Jan. 1995:

	Area (in sq. km)	*Population*	*Density per sq. km*	*Chief Town*
Groningen	2,967·10	557,995	238	Groningen
Friesland	5,740·75	609,579	181	Leeuwarden
Drenthe	2,680·49	454,864	172	Assen
Overijssel	3,420·06	1,050,389	315	Zwolle
Flevoland	2,412·29	262,325	184	Lelijstad
Gelderland	5,143·36	1,864,732	373	Arnhem
Utrecht	1,434·24	1,063,460	784	Utrecht
Noord-Holland	4,059·09	2,463,611	926	Haarlem
Zuid-Holland [1]	3,445·75	3,325,064	1,163	The Hague
Zeeland	2,931·91	365,846	204	Middelburg
Noord-Brabant	5,016·11	2,276,207	467	's-Hertogenbosch
Limburg	2,195·98	1,130,050	525	Maastricht
Total	41,447·18	15,424,122 [2]	456	

[1] Since 29 Sept. 1994 includes inhabitants of the municipality of The Hague formerly registered in the abolished Central Population Register.
[2] 7,627,482 males; 7,796,640 females.

Vital statistics for calendar years:

	Live births Total	Outside marriage	Still births	Marriages	Divorces	Deaths	Net migration
1991	198,665	23,825	1,067	94,932	28,277	129,958	+62,921
1992	196,734	24,483	1,114	93,638	30,463	129,887	+58,092
1993	195,748	25,648	1,071	88,273	30,496	137,795	+59,932
1994	195,611	27,899	1,055	82,982	36,182	133,471	+37,156

Population of municipalities with over 50,000 inhabitants on 1 Jan. 1994:

Alkmaar	92,962	Gouda	69,917	Oosterhout	50,038
Almelo	64,589	Groningen	170,535	Oss	62,141
Almere	98,444	Haarlem	150,213	Purmerend	64,506
Alphen a/d Rijn	66,143	Haarlemmermeer	103,684	Roosendaal en Nispen	62,784
Amersfoort	110,117	The Hague	445,279	Rotterdam	598,521
Amstelveen	74,059	Heerlen	95,794	Schiedam	72,515
Amsterdam	724,096	Den Helder	61,024	Smallingerland	50,440
Apeldoorn	149,449	Helmond	72,293	Spijkenisse	70,464
Arnhem	133,670	Hengelo	77,514	Tilburg	163,383
Assen	52,268	's-Hertogenbosch	95,448	Utrecht	234,106
Breda	129,125	Hilversum	84,213	Veenendaal	53,045
Capelle a/d Ijssel	59,364	Hoorn	60,979	Velsen	63,617
Delft	91,941	Kerkrade	52,848	Venlo	65,367
Deventer	69,079	Leeuwarden	87,464	Vlaardingen	73,820
Dordrecht	113,394	Leiden	114,892	Zaanstad	132,508
Ede	98,220	Lelystad	60,784	Zeist	59,258
Eindhoven	196,130	Maastricht	118,102	Zoetermeer	103,420
Emmen	93,476	Middelburg	40,118	Zwolle	99,139
Enschede	147,624	Nieuwegein	58,340		
		Nijmegen	147,018		

Urban agglomerations as at 1 Jan. 1995: Amsterdam, 1,101,407; Rotterdam, 1,078,747; The Hague, 694,249[1]; Utrecht, 547,070; Eindhoven, 395,612; Arnhem, 314,159; Heerlen-Kerkrade, 270,952; Enschede-Hengelo, 254,480; Nijmegen, 249,490; Tilburg, 237,958; Dordrecht/Zwijndrecht, 213,963; Haarlem, 212,631; Groningen, 210,708; 's-Hertogenbosch, 199,127; Leiden, 194,935; Geleen-Sittard, 186,011; Breda, 166,616; Maastricht, 164,701; Zaanstreek, 147,917; Velsen-Beverwijk, 134,973; Hilversum, 102,023.

[1] Since 29 Sept. 1994 includes inhabitants of the municipality of The Hague formerly registered in the abolished Central Population Register.

CLIMATE. A cool temperate maritime climate, marked by mild winters and cool summers, but with occasional continental influences. Coastal temperatures vary from 37°F (3°C) in winter to 61°F (16°C) in summer, but inland the winters are slightly colder and the summers slightly warmer. Rainfall is least in the months Feb. to May, but inland there is a well-defined summer maximum in July and Aug.

The Hague. Jan. 37°F (2·7°C), July 61°F (16·3°C). Annual rainfall 32·8" (820 mm). Amsterdam. Jan. 36°F (2·3°C), July 62°F (16·5°C). Annual rainfall 34" (850 mm). Rotterdam. Jan. 36·5°F (2·6°C), July 62°F (16·6°C). Annual rainfall 32" (800 mm).

ROYAL HOUSE. The reigning Queen is **Beatrix Wilhelmina Armgard,** born 31 Jan. 1938, daughter of Queen Juliana and Prince Bernhard; married to Claus von Amsberg on 10 March 1966; succeeded to the crown on 1 May 1980, on the abdication of her mother. *Offspring:* Prince Willem-Alexander, born 27 April 1967; Prince Johan Friso, born 25 Sept. 1968; Prince Constantijn, born 11 Oct. 1969.

The Queen receives an allowance from the civil list. This was 6·3m. guilders in 1992; that of Prince Claus was 1·2m. guilders and that of Crown Prince Willem Alexander, 1·5m. guilders.

Mother of the Queen: Queen Juliana Louise Emma Marie Wilhelmina, born 30 April 1909, daughter of Queen Wilhelmina (born 31 Aug. 1880, died 28 Nov. 1962) and Prince Henry of Mecklenburg-Schwerin (born 19 April 1876, died 3 July 1934); married to Prince Bernhard Leopold Frederik Everhard Julius Coert Karel Godfried Pieter of Lippe-Biesterfeld (born 29 June 1911) on 7 Jan. 1937. Abdicated in favour of her daughter, the Reigning Queen, on 30 April 1980.

Sisters of the Queen: Princess Irene Emma Elisabeth, born 5 Aug. 1939, married to Prince Charles Hugues de Bourbon-Parma on 29 April 1964, divorced 1981 (*sons:* Prince Carlos Javier Bernardo, born 27 Jan. 1970; Prince Jaime Bernardo, born 13 Oct. 1972; *daughters:* Princess Margarita Maria Beatriz, born 13 Oct. 1972; Princess Maria Carolina Christina, born 23 June 1974); Princess Margriet Francisca, born in Ottawa, 19 Jan. 1943, married to Pieter van Vollenhoven on 10 Jan. 1967 (*sons:* Prince Maurits, born 17 April 1968; Prince Bernhard, born 25 Dec. 1969; Prince Pieter-Christiaan, born 22 March 1972; Prince Floris, born 10 April 1975); Princess Maria Christina, born 18 Feb. 1947, married to Jorge Guillermo on 28 June 1975 (*sons:* Bernardo, born 17 June 1977; Nicolas, born 6 July 1979; *daughter:* Juliana, born 8 Oct. 1981).

The royal succession is in the direct female or male line in order of birth.

CONSTITUTION AND GOVERNMENT. According to the Constitution (promulgated 1814; last revision, 1983), the Kingdom consists of the Netherlands, Aruba and the Netherlands Antilles. Their relations are regulated by the 'Statute' for the Kingdom, which came into force on 29 Dec. 1954. Each part enjoys full autonomy; they are united, on a footing of equality, for mutual assistance and the protection of their common interests.

The Netherlands is a constitutional and hereditary monarchy.

The central executive power of the State rests with the Crown, while the central legislative power is vested in the Crown and Parliament (the *States-General*), consisting of 2 Chambers. The upper *First Chamber* is composed of 75 members, elected by the members of the Provincial States (*see* LOCAL GOVERNMENT, *below*). The 150-member *Second Chamber* is directly elected by proportional representation for 4-year terms. Members of the States-General must be Netherlands subjects of 21 years of age or over.

The *Council of State*, appointed by the Crown, is composed of a vice-president and not more than 28 members. The monarch is president, but the day-to-day running of the Council is in the hands of the vice-president. The Council can be consulted on all legislative matters.

The Hague is the seat of the Court, Government and Parliament; Amsterdam is the capital.

Second Chamber (elected on 6 Sept. 1989): Christian Democratic Appeal (CDA), 54; Labour Party (PVDA), 49; People's Party for Freedom and Democracy, 22; Democrats '66, 12; Green Left, 6; Calvinist Party, 3; Reformed Political Federation, 1; Calvinist Political Union, 2; Centre Democrats, 1.

The Sovereign has the power to dissolve either Chambers, subject to the condition that new elections take place within 40 days, and the new Chamber be convoked within 3 months.

Both the Government and the Second Chamber may propose Bills; the First Chamber can only approve or reject them without inserting amendments. The meetings of both Chambers are public, though each of them may by a majority vote decide on a secret session. A Minister or Secretary of State cannot be a member of Parliament at the same time.

The Constitution can be revised only by a Bill declaring that there is reason for introducing such revision and containing the proposed alterations. The passing of this Bill is followed by a dissolution of both Chambers and a second confirmation by the new States-General by two-thirds of the votes. Unless it is expressly stated, all laws concern only the realm in Europe, and not the overseas part of the kingdom, Aruba and the Netherlands Antilles.

Party affiliation in the First Chamber as elected in 1991: Labour (PVDA), 16 seats; Christian Democrats (CDA), 27; Liberals (VVD), 12; Democrats '66 (D66), 12; Green Left, 4; Calvinists, 2; Reformed Political Federation, 1; Calvinist Political Union, 1.

Elections to the Second Chamber were held on 3 May 1994. Turn-out was 78·3%. PVDA won 37 seats with 24% of votes cast (49 seats in 1989); CDA, 34 with 22·2% (54); VVD, 31 with 19·9% (22); D66, 24 with 15·5% (12); Protestants (SGP), 7 with 4·8% (6); Third Age Party (AOV), 6 with 3·6% (nil); Green Left, 5 with 3·5% (6); CD (extreme right), 3 with 2·5% (1); SP (extreme left), 2 with 1·3% (nil); Union 55+, 1 with 0·9%.

A PVDA/VVD/D66 coalition government was sworn in on 22 Aug. 1994 and in Feb. 1996 comprised:

Prime Minister: Wim Kok (PVDA).

Deputy Prime Minister, Minister of the Interior: H. Dijkstal (VVD). *Deputy Prime Minister, Minister of Foreign Affairs:* H. A. F. van Mierlo (D66). *Minister of Agriculture, Management of Nature and Fisheries:* J. van Aartsen (VVD). *Development Co-operation:* J. Pronk (PVDA). *Defence:* J. Voorhoeve (VVD). *Economic Affairs:* G. J. Wijers (D66). *Education, Culture and Science:* Dr J. M. Ritzen (PVDA). *Finance:* G. Zahn (VVD). *Housing, Planning and Environment:* M. de Boer (PVDA). *Justice:* W. Sorgdrager (D66). *Social Affairs and Employment:* A. P. Melkert (PVDA). *Transport and Public Works:* A. Jorritsma-Lebbink (VVD). *Welfare, Health and Sport:* Dr E. Borst-Eilers (D66).

National flag: Three horizontal stripes of red, white, blue.

National anthem: Wilhelmus van Nassaue; words by Philip Marnix van St Aldegonde, tune anonymous.

European Parliament. The Netherlands has 31 representatives. At the June 1994 elections turn-out was 35·6%. The CDA won 10 seats with 30·8% of votes cast (group in European Parliament: Popular European Party); the PVDA, 8 with 22·9% (European Socialist Party); the VVD, 6 with 17·9% (Liberal, Democratic and Reformist Group); D66, 4 with 11·7% (Liberal Democratic and Reformist Group); SGP, 2 with 7·8%; Greens, 1 with 3·7% (Greens).

Local Government. The kingdom is divided into 12 provinces and 636 municipalities.

Each province has its own representative body, the Provincial States. The members must be 21 years of age or over; they are directly elected for 4 years. The electoral register is the same as for the Second Chamber. Membership varies according to the population of the province. The Provincial States are entitled to issue ordinances concerning the welfare of the province, and to raise taxes pursuant to legal provisions. The provincial budgets and the provincial ordinances and resolutions relating to provincial property, loans, taxes, etc., must be approved by the Crown. The members of the Provincial States elect the First Chamber of the States-General. They meet twice a year, as a rule in public. A permanent commission composed of 6 of their members, called the 'Deputy States', is charged with the executive power and, if required, with the enforcement of the law in the province. Deputy as well as Provincial States are presided over by a Commissioner of the Queen, appointed by the Crown, who in the former assembly has a deciding vote, but attends the latter in only a deliberative capacity. He is the chief magistrate in the province. Elections to the Provincial States were held in March 1995; turn-out was 50%. VVD gained 27·2% of all votes cast; PVDA, 17·1%; D66, 9·2%.

Each municipality is governed by a Municipal Council, directly elected by residents who are 18 years of age or over, for 4 years. All Netherlands inhabitants and non-Netherlands inhabitants who meet certain requirements aged 21 or over are eligible to stand, the number of members varying according to the population. The Municipal Council may issue bye-laws and levy taxes pursuant to legal provisions; these must be approved by the Crown. The Municipal Budget and resolutions to alienate municipal property require the approbation of the Deputy States of the province. The Council meets in public as often as may be necessary, and is presided over by a Burgomaster, appointed by the Crown. The day-to-day administration is carried out by the Burgomaster and Aldermen, elected by and from the Council; this body is also charged with the enforcement of the law. In maintaining public order, the Burgomaster acts as the chief of police. Municipal council elections were held on 2 March 1994. Turn-out was 64%.

DEFENCE. Conscription is for 9 months.

Army. The 1st Netherlands Army Corps is assigned to NATO. It consists of 10 brigades and Corps troops. The active part of the Corps comprises 2 armoured brigades and 4 armoured infantry brigades, grouped in two divisions and 40% of the Corps troops. The peacetime strength of the active brigades is 80% of the war-authorized strength.

The mobilizable part of the Corps comprises 1 armoured brigade, 2 armoured infantry brigades, 1 infantry brigade and the remaining Corps troops.

The mechanized brigades comprise tank battalions (Leopard I improved and Leopard 2), armoured infantry battalions (YPR-765), medium artillery battalions (155 mm self-propelled), armoured engineer units and armoured anti armour units. Equipment includes 298 Leopard 1A4 and 445 Leopard 2 main battle tanks. The Corps troops comprise headquarters units, combat-support units, including Engineer and Corps artillery and service-support units. 5 helicopter squadrons are also available. Personnel in 1996 numbered 43,200 (24,700 conscripts).

The National Territorial Command forces consist of territorial brigades, security forces, some logistical units and staffs. The major part of these units is mobilizable. Some units in the Netherlands may be assigned to the UN as peace-keeping forces. The army is responsible for the training of these units. In time of war, the civil defence operations will be closely co-ordinated with the local civilian authorities.

There is a paramilitary Royal Military Constabulary, 3,600 strong (500 conscripts).

Navy. The principal headquarters and main base of the Royal Netherlands Navy is at Den Helder, with minor bases at Vlissingen (Flushing), Curaçao (Netherlands Antilles) and Oranjestad (Aruba). Command and control in home waters is exercised jointly with the Belgian Navy (submarines excepted).

The modern and effective combatant fleet, all built in home shipyards, and largely equipped with indigenous sensors and imported weapons, comprises 4 diesel submarines of the new Zeeleeuw class, 4 guided-missile destroyers armed with US Standard SM1-MR surface-to-air missiles, 14 frigates each with 1 or 2 Lynx anti-submarine helicopters, 10 coastal minehunters and 2 coastal minesweepers. There is 1 multi-purpose support ship (carrying up to 3 helicopters), 3 survey ships, 2 training ships and 1 torpedo tender, as well as numerous service vessels.

The Marine corps has 12 small amphibious craft, but is integrated operationally with the UK Marines for its NATO tasks.

The Naval Air Service operates 13 Orion P-3C patrol aircraft and 22 Westland Lynx SH-14D helicopters for embarked service and for search and rescue, utility and transport.

In 1995 personnel totalled 14,300, including 1,000 in the Naval Air Service and 3,000 in the Royal Netherlands Marine Corps.

Air Force. The Royal Netherlands Air Force (RNLAF) was established 1 July 1913. Its strength (1994) was 9,000 personnel (3,300 conscripts) and it has a first-line combat force of 9 squadrons of aircraft and 2 groups of surface-to-air missiles in Germany. All squadrons are operated by Tactical Air Command. The only combat types are F-16A/B (7 squadrons for air defence, ground attack and tactical reconnaissance). 5 squadrons of Alouette III, Bölkow Bö 105C and CH-47 Chinook helicopters are under control of the Royal Netherlands Army, but flown and maintained by the RNLAF for use in the communications and observation roles. Also operated is 1 squadron of F.27 Friendship/Troopship and Hercules transport aircraft, and another (based in Curaçao) with F.27 maritime patrol aircraft. AB.412 search and rescue helicopters entered service in 1994.

Basic training is carried out on the PC-7 Turbo-Trainer; pilots then go to the USA for advanced training. The surface-to-air missile force consists of 4 squadrons of Patriot with 160 missiles and 11 squadrons with Hawks, of which 7 are for airfield defence.

INTERNATIONAL RELATIONS

Membership. The Netherlands is a member of the UN, EU, OECD, Council of Europe, WEU and NATO. The Schengen Accord of June 1990 abolished border controls between the Netherlands and Austria, Belgium, France, Germany, Greece,

Italy, Luxembourg, Portugal and Spain. It came into effect (except for Austria, Greece and Italy) on 26 March 1995.

ECONOMY

Budget. The revenue and expenditure of the central government (ordinary and extraordinary) were, in 1m. guilders, for calendar years:

	1988	*1989*	*1990*	*1991*	*1992*	*1993*	*1994*
Revenue	151,904	145,034	154,310	173,078	172,608	191,436	185,575
Expenditure	173,097	168,806	177,204	189,437	192,056	198,980	185,649

The national debt, in 1m. guilders, was on 31 Dec.:

	1990	*1991*	*1992*	*1993*	*1994*
Internal funded debt	312,110	334,984	356,135	365,575	360,252
Internal floating debt	5,558	3,551	1,872	5,634	14,393
Total	317,668	338,535	358,007	371,209	374,645

VAT is 17·5% (reduced rate, 6%).

Currency. The monetary unit is the *gulden* (NLG; written as fl[orin]; in English, 'guilder') of 100 *cents*. There are coins of 5, 10 and 25 cents and 1, 2·5 and 5 guilders, and notes of 10, 25, 50, 100, 250 and 1,000 guilders. It is tied to the German Deutschmark. In March 1996 the rate of exchange was US$1 = 1·65 guilders; £1 = 2·52 guilders; DM1 = 1·12 guilders.

Banking and Finance. The central bank and bank of issue is the Netherlands Bank (*Governor*, Willem Duisenberg), founded in 1814 and nationalized in 1948. Its Governor is appointed by the government for 7-year terms. The capital amounts to 75m. guilders.

There is a stock exchange in Amsterdam.

Weights and Measures. The metric system is in use.

ENERGY AND NATURAL RESOURCES

Electricity. Production of electrical energy in 1994, 79,486m. kWh (5% nuclear). 790 windmills were installed in 1994 to produce 238m. kWh.

Gas. Production of natural gas in 1994, 79,376m. cu. metres.

Minerals. The production of crude oil began in 1943. Output in 1994, 3,437,000 tonnes (2,762,000 tonnes in 1993).

There are saltmines at Hengelo and Delfzijl; production (in 1,000 tonnes), 1991, 3,417; 1992, 3,628.

Agriculture. The net area of all holdings was divided as follows (in ha):

	1991	*1992*	*1993*	*1994*	*1995*
Field crops	796,524	804,871	801,513	796,300	796,352
Grass	1,079,857	1,063,609	1,063,788	1,050,558	1,048,234
Market gardening	75,651	77,082	76,731	75,195	72,455
Land for flower bulbs	16,570	16,699	16,830	17,106	18,086
Flower cultivation	7,377	7,625	7,699	7,951	8,017
Nurseries	9,101	9,509	9,958	10,001	9,971
Fallow land	5,882	6,227	11,232	14,421	11,340
Total	1,990,962	1,985,622	1,987,751	1,971,532	1,964,455

The net areas under special crops were as follows (in ha):

Products	*1993*	*1994*	*Products*	*1994*	*1995*
Autumn wheat	99,819	98,559	Colza	1,424	1,493
Spring wheat	18,214	23,028	Flax	4,651	4,407
Rye	7,432	5,603	Agricultural seeds	19,755	21,893
Autumn barley	4,398	2,502	Potatoes, edible [1]	110,872	117,956
Spring barley	35,657	41,169	Potatoes, industrial [2]	60,154	61,345
Oats	5,153	5,518	Sugar-beet	114,509	116,081
Peas	3,174	2,285	Fodder-beet	2,066	1,576

[1] Including early and seed pototoes. [2] Including seed potatoes.

The yield of the more important products, in tonnes, was as follows:

Crop	*1991*	*1992*	*1993*	*1994*	*1995*
Wheat	944,146	1,016,791	1,034,887	981,003	1,166,672
Rye	33,515	34,395	41,166	26,517	42,485
Barley	237,921	204,024	252,227	227,593	202,543
Oats	17,949	18,738	30,497	27,931	15,473
Field beans	9,595	8,442	7,004	3,322	2,325
Peas	31,843	22,194	13,925	9,371	4,575
Colza	20,995	13,801	7,342	4,203	4,529
Flax, unrippled	35,488	20,135	25,781	32,621	34,410
Potatoes, edible	4,842,889	5,260,645	5,062,874	4,661,903	4,811,306
Potatoes, industrial	2,106,312	2,380,380	2,635,664	2,426,513	2,529,110
Sugar-beet	7,189,203	8,251,186	7,478,571	6,149,351	6,449,412
Fodder-beet	238,799	246,209	209,252	178,159	132,144

Livestock, May 1995: 4,654,195 cattle, 14,397,463 pigs; 100,004 horses and ponies; 1,674,175 sheep, 89,561,116 poultry.

In 1994 the production of butter, under state control, declined to 128,687 tonnes; that of cheese, under state control, increased to 648,285 tonnes. Export value in 1994 (processed and unprocessed) of arable crops: 26,176m. guilders; animal produce, 20,111m. guilders and horticultural produce, 18,349m. guilders.

Fisheries. Catch in 1993: Marine, 485,258 tonnes; inland, 1,636 tonnes.

INDUSTRY. Numbers employed (in 1,000) and turnover (in 1m. guilders):

Class in industry	*Numbers employed* 1993 [1]	1994 [2]	*Turnover* 1993 [1]	1994 [2]
Mining and quarrying	9·9	9·5	. . .	. . .
Manufacturing except construction	960·0	930·8	256·7	263·0
Food, beverages and tobacco	152·1	147·4	74·9	74·6
Textiles	23·3	21·9	4·6	4·6
Clothing	10·6	10·0	1·2	1·2
Leather and footwear	4·2	3·4	0·6	0·6
Wood and wood products	18·3	18·1	2·2	2·5
Paper and paper products	24·9	24·4	7·4	8·2
Publishing and printing	82·0	80·2	16·0	16·4
Oil products	8·4	7·9	19·9	14·0
Chemicals and chemical products	87·0	83·9	37·6	43·4
Rubber and plastic products	34·5	33·3	7·5	8·6
Other non-metallic mineral products	33·5	33·2	7·4	8·5
Basic metals	28·2	27·1	7·7	9·3
Metal products (excl. machinery and equipment)	89·5	86·0	14·8	15·8
Machinery and equipment	82·8	80·8	15·4	16·0
Electrical machinery and equipment	28·0	26·3	19·4	19·7
Transport equipment	31·0	29·0	15·7	15·1
Furniture and other manufacturing	31·3	30·7	4·4	4·5
Public utilities	44·2	43·4	. . .	. . .

[1] Enterprises with 10 or more employees. [2] Enterprises with 20 or more employees.

Labour. On 1 Jan. 1995 there was a legal minimum wage of 2,163 guilders a month. Retirement age is 65 years. In Jan. 1991 job exchanges were moved from government control to joint control by employers, trade unions and local authorities.

There were 492,000 registered unemployed (i.e. persons working fewer than 12 hours per week) at the end of 1994, with 42,800 job vacancies at 30 Sept. 1994.

Trade Unions. Trade unions are grouped in 4 central federations. Total membership was 1,754,800 in 1995. In Nov. 1993 an agreement on wage restraint was concluded between the trade unions and the employers' federations, in return for an enhancement of the roles of works committees and professional training for employees.

FOREIGN ECONOMIC RELATIONS. On 5 Sept. 1944 and 14 March

1947 the Netherlands signed agreements with Belgium and Luxembourg for the establishment of a customs union. On 1 Jan. 1948 this union came into force and the existing customs tariffs of the Belgium–Luxembourg Economic Union and of the Netherlands were superseded by the joint Benelux Customs Union Tariff. It applied to imports into the 3 countries from outside sources, and exempted from customs duties all imports into each of the 3 countries from the other two.

Commerce. Imports and exports for calendar years (in 1,000 guilders):

	Imports	*Exports*		*Imports*	*Exports*
1969	39,955,406	36,205,110	1991	237,117,335	249,051,373
1979	134,885,386	127,689,416	1992	236,597,426	246,540,411
1989	221,411,909	229,409,169	1993	231,642,856	258,342,471
1990	229,706,687	239,180,621	1994	256,438,901	287,452,055

Value of trade with major partners (in 1m. guilders):

	Imports		*Exports*	
Country	*1993*	*1994*	*1993*	*1994*
Belgium–Luxembourg	27,340	30,687	33,107	38,067
France	17,746	19,438	27,327	30,851
Germany	54,661	59,758	75,391	82,881
Italy	8,710	9,506	14,433	15,988
Japan	8,792	9,148	2,482	2,943
Spain	4,158	4,653	6,221	7,535
Sweden	4,584	5,723	3,960	4,433
Switzerland	3,047	3,402	4,337	4,805
UK	21,614	24,525	24,076	28,738
USA	18,609	19,975	10,464	11,348

The main imports in 1994 (in 1m. guilders) included petroleum and products (19,639), electric machines and apparatus (20,023), cars and other vehicles (17,482), cast iron, iron and steel (10,491), plastics and products (9,908), organic chemical products (9,553), optical, measurement and precision instruments (7,893), paper and paperboard (6,734) and clothing and accessories of knit- and crochet-work (5,384). Main exports included petroleum and products (20,573), electric machines and apparatus (21,110), plastics and products (16,140), organic chemical products (14,167), optical, measurement and precision instruments (11,047), dairy products and eggs (7,942), meat and edible offal (8,722), cars and other vehicles (10,138) and plant-derived products (7,979).

Total trade between the Netherlands and UK (British Department of Trade returns, in £1,000 sterling):

	1990	*1991*	*1992*	*1993*	*1994*
Imports to UK	10,483,576	9,969,981	9,908,795	8,236,000	9,471
Exports and re-exports from UK	7,516,576	8,258,475	8,484,040	7,594,000	9,057

Tourism. There were 4·2m. foreign visitors in 1994 to hotels: 0·9m. from Germany, 0·8m. from the UK and 0·5m. from the USA. Total income from tourism, US$5,370m.

Source: Netherlands Central Bureau of Statistics.

COMMUNICATIONS

Roads. In 1992 the length of the Netherlands network of surfaced inter-urban roads was 56,030 km, of which 2,118 km were motor highways. Number of private cars (1995), 5·6m.

Railways. All railways are run by the mixed company 'N.V. Nederlandse Spoorwegen'. Route length in 1994 was 2,757 km, of which 1,991 km were electrified. Passengers carried (1994), 312m.; goods transported, 17·9m. tonnes. There is a metro (23 km) and tram/light rail network (153 km) in Amsterdam and in Rotterdam (28 km and 141 km). Tram/light rail networks operate in The Hague (122 km) and Utrecht (28 km).

Civil Aviation. There are international airports at Amsterdam (Schiphol), Rotterdam, Maastricht and Eindhoven. The Royal Dutch Airlines (KLM) was founded on 7 Oct. 1919 and had a fleet of 66 aircraft in 1994. Revenue traffic, 1994–95: Passengers, 11·9m.; freight and mail, 541m. kg. Services are also provided by 83 foreign airlines.

Sea-going Shipping. Survey of the Netherlands mercantile marine as at 1 Jan. (capacity in 1,000 GRT):

	1994		*1995*	
Ships under Netherlands flag	*Number*	*Capacity*	*Number*	*Capacity*
Passenger ships [1]	6	136	7	148
Freighters (100 GRT and over)	309	1,865	320	2,093
Tankers	52	647	58	662
	367	2,648	385	2,903

[1] With accommodation for 13 or more cabin passengers.

In 1994, 43,335 sea-going ships of 458m. gross tons entered Netherlands ports.

Total goods traffic by sea-going ships in 1994 (with 1993 figures in brackets), in 1m. tonnes, amounted to 287 (277) unloaded, of which 129 (130) tankshipping, and 88 (88) loaded, of which 24 (24) tankshipping; total seaborne freight traffic at Rotterdam was 293 (279) and at Amsterdam 29 (30).

The number of containers (including flats) at Rotterdam in 1994 (with 1993 figures in brackets) was: Unloaded from ships, 1·47m. (1,335,000) and 1,451,000 (1,402,000) loaded into ships.

Inland Shipping. The total length of navigable rivers and canals is 5,052 km, of which 2,398 km is for ships with a capacity of 1,000 and more tonnes. On 1 Jan. 1994 the inland fleet used for transport (with carrying capacity in 1,000 tonnes) was composed as follows:

	Number	*Capacity*
Self-propelled barges	4,665	4,168
Dumb barges	386	272
Pushed barges	741	1,610
	5,792	6,050

In 1993, 263m. tonnes of goods were transported on rivers and canals, of which 173m. was international traffic. Goods transport on the Rhine across the Dutch-German frontier near Lobith amounted to 114m. tonnes.

Telecommunications. On 1 Jan. 1993 there were 6·9m. telephone connexions (46 per 100 inhabitants). Number of telex lines, 22,000. *Nederlandse Omroepprogramma Stichting* (NOS) provides 5 programmes on medium-waves and FM in co-operation with broadcasting organizations. Regional programmes are also broadcast.

Advertisements are transmitted. NOS broadcasts 3 TV programmes (colour by PAL). Television sets (1 Jan. 1993) totalled 5·6m.; holders of television licences may, in addition, have radio sets. There were about 12m. radio sets in 1991.

Cinemas (1994). There were 467 cinemas with a seating capacity of 95,000.

Press (1994). There were 64 daily newspapers with a total circulation of 4·6m.

SOCIAL INSTITUTIONS

Justice. Justice is administered by the High Court (Court of Cassation), by 5 courts of justice (Courts of Appeal), by 19 district courts and by 63 cantonal courts. The Cantonal Court, which deals with minor offences, comprises a single judge; more serious cases are tried by the district courts, comprising as a rule 3 judges (in some cases one judge is sufficient); the courts of appeal are constituted of 3 and the High Court of 5 judges. All judges are appointed for life by the Sovereign (the judges of the High Court from a list prepared by the Second Chamber of the States-General). They can be removed only by a decision of the High Court.

At the district court the juvenile judge is specially appointed to try children's civil cases and at the same time charged with administration of justice for criminal actions committed by young persons between 12 and 18 years old, unless imprisonment of more than 6 months ought to be inflicted; such cases are tried by 3 judges.

Number of sentences, and cases in which prosecution was evaded by paying a fine to the public prosecutor (excluding violation of economic and tax laws):

Major offences		*Minor offences* [1]	
1992	112,815	1990	814,675
1993	132,432	1991	837,900
1994	136,943	1992	582,799
		1993	351,484
		1994	248,568

[1] Excluding an estimated 2m. minor traffic violations.

Police. In 1994 the police force was divided into 25 regions. About 29,600 police officers serve 636 municipalities. There is also a National Police Service (with about 1,600 officers), which includes the Central Criminal Investigation Office, which deals with serious crimes throughout the country, and the International Criminal Investigation Office, which informs foreign countries of international crimes.

Religion. Entire liberty of conscience is granted to the members of all denominations. The royal family belong to the Dutch Reformed Church.

According to survey estimates of 1994, the distribution of the population aged 18 years and over was: Roman Catholics, 30%; Dutch Reformed Church, 13%; Reformed Churches, 7%; other creeds, 8%; no religion, 42%.

The government of the Reformed Church is Presbyterian. On 1 July 1992 the Dutch Reformed Church had 1 synod, 9 provincial districts, 75 classes, about 160 districts and about 2,000 parishes. Their clergy numbered 1,735. The Roman Catholic Church had, Jan. 1992, 1 archbishop (of Utrecht), 6 bishops, 4 assistant bishops and about 1,750 parishes and rectorships. The Old Catholics had (1 July 1992) 1 archbishop (Utrecht), 1 bishop and 28 parishes. The Jews had, in 1992, 40 communities.

Education. Statistics for the scholastic year 1994–95:

	Full-time			Part-time		
	Schools	*Pupils/Students Total*	*Pupils/Students Female*	*Schools*	*Students Total*	*Students Female*
Basic schools	7,860	1,451,055	717,517	—	—	—
Special schools	994	116,462	37,567	—	—	—
Secondary general schools	851	666,018	347,178	—	—	—
Secondary vocational schools: [1]						
Pre—						
Combined years	383	69,828	28,165	—	—	—
Technical, nautical	326	61,260	4,170	—	—	—
Agricultural	66	21,750	9,325	—	—	—
Administration	247	11,997	7,435	—	—	—
Sales and Commerce	237	11,589	5,781	—	—	—
Home economics–health care	346	25,152	23,035	—	—	—
Other	330	8,769	7,743	—	—	—
Senior—						
Technical, nautical	82	88,053	12,859	—	—	—
Agricultural	20	16,849	5,182	—	—	—
Economics	81	97,484	48,279	—	—	—
Service trade and health care training	95	74,949	65,218	—	—	—
Other	118	12,443	7,054	—	—	—
Third level non-university training:						
Technical, nautical	24	51,860	7,633	12	3,960	350
Agricultural	8	9,161	2,757	4	332	62
Arts	20	16,272	8,957	14	2,918	1,451
Teachers' training	42	38,912	26,801	23	14,730	8,587
Economics	34	65,644	28,573	21	8,559	3,154
Health care	28	18,444	14,869	18	4,726	3,606
Other	25	27,333	21,108	22	9,015	5,892

[1] Concerning educational facilities.

Academic Year 1994–95

	Schools	Full-time Students Total	Full-time Students Female	Part-time Students Total	Part-time Students Female
University education:					
Agriculture	20	5,253	2,226	30	8
Science		13,449	4,375	278	52
Engineering		26,346	4,138	65	5
Health		17,424	10,201	643	409
Economics		27,995	7,074	657	131
Law		24,716	12,569	3,490	1,586
Behaviour and Society		30,625	19,426	4,113	2,679
Language and Culture		27,139	17,993	2,244	1,241
Education		681	370	67	23

Health. On 1 Jan. 1993 there were 39,069 doctors and (1994) 1,181 midwives; on 1 Jan. 1995 there were 60,623 licensed hospital beds (excluding mental hospitals). There were 2,484 pharmacists in 1995.

Welfare. Under the Disablement Insurance Acts (AAW) some 0·9m. persons received 17,000m. guilders in 1992, when benefits were paid up to 70% of former salary until the retirement age of 65. In 1991 the period of eligibility was capped according to the number of years beneficiaries had been in employment. 50,400m. guilders were paid in sickness benefit and 32,400m. guilders in age pensions in 1992.

Source: Netherlands Central Bureau of Statistics.

Cox, R. H., *The Development of the Dutch Welfare State: from Workers' Insurance to Universal Entitlement.* Pittsburgh Univ. Press, 1994

DIPLOMATIC REPRESENTATIVES

Of the Netherlands in Great Britain (38 Hyde Park Gate, London, SW7 5DP)
Ambassador: Jan. H. van Roijen.

Of Great Britain in the Netherlands (Lange Voorhout, 10, The Hague)
Ambassador: Sir David Miers, KBE, CMG.

Of the Netherlands in the USA (4200 Linnean Ave., NW, Washington, D.C., 20008)
Ambassador: Adriaan de Szeged.

Of the USA in the Netherlands (Lange Voorhout, 102, The Hague)
Ambassador: K. Terry Dornbush.

Of the Netherlands to the United Nations
Ambassador: Dr Nicolaas H. Biegman.

Further Reading

Centraal Bureau voor de Statistiek. *Statistical Yearbook of the Netherlands.* From 1923/24.—*Statistisch Jaarboek.* From 1899/1924.—*CBS Select (Statistical Essays).* From 1980.—*Statistisch Bulletin.* From 1945; weekly.—*Maandschrift.* From 1944; monthly bulletin.—*90 Jaren Statistiek in Tijdreeksen* (historical series of the Netherlands 1899–1989)

Nationale Rekeningen (National Accounts). From 1948–50.—*Statistische onderzoekingen.* From 1977.—*Regionaal Statistisch Zakboek* (Regional Pocket Yearbook). From 1972.—*Environmental Statistics of the Netherlands*, 1987

Staatsalmanak voor het Koninkrijk der Nederlanden. Annual. The Hague, from 1814

Staatsblad van het Koninkrijk der Nederlanden. The Hague, from 1814

Staatscourant (State Gazette). The Hague, from 1813

Anderweg, R. B. and Irwin, G. A., *Dutch Government and Politics.* London, 1993

Gladdish, K., *Governing from the Centre: Politics and Policy-Making in the Netherlands.* London, 1991

King, P. K. and Wintle, M., *The Netherlands.* [Bibliography] Oxford and Santa Barbara, 1988

Another more specialized title is listed under WELFARE, *above.*

National library: De Koninklijke Bibliotheek, Prinz Willem Alexanderhof 5, The Hague.

National statistical office: Centraal Bureau voor de Statistiek, Netherlands Central Bureau of Statistics, POB 959, 2270 AZ Voorburg.

ARUBA

KEY HISTORICAL EVENTS. Discovered by Alonzo de Ojeda in 1499, the island of Aruba was claimed for Spain but not settled. It was acquired by the Dutch in 1634, but apart from garrisons was left to the indigenous Caiquetios (Arawak) Indians until the 19th century. From 1828 it formed part of the Dutch West Indies and, from 1845, part of the Netherlands Antilles, with which on 29 Dec. 1954 it achieved internal self-government.

Following a referendum in March 1977, the Dutch government announced on 28 Oct. 1981 that Aruba would proceed to independence separately from the other islands. Aruba was constitutionally separated from the Netherlands Antilles from 1 Jan. 1986, and full independence had been promised by the Netherlands after a 10-year period. However, an agreement with the Netherlands government in June 1990 deletes, at Aruba's request, references to eventual independence.

TERRITORY AND POPULATION. The island, which lies in the southern Caribbean 29 km north of the Venezuelan coast and 68 km west of Curaçao, has an area of 193 sq. km (75 sq. miles) and a population at the 1991 census of 68,897; density, 369 per sq. km. The chief towns are Oranjestad, the capital (20,046 at 1991 census) and Sint Nicolaas. Dutch is the official language, but the language usually spoken is Papiamento, a creole language. Over half the population is of Indian stock, with the balance of Dutch, Spanish and mestizo origin.

CLIMATE. Aruba has a tropical marine climate, with a brief rainy season from Oct. to Dec. Oranjestad. Jan. 79°F (26·0°C), July 84°F (29·0°C). Annual rainfall 17" (432 mm).

CONSTITUTION AND GOVERNMENT. Under the separate constitution inaugurated on 1 Jan. 1986, Aruba is an autonomous part of the Kingdom of the Netherlands with its own legislature, government, judiciary, civil service and police force. The Netherlands is represented by a Governor appointed by the monarch (in 1995, O. Koolman). The unicameral legislature *(Staten)* consists of 21 members.

Elections were held on 29 July 1994. The electorate was some 46,000; turn-out was 85%. The Arubaanse Volkspartij (AVP) won 10 seats, the Movimento Electoral di Pueblo, 9, and the Organizacion Liberal Arubianco (OLA), 2.

An AVP-OLA coalition government was formed on 8 Aug. 1994:

Prime Minister: Hendrik Eman (AVP).

Economy: R. R. Croes. *Education and Labour:* P. E. Croes. *Finance:* A. W. Engelbrecht. *Health, Social Affairs, Culture and Sport:* L. G. Beck Martínez. *Justice and Public Works:* E. J. Vos. *Representative in the Netherlands:* A. G. Croes. *Transport and Communications:* G. F. Croes.

Flag: Blue, with 2 narrow horizontal yellow stripes, and in the canton a red 4-pointed star fimbriated in white.

ECONOMY

Budget. The 1991 budget totalled 495m. florins tax revenue.

Currency. Since 1 Jan. 1986 the currency has been the Aruban florin, at par with the Netherlands Antilles guilder. There are notes of 5, 10, 25, 50 and 100 florins. There were 76·2m. Aruban florins in circulation in 1992. Inflation was 6·9% in 1994. Foreign exchange reserves in 1992 were US$142m.; gold reserves, US$25. In March 1996, £1 = 2·74; US$1 = 1·79; DM1 = 1·21 Aruban florins.

Banking and Finance. There were 5 domestic and Dutch banks, and 1 foreign bank in 1995. There is a special tax regime for offshore banks.

ENERGY AND NATURAL RESOURCES

Electricity. Generating capacity totalled 114 MW in 1995. Production (1986) 945m. kWh.

Water. There is a desalination plant with an annual capacity of 22,000 tonnes.

INDUSTRY. The government has established 6 industrial sites at Oranjestad harbour. An oil refinery closed in 1985 was re-opened in 1991 with a capacity of 0·15m. bbls. a day.

EXTERNAL ECONOMIC RELATIONS. There are 2 free zones at Oranjestad.

Commerce. Total trade between Aruba and UK (British Department of Trade returns, in £1,000 sterling):

	1991	*1992*	*1993*	*1994*	*1995*
Imports to UK	6,365	4,495	80	5,417	3,605
Exports and re-exports from UK	18,934	27,292	41,930	47,748	58,816

Tourism. In 1994 there were 582,136 staying tourists and (1993) 251,000 cruise-ship visitors. Tourist revenue was 798m. Aruban florins in 1992.

COMMUNICATIONS

Roads. In 1984 there were 380 km of surfaced highways. In 1991 there were 26,710 passenger cars and 3,704 commercial vehicles.

Civil Aviation. There is an international airport (Queen Beatrix). Air Aruba operated 1 B-767-200, 2 B-737-300s and 1 other aircraft in 1992. Services are also provided by Aerorepublica, Air France, Alitalia, ALM, Aserca, Avenza, Avianca, British Airways, BWIA, Continental Airlines and Air Micronesia, KLM, SAM, SAS, Servivensa, TAP, United Airlines, VASP and VIASA.

Shipping. Oranjestad has a container terminal and cruise ship port. The port at Barcadera services the offshore and energy sector and a deep-water port at San Nicolas services the oil refinery.

Telecommunications. In 1996 there were 25,000 telephones. In 1995 there were 9 radio stations and 1 commercial television station (colour by NTSC). In 1993 there were 40,000 radio and 19,000 TV sets.

Press. In 1995 there were 1 Dutch-language (circulation 3,500), 1 English (circulation 5,000), 4 Papiamento dailies and 5 other newspapers.

SOCIAL INSTITUTIONS

Justice. There is a Common Court of Justice with the Netherlands Antilles. Final Appeal is to the Supreme Court in the Netherlands.

Religion. In 1990, 89% of the population were Roman Catholic and 7% Protestant.

Education. In 1991 there were 30 elementary schools with 7,191 pupils, 10 junior high schools with 3,094 pupils and 16 schools and colleges for vocational education with 2,520 students.

Health. In 1991 there were 74 doctors, 19 dentists, 11 pharmacists, 515 nursing personnel and one hospital with 263 beds.

Further Reading

Schoenhals, K., *Netherlands Antilles and Aruba.* [Bibliography] Oxford and Santa Barbara, 1993

THE NETHERLANDS ANTILLES

De Nederlandse Antillen

KEY HISTORICAL EVENTS. Bonaire and Curaçao islands, originally populated by Arawak Indians, were discovered in 1499 by Alonso de Ojeda, and claimed for Spain. They were settled in 1527, and the indigenous population exterminated and replaced by a slave-worked plantation economy. The 3 Windward

Islands, inhabited by Caribs, were discovered by Columbus in 1493. They were taken by the Dutch in 1632 (Saba and Sint Eustatius), 1634 (Curaçao and Bonaire) and 1648 (the southern part of Sint Maarten, with France acquiring the northern part). With Aruba, the islands formed part of the Dutch West Indies from 1828, and the Netherlands Antilles from 1845, with internal self-government being granted on 29 Dec. 1954. Aruba was separated from 1 Jan. 1986. At a referendum in Nov. 1993 Curaçao voted to remain part of the Netherlands Antilles.

TERRITORY AND POPULATION. The Netherlands Antilles comprise two groups of islands, the Leeward group (Curaçao and Bonaire) being situated 100 km north of the Venezuelan coast and the Windward group (Saba, Sint Eustatius and the southern portion of Sint Maarten) situated 800 km away to the north-east, at the northern end of the Lesser Antilles. The total area is 800 sq. km (308 sq. miles) and the census population in 1992 was 189,474. Estimate (1994) 202,244. Willemstad is the capital.

The areas, populations and chief towns of the islands are:

Island	*Sq. km*	*1992 Census*	*1994 Estimate*	*Chief town*
Bonaire	288	10,187	12,533	Kralendijk
Curaçao	444	144,097	149,376	Willemstad
Saba	13	1,130	1,197	The Bottom
Sint Eustatius	21	1,839	1,882	Oranjestad
Sint Maarten [1]	34	32,221	37,256	Philipsburg

[1] The northern portion (St Martin) belongs to France.

Dutch is the official language, but the languages usually spoken are Papiamento (derived from Dutch, Spanish and Portuguese) on Curaçao and Bonaire, and English in the Windward Islands.

Vital statistics (1994), Live births, 3,929; marriages, 1,269; divorces, 543; deaths, 1,340.

CLIMATE. All the islands have a tropical marine climate, with very little difference in temperatures over the year. There is a short rainy season from Oct. to Jan. Willemstad. Feb. 27·7°C, Aug. 29°C. Annual rainfall 499 mm.

CONSTITUTION AND GOVERNMENT. On 29 Dec. 1954, the Netherlands Antilles became an integral part of the Kingdom of the Netherlands but are fully autonomous in internal affairs, and constitutionally equal with the Netherlands and Aruba. The Sovereign of the Kingdom of the Netherlands is Head of State and Government, and is represented by a Governor.

The executive power in internal affairs rests with the Governor and the Council of Ministers, who together form the Government. The Ministers are responsible to a unicameral legislature *(States)* consisting of 27 members (13 from Curaçao, 3 from Bonaire, 3 from Sint Maarten, and 1 each from Saba and Sint Eustatius) elected by universal suffrage. In general elections held for the States on 25 Feb. 1994, in Curaçao 8 seats were won by the *Partido Antia Restrukturá* (PAR), 3 by the *Nationale Volkspartij* (NVP) and 2 by the *Movemiento Anti Nobo* (MAN); in Bonaire 2 by the *Partido Demokrátiko Boneriano* (PDB) and 1 by the *Union Patriótiko Boneriano* (UPB); in Sint Maarten 2 by the *Sint Maarten Patriotic Alliance* (SPA) and 1 by the *Democratic Party of Sint Maarten* (DP of Sint Maarten); in Saba 1 by the *Windward Island People's Movement* (WIPM); and in Sint Eustatius 1 by the *Democratic Party of Sint Eustatius*.

The executive power in external affairs is vested in the Council of Ministers of the Kingdom, in which the Antilles is represented by a Minister Plenipotentiary with full voting powers. On each of the insular communities, local autonomous power is divided between an Island Council (elected by universal suffrage), the Executive Council and the Lieut.-Governor, responsible for law and order.

At a referendum in Curaçao on 19 Nov. 1993, 73% of votes cast favoured maintaining the status quo of Curaçao as part of the Netherlands Antilles. The other options were: Autonomy (18%), unification with the Netherlands (8%) or complete independence (1%). At a referendum in Oct. 1994 Sint Maarten, Sint Eustatius and Saba voted to remain part of the Netherlands Antilles.

Governor: Dr Jaime M. Saleh.

The Cabinet installed in March 1994 was composed as follows in Feb. 1996:
Prime Minister: Miguel A. Pourier (PAR).

Deputy Prime Minister and Traffic and Transport: Leo A. I. Chance (SPA). *Justice:* Pedro J. Atacho (PAR). *Finance:* Harold Henriquez (PAR). *Labour and Social Affairs:* Jeffrey A. Corion. *Co-operation for Development, Women's and Humanitarian Affairs:* Edith Strauss-Mercera (PDB). *Public Health and Environmental Affairs:* Stanley H. Inderson (MAN). *Education, Sport, Culture and Youth Affairs:* Marta B. Dijkhoff (PAR).

Flag: White, with a red vertical strip crossed by a blue horizontal strip bearing 5 white stars.

ECONOMY

Budget. The central budget for 1991 envisaged 498·3m. NA guilders revenue and 536·1m. NA guilders expenditure.

Currency. The unit of currency is the *Netherlands Antilles guilder* (ANG) of 100 *cents.* There are notes of 500, 250, 100, 50, 25, 10 and 5 guilder, and coins of 2½ and 1 guilder and 50, 25, 10, 5 and 1 cent. The official rate of exchange was £1 = 2·74 NA guilders, DM1 = 1·21 NA guilders in March 1996. The NA guilder has been pegged to the US dollar at US$1 = 1·79 NA guilder since 12 Dec. 1971.

Banking and Finance. At 31 Dec. 1992 the Bank of the Netherlands Antilles had total assets and liabilities of 542·4m. NA guilders; commercial banks, 3,535m. NA guilders.

Post office savings banks had deposits of 21·2m. NA guilders in 1992.

ENERGY AND NATURAL RESOURCES

Electricity. Production (1993) totalled 907m. kWh.

Oil. The economy was formerly based largely on oil refining at the Shell refinery on Curaçao, but following an announcement by Shell that closure was imminent, this was sold to the Netherlands Antilles government in Sept. 1985, and leased to Petróleos de Venezuela to operate on a reduced scale.

Minerals. Calcium carbonate (limestone) has been mined since 1980; production (1991), 0·32m. tonnes. Production of limestone, 1990 (estimate), 0·36m. tonnes.

Agriculture. Livestock (1992 estimate): Cattle, 1,000; goats, 13,000; pigs, 3,000. (Curaçao, 1991 estimate: Cows, 290; goats, 46,000; pigs, 6,100; sheep, 10,500).

Fisheries. Catch (1991 estimate) 7,700 tonnes.

INDUSTRY AND TRADE

Industry. Curaçao has an oil refinery and a large ship-repair dry docks. Bonaire has a textile factory and a modern equipped salt plant. Sint Maarten's industrial activities are primarily based on a rum factory and a fishing factory.

Labour. In 1992 (census) the economically active population numbered 87,756 (Curaçao, 1991: 57,354).

Commerce. There is a Free Zone on Curaçao. Total imports (1992) amounted to 3,344m. (crude and petroleum products, 1,966m.) NA guilders, total exports to 2,790m. (crude and petroleum products, 2,545m.) NA guilders.

Total trade between the Netherlands Antilles and UK (British Department of Trade returns, in £1,000 sterling):

	1991	*1992*	*1993*	*1994*	*1995*
Imports to UK	29,049	7,261	28,871	28,633	14,378
Exports and re-exports from UK	18,954	19,920	17,024	17,831	18,615

Tourism. In 1993, 752,532 tourists visited the islands (Sint Maarten, 483,324; Curaçao, 214,082; Bonaire, 55,126) and there were 857,337 cruise passengers (Curaçao, 180,011; Sint Maarten, 659,943; Bonaire, 17,383).

COMMUNICATIONS

Roads. In 1989, the Netherlands Antilles had 845 km of surfaced highway distributed as follows: Curaçao, 590; Bonaire, 226; Sint Maarten, 19. Number of motor vehicles registered in 1994, 166,392.

Civil Aviation. There are international airports on Curaçao (Curaçao International Airport), Bonaire (Flamingo Airport) and Sint Maarten (Princess Juliana Airport). In 1994 Curaçao handled 1,193,091 passengers, Bonaire 296,239, Sint Maarten 3,277,208, Sint Eustatius 56,350 and Saba 45,457. The local carrier, ALM, had 6 aircraft in 1995.

Shipping (1994). 4,740 ships (totalling 30,817,000 GRT) entered the port of Curaçao; 1,006 ships (14,975,000 GRT) entered the port of Bonaire; 1,333 ships (27,094,000 GRT) entered the port of Sint Maarten. In 1994 Curaçao handled 162,335 passengers, Bonaire 12,736 and Sint Maarten 718,550.

Telecommunications. Number of telephones, 1994, 70,899. In 1994 there were 28 radio transmitters (7 on Bonaire, 15 on Curaçao, 2 on Saba and 4 on Sint Maarten) and each island had 1 cable television station. These stations broadcast in Papiamento, Dutch, English and Spanish and are mainly financed by income from advertisements. Broadcasting is administered by Landsradio, Telecommunication Administration and Tele Curaçao. In 1992 there were estimated to be 125,000 radio and 52,592 TV sets (colour by NTSC) in use. In addition, Radio Nederland and Trans World Radio have powerful relay stations operating on medium- and short-waves from Bonaire.

Press. In 1995 there were 9 daily and 2 weekly newspapers.

SOCIAL INSTITUTIONS

Justice. There is a Court of First Instance, which sits in each island, and a Court of Appeal in Willemstad.

Religion. In 1992, 73% of the population were Roman Catholics, 10% were Protestants (Sint Maarten and Sint Eustatius being primarily Protestant).

Education. In 1993 there were 22,735 pupils in primary schools, 1,643 pupils in special schools, 8,801 pupils in general secondary schools, 5,817 pupils in junior and senior secondary vocational schools, and 734 students in vocational colleges and universities.

Health. In 1994 there were 289 doctors, 66 dentists, 12 hospitals with 1,448 beds and 1,225 nursing personnel.

DIPLOMATIC REPRESENTATIVE

US Consul-General: Bernard J. Woerz (St Anna Blvd. 19, POB 158, Curaçao).

Further Reading

Central Bureau of Statistics. *Statistical Yearbook of the Netherlands Antilles*
Bank of the Netherlands Antilles. *Annual Report.*
Schoenhals, K., *Netherlands Antilles and Aruba.* [Bibliography] Oxford and Santa Barbara, 1993

NEW ZEALAND

Capital: Wellington
Population: 3·58m. (1995)
GNP per capita: US$13,190 (1994)
HDI/world rank: 0·919/17 (1992)

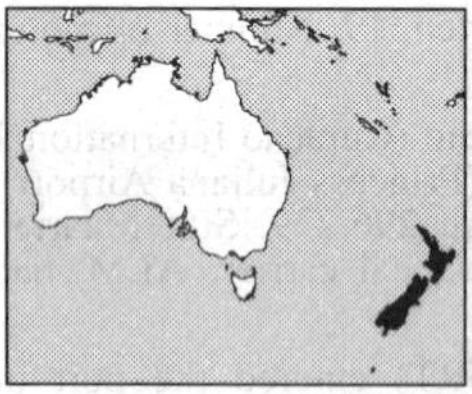

KEY HISTORICAL EVENTS. Polynesian Maoris immigrated from the eastern Pacific before and during the 14th century. The first European to discover New Zealand was Tasman in 1642. The coast was explored by Capt. Cook in 1769. From about 1800 onwards, New Zealand became a resort for whalers and traders, chiefly from Australia. By the Treaty of Waitangi in 1840 the Maori chiefs ceded sovereignty to the British Crown and the islands became a British colony. Then followed a steady stream of British settlers.

Between 1845 and 1848, and between 1860 and 1870, misunderstandings over land led to war, but peace was permanently established in 1871.

TERRITORY AND POPULATION. New Zealand lies south-east of Australia in the south Pacific, Wellington being 1,983 km from Sydney. There are two principal islands, the North and South Islands, besides Stewart Island, Chatham Islands and small outlying islands, as well as the territories overseas.

New Zealand (*i.e.*, North, South and Stewart Islands) extends over 1,750 km from north to south. Area, excluding territories overseas, 270,534 sq. km comprising North Island, 115,777 sq. km; South Island, 151,215 sq. km; Stewart Island, 1,746 sq. km; Chatham Islands, 963 sq. km. The minor islands (total area, 320 sq. miles, 829 sq. km) included within the geographical boundaries of New Zealand (but not within any local government area) are the following: Kermadec Islands (34 sq. km), Three Kings Islands (8 sq. km), Auckland Islands (606 sq. km), Campbell Island (114 sq. km), Antipodes Islands (62 sq. km), Bounty Islands (1 sq. km), Snares Islands (3 sq. km), Solander Island (1 sq. km). With the exception of meteorological station staff on Raoul Island in the Kermadec Group and Campbell Island there are no inhabitants.

The **Kermadec Islands** were annexed to New Zealand in 1887, have no separate administration and all New Zealand laws apply to them. Situation, 29° 10' to 31° 30' S. lat., 177° 45' to 179° W. long., 1,000 miles NNE of New Zealand. The largest of the group is Raoul or Sunday Island, 29 sq. km, smaller islands being Macaulay and Curtis, while Macaulay Island is 3 miles in circuit.

Growth in census population, exclusive of territories overseas:

	Total population	*Average annual increase %*		*Total population*	*Average annual increase %*
1858	115,462	—	1926	1,408,139	2·06
1874	344,984	—	1936	1,573,810	1·13
1878	458,007	7·33	1945[1]	1,702,298	0·83
1881	534,030	5·10	1951[1]	1,939,472	2·37
1886	620,451	3·05	1956[1]	2,174,062	2·31
1891	668,632	1·50	1961[1]	2,414,984	2·12
1896	743,207	2·13	1966[1]	2,676,919	2·10
1901[1]	815,853	1·89	1971[1]	2,862,631	1·34
1906	936,304	2·75	1976[1]	3,129,383	1·71
1911	1,058,308	2·52	1981[1]	3,175,737	0·20
1916[1]	1,149,225	1·50	1986[1]	3,307,084	0·82
1921	1,271,644	2·27	1991[1]	3,434,950	0·77

The census of New Zealand is quinquennial, but the census falling in 1931 was abandoned as an act of national economy, and owing to war conditions the census due in 1941 was not taken until 25 Sept. 1945.

[1] Excluding members of the Armed Forces overseas.

The populations of regional councils (all data conforms with boundaries redrawn after the 1989 re-organization of local government) at the 1991 censuses and as estimated on 31 March 1994 [1]:

Local Government Region	*Total Population* 1991 census	*Total Population* 1994 estimate	*Estimated change 1993-94 (%)*
Northland	131,620	135,400	1·0
Auckland	953,980	1,002,700	2·1
Waikata	338,959	348,200	1·0
Bay of Plenty	208,163	217,700	1·8
Gisborne	44,387	44,400	–
Hawke's Bay	139,479	141,000	0·6
Taranaki	107,222	107,900	0·4
Manuwatu-Wanganui	226,616	232,500	0·8
Wellington	402,892	410,000	0·7
Remainder North Island [1]	95	100	–
Total North Island	2,553,413	2,639,900	1·4
Tasman	34,416	38,000	1·9
Nelson	38,003	40,300	2·3
Marlborough	36,765	38,300	1·6
West Coast	33,961	33,800	0·3
Canterbury	446,114	458,800	1·6
Otago	186,067	189,100	1·2
Southland	103,442	102,600	–
Remainder South Island [2]	769	800	–
Total South Island	881,537	901,700	1·3
Total New Zealand	3,434,950	3,541,600	1·4

[1] Includes Kermadec Islands and oil rigs.
[2] Includes Chatham Islands County and Campbell Island.

New Zealand-born residents made up 84·2% of the population at the 1991 census. Foreign-born (provisional): UK and Ireland, 239,157; Australia, 48,738; Netherlands, 24,276; Samoa, 43,332; Cook Islands, 15,411; others (including USA), 155,201.

Estimated population on 31 Mar. 1995, 3,592,400 (1,822,800 females).

Maori population: 1896, 42,113; 1936, 82,326; 1945, 98,744; 1951, 115,676; 1961, 171,553; 1971, 227,414; 1981, 279,255; 1986, 294,201; 1991, 324,000. There were estimated to be some 50,000 fully-competent speakers of the Maori language in 1992. Population increase, 1991, 1·68%.

From the 1970s organisations were formed to pursue Maori grievances over loss of land and resources. The Waitangi Tribunal was set up in 1975 as a forum for complaints about breaches of the Treaty of Waitangi, and in 1984 empowered to hear claims against Crown actions since 1840. Direct negotiations with the Crown have been offered to claimants and a range of proposals to resolve historical grievances launched for public discussion in Dec. 1994. These proposals specify that all claims are to be met over 10 years with treaty rights being converted to economic assets. Recipient organizations and administration of the resources have still to be agreed.

Populations of main urban areas as at 31 March 1994 were as follows:

Auckland	929,300	Nelson	50,200
Christchurch	318,100	New Plymouth	49,500
Dunedin	112,400	Rotorua	54,700
Hamilton	153,800	Tauranga	76,100
Hastings and Napier	111,700	Timaru	27,000
		Wanganui	42,000
Palmerston North	75,200	Wellington	329,000
Gisborne	31,700	Whangarei	44,800
Invercargill	51,700		

Vital statistics for calendar years:

	Total live births	Single-parent births	Deaths	Marriages	Divorces (decrees absolute)
1992	59,266	21,759	27,249	22,018	9,114
1993	58,867	22,355	27,248	22,056	...
1994	57,435	22,180	27,092	21,858	...

Birth rate, 1994, 16·29 per 1,000; death rate, 7·68 per 1,000; marriage rate, 18·77 per 1,000; infant mortality, 7·09 per 1,000 live births. Population increase 1994, 1·5%. Expectation of life, 1992: Males, 73 years; females, 79.

In 1995 there were 67,591 immigrants (57,257 in 1994) and 45,894 emigrants (41,670 in 1994).

CLIMATE. Lying in the cool temperate zone, New Zealand enjoys very mild winters for its latitude owing to its oceanic situation, and only the extreme south has cold winters. The situation of the mountain chain produces much sharper climatic contrasts between east and west than in a north-south direction. Observations for mid-summer and mid-winter daily averages in 1990:

	Jan (°C)	July (°C)	Annual rainfall (mm) in 1993
Auckland	23·4	7·8	775
Christchurch	21·7	1·5	603
Dunedin	19·1	3·1	670
Hokitika	19·3	2·8	–
New Plymouth	21·5	5·4	–
Wellington	20·1	5·6	1,164

CONSTITUTION AND GOVERNMENT. Definition was given to the status of New Zealand by the (Imperial) Statute of Westminster of Dec. 1931, which had received the antecedent approval of the New Zealand Parliament in July 1931. The Governor-General's assent was given to the Statute of Westminster Adoption Bill on 25 Nov. 1947.

The powers, duties and responsibilities of the Governor-General and the Executive Council are set out in Royal Letters Patent and Instructions thereunder of 11 May 1917. In the execution of the powers vested in him the Governor-General must be guided by the advice of the Executive Council.

Parliament is the *House of Representatives*, since 1993 consisting of 99 members, including 4 members representing Maori electorates, elected by universal adult suffrage for 3-year terms. The 4 Maori electoral districts cover the whole country and adult Maoris of half or more Maori descent are the electors. From 1976 a descendant of a Maori is entitled to register either for a general or a Maori electoral district. In 1994 there were 136,708 persons on the Maori electoral roll.

A referendum in Oct. 1990 favoured the retention of the 3-year parliamentary term. At a referendum in Sept. 1992 on the electoral method preferred, turn-out was 55·2%. 84·7% of votes cast were in favour of changing the current first-past-the-post system, 70·3% opting for the mixed-member-proportional system (MMP).

At the elections on 6 Nov. 1993 the electorate was 2,321,664; turn-out was 83·31%. The National Party gained 50 seats with 35·05% of votes cast (48·84% in 1990), the Labour Party 45 with 34·68% (35·14%), the Alliance coalition 2 with 18·21% and New Zealand First 2 with 8·4%.

Simultaneously another referendum on the electoral system was held. A change from the existing first-past-the-post system to MMP was favoured by 53·9% of votes cast. The first MMP parliament will have 60 general seats, 55 list seats and 5 Maori seats.

Governor-General: Michael Hardie Boys (b. 1931; sworn in March 1996).

The National Party government in Nov. 1995 consisted of:

Prime Minister, Minister in charge of Security Intelligence: Jim Bolger (b.1935).

Deputy Prime Minister, Minister for Foreign Affairs and Trade, Pacific Island Affairs, Leader of the House: Don McKinnon. *Finance:* Bill Birch. *Attorney-General, Minister of State Services, Minister of Crown Health Enterprises, Minister in charge of the Audit Department:* Paul East. *Health, Women's Affairs:* Jenny Shipley. *Labour, Fisheries, Energy:* Doug Kidd. *Commerce, Industry, Trade Nego-*

tiations, State-Owned Enterprises, Railways: Vacant. *Environment, Research, Science and Technology:* Simon Upton. *Education:* Dr Lockwood Smith. *Agriculture, Forestry, Racing:* John Falloon. *Employment, Revenue:* Wyatt Creech. *Justice, Treaty of Waitangi Negotiations, Disarmament and Arms Control, Cultural Affairs:* Douglas Graham. *Tourism, Sport, Fitness and Leisure, Local Government:* John Banks. *Conservation, Lands, Survey and Land Information:* Denis Marshall. *Maori Affairs, Police:* John Luxton. *Defence, Internal Affairs, Civil Defence:* Warren Cooper. *Transport, Statistics, Communications, Information Technology:* Maurice Williamson. *Housing, Customs:* Murray McCully. *Social Welfare, Senior Citizens:* Peter Gresham. *Accident Rehabilitation and Compensation Insurance, Radio and Television:* Bruce Cliffe.

There are also 4 Ministers outside the Cabinet.

The *Speaker* is Peter Tapsell (Labour).

National flag: The British Blue Ensign, with 4 of the 5 stars of the Southern Cross in red, edged with white in the fly.

National anthem: God Defend New Zealand; words by T. Bracken, tune by J. J. Woods. There is a Maori version, words by T. H. Smith. The UK national anthem has equal status.

Local Government. Since the reform of local government in Nov. 1989 it comprises 12 regional councils, 74 territorial authorities (15 city councils, 58 district councils and 1 county council—Chatham Islands), 155 community boards and 6 special authorities. Territorial authorities and regional councils are directly elected. A city must have a minimum of 50,000 persons, be predominantly urban in character, be a distinct entity and a major centre of activity within the region. A district, on the other hand, serves a combination of rural and urban communities. There is no distinction in structural status or responsibility between a city council and a district council. There are a few other local authorities created for specific functions.

Local elections were held on 14 Oct. 1995.

Joseph, P. A., *Constitutional Law in New Zealand.* Sydney, 1993.

Mcgee, D. G., *Parliamentary Practice in New Zealand.* Wellington, 1985

Ringer, J. B., *An Introduction to New Zealand Government.* Christchurch, 1992

Robson, J. L. (ed.) *New Zealand: the Development of its Laws and Constitution.* 2nd ed. London, 1967

Scott, K. J., *The New Zealand Constitution.* OUP, 1962

Vowles, J. and Aimer, P. (eds.) *Double Decision: the 1993 Election and Referendum in New Zealand.* Victoria (Wellington) Univ. Press, 1994

DEFENCE. The control and co-ordination of defence activities is obtained through the Ministry of Defence.

The total expenditure for defence in 1994-95 was NZ$1,218,705 (2·1% of GDP). New Zealand forces serve abroad in Australia and Singapore, and with UN peacekeeping missions.

Army. The Army is organized in 2 Land Force Group Headquarters, 1 reconnaissance regiment, 2 infantry battalions, 1 artillery and 1 engineer regiment and 2 special forces squadrons. Equipment includes 26 Scorpion light tanks.

Personnel, in 1996, totalled 4,500 (500 women). There is a Territorial Army reserve 5,350-strong.

Navy. The Royal New Zealand Navy was 2,200 strong (with 400 Reserve personnel) in 1995 and includes 4 frigates of British Leander type, 1 12,400-tonne fleet replenishment ship with helicopter facilities, 1 naval sea-lift ship also fitted with helicopter deck and ro-ro facilities for army vehicles, 4 inshore patrol craft, 2 survey vessels and 1 diver support ship. The 5 Wasp helicopters for embarked service are Air Force owned and operated. The main base and Fleet headquarters is at Auckland.

Air Force. Maritime (P-3B Orion), long and medium-range transport (Boeing 727, C-130H Hercules, Andover) squadrons are based at RNZAF Base Auckland, 1 helicopter (Iroquois, Wasp) squadron at RNZAF Base Hobsonville; and offensive support (A-4 Skyhawk) at RNZAF Base Ohakea. Flying training units (Airtrainer,

MB 339, TA-4 Skyhawks, Sioux) are located at Ohakea; ground training is carried out at Auckland.

The strength in 1995 was 3,350 (700 women) personnel with 40 combat aircraft.

Rolfe, J., *Defending New Zealand.* Wellington, 1993
Thakur, R., *In Defence of New Zealand.* Wellington, 1984

INTERNATIONAL RELATIONS

Membership. New Zealand is a member of the UN, the Commonwealth, OECD, South Pacific Forum and the Colombo Plan.

ECONOMY

Budget. The following tables of revenue and expenditure relate to the Consolidated Account, which covers the ordinary revenue and expenditure of the government—*i.e.*, apart from capital items, commercial and special undertakings, advances, etc. Total revenue and expenditure of the Consolidated Account, in NZ$1m., year ended 30 June:

	1992	*1993*	*1994*	*1995*
Revenue	26,325	26,360	28,755	29,174
Expenditure	28,843	28,670	29,098	31,765

1995 tax revenue included (in NZ$1m.): Income tax, NZ$14,826; company tax, NZ$3,875; withholding taxes, NZ$1,051; domestic goods and services, NZ$6,836. Non-tax revenue was NZ$2,436m.

The gross public debt at 30 June 1995 was NZ$44,371m., of which NZ$31,036m. was held in New Zealand and NZ$13,335m. in foreign currency (US, 46%; European and other, 27%; Japanese, 27%). The gross annual interest charge on the public debt at 30 June 1993 was NZ$3,899m. (1994 estimate, NZ$3,555m.).

New Zealand System of National Accounts. National Accounts aggregates for 5 years are given in the following table (in NZ$1m.):

Year ended 31 March	*Gross domestic product*	*Gross national product*	*National income*
1992	73,213	69,700	62,839
1993	77,067	74,281	67,090
1994	80,864	77,644	70,506

Currency. The monetary unit is the *New Zealand dollar* (NZD), of 100 *cents*. There are notes of NZ$5, 10, 20, 50 and 100; and coins of 5c, 10c, 20c, 50c, NZ$1 and NZ$2. Inflation was 1·6% in 1994–95. In March 1996, £1 = NZ$2·27; US$1 = NZ$1·48; DM1 = NZ$1.

Banking and Finance. The central bank and bank of issue is the Reserve Bank (*Governor*, Dr Don Brash).

The financial system comprises a central bank (the Reserve Bank of New Zealand), registered banks, and other financial institutions. Registered banks including banks from abroad, which have to satisfy capital adequacy and managerial quality requirements. Other financial institutions include the regional trustee banks, now grouped under Trust Bank, building societies, finance companies, merchant banks and stock and station agents. The number of registered banks (1992, 20) grows as other financial institutions apply for, and satisfy the requirements for registration as a bank.

The primary functions of the Reserve Bank are the formulation and implementation of monetary policy to achieve the economic objectives set by the Government, and the promotion of the efficiency and soundness of the financial system, through the registration of banks, and supervision of financial institutions.

On 30 June 1993 the funding (financial liabilities including deposits) and claims (financial assets including loans) for all registered banks and other financial institutions were: Funding, NZ$96,996m. (foreign currency, NZ$13,116m.); claims, NZ$78,978m. (foreign currency, NZ$3,947m.).

The stock exchange in Wellington conducts on-screen trading, unifying the 3 former trading floors in Auckland, Christchurch and Wellington.

Weights and Measures. The metric system of weights and measures operates.

ENERGY AND NATURAL RESOURCES

Electricity. On 1 April 1987 the former Electricity Division of the Ministry of Energy became a state-owned enterprise, the Electricity Corporation of N.Z. Ltd., which has 39 power stations (30 hydro-electric and 9 thermal, with a total nominal capacity of 7,325 MW) producing almost 100% of the country's electricity. The remainder is generated by the Electrical Supply Authorities from 23 small plants.

Statistics for 4 years ended 31 March are:

	1990	*1991*	*1992*	*1993*	*1994*
Total sales revenue ($1m.)	1,530	1,580	1,589	1,543	...
Total sales volume (gwh)	27,374	27,892	28,660	27,753	...
Generation (gwh) (nett)	29,002	29,556	30,339	29,569	31,039
Number of employees	3,950	3,974	3,096	2,861	2,835
Production/total staff employed (gwh/person)	7·24	7·46	8·89	9·93	10·95

Oil. Crude oil production was 1·69m. tonnes in 1994.

Natural Gas. In 1993 there were 5 gasfields in production, with an output of 213,447 terajoules (198,470 in 1994).

Minerals. Output, 1993 (in tonnes): Clay for bricks and tiles, 130,004; potters' clays, 26,543; iron sand concentrate, 3,388,783; limestone for agriculture, 1,718,875; limestone for industry, 377,880; limestone and marl for cement, 1,577,367; pumice, 69,179; serpentine, 22,386; silica sand, 40,635; coal, 3,090,779; gold, 11.

Agriculture. Two-thirds of the land area is suitable for agriculture and grazing. The total area under cultivation at 30 June 1993 was 17,335,531 ha (including residential area and domestic orchards). There were 13,946,136 ha of grassland, lucerne and tussock, 94,607 ha of land for horticulture, 323,441 (1992) ha of grain or fodder crops and 1,396,758 ha of plantations of exotic timber.

The largest freehold estates are held in the South Island. The number of occupied holdings as at 30 June 1993 were as follows:

Local Territorial Authority	*No. of farms*	*Total area of farms (1,000 ha)*	*Local Territorial Authority*	*No. of farms*	*Total area of farms (1,000 ha)*
Northland	8,325	981	Marlborough	1,401	726
Auckland and Great Barrier Island	7,351	342	Nelson	163	20
Waikato	14,142	2,019	West Coast	1,284	465
Bay of Plenty	6,368	624	Canterbury	10,500	3,469
Gisborne	1,493	710	Otago	4,620	2,670
Hawke's Bay	3,573	999	Southland	5,282	1,242
Taranaki	4,515	541	Tasman	2,196	305
Wanganui and Manawatu	7,321	1,604	*Total South Island*	*25,446*	*8,896*
Wellington	2,594	551	*Total New Zealand*	*81,196*	*17,336*
Total North Island	*55,682*	*8,371*			

The area and yield for each of the principal crops are given as follows (area and yield for threshing only, not including that grown for chaff, hay, silage, etc.):

	Wheat		*Maize*		*Barley*	
Crop years	*Area (1,000 ha)*	*Yield (1,000 tonnes)*	*Area (1,000 ha)*	*Yield (1,000 tonnes)*	*Area (1,000 ha)*	*Yield (1,000 tonnes)*
1990	40·6	180·8	17·6	161·7	96·7	434·9
1991 [1]	35·5	180·7	19·0	183·4	83·7	382·0
1992	37·8	191·0	18·0	163·8	67·4	318·8
1993	40·9	219·4	15·9	133·1	79·8	389·5

[1] Area sown.

In 1993, 2,727,000 tonnes of fertilizer were spread.

Livestock 1993 (in 1,000): Dairy cattle, 3,550; beef cattle, 4,758; sheep, 50,298; deer, 1,078; goats, 353; pigs, 395. Total meat produced in the year ended 30 Sept. 1994 was estimated at 1·12m. tonnes (including 550,000 tonnes of beef and 380,000 tonnes of lamb). Total liquid milk produced in the year ended March 1994 was 9,003m. litres.

Production of wool for 1993–94, 214,000 tonnes.

Forestry. Forests cover 7·5m. ha of New Zealand's land area. Of this, 6·2m. ha are indigenous forest and 1·3m. ha planted productive forest. New planting has increased from 16,000 ha in 1991 to 61,000 ha in 1993. Introduced pines form the bulk of the large exotic forest estate and among these radiata pine is the best multi-purpose tree, reaching log size in 25–30 years. Other species planted are Douglas fir and Eucalyptus species. The table below shows production of rough sawn timber in 1,000 cu. metres for years ending 31 March:

	Indigenous			*Exotic*			*All Species*
	Rimu and Miro	*Beech*	*Total*	*Exotic Pines*	*Douglas Fir*	*Total*	*Total*
1990–91	69	7	86	1,950	224	2,199	2,283
1991–92	51	4	63	1,997	221	2,238	2,301
1992–93	55	4	67	2,379	160	2,567	2,634
1993–94	66	4	79	2,577	123	2,745	2,824

In March 1993, forest industries consisted of 260 saw-mills, 11 plywood and veneer plants, 3 particle board mills, 6 pulp and paper mills and 5 fibreboard mills.

The basic products of the pulp and paper mills are mechanical and chemical pulp which are converted into newsprint, kraft and other papers, paperboard and fibreboard. Production of woodpulp, 31 March 1994, amounted to 1·37m. tonnes and of paper (including newsprint paper and paperboard) to 835,600 tonnes.

Fisheries. The total value of New Zealand Fisheries exports during the year ended 30 June 1994 was NZ$1,101·6m. Exports: Fish, 197,603 tonnes, value NZ$762·7m.; crustaceans, 3,245 tonnes, value NZ$128·9m.

INDUSTRY. Statistics of manufacturing industries:

Production year	*Hours worked*	*Salaries and wages paid (NZ$1m.)*	*Stocks (NZ$1m.) Materials*	*Stocks (NZ$1m.) Finished goods*	*Sales and other income (NZ$1m.)*	*Ratio of total stocks to sales*
1994–95	484,761,000	7,668	2,663	3,850	49,939	...

The following is a statement of the provisional value of the products (including repairs) of the principal industries for the year 1993–94 (in NZ$1m.):

Industry group	*Purchases and operating expenses*	*Sales and other income*	*Additions to fixed tangible assets*
Primary food	9,098	10,691	391
Textiles, apparel and leathergoods	2,081	2,916	83
Wood and wood products (including furniture)	2,598	3,543	280
Paper and paper products, printing and publishing	2,974	4,440	240
Chemicals and chemical, petroleum, coal, rubber and plastic products	3,992	5,311	220
Non-metallic mineral products	771	1,130	42
Basic metal industries	1,363	1,691	88
Fabricated metal products, machinery and equipment	6,869	9,219	260
Other manufacturing industries	299	406	14
Total	34,908	45,740	1,909

Labour. There were 1,608,100 persons employed in March 1995, 706,700 females. Unemployment was 6·9% of the workforce in March 1995. The weekly average wage in Feb. 1995 was NZ$694·43 for men, NZ$511·82 for women. A minimum wage is set by the government annually. In 1994 it was NZ$245 a week. In 1994 a minimum wage was fixed for the first time for workers under 20 years at NZ$147 per week. In 1994 there were 69 industrial stoppages (58 in 1993) with 49,700 working days lost (23,800 in 1993).

Trade Unions. In 1991 there were 80 industrial unions of workers. Unions are grouped in the Council of Trade Unions (*President*, Ken Douglas). Compulsory trade union membership was made illegal in 1991, and the national wage award system was replaced by local wage agreements under the Employment Contracts Act 1991. In Dec. 1994, 375,906 persons (23·4% of the workforce) belonged to trade unions (409,112 in Dec. 1993, 603,118 in May 1991).

FOREIGN ECONOMIC RELATIONS. Foreign debt was NZ$16,660m. in June 1994. In 1990 New Zealand and Australia completed the Closer Economic Relations Agreement (initiated in 1983), which provides for mutual free trade in goods.

Commerce. Trade (excluding specie and bullion) in NZ$1m. for 12 months ended 30 June:

	Total merchandise imported (v.f.d.) [1]	*Exports of domestic produce*	*Re-exports*	*Total merchandise exported (f.o.b.)*
1991–92	14,215·0	17,205·9	684·7	17,890·6
1992-93	15,979·4	18,240·4	730·3	18,970·8
1993–94	17,019·3	19,166·4	660·7	19,827·1

[1] Value for duty.

The principal imports for the 12 months ended 30 June 1994:

Commodity	*Value (NZ$1m. v.f.d.)*
Fruit	108·5
Sugar and sugar confectionery	130·8
Beer, wine and spirits	142·5
Crude petroleum oil	702·4
Inorganic chemicals (excluding aluminium oxide)	142·3
Aluminium oxide	179·7
Knitted or crocheted fabrics and articles	205·8
Glass and glassware	119·0
Iron and steel	330·7
Articles of iron and steel	245·7
Copper and articles of copper	106·0
Aluminium and articles of aluminium	166·9
Tools, implements and articles of base metals	185·7
Machinery and mechanical appliances	2,823·7
Organic chemicals	277·9
Pharmaceutical products	505·2
Plastics and articles of plastic	757·1
Rubber and articles of rubber	229·7
Paper, paperboard and articles thereof	425·4
Printed books, newspapers etc.	304·8
Cotton yarn and fabrics	112·8
Man-made filaments and fibres	233·8
Electrical machinery and equipment	1,710·6
Motor cars, station wagons, utilities	1,205·2
Trucks, buses and vans	385·7
Aircraft	430·3
Ships and boats	72·3
Optical, photographic, technical and surgical equipment	590·4

The principal exports of New Zealand produce for the 12 months ended 30 June 1994 were:

Commodity	*Value (NZ$1m.f.o.b.)*	*Commodity*	*Value (NZ$1m.f.o.b.)*
Live animals	183·5	Butter	834·0
Meat, fresh, chilled or frozen		Cheese	528·0
Beef and veal	1,384·2	Raw hides, skins and leather	646·2
Lamb and mutton	1,250·7	Wool	1,054·1
Dairy products		Aluminium and	
Milk, cream and yoghurt	1,445·9	articles thereof	675·8

Commodity	Value (NZ$1m.f.o.b.)	Commodity	Value (NZ$1m.f.o.b.)
Casein and caseinates	558·9	Forest products	
Plastic materials and articles thereof	229·6	Sawn timber and logs	1,317·9
Sausage casings	120·2	Paper and paper products	417·0
Fish, fresh, chilled or frozen	762·7	Wood pulp	335·5
Vegetables	314·1	Iron and steel and articles thereof	442·0
Fresh kiwifruit	381·1	Machinery and mechanical appliances	635·5
Fresh apples	311·1	Electrical machinery and equipment	392·9

The following table shows the trade with different countries for the year ended 30 June (in NZ$1m.):

Countries	Imports v.f.d. from 1993	1994	Exports and re-exports f.o.b. to 1993	1994
EC countries	2,848·1	3,073·9	2,987·9	3,058·2
Australia	3,466·5	3,656·9	3,785·2	4,162·2
Bahrain	–	–	–	–
Belgium	96·8	122·9	224·8	239·1
Canada	230·4	263·1	311·9	361·9
China	458·6	516·6	368·1	528·6
Fiji	–	–	220·8	215·7
France	284·4	295·1	221·6	211·6
Germany, Fed. Rep. of	680·3	754·2	488·8	490·8
Hong Kong	217·9	207·0	412·7	481·9
Iran	–	–	131·6	72·8
Italy	361·6	448·4	200·3	265·3
Japan	2,442·4	2,693·9	2,759·1	2,886·8
Korea, Republic of	258·3	272·6	857·1	928·6
Malaysia	218·0	202·7	382·6	392·8
Netherlands	180·4	195·3	92·8	123·1
Peru	–	–	60·1	88·4
Philippines	–	–	205·3	202·1
Saudi Arabia	362·9	339·0	227·7	215·9
Singapore	224·9	279·6	289·7	269·6
Sweden	219·8	301·3	–	–
Switzerland	184·4	200·7	–	–
Taiwan	453·0	487·1	486·7	507·3
UK	995·7	1,036·5	1,216·8	1,182·3
USA	2,966·1	3,072·5	225·6	2,228·7

Total trade between New Zealand and UK was as follows (British Department of Trade returns, in £1,000 sterling):

	1991	1992	1993	1994	1995
Imports to UK	391,643	429,363	496,357	539,412	576,532
Exports and re-exports from UK	260,052	264,830	332,897	411,227	435,879

Tourism. There were 1,249,292 tourists in the year to July 1994 (including 370,760 from Australia, 154,547 from the USA, 130,947 from Japan and 112,686 from the UK). Tourist earnings for 1993 were NZ$3,400m.

COMMUNICATIONS

Roads. Total length of formed roads and streets at 30 June 1992 was 94,315 km, of which 55,313 sealed and 39,002 gravel. There were 15,612 bridges. There were 74 national and provincial state highways comprising 11,449 km of roadway, including the principal arterial traffic routes.

Total expenditure on roads, streets and bridges by the central government and local authorities combined for the financial year 1993–94 amounted to NZ$584m.

At 31 March 1994 motor vehicles licensed numbered 2,437,515, of which 1,600,499 were cars and 12,736 omnibuses, public taxis and service vehicles. Included in the remaining numbers were 57,805 motor cycles, 1,256 power cycles, 340,261 lorries and 374,110 trailers and caravans.

In 1995 there were 577 deaths in road accidents (580 in 1994).

Railways. New Zealand Rail was privatized in 1993. In 1993 there were 3,973 km of 1,067 mm gauge railway open for traffic (504 km electrified). In 1993–94, NZ rail carried 9·4m. tonnes and 10·6m. passengers. Operating revenue during 1993–94, NZ$488·55m. and operating expenses NZ$435·8m. Three rail/road ferries maintain a regular service between the North and South Islands.

Civil Aviation. There are international airports at Wellington, Auckland and Christchurch. The national carrier is Air New Zealand, which in 1995 operated 16 B-737-200 Advs, 1 B-737-200C Adv, 4 B-747-200Bs, 5 B-747-400s, 5 B-767-200ERs and 6 B-767-300ERs. Ansett New Zealand also provide services, as do Aerolíneas Argentinas, Air Calédonie International, Air Niugini, Air Pacific, Air Vanuatu, Ansett Australia, British Airways, Canadian Airlines, Cathay Pacific, Eva, Garuda Indonesia, Great Barrier Airlines, JAL, Korean Air, Malaysia Airlines, Mandarin Airlines, Polynesian Airlines, Qantas, Royal Tongan Airlines, Singapore Airlines, Solomon Airlines, Thai Airways and United Airlines. Trans-Tasman air travel is subject to agreement between Air New Zealand and Qantas.

Air New Zealand and Ansett New Zealand are the major domestic carriers. Domestic scheduled services during the 12 months ended Dec. 1990: Passengers carried, 4,502,000; freight, 47,700 tonnes. International services: Passengers carried, 3,129,000; freight, 134,074 tonnes.

Shipping. In 1995 sea-going shipping totalled 0·26m. GRT, including oil tankers, 94,169 GRT.

Entrances and clearances of vessels from overseas:

	Entrances		*Clearances*	
	No.	*Tons*	*No.*	*Tons*
1990	3,813	32,592,000	3,784	31,967,000
1991	4,365	38,069,000	4,166	36,158,000
1992	3,282	27,983,000	3,298	27,508,000
1993	4,226	37,603,000	4,012	35,138,000
1994	4,627	39,700,000	4,047	37,421,000

Telecommunications. The provision of postal and telecommunication services is the responsibility of the state-owned New Zealand Post, which began operations on 1 April 1987; the Telecom Corporation of New Zealand, formed in 1987 and privatized in 1991; and CLEAR Communications, which began operations in May 1991. There were 1,516,000 telephone subscribers in March 1993, and 685 exchanges. New Zealand Post restarted a telegram service in 1990. There are also 2 independent telegraph companies. In 1994 there were 245 post shops, 644 post centre franchises, 1,026 stamp retailers and 2,823 stamp book outlets.

Legislation of 1995 split the state-owned Radio New Zealand into a government-owned public radio broadcasting company and some 40 commercial stations. Television New Zealand operates 2 channels. A third, TV3, is commercial. There are also regional TV networks. Pay television was introduced in May 1990 – Sky Entertainment operates on 3 channels. The New Zealand Public Radio Service also includes the Radio New Zealand International service which broadcasts in 14 languages. RNZ Ltd commercial runs 35 commercial or community stations. There were, in 1993, 150 AM and 288 FM frequencies registered. There are frequencies reserved for the promotion of Maori culture; 16 Maori stations are broadcasting continuously. Number of TV receiving licences in 1992 was approximately 1,126,000.

Cinemas. There were 217 screens in 1993; attendances totalled 9·63m. in 1993.

Press. There were, in 1995, 28 daily newspapers. The *New Zealand Herald* published in Auckland has the largest daily circulation of 246,092. Other dailies range from 3,000–105,000 copies.

SOCIAL INSTITUTIONS

Justice. The judiciary consists of the Court of Appeal, the High Court and District Courts. All exercise both civil and criminal jurisdiction. Other special courts include the Maori Land Court, the Maori Appellate Court, Family Courts, the Youth

Court and the Employment Court. In Sept. 1995 the Prime Minister announced that final appeal would no longer lie to the Privy Council in London. In Nov. 1991 prisons and corrective training institutions contained 3,794 prisoners. Some 0·49m. criminal offences, including 61 murders were reported in the year ending June 1994. The death penalty for murder was replaced by life imprisonment in 1961.

The Criminal Injuries Compensation Act, 1963, which came into force on 1 Jan. 1964, provided for compensation of persons injured by certain criminal acts and the dependants of persons killed by such acts. However, this has now been phased out in favour of the Accident Compensation Act, 1982, except in the residual area of property damage caused by escapers. The Offenders Legal Aid Act 1954 provides that any person charged or convicted of any offence may apply for legal aid which may be granted depending on the person's means and the gravity of the offence etc. Since 1970 legal aid in civil proceedings (except divorce) has been available for persons of small or moderate means. The Legal Services Act 1991 now brings together in one statute the civil and criminal legal aid schemes.

Police. The police are a national body maintained by the central government. Legislation of 1994 permits the private management of prisons and prisoner escort services. The total authorized establishment at June 1994 was 6,842. The total cost of police services for the year 1994–95 was NZ$777·4m. In 1991 1,100 traffic officers merged with the police, who previously did not control traffic.

Ombudsmen. The office of Ombudsman was created in 1962. From 1975 additional Ombudsmen have been authorized. There are currently two. Ombudsmen's functions are to investigate complaints under the Ombudsman Act, the Official Information Act and the Local Government Official Information and Meetings Act from members of the public relating to administrative decisions of central, regional and local government.

During the year ended 30 June 1994, a total of 3,916 complaints were received, 82 of which were sustained and 721 were still under investigation.

Religion. No direct state aid is given to any form of religion. For the Church of England the country is divided into 7 dioceses, with a separate bishopric (Aotearoa) for the Maoris. The Presbyterian Church is divided into 23 presbyteries and the Maori Synod. The Moderator is elected annually. The Methodist Church is divided into 10 districts; the President is elected annually. The Roman Catholic Church is divided into 4 dioceses, with the Archbishop of Wellington as Metropolitan Archbishop.

Religious denomination	*Number of adherents* *1986 census*	*1991 census*	*% Intercensal change*
Church of England	791,847	732,048	–7·6
Presbyterian	587,517	540,675	–8·0
Roman Catholic (including 'Catholic' undefined)	496,389	498,612	0·4
Methodist	153,249	138,705	–9·5
Baptist	68,016	70,155	3·1
Brethren	19,755	20,337	2·9
Ratana	39,729	47,595	19·8
Buddhist	6,516	12,765	95·9
Salvation Army	16,821	19,992	18·9
Latter-day Saints (Mormon)	37,146	48,009	29·3
Pentecostal	15,714	18,765	19·4
Seventh-day Adventist	12,048	13,005	7·9
Hindu	8,148	17,664	116·8
Christian (undefined)	45,354	78,195	72·4
Jehovah's Witnesses	16,377	19,182	17·1
Assemblies of God	14,922	17,226	15·4
All other religious professions	96,192	106,392	10·6
No religion	533,790	666,609	24·9
Not specified	58,686	56,289	–4·1
Object to state	244,863	251,709	2·8
Total	3,263,283	3,373,926	3·4

Education. New Zealand has 7 universities, the University of Auckland, University of Waikato (at Hamilton), Victoria University of Wellington, Massey University (at Palmerston North), the University of Canterbury (at Christchurch), the University of Otago (at Dunedin) and Lincoln University (near Christchurch). The number of students in 1993 was 97,835. There were 5 teachers' training colleges with 10,315 students in 1992.

At 1 July 1993 there were 319 state secondary schools with 14,463 full-time teachers and 206,741 pupils. There were also 40 area high schools with 3,339 scholars in the secondary division. 88,427 students were enrolled in polytechnic courses in 1993, of these 54,376 were part-time. At 1 July 1993, 2,423 pupils received tuition from the secondary department of the correspondence school. There were 20 registered private secondary schools with 483 teachers and 11,284 pupils.

At 1 July 1993, there were 2,251 state primary schools (including intermediate schools and departments), with 402,548 pupils; the number of teachers was 19,300. A correspondence school for children in remote areas and those otherwise unable to attend school had 3,580 primary and secondary pupils. There were 86 registered private primary and intermediate schools with 430 teachers and 12,986 pupils.

Education is compulsory between the ages of 6 and 15. Children aged 3 and 4 years may enrol at the 582 free kindergartens maintained by Free Kindergarten Associations, which receive government assistance. There are also 577 play centres which also receive government subsidy. In July 1993 there were 46,030 and 21,450 children on the rolls respectively. There are also 970 child care centres with 45,148 children, 809 *kohanga reo* (providing early childhood education in the Maori language) with 14,514 children, and a number of other smaller providers of early childhood care and education.

Total budgeted expenditure in 1994–95 on education was NZ$4,804m.

The universities are autonomous bodies. All state-funded primary and secondary schools are controlled by boards of trustees. Education in state schools is free for children under 19 years of age. All educational institutions are reviewed every 3 years by teams of educational reviewers.

A series of reforms is being implemented by the government following reports of 18 working groups on tertiary education. These include a new funding system, begun in 1991 and based solely on student numbers.

Health. At 30 June 1994 there were 11,413 doctors on the medical register. In 1994 there were 16,468 public hospital beds. There are 4 regional health authorities. Total expenditure on health in 1994–95 was NZ$4,701m.

Social Welfare. Non-contributory old-age pensions were introduced in 1898. Large reductions in welfare expenditure were introduced by the government in Dec. 1990. (For previous provisions *see* THE STATESMAN'S YEAR-BOOK, 1990–91, pp. 928–30).

From 1 Oct. 1994 Family Support for families on the lowest incomes was NZ$42 for the first child aged 16 and over, NZ$35 for subsequent children aged 13–15, and NZ$27 under 13. Child allowance for single persons with one child was NZ$221·14 per week; with 2 or more children, NZ$237·47 per week.

The weekly unemployment benefit in Nov. 1994 for a single person aged 25 and over was NZ$134·69, aged 16–17 NZ$89·38 and aged 18–24 $112·23. Persons made redundant become eligible for benefit after 26 weeks. In 1991 subsidised housing was replaced by cash subsidies.

In 1993 earners of NZ$17,500 a year and less received subsidized health care; a lesser subsidy applied up to NZ$27,000; over that health care was paid for by patients.

In the budget of July 1991 it was announced that current rates of Guaranteed Retirement Income Scheme (GRI) payment would be frozen until 1 April 1993, thereafter to be on the previous year's consumer price index. On 1 April 1992 GRI was replaced by the National superannuation scheme which is income-tested. Eligibility will be gradually increased to 65 years by 2001. Universal eligibility is available at 70 years. A married couple receives NZ$348·16 per week, a single person NZ$234·14 per week.

Social Welfare Benefits and War Pensions:

Benefits	*Number in force at 30 June 1994*	*Total payments 1993–94 (NZ$1,000)*
SOCIAL WELFARE:		
Monetary—		
National Superannuation	477,400	5,102,551
Widows	9,012	86,665
Invalids	37,030	422,324
Miners	n/a	54,660
Orphans	4,093	19,185
Domestic purposes	100,256	1,228,054
Unemployment	157,182	1,498,545
Sickness	31,535	329,995
War pensions	n/a	n/a
Training	12,834	92,502
Total	842,160	8,851,866

Health benefits in 1993: Payments for private hospitals, NZ$53·25m.; primary services, NZ$299·08m.; pharmaceutical, NZ$582·93m.

Reciprocity with Other Countries. There are reciprocal arrangements between New Zealand and Australia in respect of age, invalids', widows', family, unemployment and sickness benefits, and between New Zealand and the UK in respect of family, age, superannuation, widows', orphans', invalids', sickness and unemployment benefits.

DIPLOMATIC REPRESENTATIVES

Of New Zealand in Great Britain (New Zealand Hse, Haymarket, London, SW1Y 4TQ)
High Commissioner: John Collinge.

Of Great Britain in New Zealand (Reserve Bank of New Zealand Bldg., 2 The Terrace, Wellington, 1)
High Commissioner: Robert Alston, CMG.

Of New Zealand in the USA (37 Observatory Cir., NW, Washington, D.C., 20008)
Ambassador: L. John Wood.

Of the USA in New Zealand (29 Fitzherbert Terrace, Wellington)
Ambassador: Josiah Beeman.

Of New Zealand to the United Nations
Ambassador: Colin Keating.

Further Reading

Department of Statistics. *New Zealand Official Yearbook.* (not published every year).—*Key Statistics: a monthly Abstract of Statistics.—Pocket Digest of Statistics. New Zealand Social Trends.*
Dictionary of New Zealand Biography. vol 1 (to 1868). Wellington, 1990
Encyclopaedia of New Zealand. 3 vols. Wellington, 1966
Alley, R., *New Zealand and the Pacific.* Boulder (CO), 1984
Grover, R. R., *New Zealand.* [Bibliography] Oxford and Santa Barbara, 1981
Harland, B., *On Our Own: New Zealand in a Tripolar World.* Victoria Univ. Press, 1992
Hawke, G. R., *The Making of New Zealand: an Economic History.* CUP, 1985
Massey, P., *New Zealand: Market Liberalization in a Developed Economy.* London, 1995
Oliver, W. H. (ed.) *The Oxford History of New Zealand.* OUP, 1981
Sinclair, K., *A History of New Zealand.* 2nd ed. London, 1980 –. (ed.) *The Oxford Illustrated History of New Zealand.* 2nd ed. OUP, 1994

For other more specialized titles see under CONSTITUTION AND GOVERNMENT, DEFENCE *and* INTERNATIONAL RELATIONS, *above.*
National statistical office: Department of Statistics, POB 2922, Wellington, 1.

TERRITORIES OVERSEAS

Territories Overseas coming within the jurisdiction of New Zealand consist of Tokelau and the Ross Dependency.

Tokelau. Situated some 480 km to the north of Western Samoa between 8° and 10° S. lat., and between 171° and 173° W. long., are the 3 atoll islands of Atafu, Nukunonu and Fakaofo of the Tokelau (Union) group. Formerly part of the Gilbert and Ellice Islands Colony, the group was transferred to the jurisdiction of New Zealand on 11 Feb. 1926. By legislation enacted in 1948, the Tokelau Islands were declared part of New Zealand as from 1 Jan. 1949. The area of the group is 1,011 ha; the population at the 1991 census was 1,577.

By the Tokelau Islands Act 1948 the Tokelau Group was included within the territorial boundaries of New Zealand; legislative powers are now invested in the Governor-General in Council. The inhabitants are British subjects and New Zealand citizens. In Dec. 1976 the territory was officially renamed 'Tokelau', the name by which it has customarily been known to its inhabitants. New Zealand currency and the Tokelau souvenir coin are legal tender.

From 8 Nov. 1974 the office of Administrator was invested in the Secretary of Foreign Affairs. Certain powers are delegated to the district officer in Apia, Western Samoa. The public service numbered 195 in June 1991. A *General Fono* (parliament) meets twice a year. Each village has a Council of Elders, elected every 3 years.

Tokelau's economy is based on fishing, crops and livestock, but the soil is infertile. Because of the very restricted economic and social future in the atolls, the islanders agreed to a proposal put to them by the Minister of Island Territories in 1965 that over a period of years most of the population be resettled in New Zealand. Up to March 1975, 528 migrants entered New Zealand as permanent residents under Government sponsorship. At the request of the people the scheme was suspended. Contracts in 1990 with the UN Special Committee in Decolonisation revealed that the people of Tokelau did not wish to review existing links with New Zealand.

Tokelan's budget for 1992–93 was NZ$5,332,880, of which NZ$4,300,000 came from the New Zealand Government and the remainder from locally-generated revenue.

Ross Dependency. By Imperial Order in Council, dated 30 July 1923, the territories between 160° E. long. and 150° W. long. and south of 60° S. lat. were brought within the jurisdiction of the New Zealand Government. The region was named the Ross Dependency. From time to time laws for the Dependency have been made by regulations promulgated by the Governor-General of New Zealand.

The mainland area is estimated at 400,000–450,000 sq. km and is mostly ice-covered. In Jan. 1957 a New Zealand expedition under Sir Edmund Hillary established a base in the Dependency. In Jan. 1958 Sir Edmund Hillary and 4 other New Zealanders reached the South Pole.

The main base—Scott Base—at Pram Point, Ross Island—is manned throughout the year, about 12 people being present during winter. Vanda Station in the dry ice-free Wright Valley is manned every summer.

Quartermain, L. B., *New Zealand and the Antarctic.* Wellington, 1971

SELF-GOVERNING TERRITORIES OVERSEAS

THE COOK ISLANDS

KEY HISTORICAL EVENTS. The Cook Islands, which lie between 8° and 23° S. lat., and 156° and 167° W. long., were proclaimed a British protectorate in 1888, and on 11 June 1901 were annexed and proclaimed part of New Zealand. In 1965 the Cook Islands became a self-governing territory in 'free association' with New Zealand.

TERRITORY AND POPULATION. The islands fall roughly into two groups—the scattered islands towards the north (Northern group) and the islands towards the south (Lower group). The islands with their populations at the census of 1986:

Lower Group—	*Area sq. km*	*Population*	*Northern Group—*	*Area sq. km*	*Population*
Rarotonga	67·2	9,678	Nassau	1·2	118
Mangaia	51·8	1,235	Palmerston (Avarau)	2·0	66
Atiu	26·9	955	Penrhyn (Tongareva)	9·8	496
Aitutaki	18·0	2,391	Manihiki (Humphrey)	5·4	508
Mauke (Parry Is.)	18·4	637	Rakahanga (Reirson)	4·1	283
Mitiaro	22·3	272	Pukapuka (Danger)	5·1	760
Manuae and Te au-o-tu	6·2	–	Suwarrow (Anchorage)	0·4	6
Takutea	1·3	–			
			Total	293	17,463

The population in 1994 was 18,500. Birth rate (1993, per 1,000 population), 25·8; death rate, 5·3.

CONSTITUTION AND GOVERNMENT. The Cook Islands Constitution of 1965 provides for internal self-government but linked to New Zealand by a common Head of State and a common citizenship, that of New Zealand. It provides for a ministerial system of government with a Cabinet consisting of a Premier and 6 other Ministers. The New Zealand Government is represented by a New Zealand Representative and the position of a Queen's Representative has recently been created. New Zealand is responsible for external affairs and defence, subject to consultation between the New Zealand Prime Minister and the Prime Minister. The capital is Rarotonga.

The unicameral *Parliament* comprises 25 members elected for a term of 5 years. At the elections of March 1994 the Cook Islands Party (CIP) gained 20 seats, the Democratic Coalition Party 3 and the Alliance Party, 2. There is also an advisory council composed of hereditary chiefs, the 15-member House of Ariki, without legislative powers.

Prime Minister: Sir Geoffrey A. Henry (CIP; re-elected March 1994).

ECONOMY AND TRADE

Budget. Revenue, 1994–95, NZ$78·8m.; expenditure, NZ$75·4m. Revenue is derived chiefly from customs duties which follow the New Zealand customs tariff, income tax and stamp sales.

Grants from New Zealand, mainly for medical, educational and general administrative purposes totalled NZ$8·5m. in 1991–92.

Currency. The Cook Island *dollar* is at par with the New Zealand *dollar*.

Electricity. 19·44m. kWh were generated in 1994.

Agriculture. Livestock (1991): 22,162 pigs, 5,752 goats.

Fisheries. Catch (1984) 800 tonnes.

Commerce. Exports, mainly to New Zealand, were valued at NZ$7·15m. in 1993. Main items exported were fresh fruit and vegetables, clothing and footwear. Imports totalled NZ$124·24m. Trade with the UK (British Board of Trade returns, 1995): Imports, £24,000; exports, £920,000.

COMMUNICATIONS

Roads. In 1992 there were 320 km of roads and, in 1991, 5,015 vehicles.

Civil Aviation. New Zealand has financed the construction of an international airport at Rarotonga which became operational for jet services in 1973.

Shipping. A fortnightly cargo shipping service is provided between New Zealand, Niue and Rarotonga.

Telecommunications. Radio stations are maintained at all the permanently inhabited islands. In 1992 there were 3,660 telephones. There are 2 radio stations on Rarotonga with (1991) 3,484 receivers.

Press. The *Cook Islands News* (circulation 1,500 (1994)) is the sole daily newspaper.

SOCIAL INSTITUTIONS

Justice. There is a High Court and a Court of Appeal, from which further appeal is to the Privy Council in the UK.

Religion. Some 69% of the population belong to the Cook Islands Christian Church, about 15% are Roman Catholics, and the rest chiefly Latter Day Saints and Seventh-Day Adventists.

Education. In 1995 there were 29 primary schools with 237 teachers and 2,643 pupils, and 22 secondary schools with 247 teachers and 2,095 pupils on Rarotonga, Aitutaki, Mangaia, Atiu, Mauke and Pukapuka.

Health. All Cook Islanders receive free medical and surgical treatment in their villages, the hospital and the tuberculosis sanatorium. Cook Islands Maori patients in the hospital and the sanatorium and all schoolchildren receive free dental treatment. In 1995 there were 18 doctors, 63 dentists and 103 nursing personnel; there were 66 hospitals and clinics, with 144 beds.

Further Reading

Local statistical office: Statistics Office, POB 125, Rarotonga, Cook Islands.

NIUE

Key Historical Events. Captain James Cook sighted Niue in 1774 and called it Savage Island. Christian missionaries arrived in 1846. Niue became a British Protectorate in 1900 and was annexed to New Zealand in 1901. Internal self-government was achieved in free association with New Zealand on 19 Oct. 1974, New Zealand taking responsibility for external affairs and defence. Niue is a member of the South Pacific Forum.

Territory and Population. Niue is the largest uplifted coral island in the world. Distance from Auckland, New Zealand, 1,343 miles; from Rarotonga, 580 miles. Area, 258 sq. km; height above sea-level, 220 ft. Population (census, 1991) 2,239 (1,134 males, 1,105 females); (July 1993 estimate) 1,977. During 1992 births registered numbered 31, deaths 12. Migration to New Zealand is the main factor in population change. The capital is Alofi (682 inhabitants in census, 1991).

Constitution and Government. There is a Legislative Assembly of 20 members, 14 elected from 14 constituencies and 6 elected by all constituencies. There was an election in March 1993.

Prime Minister and Minister of Finance: Frank Lui.

Budget. Financial aid from New Zealand, 1992–93, totalled NZ$7,508,890.

Agriculture. The main commercial crops of the island are coconuts, taros and yams. In 1989 there were 450 agricultural holdings with 1,527 pigs and 9,716 chickens.

Commerce. Exports, 1993, NZ$420,000; imports, NZ$3,520,000. Trade with UK (British Department of Trade returns, 1995): Imports, £31,000; exports, £652,000.

Civil Aviation. A weekly commercial air service links Niue with New Zealand.

Tourism. In 1992 there were 2,329 visitors (1,668 tourists).

Telecommunications. There is a wireless station at Alofi, the port of the island. Cable television is available. A weekly newspaper is published in English and Niuean; circulation about 400. Telephones (1992) 276.

Justice. There is a High Court under a Chief Justice, with a right of appeal to the New Zealand Supreme Court.

Religion (1991 census). 1,487 belong to the Congregational (Ekalesia Niue); Latter Day Saints (213), Roman Catholics (90), Jehovah's Witness (47), Seventh Day Adventists (27), other (63), No religion (34), not stated (1).

Education. In 1991 there was 1 primary school with 22 teachers and 337 pupils, and 1 secondary school with 27 teachers and 304 pupils.

Health. In 1992 there were 4 doctors, 1 dentist, 6 midwives and 19 nursing personnel. There is a 24-bed hospital at Alofi.

NICARAGUA

República de Nicaragua

Capital: Managua
Population: 4·4m. (1994)
GNP per capita: US$330 (1994)
HDI/world rank: 0·611/109 (1992)

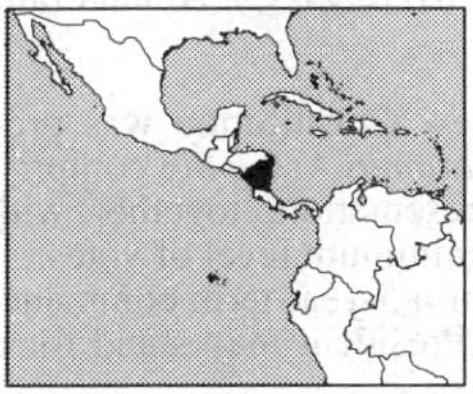

KEY HISTORICAL EVENTS. Active colonization of the Pacific coast was undertaken by Spaniards from Panama, beginning in 1523. After links with other Central American territories, and Mexico, Nicaragua became completely independent in 1838, but subject to a prolonged feud between the 'Liberals' of León and the 'Conservatives' of Granada. Mosquitia remained an autonomous kingdom on the Atlantic coast, under British protection until 1860.

A 46-year political domination of Nicaragua by the Somoza family ended on 17 July 1979, after the 17 years long struggle by the Sandinista National Liberation Front flared into civil war. A Government Junta of National Reconstruction was established by the revolutionary government on 20 July 1979 and a 51-member Council of State later created; both were dissolved on 10 Jan. 1985 following new Presidential and legislative elections.

On 9 Jan. 1987 the President signed the new Constitution, but immediately reimposed a state of emergency, suspending many of the liberties granted under the Constitution.

Rebel Sandinista activities had ceased by 1990; the last organised insurgent group negotiated an agreement with the government in April 1994.

TERRITORY AND POPULATION. Nicaragua is bounded in the north by Honduras, east by the Caribbean, south by Costa Rica and west by the Pacific. Area, 130,671 sq. km (121,428 sq. km dry land). The coastline runs 450 km on the Atlantic and 305 km on the Pacific. Population, 1971 census, 1,877,952. Estimate (1994), 4,395,000 (2·19m. females; 2·68m. urban); density, 36·2 per sq. km.

Vital statistics rates (per 1,000), 1990–95: Birth, 38·7; death, 6·6; infant mortality (per 1,000 live births) 49·8. Growth rate, 1993, 3%. Expectation of life in 1993, 66·2.

16 administrative departments are grouped in 3 zones. Areas (in sq. km.), populations (in 1,000) and chief towns in 1993:

	Area	*Population*	*Chief town*
Pacific Zone	18,429	2,622·5	
Chinandega	4,926	357·7	Chinandega
León	5,107	373·4	León
Managua	3,672	1,188·1	Managua
Masaya	590	225·1	Masaya
Granada	929	165·2	Granada
Carazo	1,050	165·2	Jinotepe
Rivas	2,155	147·8	Rivas
Central-North Zone	35,960	1,417·0	
Chontales	6,378	276·6	Juigalpa
Boaco	4,244	129·0	Boaco
Matagalpa	8,523	403·7	Matagalpa
Jinotega	9,755	190·1	Jinotega
Estelí	2,335	181·2	Estelí
Madriz	1,602	104·4	Somoto
Nueva Segovía	3,123	132·0	Ocotal
Atlantic Zone	67,039	225·3	
Rio San Juan	7,473	37·6	San Carlos
Zelaya	59,566	187·7	Bluefields

The capital is Managua with (1985) 682,111 inhabitants. Other cities: León, 100,982; Granada, 88,636; Masaya, 74,946; Chinandega, 67,792; Matagalpa,

36,983; Estelí, 30,635; Tipitapa, 30,078; Chichigalpa, 28,889; Juigalpa, 25,625; Corinto, 24,250; Jinotepe, 23,538.

The population is of Spanish and Amerindian origins with an admixture of Afro-Americans on the Caribbean coast. Ethnic groups in 1980: Mestizo, 69%; white, 14%; black, 13%; Amerindian, 4%. The official language is Spanish.

CLIMATE. The climate is tropical, with a wet season from May to Jan. Temperatures vary with altitude. Managua. Jan. 81°F (27°C), July 81°F (27°C). Annual rainfall 38" (976 mm).

CONSTITUTION AND GOVERNMENT. A new Constitution was promulgated on 9 Jan. 1987. It provides for a unicameral *National Assembly* comprising 92 members directly elected by proportional representation, together with unsuccessful presidential election candidates obtaining a minimum level of votes.

The *President* and *Vice-President* are directly elected for a 5-year term commencing on the 10 Jan. following their date of election. The President may stand for a second term, but not consecutively.

Under Article 185 of the Constitution, the President is empowered to declare a state of emergency and suspend certain of the civil rights provisions enshrined therein; this was done by the President immediately upon the promulgation of the Constitution.

Elections were held on 25 Feb 1990. The National Opposition Union (UNO) gained 51 seats, the Sandinista National Liberation Front (FSLN) 39 and independents 2.

Presidential elections were scheduled for Oct. 1996

In Dec. 1995 the government comprised:

President and Minister of Defence: Violeta Barrios de Chamorro (UNO; elected 25 Feb. 1990, took office 25 April 1990).

Vice-President: Julia Mena.

Minister of the Interior: Sergio Narvaez. *Foreign Affairs:* Ernesto Leal. *Finance:* Emilio Pereira Alegria. *Education:* Humberto Belli Pereira. *Agriculture:* Dionisio Cuadra. *Economy and Development:* Pablo Pereira. *Construction and Transport:* Pablo Vigil. *Health:* Marta Pereira. *Labour:* Francisco Rosales Arguello. *Tourism:* Fernando Guzmán. *Foreign Co-operation:* Erwin Krugger. *Environment and Natural Resources:* Milton Caldera.

National flag: Three horizontal stripes of blue, white, blue, with the national arms in the centre.

National anthem: 'Salve a ti Nicaragua' ('Hail to thee, Nicaragua'); words by S. Ibarra Mayorga, tune by L. A. Delgadillo.

Local government. There are 16 departments and 143 municipalities.

DEFENCE

Army. The Army is being reorganized. There are 5 regional commands, and in 1996 the Army comprised 2 military detachments, 1 light mechanized and 1 special forces brigade, 1 infantry, 1 security and 1 special forces battalion. Equipment included 130 T-54/-55 main battle tanks. Strength (1996) 10,000.

Navy. The Nicaraguan Navy was some 800 strong in 1995 and operates 12 inshore patrol craft of mixed Soviet and North Korean origins and 2 small inshore minesweepers.

Air Force. Formed in June 1938 as the Nicaraguan Army Air Force, the Air Force has been semi-independent since 1947. Personnel (1995) 1,200, with no combat aircraft and 15 armed helicopters. There are over 30 transport, 12 liaison and 15 trainer aircraft, some armed.

INTERNATIONAL RELATIONS

Membership. Nicaragua is a member of the UN, OAS, SELA and the Central American Common Market.

ECONOMY

Budget. Estimates for 1994: Revenue, US$405m.; expenditure, US$445m.

Currency. The monetary unit is the *córdoba* (NIO), of 100 *centavos*, which replaced the córdoba oro in 1991 at par. There are coins and notes of 1, 5, 10, 25 and 50 centavos and notes of ½, 1, 5, 10, 20, 50 and 100 córdobas. Inflation was 3·5% in 1992. In March 1996, £1 = 12·40; US$1 = 8·11; DM1 = 5·50 córdobas.

Banking and Finance. The Central Bank of Nicaragua came into operation on 1 Jan. 1961 as an autonomous bank of issue, absorbing the issue department of the National Bank. Its *Governor* is José Evenor Taboada. In July 1979 private financial banking was nationalized and branches of foreign banks were prohibited from receiving deposits, but in 1991 private banking was again permitted. 9 had opened by 1994.

Weights and Measures. The metric system is recommended. 1 manzana = 1·73 acres.

ENERGY AND NATURAL RESOURCES

Electricity. Installed capacity was 401,900 kW in 1993 (400,700 kW in 1992: 43·7% thermal; 25·8% hydroelectric; 17·5% geothermal; 10·5% gas turbine; 2·5% Aislado system). In 1993, 1,634·8m. kWh were produced.

Minerals. Production of gold in 1993 was 39,900 troy oz.; silver, 71,900 troy oz; limestone, 12,000 cu. metres.

Agriculture. Agriculture is the principal source of national wealth.

In 1991 there were 1·1m. ha arable land, 155,000 ha permanent cropland and 1·57m. ha pasture. 86,000 ha were irrigated. Production (in 1,000 tonnes) in 1993-94: Rice, 106; maize, 254; sorghum, 105; dry beans, 73; soya beans, 13; sesame seed, 8; cotton seed, 2; raw sugar, 173; bananas, 68; green coffee, 49; green tobacco, 1; raw cotton, 4.

There were about 1·68m. head of cattle in 1992 and 0·7m. pigs. Animal products (in 1,000 tonnes), 1993: Beef, 49; pork, 4; poultry, 23; milk, 47m. gallons; eggs, 34.

Forestry. The forest area in 1992 was 4·3m. ha, of which 2·1m. ha were commercially utilizable. The forests contain mahogany and cedar, three varieties of rosewoods, lignum vitae and dye-woods. Production of sawn wood in 1987, 3·77m. cu. metres (2·89m. cu. metres for fuel).

Fisheries. In 1988 the fishing fleet comprised 17 vessels of 1,917 GRT. In 1993 the catch was 5,291 tonnes.

INDUSTRY. Production in 1993 (in 1,000 tonnes): Vegetable oil, 27; wheat flour, 48; main chemical products, 13; cement, 258; metallic products, 2,483; rum, 9,868 litres; processed leather, 309 sq. yards.

Labour. The workforce in 1993 was 1,489,500 (303,000 females in 1990, 52,000 between 10 and 15 years of age). 0·43m. worked in agriculture and forestry, 0·17m. in manufacturing, 0·34m. in services and 0·19m. in trade. There were 0·32m. unemployed in 1993.

FOREIGN ECONOMIC RELATIONS. Foreign debt was US$11,000m. in 1994.

Commerce. Foreign trade in US$1m. (1993): Exports, 267, consisting of cotton, coffee, chemical products, meat, sugar; imports, 728.

Total trade between Nicaragua and UK (British Department of Trade returns, in £1,000 sterling):

	1991	*1992*	*1993*	*1994*	*1995*
Imports to UK	492	3,452	1,857	5,185	8,265
Exports and re-exports from UK	8,029	7,297	4,369	3,969	7,334

Main import suppliers in 1993 (in US$1m.): USA, 168·1; Venezuela, 83; Costa

Rica, 79; Guatemala, 70·8; Japan, 46·3. Main export markets: USA, 100·9; Canada, 28·4; Costa Rica, 24·6; Germany, 21·6; El Salvador, 15·3.

Tourism. In 1991 there were 173,208 visitors.

COMMUNICATIONS

Roads. Road length in 1993 was 15,011 km, of which 1,641 km were asphalted. In 1992 there were 72,102 motor cars, 3,408 buses, 60,553 lorries and 21,678 motor cycles. 25·52m. passengers were carried by inter-urban public transport in 1992.

Railways. The railway was closed in 1994.

Civil Aviation. The national carrier is Nica, which in 1995 operated 1 B-737-200 Adv. 47,051 passengers were carried in 1993. The Augusto Sandino international airport at Managua handled 398,010 passengers in 1993.

Shipping. The merchant marine totalled 1,483 GRT in 1995. The Pacific ports are Corinto (the largest), San Juan del Sur and Puerto Sandino through which pass most of the external trade. The chief eastern ports are El Bluff (for Bluefields) and Puerto Cabezas. In 1993, 0·2m. tonnes of cargo were loaded, and 1·07m. tonnes discharged.

Telecommunications. In 1993 there were 66,810 telephones. Broadcasting is administered by the Instituto Nicaragüense de Telecomunicaciones y Correos (Telcor). Number of radio sets in 1991 was 880,000 and television sets 210,000. There were 7 television stations at Managua (colour by NTSC) in 1994.

Press. In 1993 there were 3 daily newspapers in Managua, with a total circulation of 98,602.

SOCIAL INSTITUTIONS

Justice. The judicial power is vested in a Supreme Court of Justice at Managua, 5 chambers of second instance (León, Masaya, Granada, Matagalpa and Bluefields) and 153 judges of inferior tribunals.

Religion. The prevailing form of religion is Roman Catholic (3·75m. adherents in 1992), but religious liberty is guaranteed by the Constitution. There is 1 archbishopric and 7 bishoprics.

Education. The illiteracy rate was 12% in 1983.

Education statistics for 1992–93:

Level	*Institutions*	*Pupils/Students*	*Teachers*
Kindergarten	1,152	70,300	2,291
Primary	4,571	703,854	21,242
Secondary	417	178,342	5,009
High school	10	8,582	173
Technical college	45	19,667	696
Adult education	149	45,833	562
Workers' education	13	2,295	93
Special needs	24	3,100	227
Higher education	6	32,464	2,375

In 1994–95 there were 2 universities and 3 specialized universities (agriculture; engineering; polytechnic) with 18,585 students and 1,260 academic staff.

Health. In 1993 there were 30 hospitals with 3,460 beds, 152 health centres (26 with beds), 247 medical posts and 475 health posts. There were 2,554 doctors, 332 dentists and 1,753 qualified nurses.

DIPLOMATIC REPRESENTATIVES

Of Nicaragua in Great Britain (8 Gloucester Rd., London, SW7 4PP)
Ambassador: Veronica Lacaya de Gómez.

Of Great Britain in Nicaragua (Los Robles, Entrada Principal de la Carretera a Masaya, Cuarta Casa a Mano Derecha, Managua)
Ambassador and Consul-General: J. H. Culver.

Of Nicaragua in the USA (1627 New Hampshire Ave., NW, Washington, D.C., 20009)
Ambassador: R. Mayorga-Cortes.

Of the USA in Nicaragua (Km. 4½, Carretera Sur., Managua)
Ambassador: John F. Maisto.

Of Nicaragua to the United Nations
Ambassador: Erich Vilchez Asher.

Further Reading

Banco Central de Nicaragua. *Informe annual*
Dematteis, L. and Vail, C., *Nicaragua: a Decade of Revolution*, New York, 1991
Dijkstra, G., *Industrialization in Sandinista Nicaragua: Policy and Party in a Mixed Economy*. Boulder (Colo.), 1992
Gilbert, D., *Sandinistas: The Party and the Revolution*. Oxford, 1988
Spalding, R. J., *The Political Economics of Revolutionary Nicaragua*. London, 1987
Walker, T. W., *Nicaragua: The Land of Sandino*. 2nd ed. Boulder (Colo.), 1991
Woodward, R. L., *Nicaragua*. [Bibliography] Oxford and Santa Barbara, 1983

National library: Biblioteca Nacional, Managua
National statistical office: Dirección General de Estadística y Censos, Managua

NIGER

République du Niger

Capital: Niamey
Population: 8·8m. (1994)
GNP per capita: US$230 (1994)
HDI/world rank: 0·207/174 (1992)

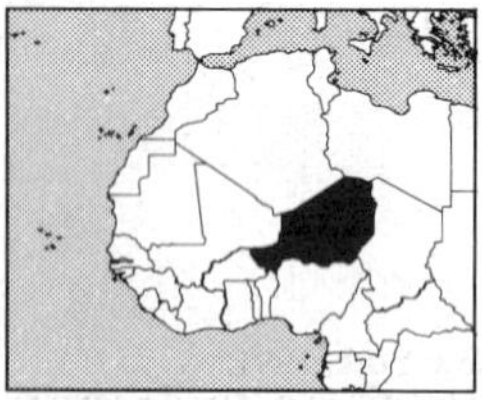

KEY HISTORICAL EVENTS. Niger was occupied by France between 1883 and 1899, and constituted a military territory in 1901, which became a part of French West Africa in 1904. It became an autonomous republic within the French Community on 18 Dec. 1958 and achieved full independence on 3 Aug. 1960.

Guerilla activity by Tuaregs of the Armed Resistance Organization (ORA) seeking local autonomy in the north continued into 1995. On 15 April a peace agreement between the Government and the ORA was initialled under the auspices of Algeria, Burkina Faso and France, but the ORA suspended the agreement on 27 Nov. 1995.

On 27 Jan. 1996 in a bloodless coup the army chief of staff Col. Barré Maïnassara deposed President Mahamane, dissolved parliament and began to rule through a National Safety Council which he headed himself.

TERRITORY AND POPULATION. Niger is bounded in the north by Algeria and Libya, east by Chad, south by Nigeria, south-west by Benin and Burkina Faso, and west by Mali. Area, 1,267,000 sq. km, with a population at the 1988 census of 7,250,383. Estimate (1994), 8,807,000 (19% urban). Population density, 6.8 per sq. km. Vital statistics rates, 1993: Growth, 3·3%; birth, 51 (per 1,000 population); death, 19; fertility, 7·1; infant mortality, 124 (per 1,000 live births); expectation of life, 47 years.

The country is divided into the capital, Niamey, an autonomous district, and 7 departments. Area, population and chief towns at the 1988 census:

Department	*Sq. km*	*Population*	*Chief town*	*Population*
Niamey	670	398,265	Niamey	392,169
Agadez	634,209	203,959	Agadez	49,361
Diffa	140,216	189,316	Diffa	–
Dosso	31,002	1,019,997	Dosso	–
Maradi	38,581	1,388,999	Maradi	109,386
Tahoua	106,677	1,306,652	Tahoua	49,941
Tillabéry	89,623	1,332,398	Tillabéry	–
Zinder	145,430	1,410,797	Zinder	119,838

The population is composed chiefly of Hausa (54%), Songhai and Djerma (23%), Fulani (10%), Beriberi-Manga (9%) and Tuareg (3%). The official language is French. Hausa is understood by 85% of the population.

CLIMATE. Precipitation determines the geographical division into a southern zone of agriculture, a central zone of pasturage and a desert-like northern zone. The country lacks water, with the exception of the south-western districts, which are watered by the Niger and its tributaries, and the southern zone, where there are a number of wells. Niamey, 95°F (35°C). Annual rainfall varies from 22" (560 mm) in the south to 7" (180 mm) in the Sahara zone. The rainy season lasts from May till Sept., but there are periodic droughts.

CONSTITUTION AND GOVERNMENT. At a referendum on 26 Dec. 1992, 89·8% of votes were in favour of a new constitution. The electorate was 3·9m.; turn-out was 56·58%. The constitution of the Third Republic accordingly became law in Jan. 1993. Under it Niger is a unitary multi-party democracy. The *President* is directly elected for a 5-year term renewable once. There is an

83-member *National Assembly* elected for a 5-year term by proportional representation.

The first round of presidential elections on 27 Feb. 1993, at which 8 candidates stood, resulted in a run-off in a second round on 27 March. Turn-out was 35%. Mahamane Ousmane was elected with 55·4% of votes cast.

Elections were held on 12 Jan. 1995 for the National Assembly. The electorate was 4·4m.; turn-out was 35%. The National Movement for a Development Society (MNSD; formerly the sole legal party) won 29 seats; the Social and Democratic Convention, 24; the Niger Party for Democracy and Socialism, 12; the Niger Alliance for Democracy and Progress, 9; the Niger Party for Unity and Democracy, 3; the Niger Social Democratic Party, 2; the Union for Democracy and Social Progress, 2; the Union of Patriots and Progressive Democrats, 1; the Niger Progressive Party, 1.

Following the deposal of President Ousmane Mahamane and the Prime Minister, Hama Amadou, on 27 Jan. 1996, the National Assembly was dissolved and political parties banned. A *National Safety Council* took control, with Col. Barré Maïnassara as head and Col. Issoufa Mamadou Maïga as his deputy. On 30 Jan. Boukari Adji was named *Prime Minister*. In a statement on 13 Feb. the deposed president, prime minister and speaker recognized the necessity of the military 'intervention' and gave their approval to a transitional period to lead up to the nomination of a new government, a constitutional referendum and elections.

National flag: Three horizontal strips of orange, white and green, with an orange disc in the middle of the white strip.

National anthem: 'Auprès du grand Niger puissant' ('By the banks of the mighty great Niger'); words by M. Thiriet, tune by R. Jacquet and N. Frionnet.

Local government: The 8 departments are each under a prefect, sub-divided into 32 *arrondissements*, each under a sub-prefect, and some 150 communes.

DEFENCE. Selective conscription for 2 years operates.

Army. There are 3 military districts. The Army consists of 4 armoured reconnaissance squadrons, 7 infantry, 1 engineer and 2 parachute companies. Equipment includes 90 AML-90 armoured cars. Strength (1996) 5,200. There are additional paramilitary forces of some 5,400.

Air Force. The Air Force had (1995) 100 personnel, 1 C-130H transport, 1 Boeing 737 VIP transport, 2 Cessna Skymasters and 2 Do 28D Skyservants and 1 Do 228 for communications duties. There are no combat aircraft.

INTERNATIONAL RELATIONS

Membership. Niger is a member of the UN, OAU and is an ACP state of the EU.

ECONOMY

Budget. In 1992 revenue (in 1,000 francs CFA) was 70·7 and expenditure, 122·8. Revenue included: Fiscal revenue, 45·9; grants, 16·4. Current expenditure, 78·9; capital expenditure, 43·9.

Currency. The unit of currency is the *franc CFA* (XAF), with a parity rate of 100 francs CFA to 1 French franc. In 1991 42,110m. francs CFA were in circulation. Foreign exchange reserves were US$225m. in 1992; gold reserves were 11,000 troy oz. For exchange rates *see* BENIN: Currency.

Banking and Finance. The regional Central Bank of West African States (BCEAO) functions as the bank of issue, and there were 6 commercial banks in 1994.

Weights and Measures. The metric system is legal, but traditional units are still in use.

ENERGY AND NATURAL RESOURCES

Electricity. Production (1990) amounted to 149·6m. kWh.

Minerals. Large uranium deposits are mined at Arlit and Akouta. Concentrate production (1992), 2,504 tonnes. Phosphates are mined in the Niger valley, and coal reserves are being exploited by open-cast mining (production, 1993, 150,000 tonnes). Tin ore production in 1989 was 100 tonnes; salt, 3,000 tonnes.

Agriculture. Production is dependent upon adequate rainfall. In 1992 there were 36·1m. ha of arable land and 80·0m. ha of permanent pasture. 45,000 ha were irrigated. Production in 1993 (in 1,000 tonnes): Millet, 1,430; maize, 1,000; sorghum, 305; groundnuts, 60; cassava, 220; sugar-cane, 140; sweet potatoes, 35·0; cotton, 3·0.

Livestock (1993): Cattle, 1·8m.; horses, 82,000; asses, 462,000; sheep, 3·5m.; goats, 5·4m.; pigs, 39,000; camels, 370,000; chickens, 2m.

Livestock products (in 1,000 tonnes), 1993: Butter, 4·4; cheese, 12.

There were 180 tractors in 1991.

Forestry. There is a government programme of afforestation as a protection from desert encroachment. There were (1990) 2·06m. ha of forest. Production (1989) 4·42m. cu. metres, mainly for fuel.

Fisheries. There are fisheries on the River Niger and along the shores of lake Chad. Catch (1986) 2,400 tonnes.

INDUSTRY. Some small manufacturing industries, mainly in Niamey, produce textiles, food products, furniture and chemicals. Output in 1989: Cement, 33,000 tonnes; flour, 7,900 tonnes; textiles, 18·2m. metres.

Labour. In 1990 the workforce was 3,619,000 (1,690,000 women). Employment (in 1,000) by branch, 1989: Agriculture, forestry and fisheries, 1·8; energy and water supply, 3·5; mining, 4·1; manufacturing, 2·9; building, 3·6; trade and tourism, 3·1; finance, 1·2; transport and communications, 2·3; public service, 5·8. In 1989 there were 24,600 registered unemployed (1,300 women).

Trade Unions. The national confederation is the *Union Syndicale des Travailleurs du Niger*, which has 15,000 members in 31 unions.

FOREIGN ECONOMIC RELATIONS. Foreign debt was US$1,711m. in 1992.

Commerce. In 1991 imports were valued at 77,100m. francs CFA and exports at 80,100m. francs CFA. Uranium and livestock are the principal exports. Major trading partners are France and Nigeria.

Total trade between Niger and UK (British Department of Trade returns, in £1,000 sterling):

	1991	*1992*	*1993*	*1994*	*1995*
Imports to UK	882	1,151	3,495	4,312	14
Exports and re-exports from UK	10,838	24,634	5,317	3,853	3,809

Tourism. There were 32,940 tourists in 1988.

COMMUNICATIONS

Roads. In 1987 there were 9,862 km of all-weather roads and 3,325 km of paved roads. Niamey and Zinder are the termini of two trans-Sahara motor routes; the Hoggar–Aïr–Zinder road extends to Kano and the Tanezrouft-Gao-Niamey road to Benin. A 648-km 'uranium road' runs from Arlit to Tahoua. There were (1987), 27,254 private cars, 2,253 buses, 5,687 lorries and 8,925 motorcycles. There were 422 traffic accidents in 1987 with 148 fatalities.

Civil Aviation. There are international airports at Niamey and Agadez. Niger is a member of Air Afrique, and there are services by Air Algérie, Air France, Air Mali, Ethiopian Airlines, Libyan Airlines and Royal Air Maroc. 84,752 passengers and

3,951 tonnes of freight passed through Niamey Airport in 1991 (174,000 passengers in 1990).

Shipping. Sea-going vessels can reach Niamey (300 km. inside the country) between Sept. and March.

Telecommunications. There were (1983) 159 post offices and (1994) about 5,000 telephones. La Voix du Sahel and Télé-Sahel under the government's Office de Radiodiffusion Télévision du Niger are responsible for radio and TV broadcasting (colour by SECAM). In 1991 there were estimated to be 0·4m. radio and 25,000 TV sets.

Press. In 1994 there was a government daily bulletin (circulation, 3,500) and several weekly/fortnightly/monthly newspapers in Hausa or French.

SOCIAL INSTITUTIONS

Justice. There are Magistrates' and Assize Courts at Niamey, Zinder and Maradi, and justices of the peace in smaller centres. The Court of Appeal is at Niamey.

Religion. In 1992 there were 6·62m. Sunni Moslems. There are some Christians, and traditional animist beliefs survive.

Education. Adult literacy was 31·2% in 1992. In 1988-89 there were 63 pre-primary schools with 9,674 pupils and 264 teachers, 108 secondary schools with 63,379 pupils ans 2,282 teachers and 5 teacher training colleges with 1,578 students. In 1989–90 there were 2,215 primary schools with 344,900 pupils and 8.462 teachers, and 2 professional training colleges with 859 students (61 women) and 69 teachers. There is a university and an Islamic university, with a total in 1994–95 of 3,980 students and 281 academic staff.

Health. In 1987 in government service there were 13 hospitals, 39 medical centres and 205 dispensaries. In 1987 there were 93 doctors, 1 dentist, 7 pharmacists, 217 midwives and 1,402 nursing personnel (577 state-registered).

DIPLOMATIC REPRESENTATIVES

Of Niger in Great Britain
Ambassador: Sandi Yacouba (resides in Paris).

Of Great Britain in Niger
Ambassador: Margaret Rothwell, CMG (resides in Abidjan).

Of Niger in the USA (2204 R. St., NW, Washington, D.C., 20008)
Ambassador: Adamou Seydou.

Of the USA in Niger (PO Box 11201, Niamey)
Ambassador: John S. Davison.

Of Niger to the United Nations
Ambassador: Adamou Seydou.

Further Reading

Fugelstad, F., *A History of Niger, 1850–1960.* OUP, 1984
Zamponi, L. F., *Niger* [Bibliography]. Oxford and Santa Barbara (CA), 1994

National statistical office: Direction de la Statistique et de l'Informatique, Ministère du Plan, Niamey.

NIGERIA

Federal Republic of Nigeria

Capital: Abuja
Population: 93·3m. (1993)
GNP per capita: US$280 (1994)
HDI/world rank: 0·406/141(1992)

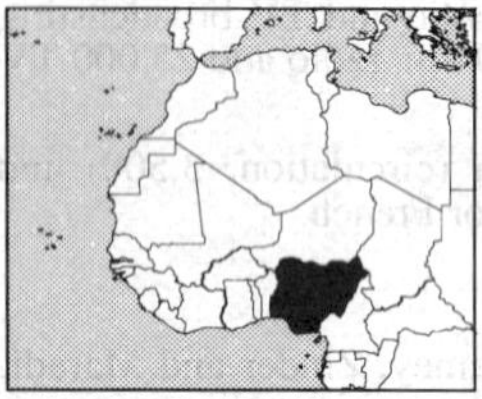

KEY HISTORICAL EVENTS. On 1 Oct. 1954 Nigeria became a federation under a Governor-General. For its previous colonial history since 1861 *see* THE STATESMAN'S YEAR-BOOK, 1993–94, p. 1031. On 1 Oct. 1960 Nigeria became sovereign and independent and a member of the Commonwealth and on 1 Oct. 1963 a republic.

Military coups took place in Dec. 1983 and Aug. 1985. Following the latter, government was assumed by an Armed Forces Ruling Council. This was dissolved in Jan. 1993 and replaced by a transitional civilian council. Presidential elections held in June 1993 were annulled. President Babangida stepped down from office on 26 Aug., nominating Ernest Shoneka as interim head of state.

On 17 Nov. 1993 Gen. Sani Abacha forced Shoneka to resign, and assumed the function of head of state himself. Moshood Abiola, who claims to have won the annulled 1993 presidential election, proclaimed himself head of state in June 1994 and was arrested for treason.

Following the execution of Ogoni separatist Ken Saro-Wiwa and 8 other civil rights activists in Nov. 1995, Nigeria was suspended from the Commonwealth.

TERRITORY AND POPULATION. Nigeria is bounded in the north by Niger, east by Chad and Cameroon, south by the Gulf of Guinea and west by Benin. It has an area of 356,669 sq. miles (923,773 sq. km). For sovereignty over the Bakassi Peninsula *see* CAMEROON: Territory and Population. Census population, 1991, 88,514,501 (43,969,970 females, urban, 36%); population density, 95·8 per sq. km. Official estimate, 1993, 93·3m. The 1991 census results show that previous estimates, such as that of 95m. based on electoral registration in 1978, were exaggerated.

Vital statistics rates, 1993: Birth, 45 (per 1,000 population); death, 14. Infantile mortality, 96 (per 1,000 live births). Expectation of life, 1991: Males, 44·5 years; females, 52·5.

There are 30 states and a Federal Capital Territory (Abuja), 9 states having been created in 1991.

Area, population and capitals of the states:

State	*Area (in sq. km)*	*Population (1991 census)*	*Capital*
Sokoto	102,535	4,392,391	Sokoto
Kebbi		2,062,226	Birnin-Kebbi
Niger	65,037	2,482,367	Minna
Kwara	66,869	1,566,469	Ilorin
Kogi		2,099,046	Lokoja
Benue	45,174	2,780,398	Makurdi
Plateau	58,030	3,283,704	Jos
Taraba	91,390	1,480,590	Jalingo
Adamawa		2,124,049	Yola
Borno	116,400	2,596,589	Maiduguri
Yobe		1,411,481	Damaturu
Bauchi	64,605	4,294,413	Bauchi
Jigawa	43,285	2,829,929	Dutse
Kano		5,632,040	Kano
Katsina	70,245	3,878,344	Katsina
Kaduna		3,969,252	Kaduna
Federal Capital Territory	7,315	378,671	Abuja
Total North	*730,885*	*47,261,959*	

State	Area (in sq. km)	Population (1991 census)	Capital
Oyo	37,705	3,488,789	Ibadan
Osun		2,203,016	Oshogbo
Ogun	16,762	2,338,570	Abeokuta
Lagos	3,345	5,685,781	Ikeja
Ondo	20,959	3,884,485	Akure
Edo	35,500	2,159,848	Benin City
Delta		2,570,181	Asaba
Rivers	21,850	3,983,857	Port-Harcourt
Abia	11,850	2,297,978	Umuahia
Imo		2,485,499	Owerri
Anambra	17,675	2,767,903	Awka
Enugu		3,161,295	Enugu
Cross River	27,237	1,865,604	Calabar
Akwa Ibom		2,359,736	Uyo
Total South	*192,883*	*41,252,542*	

Abuja replaced Lagos as the federal capital and seat of government in Dec. 1991.

Estimated population of the largest cities, 1992:

Lagos	1,347,000	Aba	270,500	Akure	146,900		
Ibadan	1,295,000	Ife	268,600	Gusau	143,000		
Kano	699,900	Ila	238,900	Ijebu-Ode	141,600		
Ogbomosho	660,600	Oyo	237,400	Effon-Alaiye	138,600		
Oshogbo	441,600	Ikerre	221,400	Kumo	134,000		
Ilorin	430,600	Benin City	207,200	Shomolu	133,700		
Abeokuta	386,800	Iseyin	197,100	Oka	129,600		
Port Harcourt	371,000	Katsina	186,900	Ikare	127,500		
Zaria	345,200	Jos	185,600	Sapele	126,000		
Ilesha	342,400	Sokoto	185,500	Minna	125,900		
Onitsha	336,600	Ilobu	180,100	Deba Habe	125,300		
Iwo	335,200	Offa	178,400	Warri	114,100		
Ado-Ekiti	325,300	Ikorodu	167,300	Bida	113,600		
Kaduna	309,600	Ilawe-Ekiti	166,900	Ikire	111,500		
Abuja (capital)	305,900	Owo	166,100	Makurdi	111,410		
Mushin	301,500	Ikirun	164,300	Lafia	110,900		
Maiduguri	289,100	Shaki	161,200	Inisa	108,300		
Enugu	286,100	Calabar	157,800	Shagamu	106,000		
Ede	277,900	Ondo	153,500	Awka	100,700		

There are about 250 ethnic groups. The 3 largest are Hausa-Fulani, Yoruba and Ibo. These, together with the Kamuri, Tiv, Edo, Nupe, Ibibio and Ijaw groups, constitute 80% of the population. The official language is English.

CLIMATE. Lying wholly within the tropics, temperatures everywhere are high. Rainfall varies very much, but decreases from the coast to the interior. The main rains occur from April to Oct. Lagos. Jan. 81°F (27·2°C), July 78°F (25·6°C). Annual rainfall 72" (1,836 mm). Ibadan. Jan. 80°F (26·7°C), July 76°F (24·4°C). Annual rainfall 45" (1,120 mm). Kano. Jan. 70°F (21·1°C), July 79°F (26·1°C). Annual rainfall 35" (869 mm). Port Harcourt. Jan. 79°F (26·1°C), July 77°F (25°C). Annual rainfall 100" (2,497 mm).

CONSTITUTION AND GOVERNMENT. Under the 1978 Constitution, Nigeria is a sovereign, federal republic comprising states and a federal capital district. As part of the process of demilitarization and democratization, in 1993 the government created 2 parties, the Social Democratic Party (SDP) and the National Republican Convention (NRC).

Voting has not been secret since March 1991; voters indicate a poster of the candidate of their choice. At the legislative and gubernatorial elections of Dec. 1991 the NRC gained 16 state governorships and the SDP 14. Parliament consists of a 593-member *House of Representatives* and a 91-member *Senate*. At the elections of 4 July 1992 the SDP gained 44 seats in the Senate and 305 in the House of Representatives, the NRC 32 and 260. Presidential primary elections in Aug. and Sept. 1992 were annulled on grounds of fraud and corruption. Primaries were eventually held on 6 March 1993. Presidential elections were held on 16 June 1993 and won by Moshood Abiola (SDP), but the results were annulled.

On stepping down from all his offices on 26 Aug. 1993 President Babangida nominated an interim government of national unity headed by Ernest Shoneka (ind).

On 17 Nov. 1993 the Minister of Defence, Gen. Sani Abacha, assumed the functions of head of state and set up an 11-member Provisional Ruling Council headed by himself. Parliament, the 30 state Executive Councils and the 2 political parties were dissolved. A 33-member cabinet, the Federal Executive Council, was appointed, chaired by Gen. Abacha. A new Executive Council wasa appointed in March 1995, which in Dec. 1995 included:

Head of State, Minister of Defence: Sani Abacha.

Minister of Agriculture: Gambo Jimeta. *Aviation:* Air Commodore Nsikak Eduok. *Commercial Tourism:* Rear-Adm. Isaac Ariola. *Communications:* Maj.-Gen. Tajudeen Olanrewaju. *Education:* Mohammed Liman. *Federal Capital Territory:* Lieut.-Gen. Jeremiah Useni. *Finance:* Anthony Ani. *Foreign Affairs:* Tom Ikimi. *Health:* Ihechukwu Madubuike. *Industry:* Lieut.-Gen. Muhammadu Haladu. *Information and Culture:* Walter Ofonagoro. *Interior:* Babagana Kingibe. *Justice and Attorney-General:* Michael Agbamuche. *Labour and Productivity:* Uba Ahmed. *National Planning:* Ayo Ogunlade. *Oil:* Dan Etete. *Power and Steel:* Bashir Dalhatu. *Solid Minerals Development:* Kaloma Ali. *Transport:* Gen. Ibrahim Gumel. *Works and Housing:* Maj.-Gen. Abdulkarim Adisa.

In June 1994 a Constitutional Conference opened with 360 participants, 90 of whom were appointed by the government. In Oct. 1994 the Conference recommended the introduction of a plurality of political parties, and the rotation of the presidency between North and South. In June 1995 the Conference submitted a proposal for a new constitution to the head of state, and the latter lifted the ban on political parties.

National flag: Three vertical strips of green, white, green.

National anthem: 'Arise, O compatriots, Nigeria's call obey'; words by a collective, tune by B. Odiase.

Local Government. Each of the 30 states is administered by a directly-elected governor, who appoints and presides over a State Executive Council. The states are subdivided into 500 local authorities, and there is a Federal Capital Territory, Abuja. Local elections took place in Dec. 1990. Turn-out was 20%. The SDP won control of 232 authorities, the NRC of 206.

DEFENCE

Army. The Army consists of 1 armoured division, 2 mechanized divisions, 1 air defence brigade and 1 composite division (motorized infantry, airborne amphibious), each with supporting artillery and engineer and reconnaissance units. Equipment includes 60 T-55 and 150 Vickers Mk 3 main battle tanks. Strength (1996) 62,000.

Navy. The Nigerian Navy comprises 1 German-built MEKO-type frigate with a helicopter and 1 frigate-type training ship, 2 British-built corvettes, 6 fast missile craft, 2 minehunters, and some 45 inshore patrol craft. There are also 2 German-built tank landing ships, 1 survey ship and some 15 service craft. The Navy has a small aviation element equipped with 2 Lynx anti-submarine helicopters. Naval personnel in 1995 totalled 5,500, including Coastguard. The main bases are at Apapa (Lagos) and Calabar.

The Coastguard operate about 10 patrol craft launches, and the police numerous boats.

Air Force. The Nigerian Air Force was established in Jan. 1964. Pilots were trained initially in Canada, India and Ethiopia. The Air Force was built up subsequently with the aid of a Federal Republic of Germany mission; much first-line equipment has since been received from the Soviet Union.

It has 12 MiG-21 supersonic jetfighters and MiG-21U fighter-trainers, and 22 Alpha Jet light attack/trainers. About 15 BO 105 twin-turbine helicopters have been acquired from the Federal Republic of Germany for search and rescue, while 1 F.27MPA is used for maritime patrol. Transport units operate 7 C-130H-30 and C-130H Hercules 4-turboprop heavy transports, 5 twin-turboprop Aeritalia G222s, 4 Super Puma helicopters, 18 Dornier 128-6 twin-turboprop and 18 DO 28D twin-piston utility aircraft, 2 Navajos and a Navajo Chieftain. Training types include 20 Bulldog primary trainers, 12 MB 339 jets for instrument training, 12 Hughes 300 helicopters and 30 L-39 Albatros advanced trainers. Personnel (1995) total about 9,500, with 52 combat aircraft and 15 armed helicopters.

INTERNATIONAL RELATIONS

Membership. Nigeria is a member of the UN, the Commonwealth (suspended Nov. 1995), ECOWAS, OAU, OPEC and is an ACP state of the EU.

ECONOMY

Policy. After 1985, 5-year plans gave way to 3-year rolling plans against a background of 15–20-year plans. There is a privatization programme.

Budget. The financial year is the calendar year. 1995 revenue, ₦350,700m. (of which ₦150,000m. from oil); expenditure, ₦204,200m. (of which ₦44,500m. capital expenditure, ₦57,000m. debt service).

Currency. The unit of currency is the *naira* (NGN) of 100 *kobo*. There are coins of 1, 10, 25 and 50 kobo and 1 naira, and notes of 1, 5, 10, 20 and 50 naira. In 1992 currency in circulation totalled ₦36,800m. Foreign exchange reserves were US$1,386m. in Aug. 1994; gold reserves were 687 troy oz. in June 1992. Government figures showed inflation at 70% at the end of 1994. In March 1992 the Central Bank ceased to fix the exchange rate and the naira was allowed to float, but in Jan. 1994 the exchange rate was again fixed, at US$1 = ₦22. Controls were again abolished in Jan. 1995. In March 1996, £1 = ₦33·62; US$1 = ₦22·00; DM1 = ₦14·90.

Banking and Finance. The Central Bank of Nigeria is the bank of issue (*Governor*, Paul Ogwuma). There were 66 commercial banks (with 2,275 branches) and 54 merchant banks in 1992 (with 116 branches) (81 banks altogether in 1989), in 20 of which central or state governments held a controlling interest.

There is a stock exchange.

Weights and Measures. The metric system is in force.

ENERGY AND NATURAL RESOURCES

Electricity. Installed capacity, 1991, 4,548m. kW. Output, 1992: 14,679·9m. kWh (5,796·1 kWh hydro-electric).

Oil. In 1992 oil production accounted for 12·7% of GDP. Production, 1995, 2,059,000 bbls. a day. There are 4 refineries.

Gas. Natural gas reserves, 1995, were estimated at 3,114,870m. cu. metres. Production, 1991, 31,300m. cu. metres.

Water. 11 River Basin Development Authorities have been established for water resources development.

Minerals. Production, 1992 (in tonnes): Tin, 149; columbite, 36; coal, 86,658; limestone, 160,493; marble, 30,661. There are large deposits of iron ore, coal (reserves estimate 245m. tonnes), lead and zinc. There are small quantities of gold and uranium. Lead production was 3,000 tonnes in 1990.

Agriculture. In 1994 agriculture accounted for 30·7% of GDP. Of the total land mass, 75% is suitable for agriculture, including arable farming, forestry, livestock husbandry and fisheries. In 1992 29·8m. ha were arable, 2·54m. ha permanent cropland and 40m. ha permanent pasture. 0·87m. ha were irrigated. Main food crops are millet and sorghum in the north, plantains and oil palms in the south, and maize, yams, cassava and rice in much of the country, the north being, however, the main food producing area. Output, 1993 (in 1,000 tonnes): Millet, 3,800; sorghum, 4,800; plantains, 1,454; maize, 2,300; yams, 20,000; groundnuts, 1,250; cotton lint, 110; palm kernel, 392,000; palm oil, 965,000; cassava, 21,000; rice, 3·40m.; cocoa, 140.

Livestock (1993): Cattle, 16·3m.; sheep, 14m.; goats, 24·5m.; pigs, 6·7m.; 120m. poultry. Products (in 1,000 tonnes), 1993: Beef and veal, 219; pork, 202; mutton and lamb, 51; goat meat, 127; poultry meat, 165; cow's milk, 380; eggs, 310.

Forestry. In 1990 there were 11·9m. ha of woodland. The most important timber species include mahogany, iroko, obeche, abwa, ebony and camwood. 1992 output (in 1,000 cu. metres): Roundwood, 108,507; saw logs, 1,168; panels, 133.

Fisheries. The total catch (1992) was (in 1,000 tonnes): Coastal fishing, 125; deep-sea, 30; fish farms, 11; other freshwater, 96.

INDUSTRY. In 1992 manufacturing contributed 8·6% of GDP. 1991 production (in 1,000 tonnes) included: Artificial fertilizer, 334; sugar, 59; butter, 8·1; cheese, 6·5; palm oil, 900; copra, 13. 1990: Charcoal, 1,497; veneer, 233; plywood, 175; paper and products, 73; newsprint, 52; palm wine, 5,121.

Labour. In 1990 the workforce (over 10 years old) was 41·86m. (14·55 females). The government doubled the minimum wage to ₦250 per month in 1991. There were 124 work stoppages in 1992 with 967,000 working days lost.

Trade Unions. All trade unions are affiliated to the Nigerian Labour Congress.

FOREIGN ECONOMIC RELATIONS. Foreign debt was US$32,530m. in Nov. 1993. The free repatriation of export profits was ended in Jan. 1994. Restrictions on foreign investors were abolished in Jan. 1995.

Commerce. Exports in 1992 were valued at ₦205,613m.; imports at ₦143,151m. Principal exports (in ₦1m.): Oil, 201,349; cocoa, 1,345; rubber, 766; urea and ammonia, 447; fish, 400. Principal imports: Machinery and transport equipment, 61,841; other manufactures, 35,072; chemicals, 22,904; foodstuffs, 12,597.

In 1993 the main export markets were: USA, 44·1%; Germany, 6·8%; Spain, 6%; India, 5·9%; France, 5·9%. Main import suppliers: UK, 14%; USA, 13·1%; Germany, 10·1%; France, 8·3%; Japan, 7·3%.

Total trade between Nigeria and UK (according to British Department of Trade returns, in £1,000 sterling):

	1991	*1992*	*1993*	*1994*	*1995*
Imports to UK	249,254	168,274	112,375	124,577	181,038
Exports and re-exports from UK	544,553	622,630	634,688	457,916	431,509

Tourism. There were 160,700 foreign visitors in 1989 (306,200 in 1988); 82·6% were from Africa.

COMMUNICATIONS

Roads (1990). There were 142,837 km of maintained roads. In 1992 there were 148,700 motor cars, 41,600 buses and 19,700 lorries. In 1990 there were 17,088 road accidents with 6,244 fatalities.

Railways. There are 3,505 route-km of line 1,067 mm gauge, which in 1991 carried 0.3m. tonnes of freight and 3·4m. passengers.

Civil Aviation. There is an international airport at Lagos (Murtala Muhammed), which handled 2·01m. passengers in 1989. The national carrier is the state-owned Nigeria Airways, which in 1995 operated 2 A310-200s, 5 B-737-200 Advs and 1 DC-10-30. In 1992, 229,000 international and 415,000 domestic passengers were carried. Services are also provided by Air Afrique, Air Gabon, Air Zaïre, Alitalia, American Trans Air, Balkan Bulgarian, British Airways, Cameroon Airlines, Egyptair, Ethiopian Airlines, Ghana Airways, KLM, Lufthansa, Middle East Airlines, Nigeria Airways, Sabena, Swissair, UTA and Varig.

Shipping. In 1995 the merchant marine totalled 0·7m. GRT, including oil tankers, 0·47m. GRT. The principal ports are Lagos, Port Harcourt, Warri and Calabar. In

1990 938,000 tonnes of cargo were loaded and 5,917,000 tonnes unloaded; 2,886 ships arrived and 2,855 departed. There is an extensive network of inland waterways.

Telecommunications. In 1991 there were 3,547 post offices. There were 492,204 telephones in 1990 and 6,724 telex sets in 1991.

The Federal Radio Corporation of Nigeria, a statutory body, broadcasts 3 national radio programmes in English, Yoruba, Hausa and Igbo, and an international service, Voice of Nigeria (5 languages). The government Nigerian Television Authority transmits a national service (colour by PAL), and 10 states have services. In 1993 there were an estimated 10m. radio and 6·1m. TV sets.

Cinemas (1974). There were 120 cinemas, with a seating capacity of 60,000. Mobile cinemas are used by the Federal and States Information Services.

Press. In 1994 there were 20 daily and 30 weekly newspapers.

SOCIAL INSTITUTIONS

Justice. The highest court is the Federal Supreme Court, which consists of the Chief Justice of the Republic, and up to 15 Justices appointed by the government. It has original jurisdiction in any dispute between the Federal Republic and any State or between States; and to hear and determine appeals from the Federal Court of Appeal, which acts as an intermediate appellate Court to consider appeals from the High Court.

High Courts, presided over by a Chief Justice, are established in each state. All judges are appointed by the government. Magistrates' courts are established throughout the Republic, and customary law courts in southern Nigeria. In each of the northern States of Nigeria there are the Sharia Court of Appeal and the Court of Resolution. Moslem Law has been codified in a Penal Code and is applied through Alkali courts.

Religion. Moslems, 48%; Christians, 34% (17% Protestants and 17% Roman Catholic); others, 18%. Northern Nigeria is mainly Moslem; Southern Nigeria is predominantly Christian and Western Nigeria is evenly divided between Christians, Moslems and animists.

Education. Adult illiteracy was 49·3% in 1990. In 1990–91 there were 34,904 primary schools with 12·82m. pupils and 302,100 teachers and 6,538 secondary and tertiary schools with 3·06m. students and 133,743 teachers.

In 1990–91 there were 48 government 'Unity' colleges with 58,300 students and 27 polytechnics with 60,500 students.

In 1994–95 there were 13 universities, 2 agricultural and 5 technological universities, 21 polytechnics, 7 colleges and 2 institutes. There were 127,358 university students and 8,336 academic staff.

Health. In 1987 there were 16,145 doctors, 999 dentists, 56,120 registered nurses, 45,852 registered midwives and 817 hospitals and 7,910 other health centres with 95,776 beds.

DIPLOMATIC REPRESENTATIVES

Of Nigeria in Great Britain (9 Northumberland Ave., London, WC2 5BX)
High Commissioner: Alhaji Abubakar Alhaji.

Of Great Britain in Nigeria (11 Eleke Cres., Victoria Island, Lagos)
High Commissioner: John T. Masefield.

Of Nigeria in the USA (1333 16th St., NW, Washington, D.C., 20036)
Ambassador: Zubair Mahmud Kazaure.

Of the USA in Nigeria (2 Eleke Cres., Lagos)
Ambassador: Walter C. Carrington.

Of Nigeria to the United Nations
Ambassador: Ibrahim Gambari.

Further Reading

Adamolekun, L., *Politics and Administration in Nigeria.* Ibadan, 1986
Burns, A., *History of Nigeria.* 8th ed. London, 1978
Crowder, M. and Abdullahi, G., *Nigeria: an Introduction to its History.* London, 1979
Forrest, T., *Politics and Economic Development in Nigeria.* Boulder (CO), 1993
Myers, R. A., *Nigeria.* [Bibliography] Oxford and Santa Barbara, 1989
Oyovbaine, S.E., *Federalism in Nigeria: A Study in the Development of the Nigerian State.* London, 1985

National statistical office: Federal Office of Statistics.

NORWAY

Kongeriket Norge

(Kingdom of Norway)

Capital: Oslo
Population: 4·3m. (1994)
GNP per capita: US$26,480 (1994)
HDI/world rank: 0·932/7 (1992)

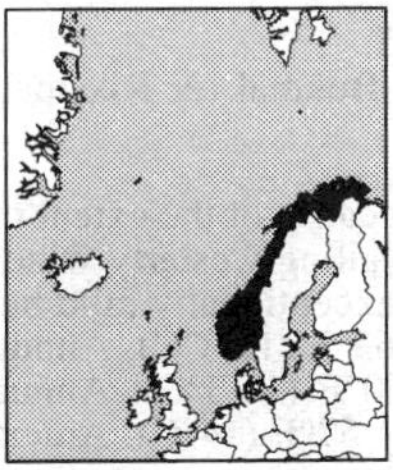

KEY HISTORICAL EVENTS. By the Treaty of 14 Jan. 1814 Norway was ceded to the King of Sweden by the King of Denmark, but the Norwegian people declared themselves independent and elected Prince Christian Frederik of Denmark as their king. The foreign Powers refused to recognize this election, and on 14 Aug. a convention proclaimed the independence of Norway in a personal union with Sweden. This was followed on 4 Nov. by the election of Karl XIII (II) as King of Norway. Sweden agreed to the repeal of the union on 26 Oct. 1905. After a plebiscite, Prince Carl of Denmark was elected King on 18 Nov. 1905, and took the name of Haakon VII.

TERRITORY AND POPULATION. Norway is bounded in the north by the Arctic Ocean, east by Russia, Finland and Sweden, south by the Skagerrak Straits and west by the North Sea.

There are 19 counties (*folk*). Area, population and densities:

	Area (sq. km)	*Population (1990 census)*	*Population (1994 estimate)*	*Density per sq. km 1994*
Oslo (City)	454	461,190	482,555	1,130·1
Akershus	4,917	417,653	434,544	94·7
Østfold	4,183	238,296	239,371	61·5
Hedmark	27,388	187,276	186,657	7·1
Oppland	25,174	182,578	183,194	7·6
Buskerud	14,927	225,172	228,506	16·5
Vestfold	2,216	198,399	203,231	95·0
Telemark	15,315	162,907	163,143	11·5
Aust-Agder	9,212	97,333	99,585	11·7
Vest-Agder	7,281	144,917	149,563	21·9
Rogaland	9,141	337,504	354,418	41·4
Hordaland	15,634	410,567	422,581	28·2
Sogn og Fjordane	18,634	106,659	107,612	6·0
Møre og Romsdal	15,104	238,409	240,215	16·5
Sør-Trøndelag	18,831	250,978	256,266	14·4
Nord-Trøndelag	22,396	127,157	127,560	6·1
Nordland	38,327	239,311	241,420	6·7
Troms	25,981	146,716	150,606	6·0
Finnmark	48,637	74,524	76,668	1·7
Mainland total	323,752 [1]	4,247,546	4,347,695	14·2

Svalbard and Jan Mayen have an area of 63,080 sq. km. Persons staying on Svalbard and Jan Mayen are registered as residents of their home Norwegian municipality.

[1] 125,001 sq. miles.

Population of the principal towns at the census of 3 Nov. 1990:

Oslo	459,292	Sandefjord	36,095	Halden	25,873
Bergen	212,944	Ålesund	35,862	Moss	24,683
Trondheim	137,846	Karmoy	35,087	Rana	24,650
Stavanger	98,109	Skedsmø	34,110	Lillehammer	22,850
Baerum	90,333	Tonsberg	31,551	Børre	22,568
Kristiansand	65,543	Ringsaker	31,377	Harstad	22,375
Drammen	51,880	Porsgrunn	31,268	Ski	22,337
Tromsø	51,218	Haugesund	27,736	Molde	22,251
Skien	47,870	Ringerike	27,384	Kongsberg	21,185
Sandnes	44,798	Fredrikstad	26,546	Oppegard	20,669
Asker	41,848	Lorenskog	26,454	Steinkjer	20,665
Bodø	36,890	Gjøvik	26,207		

Vital statistics for calendar years:

	Marriages	Divorces	Births	Still-born	Outside marriage [1]	Deaths
1992	19,266	10,209	60,109	258	25,801	44,731
1993	19,464	10,943	59,678	248	26,526	46,597
1994	...	...	59,210	...	...	43,757

[1] Excluding still-born.

Expectation of life, 1993: Males, 74·24 years; females, 80·25.

The official language is Norwegian, which has 2 versions: Bokmål (or Riksmål) and Nynorsk (or Landsmål).

CLIMATE. There is considerable variation in the climate because of the extent of latitude, the topography and the varying effectiveness of prevailing westerly winds and the Gulf Stream. Winters along the whole west coast are exceptionally mild but precipitation is considerable. Oslo. Jan. 24°F (–4·7°C), July 63°F (17·3°C). Annual rainfall 29·1" (740 mm). Bergen. Jan. 35°F (1·4°C), July 60°F (15·3°C). Annual rainfall 83" (2,108 mm). Trondheim. Jan. 26°F (–3·5°C), July 57°F (14°C). Annual rainfall 32·1" (870 mm).

ROYAL HOUSE. The reigning King is **Harald V,** born 21 Feb. 1937, married on 29 Aug. 1968 to Sonja Haraldsen. He succeeded on the death of his father, King Olav V, on 21 Jan. 1991. *Offspring:* Princess Märtha Louise, born 22 Sept. 1971; Crown Prince Haakon Magnus, born 20 July 1973.

The king receives a tax-free annual allowance of 19·8m. kroner from the civil list. Women have been eligible to succeed to the throne since 1990. There is no coronation ceremony. The royal succession is in direct male line in the order of primogeniture. In default of male heirs the King may propose a successor to the Storting, but this assembly has the right to nominate another, if it does not agree with the proposal.

CONSTITUTION AND GOVERNMENT. Norway is a constitutional and hereditary monarchy. The Constitution, voted by a constituent assembly on 17 May 1814 and modified at various times, vests the legislative power of the realm in the *Storting* (Parliament). The royal veto may be exercised; but if the same Bill passes two Stortings formed by separate and subsequent elections it becomes the law of the land without the assent of the sovereign. The King has the command of the land, sea and air forces, and makes all appointments.

The 165-member Storting is directly elected by proportional representation. The country is divided into 19 districts, each electing from 4 to 15 representatives.

The Storting, when assembled, divides itself by election into the *Lagting* and the *Odelsting*. The former is composed of one-fourth of the members of the Storting, and the other of the remaining three-fourths. Each Ting (the Storting, the Odelsting and the Lagting) nominates its own president. Most questions are decided by the Storting, but questions relating to legislation must be considered and decided by the Odelsting and the Lagting separately. Only when the Odelsting and the Lagting disagree, the Bill has to be considered by the Storting in plenary sitting, and a new law can then only be decided by a majority of two-thirds of the voters. The same majority is required for alterations of the Constitution, which can only be decided by the Storting in plenary sitting. The Storting elects 5 delegates, whose duty it is to revise the public accounts. The Lagting and the ordinary members of the Supreme Court of Justice (the *Høyesterett*) form a High Court of the Realm (the *Riksrett*) for the trial of ministers, members of the *Høyesterett* and members of the Storting. The impeachment before the *Riksrett* can only be decided by the Odelsting.

The executive is represented by the King, who exercises his authority through the Cabinet. Cabinet ministers are entitled to be present in the Storting and to take part in the discussions, but without a vote.

At the elections for the Storting held in 1993 the following parties were elected: Labour Party, 67; Centre Party, 32; Conservative Party, 28; Christian Democratic Party, 13; Socialist Left Party, 13; Progress Party 10; Liberal Party, 1; Red Electoral Alliance, 1.

In Feb. 1996 the minority Labour government comprised:

Prime Minister: Gro Harlem Brundtland (b. 1939).

Foreign Affairs: Bjørn Tore Godal. *Industry, Oil and Energy:* Jens Stoltenberg. *Defence:* Jørgen Kosmo. *Agriculture:* Gunhild Øyangen. *Local Government and Labour:* Gunnar Berge. *Environment:* Thorbjørn Berntsen. *Transport and Communications:* Kjell Opseth. *Education, Research and Church Affairs:* Gudmund Hernes. *Cultural Affairs:* Åse Kleveland. *Finance:* Sigbjørn Johnsen. *Justice:* Grete Faremo. *Trade and Shipping:* Grete Knutsen. *Family and Consumer Affairs:* Grete Berget. *Health and Social Affairs:* Hill-Marta Solberg. *Government Administration:* Nils Olav Totland. *Development Co-operation:* Kari Nordheim-Larsen. *Fisheries:* Jan Henry T. Olsen.

National flag: Red with blue Scandinavian cross edged with white.

National anthem: 'Ja, vi elsker dette landet' ('Yes, we love this land'); words by B. Bjørnson, tune by R. Nordraak.

Local Government. There are 18 counties and the urban district of Oslo, in each of which the central government is represented by a county governor. The counties are divided into 435 municipalities, each of which usually corresponds in size to a parish. The municipalities are administered by municipal councils, whose membership may vary between 25 and 85 directly-elected councillors. Elections were held in Sept. 1995; turn-out was 40%.

DEFENCE. Conscription is for 12 months, with 4 to 5 refresher training periods.

Army. There are a Northern and a Southern command, and within these the Army is organized in 4 district commands, 1 divisional headquarters and 14 territorial commands. North Command consists of 1 brigade group. South Command consists of 2 infantry battalions, including the Royal Guard. Equipment includes 170 Leopard main battle tanks. Strength (1996) 14,700 (including 9,200 conscripts). The fast mobilization reserve numbers 255,000.

Navy. The Royal Norwegian Navy has 3 components: The Navy, Coast Guard and Coastal Artillery. Main Naval combatants include 12 coastal submarines (including 6 new German-built Ula class), 4 frigates, 30 missile craft, 3 coastal minesweepers, 5 minehunters and 2 minelayers. Auxiliaries comprise 1 submarine/missile craft support ship, 1 Royal Yacht and some 10 small general-purpose tenders. The Coastal Artillery man 26 coastal batteries and other static defence systems.

The personnel of the navy totalled 6,400 in 1995, of whom 4,000 were conscripts. 1,400 served in coast artillery and 600 in coast guard. The main naval base is at Bergen (Håkonsvern), with subsidiary bases at Horten, Ramsund and Tromsø.

The naval elements of the Home Guard on mobilization can muster some 6,000 personnel, and man 2 tank landing craft, 7 torpedo craft and about 400 requisitioned fishing vessels.

The 12 Coast Guard offshore patrol vessels (of which 3 are armed, and of frigate capability) are Navy-subordinated, and assist other government agencies in rescue service, environmental patrols, surveillance and police duties. The coast guard numbered 700 in 1993.

Air Force. The Royal Norwegian Air Force comprises the Air Force and the Anti-air Artillery. The Air Force consists of 4 squadrons of F-16 Fighting Falcons, 1 squadron of F-5 fighter-bombers, 1 maritime patrol squadron of P-3N and P-3C Orions, 1 squadron of C-130 Hercules transports, 1 squadron of Falcon 20s equipped for EW duties, 1 squadron with DHC-6 Twin Otter light transports and 2 squadrons of Bell 412SP helicopters. The Anti-air Artillery deploy 4 Nike surface-to-air missile batteries and several light anti-aircraft artillery units. 6 NOAH (Norwegian adapted Hawk missiles) batteries provide area and airfield defence co-ordinated with 10 SAM batteries with the mobile missile system RBS-70. Finally 27 batteries with 40 mm Bofors AA-guns and 12·7 mm machine guns. 12 Westland Sea King helicopters are used for search and rescue duties; 5 Lynx helicopters are operated for the Coast Guard; 17 Saab Safaris are used for primary training; pilots then go to the USA for advanced training.

Total strength (1995) is about 7,900 personnel, including 4,100 conscripts.

Home Guard. The Home Guard is organized in small units equipped and trained for special tasks. Service after basic training is 1 week a year. The Home Guard consists of the Land Home Guard (strength, 1996, 71,000), Sea Home Guard and Anti-Air Home Guard organized in 18 districts. *See also under* NAVY, *above.*

INTERNATIONAL RELATIONS

Membership. Norway is a member of the UN, NATO, EFTA, OECD, the Council of Europe and the Nordic Council, and an Associate Member of the WEU.

In a referendum on 27-28 Nov. 1994 52·2% of votes cast were against joining the EU. The electorate was 3,266,182; turn-out was 88·88%.

ECONOMY

Budget. Current central government revenue and expenditure for years ending 31 Dec. (in 1m. kroner):

	1991	*1992*	*1993*	*1994*
Revenue	328,528	325,113	334,776	357,915
Expenditure	309,767	318,823	327,343	336,965

Currency. The unit of currency is the *Norwegian krone* (NOK) of 100 *øre*. There are coins of 10 and 50 øre and 1, 5 and 10 kroner, and notes of 50, 100, 200, 500 and 1,000 kroner. On 31 Dec. 1994 the nominal value of notes and coins in circulation was 40,443m. kroner. After Oct. 1990 the krone was fixed to the ecu in the EMS of the EEC in the narrow band of 2·25%, but it was freed in Dec. 1992. In March 1996, US$1 = 6·42 kroner; £1 = 9·81 kroner; DM1 = 4·35 kroner.

Banking and Finance. Norges Bank is the central bank and bank of issue. Supreme authority is vested in the Executive Board consisting of 7 members appointed by the King and the Supervisory Council consisting of 15 members elected by the Storting. The *Governor* is Kjell Storvik (b. 1930).

There are 3 major commercial banks: Den Norske Bank, Christiana and Fokus.

At the end of 1992 there were 23 private joint-stock banks. Their total amount of capital and funds was 21,284m. kroner (capital 12,029m., funds 9,255m.). Deposits amounted to 238,679m. kroner, of which 174,931m. kroner were on ordinary notice, and 63,748m. kroner on special terms.

The number of savings banks at the end of 1992 was 134. Ordinary deposits totalled 151,684m. kroner in 1993, of which 6,486m. kroner were from other banks.

There is a stock exchange in Oslo.

Weights and Measures. The metric system is obligatory.

ENERGY AND NATURAL RESOURCES

Electricity. Norway is a large producer of hydro-electric energy. The potential total hydro-electric power is estimated at 170,000m. kWh annually. Installed capacity in 1989 was 251 MW (thermoelectric) and 25,841 MW (hydro-electric). Output, 1993, 120,001m. kwh (117,062m. kWh hydro-electric in 1992).

Oil and Gas. There are enormous oil reserves in the Norwegian continental shelf. In 1966 the first exploration well was drilled. Production, 1995, 2,902,000 bbls. a day. Gas output (1994, provisional) 30·63m. cu.metres.

Minerals. Production, 1992 (in tonnes): Iron, 2,266,714; titanium, 708,149; copper, 50,099; lead 7,235; zinc, 41,410.

Agriculture. Norway is barren and mountainous. The arable area is in strips in valleys and around fiords and lakes.

In 1994 the agricultural area [1] was 1,019,300 ha, of which 583,800 ha were meadow and pasture, 178,600 ha were sown to barley, 98,700 ha to oats, 69,000 ha to wheat and 17,100 ha to potatoes. Production (in 1,000 tonnes) in 1993: Barley, 631; oats, 380; wheat, 360; potatoes, 454; hay, 3,381; vegetables, 125; meat, 227.

[1] Holdings with at least 50 ha agricultural area in use.

Livestock, 1994 [1]: 979,600 cattle (336,800 milch cows), 990,900 sheep, 59,700 goats, 746,700 pigs, 3,652,600 hens. 1993: 92,000 silver and platinum fox, 358,000 blue fox, 294,000 mink, 210,500 reindeer.

[1] Holdings with at least 50 ha agricultural area in use.

Forestry. Productive forest area, 1993, 67,309 sq. km. About 80% of the productive forest area consists of conifers and 20% of broadleaves. The annual increment (in 1993) was 20,332,000 cu. metres with bark. In 1992–93, 9·5m. cu. metres of roundwood were cut: 8·73m. cu. metres were coniferous timber (of which 4·5m. cu. metres went to sawmills and 3·56m. cu. metres to pulp industries), 0·32m. cu. metres broadleaf timber and 0·46m. cu. metres fuelwood.

Fisheries. The total number of fishermen in 1993 was 25,388, of whom 6,320 had another chief occupation. In 1994, the number of registered fishing vessels (all with motor) was 15,212, and of these 6,494 were open boats.

The catch in 1994 totalled 2,329,417 tonnes. 12,662 seals were caught in 1993. Commercial whaling was prohibited in 1988, but recommenced in 1993. 273 whales were caught in 1994, including 70 for research.

INDUSTRY. Industry is chiefly based on raw materials. Crude petroleum and natural gas production, the manufacture of paper and paper products, industrial chemicals and basic metals are the most important export manufactures. In the following table are given figures for industrial establishments in 1993 employing at least 10 persons. Electrical plants, construction and building industry are not included. The values are given in 1m. kroner.

Industries	*Establishments*	*Number of Employees*	*Gross value of production*	*Value added*
Coal and peat	3	331	163	32
Crude petroleum and natural gas	24	17,338	124,246	93,869
Metal ores	8	1,424	1,029	271
Other-mining and quarrying	73	1,785	1,974	910
Food products	859	39,694	69,327	11,558
Beverages and tobacco	36	4,915	11,187	8,407
Textiles	115	4,607	3,205	1,252
Clothing, etc.	58	1,645	1,033	408
Leather and leather products	18	726	516	173
Wood and wood products	286	10,296	9,406	2,916
Pulp, paper and paper products	82	10,151	15,028	3,906
Printing and publishing	452	29,232	19,295	8,911
Basic chemicals	50	8,231	16,340	4,772
Other chemical products	49	4,985	7,979	3,062
Coke and refined petroleum products	59	1,574	16,518	1,806
Rubber and plastic products	126	5,018	4,433	1,701
Other non-metallic mineral products	177	6,517	6,672	2,755
Basic metals	67	13,257	25,408	6,017
Metal products, except machinery/equipment	389	12,717	9,474	3,896
Machinery and equipment	294	18,114	16,463	5,912
Office machinery and computers	6	774	928	283
Electrical machinery and apparatus	119	8,272	8,709	3,272
Radio, television, communication equipment	44	3,856	3,766	1,477
Medical, precision and optical instruments	55	3,409	3,842	1,410
Motor vehicles and trailers	52	3,200	2,566	955
Other transport equipment	300	34,566	33,327	11,569
Other manufacturing industries	223	9,031	6,539	2,481
Total (all included)	4,024	255,665	419,377	183,981

Income at factor cost (in 1m. kroner):

	1990	*1991*	*1992*
Net domestic product	561,727	584,224	598,762
Less Indirect taxes	111,089	115,617	121,441
Add Subsidies	39,992	42,770	44,395
	490,630	511,377	521,718

Labour. The labour force (i.e. employed persons plus non-employed persons seeking work aged 16–74) averaged 2,151,000 persons in 1994 (979,000 females).

Distribution of employed persons by occupation in 1994 showed 533,000 in technical, physical science, humanistic and artistic work; 143,000 administrative executive work; 201,000 clerical; 213,000 sales; 106,000 agriculture, forestry, fishing etc.; 7,000 mining and quarrying; 129,000 transport and communication; 378,000 manufacturing; 286,000 service, and 39,000 military and occupation not specified.

There were 110,280 registered unemployed in 1994 (44,539 females).

There were 20 work stoppages in 1994; 97,213 working days were lost.

Trade Unions. There were 1,350,798 union members in 1994.

FOREIGN ECONOMIC RELATIONS

Commerce. Total imports and exports in calendar years (in 1,000 kroner):

	1990	*1991*	*1992*	*1993*	*1994*
Imports	169,998,400	165,181,200	161,931,000	170,991,300	192,963,000
Exports	211,579,400	220,316,300	218,374,300	226,626,100	244,475,100

Major import suppliers in 1994 (value in 1m. kroner): Sweden, 28,852; Germany, 26,758·6; UK, 19,966·2; Denmark, 14,230·9; USA, 14,150·3; Japan, 11,422·3; Netherlands, 8,150·5; France, 7,774·6; Finland, 7,016; Italy, 6,670·7. Imports from economic areas: EC, 94,726·4; Nordic countries, 50,465·6; EFTA, 40,654·3.

Major export markets 1994: UK, 50,596·4; Germany, 29,521·6; Netherlands, 23,175·5; Sweden, 23,165; France, 19,301·4; USA, 15,844·9; Denmark, 11,551·7; Canada, 8,264; Finland, 7,377·6; Italy, 7,127; Belgium, 6,903·8. Exports to economic areas: EC, 157,805·6; Nordic countries, 43,793·9; EFTA, 34,415·9.

Principal imports in 1994 (in 1m. kroner): Machinery, 21,506·9; motor vehicles, 14,835·6; electrical machinery, 9,994·3; apparel and clothing, 9,090·1; iron and steel, 8,322·1; office machines and computers, 8,313·4; metalliferous ores and metal scrap, 8,216·4; ships over 100 tonnes, 7,794·6; telecommunications and sound apparatus and equipment, 6,291·5; paper, 4,964·1; oil and products, 4,269·8; chemicals, 4,103·5; non-ferrous metals, 3,997·3; professional and scientific instruments, 3,831·1; textiles, 3,731·4; furniture, 3,404·7; medical products, 3,336·9; vegetables and fruit, 2,994·9. Principal exports in 1994 (in 1m. kroner): Oil and products, 102,598·5; fish, 18,806·2; non-ferrous metals, 18,729·5; gas, 16,608·3; machinery, 9,062·1; ships over 100 tonnes, 8,582·9; paper, 7,291·8; iron and steel, 6,723; chemicals, 5,383·1; electrical machinery, 3,534·5; primary plastics, 3,383·6.

Total trade between Norway and UK (British Department of Trade returns, in £1,000 sterling):

	1991	*1992*	*1993*	*1994*	*1995*
Imports to UK	4,232,827	3,861,771	4,170,275	3,709,666	4,325,432
Exports and re-exports from UK	1,357,299	1,419,570	1,519,473	2,020,878	1,998,499

Tourism. In 1994 there were 1,195 hotels. There were 2·83m. foreign tourists staying 5·04m. nights in 1994.

COMMUNICATIONS

Roads. In 1995 the length of public roads (including roads in towns) totalled 90,174 km. Of these, 61,101 km were hard-surfaced in 1991. Total road length included: National roads, 26,463 km; provincial roads, 27,075 km; local roads, 36,636 km. Number of registered motor vehicles, 1994: 1,653,678 passenger cars (including station wagons and ambulances), 30,547 buses, 176,528 vans, 91,240 combined vehicles, 68,011 lorries, 214,310 tractors, 38,016 snow scooters and 156,624 motor cycles and mopeds. In 1994 there were 8,406 road accidents with 283 fatalities.

Railways. The length of state railways in 1994 was 4,023 km (2,422 km electrified); of private companies, 16 km (electrified). Total receipts of the state railways in 1994 were 5,178m. kroner; total expenses, 5,380m. kroner. The state railways carried 19,997,000 tonnes of freight and 37,926,000 passengers in 1994.

There is a metro (98 km) and tram/light rail line (54 km) in Oslo.

Civil Aviation. There are international airports at Oslo (Fornebu), Bergen (Flesland) and Stavanger (Sola). Denmark and Norway hold each two-sevenths and Sweden three-sevenths of the capital of SAS (Scandinavian Airlines System), but they have joint responsibility towards third parties. At 31 Dec. 1994 there were 862 registered aircraft. 7,516,410 passengers were carried in 1993.

Services are also provided by Aeroflot, Air France, Air Malta, Air Stord, Air UK, Alitalia, Austrian Airlines, Braathens, British Airways, British Midland, Coast Air, Continental Airlines & Air Micronesia, Finnair, Hemus Air, Icelandair, KLM, Lufthansa, Muk Air, Newair, Northwest Airlines, Sabena, Sun Air, Swissair, TAP, Teddy Air, United Airlines and Wideroe's.

Shipping. The Norwegian International Shipping Registry was set up in 1987. At 31 Dec. 1994, 728 ships were registered (508 Norwegian) totalling 19·8m. GRT. There were also 914 ships totalling 1·95m. GRT on the Norwegian Ordinary Register. These figures do not include fishing boats, tugs, salvage vessels, icebreakers and similar special types of vessels.

Goods (in 1,000 tonnes) in 1993 discharged, 18,929; loaded, 108,268.

In 1993, 46·52m. passengers were carried by coastwise shipping on long distance, local and ferry services, and (excluding long distance except Bergen-Stavanger) 34·6m. tonnes of cargo.

Telecommunications. There were 2,414 post offices in 1994. Number of telephone connexions on 31 Dec. 1994 was 2,392,042. There were 0·47m. mobile telephones in use in 1994. The Norwegian Broadcasting Corporation is a non-commercial enterprise operated by an independent state organization and broadcasts 1 programme (P1) on long-, medium-, and short-waves and on FM and 1 programme (P2) on FM. Local programmes are also broadcast. It broadcasts 1 TV programme from 2,259 transmitters. Colour programmes are broadcast by PAL system. Number of television licences, 1994, 1,549,610.

Cinemas. There were 400 cinemas with a seating capacity of 96,793 in 1993, and 20 theatres and operas.

Press. There were 61 daily newspapers with a combined circulation of 2·2m. in 1994, and 91 weeklies and semi-weeklies with 0·78m.

SOCIAL INSTITUTIONS

Justice. The judicature is common to civil and criminal cases; the same professional judges preside over both. These judges are state officials. The participation of lay judges and jurors, both summoned for the individual case, varies according to the kind of court and kind of case.

The 96 city or district courts of first instance are in criminal cases composed of one professional judge and 2 lay judges, chosen by ballot from a panel elected by the local authority. In civil cases 2 lay judges may participate. These courts are competent in all cases except criminal cases where the maximum penalty exceeds 6 years imprisonment.

In every community there is a Conciliation Board composed of 3 lay persons elected by the district council. A civil lawsuit usually begins with mediation by the Board which can pronounce judgement in certain cases.

The 5 high courts, or courts of second instance are composed of 3 professional judges. Additionally, in civil cases 2 or 4 lay judges may be summoned. In serious criminal cases, which are brought before high courts in the first instance a jury of 10 lay persons is summoned to determine whether the defendant is guilty according to the charge. In less serious criminal cases the court is composed of 2 professional and 3 lay judges. In civil cases, the court of second instance is an ordinary court of appeal. In criminal cases in which the lower court does not have judicial authority, it is itself the court of first instance. In other criminal cases it is an appeal court as far as the appeal is based on an attack against the lower court's assessment of the facts when determining the guilt of the defendant. An appeal based on any other alleged mistakes is brought directly before the Supreme Court.

The Supreme Court *(Høyesterett)* is the court of last resort. There are 18 Supreme Court judges. Each individual case is heard by 5 judges. Some major cases are determined in plenary session. The Supreme Court may in general examine every aspect of the case and the handling of it by the lower courts. However, in criminal cases the Court may not overrule the lower court's assessment of the facts as far as the guilt of the defendant is concerned.

The Court of Impeachment *(Riksretten)* is composed of 5 judges of the Supreme Court and 10 members of Parliament.

All serious offences are prosecuted by the State. The Public Prosecution Authority consists of the Attorney General, 18 district attorneys and legally qualified officers of the ordinary police force. Counsel for the defence is in general provided for by the State.

Religion. There is freedom of religion, the Church of Norway (Evangelical Lutheran), however, being the national church, endowed by the State. Its clergy are nominated by the King. Ecclesiastically Norway is divided into 11 bishoprics, 96 archdeaconries and 626 clerical districts. There were 216,193 members of registered and unregistered religious communities outside the Evangelical Lutheran Church, subsidized by central government and local authorities in 1994. The Roman Catholics are under a Bishop at Oslo, a Vicar Apostolic at Trondheim and a Vicar Apostolic at Tromsø.

Education. There is free compulsory schooling in primary and lower secondary schools for 9 years starting at age 7. In 1993 there were 5,631 nursery schools for children under 7 with 173,386 children and 46,394 staff. In 1993–94 there were 3,325 primary and lower secondary schools with 466,991 pupils and 36,196 teachers; (1991–92) 75 special schools with 1,980 pupils and (1990–91) 1,099 teachers; 771 upper secondary schools with 240,506 pupils and 21,780 teachers; and 181 colleges, with 94,623 students and 4,992 teachers.

There are 4 universities (Bergen, founded 1948; Oslo, 1811; Tromsø, 1968; and Trondheim, 1910) and 10 specialized institutions of equivalent status. In 1993–94 these had 77,951 students and (Oct. 1993) 8,496 academic staff.

Health. In 1994 there were 14,497 doctors, 5,088 dentists and 61,367 nurses.

Social Security. In 1994 there were 624,512 old age pensioners who received a total of 45,715·9m. kroner, 233,688 disability pensioners who received 21,038·5m. kroner, 32,638 widows and widowers who received 1,770·1m. kroner and 46,255 single parents who received 2,324·9m. kroner. In 1993, 877,489 children received family allowances. Maternity leave is for 1 year on 80% of previous salary; unused portions may pass to a husband. In 1994 sickness benefits totalling 25,832·5m. kroner were paid: 10,442·2m. kroner in sickness allowances to 325,661 cases; 5,441·6m. kroner in confinement benefits to 73,890 cases; 9,948·7m. kroner in medical benefits.

DIPLOMATIC REPRESENTATIVES

Of Norway in Great Britain (25 Belgrave Sq., London, SW1X 8QD)
Ambassador: Tom Eric Vraalsen, GCVO.

Of Great Britain in Norway (Thomas Heftyesgate 8, 0244 Oslo, 2)
Ambassador: M. Elliott, CMG.

Of Norway in the USA (2720 34th St., NW, Washington, D.C., 20008)
Ambassador: Kjell Vibe.

Of the USA in Norway (Drammensveien 18, 0244 Oslo, 2)
Ambassador: Thomas Loftus.

Of Norway to the United Nations
Ambassador: Hans Biørn Lian.

Further Reading

Central Bureau of Statistics. *Statistisk Årbok*; *Statistical Yearbook of Norway.—Economic survey* (annual, from 1935; with English summary from 1952, now published in *Økonomiske Analyser*, annual).—*Historisk Statistikk*; *Historical Statistics.—Statistisk Månedshefte* (with English index)
Norges Statskalender. From 1816; annual from 1877
Arntzen, J. G. and Knudsen, B. B., *Political Life and Institutions in Norway.* Oslo, 1981
Derry, T. K., *A History of Modern Norway, 1814–1972.* OUP, 1973.—*A History of Scandinavia.* London, 1979
Petersson, O., *The Government and Politics of the Nordic Countries.* Stockholm, 1994
Sather, L. B., *Norway.* [Bibliography] Oxford and Santa Barbara, 1986
Selbyg, A., *Norway Today: An Introduction to Modern Norwegian Society.* Oslo, 1986

National library: The University Library, Drammensvein 42b, 0255 Oslo.
National statistical office: Central Bureau of Statistics, PB 8131 Dep., 0033 Oslo 1.

SVALBARD

An archipelago situated between 10° and 35° E. long. and between 74° and 81° N. lat. Total area, 62,000 sq. km (24,000 sq. miles). The main islands are Spitsbergen, Nordaustlandet, Edgeøya, Barentsøya, Prins Karls Forland, Bjørnøya, Hopen, Kong Karls Land and Kvitøya. The Arctic climate is tempered by mild winds from the Atlantic.

The archipelago was probably discovered by Norsemen in 1194 and rediscovered by the Dutch navigator Barents in 1596. In the 17th century whale-hunting gave rise to rival Dutch, British and Danish–Norwegian claims to sovereignty. But when in the 18th century the whale-hunting ended, the question of the sovereignty of Svalbard lost its significance; it was again raised in the 20th century, owing to the discovery and exploitation of coalfields. By a treaty, signed on 9 Feb. 1920 in Paris, Norway's sovereignty over the archipelago was recognized. On 14 Aug. 1925 the archipelago was officially incorporated in Norway.

Total population on 31 Dec. 1994 was 2,906, of whom 1,218 were Norwegians, 1,679 citizens of the former USSR, and 9 Poles. Coal is the principal product. There are 2 Norwegian and 2 Russian mining camps. 266,734 tonnes of coal were produced from Norwegian mines in 1993 valued at 71·6m. kroner.

There are research and radio stations, and an airport near Longyearbyen (Svalbard Lufthavn) opened in 1975.

Greve, T., Svalbard: Norway in the Arctic. Oslo, 1975
Hisdal, V., *Geography of Svalbard.* Norsk Polarinstitutt, Oslo, rev. ed., 1984

JAN MAYEN

This bleak, desolate and mountainous island of volcanic origin and partly covered by glaciers, is situated 71° N. lat. and 8° 30' W. long., 300 miles NNE of Iceland. The total area is 380 sq. km (147 sq. miles). Beerenberg, its highest peak, reaches a height of 2,277 metres. Volcanic activity, which had been dormant, was reactivated in Sept. 1970.

The island was possibly discovered by Henry Hudson in 1608, and it was first named Hudson's Tutches (Touches). It was again and again rediscovered and renamed. Its present name derives from the Dutch whaling captain Jan Jacobsz May, who indisputably discovered the island in 1614. It was uninhabited, but occasionally visited by seal hunters and trappers, until 1921 when Norway established a radio and meteorological station. On 8 May 1929 Jan Mayen was officially proclaimed as incorporated in the Kingdom of Norway. Its relation to Norway was finally settled by law of 27 Feb. 1930. A LORAN station (1959) and a CONSOL station (1968) have been established.

BOUVET ISLAND
Bouvetøya

This uninhabited volcanic island, mostly covered by glaciers and situated 54° 25' S. lat. and 3° 21' E. long., was discovered in 1739 by a French naval officer, Jean Baptiste Loziert Bouvet, but no flag was hoisted till, in 1825, Capt. Norris raised the Union Jack. In 1928 Great Britain waived its claim to the island in favour of Norway, which in Dec. 1927 had occupied it. A law of 27 Feb. 1930 declared Bouvetøya a Norwegian dependency. The area is 50 sq. km (19 sq. miles). From 1977 Norway has had an automatic meteorological station on the island.

PETER I ISLAND
Peter I Øy

This uninhabited island, situated 68° 48' S. lat. and 90° 35' W. long., was sighted in 1821 by the Russian explorer, Admiral von Bellingshausen. The first landing was made in 1929 by a Norwegian expedition which hoisted the Norwegian flag. On 1 May 1931 Peter I Island was placed under Norwegian sovereignty, and on 24 March 1933 it was incorporated in Norway as a dependency. The area is 180 sq. km (69 sq. miles).

QUEEN MAUD LAND
Dronning Maud Land

On 14 Jan. 1939 the Norwegian Cabinet placed that part of the Antarctic Continent from the border of Falkland Islands dependencies in the west to the border of the Australian Antarctic Dependency in the east (between 20° W. and 45° E.) under Norwegian sovereignty. The territory had been explored only by Norwegians and hitherto been ownerless. In 1957 it was given the status of a dependency.

OMAN

Saltanat 'Uman

(Sultanate of Oman)

Capital: Muscat
Population: 2·1m. (1994)
GNP per capita: US$5,200 (1994)
HDI/world rank: 0·715/91 (1992)

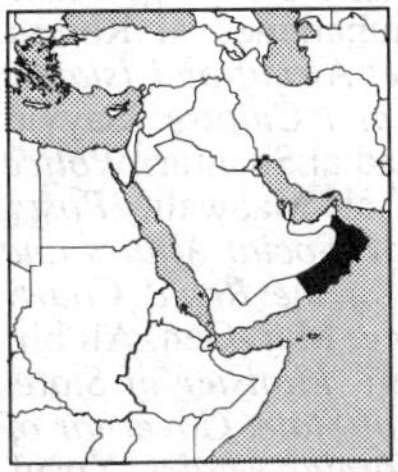

KEY HISTORICAL EVENTS. Oman was dominated by Portugal from 1507–1649. The Al-Busaid family assumed power in 1744 and have ruled to the present day. The Sultanate of Oman was known as the Sultanate of Muscat and Oman until 1970.

TERRITORY AND POPULATION. Oman is bounded in the north-east by the Gulf of Oman and south-east by the Arabian Sea, south-west by Yemen and north-west by Saudi Arabia and the United Arab Emirates. There is an enclave at the northern tip of the Musandam Peninsula between the United Arab Emirates of Ras al-Khaimah in the west and Fujairah in the south-east. An agreement of June 1995 completed the demarcation of the border with Yemen, and an agreement with Saudi Arabia of July 1995 permits the demarcation of their mutual border.

The **Kuria Muria** islands were ceded to the UK in 1854 by the Sultan of Muscat and Oman. On 30 Nov. 1967 the islands were retroceded to the Sultan of Muscat and Oman, in accordance with the wishes of the population.

The area is 309,500 sq. km. At the 1993 census the population was 2·02m. Estimated population (1994), 2,097,000, chiefly Arabs, and including 0·42m. foreign workers. Growth rate, 1994, 3·7%; infant mortality, 23 per 1,000 live births. Expectation of life was 69·1 years in 1992. Population of regions at the 1993 census (in 1,000): Muscat, 622; Batinah, 539; Sharqiyah, 248.

The country is divided into planning regions:

Region	*Population (1993 census)*	*Regional centres*	*Population (1993 census)*
Muscat	549,150	Muscat	40,856
Southern (Janubiah)	189,094	Salalah	131,802
Interior (Dakhiliah)	229,791	Nizwa,	58,582
Sharqiyah	258,344	Ibri,	93,475
Wusta	17,067	Sur	53,504
Batinah	564,677	Sohar,	90,814
		Rustaq	61,984
Dhahirah	181,224	Al-Buraimi	48,287
Musandam	28,727	Khasab	16,393

The official language is Arabic; English is in commercial use.

CLIMATE. Oman has a desert climate, with exceptionally hot and humid months from April to Oct., when temperatures may reach 47°C. Light monsoon rains fall in the south from June to Sept., with highest amounts in the western highland region. Muscat. Jan. 28°C, July 46°C. Annual rainfall 101 mm. Salalah. Jan. 29°C, July 32°C. Annual rainfall 98 mm.

RULER. The present Sultan is Qaboos bin Said (born Nov. 1940). He took over from his father Said bin Taimur, on 23 July 1970 in a palace coup.

CONSTITUTION AND GOVERNMENT. Oman is an absolute monarchy and there is no formal constitution. The Sultan legislates by decree and appoints a Cabinet to assist him; and he is also Prime Minister and Minister of Foreign Affairs, Defence and Finance. The other Ministers were in Aug. 1995:

Personal Representative of the Sultan: Sayyid Thuwiny bin Shihab al Said.

Deputy Prime Ministers: Sayyid Fahr bin Taimur bin Faisal Al Said (*Security and Defence*), Sayyid Fahd bin Mahmud bin Muhammad Al Said (*Legal Affairs*). *Agriculture and Fisheries:* Muhammed bin Abdullah bin Zaher al Hinai. *Civil Service:* Abdul Aziz al Azizi. *Commerce and Industry:* Maqbul bin Ali bin Sultan. *Communications:* Salim bin Abdullah al Ghazali. *Economy:* Ahmad bin Abdul Nabi Maki. *Education and Youth:* Saud bin Ibrahim bin Saud al Busaidi. *Electricity and Water:* Mohamed bin Ali al Qatabi. *Regional Municipalities and Environment:* Amour bin Shuwin al Hosni. *Health:* Ali bin Muhammed bin Musa al Raisi. *Housing:* Malik bin Sulaiman al Ma'mari. *Information:* Abdul Aziz bin Muhammed al Rowas. *Interior:* Sayyid Badr bin Saud bin Harib al Busaidi. *Justice, Awqaf and Islamic Affairs:* Hamid bin Abdullah al Harthi. *National Heritage and Culture:* Sayyid Faisal bin Ali al Said. *Petroleum and Minerals:* Said bin Ahmad al Shanfari. *Police and Customs Inspectorate:* Lieut.-Gen. Hilal bin Khalid al Maawali. *Posts, Telegraphs and Telephones:* Ahmad bin Suweidan al Baluchi. *Social Affairs and Labour:* Ahmed bin Mohammed al Isae. *President, Diwan of the Royal Court:* Sayyid Saif bin Hamad bin Saud. *President of the Palace Office:* Maj.-Gen. Ali bin Majid al Mamari. *Water Resources:* Hamed bin Said al Aufi. *Minister of State, Governor of Dhofar:* Sayyid Mussellam al Busaidi. *Minister of State, Governor of Muscat:* Sayyid al Mutassim al Busaidi. *Minister of State for Foreign Affairs:* Yusuf bin Alawi bin Abdullah. *Secretary-General, Ministry of Defence:* Saif bin Hamad al Batashi. *Higher Education:* Yahiya bin Mahfoud al Manthri. *Conferences:* Asaad bin Tariq al Said.

In 1991 a new consultative assembly, the *Majlis al Shura*, replaced the former State Consultative Chamber. The Majlis consists of a president and 59 representatives who are nominated one from each governorate, and ultimately approved by the Sultan. It debates domestic issues, but has no legislative or veto powers.

National flag: Red, with a white panel in the upper fly and a green one in the lower fly, and in the canton the national emblem in white.

National anthem: 'Ya Rabbana elifidh lana jalalat al Saltan' ('O Lord, protect for us his majesty the Sultan'); words and tune anonymous.

Local government. Oman is divided into 8 regional governorates and 59 districts (*wilayats*).

DEFENCE

Army. The Army consists of 1 divisional and 2 brigade headquarters, 2 armoured, 1 armoured reconnaissance, 4 artillery, 1 air defence, 8 infantry, 1 infantry reconnaissance, 1 field engineer and 1 airborne regiment and a security force. Equipment includes 6 M-60A1, 43 M-60A3, 24 Chieftain and 18 Challenger 2 main battle tanks. Strength (1996) about 25,000. (Regiments are of battalion size). The armed forces include 6,500 Royal Household troops, and the Musandam Security Force, an independent rifle company. A paramilitary tribal home guard numbers 4,000.

Navy. The Navy, which is based principally at Seeb (HQ) and Wudam comprises 4 fast missile craft, 4 coastal and 4 inshore patrol craft. Auxiliaries include 1 training ship, 1 logistic support ship, 1 troop transport and 1 survey craft. There are also 2 specially adapted amphibious ships and 5 craft. 2 new UK-built light frigates were expected to be delivered in 1996. Naval personnel in 1995 totalled 4,200.

The marine police coastguard, 400 strong in 1993, operate 6 coastal patrol craft and 2 logistics support craft.

The wholly separate Royal Yacht Squadron consists of a 3,800-tonne yacht and an 11,000-tonne support ship with helicopter and troop-carrying capability.

Air Force. The Air Force, formed in 1959, had in 1995 two strike/interceptor squadrons of Jaguars, a ground attack/interceptor squadron of Hawk 200s, a squadron of Strikemaster and Hawk 100 light jet training/attack aircraft, 1 DC-8, 3 BAC One-Eleven and 2 Gulfstream VIP transports, 3 C-130H Hercules and 14 Skyvan light transports, 30 Agusta-Bell 205, 212, 214B and JetRanger, and Bell 214 ST helicopters for security duties, 2 Super Puma VIP helicopters and 4 Bravo piston-engined trainers. Air defence force has batteries of Rapier low-level surface-to-air missiles. Personnel (1995) about 4,100, with 46 combat aircraft.

INTERNATIONAL RELATIONS. A 1982 Memorandum of Understanding with the UK provided for regular consultations on international and bilateral issues.

Membership. Oman is a member of the UN, the Arab League, the Organization of the Islamic Conference and the Gulf Co-operation Council.

ECONOMY

Policy. The fifth 5-year plan is running from 1996 to 2000. It concentrates on providing a macro-economic infrastructure to allow the private sector to develop and diversify, and encourages privatization.

Budget. Revenue (1995) OR 1,867m.; expenditure, OR 2,029m.

Currency. The unit of currency is the *Omani rial* (OMR), which replaced the *rial saidi* in 1972. It is divided into 1,000 *baiza*. There are notes of 100, 200, 250 and 500 baiza and OR 1, 5, 10, 20 and 50 and coins of 5, 10, 25, 50, 100, 250 and 500 baiza. The rial is pegged to the US dollar. Foreign exchange reserves were US$908m. in 1993. In March 1996, £1 = 0·59; US$1 = 0·39; DM1 = 0·26 rials.

Banking and Finance. The bank of issue is the Central Bank of Oman, which commenced operations in 1975 (*President*, Hamid Sangur Hasim). All banks must comply with BIS capital adequacy ratios and have a minimum capital of OR10m. In 1991 there were 25 commercial banks, of which 12 were foreign. There are 3 specialized banks.

There is a stock exchange in Muscat, which is linked with that in Bahrain.

Weights and Measures. The metric system is in operation.

ENERGY AND NATURAL RESOURCES

Electricity. Production (1994) 6,187·3m. kWh.

Oil. The economy is dominated by the oil industry, which provided 83% of Government revenue in 1990 and 49·2% of GDP. Oil in commercial quantities was discovered in 1964 and production began in 1967. Production in 1995 was 864,000 bbls. a day. Total proven reserves were estimated in 1991 to be 4,300m. bbls.

Gas. Production (1990) 4·8m. cu. metres per day. In 1989 reserves were estimated at 283,000m. cu. metres.

Water Resources. Oman relies on a combination of aquifers and desalination plants for its water, augmented by a construction programme of some 60 recharge dams. Desalination plants at Ghubriah and Wadi Adai provide most of the water needs of the capital area. In 1994 water production was 16,184·6m. gallons.

Minerals. Production of refined copper at the smelter at Sohar was 12,015 tonnes in 1990.

Agriculture. About 0·1m. ha are cultivable. The coastal plain (Batinah) north-west of Muscat is fertile, as are the Dhofar highlands in the south. In the valleys of the interior, as well as on the Batinah coastal plain, date cultivation has reached a high level, and there are possibilities of agricultural development. The crop of dates was 130,000 tonnes in 1992. Vegetable and fruit production are also important, and livestock are raised in the south where there are monsoon rains. Camels (92,000 in 1992) are bred by the inland tribes.

Fisheries. Catch (1992) 112,313 tonnes. 15,267 tonnes were taken by industrial ships, the rest by some 85,000 self-employed fishermen.

INDUSTRY. In 1990 manufacturing accounted for only 3·7% of GDP. Apart from oil production, copper mining and smelting and cement production there are light industries, mainly food processing and chemical products. The government gives priority to import substitute industries.

Labour. In 1994 there were 526,018 employees in the private sector and 105,849 persons in government service. The employment of foreign labour is being discouraged following 'Omanization' regulations of 1994.

FOREIGN ECONOMIC RELATIONS.

Total foreign debt was US$2,661m. in 1993. A royal decree of 1994 permits up to 65% foreign ownership of Omani companies with a 5-year tax and customs duties exemption.

Commerce. Total imports, 1994: OR 1,505m.; exports, OR 2,132m. (of which oil: OR 1,627m.). Principal non-oil exports are metal, metal goods, animals and products and textiles. Main export markets (% of total trade); 1993: UAE, 33·4; Japan, 19·5; South Korea, 14; China, 7. Main import suppliers: UAE, 23·7; Japan, 20·8; UK, 11·9.

Total trade between Oman and UK (British Department of Trade returns, in £1,000 sterling):

	1991	*1992*	*1993*	*1994*	*1995*
Imports to UK	73,574	83,106	82,664	78,273	74,232
Exports and re-exports from UK	237,890	240,695	305,592	362,129	447,922

COMMUNICATIONS

Roads. A network of adequate graded roads links all the main sectors of population, and only a few mountain villages are not accessible by motor vehicles. In 1994 there were 5,900 km of asphalt roads and (in 1992) 20,660 km of graded roads. In 1992 there were 254,914 vehicles on the road.

Civil Aviation. Oman has a 25% share in Gulf Air with Bahrain, Qatar and the UAE. For details *see* BAHRAIN: Civil Aviation. Gulf Air run regional services in and out of Seeb international airport (20 miles from Muscat) to Bahrain, Doha, Abu Dhabi, Dubai, Karachi, Bombay and operate daily flights to and from London. Other airlines serving Muscat are Air France, Air India, Air Lanka, Air Tanzania, Balkan Bulgarian, Biman Bangladesh, British Airways, Egyptair, Ethiopian Airlines, KLM, Kuwait Airways, Pakistan Airlines, Royal Jordanian, Saudia, Sudan Airways, Thai Airways and UTA. Domestic flights are provided by Oman Aviation Services.

Shipping. In Mutrah a deep-water port (named Mina Qaboos) was completed in 1974. The annual handling capacity is 1·5m. tonnes. Mina Raysut, the port of Salalah, has a capacity of 1m. tonnes per year. Sea-going shipping totalled 10,604 GRT in 1995.

Telecommunications. In 1989 there were 71 post offices and sub-post offices. The General Telecommunications Organization maintains a telegraph office at Muscat and an automatic telephone exchange (164,003 lines, 1994).

The government-owned Radio Oman broadcasts in Arabic and English. A colour (PAL) television service, the government-owned Oman Television, covering Muscat and the surrounding area, started transmission in 1974. A television service for Dhofar opened in 1975. In 1991 there were 7 television stations. Total number of televisions, 1,000,033 and radios, 0·9m. in 1991.

Press. There were (1991) 2 Arabic-language and 2 English-language daily newspapers.

SOCIAL INSTITUTIONS

Religion. In 1995, 87·7% of the population were Moslem.

Education. Adult literacy was 41% in 1994. In 1994–95, there were 1,045 schools with 504,261 pupils and 23,023 teachers. Plans have been implemented for the development of technical and agricultural training and craft training at intermediate and secondary level. Oman's first university, the Sultan Qaboos University, opened in 1986 and in 1994–95 there were 4,331 students and 483 academic staff.

Health. In 1994 there were 51 hospitals with 4,744 beds, 111 health centres, 2,499 doctors, 142 dentists (1992), 350 pharmacists (1992) and 6,222 nursing staff.

DIPLOMATIC REPRESENTATIVES

Of Oman in Great Britain (44A Montpelier Sq., London, SW7 1JJ)
Ambassador: Hussain Ali Abdullatif.

Of Great Britain in Oman (PO Box 300, Muscat)
Ambassador: R. J. S. Muir, CMG.

Of Oman in the USA (2342 Massachusetts Ave., NW, Washington, D.C., 20008)
Ambassador: Abdalla Bin Mohamed Al-Dhahab.

Of the USA in Oman (PO Box 52020 Madinat Qabos, Muscat)
Ambassador: David J. Dunford.

Of Oman to the United Nations
Ambassador: Salim Bin Mohammed Al-Khussaiby.

Further Reading

Carter, J. R. L., *Tribes of Oman*. London, 1981
Clements, F. A., *Oman: The Reborn Land*. London and New York, 1980.—*Oman*. [Bibliography] 2nd ed. Oxford and Santa Barbara (CA), 1994
Hawley, D., *Oman and its Rennaissance*. London, 1977
Peterson, J. E., *Oman in the Twentieth Century*. London and New York, 1978
Peyton, W. D., *Oman before 1970: The End of an Era*. London, 1985
Pridham, B. R., (ed.) *Oman: Economic, Social and Strategic Developments*. London, 1987
Shannon, M. O., *Oman and South-Eastern Arabia: A Bibliographic Survey*. Boston, 1978
Skeet, I., *Muscat and Oman: The End of an Era*. London, 1974.—*Oman: Politics and Development*. London, 1992
Wilkinson, J. C., *The Imamate Tradition of Oman*. CUP, 1987

National statistical office: Directorate General of National Statistics, POB 881, Muscat 113.

PAKISTAN

Islami Jamhuriya e Pakistan

(Islamic Republic of Pakistan) [1]

Capital: Islamabad
Population: 131·5m. (1994)
GNP per capita: US$440 (1994)
HDI/world rank: 0·483/128 (1992)

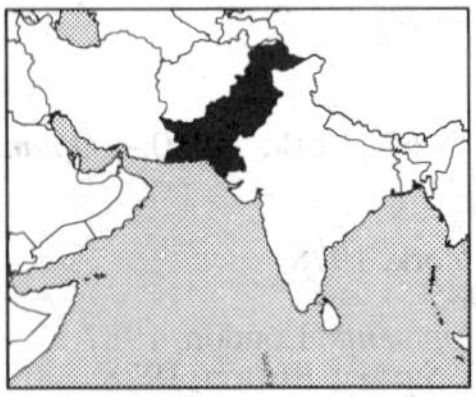

KEY HISTORICAL EVENTS. Pakistan was constituted as a Dominion on 14 Aug. 1947 comprising Baluchistan, East Bengal (including almost the whole of Sylhet, a former district of Assam), North-West Frontier, West Punjab and Sind; and those States which had acceded to Pakistan. On 23 March 1956 an Islamic republic was proclaimed. For constitutional history, 1958–70, *see* THE STATESMAN'S YEAR-BOOK, 1992–93, p. 1057

After a civil war in 1971 East Bengal declared itself an independent state, Bangladesh.

A new Constitution was adopted in 1973.

The Chief of the Army Staff, Gen. M. Zia-ul-Haq, proclaimed martial law on 5 July 1977 and the armed forces took control of the administration; scheduled elections were postponed. The Prime Minister, Z. A. Bhutto, was hanged (for conspiracy to murder) on 4 April 1979. Gen. M. Zia-ul-Haq assumed the Presidency in Sept. 1978.

On 6 Aug. 1990 the President, accusing the government of corruption and undermining the constitution, dismissed the Prime Minister, Benazir Bhutto, and all her cabinet, dissolved the National Assembly and declared a state of emergency. New governors were appointed for all 4 provinces.

On 18 April 1993 President Ghulam Ishaq Khan dismissed the next Prime Minister, Nawaz Sharif, but he was reinstated by the Constitutional Court. Both President and Prime Minister resigned on 18 July 1993, and new elections took place.

TERRITORY AND POPULATION. Pakistan is bounded in the north-west by Afghanistan, north by China, east by India and south by the Arabian Sea. The area (excluding the disputed area of Kashmir) is 307,293 sq. miles (796,095 sq. km); population (1981 census, excluding Azad, Kashmir, Baltistan, Diamir and Gilgit), 84,253,644 (females, 40·02m.). A census was scheduled for 1994. Estimate (1994) 131·5m.; density, 149·6 per sq. km. Urban population (1991), 32%. Vital statistics, 1991 (rates per 1,000 population): Birth, 41; death, 11; growth, 0·3; infant mortality (per 1,000 live births), 108. Formal registration of marriages and divorces has not been required since 1992. Expectation of life was 58·3 years in 1992.

The population of the principal cities:

Census of 1981

Islamabad	201,000	Multan	730,000	Jhang	195,000
Karachi	5,103,000	Gujranwala	597,000	Sukkur	191,000
Lahore	2,922,000	Peshawar	555,000	Bahawalpur	178,000
Faisalabad	1,092,000	Sialkot	296,000	Kasur	155,000
Rawalpindi	928,000	Sargodha	294,000	Gujrat	154,000
Hyderabad	795,000	Quetta	285,000	Okara	154,000

Population of the provinces (census of 1981) was (1,000):

[1] The name 'Pakistan' is a coinage representing 'Punjab, the Afghan border states, Kashmir, Sind and Baluchistan'.

	Area (sq. km)	*1981 census population Total*	*Male*	*Female*	*Urban*	*1981 density per sq. km (number)*	*Estimated total 1985*
North-West Frontier Province	74,521	11,061	5,761	5,300	1,665	148	12,287
Federally admin. Tribal Areas	27,219	2,199	1,143	1,056	–	81	2,467
Fed. Cap. Territory Islamabad	907	340	185	155	204	376	379
Punjab	205,344	47,292	24,860	22,432	13,051	230	53,840
Sind	140,914	19,029	9,999	9,030	8,243	135	21,682
Baluchistan	347,190	4,332	2,284	2,048	677	12	4,908

In 1994 there were still some 1·5m. Afghan refugees mainly in the North-West Frontier Province.

Urdu is the national language, though only spoken by 7·6% of the population at the 1981 census; English is used in business, higher education and in central government. In 1981 48% of the population spoke Punjabi.

CLIMATE. A weak form of tropical monsoon climate occurs over much of the country, with arid conditions in the north and west, where the wet season is only from Dec. to March. Elsewhere, rain comes mainly in the summer. Summer temperatures are high everywhere, but winters can be cold in the mountainous north. Islamabad. Jan. 50°F (10°C), July 90°F (32·2°C). Annual rainfall 36" (900 mm). Karachi. Jan. 61°F (16·1°C), July 86°F (30°C). Annual rainfall 8" (196 mm). Lahore. Jan. 53°F (11·7°C), July 89°F (31·7°C). Annual rainfall 18" (452 mm). Multan. Jan. 51°F (10·6°C), July 93°F (33·9°C). Annual rainfall 7" (170 mm). Quetta. Jan. 38°F (3·3°C), July 80°F (26·7°C). Annual rainfall 10" (239 mm).

CONSTITUTION AND GOVERNMENT. Under the 1973 Constitution, the *President* is elected for a 5-year term by a college of parliamentary deputies, senators and members of the Provincial Assemblies. Parliament is bi-cameral, comprising a *Senate*, in 1992 of 87 members (1 woman) elected mainly by Provincial Assemblies, and a *National Assembly* of 217 (2 women), directly elected with 10 religious minority representatives.

During the period of martial law (1977–85) the Constitution was in abeyance, but not abrogated. In 1985 it was amended to extend the powers of the President, including those of appointing and dismissing ministers and vetoing new legislation.

The Constitution obliges the Government to enable the people to order their lives in accordance with Islam and consolidates Islam as the basis of law. There is a *Constitutional Court.*

Following the President's dismissal of Nawaz Sharif's government in April 1993, elections were held on 6 Oct. 1993 for the 217 contestable seats in the National Assembly. Benazir Bhutto's Pakistan People's Party (PPP) gained 86 seats, the Pakistan Moslem League, 72.

Elections to 42 seats of the Senate were held in March 1991. The IDA won 30 seats, the PPP, 5.

President: Farooq Leghari (b. 1940; PPP; elected 13 Nov. 1993; sworn in 14 Nov. 1993).

In Oct. 1995 the government comprised:

Prime Minister, Minister of Finance: Benazir Bhutto (b. 1954; PPP).

Minister of Industries and Production: Brig. Muhammad Asghar. *Defence:* Aftab Shahban Mirani. *Interior:* Maj.-Gen. Nasirullah Khan Babar. *Commerce:* Ahmed Mukhtar. *Petroleum and Natural Resources:* Anwar Saifullah. *Kashmir and Northern Affairs:* Muhammad Afzal Khan. *Law and Justice:* N. D. Khan. *Foreign Affairs:* Saidar Aseff Ahmad Ali. *Population:* Julius Salek. *Social Welfare:* Dr Sher Afghan Khan Niazi. *Information and Broadcasting:* Khalid Ahmed Khan Kharal. *Education:* Khurshid Ahmed Shah. *Public Works:* Makhdum Muhammad Amin Fahin. *Food, Agriculture and Livestock:* Muhammad Yusef Talpur. *Water and*

Energy: Ghulam Mustafa Khan. *Industry and Production:* Muhammad Asghar. *Without portfolio:* Abdul Qadir Jilani.

The *Speaker* is Yussuf Raza Gillani (PPP).

National flag: Green, charged at the centre, with a white crescent and white 5-pointed star, a white vertical stripe at the mast to one-quarter of the flag.

National anthem: 'Pak sarzamin shadbad' ('Blessed be the sacred land'); words by A. Hafeez Jullandhuri, tune by A. Ghulamali Chagla.

Provincial and Local Government. Pakistan comprises the Federal Capital Territory (Islamabad), the provinces of the Punjab, the North-West Frontier (NWFP), Sind and Baluchistan, and the tribal areas of the north-west. The provincial capitals are Peshawar (NWFP), Lahore (Punjab), Karachi (Sind) and Quetta (Baluchistan). Provincial governors are appointed by the President and are assisted by elected provincial assemblies. That of Punjab has 248 seats (8 reserved for non-Moslems); Sind, 99; Baluchistan, 40; NWFP, 80. Elections were held on 8 Oct. 1993. Seats gained in the Punjab assembly: PML 106, PPP 94, PML-Junejo 18, ind 17, minor parties 5; Sind: PPP 56, Mohajir 27, PML 8, ind 5, minor parties 3; Baluchistan: minor parties 21, ind 9, PML 6, PPP 3, Awami 1; NWFP: PPP 22, Awami 20, PML 15, ind 11, minor parties 7, PML-Junejo 4. Municipal elections were held in the Punjab in Dec. 1991. Direct rule was imposed in Punjab in Sept. 1995.

Within the provinces there are divisions administered by Commissioners appointed by the President; the divisions are divided into districts and agencies administered by Deputy Commissioners or Political Agents who are responsible to the Provincial Governments.

The tribal areas (Khyber, Kurram, Malakand, Mohmand, North Waziristan, South Waziristan) are administered by political agents responsible to the federal government.

Kashmir. Pakistan controls the northern and western portions of Kashmir. Under a UN resolution of 1949 their future was to be decided by plebiscite; it is still a disputed territory.

Azad Kashmir (the west) has an area of 11,639 sq. km (4,494 sq. miles) and an estimated population (1990) of 2·58m. It has its own Assembly (48 members including 2 women), their own Council (of 14 members), High Court and Supreme Court. There is a Parliamentary form of Government with a Prime Minister as the executive head and the President as the Constitutional head. Elections to the Legislative's 40 general seats are to be held within 10 days of the general elections in Pakistan, according to a presidential proclamation of 8 Oct. 1977. The seat of government is Muzaffarabad. The elections held in June 1991 were declared invalid by the Prime Minister, Mumtaz Rathore (PPP). He was arrested in July and replaced by the President, Sardar Abdul Qayyum Khan (Islamic Conference).

The Pakistan Government is directly responsible for Gilgit, Diamir and Baltistan (the north), which have a combined area of 75,520 sq. km and an estimated population (1990) of 0·73m.

Local government elections were held in April 1992.

DEFENCE

Army. The Army is organized into 9 corps headquarters and 1 area command, and consists of 2 armoured and 19 infantry divisions; 7 independent armoured, 9 independent infantry, 9 artillery and 7 engineer brigades; 3 armoured reconnaissance regiments, 1 air defence command and 1 Special Services Group. Equipment includes 120 M-47, 50 T-54/-55, 280 M-48, 1,200 Chinese Type-59, 200 Chinese Type-69 and 200 Chinese Type-85 main battle tanks, 850 surface-to-air and 18 surface-to-surface missiles. The Army has an air component with about 140 fixed-wing aircraft for transport, reconnaissance and observation duties and 130 helicopters for anti-armour operations, transport, liaison and training. Strength (1996) 520,000. There are also 257,000 personnel in paramilitary units: National Guard, Frontier Corps, Pakistan Rangers, Coast Guard and Maritime Security.

Navy. The combatant fleet comprises 6 French-built diesel submarines, 3 midget submarines for swimmer delivery, 3 ex-US Second World War vintage destroyers and 6 ex-British Amazon and 2 Leander class frigates, 8 fast missile craft, 1 coastal and 4 inshore patrol craft, 1 French-built tripartite minehunter and 2 coastal minesweepers. Auxiliaries include 2 fleet replenishment tankers, 1 survey ship and 1 salvage tug, as well as a static ex-US repair ship. There are about a dozen minor auxiliaries.

The Air Force operates 4 Atlantic aircraft under naval control for maritime patrol duties, whilst the Navy operates 3 F-27 patrol aircraft, 6 Sea King helicopters, 3 Lynx and 4 Alouette III anti-submarine and liaison helicopters.

The principal naval base and dockyard are at Karachi. Naval personnel in 1995 totalled 22,000. There is a marine force of 1,200.

A navy-subordinated Maritime Safety Agency 2,000 strong (1995) operates 1 ex-naval destroyer and 6 fast coastal patrol craft on economic exclusion zone protection duties.

Air Force. The Pakistan Air Force came into being on 14 Aug. 1947. It has its headquarters at Peshawar and is organized within 3 air defence sectors, in the northern, central and southern areas of the country. Air defence units include 3 squadrons of F-16 Fighting Falcons, 5 squadrons of F-7P Skybolts and 3 squadrons of Chinese-built F-6s (MiG-19). Tactical units include 2 squadrons of Mirage 5 supersonic fighters and 3 with A-5 fighter-bombers, 1 squadron equipped with Mirage III-RP reconnaissance aircraft, and 1 with C-130 Hercules turboprop transports. Flying training schools are equipped with Mashshaq (Saab Supporter) armed piston-engined primary trainers, T-33 and T-37B/C jet trainers supplied by the USA, Mirage III-DPs and Chinese-built FT-5s (two-seat MiG-17s) and FT-6s (two-seat MiG-19s). A VIP transport squadron operates the Presidential F27 turboprop aircraft and Boeing 737 jet, 3 four-jet Boeing 707s, 3 twin-jet Falcon 20s and a Puma helicopter. There is a flying college at Risalpur and an aeronautical engineering college at Korangi Creek. Total strength in 1995 was 400 combat aircraft and 45,000 personnel.

INTERNATIONAL RELATIONS

Membership. Pakistan is a member of the UN, the Commonwealth (not 1972–89) and the Colombo Plan.

ECONOMY

Policy. The 7th Five-Year Plan ran from 1988 to 1993. It envisaged a fixed investment of Rs 642,000m. Since 1991 investors have no longer been required to seek government permission to set up industrial units, except in arms and alcohol production.

Budget. The financial year ends on 30 June. The consolidated federal and provincial budget for 1994–95 envisaged revenue of Rs 359,323m. (Rs 297,819m. from taxation) and expenditure of Rs 436,168m. (current expenditure, Rs 346,168; development, Rs 90,000). Provincial revenue, Rs 113,878m. (including federal transfers of Rs 94,202m.). Defence spending, Rs 101,850m.

Currency. The monetary unit is the *Pakistan rupee* (PKR) of 100 *paisas*. There are notes of R1, 2, 5, 10, 50, 100, 500 and 1,000; and coins of 5, 10, 25 and 50 paisas. Currency in circulation in March 1992, Rs 116,856m. Gold reserves in 1993 were Rs 17,204m., approved foreign exchange reserves, Rs 4,929m. The rupee was devalued 6% in July 1993. In March 1996, Rs 52·52 = £1; Rs 34·37 = US$1; Rs 23·28 = DM1.

Banking and Finance. In Jan. 1985, banks and financial institutions abandoned, in conformity with Islamic doctrine, the payment of interest on new transactions. This does not apply to international business, but does apply to the domestic business of foreign banks operating in Pakistan. Investment partnerships, between bank and customer, replaced straight loans at interest. In Dec. 1991 the Federal Shariat Court pronounced that interest or usury (*riba*) is un-Islamic and therefore illegal.

The State Bank of Pakistan is the central bank (*Governor*, Mohammad Yaqub); it came into operation as the Central Bank on 1 July 1948 and was nationalized in 1974. It was granted greater autonomy in Sept. 1993. In June 1992 total assets of the issue department amounted to Rs 161,540m. and those of the banking department Rs 149,905m.; total deposits, Rs 128,316m. It is the bank of issue, custodian of foreign exchange reserves and banker for the federal and provincial governments and for scheduled banks. It also manages the rupee public debt of federal and provincial governments. The Bank's subsidiary Federal Bank for Co-operatives makes loans to provincial co-operative banks. The National Bank of Pakistan acts as an agent of the State Bank where the State Bank has no offices of its own.

Banks were nationalized in 1974, but a federal government decision of Dec. 1990 again allows banks in the private sector. It was announced in Nov. 1990 that 51% of the equity of state-owned banks was to be privatized in 2 phases. In Nov. 1994 there were 40 banks (21 foreign) with total assets of Rs 1,467,185m.

There are stock exchanges at Karachi and Lahore.

Weights and Measures. The metric system is in general use.

ENERGY AND NATURAL RESOURCES

Electricity. Installed capacity of the state power system in 1990 was 8,430 MW. Total generated electrical energy in 1993–94, 49,889m. kWh; 19,386m. kWh of output was hydro-electric, 30,006m. kWh thermal and 497m. kWh nuclear. By March 1990 31,831 villages (of a total 43,244) had access to electric power.

Oil and Gas. Oil production in 1991 was 3·36m. tonnes. Exploitation is mainly through government incentives and concessions to foreign private sector companies. Gas production, 1992–93, 14,200m. cu. metres.

Minerals. Production (tonnes, 1993–94): Coal, 3·21m.; chromite, 10,765; limestone, 9·13m.; gypsum, 0·67m.; rock salt, 0·92m.; fire clay, 115,998; feldspar, 20,267; bauxite, 4,064; barytes, 18,334; china clay, 48,078; dolomite, 228,090; fullers' earth, 16,984. Other minerals of which useful deposits have been found are magnesite, sulphur, marble, antimony ore, bentonite, celestite, fluorite, phosphate rock, silica sand and soapstone.

Agriculture. The north and west are covered by mountain ranges. The rest of the country consists of a fertile plain watered by 5 big rivers and their tributaries. Agriculture is dependent almost entirely on the irrigation system based on these rivers. Area irrigated, 1992, 17·1m. ha. Agriculture employs half the workforce and in 1989–90 contributed 26% of GDP.

Pakistan is self-sufficient in wheat, rice and sugar. Areas harvested, 1994: Wheat, 8·03m. ha; rice, 2·19m. ha; sugar-cane, 0·96m. ha; cotton, 2·8m. ha and maize, 0·88m. ha. Production, 1994 (1,000 tonnes): Rice, 3,995; wheat, 15,213; sugar-cane, 44,427; cotton, 1,517; maize, 1,213; (1993) millet, 126; sorghum, 218 and dates, 320.

An ordinance of Jan. 1977 reduced the upper limit of land holding to 100 irrigated or 200 non-irrigated acres; it also replaced the former land revenue system with a new agricultural income tax, from which holders of up to 25 irrigated or 50 unirrigated acres are exempt. Of about 4m. farms, 89% are of less than 25 acres. In 1992, 20·65m. ha were arable land, 0·46m. ha were cropland and 12·80m. ha were pasture.

Livestock, 1993 (in 1m.): Cattle, 17·8; buffaloes, 18·7; sheep, 27·6; goats, 40·2; camels, 1·1; poultry, 95m.

Dairy products, 1993 (in 1,000 tonnes): Mutton and lamb, 288; beef and buffalo, 844; wool, 50·5; eggs, 231·9; milk, 13,192.

Forestry. In 1993–94 the forest area was 3m. ha, some 3·8% of the total land area. The government considers a 20-25% coverage desirable for economic growth and environmental stability. 0·34m. cu. metres of timber and 0·4m. cu. metres of firewood were produced by state-owned forests in 1993–94.

Fisheries. In 1992-93 the catch totalled 553,000 tonnes.

INDUSTRY. Industry is based largely on agricultural processing, with engineering and electronics. Government policy is to encourage private industry, particularly small industry. The public sector, however, is still dominant in large industries. Steel, cement, fertilizer and vegetable ghee are the most valuable public sector industries.

Production 1993–94 (tonnes): Sugar, 2,922,457; vegetable products, 670,654; jute textiles, 76,415; soda ash, 187,257; sulphuric acid, 102,341; caustic soda, 89,114; paper and board, 23,592; bicycles, 563,687 units; cotton cloth, 314·9m. sq. metres; cotton yarn, 130·96m. kg.; cement, 8·1m.; steel billets, 403,949; hot-rolled steel sheets and coils, 517,282; cold-rolled, 165,740; pig-iron, 1,252,682; motor cars, 19,514 items; tractors, 14,656 items; tea, 63,562.

Labour. In 1992 the workforce was 33·71m. (5·02m. females). 1·6m. were unemployed (0·52m. females). In 1988 51·15% were engaged in agriculture, forestry and fishing, 12·69% in manufacturing; the textile industry was the largest single manufacturing employer. Services employed 11·39%; commerce, 11·92%; construction, 6·38%; transport, storage and communication, 4·89%. In March 1993, 173,764 job seekers were registered at labour exchanges.

In 1990 there were 99 industrial disputes and 186,726 working days were lost.

FOREIGN ECONOMIC RELATIONS. Foreign debt was US$22,300m. in 1991. Most foreign exchange controls were removed in Feb. 1991. Foreign investors may repatriate both capital and profits, and tax exemptions are available for companies set up before 30 June 1995.

Commerce. In 1993–94 imports were valued at Rs 258,250m., exports at Rs 205,499m., and re-exports at Rs 811m. The value of the chief articles imported and exported (in Rs 1m.):

Imports	*1992–93*	*1993–94*	*Exports*	*1992–93*	*1993–94*
Manufactures	22,250	25,291	Raw cotton	7,001	2,383
Machinery	95,350	81,967	Cotton cloth	22,430	24,789
Food and animals	23,067	18,128	Cotton yarns	29,308	38,197
Chemicals	38,781	45,065	Rice	8,214	7,319
Minerals and fuels	41,864	46,406	Leather	5,769	6,772
Oils and fats	16,668	16,667	Carpets	4,397	4,461

Main export markets, 1992–93 (in Rs 1m.): Japan, 9,659; USA, 19,838; UK, 10,338; Germany, 11,025; Hong Kong, 10,063; Italy, 3,870; United Arab Emirates, 8,420; Saudi Arabia, 6,660. Main import suppliers: USA, 21,118; Japan, 30,625; Kuwait, 6,631; Germany, 15,475; UK, 10,776; China, 8,765; Saudi Arabia, 11,777; Malaysia, 10,425; South Korea, 8,794.

Total trade between Pakistan and UK (British Department of Trade returns, in £1,000 sterling):

	1992	*1993*	*1994*	*1995*
Imports to UK	273,324	324,335	358,879	363,068
Exports and re-exports from UK	311,771	338,581	355,058	340,382

Tourism. In 1993 there were 364,336 tourist arrivals. Foreign exchange receipts were US$156·2m. in 1990.

COMMUNICATIONS

Roads. In 1992 there were 179,752 km of roads, of which 91,985 km were all-weather roads. In 1991 there were 106,883 lorries, 88,957 buses, 32,980 taxis, 290,232 motor cars, 1,388,432 motor cycles and 525,338 other vehicles. There were 10,916 road accidents in 1993–94, with 4,511 fatalities.

Railways. Pakistan Railways had (1992) a route length of 8,163 km (of which 293 km electrified) mainly on 1,676 mm. gauge, with some metre gauge line. In 1993–94 61·72m. passengers and 8·04m. tonnes of freight were carried.

Civil Aviation. There are international airports at Karachi, Islamabad, Lahore, Peshāwar and Quetta. In 1992–93 7,951,433 domestic and 5,686,130 international passengers were handled, and 81,308 and 130,408 tonnes of freight.

The national carrier is Pakistan International Airlines (PIA; founded 1955; 56% of shares are held by the Government), which in 1995 operated 9 A300B4-200s, 6 A310-300s, 2 B-707-320Cs, 7 B-737-300s, 6 B-747-200Bs, 2 B-747-200B Combis, and 15 other aircraft. Services are also provided by Aero Asia, Aeroflot, Air China, Air Lanka, Air Liberté, Azerbaijan Hava Yollary, Bhoja Air, Biman Bangladesh, British Airways, Egyptair, Emirates, Ethiopian Airlines, Gulf Air, Indian Airlines, Iran Air, Kenya Airways, KLM, Kuwait Airways, Libyan Airlines, Lufthansa, Malaysia Airlines, Northwest Airines, Oman Air, Philippine Airlines, Qatar Airways, Royal Jordanian, Saudia, Shaheen Air, Singapore Airlines, Swissair, Syrian Airlines, Tarom, Thai Airways, Turkish Airlines, Uzbekistan Airways and Yemenia.

Shipping. In 1995, ocean-going shipping totalled 0·58m. tonnes, including oil tankers, 90,821 GRT. There are ports at Karachi and Port Qasim. Cargo handled, 1993–94, 22·57m. and 7·44m. tonnes respectively. In 1993–94 2,223 international vessels entered, and 2,196 cleared, these ports.

Telecommunications. The telegraph and telephone system is government-owned. Telephones, 1994, numbered 1,668,000. There were 13,450 telex machines in 1991. In 1993 there were 13,380 post offices. The Pakistan Broadcasting Corporation is a government body responsible for broadcasting a national radio programme in English, 3 home services and an external service, Radio Pakistan (15 languages). A separate government authority, Azad Kashmir Radio, broadcasts in Kashmir. The commercial Pakistan Television Corporation transmits on 8 channels (colour by PAL). In 1993 10m. radio and 2·08m. TV sets were in use.

Cinemas. There were 703 screens in 1994. 92 full-length films were made in 1994.

Press. In 1991 there were 451 dailies, 1,134 weeklies, 374 fortnightlies and 2,573 periodicals of greater frequencies. 3,514 titles were in Urdu, 648 in English and 10 in more than one language. Average circulation of all dailies in 1990 was 1,825,667.

SOCIAL INSTITUTIONS

Justice. The Central Judiciary consists of the Supreme Court of Pakistan, which is a court of record and has three-fold jurisdiction, namely, original, appellate and advisory. There are 4 High Courts in Lahore, Peshawar, Quetta and Karachi. Under the Constitution, each has power to issue directions of writs of *Habeas Corpus, Mandamus, Certiorari* and others. Under them are district and sessions courts of first instance in each division; they have also some appellate jurisdiction. Criminal cases not being sessions cases are tried by district magistrates and subordinate magistrates. There are subordinate civil courts also.

The Constitution provides for an independent judiciary, as the greatest safeguard of citizens' rights. There is an Attorney-General, appointed by the President, who has right of audience in all courts, and a Federal Ombudsman.

A Federal Shariat Court at the Supreme Court level has been established to decide whether any law is wholly or partially un-Islamic. In Aug. 1990 a presidential ordinance decreed that the criminal code must conform to Islamic law (Shariah), and in May 1991 parliament passed a law incorporating it into the legal system.

290,255 crimes were reported in 1993 (289,556 in 1992). Execution of the death penalty for murder, in abeyance since 1986, was resumed in 1992. There were 7,258 murders in 1993 (6,943 in 1992).

Religion. Pakistan was created as a Moslem state. The Moslems are mainly Sunni, with an admixture of 15–20% Shi'ite. Religious groups (1981 census): Moslems, 96·68%; Christians, 1·55%; Hindus, 1·51%; Parsees, Buddhists, and others. There is a Minorities Wing at the Religious Affairs Ministry to safeguard the constitutional rights of religious minorities.

Education. Adult literacy was 34% in 1992. Adult literacy programmes have been established.

The principle of free and compulsory primary education has been accepted as the responsibility of the state; duration has been fixed provisionally at 5 years. About 40% of children aged 5-9 are enrolled at school. Present policy stresses vocational and technical education, disseminating a common culture based on Islamic ideology. Figures for 1992–93:

	Students (in 1,000)	*Teachers*[1] *(in 1,000)*	*Institutions*
Primary	14,120	283·1	142,228
Middle	3,515	88·6	11,595
Secondary	1,346	177·6	11,210
Secondary vocational	561	4·9	675
Colleges	76·7	...	99
Universities	83·9	4·3	23

[1] 1991-92

Health. In 1993 there were 799 hospitals and 4,206 dispensaries (with a total of 80,047 beds) and 849 maternity and child welfare centres. There were 63,653 doctors, 6,402 dentists and 20,245 nurses.

DIPLOMATIC REPRESENTATIVES

Of Pakistan in Great Britain (35 Lowndes Sq., London, SW1X 9JN)
High Commissioner: Wajid Shamsul Hasan.

Of Great Britain in Pakistan (Diplomatic Enclave, Ramna 5, Islamabad)
High Commissioner: Sir Christopher MacRae, KCMG.

Of Pakistan in the USA (2315 Massachusetts Ave., NW, Washington, D.C., 20008)
Ambassador: Maleeha Lodhi.

Of the USA in Pakistan (Diplomatic Enclave, Ramna, 5, Islamabad)
Ambassador: Vacant.

Of Pakistan to the United Nations
Ambassador: Ahmad Kamal.

Further Reading

Federal Bureau of Statistics.—*Pakistan Statistical Yearbook.—Statistical Pocket Book of Pakistan.* (annual)
Akhtar, R., *Pakistan Year Book.* Karachi-Lahore
Bhutto, B., *Daughter of the East.* London, 1988
Burki, S. J., *Historical Dictionary of Pakistan.* Metuchen (NJ), 1991.—*Pakistan: the Continuing Search for Nationhood.* 2nd ed. Boulder (Colo.), 1992
Choudhury, G. W., *Pakistan: Transition from Military to Civilian Rule.* London, 1988
Gilmartin, D., *Empire and Islam: Punjab and the making of Pakistan.* London, 1988
Hyman, A. *et al., Pakistan: Zia and After.* London, 1989
James, W. E. and Roy, S. (eds.) *The Foundations of Pakistan's Political Economy: towards an Agenda for the 1990s.* London, 1992
Kapur, A., *Pakistan in Crisis.* London, 1991
Lamb, C., *Waiting for Allah: Pakistan's Struggle for Democracy.* London, 1991
Low, D. A. (ed.) *The Political Inheritance of Pakistan.* London, 1991
Taylor, D., *Pakistan.* [Bibliography] Oxford and Santa Barbara, 1989

National library: National Library of Pakistan, Islamabad.
National statistical office: Federal Bureau of Statistics, Statistics Division, Karachi.

PALAU

Capital: Koror
Population: 18,000 (1994)

Republic of Palau

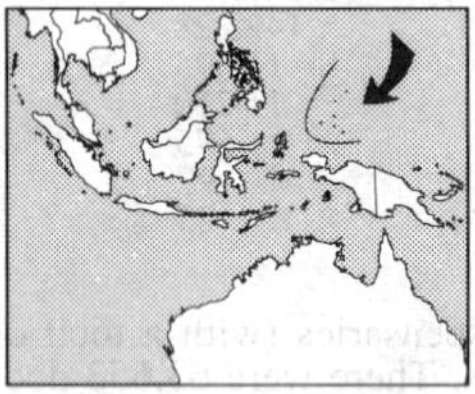

KEY HISTORICAL EVENTS. Spain acquired sovereignty over the Palau Islands in 1886, but sold the archipelago to Germany in 1899. Japan occupied the islands in 1914, and in 1921 they were mandated to Japan by the League of Nations. Captured by Allied Forces in 1944, the islands became part of the UN Trust Territory of the Pacific Islands created on 18 July 1947 and administered by the USA. Following a referendum in July 1978 in which Palauans voted against joining the new Federated States of Micronesia, the islands became an autonomous republic from 1 Jan. 1981, but acquisition of a free-association status with the USA was delayed by disputes over US intentions to base nuclear weapons on the islands. At a referendum in Nov. 1993 (the ninth of a series) 68% of votes cast favoured a Compact of Free Association with the USA, which provides US$450m. over 15 years in return for military facilities.

Palau became an independent republic on 1 Oct. 1994.

TERRITORY AND POPULATION. The archipelago lies in the Western Pacific and has a total area of 1,632 sq. km (630 sq. miles); water covers 1,172 sq. km. It comprises 26 islands and over 300 islets, the largest being Babelthuap (368 sq. km) with 3,400 inhabitants in 1980, but most inhabitants (10,493 in 1990) live on the small island of Koror (8 sq. km) to the south, containing the present headquarters (a new capital is being built in eastern Babelthuap). Estimated total population (1994), 18,000, including 5,000 foreign nationals (mainly Filipinos). some 6,000 Palauans live abroad. The local language is Palauan; both Palauan and English are official. The total population (1990 Census) was 15,122; estimate (1991) 15,450.

CONSTITUTION AND GOVERNMENT. The Constitution was adopted on 2 April 1979 and took effect from 1 Jan. 1981. The Republic has a bicameral legislature comprising a 16-member *Senate* (one from each of the Republic's 16 component states) and an 18-member *House of Delegates*, both elected for a term of 4 years as are the *President* and *Vice-President*. Customary social roles and land and sea rights are allocated by a matriarchal 16-clan system.

At the elections on 12 Nov. 1992 Kuniwo Nakamura was elected *President* by 4,841 votes to 4,707 against a single opponent.

Vice-President: Tommy Remengesau.

INTERNATIONAL RELATIONS

Membership. Palau is a member of the UN.

ECONOMY

Currency. US currency is used.

Banking and Finance. The National Development Bank of Palau is situated in Koror.

ENERGY AND NATURAL RESOURCES

Fisheries. Catch (1988) 1,400 tonnes, mainly tuna.

FOREIGN ECONOMIC RELATIONS

Commerce. Imports (1984) US$25·1m. Exports of tuna are worth US$3m. annually.

Total trade between Palau and UK (British Department of Trade returns, in £1,000 sterling): Imports to UK, nil; exports and re-exports from UK, 84.

Tourism. Tourism is a major industry. There are about 40,000 visitors a year.

COMMUNICATIONS

Roads. In 1986 there were 26 km of roads and 1,687 motor vehicles.

Shipping. In 1985, 56,000 tonnes of cargo were discharged and 2,000 tonnes were loaded.

Telecommunications. In 1988 there were 1,500 telephones. In 1993 there was a TV (colour by NTSC) station with 1,600 receivers, and a radio station with 9,000 receivers.

SOCIAL INSTITUTIONS

Justice. There is a Supreme Court and various subsidiary courts.

Religion. The majority of the population are Roman Catholic.

Education. In 1987 there were 2,784 pupils in 26 primary schools, 1,009 pupils in 6 secondary schools and 382 students (1984) in a technical school.

Health. In 1986 there were 10 doctors, 3 dentists, 1 pharmacist, 82 nursing personnel and a hospital with 70 beds.

DIPLOMATIC REPRESENTATIVE

Of Palau at the United Nations
Ambassador: Vacant.

PANAMA

República de Panamá

Capital: Panama City
Population: 2·33m. (1990)
GNP per capita: US$2,670 (1994)
HDI/world rank: 0·856/49 (1992)

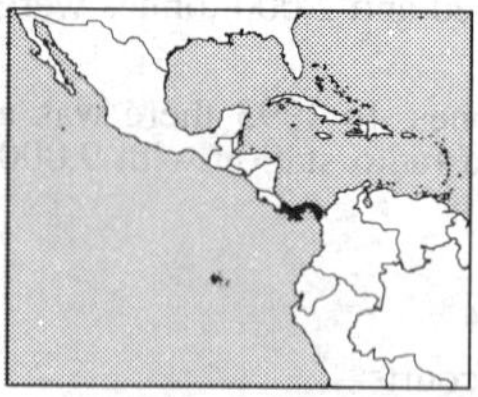

KEY HISTORICAL EVENTS. Panama had been united with Colombia, but declared its independence in 1903. Colombia recognized Panama in 1924.

In Oct. 1989 a US-backed coup attempt failed. On 15 Dec. the *de facto* leader Gen. Manuel Noriega, declared a 'state of war' with the USA. On 20 Dec. the USA invaded Panama to remove Gen. Noriega from power and he surrendered on 3 Jan. 1990. He is now serving a 40-year sentence in the USA.

TERRITORY AND POPULATION. Panama is bounded in the north by the Caribbean Sea, east by Colombia, south by the Pacific Ocean and west by Costa Rica. The area is 29,761 sq. miles (77,082 sq. km). Population at the census of 1990 was 2,329,329 (49% urban).

Vital statistics (1988): Births, 58,093; marriages, 10,112; deaths, 10,416. Crude birth rate (per 1,000): 25·0. In 1992 infant mortality was 21 per 1,000 live births; life expectancy was 72·5 years.

The largest towns (census, 1990) are Panama City, the capital, on the Pacific coast (584,803); its suburb San Miguelito (243,025); Colón, the port on the Atlantic coast (140,908); and David (102,678).

The areas and populations of the 9 provinces and the Special Territory were:

Province	*Sq. km*	*Census 1980*	*Census 1990*	*Capital*
Bocas del Toro	9,506	53,579	0,093,361	Bocas del Toro
Chiriquí	8,924	287,801	370,227	David
Veraguas	11,226	173,195	203,626	Santiago
Herrera	2,185	81,866	93,681	Chitré
Los Santos	4,587	70,200	76,947	Las Tablas
Coclé	4,981	140,320	173,190	Penonomé
Colón	7,205	166,439	202,338	Colón
San Blas (Special Territory)	3,206			El Porvenir
Panama	11,400	830,278	1,072,127	Panama City
Darién	15,458	26,497	43,832	La Palma

The official language is Spanish.

CLIMATE. A tropical climate, unvaryingly with high temperatures and only a short dry season from Jan. to April. Rainfall amounts are much higher on the north side of the isthmus. Panama City. Jan. 79°F (26·1°C), July 81°F (27·2°C). Annual rainfall 70" (1,770 mm). Colón. Jan. 80°F (26·7°C), July 80°F (26·7°C). Annual rainfall 127" (3,175 mm). Balboa Heights. Jan. 80°F (26·7°C), July 81°F (27·2°C). Annual rainfall 70" (1,759 mm). Cristóbal. Jan. 80°F (26·7°C), July 81°F (27·2°C). Annual rainfall 130" (3,255 mm).

CONSTITUTION AND GOVERNMENT. The 1972 Constitution, as amended in 1978 and 1983, provides for a *President*, 2 *Vice-Presidents* and a 72-seat *Legislative Assembly* to be elected for 5-year terms by a direct vote. To remain registered, parties must have attained at least 50,000 votes at the last election. A referendum held on 15 Nov. 1992 rejected constitutional reforms by 64% of votes cast. Turn-out was 40%.

Presidential and parliamentary elections were held on 8 May 1994. The electorate was 1,499,848; turn-out was 73·7%. Ernesto Pérez Balladares was elected President by 33·3% of votes cast against 6 opponents. Representatives of 16 parties stood for election to the Legislative Assembly, 13 grouped in alliances. The Revolutionary Democratic Party (RDP) gained 31 seats in the 'United People' alliance with the Liberal Republican Party (LRP; 1) and the Labour Party (1); the Arnulfist Party (AP) gained 15 in the 'Democratic Alliance' with the Authentic Liberal Party (4), the National Liberal Party (1) and the Democratic Independent Union (1); the Papá Egoró Movement gained 6; the Liberal Republican Nationalist Movement (MORILENA) gained 5 in the 'Change 94' alliance with the Civil Renovation Party (3) and the National Renovation Party (1); the Solidarity Party gained 2; the Christian Democrat Party gained 1.

President: Ernesto Pérez Balladares (RDP; sworn in 1 Sept. 1994).

First Vice-President: Tomas Altamirano Duque; *Second Vice-President:* Felipe Virzi.

In Sept. 1995 the government comprised:

Interior and Justice: Raul Montenegro. *Foreign Affairs:* Gabriel Lewis Galindo. *Public Works:* Luis Blanco. *Finance and Treasury:* Olmedo Miranda. *Agricultural Development:* Carlos Sousa Lennox. *Commerce and Industry:* Nitzia de Villarreal. *Health:* Aida Libia de Rivera. *Labour and Social Welfare:* Mitchel Doens. *Education:* Dr Pablo Thalassinos. *Housing:* Dr Francisco Sánchez Cardenas. *Planning and Economic Policy:* Dr Guillermo Chapman. *Minister of the Presidency:* Raul Arango.

National flag: Quarterly: first a white panel with a blue star, second red, third blue, fourth white with a red star.

National anthem: 'Alcanzamos por fin la victoria' ('We achieve victory in the end'); words by J. de la Ossa, tune by Santos Jorge.

Local Government: The 9 provinces and a Special Territory are divided into 67 municipal districts and sub-divided into 511 local authorities.

DEFENCE. The armed forces were disbanded in 1990 and constitutionally abolished in 1994. Divided between both coasts, the National Maritime Service, a coast guard rather than a navy, comprises 2 32-metre patrol craft, 4 smaller craft and 6 utility landing craft. In 1995 personnel totalled 400. For Police *see* JUSTICE, *below*.

INTERNATIONAL RELATIONS

Membership. Panama is a member of the UN, OAS and Non-aligned Movement.

ECONOMY

Budget. The 1994 budget provided for revenue of 1,929m. balboas, current expenditure of 1,416m. balboas, capital expenditure of 381m. balboas and debt service of 493m. balboas. Public sector debt was US$3,771m. in 1989.

Currency. The monetary unit is the *balboa* (PAB) of 100 *centesimos*, at parity with the US dollar. There are coins of 1, 5, 10, 25 and 50 centesimos and 1 and 100 balboas. The only paper currency used is that of the USA. US coinage is also legal tender. Inflation was 0·2% in Dec. 1993.

Banking and Finance. There is no statutory central bank. Banking is supervised and promoted by the National Banking Commission. Government accounts are handled through the state-owned *Banco Nacional de Panama.* There are 2 other state banks. The number of commercial banks was 104 in 1991.

Weights and Measures. US Customary weights and measures are in general use; the metric system is the official system.

ENERGY AND NATURAL RESOURCES

Electricity. In 1992 capacity was 958 mW, of which 551 mW were hydro-electric.

Minerals. Limestone, clay and salt are produced. There are known to be copper deposits.

Agriculture. Production in 1993 (in 1,000 tonnes): Rice, 212; maize, 94; dry beans, 5; raw sugar, 133; coffee, 12; bananas, 1,120; oranges, 33; mangoes, 4; cocoa, 1 and coconuts, 22. Livestock (1993): 1,427,000 cattle, 297,000 pigs and 8m. poultry.

Forestry. Forest and woodland coverd 3·9m. ha in 1994. There are great timber resources, notably mahogany. Production (1986) 2·05m. cu. metres.

Fisheries. The catch in 1989 was 154,895 tonnes. Shrimps are the principal species caught.

INDUSTRY. The main industry is agricultural produce processing. Other areas include oil refining, chemicals and paper-making.

Labour. In 1991 the workforce (persons 15 years and over) numbered 856,200, of whom 722,200 were employed.

Trade Unions. 77,500 workers belonged to trade unions in 1994, of whom 27,000 were members of the Confederación de Trabajadores de la República de Panamá.

FOREIGN ECONOMIC RELATIONS. The Colón Free Zone is an autonomous institution set up in 1953. 460 companies were operating there in 1993. Factories in export zones are granted tax exemption on profits for 10–20 years and exemption from the provisions of the labour code. Foreign debt was US$6,485m. in Dec. 1992.

Commerce. Trade in 1992 (in 1m. balboas): Exports, 501·5; imports, 2,023·6. Main exports: Bananas, 212·8; shellfish, 64·3; sugar, 21·3. Chief export markets: USA, 30·1%; Germany, 25·2%; Italy, 7·6%; Costa Rica, 6·2%. Chief import suppliers: USA, 37%; Japan, 8·2%; Ecuador, 6%.

Total trade between Panama and UK (British Department of Trade returns, in £1,000 sterling):

	1991	*1992*	*1993*	*1994*	*1995*
Imports to UK	1,679	7,025	12,674	7,139	2,553
Exports and re-exports from UK [1]	36,656	42,178	53,367	48,614	67,975

[1] Including new ships built for foreign owners and registered in Panama.

Tourism. In 1993, 327,000 people visited Panama.

COMMUNICATIONS

Roads. In 1989 there were 9,689 km of roads, about one-third paved or tarred. The road from Panama City westward to the cities of David and Concepción and to the Costa Rican frontier, with several branches, is part of the Pan-American Highway. The Trans-Isthmian Highway connects Panama City and Colón. In 1988 there were 176,400 registered motor vehicles.

Railways. The 1,524 mm gauge *Ferrocarril de Panama* which connects Ancón on the Pacific with Cristóbal on the Atlantic along the bank of the Panama Canal, is the principal railway. 39,000 tonnes of freight were carried in 1993. The United Brands Company runs 376 km of railway, and the Chiriquí National Railroad 171 km.

Civil Aviation. There is an international airport at Panama City (Tocumén). The national carrier is COPA, which in 1995 operated 6 B-737-200 Advs, 1 B-737-200C and 1 B-737-200C Adv. Services are also provided by Aces, Aeroflot, Aeroperlas, Aeroperú, Aerotour Dominicano, American Airlines, Avensa, Avianca, Aviateca, Continental Airlines & Air Micronesia, Cubana, Eva, Iberia, KLM, LACSA, Lloyd Aéreo Boliviano, Mexicana, SAETA, SAM, Servivensa, Taca and Viasa.

Shipping. Ships under Panamanian registry in 1995 totalled 86·46m. DWT, all foreign-owned; most of these ships elect Panamanian registry because fees are low and labour laws lenient. All the international maritime traffic for Colón and Panama runs through the Canal ports of Cristóbal, Balboa and Bahia Las Minas (Colón); Almirante is used for both the provincial and international trade. There is an oil transfer terminal at Puerto Armuelles on the Pacific coast.

Panama Canal. A 1903 USA-Panamanian treaty permitted the USA to build and operate a canal connecting the Atlantic and Pacific oceans. The treaty granted the USA in perpetuity the use, occupation and control of a Canal Zone, approximately 10 miles wide, in which the USA would possess sovereign rights 'to the entire exclusion of the exercise by the Republic of Panama of any such sovereign rights, power or authority'. In return the USA guaranteed the independence of Panama and agreed to pay $10m. and an annuity of $250,000 to commence 9 years later. The Canal was opened to shipping on 15 Aug. 1914.

Under 2 new treaties effective as of Oct. 1979 Panama assumed general territorial jurisdiction over the canal area (former Canal Zone) and became able to use portions of the area not needed for the operation and defence of the canal. Panamanian penal and civil codes became applicable. At the same time Panama assumed responsibility for commercial ship repairs and supplies, railway and pier operations, passengers, police and courts, all of which were among other areas formerly administered by the Panama Canal Company and the Canal Zone Government. The USA maintains operational control over all lands, waters and installations, including military bases, necessary to manage, operate and defend the canal until 31 Dec. 1999. A new agency of the US Government, the Panama Canal Commission, operates the canal, replacing the Panama Canal Co. A policy-making board of 5 US citizens and 4 Panamanians comprises on the Commission's board of directors. The canal administrator is a Panamanian citizen and the deputy a US citizen.

Panama's Inter-Oceanic Region Authority has been set up to take over assets on the progressive withdrawal of the US presence.

The Panama Canal Commission is concerned primarily with the operation of the Canal. Since 1 Oct. 1995, tolls assessment has been based on the Panama Canal/Universal Measurement System (PC/UMS), which incorporates the principles of the 1969 International Convention on Tonnage Measurement of Ships. Toll rates are US$2.21 a PC/UMS ton for vessels carrying passengers or cargo and US$1·76 per ton for vessels in transit in ballast. The toll rate for warships, hospital ships and supply ships, which pay on a displacement basis, is US$1·23 a ton.

The rates are set to continue the approximately break-even financial operating results after paying its own expenses.

Administrator of the Panama Canal Commission: Gilberto Guardia Fábrega.

US military personnel: Army, 9,120; Navy, 700; Marines, 120; Air Force, 2,000.

Particulars of the ocean-going commercial traffic through the canal are given as follows (vessels of 300 PC/UMS tons net and 500 displacement tons and over; cargo in long tons):

Fiscal year ending 30 Sept.	*No. of vessels transiting*	*PC/UMS net tonnage*	*Cargo in long tons*	*Tolls levied (in US$)*
1994	12,337	194,289,433	170,538,437	416,803,062
1995	13,459 [1]	215,355,914	190,303,065	460,043,676

[1] 6,933 Atlantic to Pacific; 6,526 Pacific to Atlantic.

In the fiscal year ending 30 Sept. 1995, 15,135 ships of all sizes passed through the Canal. Most numerous transits by flag: Panama, 2,563; Liberia, 1,501; Greece, 1,016; Bahamas, 1,300; Cyprus, 953; Norway, 501.

Statistical Information: The Panama Canal Commission Office of Public Affairs.

Annual Reports on the Panama Canal, by the Administrator of the Panama Canal Commission.
Rules and Regulations Governing Navigation of the Panama Canal. The Panama Canal Commission, Miami, Florida *or* Washington, DC
Cameron, I., *The Impossible Dream.* London, 1972
Le Feber, W., *The Panama Canal: The Crisis in Historical Perspective.* OUP, 1978
McCullough, D., *The Path Between the Seas.* New York and London, 1978
Major, J., *Prize Possession: the United States and the Panama Canal, 1903–1979.* CUP, 1994

Telecommunications. There were 0·2m. telephones in 1990. There are about 60 broadcasting stations, mostly commercial, grouped in the Asociación Panameña de Radiodifusión. There are 4 television channels (colour by NTSC), an educational channel, and a radio and TV network for US forces. In 1993 there were 0·45 radio and 204,539 TV sets in use. In 1988 there were 241,900 telephones.

Presss. In 1994 there were 8 dailies (1 in English).

SOCIAL INSTITUTIONS

Justice. The Supreme Court consists of 9 justices appointed by the executive. There is no death penalty. The police force numbered 11,000 in 1996, and includes a Presidential Guard.

Religion. 85% of the population is Roman Catholic, 5% Protestant, 4·5% Moslem. There is freedom of religious worship and separation of Church and State. Clergymen may teach in the schools but may not hold public office.

Education. Adult literacy was 90% in 1992. Elementary education is compulsory for all children from 7 to 15 years of age. In 1994–95 there were 2 universities and 1 technological university with a total of 67,509 students and 4,106 academic staff. There were also a nautical school, a business school and institutes of teacher training and tourism.

Health. In 1988 there were 2,761 doctors, 527 dentists and 2,514 nursing personnel. There were 58 hospitals, 178 health centres and 435 health sub-centres with a total of 7,776 beds.

DIPLOMATIC REPRESENTATIVES

Of Panama in Great Britain (119 Crawford St., London, W1H 1AF)
Ambassador: Aquilino Boyd de la Guardia.

Of Great Britain in Panama (Torre Swiss Bank, Calle 53, Apartado 889, Panama City 1)
Ambassador and Consul-General: William Stinton.

Of Panama in the USA (2862 McGill Terr., NW, Washington, D.C., 20008)
Ambassador: Ricardo Arias.

Of the USA in Panama (Apartado 6959, Panama City 5)
Ambassador: William J. Hughes.

Of Panama to the United Nations
Ambassador: Dr Jorge Illueca.

Further Reading

Statistical Information: The Comptroller-General of the Republic (Contraloria General de la República, Calle 35 y Avenida 6, Panama City) publishes an annual report and other statistical publications.

Jorden, W. J., *Panama Odyssey.* Univ. of Texas Press, 1984
Langstaff, E. DeS., *Panama.* [Bibliography]. Oxford and Santa Barbara (CA), 1982
Ropp, S. C., *Panamanian Politics.* New York, 1982
Sahota, G. S., *Poverty Theory and Policy: a Study of Panama.* Johns Hopkins Univ. Press, 1990
Other titles are listed under PANAMA CANAL, *above.*
National library: Biblioteca Nacional, Departamento de Información. Calle 22, Panama.

PAPUA NEW GUINEA

Capital: Port Moresby
Population: 3·85m. (1992)
GNP per capita: US$1,160 (1994)
HDI/world rank: 0·508/126 (1992)

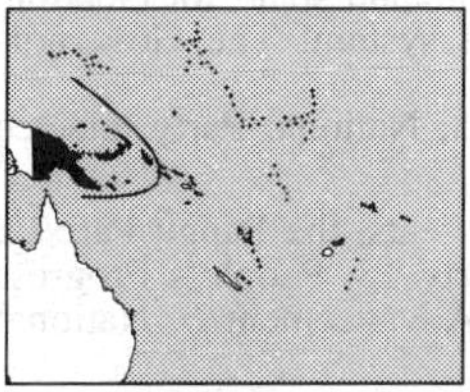

KEY HISTORICAL EVENTS. For the history of the colonial period *see* THE STATESMAN'S YEAR-BOOK 1994–95, p. 1070.

The Papua New Guinea Act 1949–1972 provided for the administration of the UN Australian Trust Territory of New Guinea in an administrative union with the Territory of Papua under the title of Papua New Guinea.

Australia granted Papua New Guinea self-government on 1 Dec. 1973 and, on 16 Sept. 1975, Papua New Guinea became a fully independent state.

Fighting between the government and the secessionist Bougaineville Revolutionary Army (BRA) continued until 3 Sept. 1994, when a peace agreement was signed. This provides for 4 neutral zones to be occupied by a Pacific peacekeeping force drawn from Fiji, Tonga and Vanuatu with logistic support from Australia and New Zealand.

TERRITORY AND POPULATION. Papua New Guinea extends from the equator to Cape Baganowa in the Louisiade Archipelago to 11° 40' S. lat. and from the border of West Irian to 160° E. long. with a total area of 462,840 sq. km. According to the census the 1990 population was 3,529,538 (excluding North Solomons, estimated 1990 population 159,500). Estimate, 1992, 3·85m. Population of main towns (1990 census): Port Moresby (National Capital District), 193,242; Lae, 80,655; Rabaul, 17,022; Madang, 27,057; Wewak, 23,224; Goroka, 17,855; Mount Hagen, 17,392. Area and population of the provinces:

Provinces	*Sq.km*	*Census 1980*	*Census 1990*	*Capital*
Milne Bay	14,000	127,975	157,288	Alotau
Northern	22,800	77,442	96,762	Popondetta
Central	29,500	116,964	140,584	Port Moresby
National Capital District	240	123,624	193,242	—
Gulf	34,500	64,120	68,060	Kerema
Western	99,300	78,575	108,705 [1]	Daru
Southern Highlands	23,800	236,052	302,724	Mendi
Enga	12,800	164,534	238,357	Wabag
Western Highlands	8,500	265,656	291,090	Mount Hagen
Chimbu	6,100	178,290	183,801	Kundiawa
Eastern Highlands	11,200	276,726	299,619	Goroka
Morobe	34,500	310,622	363,535	Lae
Madang	29,000	211,069	270,299	Madang
East Sepik	42,800	221,890	248,308	Wewak
West Sepik	36,300	114,192	135,185 [2]	Vanimo
Manus	2,100	26,036	32,830	Lorengau
West New Britain	21,000	88,941	127,547	Kimbe
East New Britain	15,500	133,197	184,408	Rabaul
New Ireland	9,600	66,028	87,194	Kavieng
North Solomons	9,300	128,794	...	Arawa

[1] Excludes 3 census divisions, estimated total 1,500.
[2] Excludes 2 census divisions, estimated total 3,000.

Vital statistics (1990, estimate): Crude birth rate, 35·2 per 1,000; crude death rate, 13·1. Life expectancy was 55 years in 1991.

The principal local languages are Neo-Melanesian (or Pidgin, a creole of English) and Hiri Motu. English is in official use.

CLIMATE. There is a monsoon climate, with high temperatures and humidity the year round. Port Moresby is in a rain shadow and is not typical of the rest of Papua

New Guinea. Jan. 82°F (27·8°C), July 78°F (25·6°C). Annual rainfall 40" (1,011 mm).

CONSTITUTION AND GOVERNMENT. A single legislative house, known as the *National Parliament*, is made up of 109 members from all parts of the country. The members are elected by universal suffrage; elections are held every 5 years. All citizens over the age of 18 are eligible to vote and stand for election. Voting is by secret ballot and follows the preferential system. The Governor-General is nominated by parliament for 6-year terms.

Governor-General: Sir Wiwa Korowi, GCMG (b. 1948; National Party; elected by Parliament to replace Sir Serei Eri, Nov. 1991).

At the elections of June 1992 independents gained 31 seats, the Pangu Pati 22, People's Democratic Movement 15, People's Action Party 13, People's Progress Party 10, Melanesian Alliance 9, League for National Advancement 5, National Party 2, Melanesian National Front 1.

In Nov. 1994 the government comprised:

Prime Minister, Minister of Foreign Affairs and Trade: Rt. Hon. Sir Julius Chan, KBE (b. 1939; sworn in 30 Aug. 1994).

Deputy Prime Minister, Minister of Finance and Planning: Chris Haiveta. *Agriculture and Livestock:* Bernard Narakobi. *Mining and Petroleum:* John Giheno. *Forests:* Andrew Posai. *Provincial Affairs and Village Development:* Castan Maibawa. *Transport:* Andrew Baing. *Justice:* Robert Timo Nagele. *Defence:* Mathias Ijape. *Communications:* John Momis. *Civil Aviation and Tourism:* Paul Pora. *Works:* Peter Yama. *Fisheries and Marine Resources:* Titus Philemon. *Correctional Services:* Sylvanius Siembo. *Environment and Conservation:* Perry Zeipi. *Education and Culture:* Joseph Onguglo. *Lands and Physical Planning:* Sir Albert Kipalan. *Health:* Peter Barter. *Labour and Employment:* Jerry Nalau. *Police:* Paul Mambei. *Home Affairs:* Nakikus Konga. *Commerce and Industry:* David Mai. *State Affairs and Administrative Services:* Paul Tohian. *Housing:* Dick Mune. *Public Services:* Bart Philemon.

The *Speaker* is Rt Hon. Rabbie Namaliu.

National flag: Diagonally ochre-red over black, on the red a bird of paradise in gold, and on the black 5 stars of the Southern Cross in white.

National anthem: 'Arise, all you sons of this land'; words and tune by T. Shacklady.

Local Government: In 1950 the first village council was formed which established the basis of an extensive local government system. A system of provincial government was introduced in 1976 and the importance of lower-level local government diminished. However, lower-level community government had replaced local government councils in some provinces by 1991.

DEFENCE. The Papua New Guinea Defence Force has a total strength of 3,800 (1996) consisting of land, maritime and air elements. The Army is organized in 2 infantry and 1 engineer battalion. The Navy, based at Port Moresby and Manus, is all of Australian build and comprises 4 inshore patrol craft, 2 tank landing craft and some boats. Personnel numbered 500 in 1995. The Defence Force has an Air Transport Squadron. Current equipment comprises 2 CN-235 transports, 1 Australian-built N22B Nomad and 4 Iroquois helicopters.

INTERNATIONAL RELATIONS

Membership. Papua New Guinea is a member of the UN, the Commonwealth, the Colombo Plan, the South Pacific Commission and the South Pacific Forum and is an observer at ASEAN and an ACP state of the EU.

ECONOMY

Budget. Budgetary income (in K1,000) for calendar years was:

Source	*1992*	*1993*	*1994* [1]
Tax revenue	721,400	666,600	732,500
Non-tax revenue	259,700	377,600	364,100
Grants	230,200	197,500	177,611
Loans	196,300	201,400	559,900
Total	1,407,600	1,443,100	1,834,111
Expenditure:			
Administration	381,500	386,900	393,100
Social	390,200	471,100	528,300
Economic	299,400	363,100	421,100
Public debt charges	256,700	269,900	328,900
Other	155,700	144,100	162,200
Total	1,483,500	1,635,100	1,833,600

[1] Estimates.

Currency. The unit of currency is the *kina* (PGK) of 100 *toea*. There are coins of 1, 2, 5, 10, 20 and 50 toea and 1 kina, and notes of 2, 5, 10, 20 and 50 kina. K141·2m. were in circulation in 1992. The kina was floated in Oct. 1994. Foreign exchange reserves were K231m. in 1992; gold reserves K11·1m. In March 1996, £1 = K2·07; US$1 = K1·35; DM1 = K1·28.

Banking and Finance. The Bank of Papua New Guinea assumed the central banking functions formerly undertaken by the Reserve Bank of Australia on 1 Nov. 1973. A national banking institution, the Papua New Guinea Banking Corporation, has been established. This bank has assumed the Papua New Guinea business of the Commonwealth Trading Bank of Australia.

There are 5 commercial banks, 3 Australian and 2 with 51% Papuan ownership. Total deposits, 1992, K1318·2m. Total savings account deposits, 1992, K226·8m.

In addition, the Agriculture Bank of Papua New Guinea had assets of K82·6m. in 1992, and finance companies and merchant banks had total assets of K198·4m.

Weights and Measures. The metric system is in force.

ENERGY AND NATURAL RESOURCES

Electricity. Production in 1990 was 1,362·3m. kWh (490·3m. kWh hydro-electric).

Oil. The Iagifu field in the Southern Highlands had (1988) potential recoverable reserves of 500m. bbls. Crude oil production (1992), 2·12m. tonnes.

Minerals. In 1991 mining produced 15% of GDP. Copper is the main mineral product. Gold, copper and silver are the only minerals produced in quantity. The Misima open-pit gold mine, first mined in 1888, was opened in 1989. Production was forecast at 0·21m. oz a year with a life of 10 years. The Porgera gold mine opened in 1990 with an expected life of 20 years. Major copper deposits in Bougainville have proven reserves of about 800m. tonnes; mining was halted by secessionist rebel activity. Copper and gold deposits in the Star Mountains of the Western Province are being developed by Ok Tedi Mining Ltd at the Mt. Fubilan mine. Production of gold commenced in 1984 and of copper concentrates in 1987. In 1986, Bougainville Copper Ltd produced 586,552 tonnes of copper concentrate containing approximately 178,593 tonnes of copper, 16,367 kg of gold and 50,385 kg of silver; Ok Tedi Mining Ltd produced 18,277 kg of gold and 5,677 kg of silver.

Agriculture. In 1991 agriculture, forestry and fishery produced 27% of GDP and employed 75% of the workforce. At 31 Dec. 1988 there were 1,024 large holdings with a total area of 415,000 ha. In 1992 there were 40,000 ha of arable land, 0·37m. ha of permanent cropland and 80,000 ha of permanent pasture. Minor commercial crops include pyrethrum, tea, peanuts and spices. Locally consumed food crops include sweet potatoes, maize, taro, bananas, rice and sago. Tropical fruits grow abundantly. There is extensive grassland. The sugar industry has made the country self-sufficient in this commodity while a beef-cattle industry is being developed.

Production (1993, in tonnes): Coffee, 63,000; copra, 120,000; coconuts, 0·79m.; cocoa beans, 37,000; rubber, 3,000.

Livestock (1993): Cattle, 105,000; pigs, 1·02m.; sheep, 4,000; goats, 2,000; poultry, 3m.

Forestry. The forest area in 1990 was 38·23m. ha. Timber production is important for both local consumption and export. In 1986, 1·7m. cu. metres of logs were cut. Production of sawn timber, 1986, 84,000 cu. metres.

Fisheries. Tuna is the major resource; in 1989 the catch was 25,240 tonnes.

INDUSTRY. Secondary and service industries are expanding for the local market. The main industries were (1988) food processing, beverages, tobacco, timber products, wood, and fabricated metal products. In 1988 there were 692 factories employing 30,503 persons. Value of output K768m.

Labour. In 1987 there were 145,331 persons in formal employment, other than public servants. In 1990 there were 40,353 public servants.

FOREIGN ECONOMIC RELATIONS. Australian aid amounts to an annual $A300m. The 'Pactra II' agreement of 1991 establishes a free trade zone with Australia and protects Australian investments. Foreign debt was K863·3m. in 1993.

Commerce. Imports (in K1,000) for calendar years:

	1988	*1989*	*1990*
Food and live animals	181,789	190,853	194,624
Beverages and tobacco	15,456	14,957	14,764
Crude materials, inedible, except fuels	8,577	7,769	8,712
Mineral fuels, lubricants and related materials	98,175	63,704	80,132
Oils and fats (animal and vegetable)	3,350	3,387	4,793
Chemicals	84,403	78,588	81,563
Manufactured goods, chiefly by material	205,654	253,251	223,045
Machinery and transport equipment	424,587	524,966	423,019
Miscellaneous manufactured articles	99,113	109,776	97,560
Commodities and transactions of merchandise trade, not elsewhere specified	12,356	12,877	13,711
Total imports	1,133,459	1,260,128	1,141,922

Exports (in K1,000) for calendar years:

	1991	*1992*	*1993*
Coconut and copra products—			
Copra	5,293	11,862	13,804
Copra (coconut) oil	11,105	24,182	15,456
Copra cake and pellets	1,671	2,501	3,832
Total	18,069	38,545	33,092
Coffee beans	79,418	67,999	92,261
Cocoa beans	34,007	34,088	33,081
Crude rubber	1,791	1,932	2,565
Tea	2,554	6,511	7,182
Pyrethrum extract	682	367	356
Forest and timber products			
Logs	62,132	92,087	255,838
Sawn timber	1,418	1,663	1,533
Other	5,456	5,052	6,851
Crocodile skins	986	1,000	1,662
Crayfish and prawns	7,532	6,469	6,173
Gold	508,286	601,909	499,362
Copper concentrate	566,445	523,197	499,116
Other domestic produce	23,085	385,714	808,726
Total domestic produce	1,562,887	2,007,320	2,541,465
Re-exports	172,947	114,446	71,304
Total exports	1,735,834	2,121,766	2,612,769

Of exports in 1993, Japan took 21%, Germany, 6·4% and Australia, 36%; of imports (1990), Australia furnished about 47%, Singapore, 8·5% and Japan, 13·3%.

Total trade between Papua New Guinea and UK (British Department of Trade returns, in £1,000 sterling):

	1991	*1992*	*1993*	*1994*	*1995*
Imports to UK	32,170	41,020	53,690	56,981	97,391
Exports and re-exports from UK	15,446	6,469	10,858	9,074	10,849

Tourism. In 1992, there were 42,816 visitors of whom 14,815 were tourists.

COMMUNICATIONS

Roads. In 1992 there were 21,433 km of roads. Motor vehicles numbered (1992) about 95,000 (65,000 commercial).

Civil Aviation. Jacksons International Airport is at Port Moresby. The state-owned national carrier, Air Niugini, operated 2 A310-300s and 12 other aircraft in 1995. Services are also provided by Qantas and Solomon Airlines. There are a total of 177 airports and airstrips with scheduled services.

Shipping. There are 12 entry and 4 other main ports served by 5 major shipping lines; the Papua New Guinea Shipping Corporation is state-owned. Sea-going shipping totalled 51,051 GRT in 1995, including oil tankers, 5,044 GRT.

Telecommunications. Telephones numbered 63,212 on 31 Dec. 1986. The National Broadcasting Commission operates 3 networks: national, provincial and commercial. A national service is relayed throughout the country. Each province has a broadcasting service, while the larger urban centres are also covered by a commercial network relayed from Port Moresby. 2 commercial television stations broadcast from Port Moresby (colour by PAL). In 1990 there were 10,000 television and 235,000 radio receivers.

Press. In 1993 there was 1 daily newspaper and a number of weeklies and monthlies.

SOCIAL INSTITUTIONS

Justice. In 1983, over 1,500 criminal and civil cases were heard in the National Court and an estimated 120,000 cases in district and local courts. The discretionary use of the death penalty for murder and rape was introduced in 1991.

Religion. In 1992 there were 2·24m. Protestants and 1·26m. Roman Catholics.

Education. Obligatory universal primary education is a government objective. In 1990 about two-thirds of eligible children were attending school. In 1990-91 there were 2,606 primary schools with 413,089 pupils, 135 secondary schools with 56,638 pupils, 101 vocational schools with 5,395 students, 7 technical colleges with 1,043 students, 9 teacher training colleges with 1,686 students and 2 universities (the University of Papua New Guinea and the Papua New Guinea University of Technology) with 5,007 students.

Health. In 1986, there were 19 hospitals, 459 health centres and 2,231 aid posts. In 1991 there was 1 doctor per 12,870 inhabitants.

DIPLOMATIC REPRESENTATIVES

Of Papua New Guinea in Great Britain (14 Waterloo Pl., London, SW1R 4AR)
High Commissioner: Sir Kina Bona.

Of Great Britain in Papua New Guinea (Kiroki St., Port Moresby)
High Commissioner: B. B. Low, CBE.

Of Papua New Guinea in the USA (1615 New Hampshire Ave., NW, Washington D.C., 20036)
Ambassador: Kepas Isimel Watangia.

Of the USA in Papua New Guinea (Armit St., Port Moresby)
Ambassador: Richard W. Teare.

Of Papua New Guinea to the United Nations
Ambassador: Utula Utuoc Samana, CMG.

Further Reading

National Statistical Office. *Summary of Statistics.* Annual.— *Abstract of Statistics.* Quarterly. —*Economic Indicators.*
Monthly Bank of Papua New Guinea. *Quarterly Economic Bulletin.*
McConnell, F., *Papua New Guinea.* [Bibliography] Oxford and Santa Barbara, 1988
Ryan, P. (ed.) *Encyclopaedia of Papua and New Guinea.* Melbourne Univ. Press, 1972
Turner, A., *Historical Dictionary of Papua New Guinea.* Metuchen (NJ), 1995
Waiko, J. D., *Short History of Papua New Guinea.* OUP, 1993

National statistical office: National Statistical Office, PO Wards Strip.

PARAGUAY

República del Paraguay

Capital: Asunción
Population: 4·5m. (1993)
GNP per capita: US$1,570 (1994)
HDI/world rank: 0·723/87 (1992)

KEY HISTORICAL EVENTS. Paraguay gained independence from Spain on 14 May 1811. In 1814 Dr José Gaspar Rodríguez de Francia was elected dictator, and in 1816 perpetual dictator, by the National Assembly. He died 20 Sept. 1840. In 1844 a new constitution was adopted, under which Carlos Antonio López (first elected in 1842, died 10 Sept. 1862) and his son, Francisco Solano López, ruled until 1870. During the devastating war against Brazil, Argentina and Uruguay (1865–70) Paraguay's population was reduced from about 600,000 to 232,000. Argentina, in Aug. 1942, and Brazil, in May 1943, voided the reparations which Paraguay had never paid. Further severe losses were incurred during the war with Bolivia (1932–35) over territorial claims in the Chaco. A peace treaty by which Paraguay obtained most of the area her troops had conquered was signed in July 1938.

Gen. Alfredo Stroessner Mattianda, the commander-in-chief of the army, assumed the presidency after a military coup in 1954. He was deposed in a further coup in Feb. 1989.

TERRITORY AND POPULATION. Paraguay is bounded in the north-west by Bolivia, north-east and east by Brazil and south-east, south and south-west by Argentina. The area is 406,752 sq. km (157,042 sq. miles).

The population (census 1992) was 4·12m. (51% urban); estimate (1993) 4·5m.; density, 10·8 per sq. km.

Vital statistics rates, 1991 (per 1,000 population): Birth, 34; death, 6; growth, 31. Expectation of life was 67·2 years in 1992.

At the 1992 census the capital, Asunción (and metropolitan area), had 637,737 inhabitants and Ciudad del Este (formerly Presidente Stroessner), 133,893.

There are 17 departments and the capital city. Area and population at the 1992 census:

Department	*Area in sq. km*	*Population*	*Department*	*Area in sq. km*	*Population*
Asunción (city)	117	502,426	Caazapá	9,496	128,550
Central	2,465	864,540	Canendiyú	14,667	96,826
Caaguazú	11,474	383,319	Amambay	12,933	97,158
Alto Paraná	14,895	403,858	Misiones	9,556	88,624
Itapúa	16,525	375,748	Neembucú	12,147	69,884
San Pedro	20,002	277,110	*Oriental*	*159,827*	*4,026,342*
Paraguari	8,705	203,012	Presidente Hayes	72,907	59,100
Cordillera	4,948	206,097	Boquerón [1]	91,669	26,292
Concepción	18,051	166,946	Alto Paraguay [2]	83,349	11,816
Guairá	3,846	162,244	*Occidental*	*246,925*	*97,208*

[1] Incorporates former department of Nueva Asunción.
[2] Incorporates former department of Chaco.

The population is mixed Spanish and Guaraní Indian. There are some 46,700 unassimilated Indians of other tribal origin, in the Chaco and the forests of eastern Paraguay. 40·1% of the population speak only Guaraní; 48·2% are bilingual (Spanish/Guaraní); and 6·4% speak only Spanish.

Mennonites who arrived in 3 groups (1927, 1930 and 1947) are settled in the Chaco and eastern Paraguay. There are also Korean and Japanese settlers.

CLIMATE. A tropical climate, with abundant rainfall and only a short dry season from July to Sept., when temperatures are lowest. Asunción. Jan. 81°F (30°C), July 64°F (17·8°C). Annual rainfall 53" (1,316 mm).

CONSTITUTION AND GOVERNMENT. On 18 June 1992 a Constituent Assembly approved a new constitution. The head of state is the *President,* elected for a non-renewable 5-year term. Parliament consists of an 80-member *Chamber of Deputies,* elected from departmental constituencies, and a 45-member *Senate,* elected from a single national constituency.

Presidential and parliamentary elections were held on 9 May 1993. Juan Carlos Wasmosy was elected President against 2 opponents with 39·5% of votes cast. The electorate was 1·6m. At the parliamentary elections the Colorado Party gained 40 seats in the Chamber of Deputies (and 20 in the Senate), the Authentic Radical Liberal Party 32 (and 17) and National Encounter 8 (and 8).

President: Juan Carlos Wasmosy (b.1938; Colorado Party; sworn in 15 Aug. 1993).

The Cabinet in Nov. 1995 comprised:

Foreign Affairs: Luis María Ramírez Boettner. *Interior:* Carlos Podesta. *Finance:* Orlando Bareiro. *Public Health and Social Welfare:* Andrés Vidovich Morales. *Justice and Labour:* Juan Manuel Morales. *Public Works and Communications:* Carlos Facetti. *Industry and Commerce:* Ubalde Scavone. *Education and Church Affairs:* Nicanor Duarte Frutos. *Defence:* Hugo Estigarribia Elizeche. *Agriculture and Livestock:* Arsenio Vasconcellos.

National flag: Red, white, blue (horizontal); the white stripe charged with the arms of the republic on the obverse, and, on the reverse, with a lion and the inscription *Paz y Justicia*—the only flag in the world with different obverse and reverse.

National anthem: '¡Paraguayos, república o muerte!' ('Paraguayans, republic or death!'); words by F. Acuña de Figueroa, tune by F. Dupuy.

Local Government. There are 17 departments with directly-elected councils and governors, and 212 municipalities. Elections were held on 9 May 1993.

DEFENCE. The army, navy and air forces are separate services under a single command. The President of the Republic is the active C.-in-C. Conscription is for 12 months (2 years in the navy).

Army. The Army is organized into 3 corps and 9 divisional headquarters and consists of 1 armoured, 2 mechanized and 4 horsed cavalry regiments, 7 infantry regiments (of battalion strength), 6 artillery groups (of battalion strength), 1 air defence and 4 engineer battalions and 20 frontier detachments. Equipment includes 5 M-4A3 main battle and 6 light aircraft. Strength (1996) 15,000 (10,400 conscripts).

Navy. The flotilla comprises 7 armoured river defence gunboats (the average age of which exceeds 50 years), 1 converted landing ship with helicopter deck, 7 river patrol boats, 1 ocean-going transport and training ship, and about 12 service craft. There are 2 counter-insurgent T-6 and 7 Cessna light aircraft and 4 helicopters. 7 new patrol craft were ordered from Spain in 1995. Personnel in 1995 totalled 3,600 including 900 marines.

Air Force. The Air Force came into being in the early thirties. There are 3 combat units, 1 with 6 Xavante light jet strike/training aircraft, 1 with armed T-33 trainers and the other with armed Tucano turboprop trainers. Other types in service include C-47 and 4 Aviocar twin-engined transports, a Twin Otter, 6 Brazilian-built Uirapuru primary trainers and 12 Chilean-built T-35 Pillan basic trainers and a number of light aircraft and helicopters. HQ and flying school are at Campo Grande, Asunción. Personnel (1995) 1,700 (600 conscripts), with 16 combat aircraft.

INTERNATIONAL RELATIONS

Membership. Paraguay is a member of the UN, OAS, Mercosur and LAIA.

ECONOMY

Policy. There is a privatization programme for large state enterprises.

Budget. In 1993 revenue (in 1m. guaranís) was 1,693,735 and expenditure, 1,929,114; in 1992 revenue was 1,564,974 and expenditure, 2,100,282.

Revenue items, 1993: Import duties, 175,725; domestic taxes, 547,959; income tax, 130,934. Items of expenditure: Public debt service, 439,454; public works, 310,862; education, 301,002; defence, 190,326; agriculture, 170,962; health, 138,645.

Currency. The unit of currency is the *guaraní* (PYG), notionally divided into 100 *céntimos.* There are coins of 1, 5, 10, 50 and 100, and notes of 100, 500, 1,000, 5,000, 10,000 and 50,000 guaranís. 366·5m. guaranís were in circulation in 1992. In 1993 foreign exchange reserves were US$700m.; gold reserves were US$12m. in 1992. Inflation was an annualized 21·6% in March 1994. In March 1996, £1 = 3,072 guaranís; US$1 = 2,010 guaranís; DM1 = 1,362 guaranís.

Banking and Finance. The Central Bank is a state-owned autonomous agency with the sole right of note issue, control over foreign exhange and the supervision of commercial banks (*Governor,* Jacinto Estigarribia). In 1994 there were 28 commercial banks (mostly foreign), 2 other banking institutions, 1 investment bank, 1 development bank and 6 building societies. Total deposits were 2,415,942m. guaranís as at 31 Dec. 1993.

A stock exchange is planned in Asunción.

Weights and Measures. The metric system was officially adopted in 1901, but some traditional measures continue in use.

ENERGY AND NATURAL RESOURCES

Electricity. There is a vast hydro-electric potential; only 2% of output is thermal. Installed capacity was 8,500 MW in 1993.

Minerals. The country is poor in minerals. Limestone, gypsum, kaolin and salt are extracted. Deposits of bauxite, iron ore, copper, manganese and uranium exist.

Agriculture. In 1992 agriculture produced 25·7% of GDP and employed 45% of the workforce. 23·8m. ha were in farming use, of which 4m. ha were cultivated.

At the agrarian census of 1991 there were 307,221 farms working 23,799,737 ha. 122,750 farms had fewer than 5 ha; 884 had over 5,000 ha.

Output (in 1,000 tonnes), 1993: Cassava, 2,680; soybeans, 1,750; maize, 500; cotton, 386; wheat, 300; rice, 50; tobacco, 11; sugar-cane, 3,000. *Yerba maté*, or strongly flavoured Paraguayan tea, continues to be produced but is declining in importance.

Livestock (1993); 8,074,000 cattle, 330,000 horses, 2,915,000 pigs, and 371,000 sheep.

Forestry. In 1993 15m. ha were forested. Palm and tung oil are produced.

INDUSTRY. In 1992 industry produced 16·9% of GDP. Production, 1988 (1,000 tons): Frozen meat, 15·5; cotton fibre, 187·4; sugar, 98·1; rice, 34·8; wheat flour, 104·5; edible oil, 39·7; industrial oil, 12·9; tung oil, 6·9; sawn timber, 629·7; cement, 255·6; soybean, peanut and coconut flour, 405; cigarettes (1m. packets), 46,598; matches (1,000 boxes), 8,979.

Labour. In 1993 there was a monthly minimum wage of 269,445 guaranís.

Trade Unions. Trade unionists number about 30,000 (*Confederación Paraguaya de Trabajadores* and *Confederación Cristiana de Trabajadores*).

FOREIGN ECONOMIC RELATIONS. Foreign debt was US1,233m. in 1994. In 1992 direct foreign investment totalled US$117m. (40% from Brazil, 19% from France, 12% from USA).

Commerce. Imports and exports (in US$1m.):

	1988	1989	1990	1991	1992
Imports	494·7	1,009·4	1,635·8	1,669·1	1,421·7
Exports	509·8	660·8	1,382·3	1,117·3	656·5

Main exports in 1992 (in US$1m.): Cotton fibre, 198·7; soya, 132·1; timber, 46·1; hides, 37; meat, 26·2. Main imports: Machinery, 231·8; vehicles, 124·7; fuel and lubricants, 99·7; beverages and tobacco, 89·5; chemicals, 58·2; foodstuffs, 43·2.

Main export markets in 1992 (in US$1m.): Brazil, 168; Netherlands, 131·3; Argentina, 45·2; USA, 33·9; Italy, 22·5; Germany, 18·8. Main import suppliers: Brazil, 208·3; Argentina, 161·8; USA, 144·3; Japan, 114·7; UK, 49·3.

Total trade between Paraguay and UK (British Department of Trade returns, in £1,000 sterling):

	1991	1992	1993	1994	1995
Imports to UK	1,488	2,514	3,113	3,321	3,468
Exports and re-exports from UK	38,229	34,149	35,797	48,935	66,430

Tourism. Visitors numbered 300,000 in 1989.

COMMUNICATIONS

Roads. In 1986 there were 23,606 km of roads, of which 2,159 were paved.

Railways. The President Carlos Antonio López (formerly Paraguay Central) Railway runs from Asunción to Encarnación, on the Río Alto Paraná, with a length of 441 km (1,435 mm gauge), and connects with Argentine Railways over the Encarnación-Posadas bridge opened in 1989. In 1994, traffic amounted to 182,000 tonnes and 24,000 passengers.

Civil Aviation. There is an international airport at Asunción (Silvio Pettirossi). The national carrier is Air Paraguay, which had 1 B-737-200 Adv in 1995. Services are also provided by Aerolineas Argentinas, Aeroperu, American Airlines, Iberia, Ladeco, Lloyd Aérea Boliviano, National Airlines, Pluna, TAM and Varig.

Shipping. Asunción, the chief port, is 950 miles from the sea. In 1995, ocean-going shipping totalled 32,226 GRT, including oil tankers, 2,850 GRT.

Telecommunications. In 1985 there were 382 post offices and 88,730 telephones. In 1993 there were 30 commercial radio stations and 2 TV stations. In 1991 there were 0·35m. television (colour by PAL) and 775,000 radio receivers.

Cinemas (1986). Cinemas numbered 6 in Asunción.

Press (1993). There were 5 daily and 6 weekly newspapers.

SOCIAL INSTITUTIONS

Justice. The 1992 constitution confers a large measure of judicial autonomy. The highest court is the Supreme Court with 5 members. Nominations for membership must be backed by 6 of the 8 members of the Magistracy Council, which appoints all judges, magistrates and the electoral tribunal. The Council comprises elected representatives of the Presidency, Congress and the bar. There are special Chambers of Appeal for civil and commercial cases, and criminal cases. Judges of first instance deal with civil, commercial and criminal cases in 6 departments. Minor cases are dealt with by Justices of the Peace.

The Attorney-General represents the State in all jurisdictions, with representatives in each judicial department and in every jurisdiction.

Religion. Religious liberty was guaranteed by the 1967 constitution. Article 6 recognized Roman Catholicism as the official religion of the country. It had 4·34m. adherents in 1992. There are Mennonite, Anglican and other communities.

Education. Adult literacy was 90·8% in 1992. Education is free and nominally compulsory. In 1987 there were 4,101 primary schools (public and private) with 579,687 pupils and 28,136 teachers. In 1985 there were 740 secondary schools with (1987) 148,516 students and (1982) 2,448 teachers. There were 11 universities (1 Roman Catholic) in 1994–95, and 1 institute of education.

Health. In 1982 there were 2,201 doctors. In 1979 there were 855 dentists, 860 pharmacists, 783 midwives and 2,636 nursing personnel. In 1985 there were 3,380 hospital beds.

DIPLOMATIC REPRESENTATIVES

Of Paraguay in Great Britain (51 Cornwall Gdns, London, SW7 4AQ)
Ambassador: Dr Washington Ashwell.

Of Great Britain in Paraguay (Calle Presidente Franco, 706, Asunción)
Ambassador and Consul-General: Graham Pirnie.

Of Paraguay in the USA (2400 Massachusetts Ave., NW, Washington, D.C., 20008)
Ambassador: Jorge Prieto.

Of the USA in Paraguay (1776 Mariscal López Ave., Asunción)
Ambassador: Robert E. Service.

Of Paraguay to the United Nations
Ambassador: José Fernández Estigarribia.

Further Reading

Gaceta Official, published by Imprenta Nacional, Estrella y Estero Bellaco, Asunción
Anuario Daumas. Asunción
Anuario Estadístico de la República del Paraguay. Asunción. Annual
Nickson, R. A., *Paraguay.* [Bibliography] Oxford and Santa Barbara, 1987

National Library: Biblioteca Nacional, De la Rosidenta, Asunción.

PERU

République del Perú

Capital: Lima
Population: 23·13m. (1994)
GNP per capita: US$1,890 (1994)
HDI/world rank: 0·709/93 (1992)

KEY HISTORICAL EVENTS. Peru declared its independence on 28 July 1821; but it was not till after a war, protracted till 1824, that the country gained its actual freedom.

On 3 Oct. 1968 a military junta overthrew the government. Civilian government was restored in July 1980. On 6 April 1992 the President suspended the constitution and dissolved the parliament. A new constitution was promulgated on 29 Dec. 1993.

TERRITORY AND POPULATION. Peru is bounded in the north by Ecuador and Colombia, east by Brazil and Bolivia, south by Chile and west by the Pacific Ocean. Area, 1,244,284 sq. km (480,041 sq. miles).

For an account of the border dispute with Ecuador *see* ECUADOR: Territory and Population. For an account of the settlement of other boundary disputes, *see* THE STATESMAN'S YEAR-BOOK, 1948, p. 1173.

Census population, 1993, 22,048,356. 1994 estimate, 23,130,300 (70·1% urban). Vital statistics 1994 (in 1,000s): Births, 619·3; deaths, 154·7; infant deaths (under 1 year) in 1989, 60,800. Growth rate, 1981–93, 2%; infantile mortality, 1994, 52·1 per 1,000 live births. Expectation of life in 1994: males, 64.9 years; females, 69·8.

Area and 1993 census population of the 24 departments and the constitutional province of Callao, together with their capitals:

Department	*Area (in sq. km)*	*Population*	*Capital*	*Population*
Amazonas	39,249	336,665	Chachapoyas	15,785
Ancash	35,826	955,023	Huaraz	66,888
Apurímac	15,666	381,997	Abancay	46,997
Arequipa	63,345	916,806	Arequipa	619,156
Ayacucho	43,814	492,507	Ayacucho	105,918
Cajamarca	33,247	1,259,808	Cajamarca	92,447
Callao [1]	147	639,729	Callao	369,768
Cusco	71,892	1,028,763	Cusco	255,568
Huancavelica	22,131	385,162	Huancavelica	31,068
Huánuco	36,938	654,489	Huánuco	118,814
Ica	21,328	565,686	Ica	161,406
Junín	44,410	1,035,841	Huancayo	258,209
La Libertad	25,570	1,270,261	Trujillo	509,312
Lambayeque	14,231	920,795	Chiclayo	411,536
Lima	34,802	6,386,308	Lima	5,706,127
Loreto	368,852	687,282	Iquitos	274,759
Madre de Dios	85,183	67,008	Puerto Naidona	31,249
Moquegua	15,734	128,747	Moquegua	38,837
Pasco	25,320	226,295	Cerro de Pasco	62,749
Piura	35,892	1,388,264	Piura	277,964
Puno	71,999	1,079,849	Puno	91,877
San Martín	51,253	552,387	Moyobamba	24,800
Tacna	16,076	218,353	Tacna	174,336
Tumbes	4,669	155,521	Tumbes	74,085
Ucayali	102,411	314,810	Pucallpa	172,286

[1] Constitutional province.

In 1991 there were some 100,000 Peruvians of Japanese origin.

The official languages are Spanish (spoken by 80·3% of the population in 1993), Quechua (16·5%) and Aymara (3%).

CLIMATE. There is a very wide variety of climate, ranging from equatorial to desert, (or perpetual snow on the high mountains). In coastal areas, temperatures vary very little, either daily or annually, though humidity and cloudiness show considerable variation, with highest humidity from May to Sept. Little rain is experienced in that period. In the Sierra, temperatures remain fairly constant over the year, but the daily range is considerable. There the dry season is from April to Nov. Desert conditions occur in the extreme south, where the climate is uniformly dry, with a few heavy showers falling between Jan. and March. Lima. Jan. 74°F (23·3°C), July 62°F (16·7°C). Annual rainfall 2" (48 mm). Cuzco. Jan. 56°F (13·3°C), July 50°F (10°C). Annual rainfall 32" (804 mm).

CONSTITUTION AND GOVERNMENT. The 1980 Constitution provided for a legislative *Congress* consisting of a *Senate* (60 members) and a *Chamber of Deputies* (180 members) and an Executive formed of the President and a Council of Ministers appointed by him. Elections were held every 5 years with the President and Congress elected, at the same time, by separate ballots. All citizens over the age of 18 are eligible to vote. Voting is compulsory.

On 5 April 1992 President Fujimori suspended the 1980 constitution and dissolved Congress. Elections were held on 22 Nov. 1992 for an 80-member Constituent Assembly. Elections were held on 9 April 1995 for President and a new 120-member single-chamber Congress to replace the Constituent Assembly. The electorate was 12m. President Fujimori was re-elected by 64·42% of votes cast. In the Congressional elections, Change 90-New Mayoralty won 67 seats with 52·1% of votes cast, Pérez de Cuellar's movement gained 17 seats, APRA 8, Popular Action 4 and the United Left 2.

A referendum was held on 31 Oct. 1993 to approve the twelfth constitution, including a provision for the president to serve a consecutive second term. 52·24% of votes cast were in favour. The constitution was promulgated on 29 Dec. 1993.

President: Alberto Fujimori (b. 1938; Change 90 Movement; sworn in 28 July 1990).

The President formed a new government in July 1995 which in Jan. 1996 comprised:

Prime Minister and Minister of Education: Dante Córdova Blanco.

Minister of Foreign Affairs: Francisco Tudela Van Breughel. *Economy and Finance:* Jorge Camet Dickman. *Interior:* Gen. Juan Briones Davila. *Justice:* Carlos Hermoza Moya. *Defence:* Gen. Tomas Castillo Meza. *Health:* Dr Eduardo Yong Motta. *Labour and Social Mobility:* Dr Augusto Antoniolli Vásquez. *Agriculture:* Absalón Vásquez Villanueva. *Energy and Mines:* Amado Yataco. *Fisheries:* Jaime Sobero Taira. *Industry, Trade, Tourism, Integration and International Commercial Negotiations:* Liliana Canale Novella. *Minister at the Presidency:* Jaime Yoshiyama.

National flag: Three vertical strips of red, white, red, with the national arms in the centre.

National anthem: 'Somos libres, seámoslo siempre' ('We are free, let us always be so'); words by J. De La Torre Ugarte, tune by J. B. Alcedo.

Local Government. There are 24 departments and 1 constitutional province divided into 192 provinces and 1,808 districts. There are also 14 administrative regions with their own authorities. Municipal elections were held on 12 Nov. 1995.

DEFENCE. There is selective conscription for 2 years.

Army. There are 6 military regions. The Army comprises (1996) approximately 75,000 personnel (50,000 conscripts) and 188,000 reserves. There are 3 armoured, 1 cavalry, 7 infantry, 1 airborne and 1 jungle division with supporting artillery, engineer and helicopter battalions, 1 Presidential Escort regiment and 1 air defence artillery group. There is an air element of 50 Mil Mi-8 and Mi-17 and 22 other helicopters, as well as about 14 fixed-wing transport and liaison aircraft. Equipment includes 300 T-54/-55 main battle tanks (perhaps 50 operational).

There is a para-military national police force of 60,000 personnel.

Navy. The principal ships of the Navy are the former Netherlands cruisers *Almirante Grau* and *Aguirre* built in 1953. *Almirante Grau*'s main armament is 8 152 mm guns and 8 Otomat surface-to-surface missiles. *Aguirre* has been converted to a helicopter cruiser and mounts only 4 152 mm guns, the two after turrets having been removed in favour of a hangar and flight deck capable of supporting 4 SH-3D Sea King helicopters.

There are 6 diesel submarines built in West Germany (1974–82). Other combatants include 1 modernized former British Daring class destroyer, 4 ex-Netherlands destroyers, 4 Italian Lupo class frigates, 6 French-built fast missile craft and 4 tank landing ships. Major auxiliaries include 5 tankers, 2 transports, 1 Antarctic patrol ship, 1 survey ship and 1 ocean tug, and 30 minor auxiliaries and service craft. A river flotilla of 9 patrol craft police the Upper Amazon, based at Puerto Maldonado and Iquitos.

The Naval Aviation branch comprises 6 S-2 Trackers and 3 EMB-111 anti-submarine aircraft based ashore, 8 Sea King and 6 AB-212 anti-submarine helicopters for service afloat and over 30 miscellaneous transport and utility aircraft.

Callao is the main base, where the dockyard is located and most training takes place. Smaller ocean bases exist at Paita and Talara.

Naval personnel in 1995 totalled 25,000 (13,500 conscripts) including 700 Naval Air Arm and 3,000 Marines. There are 3 batteries of coastal defence artillery.

The Coast Guard, 600 strong in 1995, includes 5 coastal patrol craft, 3 inshore and 10 river patrol craft.

Air Force. The operational force consists of 5 combat groups. No. 6 Group has 1 squadron of Mirage 5 jet fighters; No. 9 Group has 1 squadron of Canberra light jet bombers; No. 7 Group has 2 squadrons of A-37B light attack aircraft; No. 11 Group has Soviet-built Su-22 variable-geometry fighter bombers in 1 operational squadron; No. 4 Group has one squadron of Su-22s and one with Mirage 2000s. Other aircraft in service include medium transports (1 F.28 Fellowship, 17 An-32, 10 C-130/L-100 Hercules), light transports (16 Twin Otter, 5 Y-12, 1 twin-jet Falcon and 12 Turbo-Porter), helicopters (40 Mi-8/17, 25 Mi-24 gunships, Bell 47G, 206, 212, 214ST, 412 and UH-1, BO 105 and Alouette III), 60 training aircraft (including Aermacchi MB 339, Tucano and T-41D) and a small number of miscellaneous types for photographic and communications duties. There are military airfields at Talara, Chiclayo, Piura, Pisco, Lima (2), Iquitos and La Joya, and a float-plane base at Iquitos. In 1995 there were some 15,000 personnel (2,000 conscripts) and 90 combat aircraft and 20 armed helicopters.

INTERNATIONAL RELATIONS

Membership. Peru is a member of the UN, OAS, the Andean Group and LAIA.

ECONOMY

Policy. There is a programme of partial privatization of Aeroperú and other companies in transport, industry and mining. In 1994 a 'citizen participation' scheme was initiated to increase the extent of private shareholding in state enterprises; retirement pensions may also be taken as shares.

Budget. The budget for 1995 balanced at 21,840m. sols.

Currency. The monetary unit is the *nuevo sol* (PES), of 100 *centimos*, which replaced the inti in 1990 at a rate of 1m. intis = 1 nuevo sol. There are coins of 1, 5, 10, 20 and 50 centimos and 1 sol, and notes of 10, 20, 50 and 100 sols. Inflation was 10·2% in 1995. Foreign exchange reserves were US$6,414m. in Nov. 1995. In March 1996, £1 = 3·60 sols; US$1 = 2·36 sols; DM1 = 1·59 sols.

Banking and Finance. The bank of issue is the Banco Central de Reserva (*Governor*, Germán Suárez Chávez), which was established in 1922. The government's fiscal agent is the Banco de la Nación. There were in addition, in 1995, 17 domestic commercial, 1 foreign and 4 multinational banks.

Legislation of April 1991 permitted financial institutions to fix their own interest rates and reopened the country to foreign banks. The Central Reserve Banks sets the upper limit.

There are stock exchanges in Lima and Arequipa.

Weights and Measures. The metric system is in use.

ENERGY AND NATURAL RESOURCES

Electricity. In 1994 output was 15,862·8m. kWh (12,838m. kWh hydro-electric). Total generating capacity was 4,400 MW. 61·5% of the population were supplied with electricity in 1995.

Oil. Proven oil reserves in 1992 amounted to 362·56m. bbls. Output, 1994, 46·52m. bbls.

Minerals. Lead, copper, iron, silver, zinc and petroleum are the chief minerals exploited. Mineral production, 1994 (in 1,000 tonnes): Iron, 4,621; zinc, 682; copper, 364; lead, 227; silver, 1,780,159 kg; gold, 46,312 kg.

Agriculture. There are 4 natural zones: The Coast strip, with an average width of 80 km; the Sierra or Uplands, formed by the coast range of mountains and the Andes proper; the Montaña or high wooded region which lies on the eastern slopes of the Andes, and the jungle in the Amazon Basin, known as the Selva. 2·7m. ha were cultivated in 1991. Legislation of 1991 permits the unrestricted sale of agricultural land. Workers in co-operatives may elect to form limited liability companies and become shareholders.

Production in 1994 (in 1,000 tonnes): Potatoes, 1,745; wheat, 130; seed cotton, 168; coffee, 91; rice, 1,391; maize, 191; beans, 57; sugar-cane (1993), 4,407.

Livestock (in 1,000), 1994: Alpacas, 2,901; cattle, 4,497; pigs, 2,182; sheep, 12,141; poultry, 72,014. Livestock products (in 1,000 tonnes), 1994: Poultry meat, 353·7; mutton and lamb, 18; pork, 77·7; beef, 102·5.

Forestry. There were 84·5m. ha of forest area in 1989, made up of 74m. ha of natural forest, 253,646 ha of planted forest and 10·25m. ha of land suitable for reforestation. The forests contain valuable hardwoods; oak and cedar account for about 40%. In 1989 roundwood removals totalled 8·5m. cu metres.

Fisheries. Sardines and anchovies are caught offshore to be processed into fishmeal, of which Peru is a major producer. Production (1994, in tonnes) 10,855,500, including anchovies, 9,176,008.

INDUSTRY. About 70% of industries are located in the Lima/Callao metropolitan area. Products include pig-iron, blooms, billets, largets, round and round-deformed bars, wire rod, black and galvanized sheets and galvanized roofing sheets.

Labour. At the 1993 census the workforce (persons aged 15 and over) numbered 7,109,527 (2,104,755 females). 505,767 (157,892 females) were unemployed. In 1990 2,497,000 worked in agriculture, 176,300 in mining, 771,100 in manufacturing, 22,000 in electricity production, 271,700 in building, 1,145,700 in commerce, 323,100 in transport, 176,300 in finance and 1,960,800 in services. In Dec. 1994 the minimum monthly wage was 132 sols.

Trade Unions. Trade unions have about 2m. members (approximately 1·5m. in peasant organizations and 500,000 in industrial). The major trade union organization is the *Confederación de Trabajadores del Perú*, which was reconstituted in 1959 after being in abeyance for some years. The other labour organizations recognized by the Government are the *Confederación General de Trabajadores del Perú*, the *Confederación Nacional de Trabajadores* and the *Central de Trabajadores de la Revolución Peruana*.

FOREIGN ECONOMIC RELATIONS. An agreement of 1992 gives Bolivia duty-free transit for imports and exports through a corridor leading to the Peruvian Pacific port of Ilo from the Bolivian frontier town of Desaguadero, in return for Peruvian access to the Atlantic via Bolivia's roads and railways. Foreign debt was US$23,130·3m. in 1994.

Commerce. The value of trade has been as follows (in US$1m.):

	1989	*1990*	*1991*	*1992*	*1993*	*1994*
Imports	2,313	2,930	3,630	4,090	4,085	5,861
Exports	3,558	3,323	3,391	3,594	3,515	4,565

In 1994 the main export markets (in US$1m.) were: USA, 703·81; UK, 397·62; Japan, 382·6; China, 284·28; Germany, 278·76. Main import suppliers: USA, 1,304·2; Japan, 439·74; Brazil, 328·32; Argentina, 262·51. Main exports, 1994: Fishmeal, 2·21m. tonnes (valued at US$718m.); gold, 886,000 troy oz. (US$338m.); oil, 14m. bbls. (US$165m.).

Total trade between Peru and UK (British Department of Trade returns, in £1,000 sterling):

	1991	*1992*	*1993*	*1994*	*1995*
Imports to UK	84,034	91,804	126,482	112,911	122,645
Exports and re-exports from UK	33,061	30,775	33,031	44,580	57,500

Tourism. There were 485,169 foreign visitors in 1995.

COMMUNICATIONS

Roads. In 1994 there were 69,942 km of roads, of which 7,624 km were paved and 13,484 km gravel. In 1994 there were 760,815 registered motor vehicles, including 389,439 cars, 54,732 station wagons, 194,753 vans, 65,124 buses and 71,312 lorries.

Railways. Total length (1994), 2,121 km on 1,435- and 914-mm gauges. In 1994 railways carried 1·7m. tonnes of freight and 1·99m. passengers.

Civil Aviation. There is an international airport at Lima (Jorge Chávez). The national carrier is Faucett Perú, which in 1995 operated 4 B-727s, 3 B-727-200 Advs, 1 B-727C and 2 B-757-200s. In 1994 there were 30 other airports. 189 civil aircraft were registered in 1990, of which 163 were in commercial use. Services are also provided by the domestic airlines Aero Continente and Imperial Air, and by Aeroflot, Aerolíneas Argentinas, Aeromexico, Aerosanta, Air Paraguay, Alitalia, American Airlines, AOM, Avianca, COPA, Cubana, Expresso Aereo, Iberia, KLM, LACSA, Lan-Chile, Lloyd Aereo Boliviano, Lufthansa, SAETA, Servivensa, United Airlines, Varig and Viasa.

Shipping. In 1994 there were 30 sea-going vessels and 519 lake and river craft. In 1995, sea-going shipping totalled 0·32m. GRT, including oil tankers, 0·13m. GRT.

Telecommunications. In 1993 there were 1,363 post offices. In 1993 there were 853,839 telephones and 1,560 teleprinters. Radio broadcasting is conducted by hundreds of national, provincial and local stations grouped in the Asociación de Radiodifusores del Perú and the Unión de Radioemisores de Provincias del Perú. There are 8 TV companies (colour by NTSC). In 1993 there were 4·4m. radio and 2m. TV sets in use.

Press. There were 12 dailies in 1994 and 16 other periodicals.

SOCIAL INSTITUTIONS

Justice. The judicial system is a pyramid at the base of which are the justices of the peace who decide minor criminal cases and civil cases involving small sums of money. The apex is the Supreme Court with a President and 12 members; in between are the judges of first instance, who usually sit in the provincial capitals, and the superior courts.

The police had some 85,000 personnel in 1991.

Religion. Religious liberty exists, but the Roman Catholic religion is protected by the State, and since 1929 only Roman Catholic religious instruction is permitted in schools, state or private. There were 21·56m. adherents in 1992.

Education. Adult literacy was 87·2% at the 1993 census. Elementary education is compulsory and free between the ages of 7 and 16; secondary education is also free. In 1994–95 there were 597,800 children in pre-school education, 4,085,000 pupils in primary and 1,996,200 in secondary schools. In 1993 the number of students at the 28 state and 23 private universities was 727,200. There were 251,700 students in other forms of further education.

Health. There were in 1992, 455 hospitals and 1,083 health centres.

Social Security. An option to transfer from state social security (IPSS) to privately-managed funds was introduced in 1993.

DIPLOMATIC REPRESENTATIVES

Of Peru in Great Britain (52 Sloane St., London, SW1X 9SP)
Ambassador: Eduardo Ponce-Vivanco.

Of Great Britain in Peru (Edificio El Pacifico Washington, Ave. Arequipa, Lima)
Ambassador: John Illman.

Of Peru in the USA (1700 Massachusetts Ave., NW, Washington, D.C., 20036)
Ambassador: Ricardo V. Luna.

Of the USA in Peru (PO Box 1995, Lima)
Ambassador: Alvin P. Adams.

Of Peru to the United Nations
Ambassador: Dr Fernando Guillen Salas.

Further Reading

Instituto Nacional de Estadística e Informática.—*Anuario Estadistico del Perú.—Perú: Compendio Estadístico.* Annual.—*Boletin de Estadistica Peruana.* Quarterly
Banco Central de Reserva. Monthly Bulletin.—*Renta Nacional del Perú.* Annual, Lima

Cameron, M. A., *Democracy and Authoritarianism in Peru: Political Coalitions and Social Change.* London, 1995
Daeschner, J., *The War of the End of Democracy: Mario Vargas Llosa vs. Alberto Fujimori.* Lima, 1993
Figueroa, A., *Capitalist Development and the Peasant Economy of Peru.* CUP, 1984
Fisher, J., *Peru*: [Bibliography]. Oxford and Santa Barbara (CA), 1989
Stokes, S. C., *Cultures in Conflict: Social Movements and the State in Peru.* California Univ. Press, 1995
Strong, S., *Shining Path.* London, 1993
Thorp, R., *Economic Management and Economic Development in Peru and Colombia.* London, 1991
Vargas Llosa, A., *The Madness of Things Peruvian: Democracy under Siege.* Brunswick (NJ), 1994

National library: Avenida Abancay, Lima.
National statistical office: Instituto Nacional de Estadística e Informática, Avenida 28 de Julio, 1056 Lima

PHILIPPINES

Republika ng Pilipinas

Capital: Manila
Population: 68·62m. (1994)
GNP per capita: US$960 (1994)
HDI/world rank: 0·677/100 (1992)

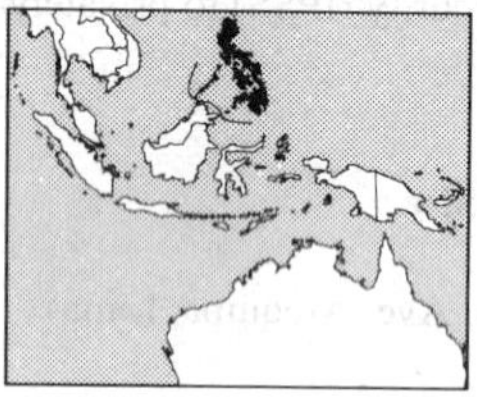

KEY HISTORICAL EVENTS. Before the Spanish discovery of the Philippines, the inhabitants came in contact with India, China and Arabia. The islands were discovered by Magellan in 1521 and conquered by Spain in 1565. Following the Spanish-American war, the islands were ceded to the USA on 10 Dec. 1898, after the Filipinos had tried in vain to establish an independent republic in 1896.

The Philippines acquired self-government as a Commonwealth of the USA on 14 May 1935, and became completely independent on 4 July 1946.

At the presidential elections of Feb. 1986 Ferdinand Marcos was opposed by Corazón Aquino. Though Marcos was proclaimed president by parliament, the elections proved to be fraudulent and Aquino became president. Marcos fled the country.

TERRITORY AND POPULATION. The Philippines is situated between 21° 25' and 4° 23' N. lat. and between 116° and 127° E. long. It is composed of 7,100 islands and islets, 3,114 of which are named. Approximate land area, 115,830 sq. miles (300,000 sq. km). The largest islands (in sq. km) are Luzon (104,688), Mindanao (94,630), Samar (13,080), Negros (12,710), Palawan (11,785), Panay (11,515), Mindoro (9,735), Leyte (7,214), Cebu (4,422), Bohol (3,865), Masbate (3,269).

Census population (1990) was 60,559,116 (30,115,929 female; 29,440,153 urban). Estimate, 1994, 68,624,247; density, 228 per sq. km.

The area and population (in 1,000) of the 15 regions (2 of them authonomous) (from north to south):

Region	*Sq. km*	*1990*	*Region*	*Sq. km*	*1990*
Ilocos	12,840	3,551	Central Visayas	14,952	4,593
Cordillera [1]	18,294	1,146	Eastern Visayas	21,432	3,055
Cagayan Valley	26,838	2,341	Northern Mindanao	28,328	3,510
Central Luzon	18,231	6,199	Southern Mindanao	31,693	4,457
National Capital	636	7,929	Central Mindanao	14,373	1,814
Southern Tagalog	46,924	8,266	Western Mindanao	16,042	2,461
Bicol	17,633	3,910	Moslem Mindanao [1]	11,638	2,056
Western Visayas	20,223	5,393			

[1] Autonomous region.

City populations (1990 census, in 1,000) are as follows; all on Luzon unless indicated in parenthesis.

Manila (the capital) [1]	1,601	Iloilo (Panay)	310
Quezon City [1]	1,670	Marikina [1]	308
Davao (Mindanao)	850	Parañaque [1]	300
Caloocan [1]	763	Las Piñas	286
Cebu (Cebu)	610	Muntilupa	278
Makati [1]	452	Malabon	277
Zamboanga (Mindanao)	442	Tagig	267
Pasig [1]	395	General Santos (Mindanao)	250
Bacolod (Negros)	364	Mandaluyong [1]	247
Pasay [1]	368	Angeles	237
Cagayan de Oro (Mindanao)	340	Butuan (Mindanao)	228
Valenzuela [1]	340	Iligan (Mindanao)	227

[1] City within Metropolitan Manila.

Olongapo	193	Cabanatuan	173
Navotas [1]	186	San Pablo	162
Batangas	185	Lipa	160
Baguio	183	Lucena	151
Mandaue (Cebu)	180		

[1] City within Metropolitan Manila.

Vital statistics: Births (1991), 1,347,700 (rate per 1,000 population, 21·4); deaths, 208,400 (3·3); marriages (1991), 445,526 (14·2). Natural increase, 1991, 1·81%; infant mortality (per 1,000 live births), 20·9 in 1991. Expectation of life in 1995: Males, 64·4 years; females, 67·8.

In 1990 the national language, Pilipino (based on Tagalog) was spoken by 55% of the population, but as a mother tongue by only 27·9%; among the 76 other indigenous languages spoken, Cebuano was spoken as a mother tongue by 24·3% and Ilocano by 9·8%.

CLIMATE. Some areas have an equatorial climate while others experience tropical monsoon conditions, with a wet season extending from May to Nov. Mean temperatures are high all year, with very little variation. Manila. Jan. 77°F (25°C), July 82°F (27·8°C). Annual rainfall 82" (2,083 mm).

CONSTITUTION AND GOVERNMENT. A new Constitution was ratified by referendum in 1987 with 78·5% of the voters endorsing it. At the elections on 11 May 1992 the electorate was 32m. Fidel Ramos was elected President against 2 opponents with 23·6% of votes cast.

Congress consists of a 24-member upper house, the *Senate*, and a 250-member *House of Representatives.* Elections were held on 8 May 1995 for 12 Senate seats and the 204 constituency-based seats in the House of Representatives. The electorate was 34m.; turn-out was 80%. A majority in both houses was gained by the pro-government coalition of National Union of Christian Democrats, Lakas ng Edsa and Laban ng Demokratikong Pilipino.

In Nov. 1995 the government comprised:

President: Fidel Ramos (sworn in 30 June 1992).

Vice President: Joseph Estrada.

Secretary for Foreign Affairs: Domingo Siazon. *Justice:* Teofisto Guingona. *Defence:* Renato de Villa. *Commerce and Industry:* Rizalino Navarro. *Finance:* Roberto de Ocampo. *Agriculture:* Roberto Sebastián. *Works and Highways:* Gregorio Vigilar. *Energy:* Francisco Viray. *Education, Culture and Sport:* Ricardo Gloria. *Labour and Employment:* Jose Brillantes. *Health:* Hilarion Ramiro. *Social Welfare and Development:* Lina Laigo. *Agrarian Reform:* Ernesto Garilao. *Interior and Local Government:* Rafael Alunan. *Tourism:* Eduardo Pilapil. *Budget and Management:* Salvador Enriquez. *Transport and Communications:* Jesús García. *Science and Technology:* William Padolina. *Director-General, National Economic Development Authority:* Cielito Habito. *Environment and Natural Resources:* Victor Ramos. *Government Spokesman:* Hector Villanueva. *Executive Secretary:* Ruben Torres.

Speaker: José de Venecia.

National flag: Horizontally blue over red, with a white triangle based on the hoist bearing a gold sun of 8 rays and 3 gold stars.

National anthem: Land of the Morning, lyric in English by M. A. Sane and C. Osias, tune by Julian Felipe; *Bayang magiliw*; Tagalog lyric by the Institute of National Language.

Local Government. The country is administratively divided into 15 regions, 76 provinces, 60 cities, 1,543 municipalities and 41,908 *barangays* (units of no fewer than 1,000 inhabitants administered by elected officials). A reform of Oct. 1991 devolved more power to local authorities, giving them 40% of local tax revenues to deliver local services. Elections were held simultaneously with the national elections on 8 May 1995 for provincial governors, city and municipal mayors and councillors.

DEFENCE. An extension of the 1947 agreement granting the USA the use of several army, navy and air force bases was rejected by the Senate in Sept. 1991. An agreement of Dec. 1994 authorizes US naval vessels to be revictualled and repaired in Philippine ports. The Philippines is a signatory of the South-East Asia Collective Defence Treaty.

Army. The Army is organized into 5 area joint-service commands, and comprises 8 infantry divisions, 3 engineer brigades, 1 special services regiment, 1 light armoured brigade, 1 scout ranger regiment, the Presidential Security Group and 8 artillery battalions. Equipment includes 41 Scorpion light tanks.

Strength (1996) 68,000, with reserves totalling 100,000.

Navy. The Navy consists principally of ex-US ships completed in 1944 and 1945, and serviceability and spares are a problem. The modernization programme in progress has been revised and delayed, but the first 22 inshore patrol craft of US design have been delivered.

The present fleet includes 1 ex-US frigate, 9 offshore patrol vesels (ex-US minesweepers and escorts) and about 38 inshore patrol craft. There are 5 tank landing ships and 2 medium landing ships, and some 30 landing craft. Auxiliaries include 1 repair ship, 2 small oilers, 3 survey ships and 2 water tankers, as well as some 20 minor auxiliaries. 8 BN Defender maritime patrol aircraft and 10 BO-105 helicopters are in use.

Navy personnel in 1995 totalled 23,000 including 8,500 marines.

Coastguard. The Coastguard is no longer part of the Navy. In 1995 there were some 60 patrol and search-and-rescue craft. Personnel, 2,000.

Air Force. The Air Force had (1995) a strength of 15,500, with 43 combat aircraft and 104 armed helicopters, and was built up with US assistance. Its fighter-bomber wing is equipped with 1 squadron of F-5As. A strike wing includes 1 squadron having OV-10 Broncos and 1 squadron, T-28s. There are 7 transport and counter-insurgency squadrons (1 with C-130/L-100 Hercules, 1 with F27s, 1 with Nomads, 1 with C-47s, 2 with UH-1 Iroquois helicopters, 1 with MD-500 helicopters and 1 with S-76 helicopters). Training aircraft include SF.260TPs, T-41s, T-34s, S.211 and T-33 jets. 2 Pumas and 1 S-70 helicopter are used as VIP transports.

Constabulary. Public order is maintained partly through the Philippine constabulary and partly through the local police forces. The constabulary is part of the Armed Forces and has some 45,000 personnel.

INTERNATIONAL RELATIONS

Membership. The Philippines is a member of the UN, ASEAN and the Colombo Plan.

ECONOMY

Policy. In 1992–95 most state assets were privatized.

Budget. Government revenue and expenditure (in 1m. pesos):

	1990	*1991*	*1992*	*1993*	*1994*	*1995*
Revenue	180,902	220,287	242,714	260,405	319,100	350,200
Expenditure	255,775	293,161	286,603	339,359	362,000	384,700

Expenditure (1994) included (in 1,000m. pesos): Defence, 33·1; education, 46·4; health, 13·1; social security, 7·7; economic development, 74·5; debt service, 117·8.

Total internal public debt was 624,600m. pesos in 1994.

Currency. The unit of currency is the *piso* (PHP) of 100 *sentimos.* There are notes of 5, 10, 20, 50, 100, 500 and 1,000 pisos and coins of 1, 5, 10, 25 and 50 sentimos and 1, 2 and 5 pisos. Total money supply, Dec. 1993, was P.133,877m. Inflation was 8·1% in 1995. Foreign exchange controls were abolished in Aug. 1992. Foreign exchange reserves were US$7,740m. in July 1994. In March 1996, £1 = 40·01 pisos; US$1 = 26·18 pisos; DM1 = 17·74 pisos.

Banking and Finance. The Central Bank (*Chairman*, Gabriel Singson) issues the currency, manages foreign exchange reserves and supervises the banking system. In 1995 there were 28 domestic commercial and 14 foreign banks. A law of May 1994 allows the entry of up to 10 foreign banks with 6 branches each in the subsequent 5 years, after which banking will be closed to further foreign participation. 70% of total bank resources must remain in Filipino hands. In 1993 there were also 653 thrift banks (for savings and mortgages) with total deposits of P.33,303m., and 1,045 rural banks (for savings and agricultural loans) with deposits of P.13,422m. In March 1994 the total number of banking institutions was 5,096, with total assets of 1,253,900m. pisos and total deposits of 786,100m. pisos.

There is a stock exchange in Manila.

Weights and Measures. The metric system was established by law in 1869 and since 1916 has come into general use, but there are local units including the picul (63·25 kg) for sugar and fibres, and the cavan (16·5 gallons) for cereals.

ENERGY AND NATURAL RESOURCES

Electricity. Total installed capacity, 6,927m. mW (1993). Output, 1993, 26,592m. kWh.

Minerals. Mineral production in 1992, (in tonnes): Nickel metal, 14,000; copper metal, 123,500; coal, 1,582,400; salt, 495,800; gold, 22,700 kg; silver, 30,900 kg; silica sand, 500,300. Other minerals include chromite, cement, rock asphalt, sand and gravel.

Agriculture. In 1990 there were 4·55m. ha of arable land, 3·42m. ha of permanent crop land and 1·26m. ha of pasture. In April 1993, 11,790,000 persons were employed in agriculture (46% of the working population).

Output (in 1,000 tonnes) in 1993: Rough rice, 9,434; coconuts, 11,317; sugarcane, 23,366; bananas, 3,110; corn, 4,798; pineapple, 1,190. Minor crops are fruits, nuts, vegetables, onions, beans, coffee, cacao, peanuts, ramie, rubber, maguey, kapok, abaca and tobacco.

Livestock, 1993 (in 1,000): Water buffaloes (carabao), 2,560; cattle, 1,910; pigs, 7,950; goats, 2,240 and poultry, 71,639 (1992).

Forestry. In 1993 forest land covered 15,882,756 ha. 19,211 ha were reafforested in 1993. Wood production, 1993 (in 1,000 cu. metres): Logs, 1,022; timber, 440; plywood, 261; veneer, 65.

Fisheries. Fish production from all sources was 2,643,200 tonnes in 1993.

INDUSTRY.

Manufacturing contributed 23·1% to GNP in 1993. Leading sectors are foodstuffs, textiles and footwear, machinery, metal products, wood and cork and chemicals. In 1990 there were 10,446 manufacturing establishments.

Labour. In 1993 the total workforce was 26·8m., of whom 15·63m. were in non-agricultural work. In 1994 25·56m. (9·34m. females) were employed, 11·8m. in agriculture, forestry and fisheries, 4·3m. in services, 3·53m. in commerce, 2·58m. in manufacturing, 1·41m. in transport and communications and 1·23m. in building work. 2·38m. persons (1m. females) were registered unemployed in 1993. 363,983 persons worked overseas in 1994.

In 1994 there were 62 strikes; 0·38m. working days were lost.

Trade Unions. In 1994 there were 6,442 trade unions with a total membership of 978,894.

FOREIGN ECONOMIC RELATIONS.

Foreign debt was US$41,600m. at the end of 1995. A law of June 1991 gave foreign nationals the right to full ownership of export and other firms, considered strategic for the economy.

Commerce. Values of imports and exports (f.o.b.) in US$1m.:

	1990	*1991*	*1992*	*1993*	*1994*
Imports	12,206	13,268	14,519	17,597	21,333
Exports	8,186	8,759	9,824	11,375	13,483

Principal exports in 1993 (in US$1m.): Garments, 2,272; electrical equipment, 3,551; coconut oil, 358; woodcraft and furniture, 308; machinery and transport equipment, 363; bananas, 226.

Main imports in 1992 (in US$1m.): Mineral fuel, 2,050; machinery and equipment, 1,804; electronics and components, 1,569; textile yarns, 1,143; electrical machinery, 979; transport equipment, 910; base metals, 885; chemicals, 466; plastics in primary and non-primary forms, 376; cereals and cereal preparations, 301.

Main export markets, 1993 (in US$1m.): USA, 4,371; Japan, 1,817; Germany, 586; Hong Kong, 548; UK, 541; Netherlands, 362. Main import suppliers: USA, 3,522; Japan, 1,817; Taiwan, 1,025; Saudi Arabia, 740; South Korea, 68; Hong Kong, 877.

Total trade between the Philippines and UK (British Department of Trade returns, in £1,000 sterling):

	1991	*1992*	*1993*	*1994*	*1995*
Imports to UK	229,955	240,732	276,820	244,346	352,425
Exports and re-exports from UK	146,571	204,962	306,146	355,131	432,397

Tourism. In 1994, 1,573,821 foreign visitors brought foreign exchange receipts of US$2,300m.

COMMUNICATIONS

Roads. In 1993 roads totalled 160,883 km; of these, 13,409 km were concrete; 13,130, asphalt; 8,504, earth; and 125,839, gravel. There were 26,594 km of national highway. In 1993, 2,125,115 motor vehicles were registered, including 498,126 private cars, 24,047 hire cars, 4,843 government cars, 165,071 lorries, 24,601 buses and 547,648 motor cycles. In 1993 there were 13,292 road accidents, with 581 fatalities.

Railways. In 1991 the National Railways totalled 499 km (1,067 mm gauge). In 1993, 5·1m. passengers and 20,000 tonnes of freight were carried. There is a light railway in Manila.

Civil Aviation. There is an international airport at Manila (Ninoy Aquino). The national carrier Philippine Airlines is 33% state-owned, and in 1995 operated 2 A300B4-100s, 7 A300B4-200s, 1 A300C4-200, 12 B-737-300s, 9 B-747-200Bs, 2 B-747-200B Combis, 3 B-747-400s and 11 other aircraft, and in 1993 carried 5,671,630 international and domestic passengers. Services were also provided by Air France, Air Nauru, Air Niugini, Alitalia, Asiana, British Air, Cathay Pacific, China Airlines, China Southern Airlines, Continental Airlines & Air Micronesia, Egyptair, Emirates, Eva Airways, Garuda Indonesia, Grand International Airways, Gulf Air, JAL, KLM, Korean Air, Kuwait Airways, Lufthansa, Malaysia Airlines, Northwest Airlines, Pakistan Airlines, Qantas, Royal Brunei Airlines, Saudia, Singapore Airlines, Swissair, Thai Airways, United Airlines and Vietnam Airlines.

Shipping. In 1993 there were 958 registered Philippine vessels totalling 3,815,261 GRT, and including 33 passenger ships, 302 cargo vessels and 27 tankers. In 1993 there were 193 public and 221 private ports. The main ports are Manila, Cebu, Iloilo and Zamboanga. In 1991, 139,969 vessels on domestic routes totalling 71,819 NRT, and in 1993, 10,714 vessels on international routes totalling 61,426 NRT entered and cleared all ports.

Telecommunications. In 1993 there were 2,101 post offices and 887,229 telephones.

In 1992 there were 502 AM and FM radio stations and 92 television stations. In 1993 there were 7m. TV sets in use.

Press. In 1995 there were 25 dailies.

SOCIAL INSTITUTIONS

Justice. There is a Supreme Court which is composed of a chief justice and 14 associate justices; it can declare a law or treaty unconstitutional by the concurrent votes of the majority sitting. There is a Court of Appeals, which consists of a presiding justice and 50 associate justices. There are 15 regional trial courts, one for each judicial region, with a presiding regional trial judge in its 720 branches. There is a metropolitan trial court in the Metropolitan Manila Area, a municipal trial court in each of the other cities or municipalities and a municipal circuit trial court in each area defined as a municipal circuit comprising one or more cities and/or one or more municipalities.

The Supreme Court may designate certain branches of the regional trial courts to handle exclusively criminal cases, juvenile and domestic relations cases, agrarian cases, urban land reform cases which do not fall under the jurisdiction of quasijudicial bodies and agencies and/or such other special cases as the Supreme Court may determine. The death penalty, abolished in 1987, was restored in 1993 for 13 offences.

In 1994 there were 96,365 police. Local police forces are supplemented by the Philippine Constabulary, which is part of the armed forces.

In 1994 the prison population was 17,315.

Religion. In 1990 there were 50,217,801 Roman Catholics, 3,287,355 Protestants, 2,769,643 Moslems, 1,590,208 Aglipayans, 1,414,393 Iglesia ni Kristo, 323,789 Born Again Christians and 736,239 members of other religions. There were 338,000 Mormons in 1994.

The Roman Catholics are organized with 2 cardinals, 23 archbishoprics, 91 bishoprics, 79 diocese, 2,328 parishes and some 20,873 chapels or missions.

Education. Public elementary education is free and schools are established almost everywhere. The majority of secondary and post-secondary schools are private. Formal education consists of an optional 1 to 2 years of pre-school education; 6 years of elementary education; 4 years of secondary education; and 4 to 5 years of tertiary or college education leading to academic degrees. 3-year post-secondary non-degree technical/vocational education is also considered formal education. In 1993–94 there were 5,035 pre-school institutions (1,892 private) with, in 1990–91, 9,644 teachers. In 1993–94 there were 35,087 elementary schools (2,052 private) and 5,880 secondary schools (2,294 private). In 1993–94 there were 10,731,453 pupils in elementary schools, 4,590,037 in secondary schools and 1,564,763 students in tertiary education.

Non-formal education consists of adult literacy classes, agricultural and farming training programmes, occupation skills training, youth clubs, and community programmes of instructions in health, nutrition, family planning and co-operatives.

In 1994–95 in the public sector there were 20 universities, 1 technological university, 1 polytechnic and 1 technological institute, and 123 other institutions of higher education. In the private sector there were 49 universities, 4 specialized universities (1 Christian; 1 Roman Catholic; 1 medical; 1 for women) and 405 other institutions of higher education.

Health. In 1993 there were 1,632 hospitals (1,095 private) with 81,647 beds. There were 1,895 dentists, 8,849 nurses and 10,831 midwives. In 1993 there were 76,913 doctors.

Welfare. The Social Security System (SSS) is a contributory scheme for employees. Disbursements in 1993 (in P.1m.): SSS (sickness, maternity, disability, survivors'; benefits), P.7,322·5m.; medicare (hospitalization), 1,721·2m.; employees' compensation (occupational accidents or sickness), 375·8m.

DIPLOMATIC REPRESENTATIVES

Of the Philippines in Great Britain (9A Palace Green, London, W8 4QE)
Ambassador: Jesus P. Tambunting.

Of Great Britain in the Philippines (6752 Ayala Avenue, Makati, Metro Manila)
Ambassador: Adrian Charles Thorpe, CMG.

Of the Philippines in the USA (1617 Massachusetts Ave., NW, Washington, D.C., 20036)
Ambassador: Raul Rabe.

Of the USA in the Philippines (1201 Roxas Blvd., Manila)
Ambassador: John D. Negroponte.

Of the Philippines to the United Nations
Ambassador: Felipe Mabilangan.

Further Reading

National Statistics Office. *Philippine Statistical Yearbook.*

Boyce, J. K., *The Political Economy of Growth and Impoverishment in the Marcos Era.* London, 1993

Bresnan, J., (ed.) *Crisis in the Philippines: The Marcos Era and Beyond.* Princeton Univ. Press, 1986

Karnow, S., *In Our Image: America's Empire in the Philippines.* New York, 1989

Kerkvliet, B. J. and Mojares, R. B. (eds.), *From Marcos to Aquino: Local Perspectives on Political Transition in the Philippines.* Hawaii Univ. Press, 1992

Larkin, J. A., *Sugar and the Origins of Modern Philippine Society.* California Univ. Press, 1993

Richardson, J. A., *Philippines.* [Bibliography] Oxford and Santa Barbara, 1989

National statistical office: National Statistics Office, POB 779, Manila

PITCAIRN ISLAND

Only settlement: Adamstown
Population: 54 (1995)

KEY HISTORICAL EVENTS. Pitcairn was discovered by Carteret in 1767, but remained uninhabited until 1790, when it was occupied by 9 mutineers of HMS *Bounty*, with 12 women and 6 men from Tahiti. Nothing was known of their existence until the island was visited in 1808.

TERRITORY AND POPULATION. Pitcairn Island (1·75 sq. miles; 4·6 sq. km) is situated in the Pacific Ocean, nearly equidistant from New Zealand and Panama (25° 04' S. lat., 130° 06' W. long.). Adamstown is the only settlement. The population in Dec. 1995 was 54. The uninhabited islands of Henderson (12 sq. miles), Ducie (1½ sq. miles) and Oeno (2 sq. miles) were annexed in 1902. Henderson is a World Heritage Site.

CLIMATE. An equable climate, with average annual rainfall of 80" (2,000 mm), spread evenly throughout the year. Mean monthly temperatures range from 75°F (24°C) in Jan. to 66°F (19°C) in July.

CONSTITUTION. The Local Government Ordinance of 1964 constitutes a *Council* of 10 members, of whom 6 are elected, 3 are nominated (1 by the 6 elected members and 2 by the Governor) and the Island Secretary is an *ex-officio* member. The Island Magistrate, who is elected triennially, presides over the Council; other members hold office for only 1 year. Liaison between Governor and Council is through a Commissioner in the Auckland, New Zealand, office of the British Consulate-General.

Governor: R. J. Alston, CMG (UK High Commissioner in New Zealand).
Island Magistrate: Jay Warren (re-elected Dec. 1993).

Flag: British Blue Ensign with the whole arms of Pitcairn in the fly.

BUDGET. For the year to 31 March 1995 revenue was $729,884 and expenditure $878,119.

CURRENCY. New Zealand currency is used.

COMMERCE. Exports from UK in 1994 (British Department of Trade returns), £989,000.

ROADS. There were (1995) 6 km of roads. In 1995 there were 38 motor cycles.

JUSTICE. The Island Court consists of the Island Magistrate and 2 assessors.

EDUCATION. In 1995 there was 1 teacher and 11 pupils.

Further Reading

A Guide to Pitcairn. Pitcairn Island Administration, Auckland, revised ed. 1990
Ball, I., *Pitcairn: Children of the Bounty.* London, 1973
Murray, S., *Pitcairn Island: the First 200 Years.* La Canada (CA), 1992

POLAND

Rzeczpospolita Polska

(Polish Republic)

Capital: Warsaw
Population: 38·58m. (1995)
GNP per capita: US$2,470 (1994)
HDI/world rank: 0·855/51 (1992)

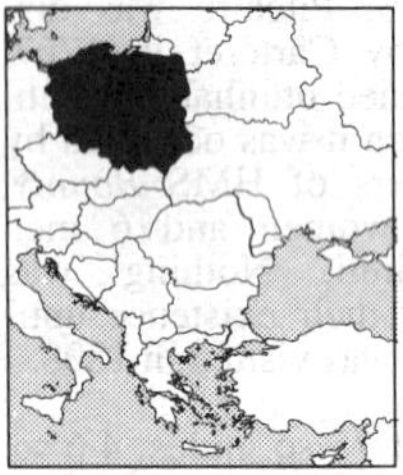

KEY HISTORICAL EVENTS. The Polish state was founded in 966 but the once-powerful kingdom was partitioned between Russia, Austria and Prussia in 1772, 1793 and 1795. For 19th century events *see* THE STATESMAN'S YEAR-BOOK 1980–81. On 10 Nov. 1918 an independent republic was proclaimed by Józef Piłsudski, and this was recognized by the Treaty of Versailles on 28 June 1919. For the collapse of the post-war Communist régime *see* THE STATESMAN'S YEAR-BOOK, 1995–96, p. 1088.

Unconditionally free parliamentary elections were held in Oct. 1991.

TERRITORY AND POPULATION. Poland is bounded in the north by the Baltic Sea and Russia, east by Lithuania, Belarus and the Ukraine, south by the Czech Republic and Slovakia and west by Germany. Poland comprises an area of 312,685 sq. km (120,628 sq. miles).

At the census of 7 Dec. 1988 the population was 37,879,000 (18·5m. males; 61·2% urban). Population July 1995, 38,581,000 (51·3% female; 61·8% urban), density, 123 per sq. km. Vital statistics, 1994 (in 1,000): Marriages, 207·7; births, 481·3; deaths, 386·4; infant deaths, 73. Rates (per 1,000 population): Marriage, 5·4; birth, 12·5; death, 10; infant mortality (per 1,000 live births), 15·1; growth rate, 2·5. A law prohibiting abortion was passed in 1993. There were 786 legal abortions in 1994. Expectation of life in 1993 was 67·4 years for males and 76 for females. In 1993 there were 21,300 emigrants and 5,900 immigrants.

The country is divided into 49 voivodships (*wojewodztwo*) and these in turn are divided into 845 towns and 2,465 wards (*gmina*). Area (in sq. km) and population (in 1,000) in 1993 (% urban in brackets).

Voivodship	*Area*	*Population*	
Biała Podlaska	5,348	309	(37)
Białystok	10,055	699	(62·8)
Bielsko–Biała	3,704	912	(48·8)
Bydgoszcz	10,349	1,127	(65·1)
Chełm	3,866	250	(43·4)
Ciechanów	6,362	435	(38·7)
Częstochowa	6,182	782	(52·9)
Elbląg	6,103	488	(62·6)
Gdańsk	7,394	1,445	(75·9)
Gorzów	8,484	508	(62·8)
Jelenia Góra	4,379	523	(66·9)
Kalisz	6,512	720	(46·8)
Katowice	6,650	3,954	(86·9)
Kielce	9,211	1,136	(47·4)
Konin	5,139	477	(41·9)
Koszalin	8,470	517	(63·8)
Kraków (Cracow)	3,254	1,235	(68·7)
Krosno	5,702	504	(35·1)
Legnica	4,037	522	(70·7)
Leszno	4,154	394	(48·4)
Łódź	1,523	1,126	(93·0)
Łomża	6,684	353	(41·5)
Lublin	6,792	1,024	(59·4)
Nowy Sącz	5,576	721	(35·7)
Olsztyn	12,327	766	(60)

Voivodship	*Area*	*Population*	
Opole	8,535	1,027	(53·2)
Ostrołęka	6,498	406	(35·5)
Piła	8,205	490	(56·4)
Piotrków	6,266	645	(50·0)
Płock	5,117	521	(49·0)
Poznań	8,151	1,347	(71·0)
Przemyśl	4,437	413	(39·1)
Radom	7,294	761	(47·7)
Rzeszów	4,397	740	(41·9)
Siedlce	8,499	659	(32·1)
Sieradz	4,869	412	(37·7)
Skierniewice	3,960	423	(47·9)
Słupsk	7,453	423	(55·4)
Suwałki	10,490	482	(56·2)
Szczecin	9,982	985	(76·3)
Tarnobrzeg	6,283	608	(39·6)
Tarnów	4,151	687	(35·6)
Toruń	5,348	668	(63·1)
Wałbrzych	4,168	742	(74·1)
Warsaw	3,788	2,413	(88·8)
Włocławek	4,402	434	(47·3)
Wrocław	6,287	1,134	(74·1)
Zamość	6,980	493	(30·3)
Zielona Góra	8,868	670	(61·9)

Population (in 1,000) of the largest towns (1993):

Warsaw	1,653·3	Katowice	366·9	Gliwice	215·7
Łódź	844·9	Lublin	352·5	Kielce	215·0
Kraków (Cracow)	751·3	Białystok	273·3	Zabrze	205·8
Wrocław (Breslau)	643·6	Sosnowiec	259·0	Toruń	202·0
Poznań	589·7	Częstochowa	258·7	Bielsko-Biala	184·4
Gdańsk (Danzig)	466·5	Gdynia	251·8	Ruda Śląska	171·6
Szczecin (Stettin)	414·2	Bytom	232·2	Olsztyn	164·8
Bydgoszcz	383·6	Radom	229·7	Rzeszów	154·8

Ethnic minorities are not identified. There were estimated to be 1·2m. Germans in 1984, and there are Ukrainians, Belorussians and Lithuanians. A Council of National Minorities was set up in March 1991. In 1992 there were 5,100 immigrants and 18,100 emigrants. There is a large Polish diaspora, some 65% in USA.

CLIMATE. Climate is continental, marked by long and severe winters. Rainfall amounts are moderate, with a marked summer maximum. Warsaw. Jan. 25°F (–3·9°C), July 66°F (18·9°C). Annual rainfall 22·1" (550 mm). Gdańsk. Jan. 29°F (–1·7°C), July 63°F (17·2°C). Annual rainfall 22" (559 mm). Kraków. Jan. 27°F (–2·8°C), July 67°F (19·4°C). Annual rainfall 29" (729 mm). Poznań. Jan. 30°F (–1·1°C), July 67°F (19·4°C). Annual rainfall 21" (523 mm). Szezecin. Jan. 30°F (–1·1°C), July 65°F (18·3°C). Annual rainfall 22" (550 mm). Wrocław. Jan. 30°F (–1·1°C), July 66°F (18·9°C). Annual rainfall 23" (574 mm).

CONSTITUTION AND GOVERNMENT. The present Constitution was adopted on 22 July 1952. Amendments were adopted in 1976 and 1983. Constitutional amendments of Aug. 1992 (the 'Small Constitution') redefined relations between the President, Government and Sejm, enhancing the powers of the President and the Prime Minister. The head of state is the *President*, who is directly elected for a 5-year term (renewable once). The President may appoint, but may not dismiss, cabinets.

The authority of the republic is vested in the *Sejm* (Parliament of 460 members), elected by proportional representation for 4 years by all citizens over 18. There is a 5% threshold for parties and 8% for coalitions, but seats are reserved for representatives of ethnic minorities even if their vote falls below 5%. 69 of the Sejm seats are awarded from the national lists of parties polling more than 7% of the vote. The Sejm elects a *Council of State* and a *Council of Ministers.* There is also an elected 100-member upper house, the *Senate.* The President and the Senate each has a power of veto which only a two-thirds majority of the Sejm can override. The Prime Minister is chosen by the President with the approval of the Sejm.

A Political Council consultative to the presidency consisting of representatives of all the major political tendencies was set up in Jan. 1991.

At the first round of the presidential elections on 5 Nov. 1995 13 candidates stood; turn-out was 64·7%. Aleksander Kwaśniewski gained 35·11% of votes cast, President Lech Wałęsa, 33.11%. At the run-off round on 19 Nov. 1995 Kwaśniewski was elected by 51·72% of votes cast; turn-out was 68%.

Parliamentary elections were held on 19 Sept. 1993. Turn-out was 52·08%. Results:

Party	*% of votes cast*	*Sejm seats*	*Sejm seats at 1991 election*	*Senate seats*
Democratic Left Alliance (DLA)	20·41%	171	60	37
Polish Peasant Party (PPP)	15·40%	132	48	36
Democratic Union	10·59%	74	62	4
Union of Labour	7·28%	41	4	2
Confederation for an Independent Poland	5·77%	22	46	nil
Non-Party Bloc for Reform	5·41%	16	–	2
German ethnic committees	0·71%	4	7	1

The following failed to surmount the 5% threshold for the Sejm, but gained Senate seats: Solidarity, 9; 9 others, 1 each.

President: Aleksander Kwaśniewski (b. 1952; DLA; elected Nov. 1995).

On 1 Feb. 1996 the President appointed Włodzimierz Cimoszewicz (DLA) *Prime Minister* and asked him to form a government.

National flag: Horizontally white over red, with the arms of Poland on the white strip.
National anthem: 'Jeszcze Polska nie zginęla' ('Poland has not yet perished'); words by J. Wybicki; tune by M. Ogiński.

Local government is carried out by councils elected every 4 years at voivodship and community level. Local government is financed partly by local taxes and partly by central government taxes. There are also district agencies which form a link between local and central government. Communities of fewer than 40,000 inhabitants elect councils on a first-past-the-post system; larger communities have a proportional party-list system. Elections were held on 19 June 1994 for 52,173 seats on 2,465 councils; turn-out was 35·8%. Administrative reforms introduced as from 1993 devolve responsibility for education and health from voivodships to municipalities, and restore districts (*powiat*) as an intermediate division.

DEFENCE. Poland is divided into 4 military districts: Warsaw, Pomerania, Kraków and Silesia.
Conscription is for 18 months. 3-year civilian duty as a conscientious alternative to conscription was introduced in 1988.

Army. The Army includes 9 mechanized divisions, 1 coastal defence, 4 artillery, 4 engineer, 1 air assault, 1 mountain infantry and 4 missile brigades; and 4 missile, 2 anti-tank and 1 artillery regiment. Equipment includes 1,035 T-55 and 717 T-72 main battle tanks. An aviation element is being formed, initially with Mi-2 and Mi-8/17 helicopters. Strength (1996) 188,200 (including 108,100 conscripts).

Navy. The fleet comprises 3 ex-Soviet diesel submarines, 1 ex-Soviet guided missile destroyer armed with SA-N-1 Goa surface-to-air and SS-N-2C Styx anti-ship missiles, 1 small frigate, 4 missile corvettes, 7 smaller fast missile craft, 3 coastal and 18 inshore patrol craft, 6 coastal and 18 inshore minesweepers, 5 medium landing ships and about 3 landing craft. Auxiliaries include 1 command ship, 4 support tankers, 2 intelligence vessels, 2 survey vessels, and 3 training ships together with about 60 minor auxiliaries.
The Fleet Air Arm comprises 2 regiments, one with 14 Iskra patrol aircraft the other with 35 Mig-21 fighter bombers, 1 squadron with 4 Mi-14 and 6 W-3 Sokol helicopters, and 1 squadron with 7 An-2 and 2 An-28 transports. Naval-manned coast defences provide 6 artillery battalions and 3 missile batteries.
Personnel in 1995 totalled 18,000 including 9,500 conscripts. 2,800 of these serve in naval aviation. Bases are at Gdynia, Gdańsk and Świnoujscie.
A para-military border guard service operates 28 inshore patrol craft and some 30 boats.

Air Force. The Air Force had a strength (1995) of 72,600 (40,300 conscripts) with 370 combat aircraft and 60 attack helicopters.
There are 6 air defence regiments (16 squadrons) with about 200 MiG-21, MiG-23 and MiG-29 supersonic interceptors, and 4 regiments (12 squadrons) operating variable-geometry Su-20 and Su-22 close-support fighters. There are also reconnaissance, ECM, transport, helicopter (including Mi-2s for observation and Mi-24 gunships) and training units. Soviet 'Guideline' 'Goa', 'Ganef', 'Gainful' and 'Gaskin' surface-to-air missiles are operational.

INTERNATIONAL RELATIONS. A treaty of friendship with Germany signed 17 June 1991 renounced the use of force, recognized Poland's western border as laid down at the Potsdam conference of 1945 (the 'Oder-Neisse line') and guaranteed minority rights in both countries.

Membership. Poland is a member of the UN, the Council of Europe, CEFTA and the NATO Partnership for Peace, and an associate partner of the WEU. Together with Austria, Croatia, the Czech Republic, Hungary, Italy, Slovakia and Slovenia,

Poland is a member of the Central European Initiative, which evolved from the Pentagonal/ Hexagonal grouping of 1990–91.

ECONOMY

Policy. For planning and privatization till 1994 *see* THE STATESMAN'S YEAR-BOOK 1994–95, p. 1098. An economic plan is running from 1994 to 1997. In 1995 15 National Investment Funds were set up to oversee the privatization of 444 state enterprises. All citizens may purchase titles to participate in these funds for 10% of their annual salary, which will enable them to buy shares in the enterprises when privatized (Mass Privatization Scheme). At a referendum on 18 Feb. 1996 on privatization, turn-out was 32%, below the 50% threshold needed to validate the results.

Budget. In 1994, revenue was (in 1m. złoty) 63,125·2, comprising: Income tax from corporations, 6,825·5; personal income tax, 17,375·9; VAT, 15,016·6; other indirect taxes, 11,870·4; dividends, 599·6; customs duties, 4,888·8; revenues from privatization, 1,599·7. Expenditure was 68,865·1, comprising: Subsidies, 537·1; housing and community, 514·5; social security, 23,590·1; internal debt service, 7,401·4; foreign debt service, 1,832·1; general subventions, 551·7; education, 1,668·1; investment, 3,082·8.

Currency. The currency unit is the *złoty* (PLZ) of 100 *groszy*. A new złoty was introduced on 1 Jan. 1995 at 1 new złoty = 10,000 old złotys. There are coins of 1, 2, 5, 10, 20 and 50 grosz and 1 and 5 złotys, and notes of 10, 20, 50, 100 and 200 złotys. Old złoty notes will be valid until 1997. Inflation was 29·5% in 1993. The złoty became convertible on 1 Jan. 1990. In 1995 the złoty was subject to a creeping devaluation of 1·2% per month; it was allowed to float in a 7% band from 16 May 1995. Foreign exchange reserves were US$3,500 in Aug. 1993. In March 1996, £1 sterling = 3·92 złotys, US$1 = 2·57 złotys; DM1 = 1·74 złotys.

Banking and Finance. The National Bank of Poland (established 1945) is the central bank and bank of issue. Its Governor is nominated by the President and approved by the Sejm. (*Governor*, Hanna Gronkiewicz-Waltz). The 9 state-owned banks established in 1989 were formed from National Bank branches and are geographically-based. They are being privatized with IMF advice. There are also specialized banks, including the state-owned Commercial (*Handlowy*) Bank, the Food Economy Bank and the Export Development Bank (the latter due for privatization). The General Savings Bank (Powszechna Kasa Oszczędności) exercises central control over savings activities.

There is a stock exchange in Warsaw.

Weights and Measures. The metric system is in general use.

ENERGY AND NATURAL RESOURCES

Electricity. Electricity production (1994) 134,831m. kWh.; installed capacity in 1991 was 31,952 MW. In 1989, 70% of electricity was produced by coal-powered thermal plants.

Oil and Gas. Total oil reserves amount to some 100m. tonnes. Crude oil production was 158,000 tonnes in 1992, natural gas 4,634m. cu. metres in 1994.

Minerals. Poland is a major producer of coal (reserves of some 120,000m. tonnes), copper (56m. tonnes) and sulphur. Production in 1993 (in tonnes): Coal, 133·63m.; brown coal, 66·77m.; sulphur, 2·14m.

Agriculture. In 1993 there were 18·64m. ha of agricultural land, comprising: Arable, 14·31m. ha; meadows, 2·44m. ha; pasture, 1·61m. ha; orchards, 0·29m. ha. 14·6m. ha were owned by private farmers, 2·59m. ha by state farms and 0·62m. ha by co-operatives. 6·69m. ha were irrigated in 1993.

Some government subsidies and guaranteed prices were restored in 1992.

Output in 1993 (in 1,000 tonnes): Wheat, 8,243; rye, 4,992; barley, 3,255; oats, 1,493; maize, 199; potatoes, 36,270; sugar-beet, 15,621.

Livestock, 1995 (in 1m.): Cattle, 7·3 (including cows, 3·58); pigs, 20·38; sheep (1992), 1·9; horses, 0·9. Milk production was 12,401m. litres; meat, 1·02m. tonnes; eggs (1992), 6,000m.

Tractors in use in 1993: 1,155,600 (in 15-h.p. units).

Forestry. In 1994, 8·72m. ha were forests (predominantly coniferous). 72·29m. ha were in the public domain, 14·92m. ha were private. 64,800 ha were afforested, and 21·63m. cu. metres of timber gained.

Fisheries. The catch was 426,000 tonnes in 1994.

INDUSTRY. In June 1995 there were 4,630 state firms, 518 firms owned by local authorities, 4,323 joint-stock firms, 96,020 private companies and 19,834 co-operatives. Production in 1994 (in 1,000 tonnes): Rolled steel, 8,586; cement, 13,888; electrolytic copper, 405; fertilizers, 1,802; paper, 1,204; refined petroleum products, 13,445; plastics, 652; metal-working machines, 6,142; cars, 338,000 units; lorries, 21,149 units; tractors, 14,000 units; fuel oil, 2,746.

Output of light industry in 1994: Cotton fabrics, 258m. cu. metres; woollen fabrics, 33·55m. metres; synthetic fibres, 138,000 tonnes; shoes, 54·5m. pairs; cleaning agents, 238,000 tonnes; washing machines, 449,000; refrigerators, 608,00;, and TV sets, 888,000.

Labour. In Dec. 1993 the population of working age was 28·38m. (14·92m. females). 17·37m. persons (8m.) were economically active, of whom 14·77m. (6·68m.) were in employment. In July 1995 there were 2·72m. registered unemployed. In 1993 3·63m. persons worked in industry, 0·86m. in building, 0·57m. in transport, 0·17m. in communications, 1·95m. in trade and 0·32m. in community services. Workers made redundant are entitled to one month's wages. Retirement age is 60 for women and 65 for men.

Trade Unions. In 1980 under Lech Wałęsa Solidarity was an engine of political reform. Dissolved in 1982 it was re-legalized in 1989 and successfully contested the parliamentary elections. It had 2·3m. members in 1991. The official union, OPZZ, had 5m. members in 1990; there were also about 4,000 small unions not affiliated to it.

FOREIGN ECONOMIC RELATIONS. Since Jan. 1989 foreign investors may own 100% of companies on Polish soil. There were 11,473 joint ventures in May 1993. Legislation of 1991 removed limits on the repatriation of profits, reduced the number of cases needing licences and ended a 10% ceiling on share purchases. Licenses are issued by the Ministry for Privatization, and are required for investment in ports, airports, arms manufacture, estate agency and legal services. In 1992 foreign investments totalled US$4,500m.

Foreign debt was US$28,700m. in April 1994.

An agreement of Dec. 1992 with the Czech Republic, Hungary and Slovakia abolishes tariffs on raw materials and goods where exports do not compete directly with locally-produced items, and envisages tariff reductions on agricultural and industrial goods in 1995–97.

Commerce. Exports (in 1m. złotys), 1994: 39,246·1; imports, 49,072·3.

Imports in 1993 included (in tonnes): Crude oil, 13·67m.; iron ore, 8·78m.; fertilizers, 0·81m.; wheat, 0·82m.; machinery and transport equipment, 14,966. Exports (in tonnes): Coal, 22·98m.; coke, 1·89m.; copper, 267,000; sulphur, 2·29m.; cement, 3·24m.; paper and products, 0·27m.

Main export markets, 1993 (in 1,000m. złotys): Germany, 93,506·5; Netherlands, 15,144·5; Italy, 13,426·5; Russia, 11,922·5; UK, 11,086·4; France, 10,753·2. Main import suppliers: Germany, 95,297·3; Italy, 26,461·6; Russia, 23,089·3; UK, 19,661·8; USA, 17,412·8; France, 14,439·4.

Total trade between Poland and UK (British Department of Trade returns £1,000 sterling):

	1991	*1992*	*1993*	*1994*	*1995*
Imports to UK	313,828	356,173	449,320	544,928	638,077
Exports and re-exports from UK	347,069	605,586	717,802	702,711	944,672

Tourism. There were 60·95m. foreign visitors in 1993 (42·57m. from Germany).

COMMUNICATIONS

Roads. In 1993 Poland had 232,000 km of hard-surfaced roads. There were 6·77m. passenger cars, 1·24m. lorries; 86,000 buses and 1·07m. motor cycles. Public road transport carried 1,215m. passengers and 303m. tonnes of freight in 1994. There were 48,901 road accidents in 1993 (6,341 fatal).

Railways. In 1993 the state railway comprised 22,655 km of 1,435 mm gauge (11,496 km electrified), 1,855 km of narrow gauges, and 659 km of 1,520 mm gauge. In 1994 railways carried 494·7m. passengers and 214·75m. tonnes of freight. Some regional railways are operated by local authorities. A 12 km metro opened in Warsaw in 1995, and there are tram/light rail networks in 13 cities.

Civil Aviation. There is an international airport at Warsaw (Okęcie). The national carrier is LOT-Polish Airlines, state-owned but with 49% of its equity scheduled for privatization. Its fleet in 1995 comprised 4 B-737-400s, 6 B-737-500s, 2 B-767-200ERs, 2 B-767-300ERs and 7 other aircrarft. 1,596,000 passengers were flown in 1994. Services are also provided by Aeroflot, Air France, Air Moldova, Air Ukraine, Alitalia, Austrian Airlines, Balkan Belavia, British Airways, Czech Airlines, Delta, El Al, Finnair, KLM, Libyan Airlines, Lithuanian Airlines, Lufthansa, Malév, Sabena, SAS, Swissair, Tarom and Tunis Air.

Shipping. The principal ports are Gdynia, Gdańsk and Szczecin. 52·38m. tonnes of cargo were handled in 1994. Ocean-going services are grouped into Polish Ocean Lines based on Gdynia and operating regular liner services, and the Polish Shipping Company based on Szczecin and operating cargo services. Poland also has a share in the Gdynia America Line. In 1994, 23·19m. tonnes of freight and 630,000 passengers were carried. In 1995 the merchant marine totalled 3·56m. GRT, including oil tankers, 0·15m. GRT.

In 1993 there were 3,997 km of navigable inland waterways. In 1990 there were 57 passenger vessels, 411 tugs and 1,337 barges. 10·12m. tonnes of freight were carried in 1994.

Telecommunications. In 1993 there were 7,975 post offices. There were 3,938,000 telephone, 39,000 telex and 23,000 fax subscribers in 1992.

Polskie Radio i Telewizja broadcasts 3 radio programmes and 2 TV programmes. There is also a commercial TV channel. Colour programmes are transmitted by the SECAM system. Links with the West are provided through the Eutelstat satellite. In 1992 independent radio and TV broadcasting were introduced under the aegis of a 9-member National Council of Radiophonics and Television. Radio licences in 1994, 10·9m.; TV licences, 10·11m.

Cinemas. In 1994 there were 705 cinemas; admissions, 14·91m. 27 full-length films were made in 1993.

Press. In 1993 there were 124 newspapers with an overall circulation of 8·09m. and 3,139 other periodicals. 9,788 book titles were published in 1993.

SOCIAL INSTITUTIONS

Justice. The penal code was adopted in 1969. Espionage and treason carry the severest penalties. For minor crimes there is provision for probation sentences and fines. In 1995 the death penalty was suspended for 5 years; it had not been applied since 1988.

There exist the following courts: 3 Supreme Courts, 21 chief administrative courts, 9 appeal courts, 177 voivodship courts, 386 district courts and 65 family consultative centres. Judges and lay assessors are elected. Judges for higher courts are appointed by the President of the Republic from candidatures proposed by the National Council of the Judiciary. Judges have life tenure. An ombudsman's office was established in 1987.

Family courts (now consultative centres) were established (1977) for cases involving divorce and domestic relations but divorce suits were transferred to ordinary courts in 1990.

Religion. Church–State relations are regulated by laws of 1989 which guarantee religious freedom, grant the Church radio and TV programmes and permit it to run schools, hospitals and old age homes. The Church has a university (Lublin), an Academy of Catholic Theology and seminaries. On 28 July 1993 the government signed a Concordat with the Vatican regulating mutual relations. The archbishop of Warsaw is the primate of Poland (since 1981, Cardinal Józef Glemp). The religious capital is Gniezno, whose archbishop will be the future primate. In Oct. 1978 Cardinal Karol Wojtyla, archbishop of Cracow, was elected Pope as John Paul II.

Statistics of major churches for 1993:

Church	*Parishes*	*Churches*	*Clergy*	*Adherents*
Roman Catholic	9,266	15,081	25,187	34,794,612
Uniate	63	105	70	110,380
Old Catholics	153	161	163	81,667
Polish Orthodox	243	410	259	570,600
Protestant (31 sects)	1,110	1,170	1,812	147,251
Moslem	9	8	10	5,246
Jewish	3	13	3	1,330
Jehovah's Witnesses	–	1,397	–	110,770

Education. Basic education from 7 to 15 is free and compulsory. Free secondary education is then optional in general or vocational schools. Primary schools are organized in complexes based on wards under one director ('ward collective schools'). In 1993–94 there were: Nursery schools, 21,178 with 984,300 pupils and 75,500 teachers; primary schools, 20,326 with 5,288,250 pupils and 323,400 teachers; secondary schools, 1,832 with 659,524 pupils and 30,300 teachers; vocational schools, 9,655 with 1,801,822 pupils and 85,600 teachers, and 140 institutions of higher education (including 11 universities, 18 polytechnics, 9 agricultural schools, 5 schools of economics, 10 teachers' training colleges and 11 medical schools) with 584,009 students and 65,300 teaching staff.

Religious (Catholic) instruction was introduced in all schools in 1990; for children of dissenting parents there are classes in ethics.

Health. Medical treatment is free and funded from the state budget. Medical care is also available in private clinics. In 1993 there were 698 hospitals and 48 psychiatric hospitals with 245,617 beds, 5,689 pharmacies and 799 drug addiction rehabilitation centres. In 1993 there were 85,367 doctors, 16,951 dentists, 17,574 pharmacists and 203,895 nurses.

Social Security. Social security benefits are administered by the State Insurance Office and funded 45% by a payroll tax and 55% from the state budget. Pensions, disability payments, child allowances, survivor benefits, maternity benefits, funeral subsidies, sickness compensation and alimony supplements are provided. In 1993 age and disability pensions were paid to 8·5m. recipients; these are index-linked to the average wage. Unemployment benefits are paid from a fund financed by a 3% payroll tax. It is indexed in various categories to the average wage and payable for 12 months. Social assistance is administered and partly-funded by local government. it provides last-resort benefits in cash and kind.

DIPLOMATIC REPRESENTATIVES

Of Poland in Great Britain (47 Portland Pl., London, W1N 3AG)
Ambassador: Ryszard Stemplowski.

Of Great Britain in Poland (Aleje Roz No. 1, 00-556 Warsaw)
Ambassador: Michael Llewellyn Smith, CMG.

Of Poland in the USA (2640 16th St., NW, Washington, D.C., 20009)
Ambassador: Jerzy Kosminski.

Of the USA in Poland (Aleje Ujazdowskie 29/31, Warsaw)
Ambassador: Nicholas A. Rey.

Of Poland to the United Nations
Ambassador: Dr Zbigniew Włosowicz.

Further Reading

The Central Statistical Office, *Rocznik Statystyczny* (annual).—*Concise Statistical Yearbook of Poland*

Bromke, A., *The Meaning and Uses of Polish History.* New York, 1987
Davies, N., *Poland, Past and Present: A Select Bibliography of Works in English.* Newtonville, 1977.—*God's Playground: A History of Poland.* 2 vols. OUP, 1981.—*Heart of Europe: a Short History of Poland.* OUP, 1984
Glazyca, G. and Rapacki, R. (eds.) *Poland into the 1990s: Economy and Society in Transition.* New York, 1991
Halecki, O., *A History of Poland.* 4th ed. London, 1983
Kaminski, B., *The Collapse of the State of Socialism: the Case of Poland.* Princeton Univ. Press, 1991
Kanka, A. G., *Poland: An Annotated Bibliography of Books in English.* New York, 1988
Kurski, J., *Lech Wałesa: Democrat or Dictator?* Boulder (CO), 1993
Leslie, R. F., (ed.) *The History of Poland since 1863.* CUP, 1980
Mitchell, K. D. (ed.) *Political Pluralism in Hungary and Poland: Perspectives on the Reforms.* New York, 1992
Sanford, G. and Gozdecka-Sanford, A., *Poland:* [Bibliography]. Oxford and Santa Barbara, 1993
Slay, B., *The Polish Economy: Crisis, Reform and Transformation.* Princeton Univ. Press, 1994
Staar, R. F., (ed.) *Transition to Democracy in Poland.* New York, 1993
Staniszkis, J., *The Dynamics of the Breakthrough in Eastern Europe: the Polish Experience.* California Univ. Press, 1991
Wałęsa, L., *A Path of Hope.* London, 1989
Wedel, J., *The Unplanned Society: Poland during and after Communism.* Columbia Univ. Press, 1992

National library: Biblioteka Narodowa, Rakowiecka 6, Warsaw.
National statistical office: Central Statistical Office, Aleje Niepodległości 208, 00-925 Warsaw.

PORTUGAL

República Portuguesa

Capital: Lisbon
Population: 9·9m. (1994)
GNP per capita: US$9,370 (1994)
HDI/world rank: 0·874/36 (1992)

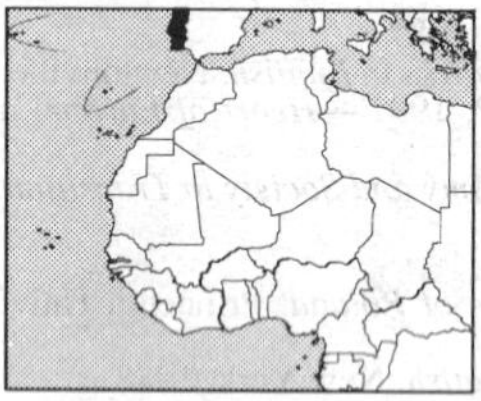

KEY HISTORICAL EVENTS. Portugal has been an independent state since the 12th century, apart from one period of Spanish rule (1580–1640). The monarchy was deposed on 5 Oct. 1910 and a republic established.

A coup on 28 May 1926 established a military government. A corporatist constitution was adopted on 19 March 1933 under which a civil dictatorship governed until a fresh coup on 25 April 1974 established a Junta of National Salvation. Following an attempted revolt on 11 March 1975, the Junta was dissolved and a Supreme Revolutionary Council formed which ruled until 25 April 1976 when constitutional government was resumed.

TERRITORY AND POPULATION. Mainland Portugal is bounded in the north and east by Spain and south and west by the Atlantic Ocean. The Atlantic archipelagoes of the Azores and of Madeira form autonomous but integral parts of the republic, which has a total area of 91,905 sq. km. Population (1991 census), 9,862,700 (5,107,500 females); density, 107·4 per sq. km. 1994 estimate: 9,902,200.

The areas and populations (in 1,000) of the districts and Autonomous Regions:

Districts	*Area (in sq. km)*	*Population (1991 census)*	*1992 estimate*	*Districts*	*Area (in sq. km)*	*Population (1991 census)*	*1992 estimate*
Aveiro	2,800	654·4	657·2	Porto	2,341	1,641·7	1,648·5
Beja	10,223	169·4	167·2	Santarém	6,707	444·9	442·6
Braga	2,695	748·2	752·6	Setúbal	5,604	712·6	715·2
Bragança	6,597	157·8	155·4	Viana do Castelo	2,210	250·1	248·7
Castelo Branco	6,616	214·9	212·6	Vila Real	4,305	236·3	233·8
Coimbra	3,917	427·7	426·0	Viseu	5,009	401·9	399·4
Evora	7,396	173·7	172·7	Total mainland	88,796	9,371·5	9,366·3
Faro	4,986	341·4	342·0				
Guarda	5,540	188·2	186·1	*Autonomous Regions*			
Leiria	3,508	426·2	426·1				
Lisbon	2,758	2,048·2	2,047·6	Azores	2,330	237·8	239·9 [1]
Portalegre	6,064	134·2	132·9	Madeira	794	253·4	256·0 [1]

[1] 1994 estimate.

In 1994 mainland Portugal was divided into 5 regions (with estimated population in 1,000): North (3,511·1); Central (1,713·8); Lisbon and Tagus Valley (3,306·2); Alentejo (530·9); Algarve (344·3).

Vital statistics for calendar years:

	Marriages	*Live births*	*Still births*	*Deaths*	*Infant deaths*	*Divorces*
1990	71,654	116,383	1,010	103,115	1,266	9,216
1991	71,808	116,415	971	104,361	1,254	10,619
1992	69,887	115,018	909	101,161	1,052	12,429
1993	68,176	114,030	887	106,384	996	12,093

Vital statistics rates, 1993 (per 1,000 population): Birth, 11·5; death, 10·7; natural increase, 0·8; infant mortality (per 1,000 live births), 6·1. Expectation of life, 1992: Males, 70·8 years; females 78·2.

In 1993 the births comprised 58,428 boys and 55,602 girls; deaths, 55,896 males and 50,488 females.

In 1993, 131,593 foreigners were legally registered: 55,786 African; 15,731 Brazilian; 9,629 British; 8,117 USA. There were 9,852 immigrants.

The chief cities are Lisbon, the capital, Oporto, Amadora, Setúbal and Coimbra.

The **Azores** islands lie in the mid-Atlantic Ocean, between 1,200 and 1,600 km west of Lisbon. They are divided into 3 widely separated groups with clear channels between, São Miguel (759 sq. km) together with Santa Maria (97 sq. km) being the most easterly; about 100 miles north-west of them lies the central cluster of Terceira (382 sq. km), Graciosa (62 sq. km), São Jorge (246 sq. km), Pico (446 sq. km) and Faial (173 sq. km); still another 150 miles to the north-west are Flores (143 sq. km) and Corvo (17 sq. km), the latter being the most isolated and primitive of the islands. São Miguel contains over half the total population of the archipelago.

Madeira comprises the island of Madeira (745 sq. km), containing the capital, Funchal; the smaller island of Porto Santo (40 sq. km), lying 46 km. to the northeast of Madeira; and two groups of uninhabited islets, Ilhas Desertas (15 sq. km), being 20 km. south-east of Funchal and Ilhas Selvagens (4 sq. m), near the Canaries.

CLIMATE. Because of westerly winds and the effect of the Gulf Stream, the climate ranges from the cool, damp Atlantic type in the north to a warmer and drier Mediterranean type in the south. July and Aug. are virtually rainless everywhere. Inland areas in the north have greater temperature variation, with continental winds blowing from the interior. Lisbon. Jan. 52°F (11°C), July 72°F (22°C). Annual rainfall 27·4" (686 mm). Porto. Jan. 48°F (8·9°C), July 67°F (19·4°C). Annual rainfall 46" (1,151 mm).

CONSTITUTION AND GOVERNMENT. A new Constitution, replacing that of 1976, was approved by the Assembly of the Republic (by 197 votes to 40) on 12 Aug. 1982 and promulgated in Sept. It abolished the (military) Council of the Revolution and reduced the role of the President under it. Portugal is a sovereign, unitary republic. Executive power is vested in the *President*, directly elected for a 5-year term (for a maximum of 2 consecutive terms). The President appoints a Prime Minister and, upon the latter's nomination, other members of the Council of Ministers.

The 230-member *National Assembly* is a unicameral legislature elected for 4-year terms by universal adult suffrage under a system of proportional representation.

At the presidential elections of 14 Jan. 1996 Jorge Sampaio was elected President by 53·8% of votes cast against former prime minister Anibal Cavaco Silva (Social Democrat).

At the parliamentary elections of 1 Oct. 1995 turn-out was 68%. The Socialist Party won 112 seats with 42·9% of votes cast (72 with 29·1% in 1991); the Social Democratic Party, 88 with 34% (135 with 50%); the Christian Democratic Party, 15 with 5·1% (5 with 4·4%); and the Communist Alliance, 15 with 8·6% (17 with 8·8%).

President: Jorge Sampaio (Socialist).

The Socialist government was composed in Dec. 1995 of:

Prime Minister: Antônio Guterres. *Minister of Agriculture, Rural Development and Fisheries:* Fernando Gomes da Silva. *Culture:* Manuel Carrilho. *Defence and the Presidency:* Antônio Vitorino. *Economy:* Daniel Bessa. *Education:* Marcal Grilo. *Environment:* Elisa Ferreira. *Finance:* Antônio Sousa Franco. *Foreign Affairs:* Jaime Gama. *Health:* Maria de Belém. *Home Affairs:* Alberto Costa. *Justice:* José Vera Jardím. *Labour:* Maria Rodrigues. *Science and Technology:* Mariano Gago. *Social Infrastructure:* Henrique Constantino. *Social Security:* Eduardo Ferro Rodrigues. *Territorial Planning:* João Cravinho. *Without portfolio:* Jorge Coelho.

The *Speaker* is António Almedia Santos (Socialist).

National flag: Vertical green and red, with the red of double width, and over all on the dividing line the national arms.

National anthem: 'Herois do mar, nobre povo' ('Heroes of the sea, noble breed'); words by Lopes de Mendonça, tune by Alfredo Keil.

European Parliament. Portugal has 25 representatives. At the June 1994 elections turn-out was 35·7%. The Socialist Party won 10 seats with 34·7% of votes cast

(Group in European Parliament: European Socialist Party); The Social Democratic Party, 9 with 34·3% (Popular European Party; Liberal, Democratic and Reformist Group); the Social Democratic Centre, 3 with 12·4% (European Democrats' Rally); the United Democratic Alliance, 3 with 11·2%.

Local Government: Since 1976, the archipelagoes of the **Azores** and of **Madeira** are Autonomous Regions with their own legislatures and governments. Elections were held in Oct. 1992. The Social Democrats gained 28 seats out of 51 in the Azores and 39 out of 55 in Madeira. Pending the formation of other regional governments, Continental Portugal is divided into 18 districts. Regions and districts are divided into 305 municipal councils and sub-divided into 4,209 parishes. Each level is governed by an assembly elected by direct universal suffrage under a system of proportional representation, with an executive body responsible to the assembly. Elections for municipal councils were held on 12 Dec. 1993. The Socialist Party gained control of 127 with 36% of votes cast, the Social Democratic Party 116 with 33·7%, the Communist Party 49 with 12·7% and the Democratic and Social Centre 13 with 8·4%.

DEFENCE. Conscription is 4–18 months.

Army. There are 5 territorial commands. The Army consists of 1 composite and 1 airborne brigade and 2 armoured cavalry, 11 infantry, 2 field, 1 military police, 1 tank and 2 engineer regiments. Equipment includes 24 M-47, 86 M-48A5 and 88 M-60A3 main battle tanks. Strength (1996) 29,700 (15,000 conscripts). Paramilitary forces are the National Republican Guard (20,900), Public Security Police (20,000), and the Border Guard (8,900).

Navy. The combatant fleet comprises 3 French-built Daphne class diesel submarines, 3 missile-armed frigates of the Vasco da Gama class of West German MEKO design which can embark 2 Lynx helicopters, 8 other small frigates, 6 offshore, 10 coastal and 13 inshore patrol vessels. Auxiliaries include 1 tanker, 2 survey ships, 1 sail training ship and 1 ocean tug. There are 10 small amphibious craft and some 20 service vessels. Naval personnel in 1995 totalled 12,500 (800 conscripts) including 2,100 marines.

Air Force. Formed in 1912, the Air Force has been independent since 1952, when it was combined with the naval air service and given equal status with the Army and Navy. In 1995, it had a strength of about 7,300 (1,800 conscripts). Equipment comprises 1 interceptor unit with F16s, 2 strike squadrons with 40 A-7P Corsair IIs; 1 squadron of P-3P Orion maritime patrol aircraft; 1 squadron of C-130H Hercules and 3 squadrons of CASA 212 Aviocars for transport and search and rescue operations; 12 Cessna 337 Skymasters and a force of Puma and Alouette III helicopters. Other aircraft in service include Falcon 20 and 50 VIP transports, Epsilon piston-engined trainers and AlphaJet advanced trainers.

INTERNATIONAL RELATIONS

Membership. Portugal is a member of the UN, EC, OECD, NATO, WEU and the Council of Europe. Portugal has adhered to the Schengen Accord abolishing border controls between Belgium, the Netherlands, Luxembourg, France, Germany, Italy and Spain. It became effective on 26 March 1995 (except for Italy).

ECONOMY

Policy. Large-scale privatization has been in train since 1989.

Budget. The 1995 budget balanced at 6,429,829,401,000 escudos. Public debt as at 31 Dec. 1993 was 7,448,297,787,000 escudos. 1995 budget (in 1m. escudos): Total income, 6,429,829·4; current income, 3,480,357·6; capital income, 2,761,131·8; local finance, 46,582·2; undeducted repayments, 25,051; current accounts, 116,706·8; total expenses, 6,429,829·4. VAT is 17% (reduced rate 5%).

Currency. The unit of currency is the *escudo* (PTE) of 100 *centavos* which has been fully convertible since Dec. 1992. 1,000 *escudos* is called a *conto*.

There are notes of 10,000, 5,000, 1,000, 500 and 100 *escudos*; cupronickel coins of 50, 25, 20, 5 and 2½ *escudos*; nickel-brass coins of 1 *escudo*; bronze coins of ½ *escudo*. Inflation was 5·3% in 1994. The escudo was devalued 3·5% within the EMS on 6 March 1995. In March 1996, £1 = 233·88; US$1 = 153·03; DM1 = 103·68 escudos.

Banking and Finance. Since 1931 the central bank and bank of issue has been the Banco de Portugal, founded 19 Nov. 1846 and nationalized on 13 Sept. 1974. Its capital is fixed at 200m. escudos. Its *Governor* is António de Sousa. Banks and insurance companies were nationalized in 1975 but are now being privatized. From Feb. 1984 new private banks were allowed to operate. The National Development Bank began operations on 4 Jan. 1960.

In 1991 there were 26 commercial banks (9 foreign), 4 investment banks and 3 savings banks. In Dec. 1992 commercial banks' total credits were 39,620,520 escudos; savings and investment banks' total credits 24,868, 530m. escudos.

There are stock exchanges in Lisbon and Oporto.

Weights and Measures. The metric system is the legal standard. The arroba (of 14·69 kg) is sometimes used locally.

ENERGY AND NATURAL RESOURCES

Electricity. Total production of electrical power in 1989 was 25,777m. kWh., of which 6,049m. was hydro-electric.

Minerals. Portugal possesses considerable mineral wealth. Production in tonnes (1987): Gold (refined) 0·320; uranium, 167; wolframite, 2,011; coal, 228,648; tin ore, 90; kaolin, 66,736. (1992): Tungsten, 1,870; copper, 609,242; non-crystalline limestone, 31,314,084; granite, 14,437,939; marble, 962,178.

Agriculture. The following figures show the area (in 1,000 ha) and production (in 1,000 tonnes) of the chief crops:

	1991		*1992*		*1993*	
Crop	*Area*	*Quantity*	*Area*	*Quantity*	*Area*	*Quantity*
Wheat	294·5 [1]	617·9 [1]	280·0 [1]	361·6 [1]	250·0 [1]	421·6 [1]
Maize	213·2 [1]	648·2 [1]	177·1 [1]	620·0 [1]	167·7 [1]	629·8 [1]
Oats	92·0	76·1	75·0	45·1	92·0	76·4
Barley	65·0 [1]	124·1 [1]	66·7 [1]	53·7 [1]	61·6	98·5
Rye	86·6	80·4	75·0	69·5	72·5	66·7
Rice	33·5	170·5	21·1	109·7	13·2	69·0
Beans	57·5 [1]	27·1 [1]	39·2 [1]	21·7 [1]	31·8 [1]	16·1 [1]
Potatoes	108·7 [1]	1,370·4 [1]	105·0 [1]	1,500·1 [1]	84·6 [1]	1,182·8 [1]

[1] Mainland only.

Fruit production on the mainland (in 1,000 tonnes), 1993: Apples, 260·5; pears, 97·9; oranges, 163·9 and peaches, 92·1.

Wine production on the mainland (in 1,000 hectolitres), 1993, 4,576·2; olive oil, 351·2.

Livestock (1993): Cattle, 1·32m.; goats, 0·84m.; sheep, 3·31m.; pigs, 2·66m. Animal products (mainland) in tonnes (1993): Meat, 664,142, of which poultry, 222,064; milk, 392,326; eggs, 88,503; cheese, 50,347.

Forestry. Pine, cork oak, oak, eucalyptus, chestnut and other species are grown.

Portugal is a major producer of cork. Estimated cork production, 1992: 154,000 tonnes. Production of resin was 28,000 tonnes in 1992.

Fisheries. The fishing industry is important. In 1993 there were 13,167 (8,322 motorized) registered fishing vessels. The sardine catch, 1993, was 90,412 tonnes valued at 4,070,309,000 escudos. Cod, mackerel, hake, crustacea, shellfish, tuna and swordfish are also caught. Total catch including estimate of frozen and salted fish, (1993) was 269,461 tonnes valued at 60,389,924,000 escudos. Registered catchers of fish, 1993, 34,454.

INDUSTRY. Output of major industrial products:

	1990	*1991*	*1992*
Concentrate of tomato (tonnes)	128,765	115,132	71,753
Tinned sardines (tonnes)	21,805	23,425	16,589
Tinned tuna (tonnes)	16,582	20,722	15,830
Refined olive oil (tonnes)	9,883	8,368	16,948
Rice (tonnes)	148,036	127,002	106,597
Wheat bread (tonnes)	266,423	243,975	240,656
Pasta (tonnes)	64,915	64,517	61,656
Refined sugar (tonnes)	305,406	281,708	297,251
Animal foodstuffs (tonnes)	3,675,951	3,501,917	3,431,060
Beer (hectolitres)	6,918,774	6,701,635	6,859,751
Soft drinks (hectolitres)	3,180,115	3,485,765	3,543,535
Cigarettes (tonnes)	16,542	16,974	15,619
Wool thread (tonnes)	3,005	3,432	...
Wool and mixed wool fabrics (tonnes)	12,014	12,179	...
Cotton thread (tonnes)	127,171	120,290	...
Cotton fabric (tonnes)	75,566	83,004	...
Knitted garments (tonnes)	24,445	26,426	44,107
Shirts (1,000)	14,943	13,122	15,571
Trousers (1,000)	22,143	20,862	...
Leather and hide footwear (1,000 pairs)	68,924	70,437	55,079
Corks (tonnes)	22,584	29,851	20,108
Cork agglomerates (tonnes)	65,396	54,381	...
Wood pulp (tonnes)	1,437,761	1,590,224	1,350,745
Sulphuric acid (tonnes)	260,433	50,885	...
Fertilizers—nitrogen based (tonnes)	554,160	505,240	...
phosphate based (tonnes)	242,790	220,360	...
Glues (tonnes)	36,297	35,769	...
Petrol (tonnes)	3,048,246	2,541,372	2,754,410
Diesel oil (tonnes)	2,963,141	2,322,695	2,959,395
Fuel oil (tonnes)	4,737,483	4,181,896	4,943,883
Butane (tonnes)	251,397	237,769	...
Tyres (1,000)	1,402	1,005	...
Glass bottles (1,000)	1,211,826	1,407,595	3,161,810
Tiles and accessories (tonnes)	615,759	593,708	...
Bricks and products (tonnes)	3,768,761	4,097,575	2,441
Cement (tonnes)	7,187,704	7,455,374	7,207,021
Files and rasps (tonnes)	591	503	...
Domestic gas appliances	200,870	196,694	...
Radios (1,000)	1,435	1,523	...
Televisions (1,000)	333	319	...
Telephones (1,000)	128	126	...
Refrigerators	463,741	543,396	...
Motorcycles	39,793	33,353	...
Motor cars	72,195	80,074	...
Vans	56,199	49,727	...

Ammonia, raw steel, tin, plate and matches are also produced.

Labour. The maximum working week was 44 hours in 1991; the minimum monthly wage for industrial and farm workers was 40,100 escudos. A minimum wage is fixed by the government. Retirement is at 65 years for men and 62 for women. In 1994, out of a working population of 4,733,000 (2,104,500 female), 4,449,200 (1,976,500 female) were employed. Unemployment was 6·8% (7·8% female). Employment (in 1,000) by sector, 1994 (females in parentheses): Agriculture, forestry and fishing, 523·1 (257·9); industry, construction, energy and water, 1,451·6 (475·3); services, 2,474·4 (1,243·1).

Trade Unions. In 1993 there were 396 unions. An agreement between trade unions, employers and the government for 1991 involved a voluntary wage ceiling, a commitment to labour peace, improvements in working conditions and a 15% increase in pension and social security payments.

FOREIGN ECONOMIC RELATIONS. As at 31 Dec. 1993 the foreign debt was 707,063m. escudos.

Commerce. Imports for consumption and exports (exclusive of coin and bullion and re-exports) for calendar years, in 1m. escudos:

	1990	*1991*	*1992*	*1993*
Imports	3,589,570	3,811,076	4,087,577	3,882,777
Exports	2,335,798	2,354,083	2,475,202	2,474,401

Principal imports, 1993, (in 1m. escudos): Chemical, petroleum, coal, rubber and plastic products, 625,950; transport equipment, 599,405; machinery except electrical, 428,494; electrical machinery and apparatus, 396,912; textiles, 278,868; food, beverages and tobacco, 263,505; crude petroleum and natural gas, 213,063; industrial chemicals, 200,683; other chemical products, 203,683; iron and steel, 89,005.

Principal exports, 1993 (in 1m. escudos): Metal products, machinery and equipment, 625,953; textiles, 386,961; clothing, 341,618; electrical machinery and apparatus, 258,999; footwear, 242,301; chemical, petroleum, coal, rubber and plastic products, 241,921; transport equipment, 186,768; food, beverages and tobacco, 165,104; wood and cork, 161,321; wood products except furniture, 134,789; paper, 117,808; china, pottery and earthenware, 56,734.

Imports and exports to main trade partners, 1990-92 (in 1m. escudos):

	Imports (c.i.f.)			*Exports (f.o.b.)*		
From or to	*1990*	*1991*	*1992*	*1990*	*1991*	*1992*
Angola	12,521	14,457	15,645	58,522	79,066	110,581
Belgium	148,416	153,935	154,902	73,191	75,725	80,911
France	412,434	454,801	525,547	362,102	337,899	351,859
Germany	570,479	570,479	615,235	389,825	450,040	473,860
Italy	357,305	390,557	418,649	96,112	93,872	95,348
Japan	96,093	110,598	125,092	23,850	20,648	18,925
Netherlands	205,130	232,195	280,166	132,136	134,899	134,976
Nigeria	78,526	46,058	53,869	1,243	1,162	1,546
Spain	514,437	602,572	677,809	309,551	351,347	366,963
Sweden	51,832	52,628	51,987	95,447	88,107	83,972
Switzerland	75,268	68,655	68,947	45,044	46,456	44,975
UK	273,105	285,418	292,211	282,915	254,244	275,110
USA	141,154	129,691	123,634	112,738	89,678	86,265

Trade in 1993 (in 1m. escudos): Germany, imports 583,328 and exports 483,887; Italy, 336,854 and 74,114; Netherlands, 191,121 and 128,808; Nigeria, 55,164 and 2,497; Sweden, 46,630 and 63,625; Switzerland, 75,829 and 51,459.

Total trade between Portugal (excluding the Azores and Madeira) and UK (British Department of Trade returns, in £1,000 sterling):

	1990	*1991*	*1992*	*1993*	*1994*
Imports to UK	1,176,161	1,043,511	1,170,815	1,143,200	1,201,900
Exports and re-exports from UK	1,033,268	1,085,084	1,164,098	1,259,000	1,173,600

Tourism. In 1992 there were 20,742,000 foreign visitors (20,579,000 in 1993), including (in 1,000) from Spain, 15,553; UK, 1,435; Germany, 877; the Netherlands, 686; Italy, 367. There were 1,777 hotel establishments with 190,892 accommodation capacity in 1992.

COMMUNICATIONS

Roads (1993). There were 9,648 km of national roads on the mainland, including 579 km of motorways. On 31 Dec. 1993 the number of light and heavy motor vehicles registered was 4,360,447; motorcycles, 180,366; tractors, 219,696; trailers, 258,253. In 1993 there were 50,745 road accidents with 2,177 victims (2,441 in 1993).

Railways. In 1994 total railway length was 3,072 km (1,668 mm and metre gauges), of which 461 km of broad-gauge was electrified. In 1994, 201·4m. passengers were carried and 7·1m. tonnes of freight. There is a metro (19 km) and tramway (94 km) in Lisbon.

Civil Aviation. There are international airports at Portela (Lisbon), Pedras Rubras (Porto), Faro (Algarve), Santa Maria and Lages (Azores) and Funchal (Madeira). The national carrier is the state-owned TAP-Air Portugal, which in 1995 operated 5 A310-300s, 6 A320-200s, 4 A340-300s, 7 B-737-200 Advs, 1 B-737-200C Adv,

8 B-737-300s and 5 other aircraft. Airlines in 1992 carried 4·5m. passengers and 42,113 tonnes of freight. Services are also provided by Aeroflot, Aero Lloyd, Air Afrique, Air Belgium, Air France, Air Inter, Air Liberté, Air Malta, Air Toulouse, Alitalia, British Airways, Condor, Delta, El Al, Finnair, Hamburg Airlines, Hapag Lloyd, Iberia, KLM, LAM, Lauda Air, LTU, Lufthansa, Luxair, Royal Air Maroc, Sabena, Swissair, TAAG, Trans World, Transavia, Transportes Aéreos de Cabo Verde, Tunis Air, Varig, Viasa and Zas.

Shipping. In 1993, 13,946 vessels of 79·55m. tonnes entered the ports; 136,583 passengers embarked and 139,249 disembarked. 14·72m. tonnes of cargo were loaded and 37·27m. tonnes unloaded. On 31 Dec. 1993 there were 323 merchant vessels of 903,604 GRT.

Telecommunications. The number of post offices was 1,016 in 1993. Portugal Telecom (PT) was formed from a merger of 3 state-owned utilities in 1994. Some 25% was scheduled for privatization in 1995. In 1993 there were 3,260,178 main and 31,745 public telephones. There were 9,064 public telexes.

Radiodifusão Portuguesa broadcasts 3 programmes on medium-waves and on FM as well as 3 regional services and an external service, Radio Portugal (English, French, Italian). There are 2 state-owned TV channels (Canal 1 and Radiotelevisão Portuguesa 2) and 2 independent channels, including 1 religious (colour by PAL). Radio Trans Europe is a high-powered short-wave station, retransmitting programmes of different broadcasting organizations. Number of receivers: Radio (1993), 2·2m.; TV set licences (1993), 1,686,513.

Cinemas (1993). There were 187 cinemas and 7·79m. admissions.

Press (1993). There were 27 daily newspapers with a combined circulation of 145,722,000 including 7 in the Azores and 1 on Madeira. There were 1,046 other periodicals with a combined circulation of 355,592,000.

SOCIAL INSTITUTIONS

Justice. There are 4 judicial districts (Lisbon, Porto, Coimbra and Evora) divided into 47 circuits. In 1993 there were 346 common courts, including 300 of the first instance (63 specialized). There are also 29 administration and fiscal courts.

There are 4 courts of appeal in each district, and a Supreme Court in Lisbon.

Capital punishment was abolished completely in the Constitution of 1976.

In 1993 there were 51 prisons. The prison population as at 31 Dec. 1993 was 11,062 including 10,191 men and 954 inmates aged under 21 years.

Religion. There is freedom of worship, both in public and private, with the exception of creeds incompatible with morals and the life and physical integrity of the people. There were 9·86m. Roman Catholics in 1992.

Education. Compulsory education has been in force since 1911. Adult illiteracy was 20% in 1990 according to official figures. In 1992–93 there were 5,409 pre-school establishments (3–6 years) with 180,667 pupils. There were 10,561 basic primary establishments (6–10 years) with 624,439 pupils and 42,584 teachers (764 private with 46,600 pupils and 2,250 teachers. There were 1,778 preparatory establishments (6–8 years) with 329,412 pupils.

In 1992–93, secondary education: General Unified schools, 430,302 pupils aged 11–14 years, complementary secondary, 193,784 pupils aged 14–16 years and 101,816 pupils aged 17–18 years; 1,786 lycées with 93,263 pupils aged 14–17 years; 31,975 pupils aged 14–16 years in technical schools; 16,358 pupils aged 15 onwards in professional schools (nursing, fisheries (aged 12–14 years) and other courses). There are also establishments for students aged 17–20 years for teaching kindergarten and basic primary pupils.

In 1994-95 there were in the public sector 12 universities, an open university, a technical university, an institute of dentistry and an institute of industrial and business studies. In the private sector there were 4 universities and 1 Roman Catholic university. There were 125,483 students and 10,066 academic staff (not including the open university).

In 1994–95 there were 62 other higher education establishments.

Welfare. In 1993, 2,361,676m. escudos were paid in social security benefits. Cash payments in escudos (and types): 725,479m. (sickness), 276,012m. (disability), 49,904m. (accidents at work), 786,384m. (age), 172,957m. (widows), 20,072m. (maternity), 107,426m. (family), 39,363m. (promotion of employment), 114,704m. (unemployment), 407m. (accommodation), 5,221m. (destitution).

Health. In 1993 there were 207 hospitals (215 with 41,814 beds in 1992), 383 clinics and 463 medical centres. There were 28,769 doctors, 973 dentists, 341 dental surgeons and 6,030 pharmacists.

DIPLOMATIC REPRESENTATIVES

Of Portugal in Great Britain (11 Belgrave Sq., London, SW1X 8PP)
Ambassador: António Costa Lobo.

Of Great Britain in Portugal (35-37 Rua de S. Domingos à Lapa, Lisbon)
Ambassador: Roger Westbrook, CMG.

Of Portugal in the USA (2125 Kalorama Rd., NW, Washington, D.C., 20008)
Ambassador: Fernando Andresen Guimarães.

Of the USA in Portugal (Ave. das Forcas Armadas, 1600 Lisbon)
Ambassador: Elizabeth Frawley Bagley.

Of Portugal to the United Nations
Ambassador: Pedro Catarino.

Further Reading

Instituto Nacional de Estatística. *Anuário Estatístico de Portugal/Statistics Year-Book.—Estatísticas do Comércio Externo.* 2 vols. Annual from 1967

Birmingham, D., *A Concise History of Portugal.* CUP, 1993

Corkill, D., *The Portuguese Economy since 1974.* Edinburgh UP, 1993

Ferreira, H. G. and Marshall, M. W., *Portugal's Revolution: Ten Years On.* CUP, 1986

Maxwell, K., *The Making of Portuguese Democracy.* CUP, 1995

Opello, W., *Portugal: from Monarchy to Pluralist Democracy.* Boulder (Colo.), 1991

Unwin, P. T. H., *Portugal.* [Bibliography] Oxford and Santa Barbara, 1987

Wheeler, D. L., *Historical Dictionary of Porgual.* Metuchen (NJ), 1994

National library: Biblioteca Nacional de Lisboa, Campo Grande, Lisbon.

National statistical office: Instituto Nacional de Estatística (INE), Avenida António José de Almeida, 1078 Lisbon Codex.

MACAO

KEY HISTORICAL EVENTS. Macao was visited by Portuguese traders from 1513 and became a Portuguese colony in 1557; it remains a Portuguese-administered territory by virtue of a Sino-Portuguese treaty of 1 Dec. 1887. It was an Overseas Province of Portugal, 1961–74. Discussions on the future of Macao took place with the People's Republic of China in 1986–87 and in 1999 Macao is scheduled to be handed to China. A Basic Law by which Macao is then to be governed, providing for the retention of the capitalist system, was enacted by the National People's Congress of the People's Republic of China on 31 March 1993.

TERRITORY AND POPULATION. The territory, which lies at the mouth of the Pearl River, comprises a peninsula (6·05 sq. km) connected by a narrow isthmus to the People's Republic of China, on which is built the city of Santa Nome de Deus de Macao, and the islands of Taipa (3·78 sq. km), linked to Macao by a 2-km bridge, and Colôane (7·09 sq. km) linked to Taipa by a 2-km causeway (total area, 17·31 sq. km. The population (1991 census) was 339,464 (174,858 females). Estimate (1994) 395,304 (202,399 females). The official language is Portuguese, but Cantonese is used by virtually the entire population.

Vital statistics, 1993: Births, 6,267 (16·2 per 1,000 population); marriages, 3,397 (8·8); deaths, 1,531 (4·0); divorces, 190 (0·5); natural increase rate, 12·2%.

In Dec. 1993, 19,305 foreigners were legally registered including 12,731 from Hong Kong.

CONSTITUTION AND GOVERNMENT. By agreement with Beijing in 1974, Macao is a Chinese territory under Portuguese administration. An 'organic statute' was published on 17 Feb. 1976. It defined the territory as a collective entity, *pessoa colectiva,* with internal legislative authority which, while remaining subject to Portuguese constitutional laws, would otherwise enjoy administrative, economic and financial autonomy. The Governor is appointed by the Portuguese President, who also appoints up to 7 Under-Secretaries on the Governor's nomination. The Legislative Assembly of 23 deputies, chosen for a 3-year term, comprises 8 members directly elected by universal suffrage, 8 indirectly elected by economic, cultural and social bodies and 7 appointed by the Governor. In April 1990 the Portuguese parliament unanimously approved laws passed by the Legislative Assembly to widen its powers and those of the governor.

At the elections held on 30 Sept. 1992 the electorate was 48,137; turn-out was 55·5%. 50 candidates stood.

Governor: Gen. Vasco Rocha Vieira.

ECONOMY

Budget. In 1992, revenue was 6,785,323,000 patacas and expenditure 6,785,323 patacas.

Currency. The unit of currency is the *pataca* (MOP) of 100 *avos* which is tied to the Hong Kong dollar at parity. There are coins of 10, 20 and 50 avos and 1 and 5 patacas, and notes of 5, 10, 50, 100, 500 and 1,000 patacas. In March 1995, £1 = 12·98 patacas; US$1 = 7·99 patacas.

Banking and Finance. The bank of issue is the Banco Nacional Ultramarino. The Monetary and Foreign Exchange Authority functions as a central bank (*Director,* Antônio dos Santos Ramos). Commercial business is handled (1993) by 20 banks with 112 branches in Macao, 6 of which are local and 14 foreign (including 4 offshore banking units). Total banks' deposits, 1993, 53,232·6m. patacas (including 4,679·7m. patacas in current and 15,198·3m. patacas in savings accounts).

ENERGY AND NATURAL RESOURCES

Electricity. Gross production (1993), 1,073m. kWh.

Fisheries. Total catch (1993) was 1,964 tonnes valued at 30,959,470 patacas.

INDUSTRY. The economy is based on gambling and tourism with a light industrial base of textiles and toy-making. In 1992 the number of firms was 1,914 and output was valued at 14,301,883 patacas. Number of firms (and value of output in 1m. patacas) per sector: textiles, 237 (2,924·40); clothing, 644 (7,316·18); food products, beverages and tobacco, 133 (214·58); paper, paper products, printing and publishing, 137 (306·91); wood and cork, 36 (20·26).

Labour. In 1991, there were 53,536 people declared employed, including 52,427 employed in manufacturing and 1,073 in services. Unemployment was 2·5% in May 1995.

FOREIGN ECONOMIC RELATIONS

Commerce. The trade, mostly transit, is handled by Chinese merchants. Imports, in 1994, were US$2,126·2m.; exports, US$1,866m., of which textiles and garments, US$1,371·6m.

In 1993, 30% of imports came from Hong Kong and 21% from China. 33% of exports went to USA, 33% to EEC (mainly Federal Republic of Germany, France and UK); clothing accounted for 63·1% of exports, textiles for 4·2% and toys 4·2%.

Total trade between Macao and UK (British Department of Trade returns, in £1,000 sterling):

	1991	*1992*	*1993*	*1994*	*1995*
Imports to UK	40,010	36,306	37,141	55,208	55,079
Exports and re-exports from UK	15,329	8,473	12,835	15,591	15,963

Tourism. In 1994 there were 7·8m. visitors, but only 2·2m. spent one night or more.

COMMUNICATIONS

Roads. In 1984 there were 90 km of roads. In 1993 there were 63,745 vehicles, of which 32,580 were passenger cars and 2,148 vans and 3,676 lorries. There were 6,185 traffic accidents.

Shipping. Macao is served by Portuguese, British and Dutch steamship lines. In 1987, 39,239 vessels of 11·5m. gross tons entered the port. In 1987, 4·84m passengers embarked and 4·7m disembarked. Regular services connect Macao with Hong Kong, 65 km to the north-east.

Telecommunications. There were 152,538 telephones in 1993 and 333 telex instruments. One government and a private commercial radio station are in operation on medium-waves broadcasting in Portuguese and Chinese. Number of receivers (1992), 0·25m. Macao receives television broadcasts from Hong Kong and in 1984 a public bilingual TV station began operating. There were (1992) 70,000 receivers (colour by PAL).

Press. In 1993, there were 11 daily newspapers (4 in Portugese and 7 in Chinese) and 16 periodicals (5 in Portuguese and 11 in Chinese).

SOCIAL INSTITUTIONS

Justice. There is a judicial district court, a criminal court and an administrative court with 13 magistrates in all. Appeals lie to the Court of Appeal and then the Supreme Court, both in Lisbon.

In 1993 there were 5,322 cases of crimes known to the police, of which 3,401 were against property. There were 546 prisoners (69 females), and 13 juvenile internees (all male).

Religion. The majority of the Chinese population are Buddhists. About 6% are Roman Catholic.

Education. In 1992–93 there were 108 schools and colleges and 3,536 teachers. Numbers of schools and colleges by category: pre-primary, 16 (7 private); pre-primary and primary, 38 (36); private pre-primary, primary and secondary, 14; primary, 10 (3); primary and secondary, 10 (8); private primary and secondary technical, 2; secondary, 8 (6); secondary and teacher training, 1; secondary and tertiary, 1; private secondary and teacher training, 1; teacher training and tertiary, 1; nurses training, 2 (1); tertiary, 7 (1). Total number of pupils and students was 88,201 (43,031 female), by category: pre-primary, 21,432; primary, 40,037; secondary, 18,634; secondary technical, 827; teacher training, 353; nurses training, 115; tertiary, 6,803. There were 9 special schools with 72 teachers and 211 enrolments. The University of East Asia, established in 1981 on Taipa, had 1,647 students and 155 teachers in 1991–92.

Health. In 1993 there were 2 general hospitals (1 private) and 41 health centres (26 private) with 892 beds. There were 319 doctors, 13 dentists, 720 nurses and 38 pharmacists.

Further Reading

Direcção de Serviços de Estatística e Censos. *Anuário Estatístico/Yearbook of Statistics Macau in Figures*. Macao, Annual.

Edmonds, R. L., *Macau.* [Bibliography] Oxford and Santa Barbara, 1989

Roberts, E. V., *Historical Dictionary of Hong Kong and Macau.* Metuchen (NJ), 1993

QATAR

Dawlat Qatar

(State of Qatar)

Capital: Doha
Population: 539,000 (1994)
GNP per capita: US$14,540 (1994)
HDI/world rank: 0·838/56 (1992)

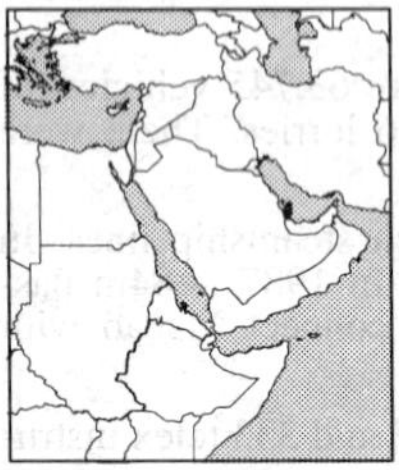

KEY HISTORICAL EVENTS. The State of Qatar declared its independence from Britain on 3 Sept. 1971, ending the Treaty of 3 Nov. 1916 which was replaced by a Treaty of friendship between the 2 countries.

On 27 June 1995 the Heir Apparent, Shaikh Hamad, deposed his father, the Amir Shaikh Khalifa bin Hamad Al-Thani.

TERRITORY AND POPULATION. Qatar is a peninsula running north into the Persian/Arabian Gulf. It is bounded in the south by the United Arab Emirates. The territory includes a number of islands in the coastal waters of the peninsula, the most important of which is Halul, the storage and export terminal for the offshore oilfields. Area, 11,437 sq. km; population census (1986) 369,079; estimate, 1994, 539,000; density 48·9 per sq. km.

Area and estimated population of municipalities, 1993:

Municipality	*Area (in sq. km)*	*Population*	*Municipality*	*Area (in sq. km)*	*Population*
Doha	131·8	339,471	Al Shamal	901·3	5,347
Al Rayyan	889·2	143,046	Al Ghwayriyah	622·3	2,517
Al Wakra	1,114·0	30,976	Al Jumayliyah	2,564·8	8,674
Umm Salal	492·6	16,785	Jarian Al Batnah	3,714·7	2,518
Al Khour	996·3	10,234			

The capital is Doha, which is the main port. Other towns are Dukhan, the centre of oil production, Umm Said, oil-terminal of Qatar, and Ruwais, Wakra, Al-Khour, Umm Salal Mohammad and Umm-Bab.

Vital statistics (1993): Live births, 10,822; deaths, 913; marriages, 1,570; divorces, 432; infant mortality, 138. Life expectancy was 70 years in 1990.

The official language is Arabic.

CLIMATE. The climate is hot and humid. Doha. Jan. 62°F (16·7°C), July 98°F (36·7°C). Annual rainfall 2·5" (62 mm).

RULER. *The Amir:* HH Shaikh Hamad bin Khalifa Al-Thani, KCMG (b. 1950) assumed power after deposing his father on 27 June 1995.

CONSTITUTION AND GOVERNMENT. There is no Parliament, but a *Council of Ministers* is assisted by a 30-member nominated Advisory Council.

After his assumption of power the Amir formed a new government which in Nov. 1995 comprised:

Prime Minister, Minister of Defence and C.-in-C. of the Armed Forces: The Amir.

Deputy Prime Minister, Minister of the Interior: Sheikh Abdullah bin Khalifa Al-Thani. *Finance, Economy and Trade:* Sheikh Mohammed bin Khalifa Al-Thani. *Foreign Affairs:* Sheikh Hamad bin Jassem bin Jabr Al-Thani. *Education:* Abdulaziz Abdullah Turki. *Justice:* Dr Najib Mohamed Al-Nuaimi. *Minister of State for Defence Affairs:* Sheikh Hamad bin Abdullah Al-Thani. *Endowments and Islamic Affairs:* Sheikh Abdullah bin Khalid Al-Thani. *Municipal Affairs and Agriculture:* Sheikh Ahmed bin Hamad Al-Thani. *Labour, Social Affairs and Housing:* Abdulrahman Saad Al-Dirham. *Communications and Transport:* Abdulla bin Saleh Al-Manna. *Public Health:* Ali Said Al-Khayarin. *Information and Culture:* Dr Hamad Abdulaziz Al-Kawari. *Minister of State, Amiri Diwan Affairs:* Sheikh

Hamad bin Suhaim Al-Thani. *Electricity and Water:* Ahmed Mohamed Ali Al-Subai. *Energy and Industry:* Abdulla bin Hamad Al-Attiyah. *Minister of State for Foreign Affairs:* Ahmed Abdullah Al-Mahmoud. *State:* Sheikh Ahmed bin Saif Al-Thani. *Cabinet Affairs:* Sheikh Mohamed bin Khalid Al-Thani.

National flag: Maroon, with white serrated border on hoist.

National anthem: There are no words, and the tune is anonymous.

Local government. Qatar is divided into 9 municipalities.

DEFENCE

Army. The Army consists of 1 Royal Guard regiment, 1 tank and 4 mechanized infantry battalions, 1 special forces company and 1 field artillery regiment. Equipment includes 24 AMX-30 main battle tanks. Personnel (1996) 8,500.

Navy. The navy expected to receive the first 2 of 4 new British-built 380-tonne fast missile craft in 1996 to add to the 3 French-built fast missile craft and 6 British-built inshore patrol craft, 1 tank landing craft and some 30 boats. There are also 4 quadruple shore-based Exocet missile batteries. Personnel in 1995 totalled 1,500 and the base is at Doha.

Air Force. The Air Force has 7 Mirage F1 fighters and 12 Commando and 14 Gazelle helicopters and 6 Alpha Jet armed trainers and Tigercat surface-to-air missile systems. Personnel (1995) 800 with 12 combat aircraft and 20 armed helicopters.

INTERNATIONAL RELATIONS

Membership. Qatar is a member of the UN, the Arab League and the Gulf Co-operation Council.

ECONOMY

Budget. Revenue (1992–93) 12,121m. riyals; expenditure 12,772m. riyals.

Currency. The unit of currency is the *Qatari riyal* (QAR) of 100 *dirhams*, introduced in 1973. There are coins of 1, 5, 10, 25 and 50 dirhams, and banknotes of 1, 5, 10, 50, 100 and 500 riyals. In March 1996, £1 = 5·56; US$1 = 3·64; DM1 = 2·47 riyals.

Banking and Finance. The Qatar Monetary Agency, which functioned as a bank of issue, became the Central Bank in 1995. In 1993 there were 6 domestic and 8 foreign banks with total deposits of 18,870·7m. riyals.

A stock exchange was established in Doha by the Amir's decree in 1995, initially to trade only in Qatari stocks.

Weights and Measures. The metric system is in general use.

ENERGY AND NATURAL RESOURCES

Electricity. Production from main power stations (1993) 5,425·8m. kWh.

Oil. Proven reserves (1986) 3,300m. bbls. Output, 1995, 474,000 bbls. a day.

Gas. The North West Dome oilfield is being developed which contains 12% of the known world gas reserves. Production (1993) 401,700m. cu. ft.

Water Resources. 2 main desalination stations have a daily capacity of 167·6m. gallons of drinkable water. A third station is planned, with a capacity of 40m. gallons a day. Total water production 1993 (well field and distillate) 20,136·1m. gallons.

Agriculture. 10% of the working population is engaged in agriculture. Percentage of total agricultural area under various crops in 1993: Vegetables, 28%; green fodder, 23%; cereals, 22%; palm dates, 20% and fruits, 7%. Government policy aims at ensuring self-sufficiency in agricultural products. In 1993 there were 875 farms. Production (1993) in tons: Cereals, 5,368; dates, 10,723; fruits, 1,038; vegetables, 36,851; meat, 2,595; poultry meat, 3,672; milk and dairy products, 29,917; eggs, 3,303.

Livestock (1993): Cattle, 11,651; camels, 42,906; sheep, 165,500; goats, 142,270; chickens, 3·0m.; horses, 1,273.

Fisheries. The state-owned Qatar National Fishing Company has 3 trawlers and its refrigeration unit processes 10 tonnes of shrimps a day. Fish production (1993) 6,994 tonnes.

INDUSTRY.

1993 output (in 1,000 tonnes): Ammonia, 763·0; urea, 825·0; reinforcing steel bars, 608·6; ethylene, 351·6; polyethylene, 181·5; sulphur, 68·2; flour, 33·0; bran, 11·5; butane, 454·7; propane, 646·1. There is an industrial zone at Umm Said.

Labour. In 1993, 604 manufacturing and mining firms with more than 10 employees employed a total of 36,456 persons.

FOREIGN ECONOMIC RELATIONS

Commerce. In 1993 exports totalled 11,578m. riyals, and imports, 6,882m. riyals. In 1993 Japan provided 16·4% of imports, the UK 10·3%, the USA 11·6% and the Federal Republic of Germany 8%.

Total trade between Qatar and UK (British Department of Trade returns, in £1,000 sterling):

	1991	*1992*	*1993*	*1994*	*1995*
Imports to UK	5,488	10,142	20,464	7,499	14,950
Exports and re-exports from UK	109,248	118,114	143,021	127,575	146,289

Tourism. In 1993 tourists stayed 340,018 nights in hotels.

COMMUNICATIONS

Roads. In 1981 there were about 800 miles of road. In 1993 there were 205,852 registered vehicles including 2,851 motorcycles and 76 fatal accidents with 84 deaths.

Civil Aviation. Gulf Air (owned equally by Qatar, Bahrain, Oman and the UAE. For details *see* BAHRAIN: Civil Aviation), operates daily services from Bahrain. There is also a Qatari airline, Qatar Airways. Services are also provided by Air India, Air Lanka, Alyemda, American Airlines, Balkan, Biman Bangladesh, Egyptair, Emirates, Iran Air, Kuwait Airways, Middle East Airlines, Pakistan Airlines, Royal Jordanian, Saudia, Sudan Airways, Syrian Airlines and Yemenia. In 1993, 704,105 passengers arrived, 702,447 departed and 346,045 were in transit; 12,607 aircraft arrived and departed, 22,873 tons cargo and mail were received and 7,852 tons were dispatched.

Shipping. In 1995, sea-going vessels totalled 0·92m. GRT, including oil tankers, 0·33m. GRT, and container ships, 91,536 GRT. In 1993, 1,383 vessels with a total tonnage of 66,255,841 GRT and 2,697,629 tonnage of cargo was discharged.

Telecommunications. There were 28 post offices in Doha and other towns in 1993. There were 177,130 telephones and 450 telex subscribers in 1992. Broadcasting is the responsibility of the state-run Qatar Broadcasting Service and Qatar Television Service. In 1991 there were 175,000 radios and 160,000 television receivers (colour by PAL).

Cinemas. In 1993 there were 3 cinemas with 281,128 attendance.

Press. In 1993 there were 4 daily, 1 weekly newspaper and 9 magazines.

SOCIAL INSTITUTIONS

Justice. The Judiciary System is administered by the Ministry of Justice which comprises three main departments: Legal affairs, courts of justice and land and real estate register. There are 5 Courts of Justice proclaiming sentences in the name of H. H. the Amir: The Court of Appeal, the Labour Court, the Higher Criminal Court, the Civil Court and the Lower Criminal Court. The death penalty is in force.

All issues related to personal affairs of Moslems under Islamic Law embodied in the Holy Quran and Sunna are decided by Sharia Courts.

Religion. The population is almost entirely Moslem.

Education. There were, in 1992-93, 34,163 pupils at 105 primary schools, 16,150 pupils at 50 preparatory schools, 10,987 pupils at 38 secondary schools and 782 male students at 3 specialist schools. There were 48 Arab and foreign private schools with 27,895 pupils and 1,692 teachers in 1992–93. The University of Qatar had 7,294 students and 881 academic staff in 1993–94.

Students abroad (1993-94) numbered 1,262. In 1992–93, 3,567 men and 2,639 women attended night schools and literacy centres.

Health. There were 3 public hospitals (including 1 for women and 1 for gynaecology and obstetrics) with a total of 1,103 beds in 1993. There were 24 health centres in 1993. In 1993 there were 644 doctors, 71 dentists, 160 pharmacists and 1,718 qualified nurses.

DIPLOMATIC REPRESENTATIVES

Of Qatar in Great Britain (27 Chesham Pl., London, SWIX 8HG)
Ambassador: Ali M. Jaidah.

Of Great Britain in Qatar (POB 3, Doha, Qatar)
Ambassador and Consul-General: P. F. Wogan, CMG.

Of Qatar in the USA (600 New Hampshire Ave., NW, Washington, D.C., 20037)
Ambassador: Abdulrahman bin Saud Al-Thani.

Of the USA in Qatar (Fariq Bin Omran, Doha)
Ambassador: Patrick N. Theros.

Of Qatar to the United Nations
Ambassador: Dr Hassan Ali Hussain Al-Ni'ma.

Further Reading

Central Statistical Organization. *Annual Statistical Abstract.*
Unwin, P. T. H., *Qatar.* [Bibliography] Oxford and Santa Barbara, 1982

National statistical office: Central Statistical Organization, Presidency of the Council of Ministers, Doha.

ROMANIA

România

Capital: Bucharest
Population: 22·76m. (1993)
GNP per capita: US$1,230 (1994)
HDI/world rank: 0·703/98 (1992)

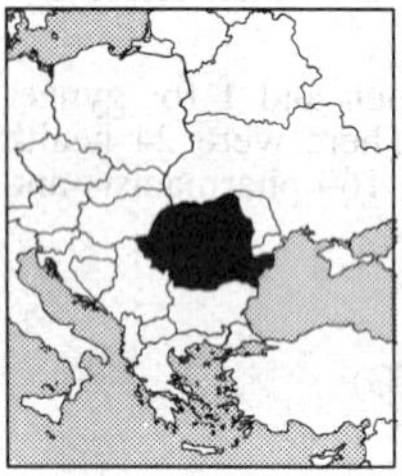

KEY HISTORICAL EVENTS. 1918 is celebrated as the year of foundation of the 'unitary national Romanian state'. For the history of the Communist period, *see* THE STATESMAN'S YEAR-BOOK, 1994–95, p. 1118.

On 26 Dec. 1989 Ion Iliescu, leader of the National Salvation Front, and Petre Român, were sworn in as President and Prime Minister respectively. The Provisional Government was at once recognized by many countries throughout the world, including the UK, USA and USSR.

TERRITORY AND POPULATION. Romania is bounded in the north by the Ukraine, in the east by Moldavia, the Ukraine and the Black Sea, south by Bulgaria, south-west by Yugoslavia and north-west by Hungary. The area is 237,500 sq. km (91,699 sq. miles). Population (1993), 22,755,260 (11,578,870 females; 54·5% urban); density, 95·8 per sq. km.

Vital statistics, 1993: Births, 249,994; deaths, 263,323; stillborn, 1,582; infantile deaths, 5,822; marriages, 161,595; divorces, 31,193. Rates (per 1,000 population): Live births, 11·0; deaths, 11·6; marriages, 7·1; divorces, 1·4; stillborn (per 1,000 live births), 6·3; infant mortality (per 1,000 live births), 22·3. Growth rate, –0·6 per 1,000. Expectation of life in 1991: Males, 66 years; females, 73. Measures designed to raise the birthrate were abolished in 1990, and abortion and contraception legalized. There were 0·62m. abortions in 1992.

Romania is divided into 41 counties (*judeţ*), of which the capital, Bucharest (Bucureşti), is one.

County	*Area in sq. km*	*Population (1993)*	*Capital*	*Population (1993)*
Bucharest	1,820	2,343,824		
Alba	6,231	410,258	Alba Iulia	72,458
Arad	7,652	484,872	Arad	188,609
Argeş	6,801	679,613	Piteşti	182,931
Bacău	6,606	741,119	Bacău	206,995
Bihor	7,535	635,894	Oradea	221,559
Bistriţa-Năsăud	5,305	328,666	Bistriţa	87,071
Botoşani	4,965	463,250	Botoşani	127,337
Braşov	5,351	643,035	Braşov	324,104
Brăila	4,724	392,946	Brăila	236,344
Buzău	6,072	516,298	Buzău	149,032
Caraş-Severin	8,503	372,850	Reşiţa	97,029
Călăraşi	5,074	337,756	Călăraşi	78,540
Cluj	6,650	727,017	Cluj-Napoca	321,850
Constanţa	7,055	745,345	Constanţa	348,985
Covasna	3,705	234,283	Sf. Gheorghe	68,282
Dîmboviţa	4,036	558,894	Tîrgovişte	98,752
Dolj	7,413	759,605	Craiova	303,520
Galaţi	4,425	641,301	Galaţi	324,234
Giurgiu	3,511	307,847	Giurgiu	74,060
Gorj	5,641	395,806	Tîrgu Jiu	96,978
Harghita	6,610	348,488	Miercurea-Ciuc	46,677
Hunedoara	7,016	548,375	Deva	77,737
Ialomiţa	4,449	305,195	Slobozia	56,209
Iaşi	5,469	812,488	Iaşi	337,643
Maramureş	6,215	541,534	Baia Mare	150,018
Mehedinţi	4,900	331,572	Drobeta-Turnu Severin	118,086
Mureş	6,696	608,464	Tîrgu Mureş	165,502
Neamţ	5,890	583,252	Piatra-Neamţ	125,157
Olt	5,507	523,160	Slatina	87,142

County	Area in sq. km	Population (1993)	Capital	Population (1993)
Prahova	4,694	876,329	Ploieşti	254,304
Satu Mare	4,405	400,041	Satu Mare	131,386
Salaj	3,850	265,790	Zalău	69,997
Sibiu	5,422	447,077	Sibiu	168,619
Suceava	8,555	706,409	Suceava	116,232
Teleorman	5,760	480,524	Alexandria	59,728
Timiş	8,692	688,890	Timişoara	325,359
Tulcea	8,430	269,538	Tulcea	97,255
Vaslui	5,297	464,176	Vaslui	79,956
Vâlcea	5,705	438,600	Râmnicu Vâlcea	114,165
Vrancea	4,863	394,879	Focşani	101,414

At the 1992 census the following ethnic minorities numbered over 100,000: Hungarians, 1,624,959 (mainly in Transylvania); Gipsies, 401,087; Germans, 119,462. A *Council of National Minorities* made up of representatives of the government and ethnic groups was set up in 1993.

The official language is Romanian.

CLIMATE. A continental climate with a large annual range of temperature and rainfall showing a slight summer maximum. Bucharest. Jan. 27°F (–2·7°C), July 74°F (23·5°C). Annual rainfall 23·1" (579 mm). Constanţa. Jan. 31°F (–0·6°C), July 71°F (21·7°C). Annual rainfall 15" (371 mm).

CONSTITUTION AND GOVERNMENT. A new Constitution was approved by a referendum on 8 Dec. 1991. Turn-out was 66%, and 77·3% of votes cast were in favour. The Constitution defines Romania as a republic where the rule of law prevails in a social and democratic state. Private property rights and a market economy are guaranteed.

The head of state is the *President*, elected by direct vote for a maximum of 2 4-year terms. He or she may not belong to a political party. The National Assembly consists of a 341-member *Chamber of Deputies* and a 143-member *Senate*; both are elected for 4-year terms from 41 constituencies by modified proportional representation, the number of seats won in each constituency being determined by the proportion of the total vote. There is a 3% threshold for admission to either house.

There is a *Constitutional Court.*

Presidential and parliamentary elections were held in Sept.–Oct. 1992. The electorate was 16,380,663. There were 6 presidential candidates. Turn-out at the first round of the presidential election was 75%, and at the second 73%. Ion Iliescu was elected with 61% of the second round votes. At the parliamentary elections of 27 Sept. turn-out was 76·28%. The Democratic National Salvation Front (since July 1993, Party of Social Democracy of Romania, PSDR) gained 117 seats in the Chamber of Deputies with 27·71% of votes cast, and 49 in the Senate with 28-29%; the Democratic Convention of Romania, 82 with 20·01%, and 34 with 20·16%; the National Salvation Front, 43 with 10·18% and 18 with 10·38%; the Party of Romanian National Unity (PRNU), 30 with 7·71% and 14 with 8·12%; the Hungarian Democratic Federation of Romania, 27 with 7·45% and 12 with 7·58%; the Greater Romania Party, 16 with 3·89% and 6 with 3·85%; the Socialist Labour Party (former Communists), 13 with 3·03% and 5 with 3·18%. The Democratic Agrarian Party won 5 Senate seats only with 3·3% of votes cast. National minority candidates won 13 seats in the Chamber of Deputies only.

President: Ion Iliescu (b. 1930; elected 20 May 1990, re-elected 11 Oct. 1992).

In Nov. 1995 the government consisted of:

Prime Minister, Nicolae Vacaroiu (b. 1943; ind).

Minister of Agriculture and Food: Valeriu Tabara (PRNU). *Communications:* Adrian Turicu (PRNU). *Culture*: Viorel Marginean (ind). *Defence*: Gheorghe Tîncă (ind). *Education:* Liviu Maior (PSDR). *Health*: Iulian Mîncu (PSDR). *Industry:* Dumitru Popescu (PSDR). *Interior*: Ioan Tăracila (ind). *Justice:* Iosif Chiuzbăian (PSDR). *Public Works and Planning*: Marin Cristea (PSDR). *Relations with the National Assembly*: Valeriu Dorneanu (ind). *Research and Technology*: Doru Pălade (ind). *Tourism*: Matei Agaton Dan (PSDR). *Trade*: Petru Crişan (PSDR). *Transport*: Aurel Novac (ind). *Water, Forests and Environment Protection*: Aurel Constantin Ilie (ind). *Youth and Sport*: Alexandru Mironov (PSDR). *Ministers of State (Chair, Council for Economic Co-ordination)*, Mîrcea Cosea (ind); *(Finance)*, Florin Georgescu (ind); *(Foreign Affairs)*, Teodor Melescănu (ind); *(Labour and Social Welfare)*, Dan Mircea Popescu (PSDR).

The *Speaker* is Adrian Năstase.

National flag: Three vertical strips of blue, yellow and red.

National anthem: 'Deşteaptăte, Române, din somnul cel de moarte' ('Wake up, Romanians, from your deadly slumber'); words by A. Mureşianu, tune by A. Pann.

Local government. This is carried out at the administrative levels of 260 towns (of which 56 are municipalities) and 2,688 wards (*comuna*). Elections were held in Feb. 1992; the NSF gained 33% of votes cast.

DEFENCE. Military service is compulsory for 12 months in the Army and Air Force and 18 months in the Navy.

Army. The 4 Army Areas consist of 2 tank and 8 motor rifle divisions; 4 mountain, 2 artillery, 3 anti-aircraft and 2 surface-to-surface missile brigades; and 4 artillery, 3 anti-tank and 4 airborne regiments. Equipment includes 146 T-34, 822 T-55, 30 T-72, 620 TR-85 and 225 TR-580 main battle tanks. Strength (1996) 128,800 (84,700 conscripts), and 400,000 reservists. The Ministry of the Interior operates a paramilitary Frontier Guard (22,300 strong), a Gendarmerie (10,000) and a Security Guard (46,800).

Navy. The fleet comprises 1 ex-Soviet diesel submarine, 1 Romanian-built missile-armed destroyer with a hangar for 2 helicopters, 5 frigates, 3 missile-armed corvettes, 6 fast missile craft, 32 fast torpedo craft, 4 offshore, and 8 inshore patrol vessels, 2 minelayer/mine countermeasure support ships and 32 small minesweepers. The Danube flotilla counts 4 river monitors (100 mm guns) and some 20 river patrol craft. Auxiliaries include 2 logistic ships, 3 small tankers, 2 oceanographic ships, 1 training ship and 2 tugs.

A force of naval infantry some 8,000 strong in 1995 is equipped with 170 tanks and some 150 artillery pieces, but lacks amphibious transport.

There is a coastal defence force numbering 1,000 (1995) organized into 4 main batteries of artillery with 32 130 mm guns and 10 anti-aircraft batteries.

Headquarters of the Navy is at Mangalia with the main base at Constanţa, and of the Danube flotilla at Brăila. Personnel in 1995 totalled 19,000 (10,000 conscripts).

Air Force. The Air Force numbered some 54,000 (10,000 conscripts), with 300 combat aircraft and 80 armed helicopters in 1995. These were organized into 12 interceptor squadrons with MiG-21, MiG-23 and MiG-29 fighters, 3 ground-attack and close-support squadrons with IAR-93 fighter-bombers, and 1 reconnaissance squadron of L-39s. There were also more than 150 training aircraft, 28 An-24/26/30 transports and more than 150 helicopters (Mi-8, Alouette and Puma). 'Guideline' and 'Gainful' surface-to-air missiles were operational, and short-range surface-to-surface missiles have been displayed.

INTERNATIONAL RELATIONS

Membership. Romania is a member of the UN, the Council of Europe, the NATO Partnership for Peace and is an Associate Partner of the WEU.

ECONOMY

Policy. There is a Council for Economic Co-ordination, chaired by a minister of state.

A privatization law of Aug. 1991 transferred state property except utilities into commercial companies held in 5 private ownership funds. These held 30% of the enterprises' capital and were reserved for Romanians, who received a free saleable certificate of ownership. 70% was held in a state ownership fund for foreign investors. It was expected to privatize some 10% of enterprises annually, but only 2 enterprises had been sold by early 1993. A second phase of privatization was initiated in Nov. 1994 by offerings of up to 20% in state firms to employees and subsequently 30% to the public purchasable by privatization vouchers. By 1995 some 4,000 of the 6,200 state companies were offered for privatization, but only 18% of these had been sold. Legislation of June 1995 offers 60% of shares in state companies to Romanian citizens in exchange for privatization coupons, and 40% to foreign investors.

Legislation of Nov. 1995 compensates former owners of 0·2m. nationalized properties. Compensation is limited to the ownership of 1 home if lived in or 50m. lei.

Budget. Revenue and expenditure (in 1m. lei) for calendar years:

	1988	*1989*	*1990*	*1991*	*1992*	*1993*
Revenue	330,968	348,421	307,066	496,779	1,363,884	3,792,352
Expenditure	286,686	288,426	310,863	537,875	1,626,908	4,128,779

In 1993 sources of revenue (in 1m. lei) included: Fiscal revenues, 3,654,410; profits tax, 750,339; tax on wages, 324,924; tax on commodity circulation, 743,905; customs duties, 269,321; non-fiscal revenues, 132,909; capital revenue, 5,033. Expenditure: Socio-cultural, 264,704; education, 605,562; health, 365,123; arts, 21,931; social assistance, 6,957; child benefit, 160,920; pensions, 92,053; defence, 419,578; public order, 219,840; state power, 173,436; economy, 1,507,755.

VAT was introduced in July 1993.

A stock exchange re-opened in Bucharest in 1995.

Currency. The monetary unit is the *leu*, pl.*lei* (ROL) notionally of 100 *bani*. There are coins of 1, 3, 5, 10, 25, 50 and 100, and notes of 100, 200, 500, 1,000, 5,000 and 10,000 lei. Annualized inflation was 33% in 1995 (62% in 1994; 300% in 1993). In March 1996, £1 = 4,394 lei; US$1 = 2,875 lei; DM1 = 1,948 lei.

Banking and Finance. The National Bank of Romania (founded 1880, nationalized 1946; *governor*, Mugur Isarescu) is the central bank and bank of issue under the Minister of Finance. It manages monetary policy. In 1991 there were 8 commercial banks and a savings bank. Total assets, 1993, 9,843,462m. lei. Savings were 617,692m. lei in 1993.

Weights and Measures. The Gregorian calendar was adopted in 1919. The metric system is in use.

ENERGY AND NATURAL RESOURCES

Electricity. Installed electric power 1993: 22,262,000 kW.; output, 1993, 55,476m. kWh (12,768m. kWh hydroelectric). A nuclear power plant is under construction at Cernăvoda.

Oil. Oil production in 1993 was 6·7m. tonnes. Oil reserves are expected to be exhausted by the mid-1990s.

Minerals. The principal minerals are oil and natural gas, salt, brown coal, lignite, iron and copper ores, bauxite, chromium, manganese and uranium. Output, 1993 (in 1,000 tonnes): Iron ore, 855; coal, 5,757; lignite, 36,083; methane gas (cu. metres, 1991), 17,252m.

Agriculture. There were 14,793,000 ha of agricultural land in 1993, including (in 1,000 ha): Arable, 9,342; meadows, 1,489; pasture, 3,363; vineyards, 2,304 and orchards and nurseries, 296. There were 3,202,800 ha of irrigated land.

Production in 1993 (in 1,000 tonnes): Wheat and rye, 5,355; barley, 1,553; oats, 554; maize, 7,988; potatoes, 3,709; sunflower seeds, 696; sugar-beet, 1,776.

Livestock, 1994 (in 1,000): Cattle, 3,597 (including milch cows, 1,979), pigs, 9,262; sheep, 11,499; goats, 776; horses, 751; poultry, 76,532. There were 158,126 tractors in 1993.

A law of Feb. 1991 provided for the restitution of collectivized land to its former owners or their heirs up to a limit of 10 ha. Land may be resold, but there is a limit of 100 ha on total holdings. Landless peasants received a distribution from the residue. State farms remain nationalized; peasants receive shares in their equity worth up to 10 ha. Collective farms may become private co-operative associations.

Forestry. Total forest area was 6·37m. ha in 1993 including 1·92m. ha coniferous, 1·9m. ha beech and 1·14m. ha oak. 10,346 ha were afforested in 1993.

INDUSTRY. In 1993 there were 23,858 industrial enterprises, of which 2,514 were state-controlled, 397 local government-controlled and 638 co-operatives. 54 enterprises employed more than 5,000 persons; 21,218 fewer than 100.

Output of main products in 1993 (in tonnes): Pig-iron, 3,189; steel, 5,446; steel tubes, 414; rolled steel, 4,092; chemical fertilizers, 1,307; sulphuric acid, 527; caustic soda, 330; paper, 285; cement, 6,240; sugar, 185; edible oils, 231; plastics, 259; chemical fibres, 101. In 1,000 units: Tractors, 26; TV sets, 431; washing machines, 166.

Labour. The employed population in 1993 was 10·1m., of whom 3·5m. worked in agriculture and 3·6m. in industry and building. In 1993 42% of the total workforce, and 58% of the industrial workforce, were women. A 5-day working week was introduced in Dec. 1989. Men retire at 62, women at 57. A law of Jan. 1991 defines unemployment, stipulates the conditions for receiving unemployment benefit, lays down rules for calculating amounts paid, establishes an unemployment fund and provides for retraining unemployed persons. Workers laid off receive 50–60% of their last wages for 180 days. A minimum monthly wage was set in 1993; it was 45,000 lei in 1994. The average monthly wage was 57,000 lei in 1993. There were 1,287,000 registered unemployed in April 1994.

Trade Unions. In June 1993 the National Confederation of Free Trade Unions (CNSLR; 1,421,790 members in 1991), which derived from the former official trade union organization, Frația (164,629 members in 1991) and Univers merged to form CNSLR-Frația, with 65 branch federations and 3·7m. members. The other major confederations in 1994 were Alfa Cartel (450,162 members in 1991) and the National Trade Union Bloc.

FOREIGN ECONOMIC RELATIONS. Foreign debt was US$3,500m. in May 1994. In Nov. 1993 the USA granted most-favoured-nation status.

Foreign investors may establish joint ventures or 100%-owned domestic companies in all but a few strategic industries. After an initial 2-year exemption, profits are taxed at 30%, dividends at 10%. Foreign investors register with the Romanian Development Agency. In May 1993 there were 25,484 joint ventures. The constitution of Nov. 1991 prohibits foreigners from owning real estate.

Commerce. In 1993 exports totalled 3,775,942m. lei (official rate) and imports 4,696,012m. lei.

Principal exports in 1990 were (in 1,000 tonnes): Petroleum products, 5,120; cement, 2,482; oilfield equipment, 4,882m. lei; equipment for chemical factories, 1,453m. lei; shipbuilding, 1,100m. lei. Principal imports (in 1,000 tonnes): Iron ore, 11,357; industrial coke, 1,106; rolled ferrous metals, 511; motor cars, 3,128.

In 1993 Romania's main export markets (trade in 1m. lei) were: Germany, 543,025; China, 307,306; Italy, 312,688; France, 168,782; Netherlands, 146,256; UK, 136,487. Main import suppliers: Germany, 806,444; Iran, 500,583; Italy, 473,200; Austria, 127,846; Egypt, 66,913.

Total trade between Romania and UK (British Department of Trade returns, in £1,000 sterling):

	1991	*1992*	*1993*	*1994*	*1995*
Imports to UK	58,531	62,814	93,289	146,375	173,844
Exports and re-exports from UK	58,735	64,388	93,843	127,059	176,770

Tourism. In 1993 10·76m. Romanians travelled abroad and 5·79m. foreign nationals visited Romania.

COMMUNICATIONS

Roads. There were in 1993, 72,816 km of roads of which 14,683 km were main roads, 12,995 km of these modernized. Freight carried, 707·5m. tonnes; passengers, 506m.

Railways. Length of standard-gauge route in 1994 was 10,887 km, of which 3,866 km were electrified; there were 427 km of narrow-gauge lines and 60 km of 1,524 mm gauge. Freight carried in 1994, 99·2m. tonnes; passengers, 206·9m. There is a metro (57 km) and tram/light rail network (353 km) in Bucharest, and tramways in 13 other cities.

Civil Aviation. Tarom (*Transporturi Aeriene Române*), the state-owned airline, operated 2 A310-300s, 1 B-707-320C, 5 B-737-300s, 26 ex-Soviet and 10 other aircraft in 1995. It also provided internal services and services to Amsterdam, Athens, Beijing, Beirut, Belgrade, Berlin, Brussels, Budapest, Cairo, Cologne, Copenhagen, Düsseldorf, Frankfurt, Istanbul, London, Moscow, Paris, Prague, Rome, Sofia, Tel Aviv, Vienna, Warsaw and Zürich. Services are also provided by Aeroflot, Air France, Alitalia, Austrian Airlines, Balkan, British Airways, Czech Airlines, Delta, El Al, Hemus Air, Iberia, JAT, KLM, Lufthansa, Malév, Royal Jordanian, Swissair, Syrian Airlines and Turkish Airlines.

Bucharest's airports are at Băneasa (internal flights) and Otopeni (international flights). Air transport in 1993 carried 1·7m. passengers and 35,000 tonnes of freight. In 1992 Tarom operated 4 B-707-320s and 86 other aircraft (68 Soviet).

Shipping. In 1995 the merchant marine comprised 297 vessels totalling 4·81m. DWT, of which 30 (20·78% of tonnage) were registered under foreign flags. Total GRT was 2·69m., including oil tankers, 0·44m. GRT, and container ships, 15,160 GRT. The main ports are Constanţa and Agigea on the Black Sea and Galaţi and Brăila on the Danube. In 1993 sea-going transport carried 6·91m. tonnes of freight; river transport, 7·1m. tonnes and 0·87m. passengers.

Telecommunications. There were 10,811 post offices in 1993. Number of telephone subscribers, 1993, 2,633,000. A law of June 1994 puts broadcasting under parliamentary control through the supervision of the National Audiovisual Council. *Radio-televiziunea Românа* broadcasts 3 radio programmes on medium-waves and FM. In March 1995, 436 cable TV stations, 66 local TV stations and 135 local radio stations were registered. There is also radio and TV transmission in Hungarian and German. There are 2 independent TV channels. Radio licences, 1993, 2·05m.; TV (colour by PAL), 3·49m.

Cinemas. There were, in 1993, 1,470 cinemas, of which 408 were for standard-sized films. These latter had 168,258 seats; admissions were 30·85m. 17 full-length films were made in 1993 (4 in 1990).

Press. The 1991 constitution abolished censorship. There were, in 1993, 100 daily papers and 987 periodicals, including 10 dailies and 96 periodicals in minority languages. 6,130 book titles were published in 1993 in 75·9m. copies (208 titles in minority languages).

SOCIAL INSTITUTIONS

Justice. Justice is administered by the Supreme Court, the 41 county courts, 81 courts of first instance and 15 courts of appeal. Lay assessors (elected for 4 years) participate in most court trials, collaborating with the judges. In 1993 there were 2,210 judges. The *Procurator-General* exercises 'supreme supervisory power to ensure the observance of the law' by all authorities, central and local, and all citizens. The Procurator's Office and its organs are independent of any organs of justice or administration, and only responsible to the Grand National Assembly (which appoints the Procurator-General for 4 years) and between its sessions, to the State Council. The Ministry of the Interior is responsible for ordinary police work. State security is the responsibility of the State Security Council. The death penalty was abolished in Jan. 1990 and is forbidden by the 1991 constitution. In 1991 criminal sentences were awarded to 83,247 persons (8,957 females, 6,940 juveniles) and 27,252 persons were imprisoned.

Religion. The State Secretariat for Religious Denominations oversees religious affairs. Churches' expenses and salaries are paid by the State. There are 14 Churches, the largest being the Romanian Orthodox Church. It is autocephalous, but retains dogmatic unity with the Eastern Orthodox Church. It is organized into 12 dioceses grouped into 5 metropolitan bishoprics and headed by Patriarch Teoctist Arapașu. There are some 11,800 churches, 2 theological colleges and 6 'schools of cantors', as well as seminaries.

The Uniate (Greek Catholic) Church (which severed its connexion with the Vatican in 1698) was suppressed in 1948 but in 1990 was re-legalized. Property seized by the state in 1948 was restored to it, but not property which had passed to the Orthodox Church.

Religious affiliation at the 1992 census: Romanian Orthodox, 19,762,135; Roman Catholic, 1,144,820; Protestant, 801,577; Uniate, 228,377; Pentecostal, 220,051; Baptist, 109,677; Seventh Day Adventist, 78,658; Unitarian, 76,333; Moslem, 55,988.

Education. Education is free and compulsory from 6 to 16, consisting of 8 years of primary school and 2 years of secondary (gymnasium). Further secondary education is available at *lycées*, professional schools or advanced technical schools.

In 1993–94 there were 12,715 kindergartens with 37,303 teachers and 712,136 children; 13,945 primary and secondary schools with 164,780 teachers and 2,533,491 pupils; 1,277 *lycées* with 59,488 teachers and 722,421 pupils; 739 professional schools with 6,222 teachers and 300,413 pupils; and 636 advanced technical institutes with 1,698 teachers and 50,707 students. In 1993–94 primary and secondary education in Hungarian was given to 155,955 pupils by 11,220 teachers and in German to 12,084 pupils by 693 teachers.

In 1994–95 there were 19 universities, 16 specialized universities (agriculture, 4; medicine and pharmacy, 5; petroleum and gas, 1; technical, 6), a polytechnic institute, a merchant navy institute, a school of political and administrative studies and 9 specialized academies (architecture; dramatic art; economics; fine arts; 2 music; physical education and sport; theatre and film; visual arts).

Health. In 1991 there were 215,629 hospital beds and in 1993 46,591 doctors (including 6,326 dentists).

Social Security. In 1993 pensioners comprised 3·85m. old age and retirement, 304,000 disability, 567,000 successor allowance, 62,000 war invalidity and dependents, 22,000 social assistance, 985,400 retired collective farmers and 22,000 retired private farmers. These drew average monthly pensions ranging from 3,834 to 33,587 lei.

DIPLOMATIC REPRESENTATIVES

Of Romania in Great Britain (4 Palace Green, London, W8 4QD)
Ambassador: Sergiu Celac.

Of Great Britain in Romania (24 Strada Jules Michelet, Bucharest)
Ambassador: Christopher Crabbe, CMG.

Of Romania in the USA (1607 23rd St., NW, Washington, D.C., 20008)
Ambassador: Vacant.

Of the USA in Romania (7–9 Strada Tudor Arghezi, Bucharest)
Ambassador: Alfred H. Moses.

Of Romania to the United Nations
Ambassador: Ion Gorița.

Further Reading

Comisia Națională pentru Statistică. *Anuarul Statistic al României/Romanian Statistical Yearbook.* Bucharest, annual.—*Revista de Statistică.* Monthly

Deletant, A. and D., *Romania* [Bibliography]. Oxford and Santa Barbara (CA), 1985
Gallagher, T., *Romania after Ceauşescu; the Politics of Intolerance.* Edinburgh Univ. Press, 1995
Gilberg, T., *Nationalism and Communism in Romania: the Rise and Fall of Ceauşescu's Personal Dictatorship.* Oxford, 1990
Rady, M., *Romania in Turmoil: a Contemporary History.* London, 1992
Ratesh, N., *Romania: the Entangled Revolution.* New York, 1991

National statistical office: Comisia Naţională pentru Statistică, Bucharest

RUSSIA

Rossiiskaya Federatsiya

Capital: Moscow
Population: 148·4m. (1994)
GNP per capita: US$2,650 (1994)
HDI/world rank: 0·849/52 (1992)

KEY HISTORICAL EVENTS. After the dissolution of the USSR in Dec. 1991, Russia became one of the founding members of the Commonwealth of Independent States. Boris Yeltsin was elected President in June 1991. A period of confrontation in 1992–93 between President Yeltsin and parliament culminated on 21 Sept. in a presidential decree on 'gradual constitutional reform' which suspended the operations of parliament, called new parliamentary elections for Dec. and assumed emergency executive powers. Parliament and the Constitutional Court rejected this action, and parliament proclaimed Vice-President Rutskoi acting president. The USA, the EC and other countries expressed support for President Yeltsin, as did the Ukraine and Belarus. Many deputies refused to leave the parliament building and mounted an armed guard which was cordoned off by pro-Yeltsin forces. Public demonstrations and counter-demonstrations began on 26 Sept. After a week in which deputies remained in the parliament building, some thousands of armed anti-Yeltsin demonstrators assembled on 3 Oct. and were urged to seize the Kremlin and television centre. Shots were fired and there were fatal casualties. On 4 Oct. troops took the parliament building by storm after a 10-hour assault in which 140 people died. Vice-President Rutskoi and Speaker Khasbulatov were stripped of their offices and arrested.

In Feb. 1994 parliament amnestied not only those arrested after the occupation of the parliament building in Sept.–Oct. 1993, but also the instigators of the failed coup against the Soviet government in Aug. 1991.

TERRITORY AND POPULATION. Russia occupies 17,075,400 sq. km from the Far North to the Black Sea in the south and from the Far East to the exclave of Kaliningrad in the west. Its 1989 census population was 147,021,869 (53·3% female, 73·6% urban), of whom 81·5% were Russians, 3·8% Tatars, 3% Ukrainians, 1·2% Chuvash, 0·9% Bashkir, 0·8% Belorussians, and 0·7% Mordovians. Chechens, Germans, Udmurts, Mari, Kazakhs, Avars, Jews and Armenians all numbered 0·5m. or more. Population estimate, 1994, 148·4m. (female, 53%; urban, 73%).

Vital statistics rates, 1993 (per 1,000 population): Birth, 9·4; death, 14·5; marriage, 7·5; divorce, 4·5; natural increase, –5·1; infant mortality (per 1,000 live births), 19·9. There were 3·5m. induced abortions in 1992. Life expectancy: Males, 59 years; females, 72.

There were 0·9m. immigrants in 1993, mainly from the former Soviet republics, and 0·5m. emigrants. In Jan. 1994 there were 447,933 refugees, mostly from Tajikistan, Georgia, Azerbaijan, Chechernia and Ingushetia.

The 2 principal cities are Moscow, the capital, with a population (Jan. 1994) of 8,793,000 and St Petersburg (formerly Leningrad), 4,883,000. In 1994 the following cities had populations over 200,000:

	Population (in 1,000)		*Population (in 1,000)*		*Population (in 1,000)*
Nizhni Novgorod	1,425	Samara	1,223	Kazan	1,092
Novosibirsk	1,418	Omsk	1,161	Ufa	1,092
Yekaterinburg	1,347	Chelyabinsk	1,125	Perm	1,086

	Population (in 1,000)		Population (in 1,000)		Population (in 1,000)
Rostov-on-Don	1,023	Bryansk	460	Taganrog	291
Volgograd	1,000	Tver	454	Dzerzhinsk	286
Krasnoyarsk	914	Cheboksary	446	Volzhsky	286
Voronezh	905	Murmansk	444	Kostroma	283
Saratov	899	Magnitogorsk	439	Petrozavodsk	279
Togliatti	689	Kursk	439	Orsk	274
Simbirsk	670	Nizhni Tagil	429	Angarsk	267
Izhevsk	653	Kaliningrad	415	Prokopevsk	266
Krasnodar	638	Arkhangelsk	407	Surgut	259
Vladivostok	637	Chita	367	Bratsk	258
Irkutsk	632	Ulan-Ude	365	Petropavlovsk-Kamchatsky	256
Yaroslavl	631	Grozny	364[1]		
Khabarovsk	609	Kurgan	362	Sterlitamak	256
Barnaul	596	Smolensk	353	Rybinsk	249
Novokuznetsk	593	Sochi	353	Yoshkar-Ola	248
Orenburg	558	Orel	346	Severodvinsk	243
Penza	551	Kaluga	345	Nizhnevartovsk	241
Tula	535	Vladimir	338	Nalchik	239
Ryazan	526	Stavropol	337	Biysk	233
Naberezhnye Chelny	524	Makhachkala	327	Novgorod	233
		Saransk	320	Shakhty	229
Kemerovo	513	Cherepovets	319	Syktyvkar	227
Astrakhan	512	Belgorod	318	Blagoveshchensk	214
Tomsk	496	Tambov	313	Kamensk-Uralsky	207
Tyumen	491	Komsomolsk-on-Amur	311	Pskov	207
Kirov	491			Zlatoust	206
Ivanovo	476	Vladikavkaz	311	Balakovo	206
Lipetsk	470	Vologda	296	Podolsk	204

[1] 1993

The Russian Federation consists of:

(1) *21 Republics:* Adygeya, Altai, Bashkortostan, Buryatia, Chechenia [1], Chuvashia, Dagestan, Ingushetia, Kabardino-Balkaria, Kalmykia, Karachai-Cherkessia, Karelia, Khakassia, Komi, Mari El, Mordovia, North Ossetia (Alania), Sakha, Tatarstan, Tuva, Udmurtia.

(2) *6 Territories (krai):* Altai, Khabarovsk, Krasnodar, Krasnoyarsk, Primorye, Stavropol.

(3) *49 Provinces (oblast):* Amur, Arkhangel, Astrakhan, Belgorod, Bryansk, Chelyabinsk, Chita, Irkutsk, Ivanovo, Kaluga, Kaliningrad, Kamchatka, Kemerovo, Kirov, Kostroma, Kurgan, Kursk, Lipetsk, Magadan, Moscow, Murmansk, Nizhni Novgorod, Novgorod, Novosibirsk, Omsk, Orel, Orenburg, Penza, Perm, Pskov, Rostov, Ryazan, St Petersburg, Sakhalin, Samara, Saratov, Smolensk, Sverdlovsk,Tambov, Tomsk, Tula, Tver, Tyumen, Ulyanovsk, Vladimir, Volgograd, Vologda, Voronezh, Yaroslavl.

(4) *10 Autonomous Areas (avtonomny okrug):* Agin-Buryat, Chukot, Evenki, Khanty-Mansi, Komi-Permyak, Koryak, Nenets, Taimyr (Dolgano-Nenets), Ust-Ordyn-Buryat, Yamalo-Nenets.

(5) *2 Cities of federal status:* Moscow, St Petersburg.

(6) The Jewish Autonomous Region (Birobijan).

[1] Since 1995 Chechenia has been in armed rebellion against Russia.

CLIMATE. Moscow. Jan. –9·4°C, July 18·3°C. Annual rainfall 630 mm. Arkhangelsk. Jan. –15°C, July 13·9°C. Annual rainfall 503 mm. St. Petersburg. Jan. –8·3°C, July 17·8°C. Annual rainfall 488 mm. Vladivostok. Jan. –14·4°C, July 18·3°C. Annual rainfall 599 mm.

CONSTITUTION AND GOVERNMENT. The Russian Soviet Federative Socialist Republic (RSFSR) adopted a constitution in April 1978. In June 1990, pending the promulgation of a new constitution, it adopted a declaration of republican sovereignty by 544 votes to 271. It became a founding member of the CIS in Dec. 1991, and adopted the name 'Russian Federation'.

A law of Nov. 1991 extended citizenship to all who lived in Russia at the time of its adoption and to those in other Soviet republics who requested it.

There is a 19-member *Constitutional Court*, whose functions under the 1993 Constitution include making decisions on the constitutionality of federal laws, presidential and government decrees, and the constitutions and laws of the subjects of the Federation. It is governed by a Law on the Constitutional Court, adopted in July 1994. Judges are elected for non-renewable 12-year terms.

At a referendum on 25 April 1993 the electorate was 107·3m.; turn-out was 69·2m. 4 questions were put: Confidence in President Yeltsin (58·7% of votes cast); approval of economic reforms (53% of votes cast); early presidential elections (31·7% of the electorate); early parliamentary elections (43·1% of the electorate).

Voting was held on 12 Dec. 1993 on the adoption of a new constitution and the election of a new parliament for a 2-year term. The electorate was 106,170,335. The reported turn-out was 54·8%. The constitution was approved by 58·4% of votes cast, and came into effect on 24 Dec. 1993.

According to the 1993 Constitution the Russian Federation is a 'democratic federal legally-based state with a republican form of government'. The state is a secular one, and religious organizations are independent of state control. Individuals have freedom of movement within or across the boundaries of the Federation; there is freedom of assembly and association, and freedom to engage in any entrepreneurial activity not forbidden by law. Censorship as such is forbidden. All citizens have a right to housing, to free medical care, and to a free education. The state itself is based upon a separation of powers and upon federal principles, including a Constitutional Court. The most important matters of state are reserved for the federal government, including socio-economic policy, the budget, taxation, energy, foreign affairs and defence. Other matters, including the use of land and water, education and culture, health and social security, are for the joint management of the federal and local governments, which also have the right to legislate within their spheres of competence. A central role is accorded to the *President*, who defines the 'basic directions of domestic and foreign policy' and represents the state internationally. The President is directly elected for a 4-year term, and for not more than 2 consecutive terms; he or she must be at least 35 years old, a Russian citizen, and a resident in Russia for at least the previous 10 years. 1m. signatures are needed to validate a presidential candidate, no more than 7% of which may come from any one region. The President has the right to appoint the prime minister, and (on his nomination) to appoint and dismiss deputy prime ministers and ministers, and may dismiss the government as a whole. In the event of the death or incapacity of the President, the Prime Minister becomes head of state.

Boris Yeltsin became President for a 5-year term at the elections of 12 June 1991, gaining 57·3% of the votes cast against 5 opponents. Turn-out was 74%. Aleksandr Rutskoi became Vice-President at the same time.

Parliament is known as the *Federal Assembly*. The 'representative and legislative organ of the Russian Federation', it consists of 2 chambers: the *Council of the Federation* and the *State Duma*. The Council of the Federation, or upper house, consists of 178 deputies, 2 from each of the 89 subjects of the Federation. The State Duma, or lower house, consists of 450 deputies chosen for a 4-year term. 225 of these are elected from single-member constituencies on the first-past-the-post system, the remainder from party lists by proportional representation. To qualify for candidacy an individual must obtain signatures from at least 1% of voters in the constituency; a party or electoral alliance must obtain a minimum of 100,000 supporting signatures from at least 7 regions, but not more than 15% from any one region. There is a 5% threshold for the party-list seats. Parties which gain at least 35 seats may register as a faction, which gives them the right to join the Duma Council and chair committees. Any citizen aged over 21 may be elected to the State Duma, but may not at the same time be a member of the upper house or of other representative bodies, and all deputies work on a 'permanent professional basis'. Both houses elect a chair, committees and commissions. The Council of the Federation considers all matters that apply to the Federation as a whole, including state boundaries, martial law, and the deployment of Russian forces elsewhere. The Duma approves nominations for prime minister, and adopts federal laws (they are also considered by the Council of the Federation, but any objection may be overridden by a two-thirds majority; objections on the part of the President may be overridden by both houses on the same basis). The Duma for its part can reject nominations for prime minister, but after the third such rejection it is automatically dissolved. It is also dissolved if it twice votes a lack of confidence in the government as a whole, or if it refuses to express confidence in the government when the matter is raised by the prime minister.

Elections for the State Duma were held on 17 Dec. 1995. The electorate was 105m.; turn out was 72·66% 2,687 candidates stood representing 43 parties or groups. 4 parties exceeded the 5% threshold for party-list seats: Communist Party, 99 seats; Liberal Democratic Party (of Vladimir Zhirinovsky), 50; Our Home is Russia, 45; Yabloko, 31. Total seats gained: Communist Party, 157 with 22·3% of votes cast (48 with 12·4% in 1993); Our Home is Russia, 55 with 10·13%; Liberal Democratic Party, 51 with 11·18% (64 with 22·92% in 1993); Yabloko, 45 with 6·89% (23 with 7·86% in 1993); Agrarian Party , 20 with 3·78% (33 wtih 7·99% in 1993); Power to the People, 9 with 1·61%, Russia's Democratic Choice, 9 with 3·86% (70 with 15·51% in 1993); Congress of Russian Communities, 5 with 4·31%; Women of Russia, 3 with 4·61% (23 with 8·13% in 1993); Forward Russia, 3 with 1·94%; Ivan Rybkin's Bloc, 3 with 1·11%; Pamfilova-Gurev-Lysenko, 2 with 1·6%. 77 seats went to independents (141 in 1993) and 11 to minor parties. The Communist Party delegated some seats to the Agrarian Party to enable it to register as a faction. Registered factions (with seats held) in Jan. 1996: Communist Party (149), Our Home is Russia (55), Liberal Democratic Party (51), Yabloko (46), Russian Regions (42), Power to the People (37), Agrarian Party (35).

President: Boris Yeltsin (b. 1931; sworn in 10 July 1991).

Head of the Presidential Administration: Sergei Filatov.

The members of the government in Jan. 1996 were:

Prime Minister: Viktor Chernomyrdin (b. 1938).

First Deputy Prime Minister for the Economy and Finance: Vladimir Kadannikov. *First Deputy Prime Minister:* Oleg Soskovets. *Deputy Prime Minister for Foreign Economic Relations:* Oleg Davydov. *Deputy Prime Minister for Agriculture:* Viktor Zaveryukha. *Deputy Prime Minister for Social Policy:* Yuri Yarov. *Deputy Prime Minister for Relations with CIS:* Aleksei Bolshakov. *Minister for Nationalities and Regional Policy:* Vyacheslav Mikhailov. *Minister for the Economy:* Yevgeni Yasin. *Justice:* Vacant. *Communications:* Vladimir Bulgak. *Culture:* Yevgeni Sidorov. *Health:* Eduard Nechaev. *Environment and Natural Resources:* Viktor Danilov-Danilyan. *Education:* Yevgeni Tkachenko. *Internal Affairs:* Gen. Anatoli Kulikov. *Defence:* Gen. Pavel Grachev. *Finance:* Vladimir Panskov. *Foreign Affairs:* Yevgeni Primakov. *Agriculture:* Viktor Khlystun. *Fuel and Energy:* Yuri Shafranik. *Labour:* Gennadi Melikyan. *Nuclear Power:* Viktor Mikhailov. *Railways:* Gennadi Fadeev. *Civil Defence:* Maj.-Gen. Sergei Shoigu. *Chair, State Committee on the Press:* Sergei Gryzunov. *Science:* Boris Saltykov. *Transport:* Nikolai Tsakh.

Speaker, Council of the Federation: Vladimir Shumeiko; *Speaker, State Duma:* Gennadi Selezne.

National flag: 3 horizontal stripes of white, blue and red.

National anthem: No words, tune from an opera by M. Glinka.

Local Government: There are 1,852 regions (*rayon*), 1,059 towns, 339 urban districts, 2,066 urban settlements and 23,976 rural settlements.

A presidential decree of Oct. 1993 established a new regime for local authorities. Their membership is limited to 50. Regulations passed are subject to the approval of the presidentially-appointed heads of the authorities.

DEFENCE. The President of the Republic is C.-in-C. of the armed forces. Conscription was raised from 18 months to 2 years in April 1995.

Army. A Russian Army was created by presidential decree in March 1992. In 1996 forces numbered 0·67m. (0·21m. conscripts). The Army is deployed in 8 military districts and 1 Group of Forces, and comprises: 14 Army and 8 Corps headquarters, 17 tank, 47 motor rifle, 5 airborne, 7 machine gun/artillery and 4 artillery divisions, and some 47 artillery, 4 heavy artillery, 6 airborne, 7 special forces, 24 surface-to-surface missile, 1 independent tank, and 15 independent motor rifle brigades, and 20 anti-tank and 28 surface-to-air missile regiments. Equipment includes some 19,000 main battle tanks, including T-54/-55, T-62, T-64A/-B, 11,000 T-72L/-M and T-80/-M9, 200 PT-76 light tanks, 2,500 multiple rocket launchers, 600 surface-to-surface nuclear-capable missile launchers and 500 surface-to-air missiles.

The Army air element has some 3,000 helicopters in the inventory, including 2,000 Mi-8/17 transport, assault and battlefield electronic countermeasures and electronic intelligence machines and 1,000 armed Mi-24s. There is a small number of Mi-26 heavy-lift helicopters.

Strategic Nuclear Ground Forces. In 1995 there were 5 rocket armies, each with launcher groups, 10 silos and 1 control centre. Inter-continental ballistic missiles numbered 928. Personnel, 100,000 (50,000 conscripts).

Navy. The Russian Navy continues to reduce steadily and levels of sea-going activity remain very low. The safe deployment and protection of the reduced force of strategic missile-firing submarines remains its first priority; and the defence of the Russian homeland its second. The strategic missile submarine force operates under command of the Strategic Nuclear Force commander whilst the remainder come under the Main Naval Staff in Moscow, through the Commanders of the fleets.

The Northern and Pacific fleets count the entirety of the ballistic missile submarine force, all nuclear-powered submarines, the sole aircraft carrier and most major surface warships. The Baltic Fleet organization is based in the St Petersburg area and in the Kaliningrad exclave. Some minor war vessels have been ceded to the Baltic republics.

The Black Sea Fleet continues to be the object of wrangling between Russia and the Ukraine, and remains to some extent operationally paralyzed by the dispute. While a political decision has been made to divide the fleet between the nations, the practical and personnel issues remain unresolved. The small Caspian Sea flotilla, formerly a sub-unit of the Black Sea Fleet, is similarly to be divided between Azerbaijan (25%), and Russia, Kazakhstan and Turkmenistan, the littoral republics (75%).

The material state of all the fleets is suffering from continued inactivity and lack of spares and fuel. The nuclear submarine refitting and refuelling operations in the Northern and Pacific Fleets remain in disarray, given the large numbers of nuclear submarines awaiting defuelling and disposal.

The strength of the submarine force has now essentially stabilized, but there are still large numbers of decommissioned vessels awaiting their turn for scrapping in a steadily deteriorating state.

The aircraft carrier *Admiral Kuznetsov* is now judged operational, albeit with a limited aviation capability, and she deployed to the Mediterranean in Dec. 1995.

The overall strength of the Navy at the end of the indicated year was as follows:

Category	*1990*	*1991*	*1992*	*1993*	*1994*	*1995*
Strategic Submarines	61	59	55	50	46	38
Nuclear Attack Submarines	104	100	95	80	63	66
Diesel Submarines	86	80	75	70	62	55
Aircraft Carriers	5	5	4	3	1	1
Cruisers	40	38	33	31	25	26
Destroyers	32	29	26	22	22	21
Frigates	148	146	129	114	112	101

The strength of the disputed Black Sea Fleet at the end of 1995 was 15 diesel-powered submarimes, 1 helicopter cruiser, 4 other cruisers, 5 destroyers and 21 frigates, as well as some 30 mine warfare amphibious ships and 100 support units. For nomenclature and NATO nicknames for former Soviet ship classes and weapons *see* THE STATESMAN'S YEAR-BOOK, 1993–94, p. 384.

The force of Strategic Submarines is constituted as follows:

Class	*No.*	*Tonnage*	*Speed*	*Missiles*	*Other Weapons*
Typhoon	6	27,000	27	20 SS-N-20	Torpedoes
Delta-IV	7	12,350	24	16 SS-N-23	Torpedoes
Delta-III	13	11,900	24	16 SS-N-18	Torpedoes
Delta-II	4	11,500	24	16 SS-N-8	Torpedoes
Delta-I	8	11,000	25	12 SS-N-8	Torpedoes

The SS-N-20 'Sturgeon' missile carried by the Typhoon carries 6 warheads to a maximum range of 4,500 nautical miles, while the SS-N-23 'Skiff' in the other modern class, the 'Delta-IV', carries 10 warheads over the same range. The other older missiles carry 1 to 3 warheads over ranges varying between 1,300 and 4,000 nautical miles.

The attack submarine fleet comprises a wide range of classes, from the enormous 16,250 tonne 'Oscar' nuclear-powered missile submarine to diesel boats of around 2,000 tonnes. The inventory of anti-ship missile-firing submarines comprises 12 'Oscar I' and 'II' built 1982–1994, 24 SS-N-19 'Shipwreck' missiles, 2 'Charlie-I', 1967–72, 8 SS-N-7 'Starbright'; and 1 'Echo-II', 1961–67, 8 SS-N-3 'Shaddock' or SS-N-12 'Sandbox', all nuclear-propelled. Finally, there are 3 former strategic 'Yankee'-class submarines converted to fire the SS-N-21 'Sampson' land-attack cruise missile, which has a range of 1,600 nautical miles. Torpedo-firing boats currently building are the 'Akula' class, nuclear-powered and of 8,100 tonnes, of which there are 13, and the 'Sierra' class, nuclear-powered, 7,700 tonnes now numbering 4. The 'Victor-III' class, nuclear-powered, 6,400 tonnes, is now complete at a total of 26. The diesel-powered 'Kilo' class, of which the Navy operates 24, is still building at a reduced rate mostly for export. There are a further 6 nuclear-powered and 31 diesel submarines nominally on the active list.

Cruisers (7,500–8,000 tonnes full load and upwards) are divided into 2 categories; those optimized for anti-submarine warfare (ASW) are classified as 'Large Anti-Submarine Ships' and those primarily configured for anti-surface ship operations are classified 'Rocket Cruisers'. The principal surface ships of the Russian Navy include the following classes:

Aircraft Carrier. The *Admiral Kuznetsov* of 65,000 tonnes was completed in 1989, is capable of 30 knots, and armed with 12 SS-N-19 'Shipwreck' anti-ship missiles and SA-N-9 anti-air missiles, is capable of embarking 25–30 aircraft and 8–10 helicopters. All other aircraft carriers have been decommissioned or scrapped.

Anti-Shipping Rocket Cruisers. The ships of this classification are headed by the 3 ships of the Admiral Ushakov (formerly Kirov) class, the largest combatant warships, apart from aircraft carriers, to be built since the Second World War. *Admiral Ushakov* (1980), *Admiral Lazarev* (1984), *Admiral Nakhimov* (1988) and *Petr Velikii* (1995). They displace 28,400 tonnes and are capable under combined nuclear and oil-fired steam propulsion of 33 knots and are armed with 20 SS-N-19 anti-ship missiles, 12 batteries of SA-N-6 anti-air missiles, 3 helicopters and a wide range of lesser armaments. There are 4 Slava class: *Slava* (1982), *Marshall Ustinov* (1986), *Chervona Ukraina* (1988) and *Admiral Lobov* (1995), each of 12,700 tonnes capable of 34 knots, and armed with 16 SS-N-12 anti-ship missiles, 8 batteries of SA-N-6 anti-air missiles, 8 torpedo tubes and a single helicopter. Finally in this category is the single remaining ship of the Admiral Zozulya ('Kresta I') class, displacing 7,700 tonnes.

Anti-Submarine Cruisers. The largest of this classification is the Nikolaev ('Kara') class now reduced to 4 ships, displacing 9,800 tonnes, capable of 34 knots, completed 1973–79, and armed with SS-N-14 anti-submarine missiles with a secondary anti-ship role, SA-N-3 anti-air missiles, torpedo-tubes and a single helicopter. The most modern class in this category, the Udaloy class, numbering 12, the first of which entered service in 1981, displace 8,600 tonnes, are capable of 30 knots and are armed with SS-N-14 missiles, torpedo tubes and 100 mm guns, but carry 2 helicopters. There is also a single Moskva class helicopter cruiser, displacing 16,500 tonnes and deploying a force of 14 anti-submarine helicopters.

Smaller ships include the 17 Sovremenny class guided missile destroyers and the single remaining 'modified Kashin' class. There are a further 3 'Kashin', 26 large frigates including the first of a new class, the *Neustrashimy*, and 75 smaller frigates.

The coastal defence force includes 80 missile corvettes, 20 fast missile craft, 30 hydrofoil fast torpedo craft and 15 patrol craft (many more are laid up). Mine warfare forces include 3 minelayers and 33 offshore, 85 coastal and about 65 inshore mine countermeasure vessels.

Amphibious ships include 3 large dock landing ships of the Ivan Rogov class, 22 Ropucha and 7 Alligator class tank landing ships, 20 medium landing ships, as well as some 80 minor craft.

Amphibious landing forces are found from the Naval Infantry, 15,000 strong, units of which are assigned to all fleets. Organized into a single division, 7,000 strong, and 3 active independent brigades, its principal equipment includes 240 main battle tanks, 100 amphibious light tanks, 300 artillery pieces and about 900 armoured personnel carriers. A separate force of almost 9,000 Coastal Defence troops man artillery and missile batteries as well as conventional mechanized units positioned to defend the main naval bases and ports.

The operational reach of the Navy is poor; there is just 1 multi-purpose underway replenishment ship, the *Berezina*, an additional 6 dual-purpose stores and fuel replenishment ships, 6 purpose-built tankers, and 20 other tankers converted from a commercial design with limited underway replenishment capability. Second line support is provided by 12 tankers, and about 230 maintenance and logistic ships, 60 electronic intelligence gatherers, 70 other special-purpose auxiliaries, and 210 survey, research and space support ships.

The Russian Naval Air Force includes some 100 bombers, 150 maritime patrol, 200 fighter/ground attack aircraft and 250 helicopters. Maritime reconnaissance and anti-submarine tasks are performed by 65 Tu-95 and Tu-142 'Bear' with numerous shorter range aircraft tasked to anti-submarine operations, electronic countermeasures, intelligence gathering, and tankers. The helicopter force includes 200 anti-submarine, 25 combat assault, and 15 mine countermeasures aircraft.

Personnel in 1995 numbered 200,000, of whom 40,000 were conscripts. Some 13,000 serve in the strategic submarine force, 24,000 in naval aviation, 15,000 marines or naval infantry, and 9,000 in coastal artillery and coastal defence troops.

Coastguard, customs and border patrol duties are performed by the substantial maritime element of the Committee for the Protection of State Borders, which operates some 7 large helicopter-carrying frigates of a modified naval 'Krivak' class, 18 small frigates, 32 coastal and 155 inshore patrol craft among all the Russian coastal areas.

Air Force. Russia has both Air Force and Air Defence Forces. Under the terms of the Conventional Forces in Europe (CFE) treaty, Russia is allowed to have up to 3,450 combat aircraft, 890 helicopters and 300 naval combat aircraft.

Russia claimed control of all former Soviet forces stationed abroad and is now repatriating them, a task scheduled for completion by 1995.

The Air Force is organized into 4 main Commands: Long-Range Aviation, Frontal Aviation, Military Transport Aviation and Reserve and Training Command. Air defence forces are kept separate.

Long-Range Aviation is reported to have 10 Tu-160, 200 Tu-22M, 140 Tu-95, 130 Tu-22 and over 200 Tu-16 bombers, some equipped to carry nuclear weapons. There are 70 Tu-16s equipped for electronic countermeasures and electronic intelligence missions and 30 Il-78 tanker aircraft. Frontal Aviation has over 3,500 combat and 1,800 support aircraft and is divided into 8 Air Armies, 7 in Russia and 1 in Trans-Caucasia. The main bomber type is the Su-24 of which 800 are available, including some assigned to reconnaissance duties. The MiG-23/27, Su-17/20 and Su-25 serve for fighter and attack missions. There are also MiG-25s (some for reconnaissance) and MiG-29s for air defence duties. The MiG-21 has been withdrawn from service. Military Transport Aviation has over 300 Il-76s, which have largely replaced An-12s for heavy-lift operations. The other main transport type is the An-2 of which over 500 are available, although there are about 100 An-24/26/32 medium transports and 15 An-124 and 30 An-22 very heavy-lift aircraft. 30-plus Il-62, Tu-134, Tu-154 and Yak-40 aircraft are assigned to VIP transport. Reserve and Training Command uses Yak-18 and Yak-52 primary trainers and L-29s and L-39s for jet conversion, plus two-seat models of many front-line types, such as the MiG-23, MiG-25, MiG-29, Su-17/20 and Su-25. It is scheduled to be reorganized and slimmed down. Strength (1994), 170,000 (85,000 conscripts).

Air Defence Forces remain independent of the other Russian Air Forces and have over 1,000 interceptor fighters. These include 400 MiG-23s, 300 MiG-25s, over 200 MiG-31s and 250 Su-27s. They are supported by more than a dozen Il-76 airborne warning and control aircraft. Strength (1995), 130,000 (40,000 conscripts).

The Border Guards have their own aviation component to patrol Russia's borders. It has An-24 fixed-wing aircraft, now being succeeded by armed An-72Ps and Mi-8 and armed Mi-24 helicopters.

INTERNATIONAL RELATIONS

Membership. Russia is a member of the UN (Security Council), CIS, the Council of Europe and the NATO Partnership for Peace.

ECONOMY

Policy. In Oct. 1991 the President announced an economic programme whose aim was the establishment of a 'healthy mixed economy with a powerful private sector'. As part of this programme the prices of most commodities were freed on 2 Jan. 1992

A bankruptcy law of Nov. 1992 permits the winding-up of indebted enterprises; further legislation came into force in April 1993. Centralized distribution of resources to enterprises was abolished from 1993.

Privatization is overseen by the State Committee on the Management of State Property, and began with small and medium-sized enterprises. Enterprises in oil, gas and pharmaceuticals, or employing more than 10,000 workers, or with assets over 200m. rubles on 1 Jan. 1992 required government permission to be privatized. A state programme of privatization of state and municipal enterprises was approved by parliament in June 1992, and vouchers worth 10,000 rubles each began to be distributed to all citizens in Oct. 1992. These may be sold or exchanged for shares. Employees have the right to purchase 51% of the equity of their enterprises. 25 categories of industry (including raw materials and arms) remain in state ownership. By Jan. 1994 a total of 89,000 enterprises had been privatized including 58,700 in trade and services (72% of the total), about three-quarters of large or medium sized enterprises producing 47% of industrial output, and 8·6m. apartments or 24% of the total. The voucher phase of privatization ended on 30 June 1994. A post-voucher stage authorized by presidential decree of 22 July 1994 provides for firms to be auctioned for cash following the completion of the sale of up to 70% of manufacturing industry for vouchers.

Budget. Budgetary incomes in 1993 were valued at 49,730,400m. roubles (in 1992, 5,327,600m.). The main sources of revenue were taxes on profits (16,785,900m.), value added tax (11,213,800m.), income tax (4,394,500m.), income from foreign trade (2,345,100m.) and excise duties (1,779,600m. roubles). Budgetary expenditures were valued at 57,674,000m. roubles (in 1992, 5,969,500m.). Items of expenditure included: National economy, 2,228,100m.; education, 6,917,800m.; health, 5,414,600m.; social security, 939,600m.; defence, 7,212,500m.; law enforcement and government, 4,200,200m. roubles. There was a budgetary deficit of 7,943,600m. roubles (in 1992, 641,900m.).

Currency. The unit of currency is the *rouble* (RUR), notionally of 100 *kopeks*. Banknotes are in denominations of 100, 200, 500, 1,000, 5,000, 10,000, 20,000 and 50,000 roubles. In July 1993 the State Bank abruptly withdrew pre-1993 currency from circulation. Gold reserves were 350 tonnes in 1994. Convertibility of the rouble was initiated in July 1992. Foreign currency shops were closed in 1993. Until June 1996 the rouble had a fluctuation rate of 4,550-5,150 against the US dollar. Inflation was 9,400% in 1993. In March 1996, £1 = 0·99 roubles; US$1 = 0·65 roubles; DM1 = 0·44 roubles (official rate); £1 = 7,397 roubles; US$1 = 4,840 roubles; DM1 = 3,279 roubles (market rate).

Banking and Finance. The central bank and bank of issue is the State Bank of Russia (*Governor*, Sergei Dubinin). The Russian Bank for Reconstruction and Development and the State Investment Company were created in 1993 to channel foreign and domestic investment. In June 1994 there were some 2,214 commercial banks, about 80% of which were state-owned through ministries or state enterprises. Total assets of commercial banks in May 1992 were 1,665,000m. roubles. Foreign bank branches have been operating since Nov. 1992. In 1995, the top 6 banks in terms of assets (in US$1m.) were: Sberbank, 12·5; Foreign Trade Bank, 5·3; Agriculture and Industry Bank, 5·2; External Commercial Bank, 2·6; Russian Credit, 2·2; Universal Import-Export, 2.

The state savings bank Sberbank held 3,966,800m. roubles in 210·9m. individual deposits in Jan. 1994. The average deposit was 18,811 roubles.

By Jan. 1994, 180 exchanges had been licensed, and some 36,100 firms of brokers.

In 1993 all forms of investment were valued at 27,124,000m. roubles (16% less than in 1992), of which 17·5% was provided by the state budget, 15·1% by local authorities and 59·8% by enterprises themselves. 36·3% of investment was in industry, 24% in housing, 10·1% in transport and 7·2% in agriculture.

There are stock exchanges in St Petersburg and Vladivostok.

Weights and Measures. The metric system is in use. The Gregorian Calendar was adopted as from 14 Feb. 1918.

ENERGY AND NATURAL RESOURCES

Electricity. In 1993, 956,600m. kWh of electricity was produced, including 175,000m. kWh hydro-electric and 119,000m. kWh nuclear.

Minerals. Russia contains great mineral resources: Iron ore in the Urals, the Kerch Peninsula and Siberia; coal in the Kuznets Basin, Eastern Siberia, Urals and the sub-Moscow Basin; oil in the Urals, Azov-Black Sea area, Bashkiria, and West Siberia. It also has abundant deposits of gold, platinum, copper, zinc, lead, tin and rare metals. Output (in tonnes), 1993: Coal, 306m.; peat, 2·5m.; shale, 3·3m.; iron ore, 76·1m.; gold, 136·2.

Oil. Output of oil was 354m. tonnes in 1993 (399m. in 1992).

Gas. Output of natural gas in 1993 was 618,000m. cu. metres (in 1992, 641,000m.).

Agriculture. A presidential decree of Dec. 1991 authorized the private ownership of land on a general basis; a further decree of March 1996 authorized its free sale. Collective and state farms which wish to start private farming are required to re-register as co-operatives or share companies. By Jan. 1994, 24,344 state and collective farms had been reorganized and 81,628 private farms created. 8,373 state or collective farms retained their previous status. In Jan. 1993 there were some 26,900 agricultural enterprises of all kinds, employing 8·1m. In 1994 the total cultivated area was 111·8m. ha, of which individual farmers' plots accounted for 3·9m. ha and commercial farms for 5m. ha.

A presidential decree of 28 Oct. 1993 permits the free sale of land, and the raising of mortgages with land as collateral. Members of collectives may withdraw with a certificate of land ownership and a share of the collective's equipment or compensation in lieu; members may also elect to remain in co-operatives voluntarily. The decree permits foreign nationals to own land through joint ventures.

The total value of agricultural output in 1993 was 22,418,000m. roubles, of which 62% was accounted for by state and collective farms, 36% by the private plots of farmers and other citizens (particularly potatoes and vegetables), and 2% by newly formed commercial farms.

Output in 1993 (in tonnes) included: Grain, 99·1m.; flax, 58,000; sunflower seeds, 2·8m.; potatoes, 37·7m.; other vegetables, 9·8m.; fruit and berries, 3·2m.; tea, 7·8m.

Livestock, Jan. 1994: Cows, 19·8m.; sheep and goats, 43·7m.; pigs, 28·6m. Livestock products in 1993 (in tonnes): Meat, 7·5m.; milk, 46·5m.; wool, 158,000; (in units) eggs, 40,300m.

Forestry. 175m. cu. metres of timber were produced in 1993.

INDUSTRY. Output in 1993 accounted for over 30% of GNP and (in tonnes) included: Cast-iron, 40·5m.; steel, 58·3m.; rolled iron, 42·7m.; steel pipe, 5·8m.; caustic soda, 1·4m.; synthetic fibre, 349,000; soap, 81,900; cellulose, 4·3m.; paper, 2·9m.; cement, 52·2m.; confectionery, 1·8m.; (in sq. metres) glass, 103m.; bricks, 19,500m.; (in units) machine tools, 38,700; forges, 7,400; tractors, 88,900; combine harvesters, 33,000; bulldozers, 6,500; tins of food, 4,405m. Total output in physical terms was 83·8% of the 1992 total, and valued at 113,000m. roubles.

Labour. In 1993 incomes were increasingly differentiated, and (according to official sources) about a third of the population earned less than the subsistence minimum. In June 1995 the minimum wage was 55,000 roubles a month; the average wage was 495,000 roubles a month. A State Employment Service was set up in 1992. Unemployment benefits are paid for 15 months: 3 months at full salary, 3 months at 75% and a final 9 months at a progressively reducing rate. Annual paid leave is 24 working days. The workforce was 71m. in 1993, of whom 29·5m. were employed outside the state sector; 29·3% were employed in industry and 20·5% in health, education and science. In Jan. 1994, 4·4m. (5·9% of the labour force) were unemployed, and a further 4·4m. were on short time (accordingly 11·7% were wholly or partly unemployed). Of these, 1m. were registered with the authorities, of whom 67·9% were women. Retirement age is 55 years for women, 60 for men.

Trade Unions. The Federation of Independent Trade Unions (founded 1990) is the successor to the former Communist official union organization. In 1993 it comprised 77 regional and 46 sectoral trade unions, with a total membership of 60m.

FOREIGN ECONOMIC RELATIONS. Most CIS republics have given up claims on Soviet assets in return for Russia's assuming their portion of foreign debt. Foreign debt was US$80,000m. in June 1994.

A Foreign Investment Agency was set up in Dec. 1992. In Jan. 1994 there were 6,359 joint enterprises in operation, employing 304,000 and accounting for 8% of foreign trade.

Commerce. In 1993, exports to non-CIS countries were valued at US$44,297m., and imports at US$26,807m. Germany was the main trading partner, followed (for exports) by the UK, China and Italy, and (for imports) by China, the USA and Japan. Of exports, 46·7% by value were minerals and 23·2% metals and precious stones. Of imports, 33·8% by value was machinery, 22·2% foodstuffs and 13·9% textiles. Total trade between Russia and UK (British Department of Trade returns, in £1,000 sterling):

	1993	*1994*	*1995*
Imports to UK	822,125	804,817	965,870
Exports and re-exports from UK	551,873	707,599	870,387

Tourism. In 1994 there were 5·4m. foreign visitors (2·2m. on business and 1·5m. tourists), and 8·5m. Russian citizens travelled abroad (2·8m. on business, 1·6m. tourists, 3m. by private invitation).

COMMUNICATIONS

Roads. In 1993 there were 726,000 km of hard-surfaced motor roads. 10,225m. tonnes of freight were carried in 1993. 24,124m. passengers were carried by bus services, 9,102m. by trolley buses and 8,125m. by trams.

Railways. Length of railways in 1993 was 87,576 km of 1,520 mm gauge (of which 37,365 km were electrified). 2,324m. passengers were carried in 1993 and 1,346m. tonnes of freight. There are metro services in 6 cities.

Civil Aviation. There are international airports at Moscow (Sheremetevo) and St Petersburg (Pulkovo). The national carrier is Aeroflot International Russian

Airlines, which is 51% state- and 49% employee-owned. In 1995 it had a fleet of 2,643 ex-Soviet aircraft. There are 11 other Russian airlines. Services are also provided by Adria, Aerosweet, Air Algérie, Air China, Air France, Air India, Air Koryo, Air Moldova, Air Ukraine, Alitalia, All Nippon Airways, Arax, Austrian Airlines, Azerbaijan Hava Yollary, Balkan, Bashkir Airlines, Belavia, British Airlines, Croatia Airlines, Cubana, Cyprus Airways, Czech Airlines, Delta, Donavia, Egyptair, El Al, Estonian Air, Finnair, Iberia, Iran Air, JAL, JAT, Kazakhstan Airlines KLM, Korean Air, Libyan Airlines, Lithuanian Airlines, LOT, Lufthansa, Malév, Mongolian Airlines, Northwest Airlines, Orbi, Pakistan Airlines, Palair Macedonian, Royal Jordanian, SAS, Swissasir, Syrian Airlines, TAAG, Tarom, Transaero, Turkish Airlines, Uzbekistan Airways, Vietnam Airlines, Xinjiang Airlines and Yemenia. In 1993, 42m. passengers and 0·9m. tonnes of freight were carried on domestic flights, and 4·7m. passengers and 0·1m. tonnes of freight on international flights.

Shipping. In 1995, the merchant fleet comprised 2,991 vessels totalling 20·38m. DWT, and representing 3·08% of the world's total fleet tonnage. 236 vessels (24% of tonnage) were registered under foreign flags, Total GRT, 16·54m., including oil tankers, 2·38m. GRT, and container ships, 0·46m. GRT. In 1993, 215m. tonnes of freight and 40m. passengers were carried on the 101,000 km of inland waterways; about two-thirds was building materials. Kaliningrad was opened to shipping in May 1991. In 1993, 83m. tonnes of cargo were carried by the merchant marine.

Telecommunications. In Jan. 1994 there were 51,400 post office (34,200 in rural areas) and 25·4m. telephones (3·5m. in rural areas; 17m. domestic in 35% of all households).

Television broadcasting in still largely state-controlled, although an independent service began in 1993. There are 2 major channels, Ostankino and Russian Television (colour by SECAM). In 1994, 98·8% of the population could receive TV broadcasts. There are also local city channels (e.g. 6 in Moscow in 1993). Access to cable TV varies with locality; satellite TV reached about 5% of the population in 1993. In 1993 there were 50m. radios in use.

Cinemas. There were about 0·12m. screens in 1993; attendances totalled about 2,000m. in 1993.

Press. In 1993 there were 4,650 newspapers, 4,331 of them in Russian. Daily circulation of Russian-language newspapers, 84m.; other languages, 2m. A presidential decree of 22 Dec. 1993 brought the press agencies ITAR-TASS and RIA-Novosti under state control.

SOCIAL INSTITUTIONS

Justice. The Supreme Court is the highest judicial body on civil, criminal and administrative law. The Supreme Abritration Court deals with economic cases. The KGB, and the Federal Security Bureau which succeeded it, were replaced in Dec. 1992 by the Federal Counter-Intelligence Service.

A new civil code was introduced in 1993 to replace the former Soviet code. It guarantees the inviolability of private property and includes provisions for the freedom of movement of capital and goods. 12-member juries were introduced in a number of courts after Nov. 1993.

In 1995, 2,755,669 crimes were reported (2,632,708 in 1994); 31,703 were cases of murder or attempted murder. In 1993, 792,400 sentences were passed, of which 37% involved imprisonment.

Religion. The Russian Orthodox Church, represented by the Patriarchate of Moscow, had, in 1994, an estimated 35-40m. adherents, over 14,000 parishes (half of them in Russia), 136 monasteries, and 26 secondary and higher educational institutions. There are still many Old Believers, whose schism from the Orthodox Church dates from the 17th century. The Russian Church is headed by the Patriarch of Moscow and All Russia (Metropolitan Aleksei II (b. 1929) of St Petersburg and Novgorod, elected June 1990), assisted by the Holy Synod, which has 7 members–the Patriarch himself and the Metropolitans of Krutitsy and Kolomna (Moscow),

St Petersburg and Kiev *ex officio*, and 3 bishops alternating for 6 months in order of seniority from the 3 regions forming the Moscow Patriarchate. The Patriarchate of Moscow maintains jurisdiction over 119 eparchies, of which 59 are in Russia; there are parishes of Russian Orthodox abroad, in Belorussia, Ukraine, Kazakhstan, Moldavia, Uzbekistan, the Baltic states, and in Damascus, Geneva, Prageu, New York and Japan. There is a spiritual mission in Jerusalem, and a monastery at Mt Athos in Greece. There are Jewish communities in Moscow and St Petersburg.

Education. In 1993–94 there were 21·1m. pupils in 70,000 primary and secondary schools; 2,542,900 students in 548 higher educational establishments (including 748,000 correspondence students) and 1,993,800 students in 2,607 technical colleges of all kinds (including correspondence students); 6·8m. children (57% of those eligible) were attending pre-school institutions. In 1993–94 there were 743 grammar schools and 418 *lycées* with a combined total of 833,000 students. In addition there were 368 private schools with 33,000 puils.

In 1957 a Siberian branch of the Academy of Sciences was organized. Pre-dating the foundation of a Russian Academy of Sciences, St Petersburg and Urals branches were founded in 1990 and 1991 respectively. The Soviet became the Russian Academy of Sciences in Dec. 1991. In Jan. 1994 there were 4,540 scientific institutes, of which 3,014 were independent research institutes or experimental factories; 973,100 scientific and technological staff were employed.

Health. Doctors in Jan. 1994 numbered 668,500, and hospital beds 1·9m. There were 12,500 hospitals. In Jan. 1994 there were 133 cases of AIDS (85 deaths since 1987).

Welfare. Vouchers are issued to cover basic health care and pensions contributions. These may be topped up to buy better services. A transition from state-financed to insurance-based health care is taking place.

There were 36·1m. pensioners in Jan. 1994, of whom 29m. were old age pensioners. Age pensions are indexed for inflation. The minimum age pension in 1994 was 19,000 roubles a month. The average monthly pension in June 1995 was 201,874 roubles.

A lump sum of 2,700 rubles was payable in 1992 to parents on the birth of a child. From Dec. 1993 the minimum pension was 26,320 rubles a month, indexed to inflation quarterly.

Personal pensions conferred by the former Communist régime conferring special benefits on party or state personnel or awarded for services rendered were abolished in 1992.

DIPLOMATIC REPRESENTATIVES

Of Russia in Great Britain (13 Kensington Palace Gdns., London W8 4QX)
Ambassador: Anatoli Adamishin.

Of Great Britain in Russia (Sofiiskaya Naberezhnaya, 109072 Moscow)
Ambassador: Andrew Wood, CMG.

Of Russia in the USA (1125 16th St., NW, Washington, D.C., 20036)
Ambassador: Yuli Vorontsov.

Of the USA in Russia (Novinski Bulvar 19, Moscow)
Ambassador: Thomas Pickering.

Of Russia to the United Nations
Ambassador: Sergei Lavrov.

Further Reading

Rossiiskii Statisticheskii Ezhegodnik. Moscow, annual (title varies)
Aslund, A. (ed.) *Economic Transformation in Russia.* New York, 1994
Cambridge Encyclopedia of Russia and the Former Soviet Union. CUP, 1995
Dukes, P., *A History of Russia: Medieval, Modern, Contemporary.* 2nd ed. London, 1990
Kochan, L., *The Making of Modern Russia.* 2nd ed, revised by R. Abraham. London, 1994
Pares, B., *A History of Russia.* London, 1962

Paxton, J., *Encyclopedia of Russian History.* Denver (CO), 1993
Pitman, L., *Russia/USSR.* [Bibliography]. 2nd ed. Oxford and Santa Barbara (CA), 1994
Riasanovsky, N. V., *A History of Russia.* 5th ed. OUP, 1993
Roxburgh, A., *The Second Russian Revolution: the Struggle for Power in the Kremlin.* London, 1992
Sakwa, R., *Russian Politics and Society.* London, 1993
Smith, H., *The New Russians.* London, 1990
Treadgold, D. W., *Twentieth Century Russia.* 6th ed. Boston, 1987
Westwood, J. N., *Endurance and Endeavour: Russian History, 1812–1992.* 4th ed. OUP, 1993
White, S. *et al.* (eds.) *Developments in Russian and Post-Soviet Politics.* London, 1994
Yeltsin, B., *The View from the Kremlin* (in USA *The Struggle for Russia*). London and New York, 1994

National statistical office: Gosudarstvennyi Komitet po Statistike (*Goskomstat*), Moscow.

THE REPUBLICS

Status. The 21 republics that with Russia itself constitute the Russian Federation were part of the RSFSR in the Soviet period. On 31 March 1992 the federal government concluded treaties with the then 20 republics, except Checheno-Ingushetia and Tatarstan, defining their mutual responsibilities. The *Council of the Heads of the Republics* is chaired by the Russian President and includes the Russian Prime Minister. Its function is to provide an interaction between the federal government and the republican authorities.

ADYGEYA

Part of Krasnodar Territory. Area, 7,600 sq. km (2,934 sq. miles); population (Jan. 1991), 449,000. Capital, Maikop (149,000). Established 27 July 1922; granted republican status in 1991.

President: Aslan Dzharimov.

Chief industries are timber, woodworking, food processing and there is some engineering. Agriculture consists primarily of crops (beets, wheat, maize), on partly irrigated land. Industrial output was valued in 1993 at 112,000m. rubles, agricultural output at 68,000m. rubles.

In 1991–92 there were 165 schools with 62,000 pupils, 6 technical colleges with 6,600 students and a pedagogical institute with 5,300 students.

In 1991 there were 33·5 doctors and 122 hospital beds per 10,000 population.

ALTAI

Part of Altai Territory. Area, 92,600 sq. km (35,740 sq. miles); population (Jan. 1994), 198,300. Capital, Gorno-Altaisk (39,000). Established 1 June 1922 as Oirot Autonomous Region; renamed 7 Jan. 1948; granted republican status in 1991 and renamed in 1992.

Chief industries are clothing and footwear, foodstuffs, gold mining, timber, chemicals and dairying. Cattle breeding predominates; pasturages and hay meadows cover over 1m. ha, but 142,000 ha are under crops. Industrial output was valued at 19,900m. rubles in 1993, agricultural output at 43,000m. rubles.

In 1991–92 there were 37,000 pupils in 194 schools; 5 technical colleges had 3,800 students and 3,000 students were attending a pedagogical institute.

In 1991 there were 32·7 doctors and 143 hospital beds per 10,000 population.

BASHKORTOSTAN

Area 143,600 sq. km (55,430 sq. miles), population (Jan. 1994) 4,055,300. Capital, Ufa (1989 census population 1·1m.). Bashkiria was annexed to Russia in 1557. It was constituted as an Autonomous Soviet Republic on 23 March 1919. A declaration of republican sovereignty was adopted in 1990, and a declaration of independence on 28 March 1992. A treaty of Aug. 1994 with Russia preserves the common legislative framework of the Russian Federation while defining mutual areas of competence. The population, census 1989, was 39·3% Russian, 28·4% Tatar, 21·9% Bashkir, 3% Chuvash and 2·7% Mari.

A constitution was adopted on 24 Dec. 1993. It states that Bashkiria conducts its own domestic and foreign policy, that its laws take precedence in Bashkiria, and that it forms part of the Russian Federation on a voluntary and equal basis.

The *President* is Murtaza Rakhimov.

Flag. 3 equal stripes of blue, white and green, in the centre a stylized 7-petalled flower.

Industrial production was valued at 4,188,000m. rubles in 1993, agricultural output at 617,000m. rubles. The most important industries are oil and oil products; there are also engineering, glass and building materials enterprises. Agriculture specializes in wheat, barley, oats and livestock.

In 1991–92 there were 590,000 pupils in 3,245 schools. There is a state university and a branch of the Academy of Sciences with 8 learned institutions (511 research workers). There were 62,900 students in 72 technical colleges and 52,300 in 9 higher educational establishments.

In 1991 there there 36 doctors and 134 hospital beds per 10,000 population.

BURYATIA

Area is 351,300 sq. km (135,650 sq. miles). The Buryat Republic, situated to the south of Sakha, adopted the Soviet system 1 March 1920. This area was penetrated by the Russians in the 17th century and finally annexed from China by the treaties of Nerchinsk (1689) and Kyakhta (1727). The population (Jan. 1994) was 1,052,800. Capital, Ulan-Ude (1989 census population, 353,000). The population (1989 census) was 69·9% Russian, 24% Buryat, 2·2% Ukrainian, 1% Tatar and 0·5% Belorussian.

There is a 65-member parliament, the *People's Hural.* Presidential and parliamentary elections were held on 16 June 1994.

Leonid Potapov was elected *President* by 46% of votes cast in a first round against 3 opponents, necessitating a second round.

The main industries are engineering, brown coal and graphite, timber, building materials, sheep and cattle farming. Industrial production was valued at 384,000m. rubles in 1993, agricultural output at 181,000m. rubles.

In 1991–92 there were 595 schools with 190,000 pupils, 20 technical colleges with 16,000 students and 4 higher educational institutions with 20,800 students. A branch of the Siberian Department of the Academy of Sciences had 4 institutions with 281 research workers.

In 1991 there were 40·4 doctors and 136 hospital beds per 10,000 population.

CHECHENIA (CHECHNYA)

The area of the former Checheno-Ingush Republic was 19,300 sq. km (7,350 sq. miles); population (Jan. 1992), 1,308,000. Capital, Grozny (1989 census population, 401,000). The Chechens and Ingushes were conquered by Russia in the late 1850s. In 1918 each nationality separately established its 'National Soviet' within the Terek Autonomous Republic, and in 1920 (after the Civil War) were constituted areas within the Mountain Republic. The Chechens separated out as an Autonomous Region on 30 Nov. 1922 and the Ingushes on 7 July 1924. In Jan. 1934 the two regions were united, and on 5 Dec. 1936 constituted as an Autonomous Republic. This was dissolved in 1944 and the population was deported en masse, allegedly for collaboration with the German occupation forces. It was reconstituted on 9 Jan. 1957: 232,000 Chechens and Ingushes returned to their homes in the next 2 years. The population (1989 census) included 70·7% Chechens and Ingushes, 23·1% Russians, 1·2% Armenians and 1% Ukrainians.

A Chechen Republic was declared in 1991, which declared its independence in Nov. 1991. (A separate Ingush Republic was declared in June 1993).

In April 1993 President Dudaev dissolved parliament. Hostilities continued throughout 1994 between the government and forces loosely grouped under the 'Provisional Chechen Council'.

The Russian government, which had never recognized the Chechen declaration of independence of Nov. 1991, moved troops and armour into Chechenia on 11 Dec. 1994 'to re-establish constitutional order'. Grozny was bombed and attacked by Russian ground forces at the end of Dec. 1994 and the presidential palace was captured on 19 Jan. 1995, but fighting continued, outside the capital. On 30 July 1995 the Russian and Chechen authorities signed a ceasefire.

On 8 Dec. 1995 an agreement between the Russian and Chechen prime ministers amnestied insurgents who laid down their arms and stipulated that Chechenia should have its own consulates and trade missions abroad. However, hostilities, raids and hostage-taking continued. President Dudaev was killed during fighting in April 1996.

An election for the 'head of the republic' was held on 17 Dec. 1995.

President: Vacant.

Prime Minister: Doku Zavgaev.

Minister of Information: Movladi Udugov. *Finance:* Taimaz Abubakarov.

Ingush desire to separate from Chechenia led to fighting along the Chechen-Ingush border and a deployment of Russian troops. An agreement to withdraw was reached between Russia and Chechenia on 15 Nov. 1992. The separation of Chechenia and Ingushetia was formalized by an amendment of Dec. 1992 to the Russian Constitution.

Checheno-Ingushetia had a major oilfield, and a number of engineering works, chemical factories, building materials works and food canneries. There was a timber, woodworking and furniture industry. Industrial output in the two republics was valued at 213,000m. rubles in 1993, agricultural output at 79,000m. rubles.

There were, in 1991–92, 548 schools with 258,000 pupils, 12 technical colleges with 13,900 students and 3 places of higher education with 16,800 students.

In 1992 it was decided to revert to the Roman alphabet (which had replaced Arabic script in 1927 and been itself replaced by Cyrillic in 1938).

In 1991 there were 25·8 doctors and 102 hospital beds per 10,000 population.

CHUVASHIA

Area, 18,300 sq. km (7,064 sq. miles); population (Jan. 1994), 1,359,000. Capital, Cheboksary (1989 census population, 420,000). The territory was annexed by Russia in the middle of the 16th century. On 24 June 1920 it was constituted as an Autonomous Region, and on 21 April 1925 as an Autonomous Republic. The population (1989 census) was 67·8% Chuvash, 26·7% Russian, 2·7% Tatar and 1·4% Mordovian. Republican sovereignty was declared in Sept. 1990.

Nikolai Fedorov was elected *President* on 26 Dec. 1993 against 6 opponents.

The timber industry antedates the Soviet period. Other industries today include railway repair works, electrical and other engineering industries, building materials, chemicals, textiles and food industries; timber felling and haulage are largely mechanized. Grain crops account for nearly two-thirds of all sowings and fodder crops for nearly a quarter. Fruit and wine-growing are a developing branch of agriculture. Industrial output was valued at 641,000m. rubles in 1993, agricultural output at 224,000m. rubles.

In 1991–92 there were 209,000 pupils at 718 schools, 21,100 students at 26 technical colleges and 18,700 students at 3 higher educational establishments.

In 1991 there were 37·1 doctors and 134 hospital beds per 10,000 population.

DAGESTAN

Area, 50,300 sq. km (19,416 sq. miles); population (Jan. 1994), 1,953,000. Capital, Makhachkala (1989 census population, 315,000). Over 30 nationalities inhabit this republic apart from Russians (9·2% at 1989 census); the most numerous are the Avartsy, Dargintsy, Lezginy, Kumyki, Laki, Tabasarany and other Dagestani nationalities (80·2%), Azerbaijanis (4·2%), Chechens (3·22%) and Jews (0·5%). Annexed from Persia in 1723, Dagestan was constituted an Autonomous Republic on 20 Jan. 1921.

210 deputies were elected to the republican Supreme Soviet on 24 Feb. 1985, 84 of them women. In 1991 the Supreme Soviet declared the area of republican, rather than autonomous republican, status.

There are engineering, oil, chemical, woodworking, textile, food and other light industries. Agriculture is varied, ranging from wheat to grapes, with sheep farming and cattle breeding. Industrial output was valued at 136,000m. rubles in 1993, agricultural output at 155,000m. rubles. A chain of power stations is under construction in the Sulak River (total capacity 2·5m. kw.).

In 1991–92 there were 1,568 schools with 397,000 pupils, 21,000 students at 27 technical colleges and 5 higher education establishments with 28,000 students; and a branch of the USSR Academy of Sciences with 4 learned institutions (373 research workers). In 1991 there were 42·9 doctorsand 119 hospital beds per 10,000 population.

INGUSHETIA

The history of Ingushetia is interwoven with that of Chechenia (*see above*). Ingush desire to separate from Chechenia led to fighting along the Chechen-Ingush border and a deployment of Russian troops. The separation of Ingushetia from Chechenia was formalized by an amendment of Dec. 1992 to the Russian Constitution. On 15 May 1993 an extraordinary congress of the peoples of Ingushetia adopted a declaration of state sovereignty within the Russian Federation.

The capital is Nazran.

There is a 27-member parliament.

On 27 Feb. 1994 presidential elections and a constitutional referendum were held. Turn-out was 70%. *President* Ruslan Aushev was re-elected by 94% of votes cast. At the referendum 97% of votes cast approved a new constitution stating that Ingushetia is a democratic law-based secular republic forming part of the Russian Federation on a treaty basis.

Vice President: Boris Agapov.

Prime Minister: Ruslan Takiev.

KABARDINO-BALKARIA

Area, 12,500 sq. km (4,825 sq. miles); population (Jan. 1991) 785,800. Capital, Nalchik (1989 census population, 235,000). Kabarda was annexed to Russia in 1557. The republic was constituted on 5 Dec. 1936. Population (1979 census) included Kabardinians and Balkars (57·6%), Russians (31·9%), Ukrainians (1·7%), Ossetians (1·3%) and Germans (1·1%).

A treaty with Russia of 1 July 1994 defines their mutual areas of competence within the legislative framework of the Russian Federation.

President: Valeri Kokov.

Main industries are ore-mining, timber, engineering, coal, food processing, timber and light industries, building materials. Grain, livestock breeding, dairy farming and wine-growing are the principal branches of agriculture. Industrial output was valued at 176,000m. rubles in 1993, agricultural output at 113,000m. rubles.

In 1991–92 there were 248 schools with 130,000 pupils, 9,200 students in 10 technical colleges and 12,600 students at 2 higher educational establishments. In 1991 there were 48·6 doctors and 126 hospital beds per 10,000 population.

KALMYKIA

Area, 76,100 sq. km (29,382 sq. miles); population (Jan. 1994), 320,600. Capital, Elista (85,000). The population (1989 census) was 45·4% Kalmyk, 37·7% Russian, 2·6% Chechen, 1·9% Kazakh and 1·7% German.

The Kalmyks migrated from western China to Russia (Nogai Steppe) in the early 17th century. The territory was constituted an Autonomous Region on 4 Nov. 1920, and an Autonomous Republic on 22 Oct. 1935; this was dissolved in 1943. On 9 Jan. 1957 it was reconstituted as an Autonomous Region and on 29 July 1958 as an Autonomous Republic once more. In Oct. 1990 the republic was renamed the Kalmyk Soviet Socialist Republic; it was given its present name in Feb. 1992.

At the presiential elections of 11 April 1993 turn-out was 82%. Kirsan Ilyumzhinov (b. 1962) was elected with 65% of votes cast against 2 opponents.

In April 1993 the Supreme Soviet was dissolved and replaced by a professional parliament consisting of 25 of the former deputies. On 5 April 1994 a specially-constituted 300-member constituent assembly adopted a 'Steppe Code' as Kalmykia's basic law. This is not a constitution and renounces the declaration of republican sovereignty of 18 Oct. 1990. It provides for a *President* elected for 5-year terms with the power to dissolve parliament, and a 27-member parliament, the *People's Hural*, elected every 4 years. It stipulates that Kalmykia is an equal member and integral part of the Russian Federation, functioning in accordance with the Russian constitution.

Local government Soviets were abolished in April 1993.

Main industries are fishing, canning and building materials. Cattle breeding and irrigated farming (mainly fodder crops) are the principal branches of agriculture. Industrial output was valued at 35,600m. rubles in 1993, agricultural output at 89,000m. rubles.

In 1991–92 there were 57,000 pupils in 255 schools, 4,800 students in 7 technical colleges and 5,000 in higher education. In 1991 there were 47·2 doctors and 165 hospital beds per 10,000 population.

KARACHAI-CHERKESSIA

Part of Stavropol Territory. Area, 14,100 sq. km (5,442 sq. miles); population (Jan. 1994), 434,100. Capital, Cherkessk (113,000). A Karachai Autonomous Region was established on 26 April 1926 (out of a previously united Karachaevo-Cherkess Autonomous Region created in 1922), and dissolved in 1943. A Cherkess Autonomous Region was established on 30 April 1928. The present Autonomous Region was re-established on 9 Jan. 1957. The Region declared itself a Soviet Socialist Republic in Dec. 1990.

There are ore-mining, engineering, chemical and woodworking industries. The Kuban-Kalaussi irrigation scheme irrigates 200,000 ha. Livestock breeding and grain growing predominate in agriculture. Industrial output was valued at 114,000m. rubles in 1993, agricultural output at 92,000m. rubles.

In 1991–92 there were 71,000 pupils in 182 secondary schools, 6 technical colleges with 4,700 students and 1 institute with 4,300 students. In 1991 there were 28·4 doctors and 110 hospital beds per 10,000 population.

KARELIA

The Karelian Republic, capital Petrozavodsk (1989 census population, 270,000), covers an area of 172,400 sq. km, with a population of 794,200 (Jan. 1994). Karelians represent 10% of the population, Russians, 73·6%, Belorussians 7% and Ukrainians 3·6% (1989 census).

Karelia (formerly Olonets Province) became part of the RSFSR after 1917. In June 1920 a Karelian Labour Commune was formed and in July 1923 this was transformed into the Karelian Autonomous Soviet Socialist Republic (one of the autonomous republics of the RSFSR). On 31 March 1940, after the Soviet–Finnish war, practically all the territory (with the exception of a small section in the neighbourhood of the Leningrad area) which had been ceded by Finland to the USSR was added to Karelia and the Karelian Autonomous Republic was transformed into the Karelo-Finnish Soviet Socialist Republic as the 12th republic of the USSR. In 1946, however, the southern part of the republic, including its whole seaboard and the towns of Viipuri (Vyborg) and Keksholm, was attached to the RSFSR, reverting in 1956 to autonomous republican status within the RSFSR. In Nov. 1991 it declared itself the 'Republic of Karelia'.

Karelia has a wealth of timber, some 70% of its territory being forest land. It is also rich in other natural resources, having large deposits of mica, diabase, spar, quartz, marble, granite, zinc, lead, silver, copper, molybdenum, tin, baryta and iron ore. Its lakes an rivers are rich in fish.

There are timber mills, paper-cellulose works, mica, chemical plants, power stations and furniture factories. Output, 1986: Timber, 11·1m. cu. metres; paper, 1·3m. tonnes; cellulose, 826,000 tonnes; electricity, 3,634m. kwh.; iron ore, 9·5m. tonnes. Industrial output was valued at 520,000m. rubles in 1993, agricultural output at 97,000m. rubles.

A railway between Petrozavodsk and Suoyarvi connects the capital and the Murmansk Railway with the main railway line Sortavala–Vyborg. A railway line was also laid between Kandalaksha and Kuolayarvi. Length of track, 1,600 km.

In 1991–92 there were 118,000 pupils in 334 schools. There were 10,200 students in 3 institutions of higher education and 12,500 in 16 technical colleges.

In 1991 there were 50·2 doctors and 148 hospital beds per 10,000 population.

KHAKASSIA

Part of Krasnoyarsk Territory. Area, 61,900 sq. km (23,855 sq. miles); population (Jan. 1994), 584,000. Capital, Abakan (1989 census, 154,000). Established 20 Oct. 1930; granted republican status in 1991.

President: V. Shtygashev (elected 1992).

There are coal- and ore-mining, timber and woodworking industries. The region is linked by rail with the Trans-Siberian line. Industrial output was valued at 545,000m. rubles in 1993, agricultural output at 83,000m. rubles.

In 1991–92 there were 94,000 pupils in 276 secondary schools, 7,500 students in 7 technical colleges and 6,100 students at a higher education institution.

In 1991 there were 34·4 doctors and 142 hospital beds per 10,000 population.

KOMI

Area, 415,900 sq. km (160,540 sq. miles); population (Jan. 1994), 1,228,100. Capital, Syktyvkar (1989 census population, 233,000). Annexed by the princes of Moscow in the 14th century, the territory was constituted as an Autonomous Region on 22 Aug. 1921 and as an Autonomous Republic on 5 Dec. 1936. The population (1989 census) was 57·7% Russian, 23·3% Komi, 8·3% Ukrainian and 2·1% Belorussian.

A declaration of sovereignty was adopted by the republican parliament in Sept. 1990, and the designation 'Autonomous' dropped from the republic's official name.

Flag: 3 horizontal stripes of blue, green and white.

There are coal, oil, timber, gas, asphalt and building materials industries, and light industry is expanding. Livestock breeding (including dairy farming) is the main branch of agriculture. Crop area, 92,000 ha. Industrial output was valued at 1,038,000m. rubles in 1993, agricultural output at 134,000m. rubles.

In 1991–92 there were 200,000 pupils in 589 schools, 10,700 students in 3 higher educational establishments, 15,400 students in 20 technical colleges; and a branch of the Academy of Sciences with 4 institutions (297 research workers).

In 1991 there were 41 doctors and 143 hospital beds per 10,000 population.

MARI EL

Area, 23,200 sq. km (8,955 sq. miles); population (Jan. 1994), 764,700. Capital, Yoshkar-Ola (1989 census population, 242,000). The Mari people were annexed to Russia, with other peoples of the Kazan Tatar Khanate, when the latter was overthrown in 1552. On 4 Nov. 1920 the territory was constituted as an Autonomous Region, and on 5 Dec. 1936 as an Autonomous Republic. The republic renamed itself the Mari Soviet Socialist Republic in Oct. 1990, and adopted a new constitution in June 1995. In Dec. 1991 Vladislav Zotin was elected the first president. The population (1989 census) was 47·5% Russian, 43·3% Mari, and 5·9% Tatar.

There are over 300 factories. The main industries are metalworking, timber, paper, woodworking and food processing. Over 69% of cultivated land is grain, but flax, potatoes, fruit and vegetables are also expanding branches of agriculture, as is also livestock farming. Industrial output was valued at 257,000m. rubles in 1993, agricultural output at 153,000m. rubles.

Estimated reserves of the Pechora coalfield are 260,000m. tonnes.

In 1991–92 there were 435 schools with 118,000 pupils; 14 technical colleges and 3 higher education establishments had 9,500 and 14,600 students respectively.

In 1991 there were 33·1 doctors and 135 hospital beds per 10,000 population.

MORDOVIA

Area, 26,200 sq. km (10,110 sq. miles); population (Jan. 1994), 962,700. Capital, Saransk (1989 census population, 312,000). By the 13th century the Mordovian tribes had been subjugated by Russian princes. In 1928 the territory was constituted as a Mordovian Area within the Middle-Volga Territory, on 10 Jan. 1930 as an Autonomous Region and on 20 Dec. 1934 as an Autonomous Republic. The population (1989 census) was 60·8% Russian, 32·5% Mordovian and 4·9% Tatar.

175 deputies were elected to the republican Supreme Soviet on 24 Feb. 1985, 74 of them women. Vasilii Guslyannikov was the elected president, but in April 1993 the Supreme Soviet abolished the presidency and appointed Valeri Shvetsov *Prime Minister.*

The republic has a wide range of industries: Electrical, timber, cable, building materials, furniture, textile, leather and other light industries. Agriculture is devoted chiefly to grain, sugar-beet, sheep and dairy farming. Industrial output was valued at 457,000m. rubles in 1993, agricultural output at 185,000m. rubles.

In 1991–92 there were 132,000 pupils in 820 schools, 14,800 students in 21 technical colleges and 22,200 attending 2 higher educational institutions.

In 1991 there were 41·9 doctors and 151 hospital beds per 10,000 population.

NORTH OSSETIA (ALANIA)

Area, 8,000 sq. km (3,088 sq. miles); population (Jan. 1994), 650,400. Capital, Vladikavkaz (1989 census population, 300,000). North Ossetia was annexed to Russia after the latter's treaty of Kuchuk-Kainardji with Turkey and named Terek region in 1861. On 4 March 1918 the latter was proclaimed an Autonomous Soviet Republic, and on 20 Jan. 1921 this territory with others was set up as the Mountain Autonomous Republic, with North Ossetia as the Ossetian (Vladikavkaz) Area within it. On 7 July 1924 the latter was constituted as an Autonomous Region and on 5 Dec. 1936 as an Autonomous Republic. A new Constitution was adopted on

12 Nov. 1994 under which the republic reverted to its former name, Alania. The population (1989 census) was 53% Ossentian, 29% Russian, 5·2% Chechen, 1·9% Armenian and 1·6% Ukrainian.

At elections held on 16 Jan. 1994 turn-out was 55%. Akhsarbek Galazov (b. 1930) was elected *President* against 1 opponent by 60% of votes cast.

Flag: 3 equal horizontal stripes of white, purple and gold.

The main industries are non-ferrous metals (mining and metallurgy), maize-processing, timber and woodworking, textiles, building materials, distilleries and food processing. There is also a varied agriculture. Industrial output was valued at 167,000m. rubles in 1993, agricultural output at 175,000m. rubles.

There were in 1991–92, 106,000 children in 213 schools, 11,600 students in 13 technical colleges and 17,900 students in 4 higher educational establishments (pedagogical, agriculture, medical and mining-metallurgical institutes).

In 1991 there were 63·2 doctors and 120 hospital beds per 10,000 population.

SAKHA

The area is 3,103,200 sq. km (1,197,760 sq. miles); population (Jan. 1994), 1,060,700. Capital, Yakutsk (187,000). The Yakuts were subjugated by the Russians in the 17th century. The territory was constituted an Autonomous Republic on 27 April 1922. The population (1989 census) was 50·3% Russian, 33·4% Yakut, 7% Ukrainian and 1·6% Tatar.

The *President* (elected in 1991) is Mikhail Nikolaev. *Vice-President and Prime Minister:* Vyacheslav Shtyrov.

The principal industries are mining (gold, tin, mica, coal) and livestock-breeding. Silver- and lead-bearing ores and coal are worked. Large diamond fields have been opened up; Sakha produces most of the Russian Federation's output. Timber and food industries are developing. Trapping and breeding of fur-bearing animals (sable, squirrel, silver fox) are an important source of income. Industrial production was valued at 1,771,000m. rubles in 1993, agricultural output at 373,000m. rubles.

In 1991–92 there were 206,000 pupils in 703 secondary schools, 10,500 students at 19 technical colleges and 8,100 attending 2 higher education institutions.

In 1991 there were 45 doctors and 160 hospital beds per 10,000 population.

TATARSTAN

Area, 68,000 sq. km (26,250 sq. miles); population (Jan. 1994), 3,743,600. Capital, Kazan (1989 census population 1·1m.). From the 10th to the 13th centuries this was the territory of the Volga-Kama Bulgar State; conquered by the Mongols, it became the seat of the Kazan (Tatar) Khans when the Mongol Empire broke up in the 15th century, and in 1552 was conquered again by Russia. On 27 May 1920 it was constituted as an Autonomous Republic. The population (1989 census) was 48·5% Tatar, 43·3% Russian, 3·7% Chuvash, 0·9% Ukrainian and 0·8% Mordovian.

In Oct. 1991 the Supreme Soviet adopted a declaration of independence. At a referendum in March 1992 61·4% of votes cast were in favour of increased autonomy. A Constitution was adopted in April 1992, which proclaims Tatarstan a sovereign state which conducts its relations with the Russian Federation on an equal basis. On 15 Feb. 1994 the Russian and Tatar presidents signed a treaty defining Tatarstan as a state united with Russia on the basis of the constitutions of both, but the Russian parliament has not ratified it.

The *President* is Mintimir Shaimiev.
Prime Minister: is Mukhammat Sabirov.
Speaker: Farid Mukhametshin.

The republic has engineering, oil and chemical, timber, building materials, textiles, clothing and food industries. Industrial production was valued at 2,955,000m. rubles in 1993, agricultural output at 532,000m. rubles.

In 1991–92 there were 2,388 schools with 517,000 pupils, 65 technical colleges with 57,800 students and 14 higher educational establishments with 69,100 students (including a state university). There is a branch of the USSR Academy of Sciences with 5 institutions (512 research workers).

In 1991 there were 38·4 doctors and 128 hospital beds per 10,000 population.

TUVA

Area, 170,500 sq. km (65,810 sq. miles); population (Jan. 1994), 306,300. Capital, Kyzyl (80,000). Tuva was incorporated in the USSR as an autonomous region on 11 Oct. 1944 and elevated to an Autonomous Republic on 10 Oct. 1961. It is bounded to the east, west and north by Siberia, and to the south by Mongolia. The Tuvans are a Turkic people, formerly ruled by hereditary or elective tribal chiefs. (For the earlier history of the former Tannu-Tuva Republic, *see* THE STATESMAN'S YEAR-BOOK, 1946, p. 798.) The population (1989 census) was 64·3% Tuvans and 32% Russian. Tuva renamed itself the 'Republic of Tuva' in Oct. 1991 and elected its first *President*, Sherig-Ool Oorzhak, in March 1992.

A new constitution was promulgated on 22 Oct. 1993 which adopts the name 'Tyva' for the republic. This constitution provides for a 32-member parliament (*Supreme Hural*) and a *Grand Hural* alone empowered to change the constitution, asserts the precedence of Tuvan law and adopts powers to conduct foreign policy. It was approved by 62·2% of votes cast at a referendum on 12 Dec. 1993.

Tuva is well-watered and hydro-electric resources are important. The Tuvans are mainly herdsmen and cattle farmers and there is much good pastoral land, but, in 1983, 371,000 ha were under crops. There are deposits of gold, cobalt and asbestos. The main exports are hair, hides and wool. There are mining, woodworking, garment, leather, food and other industries. Industrial production was valued at 25,800m. rubles in 1993, agricultural output at 44,000m. rubles.

In 1991–92 there were 159 schools with 62,000 pupils; 5 technical colleges with 3,800 students, and 1 higher education institution with 2,900 students.

In 1991 there were 38·4 doctors and 192 hospital beds per 10,000 population.

UDMURTIA

Area, 42,100 sq. km (16,250 sq. miles); population (Jan. 1994), 1,640,700. Capital, Izhevsk (1989 census population 635,109). The Udmurts (formerly known as 'Votyaks') were annexed by the Russians in the 15th and 16th centuries. On 4 Nov. 1920 the Votyak Autonomous Region was constituted (the name was changed to Udmurt in 1932), and on 28 Dec. 1934 was raised to the status of an Autonomous Republic. The population (1989 census) was 58·9% Russian, 30·9% Udmurt, 6·9% Tatar, 0·9% Ukrainian and 0·6% Mari. A declaration of sovereignty and the present state title were adopted in Sept. 1990.

A new parliament was established in Dec. 1993 consisting of a 50-member upper house, the *Council of Representatives*, and a full-time 35-member lower house.

Heavy industry includes the manufacture of locomotives, machine tools and other engineering products, most of them for the defence industries, as well as timber and building materials. There are also light industries: Clothing, leather, furniture and food. Industrial production was valued at 958,000m. rubles in 1993, agricultural output at 368,000m. rubles.

In 1991–92 there were 871 schools with 250,000 pupils; there were 22,400 students at 30 technical colleges and 24,800 at 5 higher educational institutions.

In 1991 there were 46·6 doctors and 136 hospital beds per 10,000 population.

JEWISH AUTONOMOUS REGION (BIROBIJAN)

Part of Khabarovsk Territory. Area, 36,000 sq. km (13,895 sq. miles); population (Jan. 1994),217,800 (1989 census, Russians, 83·2%;Ukrainians, 7·4%; Jews,4·2%).

Capital, Birobijan (82,000). Established as Jewish National District in 1928, became an Autonomous Region 7 May 1934. In Oct. 1991 the region declared itself an Autonomous Republic.

Chief industries are non-ferrous metallurgy, building materials, timber, engineering, textiles, paper and food processing. There were 161,000 ha under cultivation in 1983; main crops are wheat, soya, oats, barley. Industrial production was valued at 74,500m. rubles in 1993, agricultural output at 73,000m. rubles.

In 1991–92 there were 35,000 pupils in 111 schools; students in 6 technical colleges numbered 4,900. There is a Yiddish national theatre, a Yiddish newspaper and a Yiddish broadcasting service.

In 1991 there were 37·5 doctors and 162 hospital beds per 10,000 poulation.

AUTONOMOUS AREAS

Agin-Buryat Situated in Chita region (Eastern Siberia); area, 19,000 sq. km, population (Jan. 1994), 79,400. Capital, Aginskoe. Formed 1937, its economy is basically pastoral.

Chukot Situated in Magadan region (Far East); area, 737,700 sq. km. Population (Jan. 1994), 113,100. Capital, Anadyr. Formed 1930. Population chiefly Russian, also Chukchi, Koryak, Yakut, Even. Minerals are extracted in the north, including gold, tin, mercury and tungsten.

Evenki Situated in Krasnoyarsk territory (Eastern Siberia); area, 767,600 sq. km, population (Jan. 1994) 22,600, chiefly Evenks. Capital, Tura. Formed 1930.

Khanty-Mansi Situated in Tyumen region (Western Siberia); area, 523,100 sq. km, population (Jan. 1994) 1,312,600, chiefly Russians but also Khants and Mansi. Capital, Khanti-Mansiisk. Formed 1930.

Komi-Permyak Situated in Perm region (Northern Russia); area, 32,900 sq. km, population (Jan. 1994) 160,300, chiefly Komi-Permyaks. Formed 1925. Capital, Kudymkar. Forestry is the main occupation.

Koryak Situated in Kamchatka; area, 301,500 sq. km, population (Jan. 1994) 35,400. Capital, Palana. Formed 1930.

Nenets Situated in Archangel region (Northern Russia); area, 176,700 sq. km, population (Jan. 1994) 50,900. Capital, Naryan-Mar. Formed 1929.

Taimyr Situated in Krasnoyarsk territory, this most northerly part of Siberia comprises the Taimyr peninsula and the Arctic islands of Severnaya Zemlya. Area, 862,100 sq. km, population (Jan. 1994) 49,200, excluding the mining city of Norilsk which is separately administered. Capital, Dudinka. Formed 1930.

Ust-Ordyn-Buryat Situated in Irkutsk region (Eastern Siberia); area, 22,400 sq. km, population (Jan. 1994) 142,500. Capital, Ust-Ordynsk. Formed 1937.

Yamalo-Nenets Situated in Tyumen region (Western Siberia); area, 750,300 sq. km, population (Jan. 1994) 468,800. Capital, Salekhard. Formed 1930.

RWANDA

Republika y'u Rwanda

Capital: Kigali
Population: 7·46m. (1993)
GNP per capita: US$210 (1993)
HDI/world rank: 0·332/156 (1992)

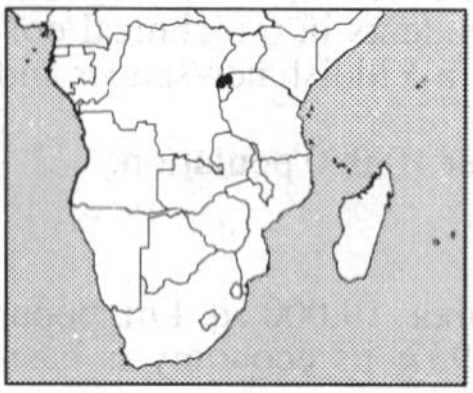

KEY HISTORICAL EVENTS. From the 16th century to 1959 the Tutsi kingdom of Rwanda shared the history of Burundi. In 1959 an uprising of the Hutu destroyed the Tutsi feudal hierarchy and overthrew the monarchy. Elections and a referendum under the auspices of the UN in Sept. 1961 resulted in an overwhelming majority for the republican party, the Parmehutu (*Parti du Mouvement de l'Emancipation du Bahutu*), and the rejection of the monarchy. The republic proclaimed by the Parmehutu on 28 Jan. 1961 was recognized by the Belgian administration (but not by the UN) in Oct. 1961. Internal self-government was granted on 1 Jan. 1962, and by decision of the General Assembly of the UN the Republic of Rwanda became independent on 1 July 1962.

In Oct. 1990 rebel Tutsi forces of the Rwandan Patriotic Front (RPF) invaded from Uganda. An agreement was signed on 14 Aug. 1992 to end the civil war, but fighting continued. Rebels and government agreed to merge their forces at peace talks in March 1993. A peace agreement was signed on 4 Aug. 1993 at Arusha (Tanzania). On 5 Oct. the UN Security Council unanimously decided to send a peacekeeping force to oversee the establishment of transitional organs in line with the Aug. agreement. However, President Habyarimana was killed, possibly assassinated, on 6 April 1994. Fatalities in the fighting which broke out included the Prime Minister and UN personnel. Rebel Tutsi forces of the RPF began an attack from the north of the country.

An interim government was formed on 10 April with the Speaker Théodore Sindikubwabo (National Republican Movement for Development; MRND) as President and Jean Kambada (Democratic Republican Movement; MDR) as Prime Minister.

Most UN forces were withdrawn during the fighting and massacres of April 1994, but following a UN Security Council resolution of 17 May 1994 a new force of 5,500 was sent in.

By May 1994 an estimated 0·86m. refugees had fled into neighbouring countries.

On 22 June 1994 the UN Security Council approved France's dispatch of 2,000 troops on a humanitarian mission. The RPF, however, said it would treat the force as invaders. The French forces maintained a 'safe zone' for refugees in the south-west of Rwanda until their withdrawal on 21 Aug. 1994.

Under the aegis of the OAU at Tunis representatives of the Rwandan interim government and the RPF agreed a ceasefire.

At the request of the RPF on 6 July 1994 in Brussels Faustin Twagiramungu agreed to form a 22-member government of national unity in which 8 posts were held by the RPF.

On 8 Nov. 1994 the UN Security Council resolved by 13 votes (China abstaining and Rwanda opposing) to set up an international tribunal to try crimes of genocide in Rwanda. It was inaugurated on 27 June 1995 and subsequently merged with that for Yugoslavia.

UN forces (UNAMIR) left Rwanda on 8 March 1996.

TERRITORY AND POPULATION. Rwanda is bounded south by Burundi, west by Zaïre, north by Uganda and east by Tanzania. A mountainous state of 26,338 sq. km (10,169 sq. miles), its western third drains to Lake Kivu on the border with Zaïre and thence to the Congo river, while the rest is drained by the Kagera river into the Nile system.

The population was 7,164,994 at the 1991 Census, of whom over 90% were Hutu,

9% Tutsi and 1% Twa (pygmy); estimate (1993) 7,459,000 (8% urban); density, 282·1 per sq. km. Expectation of life, 1991, 46 years.

The areas and populations of the 10 prefectures are:

Prefecture	Area (in sq. km)	Population (1991 census)	Prefecture	Area (In sq. km)	Population (1991 census)
Cyangugu	1,845	515,129	Kigali	3,118	1,156,651
Kibuye	1,705	470,747	Kibungo	4,046	655,368
Gisenyi	2,050	734,697	Gitarama	2,189	851,516
Ruhengeri	1,663	766,112	Gikongoro	2,057	464,585
Byumba	4,761	783,350	Butare	1,837	766,839

Kigali, the capital, had 234,500 inhabitants in 1993; other towns being Butare, Ruhengeri and Gisenyi.

Kinyarwanda, the language of the entire population, French and English (since 1996) are the official languages. Swahili is spoken in the commercial centres.

CLIMATE. Despite the equatorial situation, there is a highland tropical climate. The wet seasons are from Oct. to Dec. and March to May. Highest rainfall occurs in the west, at around 70" (1,770 mm), decreasing to 40–55" (1,020–1,400 mm) in the central uplands and to 30" (760 mm) in the north and east. Kigali. Jan. 67°F (19·4°C), July 70°F (21·1°C). Annual rainfall 40" (1,000 mm).

CONSTITUTION AND GOVERNMENT. Under the 1978 Constitution the MRND was the sole political organization.

A new Constitution was promulgated in June 1991 which permits multi-party democracy.

The Arusha Agreement of Aug. 1994 provided for a transitional 70-member National Assembly, which began functioning in Nov. 1994. The seats won by the MRND were taken over by other parties on the grounds that the MRND was culpable of genocide.

President: Pasteur Bizimungu (b. 1950; RPF; installed 19 July 1994).

In Nov. 1995 the government comprised:

Vice President and Minister of Defence: Paul Kagame (RPF).

Prime Minister: Pierre-Célestin Rwigyema (MDR).

Minister of Agriculture, Livestock and Forestry: Augustine Iyamuremye (PSD). *Civil Service:* Abdulkarim Habimana (RPF). *Commerce, Industry and Handicrafts:* Prosper Higiro (PL). *Environment and Tourism:* Jean Nayinzira (PCD). *Family and Women's Affairs:* Aloyise Inyumba (RPF). *Finance:* Marc Rugenara (PSD). *Foreign Affairs:* Anastase Gasana (MDR). *Health:* Joseph Kalemera (RPF). *Higher Education, Research and Culture:* Joseph Nsengimana (PL). *Information:* Jean-Pierre Bizimana (MDR). *Interior and Community Development:* Alexis Kanyarengwe (RPF). *Justice:* Marthe Mukamurenzi (ind). *Labour and Social Affairs:* Pie Mugabo (PL). *Planning:* Jean-Berchmans Birara (ind). *Primary and Secondary Education:* Laurien Ngirabanzi (MDR). *Public Works and Energy:* Charles Ntakirutinka (PSD). *Refugee Rehabilitation:* Patriok Mazimpaka (RPF). *Transport and Communications:* Charles Muligande (RPF). *Youth and Sport:* Jacques Bihozagara (RPF).

National flag: Three equal vertical panels of red, yellow and green (left to right), the letter 'R' in black superimposed on the centre panel.

National anthem: 'Rwanda rwacu, Rwanda gihugu cyambyage' ('My Rwanda, Rwanda who gave me birth'); words by a collective, tune traditional.

Local government. The 10 prefectures, each under an appointed Prefect, are divided into 143 communes, each with an appointed Burgomaster and an elected Council.

DEFENCE. There has been no reliable information since the civil was in 1994.

Army. The Army consisted of 1 commando battalion, 1 reconnaissance, 8 infantry and 1 engineer company. Equipment included 12 AML-60 armoured cars. Strength (1994) about 5,000. There was a paramilitary gendarmerie of some 1,200.

Air Force. The Air Force operated 1 Guerrier armed light aircraft, 2 Noratlas and 1 Islander light transports and 6 Gazelle and 6 Alouette III helicopters. Current status is not known. Personnel (1993) 200.

INTERNATIONAL RELATIONS

Membership. Rwanda is a member of the UN, OAU and is an ACP state of the EU.

ECONOMY

Budget. In 1991 total revenue (in 1m. Rwanda francs) was 23,217; expenditure was 41,468, of which 2,434 was development expenditure.

Currency. The unit of currency is the *Rwanda franc* (RWF) notionally of 100 *centimes*. There are coins of 1, 2, 5, 10, 20 and 50 and notes of 100, 500, 1,000 and 5,000 Rwanda francs. On 3 Jan. 1995 500-, 1,000- and 5,000-Rwanda franc notes were replaced by new issues, demonetarizing the currency taken abroad by exiles. The currency is not convertible. Foreign exchange reserves were US$40m. in July 1994. There are no gold reserves. In March 1996, £1 = 336·25 Rwanda francs; US$1 = 220 Rwanda francs; DM1 = 149 Rwanda francs.

Banking and Finance. The central bank is the National Bank of Rwanda (founded 1960; *Governor* Augustin Ruzidana) which became the bank of issue in 1964. There are 4 commercial banks (independent with state equity participation, the Economic Community of the Great Lakes Bank, and a state-run savings bank and development bank).

ENERGY AND NATURAL RESOURCES

Electricity. 4 hydro-electric installations and 1 thermal plant produced 110m. kWh in 1986, but over half of the country's needs come from Zaïre.

Minerals. Production (1991): Cassiterite, 871 tonnes; wolfram, 212 tonnes. About 1m. cu. metres of natural gas are obtained from under the lake each year.

Agriculture. Subsistence agriculture accounts for most of the GNP. Staple food crops (production 1992, in 1,000 tonnes) are sweet potatoes (770), cassava (400), dry beans (200), sorghum (175), potatoes (280), maize (100), peas (18) and groundnuts (12). The main cash crops are coffee (35), tea (14) and pyrethrum. There is a pilot rice-growing project.

Long-horned Ankole cattle play an important traditional role. Efforts are being made to improve their present negligible economic value. There were (1992) 0·61m. cattle, 1·10m. goats, 0·39m. sheep and 1·42m. pigs.

INDUSTRY. There are about 100 small-sized modern manufacturing enterprises in the country. Food manufacturing is the dominant industrial activity (64%) followed by construction (15·3%) and mining (9%). There is a large modern brewery.

FOREIGN ECONOMIC RELATIONS. With Burundi and Zaïre Rwanda forms part of the Economic Community of the Great Lakes. Foreign debt was US$844·6m. in 1991.

Commerce. In 1991 exports amounted to US$94m. and imports US$267m. Major exports are coffee, tea and tin. Main export markets: 1991: Germany, 21·3%; Netherlands, 18·8%; Belgium, 11·8%; UK, 6·4%. Main import suppliers: Belgium, 17·1%; Kenya, 13·4%; South Africa, 10·4%; France, 6·8%.

Total trade between Rwanda and UK (British Department of Trade returns, in £1,000 sterling):

	1991	*1992*	*1993*	*1994*	*1995*
Imports to UK	2,193	2,582	1,892	1,666	1,841
Exports and re-exports from UK	2,334	1,552	3,337	2,542	4,825

COMMUNICATIONS

Roads. There were (1993) 3,100 km of main roads and 4,900 km of secondary roads (979 km asphalt. There are road links with Burundi, Uganda, Tanzania and Zaïre. There were in 1990 7,868 cars and 18,600 other vehicles.

Civil Aviation. There are international airports at Kanombe, for Kigali, and at Kamembe. The national carrier is Air Rwanda, which operated 1 B-707-320C and 1 other aircraft in 1995.

Telecommunications. Telephone provision, 1993, 1 per 1,000 population. The state-controlled Radiodiffusion de la République Rwandaise is responsible for broadcasting. There is no television. There were about 630,000 radio sets in 1993.

Press. There were 60 newspapers and periodicals in 1992.

SOCIAL INSTITUTIONS

Justice. A system of Courts of First Instance and provincial courts refer appeals to Courts of Appeal and a Court of Cassation situated in Kigali.

Religion. In 1989 there were 4·54m. Roman Catholics, 0·63m. Protestants and 0·63m. Moslems. Some of the population follow traditional animist religions. Before the civil war there were 9 Roman Catholic bishops and 370 priests. By the end of 1994 3 bishops had been killed and 3 reached retiring age; 106 priests had been killed and 130 had sought refuge abroad.

Education. In 1985 there were 790,198 pupils attending primary schools with 14,005 teachers. There were secondary, technical and teacher-training schools with 45,000 students and 1,082 teachers. In 1994 there were 2 universities and an Adventist university.

Health. In 1983 there were 170 hospitals and health centres with (1980) 9,015 beds; there were also 164 doctors, 1 dentist, 10 pharmacists, 464 midwives and 525 nursing personnel.

There were 10,786 reported cases of AIDS by Nov. 1993, and 1·38m. reported of malaria in 1992.

DIPLOMATIC REPRESENTATIVES

Of Rwanda in Great Britain (42 Aylmer Rd, London N2)
Ambassador: Gideon Kayinamura.

Of Great Britain in Rwanda
Ambassador: Kaye Oliver, OBE (resides in Kampala).

Of Rwanda in the USA (1714 New Hampshire Ave., NW, Washington, D.C., 20009)
Ambassador: Vacant.

Of the USA in Rwanda (Blvd. de la Révolution, Kigali)
Ambassador: David P. Rawson.

Of Rwanda to the United Nations
Ambassador: Manzi Bakuramutsa.

Further Reading

Braeckman, C., *Rwanda: Histoire d'un Génocide.* Paris, 1994
Dorsey, L., *Historical Dictionary of Rwanda.* Metuchen (NJ), 1995
Prunier, G., *The Rwanda Crisis: History of a Genocide.* Farnborough, 1995

ST HELENA

Capital: Jamestown
Population: 5,700 (1992)

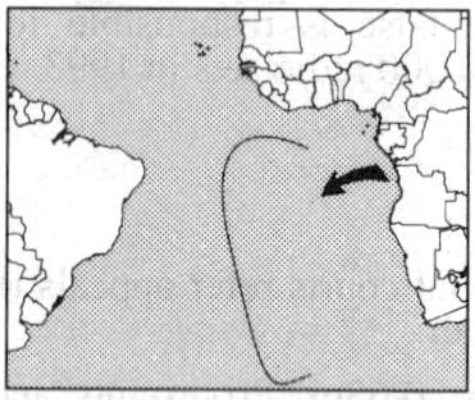

KEY HISTORICAL EVENTS. The island was uninhabited when discovered by the Portuguese in 1502. It was administered by the East India Company from 1659 and became a British colony in 1834.

TERRITORY AND POPULATION. St Helena, of volcanic origin, is 1,200 miles from the west coast of Africa. Area, 47 sq. miles (121·7 sq. km), with a cultivable area of 243 ha. Population (1992) 5,700. The port is Jamestown, population (1992) 1,500.

CLIMATE. A mild climate, with little variation. Temperatures range from 75–85°F (24–29°C) in summer to 65–75°F (18–24°C) in winter. Rainfall varies between 13" (325 mm) and 37" (925 mm) according to altitude and situation.

GOVERNMENT. The *Legislative Council* consists of the Governor, 2 *ex-officio* members (the Government Secretary and the Treasurer) and 12 elected members. The Governor is assisted by an *Executive Council* consisting of the 2 *ex-officio* members and the chairs of the 6 Council Committees.

Governor and C.-in-C.: D.L. Smallman, LVO.
Chief Secretary: J. G. Perrott.

Flag: The British Blue Ensign with the shield of the colony in the fly.

FINANCE AND TRADE

Budget. A National Development Plan covered 1990–91 to 1994–95.

Commerce. The economy is dependent on UK and EU aid. Total trade between Ascension and St Helena and UK (British Department of Trade returns, in £1,000 sterling):

	1991	*1992*	*1993*	*1994*	*1995*
Imports to UK	820	691	412	496	446
Exports and re-exports from UK	6,980	7,336	6,564	10,423	9,144

COMMUNICATIONS

Roads. There were (1988) 94 km of all-weather motor roads. There were 1,301 vehicles in 1987.

Shipping. There is a service from Cardiff (UK) 6 times a year, and links with South Africa and neighbouring islands.

Telecommunications. The Cable & Wireless Ltd cable connects St Helena with Cape Town and Ascension Island. St Helena Government Broadcasting Station, Radio St Helena, broadcasts daily and relays BBC programmes. Number of radio receivers (1993), 2,500.

SOCIAL INSTITUTIONS

Justice. Police force, 32; cases are dealt with by a police magistrate.

Religion. There are 10 Anglican churches, 4 Baptist chapels, 3 Salvation Army halls, 1 Seventh Day Adventist church and 1 Roman Catholic church.

Education. 3 pre-school playgroups, 7 primary and 1 comprehensive school controlled by the Government had 1,188 pupils in 1987. The Prince Andrew School (opened in 1989) offers vocational courses leading to British qualifications.

Health. There were 3 doctors, 1 dentist and 1 hospital in 1992.

Ascension is a small island of volcanic origin, of 34 sq. miles (88 sq. km), 700 miles north-west of St Helena. There are 120 ha providing fresh meat, vegetables and fruit. Population, 31 March 1993, was 1,117 (excluding military personnel).

The island is the resort of sea turtles, rabbits, the sooty tern or 'wideawake' and feral donkeys.

A cable station connects the island with St Helena, Sierra Leone, St Vincent, Rio de Janeiro and Buenos Aires. There is an airstrip (Miracle Mile) near the settlement of Georgetown; the Royal Air Force maintains an air link with the Falkland Islands.

Administrator: Roger Huxley.

Tristan da Cunha, is the largest of a small group of islands in the South Atlantic lying 1,320 miles (2,124 km) south-west of St Helena, of which they became dependencies on 12 Jan. 1938. Tristan da Cunha has an area of 98 sq. km and a population (1988) of 313, all living in the settlement of Edinburgh. Inaccessible Island (10 sq. km) lies 20 miles west and the 3 Nightingale Islands (2 sq. km) lie 20 miles south of Tristan da Cunha; they are uninhabited. Gough Island (90 sq. km) is 220 miles south of Tristan and has a meteorological station.

Tristan consists of a volcano rising to a height of 6,760 ft, with a circumference at its base of 21 miles. The volcano, believed to be extinct, erupted unexpectedly early in Oct. 1961. The whole population was evacuated without loss and settled temporarily in the UK; in 1963 they returned to Tristan. Potatoes remain the chief crop, cattle, sheep and pigs are now reared, and fish are plentiful.

Population in 1992, 295. The original inhabitants were shipwrecked sailors and soldiers who remained behind when the garrison from St Helena was withdrawn in 1817.

At the end of April 1942 Tristan da Cunha was commissioned as HMS *Atlantic Isle*, and became an important meteorological and radio station. In Jan. 1949 a South African company commenced crawfishing operations. An Administrator was appointed at the end of 1948 and a body of basic law brought into operation. The Island Council, which was set up in 1932, consists of a Chief Islander, 3 nominated and 8 elected members (including 1 woman) under the chairmanship of the Administrator.

Administrator: B. G. Dalley.

Further Reading

Crawford, A., *Tristan da Cunha and the Roaring Forties.* Edinburgh, 1982
Cross, A., *Saint Helena.* Newton Abbot, 1980
Munch, P. A., *Sociology of Tristan da Cunha.* Oslo, 1945.—*Crisis in Utopia.* New York, 1971

ST KITTS AND NEVIS

Federation of St Kitts and Nevis

Capital: Basseterre
Population: 43,520 (1993)
GNP capita: US$4,760 (1994)
HDI/world rank: 0·873/37 (1992)

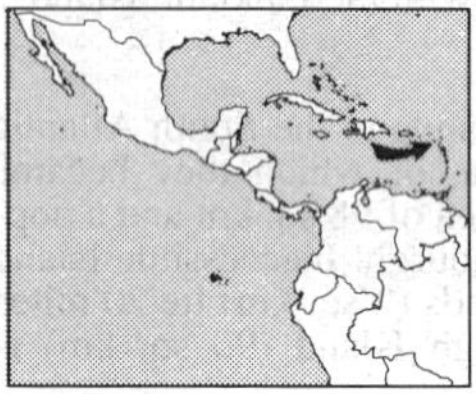

KEY HISTORICAL EVENTS. The islands of St Kitts (formerly St Christopher) and Nevis were discovered and named by Columbus in 1493. They were settled by Britain in 1623 and 1628 respectively, but ownership was disputed with France until 1783. They formed part of the Leeward Islands Federation from 1871 to 1956, and part of the Federation of the West Indies from 1958 to 1962. In Feb. 1967 the colonial status was replaced by an 'association' with Britain, giving the islands full internal self-government. St Kitts and Nevis became fully independent on 19 Sept. 1983.

TERRITORY AND POPULATION. The 2 islands of St Kitts and Nevis are situated at the northern end of the Leeward Islands in the Eastern Caribbean. Nevis lies 3 km to the south-east of St Kitts. Population, census (1991) 40,618. Estimate, 1993, 43,520, vital statistics: Live births registered, 1993, 915; birthrate, 20·9 per 1,000 inhabitants; deaths registered, 1991, 397; death rate, 9·7 per 1,000. Life expectancy, 1993: Males, 67·86 years; females, 71·14.

	sq. km	*Census 1980*	*Census 1991*	*Chief town*	*1994 estimate*
St Kitts	168·4	33,881	31,824	Basseterre	12,605
Nevis	93·2	9,428	8,794	Charlestown	1,411
	261·6	43,309	40,618		

In 1991, 94·9% of the population were Black. English is the official and spoken language.

CLIMATE. Temperature varies between 17–33°C, with a sea breeze throughout the year, low humidity. Average annual rainfall is 1,300 mm.

CONSTITUTION AND GOVERNMENT. The 1983 Constitution described the country as 'a sovereign democratic federal state'. The Queen of the UK is the head of state, represented by a Governor-General. It allowed for a unicameral Parliament consisting of 11 elected Members (8 from St Kitts and 3 from Nevis) and 3 appointed Senators. Nevis was given its own Island Assembly and the right to secession from St Kitts. At the elections on 3 July 1995 the Labour Party gained 7 seats, the People's Action Movement 1, the Concerned Citizens Movement 2 and the Nevis Reformation Party 1.

Governor-General: Sir Cuthbert Montraville Sebastian, OBE.

In Jan. 1996 the government comprised:

Prime Minister and Minister of Nationa Security, Foreign Affairs Finance, Planning and Information: Dr Denzil Douglas.

Deputy Prime Minister of Trade, Industry and CARICOM Affairs, Youth, Sports and Community Affairs: Sam Condor. *Health and Women's Affairs:* Dr Earl Asim Martin. *Tourism, Culture and Environment:* G.A. Dwyer Astaphan. *Education, Labour and Social Security:* Rupert Herbert. *Communications, Works and Public Utilities:* Cedric Liburd. *Agriculture, Lands and Housing:* Timothy Harris. *Attorney General:* Delano Bart.

The *Speaker* is Walford Gumbs.

The Premier of *Nevis* is Vance Amory.

The *Nevis Island* legislature comprises an Assembly of 3 nominated members and elected members from each electoral district on the Island, and an Administration consisting of the Premier and 2 other persons appointed by the Deputy Governor-General.

National flag: Diagonally green, black, red, with the black fimbriated in yellow and charged with two white stars.

National anthem: 'O Land of beauty! Our country where peace abounds'; words and tune by K. A. Georges.

INTERNATIONAL RELATIONS

Membership. St Kitts and Nevis is a member of the UN, the OAS, the Commonwealth and is an ACP state of the EU.

ECONOMY

Budget. The 1993 budget envisaged recurrent expenditure at EC$117,373,838 and revenue at EC$122,493,650.

Currency. The East Caribbean *dollar* (XCD) (of 100 *cents*) is in use. There are notes of EC$1, 5, 20 and 100, and coins of 1, 2, 5, 10, 25 and 50 cents and EC$1. In March 1996, £1 = EC$4·13; US$1 = EC$2·70; DM1 = EC$1·83.

Banking and Finance. The East Caribbean Central Bank (*Governor,* K. Dwight Venner) is the bank of issue. Operates 4 branches in St. Kitts and Nevis. The main office is located in Basseterre. There are 7 commercial banks, including 3 foreign. Commercial banks' assets (Dec. 1992) EC$646·47m.; deposits EC$481·28.

ENERGY AND NATURAL RESOURCES

Electricity. Production (1990) 46·5m. kWh. (St Kitts only).

Agriculture. The main crops are sugar, coconut, copra and cotton. In 1995, 8,220 acres were sown to sugar-cane. Most of the farms are small-holdings and there are a number of coconut estates amounting to some 1,000 acres under public and private ownership. Production, 1992 (in 1,000 tonnes): Sugar, 20; sugar-cane, 200 tonnes; coconuts, 2; fruit and vegetables, 3; cotton (1990), 20 tons.

Livestock (1992): Cattle, 5,000; pigs, 2,000; sheep, 15,000; goats, 10,000; poultry, (1987) 50,116.

Fisheries. Catch (1988) 2·5m. lbs.

INDUSTRY. The main industries are the assembly of electronic equipment and food and drink processing, particularly sugar and cane spirit. 180,285 tonnes of sugar were produced in 1995.

FOREIGN ECONOMIC RELATIONS

Commerce. Imports, (1992) EC$259·4m., mainly from the USA (EC$100·4m.); exports, EC$65·1m, mainly to the UK (EC$31·7m.). The chief export is sugar.

Total trade between St Kitts–Nevis and UK (British Department of Trade returns, in £1,000 sterling):

	1991	*1992*	*1993*	*1994*	*1995*
Imports to UK	6,476	7,052	8,996	6,505	8,671
Exports and re-exports from UK	5,765	6,074	8,735	6,915	9,104

Tourism. In 1994, there were 209,313 visitors, including 115,128 cruise ship passengers. In 1995 there were 31 hotels with 1,593 rooms.

COMMUNICATIONS

Roads. There were (1993) about 186·4 km of roads, of which 86·4 were surfaced, and 6,848 licensed vehicles.

Railways. There are 36 km of railway operated by the sugar industry.

Civil Aviation. There is an international airport at Golden Rock (4 km from Basseterre). 123,195 passengers arrived by air in 1992. Services are provided by American Airlines, BWIA, Canadian Airlines, LIAT, Virgin Islands Airways and Windward Islands Airways. There is an airfield on Nevis (Newcastle).

Shipping. There is a deep-water port at Bird Rock (Basseterre). 148,084 tons of cargo were unloaded in 1994 and 33,820 tons loaded. The government maintains a commercial motor boat service between the islands.

Telecommunications. There are 2 post offices with 7 branches. There were 11,121 telephone subscribers in 1992. There is a government-owned radio and TV station; Nevis has a privately-owned radio station and a TV station as well. In 1993 there were 9,500 television (colour by NTSC) and 25,000 radio receivers.

SOCIAL INSTITUTIONS

Justice. Justice is administered by the Supreme Court and by Magistrates' Courts.They have both civil and criminal jurisdiction.

Religion. In 1994, 27·5% of the population were Anglican, 25·3% Methodist, 6·9% Roman Catholic, 5·5% Pentecostal, 3·9% Baptist and 3·9% Church of-God.

Education. Adult literacy was 95% in 1993. Primary education is compulsory between the ages of 5 and 14, but no pupil is required to leave school before the age of 16. There is an Extra-Mural Department of the University of the West Indies, a Technical College and a Teachers' Training College. In 1993–94 there were 2,203 pupils and 156 teachers in 45 pre-primary schools, In 1990–91 there were 5,957 pupils and 302 teachers in 23 primary schools, 4,236 pupils and 304 teachers in 7 secondary schools, and 1,299 pupils and 76 teachers in 8 private schools. In 1989 there were 211 students in the Technical and Teacher's Training Colleges.

Health. In 1990 there were 28 doctors, 4 hospitals with 258 beds and 17 health clinics.

DIPLOMATIC REPRESENTATIVES

Of St Kitts and Nevis in Great Britain (10 Kensington Ct., London W8 5DL)
High Commissioner: Aubrey Hart.

Of Great Britain in St Kitts and Nevis
High Commissioner: R. Thomas, CMG (resides at Bridgetown).

Of St Kitts and Nevis in the USA (2100 M. St., NW, Washington, D.C., 20037)
Ambassador: Erstein M. Edwards.

Of the USA in St Kitts and Nevis
Ambassador: Jeanette Hyde (resides in Bridgetown).

Of St Kitts and Nevis to the United Nations
Ambassador: Lee L. Moore, QC.

Further Reading

Statistics Division. *National Accounts.* Annual.—*St Kitts and Nevis Quarterly.*
Gordon, J., *Nevis: Queen of the Caribees.* London, 1985
Moll, V. P., *St Kitts and Nevis.* [Bibliography]. Oxford and Santa Barbara (CA), 1995

National library: Public Library, Basseterre.
National statistical office: Statistics Division, Ministry of Development, Basseterre.

ST LUCIA

Capital: Castries
Population: 136,000 (1993)
GNP per capita: US$3,450 (1994)
HDI/world rank: 0·732/84 (1992)

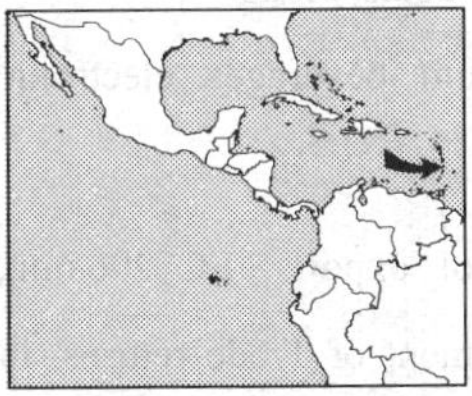

KEY HISTORICAL EVENTS. Attempts to colonize the island by the British took place in 1605 and 1638. The French settled in 1650 and St Lucia was ceded to Britain in 1814. Self-government was achieved in 1967 and independence on 22 Feb. 1979.

TERRITORY AND POPULATION. St Lucia is an island of the Lesser Antilles situated in the Eastern Caribbean between Martinique and St Vincent, with an area of 238 sq. miles (617 sq. km); population (census, 1991) 133,308. Estimate, 1993, 136,000 (46% urban); density, 216·1 per sq. km. The capital is Castries (population, 1992, 53,883), and Vieux Fort, the second town and port (13,140). Life expectancy (1992) was 69·3 (men) and 74 (women).

CLIMATE. The climate is tropical, with a dry season lasting from Jan. to April, a wet season from May to Aug., followed by an Indian summer for two months, but most rain falls in Nov. and Dec. Amounts vary over the year, according to altitude, from 60" (1,500 mm) to 138" (3,450 mm). Temperatures are uniform at about 80°F (26·7°C).

CONSTITUTION AND GOVERNMENT. There is a 17-seat *House of Assembly* elected for 5 years; an 11-seat *Senate* appointed by the Governor-General, 6 on the advice of the Prime Minister, 3 on the advice of the Leader of the Opposition, and 2 'after consultation with appropriate religious, economic or social bodies or associations'.

At the elections of April 1992 the United Workers' Party gained 11 seats and the St Lucia Labour Party 6.

Governor-General: Sir Anthony Stanislaus James, GCSL, GCMG, OBE.

In Nov. 1995 the government comprised:

Prime Minister, Minister of Finance, Planning, Development, Information and Broadcasting: Rt Hon. John George Melvin Compton.

Deputy Prime Minister and Minister of Home Affairs, Foreign Affairs, Trade and Industry: George Mallet. *Education, Culture and Labour:* Louis George. *Community Development, Social Affairs, Youth and Sport and Co-operatives:* Desmond Braithwaite. *Agriculture, Lands, Fisheries and Forestry:* Ira D'Auvergne. *Communications, Works and Transport:* Gregory Avril. *Attorney-General and Minister of Legal Affairs:* Lorraine Williams. *Tourism, Public Utilities and National Mobilization:* Romanus Lansiquot. *Health and Local Government:* Stephenson King. *Ministers of State:* Rufus Bousquet (*Trade and Industry*); Edward Innocent (*Youth, Sports and Co-operatives*); Michael Pilgrim (*Housing, Urban Development and Renewal*).

National flag: Blue with a design of a black triangle edged in white, bearing a smaller yellow triangle, in the centre.

National anthem: 'Sons and daughters of St Lucia'; words by C. Jesse, tune by L. F. Thomas.

Local Government. There are 8 administrative regions.

INTERNATIONAL RELATIONS

Membership. St Lucia is a member of the UN, OAS, Caricom, the Commonwealth and is an ACP state of the EU.

ECONOMY

Budget. The budget in 1993–94 amounted to EC$542·8m. expenditure; revenue, EC$375·8m.

Banking and Finance. There are 3 domestic and 4 foreign banks.

AGRICULTURE. Bananas, cocoa, breadfruit and mango are the principal crops. Livestock (1992): Cattle, 3,000; pigs, 8,000; sheep, 5,000; goats, 3,000.

INDUSTRY. In 1992, laundry soap, coconut meal, rum, beverages, electronic assembly and clothing were the chief products.

FOREIGN ECONOMIC RELATIONS

Commerce. Value of imports (1991), EC$797·4m.; of exports, EC$296·6m., including coconut oil, cocoa beans, copra and bananas.

Total trade between St Lucia and UK (British Department of Trade returns, in £1,000 sterling):

	1991	*1992*	*1993*	*1994*	*1995*
Imports to UK	44,852	53,820	53,663	41,294	45,993
Exports and re-exports from UK	19,025	19,586	19,559	42,496	70,076

Tourism. The total number of visitors during 1992 was 348,869.

COMMUNICATIONS

Roads. The island has 500 miles of main and secondary roads, and 2,084 commercial vehicles and 8,629 cars in 1986.

Civil Aviation. There is an international airport at Hewanorra. The island is served by Air Canada, Air Martinique, American Airlines British Airways, BWIA, Condor, Helenair and LIAT.

Shipping. There are 2 ports, Castries and Vieux Fort.

Telecommunications. There were (1992) 26,000 telephones, 68 telex and 560 fax machines. In 1993 there were 2 private radio stations, 2 privately-owned local TV stations and a cable TV service. There were 24,334 TV and 35,269 radio receivers in 1991.

Cinemas. There were 8 cinemas in 1986.

Press. In 1993 there were 3 newspapers with a nation-wide circulation.

SOCIAL INSTITUTIONS

Justice. The island is divided into 2 judicial districts, and there are 9 magistrates' courts. Appeals lie to the Eastern Caribbean Supreme Court of Appeal.

Religion. In 1989 over 82% of the population was Roman Catholic. The main Protestant denominations are Anglican and Methodist.

Education (1992–93). 84 primary schools, with 32,204 pupils on roll. Primary education is free and compulsory by law, but the legislation is not enforced. There are 14 secondary schools with 7,612 pupils. There is 1 community college with divisions of art and general studies (244 students), teacher education (135), technical education (269), nursing education (60) and continuing education (417).

Health. In 1992 there were 64 doctors, 6 dentists and 256 nursing personnel employed by the government, 4 hospitals with 435 beds and 34 health centres.

DIPLOMATIC REPRESENTATIVES

Of St Lucia in Great Britain (10 Kensington Ct., London, W8 5DL)
High Commissioner: Aubrey E. Hart.

Of Great Britain in St Lucia
High Commissioner: R. Thomas, CMG.

Of St Lucia in the USA (2100 M St., NW, Washington, D.C., 20037)
Ambassador: Dr Joseph E. Edmunds.

Of the USA in St Lucia
Ambassador: Jeanette Hyde (resides in Bridgetown).

Of St Lucia to the United Nations
Ambassador: George Odlum.

Further Reading

Ellis, G., *St Lucia: Helen of the West Indies.* London, 1985
Mommsen, J. H., *St Lucia.* [Bibliography]. Oxford and Santa Barbara (CA), 1996

Library: The Central Library, Castries.

ST VINCENT AND THE GRENADINES

Capital: Kingstown
Population: 109,000 (1994)
GNP per capita: US$2,120 (1994)
HDI/world rank: 0·761/79 (1992)

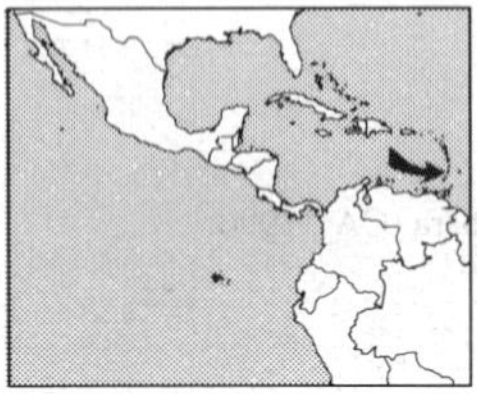

KEY HISTORICAL EVENTS. The date of discovery of St Vincent was 22 Jan. 1498. In 1969 St Vincent and the Grenadines became a self-governing Associated State of UK and acquired full independence on 27 Oct. 1979.

TERRITORY AND POPULATION. St Vincent is an island of the Lesser Antilles, situated in the Eastern Caribbean between St Lucia and Grenada, from which latter it is separated by a chain of small islands known as the Grenadines. The total area of 388 sq. km (150 sq. miles) comprises the island of St Vincent itself (345 sq. km) and those of the Grenadines attached to it (43 sq. km) of which the largest are Bequia, Mustique, Canouan, Mayreau and Union.

The population at the 1991 Census was 106,499, of whom 8,367 lived in the St Vincent Grenadines. 1994 estimate, 109,000 (24·6% urban); density, 280 per sq. km. The capital, Kingstown, had 26,223 inhabitants in 1991 (including suburbs). The population is mainly of black (82%) and mixed (13·9%) origin, with small white, Asian and Amerindian minorities.

Vital statistics (1994): Live births, 2,549; deaths, 768; marriages, 458.

CLIMATE. The climate is tropical marine, with north-east Trades predominating and rainfall ranging from 150" (3,750 mm) a year in the mountains to 60" (1,500 mm) on the south-east coast. The rainy season is from June to Dec., and temperatures are equable throughout the year.

CONSTITUTION AND GOVERNMENT. The head of state is Queen Elizabeth II, represented by a *Governor.* Parliament is unicameral and consists of a 21-member *House of Assembly,* 15 of which are directly elected for a 5-year term from single-member constituencies. The remaining 6 are senators appointed by the Governor (4 on the advice of the Prime Minister and 2 on the advice of the Leader of the Opposition). At the elections in Feb. 1994, the New Democratic Party won 12 seats and the alliance of the St Vincent Labour Party and the Movement for National Unity (which have in 1995 merged to form the Unity Labour Party) 3.

Governor: Sir David Jack, GCMG, MBE.

In Jan. 1996 the government comprised:

Prime Minister and Minister of Finance and Planning: Rt. Hon. James Fitz-Allen Mitchell.

Attorney-General and Minister of Justice: Carlyle Dougan, QC. *Education, Culture, Women's Affairs and Ecclesiastical Affairs:* John Horne. *Agriculture and Labour:* Allan Cruickshank. *Communications and Works:* Jeremiah Scott. *Housing, Local Government, Youth, Sports and Community Development:* Louis Jones. *Health and Environment:* Yvonne Francis-Gibson. *Trade, Industry and Consumer Affairs:* Bernard Wyllie. *Foreign Affairs and Tourism:* Alpian Allen.

There are 2 Ministers of State.

National flag: Three vertical stripes of blue, yellow, green, with the yellow of double width and charged with three green diamonds.

National anthem: 'St Vincent, land so beautiful'; words by Phyllis Punnett, tune by J. B. Miguel.

INTERNATIONAL RELATIONS

Membership. St Vincent and the Grenadines is a member of UN, OAS, CARICOM, the Commonwealth and is an ACP state of the EU.

ECONOMY

Budget. The 1993–94 budget envisaged current expenditure of US$68·4m., capital expenditure of US$29·3m. and current revenue of US$68·5m.

Currency. The currency in use is the *East Caribbean dollar* (XCD). Foreign exchange reserves were US$27·9m. in Sept. 1993. In March 1996, £1 = EC$4·13; US$1 = EC$2·70; DM1 = EC$1·83.

Banking and Finance. The East Caribbean Central Bank is the bank of issue. There are branches of Barclays Bank PLC, the Caribbean Banking Corporation, the Canadian Imperial Bank of Commerce, the Bank of Nova Scotia. Locally-owned banks: First St Vincent Bank, the National Commercial Bank and St Vincent Co-operative Bank.

ENERGY AND NATURAL RESOURCES

Electricity. Production (1991) was 53,024,788 kWh.

Agriculture. Agriculture accounted for 18·9% of GDP in 1990. According to the 1985–86 census of agriculture, 29,649 acres of the total acreage of 85,120 were classified as agricultural lands; 5,500 acres were under forest and woodland and all other lands accounted for 1,030 acres. The total arable land was about 8,932 acres, of which 4,016 acres were under temporary crops, 2,256 acres under temporary pasture, 2,289 acres under temporary fallow and other arable land covering 371 acres. 16,062 acres were under permanent crops, of which approximately 5,500 acres were under coconuts and 7,224 acres under bananas; the remainder produce cocoa, citrus, mangoes, avocado pears, guavas and miscellaneous crops. The sugar industry was closed down in 1985 although some sugar-cane is grown for rum production. Production (1991, in tonnes): Bananas, 64,779.

Livestock (1991): Cattle, 8,000; pigs, 9,000; sheep, 15,000; goats, 5,000.

INDUSTRY. Industries include assembly of electronic equipment, manufacture of garments, electrical products, animal feeds and flour, corrugated galvanized sheets, exhaust systems, industrial gases, concrete blocks, plastics, soft drinks, beer and rum, wood products and furniture, and processing of milk, fruit juices and food items.

Labour. The Department of Labour is charged with looking after the interest and welfare of all categories of workers, including providing advice and guidance to employers and employees and their organizations and enforcing the labour laws.

FOREIGN ECONOMIC RELATIONS. Foreign debt was US$62·6m. in 1992.

Commerce (1994). Imports, EC$365·1m.; exports, EC$126·5m.

Principal exports, 1994 (in EC$1,000): Eddoes, 1,720; dasheen, 845; sweet potatoes, 1,160; tannias, 144; bananas, 43,401; coconut, 302; plantain, 671; ginger, 240; flour, 23,352.

Total trade between St Vincent and the Grenadines and UK (British Department of Trade returns, in £1,000 sterling):

	1991	*1992*	*1993*	*1994*	*1995*
Imports to UK	29,259	26,546	25,891	14,312	22,242
Exports and re-exports from UK	7,316	9,469	7,959	7,652	7,215

Tourism. There were 157,532 visitors in 1990.

COMMUNICATIONS

Roads. There were (1991) 60 miles of highway, 34 miles of concrete road, 296 miles of oiled asphalt road and 196 miles of earth track. Vehicles registered (1992) 9,867.

Civil Aviation. There is an airport (E. T. Joshua) on mainland St Vincent. Scheduled services are operated daily by LIAT and Air Martinique. Airports on Bequia, Union, Mustique and Canolian have regular scheduled services.

Shipping. In 1994 there were some 200 ships in the Vincentian open register. In 1991 943 motor vessels of 919,846 NRT entered and cleared and 73 tankers of 84,367 NRT bringing 23,974 tons of fuel entered.

Telecommunications. There is a General Post Office at Kingstown and 56 district post offices. There is a fully digital automatic telephone system with (1992) 14,600 subscribers; 17,500 stations and digital radio links to Bequia, Mustique, Union, Petit St Vincent and Palm Island. The telephone network has almost 100% geographical coverage. The National Broadcasting Corporation is part government-owned and part commercial. In 1992 there were 65,000 radio and 20,600 TV sets (colour by NTSC).

Cinemas. There were 2 cinemas in 1987 with a seating capacity of 1,825.

SOCIAL INSTITUTIONS

Justice. Law is based on UK common law as exercised by the Eastern Caribbean Supreme Court on St Lucia. Final appeal lies to the UK Privy Council. In 1995 there were 4,700 criminal matters disposed of in the 3 magisterial districts which comprise 11 courts. 62 cases were dealt with in the Criminal Assizes in the High Court. Strength of police force (1995), 663 (including 19 gazetted officers).

Religion. At the 1980 Census, 42% of the population was Anglican, 21% Methodist and 12% Roman Catholic.

Education. In 1989 there were 64 primary schools (52 rural) with 25,152 pupils, 21 secondary schools (13 rural) and 1 school for special needs.

Health. In 1992 there was a general hospital in Kingstown with 207 beds, 6 rural hospitals, 2 private hospitals and 38 clinics. There were 40 doctors, 6 dentists, 224 registered nurses, 144 nursing assistants and 39 community health aides.

Library: St Vincent Public Library, Kingstown. *Librarian:* Mrs Pearl Herbert.

DIPLOMATIC REPRESENTATIVES

Of St Vincent and the Grenadines in Great Britain (10 Kensington Ct, London, W8 5DL)
High Commissioner: Aubrey Hart.

Of Great Britain in St Vincent and the Grenadines (POB 132, Granby St., Kingstown)
High Commissioner: R. Thomas, CMG.

Of St Vincent and the Grenadines in the USA
Ambassador: Kingsley C. A. Layne.

Of the USA in St Vincent and the Grenadines
Ambassador: Jeanette Hyde (resides in Bridgetown).

Of St Vincent and the Grenadines to the United Nations
Ambassador: Herbert G. Young.

Further Reading

Jenkins, D. and Bobrow, J., *St Vincent and the Grenadines: a Plural Country*. St Vincent, 1985
Potter, R. B., *St Vincent and the Grenadines*. [Bibliography]. Oxford and Santa Barbara (CA), 1992
Price, N., *Behind the Planter's Back*. London, 1988
Sutty, L., *St Vincent and the Grenadines*. London, 1993

SAN MARINO

Repubblica di San Marino

Capital: San Marino
Population: 24,003 (1993)

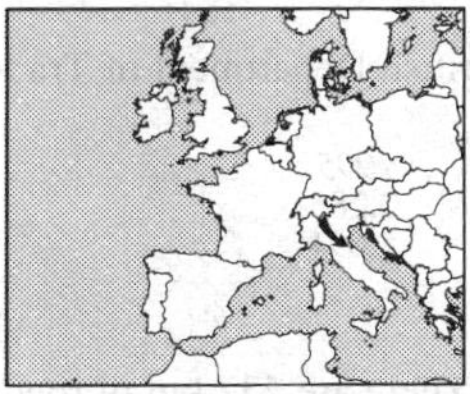

KEY HISTORICAL EVENTS. On 22 March 1862 San Marino concluded a treaty of friendship and co-operation, including a *de facto* customs union with Italy. The treaty was renewed on 27 March 1872, 28 June 1897 and 31 March 1939, with several amendments 1942–87.

TERRITORY AND POPULATION. San Marino is a land-locked state in central Italy, 20 km from the Adriatic. Area is 61·19 sq. km (23·6 sq. miles) and the population (1993), 24,003 (90·5% urban); some 13,000 citizens live abroad. Population density, 393 per sq. km. The capital, San Marino, had 4,335 inhabitants (1993); the largest town is Serravalle (7,264 in 1991), an industrial centre in the north.

CONSTITUTION AND GOVERNMENT. The legislative power is vested in the *Great and General Council* of 60 members elected every 5 years by popular vote, 2 of whom are appointed every 6 months to act as *Captains Regent*, who are the heads of state.

At the elections of 30 May 1993 the Christian Democrats gained 41·4% of votes cast and the Socialist Party 18%, forming a coalition government with 40 seats in the Great and General Council. The Progressive Democrats (former Communists) gained 28·7% of votes cast and 11 seats, the Popular Democratic Alliance 4 seats, the Democratic Movement 3 seats and the Refounded Communists 2.

Executive power is exercised by the 10-member *Congress of State*, presided over by the Captains Regent. The *Council of Twelve*, also presided over by the Captains Regent, is appointed by the Great and General Council to perform administrative functions and is a court of third instance.

In Dec. 1995 the Congress of State comprised:

Minister of Foreign and Political Affairs: Gabriele Gatti. *Finance, Budget, Planning and Information:* Clelio Galassi. *Home Affairs:* Antonio Volpinari. *Industry and Handicraft:* Fiorenzo Stolfi. *Territory, Environment and Agriculture:* Emma Rossi. *Commerce and Relations with Local Councils:* Ottaviano Rossi. *Health and Social Security:* Sante Canducci. *Education, Culture, University and Justice:* Pier Marino Menicucci. *Labour and Co-operation:* Claudio Podeschi. *Communications, Transport, Tourism and Sport:* Augusto Casali.

National flag: Horizontally white over light blue, with the national arms over all in the centre.

National anthem: No words, tune monastic, transcribed by F. Consolo.

Local Government. There are 9 districts (*castelli*), each run by a board elected every 5 years.

DEFENCE. Military service is not obligatory, but all citizens between the ages of 16 and 55 can be called upon to defend the State. They may also serve as volunteers in the Military Corps. There is a paramilitary Gendarmerie.

INTERNATIONAL RELATIONS. San Marino maintains a traditional neutrality, e.g. in the First and Second World Wars.

Membership. San Marino is a member of the UN and the Council of Europe.

ECONOMY. The budget (ordinary and extraordinary) for the financial year ending 31 Dec. 1995 balanced at 521m. lire.

3,940 ha of land area are arable. Wheat, barley, maize and vines are grown. The chief exports are wood machinery, chemicals, wine, textiles, tiles, varnishes and ceramics.

Italian currency is in use, but the republic issues its own coins.

In 1994, 3m. tourists visited San Marino.

FOREIGN ECONOMIC RELATIONS

Commerce. Total trade between San Marino and UK (British Department of Trade returns, in £1,000 sterling):

	1995
Imports to UK	2,285
Exports and re-exports from UK	5,091

COMMUNICATIONS

Roads. A bus service connects San Marino with Rimini. There are 237 km of roads and (1987) 16,540 passenger cars and 3,225 commercial vehicles.

Telecommunications. In 1995 there were 15,000 telephones and 9 post offices. In 1987 there were 6,608 television receivers. San Marino RTV is the state broadcasting company. Radio Titano is a private station. There were 12,535 radio receivers in 1991.

Cinemas. In 1987 there were 7 cinemas with a seating capacity of 1,000.

SOCIAL INSTITUTIONS

Justice. Judges are appointed permanently by the Great and General Council; they may not be San Marino citizens. Petty civil cases are dealt with by a justice of the peace; legal commissioners deal with more serious civil cases and all criminal cases and appeals lie to them from the justice of the peace. Appeals against the legal commissioners lie to an appeals judge, and the Council of the Twelve functions as a court of third instance.

Religion. The great majority of the population are Roman Catholic.

Education. Education is compulsory up to 16 years of age. In 1994 there were 15 nursery schools with 811 pupils and 102 teachers, 14 elementary schools with 1,166 pupils and 219 teachers, 3 junior high schools with 772 pupils and 133 teachers, and 1 high school with 274 pupils and 44 teachers. The University of San Marino began operating in 1988.

Health. In 1987 there were 149 hospital beds and 60 doctors.

DIPLOMATIC REPRESENTATIVES

British Consul-General (resides at Florence): R. J. Griffiths, OBE.

Of San Marino to the United Nations
Ambassador: Pietro Giacomini.

Further Reading

Matteini, N., *The Republic of San Marino.* San Marino, 1981
Packett, C. N., *Guide to the Republic of San Marino.* Bradford, 1970

Information: Office of Cultural Affairs and Information of the Department of Foreign Affairs.

SÃO TOMÉ E PRÍNCIPE

República Democrática de São Tomé e Príncipe

Capital: São Tomé
Population: 131,100 (1995)
GNP per capita: US$250 (1994)
HDI/world rank: 0·451/133 (1992)

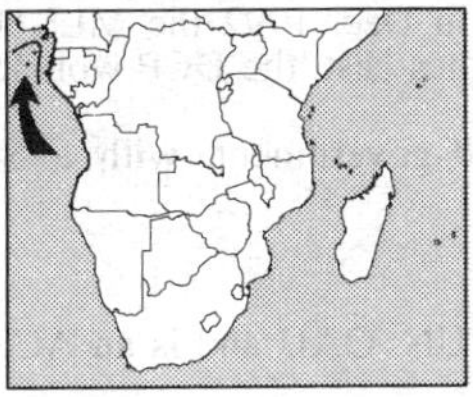

KEY HISTORICAL EVENTS. The islands of São Tomé and Príncipe were discovered in 1471 and from 1522 were a Portugese colony; this became an overseas province of Portugal in 1951. Independence was gained on 12 July 1975.

TERRITORY AND POPULATION. The republic, which lies about 200 km off the west coast of Gabon, in the Gulf of Guinea, comprises the main islands of São Tomé (845 sq. km) and Príncipe and several smaller islets including Pedras Tinhosas and Rolas. It has a total area of 1,001 sq. km (387 sq. miles). Population (census, 1991) 120,146. Estimate (1995) 131,100.

The areas and populations of the 2 provinces:

Province	*Sq. km*	*Census 1991*	*Estimate 1995*	*Chief town*	*Census 1991*
São Tomé	859	114,507	125,200	São Tomé	43,420
Príncipe	142	5,639	5,900	São António	1,000

Vital statistics (1985): Births, 3,700; deaths, 900. Rates (per 1,000 population): Birth (1988), 36·7; death (1988), 11·5; infant mortality (per 1,000 live births, 1990), 74. Expectation of life, 1990: Males, 60·7 years; females, 63·1.

The official language is Portuguese. Lungwa Sao Tome, a Portuguese creole, and Fang, a Bantu language are the spoken languages.

CLIMATE. The tropical climate is modified by altitude and the effect of the cool Benguela current. The wet season is generally from Oct. to May, but rainfall varies very much, from 40" (1,000 mm) in the hot and humid north-east to 150–200" (3,800–5,000 mm) on the plateau. São Tomé Jan. 79°F (26·1°C), July 75°F (23·9°C). Annual rainfall 38" (951 mm).

CONSTITUTION AND GOVERNMENT. The 1990 constitution was approved by 72% of votes at a referendum of Aug. 1990. It abolished the monopoly of the Movement for the Liberation of São Tomé e Príncipe (MLSTP). The *President* must be over 34 years old, and is elected by universal suffrage for one or two (only) 5-year terms. He or she is also head of government and appoints a Council of Ministers. The 55-member *National Assembly* is elected for 4 years.

At the presidential elections of Feb. 1991 the sole candidate, Miguel Trovoada, was elected by 82% of votes cast. Turn-out was 60%. Presidential elections were scheduled for March 1996.

At the elections on 2 Oct. 1994 the electorate was some 57,000; turn-out was 79%. The MLSTP/Social Democratic Party won 27 seats, the Democratic Convergence Party (DCP), 14 and Independent Democratic Action (IDA), 14.

President, C.-in-C.: Miguel Trovoada (b. 1946; IDA).

In Jan. 1996 the government comprised:

Prime Minister Armindo Vaz d'Almeida.

Minister of Foreign Affairs and Co-operation: Guilherme Posser da Costa. *Economic Affairs:* Joaquim Rafael Branco. *Planning and Finance:* Carlos Quaresma Batisa de Souza. *Interior and Security:* Alberto Paulino. *Justice, Public Administration, Employment and Social Security:* Manuel Vaz Afonso Fernandes. *Social Amenities:* Alcino Martinho de Barros Pinto. *Education, Youth and Sports:*

Guilherme Octaviano Viegas. *Health:* Fernando da Conceicao Silvera. *Minister-delegate for the Region of Príncipe:* Zeferino Vaz dos Santos dos Prazeres.

National flag: 3 horizontal stripes of green, yellow, green, with the yellow of double width and bearing 2 black stars; in the hoist a red triangle over all.

National anthem: 'Independência total, glorioso canto do povo' ('Total independence, glorious song of the people'); words by A. N. do Espírito Santo, tune by M. de Sousa e Almeida.

Local Government. São Tomé province comprises 6 districts. Districts have assemblies elected universally for 3-year terms. In elections in Dec. 1992 the MLSTP won 38 of the 59 district assembly seats with 70% of votes cast, the DCP won 15 seats, IDA 6.

Since April 1995 **Príncipe** has enjoyed internal self-government, with a 5-member regional government and an elected assembly.

INTERNATIONAL RELATIONS

Membership. São Tomé e Príncipe is a member of the UN, OAU and is an ACP state of the EU.

ECONOMY

Policy. Most branches of the economy were nationalized after independence, but economic liberalization began in 1985 and was increased in 1991.

Budget. In 1993 the revenue was 4,000m. dobras and expenditure 6,300m. dobras. The 1994 budget sets expenditure at 18,000m. dobras. 13,000m. dobras is earmarked for servicing foreign debt, 1,500m. dobras for health and education, 400m. dobras for embassies abroad, 350m. dobras for defence, 285m. dobras for financial administration, 160m. dobras for justice and 130m. dobras for social development.

Currency. The unit of currency is the *dobra* (STD) of 100 *centimos*. There are coins of 50 centimos and 1, 2, 5, 10 and 20 dobras, and notes of 50, 100, 500, 1,000, 2,000 and 5,000 dobras. In March 1996, £1 = 2,830·80 dobras; US$1 = 1,852·13 dobras; DM1 = 1,058·12 dobras.

Banking and Finance. In 1991 the Banco Central de São Tomé e Príncipe replaced the Banco Nacional as the central bank and bank of issue. A private commercial bank, the Banco Internacional de São Tomé e Príncipe, began operations in 1993.

Weights and Measures. The metric system is in use.

ENERGY AND NATURAL RESOURCES

Electricity. Installed capacity, 1992, 7·2m. kW; output, 4·6m. kWh. 30% of supply is hydroelectric.

Agriculture. In 1992 agriculture produced 25% of GDP. After independence all landholdings over 200 ha were nationalized into 15 state farms. These were partially privatized in 1985 by granting management contracts to foreign companies, and distributing some state land as small private plots. Production (1992 in tonnes): Coconuts, 42,000; cocoa, 3,858; copra, 3,000; bananas, 3,000; palm oil, 250. Food crops include cassava, sweet potatoes and yams. In 1992 there were 4,000 goats, 2,000 sheep, 3,000 pigs and 4,000 cattle.

Forestry. Forests cover 60% of the land area. In 1988 6,000 cu. metres of timber were cut.

Fisheries. There are rich tuna shoals. Catch (1991) 2,996 tonnes.

INDUSTRY. In 1992 manufacturing contributed 6·9% of GDP. There are a few small factories in agricultural and timber processing, bricks, ceramics, printing, textiles and soap-making.

Labour. In 1987 the economically active population was 31,900. There were 6,430 registered unemployed. There is a minimum monthly wage of 7,000 dobras.

FOREIGN ECONOMIC RELATIONS. Foreign debt was US$189·9m. in 1992.

Commerce. Imports in 1992 amounted to 10,089·4m. dobras and exports to 1,739·8m. dobras, the main exports being cocoa (80%), copra (15%), coffee, bananas and palm-oil.

Total trade between São Tomé e Príncipe and UK (British Department of Trade returns, in £1,000 sterling):

	1991	*1992*	*1993*	*1994*	*1995*
Imports to UK	1	4	–	3	85
Exports and re-exports from UK	1,020	1,117	3,433	2,313	2,297

Main export markets, 1990: Germany, 44·8%; Netherlands, 31·1%. Main import suppliers: Portugal, 39·5%; Spain, 12·3%; Belgium, 12·1%.

Tourism. Exit visas for citizens were abolished in 1994.

COMMUNICATIONS

Roads. There were 380 km of roads in 1994, 250 km asphalted.

Civil Aviation. São Tomé airport is linked by regular services to Lisbon, Luanda, and Libreville. There is a light aircraft service to Príncipe. The national carrier is Air São Tomé in which the government has a 35% stake. 40% is owned by TAP-Air Portugal, who operate most international routes.

Shipping. São Tomé is the main port, but it lacks a deep water harbour. Neves handles oil imports and is the main fishing port. Portuguese shipping lines run routes to Lisbon, Oporto, Rotterdam and Antwerp.

Telecommunications. There were (1991) 3,105 telephones. Radio broadcasting is conducted by the government-controlled Rádio Nacional. There is a Voice of America radio station, a religious station and a private German station. There were about 31,000 radio sets in 1991. There is an experimental TV service at weekends.

Press. In 1986 there were 2 weekly newspapers.

SOCIAL INSTITUTIONS.

Justice. Members of the Supreme Court are appointed by the National Assembly. There is no death penalty.

Religion. About 80% of the population are Roman Catholic. There is a small Protestant church and a Seventh Day Adventist school.

Education. Adult literacy was 60% in 1992. Education is free and compulsory. In 1993 there were 85 primary and 5 secondary schools. 90% of primary age children were attending school. There is a vocational centre, a school of agriculture and a pre-university *lycee.*

Health. In 1988 there were 50 doctors.

DIPLOMATIC REPRESENTATIVES

Of São Tomé and Príncipe in Great Britain (resides in Brussels)
Ambassador: Vacant.

Of Great Britain in São Tomé and Príncipe
Ambassador: Roger Hart (resides in Luanda).

Of São Tomé and Príncipe in the USA and to the United Nations
Ambassador: Vacant.

Of the USA in São Tomé and Príncipe
Ambassador: Elizabeth Raspolic.

Of São Tomé and Príncipe to the United Nations
Ambassador: Vacant.

Further Reading

Shaw, C. S., *São Tomé e Príncipe.* [Bibliography] Oxford and Santa Barbara (CA), 1994

SAUDI ARABIA

Mamlaka al-'Arabiya as-Sa'udiya

(Kingdom of Saudi Arabia)

Capital: Riyadh
Population: 16·9m. (1992)
GNP per capita: US$7,240 (1994)
HDI/world rank: 0·762/76 (1992)

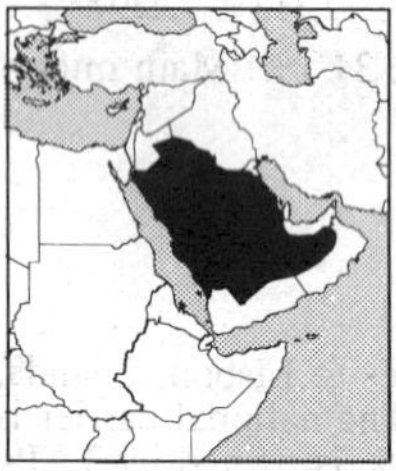

KEY HISTORICAL EVENTS. Saudi Arabia was founded by Abdul Aziz ibn Abdur-Rahman al-Faisal Al Sa'ud, proclaimed King of the Hejaz on 8 Jan. 1926. By a treaty of 20 May 1927 the UK recognized the independence of Hejaz, Nejd, Asir and Al-Hasa, which became the State of the Kingdom of Saudi Arabia by decree of 23 Sept. 1932.

TERRITORY AND POPULATION. Saudi Arabia, which occupies over 70% of the Arabian peninsula, is bounded in the west by the Red Sea, east by the Arabian/Persian Gulf and the United Arab Emirates, north by Jordan, Iraq and Kuwait and south by Yemen and Oman. For the border dispute with Yemen *see* YEMEN: Territory and Population. The total area is estimated to be 849,400 sq. miles (2·2m. sq. km). Riyadh is the political, and Mecca the religious, capital.

The total population was (1974 census) 7,012,642, of which 5,128,655 were categorized as settled and 1,883,987 as nomadic. Estimate (1992) 16·9m., of whom 12·3m. were Saudi Arabians.

Annual growth rate of the indigenous population was 3·7% in 1990. Expectation of life was 68·7 years in 1992. Infant mortality was 30 per 1,000 live births in 1989.

Principal cities with 1991 population estimates (in 1m.): Riyadh, 1·8; Jiddah, 1·5; Mecca, 0·63; Taif, 0·41; Medina, 0·4; Dammam, 0·35.

The Neutral Zone (3,560 sq. miles, 5,700 sq. km.), jointly owned and administered by Kuwait and Saudi Arabia from 1922 to 1966, was partitioned between the two countries in 1966, but the exploitation of the oil and other natural resources continues to be shared.

CLIMATE. A desert climate, with very little rain and none at all from June to Dec. The months May to Sept. are very hot and humid, but winter temperatures are quite pleasant. Riyadh. Jan. 58°F (14·4°C), July 108°F (42°C). Annual rainfall 4" (100 mm). Jiddah. Jan. 73°F (22·8°C), July 87°F (30·6°C). Annual rainfall 3" (81 mm).

ROYAL HOUSE. The reigning King is **Fahd ibn Abdul Aziz al Saud** (b. 1922), Custodian of the two Holy Mosques, succeeded in May 1982, after King Khalid's death. *Crown Prince:* Prince Abdullah ibn Abdul Aziz, half-brother of the King.

CONSTITUTION AND GOVERNMENT. Constitutional practice derives from Sharia law. There is no formal Constitution, but 3 royal decrees of 1 March 1992 established a Basic Law which defines the systems of central and municipal government, and set up a 60-man Consultative Council (*Majlis ash-Shura*) of royal nominees in Aug. 1993. *Speaker* is Muhammad ibn Jubair.

It was decreed in Aug. 1993 that ministers in post would serve a further 2 years, and thereafter ministers would hold office for 4-year terms.

Saudi Arabia is an absolute monarchy, but executive power is discharged through a *Council of Ministers.*

The King has the post of *Prime Minister*, and can veto any decision of the Council of Ministers within 30 days.

In Jan. 1996 the Council of Ministers comprised:

Deputy Prime Minister and Commander of the National Guard: Crown Prince Abdullah ibn Abdul Aziz (b. 1923). *Second Deputy Prime Minister and Minister of Defenceand Aviation, and Inspector General:* Prince Sultan ibn Abdul Aziz. *Public Works and Housing:* Prince Miteb ibn Abdul Aziz. *Interior:* Prince Naif ibn Abdul Aziz. *Foreign Affairs:* Prince Saud al Faisal. *Labour and Social Affairs:* Mousaed bin Muhammad al Sanani. *Communications:* Nazer bin Muhammad al Saloum. *Finance and National Economy:* Ibrahim Abdul Aziz al Asaf. *Information:* Fouad bin Abdul Salaam bin Muhammad Farisi. *Industry and Electricity:* Hisham bin Abdullah bin Hisham Yamani. *Commerce:* Osama bin Jaafar bin Ibrahim Faqih. *Justice:* Muhammad Ibrahim al Shaikh. *Education:* Muhammad bin Ahmad al Rashid. *Higher Education:* Khalid al Angari. *Petroleum and Mineral Resources:* Ali bin Ibrahim al Nuaimi. *Islamic Affairs, Awqafs and Guidance:* Dr Abdul Muhsin al Turki. *Pilgrimage:* Dr Mahmoud Safr. *Municipal and Rural Affairs:* Muhammad al Shaikh. *Planning:* Abdul Wahhab al Attar. *Agriculture and Water:* Abdullah bin Abdul Aziz bin Muammar. *Health:* Osama bin Abdul Majed Shoboksi. *Posts and Telecommunications:* Ali bin Talal al Jehani.

National flag: Green, with the text 'There is no God but Allah and Mohammed is his prophet' in white Arabic script, and beneath this a white sabre.

National anthem: 'Sarei lil majd walaya' ('Hasten to glory and supremacy'); words by Ibrahim Khafaji, tune by Abdul Rahman al Katib.

Local Government. 13 provinces were designated in 1993, each governed by an emir with ministerial rank appointed by the King. Each province has a consultative council which meets every 3 months and consists of provincial government officials *ex officio* and at least 10 Saudi citizens recommended by the emir for the King's appointment. Council members serve 4 years and meet once every 2 weeks.

DEFENCE. The USA stations Air Force units on rotational detachment. The Peninsular Shield Force of about 7,000 comprises units from all Gulf Co-operation Council countries.

Army. The Army comprises 3 armoured brigades, 5 mechanized brigades, 1 airborne brigade, 1 Royal Guard regiment and 8 artillery battalions. Equipment includes 315 M-1A2, 290 AMX-30, 450 M-60A3 main battle tanks and 10 surface-to-surface missiles. The Army Aviation Command disposes of nearly 50 Blackhawk, Dauphin and armed AH-64A Apache and Bell 406 helicopters. Strength (1996) was approximately 70,000. There is a para-military Frontier Force (approximately 10,500).

Navy. The Royal Saudi Naval Forces comprise 4 French-built 2,900-tonnes frigates armed with Otomat anti-ship missiles, 4 smaller US-built missile frigates, 9 US-built fast missile craft, 2 German-built torpedo craft, 4 US-built coastal minesweepers and the first 3 of 6 UK-built Sandown class minehunters. Auxiliaries include 2 French-built replenishment tankers each embarking 2 helicopters, 3 ocean tugs and a Royal Yacht. There are numerous minor auxiliaries and boats.

Naval Aviation forces operate 6 Super Puma armed with Exocet missiles, 6 for search-and rescue and 21 Dauphin helicopters, both ship and shore based, and there is a regiment of some 3,000 marines.

The main naval bases are at Jiddah (Red Sea) and Jubail (The Gulf). Naval personnel in 1995 totalled 13,500.

The Coast Guard operates some 35 inshore patrol craft, 24 hovercraft and over 300 boats of various types.

Air Force. Formed as a small army support unit in 1932, the Air Force has been built up considerably with British and US assistance since 1946. Complete re-equipment began in 1966 and delivery of 58 F-15 Eagles to equip 3 air superiority squadrons was made in 1982–84; they operate in conjunction with 5 E-3A Sentry AWACS aircraft and 8 KC-707 flight refuelling tankers. The US government has delivered 36 more F-15 Eagles and another 17 C-130 Hercules. Current combat units include 4 squadrons of F-5E Tiger II supersonic fighter-bombers and RF-5E Tigereye reconnaissance aircraft, supported by a conversion unit with F-5B/F combat trainers. 2 squadrons operate Tornado strike aircraft and another 2 have Tornado interceptors. 1 squadron of Hawk light jet attack/trainers is based at the Al Kharj and a second at King Faisal Air Academy, Riyadh, together with 12 Reims/Cessna FR172 piston-engined primary trainers, PC-9 basic trainers and Jetstream navigation trainers. Other types in current service include 60 C-130E/H and KC-130H Hercules transports and tankers, 1 Boeing 747 SP, 1 Boeing 747-200, 1 Boeing 737, 3 Boeing 707, 4 CN-235s, 12 BAe-125s, 3 Learjets and 2 JetStar VIP jet transports, more than 80 Agusta-Bell 205, 212 and JetRanger and KV-107 helicopters, 2 Agusta AS-61A-4 VIP transport helicopters and communications aircraft. Personnel (1995), about 18,000 with 295 combat aircraft.

Air Defence Force. This separate Command was formerly part of the Army, which retains a point air defence capability. In 1995 it had 33 surface-to-air missile batteries and a strength of 4,000.

National Guard. The National Guard comprises 2 mechanized and 6 infantry brigades and 1 ceremonial cavalry squadron. Additionally there are a number of regular and irregular units, the total strength of the National Guard amounting to approximately 77,000 (57,000 active, 20,000 tribal levies). The National Guard's primary role is the protection of the Royal Family and vital points in the Kingdom. It is directly under royal command. The UK provides small advisory teams to the National Guard in the fields of general training and communications.

INTERNATIONAL RELATIONS

Membership. Saudi Arabia is a member of the UN, the Arab League, the Gulf Co-operation Council and OPEC.

ECONOMY

Policy. The sixth 5-year development plan (1995–99) continues the emphasis on developing the private sector, and aims to increase and indigenize the workforce, enhance defence capacity, achieve a balanced economic development and protect the environment.

Budget. In 1986 the financial year became the calendar year. Estimated revenue, 1995 (and 1994): 135,000m. rials (120,000m. rials); expenditure, 150,000m. rials (160,000m. rials).

Oil sales account for 90% of state income. Estimated 1993 expenditure (in 1m. rials): Defence and security, 61·6; education, 34·1; health and social welfare, 14·1; economic and social subsidies, 9·2; transport and communications, 9·1.

Currency. The unit of currency is the *rial* (SAR) of 100 *halalas*. 1 *qurush* = 5 halalas. There are coins of 1, 5, 10, 25 and 50 halalas and 1 and 2 qurush, and notes of 1, 5, 10, 50, 100 and 500 rials. In Oct. 1994, foreign exchange reserves totalled US$7,241m.; gold reserves in 1993 were US$1,290m. Inflation was 5% in March 1995. In March 1996, £1 = 5·73; US$1 = 3·75; DM1 = 2·54 rials.

Banking and Finance. The Saudi Arabian Monetary Agency (*governor*, Hamad Saud al Sayari), established in 1953, functions as the central bank and the government's fiscal agent. There were 12 commercial banks with 958 branches, 5 special credit institutions and a variety of other financial institutions in 1995. Sharia forbids the charging of interest; Islamic banking is based on sharing clients' profits and losses and imposing service charges. The Saudi Arabian Agricultural Bank with 70 branches and offices extended 755m. rials in credit services to farmers during 1989. In 1989 total deposits in commercial banks were US$146,300m. and total assets were 233,600m. rials.

There is a stock exchange.

ENERGY AND NATURAL RESOURCES

Electricity. By 1995 the over 100 electricity producers had been amalgamated into 4 companies. Installed capacity was 18,200 MW in 1993. All electricity is thermally generated. 63,632m. kWh. were generated in 1990-91.

Oil. Proven reserves (1994) 258,703m. bbls (25% of world resources). Oil production began in 1938 by Aramco, which is now 100% state-owned and accounts for about 97% of total crude oil production.

Estimated crude oil production in 1995 was 8,083,000 bbls. a day.

Production comes from 14 major oilfields, mostly in the Eastern Region and offshore, and including production from the Neutral Zone.

Gas. In 1989 production of liquefied natural gas from oilfield—associated and dissolved gas was 420,946 bbls per day.

Water. Efforts are underway to provide adequate supplies of water for urban, industrial, rural and agricultural use. Most investment has gone into sea-water desalination. In 1991 28 plants had the capacity to produce 1·9m. cu. metres a day. Annual consumption is about 14,000m. cu. metres. 90% goes on agriculture (from fossil reserves, since desalinated water is still too saline).

Minerals. Production began in 1988 at Mahd Al-Dahab gold mine. Deposits of iron, phosphate, bauxite, uranium and copper have been found.

Agriculture. Since 1970 the Government has spent substantially on desert reclamation, irrigation schemes, drainage and control of surface water and control of moving sands. Undeveloped land has been distributed to farmers and there are research and extension programmes. Large scale private investment has concentrated on wheat, poultry and dairy production.

In 1990 agriculture contributed 8% of GDP. 1·2m. ha of land were cultivated and 85m. ha in pastoral use. There were some 152,000 farms in 1992; the agricultural workforce was 1,877,000 in 1993.

Date production in 1993 was 560,000 tonnes; wheat, 3·6m. tonnes. About 1·10m. tonnes of barley are produced annually as animal fodder. Estimated production of other crops, 1993 (in 1,000 tonnes): Tomatoes, 490; water melons, 420; grapes, 120; cows' milk, 303; poultry meat, 319; eggs, 112·75.

Livestock estimates (1993, in 1,000) include 210 cattle, 420 camels, 7,100 sheep and 3,400 goats.

Fisheries. Saudi Fisheries, established in 1981, has introduced a wide variety of fish to the domestic market and opened up a thriving export business in shrimps. Annual catch, 10,000 tonnes.

INDUSTRY. The Government encourages the establishment of manufacturing industries. Its policy includes the provision of industrial estates and loans covering 50% of capital investment. It has established 2 industrial poles at Jubail and Yanbu, linked by gas and oil pipelines, to be the focus of heavy industrial development. Both have petrochemical complexes producing ethylene and methanol. In 1988 there were 12 major industries (petrochemical, urea and ammonia fertilizer, steel, gas and plastics) and over 65 support and light manufacturing businesses in operation in Jubail, and 8 heavy industries (natural gas liquids fractionation, refining, petrochemical, lube additives, crude oil and chemical terminals) and 21 light and support industries in operation in Yanbu. 2,000 factories were in operation in 1992.

Labour. In 1988, 95% of the total labour force was employed in the non-oil sector. There were 4m. foreign workers in 1995.

FOREIGN ECONOMIC RELATIONS. In 1992, foreign debt totalled US$17,089m.

Commerce. In 1993 imports totalled 127,926m. rials and exports 174,996m. rials (154,867m. rials oil and products). Exports in 1994 were some 155,500m. rials (oil, 139,800m. rials). The principal export is crude oil; refined oil, petro-chemicals and wheat are other major exports. Share of exports: Japan, 17·1%; USA, 16·2%; Singapore, 5·7%; France, 5·2%. Imports: USA, 20·6%; Japan, 12·7%; UK, 8·5%; Germany, 7·2%.

Total trade between Saudi Arabia and UK (British Department of Trade returns, in £1,000 sterling):

	1991	*1992*	*1993*	*1994*	*1995*
Imports to UK	963,919	963,607	1,274,480	739,601	720,783
Exports and re-exports from UK	2,228,965	1,967,625	1,826,121	1,515,252	1,644,356

Tourism. In 1989 there were 774,560 pilgrims to Mecca from abroad.

COMMUNICATIONS

Roads. In 1992 there were 34,837 km of main and secondary roads and 88,528 km or rural roads. In 1991, 5m. vehicles were registered. Women may not drive.

Railways. Single track, 1,435 mm gauge lines link Riyadh and Dammam and Riyadh with Hofuf. In 1992 railways carried 0·4m. passengers and 1·9m. tonnes of freight.

Civil Aviation. The national carrier is the state-owned Saudia, which in 1995 operated 11 A300B4-600s, 17 B-737-200 Advs, 2 B-737-200C Advs, 2 B747-100s, 8 B-747-100Bs, 1 B-747-200B(F), 1 B-747-200F, 10 B-747-300s, 1 B-747SP and 33 other aircraft. Services are also provided by 42 foreign airlines. There are 3 major international airports at Jiddah (King Abdulaziz), Dhahran and Riyadh (King Khaled) and 20 domestic airports. King Fahd International Airport in Eastern Province is under construction. In 1990, 21·3m. passengers passed through Saudi airports.

Shipping. The ports of Dammam and Jubail are on the Arabian/Persian Gulf and Jiddah, Yanbu and Jizan on the Red Sea. There is a deepwater oil terminal at Ras Tanura, and 14 minor ports. In 1995 the merchant marine comprised 110 vessels totalling 8·2m. DWT, representing 1·24% of the world's total fleet tonnage. 49 vessels (89·13% of tonnage) were registered under foreign flags. GRT totalled 1·08m; including oil tankers, 210,370 GRT, and container ships, 67,599 GRT.

Telecommunications. Number of telephones (1990), 1·36m., including 15,590 mobile. There were 10,100 telex machines. Number of post offices (1988) 603. The government-controlled Broadcasting Service of the Kingdom of Saudi Arabia and Saudi Arabian Television are responsible for broadcasting. Radio programmes include 2 home services, 2 religious services, services in English and French and an external serivce. Aramco Oil have a private station. There are TV programmes in Arabic and English; Channel 3 TV is a non-commercial independent. Colour is by SECAM and PAL. In 1993 there were estimated to be 5m. radio and 4·5m. TV sets.

Press. In 1991 there were 3 daily newspapers in Arabic and 3 in English and 2 Arabic and 2 English weeklies.

SOCIAL INSTITUTIONS

Justice. The religious law of Islam (Sharia) is the common law of the land, and is administered by religious courts, at the head of which is a chief judge, who is responsible for the Department of Sharia Affairs. Sharia courts are concerned primarily with family inheritance and property matters. The Committee for the Settlement of Commercial Disputes is the commercial court. Other specialized courts or committees include one dealing exclusively with labour and employment matters; the Negotiable Instruments Committee, which deals with cases relating to cheques, bills of exchange and promissory notes, and the Board of Grievances, whose preserve is disputes with the government or its agencies and which also has jurisdiction in trademark-infringement cases and is the authority for enforcing foreign court judgements.

The death penalty is in force for murder, rape, sodomy, armed robbery, sabotage, drug trafficking, adultery and apostasy; executions may be held in public. There were 58 executions in 1994.

Religion. About 92% are Sunni Moslems and 8% Shiites. The *Grand Mufti*, Abdul Aziz ben Baz, has cabinet rank. A special police force, the Mutaween, exists to enforce religious norms.

Education. Adult literacy was 64·1% in 1992 Schooling is in three stages, primary, intermediate and secondary which is to prepare older pupils for university; pre-primary schools are being introduced. Education is free in all these stages. Girls' education is administered separately. In 1990–91 there were 17,278 schools with 1,398,281 pupils and 92,716 teachers. In 1991–92 there were 38 special schools for the handicapped with 4,894 students.

In 1995-96 there were 4 universities, 2 Islamic universities and 1 university of petroleum and minerals. There were 90,207 students and 7,352 academic staff.

Health. In 1991 there were 818 private and 1,639 primary health centres. In 1988 there were some 19,100 doctors and 56,628 medical personnel. There were 253 hospitals in 1989.

Welfare. In 1988 there were 224 hospitals with 35,797 beds, 2,258 primary health care centres and in 1988, 18,048 doctors, 38,434 nurses and midwives, 8,858 technical assistants. There were also 73 private hospitals (10,244 beds) employing 6,096 doctors. At Jiddah there is a quarantine centre for pilgrims.

DIPLOMATIC REPRESENTATIVES

Of Saudi Arabia in Great Britain (30 Charles St., London, W1A 7PM)
Ambassador: Dr Ghazi Al-Ghossaibi.

Of Great Britain in Saudi Arabia (PO Box 94351, Riyadh 11963)
Ambassador: Andrew Green, CMG.

Of Saudi Arabia in the USA (601 New Hampshire Ave., NW, Washington, D.C., 20037)
Ambassador: HRH Prince Bandar bin Sultan.

Of the USA in Saudi Arabia (PO Box 9041, Riyadh)
Ambassador: Raymond E. Mabus.

Of Saudi Arabia to the United Nations
Ambassador: Vacant.

Further Reading

Azzam, H., *Saudi Arabia: Economic Trends, Business Environment and Investment Opportunities.* London, 1993
Clements, F. A., *Saudi Arabia.* [Bibliography] Oxford and Santa Barbara (CA), 1988
Holden, D. and Johns, R., *The House of Saud.* London and New York, 1981
Kostiner, J., *The Making of Saudi Arabia: from Chieftaincy to Monarchical State.* OUP, 1994
Peterson, J. E., *Historical Dictionary of Saudi Arabia.* Metuchen (NJ), 1994

National statistical office: Ministry of Finance and National Economy, Department of Statistics, Riyadh.

SENEGAL

République du Sénégal

Capital: Dakar
Population: 7·97m. (1993)
GNP per capita: US$610 (1994)
HDI/world rank: 0·340/152 (1992)

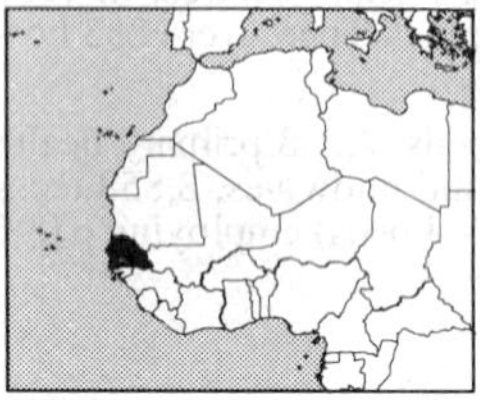

KEY HISTORICAL EVENTS. France established a fort at Saint-Louis in 1659 and later acquired other coastal settlements from the Dutch; the interior was occupied in 1854–65. Senegal became a territory of French West Africa in 1902 and an autonomous state within the French Community on 25 Nov. 1958. On 4 April 1959 Senegal joined with French Sudan to form the Federation of Mali, which achieved independence on 20 June 1960, but on 22 Aug. Senegal withdrew from the Federation and became a separate independent republic. Senegal was a one-Party state from 1966 until 1974, when a pluralist system was re-established.

TERRITORY AND POPULATION. Senegal is bounded by Mauritania to the north and north-east, Mali to the east, Guinea and Guinea-Bissau to the south and the Atlantic to the west with The Gambia forming an enclave along that shore. Area, 197,161 sq. km; population (census, 1988), 6,982,084; (estimate, 1993) 7·97m. (3·98m. female; 40% urban). Population density, 40·5 per sq. km. Growth rate (1992), 2·9%; infant mortality (1991), 81 per 1,000 live births; birth rate (1991) per 1,000 population, 43; death rate, 16. Life expectancy in 1992 was 48·3 years for men and 50·3 for women.

The areas, populations and capitals of the 10 regions:

Region	*Area (in sq. km)*	*1988 Census*	*Capital*
Dakar	550	1,571,614	Dakar
Diourbel	4,359	620,197	Diourbel
Fatick	7,935	507,651	Fatick
Kaolack	16,010	805,859	Kaolack
Kolda	21,011	593,199	Kolda
Louga	29,188	507,572	Louga
Saint-Louis	44,127	656,941	Saint-Louis
Tambacounda	57,602	383,572	Tambacounda
Thiès	6,601	937,412	Thiès
Ziguinchor	7,339	398,067	Ziguinchor

The largest cities (with 1992 estimated population) are: Dakar, the capital (1,729,823), Kaolack (179,894), Saint-Louis (125,717), Thiès (201,350) and Ziguinchor (148,831).

Ethnic groups are the Wolof (40% of the population), Serer (20%), Fulani (15%), Tukulor (10%), Diola (8%), Malinké (6%), Bambara (6%) and Sarakole (2%).

The official language is French; Wolof is widely spoken.

CLIMATE. A tropical climate with wet and dry seasons. The rains fall almost exclusively in the hot season, from June to Oct., with high humidity. Dakar. Jan. 72°F (22·2°C), July 82°F (27·8°C). Annual rainfall 22" (541 mm).

CONSTITUTION AND GOVERNMENT. The head of state is the *President*, elected by universal suffrage for not more than two 7-year terms. For the unicameral 120-member National Assembly 60 members are elected in single-member constituencies and 60 by a form of proportional representation for 5-year terms. It was announced in Dec. 1995 that a senate would be established to represent territorial collectives in parliment.

At the presidential elections of 21 Feb. 1993 there were 8 candidates; turn-out was 51·46%. Abdou Diaf was re-elected with 58·4% of votes cast.

President: Abdou Diouf (took office in Jan. 1981, re-elected 1983, 1988 and 1993).

At the elections of 9 May 1993 the electorate was 2·5m.; turn-out was 40·74%. 1,282 candidates representing 6 parties stood. The Socialist Party (SP) gained 84 seats, the Senegalese Democratic Party 27, the Democratic League 3, the Japoo coalition 3, the African Party of Independence and Labour 2 and the Senegalese Democratic Union – Renovation 1.

The Cabinet appointed in April 1991 was composed as follows in Jan. 1996:

Prime Minister: Habib Thiam.

Ministers of State: Moustapha Niasse (*Foreign Affairs and Expatriates*); Robert Sagna (*Agriculture*); Abdoulaye Wade (*Presidency*); Ousmane Dieng (*Presidential Services*). *Minister of the Armed Forces*: Cheikh Hamidou. *Communications:* Serigne Diop. *Culture:* Abdoulaye Kane. *Economy, Finance and Planning:* Pape Ousmane Sakho. *Employment, Labour and Professional Training:* Assane Diop. *Education:* André Sonkho. *Energy, Minerals and Industry:* Magued Diouf. *Environment and Conservation of Nature:* Aboulaye Bathily. *Equipment and Land Transport:* Landing Sone. *Fisheries and Marine Transport:* Allassawne N'Diaye. *Health and Social Welfare:* Assane Diop. *Justice:* Jacques Baudin. *Modernization and Technology:* Nene Mbaye. *Tourism and Civil Aviation:* Tidiane Sylla. *Towns:* Daour Cisse. *Trades and Crafts:* Idrissa Seck. *Water Resources:* Mamadou Faye. *Women, Children and Family Welfare:* Aminata N'Diaye. *Youth and Sport:* Ousmane Paye. *Interior:* Abdourahmane Sow. *Health and Social Action:* Ousmane Ngom. *Research and Technology:* Marie-Louise Corea.

The Speaker is Sheikh Abdul Khadre Cissokho (SP).

National flag: Three vertical strips of green, yellow, red, with a green star in the centre.

National anthem: 'Pincez tous vos koras, frappez les balafos' ('All pluck the koras, strike the balafos'); words by Léopold Sédar Senghor, tune by Herbert Pepper.

Local Government. Senegal is divided into 10 regions, each with an appointed governor and an elected regional assembly. They are divided into 30 departments, each under an appointed prefect, and thence into 99 *arrondissements.*

DEFENCE. There is selective conscription for 2 years.

Army. There are 4 military zones. The Army had a strength of 12,000 (mostly conscripts) in 1996, organized in 6 infantry battalions, 1 engineer, 1 armoured, 1 airborne, 1 commando and 1 artillery battalion, 1 horsed Presidential Guard and 3 construction companies. Equipment includes 67 armoured cars. There is also a paramilitary force of gendarmarie and customs.

Navy. The flotilla includes 2 coastal patrol craft, 8 inshore patrol craft, 1 tank landing craft, 2 smaller amphibious craft, and about 6 service craft. Personnel (1995) totalled 700, and bases are at Dakar and Casamance.

Air Force. The Air Force, formed with French assistance, has 3 Rallye Guerrier and 5 Magister armed trainers, 5 F.27 twin-turboprop transports, 2 Puma, 1 Gazelle and 2 Alouette II helicopters, plus 2 Rallye trainers. Personnel (1995) 650, with 8 combat aircraft.

INTERNATIONAL RELATIONS

Membership. Senegal is a member of the UN, OAU and is an ACP state of the EU.

ECONOMY

Policy. An austerity programme was adopted in 1993.

Budget. Since Jan. 1993 the fiscal year has been the calendar year. It was preceded by a fiscal year from July 1991 to Dec. 1992. The 1994 budget envisaged revenue of 272,700m. francs CFA and current expenditure of 309,400m. francs CFA.

Currency. The currency is the *franc CFA* (XOF) at a parity of 100 *francs CFA* to 1 French *franc*. Currency in circulation, 1992: 96,610m. francs CFA. In 1992 gold reserves were 29,000 troy oz., and foreign exchange reserves US$8·7m.

Banking and Finance. The bank of issue is the *Banque Centrale des États de l'Afrique de l'Ouest*. The principal commercial bank is the *Union Sénégalaise de la Banque pour le Commerce et l'Industrie* (established 1961 with assistance from Crédit Lyonnais) in which the Senegalese government has the majority shareholding; also state controlled is the *Banque Nationale de Développement du Sénégal*. There are 5 private banks. In 1992 bank deposits totalled 102,800m. francs CFA and term deposits 171,690m. francs CFA. Savings bank deposits were 4,570m. francs CFA in 1991.

ENERGY AND NATURAL RESOURCES

Electricity. In 1993 installed capacity was 215 MW. Output was 868m. kWh in 1989.

Minerals. 1,128,000 tonnes of calcium phosphate were produced in 1992 and 93,000 tonnes of aluminium phosphate in 1989.

Agriculture. Most land is owned under customary rights and holdings tend to be small. In 1992 2·35m. ha were used as arable land, 0·16m. ha for permanent crops and 3·1m. ha for permanent pasture. Production, 1993 (in tonnes): Groundnuts, 628,000; cotton, 50,000; sorghum, 98,000; rice paddy, 89,000; millet, 657; maize, 125,000; cassava, 43,000.

Livestock (1993, in 1,000): 4,400 sheep, 3,118 goats, 2,750 cattle, 320 pigs, 364 asses, 15 camels and 498 horses. Animal products, 1993 (1,000 tonnes): Beef and veal, 45; pork, 7; horseflesh, 6; mutton and lamb, 15; goat meat, 13; poultry meat, 52; milk, 103; eggs, 27.

In 1992 there were 550 tractors.

Forestry. There were (1991) 10·55m. ha of forest. Production (1990) amounted to 4·48m. cu. metres.

Fisheries. In 1992 the fishing fleet comprised 167 vessels totalling 40,600 GRT. In 1990 18,500 tonnes of freshwater and 258,900 tonnes of sea fish (mainly sardines) were caught, and 22,300 tonnes of shellfish.

INDUSTRY. 1991 output (in 1,000 tonnes): Cement, 503; artificial fertilizer, 65·7; sugar, 90; palm-oil, 6; butter, 435 tonnes.

Labour. The workforce (10 years and over) in 1990 was 2,433,000 (633,000 females). In 1990 269,634 children under 10 were employed (92,457 girls). In 1988 there were 276,900 registered unemployed. In 1991 the legal hourly minimum wage was 201·60 francs CFA.

Trade Unions. There are two major unions, the *Union Nationale des Travailleurs Sénégalais* (government-controlled) and the *Confédération Nationale des Travailleurs Sénégalais* (independent) which broke away from the former in 1969 and in 1994 comprised 75% of salaried workers.

FOREIGN ECONOMIC RELATIONS. Foreign debt was US$3,522m. in 1991.

Commerce. In 1991 imports totalled US$1,306m. and exports US$883m. Value of exports, 1990 (US$1m.): Foodstuffs and live animals, 270·6; animal fat, vegetable oil and wax, 130·1; chemicals, 116·7. Imports: Foodstuffs and live animals, 403; mineral fuel, 258·7; chemicals, 157·6; manufactures, 259·8; machinery, 344·5. Main export markets, 1992: France, 24·6%; India, 15·3%; Italy, 9·3%; Mali, 5·6%. Main import suppliers: France, 35·7%; USA, 6·4%; Côte d'Ivoire, 5·4%; Italy, 5·3%.

Total trade between Senegal and UK (British Department of Trade returns, in £1,000 sterling):

	1991	*1992*	*1993*	*1994*	*1995*
Imports to UK	5,025	3,519	4,012	7,625	8,485
Exports and re-exports from UK	13,960	13,345	14,615	20,933	32,217

Tourism. In 1991 there were 269,300 tourist arrivals bringing in a revenue of 37,900m. francs CFA.

COMMUNICATIONS

Roads. The length of roads (1993) was 13,850 km of which 3,900 km were bitumenized. In 1987 there were 81,855 passenger cars, 30,454 lorries and 8,843 buses.

Railways. There are 4 railway lines: Dakar-Kidira (continuing in Mali), Thiès-Saint-Louis (193 km), Guinguinéo-Kaolack (22 km), and Diourbel-Touba (46 km). Total length (1993), 1,225 km (metre gauge). In 1990 railways carried 0·98m. passengers and 3·15m. tonnes of freight.

Civil Aviation. The international airport is Dakar Yoff. 603,000 passengers passed through Yoff in 1991. Air Sénégal is 50% state-owned, had 3 aircraft in 1995. Services are also provided by Aeroflot, Air Afrique, Air Algérie, Air France, Air Gabon, Air Guinée, Air Liberté, Air Mauritanie, Alitalia, Condor, Ethiopian Airlines, Gambia Airways, Ghana Airways, Iberia, Royal Air Maroc, Sabena, Saudia, Swissair, TAP and Tunis Air.

Shipping. In 1995 the merchant totalled 27,640 GRT. 1,786,200 tonnes of freight were loaded in the port of Dakar in 1991 and 1,797,600 tonnes unloaded. There is a river service on the Senegal from Saint-Louis to Podor (363 km) open throughout the year, and to Kayes (924 km) open from July to Oct. The Senegal River is closed to foreign flags. The Saloum River is navigable as far as Kaolack, the Casamance River as far as Ziguinchor.

Telecommunications. There were, in 1983, 530 post offices. Telephones in 1990 numbered 44,300. The government-owned Office de Radio-Télévision du Sénégal broadcasts a national and an international radio service from 10 main transmitters. There are also regional services. There is also a TV service (colour by SECAM). In 1993 there were 0·85m. radio and 61,000 TV sets.

Press. The main daily is *Le Soleil,* circulation (1989) 30,000.

SOCIAL INSTITUTIONS

Justice. There are *juges de paix* in each *département* and a court of first instance in each region. Assize courts are situated in Dakar, Kaolack, Saint-Louis and Ziguinchor, while the Court of Appeal resides in Dakar. The death penalty is authorized.

Religion. The population (1993) was 90% Sunni Moslem, the remainder being Christian (mainly Roman Catholic) or animist.

Education. Adult literacy was 38·3% in 1990. In 1989-90 there were 682,900 pupils and 11,859 teachers in 2,422 primary schools and 166,700 pupils and 4,791 teachers in secondary schools. In 1989–90 there were 5,658 students (1,689 female) in vocational training schools, with 179 teachers and 723 students (129 female) and 87 teachers in teacher training colleges. In 1988–89 there were 14,833 students (3,136 female) and 770 teachers at university level. There are 2 universities with 16,654 students and 889 academic staff in 1995-96, and 19 other insitiutions of higher education.

Health. In 1988 there were 16 government hospitals with 4,064 beds, 529 maternity homes, 47 health centres, 661 clinics and 13 leprosy clinics. There were 407 doctors (258 in government service), 58 dentists (27), 474 midwives (458), and 934 other medical personnel (879). There were 200 pharmacists.

DIPLOMATIC REPRESENTATIVES

Of Senegal in Great Britain (11 Phillimore Gdns., London, W8 7QG)
Ambassador: Gabriel Alexandre Sar.

Of Great Britain in Senegal (20 Rue du Docteur Guillet, Dakar)
Ambassador: A. E. Furness, CMG.

Of Senegal in the USA (2112 Wyoming Ave., NW, Washington, D.C., 20008)
Ambassador: Mamadou Mansour Seck.

Of the USA in Senegal (Ave. Jean XXIII, Dakar)
Ambassador: Mark Johnson.

Of Senegal to the United Nations
Ambassador: Kéba Birane Cisse.

Further Reading

Centre Français du Commerce Extérieur. *Sénégal: un Marché.* Paris, 1993
Delgado, C. L. and Jammeh, S., *The Political Economy of Senegal under Structural Adjustment.* New York, 1991
Dilley, R. M. and Eades, J. S., *Senegal.* [Bibliography] Oxford and Santa Barbara (CA), 1994
Gellar, S., *Senegal.* Boulder (Colo.), 1982.—*Senegal: an African Nation between Islam and the West.* Aldershot, 1983
Phillips, L. C., *Historical Dictionary of Senegal.* 2nd ed, revised by A. F. Clark. Metuchen (NJ), 1995

National statistical office: Direction de la Statistique, BP 116, Dakar.

SEYCHELLES

Republic of Seychelles

Capital: Victoria
Population: 72,253 (1993)
GNP per capita: US$6,210 (1994)
HDI/world rank: 0·810/62 (1992)

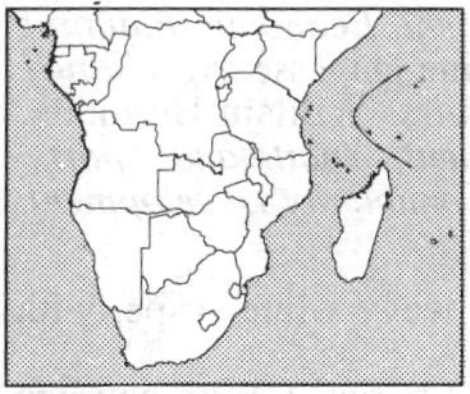

KEY HISTORICAL EVENTS. The islands were first colonized by the French in 1756, in order to establish plantations of spices to compete with the Dutch monopoly. They were captured by the English in 1794 and incorporated as a dependency of Mauritius in 1814. In Nov. 1903 the Seychelles archipelago became a separate colony. Internal self-government was achieved on 1 Oct. 1975 and independence as a republic within the Commonwealth on 29 June 1976. The first President, James Mancham, was deposed in a coup on 5 June 1977 and replaced by his Prime Minister.

TERRITORY AND POPULATION. The Seychelles consists of 115 islands in the Indian Ocean, north of Madagascar, with a combined area of 175 sq. miles (455 sq. km) in two distinct groups. The Granitic group of 32 islands cover 92 sq. miles (239 sq. km); the principal island is Mahé, with 59 sq. miles (153 sq. km) and 59,500 inhabitants at the 1987 census, the other inhabited islands of the group being Praslin, La Digue, Silhouette, Fregate and North, which together had 7,100 inhabitants.

The Outer or Coralline group comprises 83 islands spread over a wide area of ocean between the Mahé group and Madagascar, with a total land area of 83 sq. miles (214 sq. km) and a population of about 400. The main islands are the Amirante Isles (including Desroches, Poivre, Daros and Alphonse), Coetivy Island and Platte Island, all lying south of the Mahé group; the Farquhar, St Pierre and Providence Islands, north of Madagascar; and Aldabra, Astove, Assumption and the Cosmoledo Islands, about 1,000 km south-west of the Mahé group. Aldabra (whose lagoon covers 55 sq. miles), Farquhar and Desroches were transferred to the new British Indian Ocean Territory in 1965, but were returned by Britain to the Seychelles on the latter's independence in 1976. Population (1987 census), 68,499 (1993, estimate) 72,253. Vital statistics (1993): Births, 1,689; deaths, 597. Life expectancy was 71 years in 1993; infant mortality, 13 per 1,000 live births.

The official languages are Creole, English and French but 95% of the population speak Creole.

CLIMATE. Though close to the equator, the climate is tropical. The hot, wet season is from Dec. to May, when conditions are humid, but south-east trades bring cooler conditions from June to Nov. Temperatures are high throughout the year, but the islands lie outside the cyclone belt. Victoria. Jan. 80°F (26·7°C), July 78°F (25·6°C). Annual rainfall 95" (2,375 mm).

CONSTITUTION AND GOVERNMENT. Under the 1979 Constitution the Seychelles People's Progressive Front (SPPF) was the sole legal Party. A constitutional amendment of Dec. 1991 legalized other parties. A commission was elected in July 1992 to draft a new constitution. The electorate was some 50,000; turn-out was 90%. The SPPF gained 14 seats on the commission, the Democratic Party, 8; the latter, however, eventually withdrew. At a referendum in Nov. 1992 the new draft constitution failed to obtain the necessary 60% approval votes. The commission was reconvened in Jan. 1993. At a further referendum on 18 June 1993 the constitution was approved by 73·6% of votes cast.

There is a unicameral *People's Assembly* comprising 33 members elected for 5 years. There is an *Executive President* directly elected for a 5-year term, who nominates and leads a Council of Ministers.

At the presidential and parliamentary elections of 23 July 1993 turn-out was 60%. President René was re-elected against 2 opponents by 59·5% of votes cast. The SPPF gained 28 seats, the Democratic Party, 4 and the United Opposition, 1.

The Government in Nov. 1995 comprised:

President: France Albert René (b. 1935; SPPF; re-elected for a 4th term and sworn in 26 July 1993).

Finance, Communications and Defence: James Michel. *Administration and Manpower:* Joseph Belmont. *Industry:* Ralph Adam. *Environment, Economic Planning and Foreign Affairs:* Danielle de St Jorre. *Health:* Jacqueline Dugasse. *Agriculture and Fisheries:* Esmé Jumeau. *Employment and Social Affairs:* William Herminie. *Tourism and Transport:* Simone Testa. *Local Government, Youth and Sports:* Sylvette Frichot. *Education and Culture:* Patrick Pillay. *Community Development:* Dolor Ernesta.

National flag: Divided horizontally red over green by a wavy white stripe, with red of double width.

National anthem: 'Avec couraz e disipline nou ti briz tout barier' ('With courage and discipline we have broken down all barriers'); words collective, tune P. Dastros-Gèze.

A competition for a new flag and anthem was held in 1994.

DEFENCE. The Defence Force comprises all services. Personnel (1996) 300 organized in 1 infantry battalion and 2 artillery troops and a Coastguard element, 300 strong (1995), based at Port Victoria, which operates 4 fast inshore patrol craft and a tank landing craft and 1 Defender helicopter. The Air Wing has been disbanded. There is also a National Guard (1,000).

INTERNATIONAL RELATIONS

Membership. Seychelles is a member of the UN, Commonwealth and OAU and is an ACP state of the EU.

ECONOMY

Policy. There was a 1990–94 development plan.

Budget. Budget in 1m. rupees, for calendar years:

	1989	*1990*	*1991*	*1992*	*1993*
Recurrent revenue	898·7	989·2	961·5	1,097·6	1,209·5
Recurrent expenditure	793·9	825·9	870·5	1,014·7	1,122·2

Currency. The unit of currency is the *Seychelles rupee* (SCR) divided into 100 *cents.* There are coins of 5, 10 and 25 cents and 1 and 5 rupees, and notes of 10, 25, 50 and 100 rupees. In March 1996, £1 = 7·55; US$1 = 4·94; DM1 = 3·35 rupees.

Banking and Finance. Central Bank of Seychelles (the bank of issue), Development Bank of Seychelles, Seychelles Savings Bank and Seychelles International Bank have head offices and Barclays Bank, Banque Francaise Commerçiale, Habib Bank and Bank of Baroda, have branches in Victoria and Mahé. Total assets and liabilities of commercial banks at 31 Dec. 1993, 1,438·4m. rupees.

ENERGY AND NATURAL RESOURCES

Electricity. Production (1993) 117·6m. kWh.

Agriculture. Coconuts are the main cash crop (production, 1992, 7,000 tonnes). Other main crops produced for export are cinnamon bark (1993, 435 tonnes) and copra (1993, 181 tonnes). Tea production, 1993, 246 tonnes (green leaf). Crops grown for local consumption include cassava, sweet potatoes, yams, sugar-cane, bananas and vegetables. The staple food crop, rice, is imported.

Livestock (1992): Cattle, 2,000; pigs, 19,000; goats, 5,000.

Fisheries. Seychelles is located in abundant tuna fishing grounds, and fishing is a major industry. Catch (1993) 5,447 tonnes.

INDUSTRY. Local industry is expanding, the largest development in recent years being the brewery (output, 1993, 6,523,000 litres of beer and stout and 7,045,000 litres of soft drinks). Other main activities include production of cigarettes (65m. in 1993), tuna canning (4,531 tonnes in 1993) and paints, dairy, processing of cinnamon and coconuts.

FOREIGN ECONOMIC RELATIONS

Commerce. Total trade, in 1m. rupees, for calendar years:

	1989	*1990*	*1991*	*1992*	*1993*
Imports (less re-exports)	930·2	993·8	910·4	980·9	1,234·9
Domestic exports	70·1	73·1	87·6	93·2	78·8

Principal imports (1993): Manufactured goods, Rs 405m.; food, beverages and tobacco, Rs 237m.; petroleum products, Rs 176m., machinery and transport equipment, Rs 310m. mainly from UK (13·3%), Singapore (13·1%), South Africa (12·8%), USA (7·7%) and France (6·2%). Principal exports (1993): Fresh and frozen fish, Rs 9·2m.; shark fins, Rs 3·1m.; canned tuna, Rs 58·3m.; frozen prawns, Rs 2·8m.; cinnamon bark, Rs 2·3m. mainly to UK, France, Réunion and Singapore.

Total trade between Seychelles and UK (British Department of Trade returns, in £1,000 sterling):

	1991	*1992*	*1993*	*1994*	*1995*
Imports to UK	3,457	2,891	6,598	9,159	9,827
Exports and re-exports from UK	10,513	12,352	17,821	20,065	19,217

Tourism. Tourism is the main foreign exchange earner. Visitor numbers were 116,180 in 1993, (98,547 in 1992).

COMMUNICATIONS

Roads. In 1994 there were 219 km of surfaced roads and 102 km of earth roads. In 1993 there were 6,153 passenger cars, 350 buses, 1,848 commercial vehicles and 148 motor cycles.

Civil Aviation. There is an international airport on Mahé. 374,000 passengers were handled in 1993. Air Seychelles operated 1 B-757-200ER, 1 B-767-200ER and 4 other aircraft in 1995. Services are also provided by Aeroflot, Air Austral, Air France, Air Madagascar, British Airways, Condor, Inter Aviation and Kenya Airways.

Shipping. The main port is Victoria, which is also a tuna-fishing and fuel and services supply centre. Shipping (1993), goods unloaded, 436,000 tonnes, goods loaded, 14,300 tonnes.

Telecommunications. Services operated by Cable & Wireless Ltd provide telegraphic communications with all parts of the world by satellite. Telephone lines in Dec. 1993 numbered 10,909. Broadcasting is under the auspices of the Seychelles Broadcasting Corporation, an independent body. There is a radio programme in English, French and Creole. There is also a religious station. TV colour is by PAL. In 1991 there were 30,000 radio and 8,200 TV sets.

Cinemas. In 1989 there was 1 cinema with seating capacity of 200.

Press. In 1990 there was 1 daily newspaper.

SOCIAL INSTITUTIONS

Justice. In 1993, 3,081 criminal and other offences were recorded by the police.

Religion. 92% of the inhabitants are Roman Catholic and 6% Anglican.

Education. Adult literacy was 85% in 1991. Education is free from 6 to 15 years in primary schools, 16 to 18 in secondary schools and 18 to 21 in polytechnics. In 1994 there were 16,082 pupils and 1,000 teachers in primary schools, 1,181 pupils and 122 teachers in secondary schools and 1,702 students and 201 teachers in the Polytechnic.

Health. In 1993 there were 70 doctors, 10 dentists, 308 nurses and 424 hospital beds. The health service is free.

DIPLOMATIC REPRESENTATIVES

Of Seychelles in Great Britain (111 Baker St., London, W1M 1FE)
High Commissioner: John Philip Mascarenhas.

Of Great Britain in Seychelles (Victoria Hse., Victoria, Mahé)
High Commissioner: P. A. B. Thomson, CVO.

Of Seychelles in the USA
Ambassador: Marc M. Marengo.

Of the USA in Seychelles (Victoria Hse., Victoria, Mahé)
Ambassador: Carl Burton Stokes.

Of Seychelles to the United Nations
Ambassador: Marc M. Marengo.

Further Reading

Statistical Information: Information Office, 52 Kingsgate House, Victoria, Mahé.
Seychelles in Figures. Statistics Division, Mahé, 1989
Benedict, M. and Benedict, B., *Men, Women and Money in Seychelles.* Univ. of California Press, 1983
Bennett, G. and Bennett, P. R., *Seychelles.* [Bibliography] Oxford and Santa Barbara, 1993
Franda, M., *The Seychelles: Unquiet Islands.* Boulder (CO), 1982
Lionnet, G., *The Seychelles.* Newton Abbot, 1972
Mancham, J. R., *Paradise Raped: Life, Love and Power in the Seychelles.* London, 1983

SIERRA LEONE

Republic of Sierra Leone

Capital: Freetown
Population: 4·46m. (1993)
GNP per capita: US$150 (1994)
HDI/world rank: 0·221/173 (1992)

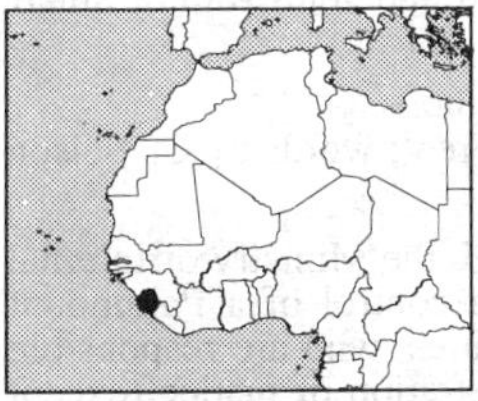

KEY HISTORICAL EVENTS. The Colony of Sierra Leone originated in the sale and cession, in 1787, by native chiefs to English settlers, of a piece of land intended as a home for natives of Africa who were waifs in London, and later it was used as a settlement for freed African slaves. The hinterland was declared a British protectorate on 21 Aug. 1896. Sierra Leone became independent as a member state of the Commonwealth on 27 April 1961, and a republic on 19 April 1971.

A military coup on 29 April 1992 deposed the President and set up a National Provisional Ruling Council. The chairman of this, Captain Valentine Strasser, was in turn deposed in a bloodless military coup on 16 Jan. 1996, and Gen. Julius Maada Bio assumed power.

There is an insurrection in the south-east (adjoining Liberia) led by the Revolutionary United Front.

TERRITORY AND POPULATION. Sierra Leone is bounded on the north-west, north and north-east by Guinea, on the south-east by Liberia and on the south-west by the Atlantic Ocean. The area is 27,925 sq. miles (73,326 sq. km). Population (census 1985), 3,517,530, of whom about 2,000 were Europeans, 3,500 Asiatics and 30,000 non-native Africans. Estimate (1993), 4,460,000 (32% urban); density, 64·3 per sq. km. The capital is Freetown, with 469,776 inhabitants in 1985.

Vital statistics rates (1993, per 1,000 population); Birth, 48·2; death, 21·6; growth rate, 2·7%. Infant mortality was 143 per 1,000 live births in 1990; expectation of life was 43 years.

Sierra Leone is divided into 4 provinces:

	Sq. km	*Census 1985*	*Capital*	*Estimate 1988*
Western Province	557	554,243	Freetown	469,776
Southern Province	19,694	740,510	Bo	26,000
Eastern Province	15,553	960,551	Kenema	13,000
Northern Province	35,936	1,262,226	Makeni	12,000

The provinces are divided into districts as follows: Bo, Bonthe, Moyamba, Pujehun (Southern Province); Kailahun, Kenema, Kono (Eastern Province); Bombali, Kambia, Koinaduga, Port Loko, Toukolili (Northern Province).

The principal peoples are the Mendes (34% of the total) in the south, the Temnes (31%) in the north and centre, the Konos, Fulanis, Bulloms, Korankos, Limbas and Kissis. English is the official language; a Creole (Krio) is spoken.

CLIMATE. A tropical climate, with marked wet and dry seasons and high temperatures throughout the year. The rainy season lasts from about April to Nov., when humidity can be very high. Thunderstorms are common from April to June and in Sept. and Oct. Rainfall is particularly heavy at Freetown because of the effect of neighbouring relief. Freetown. Jan. 80°F (26·7°C), July 78°F (25·6°C). Annual rainfall 135" (3,434 mm).

CONSTITUTION AND GOVERNMENT. In a referendum in Sept. 1991 some 60% of the 2·5m. electorate voted for the introduction of a new constitution instituting multi-party democracy. There is a 68-member *National Assembly.*

Following the ouster of its chairman, Captain Valentine Strasser, on 16 Jan. 1996, Gen. Julius Maada Bio (b.1963) formed a new National Provisional Ruling Council and a government on 19 Jan., the latter mainly civilian, and was sworn in as

President on 17 Jan. There is a *Supreme Council of State (SCS)*, and a *Council of State Secretaries*.

Presidential and National Assembly elections were held on 26-27 Feb. 1996. 13 parties stood. Turn-out was 60%. Ahmad Tejan Kabbah (Sierra Leone People's Party) gained 35·8% of votes cast for the presidency in a first round. There was a qualifying threshold of 55% of votes for outright election in this round; a second round is scheduled to take place between Ahmad Kabbah and John Karefa-Smart (United National People's Party).

National flag: Three horizontal stripes of green, white, blue.

National anthem: 'High We Exalt Thee, Realm of the Free'; words by C. Nelson Fyle, tune by J. J. Akar.

Local Government. The provinces are administered through the Ministry of Internal Affairs and divided into 148 Chiefdoms, each under the control of a Paramount Chief and Council of Elders known as the Tribal Authorities, who are responsible for the maintenance of law and order and for the administration of justice (except for serious crimes). All of these Chiefdoms have been organized into local government units, empowered to raise and disburse funds for the development of the Chiefdom concerned.

DEFENCE

Army. The Army consists of 4 infantry battalions, 2 artillery batteries and 1 engineer squadron. Strength (1996), about 6,000.

Navy. The small flotilla comprises 2 ex-Chinese fast inshore patrol craft, 1 small inshore craft and 3 utility landing craft. Personnel in 1995 totalled 200.

Air Force. An air wing was created in 1995 with South African assistance. It operates 1 Mi-24 gunship and 2 Mi-17 transport helicopters.

INTERNATIONAL RELATIONS

Membership. Sierra Leone is a member of the UN, OAU, ECOWAS and the Commonwealth and is an ACP state of the EU.

ECONOMY

Budget. The financial year ends on 30 June. Revenue, 1993–4, 65,811m. leones; expenditure, 96,593m. leones.

Currency. The unit of currency is the *leone* (SLL) of 100 *cents*. There are notes of 1, 2, 5, 10, 20, 50 100, 500, 1,000 and 5,000 leones, and coins of 1, 5, 10, 20 and 50 *cents*. 15,650m. leones were in circulation in 1992. Foreign exchange reserves were US$34·8m. in 1993. Exchange controls were liberalized in 1993. In March 1996, £1 = 1,360·28 leones; US$1 = 890 leones; DM1 = 603 leones.

Banking and Finance. The bank of issue is the Bank of Sierra Leone (established 1964). There are 4 commercial banks (2 foreign).

Weights and Measures. The metric system is in use.

ENERGY AND NATURAL RESOURCES

Electricity. Installed capacity was 126 MW in 1991. Production (1990) 224m. kWh.

Minerals. The chief minerals mined are gold (12,900 troy oz, 1990), diamonds (10,000 carats), bauxite (1·4m. tonnes), and rutile (144,000 tonnes).

Agriculture. Agriculture contributed 31·7% of GDP in 1990, and engaged 65% of the workforce, mainly in small-scale peasant production. Cattle production is important in the north. Production (1993, in 1,000 tonnes): Rice, 486; cassava, 97; palm oil, 50; palm kernels, 35; coffee, 36; cocoa, 24.

Livestock (1993): Cattle, 333,000; goats, 153,000; sheep, 278,000; chickens, 6m.

Fisheries. In 1992 there were 47 fishing vessels over 100 GRT totalling 18,773 GRT, 30,900 tonnes of sea fish and 15,000 tonnes of freshwater fish were caught in 1991.

INDUSTRY. Manufacturing contributed 6% of GDP in 1990. There are palm-oil and rice mills; sawn timber, joinery products and furniture are produced.

Labour. The workforce was 1,438,000 in 1990. 14,800 persons were registered unemployed in 1992. About 125,000 workers are in wage-earning employment.

FOREIGN ECONOMIC RELATIONS. Foreign debt was US$1,291m. in 1991.

Commerce. Total trade (in 1m. leones) for 1992: Imports, 51,834·1; exports, 55,217.

Main exports, 1989: Rutile, 139,600 tonnes; bauxite, 1,557,200 tonnes; diamonds, 131,700 carats; gold, 7160·2 oz; coffee, 5,163 tonnes; cocoa, 7,572 tonnes.

Main export markets, 1991: USA, 33·5%; Belgium, 21·7%; UK, 13·1%; Germany, 11·7%. Main import suppliers: Nigeria, 23·9%; UK, 14·2%; USA, 11%; Germany, 9·4%.

Total trade between Sierra Leone and UK (British Department of Trade returns, in £1,000 sterling):

	1991	*1992*	*1993*	*1994*	*1995*
Imports to UK	5,516	9,424	16,219	19,743	4,774
Exports and re-exports from UK	17,926	15,450	20,169	20,241	26,319

Tourism. In 1990 there were 100,000 tourists, mainly French.

COMMUNICATIONS

Roads. There were (1989) about 7,500 miles of main roads, of which 1,500 miles were surfaced with bitumen. In 1988 there were 29,012 passenger cars and 10,173 commercial vehicles.

Civil Aviation. Freetown Airport (Lungi) is the international airport. The airport is served by Air Afrique, British Airways, Ghana Airways and KLM.

Shipping. The port of Freetown has a very large natural harbour. Iron ore is exported through Pepel, and there are small ports at Bonthe and Sulima. In 1995 the merchant fleet totalled 15,100 GRT, including oil tankers, 1,835 GRT. 1·8m. tonnes of cargo were loaded in 1990 and 0·53m. tonnes discharged.

Telecommunications. Telephone provision, 1991, 4·1 per 1,000 population. There were (1983) 37 post offices and 76 postal agencies. Broadcasting is under the auspices of the government-controlled Sierra Leone Broadcasting Service and Sierra Leone Television, which is part commercial. In 1991 there were 925,000 radio and 25,000 TV sets (colour by PAL).

Press. In 1987 there was one daily newspaper with a circulation of 12,000.

SOCIAL INSTITUTIONS

Justice. The High Court has jurisdiction in civil and criminal matters. Subordinate courts are held by magistrates in the various districts. Native Courts, headed by court Chairmen, apply native law and custom under a criminal and civil jurisdiction. Appeals from the decisions of magistrates' courts are heard by the High Court. Appeals from the decisions of the High Court are heard by the Sierra Leone Court of Appeal. Appeal lies from the Sierra Leone Court of Appeal to the Supreme Court which is the highest court.

Religion. There were 1·72m. Moslems in 1992. Traditional animist beliefs persist.

Education. Adult literacy was 23·7% in 1992. Primary education is partially free but not compulsory. In 1990–91 there were 2,072 primary schools with 414,200 pupils and 14,972 teachers, 227 secondary schools with 116,648 pupils and 5,610 teachers, 19 vocational training colleges with 4,530 students and 326 staff, and

6 teacher training schools. There were 5 institutes of higher education with 4,742 students and 600 teachers. Fourah Bay College and Njala University College are the 2 constituent colleges of the University of Sierra Leone. They had 2,571 students and 257 academic staff in 1990–91.

Health. In 1988 there were 300 doctors and 4,025 hospital beds.

DIPLOMATIC REPRESENTATIVES

Of Sierra Leone in Great Britain (33 Portland Pl., London, W1N 3AG)
High Commissioner: Alhaji Haroun Buhari.

Of Great Britain in Sierra Leone (Standard Chartered Bank of Sierra Leone Ltd Bldg., Lightfoot Boston St., Freetown)
High Commissioner: I. McCluney, CMG.

Of Sierra Leone in the USA (1701 19th St., NW, Washington, D.C., 20009)
Ambassador: Thomas K. Kargbo.

Of the USA in Sierra Leone (Corner Walpole and Siaka Stevens St., Freetown)
Ambassador: John L. Hirsch.

Of Sierra Leone to the United Nations
Ambassador: Alimamy P. Bangura.

Further Reading

Binns, M. and Binns, T., *Sierra Leone* [Bibliography]. Oxford and Santa Barbara (CA), 1992
Fyfe, C., *A History of Sierra Leone*. OUP, 1962

SINGAPORE

Republic of Singapore

Population: 2·93m. (1994)
GNP per capita: US$23,360 (1994)
HDI/world rank: 0·878/35 (1992)

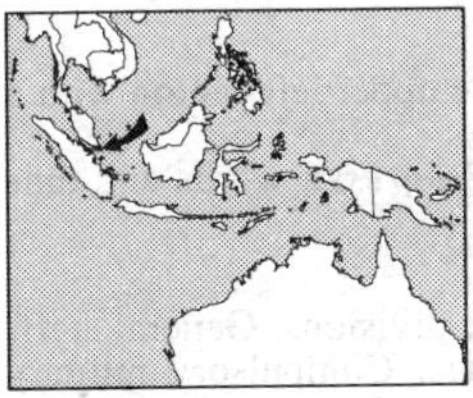

KEY HISTORICAL EVENTS. For the early history of the settlement (1819) and colony (1867) *see* THE STATESMAN'S YEAR-BOOK, 1959, pp. 246 f.

By an agreement with Malaysia of 1965, Singapore ceased to be one of the states of the Federation of Malaysia and became an independent sovereign state. On 22 Dec. 1965 it became a republic.

Singapore accepted responsibility for international agreements entered into by the Malaysian Government on its behalf.

TERRITORY AND POPULATION. The Republic of Singapore consists of Singapore Island itself, and 60 islets. Singapore Island is situated off the southern extremity of the Malay peninsula, to which it is joined by a 1,056-metre causeway carrying a road, railway and water pipeline. The Straits of Johore between the island and the mainland are about three-quarters of a mile wide. The island is 247·6 sq. miles (641·4 sq. km) in area, including the 60 adjacent islets, 20 of which are inhabited.

Census of population (1990): 2,089,400 Chinese, 380,600 Malays, 191,000 Indians and 29,200 others; total 2,690,200. Estimate (1994), 2,269,600 Chinese, 415,900 Malays, 209,400 Indians and 35,300 others; total 2,930,200. Density, 4,568 per sq. km; growth rate, 2%; infant mortality, 1993, 5 per 1,000 live births; life expectancy, 1993, 76 years.

Malay, Chinese (Mandarin), Tamil and English are the official languages; Malay is the national language and English is the language of administration.

CLIMATE. The climate is equatorial, with uniformly high temperatures and no defined wet or dry season, rain being plentiful throughout the year, especially from Nov. to Jan., generally the cooler months. Jan. 78·1°F (25·6°C), July 80·8°F (27·1°C). Annual rainfall 2,352 mm.

CONSTITUTION AND GOVERNMENT. *Parliament* is unicameral consisting of 81 members, elected by secret ballot from single-member and group representation constituencies. With the customary exception of those serving criminal sentences, all citizens over 21 are eligible to vote. Voting in an election is compulsory. At the general election on 31 Aug. 1991, there were 36 electoral divisions, of which 21 were single-member constituencies and 15 were group representation constituencies (GRC). Each GRC returns 4 Members of Parliament, one of whom must be from the Malay community, the Indian and other minority communities. There is a common roll without communal electorates.

A Presidential Council to consider and report on minorities' rights was established in 1970.

At the elections of Aug. 1991 opposition parties contested only 40 of the 81 seats in parliament. The People's Action Party (PAP) gained 61% of votes cast and 77 seats (63·2% and 80 in 1988); the Singapore Democratic Party gained 3 seats (1 in 1988) and the Workers' Party 1 seat.

At the presidential elections of 28 Aug. 1993 there were 2 PAP candidates. Ong Teng Cheong was elected by 58·7% of votes cast.

President: Ong Teng Cheong (sworn in 1 Sept. 1993).

The People's Action Party Cabinet at Sept. 1995 was composed as follows:
Prime Minister: Goh Chok Tong (b. 1941).

Senior Minister, Prime Minister's Office: Lee Kuan Yew, GCMG, CH. *Deputy Prime Ministers:* Lee Hsien Loong; Dr Tony Tan Keng Yam (*Defence*). *Trade and Industry:* Yeo Cheow Tong. *Finance:* Dr Richard Hu Tsu Tau. *Education:* Lee Yock Suan. *Law and Foreign Affairs:* S. Jayakumar. *Labour:* Dr Lee Boon Yang. *Home Affairs:* Wong Kan Seng. *Health, Information and the Arts:* George Yeo Yong Boon. *Community Development:* Abdullah Tarmugi. *Communications:* Mah Bow Tan. *Environment:* Teo Chee Hean. *National Development:* Lim Heng Kiang. *Without portfolio:* Lim Boon Heng.

National flag: Horizontally red over white, charged in the upper left canton with a crescent and a circle of 5 stars, all in white.

National anthem: Majulah Singapura (*May Singapore Progress*); words and tune by Zubair Said.

DEFENCE. The Ministry of Defence comprises 5 major divisions: General staff, manpower, logistics, security and intelligence and finance. Compulsory military service in peace-time for all male citizens and permanent residents was introduced in 1967. Periods of service are officers and non-commissioned officers 30 months, other ranks 24 months. Reserve liability is to age 40 for men, 50 for officers.

An agreement with the USA in Nov. 1990 provided for an increase in US use of naval and air force facilities.

Singapore is a member of the Five Powers Defence Arrangement, with Australia, New Zealand, Malaysia and the UK.

Army. The Army consists of 3 Combined Arms Divisions, 2 People's Defence Force (PDF) Commands and some non-divisional units. Strength (1996) 45,000 (including 30,000 conscripts) and 210,000 reserves.

Navy. The small, relatively modern Navy operates the first of a new class of 6 500-tonne anti-submarine partolcraft, 6 German-designed fast missile corvettes, 12 inshore patrol craft, 4 Swedish-built coastal minehunters, 1 ex-UK and 4 ex-US tank landing ships, 10 small landing craft and 1 training ship. A small ex-Swedish submarine has been acquired but was not operational in 1995. Naval personnel in 1995 numbered 3,000 (800 conscripts) and the naval bases are on Pulau Brani and at Jurong.

The Marine Police operates 4 inshore patrol craft and some 80 patrol boats, some armed.

Air Force. The Air Force has 2 squadrons of F-5E supersonic fighters and 1 squadron of RF-5E reconnaissance aircraft supported by 2-seat F-5Fs; 3 fighter-bomber squadrons equipped with A-4S Skyhawks, supported by TA-4S 2-seat trainers; 1 squadron of F-16 jet fighters, supported by 2-seat trainers; a squadron of E-2C Hawkeye AEW aircraft; a radar unit, anti-aircraft guns and Bloodhound, Rapier and Hawk surface-to-air missile squadrons; a transport squadron of C-130 Hercules (including 4 equipped as flight refuelling tankers); a squadron of Fokker 50s equipped for search and rescue and maritime patrol; a squadron of Bell UH-1s, 2 squadrons of AS 332M Super Puma helicopters and 2 squadrons of AS-550A2 helicopters; and training units equipped with SF.260MS piston-engined basic trainers, SIAI-Marchetti S.211 jet-powered advanced trainers and AS 350 Ecureuil helicopters. Personnel strength (1995) about 6,000 (3,000 conscripts), with 155 combat aircraft and 20 armed helicopters.

INTERNATIONAL RELATIONS

Membership. Singapore is a member of the UN, the Commonwealth, the Colombo Plan and ASEAN.

ECONOMY

Performance. The GNP at current market prices for 1994, was S$104,879·6m., an increase of 11·3% over 1993.

Budget. Public revenue and expenditure for financial years (in S$1m.):

	1991	*1992*	*1993*	*1994*
Revenue	17,225·7	16,779·0	18,188·9	24,252·4
Expenditure	11,774·0	13,114·0	14,075·0	15,282·1

Currency. The unit of currency is the *Singapore dollar* (SGD) of 100 *cents*. There are coins of 1, 5, 10, 20 and 50 cents and S$1, and notes of S$1, 2, 5, 10, 20, 50, 100, 500, 1,000 and 10,000. Gross circulation in 1994 was S$10,170m. Foreign exchange reserves in 1994 were S$85,166m. In March 1996, £1 = 2·16 dollars; US$1 = 1·41 dollars; DM1 = 0·96 dollars.

Banking and Finance. The Monetary Authority of Singapore performs the functions of a central bank, except the issuing of currency which is the responsibility of the Board of the Commissioners of Currency.

The Development Bank of Singapore was established as a fully licensed bank in 1968, and is the largest local bank in terms of assets. Primarily it provides long-term financing of manufacturing and other industries. In 1994 it had a paid up capital of S$1,124·9m. and shareholders' funds amounting to S$4,934m.

There were 132 commercial banks with 446 banking offices operating in 1994. The total assets/liabilities amounted to S$201,952·5m. in 1994. Total deposits of non-bank customers amounted to S$99,032·2m. and advances including bills financing, totalled S$90,974·2m. in 1994. There were 77 merchant banks as at March 1995.

In Dec. 1994, the Singapore Post Office Savings Bank had 4,980,999 savings accounts and a total deposit balance of all accounts of S$20,268·9m.

There is a stock exchange.

Weights and Measures. The metric system is in use.

ENERGY AND NATURAL RESOURCES

Electricity. The Public Utilities Board is responsible for the provision of electricity, piped gas and water. Electrical power is generated by 4 oil-fired power stations, with a total generating capacity of 4,513 MW in 1994. Production (1994) 20,675m. kWh.

Agriculture. Only about 1·7% of the total area is used for farming. Most food is imported but Singapore is self-sufficient in eggs, and 5,644 tonnes of vegetables were produced for domestic consumption in 1994.

Agro-technology parks house large-scale intensive farms to improve production of fresh food.

Fisheries. The total local supply of fresh fish in 1994 was 13,638 tonnes.

INDUSTRY.

INDUSTRY. The largest industrial area is the Jurong Industrial Estate with 6,467 companies employing 333,099 workers in 1994.

Production, 1993 (in S$1m.), totalled 87,653·3, including machinery and appliances, 47,347·6; petroleum, 11,329·6; chemical products, 5,061·2; transport equipment, 4,353·5; fabricated metal products, 4,533·4; food, beverages and tobacco, 3,179; paper products and printing, 3,128·6; wearing apparel, 1,436·9.

Labour. In June 1994, 1,649,300 persons were employed, of whom 1,424,000 were employees, 95,500 were employers and 129,800 were own account/contributing family workers. The majority were working in manufacturing, 422,500; trade, 376,900.

Legislation regulates the principal terms and conditions of employment such as hours of work, sick leave and other fringe benefits. Youths of 14-16 years may work in industrial establishments, and children of 12–14 years may be employed in approved apprenticeship schemes. A trade dispute may be referred to the Industrial Arbitration Court.

The Ministry of Labour operates an employment service and provides the handicapped with specialized on-the-job training. The Central Provident Fund was established in 1955 to make provision for employees in their old age. At the end of 1994 there were 2·52m. members with S$57,649m. standing to their credit in the fund.

Trade Unions. There were 85 registered trade unions comprising 82 employee unions and 3 employer unions in 1994. The total membership of employee unions numbered 232,927. Members of employer unions numbered 1,088.

FOREIGN ECONOMIC RELATIONS.

Foreign investment in up to 40% of the equity of domestic banks is permitted. Foreign investments totalled S$3,900m. in 1993 (S$3,500m. in 1992).

Commerce. Imports and exports (in S$1m.), by country, 1994:

	Imports (c.i.f.)	*Exports (f.o.b.)*
Australia	2,392·9	3,490·3
China	4,412·0	3,206·7
France	3,318·0	1,998·6
Germany	5,296·6	5,229·8
Hong Kong	5,285·4	12,614·2
Italy	2,208·9	1,050·3
Japan	34,422·1	18,342·6
Malaysia	25,600·0	29,069·5
Saudi Arabia	5,607·0	503·2
Taiwan	6,918·2	5,939·5
Thailand	7,470·8	8,189·3
UK	4,325·7	3,985·0
USA	23,901·9	27,637·0

The major trading countries for 1994 were Malaysia (18·01%), USA (16·97%) and Japan (14·74%). Total imports increased to S$156,396m. in 1994 from S$137,603m. in 1993. Exports increased to S$147,327m. in 1994 from S$119,473m. in 1993.

Exports (1994, in S$1m.): Machinery and transport equipment, 94,199 (69,640·6 in 1993, of which electrical machinery, 45,949; transport equipment, 3,154; non-electric machinery, 45,096); mineral fuels, 14,075; raw materials, 2,193 (including rubber); chemicals, 8,418; food, beverages and tobacco, 5,990; clothing, 2,322; animal and vegetable oils, 574; textiles, 2,154; scientific and optical instruments, 3,288; metal goods, 1,614; iron and steel, 1,083; orchids and other plants, 40; aquarium fish, 81.

Imports (1994, in S$1m.): Machinery and transport equipment, 88,306 (69,641 in 1993, of which electrical machinery, 47,902; transport equipment, 7,661; non-electric machinery, 32,744); mineral fuels, 13,788; food, beverages and tobacco, 7,359; chemicals, 10,114; crude materials, 1,939 (of which rubber, 533); textiles, 3,072; iron and steel, 3,222; animal and vegetable oils, 641; metal goods, 2,697; scientific and optical instruments, 4,843; non-metal mineral goods, 2,268; paper and paperboard and related articles, 1,408.

In the following table (British Department of Trade returns, in £1,000 sterling) the imports include produce from Sabah, Sarawak and other eastern places, transhipped at Singapore, which is thus entered as the place of export:

	1991	*1992*	*1993*	*1994*	*1995*
Imports to UK	1,134,365	1,192,803	1,615,210	1,896,892	2,205,799
Exports and re-exports from UK	1,018,419	1,145,058	1,429,660	1,768,541	2,068,581

Tourism. There were 6·9m. visitors in 1994. In 1994 there were 75 gazetted hotels with a total of 25,322 rooms.

COMMUNICATIONS

Roads. There were (1994) 3,027 km of public roads, of which 2,943 km are asphalt-paved. In 1994 motor vehicles numbered 611,611, of which 321,556 were private cars, 10,198 buses, 126,156 motor cycles and scooters, 19,091 public cars including taxis, school taxis and private hire cars.

Railways. A 25·8-km main line runs through Singapore, connecting with the States of Malaysia and as far as Bangkok. Branch lines serve the port of Singapore and the industrial estate at Jurong. The Singapore metro extended to 67 km in 1993.

Civil Aviation. In 1994 Singapore Airlines (54% state-owned) flew to 85 destinations in 42 countries. At March 1995 it operated 1 B-747-200, 10 B-747-300s, 28 B-747-400s, 17 A310-300s and 5 A310-200s. 66 international airlines operated more than 2,800 scheduled flights a week, totalling 145,334 commercial aircraft movements at Singapore International Airport in Changi ('Airtropolis') in 1994. Services are provided by Aeroflot, Air China, Air France, Air India, Air Lanka, Air Mauritius, Air New Zealand, Air Niugini, Air Seychelles, Alitalia, All Nippon Airways, Asiana, Buman Bangladesh, British Airways Cathay Pacific, China Airlines, China Eastern Airlines, China Southern Airlines, China Southwest Airlines, Czech Airlines, Delta, Egyptair, Emirates, Eva, Finnair, Garuda Indonesia, Gulf Air, Indian Airlines, JAL, JAT, KLM, Korean Air, Kuwait Airways, Lauda Air, Lufthansa, Malaysia Airlines, Middle East Airlines, Myanma Airways, Northwest Airlines, Pakistan Airlines, Philippine Airlines, Qantas, Royal Air, Cambodge, Royal Brunei Airlines, Royal Jordanian, Royal Nepal Airlines, SAA, SAS, Saudia, Swissair, Thai Airways, Turkish Airlines, United Airlines, Vietnam Airlines and Yunnan Airlines. In 1994, 21·64m. passengers and 1,009,764 tonnes of freight were handled.

Shipping. Singaprore is a large container port. The economy is dependent on shipping and entrepôt trade. A total of 101,000 vessels of 697m. GRT entered Singapore during 1994. In 1995 the merchant marine comprised 547 vessels totalling 10·24m. DWT, representing 1·55% of the world's total fleet tonnage. 202 vessels (31·88% of total tonnage) were registered under foreign flags. Total GRT, 11·89m., including oil tankers, 4·96m. GRT, and container ships, 1·33m. GRT.

Telecommunications. In 1994, 95 post offices and 54 postal agencies were in operation. Telephones numbered 1·31m. in 1994 and fax machines 39,354 in 1992. On 1 Oct. 1994, Singapore Broadcasting Corporation was privatized with the formation of a group of companies, Singapore International Media, within which Television Corporation of Singapore broadcasts mainly English and Chinese programmes and Television 12 broadcasts Malay and Tamil programmes as well as sports, documentaries and arts programmes. In 1994 there were 210,370 radio and 645,529 TV licences (colour by PAL).

Cinemas. (1994). There were 107 cinemas with a total seating capacity of 55,000.

Press. (1994). There were 8 daily newspapers, in 4 languages, with a total daily circulation of 1,029,043.

SOCIAL INSTITUTIONS

Justice. There is a Supreme Court in Singapore which consists of the High Court, the Court of Appeal and the Court of Criminal Appeal. The Supreme Court is composed of a Chief Justice and 12 Judges. An appeal from the High Court lies to the Court of Appeal in civil matters and to the Court of Criminal Appeal in criminal matters. The High Court has original civil and criminal jurisdiction as well as appellate civil and criminal jurisdiction in respect of appeals from the Subordinate Courts. There are 30 district courts, 7 magistrates' courts, 1 juvenile and 1 coroner's court and a small claims tribunal. The right of appeal to the UK Privy Council was abolished in 1994.

Penalties for drug trafficking and abuse are severe, including a mandatory death penalty.

Religion. In 1990, 53·9% of the population aged 15 years and above were Buddhists and Taoists, 12·6% Christians, 15·4% Moslems and 3·6% Hindus.

Education. The general literacy rate rose from 84% in 1980 to an estimated 91·3% in 1994. Kindergartens are private and fee-paying. Compulsory primary state education starts at 6 years and culminates at 11 or 12 years with an examination which influences choice of secondary schooling. There are 12 autonomous and 8 private fee-paying secondary schools. Tertiary education at 16 years is divided into 3 branches: Junior colleges leading to university; 4 polytechnics with 42,303 students in 1993–94; and 11 technical institutes with 124,952 students in 1993–94. Statistics of schools at end June 1994:

	Schools	*Pupils*	*Teachers*
Primary schools	187	261,402	11,058
Secondary schools	137	156,522	7,715 [1]
Pre-university centres and centralized institutes	14	22,732	
Junior colleges	14		1,648 [2]

[1] Teachers teaching in pre-university centres are included under secondary schools.
[2] Teachers teaching in centralized institutes are included under junior colleges.

There are 2 universities: the National University of Singapore (established 1980) with 16,137 students in 1994–95, and the Nanyang Technological University (established 1991) with 11,052 in 1994–95.

Health. There were 13 government and government-restructured hospitals with about 8,346 beds in 1994. There were 4,133 doctors, 750 dentists and 12,200 nurses registered. There were 11 private hospitals with 2,100 beds.

Social Security. The Central Provident Fund makes provision for retired employees. In 1994 there were 2,521,750. members and the Fund held US$57,649·2m.

DIPLOMATIC REPRESENTATIVES

Of Singapore in Great Britain (9 Wilton Cres., London, SW1X 8SA)
High Commissioner: J. Y. Pillay.

Of Great Britain in Singapore (Tanglin Rd, Singapore 247919)
High Commissioner: Gordon Duggan.

Of Singapore in the USA (1824 R. St., NW, Washington, D.C., 20009)
Ambassador: S. R. Nathan.

Of the USA in Singapore (30 Hill St., Singapore 179360)
Ambassador: Timothy Chorba.

Of Singapore to the United Nations
Ambassador: Bilahari Kausikan.

Further Reading

Department of Statistics. *Monthly Digest of Statistics.– Yearbook of Statistics.*

The Constitution of Singapore. Singapore, 1992
Information Division, Ministry of Information and the Arts. *Singapore Yearbook.*
Ministry of Trade and Industry, *Economic Survey of Singapore.* (Quarterly and Annual)
Chew, E. C. T., *A History of Singapore.* Singapore, 1992
Clammer, J. R., *Singapore: Ideology, Society, Culture.* Singapore, 1985
Huff, W. G., *Economic Growth of Singapore: Trade and Development in the Twentieth Century.* CUP, 1994
Myint, S., *The Principles of Singapore Law.* 2nd ed. Singapore, 1992
National Library. *Books about Singapore.* Singapore, irregular
Quah, J. S. T., *Government and Politics of Singapore.* OUP, 1985
Quah, S. R. and Quah, J. S. T., *Singapore* [Bibliography] Oxford and Santa Barbara (CA), 1988
Tan, C. H., *Financial Markets and Institutions in Singapore.* 7th ed. Singapore, 1992
Turnbull, C. M., *A History of Singapore, 1819–1988.* 2nd ed. OUP, 1989
Vasil, R. K., *Governing Singapore.* Singapore, 1992

National library: National Library, Stamford Rd, Singapore, 178896.
National statistical office: Department of Statistics, Minister of Trade and Industry, Singapore 068811.

SLOVAKIA

Slovenská Republika

Capital: Bratislava
Population: 5·3m. (1993)
GNP per capita: US$2,230 (1994)
HDI/world rank: 0·872/40 (1992)

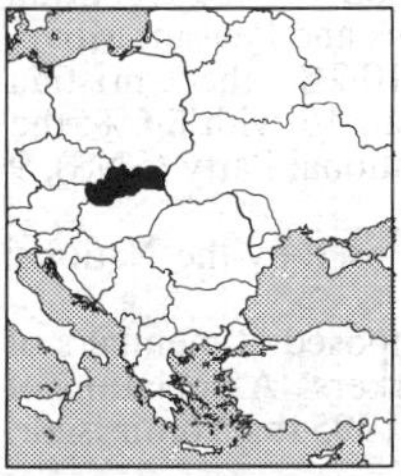

KEY HISTORICAL EVENTS. For Slovakia's history when part of Czechoslovakia *see* THE STATESMAN'S YEAR-BOOK, 1994–95, p. 1172.

At the Czechoslovak 1992 elections the Movement for Democratic Slovakia led by Vladimír Mečiar campaigned on the issue of Slovak independence, and on 17 July the Slovak National Council adopted a declaration of sovereignty by 113 to 24 votes.

On 1 Sept. 1992 the Slovak National Council adopted, by 114 votes to 16 with 4 abstentions (and a boycott by the Hungarian deputies), a Constitution for an independent Slovakia which came into being on 1 Jan. 1993.

Economic property was divided between Slovakia and the Czech Republic in accordance with a Czechoslovakian law of 13 Nov. 1992. Real estate became the property of the republic in which it was located. Other property was divided by specially-constituted commissions in the proportion of 2 (Czech Republic) to 1 (Slovakia) on the basis of population size. Military materiel was divided on the 2:1 principle. Regular military personnel were invited to choose which armed force they would serve in.

TERRITORY AND POPULATION. Slovakia is bounded in the north-west by the Czech Republic, north by Poland, east by the Ukraine, south by Hungary and south-west by Austria. Minor exchanges of territory to straighten their mutual border were agreed between Slovakia and the Czech Republic on 4 Jan. 1996.Its area is 49,035 sq. km. At the census of 11 Nov. 1980 the population was 4,991,168. Estimated population in 1993, 5,324,632. Density, 1991, 108 per sq. km. There are 4 administrative regions *(Kraj)*, one of which is the capital, Bratislava.

Region	*Chief city*	*Area in sq. km*	*Population 1990*
Bratislava	—	368	440,421
Západoslovenský	Bratislava	14,492	1,727,800
Středoslovenský	Banská Bystrica	17,982	1,615,438
Východoslovenský	Košice	16,193	1,503,421

Vital statistics, 1993: Births, 74,640; deaths, 52,707; marriages, 30,771; divorces, 8,143; infantile deaths, 779. Rates (per 1,000 population), 1993: Birth, 13·8; death, 9.9; marriage, 5·8; divorce, 1·5; infant mortality (per 1,000 live births), 4·8.

The population of the principal towns in 1993 (in 1,000): Bratislava, 448; Banská Bystrica, 85; Žilina, 86; Trnava, 72; Košice, 239; Nitra, 87; Prešov, 91; Martin, 60.

There was a Hungarian minority of 567,000 in 1996.

Minority languages could once be used for official business if its speakers made up at least 20% of the population, but a law of Nov. 1995 makes Slovak the sole official language.

CLIMATE. A humid continental climate, with warm summers and cold winters. Precipitation is generally greater in summer, with thunderstorms. Autumn, with dry, clear weather and spring, which is damp, are each of short duration. Bratislava, Jan. –0·7°C. June 19·1°C. Annual rainfall 649mm.

CONSTITUTION AND GOVERNMENT. Parliament is the *National Council*, which descends from the legislature responsible for Slovakia's affairs in federal Czechoslovakia. It has 150 members elected by proportional representation.

There is a *Constitutional Court* whose judges are normally nominated by the President.

Citizenship belongs to all citizens of the former federal Slovak Republic; other residents of 5 years standing may apply for citizenship. Slovakia grants dual citizenship to Czechs.

Elections to the National Council were held on 30 Sept.–1 Oct. 1994. The electorate was 3·9m.; turn-out was 75·7%. The Movement for a Democratic Slovakia (HZDS) gained 61 seats with 35% of votes cast; the Common Choice Coalition (Party of the Democratic Left and Social Democrats and Greens and Peasant Movement), 18 with 10·4%; the Hungarian Coalition, 17 with 10·2%; the Christian Democratic Movement, 17 with 10·1%; the Democratic Union, 15 with 8·6%; the Union of Slovak Workers (ZRS), 13 with 7·3%; the Slovak National Party (SNS), 9 with 5·4%.

The *President* is Mihal Kováč (b. 1936; ind), elected unopposed by the National Council on 15 Feb. 1993 and sworn in on 2 March.

A coalition government was appointed on 13 Dec. 1994 composed of members of the Movement for a Democratic Slovakia (HZDS), the Workers' Association of Slovakia (ZRS) and the Slovak National Party (SNS). In Nov. 1995 this comprised:

Prime Minister: Vladimír Mečiar (b. 1942; HZDS).

Deputy Prime Minister for Legislature and Media Policy: Katarína Tóthová (HZDS). *Deputy Prime Minister for the Economy and Minister of Finance:* Sergej Kozlík (HZDS). *Deputy Prime Minister for Social, Industrial and Trade Union Relations:* Jozef Kalman (ZRS). *Minister of Foreign Affairs:* Juraj Schenk (HZDS). *Defence:* Ján Sitek (SNS). *The Economy:* Ján Ducky (HZDS). *Privatization:* Peter Bisák (ZRS). *Interior;* Ludovít Hudek (HZDS). *Labour, Social Affairs and the Family:* Olga Keltošová. *Culture:* Ivan Hudec (HZDS). *Justice:* Jozef Liščák (ZRS). *Education and Science:* Eva Slavkovská (SNS). *Health:* Lubomír Javorský (HZDS). *Agriculture:* Peter Baco (HZDS). *Transport and Communications:* Alexander Rezes (HZDS). *Environment:* Jozef Zlocha (ZRS). *Without portfolio:* Ján Mráz (ZRS).

National flag: 3 horizontal stripes of white, blue and red, with the arms over all three-tenths of the distance from the hoist.

National anthem: 'Nad Tatru sa blýska' ('Over Tatra it lightens'); words by J. Matuška, tune anonymous.

Local Government. The local authorities are the district bureaux with the power to raise local taxes and with responsibility for roads, schools, utilities and public health. Elections for 2,853 mayors and 35,524 municipal councillors were held on 18–19 Nov. 1994. Turn-out was 52%. Independents gained 28·5% of the mayoralties, the Democratic Left 17·9%; HZDS 15·9%; Christian Democrats 14·8%. HZDS gained 22·8% of the councillor posts, Christian Democrats 19·7%; Party of the Democratic Left 15·7%.

DEFENCE. Conscription is for 18 months.

Army. There is 1 mechanized infantry division. Equipment includes 912 T-72M and T-54/-55 main battle tanks. Personnel (1996), 33,000.

Air Force. There are 130 combat aircraft, including 30 Su-22 and Su-25, 60 MiG-21 and 23 MiG-29 fighters and 19 attack helicopters. Transport equipment includes 13 fixed-wing aircraft and 30 Mi-8/17 helicopters, while 18 Mi-2s are used for liaison duties. Personnel (1995), 14,000.

INTERNATIONAL RELATIONS

Membership. Slovakia is a member of the UN, CEFTA, the NATO Partnership for Peace and is an Associate Partner of the WEU. Together with Austria, Croatia, the Czech Republic, Hungary, Italy, Poland and Slovenia, it is also a member of the Central European Initiative which evolved from the Pentagonal/Hexagonal grouping of 1990–91. An application to join the EU was made in June 1995.

ECONOMY

Policy. Privatization was proceeding by the issue of vouchers and direct sale. By the end of 1992, 503 large joint stock companies had been privatized by the voucher scheme, and 330 large firms and 9,676 small businesses had been sold off. 3·2m. persons had invested in privatization vouchers by the end of 1994. Legislation of July 1995 ended privatization by vouchers, which became exchangeable instead against state securities.

Budget. In 1993, revenue was Ks. 169,787m. and expenditure, Ks. 191,130m.

VAT, personal and company income tax, real estate taxes and inheritance taxes came into force in Jan. 1993.

Currency. The unit of currency is the *Slovak koruna* or crown (SKK) of 100 *haliers*, introduced on 8 Feb. 1993. There are coins of 10, 20 and 50 haliers and Ks. 1, 2, 5 and 10, and notes of Ks. 20, 50, 100, 200, 500, 1,000 and 2,000. The koruna was revalued 4% in May 1995. Year-on-year inflation was 7·6% in Nov. 1995. Foreign exchange reserves were US$3,000m. in Dec. 1995.

In March 1996, £1 = Ks. 45·99; US$1 = Ks. 30·09; DM1 = Ks. 20·39.

Banking and Finance. The central bank and bank of issue is the Slovak National Bank, founded in 1993 (*Governor,* Vladímir Masár). It has an autonomous statute modelled on the German Bundesbank, with the duties of maintaining control over monetary policy and inflation, ensuring the stability of the currency, and supervising commercial banks. Decentralization of the banking system began in 1991, and private banks began to operate. Foreign investors may acquire up to 25% of major banks' assets (100% of small banks), but no single investor may acquire more than 10%. There were 26 commercial banks in 1993, and 9 foreign bank branches. Total subscribed bank capital was Ks. 11,800m. in 1993. Savings accounts totalled Kčs. 94,859m. in 1992.

There is a stock exchange in Bratislava.

Weights and Measures. The metric system is in force.

ENERGY AND NATURAL RESOURCES

Electricity. There is a nuclear power station at Bohunice, and a hydro-electric dam at Gabčikovo on the Danube, from which Hungary has withdrawn. Output, 1993, 24,429 MWh. In 1995 about 55% of electricity was nuclear-generated.

Minerals. In 1993 2·81m. tonnes of brown coal and in 1991 1·34m. tonnes of lignite were produced. 1·09m. tonnes of iron ore were extracted in 1993.

Agriculture. In 1993 there were 1·48m. ha of arable land. In 1993 agriculture produced about 20% of GDP.

A federal law of May 1991 returned land seized by the Communist regime to its original owners, to a maximum of 150 ha of arable to a single owner.

Livestock in the state and co-operative sectors in 1993: Cattle, 1·89m. (0·34m. milch cows); pigs, 1·62m; sheep, 0·23m.; poultry, 3·99m. Livestock products, 1993: Meat, 477,565 tonnes; eggs, 1,527,000; milk, 1,214,000 litres.

INDUSTRY. In Czechoslovakia Slovakia was less industrialized than the Czech Republic, though there are concentrations of heavy engineering and munitions plants. Consumer industries include textiles and footwear. 1993 output included (in 1m. tonnes): Pig iron, 3·21; crude steel, 3·92; iron and steel plates, 2·86; zinc (1991), 0·81; plastics, 0·37; TV receivers (1991), 201,851.

Labour. In 1993, 2,166,000 persons were employed, and 368,095 registered unemployed. 539,711 persons were employed in industry, 259,000 in agriculture, forestry and hunting, 250,000 in commerce and 133,000 in building. The average monthly wage in Oct. 1993 was Ks. 5,348. Unemployment was 14·4% in Dec. 1993.

FOREIGN ECONOMIC RELATIONS. A memorandum envisaging a customs union and close economic co-operation was signed with the Czech Republic in Oct. 1992. An agreement of Dec. 1992 with the Czech Republic, Hungary and Poland abolishes tariffs on raw materials and goods where exports do not compete directly with locally-produced items, and envisages tariff reductions on agricultural and industrial goods in 1995–97.

Tax holidays of up to 7 years are available to foreign investors.

Foreign debt was US$3,600m. in 1993. By Sept. 1994 total foreign investments since 1990 amounted to US$416m.

Commerce. In 1992 (and 1993) exports totalled US$3,321m. (US$2,999m.) and imports US$3,550m. (US$4,049m.).

Total trade between Slovakia and the UK (British Department of Trade returns, in £1,000 sterling):

	1993	*1994*	*1995*
Imports to UK	2,392	56,654	67,509
Exports and re-exports from UK	10,628	44,666	76,764

COMMUNICATIONS

Roads. In 1992 there were 198 km of motorways and 17,668 km of main roads. In 1993 there were 994,933 private cars, 84,491 lorries, 17,061 vans, 12,655 buses and 233,705 motorcycles.

Railways. In 1994 the length of railway routes was 3,664 km of 1,435mm gauge (1,378 km electrified). In 1994 railways carried 99·1m. passengers and 58·9m. tonnes of freight. There are tram/light rail networks in Bratislava and Košice.

Civil Aviation. There is an international airport at Bratislava (M.R. Stefánik). Services are provided by Aeroflot, Czech Airlines, Hemus and Tatra Air.

Telecommunications. In 1993 there were 1,620 post offices and 1,424,928 telephones. Broadcasting is the responsibility of the government-controlled Slovak Broadcasting Council. Former Czechoslovakian radio and TV stations became a second channel to the existing Slovak networks. The state-run Slovak Radio broadcasts on 4 wavelengths, and there are 12 private regional stations. Slovak Television is a public corporation. It transmits on 2 channels (colour by SECAM), the second being shared with a commercial station. There are several independent local TV stations, and 2 cable networks. In 1994 there were 1·6m. TV sets in use.

Cinemas. There were 767 cinemas in 1990. 1 full-length film was made in 1993.

Press (1993). There were 22 daily newspapers.

SOCIAL INSTITUTIONS

Justice. The post-Communist judicial system was established by a federal law of July 1991. This provided for a unified system of 4 types of court: civil, criminal, commercial and administrative. Commercial courts arbitrate in disputes arising from business activities. Administrative courts examine the legality of the decisions of state institutions when appealed by citizens. In addition, there are military courts which operate under the jurisdiction of the Ministry of Defence. There is a Supreme Court, and a hierarchy of courts under the Ministry of Justice at republic, region and district level. District courts are courts of first instance. Cases are usually decided by senates comprising a judge and 2 associate judges, though occasionally by a single judge. (Associate judges are citizens in good standing over the age of 25 who are elected for 4-year terms). Regional courts are courts of first instance in more serious cases and also courts of appeal for district courts. Cases are usually decided by a senate of 2 judges and 3 associate judges, although again occasionally by a single judge. The Supreme Court interprets law as a guide to other courts and functions also as a court of appeal. Decisions are made by senates of 3 judges. The judges of the Supreme Court are nominated by the President; other judges are appointed by the National Council.

Religion. A federal Czechoslovakian law of July 1991 provides the basis for church-state relations and guarantees the religious and civic rights of citizens and churches. Churches must register to become legal entities but operate independently of the state. A law of 1993 restored confiscated property to churches and religious communities unless it had passed into private hands, co-operative farms or trading companies.

At a census in March 1991 there were 3,187,383 Roman Catholics. In 1995 there were 220,000 Uniates and 22,000 Orthodox. 7% of the population were Lutheran.

Education. In 1993-94 there were 3,482 pre-school institutions with 183,972 children and 15,834 teachers; 2,483 9-year primary schools with 690,189 pupils and 38,874 teachers; 28 independent church schools with 9,384 pupils and 556 teachers; 175 grammar schools with 68,102 pupils and 4,815 teachers; 26 independent grammar schools (19 church-run) with 4,888 pupils and 112 teachers; 339 vocational schools with 113,816 pupils and 8,494 teachers; and 14 institutes of higher education with 69,608 students and 7,769 teachers. In 1995-96 there were 3 universities and 5 specialized universities (ecomonics, transport and communications, veterinary medicine and 2 technical), with 46,676 students and 5,809 academic staff.

Health. In 1993 there were 18,556 doctors and 80 hospitals with 41,926 beds.

DIPLOMATIC REPRESENTATIVES

Of Slovakia in Great Britain (25 Kensington Palace Gdns., London W8 4QY)
Ambassador: Ján Vilikovský.

Of Great Britain in Slovakia (35 Grosslingová, 81109 Bratislava)
Ambassador: Peter Harborne.

Of Slovakia in the USA
Ambassador: Dr Branislav Lichardus.

Of the USA in Slovakia (4 Hviezdoslavovo Namestie, 81102 Bratislava)
Ambassador: Theodore E. Russell.

Of Slovakia to the United Nations
Ambassador: Vacant.

Further Reading

Kirschbaum, S. J., *A History of Slovakia: the Struggle for Survival.* London and New York, 1995
Krejčí, J., *Czechoslovakia at the Crossroads of History.* London, 1990
Leff, C. S., *National Conflict in Czechoslovakia: The Making and Remaking of a State, 1918–1987.* Princeton Univ. Press, 1988
Short, D., *Czechoslovakia.* [Bibliography] Oxford and Santa Barbara, 1986
Stone, N. and Strouhal, E., (eds.) *Czechoslovakia: Crossroads and Crises, 1918-88.* London, 1989
Wheaton, B. and Kavan, Z., *Velvet Revolution: Czechoslovakia 1988-91.* Boulder (Colo.), 1992

SLOVENIA

Republika Slovenija

Capital: Ljubljana
Population: 2m. (1992)
GNP per capita: US$7,140 (1994)

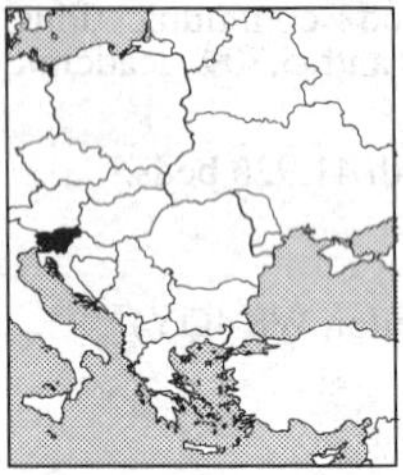

KEY HISTORICAL EVENTS. The lands originally settled by Slovenes in the 6th century were steadily encroached upon by Germans. Slovenia developed as part of Austria-Hungary, after the defeat of the latter in the First World War becoming part of the Kingdom of the Serbs, Croats and Slovenes (Yugoslavia) on 1 Dec. 1918.

A legal opposition group, the Slovene League of Social Democrats (leader, France Tomsič), was formed in Jan. 1989. In Oct. 1989 the Slovene Assembly voted a consitutional amendment giving it the right to secede from Yugoslavia. On 2 July 1990 the Assembly adopted a 'declaration of sovereignty' by 187 votes to 3, and in Sept. proclaimed its control over the territorial defence force on its soil. At a referendum on 23 Dec. 88·5% of participants voted for independence, which was formally declared on 26 Dec.

In Feb. 1991 parliament ruled that henceforth Slovenian law took precedence over federal. On 25 June Slovenia declared independence, but agreed to suspend this for 3 months at peace talks sponsored by the EC. Federal troops moved into Slovenia on 27 June to secure Yugoslavia's external borders, but after some fighting finally withdrew by the end of July. The 3-month moratorium agreed at the EC having expired, Slovenia (and Croatia) declared their complete independence of the Yugoslav federation on 8 Oct. 1991. They were recognized as independent states by Germany on 23 Dec. and by the EC on 15 Jan. 1992.

TERRITORY AND POPULATION. Slovenia is bounded in the north by Austria, in the north-east by Hungary, in the south-east by Croatia and in the west by Italy. There is a small strip of coast south of Trieste. Its area is 20,251 sq. km. The capital is Ljubljana. Population (1991 census), 1,965,986 (females, 1,013,375), density per sq. km, 97·5. 1992 estimate, 1,996,800.

Vital statistics:

	Live births	*Marriages*	*Deaths*	*Growth rate per 1,000*
1990	23,447	8,517	18,555	2·50
1991	21,583	8,193	19,324	1·15
1992	19,382	9,119	19,333	0·33

Rates, 1992 (per 1,000 population): Birth, 9·8; death, 9·8; marriage, 4·6; growth, 2; infant mortality, 8·9 (per 1,000 live births).

Population (1991, in 1,000) of the principal cities: Ljubljana, 268; Maribor, 105·4; Celje, 42; Kranj, 37·1.

The population is predominantly Slovene. The official language is Slovene.

CONSTITUTION AND GOVERNMENT. There is a bicameral parliament consisting of a 90-member *National Assembly*, elected for 4-year terms by proportional representation with a 3% threshold; and a 40-member *State Council*, elected for 5-year terms by interest groups. It has veto powers over the National Assembly. Presidential and parliamentary elections were held on 6 Dec. 1992. The electorate was 1·5m; turn-out was 75%. Milan Kučan was re-elected President against 7 opponents by 64% of votes cast. At the parliamentary elections the Liberal Democratic Party (LDP) won 22 seats with 23·3% of votes cast, the Christian Democratic Party (CDP) 15 with 14·5%, the Associated List (a coalition including the United League, former Communists) 14 with 13·6%, the National Party 12 with 9·9%, the People's Party 10 with 8·8%, the Democratic Party 6 with 5%, the Greens 5 with 3·7% and the Social Democratic (SDP) Party 4 with 3·3%.

President: Milan Kučan (b.1941; elected 6 Dec. 1992).

In Jan. 1993 a LDP-CDP-UL-Green–SDP coalition government was formed which in Sept. 1995 comprised:

Prime Minister: Janez Drnovšek (b. 1950; LDP).

Deputy Prime Minister, Foreign Minister: Zoran Thaler (LDP). *Finance:* Mitja Gaspari (UL). *Interior:* Andrej Šter (CDP). *Justice:* Meta Župančič (ind). *Defence:* Jelko Kačin (SDP). *Economy and Development:* Janko Deželak (CDP). *Education and Sport:* Slavko Gaber (LDP). *Transport and Communications:* Igor Umek (CDP). *Agriculture and Forestry:* Jože Osterc (CDP). *Health:* Božidar Voljč (UL). *Science and Technology:* Rado Bohinc (UL). *Labour, Family and Social Affairs:* Rina Klinar (SDP). *Culture:* Sergij Pelhan (UL). *Economic Activities:* Maks Tajnikar (UL). *Environment:* Dr Pavle Gantar (LDP).

National flag: 3 horizontal stripes of white, blue and red, with the arms over all in the canton.

National anthem: 'Prijateli obrodile so trte vince nam sladko' ('Friends, the vines have produced wine sweet to us'); words by France Prešeren, tune by S. Premrl.

Local Government. There are 62 administrative districts. Municipal elections were held in 2 rounds on 4 and 18 Dec. 1994 for 147 mayoralties. Turn-out was 50%.

DEFENCE. There is conscription for 7 months.

Army. There are 6 military districts. The Army is organized in 7 infantry and 1 surface-to-air missile brigades and 2 independent mechanized battalions. Equipment includes some 42 M-84 and 40 T-55 main battle tanks. Personnel (1996), 8,400 (5,500 conscripts). There is a paramilitary police force of 4,500 with 5,000 reserves.

Navy. The force, some 50 strong (with 400 reserves) in 1995, operates 2 inshore patrol craft based at Koper.

Air Force. The Air Force in 1996 had 7 fixed-wing transports and trainers, a dozen Bell helicopters and an A.109.

INTERNATIONAL RELATIONS

Membership. Slovenia is a member of the UN, CEFTA and the NATO Partnership for Peace.

ECONOMY

Policy. A reform plan for 1992–93 aimed at closer co-operation between economic organs, imposed stricter fiscal restrictions and gave the government a more active role in economic restructuring. Privatization is being carried out in 2 stages, beginning with small businesses, by transferring the capital to an investment fund to act as intermediary. 20% of the capital is to be transferred to savings banks, 10–20% to commercial banks, 20% to wage-earners and 10% to former owners.

Budget. Revenue in 1992 was 234,215m. tolars.

Currency. The unit of currency is the *tolar* (SLT) of 100 *stotinas*, which replaced the Yugoslav dinar. There are coins of 10, 20 and 50 stotinas and 1, 2 and 5 tolars, and notes of 1, 2, 5, 10, 50, 100, 200, 500, 1,000, 5,000 and 10,000 tolars. It is based on the ecu according to a floating exchange rate, and became convertible on 1 Sept. 1995. Inflation was 1% in April 1993. Foreign exchange reserves were US$1,200m. in 1993. In March 1996, £1 = 203·39 tolars; US$1 = 133·07 tolars; DM1 = 90.16 tolars.

Banking and Finance. A central bank and bank of issue, the Bank of Slovenia, was founded in June 1991. Its *Governor* is Franc Arhar.

There is a stock exchange in Ljubljana.

ENERGY AND NATURAL RESOURCES

Electricity. Output in 1992 was 12,026m. kWh. There is 1 nuclear power station. In 1992 3,971 kWh were nuclear-produced, 4,681 kWh thermal and 3,374 kWh hydro-electric.

Minerals. Brown coal and lignite production was 5,556,000 tonnes in 1992.

Agriculture. Agriculture contributed 4·5% of GDP in 1991. In 1992 agricultural land totalled 0·87m. ha (0·24m. ha arable, 0·21m. ha pasture, 21,980 ha vineyards). The cultivated area was 649,285 ha. Yields (in 1,000 tonnes) in 1992: Wheat, 178; maize, 207; sugar-beet, 36; potatoes, 368; cabbage, 368.

Livestock in 1993 (in 1,000): Cattle, 504; sheep, 21; pigs, 602; poultry, 11,424. Livestock products, 1992: Meat, 142,300 tonnes; milk, 563m. litres.

Forestry. 2·09m. cu. metres of timber were cut in 1991.

Fisheries. There were 46 sea fishing vessels in 1989. Total catch (1992) was 4,706 tonnes (978 tonnes freshwater).

INDUSTRY. There were 14,541 enterprises in 1991, of which 33 were public, 1,336 social, 125 private, 12,770 limited companies, 131 share companies and 59 co-operatives. Industry contributed 56% of GDP in 1991. Traditional industries are metallurgy, furniture-making and sports equipment. The manufacture of electric white goods and transport equipment is being developed.

Production, 1992 (in 1,000 tonnes): crude steel, 297; cement, 801; aluminium, 84·8; paper and allied products, 263; machinery, 22·7; cotton fabrics, 108m. sq. metres; woollens, 13·1m. sq. metres; 74,000 cars; 360 lorries; (1991) 191,000 TV sets.

Labour. The population of working age (15–64 males; 15–59 females) in 1989 was 1,262,625. The non-agricultural workforce in 1992 was 918,180. There were 102,593 registered unemployed in 1993.

FOREIGN ECONOMIC RELATIONS. Foreign debt was US$1,700m. in 1993.

Commerce. Exports in 1992 were worth 540,804m. tolars; imports, 504,442m. tolars. Major exports included: Raw materials, semi-finished goods, machinery, electric motors, transport equipment, foodstuffs, clothing, pharmaceuticals and cosmetics. Major imports: Raw materials, semi-finished goods, machinery, foodstuffs. Share of exports to principal markets in 1992: Germany, 27·1%; Italy, 13·1%; France, 9·3%; Austria, 5·1%; USA, 2·9%. Imports: Germany, 22·8%; Italy, 13·8%; Austria, 8·2%; France, 8%; USA, 2·7%.

Total trade between Slovenia and the UK (British Department of Trade returns, in £1,000 sterling):

	1993	*1994*	*1995*
Imports to UK	53,344	93,529	113,956
Exports and re-exports from UK	56,713	89,690	122,397

Tourism. 5,098,000 tourist nights were spent in 1991. Revenue was 1,313m. dinars in 1989.

COMMUNICATIONS

Roads. In 1992 there were 14,794 km of roads, including 1,356 km of main roads and 11,130 km of hard-surfaced roads. There were 606,820 passenger cars in 1992. In 1992 there were 2,676 buses, 31,281 lorries and 13,568 motorcycles. 146m. passengers and 6·4m. tonnes of freight were carried in 1992.

There were 5,779 traffic accidents in 1989 in which 553 persons were killed.

Railways. In 1992 there were 1,201 km of 1,435 mm gauge, of which 489 km were electrified. In 1993 11·9m. passengers and 12·6m. tonnes of freight were carried.

Civil Aviation. There are international airports at Ljubljana (Brnik) and Maribor. The national carrier is Adria Airways. In 1995 it had 2 A320-200s, and 6 other aircraft. Services were also provided by Aeroflot, Air France, Austrian Airlines, Croatia Airlines, Czech Airlines, Macedonian Airlines and Swissair. In 1992, 274,000 passengers and 3,129 tonnes of freight were flown.

Shipping. There is a port at Koper. Sea-going shipping totalled 9,061 GRT in 1995.

Telecommunications. In 1992 there were 505 post offices and 0·77m. telephones. The government-controlled Radiotelevizija Slovenija broadcasts 1 national and local radio programme, and also programmes in German and Italian. In all there were in 1995 6 nationwide radio networks as well as regional and local stations. Public television transmission is carried out by the 2 stations of Televizija Slovenija (colour by PAL). There are also a national independent TV network, a network serving Ljubljana and district and several local stations.

Cinemas. There were 158 cinemas with a total of 45,000 seats in 1989.

Press. In 1995 there were 5 national dailies, 1 national evening and 20 weekly newspapers. In 1989, 1,932 book titles were published in a total of 7·09m. copies.

SOCIAL INSTITUTIONS

Justice. There are 8 courts of first instance, 4 higher courts and a supreme court.

Religion. 94% of the population were Roman Catholic at the 1994 census.

Education. In 1992–93 there were 843 primary schools with 220,879 pupils and 14,936 teachers and 226 secondary schools with 94,423 pupils and 8,688 teachers. Pupils in 1991–92: Primary, 231,800; secondary, 103,400; tertiary, 3,200. In 1989–90 there were 27 institutions of higher education with 34,208 students and 2,569 academic staff. There were 2 universities with 45,314 students and 2,422 academic staff in 1994-95.

Health. In 1991 there were 4,086 doctors and 11,881 hospital beds.

Welfare. There were 594,150 pensioners in 1992, including 248,974 old age pensioners. Benefits totalled 419,805m. tolars.

DIPLOMATIC REPRESENTATIVES

Of Slovenia in Great Britain (11–15 Wigmore St., London W1H 9LA)
Ambassador: Matjaž Šinkovec

Of Great Britain in Slovenia (3 Trg Republike, 61000 Ljubljana)
Ambassador: G. M. Johnston.

Of Slovenia in the USA
Ambassador: Ernest Petrič

Of the USA in Slovenia (4 Pražakova, 61000 Ljubljana)
Ambassador: Victor Jackovich.

Of Slovenia to the United Nations
Ambassador: Danilo Türk.

Further Reading

Benderly, J. and Kraft, E. (eds.) *Independent Slovenia: Origins, Movements, Prospects.* London, 1995

National statistical office: National Statistical Office, Vožarski Pot 12, Ljubljana

SOLOMON ISLANDS

Capital: Honiara
Population: 349,500 (1993)
GNP per capita: US$800 (1994)
HDI/world rank: 0·511/125 (1992)

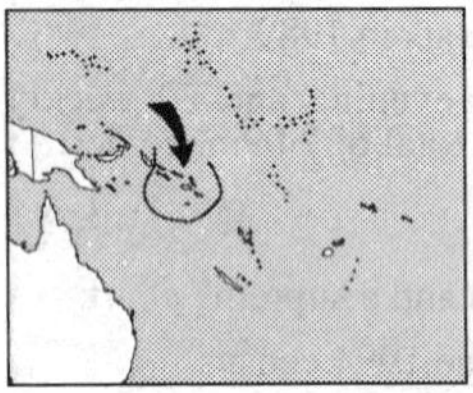

KEY HISTORICAL EVENTS. The Solomon Islands were discovered by Europeans in 1568; 200 years passed before contact was made again. The southern Solomon Islands were placed under British protection in 1893; the eastern and southern outliers were added in 1898 and 1899. Santa Isabel and the other islands to the north were ceded by Germany in 1900. Full internal self-government was achieved on 2 Jan. 1976 and independence on 7 July 1978.

TERRITORY AND POPULATION. The Solomon Islands lie within the area 5° to 12° 30' S. lat. and 155° 30' to 169° 45' E. long. The group includes the main islands of Guadalcanal, Malaita, New Georgia, San Cristobal (now Makira), Santa Isabel and Choiseul; the smaller Florida and Russell groups; the Shortland, Mono (or Treasury), Vella La Vella, Kolombangara, Ranongga, Gizo and Rendova Islands; to the east, Santa Cruz, Tikopia, the Reef and Duff groups; Rennell and Bellona in the south; Ontong Java or Lord Howe to the north; and many smaller islands. The land area is estimated at 10,954 sq. miles (28,370 sq. km). The larger islands are mountainous and forest clad, with flood-prone rivers of considerable energy potential. Guadalcanal has the largest land area and the greatest amount of flat coastal plain. Population was (census, 1986) 285,796. 1993 estimate, 349,500; density, 12·3 per sq. km. Growth rate, 1992, 3·1%.

The islands are administratively divided into a Capital Territory and 7 provinces. Area and population:

Province	*Sq.km*	*Census 1986*	*Estimate 1991*	*Capital*
Western	9,312	55,250	64,732	Gizo
Isabel	4,136	14,616	16,526	Buala
Central	1,286	18,457	20,914	Tulagi
Capital Territory	22	30,413	36,919	...
Guadalcanal	5,336	49,831	60,692	Honiara
Malaita	4,225	80,032	86,710	Auki
Makira and Ulawa	3,188	21,796	25,307	Kirakira
Temotu	895	14,781	16,500	Lata (Santa Cruz)

The capital, Honiara, on Guadalcanal, is the largest urban area, with an estimated population in 1989 of 33,749.

English is the official language. Melanesian languages are spoken by 85% of the population, Papuan languages by 9% and Polynesian languages by 4%.

CLIMATE. An equatorial climate with only small seasonal variations. South-east winds cause cooler conditions from April to Nov., but north-west winds for the rest of the year bring higher temperatures and greater rainfall, with annual totals ranging between 80" (2,000 mm) and 120" (3,000 mm).

CONSTITUTION AND GOVERNMENT. The Solomon Islands is a constitutional monarchy with the British Sovereign (represented locally by a Governor-General, who must be a Solomon Island citizen) as Head of State. Legislative power is vested in the single-chamber *National Parliament* composed of 47 members, elected by universal adult suffrage for 4 years. Executive authority is effectively held by the Cabinet, led by the Prime Minister.

The Governor-General is appointed for up to five years, on the advice of Parliament, and acts in almost all matters on the advice of the Cabinet. The Prime Minister is elected by and from members of Parliament. Other Ministers are appointed by the Governor-General on the Prime Minister's recommendation, from members of Parliament. The Cabinet is responsible to Parliament. Emphasis is laid on the devolution of power to provincial governments, and traditional chiefs and leaders have a special role within the arrangement.

At the elections of 26 May 1993 the electorate was 165,000; 280 candidates stood. A coalition of the People's Alliance Party, the United Party, the National Front for Progress and the Liberation Party gained 24 seats.

Governor General: Sir Moses Pitakaka, GCMG.

In Oct. 1995 the government comprised:

Prime Minister: Solomon Mamaloni.

Deputy Prime Minister, Minister for Home Affairs: Dennis Lulei. *Agriculture and Fisheries:* Edmond Adresen. *Commerce, Employment and Trade:* George Luilamo. *Development Planning:* David Sitai. *Culture and Tourism:* William Haomae. *Education and Training:* Alfred Martin. *Finance:* Christopher Abe. *Health and Medical Services:* Gordon Mars. *Foreign Affairs:* Danny Philip. *Justice:* Oliver Zapo. *Provincial Government and Rural Development:* Allan Qurugu. *Post and Communication:* John Masuota. *Transport, Works and Utilities:* John Fieango. *Lands and Housing:* Francis Orodani. *Forestry, Environment and Conservation:* Allan Kemakeza. *Energy, Minerals and Mines:* Eric Serl. *Sports, Youth and Women's Development:* Brown Beu. *Police and National Security:* Victor Ngele.

National flag: Divided blue over green by a diagonal yellow band, and in the canton 5 white stars.

National anthem: 'God save our Solomon Islands from shore to shore'; words and tune by P. Balekana.

DEFENCE. The marine wing of the police operates 4 inshore patrol craft and 2 small landing craft with about 80 personnel in 1995.

INTERNATIONAL RELATIONS

Membership. The Solomon Islands is a member of the UN, the Commonwealth, South Pacific Forum and is an ACP state of the EU.

ECONOMY

Policy. The Government's Programme of Action for 1990–94 aimed for economic and constitutional reforms, emphasizing the needs of national resource management, health and education.

Budget. The budget for 1989 envisaged expenditure of SI$115m. and revenue of SI$110·5m.

Currency. The *Solomon Island dollar* (SBD) of 100 *cents* was introduced in 1977. There are coins of 1, 2, 5, 10, 20 and 50 cents and SI$1, and notes of SI$2, 5, 10, 20 and 50. In March 1996, £1 = 5·35 dollars; US$1 = 3·50 dollars; DM1 = 2·37 dollars.

Banking and Finance. The Central Bank of Solomon Islands is the bank of issue. There are 3 commercial banks.

Weights and Measures. The metric system is in force.

ENERGY AND NATURAL RESOURCES

Electricity. Production (1987) 24,205,117 kWh.

Minerals. There are reserves of bauxite and phosphate, and there is a small industry extracting gold (36,241 grams refined, in 1989) and silver (7,414) by panning.

Agriculture. Land is held either as customary land (88% of holdings) or registered land. Customary land rights depend on clan membership or kinship. Only Solomon Islanders own customary land; only Islanders or government members may hold perpetual estates of registered land. Coconuts, cocoa, rice and other minor crops are grown. Main food crops: coconut, cassava, sweet potato, yam, taro and banana. Production of copra (1994), 20,724 tonnes; palm oil, 25,855; cocoa, 2,063; palm kernels, 5,690.

Livestock (1991): Cattle, 13,000; pigs, 53,000.

Forestry. Forests cover about 2·4m. ha. Production (1994) of sawn timber, 372 cu. metres.

Fisheries. Total catch, 1994, 30,179 tonnes.

INDUSTRY. Industries include palm oil milling, rice milling, fish canning, fish freezing, saw milling, food, tobacco and soft drinks. Other products include wood and rattan furniture, fibreglass articles, boats, clothing and spices.

FOREIGN ECONOMIC RELATIONS. The Government's Programme of Action for 1990–94 aimed to encourage foreign investment, particularly in manufacturing and tourism.

Commerce. Imports (1994), SI$468·12m.; exports, SI$467·88m. Main imports (in SI$1,000): Rice, 25,840; distillate, 21,408; motor spirits, 6,891; outboard motors, 3,770; passenger cars, 3,675; cement, 3,463; meat preparations, 3,360; refined sugar, 3,209. Main exports: Timber, 276,856; fish products, 99,068; oil palm products, 44,215; copra, 19,770; cocoa, 12,549; coconut oil, 2,013. In 1994 the principal suppliers were Australia (37·2%), Japan (17·1%), New Zealand (9·6%) and Singapore (8·4%); the principal export markets were Japan (41·1%), South Korea (14·1%) and UK (13·1%).

Total trade between Solomon Islands and UK (British Department of Trade returns, in £1,000 sterling):

	1991	*1992*	*1993*	*1994*	*1995*
Imports to UK	6,846	5,691	2,339	2,719	8,602
Exports and re-exports from UK	1,170	606	1,681	1,059	1,014

Tourism. In 1988, there were 10,679 visitors of whom 50·3% were tourists.

COMMUNICATIONS

Roads. In 1987 there were 1,300 km of motorable roads of which 100 km were bitumen-topped; the rest were coral or gravel. In 1986 there were 3,629 vehicles, of which about 1,827 were commercial vehicles.

Civil Aviation. The international airport at Honiara (Henderson) is served by Air Nauru, Air Niugini, Air Pacific, Qantas and Western Pacific. The national carrier is the state-owned Solomon Airlines, which in 1995 operated 2 aircraft. There are 27 airfields. Solomon Airlines also provides inter-island transport and scheduled flights to Kieta in Papua New Guinea.

Shipping. There are international ports at Honiara, and Yandina in the Russell group. In 1995 the merchant marine totalled 5,746 GRT.

Telecommunications. There are 14 post offices and 95 postal agencies. Number of telephones (1988), 2,500. Solomon Islands Broadcasting Corporation is a statutory authority which broadcasts radio programmes from Honiara, Gizo and Lata. In 1993 there were about 38,000 radio receivers. There is no television.

Press. In 1988 there were 3 weekly newspapers.

SOCIAL INSTITUTIONS

Justice. Civil and criminal jurisdiction is exercised by the High Court of Solomon Islands, constituted 1975. A Solomon Islands Court of Appeal was established in 1982. Jurisdiction is based on the principles of English law (as applying on 1 Jan. 1981). Magistrates' courts can try civil cases on claims not exceeding $2,000, and criminal cases with penalties not exceeding 14 years' imprisonment. Certain crimes, such as burglary and arson, where the maximum sentence is for life, may also be tried by magistrates. There are also local courts, which decide matters concerning customary titles to land; decisions may be put to the Customary Land Appeal Court. There is no capital punishment.

Religion. At the 1986 census, 33·9% of the population were Anglican, 19·2% Roman Catholic, 17·6% South Sea Evangelical and 23·5% other Protestant.

Education. In 1989 there were 51,436 pupils and 2,248 teachers in 468 primary schools, and 5,556 pupils and 307 teachers in 12 provincial and 8 national secondary schools.

Training of teachers and trade and vocational training is carried out at the college of Higher Education. The University of the South Pacific Centre is at Honiara.

Health. In 1988 there were 8 hospitals, 31 doctors, 464 registered nurses and 283 nursing aides.

DIPLOMATIC REPRESENTATIVES

Of the Solomon Islands in Great Britain (resides in Brussels).
High Commissioner: Levi Malau Laka.

Of Great Britain in the Solomon Islands (Telekon House, Mendana Ave., Honiara)
High Commissioner: Brian Connelly.

Of the USA in the Solomon Islands
Ambassador: Richard W. Teare (resides in Port Moresby).

Of the Solomon Islands in the USA and to the United Nations
Ambassador: Rex Horoi.

Further Reading

Bennett, J. A., *Wealth of the Solomons: A History of a Pacific Archipelago, 1800–1978*. Univ. of Hawaii Press, 1987
Kent, J., *The Solomon Islands*. Newton Abbot, 1972

SOMALIA

Jamhuriyadda Dimugradiga
ee Soomaaliya

(Somali Democratic Republic)

Capital: Mogadishu
Population: 9·2m. (1992)
GNP per capita: US$170 (1989)
HDI/world rank: 0·246/166 (1992)

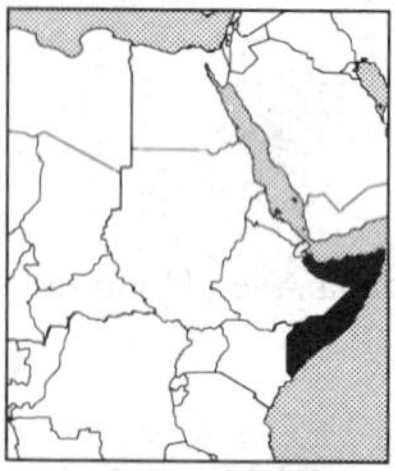

KEY HISTORICAL EVENTS. The Somali Republic came into being on 1 July 1960 as a result of the merger of the British Somaliland Protectorate, which became independent on 26 June 1960, and the Italian Trusteeship Territory of Somalia. On 21 Oct. 1969 Maj.-Gen. Mohammed Siyad Barre took power in a coup and formed a Supreme Revolutionary Council to administer the country, which was renamed the Somali Democratic Republic. After 12 years of civil war involving 5 factions, prominent amongst them the United Somali Congress (USC), the Somali National Movement (SNM) and the Somali Patriotic Movement (SPM), rebel forces had fought their way into Mogadishu by the end of 1990. Mohamed Siyad Barre fled on 27 Jan. 1991. Ali Mahdi Muhammad (USC) became president in Aug. 1991 but interfactional fighting continued. A UN-sponsored truce was signed in March 1992.

In Aug. 1992 a new coalition government agreed a UN military presence to back up relief efforts to help the estimated 1·5-2m. victims of famine. In accordance with a unanimous UN Security Council resolution of 3 Nov. 1992 troops from the USA and other countries mounted a mission to ensure the supply of aid to victims of the civil war and drought. On 11 Dec. 1992 the leaders of the two most prominent of the 15 warring factions, Ali Mahdi Muhammad and Muhammad Farah Aidid, agreed to a peace plan under the aegis of the UN, and a pact was signed on 15 Jan. 1993. At the end of March, the warring factions agreed to disarm and form a 74-member National Transitional Council.

Following the killing of 24 Pakistani soldiers of the UN 29-nation peacekeeping force on 17 June 1993, UN troops attacked and seized the stronghold of Mohamed Aidid and sought his arrest. After an escalation of violence in which hundreds of Somalis were killed, an envoy from the US President negotiated the release of hostages from Gen. Aidid and it was agreed to set up an independent commission to investigate the killing of the 24 Pakistani soldiers. On 16 Nov. 1993 the UN Security Council unanimously resolved to cease seeking the arrest of Aidid and to set up the commission of enquiry. After Dec. 1993 various national contingents began to leave the peacekeeping force, including US forces in March 1994. A unanimous UN Security Council resolution of 4 Feb. 1994 laid stress on the need for reconciliation and the promotion of democratic government, and scaled down the number of UN forces in the country. On 4 Nov. 1994 the UN Security Council unanimously decided to withdraw UN forces; the last of these left on 2 March 1995.

The principal insurgent group in the north of the country, the SNM, declared the secession of an independent **'Somaliland Republic'** on 17 May 1991, based on the territory of the former British protectorate, with a capital at Hargeisa and a port at Berbera. Its president is Mohamed Ibrahim Egal. The Somalian government rejected the secession. Clan warfare broke out in Hargeisa in Nov. 1994, and Mohammed Aidid's forces launched a campaign to reoccupy the 'Republic' in Jan. 1996.

TERRITORY AND POPULATION. Somalia is bounded north by the Gulf of Aden, east and south by the Indian ocean, and west by Kenya, Ethiopia and Djibouti. Total area 637,657 sq. km (246,201 sq. miles). Census population (1975) 3,253,024 of whom 15% urban. Estimate, 1992, 9·2m. (25% urban). 50% of the population is nomadic. Density, 12 per sq. km. Vital statistics (rates per 1,000),

1990: Birth, 50·8; death, 20·2; infant mortality, 132; growth, 10·1. Life expectancy in 1991, 48 years.

The country is administratively divided into 18 regions (with chief cities): Awdal (Saylac), Bakol (Xuddur), Bay (Baydhabo), Benadir (Mogadishu), East (Boosaso), Galgudug (Duusa Marreeb), Gedo (Garbahaarrey), Hiran (Beledweyne), Central Juba (Jilib), Lower Juba (Kismaayo), Mudug (Gaalkacyo), Nogal (Gaarowe), North-West (Hargeysa), Sanaag (Ceerigabo), Central Shabele (Jawhar), Lower Shabele (Marka), Sol (Las Anod), Togder (Burao). The capital is Mogadishu (1987 population, 1m.). Other large towns are Hargeysa (0·4m.), Kismayo (0·2m.), Marka (0·1m.) and Berbera.

The national language is Somali. Arabic is also an official language and English and Italian are extensively spoken.

CLIMATE. Much of the country is arid, though rainfall is more adequate towards the south. Temperatures are very high on the northern coasts. Mogadishu. Jan. 79°F (26·1°C), July 78°F (25·6°C). Annual rainfall 17" (429 mm). Berbera. Jan. 76°F (24·4°C), July 97°F (36·1°C). Annual rainfall 2" (51 mm).

CONSTITUTION AND GOVERNMENT. The Constitution came into force in 1984. The sole legal Party was the Somali Revolutionary Socialist Party (SRSP). The Executive President was elected for a 7-year term by direct popular vote. The People's Assembly consisted of 171 members elected for a 5-year term from a single list of 171 SRSP candidates.

Following the deposition of President Barre, Ali Mahdi Muhammad (USC) was sworn in as *President* for a 2-year term in Aug. 1991.

A coalition government of the USC, Southern Somali Democratic Movement, the SPM and the Somali Democratic Movement was formed in Aug. 1992 under the chairmanship of Gen. Muhammad Farah Aidid.

National flag: Light blue with a white star in the centre.

Local Government. The 18 regions are sub-divided into 84 districts.

DEFENCE. The breakdown of government following the 1991 revolution means no national armed forces have yet been established.

INTERNATIONAL RELATIONS

Membership. Somalia is a member of the UN, OAU, the Arab League, the Organization of the Islamic Conference and is an ACP state of the EU.

ECONOMY

Budget. Budget for 1990: Revenue, Som.Sh. 49,264m.; expenditure, Som.Sh. 68,970m.

Currency. The unit of currency is the *Somali shilling* (SOS) of 100 *cents.* There are notes of 5, 10, 20, 100, 500 and 1,000 shillings and coins of 1, 5, 10, 50 cents and 1 shilling. Som.Sh. 70,840m. were in circulation in 1990. In 1990 foreign exchange reserves were US$11,400m.; gold reserves were 19,000 troy oz. In March 1996, £1 = 4,004·41 Som.Sh.; US$1 = 2,620 Som.Sh.; DM1 = 1,775·19 Som.Sh.

Banking and Finance. The bank of issue is the Central Bank of Somalia (founded in 1960 as the Somali National Bank). All banks were nationalized in 1970. The Commercial and Savings Bank was closed in 1990. The Somali Development Bank (founded 1983) and the Commercial Bank of Somalia, are the only other banks.

Weights and Measures. The metric system is in use.

ENERGY AND NATURAL RESOURCES

Electricity. Installed capacity, 1987, 145·6m. kW. Production (1986) was 137m. kWh.

Minerals. There are deposits of chromium, coal, copper, gold, gypsum, lead, limestone, manganese, nickel, silver, titanium, tungsten, uranium and zinc.

Agriculture. Somalia is essentially a pastoral country, and about 80% of the inhabitants depend on livestock-rearing (cattle, sheep, goats and camels). Half the population is nomadic. Arable and permanent crop land in 1990 were 1·0m. ha and 0·01m. ha. Estimated production, 1991 (in 1,000 tonnes): Sugar-cane, 240; bananas, 110; maize, 100; sorghum, 145; grapefruit, 29; seed cotton, 3.

Livestock (1991): 20·5m. goats; 13·8m. sheep; 6·86m. camels; 4·9m. cattle; 1,000 horses, 25,000 asses and 24,000 mules.

Forestry. 60% of the country is woodland. Wood and charcoal are the main energy sources. Frankincense and myrrh are produced.

Fisheries. In 1988 the fishing fleet comprised 28 vessels totalling 5,188 DWT. 20,500 tonnes were caught in 1988.

INDUSTRY. A few small industries existed in 1986 including sugar refining, food processing, textile and petroleum refining. Production (1988): Textiles, 6·2m. yards; tinned meat and fish, 21·5m. tins.

Labour. 2,143,000 persons (828,000 females) were employed in 1990. 167,000 were between 10 and 15 years of age. 34·6% were labourers, 21·4% worked in trade and 14·3% in services.

FOREIGN ECONOMIC RELATIONS. Foreign debt was US$2,447m. in 1992.

Commerce. Exports in 1991 totalled US$52·3m.; imports, US$238·1m.

Principal exports: Livestock, hides and skins, bananas. Main export markets in 1992 (trade in US$1m.): Saudi Arabia, 24·9; Italy, 11. Main import suppliers: Saudi Arabia, 12·9; USA, 10·9; Italy, 10·6.

Total trade between the Somali Republic and UK (British Department of Trade returns, in £1,000 sterling):

	1991	*1992*	*1993*	*1994*	*1995*
Imports to UK	42	118	246	1,508	23
Exports and re-exports from UK	3,152	3,436	3,540	7,502	3,714

COMMUNICATIONS

Roads. In 1988 there were 22,281 km of roads (3,010 km were tarmacadamed).

Civil Aviation. There are international airports at Mogadishu and Berbera and 5 domestic airports. The national airline, Somali Airlines, which transported 105,000 passengers in 1988, had 1 aircraft in 1995. Mogadishu airport was used by Air Tanzania, Alitalia, Alyemda, Kenya Airways, PIA and Saudia.

Shipping. There are deep-water harbours at Kismayo, Berbera, Marka and Mogadishu. The merchant fleet (1995) totalled 17,288 GRT.

Telecommunications. Number of telephones (1987), about 7,000. The state radio stations transmit in Somali, Arabic, English and Italian from Mogadishu, and Hargeisa. TV broadcasting has ceased. There were 95,000 radios in 1993.

SOCIAL INSTITUTIONS

Justice. There are 84 district courts, each with a civil and a criminal section. There are 8 regional courts and 2 Courts of Appeal (at Mogadishu and Hargeysa), each with a general section and an assize section. The Supreme Court is in Mogadishu.

Religion. The population is almost entirely Sunni Moslems.

Education. The nomadic life of a large percentage of the population inhibits education progress. In 1985 adult literacy was only 11·6%. In 1985 there were 194,335 pupils and 9,676 teachers in primary schools, there were 37,181 pupils and 2,320 teachers in secondary schools, and in 1984 613 students with 30 teachers at teacher-training establishments. The National University of Somalia in Mogadishu (founded 1959) had 4,650 students and 550 academic staff in 1994–95.

Health. In 1986 there were 88 hospitals, 358 doctors, 113 pharmacists, 2 dentists, 556 midwives and 1,834 nursing personnel.

DIPLOMATIC REPRESENTATIVES

The Embassy of Somalia in Great Britain closed on 2 Jan. 1992.

Of Great Britain in Somalia (Waddada Xasan Geedd Abtoow 7/8, Mogadishu)
Staff temporarily withdrawn.

The Embassy of Somalia in the USA closed on 8 May 1991. A liaison office opened in March 1994, and withdrew to Nairobi in Sept. 1994.

Of Somalia to the United Nations
Ambassador: Vacant.

Further Reading

Abdisalam, M. I.-S., *The Collapse of the Somali State*. London, 1995
DeLancey, M. W., *et al. Somalia.* [Bibliography] Oxford and Santa Barbara (CA), 1988
Ghalib, J. M., *The Cost of Dictatorship: the Somali Experience.* New York, 1995
Lewis, I. M., *Blood and Bone: the Call of Kinship in Somali Society*. Lawrenceville (NJ), 1995.—*Understanding Somalia: a Guide to Culture, History and Social Insitutions*. 2nd ed. London 1995
Omar, M. O., *The Road to Zero: Somalia's Self-Destruction*. London, 1995
Samatar, A. I. (ed.) *The Somali Challenge: from Catastrophe to Renewal?* Boulder (CO), 1994

National statistical office: Central Statistical Department, State Planning Commission, Mogadishu.

SOUTH AFRICA

Republic of South Africa

Capital: Pretoria
Seat of Government: Cape Town
Population: 41·24m. (1995)
GNP per capita: US$3,010 (1994)
HDI/world rank: 0·705/95 (1992)

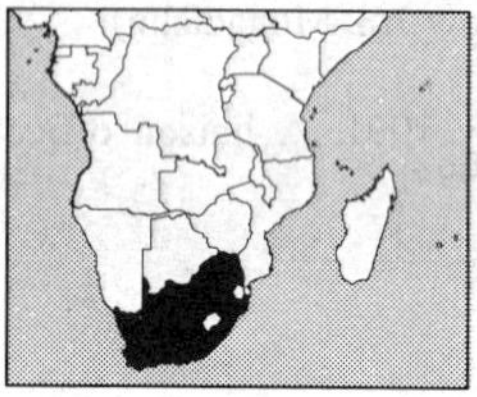

KEY HISTORICAL EVENTS. The Union of South Africa was formed in 1910 and comprised the former self-governing British colonies of the Cape of Good Hope, Natal, the Transvaal and the Orange Free State. The Union became a republic on 31 May 1961, and embarked on a formal policy of political and social racial segregation (*apartheid*).

By 1989 the restrictions of apartheid (racial segregation) began to be removed, and the government announced its willingness to consider the extension of Black South Africans' political rights. In Feb. 1990 a 30-year ban on the African National Congress (ANC) was lifted and its leader, Nelson Mandela, released from prison.

At the Whites-only referendum on 17 March 1992 on the granting of constitutional equality to all races turn-out was 85·6%. 1,924,186 (68·7%) votes were in favour; 875,619 against.

On 22 Dec. 1993 parliament approved (by 237 votes to 45) a Transitional Constitution paving the way for a new multi-racial parliament which was elected on 26–29 April 1994.

TERRITORY AND POPULATION. South Africa is bounded in the north by Namibia, Botswana and Zimbabwe, north-east by Mozambique and Swaziland, east by the Indian Ocean and south and west by the South Atlantic with Lesotho forming an enclave. Area: 1,224,691 sq. km. This area includes the uninhabited Prince Edward Island (41 sq. km) and Marion Island (388 sq. km) lying 1,900 km south-east of Cape Town and taken possession of in Dec. 1947.

On 28 Feb. 1994 Walvis Bay was ceded to Namibia. In May 1994 the former TBVC countries (Transkei, Bophuthatswana, Venda and Ciskei) were re-integrated into South Africa.

At the census of 1991 the population was 37,713,951 (19,055,846 females; 5,061,242 Whites).

Official population estimate, 30 June 1995, (in 1,000): 41,244 (Whites, 5,224; Coloureds, 3,508; Asians, 1,015; Blacks, 31,461). Growth rate, 1994, 2·04%. Urban population was 48·8% in 1994.

Vital statistics for calendar years:

	Births	*Still Births*	*Deaths*	*Marriages*	*Immigrants*	*Emigrants*
1992	501,461	...	177,841	111,557	8,686	4,289
1993	557,995	6,879	201,273	120,159	10,306	8,078
1994	677,107	6,968	213,279	133,309	6,398	10,235

Due to under-registration and the high percentage of late registration, the collection of Black birth information was discontinued in 1981–89. As from 1991 no distinction between racial groups was made. The 1994 live birth figure includes 430,762 late registrations of births which actually took place between 1987–93.

Infant deaths in 1993, 17,851. Divorces in 1994: Whites, 18,250; Coloureds, 5,190; Asians, 1,684; Mixed, 117; Blacks, 4,754.

Of the 6,398 immigrants in 1994, 2,784 were from Europe (of whom 1,047, UK); 1,645 from Asia (of whom 584, Taiwan); 1,628 from Africa, 249 from the Americas and 80 from Oceania. Of the 10,235 emigrants in 1994, 4,198 went to Europe (of whom 2,880 to UK); 2,766 to Oceania (of whom 1,298, Australia); 1,744 to the Americas; 942 to Africa and 531 to Asia.

In 1995 there were also estimated to be 8·5m. illegal immigrants, 3m. of whom had arrived since 1994.

In 1994 the provinces of the Cape of Good Hope, Natal, the Orange Free State and the Transvaal, as well as the TBVC countries [1], were replaced by 9 new provinces. On 30 June 1995 their areas, estimated populations, population densities and capitals were:

Province	*Area (in sq. km)*	*Population*	*Population Density (per sq. km)*	*Capital*
Eastern Cape	169,600	6,481,300	38·2	Bisho
Free State	129,480	2,782,500	21·5	Bloemfontein
Gauteng	18,810	7,048,300	374·7	Johannesburg
KwaZulu-Natal	92,180	8,713,100	94·5	Pietermaritzburg
Mpumalanga	78,370	3,007,100	38·4	Nelspruit
Northern Cape	361,800	742,000	2·1	Kimberley
Northern Province	123,280	5,397,200	43·8	Pietersburg
North-West	116,190	3,351,800	28·8	Mmabatho
Western Cape	129,370	3,721,200	28·8	Cape Town

[1] Transkei and Ciskei were integrated into Eastern Cape, Venda into Northern Province and Bophuthatswana into Free State, Mpumalanga and North-West.

Urban areas, according to the 1991 census:

Urban Area	*Total*	*White*	*Coloured*	*Asian*	*Black*
Johannesburg/Randburg	1,916,063	538,728	131,047	66,176	1,180,112
Cape Peninsula	2,350,157	612,200	1,256,290	27,058	454,609
Durban/Pinetown/Inanda/ Chatsworth	1,137,378	328,183	64,876	575,268	169,051
East Rand	1,378,792	445,160	37,289	17,951	878,392
Pretoria/Wonderboom/ Soshanguve	1,080,187	529,732	25,728	20,516	504,211
Port Elizabeth/Uitenhage	853,204	183,901	204,504	9,548	455,251
West Rand	870,066	263,168	30,473	24,812	551,613
Vanderbijlpark/Vereeniging/ Sasolburg	773,594	187,771	24,794	7,962	553,067
Bloemfontein	300,150	111,374	25,100	442	163,234
Pietermaritzburg	228,549	61,104	15,862	64,506	87,077
Free State Goldfields	427,569	77,200	8,159	129	342,081
Kimberley	167,060	34,066	57,853	1,475	73,666
East London/Bisho	270,127	90,486	35,880	4,125	139,635

There are 11 official languages (with numbers of home speakers at the 1991 census, including the former TBVC countries): Zulu (8,457,022); Xhosa (6,596,882); Afrikaans (5,689,131); Pedi (3,694,950); English (3,417,263); Tswana (2,715,419); Sotho (2,604,048); Tsonga (1,603,364); Swazi (975,827); Venda (645,315); Ndebele (562,463). The use of any of these is a constitutional right 'wherever practicable'. Each province may adopt any of these as its official language.

At the 1991 census 67,387 persons declared themselves bilingual in Afrikaans and English, and 685,120 spoke other languages, 8 of which are recognized by the Constitution and promoted by a special board.

CLIMATE. The climate is healthy and invigorating, with abundant sunshine and relatively low rainfall. The factors controlling this include the latitudinal position, the oceanic location of much of the country, and the existence of high plateaus. The south-west has a Mediterranean climate, with rain mainly in winter, but most of the country has a summer maximum, though quantities show a clear decrease from east to west. Temperatures are remarkably uniform over the whole country. Pretoria. Jan. 72·5°F (22·5°C), July 52·3°F (11·3°C). Annual rainfall 29·5" (750 mm). Bloemfontein. Jan. 73°F (22·8°C), July 47°F (8·3°C). Annual rainfall 23" (564 mm). Cape Town. Jan. 69°F (20·6°C), July 54°F (12·2°C). Annual rainfall 20" (508 mm). Durban. Jan. 75°F (23·9°C), July 62°F (16·7°C). Annual rainfall 40" (1,008 mm). Johannesburg. Jan. 68°F (20°C), July 51°F (10·6°C). Annual rainfall 28" (709 mm).

CONSTITUTION AND GOVERNMENT. A Transitional Constitution was adopted on 27 April 1994 to be in force for 5 years. Under it the National Assembly and Senate form a *Constitutional Assembly* (chaired by Cyril Ramaphosa, b. 1952; ANC) which has the task of adopting a definitive constitution by a two-thirds majority by 1996. The 1994 Constitution provides for an executive *President*, elected by parliament, *Deputy Presidents*, nominated one each by parties gaining at least 20% of electoral votes, and a parliament of 2 houses: a National Assembly and a Senate.

A *Constitutional Court*, consisting of a president and 10 other judges, of whom 6 are appointed by the President of the Republic on the advice of the Judicial Service Commission, and 4 are appointed from among the judges of the Supreme Court, was inaugurated in Feb. 1995. It reviews the actions of the legislature, executive and judiciary in the light of the Bill of Rights, and can overturn legislation. Its remit includes approval of the post-1999 constitution prior to its adoption by parliament.

The *National Assembly* is a legislature consisting of 400 members directly elected for 5 years, 200 from a national list, and 200 from provincial lists in the following proportions: Eastern Cape, 28; Free State, 14; Gauteng, 44; KwaZulu-Natal, 42; Mpumalanga, 11; Northern Cape, 4; Northern Province, 25; North-West, 12; Western Cape, 20. Parties gaining at least 5% of votes are entitled to Cabinet representation. The 9 provincial parliaments are elected at the same time, and candidates may stand for both, choosing if elected to both whether to sit in the national or provincial assembly; in the former case the runner-up is elected to the provincial assembly. The *Senate* consists of 90 members (10 from each province) indirectly elected by the provincial legislatures by proportional representation.

Bills may be introduced in either house, but must be passed by both. If a bill is rejected by one house, it is referred back to both after consideration by a joint National Assembly-Senate committee. Bills relating to the provinces must be passed by the Senate.

Parliamentary elections were held on 26–28 April 1994 (extended to 29 April in some areas). The electorate was 22·7m.; turn-out was 86%. 19 parties stood. The African National Congress (ANC) gained 252 seats with 62·7% of votes cast, the National Party (NP) 82 with 20·4%, the Inkatha Freedom Party (IFP) 43 with 10·5%, the Freedom Front (FF) 9 with 2·2%, the Democratic Party 7 with 1·7%, the Pan-Africanist Congress (PAC) 5 with 1·2% and the African Christian Democratic Party 2 with 0·5%.

The party composition of the Senate in Dec. 1994 was: ANC, 10; NP, 17; IFP, 5; FF, 5; DP,3. Its *President* is Dr Kobie Coetsee.

A Government of National Unity took office on 6 May 1994 which in Feb. 1996 comprised:

President: Nelson Mandela (b. 1919; ANC; elected 9 May 1994, sworn in 10 May).

First Deputy President: Thabo Mbeki (ANC). *Second Deputy President:* Frederik Willem de Klerk (NP).

Minister of Agriculture: Dr A. van Niekerk (NP). *Arts, Culture, Science and Technology:* Dr Ben Ngubane (IFP). *Correctional Services:* Sipho Mzimela (IFP). *Defence:* Joe Modise (ANC). *Education:* Sibusiso Bengu (ANC). *Environmental Affairs and Tourism:* Dr Dawie de Villiers. *Finance:* Chris Liebenberg (ind). *Foreign Affairs:* Alfred Nzo (ANC). *General Affairs:* Chris Fismer (NP). *Health:* Dr Nkosazana Zuma (ANC). *Home Affairs:* Dr Mangosuthu Buthelezi (IFP). *Housing:* Sankie Mthembi-Nkondo (ANC). *Justice:* Dr Dullah Omar (ANC). *Labour:* Tito Mboweni (ANC). *Land Affairs:* Derek Hanekom (ANC). *Mineral and Energy Affairs:* Roelf 'Pik' Botha (NP). *Posts, Telecommunications and Broadcasting:* Dr Pallo Jordan (ANC). *Provincial Affairs and Constitutional Development:* Roelf Meyer (NP). *Public Enterprises:* Stella Sigcau (ANC). *Public Service and Administration:* Dr Zola Skweyiya (ANC). *Public Works:* Jeff Radebe (ANC). *Safety and Security:* F. Sidney Mufamadi (ANC). *Sport and Recreation:* Steve Tshwete (ANC). *Trade and Industry:* Trevor Manuel (ANC). *Transport:* S. 'Mac' Maharaj (ANC). *Water Affairs and Forestry:* Kadar Asmal (ANC). *Welfare and Population Development:* Abe Williams (NP). *Minister without portfolio in the President's*

Office with responsibility for the Reconstruction and Development Programme: Jay Naidoo (ANC).

The *Speaker* is Dr Frene Ginwala.

National flag: A horizontal green Y birfurcating the hoist enclosing in its arms a black triangle bordered in yellow. The upper fly is red, the lower blue, both bordered in white.

National anthem: The former *Die Stem van Suid-Afrika/The Call of South Africa* (words by C. J. Langenhoven; tune by M. L. de Villiers) and the ANC anthem *Nkosi sikelel' iAfrika/God bless Africa* were both in use in 1996.

Provincial Government. The 1994 Transitional Constitution provides for 9 provinces, which may with a two-thirds majority adopt a constitution for the province in question. A provincial constitution may not be inconsistent with the provisions of the transitional Constitution except that different legislative and executive structures may be provided for. A provincial constitution only becomes effective after the Constitutional Court has certified that it is in accordance with the provisions of the Constitution. Each province has a provincial legislature in which the legislative authority of that province vests and which accordingly has the power to make laws for the province. A provincial legislature must consist of a minimum of 30 and a maximum of 100 members elected by proportional representation. A provincial legislature is elected for 5 years or less in certain circumstances. If a legislature adopts a motion of no-confidence in the executive council of the province, including the Premier, the Premier must resign or dissolve the legislature for an election.

The executive council of a province consists of the Premier as chairperson and a maximum of 10 members who are proportionally divided between all parties holding at least 10% of the seats in the provincial legislature. The Premier allocates portfolios to the parties in question after consultation with the respective leaders and appoints members of the council.

A provincial legislature has legislative authority and an executive council has executive authority with regard to the following functional areas or topics: Agriculture, education (excluding universities and technikons), health service, welfare services, housing, local government, police, cultural affairs, nature conservation, soil conservation, the environment, animal control and diseases, abattoirs, markets and pounds, gambling, language policy, public media, regional airports, transport, road traffic, regional planning and development, provincial sport and recreation, tourism, trade and industrial promotion, consumer protection, indigenous law and customary law, traditional authorities, and urban and rural development. A province does not automatically enjoy authority over these matters. Existing laws on these topics are administered by the national government until a province requests a transfer of them. The condition for such a transfer is that the province must have the administrative capacity to perform the powers and functions in question.

(For details of the individual provinces *see below*).

Local Government. Elections were held on 1 Nov. 1995 for 688 metropolitan, town and rural councils. The electorate was 12·3m.; it is estimated that only 75% of eligible voters were registered. The ANC gained 66·37% of all votes cast and a majority in some 400 councils; the NP, 16·22%; the Freedom Front, 5%. Elections in Cape Town and KwaZulu-Natal were postponed until 27 March 1996 to allow for the settlement of boundary questions.

DEFENCE. The South African Defence Force was replaced by the South African National Defence Force in May 1994. It comprises a Permanent Force, a Citizen Force and a Commando organization. The Permanent Force consists of professional soldiers, airmen and seamen who are responsible for the administration and training of the whole Defence Force in peace-time, but who are gradually absorbed into the Citizen Force in time of war. The Permanent Force and the Citizen Force consist of Army, Air Force, Naval and Medical Services components; the Commando organization is an army and air organization. The new constitutional dispensation brought about a Defence Secretariat. The Secretariat is a component of the Department of

Defence. It advises the Minister of Defence on defence policy, plan, programme and budget. It performs the accounting officer's function for the Department of Defence as well as monitoring compliance with directives issued by the President or the Minister to the Chief of the South African National Defence Force. It also performs any additional duties imposed by the Minister of Defence.

Army. South Africa is divided into 10 territorial commands. Within the commands are group headquarters, full-time territorial combat units, part-time territorial combat units and support units. The Commando's (205 units) are manned by volunteers and are utilised for area protection. The SA Army's mobile forces consist of one part-time operational division, one mechanised full-time brigade, one part-time/full-time parachute brigade as well as one full-time special forces brigade. Within the various commands are training units and other establishments of which permanent force members form the permanent staff. Equipment includes some 232 Mk 1A Olifant main battle tanks of which some 44 were upgraded to Mk 1B status, about 130 tank transport vehicles and about 180 Rooikat armoured combat vehicles. The total strength of the SA Army, including civilian members, is about 66,600.

There is a paramilitary South African Police Service 140,000-strong.

Navy. The Navy has its headquarters at Pretoria from where operational control is exercised directly. The Navy includes 3 French-built diesel submarines, 6 fast missile armed patrol craft (3 more in reserve), 8 coastal minesweepers, 3 inshore patrol craft, 1 British-built survey ship, 1 fleet replenishment ship and a naval-manned Antarctic supply ship, the latter 2 with helicopter facilities. There are additionally some 6 service craft. Forces are based at Simonstown and Durban and 6 reserve units are situated in major centres.

Navy personnel in 1995 totalled 4,500.

Air Force. There is 1 fighter-bomber squadron with 30 Mirage F1-AZ ground attack aircraft and another with Atlas Cheetahs (locally modified Mirage IIIs) including some equipped for reconnaissance; and 1 coastal patrol squadron with C-47s. Transport squadrons have 7 C-130B Hercules, more than 20 C-47s, 12 Caravan 1s, 4 Boeing 707s and 3 twin-jet HS.125s. 3 helicopter squadrons have 70 Alouette IIIs and 60 Oryx. PC-7s are used for primary training, followed by advanced training on Impalas and Atlas Cheetahs, weapons training on Impalas, and multiengine crew training on C-47s. There is 1 squadron of Caravan 1 light transports. Total strength (1995) was about 10,000, 135 combat aircraft and at least 20 armed helicopters.

South African Medical Services (SAMS). The SAMS line functions are exercised on a decentralized basis through a system of 10 regional commands. Also included in the line functions are the specialist permanent force units under the direct command of the SAMS Headquarters. These are 7 Medical Battalion Group, Medical Command Post Army Battle School, Institute for Aviation Medicine and the Military Psychological Institute. Hospitals and other medical units are as follows: 3 military hospitals, 6 military base hospitals, 48 sickbays, 53 military medical clinics, 11 veterinary clinics. SAMS part-time force units consist of 1, 3 and 6 Medical Battalion Groups. The total personnel of 8,600 are utilized in more than 50 medical, medically-related and other occupational groups. The part-time force numbers approximately 35,800.

INTERNATIONAL RELATIONS

Membership. South Africa is a member of the UN, the Commonwealth (except during 1961–94), SADC and the OAU.

ECONOMY

Policy. A Reconstruction and Development Programme (RDP) was instituted under a government minister in 1994 to run until 1999. Its policy aims are to meet basic needs, develop human resources, build the economy and democratize the state and society, and include as targets: Redistributing 30% of agricultural land; raising the annual number of houses built from 50,000 to 300,000; providing safe drinking water for 12m. persons; providing sanitation for 21m.; creating 300,000 non-agricultural jobs; reversing privatization 'contrary to the public interest'; introducing anti-trust legislation; 'de-racializing' business ownership; improving industrial relations. The government budget for 1995–96 earmarked R5,000m. for RDP.

Budget. Total revenue and expenditure of the central government's State Revenue Account in R1m.:

	1992–93	*1993–94*	*1994–95*	*1995–96*
Revenue	84,749	88,210	111,950	124,191
Expenditure	100,676	114,154	140,231	153,248

The main sources of State Revenue Fund, 1995–96, were: Income tax, R49,755m.; general sales tax and VAT, R32,750m.; excise duties, R6,111m.; customs duties, R4,700m. Consolidated main expenditure of government: Education, R32,616m.; defence, R11,025m.; economic services, R15,655m.; interest on public debt, R28,608m.; health, R16,885m.; other social, R22,558m.

From Sept. 1991 VAT at 10% replaced the 13% general sales tax. From 7 April 1993 the rate at which VAT is levied was increased from 10% to 14%. Corporate tax was reduced from 50% to 48% as from April 1991. In the March 1993 Budget the company tax rate was lowered from 48% to 40% of taxable income, but an additional tax of 15% on distributed profits was introduced.

Public debt on 31 March 1995, R244,605m., of which R8,774m. was foreign debt; internal debt, R235,831m.

Currency. The unit of currency is the *rand* (ZAR) of 100 *cents*. There are notes of R10, R20, R50, R100 and R200 and coins of 1c, 2c, 5c, 10c, 20c, 50c, R1, R2 and R5. Gold and foreign exchange reserves totalled R11,904m. on 31 Aug. 1995. A single free-floating exchange rate replaced the former 2-tier system on 13 March 1995. In March 1996, £1 = R5·95; US$1 = R3·90; DM1 = R2·64.

Banking and Finance. The central bank and bank of issue is the South African Reserve Bank (established 1920), which functions independently. Its *Governor* is Dr Chris Stals. Total deposits, 31 March 1994, R3,702m.; assets, R30,639m.

At 30 Nov. 1995 there were 42 registered banks, 3 mutual banks and 4 branches of foreign banks, collectively having total monthly average deposits of R325,520m. and total monthly average assets of R369,717m. There were 44 foreign banks with representative offices as at 30 Nov. 1995. Post Office Savings Bank deposits (31 Dec. 1993), R1,191m.

The Banks Act, 1990 (Act No. 94 of 1990) governs the operations and prudential requirements of banks. As at 1 Dec. 1995 the minimum capital adequacy ratio was 8%.

There is a stock exchange at Johannesburg (JSE). Foreign nationals have been eligible for membership since March 1996.

Weights and Measures. The metric system is in force.

ENERGY AND NATURAL RESOURCES

Electricity. There were (1994) 22 thermal power stations, 1 nuclear, 2 hydro-electric, 2 pump storage and 3 gas-turbine. Production (1994) was 167,609m. kWh.

Oil and Gas. In 1994 reserves were sufficient to yield 30,000 bbls a day of refined petroleum products until 2001 from gas produced at sea and converted on land.

Water. South Africa's average annual rainfall of about 470 mm is well below the world average. The unevenly distributed rainfall and high evaporation rate greatly affects the reliability and variability of river flow. Only about 62% or 33,000m. cu. metres of the mean annual run-off can be exploited economically. In addition about 5,400m. cu. metres may be obtainable from underground sources. Government activities are governed by the Water Act, 1956 (as amended). It is administered by the Department of Water Affairs and Forestry which manages water quantity and quality as well as the demand for the resource. A Water Research Commission was established in 1971 to co-ordinate and promote water research. Water availability is distributed poorly in relation to regions of economic growth and major inter-basin water transfer schemes are therefore a feature of the South African infra-structure. The latest such scheme under construction is the Lesotho Highlands Water Project which will divert the Orange River headwaters within Lesotho through tunnels into the Vaal River System which serves an area where about 60% of the industrial production of the country is generated. Lesotho is to receive royalties in exchange.

Minerals. Value of the main mineral production sales (in R1,000):

	1991	*1992*	*1993*	*1994*
Asbestos	167,757	170,114	142,695	140,238
Chrome ore	472,313	384,098	355,769	400,056
Coal	8,777,548	9,331,843	9,713,960	10,332,818
Copper	1,173,227	1,077,418	1,035,360	1,254,819
Fluorspar	91,621	86,434	82,789	85,990
Gold	19,296,121	19,512,563	23,239,318	24,953,110
Iron ore	1,161,742	1,127,577	1,278,879	1,400,240
Lime and limestone	487,072	502,599	536,122	604,767
Manganese	767,079	599,769	549,040	644,921
Silver	38,329	55,816	67,923	78,127

Total value of all minerals sold: (1993), R50,219m.; (1994), R53,526m.

Mineral production (tonnes) 1994: Coal, 195·8m.; iron ore, 32·3m.; manganese, 2·9m.; chrome ore, 3·6m.; asbestos, 92,130; copper, 165,213; lime and limestone, 19·5m.; fluorspar, 174,258; gold, 579,909 kg; silver, 195,754 kg; diamonds, 10,853,653 carats.

South Africa is a major producer of gold. Reserves were estimated at 39,933 tonnes in 1994. Value of gold production (1994) was R24,953m.

Agriculture. The redistribution of 30% of land, expropriated since 1913, is envisaged by the Reconstruction and Development Programme. By 1994 1·2m. Black farmers were farming 17m. ha and 55,000 Whites with 1·1m. Black labourers were farming 102m. ha. Dispossessed landowners are entitled to restitution from the state, though the rights of present landowners must be respected and compensation paid.

Much of the land suitable for mechanized farming has unreliable rainfall. Of the total area natural pasture occupies 69% (58·2m. ha) and planted pasture 2% (2m. ha). Annual crops and orchards are cultivated on 9·9m. ha of dry land and 1·1m. ha under irrigation. There were 61,899 farms in 1993.

In 1994, agriculture, forestry and fisheries contributed 5·1% of GDP.

Production (1993, in 1,000 tonnes): Maize, 9,668; sorghum, 478; wheat, 1,984; groundnuts, 132; sunflower seed, 349; sugar-cane, 11,244; oranges, 635; potatoes, 1,269; other vegetables, 1,922; grapes, 109; apples, 586.

Livestock, in 1,000 (1993): 8,337 cattle, 25,470 sheep, 2,341 goats, 1,194 pigs.

The 1993 production of red meat was 944,000 tonnes, poultry meat, 781,000 tonnes, wool, 77,573 tonnes, eggs, 231,000 tonnes, milk, 2·3m. tonnes.

Cotton-growing is undertaken by some farmers, the plant being found a better drought resistant than either tobacco or maize. Viticulture and fruit-growing are important, and were valued at R2,996m. for 1993-94.

In 1993–94 the gross value of agricultural production was R26,614m. (field crops, R9,683m.; livestock products, R11,494m.; horticultural products, R5,437m.).

Forestry. The commercial forests occupy about 1·26m. ha as well as 148,000 ha of protected indigenous trees. On 31 March 1990 there were 671,562 ha of pines, 538,485 ha of eucalypts, 115,198 ha of wattles and 7,991 ha of other hardwoods.

Production, 1989-90, of sawn timber, 1·66m. cu. metres (value R313m.); pulp, paper and paperboard, 1·39m. tonnes (R1,227m.).

Fisheries. In 1992 sea fisheries landed 608,000 tonnes of fish, shell-fish, seaweed and guano. Total output, wholesale value, 1993, R1,190m. The fishing fleet consisted of 3,969 vessels in 1994.

INDUSTRY. Net value of sales of the principal groups of industries (in R1m.) in 1994: Processed food, 37,034; beverages and tobacco, 16,353; vehicles, 25,011; basic metals, 20,478; petroleum products, 14,116; chemicals and products, 26,381;

non-electrical machinery, 13,370; electrical machinery, 10,737; fabricated metal products except machinery, 17,437; printing and publishing, 8,037; wood and cork products except furniture, 3,951; clothing, 6,586; paper and products, 11,852; textiles, 9,016; total net value including other groups, 253,002. Manufacturing industry contributed R90,177m. (23·4%) of GDP of R385,092m. in 1994.

Labour. The *National Economic Development and Labour Council* (*Nedlac*) is a forum for obtaining consensus between ministries, employers and trade unions on issues before legislation is submitted to parliament. Legislation of 1995 provides a framework for industrial relations, and sets out rules pertaining to collective bargaining, strikes and lock-outs; the rights of employers and employees; and dismissals, disputes and compensation. It envisages the establishment of a Labour Court, and independent conciliation and arbitration commission and workplace forums with elected worker representatives (where at least 100 persons are employed) to allow for joint decision-making with employers. In 1995 the economically active population numbered (in 1,000; females in parentheses) 14,497 (6,416), including: Blacks, 10,078 (4,565); Whites, 2,496 (1,033); Coloureds, 1,509 (673); Asians, 414 (145). Unemployed in 1993, 3,586 (1,903).

Industrial employment (except mining) at Dec. 1994: Manufacturing employed 1,409,977 workers; construction, 355,114; trade and accommodation services, 740,094. In 1994, 610,294 persons were employed in mining, including 392,185 in gold mining.

Average monthly earnings (excluding agriculture and mining) of employees, 1994, R2,879.

Trade Unions. In 1994 there were 213 registered and 65 unregistered trade unions. Total membership of all trade unions (registered and unregistered) represented about 23·7% of the economically active population. There were 9 trade union federations, but most unions were not affiliated to these. The Congress of South African Trade Unions (COSATU; *General Secretary*, Sam Shilowa) has formed links with the ANC. It had 1·3m. members in 1994.

A draft Labour Relations Act was released in 1995. Designed to move industrial relations from an adverserial approach towards co-operation, it encourages the establishment or workplace forums.

FOREIGN ECONOMIC RELATIONS.

International sanctions on trade with South Africa were lifted by 1993.

Commerce. South Africa, Botswana, Lesotho, Namibia and Swaziland are members of a customs union and the foreign trade statistics shown below represent the combined imports and exports of these countries. The total value of the imports and exports was as follows (in R1m.):

	Imports		*Exports*
1991	48,209	1991	64,355
1992	52,978	1992	67,508
1993	59,079	1993	79,481

The main imports (in R1m.) in 1993 were: Machinery and mechanical appliances, electrical equipment and parts, sound and television recorders and reproducers and parts, 17,131; vehicles, aircraft, vessels and equipment, 8,916; chemical and allied products, 6,599; optical, photographic, measuring, medical and other instruments and apparatus, clocks and watches, musical instruments, and parts, 2,716; textiles and articles thereof, 2,654; plastics and rubber and articles thereof, 2,639; base metals and articles thereof, 2,606; vegetable products, 1,928; pulp of wood etc., paper and paperboard and articles thereof, 1,740; natural cultured pearls, precious and semi-precious stones, precious metals, coins and imitation jewellery, 1,467.

The main exports (in R1m.) in 1993 were: Natural cultured pearls, precious and semi-precious stones, precious metals, coins and imitation jewellery, 10,138; base metals and articles thereof, 9,905; mineral products, 8,444; chemical and allied products, 3,378; machinery and mechanical appliances, electrical equipment and parts, sound recorders and reproducers, and parts, 2,811; vehicles, aircraft and equipment,

2,701; vegetable products, 2,437; pulp of wood etc., paper and paperboard and articles thereof, 1,937; textiles and articles thereof, 1,812.

Total trade between South Africa and UK (British Department of Trade returns, in £1,000 sterling):

	1991	*1992*	*1993*	*1994*	*1995*
Imports to UK	954,676	865,328	998,437	970,718	1,113,064
Exports and re-exports from UK	1,023,469	1,078,697	1,124,424	1,410,878	1,830,397

Tourism. In 1993, 3,358,193 tourists visited South Africa, of whom 2,700,415 were from African countries [1] and 430,036 from Europe (154,238 from the UK and 107,755 from Germany).

[1] Travellers to and from Botswana, Lesotho and Swaziland included only since Oct. 1991.

COMMUNICATIONS. In 1990 South African Transport Services became Transnet, a public company comprising railways, harbours, pipelines and road transport, set up, with the government as sole shareholder, as a first step to possible privatization.

Roads. In 1995 there were 360,522 km of national and provincial rural roads (61,679 km surfaced). In 1993, private firms and local authorities transported 511,264 passengers; Transnet carried 2·4m. tonnes of freight and private firms, 406,807 tonnes. Motor vehicles in operation (1993) included 3,813,904 passenger cars, 1,345,610 commercial vehicles, 228,318 minibuses, 22,884 buses and 273,244 motorcycles.

Railways. With the formation of the Union in 1910, the state-owned lines in the 4 provinces (12,194 km) were amalgamated into one state undertaking. In 1990 South African Railways, renamed Spoornet, became part of Transnet.

In 1992 there were 20,995 km of 1,065 mm gauge (9,078 km electrified) and 314 km of 762 mm gauge. In 1993–94, railways carried 1·7m. long-distance passengers and 164m. tonnes of freight. In 1990 the South African Rail Commuter Corporation was set up to run commuter trains in major cities; it carried 409m. passengers in 1993–94.

Civil Aviation. Civil aviation is controlled by the Ministry of Transport. Airports and air traffic and navigation services were commercialized in 1993. The Airports Company controls the major airports. There are internatinal airports at Cape Town, Durban and Johannesburg.

South African Airways (SAA), Comair, Sun Air and SA Express operate scheduled international air services within Africa and to Europe, Latin America and the Middle and Far East. The Alliance airline was founded in Dec. 1994 as a joint venture between SAA and the governments and national carriers of Tanzania and Uganda. 13 independent operators provide internal flights which link up with SAA's, Comair's and SA Express's internal network. During 1992 SAA carried 4,686,422 passengers (843,981 on internal flights) and 55,377 tonnes of freight and mail. In 1995 SAA's fleet comprised 4 A300B2-200s, 2 A300B4-200s, 1 A300F4-200, 7 A320-200s, 12 B-737-200 Advs, 1 B-737-400 Adv (F), 5 B-747-200Bs, 1 B-747-200B Combi, 2 B-747-300s, 4 B-747-400s, 2 B-747SPs and 1 B-767-200ER.

Services were also provided by Aero Zambia, Aeroflot, Aerolíneas Argentinas, Air Afrique, Air Austral, Air Botwana, Air France, Air Gabon, Air India, Air Madagascar, Air Malaŵi, Air Mauritius, Air Namibia, Air Seychelles, Air Tanzania, Air Zimbabwe, Airlink, Alitalia, American Airlines, Austrian Airlines, Balkan, British Airways, Cameroon Airlines, Care Airlines, Cathay Pacific, China Airlines, Commercial Airways, Egyptair, El Al, Emirates, Ethiopian Airlines, Ghana Airways, Gulf Air, Kenya Airways, LAM, Lesotho Airways, LTU, Lufthansa, Malaysia Airlines, Metavia Airlines, Northwest Airlines, Olympic Airways, Qantas, Royal Air Maroc, Royal Swazi Airways, Sabena, Singapore Airlines, Sudan Airways, Swissair, TAAG, TAP, Uganda Airlines and Varig.

In Oct. 1994 there were 375 licensed aerodromes, of which 212 were public and 74 private, and 180 approved helistops. 6,182 civil aircraft were registered in Dec. 1995.

Shipping. In 1995 sea-going shipping totalled 0·28m. GRT, including oil tankers, 2,203 GRT and container ships, 0·2m. GRT. The main ports are Durban, Cape Town, Saldanha and Richards Bay. Smaller ports are Mossel Bay, Port Elizabeth and East London. During 1995 the main ports handled 129·5m. tonnes of cargo.

Telecommunications. In 1991 the former Department of Posts and Telecommunications was divided into 2 independent public companies, the South African Post Office and Telkom SA Ltd. In 1993 there were 2,105 post offices and postal agencies. In 1994 there were 7,300 telex subscribers. Line capacity of automatic telephone exchanges (1993), 4,406,795; there were (1993) 5,206,235 telephones. There were 12,228 (combined accounts) users of data services.

Broadcasting is supervised by the Independent Broadcasting Authority, set up in 1993 to establish a system free from political control. The South African Broadcasting Corporation broadcast (1990) 23 radio services in 16 languages and 4 TV services in 7 languages (colour by PAL). An external radio service broadcasts in 7 languages. There were (1990) about 10m. radio and 3·45m. TV sets. An independent TV company, M-Net, was permitted to broadcast news from 1 Jan. 1991.

Cinemas (1990). There were approximately 1,200.

Press (1994). There were 29 main newspapers, of which 5 were Afrikaans, 21 English and 2 bilingual. There were 3 Afrikaans and 14 English daily newspapers.

SOCIAL INSTITUTIONS

Justice. The common law of the republic is the Roman–Dutch law—that is, the uncodified law of Holland as it was at the date of the cession of the Cape in 1806. The law of England as such is not recognized as authoritative, though by statute the principles of English law relating to evidence and to mercantile matters, *e.g.*, companies, patents, trademarks, insolvency and the like, have been introduced. In shipping and insurance, English law is followed in the former Cape Province, and it has also largely influenced civil and criminal procedure throughout the republic. In all other matters, family relations, property, succession, contract, etc., Roman–Dutch law rules, English decisions being valued only so far as they agree therewith.

The Supreme Court of South Africa is constituted as follows: (i) The Appellate Division, consisting of the Chief Justice and as many Judges of Appeal as the President may stipulate, is the highest court and its decisions are binding on all courts. Except for contempt of court in *faciae curiae*, it has no original jurisdiction, but is purely a Court of Appeal. (ii) The Provincial Divisions: In each province there is at least 1 provincial division of the Supreme Court. The Judge President of a provincial division may divide the area under his jurisdiction into circuit districts. In each such district there shall be held at least twice in every year and at such times and places determined by the Judge President, a court which shall be presided over by a judge of the division in which that district is situated. Such a court is known as the circuit local division for the district in question and is deemed to be a local division. (iii) The Local Divisions. The judges hold office till they attain the age of 70 years. A judge is expected to be available to perform service for an aggregate of 3 months a year until the age of 75. No judge can be removed from office except by the President upon an address from each of the respective Houses of Parliament on the ground of misbehaviour or incapacity.

Black divorce courts have jurisdiction to some extent concurrent with that of the Supreme Court in cases in which the parties are Black.

The provinces are further divided into 431 magisterial districts, each with a magistrate's court having a prescribed civil and criminal jurisdiction. There were 1,758 magistrates in 1995. From this court there is an appeal to the provincial divisions of the Supreme Court, and thence to the appellate division. Magistrates' convictions carrying sentences above a prescribed limit are subject to automatic review by a judge. In addition, several regional divisions consisting of a number of districts have been constituted. Convictions of such courts are not subject to automatic review by a judge, but to appeal in the normal way.

Courts of Black affairs commissioners were abolished in 1984. All criminal and civil cases are dealt with by judges (in the Supreme Courts) and magistrates (in the lower courts). Judges and magistrates are entitled to take judicial cognizance of customary (indigenous) laws and must, where relevant, apply them. A limited civil and criminal jurisdiction is conferred upon the Black chief or headman over his own tribe.

In 1994 there were 160 small claims courts, which have been introduced in a number of areas since 1985. These courts (where Commissioners preside) have civil jurisdiction only, limited by the quantum of damages and the nature of the claim.

The death penalty was abolished in June 1995. No executions had taken place since 1989.

Religion. 1991 census results (excluding the former TBVC countries) as regards religious denominations: *Christian churches:* Nederduits Gereformeerde Kerk, 3,212,693; Roman Catholics, 2,343,944; Methodists, 1,813,365; Zion Christian Church, 1,517,021; other Black independent churches, 5,366,925; Anglicans, 836,015; Lutherans, 773,631; Presbyterians, 402,198; Apostolic Faith Mission of Southern Africa, 402,621; other Apostolic churches, 423,505; United Congregational Church of Southern Africa, 383,622; Nederduitsch Hervormde Kerk, 266,754; Baptists, 249,028; Full Gospel Church, 201,909; Church of England, 162,429; Gereformeerde Kerk, 159,826; Assemblies of God, 152,218; New Apostolic Church, 144,727; Church of the Province of South Africa, 137,437; Seventh Day Adventists, 84,112; Pentecostal Protestants, 70,344; Swiss Church, 42,610; Church of England in South Africa, 39,836; Afrikaanse Protestantse Kerk, 32,175; Salvation Army, 32,629; Greek Orthodox, 26,673; Mormons, 7,844; Pentecostal Church, 22,185; other Christian churches, 1,274,518.

In 1992 the Anglican Church of Southern Africa voted by 79% of votes cast for the ordination of women.

Non-Christian religions: Hindus, 389,573; Moslems, 338,142; Jews, 67,654; Buddhists, 2,391; Confucians, 1,498; other non-Christian religions, 24,212.

Education. Until April 1994 the provision of education was assigned to various state departments responsible for executing education policy, which was determined by the Minister of National Education. These state departments were largely racially-based, in accordance with the tricameral system then in effect.

The 1994 Transitional Constitution introduced a new education system. Education up to tertiary level falls within the legislative authority of the provinces, though the national parliament may legislate in this field to ensure nationwide uniform standardization and effective implementation.

In 1994 the Council of Education Ministers was set up to oversee the operation of the new system. It comprises the national Minister and Deputy Minister of Education and the members of the provincial executive councils responsible for education. The Council meets once a month.

It is intended that the first 10 years of schooling should be free and compulsory, but for economic reasons only the first year's primary schooling was free in 1995.

There is a policy to change syllabuses to remove bias, factual incorrectness and insensitivity without replacing textbooks.

Primary and Secondary Education. In 1994 there were 11,614,857 children and 387,323 teachers in public ordinary schools, 45,517 children and 11,290 teachers in special schools and 171,692 children and 20,076 teachers in private ordinary schools.

Higher Education. In 1994 a Commission on Higher Education was appointed to investigate this sector in the light of the new goals and policies.

In 1994–95, there were 16 universities, 1 Christian university and 1 medical university, with 166,793 students and 10,747 academic staff. There are also 2 open (distance) universities, and 30 institutes of higher education (12 in agriculture, 4 in nursing and 14 technikons).

All the universities are open to all population groups but each has a different cultural ethos and the medium of instruction is English and/or Afrikaans. Technikons provide education at an advanced tertiary level for a variety of technical, commercial and general courses of study. They have the right to confer degrees. Technical colleges are mainly responsible for the training of apprentices and the education, on a part-time basis, of persons not subject to compulsory school attendance.

In 1993 there were 93,044 students and 3,735 teachers in technical colleges, 59,918 students and 4,865 teachers in teacher training colleges and 137,168 students and 2,415 teachers in technikons.

Health. In 1994 there were 26,452 medical practitioners of whom 7,167 had specialist qualifications, 4,029 dentists, 331 dental specialists, 9,622 pharmacists and 158,538 nurses and midwives. In 1995 there were 834 hospitals with about 150,000 beds, of which 18% were provided by private medical care.

Treatment in the public health service covers 75–80% of the population and is free of charge for the indigent, children under 6 years and pregnant mothers. Other patients are charged on a sliding scale based on their means. 60% of private health care is funded by medical insurance schemes and the remainder by privately paying patients. The free medical treatment scheme amounts to about R500m.

Welfare. Under the Social Assistance Act, 1992, grants are made to the aged, war veterans, blind and disabled, as well as maintenance grants to single mothers with inadequate income, and foster child grants. Assistance in the form of social relief is given to individuals and families unable to meet their primary needs.

The social welfare service is a partnership between the private and the public sectors. Services are delivered by private welfare organizations which are subsidized by the state.

In 1993 there were 1,742 registered private welfare organizations, partially funded by the state for services rendered. All are registered under the National Welfare Act, 1978.

The changing political situation necessitated the development of a new welfare dispensation to cope with the demands of the 'new' South Africa. Welfare services are divided into service fields, namely, family and child care, care of the aged, care of the disabled, drug dependent care, care of offenders and social security.

The Child Care Act, 1983 (as amended in 1991) is designed to protect children against neglect, abuse, ill-treatment and exploitation. The Act provides for preventive child care services, foster care and also for various children's allowances and financial assistance to children's homes and creches. The Primary School Nutrition Scheme was set up in 1994 to alleviate hunger which affects school attendance and concentration. It is administered jointly by the Department of Health and the Department of Education.

Policy regarding aging has moved away from care of the aged to age management. A national Discussion Group on Aging was instituted in 1994 to advise the Department of Welfare on legislation, policy, standards and criteria on financing. The consumers of services are involved in the design of affordable, accessible and equitable age management.

The National Strategy against the Abuse of Alcohol and other Drugs directs research into drug abuse. The Drug Advisory Board advises the Minister of Welfare and Population Development and brings together the voluntary and government agencies working on drug abuse.

The Committee for Marriage and Family Life of the South African Welfare Council was commissioned by the government to promote the quality of family life.

Excessive population growth and widespread illegal immigration and a low rate of economic development are seen as two facets of the same problem. The Chief Directorate Population Development is located in the Department of Welfare to ensure that population factors and objectives (accommodating to increasing population size, influencing demographic processes—especially high fertility) are integrated in overall socio-economic development policy. These are embodied in the government's Reconstruction and Development Programme (RDP).

DIPLOMATIC REPRESENTATIVES

Of South Africa in Great Britain (South Africa Hse., Trafalgar Sq., London, WC2N 5DP)
High Commissioner: Mendi Msimang.

Of Great Britain in South Africa (255 Hill St., Arcadia, Pretoria, 0002)
High Commissioner: Sir Anthony Reeve, KCMG, KCVO.

Of South Africa in the USA (3051 Massachusetts Ave., NW, Washington, D.C., 20008)
Ambassador: Franklin Sonn.

Of the USA in South Africa (877 Pretorius St., Pretoria)
Ambassador: James Joseph.

Of South Africa to the United Nations
Ambassador: Khiphusizi Jele.

Further Reading

Beinart, W., *Twentieth Century South Africa.* OUP, 1994
Benson, M., *Nelson Mandela: The Man and the Movement.* New York, 1986
Brewer, J., (ed.) *Restructuring South Africa.* London, 1994
Davenport, T. R. H., *South Africa: A Modern History.* 4th ed. CUP, 1991
Davies, G. V., *South Africa.* [Bibliography]. 2nd ed. Oxford and Santa Barbara (CA), 1994
Hough, M. and Du Plessis, A., (eds.) *Selected Documents and Commentaries on Negotiations and Constitutional Development in the RSA, 1989–1994.* Pretoria Univ., 1994
Johnson, R. W. and Schlemmer, L. (eds.). *Launching Democracy in South Africa: the First Open Election, 1994.* Yale Univ. Press, 1996
Mandela, N., *Long Walk to Freedom: the Autobiography of Nelson Mandela.* London, 1994
Meredith, M., *South Africa's New Era: the 1994 Election.* London, 1994
Mostert, N., *Frontiers: the Epic of South Africa's Creation and the Tragedy of the Xhosa People.* London, 1992
Nattrass, N. and Ardington, E. (eds.), *The Political Economy of South Africa.* Cape Town and OUP, 1990
Oxford History of South Africa. OUP, 1969
Riley, E., *Major Political Events in South Africa, 1948–1990.* Oxford, 1991
Taylor, R., *South Africa: an Introduction.* Hemel Hempstead, 1993
Thompson, L., *A History of South Africa.* 2nd ed. Yale Univ. Press, 1996
Who's Who in South African Politics. 5th ed. London, 1995

National statistical office: Central Statistical Service, Private Bag X44, Pretoria 0001.

THE PROVINCES

EASTERN CAPE

Territory and Population. The area is 169,600 sq. km and the population was estimated at 6,481,300 in 1995 (3·51m. females; 5·65m. Blacks; 0·44m. Coloured; 0·37m. Whites; 16,300 Asians). At the 1991 Census, 82·6% spoke Xhosa as their home language, 9·6% Afrikaans, 4·2% English and 2·1% Sotho.

Constitution and Government. Eastern Cape comprises 77 administrative districts (including Umzimkulu district, an enclave within KwaZulu-Natal). The provincial capital is to be either Bisho or Umtata. There is a 56-seat provincial legislature; at the provincial elections held 27–29 April 1994, 48 seats were won by the ANC (with 84·6% of votes cast), 6 by the NP (with 9·9%), 1 by the DP (with 2·1%) and 1 by the PAC (with 2·0%).

In Feb. 1996 the Executive Council comprised:
Premier: Raymond Mhlaba (ANC).

Agriculture and Environment: Ezra Sigwela (ANC). *Public Service and Administration:* Mandisa Marasha (ANC). *Economic Affairs:* Smuts Ngonyama (ANC). *Finance:* Shepherd Mayatula (ANC). *Health and Welfare:* Dr Trudie Thomas (ANC). *Education and Culture:* Ziziwe Balindlela (ANC). *Justice and Police Services:* Dr Malizo Mphehle (ANC). *Public Works:* Thobile Mhlahlo. *Housing and Local Government:* Maxwell Mamase (ANC). *Transport:* Dr Tertius Delport (NP). *Safety and Security:* Denis Neer.

Agriculture. In 1988 (excluding the former Ciskei and Transkei now within the province) there were 6,588 farms with 105,585 agricultural workers; gross farming income amounted to R908·1m.

Labour. In 1991 (including the former Ciskei and Transkei) the economically active population numbered 1,296,427 (21·2% of the total provincial population). Of those employed (excluding Ciskei and Transkei), 15·5% were in agriculture, 0·3% in mining, 17·3% in manufacturing, 15·8% in trade and 33·7% in services; the unemployment rate (Oct. 1993) was 24·1%.

Education. In 1993 there were 16,336 pupils in pre-primary schools, 4,289 pupils in special schools, 1,602,255 pupils in primary schools and 694,688 in secondary schools, with altogether 56,462 teachers; there were also 574 lecturers and 7,630 students in technical colleges, and 1,175 lecturers and 14,373 students in teachers' training establishments.

Roads. Motor vehicles registered (1991, excluding Ciskei and Transkei) totalled 341,759, including 197,151 passenger cars and 71,985 commercial vehicles.

Health. In 1992 there were 2,043 medical practitioners, 21,416 nurses, 586 hospitals and clinics and 29,806 hospital beds.

FREE STATE

Territory and Population. The area is 129,480 sq. km and the population was estimated at 2,782,500 in 1995 (1·31m. females; 2·33m. Blacks; 0·37m. Whites; 73,000 Coloureds; 3,200 Asians). At the 1991 Census, 57·4% of the population spoke Sotho as their home language, 14·7% Afrikaans, 9·4% Xhosa, 6·4% Tswana, 5·2% Zulu, 1·5% English and 1·1% Pedi.

Free State comprises 52 administrative districts. The provincial capital is Bloemfontein.

Constitution and Government. There is a 30-seat provincial legislature; at the provincial elections held 27–29 April 1994, 24 seats were won by the ANC (with 77·5% of the 1,339,251 votes cast), 4 by the NP (with 12·7%) and 2 by the FF (with 6·1%).

In Feb. 1995 the government comprised:

Premier: Patrick Lekota (ANC).

Finance and Expenditure: Tate Makgoe (ANC). *Education and Culture:* T. Saki Belot (ANC). *Safety and Security:* Dr D. A, Kganase (ANC). *Public Works and Roads:* Gregory Nthatisi (ANC). *Health and Welfare:* Senorita Nthlabathi (ANC). *Agriculture and Environment Affairs:* Cas Human (ANC). *Economic Affairs and Tourism:* Ace Magushule (ANC). *Public Transport:* Dr Louis van der Watt (NP). *Housing:* Vax Mayekiso (ANC). *Local Government Management:* Ouma Motsumi (ANC).

Agriculture. In 1988 (excluding the TBVC countries now within the province) there were 10,926 farms with 200,559 agricultural workers; gross farming income amounted to R2,473·6m.

Labour. In 1991 (including that part of the former Bophuthatswana now within the province) the economically active population numbered 1,056,828. Of those employed (excluding Bophuthatswana), 17·2% were in agriculture, 27·5% in mining, 7·0% in manufacturing, 10·5% in trade and 27·2% in services; the unemployment rate (Oct. 1993) was 26·7%.

Education. In 1993 there were 19,392 pupils in pre-primary schools, 3,414 pupils in special schools, 457,060 pupils in primary schools and 279,153 in secondary schools, with altogether 23,338 teachers; there were also 215 lecturers and 3,549 students in technical colleges, and 447 lecturers and 4,091 students in teachers' training establishments.

Roads. Motor vehicles registered (1991, excluding Bophuthatswana) totalled 444,023 including 188,497 passenger cars and 93,648 commercial vehicles.

Health. In 1992 there were 1,303 medical practitioners, 10,723 nurses, 453 hospitals and clinics and 11,075 hospital beds.

GAUTENG

Territory and Population. The area is 18,810 sq. km and the population was estimated at 7,048,300 in 1995 (3·27m. females; 4·44m. Blacks; 2·15m. Whites; 0·28m. Coloureds; 0·17m. Asians). At the 1991 Census, 20·5% spoke Afrikaans as their home language, 18·4% Zulu, 16·1% English, 11·2% Sotho, 8·8% Pedi, 7·2% Tswana, 6·2% Xhosa, 3·8% Tsonga, 1·4% Ndebele, 1·3% Swazi and 1·1% Venda.

The province of Gauteng (at first called Pretoria-Witwatersrand-Vereeniging (PWV) comprises 23 administrative districts. The provincial capital is Johannesburg.

Constitution and Government. There is an 86-seat provincial legislature; at the provincial elections held 27–29 April 1994, 50 seats were won by the ANC (with 58·4% of the 4,143,901 votes cast), 21 by the NP (with 24·2%), 5 by the FF (6·2%), 5 by the DP (5·4%), 3 by the IFP (3·7%), and 1 each by the PAC (1·5%) and ACDP (0·6%).

In Feb. 1995 the government comprised:

Premier: Tokyo Sexwale (ANC).

Economic Affairs and Finance: Jabu Moleketi (ANC). *Health:* Amos Masondo (ANC). *Education:* Mary Metcalf (ANC). *Social Welfare:* Johannes Blanche (NP). *Housing and Local Government:* Daniel Mofokeng (ANC). *Urban, Rural Development and the Environment:* Sicelo Shiceka (ANC). *Public Transport:* Olaus van Zyl (NP). *Public Safety and Security:* Jesse Duarte (ANC). *Conservation and Agriculture:* John Masuvo (NP). *Sports, Recreation, Arts and Culture:* Peter Skosana (ANC).

Agriculture. In 1988 there were 2,960 farms with 49,759 agricultural workers; gross farming income amounted to R890·9m.

Labour. In 1991 the economically active population numbered 3,431,126. Of those employed, only 2·4% were in agriculture, with 8·6% in mining, 19·5% in manufacturing, 16·7% in trade and 30·9% in services. The unemployment rate (Oct. 1993) was 26·6%.

Education. In 1993 there were 45,522 pupils in pre-primary schools, 15,296 pupils in special schools, 903,157 pupils in primary schools and 692,783 in secondary schools, with altogether 59,804 teachers; there were also 1,196 lecturers and 21,639 students in technical colleges, and 1,094 lecturers and 12,361 students in teachers' training establishments.

Roads. Motor vehicles registered (1991) totalled 2,328,273 including 1,479,537 passenger cars and 404,468 commercial vehicles.

Health. In 1992 there were 8,720 medical practitioners, 42,339 nurses, 1,167 hospitals and clinics and 43,548 hospital beds.

KWAZULU-NATAL

Territory and Population. The area is 92,180 sq. km and the population was estimated at 8,713,100 in 1995 (4·55m. females; 7·21m. Blacks; 0·8m. Asians; 0·6m. Whites; 0·12m. Coloureds). At the 1991 Census, 79·3% spoke Zulu as their home language, 16·0% English, 1·9% Afrikaans and 1·2% Xhosa.

Constitution and Government. KwaZulu-Natal comprises 66 administrative districts. The provincial capital was initially Pietermaritzburg, and a referendum held at the end of 1995 to decide between Ulundi (the former capital of KwaZulu) and Pietermaritzburg (the former capital of Natal) as the permanent capital confirmed this. There is an 81-seat provincial legislature; at the provincial elections held on 27–29 April 1994, 41 seats were won by the IFP (with 52·2% of votes cast), 26 by the ANC (with 33·4%), 9 by the NP (with 11·6%), 2 by the DP (with 2·2%) and 1 each by the PAC (0·8%), the African Christian Democratic Party (0·7%) and Minority Front (1·4%).

In Feb. 1995 the government comprised:

Premier: Frank Mdlalose (IFP).

Finance: Senzele Mhlungu (IFP). *Housing and Local Government:* Peter Miller (IFP). *Economic Affairs amd Tourism:* Jacob Zuma (ANC). *Police Services:* Celani Mtetwa (IFP). *Nature Conservation, Environment Affairs and Traditional Authority:* Nyanga Ngubane (IFP). *Agriculture:* George Bartlett (NP). *Health:* Dr Zweli Mkhize (ANC). *Roads, Transportation and Traffic Control:* J. S'bu Ndebele (ANC). *Social Welfare:* Prince Gideon Zulu (IFP). *Education and Culture:* Dr Vincent Zulu (IFP).

Agriculture. In 1988 there were 6,305 farms with 211,471 agricultural workers; gross farming income amounted to R2,078·8m.

Labour. In 1991 the economically active population numbered 2,421,905. Of those employed, 13·3% were in agriculture, 1·9% in mining, 20·4% in manufacturing, 16·7% in trade and 30·0% in services. The unemployment rate (Oct. 1993) was 34·7%.

Education. In 1993 there were 38,127 pupils in pre-primary schools, 2,465 pupils in special schools, 1,481,712 pupils in primary schools and 818,976 in secondary schools, with altogether 63,921 teachers; there were also 717 lecturers and 9,188 students in technical colleges, and 1,062 lecturers and 12,147 students in teachers' training establishments.

From 1995 education will be provided by a unified KwaZulu-Natal Education Department (KZNED). In 1993-94 there were 12,155,000 pupils in KwaZulu-Natal schools but this number is expected to increase to between 2·5m. and 2·8m. because of the estimated number of pupils not attending school before 1995.

Roads. Motor vehicles registered (1991) totalled 964,917, including 550,380 passenger cars and 200,317 commercial vehicles.

Health. In 1992 there were 4,576 medical practitioners, 36,921 nurses, 782 hospitals and clinics and 48,843 hospital beds.

MPUMALANGA

Territory and Population. The area is 78,370 sq. km and the population was estimated at 3,007,100 in 1995 (1·47m. females; 2·69m. Blacks; 0·3m. Whites; 15,100 Coloureds; 11,900 Asians). At the 1991 Census, 30·2% spoke Swazi as their home language, 24·2% Zulu, 11·3% Ndebele, 10·2% Pedi, 9·3% Afrikaans, 3·8% Tsonga, 2·6% Tswana, 2·0% English, 1·9% Sotho and 1·7% Xhosa.

Mpumalanga comprises 28 administrative districts. The provincial capital is Nelspruit.

Constitution and Government. There is a 30-seat provincial legislature; at the provincial elections held 27–29 April 1994, 25 seats were won by the ANC (with 81·5% of votes cast), 3 by the NP (with 9·1%) and 2 by the FF (with 5·7%).

In Feb. 1995 the governent comprised:

Premier: Matthew Phosa (ANC).

Economic Affairs: Jacob Mabena (ANC). *Finance:* Jacques Modipane (ANC). *Local Government:* January Che Masilela (ANC). *Environmental Affairs:* David

Mkhwanazi (ANC). *Education and Training:* David Mabuza (ANC). *Public Works, Roads and Transport:* Ntimane Mathebula (ANC). *Safety and Security:* Jabulane Mabona (ANC). *Housing:* Craig Padayachee (ANC). *Agriculture:* Dr Lucas Nel (NP). *Health:* Candith Mashego (ANC). *Without Portfolio (Youth):* Steven Mbuyisa (ANC). *Without Portfolio (RDP):* Joseph Mbazima (ANC).

Agriculture. In 1988 (excluding that part of the former Bophuthatswana now within the province) there were 6,386 farms with 182,645 agricultural workers; gross farming income amounted to R2,186m.

Labour. In 1991 (including that part of the former Bophuthatswana now within the province) the economically active population numbered 873,951. Of those employed (excluding Bophuthatswana), 26·6% were in agriculture, 14·1% in mining, 10·1% in manufacturing, 11·2% in trade and 22·0% in services. The unemployment rate (Oct. 1993) was 30·2%.

Education. In 1993 there were 6,731 pupils in pre-primary schools, 2,006 pupils in special schools, 471,079 pupils in primary schools and 285,345 in secondary schools, with altogether 21,952 teachers; there were also 250 lecturers and 3,884 students in technical colleges, and 302 lecturers and 3,628 students in teachers' training establishments.

Roads. Motor vehicles registered (mid 1991, excluding Bophuthatswana) totalled 381,346 including 158,587 passenger cars and 100,546 commercial vehicles; new vehicles registrations in the year to mid 1992 totalled 15,307 including 6,893 passenger cars and 4,184 commercial vehicles.

Health. In 1992 there were 825 medical practitioners and 7,738 nurses; 391 hospitals and clinics had 6,501 hospital beds; there were 149,842 admissions and 701,137 outpatients.

NORTHERN CAPE

Territory and Population. The area is 361,800 sq. km. The population was estimated at 742,000 in 1995 (0·37m. females; 0·4m. Coloureds; 0·22m. Blacks; 0·12m. Whites; 1,900 Asians). At the 1991 Census, 66·0% spoke Afrikaans as their home language, 19·0% Tswana, 6·2% Xhosa and 2·6% English.

Northern Cape comprises 26 administrative districts. The provincial capital is Kimberley.

Constitution and Government. There is a 30-seat provincial legislature; at the provincial elections held 27–29 April 1994, 15 seats were won by the ANC (with 50·0% of votes cast), 12 by the NP (with 40·7%), 2 by the FF (with 6·0%) and 1 by the DP (1·9%). An ANC-NP coalition government was formed.

In Feb. 1996 the government comprised:

Premier: Manne Dipico (ANC).

Economic Affairs, Trade and Industry: Goolam Akharwaray (ANC). *Education and Culture:* Tina Joemat (ANC). *Health and Welfare:* Dr Modise Matlaopane (ANC). *Local Government, Housing and Land Reform:* Ouneas Dikgetsi (ANC). *Safety and Security:* Eunice Komane (ANC). *Agriculture:* Jacobus Marais (NP). *Finance:* Jan Brazelle (NP). *Public Works:* Peggy Hollander (NP). *Transport:* Charl van Wyk (NP). *Youth and Sports Affairs:* Jozef Henning (FF).

Agriculture. In 1988 there were 6,857 farms with 80,900 agricultural workers; gross farming income amounted to R688·5m.

Labour. In 1991 the economically active population numbered 277,591. Of those employed, 26·2% were in agriculture, 12·9% in mining, 3·9% in manufacturing, 11·1% in trade and 30·4% in services. The unemployment rate (Oct. 1993) was 25·8%.

Education. In 1993 there were 1,666 pupils in pre-primary schools, 1,801 pupils in special schools, 118,851 pupils in primary schools and 69,470 in secondary schools, with altogether 7,677 teachers; there were also 103 lecturers and 1,599 students in technical colleges, and 83 lecturers and 763 students in teachers' training establishments.

Roads. Motor vehicles registered (1991) totalled 143,315, including 63,504 passenger cars and 44,042 commercial vehicles.

Health. In 1992 there were 287 medical practitioners, 3,302 nurses, 295 hospitals and clinics and 4,064 hospital beds.

NORTHERN PROVINCE

Territory and Population. The area is 123,280 sq. km and the population was estimated at 5,397,200 in 1995 (2·9m. females; 5·24m. Blacks; 0·15m. Whites; 6,900 Coloureds; 4,600 Asians). At the 1991 Census (including the former Venda), 56·7% spoke Pedi as their home language, 22·7% Tsonga, 11·8% Venda, 2·6% Afrikaans and 1·6% Ndebele.

Northern Province comprises 32 administrative districts. The provincial capital is Pietersburg.

Constitution and Government. There is a 40-seat provincial legislature; at the provincial elections held 27–29 April 1994, 38 seats were won by the ANC (with 92·3% of votes cast) and 1 each by the NP (3·3%) and the FF (2·2%).

In Feb. 1995 the government comprised:

Premier: Ngoako Ramathlodi (ANC).

Economic Affairs, Trade and Industry: Thaba Mufamadi (ANC). *Education, Training and Culture:* Dr P. Aaron Motsoaledi (ANC). *Agriculture and Forestry:* Tiny Burgers (ANC). *Land, Housing and Local Government:* John Dombo (ANC). *Environment, Water Affairs and Tourism:* Maris-Stella Sexwale-Mabitjie (ANC). *Public Works:* Dikeledi Magadzi (ANC). *Police and Protection Services:* Seth Nthai (ANC). *Finance and Expenditure:* C. Edgar Mushwane (ANC). *Public Transport:* Johan Kriek (FF). *Health and Welfare:* Dr M. Joe Phaahla (ANC).

Agriculture. In 1988 (excluding the former Venda now within the province) there were 5,455 farms with 127,497 agricultural workers; gross farming income amounted to R936·6m.

Labour. In 1991 (including the former Venda homeland) the economically active population numbered 810,117. Of those employed (excluding Venda), 25·4% were in agriculture, 9·2% in mining, 6·3% in manufacturing, 13·4% in trade and 32·9% in services; the unemployment rate (Oct. 1993) was 50·4%.

Education. In 1993 there were 72,805 pupils in pre-primary schools, 1,185 pupils in special schools, 1,043,566 pupils in primary schools and 757,058 in secondary schools, with altogether 53,026 teachers; there were also 387 lecturers and 3,123 students in technical colleges, and 1,532 lecturers and 20,085 students in teachers' training establishments.

Roads. Motor vehicles registered (1991, excluding Venda) totalled 240,801, including 95,627 passenger cars and 81,237 commercial vehicles.

Health. In 1992 there were 796 medical practitioners, 15,014 nurses, 849 hospitals and clinics and 23,122 hospital beds.

NORTH-WEST

Territory and Population. The area is 116,190 sq. km and the population was estimated at 3,351,800 in 1995 (1·62m. females; 3m. Blacks; 0·27m. Whites; 60,500 Coloureds; 10,600 Asians). At the 1991 Census (including the former Bophuthatswana), 59·0% spoke Tswana as their home language, 8·8% Afrikaans,

6·3% Xhosa, 5·4% Tsonga, 5·2% Pedi, 5·0% Sotho, 2·7% Zulu, 2·6% Ndebele, 1·0% English and 1·0% Swazi.

Constitution and Government. North-West Province comprises 32 administrative districts. The provincial capital is Mmabatho. There is a 30-seat provincial legislature; at the provincial elections held 27–29 April 1994, 26 seats were won by the ANC (with 83·5% of the 1,568,574 votes cast), 3 by the NP (with 8·9%) and 1 by the FF (with 4·6%).

In Feb. 1995 the government comprised:

Premier: Popo Molefe (ANC).

Education: Mamokoena Gaoretelelwe (ANC). *Health and Social Welfare:* Dr Molefi Paul Sefularo (ANC). *Local Government and Housing:* Darkey Ephraim Africa (ANC). *Finance:* Martin Kuscus (ANC). *Public Works:* Zacharia Pitso Tolo (ANC). *Transport and Aviation:* Frans Vilakazi (ANC). *Agriculture and Environment:* Johannes Oabetswe Tselapedi (ANC). *Economic Affairs:* Abraham Adriaan Venter (NP). *Media:* Riani de Wet (ANC). *Public Safety:* Satish Roopa (ANC).

Agriculture. In 1988 (excluding the TBVC countries now within the province) there were 8,203 farms with 152,181 agricultural workers; gross farming income amounted to R1,326·3m.

Labour. In 1991 (including that part of the former Bophuthatswana homeland now within the province) the economically active population numbered 957,470. Of those employed (excluding Bophuthatswana), 24·8% were in agriculture, 30·7% in mining, 4·3% in manufacturing, 9·4% in trade and 22·5% in services; the unemployment rate (Oct. 1993) was 20·4%.

Education. In 1993 there were 22,261 pupils in pre-primary schools, 2,708 pupils in special schools, 400,436 pupils in primary schools and 233,436 in secondary schools, with altogether 21,750 teachers; there were also 110 lecturers and 1,684 students in technical colleges, and 274 lecturers and 3,275 students in teachers' training establishments.

Roads. Motor vehicles registered (1991, excluding Bophuthatswana) totalled 319,805 including 140,802 passenger cars and 71,237 commercial vehicles.

Health. In 1992 there were 780 medical practitioners, 9,393 nurses, 457 hospitals and clinics and 15,409 hospital beds.

WESTERN CAPE

Territory and Population. The area is 129,370 sq. km and the population was estimated at 3,721,200 in 1995 (1·85m. females; 2·12m. Coloureds; 0·89m. Whites; 0·68m. Blacks; 35,100 Asians). At the 1991 Census, 62·2% spoke Afrikaans as their home language, 20·0% English and 15·3% Xhosa.

Western Cape comprises 41 administrative districts. The provincial capital is Cape Town.

Constitution and Government. There is a 42-seat provincial legislature; at the provincial elections held 27–29 April 1994, 23 seats were won by the NP (with 54·2% of votes cast), 14 by the ANC (with 33·6%), 3 by the DP (with 6·8%), and 1 each by the FF (2·1%) and African Christian Democratic Party (1·2%).

In Feb. 1996 the government comprised:

Premier: Hernus Kriel (NP).

Housing, Leader of the House: Gerald Morkel (NP). *Finance and Environment Affairs:* Kobus Meiring (NP). *Economic Affairs and Reconstruction and Development Programme:* Chris Nissen (ANC). *Agriculture, Planning and Tourism:* Lampie Fick (NP). *Roads, Transport and Public Works:* Leonard Ramatlakane (ANC). *Local Government and Development Management:* Peter Marais (NP). *Education and Cultural Affairs:* Martha Olckers (NP). *Health and Social Services:*

Ebrahim Rasool (ANC). *Sport and Recreation:* Lerumo Kalako (ANC). *Police Services:* Patrick MacKenzie (NP).

Agriculture. In 1994 there were 8,747 farms with 186,863 agricultural workers; gross farming income amounted to R6,255·2m.

Labour. In 1991 the economically active population numbered 1,534,579. Of those employed, 15·4% were in agriculture, 0·6% in mining, 18·7% in manufacturing, 16·7% in trade and 27·1% in services; the unemployment rate (Oct. 1993) was 17·3%.

Education. In 1995 there were 789 pupils in pre-primary schools, 13,472 pupils in special schools, 499,659 pupils in primary schools, 77,250 in intermediate classes, 235,927 in secondary schools and 23,727 in combined schools, with altogether 32,898 teachers; there were also 816 lecturers and 20,692 students in technical colleges, and 210 lecturers and 3,306 students in teachers' training establishments.

Roads. Motor vehicles registered (1995) totalled 986,780, including 689,099 passenger cars, 228,973 light commercial vehicles, 41,386 heavy commercial vehicles and 27,322 motorcycles.

Health. In 1995 there were 2,487 medical practitioners, 16,614 nurses, 60 hospitals, 186 clinics and 15,290 hospital beds.

SOUTH GEORGIA AND SOUTH SANDWICH ISLANDS

KEY HISTORICAL EVENTS. The first landing and exploration was undertaken by Captain James Cook, who formally took possession in the name of George III on 17 Jan. 1775. British sealers arrived in 1788 and American sealers in 1791. Sealing reached its peak in 1800. A German team was the first to carry out scientific studies there in 1882–83. Whaling began in 1904 and ceased in 1966, and the civil administration was withdrawn. Argentine forces invaded South Georgia on 3 April 1982. A British naval task force recovered the Island on 25 April 1982.

TERRITORY AND POPULATION. South Georgia lies 800 miles south-east of the Falkland Islands and has an area of 1,450 sq. miles. The South Sandwich Islands are 470 miles south-east of South Georgia and have an area of 130 sq. miles. In 1993 crown sovereignty and jurisdiction were extended from 12 to 200 miles around the islands. There is no permanent population. There is a small military garrison. The British Antarctic Survey have a biological station on Bird Island. The South Sandwich Islands are uninhabited.

CLIMATE. The climate is wet and cold with strong winds and little seasonal variation. 15°C is occasionally reached on a windless day. Temperatures below –15°C at sea level are unusual.

CONSTITUTION AND GOVERNMENT. Under the new Constitution which came into force on 3 Oct. 1985 the Territories ceased to be dependencies of the Falkland Islands. Executive power is vested in a Commissioner who is the officer for the time being administering the Government of the Falkland Islands. The Commissioner is obliged to consult the officer for the time being commanding Her Majesty's British Forces in the South Atlantic on matters relating to defence and internal security (except police). The Commissioner whenever practicable consults the Executive Council of the Falkland Islands on the exercise of functions that in his opinion might affect the Falkland Islands. There is no Legislative Council. Laws are made by the Commissioner.

Commissioner: D. Tatham, CMG.

Economy. The total revenue of the Territories (estimate, 1988–89) £268,240, mainly from philatelic sales and investment income. Expenditure estimate £194,260.

Communications. There is occasional direct sea communication between the Falkland Islands and South Georgia and the South Sandwich Islands by means of the Royal Research Ships *James Clarke Ross* and *Bransfield* and the ice patrol vessel *HMS Endurance*. Royal Fleet Auxiliary ships, which serve the garrison, run regularly to South Georgia. Mail is dropped from military aircraft.

Justice. There is a Supreme Court for the Territories and a Court of Appeal in the United Kingdom. Appeals may go from that court to the Judicial Committee of the Privy Council. There is no magistrate permanently in residence. The Officer Commanding the garrison is usually appointed a magistrate.

Further Reading

Headland, R. K., *The Island of South Georgia*. CUP, 1985

SPAIN

Reino de España

(Kingdom of Spain)

Capital: Madrid
Population: 39·19m. (1994)
GNP per capita: US$13,280 (1994)
HDI/world rank: 0·930/9 (1992)

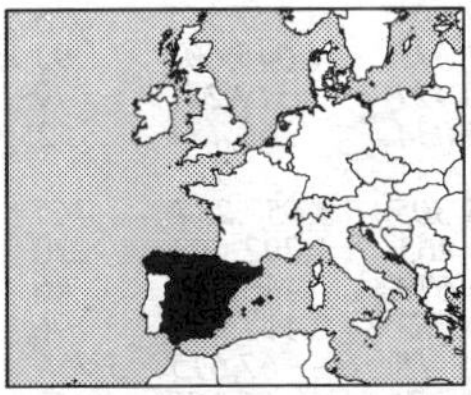

KEY HISTORICAL EVENTS. Although Spain has traditionally been a monarchy there have been two republics, the first in 1873, which lasted for 11 months, and the second in 1931–39; both were democratically and peacefully proclaimed. Part of the army rebelled against the Republican government on 18 July 1936, thus beginning the Spanish Civil War (*see* THE STATESMAN'S YEAR-BOOK, 1939, pp. 1325–26). The new regime was led by Gen. Francisco Franco y Bahamonde as Head of State and Government, and its institutions were based on single party rule, with the *Falange* as the only legal political organization.

In July 1969, Prince Don Juan Carlos de Borbón y Borbón, grandson of Alfonso XIII, was sworn in as successor to the Head of State and he had the title of HRH Prince of Spain until he became King. Gen. Franco died on 20 Nov. 1975 and on 22 Nov. Prince Juan Carlos took the oath as Juan Carlos I, King of Spain.

TERRITORY AND POPULATION. Spain is bounded in the north by the Bay of Biscay and the Pyrenees (which form the frontier with France and Andorra), east and south by the Mediterranean and the Straits of Gibraltar, south-west by the Atlantic and west by Portugal and the Atlantic. Continental Spain has an area of 492,592 sq. km, and including the Balearic and Canary Islands and the towns of Ceuta and Melilla 504,750 sq. km (194,884 sq. miles). Population (census, 1 March 1991), 38,872,268 (19,835,822 female). Estimate (1994), 39·19m.

The growth of the population has been as follows:

Census year	*Population*	*Rate of annual increase*	*Census year*	*Population*	*Rate of annual increase*
1860	15,655,467	0·34	1950	27,976,755	0·81
1910	19,927,150	0·72	1960	30,903,137	0·88
1920	21,303,162	0·69	1970	33,823,918	0·94
1930	23,563,867	1·06	1981	37,746,260	1·15
1940	25,877,971	0·98	1991	38,872,268	0·29

Area and population of the autonomous communities and provinces, on 1 March 1991 (census):

Autonomous community / *Province*	*Area (sq. km)*	*Population*	*Per sq. km*
Andalusia	*87,268*	*6,940,522*	*79*
Almería	8,774	455,496	51
Cádiz	7,385	1,078,404	146
Córdoba	13,718	754,452	54
Granada	12,531	790,515	63
Huelva	10,085	443,476	43
Jaén	13,498	637,633	47
Málaga	7,276	1,160,843	159
Sevilla	14,001	1,619,703	115
Aragón	*47,669*	*1,188,817*	*24*
Huesca	15,671	207,810	13
Teruel	14,804	143,680	9
Zaragoza	17,194	837,327	48
Asturias	*10,565*	*1,093,937*	*103*

Autonomous community / *Province*	*Area (sq. km)*	*Population*	*Per sq. km*
Baleares	*5,014*	*709,138*	*141*
Basque Country, The	*7,261*	*2,104,041*	*289*
Álava	3,047	272,447	89
Guipúzcoa	1,997	676,488	338
Vizcaya	2,217	1,155,106	521
Canary Islands	*7,273*	*1,493,784*	*205*
Palmas, Las	4,065	767,969	188
Santa Cruz de Tenerife	3,208	725,815	226
Cantabria	*5,289*	*527,326*	*99*
Castilla-La Mancha	*79,226*	*1,658,446*	*20*
Albacete	14,858	342,677	23

Autonomous community Province	Area (sq. km)	Population	Per sq. km
Ciudad Real	19,749	475,435	24
Cuenca	17,061	205,198	12
Guadalajara	12,190	145,593	11
Toledo	15,368	489,543	31
Castilla y León	*94,147*	*2,545,926*	*27*
Ávila	8,048	174,378	21
Burgos	14,269	352,772	24
León	15,468	525,896	33
Palencia	8,029	185,479	23
Salamanca	12,336	357,801	29
Segovia	6,949	147,188	21
Soria	10,287	94,537	9
Valladolid	8,202	494,207	60
Zamora	10,559	213,668	20
Catalonia	*31,930*	*6,059,454*	*191*
Barcelona	7,773	4,654,407	598
Gerona	5,886	509,628	86
Lérida	12,028	353,455	29
Tarragona	6,283	542,004	86
Extremadura	*41,602*	*1,061,852*	*25*
Badajoz	21,657	650,388	30
Cáceres	19,945	411,464	20
Galicia	*29,434*	*2,731,669*	*92*
Coruña, La	7,876	1,096,966	139
Lugo	9,803	384,365	39
Orense	7,278	353,491	48
Pontevedra	4,477	896,847	200
Madrid	*7,995*	*4,947,555*	*618*
Murcia	*11,317*	*1,045,601*	*92*
Navarra	*10,421*	*519,227*	*49*
Rioja, La	*5,034*	*263,434*	*52*
Valencian Community	*23,305*	*3,857,234*	*165*
Alicante	5,863	1,292,563	220
Castellón	6,679	446,744	66
Valencia	10,763	2,117,927	196
Ceuta [1]	*18*	*67,615*	*3,756*
Melilla [1]	*14*	*56,600*	*4,042*
Total	*504,750*	*38,872,268*	*77*

[1] Ceuta and Melilla are on the northern coast of Morocco.

The capitals of the autonomous communities are: Andalusia: Seville; Aragón: Zaragoza (Saragossa); Asturias: Oviedo; Baleares (Balearic Islands): Palma de Mallorca; The Basque Country: Vitoria; Canary Islands, dual and alternative capital, Las Palmas and Santa Cruz de Tenerife; Cantabria: Santander; Castilla-La Mancha (Castile-La Mancha): Toledo; Castilla y León (Castile and Leon): Valladolid; Catalonia: Barcelona; Extremadura: Mérida; Galicia: Santiago de Compostela; Madrid: Madrid; Murcia: Murcia (but regional parliament in Cartagena); Navarra (Navarre): Pamplona; La Rioja: Logroño; Valencian Community: Valencia.

The capitals of the provinces are in the towns from which they take the name, except in Álava (capital Vitoria), Asturias (Oviedo), Baleares (Palma de Mallorca), Cantabria (Santander), Guipúzcoa (San Sebastián), La Rioja (Logroño), Navarra (Pamplona) and Vizcaya (Bilbao).

The islands which form the Canary Archipelago are divided into 2 provinces, under the name of their respective capitals: Santa Cruz de Tenerife and Las Palmas de Gran Canaria. The province of Santa Cruz de Tenerife is constituted by the islands of Tenerife, La Palma, Gomera and Hierro, and that of Las Palmas by Gran Canaria, Lanzarote and Fuerteventura, with the small barren islands of Alegranza, Roque del Este, Roque del Oeste, Graciosa, Montaña Clara and Lobos. The area of the islands is 7,273 sq. km; population (census, March 1991), 1,493,784. Places under Spanish sovereignty in Morocco are: Alhucemas, Ceuta, Chafarinas, Melilla and Peñón de Vélez.

Populations of principal towns on 1 March 1991 (census):

Town	*Population*
Albacete	128,718
Alcalá de Henares	159,355
Alcobendas	78,825
Alcorcón	139,641
Algeciras	101,063
Alicante	261,255
Almería	153,288
Avilés	84,787
Badajoz	121,924
Badalona	206,585
Baracaldo	104,883
Barcelona	1,625,542
Bilbao	368,710
Burgos	160,381
Cáceres	71,745
Cádiz	153,550
Cartagena	166,736
Castellón de la Plana	133,180
Córdoba	300,229
Cornellá de Llobregat	83,783
Coruña, La	245,459
Coslada	73,440
Elche	181,658
Ferrol, El	82,371
Fuenlabrada	144,723
Getafe	138,704
Gijón	259,054
Granada	254,034
Guecho	79,577
Hermanas, Dos	76,923
Hospitalet	269,241
Huelva	141,041
Jaén	101,938
Jerez de la Frontera	182,939
Laguna, La	109,485
Leganés	171,400
León	144,137
Lérida	111,880
Logroño	121,066
Lugo	86,658
Madrid	2,909,792
Málaga	512,136
Marbella	76,823

Town	Population	Town	Population	Town	Population
Mataró	101,501	San Baudilio del Llobregat	77,650	Tarragona	110,003
Móstoles	192,018	San Fernando	85,191	Tarrasa	154,300
Murcia	318,838	San Sebastián	169,933	Telde	75,594
Orense	101,623	Santa Coloma de Gramanet	132,173	Torrejón de Ardoz	81,072
Oviedo	194,919	Santa Cruz de Tenerife	189,317	Valencia	752,909
Palencia	77,752	Santander	189,069	Valladolid	328,365
Palma de Mallorca	296,754	Santiago de Compostela	87,472	Vigo	274,629
Palmas, Las	342,030	Sevilla	659,126	Vitoria	204,961
Pamplona	179,251			Zaragoza	586,219
Reus	86,864				
Sabadell	184,460				
Salamanca	162,544				

Vital statistics for calendar years:

	Marriages	Births	Deaths
1992	217,512	390,272	329,454
1993	201,463	380,564	338,666
1994	196,062	365,124	335,843

In 1995 the number of foreigners legally registered was 461,658 (largest foreign communities: Moroccan, 63,939; British, 62,317).

Languages. The Constitution states that 'Castilian is the Spanish official language of the State', but also that 'All other Spanish languages will also be official in the corresponding Autonomous Communities'.

Catalan is spoken by a majority of people in Catalonia (68%, 1991) and Baleares (66·9%), and by one half in Valencian Community (51%, where it is frequently called Valencian); in Aragón, a narrow strip close to Catalonia and Valencian Community boundaries, speaks Catalan. Galician, a language very close to Portuguese, is spoken by a majority of people in Galicia (91%, 1991); Basque, by a significant minority in the Basque Country (26·3%). Basque is also spoken by a small minority in north-west Navarra (12%).

In bilingual communities, both Spanish and the regional language are taught in the schools and universities.

CLIMATE. Most of Spain has a form of Mediterranean climate with mild, moist winters and hot, dry summers, but the northern coastal region has a moist, equable climate, with rainfall well-distributed throughout the year, mild winters and warm summers, though having less sunshine than the rest of Spain.

Madrid. Jan. 41°F (5°C), July 77°F (25°C). Annual rainfall 16·8" (419 mm). Barcelona. Jan. 46°F (8°C), July 74°F (23·5°C). Annual rainfall 21" (525 mm). Cartagena. Jan. 51°F (10·5°C), July 75°F (24°C). Annual rainfall 14·9" (373 mm). La Coruña. Jan. 51°F (10·5°C), July 66°F (19°C). Annual rainfall 32" (800 mm). Sevilla. Jan. 51°F (10·5°C), July 85°F (29·5°C). Annual rainfall 19·5" (486 mm). Palma de Mallorca (Balearic Islands). Jan. 51°F (11°C), July 77°F (25°C). Annual rainfall 13·6" (347 mm). Santa Cruz de Tenerife (Canary Islands). Jan. 64°F (17·9°C), July 76°F (24·4°C). Annual rainfall 7·72" (196 mm).

ROYAL HOUSE. The reigning King is **Juan Carlos I,** born 5 Jan. 1938. The eldest son of Don Juan, Conde de Barcelona. Juan Carlos was given precedence over his father as pretender to the Spanish throne in an agreement in 1954 between Don Juan and Gen. Franco. Don Juan, who resigned his claims to the throne in May 1977, died on 1 April 1993. King (then Prince) Juan Carlos married, in 1962, Princess Sophia of Greece, daughter of the late King Paul of the Hellenes and Queen Frederika. *Offspring:* Elena, born 20 Dec. 1963, married 18 March 1995 Jaime de Marichalar; Cristina, 13 June 1965; Felipe, Prince of Asturias, Heir to the throne, 30 Jan. 1968.

The King receives an allowance, part of which is taxable, approved by parliament each year. In 1995 it was 956m. pesetas. There is no formal court; the (private) *Diputación de la Grandeza* represents the interests of the aristocracy.

CONSTITUTION AND GOVERNMENT. Following the death of Gen. Franco the parliament was freely elected on 15 June 1977. A new Constitution was approved by referendum on 6 Dec. 1978, and came into force 29 Dec. 1978. It established a parliamentary monarchy, with King Juan Carlos I as head of state. Legislative power is vested in the *Cortes Generales*, a bicameral parliament composed of the *Congress of Deputies* (lower house) and the *Senate* (upper house). The Congress of Deputies has not less than 300 nor more than 400 members (350 in the general elections of 1977, 1979, 1982, 1986, 1989 and 1993) elected in a proportional system under which electors choose between party lists of candidates in multi-member constituencies. The Senate has 252 members of whom 208 are elected by a majority system: The 47 mainland provinces elect 4 senators each, regardless of population; the island provinces electing 5 (Baleares, Las Palmas) or 6 (Santa Cruz de Tenerife); and Ceuta and Melilla, 2 senators each. To these are added 44 senators elected by the parliaments of the autonomous communities. There is also a *Council of State* (president, Fernando Ledesma). Deputies and senators are elected by universal secret suffrage for 4-year terms. Executive power is vested in the Prime Minister and a Cabinet; the Prime Minister is elected by the Congress of Deputies.

The *Constitutional Court* is empowered to solve conflicts between the State and the Autonomous Communities, to determine if legislation passed by the Cortes is contrary to the Constitution and to protect the constitutional rights of individuals violated by any authority. Its 12 members are appointed by the monarch in the following way: 4, on the proposal of the Congress of Deputies; 4, on the proposal of the Senate; 2 on the proposal of the General Council of the Judicial Power (*see under* JUSTICE, *below*); and 2 on the proposal of the Cabinet. It has a 9-year term, a third of the membership being renewed every 3 years.

A general election took place on 3 March 1996 (*see* ADDENDA).

National flag: 3 horizontal stripes of red, yellow, red, with the yellow of double width, and charged near the hoist with the national arms.

National anthem: Marcha Real (*Royal march*); no words, tune anonymous.

European Parliament. Spain has 64 representatives. At the June 1994 elections turn-out was 59·6%. The PP won 28 seats with 40·2% of votes cast (group in European Parliament: Popular European Party); the PSOE, 22 with 30·6% (European Socialist Party); the IU, 9 with 13·4%; the CiU, 3 with 4·6% (Popular European Party; Liberal, Democratic and Reformist Group); the Nationalist Coalition, 2 with 2·8% (Popular European Party).

Regional and Local Government. The Constitution of 1978 establishes a semifederal system of regional administration, with the *autonomous community (comunidad autónoma)* as its basic element. There are 17 autonomous communities, each of them having a Parliament, elected by universal vote, and a regional government; all possess exclusive legislative and executive power in many matters, as listed in the national Constitution and in their own fundamental law *(estatuto de autonomía).*

In Sept. 1994 Ceuta and Melilla gained a limited autonomous status, with legislative assemblies replacing their municipal councils.

Date of last elections and party composition of the autonomous communities: *Andalusia* (March 1996), PSOE 52, PP 40, United Left, 13, Andalusian Party 4; *Aragón* (May 1995), PP 27, PSOE 19, Aragonese Regionalist Party 14, IU 5, others 2; *Asturias* (May 1995), PP 21, PSOE 17, IU 6, others 1; *Baleares* (May 1995), PP 30, PSOE 16, nationalists 6, IU 3, others 4; *Basque Country* (Oct. 1994), Basque Nationalist Party 22, PSOE-Euskadiko Ezquerra 12, Herri Batasuna 11, PP 11, Eusko Alkartasuna 8, United Left-Ezker Batua 6, Alavese Unity 5; *Canary Islands* (May 1995), PP 18, PSOE 16, Canarian Coalition 22, others 4; *Cantabria* (May 1995), PP 13, PSOE 10, regionalists 6, IU 3, others 7; *Castile-La Mancha* (May 1995), PSOE 24, PP 22, IU 1; *Castile and Leon* (May 1995), PP 50, PSOE 27, IU 5, others 2; *Catalonia* (Nov. 1995), Convergència i Unió 60, PSOE 34, PP 17, Esquerra Republicana de Catalunya 13, Iniciativa per Catalunya 11; *Extremadura* (May 1995), PSOE 31, PP 27, IU 6, others 1; *Galicia* (Oct. 1993), PP 43, PSOE 19, Galician National Block 13; *La Rioja* (May 1995), PP 17, PSOE 12, regionalists 2,

IU 2; *Madrid* (May 1995), PP 54, PSOE 32, IU 17; *Murcia* (May 1995), PP 26, PSOE 15, IU 4; *Navarre* (May 1995), PP 17, PSOE 11, regionalists 10, Herri Batasuna (Basque nationalists) 5, Eusko Alkartasuna 2, IU 5; *Valencian Community* (May 1995), PP 42, PSOE 32, Valencian Union (regionalists) 5, IU 10.

There are 7 autonomous communities composed of only one province: Asturias, Baleares, Cantabria, La Rioja, Madrid, Murcia and Navarra. The other 10 are formed by 2 or more provinces. In all, there are in Spain 50 provinces, since the administrative division established in 1833. The *Provincial Council (Diputación Provincial)* is the administrative organ of the province, except in the 7 autonomous communities composed of only one province, where there are only the regional legislative and executive powers. The provincial council is indirectly elected. Each of the 7 main islands of the Canaries (provinces of Las Palmas and Santa Cruz de Tenerife) has a directly elected corporation, the *Cabildo Insular,* to rule its special interests; in the main islands of the Balearics there is also an elected *Consell Insular*.

The provinces are constituted by the association of municipalities (8,077 in 1991). Municipalities are autonomous in their own sphere. At their head stands the municipal council *(Ayuntamiento),* members of which are elected in a universal ballot every 4 years, and they, in turn, elect one of them as Mayor *(Alcalde).* In 1991 6,216 municipalities had fewer than 3,000 inhabitants; such resource-poor municipalities may form associations to share services (*mancomunidades*).

Elections were held in May 1995 for 65,732 municipal councillors. The electorate was 32,019,932. Turn-out was 69·79%. The Popular Party won 35·2% of votes cast (25·1% in the 1991 elections), the PSOE 30·8% (38·5%), and the United Left Coalition (Communists) 11·6% (8·5%).

DEFENCE. Conscription is for 9 months. Civilian service may be offered as an alternative. Recruits to the national police are exempt from conscription. Since 1989 women have been accepted in all sections of the armed forces.

Army. The Army is divided into 8 Regional Operation Commands (including 2 overseas) and consists of 1 mechanized division, 2 armoured cavalry, 1 mountain, 3 light infantry, 1 airborne, 1 artillery, 1 engineer and 1 air-portable brigade; 3 island garrisons, 3 special operations battalions and the Spanish Legion, A Rapid Reaction Force is formed from the Spanish Legion and the airborne and air-portable brigades. There is also an Army Aviation brigade. Equipment includes 210 AMX-30, 164 M-48A5E and 294 M-60 main battle tanks. The Aviation Brigade consists of 170 helicopters (28 attack). Strength (1996) 144,700 (including 97,000 conscripts). Of these 2,500 are stationed on the Balearic Islands, 6,500 on the Canary Islands and 10,000 in Ceuta and Melilla. The paramilitary *Guardia Civil* numbers 72,000 (2,200 conscripts).

Navy. The principal ship of the Navy is the 17,000-tonne *Príncipe de Asturias*, a light vertical/short take-off and landing aircraft carrier built to a US design and commissioned in 1989. Her air group comprises 8 AV-8S Matador, 8 Sea King anti-submarine helicopters, 2 Sea King early warning helicopters and about 4 AB-212 light helicopters.

There are also 8 French-designed submarines (4 Daphne class, 4 Agosta class), 6 US-design Santa María guided missile frigates with Standard SM-1 surface-to-air missiles, 5 other guided missile frigates, and 6 smaller frigates, 5 offshore patrol vessels, 10 coastal and 16 inshore patrol craft, 4 ocean minesweepers, 8 coastal minesweepers, 2 amphibious troop transports, 2 tank landing ships and 13 landing craft. Major auxiliaries include 2 tankers, 2 transports, 5 ocean tugs, 1 training ship, 4 water carriers and 6 survey ships. There are about 80 minor auxiliaries and service craft.

The Naval Air Service operates 20 AV-8S Matador and EAV-8B Harrier-II attack aircraft, 34 S-70B Seahawk, Sea King, SH 60B, AB-212 and Hughes 500 anti-submarine helicopters, 3 radar early warning Sea Kings and a few additional training and utility aircraft. The Air Force operates 7 Orion maritime patrol aircraft on anti-submarine tasks.

There are 7,000 marines, who provide 1 amphibious regiment and garrison regiments at the main bases. Main naval bases are at Ferrol, Rota, Cádiz, Cartagena, Palma de Mallorca, Mahón and Las Palmas (Canary Islands).

In 1995 personnel totalled 31,900 (16,900 conscripts) including the marines and 1,000 naval air arm.

Air Force. The Air Force is organized as an independent service, dating from 1939. It is administered through 4 operational commands. These are geographically oriented following a reorganization in 1991 and comprise Central Air Command, Straits Air Command, Eastern Air Command and Air Command of the Canaries. Strength (1995) 29,400 (12,100 conscripts).

The Tactical Air Command has 2 fighter-bomber squadrons of Spanish-built Northrop SF-5s and 1 aero-naval co-operation squadron with P-3 Orion anti-submarine aircraft. Air Combat Command has 1 squadron of RF-4C Phantom IIs, 4 squadrons of F-18 Hornets and 3 squadrons of Mirage F-1s. 5 KC-130H tankers support the fighter squadrons. 3 wings of Air Transport Command operate C-130 Hercules, CN-235s and Spanish-built CASA Aviocars. Air Command of the Canaries has 3 squadrons, equipped with Aviocar transports; Mirage F1 fighter-bombers; F27 Maritime aircraft and Super Puma helicopters for search and rescue. Other equipment includes 3 Boeing 707s, 8 Falcons and helicopters for VIP transport; and aircraft for photographic, firefighting, target towing and research duties. Air-sea rescue units have Aviocars and Super Puma helicopters.

American-built F33 Bonanza and Chilean-built Pillan piston-engined aircraft are used for basic training, after which pupil pilots progress to CASA C-101 jet aircraft. Two-seat versions of operational types are used as advanced trainers. Other training types S-76 helicopters.

INTERNATIONAL RELATIONS

Membership. Spain is a member of the UN, the Council of Europe, NATO, WEU, the EU and OECD and the Schengen Accord, which abolished frontier controls between Austria, Belgium, France, Germany, Greece, Italy, Luxembourg, the Netherlands, Portugal and Spain, and came into effect (except for Austria, Greece and Italy) on 26 March, 1995.

ECONOMY

Budget. Revenue and expenditure in 1m. pesetas:

	1991	*1992*	*1993*	*1994*	*1995*
Revenue	13,427,714	15,382,724	16,894,964	19,001,429	19,402,252
Expenditure	13,427,714	15,382,724	16,894,964	19,001,429	19,402,252

The budget is made up as follows (in 1m. pesetas):

Revenue (1995)		*Revenue (1995) continued*	
Direct taxes	6,883,700	Sale on real investments	7,900
Indirect taxes	5,563,700	Capital transfers	272,400
Levies and various revenues	341,200	Financial assets	64,439
Current transfers	521,333	Deficit	5,188,613
Income on assets	759,267		

Expenditure (1995)		*Expenditure (1995) continued*	
H.M. House	956	Ministry of Public Works, Transport and Environment	1,315,581
Cortes (Parliament)	17,397	,, Education and Science	1,151,941
Court of Accounts	5,315	,, Labour and Social Security	1,928,817
Constitutional Court	1,680	,, Industry and Energy	200,322
Council of State	1,125	,, Agriculture, Fisheries and Food	199,427
Public Debt	4,217,159	,, Culture	71,505
Civil Service Pensions	883,495	,, Public Administration	38,107
General Council of the Judicial Power	3,053	,, Health and Consumer Affairs	2,535,233
Ministry of Foreign Affairs	108,841		
,, Justice and Interior	794,754		
,, Defence	866,499		
,, Finance	529,949		

Expenditure (1995) continued		*Expenditure (1995) continued*	
Ministry of Social Affairs	58,809	Regional governments	3,165,458
,, Commerce and Tourism	64,070	Regional Compensation Fund	128,845
,, the Presidency	53,285	Expenses in several ministries	253,132
		Financial relations with EEC	856,997

VAT is normally 16%, with a rate of 7% on certain items.

Currency. The unit of currency is the *peseta* (ESP), notionally divided into 100 *céntimos* (not in use since 1984).

Bank-notes of 10,000, 5,000, 2,000 and 1,000 pesetas and coins of 1, 2, 5, 10, 25, 50, 100, 200, 500 and 2,000 pesetas are in circulation. On 1 Jan. 1992 the circulation of bank-notes and coins was 6,506,500m. pesetas and of coins, 249,800m. pesetas. Inflation was 4·3% in Dec. 1995 (4·3% in 1993). The peseta was devalued by 7% within EMS on 6 March 1995. In March 1996, £1 = 189·76 pesetas; US$1 = 124·16 pesetas; DM1 = 84·12 pesetas.

Banking and Finance. The central bank is the Bank of Spain (*Governor*, Luis Ángel Rojo) which gained autonomy under an ordnance of 1994. Its governor is appointed for a 6-year term. The Banking Corporation of Spain, *Argentaria*, groups together the shares of all state-owned banks, and competes in the financial market with private banks. In Sept. 1993 the government sold 49·9% of the capital of *Argentaria*.

The largest banks are: Banco Bilbao Vizcaya; Banco Central Hispano Americano; Banco Santander; Banco Español de Crédito (BANESTO); Banco Exterior de España; Caja Postal; Banco Hipotecario de España; Banco Popular Español. All are privately owned except the Banco Exterior de España. BANESTO was taken over by Banco Santander in 1994.

Spanish banks deposits, Sept. 1994, amounted to 31,838,181m pesetas. Breakdown of other bank deposits in 1994: Foreign banks, 735,141m.; savings banks, 27,363,046m.; rural (farmers) savings banks, 2,518,900m.

There are stock exchanges in Madrid, Barcelona, Bilbao and Valencia.

Weights and Measures. The metric system was introduced in 1859.

ENERGY AND NATURAL RESOURCES

Electricity. Electric power-stations in 1991 had a total installed capacity of 45·2m. kW. The total output in 1994, amounted to 165,434m. kWh of which 28,725m. was hydroelectric and 55,316m. nuclear. There were 9 nuclear power stations, with a net capacity of 7·3m. kW (1991), which produced 33·4% of electricity in 1994. The government announced in 1991 that no new nuclear power stations would commence operating before 2000.

Oil. Crude oil production (1994) 816,000 tonnes.

Gas. Production of natural gas in 1994 was 753m. cu. metres.

Minerals. Spain has a relatively wide range of minerals but most of them are found in small or moderate quantities. Production of the principal minerals (in 1,000 tonnes; net metal content):

	1991	*1992*		*1991*	*1992*
Anthracite	5,640	6,177	Copper	8	9
Coal	8,602	8,464	Lead	46	30
Lignite	19,636	18,689	Zinc	261	205
Uranium [1]	257	862	Tin [1]	12	7
Iron	1,763	1,334	Fluorspar	112	97
Pyrites	628	406	Potassium salts	1,267	594

[1] Tonnes.

Agriculture. In 1994 the total value of agricultural produce was 3,508m. pesetas; of livestock, 1,435·3m. 19,656,600 ha were under cultivation in 1993, including 3,208,000 ha (1992) under irrigation; 6,494,000 ha were dedicated to pastures. On 1 Jan. 1991, 755,743 tractors, 280,904 motor ploughs and 51,703 harvesters were in use.

Principal crops	Area (in 1,000 ha) 1991	1992	1993	1994	Yield (in 1,000 tonnes) 1991	1992	1993	1994
Wheat	2,257	2,296	2,025	1,994	5,392	4,464	4,989	4,311
Barley	4,372	4,021	3,499	3,602	9,141	5,994	9,532	7,596
Oats	323	296	326	346	410	320	400	402
Rye	198	185	170	155	242	230	300	220
Rice	94	82	50	63	582	557	315	394
Maize	483	411	284	342	3,151	2,609	1,673	2,266
Potatoes	273	262	213	207	5,218	5,237	3,922	4,074
Sugar-beet	166	161	181	175	6,867	7,476	8,226	8,004
Sunflower	1,111	1,453	2,264	1,349	979	1,359	1,214	984

In 1991, 1,430,500 ha were under vines; production of wine was (1994) 19,584,200 hectolitres. The area under onions in 1994 was 27,400 ha, yielding 1,016,600 tonnes. Production in tonnes of other significant crops (ha in 1991): Oranges and mandarines, 4,366,000 (215,500 ha); lemons, 596,000 (46,200 ha); tomatoes, 2,894,000 (56,600 ha). Other products are esparto, flax, hemp and pulse. Spain has important industries connected with the preparation of wine and fruits.

Industrial crops (1994 in 1,000 tonnes): Raw cotton, 115; olive oil, 462.

Livestock products (1994 in 1,000 tonnes): Pork, 2,107; beef, 478·15; mutton, 224·3; poultry meat, 873·8; goat meat, 16·04; rabbit meat, 99·8. Milk and eggs (1991): cows' milk, 5,650m. litres; sheep's milk, 309m. litres; goats' milk, 454m. litres; eggs, 888·3m. dozen; honey, 24,000 tonnes.

Livestock (1991): Horses, 248,000; asses, 0·14m.; mules, 0·11m.; cattle, 5·06m.; sheep, 23·3m.; goats, 2·9m.; pigs, 17·1m.; poultry (1990), 51m.

Forestry. Total forests (1993) 16,136,800 ha; production, 1991, 10,937,000 cu. metres of wood. Other forest products (1991 in tonnes): Resins, 1,759; cork, 72,146; esparto, 1,522. Value of forest products, 1991: 98m. pesetas.

Fisheries. The total catch amounted in 1993 to 866,831 tonnes, including 552,113 tonnes of fresh and salty fish, 238,456 tonnes of frozen fish and 76,262 tonnes from nurseries; total value, 229,105m. pesetas. The main fishing region is the North-West (Galicia), with 52·9% of the catch. Fishing vessels had a total tonnage of 579,189 tonnes in 1992.

INDUSTRY. The industrial sector represented around 70% of export value, 30·9% of GNP and 21·1% of employment in 1993. In 1992, the principal textile productions were (in 1,000 tonnes): Wool yarn, 25; cotton yarn, 96; fabrics yarn, 134; wool cloth, 10; cotton cloth, 95; fabrics cloth, 58. In 1992, 7·8m. tonnes of writing, printing, packing and other paper were produced. The production of cement reached 22,789,000 tonnes in 1993. Steel production (1994) 13,479,000 tonnes. Sulphuric acid production (1992), 1,724,000 tonnes; nitrogenous fertilizers, 842,000 tonnes; plastics, 2,252,000 tonnes. The 9 oil refineries refined (1993) 31·9m. tonnes of crude oil. In 1992, 2·5m. TV sets, 1·3m. refrigerators and freezers and 1·7m. washing machines, dishwashers and clothes driers were manufactured. There are important toy and shoe industries. Shipyards launched 344,647 GRT in 1993. In 1993, 1,505,923 cars, 148,536 lorries and vans, 144,807 industrial vehicles and 446 buses were manufactured.

Labour. The monthly minimum wage for adults was 64,920 pesetas (Jan. 1996). The average monthly wage for workers in industry and services was 181,700 pesetas in 1994. The economically active population numbered 15·5m. in May 1995. Of these, 12,027,400 were employed: 1,358,300 in agriculture and fishing, 2,701,100 in manufacturing, 166,300 in energy and mining, 1,473,500 in construction industry and 7,412,700 in trade, transport and other public and personal services. 15·1% of the active population was unemployed at the end of 1995 (2,377,951 persons). Retirement age is 65 years.

Trade Unions. The Constitution guarantees the establishment and activities of trade unions provided they have a democratic structure. The two most important trade unions are *Unión General de Trabajadores* (UGT), founded in 1888 by Pablo

Iglesias (who had founded in 1879 the Spanish Workers Socialist Party, PSOE), and *Comisiones Obreras*, which was gradually established 1958–63, then as a clandestine labour organization.

FOREIGN ECONOMIC RELATIONS. Foreign debt was US$79,784m. at the end of 1992, of which US$16,223m. was government debt.

Commerce. Foreign trade of Spain (Peninsula, Baleares, Canaries, Ceuta, Melilla) (in 1m. pesetas):

	1989	*1990*	*1991*	*1992*	*1993*
Imports	8,458,361	8,914,741	9,672,149	10,205,013	10,482,688
Exports	5,257,628	5,257,628	6,225,670	6,581,175	7,982,704

In 1993 the most important groups of imports were (in US$1m.): Vehicles and other transport equipment, 12,061 (14·5% of total); agrarian products, 11,524 (14·03%); mechanical engineering, 11,089 (13·41%); chemicals, 10,924 (13·22%); crude petroleum and other fuels, 8,760 (10·63%); electric engineering, 6,480 (7·87%); metallic products, 5,263 (6·37%); textiles, 4,387 (5·3%); optical instruments and tools, 2,764 (3·34%); minerals, 1,049 (1·28%).

The most important groups of exports in 1993 (in US$1m.) were: Vehicles and other transport equipment, 15,791 (25·09%); agrarian products, 10,492 (16·66%); chemical, 6,871 (10·93%); mechanical engineering, 5,971 (9·51%); metallic products, 5,769 (9·15%); electric engineering, 3,965 (6·34%); textiles, 2,539 (4·03%); products of petroleum and other fuels, 1,834 (2·92%); footwear, 1,364 (2·17%).

Distribution of trade (in 1m. pesetas) by origin and destination:

	Imports		*Exports*	
	1993	*1994*	*1993*	*1994*
EU[1]	6,396,374	7,514,476	5,445,929	6,726,962
France	1,775,248	2,155,714	1,519,687	1,971,236
Germany	1,637,195	1,803,725	1,198,982	1,390,410
Italy	945,961	1,104,533	742,065	902,181
UK	802,847	969,150	673,495	804,638
Netherlands	380,087	481,429	306,267	407,238
Belgium–Luxembourg	367,420	412,617	244,114	292,970
Portugal	281,283	343,201	609,263	762,583
USA	715,734	901,041	372,438	481,864
Japan	405,784	439,978	68,089	131,651
Latin America	447,400	452,545	439,199	484,807
Mexico	128,177	128,190	149,697	184,150
Brazil	108,963	123,717	31,209	48,651
Switzerland	213,857	182,016	98,756	118,434
Eastern Europe	203,359	235,921	117,412	150,437
Nigeria	96,587	143,202	12,737	10,880
Libya	115,031	135,202	10,027	15,912
Saudi Arabia	135,880	148,916	57,694	69,225
Iran	74,755	88,871	14,037	17,949
Algeria	100,754	111,743	99,796	114,082

[1] 1994 figures include Austria, Finland and Sweeden.

Total trade between Spain and UK (British Department of Trade returns, in £1,000 sterling):

	1991	*1992*	*1993*	*1994*
Imports to UK	2,627,857	2,938,716	2,954,000	3,439,000
Exports and re-exports from UK	4,278,767	4,405,290	3,994,500	4,749,400

Total trade of the Spanish territories and UK (British Department of Trade returns, in £1,000 sterling):

	Imports to UK			*Exports from UK*		
	1993	*1994*	*1995*	*1993*	*1994*	*1995*
Canary Islands	48,276	91,191	112,087	104,630	125,559	126,153
North Africa	4,320	nil	nil	7,089	7,022	9,040

Tourism. In 1994, 61,428,000 tourists visited Spain (from France, 22·2%; Portugal, 16·01%; Germany, 15·7%; UK, 14·9%; Italy, 4·5%). Receipts of foreign currency (1993) US$18,767,000. Hotel beds, 1,009,241 (Jan. 1994).

COMMUNICATIONS

Roads. In 1993 the total length of highways and roads was 160,136 km. The main network in 1994 comprised 7,404 km of motorways and four-lane highways (1,991 km toll motorways), and 21,576 km of first class roads. Number of cars (1993) was 13,440,694, lorries and vans, 2,735,144, buses, 47,028 and motorcycles, 1,278,695. 4,083 persons were killed in road accidents in 1994.

Railways. The total length of the state railways in 1994 was 14,589 km, mostly broad (1,668-mm) gauge (6,736 km electrified in 1993). State railways are run by the *Red Nacional de Ferrocarriles Españoles* (National Spanish Railway Network; RENFE). The differential gauge had strategic origins; passengers change at the French frontier unless aboard variable-gauge trains. A high-speed standard-gauge (1,435 mm) railway, 471 km in length, from Madrid to Seville began operating in 1992. In 1994 freight carried was 24·9m. tonnes and 465m. passengers, including FEVE (narrow gauge) and regional railways (Basque Country, Catalonia). There are metros in Madrid (112 km), Barcelona (72 km) and Bilbao (26 km), and a light railway in Valencia.

Civil Aviation. There are international airports at Madrid (Barajas), Barcelona (Prat del Llobregat), Alicante, Bilbao, Gerona, Gran Canaria, Ibiza, Lanzarote, Málaga, Palma de Mallorca, Santiago de Compostela, Seville, Tenerife (Los Rodeos and Reina Sofía), Valladolid, Valencia and Zaragoza. The national carrier is Iberia Airlines, 99·8% state-owned. Its fleet in 1995 comprised 6 A300B4-100s, 2 A300B4-200s, 22 A320-200s, 30 B-727-200 Advs, 6 B-747-200Bs, 1 B-747-200B Combi, 8 B-757-200s and 36 other aircraft. There are 3 other regular carriers: Air España, Aviaco and Viva Air. Services are also provided by 66 foreign airlines. There are 43 airports open to civil traffic. A small airport in Seo de Urgel is used for the air service of Andorra.

Aircraft movements in 1993, 459,819 internal and 400,680 international. In 1993, 81·4m passengers and 379,110 tonnes of freight were carried.

Shipping. The merchant navy in 1993 had 1,151 vessels of a gross tonnage of 0·9m.

In 1993, 104,254 ships entered Spanish ports; 7·6m. passengers disembarked and 7·5m. embarked; total cargo discharged and loaded, 236m. tonnes.

Telecommunications. The receipts of the post office in 1992 were 137,374m. pesetas; expenses, 165,853m. pesetas. In 1992 there were 11,850 post offices. In 1994 there were 14·08m. telephone lines, all privately operated, and 335,000 mobile telephones were in use.

Radio Nacional de España broadcasts 5 programmes on medium-waves and FM, as well as many regional programmes; it has one commercial programme. The greatest radio audience is that of an independent network, *Sociedad Española de Radiodifusión* (SER); *Cadena de Ondas Populares Españolas* (COPE) belongs to the Roman Catholic church. Two independent radio networks were established in 1982 covering the whole of Spain, *Antena 3* and *Radio 80* (taken over by SER in 1992). *Televisión Española* broadcasts 2 programmes (TVE1 and TVE2). There were in 1994 the following regional TV networks: *TV3* (1983) and *Canal 33* (1989), both broadcasting in Catalan; *ETB1* (1983) and *ETB2* (1987), both Basque, the first one broadcasting in Basque; *Televisión de Galicia* (1985), in Galician; *TM3* (1989), for the area of Madrid; *Canal 9* (1989), mostly in Valencian (Catalan); and *Tele-Sur* (1989), for Andalusia. *Radio Exterior* broadcasts abroad, and *Televisión Española* has an international channel. There are 3 nationwide commercial TV networks: Antena 3, Tele 5 and the pay-TV channel Canal Plus. Colour transmissions are carried by PAL system. Number of receivers (1992): Radio, 12m.; television, 19·07m.

Cinemas (1993). There were 1,602 cinemas with an audience of 50,056,785.

Press In 1994 there were about 90 daily newspapers with a total daily circulation of 4m. copies. In 1994, 57,697 book titles were published, including 11,696 translations . 42,738 titles were in Castilian, 5,281 in Catalan, 1,076 in Basque and 933 in Galician.

SOCIAL INSTITUTIONS

Justice. Justice is administered by Tribunals and Courts, which jointly form the Judicial Power. Judges and magistrates cannot be removed, suspended or transferred except as set forth by law. The Constitution of 1978 established the *General Council of the Judicial Power*, consisting of a President and 20 magistrates, judges, attorneys and lawyers, governing the Judicial Power in full independence from the state's legislative and executive organs. Its members are appointed by the Cortes Generales. Its President is that of the Supreme Court.

The Judicature is composed of the Supreme Court; 17 Higher Courts of Justice, 1 for each autonomous community; 52 Provincial High Courts; Courts of First Instance, Courts of Judicial Proceedings, not passing sentences, and Penal Courts, passing sentences.

The Supreme Court consists of a President (appointed by the monarch, on the proposal of the General Council of the Judicial Power) and various judges distributed among 7 chambers: 1 for trying civil matters, 3 for administrative purposes, 1 for criminal trials, 1 for social matters and 1 for military cases. The Supreme Court has disciplinary faculties; is court of appeal in all criminal trials; for administrative purposes decides in first and second instance disputes arising between private individuals and the State, and in social matters makes final decisions.

A new penal code came into force in May 1996, replacing the code of 1848. It provides for a maximum of 30 years imprisonment in specified exceptional cases, with a normal maximum of 20 years. Sanctions with a rehabilitative intent include fines adjusted to means, community service and week-end imprisonment. New offences include money laundering, misleading publicity, sexual harassment, damage to the environment, defamation in the press, sexual, racial, political or religious discrimination and incitation to genocide.

A juvenile criminal law of 1995 lays emphasis on rehabilitation. It raised the age of responsibility from 12 to 14 years. Criminal conduct on the part of children under 14 is a matter for legal protection and custody. 14- and 15-year-olds are classified as 'minors', 16- and 17-year-olds as 'young persons', and the legal majority for criminal offences is set at 18 years. Persons up to the age of 21 may, at the courts' discretion, be dealt with as juveniles.

A jury system commenced operating in Nov. 1995 in criminal cases. Juries consist of 9 members.

The *Audiencia Nacional* deals with terrorism, monetary offences and drug-trafficking where more than one province is involved. Its president is appointed by the General Council of the Judicial Power. There is an *Ombudsman*; 18,594 complaints were received in 1994 (22,372 in 1993).

The death penalty was abolished by the 1978 Constitution.

901,696 criminal offences were reported in 1994 (938,612 in 1993). The prison population was, in Nov. 1994, 41,303.

Religion. There is no official religion. Roman Catholicism is the religion of the majority. There are 11 metropolitan sees and 52 suffragan sees, the chief being Toledo, where the Primate resides. The archdioceses of Madrid-Alcalá and Barcelona depend directly from the Vatican. The government contributes some 15,000m. pesetas to the Roman Catholic church annually.

There are about 0·25m. other Christians, including several Protestant denominations, Jehovah Witnesses (about 60,000) and Mormons.

The first synagogue since the expulsion of the Jews in 1492 was opened in Madrid on 2 Oct. 1959. The number of Jews is estimated at about 15,000.

There is a growing Moslem community, with about 0·45m. members. Most of them are foreign citizens, but there are also Spanish Moslems, mainly in Ceuta and Melilla.

Education. Until Sept. 1991, primary education was compulsory and free between 6 and 14 years of age. In Sept. 1991 the General Regulation of the Educational System Act came into force. This Act gradually extends the school-leaving age to 16 years and determines the following levels of education: Infants (3–5 years of age), primary (6–11), secondary (12–15) and baccalaureate or vocational and technical

(16–17). Primary and secondary levels of education are now compulsory and free. Religious instruction is optional.

In 1994–95 pre-primary education (under 6 years) was undertaken by 49,772 schools, with 1,085,198 pupils. Primary or basic education (6 to 14 years): 167,815 schools, with 4,075,043 pupils. There were 210,962 teachers in pre-primary and primary schools. Secondary education (14-17 years), including high schools and technical schools, was conducted at 5,159 schools, with 2,705,753 pupils and 136,790 teachers.

In 1995–96 there were in all 48 universities: 34 public State Universities, 4 Polytechnic Universities, 2 Autonomous Universities, 4 Catholic (private) universities, 3 private universities, and the *Universidad Nacional de Educación a Distancia* (Open University), which teaches by mail, radio and TV, (109,670 students in June 1994). In 1994–95 there were 1,460,757 students at all universities; 53,325 at private universities.

Health. In 1994 there were 159,291 doctors, 12,247 dentists, 39,608 pharmacists and 167,894 nurses (including 6,210 midwives). In 1991 there were 813 hospitals with 164,451 beds.

Welfare. The social security budget was 10,850,401m. pesetas in 1995, and covered retirement pensions (58·5% of that budget), health and hospital services (30·5%) and other allowances and aids. The minimum monthly pension in 1995 was 34,070 pesetas, for those low-income citizens who had not contributed to the social security.

In 1996 the system of contributions to the social security and employment scheme was: For pensions, sickness, invalidity, maternity and children, a contribution of 28·3% of the basic wage (23·6% paid by the employer, 4·7% by the employee); for unemployment benefit, a contribution of 7·8% (6·2% paid by the employer, 1·6% by the employee). There are also minor contributions for a Fund of Guaranteed Salaries, working accidents and professional sicknesses, and vocational training.

DIPLOMATIC REPRESENTATIVES

Of Spain in Great Britain (Portland House, Stag Pl., London SW1E 5SE)
Ambassador: Alberto Aza Arias.

Of Great Britain in Spain (Calle de Fernando el Santo, 16, Madrid, 4)
Ambassador: A. D. Brighty, CMG, CVO.

Of Spain in the USA (2700 15th St., NW, Washington, D.C., 20009)
Ambassador: Jaime de Ojeda y Eiseley.

Of the USA in Spain (Serrano 75, 28006 Madrid)
Ambassador: Richard N. Gardner.

Of Spain to the United Nations
Ambassador: Juan Antonio Yáñez-Barnuevo.

Further Reading

Donaghy, P. J. and Newton, M. T., *Spain: a Guide to Political and Economic Institutions*. CUP, 1987
Harrison, J., *The Spanish Economy in the Twentieth Century*. London, 1985
Heywood, P., *The Government and Politics of Spain*. London, 1995
Hooper, J., *The New Spaniards*. 2nd ed. [of *The Spaniards*] London, 1995
Péréz-Díaz, V. M., *The Return of Civil Society: the Emergence of Democratic Spain*. Harvard Univ. Press, 1993
Powell, C., *Juan Carlos of Spain: Self-Made Monarch*. London and New York, 1996
Preston, P., *The Triumph of Democracy in Spain*. London and New York, 1986
Shields, G. J., *Spain*. [Bibliography] 2nd ed.Oxford and Santa Barbara (CA), 1994
Shubert, A., *A Social History of Modern Spain*. London, 1990

National library: Biblioteca Nacional, Madrid.
National statistical office: Instituto Nacional de Estadística (INE), Paseo de la Castellana, 183, Madrid.

SRI LANKA

Sri Lanka Prajathanthrika Samajavadi Janarajaya

(Democratic Socialist Republic of Sri Lanka)

Capital: Colombo
Population: 17·4m. (1992)
GNP per capita: US$640 (1994)
HDI/world rank: 0·704/97 (1992)

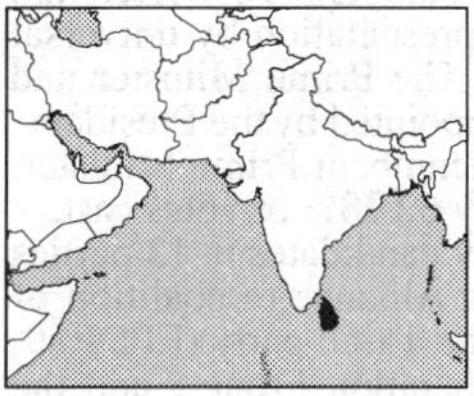

KEY HISTORICAL EVENTS. In 1505 the Portuguese had formed settlements in the west and south, which were taken from them in the middle of the next century by the Dutch. In 1796 the British Government annexed the foreign settlements to the presidency of Madras. In 1802 Ceylon was constituted a separate colony. In the beginning of the 19th century the British subjugated the Kandyan Kingdom in the central highlands.

Ceylon became an independent Commonwealth state on 4 Feb. 1948 and became republic in 1972 as Sri Lanka.

War between northern Tamil separatists and government forces began in 1983. A state of emergency ended on 11 Jan. 1989, but violence continued. President Ranasinghe Premadasa was assassinated on 1 May 1993. A ceasefire was signed on 3 Jan. 1995.

TERRITORY AND POPULATION. Sri Lanka is an island in the Indian Ocean, south of the Indian peninsula from which it is separated by the Palk Strait. On 28 June 1974 the frontier between India and Sri Lanka in the Palk Strait was re-defined, giving to Sri Lanka the island of Kachchativu.

Area (in sq. km.) and census population on 17 March 1981:

Provinces	*Area*	*Population*	*Provinces*	*Area*	*Population*
Western	3,708·61	3,919,807	North-Central	10,723·59	849,492
Central	5,583·50	2,009,248	Uva	8,487·91	914,522
Southern	5,559·15	1,882,661	Sabaragamuwa	4,901·55	1,482,031
Northern	8,882·11	1,109,404			
Eastern	9,951·26	975,251	Total	65,609·86	14,846,750
North-Western	7,812·18	1,704,334			

Population (1981 census), 14,846,750, an increase of 17% since 1971. Population (in 1,000) according to ethnic group and nationality at the 1981 census: 10,980 Sinhalese, 1,887 Sri Lanka Tamils, 1,047 Sri Lanka Moors, 39 Burghers, 47 Malays, 819 Indian Tamils, 28 others. Non-nationals of Sri Lanka totalled 635,150. Population, 1992, 17,405,000.

Vital statistics, 1991 (provisional): Birth-rate (per 1,000 population), 21; death-rate, 5·5; infant mortality (1990, per 1,000 live births), 19·3.

The urban population was 21·5% of the total in 1981. The principal towns and their population according to the census of 1981 are: Colombo (the capital), 587,647; Dehiwela-Mt. Lavinia, 173,529; Moratuwa, 134,826; Jaffna, 118,224; Kotte, 101,039; Kandy, 97,872; Galle, 76,863; Negombo, 60,762; Trincomalee, 44,313; Batticaloa, 42,963; Matara, 38,843; Ratnapura, 37,497; Anuradhapura, 35,981; Badulla, 33,068; Kalutara, 31,503. Population of the Greater Colombo area, 1980, about 1m.

Sinhala and Tamil are the official languages; English is in use.

CLIMATE. Sri Lanka, which has an equatorial climate, is affected by the North-east Monsoon (Dec. to Feb.), the South-west Monsoon (May to Sept.) and 2 inter-monsoons (March to April and Oct. to Nov.). Rainfall is heaviest in the south-west highlands while the north-west and south-east are relatively dry. Colombo. Jan.

79·9°F (26·6°C), July 81·7°F (27·6°C). Annual rainfall 95·4" (2,424 mm). Trincomalee. Jan. 78·8°F (26°C), July 86·2°F (30·1°C). Annual rainfall 62·2"(1,580 mm). Kandy. Jan. 73·9°F (23·3°C), July 76·1°F (24·5°C). Annual rainfall 72·4" (1,840 mm). Nuwara Eliya. Jan. 58·5°F (14·7°C), July 60·3°F (15·7°C). Annual rainfall 75" (1,905 mm).

CONSTITUTION AND GOVERNMENT. A new constitution for the Democratic Socialist Republic of Sri Lanka was promulgated in Sept. 1978.

The Executive *President* is directly elected for a 6-year term renewable once.

Parliament consists of one chamber, composed of 225 members (196 elected and 29 from the National List). Election is by proportional representation by universal suffrage at 18 years. The term of Parliament is 6 years. The Prime Minister and other Ministers, who must be members of Parliament, are appointed by the President.

Presidential elections were held on 9 Nov. 1994. The incumbent Prime Minister, Chandrika Kumaratunga, was elected against 1 opponent by 62·28% of votes cast.

Parliamentary elections were held on 16 Aug. 1994. 1,449 candidates in 13 parties and 26 independent groups stood for office. The People's Alliance (a coalition of 9 parties) gained 105 seats, the United National Party 94, the Tamil party (EPDP) 9, the Sri Lanka Moslem Congress 7, the Tamil United Liberation Front 5 and the Democratic People's Liberation Front 3.

In Oct 1995 the government comprised:

President, Minister of Finance, Minister of Defence: Chandrika Kumaratunga (b. 1945; Sri Lanka Freedom Party; sworn in 12 Nov. 1994).

Prime Minister: Sirima Bandaranaike (b. 1916).

Minister of Public Admistration, Local Government, Plantations: Ratnasiri Wickremanayke. *Power and Energy, Irrigation:* Col. Anuruddha Ratwatte. *Home Affairs, Provincial Councils and Co-operatives:* Amarasiri Dodangoda. *Foreign Affairs:* Laksham Kadirgamar. *Cultural and Religious Affairs:* Laksham Jayakody. *Science, Technology and Human Resources Development:* Bernard Soysa. *Agriculture, Lands and Forests:* D.M. Jayaratna. *Labour and Vocational Training:* Mahinda Rajapakse. *Shipping, Ports, Rehabilitation and Reconstruction:* M.H.M. Ashraff. *Information, Tourism and Aviation:* Dharmasiri Senanayake. *Trade, Commerce and Food:* Kingsley Wickremaratna. *Industrial Development:* C. V. Gunaratna *Education and Higher Education:* Richard Pathirana. *Housing, Construction and Public Utilities:* Nimal Siripala De Silva. *Posts and Telecommunications:* Mangala Samaraweera. *Youth Affairs, Sports and Rural Development:* D.S. Dissanayaka. *Transport, Highways, Environment and Women's Affairs:* Srimani Athulathmudali. *External Trade, Justice and Constitutional Affairs:* G.L. Peiris. *Health and Social Services:* A.H.M. Fowzie. *Fisheries:* Indika Gunawardena.

National flag: A yellow field bearing 2 panels; in the hoist 2 vertical strips of green and orange; in the fly, dark red with a gold lion holding a sword and in each corner a gold 'bo' leaf.

National anthem: 'Sri Lanka Matha, Apa Sri Lanka' ('Mother Sri Lanka, thee Sri Lanka'); words and tune by A. Samarakone. There is a Tamil version, 'Sri Lanka thaaya, nam Sri Lanka'; words anonymous.

Local Government. Sri Lanka is divided into 25 districts, administered by government agents. There are 12 municipal councils, 39 urban councils and 257 pradeshiya sabas. There are 9 provincial councils, consisting of a governor, appointed by the President, a Chief Minister, a Board of Ministers and members elected for 5-year terms. At elections in May 1991 3,533 representatives were elected to 236 municipal and urban councils and pradeshiya sabas in 7 of 9 provinces. Polls were not held in Northern Province and Eastern Province because of the Tamil rebellion there in May 1991, but were held eventually in Eastern province in March 1994 to 40 councils. The United National Party gained control of 18 of these, Tamil Nationalist groups 12, the Sri Lanka Moslem Congress 6 and the Sri Lanka Freedom Party 4. The United National Party gained control of 6 provincial councils and 190 of 237 local councils and the Sri Lanka Freedom Party 36.

DEFENCE

Army. The Army consists of 3 divisional and 4 task force headquarters, 1 independent special forces, 23 infantry, 1 mechanized infantry and 1 air mobile brigade and 3 armoured reconnaissance, 4 field artillery and 1 armoured regiment. Equipment includes 25 T-54/-55 main battle tanks. Strength (1996), 105,000. Paramilitary forces consist of the Ministry of Defence Police (40,000, including 1,000 women and a 3,000-strong anti-guerilla force), the Home Guard (15,200) and the National Guard (some 15,000).

Navy. The naval force comprises 2 Surveillance Command Ships (ex-mercantile), 1 locally-built coastal patrol craft, 40 inshore patrol craft of varying types as well as about 30 small fast patrol boats and service craft. There are 2 mechanized landing craft of 270 tonnes full load. The main naval base is at Trincomalee. Personnel in 1995 numbered 10,300, with a reserve of about 1,100.

Air Force. The Air Force was formed on 10 Oct. 1950. Its flying bases are at Anuradhapura, Katunayake, Ratmalana, Vavuniya and China Bay, Trincomalee. Equipment of 8 squadrons and wings comprises 4 F-7 fighters, 10 SF.260 and 2 Cessna 150 trainers, 2 Pucara light strike aircraft, 1 HS748, 8 Chinese-built Y-12s, 1 An-32, 1 Chinese-built Y-8 (An-12), 1 Super King Air, 5 Cessna Skymasters, 1 Cessna 421 and 12 Bell 212, 4 Bell 412, 6 Mi-17, 3 Mi-24 and 6 JetRanger helicopters for internal security operations. Total strength (1995) about 10,000 with 27 combat aircraft and 26 armed helicopters.

INTERNATIONAL RELATIONS

Membership. Sri Lanka is a member of the UN, the Commonwealth, and the Colombo Plan.

ECONOMY

Policy. The 1993–97 plan aims at a 6·4% annual growth rate. Investment allocated is mainly for completion of projects in priority areas such as power, irrigation, road rehabilitation, water supply and telecommunications. Total public investment is about Rs 325,000m.

Budget. Revenue and expenditure of central government in Rs 1m. for financial years ending 31 Dec.:

		Expenditure		
Year	*Revenue*	*Recurrent*	*Capital*	*Total*
1990	70,849	72,374	40,836	113,210
1991	80,173	87,264	53,979	141,243
1992 [1]	93,711	89,278	60,801	150,079

[1] Estimate.

The principal sources of revenue in 1992 were (in Rs 1m.): General sales and tax, 24,379; import levies, 21,391; export duties, 594; selective sales taxes, 14,550; property transfer taxes, 2,672; taxes on personal and corporate income, 11,561.

The principal items of recurrent expenditure in 1992 (in Rs 1m.): Finance, 30,719; defence, 15,627; public administration, 16,583; education, 5,919; agriculture, 585; health, 2,800. Capital expenditure on finance, 30,078; Mahaweli development, 3,924; power and energy, 2,358; transport and highways, 4,989.

Currency. The unit of currency is the *Sri Lankan rupee* (LKR) of 100 *cents*. There are coins of 1, 2, 5, 10, 25 and 50 cents and Rs 1, 2 and 5, and notes of Rs 5, 10, 20, 50, 100, 500 and 1,000. The total circulation was Rs 30,496m. on 31 Dec. 1992. Inflation was an annualized 10% in 1994. In March 1996, £1 = Rs 82·05; US$1 = Rs 53·69; DM1 = Rs 36·37.

Banking and Finance. The Central Bank of Sri Lanka is the bank of issue. 2 state-owned commercial banks, the Bank of Ceylon and the People's Bank, account for about 70% of bank lending. There are also 21 private banks (17 foreign). Total assets of commercial banks at 31 Dec. 1992, Rs 184,507·1m.

Sri Lanka National Savings Bank at 31 Dec. 1992 had a balance to depositors' credit of Rs 34,281·1m. There are 5 main long-term credit institutions.

There is a stock exchange in Colombo.

Weights and Measures. The metric system has been established.

ENERGY AND NATURAL RESOURCES

Electricity. Installed capacity (1992), 1,289,650 kW. Energy produced, 3,540m. kWh; the main source was hydro power (2,900m. kWh).

Water. The Mahaweli Ganga scheme irrigates 90,113 ha of new land and (1992) 100,653 ha of land already cultivated.

Minerals. Gems are among the chief minerals mined and exported. Graphite is also important; production in 1992 was 3,307 tonnes. Production of ilmenite, 1992, 38,296 tonnes. Some rutile is also produced (2,741 tonnes in 1992). Salt extraction is the oldest industry. The method is solar evaporation of sea-water. Production, 1992, 115,665 tonnes.

Agriculture. Agriculture accounted for 24% of GDP in 1992. About 2·5m. ha are under cultivation. Agriculture engages 47·5% of the labour force. Main crops in 1992: Paddy (2,339,700 tonnes from 803,174 ha), rubber (106,149 tonnes), tea (178,870 tonnes) and coconuts (2,296m. nuts). Tea plantations are being returned to the private sector after nationalization in 1975.

Livestock in 1992 (estimate): 1,603,400 cattle, 896,500 buffaloes, 91,200 swine, 528,000 goats, 22,300 sheep, 8,851,800 poultry.

Fisheries. Production in 1992 was 206,168 tonnes including 163,168 tonnes of coastal water fish, 21,000 tonnes of fresh water fish and 22,000 tonnes from off-shore and deep-sea fisheries. In 1992 there were 27,435 fishing craft, of which 15,637 were not motorized.

INDUSTRY. The main industries are food, beverages and tobacco; textiles, clothing and leather goods; chemicals, petroleum, rubber and plastics.

Trade Unions. In 1992 there were 1,039 registered trade unions.

FOREIGN ECONOMIC RELATIONS. Foreign debt in 1992 was Rs 234,851m.

Commerce. The values of total imports and exports (imports excluding bullion, specie and postal articles; exports, including re-exports and ship's stores) for calendar years (in Rs 1,000):

	1988	*1989*	*1990*	*1991*	*1992*
Imports	70,320,427	75,352,750	105,559,159	127,830,821	149,780,179
Exports	47,092,044	55,511,162	76,623,713	82,224,847	107,508,538

Principal exports in 1992 (in Rs 1m.): Tea, 14,893; rubber, 2,960; copra, coconut oil and desiccated coconut, 2,665; other crops, 4,841; textiles and garments, 52,588; precious and semi-precious stones, 7,170.

Principal imports (Rs 1m.) in 1992 were petroleum, 13,938m.; machinery and equipment, 17,200m.; vehicles and transport equipment, 7,963; food and beverages, 37,995.

In 1992 the principal sources of imports were (in Rs 1m.): Japan, 18,214; USA, 6,985; UK, 7,575; Iran, 5,129; Hong Kong, 10,581; Singapore, 10,416; Taiwan, 9,379; India, 13,230; Malaysia, 5,591; China, 5,302.

Principal export destinations 1992 were (in Rs 1m.): USA, 36,711; Germany, 9,284; Japan, 5,610; UK, 7,460; Egypt, 1,535; Belgium, 5,911; Iran, 2,116.

Total trade between Sri Lanka and UK (British Department of Trade returns, in £1,000 sterling):

	1991	*1992*	*1993*	*1994*	*1995*
Imports to UK	74,460	93,045	142,478	185,784	205,662
Exports and re-exports from UK	128,565	103,214	126,243	152,850	156,409

Tourism. 393,669 tourists visited the country in 1992, bringing in foreign exchange earnings of US$198·5m.

COMMUNICATIONS

Roads. There were (1992) 25,952 km of motorable roads, of which 10,961 km are blacktopped, first-class nationally-maintained roads. Number of motor vehicles, 31 Dec. 1992, 1,003,047, comprising 189,477 private cars and cabs, 113,739 lorries, 98,555 tractors, 516,205 motor cycles and 46,162 buses.

Railways. In 1993 there were 1,434 km of railway (1,676 mm gauge). In 1993 77·2m. passengers and 1·5m. tonnes of freight were carried.

Civil Aviation. There is an international airport at Colombo (Katunayake). The national carrier is Air Lanka, which operated 2 A320-200s, 3A340-300s and 3 other aircraft in 1995, and flew to 30 destinations in 20 countries. Services are also provided by Aeroflot, Air Maldives, AOM, Balkan, British Airways, Cathay Pacific, Condor, Emirates, Gulf Air, Indian Airlines, KLM, Kuwait Airways, LTU, Malaysia Airlines, Middle East Airlines, Northwest Airlines, Oman Air, Pakistan Airlines, Qatar Airways, Royal Jordanian, Saudia, Singapore Airlines and Thai Airways.

Shipping. In 1995, sea-going shipping totalled 0·45m. GRT, including oil tankers, 0·13m. GRT. Colombo is a modern container port; Trincomalee and Galle are natural harbours. In 1992, 3,438 merchant vessels totalling 45·4m. GRT entered the ports.

Telecommunications. In 1992 there were 527 post offices, 3,357 sub-post offices and 98 agency post offices. In 1989 there were 1,583 telex lines and in 1991 175,000 telephones. Direct dialling was available to 85 countries in 1992. Broadcasting is provided by the Sri Lanka Broadcasting Corporation. In 1993 there were 2·2m. radio and 0·7m. TV sets (colour by PAL).

Cinemas. In 1992 there were 258 cinemas and 27,605,949 admissions. Films released, 1992, 97.

Press. In 1992 there were 4 daily and 3 weekly papers in Sinhala; 2 daily and 3 weekly in Tamil; 3 daily and 3 weekly in English.

SOCIAL INSTITUTIONS

Justice. The systems of law which obtain are Roman-Dutch, English, Tesawalamai, Islamic and Kandyan.

Kandyan law applies in matters relating to inheritance, matrimonial rights and donations; Tesawalamai law applies in Jaffna as above and in sales of land. Islamic law is applied to all Moslems in respect of succession, donations, marriage, divorce and maintenance. These customary and religious laws have been modified by local enactments.

The courts of original jurisdiction are the High Court, Provincial Courts, District Courts, Magistrates' Courts and Primary Courts. District Courts have unlimited civil jurisdiction. The Magistrates' Courts exercise criminal jurisdiction. The Primary Courts exercise civil jurisdiction in petty disputes and criminal jurisdiction in respect of certain offences.

The Constitution of 1978 provided for the establishment of two superior courts, the Supreme Court and the Court of Appeal.

The Supreme Court is the highest and final superior court of record and exercises jurisdiction in respect of constitutional matters, jurisdiction for the protection of fundamental rights, final appellate jurisdiction in election petitions and jurisdiction in respect of any breach of the privileges of Parliament. The Court of Appeal has appellate jurisdiction to correct all errors in fact or law committed by any court, tribunal or institution.

Police. The strength of the police service in 1992 was 30,642.

Religion. In 1994 the population was 73% Buddhist, 15% Hinduist, 7% Moslem and 5% Christian.

Education. Education is free from school year 1 to university and is imparted in the medium of the mother tongue. In 1991 about 88% of the population (10 years old and older) was literate.

In 1992 there were 10,590 schools including 10,042 government schools, 478 Pirivenas and 70 private schools. The government schools had 175,682 teachers and 4·16m. students from year 1 to 13. Ministry of Education expenditure (1992), Rs 5,728m.

In 1994-95 there were 8 universities, 1 open (distance) university and 1 Buddhist and Pali university, with 26,973 students and 2,005 academic staff.

Health. In 1992 there were 506 hospitals, including 84 maternity homes, and 350 central dispensaries. The hospitals had 48,061 beds. There were 3,345 Department of Health doctors. Total state budget expenditure on health, 1992, Rs 6,967·1m.

Social Welfare. The activities of the Department of Social Services include: Payment of Public Assistance, monthly allowance, financial assistance to needy tuberculosis, leprosy and cancer patients and their dependants; relief of those affected by widespread distress, such as floods, drought, cyclone; custodial care and welfare services to the elderly and infirm; vocational training, aids and appliances for the physically and mentally handicapped; custodial care, vocational training and rehabilitation for socially handicapped persons; community-based rehabilitation of treated drug addicts; registration of and financial assistance to voluntary organizations which engage in social welfare activities.

The government's Poverty Alleviation ('Janasaviya') Programme targets 0·35m. of the neediest families, who received a monthly Rs 1,458 (in 1992) in return for 20 days community service. Total budget was Rs 4,900m. in 1992.

DIPLOMATIC REPRESENTATIVES

Of Sri Lanka in Great Britain (13 Hyde Park Gdns., London, W2 2LU)
High Commissioner: Sarath Kusum Wickremesinghe.

Of Great Britain in Sri Lanka (190 Galle Rd., Kollupitiya, Colombo 3)
High Commissioner: E. John Field, CMG.

Of Sri Lanka in the USA (2148 Wyoming Ave., NW, Washington, D.C., 20008)
Ambassador: Jayantha Dhanapala.

Of the USA in Sri Lanka (210 Galle Rd., Kollupitiya, Colombo 3)
Ambassador: Vacant.

Of Sri Lanka to the United Nations
Ambassador: Herman de Silva.

Further Reading

De Silva, C. R. *Sri Lanka: a History.* Delhi, 1991
Johnson, B. L. C. and Scrivenor, M. le M., *Sri Lanka: Land, People and Economy.* London, 1981
Manogaran, C., *Ethnic Conflict and Reconciliation in Sri Lanka.* Univ. Hawaii Press, 1987
Manor, J., *Sri Lanka: In Change and Crisis.* London, 1984
McGowan, W., *Only Man is Vile: the Tragedy of Sri Lanka.* New York, 1992
Moore, M., *The State and Peasant Politics in Sri Lanka.* CUP, 1985
Samaraweera, V., *Sri Lanka.* [Bibliography] Oxford and Santa Barbara, 1987
Schwarz, W., *The Tamils of Sri Lanka.* London, 1983
Tambiah, S. J., *Sri Lanka: Ethnic Fratricide and the Dismantling of Democracy.* London, 1986
Wilson, A. J., *The Break-Up of Sri Lanka: The Sinhalese-Tamil Conflict.* London, 1988

National statistical office: Department of Census and Statistics, POB 563, Colombo 7.

SUDAN

Jamhuryat es-Sudan

(Republic of Sudan)

Capital: Khartoum
Population: 28·2m. (1994)
GNP per capita: US$400 (1990)
HDI/world rank: 0·379/144 (1992)

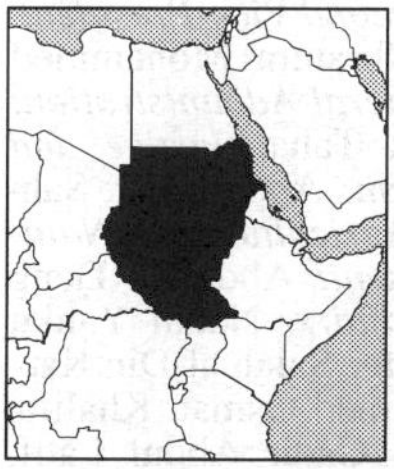

KEY HISTORICAL EVENTS. In Dec. 1955 the Sudanese parliament passed unanimously a declaration that an independent state should be set up, and a Council of State of 5 should temporarily assume the duties of Head of State. The Codomini, the UK and Egypt, gave their assent on 31 Dec. 1955 and Sudan was proclaimed a sovereign independent republic on 1 Jan. 1956.

For the history of the Condominium and the steps leading to independence, *see* THE STATESMAN'S YEAR-BOOK, 1955, pp. 340–341; for subsequent political history *see* THE STATESMAN'S YEAR-BOOK, 1990–91, pp. 1135–36.

On 30 June 1989 Brig.-Gen. (later Lieut.-Gen.) Omar Hassan Ahmad al-Bashir overthrew the civilian government in a military coup.

The rebel Sudanese People's Liberation Army maintains guerilla activities in the south.

TERRITORY AND POPULATION. Sudan is bounded in the north by Egypt, north-east by the Red Sea, east by Eritrea and Ethiopia, south by Kenya, Uganda and Zaïre, west by the Central African Republic and Chad, and north-west by Libya. Its area is 967,500 sq. miles (2,505,813 sq. km). Population (1983 census), 20,564,364; estimate (1994), 28·2m. Infant mortality, 1994, 120 per 1,000 live births; expectation of life, 1990, 51 years.

In Feb. 1994 the former 9 regions were subdivided to form 26 federal states as follows:

Former region	*New states*
Khartoum	Khartoum
Bahr al-Ghazal	Western Bahr al-Ghazal; Northern Bahr al-Ghazal; Lakes
Central	Gezira; White Nile; Sinnar; Blue Nile
Dafur	Northern Dafur; Southern Dafur; Western Dafur
Eastern	Red Sea; Gedaref; Kassala
Equatoria	Eastern Equatoria; Western Equatoria; Bahr al-Jabal
Kurdufan	Northern Kurdufan; Southern Kurdufan; Western Kurdufan
Northern	Nile; Northern State
Upper Nile	Northern Upper Nile; Unity State

The chief cities (census, 1983) are the capital, Khartoum (476,218), its suburbs Omdurman (526,287) and Khartoum North (341,146), Port Sudan (206,727), Wadi Medani (141,065), al-Obeid (140,024), Kassala (98,751 in 1973), Atbara (73,009), al-Qadarif (66,465 in 1973), Kosti (65,257 in 1973) and Juba (56,737 in 1973).

The northern and central thirds of the country are populated by Arab and Nubian peoples, while the southern third is inhabited by Nilotic and Bantu peoples; Arabic, the official language, is spoken by 60% of inhabitants.

CLIMATE. Lying wholly within the tropics, the country has a continental climate and only the Red Sea coast experiences maritime influences. Temperatures are generally high throughout the year, with May and June the hottest months. Winters are virtually cloudless and night temperatures are consequently cool. Summer is the rainy season inland, with amounts increasing from north to south, but the northern areas are virtually a desert region. On the Red Sea coast, most rain falls in winter. Khartoum. Jan. 74°F (23·3°C), July 89°F (31·7°C). Annual rainfall 6" (157 mm). Juba. Jan. 83°F (28·3°C), July 78°F (25·6°C). Annual rainfall 39" (968 mm). Port Sudan. Jan. 74°F (23·3°C), July 94°F (34·4°C). Annual rainfall 4" (94 mm). Wadi Halfa. Jan. 60°F (15·6°C), July 90°F (32·2°C). Annual rainfall 0·1" (2·5 mm).

CONSTITUTION AND GOVERNMENT. The constitution was suspended after the 1989 coup and a 12-member Revolutionary Council has ruled. A 300-member Provisional National Assembly was appointed in Feb. 1992 as a transitional legislature pending elections.

In Nov. 1994 the government comprised:

President and Minister of Defence: Lieut.-Gen. Omar Hassan Ahmad al-Bashir (appointed Oct. 1993).

First Vice-President: Brig.-Gen. Zubir Mohammed Saleh. *Second Vice-President:* George Kengor Arop. *Minister of the Interior:* El Tayyib Ibrahim Mohammed Kheir. *Presidential Affairs:* Brig. Abd al-Rahim Hussain. *Federal Administration:* Dr Ali al-Hajj Mohammed. *Foreign Affairs:* Ali Uthman Taha. *Justice and Attorney-General:* Abdel-Aziz Shiddo. *Culture and Information:* Abdel-Basit Sahdarat. *Planning and Investment:* Mohammed Khair al-Zubeir. *Agriculture and Natural Resources:* Abdul-Gasim Shammo. *Peace and Development:* Abdallah Deng Niyal. *Local Government and Co-ordination of Provincial Affairs:* Natali Yanku Ambu. *Irrigation:* Yacoub Abu Shura Musa. *Energy and Mining:* Salah al-Din Karrar. *Industry:* Badr Eddin Suleiman. *Social Planning:* Mohammed Osman Khalifa. *Housing, Construction and Public Utilities:* Osman Abdoul Gadir Abdul Latif. *Higher Education and Scientific Research:* Dr Ibrahim Ahmed Omer. *Tourism and Environment:* Mohammed Tahir Eilla. *Commerce:* Tag al-Sir Mustafa. *Education:* Kabosho Kuku. *Aviation and Survey:* Al Tigania Adam Tahir. *Transport:* Al-Fatih Mohammed. *Roads and Communications:* Uthman Abd al-Qadir al-Latif. *Labour and Administrative Reform:* Gen. Dominic Kassiano. *Health:* Lieut. Col. Galwuk Deng Garang.

National flag: Three horizontal stripes of red, white, black, with a green triangle based on the hoist.

National anthem: 'Nahnu Djundullah' ('We are God's army'); words by A. M. Salih, tune by A. Murjan.

Regional and Local Government. In Feb. 1994 a federal system of 26 states was set up, each under a governor, a deputy governor and a cabinet of ministers. The states are subdivided into 66 provinces and 218 districts.

DEFENCE. There is conscription for 3 years.

Army. The Army is organized in 1 armoured, 1 engineer, 1 airborne and 6 infantry divisions, 1 mechanized infantry, 24 infantry, 10 artillery, 1 reconnaissance and 12 air defence artillery brigades and 3 artillery regiments. Equipment includes 250 T-54/T-55, 20 M-60A3 and 50 Ch Type-59 main battle tanks. Strength (1996) 115,000 (30,000 conscripts). There is a paramilitary People's Defence Force of about 15,000.

Navy. The Navy operates in the Red Sea and also on the River Nile. It comprises 3 inshore patrol craft, 4 riverine patrol craft, 7 ex-Yugoslav landing craft and some armed boats. The flotilla suffers from lack of maintenance and spares. Personnel in 1995 were believed to number 1,000.

Air Force. The Air Force was built up with Soviet and Chinese assistance. 2 combat squadrons are equipped with about 6 MiG-21 fighters, 8 F-6 (Chinese-built MiG-19) fighter-bombers. There is 1 transport squadron with 3 C-130H Hercules, 6 Aviocars and 2 DHC-5D Buffalo turboprop transports; 2 helicopter squadrons have 6 AB.212s, 9 Romanian-built Pumas, 5 Mi-8s; there are 2 Mig-21U conversion trainers. Personnel totalled (1995) about 3,000, with 16 combat aircraft. Effectiveness is reduced by economic problems and insurgency.

INTERNATIONAL RELATIONS

Membership. Sudan is a member of the UN, OAU, the Arab League and is an ACP state of the EU.

ECONOMY

Policy. Subsidies on consumer staples including sugar and fuel were abolished in Oct. 1991.

Budget. The 1992–93 budget envisaged revenue of £S64,800m., current expenditure of £S69,200m. and capital expenditure of £S47,187m.

Currency. The monetary unit was the *Sudanese pound* (SDP) of 100 *piastres* and 1,000 *milliemes*. This was replaced in May 1992 by the *dinar* at a rate of 1 dinar = £S10. There are notes of 5, 10, 25 and 50 dinars. Sudanese pounds remain legal tender. Foreign exchange reserves were £S41·2m. in 1993. In March 1995 the commercial exchange rates were, £1 = 132·21; US$1 = 86·50; DM1 = 56·61 dinars.

Banking and Finance. The Bank of Sudan opened in Feb. 1960 with an authorized capital of £S1·5m. as the central bank and bank of issue. Banks were nationalized in 1970 but in 1974 foreign banks were allowed to open branches. The application of Islamic law from 1 Jan. 1991 put an end to the charging of interest in official banking transactions, and 7 banks are run on Islamic principles. Mergers of 7 local banks in 1993 resulted in the formation of the Khartoum Bank, the Industrial Development Bank and the Savings Bank. In 1994 there were 27 commercial and private banks.

A stock exchange opened in 1995.

Weights and Measures. The metric system is in use.

ENERGY AND NATURAL RESOURCES

Electricity. Installed capacity was 500 MW in 1991. Production (1986) 1,210m. kWh.

Oil. Two oil wells in the south-west produce 15,000 bbls per day of high quality oil. Production of petrol products (1985) 1,019 tonnes.

Minerals. Mineral deposits include graphite, sulphur, chromium, iron, manganese, copper, zinc, fluorspar, natron, gypsum and anhydrite, magnesite, asbestos, talc, halite, kaolin, white mica, coal, diatomite (kieselguhr), limestone and dolomite, pumice, lead, wollastonite, black sands and vermiculite pyrites. Chromite and gold are mined.

Agriculture. 80% of the population depends on agriculture. Land tenure is based on customary rights; land is ultimately owned by the government.

Production (1992) in 1,000 tonnes: Sorghum, 4,320; sugar-cane, 4,600; groundnuts, 454; seed cotton, 261; millet, 424; wheat, 895; sesame, 330; cotton seed, 170; fruit, 852.

One of the largest sugar complexes in the world was opened at Kenana in March 1981. It is capable of processing 330,000 tonnes a year. Production in 1992 was 513,000 tonnes.

Livestock (1992): Cattle, 21·6m.; sheep, 22·6m.; goats, 18·7m.; poultry, 35m.

Forestry. Forest reserves were 1,278,165 ha.

INDUSTRY. Manufacturing contributes about 9% of GDP and employs 4% of the workforce. Output: Sugar (1990–91), 432,300 tonnes; cement (1988–89), 149,100 tonnes.

FOREIGN ECONOMIC RELATIONS. Foreign debt was US$16,000m. in 1994.

Commerce. Total trade for calendar years, in US$1m.:

	1989	*1990*	*1991*	*1992*	*1993*
Imports	1,301	1,216	880	810	600
Exports	585	555	450	213	185

The main exports are cotton, sesame, gum arabic, sorghum, livestock, hides and skins. Main export markets, 1991: Thailand, 17·3%; Saudi Arabia, 10%; Italy,

9·5%; Germany, 8·8%; Japan, 7·8%. Main import suppliers: Saudi Arabia, 13·5%; UK, 10·3%; Italy, 8·5%; Germany, 7·8%; China, 7·6%.

Total trade between Sudan and UK (British Department of Trade returns, in £1,000 sterling):

	1991	*1992*	*1993*	*1994*	*1995*
Imports to UK	6,168	5,250	8,174	7,301	10,183
Exports and re-exports from UK	75,460	52,304	45,399	45,603	44,222

Tourism. There were 42,000 visitors in 1986.

COMMUNICATIONS

Roads. In 1982 there were about 3,000 km of tarmac roads, including the new 1,190 km road from Khartoum to Port Sudan, and 45,000 km of tracks. There were 99,400 passenger cars and 17,500 commercial vehicles in 1985.

Railways. The total length of line open for traffic (1990) was 4,874 km. The gauge is 1,067 mm. In 1992, the railways carried 0·5m. passengers and 1m. tonnes of freight.

Civil Aviation. There is an international airport at Khartoum. Sudan Airways, the government-owned national carrier operating domestic and international services, had 1 A300B4-600, 2 A310-300s, 1 A320-200, 3 B-707-320Cs, 2 B-737-200C Advs and 5 other aircraft in 1995.

Shipping. Supplementing the railways are regular river steamer services of the Sudan Railways. Port Sudan is the major seaport; another port at Suakin was opened in 1991. Traffic on the River Nile has ceased owing to the civil war. Seagoing shipping totalled 72,752 GRT in 1995, including oil tankers, 1,222 GRT.

Telecommunications. Number of telephones in 1993 was 66,000 (70% in Greater Khartoum). Broadcasting is controlled by the Sudan National Broadcasting Corporation and Sudan Television (Colour by PAL). In 1991 there were some 6m. radio and 0·25m. TV sets.

Cinemas. In 1975 there were 58, seating capacity 112,000 and also 43 mobile units.

Press. In 1985 there were 2 daily newspapers with a circulation of 120,000.

SOCIAL INSTITUTIONS

Justice. The judiciary is a separate and independent department of state directly and solely responsible to the President of the Republic. The general administrative supervision and control of the judiciary is vested in the High Judicial Council.

Civil Justice is administered by the courts constituted under the Civil Justice Ordinance, namely the High Court of Justice—consisting of the Court of Appeal and Judges of the High Court, sitting as courts of original jurisdiction—and Province Courts—consisting of the Courts of Province and District Judges. The law administered is 'justice, equity and good conscience' in all cases where there is no special enactment. Procedure is governed by the Civil Justice Ordinance.

Justice for the Moslem population has always been administered by the Islamic law courts, which form the Sharia Divisions of the Court of Appeal, High Courts and Kadis Courts; President of the Sharia Division is the Grand Kadi. In Dec. 1990 the government announced that Sharia would be applied in the non-Moslem southern parts of the country as well.

Criminal Justice is administered by the courts constituted under the Code of Criminal Procedure, namely major courts, minor courts and magistrates' courts. Serious crimes are tried by major courts, which are composed of a President and 2 members and have the power to pass the death sentence. Major Courts are, as a rule, presided over by a Judge of the High Court appointed to a Provincial Circuit or a Province Judge. There is a right of appeal to the Chief Justice against any decision or order of a Major Court, and all its findings and sentences are subject to confirmation by him.

Lesser crimes are tried by Minor Courts consisting of 3 Magistrates and presided over by a Second Class Magistrate, and by Magistrates' Courts.

Religion. Islam is the state religion. In 1992 there were 21·9m. Sunni Moslems, concentrated in the north, and 2·4m. Christians and some 5m. traditionalist animists in the south.

Education (1985). 6,707 primary schools had 1·7m. pupils; there were 490,583 pupils in 2,167 secondary schools and 28,985 in tertiary education. In 1995-96 there were 17 universities, 2 Islamic universities, 1 university of science and technology and an institute of advanced banking. There were also 14 colleges or other institutions of higher education.

Health. In 1981 the Ministry of Health maintained 158 hospitals (with 17,205 beds), 887 dispensaries, 1,619 dressing stations and 220 health centres. There were 2,122 doctors and 12,871 nurses.

DIPLOMATIC REPRESENTATIVES

Of Sudan in Great Britain (3 Cleveland Row, London, SW1A 1DD)
Ambassador: Omer Bireedo.

Of Great Britain in Sudan (PO Box No. 801, Khartoum)
Ambassador: Alan Goulty.

Of Sudan in the USA (2210 Massachusetts Ave., NW, Washington, D.C., 20008)
Ambassador: Vacant.

Of the USA in Sudan (Sharia Ali Abdul Latif POB 699, Khartoum)
Ambassador: Timothy M. Carney.

Of Sudan to the United Nations
Ambassador: Sayed Ali Mohamed Osman Yassin.

Further Reading

Craig, G. M. (ed.) *Agriculture of the Sudan.* OUP, 1991
Daly, M. W., *Sudan.* [Bibliography] Oxford and Santa Barbara (CA), 1983
Gurdon, C., *Sudan in Transition: A Political Risk Analysis.* London, 1986
Halasa, A., *et al. The Return to Democracy in Sudan.* Geneva, 1986
Holt, P. M., *A Modern History of the Sudan.* New York, 3rd ed. 1979
Khalid, M., *The Government They Deserve: the Role of the Elite in Sudan's Political Evolution.* London, 1990
Woodward, P., *Sudan, 1898-1989: the Unstable State.* London, 1991

SURINAME

Republic of Suriname

Capital: Paramaribo
Population: 402,900 (1994)
GNP per capita: US$870 (1994)
HDI/world rank: 0·762/77 (1992)

KEY HISTORICAL EVENTS. For the colonial history of Suriname *see* THE STATESMAN'S YEAR-BOOK, 1991–92, p. 1154. On 25 Nov. 1975, Suriname gained independence. Following a period of military rule, Suriname returned to democracy in Jan. 1988 following elections in Nov. 1987, but on 24 Dec. 1990 a further military coup deposed the government. Ronald Venetiaan was elected President in Sept. 1991.

The government and rebel guerilla groups reached a peace agreement in Aug. 1992.

TERRITORY AND POPULATION. Suriname is bounded in the north by the Atlantic Ocean, east by French Guiana, west by Guyana, and south by Brazil. Area, 163,820 sq. km. Census population (1980), 355,240. Estimate (1994) 402,900. The capital, Paramaribo, had (1993 estimate) 200,970 inhabitants.

Suriname is divided into 10 districts (with chief town): Brokopondo (Brokopondo), Commewijne (Nieuw Amsterdam), Coronie (Totness), Marowijne (Albina), Nickerie (Nieuw Nickerie), Para (Onverwacht), Paramaribo (Paramaribo), Saramacca (Groningen), Sipalwini (local authority in Paramaribo), Wanica (Lelydorp).

Major ethnic groups in percentages of the population in 1991: Creole, 35%; Indian, 33%; Javanese, 16%; Bushnegroes (Blacks),10%; Amerindian, 3%.

The official language is Dutch. English is widely spoken next to Hindi, Javanese and Chinese as inter-group communication. A vernacular, called 'Sranan' or 'Surinamese', is used as a lingua franca. In 1976 it was announced that Spanish would become the nation's principal working language.

CLIMATE. The climate is equatorial, with uniformly high temperatures and rainfall. There is no recognized dry season. Paramaribo. Jan. 80°F (26·7°C), July 81°F (27·2°C). Annual rainfall 3083·6 mm.

CONSTITUTION AND GOVERNMENT. A new Constitution was approved by referendum in Sept. 1987.

Elections were held in May 1991. The electorate was 0·2m. The New Front Coalition won 30 seats, the National Democratic Party (supported by the Army), 12, and the new coalition of smaller parties, the Democratic Alternative '91, 9. As the two-thirds majority necessary to elect the president was not attained, an electoral assembly of 860 national and local representatives was elected, which elected Ronald Venetiaan by 645 votes against 2 opponents to become *President* for a 5-year term on 16 Sept. 1991.

In Jan. 1996 the government consisted of:

President: Ronald Venetiaan (b. 1936; Front for Democracy Coalition).

Vice-President: Jules Ajodhia.

Labour: J. Kross. *Foreign Affairs:* Subhas Mungra. *Defence:* Siegfried Gilds. *Finance:* Humphrey Hildenberg. *Justice and Police:* Soeshiel Girjasing. *Natural Resources:* Franco Demon. *Education:* Gerard Hiwat. *Public Works:* Radj Koemar Randjietsing. *Planning and Development Co-operation:* R. Assen. *Regional Affairs:* R. van Russel. *Agriculture, Animal Husbandry and Fisheries:* J. Sisal. *Transport, Communications and Tourism:* John Defares. *Public Health:* Mohamed Khudabux. *Home Affairs:* S. Sabiran. *Social Affairs:* W. Soemita. *Trade and Industry:* Richard Kalloe.

National flag: Horizontally green, red and green with the red of double width with a yellow 5-pointed star in the centre of the red bar.

National anthem: 'God zij met ons Suriname' ('God be with our Suriname'); words by C. A. Hoekstra, tune by J. C. de Puy. There is a Sranan version, 'Opo kondreman oen opo Sranan'; words by H. de Ziel.

DEFENCE

Army. The armed forces consist of 1 infantry and 1 military police battalion and 1 mechanized cavalry squadron with a total strength of about 1,400 in 1996. Equipment includes 1 PC-7 armed trainer, 3 Defender and 1 Cessna 310 twin-engined light transports operated alongside 1 Alouette III and 1 Cessna 172 liaison aircraft. Officers' ranks were abolished in Feb. 1986.

Navy. The flotilla comprises 5 inshore patrol craft, as well as 3 river patrol boats, all built in the Netherlands. In 1995 personnel totalled 240.

INTERNATIONAL RELATIONS

Membership. Suriname is a member of the UN, OAS, CARICOM and is an ACP state of the EU.

ECONOMY

Budget. 1993 revenue was (in 1m. Sf) 2,097·7, made up of direct taxes, 539·1; indirect taxes, 383; bauxite levy and other revenues, 314·2; aid, 861·4. Total expenditure was 2,912·8, made up of wages and salaries, 1,063·7; materials, 701·8; transfers, 585·7; interest, 219·2; development expenditure, 335·8; loans, 6·6.

Currency. The unit of currency is the *Suriname guilder* (SRG; written as Sf[lorin]) of 100 *cents*. There are coins of 1, 5, 10 and 25 cents and 1 and 2·5 Sf, and notes of 5, 10, 25, 100, 250, 500 and 1,000 Sf. In March 1996, £1 sterling = 626·64 Sf; US$1 = 410·00 Sf; DM1 = 277·78 Sf.

Banking and Finance. The Central Bank of Suriname is a bankers' bank and also the bank of issue. There are 3 commercial banks; the Suriname People's Credit Bank operates under the auspices of the Government. There is a post office savings bank, a mortgage bank, an investment bank, a long-term investments agency, a National Development Bank and an Agrarian Bank.

Weights and Measures. The metric system is in force.

ENERGY AND NATURAL RESOURCES

Electricity. Production (1994) 1,352m. kWh.

Oil. Crude oil production (1992) 0·2m. tonnes.

Minerals. Bauxite is the most important mineral. Production (1994), 3,703,000 tonnes.

Agriculture. Agriculture is restricted to the alluvial coastal zone; cultivated area in 1992, 87,120 ha. The staple food crop is rice; 68,750 ha of paddy were planted in 1992. Production (1994, in 1,000 tonnes): Paddy, 217·9; rice, 80·6; oranges, 15·1; grapefruit, 1·2; other citrus fruit, 2·9; bananas, 18·2; plantains, 47·5; vegetables, 38·3; coconuts, 10·9; cassava, 6·4; rootcrops, 8·7.

Livestock (1994, in 1,000): Cattle, 86·7; sheep and goats, 13·7; pigs, 29·3; poultry, 3,100.

Forestry. Forests cover 14·9m. ha. Production in 1994 was 100,497 cu. metres.

Fisheries. The fish catch in 1993 amounted to 12,111 tonnes.

INDUSTRY. There are aluminium smelting, food-processing and wood-using industries. Production, 1994: Cement, 24,665 tons[1]; palm oil, 1,051,000 litres[1];

beer (1993), 10,685,000 litres; alumina, 1,498,000 tonnes; aluminium, 26,700 tonnes; cigarettes, 443m.; shoes, 98,990 pairs[1]; plywood, 6,864 sq. metres.

[1]Estimate.

FOREIGN ECONOMIC RELATIONS

Commerce. In 1993 (provisional) imports totalled 1,798·4m. Sf. and exports, 2,142·2m. Sf. Principal imports, 1993 (in 1m. Sf): Raw materials and semi-manufactured goods, 661·5; fuels and lubricants, 593·4; investment goods, 277·6; foodstuffs, 45·1; cars and motorcycles, 37·9; textiles, 10. Principal exports, 1993 (in 1m. Sf.): Alumina, 1,701·8; aluminium, 258·8; shrimps, 62·8; rice, 48·8; bananas and plantains, 14·6; wood and wood products, 3·3.

In 1993 (provisional) exports, including re-exports, (in 1m. Sf) were mainly to the USA (616·1), Netherlands (601·4), Norway (486·8), Brazil (365·9), Japan (53·5) and UK (13·8); imports were mainly from the USA (787·6), Trinidad and Tobago (333·7), Netherlands Antilles (231), Japan (27·9), Netherlands (23·1), Brazil (14·2) and UK (10·2).

Total trade between Suriname and UK (British Department of Trade returns, in £1,000 sterling):

	1991	*1992*	*1993*	*1994*	*1995*
Imports to UK	9,922	11,531	14,232	17,447	22,992
Exports and re-exports from UK	7,896	11,521	6,289	9,163	7,536

COMMUNICATIONS

Roads. There are 1,335 km of main roads. In 1994 there were 42,169 passenger cars, 15,360 goods vehicles, 1,629 buses, 832 motor cycles and 24,294 mopeds.

Railways. There are 2 single-track railways.

Civil Aviation. There is an international airport at Paramaribo (Johan Adolf Pengel). The national carrier is Suriname Airways, which had 3 aircraft in 1995. Services are also maintained by Air Aruba, Air France, Cruzeiro Gamair and KLM. In 1994 there were 68,221 passenger arrivals and 72,952 departures.

Shipping. The Royal Netherlands Steamship Co. operates services to the Netherlands, the USA and regionally. The Suriname Navigation Co. maintains services from Paramaribo to Georgetown, Cayenne and the Caribbean area.

Telecommunications. In 1994 there were 50,134 telephones. The government controls the partly commercial Stichting Radio Omroep Suriname and Radio Suriname Internationaal, and Surinaamse Televisie. In 1991 there were 0·25m. radio and 40,000 TV sets (colour by NTSC). There are 6 broadcasting and 1 television stations.

Press (1987). There were 2 daily newspapers.

SOCIAL INSTITUTIONS

Justice. There is a court of justice, whose members are nominated by the President. There are 3 cantonal courts.

Religion. There is entire religious liberty. At the 1980 census the main religious bodies were: Hindus, 97,170; Roman Catholics, 80,922; Moslems, 69,638; Moravian Brethren, 55,625; Reformed, 6,265; Lutheran, 2,695; Jehovah's Witnesses, 1,626; Seventh Day Adventists, 1,061; others, 24,627.

Education. In 1992–93 there were 223 primary schools with 3,079 teachers and 71,246 pupils, and there were 1,401 teachers and 22,886 pupils at 86 secondary schools. In 1995–96 the university had 1,335 students and 155 academic staff. There is a training college with (1991–92) 1,478 students.

Health. There were (1994) 1,390 general hospital beds and 251 physicians.

DIPLOMATIC REPRESENTATIVES

Of Suriname in Great Britain
Ambassador: Evert Azimullah (resides in The Hague).

Of Great Britain in Suriname
Ambassador: D. J. Johnson (resides in Georgetown).

Of Suriname in the USA (4301 Connecticut Ave., NW, Washington, D.C., 20008)
Ambassador: Willem A. Udenhout.

Of the USA in Suriname (Dr Sophie Redmondstraat 129, Paramaribo)
Ambassador: Roger Gamble.

Of Suriname to the United Nations
Ambassador: Vacant.

Further Reading

Dew, E. M., *Trouble in Suriname, 1975–1993*. New York, 1995
Hoefte, R. A. L., *Suriname*: [Bibliography]. Oxford and Santa Barbara (CA), 1990

National statistical office: Algemeen Bureau voor de Statistiek, POB244, Paramaribo.

SWAZILAND

Umbuso weSwatini—
Kingdom of Swaziland

Capital: Mbabane
Population: 818,000 (1993)
GNP per capita: US$1,160 (1994)
HDI/world rank: 0·522/124 (1992)

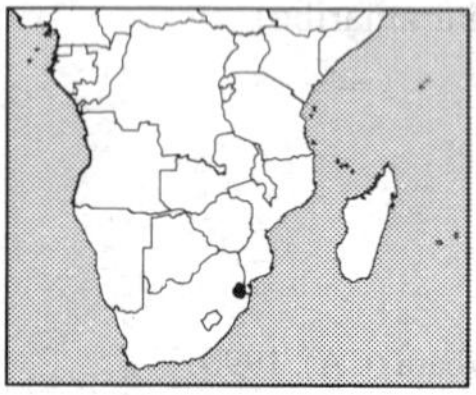

KEY HISTORICAL EVENTS. Swaziland became independent on 6 Sept. 1968 (For pre-independence history *see* THE STATESMAN'S YEAR-BOOK, 1994–95, p. 1239).

TERRITORY AND POPULATION. Swaziland is bounded on the north, west and south by South Africa, and on the east by Mozambique. The area is 6,705 sq. miles (17,400 sq. km). Population (census 1986), 681,059. 1993 estimate, 818,000. Main urban areas with 1986 census populations: Mbabane, the administrative capital (38,290); Manzini (18,084); Big Bend (9,676); Mhlume (6,509); Havelock Mine (4,850); Nhlangano (4,107). The legislative capital is Lobamba.

The population is 84% Swazi and 10% Zulu. The official languages are Swazi and English.

CLIMATE. A temperate climate with two seasons. Nov. to March is the wet season, when temperatures range from mild to hot, with frequent thunderstorms. The cool, dry season from May to Sept. is characterised by clear, bright sunny days. Mbabane. Jan. 68°F (20°C), July 54°F (12·2°C). Annual rainfall 56" (1,402 mm).

ROYAL HOUSE. The reigning King is **Mswati III** (b. 1968; crowned 25 April 1986), who succeeded his father, King Sobhuza II (reigned 1921–82). The King rules in conjunction with the Queen Mother (his mother, or a senior wife).

CONSTITUTION AND GOVERNMENT. There is a *House of Assembly* of 65 members, 55 of whom are elected and 10 appointed by the King, and an *Upper House* of 30 senators, 10 of whom are elected by the House of Assembly and 20 appointed by the King. Elections are held in 2 rounds, the second being a run-off between the 5 candidates who come first in each constituency.

There is also a traditional Swazi National Council headed by the King and Queen Mother at which all Swazi men are entitled to be heard.

At the elections of 26 Sept. and 11 Oct. 1993 the electorate was 283,693. There were 2,094 candidates.

In March 1996, the Cabinet was composed as follows:

Prime Minister: Prince Mbilini Dlamini.

Deputy Prime Minister: Dr Sishayi Nxumalo. *Foreign Affairs:* Auther Khoza. *Labour and Public Service:* Albert Shabangu. *Agriculture:* Chief Dambuza Lukhele. *Commerce and Industry:* Majahenkhaba Dlamini. *Works and Construction:* Prince Mahlalengangeni Dlamini. *Education:* Solomon Dlamini. *Health:* Muntu Mswane. *Justice:* Chief Maweni Simelane. *Home Affairs:* Prince Sobandla Dlamini. *Natural Resources, Land Utilization and Energy:* Absalom Dlamini. *Transport and Communications:* Ephraem Magagula. *Broadcasting, Information and Tourism:* Prince Khuzulwandle Dlamini. *Economic Planning and Development:* Themba Masuku. *Finance:* Derek Von Wissel. *Housing and Township Development:* John Carmichael.

National flag. Horizontally 5 unequal stripes of blue, yellow, crimson, yellow, blue; in the centre of the crimson strip an African shield of black and white, behind which are 2 assegais and a staff, all laid horizontally.

National anthem. 'Nkulunkulu mnikati wetibusiso temaSwati' ('O Lord our God bestower of blessings upon the Swazi'); words by A. E. Simelane, tune by D. K. Rycroft.

Local Government. The country is divided into the 4 regions of Shiselweni, Lubombo, Manzini and Hhohho. They are administered by Regional Administrators.

DEFENCE

Army Air Wing. There are 2 Israeli-built Arava light twin-turboprop transports with underwing weapon attachments for light attack duties.

INTERNATIONAL RELATIONS

Membership. Swaziland is a member of the UN, OAU, SADC, the Commonwealth and is an ACP state of the EU.

ECONOMY

Budget. Revenue and expenditure (in 1m. emalangeni) for financial years ending 31 March:

	1990–91	*1991–92*	*1992–93*	*1993–94*
Revenue	756·4	816·1	890·3	1,089·4
Expenditure	755·8	794·9	932·6	1,209·3

Currency. The unit of currency is the *lilangeni* (plural *emalangeni*) (SZL) of 100 *cents* but Swaziland remains in the Common (formerly Rand) Monetary Area and the South African rand is legal tender. There are coins of 1, 2, 5, 10, 20, 50 and 100 cents and notes of 2, 5, 10, 20 and 50 emalangeni. In 1990 48·2m. emalangeni were in circulation. In March 1996, £1 = 5·95; US$1 = 3·90; DM1 = 2·64 emalangeni.

Banking and Finance. The central bank and bank of issue is the Central Bank of Swaziland, established in 1974. There were 24 commercial banks in 1992. Foreign banks include Barclay's, Standard Chartered and Meridien. The Swaziland Development and Savings Bank concentrates on agricultural and housing loans. Total assets of the above were 1·05m. emalangeni in 1992. The Swaziland Building Society had assets of 84·6m. emalangeni in 1990–91.

In 1990 Swaziland Stock Brokers was established to trade in stocks and shares for institutional and private clients.

ENERGY AND NATURAL RESOURCES

Electricity. Production (1993), 366m. kWh.

Minerals. Output (in tonnes) in 1994: Coal, 227,730; asbestos, 26,720; quarry stone, 185,401 cu. metres. Diamond production was worth 15·2m. emalangeni in 1990 (20m. in 1989).

Agriculture. In 1993–94 the cultivated area was 178,121 ha and the grazing area 1,452,116 ha. Production (1993–94, in tonnes): Sugar-cane, 3,647,244; citrus, 88,263; pineapples, 19,700; tobacco, 394; seed cotton, 6,294; maize, 85,748; sorghum, 1,830; tomatoes, 242.

Livestock (1994): Cattle, 626,400; goats, 495,200; sheep, 27,000; poultry, 0·9m.

Forestry. The commercial forest area was 96,300 ha in 1993-94. Wood pulp output was 170,846 tonnes in 1993.

INDUSTRY. Most industries are based on processing agricultural products and timber. Footwear and textiles are also manufactured, and some engineering products.

Labour. The formal labour force numbered 93,496 in 1993; 20,041 Swazis worked in gold mines in South Africa.

Trade Unions. In 1992 there were 18 unions grouped in the Swaziland Federation of Trade Unions.

FOREIGN ECONOMIC RELATIONS. Swaziland has a customs union with South Africa and receives a *pro rata* share of the dues collected.

Commerce. In 1993 exports (in E1,000) were 2,156,075; imports, 3,593,041. Exports in 1991 included sugar, 411,572; unbleached wood pulp, 189,130; canned fruits, 67,273; asbestos, 13,762. Imports in 1993 included machinery and transport equipment, 802,241; minerals, fuels and lubricants, 309,948; manufactured items, 528,313; food and live animals, 451,543.

Total trade between Swaziland and UK (British Department of Trade returns, in £1,000 sterling):

	1991	*1992*	*1993*	*1994*	*1995*
Imports to UK	39,607	40,101	42,187	42,034	39,714
Exports and re-exports from UK	4,336	3,226	2,887	3,287	3,023

Tourism. There were 287,023 visitors in 1993.

COMMUNICATIONS

Roads. Total length of roads (1994), 2,885 km, of which 814 km were tarred.

Railways. In 1995 the system comprised 301 km of route, and carried 4,287,000 tonnes of freight in 1994–95.

Civil Aviation. There is an international airport at Manzini (Matsapha). The national carrier, Royal Swazi National Airways is 50% state-owned, and had 2 aircraft in 1995. Services are also provided by Air Zimbabwe, Commercial Airways and LAM.

Telecommunications. There were (1987) 71 post offices, 2 telegraph stations and 29 postal agencies. In 1994 there were 35,534 telephones, 18,605 exchange connexions and 239 telex exchange connexions. The Broadcasting Corporation and Swaziland Television Authority are government-owned. Swaziland Broadcasting Services run on a semi-commercial basis. In 1992 there were some 60,000 radio and 12,500 television receivers (colour by PAL).

Cinemas. There were 5 cinemas in 1980 with a total seating capacity of 1,625.

Press. In 1992 there were 3 daily and 3 weekly newspapers and several periodicals, all in English except 1 daily in Swazi.

SOCIAL INSTITUTIONS

Justice. The constitutional courts practice Roman-Dutch law. The judiciary is headed by the Chief Justice. There is a High Court and various Magistrates and Courts. A Court of Appeal with a President and 3 Judges deals with appeals from the High Court. There are 16 courts of first instance. There are also traditional Swazi National Courts.

Religion. In 1984 there were about 0·12m. Christians and about 30,000 adults holding traditional beliefs.

Education. Education is not compulsory, but government-funded primary schools (for 6 to 13-year olds) are within reach of every child. About half the children of secondary school age attend school. There are also private schools. In 1994 there were 686 schools with 192,599 pupils in primary and 52,571 in secondary and high school classes.

The University of Swaziland, at Matsapha, had 2,132 students in 1994–95. There are 3 teacher training colleges (total enrolment in 1994–95, 857) and 8 vocational institutions (1,150 students and 147 teachers in 1991). There is also an institute of management.

Health. In 1984 there were 80 doctors, 13 dentists and 1,608 hospital beds.

DIPLOMATIC REPRESENTATIVES

Of Swaziland in Great Britain (58 Pont St., London SW1X 0AE)
High Commissioner: Percy Mngomezulu.

Of Great Britain in Swaziland (Allister Miller St., Mbabane)
High Commissioner: John Doble.

Of Swaziland in the USA (3400 International Dr., NW, Washington, D.C., 20008)
Ambassador: Mary M. Khanya.

Of the USA in Swaziland (PO Box 199, Mbabane)
Ambassador: John T. Sprott.

Of Swaziland to the United Nations
Ambassador: Mathendele Dlamini.

Further Reading

Booth, A., *Swaziland: Tradition and Change in a Southern African Kingdom.* Aldershot and Boulder (CO), 1984

Funnell, D. C., *Under the Shadow of Apartheid: Agrarian Transformation in Swaziland.* Avebury, 1991

Grotpeter, J. J., *Historical Dictionary of Swaziland.* Metuchen, 1975

Matsebula, J. S. M., *A History of Swaziland.* 3rd ed. London, 1992

Nyeko, B., *Swaziland.* [Bibliography] 2nd ed. Oxford and Santa Barbara (CA), 1994

National statistical office: Central Statistical Office, POB 456, Mbabane.

SWEDEN

Konungariket Sverige
(Kingdom of Sweden)

Capital: Stockholm
Population: 8·82m. (1995)
GNP per capita: US$23,630 (1994)
HDI/world rank: 0·929/10 (1992)

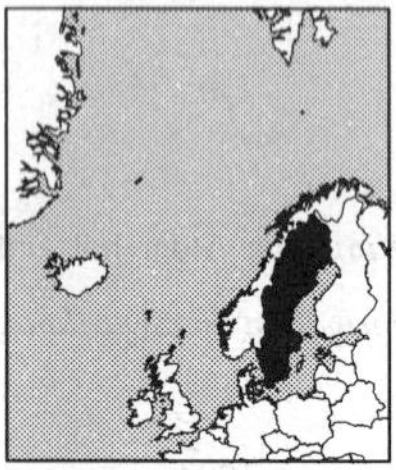

KEY HISTORICAL EVENTS. Organized as an independent unified state in the 10th century, Sweden became a constitutional mon-archy in 1809. In 1809 Finland was ceded to Russia. In 1815 German lands were ceded to Prussia. Sweden was united with Norway until 1905.

TERRITORY AND POPULATION. Sweden is bounded in the west and north-west by Norway, east by Finland and the Gulf of Bothnia, south-east by the Baltic Sea and south-west by the Kattegat. The area is 449,964 sq. km. At the 1990 census the population was 8,587,353. Estimate, 31 Dec. 1994, 8,816,381 (4,460,127 females). About 80–85% of the population live in the densely populated areas.

Area, population and population density of the 24 counties (*län*).

	Land area (in sq. km)	*Population (1985 census)*	*Estimated population 31 Dec. 1994*	*Density per sq. km 31 Dec. 1994*
Stockholm	6,490	1,577,596	1,708,502	263
Uppsala	6,989	251,754	286,642	41
Södermanland	6,062	249,885	259,793	43
Östergötland	10,562	393,668	415,603	39
Jönköping	9,944	300,892	312,494	31
Kronoberg	8,458	174,025	180,747	21
Kalmar	11,171	238,406	244,057	22
Gotland	3,140	56,180	58,237	19
Blekinge	2,941	151,055	153,016	52
Kristianstad	6,089	280,516	294,571	48
Malmöhus	4,938	750,294	811,415	164
Halland	5,454	240,090	268,067	49
Göteborg and Bohus	5,141	747,849	764,594	149
Älvsborg	11,395	426,769	449,767	39
Skaraborg	7,937	270,530	279,921	35
Värmland	17,586	279,503	285,498	16
Örebro	8,517	270,384	276,828	33
Västmanland	6,302	254,858	261,753	42
Kopparberg	28,193	284,029	291,203	10
Gävleborg	18,192	289,452	289,654	16
Västernorrland	21,678	262,555	260,295	12
Jämtland	49,443	134,161	136,301	3
Västerbotten	55,401	245,302	259,775	5
Norrbotten	98,911	262,443	267,648	3

There are some 17,000 Sami (Lapps). A parliament, the *Sameting*, was instituted for these in 1993.

On 31 Dec. 1994 aliens in Sweden numbered 537,441. Of these, 106,682 were Finns, 47,673 Bosnians, 40,368 Yugoslavs, 32,985 Norwegians, 32,670 Iranians, 26,674 Danes, 21,995 Turks, 16,070 Poles, 14,097 Chileans, 13,092 Germans, 10,991 Britons, 10,480 Somalis, 9,101 Americans, 7,681 Ethiopians, 6,640 Lebanese, 4,919 Icelanders, 4,823 Greeks and 4,706 Romanians.

Vital statistics for calendar years:

	Total living births	*To mothers single, divorced or widowed*	*Stillborn*	*Marriages*	*Divorces*	*Deaths exclusive of still-born*
1992	122,848	60,771	396	37,173	22,571	94,710
1993	117,998	59,489	400	34,005	22,296	97,008
1994	112,257	57,927	348	34,203	22,740	91,844

Expectation of life in 1994: Males, 75 years; females, 81.

Immigration: 1992, 45,348; 1993, 61,872; 1994, 83,598. Emigration: 1992, 25,726; 1993, 29,874; 1994, 32,661.

Population of the 50 largest communities, 31 Dec. 1994:

Stockholm	703,627	Södertälje	81,890	Kalmar	58,070
Göteborg	444,553	Karlstad	78,915	Falun	55,014
Malmö	242,706	Skellefteå	75,822	Solna	54,159
Uppsala	181,191	Huddinge	76,379	Mölndal	53,859
Linköping	130,489	Kristianstad	73,543	Sollentuna	53,897
Örebro	118,606	Växjö	72,432	Trollhättan	52,275
Västerås	122,998	Luleå	70,694	Varberg	54,412
Norrköping	123,240	Botkyrka	69,195	Hässleholm	49,824
Jönköping	114,811	Nacka	69,121	Norrtälje	49,975
Helsingborg	113,411	Haninge	64,676	Skövde	49,164
Borås	96,123	Karlskrona	60,642	Uddevalla	48,859
Umeå	99,249	Östersund	59,730	Nyköping	48,674
Sundsvall	94,815	Kungsbacka	60,329	Borlänge	48,171
Lund	95,895	Örnsköldsvik	58,663	Motala	42,811
Eskilstuna	89,761	Täby	58,686	Piteå	41,021
Gävle	90,270	Gotland	58,237	Västervik	39,770
Halmstad	83,080	Järfälla	58,196		

Source: Statistics Sweden

CLIMATE. The north has severe winters, with snow lying for 4–7 months. Summers are fine but cool, with long daylight hours. Further south, winters are less cold, summers are warm and rainfall well-distributed throughout the year, with a slight summer maximum. Stockholm. Jan. 3·2°C, July 18·4°C. Annual rainfall 385 mm.

ROYAL FAMILY. The reigning King is **Carl XVI Gustaf**, b. 30 April 1946, succeeded on the death of his grandfather Gustaf VI Adolf, 15 Sept. 1973, married 19 June 1976 to *Silvia* Renate Sommerlath, b. 23 Dec. 1943 (Queen of Sweden). *Daughter* and *Heir Apparent:* Crown Princess Victoria Ingrid Alice Désirée, Duchess of Västergötland, b. 14 July 1977; *son:* Prince Carl Philip Edmund Bertil, Duke of Värmland, b. 13 May 1979; *daughter:* Princess Madeleine Thérèse Amelie Josephine, Duchess of Hälsingland and Gästrikland, b. 10 June 1982.

Sisters of the King. Princess Margaretha, b. 31 Oct. 1934, married 30 June 1964 to John Ambler; Princess Birgitta (Princess of Sweden), b. 19 Jan. 1937, married 25 May 1961 (civil marriage) and 30 May 1961 (religious ceremony) to Johann Georg, Prince of Hohenzollern; Princess Désirée, b. 2 June 1938, married 5 June 1964 to Baron Niclas Silfverschiöld; Princess Christina, b. 3 Aug. 1943, married 15 June 1974 to Tord Magnuson.

Uncles of the King. Count Sigvard Bernadotte of Wisborg, b. on 7 June 1907; Prince Bertil, Duke of Halland, b. on 28 Feb. 1912, married 7 Dec. 1976 to Lilian May Davies, b. 30 Aug. 1915 (Princess of Sweden, Duchess of Halland); Count Carl Johan, Bernadotte of Wisborg, b. on 31 Oct. 1916.

Aunt of the King. Princess Ingrid (Princess of Sweden, Dowager Queen of Denmark), b. 28 March 1910, married 24 May 1935 to Frederik, Crown Prince of Denmark (King Frederik IX), died 14 Jan. 1972.

The royal family receive a tax-free annual allowance of 10m. krona from the civil list; this does not include the maintenance of the royal palaces, furniture or royal art collections.

CONSTITUTION AND GOVERNMENT. Under the 1975 Constitution Sweden is a representative and parliamentary democracy. The King is Head of State, but does not participate in government. Parliament is the single-chamber *Riksdag* of 349 members elected for a period of 4 years in direct, general elections.

The manner of election to the *Riksdag* is proportional. The country is divided into 29 constituencies. In these constituencies 310 members are elected. The remaining 39 seats constitute a nation-wide pool intended to give absolute proportionality to parties that receive at least 4% of the votes. A party receiving less than 4% of the votes in the country is, however, entitled to participate in the distribution of seats in a constituency, if it has obtained at least 12% of the votes cast there.

At the elections of 18 Sept. 1994 turn-out was 86%. The Social Democratic Party (SDP) won 162 seats with 45·3% of votes cast (138 with 37·6% in 1991), the Moderate Party 80 with 22·4% (80 with 21·9%), the Centre Party 27 with 7·7% (31 with 8·5%), the Liberal Party 26 with 7·2% (33 with 9·1%), the Left Party (ex-Communists) 22 with 6·2% (16 with 4·5%), the Green Party 18 with 5% and the Christian Democratic Party 14 with 4·1% (26 with 7·1%).

A minority Social Democratic government was formed in Oct. 1994, which in May 1996 comprised:

Prime Minister: Göran Persson (b.1949).

Minister with Special Responsibility for Co-ordination: Jan Nygren. *Justice:* Laila Freivalds. *Foreign Affairs:* Lena Hjelm-Wallén. *International Development Co-operation with Special Responsibility for support to Central and Eastern Europe:* Pierre Schori. *Defence:* Thage G. Peterson. *Health and Social Affairs:* Ingela Thalén. *Transport and Communications:* Ines Uusmann. *Finance:* Erik Åsbrink. *Education:* Carl Tham. *Schools and Adult Education:* Ylva Johansson. *Agriculture:* Vacant. *Labour:* Margareta Winberg. *Minister with Special Responsibility for Refugee and Immigration Policy:* Leif Blomberg. *Industry and Commerce:* Sten Heckscher. *Minister with Special Responsibility for Housing and Energy Policy:* Jörgen Andersson. *Public Administration:* Marita Ulvskog. *Environment and Physical Planning:* Anna Lindh. *Cultural Affairs:* Margot Wallström.

The *Speaker* is Birgitta Dahl.

The main function of government ministries is to prepare the decisions of the Cabinet; such decisions may concern bills for the *Riksdag,* general government directives and higher appointments. Only to a small extent does the Cabinet make individual administrative decisions.

National flag: Blue with a yellow Scandinavian cross.

National anthem: 'Du gamla, du fria, du fjällhöga nord' ('Thou ancient, thou free, thou mountainous north'); words by R. Dybeck; folk-tune.

The official language is Swedish. The capital is Stockholm.

Regional and Local Government. The country is divided into 24 counties (*län*), in each of which the central government is represented by a state county administrative board (*länsstyrelse*). The governor (*landshövding*), appointed by the government, is chairman of the board, which in addition to the governor has 14 members elected by the county council.

Local government and the levying of local taxes are based on the Constitution and regulated by the local government act and special acts. According to the local government act Sweden is divided into municipalities with elected councils. The number of municipalities has, since 1951, been reduced from about 2,500 to 288 in 1995. The municipalities deal with social welfare, education and culture, public health, town planning, housing etc. Each county, except Gotland, which consists of only one municipality, has an elected county council (*landsting*). The county councils chiefly administer the health services and medical care. The municipalities of Göteborg and Malmö do not belong to county councils. The parishes, 2,545 in 1995, are the local units of the Church of Sweden and have the same status in public law as the municipalities. The parochial church council (*kyrkofullmäktige*) is the supreme decision-making body in most parishes, whose members are publicly elected. Small parishes have instead the parish meeting, a form of direct democracy.

Regional and local elections took place simultaneously with the parliamentary elections on 18 Sept. 1994.

DEFENCE. A Supreme Commander is, under the Government, in command of the three services. He is assisted by the Swedish Armed Forces HQ.

There is conscription for males of 7½-15 months. Refresher training (3–34 days) is obligatory.

Army. The peace-time Army consists for training purposes of 38 armoured, cavalry, infantry, artillery and other units. On mobilization to a war footing the Field Army comprises 6 divisional HQs, 6 infantry, 4 Arctic, 1 mechanized Arctic, 2 armoured and 3 mechanized brigades and 7 artillery regiments. There are also Territorial Defence units. Equipment includes 338 Centurion and 289 Strv-103B main battle tanks. The Army Aviation Corps comprises 2 battalions operating 6 Bulldog aircraft and 18 JetRanger helicopters for observation, 20 armed BO 105 helicopters, 10 AB.204B and 5 AB.412 transport helicopters, plus 26 Hughes 300C helicopters for training and observation duties.

There is a voluntary Home Guard with a strength of 125,000, ready for action within 2 hours.

The active personnel of the Army comprised (1996) about 45,000 (23,700 conscripts).

Navy. Naval forces are divided between 2 branches: Navy, and Coastal Artillery. There are 4 Naval Command Areas, covering southern, eastern, western and northern coasts.

The Navy operates 13 diesel submarines, 4 Göteborg and 2 Stockholm class corvettes, 27 other missile craft, 12 inshore patrol craft, 2 minelayers, 7 minehunters, 1 coastal minesweeper and 16 inshore minesweepers. Auxiliaries include 2 mine countermeasures support ships, 1 electronic intelligence gatherer, 1 surveying vessel, 7 icebreakers, 2 tugs and 1 salvage vessel, as well as numerous service craft and boats.

The Coastal Artillery have 2 main tasks: Fixed coastal defence and mobile coastal defence. The fixed coastal defence is organized in Coast Artillery Brigades consisting of artillery up to 152 mm calibre and land-sea missiles. The mobile coastal artillery consists of 3 Mobile Artillery Battalions, 1 Missile Battalion and 6 Amphibious Battalions. The Coastal Artillery operates 9 coastal and 16 inshore minelayers, 18 small patrol craft and some 140 small amphibious craft.

The Naval Air Arm comprises 10 Boeing Vertol 107 helicopters and 8 AB-206 Jet-Ranger helicopters, and also 1 Aviocar fixed-wing aircraft for anti-submarine warfare and electronic surveillance.

The personnel of the Navy in 1996 totalled 9,000 (4,100 conscripts) of whom 2,400 serve in Coastal Defence.

A separate civil Coast Guard, 600 strong, operates some 70 inshore cutters, patrol boats and service craft and 4 aircraft.

Air Force. There are 3 air commands. After mobilization to a war footing the Air Force consists of 10 fighter, 6 medium attack/reconnaissance, 4 light attack, 4 central transport and 8 regional transport squadrons, 7 helicopter units, 24 air-base and 9 combat command control and air surveillance battalions. Combat aircraft include AJ 37, JA 37 and S 37 Viggens, J 35 Drakens, SK 60 trainers and 15 search-and-rescue helicopters. 6 JA 39 Gripen aircraft are delivered but were not yet deployed with units in 1996.

Strength (1996) 9,000 (4,100 conscripts), with 390 combat aircraft.

INTERNATIONAL RELATIONS

Membership. Sweden is a member of the UN, EU and the NATO Partnership for Peace.

ECONOMY

Budget. Revenue and expenditure of the total budget (Current and Capital) for financial years ending 30 June (in 1m. kr.):

	Revenue	*Expenditure*		*Revenue*	*Expenditure*
1990–91	403,487	437,987	1993–94	376,925	554,023
1991–92	397,725	478,483	1994–95	423,183	579,421
1992–93	377,743	565,548	1995–96	723,053	938,010

The revenue and expenditure for the financial year 1 July 1992 to 30 June 1993 was as follows (in 1m. kr.):

Revenue		*Expenditure*	
Taxes:		Royal Household and residences	65
Taxes on income, capital gains and profits	30,443	Justice	18,196
Statutory social security fees	64,677	Foreign Affairs	17,689
Taxes on property	25,520	Defence	38,191
Value-added tax and other taxes on goods and services	195,075	Health and Social Affairs	129,057
Total revenue from taxes	315,716	Transport and Communications	26,634
Non-tax revenue	29,779	Finance	125,520
Capital revenue	11,382	Education	36,191
Loan repayment	9,028	Agriculture	6,915
Computed revenue	11,020	Labour	39,882
Total revenue	376,925	Cultural Affairs	14,888
		Industry	4,306
		Civil Service Affairs	2,122
		Environment	2,180
		Parliament and agencies	706
		Interest on National Debt, etc.	94,736
		Unforeseen expenditure	6
		Total expenditure	554,023

In 1994-95 the national debt amounted to 1,370,401m. kr. VAT is 25% (reduced rate, 12%).

Currency. The unit of currency is the *krona* (SEK), of 100 *öre*. There are coins of 10 and 50 öre and 1 and 5 kronor, and notes of 10, 20, 50, 100, 500 and 1,000 kronor. Inflation was 1·9% in Dec. 1992. In March 1996, £1 = 10·34 kronor; US$1 = 6·76 kronor; DM1 = 4·58 kronor.

Banking and Finance. The central bank and bank of issue is the *Sveriges Riksbank*, whose *Governor* is appointed for 5 years by 8 trustees, 7 of whom are appointed by Parliament. The *Governor* is Urban Backström. The bank's capital and reserve fund are provided by its constitution. On 31 Dec. 1994 its note circulation amounted to 72,992m. kr.; its gold and foreign-exchange reserves totalled 177,964m. kr. In 1994 there were 23 commercial banks. On 31 Dec. 1994 their total deposits amounted to 743,859m. kr.; advances to the public amounted to 739,300m. kr. Of the 5 largest, Nordbanken and Gota Bank were merged into a single state-owned institution in 1993; the other 3 (Skandinavska Enskilda Bank, Swedbank and Svenska Handelsbank) remain private.

On 31 Dec. 1994 there were 91 savings banks.

There is a stock exchange in Stockholm.

Weights and Measures. The metric system is obligatory.

ENERGY AND NATURAL RESOURCES

Electricity. Sweden is rich in hydro-power resources. Electricity net production in 1994 was 137,651m. kWh. In 1993, 16,578 MW were produced in hydro-electric plants, 10,302 MW in nuclear plants and 8,761 MW in thermal plants. A referendum of 1980 called for the phasing out of nuclear power by 2010.

Minerals. Sweden is one of the leading producers of iron ore. There are also deposits of copper, lead and zinc. The total production of iron ores amounted to 10·3m. tonnes in 1993; the production of copper ore was 332,013 tonnes. In 1989, the production of lead ore was 215,490 tonnes, and of zinc ore 204,087 tonnes. In southern Sweden there are deposits of alum shale, containing oil and uranium.

Agriculture. According to the farm register which is revised annually the following data were provided for 1994: The number of farms in cultivation of more than 2 ha of arable land, was 90,102; of these there were 50,600 of 2–20 ha; 35,161 of 20–100 ha; 4,241 of above 100 ha. Of the total land area, 2,780,077 [1] ha were arable land and 339,156 [1] ha pasture.

[1] Figures refer to holdings of more than 2 ha of arable land.

Chief crops	*Area (1,000 ha)* [1] *1992*	*1993*	*1994*	*Production (1,000 tonnes) 1992*	*1993*	*1994*
Wheat	270·3	304·4	251·8	1,406	1,746	1,345
Rye	34·6	46·4	38·96	136	230	173
Barley	454·1	420·4	473·0	1,261	1,671	1,661
Oats	360·9	322·0	341·4	807	1,295	991
Potatoes	39·2	36·3	33·0	1,253	976	763
Sugarbeet	48·0	51·3	53·4	2,136	2,535	2,350
Tame hay	708·4	771·2	780·0	4,116	...	3,156
Oil seed	137·4	145·5	128·5	284	...	...

[1] Figures refer to holdings of more than 2 ha of arable land.

Total production of milk (in 1,000 tonnes): 1992, 3,201; 1993, 3,352; 1994, 3,421. Butter production in the same years was (in 1,000 tonnes): 62, 66, 66; and cheese 117, 126, 133.

Livestock (1994): Cattle, 1,826,489; sheep and lambs, 483,428; pigs, 2,328,405; poultry, 12,564,182. There were 279,869 reindeer in Sami villages in 1994.

Number of farm tractors in 1990, 183,000; combines in 1990, 47,000.

The number of pelts produced in 1989–90 (and in 1988–89) was: Fox, 33,472 (43,245); mink, 1·28m. (1·57m.); others, 6,190 (6,013).

Forestry. Forests form one of the country's greatest natural assets. The growing stock consists of 45% Norway spruce, 39% Scots pine and 15% deciduous trees. In 1992 forests covered 23,232,000 ha. Municipal and State ownership accounts for 37% of the forests, companies own 13%, and the remaining half is in private hands. In 1992–93, 50·8m. cu. metres (solid volume excluding bark) of wood were removed, including 25m. cu. metres of sawlogs and 21·5m. cu. metres of pulpwood. The production of woodpulp in 1992 was 9·6m. tonnes (dry weight).

Fisheries. In 1994 the total catch of the sea fisheries was 379,014 tonnes.

INDUSTRY. The most important manufacturing sector is the production of metals, metal products, machinery and transport equipment, covering almost half of the total value added by manufacturing. Production of high-quality steel is an old speciality. The production of ordinary steel is decreasing and is short of domestic demand. Aluminium, lead and copper are also produced. Metallurgy forms a base for the production of machinery of many sorts and transport equipment.

Another important manufacturing sector is based on forest resources. This sector includes saw-mills, plywood factories, joinery industries, pulp- and paper-mills, wallboard and particle board factories. A fast increasing sector is the chemical industry, especially the petro-chemical branch. Minerals industries include production of building materials and decorative arts products of glass and china.

Industry groups	*No. of establishments 1993*	*1992*	*Average no. of wage-earners 1993*	*1992*	*Sales value of production (gross) in 1m. kr. 1993*	*1992*
Mining and quarrying	*153*	*158*	*5,219*	*5,901*	*8,843*	*8,229*
Metal-ore mining	24	28	3,643	4,221	5,995	5,827
Other mining	129	130	1,576	1,680	2,848	2,403
Manufacturing	*8,109*	*8,835*	*371,958*	*415,231*	*787,704*	*635,314*
Manufacture of food, beverages and tobacco	848	858	44,420	45,771	110,699	90,039
Textile, wearing apparel and leather industries	318	371	9,662	11,661	10,432	9,452
Manufacture of wood and wood products including furniture	953	1,080	30,564	35,038	43,932	41,167
Manufacture of paper and paper products, printing and publishing	1,098	1,199	51,737	56,980	114,061	101,612
Manufacture of chemicals, petroleum, coal, rubber and plastic products	736	771	29,306	32,016	108,445	82,981

Industry groups	No. of establishments 1993	1992	Average no. of wage-earners 1993	1992	Sales value of production (gross) in 1m. kr. 1993	1992
Manufacture of non-metallic mineral products, except products of petroleum and coal	364	382	10,840	13,086	15,990	14,087
Basic metal industries	168	170	24,128	26,013	52,664	40,825
Manufacture of fabricated metal products, machinery and equipment	3,557	3,922	169,783	192,782	329,104	253,084
Other manufacturing industries	67	82	1,518	1,884	2,378	2,066

Source: Statistics Sweden

Labour. In 1994 there were 4·27m. persons in the labour force, of whom 3,927,000 were employed: 1,589,000 in service industries; 762,000 in mining, manufacturing, electricity and water services; 568,000 in trade, restaurants and hotels; 379,000 in finance, insurance, real estate and business services; 271,000 in transport and communication; 219,000 in construction; 135,000 in agriculture, forestry, hunting and fishing.

Trade Unions. The Swedish Trade Union Confederation (LO) had 21 member unions with a total membership of 2,230,490 at 31 Dec. 1994; the Central Government Organization of Salaried Employees (TCO) had 20, with 1,308,482; the Swedish Confederation of Professional Associations (SACO) had 25, with 384,773; the Central Organization of Swedish Workers had 12,390 members.

FOREIGN ECONOMIC RELATIONS. A policy of reducing foreign aid as an economy measure was announced in Sept. 1992. Since Jan. 1991 restrictions on foreign investment have been abolished, and an economic reform programme of Nov. 1991 permits foreigners to buy Swedish companies. Permission to operate in Sweden has not been needed since July 1992.

Commerce. Imports and exports (in 1m. kr.):

	1990	*1991*	*1992*	*1993*	*1994* [1]
Imports	323,875	301,290	290,929	334,257	397,741
Exports	339,852	332,779	326,031	388,290	471,217

[1] Provisional.

Breakdown by Standard International Trade Classification (SITC, revision 3) categories (value in 1m. kr; 1994 figures are provisional):

	Imports 1993	1994	*Exports* 1993	1994
0. Food and live animals	20,947	24,997	6,001	7,644
1. Beverages and Tobacco	3,585	4,778	965	1,862
2. Raw Materials	11,022	14,339	30,747	37,034
3. Fuels and lubricants	30,557	30,043	13,155	11,898
4. Animal and vegetable oils	750	1,005	670	884
5. Chemicals	38,186	45,083	38,590	44,633
6. Manufactured materials	51,916	64,896	94,575	114,046
7. Machinery and transport equipment	120,937	150,342	168,080	212,268
8. Manufactured items	54,786	61,071	34,638	40,040
9. Other	1,571	1,187	869	908

Principal exports in 1994 (in tonnes): Paper and board, 5,762,600; lumber, sawn and planed, 10·42m. sq. metres; power-generating non-electrical machinery, 113,413; chemical wood pulp, 2,215,800; newsprint, 2,030,200; mechanical handling equipment, 128,841; flat-rolled products of alloy steel, 743,000; pumps and centrifuges, 49,154.

Imports and exports by countries (in 1m. kr.):

	Imports from		*Exports to*	
	1993	*1994* [1]	*1993*	*1994* [1]
Belgium	11,524	13,877	16,144	23,179
Denmark	24,432	26,973	25,769	32,621
Finland	20,705	25,014	17,780	22,537
France	17,947	22,192	20,875	24,112
Germany	59,888	73,307	55,783	62,769
Italy	11,934	15,284	14,449	17,837
Netherlands	15,453	16,211	19,716	24,939
Norway	21,533	24,267	31,632	38,352
Switzerland	6,769	7,609	7,302	9,119
UK	31,618	38,133	39,814	47,910
USA	30,372	34,083	32,612	37,636

[1] Provisional.

Source: Statistics Sweden

Total trade between Sweden and UK (British Department of Trade returns, in £1,000 sterling):

	1990	*1991*	*1992*	*1993*	*1994*
Imports to UK	3,594,547	3,142,449	3,283,739	3,622,621	4,159,883
Exports and re-exports from UK	2,712,775	2,471,539	2,438,972	2,892,123	3,348,029

Tourism. In 1994 foreign visitors stayed 3,320,091 nights in hotels and 854,967 in holiday villages and youth hostels.

COMMUNICATIONS

Roads. On 1 Jan. 1995 there were 0·21m. km of public roads comprising state-administered roads, 97,931 km, municipal, 38,352 km, private roads with subsidies, 73,717 km, of which 74,080 km were surfaced. Motor vehicles on 31 Dec. 1994 included 3,594 passenger cars, 318,000 buses and lorries and 115,000 motor cycles.

Railways. Total length of railways at 31 Dec. 1994 was 10,798 km (7,266 km electrified). The state railway operator SJ carried 95·2m. passengers and 55m. tonnes of freight in 1994. Some lines are run under contract by private operators. There is a metro in Stockholm (108 km), and tram/light rail networks in Stockholm, Göteborg (81 km) and Norrköping.

Civil Aviation. There are international airports at Stockholm (Arlanda) and Göteborg (Landvetter). Commercial air traffic is maintained in Sweden and other parts of the world by Scandinavian Airlines System (SAS), of which AB Aerotransport (ABA = Swedish Air Lines) is the Swedish partner (DDL = Danish Air Lines and DNL = Norwegian Air Lines being the other two). SAS has a joint paid-up capital of 9,915m. Sw. kr. Capitalization of ABA, 3,029m. Sw. kr., of which 50% is owned by the Government and 50% by private enterprises.

In 1994, the total distance flown was 98·9m. km; passenger-km, 8,203·5m.; goods, 188·7m. tonne-km. These figures represent the Swedish share of the SAS traffic (Swedish domestic and three-sevenths of international traffic). Services are also provided by Aeroflot, Air China, Air France, Alitalia, American Airlines, Austrian Airlines, Balkan, Braathens Safe, British Airways, Czech Airlines, Egyptair, Estonia Air, Finnair, Iberia, Icelandair, Kenya Airways, KLM,, Latvian Airlines, Lithuanian Airlines, LOT, Lufthansa, Maersk Air, Malév, Royal Air Maroc, Sabena, Sterling Airways, Swissair, TAP, Thai Airways and Turkish Airlines.

Shipping. There are major ports at Helsingborg, Malmö, Stockholm and Göteborg. The mercantile marine consisted on 31 Dec. 1994 of 413 vessels of 2·71m. gross tonnes (only vessels of at least 100 gross tonnes, and excluding fishing vessels and tugs).

Vessels entered from and cleared for foreign countries, exclusive of passenger liners and ferries, with cargoes and in ballast, in 1994, were as follows (only vessels of at least a net tonnage of 40): With cargoes, 26,836 with a gross tonnage of 137·4m.; in ballast, 15,413 with a gross tonnage of 64·1m.

Telecommunications. There were 1,878 post offices at the end of 1994. In 1993 there were 6,790 telephone exchanges and 5,967,000 telephones. 1·04m. mobile telephones were in use in 1994.

3,352,000 combined radio and TV reception fees were paid in 1994. *Sveriges Radio AB* is a non-commercial semi-governmental corporation, transmitting 3 national programmes and regional programmes. It also broadcasts 2 TV programmes (colour by PAL). There are 3 commercial satellite channels (TV3, TV4 and Nordic), and legislation was in process in 1992 to authorize a land-based commercial channel.

Cinemas (1995). There were 1,172 cinemas.

Press (1995). There were 174 daily newspapers with an average week-day net circulation of 4,544,000.

SOCIAL INSTITUTIONS

Justice. The administration of justice is independent. The Attorney-General (appointed by the Government) and 3 Ombudsmen exercise a check on judicial affairs administration. In 1994–95 the Ombudsmen received altogether 4,891 cases; of these, 127 were instituted on their own initiative.

There is a 3-tier hierarchy of courts: The Supreme Court; 6 intermediate courts of appeal and 97 district courts. Of the district courts 27 also serve as real estate courts and 6 as water rights courts.

District courts are courts of first instance and deal with both civil and criminal cases. Petty cases are tried by 1 judge. Civil and criminal cases are tried as a rule by 3 to 4 judges or in minor cases by 1 judge. Disputes of greater consequence relating to the Marriage Code or the Code relating to Parenthood and Guardianship are tried by a judge and a jury of 3–4 lay assessors. More serious criminal cases are tried by a judge and a jury of 5 members (lay assessors) in felony cases, and of 3 members in misdemeanour cases. The cases in courts of appeal are generally tried by 4 or 5 judges, but the same cases, which are tried with a judge and a jury in the first instance, are tried by 3 or 4 judges and a jury of 2–3 members.

Those with low incomes can receive free legal aid out of public funds. In criminal cases a suspected person has the right to a defence counsel, paid out of public funds.

The Attorney-General and the Judicial Commissioner for the Judiciary and Civil Administration supervise the application in the public sector of acts of Parliament and regulations. The Attorney-General is the government's legal adviser and also the Public Prosecutor.

There were 76 penal and correctional institutions for offenders in 1994 with an average population of 6,021 inmates (including offenders in remand prison).

Religion. The overwhelming majority of the population belong to the Evangelical Lutheran Church, which is the established national church. In 1995 there were 13 bishoprics (Uppsala being the metropolitan see) and 2,552 parishes. The clergy are chiefly supported from the parishes and the proceeds of the church lands. The non-conformists mostly still adhere to the national church. The largest denominations, on 1 Jan. 1994, were: Pentecostal Movement, 93,505 members; The Mission Covenant Church of Sweden, 74,148; Salvation Army, 26,974; Orebo Missionary Society, 22,693; Swedish Evangelical Mission, 20,617; The Baptist Union of Sweden, 19,442; Swedish Alliance Missionary Society, 12,975; Holiness Mission, 6,374.

There were also 154,698 Roman Catholics (under a Bishop resident at Stockholm).

Education. In 1994–95 there were 618,730 pupils in primary education (grades 1–6 in compulsory comprehensive schools); secondary education at the lower stage (grades 7–9 in compulsory comprehensive schools) comprised 297,931 pupils. In secondary education at the higher stage (the integrated upper secondary school), there were 59,285 pupils in Oct. 1994 (excluding pupils in the fourth year of the technical course regarded as third-level education). The folk high schools, 'people's colleges', had 19,210 pupils in courses of more than 15 weeks in 1993–94.

In municipal adult education there were 146,474 students in 1994.

There are also special schools for pupils with visual and hearing handicaps (716 pupils in 1994) and for those who are mentally retarded (12,850 pupils).

In 1993–94 there were in integrated institutions for higher education 256,442 students enrolled for undergraduate studies. The number of students enrolled for post-graduate studies in 1994 was 15,749.

Source: Statistics Sweden

Health. In 1994 there were 22,400 doctors, 4,800 dentists, 74,900 nurses and midwives and 45,537 hospital beds. In 1993 the total cost of health care was 109,972m. Kr., representing 8% of GDP

Welfare. Social insurance benefits are granted mainly according to uniform statutory principles. All persons resident in Sweden are covered, regardless of citizenship. All schemes are compulsory, except for unemployment insurance. Benefits are usually income-related. Most social security schemes are at present undergoing extensive discussion and changes. Recent proposals include the introduction of a new pension scheme.

Type of scheme	*Beneficiaries*	*Expenditure 1994 (in 1m. kr)*
Sickness and parental insurance	All residents	53,800
Work injury insurance	All gainfully occupied persons	7,999
Unemployment insurance	Members of unemployment insurance societies	36,286
Basic and supplementary pensions (old-age, disability, survivors)	All resident or gainfully occupied persons (2,076,000)	177,630
Partial pensions	All gainfully occupied persons between 60 and 65 (51,000)	2,564
Child allowance	All children below 16 (1,758,000)	17,260

The total social expenditure, including also health care and social assistance, amounted to 573,290m. kr. in 1993, representing 39·8% of GDP.

DIPLOMATIC REPRESENTATIVES

Of Sweden in Great Britain (11 Montagu Pl., London, W1H 2AL)
Ambassador: Lars-Åke Nilsson.

Of Great Britain in Sweden (Skarpögatan 6-8, 115 27 Stockholm)
Ambassador: Roger Bone, CMG.

Of Sweden in the USA (600 New Hampshire Ave., NW, Washington, D.C., 20037)
Ambassador: Carl Liljegren.

Of the USA in Sweden (Strandvägen 101, 115 27 Stockholm)
Ambassador: Thomas L. Siebert.

Of Sweden to the United Nations
Ambassador: Peter Osvald.

Further Reading

Statistics Sweden. *Statistik Årsbok/Statistical Yearbook of Sweden.—Historisk statistik för Sverige* (Historical Statistics of Sweden). 1955 ff.—*Allmän månadsstatistik* (Monthly Digest of Swedish Statistics).—*Statistiska meddelanden* (Statistical Reports). From 1963

Andersson, L., *A History of Sweden.* Stockholm, 1962
Grosskopf, G., *The Swedish Tax System.* Stockholm, 1986
Gustafsson, A., *Local Government in Sweden.* Stockholm, 1988
Hadenius, S., *Swedish Politics during the Twentieth Century.* Stockholm, 1988
Heelo, H. and Madsen, H., *Policy and Politics in Sweden: Principled Pragmatism.* Philadelphia, 1987
Henrekson, M., *An Economic Analysis of Swedish Government Expenditure.* Aldershot, 1992
Lindström, E., *The Swedish Parliamentary System.* Stockholm, 1983
Olsson, S. E., *Social Policy and Welfare State in Sweden.* Lund, 1990
Peterson, C.-G., *Local Self-Government and Democracy in Transition.* Stockholm, 1989

Petersson, O., *Swedish Government and Politics.* Stockholm, 1994
Sather, L. B. and Swanson, A., *Sweden.* [Bibliography] Oxford and Santa Barbara, 1987
Scott, F. D., *Sweden: The Nation's History.* Univ. of Minnesota Press, 1983
Sveriges statskalender. Published by Vetenskapsakademien. Annual, from 1813

National library: Kungliga Biblioteket, Stockholm.
National statistical office: Statistics Sweden, S-11581 Stockholm.

SWITZERLAND

Schweizerische Eidtgenossenschaft—
Confédération Suisse—
Confederazione Svizzera [1]

Capital: Berne
Population: 7·02m. (1995)
GNP per capita: US$37,180 (1994)
HDI/world rank: 0·925/13 (1992)

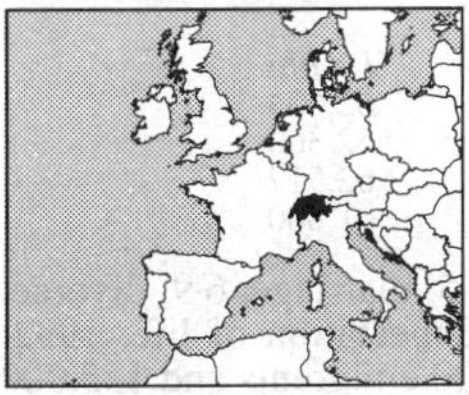

KEY HISTORICAL EVENTS. For Switzerland's history until the Napoleonic period *see* THE STATESMAN'S YEAR-BOOK, 1994-95, p.1255. In 1815 the perpetual neutrality of Switzerland and the inviolability of her territory were guaranteed by Austria, France, Great Britain, Portugal, Prussia, Russia, Spain and Sweden, and the Federal Pact, which included 3 new cantons, was accepted by the Congress of Vienna. In 1848 a new Constitution was passed. The 22 cantons set up a Federal Government and a Federal Tribunal. This Constitution was on 29 May 1874 superseded by the present Constitution. A new canton, Jura, was established on 1 Jan. 1979.

TERRITORY AND POPULATION. Switzerland is bounded in the west and north-west by France, north by Germany, east by Austria and south by Italy. Area and population by canton (with date of establishment), according to the census held on 1 Dec. 1980 and estimate 31 Dec. 1994:

Canton	*Area (sq. km)*	*Census 1 Dec. 1980*	*Estimate (in 1,000) 31 Dec. 1994*
Zurich (1351)	1,729	1,122,839	1,167·6
Berne (1553)	6,050	912,022	943·6
Lucerne (1332)	1,493	296,159	337·7
Uri (1291)	1,077	33,883	35·9
Schwyz (1291)	908	97,354	120·6
Obwalden (1291)	490	25,865	31·1
Nidwalden (1291)	276	28,617	36·0
Glarus (Glaris) (1352)	685	36,718	39·3
Zug (1352)	239	75,930	90·3
Fribourg (Freiburg) (1481)	1,671	185,246	222·1
Solothurn (Soleure) (1481)	791	218,102	237·1
Basel-Town (Bâle-V.) (1501)	37	203,915	197·7
Basel-Country (Bâle-C.) (1501)	428	219,822	251·4
Schaffhausen (Schaffhouse) (1501)	299	69,413	74·0
Appenzell-Outer Rhoden (1513)	243	47,611	54·4
Appenzell-Inner Rhoden (1513)	173	12,844	14·7
St Gallen (St Gall) (1803)	2,026	391,995	440·7
Graubünden (Grisons) (1803)	7,105	164,641	184·3
Aargau (Argovie) (1803)	1,404	453,442	524·1
Thurgau (Thurgovie) (1803)	991	183,795	220·4
Ticino (Tessin) (1803)	2,812	265,899	302·4
Vaud (Waadt) (1803)	3,212	528,747	601·6
Valais (Wallis) (1815)	5,225	218,707	269·6
Neuchâtel (Neuenburg) (1815)	803	158,368	164·5
Geneva (1815)	282	349,040	391·1
Jura (1979)	836	64,986	69·0
Total	41,129	6,365,960	7,021·2

In 1994 there were 3,591,600 females and 1,331,600 resident foreign nationals.

German, French and Italian are the official languages; Romansch (spoken mostly in Graubünden) is a national language. German is spoken by the majority of inhabi-

[1] The Latin 'Confoederatio Helvetica' is also in use.

tants in 19 of the 26 cantons, French in Fribourg, Vaud, Valais, Neuchâtel, Jura and Geneva, and Italian in Ticino. At the 1990 census 63·6% of the population gave German as their mother tongue, 19·2% French, 7·6% Italian, 0·6% Romansch and 8·9% other languages.

At the end of 1994 the 5 largest cities were Zürich (353,361); Basel (179,639); Geneva (174,363); Berne (134,129); Lausanne (123,266). At the end of 1990 the population figures of conurbations were: Zürich, 841,100; Geneva, 394,800; Basel, 360,400; Berne, 299,500; Lausanne, 263,600; other towns 1994, (and their conurbations 1992), Winterthur, 88,168 (109,800); St Gallen, 75,541 (127,400); Lucerne, 61,656 (161,000); Biel, 52,197 (83,000).

Vital statistics for calendar years:

	Live births	*Marriages*	*Divorces*	*Deaths*
1991	86,200	47,600	13,627	62,634
1992	86,900	45,000	14,500	62,300
1993	83,762	43,257	15,053	62,512
1994	82,900	42,400	15,600	61,800

Rates (1990, per 1,000 population): Birth, 12·5; death, 9·5; marriage, 6·9; divorce, 2·0. Infant mortality, 1992 (per 1,000 live births), 6·4. Expectation of life, 1992: Males, 74·3 years; females, 81·2. In 1988 there were 91,500 emigrants and 125,000 immigrants.

CLIMATE. The climate is largely dictated by relief and altitude and includes continental and mountain types. Summers are generally warm, with quite considerable rainfall; winters are fine, with clear, cold air. Berne. Jan. 32°F (0°C), July, 65°F (18·5°C). Annual rainfall 39·4" (986 mm).

CONSTITUTION AND GOVERNMENT. Switzerland is a republic. The highest authority is vested in the electorate, *i.e.*, all Swiss citizens over 18 (20 until a referendum of March 1991). This electorate—besides electing its representatives to the Parliament—has the voting power on amendments to, or on the revision of, the Constitution. It also takes decisions on laws and international treaties if requested by 50,000 voters or 8 cantons (facultative referendum), and it has the right of initiating constitutional amendments, the support required for such demands being 100,000 voters (popular initiative).

The Federal Government is supreme in matters of peace, war and treaties; it regulates the army, the railway, telecommunication systems, the coining of money, the issue and repayment of bank-notes and the weights and measures of the republic. It also legislates on matters of copyright, bankruptcy, patents, sanitary policy in dangerous epidemics, and it may create and subsidize, besides the Polytechnic School at Zürich and at Lausanne, 2 federal universities and other educational institutions. There has also been entrusted to it the authority to decide concerning public works for the whole or great part of Switzerland, such as those relating to rivers, forests and the construction of national highways and railways. By referendum of 13 Nov. 1898 it is also the authority in the entire spheres of common law. In 1957 the Federation was empowered to legislate on atomic energy matters and in 1961 on the construction of pipelines of petroleum and gas.

The legislative authority is vested in a parliament of 2 chambers: the Council of States (*Ständerat/Conseil des États*) and the National Council (*Nationalrat/Conseil National*). The Council of States is composed of 46 members, chosen and paid by the 23 cantons of the Confederation, 2 for each canton. The mode of their election and the term of membership depend on the canton. 3 of the cantons are politically divided—Basel into Town and Country, Appenzell into Outer-Rhoden and Inner-Rhoden, and Unterwalden into Obwalden and Nidwalden. Each of these 'half-cantons' sends 1 member to the State Council.

The National Council has 200 members directly elected for 4 years, in proportion to the population of the cantons, with the proviso that each canton or half-canton is represented by at least 1 member. The members are paid from federal funds. The parliament sits for 16 three-day sessions annually.

The 200 members are distributed among the cantons as follows:

Zurich	35	Appenzell—Outer- and Inner-Rhoden	3
Berne	29	St Gallen (St Gall)	12
Lucerne	9	Graubünden (Grisons)	5
Uri	1	Aargau (Argovie)	14
Schwyz	3	Thurgau (Thurgovie)	6
Unterwalden–Upper and Lower	2	Ticino (Tessin)	8
Glarus (Glaris)	1	Vaud (Waadt)	17
Zug	2	Valais (Wallis)	7
Fribourg (Freiburg)	6	Neuchâtel (Neuenburg)	5
Solothurn (Soleure)	7	Geneva	11
Basel (Bâle)—town and country	13	Jura	2
Schaffhausen (Schaffhouse)	2		

A general election takes place by ballot every 4 years. Every citizen of the republic who has entered on his 18th year is entitled to a vote, and any voter, not a clergyman, may be elected a deputy. Laws passed by both chambers may be submitted to direct popular vote, when 50,000 citizens or 8 cantons demand it; the vote can be only 'Yes' or 'No'. This principle, called the *referendum*, is frequently acted on.

On 22 Oct. 1995 elections were held for both chambers of the federal parliament; turn-out was 42%. In the Council of States, the Radical Democratic Party (RDP) gained 17 seats (18 in 1991); the Christian Democratic Party (CDP), 16 (16); the Swiss Socialist Party (SSP), 5 (nil); the Swiss People's Party or Democratic Centre Union (SPPDCU), 5 (4); others, 3. In the National Council, SSP gained 54 seats (41 in 1991); RDP,45 (44); CDP, 34 (35); SPPDCU, 29 (25); others, 38.

The chief executive authority is deputed to the *Bundesrat*, or Federal Council, consisting of 7 members, elected from 7 different cantons for 4 years by the *United Federal Assembly*, *i.e.*, joint sessions of both chambers. The members of this council must not hold any other office in the Confederation or cantons, nor engage in any calling or business. In the Federal Parliament legislation may be introduced either by a member, or by either chamber, or by the Federal Council (but not by the people). Every citizen who has a vote for the National Council is eligible to become a member of the executive.

The *President* of the Federal Council (called President of the Confederation) and the Vice-President are the first magistrates of the Confederation. Both are elected by the United Federal Assembly for 1 calendar year from among the Federal Councillors. and are not immediately re-eligible to the same offices. The Vice-President, however, may be, and usually is, elected to succeed the outgoing President.

President of the Confederation (1996): Jean-Pascal Delamuraz (RDP).

The 7 members of the Federal Council act as ministers, or chiefs of the 7 administrative departments of the republic. The city of Berne is the seat of the Federal Council and the central administrative authorities.

In March 1996 the Federal Council comprised:

Foreign Affairs: Flavio Cotti (CDP). *Interior:* Ruth Dreifuss (SSP). *Justice and Police:* Arnold Koller (CDP). *Military:* Adolf Ogi (SPPDCU). *Finance:* Kaspar Villiger (RDP). *Public Economy:* Jean-Pascal Delamuraz (RDP). *Transport, Communications and Energy:* Moritz Leuenberger (SSP).

National flag: Red with a white couped cross.

National anthem: 'Trittst im Morgenrot daher'/'Sur nos monts quand le soleil'/ 'Quando il ciel' di porpora' ('Step into the rosy dawn'); German words by Leonard Widmer, French by C. Chatelanat, Italian by C. Valsangiacomo, tune by Alberik Zwyssig.

Cantonal and Local Government. Each of the 26 cantons and demi-cantons is sovereign, so far as its independence and legislative powers are not restricted by the federal constitution; all cantonal governments, though different in organization (membership varies from 5 to 11, and terms of office from 1 to 5 years), are based on the principle of sovereignty of the people.

In 21 cantons a body chosen by universal suffrage, usually called the *Great Council*, or *Canton Council*, exercises the functions of a parliament. In all the cantonal constitutions except those of the 5 cantons which have a *Landsgemeinde*, the referendum has a place. By this principle, where it is most fully developed, as in Zurich, all laws and concordats, or agreements with other cantons, and the chief matters of finance, as well as all revisions of the Constitution, must be submitted to the popular vote. In the 5 cantons of Appenzell, Glarus and Unterwalden the people exercise their powers direct in the *Landsgemeinde*, *i.e.*, the assembly in the open air of all citizens of full age. In all the cantons the *popular initiative* for constitutional affairs, as well as for legislation, has been introduced, except in Lucerne, where the *initiative* exists only for constitutional affairs. In most cantons there are districts (*Amtsbezirke*) consisting of a number of communes grouped together, each district having a Prefect (*Regierungsstatthalter*) representing the cantonal government. In the larger communes, for local affairs, there is an Assembly (legislative) and a Council (executive) with a president, mayor or syndic, and not less than 4 other members. In the smaller communes there is a council only, with its officials.

DEFENCE. There are fortifications in all entrances to the Alps and on the important passes crossing the Alps and the Jura. Large-scale destructions of bridges, tunnels and defiles are prepared for an emergency.

Army. There are about 3,400 regular soldiers, but some 400,000 conscripts undergo training annually in the following phases: At 20 years of age, 15 weeks recruit training; between 21 and 32, reservist refresher training (*Auszug*); between 33 and 42, 39 days training for the Militia (*Landwehr*). Proposals ('Army 95') implemented in 1995 envisaged a more flexible army to protect the population against military or natural catastrophes, combat terrorism and take part in international peacekeeping. The conscript sign-off age was reduced to 42 years, the number of conscripts reduced to 400,000, and the number of regular soldiers (including women) increased.

The Army is divided into 3 field corps each of 1 armoured and 2 infantry divisions and support groups, a corps with 3 mountain divisions, and independent redoubt-, fortress- and territorial-brigades. Strength on mobilization (1996): 363,800, and 396,300 reserves (all services).

The administration of the Swiss Army is partly in the hands of the Cantonal authorities, who can promote officers up to the rank of captain. But the Federal Government is concerned with all general questions and makes all the higher appointments.

In peace-time the Army has no general; in time of war the Federal Assembly in joint session of both Houses appoints a general.

Equipment includes about 380 Leopard, 117 Pz-61, 186 Pz-68 and 186 Pz-68/88 main battle tanks.

Air Corps. The Air Corps is part of the Army. It has 3 flying regiments. The fighter squadrons are equipped with Swiss-built F-5E Tiger IIs (7 squadrons), Mirage IIIS supersonic interceptor/ground-attack (2 squadrons), Mirage IIIRS fighter/reconnaissance (1 squadron), and Bloodhound surface-to-air missile batteries are operational.

Training aircraft are Pilatus PC-7 Turbo-Trainers and Hawks; there are also communications and transport aircraft and helicopters. Personnel (1995), 32,500 on mobilization, with 153 combat aircraft.

INTERNATIONAL RELATIONS

Membership. Switzerland is a member of OECD, EFTA and the Council of Europe, and applied to join the EU on 26 May 1992. In referendums in 1986 the electorate voted against joining the UN, and in Dec. 1992 the European Economic Area.

ECONOMY

Budget. Revenue and expenditure of the Confederation, in 1m. francs, for calendar years:

	1990	*1991*	*1992*	*1993*	*1994*	*1995*
Revenue	32,674	33,490	34,953	32,782	36,239	36,319
Expenditure	31,616	35,501	37,816	40,600	41,341	42,399

Sources of revenue, 1995: Direct federal taxes, 8,650; VAT, 7,700; corporation tax, 3,000; settlement taxes, 2,900; stamp duty, 1,850. Expenditure: Social security, 10,955; defence, 5,952; transport, 6,351; agriculture, 3,461; education and research, 3,233.

Currency. The unit of currency is the *Swiss franc* (CHF) of 100 *centimes* or *Rappen*. There are coins of 5, 10, 20 and 50 centimes and 1, 2 and 5 francs, and notes of 10, 20, 50, 100, 500 and 1,000 francs. Notes in circulation, 1991, 29,220m. francs; international exchange reserves, 52,350m. francs; gold reserves, 11,900m. francs. In March 1996, £1 = 1·84 francs; US$1 = 1·20 francs; DM1 = 0·82 francs.

Banking and Finance. The National Bank, with headquarters divided between Berne and Zurich, opened on 20 June 1907. It has the exclusive right to issue banknotes. The *Governor* is Marcus Lusser.

On 31 Dec. 1993 there were 419 banks (excluding branches of foreign banks and private banks) with total assets of 1,177,805m. Swiss francs. They included 28 cantonal banks (253,080m. francs), 4 big banks (611,841m.), 155 regional and saving banks (83,460m.), 2 associations (consisting of 1,229 member banks in 1992) of loan and *Raiffeisen* banks (42,579m.) and 230 other banks (186,845m.). In 1991 the 10 largest banks in order of capitalization were: Union Bank of Switzerland, Swiss Bank Corporation, Crédit Suisse, Swiss Volksbank, Zürcher Kantonalbank, Bank Leu, Banca della Svizzera Italiana, Banque Cantonale Vaudoise, Bank Julius Baer.

Money laundering was made a criminal offence in Aug. 1990. Complete secrecy about clients' accounts remains intact, but anonymity was abolished in July 1991.

On 31 Dec. 1989 the total amount of savings deposits, deposit and investment accounts was 180,600m. francs.

The stock exchange system is being reformed under federal legislation of 1990 on securities trading and capital market services. The 4 smaller exchanges have been closed and activity concentrated on the major exchanges of Zurich, Basel and Geneva, which are increasingly harmonizing their operations in preparation for the introduction of a new Swiss Stock Exchange (SSE). Zurich is a major international insurance centre.

Weights and Measures. The metric system is legal.

ENERGY AND NATURAL RESOURCES

Electricity. The Energy 2000 programme aims to stabilize consumption. The total production of energy amounted to 54,074m. kWh in 1990 of which 30,675m. kWh were hydro-electric, 22,298m. kWh nuclear and 1,101m. kWh thermal. In 1993 37·2% was nuclear-produced, but in Sept. 1990 54% of citizens voted for a 10-year moratorium on the construction of new nuclear plants.

Minerals. Salt is mined.

Agriculture. The country is self-sufficient in wheat and meat. Agriculture is protected by subsidies, price guarantees and import controls. Farmers are guaranteed an income equal to industrial workers. Agriculture occupied 6·5% of the total workforce and contributed 2·5% to GDP in 1990. The agricultural area, in 1990, totalled 1,071,346 ha, of which 312,372 ha were arable, 13,245 ha vineyards, 90,338 ha cultivated grassland and 638,904 ha natural grassland and pasture. In 1991 there were 108,296 farms (40% in mountain or hill regions), of which 23,493 were under 1 ha, 13,953 over 20 ha and 45,492 part-time.

Area harvested, 1988 (in 1,000 ha): Cereals, 186; coarse grains, 92; potatoes, 19; sugar-beet, 15. Production, 1988 (in 1,000 tonnes): Potatoes, 748; sugar-beet, 923; wheat, 553; barley, 299; maize, 237; tobacco, 1. Fruit production (in 1,000 tonnes) in 1988 was: Apples, 540; pears, 229; plums, 33; cherries, 35; nuts, 6.

Wine is produced in 18 of the cantons. In 1988 vineyards yielded 117 tonnes of wine.

Livestock, 1993: Cattle, 1,745,087 (including milch cows, 762,450); pigs, 1,691,781; horses, 54,527; sheep, 424,027; goats, 56,687.

Forestry. The forest area was 1,204,047 ha in 1993. Production (1993) 4,338 cu. metres of timber (73·1% coniferous and 26·9% broadleaved).

INDUSTRY. There were 347,500 firms in 1991, of which 84·9% employed fewer than 10 persons. The chief food producing industries, based on Swiss agriculture, are the manufacture of cheese, butter, sugar and meat.

Among the other industries, the manufacture of textiles, clothing and footwear, chemicals and pharmaceutical products, the production of machinery (including electrical machinery and scientific and optical instruments) and watch and clock making are the most important.

Labour. In 1994, the total working population was 3,776,000, of whom 145,000 were active in agriculture and forestry, 1,092,000 in manufacture and construction and 2,539,000 in services. 164,378 persons (44% female) were registered unemployed in Dec. 1994.

The foreign labour force with permit of temporary residence was 939,000 in Aug. 1995 (326,600 women). Of these 261,400 were Italian, 146,700 Yugoslav, 108,600 French, 103,400 Portuguese and 89,600 German.

Trade Unions. The Swiss Federal Union of Administrative and Public Service Workers had, in 1985, a membership of 123,300. The Federation of Trade Unions had about 443,000 members.

FOREIGN ECONOMIC RELATIONS. Legislation of 1991 increased the possibilities of foreign ownership of domestic companies.

Commerce. Imports and exports, excluding gold (bullion and coins) and silver (coins), were (in 1m. Swiss francs):

	1988	*1989*	*1990*	*1991*	*1992*	*1993*	*1994*
Imports	82,399	95,209	96,610	95,032	92,330	89,830	92,608
Exports	74,064	84,268	88,260	87,947	92,142	93,289	95,827

Main import suppliers in 1994 (in 1m. francs): Germany, 30,407; France, 10,174; Italy, 9,160; UK, 6,140; USA, 5,704; Japan, 3,131. Main export markets: Germany, 22,440; France, 8,802; USA, 8,673; Italy, 7,135; UK, 6,360; Japan, 3,713.

Main imports in 1994 (in 1m. francs): Raw materials and semi-manufactures, 31,952; consumer goods, 35,263; producers' goods, 22,349. Exports: Machinery and apparatus, 26,123; chemicals, 23,492; precision instruments, clocks and watches and jewellery, 19,994; metals, 7,780; textiles, clothing and shoes, 4,292.

Total trade between Switzerland (including Liechtenstein) and UK for calendar years (British Department of Trade, in £1,000 sterling):

	1991	*1992*	*1993*	*1994*	*1995*
Imports to UK	3,754,586	3,918,936	4,721,923	4,817,153	5,152,985
Exports and re-exports from UK	2,105,656	1,844,610	2,273,423	2,455,847	2,749,033

Tourism. Tourism is an important industry. In 1994, overnight stays by tourists totalled 74,788,000. There were 9·9m. foreign visitors in 1993, bringing receipts of 12,820m. francs. 9·56m. Swiss citizens travelled abroad in 1993.

COMMUNICATIONS

Roads. There were (1993) 71,045 km of main roads, including 1,530 km of national highways, 18,318 km of cantonal roads and 51,197 km of local roads. Motor vehicles in 1991 (in 1,000): Private cars, 3,066; lorries, 277; buses, 34; motor cycles, 323. Goods transport by road, 1992, was 10,374m. tonne-km. There were 83,379 road accidents in 1993, with 723 fatalities.

Railways. In 1993 the length of the general traffic railways was 5,029 km, and of special lines (funiculars etc.), 814 km. In 1994 the Federal Railway carried 264m. passengers and 47·5m. tonnes of freight. There are tram/light rail networks in Basel, Berne, Bex, Geneva, Lausanne, Neuchâtel and Zurich.

There are many other lines, the most important of which are the Berne–Lotschberg–Simplon (115 km) and Rhaetian (363 km) networks.

Civil Aviation. There are international airports at Berne (Belp), Basel (which also serves Mulhouse in France), Geneva and Zurich. Swissair is the national carrier. In

1995 it had 3 A310-200s, 5 A310-300s, 1 A320-200, 4 A321-100s, 2 B-747-300s, 3 B-747-300 Combis and 47 other aircraft. In 1991 Swissair carried 7·9m. passengers and 271,000 tonnes of freight. Services are also provided by 78 foreign airlines.

Shipping. In 1989 there were 1,208 km of navigable waterways. 13·3m. tonnes of freight were transported. A merchant marine was created in 1941, the place of registry of its vessels being Basel. In 1995 it consisted of 174 vessels with a total of 4·36m. DWT. GRT totalled 0·38m.

Telecommunications. In 1989 there were 3,835 post offices, 29,600 telex and 19,151 fax subscribers. In 1993 there were 4,266,000 primary telephones and (1994) 307,000 mobile telephones, and (1990) 23,953 fax and 24,300 telex machines.

Schweizerische Radio- und Fernsehgesellschaft/Société Suisse de Radiodiffusion et Télévision/Società Svizzera di Radiotelevisione is a non-profit-making company responsible for radio and television services. There are German, French and Italian radio and TV networks (colour by PAL). The German radio service has 3 programmes, local programmes and also broadcasts in Romansch; the French service ('Suisse Romande') has 3 programmes, as does the Italian. There is an external service, Swiss Radio International (Arabic, English, Spanish) and 4 city-based private stations. The UN and the Red Cross have radio stations. In 1994 there were 2,727,000 radio and 2,513,000 TV sets in use.

Cinemas. There were 406 screens in 1993.

Press (1993). There were 96 daily newspapers (76 German language, 16 French and 4 Italian) with a total circulation of 2,795,386. 10,274 book titles were published in 1992 (10·9% in English).

SOCIAL INSTITUTIONS

Justice. The Federal Court which sits at Lausanne, consists of 30 judges, 15 supplementary judges and 15 temporary supplementary judges, elected by the Federal Assembly for 6 years and eligible for re-election; the President and Vice-President serve for 2 years and cannot be re-elected. The Tribunal has original and final jurisdiction in suits between the Confederation and cantons; between cantons and cantons; between the Confederation or cantons and corporations or individuals; between parties who refer their case to it; in such suits as the constitution or legislation of cantons places within its authority; and in many classes of railway suits. It is a court of appeal against decisions of other federal authorities, and of cantonal authorities applying federal laws. The Tribunal comprises 2 courts of public law, 2 civil courts, a chamber of bankruptcy, a chamber of prosecution, a court of criminal appeal, a court of extraordinary appeal, a federal criminal court, and a criminal chamber for cases of treason (sits very rarely). The jurors who serve in the Assize Courts are elected by the people, and are paid a daily allowance.

A Federal Insurance Court sits in Lucerne, and comprises 9 judges and 9 supplementary judges elected for 6 years by the Federal Assembly.

A federal penal code replaced cantonal codes in 1942. It abolished capital punishment except for offences in war-time; this latter proviso was abolished in 1991.

There were 64,151 adult criminal convictions in 1992 (13·4% female; 44·4% foreign).

Religion. There is liberty of conscience and of creed. At the 1990 census 47·3% of the population were Protestant, 46·2% Roman Catholic and 7·4% without religion. In 1992 the proportions were: Roman Catholics, 47·6%; Protestants, 44·3%.

Education. Education is administered by the cantons and communes and is free and compulsory for 9 years. Compulsory education consists of 4 (Berne, Basel-Town, Jura Vaud), 5 (Aargau, Basel-Country, Neuchâtel) or 6 (other cantons except Ticino, which has 9) years of primary education and the balance in Stage I secondary education. This may be followed by 5 years of Stage II secondary education of general or vocational schools. Tertiary education is at universities, higher vocational schools and advanced vocational training institutes.

In 1994–95 there were 154,850 children in nursery schools. There were 764,274 pupils in compulsory education (437,444 at primary, 284,516 at lower secondary and 42,314 at special schools), 85,922 in Stage II general secondary education, 192,403 in Stage II vocational secondary education, and 148,154 students in higher education, including 89,262 at university.

There are 7 universities (date of foundation and students in 1989–90): Basel (1460, 6,763), Berne (1528, 9,511), Fribourg (1889, 5,814), Geneva (1559, 12,028), Lausanne (1537, 6,942), Neuchâtel (1866, 2,512), Zurich (1523, 20,690); and 5 institutions of equivalent status: Lucerne Theological Faculty (199), St Gallen PHS (171), St Gallen School of Economics and Social Science (3,952), Lausanne Federal Institute of Technology (3,495), Zurich Federal Institute of Technology (11,200).

Health. Medical facilities (number per 0·1m. population in 1992): General hospitals, 605·7; psychiatric clinics, 162·7; old people's and nursing homes, 1,165·3; doctors in private practice, 160·2; dentists, 48·5; pharmacies, 22·5.

New cases of infectious diseases, 1992: Tuberculosis, 987; AIDS, 569; malaria, 261.

Welfare. The Federal Insurance Law against illness and accident, of 13 June 1911, entitles all citizens to insurance against illness; foreigners may be admitted to the benefits. Compulsory insurance against illness does not exist, but cantons and communities are entitled to declare insurance obligatory for certain classes or to establish public benefit (sick fund) associations, and to make employers responsible for the payment of the premiums of their employees.

Unemployment insurance is compulsory for all wage-earners. Insurance against accident is compulsory for all officials, employees and workmen of all the factories, trades, etc., which are under the federal liability law.

Old age and widows and widowers insurance has been compulsory since 1948.

In 1993 the following amounts (in 1m. francs) were paid in social security benefits: Federal old age pensions, 23,047; supplementary benefits, 1,541; federal disability insurance, 5,987; loss of earnings insurance, 831; unemployment insurance, 5,986; family allowances, 1,144.

DIPLOMATIC REPRESENTATIVES

Of Switzerland in Great Britain (16–18 Montagu Pl., London, W1H 2BQ)
Ambassador: François Nordmann.

Of Great Britain in Switzerland (Thunstrasse 50, 3005 Bern)
Ambassador: David Beattie, CMG.

Of Switzerland in the USA (2900 Cathedral Ave., NW, Washington, D.C., 20008)
Ambassador: Carlo Jagmetti.

Of the USA in Switzerland (Jubilaeumstrasse 93, 3005, Bern)
Ambassador: M. Larry Lawrence.

Further Reading

Office Fédéral de la Statistique. *Annuaire Statistique de la Suisse.*

Hilowitz, J. E., (ed.) *Switzerland in Perspective.* New York, 1991
Meier, H. K. and Meier, R. A., *Switzerland.* [bibliography] London and Santa Barbara, 1990
Wildblood, R., *What makes Switzerland tick?* London, 1988

National library: Bibliothèque Nationale Suisse, Hallwylstr. 15, 3003 Berne.
National statistical office: Office Fédéral de la Statistique, Hallwylstr. 15, 3003 Berne.

SYRIA

Jumhuriya al-Arabya as-Suriya

(Syrian Arab Republic)

Capital: Damascus
Population: 14·19m. (1995)
GNP per capita: US$1,110 (1991)
HDI/world rank: 0·761/78 (1992)

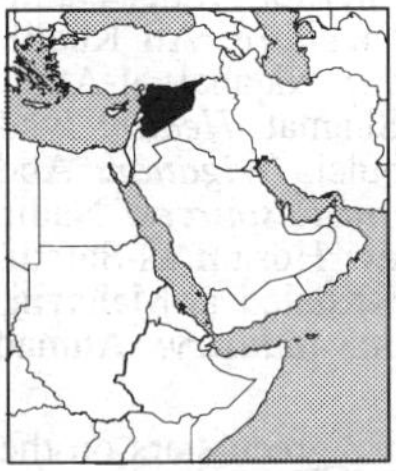

KEY HISTORICAL EVENTS. Independence was achieved on 12 Apr. 1946. Syria merged with Egypt to form the United Arab Republic from 2 Feb. 1958 until 29 Sept. 1961, when independence was resumed following a coup the previous day. Lieut.-Gen. Hafez al-Assad became Prime Minister following the fifth coup of that decade on 13 Nov. 1970, and assumed the Presidency on 22 Feb. 1971.

TERRITORY AND POPULATION. Syria is bounded by the Mediterranean and Lebanon on the west, by Israel and Jordan on the south, by Iraq on the east and by Turkey on the north. The frontier between Syria and Turkey was settled by the Franco-Turkish agreement of 22 June 1929.

The area is 185,180 sq. km (71,498 sq. miles). The census of 1984 gave a population of 13,812,284 (47% urban). Estimate (1995), 14,186,074 (50% urban); density, 74 per sq. km. There was a census in 1994. Life expectancy was 66·4 years in 1992.

Area and population (1995 estimate, in 1,000) of the 14 districts *(mohafaza)*:

	Sq. km	*Population*		*Sq. km*	*Population*
Damascus (City)	105	1,489	Idlib	6,097	922
Damascus (District)	18,032	1,730	Hasakah	23,334	1,050
Aleppo	18,500	3,035	Raqqah	19,616	566
Homs	42,223	1,247	Suwaydá	5,550	270
Hama	8,883	1,120	Dará	3,730	623
Lattakia	2,297	766	Tartous	1,892	596
Dayr az-Zawr	33,060	722	Qunaytirah	1,861	50

Principal towns (population, 1993 in 1,000): Damascus (the capital), 1,497; Aleppo, 1,494; Homs, 537; Lattakia, 293; Hama, 229.

Vital statistics, 1994: Births, 407,395; deaths, 43,981; marriages, 115,994; divorces, 9,982. Infant mortality was 33 per 1,000 live births in 1992.

Arabic is the official language, spoken by 89% of the population, while 6% speak Kurdish (chiefly Hasakah governorate), 3% Armenian and 2% other languages.

CLIMATE. The climate is Mediterranean in type, with mild wet winters and dry, hot summers, though there are variations in temperatures and rainfall between the coastal regions and the interior, which even includes desert conditions. The more mountainous parts are subject to snowfall. Damascus. Jan. 38·1°F (3·4°C), July 77·4°F (25·2°C). Annual rainfall 8·8" (217 mm). Aleppo. Jan. 36·7°F (2·6°C), July 80·4°F (26·9°C). Annual rainfall 10·2" (258 mm). Homs. Jan. 38·7°F (3·7°C), July 82·4°F (28°C). Annual rainfall 3·4" (86·7 mm).

CONSTITUTION AND GOVERNMENT. A new Constitution was approved by plebiscite on 12 March 1973 and promulgated on 14 March. It confirmed the Arab Socialist Renaissance *(Ba'ath)* Party, in power since 1963, as the 'leading party in the State and society'. Legislative power is held by a 250-member *People's Council*, renewed every 4 years. 120 seats are allotted to Ba'ath Party members, 40 to the National Progressive Front and 90 independents are elected. Elections were held on 24–25 Aug. 1994.

At a referendum on 2 Dec. 1991 Lieut.-Gen. Hafez al-Assad (b.1930), the sole candidate, was confirmed as *President* for a fourth 5-year term.

First Vice-President: Abdul Halim Khaddam *(Political and Foreign Affairs). Second Vice-President:* Rifaat al-Assad *(Defence and Security). Third Vice-President:* Mohammed Zuhair Mashariqa *(Party Affairs).*

A government was formed in June 1992 which in Oct. 1995 comprised:
Prime Minister: Mahmoud al-Zubi.

Deputy Prime Ministers: Gen. Mustafa Tlass *(Defence)*; Dr Salim Yassin *(Economic Affairs)*; Rashid Akhtarim *(Public Affairs). Education:* Ghassan Halabi. *Higher Education:* Salha Sounkour. *Interior:* Mohammad Harbah. *Information:* Mohammad Salman. *Local Administration:* Yahya Abu Asali. *Supply and Internal Trade:* Nadin Akkash. *Transport:* Mufid Abdul Karim. *Labour and Social Welfare:* Ali Khalil. *Economy and Foreign Trade:* Mohammad al-Imadi. *Culture:* Najahal al-Attar. *Foreign Affairs:* Farouk ash-Sharaa. *Tourism:* Amin Abdul Shamat. *Health:* Iyad al-Shatti. *Waqfs (Religious Endowments):* Abdel-Majid Tarabulsi. *Irrigation:* Abd ar-Rahman Madani. *Electricity:* Munib Daher. *Oil and Mineral Resources:* Nadir Nabulsi. *Construction:* Majid Rhaibani. *Housing and Utilities:* Hosam as-Safadi. *Agriculture and Agrarian Reform:* Assad Mustafa. *Finance:* Khaled al-Mahayni. *Communications:* Radwan Martini. *Justice:* Hussein Hassun. *Industry:* Ahmad Nezamuldin. *Presidential Affairs:* Wahib Fadil.

National flag: 3 horizontal stripes of red, white, black, with 2 green stars on the white stripe.

National anthem: 'Humata al Diyari al aykum salaam' ('Defenders of the Realm, on you be peace'); words by Khalil Mardam Bey, tune by M. S. and A. S. Flayfel.

Local Government. Syria is administratively divided into 14 districts *(mohafaza)*. These are divided into 59 *mantika*, which are subdivided into 179 smaller administrative units *(nahia)*, each covering a number of villages.

DEFENCE. Military service is compulsory for a period of 30 months.

Army. The Army is organized into 6 armoured and 3 mechanized divisions, a Republican Guard division, 1 special forces division, 8 independent special forces regiments, 3 independent infantry brigades, 2 independent artillery, 3 surface-to-surface missile, 2 independent anti-tank and 1 coastal defence surface-to-surface missile brigade and 1 independent tank regiment. Equipment includes 2,100 T-54/-55, 1,000 T-62 and 1,500 T-72/-72M main battle tanks. Strength (1996) about 315,000 (including 250,000 conscripts).

Navy. The Navy includes 1 ex-Soviet 'Romeo'-class diesel submarine, 2 small frigates, 18 fast missile craft, 11 inshore patrol craft, 2 coastal and 5 inshore minesweepers, and 3 medium landing ships (all ex-Soviet). A small naval aviation branch operates 16 Soviet-built anti-submarine helicopters. Personnel in 1995 numbered 8,000. The main base is at Tartus.

Air Force. The Air Force, including Air Defence Command, had (1995) about 40,000 personnel, 579 combat aircraft and 100 armed helicopters, including about 180 MiG-21, 80 MiG-23, 20 MiG-25 and 40 MiG-29 supersonic interceptors, 60 MiG-23, 60 Su-22 and 20 Su-24 fighter-bombers, as well as some MiG-25 reconnaissance aircraft. Training units have Spanish-built Flamingo and Pakistani-built Mushshak piston-engined primary trainers and Czechoslovakian L-29 Delfin and L-39 jet basic trainers. There are also transport units with Il-76, An-12, An-24/26 and other types, and helicopter units with Soviet-built Mi-6s, Mi-8/17s and Mi-24 gunships, Polish-built Mi-2s and French-built Gazelles. 'Guideline', 'Goa', 'Gainful' and 'Gaskin' surface-to-air missiles are widely deployed in Syria by Air Defence Command, and 'Gammon' long-range surface-to-air missiles in Lebanon.

INTERNATIONAL RELATIONS. A Treaty of Brotherhood, Co-operation and Co-ordination with Lebanon of May 1991 provides for close relations in the fields of foreign policy, the economy, military affairs and security. By the treaty the Lebanese government's decisions are subject to review by 6 joint Syrian-Lebanese bodies.

Membership. Syria is a member of the UN and Arab League.

ECONOMY

Policy. State control of prices and imports is being relaxed and new investment encouraged.

Budget. The consolidated budget for the calendar year 1995 balanced at £Syr.162,040m.

Currency. The monetary unit is the *Syrian pound* (SYP) of 100 *piastres*. There are coins of 5, 10, 25, 50 and 100 piastres and £Syr.1, and notes of £Syr. 1, 5, 10, 25, 50, 100 and 500. Inflation was 12% in 1992. There are 2 exchange rates. In March 1996, £1 = £Syr.64·04; US$1 = £Syr.41·90; DM1 = £Syr.28·39.

Banking and Finance. The Central Bank is the bank of issue. Commercial banks were nationalized in 1963.

Weights and Measures. The metric system is legal, though former weights and measures may still be in use: 1 *okiya* = 0·47 lb.; 6 *okiyas* = 1 *oke* = 2·82 lb.; 2 *okes* = 1 *rottol* = 5·64 lb.; 200 *okes* = 1 *kantar.*

ENERGY AND NATURAL RESOURCES

Electricity. Production (1994), 14,036m. kWh.

Oil. Estimated crude oil production (1994), 32·43m. cubic ft. Reserves (1983) 1,521m. bbls.

Gas. Gas reserves (1982), 700,000m. cubic ft. Production (1983), 75·86m. cu. metres.

Water. In 1992 there were 5 main dams and 127 surface dams. Production of drinking water, 1994, 687·08m. cu. metres.

Minerals. Phosphate deposits have been discovered. Production, 1994, 1,202,000 tonnes; other minerals were salt, 100,000 tonnes and gypsum 304,000 tonnes. There are indications of lead, copper, antimony, nickel, chrome and other minerals widely distributed. Sodium chloride and bitumen deposits are being worked.

Agriculture. In 1992 agriculture accounted for 26·1% of GDP. The arable area in 1994 was 5,971,000 ha, there were 4,852,000 ha of crop-land and 8,299,000 ha of pasture. In 1994 there were 78,150 tractors.

Production of principal crops, 1994 (in 1,000 tonnes): Wheat, 3,703; barley, 1,482; maize, 204; seed cotton, 535; olives, 518; lentils, 116; millet, 4; sugar-beet, 1,452; potatoes, 362; tomatoes, 426; grapes, 362.

Production of animal products, 1994 (in tonnes): Milk, 1,227,000; butter, 12,402; cheese, 64,136; honey, 831; 2,050m. eggs.

Livestock (1994, in 1,000): Cattle, 721; horses, 27; mules, 18; asses, 201; sheep, 11,257; goats, 1,035; poultry, 18,482.

Forestry. In 1994 there were 487,000 ha of forest. The artificial forestry area was 24,177 ha, producing 28,400,000 woody plants, 2,770 tonnes of charcoal, 5,375 tonnes of firewood and 16,125 tonnes of industrial wood in 1994.

Fisheries. The total catch in 1994 was 9,915 tonnes.

INDUSTRY. Public sector industrial production in 1994 included (in tonnes): Cotton yarn, 37,280; cotton and mixed textiles, 15,156; mixed woollen yarn, 1,571; manufactured tobacco, 7,773; iron bars, 33,037; asbestos, 13,923; vegetable oil, 28,217; 62,487 electrical engines; 64,127 refrigerators; 100,200 water meters; woollen carpets, 514,000 sq. metres.

Trade Unions. In 1994 there were 199 trade unions with 417,732 members.

FOREIGN ECONOMIC RELATIONS. Legislation of 1991 permits foreign investors a 10-year tax exemption duty-free import of equipment and repatriation of profits. Foreign debt was US$16,400m. in 1990.

Commerce. Imports in 1994 totalled US$5,455m. (US$4,131m. in 1993); exports, US$3,555m. (US$3,153m. in 1993).

Main imports, 1994 (in US$1,000) included: Petroleum and products, 64,437; wheat, 11,364 (in 1993); iron and steel bars and rods, 285,526; cane sugar, 116,176; yarn of continuous synthetic fibres, 91,276; alternating current motors and generators, 61,546; passenger transport motor vehicles, 67,310. Main exports included: Petroleum and products, 1,999,191; raw cotton, 194,741; printed woven cotton fabrics, 4,428; natural phosphate, 17,015.

In 1992 imports came mainly from France, UK, Belgium, Germany, Italy, Romania and USA. Exports went mainly to Italy, France, Germany and Romania.

Total trade between Syria and UK (British Department of Trade returns, in £1,000 sterling):

	1991	*1992*	*1993*	*1994*	*1995*
Imports to UK	42,459	53,211	105,311	97,990	89,768
Exports and re-exports from UK	49,791	64,598	74,551	101,988	84,593

Tourism. In 1994, there were 2,012,297 visitors.

COMMUNICATIONS

Roads. In 1994 there were 26,993 km of asphalted roads, 8,384 km of paved non-asphalted road and 2,098 km of earth roads. In 1994 there were 440,976 motor vehicles, including 130,829 cars and taxis, 5,282 buses, 23,034 mini-buses, 45,228 goods vehicles and 87,070 motorcycles.

Railways. In 1994 the network totalled 1,934 km of 1,435 mm gauge (Syrian Railways) and 327 km of 1,050 mm gauge (Hedjaz-Syrian Railway). In 1994 Syrian Railways carried 2m. passengers and 4·9m. tonnes of freight.

Civil Aviation. The international airport is at Damascus. In 1994, 12,694 aircraft arrived at Damascus, Aleppo, Al-Kamishli, Lattakia and Deir Ez-Zor airports; 705,093 passengers arrived, 735,105 departed and 92,734 were in transit; 9,689 tonnes of freight was unloaded and 10,876 tonnes loaded. The national carrier is the state-owned Syrian Arab Airlines, which in 1995 had a fleet of 6 B-727-200 Advs, 2 B-747SPs, 7 ex-Soviet and 2 other aircraft. Services were also provided by Aeroflot, Air Algérie, Air France, Air Malta, Air Ukraine, Alitalia, Alyemda, Austrian Airlines, Balkan, British Airways, British Mediterranean Airways, Cyprus Airways, Czech Airlines, Egyptair, Emirates, Gulf Air, Iran Air, KLM, Kuwait Airways, Libyan Airlines, LOT, Lufthansa, Malév, Pakistan Airlines, Qatar Airways, Royal Jordanian, Saudia, Sudan Airways, Tarom, Tunis Air, Turkish Airlines and Yemenia.

Shipping. In 1995 the merchant marine totalled 0·45m. GRT.

Telecommunications. Number of telephones (1994), 699,589; of these, 250,266 were in Damascus and 115,825 in Aleppo. Broadcasting is controlled by the government Syrian Broadcasting and Television Organization. There are 2 national radio programmes and an external service and 2 TV programmes (colour by SECAM and PAL). In 1993 there were 2·85m. radio and 0·7m. TV sets.

Cinemas. In 1994 there were 49 cinemas with 25,111 seats.

Press. There were (1984) 3 national daily newspapers in Damascus; other dailies and periodicals appear in Hama, Homs, Aleppo and Lattakia.

SOCIAL INSTITUTIONS

Justice. Syrian law is based on both Islamic and French jurisprudence. There are 2 courts of first instance in each district, one for civil and 1 for criminal cases. There is also a Summary Court in each sub-district, under Justices of the Peace. There is a Court of Appeal in the capital of each governorate, with a Court of Cassation in Damascus. The death penalty is in force, and executions may be held in public.

Religion. In 1992 there were 11·61m. Moslems (namely Sunni with some Shi'ites and Ismailis). There are also Druzes and Alawites. Christians (1·15m. in 1992) include Greek Orthodox, Greek Catholics, Armenian Orthodox, Syrian Orthodox, Armenian Catholics, Protestants, Maronites, Syrian Catholics, Latins, Nestorians and Assyrians. There are also Jews and Yezides.

Education. In 1994 there were 1,046 kindergartens with 90,530 children; 10,219 primary schools with 110,580 teachers and 2,624,594 pupils; 2,433 intermediate and secondary schools with 49,951 teachers and 846,550 pupils. In 1994, 15 teachers' colleges had 750 teachers and 4,642 students; 296 schools for technical education had 10,279 teachers and 69,215 students.

In 1994–95 there were 4 universities and a higher institution of political science, with 161,152 students and 5,190 academic staff.

Health. In 1994 there were 15,050 beds in 277 hospitals, and 731 health centres. In 1994 there were 14,250 doctors, 7,738 dentists, 5,006 pharmacists, 5,635 midwives and 20,909 nursing personnel.

DIPLOMATIC REPRESENTATIVES

Of Syria in Great Britain (8 Belgrave Square, London SW1X 8PH)
Ambassador: Mohammad Khodor.

Of Great Britain in Syria (11 Mohammad Kurd Ali St., Damascus POB 37)
Ambassador: J. Sindall, CMG.

Of Syria in the USA (2215 Wyoming Ave., NW, Washington, D.C., 20008)
Ambassador: Walid Al-Moualem.

Of the USA in Syria (Abu Rumaneh, Al Mansur St., Damascus)
Ambassador: Christopher W. Ross.

Of Syria to the United Nations
Ambassador: Vacant.

Further Reading

Choueiri, Y., *State and Society in Syria and Lebanon.* Exeter Univ. Press, 1994
Devlin, J. F., *Syria: Modern State in an Ancient Land.* Boulder, 1983
Maoz, M. and Yaniv, A., *Syria under Assad.* New York, 1986
Seale, P., *The Struggle for Syria.* London, 1986.—*Asad of Syria: the Struggle for the Middle East.* London, 1989
Seccombe, I. J., *Syria.* [Bibliography] Oxford and Santa Barbara (CA), 1987

National statistical office: Central Bureau of Statistics, Office of the Prime Minister, Damascus.

TAJIKISTAN
Jumkhurii Tojikiston

Capital: Dushanbe
Population: 5·7m. (1994)
GNP per capita: US$350 (1994)
HDI/world rank: 0·643/103 (1992)

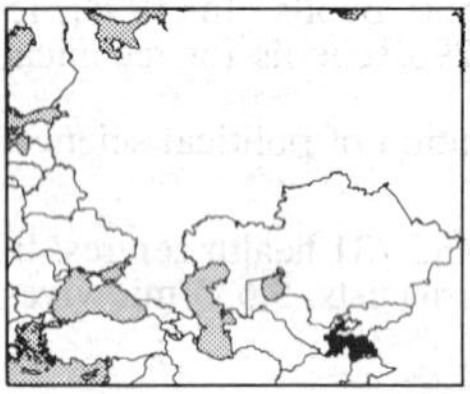

KEY HISTORICAL EVENTS. The Tajik Soviet Socialist Republic was formed from those regions of Bokhara and Turkestan where the population consisted mainly of Tajiks. It was admitted as a constituent republic of the Soviet Union on 5 Dec. 1929. In Aug. 1990 the Tajik Supreme Soviet adopted a declaration of republican sovereignty, and in Dec. 1991 the republic became a member of the CIS.

After demonstrations and fighting the Communist government was replaced by a Revolutionary Coalition Council on 7 May 1992. Following further demonstrations President Nabiev was ousted on 7 Sept. Civil war broke out, and the government resigned on 10 Nov. On 30 Nov. it was announced that a CIS peacekeeping force would be sent to Tajikistan. A state of emergency was imposed in Jan. 1993.

TERRITORY AND POPULATION. Tajikistan is bordered in the north and west by Uzbekistan and Kyrgyzstan; in the east by China and in the south by Afghanistan. Area, 143,100 sq. km (55,240 sq. miles). It includes 2 provinces (Khudzand and Khatlon) and 43 rural districts, 18 towns and 49 urban settlements, together with the Gorno-Badakhshan Autonomous Region. Its highest mountain is 7,495 metres high. Even the lowest valleys in the Pamirs are not below 3,500 metres above sea-level. Of the 1989 census population of 5,092,603, 62·3% were Tajik, 23·5% Uzbek and 7·6% Russian. Population (Jan. 1994 estimate), 5,704,000 (50·4% female; 29·6% urban). Vital statistics rates, 1993 (per 1,000 population): Births, 33·1; deaths, 8·7; natural increase, 24·4; infant mortality (per 1,000 live births), 47.

The capital is Dushanbe (1991 population estimate, 592,000). Other large towns are Khudzand (formerly Leninabad), Kurgan-Tyube and Kulyab.

The official language is Tajik, written in Arabic script until 1930 and after 1992 (the Roman alphabet was used 1930–40; the Cyrillic, 1940–92).

CONSTITUTION AND GOVERNMENT. In Nov. 1994 a new Constitution was approved by a 90% favourable vote by the electorate which enhanced the President's powers. At elections in Nov. 1991 Rakhmon Nabiev was elected President with 56·9% of votes cast. Following his resignation under pressure on 7 Sept. 1992 the Speaker, Imamali Rakhmonov, assumed the functions of president. At presidential elections on 6 Nov. 1994 the electorate was 2·6m.; turn-out was 90%. President Rakhmonov was re-elected by 58·3% of votes cast against 1 opponent.

At the elections of 26 Feb. 1995 for the 181-member parliament the electorate was 2·6m.; turn-out was officially put at 84%. 40% of the seats were uncontested.

In Feb. 1996 the government comprised:

Prime Minister: Yakhyo Azimov.

Deputy Prime Ministers: Kadriddin Glyasov; Jamoliddin Mansurov; Okil Okilov; Kholisjon Temurjanov. *Minister of Agriculture:* Khabiballo Tabarov. *Commerce and Material Resources:* Khakim Saliev. *Communications:* Ibrakhim Usmanov. *Construction:* Odil Ochilov. *Culture:* Ato Khodjaev. *Defence:* Maj.-Gen. Sherali Khairulloev. *Environment:* Sadullo Khairulloev. *Finance:* Makhmad Yunusov. *Foreign Affairs:* Rashid Olimov. *Foreign Economic Relations:* Izatullo Khayoev. *Health:* Alamkhon Akhmedov. *Industry:* Shavkat Umarov. *Interior:* Saidamin Gafurov. *Justice:* Shavkat Ishmoilev. *Land Improvement and Water Resources:* Vakhid Shafov. *Press and Information:* Bobokhon Makhmadov. *Public Security:* Saidanvar Kamolov. *Social Security:* Abdusaer Jaburov. *Transport:* Fariddun Mukhiddinov.

National flag: 3 horizontal stripes of red, white and green in the proportions 1:2:1. In the centre a gold crown under an arc of 7 stars.

Local and Regional Government. Elections to the district, urban and rural Soviets and the regional Soviet of Gorno-Badakhshan were held in Dec. 1989.

DFENCE. No military units had been formed by 1995. It is planned to form an Air Force squadron. 5 Mi-24s and 10 Mi-8s have been procured. 15,000 Russian troops are stationed in the country.

INTERNATIONAL RELATIONS

Membership. Tajikistan is a member of the UN.

ECONOMY

Budget. Budgetary income in 1993 was 406,800m. rubles; expenditure was 329,100m. rubles.

Currency. The unit of currency is the *Tajik rouble* (TJR) of 100 *tanga*, which replaced the Russian rouble on 10 May 1995 at 1 Tajik rouble = 100 Russian roubles.

Banking and Finance. The *Chairman* of the National Bank is Kayum Navmidinov.

ENERGY AND NATURAL RESOURCES

Electricity. Output in 1993 was 17,700m. kWh.

Oil and Gas. In 1993 oil production (including gas concentrate) was 40,000 tonnes; natural gas, 50m. cu. metres.

Minerals. There are rich deposits of brown coal, lead, zinc, uranium, radium, arsenic and bismuth. Asbestos, mica, corundum and emery, lapis lazuli, potassium salts, sulphur and other minerals are also found. Coal production was 0·2m. tonnes in 1993.

Agriculture. Area under cultivation in 1993, was 4·3m. ha, of which 75,200 ha was accounted for by private subsidiary agriculture and 19,000 ha by commercial agriculture. Private and commercial agriculture accounted for 37% of the value of output in 1992; total output was valued at 1,600m. rubles (in constant 1983 prices) in 1993, 98% of the 1992 figure.

Tajikistan grows apricots, figs, olives, pomegranates, a local variety of lemons and oranges, and sugar-cane. Eucalyptus and geranium are grown for the perfumery industry. Jute, rice and millet are also grown.

Tajikistan contains rich pasture lands, and cattle breeding is important. Livestock on 1 Jan. 1994: 1·3m. cattle, 2·9m. sheep and goats and 0·04m. pigs.

Output of main agricultural products (in 1,000 tonnes) in 1993: Grain, 254; cotton, 524; potatoes, 147; vegetables, 485; fruit and berries, 148; meat, 69; milk, 432; and 154m. eggs.

INDUSTRY. Industrial enterprises include mining, engineering, food, textile, clothing and silk factories. Output was valued at 735,000m. rubles in current prices in 1993, 80·5% of the 1992 figure.

Output, 1993 (in tonnes): Mineral fertilizer, 20,000; cement, 0·3m.; fabrics, 114m. cu. metres; footwear, 3·9m. pairs; 1,100 lathes; 18,000 refrigerators and freezers.

Labour. In 1993 the population of working age was 2·75m., of whom 1·86m. were employed, 55·3% in the state sector, 25·12% in the private sector and 18·4% in co-operatives. In Jan. 1994 there were 21,500 registered unemployed (1·1% of the labour force), of whom 5,000 were receiving benefits. Average monthly salaries in 1994 were 14,336 roubles. The monthly minimum wage was 14,400 Tajik roubles in 1995.

FOREIGN ECONOMIC RELATIONS

Commerce. In 1993 imports were valued at US$373·8m. and exports at US$263·1m. Total trade between Tajikistan and UK (British Department of Trade returns, in £1,000 sterling):

	1993	*1994*	*1995*
Imports to UK	157	142	138
Exports and re-exports from UK	19,486	4,266	4,754

COMMUNICATIONS

Roads. In Jan. 1990 there were 28,500 km of motor roads. (17,700 km hard surface). In 1993, 139·9m. passengers and 12·3m. tonnes of freight were carried.

Railways. A railway line between Termez and Dushanbe (258 km) connects the republic with the railway system of the CIS. The mountainous nature of the republic makes ordinary railway construction difficult; accordingly 345 km of narrow gauge railways have been constructed (Kurgan–Tyube–Piandzh and Dushanbe–Kurgan–Tyube, connecting Dushanbe with the cotton-growing Vakhsh valley are particularly important). Length of railways, 1990, 480 km. In 1993, 1·2m. passengers and 1·2m. tonnes of freight were carried.

Civil Aviation. There is an international airport at Dushanbe. The national carrier is Tajikistan Airlines, which operated 4 ex-Soviet aircraft in 1995. In 1993, 0·2m. passengers and 2,100 tonnes of freight were carried.

Shipping. A steamship line on the Amu-Darya runs between Termez, Sarava and Jilikulam on the river Vakhsh (200 km).

Telecommunications. Broadcasting is controlled by the State Teleradio Broadcasting Company. Tadjik Radio broadcasts 3 national programmes, a Radio Moscow relay and a foreign service (Dari, Iranian).

Press (1989). There were 74 newspapers, 63 in Tajik. Daily circulation of Tajik-language newspapers, 1,208,000; in all languages, 1,598,000.

SOCIAL INSTITUTIONS

Religion. The Tajiks are predominantly Sunni Moslems.

Education. In 1993–94 there were 3,179 primary and secondary schools with 1·3m. pupils, 13 higher educational institutions with 69,000 students and 43 technical colleges with 38,400 students. In Jan. 1992, 14% of eligible children were attending pre-school institutions.

There is 1 university, which had 7,220 students in 1994–95.

Health. In Jan. 1994 there were 374 hospitals with 60,000 beds, 13,000 doctors and 42,800 junior medical personnel.

Welfare. In Jan. 1994 there were 0·41m. age pensioners and 0·2m. other pensioners.

BADAKHSHAN AUTONOMOUS REPUBLIC

Comprising the Pamir massif along the borders of Afghanistan and China, the province was set up on 2 Jan. 1925, initially as the Special Pamir Province. Area, 63,700 sq. km (24,590 sq. miles). The population at the 1989 census was 161,000 (89·5% Tajik, 6·7% Kirghiz). Estimate, 1990, 164,300. Capital, Khorog (14,800). The inhabitants are predominantly Ismaili Moslems. Mining industries are developed (gold, rock-crystal, mica, coal, salt). Wheat, fruit and fodder crops are grown and cattle and sheep are bred in the western parts. In 1990 there were 74,200 cattle and 329,500 sheep and goats. Total area under cultivation, 18,400 ha. In 1990-91 there were 47,600 students at all levels of education. There were 140 doctors and 1,400 junior medical personnel in 1991.

DIPLOMATIC REPRESENTATIVES

Of Great Britain in Tajikistan
Ambassador: Alexander Bergne (resides in Tashkent).

Of the USA in Tajikistan (39 Ainii St., Dushanbe)
Ambassador: R. Grant Smith.

Of Tajikistan to the United Nations
Ambassador: Rashid Alimov.

TANZANIA

Jamhuri ya Muungano wa Tanzania—United Republic of Tanzania

Capital: Dodoma
Population: 29·7m. (1994)
GNP per capita: US$90 (1994)
HDI/world rank: 0·364/147 (1992)

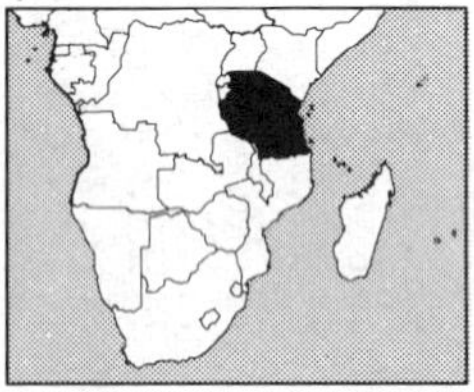

KEY HISTORICAL EVENTS. Tanganyika achieved responsible government in Sept. 1960 and full self-government on 1 May 1961. On 9 Dec. 1961 Tanganyika became a sovereign independent member state of the Commonwealth of Nations. It adopted a republican form of government on 9 Dec. 1962. For history from the end of the 17th century until 1960 *see* THE STATESMAN'S YEAR-BOOK, 1991–92, p. 1183.

On 24 June 1963 Zanzibar became an internal self-governing state and on 9 Dec. 1963 independent. On 12 Jan. 1964 its sultanate was overthrown by the Afro-Shirazi Party who established the People's Republic of Zanzibar.

On 26 April 1964 Tanganyika, Zanzibar and Pemba combined to form the United Republic of Tanganyika and Zanzibar (named Tanzania on 29 Oct.). In 1993 regional parliaments for Zanzibar and mainland Tanzania (Tanganyika) were set up.

TERRITORY AND POPULATION. Tanzania is bounded in the north-east by Kenya, north by Lake Victoria and Uganda, north-west by Rwanda and Burundi, west by Lake Tanganyika, south-west by Zambia and Malaŵi and south by Mozambique. Total area 945,037 sq. km (364,881 sq. miles) including the offshore islands of Zanzibar (1,660 sq. km) and Pemba (984 sq. km) and inland water surfaces (59,050 sq. km)). The census of 1988 gave a total population of 23,174,336 (22,533,758 in mainland Tanzania and 640,578 in Zanzibar and Pemba). Estimate (1994), 29·7m.; density, 31·5 per sq. km.

The chief towns (1988 census populations) are Dar es Salaam, the chief port and former capital (1,360,850), Mwanza (223,013), Dodoma, the new capital (203,833), Tanga (187,634), Zanzibar Town (157,634), Tabora and Mbeya.

The United Republic is divided into 25 administrative regions of which 20 are in mainland Tanzania, 3 in Zanzibar (Zanzibar North, Zanzibar West, Zanzibar South) and 2 in Pemba (Pemba North, Pemba South). Areas and 1988 census populations of the regions:

Region	*Sq. km*	*Population*	*Region*	*Sq. km*	*Population*
Arusha	82,306	1,351,675	Pwani (Coast)	32,407	638,015
Dar es Salaam	1,393	1,360,850	Rukwa	68,635	694,974
Dodoma	41,311	1,237,819	Ruvuma	63,498	783,327
Iringa	56,864	1,208,914	Shinyanga	50,781	1,772,549
Kagera	28,388	1,326,183	Singida	49,341	791,814
Kigoma	37,037	854,817	Tabora	76,151	1,036,293
Kilimanjaro	13,309	1,108,699	Tanga	26,808	1,283,636
Lindi	66,046	646,550	*Zanzibar & Pemba*	*2,460*	*640,578*
Mara	19,566	970,942	Pemba North	574	137,399
Mbeya	60,350	1,476,199	Pemba South	332	127,640
Morogoro	70,799	1,222,737	Zanzibar North	470	97,028
Mtwara	16,707	889,494	Zanzibar South	854	70,184
Mwanza	19,592	1,878,271	Zanzibar West	230	208,327

The official languages are English and Swahili (spoken as a mother tongue by only 8·8% of the population, but used as a lingua franca by 90%).

CLIMATE. The climate is very varied and is controlled very largely by altitude and distance from the sea. There are three climatic zones: the hot and humid coast, the drier central plateau with seasonal variations of temperature, and the semi-temperate mountains. Dodoma. Jan. 75°F (23·9°C), July 67°F (19·4°C). Annual rainfall 23" (572 mm). Dar es Salaam. Jan. 82°F (27·8°C), July 74°F (23·3°C). Annual rainfall 43" (1,064 mm).

CONSTITUTION AND GOVERNMENT. The country was a one-party state, but a law of May 1992 introduced multi-party democracy.

The *President* is head of state, chairman of the party and commander-in-chief of the armed forces. The second Vice-President is head of the executive in Zanzibar. The Prime Minister and first Vice-President is also the leader of government business in the National Assembly.

According to the Constitution of 1977, as amended in Oct. 1984, the *National Assembly* is composed of a total of 244 members: 169 Members of Parliament elected from the Constituencies (119 from the mainland and 50 from Zanzibar); 15 National Members elected by the National Assembly; 15 women members elected by the National Assembly, 5 from Zanzibar; 5 members elected by the House of Representatives in Zanzibar; 25 ex-officio Members (20 Regional Commissioners from the mainland and 5 from Zanzibar) and 15 Nominated Members (by the President), 5 from Zanzibar.

In Dec. 1979 a separate Constitution for Zanzibar was approved. Although at present under the same Constitution as Tanzania, Zanzibar has, in fact, been ruled by decree since 1964.

Presidential and parliamentary elections were held on 29 Oct. 1995, in many places postponed or extended because of administrative problems or faults. On 11 Nov. all opposition candidates withdrew from the presidential elections because of alleged irregularities. Benjamin Mkapa was elected President with 61·8% of votes cast.

The Government in Oct. 1995 consisted of:

President and Minister of Defence: Benjamin Mkapa (Chama Cha Mapinduzi; sworn in 30 Nov. 1995).

Prime Minister and First Vice-President: Cleopa Msuya.

Second Vice-President: Dr Salmin Amour. *Minister of Home Affairs:* Ernest Nyanda. *Finance:* Jakaya M. Kikwete. *Foreign Affairs and International Co-operation:* Joseph Rwegasira. *Agriculture:* Frederick Sumaye. *Labour and Youth Development:* Basil Mramba. *Education and Culture, Communication and Transport:* Philemon Sarungi. *Tourism, Natural Resources and Environment:* Juma Hamad Omar. *Industry and Trade:* Kighoma Malima. *Health:* Amran Mayagila. *Information and Broadcasting:* Philip Sangoka Marmo. *Science, Technology and Higher Education:* Vacant. *Community Development, Women and Children:* Anna Makinda. *Energy, Minerals and Water:* Jackson Makweta. *Works:* Nalaila Kiula. *Justice and Constitutional Affairs:* Samuel J. Sitta. *Without portfolio:* K. Ngombale Mwiru, John Malecela.

National flag: Divided diagonally green, black, blue, with the black strip edged in yellow.

National anthem: 'God Bless Africa/Mungu ibariki Afrika'; words collective, tune (same as that for Zambia and Zimbabwe) by M. E. Sontanga.

Regional and Local Government. There are regional parliaments for Zanzibar and mainland Tanzania (Tanganyika), and Zanzibar has a President, who is *ex officio* a Vice-President of Tanzania. Elections were held on 22 Oct. 1995. Salmin Amour (Chama Cha Mapinduzi) was elected *President* by 50·2% of votes cast against 1 opponent. Chama Cha Mapinduzi gained 26 seats; the Civic United Front, 24.

DEFENCE. Conscription is for 2 years, which may include civilian service.

Army. The Army consists of 5 infantry and 1 tank brigade and 2 artillery, 2 anti-aircraft, 2 mortar, 2 anti-tank and 1 engineer battalion. Equipment includes 30 Chinese Type-59 and 35 T-54 main battle tanks. Strength (1996), 30,000. There is also a Citizen's Militia of 80,000.

Navy. There are 4 ex-Chinese torpedo-armed hydrofoils and 14 inshore patrol craft of mixed Chinese and North Korean origins. 4 further British-built inshore patrol craft are based permanently in Zanzibar and 4 armed patrol boats on Lake Victoria Nyanza. Personnel in 1995 totalled about 1,000.

Air Force. The Tanzanian People's Defence Force Air Wing was built up initially with the help of Canada, but combat equipment has been acquired from China. Personnel totalled 3,600 in 1995 (including some 2,600 air defence troops), with about 10 F-7 (MiG-21) and 10 F-6 (MiG-19); 4 Buffalo twin-engined short-take-off-and-land transports; 1 HS 748 turboprop transport; 2 Chinese-built Y-12 transports; 2 Cessna 404 liaison aircraft; 6 Agusta-Bell AB.205 transport helicopters, and 2 JetRanger helicopters.

INTERNATIONAL RELATIONS

Membership. Tanzania is a member of the UN, OAU, the Commonwealth, SADC and is an ACP state of the EU.

ECONOMY

Budget. The fiscal year ends 30 June. The 1992–93 budget balanced at Sh. 353,605m. Recurrent revenue was Sh.215,617m.; foreign loans and grants, Sh. 140,988m. Recurrent expenditure was Sh. 251,543; capital expenditure, Sh. 102,062m.

Currency. The monetary unit is the *Tanzanian shilling* (TZS) of 100 *cents*. There are coins of 5, 10, 20, 50 cents and Sh.1, 5, 10 and 20, and notes of Sh. 10, 20, 50, 100, 200, 500 and 1,000. Sh. 63,600m. were in circulation in 1991. Foreign exchange reserves were US$374·9m. in March 1993. In March 1996, £1 = Sh. 817·96; US$ = Sh. 535·00; DM1 = Sh. 18·63.

Banking and Finance. On 14 June 1966 the central bank, the Bank of Tanzania (*Governor*, Idris Rashid), with a government-owned capital of Sh. 20m., began operations.

On 6 Feb. 1967 all commercial banks with the exception of National Co-operative Banks were nationalized and their interests vested in the National Bank of Commerce on the mainland and the Peoples' Bank in Zanzibar. However, in 1993 private-sector commercial banks were allowed to open; there were 4 in 1994.

A stock exchange was scheduled to open in Dar es Salaam in 1996.

Weights and Measures. The metric system is in force.

ENERGY AND NATURAL RESOURCES

Electricity. Installed capacity was 490 MW in 1992. Production (1991) 1,581m. kWh.

Minerals. Production (1991): Diamonds, 92,000 carats; gold, 3,018 kg; gemstones, 7,873 kg. Large deposits of coal and tin exist but mining is on a small scale.

Agriculture. 80% of the workforce are engaged in agriculture, chiefly in subsistence farming. Production of main agricultural crops in 1992 (in 1,000 tonnes) was: Sisal, 35; seed cotton, 218; sugar-cane, 1,410; coffee, 56; tobacco, 17; maize, 2,226; millet, 263; sorghum, 587; wheat, 64; cashew nuts, 40; citrus, 34. Zanzibar is a major producer of cloves.

Livestock (1992): 13·2m. cattle, 3·7m. sheep, 9m. goats, 25m. chickens. Livestock products (1992): Honey, 15,500 tonnes.

Forestry. Forests cover 43m. ha.

Fisheries. Catch (1991) 400,300 tonnes of which, inland waters, 345,000 tonnes.

INDUSTRY. Industry is limited and is mainly textiles, petroleum and chemical products, food processing, tobacco, brewing and paper manufacturing.

FOREIGN ECONOMIC RELATIONS.
Foreign debt was US$6,715m. in 1992.

Commerce. Total trade (in US$1m.):

	1989	*1990*	*1991*	*1992*	*1993*
Imports	691	1,444	1,477	1,510	1,550
Exports	318	407	362	300	350

Principal exports, 1991 (in US$1m.): Coffee, 77·3; manufactures, 70·3; cotton, 63·3; minerals, 41·6; tea, 21·7; tobacco, 16·7; cashew nuts, 16·7; petroleum products, 7·3. Principal imports: Machinery, 254·2; transport equipment, 247·7; crude oil and products, 168·5; building materials, 110·7. Main export markets, 1992: Germany, 15·6%; UK, 11·3%; India, 11·5%; Netherlands, 6·7%; Belgium, 11·4%; Japan, 9·8%. Main import suppliers: UK, 9·8%; Japan, 7·7%; Italy, 4·8%; Oman, 2·7%; Germany, 8·0%.

Total trade between Tanzania and UK (British Department of Trade returns, in £1,000 sterling):

	1991	*1992*	*1993*	*1994*	*1995*
Imports to UK	20,938	21,140	25,633	22,452	27,480
Exports and re-exports from UK	72,822	78,545	108,943	82,312	87,412

Tourism. In 1991 there were 146,700 visitors spending 394,800 nights and bringing receipts of US$62·6m.

COMMUNICATIONS

Roads. In 1994 there were 55,500 km of classified roads, of which 3,660 km were tarred.

Railways. In 1977 the independent Tanzanian Railway Corporation was formed. The network totals 2,600 km (metre-gauge), excluding the joint Tanzanian Zambian (Tazara) railway's 969 km in Tanzania (1,067 mm gauge) operated by a separate administration. In 1994, the state railway carried 1·2m. passengers and 1·2m. tonnes of freight and in 1991 the Tazara carried 1·6m. passengers and 1m. tonnes of freight.

Civil Aviation. There are 3 international airports (Dar es Salaam, Zanzibar and Kilimanjaro). Air Tanzania, the state-owned national carrier, had 2 B-737-200C Advs and 1 other aircraft in 1995, and provided domestic services and services to Mozambique, Zambia, Seychelles, Comoros, Rwanda, Burundi, Madagascar and (with Air Malaŵi) South Africa. Tanzania is a partner with Uganda and South African Airways in Alliance Airline. Services are also provided by Aeroflot, Air France, Air India, Air Malaŵi, Air Zimbabwe, Alyemda, British Airways, Egyptair, Ethiopian Airlines, Gulf Air, Kenya Airways, KLM, Lufthansa, Royal Swazi, SAA, Swissair and Uganda Airlines. 286,000 passengers were carried in 1991.

Shipping. In 1995, the merchant marine totalled 49,433 GRT, including oil tankers, 7,173 GRT. The main seaports are Dar es Salaam, Mtwara, Tanga and Zanzibar. There are also ports on the lakes. In 1991, 1,000,000 tonnes of freight were loaded and 2·9m. unloaded.

Telecommunications. In 1989 there were 137,000 telephones and 3,350 telex lines. The government-controlled Radio Tanzania and Sauti ya Tanzania Zanzibar are responsible for radio broadcasting on the mainland and on Zanzibar respectively. On the mainland there is a national service and a commercial programme in Swahili and an external service in English. There is television only on Zanzibar provided by the government-run Television Zanzibar (colour by PAL). There were about 4m. radio and 80,000 TV sets in 1992.

Press (1994). There were 2 dailies (1 in English, 1 in Swahili), 2 weeklies and several monthly magazines.

SOCIAL INSTITUTIONS

Justice. The Judiciary is independent in both judicial and administrative matters and is composed of a 4-tier system of Courts: Primary Courts; District and Resident

Magistrates' Courts; the High Court and the Court of Appeal. The Chief Justice is head of the Court of Appeal and the Judiciary Department. The Court's main registry is at Dar es Salaam; its jurisdiction includes Zanzibar. The Principal Judge is head of the High Court, also headquartered at Dar es Salaam, which has resident judges at 7 regional centres.

Religion. In 1992 there were 8·4m. Roman Catholics, Anglicans and Lutherans and 9m. Moslems. Moslems are concentrated in the coastal towns; Zanzibar is 96% Moslem and 4% Hindu. Some 23% follow traditional religions.

Education. In 1991 there were 10,505 primary schools with 3,408,000 pupils, and 133 state secondary schools (175 private in 1988) with 66,472 students.

Technical and vocational education is provided at several secondary and technical schools and at the Dar es Salaam Technical College.

There were, in 1991, 42 teachers' colleges, including the college at Chang'ombe for secondary-school teachers, with 16,890 students.

In 1994–95 there was 1 university, 1 university of agriculture and 1 open university, with a total of 5,591 students and 890 academic staff. There were also 9 other institutions of higher education.

Health. In 1991 there were 1,112 doctors and dentists and 173 hospitals with 24,130 beds.

DIPLOMATIC REPRESENTATIVES

Of Tanzania in Great Britain (43 Hertford St., London, W1)
High Commissioner: Dr Abdul-Kader Shareef.

Of Great Britain in Tanzania (Hifadhi Hse., Samora Ave., Dar es Salaam)
High Commissioner: Alan Montgomery, CMG.

Of Tanzania in the USA (2139 R. St., NW, Washington, D.C., 20008)
Ambassador: Vacant.

Of the USA in Tanzania (36 Laibon Rd., Dar es Salaam)
Ambassador: J. Brady Anderson.

Of Tanzania to the United Nations
Ambassador: Daudi Ngelautwa Mwakawago.

Further Reading

Ayany, S. G., *A History of Zanzibar.* Nairobi, 1970
Coulson, A., *Tanzania: A Political Economy.* OUP, 1982
Darch, C., *Tanzania.* [Bibliography] 2nd ed. Oxford and Santa Barbara (CA), 1996
Hood, M., (ed.) *Tanzania and Nyerere.* London, 1988
Nyerere, J., *Freedom and Development.* New York, 1976
Resnick, I. N., *The Long Transition: Building Socialism in Tanzania.* New York and London, 1981
Yeager, R., *Tanzania: An African Experiment.* Aldershot, 1982

National statistical office: Bureau of Statistics, Dar es Salaam.

THAILAND

Prathet Thai

(Kingdom of Thailand)

Capital: Bangkok
Population: 58·34m. (1993)
GNP per capita: US$2,210 (1994)
HDI/world rank: 0·827/58 (1992)

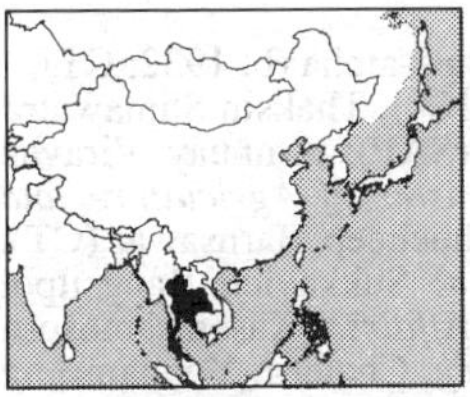

KEY HISTORICAL EVENTS. Until 24 June 1932 Siam was an absolute monarchy. A coup of that date resulted in the constitution of 1932. Numerous coups have followed.

On 23 Feb. 1991 a military junta seized power, deposing the prime minister.

Following the appointment of Gen. Suchinda Kraprayoon as Prime Minister on 17 April 1992 there were massive anti-government demonstrations over several weeks in the course of which many demonstrators were killed. Gen. Suchinda resigned, and in May the legislative assembly voted that future prime ministers should be elected by its members rather than appointed by the military. A new government was elected on 13 Sept.

TERRITORY AND POPULATION. Thailand is bounded in the west by Burma, north and east by Laos and south-east by Cambodia. In the south it becomes a peninsula bounded in the west by the Indian Ocean, south by Malaysia and east by the Gulf of Thailand. Area is 513,115 sq. km (198,114 sq. miles).

At the census taken in 1990 the total population (preliminary) was 54,532,300, of whom 17,947,700 lived in the Central region, 19,037,300 in the North-East region, 6,964,000 in the South region, 10,583,300 in the North region. Population (census 1993): 58,336,072 (29,130,986 females); density of population, 113·69 per sq. km.

Vital statistics, 1991: Births, 960,556 (466,803 females); deaths, 264,350 (109,152 females). Expectation of life (1989), 66 years.

Thailand is divided into 4 regions, 73 provinces and Bangkok, the capital.

Population of Bangkok (1993 census), 5,572,712. Other towns (1991 estimate): Nonthaburi (264,201), Nakhon Ratchasima (202,503), Chiangmai (161,541), Hat Yai (142,351), Khon Kaen, (131,478), Nakhon Sawan (108,569).

Thai is the official language, spoken by 53% of the population as their mother tongue. 27% speak Lao (mainly in the north-east), 12% Chinese (mainly in urban areas), 3·7% Malay (mainly in the south) and 2·7% Khmer (along the Cambodian border).

CLIMATE. The climate is tropical, with high temperatures and humidity. Over most of the country, 3 seasons may be recognized. The rainy season is June to Oct., the cool season from Nov. to Feb. and the hot season is March to May. Rainfall is generally heaviest in the south and lightest in the north east.

Bangkok. Jan. 78°F (25·6°C), July 83°F (28·3°C). Annual rainfall 56" (1,400 mm).

ROYAL HOUSE. The reigning King is **Bhumibol Adulyadej,** born 5 Dec. 1927. King Bhumibol married on 28 April 1950 Princess Sirikit, and was crowned 5 May 1950. Children: Princess Ubol Ratana (born 5 April 1951, married Aug. 1972 Peter Ladd Jensen), Crown-Prince Vajiralongkorn (born 28 July 1952, married 3 Jan. 1977 Soamsawali Kitiyakra), Princess Maha Chakri Sirindhorn (born 2 April 1955), Princess Chulabhorn (born 4 July 1957, married 7 Jan. 1982 Virayudth Didyasarin).

CONSTITUTION AND GOVERNMENT. Parliament consists of a 270-member *Senate*, appointed by the King, and a 391-member *House of Representatives*, elected for 4-year terms. In May 1992 the legislative assembly voted (by 533 votes to 9) a constitutional amendment whereby future prime ministers should be elected by its members, and not appointed by the military. Constitutional amendments of Jan. 1995 lowered the voting age from 20 to 18 and restricted to two-thirds the proportion of the military in the House of Representatives.

At the elections of 2 July 1995 the electorate was 39m. Chart Thai (CT, i.e. 'Thai Nation') gained 93 seats; the Democratic Party, 86; New Aspiration (NA), 56; Chart Pattana, 53; Palang Dharma (PD), 23; the Social Action Party, 23; Prachakorn Thai (PT), 18; Nam Thai (NT), 18; Muanchon (M), 3.

A 7-party coalition government was formed on 18 July 1995, which in Feb. 1996 comprised:

Prime Minister and Minister of the Interior: Banharn Silapa-archa (b. 1932; CT).

Deputy Prime Ministers: Gen. Chavalit Yongchaiyudh (NA); Thaksin Shinawatra (PD); Samak Sundaravej (PT); Boonphan Kaewattana (SAP); Amnuay Viravan (NT); Air Chief Marshal Somboon Rahong (CT). *Minister of Agriculture and Co-operatives:* Montree Pongpanit (SAP). *Commerce:* Chucheep Harnsawat (CT). *Defence:* Gen. Chavalit Yongchaiyudh (NA). *Education:* Sukkavich Rangsitpol (NA). *Finance:* Surakiat Sathirathai (CT). *Foreign Affairs:* Kasemsamosorn Kasemsri (NT). *Industry:* Chaiwat Sinsuwong (PD). *Justice:* Chalerm Yoobamrung (M). *Public Health:* Sanoh Thienthong (CT). *Science, Technology and the Environment:* Yingphan Manasikarn (PT). *Transport and Communications:* Wan Muhammadnor Matha (NA). *University Affairs:* Boonchu Trithong (CT). *Labour and Social Welfare:* Phisan Moonlasartsathorn (NA).

The *Speaker* is Boon-Ua Prasertsuwan.

National flag: 5 horizontal stripes of red, white, blue, white and red, the blue stripe occupying the central one-third of the whole area.

National anthem: 'Prathet Thai ruam nua chat chua Thai' ('Thailand, cradle of Thais wherever they may be'); words by Luang Saranuprapan, tune by Phrachen Duriyang.

Local Government. Thailand is divided into 76 provinces *(changwads)*, each under the control of a *changwad* governor. The *changwads* are subdivided into 744 districts *(amphurs)* and 81 sub-districts *(king amphurs)*, 7,307 communes *(tambons)* and 65,277 villages *(moobans)*.

DEFENCE. Conscription is for 2 years.

Army. The Army is organized in 4 regions and includes 1 armoured, 1 cavalry, 2 mechanized infantry, 7 infantry (including the Royal Guard), 2 special forces and 1 artillery division; 19 engineer and 8 independent infantry battalions; 1 independent cavalry and 1 armoured air cavalry regiment and 3 reconnaissance companies. Equipment includes 150 M-48A5, 53 M-60 and about 50 Chinese Type-69 main battle tanks. There is also an Army Aviation force including more than 100 UH-1 transport helicopters, and over 60 O-1 Bird Dog observation aircraft and about 20 fixed-wing transports. Strength (1996) 150,000 (80,000 conscripts, with 200,000 reserves for all the armed forces).

Navy. The Royal Thai Navy is, next to the Chinese, the most significant naval force in the South China Sea. The combatant fleet includes 6 missile-armed and 4 other frigates, 3 modern missile-armed 950-tonne corvettes and 2 anti-submarine corvettes, 6 German and Italian-built fast missile craft, 11 coastal and 40 inshore patrol craft, and about 40 riverine patrol boats. There is 1 mine countermeasures support vessel, 2 coastal minehunters and 3 coastal minesweepers. Amphibious capability is provided by 7 tank landing ships and 2 medium landing ships as well as 50 landing craft. Major auxiliaries are 1 small tanker, 3 surveying ships and 3 training ships. Minor auxiliaries and service craft number about 12.

The Naval air element, all shore based, includes 3 P-3T Orion, 6 F-27 Maritime and 3 DO228 for maritime patrol, 4 F-27 Friendship transports, 9 Cessna T-337 armed light transports and 16 Bell anti-submarine and 14 utility and search-and-rescue helicopters.

Naval personnel in 1995 totalled 65,000 including 20,000 marines and 1,500 Naval Air Arm. The main bases are at Bangkok, Sattahip, Songkla and Phang Nga, with the riverine forces based at Nakhon Phanom.

A separate coast guard force, the Royal Thai Marine Police, numbers 2,500 and operates 3 coastal patrol craft, 32 riverine and inshore craft and numerous boats.

Air Force. The Royal Thai Air Force was reorganized with the assistance of a US Military Air Advisory Group. It had a strength (1995) of 43,000 personnel and 170 combat aircraft, and is made up of a headquarters and Combat, Logistics Support, Training and Special Services Groups. Combat units comprise 2 squadrons of F-6s, 2 squadrons of F-5E/F interceptors, 4 squadrons with L-39 light strike aircraft, 1 squadron with A-37B light jet attack aircraft, 1 with OV-10 Bronco light reconnaissance/attack aircraft, and 2 with AU-23A Peacemakers and 1 squadron with Nomads for security duties. 3 Aravas are used for electronic intelligence gathering and 3 Learjets for combat support. There are transport units equipped with a total of about 70 C-130H/H-30 Hercules, HS 748, C-123B Provider, C-47, G.222 and smaller aircraft, including Australian-built Missionmasters; there are 30 UH-1H and 17 S-58T helicopters; training units with Airtrainer CT/4 primary trainers built in New Zealand, Italian-built SF.260MTs, and PC-9 and intermediate trainers.

INTERNATIONAL RELATIONS

Membership. Thailand is a member of the UN, ASEAN and the Colombo Plan.

ECONOMY

Policy. The Sixth 5-year Development Plan (1987–91) envisaged emphasis on development of the production system, with specific attention being paid to providing employment and expanding the industrial base. The Seventh Plan covered 1992–96.

Budget. The fiscal year starts in Oct. The draft budget for 1995–96 balanced at 832,200m. baht.

Currency. The unit of currency is the *baht* (THB) of 100 *satang*. There are coins of 25 and 50 satangs and 1, 2, 5 and 10 baht, and notes of 10, 20, 50, 100, 500 and 1,000 baht. In April 1991 the total amount of notes in circulation was 151,306m. baht. Foreign exchange reserves were US$30,000m. in 1994. Inflation was 5% in 1995. In March 1996, £1 = 38·55 baht; US$1 = 25·22 baht; DM1 = 17·09 baht.

Banking and Finance. The Bank of Thailand (founded in 1942) is the central bank and bank of issue, an independent body although its capital is government-owned. Its assets and liabilities in Dec. 1991 were 580,844·5m. baht. Its *Governor* is Vijit Sukpinit. In 1994 there were 15 domestic commercial banks, 14 foreign banks with branch licenses and 22 foreign banks with representative offices. Total credits of commercial banks, Dec. 1995, 4,144,000m. baht. Deposits, Dec. 1995, 3,141,500m. baht. There is a Government Savings Bank.

There is a stock exchange (SET) in Bangkok.

Weights and Measures. The metric system was made compulsory in 1923. Units of weight: 1 *standard picul* = 60 kg; 1 *standard catty* (1/100 picul) = 600 grammes; 1 *standard carat* = 20 centigrammes. Units of length: 1 *sen* = 40 metres; 1 *wah* (1/20 sen) = 2 metres; 1 *sauk* (1/2 wah) = 0·50 metre; 1 *keup* (1/2 sauk) = 0·25 metre. Units of square measure: 1 *rai* (1 sq. sen) = 1,600 sq. metres: 1 *ngan* (1/4 rai) = 400 sq. metres; 1 *sq. wah* (1/100 ngan) = 4 sq. metres. Units of capacity: 1 *standard kwien* = 2,000 litres; 1 *standard ban* (1/2 kwien) = 1,000 litres; 1 *standard sat* (1/50 ban) = 20 litres; 1 *standard tannan* (1/20 sat) = 1 litre.

The year of the Buddhist era (B.E.) 2484 began on 1 Jan. 1941.

ENERGY AND NATURAL RESOURCES

Electricity. Installed capacity, 1988, was 6,997 MW (3,608 MW thermal, 2,268 MW hydro-electric, 267 MW gas turbine and 82 MW diesel). Output: 32,464·4m. kWh (22,966·8m. kWh thermal, 3,779m. kWh hydro-electric, 763·7m. kWh gas turbine and 20·9m. kWh diesel).

Oil. Proven oil reserves in 1987 were less than 160m. bbls. Estimated production of crude oil (1993) 8,544 bbls.

Gas. Production of natural gas (1993) 343,581m. cu. ft. Estimated reserves, 1986, 12,922,000m. cu. ft.

Minerals. The mineral resources include cassiterite (tin ore), wolfram, scheelite, antimony, coal, copper, gold, iron, lead, manganese, molybdenum, rubies, sapphires, silver, zinc and zircons. Production, 1993 (in 1,000 tonnes): Iron ore, 208·9; manganese ore, 6·5; tin concentrates, 6·4; lead ore, 14·3; antimony ore, 1·5; zinc ore, 445·8; lignite, 15,592·8; gypsum, 7,454·8; wolfram ore (tungsten), 0·2; fluorite ore, 48·4; marl, 563·7.

Agriculture. In 1992 agriculture produced 11·9% of GDP. The chief produce is rice, a staple of the national diet. Output of the major crops in 1993 was (in 1,000 tonnes): Paddy, 19,440; maize, 3,300; sugar-cane, 38,500; jute and kenaf, 144·4; tobacco leaves, 28·7; tapioca-root, 19,487; soybeans, 500; coconut, 1,170; mung beans, 258; cotton, 94; groundnuts, 153; sesame, 32·8; castor seeds, 32·4; kapok and bambax fibre, 39·7; sorghum (1992), 140.

Livestock, 1991 (in 1,000): Horses, 18; buffaloes, 4,743; cattle, 6,052; pigs, 5,000; sheep, 178; goats, 140; poultry, 114m.

Forestry. About 14·4m. ha was under forest in 1988. Teak and other hardwoods grow in the deciduous forests of the north; elsewhere tropical evergreen forests are found, with the timber yang the main crop (a source of yang oil).

Output of main forestry products in 1992: Teak, 1,000 cu. metres; yang and other woods, 109,000 cu. metres. By-products in 1992: Firewood, 285,100 cu. metres; charcoal, 141,900 cu. metres.

Rubber production in 1993: 1·58m. tonnes.

Fisheries. In 1992 the catch of sea fish was 2,622,000 tonnes including marine prawns, shrimps and other shellfish, 313,000 tonnes; of freshwater fish, 233,000 tonnes.

INDUSTRY. In 1991 manufacturing produced 36·4% and services 49·8% of GDP. Production of manufactured goods in 1990 included 18,053,899 tonnes of cement, 263,482,000 litres of beer, 905m. litres of soft drinks, 38,180 tonnes of cigarettes, 208,483 tonnes of galvanized iron sheets, 173,111 tonnes of tin plate, 305,145 automobiles, 715,115 motorcycles, 65,319 tonnes of tyres, 225,017 tonnes of synthetic fibre, 152,263 tonnes of jute products, 157,600 tonnes of paper, 150,946 tonnes of detergent, 13,983m. litres of petroleum products and 5,106,000 tonnes of sugar (1992).

Labour. In 1992 the labour force (aged 13 and over) was 32·4m. Employed persons totalled 31·4m., of whom 18·8m. were in agriculture and 3·6m. in manufacturing. The unemployment rate was 3·1%.

FOREIGN ECONOMIC RELATIONS. Foreign debt was US$62,100m. in 1994.

Commerce. Tariffs on raw materials and semi-manufactures were reduced on 1 Jan. 1995. The foreign trade (in 1,000m. baht) was as follows:

	1992	*1993*	*1994*	*1995*
Imports (c.i.f.)	1,033·2	1,143·1	1,337·0	1,543·0
Exports (f.o.b.)	824·6	921·4	1,096·5	1,277·8

Main exports by category in 1991, in 1m. baht: Manufactures, 286,148; food, 191,973; machinery, 176,626; raw materials, 35,465. Imports: Machinery, 394,611; manufactures, 267,887; chemicals, 88,631; mineral fuel and lubricant, 87,580; raw materials, 58,987.

In 1993 exports (in 1m. baht) went mainly to USA (202,227), Japan (159,479), Singapore (112,844), Hong Kong (49,583) and Germany (37,457); imports were mainly from Japan (353,507), USA (136,045), Singapore (75,188), Germany (62,846) and Taiwan (59,127).

Total trade between Thailand and UK (British Department of Trade returns, in £1,000 sterling):

	1991	*1992*	*1993*	*1994*	*1995*
Imports to UK	625,374	641,886	770,677	913,135	1,039,849
Exports and re-exports from UK	463,449	476,368	659,376	745,587	836,622

Tourism. In 1990, 5·37m. foreigners visited Thailand. Tourist revenue was 110,000m. baht.

COMMUNICATIONS

Roads. In 1991 there were 17,920 km of state highways and 28,127 km of provincial highways. In 1989 there were 1,523,361 commercial vehicles and 655,927 private cars.

Railways. In 1994 the State Railway totalled 3,870 route km (metre gauge), excluding the Mae Klong line. In 1994 it carried 87m. passengers and 7·6m. tonnes of freight.

Civil Aviation. There are international airports at Bangkok, Chiangmai, Phuket, Hat Yai and U-tapao. The national carrier is Thai Airways International, 92·85% state-owned, which in 1995 operated 6 A300B4-100s, 4 A300B4-200s, 6 A300B4-600s, 10 A300B4-600Rs, 1 A300C4-200, 2 A310-200s, 6 A330-300s, 7 B-737-400s, 6 B-747-200Bs, 2 B-747-300s and 8 B-747-400s. Services were also provided by Aeroflot, Air China, Air France, Air India, Air Koryo, Air Lanka, Air Liberté, Air New Zealand, Alitalia, All Nippon, AOM, Asiana, Balkan, Biman Bangladesh, British Airways, Canadian Airlines, Cathay Pacific, China Airlines, China Eastern Airlines, China Southern Airlines, China Southwest Airlines, Condor, Czech Airlines, Delta, Dragonair, Druk-Air, Egyptair, El Al, Emirates, Ethiopian Airways, Eva, Finnair, Garuda Indonesia, Gulf Air, Indian Airlines, JAL, KLM, Korean Air, Kuwait Airways, Lao Aviation, Lauda Air, LOT, LTU, Lufthansa, Malaysia Airlines, Myanma Airways, Northwest Airlines, Olympic Airways, Pakistan Airlines, Philippine Airlines, Qantas, Royal Air Cambodge, Royal Brunei Airlines, Royal Jordanian, Royal Nepal Airlines, SAA, SAS, Saudia, Singapore Airlines, Swissair, Tarom, Turkish Airlines, United Airlines, Uzbekistan Airways, Varig, Vietnam Airlines and Yunnan Airlines.

Shipping. In 1995 sea-going shipping totalled 2·11m. GRT, including oil tankers, 0·36m. GRT, and container ships, 0·11m. GRT. In 1988, 5,020 vessels of 24,758,487 NRT entered and 4,854 of 24,295,440 NRT cleared the port of Bangkok.

Telecommunications. In 1994 there were 1,553,200 telephones.

The Radio and Television Executive Committee controls the administrative, legal, technical and programming aspects of broadcasting, and consists of representatives of various government bodies. All radio stations are operated by, or under the supervision of, government agencies. Radio Thailand broadcasts 3 national programmes, provincial programmes, an educational service and an external service (9 languages) and the Voice of Free Asia. Television of Thailand is the state service (colour by PAL). There are 3 commercial channels and an Army service. In 1993 there were 10m. radio and 3·3m. TV sets in use.

Cinemas (1993). There were 600 cinemas with a seating capacity of 380,011.

Press (1989). There are 23 daily newspapers in Bangkok, including 2 in English and 7 in Chinese, with a combined circulation of about 2m.

SOCIAL INSTITUTIONS

Justice. The judicial power is exercised in the name of the King, by *(a)* courts of first instance, *(b)* the court of appeal *(Uthorn)* and *(c)* the Supreme Court *(Dika)*. The King appoints, transfers and dismisses judges, who are independent in conducting trials and giving judgment in accordance with the law.

Courts of first instance are subdivided into 20 magistrates' courts *(Kwaeng)* with limited civil and minor criminal jurisdiction; 85 provincial courts *(Changwad)* with unlimited civil and criminal jurisdiction; the criminal and civil courts with exclusive jurisdiction in Bangkok; the central juvenile courts for persons under 18 years of age in Bangkok.

The court of appeal exercises appellate jurisdiction in civil and criminal cases from all courts of first instance. From it appeals lie to Dika Court on any point of law and, in certain cases, on questions of fact.

The Supreme Court is the supreme tribunal of the land. Besides its normal appellate jurisdiction in civil and criminal matters, it has semi-original jurisdiction over general election petitions. The decisions of Dika Court are final. Every person has the right to present a petition to the Government who will deal with all matters of grievance.

Religion. In 1993 there were 54·53m. Buddhists, 2·31m. Moslems, 0·29m. Christians and 0·69m. others.

Education. Education is compulsory for children for 9 years and free in local municipal schools. In 1992 there were 1,390,417 pupils enrolled at pre-primary level, 6,757,437 at primary level, 1,772,469 at lower secondary level, 944,970 at upper secondary level and 973,681 in higher education. In 1992 there were 36 teachers' training colleges with 6,498 teachers and 51,237 students. In 1995–96 there were 13 universities, 2 open (distance) universities, 4 institutes of technology and 1 institute of development administration in the public sector, and 9 universities and 1 institute of technology in the private sector.

Health. The Primary Health Care Programme had provided health services in 95% of villages in 1986. In 1990 there were 959 hospitals and 7,828 health centres. In 1990 there were 12,520 physicians, 2,285 dentists, 4,168 pharmacists, 77,186 nurses and 10,796 midwives.

DIPLOMATIC REPRESENTATIVES

Of Thailand in Great Britain (29–30 Queen's Gate, London, SW7 5JB)
Ambassador: Vidhya Rayananonda.

Of Great Britain in Thailand (Thanon Witthayu, Bangkok)
Ambassador: C. C. W. Adams, CMG.

Of Thailand in the USA (2300 Kalorama Rd., NW, Washington, D.C., 20008)
Ambassador: Nitya Pibulsonggram.

Of the USA in Thailand (95 Thanon Witthayu, Bangkok)
Ambassador: R. Itoh.

Of Thailand to the United Nations
Ambassador: Asda Jayanama.

Further Reading

National Statistical Office *Thailand Statistical Yearbook.*
Girling, J. I. S., *Thailand: Society and Politics.* Cornell Univ. Press, 1981
Krongkaew, M. (ed.) *Thailand's Industrialization and its Consequences.* London, 1995
Kulick, E. and Wilson, D., *Thailand's Turn: Profile of a New Dragon.* London and New York, 1993 (NY, 1994)
Watts, M., *Thailand.* [Bibliography] Oxford and Santa Barbara (CA), 1986

National statistical office: National Statistical Office, Thanon Lan Luang, Bangkok 10100.

TOGO

République Togolaise

Capital: Lomé
Population: 3·5m. (1991)
GNP per capita: US$320 (1994)
HDI/world rank: 0·409/140 (1992)

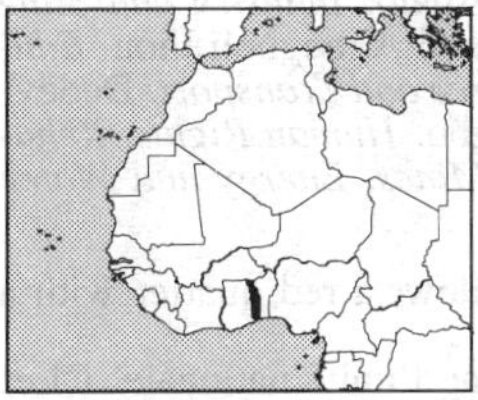

KEY HISTORICAL EVENTS. Togo became independent on 27 April 1960. (For its colonial history *see* THE STATESMAN'S YEAR-BOOK, 1991–92, p. 1194).

On 13 Jan. 1963 the first President, Sylvanus Olympio was murdered by soldiers. His successor, Nicolas Grunitzky, was deposed in a bloodless military coup in Jan. 1967 and on 14 April 1967 Gen. (then Col.) Gnassingbé Eyadéma assumed the Presidency. Following a general strike in June 1991 the government agreed to hold a National Conference, and this elected an interim Supreme Republican Council. A new constitution was approved in 1992.

TERRITORY AND POPULATION. Togo is bounded west by Ghana, north by Burkina Faso, east by Benin and south by the Gulf of Guinea. The area is 56,785 sq. km. The population of Togo in 1981 (census) was 2,700,982; 1991 (estimate) 3,455,000 (1,747,000 females), 25·7% urban. Population density, 60·8 per sq. km. The capital is Lomé (population, 1990, 0·45m.), other towns being Sokodé (55,000), Kpalimé (31,000), Atakpamé (30,000), Tsévié (26,000), Bassar (19,000) and Aného (16,000).

Population growth in 1990 was 3% per annum; infant mortality was 10%; life expectancy, 54 years.

Area, population and chief town of the 5 regions:

Region	*Area in sq. km*	*Population (1981 census)*	*Population (1984 estimate)*	*Chief town*
Des Savanes	8,602	326,826	358,700	Dapaong
De La Kara	11,630	432,626	444,200	Kara
Centrale	13,182	269,174	310,500	Sokodé
Des Plateaux	16,975	561,656	708,100	Atakpamé
Maritime	6,396	1,039,700	1,147,800	Lomé

There are 37 ethnic groups. The south is largely populated by Ewe-speaking peoples (forming 44% of the population) and related groups, while the north is mainly inhabited by Hamitic groups speaking Kabre (27%), Gurma (14%) and Tem (4%). The official language is French but Ewe and Kabre are also taught in schools.

CLIMATE. The tropical climate produces wet seasons from March to July and from Oct. to Nov. in the south. The north has one wet season, from April to July. The heaviest rainfall occurs in the mountains of the west, south-west and centre. Lomé. Jan. 81°F (27·2°C), July 76°F (24·4°C). Annual rainfall 35" (875 mm).

CONSTITUTION AND GOVERNMENT. A referendum on 27 Sept. 1992 approved a new constitution by 98·11% of votes cast. Under this the *President* and the *National Assembly* are directly elected for 5-year terms. The latter has 81 seats and is elected in 2 rounds on a first-past-the-post system.

At the presidential election of 25 Aug. 1993 turn-out was 39·5%. President Eyadéma was re-elected against 2 opponents by 96·49% of votes cast.

At the parliamentary elections in Feb. 1994 the electorate was 2m. 352 candidates stood. The Togolese People's Assembly (RPT, the former sole party) gained 38 seats, the Action Committee for Renewal 36 and the Togolese Union for Democracy (UTD) 7.

President: Gen. Gnassingbé Eyadéma (re-elected 25 Aug. 1993).

On 25 May 1994 an RPT-UDT coalition government was formed, which in Sept. 1995 comprised:

Prime Minister: Edem Kodjo (b. 1939; UDT).

Economy and Finance: Elome Dadzie. *Foreign Affairs and Co-operation:* Vacant. *Planning and Territorial Development:* Yandjia Yentchabre. *Equipment:* Tchamdja Andjo. *Justice:* Kagni Gabriel. *Territorial Administration and Security:* Seyi Memene. *Communications and Culture:* Atsutse Agbobli. *Tourism, Rural Development and Environment:* Yao Do Felli. *Health:* Afatbao Amédomé. *Welfare and National Solidarity:* Were Gazaro. *Defence:* Alfa Abalo. *Industry and State Companies:* Payadowa Boukpessi. *Youth and Sport:* Kouami Agbogboli Ihou. *Education and Scientific Research:* Komlavi Seddoh. *Commerce and Transport:* Dedevi Michele Ekue. *Interior and Decentralization:* Kodjo Sagbo. *Human Rights, Rehabilitation and Relations with Parliament:* Djovi Gally. *Mines, Energy and Water Resources:* Anato Agbodouhoue.

National flag: Five horizontal stripes of green and yellow, a red quarter with a white star.

National anthem: 'Ecartons tout mauvais esprit qui gêne l'unité nationale' ('Let us sweep aside all ill feelings which foil the national unity'); words and tune collective.

Local Government: There are 5 regions, each under an inspector appointed by the President; they are divided into 31 *prefectures* and the capital Lomé, each administered by a district chief assisted by an elected district council.

DEFENCE. There is selective conscription for 2 years.

Army. The Army consists of 2 infantry, 1 Presidential Guard, 1 parachute commando and 1 support regiment. Equipment includes 2 T-54/-55 main battle tanks. Strength (1996) 6,500, with a further 750 in a paramilitary gendarmerie.

Navy. In 1995 the Naval wing of the armed forces operated 2 inshore patrol craft from the naval base at Lomé. Naval personnel number 115.

Air Force. An Air Force, established with French assistance, has 4 Brazilian-built EMB-326 Xavante (Aermacchi MB.326) armed jet trainers; 5 Alpha Jet advanced trainers, with strike capability, 2 turboprop Buffalo transports; 2 Beech King Air 200s and 1 Cessna 337 for liaison; 3 Epsilon armed trainers; 2 Lama helicopters. Personnel (1995), 250, with 9 combat aircraft.

INTERNATIONAL RELATIONS

Membership. Togo is a member of the UN, OAU and ECOWAS, and is an ACP state of the EU.

ECONOMY

Policy. A Sixth 5-year plan was drawn up for 1991–95.

Budget. At the 1993 budget revenue was 90,000m. francs CFA. Expenditure was 92,000m. francs CFA in 1991.

Currency. The unit of currency is the *franc* CFA with a parity rate of 100 francs CFA to 1 French franc. Gold reserves were US$3·3m. in 1992. Foreign exchange reserves were US$272·5m.; 28,000m. francs CFA were in circulation in 1993. The rate of exchange (March 1996) was 772·97 francs CFA to £1; US$1 = 505·74 francs CFA; DM1 = 342·67 francs CFA.

Banking and Finance. The bank of issue is the Central Bank of West African States (BCEAO). 7 commercial and 3 development banks are based in Lomé. Bank deposits totalled 168,700m. francs CFA in 1989.

Weights and Measures. The metric system is in use.

ENERGY AND NATURAL RESOURCES

Electricity. Installed capacity was 65,500 kWh in 1987 (35,500 kWh hydroelectric). Production (1988) 339·5m. kWh. There is a hydro-electric plant at Kpalimé.

Minerals. Output of phosphate rock (1992) 2,079,000 tonnes. Other minerals are limestone, iron ore (550m. tonnes) and marble.

Agriculture. Agriculture supports about 80% of the population and produces 30% of GDP. Most food production comes from individual holdings under 3 ha. Inland the country is hilly; dry plains alternate with arable land. There are considerable plantations of oil and cocoa palms, coffee, cacao, kola, cassava and cotton. Production, 1992 (in 1,000 tonnes): Cassava, 480; tomatoes, 9; yams, 393; maize, 239; sorghum, 109; millet, 82; seed cotton, 97; rice, 26; groundnuts, 22; coffee, 13.

Livestock (1992, in 1,000): Cattle, 320; sheep, 1,500; pigs, 800; goats, 2,000.

Forestry. In 1991 the wooded area was 1·6m. ha. In 1994 teak plantations covered 8,600 ha. Annual production for fuel, 1·3m. cu. metres.

Fisheries. Fishery is on a small scale. The annual catch averages 15,000 tonnes (65% marine).

INDUSTRY. Industry is small-scale. Cement and textiles are produced and food processed.

Labour. In 1990 the workforce was 1,396,000 (508,000 female, 54,000 aged 10–15). In 1994 the statutory minimum wage was 75·60 francs CFA per hour.

Trade Unions. With the abandonment of single-party politics the former monolithic Togo National Workers Confederation (CNTT) has split into several federations and independent trade unions.

FOREIGN ECONOMIC RELATIONS. A free trade zone was established in 1990. Foreign debt was US$1,356m. in 1992.

Commerce (in 1m. francs CFA):

	1984	*1985*	*1986*	*1987*	*1988*	*1989*
Imports	118,460	129,406	107,983	127,308	145,170	150,554
Exports	83,588	85,380	70,551	73,212	72,209	78,188

In 1989 the main imports (in 1m. francs CFA) were: Textiles, 15,430; motor vehicles and spares, 9,494; cigarettes, 5,655; antibiotics, 4,235. Exports: Phosphates, 41,607; cotton, 12,328; coffee, 7,055; cocoa, 3,934. The main import suppliers in 1992 were: France, 21·4%; China, 8·8%; Thailand, 7·3%; Netherlands, 5·8%; Côte d'Ivoire, 5·3%. Main export markets: Canada, 9·3%; Burkina Faso, 5·9%; France, 4·6%; India, 3·8%; Italy, 3·6%.

Total trade between Togo and UK (British Department of Trade returns, in £1,000 sterling):

	1991	*1992*	*1993*	*1994*	*1995*
Imports to UK	1,820	4,066	901	3,176	2,671
Exports and re-exports from UK	20,932	7,658	4,769	7,278	11,781

Tourism. There were 123,550 tourists in 1990; receipts were 7,000m. francs CFA.

COMMUNICATIONS

Roads. There were, in 1990, 7,870 km of roads, of which 1,570 km were paved. In 1988 there were 47,083 passenger cars, 29,179 motorcycles and 22,611 commercial vehicles.

Railways. There are 4 metre-gauge railways connecting Lomé, with Aného (continuing to Cotonou in Benin), Kpalimé, Tabligbo and (via Atakpamé) Blitta; total length 525 km. In 1994 the railways carried 5·7 tonne-km and 0·6m. passengers.

Civil Aviation. The national carrier is Air Togo. Air services connect Tokoin airport, near Lomé, with Paris, Dakar, Abidjan, Douala, Accra, Lagos, Cotonou and Niamey and by internal services with Sokodé, Mango, Dapaong, Atakpamé and Niamtougou. 309,200 passengers and 3,796 tonnes of freight were handled in 1987.

Shipping. In 1987, 1,195 vessels unloaded 1,149,800 tonnes of freight and loaded 195,200 tonnes at Lomé. The merchant marine comprised (1985) 11 vessels of 77,989 DWT. In 1981 some 2·2m. tonnes of phosphate were loaded at the port of Kpéme.

Telecommunications. There were (1983) 388 post offices and 11,105 telephones. Broadcasting is provided by the government-controlled Radiodiffusion-Télévision Togolaise. There were 0·7m. radio and 23,000 TV receivers (colour by SECAM) in 1991.

Press. There was (1993) 1 government-controlled daily newspaper (circulation 10,000).

SOCIAL INSTITUTIONS

Justice. The Supreme Court and two Appeal Courts are in Lomé, one for criminal cases and one for civil and commercial cases. Each receives appeal from a series of local tribunals.

Religion. In 1994, 18% of the population were Christian and 2% Moslem (chiefly in the north). Many follow traditional animist religions.

Education. Adult literacy was 43% in 1990. In 1986 there were 474,998 pupils and 10,209 teachers in 2,345 primary schools, 86,327 pupils in secondary schools, and 5,050 students and 198 teachers in technical schools and 374 students and 22 teachers at the teacher-training college. In 1990 about 50% of children of school age were attending school. The University of Benin at Lomé (founded in 1970) had 9,139 students and 134 academic staff in 1994–95.

Health. In 1988 there were 28 hospitals and 348 health centres with 5,275 beds and 278 doctors, 25 pharmacists, 348 midwives and 1,285 nursing staff.

DIPLOMATIC REPRESENTATIVES

The Embassy of Togo in Great Britain closed on 30 Sept. 1991.

Of Great Britain in Togo
Ambassador and Consul-General: D. C. Walker, CMG, CVO (resides in Accra).

Of Togo in the USA (2208 Massachusetts Ave., NW, Washington, D.C., 20008)
Ambassador: Vacant.

Of the USA in Togo (Rue Pelletier Caventou, Lomé)
Ambassador: Johnny Young.

Of Togo to the United Nations
Ambassador: Vacant.

Further Reading

Cornevin, R., *Histoire du Togo.* 3rd ed., Paris, 1969
Decalo, S., *Togo.* [Bibliography] Oxford and Santa Barbara (CA), 1995
Feuillet, C., *Le Togo en Général.* Paris, 1976

TONGA

Kingdom of Tonga

Capital: Nuku'alofa
Population: 103,000 (1991)
GNP per capita: US$1,640 (1994)

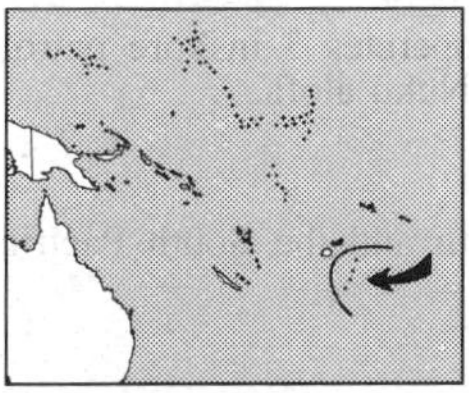

KEY HISTORICAL EVENTS. The Tongatapu group was discovered by Tasman in 1643.

A British protectorate was proclaimed on 18 May 1900. (For previous history *see* THE STATESMAN'S YEAR-BOOK, 1991–92, p. 1198). On 4 June 1970 Tonga became independent within the Commonwealth.

TERRITORY AND POPULATION. The Kingdom consists of some 169 islands and islets with a total area of 289 sq. miles (748 sq. km; including inland waters), and lies between 15° and 23° 30' S. lat and 173° and 177° W. long., its western boundary being the eastern boundary of Fiji. The islands are split up into the following groups reading from north to south: The Niuas, Vava'u, Ha'apai, Tongatapu and 'Eua. The 3 main groups, both from historical and administrative significance, are Tongatapu in the south, Ha'apai in the centre and Vava'u in the north.

The capital is Nuku'alofa on Tongatapu, population (1986) 29,018.

There are 5 divisions comprising 23 districts:

Division	*Sq. km*	*Census 1986*	*Capital*
Niuas	72	2,368	Hihifo
Vava'u	119	15,175	Neiafu
Ha'apai	110	8,919	Pangai
Tongatapu	261	63,794	Nuku'alofa
'Eua	87	4,393	Ohonua

Census population (1986) 94,649 (males, 47,611); estimate (1991) 103,000.

CLIMATE. Generally a healthy climate, though Jan. to March is hot and humid, with temperatures of 90°F (32·2°C). Rainfall amounts are comparatively high, being greatest from Dec. to March. Nuku'alofa. Jan. 25·8°C, July 21·3°C. Annual rainfall 1,643 mm. Vava'u. Jan. 27·3°C, July 23·4°C. Annual rainfall 2,034 mm.

ROYAL HOUSE. The reigning King is **Taufa'ahau Tupou IV**, GCVO, GCMG, KBE, born 4 July 1918, succeeded on 16 Dec. 1965 on the death of his mother, Queen Salote Tupou III; his coronation took place on 4 July 1967.

CONSTITUTION AND GOVERNMENT. The present Constitution is almost identical with that granted in 1875 by King George Tupou I. There is a Privy Council, Cabinet, Legislative Assembly and Judiciary. The 30-member *Legislative Assembly*, which meets annually, is composed of the King, 9 nobles elected by their peers, 9 elected representatives of the people and the Privy Councillors (numbering 11); the King appoints one of the 9 nobles to be the Speaker. The elections are held triennially.

Elections were held in Feb. 1993. The electorate of commoners was 45,000; there were 55 candidates. 6 seats were won by pro-democracy candidates.

In Nov. 1995 the government comprised:

Prime Minister and Minister of Agriculture, Fisheries, Forests and Marine Affairs: The Hon. Baron Vaea.

Deputy Prime Minister and Minister of Education, Works and Civil Aviation: The Hon. Dr S. Langi Kavaliku. *Finance, Labour, Commerce and Industry:* Tutoatasi Faka-Fanua. *Foreign Affairs and Defence:* HRH The Crown Prince Tupouto'a. *Health:* Dr Sione Tapa. *Attorney-General and Minister of Justice:* Tevita Tupou. *Police, Prisons and Fire Services:* The Hon. George 'Akauola. *Lands, Surveys and Natural Resources:* Dr S. Ma'afu Tupou. *Without Portfolio:* The Hon. Ma'afu

Tuku'i'aulahi. *Governor of Ha'apai:* The Hon. Fakafanua. *Governor of Vava'u:* The Hon. Tu'i'afitu.

National flag: Red with a white quarter bearing a red couped cross.

National anthem: ''E 'Otua, Mafimafi, ko ho mau 'eiki Koe' ('Oh Almighty God above, thou art our Lord and sure defence'); words by Prince Uelingtoni Ngu Tupoumalohi, tune by K. G. Schmitt.

DEFENCE. A naval force some 125 strong in 1995 operates 3 inshore patrol craft, and 1 ex-Australian amphibious craft base at Tuliki, Nuku'alofa.

INTERNATIONAL RELATIONS

Membership. Tonga is a member of the Commonwealth and the South Pacific Forum, and is an ACP state of the EU.

ECONOMY

Budget. Recurrent revenue and expenditure in T$1,000:

	1990–91	*1991–92*	*1992–93*	*1993-94*
Revenue	47,442	46,229	52,287	54,766
Expenditure	47,438	51,984	49,928	52,230

Currency. The unit of currency is the *pa'anga* (TOP) of 100 *seniti*. There are notes of T$50, 20, 10, 5, 2 and 1 and coins of *seniti* 50, 20, 10, 5, 2 and 1. In March 1996, £1 = T$2·01; US$1 = T$1·31; DM1 = T$0·89.

Banking and Finance. The National Reserve Bank of Tonga was established in 1989 as a bank of issue and to manage foreign reserves. The Bank of Tonga and the Tonga Development Bank are both situated in Nuku'alofa with branches in the main islands.

ENERGY AND NATURAL RESOURCES

Electricity. Production (1986) 8m. kWh.

Agriculture. Production (1992, in 1,000 tonnes): Coconuts, 25; fruit and vegetables, 28; copra, 2; cassava, 15.

Livestock (1992, in 1,000): Cattle, 10; horses, 12; pigs, 97; goats, 16.

Fisheries. Catch (1982) 2,500 tonnes.

FOREIGN ECONOMIC RELATIONS

Commerce. In 1991, imports were valued at T$76,817,269 while exports and re-exports were T$20,610,860 and T$854,263.

Main exports (1991, in T$): Coconut oil 417,713, vanilla beans 2,857,089, dessicated coconut 1,745, water melons 158,012, knitted clothes 479,560, taros 105,435; cassava 126,414, yams and sweet potatoes, 80,260, kape 27,380, footwear 104,733, tapa cloth 50,020, mato 65,375.

Principal destinations for Tongan exports/re-exports in 1991 (in T$) were: Japan, 12,456,884; USA, 2,679,277; Australia, 1,918,919; New Zealand, 1,840,694; UK, 13,600. Of 1991 imports (in T$), New Zealand furnished 22,723,894; Australia, 19,609,346; Fiji, 11,916,618; USA, 6,966,313.

Total trade between Tonga and UK (British Department of Trade returns, in £1,000 sterling):

	1991	*1992*	*1993*	*1994*	*1995*
Imports to UK	20	294	55	341	113
Exports and re-exports from UK	944	482	1,463	686	3,010

Tourism. There were 39,550 visitors in 1987.

COMMUNICATIONS

Roads. In Dec. 1991 there were 7,364 registered motor vehicles and approximately 415 km of paved roads.

Civil Aviation. There is an international airport at Fua'Amotu. The national carrier is the state-owned Royal Tongan Airlines, which operated 2 aircraft in 1995 and had services to Fiji and New Zealand. Services also provided by Air New Zealand, Air Pacific and Polynesian Airlines.

Shipping. In 1995, sea-going shipping totalled 12,307 GRT. 2 shipping lanes provide monthly services to American Samoa, Australia, Fiji, Kiribati, New Caledonia, New Zealand, Tuvalu and Western Samoa.

Telecommunications. Telephones numbered 3,500 in 1986. The operation of the International Telecommunication Services is undertaken by Cable and Wireless, under an agreement between the Company and the Government. The operation and development of the National Telecommunication Network and Services are the responsibilities of the Tonga Telecommunication Commission. The Tonga Broadcasting Commission is an independent statutory board which operates 2 programmes. There is also a religious service. There were about 66,000 radio sets in 1993. There are 2 television channels.

SOCIAL INSTITUTIONS

Justice. The judiciary is presided over by the Chief Justice. The enforcement of justice is the responsibility of the Attorney-General and the Minister of Police. In 1994 the UK ceased appointing Tongan judges and subsidizing their salaries.

Religion. The Tongans are Christian, 40,516 (1986) being adherents of the Free Wesleyan Church.

Education. In 1991 there were 104 government and 11 denominational primary schools, with a total of 16,655 pupils. There were 7 government and 32 mission schools and 1 private school offering secondary education, with a total roll of 13,839. There is an extension centre of the University of the South Pacific at Nuku'alofa, a teacher training college and 3 technical institutes.

Health. In 1988–89 there were 45 doctors, 11 dentists, 2 pharmacists, 37 midwives, 266 nursing personnel and 4 hospitals with 307 beds.

DIPLOMATIC REPRESENTATIVES

Of Tonga in Great Britain (36 Molyneux St., London, W1H 6AB)
High Commissioner: Sione Kité.

Of Great Britain in Tonga (POB 56 Nuku'alofa)
High Commissioner: A. J. Morris.

Of Tonga in the USA
Ambassador: Sione Kité (resident in London)

Of the USA in Tonga
Ambassador: Vacant (resident in Suva)

Further Reading

Campbell, I. C., *Island Kingdom: Tonga, Ancient and Modern.* Canterbury (NZ) Univ. Press, 1994

TRINIDAD AND TOBAGO

Republic of Trinidad and Tobago

Capital: Port-of-Spain
Population: 1·25m. (1991)
GNP per capita: US$3,740 (1994)
HDI/world rank: 0·872/39 (1992)

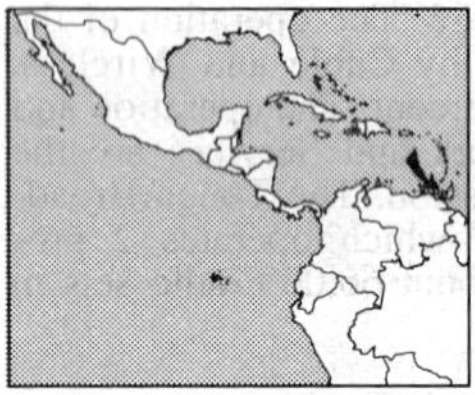

KEY HISTORICAL EVENTS. Trinidad was discovered by Columbus in 1498 and colonized by the Spaniards in the 16th century. For colonial history *see* THE STATESMAN'S YEAR-BOOK, 1991–92, p. 1201. Trinidad and Tobago were joined in 1889.

On 31 Aug. 1962 Trinidad and Tobago became an independent member state of the Commonwealth. A Republican Constitution was adopted on 1 Aug. 1976.

During an attempted coup in July 1990 by a Moslem sect the prime minister was taken hostage and wounded.

TERRITORY AND POPULATION. The island of Trinidad is situated in the Caribbean Sea, about 12 km off the north-east coast of Venezuela; several islets, the largest being Chacachacare, Huevos, Monos and Gaspar Grande, lie in the Gulf of Paria which separates Trinidad from Venezuela. The smaller island of Tobago lies 30·7 km further to the north-east. Altogether, the islands cover 5,124 sq. km (1,978 sq. miles) of which Trinidad (including the islets) has 4,821 sq. km (1,861 sq. miles) and Tobago 303 sq. km (117 sq. miles). Population (census 1990) 1,169,600 (Trinidad, 1,123,200; Tobago, 46,400); estimate (1991) 1·25m. Capital, Port-of-Spain (1990 census, 58,400); other important towns, San Fernando (30,100), Arima (29,700) and Point Fortin (20,000). The main town on Tobago is Scarborough. Those of African descent are 40·8% of the population, Indians, 40·7%, mixed races, 16·3%, European, Chinese and others, 2·2%. English is spoken generally.

Growth rate, 1992, 0·81%; infantile mortality, 12·7 per 1,000 live births; expectation of life, 72 years.

CLIMATE. A tropical climate cooled by the north-east trade winds. The dry season runs from Jan. to June, with a wet season for the rest of the year. Temperatures are uniformly high the year round. Port-of-Spain. Jan. 78°F (25·6°C), July 79°F (26·1°C). Annual rainfall 1,556 mm.

CONSTITUTION AND GOVERNMENT. The 1976 Constitution provides for a bicameral legislature of a *Senate* and a *House of Representatives*, who elect the *President*, who is head of state. The *Senate* consists of 31 members, 16 being appointed by the President on the advice of the Prime Minister, 6 on the advice of the Leader of the Opposition and 9 at the discretion of the President.

The *House of Representatives* consists of 36 (34 for Trinidad and 2 for Tobago) elected members and a Speaker elected from within or outside the House.

Executive power is vested in the Prime Minister, who is appointed by the President, and the Cabinet.

At the general election of 6 Nov. 1995 the People's National Movement (PNM) won 17 seats with 50% of votes cast, the United National Movement (UNM), 17 with 45% and the National Alliance for Reconstruction (NAR), 2 (the Tobago seats) with 5%. In 1990 the UNC (founded in 1989) became the official Opposition.

President: Noor Mohammed Hassanali (re-elected Feb. 1992).

In Sept. 1995 the Cabinet comprised:
Prime Minister: Patrick Manning (b.1946; PNM).
Finance and Tourism: Wendell Mottley. *Attorney General and Minister of Legal Affairs:* Keith Sobion. *Energy and Energy Industries:* Barry Barnes.

Public Utilities: Ralph Maraj. *Trade and Industry:* Kenneth Valley. *National Security:* John Eckstein. *Foreign Affairs, Public Administration and Information:* Gordon Draper. *Sport and Youth Affairs:* Jean Pierre. *Consumer Affairs:* Camille Robinson-Regis. *Social Development:* Russell Huggins. *Local Government, Works and Transport:* Colm Imbert. *Education:* Augustus Ramrekersingh. *Health:* Dr Linda Baboolal. *Science, Technology, Higher Education, Planning and Development:* Dr Lenny Saith. *Labour and Co-operatives:* Kenneth Collis. *Community Development, Culture and Women's Affairs:* Joan Yuille-Williams. *Agriculture, Lands and Marine Resources:* Dr Keith Rowley. *Housing and Settlements:* Dr Vincent Lasse.

The *Speaker* is Occah Seapaul.

Leader of the Opposition: Basdeo Panday.

National flag: Red with a diagonal black strip edged in white.

National anthem: 'Forged from the love of liberty'; words and music by P. Castagne.

Local Government. Trinidad is divided into 9 regional corporations, 2 city corporations, 3 borough corporations and Tobago, which has a 15-member elected House of Assembly with limited powers of self-government. Elections were held on 28 Sept. 1992. The electorate was 774,191; turn-out was 39·76%. The PNM gained 50·29% of votes cast, the UNC 36·86%, the NAR 11% and independents 0·82%.

DEFENCE. The Defence Force has 2 infantry battalions and 1 support battalion. The small air element was disbanded in 1994. Security aircraft are operated by the police. Personnel in 1996 totalled 2,100.

The Coast Guard of 700 (1995) operates 9 inshore patrol craft, a number of boats and had 3 Cessna light aircraft for patrol duties.

The paramilitary police had 4,800 personnel.

INTERNATIONAL RELATIONS

Membership. Trinidad and Tobago is a member of the UN, the Commonwealth, OAS, CARICOM and is an ACP state of the EU.

ECONOMY

Budget. In 1992 the fiscal year was changed from the calendar year to 1 Oct.–30 Sept.

In 1993 government revenue was TT$9,591·9m. and expenditure was TT$8,828·8m. The budget envisaged recurrent expenditure as TT$6,686·7m. and capital expenditure as TT$1,658·7m.

Currency. The unit of currency is the *Trinidad and Tobago dollar* (TTD) of 100 *cents*. There are coins of 1, 5, 10, 25 and 50 cents and TT$1, and banknotes of TT$1, 5, 10, 20 and 100. TT$747·8m. were in circulation in 1991. Foreign exchange reserves were TT$101·2m. in Dec. 1991. Inflation was 12% at the end of 1991. In April 1994 the TT dollar was floated. In March 1996, £1 = TT$8·74; US$1 = TT$5·72; DM1 = TT$3·87.

Banking and Finance. A Central Bank began operations in 1964 (*Governor*, Thomas Harewood). Its total assets were TT$6,722m. in 1992. There are 6 commercial banks. Government savings banks are established in 69 offices, with a head office in Port-of-Spain. The stock exchange in Port-of-Spain participates in the regional Caribbean exchange.

ENERGY AND NATURAL RESOURCES

Electricity. In 1993, 3,817m. kWh was generated.

Oil. Oil production is one of Trinidad's leading industries. Commercial production began in 1909; production of crude oil in 1992 was 7·13m. tonnes. Crude oil is also imported for refining. The 'Pitch Lake' is an important source of asphalt.

Gas. In 1991 production was 7,405m. cu. metres.

Agriculture. Sugar production in 1993 was 137,000 tonnes.

Livestock (1992 in 1,000): Cattle, 60; sheep, 14; goats, 52; pigs, 50; poultry, 10m. Livestock products, 1993: Beef, 1,007 tonnes; pork, 1,938 tonnes; poultry, 14·77m. birds.

Fisheries. The catch in 1986, 14,800 tonnes.

INDUSTRY. In 1991, 654,000 tonnes of iron and steel were produced. Other manufacturing includes ammonia and urea (production, 1991, 1,768,400 tonnes), methanol (1991, 452,881 tonnes), cement (1992, 385,100 tonnes), spirits (1991, 3,761,000 proof gallons), beer (1992, 35,507,000 litres), cigarettes (1992, 656,000 kg), passenger cars (1992, 2,157), commercial vehicles (1991, 1,711), sugar (1991, 135,100 tonnes).

Labour. The working population in 1993 was 504,500. The number of unemployed in 1993 was 99,900.

Trade Unions. About 30% of the labour force belong to unions, which are grouped under the National Trade Union Centre.

FOREIGN ECONOMIC RELATIONS. The Foreign Investment Act of 1990 permits foreign investors to acquire land and shares in local companies, and to form companies. External debt was TT$5,755·7m. in 1992.

Commerce. Exports in 1993 were TT$8,800m. of which TT$5,070m. was mineral fuels and products. Imports totalled TT$7,495·3m. of which TT$2,463·5m. was for machinery and transport equipment. The USA was the principal trading partner.

Total trade of Trinidad and Tobago with UK (British Department of Trade returns, in £1,000 sterling):

	1991	*1992*	*1993*	*1994*	*1995*
Imports to UK	41,664	35,187	43,077	48,287	43,600
Exports and re-exports from UK	62,491	59,083	70,700	72,270	103,434

Tourism. There were 192,660 visitors in 1990.

COMMUNICATIONS

Roads. In 1994 there were 6,435 km of main and local roads. Motor vehicles registered in 1992 totalled 278,405.

Civil Aviation. There is an international airport at Port-of-Spain (Piarco). The national carrier is BWIA International Trinidad & Tobago Airways, which in 1995 operated 12 aircraft. Services are also provided by Air Canada, Air Caribbean, American Airlines, Carib Express, LIAT and Surinam Airways.

Shipping. Sea-going shipping totalled 17,037 GRT in 1995. In 1991, 13·5m. tonnes of cargo were handled. A deep-water harbour at Scarborough (Tobago) was opened in 1991. The other main harbours are Point Lisas and Port-of-Spain.

Telecommunications. International communications to all parts of the world are provided by Trinidad and Tobago External Telecommunications Co. Ltd (TEXTEL) by means of a satellite earth station and various high quality radio circuits. The marine radio service is also maintained by TEXTEL. Number of post offices (1993), 76; postal agencies, 77; number of telephones (1992), 0·17m. Radio programmes are overseen by the Telecommunications Authority. There are 8 commercial stations. There is an independent television company (colour by NTSC). There are 3 TV stations, as well as community and cable services. There were 0·7m radio and 0·25m television receivers in 1993.

Cinemas (1993). There were 26 cinemas and 2 drive-in cinemas.

Press (1993). There were 3 daily newspapers with a total daily circulation of 96,000, 4 Sunday newspapers with a total circulation of 116,000, and 6 weekly and 1 bi-weekly newspapers.

SOCIAL INSTITUTIONS

Justice. The High Court consists of the Chief Justice and 11 puisne judges. In criminal cases a judge of the High Court sits with a jury of 12 in cases of treason and murder, and with 9 jurors in other cases. The Court of Appeal consists of the Chief Justice and 3 Justices of Appeal; there is a limited right of appeal from it to the Privy Council. There are 3 High Courts and 12 magistrates' courts. There is an *Ombudsman*. The death penalty is authorized.

Religion. In 1990, 10·9% of the population were Anglicans (under the Bishop of Trinidad and Tobago), 29·4% Roman Catholics (under the Archbishop of Port-of-Spain), 23·8% Hindus and 5·8% Moslems.

Education. In 1992–93 there were 196,848 pupils enrolled in primary schools, 12,278 in government secondary schools, 19,417 in assisted secondary schools, 36,855 in junior secondary schools, 23,152 in senior comprehensive schools, 7,737 in composite schools and 4,483 in technical and vocational schools. The University of the West Indies campus in St Augustine had 4,769 students and 440 academic staff in 1994–95. 709 of the students were from other countries.

Health. In 1993 there were 1,051 physicians, 136 dentists, 529 pharmacists and 60 hospitals and nursing homes with 4,216 beds. There were 2,260 nurses and midwives and 1,259 nursing assistants in government institutions.

DIPLOMATIC REPRESENTATIVES

Of Trinidad and Tobago in Great Britain (42 Belgrave Sq., London, SW1X 8NT)
High Commissioner: Vacant.

Of Great Britain in Trinidad and Tobago (19 St Clair Ave., Port-of-Spain)
High Commissioner: R. A. Neilson, CMG, LVO.

Of Trinidad and Tobago in the USA (1708 Massachusetts Ave., NW, Washington, D.C., 20036)
Ambassador: Corinne McKnight.

Of the USA in Trinidad and Tobago (15 Queen's Park West, Port-of-Spain)
Ambassador: Brian J. Donnelly.

Of Trinidad and Tobago to the United Nations
Ambassador: Annette Des Iles.

Further Reading

Chambers, F., *Trinidad and Tobago.* [Bibliography] Oxford and Santa Barbara, 1986
Cooper, St G. C. and Bacon, P. R. (eds.) *The Natural Resources of Trinidad and Tobago.* London, 1981

Central library: The Central Library of Trinidad and Tobago, Queen's Park East, Port-of-Spain.
National statistical office: Central Statistical Office, 2 Edward St., Port-of-Spain.

TUNISIA

Jumhuriya at-Tunisiya

(Republic of Tunisia)

Capital: Tunis
Population: 8·8m. (1994)
GNP per capita: US$1,800 (1994)
HDI/world rank: 0·763/75 (1992)

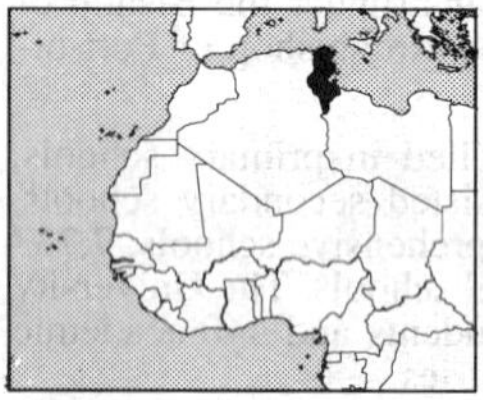

KEY HISTORICAL EVENTS. Tunisia was a French protectorate from 1883 and achieved independence on 20 March 1956. The Constituent Assembly, elected on 25 March 1956, abolished the monarchy (of the Bey of Tunis) on 25 July 1957 and proclaimed a republic.

TERRITORY AND POPULATION. Tunisia is bounded in the north and east by the Mediterranean Sea, west by Algeria and south by Libya. The area is 164,150 sq. km (63,378 sq. miles). At the census of 1984 the population was 6,966,173 (3,419,026 females) of whom 52·8% were urban. Estimate (1994) 8·8m. (54% urban); density, 51·1 per sq. km. There was a census in 1994.

Vital statistics rates (1993): Birth, 24·4 per 1,000 population; death, 6·1. Expectation of life was 67·1 years in 1992. Growth rate, 1993, 1·9%.

The 1984 census populations of the 23 governorates:

	Area in sq. km	*Population*		*Area in sq. km*	*Population*
Aryanah	1,558	374,192	Qasrayn (Kassérine)	8,066	297,959
Bajah (Béja)	3,558	274,706	Qayrawan (Kairouan)	6,712	421,607
Banzart (Bizerta)	3,685	394,670	Qibili (Kebili)	22,084	95,371
Bin Arus	761	246,193	Safaqis (Sfax)	7,545	577,992
Jundubah (Jendouba)	3,102	359,429	Sidi Bu Zayd (Sidi Bouzid)	6,994	288,528
Kaf (Le Kef)	4,965	247,672	Silyanah (Siliana)	4,631	222,038
Madaniyin (Médénine)	8,588	295,889	Susah (Sousse)	2,621	322,491
Mahdiyah (Mahdia)	2,966	270,435	Tatawin (Tataouine)	38,889	100,329
Munastir (Monastir)	1,019	278,478	Tawzar (Tozeur)	4,719	67,943
Nabul (Nabeul)	2,788	461,405	Tunis	346	774,364
Qabis (Gabès)	7,175	240,016	Zaghwan (Zaghouan)	2,768	118,743
Qafsah (Gafsa)	8,990	235,723			

Tunis, the capital, had (1994 census, in 1,000) 674·1 inhabitants: Sfax, 230·9; Aryanah, 152·7; Ettadhamen, 149·2; Sousse, 125; Kairouan, a holy city of the Moslems, 102·6; Gabès, 98·9; Bizerta, 98·9; Bardo, 72·7; Gafsa, 71·1.

The official language is Arabic but the use of French is widespread.

CLIMATE. The climate ranges from warm temperate in the north, where winters are mild and wet and the summers hot and dry, to desert in the south. Tunis. Jan. 48°F (8·9°C), July 78°F (25·6°C). Annual rainfall 16" (400 mm). Bizerta. Jan. 52°F (11·1°C), July 77°F (25°C). Annual rainfall 25" (622 mm). Sfax. Jan. 52°F (11·1°C), July 78°F (25·6°C). Annual rainfall 8" (196 mm).

CONSTITUTION AND GOVERNMENT. The Constitution was promulgated on 1 June 1959. The *President* and the *National Assembly* are elected simultaneously by direct universal suffrage for a period of 5 years. The President cannot be re-elected more than 3 times consecutively.

The National Assembly has 153 seats, 144 directly elected by the first-past-the-post system and 19 distributed nationally by proportional representation: 10 to the Socialist Democratic Movement, 4 to the Renovation Movement, 3 to the Democratic Unionist Union and 2 to the Party of Popular Unity.

Presidential and parliamentary elections were held on 20 March 1994; turn-out was 93%. President Zine El Abidine Ben Ali, the sole candidate, was re-elected by

99·8% of votes cast. The Constitutional Democratic Assembly (CDA) won all 144 of the directly-elected National Assembly seats with 97·73% of votes cast.

President: Zine El Abidine Ben Ali (appointed 2 April 1989, re-elected 20 March 1994).

The Cabinet in Nov. 1995 comprised:

Prime Minister: Hamed Karoui.

Justice: Sadok Chaabane. *Foreign Affairs:* Habib Ben Yahia. *Secretary General of the Presidency:* Mohamed El Jeri. *Defence:* Dr Abdelaziz Ben Dhia. *Interior:* Mohamed Jegham. *International Co-operation and Foreign Investment:* Mohamed Ghannouchi. *Finance:* Nouri Zorgati. *Economic Development:* Nabli Mustapha Kamel. *Transport:* Mondher Zenaidi. *Equipment and Housing:* Ali Chaouch. *Tourism and Handicrafts:* Slaheddine Maaoui. *Social Affairs:* Sadok Rabah. *Education:* Hatem Ben Othman. *Higher Education and Scientific Research:* Daly Jazi. *Professional Training and Employment:* Moncer Rouissi. *Public Health:* Hedi Henni. *Youth and Infancy:* Abderrahim Zouari. *Culture:* Salah Baccari. *Environment, Town and Country Planning:* Mohamed Mehdi Melika. *Secretary General of the Government:* Ridha Grira. *Agriculture:* Mohamed Ben Rajab. *State Property:* Mustapha Bouaziz. *Communications:* Habib Ammar. *Religious Affairs:* Ali Chebbi. *Industry:* Slaheddine Bouguerra. *Commerce:* Slaheddine Ben M'Barek. *Family and Women's Affairs:* Neziha Zarrouk.

The *Speaker* is Habib Boulares.

National flag: Red with a white circle in the middle, on which is a 5-pointed red star encircled by a red crescent.

National anthem: 'Humata al Hima' ('Defenders of the Homeland'); words by Mustapha al Rafi, tune by M. A. Wahab.

Local Government. The country is divided into 23 governorates, sub-divided into 199 districts and then into communes and imadas. On 21 May 1995 elections were held for the 3,774 seats on the 257 local councils. The CDA gained control of all councils.

DEFENCE.
Selective conscription is 1 year.

Army. The Army consists of 3 mechanized, 1 Sahara and 1 special forces brigade; and 1 engineer regiment. Equipment includes 54 M-60A3 and 30 M-60A1 main battle tanks. Strength (1996) 27,000 (25,000 conscripts). There are also the paramilitary Police (13,000) and National Guard (10,000).

Navy. The Navy consists of 3 1985-built fast missile craft and 3 older craft with short range missiles, 17 inshore patrol craft, 1 survey/training ship and 1 large tug. In 1995 naval personnel totalled 5,000. Forces are based at Bizerta, Sfax and Kelibia.

The Coast Guard operates 4 coastal and 19 inshore patrol craft.

Air Force. Equipment of the Air Force, acquired from various Western sources, includes 1 squadron of Aermacchi M.B.326K/L and 1 squadron of L-59 jet light attack aircraft; 1 squadron of F-5E/F Tiger II fighters; 10 SF.260W piston-engined light trainer/attack aircraft; 3 C-130 Hercules transports, 3 L-410 light transports and 2 S.208 liaison aircraft, 6 SF.260C trainers, 18 UH-1H, 18 AB.205, 6 Ecureuil and about 6 Alouette III helicopters. Personnel (1995) about 3,500 (700 conscripts), with 32 combat aircraft and 7 armed helicopters.

INTERNATIONAL RELATIONS

Membership. Tunisia is a member of the UN, OAU, the Islamic Conference and the Arab League.

ECONOMY

Policy. The eighth 5-year development plan began in 1992.

Currency. The unit of currency is the *Tunisian dinar* (TND) of 1,000 *millimes*. There are coins of 5, 10, 20, 50, 100 and 500 millimes and 1 dinar, and notes of 1, 5, 10 and 20 dinars. The currency was made convertible on 6 Jan. 1993. Foreign exchange reserves were 853·8m. dinars in 1993. Inflation was 3% in 1994. In March 1996, £1 = 1·470 dinars; US$1 = 0·962 dinars; DM1 = 0·652 dinars.

Banking and Finance. The Central Bank of Tunisia is the bank of issue. In 1988 there were 9 development banks, 10 deposit banks and 9 off-shore banks.

There is a small stock exchange (16 companies trading in 1993).

Weights and Measures. The metric system is legal. Some traditional weights are still in use: 12 *sa* = 1 *wiba* = 1 bushel; 16 *wiba* = 1 *kfiz*; 1 *ounce* = 31·487 grammes.

ENERGY AND NATURAL RESOURCES

Electricity. Electrical energy generated was 5,095m. kWh in 1991.

Oil and Gas. Crude oil production (1992) was 5·35m. tonnes. Gas production (1991) was 387m. cu. metres.

Water. In 1993 there were 20 large dams, 250 hillside dams and some 1,000 artificial lakes. In 1986, 257,000 ha were irrigated.

Minerals. Mineral production (in 1,000 tonnes) in 1991: Calcium phosphate, 6,352; iron ore, 295; lead ore (concentrated), 1·3; zinc ore (concentrated), 9·4; sea salt, 406; spath fluor, 38.

Agriculture. There are 5 agricultural regions: The *north*, mountainous with large fertile valleys; the *north-east*, with the peninsula of Cap Bon, suited for the cultivation of oranges, lemons and tangerines; the *Sahel*, where olive trees abound; the *centre*, a region of high table lands and pastures, and the *desert* of the south, where dates are grown.

Some 40% of the population are employed in agriculture, which contributed 12·2% of GDP in 1989. Large estates predominate; smallholdings are tending to fragment, partly owing to inheritance laws. There were some 0·4m. farms in 1990 (0·32m. in 1960). Of the total area of 15,583,000 ha, about 9m. ha are productive, including 2m. under cereals, 3·6m. used as pasturage, 0·9m. forests and 1·3m. uncultivated. The main crops are cereals and olive oil. Production, 1993 (in 1,000 tonnes): Wheat, 1,413; barley, 478; olive oil, 204; olives, 630; dates, 90; almonds, 47; potatoes, 199; tomatoes, 452; peppers, 170; melons, including watermelons, 354; apples, 75; apricots, 24; citrus fruits, 271; pears, 42; peaches and nectarines, 59; plums 11; chickpeas, 27; sugar-beet, 246; tobacco, 6; wine, 34; grapes, 108.

Livestock, 1993 (in 1,000): Horses, 56; asses, 231; mules, 81; cattle, 659; sheep, 7,110; goats, 1,417; camels, 231; pigs, 6. Livestock products, 1993 (in 1,000 tonnes): Meat, 141; milk, 441; eggs, 53·7.

Fisheries. In 1991 the catch amounted to 90,000 tonnes.

INDUSTRY. Production, 1991 (in 1,000 tonnes): Superphosphate, 714; phosphoric acid, 806; cement, 4,196; lime, 578. 2,010 cars, 450 lorries, 1,240 vans, 220 buses and coaches, 330 tractors, 23,320 radio and 58,460 television sets were produced in 1987.

Labour. Unemployment was 15·8% in 1992.

Trade Unions. The Union Générale des Travailleurs Tunisiens won 27 seats in the parliamentary elections (1 Nov. 1981). There are also the Union Tunisienne de l'Industrie, du Commerce et de l'Artisanat (UTICA, the employers' union) and the Union National des Agriculteurs (UNA, farmers' union).

FOREIGN ECONOMIC RELATIONS. In Feb. 1989 Tunisia signed a treaty of economic co-operation with the other countries of Maghreb: Algeria, Libya, Mauritania and Morocco. Foreign debt was US$9,200m. in 1993.

Commerce. The imports and exports for calendar years (US$1m.):

	1990	*1991*	*1992*	*1993*	*1994*
Imports	5,476	5,190	6,077	6,213	6,600
Exports	3,498	3,714	4,033	3,803	4,600

Main exports in 1991 (in 1,000 tonnes): Crude oil, 3,993; textiles, 90; olive oil, 158; phosphates, 808; fertilizers, 1,471; fruit, 48; leather and shoes, 5·7; fishery products, 13·6; machinery and electrical appliances, 13·1.

Main imports in 1991 (in 1,000 tonnes): Oil and by-products, 2,404; natural gas, 639; vegetable oil, 136; dairy products, 20; coffee, tea and spices, 21; cereals, 922; sugar, 168.

Exports and imports in 1991 by country (in 1m. dinars): France, 862·7, 1,247·5; Italy, 674·4, 835·6; Germany, 561·1, 682·4; Belgium, 213·5, 256·7.

Total trade between Tunisia and UK (British Department of Trade returns, in £1,000 sterling):

	1991	*1992*	*1993*	*1994*	*1995*
Imports to UK	25,613	48,445	39,383	46,000	55,690
Exports and re-exports from UK	43,651	50,685	62,210	81,056	83,667

Tourism. Tourism is important. In 1994 there were 3·85m. visitors.

COMMUNICATIONS

Roads. In 1987 there were 18,952 km of roads. Number of motor vehicles, 1987, 506,000.

Railways. In 1994 there were 2,152 km of railways (468 km of 1,435 mm gauge and 1,684 km of metre-gauge), of which 110 km were electrified. 28·3m. passengers and 11·8m. tonnes of freight were carried in 1994. There is a light rail network in Tunis (52 km).

Civil Aviation. The national carrier, Tunis Air, is 84·86% state-owned, and in 1995 had a fleet comprising 1 A300B4-100, 1 A300B4-200, 8 A320-200s, 1 B-727-200, 6 B-727-200 Advs, 3 B-737-200 Advs, 1 B-737-200C Adv and 4 B-737-500s. There are 5 international airports, the main one at Tunis-Carthage. In 1987, 4,429,000 passengers and 21,688 tonnes of freight were carried. Services are also provided by Aeroflot, Air Algérie, Air France, Air Inter, Air Liberté, Air Malta, Air Ukraine, Alitalia, Balkan, British Airways, Czech Airlines, Egyptair, Iberia, KLM, Libyan Airlines, Lufthansa, Middle East Airlines, Royal Air Maroc, Royal Jordanian, Saudia, Swissair, Syrian Airlines and Turkish Airlines.

Shipping. The main port is Tunis, and its outer port is Tunis-Goulette. These two ports and Sfax, Sousse and Bizerta are directly accessible to ocean-going vessels. The ports of La Skhirra and Gabès are used for the shipping of Algerian and Tunisian oil. In 1995, sea-going shipping totalled 0·18m. GRT, including oil tankers, 9,976 GRT.

Telecommunications. There were, in 1983, 218,808 telephones. The government-controlled Radiodiffusion-Télévision Tunisienne provides broadcasting. There is a national radio programme, an international service; Radio Tunisie Internationale (French and Italian) and 2 regional programmes. There are Arabic and French TV networks (colour by SECAM). In 1991 there were 1,693,527 radio and 0·65m. TV sets.

Cinemas (1987). There were 80 cinemas.

Press. In 1993 there were 20 daily and weekly newspapers (4 in French).

SOCIAL INSTITUTIONS

Justice. There are 51 magistrates' courts, 13 courts of first instance, 3 courts of appeal (in Tunis, Sfax and Sousse) and the High Court in Tunis.

A Personal Status Code was promulgated on 13 Aug. 1956 and applied to Tunisians from 1 Jan. 1957. This raised the status of women, made divorce subject to a court decision, abolished polygamy and decreed a minimum marriage age.

Religion. The constitution recognizes Islam as the state religion. In 1992 there were 8·36m. Sunni Moslems. There are about 20,000 Roman Catholics, under the Prelate of Tunis.

Education. Adult literacy was 65% in 1993. All education is free from primary schools to university. There are a teachers' training college, a school of law, 2 centres of economic studies, 2 schools of engineering, 2 medical schools, a faculty of agriculture, 2 institutes of business administration and 1 school of dentistry.

In 1987–88 there were 3,605 primary schools with 43,189 teachers and 1,338,905 pupils; 436 secondary schools with 22,373 teachers and 437,604 pupils. In 1980–81 there were 60,137 students at technical and vocational schools and 4,101 students in teacher-training.

In 1995–96, there were 6 universities, 3 of them (Tunis I, Tunis II, Tunis III) being specialized by faculty,

Health. In 1987 there were 36 general hospitals (22 university and 14 regional), 20 specialized institutions, centres and university hospitals, and (1988) 92 district hospitals. In 1986 there were 15,814 beds.

Social Security. A system of social security was set up in 1950 (amended 1963, 1964 and 1970).

DIPLOMATIC REPRESENTATIVES

Of Tunisia in Great Britain (29 Prince's Gate, London, SW7 1QG)
Ambassador: Dr Mohamed Lessir.

Of Great Britain in Tunisia (5 Place de la Victoire, Tunis)
Ambassador and Consul-General: Richard Edis CMG.

Of Tunisia in the USA (1515 Massachusetts Ave., NW, Washington, D.C., 20005)
Ambassador: Azouz Ennifar.

Of the USA in Tunisia (144 Ave. de la Liberté, Tunis)
Ambassador: Mary A. Casey.

Of Tunisia to the United Nations
Ambassador: Slaheddine Abdellah.

Further Reading

Lawless R. I. *et al.*, *Tunisia.* [Bibliography] Oxford and Santa Barbara (CA), 1982
Salem, N., *Habib Bourguiba, Islam and the Creation of Tunisia.* London, 1984

National statistical office: Institut National de la Statistique, 27 Rue de Liban, Tunis.

TURKEY

Türkiye Çumhuriyeti

(Republic of Turkey)

Capital: Ankara
Population: 61·18m. (1994)
GNP per capita: US$2,450 (1994)
HDI/world rank: 0·792/66 (1992)

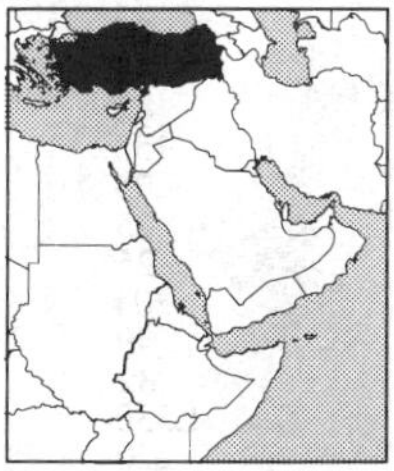

KEY HISTORICAL EVENTS. Turkey became a republic on 29 Oct. 1923. (For the transition from the Ottoman Empire *see* THE STATESMAN'S YEAR-BOOK, 1991–92, p. 1210). Religious courts were abolished in 1924, Islam ceased to be the official state religion in 1928, women were given the franchise and western-style surnames were adopted in 1934.

On 27 May 1960 the Army overthrew the government. A new constitution was approved in a referendum held on 9 July 1961 and general elections were held. On 12 Sept. 1980, the Army again overthrew the government. The Constituent Assembly was convened in Oct. 1981, and prepared a new Constitution which was enforced after a national referendum on 7 Nov. 1982.

TERRITORY AND POPULATION. Turkey is bounded in the west by the Aegean Sea and Greece, north by Bulgaria and the Black Sea, east by Georgia, Armenia and Iran, and south by Iraq, Syria and the Mediterranean.

The area (including lakes) is 779,452 sq. km (300,947 sq. miles). Area in Europe (Thrace), 23,764 sq. km. Area in Asia (Anatolia), 755,688 sq. km.

The census population is given as follows:

	Total		*Total*		*Total*
1927	13,648,270	1955	24,064,763	1975	40,347,719
1935	16,158,018	1960	27,754,820	1980	44,736,957
1945	18,790,174	1965	31,391,421	1985	50,664,458
1950	20,947,188	1970	35,605,176	1990	56,473,035

Population estimate (1994), 61,183,000 (30,197,000 females). Urban population (1990 census), 33,326,351 (59·1%); density, 73 per sq. km.

Vital statistics, 1991: Marriages, 459,624; divorces, 27,167; deaths, 165,218 (in 1990). Expectation of life (1990) 65 years. There were 3,269 immigrants in 1992.

Some 12m. Kurds live in Turkey. Limited use of the Kurdish language (not in schools or publications) was sanctioned in Feb. 1991.

The area, population and population density of the provinces at the census of 1990:

	Area in sq.km.	*Population*	*Density per sq.km.*
Adana	17,562	1,934,907	111
Adiyaman	7,423	513,131	70
Afyonkarahisar	14,295	739,223	52
Ağri	11,066	437,093	40
Aksaray	7,626	326,399	43
Amasya	5,452	357,191	66
Ankara	25,614	3,236,626	126
Antalya	20,815	1,132,211	55
Artvin	7,436	212,833	29
Aydin	7,870	824,816	105
Balikesir	14,456	973,314	68
Batman	4,694	344,669	74
Bayburt	3,652	107,330	30
Bilecik	4,321	175,526	40
Bingöl	8,319	250,966	30
Bitlis	8,010	330,115	41
Bolu	10,575	536,869	51
Burdur	7,167	254,899	36
Bursa	10,990	1,603,137	146

	Area in sq.km.	Population	Density per sq.km.
Çanakkale	9,950	432,263	44
Çankırı	8,659	279,129	33
Çorum	12,729	609,863	49
Denizli	11,874	750,882	64
Diyarbakir	14,908	1,094,996	73
Edirne	6,174	404,599	65
Elazığ	9,455	498,225	53
Erzincan	11,413	299,251	27
Erzurum	25,133	848,201	34
Eskişehir	13,477	641,057	48
Gaziantep	8,015	1,140,594	153
Giresun	6,965	499,087	75
Gümüşhane	6,748	169,375	25
Hakkâri	7,121	172,479	25
Hatay	5,570	1,109,754	204
Isparta	8,847	434,771	49
İçel	15.448	1,266,995	82
İstanbul	5,591	7,309,190	1,330
İzmir	12,263	2,694,770	220
Karaman	9,163	217,536	24
Kars	18,841	662,155	35
Kastamonu	12,982	423,611	33
Kayseri	16,537	943,484	57
Kırıkkale	4,365	349,396	84
Kırklareli	6,378	309,512	49
Kirşehir	6,501	256,862	40
Kocaeli	3,578	936,163	260
Konya	40,451	1,750,303	43
Kütahya	11,661	578,020	51
Malatya	11,752	702,055	57
Manisa	13,237	1,154,418	87
K. Maraş	14,680	892,952	61
Mardin	8,594	557,727	65
Muğla	12,504	562,809	45
Muş	8,413	376,543	45
Nevşehir	5,540	289,509	52
Nigde	7,831	305,861	39
Ordu	6,142	830,105	137
Rize	3,920	348,776	91
Sakarya	4,821	683,061	140
Samsun	9,739	1,158,400	120
Siirt	6,176	243,435	40
Sinop	5,657	265,153	48
Şirnak	7,172	262,006	40
Sivas	28,568	767,481	28
Tekirdağ	6,333	468,842	74
Tokat	9,869	719,251	73
Trabzon	4,498	795,849	180
Tunceli	7,954	133,143	17
Urfa	19,271	1,001,455	52
Uşak	5,389	290,283	54
Van	21,095	637,433	30
Yozgat	13,597	579,150	43
Zonguldak	8,560	1,073,560	126

65% of the population was urban in 1990.

Population of urban areas and towns of over 120,000 inhabitants:

	Urban area	Town		Urban area	Town
İstanbul	6,407,215	6,293,397	İçel	700,851	414,308
Ankara	3,022,236	2,541,899	Kayseri	587,793	461,415
İzmir	2,665,105	2,319,188	Diyarbakir	560,347	371,038
Adana	1,429,677	972,318	Manisa	556,787	158,426
Bursa	1,030,737	775,388	Şanliurfa	520,533	239,604
Konya	1,015,415	543,460	Antalya	514,264	353,149
Gaziantep	759,893	573,968	Kocaeli	498,646	271,132

	Urban area	*Town*		*Urban area*	*Town*
Hatay	481,560	118,443	Elaziğ	275,342	218,121
Samsun	462,836	277,222	Kırıkkale	267,379	233,008
Balikesir	461,618	172,570	Sakarya	255,112	170,231
Eskişehir	455,478	415,831	Kütahya	232,632	135,432
Erzurum	409,095	297,544	Van	217,442	126,010
Kahramanmaraş	395,872	237,456	İsparta	204,311	113,693
Zonguldak	381,824	124,862	İskenderun	...	175,998
Malatya	367,765	304,760	Tarsus	...	168,654
Sivas	350,564	219,949	Batman	...	131,812
Trabzon	288,118	173,354	Osmaniye	...	121,188
Denizli	285,836	199,360			

CLIMATE. Coastal regions have a Mediterranean climate, with mild, moist winters and hot, dry summers. The interior plateau has more extreme conditions, with low and irregular rainfall, cold and snowy winters and hot, almost rainless summers. Ankara. Jan. 32·5°F (0·3°C), July 73°F (23°C). Annual rainfall 14·7" (367 mm). Istanbul. Jan. 41°F (5°C), July 73°F (23°C). Annual rainfall 28·9" (723 mm). Izmir. Jan. 46°F (8°C), July 81°F (27°C). Annual rainfall 28" (700 mm).

CONSTITUTION AND GOVERNMENT. On 7 Nov. 1982 a referendum established that 98% of the electorate were in favour of new Constitution. The President is elected for 7-year terms. The Presidency is not an executive position, and the President may not be linked to a political party. There is a 550-member *Grand National Assembly*, elected by universal suffrage (at 18 years and over) for 5-year terms by proportional representation.

There is a Constitutional Court consisting of 15 regular and 5 alternating members.

Elections were held in Dec. 1995. The electorate was 34,155,981; turn-out was 85·2%. The Prosperity Party (Islamic) gained 158 seats with 21·38% of votes cast (62 with 16·9% in 1991); the True Path Party (TPP), 135 with 19·18% (178 with 27%); the Motherland Party (MP), 132 with 19·65% (115 with 27%); the Democratic Left, 76 with 14·64% (7 with 10·8%); and the Republican Populist Party, 49 with 10·71%.

President: Suleyman Demirel (b. 1924; sworn in 16 May 1993).

In March 1996 a TPP-MP coalition government was formed with rotation of Prime Ministers, Tansu Çiller (b. 1946; TPP) to hold office in 1997–98. The government included:

Prime Minister: Mesut Yilmaz (MP).

Deputy Prime Minister: Nahit Menteşe (TPP). *Minister of Finance:* Lütfullah Kayalar (MP). *Defence:* Oltan Sungurlu (MP). *Interior:* Ulkü Güney (MP). *Foreign Affairs:* Emre Gönensay (TPP). *Justice:* Mehmet Agar (TPP). *Industry:* Yalim Erez (TPP). *Health:* Yildirim Aktuna. *Tourism:* Isilay Saygin.

The *Speaker* is Mustafa Kalemli (MP).

National flag: A white crescent and star on red.

National anthem: 'Korkma! Sönmez bu şafaklarda yüzen al sancak' ('Be not afraid! Our flag will never fade'); words by Mehmed Akif Ersoy, tune by Zeki Güngör.

Local Government. The 73 provinces have elected councils, as do municipalities. Mayors (of metropolitan areas and municipalities) and village heads and councils of elders are also elected. At partial municipal elections on 4 June 1995 the TPP gained 22 of 36 seats with 39·6% of votes cast, the Republican Populist Party gained 20·36%, the Prosperity Party 17·4%.

DEFENCE. There is a Supreme Council of National Security, under the chairmanship of the Prime Minister, which co-ordinates the resources in case of war. Besides the Minister of National Defence and the Chief of the General Staff, the heads of economic Ministries are members of this council.

Conscription is 18 months.

Army. The Army consists of 1 mechanized divisional HQ, 1 mechanized and 1 infantry division, 9 infantry, 14 armoured, 17 mechanized and 4 commando brigades, 1 armoured, 1 Presidential Guard and 5 coastal defence regiments and 26 frontier defence battalions. Equipment includes 75 M-47, 2,876 M-48, 932 M-60 and 397 Leopard main battle tanks. Army Aviation has over 300 aircraft and helicopters. Strength (1996) 400,000 (352,000 conscripts), and reserves number 258,700. There is also a paramilitary gendarmerie cum national guard of 180,000 with its own fleet of over 50 transport and observation helicopters.

Navy. Current strength includes 15 diesel submarines (7 reasonably modern, of German design and 8 very old ex-US built 1944–45), 5 ex-US destroyers (1943–46), 17 frigates of which 5 are modern German MEKO-type, 8 ex-US Knox class, 1 ex-German Type 120 Köln class, and 2 locally built in the 1970s. Light forces comprise 17 fast missile craft, 10 coastal and 17 inshore patrol craft. Mine warfare forces include 2 minelayers, 17 coastal and 4 inshore minesweepers. Amphibious lift is provided by 8 tank landing ships and about 60 landing craft. Major auxiliaries in service are 1 replenishment and 5 support tankers, 5 depot ships, 3 salvage/rescue ships, 2 survey ships and 1 training ship. Minor auxiliaries, coastal freighters and service craft number about 120.

The main naval base is at Gölcük in the Gulf of Izmit. There are others at Iskenderun, Eregli, Aksaz Karaağaç Mersin and Izmir. There are 3 naval shipyards: Gölcük, Taşkizak and Izmir.

The naval air component operates 10 S-2 mixed Air Force and Naval-manned Tracker anti-submarine aircraft and 20 helicopters for anti-submarine and patrol duties. There is a Marine Regiment some 3,000 strong.

Personnel in 1995 totalled 51,000 (34,500 conscripts) including marines.

The separate Coast Guard numbers about 1,100 and performs coastal police duties with a force of 28 inshore patrol vessels, 4 transports and numerous boats.

Air Force. The Air Force is under the control of the General Staff and, operationally, under 6 ATAF. It is organized as 2 tactical air forces, with headquarters at Eskisehir and Diyarbakir, each having a flight of UH-1H helicopters and T-33s. Combat aircraft comprise F-5As in 2 squadrons; F-16A/Bs in 8 squadrons; F-4E and RF-4E Phantoms in 8 squadrons; plus Nike-Hercules surface-to-air missile batteries. The 4 transport squadrons are equipped with Transall C-160, C-130 Hercules, Citation, Gulfstream and CN-235 aircraft, and UH-1H helicopters. Training types include T-33A, T-37 and T-38 advanced trainers, SF.260 basic and T-41 primary trainers. Personnel strength (1995), 56,800 (28,700 conscripts), with about 500 combat aircraft.

INTERNATIONAL RELATIONS

Membership. Turkey is a member of the UN, OECD, NATO and Council of Europe and an Associate Member of the WEU.

ECONOMY

Policy. The state had a stake in 235 enterprises in 1992, but privatization is in train and is co-ordinated by the Public Participation Fund.

Budget. Budgets (in TL1,000m.):

	1992	*1993*	*1994*
Revenue	174,224	351,392	753,440
Expenditure	221,658	485,249	899,375

Tax revenues were TL971,346,000m. in 1994.

Currency. The unit of currency is the *Turkish lira* (TRL) notionally of 100 *kuruş*. There are coins of TL500, 1,000, 2,500, 5,000, 10,000 and 25,000 and notes of TL20,000, 50,000, 100,000, 250,000 and 1m. In Sept. 1994 gold reserves were US$1,439m., and foreign exchange reserves, US$15,197m. The lira is fully convertible; it was devalued 13·6% in Jan. 1994. TL6,840,600m. were in circulation in 1989. Annualized inflation was 125% in 1994. In March 1996, £1 = TL102,165; US$1 = TL66,845; DM1 = TL45,291.

Banking and Finance. The Central Bank (Merkez Bankası; *Acting Governor*, Osman Cavit Ertan) is the bank of issue. In 1995 there were 55 commercial banks (6 state-owned, 29 private, 20 foreign), and 12 development and investment banks. The Central Bank's assets were TL647,911m. in Sept. 1994. The assets and liabilities of deposit money banks were TL1,538,084m.

There is a stock exchange in Istanbul (ISE).

Weights and Measures. The metric system is in use. The Gregorian calendar has been in exclusive use since 26 Dec. 1925.

ENERGY AND NATURAL RESOURCES

Electricity. In 1993 installed capacity was 20,335·1 MW (7,113·6 MW hydro-electric in 1992). Production was 69,864·7m. kWh.

Oil and Gas. Crude oil production (1992) was 4·3m. tonnes. Total refining capacity is 24m. tonnes a year. 212·49m. cu. metres of natural gas were produced in 1990.

Minerals. Turkey is rich in minerals, and is a major producer of chrome.

Production of principal minerals (in 1,000 tonnes) was:

	1987	*1988*	*1989*	*1990*
Coal	7,084	6,688	6,259	5,629
Lignite	46,481	39,025	52,567	46,892
Chrome	1,049	1,157	1,598	1,205
Copper concentrate	137	168	167	184
Bauxite	259	269	534	773
Iron	5,366	5,481	4,518	4,925
Boron	1,629	2,044	1,979	2,063
Salt	1,202	1,358	1,739	1,889

Agriculture. At the 1991 census of agriculture there were 4,091,530 households engaged in farming, of which 148,190 were engaged purely in animal farming. Holdings are increasingly fragmented by the custom of dividing land equally amongst sons. There are government price supports to cereal growers. The sown area in 1993 was 18,922,000 ha; 4,887,000 ha was fallow; vineyards, orchards and olive groves occupied 3,054,000 ha.

The soil for the most part is very fertile; the principal products are cotton, tobacco, cereals (especially wheat), figs, silk, dried fruits, liquorice root, nuts, almonds, mohair, skins and hides, furs, wool, gums, canary seed, linseed and sesame. The South-Eastern Anatolian Irrigation Project (GAP) is expected to produce 1·6m. ha of fertile land.

Production (in 1,000 tonnes) of principal crops:

	1989	*1990*	*1991*	*1992*	*1993*
Wheat	16,200	20,000	20,400	19,318	21,000
Barley	4,500	7,300	7,800	6,900	7,500
Maize	2,000	2,100	2,180	2,100	2,500
Rye	191	240	256	225	235
Tobacco	270	288	233	320	...
Oats	216	270	255	250	245
Rice	198	138	124	215	135

Other produce, 1992 (in 1,000 tonnes): Dry beans, 205; lentils, 600; chick peas, 810; cotton lint, 605; sugar-beet, 14,800; sunflower seeds, 950; cotton seed, 968; soya beans, 95; onions, 1,700; potatoes, 4,500; pears, 415; apples, 2,000; figs, 314 (1991); apricots, 378; grapes, 3,460; oranges, 824; tangerines, 370; lemons and limes, 420; nuts, 787; tea, 142; olives, 630; olive oil, 121.

Livestock, 1992 (in 1,000): Horses, 496; mules, 188; asses, 980; cattle, 11,973; sheep, 40,433; goats, 10,764. Livestock products, 1992 (in 1,000 tonnes): Total meat, 1,009; milk, 6,106; greasy wool, 42; goat hair and mohair (1991), 5,330 tonnes; eggs, 390; honey, 55.

Forestry. In 1993 total forest land was 20,199,000 ha. Produce (1,000 cu. metres) in 1992: Logs, 3,064; industrial wood, 676.

Fisheries. Catch (1993): Sea fish, 453,123 tonnes; crustaceans and molluscs, 48,908 tonnes; fresh water fish, 41,575 tonnes. Aquaculture production, 1993, 12,438 tonnes (mainly carp and trout). There were (1989) 8,488 fishing boats.

INDUSTRY. In 1990, 55 state enterprises accounted for about 30% of production. In 1991 there were 8,258 industrial enterprises. Production in 1992 (in 1,000 tonnes): Ammonia, 419; sulphuric acid, 642; PVC, 150; polyethylene, 261; ethylene, 382; fertilizers, 3,081; cotton yarn, 225; woollen yarn, 58; cotton fabrics, 596·9m. metres; woollen textiles, 19·7m. metres; carpets, 10,961,108 sq. metres; paper, 471; cement, 28,552; pig-iron, 428; crude iron, 4,508; crude steel, 10,343; coke, 3,250; iron and steel bars, 1,148; sugar, 1,572; lorries, 20,750 units; motor cars, 265,094 units.

Labour. Economically active population aged 12 and over, 1991, 39,035,751 (19,584,055 females) of whom 9,524,278 were engaged in agriculture, forestry, hunting and fishing, 2,896,242 in manufacturing, 2,173,448 in trade, restaurants and hotels and 2,675,315 in services. 1,931,000 were unemployed in Oct. 1994.

Trade Unions. The trade-union movement began in 1947. There are 4 national confederations (including Türk-Iş and Disk) and 6 federations. There are 35 unions affiliated to Türk-Iş and 17 employers' federations affiliated to Disk, whose activities were banned on 12 Sept. 1980. In 1992, labour unions totalled 106 and employers' unions, 51. Some 2·2m. workers belonged to unions in 1990. Membership is forbidden to civil servants (including schoolteachers). There were 98 strikes in 1992 with 1,153,578 working days lost and 11 lockouts with 158,545 working days lost.

FOREIGN ECONOMIC RELATIONS. Total foreign debt in 1994 was US$73,779m. A customs union with the EU came into force on 1 Jan. 1996.

Commerce. Imports and exports (in US$1m.) for calendar years:

	1990	*1991*	*1992*	*1993*	*1994*
Imports	22,302	21,047	22,871	29,428	23,270
Exports	12,959	13,593	14,715	15,345	18,105

Exports (1992) in US$1m.: Vegetable produce, 2,055; livestock products, 140; fishery produce, 50; timber and processed wood, 14; non-metallic quarrying, 212; metal ores, 49; fuel, 1; processed agricultural products, 1,241; refined petroleum and products, 231; manufactures, 10,718.

Imports (1992) in US$1m.: Machinery, 6,774; building materials, 792; animal husbandry, 95; consumer goods, 2,971; raw materials, 13,126.

The main export markets in 1994 (in US$1m.) were: Germany, 3,934; USA, 1,520; Italy, 1,034; UK, 889; France, 851; Russia, 820. Main import suppliers: Germany, 3,646; USA, 2,429; Italy, 2,009; France, 1,458; Saudi Arabia, 1,229; UK, 1,170.

Total trade between Turkey and UK (British Department of Trade returns, in £1,000 sterling):

	1991	*1992*	*1993*	*1994*	*1995*
Imports to UK	402,770	457,000	532,007	628,109	794,890
Exports and re-exports from UK	729,988	691,738	1,046,504	813,522	1,157,777

Tourism. The number of foreign visitors was 6,500,294 in 1993. Earnings from tourism in 1994, US$4,321m. 3,311,313 Turks travelled abroad in 1993. There were 0·6m. tourist beds in 1993.

COMMUNICATIONS

Roads. In 1993 there were 31,424 km of state highways (including 125 km of motorway) and 28,346 km of provincial roads. In 1992 there were 2,181,388 cars, 595,340 lorries and pick-ups, 75,592 buses, 145,312 minibuses and 655,347 motorcycles. There were 171,741 road accidents in 1992, with 6,215 fatalities.

Railways. Total length of railway lines in 1993 was 10,386 km (1,435 mm gauge) of which 1,093 km were electrified; 119m. passengers and 14·6m. tonnes of freight were carried.

Civil Aviation. There are international airports at Istanbul (Atatürk), Dalaman and Ankara (Esenboga). The national carrier is Turkish Airlines, which is 98·2% state-owned, and in 1995 had a fleet of 7 A310-200s, 7 A310-300s, 3 A340-300s, 8 B-727-200 Advs, 28 B-737-400s, 2 B-737-500s and 8 other aircraft. In 1992 it flew 4,089,213 passengers (1,686,260 on international flights) and carried 397,191 tonnes (181,721) of freight. Services are also provided by Adria, Aeroflot, Air Algérie, Air France, Air Malta, Air Moldova, Air Ukraine, Albanian Airlines, Alitalia, AOM, Austrian Airlines, Azerbayan Hava Yollary, Balkan, British Airways, Croatia Airlines, Cyprus Turkish Airlines, Czech Airlines, Delta, Donavia, Egyptair, El Al, Emirates, Finnair, Gulf Air, Hapag Lloyd, Iberia, Iran Air, Kazakhstan Airlines, KLM, Kuwait Airways, Kyrgyzstan Airlines, Latvian Airlines, Libyan Airlines, Lithuanian Airlines, LOT, LTU, Lufthansa, Malaysia Airlines, Malév, Middle East Airlines, Olympic Airways, Orbi, Pakistan Airlines, Palair Macedonian, Royal Air Maroc, Royal Jordanian, Sabena, SAS, Saudia, Singapore Airlines, Swissair, Syrian Airlines, Tarom, Thai Airways, Top Air, Tunis Air and Uzbekistan Airways.

Shipping. In 1992 there were 3,038 cargo ships totalling 3,045,384 GRT, 221 tankers totalling 965,390 GRT and 1,319 passenger ships totalling 236,417 GRT. The main ports are: Istanbul, Izmir, Samsun, Mersin, Iskenderun and Trabzon.

Coastal shipping, 1992: 22,136 vessels handled; 314,813 passengers entered, and 33,308 cleared; 17·3m. tonnes of goods entered, 14·1m. cleared. International shipping: 17,118 vessels handled; 547,484 passengers entered, 546,208 cleared; 53·2m. tonnes of goods entered, 26·6m. cleared.

Telecommunications. In 1992 there were 41,623 post offices. In 1990 there were 6·89m. telephones.

The Turkish Radio-Television Corporation (TRT) broadcasts 4 national radio tourist programmes in English, French and German, 2 regional programmes and a foreign service, Voice of Turkey (English, French, German).

The government monopoly of broadcasting was abolished in 1993, and there are about 800 independent radio and 84 TV stations. TRT transmits on 5 channels (colour by PAL). In 1993 there were 7·1m. radio and 10 ·53m. TV sets in use. There were 7·5m. radio and 13m. TV sets registered in 1990.

Cinemas. In 1992 there were 312 cinemas. Attendances totalled 13,241,399.

Press. In 1991 there were 54 dailies and 3,033 periodicals. 6,151 book titles were published in 1992. There were 910 public libraries serving a readership of 19,297,767 in 1992.

SOCIAL INSTITUTIONS

Justice. The unified legal system consists of: (1) justices of the peace (single judges with limited but summary penal and civil jurisdiction); (2) courts of first instance (single judges, dealing with cases outside the jurisdiction of (3) and (4)); (3) central criminal courts (a president and 2 judges, dealing with cases where the crime is punishable by imprisonment over 5 years); (4) commercial courts (3 judges); (5) state security courts, to prosecute offences against the integrity of the state (a president and 4 judges, 2 of the latter being military).

The civil and military High Courts of Appeal sit at Ankara. The Council of State is the highest administrative tribunal; it consists of 5 chambers. Its 31 judges are nominated from among high-ranking personalities in politics, economy, law, the army, etc. The Military Administrative Court deals with the judicial control of administrative acts and deeds concerning military personnel. The Court of Jurisdictional Disputes is empowered to resolve disputes between civil, administrative and military courts. The Supreme Council of Judges and Public Prosecutors appoints judges and prosecutors to the profession and has disciplinary powers.

The Civil Code and the Code of Obligations have been adapted from the corresponding Swiss codes. The Penal Code is largely based upon the Italian Penal Code, and the Code of Civil Procedure closely resembles that of the Canton of Neuchâtel. The Commercial Code is based on the German.

Prison population (1991), 10,893 (237 females; 214 juveniles).

Religion. Islam ceased to be the official religion in 1928 and Turkey is now a secular state. Freedom of religion is guaranteed by the Constitution. A law of 1934 forbids the wearing of clerical garb for those other than religious leaders except in places of worship and during divine service. The constitution forbids the political exploitation of religion or any impairment of the secular character of the republic.

In 1992 there were 58·12m. Moslems, two-thirds Sunni and one-third Shi'ite (Alevis). The administration of the Sunni Moslem religious organizations is the responsibility of the Department of Religious Affairs, attached to the Prime Minister's office.

Istanbul is the seat of the Patriarch of the Greek Orthodox Church in Turkey. The Armenian Church (Gregorian) is ruled by a Patriarch in Istanbul who is subordinate to the Katholikos of Etchmiadzin, the spiritual head of all Armenians. The Armenian Apostolic Church is ruled by the Patriarch of Cilicia. The Chaldeans (Nestorian Uniats) have a Bishop at Mardin. The Syrian Uniats have a See of Mardin and Amida, but it is united with their Patriarchate of Antioch (residence, Damascus). Greek Uniats (Byzantine Rite) have as their Ordinary in Istanbul, the Titular Bishop of Gratianopolis. Roman Catholics have a Nuncio in Ankara and a Bishop in Istanbul. There are Protestant chapels in Istanbul. There is a Grand Rabbi in Istanbul for the Jews, who number some 20,000.

Education. Adult literacy was 82·5% in 1994. Primary education from 6 to 14 is compulsory and co-educational and, in state schools, free. In 1990–91 78% of school-age children attended school.

Religious instruction (Sunni Moslem) in state schools having been first prohibited and then made optional is now compulsory. In 1991 there were 5,197 religious secondary schools with 0·29m. pupils up to 14 years.

Statistics for 1991–92	*Number*	*Teachers*	*Students*
Pre-school institutions	4,454	7,976	132,724
Primary schools	50,701	234,961	6,878,923
Junior high schools	6,177	50,913	2,116,625
High schools	1,887	66,789	894,047
Vocational and technical junior high schools	847	563	288,710
Vocational and technical high schools	2,124	56,862	688,300
Higher education institutes	424	35,132	751,057

In 1992–93 there were 29 universities (with numbers of teachers and students in 1991–92): Akdeniz (663; 9,642); Anatolia (1,146; 307,272); Ankara (3,073; 33,028); Atatürk (1,293; 16,528); Bilkent (541; 6,740); Boğaziçi (543; 8,759); Cumhuriyet (626; 7,522); Cukurova (1,135; 16,225); Dicle (770; 8,305); 9 Eylül (1,414; 26,734); Ege (1,939; 19,072); Erciyes (730; 9,518); Firat (616; 6,149); Gazi (2,193; 35,835); Gaziantep (275; 4,016); Hacettepe (2,771; 24,767); Inönü (322; 5,700); Istanbul (2,876; 45,951); Istanbul Technical (1,819; 19,270); Karadeniz (879; 14,218); Marmara (1,721; 22,856); Mimar Sinan (443; 3,856); 19 Mayis (668; 9,779); Middle East Technical (1,809; 16,540); Selçuk (1,088; 19,038); Trakya (541; 13,347); Uludağ (1,212; 20,683); Yildiz (855; 15,125); Yüzüncü Yil (319; 2,352). A French-speaking university opened at Galatasaray (Istanbul) in 1994.

In 1992 20,519 students were studying abroad.

Health. In 1992 there were 20,204 general practitioners, 8,974 specialist doctors, 1,844 dentists, 1,040 pharmacists attached to the Ministry of Health and 32,631 nurses. In 1994 there were 810 hospitals and 152 health centres.

Social Security. In 1992, 989,492 beneficiaries received TL15,011,934m. from the Government Employees Retirement Fund; 1,856,523 beneficiaries received TL31,658,047m. from the Social Insurance Institution; and 664,621 beneficiaries received TL3,369,195m. from the Independent Insurance System.

DIPLOMATIC REPRESENTATIVES

Of Turkey in Great Britain (43 Belgrave Sq., London, SW1X 8PA)
Ambassador: Özdem Sanberk.

Of Great Britain in Turkey (Sehit Ersan Caddesi 46/A, Cankaya, Ankara)
Ambassador: Sir Kieran Prendergast, KCVO, CMG.

Of Turkey in the USA (1606 23rd St., NW, Washington, D.C., 20008)
Ambassador: Nüzhet Kandemir.

Of the USA in Turkey (110 Ataturk Blvd., Ankara)
Ambassador: Marc Grossman.

Of Turkey to the United Nations
Ambassador: Hüseyin Çelem.

Further Reading

State Institute of Statistics. *Türkiye İstatistik Yıllığı/Statistical Yearbook of Turkey.—Diş Ticaret İstatistikleri/Foreign Trade Statistics* (Annual).—*Aylık İstatistik Bülten* (Monthly).

The Turkish Constitution, 1971. Ankara, 1972
Central Bank. *Üç Aylık Bülten/Quarterly Bulletin*
Ahmad, F., *The Making of Modern Turkey.* London, 1993
Barchard, D., *Turkey and the West.* London, 1985
Birand, M. A., *Shirts of Steel: an Anatomy of the Turkish Armed Forces.* London, 1991
Dodd, C. H., *The Crisis of Turkish Democracy.* Beverley, 1983
Güclü, M., *Turkey.* [Bibliography] Oxford and Santa Barbara (CA), 1981
Hale, W., *The Political and Economic Development of Modern Turkey.* London, 1981
Hesper, M., *The State Tradition in Turkey.* Beverley, 1985
Kazancigil, A. and Ozbudun, E., (eds.) *Atatürk: Founder of a Modern State.* London, 1981
Kinross, Lord, *Atatürk.* London, 1964
Lewis, B., *The Emergence of Modern Turkey.* OUP, 1968
Özal, T., *Turkey in Europe and Europe in Turkey.* Nicosia, 1992
Tachau, F., *Turkey: The Politics of Authority, Democracy and Development.* New York, 1984
Weiker W., *The Modernization of Turkey.* New York, 1981
Zürcher, E. J., *Turkey: a Modern History.* London and New York, 1993 (NY, 1994)

State library: MilliKütüphane Müdürlüğü, Ankara.
National statistical office: State Institute of Statistics, Prime Ministry, Ankara. *President:* Dr Orhan Güvenen.

TURKMENISTAN

Turkmenostan Respublikasy

Capital: Ashgabat
Population: 4·4m. (1994)
GNP per capita: US$1,270 (1992)
HDI/world rank: 0·731/86 (1992)

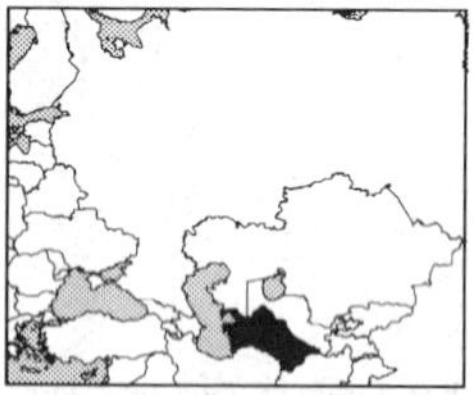

KEY HISTORICAL EVENTS. The country passed under Russian control in 1881. The Turkmen Soviet Socialist Republic was formed on 27 Oct. 1924 and covers the territory of the former Trans-Caspian Region of Turkestan, the Charjiui vilayet of Bokhara and a part of Khiva situated on the right bank of the Oxus. In May 1925 the Turkmen Republic entered the Soviet Union as one of its constituent republics. In Aug. 1990 the Turkmen Supreme Soviet unanimously adopted a declaration of sovereignty.

In Oct. 1991, following 94·1% support in a referendum, it adopted a declaration of independence. It became a member of the CIS in Dec. 1991.

TERRITORY AND POPULATION. Turkmenistan is bounded in the north by Kazakhstan, in the north and north-east by Uzbekistan, in the south-east by Afghanistan, in the south-west by Iran and in the west by the Caspian Sea. Area, 448,100 sq. km (186,400 sq. miles).

According to the 1989 census 72% of the 3,522,717 population were Turkmenians; Russians accounted for 9·5%; 9% were Uzbek and 2·5% Kazakh.

Population estimate (Jan. 1994) 4,358,000 (50·6% female; 45·4% urban). Vital statistics rates (per 1,000 population), 1993: Births, 33·1; deaths, 7·9; natural increase, 25·2; infant mortality (per 1,000 live births), 45·9.

There are 5 regions: Chardzhou, Mary, Ashgabat, Tashauz and Krasnovodsk, comprising 42 rural districts, 15 towns and 74 urban settlements. The capital is Ashgabat (formerly Ashkhabad; 1990 population, 411,000); other large towns are Chardzhou, Mary (Merv), Nebit-Dag and Krasnovodsk.

There is a dual citizenship agreement with Russia.

CONSTITUTION AND GOVERNMENT. A new constitution was adopted in 1992. It provides for a strongly executive head of state, the *Turkmenbashi* (*Leader of Turkmens*).

At the presidential elections of June 1992 the electorate was 1·86m. Saparmurad Niyazov was re-elected unopposed by 99·5% of votes cast. At a referendum on 16 Jan. 1994 99·99% of votes cast were in favour of prolonging President Niyazov's term of office to 2002.

A new parliament was instituted in Dec. 1994, the 50-member *Majlis.* Parliamentary elections were held on 11 Dec. 1994. The only party standing was the Democratic Party (DP; former Communists). 1 candidate stood in each constituency, but to be elected had to receive 51% of the vote. Turn-out was said to be 99·8%.

In Nov. 1995 the government comprised:

Head of State and Prime Minister: Saparmurad Niyazov (b. 1940; DP).

Deputy Prime Ministers: Orasgeldy Ajdogdev; Matkarim Rajapov; Reedjep Saparov; Klehim Ishanov; Batyr Ovezov. *Deputy Prime Minister and Minister of the Interior, National Security and Justice:* Batyr Sarjaev. *Deputy Prime Minister and Foreign Minister:* Boris Shikmuradov. *Deputy Prime Minister and Minister for Construction, Transport and Communications:* Yagmur Ovezov. *Defence:* Dangatar Kopekov. *Trade:* Halnazar Agahanov. *Economy and Finance:* Muhamed Abalakov. *Justice:* Tagandurdy Hallev. *Culture and Tourism:* Geldymurad Nurmuhamedov. *Health:* Gurbangeldy Kadamov. *Communications:* Amanmurad Jummiev. *Oil and Gas:* Aman Ezenov. *Agriculture and Foodstuffs:* Tagandurdy Nurev. *Social Affairs:* Halykberdy Atav. *Construction and Architecture:* Allaberdy Tekaev. *Education:*

Rejepdurdye Karaev. *Water Conservancy:* Amannazar Ilamanov. *Automobile Transport and Roads Maintenance:* Senkuly Rahmanov. *Foreign Economic Relations:* Chary Kuliev. *Environment:* Dortkuli Kurbanov. *Industry:* Halmuhamed Orazsahatov. *Consumer Goods:* Ashir Ataev. *Grain Produce:* Amageldy Chariyarov. *Power Engineering and Industry:* Saparmurad Nurev.

National flag: Green, with a white crescent and 5 white stars, and a red, white and black strip of 5 carpet patterns near the hoist.

Local Government. Elections to regional, district, urban and rural Soviets were held on 7 Jan. 1990.

DEFENCE. Armed forces are under joint Russo-Turkmenistan control. In 1996 the Army was 11,000 strong and organized in 3 motor rifle divisions, 1 artillery and 1 engineer brigade and 1 multiple rocket launcher, 1 anti-tank and 3 engineer regiments. Equipment includes 570 T-72 main battle tanks. Air forces comprise 60 MiG-27s and Su-17s and 2 air defence regiments of 85 MiG-23s and 30 MiG-25s. That part of the former Soviet Caspian Sea Flotilla (some 75%) not ceded to Azerbaijan and amounting to some 30 small warships has been relocated to Astrakhan, and operates under joint Russian, Kazakhstan and Turkmenistan command.

INTERNATIONAL RELATIONS

Membership. Turkmenistan is a member of the UN and the NATO Partnership for Peace.

ECONOMY

Policy. A privatization programme was launched on 1 June 1994. Enterprises with fewer than 100 employees are being sold to the employees or auctioned to citizens or foreign nationals. Large enterprises are to become joint stock companies, with the state retaining a controlling number of shares.

Budget. Budgetary income in 1993 was 2,000m. manat; expenditure was 1,900m. manat.

Currency. The unit of currency is the *manat* (TMM) of 100 *tenesi.* There are notes of 1, 5, 10, 20, 50, 100, 500 and 1,000 manat. On 1 Nov. 1993 the *manat* was introduced at a rate of 1 manat = US$0.50 = 500 roubles. Foreign exchange reserves were US$300m. in 1993. The manat was twice devalued in 1994, at first to a commercial rate of US$1 = 75 manat and an official rate of US$1 = 10 manat, and subsequently to an official rate of US$1 = 230 manat.

Banking and Finance. The *governor* of the Central Bank is Khudaiderdy Ozerov.

ENERGY AND NATURAL RESOURCES

Electricity. Output was 12,600m. kWh in 1993.

Oil and Gas. In 1994 gas reserves were estimated at 8,000,000m. cu. metres and oil reserves at 700m. tonnes. In 1993 crude oil production (including gas concentrate) was 5m. tonnes; natural gas, 65,300m. cu. metres.

Minerals. Turkmenistan is rich in minerals, such as coal, sulphur, magnesium and salt. 0·7m. tonnes of salt were produced in 1991.

Agriculture. The main economic sector is agriculture, based on irrigation by the Kara-Kum Canal. Turkmenistan produces cotton, wool, Astrakhan fur and carpets, and a breed of Turkoman horse and Karakul sheep. Output was valued at 2,700m. rubles (in constant 1983 prices) in 1993, 109% of the 1992 figure.

The main grain grown is maize. Sericulture, fruit and vegetable growing are also important; dates, olives, figs, sesame and other southern plants are grown. Area under cultivation in 1993 was 32·3m. ha, of which 74,100 ha was accounted for by private subsidiary agriculture, and 500 ha by commercial agriculture on some 100 farms. Private and commercial agriculture accounted for 22% by value of output in 1992.

Livestock on 1 Jan. 1994: Cattle, 1·1m.; pigs, 0·1m.; sheep and goats, 6·3m.

Output of main agricultural products (in 1,000 tonnes) in 1993: Grain, 900; cotton, 1,341; potatoes, 30; vegetables, 300; fruit and berries (1992), 48; meat, 109; milk, 507; and 267m. eggs.

Forestry. 67,000 cu. metres of sawn timber were produced in 1989.

Fisheries. There are fisheries in the Caspian Sea.

INDUSTRY. Output was valued at 5,800m. manat in current prices in 1993. Output, 1993 (in tonnes): Cement, 1·1m.; mineral fertilizer, 0·13m.; fabrics, 48·3m. sq. metres; footwear, 3·4m. pairs.

Labour. In 1993 the population of working age was 2·05m., of whom 1·6m. were employed, 53·8% in the state sector, 19·7% in the private sector and 25·9% in co-operatives. Average monthly wage in 1994 was 1,000 manat.

FOREIGN ECONOMIC RELATIONS

Commerce. In 1993 imports were valued at US$501·2m. and exports at US$1,049m.

Total trade between Turkmenistan and UK (British Department of Trade returns, in £1,000 sterling):

	1993	*1994*	*1995*
Imports to UK	25	837	738
Exports and re-exports from UK	14,619	4,382	3,902

COMMUNICATIONS

Roads. Length of motor roads in Jan. 1990, 22,600 km (17,800 km hard surface). In 1993, 273·1m. passengers and 46·3m. tonnes of freight were carried.

Railways. Length of railways, 2,187 km of 1,520 mm gauge. In 1993, 4·9m. passengers and 18·5m. tonnes of freight were carried.

Civil Aviation. The national carrier is the state-owned Turkmenavia, which operated 3 B-737-300s, 1 B-757-200 and 32 ex-Soviet aircraft in 1995. Airlines carried 1·7m. passengers and 14,900 tonnes of freight in 1993.

Shipping. In 1995, sea-going shipping totalled 15,812 GRT, including oil tankers, 1,621 GRT.

Inland Waterways. Waterways extended over 1,300 km in 1990. In 1993, 1·1m. tonnes of freight were carried.

Telecommunications. Turkmen Radio is government-controlled. It broadcasts 2 national and 1 regional programme, a Moscow Radio relay and a foreign service, Voice of Turkmen. There is 1 state-run TV station.

Press. Newspapers are subject to censorship. In 1995 there were 130 newspapers and periodicals.

SOCIAL INSTITUTIONS

Religion. Many of the population are Sunni Moslems.

Education. In 1993–94 there were 1,900 primary and secondary schools with 874,000 pupils, 11 higher educational institutions with 38,900 students, 41 technical colleges with 29,000 students, and 11 music and art schools.

In Jan. 1994, 0·2m. children (29·5% of those eligible) were attending pre-school institutions.

Health. In Jan. 1994 there were 14,000 doctors, 43,000 junior medical personnel and 368 hospitals with 46,100 beds.

Welfare. In Jan. 1994 there were 0·3m. age and 0·16m. other pensioners.

DIPLOMATIC REPRESENTATIVES

Of Great Britain in Turkmenistan (Suite 220, Ashgabat Business Centre, Berzengi, Ashgabat)
Ambassador: Neil Hook, MVO.

Of Turkmenistan in the USA
Ambassador: Halil Ugar.

Of the USA in Turkmenistan
Ambassador: Michael W. Cotter.

Of Turkmenistan to the United Nations
Ambassador: Aksoltan Ataeva.

THE TURKS AND CAICOS ISLANDS

Capital: Grand Turk
Population: 14,000 (1993)

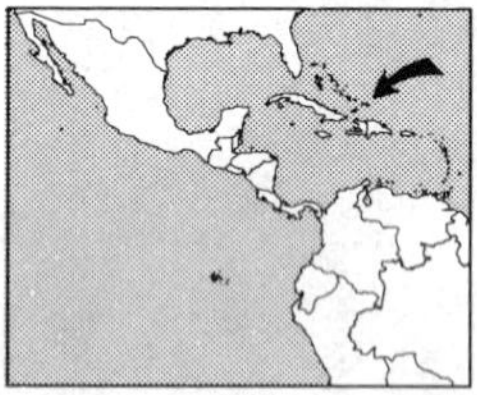

KEY HISTORICAL EVENTS. After a long period of rival French and Spanish claims the islands were eventually secured to the British Crown by the appointment in 1766 of a Resident British Agent, and became a separate colony in 1973 after association at various times with the colonies of the Bahamas and Jamaica.

TERRITORY AND POPULATION. The Turks and Caicos Islands are situated between 21° and 22°N. lat. and 71° and 72°W. long., about 50 miles east of Inagua in the Bahamas, of which they are geographically an extension. There are over 40 islands, covering an estimated area of 192 sq. miles (497 sq. km). Only 8 are inhabited: Grand Caicos, the largest, is 30 miles long by 2 to 3 miles broad; Grand Turk, the capital and main political and administrative centre, is 7 miles long by 1·25 broad. Population, 1990 census, 12,350; Grand Turk, 3,761; Providenciales, 5,586; South Caicos, 1,220; Middle Caicos, 275; North Caicos, 1,305; Salt Cay, 213. Estimate, 1993, 14,000.

Vital statistics (1989): Births, 192; deaths, 58.

CLIMATE. An equable and healthy climate as a result of regular trade winds, though hurricanes are sometimes experienced. Grand Turk. Jan. 76°F (24·4°C), July 83°F (28·3°C). Annual rainfall 21".

CONSTITUTION AND GOVERNMENT. A new Constitution was introduced in 1988 and amended in 1992. The Governor has responsibility for external affairs, internal security, defence and certain other matters. The Executive Council comprises 2 official members: The Chief Secretary and the Attorney-General; a Chief Minister and 5 other ministers from among the elected members of the Legislative Council; and is presided over by the Governor. The Legislative Council consists of a Speaker, the 2 official members of the Executive Council, 13 elected members and 3 appointed members.

At general elections held on 31 Jan. 1995 for the 13 elective seats on the Legislative Council, the People's Democratic Movement gained 8 seats; the People's National Party, 4; and ind, 1.

Governor: Martin Bourke.
Chief Minister: Derek Taylor.

Flag: British Blue Ensign with the shield of the Colony in the fly.

INTERNATIONAL RELATIONS

Membership. The Islands are a member of CARICOM.

ECONOMY

Budget. 1993–94 recurrent revenue was US$27·3m. and expenditure, US$28·5m. Forecast for 1994–95: Revenue, US$31·2m.; expenditure, US$31m.

Currency. The US dollar is the official currency.

Banking and Finance. There are 4 commercial banks. Offshore finance is a major industry.

INDUSTRY

Labour. In 1989, out of a total population of 4,885 aged 14 or over, 4,043 were working, 573 unemployed and 269 economically inactive.

FOREIGN ECONOMIC RELATIONS

Commerce. Exports, 1992–93, US$6·47m.; imports, US$39,835,000. The main export is dried, frozen and processed fish.

Total trade between Turks and Caicos Islands and UK (British Department of Trade returns, in £1,000 sterling):

	1991	*1992*	*1993*	*1994*	*1990*
Imports to UK	12	1,127	528	104	58
Exports and re-exports from UK	1,732	722	758	1,492	1,437

Tourism. Number of visitors, 1994, 70,946.

COMMUNICATIONS

Civil Aviation. The international airports are on Grand Turk and Providenciales. Turks and Caicos Airways had 2 aircraft in 1995. Services are also provided by American Airlines and Carnival Airlines. An internal air service provides regular daily flights between the inhabited islands.

Shipping. The main ports are at Grand Turk, Cockburn Harbour and Providenciales. There is a service to Miami. Registered shipping (1985), 168 sailing vessels of 2,445 tons and 49 motor vessels of 5,517 tons.

Telecommunications. There are internal and international cable, telephone, telex, telegraph and fax services. There were (1988) 1,359 telephones. The Government operates the semi-commercial Radio Turks and Caicos. There are also 2 commercial and 1 religious station. In 1995 there were about 6,000 radio sets. There is cable and satellite TV.

Press. There is 1 weekly and 1 bi-weekly newspaper.

SOCIAL INSTITUTIONS

Justice. Laws are a mixture of Statute and Common Law. There is a Magistrates Court and a Supreme Court. Appeals lie from the Supreme Court to the Court of Appeal which sits in Nassau, Bahamas. There is a further appeal in certain cases to the Privy Council in London. In 1989 the prison population was 159.

Religion. The Christian faith predominates with Anglican, Methodist, Baptist and evangelists groups.

Education. Education is free between the ages of 5 and 14 in the 10 government primary schools; there are also 4 private primary schools. In March 1993 the average number of pupils in the 4 government secondary schools was 1,075.

Health. In 1995 there were 6 doctors, 1 dentist, 56 nurses and midwives and 36 hospital beds.

Further Reading

Boultbee, P. G., *Turks & Caicos Islands.* [Bibliography]. Oxford and Santa Barbara (CA), 1991

TUVALU

Capital: Fongafale
Population: 10,090 (1991)

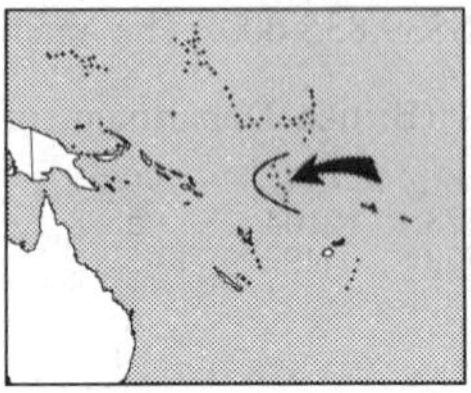

KEY HISTORICAL EVENTS. Formerly the Ellice Islands in the Gilbert and Ellice Islands, a British Protectorate since 1892. After a referendum the island group was separated from the Gilbert Islands in Oct. 1975. Independence was achieved on 1 Oct. 1978.

TERRITORY AND POPULATION. Tuvalu lies between 5° 30' and 11° S. lat. and 176° and 180° E. long. and comprises Nanumea, Nanumanga, Niutao, Nui, Vaitupu, Nukufetau, Funafuti (administrative centre), Nukulaelae and Niulakita. Population (census 1991) 10,090, of whom 1,097 were working abroad, mainly in Nauru. Area approximately $9^1/_2$ sq. miles (24 sq. km). The population is of a Polynesian race.

CLIMATE. A pleasant but monotonous climate with temperatures averaging 86°F (30°C), though trade winds from the east moderate conditions for much of the year. Rainfall ranges from 120" (3,000 mm) to over 160" (4,000 mm). Funafuti. Jan. 84°F (28·9°C), July 81°F (27·2°C). Annual rainfall 160" (4,003 mm).

CONSTITUTION AND GOVERNMENT. The Constitution provides for a Prime Minister and 4 other Ministers to be elected from among the 12 elected members of the *House of Parliament.*

Governor-General: HE Tulaga Manuella.

In Nov. 1995 the Cabinet comprised:

Prime Minister, Minister of Foreign Affairs and Economic Planning: Kamuta Latasi.

Deputy Prime Minister, Minister of Natural Resources, Home Affairs and Rural Development: Otinielu Tausi. *Finance, Trade, Commerce and Public Corporations:* Koloa Talake. *Health and Human Resources Development:* Faimalaga Luka, OBE. *Labour, Works and Communications:* Houati Iele. *Attorney-General:* Feleti Teo [1]. *Secretary to the Government:* Taausa Taafaki [1].

Speaker: Dr Tomasi Puapua.

[1] Ex-officio members of the Cabinet and House of Parliament.

National flag: A new flag was adopted on 1 Oct. 1995: 3 horizontal stripes of red, blue, red in the proportions 1:3:1 with the blue fimbriated in white and having inserted at the hoist a white triangle containing the coat of arms, with 8 white stars in the fly.

National anthem: 'Tuvalu mo te Atua' ('Tuvalu for the Almighty'); words and tune by A. Manoa.

Local Government. There is a town council on Funafuti and island councils on the 7 other atolls, each consisting of 6 elected members including a president. Since 1966 Members of Parliament have been *ex-officio* members of Island Councils. The island of Niulakita is administered as part of Niutao.

INTERNATIONAL RELATIONS

Membership. Tuvalu is a member of the Commonwealth and the South Pacific Forum and is an ACP state of the EU.

ECONOMY

Budget. In 1994 the budget envisaged revenue of $A9·4m.

Currency. The unit of currency is the Australian *dollar* although Tuvaluan coins up to $A1 are in local circulation.

Banking and Finance. The Tuvalu National Bank was established at Funafuti in 1980 and is a joint venture between the Tuvalu Government and Wespac International.

ENERGY AND NATURAL RESOURCES

Electricity. Production (1992) 1·3m. kWh.

Agriculture. Coconut palms are the main crop. Production of coconuts (1991), 4,000 tonnes. Fruit and vegetables are grown for local consumption.

Fisheries. Sea fishing is excellent but is largely unexploited although in 1988 Japanese, Taiwanese and South Korean vessels were granted licences to fish.

FOREIGN ECONOMIC RELATIONS

Commerce. Commerce is dominated by co-operative societies, the Tuvalu Co-operative Wholesale Society being the main importer. Main sources of income are copra, stamps, handicrafts and remittances from Tuvaluans abroad.

Total trade between Tuvalu and UK (British Department of Trade returns, in £1,000 sterling):

	1991	*1992*	*1993*	*1994*	*1995*
Imports to UK	1	—	1	1	—
Exports and re-exports from UK	107	170	74	134	268

COMMUNICATIONS

Civil Aviation. Fiji Air and Air Marshal operate services to Kiribati and Fiji.

Shipping. Funafuti is the only port and a deep-water wharf was opened in 1980.

Telecommunications. The government broadcasting service, Radio Tuvalu transmits daily in Tuvaluan and English and all islands have daily radio communication with Funafuti. There were about 4,000 radio receivers in 1993.

SOCIAL INSTITUTIONS

Justice. There is a High Court presided over by the Chief Justice of Fiji. A Court of Appeal is constituted if required.

Religion. The majority of the population are Christians, mainly Protestant but with small groups of Roman Catholics, Seventh Day Adventists, Jehovah's Witnesses and Mormons. There are some Moslems and Baha'is.

Education. There are 9 state primary, 1 secondary and 1 church secondary school.

Health. In 1984 there was 1 central hospital with 36 beds situated at Funafuti. There were 4 doctors.

DIPLOMATIC REPRESENTATIVES

Of Great Britain in Tuvalu
High Commissioner: Michael Peart, CMG, LVO (resides in Suva).

Of Tuvalu in the USA
Ambassador: (Vacant).

Of the USA in Tuvalu
Ambassador: Vacant (resides in Suva).

UGANDA

Republic of Uganda

Capital: Kampala
Population: 16·6m. (1991)
GNP per capita: US$200 (1994)
HDI/world rank: 0·329/158 (1992)

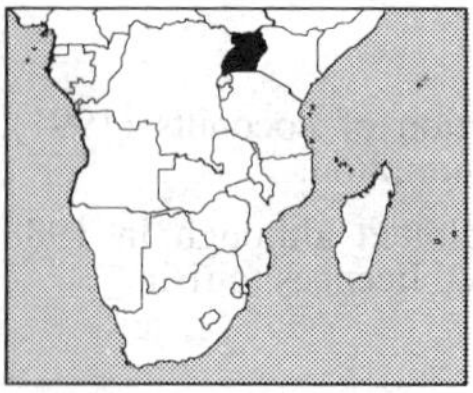

KEY HISTORICAL EVENTS. Uganda became a British Protectorate in 1894, the province of Buganda being recognized as a native kingdom under its Kabaka. In 1961 Uganda was granted internal self-government with federal status for Buganda.

Uganda became a fully independent member of the Commonwealth on 9 Oct. 1962. Full sovereign status was granted by the Uganda Independence Act, 1962. Uganda became a republic on 8 Sept. 1967.

In 1971, President Milton Obote was overthrown by troops led by Gen. Idi Amin.

In April 1979 a force of the Tanzanian Army and Ugandan exiles advanced into Uganda taking Kampala on 11 April. On 14 April Dr Yusuf Lule was sworn in as President and the country was administered, initially, by the Uganda National Liberation Front. Godfrey Lukongwa Binaisa was appointed President by the National Consultative Council on 20 June 1979. He was deposed in May 1980 by the Military Commission, the military arm of Uganda National Liberation Front.

Milton Obote again became President when the Uganda People's Congress won the elections of Dec. 1980; he was deposed on 27 July 1985.

Lieut.-Gen. Tito Okello became Head of State on 29 July 1985 but the National Resistance Army (NRA) of Yoweri Museveni, the armed wing of the National Resistance Movement, was not prepared to co-operate with the new regime. After an abortive ceasefire between the NRA and government forces on 17 Dec. 1985 the NRA fought its way into Kampala and Yoweri Museveni was installed as President on 27 Jan. 1986.

TERRITORY AND POPULATION. Uganda is bounded on the north by Sudan, on the east by Kenya, on the south by Tanzania and Rwanda, and the west by Zaïre. Total area 241,038 sq. km, including 43,938 sq. km of water.

At the 1991 census (provisional) the population was 16,582,700 (8,457,900 females; 11·3% (1,876,000) lived in urban areas, the largest towns being Kampala, the capital (773,463), Jinja (60,979), Mbale (53,634), Masaka (49,070), Gulu (42,841), Entebbe (41,638), Soroti (40,602) and Mbarara (40,383). Density, 84 per sq. km. Vital statistics rates per 1,000, 1985–90: Birth, 50·1; death, 15·4; infant mortality, 103; population growth, 0·35. Expectation of life in 1990 was: Males, 49·4 years; females, 52·7.

The country is administratively divided into 38 districts, which are grouped in 4 geographical regions (which do not have administrative status). Area and population in 1991:

Region/District	*Area in sq. km.*	*Population in 1,000*	*Region/District*	*Area in sq. km.*	*Population in 1,000*
Central Region	61,510	4,822·3	*Eastern Region*	39,953	4,110·3
Kalangala	5,716	16·4	Iganga	13,113	944·0
Kampala	238	773·5	Jinja	734	284·9
Kiboga	3,774	140·8	Kamuli	4,348	480·7
Luwero	9,198	449·2	Kapchorwa	1,738	116·3
Masaka	10,611	831·3	Kumi	2,861	237·0
Mpigi	6,222	915·4	Mbale	2,546	706·6
Mubende	6,536	497·5	Pallisa	1,919	356·0
Mukono	14,242	816·2	Soroti	10,060	430·9
Rakai	4,973	382·0	Tororo	2,634	554·0
Western Region	54,917	4,521·0	*Northern Region*	84,658	3,129·1
Bundibugyo	2,338	116·0	Apac	6,488	460·7
Bushenyi	5,396	734·8	Arua	7,830	624·6

Region/District	*Area in sq. km.*	*Population in 1,000*	*Region/District*	*Area in sq. km.*	*Population in 1,000*
Western Region (contd)			*Northern Region (contd)*		
Hoima	5,492	197·8	Gulu	11,735	338·7
Kabale	1,827	412·8	Kitgum	16,136	350·3
Kabalore	8,361	741·4	Kotido	13,208	190·7
Kasese	3,205	343·0	Lira	7,251	498·3
Kibaale	4,718	219·3	Moroto	14,113	171·5
Kisoro	662	184·9	Moyo	5,006	178·5
Masindi	9,326	253·5	Nebbi	2,891	315·9
Mbarara	10,839	929·6			
Rukungiri	2,753	388·0			

The official language is English, but Kiswahili is used as a lingua franca. About 70% of the population speak Bantu languages; Nilotic languages are spoken in the north and east.

CLIMATE. Although in equatorial latitudes, the climate is more tropical, because of its elevation, and is characterized by 2 distinct rainy seasons March-May and Sept.-Nov. June-Aug. and Dec.-Feb. are comparatively dry. Temperatures vary little over the year. Kampala. Jan. 74°F (23·3°C), July 70°F (21·1°C). Annual rainfall 46·5" (1,180 mm). Entebbe. Jan. 72°F (22·2°C), July 69°F (20·6°C). Annual rainfall 63·9" (1,624 mm).

KABAKA. Having lapsed in 1966, the kabakaship was revived as a ceremonial office in 1993. Ronald Muwenda Mutebi was crowned Mutebi II, 36th Kabaka, on 31 July 1993.

CONSTITUTION AND GOVERNMENT. The *President* is head of state and head of government and is elected for a 5-year term by the National Assembly. The national legislature was the 278-member National Resistance Council. This was replaced by a 278-member *Constituent Assembly* in March 1994, 214 of whose members were directly elected, 10 nominated by the President, 10 by the military and 39 (women) by women's associations. A new constitution was adopted on 8 Oct. 1995. It prolongs the monopoly of the National Resistance Movement for a further 5 years, after which multi-party democracy is envisaged.

Elections were scheduled for 1996.

In Dec. 1995 the government comprised:

President, Minister of Defence: Yoweri Museveni (b. 1945; sworn in 27 Jan. 1986).

Vice-President, Minister of Gender and Community Development: Specîosa Wandira Kazibwe.

Prime Minister: Kintu Musoke.

First Deputy Prime Minister: Eriya Kategaya. *Second Deputy Prime Minister and Minister of Public Service:* Dr Paul K. Ssemogerere. *Third Deputy Prime Minister and Minister of Lands, Housing and Urban Development:* Eric Adriko. *Finance and Economic Planning:* Joshua Mayanja Nkangi. *Commerce, Industry and Co-operatives:* Richard Kaijuka. *Agriculture, Animal Industry and Fisheries:* Victoria Ssekitoleko. *Health:* Dr James Makumbi. *Works, Transport and Communications:* Ali Kirunda Kivejinja. *Information:* Paul Etyang. *Natural Resources:* Henry Kajura. *Tourism, Wildlife and Antiquities:* Brig. Moses Ali. *Education and Sports:* Amanya Mushega. *Local Government:* Jaberi Bidandi Ssali. *Labour and Social Affairs:* Stephen Chebrot. *Interior:* Crispus Kiyonga. *Foreign Affairs:* Dr Ruhakana Rugunda. *Justice:* Joseph Ekemu.

National flag: Six horizontal stripes (black, yellow, red, black, yellow, red), with in the centre a small white disc bearing a representation of a Balearic Crested Crane.

National anthem: 'Oh, Uganda, may God uphold thee'; words and tune by G. W. Kakoma.

Local Government. The 38 districts are divided into 154 counties, which are in turn divided into sub-counties which form the basic administrative units.

DEFENCE

Army. The National Resistance Army had a strength of about 50,000 in 1996. Equipment includes 20 T-54/-55 main battle tanks. Efforts are being made to reduce the size of the army and convert it to a specialized force.

Navy. A Marine unit of the police (400 strong in 1995) operates 8 small patrol craft.

Air Force. Since 1979, the service has been in a period of decline. Some aircraft of Western European origin are still serviceable, including a small number of AS.202 Bravo and SF.260 trainers and about 4 Agusta-Bell helicopters. The Police Air Wing still operates 2 fixed-wing aircraft and 10 Bell helicopters.

INTERNATIONAL RELATIONS

Membership. Uganda is a member of UN, OAU, Islamic Conference Organization, the Commonwealth and is an ACP state of EU.

ECONOMY

Policy. A privatization programme was instituted in 1991 managed by the Public Enterprise Reform and Divestiture Secretariat. The state is to retain ownership of certain utilities, national parks and the development bank. About 100 enterprises are in state ownership, but few had been privatized by 1995.

Budget. In 1991–92 revenue (excluding grants) was 182,340m. Uganda Sh. and expenditure, 410,310m. Uganda Sh. Sources of revenue included (in 1m. Uganda Sh.): Tax, 176,180; export duties, 2,120; customs duties, 74,740. Expenditures included: Agriculture, animal industry and fisheries, 8,192; education, 38,009; health, 3,306; defence, 63,421.

Currency. The monetary unit is the *Uganda shilling* (UGS) notionally divided into 100 *cents*. In 1987 the currency was devalued by 77% and a new 'heavy' shilling was introduced worth 100 old shillings. There are notes of 50, 100, 200, 500, 1,000 and 5,000 shillings. In March 1996, £1 = 1,537·57 shillings; US$1 = 1,006 shillings; DM1 = 681·62 shillings.

Banking and Finance. The Bank of Uganda (established 1966) is the central bank and bank of issue. The Uganda Credit and Savings Bank, established in 1950, was on 9 Oct. 1965 reconstituted as the Uganda Commercial Bank, with its capital fully owned by the Government. In 1992 it had 188 branches. In addition there were 4 foreign, 2 private and 2 development banks and 1 co-operative bank.

A stock exchange was scheduled to open in Kampala in 1996

ENERGY AND NATURAL RESOURCES

Electricity. Installed capacity, 1992, was 168 MW, of which the Owen Falls hydro-electric scheme provided 162 MW. Production (1991) 782·4m. kWh.

Agriculture. In 1991 the agricultural area included 5·02m. ha of arable, 1·7m. ha of permanent crops and 1·8m. ha of pasture. In 1989, agriculture was one of the priority areas for increased production, with many projects funded both locally and externally. Agriculture provided 68·6% of GDP in 1989. Production (1993) in 1,000 tonnes: Tobacco, 5; coffee, 177; cotton lint, 7; tea, 12; unrefined sugar, 60; plantains, 7,806; millet, 652; maize, 681; sorghum, 382; cassava, 3,982; dry beans, 441.

Livestock (1993): Cattle, 5·2m.; sheep, 1·76m.; goats, 3·4m.; pigs, 0·9m.; poultry, 20m. Livestock products, 1993 (in 1,000 tonnes): Beef and veal, 86; pork, 49; poultry meat, 34; eggs, 16; honey, 250; milk, 455.

Forestry. Woodland covers 5·56m. ha (1990) and exploitable forests consist almost entirely of hardwoods. 13·87m. cu. metres of wood were cut or gathered in 1988, 1·8m. for timber.

Fisheries. Uganda possesses one of the largest fresh-water fisheries in the world. In 1989 fish production was 213,500 tonnes. Fish farming (especially carp and tilapia) is a growing industry.

INDUSTRY. Production (in 1,000 tonnes) in 1988: Cement, 17·38; soap, 26·87; wheat flour, 13·87; sugar, 15·86; beer, 19·52m. litres.

Labour. The workforce was 8·13m. in 1990 (3·34m. female; 0·88m. between 10 and 15 years).

FOREIGN ECONOMIC RELATIONS. Foreign debt was US$2,700m. in 1994.

Commerce. In 1989 commerce provided 20% of GDP. In 1991 imports were US$610m. and exports, US$180m.

Coffee, cotton, tea and tobacco are the principal exports.

Total trade between Uganda and UK (British Department of Trade returns, in £1,000 sterling):

	1991	*1992*	*1993*	*1994*	*1995*
Imports to UK	6,730	9,398	7,601	15,491	11,136
Exports and re-exports from UK	35,718	26,682	30,439	40,779	49,105

Tourism. There were 90,770 tourists in 1991.

COMMUNICATIONS

Roads. There were (1985) 7,582 km of all-weather roads maintained by the Ministry of Works, of which 1,934 km are two-lane bitumenized highways, and some 19,640 km of other roads, maintained by district governments. There were 34,938 motor vehicles in 1989, including 12,964 passenger cars, 7,410 vans, 3,700 lorries, 2,984 buses and 4,240 motorcycles.

Railways. The Uganda Railways network totals 1,241 km (metre gauge). In 1994 railways carried 221,000 passengers and 780,000 tonnes of freight.

Civil Aviation. There is an international airport at Entebbe. The national carrier is the state-owned Uganda Airlines, which operated 1 B-737-200 Adv, and 1 other aircraft in 1995. Uganda and Tanzania are partners with South African Airways in Alliance Airline. Services are also provided by Air Burundi, Air Rwanda, Air Tanzania, British Airways, Egyptair, Ethiopian Airlines, Gulf Air, Inter Aviation, Kenya Airways, Royal Swazi, Sabena and Sudan Airways. Uganda Airlines carried 45,000 international and 16,000 domestic passengers in 1988. 130,000 passengers and 7,791 tonnes of freight were handled at Entebbe in 1989.

Telecommunications. There were 54,900 telephones in use in 1989. The government runs Radio Uganda, which has 10 stations and transmits 3 regional programmes, and Uganda Television with 9 stations and 1 programme. Colour is by PAL. There were about 0·5m. radio receivers and about 0·25m. television sets in 1992.

Press. There were 4 daily newspapers in 1992 with a fluctuating circulation of 45,000-55,000, and 12 weekly, 1 bi-weekly and 5 monthly newspapers and magazines.

SOCIAL INSTITUTIONS

Justice. The High Court of Uganda, presided over by the Chief Justice and 29 puisne judges, exercises original and appellate jurisdiction throughout Uganda. Subordinate courts, presided over by Chief Magistrates and Magistrates of the first, second and third grade, are established in all areas: Jurisdiction varies with the grade of Magistrate. Chief and first-grade Magistrates are professionally qualified; second- and third-grade Magistrates are trained to diploma level at the Law Development Centre, Kampala. Chief Magistrates exercise supervision over and hear appeals from second- and third-grade courts and village courts.

The Supreme Court of Uganda hears appeals from the High Court.

Religion. In 1992 there were 8·53m. Roman Catholics, 4·5m. Anglicans and 1·13m. Moslems.

Education. In 1989 there were 2,633,764 pupils in 7,905 primary schools (of which 7,420 were Government-aided schools and 485 private schools); 240,334 students in 774 secondary schools; 13,174 students in 94 primary teacher training colleges; 3,208 students in 24 technical institutes; 1,819 students in 10 national teachers colleges; 1,009 students in technical colleges; 1,628 students in 5 colleges of commerce; 1,037 students in the Institute of Teacher Education, Kyambogo; 504 students in the Uganda Polytechnic, Kyambogo; 800 students in the National College of Business Studies, Nakawa. In 1995–96 there was 1 university and 1 university of science and technology in the public sector, and 2 universities, 1 Christian, 1 Roman Catholic and 1 Islamic university in the private sector.

Health. In 1988 there were 980 health centres (217 private), and in 1989 there were 81 hospitals and 20,136 hospital beds. The Ministry of Health has 16 schools for training nurses and other health staff, 105 health centres, 89 dispensaries with maternity units, 87 dispensaries, 35 maternity units, 371 sub-dispensaries, 14 leprosy centres and 169 aid posts. In 1984 there were about 700 doctors.

DIPLOMATIC REPRESENTATIVES

Of Uganda in Great Britain (Uganda Hse., Trafalgar Sq., London, WC2N 5DX)
High Commissioner: George Kirya.

Of Great Britain in Uganda (10/12 Parliament Ave., Kampala)
High Commissioner: Edward Clay, CMG.

Of Uganda in the USA (5909 16th St., NW, Washington, D.C., 20011)
Ambassador: Stephen Katenta-Apuli.

Of the USA in Uganda (Parliament Ave., Kampala)
Ambassador: E. Michael Southwick.

Of Uganda to the United Nations
Ambassador: Perezi Karukubiro Kamunanwire.

Further Reading

Collison, R. L., *Uganda.* [Bibliography] Oxford and Santa Barbara (CA), 1981
Jørgensen, J. J., *Uganda: A Modern History.* London, 1981
Museveni, Y., *What is Africa's Problem?* London, 1993
Mutibwa, P., *Uganda since Independence: a Story of Unfulfilled Hopes.* London, 1992

National statistical office: Statistical Department, Ministry of Finance and Economic Planning, Kampala.

UKRAINE

Ukraina

Capital: Kiev
Population: 52·14m. (1994)
GNP per capita: US$1,570 (1994)
HDI/world rank: 0·843/54 (1992)

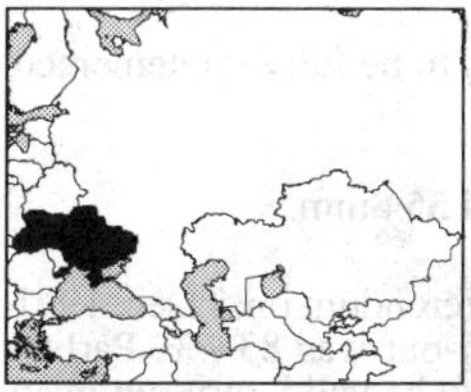

KEY HISTORICAL EVENTS. The Ukrainian Soviet Socialist Republic was proclaimed on 25 Dec. 1917 and was finally established in Dec. 1919. In Dec. 1920 it concluded a military and economic alliance with the RSFSR and on 30 Dec. 1922 formed, together with the other Soviet Socialist Republics, the Union of Soviet Socialist Republics. On 1 Nov. 1939 Western Ukraine (about 88,000 sq. km) was incorporated in the Ukrainian SSR. On 2 Aug. 1940 Northern Bukovina (about 6,000 sq. km) ceded to the USSR by Romania 28 June 1940, and the Khotin, Akkerman and Izmail provinces of Bessarabia were included in the Ukrainian SSR, and on 29 June 1945 Ruthenia (Sub-Carpathian Russia), about 7,000 sq. km, was also incorporated. From the new territories 2 new regions were formed, Chernovits and Izmail.

On 5 Dec. 1991 the Supreme Soviet unanimously repudiated the 1922 Treaty of Union and declared Ukraine's independence. Ukraine was one of the founder member of the CIS in Dec. 1991.

TERRITORY AND POPULATION. The Ukraine is bounded in the east by Russia, the north by Belarus, the west by Poland, Slovakia, Hungary, Romania and Moldova, and the south by the Black Sea and the Sea of Azov. Area, 603,700 sq. km (231,990 sq. miles).

The 1989 census population was 51,452,034 of whom 72·7% were Ukrainians, 22·1% Russians, 1% Jews and 0·92% Belorussians. Estimate, Jan. 1994, 52,114,000 (53·5% female; 67·9% urban).

Vital statistics rates (per 1,000 population), 1993: Births, 10·7; deaths, 14·2; growth, –3·5; infant mortality (per 1,000 live births), 14·9.

The Ukraine is divided into 24 provinces and the Crimea, which has a degree of autonomy. Area and population of the provinces in 1991:

	Area (sq. km)	*Population (in 1,000)*		*Area (sq. km)*	*Population (in 1,000)*
Cherkasy	20,900	1,530·9	Lviv (Lvov)	21,800	2,764·4
Chernihiv	31,900	1,405·8	Mykolaïv	24,600	1,342·4
Chernivtsi	8,100	938·6	Odessa	33,300	2,635·3
Dnipropetrovsk	31,000	3,908·7	Poltava	28,800	1,756·9
Donetsk	26,500	5,346·7	Rivne (Rovno)	20,100	1,176·8
Ivano-Frankivsk	13,900	1,442·9	Sumy	23,800	1,430·2
Kharkov	31,400	3,194·8	Ternopil	13,800	1,175·1
Kherson	28,500	1,258·7	Vinnytsya	26,500	1,914·4
Khmelnytsky	20,600	1,520·6	Volyn	20,200	1,069·0
Kiev	28,900	4,589·8	Zakarpatska	12,800	1,265·9
Kirovohrad	24,600	1,245·3	Zaporizhya	27,200	2,099·6
Luhansk	26,700	2,871·1	Zhytomyr	29,900	1,510·7

The capital is Kiev (population 2·6m. in 1993). Other towns with 1991 populations over 0·2m. are:

	Population (in 1,000)		*Population (in 1,000)*		*Population (in 1,000)*
Kharkov	1,623	Zaporizhzhya	897	Mykolaïv	512
Dnipropetrovsk	1,189	Lviv (Lvov)	802	Luhansk	504
Donetsk	1,121	Kryvy Rih	724	Makiïvka	424
Odessa	1,101	Mariupol	522	Vinnytsya	381

	Population (in 1,000)		Population (in 1,000)		Population (in 1,000)
Sevastopol	366	Sumy	301	Rivne (Rovno)	239
Kherson	365	Zhytomyr	298	Ivano-Frankivsk	226
Simferopol	353	Dniprodzerzhynsk	284	Ternopil	218
Horlivka	337	Kirovohrad	278	Lutsk	210
Poltava	320	Chernivtsi	259	Bila Tserkva	204
Chernihiv	306	Kremenchuk	241	Kramatorsk	201
Cherkasy	302				

A law of Oct. 1989 made Ukrainian the official language, to be fully implemented within 3 to 10 years.

CLIMATE. Kiev. Jan. –6·1°C, July 20°C. Annual rainfall 554 mm.

CONSTITUTION AND GOVERNMENT. In a referendum on 1 Dec. 1991 90·3% of votes cast were in favour of independence. Turn-out was 83·7%. Parliament (the *Supreme Council*) has 450 seats. For an election to be valid, turn-out in an electoral district must reach 50%. Elections were held in 4 rounds in March, April, July and Nov. 1994 with run-offs in Aug. 1994. The electorate was 38,204,100. 5,833 candidates stood initially, of whom 3,633 were nominated by groups of voters, 1,557 by workers' collectives and 643 by political parties. The Communist Party gained 91 seats; Agrarian Party, 52; Centre Party, 37; Unity Party, 34; Inter-Regional Bloc for Reform, 34; Reform Party, 31; Statist Party, 30; Socialist Party, 30; Rukh, 27; ind, 34.

The *State Council* is chaired by the President. On 18 May 1995 the President renounced his right to dissolve parliament and parliament renounced its right to dismiss the President

Presidential elections were held in 2 rounds on 26 June and 10 July 1994. At the first round, turn-out was 69%. President Leonid Kravchuk gained 37·8% of votes cast against 6 opponents. At the 2nd round, turn-out was 71·6%. Leonid Kuchma was elected against President Kravchuk by 51·5% of votes cast.

President: Leonid Kuchma (sworn in 19 July 1994).

In March 1996 the government comprised:

Prime Minister: Ievheni Marchuk (b. 1941).

First Deputy Prime Minister: Pavel Lazarenko. *Deputy Prime Ministers:* Vasyl Durdynets (*Security, Emergencies, Combating Organized Crime*); Petro Sabluk (*Agro-Industries*); Roman Shpek (*Economy*); Ivan Kuras (*Humanitarian Policy*); Anatoli Kinakh (*Industry*). *Minister of Defence:* Valeri Shmarov. *Foreign Affairs:* Hennadi Udovenko. *Foreign Economic Relations and Trade:* Serhii Osyka. *Interior:* Yuri Kravchenko. *Health:* Ievheni Korolenko. *Environmental and Nuclear Safety:* Yuri Kostenko. *Economy:* Vasyl Hureiev. *Education:* Mykhailo Zhurovsky. *Industry:* Valeri Mazur. *Finance:* Petro Hermanchuk. *Communications:* Oleh Prozhivalsky. *Agriculture:* Yuri Karasik. *Justice:* Vasyl Onopenko. *Social Security:* Arkadi Yershov. *Transport:* Orest Klimpush. *Labour:* Mykhailo Kaskevych. *Youth and Sport:* Valeri Borzov. *Ethnic Groups:* Oleksandr Iemets. *Press and Information:* Mykhailo Onufriichuk. *Construction:* Yuri Serbyn. *Forestry:* Valeri Samoplavsky. *Energy:* Vylem Semenyuk. *Defence Industries:* Vyktor Petriv.

Speaker: Oleksandr Moroz.

National flag: Blue over yellow horizontally.

National anthem: 'Shche ne vmerla, Ukraïna' ('Thou hast not perished, Ukraine'); words by P. Chubynsky, tune by M. Verbytsky.

Local Government: The 24 provincial councils are subordinate to the President. Lower-level councils are subordinate to the provincial authorities. Elections were held on 4 March 1990.

DEFENCE. An agreement of Jan. 1994 (to be ratified by the Ukrainian parliament) between the presidents of Russia, the Ukraine and the USA provides for the removal of all former Soviet nuclear missiles from Ukrainian territory. Conscription is for 18 months.

Army. In 1996 ground forces numbered about 212,600 organized as follows: Ministry of Defence troops comprised 1 training tank brigade, 1 training artillery division, 1 artillery, 1 anti-tank and 3 engineer brigades; Western Operations Command comprised 1 artillery division, 1 training tank division, 1 surface-to-surface missile brigade and 1 engineer regiment, and 3 corps (1 with 2 motor rifle divisions, 2 mechanized, 1 artillery and 1 engineer brigade, 1 multiple rocket launcher and 1 anti-tank regiment; 1 with 2 mechanized divisions, 1 mechanized and 1 artillery brigade, 1 reserve anti-tank and 1 reserve multiple rocket launcher regiment; and 1 with 1 tank division and 1 anti-tank regiment); Southern Operations Command comprised 2 mechanized, 1 air mobile and 1 artillery division, 1 surface-to-surface missile, 2 surface-to-air missile and 2 artillery brigades, and 3 corps (1 with 2 mechanized and 1 artillery brigade and 1 anti-tank, 1 multiple rocket launcher and 2 reserve artillery brigades; 1 with 1 reserve motor rifle and 1 mechanized division, and 1 multiple rocket launcher and 1 reserve anti-tank regiment; and 1 with 1 tank and 2 mechanized divisions, 1 artillery brigade and 1 anti-tank and 1 multiple rocket launcher regiment); 2 special forces units. Equipment includes 4,775 main battle tanks (680 T-54/-55, 85 T-62, 2,345 T-64, 1,320 T-72 and 345 T-80), 640 medium-range launchers and 132 surface-to-surface missiles.

Navy. The former Soviet Black Sea Fleet continues to be the object of wrangling between Russia and the Ukraine, and remains to some extent operationally paralyzed by the dispute. While a political decision has been made to divide the fleet between the nations, the practical and personnel issues remain unresolved. In 1995, the undisputed Ukrainian elements numbered 16,000, including 7,000 Naval Aviation and 4,000 in coastal defence, with fleet units based at Sevastopol and Odessa. The operational forces include 2 Krivak-3 frigates, 2 smaller frigates and some 40 patrol craft.

The aviation forces of the former Soviet Black Sea Fleet under Ukrainian command constitute about 50 bombers, 100 fighter/ground attack, and about 40 anti-submarine and maritime reconnaissance aircraft. Main bomber types are Tu-26 'Backfire' and Tu-16 'Badger' armed principally with stand-off anti-ship missiles. There are also some 60 armed helicopters, most of seagoing types. The personnel of the Ukrainian Naval Aviation Force numbered (1995) about 7,500.

Air Force. The Ukraine has taken over more than 2,000 ex-Soviet aircraft, nearly 1,500 of them combat equipment. It is limited to 1,090 combat aircraft and 330 armed helicopters under the Conventional Forces in Europe agreement and will have to dispose of some materiel. Equipment includes 190 MiG-29 and 60 Su-27 interceptors, several hundred MiG-23/27 and Su-17 fighter-bombers, 200 Su-24 strike aircraft, Tu-22M strategic bombers and 30 Il-76 tankers. Support equipment includes 200 Il-76 transports and 250 armed Mi-24 and 400 transport helicopters. Personnel (including Air Defence), 1995, 151,000.

INTERNATIONAL RELATIONS

Membership. The Ukraine is a member of the UN, the Council of Europe and the NATO Partnership for Peace.

ECONOMY

Policy. Subsidies were removed and prices allowed to find their market level in Jan. 1992, but presidential decrees of Nov. 1993 brought back measures of price control, limitation of profits and hard currency restrictions. Privatization is overseen by the government-controlled State Property Fund. An economic state of emergency was declared in June 1993 and an Extraordinary Committee for the Management of the Economy was set up headed by the Prime Minister.

Budget. 1993 budget (in 1,000m. karbovanets): Revenue, 49,621·8; expenditure, 57,248·8. Sources of revenue included: VAT, 17,206·5; profits tax, 14,473·6.

Expenditure included: Welfare, 13,825·1; subsidies to state enterprises, 11,039·8; defence, 2,765·7; administration, 1,261·1.

Currency. The unit of currency is the *karbovanets* (UAK), although it is intended to replace this with a new unit of currency, the *hryvna.* There are notes of 1,000, 2,000, 5,000, 10,000, 20,000, 50,000 and 100,000 karbovanets. The use of foreign currencies in domestic transactions was prohibited in Aug. 1995. In March 1996, £1 = 289,326; US$1 = 189,300; DM1 = 128,261 karbovanets.

Banking and Finance. A National Bank was founded in March 1991. It operates under government control. Its *governor* is Viktor Yushchenko.

ENERGY AND NATURAL RESOURCES

Electricity. Power output was 227,000m. kWh in 1993. In 1993 there were 5 nuclear power stations producing 27% of output. The Chernobyl nuclear power station, which suffered an explosion in 1986, remained in operation after being scheduled for closure in 1993. There was a moratorium on constructing further nuclear installations until 1995.

Oil and Gas. In 1993 output of crude oil and gas concentrate was 4·2m. tonnes, and of natural gas 19,200m. cu. metres.

Minerals. Coal in the Donets field yielded, in 1988, 192m. tonnes—about 25% of the USSR production. Output in 1993, 116m. tonnes. Iron ore, 1990, 220m. tonnes.

The Ukraine also contains rich deposits of salt and various important chemicals.

In Northern Bukovina there are deposits of gypsum, oil, alabaster and brown coal.

Agriculture. The Ukraine contains rich agricultural land. It raises wheat, buck-wheat, beet, sunflower, cotton, flax, tobacco, soya, hops, the rubber plant kok-sagyz, fruit and vegetables. The area under cultivation was 40·4m. ha in 1993. Agricultural production was valued at 38,500m. rubles in 1993 in constant 1983 prices (99% of the 1992 figure).

A presidential decree of Nov. 1994 authorizes state farm members to leave and receive a portion of land free of charge. The land may be resold.

Output (in 1m. tonnes) in 1993: Grain, 45·6; sugar-beet, 33·6; potatoes, 20·9; vegetables, 5·8; fruit and berries, 2·9; meat, 2·9; milk, 18·1; 11,766m. eggs.

On 1 Jan. 1994 there were 21·6m. cattle, 15·3m. pigs, 6·9m. sheep and goats.

Forestry. In 1991, 7·8m. cu. metres of timber were produced.

INDUSTRY. Combining coal from the Donets field with the iron-ore from the mines in Krivoi Rog has made possible the development of a large ferrous metal-lurgical industry. Industrial output was valued at 35,593,000m. rubles in 1993, 90% of the 1992 figure; there were 9,100 industrial enterprises.

Output, 1993, (in tonnes): Rolled ferrous metals, 24m.; mineral fertilizer, 2·5m.; synthetic fibre, 80,000; paper, 181,000; cement, 15,000; lathes, 25,800 units; motor cars, 140,000 units; tractors, 55,500 units.

Consumer goods and food industries are important. Output, 1993: Sugar, 3·8m. tonnes; milk products, 2·7m. tonnes; processed meats, 1·1m. tonnes; butter, 706,000 tonnes; fabrics, 574m. sq. metres; footwear, 101m. pairs; TV sets, 1·9m.; refrigerators and freezers, 0·76m.

Labour. In 1993, 29·4m. persons were of working age, of whom 23·9m. were in paid employment (18·2m. in the state sector and 1·2m. in the private sector). Average wages were 159,800 karbovanets a month in 1993. In July 1994, 91,900 persons were registered as unemployed.

Trade Unions. There are 13 trade unions grouped in a Trades Union Federation (*Chair*, Oleksandr Stoyan).

FOREIGN ECONOMIC RELATIONS. In June 1994 total foreign debt was US$6,000m.

Commerce. In 1993 exports were valued at US$3,115·8m. and imports at US$2,431m.

Total trade between Ukraine and UK (British Department of Trade returns, in £1,000 sterling):

	1993	*1994*	*1995*
Imports to UK	12,462	18,072	22,941
Exports and re-exports from UK	73,091	86,284	111,106

COMMUNICATIONS

Roads. In 1990 there were 227,000 km of hard-surfaced motor roads. In 1993 492m. passengers and 439m. tonnes of freight were transported.

Railways. Total length was 23,631 km of 1,520 mm gauge in 1992, of which 8,415 km were electrified. In 1993 railways carried 667m. passengers and 554m. tonnes of freight.

Civil Aviation. There is an international airport at Kiev (Boryspol). The national carrier, Air Ukraine, operated 1 B-737-200 Adv and 94 ex-Soviet aircraft in 1995. Services are also provided by Aeroflot, Aerosweet, Air France, Austrian Airlines, Aviaprima-Sochi Airlines, Balkan, Czech Airlines, Delta, Egyptair, Estonian Air, Finnair, Iberia, JAT, KLM, LOT, Lufthansa, Malév, Northwest Airlines, Swissair, Tarom, Transaero and Turkish Airlines. In 1993, 1·7m. passengers and 0·2m. tonnes of freight were carried.

Shipping. In 1993, 8m. passengers and 25m. tonnes of freight were carried by inland waterways. In 1995 there were 649 ocean-going vessels, totalling 5·83m. DWT. 38 vessels (5·09% of total tonnage) were registered under foreign flags. GRT totalled 5·29m., including oil tankers, 84,276 GRT, and container ships, 139,187 GRT.

Telecommunications. Broadcasting is administered by the government State Teleradio Company of the Ukraine. The state-controlled Ukrainian Radio broadcasts 3 national and various regional programmes, a shared relay with Radio Moscow, and a foreign service (Ukrainian, English, German and Romanian). There were 4 independent stations in 1993. The state-controlled Ukrainian Television broadcasts on 2 channels (colour by SECAM).

Press (1989). Out of 1,763 newspapers, 1,241 were in Ukrainian. Daily circulation of Ukrainian-language newspapers, 15·9m., other languages, 8·2m.

SOCIAL INSTITUTIONS

Religion. The majority faith is the Orthodox Church, which in 1996 was split into 3 factions: The Ukrainian Orthodox Church, which owes obedience to the Russian Orthodox Church in Moscow, and is headed by Volodymyr, Patriarch of Kiev and All Rus-Ukraine; the Autocephalous Ukrainian Orthodox Church, which served émigrés and dissidents during the Soviet era, headed by Patriarch Mstyslav; and the Kiev Patriarchate Ukrainian Orthodox Church, headed by Metropolitan Filaret, which was unified with the Autocephalous Church in the period 1991–92.

The Uniate (Greek Catholic) Church, which practises the Orthodox rite but acknowledges the Pope of Rome, was banned in 1946 but re-legalized in 1991. Its main support is in Western Ukraine. Its head is Cardinal Myroslav Lubachivsky (b. 1914), Archbishop-Major of Lviv. The hierarchy was restored by the Pope's confirmation of 10 bishops in Jan. 1991. There are also some 70,000 Reformed Protestants in the Transcarpathian region and a Jewish community in Kiev. There are Roman Catholics in Western Ukraine.

Education. In 1993–94 the number of pupils in 21,700 primary and secondary schools was 7·1m.; 159 higher educational establishments had 829,200 students, and 754 technical colleges, 680,700 students; 47% of eligible children were attending pre-school institutions.

In 1995–96 there were 7 universities and an international university of science and technology.

Health. Doctors numbered 230,000 in Jan. 1994 and junior medical personnel, 600,000. There were 0·68m. beds in 3,900 hospitals.

Welfare. There were 10·9m. age pensioners in Jan. 1994 and 3·6m. other pensioners.

DIPLOMATIC REPRESENTATIVES

Of the Ukraine in Great Britain (78 Kensington Park Rd., London W11 2PL)
Ambassador: Sergui Komissarenko.

Of Great Britain in the Ukraine (9 Desyatinna, 252025 Kiev)
Ambassador: Roy Reeve.

Of the Ukraine in the USA (L Street, NW, Washington DC 20036)
Ambassador: Yuri Shcherbak.

Of the USA in the Ukraine (10 Yuria Kotsyubinskoho, 252053 Kiev 53)
Ambassador: William Miller.

Of the Ukraine to the United Nations
Ambassador: Anatoli Zlenko.

Further Reading

Encyclopedia of Ukraine, 5 vols. Toronto, 1984–93
Koropeckyj, I. S., *The Ukrainian Economy: Achievements, Problems, Challenges.* Harvard Univ. Press, 1993
Kuzio, T. and Wilson, A., *Ukraine: Perestroika to Independence.* London, 1994
Marples, D., *Ukraine under Perestroika: Ecology, Economics and the Workers' Revolt.* London, 1991
Motyl, A. J., *Dilemmas of Independence: Ukraine after Totalitarianism.* New York, 1993
Nahaylo, B., *Ukrainian Resurgence.* Farnborough, 1993
Solchanyk, R., (ed.) *Ukraine: from Chernobyl to Sovereignty.* London, 1991
Subtelny, O., *Ukraine: a History.* Toronto, 1989

CRIMEA

The Crimea is a peninsula extending southwards into the Black Sea with an area of 25,881 sq. km. Population (1991 estimate), 2,549,800 (Ethnic groups, Sept. 1993: Russians, 61·6%; Ukrainians, 23·6%; Tatars, 9·6%). The capital is Simferopol.

It was occupied by Tatars in 1239, conquered by Ottoman Turks in 1475 and retaken by Russia in 1783. In 1921 after the Communist revolution it became an autonomous republic, but was transformed into a province (*oblast*) of the Russian Federation in 1945 after the deportation of the Tatar population in 1944 for alleged collaboration with the German invaders in the Second World War. It was transferred to the Ukraine in 1954 and became an autonomous republic in 1991. About half the surviving Tatar population of 0·4m. had returned from exile by mid-1992.

In April 1992 the Ukrainian government defined the Crimea as an autonomous part of the Ukraine, an economic free zone with full ownership of property on its territory and continental shelf.

There is a 94-member local parliament. At elections held in 2 rounds on 16 and 30 Jan. 1994 Yuri Meshkov was elected *President* for a 4-year term by 38·5% and 72% of votes cast against 5 opponents. The electorate was 1·8m.; turn-out was 75% in the first round.

Parliamentary elections were held on 27 March 1994. The Russia Bloc gained 54 seats, Kurultai (Tatars) 14, ind 21.

Parliament declared sovereignty on 20 May 1994 and voted to restore the 1992 constitution, but on 6 June delegations of the Ukrainian and Crimean parliaments signed a text recognizing the territorial integrity of the Ukraine. Legislation of 17 March 1995 empowered the Ukrainian government to dissolve the Crimean parliament. In April President Meshkov was unseated and the Ukrainian President Kuchma assumed direct control. On 2 Nov. 1995 parliament adopted a new constitution which defines the Crimea as 'an autonomous republic forming an integral part of the Ukraine'.

UNITED ARAB EMIRATES (UAE)

Imarat al-Arabiya al-Muttahida

Capital: Abu Dhabi
Population: 2·1m. (1993)
GNP per capita: US$22,220 (1992)
HDI/world rank: 0·771/62 (1992)

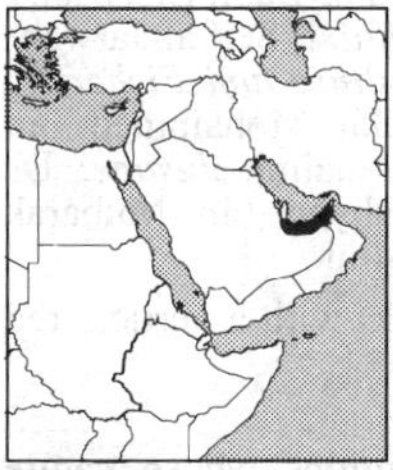

KEY HISTORICAL EVENTS. British forces withdrew from the Persian Gulf in 1971 and the treaties whereby the UK had been responsible for the defence and foreign relations of the Trucial States (*see* THE STATESMAN'S YEAR-BOOK, 1991–92, p. 1292) were terminated, being replaced on 2 Dec. 1971 by a treaty of friendship between the UK and the United Arab Emirates. The United Arab Emirates (formed 2 Dec. 1971) consists of the former Trucial States: Abu Dhabi, Dubai, Sharjah, Ajman, Umm al Qaiwain, Ras al-Khaimah (joined in Feb. 1972) and Fujairah. The small state of Kalba was merged with Sharjah in 1952.

TERRITORY AND POPULATION. The Emirates are bounded in the north by the Persian (Arabian) Gulf, north-east by Oman, east by the Gulf of Oman and Oman, south and west by Saudi Arabia, and north-west by Qatar. Their area is approximately 32,300 sq. miles (83,657 sq. km), excluding over 100 offshore islands. The total population at census (1985), 1,622,464. Estimate (1993) 2,083,000 (803,000 females). About one-tenth are nomads. Infant mortality rate, 1992, 11·7 per 1,000 live births. Life expectancy in 1992: Males, 70 years; females, 78.

Population of the 7 Emirates, 1985 census: Abu Dhabi, 670,125; Ajman, 64,318; Dubai, 419,104; Fujairah, 54,425; Ras al-Khaimah, 116,470; Sharjah, 268,722; Umm al Qaiwain, 29,229.

The chief cities are Abu Dhabi, the federal capital, Dubai, Sharjah and Ras al-Khaimah.

The official language is Arabic; English is widely spoken.

CLIMATE. The country experiences desert conditions, with rainfall both limited and erratic. The period May to Sept. is generally rainless. Dubai. Jan. 74°F (23·4°C), July 108°F (42·3°C). Annual rainfall 2·4" (60 mm). Sharjah. Jan. 64°F (17·8°C), July 91°F (32°C). Annual rainfall 4·2" (105 mm).

CONSTITUTION AND GOVERNMENT. The Emirates is a federation, headed by a *Supreme Council of Rulers* which is composed of the 7 rulers which elects from among its members a *President* for 5-year terms and appoints a *Council of Ministers.* The Council of Ministers drafts legislation and a federal budget; its proposals are submitted to a *Federal National Council* of 40 elected members which may propose amendments but has no executive power. There is a *National Consultative Council* made up of citizens.

Members of the Supreme Council of Rulers:

President: HH Sheikh Zayed bin Sultan al-Nahyan, Ruler of Abu Dhabi (re-elected Oct. 1991).

HH Sheikh Maktoum bin Rashid al-Maktoum, *Vice President, Prime Minister,* Ruler of Dubai.

HH Dr Sheikh Sultan bin Mohammed al-Qassimi, Ruler of Sharjah.
HH Sheikh Saqr bin Mohammed al-Qassimi, Ruler of Ras al-Khaimah.
HH Sheikh Hamad bin Mohammed al-Sharqi, Ruler of Fujairah.
HH Sheikh Humaid bin Rashid al-Nuaimi, Ruler of Ajman.
HH Sheikh Rashid bin Ahmed al-Mualla, Ruler of Umm al Qaiwain.

The Council of Ministers in Dec. 1995 was:

Prime Minister: HH Sheikh Maktoum bin Rashid al-Maktoum.

Deputy Prime Minister: HH Sheikh Sultan bin Zayed al-Nahyan. *Interior:* Lieut.-Gen. Dr Mohammed Saeed al-Badi. *Finance and Industry:* HH Sheikh Hamdan bin Rashid al-Maktoum. *Defence:* Gen. Sheikh Mohammed bin Rashid al-Maktoum. *Economy and Commerce:* Saeed Ghobash. *Information and Culture:* Khalfan bin Mohammed al-Roumi. *Communications:* Mohammed Saeed al-Mulla. *Public Works and Housing:* Rakad bin Salem bin Rakad. *Education:* Hamad Abdul Rahman al-Madfa. *Petroleum and Mineral Resources:* Ahmed bin Saeed al-Badi. *Electricity and Water:* Humaid bin Nasser al-Owais. *Labour and Social Affairs:* Seif al-Jarwan. *Planning:* HH Sheikh Humaid bin Ahmed al-Mualla. *Agriculture and Fisheries:* Saeed al-Ragabani. *Islamic Affairs and Endowments:* Sheikh Mohammed bin Ahmed al-Khazraji. *Foreign Affairs:* Rashid Abdullah al-Nuaimi. *Justice:* Dr Abdullah Omran Taryam. *Higher Education:* Sheikh Nahyan bin Mubarak al-Nahyan. *Youth and Sports:* Sheikh Faisal bin Khaled al-Qassimi.

National flag: Three horizontal stripes of green, white, black, with a vertical red strip in the hoist.

National anthem: There are no words, tune by M. A. Wahab.

Local Government. Each Emirate has its own local institutions whose nature depends on size and population. Abu Dhabi has an Executive Council chaired by the Crown Prince.

DEFENCE

Army. The Army consists of 1 Royal Guard, 1 armoured, 1 mechanized infantry, 2 infantry and 1 artillery brigade. There are also 2 unintegrated infantry brigades in Dubai. Equipment includes 95 AMX-30 and 36 Lion OF-40 Mk 2 main battle tanks. The strength was (1996) 65,000.

Navy. The combined naval flotilla of the Emirates includes 1 leased ex-US guided missile frigate, 2 German-built missile corvettes, 8 German-built fast missile craft, 9 British-built inshore patrol craft, 3 tank landing craft, 2 transports, 1 maintenance ship and 3 service craft. Personnel in 1995 numbered 2,000 officers and ratings. The main base is at Taweela (Sharjah), with minor bases in the other Emirates.

The Coast Guard flotilla comprises 40 inshore patrol craft and some 30 boats.

Air Force. Formation of an air wing in Abu Dhabi, to support land forces, began in 1968 with the purchase of some light short-take-off-and-land transports and helicopters. Expansion has been rapid. Current equipment includes 21 Mirage 2000 and 23 Mirage 5 supersonic fighter-bombers, 8 Mirage 2000R and 3 Mirage 5R tactical reconnaissance aircraft, 5 Mirage 2000D and 3 Mirage 5D 2-seat trainers; 4 C-130 Hercules turboprop transports; 4 CASA C-212 Aviocar electronic countermeasures and intelligence aircraft; 20 Apache armed helicopters; about 50 Gazelle, Alouette III, Puma, Super Puma and Ecureuil transport and liaison helicopters; 23 PC-7 Turbo-Trainers and 40 Hawk light attack/trainers. Initial personnel were mostly British but considerable assistance is now being received from Arab countries and from Pakistan. The air wing became the Air Force of Abu Dhabi in 1972, in which year 3 JetRanger helicopters were transferred to the air wing of the Union Defence Force, since combined with the Dubai Police Air Wing to form a single component of the United Emirates Air Force. Current equipment of the Dubai Air Wing of the UEAF, bought mainly in Italy, comprises 3 Aermacchi MB 326K jet light attack aircraft, 1 piston-engined SF.260W armed basic trainer, 5 SF.260TP turboprop trainers, and 2 MB 326L, 4 MB 339 and 8 Hawk jet trainers, 6 Bell 205A-1, 3 Bell 212, 8 Bell 214 and 6 JetRanger helicopters and 1 Cessna 182 liaison aircraft, plus 2 L-100-30 Hercules transports and a variety of other types for VIP and transport use. The Sharjah aviation force has been transferred to the central UAE Air Force. Personnel (1995) 3,500 including Dubai, 700, with 97 combat aircraft and 42 armed helicopters.

INTERNATIONAL RELATIONS

Membership. The UAE is a member of the UN, Gulf Co-operation Council and of the Arab League.

ECONOMY

Budget. Revenue is principally derived from oil-concession payments. Federal expenditure (1993) was DH 17,300m. (excluding defence) and revenue 15,900m.

Currency. The unit of currency is the *dirham* (AED) of 100 *fils*. There are notes of 5, 10, 50, 100 and 500 dirhams and coins of 1 and 5 dirhams and 1, 5, 10, 25 and 50 fils. Inflation was 3·5% in Sept. 1993. Rate of exchange, March 1995, £1 = 5·97 dirhams; US$1 = 3·67 dirhams.

Banking and Finance. The UAE Central Bank was established in 1980 (*Governor*, Sultan al-Suweidi). In 1994 there were 47 local and foreign banks with 300 branches. Foreign banks are restricted to 8 branches each.

ENERGY AND NATURAL RESOURCES

Electricity. Production (1990) 16,189m. kWh.

Oil. Oil and gas provide about 50% of GDP. Reserves of crude oil (1993) 200,000m. bbls.

Abu Dhabi. Proven reserves (1988) 31,000m. bbls. Estimated oil production, 1992, 91·28m. tonnes.

Dubai. In 1975 Dubai took control of foreign oil and gas operations and a Dubai producing group was set up to comprise the foreign interests. Estimated oil production (1992) 19·37m. tonnes.

Sharjah. Oil production, 1992, 1·92m. tonnes.

Ras al-Khaimah. Oil production (1990) 400,000 tonnes.

Gas. Abu Dhabi has reserves of natural gas, nationalized in 1976. There is a gas liquefaction plant on Das Island. Gas proven reserves (1993) were 200,000,000m. cu. ft.

Water. Production of drinking water by desalination of sea water (1992) was 90,000m. gallons.

Agriculture. The fertile Buraimi Oasis, known as Al Ain, is largely in Abu Dhabi territory. By 1992, 20,424 farms had been set up on land reclaimed from sand dunes. Owing to lack of water and good soil there are few natural opportunities for agriculture, but there is a programme of fostering agriculture by desalination of water and tree-planting, and strawberries, flowers and dates are now cultivated for export. In 1993 there were 0·28m. ha of agricultural land. In 1990 there were 29,000 ha arable land, 10,000 ha of crop-land and 200,000 ha of pasture. Output, 1992 (in 1,000 tonnes): Dates, 237·5; other fruit, 58·3; vegetables, 379·1; animal feed, 479·2. Livestock products: Red meat, 14·5; poultry, 15·6; eggs, 217·7m.; milk, 79·2.

Livestock (1991, in 1,000): Cattle, 53; camels, 118; sheep, 270; goats, 590.

Fisheries. In 1992 there were 3,536 fishing boats and 11,074 fishermen. Catch (1992) 95,049 tonnes.

INDUSTRY. In 1993 there were 904 industrial firms. Products include aluminium, cable, cement, chemicals, fertilizers (Abu Dhabi), rolled steel and plastics (Dubai, Sharjah) and tools and clothing (Dubai).

FOREIGN ECONOMIC RELATIONS. There are free trade zones at Jebel Ali (administered by Dubai), Sharjah and Fujairah. Foreign companies may set up wholly-owned subsidiaries. In 1991 there were 400 companies in the Jebel Ali zone.

Commerce. Imports in 1993 totalled DH46,900m., exports DH85,200m. Oil exports accounted for DH28,000m in 1988.

Total trade between the UAE (excluding Abu Dhabi) and UK (British Department of Trade returns, in £1,000 sterling):

	1990	*1991*	*1992*	*1993*	*1994*
Imports to UK	105,072	122,878	215,416	155,354	159,699
Exports and re-exports from UK	494,559	529,572	613,621	774,193	780,588

Total trade between Abu Dhabi and UK (British Department of Trade returns, in £1,000 sterling):

	1990	*1991*	*1992*	*1993*	*1994*
Imports to UK	76,414	109,043	116,512	96,099	70,971
Exports and re-exports from UK	170,165	220,088	312,936	540,385	332,990

Tourism. In 1991 there were 189 hotels which had 348,000 visitors.

COMMUNICATIONS

Roads. In 1990 there were 2,876 km of roads and 230,000 vehicles.

Civil Aviation. There are international airports at Abu Dhabi, Al Ain (Fujairah), Dubai, Ras al-Khaimah and Sharjah. 70m. passengers were handled in 1990. Gulf Air is run by a consortium of Abu Dhabi, Bahrain, Doha and Muscat. Dubai set up its own airline, Emirates Air, in 1985. It now operates internationally; in 1995 its fleet comprised 6 A300B4-600Rs, 10 A310-300s and 1 B-727-200 Adv. Services are also provided by Aeroflot, Air Algérie, Air France, Air India, Air Lanka, Air Malta, Air Seychelles, Air Tanzania, Air Ukraine, Alitalia, Alyemda, American Airlines, Avia-Sochi Airlines, Azerbaijan Hava Yollary, Balkan, Biman Bangladesh, British Airways, Cathay Pacific, China Airlines, Condor, Cyprus Airways, Czech Airlines, Daallo, Egyptair Ethiopian Airlines, Eva, Finnair, Garuda Indonesia, Indian Airlines, Iran Air, JAT, Kenay Airways, KLM, Kuwait Airways, Libyan Airlines, Lithuanian Airlines, LOT, LTU, Lufthansa, Malaysia Airlines, Mandarin, Middle East Airlines, Northwest Airlines, Olympic Airways, Oman Air, Pakistan Airlines, Philippine Airlines, Qatar Airways, Royal Air Maroc, Royal Brunei Airlines, Royal Jordanian, Royal Nepal Airlines, SAA, Saudia, Singapore Airlines, Sudan Airways, Swissair, Syrian Airlines, Tarom, Thai Airways, Tunis Air, Turkish Airlines, Uganda Airlines, United Airlines, Uzbekistan Airways, Vietnam Airlines, Virgin Atlantic, Yemenia and Zas.

Shipping. There are 5 ports on the Persian (Arabian) Gulf (Zayed in Abu Dhabi, Rashid and Jebel Ali in Dubai, Khalid in Sharjah and Saqr in Ras al-Khaimah) and 2 on the Gulf of Oman: Fujairah and Khor Fakkan. Rashid and Fujairah are important container terminals. 35m. tonnes of cargo were handled in 1993. In 1995, sea-going vessels totalloed 1·6m. GRT, including oil tankers, 0·92m. GRT, and containers ships, 0·21m. GRT.

Telecommunications. In 1993 there were 58 post offices, 128 postal agencies, 677,973 telephones, 536,606 fax machines and some 60,000 mobile telephones.

There are several government authorities providing broadcasting nationally (Voice of the United Arab Emirates, Capital Radio, which is partly commercial and United Arab Emirates Television Service) and regionally (UAE Radio and Television-Dubai, Ras al-Khaimah Broadcasting, Umm al Qaiwain Broadcasting, and Sharjah TV). In 1993 there were 0·42m. radio and 0·17m. TV sets (colour by PAL).

Press (1993). There are dailies and weeklies in Arabic and English.

SOCIAL INSTITUTIONS

Justice. The basic principles of the law are Islamic. Legislation seeks to promote the harmonious functioning of society's multi-national components while protecting the interests of the indigenous population. Each Emirate has its own penal code. A federal code takes precedence and ensures compatibility. There are federal courts with appellate powers which function under federal laws. Emirates have the option to merge their courts with the federal judiciary.

The death penalty for drug smuggling was introduced in April 1995.

Religion. Nearly all the inhabitants are Moslem of the Sunni, and a small minority of the Shi'ite, sects.

Education In 1991–92 there were 152,790 pupils in primary schools, 56,848 in preparatory schools and 32,951 in secondary schools. There were 1,501 students in religious schools and about 740 in technical schools. In 1993–94 there were 10,922 students at the Emirates University and 1,800 students in 3 higher colleges of technology. Adult illiteracy was 16·8% in 1993.

Health. In 1993 there were 35 hospitals (29 government and 6 private) with 4,314 beds, 96 government health centres, a herbal medicine centre, 500 private clinics, 3,000 doctors, 400 dentists and 8,000 nurses.

DIPLOMATIC REPRESENTATIVES

Of the UAE in Great Britain (30 Prince's Gate, London, SW7 1PT)
Ambassador: Easa Saleh Al-Gurg, CBE.

Of Great Britain in the UAE (POB 248, Abu Dhabi)
Ambassador: A. D. Harris, LVO.

Of the UAE in the USA (600 New Hampshire Ave., NW, Washington, D.C., 20037)
Ambassador: Mohammed bin Hussein Al-Shaali.

Of the USA in the UAE (POB 4009, Abu Dhabi)
Ambassador: William A. Rugh.

Of the UAE to the United Nations
Ambassador: Mohammed Jassim Samhan.

Further Reading

Alkim, H. al.-, *The Foreign Policy of the UAE.* Saqi, 1989
Clements, F. A., *United Arab Emirates.* [Bibliography] Oxford and Santa Barbara (CA), 1983
Heard-Bey, F., *From Trucial States to United Arab Emirates.* London, 1982
Taryam, A. O., *The Establishment of the United Arab Emirates.* London, 1987

UNITED KINGDOM OF GREAT BRITAIN AND NORTHERN IRELAND

Capital: London
Population: 58·78m. (1996)
GNP per capita: US$18,410 (1994)
HDI/world rank: 0·916/18 (1992)

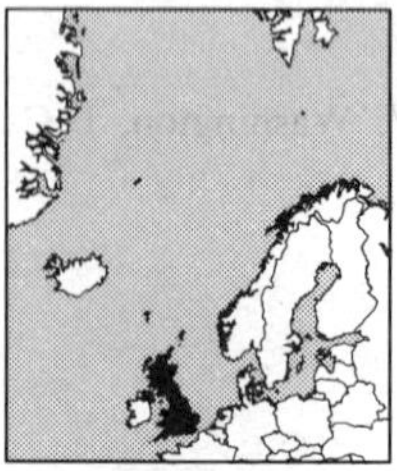

'Great Britain' is the geographical name of that island of the British Isles which comprises England, Scotland and Wales (so called to distinguish it from 'Little Britain' or Brittany). By the Act of Union, 1801, Great Britain and Ireland formed a legislative union as the United Kingdom of Great Britain and Ireland. Since the separation of Great Britain and Ireland in 1921 Northern Ireland remained within the Union which is now the United Kingdom of Great Britain and Northern Ireland. The United Kingdom (UK) does not include the Channel Islands or the Isle of Man which are direct dependencies of the Crown with their own legislative and taxation systems. England and Wales form an administrative entity, with some special arrangements for Wales (*see* LOCAL GOVERNMENT: ENGLAND AND WALES, *below*).

GREAT BRITAIN

TERRITORY AND POPULATION. Area (in sq. km) and population (present on census night) at the census taken 21 April 1991:

Divisions	*Area*	*Population*
England	130,423	46,382,050
Wales	20,766	2,811,865
Scotland	77,167	4,962,152
	228,356	54,156,067

Population (present on census night) at the 4 previous decennial censuses:

Divisions	*1951*	*1961*	*1971*	*1981*
England [1]	41,159,213	43,460,525	46,018,371	46,226,100 [2]
Wales	2,598,675	2,644,023	2,731,204	2,790,500 [2]
Scotland	5,096,415	5,179,344	5,228,963	5,130,735
Great Britain	48,854,303	51,283,892	53,978,538	54,147,300 [2]

[1] Areas now recognised as part of Gwent, Wales, formed the English county of Monmouthshire until 1974. [2] The final counts for England and Wales are believed to be over-stated as a result of an error in processing. The preliminary counts presented here rounded to the nearest hundred are thought to be more accurate.

UK population estimate, 1996, 58,784,000 (29,930,000 females); density, 240 per sq. km.

UK vital statistics: Births, 1993, 761,713 (242,000 outside marriage); deaths, 1992, 308,535; marriages, 1992, 356,013.

Population (usually resident) at the census of 1991:

Divisions	*Males*	*Females*	*Total*
England	22,812,889	24,242,315	47,055,204
Wales	1,370,104	1,464,969	2,835,073
Scotland	2,391,961	2,606,606	4,998,567
Great Britain	26,574,954	28,313,890	54,888,844

In 1991 in Wales 508,098 persons were able to speak Welsh. In Scotland in 1991, 65,978 of the usually resident population could speak Gaelic (79,307 in 1981).

Private households at the 1991 census: England, 19,984,500; Wales, 1,201,700; Scotland, 2,164,081.

The age distribution in 1991 of the 'usually resident' population of England and Wales and Scotland was as follows (in 1,000):

Age-group	*England and Wales*	*Scotland*	*Great Britain*
Under 5	3,316	317	3,633
5 and under 10	3,123	318	3,440
10 " 15	2,988	312	3,299
15 " 20	3,205	332	3,547
20 " 25	3,731	375	4,106
25 " 35	7,594	768	8,361
35 " 45	6,970	695	7,665
45 " 55	5,793	578	6,372
55 " 65	5,126	537	5,663
65 " 70	2,491	247	2,737
70 " 75	2,014	193	2,208
75 " 85	2,776	259	3,035
85 and upwards	763	68	831

Population densities (persons per ha), 1991 census: Great Britain, 2·4; England, 3·6; Wales, 1·4; Scotland. 0·6.

England and Wales: The census population, (present on census night) of England and Wales 1801 to 1991:

Date of enumeration	*Population*	*Pop. per sq. mile*	*Date of enumeration*	*Population*	*Pop. per sq. mile* [1]
1801	8,892,536	152	1901	32,527,843	558
1811	10,164,256	174	1911	36,070,492	618
1821	12,000,236	206	1921	37,886,699	649
1831	13,896,797	238	1931	39,952,377	685
1841	15,914,148	273	1951	43,757,888	750
1851	17,927,609	307	1961	46,104,548	791
1861	20,066,224	344	1971	48,749,575	323
1871	22,712,266	389	1981	49,016,600	325
1881	25,974,439	445	1991	49,193,915	330
1891	29,002,525	497			

[1] Per sq. km from 1971.

Estimated population, 1996, 51,997,000 (26,445,000 females; 2,930,000 in Wales).

The birth places of the 1991 'usually resident' population were: England, 42,897,179; Wales, 2,747,790; Scotland, 5,221,038; Northern Ireland, 244,914; Ireland, 592,020; Commonwealth, 1,865,751; foreign countries, 1,287,821.

Ethnic Groups. The 1991 census was the first to include a question on ethnic status.

Ethnic groups as enumerated:

	Total	*Females*	*Total born in UK*
White	51,873,794	26,807,415	49,703,681
Indian	840,225	417,364	352,448
Black Caribbean	499,964	260,480	268,318
Pakistani	476,555	230,983	240,552
Black African	212,362	105,562	77,315
Black Other	178,401	90,888	150,638
Bangladeshi	162,835	77,891	56,678
Chinese	156,938	79,269	44,635
Other Asian	197,534	103,929	43,265
Other	290,206	140,109	173,518

11 'Standard Regions' (also classified as 'level 1 regions' for EC purposes) are identified in the UK as economic planning regions. They have no administrative significance. They are: Northern Ireland, Scotland, Wales, and 8 regions of England. Population of the English regions (in 1,000) at the 1991 census: East Anglia, 2,019; East Midlands, 3,920; West Midlands, 5,089; North, 3,019; North

West, 6,147; South East, 16,794 (including Greater London, 6,394); South West, 4,600; Yorkshire and Humberside, 4,797.

England and Wales are divided (apart from Greater London) into 53 counties (6 of them 'metropolitan') subdivided into 369 districts. Greater London comprises 32 boroughs and the City of London.

Area in sq. km of counties and usually resident population at the 1991 census:

	Area sq. km	*Population*
Metropolitan counties		
ENGLAND		
Greater Manchester	1,286	2,499,441
Merseyside	655	1,403,642
South Yorkshire	1,559	1,262,630
Tyne and Wear	537	1,095,152
West Midlands	899	2,551,671
West Yorkshire	2,034	2,013,693
Non-metropolitan counties		
ENGLAND		
Avon	1,332	932,674
Bedfordshire (Beds)	1,236	524,105
Berkshire (Berks)	1,256	734,246
Buckinghamshire (Bucks)	1,877	632,487
Cambridgeshire (Camb)	3,400	645,125
Cheshire	2,331	956,616
Cleveland	597	550,293
Cornwall and Isles of Scilly	3,530	468,425
Cumbria	6,817	483,163
Derbyshire	2,629	928,636
Devon	6,703	1,009,950
Dorset	2,653	645,166
Durham	2,429	593,430
East Sussex	1,794	690,447
Essex	3,675	1,528,577
Gloucestershire (Gloucs)	2,653	528,370
Hampshire (Hants)	3,779	1,541,547
Hereford and Worcester	3,923	676,747
Hertfordshire (Herts)	1,639	975,829
Humberside (Humb)	3,508	858,040
Non-metropolitan counties—contd.		
Isle of Wight (IOW)	380	124,577
Kent	3,735	1,508,873
Lancashire (Lancs)	3,070	1,383,998
Leicestershire (Leics)	2,551	867,521
Lincolnshire (Lincs)	5,921	584,536
Norfolk	5,372	745,613
Northamptonshire (Northants)	2,367	578,807
Northumberland	5,026	304,694
North Yorkshire (N. Yorks)	8,309	702,161
Nottinghamshire (Notts)	2,160	993,872
Oxfordshire (Oxon)	2,583	547,584
Shropshire (Salop)	3,488	406,387
Somerset (Som)	3,452	460,368
Staffordshire (Staffs)	2,715	1,031,135
Suffolk	3,798	632,266
Surrey	1,677	1,018,003
Warwickshire	1,979	484,247
West Sussex	1,988	702,290
Wiltshire (Wilts)	3,476	564,471
WALES		
Clwyd	2,430	408,090
Dyfed	5,766	343,543
Gwent	1,377	442,212
Gwynedd	3,863	235,452
Mid Glamorgan (M. Glam)	1,017	534,101
Powys	5,072	117,647
South Glamorgan (S. Glam)	416	392,780
West Glamorgan (W. Glam)	820	361,428

County districts with populations of over 90,000 (1991 census):

ENGLAND	
Allerdale (Cumbria)	95,702
Amber Valley (Derbyshire)	111,897
Arun (W. Sussex)	129,357
Ashfield (Notts)	108,364
Ashford (Kent)	92,331
Aylesbury Vale (Bucks)	145,931
Barnsley (S. Yorks)	220,937
Basildon (Essex)	161,124
Basingstoke and Deane (Hants)	144,790
Bassetlaw (Notts)	103,979
Beverley (Humberside)	111,699
Birmingham (W. Midlands)	961,041
Blackburn (Lancs)	136,612
Blackpool (Lancs)	146,069
Bolton (Greater Manchester)	258,584
Bournemouth (Dorset)	151,302
Bracknell Forest (Berks)	95,949
Bradford (W. Yorks)	457,344
Braintree (Essex)	118,883
Breckland (Norfolk)	107,167
ENGLAND—*contd.*	
Brighton (E. Sussex)	143,582
Bristol (Avon)	376,146
Broadland (Norfolk)	106,292
Bromsgrove (Hereford and Worcester)	91,544
Broxtowe (Notts)	107,137
Burnley (Lancs)	91,130
Bury (Greater Manchester)	176,760
Calderdale (W. Yorks)	191,585
Cambridge	91,933
Canterbury (Kent)	123,947
Carlisle (Cumbria)	100,562
Charnwood (Leics)	141,806
Chelmsford (Essex)	152,418
Cheltenham (Gloucs)	103,115
Cherwell (Oxon)	117,832
Chester (Cheshire)	115,971
Chesterfield (Derbyshire)	99,403
Chichester (W. Sussex)	101,358
Chorley (Lancs)	96,504

ENGLAND—*contd.*

Colchester (Essex)	142,515
Coventry (W. Midlands)	294,387
Crewe and Nantwich (Cheshire)	103,164
Dacorum (Herts)	132,240
Darlington (Durham)	98,906
Derby	218,802
Doncaster (S. Yorks)	288,854
Dover (Kent)	103,216
Dudley (W. Midlands)	304,615
Easington (Durham)	97,824
East Devon	115,873
East Hampshire	103,460
East Hertfordshire	115,818
Eastleigh (Hants)	105,999
East Lindsey (Lincs)	116,957
East Staffordshire	97,105
Elmbridge (Surrey)	114,479
Epping Forest (Essex)	116,027
Erewash (Derbyshire)	106,101
Exeter (Devon)	98,125
Fareham (Hants)	99,262
Gateshead (Tyne and Wear)	199,588
Gedling (Notts)	110,133
Gillingham (Kent)	95,358
Gloucester	101,608
Gravesham (Kent)	92,454
Great Grimsby (Humberside)	90,517
Guildford (Surrey)	122,378
Halton (Cheshire)	123,716
Harrogate (N. Yorks)	143,526
Hartlepool (Cleveland)	90,409
Havant (Hants)	119,697
Hinckley and Bosworth (Leics)	96,201
Horsham (W. Sussex)	108,562
Huntingdonshire (Cambs)	144,075
Ipswich (Suffolk)	116,956
King's Lynn and West Norfolk	130,462
Kingston upon Hull (Humberside)	254,117
Kirklees (W. Yorks)	373,127
Knowsley (Merseyside)	152,091
Lancaster	123,856
Langbaurgh on Tees (Cleveland)	145,123
Leeds (W. Yorks)	680,722
Leicester	270,493
Lichfield (Staffs)	92,679
Liverpool (Merseyside)	452,450
Luton (Beds)	171,671
Macclesfield (Cheshire)	151,590
Maidstone (Kent)	136,209
Manchester	404,861
Mansfield (Notts)	100,386
Mendip (Som)	95,603
Mid-Bedfordshire	109,801
Middlesbrough (Cleveland)	140,849
Mid-Sussex (W. Sussex)	121,193
Milton Keynes (Bucks)	176,330
Newark and Sherwood (Notts)	102,784
Newbury (Berks)	136,700
Newcastle under Lyme (Staffs)	119,091
Newcastle upon Tyne (Tyne and Wear)	259,541
New Forest (Hants)	160,456
Northampton	180,567
Northavon (Avon)	130,647
North Bedfordshire	133,692
North-East Derbyshire	97,570

ENGLAND—*contd.*

North Hertfordshire	111,994
North Norfolk	90,461
North Tyneside (Tyne and Wear)	192,286
North Wiltshire	111,974
Norwich (Norfolk)	120,895
Nottingham	263,522
Nuneaton and Bedworth (Warwickshire)	117,052
Oldham (Greater Manchester)	216,531
Oxford	110,103
Peterborough (Cambs)	153,166
Plymouth (Devon)	243,373
Poole (Dorset)	133,050
Portsmouth (Hants)	174,697
Preston (Lancs)	126,082
Reading (Berks)	128,877
Reigate and Banstead (Surrey)	117,777
Rochdale (Greater Manchester)	202,164
Rochester upon Medway (Kent)	144,870
Rotherham (S. Yorks)	251,637
Rushcliffe (Notts)	97,567
Ryedale (N. Yorks)	90,746
St Albans (Herts)	126,202
St Edmundsbury (Suffolk)	91,731
St Helens (Merseyside)	178,764
Salford (Greater Manchester)	220,463
Salisbury (Wilts)	105,318
Sandwell (W. Midlands)	290,091
Scarborough (N. Yorks)	106,221
Sedgefield (Durham)	90,530
Sedgemoor (Som)	97,763
Sefton (Merseyside)	289,542
Sevenoaks (Kent)	108,828
Sheffield (S. Yorks)	501,202
Shepway (Kent)	91,486
Shrewsbury and Atcham (Salop)	91,749
Slough (Berks)	101,066
Solihull (W. Midlands)	199,859
Southampton (Hants)	196,864
South Bedfordshire	108,941
South Cambridgeshire	121,109
Southend on Sea (Essex)	158,517
South Kesteven (Lincs)	108,945
South Lakeland (Cumbria)	96,897
South Norfolk	102,612
South Oxfordshire	119,476
South Ribble (Lancs)	102,001
South Somerset	141,655
South Staffordshire	105,487
South Tyneside (Tyne and Wear)	154,697
Stafford	117,788
Staffordshire Moorlands	95,450
Stockport (Greater Manchester)	284,395
Stockton on Tees (Cleveland)	173,912
Stoke on Trent (Staffs)	244,637
Stratford on Avon (Warwickshire)	105,586
Stroud (Gloucs)	103,622
Suffolk Coastal	107,970
Sunderland (Tyne and Wear)	289,040
Swale (Kent)	115,769
Tameside (Greater Manchester)	216,431
Taunton Deane (Som)	93,969
Teignbridge (Devon)	108,258
Tendring (Essex)	125,818
Test Valley (Hants)	101,428

ENGLAND—*contd.*	
Thamesdown (Wilts)	170,850
Thanet (Kent)	123,665
Thurrock (Essex)	127,819
Tonbridge and Malling (Kent)	101,763
Torbay (Devon)	119,674
Trafford (Greater Manchester)	212,731
Tunbridge Wells (Kent)	99,538
Vale of White Horse (Oxon)	109,922
Vale Royal (Cheshire)	114,092
Wakefield (W. Yorks)	310,915
Walsall (W. Midlands)	259,488
Warrington (Cheshire)	182,685
Warwick	116,299
Waveney (Suffolk)	106,751
Waverley (Surrey)	113,212
Wealden (E. Sussex)	130,214
Welwyn Hatfield (Herts)	92,366
West Lancashire	107,978
West Oxfordshire	90,251
West Wiltshire	107,803
Wigan (Greater Manchester)	306,521
Winchester (Hants)	96,386
Windsor and Maidenhead (Berks)	132,465
Wirral (Merseyside)	330,795
Wokingham (Berks)	139,189
Wolverhampton (W. Midlands)	242,190
Woodspring (Avon)	177,472
Worthing (W. Sussex)	96,157
The Wrekin (Salop)	139,516
Wychavon (Hereford and Worcester)	101,716
Wycombe (Bucks)	157,906
Wyre (Lancs)	101,818
Wyre Forest (Hereford & Worcester)	94,814
York (N. Yorks)	98,745

WALES	
Cardiff (S. Glam)	279,055
Newport (Gwent)	133,318
Ogwr (Mid-Glam)	132,442
Rhymney Valley (Mid-Glam)	103,400
Swansea (W. Glam)	181,906
Taff Ely (Mid-Glam)	95,427
Torfaen (Gwent)	90,527
Vale of Glamorgan	113,725
Wrexham Maelor (Clwyd)	115,251

The following table shows the distribution of the urban and rural population of England and Wales (persons present) in 1951, 1961, 1971, and 1981.

		Population		Percentage	
	England and Wales	*Urban districts* [1]	*Rural districts* [1]	*Urban*	*Rural*
1951	43,757,888	35,335,721	8,422,167	80·8	19·2
1961	46,071,604	36,838,442	9,233,162	80·0	20·0
1971	48,755,000	38,151,000	10,598,000	78·2	21·5
1981	49,011,417	37,686,863	11,324,554	76·9	23·1

[1] As existing at each census.

Urban and rural areas were re-defined for the 1981 and 1991 censuses on a land use basis. In Scotland 'localities' correspond to urban areas. The 1981 census gave the usually resident population of England and Wales as 48,521,596, of which 43,599,431 were in urban areas; and of Scotland as 5,035,315, of which 4,486,140 were in localities.

Greater London Boroughs. Total area 1,580 sq. km. Usually resident total population at the 1991 census, 6,679,699 (inner London, 2,504,451). By borough:

Barking and Dagenham	143,681
Barnet	293,564
Bexley	215,615
Brent	243,025
Bromley	290,609
Camden [1]	170,444
Croydon	313,510
Ealing	275,257
Enfield	257,417
Greenwich	207,650
Hackney [1]	181,248
Hammersmith and Fulham [1]	148,502
Haringey [1]	202,204
Harrow	200,100
Havering	229,492
Hillingdon	231,602
Hounslow	204,397
Islington [1]	164,686
Kensington and Chelsea [1]	138,394
Kingston upon Thames	132,996
Lambeth [1]	244,834
Lewisham [1]	230,983
Merton	168,470
Newham [1]	212,170
Redbridge	226,218
Richmond upon Thames	160,732
Southwark [1]	218,541
Sutton	168,880
Tower Hamlets [1]	161,064
Waltham Forest	212,033
Wandsworth [1]	252,425
Westminster, City of [1]	174,718

[1] Inner London borough.

The City of London (677 acres) is administered by its Corporation which retains some independent powers. Resident population (1991 census) 4,142.

Scotland: Area 78,762 sq. km, including its islands, 186 in number, and inland water 1,580 sq. km.

Population (including military in the barracks and seamen on board vessels in the harbours) at the dates of each census:

Date of enumeration	*Population*	*Pop. per sq. mile* [1]	*Date of enumeration*	*Population*	*Pop. per sq. mile*
1811	1,805,864	60	1901	4,472,103	150
1821	2,091,521	70	1911	4,760,904	160
1831	2,364,386	79	1921	4,882,497	164
1841	2,620,184	88	1931	4,842,980	163
1851	2,888,742	97	1951	5,096,415	171
1861	3,062,294	100	1961	5,179,344	174
1871	3,360,018	113	1971	5,229,963	68
1881	3,735,573	125	1981	5,130,735	66
1891	4,025,647	135	1991	4,998,567	60

[1] Per sq. km from 1971.

The 1991 census population included 2,606,606 males.

Until April 1996 Scotland was divided into 9 regions (subdivided into 53 districts) and 3 island authority areas. Area of regions and usually resident population figures of regions and districts at the 1991 census:

Regions (area sq. km) and Districts	*Population*
Borders (4,713)	103,881
Berwickshire	19,174
Ettrick and Lauderdale	34,038
Roxburgh	35,346
Tweeddale	15,323
Central (2,635)	267,492
Clackmannan	47,679
Falkirk	140,980
Stirling	78,833
Dumfries and Galloway (6,396)	147,805
Annandale and Eskdale	37,087
Nithsdale	57,012
Stewartry	23,629
Wigtown	30,077
Fife (1,312)	341,199
Dunfermline	127,258
Kirkcaldy	147,053
North East Fife	66,888
Grampian (8,698)	503,888
Aberdeen City	204,885
Banff and Buchan	85,303
Gordon	76,642
Kincardine and Deeside	53,442
Moray	83,616
Highland (25,398)	204,004
Badenoch and Strathspey	11,008
Caithness	26,710
Inverness	62,186
Lochaber	19,310
Nairn	10,623
Ross and Cromarty	49,197
Skye and Lochalsh	11,754
Sutherland	13,216
Lothian (1,716)	726,010
East Lothian	84,114
Edinburgh City	418,914
Midlothian	78,845
West Lothian	144,137
Strathclyde (13,503)	2,248,706
Argyll and Bute	65,140
Bearsden and Milngavie	40,612
Clydebank	45,717
Clydesdale	57,588
Cumbernauld and Kilsyth	62,412
Cumnock and Doon Valley	42,594
Cunninghame	136,875
Dumbarton	77,173
East Kilbride	82,777
Eastwood	59,959
Glasgow City	662,853
Hamilton	105,202
Inverclyde	90,103
Kilmarnock and Loudoun	79,861
Kyle and Carrick	112,658
Monklands	102,379
Motherwell	142,632
Renfrew	196,980
Strathkelvin	85,191
Tayside (7,942)	383,848
Angus	94,480
Dundee City	165,873
Perth and Kinross	123,495
Island Authority Areas	
Orkney Islands (976)	19,612
Shetland Islands (1,433)	22,522
Western Isles (2,898)	29,600

In April 1996 29 new unitary authority areas came into being: Aberdeen, Aberdeenshire, Angus, Argyll and Bute, Borders, Clackmannan, Dumbarton and Clydebank, Dumfries and Galloway, Dundee, East Ayrshire, East Dunbartonshire, East Lothian, East Renfrewshire, Edinburgh, Falkirk, Fife, Glasgow, Highland, Inverclyde, Midlothian, Moray, North Ayrshire, North Lanarkshire, Perth and Kinross, Renfrewshire, South Ayrshire, South Lanarkshire, Stirling, West Lothian. The Island Authority Areas (Orkney, Shetland, Western Isles) remained as they were.

The birthplaces of the 1991 usually resident population were: Scotland, 4,454,065; England, 354,268; Wales, 4,710; Northern Ireland, 26,393; Ireland 22,773; Commonwealth, 59,134; foreign countries, 148,987.

Vital statistics. For England and Wales:

	Total live births	Live births outside marriage	Total deaths	Deaths under 1 year	Marriages	Divorces, annulments and dissolutions
1989	687,725	185,804	576,872	5,808	346,697	150,872
1990	706,140	199,999	564,846	5,564	331,150	153,386
1991	698,885	211,237	568,108	5,105	306,756	158,745
1992	689,307	215,179	556,448	4,484	311,564	160,385

There were 3,145 stillbirths in 1992. In 1993 there were 673,467 total live births (216,548 outside marriage).

Birth rate, 1993, per 1,000 population, 13·1; death rate (1990), 11·1; marriage rate (1989), 13·7; divorce rate (1989) per 1,000 married couples, 12·7; infant mortality per 1,000 live births, 7·9; sex ratio, 1993, 1,056 male births to 1,000 female. Average age of first marriage, 1989: Males, 27, females, 25.

Vital statistics. For Scotland:

	Estimated resident population at 30 June [1]	Total births	Live births outside marriage	Deaths	Marriages	Divorces, annulments and dissolutions
1990	5,102,400	65,973	17,873	61,527	34,672	12,272
1991	5,107,000	67,024	19,517	61,041	33,762	12,399
1992	5,111,200	65,789	19,950	60,937	35,057	12,479
1993	5,120,200	63,337	19,855	64,049	33,366	12,787
1994	5,132,400	61,656	19,224	59,328	31,480	13,133

[1] Includes merchant navy at home and forces stationed in Scotland.

Birth rate, 1994, per 1,000 population, 12; death rate, 11·6; marriage, 6·1; infant mortality per 1,000 live births, 6·2; sex ratio, 1,038 male births to 1,000 female. Average age of marriage in 1994: Males, 32, females, 29·8. Expectation of life, 1994: Males, 72·1 years, females, 77·6.

Emigration and Immigration. During the last hundred years the UK has most often been a net exporter of population. Throughout the period 1881–1931 there was a consistent net loss from migration, though the fifteen years 1931–46 brought a reversal of the trend as a result of immigration from Europe. Since the Second World War the loss has largely continued. However, during the five years 1956–1961, increased immigration particularly from the new Commonwealth and Pakistan, resulted in a net gain.

Since 1964 migration figures have been available from the International Passenger Survey (IPS). This was a sample survey conducted by the former Office of Population Censuses and Surveys, covering all the principal air and sea routes between the UK and overseas, except those to and from the Republic of Ireland. It is highly likely that the IPS data also exclude persons seeking asylum after entering the country and short-term visitors granted extensions of stay, for example as students or on the basis of marriage. After taking account of persons leaving the UK for a short-term period who stayed overseas for periods longer than originally intended, the adjustment needed to net migration ranges from about 10,000 in 1981 to 50,000, an average of approximately 20,000. The adjustment for 1993, the latest year available, is about 40,000. For the years 1974–83 the survey shows an average annual net loss for the UK of 37,000; and for 1984–93, an average annual net gain of 21,000.

In 1994, 32,821 persons applied for political asylum in the UK (2,905 in 1984).

Acceptances for settlement in the UK totalled 55,650 in 1993 (52,570 in 1992), including 31,060 (30,840) from the Commonwealth.

The table below, derived from the IPS, summarizes migration statistics for 1993 (in 1,000):

By country of last or future intended residence	Into UK	Out from UK	Balance
All countries	209	213	−3
EU	51	62	−12
Australia, Canada, New Zealand	35	48	−12
India, Bangladesh, Sri Lanka, Pakistan	20	6	+14

By country of last or future intended residence		*Into UK*	*Out from UK*	*Balance*
Other Commonwealth		27	25	+2
USA		23	33	−10
South Africa		9	3	+6
Rest of world		44	36	+9
By sex/age in 1993				
Males	0–14	17	20	−3
	15–24	27	20	+7
	25–44	43	55	−12
	45 and over	11	17	−6
	All ages	98	112	−13
Females	0–14	17	11	+6
	15–24	44	29	+15
	25–44	42	50	−8
	45 and over	8	11	−3
	All ages	111	101	+10

Coleman, D. and Salt, J., *The British Population: Patterns, Trends and Processes.* OUP, 1992

CLIMATE. The climate is cool temperate oceanic, with mild conditions and rainfall evenly distributed over the year, though the weather is very changeable because of cyclonic influences. In general, temperatures are higher in the west and lower in the east in winter and rather the reverse in summer. Rainfall amounts are greatest in the west, where most of the high ground occurs.

London. Jan. 40°F (4·5°C), July 64°F (18°C). Annual rainfall 24" (600 mm). Aberdeen. Jan. 39°F (4°C), July 57°F (14°C). Annual rainfall 33" (823 mm). Belfast. Jan. 40°F (4·5°C), July 61°F (16·1°C). Annual rainfall 34·6" (865 mm). Birmingham. Jan. 38°F (3·3°C), July 61°F (16·1°C). Annual rainfall 30" (749 mm). Cardiff. Jan. 40°F (4·4°C), July 61°F (16·1°C). Annual rainfall 42·6" (1,065 mm). Edinburgh. Jan. 38°F (3·5°C), July 58°F (14·5°C). Annual rainfall 28" (708 mm). Glasgow. Jan. 39°F (4°C), July 60°F (15·5°C). Annual rainfall 37·2" (930 mm). Manchester. Jan. 41°F (5°C), July 62°F (16·5°C). Annual rainfall 34·1" (853 mm).

THE ROYAL FAMILY. The reigning Queen, Head of the Commonwealth, is **Elizabeth II** Alexandra Mary, b. 21 April 1926, daughter of King George VI and Queen Elizabeth; married on 20 Nov. 1947 Lieut. Philip Mountbatten (formerly Prince Philip of Greece), created Duke of Edinburgh, Earl of Merioneth and Baron Greenwich on the same day and created Prince Philip, Duke of Edinburgh, 22 Feb. 1957; succeeded to the crown on the death of her father, on 6 Feb. 1952. Offspring: **Prince Charles Philip Arthur George, Prince of Wales** (Heir Apparent), b. 14 Nov. 1948, married Lady Diana Frances Spencer on 29 July 1981; separated 9 Dec. 1992; announced divorce proceedings in Feb. 1996. Offspring: *William* Arthur Philip Louis, b. 21 June 1982; *Henry* Charles Albert David, b. 15 Sept. 1984. **Princess Anne Elizabeth Alice Louise, the Princess Royal,** b. 15 Aug. 1950, married Mark Anthony Peter Phillips on 14 Nov. 1973; divorced, 1992; married Cdr Timothy Laurence on 12 Dec. 1992. Offspring of first marriage: *Peter* Mark Andrew, b. 15 Nov. 1977; *Zara* Anne Elizabeth, b. 15 May 1981. **Prince Andrew Albert Christian Edward, created Duke of York,** 23 July 1986, b. 19 Feb. 1960, married Sarah Margaret Ferguson on 23 July 1986; formally separated, 28 June 1993. Offspring: Princess *Beatrice* Mary, b. 8 Aug. 1988; Princess *Eugenie* Victoria Helena, b. 23 March 1990. **Prince Edward Antony Richard Louis,** b. 10 March 1964.

The Queen Mother: Queen *Elizabeth* Angela Marguerite, b. 4 Aug. 1900, daughter of the 14th Earl of Strathmore and Kinghorne; married the Duke of York, afterwards King George VI, on 26 April 1923.

Widow of the Uncle of the Queen: Princess *Alice* Christabel, Duchess of Gloucester, b. 25 Dec. 1901, married the late Duke of Gloucester 6 Nov. 1935.

Sister of the Queen: Princess *Margaret* Rose, Countess of Snowdon, b. 12 Aug. 1930; married Antony Armstrong-Jones (created Earl of Snowdon, 3 Oct. 1961) on 6 May 1960; divorced, 1978. Offspring: *David* Albert Charles (Viscount Linley),

b. 3 Nov. 1961, married Serena Alleyne Stanhope on 8 Oct. 1993; Lady *Sarah* Frances Elizabeth Chatto, b. 1 May 1964, married Daniel Chatto on 14 July 1994.

Cousins of the Queen

Richard Alexander Walter George, Duke of Gloucester, b. 26 Aug. 1944, married Birgitte van Deurs on 8 July 1972 (offspring: *Alexander* Patrick Gregers Richard, Earl of Ulster, b. 24 Oct. 1974; Lady *Davina* Elizabeth Alice Benedikte Windsor, b. 19 Nov. 1977; Lady *Rose* - Victoria Birgitte Louise Windsor, b. 1 March 1980).

Edward George Nicholas Paul Patrick, Duke of Kent, b. 9 Oct. 1935; married Katharine Worsley on 8 June 1961 (offspring: *George* Philip Nicholas, Earl of St Andrews, b. 26 June 1962, married Sylvania Tomaselli on 9 Jan. 1988 (offspring: *Edward* Edmund Maximilian George, Baron Downpatrick, b. 2 Dec. 1988; Lady *Marina* Charlotte Alexandra Katharine Windsor, b. 30 Sept. 1992); Lady *Helen* Marina Lucy Windsor, b. 28 April 1964, married 18 July 1992 Timothy Verner Taylor (offspring: *Columbus* George Donald Taylor, b. 6 Aug. 1994); Lord *Nicholas* Charles Edward Jonathan Windsor, b. 25 July 1970). **Princess Alexandra Helen Elizabeth Olga Christabel, the Hon. Lady Ogilvy** b. 25 Dec. 1936; married 24 April 1963 Sir Angus Ogilvy (offspring: *James* Robert Bruce, b. 29 Feb. 1964, married 30 July 1988, Julia Rawlinson; Lady *Marina* Victoria Alexandra, Mrs Mowatt, b. 31 July 1966, married 2 Feb. 1990 Paul Mowatt (offspring: *Zenouska* May Mowatt, b. 26 May 1990; *Christian* Alexander Mowatt, b. 4 June 1993). **Prince Michael George Charles Franklin**, b. 4 July 1942; married Baroness Marie-Christine von Reibnitz on 30 June 1978 (offspring: Lord *Frederick* Michael George David Louis Windsor, b. 6 April 1979; Lady *Gabriella* Marina Alexandra Ophelia Windsor, b. 23 April 1981).

The Queen's legal title rests on the statute of 12 and 13 Will. III, ch. 3, by which the succession to the Crown of Great Britain and Ireland was settled on the Princess Sophia of Hanover and the 'heirs of her body being Protestants'. By proclamation of 17 July 1917 the royal family became known as the House and Family of Windsor. On 8 Feb. 1960 the Queen issued a declaration varying her confirmatory declaration of 9 April 1952 to the effect that while the Queen and her children should continue to be known as the House of Windsor, her descendants, other than descendants entitled to the style of Royal Highness and the title of Prince or Princess, and female descendants who marry and their descendants should bear the name of Mountbatten-Windsor.

Lineage to the throne: 1. Prince of Wales. 2. Prince William of Wales. 3. Prince Henry of Wales. 4. Duke of York. 5. Princess Beatrice of York. 6. Princess Eugenie of York.

For the Royal Style and Titles of Queen Elizabeth *see* Commonwealth section. By letters patent of 30 Nov. 1917 the titles of Royal Highness and Prince or Princess are restricted to the Sovereign's children, the children of the Sovereign's sons and the eldest living son of the eldest son of the Prince of Wales.

Provision is made for the support of the royal household, after the surrender of hereditary revenues, by the settlement of the Civil List soon after the beginning of each reign. (For historical details, *see* THE STATESMAN'S YEAR-BOOK, 1908, p. 5, and 1935 p. 4). The Civil List Act of 1 Jan. 1972 provided for a decennial, and the Civil List (Increase of Financial Provision) Order 1975 for an annual review of the List, but in July 1990 it was again fixed for one decade.

The Civil List of 1991–2000 provided for an annuity of £7,900,000 to the Queen; £360,000 to Prince Philip; £640,500 to Queen Elizabeth (the Queen Mother); £230,500 to the Princess Royal; £220,000 to the Princess Margaret; £250,000 to the Duke of York; £100,000 to Prince Edward; £90,000 to Princess Alice. However, since April 1993 only the Queen, Prince Philip and the Queen Mother have received payments from the Civil List. The income of the Prince of Wales derives from the Duchy of Cornwall. The Civil List was exempted from taxation in 1910. The Queen has paid income tax on her private income since April 1993.

Sovereigns of Great Britain, from the Restoration (with dates of accession):

House of Stewart		*House of Stewart-Orange*	
Charles II	29 May 1660	William and Mary	13 Feb. 1689
James II	6 Feb. 1685	William III	28 Dec. 1694

House of Stewart		*House of Saxe-Coburg and Gotha*	
Anne	19 March 1702	Edward VII	22 Jan. 1901
House of Hanover		*House of Windsor*	
George I	1 Aug. 1714	George V	6 May 1910
George II	11 June 1727	Edward VIII	20 Jan. 1936
George III	25 Oct. 1760	George VI	11 Dec. 1936
George IV	29 Jan. 1820	Elizabeth II	6 Feb. 1952
William IV	26 June 1830		
Victoria	20 June 1837		

CONSTITUTION AND GOVERNMENT. The supreme legislative power is vested in Parliament, which consists of the Crown, the House of Lords and the House of Commons and dates in its present form from the middle of the 14th century. A Bill which is passed by both Houses and receives Royal Assent becomes an Act of Parliament and part of statute law.

Parliament is summoned, and a General Election is called, by the sovereign on the advice of the Prime Minister. A Parliament may last up to 5 years, normally divided into annual sessions. A session is ended by prorogation, and all Public Bills which have not been passed by both Houses then lapse. A Parliament ends by dissolution, either by will of the sovereign or by lapse of the 5-year period.

Under the Parliament Acts 1911 and 1949, all Money Bills (so certified by the Speaker of the House of Commons), if not passed by the Lords without amendment, may become law without their concurrence within 1 month of introduction in the Lords. Public Bills, other than Money Bills or a Bill extending the maximum duration of Parliament, if passed by the Commons in 2 successive sessions and rejected each time by the Lords, may become law without being passed by the Lords provided that 1 year has elapsed between Commons second reading in the first session and third reading in the second session, and that the Bill reaches the Lords at least 1 month before the end of the second session. In 1991 the War Crimes Act was passed in this way. This was the first time since 1949, because the Lords today respect the privileges of the elected House, especially as regards taxes and public spending, and act mainly as a revising chamber.

Peerages are created by the sovereign, with no limits on their number. There are 4 types of Lord: 1) *Lords Spiritual*, comprising 2 archbishops and 24 diocesan bishops of the Church of England, who leave the House when they retire; 2) *hereditary peers* – as at 31 Dec. 1995 there were 755 peers (16 of whom were women) who had succeeded to a peerage on the death of a relative and 14 who had themselves been granted a hereditary peerage; 3) *life peers* – there were 374 lords (65 of whom were women) who had been given a peerage for their own lifetime only under the Life Peerages Act 1958; 4) *Lords of Appeal* (both active and retired) – there were 24 peers, granted a peerage for life under the Appellate Jurisdiction Act 1876, in order to enable them to hear appeal cases in the House of Lords. The full House thus consists of 1,198 lords, of whom 83 are women. The average attendance at each sitting of the House is approximately 380.

The House of Commons consists of members (of both sexes) representing constituencies determined by the Boundary Commissions. Persons under 21 years of age, Clergy of the Church of England and of the Scottish Episcopal Church, Ministers of the Church of Scotland, Roman Catholic clergymen, civil servants, members of the regular armed forces, policemen, most judicial officers and other office-holders named in the House of Commons (Disqualification) Act are disqualified from sitting in the House of Commons. No peer eligible to sit in the House of Lords can be elected to the House of Commons unless he has disclaimed his title, but Irish peers and holders of courtesy titles, who are not members of the House of Lords, are eligible.

The Representation of the People Act 1948, abolished the business premises and University franchises, and the only persons entitled to vote at Parliamentary elections are those registered as residents or as service voters. No person may vote in more than one constituency at a general election. Persons may apply on certain grounds to vote by post or by proxy. Elections are held on the first-past-the-post system, in which the candidate who receives the most votes is elected.

All persons over 18 years old and not subject to any legal incapacity to vote and who are either British subjects or citizens of Ireland are entitled to be included in the register of electors for the constituency containing the address at which they were residing on the qualifying date for the register and are entitled to vote at elections held during the period for which the register remains in force.

Members of the armed forces, Crown servants employed abroad, and the wives accompanying their husbands, are entitled, if otherwise qualified, to be registered as 'service voters' provided they make a 'service declaration'. To be effective for a particular register, the declaration must be made on or before the qualifying date for that register. In certain circumstances, British subjects living abroad may also vote.

The Parliamentary Constituencies Act 1986, as amended by the Boundary Commissions Act 1992, provided for the setting up of Boundary Commissions for England, Wales, Scotland and Northern Ireland. The Commissions' last reports were made in 1995, and thereafter reports are due at intervals of not less than 8 and not more than 12 years, and to submit reports from time to time with respect to the area comprised in any particular constituency or constituencies where some change appears necessary. Any changes giving effect to reports of the Commissions are to be made by Orders in Council laid before Parliament for approval by resolution of each House. The Parliamentary electorate of the United Kingdom and Northern Ireland in the register in 1994 numbered 43,786,734, of whom 36,455,151 were in England, 2,222,091 in Wales, 3,947,157 in Scotland and 1,162,335 in Northern Ireland. It is officially estimated that 7·1% of persons eligible to vote failed to register on the electoral roll in 1991.

At the general election held in 1992, 651 members were returned, 524 from England, 72 from Scotland, 38 from Wales and 17 from Northern Ireland. Every constituency returns a single member.

In Aug. 1911 provision was first made for the payment of a salary of £400 per annum to members of the Commons, other than those already in receipt of salaries as officers of the House, as Ministers or as officers of Her Majesty's household. As from 1 Jan. 1995 the salaries of members are £33,189 per annum. There is an office costs allowance of up to £41,308 per annum. Members whose constituencies are outside inner London are entitled to additional expenses incurred in staying overnight away from home whilst performing parliamentary duties within an annual maximum of £11,268. Members of the House of Lords are unsalaried but may recover expenses incurred in attending sittings of the House within maxima for each day's attendance of £32 for day subsistence, £71.50 for night subsistence and £32 for secretarial and research assistance and office expenses. Additionally, Members of the House who are disabled may recover the extra cost of attending the House incurred by reason of their disablement. In connection with attendance at the House and parliamentary duties within the UK Lords may also recover the cost of travelling to and from home.

The following is a table of the duration of Parliaments called since Aug. 1945:

Reign	*When met*	*When dissolved*	*Duration (years*	*and days)*
George VI	1 Aug. 1945	3 Feb. 1950	4	188
,,	1 Mar. 1950	5 Oct. 1951	1	219
George VI and Elizabeth II	31 Oct. 1951	6 May 1955	3	188
Elizabeth II	7 June 1955	18 Sept. 1959	4	105
,,	20 Oct. 1959	25 Sept. 1964	4	341
,,	27 Oct. 1964	10 Mar. 1966	1	134
,,	18 Apr. 1966	29 May 1970	4	81
,,	29 June 1970	8 Feb. 1974	3	225
,,	12 Mar. 1974	20 Sept. 1974	0	224
,,	22 Oct. 1974	7 April 1979	4	167
,,	9 May 1979	13 May 1983	4	4
,,	15 June 1983	18 May 1987	3	338
,,	25 June 1987	16 March 1992	4	266
,,	27 April 1992	—	—	—

The executive government is vested nominally in the Crown, but practically in a committee of Ministers, called the Cabinet, which is dependent on the support of a majority in the House of Commons. The head of the Ministry is the Prime Minister, a position first constitutionally recognized in 1905. His colleagues in the Ministry are appointed on his recommendation, and he dispenses the greater portion of the patronage of the Crown.

Heads of the Administrations since 1937 (C. = Conservative, L. = Liberal, Lab. = Labour, Nat. = National, Coal. = Coalition, Care. = Caretaker):

N. Chamberlain (Nat.)	28 May 1937	Sir Alec Douglas-Home (C.)	18 Oct. 1963
W. S. Churchill (Coal.)	10 May 1940	H. Wilson (Lab.)	16 Oct. 1964
W. S. Churchill (Care.)	23 May 1945	E. Heath (C.)	19 June 1970
C. R. Attlee (Lab.)	26 July 1945	H. Wilson (Lab.)	12 Mar. 1974
W. S. Churchill (C.)	26 Oct. 1951	J. Callaghan (Lab.)	5 Apr. 1976
Sir Anthony Eden (C.)	6 Apr. 1955	M. Thatcher (C.)	4 May 1979
H. Macmillan (C.)	10 Jan. 1957	J. Major (C.)	22 Nov. 1990

At the general election of 9 April 1992 33,145,074 votes were cast. The Conservative Party gained 336 seats with 42·8% of votes cast (376 with 42·3% in 1987); the Labour Party 271 with 35·2% (229 with 32%), the Liberal Democratic Party 20 with 18·3% (19 with 23·1%). The Ulster Unionist Party gained 9 seats, Plaid Cymru (Welsh nationalist) 4, the Social and Democratic Labour Party 4, the Scottish National Party 3, the Democratic Unionist Party 3, the Ulster Popular Unionist Party 1.

In 15 by-elections after the 1992 general election Labour won 9 seats, the Liberal Democrats 4, the Scottish National Party 1 and the United Kingdom Unionist Party 1.

In March 1996 the Government consisted of the following ('Rt Hon.' – Right Honourable – signifies a member of the Privy Council):

(a) 23 MEMBERS OF THE CABINET

Prime Minister, First Lord of the Treasury and Minister for the Civil Service: Rt Hon. John Major, MP, b. 1943. (Salary £58,557 per annum.)

First Secretary of State and Deputy Prime Minister: Rt Hon. Michael Heseltine, MP, b. 1933. (£43,991.)

Lord Chancellor: Rt Hon. The Lord Mackay of Clashfern, QC, b. 1927. (£126,138.)

Secretary of State for Foreign and Commonwealth Affairs: Rt Hon. Malcolm Rifkind, QC, MP, b. 1946. (£43,991.)

Chancellor of the Exchequer: Rt Hon. Kenneth Clarke, QC, MP, b. 1940. (£43,991.)

Secretary of State for the Home Department: Rt Hon. Michael Howard, QC, MP, b. 1941. (£43,991.)

Secretary of State for Trade and Industry and President of the Board of Trade: Rt Hon. Ian Lang, MP, b. 1940. (£43,991.)

Secretary of State for Transport: Rt Hon. Sir George Young, Bt, MP, b. 1941. (£43,991.)

Secretary of State for Defence: Rt Hon. Michael Portillo, MP, b. 1953. (£43,991.)

Lord Privy Seal and Leader of the House of Lords: Rt Hon. Viscount Cranborne, b. 1946. (£57,161.)

Lord President of the Council, Leader of the House of Commons: Rt Hon. Tony Newton, OBE, MP, b. 1937. (£43,991.)

Minister of Agriculture, Fisheries and Food: Rt Hon. Douglas Hogg, QC, MP, b. 1945. (£43,991.)

Secretary of State for the Environment: Rt Hon. John Gummer, MP, b. 1939. (£43,991.)

Secretary of State for Wales: Rt Hon. William Hague, MP, b. 1961. (£43,991.)

Secretary of State for Social Security: Rt Hon. Peter Lilley, MP, b. 1943. (£43,991.)

Chancellor of the Duchy of Lancaster: Rt Hon. Roger Freeman, MP, b. 1942. (£43,991.)

Secretary of State for Scotland: Rt Hon. Michael Forsyth, MP, b. 1954. (£43,991.)

Secretary of State for National Heritage: Rt Hon. Virginia Bottomley, MP, b. 1948. (£43,991.)

Secretary of State for Northern Ireland: Rt Hon. Sir Patrick Mayhew, QC, MP, b. 1929. (£43,991.)

Secretary of State for Education and Employment: Rt Hon. Gillian Shepherd, MP, b. 1940. (£43,991.)

Secretary of State for Health: Rt Hon. Stephen Dorrell, MP, b. 1952. (£43,991.)

Chief Secretary to the Treasury: Rt Hon. William Waldegrave, MP, b. 1946. (£43,991.)

Minister without Portfolio: Rt Hon. Dr Brian Mawhinney, MP, b. 1940. (£43,991.)

(*b*) 4 Law Officers

Attorney-General: Rt Hon. Sir Nicholas Lyell, QC, MP, b. 1938. (£46,745.)

Lord Advocate: Lord Mackay of Drumadoon, QC, b. 1946. (£57,241.)

Solicitor-General: Sir Derek Spencer, QC, MP, b. 1936. (£38,329.)

Solicitor-General for Scotland: Paul Cullen, QC, b. 1948. (£48,985.)

(*c*) 28 Ministers not in the Cabinet

Parliamentary Secretary, Treasury (Chief Whip): Rt Hon. Alastair Goodlad, MP, b. 1943. (£36,613.)

Minister of State, Foreign and Commonwealth Office: Rt Hon. Jeremy Hanley, MP, b. 1945. (£31,125.)

Minister of State, Foreign and Commonwealth Office: Rt Hon. Sir Nicholas Bonsor, Bt, MP, b. 1942. (£31,125.)

Minister of State, Foreign and Commonwealth Office: David Davis, MP, b. 1948. (£31,125.)

Minister of State, Foreign and Commonwealth Office, Minister for Overseas Development: Rt Hon. Baroness Chalker of Wallasey, b. 1942. (£50,328.)

Financial Secretary, Treasury: Michael Jack, MP, b. 1946. (£31,125.)

Minister of State, Northern Ireland Office: Rt Hon. Michael Ancram, MP, b. 1945. (£31,125.)

Minister of State, Northern Ireland Office: Rt Hon. Sir John Wheeler, JP, MP, b. 1940. (£31,125.)

Minister of State, Home Office: Ann Widdecombe, MP, b. 1947. (£31,125.)

Minister of State, Home Office: Rt Hon. David MacLean, MP, b. 1953. (£31,125.)

Minister of State, Home Office: Rt Hon. Baroness Blatch, CBE, b. 1937. (£50,328.)

Minister of State, Ministry of Defence: Hon. Nicholas Soames, MP, b. 1948. (£31,125.)

Minister of State, Ministry of Defence: Rt Hon. James Arbuthnot, MP, b. 1952. (£31,125.)

Minister of State, Department of Trade and Industry: Rt Hon. Lord Fraser of Carmyllie, QC, b. 1945. (£50,328.)

Minister of State, Department of Trade and Industry: Tim Eggar, MP, b. 1951. (£31,125.)

Minister of State, Department of Trade and Industry: Rt Hon. Anthony Nelson, MP, b. 1948. (£31,125.)

Minister of State, Department of Health, Minister of Health: Gerald Malone, MP, b. 1950. (£31,125.)

Minister of State, Department of Education: Eric Forth, MP, b. 1944. (£31,125.)

Minister of State, Scottish Office: Lord James Douglas-Hamilton, MP, b. 1942. (£31,125.)

Minister of State, Department of Transport: John Watts, MP, b. 1947. (£31,125.)

Minister of State, Department of Social Security, Minister for Social Security and Disabled People: Alistair Burt, MP, b. 1955. (£31,125.)

Minister of State, Department of Social Security: Lord Mackay of Ardbrecknish, b. 1938. (£50,328.)

Minister of State, Department of the Environment, Minister for the Environment and Countryside: Rt Hon. Earl Ferrers, b. 1929. (£50,328.)

Minister of State, Department of the Environment, Minister for Local Government, Housing and Urban Regeneration: David Curry, MP, b. 1944. (£31,125.)

Minister of State, Department of the Environment, Minister for Construction, Planning and Energy Efficiency: Robert Jones, MP, b. 1950. (£31,125.)

Minister of State, Department of Education and Employment: Eric Forth, MP, b. 1944. (£31,125.)

Minister of State, Department of Education and Employment: The Lord Henley, b. 1953. (£50,328.)

Minister of State, Ministry of Agriculture, Fisheries and Food: Tony Baldry, MP, b. 1950. (£31,125.)

There are also 33 Under-Secretaries of State.

Leader of the Opposition in the House of Commons: Rt Hon. Tony Blair, MP, b. 1953. (£40,322.)

Leader of the Opposition in the House of Lords: The Lord Richard, b. 1932. (£42,361.)

Cabinet Ministers, Ministers of State, Parliamentary Secretaries and the Leader of the Opposition who are also Members of Parliament, receive additionally a reduced Parliamentary salary of £25,660.

The Privy Council: Before the development of the Cabinet System, the Privy Council was the chief source of executive power, but now its functions are largely formal. It advises the monarch to approve Orders in Council and on the issue of royal proclamations, and has some independent powers such as the supervision of the registration of the medical profession. It consists of all Cabinet members, the Archbishops of Canterbury and York, the Speaker of the House of Commons and senior British and Commonwealth statesmen. There are a number of advisory Privy Council committees. The *Judicial Committee* is the final court of appeal from courts of the UK dependencies, the Channel Islands and the Isle of Man, and some Commonwealth countries.

Ball, A., *British Political Parties: The Emergence of a Modern Party System.* 1981
Boulton, C. J. (ed.), *Erskine May's Treatise on the Law Privileges, Proceedings and Usage of Parliament.* 21st ed. London, 1990
Bruce, A., *et al. The House of Lords: 1,000 Years of British Tradition.* London, 1994
Butler, D. and Butler, G., *British Political Facts, 1900–1994.* London, 1994
Butler, D. and Kavanagh, D., *The British General Election of 1992.* London, 1992
Dod's Parliamentary Companion. London [published after elections]

Drewry, G. (ed.), *The New Select Committees*. OUP, 1985
Griffith, J. A. G. and Ryle, M., *Parliament: Functions, Practices and Procedures*. London, 1990
Hanson, A. H. and Walles, M., *Governing Britain: a Guidebook to Political Institutions*. 5th ed. London, 1990
Hennessy, P., *Whitehall*. London, 1989
King, A. (ed.), *The British Prime Minister*. Rev. ed. London, 1985.—*British Members of Parliament*. London, 1974
Norton, P., *Parliament in the 1980s*. Oxford, 1985
Parker, F. K., *Conduct of Parliamentary Elections*. London, 1983
Shell, D., *The House of Lords*. 2nd ed. Hemel Hempstead, 1992
Silk, E. P., *How Parliament Works*. London, 1987
The Times Guide to the House of Commons. London, [published after elections]
Waller, R., *The Almanac of British Politics*. 4th ed. London, 1991

National flag: The combined crosses of St George (red), St Andrew (white) and St Patrick (red), the red fimbriated in white, all on a blue ground.

National anthem: God Save the Queen (King) (words and tune anonymous; earliest known printed source, 1744).

European Parliament: The United Kingdom has 87 representatives. At the June 1994 elections turn-out was 36·4%. The Labour Party won 62 seats with 44·2% of votes cast (group in European Parliament: European Socialist Party); the Conservative Party, 18 with 27·8% (Popular European Party); the Liberal Democratic Party, 2 with 16·7% (Liberal, Democratic and Reformist Group); the Scottish National Party, 2 with 3·2% (European Radical Alliance). Voting for these parties was on the first-past-the-post system. Voting in Northern Ireland was by the single transferable vote system: the Democratic Ulster Unionist Party, the Social Democrat and Labour Party (European Socialist Party) and the Official Ulster Union Party (Popular European Party) gained 1 seat each.

Local Administration: This is carried out by 4 different types of bodies, namely: (i) local branches of some central ministries, such as the Departments of Health and Social Security; (ii) local sub-managements of nationalized industries; (iii) specialist authorities such as the National Rivers Authority; and (iv) the system of local government described below. The phrase 'local government' has come to mean that part of the local administration conducted by elected councils. There are 2 separate systems, one for England and Wales and one for Scotland. For local government finance *see* Budget: *Local Taxation*, below.

The Local Government Act 1992 established a Local Government Commission, which completed its report in 1996 on whether the two-tier local government structure should be replaced by unitary authorities in some areas. It recommended the creation of 8 new unitary councils within the existing two-tier system of counties and districts: Blackburn, Blackpool, Gillingham and Rochester, Halton, Peterborough, Thurrock, Warrington, the Wrekin.

Local Government: England and Wales—*Outside London*. England and Wales have slightly differing systems. Each country has three types of councils namely, county, district and English parish or Welsh Community Councils. In addition, England has some metropolitan district councils.

Councillors are elected by their local electors for 4 years. The chair of the council is one of the councillors elected by the rest. In a district with the status of borough his or her title is mayor. Mayors of cities may have the title of lord mayor conferred on them. 51 towns in England and Wales have the status of city. This status is granted by the personal command of the monarch and confers no special privileges or powers. Any parish or community council can by simple resolution adopt the style 'town council' and the status of town for the parish or community. The chairman of the council will be known as the town mayor.

Counties and Districts: There are 47 non-metropolitan counties (of which 8 are in Wales). The 6 metropolitan counties (Greater Manchester, Merseyside, South Yorkshire, Tyne and Wear, West Yorkshire and West Midlands) have no councils, the metropolitan districts having most of the county functions. Within the counties there are 369 districts (36 metropolitan and 333 non-metropolitan, of which 37 are in Wales).

Elections for one third of the seats on the councils of the 32 London boroughs, 36 metropolitan districts and 118 non-metropolitan districts were held on 5 May 1994. The Labour Party gained control of 93 councils; the Liberal Democratic Party, 19; the Conservative Party, 15; ind, 5. There was no overall majority in 54 councils.

Elections were held outside the metropolitan areas ('the shires') on 4 May 1995. Labour made a net gain of 155 councils, the Liberal Democrats 45 and the Conservatives lost 51.

Parishes and Communities: There are some 10,000 parishes within the English districts, of which 8,000 or so have councils. About 300 are former small boroughs or urban districts which became successor parishes.

In Wales, parishes are known as communities. Unlike England, where some urban areas are not in any parish, communities have been established for the whole of Wales. There is one for each former parish, county borough, borough or urban district (or part thereof where the former area is divided by a new boundary). There are about 1,000 communities altogether, of which 800 or so have councils.

The Local Government Act 1972 laid down the boundaries for all the counties and districts in England and Wales except the English non-metropolitan districts.

Permanent Local Government Boundary Commissions for England and for Wales advise the Secretaries of State on boundaries and electoral arrangements.

Local government functions may be classified into county, district and parish or community functions, but whereas county and district functions are distinct, the parish and community functions are mostly concurrent with those of the districts. Arrangements may, however, be made so that any council may discharge functions of any other as its agent.

The following is the classification of powers given above: *Parish and Community Functions.* Allotments, burial and cremation, halls, meeting places and entertainments, facilities for exercise and recreation, public lavatories, street lighting, offstreet vehicle parking, footpaths, the support of local arts and crafts, the encouragement of tourism and the right to be consulted by the district council on planning applications and certain byelaws. *District Functions.* In addition to the Parish and Community functions, aerodromes, civic restaurants, housing, markets, refuse collection, the administration of planning control, the formulation of local plans, sewerage on behalf of the water authority, museums, the licensing of places of entertainment and refreshment, and the constitutional oversight of parishes and communities. *County Functions.* The formulation of structure plans, traffic, transportation and roads, education, public libraries and museums, youth employment and social services.

There are, in addition, a number of special arrangements. Four district councils in Wales are designated as library authorities and Welsh district councils have powers in relation to allotments currently with community councils. The county councils in England and Wales separately or jointly appoint the fire and police authorities, and the bodies responsible for national parks. In Metropolitan counties, there are no county councils and all functions are performed by the districts (in some cases jointly). The total number of local government electors in England and Wales was 38,660,999 in 1994.

Greater London. From 1965–86 London was governed by the Greater London Council, covering the whole metropolitan area, and by 32 London boroughs and the Corporation of the City of London, each with responsibilities in its own area. The GLC was abolished on 1 April 1986. The individual borough councils are the education authorities. Fire services in Greater London are the responsibility of the London Fire and Civil Defence Authority, whose members are appointed by the boroughs and the City. Flood prevention is the responsibility of the Thames Water Authority. Waste regulation for the whole of Greater London is the function of the London Waste Regulation Authority. Waste collection is the responsibility of the boroughs. Waste disposal is the responsibility of the boroughs acting individually or in groups. Except in the City, the police authority is the Metropolitan Police, which is responsible to central government. London Regional Transport is likewise responsible to central government for passenger transport. Other local government functions are the responsibility of the boroughs, acting either individually or jointly, and the City.

Local Government: Scotland. For local government purposes, mainland Scotland was divided on a two-tier basis into 9 regions and 53 districts, but these were replaced in April 1996 by 29 single-tier, or unitary, councils. (*For list see* TERRITORY AND POPULATION: Scotland, *above*). The 3 islands areas of Orkney, Shetland and the Western Isles already had single-tier councils responsible for virtually all functions.

Over 1,000 community councils have been established under schemes drawn up by district and island councils. These community councils cannot claim public funds as of right nor do they have specific powers conferred by statute: Consequently they are not local authorities in the sense that English parish councils or Welsh community councils are.

As in England and Wales, a permanent Local Government Boundary Commission advises the Secretary of State on local authority boundaries and electoral constituencies.

The total number of local government electors in Scotland was 3,960,657 in 1995.

On 6 April 1995 elections were held for the 29 newly-created unitary councils. 1,161 seats were contested. Labour won 614 seats with 47% of votes cast, and gained control of 20 of the councils; the Scottish National Party won 181 seats with 26% and gained 3 councils; the Liberal Democrats won 123 seats with 10%; the Conservative Party won 81 seats with 11%. Independents gained control of 3 councils, and 3 councils had no overall control.

The next elections were scheduled for 1999.

DEFENCE. The Defence Council was established on 1 April 1964 under the chairmanship of the Secretary of State for Defence, who is responsible to the Sovereign and Parliament for the defence of the realm. Vested in the Defence Council are the functions of commanding and administering the Armed Forces. The Secretary of State heads the Ministry of Defence as a Department of State. There are 3 subordinate Ministers; 2 Ministers of State and 1 Parliamentary Under-Secretary of State.

Defence Council membership comprises the Secretary of State, the 3 Ministers mentioned above, the Chief of the Defence Staff, the 3 single Service Chiefs of Staff, the Vice-Chief of Defence Staff, the Chief of Defence Procurement, the Chief Scientific Adviser, the Permanent Under-Secretary of State and the Second Permanent Under Secretary of State.

There are 3 Service Boards, each of which enjoys delegated powers for the administration of matters relating to the naval, military and air forces respectively.

Defence policy decision making is a collective Governmental responsibility. Important matters of policy are considered by the full Cabinet or, more frequently, by the Defence and Oversea Policy Committee under the chairmanship of the Prime Minister. Other members of this Committee include the Secretary of State for Defence, the Foreign and Commonwealth Secretary and the Home Secretary.

The ban on homosexuals serving in the armed forces was upheld by the Court of Appeal in Nov. 1995.

The Procurement Executive. An important development in 1971 was the creation of a Procurement Executive to combine the Defence Procurement responsibilities of the Ministry of Defence and the former Ministry of Aviation Supply.

Total armed forces, 1993: Active, 274,800 (including 18,900 women and about 8,000 persons enlisted abroad); reserves, 349,300.

Defence Budget (Plans): 1993–94, £23,523m.; 1994–95, £23,750m.; 1995–96 £23,220m.

Army. Control of the British Army is vested in the Defence Council and is exercised through the Army Board. The Secretary of State for Defence is Chairman of the Army Board. The other civilian members are the 3 subordinate Ministers and the Second Permanent Under Secretary of State.

The Military members of the Army Board are the Chief of the General Staff, the Adjutant General, the Quartermaster General, the Master General of the Ordnance, the C.-in-C. UK Land Command and the Assistant Chief of General Staff. The Chief of the General Staff is the professional head of his Service and the professional adviser to Ministers on the Army aspects of military matters. He is responsible for the fighting efficiency of his Service; for Army advice on the conduct of operations; and for the issuing of such single Service operational orders as may be appropriate resulting from defence policy decisions. He is also responsible for the Territorial Army. The Chief of the General Staff is a member of the Chiefs of Staff Committee which is chaired by the Chief of the Defence Staff, who is responsible to HM Government for professional advice on strategy and military operations and on the military implication of defence policy. The Adjutant-General is responsible for recruiting and selection of army manpower; for the administration and individual training of military personnel; for the discipline of the Army; for pay and allowances and pensions; for legal services; for the veterinary and remount services; for the Army Cadet Forces; for questions of Army welfare and education including school children overseas; and for resettlement and sports. The Quartermaster-General is responsible for logistic planning for the Army; for the storage, distribution, maintenance, repair and inspection of equipment, stores and ammunition; for development of stores; for supply, transport and accommodation; for the development, production and inspection of clothing; for military movements and transportation; for the Army postal, catering, salvage and fire services; and for questions connected with canteens, institutes and military labour. The Master General of the Ordnance is a member of both the Army Board and of the Procurement Executive Management Board. He is responsible to the Chief of Defence Procurement for the financial and technical management of the approved programme for the procurement of land service equipment for the Armed Services, and to the Army Board for the co-ordination of the Army's total equipment programme.

The Army is organized in 1 Land Command Headquarters, 3 military districts, 3 divisional headquarters and 1 UK Support Command (Germany) – UKSC(G) and comprises: 1 armoured division with 3 armoured brigades, 3 artillery, 4 engineer, 1 aviation and 1 air defence regiment; 1 division with 2 mechanized and 1 airborne brigade and 3 artillery, 2 engineer, 1 aviation and 1 air defence regiment; UKSC(G) troops consisting of 2 armoured reconnaissance, 3 multiple launch rocket system, 2 air defence and 1 engineer regiment; 1 air mobile and 13 infantry brigades; and the following summary combat arm units: 9 armoured regiments, 2 armoured reconnaissance regiments, 4 mechanized infantry battalions, 8 armoured infantry battalions, 26 infantry battalions, 3 airborne battalions, 1 special forces regiment (SAS), 12 artillery, 4 air defence, 10 engineer and 5 aviation regiments and 6 Home Service infantry battalions (Northern Ireland deployment only).

Headquarters Land at Wilton commands all Army units in UK and Germany except Ministry of Defence controlled units. The Ministry of Defence retains direct operational control of units in Northern Ireland. There are 2 major overseas Commands: Hong Kong and Cyprus. There are also garrisons in the Falkland Islands and Brunei. The Army Air Corps has some 300 helicopters and 17 fixed-wing aircraft.

The strength of the Regular Army in 1995 was 116,000 (including 6,600 women and 4,400 in the Brigade of Gurkhas). Strength of reserve forces were: Regular reserves, 260,300; Territorial Army, 59,700.

The Territorial Army (TA) role is to provide a national reserve for employment on specific tasks at home and overseas and to meet the unexpected when required; and, in particular, to complete the Army Order of Battle of NATO committed forces and to provide certain units for the support of NATO Headquarters, to assist in maintaining a secure UK base in support of forces deployed on the Continent of Europe and to provide a framework for any future expansion of the Reserves. In addition, men who have completed service in the Regular Army normally have some liability to serve in the Regular Reserve. All members of the TA and Regular

Reserve may be called out by a Queen's Order in time of emergency of imminent national danger and most of the TA and a large proportion of the Regular Reserve may be called out by a Queen's Order when warlike operations are in preparation or in progress. The Home Service Battalions of the Royal Irish Regiment are only liable for service in Northern Ireland.

Men, women and juniors enlist in the Army for 22 years' active and reserve service. Soldiers enlist for a minimum of 3 years and can leave active service thereafter on one year's notice. Bonuses are paid to those who serve for certain periods and there are manning control points at which the Army may require soldiers to terminate their service, again on one year's notice. Those enlisting in certain technical trades must agree to serve for a minimum of 6 years. Recruits under the age of 17½ on reaching the age of 18 are entitled either to confirm their original engagement or to reduce their period of service to 3 years.

Equipment includes 426 Challenger and 60 Chieftain main battle tanks and 526 surface-to-air missiles.

Women serve throughout the Army in the same regiments and corps as men. There are only a few roles in which they are not employed such as the Infantry and Royal Armoured Corps.

Chandler, D. (ed.) *The Oxford Illustrated History of the British Army*. OUP, 1995

Navy. Control of the Royal Navy is vested in the Defence Council and is exercised through the Admiralty Board, chaired by the Secretary of State for Defence. The other civilian members are the Ministers of State for the Armed Forces and Defence Procurement, the Parliamentary Under Secretary for Defence and the Second Permanent Under Secretary of State. The naval members are the Chief of Naval Staff (First Sea Lord) responsible for management, fighting efficiency, planning and operational advice; the combined Second Sea Lord and C.-in-C. Naval Home Command, responsible for the manning of the Fleet and all personnel aspects; the Controller of the Navy, responsible for procurement of ships, their weapons and equipment; the Chief of Fleet Support, responsible for logistic support, stores, fuels and transport, naval dockyards and the auxiliary services; the C.-in-C. Fleet, and the Assistant Chief of Naval Staff, responsible for co-ordinating advice on certain policy and operational matters. The Navy Board, an executive sub-committee of the Admiralty Board, is responsible for the professional management of the service.

In 1995 changes in management structure, reductions in strength, base closures and rationalization continued. The Chief of Fleet Support and Controller of the Navy are now located in the Bath area. The naval bases at Rosyth and Portland have closed, although the dockyard at Rosyth remains operational.

The C.-in-C. Fleet, headquartered at Northwood, is responsible for the command of the fleet, while command of naval establishments in the UK is exercised by the C.-in-C. Naval Home Command from Portsmouth. Main naval bases are at Devonport, Portsmouth and Faslane, and minor bases overseas at Hong Kong (closing 1997) and Gibraltar.

The Royal Naval Reserve (RNR) and the Royal Marines Reserve (RMR) are volunteer forces which in 1995 numbered some 2,900 and 1,000 respectively. The RNR provides trained personnel in war to supplement regular forces. The main roles of the RMR are reinforcement and other specialist tasks with the UK-Netherlands Amphibious Force. In addition, men who have completed service in the Royal Navy and the Royal Marines have a commitment to serve in the Royal Fleet Reserve, currently 22,100 strong.

Royal Navy and Queen Alexandra's Royal Naval Nursing Service (QARNNS) ratings, both male and female, and Royal Marine ranks enlist on the 'Open Engagement' to complete 22 years active service with the option to leave at 18 months notice on completion of a minimum of 2 and a half years productive service. Those who leave before completing 22 years have a liability for up to 3 years service in the Royal Fleet Reserve.

The roles of the Royal Navy are first, to deploy the national strategic nuclear deterrent, second to provide maritime defence of the UK and its dependent territories, third to contribute to the maritime elements of NATO's force structure and fourth to meet national maritime objectives outside the NATO area. Personnel strength has reduced steadily over the past 5 years and should stabilize at about 50,000 (including Royal Marines) in 1996, with operational strength at 12 nuclear attack submarines, 2 aircraft carriers and about 35 destroyers and frigates.

The strategic deterrent is now borne principally by the new Trident submarines, of which the first 2 of 4, *Vanguard* and *Victorious*, each of 15,250 tonnes, and deploying 16 US–built Trident-2 D5 UGM-133A missiles with British warheads, are now operational. The third ship, *Vigilant*, will become operational in 1997, and the fourth, *Vengeance* in 1999. The last missile submarine of the Resolution class, *Renown*, deploying 16 Polaris A-3TK missiles is due to decommission in mid-1996.

The strength of the fleet's major non-strategic units at the end of each of the last 6 years was as follows:

	1990	*1991*	*1992*	*1993*	*1994*	*1995*
Strategic Submarines	4	4	4	4	3	3
Nuclear Submarines	14	15	13	13	12	12
Diesel Submarines	6	6	4	4	nil	nil
Aircraft Carriers	2 [1]	2 [1]	2 [1]	2 [1]	2 [1]	2 [1]
Destroyers	13	12	12	12	12	12
Frigates	33	33	30	25	24	23

[1] Following Government policy, of the 3 Carriers held, only 2 are kept in operational status.

The nuclear-powered submarine force numbers 12, of 2 classes, armed with torpedoes and Harpoon anti-ship missiles. There are 7 Trafalgar class, (5,300 tonnes) completed 1983–1991 and 5 Swiftsure (4,900 tonnes) completed 1973–79. The 4 diesel-electric submarines of the Upholder class were decommissioned in 1994.

The principal surface ships are the Light vertical/short take-off and landing Aircraft Carriers of the Invincible class, (*Invincible, Illustrious* and *Ark Royal*), 20,900 tonnes, completed 1980-85, embarking an air group of 8 Sea Harrier vertical/short take-off and landing fighters, 9 anti-submarine Sea King and 3 radar early warning Sea King helicopters, armed with 1 twin Sea Dart surface-to-air missile system. 2 of these ships are maintained in the operational fleet, with the third (currently *Ark Royal*) either in refit or reserve.

The 12 destroyers are all Type 42 (completed 1976–85), armed with 1 twin Sea Dart surface-to-air missile system. Frigates comprise 12 Type 22 (completed 1979–89) and 11 Norfolk class (Type 23) completed 1989–96.

The lightly-armed patrol force comprises 1 ice patrol ship, 16 other offshore patrol vessels (including 3 in the Hong Kong squadron) and 16 inshore patrol craft mostly employed in training. Mine countermeasures capability is provided by 13 offshore hunter/sweepers and 5 coastal minehunters. Amphibious lift for the Royal Marines is provided by 1 dock landing ship (with a second in reserve) and 5 tank landing ships (civil manned, and in peacetime employed on army freighting), supported by about 32 small amphibious craft.

Comprehensive support to the fleet is provided by 28 major auxiliaries including 5 replenishment and 4 support tankers, 2 multi-purpose fuel and ammunition ships, 3 ammunition and stores ships, 1 repair ship, 3 ocean tugs, 5 survey ships, 1 trials ship, 1 aviation training ship, 2 armament transports and the Royal Yacht. Second-line support is provided by about 200 harbour and coastal service craft and minor auxiliaries.

The Fleet Air Arm, 7,000 strong in 1995, has some 300 aircraft, in 19 operational, training and search-and-rescue squadrons, including 40 Sea Harrier vertical/short take-off and landing fighter aircraft, 70 Sea King and 76 Lynx anti-submarine helicopters, 10 Sea King airborne early warning helicopters and 36 Sea King (commando transports) and 70 miscellaneous support and training craft.

The total number of male and female personnel (including Royal Marines) was (in 1,000) on 31 March: 1992, 62·1; 1993, 59·4; 1994, 55·8; 1995, 50·9; 1996 (estimated), 49·8.

Air Force. In May 1912 the Royal Flying Corps first came into existence with military and naval wings, of which the latter became the independent Royal Naval Air Service in July 1914. On 2 Jan. 1918 an Air Ministry was formed, and on 1 April 1918 the Royal Flying Corps and the Royal Naval Air Service were amalgamated, under the Air Ministry, as the Royal Air Force (RAF).

In 1937 the units based on aircraft carriers and naval shore stations again passed to the operational and administrative control of the Admiralty, as the Fleet Air Arm. In 1964 control of the RAF became a responsibility of the Ministry of Defence.

The RAF is administered by the Air Force Board, of which the Secretary of State for Defence is Chairman. The Minister of State for the Armed Forces is Vice-Chairman, and normally acts as Chairman on behalf of the Secretary of State. Other members of the Board are the Minister of State for Defence Procurement, the Under-Secretary of State for Defence, the Chief of the Air Staff, Air Member for Personnel, Air Member for Logistics, Air Officer Commanding-in-Chief Strike Command, Controller of Aircraft and the Second Permanent Under-Secretary of State.

The RAF is organized into 3 commands: Strike Command, Personnel and Training Command and Logistics Command.

Strike Command is responsible for all of the RAF's frontline forces, although day-to-day control of most operations is delegated to its 3 Groups. No 1 Group is responsible for strike/attack, offensive air support, support helicopters and reconnaissance. Tornado GR1s and Tornado GR1As are used in the strike, attack and reconnaissance roles, while Tornado GR1Bs are used primarily in the maritime attack role. Jaguars are used in the attack, reconnaissance and light anti-shipping roles. Battlefield support forces comprise Harrier GR7s, as well as Chinook, Puma and Wessex helicopters. No 1 Group also operates Canberra aircraft in the strategic photographic reconnaissance role. No 11/18 Group controls the air defence forces, Tornado F3 fighters and Boeing E-3D Airborne Early Warning aircraft, together with ground environment radars, associated communications systems and the Ballistic Missile Early Warning System at Fylingdales. No 11/18 Group also controls the reserve force of Hawk trainers which, in wartime, would supplement the Tornado F3 fighters. Maritime air operations, together with the RAF's search and rescue flights, are also under the operational control of No 11/18 Group. A maritime patrol and anti-submarine warfare capability is provided by Nimrod aircraft, which also have a capability against surface ships. The search and rescue flights are equipped with Sea King helicopters. Additionally No 11/18 Group operates Nimrod Reconnaissance aircraft. No 38 Group is responsible for air-to-air refuelling and strategic air transport, which is carried out by VC10, Tristar and Hercules aircraft. No 38 Group also controls the aircraft of No 32 (The Royal) Squadron, comprising British Aerospace 146 and 125 aircraft and Wessex and Twin Squirrel helicopters. RAF forces in Germany, which are made up of Tornado GR1s, Harrier GR7s and Chinook and Puma helicopters, are under the day-to-day control of No 1 Group. The Military Air Traffic Operations organization also has the status of a Group.

The RAF Regiment, which is under the control of No 38 Group, has field squadrons in service with No 1 Group and short-range air defence squadrons armed with Rapier in service with No 1 Group and No 11/18 Group.

As well as the forces in Germany, the RAF has a flight of Tornado F3s, a flight of Hercules and a squadron of Chinook and Sea King helicopters based in the Falkland Islands, and a squadron of Wessex helicopters in both Hong Kong and Cyprus. In addition, Strike Command forces are deployed overseas in support of UN/WEU and Coalition operations.

Headquarters RAF Strike Command is based at RAF High Wycombe.

Personnel and Training Command was formed at RAF Innsworth on 1 April 1994.

The RAF College, which trains all candidates for commissions, is at Cranwell. The RAF Staff College at Bracknell provides all subsequent command and staff training for officers. The College is due to close with the creation of a new Joint Service Command and Staff College at Camberley in 1997. Each of the main training bases have Central Flying School squadrons. Proposals have been announced to establish a tri-Service Helicopter Flying School at RAF Shawbury in 1997. The Air Training Corps and the Air Sections of the Combined Cadet Force are under the administrative control of Personnel and Training Command. The closures of RAF Scampton, RAF Finningley and the Queen's University Air Squadron in Belfast are due to take place in 1996 and RAF Locking in 1998.

Personnel and Training Command is equipped with the following aircraft types: Bulldog and Slingsby Firefly as primary trainers, Tucano as basic trainers, Hawk as advanced trainers, Jetstreams for multi-engine pilot training, twin-jet Dominies for training navigators and other non-pilot aircrew, and Gazelle and Wessex helicopters.

Logistics Command was formed at RAF Brampton on 1 April 1994. The Command is responsible for providing the full range of logistics support activities to all RAF units worldwide and Joint Service support to Royal Navy and Army units for rationalized equipment ranges. It is responsible for: Support chain management, including the provisioning, storage, distribution and disposal of equipment; repair, overhaul, maintenance and modification programmes at 3rd and 4th line; provision and management of communications and information systems; RAF catering.

RAF personnel, 1 Jan. 1996, 68,164 (including 5,926 women). The Women's Royal Air Force (WRAF) was merged with the RAF in 1994. Since 1992 women have been eligible to fly combat aircraft. Total trained personnel in Jan. 1996, 65,964.

Brereton, J. M., *The British Soldier*. London, 1985
Jane's Fighting Ships. London, annual
McIntosh, M., *Managing British Defence*. London, 1990
Strawson, J., *Gentlemen in Khaki: the British Army, 1890–1990*. London, 1989

INTERNATIONAL RELATIONS

Membership. The UK is a member of the UN, Commonwealth, the EU, OECD, the Council of Europe, WEU and NATO.

ECONOMY

Budget. The fiscal year starts on 1 April. Until 1993 statements of revenue had been contained in the Budget presented annually in March, and expenditure in the previous year's Autumn Statement. The last March Budget (for 1993-94) was in 1993. Starting with that of Nov. 1993, Budgets have combined statements of revenue and expenditure, and are presented annually in Nov.

Revenue and expenditure for years ending 31 March, in £1m. sterling:

Revenue	*Estimated in the Budgets*	*Actual receipts into the Exchequer*
1993	229,800	223,300
1994	229,200	229,700
1995	252,400	252,500
1996	278,700	271,900

The Budget estimate of general government receipts for 1996–97 was £284,800m.

Expenditure	*Budget and supplementary estimates*	*Actual payments out of the Exchequer*
1993	258,500	259,900
1994	280,300	280,700
1995	291,800	288,900
1996	301,800	302,100

The Budget estimate of general government expenditure for 1996–97 was £308,300m.

Figures for general government expenditure, both actual and estimated, include a deduction for privatization proceeds. In 1995–96 this sum was £3,000m.

Public sector borrowing requirement (PSBR): 1995–96, £29,000m.; 1996–97, £22,400m.

Sources of revenue (in £1m.):	*Receipts 1994–95*	*Budget estimate 1995–96*	*Budget estimate 1996–97*
Inland Revenue:			
Income tax	63,100	68,900	70,200
Corporation tax	19,400	24,700	26,600
Petroleum revenue tax	700	900	1,000
Capital Gains tax	900	900	1,000

Sources of revenue (in £1m.):	Receipts 1994–95	Budget estimate 1995–96	Budget estimate 1996–97
Inland Revenue:			
Inheritance tax	1,400	1,500	1,500
Stamp duties	1,800	2,000	2,400
Total Inland Revenue	87,300	98,800	102,600
Customs and Excise:			
VAT	41,800	44,000	47,900
Fuel duties	14,000	15,500	17,400
Tobacco duties	7,400	7,200	7,700
Alcohol duties	5,500	5,500	5,700
Betting and gaming duties	1,200	1,600	1,700
Customs duties	2,000	2,300	2,400
Agricultural levies	200	100	200
Air passenger duty	100	300	300
Insurance premium tax	100	600	700
Landfill tax	–	–	100
Total Customs and Excise	72,300	77,400	84,100
Vehicle Excise duties	3,800	4,100	4,300
Oil royalties	500	600	500
Business rates	12,700	13,600	14,700
Social Security receipts	42,100	44,400	46,900
Council Tax	9,100	9,200	9,900
Interest and dividends	5,000	5,200	4,800
Other receipts	17,400	18,700	17,000

Major branches of expenditure for year ended 31 March 1996 and the estimates for the year 1996–97 (in £1m.):

	Expenditure 1995–96	Budget estimate 1996–97
Social Security	73,730	76,810
Cyclical social security[1]	14,000	13,900
Health	32,930	33,750
Defence	21,210	21,420
Overseas Development	2,370	2,290
Agriculture, Fisheries and Food	2,930	3,020
Trade and Industry	3,670	2,910
Transport	4,620	4,180
Housing	6,700	5,840
Environment	2,370	2,400
Home Office	6,600	6,520
Education and Employment	4,190[2]	4,040
Scotland	14,470	14,550
Wales	6,720	6,800
Northern Ireland	7,820	8,010
EU	2,890	2,300
Debt interest	20,500	22,300
Local authorities	74,400	74,500
Nationalized industries	–70	–840

[1] Jobseekers' Allowance and Income Support paid to persons of working age.
[2] Before 1995–96 Employment was treated separately.

A single graduated income tax came into operation on 6 April 1973.

Rates of Personal Tax from 6 April 1996	%
Income between	
£0–3,900 (lower rate)	20
£3,901–£25,500 (basic rate)	24
Over £25,500 (higher rate)	40

Income from interest on savings accounts is taxed at 20% for basic rate taxpayers and 40% for higher rate taxpayers.

Under the tax system, the amounts of the personal allowances are adjusted so that they retain their equivalent in relation to earned income. Independent taxation of husband and wife was introduced on 6 April 1990.

	1996–97
Allowances	£
Personal allowance	3,765
Married couple's allowance	1,790
Blind person's allowance	1,250
Age allowance (age 65 to 74):	
Single	4,910
Married couple's allowance	3,115
Age allowance (age 75 or over):	
Single	5,090
Married couple's allowance	3,155

There is an income limit of £15,200 for age-related allowances. Tax relief for the married couple's allowance is restricted to 15%. Tax relief for mortgage interest repayments is 15% (25% for those aged 65 or over). Mortgage protection, permanent health and long-term care insurance benefits are exempt from tax.

Deductions of tax under PAYE ('pay as you earn') extend over the full range of unified tax rates and not merely the basic rate. Similarly, assessment on business profits and on other income which was directly assessed to tax, such as rents and interest on bank deposits, are made by reference to the full scale of rates, including where appropriate the investment income surcharge.

The basic rate of 24% is the rate at which tax is deducted from payments of interest, etc., and corresponds under the corporation tax system, to the tax credit on dividends. Where an individual's total income is such that he is liable on this taxed investment income at rates exceeding 24%, or if his investment income is high enough to make him liable to the surcharge, the higher rate or surcharge liability on this taxed investment income will in general be assessed separately after the end of the tax year.

The assessment and collection of income tax was reformed from 1996–97 with the introduction of self assessment for non-PAYE taxpayers, estimated to number 9m. The main measures abolish the 'preceding year' basis of assessment for the self employed, and tax income as it arises from 1997–98, with a transitional year in 1996–97; align payment dates for assessed income tax from all sources and for capital gains tax; introduce separate assessment for partners; and introduce clear rules for filing tax returns, allowing taxpayers the option of calculating their own tax, and for the payment of tax, and clear sanctions for failing to comply with them.

Insurance Premium Tax. This was introduced from 1 Oct. 1994 at 2·5%. It does not apply to life insurance, pensions or export credit insurance.

Corporation Tax. Corporation Tax applies, with certain exceptions, to trades or businesses carried on by bodies corporate or by unincorporated societies or other bodies. The full rate of Corporation Tax was 33% for 1996–97. Small companies (i.e. with profits under £0·3m.), 1996–97, 24%.

Capital Gains Tax. Gains resulting from the disposal of capital assets (other than British Government and Government guaranteed securities and certain exempted forms of property such as a private car and personal residences) are taxed under the Finance Act 1965. In 1996–97 exemption was granted for all gains made in a financial year which in total did not exceed £6,300 and most trusts on the first £3,150. In 1988 the base was brought forward from 1965 to 1982. Persons selling their own businesses qualify for retirement relief (100% on the first £0·25m. of gains, 50% on £0·25m.–£1m.) at the age of 50.

Inheritance Tax. Transfers before 7 years of death, and between spouses, are exempt. From 1989 a flat rate of 40% was introduced with a threshold in 1996–97 of £200,000. Most family business assets were exempted in 1992–93.

Value Added Tax. Value Added Tax (VAT) was introduced from 1 April 1973 at the rate of 10% on the supply of goods (with certain exceptions) and services. It was raised to 17·5% from 1 April 1991. VAT was imposed on domestic fuel and power at 8% and was to have been imposed at the standard rate from 1 April 1995, but following a Government defeat in the House of Commons this second phase was withdrawn. The shortfall was made up by raising taxes on petrol, alcohol and tobacco. From 29 Nov. 1995 the turnover threshold above which traders are required to register became £47,000 per annum.

National Lottery. The National Lottery was launched in Nov. 1994 and is administered by a private company under the regulation of a State Director General. Distribution of net proceeds: Prizes, 50%; good causes (the arts, charities, millenium projects, national heritage and sport), 28%; tax, 12%; operator's costs and profit, 5%; retailers' commission, 5%. Spending of National Lottery money counts as general Government expenditure. It was expected to provide some £1,250m. in 1996–97 for good causes.

Local Taxation. The Community Charge ('poll tax') was introduced in Scotland in 1989 and in England and Wales in 1990, and was replaced by the Council Tax when the Local Government Finance Act came into force on 1 April 1993. For details of the Community Charge *see* THE STATESMAN'S YEAR-BOOK, 1993–94, p. 1339. The Council Tax reverts to the relative value of property within an individual authority as a basis for assessing the amount payable, but also takes account of personal circumstances to enable a discount of 25% for single households, with further reliefs available rebating liability by up to 100%. The value of residential property is assessed by the Inland Revenue within one of 8 valuation bands. Second residences are liable to 50% of the Council Tax. A uniform business rate applies nationally to business premises. 5-yearly revaluations of non-domestic properties began in 1995.

Local authority receipts for 1994–95 (and forecasts for 1995–96 and 1996–97) were £75,300m. (£77,500m. and £79,600m.), made up of: Council Tax, £8,800m. (£9,100m. and £10,000m.); current grants from central government (including non-domestic rate income), £56,500m. (£57,200m. and £58,400m.); capital grants from central government, £2,800m. (£3,300m. and £3,300m.); other, £7,300m. (£7,800m. and £7,900m.). Expenditure was £76,800m. (£78,400m. and £79,200m.), made up of: Current expenditure on goods and services, £51,800m. (£52,600m. and £54,000m.); current grants and subsidies, £13,800m. (£14,100m. and £14,700m.); interest, £4,200m. (£4,100m. and £4,100m.); capital expenditure before depreciation, £7,100m. (£7,700m. and £6,300m.).

Local authority spending is determined by the authorities themselves in the light of central government support, finance available from their own resources and the implications for local taxation. The government retains powers, however, to cap local authority budgets. The amount which the government thought local authorities in England, should spend on revenue expenditure—the Total Standard Spending (TSS)—was £42,660m. in 1994–95, £43,511m. for 1995–96 and £44,900m. in 1996–97.

Expenditure by local authorities (in £1m.):

	1994–95	*1995–96 estimate*	*1996–97 forecast*
Self-financed	11,761	12,300	12,500
Government-financed	61,254	62,100	62,000

In Scotland, revenue support grant replaced rate support grants when the Community Charge was introduced, and is now a component of Aggregate External Finance. For 1994–95 Aggregate External Finance amounted to £5,299m., for 1995–96 it was estimated at £5,320m. and for 1996–97 it was planned to be £5,380m.

Gross National Product:

	1990	*1991*	*1992*	*1993*	*1994*
Expenditure (£*1m.*)					
Consumers' expenditure	347,527	365,057	382,696	405,639	428,084
Central and local government final consumption	112,934	124,205	132,378	138,224	144,084
Gross domestic fixed capital formation	106,776	96,534	92,892	94,715	100,075
Value of physical increase in stocks and work in progress	−1,118	−5,069	−1,992	−197	3,303

Gross National Product:

	1990	*1991*	*1992*	*1993*	*1994*
Expenditure (£*1m.*)					
Total domestic expenditure at market prices	566,119	580,727	605,974	638,381	675,546
Exports of goods and services	133,284	134,148	139,827	157,999	173,925
Less Imports of goods and services	–148,285	–140,775	–149,164	–166,266	–180,729
Less Taxes on expenditure	–78,298	–84,816	–87,679	–91,361	–96,950
Subsidies	6,066	5,995	6,108	7,458	7,224
Gross domestic product at factor cost	478,886	494,824	514,594	546,120	579,140
Factor incomes (£*1m.*)					
Income from employment	312,358	328,257	341,009	352,896	...
Income from self-employment [1]	61,138	58,533	58,060	61,346	...
Gross trading profits of companies [1]	64,748	61,409	64,574	73,397	...
Gross trading surplus of public corporations [1]	3,801	1,809	1,813	3,415	...
Gross trading surplus of other public enterprises [1]	12	–36	89	294	...
Rent [2]	38,569	43,021	46,846	52,872	...
Total domestic income before providing for depreciation and stock appreciation	485,017	497,356	516,598	548,162	...
Less Stock appreciation	–6,131	–2,522	–2,216	–2,359	...
Income adjustment	–	0	212	317	...
Gross domestic product at factor cost	478,886	494,824	514,594	546,120	579,140
Net property income from abroad	1,630	320	5,777	3,062	10,519
Gross national product	480,516	495,144	520,371	549,182	589,659
Less Capital consumption	–61,200	–63,510	–63,984	–65,023	–68,150
National income	419,316	431,634	456,387	484,159	521,509

[1] Before providing for depreciation and stock appreciation.
[2] Before providing for depreciation.

Currency. The unit of currency is the *pound sterling* (GBP) of 100 *pence.* (Before decimalization on 15 Feb. 1971 £1 = 20 shillings (*s*) of 12 pence (*d*). A gold standard was adopted in 1816, the sovereign or twenty-shilling piece weighing 7·98805 grammes 0·916⅔ fine. Currency notes for £1 and 10*s*. were first issued by the Treasury in 1914, replacing the circulation of sovereigns. The issue of £1 and 10*s*. notes was taken over by the Bank of England in 1928. 10*s*. notes were withdrawn in 1970 and £1 notes (in England and Wales) in 1988. The UK is a member of the EU European Monetary System (EMS), but on 16 Sept. 1992 it suspended its membership of the Exchange Rate Mechanism (ERM), which it had entered on 8 Oct. 1990. Inflation was 2·9% in Dec. 1994 (1·9% in Dec. 1993). In March 1996, £1 = US$ 1·53; US$1 = £0·65; DM1 = £0·44.

Coinage. The sovereign (£1) weighs 123·27447 grains, or 7·98805 grammes, 0·916⅔ (or eleven-twelfths) fine, and consequently it contains 113·00159 grains or 7·32238 grammes of fine gold. There are coins of £1 (22·5 mm diameter, 9·5 grammes weight); 50p (equilateral curved heptagon, 30 mm diameter, 13·5 grammes); 20p (equilateral curved heptagon 21·4 mm diameter, 5 grammes); 10p (24·5 mm, 6·5 grammes); 5p (18·0 mm, 3·25 grammes); 2p (25·9 mm, 7·12 grammes) and 1p (20·3 mm, 3·56 grammes). The Decimal Currency Act, 1967 and the Royal Proclamation of 20 Dec. 1968 determined the specification and design for a 50p coin. The 1967 Act and the Coinage Act, 1971, determined the specification of the 10p, 5p, 2p, 1p and ½p coins. The Royal Proclamation of 14 Feb. 1968 determined the new designs for these coins. The Royal Proclamation of 15 July 1992 required that the 2p and 1p be made of mild steel coated with copper. The Decimal Currency Act, 1969, provided that the coins of the Queen's Maundy Money should continue to be made in silver to a millesimal fineness of 925.

By Proclamation dated 28 July 1971, which came into force on 30 Aug. 1971, the crown, double-florin, the florin, the shilling and the sixpence were treated as coins of the new currency and as being of the denominations respectively of 25, 20, 10, 5 and 2½ new pence. The sixpence was demonetized on 30 June 1980, the ½p on 31 Dec. 1984, the 5p/shilling on 31 Dec. 1990 and the 10p/florin on 30 June 1993. A smaller 5p coin was issued on 27 June 1990 and a smaller 10p coin on 30 Sept. 1992.

The Coinage Act, 1971, specified that the legal tender limits for coins were: Gold coins (face value only), for payment of any amount; coins of cupro-nickel and silver of denominations of more than 10p, for payment of any amount not exceeding £10; coins of cupro-nickel and silver of not more than 10p, for payment of any amount not exceeding £5; coins of bronze and copper-plated steel, for payment of any amount not exceeding 20p. The £1 coin is legal tender for any amount.

There are in addition Britannia gold bullion coins with a face value of £100, £50, £20 and £10, and commemorative £5 crowns and £2 coins.

Coins in circulation at 31 Dec. 1995: £1, 1,033m.; 50p, 480m.; 20p, 1,543m.; 10p, 1,360m.; 5p, 2,800m.; 2p, 4,135m.; 1p, 6,799m.

Bank-notes. The Bank of England issues notes in denominations of £5, £10, £20 and £50 for the amount of the fiduciary issue. Under the provisions of the Currency Act, 1983, which came into force on 28 March 1983, the amount of the fiduciary issue was limited to £13,500m., but this figure can be altered by direction of HM Treasury on the advice of the Bank of England.

In Scotland the Bank of Scotland, Clydesdale Bank and the Royal Bank of Scotland have note-issuing powers. There is a £1 note in Scotland.

The total amount of Bank of England notes issued at 28 Dec. 1994 was £20,460m., of which £20,448m. represented notes with other banks and the public, and £12m. notes in the Banking Department of the Bank of England.

Banking and Finance. The Bank of England, Threadneedle Street, London, is the Government's banker and the 'banker's bank'. It has the sole right of note issue in England and Wales and manages the National Debt. It was founded by Royal Charter in 1694 and nationalized in 1946. The capital stock has, since 1 March 1946, been held by HM Treasury. The *Governor* (appointed for 5-year terms) is Eddie George (b. 1938; took office 1993).

The statutory Bank Return is published weekly. End-Dec. figures for the past 4 years are as follows (in £1m.):

	Notes in circulation	*Notes and coin in Banking Department*	*Public deposits (government)*	*Other deposits* [1]
1992	18,558	12	99	5,649
1993	19,378	12	3,300	7,890
1994	20,448	12	1,027	5,198

[1] Including Special Deposits.

Official reserves of gold and convertible currencies, SDR and reserve position in the IMF at the end of Dec. 1993 were US$42,926m. The value of paper-based credit transfers for 1993 was 432·2m. (volumes); of paperless credit transfers, 935·7m. (volumes); of direct debits, 1,046m. (volumes).

Major British Banking Groups' statistics at 31 Dec. 1995: Total deposits (sterling and currency), £566,487m.; sterling market loans, £91,606m.; market loans (sterling and currency), £164,532m.; advances (sterling and currency), £346,633m.; sterling investments, £44,122m.

National Savings Bank. Statistics for 1993 and 1994:

	Ordinary accounts		*Investment accounts*	
	1993	*1994*	*1993*	*1994*
Accounts open at 31 Dec.	15,955,955 [1]	15,988,061 [1]	4,708,030	4,590,238
Amounts—	*£1,000*	*£1,000*	*£1,000*	*£1,000*
Received	635,100	636,912	1,305,885	1,439,905
Interest credited	46,231 [2]	39,841 [2]	556,065	519,585
Paid	671,211	680,871	1,674,217	1,813,168
Due to depositors at 31 Dec.	1,438,116	1,433,998	9,163,522	9,309,844
Average amount due to each depositor in active accounts	£90·13	£89·69	£1,946·36	£2,028·18

[1] Excluding non-computerized accounts, amounting to £99·9m. in 1993 and £100m. in 1994.

[2] The interest credited to depositors for the Ordinary account for 1994 has altered. Interest of 3·25% a year is payable on accounts with a minimum balance of £500 and 2% on accounts with a minimum balance of less than £500. Interest is earned on each whole pound on deposit for complete calendar months.

The amount due to depositors on Ordinary Accounts on 1 Jan. 1996 was approximately £1,438,748,142 and in Investment Accounts £9,279,701,995.

There are stock exchanges in Belfast, Birmingham, Glasgow and Manchester, which function mainly as representative offices for the London Stock Exchange (called International Stock Exchange until May 1991). In July 1991 the 91 shareholders voted unanimously for a new memorandum and articles of association which devolves power to a wider range of participants in the securities industry and replaces the Stock Exchange Council with a 14-member board.

Roberts, R. and Kynaston, D. (eds.) *The Bank of England: Money, Power and Influence, 1694–1994*. OUP, 1995

Weights and Measures. Conversion to the metric system, which replaced the imperial system, became obligatory on 1 Oct. 1995. The use of the pint for milk deliveries and bar sales, and use of miles and yards in road signs, is exempt indefinitely, and the use of the pound (weight) in selling greengrocery is exempt until 1999.

ENERGY AND NATURAL RESOURCES

Electricity. The Electricity Act of 1989 implemented the restructuring and transfer to the private sector of the electricity supply industry.

The Office of Electricity Regulation (Offer) was set up under the Act to protect consumer interests following privatization.

Generators. Under the provisions of the 1989 Electricity Act, National Power and PowerGen took over the fuel-fired and hydro-electric power stations, and were privatized in 1991. Nuclear Electric, responsible for operating the 12 nuclear power stations, and Scottish Nuclear were merged as a single holding company in 1996 with 2 new operating subsidiaries, Magnox Electric and British Energy. These were scheduled for privatization in 1996. Under licence generating companies may also be involved in electricity supply.

A levy (Non-Fossil Fuel Obligation) is being imposed on generators until 1998 to fund the decommissioning of ageing nuclear plant and finance renewable energy sources, mainly wind generation, which in 1994 supplied 1·5% of demand.

Suppliers. The 12 Area Electricity Boards were replaced under the 1989 Electricity Act by 12 successor companies which were privatized in 1990. These are Eastern Group; East Midlands Electricity; London Electricity; Manweb; Midlands Electricity; Northern Electric; NORWEB; SEEBOARD; Southern Electric; SWALEC; South Western Electricity; Yorkshire Electricity. The companies are responsible for maintaining and operating their local distribution networks, and have a statutory duty to supply electricity to their tariff customers. Their main business, therefore, is in electricity supply. Most of the companies are involved in the retailing of electrical goods and electrical contracting. Some have diversified into other business activities.

The *Electricity Association* is the trade association of the UK electricity companies, providing a forum for members to discuss matters of common interest, a collective voice for the electricity industry when needed and specialist research and professional services.

The National Grid Company is responsible for operating the transmission system and for co-ordinating the operation of power stations connected to it. The company also operates the cross-Channel link with France and the interconnection with the Scottish power system.

In Scotland there are 3 main electricity companies. ScottishPower and Scottish Hydro-Electric are vertically-integrated companies carrying out generation, transmission, distribution and supply of electricity within their areas. Scottish Nuclear, responsible for operating the 2 Scottish nuclear power stations was merged with Nuclear Electric in 1996.

The electricity industry accounts for 1·5% of GDP. Output capacity of all UK power stations as at the end of March 1995 was 68,937 MW, of which 61% was conventional fossil generation, 17·5% was nuclear, 12·5% combined-cycle gas turbine, 6% hydro-electric, 2% gas-turbine and oil-engine and about 0·5% other renewable. 284,439,000 MWh were supplied to 26·2m. customers in 1994, of which domestic users took 35%, industrial users 33% and commercial and other users 32%. Electricity generated in 1994, 302,807m. kWh.

Electricity Association. *UK Electricity*. Annual

Oil. Production in 1,000 tonnes, in 1993 (and 1992): Throughput of crude and process oils, 96,273 (92,334); refinery use, 6,383 (6,080). Refinery output: Gases, 1,737 (1,755); naphtha, 2,696 (3,040); motor spirit, 28,394 (27,980); kerosene, 11,048 (10,131); diesel oil, 27,361 (25,649); fuel oil, 13,183 (12,388); lubricating oils, 1,264 (1,163); bitumen, 2,450 (2,336). Total output of refined products, 89,584 (85,783). Crude oil production, 1993, 100·1m. tonnes; 1994 (provisional), 126·9m. tonnes. Estimated production, 1995, 2,672,000 bbls. a day.

Gas. Following the Gas Act of 1986, British Gas plc became the successor company to the British Gas Corporation. It conducts its operations under 3 business units: the UK gas business, exploration and production worldwide and Global Gas. The UK gas business has a headquarters and 12 regions.

British Gas is expanding its exploratory and productive activities (in oil as well as gas) both in the UK and overseas, and in 1993 was active in some 20 countries. The main aim of Global Gas is to participate in the development of gas business and the design, construction and operation of power generation facilities in the UK and abroad.

In 1993, British Gas sold 569,000m. kwh of gas to over 18m. customers. Its turnover totalled £10,386m. and it employed 76,500 persons. Gas reserves are some 590,000m. cu. metres.

The Office of Gas Supply (Ofgas) is a ‘regulator’ charged with protecting consumer interests after privatization. During 1994 the UK gas operations were scheduled for reorganization into 5 business streams: Transportation and Storage; Public Gas Supply; Contract Trading; Retailing; and Service and Installation. Transportation and Storage and Public Gas Supply continue to be regulated by Ofgas. The government propose to open up to competition 5% of the (largely domestic) market served by Public Gas Supply in each year 1996 and 1997, and leading ultimately to a completely open market.

Wind. In 1993 there were 19 wind farms with a total of about 400 wind turbines for the generation of electricity.

Water. The Water Act of Sept. 1989 privatized the 10 water authorities in England and Wales: Anglian; North West; Northumbrian; Severn Trent; South West; Southern; Thames; Welsh; Wessex; Yorkshire. The Act also inaugurated the National Rivers Authority, with environmental and resource management responsibilities, and the ‘regulator’ Office of Water Services (Ofwat), charged with protecting consumer interests.

In Scotland water supply is the responsibility of the Regional and Island local authorities. 7 river purification boards are responsible for environmental management.

Minerals. Coal. Legislation to privatize the coal industry was introduced in 1994 and the mining assets were sold to the private sector in Dec. Non-mining assets (land, smokeless fuel products, distribution networks) are being sold separately. The mining assets comprised 16 operating deep mines and 32 opencast sites and 7 mothballed pits. Private mining operators are to be licensed by a newly-established Coal Authority. The number of British Coal Corporation (BCC) producing collieries at 25 March 1995 was 15 (65 in 1991). Statistics of the coalmining industry for recent years:

Output, 1m. tonnes:	*1990*	*1991*	*1992*	*1993*
Deep-mined coal	72·9	73·4	65·8	50·5
Opencast coal	18·8	19·4	18·4	17·0
Recovered slurry, etc.	1·7	2·2	0·6	0·7
Employees, 1,000 [1]:	60·9	52·3	38·4	19·4
Output per shift (in tonnes):	4·7	5·3	6·3	8·8
Home consumption (in 1m. tonnes):	108·3	107·5	100·6	87·5
Electricity supply	84·5	84·0	79·0	66·2
Coke ovens	10·9	10·0	9·0	8·5
Industry	5·7	6·0	6·1	5·3
Domestic users	4·3	4·8	4·2	5·2

[1] At BCC collieries.

Stocks of coal at the end of 1993 amounted to 45·4m. tonnes, including 29·9m. tonnes distributed, 12·2m. tonnes at collieries and 3·3m. tonnes at opencast sites.

BCC's production of coke (including coke breeze), 1990–91, 1m. tonnes.

Output of non-fuel minerals in Great Britain, 1993 (in 1,000 tonnes): Limestone, 90,069; sandstone, 12,100; igneous rock, 49,209; clay and shale, 10,891; industrial sand, 3,587; chalk, 9,076; china clay, 2,852; sand and gravel, 89,470.

The UK is a major producer of steel. Output in recent years (in 1m. tonnes):

	Pig-iron	*Crude steel*	*Finished steel products*	*Home consumption Crude steel equivalent*
1992	11·7	16·2	13·0	13·5
1993	11·6	16·6	13·3	13·2
1994	11·9	17·3	14·4	...

The number of UK employees at 31 Dec. 1993 was some 39,100. British Steel plc produces about 75% of the UK's production of crude steel, whilst some 40 other members of the British Independent Steel Producers Association (BISPA) mainly concentrate on wire, engineering and stainless products.

Production of non-ferrous metals (in 1,000 tonnes) in 1992 (and 1993): Refined copper, 42·1 (46·5); refined lead, 346·8 (363·8); tin ore, 2 (2); primary aluminium, 244·4 (239·1); slab zinc, 96·8 (102·4).

Agriculture. In 1992 (and 1993) agricultural land in the UK totalled (in 1,000 ha) 18,411 (18,530), comprising common grazing, 1,231 (1,229), and agricultural holdings, 17,180 (17,301). Land use of the latter: All grasses 6,759 (6,775); crops, 4,993 (4,566); rough grazing, 4,592 (4,610); bare fallow, 46 (47); other, 789 (740). Area sown to crops: Cereals, 3,493 (3,031); fodder crops, 340 (388); horticultural crops, 198 (177); others, 798 (787).

The number of workers employed in agriculture in the UK was, in June 1993 (in 1,000), 255·8. Of these, 167·3 (13·6 females) were engaged full-time, 57·3 (25·5 females) part-time, and 85 (30·4 females) were seasonal or casual workers. These figures do not include farmers, partners, directors or their spouses. There were some 244,300 farm holdings in 1994, about 66% owner-occupied. Average size of holdings, 70·1 ha.

Principal crops in the UK:

	Wheat	Barley	Oats	Potatoes	Sugar-beet	Oilseed rape
			Area (1,000 ha)			
1990	2,013	1,515	107	177	194	–
1991	1,980	1,393	103	177	196	–
1992	2,072	1,309	101	179	197	421
1993	1,759	1,164	92	170	197	418
1994	1,811	1,106	109	164	195	496
			Total product (1,000 tonnes)			
1990	14,033	7,911	530	6,480	7,900	–
1991	14,363	7,627	523	6,279	...	–
1992	14,092	7,366	504	7,826	...	1,166
1993	12,890	6,038	479	7,065	8,988	1,136
1994	13,164	5,862	606	6,445	8,016	1,265

Horticultural crops. 1993 output (in 1,000 tonnes): Cabbage, 660; carrots, 638; onions, 346; tomatoes, 134; apples, 276; soft fruit, 81.

Livestock in the UK as at June in each year (in 1,000):

	1989	1990	1991	1992	1993
Cattle	11,977	12,057	11,866	11,778	11,751
(dairy)	(2,865)	(2,847)	(2,770)	(2,682)	(2,667)
(beef)	(1,495)	(1,599)	(1,666)	(1,699)	(1,751)
Sheep	42,967	43,789	43,621	43,973	43,901
Pigs	7,509	7,447	7,596	7,608	7,756
Poultry	120,198	124,384	127,228	123,992	...

Livestock products, 1992 (in 1,000 tonnes): Milk products, 868; animal meat, 2,255; poultry meat, 1,069.

In March 1996 the government acknowledged the possibility that bovine spongiform encephalopathy (BSE) might be transmitted to humans as a form of Creutzfeldt-Jakob disease via the food chain. Cases of BSE in cattle in the UK: 1988, 1,954; 1989, 6,955; 1990, 13,042; 1991, 22,939; 1992, 35,269; 1993, 37,020; 1994, 26,087.

Forestry. On 31 March 1995 the area of productive woodland in Britain was 2,182,000 ha, of which the Forestry Commission managed 815,000 ha and the private sector 1,367,000 ha. The Forestry Commission employed 6,650 staff in 1995. In addition a further 10,400 were employed in private forestry with an estimated 11,215 engaged in the wood processing industry. In 1994–95 a total of 7·7m. cu. metres of timber was thinned and felled.

New planting (1994–95), 19,400 ha (2,900, Forestry Commission; 18,500, private woodlands).

Forestry Commission. *Forestry Facts and Figures.* Annual
James, N. D. G., *A History of English Forestry.* London, 1981

Fisheries. Quantity (in 1,000 tonnes) and value (in £1,000) of fish of British taking landed in Great Britain (excluding salmon and sea-trout):

Quantity	1989	1990	1991	1992	1993
Wet fish	580·4	528·4	477·7	505·6	536·2
Shell fish	91·3	93·1	84·6	108·0	102·5
	671·8	621·5	562·3	613·7	638·7
Value					
Wet fish	299,354	329,491	310,042	309,470	317,800
Shell fish	94,992	101,012	86,427	95,743	107,163
	394,346	430,503	396,469	405,213	423,963

In Dec. 1993 the fishing fleet of England and Wales comprised 9,588 registered vessels and that of Scotland, 2,495 vessels. Major fishing ports: (England) Fleetwood, Grimsby, Hull, Lowestoft, North Shields; (Wales) Milford Haven; (Scotland) Aberdeen, Mallaig, Lerwick, Peterhead.

Domestic Tourism. In 1994, 110m. residents made trips within the UK, passing

416·5m. nights in accommodation and spending £14,495m. Of these, 63m. were holiday-makers spending £9,345m.

INDUSTRY. In 1994 there were 184,182 manufacturing units, of which 324 employed 1,000 or over persons, and 129,847, 9 or fewer. Statistics (UK, unless otherwise stated) of a cross-section of industrial production (in 1,000 tonnes):

	1990	*1991*	*1992*	*1993*
Sulphuric acid	1,996	1,852	...	...
Synthetic rubber	292	258	271	...
Cotton single yarn	23	13	9	7·3
Woollen yarn	73	66	68	67
Man-made fibres (rayon, nylon, etc.)	273	267	262	...
Cement	14,740	12,297	11,006	...
Fertilizers	4,892	4,474	3,733	2,216
Motor cars (units)	1,295,160	1,236,900	1,291,880	1,375,524

Engineering. Manufacturers' sales (in £1m.) for 1992 (and 1991): Motor vehicles and engines, 13,565 (12,170); railway and tramway vehicles, 868 (799); boilers and process plant, 2,265 (2,308); mechanical lifting and handling equipment, 2,471 (2,612); refrigerating, space-heating, ventilating and air conditioning equipment, 1,955 (2,415); construction and earth-moving equipment, 1,120 (1,700), wheeled tractors, 1,041 (865); industrial (including marine) engines, 1,220 (1,422).

Electrical Goods. Manufacturers' sales (in £1m.) for 1992 (and 1991): Radio and electronic capital goods, 3,479 (3,882); basic electrical equipment, 3,999 (3,770); radio and electronic data capital goods, 3,479 (3,882); telephone and telegraph apparatus and equipment, 1,615 (2,354); domestic electrical appliances, 1,589 (1,815).

Textile Manufacturers. Production of woven cloth for 1992 (and 1993): Cotton (1m. metres), 142 (109); man-made fibres (1m. metres), 181 (191); woven woollen and worsted fabrics (1m. sq. metres), deliveries, 72 (70).

Construction. Total value (in £1m.) of constructional work in Great Britain in 1993 (and 1992) was 46,323 (51,078), including new work, 23,556 (27,713), of which housing, 6,628 (5,719). Housing for public authorities, 5,439 (4,933); for private sector, 7,370 (8,049).

Labour. In June 1994 the UK workforce (*i.e.* all persons in employment plus the claimant unemployed) totalled (in 1,000) 27,875 (12,179 females), of whom 25,232 (11,559 females) were in employment, 21,397 (10,661 females) were employees, 3,266 (814 females) were self-employed and 250 (18 females) were in HM Forces. UK employees by form of employment in 1994 (in 1,000): Agriculture, forestry and fishing, 266; energy and water supply, 313; manufacturing industry, 4,328; construction, 786; distributive and catering trades, 4,668; transport and communications, 1,231; business and finance, 2,707; public administration, 1,372; education, 1,901; health, 1,619; other services, 1,722. Registered unemployed in UK as at July (in 1,000; figures adjusted for seasonality and discontinuities): 1990, 1,612 (females, 423); 1991, 2,294 (554); 1992, 2,723 (634); 1993, 2,912 (674); 1994, 2,632. In Dec. 1992, 955,600 persons (165,200 females) had been unemployed for more than a year. In July 1994 there were 157,000 vacancies at Jobcentres.

Workers (in 1,000) involved in industrial stoppages (and working days lost): 1990, 298 (1·9m.); 1991, 176 (0·76m.); 1992, 148 (0·53m.); 1993, 385 (0·69m.).

The Wages Councils set up in 1909 to establish minimum rates of pay (in 1992 of 2·5m. workers) were abolished in 1993.

Trade Unions. In Jan. 1995 there were 68 unions affiliated to the Trades Union Congress (TUC) with a total membership of 6,898,106 (7,298,262 in 1994) (2·6m. of them women). The unions affiliated to the TUC in 1994 ranged in size from UNISON with 1·4m. members, to the Sheffield Wool Shear Workers' Union with 13 members. The 4 largest unions, however, account for more than half the total membership. In 1994, 62% of public sector employees and 23% of private sector employees were unionized. 48% of employees were in workplaces where trade unions were recognized for collective bargaining.

The TUC's executive body, the General Council, is elected at the annual Congress. Congress consists of representatives of all unions according to the size of the organization, and is the principal policy-making body.

The General Secretary (John Monks, b. 1945) is elected by the Congress but is not subject to annual re-election. The TUC draws up policies and promotes and publicizes them. It makes representations to government, employers and international bodies. The TUC also carries out research and campaigns and provides a range of services to unions including courses for union representatives. In March 1994 it abolished all its specialist committees, reduced General Council meetings to 6 a year and established an Executive Committee to meet monthly, its aim being to concentrate resources on campaigns and services for unions.

The TUC is affiliated to the International Confederation of Free Trade Unions, the Trade Union Advisory Committee of OECD, the Commonwealth Trade Union Council and the European Trade Union Confederation. The TUC provides a service of trade union education. It provides members to serve, with representatives of employers, on the managing boards of such bodies as the Health and Safety Commission and the Advisory, Conciliation and Arbitration Service.

Clegg, H. A., *A History of British Trade Unions since 1889* [until 1951]. 3 vols. Oxford, 1994
Pelling, H., *A History of British Trade Unionism.* 5th ed. London, 1992.
Willman, P. *et al., Union Business: Trade Union Organization and Financial Reform in the Thatcher Years.* CUP, 1993

FOREIGN ECONOMIC RELATIONS

Commerce. Value of the imports and exports of merchandise (excluding bullion and specie and foreign merchandise transhipped under bond) of the UK for 6 recent years (in £1,000):

	Total imports	*Total exports*		*Total imports*	*Total exports*
1989	120,787,729	93,249,123	1992	125,843,872	108,289,964
1990	126,165,755	103,910,969	1993	137,403,703	120,935,514
1991	118,871,355	104,818,449	1994	148,360,300	133,860,500

The value of goods imported is generally taken to be that at the port and time of entry, including all incidental expenses (cost, insurance and freight) up to the landing on the quay. For goods consigned for sale, the market value in this country is required and recorded in the returns. For exports, the value at the port of shipment (including the charges of delivering the goods on board) is taken. Imports are entered as from the country whence the goods were consigned to the UK, which may, or may not, be the country whence they were last shipped. Exports are credited to the country of ultimate destination as declared by the exporters.

Until 1992 all overseas trade statistics were compiled from Customs declarations. With the inception of the Single Market on 1 Jan. 1993, however, the requirement for Customs declarations in intra-EU trade was removed; trade figures for EU countries since 1993 are compiled from VAT returns. The totals given in the table below include figures for 'Below Threshold Trade' (minimal) and a non-response estimate.

In 1995 the UK's trade with non-EU countries was: Imports, £75,143,978; exports, £64,705,195.

Provisional figures for trade by countries and groups of countries (in £1,000):

	Imports from		*Exports to*	
EU countries	*1993*	*1994*	*1993*	*1994*
EU	67,482,800	74,780,300	63,365,000	63,506,900
Austria	971,100	1,017,900	911,700	1,034,900
Belgium and Luxembourg	6,123,700	6,742,800	6,429,700	6,971,700
Denmark and Faroe Islands	1,954,100	2,024,400	1,476,200	1,685,000
Finland	1,904,700	2,253,300	1,129,700	1,297,300
France	12,555,700	14,343,000	11,100,000	12,779,100
Germany	18,349,100	20,862,400	14,641,300	16,389,100
Greece	296,900	331,900	830,700	871,700
Ireland	4,951,900	5,529,200	5,803,100	6,447,000
Italy	6,152,800	6,843,000	5,572,100	6,461,600
Netherlands	8,236,000	9,471,100	7,594,900	9,057,200

	Imports from		Exports to	
EU countries—(contd.)	*1993*	*1994*	*1993*	*1994*
Portugal, Azores and Madeira	1,143,200	1,201,900	1,259,000	1,173,600
Spain	2,954,000	3,439,000	3,994,500	4,749,400
Sweden	3,622,600	4,159,900	2,892,100	3,348,000
Other foreign countries	*1994*	*1995*	*1994*	*1995*
Europe—				
EEA/EFTA	16,197,106	9,734,828	10,266,611	4,896,313
Albania	220	1,017	5,607	7,555
Andorra	298	8	12,070	13,043
Belarus	12,035	20,981	11,097	22,570
Bosnia-Hercegovina	191	240	3,120	4,084
Bulgaria	69,927	118,550	86,138	104,224
Croatia	41,238	36,725	142,338	231,512
Czech Republic	278,301	321,497	374,453	567,923
Estonia	58,830	111,840	15,285	29,665
Hungary	240,075	371,571	259,189	295,859
Iceland	239,275	251,887	109,693	138,103
Latvia	222,378	170,411	30,696	40,058
Lithuania	155,387	173,228	24,080	49,435
Macedonia	5,897	5,323	14,166	18,079
Moldova	793	301	1,686	2,248
Norway	3,709,666	4,325,432	2,020,878	1,998,499
Poland	544,920	638,077	702,711	944,672
Romania	146,375	173,844	127,059	176,770
Russia	804,817	965,870	707,599	870,387
Slovakia	56,654	67,509	44,660	76,764
Slovenia	93,529	113,956	89,690	122,397
Switzerland and Liechtenstein	4,817,153	5,157,507	2,455,047	2,759,325
Turkey	628,109	794,890	813,522	1,157,777
Ukraine	18,072	22,941	86,284	111,106
Yugoslavia	44	560	4,253	9,970
Africa—				
Algeria	182,853	244,279	47,257	64,277
Angola	12,173	22,408	23,681	29,387
Burundi	4,251	3,670	3,288	3,339
Cameroon	34,889	31,328	15,452	25,234
Côte d'Ivoire	65,958	101,737	27,057	49,428
Egypt	252,203	246,619	368,000	383,541
Ethiopia	13,128	15,928	48,236	53,337
Liberia	254	544	8,510	8,456
Libya	148,151	131,787	194,905	227,369
Mali	477	225	10,841	24,074
Mauritania	10,978	14,579	9,949	6,026
Morocco	200,583	253,752	193,665	271,114
Mozambique	2,903	1,922	35,489	13,274
Rwanda	1,666	1,841	2,542	4,825
Senegal	7,625	8,485	20,933	32,217
Sudan	7,301	10,183	45,603	44,222
Tunisia	46,000	55,690	81,056	83,667
Zaïre	10,973	11,350	12,058	15,671
Asia and Oceania—				
Afghanistan	4,096	1,165	7,830	7,156
Bahrain	25,380	26,379	150,378	150,757
Burma	14,004	9,283	13,011	15,244
China	1,641,798	1,937,869	844,865	824,403
China (Taiwan)	1,580,880	1,726,761	735,287	961,933
Fiji	80,642	82,020	6,179	6,770
Indonesia	782,546	903,867	366,035	525,499
Iran	132,650	125,834	289,062	332,614
Iraq	122	164	9,581	5,044
Israel	572,375	692,156	1,031,644	1,108,455
Japan	8,841,577	9,613,810	2,991,159	3,782,955
Jordan	24,034	20,894	114,716	119,597
Korea (South)	1,096,209	1,561,755	970,978	1,153,116
Kuwait	239,359	151,377	312,037	550,870

	Imports from		*Exports to*	
Foreign countries—(contd.)	*1994*	*1995*	*1994*	*1995*
Asia and Oceania—(contd.)				
Lebanon	7,282	14,198	138,616	175,132
Oman	78,273	74,232	362,129	447,922
Philippines	244,346	352,425	355,181	432,397
Qatar	7,499	14,950	127,575	146,289
Saudi Arabia	739,601	720,783	1,515,252	1,644,356
Syria	97,990	89,768	101,088	84,593
Thailand	913,135	1,039,849	745,587	836,622
United Arab Emirates	230,670	281,041	1,113,578	1,184,136
America—				
Argentina	170,970	252,265	224,942	233,682
Bolivia	16,780	14,732	10,147	17,042
Brazil	919,360	986,520	525,240	674,502
Chile	194,555	299,959	152,839	170,949
Colombia	191,449	174,109	231,445	145,244
Costa Rica	76,795	78,515	20,930	23,271
Cuba	10,634	8,184	26,456	19,160
Dominican Republic	20,687	24,343	24,708	27,946
Ecuador	22,891	20,390	65,290	52,825
El Salvador	7,200	3,419	19,217	22,737
Guatemala	14,683	14,898	22,886	31,103
Haiti	539	1,254	7,754	13,466
Honduras	19,157	18,130	13,861	15,537
Mexico	239,740	298,124	389,299	276,753
Nicaragua	5,185	8,265	3,969	7,334
Panama	7,139	2,553	48,614	67,975
Paraguay	3,321	3,468	48,935	66,430
Peru	112,911	122,645	44,580	57,500
Puerto Rico	77,236	81,961	309,154	466,196
Uruguay	52,173	62,379	51,546	56,833
USA	17,727,680	20,268,863	16,783,484	17,949,473
Venezuela	133,589	204,167	196,787	178,784
Total, foreign countries (including some not specified above)	59,798,856	58,285,098	49,365,737	47,456,375
Commonwealth countries				
In Europe—				
Cyprus	120,857	156,451	245,192	307,438
Gibraltar	4,819	10,598	74,866	79,579
Malta	75,096	79,790	205,463	284,346
In Africa—				
West Africa:				
Gambia	4,638	3,119	16,521	13,591
Ghana	138,814	163,812	190,625	240,081
Nigeria	124,577	181,038	454,911	431,509
Sierra Leone	19,743	4,774	20,241	26,319
Southern Africa:				
Botswana	19,618	23,647	22,461	25,837
Lesotho	1,605	399	665	1,324
Malawi	25,816	16,188	19,594	13,449
Namibia	26,723	26,635	4,530	5,983
South Africa	970,718	1,113,064	1,410,878	1,830,397
Swaziland	42,034	39,714	3,207	3,033
Zambia	13,038	19,460	44,523	49,819
Zimbabwe	145,640	149,344	104,690	87,696
East Africa:				
Kenya	167,152	162,198	195,880	244,347
Mauritius	292,504	345,149	75,182	71,018
Tanzania	22,452	27,480	82,312	87,412
Uganda	15,491	11,136	40,779	49,105
Maldives	7,404	8,879	2,580	3,850
Seychelles	9,159	9,827	20,065	19,217
St Helena	496	446	10,423	9,144

Commonwealth countries—(contd.)	Imports from 1994	1995	Exports to 1994	1995
In Asia—				
Bangladesh	156,004	231,644	55,678	89,145
Hong Kong	3,079,611	3,538,821	2,297,561	2,656,583
India	1,288,939	1,435,481	1,311,495	1,682,709
Malaysia	1,204,026	1,487,884	1,305,201	1,189,582
Pakistan	358,879	363,068	355,058	340,382
Singapore	1,896,892	2,205,799	1,768,541	2,068,581
Sri Lanka	185,784	205,662	153,850	156,409
In Oceania—				
Australia	1,063,253	1,110,448	1,914,442	2,121,352
New Zealand	539,412	576,532	411,227	435,879
Papua New Guinea	56,981	97,391	9,074	10,849
Western Samoa	12	16	1,115	567
In America—				
Bahamas	25,628	33,029	30,580	30,912
Barbados	15,906	25,639	30,992	101,144
Belize	42,504	47,010	12,767	14,261
Bermuda	6,309	3,085	23,512	17,316
Canada	1,880,941	2,379,624	1,916,664	1,811,964
Falkland Islands	4,516	4,721	9,360	15,665
Guyana	71,717	72,821	26,922	33,946
Jamaica	133,963	149,076	56,354	69,771
Trinidad and Tobago	48,287	43,600	72,270	103,434
Total, Commonwealth countries (including some not specified above)	13,781,214	16,858,880	14,141,160	17,248,820

Provisional figures for imports and exports classified by the sections of the 3rd revision of the Standard International Trade Classification (in £1,000):

	Imports from EU countries 1993	Imports (excluding EU countries) 1993	Exports to EU countries 1993	Exports (excluding EU countries) 1993
0. *Food and Live Animals*				
Live animals (excluding zoo animals, dogs and cats)	89,200	65,317	206,200	101,877
Meat and meat preparations	1,450,700	490,668	850,100	82,954
Dairy products and eggs	834,700	183,761	486,100	154,302
Fish and fish preparations	205,800	779,112	515,500	81,533
Cereals and cereal preparations	843,200	157,946	824,800	389,905
Fruit and vegetables	1,857,600	1,262,498	222,000	80,081
Sugar, sugar preparations, honey	229,400	566,589	162,100	171,442
Coffee, tea, cocoa, spices	434,400	560,205	264,700	314,035
Feeding stuff for animals	409,500	404,307	229,600	86,577
Miscellaneous food preparations	662,200	78,917	242,000	143,899
Total of Section 0	7,016,800	4,549,319	4,003,000	1,606,605
1. *Beverages and Tobacco*				
Beverages	1,404,000	290,079	964,100	1,648,330
Tobacco and tobacco manufactures	173,700	258,383	84,400	564,331
Total of Section 1	1,577,700	548,462	1,048,500	2,212,661
2. *Crude Materials, Inedible, except Fuels*				
Hides, skins and furskins, undressed	50,000	39,461	83,900	63,905
Oil seeds, oil nuts and oil kernels	83,600	183,030	20,600	4,521
Crude rubber (including synthetic and reclaimed)	106,200	126,124	139,300	77,918
Wood and cork	107,300	1,000,335	15,600	6,505
Pulp and waste paper	64,900	469,726	19,300	5,970

	Imports from EU countries 1993	*Imports (excluding EU countries) 1993*	*Exports to EU countries 1993*	*Exports (excluding EU countries) 1993*
2. *Crude Materials, Inedible, except Fuels—contd.*				
Textile fibres and their waste	221,800	257,263	243,200	248,336
Crude fertilizers and crude minerals (excluding fuels)	121,900	378,924	220,500	212,777
Metalliferous ores and metal scrap	223,900	942,324	271,800	338,052
Crude animal and vegetable materials, not elsewhere specified	385,600	187,648	70,000	43,814
Total of Section 2	1,365,200	3,584,836	1,084,100	1,001,798
3. *Mineral Fuels, Lubricants and Related Materials*				
Coal, coke and briquettes	98,200	609,383	55,300	23,649
Petroleum and petroleum products	836,000	4,909,982	4,472,900	3,319,694
Gas, natural and manufactured	33,600	387,256	328,000	33,190
Electric current	426,200	nil	nil	nil
Total of Section 3	1,394,000	5,906,621	4,856,300	3,376,533
4. *Animal and Vegetable Oils and Fats*				
Animal oils and fats	50,200	31,177	12,600	6,856
Vegetable fats and oils	189,500	129,470	38,900	24,658
Processed oils and fats	32,300	36,313	22,100	8,514
Total of Section 4	272,000	196,961	73,600	40,027
5. *Chemicals*				
Organic chemicals	2,142,500	952,786	2,585,600	1,750,411
Inorganic chemicals	558,200	403,133	713,600	490,149
Dyeing, tanning and colouring materials	590,500	279,281	654,700	740,249
Medicinal and pharmaceutical products	1,222,400	791,068	1,638,600	2,046,646
Essential oils and perfume; toilet and cleansing preparations	729,400	281,471	894,400	796,246
Fertilizers, manufactured	125,400	114,365	58,000	22,623
Primary plastics	1,683,300	746,565	952,800	912,679
Non-primary plastics	788,100	294,749	565,200	372,811
Other chemical products	977,900	406,843	989,700	1,373,275
Total of Section 5	8,817,700	3,975,515	9,052,500	8,132,278
6. *Manufactured Goods Classified Chiefly by Material*				
Leather and dressed furs	98,700	92,930	96,200	196,021
Rubber	654,800	406,573	685,800	384,622
Wood and cork (excluding furniture)	294,900	594,818	83,800	45,614
Paper, paperboard	1,574,700	2,199,359	1,126,100	704,197
Textile yarn, fabrics	2,230,200	1,748,678	1,509,900	1,091,731
Non-metallic mineral manufactures	1,332,200	2,513,683	2,357,800	1,749,620
Iron and steel	1,767,600	754,826	1,604,600	1,525,093
Non-ferrous metals	1,007,900	1,908,678	1,015,000	909,508
Manufactures of metal, not elsewhere specified	1,386,900	1,160,519	1,103,300	1,152,495
Total of Section 6	10,347,800	11,380,065	9,582,600	7,758,899
7. *Machinery and Transport Equipment*				
Power generating machinery	1,357,000	2,580,102	2,038,900	3,963,771
Machinery for particular industries	1,836,000	1,331,774	1,349,900	2,747,002

	Imports from EU countries 1993	*Imports (excluding EU countries) 1993*	*Exports to EU countries 1993*	*Exports (excluding EU countries) 1993*
7. *Machinery and Transport Equipment—contd.*				
Metal working machinery	228,200	360,386	215,900	453,495
General industrial machinery	2,585,200	1,926,535	1,985,000	2,895,620
Office machinery	4,415,300	5,667,511	5,246,200	2,954,001
Telecommunications and sound recording apparatus	1,084,400	3,013,709	1,989,300	1,675,819
Electrical machinery	3,928,200	5,244,930	4,389,200	3,712,099
Road vehicles	11,125,600	3,247,934	5,540,800	2,738,925
Other transport equipment	912,300	5,634,635	1,518,300	2,820,191
Total of Section 7	27,472,300	25,759,581	24,273,500	23,960,922
8. *Miscellaneous Manufactured Articles*				
Prefabricated buildings, sanitary, plumbing, heating and lighting fixtures	261,800	125,067	138,400	140,121
Furniture	601,400	403,944	338,800	256,554
Travel goods, handbags and similar articles	71,600	287,517	51,400	46,224
Clothing	1,275,900	3,461,114	1,467,600	825,688
Footwear	667,900	549,888	196,500	201,155
Scientific instruments	937,900	1,909,703	1,271,900	2,034,261
Photographic apparatus, optical goods, clocks	735,700	1,098,793	726,300	736,259
Miscellaneous manufactured articles, not elsewhere specified	2,648,500	5,081,850	2,691,100	3,778,617
Total of Section 8	7,200,500	12,917,876	6,881,900	8,018,879
9. *Commodities and Transactions not Classified According to Kind*				
Total of Section 9	2,018,800	1,101,666	2,509,100	1,461,912
Total of all classes	67,482,800	69,920,903	63,365,000	57,570,514

Foreign Tourism. There were 21·03m. overseas visitors in 1994 spending £9,915m. 26·25m. UK residents journeyed abroad. The main countries of origin for foreign visitors in 1994 were: USA (2·98m.), France (2·78m.), Germany (2·52m.), Ireland (1·68m.) and the Netherlands (1·2m.).

COMMUNICATIONS

Roads. Responsibility for the construction and maintenance of trunk roads belongs to central government (in England, the Department of Transport, in Wales the Welsh Office and in Scotland the Scottish Office). Roads not classified as trunk roads are the responsibility of county, metropolitan district or London borough councils (in Scotland regional or island councils).

In 1993 there were 364,477 km of public road in Great Britain, classified as: Motorways, 3,141 km; trunk roads, 12,229 km; principal roads, 35,903 kim; others, 313,204 km.

Motor vehicles for which licences were current at 31 Dec. 1993, numbered (in 1,000) 24,826, including 20,102 private cars, 650 mopeds, scooters and motor cycles, 106 public transport vehicles and 428 goods vehicles. New vehicle registrations in 1993, 2,074. Driving tests, 1993 (in 1,000): Applications, 1,611·9; tests held, 1,511; tests passed, 730. The driving test was extended in 1996 to include a written examination.

Road casualties in Great Britain, 1993, 306,020 including 3,814 killed (the lowest figure since records began in 1926); in 1992, 310,673 (4,229 killed).

Inter- and intra-urban bus and coach journeys average 44,000m. passenger-km annually. For London buses *see* London Transport under RAILWAYS, *below*.

Railways. After April 1994, Britain's railway network was restructured to allow for privatization. Ownership of the track, stations and infrastructure was vested in a new government-owned company, Railtrack, which in 1996 was in the process of flotation on the Stock Exchange. The British Railways Board remained as principal train operator and provided various other services such as train and track maintenance pending the privatization of these units.

Passenger operations have been reorganized into 25 train-operating companies, wholly-owned subsidiaries of the British Railways Board, which pay Railtrack for access to the rail network, and lease their rolling stock from 3 private sector companies. These are gradually being let as franchises to the private sector. Freight operations have been split between 5 companies, with a sixth operating postal trains. These and other divisions of British Railways providing engineering and service functions are being progressively sold to the private sector. Eurotunnel PLC holds a concession from the government to operate the Channel Tunnel, through which frequent vehicle-carrying trains are run.

European Passenger Services, which jointly operates Eurostar trains through the Channel Tunnel (49·4 km) with French and Belgian railways, is a separate government-owned company. This, and the project company Union Railways, is scheduled for transfer to a private consortium which is to build a new rail link between London and the Channel Tunnel.

In the year ended 31 March 1995, British Railways Group turnover was £6,241·6m. and 100,264 staff were employed. Total train miles operated, 1994–95, 251·6m.

	1993–94	*1994–95*
Passenger Receipts and Traffic		
Receipts	£2,165·8m.	£2,152·9m.
Passenger journeys	713·2m.	702·2m.
Passenger miles (estimated)	18,867·0m.	17,806·0m.
Freight receipts and traffic		
Receipts	£565·4m.	£645·3m.
Traffic	103·3m. tonnes	97·4m. tonnes
Net tonne miles (trainload and wagonload)	8,553m.	8,073m.
Rolling Stock		
Locomotives		
Diesel	1,428	1,422
Electric	260	258
High Speed Trains		
Power cars	197	197
Passenger carriages	712	712
Coaching vehicles	11,090	10,771
Freight vehicles (excluding brake vans)	13,871	13,339
Stations and Route		
Stations [1]	2,553	2,565
Route open for traffic	16,536 km	16,542 km
Of which electrified	4,925 km	4,925 km

[1] Including freight-only stations.

London Transport is responsible to the Secretary of State for Transport for the operation of the capital's metro, London Underground, and for the planning and regulation of bus services. In 1995, London Underground, its wholly-owned subsidiary, carried 2·5m. passengers a day to and from 266 stations (including 21 managed by Railtrack) on 12 lines. Some 5,000 buses run under contract to London Transport by independent companies carried 3·7m. passengers a day on some 700 routes.

The Docklands Light Railway is operated in east inner London by the London Docklands Development Corporation.

There are metros in Glasgow and Newcastle, and light rail systems in Manchester and Sheffield.

Civil Aviation. Airports at Birmingham, Bristol, Cardiff, Derby (East Midlands), Edinburgh, Glasgow, Leeds/Bradford, Liverpool, London (Gatwick), London (Heathrow), London (Luton), London (Stansted), London City, Manchester, Newcastle and Southampton handled more than 5,000 international passengers in 1995.

Following the Civil Aviation Act 1971, the Civil Aviation Authority (CAA) was established as an independent public body responsible for the economic and safety regulation of British civil aviation. A CAA wholly-owned subsidiary, National Air Traffic Services operates air traffic control. Highlands and Islands Airports Ltd is owned by the Scottish Office and operates 8 airports in the Scottish Highlands and Islands.

Operating and traffic statistics of UK airlines on scheduled services during the calendar year 1993 (and 1994): Aircraft–km flown, 584m. (636m.); revenue passengers carried, 40m. (43·9m.); cargo (freight and mail) carried 541,986 (618,067) tonnes. Traffic between UK airports and places abroad in 1993 (and 1994) on all services included 880,162 (932,499) air transport aircraft movements.

There were 15,059 civil aircraft registered in the UK at 31 Dec. 1995.

British Airways is the largest UK airline. It operates long and short haul international services, as well as an extensive domestic network. In 1995 it operated 5 A320-100s, 5 A320-200s, 33 B-737-200 Advs, 34 B-737-400s, 15 B-747-100s, 13 B-747-200Bs, 3 B-747-200B Combis, 32 B-747-400s, 42 B-757-200s, 23 B-767-300ERs, 14 BAe ATPs, 7 Concordes, and 6 DC-10-30s. Other airlines operating scheduled flights in 1995 (with numbers of aircraft): Air Belfast (2); Air UK (41); British Midland Airways (39); GB Airways (6); Manx Airlines (21); Monarch Airlines (21); Virgin Atlantic Airways (12).

Shipping. The UK-owned merchant fleet (trading vessels over 100 GRT) in Dec. 1995 totalled 678 ships of 12·8m. DWT and 9m. GRT. The UK-registered fleet totalled 373 ships of 3·3m. DWT and 3·2m. GRT.

The average age of the UK-owned fleet was 15·4 years, while that of the world fleet was 13·5 years. Total gross international revenue in 1994 was £4,342m. The net contribution to the UK balance of payments was £1,008m.; there were import savings of £1,309m., giving a total contribution of £2,317m. The container and roll-on-roll-off (RoRo) shipping sectors are the leading revenue earners.

The principal ports are (with 1m. tonnes of cargo handled in 1994): London (51·8), Forth (44·4), Tees and Hartlepool (43), Grimsby and Immingham (42·9), Sullom Voe (38·6), Milford Haven (34·3), Southampton (31·5), Liverpool (29·5), Felixstowe (22·1), Medway (14·7), Dover (14·1), Orkneys (14·1), Port Talbot (11·1), Hull (10·2) and Belfast (9·9).

Inland Waterways. There are approximately 3,500 miles of navigable canals and river navigations in Great Britain. Of these, the publicly-owned British Waterways Board (BW) is responsible for some 385 miles (620 km) of commercial waterways (maintained for freight traffic) and some 1,160 miles (1,868 km) of cruising waterways (maintained for pleasure cruising, fishing and amenity). BW is also responsible for a further 450 miles (732 km) of canals, some of which are not navigable. BW's external turnover for the year to 31 March 1995 was £36·6m. This comprised principally Freight Activities (£2·9m.), Leisure (£9·9m.), the Estate (£12·4m.) and Water Charges (£3m.).

The most important of the river navigations and canals managed by other authorities include the rivers Thames, Great Ouse and Nene, the Norfolk Broads and the Manchester Ship Canal.

Postal Services. The Post Office operates as a group of 3 distinct businesses: Royal Mail (letter delivery), Parcelforce (parcel delivery), and Post Office Counters (retailing and agency services). Every area of the country is served by regional offices for each of the businesses. Royal Mail collects and delivers 67m. letters a day to the 25m. UK addresses. Other services include electronic mail, guaranteed parcel deliveries (same-day and overnight to UK addresses) and swift deliveries to 100 other countries. The British Postal Consultancy Service provides advice to administrations abroad.

In 1995 there were some 20,000 post offices, 700 operated directly by the Post

Office, the remainder (sub-post offices) on a franchise or agency basis and 120,000 posting boxes. Staff numbered 189,000 in 1994–95. 16,751m. letters were posted in 1994–95.

The Post Office has a monopoly on the carriage of letters within the UK, but the government has suspended this subject to a minimum delivery charge of £1 and licensed mail transferred between document exchanges. Private services are permitted to handle door-to-door deliveries subject to a minimum fee of £1.

Telecommunications. British Telecom was established in 1981 to take over the management of telecommunications from the Post Office. In 1984 it was privatized as British Telecommunications plc, changing its trading name from British Telecom to BT in 1991.

In 1994 there were 7,327 digital or electronic analogue exchanges serving 84% of BT's customers' lines. The trunk network is completely digital. More than 2·2m. km of optical fibre have been installed. In 1995 there were 20·5m. residential and 6·3m. business lines, 132,000 public payphones, 200,000 private rented payphones and 30,000 UK telex connections. BT handles a daily average of 93m. telephone calls a day and 22m. calls to emergency fire, police or ambulance service a year. In 1991 there were 0·9m. fax terminals. Electronic services include electronic mail ('email') and a complete corporate global messaging network. BT telephone, television and business services are carried by 15–20 satellites. In 1995 BT had some 20 offices worldwide and employed 137,561 persons.

Other companies offering telecommunications services include Mercury Communications, cable TV networks, and 4 providers of national cellular radio ('mobile') telephone systems with a total of 2·72m. users at the end of 1994. Hull (Humberside) has always had its own telephone system, now called Kingston Communications. Some electricity companies use their pylons network to provide a fibre-optic telecoms system.

Broadcasting. Radio and television services are provided by the British Broadcasting Corporation (BBC), by licensees of the Radio Authority and the Independent Television Commission (ITC) and by the Welsh-language Sianel Pedwar Cymru (S4C, Channel 4 Wales). The BBC, constituted by Royal Charter until 31 Dec. 1996, has responsibility for providing domestic and external broadcast services, the former financed from the television licence revenue, the latter by Government grant. The domestic services include 2 national television services, 5 national radio network services and a network of local radio stations. Government proposals for the future of the BBC after 1996 were published in July 1994.

The ITC is responsible for licensing and regulating all non-BBC TV services (except S4C), including ITV (regional and breakfast-time licensees), Channel 4, Channel 5, cable and satellite and additional services, such as teletext, carried on the spare capacity of TV signals. The Radio Authority is responsible for licensing and regulating independent national and local radio services. S4C is transmitted in Wales, and is funded by the government. It acts as both broadcaster and regulator.

The BBC's domestic radio services are available on Long Wave, MF and VHF; those of the Radio Authority on MF and VHF. Television services other than those only on cable and satellite are broadcast at UHF in 625-line definition and in colour (by PAL). The BBC World Service, which started life in 1932 as the Empire Service, broadcast in 42 languages to an audience estimated at 133m. in 1995. As the self-financed BBC Worldwide TV, the BBC is also involved in commercial joint ventures to provide international television services.

The broadcasting authorities, whose governing bodies are appointed (by HM the Queen in the case of the BBC and by the Secretary of State for National Heritage in the case of the ITC, the Radio Authority and S4C) as trustees for the public interest in broadcasting, are independent of government and are publicly accountable to Parliament for the discharge of their responsibilities. Their duties and powers are laid down in the BBC Royal Charter and the Broadcasting Act 1990.

All independent (non-BBC) radio and television services other than S4C are financed by the sale of broadcasting advertising time, commercial sponsorship, or, in some cable and satellite services, by subscription.

In 1981 the Broadcasting Complaints Commission was set up to consider and adjudicate upon complaints of unfair or unjust treatment in broadcast programmes or of unwarranted infringement of privacy in or in the making of programmes. These statutory functions have been continued in the Broadcasting Act of 1990. The Broadcasting Standards Council was set up in 1988 to act as a focus for public concern about the portrayal of violence and sex on television and radio. The Council's role is to monitor programmes, receive and examine complaints from the public, undertake and commission research, and to draw up a code of practice on the portrayal of sex and violence, and on matters of taste and decency. The Broadcasting Act 1990 requires the broadcasters to reflect the Council's code in their programme guidelines. It also empowers the Council to consider and adjudicate upon complaints and publish their findings.

The number of television receiving licences in force on 31 March 1995 was 21,046,000, including 20,245,000 for colour. There were 779,461 cable television subscribers in 1994.

Cinemas. In 1994 cinemas had 1,969 screens. Admissions were 123m. in 1994 (114m. in 1993, from a low point of 54m. in 1984). 35 full-length films were made in 1994.

Press. In 1995 there were 11 national dailies with a combined average circulation in March of 14,428,566, and 9 national Sunday newspapers (15,382,124). There were also about 100 morning, evening and Sunday regional newspapers and 2,000 weeklies (about 1,000 of these for free distribution). There were about 7,000 other commercial periodicals.

In Jan. 1991 the Press Complaints Commission replaced the former Press Council. It has 15 members and a chair (Lord McGregor of Durris) including 7 editors. It is funded by the newspaper industry.

SOCIAL INSTITUTIONS

Justice. *England and Wales.* The legal system of England and Wales, divided into civil and criminal courts has at the head of the superior courts, as the ultimate court of appeal, the House of Lords, which hears each year a number of appeals in civil matters, including a certain number from Scotland and Northern Ireland, as well as some appeals in criminal cases. In order that civil cases may go from the Court of Appeal to the House of Lords, it is necessary to obtain the leave of either the Court of Appeal or the House itself, although in certain cases an appeal may lie direct to the House of Lords from the decision of the High Court. An appeal can be brought from a decision of the Court of Appeal or the Divisional Court of the Queen's Bench Division of the High Court in a criminal case provided that the Court is satisfied that a point of law 'of general public importance' is involved, and either the Court or the House of Lords is of the opinion that it is desirable in the public interest that a further appeal should be brought. As a judicial body, the House of Lords consists of the Lord Chancellor, the Lords of Appeal in Ordinary, commonly called Law Lords, and such other members of the House as hold or have held high judicial office. The final court of appeal for certain of the Commonwealth countries is the Judicial Committee of the Privy Council which, in addition to Privy Counsellors who are or have held high judicial office in the UK, includes others who are or have been Chief Justices or Judges of the Superior Courts of Commonwealth countries.

Civil Law. The main courts of original civil jurisdiction are the High Court and county courts.

The High Court has exclusive jurisdiction to deal with specialist classes of case e.g. Judicial Review. It has concurrent jurisdiction with county courts in cases involving contract and tort although it will only hear those cases where the issues are complex or important. The High Court also has appellate jurisdiction to hear appeals from lower tribunals.

The judges of the High Court are attached to one of its 3 divisions: Chancery, Queen's Bench and Family; each with its separate field of jurisdiction. The Heads of the 3 divisions are the Lord Chief Justice (Queen's Bench), the Vice-Chancellor

(Chancery) and the President of the Family Division. In addition there are 95 High Court judges. For the hearing of cases at first instance, High Court judges sit singly. Appellate jurisdiction is usually exercised by Divisional Courts consisting of 2 (sometimes 3) judges, though in certain circumstances a judge sitting alone may hear the appeal. High Court business is dealt with in the Royal Courts of Justice and by over 130 District Registries outside London.

County courts can deal with all contract and tort cases and recovery of land actions, regardless of value. They have upper financial limits to deal with specialist classes of business such as equity and Admiralty cases. Certain county courts have been designated to deal with family, bankruptcy, patents and discrimination cases.

There are about 260 county courts located throughout the country each with its own district. A case may be heard by a Circuit Judge or by a District Judge, (the latter generally being restricted to cases valued at £5,000 or less). County courts have a small claims jurisdiction for actions for money worth £7,000 or less; this is an informal procedure where parties are encouraged to present cases without the need for legal representation.

The Restrictive Practices Court was set up in 1956 under the Restrictive Trade Practices Act and is responsible for deciding whether a restrictive trade agreement is in the public interest. It is presided over by a High Court judge, but laymen sit on the bench also. Another specialist court is the Employment Appeal Tribunal, with similar composition, which hears appeals in employment cases from lower tribunals.

The Court of Appeal (Civil Division) hears appeals in civil actions from the High Court and county courts and certain special courts such as the Restrictive Practice Court and Employment Appeal Tribunal. Its President is the Master of the Rolls, aided by up to 29 Lords Justices of Appeal setting in 6 or 7 divisions of 2 or 3 judges each.

Civil proceedings are instituted by the aggrieved person, but as they are a private matter, they are frequently settled by the parties through their lawyers before the matter comes to trial. In very limited classes of dispute (e.g. libel and slander), a party may request a jury to sit to decide questions of fact and the award of damages.

Criminal Law. At the base of the system of criminal courts in England and Wales are the magistrates' courts which deal with over 97% of criminal cases. In general, in exercising their summary jurisdiction, they have power to pass a sentence of up to six months imprisonment and to impose a fine of up to £5,000 on any one offence. They also deal with the preliminary hearing of cases triable at the Crown Court. In addition to dealing summarily with over 2m. cases, which include thefts, assaults, road traffic infringements, drug abuse, etc, they also have a limited civil jurisdiction.

Magistrates' courts normally sit with a bench of 3 lay justices. Although unpaid they are entitled to loss of earnings and travel and subsistence allowance. They undergo training after appointment and they are advised by a professional justices' clerk. In central London and in some provincial areas full-time stipendiary magistrates have been appointed. Generally they possess the same powers as the lay bench, but they sit alone. On 1 Jan. 1996 the total strength of the lay magistracy was 30,326 including 14,375 women. Justices are appointed on behalf of the Queen by the Lord Chancellor, except in Greater Manchester, Merseyside and Lancashire where they are appointed by the Chancellor of the Duchy of Lancaster.

Justices are selected and trained specially to sit in Youth and Family Proceedings Courts. Youth Courts deal with cases involving children and young persons up to the age of 18 charged with criminal offences (other than homicide and other grave offences). These courts normally sit with 3 justices, including at least one man or one woman, and are accommodated separately from other courts.

Family Proceedings Courts deal with matrimonial applications, Children Act matters, including care, residence and contact and adoption. These courts normally sit with three justices including at least one man and one woman.

Above the magistrates' courts is the Crown Court. This was set up by the Courts Act 1971 to replace quarter sessions and assizes. Unlike quarter sessions and assizes, which were individual courts, the Crown Court is a single court which is capable of sitting anywhere in England and Wales. It has power to deal with all trials on indictment and has inherited the jurisdiction of quarter sessions to hear appeals, proceedings on committal of persons from the magistrates' courts for sentence, and certain original proceedings on civil matters under individual statutes.

The jurisdiction of the Crown Court is exercisable by a High Court judge, a Circuit judge or a Recorder or Assistant Recorder (part-time judges) sitting alone, or, in specified circumstances, with justices of the peace. The Lord Chief Justice has given directions as to the types of case to be allocated to High Court judges (the more serious cases) and to Circuit judges or Recorders respectively.

Appeals from magistrates' courts go either to a Divisional Court of the High Court (when a point of law alone is involved) or to the Crown Court where there is a complete re-hearing on appeals against conviction and/or sentence. Appeals from the Crown Court in cases tried on indictment lie to the Court of Appeal (Criminal Division). Appeals on questions of law go by right, and appeals on other matters by leave. The Lord Chief Justice or a Lord Justice sits with judges of the High Court to constitute this court.

There remains as a last resort the invocation of the royal prerogative exercised on the advice of the Home Secretary. In 1965 the death penalty was abolished for murder.

All contested criminal trials, except those which come before the magistrates' courts, are tried by a judge and a jury consisting of 12 members. The prosecution or defence may challenge any potential juror for cause. The jury decides whether the accused is guilty or not. The judge is responsible for summing up on the facts and explaining the law; he sentences convicted offenders. If, after at least 2 hours and 10 minutes of deliberation, a jury is unable to reach a unanimous verdict it may, on the judge's direction, provided that in a full jury of 12 at least 10 of its members are agreed, bring in a majority verdict. The failure of a jury to agree on a unanimous verdict or to bring in a majority verdict may involve the retrial of the case before a new jury.

The Employment Appeal Tribunal. The Employment Appeal Tribunal which is a superior Court of Record with the like powers, rights, privileges and authority of the High Court, was set up in 1976 to hear appeals on questions of law against decisions of industrial tribunals and of the Certification Officer. The appeals are heard by a High Court Judge sitting with 2 members (in exceptional cases 4) appointed for their special knowledge or experience of industrial relations either on the employer or the trade union side, with always an equal number on each side. The great bulk of their work is concerned with the problems which can arise between employees and their employers.

Military Courts. Offences committed by persons subject to service law under the Army Act 1955, the Air Force Act 1955 or the Naval Discipline Act 1957 may be dealt with either summarily or by courts-martial.

The Personnel of the Law. All judicial officers except the Lord Chancellor (who is a member of the Cabinet) are independent of Parliament and the Executive. They are appointed by the Crown on the advice of the Prime Minister or the Lord Chancellor, or by the Lord Chancellor, and hold office until retiring age. Under the Judicial Pensions and Retirement Act 1993 judges normally retire at age 70 years, though they may be called upon by the Lord Chancellor to serve till age 75. The legal profession is divided; barristers, who advise on legal problems and can conduct cases before all courts, usually act for the public only through solicitors, who deal directly with the legal business brought to them by the public and have rights to present cases before certain courts. Long-standing members of both professions are eligible for appointment to most judicial offices.

In 1994 the Lord Chancellor introduced developments to the procedures for making all judicial appointments below the level of the High Court. Suitably qualified practitioners are invited to apply for advertised vacancies, and shortlisted applicants are interviewed by a panel consisting of a judge, an official and a lay member. Panels make recommendations to the Lord Chancellor, who retains the right of final recommendation to the Sovereign or appointment, as appropriate. All vacancies for the full-time offices of Circuit Judge, District Judge and Master or Registrar of the Supreme Court are now filled under this procedure. The new procedures are now being extended to part-time judicial appointments, beginning with that of Assistant Recorder.

Legal Aid. Broadly there are 3 kinds of legal aid available in England and Wales. Firstly there is legal advice and assistance, otherwise known as the 'Green Form' scheme. This includes advice and assistance on almost any question of English law, both civil and criminal, but does not normally cover any form of representation before a court or tribunal. Qualification for 'Green Form' is dependent on the means of the applicant. As an extension of the scheme, however, assistance by way of representation is available for certain proceedings, chiefly civil, in magistrates' courts. Assistance by way of representation is also means-tested. In 1994–95 there were 1·6m. payments under the Legal Advice and Assistance Scheme. The net cost to the Legal Aid Fund of this part was £152·2m., of which £13·4m. was accounted for by assistance by way of representation. Legal advice and assistance also provides for duty solicitor schemes at magistrates' courts and police stations. Under the magistrates' courts scheme, initial advice, and representation where necessary, is available to unrepresented defendants at court from duty solicitors either in attendance at courts or on call. The scheme covers advice to a defendant in custody, making a bail application, representing a defendant in custody on a guilty plea, and certain other cases. The advice and assistance at police stations scheme enables any person who has been arrested and taken to a police station, or who is assisting the police with their enquiries, to receive advice and assistance, from either a duty solicitor or the person's own solicitor. The cost of these schemes, which are not subject to means test or contribution, is met from the Legal Aid Fund and in 1994–95 amounted to £80·5m. Secondly, under Part IV of the Legal Aid Act 1988, there is legal aid for civil court proceedings. Under regulations, aid is available to those of low or moderate means either free or subject to a contribution, depending on means. In 1994–95, 385,955 civil legal aid certificates were issued. The cost of legal aid is met from (*a*) contributions from assisted persons; (*b*) the operation of the statutory charge which gives the Legal Aid Board a first charge on money or property recovered or preserved for an assisted person; (*c*) costs recovered from opposing parties and (*d*) a grant from the Exchequer. The net cost of civil legal aid to the state (excluding administration costs of the scheme) in 1994–95 amounted to £601·6m. Thirdly under Part V of the Legal Aid Act 1988 a court dealing with criminal proceedings may order legal aid to be given if it considers it is desirable in the interests of justice and if it also considers that the defendant (or appellant) requires financial assistance in meeting the costs he or she may incur. The factors to be taken into account when determining whether it is in the interests of justice that criminal legal aid be granted are defined by statute to include cases where, for example, the defendant is likely to be deprived of his or her liberty, consideration of a substantial question of law may be involved, or the defendant may be unable to understand the proceedings or to state his or her case due to inadequate knowledge of English, mental illness or other mental or physical disability. Legal aid must be granted, subject to means, in the following circumstances: Where a person is committed for trial on a charge of murder, where the prosecutor appeals or applies for leave to appeal from the criminal division of the Court of Appeal or the Courts-Martial Appeal Court to the House of Lords, and in certain circumstances where the court is considering depriving a defendant of his liberty.

The costs of legal aid in criminal proceedings are paid by the central government, but courts have power to require legally aided persons to contribute towards the cost of legal aid given to them. The net cost of legal aid in criminal proceedings in 1994–95 was £464·3m. £262·3m. of this was for legal aid in the higher courts which is paid for out of the Lord Chancellor's vote, and £202m. for legal aid in the magistrates' courts which is paid from the Legal Aid Fund.

Police. In April 1995 the Home Office gave up central control of police manpower and authorized establishments of police no longer exists. Instead, Chief Constables recruit according to their budgets. The Home Office collates police strength in March and Sept. each year. The actual strength of the police service in England and Wales in Sept. 1995 was 126,808 (including 17,890 women). In addition there were

19,655 special constables (including 6,904 women). The estimated total revenue expenditure on the police service for 1994–95 was £6,433m.

SCOTLAND. The High Court of Justiciary is the supreme criminal court in Scotland and has jurisdiction in all cases of crime committed in any part of Scotland, unless expressly excluded by statute. It consists of the Lord Justice-General, the Lord Justice-Clerk and 24 other judges, who are the same judges as of the Court of Session, the Scottish supreme civil court. One judge is seconded to the Scottish Law Commission. The Court, which is presided over by the Lord Justice-General, whom failing, the Lord Justice-Clerk, exercises an appellate jurisdiction as well as one of first instance, sits as business requires in Edinburgh both as a Court of Appeal (the *quorum* being 2 judges if appeal against sentence or other disposals, 3 in all other cases) and as a court of first instance and on circuit as a court of first instance. The decisions of the Court are not subject to review by the House of Lords. One judge sitting with a jury of 15 persons can, and usually does, try cases, but 2 or more (with a jury) may do so in important or complex cases. It has a privative jurisdiction over cases of treason, murder, rape, incest, deforcement of messengers, breach of duty by magistrates and offences under the Official Secrets Act. It also, in practice, is the only court which tries serious crimes against person or property and generally those cases in which a sentence greater than imprisonment for 3 years is likely to be imposed. Moreover, the Court has inherent power to try and to punish all acts which are plainly criminal though previously unknown and not dealt with by any statute.

The appellate jurisdiction of the High Court of Justiciary extends to all cases tried on indictment, whether in the High Court or the Sheriff Court, and persons so convicted may appeal to the Court against conviction or sentence or both except where the sentence is fixed by law. By such an appeal, a person may bring under review any alleged miscarriage of justice including any alleged miscarriage of justice on the basis of the existence of significant additional evidence which was not heard at the trial and which was not available and could not reasonably have been made available at the trial. It is also a court of review from courts of summary jurisdiction, and on the final determination of any summary prosecution the convicted person may appeal to the Court by way of stated case on questions of law, etc., but not on questions of fact, except in relation to a miscarriage of justice alleged by the person accused on the basis of the existence and significance of additional evidence which was not heard at the trial and which was not available and could not reasonably have been made available at the trial. However, before cases proceed to a full hearing, leave to appeal must first be granted. Grounds of appeal and any relevant reports are considered by a 'sift' judge sitting alone in chambers, who will decide if there is merit in the appeal. Should leave to appeal be refused, this decision may be appealed to the High Court within 14 days, when the matter will be reviewed by 2 judges, again sitting in chambers. The Lord Advocate is entitled to appeal to the High Court against any sentence passed on indictment on the ground that it is unduly lenient, or on a point of law. A further or complementary form of process of review which can be resorted to by convicted persons in these courts is by Bill of Suspension (and Liberation), but it is of strictly limited application, and cannot be used to appeal any conviction, sentence, judgment or order pronounced in any proceedings on indictment. A prosecutor in cases tried on indictment or under summary criminal procedure may also bring under review a decision in law, prior to final judgment of the case, by way of Bill of Advocation. The Court also hears appeals under the Courts-Martial (Appeals) Act 1951.

The Sheriff Court has an inherent universal criminal jurisdiction (as well as an extensive civil one) limited in general to crimes and offences committed within a sheriffdom (a specifically defined region), which has, however, been curtailed by statute or practice under which the High Court of Justiciary has exclusive jurisdiction in relation to the crimes above-mentioned. This Court is presided over by a Sheriff-Principal or Sheriff, who when trying cases on indictment sits with a jury of 15 persons. His powers of awarding punishment involving imprisonment are restricted to 3 years maximum, but he may under certain statutory powers remit the prisoner to the High Court for sentence if this is felt to be insufficient. The Sheriff also exercises a wide summary criminal jurisdiction and when doing so sits without a jury; and he has concurrent jurisdiction with every other court within his Sheriff Court District in regard to all offences competent for trial in summary courts. The great majority of offences which come before the courts are of a minor nature and, as such, are disposed of in the Sheriff Summary Courts or in the District Courts (*see* below). In cases to be tried on indictment either in the High Court of Justiciary or in the Sheriff Court, the judge may, before the trial, hold a preliminary or first diet to decide questions of a preliminary nature, whether to the competency or relevancy or otherwise. Any decision at a preliminary diet (other than a decision to adjourn the first or preliminary diet or discharge the trial diet) can be the subject of an appeal to the High Court of Justiciary prior to the trial.

In cases to be tried on indictment in the Sheriff Court by Sheriff and Jury trial a first diet is mandatory before the trial diet to decide questions of a preliminary nature ie to the competency or relevancy or otherwise, and to identify cases which are unlikely to go to trial on the date programmed. Likewise, in summary proceedings, an intermediate diet is again mandatory before trial. In High Court cases such matters may be dealt with at a preliminary diet.

District Courts in each local authority district have jurisdiction in minor offences occurring within the district. These courts are presided over by lay magistrates, known as Justices, who have limited powers of fine and imprisonment. In Glasgow District there are also 4 Stipendiary Magistrates who have the same sentencing powers as Sheriffs.

The Court of Session, presided over by the Lord President (the Lord Justice-General in criminal cases), is divided into an Inner House comprising 2 divisions of 4 judges each with mainly appellate function, and an Outer House comprising 18 single judges, sitting individually at first instance; it exercises the highest civil jurisdiction in Scotland, with the House of Lords as a court of appeal.

Police. The police forces in Scotland at the end of 1994 had an authorized establishment of 14,209; the actual strength was 12,634 men and 1,679 women. There were 1,992 special constables. The total police net expenditure in Scotland was £514m. for 1992–93.

CIVIL JUDICIAL STATISTICS

ENGLAND AND WALES	*1992*	*1993*
Appellate Courts		
Judicial Committee of the Privy Council	63	56
House of Lords	96	62
Court of Appeal	1,651	1,860
High Court of Justice (appeals and special cases from inferior courts)	3,562 [1]	3,937
Courts of First Instance (excluding Magistrates' Courts and Tribunals)		
High Court of Justice:		
Chancery Division [2]	47,597	43,306
Queen's Bench Division [3]	270,305 [6]	211,854
Official Referee's	1,266	1,115
County courts: Matrimonial suits [4]	192,298	187,357
Other [5]	3,555,256	3,028,143
Restrictive Practices Court	1	3

SCOTLAND	*1993*	*1994*
House of Lords (Appeals from Court of Session)	2	6
Court of Session—		
General Department	4,906	4,193
Petition Department	1,276	1,342
Sheriff's Ordinary Cause	55,333	44,190
Sheriff's Summary Cause	38,346	35,646
Small Claims	72,714	64,002

[1] Includes an estimated figure of 177 Family Division appeals entered for which 1992 data were not available.

[2] Including Companies Court, Bankruptcy petitions and Patents Court.
[3] Including Admiralty Court.
[4] Including petitions filed at Principal Registry.
[5] Plaint, Admiralty, Bankruptcy and Companies, Adoption, Guardianship and miscellaneous.
[6] The decrease in Queen's Bench actions is due to the increased jurisdiction of county courts from 1 July 1991 to deal with all matters in contract and tort regardless of value.

CRIMINAL STATISTICS

ENGLAND AND WALES

	Total number of offenders		*Indictable offences* [1]	
	1993	*1994*	*1993*	*1994*
Aged 10 and over [2]				
Proceeded against in magistrates' courts [3]	1,956,271	1,947,165	478,808	497,326
Found guilty at magistrates' courts	1,359,287	1,340,060	243,471	248,513
Found guilty at the Crown Court	66,027	67,563	64,113	65,635
Cautioned [4]	311,299	308,431	209,554	209,767
Aged 10 and under 18				
Proceeded against in magistrates' courts [3]	91,136	102,293	59,792	68,485
Found guilty at magistrates' courts	53,184	59,906	33,345	38,221
Found guilty at the Crown Court	2,174	2,156	2,117	2,103
Cautioned [4]	121,582	124,654	94,063	95,487

[1] Includes offences which can be tried either at the Crown Court or at magistrates' courts.
[2] Includes other offenders, e.g. companies, public bodies.
[3] Almost all defendants are initially proceeded against at magistrates' courts.
[4] Offenders who, on admission of guilt, are given an oral caution by or on the instruction of a senior police officer as an alternative to court proceedings. Such cautions are not given for motoring offences.
[5] 1992 figures relate to the age group aged 10 and under 17.

CRIMINAL STATISTICS

SCOTLAND

	All Crimes and Offences		*Crimes* [1]	
	1991	*1992*	*1991*	*1992*
All persons and companies				
Proceeded against in all courts	190,837	197,724	59,555	65,416
Charge proved	170,492	176,160	49,574	54,314
Children (aged 8–15)				
Proceeded against in all courts	225	177	154	117

[1] Crimes are generally the more serious criminal acts and offences the less serious. 'Crimes' are not equivalent in coverage to 'indictable/triable either way offences'.

In March 1995 the population in prisons, youth custody centres and detention centres in England and Wales was 51,243 (the highest level ever recorded); in Scotland (1993), 5,637.

Religion. The Anglican Communion has originated from the Church of England and parallels in its fellowship of autonomous churches the evolution of British influence beyond the seas from colonies to dominions and independent nations. The Archbishop of Canterbury presides as *primus inter pares* at the decennial meetings of the bishops of the Anglican Communion at the Lambeth Conference and at the biennial meetings of the Primates and the Anglican Consultative Council. The last Conference was held in Canterbury in 1988 and was attended by 518 bishops.

The Anglican Communion consists of 33 member Churches or Provinces. These are Australia, Brazil, Burma, Burundi, Rwanda and Zaïre, Canada, Central Africa, Ceylon, England, Indian Ocean, Ireland, Japan, Jerusalem and the Middle East, Kenya, Korea, Melanesia, Mexico, New Zealand, Nigeria, Papua New Guinea, the Philippines, Scotland, Southern Africa, Southern Cone of America, Sudan,

Tanzania, Uganda, USA, Wales, West Africa, West Indies. There are also areas which come under the metropolitical jurisdiction of the Archbishop of Canterbury. These are Bermuda, the Diocese in Europe, Falkland Islands, The Council of the Churches of East Asia, The Diocese of Hong Kong and Macao, Sabah, Kuching, Singapore, West Malaysia, The Lusitanian Church (Portugal) and The Spanish Reformed Episcopal Church.

England and Wales. The established Church of England, which baptizes about 25% of the children born in England (*i.e.* excluding Wales but including the Isle of Man and the Channel Islands), is Anglican. Civil disabilities on account of religion do not attach to any class of British subject. Under the Welsh Church Acts, 1914 and 1919, the Church in Wales and Monmouthshire was disestablished as from 1 April 1920, and Wales was formed into a separate Province.

The Queen is, under God, the supreme governor of the Church of England, with the right, regulated by statute, to nominate to the vacant archbishoprics and bishoprics. The Queen, on the advice of the First Lord of the Treasury, also appoints to such deaneries, prebendaries and canonries as are in the gift of the Crown, while a large number of livings and also some canonries are in the gift of the Lord Chancellor.

There are 2 archbishops (at the head of the 2 Provinces of Canterbury and York), and 42 diocesan bishops including the bishop of the diocese in Europe, which is part of the Province of Canterbury. Dr George Carey was enthroned as *Archbishop of Canterbury* in April 1991. Each archbishop has also his own particular diocese, wherein he exercises episcopal, as in his Province he exercises metropolitan, jurisdiction. In Dec. 1995 there were 66 suffragan and assistant bishops, 40 deans and provosts of cathedrals and 103 archdeacons. The *General Synod*, which replaced the Church Assembly in 1970 in England, consists of a House of Bishops, a House of Clergy and a House of Laity, and has power to frame legislation regarding Church matters. Each House has a veto over the others. The first two Houses consist of the members of the Convocations of Canterbury and York, each of which consists of the diocesan bishops and elected representatives of the suffragan bishops, 6 for Canterbury province and 3 for York (forming an Upper House), deans, provosts, and archdeacons, and a certain number of proctors elected as the representatives of the inferior clergy, together with, in the case of Canterbury Convocation, 4 representatives of the Universities of Oxford, Cambridge, London and the Southern Universities and in the case of York 2 representatives for the Universities of Durham and Newcastle and the other Northern Universities; 3 archdeacons to the Armed Forces, the Chaplain General of Prisons and 2 representatives of the Religious Communities (forming the Lower House). The House of Laity is elected by the lay members of the Deanery Synods but also includes 3 representatives of the Religious Communities and *ex-officio* Church Commissioners and Ecclesiastical Judges. Every Measure passed by the General Synod must be submitted to the Ecclesiastical Committee, consisting of 15 members of the House of Lords nominated by the Lord Chancellor and 15 members of the House of Commons nominated by the Speaker. This committee reports on each Measure to Parliament, and the Measure receives the Royal Assent and becomes law if each House of Parliament resolves that the Measure be presented to the Queen.

Parochial affairs are managed by annual parochial church meetings and parochial church councils. At 31 July 1995 there were 13,025 ecclesiastical parishes, inclusive of the Isle of Man and the Channel Islands. These parishes do not, in many cases, coincide with civil parishes. Although most parishes have their own churches, not every parish nowadays can have its own incumbent or minister. In Dec. 1995 there were 5,897 beneficed clergy excluding dignitaries, 1,769 other clergy of incumbent status and 1,907 assistant curates working in the parishes.

Women have been admitted to Holy Orders (but not the Episcopate) as deacons since 1987 and as priests since 1994. On 11 Nov. 1992 the General Synod voted for the ordination of women to the priesthood (the Upper House, by 39 votes to 13; the Lower House, by 176 to 74; the House of Laity, by 169 to 82). The legislation received the Royal Assent on 5 Nov. 1993 and the Canon permitting women's ordination came into effect on 22 Feb. 1994. At 31 Dec. 1995 there were 820 full-time stipendiary women clergy, 762 of whom were in the parochial ministry. In July 1995 the General Synod stated that 304 clergymen had left the Church of England because they disagreed with the ordination of women, and that perhaps 75% of these had joined the Roman Catholic Church.

Private persons possess the right of presentation to over 2,000 benefices; the patronage of the others belongs mainly to the Queen, the bishops and cathedrals, the Lord Chancellor, and the universities of Oxford and Cambridge. In addition to the 6,147 dignitaries and parochial incumbents, there were (1995) 126 cathedral, 3,673 parochial and 314 non-parochial clergy working within the diocesan framework. Although these figures account for the majority of active clergy in England, there are many others serving in parishes and institutions who cannot be quantified with any certainty. They include some 1,500 full-time hospital, Forces, prison, industrial and school and college chaplains. Over 1,000 non-stipendiary clergy hold a bishop's licence to officiate at services.

In 1993 there were estimated to be 1·3m. Easter Day and 1·5m. Christmas Communicants. Usual Sunday attendances at all services were 1·1m.

Of the 40,397 buildings registered for the solemnization of marriages at 30 June 1994, (statistics from the Office of Population Censuses and Surveys) 16,538 belonged to the Established Church and the Church in Wales and 23,859 to other religious denominations (Methodist, 6,739; Roman Catholic, 3,331; Baptist, 3,109; United Reformed, 1,689; Congregational, 1,264; Calvinistic Methodist, 1,093; Jehovah's Witnesses, 786; Brethren, 744; Salvation Army, 737; Unitarians, 165; other Christian, 3,857; Sikhs, 129; Moslems, 90; other non-Christian, 126). Of the 306,756 marriages celebrated in 1991 (331,150 in 1990), 102,840 were in the Established Church and the Church in Wales, 52,583 in other denominations and 151,333 were civil marriages in Register Offices.

Roman Catholics in England and Wales were estimated at 4,404,690 in 1995. There were 5 archdioceses and 18 dioceses, 6,184 clergy and 2,829 parish churches and 974 other churches open to the public. Convents, 1,278.

Membership of other denominations in the UK in 1991 (and 1975):

Presbyterians, 1,291,672 (1·65m.); Methodists, 483,387 (0·61m.); Baptists, 241,842 (0·27m.); other Protestants, 123,677; independent churches, 408,999; Orthodox, 265,258 (0·2m.); Afro-Caribbean churches, 69,658; Mormons (1994), 163,800; Jehovah's Witnesses, 0·12m.; Spiritualists, 60,000; Moslems, 0·99m. (0·4m.); Sikhs, 0·39m. (0·12m.); Hindus, 0·14m. (0·1m.); Jews, 108,400 (0·11m.).

The Salvation Army is established in 94 countries. In 1991 in the UK and Ireland it had 1,792 ministers, 55,000 members and 837 churches.

There is a 400-member Board of Deputies of British Jews. The *Chief Rabbi* is Jonathan Sacks.

Scotland. The Church of Scotland, which was reformed in 1560, subsequently developed a presbyterian system of church government which was established in 1690 and has continued to the present day.

The supreme court is the General Assembly, which now consists of some 1,250 members, ministers and elders in equal numbers, together with members of the diaconate commissioned by presbyteries. It meets annually in May, under the presidency of a Moderator appointed by the Assembly. The Queen is normally represented by a Lord High Commissioner, but has occasionally attended in person. The royal presence in a special throne gallery in the hall but outside the Assembly symbolises the independence from state control of what is nevertheless recognised as the national Church in Scotland.

There are also 46 presbyteries in Scotland, roughly co-terminous with District Councils, together with 1 presbytery of England, 1 presbytery of Europe, and 1 presbytery of Jerusalem. At the base of this conciliar structure of Church courts are the kirk sessions, of which there were 1,656 on 1 Dec. 1992, with a total of 752,719 members.

The Episcopal Church of Scotland is a province of the Anglican Church and is one of the historic Scottish churches. It consists of 7 dioceses. As at 31 Dec. 1995 it had 243 churches and missions, 287 clergy and 54,495 members, of whom 34,266 were communicants.

There are in Scotland some small outstanding Presbyterian bodies and also Baptists, Congregationalists, Methodists and Unitarians.

The Roman Catholic Church which celebrated the centenary of the restoration of the Hierarchy in 1978, had in Scotland (1993) 2 archbishops, 6 diocesan bishops, 1 auxiliary bishop, 992 clergy, 462 parishes, and (in 1992) 744,600 adherents.

The proportion of marriages in Scotland according to the rites of the various Churches in 1994 was: Church of Scotland, 37·4%; Roman Catholic, 9·6%; Episcopal, 1·7%; others, 5·3%; civil, 46%.

Bradley, I., *Marching to the Promised Land: Has the Church a Future?*. London, 1992.
De La Noy, M., *The Church of England: a Portrait.* London, 1993.

Education (England and Wales). *The Publicly Maintained System of Education:* Compulsory schooling begins at the age of 5 and the minimum leaving age for all pupils is 16. No tuition fees are payable in any publicly maintained school (but it is open to parents, if they choose, to pay for their children to attend other schools). The post-school or tertiary stage, which is voluntary, includes universities, further education establishments and other higher education establishments (including those which provide courses for the training of teachers), as well as adult education centres and the youth service. Financial assistance (grants and loans) is generally available to students on higher education courses in the university and non-university sectors and to some students on other courses in further education.

National Curriculum. The Education Reform Act 1988 established a national curriculum for gradual introduction into primary and secondary schools. It was revised in 1994. Statutory subjects at 5 to 11 years: English (and Welsh in Wales), mathematics, science (core subjects); technology (including information technology), geography, history, art and music (foundation subjects). At 11 to 14 years a foreign language is added. Physical and religious education are not prescribed in the curriculum but are requirements; parents may withdraw their children from the latter.

Nursery Education. Provision for children under 5 is made in either nursery schools or in nursery or infant classes in primary schools. In the public sector no fees are payable. In Jan. 1992 there were 563 public sector nursery and 2,263 private schools and 4,874 primary schools with nursery classes in England. In 1992 there were 52,066 pupils under 5 attending nursery schools and 577,000 pupils under 5 in nursery and infant classes in primary schools. About 48% of all these children were attending part-time. In Wales there were 52 maintained nursery schools in 1995 and 52,360 pupils under 5 years provided for in nursery or infant classes in primary schools.

Primary Schools. These provide for pupils from the age of 5 up to the age of 11. In Jan. 1993 there were 18,828 primary schools in England of which 2,545 were infant schools providing for pupils up to the age of about 7, the remainder mainly taking pupils from age 5 through to 11. Nearly all primary schools take both boys and girls. 19% of primary schools had 100 full time pupils or less.

In Jan. 1995 there were 1,691 primary schools in Wales. In those primary schools (and some secondary schools) which are in the predominantly Welsh-speaking areas, the main language of instruction is Welsh. There are also 'Welsh', or, more accurately, bilingual schools in mainly English-speaking parts of Wales. Generally children transfer from primary to secondary schools at 11.

Middle Schools. A number of local education authorities operate a middle school system. These provide for pupils from the age of 8, 9 or 10 up to the age of 12, 13 or 14. In Jan. 1992 there were 1,036 middle schools in England deemed either primary or secondary according principally to the age range of the school concerned.

Secondary Schools. These usually provide for pupils from the age of 11 upwards. In Jan. 1993 there were 3,773 secondary schools in England and (in 1995) 227 in Wales. In England some local education authorities have retained selection at age 11 for entry to grammar schools of which there were 157 in 1992. There were a small number of technical schools in 1992 which specialise in technical studies. There were 179 secondary modern schools in 1992 providing a general education up to the minimum school leaving age of 16, although exceptionally some pupils stay on beyond that age.

Almost all local education authorities operate a system of comprehensive schools to which pupils are admitted without reference to ability or aptitude. In Jan. 1992 there were 2,872 such schools in England with just under 2·4m. pupils. With the development of comprehensive education various patterns of secondary schools have come into operation. Principally these are: 1. all through schools with pupils aged 11 to 18 or 11 to 16; pupils over 16 being able to transfer to an 11 to 18 school or a sixth form college providing for pupils aged 16 to 19. (There were 115 sixth form colleges in England in 1992). 2. local education authorities operating a three-tier system involving middle schools where transfer to secondary school is at ages 12, 13 or 14. These correspond to 12 to 18, 13 to 18 and 14 to 18 comprehensive schools respectively; or 3. in areas where there are no middle schools a two-tier system of junior and senior comprehensive schools for pupils aged 11 to 18 with optional transfer to these schools at age 13 or 14.

The majority of secondary schools in Wales are classified as comprehensive. In 1995, 48 schools used Welsh as a teaching medium.

Grant Maintained Schools. Local education authority maintained secondary, middle and primary schools can apply for Grant Maintained (GM) status as self-governing state schools. Under GM status schools receive funding directly from the Funding Agency for Schools or, in Wales, from the Welsh Office. Their governing bodies are responsible for all aspects of school management, including the deployment of funds, employment of staff and provision of most of the educational support services for staff and pupils. The first GM primary schools were incorporated in 1991. By Jan. 1995 there were 1,032 GM schools in England (410 primary and 622 secondary) and by Jan. 1996, 5 GM primary and 11 secondary schools in Wales.

City Technology Colleges. New legislation in 1988 enabled the Secretary of State for Education and Science, in partnership with sponsors from business and industry, to fund the establishment of City Technology Colleges. In 1995 there were 15 of these secondary schools for 11-18 year olds, which have a broad curriculum with an emphasis on science and technology. The schools are independent of local education authorities. Their capital costs are shared between central Government and sponsors with Government meeting all recurrent costs. They teach children of all abilities and do not charge fees.

Assisted Places Scheme. In order to give able children a wider range of educational opportunity the Government set up, in 1981, the Assisted Places Scheme to give help with tuition fees at certain independent schools to parents who could not otherwise afford them. In the school year 1993–94 there were 295 participating schools in England and (in 1995–96) 8 in Wales offering a total of 5,922 assisted places, 4,908 for entry at age 11, 12, and 13, and 1,014 for entry at sixth form level.

Special Education. Under the Education Act 1993, children have special educational needs if they have a learning difficulty which calls for special educational provision to be made for them. It has been estimated that, nationally, some 20% of the school population will have special educational needs at some time during their school career. In a minority of cases, perhaps just over 2% of children, the Local Education Authority will need to make a statutory assessment of special educational needs under the Education Act 1993, which may ultimately lead to a 'statement'. In England the total number of pupils with statements in 1994 was about 196,800 (14,521 in Wales in 1995). In England in 1994 there were 1,200 maintained special schools, 73 non-maintained special schools and 38 hospital special schools.

The Education Act 1993 and regulations made thereunder build upon the principles and practices first set out in the 1981 Education Act. They place duties and responsibilities on Local Education Authorities and schools, and all those who help them work with children with special educational needs. Maintained schools must use their best endeavours to make provision for such pupils. The Code of Practice on the Identification and Assessment of Special Educational Needs, which came into force on 1 Sept. 1994, gives practical guidance to these bodies as to how they fulfil their duties. Provision for all children with special educational needs will be made by the most appropriate agency, which in most cases will be the child's mainstream school. However, the Code of Practice recognizes that there is a continuum of needs and a continuum of provision, which may be made in a variety of different forms. However, even before reaching statutory school age, a child may have special educational needs requiring the intervention of the Local Education as well as the Health Authority.

Some pupils with statements remain in school after the age of 16. Local Education Authorities remain responsible for such pupils until they are 19. Others with statements leave school at 16, moving perhaps to a college within the further education sector, or to social services provision.

Ancillary Services. Local Education Authorities and the governing bodies of GM schools may provide registered pupils at schools maintained by them with milk, meals and refreshment and they may make such charges as they think fit. For pupils whose parents or they themselves are in receipt of income support, however, they are required to ensure that such provision is made for the pupil at mid-day as appears to them to be requisite and anything which is provided must be free of charge.

Further Education (Non-University). In 1995–96 there were some 500 institutions in England providing further education in institutions of further and higher education. Course enrolments in 1994–95 numbered some 772,000 full-time (including sandwich) students and 2·8m. part-time and evening students. There are in addition adult education centres providing mainly part-time courses of non-advanced general education. In 1994–95, 1·4m. students attended these centres. On 1 April 1993, further education and sixth-form colleges left local authority control and were brought together under the Further Education Funding Council (England) and the Further Education Funding Council for Wales to create a new sector of publicly-funded further education. In 1994–95, 72% of 16-year-olds were participating in some form of full-time education and 8% part-time. 58% of 17-year-olds were following full-time education and 9% part-time.

Education at institutions of further education is not free, but fees are generally low, and are not charged for students under the age of 19.

In Wales in Nov. 1995 there were 29 institutions in the further education sector and 169,995 students.

The Youth Service. The Youth Service forms part of the education system and is concerned with promoting the personal development and social education of young people through a wide range of leisure-time activities. A duty is laid upon local education authorities by the provisions of the Education Act 1944, as amended by the Further and Higher Education Act 1992, to secure adequate provision of further education which includes the Youth Service. To this end they either provide, maintain and staff youth clubs, centres and other facilities themselves or assist voluntary agencies to do so.

The Youth Service Unit of the Department for Education awards grant to the Headquarters of National Voluntary Youth Organizations (NVYO) for approved national programmes of work which are designed to promote the personal and social education of young people. Only organizations registered under the NVYO scheme are eligible to apply. Over the years 1993–94 to 1995–96 successful applicants are to receive some £8·6m. in total grant. In addition, the National Youth Agency administers on the Department's behalf the Youth Work Development Scheme, which is designed to promote youth work which is developmental and local or regional in nature.

Awards to Students. Local education authorities in England and Wales are responsible for making mandatory awards to suitably qualified students taking first-degree and comparable courses, courses of initial teacher-training and certain other advanced level courses. These awards cover fees and maintenance but the maintenance grants are subject to the income of the student and his or her parents or spouse. In addition studentships may be available both from universities and other sources.

The authorities may also give discretionary awards to students who do not qualify for mandatory awards including those taking non-degree level courses. Grants will be reduced by between 5·3% and 8·6% in 1995–96, depending on students' circumstances.

The Student Loans scheme was introduced by the Government in 1990 to supplement mandatory awards which are now frozen at 1990 levels. Eligible students apply for loans to the Student Loans Company Limited which is funded wholly by the Government. On leaving higher education former students begin to repay loans over a 5-year period when they reach an income threshold of 85% of average earnings. In 1992–93 the Government provided further and higher education institutions with £26·7m. for Access Funds to help students with severe financial difficulties. In 1993–94 47% of students took out loans averaging £747.

In Scotland the Student Awards Agency for Scotland administers the Students' Allowance Scheme and the Postgraduate Students' Allowances Scheme, which offer means-test grants to personally eligible students in full-time, further or higher education. A limited number of grants are also available under the Scottish Studentship Scheme for postgraduate study in the arts and humanities.

Awards known as state studentships are offered on a competitive basis by the Department for Education and the Students Awards Agency for Scotland to candidates considered by the universities and other higher education institutions to be qualified for postgraduate studies in the humanities; similar awards, tenable at universities or other higher education institutions are offered by the Research Councils to students studying topics within the broad spectrum of agriculture and food; the biological sciences; man's natural environment; science and engineering and the social sciences at postgraduate level.

The 5 Research Councils made over 7,300 new awards in 1990-91 and there were more than 15,000 current awards in that academic year. In 1992–93 the British Academy gave 924 new awards and the Department 437 state bursaries, 204 library bursaries and 25 state studentships.

Teachers. To attain qualified teacher status, for work in maintained schools in England and Wales, teachers must have successfully completed a course of professional training. This can be achieved either by completing a programme of initial training for teachers in schools, conforming to arrangements set out in the current Education (Teachers) Regulations or, in the case of mature entrants with a certain level of higher education and teachers who have trained abroad, a period of 'on the job' training as a licensed teacher or overseas trained teacher. School teachers from Scotland or Northern Ireland may be entitled to qualified teacher status if they have successfully completed a course of initial teacher training, or are recognized as teachers in those countries. Teachers who are nationals of participating member states of the European Economic Area may be entitled to qualified teacher status if they meet the requirements on the mutual recognition of qualifications.

In 1993–94 there were about 33,250 students on initial teacher-training courses; this figure includes students on the Open University courses and school-centred courses.

On 1 Jan. 1994, 436,898 teachers were employed by local education authorities in maintained nursery, primary and secondary schools and by Grant-Maintained Schools in England and Wales.

Finance. Total current and capital expenditure on education in England (including Universities GB, and Mandatory Awards England and Wales) from public funds is estimated at £27,061m. for 1993–94 as compared with £25,359m. for 1992–93.

Education (Scotland). The statistics on schools relate to education authority and grant-aided schools. All teachers employed in these schools require to be qualified; figures given are full-time equivalents.

Nursery Education. In Sept. 1995 there were 784 nursery schools and departments, with a total enrolment of 49,760 pupils.

Primary Education. In Sept. 1995 there were 2,336 primary schools and departments and the number on the registers was 438,010. In Sept. 1994, 22,638 teachers were employed in primary schools and departments.

Secondary Education. In Sept. 1995 there were 405 secondary schools with 314,907 pupils. All but 31 schools provided a full range of Scottish Certificate of Education courses and non-certificate courses. Pupils who start their secondary education in schools which do not cater for a full range of courses may be transferred at the end of their second or fourth year to schools where a full range of courses is provided. There were 24,487 full-time equivalent teachers in secondary schools at Sept. 1995.

Special Schools. In Sept. 1995 there were 318 special schools and departments. 8,712 children were under instruction.

Further Education. Under the Further and Higher Education (Scotland) Act 1992 funding of further education colleges was transferred to central government on 1 April 1993.

There are 43 incorporated colleges in Scotland as well as the education centres in Orkney and Shetland which are run by the education authorities but funded by direct payments from the Scottish Office Education Department. The colleges offer training in a wide range of vocational areas and co-operate with the Scottish Vocational Education Council and the Scottish Office Education Department in the development of new courses. Scottish Vocational Qualifications (SVQs) were introduced in 1989 and the general SVQs were piloted in 1993. Both qualifications aim to improve the skills of the nation's workforce and increase the country's competitiveness. The colleges benefit from co-operation with industry, both by the involvement of Industry Lead Bodies in developing SVQs and by membership of the college boards of management.

Independent Schools. Outside the state system of education there were in England 2,266 independent schools in Jan. 1994, ranging from large 'public' schools to small local ones. There were (Jan. 1994) 555,900 pupils in these schools. In Wales (1994) 10,672 full-time pupils attended 64 independent schools. Fees are charged by all these schools, which receive no grant from central government sources. All independent schools in England (and Wales) are required to be registered by the Department for Education (and the Welsh Office) and are liable to the inspection by HM Inspectors. The term 'public schools' refers to independent schools in membership of the Headmasters' Conference, Governing Bodies Association or the Governing Bodies of Girls' Schools Association. Qualifications under which a school may be represented at the Headmasters' Conference include the measure of independence enjoyed by the governing body and the amount of advanced courses undertaken. Some of these schools are for boarders only, but the majority include non-resident 'day-pupils'. In Scotland there were 113 independent schools, with a total of 32,303 pupils in Sept. 1995. A small number of the Scottish independent schools are of the 'public school' type but they are not known as 'public schools' since in Scotland this term is used to denote education authority (*i.e.*, state) schools.

The earliest of the schools were founded by, and attached to, medieval churches. Many were founded as 'grammar' (classical) schools in the 16th century, receiving charters from the reigning sovereign. Reformed mainly in the middle of the 19th century, among the best-known are Eton College, founded in 1440 by Henry VI; Winchester College (1394) founded by William of Wykeham, Bishop of Winchester; Harrow School, founded in 1560 as a grammar school by John Lyon, a yeoman; and Charterhouse (1611). Among the earliest foundations are King's School, Canterbury, founded 600; King's School, Rochester (604) and St Peter's, York, (627).

Higher Education. The Further and Higher Education Act 1992 removed the polytechnics from local authority funding and gave them university title. The Act created the Higher Education Funding Council for England (HEFCE), the Higher Education Funding Council for Wales (HEFCW) and the Scottish Higher Education Funding Council (SHEFC) to be responsible as from 1 April 1993 for the funding of universities and other higher education institutions and prescribed courses of higher education in further education colleges. The higher education funding councils are non-departmental public bodies operating within a policy and funding context set by the government. Their task is to advise the Secretary of State on the funding needs of institutions and to distribute the funds that the Secretary makes available for the provision of education and the undertaking of research.

University status is granted by the Higher Education Quality Council.

Polytechnics created universities by the 1992 Act (P = Polytechnic): Anglia P became Anglia P Univ.; Birmingham P, Univ. of Central England in Birmingham; Bournemouth P, Bournemouth Univ.; Brighton P, Univ. of Brighton; Bristol P, Univ. of the West of England, Bristol; City of London P, London Guildhall Univ.; Coventry P, Coventry Univ.; Derby P, Univ. of Derby; Hatfield P, Univ. of Hertfordshire; Huddersfield P, Univ. of Huddersfield; Humberside P, Univ. of Humberside; Kingston P, Kinston Univ.; Leeds P, Leeds Metropolitan Univ.; Lancashire P, Univ. of Central Lancashire; Leicester P, De Montfort Univ.; Liverpool P, Liverpool John Moores Univ.; Manchester P, Manchester Metropolitan Univ.; Middlesex P, Middlesex Univ.; Newcastle P, Univ. of Northumbria at Newcastle; Nottingham P, Nottingham Trent Univ.; Oxford P, Oxford Brookes Univ.; P of Central London, Univ. of Westminster; P of East London, Univ. of East London; P of North London, Univ. of North London; P South West, Univ. of Plymouth; P of West London, Thames Valley Univ.; Portsmouth P, Univ. of Portsmouth; Sheffield City P, Sheffield Hallam Univ.; South Bank P, South Bank Univ.; Staffordshire P, Staffordshire Univ.; Sunderland P, Univ. of Sunderland; Teesside P, Univ. of Teesside; Thames P, Univ. of Greenwich; Wolverhampton P, Univ. of Wolverhampton.

In *England* in 1995–96 there were 137 institutions of higher education directly funded by the HEFCE, of which 70 were universities. In 1995–96 the HEFCE distributed £3,207m. in funding: £2,270m. for teaching, £636m. for research, £287m. of non-formula money and £14m. transitional funding. There were 1,137,000 students in funded institutions, including 727,000 full-time.

a) *Universities*

Name (Location)	*No. of students (1994–95)*	*No. of academic staff (1994–95)*
Anglia Polytechnic Univ. (Chelmsford)	12,006	517
Aston Univ. (Birmingham)	4,950	...
Univ. of Bath	7,031	377
Univ. of Birmingham	17,393	2,379
Bournemouth Univ. (Poole)	9,709	420
Univ. of Bradford	7,980	400
Univ. of Brighton	6,235	500
Univ. of Bristol	10,627	841
Brunel Univ. (Uxbridge)	7,374	267
Univ. of Cambridge	13,920	1,260
Univ. of Central England in Birmingham	6,000	650
Univ. of Central Lancashire (Preston)	16,990	516
City Univ. (London)	6,373	360
Coventry Univ.	8,345	550
Cranfield Univ. (Bedford)	2,090	...
De Montfort Univ. (Leicester)	26,000	600
Univ. of Derby	11,368	...
Univ. of Durham	5,600	435
Univ. of East Anglia (Norwich)	4,600	360
Univ of East London (London)	10,000	500
Univ. of Essex (Colchester)	3,650	300
Univ. of Exeter	9,031	530
Univ. of Greenwich (London)	17,376	500
Univ. of Hertfordshire (Hatfield)	8,000	480
Univ. of Huddersfield	6,816[1]	...
Univ. of Hull	8,884	456
Univ. of Humberside (Hull)	12,580	362
Univ. of Keele	3,750	320
Univ. of Kent at Canterbury	5,981	403
Kingston Univ. (Kingston upon Thames)	6,868	430
Univ. of Lancaster	5,860	450
Univ. of Leeds	17,505	1,100
Leeds Metropolitan Univ.	16,800	1,260
Univ. of Leicester	9,357	603

a) *Universities–Contd.*

Name (Location)	*No. of students (1994–95)*	*No. of academic staff (1994–95)*
Univ. of Liverpool	13,712	1,007
Liverpool John Moores Univ.	9,940[1]	...
Univ. of London	59,427[1]	...
London Guildhall Univ.	5,496[1]	...
Loughborough Univ. of Technology	9,963	564
Luton Univ.	14,000	700
Univ. of Manchester	16,086	2,050
Univ. of Manchester Institute of Science and Technology	6,030	463
Manchester Metropolitan Univ.	29,891	900
Middlesex Univ. (London)	11,570	410
Univ. of Newcastle upon Tyne	12,870	1,852
Univ. of North London	8,500	525
Univ. of Northumbria at Newcastle	18,174	780
Univ. of Nottingham	12,960	1,062
Nottingham Trent Univ.	9,620	755
Univ. of Oxford	16,080	1,650
Oxford Brookes Univ.	11,000	590
Univ. of Plymouth	16,489	595
Univ. of Portsmouth	7,100	630
Univ. of Reading	9,700	760
Univ. of Salford	4,325	390
Univ. of Sheffield	13,288[1]	...
Sheffield Hallam Univ.	18,645	927
Univ. of Southampton	9,238	740
South Bank Univ. (London)	19,674	545
Staffordshire Univ. (Stoke on Trent)	13,359	523
Univ. of Sunderland	4,380	400
Univ. of Surrey (Guildford)	5,301	376
Univ. of Sussex (Brighton)	8,905	520
Univ. of Teesside (Middlesbrough)	4,902[1]	...
Thames Valley Univ. (London)	3,877[1]	...
Univ. of Warwick (Coventry)	13,800	637
Univ. of Westminster (London)	19,246	395
Univ. of the West of England, Bristol	18,328	673
Univ. of Wolverhampton	21,384	453
Univ. of York	4,380	360

[1] 1993–94.

b) *Other Institutions*

Bath College of Higher Education[1]; Bishop Grosseteste College (Lincoln); Bolton Institute of Higher Education[1]; Bretton Hall (Wakefield); Buckinghamshire College of Higher Education (High Wycombe); Central School of Speech and Drama (London); Canterbury Christ Church College; Cheltenham and Gloucester College of Higher Education[1]; Chester College of Higher Education; College of Guidance Studies (Swanley); College of Ripon and York St. John (York); College of St. Mark and St. John (Plymouth); Dartington College of Arts (Totnes); Edge Hill College of Higher Education (Ormskirk); Falmouth School of Art and Design; Harper Adams Agricultural College (Newport); Homerton College (Cambridge); Institute of Advanced Nursing Education (London); Kent Institute of Art and Design (Maidstone); King Alfred's College, Winchester; La Sainte Union College of Higher Education (Southampton); Liverpool Institute of Higher Education; London Business School; The London Institute; Loughborough College of Art and Design; Nene College (Northampton); Newman College (Birmingham); North Riding College (Scarborough); Ravensbourne College of Design and Communication (Bromley); Roehampton Institute (London); Rose Bruford College of Speech and Drama (Sidcup); Royal Academy of Music (London); Royal College of Art (London); Royal College of Music (London); Royal Northern College of Music (Manchester); St. Martin's College (Lancaster); St. Mary's College (Twickenham); Salford College of Technology; Southampton Institute of Higher Education; Trinity and All Saints (Leeds); Trinity College of Music (London); Westhill College (Birmingham); West London Institute of Higher Education; Westminster College, Oxford; West Surrey College of Art and Design (Farnham)[1]; West Sussex Institute of Higher Education (Chichester); Wimbledon School of Art; Winchester School of Art; Worcester College of Higher Education.

[1] May award degrees

In *Wales* in 1995 there were 15 institutions of higher education funded by the HEFCW, including 2 universities: the Univ. of Wales (1993–94, 32,022 full-time and sandwich students), with 6 constituent colleges (University College of Wales Aberystwyth; University College of North Wales Bangor; Univ. of Wales College of Cardiff; St David's University College Lampeter; University College of Swansea; Univ. of Wales College of Medicine, in Cardiff); and the Univ. of Glamorgan (Pontypridd) (1993–94, 8,067 full-time and sandwich students), formed from the Polytechnic of Wales in 1992. The other institutions were: Cardiff Institute of Higher Education, Coleg Normal Bangor, Gwent College of Higher Education (Newport), North East Wales Institute (Wrexham), Swansea Institute of Higher Education, Trinity College Carmarthen, Welsh College of Music and Drama (Cardiff). The Welsh Agricultural College merged with University College of Wales Aberystwyth on 1 March 1995. In 1993–94 there was a total of 15,193 full-time and sandwich students at these colleges. In 1994–95, the Univ. of Glamorgan had 14,425 students and 450 academic staff, and the University of Wales had 36,567 students.

In *Scotland* in 1995 there were 21 institutions of higher education funded by the SHEFC, of which 5 were universities formed from former central institutions (*cf.* English polytechnics): Abertay Dundee Univ., Glasgow Caledonian Univ., Napier Univ. (Edinburgh), Univ. of Paisley, The Robert Gordon Univ. (Aberdeen); and 8 were already-existing universities:

a) *Universities*

Name (and Location)	*Full-time and sandwich students (1994–95)*	*Full-time academic staff (1994–95)*
Aberdeen Univ.	9,009	525
Abertay Dundee Univ.	3,630	100
Dundee Univ.	5,474	700
Edinburgh Univ.	15,389	1,186
Glasgow Univ.	15,097	1,233
Glasgow Caledonian Univ.	8,016	513
Heriot-Watt Univ. (Edinburgh)	4,392	600
Napier Univ. (Edinburgh)	6,825	486
Paisley Univ.	5,831	290
Robert Gordon Univ. (Aberdeen)	5,809	400
St Andrews Univ.	5,184	325
Stirling Univ.	5,252	360
Strathclyde Univ. (Glasgow)	13,493	1,127
Total	*103,401*	*7,845*

b) *Other Institutions*

Edinburgh College of Art, Glasgow School of Art, Moray House Institute of Education (Edinburgh), Northern College of Education (Aberdeen and Dundee), Queen Margaret College (Edinburgh), Royal Scottish Academy of Music and Drama (Glasgow), Scottish College of Textiles (Galashiels), St. Andrew's College of Education (Glasgow).

The Scottish Agricultural College (Perth) is funded by the Scottish Office Agriculture and Fisheries Department.

In 1994–95 there were 115,514 full-time and sandwich students at the institutions funded by SHEFC (57,034 female).

All the higher education institutions are independent and self-governing. In addition to funding through the higher education funding councils they receive tuition fees through local education authorities for students domiciled in England and Wales, and from the Students Awards Agency for Scotland for students domiciled in Scotland. Institutions which carry out research may also receive funding through the 5 Research Councils administered by the Office of Science and Technology.

The *Open University* received its Royal Charter on 1 June 1969 and is an independent, self-governing institution, awarding its own degrees at undergraduate and postgraduate level. It is financed by the Government through the HEFCE and by the receipt of students' fees. Tuition is by means of correspondence textbooks, audio and video cassettes, radio and television broadcasts and residential schools. Some courses require access to a personal computer. There are also over 290 local study centres where face-to-face tutorials and counselling services may be offered. No formal qualifications are required for entry to undergraduate or associate student courses. Residents from most countries of Western Europe aged 18 or over may apply, though some courses are not available outside the UK. There are over 130 undergraduate courses; many are available on a one-off basis to associate students. In 1994 there were over 90,000 undergraduates, over 8,000 postgraduates and over 30,000 short course and associate students, The university has some 3,000 full-time staff working at its Milton Keynes headquarters and in 13 regional centres throughout the country. There are over 6,000 part-time tutors and counsellors.

One university is independent of the state system, the *University of Buckingham*, which opened in 1976 and received a Royal charter in 1983. It offers 2-year courses towards its own honours degrees, the academic year commencing in Jan. and consisting of four 10-week terms. There are 4 Schools of Studies with 11 academic departments: Business; Humanities; Law; and Sciences. Postgraduate opportunities are offered in all the schools of studies. In 1995, there were 1,009 full-time students and 105 teachers (22 part-time).

All universities charge fees, but financial help is available to students from several sources (*see Awards to Students* above), and the majority of students receive some form of financial assistance.

Number of women students 1990–91: England, 118,174; Scotland, 23,739; Wales (1992–93), 35,035. There are colleges exclusively for women at Oxford and Cambridge. Total number of full-time or sandwich students, 1990–91 England, 274,830; Scotland, 54,042; Wales (1992–93), 49,965.

The British Council. The British Council promotes cultural, educational and technical co-operation between Britain and other countries. Established in 1934 and incorporated by Royal Charter in 1940, it is Britain's principal agency for cultural relations overseas. An independent, non-political organization, it is represented in 100 countries, running a mix of offices, libraries, resource centres and English-teaching operations. Its headquarters are in London and Manchester with regional centres in Belfast, Cardiff and Edinburgh.

The British Council's total expenditure in 1994–95 was £426·9m. This was made up of government grants (£139·8m.), revenues from English language teaching and client-funded education services (£115·5m.) and development programmes, principally in education and training, which are managed on behalf of the British Government and other clients (£171·6m.).

The British Council seeks to maximize Britain's role in the world. It does this by extending the use and improving the teaching of English; promoting international partnerships in cultural, educational and scientific fields; demonstrating the achievements of British arts; extending Britain's contribution to overseas development; and promoting, in response to overseas demand, the use of British goods and services in education and training.

Chairman: Sir Martin Jacomb.
Director-General: Sir John Hanson, KCMG, CBE.
Headquarters: 10 Spring Gdns., London, SW1A 2BN.

Donaldson, F., *The British Council: the First Fifty Years.* London, 1984.

National Insurance. The National Insurance Act 1946 came into operation on 5 July 1948, repealing the existing schemes of health, pensions and unemployment insurance. This Act, along with later legislation, was consolidated as the National

Insurance Act 1965. The scheme now operates under the Social Security Contributions and Benefits Act 1992 and the Social Security Administration Act 1992.

Since 1975, Class 1 contributions have been related to the employee's earnings and are collected with PAYE income tax, instead of by affixing stamps to a card. Class 2 and Class 3 contributions remain flat-rate, but, in addition to Class 2 contributions, those who are self-employed may be liable to pay Class 4 contributions, which for the year 1996–97 are at the rate of 6% on profits or gains between £6,860 and £23,660, which are assessable for income tax under Schedule D. The non-employed and others whose contribution record is not sufficient to give entitlement to benefits are able to pay a Class 3 contribution of £5·95 per week in 1996–97 voluntarily to qualify for a limited range of benefits. Class 2 weekly contributions for 1996–97 for men and women are £6·05. Class 1A contributions are paid by employers who provide employees with a car and fuel for their private use.

From 6 April 1978 the Social Security Pensions Act 1975 introduced earnings-related retirement, invalidity and widows' pensions. Members of occupational pension schemes may be contracted out of the earnings-related part of the state scheme relating to retirement and widows' benefits. Employee's national insurance contribution liability depends on whether he/she is in contracted-out or not contracted-out employment.

Full rate contributions for non-contracted-out employment in 1996–97:

Weekly earnings (in £1)	*Yearly earnings (in £1)*	*Employee pays*	*Employer pays*
Nil–60	Nil–3,171	Nil	Nil
61–109	3,172–5,719	10%[1]	3%
110–154	5,720–8,059	10%[1]	5%
155–209	8,060–10,919	10%[1]	7%
210–454	10,920–23,659	10%[1]	10·2%
Over 455	Over 23,660	10%[1]	10·2%

[1] Plus 2% of £61.

Where earnings exceed £60 per week the employee contributes 2% of earnings up to £61 and 10% thereafter.

For contracted-out employment the employees' contributions are as above but 8·2% on weekly earnings of £61–£455. The employer's rates are reduced by 3%.

From April 1996 employers who engage a trainee, or a person who has been unemployed for at least 2 years are eligible for a year's rebate of contributions.

Contributions together with interest on investments form the income of the *National Insurance Fund* from which benefits are paid. A Treasury grant was instituted in 1993.

Receipts, 1993–94 (in £1m.), 47,771·38, including: Contributions, 35,089·75; compensation from Consolidated Fund for recoveries, 1,122; investment income, 469·8. Disbursements, 43,222·73, including: Unemployment Benefit, 1,651·76; Sickness Benefit, 365; Invalidity Benefit, 7,067·82; Maternity Allowances, 33; Widow's Benefit, 1,040; Guardian's Allowances, 1; Retirement Pensions, 28,183·11; Pensioners' Lump Sums, 122·1; Personal Pensions, 2,859·53; transfers to Northern Ireland, 40; administration, 1,555·39; redundancy payments, 268·97.

Statutory Sick Pay (SSP). Employers are responsible for paying statutory sick pay (SSP) to their employees for up to 28 weeks in any period of incapacity for work. Basically, all employees aged between 16 and 65 (60 for women) with earnings above the Lower Earnings Limit are covered by the scheme whenever they are sick for 4 or more days consecutively. There are 2 weekly rates, £47·80 or £52·50 depending on average weekly earnings. For most employees SSP completely replaces their entitlement to state incapacity benefit which is not payable as long as any employer's responsibility for SSP remains.

Pregnant working women may be eligible to receive statutory maternity pay directly from their employer for a maximum of 18 weeks. There are 2 rates: Where a woman has been working for the same employer for at least 2 years, she is entitled to 90% of her average weekly earnings for the first 6 weeks and to the lower rate of £52·50 a week for the remaining 12 weeks; and where a woman has been employed for between 26 weeks and 2 years, she is entitled to payments for up to 18 weeks at the lower rate. Employers are reimbursed by the state for 92% of the amount they pay.

Women who are not eligible for statutory maternity pay, those who are self-employed, have recently changed jobs or given up their job, may qualify for a weekly maternity allowance of £44·55, which is payable for up to 18 weeks.

All pregnant employees have the right to take 14 weeks' maternity leave.

A payment of £100 from the social fund may be available if the mother or her partner are receiving income suport, family credit or disability working allowance. It is also available if a woman adopts a baby.

Contributory benefits. Qualification for these depends upon fulfilment of the appropriate contribution conditions, except that persons who are incapable of work as the result of an industrial accident may receive incapacity benefit followed by invalidity benefit without having to satisfy the contributions conditions. Employed persons may qualify for all the benefits; self-employed persons may not qualify for unemployment benefit.

Unemployment Benefit (renamed *Jobseekers' Allowance* after April 1996) is payable for up to 1 year in any one period of unemployment. The rate is £46·45 a week, £75·10 a week for a couple. Benefit is not payable to persons who left their job voluntarily or through misconduct. In 1994–95, there were some 445,000 beneficiaries.

Incapacity benefit. This replaced the former sickness benefit and invalidity benefit on 13 April 1995. Entitlement begins when entitlement to SSP (if any) ends. There are 3 rates: A lower rate of £44·40 a week for the first 28 weeks; a higher rate of £52·50 a week between the 29th and 52nd week; and a long-term rate of £58·85 a week from the 53rd week of incapacity. It also comprises certain age additions and increases for adult and child dependants. A more objective medical test of incapacity for work was introduced for incapacity benefit as well as for other social security benefits paid on the basis of incapacity for work. This test applies after 28 weeks' incapacity for work and assesses ability to perform a range of work-related activities rather than the ability to perform a specific job. Some 1,999,000 claims were met in 1994–95.

Maternity Benefit. Women who do not qualify for statutory maternity pay may be entitled to maternity allowance if they satisfy a test of recent work and contributions paid. The weekly rate is £44·55. Maternity allowance can be paid for up to 18 weeks. Payment can start at the earliest 11 weeks before the expected week of confinement but the woman has some choice in deciding when to give up work and still retain title to the full 18 weeks.

Widow's Benefits. From 11 April 1988 the three main widow's benefits are: Widow's payment, widowed mother's allowance, widow's pension.

A widow cannot get any widow's benefits based on her husband's NI if: She had been divorced from the man who has died; or she was living with the man as if she were married to him, but without being legally married to him; or she is living with another man as if she is married to him; or she was in prison or held in legal custody. A widow can only get widow's benefits if her husband has paid enough NI contributions. *Widow's Payment* is a single tax-free payment of £1,000. A widow may be able to get this benefit if her husband has paid enough NI contributions and she was under 60 when her husband died; or her husband was not getting a State Retirement Pension when he died. *Widowed Mother's Allowance:* A widow may be able to get a widowed mother's allowance if her husband has paid enough NI contributions and she is receiving child benefit for one of her children, or her husband was receiving child benefit, or she is expecting her husband's baby, or if she was widowed before 11 April 1988 and has a young person under 19 living with her for whom she was receiving Child Benefit. A widow entitled to a widowed mother's allowance will get an amount based on her husband's NI contributions. The maximum will be £58·85 a week. She will also get £9·85 a week for her eldest dependent child and £11·05 for each subsequent child and she may also get an additional pension based on her husband's earnings since 1978. Widowed mother's allowance is usually paid as long as the widow is getting child benefit. It is taxable. *Widow's Pension:* A widow may be able to get a widow's pension if her husband has paid enough NI contributions. She must be 45 or over (40 or over if widowed before 11 April 1988) when her husband died or when her widowed mother's allowance ends. A widow cannot get a widow's pension at the same time as a widowed mother's allowance. A widow who is entitled to a widow's pension will get an amount that depends on her age when her husband died or when her widowed mother's allowance ends. If she was 55 or over (50 or over if widowed before 11 April 1988) she will get the full rate of widow's pension. The maximum amount of widow's pension will be £58·85 a week. She may also get an additional pension based on her husband's earnings since 1978. If her late husband was a member of a contracted-out occupational scheme or a personal pension scheme that scheme is responsible for paying the whole or part of the additional pensions. Widow's pension is usually paid until the widow is entitled to state retirement pension, when she is 60 or older. Widow's pension is taxable. There were some 313,000 pensioners in 1994–95.

Retirement Pension. The state retirement ('old age') pension scheme has 2 components: A basic pension and an earnings-related pension (State Earnings Related Pension — SERPS). The amount of the first is, subject to National Insurance contributions made; SERPS is 1·25% of average earnings between the lower weekly earnings limit for Class I contribution liability and the upper earnings limit for each year of such earnings. Pensions are payable, to women at 60 years of age and men at 65, but the age differential will be progressively phased out starting in April 2010. Women born before 6 April 1950 will be unaffected; women born after 5 March 1955 will receive their pension at 65; pension age for women between these dates will move up gradually from 60 to 65. The standard rates of basic pensions are £58·85 a week for a man or woman on his or her own contributions and £94·10 for a married couple. Proportionately reduced pensions are payable where contribution records are deficient.

Employees in an occupational scheme may be contracted out of SERPS provided that the occupational scheme provides a pension not less than the 'guaranteed minimum pension'. Self-employed persons, and also employees, may substitute personal pension schemes for SERPS. An independent statutory body, the Occupational Pension Board, is responsible for supervising contracted-out schemes.

Persons who defer claiming their pension during the 5 years following retirement age are paid an increased amount. In addition, a man who had paid graduated contributions receives 7·64p per week for every £7·50 of graduated contributions paid, and a woman 7·64p per week for every £9 paid. Although no further graduated contributions have been paid after April 1975, pension already earned will be paid along with the basic pension in the normal way. In 1994–95 there were some 10,087,000 persons were receiving pensions. Since 1 Oct 1989 the pension for which a person has qualified may be paid in full whether a person continues in work or not irrespective of the amount of earnings.

At the age of 80 an age addition of £0·25 a week is payable. In addition non-contributory pensions are now payable, subject to residence conditions, to persons aged 80 and over who do not qualify for a retirement pension or qualify for one at a low rate. The rates of these pensions, which are financed by Exchequer funds, are £35·25 a week. These amounts do not include the £0·25 age addition.

Pensioners whose pension is insufficient to live on may qualify for Income Support.

Non-Contributory Benefits.

Child Benefit. Child benefit is a tax-free cash allowance for children normally paid to the mother. The weekly rates are £10·40 for the eldest qualifying child and £8·45 for each other child. Child benefit is payable for children under 16, for 16 and 17 year olds registered for work or training and for those under 19 receiving full-time non-advanced education. Some 12,685,000 children in 6,950,000 families received benefit in 1994–95.

One Parent Benefit is a tax-free cash allowance for certain people bringing up children alone. It is payable for the first or only child in the family in addition to child benefit. The weekly rate is £6·30. There were some 938,000 beneficiaries in 1994–95.

Child Support Agency. The Agency, which started work in April 1993, will, over a 4-year phased timetable, replace the court system for obtaining maintenance for children being brought up by single parents. The Agency is responsible for assessing, collecting and enforcing child maintenance payments and for tracing absent parents. Assessments are made using a formula which takes into account each parent's income and essential outgoings. Changes to the child support arrangements were introduced in Feb. 1994 to take account of concerns raised by members of the public and MPs. These are designed to reduce the amount of child maintenance that many absent parents are required to pay and to give some families more time to adjust to increased bills. In 1994–95 the Agency took on 398,584 new cases and completed 568,149 assessments.

Family Credit. Family Credit is a tax-free benefit for working families with children. To be able to get Family Credit there must be at least one child under 16 in the family (or under 19 if in full-time education up to, and including, A level or equivalent standard). The claimant or partner (if there is one) must be working at least 16 hours a week to qualify. They may be employed or self-employed, a lone parent or a couple. The claim should be made by the woman in two-parent families. The amount of Family Credit payable depends on the income of the claimant and partner, how many children there are in the family and their ages. The same rates of benefit are paid for one-parent families as for two-parent families. A maximum award, consisting of an adult rate of £45·10 a week plus a rate for each child varying with age is payable if the family's income does not exceed £73·00 a week. The award is reduced by £0·70 for each extra £1 earned. Family Credit is not payable if the claimant (or claimant and partner together) have savings or capital of over £8,000. Benefit is reduced if savings or capital of more than £3,000 is held. Family Credit is paid at the same rate for 26 weeks. The amount of the award will usually stay the same even if earnings, or other circumstances, change during that period. There were some 591,000 recipients in 1994–95.

Guardian's Allowance. A person responsible for an orphan child may be entitled to a guardian's allowance of £11·05 a week in addition to child benefit. Normally both the child's parents must be dead but when they never married or were divorced, or one is missing, or serving a long sentence of imprisonment, the allowance may be paid on the death of one parent only.

Attendance Allowance. This is a tax-free Social Security benefit for disabled people over 65 who need help with personal care. Current rate, £31·20 a week (£46·70 a week for the terminally ill). There were some 1,084,000 recipients in 1994–95.

Invalid Care Allowance. This is a taxable benefit which may be paid to those who forgo the opportunity of full-time work to care for a person who is receiving attendance allowance, constant attendance allowance or the highest or middle-core component of Disability Living Allowance. Current rate £35·25 a week, with increases for dependants.

Disability Living Allowance. This is a non-taxable benefit available to people disabled before the age of 65 who need help with getting around or with personal care for at least 3 months. The mobility component has 2 weekly rates: £32·65 or £12·40; the care component has 3: £46·70, £31·20 or £12·40. There were some 1,420,000 recipients in 1994–95.

Disability Working Allowance. This is a tax-free benefit for people with an illness or disability which puts them at a disadvantage in getting a job. It is income-related and is intended for people who are starting work or already working at least 16 hours a week. The allowance is not payable if assets exceed £16,000. About 5,000 people received the allowance in 1994–95.

Industrial Injuries Disablement and Death Benefits. The Industrial Injuries Act, which also came into operation on 5 July 1948, with its later amending Acts, was consolidated as the National Insurance (Industrial Injuries) Act, 1965. This legislation was incorporated in the Social Security Act, 1975. The scheme provides a system of insurance against 'personal injury by accident arising out of and in the course of employment' and against certain prescribed diseases and injuries due to the nature of the employment. It takes the place of the Workmen's Compensation Acts and covers persons who are employed earners under the Social Security Act. There are no contribution conditions for the payment of benefit. Three types of benefit are provided:

Disablement benefit. This is payable where, as the result of an industrial accident or prescribed disease, there is a loss of physical or mental faculty. The loss of faculty will be assessed as a percentage by comparison with a person of the same age and sex whose condition is normal. If the assessment is between 14–100% benefit will be paid as weekly pension; 14–19% are payable at the 20% rate. The rates vary from £19·06 (20% disabled) to £95·30 (100% disablement). Assessments of less than 14% do not normally attract basic benefit except for certain progressive chest diseases. Pensions for persons under 18 are at a reduced rate. When injury benefit was abolished for industrial accidents occurring and prescribed diseases commencing on or after 6 April 1983, a common start date was introduced for the payment of disablement benefit 90 days (excluding Sundays) after the date of the relevant accident or onset of the disease. The following increases can be paid with disablement benefit: Constant attendance allowance – where the disability for which the claimant is receiving disablement benefit is assessed at 100% and is so severe that they need constant care and attention. There are 4 rates depending on the amount of attendance needed. Exceptionally severe disablement allowance – where the claimant is in receipt of constant attendance allowance at one of the two higher rates and the need for attendance is likely to be permanent.

Reduced earnings allowance (REA) is a separate benefit. Entitlement exists if the claimant has not retired and cannot go back to their normal job or do another job for the same pay because of the effects of the disability caused by an accident or disease which occurred on or before 30 Sept. 1990. It can be paid whether or not disablement benefit is paid, providing the disablement benefit assessment is 1% or more (*e.g.* where disablement is assessed at less than 14%) and on top of 100% disablement benefit. From 1 Oct. 1989, if a claimant is of pensionable age (60 for a woman, 65 for a man) they can continue to receive REA if they are in regular employment, or in some cases if they are receiving Sickness Benefit, Invalidity Benefit or Unemployment Benefit. It will not matter whether or not they receive State Retirement Pension. If they are not in regular employment then entitlement to REA will cease. In most cases it will be replaced by Retirement Allowance.

Death Benefit. This is payable to the widow of a person who died before 11 April 1988 as the result of an industrial accident or a prescribed disease. Deaths which occurred on or after 11 April 1988 – a widow is entitled to full widow's benefits even if her late husband did not satisfy the contribution condition, if he died as a result of an industrial accident or prescribed disease.

Allowances may be paid to people who are suffering from pneumoconiosis or byssinosis or certain other slowly developing diseases due to employment before 5 July 1948. They must not at any time have been entitled to benefit for the disabled under the Industrial Injuries provision of the Social Security Act or compensation under Workmen's Compensation Acts or received damages through the courts.

In certain cases supplementation allowances are payable to people who are getting or are entitled to compensation under the Workmen's Compensation Acts.

War Pensions. Pensions are payable for disablement or death as a result of service in the armed forces, Merchant Navy or Civil Defence during war, or to civilians injured by enemy action. The amount depends on the degree of disablement. The maximum is £101·10 a week; war widows, £76·35. Various supplements may apply.

Severe Disablement Allowance. A severe disablement allowance of £35·55 plus an age-related addition of up to £12·40 a week may be payable to people under pensionable age who have been continuously incapable of work for at least 28 weeks but who do not qualify for incapacity benefit. Those over 20 who are unable to work and are 80% disabled but do not qualify for the National Insurance invalidity pension because they have not paid sufficient contributions may be entitled to severe disablement allowance. Additions for adult dependants and for children may also be paid. There were some 342,000 beneficiaries in 1994–95.

Housing Benefit. The housing benefit scheme assists persons who need help to pay their rent, using general assessment rules and benefit levels similar to those for the income support scheme. People whose net income is below certain specified levels qualify for housing benefit of up to 100% of their rent. The scheme sets a limit of £16,000 on the amount of capital a person may have and still remain entitled. Restrictions on the granting of benefit to persons under 25 were introduced in 1995.

Council Tax Benefit. The scheme offers help to those claiming income support and others with low incomes. Subject to rules broadly similar to those governing the provision of income support and housing benefit, people may receive rebates of up to 100% of their council tax. In 1994–95 some 5,641,000 households received such help. A person who is liable for the council tax may also claim benefit (called 'second adult rebate') for a second adult who is not liable to pay the council tax and who is living in the home on a non-commercial basis.

Income Support. Under the Social Security Act, 1986, benefit is payable to any persons in Great Britain aged 18 years or over (excluding persons at school or college or anyone directly involved in a trade dispute) who are not in full-time work or who work for less than 16 hours per week and who are without resources, or whose resources (including national insurance benefits) need to be supplemented in order to meet their requirements. Income Support is not payable if the claimant (or claimant and partner together) have savings or capital over £8,000. Benefit is reduced if savings or capital of more than £3,000 is held. A person who is excluded from benefit under the normal rules may, in certain limited circumstances, receive payments to meet urgent need. Current rates range from £28·00 a week for a single person under 18 to £73·00 for a couple, both over 18. Additional sums, known as premiums, are available to families, lone parents, pensioners, long-term sick and disabled people, and those caring for them who qualify for the invalid care allowance.

The Social Fund. The Fund makes payments and loans to help recipients meet intermittent expenses. 'Regulated payments' comprise *Maternity Payments* (a payment of up to £100 for each baby expected, born or adopted, payable to persons receiving income support, disability working allowance or family credit); *Funeral Payments* (a payment of reasonable funeral expenses incurred by persons receiving income support, disability working allowance or family credit; recoverable from the estate of the deceased); *Cold Weather Payments* (a payment of £8·50 for any consecutive 7 days when the temperature is below freezing to persons receiving income support who are pensioners, disabled or have a child under 5). 'Discretionary Payments' comprise: *Community Care Grants* (payments to help persons receiving income support to move into the community or avoid institutional care); *Budgeting Loans* (interest-free loans to persons receiving income support for expenses difficult to budget for); *Crisis Loans* (interest-free loans to anyone without resources in an emergency where there is no other means of preventing serious risk to health or safety). Savings over £500 (£1,000 for persons aged 60 or over) are taken into account before payments are made.

Barr, N., *et al. The State of Welfare: the Welfare State in Britain since 1974.* Oxford, 1990
Hill, M., *The Welfare State in Britain: a Political History since 1945.* Aldershot, 1993
Timmins, N., *The Five Giants: a Biography of the Welfare State.* London, 1995

National Health. The National Health Service (NHS) in England and Wales started on 5 July 1948 under the National Health Service Act, 1946. There are separate Acts for Scotland and for Northern Ireland, where the Health Services are run on similar lines to those in England and Wales.

The NHS is a charge on the national income in the same way e.g. as the armed forces. Every person normally resident in the UK is entitled to use any complete part of the services, and no insurance qualification is necessary.

Since 1948 a weekly NHS contribution has been payable by employees and the self-employed. In 1957 this contribution was extended to employers. For convenience this contribution is collected with the National Insurance contribution and amounts to 1·05% of the latter for employees and 0·9% for employers. The NHS is funded 13% by these contributions, 83% by general taxation and 3·5% by charges for drugs and dental treatment and the rest from other receipts. Health authorities may raise funds from voluntary sources; hospitals may take private paying patients.

Organization. The National Health Service and Community Care Act, 1990, provided for a major restructuring of the NHS. From 1 April 1991, health authorities became the purchasers of health care, concentrating on their responsibilities to plan and obtain services for their local residents by the placement of health service contracts with the appropriate units. Day-to-day management tasks became the responsibility of hospitals and other units, with whom the contracts are placed, in their capacity as providers of care.

In April 1996 the Regional Health Authorities were replaced by 8 regional offices of the NHS Executive. The District Health Authorities and Family Health Service Authorities were replaced by comprehensive Health Authorities directly financed by central governments Hospital and Community Health Services funds. The budget for 1996–97 was £2,260m.

The key responsibility of Health Authorities is to ensure that the health needs of their local communities are met. They have the purchasing power to commission hospital and community health services for their residents. In doing so they have a duty to ensure that high standards are maintained and that they are securing the best possible value for money.

The Health Authorities manage the Family Doctor (or General Medical) Service and also organize the general dental, pharmaceutical and ophthalmic services for their areas. Any doctor may take part in the Family Doctor Service, and are paid for their NHS work; they may also take private fee-paying patients.

NHS Trusts are established as self-governing units within the NHS. Trusts are responsible for the ownership and management of the hospitals or other establishments or facilities vested in them, and for carrying out the individual functions set out in their establishment orders. In April 1995 there were 433 Trusts, representing most hospitals.

General practitioners (GPs) may apply for fundholding status, responsible for their own NHS budget for a specified range of goods and services. There are 2 types of fundholder: Standard fundholders for practices with at least 5,000 patients, who purchase the full range of in- and out-patient services; and Community fundholders, for smaller practices of at least 3,000 patients, who purchase only community nursing services and diagnostic tests. In 1995 there were 2,007 fundholding units comprising 2,603 practices.

Services. The NHS broadly consists of hospital and specialist services, general medical, dental and ophthalmic services, pharmaceutical services, community health services and school health services. All these services are free of charge except for such things as prescriptions, spectacles, dental and optical examination, dentures and dental treatment, amenity beds in hospitals and for some of the community services, for which charges are made with certain exemptions.

The total cost of the NHS was estimated at £39,876m. for 1995–96.

The number of abortions performed in England and Wales in 1992 under the provisions of the Abortion Act, 1967, was 172,063 (179,522 in 1991). Of these, 160,495 abortions were to England and Wales residents, of which 105,630 were to single women, 36,349 to married women, and 18,471 were to widowed, divorced or separated women and to women who did not state their marital status.

The number of abortion notifications received in Scotland in 1993 (provisional figures) under the provisions of the Abortion Act, 1967, was 11,069, of which 7,549 related to single women, 2,194 to married women, and 1,326 were to widowed, divorced or separated women and to women who did not state their marital status.

In Great Britain in 1993 there were 34,135 general medical practitioners (GPs) and 18,466 general dental practitioners and (1992) 300,698 qualified nurses and midwives. There were (1990) 338,630 average daily available hospital beds in the UK.

In the UK in 1995 there were 193 public and private hospices for the terminally ill with 2,982 beds.

Personal Social Services. Under the Local Authority Social Services Act, 1970, and in Scotland the Social Work (Scotland) Act, 1968, the welfare and social work services provided by local authorities were made the responsibility of a new local authority department—the Social Services Department in England and Wales, and Social Work Departments in Scotland headed by a Director of Social Work, responsibility in Scotland passing in 1975 to the local authorities. The social services thus administered include: the fostering, care and adoption of children, welfare services and social workers for people with learning difficulties and the mentally ill, the disabled and the aged, and accommodation for those needing residential care services. In Scotland the Social Work Departments' functions also include the supervision of persons on probation, of adult offenders and of persons released from penal institutions or subject to fine supervision orders.

The total cost of personal social services was estimated at £462m. for 1995–96.

DIPLOMATIC REPRESENTATIVES

Of the USA in Great Britain (Grosvenor Sq., London, W1A 1AE)
Ambassador: Adm. William Crowe.

Of Great Britain in the USA (3100 Massachusetts Ave., NW, Washington, D.C., 20008)
Ambassador: Sir John Kerr, KCMG.

Of Great Britain to the United Nations
Ambassador: Sir David Hannay, KCMG.

Great Britain's permanent representative to the European Union
Ambassador: Sir John Weston, KCMG.

Further Reading

Government publications are published by HM Stationery Office (HMSO).
Office of National Statistics. *Annual Abstract of Statistics.* HMSO.—*Monthly Digest of Statistics.* HMSO.—*Social Trends.* HMSO.—*Regional Statistics.* HMSO
Central Office of Information. *Britain: An Official Handbook.* HMSO, annual.—*The Monarchy.* 1992
Directory of British Associations. Beckenham, annual
Cairncross, A., *The British Economy since 1945: Economic Policy and Performance, 1945–1995.* 2nd ed. London, 1995
Catterall, P., *British History, 1945–1987: an Annotated Bibliography.* Oxford, 1991
Gamble, A., *Britain in Decline: Economic Policy, Political Strategy and the British State.* 3rd ed. London, 1990
Gascoigne, B. (ed.) *Encyclopedia of Britain.* London, 1994
Harbury, C. D. and Lipsey, R. G., *Introduction to the UK Economy.* 4th ed. Oxford, 1993
Institute of Contemporary British History. *Contemporary Britain: an Annual Review.* Oxford, from 1990
Irwin, J. L., *Modern Britain: an Introduction.* 3rd ed. London, 1994
Marr, A., *Ruling Britannia: the Failure and Future of British Democracy.* London, 1995
Mitchell, B. R., *Abstract of British Historical Statistics.* OUP, 1962
Morgan, K.O., *The People's Peace: British History, 1945-89.* OUP, 1990
Oakland, J., *British Civilization: an Introduction.* 3rd ed. London, 1995
Oxford History of England. 16 vols. OUP, 1936–91
Palmer, A. and Palmer, V., *The Chronology of British History.* London, 1995
Sked, A. and Cook, C., *Post-War Britain: a Political History.* 4th ed. London, 1993
Thompson, F. M. L. (ed.) *The Cambridge Social History of Britain, 1750-1950.* 3 vols. CUP, 1990
20th-Century Britain: an Encyclopedia, edited by F. M. Leventhal. New York, 1995

Other more specialized titles are listed under TERRITORY AND POPULATION; CONSTITUTION AND GOVERNMENT; DEFENCE; ELECTRICITY; FORESTRY; TRADE UNIONS; RELIGION; THE BRITISH COUNCIL; *and* NATIONAL INSURANCE, *above.*

England

Day, A., *England.* [Bibliography]. Oxford and Santa Barbara (CA), 1993
Lloyd, T. O., *Empire, Welfare State, Europe: English History, 1906–1992.* 4th ed. OUP, 1993

Scotland

Scottish Office. *Scottish Economic Bulletin.* HMSO (quarterly).—*Scottish Abstract of Statistics.* HMSO (annual)
Dennistoun, R. and Linklater, M. (eds.) *Anatomy of Scotland.* Edinburgh, 1992
Donaldson, G. (ed.) *The Edinburgh History of Scotland.* 4 vols. Edinburgh, 1965–75
Grant, E., *Scotland.* [Bibliography] Oxford and Santa Barbara (CA), 1982
Harvie, C., *Scotland and Nationalism: Scottish Society and Politics, 1707–1994.* 2nd ed. London, 1994
Hogg, A. and Hutcheson, A. MacG., *Scotland and Oil.* 2nd ed. Edinburgh, 1975
Kellas, J. G., *The Scottish Political System.* 3rd ed. CUP, 1984
Lynch, M., *Scotland: a New History.* London, 1991
Monies, G., *Local Government in Scotland.* Edinburgh, 1985

Wales

Digest of Welsh Statistics. HMSO (annual)
Davies, J., *History of Wales.* London, 1993
History of Wales. vols. 3, 4 (1415–1780). 2nd ed. OUP, 1993
Huws, G. and Roberts, H., *Wales* [Bibliography]. Oxford and Santa Barbara, 1990
Jenkins, G. H., *The Foundations of Modern Wales 1642–1780.* Oxford, 1988
Jenkins, P.A., *A History of Modern Wales, 1536-1990.* Harlow, 1991
Jones, G. E., *Modern Wales: a Concise History.* 2nd ed. CUP, 1994
May, J. (ed.) *Reference Wales.* Wales Univ. Press, 1994

National Statistical Office: Office for National Statistics (ONS), Great George St., London SW1P 3AQ. ONS was formed from a merger of the former Central Statistical Office and the Office of Population Censuses and Surveys on 1 April 1996. *Director:* Dr Tim Holt.

NORTHERN IRELAND

TERRITORY AND POPULATION. Area (revised by the Ordnance Survey Department) and population were as follows:

District	*Population (usually resident) 1991 Census*	*Population present on 21 April 1991*	*Area in ha. (including inland water)*
Antrim	44,516	44,322	57,793
Ards	64,764	64,026	38,067
Armagh	51,817	51,331	67,128
Ballymena	56,641	56,032	63,195
Ballymoney	24,198	23,984	41,855
Banbridge	33,482	33,102	44,556
Belfast	279,237	283,746	11,489
Carrickfergus	32,750	32,439	8,193
Castlereagh	60,799	60,649	8,500
Coleraine	50,438	51,062	48,555
Cookstown	31,082	30,808	62,171
Craigavon	74,986	74,494	37,925
Derry (Londonderry)	95,371	94,918	38,742
Down	58,008	57,511	64,953
Dungannon	45,428	45,322	78,323
Fermanagh	54,033	54,062	187,677
Larne	29,419	29,181	33,646
Limavady	29,567	29,201	58,635
Lisburn	99,458	99,162	44,638
Magherafelt	36,293	35,874	57,239
Moyle	14,789	14,617	49,440
Newry and Mourne	82,943	82,288	90,937

District	*Population (usually resident) 1991 Census*	*Population present on 21 April 1991*	*Area in ha. (including inland water)*
Newtownabbey	74,035	73,832	15,069
North Down	71,832	70,308	8,158
Omagh	45,809	45,343	112,990
Strabane	36,141	35,668	86,165
Northern Ireland	1,577,836	1,573,282	1,416,039

Chief town (population present on 21 April 1991): Belfast, 283,746.
Vital statistics for calendar years:

	Marriages	*Divorces*	*Births*	*Deaths*
1992	9,392	2,280	25,572	14,988
1993	9,045	2,213	24,909	15,633
1994	8,683	2,303	24,289	15,114

CONSTITUTION AND GOVERNMENT. Northern Ireland is part of the United Kingdom. The Government of Ireland Act 1920 granted Northern Ireland its own bicameral parliament (Stormont), and between 1921 and 1972 it had full responsibility for local affairs except for such matters as defence, and the armed forces, foreign and trade policies, and taxation and customs. However, in the late 1960s a Civil Rights campaign and reactions to it escalated into serious rioting and sectarian violence involving the Irish Republican Army (IRA, an illegal organization aiming to unify Northern Ireland with the Republic of Ireland) and loyalist paramilitary organizations. The Northern Ireland government resigned and direct rule by the UK government began in 1972. The Northern Ireland parliament was abolished in 1973. The Northern Ireland Constitution Act 1973 provided for devolved government on a power-sharing basis, but this collapsed in May 1974.

Under the Northern Ireland Act 1974 the UK parliament approves all laws for Northern Ireland and the Northern Ireland departments are under the direction and control of a UK Cabinet Minister, the Secretary of State for Northern Ireland.

Attempts have been made by successive governments to find a means of restoring greater power to Northern Ireland's political representatives on a widely acceptable basis, including through a Constitutional Convention (1975–76), a Constitutional Conference (1979–80) and 78-member Northern Ireland Assembly elected by proportional representation in 1982. This was dissolved in 1986, partly in response to Unionist reaction to the Anglo-Irish Agreement signed by the governments of the UK and the Republic of Ireland on 15 Nov. 1985. The Agreement committed both the UK and the Irish governments to the principle that Northern Ireland should remain part of the UK for as long as that were the wish of the majority of population in Northern Ireland, that there was at present no wish for change, but if there were such a desire in the future, legislation would be introduced to give it effect. The Agreement established an Intergovernmental Conference of British and Irish ministers to monitor political, security, legal and other issues of concern to the nationalist community, and through which the Irish government could put forward views and proposals on specific matters affecting Northern Ireland affairs. There was to be no derogation from the sovereignty of the UK or Irish governments as a result of the Agreement.

Since 1990 the UK government has sought, through dialogue, to secure a political settlement encompassing all the relevant relationships: Those within Northern Ireland, those within the island of Ireland and those between the UK and Irish governments. In 1991 and 1992 round table talks were held between the two governments and the Northern Ireland parties. Since then the search for a settlement has continued through bilateral discussions.

On 15 Dec. 1993 the Prime Ministers of the UK and the Republic of Ireland (John Major and Albert Reynolds) issued a joint declaration as a basis for all-party talks to achieve a political settlement, inviting Sinn Féin ('Ourselves Alone', pro-Republican nationalist party and the political wing of the IRA) to join the talks in an All-Ireland Forum 3 months after the cessation of terrorist violence. The declaration stated that both the UK and Irish governments affirmed that the status of Northern Ireland could only be changed with the consent of a greater number of its people;

that the future of Ireland was to be decided by the people of the North and South alone; that the UK would give legislative effect to a united Ireland if a majority in the North so decided; and that the Irish government would abandon its constitutional claim to all the island of Ireland if there were a political settlement.

The IRA announced 'a complete cessation of military operations' from midnight on 31 Aug. 1994. On 13 Oct. 1994 the anti-IRA Combined Loyalist Military Command also announced a ceasefire 'dependent upon the continued cessation of all nationalist republican violence'.

Talks between UK government officials and Sinn Féin, and also with the political representatives of the loyalists, i.e. the Ulster Democratic Party and the Progressive Unionist Party began in Dec. 1994 and continued at ministerial level in March and May 1995.

On 22 Feb. 1995 the British and Irish Prime Ministers (John Major and John Bruton) announced new joint UK-Irish proposals for a settlement in Northern Ireland contained in 2 documents: *A Framework for Accountable Government in Northern Ireland*, drawn up by the UK government, and *A New Framework for Agreement*, agreed by the UK and Irish governments.

The proposals envisaged: An elected single-chamber 90-member Northern Ireland assembly; a north-south body comprising members of this assembly and representatives of the Irish government and accountable to both. This body would have executive, harmonizing or consultative functions in matters designated by the UK and Irish parliaments, its decisions being reached by consensus; a standing inter-governmental conference to consider matters not transferred to the above proposed bodies; changes to the Irish constitution to withdraw the Republic's territorial claim to Northern Ireland if it were contrary to the will of a majority of its people; amendments to UK legislation to enable Northern Ireland's future status to be determined by a majority decision of its people; an undertaking by both governments to ensure the 'systematic and effective protection of common specified civil, political, social and cultural rights'.

On 28 Nov. 1995 the British and Irish Prime Mininsters (John Major and John Bruton) agreed on a formula which would allow preliminary talks involving Northern Ireland's main political parties to start while a 3-member international body headed by former US Senator George Mitchell prepared a report on 'the arrangements necessary for the removal from the political equation' of paramilitary arms. The Mitchell commission report, published on 24 Jan. 1996, set out 6 principles to which all parties should adhere, including a commitment to renounce violence, verifiable disarmament of all paramilitaries and a pledge to adhere to any agreement reached through all-party negotiations. Concluding that the paramilitaries 'will not decommission any arms prior to all-party negotiations', the commission recommended that negotiations and decommissioning of weapons should proceed at the same time, and proposed a number of measures including an elective process. However, the British Prime Minister stated that, 'In the absence of prior decommissioning, there may well be another way forward', proposing elections to a temporary body which could be used as a forum for negotiations.

On 9 Feb. 1996 the IRA exploded a bomb in the Docklands area of London (the first of several incidents) and announced the end of their ceasefire.

On 28 Feb. the British and Irish Prime Ministers agreed that all-party negotiations should start on 10 June. On 21 March the British Prime Minister announced that elections would be held on 30 May to produce a 110-member forum to run for a year in parallel with the negotiations. Each of the 18 Northern Ireland constituencies would return 5 delegates. The 10 parties receiving the most votes would receive 2 extra delegates. Leaders of parties represented in the forum are to select a team for the negotiations starting on 10 June. Sinn Féin may participate in the forum, but not in the negotiations until the IRA restores its ceasefire.

Secretary of State for Northern Ireland: Rt Hon. Sir Patrick Mayhew, QC, MP.

Local Government. Northern Ireland has a single-tier system of 26 district councils based on main centres of population. Elections were held on 19 May 1993 for the 582 council seats. The Ulster Unionist Party gained 201 seats with 34·5% of votes cast, the Social Democratic and Labour Party 127 with 21·8%, the Democratic Unionist Party 102 with 17·5%, Sinn Féin 51 with 8·8%, the Alliance 44 with 7·6%, the Conservative Party 6 with 1·8%, others 22. Independents gained 29 seats with 5%.

The district councils are responsible for the provision of a wide range of local services including refuse collection and disposal, street cleansing, litter prevention, consumer protection, environmental health, miscellaneous licensing including dog control, the provision and management of recreational and cultural facilities, the promotion of tourist development schemes and the enforcement of building regulations. They have in addition both a representative role in which they send forward representatives to sit as members of statutory bodies including the Northern Ireland Housing Council, the Fire Authority and the Area Boards for health and personal social services and education and libraries; and a consultative role under which the Department of Environment (NI) and the Northern Ireland Housing Executive, among others, have an obligation to consult them regarding the provision of the regional services for which these bodies are responsible.

ECONOMY

Policy. The Department of the Environment for Northern Ireland is the unitary planning authority for the region. It is responsible not only for formulating planning policy but also for making development plans, controlling development, designating Conservation Areas and preparing comprehensive development schemes, all of which in Great Britain are local authority responsibilities. In Sept. 1993, the Department published *A Planning Strategy for Rural Northern Ireland.* This document presents a comprehensive range of planning policies which apply to the towns, villages and countryside of Northern Ireland, outside the Belfast conurbation and the city of Londonderry. It has recently embarked upon a study of the Belfast City Region, the area within 25 to 30 miles of the city centre. This study will look strategically at land-use patterns including the location of new housing and transport networks. An options paper was issued in Jan. 1996 inviting responses from elected representatives, interested organizations and the general public to different methods of accommodating long-term change and development. The Department's strategic policy documents provide a broad framework within which development plans are prepared for individual areas. Development plans set down proposals for the development and use of land over a period of up to 15 years ahead. Plans covering almost all of Northern Ireland have been published and work is progressing on the remaining areas, together with reviews of some earlier plans.

The Department deals with up to 20,000 planning applications each year. Applications vary in scale, importance and complexity from electricity lines and house extensions to major industrial, commercial and residential developments and infrastructure projects.

The main Northern Ireland government department concerned with economic development is the Department of Economic Development (DED). The department and its agencies have responsibility for the promotion of inward investment and the development of larger home industry (Industrial Development Board, IDB); promotion of enterprise and small business (Local Enterprise Development Unit, LEDU); training and employment matters (Training and Employment Agency, T&EA); promotion of industrially-relevant research and development and technology transfer (Industrial Research and Technology Unit, IRTU); promotion and development of tourism (Northern Ireland Tourist Board, NITB); energy matters; mineral development; company regulation; consumer protection; health and safety at work; industrial relations; and equality of opportunity in employment.

The IDB's main aim is to play a supporting role in assisting the profitable growth of the manufacturing and internationally tradeable service sectors through the development of existing companies and by securing new investment overseas. During 1994–95, 10 inward investment projects were brought to Northern Ireland offering the prospect of almost 2,000 new jobs. 66 investment projects from established companies aimed at improving their international competitiveness were assisted.

The LEDU is the small business agency (for companies employing fewer than

50 people). It aims to strengthen the economy by encouraging enterprise and new business start-ups and by helping established small businesses achieve export-orientated, profitable growth. In 1994–95 LEDU assisted 1,501 new business start-ups and turnover amongst LEDU-assisted firms increased by 11% in real terms, compared with 9·5% in 1993–94.

The T&EA is an Executive Agency within DED. It assists economic development and helps people find work through training and employment services on the basis of equality of opportunity. It works closely with employers and business interests, and with the other economic development agencies in making training relevant to local needs. In 1994–95 T&EA placed 33,786 people in employment. Over 350 companies were assisted in developing their management and workforce skills through the Company Development Programme, and almost 40% of trainees on the new Jobskills programme achieved a full national vocational qualification (NVQ) of 2 or above.

The IRTU, an Executive Agency within DED, provides the focus for all aspects of industry-related technology and innovation policy, including grants for industrial research and development, information, advice, scientific testing and analysis services. In 1994–95 IRTU disbursed £13m. of Government funding to Research and Development projects; in addition, IRTU enabled companies to obtain support under EU programmes.

Currency. Banknotes are issued by Allied Irish Banks, Bank of Ireland, First Trust Bank, Northern Bank and Ulster Bank.

Public Finance. The Finance Department is responsible for control of the expenditure of Northern Ireland departments, liaison with HM Treasury and the Northern Ireland Office on financial matters, economic and social research and analysis, Citizens Charter Unit, the Valuation and Lands Agency, the Government Purchasing Service (Northern Ireland) and the Legal Services.

It is also responsible for developing, formulating, co-ordinating and monitoring the Equal Opportunities policy for the Northern Ireland Civil Service and formulating policy and co-ordinating arrangements for personnel management, including recruitment, training, promotion, general career management, welfare and retirement. Other responsibilities include the size and deployment of personnel, pensions, conditions of service and the co-ordination of pay policies in the Civil Service. It also provides a central efficiency and information technology service for the Northern Ireland Civil Service. The Department provides the staff for the Civil Service Commission, an independent body responsible for the recruitment of all non-industrial staff for the Northern Ireland Civil Service. The Commissioners are appointed by the Queen. They act under an Order-in-Council and are completely independent.

Since the financial year 1992–93 the income of the Northern Ireland Consolidated Fund has been as follows (in £1,000 sterling):

	1993–94	*1994–95*	*1995–96*
Attributed share of UK taxes	3,090,256	4,052,593	3,431,800
Grant in Aid from UK Government	2,391,600	1,649,900	2,261,700
Regional and district rates	203,091	224,975	343,700
Other receipts	329,519	307,401	313,800
Total	6,014,068	6,234,870	6,651,000

The public debt at 31 March 1995 was as follows: Ulster Savings Certificates, £115,562,835; Ulster Development Bonds, £15,585; borrowing from UK Government, £1,666,319,612; borrowing from Northern Ireland Government Funds, £136,085,270; European Investment Bank Loan, £5,775,365; external short-term total, £1,797,397,029.

The above amount of public debt is offset by equal assets in the form of loans from Government to public and local bodies and of cash balances.

ENERGY AND NATURAL RESOURCES

Electricity. There are 4 power stations with an installed capacity of some 2,400 MW.

The generating stations were privatized in 1992, and Northern Ireland Electricity, responsible for transmission, distribution and supply, in 1993. Sales of electricity for the year ended 31 March 1992 amounted to some 6,000m. units supplied to about 606,000 customers.

Gas. British Gas, which purchased Ballylumford power station, has plans to convert it to gas firing. This will involve the construction of an undersea pipeline from Scotland and will enable the eventual supply of natural gas to the wider Northern Ireland energy market.

Water. The Department of the Environment Water Service Agency is responsible for water supply and sewerage. Some 700 megalitres of water are supplied per day to approximately 98% of the population. Approximately 85% of the population live in property which is connected to sewers or modern septic tanks.

The Department is also responsible for the conservation and planned development of water resources.

Minerals. Output of minerals (in 1,000 tonnes), 1992: Basalt and igneous rock (other than granite), 9,024; grit and conglomerate, 3,304; limestone, 3,398; sand and gravel, 3,696; other minerals (rocksalt, fireclay, diatomite, granite, chalk, clay and shale), 633. There are lignite deposits of 1,000m. tonnes which have not yet been developed.

Agriculture. Provisional gross output in 1994:

	Quantity (1,000)	*Value (£1m.)*		*Quantity (1,000)*	*Value (£1m.)*
Finished cattle and calves	502	412·0	Other crops (tonnes)	19	2·1
Finished sheep and lambs	1,501	90·8	Fruit (tonnes)	36	4·9
Finished pigs	1,249	82·4	Vegetables (tonnes)	40	6·0
Poultry (tonnes)	104	77·2	Mushrooms (tonnes)	15	16·3
Eggs: for human consumption (dozen)	75,600	35·4	Flowers	...	8·1
Wool (tonnes)	4	2·9	Other items	...	14·3
Milk (litres)	1,376,000	289·2	Total receipts		1,088·4
Other livestock products	...	9·3	Value of changes in stocks due to volume		–7·2
Potatoes	179	22·3			
Barley	62	10·6	Gross output		1,081·2
Wheat	31	4·5			

Area (in 1,000 ha) of crops at June census:

	1994	*1995*		*1994*	*1995*
Barley	33·4	32·7	Fruit	1·8	1·7
Wheat	7·0	6·4	Other crops	6·7	7·7
Oats	2·4	2·5	Grass	774·3	778·5
Potatoes	8·4	8·7	Rough grazing	179·0	173·6
Vegetables	1·4	1·4			

Livestock (in 1,000) at June census:

	1994	*1995*		*1994*	*1995*
Cattle	1,580·8	1,592·0	Pigs	562·3	548·2
Dairy	274·2	271·5	Sows	57·8	56·6
Beef	278·5	278·3	Poultry	13,643·0	14,946·6
Sheep	2,530·8	2,470·4	Laying hens	3,195·4	3,095·6
Ewes	1,218·3	1,184·9	Broilers	7,595·7	8,618·3

INDUSTRY

Labour. The main sources of employment statistics are the Census of Employment, conducted every 2 years, and the Quarterly Employment Survey. In June 1995 there were 569,670 employees in employment, of whom 284,550 were males. The average level of seasonally-adjusted unemployment between Jan. and Sept. 1995 was 11·7% of the workforce, 88,600. In June 1995 employment in manufacturing and construction amounted to 127,010, just over 22% of the total employees in employment. In June 1994, 19,290 persons were engaged in the food, drink and tobacco industries, 14,800 in clothing and footwear, 10,110 in textiles, 8,690 in aircraft, shipbuilding and other transport equipment (except motor vehicles), 21,560 in construction and 47,990 in other sectors of manufacturing.

Tourism. 1·29m. visitors came to Northern Ireland in 1994 producing £183m. in revenue. The Northern Ireland Tourist Board is responsible for encouraging tourism and tourist amenities. It advises the DED on tourism policy.

9 Areas of Outstanding Natural Beauty and 44 National Nature Reserves have been declared, and there are country and regional parks.

COMMUNICATIONS

Roads. Ulsterbus Ltd runs services throughout Northern Ireland and Citybus Ltd runs services in the Belfast area.

The Department of the Environment (NI) administers a licensing system for professional hauliers with the objective of maintaining standards and conditions necessary for the safe operation of vehicles and fair competition between hauliers. The level of services provided and the rates charged by the industry are determined by the normal economic forces of supply and demand. At 31 March 1995 there were 1,921 professional hauliers and 4,356 vehicles licensed to engage in road haulage.

The number of motor vehicles licensed at 31 Dec. 1994 was 595,951, comprising private cars, 514,760; motor cycles, scooters and mopeds, 8,775; hackney vehicles, 3,078; goods vehicles, 20,714; special machines, 7,671. In addition, there were 40,953 vehicles which were not subject to licence duty.

At 1 April 1993 the total mileage of roads was 15,060, graded for administrative purposes as follows: Motorway 70 miles; Class I dual carriageway, 95 miles; Class I single carriageway, 1,287 miles; Class II, 1,770 miles; Class III, 2,935 miles; unclassified, 8,903 miles.

Railways. All train services are operated by the Northern Ireland Railways Co. Ltd which is a subsidiary of the Northern Ireland Transport Holding Co. The number of track-km operated is 478·8. In 1994–95 railways carried 6·1m. passengers.

Civil Aviation. There are scheduled air services to 3 airports in Northern Ireland. Belfast International Airport is the main airport. Services are provided by Aer Lingus, Air Belfast, American Transair, British Airways, British Midland, Night Air, KLM and Maersk Air. In 1994, it handled 2·1m. passengers and 37,722 tonnes of freight and mail. Belfast City Airport offers commuter services to 15 regional airports in Great Britain as well as services to London-Heathrow, -Gatwick and -Luton and to the Isle of Man and Channel Islands. In 1994 it handled 1·2m. passengers. Eglinton Airport, situated 16 km from Londonderry, provides services from the north-west of Ireland to Glasgow and Manchester. In 1994, 34,000 passengers were handled. There are two other licensed airfields at St Angelo and Newtownards, used principally by flying clubs, private owners and air taxi businesses.

Shipping. There are passenger services from Belfast to Liverpool and Stranraer and from Larne to Cairnryan. Drive-on/drive-off cargo services operate from Belfast and Larne to other UK ports. Belfast, Londonderry and Warrenpoint offer conventional cargo services. A new port at Londonderry opened in 1993.

SOCIAL INSTITUTIONS

Justice. The Lord Chancellor has responsibility for the administration of all courts in Northern Ireland through the Northern Ireland Court Service, and is responsible for the appointment of judges and resident magistrates.

The court structure in Northern Ireland has 3 tiers–the Supreme Court of Judicature of Northern Ireland (comprising the Court of Appeal, the High Court and the Crown Court), the County Courts and the Magistrates' Courts. There are 21 Petty Sessions districts which when grouped together for administration purposes form 7 County Court Divisions and 4 Crown Court Circuits.

The County Court has general civil jurisdiction subject to an upper monetary limit of £15,000. Appeals from the Magistrates' Courts lie to the County Court, or to the Court of Appeal on a point of law or an issue as to jurisdiction, while appeals from the County Court lie to the High Court or, on a point of law, to the Court of Appeal by way of case stated. District Judges have jurisdiction to deal with most defended actions up to £3,000 and most undefended actions up to £15,000. They also deal, by an informal arbitration procedure, with small claims where the value does not exceed £1,000. Grounds of appeal from a District Judge's decision in a small claims case are limited.

Police. The police force consists of the Royal Ulster Constabulary, supported by the Royal Ulster Constabulary Reserve, a mainly part-time force.

Religion. According to the census of 1991 there were: Roman Catholics, 605,639; Presbyterians, 336,891; Church of Ireland, 279,280; Methodists, 59,517. Those belonging to other denominations numbered 122,448; to none, 59,234. 114,827 persons did not answer the voluntary question on religion.

Education. Public education, other than university education, is administered centrally by the *Department of Education for Northern Ireland* and locally by 5 Education and Library boards. The Department is concerned with the whole range of education from nursery education through to higher education and continuing education; for sport and recreation; for youth services; for the arts and culture (including libraries) and for the development of community relations with and between schools.

Each *Education and Library Board* is the local education authority for its area. Boards were first appointed in 1973, the year of local government reorganization, and are reappointed every 4 years following the District Council elections. Boards were last reconstituted on 1 July 1993. The membership of each Board consists of District councillors, representatives of transferors of schools, representatives of trustees of maintained schools and other persons who are interested in the service for which the Board is responsible. Boards have a duty, amongst other things, to ensure that there are sufficient schools of all kinds to meet the needs of their areas. The Boards are responsible for costs associated with capital works at controlled schools. Voluntary schools, including maintained and voluntary grammar schools, can receive grant-aid from the Department of Education toward capital works of up to 85%, or 100% if they have opted to change their management structures so that no single interest group has a majority of nominees. Most voluntary grammar schools can receive the same rate of grant on the purchase of equipment. The Boards award university and other scholarships; they provide school milk and meals; free books and transport for pupils; they enforce school attendance; provide a curriculum advisory and support service to all schools in their area; regulate the employment of children and young people; and secure the provision of youth and recreational facilities. They are also required to develop a comprehensive and efficient library service for their area. Board expenditure is funded at 100% by the Department of Education. Integrated schools receive 100% funding for recurrent costs from the Department of Education, and, where long-term viability has been established, for capital works.

The Education Reform (NI) Order 1989 made provision for the setting up of a *Council for Catholic Maintained Schools* with effect from April 1990. The Council has responsibility for all maintained schools under Roman Catholic Management which are under the auspices of the diocesan authorities and of religious orders. The main objective of the Council is to promote high standards of education in the schools for which it is responsible. Its functions include providing advice on matters relating to its schools, the employment of teaching staff and administration of appointment procedures, the promotion of effective management and the promotion and co-ordination of effective planning and rationalization of school provision in the Catholic Maintained sector. The membership of the Council consists of trustee representatives appointed by the Northern Roman Catholic Bishops, parents, teachers, and persons appointed by the Head of the Department of Education in consultation with the Bishops.

Integrated Schools. In recent years a small number of integrated schools have been established at primary and post-primary levels with the aim of providing education for Roman Catholic and Protestant children together. These schools began as independent schools and qualified for public funding (on the same basis as other non-state schools) when their longer-term viability had been adequately demonstrated.

The Education Reform (NI) Order 1989 has introduced new measures whereby new integrated schools may receive public funding right from the start. Grant Maintained Integrated schools are eligible for grants on capital works, including purchase of sites and buildings and equipment, at the rate of 100%. At Oct. 1995 there were 28 integrated schools with total enrolments of some 5,000 pupils, about 2% of all pupils.

Nursery Education is provided in nursery schools or nursery classes in primary schools. There were 91 nursery schools in 1994–95, with 5,334 pupils and 168 teachers.

Primary Education is from 4 to 11 years. In 1994–95 there were 938 primary schools with 186,624 pupils and 8,658 teachers. There were also 25 preparatory departments of grammar schools with 3,596 pupils and 169 teachers.

Secondary Education is from 11 to 18 years. In 1994–95 there were 71 grammar schools with 60,502 pupils and 3,694 teachers and 161 secondary schools with 89,534 pupils and 6,308 teachers.

Further Education. There were 17 institutions of further education in 1994–95 with 2,171 full-time and 3,205 part-time teachers and an enrolment of 23,675 full-time, 26,439 part-time day and 29,135 evening students on vocational courses; and 47,138 students on non-vocational (mostly evening) courses.

Special Education. The Education and Library Boards provide for children with special educational needs up to the age of 19. This provision may be made in ordinary classes in primary or secondary schools or in special units attached to those schools or in special schools. In 1994–95 there were 50 special schools with 4,765 pupils. This includes 3 hospital schools.

Universities. There are 2 universities: The Queen's University of Belfast (founded in 1849 as a college of the Queen's University of Ireland and reconstituted as a separate university in 1908) had 127 professors, 248 readers and senior lecturers, 339 lecturers, 13 other grades of academic staff and 10,576 full-time students in 1993–94 academic year. The University of Ulster, formed on 1 Oct. 1984, has campuses in Belfast, Coleraine, Jordanstown and Londonderry. In 1993–94 academic year the University had 81 professors, 250 readers and senior lecturers, 496 lecturers, 11 other grades of academic staff and 12,163 full-time students.

Teacher training takes place at both universities and at 2 colleges of education: Stranmillis, and St. Mary's, the latter mainly for the primary school sector, in respect of which 4-year (Hons) BEd courses and one-year Postgraduate Certificate in Education (PGCE) courses are available. The training of teachers for secondary schools is provided, in the main, in the education departments of the 2 universities, but 4-year (Hons) BEd courses are also available in the colleges for intending secondary teachers of religious education, business studies and craft, design and technology. Part-time PGCE courses (primary and secondary) are available through the Open University. There were a total of 1,866 students (1,478 women) in training at the 2 colleges and the 2 universities during 1994–95. The principal initial teacher-training courses are the Bachelor of Education (4-year honours), BA (Hons) with education (4-year) and the one year Certificate of Education for graduates.

Expenditure by the Department of Education (1994–95) was £1,300m.

Health and Personal Social Services. The Department of Health and Social Services is responsible for the provision of integrated health and personal social services in Northern Ireland, designed to promote the physical and mental health of the people of Northern Ireland through the prevention, diagnosis and treatment of illness, and also to promote their social welfare. 4 Health and Social Services Boards are responsible for assessing the health and personal social services requirements of their resident populations and for purchasing appropriate services from a range of providers designed to meet these needs. Since 1 April 1996 services have been delivered exclusively by HSS trusts (similar to NHS trusts in the rest of the UK) established under the Health and Personal Social Services (NI) Order 1991. A total of 20 HSS trusts are fully operational. 8 HSS Trusts based on acute hospitals and the regional Northern Ireland Ambulance Service are identical in structure and management to NHS Trusts in Great Britain. The remaining 11 provide also the whole range of community health and personal social services, reflecting the integrated nature of these services in Northern Ireland.

Social Security. Social security schemes are similar to those in Great Britain.

National Insurance. During the year ended 31 March 1995 the expenditure of the National Insurance Fund at £1,095·4m. exceeded contributions by £224·3m. The shortfall in income was made up by a Treasury Grant, investment income and a transfer from the Great Britain Fund.

Total benefit expenditure was £1,015·8m., excluding £3·5m. which was subsequently recovered from damages paid to recipients of National Insurance Fund Benefits.

£8·9m. was paid in Sickness Benefit and employers received £3·2m. reimbursement in respect of Statutory Sick Pay paid to their employees. £31·4m. was paid in Unemployment Benefit. Widows Benefit amounted to £35·4m. and Retirement Pensions to £631·6m. Invalidity Pensions and allowances totalled £304·2m. Maternity Allowance of £1·2m. was paid and employers were reimbursed £15·5m. in respect of Statutory Maternity Pay. £33·8m. was given to personal pension plan providers.

Child Benefit. During the year ended 31 March 1995, £221·1m. was paid.

Income Support. In 1994–95, £656·6m. was paid.

Family Credit. In 1994–95, £61·9m. was paid.

Further Reading

Arthur, P. and Jeffery, K., *Northern Ireland since 1968.* Oxford, 1988

Bow, P. and Gillespie, G., *Northern Ireland: a Chronology of the Troubles, 1968–1993.* Dublin, 1993

Cormack, R. J. and Osborne, R. D. (eds.) *Discrimination and Public Policy in Northern Ireland.* OUP, 1991

Cunningham, M. J., *British Government Policy in Northern Ireland, 1969–89.* Manchester Univ. Press, 1991

Irvine, M., *Northern Ireland: Faith and Faction.* London, 1991

Keogh, D. and Haltzel, M. (eds.) *Northern Ireland and the Politics of Reconciliation.* CUP, 1994

McGarry, J. and O'Leary, B., (eds.) *The Future of Northern Ireland.* Oxford, 1991. — *Explaining Northern Ireland: Broken Images.* Oxford, 1995

Roche, P. J. and Barton, B., (eds.) *The Northern Ireland Question: Myth and Reality.* London, 1991

Shannon, M. O., *Northern Ireland.* [Bibliography] Oxford and Santa Barbara (CA), 1991

Whyte, J., *Interpreting Northern Ireland.* Oxford Univ. Press, 1990

ISLE OF MAN

TERRITORY AND POPULATION. Area, 221 sq. miles (572 sq. km); resident population census April 1991, 69,788. The principal towns are Douglas (population, 22,214), Ramsey (6,496), Peel (3,829), Castletown (3,152). The island is divided into 6 sheadings (Ayre, Garff, Glenfaba, Michael, Middle and Rushen) each subdivided 3 parishes except Garff, which has 2.

Vital statistics, 1994: Births, 883; deaths, 902; marriages, 452.

CONSTITUTION AND GOVERNMENT. The Isle of Man is a Crown dependency administered in accordance with its own laws by the High Court of *Tynwald*, consisting of the President of Tynwald, elected by the Court, and the *Legislative Council*, composed of the Lord Bishop of Sodor and Man, the Attorney-General (who does not vote) and 8 members selected by the *House of Keys*; and the House of Keys, a representative assembly of 24 members chosen by adult suffrage on the single transferable vote system with the option of voting for a single candidate. The Isle of Man is not bound by Acts of the UK Parliament unless specially mentioned in them or applied by Order in Council although the UK is responsible for conducting its foreign affairs. The Lieutenant Governor presided over Tynwald until 1990 when he was replaced by an elected President of Tynwald.

A Council of Ministers was instituted in 1990. This replaced the former Executive Council and consists of the Chief Minister (elected for a 5-year term) and the ministers of the 9 major departments of Government. Elections for the House of Keys were held on 21 Nov. 1991. 73 candidates stood, mostly independents. Turn-out was 69·5%.

Lieut.-Governor: Sir Timothy Daunt.
President: Sir Charles Kerruish (elected July 1990).
Chief Secretary: J. F. Kissack.
In Sept. 1995 the *Chief Minister* was Miles Walker. *Finance Minister:* Donald Gelling.

Flag: Red, with 3 steel-coloured legs armoured and spurred (knees and spurs, yellow) in the centre.

ECONOMY

Budget. The Isle of Man levies its own taxes. Revenue is derived from customs duties, VAT and income tax. In the 1995–96 budget expenditure was estimated at £211·3m. to be balanced by income of £208·6m. and £2·8m. of unspent capital brought forward from 1994–95.

Income tax is 15% of the first £8,750 of taxable (over £6,400) income for a single person and of the first £17,500 (over £12,800) for a married couple, and 20% on the remainder. There are no death or estate duties, gifts or inheritance taxes or capital gains taxes. Companies and trusts are liable at 20% on the whole of their taxable income. There is a duty of £600 on every company incorporated in the Isle of Man which trades and is controlled outside the island.

Currency. The Isle of Man Government issues its own notes and coin on a par with £ sterling. £50, £20, £10, £5, £1, and £5, £2, £1, 50p, 20p, 10p, 5p, 2p and 1p coins are issued. Various commemorative coins have been minted together with legal tender gold coins and a platinum bullion coin. Inflation was 2·9% in Sept. 1995.

Banking and Finance. Government regulation of the banking sector is exercised through the Financial Supervision Commission. The Commission was established in 1983 and is responsible for the licensing and supervision of banks, deposit-takers and certain financial intermediaries giving financial advice and receiving client monies for investment and management. As at Nov. 1995 there were 60 licensed banking institutions, 70 investment businesses and 6 UK Building Societies with Isle of Man licences. As at June 1995 the deposit base was £14,100m. The Isle of Man has designated status under the UK Financial Services Act. A compensation fund to protect depositors was set up in Feb. 1991 under the Isle of Man Financial Supervision Commission. Financial business contributes some 35% of national income.

Agriculture. The area farmed is about 113,000 acres out of a total land area of around 0·14m. acres. About 65,000 acres is devoted to grass whilst a further 36,000 acres are accounted for by rough grazing. Barley accounts for most of the remaining land under cultivation and some barley is exported. There are approximately 0·16m. sheep, 33,000 cattle, 27,000 poultry and 5,000 pigs on farms. Agriculture contributes 2% of the Island's GNP.

Labour. The economically active population in 1991 was 33,189 (14,024 females) of whom 5,237 were self-employed. Employment by sector: Professional, 17·1%; finance, 13·7%; building, 10·7%; manufacturing, 10·5%; retailing, 9·4%. 1,410 persons were unemployed in Sept. 1995.

External Economic Relations. A special relationship exists with the EU providing for free trade and the adoption of external trade policies with third countries.

Tourism. In 1993–94 tourism contributed around 6% of national income; there were approximately 0·23m. visitors during 1994.

COMMUNICATIONS

Roads. There are 500 miles of good roads. The International TT Motor Cycle Races and cycle races take place annually. Omnibus services operate to all parts of the island.

In 1994–95 there were 52,145 licensed vehicles on the roads, of which 42,739 were private cars.

Railways. Several novel transport systems operate on the Island during the summer season, including 100-year-old horse-drawn trams, and the Manx Electric Railway, linking Douglas, Ramsey and Snaefell Mountain (2,036 ft). The Isle of Man Steam Railway also operates between Douglas and Port Erin.

Civil Aviation. Ronaldsway Airport handles scheduled services operated by Manx Airlines and Jersey European to and from London, Manchester, Belfast, Dublin, Glasgow, Liverpool, Blackpool, Birmingham, Leeds, Luton, Newcastle, Cardiff and Jersey. Air taxi services also operate.

Shipping. Car ferries link the Island with Heysham throughout the year and Liverpool, Fleetwood, Dublin and Belfast during the summer. The Manx Marine Administration oversees the Marine Register on which were 160 vessels in 1995 totalling 2·3m. tonnes.

Telecommunications. Manx Radio is a commercial broadcaster operated by the Government from Douglas.

Press. In 1995 there were 4 weekly newspapers.

SOCIAL INSTITUTIONS

Justice. The judiciary is headed by the First Deemster. The police force numbered 213 all ranks in 1994.

Education. Education is compulsory between the ages of 5 and 16. In 1995 there were 5,976 pupils in the 34 primary schools and 4,608 pupils in the 5 secondary schools operated by the Department of Education. In addition, there was a private primary school (208 pupils) and a private secondary school (308 pupils). The Department also runs a college of further education and a special school.

Social Security. Numbers receiving certain benefits at 31 March 1994: Retirement Pension, 14,919; Unemployment Benefit, 565; Invalidity Benefit, 1,308; Child Benefit, 14,786 children; Supplementary Benefit, 4,692; Attendance, Mobility and Disability Living Allowances, 1,475. Total benefit expenditure, 1993–94 (in £1,000), 85,151, made up of: Elderly People, 53,961; Family, 13,335; Sick and Disabled, 11,240; Unemployed, 5,148; Widows and Orphans, 1,467.

Further Reading

Additional information is available from: Economic Affairs Division, 2 Circular Rd, Douglas, Isle of Man IM1 1PQ.

Publications: *Isle of Man Key Facts 1995, Isle of Man Digest of Economic and Social Statistics 1994, Isle of Man Census Reports 1991, Isle of Man Family Expenditure Survey, Isle of Man Passenger Survey Reports 1985–1994, Isle of Man National Income Estimates, Isle of Man General Index of Retail Prices* (Monthly), *Isle of Man Earnings Survey* (Annual).

Kinvig, R. H., *History of the Isle of Man.* Oxford, 1945.—*The Isle of Man: A Social, Cultural and Political History.* Liverpool Univ. Press, 1975

Robinson, V. and McCarroll, D., (eds.) *The Isle of Man: Celebrating a Sense of Place.* Liverpool Univ. Press, 1990

Solly, M., *Government and Law in the Isle of Man.* London, 1994

Stenning, E. H., *Portrait of the Isle of Man.* London, 1984

CHANNEL ISLANDS

TERRITORY. The Channel Islands are situated off the north-west coast of France and are the only portions of the 'Duchy of Normandy' now belonging to the Crown of England, to which they have been attached since the Conquest. They consist of Jersey (28,717 acres), Guernsey (15,654 acres) and the following dependencies of Guernsey–Alderney (1,962), Brechou (74), Great Sark (1,035), Little Sark (239), Herm (320), Jethou (44) and Lihou (38), a total of 48,083 acres, or 75 sq. miles (194 sq. km).

CLIMATE. The climate is mild, with an average temperature for the year of 11·5°C. Average yearly rainfall totals: Jersey, 862·9mm; Guernsey, 858·9mm. The wettest months are in the winter. Highest temperatures recorded: Jersey, 34·8°C.; Guernsey, 31·7°C. Maximum temperatures usually occur in July and Aug. (daily maximum 20·8°C. in Jersey, slightly lower in Guernsey). Lowest temperatures recorded: Jersey, 10·3°C.; Guernsey, –7·4°C. Jan. and Feb. are the coldest months (mean temperature approximately 6°C.).

CONSTITUTION. The Lieut.-Governors and Cs.-in-C. of Jersey and Guernsey are the personal representatives of the Sovereign, the Commanders of the Armed Forces of the Crown and the channel of communication between the Crown and the insular governments. They are appointed by the Crown and have a voice but no vote in the Assemblies of the States (the insular legislatures). The Secretaries to the Lieut.-Governors are their staff officers.

The Bailiff is appointed by the Crown and is President both of the Assembly of the States and of the Royal Courts of Jersey and Guernsey. The Baliff has a casting vote in the States. The official languages are French and English, but English is the main language. In the country districts of Jersey and Guernsey and throughout Sark some people also speak a Norman-French dialect; that of Alderney has died out.

EXTERNAL ECONOMIC RELATIONS. The Channel Islands are not members of the EC, but participate in ERM through their monetary union with the UK. From 1958 the trade of the Channel Islands with the UK has been regarded as internal trade.

COMMUNICATIONS

Roads. Omnibus services operate in all parts of Jersey and Guernsey.

Civil Aviation. Scheduled air services are maintained by Aer Lingus, Air Corbière, Air UK, Aurigny Air Services, British Airways, British Midland, Crossair, Delta, Gill Aviation, Jersey European Airways, KLM, Loganair, Lufthansa and Manx Airlines.

Shipping. Passenger and cargo services between Jersey, Guernsey and England are maintained by British Channel Island Ferries; between Guernsey, Jersey and England and St Malo by the Commodore Shipping Co., Emeraude Ferries connect Jersey with St Malo; between Guernsey, Jersey, Alderney, England and France by Condor Ltd (hydrofoil), and between Guernsey and Alderney and England and Guernsey and Sark by local companies.

Telecommunications. Postal and overseas telephone and telegraph services are maintained by the respective Postal Administrations of each bailiwick. The local telephone services are maintained by the insular authorities. There were, in 1990, 47,647 telephone lines in Jersey and 57,201 rented telephones in Guernsey.

There is an independent television station in Jersey and local radio stations, BBC Radio Jersey and Guernsey, opened in 1982.

SOCIAL INSTITUTIONS

Justice. Justice is administered by the Royal Courts of Jersey and Guernsey, each oF which consists of the Bailiff and 12 Jurats, the latter being elected by an electoral college. There is an appeal from the Royal Courts to the Courts of Appeal of

Jersey and of Guernsey. A final appeal lies to the Privy Council in certain cases. A stipendiary magistrate in each, Jersey and Guernsey, deals with minor civil and criminal cases.

Church. Jersey and Guernsey each constitutes a deanery under the jurisdiction of the Bishop of Winchester. The rectories (12 in Jersey; 10 in Guernsey) are in the gift of the Crown. The Roman Catholic and various Nonconformist Churches are represented.

Further Reading

Coysh, V., *The Channel Islands: A New Study.* Newton Abbot, 1977

Cruickshank, C., *The German Occupation of the Channel Islands.* London, 1975

Jee, N., *The Landscape of the Channel Islands.* Chichester, 1982

Lempriere, R., *Portrait of the Channel Islands.* London, 1970.—*History of the Channel Islands.* Rev. ed. London, 1980

Uttley, J., *The Story of the Channel Islands.* London, 1966

JERSEY

TERRITORY AND POPULATION. The area is 116·2 sq. km (44·9 sq. miles). Resident population (1991 census), 84,082 (43,220 females); density, 724 per sq. km. In the year ended 31 Dec. 1991 there were 1,057 births (rate, 12·5 per 1,000 population) and 832 deaths (9·9). The chief town is St Helier on the south coast. The official language is English (French until 1960).

CONSTITUTION AND GOVERNMENT. The States consist of 12 Senators (elected for 6 years, 6 retiring every third year), 12 Constables (triennial) and 29 Deputies (triennial), all elected on universal suffrage by the people.

The island parliament is 'The States of Jersey'. The States comprises the Bailiff, the Lieut.-Governor, the Dean of Jersey, the Attorney-General and the Solicitor-General, and 53 members elected by universal suffrage: 12 Senators, the Constables of the 12 parishes of the island and 29 Deputies. They all have the right to speak in the Assembly, but only the 53 elected members have the right to vote; the Bailiff has a casting vote. Senators are elected in Oct. every third year for 6-year terms, 6 retiring every third year. Constables are elected by the electors of their parishes for 3-year terms. Deputies are elected on a constituency basis in Nov. every third year. Except in specific instances, enactments passed by the States require the sanction of The Queen-in-Council. The Lieut.-Governor has the power of veto on certain forms of legislation.

Administration is carried out by Committees of the States.

Flag: White with a red diagonal cross. In the top centre of the flag a shield of the arms of Jersey ensigned with the Plantagenet Crown.

Lieut.-Governor and C.-in-C. of Jersey: Gen. Sir Michael Wikes, KCB, CBE.

Secretary and ADC to the Lieut.-Governor: Lieut.-Colonel C. Woodrow, OBE, MC, QGM.

Bailiff of Jersey and President of the States: P. Bailhache.

ECONOMY

Budget (year ending 31 Dec. 1991). Revenue, £354,010,485; revenue expenditure, £297,812,924; capital expenditure, £62,701,000; net public debt, nil. The standard rate of income tax is 20p in the pound. No super-tax or death duties are levied. Parochial rates of moderate amount are payable by owners and occupiers.

Currency. The States issue bank-notes in denominations of £50, £20, £10, £5 and £1. Coinage from 1p to 50p is struck in the same denominations as the UK. £32·1m. were in circulation in 1991.

Banking and Finance. Financial services contributed 47% of GDP in 1991. Bank deposits and balances due to parent companies, 1992, totalled £45,271m.

AGRICULTURE AND FISHERIES. In 1991 there were 568 farms totalling 16,020 acres. Livestock, 1991: Cattle, 6,517 (milch cows, 4,583). The catch of fish in 1991 was 4,473 tonnes.

INDUSTRY. Principal activities: Tourism; total number of hotel and guesthouse bedrooms (1990), 23,069; expenditure of tourists (1990), £270m. Agriculture, total output (1988), £36·4m. and total exports, £30·7m. Light industry, mainly electrical goods, textiles and clothing. In 1991 47,547 persons were economically active (20,529 females). 912 persons were registered unemployed in Oct. 1992.

Commerce. Since 1980 the Customs have ceased recording imports and exports. Principal imports: Machinery and transport equipment, manufactured goods, food, mineral fuels, and chemicals. Principal exports: Machinery and transport equipment, food, and manufactured goods.

Tourism. In 1991 tourism accounted for 27% of GDP. There were 1·38m. passenger arrivals, of whom 701,000 were staying visitors and 145,000 non-UK day-trip visitors. Tourist revenue was £254m.

COMMUNICATIONS

Roads. In 1991 there were 51,131 private cars, 8,335 hire cares, 5,231 vans, 2,047 lorries, 65 buses, 662 coaches and 3,880 motorcycles and scooters.

Civil Aviation. The Jersey airport is situated at St Peter. It covers approximately 375 acres. Number of aircraft movements excluding local flying (1990) 60,107; number of passengers: 1,890,714; cargo and mail, 8,792 tonnes.

Shipping (1990). All vessels arriving in Jersey from outside Jersey waters report at St Helier or Gorey on first arrival. There is a harbour of minor importance at St Aubin. Number of commercial vessels entering St Helier in 1990, 26,472; number of visiting yachts (1990), 12,097. Passengers arrived in 1990, 491,145.

Telecommunications. Postal, and overseas telephone and telegraph services are maintained by the Postal Administration of Jersey. The local telephone service is maintained by the Insular Authority. In 1989 there were 43,880 telephones and 24 post offices.

JUSTICE. Justice is administered by the Royal Court, consisting of the Bailiff and 12 Jurats (magistrates). There is a final appeal in certain cases to the Sovereign in Council. There is also a Court of Appeal, consisting of the Bailiff and 2 judges. Minor civil and criminal cases are dealt with by a stipendiary magistrate.

EDUCATION (1992). There were 5 States secondary schools and 1 high school, and 24 States primary schools; 4,753 pupils attended the primary schools, 3,667 the secondary schools. There were 8 private primary schools with 1,297 pupils and 8 private secondary schools with 833 pupils. There were 382 full-time students at the further education college.

HEALTH. In 1992 there were 88 doctors and 343 hospital beds.

SOCIAL SECURITY. In 1991 income was £60,854,872. Benefits paid totalled £52,810,857 (long-term benefits, £41,566,023; sickness, £4,484,999; invalidity, £3,582,915. 1,843 families totalling 3,313 children were receiving family allowances.

Further Reading

Balleine, G. R., *Biographical Dictionary of Jersey.* London, 1948.—*A History of the Island of Jersey.* Rev. ed. Chichester, 1981.—*The Bailiwick of Jersey.* 3rd ed. London, 1970

Bois, F. de L., *The Constitutional History of Jersey.* Jersey, 1970

States of Jersey Library: Halkett Place, St Helier.

GUERNSEY

POPULATION. Census population (1991) 58,867. Births during 1994 were 676; deaths, 591. The town is St Peter Port.

CONSTITUTION. The government of the island is conducted by committees appointed by the States.

The States of Deliberation, the Parliament of Guernsey, is composed of the following members: The Bailiff, who is President *ex officio;* 12 Conseillers elected by popular franchise; H.M. Procureur and H.M. Comptroller (Law Officers of the Crown), who have a voice but no vote; 33 People's Deputies elected by popular franchise; 10 Douzaine Representatives elected by their Parochial Douzaines; 2 representatives of the States of Alderney.

Elections for People's Deputies were held on 20 April 1994.

The States of Election, an electoral college, elects the Jurats. It is composed of the following members: The Bailiff (President *ex officio*); the 12 Jurats or 'Jurés-Justiciers'; the 12 Conseillers; H.M. Procureur and H.M. Comptroller; the 33 People's Deputies and 34 Douzaine Representatives.

Since Jan. 1949 all legislative powers and functions (with minor exceptions) formerly exercised by the Royal Court have been vested in the States of Deliberation. Projets de Loi (Bills) require the sanction of The Queen-in-Council.

Flag: White bearing a red cross of St George, with an argent with a cross gules superimposed on the cross.

Lieut.-Governor and C.-in-C. of Guernsey and its Dependencies: Vice-Admiral Sir John Coward, KCB, DSO.

Secretary and ADC to the Lieut.-Governor: Capt. D. P. L. Hodgetts.

Bailiff of Guernsey and President of the States: Sir Graham Dorey.

Deputy Bailiff of Guernsey: de V. G. Carey.

BANKING AND FINANCE (year ended 31 Dec. 1994). Revenue, including Alderney, £168,368,350; expenditure, including Alderney, £153,927,201. The standard rate of income tax is 20p in the pound. States and parochial rates are very moderate. No super-tax or death duties are levied.

There were 75 banks in 1994.

COMMERCE (1994). Principal imports: Petrol and oils, 157,092,000 litres. Principal exports: Tomatoes, £3·6m.; flowers and fern, £21m.; flowers by post, £4m.; vegetables, £2·1m.; plants, £2·7m.

COMMUNICATIONS

Civil Aviation. The airport in Guernsey, situated at La Villiaze, has a landing area of approximately 124 acres and a tarmac runway of 4,800 ft. In 1994, passenger arrivals totalled 790,592.

Shipping. The principal harbour is that of St Peter Port, and there is a harbour at St Sampson's (used mainly for commercial shipping). In 1994 passenger arrivals totalled 326,048. Ships registered in Guernsey at 31 Dec. 1995 numbered 1,945 and 326 fishing vessels. In 1994, 11,927 yachts visited Guernsey.

EDUCATION. There are 2 public schools in the island: Elizabeth College, founded by Queen Elizabeth in 1563, for boys, and the Ladies' College, for girls. The States grammar school provides for education up to University entrance requirements, and there are numerous modern secondary and primary schools and a College of Further Education. The total number of school children was (1993) 8,339. Facilities are available for the study of art, domestic science and many other subjects of a technical nature. There is also a convent school with boarding facilities for girls.

HEALTH. Guernsey is not covered by the UK National Health Service. Public health is overseen by the States of Guernsey Insurance Authority and Board of Health. A private medical insurance scheme to provide specialist cover for all residents was implemented by the States on 1 Jan. 1996.

ALDERNEY. Population (1986 census, 2,130; 1994 estimate, 2,375). The island has an airport. The Constitution of the island (reformed 1987) provides for its own popularly elected President and States (12 members), and its own Court. Elections were held for the President and 4 members of the States in Dec. 1993. The town is St Anne's.

Flag: White with a red cross with the island badge in the centre.

President of the States: George W. Baron.
Clerk of the States: D. V. Jenkins.
Clerk of the Court: A. Johnson.

Alderney levies its taxes at Guernsey rates and passes the revenue to Guernsey, which charges for the services it provides.

SARK. Population (1986 estimate, 550). The Constitution is a mixture of feudal and popular government with its Chief Pleas (parliament), consisting of 40 tenants and 12 popularly elected deputies, presided over by the Seneschal. The head of the island is the Seigneur. Sark has no income tax. Motor vehicles, except tractors, are not allowed.

Flag: White with a red cross and a red first quarter bearing two gold lions.

The Seigneur: J. M. Beaumont.
Seneschal: L. P. de Carteret.

Further Reading

Carteret, A. R. de, *The Story of Sark.* London, 1956
Coysh, V., *Alderney.* Newton Abbot, 1974
Hathaway, S., *Dame of Sark: An Autobiography.* London, 1961
Le Huray, C. P., *The Bailiwick of Guernsey.* London, 1952
Marr, L. J., *A History of Guernsey.* Chichester, 1982

UNITED STATES OF AMERICA

Capital: Washington, D.C.
Population: 263·43m. (1995)
GNP per capita: US$25,860 (1994)
HDI/world rank: 0·937/2 (1992)

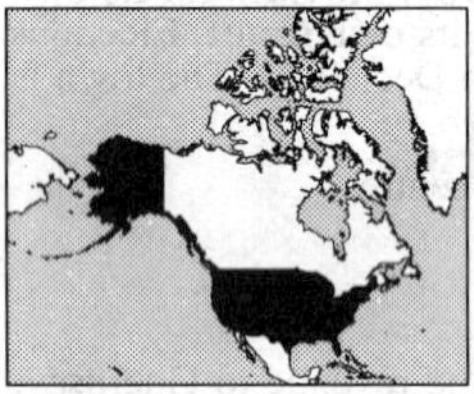

KEY HISTORICAL EVENTS. The Declaration of Independence of the 13 states of which the American Union then consisted was adopted by Congress on 4 July 1776. On 30 Nov. 1782 Great Britain acknowledged the independence of the USA, and on 3 Sept. 1783 the treaty of peace was concluded and was ratified by the USA on 14 Jan. 1784.

TERRITORY AND POPULATION. Population at each census from 1790 to 1990 (including Alaska and Hawaii from 1960). Figures do not include Puerto Rico, Guam, American Samoa or other Pacific islands, or the US population abroad. Residents of Indian reservations not included before 1890.

	White	*Black* [1]	*Other races* [2]	*Total*	*Decennial increase %*
1790	3,172,464 [3]	757,208	—	3,929,672	—
1800	4,306,446	1,002,037	—	5,308,483	35·1
1810	5,862,073	1,377,808	—	7,239,881	36·4
1820	7,866,797	1,771,562	—	9,638,359	33·1
1830	10,537,378	2,328,642	—	12,866,020	33·5
1840	14,195,805	2,873,648	—	17,069,453	32·7
1850	19,553,068	3,638,808	—	23,191,876	35·9
1860	26,922,537	4,441,830	78,954 [4]	31,443,321	35·6
1870 [5]	33,589,377	4,880,009	88,985	38,558,371	22·6
1870 [5]	*34,337,292*	*5,392,172*	*88,985*	*39,818,449*	*26.6*
1880	43,402,970	6,580,793	172,020	50,155,783	30·1
1890	55,101,258	7,488,676	357,780	62,947,714	25·5
1900	66,868,508	8,834,395	509,265	76,212,168	21·0
1910	81,812,405	9,828,667	587,459	92,228,531	21·0
1920	94,903,540	10,463,607	654,421	106,021,568	14·9 [6]
1930	110,395,753 [7]	11,891,842	915,065	123,202,660	16·1 [6]
1940	118,357,831	12,865,914	941,384	132,165,129	7·3
1950	135,149,629	15,044,937	1,131,232	151,325,798	14·5
1960 [8]	158,831,732	18,871,831	1,619,612	179,323,175	18·5
1970	177,748,975	22,580,289	2,882,662	203,211,926	13·3
1980	188,371,622	26,495,025	11,679,158	226,545,805	11·4
1990	199,686,070	29,986,060	19,037,743	248,709,873	9·8

[1] Seventeen southern states (including D.C.) in 1900 had 7,922,969 Blacks (89·7% of the total Black population); in 1920, 8,912,231 (85·2%); in 1940, 9,904,619 (77%); in 1950, 10,225,407 (68%); in 1960, 11,311,607 (59·9%); in 1970, 11,969,961 (53%); in 1980, 14,048,000 (53%).

[2] *1870*, 63,199 Chinese, 55 Japanese and 25,731 Indians; *1880*, 105,465 Chinese, 148 Japanese and 66,407 Indians; *1890*, 107,488 Chinese, 2,039 Japanese and 248,253 Indians; *1900*, 118,746 Chinese, 85,716 Japanese, 237,196 Indians, 67,607 other races; *1910*, 94,414 Chinese, 152,745 Japanese, 276,927 Indians, 2,767 Filipino, 60,606 other races; *1920*, 85,202 Chinese, 220,596 Japanese, 244,437 Indians, 26,634 Filipino, 77,552 other races; *1930*, 343,352 Indians, 102,159 Chinese, 278,743 Japanese, 108,424 Filipino, 82,387 other races; *1940*, 345,252 Indians, 106,334 Chinese, 285,115 Japanese, 98,535 Filipino, 106,148 other races; *1950*, 357,499 Indians, 326,379 Japanese, 150,005 Chinese, 122,707 Filipino, 174,642 other races; *1960*, 523,591 Indians, 464,332 Japanese, 237,292 Chinese, 176,310 Filipino, 218,087 other races; *1970*, 792,730 Indians, 591,290 Japanese, 435,062 Chinese, 343,060 Filipino, 720,520 other races; *1980*, 1,364,033 Indians, 700,974 Japanese, 806,040 Chinese, 774,652 Filipino, 8,033,459 other races; *1990*, 7,273,662 Asians or Pacific Islanders, 1,952,234 Indians, 9,804,847 other races.

[3] Made up of Anglo-Scottish, 89·1%; German, 5·6%; Dutch, 2·5%; Irish, 1·9%; French, 0·6%.

[4] 34,933 Chinese and 44,021 Indians.

[5] Enumeration in 1870 incomplete. Figures in italics represent estimated corrected population.

[*Footnotes continued on next page.*]

Urban population (persons living in places with at least 2,500 inhabitants) at the 1990 census was 187,053,487 (75·2%); rural, 61,656,386. In 1980 the urban population was 73·7%; in 1970, 73·6%.

Sex distribution by race of the population at the 1990 census:

	Total population	*White*	*Black*	*American Indian*	*Asian or Pacific*	*Other*
Males:	121,239,418	97,475,880	14,170,151	967,186	3,558,038	5,068,163
Females:	127,470,455	102,210,190	15,815,909	992,048	3,715,624	4,736,684

Alongside these racial groups, and applicable to all of them, a category of 'Hispanic origin' comprised 22,354,059 persons (11,388,059 males; 10,966,000 females).

Age distribution by sex of the population at the 1990 census:

Age-group	*Male*	*Female*	*Total*
Under 5	9,392,409	8,962,034	18,354,443
5–9	9,262,527	8,836,652	18,099,179
10–14	8,767,167	8,347,082	17,114,249
15–19	9,102,690	8,651,317	17,754,015
20–24	9,675,596	9,344,716	19,020,312
25–29	10,695,936	10,617,109	21,313,045
30–34	10,876,933	10,985,954	21,862,887
35–39	9,902,243	10,060,874	19,963,117
40–44	8,691,984	8,923,802	17,615,786
45–49	6,810,597	7,061,976	13,872,573
50–54	5,514,738	5,835,775	11,350,513
55–59	5,034,370	5,497,386	10,531,756
60–64	4,947,047	5,669,120	10,616,167
Over 65	12,565,173	18,676,658	31,241,831

US population abroad at the time of the 1990 census was 925,845.

At the 1990 census there were 91,947,410 households.

Population in July 1995 as estimated by the US Bureau of the Census: 263,434,000 (134,749,000 females).

The 1990 census showed that 31·8m. persons 5 years and over spoke a language other than English in the home, including Spanish by 17·3m.; French, 1·7m.; German, 1·5m.; Italian, 1·3m.; Chinese, 1·2m.

The following table includes population statistics, the year in which each of the original 13 states (Connecticut, Delaware, Georgia, Maryland, Massachusetts, New Hampshire, New Jersey, New York, North Carolina, Pennsylvania, Rhode Island, South Carolina, Virginia) ratified the constitution, and the year when each of the other states was admitted into the Union. Traditional abbreviations for the names of the states are shown in brackets with postal codes for use in addresses. The area of the USA in 1995 was 3,787,319 sq. miles (9,809,155 sq. km), of which 3,536,338 sq. miles (9,159,116 sq. km) were land.

The USA is divided into 4 geographic regions comprising 9 divisions. These are, with their 1990 census populations: Northeast (comprising the New England and Middle Atlantic divisions), 50,809,229; Midwest (East North Central, West North Central), 59,668,632; South (South Atlantic, East South Central, West South Central), 85,445,930; West (Mountain, Pacific), 52,786,082.

Geographic divisions and states	*Land area: sq. miles 1990*	*Census population 1 April 1990*	*Pop. per sq. mile, 1990*
United States	3,536,338	248,709,873	70·3

[6] Between the 1910 census (15 April 1910) and the 1920 census (1 Jan. 1920), the period covered was 116 months (less than a full decade). Adjusting for this, the exact rate of increase for the decade was 15·4%. Similarly correcting for the 123 months between the 1920 and 1930 censuses, the true rate of increase was 15·7%.

[7] Figures for 1930 have been revised to include Mexicans (1,422,533), who were classified with 'Other Races' in the 1930 census reports.

[8] Figures for 1960 strictly comparable with those given for other years (*i.e.*, excluding Alaska and Hawaii) are: White, 158,454,956; Black, 18,860,117; other races, 1,149,163; total, 178,464,236; decennial increase, 18·4%.

Geographic divisions and states		Land area: sq. miles 1990	Census population 1 April 1990	Pop. per sq. mile, 1990
New England		62,812	13,206,943	210·3
Maine (1820)	*(Me./ME)*	30,865	1,227,928	39·8
New Hampshire (1788)	*(N.H./NH)*	8,969	1,109,252	123·7
Vermont (1791)	*(Vt./VT)*	9,249	562,758	60·8
Massachusetts (1788)	*(Mass./MA)*	7,838	6,016,425	767·6
Rhode Island (1790)	*(R.I./RI)*	1,045	1,003,464	960·3
Connecticut (1788)	*(Conn./CT)*	4,845	3,287,116	678·4
Middle Atlantic		99,462	37,602,286	378·1
New York (1788)	*(N.Y./NY)*	47,224	17,990,455	381·0
New Jersey (1787)	*(N.J./NJ)*	7,419	7,730,188	1,042·0
Pennsylvania (1787)	*(Pa./PA)*	44,820	11,881,643	265·1
East North Central		243,539	42,008,942	172·5
Ohio (1803)	*(Oh./OH)*	40,953	10,847,115	264·9
Indiana (1816)	*(Ind./IN)*	35,870	5,544,159	154·6
Illinois (1818)	*(Ill./IL)*	55,593	11,430,602	205·6
Michigan (1837)	*(Mich./MI)*	56,809	9,295,297	163·6
Wisconsin (1848)	*(Wis./WI)*	54,314	4,891,769	90·1
West North Central		504,981	17,659,690	35·0
Minnesota (1858)	*(Minn./MN)*	79,617	4,375,099	55·0
Iowa (1846)	*(Ia./IA)*	55,875	2,776,755	49·7
Missouri (1821)	*(Mo./MO)*	68,898	5,117,073	74·3
North Dakota (1889)	*(N.D./ND)*	68,994	638,800	9·3
South Dakota (1889)	*(S.D./SD)*	75,896	696,004	9·2
Nebraska (1867)	*(Nebr./NE)*	76,878	1,578,385	20·5
Kansas (1861)	*(Kans./KS)*	81,823	2,477,574	30·3
South Atlantic		266,160	43,566,853	163·2
Delaware (1787)	*(Del./DE)*	1,955	666,168	340·8
Maryland (1788)	*(Md./MD)*	9,775	4,781,468	489·2
Dist. of Columbia (1791)	*(D.C./DC)*	61	606,900	9,884·4
Virginia (1788)	*(Va./VA)*	39,598	6,187,358	156·3
West Virginia (1863)	*(W. Va./WV)*	24,087	1,793,477	74·5
North Carolina (1789)	*(N.C./NC)*	48,718	6,628,637	136·1
South Carolina (1788)	*(S.C./SC)*	30,111	3,486,703	115·8
Georgia (1788)	*(Ga./GA)*	57,919	6,478,216	111·9
Florida (1845)	*(Fla./FL)*	53,997	12,937,926	239·6
East South Central		178,616	15,176,284	85·0
Kentucky (1792)	*(Ky./KY)*	39,732	3,685,296	92·8
Tennessee (1796)	*(Tenn./TN)*	41,220	4,877,185	118·3
Alabama (1819)	*(Al./AL)*	50,750	4,040,587	79·6
Mississippi (1817)	*(Miss./MS)*	46,914	2,573,216	54·8
West South Central		426,234	26,702,793	62·6
Arkansas (1836)	*(Ark./AR)*	52,075	2,350,725	45·1
Louisiana (1812)	*(La./LA)*	43,566	4,219,973	96·9
Oklahoma (1907)	*(Okla./OK)*	68,679	3,145,585	45·8
Texas (1845)	*(Tex./TX)*	261,914	16,986,510	64·9
Mountain		856,121	13,658,776	16·0
Montana (1889)	*(Mont./MT)*	145,556	799,065	5·5
Idaho (1890)	*(Id./ID)*	82,751	1,006,749	12·2
Wyoming (1890)	*(Wyo./WY)*	97,105	453,588	4·7
Colorado (1876)	*(Colo./CO)*	103,729	3,294,394	31·8
New Mexico (1912)	*(N. Mex./NM)*	121,365	1,515,069	12·5
Arizona (1912)	*(Ariz./AZ)*	113,642	3,665,228	32·3
Utah (1896)	*(Ut./UT)*	82,168	1,722,850	21·0
Nevada (1864)	*(Nev./NV)*	109,806	1,201,833	10·9

Geographic divisions and states		*Land area: sq. miles 1990*	*Census population 1 April 1990*	*Pop. per sq. mile, 1990*
Pacific		895,354	39,127,306	43·7
Washington (1889)	*(Wash./WA)*	66,581	4,866,692	73·1
Oregon (1859)	*(Oreg./OR)*	96,003	2,842,321	29·6
California (1850)	*(Calif./CA)*	155,973	29,760,021	190·8
Alaska (1959)	*(Ak./AK)*	570,374	550,043	1·0
Hawaii (1960)	*(Hi./HI)*	6,423	1,108,229	172·5

Geographic divisions and states	*Land area: sq. miles 1990*	*Estimated population 1 July 1988 (in 1,000)*	*Census population 1 April 1990*	*Pop. per sq. mile, 1990*
Outlying Territories, total	4,691	...	3,862,431	760
Puerto Rico (1898)	3,427	3,291	3,522,037	1,028
Virgin Islands (1917)	134	103·2	101,809	761
American Samoa (1900)	77	39·5	46,773	607
Guam (1898)	209	133	133,152	637
Northern Marianas (1947)	184	21·2	43,345	235
Palau (1947)	192	...	15,122	79
Midway Islands (1867)	3	...	13	5
Wake Island (1898)	3	...	7	3
Johnston Atoll (1858)	1	...	173	157

The 1990 census showed 19,767,316 foreign-born persons, by continent of origin: Latin America, 8,407,831 (42·5%); North America, 8,124,251 (41·1%); Asia, 4,979,043 (25·2%); Europe, 4,016,678 (20·3%); Africa, 363,819 (1·8%); Pacific, 104,145 (0·5%). The 9 countries contributing the largest numbers who were foreign-born were Mexico, 4,298,014; Philippines, 912,674; Canada, 744,830; Cuba, 736,971; Germany, 711,929; UK, 640,145; Italy, 580,592; South Korea, 568,397; Vietnam, 543,262.

Increase or decrease of native White, and foreign-born White, population from 1870 to 1990, by decades:

	Native White			*Foreign-born White*		
	Total	*Increase*	*Per cent increase*	*Total*	*Increase or decrease (–)*	*Per cent. change*
1870	28,095,665	5,269,881	23·1	5,493,712	1,396,959	34·1
1880	36,843,291	8,747,626	31·1	6,559,679	1,065,967	19·4
1890	45,979,391	9,018,732 [1]	24·5	9,121,867	2,562,188	39·1
1900	56,595,379	10,615,988	23·1	10,213,817	1,091,950	12·0
1910	68,386,412	11,791,033	20·8	13,345,545	3,131,728	30·7
1920	81,108,161	12,721,749	18·6	13,712,754	367,209	2·8
1930	96,303,335	15,195,174	18·7	13,983,405	270,651	2·0
1940	106,795,732	10,492,397	10·9	11,419,138	–2,564,267	–18·3
1950	124,780,860	17,985,128	16·8	10,161,168	–1,257,970	–11·0
1960	149,543,638	24,762,778	19·8	9,293,992	– 867,176	– 8·5
1970	169,385,451	19,841,813	13·3	8,733,770	– 560,222	– 6·0
1980	179,711,066	10,325,615	6·0	9,323,946	590,176	6·7
1990	189,663,258	9,952,192	5·5	10,022,812	698,866	7·5

[1] Exclusive of population specially enumerated in 1890 in Indian Territory and on Indian reservations.

Population of cities with over 100,000 inhabitants at the censuses of 1980 and 1990:

Cities	*Census 1980*	*Census 1990*	*Cities*	*Census 1980*	*Census 1990*
New York, N.Y.	7,071,639	7,322,564	Detroit, Mich.	1,203,369	1,027,974
Los Angeles, Calif.	2,968,528	3,485,398	Dallas, Tex.	904,599	1,006,877
Chicago, Ill.	3,005,072	2,783,726	Phoenix, Ariz.	790,183	983,403
Houston, Tex.	1,611,382	1,630,553	San Antonio, Tex.	810,353	935,933
Philadelphia, Pa.	1,688,210	1,585,577	San José, Calif	629,400	782,248
San Diego, Calif.	875,538	1,110,549	Indianapolis, Ind.	711,539	741,952

Cities	*Census 1980*	*Census 1990*
Baltimore, Ma.	786,741	736,014
San Francisco, Calif.	678,974	723,959
Jacksonville, Fla.	571,003	672,971
Columbus, Ohio	565,021	632,910
Milwaukee, Wis.	636,297	628,088
Memphis, Tenn.	646,174	610,337
Washington, D.C.	638,432	606,900
Boston, Mass.	562,994	574,283
Seattle, Wash.	493,846	516,259
El Paso, Tex.	425,259	515,342
Nashville-Davidson, Tenn.	477,811	510,784
Cleveland, Ohio	573,822	505,616
New Orleans, La.	557,927	496,938
Denver, Colo.	492,686	467,610
Austin, Tex.	345,890	465,622
Fort Worth, Tex.	385,164	447,619
Oklahoma City, Okla.	404,014	444,719
Portland, Ore.	368,148	437,319
Kansas City, Mo.	448,028	435,146
Long Beach, Calif.	361,498	429,433
Tucson, Ariz.	330,537	405,390
St. Louis, Mo.	452,804	396,685
Charlotte, NC	315,474	395,934
Atlanta, Ga.	425,022	394,017
Virginia Beach, Va.	262,199	393,069
Albuquerque, N.M.	332,920	384,736
Oakland, Calif.	339,337	372,242
Pittsburgh, Pa.	423,959	369,379
Sacramento, Calif.	275,741	369,365
Minneapolis, Minn.	370,951	368,383
Tulsa, Okla.	360,919	367,302
Honolulu, Hi.	365,048	365,272
Cincinnati, Ohio.	385,409	364,040
Miami, Fla.	346,681	358,548
Fresno, Calif.	217,491	354,202
Omaha, Nebr.	313,939	335,795
Toledo, Ohio	354,635	332,943
Buffalo, N.Y.	357,870	328,123
Wichita, Kan.	279,838	304,011
Santa Ana, Calif.	204,023	293,742
Mesa, Ariz.	152,404	288,091
Colorado Springs, Colo.	215,105	281,140
Tampa, Fla.	271,577	280,015
Newark, N.J.	329,248	275,221
St. Paul, Minn.	270,230	272,235
Louisville, Ky.	298,694	269,063
Anaheim, Calif.	219,494	266,406
Birmingham, Ala.	284,413	265,968
Arlington, Tex.	160,113	261,721
Norfolk, Va.	266,979	261,229
Las Vegas, Nev.	164,674	258,295
Corpus Christi, Tex.	232,134	257,453
St. Petersburg, Fla.	238,647	238,629
Rochester, N.Y.	241,741	231,636
Jersey City, N.J.	223,532	228,537
Riverside, Calif.	170,591	226,505
Anchorage, Ak.	174,431	226,338
Lexington-Fayette, Ky.	204,165	225,366
Akron, Ohio	237,177	223,019
Aurora, Colo.	158,588	222,103
Baton Rouge, La.	220,394	219,531
Stockton, Calif.	148,283	210,943
Raleigh, N.C.	150,255	207,951
Richmond, Va.	219,214	203,056
Shreveport, La.	206,989	198,525
Jackson, Miss.	202,895	196,637
Mobile, Ala.	200,452	196,278
Des Moines, Ia.	191,003	193,187
Lincoln, Nebr.	171,932	191,972
Madison, Wis.	170,616	191,262
Grand Rapids, Mich.	181,843	189,126
Yonkers, N.Y.	195,351	188,082
Hialeah, Fla.	145,254	188,004
Montgomery, Ala.	177,857	187,106
Lubbock, Tex.	174,361	186,206
Greensboro, N.C.	155,642	183,521
Dayton, Ohio	193,536	182,044
Huntington Beach, Calif.	170,505	181,519
Garland, Tex.	138,857	180,650
Glendale, Calif.	139,060	180,038
Columbus, Ga.	169,441	179,278
Spokane, Wash.	171,300	177,196
Tacoma, Wash.	158,501	176,664
Little Rock, Ariz.	159,159	175,795
Bakersfield, Calif.	105,611	174,820
Fremont, Calif.	131,945	173,339
Fort Wayne, Ind.	172,391	173,072
Newport News, Va.	144,903	170,045
Worcester, Mass.	161,799	169,759
Knoxville, Tenn.	175,045	165,121
Modesto, Calif.	106,963	164,730
Orlando, Fla.	128,291	164,693
San Bernardino, Calif.	118,794	164,164
Syracuse, N.Y.	170,105	163,860
Providence, R.I.	156,804	160,728
Salt Lake City, Utah	163,034	159,936
Huntsville, Ala.	142,513	159,789
Amarillo, Tex.	149,230	157,615
Springfield, Mass.	152,319	156,983
Irving, Tex.	109,943	155,037
Chattanooga, Tenn.	169,514	152,466
Chesapeake, Va.	114,486	151,976
Kansas City, Kan.	161,148	149,767
Fort Lauderdale, Fla.	153,279	149,377
Glendale, Ariz.	97,172	148,134
Warren, Mich.	161,134	144,864
Winston-Salem, N.C.	131,885	143,485
Garden Grove, Calif.	123,307	143,050
Oxnard, Calif.	108,195	142,216
Tempe, Ariz.	106,919	141,865
Bridgeport, Conn.	142,546	141,686
Paterson, N.J.	137,970	140,891
Flint, Mich.	159,611	140,761
Springfield, Mo.	133,116	140,494
Hartford, Conn.	136,392	139,739
Rockford, Ill.	139,712	139,426
Savannah, Ga.	141,654	137,560
Durham, N.C.	101,149	136,611
Chula Vista, Calif.	83,927	135,163
Reno, Nev.	100,756	133,850
Hampton, Va.	122,617	133,793
Ontario, Calif.	88,820	133,179
Torrance, Calif.	129,881	133,107
Pomona, Calif.	92,742	131,723
Pasadena, Calif.	18,072	131,591
New Haven, Conn.	126,089	130,474
Scottsdale, Ariz.	88,622	130,069
Plano, Tex.	72,331	128,713

Cities	Census 1980	Census 1990	Cities	Census 1980	Census 1990
Oceanside, Calif.	76,698	128,398	Inglewood, Calif.	94,162	109,602
Lansing, Mich.	130,414	127,321	Ann Arbor, Mich.	107,969	109,592
Lakewood, Colo.	113,808	126,481	Vallejo, Calif.	80,303	109,199
Evansville, Ind.	130,496	126,272	Waterbury,Conn.	103,266	108,961
Boise, Idaho	102,249	125,738	Salinas, Calif.	80,479	108,777
Tallahassee, Fla.	81,548	124,773	Cedar Rapids, Ia.	110,243	108,751
Laredo, Tex.	91,449	122,899	Erie, Pa.	119,123	108,718
Hollywood, Fla.	121,323	121,697	Escondido, Calif.	64,355	108,635
Topeka, Kan.	118,690	119,883	Stamford, Conn.	102,466	108,056
Pasadena, Tex.	112,560	119,363	Salem, Ore.	89,091	107,786
Moreno Valley, Calif.	...	118,779	Abilene, Tex.	98,315	106,654
Sterling Heights, Mich.	108,999	117,810	Macon, Ga.	116,896	106,612
Sunnyvale, Calif.	106,618	117,229	El Monte, Calif.	79,494	106,209
Gary, Ind.	151,968	116,646	South Bend, Ind.	109,727	105,511
Beaumont, Tex.	118,102	114,323	Springfield, Ill.	100,054	105,227
Fullerton, Calif.	102,246	114,144	Allentown, Pa.	103,758	105,090
Peoria, Ill.	124,160	113,504	Thousand Oaks, Calif.	77,072	104,352
Santa Rosa, Calif.	82,658	113,313	Portsmouth, Va.	104,577	103,907
Eugene, Ore.	105,664	112,669	Waco, Tex.	101,261	103,590
Independence, Mo.	111,797	112,301	Lowell, Mass.	92,418	103,439
Overland Park, Kan.	81,784	111,790	Berkeley, Calif.	103,328	102,724
Hayward, Calif.	93,585	111,498	Mesquite, Tex.	67,053	101,484
Concord, Calif.	103,763	111,348	Rancho Cucamonga, Calif.	55,250	101,409
Alexandria, Va.	103,217	111,183	Albany, N.Y.	101,727	101,082
Orange, Calif.	91,450	110,658	Livonia, Mich.	104,814	100,850
Santa Clarita, Calif.	...	110,642	Sioux Falls, S.D.	81,343	100,814
Irvine, Calif.	62,134	110,330	Simi Valley, Calif.	77,500	100,217
Elizabeth, N.J.	106,201	110,002			

Vital Statistics: Vital statistics are based on records of births, deaths, fetal deaths, marriages and divorces filed with registration officials of states and cities. Figures for the US include Alaska beginning with 1959 and Hawaii beginning with 1960.

Annual collection of mortality records from a national death-registration area was inaugurated in 1900. A national birth-registration area was established in 1915. These areas, which at their inception comprised 10 states and the District of Columbia, expanded gradually until 1933, when both the birth- and death-registration areas covered the entire continental US. Marriage and divorce statistics are compiled from reports furnished by state and local officials. Data on annulments are included in the divorce statistics. The marriage-registration area was established in 1957 with 30 states and 3 other areas. The divorce-registration area was established in 1958 with 14 states and 2 other areas. In 1995 the marriage-registration area included 42 states and D.C., and the divorce-registration area included 31 states.

	Live births [1]	Deaths [2]	Marriages [3]	Divorces [4]	Deaths under 1 year [5]
1900	—	343,217	709,000	56,000	—
1910	2,777,000	696,856	948,000	83,000	—
1920	2,950,000	1,118,070	1,274,476	170,505	170,911
1930	2,618,000	1,327,240	1,126,856	195,961	143,201
1940	2,559,000	1,417,269	1,595,879	264,000	110,984
1950	3,632,000	1,452,454	1,667,231	385,144	103,825
1960	4,257,850 [6]	1,711,982	1,523,000	393,000	110,873
1970	3,731,386 [6]	1,921,031	2,158,802	708,000	74,667
1980	3,612,258	1,989,841	2,390,252	1,189,000	45,526
1988	3,913,000	2,171,000	2,389,000	1,183,000	38,910
1989	4,021,000	2,155,000	2,419,236	1,007,538	39,655
1990	4,179,000	2,162,000	2,448,000	1,175,000	38,351
1991	4,111,000	2,165,000	2,371,100	1,187,000	36,766
1992	4,065,014	2,177,000	2,362,000	1,215,000	34,400
1993	4,000,240	2,268,000	2,334,000	1,187,000	33,900
1994	3,979,000	2,286,000	2,362,000	1,191,000	33,100

[1] Figures through 1959 include adjustment for under-registration (the 1959 registered count was 4,244,796); beginning 1960 figures represent number registered.

[*Footnotes continued on next page.*]

1,528,930 abortions were reported in 1992 (1,556,510 in 1991).

Rates (per 1,000 population):

	Birth	*Death*	*Marriage*	*Divorce*
1991	16·3	8·6	9·4	4·7
1992	16·0	8·5	9·3	4·8

The crude birth rate, based on total live-birth estimates per 1,000 total population, fell from 29·5 in 1915 to 18·4 in 1933; it rose to a peak of 26·6 in 1947—its highest for 25 years. This peak reflects demobilization (1945–46), the record marriage rate that followed, and the high levels of employment and income. The decrease in the following 3 years was moderate. In 1951 the rate moved upward and levelled off in 1957 at about 25 per 1,000 population. Since 1957 the crude birth rate declined every year to 4·6 live births per 1,000 population in 1975. Since 1985 it rose from 15·7 to 16·7 in 1990, declining ever since: to 15·5 in 1993 and 15·3 in 1994. Estimated number of births to unmarried women in 1992 was 1,225,000 (30·1% of all births, 22·6% of White births, 68·1% of Black births).

Deaths, excluding fetal deaths (per 1,000 population), declined from 17·2 in 1900 to 10 in 1946. The death rate has been below 10 per 1,000 since 1947, fluctuating slightly from year to year, mainly under the impact of occurrences of outbreaks of severe respiratory diseases. The rate for 1970, 9·5; 1980, 8·8; 1990, 8·6; 1992, 8·6; 1993, 8·8.

The marriage rates per 1,000 population for selected years: 1920, 12; 1932, 7·9; 1946, 16·4; 1951, 10·4; 1961, 8·5; 1970, 10·6; 1975, 10; 1980, 10·6; 1985, 10·1; 1986, 10; 1988, 9·7; 1990, 9·8; 1993, 9. The divorce rates per 1,000 population for selected years are: 1920, 1·6; 1946, 4·3; 1951, 2·5; 1961, 2·3; 1971, 3·7; 1980, 5·2; 1985, 5; 1990, 4·7; 1992, 4·7; 1993, 4·6.

The infant mortality rates, per 1,000 live births: 1915–19, 95·7; 1920–24, 76·7; 1925–29, 69; 1930–34, 60·4; 38·3 in 1945; 29·2 in 1950; 26·4 in 1955; 26 in 1960; 20 in 1970; 16·1 in 1975; 12·6 in 1980; 10·6 in 1985; 10·4 in 1986; 10 in 1987; 10 in 1988; 8·9 in 1991; 8·8 in 1992.

Expectation of life, 1995: Males, 72·8 years; females, 79·7 years.

Numbers of deaths by principal causes, 1994 (and as a percentage of all deaths): Heart disease, 734,090 (32·1%); cancer, 536,860 (23·5%); stroke, 154,350 (6·8%); obstructive lung disease, 101,870 (4·5%); accidents, 90,140 (3·9%); pneumonia and influenza, 82,090 (3·6%); diabetes mellitus, 55,390 (2·4%); AIDS, 41,930 (1·8%); suicide, 32,410 (1·4%); liver disease, 25,730 (1·1%). There were 25,470 homicides in 1993.

Immigration: The Immigration and Nationality Act, as amended, provides for the numerical limitation of most immigration. The Immigration Act of 1990 established major revisions in the numerical limits and preference system regulating legal immigration. The numerical limits are imposed on visas issued and not admissions. The maximum number of visas allowed to be issued under the preference categories in 1994 was 369,213: 226,000 for family-sponsored immigrants and 143,213 for employment-based immigrants. There are 9 categories among which the family-sponsored and employment-based immigrant visas are distributed. The family-sponsored preferences are: 1) unmarried sons and daughters of US citizens; 2) spouses, children, and unmarried sons and daughters of permanent resident aliens; 3) married sons and daughters of US citizens; 4) brothers and sisters of US citizens. The employment-based preferences are: 1) priority workers (persons of

---

[2] Excluding fetal deaths and deaths among the armed forces overseas.

[3] Estimates for all years except 1970.

[4] Includes reported annulments. Estimated for all years.

[5] Deaths for 1979–81 (Ninth Revision, International Classification of Diseases, 1975). Deaths from complications of pregnancy, childbirth and the puerperium. Deaths for 1968–78 were classified according to the Eighth Revision, International Classification of Diseases, adopted, 1965. Deaths for 1958–67 were classified according to the Seventh Revision of the International Lists of Diseases and Causes of Death, those for 1949–57 according to the Sixth Revision and those for 1939–48, according to the Fifth Revision.

[6] Based on a 50% sample. [7] Provisional.

extraordinary ability, outstanding professors and researchers, and certain multinational executives and managers); 2) professionals with advanced degrees or aliens with exceptional ability; 3) skilled workers, professionals (without advanced degrees), and needed unskilled workers; 4) special immigrants; and 5) employment creation immigrants (investors). Within the overall limitations the per-country limit for independent countries is set to 7% of the total family and employment limits, while dependent areas are limited to 2% of the total. The 1994 limit allowed no more than 25,844 preference visas for any independent country and 7,384 for any dependency. Prior to fiscal year 1992, visas were allocated under a system of 6 preference categories, 4 of which are designed to reunite close relatives of US citizens and resident aliens of the US, and 2 for skilled and professional workers. Visa numbers not used in the preference categories are made available to qualified non-preference immigrants. The non-preference visas had not been issued since 1978 due to high demand in other categories. Beginning in 1987, additional visas were issued under the non-preference category to persons from countries adversely affected by the Immigration Amendments of 1965. The non-preference category was eliminated by the Immigration Act of 1990. Immigrants not subject to any numerical limitation are spouses, children, and parents of US citizens who are 21 years of age or older; certain former US citizens; ministers of religion; certain long-term US government employees; refugees and asylum-seekers adjusting to immigrant status; and certain other groups of immigrants.

Immigration data for 1994 include 6,022 aliens who were admitted as permanent residents under the legalization programme created by the Immigrant Reform and Control Act of 1986. These aliens have resided in the USA since before 1982 or were agricultural workers on perishable crops and have qualified as temporary residents under the first phase of the legalization programme; in the fiscal year 1989, they began qualifying for permanent status.

Immigrant aliens admitted to the USA for permanent residence, by country or region of birth, for fiscal years:

Country or region of birth	*Immigrants admitted* 1991	1992	1993	1994
All countries	1,827,167	973,977	904,292	804,416
Europe	135,234	145,392	158,254	160,916
Germany	6,509	9,888	7,312	6,992
Greece	2,079	1,858	1,884	1,440
Italy	2,619	2,592	2,487	2,305
Poland	19,199	25,504	27,846	28,048
Portugal	4,524	2,748	2,081	2,169
Spain	1,849	1,631	1,388	1,418
UK	13,903	19,973	18,783	16,326
Yugoslavia	2,713	2,604	2,809	3,405
Other Europe	81,839	78,594	93,664	98,813
Asia	358,533	356,955	358,047	292,589
China and Taiwan	46,299	55,251	79,907	64,017
Hong Kong	10,427	10,452	9,161	7,731
India	45,064	36,755	40,121	34,921
Japan	5,049	11,028	6,908	6,093
Korea (North and South)	26,518	19,359	18,026	16,011
Philippines	63,596	61,022	63,457	53,535
Thailand	7,397	7,090	6,654	5,489
Other Asia	154,183	155,998	148,142	104,792
North America	1,210,981	384,047	301,380	272,226
Canada	13,504	15,205	17,156	16,068
Mexico	946,167	213,802	126,561	111,398
Cuba	10,349	11,791	13,666	14,727
Dominican Republic	41,405	41,969	45,420	51,189
Haiti	47,527	11,002	10,094	13,333
Jamaica	23,828	18,915	17,241	14,349
Trinidad and Tobago	8,407	7,008	6,577	6,292
Other Caribbean	8,623	6,728	6,440	4,914
Central America	111,093	57,558	58,162	39,908
Other North America	78	69	63	48

Country or region of birth	Immigrants admitted 1991	1992	1993	1994
South America	79,934	55,308	53,921	47,377
Colombia	19,702	13,201	12,819	10,847
Ecuador	9,958	7,286	7,324	5,906
Other South America	50,274	34,821	33,778	30,624
Africa	36,179	27,086	27,783	26,712
Australia and New Zealand	2,471	3,205	3,372	2,967
Other countries	3,835	1,984	1,535	1,629

The total number of immigrants admitted from 1820 up to 30 Sept. 1994 was 61,503,866; this included 7,126,132 from Germany, and 5,421,949 from Italy.

Aliens coming to the USA for temporary periods of time are classified as non-immigrants. During fiscal year 1994, a total of 22,118,706 non-immigrants were admitted. This total includes multiple entries but excludes border crossers, crewmen and insular travellers. Tourists numbered 17,154,834, with 9,573,609 coming from the Caribbean, Germany, Japan, Mexico and the UK. There were 1,068,170 aliens expelled during fiscal year 1994. Of this number, 39,620 were deported and 1,028,550 were required to depart without formal orders of deportation.

During fiscal year 1994, 407,398 persons became US citizens through naturalization, including 342,863 naturalized under the general provisions of 5-year residence in the USA, 32,659 spouses and children of US citizens and 5,713 members of the US Armed Forces. The new citizens included 30,278 from China and Taiwan, 15,896 from Cuba, 5,622 from Italy, 12,173 from Jamaica, 11,389 from Korea, 39,310 from Mexico, 37,304 from the Philippines and 26,833 from Vietnam.

The refugee admissions ceiling for the fiscal year 1994 was fixed at 112,000, including 48,000 from Eastern Europe and the former USSR and 40,000 from South-East Asia.

National Urban League. *The State of Black America.* New York, annual
Sklare, M., *The Jew in American Society.* New York, 1974

CLIMATE. For temperature and rainfall figures, *see* entries on individual states as indicated by regions, below, of mainland USA.

Pacific Coast. The climate varies with latitude, distance from the sea and the effect of relief, ranging from polar conditions in North Alaska through cool to warm temperate climates further south. The extreme south is temperate desert. Rainfall everywhere is moderate. *See* Alaska, California, Oregon, Washington.

Mountain States. Very varied, with relief exerting the main control; very cold in the north in winter, with considerable snowfall. In the south, much higher temperatures and aridity produce desert conditions. Rainfall everywhere is very variable as a result of rain-shadow influences. *See* Arizona, Colorado, Idaho, Montana, Nevada, New Mexico, Utah, Wyoming.

High Plains. A continental climate with a large annual range of temperature and moderate rainfall, mainly in summer, although unreliable. Dust storms are common in summer and blizzards in winter. *See* Nebraska, North Dakota, South Dakota.

Central Plains. A temperate continental climate, with hot summers and cold winters, except in the extreme south. Rainfall is plentiful and comes at all seasons, but there is a summer maximum in western parts. *See* Mississippi, Missouri, Oklahoma, Texas.

Mid-West. Continental, with hot summers and cold winters. Rainfall is moderate, with a summer maximum in most parts. *See* Indiana, Iowa, Kansas.

Great Lakes. Continental, resembling that of the Central Plains, with hot summers but very cold winters because of the freezing of the lakes. Rainfall is moderate with a slight summer maximum. *See* Illinois, Michigan, Minnesota, Ohio, Wisconsin.

Appalachian Mountains. The north is cool temperate with cold winters, the south warm temperate with milder winters. Precipitation is heavy, increasing to the south but evenly distributed over the year. *See* Kentucky, Pennsylvania, Tennessee, West Virginia.

Gulf Coast. Conditions vary from warm temperate to sub-tropical, with plentiful rainfall, decreasing towards the west but evenly distributed over the year. *See* Alabama, Arkansas, Florida, Louisiana.

Atlantic Coast. Temperate maritime climate but with great differences in temperature according to latitude. Rainfall is ample at all seasons; snowfall in the north can be heavy. *See* Delaware, District of Columbia, Georgia, Maryland, New Jersey, New York, North Carolina, South Carolina, Virginia.

New England. Cool temperate, with severe winters and warm summers. Precipitation is well distributed with a slight winter maximum. Snowfall is heavy in winter. *See* Connecticut, Maine, Massachusetts, New Hampshire, Rhode Island, Vermont. *See* also Hawaii and Outlying Territories.

CONSTITUTION AND GOVERNMENT. The form of government of the USA is based on the constitution of 17 Sept. 1787.

By the constitution the government of the nation is composed of three co-ordinate branches, the executive, the legislative and the judicial.

The Federal Government has authority in matters of general taxation, treaties and other dealings with foreign countries, foreign and inter-state commerce, bankruptcy, postal service, coinage, weights and measures, patents and copyright, the armed forces (including, to a certain extent, the militia), and crimes against the USA; it has sole legislative authority over the District of Columbia and the possessions of the USA.

The 5th article of the constitution provides that Congress may, on a two-thirds vote of both houses, propose amendments to the constitution, or, on the application of the legislatures of two-thirds of all the states, call a convention for proposing amendments, which in either case shall be valid as part of the constitution when ratified by the legislatures of three-fourths of the several states, or by conventions in three-fourths thereof, whichever mode of ratification may be proposed by Congress. Ten amendments (called collectively 'the Bill of Rights') to the constitution were added 15 Dec. 1791; two in 1795 and 1804; a 13th amendment, 6 Dec. 1865, abolishing slavery; a 14th in 1868, including the important 'due process' clause; a 15th, 3 Feb. 1870, establishing equal voting rights for white and coloured; a 16th, 3 Feb. 1913, authorizing the income tax; a 17th, 8 April 1913, providing for popular election of senators; an 18th, 16 Jan. 1919, prohibiting alcoholic liquors; a 19th, 18 Aug. 1920, establishing woman suffrage; a 20th, 23 Jan. 1933, advancing the date of the President's and Vice-President's inauguration and abolishing the 'lameduck' sessions of Congress; a 21st, 5 Dec. 1933, repealing the 18th amendment; a 22nd, 26 Feb. 1951, limiting a President's tenure of office to 2 terms, or to 2 terms plus 2 years in the case of a Vice-President who has succeeded to the office of a President; a 23rd, 30 March 1961, granting citizens of the District of Columbia the right to vote in national elections; a 24th, 4 Feb. 1964, banning the use of the poll-tax in federal elections; a 25th, 10 Feb. 1967, dealing with Presidential disability and succession; a 26th, 22 June 1970, establishing the right of citizens who are 18 years of age and older to vote; a 27th, 7 May 1992, providing that no law varying the compensation of Senators or Representatives shall take effect until an election has taken place.

National flag: Seven red and 6 white alternating stripes, horizontal; with a blue canton, extending down to the lower edge of the 4th red stripe from the top, and displaying 50 white 5-pointed stars, one for each state. The stars have one point directed vertically upward, and they are arranged in 6 rows of 5 each, alternating with 5 rows of 4 each. On the admission of additional states, stars are added, effective on 4 July following the date of admission. Congress, by law of 22 Dec. 1942, has codified 'existing rules and customs' pertaining to the display of the flag, for civilians.

National anthem: The Star-spangled Banner, 'Oh say, can you see by the dawn's early light'; words by F. S. Key, 1814, tune by J. S. Smith; formally adopted by Congress 3 March 1931.

National motto: 'In God we trust'; formally adopted by Congress 30 July 1956.

Presidency. The executive power is vested in a president, who holds office for 4 years, and is elected, together with a vice-president chosen for the same term, by electors from each state, equal to the whole number of senators and representatives to which the state may be entitled in the Congress. The President must be a natural-born citizen, resident in the country for 14 years, and at least 35 years old.

The presidential election is held every fourth (leap) year on the Tuesday after the first Monday in November. Technically, this is an election of presidential electors, not of a president directly; the electors thus chosen meet and give their votes (for the candidate to whom they are pledged, in some states by law, but in most states by custom and prudent politics) at their respective state capitals on the first Monday after the second Wednesday in December next following their election; and the votes of the electors of all the states are opened and counted in the presence of both Houses of Congress on the sixth day of January. The total electorate vote is one for each senator and representative. Electors may not be a member of Congress or hold federal office. If no candidate secures the minimum 270 college votes needed for outright victory, the 12th Amendment to the Constitution applies, and the House of Representatives chooses a president from among the first 3 finishers in the electoral college. (This last happened in 1824).

If the successful candidate for President dies before taking office the Vice-President-elect becomes President; if no candidate has a majority or if the successful candidate fails to qualify, then, by the 20th amendment, the Vice-President acts as President until a president qualifies. The duties of the Presidency, in absence of the President and Vice-President by reason of death, resignation, removal, inability or failure to qualify, devolve upon the Speaker of the House under legislation enacted 18 July 1947. And in case of absence of a Speaker for like reason, the presidential duties devolve upon the President *pro tem.* of the Senate and successively upon those members of the Cabinet in order of precedence, who have the constitutional qualifications for President.

The presidential term, by the 20th amendment to the constitution, begins at noon on 20 Jan. of the inaugural year. This amendment also instals the newly elected Congress in office on 3 Jan. instead of—as formerly—in the following December. The President's salary is $200,000 per year (taxable), with in addition $50,000 to assist in defraying expenses resulting from official duties. Also he may spend up to $100,000 non-taxable for travel and $20,000 for official entertainment. The office of Vice-President carries a salary of $171,500 and $10,000 allowance for expenses, all taxable. The Vice-President is *ex-officio* President of the Senate, and in the case of 'the removal of the President, or of his death, resignation, or inability to discharge the powers and duties of his office', he becomes the President for the remainder of the term.

President of the United States: William (Bill) Jefferson Blythe IV Clinton, of Arkansas, b. 1946. (Governor of Arkansas, 1979–81, 1983–92).
Vice President: Albert Gore, of Tennessee, b. 1948 (House of Representatives, 1977–85; Senate, 1985–).

At the Presidential election on 3 Nov. 1992 turn-out was 55·9% (50·1% in 1988). Bill Clinton (D.) received 44,908,254 votes (43%), George Bush (R.) 39,102,343 (37·4%) and Ross Perot 19,741,065 (18.9%). Electoral college votes: Clinton, 370; Bush, 168; Perot, nil.

Voting percentages and electoral college votes by state:

a) Majority for Clinton

State	*Clinton (%)*	*Bush (%)*	*Perot (%)*	*Electoral College (votes)*
Arkansas	53	36	11	6
California	47	32	21	54
Colorado	40	36	23	8
Connecticut	42	36	22	8
Delaware	44	36	21	3
DC	86	9	4	3
Georgia	44	43	13	13
Hawaii	49	37	14	4
Illinois	48	35	17	22
Iowa	44	37	19	7

State	Clinton (%)	Bush (%)	Perot (%)	Electoral College (votes)
Kentucky	45	42	14	8
Louisiana	46	42	12	9
Maine	39	31	30	4
Maryland	50	36	14	10
Massachusetts	48	29	23	12
Michigan	44	36	20	18
Minnesota	44	32	24	10
Missouri	44	34	22	11
Montana	38	36	26	3
Nevada	38	35	27	4
New Hampshire	39	38	23	4
New Jersey	43	41	16	15
New Mexico	46	38	16	5
New York	50	35	16	33
Ohio	40	39	21	21
Oregon	43	32	25	7
Pennsylvania	45	36	18	23
Rhode Island	48	29	22	4
Tennessee	47	43	10	11
Vermont	46	31	23	3
Washington	44	31	24	11
West Virginia	49	35	16	5
Wisconsin	41	37	22	11

b) Majority for Bush

	Bush	Clinton	Perot	
Alabama	48	41	11	9
Alaska	41	32	28	3
Arizona	39	37	24	8
Florida	41	39	20	25
Idaho	43	23	28	4
Indiana	43	37	20	12
Kansas	39	34	27	6
Mississippi	50	41	9	7
Nebraska	47	30	23	5
North Carolina	44	43	13	14
North Dakota	45	32	23	3
Oklahoma	43	34	23	8
South Carolina	48	40	12	8
South Dakota	41	37	22	3
Texas	40	37	22	32
Utah	45	26	29	5
Virginia	45	41	14	13
Wyoming	40	34	26	3

PRESIDENTS OF THE USA

Name	From state	Term of service	Born	Died
George Washington	Virginia	1789–97	1732	1799
John Adams	Massachusetts	1797–1801	1735	1826
Thomas Jefferson	Virginia	1801–09	1743	1826
James Madison	Virginia	1809–17	1751	1836
James Monroe	Virginia	1817–25	1759	1831
John Quincy Adams	Massachusetts	1825–29	1767	1848
Andrew Jackson	Tennessee	1829–37	1767	1845
Martin Van Buren	New York	1837–41	1782	1862
William H. Harrison	Ohio	Mar.–Apr. 1841	1773	1841
John Tyler	Virginia	1841–45	1790	1862
James K. Polk	Tennessee	1845–49	1795	1849
Zachary Taylor	Louisiana	1849–July 1850	1784	1850
Millard Fillmore	New York	1850–53	1800	1874
Franklin Pierce	New Hampshire	1853–57	1804	1869
James Buchanan	Pennsylvania	1857–61	1791	1868

Name	*From state*	*Term of service*	*Born*	*Died*
Abraham Lincoln	Illinois	1861–Apr. 1865	1809	1865
Andrew Johnson	Tennessee	1865–69	1808	1875
Ulysses S. Grant	Illinois	1869–77	1822	1885
Rutherford B. Hayes	Ohio	1877–81	1822	1893
James A. Garfield	Ohio	Mar.–Sept. 1881	1831	1881
Chester A. Arthur	New York	1881–85	1830	1886
Grover Cleveland	New York	1885–89	1837	1908
Benjamin Harrison	Indiana	1889–93	1833	1901
Grover Cleveland	New York	1893–97	1837	1908
William McKinley	Ohio	1897–Sept. 1901	1843	1901
Theodore Roosevelt	New York	1901–09	1858	1919
William H. Taft	Ohio	1909–13	1857	1930
Woodrow Wilson	New Jersey	1913–21	1856	1924
Warren Gamaliel Harding	Ohio	1921–Aug. 1923	1865	1923
Calvin Coolidge	Massachusetts	1923–29	1872	1933
Herbert C. Hoover	California	1929–33	1874	1964
Franklin D. Roosevelt	New York	1933–Apr. 1945	1882	1945
Harry S Truman	Missouri	1945–53	1884	1972
Dwight D. Eisenhower	New York	1953–61	1890	1969
John F. Kennedy	Massachusetts	1961–Nov. 1963	1917	1963
Lyndon B. Johnson	Texas	1963–69	1908	1973
Richard M. Nixon	California	1969–74	1913	1994
Gerald R. Ford	Michigan	1974–77	1913	—
James Earl Carter	Georgia	1977–81	1924	—
Ronald W Reagan	California	1981–89	1911	—
George H Bush	Texas	1989–93	1924	—
Bill (William J.) Clinton	Arkansas	1993–	1946	—

VICE-PRESIDENTS OF THE USA

John Adams	Massachusetts	1789–97	1735	1826
Thomas Jefferson	Virginia	1797–1801	1743	1826
Aaron Burr	New York	1801–05	1756	1836
George Clinton	New York	1805–12 [1]	1739	1812
Elbridge Gerry	Massachusetts	1813–14 [1]	1744	1814
Daniel D. Tompkins	New York	1817–25	1774	1825
John C. Calhoun	South Carolina	1825–32 [1]	1782	1850
Martin Van Buren	New York	1833–37	1782	1862
Richard M. Johnson	Kentucky	1837–41	1780	1850
John Tyler	Virginia	Mar.–Apr. 1841 [1]	1790	1862
George M. Dallas	Pennsylvania	1845–49	1792	1864
Millard Fillmore	New York	1849–50 [1]	1800	1874
William R. King	Alabama	Mar.–Apr. 1853 [1]	1786	1853
John C. Breckinridge	Kentucky	1857–61	1821	1875
Hannibal Hamlin	Maine	1861–65	1809	1891
Andrew Johnson	Tennessee	Mar.–Apr. 1865 [1]	1808	1875
Schuyler Colfax	Indiana	1869–73	1823	1885
Henry Wilson	Massachusetts	1873–75 [1]	1812	1875
William A. Wheeler	New York	1877–81	1819	1887
Chester A. Arthur	New York	Mar.–Sept. 1881 [1]	1830	1886
Thomas A. Hendricks	Indiana	Mar.–Nov. 1885 [1]	1819	1885
Levi P. Morton	New York	1889–93	1824	1920
Adlai Stevenson	Illinois	1893–97	1835	1914
Garret A. Hobart	New Jersey	1897–99 [1]	1844	1899
Theodore Roosevelt	New York	Mar.–Sept. 1901 [1]	1858	1919
Charles W. Fairbanks	Indiana	1905–09	1855	1920
James S. Sherman	New York	1909–12 [1]	1855	1912
Thomas R. Marshall	Indiana	1913–21	1854	1925

[1] Position vacant thereafter until commencement of the next presidential term.

VICE-PRESIDENTS OF THE USA

Calvin Coolidge	Massachusetts	1921–Aug. 1923 [1]	1872	1933
Charles G. Dawes	Illinois	1925–29	1865	1951
Charles Curtis	Kansas	1929–33	1860	1935
John N. Garner	Texas	1933–41	1868	1967
Henry A. Wallace	Iowa	1941–45	1888	1965
Harry S Truman	Missouri	1945–Apr. 1945 [1]	1884	1972
Alben W. Barkley	Kentucky	1949–53	1877	1956
Richard M. Nixon	California	1953–61	1913	1994
Lyndon B. Johnson	Texas	1961–Nov. 1963 [1]	1908	1973
Hubert H. Humphrey	Minnesota	1965–69	1911	1978
Spiro T. Agnew	Maryland	1969–73	1918	—
Gerald R. Ford	Michigan	1973–74	1913	—
Nelson Rockefeller	New York	1974–77	1908	1979
Walter Mondale	Minnesota	1977–81	1928	—
George Bush	Texas	1981–89	1924	—
Danforth Quayle	Indiana	1989–93	1947	—
Albert Gore	Tennessee	1993–	1948	—

[1] Position vacant thereafter until commencement of the next presidential term.

Cabinet. The administrative business of the nation has been traditionally vested in several executive departments, the heads of which, unofficially and *ex officio*, formed the President's Cabinet. Beginning with the Interstate Commerce Commission in 1887, however, an increasing amount of executive business has been entrusted to some 60 so-called independent agencies, such as the Housing and Home Finance Agency, Tariff Commission, etc.

All heads of departments and of the 60 or more administrative agencies are appointed by the President, but must be confirmed by the Senate.

The Cabinet consisted of the following (March 1995):

1. *Secretary of State* (created 1789). Warren Christopher, of North Dakota; lawyer, government official; Deputy Attorney-General, 1963–69; Deputy Secretary of State, 1977–81; b. 1925.

2. *Secretary of the Treasury* (1789). Robert Rubin, of New York; economist, investment banker; head of the National Economic Council; Economic Adviser to the President; b. 1938.

3. *Secretary of Defense* (1947). Dr William Perry, of Pennsylvania; mathematical scientist; electronic defence industrialist; technical consultant, Defense Department, 1967-77; Under-Secretary of Defense, 1977-81; Deputy Secretary of Defense, 1993-94; b. 1927.

4. *Attorney-General* (Department of Justice, 1870). Janet Reno, of Florida; lawyer; State Attorney of Dade County (FL), 1978–92; b. 1938.

5. *Secretary of the Interior* (1849). Bruce Babbitt, of California; lawyer; Attorney-General of Arizona, 1975–78; Governor of Arizona, 1978–87; b. 1938.

6. *Secretary of Agriculture* (1889). Dan Glickman, of Kansas; lawyer; Congressman, 1977–94; member of House Agriculture, Judiciary and Science, Space and Technology Committees, chair Select Committee on Intelligence, 1993–94; b. 1944.

7. *Secretary of Commerce* (1903). Vacant.

8. *Secretary of Labor* (1913). Robert Reich, of Pennsylvania; government service, political economics educator at Harvard Univ., 1981–92; b. 1946.

9. *Secretary of Health and Human Services* (1953). Dr Donna Shalala of Ohio; political scientist, educator; US Housing Department, 1977–81; President of Hunter College (NY), Chancellor of the Univ. of Wisconsin, 1988–92; b. 1941.

10. *Secretary of Housing and Urban Development* (1966). Henry Cisneros, of Texas; urban studies educator; city government official; Mayor of San Antonio, 1981–89; b. 1947.

11. *Secretary of Transportation* (1967). Federico Pena, of Texas; lawyer; Congress as Representative for Colorado; House Democratic Leader; b. 1949.

12. *Secretary of Energy* (1977). Hazel O'Leary, of Virginia; lawyer; service in the US Department of Energy; vice-president of an electricity company; b. 1937.

13. *Secretary of Education* (1979). Richard Riley, of South Carolina; lawyer; South Carolina state representative, 1963–66; state senator, 1966–76; Governor of South Carolina, 1979–87; b. 1933.

14. *Veterans' Affairs Administrator* (1989). Jesse Brown; US Marines; director, Disabled American Veterans; b. 1944.

Each of the above Cabinet officers receives an annual salary of $148,400 and holds office during the pleasure of the President.

The Administrator of the Environmental Protection Agency, Carol Browner, the US Trade Representative, Mickey Kantor, the Office of Management and Budget Director, Leon Panetta, and the US ambassador to the United Nations, Madeleine Albright, have Cabinet rank.

Congress: The legislative power is vested by the Constitution in a Congress, consisting of a Senate and House of Representatives.

Electorate: By amendments of the constitution, disqualification of voters on the ground of race, colour or sex is forbidden. The electorate consists of all citizens over 18 years of age. Literacy tests have been banned since 1970. In 1972 durational residency requirements were held to violate the constitution. In 1973 US citizens abroad were enfranchised.

With limitations imposed by the constitution, it is the states which determine voter eligibility. In general states exclude from voting: Persons who have not established residency in the jurisdiction in which they wish to vote; persons who have been convicted of felonies whose civil rights have not been restored; persons declared mentally incompetent by a court.

Illiterate voters are entitled to receive assistance in marking their ballots. Minority-language voters in jurisdictions with statutorily prescribed minority concentrations are entitled to have elections conducted in the minority language as well as English. Disabled voters are entitled to accessible polling places. Voters absent on election days or unable to go to the polls are generally entitled under state law to vote by absentee ballot.

The Constitution guarantees citizens that their votes will be of equal value under the 'one person, one vote' rule.

Senate: The Senate consists of 2 members from each state, chosen by popular vote for 6 years, approximately one-third retiring or seeking re-election every 2 years. Senators must be no less than 30 years of age; must have been citizens of the USA for 9 years, and be residents in the states for which they are chosen. The Senate has complete freedom to initiate legislation, except revenue bills (which must originate in the House of Representatives); it may, however, amend or reject any legislation originating in the lower house. The Senate is also entrusted with the power of giving or withholding its 'advice and consent' to the ratification of all treaties initiated by the President with foreign Powers, a two-thirds majority of senators present being required for approval. (However, it has no control over 'international executive agreements' made by the President with foreign governments; such 'agreements' cover a wide range and are more numerous than formal treaties.) It also has the power of confirming or rejecting major appointments to office made by the President, but it has no direct control over the appointment by the President of 'personal representatives' or 'personal envoys' on missions abroad. Members of the Senate constitute a High Court of Impeachment, with power, by a two-thirds vote, to remove from office and disqualify any civil officer of the USA impeached by the House of Representatives, which has the sole power of impeachment.

The Senate has 17 Standing Committees to which all bills are referred for study, revision or rejection. The House of Representatives has 19 such committees. In both Houses each Standing Committee has a chairman and a majority representing the majority party of the whole House; each has numerous sub-committees. The jurisdictions of these Committees correspond largely to those of the appropriate executive departments and agencies. Both Houses also have a few select or special Committees with limited duration; there were (1995) 4 Joint Senate-House Committees.

House of Representatives: The House of Representatives consists of 435 members elected every second year. The number of each state's representatives is determined by the decennial census, in the absence of specific Congressional legislation affecting the basis. The states, in 1996, had the following numbers of representatives:

Alabama	7	Indiana	10	Nebraska	3	South Carolina	6
Alaska	1	Iowa	5	Nevada	2	South Dakota	1
Arizona	6	Kansas	4	New Hampshire	2	Tennessee	9
Arkansas	4	Kentucky	6	New Jersey	13	Texas	30
California	52	Louisiana	7	New Mexico	3	Utah	3
Colorado	6	Maine	2	New York	31	Vermont	1
Connecticut	6	Maryland	8	North Carolina	12	Virginia	11
Delaware	1	Massachusetts	10	North Dakota	1	Washington	9
Florida	23	Michigan	16	Ohio	19	West Virginia	3
Georgia	11	Minnesota	8	Oklahoma	6	Wisconsin	9
Hawaii	2	Mississippi	5	Oregon	5	Wyoming	1
Idaho	2	Missouri	9	Pennsylvania	21		
Illinois	20	Montana	1	Rhode Island	2		

The constitution requires congressional districts within each state to be substantially equal in population. Final decisions on congressional district boundaries are taken by the state legislatures and governors. By custom the representative lives in the district from which he is elected. Representatives must be not less than 25 years of age, citizens of the USA for 7 years and residents in the state from which they are chosen.

In addition, 5 delegates (1 each from the District of Columbia, American Samoa, Guam, the US Virgin Islands and Puerto Rico) are also members of Congress. They have a voice but no vote, except in committees. The delegate from Puerto Rico is the resident commissioner. Puerto Ricans vote at primaries, but not at national elections. Each of the two Houses of Congress is sole 'judge of the elections, returns and qualifications of its own members'; and each of the Houses may, with the concurrence of two-thirds, expel a member. The period usually termed 'a Congress' in legislative language continues for 2 years, terminating at noon on 3 Jan.

The salary of a senator is $133,600 per annum, with tax-free expense allowance and allowances for travelling expenses and for clerical hire. The salary of the Speaker of the House of Representatives is $171,500 per annum, with a taxable allowance. The salary of a Member of the House is $133,600 ($148,400 for the Majority Leader and Minority Leader).

No senator or representative can, during the time for which he is elected, be appointed to any *civil* office under authority of the USA which shall have been created or the emoluments of which shall have been increased during such time; and no person holding *any* office under the USA can be a member of either House during his continuance in office. No religious text may be required as a qualification to any office or public trust under the USA or in any state.

The 104th Congress (1995–97) was constituted (Oct. 1995) as follows: Senate, 53 Republicans, 46 Democrats, 1 vacant; House of Representatives, 233 Republicans, 199 Democrats, 1 independent, 2 vacant.

Following the mid-term elections of 8 Nov. 1994, the 104th Congress (1995–97) was constituted as follows: Senate, 53 Republicans, 47 Democrats; House of Representatives, 230 Republicans, 204 Democrats, 1 independent. Turn-out was 38%.

The *Speaker* of the House of Representatives is Newt Gingrich (R). The *Majority Leader* of the Senate is Robert Dole (R).

Indians: By an Act passed on 2 June 1924 full citizenship was granted to all Indians born in the USA, though those remaining in tribal units were still under special federal jurisdiction. The Indian Reorganization Act of 1934 gave the tribal Indians, at their own option, substantial opportunities of self-government and the establishment of self-controlled corporate enterprises empowered to borrow money and buy land, machinery and equipment; these corporations are controlled by democratically elected tribal councils. Recently a trend towards releasing Indians from federal supervision has resulted in legislation terminating supervision over specific tribes. In 1988 the federal government recognized that it had a special relationship with, and a trust responsibility for, federally-recognized Indian entities in continental USA and tribal entities in Alaska. In 1993 the Bureau of Indian Affairs listed 552 'Indian Entities Recognized and Eligible to Receive Services'. Indian lands (1991) amounted to 52,092,247 acres, of which 41,868,582 was tribally owned and 10,233,665 in trust allotments. Indian lands are held free of taxes. Total Indian population at the 1990 census was 1,959,000, of which Oklahoma, Arizona, California and New Mexico accounted for 832,466.

McNickle, D., *The Indian Tribes of the United States.* OUP, 1962.—*Native American Tribalism.* OUP, 1963.

State and Local Government: The Union comprises 13 original states, 7 states which were admitted without having been previously organized as territories, and 30 states which had been territories—50 states in all. Each state has its own constitution (which the USA guarantees shall be republican in form), deriving its authority, not from Congress, but from the people of the state. Admission of states into the Union has been granted by special Acts of Congress, either (1) in the form of 'enabling Acts' providing for the drafting and ratification of a state constitution by the people, in which case the territory becomes a state as soon as the conditions are fulfilled, or (2) accepting a constitution already framed, and at once granting admission.

Each state is provided with a legislature of two Houses (except Nebraska, which since 1937 has had a single-chamber legislature), a governor and other executive officials, and a judicial system. Both Houses of the legislature are elective, but the senators (having larger electoral districts usually covering 2 or 3 counties compared with the single county or, in some states, the town, which sends 1 representative to the Lower House) are less numerous than the representatives, while in 38 states their terms are 4 years; in 12 states the term is 2 years. Of the 4-year senates, Illinois, Montana and New Jersey provide for two 4-year terms and one 2-year term in each decade. Terms of the lower houses are usually shorter; in 45 states, 2 years.

Members of both Houses are paid at the same rate, which varies from $200 a year in New Hampshire to $57,500 a year in New York. The trend is towards annual sessions of state legislatures; in 1995, 43 met annually (in 1939, only 4), and 7 (Arkansas, Kentucky, Montana, Nevada, North Dakota, Oregon and Texas) biennially.

The Governor has power to summon an extraordinary session, but not to dissolve or adjourn. The duties of the two Houses are similar, but in many states money bills must be introduced first in the Lower House. The Senate sits as a court for the trial of officials impeached by the other House, and often has power to confirm or reject appointments made by the Governor.

State legislatures are competent to deal with all matters not reserved for the federal government by the federal constitution nor specifically prohibited by the federal or state constitutions. Among their powers are the determination of the qualifications for the right of suffrage, and the control of all elections to public office, including elections of members of Congress and electors of President and Vice-President; the criminal law, both in its enactment and in its execution, with unimportant exceptions, and the administration of prisons; the civil law, including all matters pertaining to the possession and transfer of, and succession to, property; marriage and divorce, and all other civil relations; the chartering and control of all manufacturing, trading, transportation and other corporations, subject only to the right of Congress to regulate commerce passing from one state to another; labour; education; charities; licensing; fisheries within state waters, and game laws (apart from the hunting of migratory birds, which is a federal concern under treaties with Canada and Mexico). Taxes on income were left to the states until 1913, when the

16th amendment authorized the imposition of federal taxes on income without regard to apportionment.

The Governor is elected by direct vote of the people over the whole state for a term of office varying in the several states from 2 to 4 years, and with a salary ranging from $60,000 (Arkansas) to $130,000 (New York). His duty is to see to the faithful administration of the law, and he has command of the military forces of the state. He may recommend measures but does not present bills to the legislature. In some states he presents estimates. In all but one of the states (North Carolina) the Governor has a veto upon legislation, which may, however, be overridden by the two Houses, in some states by a simple majority, in others by a three-fifths or two-thirds majority. In some states the Governor, on his death or resignation, is succeeded by a Lieut.-Governor who was elected at the same time and has been presiding over the state Senate. In several states the Speaker of the Lower House succeeds the Governor.

The chief officials by whom the administration of state affairs is carried on (secretaries, treasurers, members of boards of commissioners, etc.) are usually chosen by the people at the general state elections for terms similar to those for which governors hold office.

At the 2 state gubernatorial elections on 7 Nov. 1995 the Republicans won 1 governorship and the Democrats 1, making a nationwide tally of 30 Republicans, 19 Democrats and 1 independent.

Local Government. The chief unit of local government is the county, of which there were (1995) 2,994 with definite functions; in addition, Rhode Island has 5 'counties' which have no functions; Alaska does not have counties but 25 divisions and, since Oct. 1960, there has been no active county government in Connecticut. Louisiana has 64 'parishes'. The counties maintain public order through the sheriff and his deputies, who may, in a crisis, be drawn temporarily from willing citizens; in many states the counties maintain the smaller local highways; other functions are the granting of licences and the apportionment and collection of taxes. In a few states they also manage the schools.

The unit of local government in New England is the rural township, governed directly by the voters, who assemble annually or oftener if necessary, and legislate in local affairs, levy taxes, make appropriations and appoint and instruct the local officials. Townships are grouped to form counties. Where cities exist, the township government is superseded by the city government.

319 mayoral elections were held on 7 Nov. 1995.

The **District of Columbia,** ceded by the State of Maryland for the purposes of government in 1791, is the seat of the US Government. It includes the city of Washington, and embraces a land area of 61 sq. miles. The Reorganization Plan No. 3 of 1967 instituted a Mayor Council form of government with appointed officers. In 1973 an elected Mayor and elected councillors were introduced; in 1974 they received power to legislate in local matters. Congress retains power to enact legislation and to veto or supersede the Council's acts. Since 1961 citizens have had the right to vote in national elections. On 23 Aug. 1978 the Senate approved a constitutional amendment giving the District full voting representation in Congress. This has still to be ratified.

The **Commonwealth of Puerto Rico, American Samoa, Guam and the Virgin Islands** each have a local legislature, whose acts may be modified or annulled by Congress, though in practice this has seldom been done. Puerto Rico since its attainment of commonwealth status on 25 July 1952, enjoys practically complete self-government, including the election of its governor and other officials. The conduct of foreign relations, however, is still a federal function and federal bureaux and agencies still operate in the island.

General supervision of territorial administration is exercised by the Office of Territories in the Department of Interior.

Congress and the Nation, 4 vols., Congressional Quarterly, Washington, from 1965.—*Congressional Ethics,* Rev. ed., 1980.—*Congressional Quarterly Almanac,* annual

Constitution of the US, National and State. 2 vols. [with subsequent amendments]. Dobbs Ferry, 1962
Bowles, N., *The Government and the Politics of the United States.* London, 1993
Encyclopedia of the United States Congress. New York, 1994
Kelly, A. H. *et al. The American Constitution: its Origins and Development.* 7th ed. New York, 1991
King, A. (ed). *The New American Political System.* 2nd ed. Washington (DC), 1990
Lees, J. D. *et al. American Politics Today.* 4th ed revised by R. A. Maidment. Manchester Univ. Press, 1994
Maisel, L. S. (ed). *Political Parties in the United States: an Encyclopedia.* Camden (CT), 1991
Neustadt, R. E., *Presidential Power and the Modern Presidents: the Politics of Leadership from Roosevelt to Reagan.* New York, 1991
Peele, G. *et al.* (eds). *Developments in American Politics.* 2nd ed. London, 1994
Political profiles. 5 vols. New York, from 1978

DEFENCE. The President is C.-in-C. of the Army, Navy and Air Force.

The National Security Act of 1947 provides for the unification of the Army, Navy and Air Forces under a single Secretary of Defense with cabinet rank. The President is also advised by a National Security Council and the Office of Civil and Defense Mobilization.

The major components of the Department of Defense are the Office of the Secretary of Defense and the Joint Chiefs of Staff, who provide immediate staff assistance and advice to the Secretary; the departments of the Army, Navy and Air Force, each separately organized under a civilian head (not of cabinet rank); and the unified and specified commands.

Army. *Secretary of the Army:* Togo West.

Central Administration. The Secretary of the Army is the head of the Department of the Army. Subject to the authority of the President as C.-in-C. and of the Secretary of Defense, he is responsible for all affairs of the Department.

The Secretary of the Army is assisted by the Under Secretary of the Army, 5 Assistant Secretaries of the Army (Civil Works, Financial Management, Installations, Logistics and Environment, Manpower and Reserve Affairs, Research, Development and Acquisition), General Counsel, Administrative Assistant, Director for Information Systems for Command, Control, Communications and Computers, Inspector General, Auditor General, Chief of Legislative Liaison, Chief of Public Affairs, Director for Small and Disadvantaged Business Utilization, Chairman of the Army Reserve Forces Policy Committee and the Army Staff headed by the Chief of Staff, US Army. The Office of the Under Secretary of the Army includes a Deputy Under Secretary (Operations Research).

The Chief of Staff, Army, in his role as a member of the Joint Chiefs of Staff, takes part in the planning and supervision of the operational forces under the command of the Commanders-in-Chief. The Vice Chief of Staff assists and advises the Chief of Staff.

The Army General Staff is the principal element of the Army Staff and includes the Offices of the Chief of Staff, Deputy Chief of Staff for Operations and Plans, Deputy Chief of Staff for Personnel, Deputy Chief of Staff for Logistics, and Deputy Chief of Staff for Intelligence. Other elements of the Army Staff are the offices of the Judge Advocate General, Surgeon General, Chief of Chaplains, Chief, Army Reserve, Chief, National Guard Bureau, and Chief of Engineers.

The Army consists of the Active Army, the Army National Guard of the US, the Army Reserve and civilian workforce; and all persons appointed to or enlisted into the Army without component; and all persons serving under call or conscription, including members of the National Guard of the States, etc., when in the service of the US. The strength of the Active Army was (30 June 1995) 524,900 (including 69,800 women).

The US Army Forces Command, with headquarters at Fort McPherson, Georgia, commands the Third US Army; 4 continental US Armies, and all assigned Active Army and US Army Reserve troop units in the continental US, the Commonwealth of Puerto Rico, and the Virgin Islands of the USA. The headquarters of the continental US Armies are: First US Army, Fort George G. Meade, Maryland; Second

US Army, Fort Gillem, Georgia; Fifth US Army, Fort Sam Houston, Texas; Sixth US Army, Presidio of San Francisco, California. The US Army Training and Doctrine Command, with headquarters at Fort Monroe, Virginia, co-ordinates and integrates the total combat development effort of the Army as well as developing, managing, establishing and verifying the training of individuals of the US Army and authorized foreign nationals. The US Army Health Services Command, with headquarters at Fort Sam Houston, Texas, provides health services in the continental US for the US Army and provides professional education and training for medical personnel of the US Army and authorized foreign national personnel. The US Army Materiel Command, with headquarters in Alexandria, Virginia, is responsible for US Army activities dealing with equipment development, procurement, delivery, supply and maintenance. The US Army Information Systems Communications Command, with headquarters at Fort Huachuca, Arizona, provides worldwide communication automation support to the Department of the Army and supports the Defense Communications Systems. The US Army Military District of Washington, with headquarters at Fort McNair, Washington, DC, provides support to the Department of the Army and the Department of Defense at the seat of Government. The US Army Space Command, with headquarters in Colorado Springs (CO), is the Army component to the US Space Command.

Approximately 32% of the Active Army is deployed outside the continental USA. Several divisions, which are located in the USA, keep equipment in Germany and can be flown there in 48–72 hours. Headquarters of US Seventh and Eighth Armies are in Europe and Korea respectively.

Operational Commands and Weapons. The larger commands are the theater army and corps. The typical theater army may consist of a variable number of corps composed of combat forces of armour, infantry, air defense artillery, aviation and field artillery units; combat support forces of aviation, engineer, intelligence and signal elements; and combat service support forces. A typical corps consists of a variable number and mixture of infantry, mechanized infantry, armoured, air assault, or airborne divisions; one or more separate infantry, mechanized infantry or armoured brigades; one or more armoured cavalry regiments; corps artillery (155-mm howitzer, 203-mm howitzer, multiple launch rocket system (MLRS); corps air defense brigade (*Hawk, Chaparral, Patriot* and *Avenger* battalions), corps aviation brigade and combat support and combat service support forces.

US Army Divisions have a common base (containing command, divisional artillery, air defense artillery, combat support and combat service support units) aviation brigade, and a varying mixture of combat manoeuvre battalions (usually 9 or 10 in number in 3 brigades) to make up airborne, infantry, armoured, mechanized infantry and air assault divisions. Divisions can in this way be 'tailored' to fit a variety of strategic or tactical situations. A mechanized infantry division, with about 17,300 soldiers, may have 5 mechanized infantry battalions and 4 armoured battalions; an armoured division, with about 17,300 soldiers, may have 4 mechanized infantry battalions and 5 armoured battalions; an airborne division, with 13,100 soldiers, may have 9 infantry (airborne) battalions. The air assault division is a highly specialized force capable of battlefield helicopter operations for infantry, field artillery, air defense artillery and necessary support forces.

The 10,800-man light infantry divisions consist of 9 infantry battalions and offer rapid strategic force projection. Light divisions can operate in all environments and are general purpose forces. Special operations forces consist of special forces, rangers, special operations aviation psychological operations, and civil affairs units. The units are designed, equipped, and trained for special missions.

Small arms include the M-9 (9mm pistol), the M-16 series rifle and the M-249 Squad Automatic Weapon both of which fire a 5·56-mm cartridge. The standard generalpurpose machine-gun is the M-60 (23 lb.; 550 rounds of 7·62-mm per minute). Infantry weapons also include M-203 grenade launcher attachment for the M-16A1 rifle, which fire a 40-mm grenade up to 400 metres, the *TOW* and *Dragon* anti-tank missile systems, and the M-72 rocket, a light anti-tank weapon.

Combat vehicles of the US Army are the tank, armoured personnel carrier, infantry fighting vehicle, and the armoured command vehicle. The first-line tanks are the

M1A1 Abrams tank with a 120mm main gun, and the M1 Abrams. The standard armoured infantry personnel carrier is the M2 Bradley Fighting Vehicle (BFV), which is replacing the older M113. Both carry a mechanized infantry squad, but the BFV mounts a 25-mm Bushmaster gun and *TOW* missile launchers. The M3 version of the BFV is being used as the ground scout vehicle in armoured cavalry regiments, armoured and mechanized infantry divisional cavalry squadrons and in scout platoons of armoured and mechanized infantry battalions.

The approved calibres of artillery are: Light, 105-mm howitzer, medium 155-mm howitzer; the heavy, 203-mm howitzer. The Multiple Launch Rocket System (MLRS) is a 227-mm rapid fire rocket system used in a non-nuclear counterfire, reinforcing and deep fires roles. The 107-mm mortar, the 81-mm mortar and the 60-mm mortar are used by the combat manoeuvre elements. The 120mm mortar will replace the 107mm mortar. The *TOW* is the primary anti-tank weapon. Forward-area air-defence weapons, including the *Chaparral, Stinger* and *Avenger* 20-mm gun, provide the capability of low-altitude defence against high-performance aircraft.

The Army has three categories of missiles—surface-to-surface (field artillery) and surface-to-air (air defence artillery) and anti-tank. Surface-to-surface missiles are now limited to the Army Tactical Missile System (ATACMS; fielded) and the Tri-Service Stand-Off Attack Missile (TSSAM; EMD). ATACMS is a semi-ballistic missile capable of carrying a variety of warheads to ranges in excess of 150 km. Planned improvements include an extended range variant with a range of 300+ km. TSSAM is a joint Army, Air Force, Navy cruise missile program. TSSAM carries the Bat submunition (anti-tank) to distances in excess of 200 km. Planned improvements modify Bat submunition for targets other than armour. Surface-to-air missiles, for air defence, are: *Patriot*, guided, conventional warhead, operational; *Hawk*, homing type, low-to-mid-altitude, field operational (product improvements continue to improve the effectiveness of the system); *Chaparral*, infra-red homing, low-altitude, forward area, operational (improvements to the basic system are under development); *Stinger*, hand-held or mobile-launched, infra-red homing, low-altitude, forward area, operational. Anti-tank missiles are: *TOW*, tube launched, optically tracked, wire guided, anti-armour, forward area, operational; *Hellfire*, laser-guided, anti-armour, operational and *Dragon*, wire-guided, medium anti-armour, forward area, operational.

The Army employs rotary- and fixed-wing aircraft as organic elements of its ground formations where their use is required on a full-time basis and their immediate and constant availability is essential. The front line commander exploits the benefits of aviation technology to perform traditional land battle tasks in the third dimension. This concept of airmobility for ground formation utilizes aerial vehicles as a highly integrated team to perform all five functions of land combat: reconnaissance, command and control, logistics and that inseparable combination, firepower and manoeuvre.

The Army has some 7,000 aircraft, all but about 400 of them helicopters. The principal types are 1,500 UH-1 Iroquois Huey and 1,500 UH-60 Black Hawk utility helicopters, 1,500 OH-58 Kiowa observation helicopters, 700 AH-1 Cobra and 700 AH-64 Apache attack helicopters, and 450 CH-47 Chinook cargo helicopters.

Enlistment, Terms of Service. Since 1974 the Army has operated an 'all volunteer' system making it, in effect, an all-regular force both regular and reserve components. Terms of service may be 2, 3, 4, 5 or 6 years. Men and women who enlist incur an 8-year obligation and must serve in the reserve components any part of the period not served on active duty. Over 95% of recruits enlisting in the Army have a high school education and over 50% of the Army is married. Women serve in both combat support and combat service support units.

The National Guard is a reserve military component with both a state and a federal rôle. Enlistment is voluntary. The members are recruited by each state, but are equipped and paid by the federal government (except when performing state missions). Training is supervised by the active Army (FORSCOM), and unit organization parallels that for the active army; training facilities are made available by the USA and each state. As the organized militia of the several states, the District of Columbia, Puerto Rico and the Territories of the Virgin Islands and Guam, the

Guard may be called into service for local emergencies by the chief executives in those jurisdictions; and may be called into federal service by the President to thwart invasion or rebellion or to enforce federal law. In its role as a reserve component of the Army, the Guard is subject to the order of the President in the event of national emergency. In 1995 it numbered 502,580 (Army, 387,000; Air Force, 115,580).

The Army Reserve is designed to supply qualified and experienced units and individuals in an emergency. US Army Forces Command is charged with the command, support and training supervision of US Army Reserve units. Members of units are assigned to the Ready Reserve, which is subject to call by the President in case of national emergency without declaration of war by Congress. The Standby Reserve and the Retired Reserve may be called only after declaration of war or national emergency by Congress. In 1995 the Army Reserve numbered 654,000 (119,000 women).

Navy. *Secretary of the Navy:* John Dalton.

The Department of the Navy is administered under the Defense Secretary by the Secretary of the Navy, assisted by the Under Secretary and 4 Assistant Secretaries (for Financial Management; Installation and Environment; Manpower and Reserve Affairs; and Research, Development and Acquisition). Other divisions of the Department of the Navy are those of: Legislative Affairs, Information, the Judge Advocate General, Program Appraisal, the General Counsel, and the Inspector General of the Navy.

The professional head of the Navy is the Chief of Naval Operations, whose staff includes the Vice Chief, 4 Deputy Chiefs responsible for Manpower and Personnel; Plans, Policy and Operations; Logistics; and Resources, Warfare Requirements and Assessments. There are 3 major staff directorates for Intelligence; Training; and Space and electronic warfare and 5 specialist divisions.

The Operating Forces include the Atlantic Fleet divided between the 2nd fleet (home waters) and 6th fleet (Mediterranean); the Pacific Fleet is similarly divided between the 3rd fleet (home waters), 7th fleet (West Pacific) and the 5th fleet (Indian Ocean) formally activated in 1995 is maintained by units from both Pacific and Atlantic. All fleets include associated Fleet Marine Forces. Other operational commands include the Military Sealift Command, U.S. Naval Forces Europe, the Mine Warfare Command and the Operational Test and Evaluation Force.

The authorized budget for the Department of the Navy (which includes funding both for the Navy and Marine Corps) for current and recent fiscal years: 1992, $84,800m.; 1993, $82,600m.; 1994, $77,100m.; 1995, $78,200m.; budget request for 1996, $75,600m.

Funding, personnel and fleet strength have continued to decline through 1995, but were expected to stabilize in 1996. The '600-ship navy' planned in the late 1980s had reduced to 443 by Oct. 1993 and to 367 by Oct. 1995 and the eventual figure is likely to be about 350.

The Navy personnel total in 1995 was 428,000, including 50,000 women who are eligible to serve at sea in support ships.

The operational strength of the Navy at the end of the year indicated:

Category	*1989*	*1990*	*1991*	*1992*	*1993*	*1994*	*1995*
Strategic Submarines	36	34	24	23	22	16	17
Nuclear Attack Submarines	97	93	89	87	86	85	78
Diesel Submarines	3	nil	nil	nil	nil	nil	nil
Aircraft Carriers	14	14	14	12	13	12	13[1]
Amphibious Carriers	12	13	13	13	14	13	11
Battleships	4	4	2	nil	nil	nil	nil
Cruisers	38	41	44	46	49	44	31
Destroyers	68	68	58	51	40	39	46
Frigates	112	100	98	90	67	59	46

[1] Includes the USS *John F. Kennedy* as 'operational and training reserve carrier' until replacing the USS *America* on decommissioning in late 1996.

Ships in inactive reserve are not included; but those serving as Naval Reserve Force training ships are. Amphibious Carriers are those ships of the Wasp, Tarawa, and Iwo Jima classes capable of operating AV-8 Harrier-type aircraft as well as helicopters.

Submarine Forces. A principal part of the US naval task is to deploy the seaborne strategic deterrent from nuclear-powered ballistic missile-carrying submarines (SSBN), of which there were, in 1995, 17, all of the Ohio class, the first of which entered service in 1981. These ships are of 19,000 tonnes submerged displacement, and capable of 24 knots. They are designed to deploy the Trident-2 D-5 missile, with a maximum range of 6,500 nautical miles, carrying about 8 warheads with substantially improved targeting accuracy over the Trident-1 C-4 missile, which has a range of 4,000 nautical miles, and is deployed in the first 8 ships of the class. The first submarine deployed the Trident-2 operationally in 1990. The first 8 ships may be retrofitted with the Trident-2 in due course, and building will cease after the eighteenth. The last of the Franklin class first generation strategic missile submarines was withdrawn in 1995.

The listed total of 78 nuclear-powered attack submarines (SSN) comprises 58 of the Los Angeles class (7,040 tonnes) in three major batches: A basic design (27 ships) completed 1976-85, a small group of 8 ships additionally equipped with vertical-launch missile tubes for Tomahawk cruise missiles completed 1985-89, and the current building programme of which 23 ships have been completed, known as 'Improved' Los Angeles, incorporating cruise missile tubes, a new command system, and several important additional technical modifications. There are also 19 Sturgeon class (5,040 tonnes) completed 1967-75, and 1 other.

Surface Forces. The surface fleet is headed by the force of large aircraft carriers, the first class of which entered service in the late 1950s carrying nuclear bombers as the naval contribution to the strategic deterrent. When this role passed to the ballistic missile submarine force, the carrier force was gradually reoriented to its current tasks, which relate more to limited and littoral warfare. The target of "15 deployable carriers" set in 1986 was officially amended to 14 as a result of budgetary pressure in 1989, and has now fallen to 12 of which 11 are in operational service and 1 is used for training and reserve forces.

There are 7 Nimitz and improved Nimitz class ships, of about 88,000 tonnes, completed between 1975 and 1995, nuclear-powered and capable of 33 knots. The USS *Enterprise,* completed in 1961, displacing 81,000 tonnes was the prototype nuclear-powered carrier and is also capable of 33 knots. The 4 ships of the Kitty Hawk and John F. Kennedy classes are from 73,000 tonnes, were completed between 1961 and 1968, and represent the last oil-fuelled carriers built by the US Navy. The force is completed by the remaining ships of the Forrestal class, completed in 1955, of about 82,000 tonnes.

All carriers deploy an air group which comprises on average 2 squadrons each of 10 F-14 Tomcat fighters, 2 squadrons each of 10 F/A-18 Hornet fighter/ground attack aircraft and 1 squadron of 10 A-6E Intruder medium bombers. They also carry a squadron of 4 E-2C Hawkeye early warning aircraft, 4 KA-6 airborne tankers, 4 EA-6B Prowler electronic combat aircraft, 6 S-3B Viking anti-submarine aircraft and 6 SH-3D Sea King, or SH-60F Oceanhawk anti-submarine helicopters.

The cruiser force continues to reduce, with 23 ships withdrawn from service in 1994–95. The force comprises the 27 ships of the Ticonderoga class commissioned between 1983 and 1993, of 9,600 tonnes, capable of 30 knots, equipped with the highly-capable Aegis air-defence control system and armed with Standard SM-2ER surface-to-air missiles (SAM), 2 127mm guns and 2 SH-60B Seahawk LAMPS-III helicopters. All but the first 5 ships are equipped with 2 x 61-cell vertical launch system for their missiles, which additionally allows them to launch Harpoon anti-ship missiles and Tomahawk sea-launched cruise missles (SLCM). The 2 nuclear-powered vessels of the Virginia class and 2 similar California class, completed between 1973 and 1980, are of 11,400 tonnes and 10,700 tonnes respectively, capable of 31 knots and armed with 2 twin Standard SAM launchers, 8 Harpoon anti-surface ship missiles, ASROC anti-submarine missiles, and (Virginia class only) 8 Tomahawk SLCM. Neither class carries a helicopter.

In addition, there are 17 guided-missile destroyers including 13 of the new Arleigh

Burke class currently building, and equipped with the Aegis air-defence system and 4 Kidd class, 31 anti-submarine destroyers of the Spruance class, 46 guided-missile frigates of the Oliver Hazard Perry class and 24 inshore patrol craft. Mine warfare ships include 14 new mine counter-measure vessels of the Avenger class and the first 5 of a new Osprey class coastal minehunter.

Amphibious Warfare. Amphibious capability comprises some 51 ships. The 4 Wasp (LHD-1) class and the 5 ships of the Tarawa (LHA-1) class are in many respects similar to the vertical/short take off and landing aircraft carriers in other principal navies and are capable of sea control tasks. The Wasp class, completed from 1989 to 1995 and still building, are of 41,200 tonnes, capable of 23 knots, equipped with an air group of some 6-8 Harrier AV-8B aircarft, and up to 42 mixed helicopters, and accommodating 1,900 troops. The 5 ships of the Tarawa class are of 40,000 tonnes, were completed between 1976 and 1981, deploy a similar air group and carry 1,700 troops. The 2 remaining ships of the Iwo Jima class are also capable of operating vertical/short take-off and landing aircraft but do not normally do so. They are of 18,800 tonnes, were built between 1961 and 1970, are capable of 21 knots and normally carry 20 mixed helicopters and accommodate 1,750 troops. Additionally there are 2 amphibious command ships, 26 dock landing ships and 2 tank landing ships. There are some 115 amphibious craft including 80 air-cushion landing craft (hovercraft) and 35 others, and several hundred minor personnel and vehicle transports. The total oceanic lift capability of the amphibious forces amounts to over 50,000 men, 1,000 main battle tank equivalents, and operating facilities for about 180 helicopters.

Underway Support. The Navy is provided with global, long-term sustainability through a force of some 46 underway replenishment ships, including 20 tankers, 8 multi-purpose fast replenishment ships, 7 stores ships and 11 ammunition ships. Second-line support is provided by 12 depot ships, 10 support tankers, 10 tugs and 2 hospital ships. Special purpose auxiliaries include 2 command ships, 18 ocean surveillance ships, 4 missile and space support ships, and 16 survey and oceanographic vessels. Of these major auxiliaries, about half are operated by the civilian-manned Military Sealift Command. In addition there are some hundreds of minor auxiliaries, and several thousand service craft.

Shipbuilding. Major warship building yards involved in the current building programme are located at Groton, Conn. (submarines), Newport News, Va., (submarines and aircraft carriers), Pascagoula, Miss. (cruisers and amphibious ships), Bath, Me. (cruisers and destroyers) and New Orleans, La., (amphibious and auxiliary ships).

Naval Aviation. The principal function of the naval aviation organization (80,000 strong in 1995) is to provide and train the 11 Air Wings maintained for service in the Aircraft Carriers. These usually consist of 80 fixed wing and 6 rotary wing aircraft. In addition, 1 carrier air wing is provided from the reserves, in some cases with slightly older aircraft. The main carrier-borne combat aircraft on inventory are 360 F-14 fighters, 150 A-6E Intruder attack aircraft, 780 F/A-18 Hornet dual-purpose fighter/attack aircraft and 150 S-3A Viking anti-submarine aircraft. Supporting roles are performed by 100 EA-6B electronic warfare aircraft, 90 E-2C Hawkeye airborne early warning aircraft, 50 KA-6D tankers, and 40 SH-3 Sea King and 70 SH-60F Oceanhawk helicopters for inner-zone anti-submarine defence. Helicopters held for embarkation in cruisers and below are of 2 types, the older SH-2F Seasprite aircraft of which there are some 40 and the SH-60B Seahawk of which there are 155. The principal tasks of the shore-based elements of US naval aviation are maritime reconnaissance and anti-submarine warfare, for which there are holdings of about 250 P-3C Orion aircraft. Additional tasks include electronic warfare (12 EP-3), electronic intelligence (16 ES-3) and mine countermeasures for which 50 MH- and RH-53 helicopters are held. Finally there are some 600 training aircraft of types not previously mentioned, and 100 aircraft and 90 helicopters for transport and other miscellaneous duties.

The Marine Corps. While administratively part of the Department of the Navy, the Corps ranks as a separate armed service, with the Commandant serving in his own right as a member of the Joint Chiefs of Staff, and responsible directly to the Secretary of the Navy. Its strength had stabilized at about 175,000 by late 1995.

The role of the Marine Corps is to provide specially trained and equipped amphibious expeditionary forces. It is organized into 3 divisions each some 50,000 strong, subdivided into Marine Expeditionary Brigades (17,000) and Marine Expeditionary Units (some 5,000 strong). In peacetime, Marine Expeditionary Units are permanently deployed afloat in the Eastern Atlantic/Mediterranean and the West Pacific/Indian Ocean. The principal equipment of the Corps consists of 270 M-1A1 Abrams and 150 M60-A1 tanks, 600 LAV-25 armoured infantry fighting vehicles, 1,300 armoured personnel carriers and over 1,000 artillery pieces of calibres between 105mm and 203mm. Additional heavy equipment for US-based Marine forces units, beyond that which can be embarked in the amphibious shipping, is provided in 2 squadrons each of 13 large cargo ships prepositioned at Diego Garcia (Indian Ocean) and in the Mediterranean. In addition the Corps includes an autonomous aviation element numbering some 400 combat aircraft and 515 helicopters. There are 260 F/A 18 Hornet, 175 AV-8B Harriers, 25 EA-6B electronic warfare aircraft, 65 KC-130 tankers, and a miscellany of other support and training aircraft. Helicopters include 230 CH-46E and 165 CH-53 transport, as well as 180 AH-1 Cobra attack helicopters of various types. Harriers and helicopters are normally employed afloat in the amphibious aircraft carriers and other suitable ships. The Hornets and other fixed wing aircraft are normally based ashore, but may be embarked in other aircraft carriers, given the operational need.

The US Coast Guard operates under the Department of Transportation in time of peace and as a part of the Navy in time of war or when directed by the President. The act of establishment stated the Coast Guard 'shall be a military service and branch of the armed forces of the United States at all times'. It comprises 230 ships including cutters of destroyer, frigate, corvette and patrol vessel types, 3 powerful icebreakers, and various auxiliaries and tenders, as well as over 1,400 rescue and utility craft. It also maintains 70 fixed-wing aircraft and 134 helicopters. The active-duty workforce in 1995 was 33,284. The auxiliary workforce is comprised of 35,659 volunteer civilians that operate their own vessels on their own time and, for the most part at their own expense. The Auxiliary assists the Coast Guard in search and rescue missions and offers Courtesy Marine Examinations and Public Education courses ranging from boat handling to rules of the road.

The Coast Guard missions include maintenance of aids to navigation, boating safety, defence operations, environmental response (oil spills), ice operations, maritime law enforcement, marine inspection, marine licensing, marine science, port safety and security, search and rescue and waterways management.

Air Force. *Secretary of the Air Force:* Dr Sheila E. Widnall.

The Department of the Air Force was activated within the Department of Defense on 18 Sept. 1947, under the terms of the National Security Act of 1947. It is administered by the Secretary of the Air Force, assisted by an Under Secretary, a Deputy for International Affairs and 4 Assistant Secretaries (Acquisition; Space; Manpower, Reserve Affairs, Installations and Environment; and Financial Management and Comptroller). The USAF, under the administration of the Department of the Air Force, is supervised by a Chief of Staff, who is a member of the Joint Chiefs of Staff. He is assisted by a Vice Chief of Staff, Assistant Vice Chief of Staff, 4 Deputy Chiefs of Staff (Personnel; Plans and Operations; Logistics; Command, Control, Communications and Computers) and an Assistant Chief of Staff for Intelligence.

The USAF consists of active duty Air Force officers and enlisted personnel, civilian employees, the Air National Guard and the Air Force Reserve. The USAF has undergone a major reorganization as a result of the changes in the international situation and of the need to reduce the national defence budget, and has adopted a re-defined mission to defend the USA through control and exploitation of air and space. This became effective on 1 Jan. 1992. For operational purposes the service is divided into 8 major commands, 35 field operating agencies and 3 direct-reporting units. Under these organizations there are 108 major and 29 minor facilities worldwide as well as 86 National Guard and Reserve bases.

Major commands are organized on a functional basis in the USA and a geographic basis overseas. They accomplish designated phases of Air Force worldwide activities. They also organize, administer, equip and train their subordinate elements for the accomplishment of assigned missions. Major commands are generally assigned specific responsibilities based on functions. In descending order of command, elements of major commands include numbered air forces, wings, groups, squadrons and flights.

The bulk of the combat forces are grouped under the Air Combat Command, which controls strategic bombing, tactical strike, air defence and reconnaissance assets in the USA. Under the Air Force's realignment, the Air Mobility Command provides air lift, air refuelling, special air mission and aeromedical evacuation for US forces. The newest major command is the Air Education and Training Command which provides a wide variety of training from initial to advanced degree-granting education.

The other major commands are the Air Force Materiel Command, Air Force Special Operations Command, Air Force Space Command, Pacific Air Forces and United States Air Forces in Europe. The Pacific (PAF) and European (USAFE) are responsible for offensive and defensive air operations in the Pacific and Asia and Europe and the Mediterranean respectively.

The field operating agencies are (AF = Air Force): the AF Audit Agency, AF Base Disposal Agency, AF Center for Environmental Excellence, AF Civil Engineering Support Agency, AF Civilian Personnel Management Center, AF Combat Operations Staff, AF Command, Control, Communications and Computer Agency, AF Cost Analysis Agency, AF Flight Standards Agency, AF Frequency Management Agency, AF Historical Research Agency, AF Inspection Agency, AF Intelligence Command, AF Intelligence Support Agency, AF Legal Services Agency, AF Logistics Management Agency, AF Management Engineering Agency, AF Medical Operations Agency, AF Medical Support Agency, AF Military Personnel Center, AF Morale, Welfare, Recreation and Services Agency, AF News Agency, AF Office of Special Investigations, AF Program Executive Office, AF Real Estate Agency, AF Review Boards Agency, AF Safety Agency, AF Security Police Agency, AF Studies and Analyses Agency, AF Technical Applications Center, Air Reserve Personnel Center, Air Weather Service, Center for Air Force History, Joint Services Survival, Evasion, Resistance and Escape Agency, and 7th Communications Group.

The direct-reporting units are: AF Academy, AF District of Washington and AF Operational Test and Evaluation Center.

Air Force aircraft are categorized as bombers, fighters, attack and observation aircraft, reconnaissance and special duty aircraft, transports and tankers, trainers and helicopters. The bombers are the B-1B Lancer, a supersonic inter-continental, nuclear and conventional aircraft; the B-2A, a subsonic, multi-role strategic bomber; and the B-52G/H Stratofortress, which has been the primary manned strategic bomber for over 35 years.

In the fighter category are the F-15 Eagle for air superiority tactical missions; the F-16 Fighting Falcon, a compact, multi-role fighter and attack aircraft; the F-111, a multi-purpose tactical fighter-bomber; the F-117A, the world's first operational aircraft to exploit low-observable stealth technology; the A-10/OA-10 Thunderbolt II attack aircraft; and the AC-130H/U for counter-insurgency.

Under the reconnaissance and special duty heading are the U-2R/RT for reconnaissance; the EC-130E/H Commando/Compass Call and the EF-111A Raven for electronic countermeasures; the E-3B/C Sentry, the E-4B and E-8 Joint Surveillance and Target Attack Radar System for command and control functions; the E-9A for telemetry relay; and the WC-130E/H for weather reconnaissance.

The primary transporters are the C-5A/B Galaxy for long-range heavy loads; the C-9A/C Nightingale for aeromedical evacuation; the C-17A Globemaster III for cargo and tactical air lift, the C-141A/B Starlifter for long-range troop and cargo; and the C-130 Hercules for theatre tactical air lift. The 2 refuelling aircraft are the KC-135 Stratotanker and the KC-10A Extender.

Strategic missiles in the Air Force's inventory include the LGM-30F/G Minuteman, the LGM-118A Peacekeeper, the AGM-69A Short-Range Attack Missile and the AGM-86B/C Air-Launched Cruise Missile.

In 1994 the Air Force had approximately 426,000 military personnel. Approximately 66,300 Air Force members are women. Since 1991 women have been authorized to fly combat aircraft, but not until 1993 were they allowed to fly fighters.

Deployment of US forces abroad: 22,754 personnel were deployed abroad on 11 Jan. 1994 (Arabian/Persian Gulf, 6,360; Haiti, 6,063; Cuba, 4,252; Panama, 3,531; Bosnia-Hercegovina, 3,330; former Yugoslavia, 870; Somalia, 2,600). Forces were withdrawn from Somalia in March 1995.

Coker, C., *US Military Power in the 1980s.* London, 1984
Howarth, S., *To Shining Sea: a History of the United States Navy, 1775–1991.* London, 1991
Kinnell, S., *Military History of the United States: an Annotated Bibliography.* Oxford and Santa Barbara (CA), 1986

INTERNATIONAL RELATIONS

Membership. The USA is a member of the UN, OAS, NATO, OECD and the Colombo Plan.

ECONOMY

Budget. The budget covers virtually all the programmes of federal government, including those financed through trust funds, such as for social security, Medicare and highway construction. Receipts of the Government include all income from its sovereign or compulsory powers; income from business-type or market-orientated activities of the Government is offset against outlays. The fiscal year ends on 30 Sept. (before 1977 on 30 June). Budget receipts and outlays (in $1m.):

Fiscal year ending in	*Receipts*	*Outlays*	*Surplus* (+) *or deficit* (–)
1950	39,443	42,562	– 3,119
1960	92,492	92,191	+ 301
1970	192,807	195,649	– 2,842
1980	517,112	590,947	–73,835
1990	1,031,321	1,252,515	–221,194
1994	1,257,737	1,460,841	–203,104
1995	1,354,213	1,519,133	–163,920
1996 [1]	1,426,775	1,572,411	–145,636

[1] Estimates.

Budget and off-budget receipts, by source, for fiscal years (in $1m.):

Source	*1994*	*1995*	*1996* [1]
Individual income taxes	543,055	590,244	630,873
Corporation income taxes	140,385	157,004	167,108
Social insurance taxes and contributions	461,475	484,473	507,535
Excise taxes	55,225	57,484	53,886
Other	57,597	66,008	67,373
Total	1,257,737	1,355,213	1,426,775

[1] Estimates.

Budget and off-budget outlays, by function, for fiscal years (in $1m.):

Function	*1994*	*1995*	*1996* [1]
National defence	281,842	272,066	265,556
International affairs	17,083	16,434	14,830
General science, space and technology	16,227	16,724	16,877
Energy	5,219	4,936	3,217
Natural resources and environment	21,064	22,105	21,550
Agriculture	15,046	9,773	7,718
Commerce and housing credit	–5,118	–14,441	–10,744
Transportation	38,066	39,350	39,769
Community and regional development	10,454	10,641	12,878
Education, training, employment and social services	46,307	54,263	54,131
Health	107,122	115,418	121,211
Medicare	144,747	159,855	177,586

Function	*1994*	*1995*	*1996* [1]
Income security	214,031	220,449	228,342
Social Security	319,565	335,846	350,924
Veterans' benefits and services	37,642	37,938	37,748
Administration of justice	15,256	16,223	18,764
General government	11,303	13,835	13,590
Net interest	202,957	232,173	241,059
Allowances	–	–	–327
Undistributed offsetting receipts	–37,772	–44,455	–42,268
Total	1,460,841	1,519,133	1,572,411

[1] Estimates.

Budget and off-budget outlays, by agency, for fiscal years (in $1m.):

Agency	*1994*	*1995*	*1996* [1]
Legislative branch	2,552	2,625	2,695
The Judiciary	2,677	2,910	3,297
Executive Office of the President	229	214	206
Funds appropriated to the President	10,511	11,161	10,445
Agriculture	60,753	56,665	54,840
Commerce	2,915	3,401	3,789
Defence—Military	268,646	259,556	254,325
Defence—Civil	30,407	31,669	32,255
Education	24,699	31,322	30,404
Energy	17,839	17,617	14,678
Health and Human Services	278,901	303,081	327,429
Housing and Urban Development	25,845	29,044	26,432
Interior	6,900	7,405	6,939
Justice	10,005	10,788	12,964
Labor	37,047	32,090	34,404
State	5,718	5,344	5,500
Transportation	37,228	38,777	38,994
Treasury	307,577	348,579	364,956
Veterans Affairs	37,401	37,771	37,606
Environmental Protection Agency	5,855	6,351	6,329
General Services Administration	334	707	469
National Aeronautics and Space Administration	13,695	13,378	14,190
Office of Personnel Management	38,596	41,276	42,374
Small Business Administration	779	677	957
Social Security Administration	345,817	362,123	377,255
Other independent agencies	11,384	2,230	9,192
Allowances	–	–	–647
Undistributed offsetting receipts	–123,469	–137,628	–139,866
Total	1,460,841	1,519,133	1,572,411

[1] Estimates.

National Debt: Federal debt held by the public (in $1m.), and *per capita* debt (in $1) on 30 June to 1976 and then on 30 Sept.:

	Public debt	*Per capita*		*Public debt*	*Per capita*
1919	25,485	243	1980	709,838	3,117
1920	24,299	228	1990	2,410,722	9,646
1930	16,185	132	1991	2,688,137	10,640
1940	42,772	325	1992	2,998,834	11,741
1950	219,023	1,438	1993	3,247,471	12,581
1960	236,840	1,311	1994	3,432,123	13,168
1970	283,198	1,381	1995	3,603,412	13,750

State and Local Finance: Revenue of the 50 states and 86,692 local governments from their own sources amounted to $793,269m. in 1991–92; in addition they received $179,184m. in revenue from fiscal aid, shared revenues and reimbursements from the federal government, bringing total revenue from all sources to $1,085,060m. Of the revenue from state and local sources, taxes provided $555,479m., of which property taxes (mainly imposed by local governments) yielded $178,406m. of all tax revenue; and sales taxes, both general sales taxes and selective excises, provided $196,150.

State tax revenue totalled $328,380m. in 1991–92. Largest sources of state tax revenue are general sales taxes (imposed during 1992 by 45 states), motor fuel sales taxes (all states), individual income (44 states), motor vehicle and operators' licences (46 states), corporation income (46 states), tobacco products (all states) and alcoholic beverage sales taxes (all states).

General revenue of local units from own sources in 1991–92 totalled $357,278m. In addition they received $216,305m. from state and federal aids. Property taxes provided $171,723m.

Total expenditures of state and local governments were $1,150,454m. in 1991–92, of which $823,706m. were for current operation. Education took $326,770m. in current and capital expenditure; highways, $66,689m.; public welfare, $154,234m.; health, $29,344m. and hospitals, $58,768m. Capital outlays (construction, equipment and land purchases) totalled $116,914m.

Gross debt of state and local governments totalled $970,043m. Total cash and investment assets of state and local governments were $1,652,452m. ($815,420m. in employee retirement funds).

US Bureau of the Census. *Government Finances.* Washington, DC, Annual

National Income. The Bureau of Economic Analysis of the Department of Commerce prepares detailed estimates on the national income and product. In 1991 the Bureau revised these accounts back to 1929, notably by the use of GDP instead of GNP as a primary measure of production. The principal tables are published monthly in *Survey of Current Business;* the complete set of national income and product tables are published in the *Survey* normally each July, showing data for recent years. *The National Income and Product Accounts of the United States* (vol. 1, 1929–58; vol. 2, 1959–88) and the July 1992, Aug. 1993 and July 1994 *Surveys* contain complete sets of tables from 1929 through 1993. The conceptual framework and statistical methods underlying the accounts are described in National Income and Product Account (NIPA) Methodology Papers 1–6. Subsequent limited changes were described in the Dec. 1991, July 1992, Aug. 1993 and July 1994 *Surveys.*

Figures (in $1,000m.) for 1929 (as the peak year between the First and Second World War), 1933 (as the low point of the inter-war depression), decennial years and the 2 most recent years for which data are available (Statistics for Alaska and Hawaii are included from 1960, but this does not significantly affect the comparability of the data):

	1929	*1933*	*1970*	*1980*	*1990*	*1992*	*1993*
I. Gross Domestic Product	103·1	55·6	1,010·7	2,708·0	5,546·1	6,020·2	6,343·3
(*a*) Personal consumption expenditures	77·5	45·9	646·5	1,748·1	3,761·2	4,136·9	4,378·2
(*b*) Gross private domestic investment	16·7	1·7	150·3	467·6	808·9	788·3	882·0
(*c*) Net exports of goods and services	0·4	0·1	1·2	−14·7	−71·4	−30·3	−65·3
(*d*) Government purchases	8·6	7·9	212·7	507·1	1,047·4	1,125·3	1,148·4
1. GDP *plus* net receipts of factor income from the rest of the world *less* consumption of fixed capital, indirect business tax and non-tax liability, business transfer payments, statistical discrepancy, *plus* subsidies less current surplus of government enterprises, equals:							
2. National Income which, *less* corporate profits with inventory valuation and capital consumption adjustments, net interest, contributions for social insurance, wage accruals less disbursements, *plus* personal interest income, personal dividend income, government transfer payments to persons, equals:	85·3	40·2	833·5	2,198·2	4,491·0	4,829·5	5,131·4
3. Personal income whereof	84·2	46·0	831·0	2,265·4	4,673·8	5,154·3	5,375·1
4. Personal tax and non-tax payments take leaving	2·3	1·2	109·0	312·4	623·3	648·6	686·4

	1929	*1933*	*1970*	*1980*	*1990*	*1992*	*1993*
5. Disposable personal income divided into	81·8	44·8	722·0	1,952·9	4,050·5	4,505·8	4,688·7
(e) Personal outlays [1]	79·4	46·6	664·5	1,799·1	3,880·6	4,257·8	4,496·2
(f) Personal saving	2·5	−1·7	57·5	153·8	170·0	247·9	192·6
IA. GDP in constant (1987) dollars	821·8	587·1	2,873·9	3,776·3	4,897·3	4,979·3	5,134·5
(a) Personal consumption expenditures	554·5	447·4	1,813·5	2,447·1	3,272·6	3,349·5	3,458·7
(b) Gross private domestic investment	152·8	26·6	429·7	594·4	746·8	725·3	819·9
(c) Net exports of goods and services	1·9	−3·0	−35·2	30·7	−54·7	−32·3	−73·9
(d) Government purchases	112·6	116·1	665·8	704·2	932·6	936·9	929·8
II. National Income composed of	85·3	40·2	833·5	2,198·2	4,491·0	4,829·5	5,131·4
Compensation of employees	*51·1*	*29·6*	*618·3*	*1,644·4*	*3,297·6*	*3,591·2*	*3,780·4*
(e) Salaries and wages	50·5	29·0	551·5	1,376·6	2,745·0	2,954·8	3,100·8
(f) Supplements to wages and salaries	0·7	0·6	66·8	267·8	552·5	636·4	679·6
Proprietors' income [2]	*14·5*	*5·5*	*79·9*	*171·8*	*363·3*	*418·7*	*441·6*
(g) Farm [2]	6·1	2·5	14·6	11·5	41·9	44·4	37·3
(h) Business and professional [2]	8·4	3·0	65·3	160·3	321·4	374·4	404·3
Personal income from rents [3]	*4·9*	*2·0*	*17·8*	*13·2*	*−14·2*	*−5·5*	*24·1*
Net interest	*4·6*	*3·9*	*40·0*	*191·2*	*463·7*	*420·0*	*399·5*
Corporate profits [2]	*10·2*	*−0·7*	*89·6*	*177·7*	*380·6*	*405·1*	*485·8*
(i) Tax liabilities	1·4	0·5	39·7	84·8	138·7	139·7	173·2
(j) Inventory valuation adjustment	0·5	−2·1	−5·9	−43·0	−11·0	−6·4	−6·2
(k) Capital consumption adjustment	−0·9	−0·3	6·4	−20·2	25·9	15·7	29·5
(l) Dividends	5·8	2·0	25·2	59·0	153·5	171·1	191·7
(m) Undistributed profits	3·4	−0·8	24·1	97·1	73·6	85·1	97·5

[1] Includes personal consumption expenditures, interest paid by persons and personal transfer payments to the rest of the world (net).
[2] With inventory valuation and capital consumption adjustments.
[3] With capital consumption adjustment.

Currency. The unit of currency is the *dollar* (USD) of 100 *cents*. Prior to the banking crisis that occurred early in 1933, the monetary system had been on the gold standard for more than 50 years. An Act of 14 March 1900 required the Secretary of the Treasury to maintain at a parity with gold all forms of money issued by the USA. For a description of these, *see* THE STATESMAN'S YEAR-BOOK, 1934. For information 1934–74 *see* THE STATESMAN'S YEAR-BOOK, 1988–89.

Under the Coinage Act of 1965, all coins and currencies of the USA, regardless of when coined or issued, are legal tender for all debts, public and private. Most currency in use now is issued by the 12 Federal Reserve Banks, which are denoted by a branch letter (A = Boston, MA; B = New York, NY; C = Philadelphia, PA; D = Cleveland, OH; E = Richmond, VA; F = Atlanta, GA; G = Chicago, IL; H = St Louis, MO; I = Minneapolis, MN; J = Kansas City, MO; K = Dallas, TX; L = San Francisco, CA). There are coins of 1, 5 ('nickels'), 10 ('dimes'), 25 ('quarters') and 50 ('halves') cents, and notes of $1, 2, 5, 10, 20, 50 and 100. Notes ($500, 1,000, 5,000 and 10,000) issued by the 'United States of America' are legal tender, but are retained when deposited in a bank.

The following outmoded units are still redeemable: Fractional currency of 1862–74; United States notes of 1862–1966; Gold Certificates of 1863–1923; Silver Certificates of 1878–1957; Interest-Bearing Notes of 1861–64; Compound Interest Treasury Notes of 1864–65; Refunding Certificates of 1879; Coin notes of 1890–91; Federal Reserve Notes since 1914; National Bank Notes.

Federal Reserve notes are obligations of the USA and a first lien on the assets of the Federal Reserve Banks, through which they are issued. Each of the 12 banks issues them against the security of an equal volume of collateral.

Inflation was 4·5% in 1991 (6·1% in 1990, 4·6% in 1989).

In March 1996, $1 = £0·65; £1 = $1·53; DM1 = $0·44.

Banking and Finance. The Federal Reserve System, established under The Federal Reserve Act of 1913, comprises the Board of 7 Governors, the 12 regional Federal Reserve Banks with their 25 branches, and the Federal Open Market Committee. The 7 members of the Board of Governors are appointed by the President with the consent of the Senate. Each Governor is appointed to a full term of 14 years or an unexpired portion of a term, one term expiring every 2 years. The Board exercises broad supervisory authority over the operations of the 12 Federal Reserve Banks, including approval of their budgets and of the appointments of their presidents and first vice presidents; it designates 3 of the 9 directors of each Reserve Bank including the Chairman and Deputy Chairman. The *Chairman* of the Federal Reserve Board is appointed by the President for 4-year terms. The Chairman for 1996–2000 is Alan Greenspan. The Board has supervisory and regulatory responsibilities over banks that are members of the Federal Reserve System, bank holding companies, bank mergers, Edge Act and agreement corporations, foreign activities of member banks, international banking facilities in the U.S., and activities of the U.S. branches and agencies of foreign banks. Legislation of 1991 requires foreign banks to prove that they are subject to comprehensive consolidated supervision by a regulator at home, and have the Board's approval to establish branches, agencies and representative offices. The Board also assures the smooth functioning and continued development of the nation's vast payments system. Another area of the Boards responsibilities involves the implementation by regulation of major federal laws governing consumer credit.

The 12 members of the Federal Open Market Committee (FOMC) include the 7 members of the Board of Governors and 5 of the 12 Federal Reserve Bank presidents. The latter serve 1-year terms on the FOMC in rotation except for the President of the Federal Reserve Bank of New York, who is a permanent member. The FOMC has an essential role in the formulation of monetary policy. It influences credit market conditions, money and bank credit, by buying or selling US Government securities; and it also supervises System operations in foreign currencies for the purpose of helping to safeguard the value of the dollar in international exchange markets and facilitating co-operation and efficiency in the international monetary system. The Board of Governors also influences credit conditions through powers to set reserve requirements, to approve discount rates at Federal Reserve Banks, and to fix margin requirements on stock-market credit.

The Reserve Banks advance funds to depository institutions, issue Federal Reserve notes, which are the principal form of currency in the US, act as fiscal agent for the Government, and afford nationwide cheque-clearing and fund transfer arrangements. They may increase or reduce the country's supply of reserve funds by buying or selling Government securities and other obligations at the direction of the FOMC. The purchase and sale of securities in the open market is conducted by the Federal Reserve Bank of New York. Their capital stock is held by the member banks, but it carries no voting rights except in the election of directors.

From 1968, the Congress passed a number of consumer financial protection acts, the first of which was the Truth in Lending Act, for which it has directed the Board to write implementing regulations and assume partial enforcement responsibility. Others include the Equal Credit Opportunity Act, Home Mortgage Disclosure Act, Consumer Leasing Act, Fair Credit Billing Act, Truth in Savings Act and Electronic Fund Transfer Act. To manage these responsibilities the Board has established a Division of Consumer and Community Affairs. To assist it, the Board consults with a Consumer Advisory Council, established by the Congress in 1976 as a statutory part of the Federal Reserve System.

Another statutory body, the Federal Advisory Council, consists of 12 members (one from each district); it meets in Washington four times a year to advise the Board of Governors on economic and banking developments. Following the passage of the Monetary Control Act of 1980, the Board of Governors established the Thrift Institutions Advisory Council to provide information and views on the special needs and problems of thrift institutions. The group is comprised of representatives of mutual savings banks, savings and loan associations, and credit unions.

All depository institutions (commercial and savings banks, savings and loan associations, credit unions, US agencies and branches of foreign banks, and Edge Act and agreement corporations) must meet reserve requirements set by the Federal Reserve and hold the reserves in the form of vault cash or deposits at Federal Reserve Banks.

Banks which participate in the federal deposit insurance fund have their deposits insured against loss up to $100,000 for each account. The fund is administered by the Federal Deposit Insurance Corporation established in 1933; it obtains resources through annual assessments on participating banks. All members of the Federal Reserve System are required to insure their deposits through the Corporation, and non-member banks may apply and qualify for insurance.

The Federal Deposit Insurance Corporation Improvement Act of 1992 originated with bank reform initiatives. It imposed new capital rules on banks, new reporting requirements and a code of 'safety and soundness' standards. The main aim of the Act is to reduce risk through rigorous enforcement of capital requirements. Regulators are required to take action where banks fail to observe these standards.

At 30 June 1995 the 10 major banks in terms of assets ($1,000m.) were: Chemical Banking-Chase Manhatten, 297·3; Citicorp, 257; BankAmerica, 226·6; NationsBank, 184·2; J. P. Morgan, 166·6; First Chicago-NBD, 123·4; First Union-First Fidelity, 118·4; Bankers Trust, 102·9; BancOne, 86·8; KeyCorp, 67·5.

There is a stock exchange in New York (NYSE), an American Stock Exchange (ASE), a Midwest stock exchange and a Pacific Stock Exchange in San Francisco.

Board of Governors of the Federal Reserve System. *The Federal Reserve System: Purposes and Functions.* 8th ed., 1994.—*Federal Reserve Bulletin.* Monthly.—*Annual Report.*—*Annual Statistical Digest.*—*The Federal Reserve Act, As Amended Through August 1990*

Meulendyke, A.-M., *U.S. Monetary Policy and Financial Markets.* New York, 1989

Timberlake, R. H., *The Origins of Central Banking in the United States.* Cambridge, Massachusetts, 1978

Weights and Measures. The US Customary System derives from the British Imperial System. It differs in respect of the *gallon* (=0·83268 Imperial gallon); *bushel* (= 0·969 Imperial bushel); *hundredweight* (= 100 lbs); and the *short* or *net ton* (= 2,000 lbs). The metric system is to be introduced in the 1990s.

ENERGY AND NATURAL RESOURCES

Electricity. In 1994, 22% of electricity was produced by 109 nuclear reactors. (The last one was built in 1989.) Production (public utilities only, 1994) 2,910,712m. kWh.

Oil and Gas. Crude oil production, 1994, 8,645,000 bbls. a day; 1995, 8,371,000 bbls. a day. Proven reserves were 22,457m. bbls. at 31 Dec. 1994. 1994 output was valued at $31,910m. Natural gas production, 1994, was 9,635,000m. cu. ft. 1993 production of 19,305,000m. cu. ft. was valued at $39,185m.

Coal. Demonstrated coal reserves were 474,100m. short tons in 1993. 1994 output (in 1m. short tons): 1,033·5, including bituminous coal, 640·5; sub-bituminous coal, 300·5; lignite, 88·1; anthracite, 4·7. Output from opencast workings, 634·4; underground mines, 399·1. Value of total output, 1994, $36,180m.

Non-Fuel Minerals. The USA is wholly dependent upon imports for columbium, bauxite, mica sheet, manganese, strontium and graphite, and imports over 80% of its requirements of industrial diamonds, fluorspar, platinum, tantalum, tungsten, chromium and tin.

Total value of non-fuel minerals produced in 1992 was $32,033m. ($33,464m. in 1990). Details are given in the following tables.

Production of metals:

		Quantity		*Value ($1m.)*	
	Unit	*1993*	*1994*	*1993*	*1994*
Copper	1,000 tonnes	1,800	1,840	3,636	4,382
Gold	tonnes	331	330	3,841	3,843
Iron ore	1m. tonnes	56·3	57	1,643	1,700
Lead	1,000 tonnes	362	365	249	286
Magnesium metal	1,000 tonnes	132	135	377	...
Molybdenum	1,000 tonnes	37	40	165	215
Nickel	tonnes	2,500	...	...	...
Silver	tonnes	1,645	1,400	227	192
Zinc	1,000 tonnes	488	540	497	549
Total metals				*11,876*	

Figures for some metals are withheld to avoid disclosing company data. Latest figures available: Bauxite, 1988, 588,000 tonnes; manganiferous ore, 1986, 14,000 short tons; tungsten, 1986, 817 tonnes; vanadium, 1980, 4,806 short tons.

Precious metals are mined mainly in Nevada, California, and Utah (gold) and Nevada, Arizona and Idaho (silver).

Production of non-metals:

		Quantity		*Value ($1m.)*	
	Unit	*1993*	*1994*	*1993*	*1994*
Barite	1,000 tonnes	315	340	19	13
Boron	1,000 tonnes	1,055	560	373	370
Bromine	1,000 tonnes	177	197	123	157
Cement	1m. short tons	81·9	87·6	4,145	4,419
Clays	1,000 tonnes	41,074	42,300	1,488	1,597
Diatomite	1,000 tonnes	599	596	150	162
Feldspar	1,000 tonnes	770	740	31	30
Fluorspar	1,000 tonnes	60	50	...	...
Garnet (industrial)	tonnes	43,995	46,500	4	5
Gypsum	1m. short tons	17·4	19·1	107	118
Lime	1m. short tons	18·7	19·1	977	996
Phosphate rock	1m. tonnes	35	41	759	902
Pumice	1,000 tonnes	469	485	12	14
Salt	1,000 tonnes	38,665	38,600	894	906
Sand and gravel	1m. tonnes	895	949	3,988	4,293
Sodium sulphate	1,000 tonnes	322	300	...	25
Stone (crushed)	1m. tonnes	1,116	1,195	5,770	6,731
Sulphur (all forms)	1,000 tonnes	1,904	2,700	101	135

Agriculture. Agriculture in the USA is characterized by its ability to adapt to widely varying conditions, and still produce an abundance and variety of agricultural products. From colonial times to about 1920 the major increases in farm production were brought about by adding to the number of farms and the amount of land under cultivation. During this period nearly 320m. acres of virgin forest were converted to crop land or pasture, and extensive areas of grass lands were ploughed. Improvident use of soil and water resources was evident in many areas.

During the next 20 years the number of farms reached a plateau of about 6·5m., and the acreage planted to crops held relatively stable around 330m. acres. The major source of increase in farm output arose from the substitution of power-driven machines for horses and mules. Greater emphasis was placed on development and improvement of land, and the need for conservation of basic agricultural resources was recognized. A successful conservation programme, highly co-ordinated and on a national scale—to prevent further erosion, to restore the native fertility of damaged land and to adjust land uses to production capabilities and needs—has been in operation since early in the 1930s.

Following the Second World War the uptrend in farm output has been greatly accelerated by increased production per acre and per farm animal. These increases are associated with a higher degree of mechanization; greater use of lime and fertilizer; improved varieties, including hybrid maize and grain sorghums; more effective control of insects and disease; improved strains of livestock and poultry; and wider use of good husbandry practices, such as nutritionally balanced feeds, use of superior sites and better housing. During this period land included in farms decreased slowly, crop land harvested declined somewhat more rapidly, but the number of farms declined sharply.

All land in farms totalled less than 500m. acres in 1870, rose to a peak of over 1,200m. acres in the 1950s and declined to 975m. acres in 1994, even with the addition of the new States of Alaska and Hawaii in 1960. The number of farms declined from 6·35m. in 1940 to 2·04m. in 1994, as the average size of farms doubled. The average size of farms in 1994 was 478 acres, but ranged from a few acres to many thousand acres. In 1992, 554,000 farms (595,000 in 1987) were less than 50 acres; 584,000 (645,000), 50–179 acres; 614,000 (678,000), 180–999 acres; and 173,000 (169,000) 1,000 acres or more.

Farms operated by owners in 1992 were 1,112,000; by part-owners, 597,000; by tenants, 217,000.

Value of land and buildings in 1994 was $725,711m.

At the 1990 census 66,964,000 persons (22·5% of the population) were rural, of whom 4,591,000 (under 2%) lived on farms. In 1994 there were 1,453,000 farm operators and managers and 1,992,000 persons in other agricultural and related occupations, of which 748,000 were farm workers.

Cash receipts from farm marketings and government payments (in $1m.):

	Crops	*Livestock and livestock products*	*Government payments*	*Total*
1991	82,060	86,735	8,200	176,995
1992	84,853	86,350	9,169	180,372
1993	84,497	90,555	13,402	184,454

Gross farm income (including government payments), in $1m., was 200,213 in 1992 and 201,431 in 1993; net farm income amounted to 50,074 in 1992 and 43,401 in 1993. Farm real estate debt, excluding debt in operator dwellings, was $78,305m. in 1990, $80,420 in 1991 and $80,740m. in 1992.

Total area of farm land under irrigation in 1992 was 49,404,000 acres. Water consumption was 137,000m. gallons a day in 1990.

Acreage and specified values of farms (area in 1m. acres; value in $1m.; cash receipts in $1m.):

	Farm area	*Crop land used for crops*	*Value of land and buildings*	*Cash receipts*
1990	987	341	658,187	169,974
1991	983	337	...	168,795
1992	980	340	687,432	171,202
1993	978	332	682,039	175,052
1994	875	340	725,711	...

The areas and production of the principal crops for 3 years were:

	1992			*1993*			*1994*[1]		
	Harvested 1m. acres	*Production 1m.*	*Yield per acre*	*Harvested 1m. acres*	*Production 1m.*	*Yield per acre*	*Harvested 1m. acres*	*Production 1m.*	*Yield per acre*
Corn for grain (bu.)	72·1	9,477	131·5	62·9	6,336	100·7	72·9	10,103	138·6
Soybeans (bu.)	58·2	2,190	37·6	57·3	1,871	32·6	61·1	2,558	41·9
Wheat (bu.)	62·8	2,467	39·3	62·7	2,396	38·2	61·8	2,321	37·6
Cotton (bales)[2]	11·1	16·2	700	12·8	16·1	606	13·3	19·7	708
Tobacco (lbs.)	0·8	1,722	2,195	0·7	1,614	2,159	0·7	1,582	2,345
Potatoes (cwt.)	1·3	425	323	1·3	429	326	1·4	459	334
Sorghum for grain (bu.)	12·1	875	72·6	8·9	534	59·9	9	655	73
Rice (cwt.)[2]	3·1	180	5,736	2·8	156	5,510	3·3	198	5,964

[1] Preliminary. [2] Yield in lbs.

Fruit. Production:

	1992	*1993*	*1994*
Apples (1m. lbs)	10,474	10,605	10,733
Citrus Fruit (1m. boxes[1])	298	362	343
Grapes (1,000 tons)	6,032	6,018	5,923

[1] Average net weight per box 65–95 lbs.

Dairy produce. In 1994, production of milk was 153,600m. lbs.; cheese, 6,730m. lbs.; butter, 1,296m. lbs.; ice-cream, 876m. gallons; non-fat dry milk, 1,227m. lbs.; cottage cheese, 410m. lbs.

Livestock. In 1995 livestock numbered (in 1m.): Cattle and calves (including milch cows), 103·3; sheep and lambs, 8·9; hogs and pigs, 59·6.

In 1994 there were 7,018m. broilers and 289m. turkeys. Eggs produced, 1994, 73,900m.

Value of production (in $1m.) was:

	1992	*1993*	*1994*
Cattle and calves	28,633	30,330	28,702
(of which milch cows)	19,994	19,484	20,167

	1992	1993	1994
Hogs and pigs	9,854	10,628	9,691
Broilers	9,174	10,417	11,374
Turkeys	2,396	2,509	2,672
Eggs	3,397	3,800	3,777

Value of livestock (in $1m.), 1995: Cattle, 63,600; hogs and pigs, 3,200; sheep and lambs, 664.

Forestry. In 1992 the gross area of National forest was 231·5m. acres (93·7m. ha), within which 191·5m. acres (77·5m. ha) were Federally owned ('National forest system'). Timber cut in 1993 was 5,917m. board ft with a value of $918m. In 1992 total forest land was 732m. acres (298m. ha), of which 490m. acres was timberland (97m. acres Federally owned or managed, 35m. acres, state, county or municipality owned, 358m. acres private). In 1991, 33,250m. board ft of softwoods and 6,781m. board ft of hardwoods were produced.

Fisheries. In 1993 the domestic catch was 10,467m. lbs, valued at $3,471m. (including 1,468m. lbs of shellfish valued at $1,587m.). Main species landed in terms of value ($1m.): Crab, 510; salmon, 424; shrimp, 413; Alaska pollock, 358; cod, 161. Disposition of the domestic catch (1m. lbs): Fresh or frozen, 7,744; tinned, 649; cured, 115; reduced to meal or oil, 1,959.

The fishing fleet in 1992 comprised 31,092 vessels over 5 NRT.

Tennessee Valley Authority. Established by Act of Congress, 1933, the TVA is a multiple-purpose federal agency which carries out its duties in an area embracing some 41,000 sq. miles in the 7 Tennessee River Valley states: Tennessee, Kentucky, Mississippi, Alabama, North Carolina, Georgia and Virginia. In addition, 76 counties outside the Valley are served by TVA power distributors. Its 3 directors are appointed by the President, with the consent of the Senate; headquarters are in Knoxville (TN). There were 16,587 employees in May 1995. Under a policy announced in Dec. 1994 the TVA is subject to a debt ceiling of $30,000m., and is to stop adding to its total debt before Oct. 1997. Total debt in 1994 was $26,000m.

The primary task of the TVA was the multipurpose development of the Tennessee River for flood control, navigation, and electric power production. In 1994 3 nuclear reactors were in operation.

The TVA has also contributed to controlling erosion on the land, introducing better fertilizers and new farming practices, eradicating malaria, demonstrating ways electricity could lighten the burdens in the home and increase production on the farm, and the creation of potential job-producing enterprises.

Annual Report of the TVA. Knoxville, 1934 to date

Hargrove, E. C., *Prisoners of Myth: the Leadership of the Tennessee Valley Authority, 1933–1990.* Princeton Univ. Press, 1994

Tennessee Valley Authority. *A History of the Tennessee Valley Authority.* Knoxville (TN) 1982

INDUSTRY. The following table presents industry statistics of manufactures as reported at various censuses from 1909 to 1987 and from the Annual Survey of Manufactures for years in which no census was taken.

The annual Surveys of Manufactures carry forward the key measures of manufacturing activity which are covered in detail by the Census of Manufactures. The large plants in the surveys account for approximately two-thirds of the total employment in operating manufacturing establishments in the US.

	Number of establishments	*Production workers (average for year)*	*Production workers' wages total ($1,000)*	*Value added by manufacture ($1,000)*
1909	264,810	6,261,736	3,205,213	8,160,075
1919	270,231	8,464,916	9,664,009	23,841,624
1929	206,663	8,369,705	10,884,919	30,591,435
1933	139,325	5,787,611	4,940,146	14,007,540
1939	173,802	7,808,205	8,997,515	24,487,304
1950	260,000	11,778,803	34,600,025	89,749,765
1960	...	12,209,514	55,555,452	163,998,531
1970	...	13,528,000	91,609,000	300,227,600

	Number of establishments	Production workers (average for year)	Production workers' wages total ($1,000)	Value added by manufacture ($1,000)
1980	...	13,900,100	198,164,000	773,831,300
1982	358,061	12,400,600	204,787,200	824,117,700
1984	...	12,572,800	231,783,900	983,227,700
1986	...	11,800,000	237,000,000	1,035,000,000
1988	...	12,400,000	264,000,000	1,262,000,000
1989	...	12,300,000	269,000,000	1,308,000,000
1990	...	12,100,000	272,000,000	1,326,000,000
1991	...	11,500,000	266,000,000	1,314,000,000
1992	382,000	11,654,000	282,000,000	1,428,707,000

In 1992 (and 1991) the total number of employees was 18·3m. (18·1m.).

In 1992 the principal commodities produced (by value of shipments, in $1m.) were: Motor vehicles and equipment, 240,110; refined petroleum, 136,265; aircraft and parts, 104,730; meat products, 93,466; electronic components and accessories, 74,604; drugs, 67,969; computer and office equipment, 66,149; industrial organic chemicals, 64,525; blast furnace and basic steel products, 58,713; beverages, 56,983; commercial printing, 56,415; dairy products, 54,096; grain mill products, 49,169; plastics materials and synthetics, 48,535; miscellaneous converted paper products, 45,977; fabricated structural metal products, 45,252; preserved fruits and vegetables, 45,192; soap, cleaners and toilet goods, 43,404; rolled and drawn non-ferrous metals, 39,906; medical instruments and supplies, 39,365; search and navigation equipment, 36,185; miscellaneous foods and kindred products, 34,244; newspapers, 34,203; measuring and controlling devices, 34,173; paper, 32,817; paperboard containers and boxes, 32,577; general industrial machinery, 31,686; metal forgings and stampings, 30,668; miscellaneous fabricated metal products, 30,620; cigarettes, 29,746; bakery products, 28,629; construction and related machinery, 27,675; guided missiles, space vehicles, parts, 27,302; refrigeration and service machinery, 27,253; industrial inorganic chemicals, 27,167; metalworking machinery, 26,589; other industrial machinery, 25,359; millwork, plywood and structural members, 24,865; sawn and planed lumber, 23,210; concrete, gypsum and plaster products, 22,718; miscellaneous electical equipment and supplies, 22,275; photographic equipment and supplies, 22,093; periodicals, 21,976; books, 21,854; women's and misses' outerwear, 21,610; special industrial machinery, 21,263; household furniture, 20,707; miscellaneous chemical products, 20,389.

In 1992 the first 20 industries in terms of value added by manufacture (in $1m.) were: Motor vehicles, 44,632; pharmaceutical preparations, 37,435; motor vehicle parts, 32,262; newspapers, 27,264; search and navigation equipment, 25,213; aircraft, 25,173; printing, 24,885; cigarettes, 24,802; semiconductors, 23,296; industrial organic chemicals, 22,489; petroleum refining, 19,104; blast furnaces and steel mills, 16,633; periodicals, 15,763; computers, 15,691; paper, 14,872; photographic, 14,843; toilet preparations, 13,109; plastic materials, 12,971; telephone and telegraph apparatus, 12,964; industrial machinery, 12,845.

Iron and Steel: Output of the iron and steel industries (in 1,000 net tons of 2,000 lb.), according to figures supplied by the American Iron and Steel Institute, was:

	Pig-iron (including ferro-alloys)	Raw steel	Steel by method of production [1]			
			Open hearth	Bessemer	Electric [2]	Basic Oxygen
1932 [3]	9,835,227	15,322,901	13,336,210	1,715,925	270,044	...
1939	35,677,097	52,798,714	48,409,800	3,358,916	1,029,067	...
1944 [4]	62,866,198	89,641,600	80,363,953	5,039,923	4,237,699	...
1950	66,400,311	96,336,075	86,262,509	4,534,558	6,039,008	...
1970	87,933	131,514	48,022	—	20,162	63,330
1980	70,329	111,835	13,054	—	31,166	67,617
1990	54,750	98,906	3,469	—	36,939	58,471
1993	53,082	97,877	—	—	38,524	59,353
1994	54,426	100,579	—	—	39,551	61,028

[1] The sum of these 4 items should equal the total in the preceding column; any difference

appearing is due to the very small production of crucible steel, omitted prior to 1950.
[2] Includes crucible production beginning 1950. [3] Low point of the depression.
[4] Peak year of war production.

The iron and steel industry in 1994 employed 92,587 wage-earners who worked an average of 42 hours per week and earned an average of $21.96 per hour: total employment costs were $6,744m. and total employment costs for 33,031 salaried employees were $2,466m.

Annual Statistics Report. American Iron and Steel Institute

Labour. The Bureau of Labor Statistics estimated that in 1995 the civilian labour force was 132,304,000 (66·6% of those 16 years and over), of whom 124,900,000 were employed and 7,404,000—or 5·6%—were unemployed. Employment by industry in 1995:

Industry Group	*Male*	*Female*	*Total*	*Percentage distribution*
Employed (1,000 persons):	67,377	57,523	124,900	100·0
Agriculture, forestry and fisheries	2,681	911	3,592	2·9
Mining	543	84	627	0·5
Construction	6,906	762	7,668	6·1
Manufacturing:				
Durable goods	8,930	3,084	12,015	9·6
Non-durable (including not specified)	5,090	3,389	8,478	6·8
Transportation, communication and other public utilities	6,195	2,513	8,709	7·0
Wholesale and retail trade	13,759	12,312	26,071	20·9
Finance, insurance and real estate	3,332	4,651	7,983	6·4
Services	16,610	27,190	43,801	35·1
Private households	101	870	971	0·8
Other services	16,509	26,321	42,830	34·3
Professional services	9,219	20,442	29,661	23·7
Public administration	3,331	2,626	5,957	4·8

A total of 45 strikes and lockouts of 1,000 workers or more occurred in 1994, involving 322,000 workers and 5m. idle days; the number of idle days was 0·02% of the year's total working time of all workers.

The Federal Mediation and Conciliation Service, the National Labor Relations Board, the National Mediation Board and the National Railroad Adjustment Board provide formal machinery for the settlement of labour disputes.

In 1995 there was a federal hourly minimum wage of $4.25.

Labour relations are legally regulated by the National Labor Relations Act, amended by the Labor–Management Relations (Taft–Hartley) Act, 1947 as amended by the Labor–Management Reporting and Disclosure Act, 1959, again amended in 1974, and the Railway Labor Act of 1926, as amended in 1934 and 1936.

Trade Unions. The labour movement comprises 78 national and international labour organizations as well as a large number of small independent local or single-firm labour organizations. The American Federation of Labor and the Congress of Industrial Organizations merged into one organization, the AFL–CIO, in 1955, with 13m. members in 1995. Its *President* is John Sweeney, elected 1995.

Unaffiliated or independent labour organizations, inter-state in scope, had an estimated total membership excluding all foreign members (1993) of about 3m.

Labour organizations represented 17·5% (18·9m.) of wage and salary workers in 1994; A newly-developing 'associative unionism' is not based on the workplace, but provides representation for employees which is portable throughout their work history. 15·5% (16·7m.) were actual members of unions. 35% of employees in the public sector, and 11% in the private sector, were members of unions in 1995. Strongholds of organized labour are, industry-wise, iron and steel, railways, coal mining and car building; region-wise, East coast cities and the mid-West industrial belt.

FOREIGN ECONOMIC RELATIONS. The North American Free Trade Agreement (NAFTA) between the USA, Canada and Mexico was signed on 7 Oct.

1992 and came into effect on 1 Jan. 1994. The UK has had 'most-favoured-nation' status since 1815. In 1994, foreign investment totalled $47,200m., including from UK, £19,000m.; Switzerland, $5,700m.; Germany, $3,600m.; Canada, $3,600m.; Japan, $2,000m.

Commerce. Total value of imports, exports and re-exports (in $1m.):

	Exports		*General*
	Total	*US merchandise*	*imports*
1992	448,164	425,377	532,665
1993	465,091	439,282	580,659
1994	512,521	482,141	663,829

Imports and exports of gold and silver refined bullion (in $1m.):

	Gold		*Silver*	
	Exports	*Imports*	*Exports*	*Imports*
1991	2,039	1,722	115	339
1992	2,877	1,568	126	341
1993	7,611	1,495	100	297

Exports and imports (in $1m.), 1994:

	Exports	*Imports*
Agricultural commodities	44,951	25,949
Animal feeds	3,348	436
Bulbs	112	238
Cereal flour	1,164	970
Cocoa	34	698
Coffee	53	2,270
Corn	4,187	85
Cotton, raw and linters	2,676	21
Dairy products, eggs	717	583
Fur skins, raw	131	78
Grains, unmilled	694	181
Hides and skins	1,392	126
Live animals	587	1,392
Meat and preparations	5,191	2,629
Oils/fats, animal	567	22
Oils/fats, vegetable	962	1,051
Plants	117	105
Rice	1,008	130
Seeds	315	152
Soybeans	4,353	46
Sugar	5	551
Tobacco, unmanufactured	1,303	698
Vegetables and fruit	6,752	6,074
Wheat	4,057	286
Other agricultural	5,227	7,128
Manufactured goods	402,106	557,871
ADP equipment, office machinery	30,879	52,118
Airplanes	18,824	3,805
Airplane parts	9,841	2,743
Aluminium	2,776	4,947
Artwork/antiques	1,185	2,427
Basketware, etc.	1,817	2,590
Chemicals – cosmetics	3,536	1,995
Chemicals – dyeing	2,323	1,868
Chemicals – fertilizers	2,699	1,296
Chemicals – inorganic	4,068	4,105
Chemicals – medicinal	6,093	4,680
Chemicals – organic	12,826	10,799
Chemicals – plastics	12,486	5,933
Chemicals – other	7,570	3,238
Clothing	5,464	36,744
Copper	1,268	2,296
Electrical machinery	44,309	57,672
Footwear	647	11,716
Furniture and parts	3,127	7,567

	Exports	*Imports*
Gem diamonds	183	5,740
General industrial machinery	21,783	21,337
Glass	1,459	1,351
Glassware	560	1,157
Gold, nonmonetary	5,644	1,932
Iron and steel mill products	3,548	12,876
Lighting, plumbing	1,252	2,024
Metal manufactures	7,012	8,848
Metalworking machinery	3,899	4,614
Motorcycles, bicycles	1,518	2,323
Nickel	209	735
Optical goods	965	1,816
Paper and paperboard	7,450	9,065
Photographic equipment	3,017	4,678
Plastic articles	3,573	4,513
Platinum	304	1,324
Pottery	105	1,556
Power generating machinery	20,270	19,561
Printed materials	3,973	2,232
Records/magnetic media	5,867	3,611
Rubber articles	785	1,251
Rubber tyres and tubes	1,614	3,035
Scientific instruments	16,463	9,964
Ships, boats	1,166	806
Silver and bullion	247	488
Spacecraft	444	219
Specialized industrial machinery	19,695	16,755
Telecommunications equipment	15,845	32,457
Textile yarn, fabric	6,429	9,208
Toys/games/sporting goods	3,086	11,824
Travel goods	233	3,080
Vehicles/new cars – Canada	7,420	22,081
Vehicles/new cars – Japan	1,724	23,973
Vehicles/new cars – other	5,287	14,559
Vehicles/trucks	5,126	10,348
Vehicles/chassis/bodies	428	428
Vehicles/parts	21,163	19,610
Watches/clocks/parts	277	2,643
Wood manufactures	1,543	3,387
Zinc	47	787
Other manufactured goods	28,758	41,135
Mineral fuel	8,895	56,412
Coal	2,962	646
Crude oil	44	38,464
Petroleum preparations	3,161	10,242
Liquefied propane/butane	195	873
Natural gas	254	4,014
Electricity	30	960
Other mineral fuels	2,248	1,213
Selected commodities:		
Fish and preparations	3,033	6,593
Cork, wood, lumber	5,554	6,683
Pulp and waste paper	3,793	2,315
Metal ores, scrap	3,734	3,253
Crude fertilizers	1,445	1,027
Cigarettes	4,965	71
Alcoholic beverages, distilled	356	1,826
All other	3,243	1,829

Total trade beween the USA and the UK (British Department of Trade returns, in £1,000 sterling):

	1992	*1993*	*1994*	*1995*
Imports to UK	13,711,323	16,357,928	17,727,680	20,268,863
Exports and re-exports from UK	12,225,877	15,354,306	16,783,484	17,949,473

Imports and exports by selected countries for the calendar years 1993 and 1994 (in $1m.):

Country	General imports 1993	General imports 1994	Exports incl. re-exports [1] 1993	Exports incl. re-exports [1] 1994
UK	21,730	25,063	26,438	26,833
France	15,279	16,775	13,267	13,622
Germany	28,562	31,749	18,932	19,237
Italy	13,216	14,711	6,464	7,193
Netherlands	5,443	6,015	12,839	13,591
Russia	1,743	3,235	2,970	2,579
Canada	111,216	128,948	100,444	114,441
Mexico	39,917	49,493	41,581	50,840
China	31,540	38,781	8,763	9,287
Japan	107,246	119,149	47,982	53,481
South Korea	17,118	19,658	14,782	18,028
Taiwan	25,102	26,711	16,168	17,078
Australia	3,297	3,200	8,277	9,781
Hong Kong	9,554	9,698	9,874	11,445
Singapore	12,798	15,361	11,678	13,022

[1] 'Special category' exports are included in these totals.

Tourism. In 1993, 45,779,000 visitors travelled to the USA, of whom 16,900,459 were classified as tourists. Visitors spent US$57,621m. (excluding transportation paid to US international carriers), and came mainly from Canada (17·29m.), Mexico (9·82m.) and Europe (8·63m.). Tourists came mainly from Europe (7·34m., of which UK 2·56m. and Germany 1·66m.), Japan (3·18m.), Mexico (1·26m.) and the Caribbean (0·88m.). Expenditure by US travellers in foreign countries for 1993 was US$40,564m. (excluding transportation paid to foreign flag international carriers).

COMMUNICATIONS

Roads. On 31 Dec. 1993 the total public road mileage (rural and urban), amounted to 3,904,721 miles, of which 3,554,235 miles were surfaced roads. The total mileage cited includes about 675,000 miles of rural roads under control of the states, about 2,247,000 miles of local rural roads, about 0·18m. miles of federal park and forest roads, and 803,078 miles of urban roads. Expenditure on highway administration and maintenance amounted to $86,539m. in 1993, of which $923m. were provided by the federal government. On 1 Jan. 1990, toll roads administered by state and local toll authorities, totalled 4,721 miles.

Motor vehicles registered in 1993: 194,063,000, including 146,314,000 automobiles, 654,000 buses, 41,075,000 trucks and 4,065,000 motorcycles. There were 175·13m licensed drivers in 1994 (86·13m. females). Inter-city trucks (private and for hire) averaged 735,000m. revenue net ton-miles in 1990. Of the buses in service in 1990, 508,261 were school buses. Inter-city service operated a total of 19,800 buses and carried a total of 322m. revenue passengers in 1990.

There were 40,115 deaths in road accidents in 1993.

Railways. Railway history in the USA commences in 1828, but the first railway to convey both freight and passengers in regular service (between Baltimore and Ellicott's Mills (MD), 13 miles) dates from 24 May 1830. Mileage rose to a peak of 266,381 miles in 1916, falling thereafter to 222,164 in 1969 (these include some duplication under trackage rights and some mileage operated in Canada by US companies). The ordinary gauge is 4 ft 8½ in. (about 99·6% of total mileage).

Freight service is provided by 13 major independent railroad companies and several hundred smaller operators. Long-distance passenger trains are run by the National Railroad Passenger Corporation (Amtrak), which is federally-assisted. Amtrak was set up in 1971 to maintain a basic network of long-distance passenger trains, and is responsible for almost all non-commuter services over some 38,000 route-km, of which it owns only 1,256 km (555 km electrified). Outside the major conurbations, there are almost no regular passenger services other than those of Amtrak, which carried 21·8m passengers in 1994.

Civil Aviation. There are international airports at Anchorage, Atlanta (Hartsfield), Baltimore (Baltimore/Washington), Boston (Logan), Chicago (O'Hare), Cincinnati (Northern Kentucky), Cleveland (Hopkins), Dallas/Fort Worth, Denver (Stapleton), Detroit Metropolitan, Honolulu, Houston Intercontinental, Kansas City, MO, Las

Vegas (McCarran), Los Angeles, Miami, Minneapolis/St Paul, New Orleans, New York (John F. Kennedy), New York (La Guardia), New York (Newark), Orlando, Philadelphia, Phoenix (Sky Harbor), Pittsburgh, Portland, St Louis (Lambert), Salt Lake City, San Diego (Lindbergh Field), San Francisco, Seattle-Tacoma, Tampa, Washington DC (Dulles) and Washington DC (National).

The principal airlines (with numbers of aircraft in service) in 1993 were: Air Wisconsin (38), Alaska Airlines (70), Aloha Airlines (23), American Airlines (672), American Trans Air (23), America West Airlines (86), Continental Airlines (325), Delta Air Lines (554), Emery Worldwide (59), Evergreen (32), Federal Express (496), Hawaiian (30), Horizon Air Industries (56), Northwest Airlines (373), Southwest Airlines (141), Trans World (172), United Airlines (539), USAir (502), Westair (52).

Statistics from the Department of Transportation indicate that for 1992 US flag carriers in scheduled international service had 43·4m. enplanements with 764·6m. aircraft miles (excluding all-cargo) for a total of 130,578m. revenue passenger-miles. Non-scheduled services had a total of 12,212m. revenue passenger-miles internationally and domestically. Domestically, US scheduled airlines in 1992 had 429·9m. enplanements with a total of 3,671m. aircraft miles for 347,503m. revenue passenger-miles.

Shipping. On 1 Oct. 1995 the US merchant marine included 512 sea-going vessels of 1,000 gross tons or over, with an aggregate 18·8 DWT. This included 182 tankers of 11·1 DWT.

On 1 Oct. 1994, US merchant ocean-going vessels were employed as follows: Active, 345 of 15·2m. DWT, of which 132 of 4·7m. DWT were foreign trade, 129 of 7·3m. DWT in domestic trade and 24 of 1·8m. DWT in foreign to foreign operations. Inactive vessels totalled 4·7m. DWT; 26 of 1·4m. DWT privately owned were laid up and 136 of 2·7m. DWT were Government-owned National Defense reserve fleet. Of the total vessels in the US fleet, 333 of 15·1m. DWT were privately owned.

US exports and imports carried on dry cargo and tanker vessels in 1994 totalled 899·1m. long tons, of which 35m. long tons were carried in US flag vessels. In 1993, 54,838 vessels entered, and 53,637 cleared, all US ports.

Telecommunications. The US Postal Service superseded the Post Office Department on 1 July 1971.

Postal business for the years ended 30 Sept. included the following items:

	1991	*1992*	*1993*	*1994*
Number of post offices	39,985	39,595	39,392	39,372
Operating revenue ($1,000)	43,884,472	46,695,800	47,582,000	49,383,400
Operating expenses ($1,000)	43,290,783	45,652,878	46,216,000	48,455,200

Regional private companies formed from the American Telephone and Telegraph Co. after its dissolution in 1995 ('Baby Bells') operates the telephone, telegraph, telex and electronic transmission services system at the national and local levels. Total domestic access lines in 1993, 147m.

Legislation on the media and telecommunications of 1995 deregulates the market while preserving safeguards against over-concentration of individual ownership: a single company may not control a network reaching more than 35% of TV viewers, or produce a newspaper and a television service in the same market. Local companies are now permitted to operate long-distance telephone services and also cable TV services.

The licensing agency for broadcasting stations is the Federal Communications Commission, an independent federal body composed of 5 Commissioners appointed by the President. Its regulatory activities comprise: Allocation of spectrum space; consideration of applications to operate individual stations; and regulation of their operations. In 1994 there were 10,022 commercial radio stations, 1,145 commercial TV stations, 367 non-commercial TV stations and 11,230 cable TV systems. Programming is targeted to appeal to a given segment of the population or audience taste. There are 5 national TV networks (3 commercial; colour by NTSC) with 46 national cable networks. All major cities have network affiliates and additional commercial stations.

Broadcasting to countries abroad is conducted by The Voice of America, Radio Liberty and Radio Free Europe, which are grouped under a 7-member council nominated by the President and reviewed by Congress.

In 1993 there were 520m. radio and 215m. TV receivers in use.

Cinemas. In Jan. 1994 there were 25,737 screens (25,105 in 1993), including 850 drive-ins. Attendance in 1993 was 1,244m. (1,173m. in 1992). 431 full-length films were made in 1993.

Press. In 1994 there were 1,556 daily papers with an average circulation of 59,811,594. These included 623 morning papers, 954 evening papers and 884 Sunday papers (circulation, 62,565,574).

SOCIAL INSTITUTIONS

Justice. Legal controversies may be decided in two systems of courts: The federal courts, with jurisdiction confined to certain matters enumerated in Article III of the Constitution, and the state courts, with jurisdiction in all other proceedings. The federal courts have jurisdiction exclusive of the state courts in criminal prosecutions for the violation of federal statutes, in civil cases involving the government, in bankruptcy cases and in admiralty proceedings, and have jurisdiction concurrent with the state courts over suits between parties from different states, and certain suits involving questions of federal law.

The highest court is the Supreme Court of the US, which reviews cases from the lower federal courts and certain cases originating in state courts involving questions of federal law. It is the final arbiter of all questions involving federal statutes and the Constitution; and it has the power to invalidate any federal or state law or executive action which it finds repugnant to the Constitution. This court, consisting of 9 justices appointed by the President who receive salaries of $164,100 a year (the Chief Justice, $171,500), meets from Oct. until June every year. For the term ended June 1995 it disposed of 7,136 cases, deciding 160 on their merits. In the remainder of cases it either summarily affirms lower court decisions or declines to review. A few suits, usually brought by state governments, originate in the Supreme Court, but issues of fact are mostly referred to a master.

The US courts of appeals number 13 (in 11 circuits composed of 3 or more states and 1 circuit for the District of Columbia and 1 Court of Appeals for the Federal Circuit); the 179 circuit judges receive salaries of $141,700 a year. Any party to a suit in a lower federal court usually has a right of appeal to one of these courts. In addition, there are direct appeals to these courts from many federal administrative agencies. In the year ending 30 June 1995, 51,518 appeals were filed in the courts of appeals, including 1,847 in the Federal Circuit.

The trial courts in the federal system are the US district courts, of which there are 89 in the 50 states, 1 in the District of Columbia and 1 each in the Commonwealth of Puerto Rico and the Territories of the Virgin Islands, Guam and the Northern Marianas. Each state has at least 1 US district court, and 3 states have 4 apiece. Each district court has from 1 to 28 judgeships. There are 649 US district judges ($133,600 a year), who received 239,013 civil cases and 63,310 criminal defendants from 1 July 1994 to 30 June 1995.

In addition to these courts of general jurisdiction, there are special federal courts of limited jurisdiction. The US Court of Federal Claims (16 judges at $133,600 a year) decides claims for money damages against the federal government in a wide variety of matters; the Court of International Trade (9 judges at $133,600) determines controversies concerning the classification and valuation of imported merchandise.

The judges of all these courts are appointed by the President with the approval of the Senate; to assure their independence, they hold office during good behaviour and cannot have their salaries reduced. This does not apply to judges in the Territories, who hold their offices for a term of 10 years or to judges of the US Court of Federal Claims. The judges may retire with full pay at the age of 70 years if they have served a period of 10 years, or at 65 if they have 15 years of service, but they are subject to call for such judicial duties as they are willing to undertake. 11 US judges up to 1995 have been involved in impeachment proceedings, of whom 7 were convicted and removed from office.

In 1995, of the 239,013 civil cases filed in the district courts, 155,601 arose under various federal statutes (such as labour, social security, tax, patent, securities, antitrust and civil rights laws); 44,511 involved personal injury or property damage claims; 31,619 dealt with contracts; and 7,282 were actions concerning real property.

Among the 63,310 criminal defendants (44,184 criminal cases) filed in 1995 in the district courts, 22,329 persons were charged with alleged infractions of drug laws; 11,040 persons were charged with miscellaneous general offences; 11,722 with embezzlement and fraud; 3,359 for larceny and theft; 3,396 were charged with immigration violations; 1,393 with robbery; and 1,350 with forgery and counterfeiting and fraud.

Persons convicted of federal crimes may be fined, released on probation under the supervision of the probation officers of the federal courts, confined in prison, or confined in prison with a period of supervised release to follow, also under the supervision of probation officers of the federal courts. Federal prisoners are confined in 77 institutions incorporating various security levels that are operated by the Bureau of Prisons. Prisoners confined in Federal and State Prisons at June 1995, numbered 1,104,074 (6·1% women).

The state courts have jurisdiction over all civil and criminal cases arising under state laws, but decisions of the state courts of last resort as to the validity of treaties or of laws of the US, or on other questions arising under the Constitution, are subject to review by the Supreme Court of the US. The state court systems are generally similar to the federal system, to the extent that they generally have a number of trial courts and intermediate appellate courts, and a single court of last resort. The highest court in each state is usually called the Supreme Court or Court of Appeals with a Chief Justice and Associate Justices, usually elected but sometimes appointed by the Governor with the advice and consent of the State Senate or other advisory body; they usually hold office for a term of years, but in some instances for life or during good behaviour. The lowest tribunals are usually those of Justices of the Peace; many towns and cities have municipal and police courts, with power to commit for trial in criminal matters and to determine misdemeanours for violation of the municipal ordinances; they frequently try civil cases involving limited amounts of damages.

There were no executions from 1968 to 1976. The US Supreme Court had held the death penalty, as applied in general criminal statutes, to contravene the eighth and fourteenth amendments of the US constitution, as a cruel and unusual punishment when used so irregularly and rarely as to destroy its deterrent value.

The death penalty was reinstated by the Supreme Court in 1976, but has not been authorized in Alaska, the District of Columbia, Hawaii, Iowa, Kansas, Maine, Massachusetts, Michigan, Minnesota, North Dakota, Rhode Island, Vermont, West Virginia and Wisconsin.

A Guide to Court Systems. Institute of Judicial Administration. New York, 1960
The United States Courts. Administrative Office of the US Courts, Washington, D.C., 20544
Hall, K. L. (ed.) *The Oxford Companion to the Supreme Court of the United States.* OUP, 1993
Huston, L. A. and others, *Roles of the Attorney General of the United States.* New York, 1968
McCloskey, R. G., *The Modern Supreme Court.* Harvard Univ. Press, 1972
McLauchlan, W. P., *American Legal Processes.* New York, 1977
Walker, S. E., *Popular Justice.* New York, 1980

Religion. *The Yearbook of American and Canadian Churches for 1994,* published by the National Council of the Churches of Christ in the USA, New York, gave the following figures available from official statisticians of church bodies: The principal religious bodies (numerically or historically) or groups of religous bodies are shown below:

Protestant Churches	*No. of churches*	*Membership (in 1,000)*
Baptist bodies		
Southern Baptist Convention	38,401	15,359
National Baptist Convention, USA	33,000	8,200
National Baptist Convention of America, Inc.	2,500	3,500

Protestant Churches	*No. of churches*	*Membership (in 1,000)*
Baptist bodies—contd.		
American Baptist Churches in the USA	5,845	1,534
American Baptist Association	1,705	250
Conservative Baptist Association of America	1,084	200
Free Will Baptists	2,495	209
Baptist Missionary Association of America	1,362	237
Christian Church (Disciples of Christ)	3,996	663
Christian Churches and Churches of Christ	5,579	1,012
Church of the Nazarene	5,172	574
Churches of Christ	13,354	1,685
The Episcopal Church	7,367	2,472
Jehovah's Witnesses	9,890	914
Latter-Day Saints:		
Church of Jesus Christ of Latter-Day Saints	9,654	4,612
Reorganized Church of Jesus Christ of Latter-Day Saints	1,001	150
Lutheran bodies		
Evangelical Lutheran Church in America	11,055	5,236
The Lutheran Church-Missouri Synod	5,369	2,610
Wisconsin Evangelical Lutheran Synod	1,211	420
Mennonite churches:		
Mennonite Church	1,056	99
Old Order Amish	873	79
Methodist bodies:		
United Methodist Church	37,100	8,789
African Methodist Episcopal Church	8,000	3,500
African Methodist Episcopal Zion Church	3,000	1,200
Wesleyan Church (USA)	1,612	114
Pentecostal bodies:		
The Church of God in Christ	15,300	5,500
Assemblies of God	11,689	2,258
Church of God (Cleveland, Tenn.)	5,776	672
United Pentecostal Church International	3,728	550
Presbyterian bodies:		
Presbyterian Church (USA)	11,456	3,758
Presbyterian Church in America	1,212	240
Reformed Churches:		
Reformed Church in America	927	275
Christian Reformed Church in North America	736	224
The Salvation Army	1,151	446
Seventh-day Adventist Church	4,261	749
United Church of Christ	6,264	1,555
Roman Catholic Church	19,863	59,221
Orthodox Churches	19,000	3,416,364
Non-Christian Religions:		
Hindus	–	340,000
Baha'i	1,700	50,000
Islam [1]	–	3,332,000
Jews	2,848	4,300

[1] Figures include Canada.

Greeley, A., *Religious Change in America.* Harvard Univ. Press, 1989

Education. Elementary and secondary education is mainly a state responsibility. Each state and the District of Columbia has a system of free public schools, established by law, with courses covering 12 years plus kindergarten. There are 3 structural patterns in common use; the K8-4 plan, meaning kindergarten plus 8 elementary grades followed by 4 high school grades; the K6–3–3 plan, or kindergarten plus 6 elementary grades followed by a 3-year junior high school and a 3-year senior high school; and the K5-3-4 plan, kindergarten plus 5 elementary grades followed by a 3-year middle school and a 4-year high school. All plans lead to high-school graduation, usually at age 17 or 18. Vocational education is an integral part of secondary education. Some states also have 2-year colleges in which education is provided at a nominal cost. Each state has delegated a large degree of control of the educational programme to local school districts (numbering 14,881 in school year 1993–94), each with a board of education (usually 3 to 9 members) selected locally and serving mostly without pay. The school policies of the local school districts must be in accord with the laws and the regulations of their state Departments of Education. While regulations differ from one jurisdiction to another, in general it may be said that school attendance is compulsory from age 7 to 16.

'Charter schools' are legal entities outside the school boards administration. They retain the basics of public school education, but may offer unconventional curricula and hours of attendance. Founders may be parents, teachers, public bodies or commercial firms. Organization and conditions depend upon individual states' legislation. The first charter schools were set up in Minnesota in 1991.

The Census Bureau estimates that in Nov. 1979 only 1m. or 0·6% of the 170m. persons who were 14 years of age or older were unable to read and write; in 1930 the percentage was 4·8. In 1940 a new category was established—the 'functionally illiterate', meaning those who had completed fewer than 5 years of elementary schooling; for persons 25 years of age or over this percentage was 1·9 in March 1994 (for the Black population alone it was 2·8%); it was 0·8% for white and 0·6% for Blacks in the 25–29-year-old group. The Bureau reported that in March 1994 the median years of school completed by all persons 25 years old and over was 12·9, and that 22·2% had completed 4 or more years of college. For the 25–29-year-old group, the median school years completed was 13 and 23·3% had completed 4 or more years of college.

In the autumn of 1994, 14,279,000 students (7,907,000 women) were enrolled in 3,642 colleges and universities; 2,133,000 were first-time students. About 34% of the population between the ages of 18 and 24 were enrolled in colleges and universities.

Public elementary and secondary school revenue is supplied from the county and other local sources (47·4% in 1992–93), state sources (45·6%) and federal sources (6·9%). In 1994–95 expenditure for public elementary and secondary education totalled about $283,000m., including $253,000m. for current operating expenses, $24,000m. for capital outlay and $6,000m. for interest on school debt. The current expenditure per pupil in average daily attendance was $5,730. The total cost per pupil, also including capital outlay and interest, amounted to about $6,850. Estimated total expenditures, for private elementary and secondary schools in 1994–95 were about $23,600m. In 1994–95 college and university spending totalled about $200,800m., of which about $126,600m. was spent by institutions under public control. The federal government contributed about 12% of total current-fund revenue; state governments, 24%; student tuition and fees, 27%; and all other sources, 37%.

Vocational education below college grade, including the training of teachers to conduct such education, has been federally aided since 1918. Federal support for vocational education in 1993–94 amounted to about $993m. Many public high schools offer vocational courses in addition to their usual academic programmes.

Summary of statistics of regular schools (public and private), teachers and pupils for 1993–94 (compiled by the US National Center for Education Statistics):

Schools by level	*Number of schools* [1]	*Teachers (in 1,000)*	*Enrolment (in 1,000)*
Elementary schools:			
Public	62,726	1,510	28,533
Private	23,543	262	4,280
Secondary schools:			
Public	22,733	995	14,943
Private	10,555	104	1,191
Higher education:			
Public	1,625	575	11,189
Private	2,007	251	3,116
Total	123,189	3,697	63,252

[1] Schools with both elementary and secondary grades are counted twice, once with the elementary and once with the secondary schools.

Most of the private elementary and secondary schools are affiliated with religious denominations. In 1993–94 there were 7,114 Roman Catholic elementary schools with 1·86m. pupils and 112,000 full- and part-time teachers, and 1,231 secondary schools with 585,000 pupils and 45,002 full- and part-time teachers.

During the school year 1994–95 high-school graduates numbered about 2,564,000 (of whom 2·3m. were from public schools). Institutions of higher education conferred about 1,192,000 bachelor's degrees during the year 1994–95, 0·53m. associate's degrees; 405,000 master's degrees; 43,000 doctorates; and 77,000 first professional degrees. In 1993–94 the federal government provided $7,713m. in grants and work-study programmes and $9,688m. in loans and other financial assistance to students.

During the academic year, 1993–94, 0·45m. foreign students were enrolled in American colleges and universities. The countries with the largest numbers of students in American colleges were: China, 44,400; Japan, 43,800; Taiwan, 37,600; India, 34,800; South Korea, 31,100; Canada, 22,700.

School enrolment, Oct. 1993, embraced 95·4% of the children who were 5 and 6 years old; 99·5% of the children aged 7–13 years; 98·9% of those aged 14–15, 94% of those aged 16–17 and 61·6% of those aged 18–19.

The US National Center for Education Statistics estimates the total enrolment in the autumn of 1995 at all of the country's elementary, secondary and higher educational institutions (public and private) at 65·1m. (63·9m. in the autumn of 1994).

The number of teachers in regular public and private elementary and secondary schools in the autumn of 1995 was expected to increase slightly to 2·97m. The average annual salary of the public school teachers was about $36,930 in 1994–95.

Health. Admission to the practice of medicine (for both doctors of medicine and doctors of osteopathic medicine) is controlled in each state by examining boards directly representing the profession and acting with authority conferred by state law. Although there are a number of variations, the usual time now required to complete training is 8 years beyond the secondary school with up to 3 or more years of additional graduate training. Certification as a specialist may require between 3 and 5 more years of graduate training plus experience in practice. In Jan. 1992 the estimated number of active physicians (MD and DO—in all forms of practice) in the USA, Puerto Rico and outlying US areas was 653,062.

Active dentists in Dec. 1988 numbered 146,800.

Number of hospitals listed by the American Hospital Association in 1994 was 6,374, with 1,128,066 beds and 33,125,492 admissions during the year; average daily census was 745,011. Of the total, 307 hospitals with 83,823 beds were operated by the federal government; 1,371 with 164,445 beds by state and local government; 3,139 with 636,949 beds by non-profit organizations (including church groups); 719 with 100,667 beds are proprietary. The categories of non-federal hospitals are 5,256 short-term general and special hospitals with 903,719 beds; 110 non-federal long-term general and special hospitals with 19,431 beds; 696 psychiatric hospitals with 120,575 beds; 5 tuberculosis hospitals with 518 beds.

Source: AHA *Hospital Statistics,* 1995–96 ed. Copyright by the American Hospitals Association.

Personal health-care costs in 1994 totalled $832,500m., distributed as follows: Hospital care, $341,700m.; doctors, $182,700m.; nursing-home care, $74,200m.; drugs, $79,000m.; dentists, $40,000m.; medical durables, $13,200m.; home health care, $24,200m.; other personal health care, $20,900m.

Welfare. Social welfare legislation was chiefly the province of the various states until the adoption of the Social Security Act of 14 Aug. 1935. This as amended provides for a federal system of old-age, survivors and disability insurance; health insurance for the aged and disabled; supplemental security income for the aged, blind and disabled; federal state unemployment insurance; and federal grants to states for public assistance (medical assistance for the aged and aid to families with dependent children generally and for maternal and child-health and child-welfare services). The Social Security Administration (formerly part of the Department of Health and Human Services but an independent agency since March 1995) has responsibility for the programmes—old-age, survivors and disability insurance and supplemental security income. The Administration for Children and Families (ACF), an agency of the Department of Health and Human Services, is responsible for federal programmes which promote the economic and social well-being of families, children, individuals and communities. ACF has federal responsibility for the following programmes: The Aid to Families with Dependent Children Program (providing cash assistance to family and children in the 50 states, the District of Columbia, Guam, Puerto Rico and the Virgin Islands); low income energy assistance; Head Start; child care; child protective services; and a community services block grant. The ACF also has federal responsibility for social service programmes for children, youth, native Americans and persons with developmental disabilities.

The Administration of Aging (AOA), an agency of the Department of Health and Human Services, serves older persons and their families with social, nutritional, education, and aging-related research and demonstration projects through the administration of the Older Americans Act. In addition, AOA is the focal point for aging policy within the Federal government. The Assistant Secretary for Aging is the primary advocate for the elderly in the USA. In 1993–94, $872m. was expended through a network of 57 State Units on Aging, 670 Area Agencies on Aging, 227 tribal organizations, 6,000 senior centres, and more than 25,000 service providers. More than 250m. meals were also provided through this programme.

The Health Care Financing Administration, an agency of the Health and Human Services Department, has federal responsibility for health insurance for the aged and disabled. Unemployment insurance is the responsibility of the Department of Labor.

In 1994 an average of 14·2m. persons (adults and children) were receiving payments under Aid to Families with Dependent Children (average monthly payment, $376 per family). Total payments under Aid to Families with Dependent Children were $22,800m. in 1994. The role of Child Support Enforcement is to ensure that children are supported by their parents. Money collected is for children who live with only one parent because of divorce, separation or out-of-wedlock birth. In 1993, nearly $9,000m. was collected on behalf of these children.

In 1994, federal appropriations for the social services block grant amounted to $2,800m. In addition, 1994 federal appropriations for child care totalled $893m. Included in this amount were $109m. for persons with developmental disabilities and $38·6m. for native Americans.

The Social Security Act provides for protection against the cost of medical care through Medicare, a two-part programme of health insurance for people age 65 and over, people of any age with permanent kidney failure, and for certain disabled people under age 65 who receive Social Security disability benefits. In 1994, payments totalling $103,200m. were made under the hospital portion of Medicare on behalf of 36m. people. During the same period, $58,600m. was paid under the voluntary medical insurance portion of Medicare on behalf of 35·1m. people.

In 1994, 139m. persons worked in employment covered by old-age, survivors and disability insurance.

In 1994 about 43m. beneficiaries were on the rolls, and the average benefit paid to a retired worker (not counting any benefits paid to his/her dependants) was about $699 per month. Full retirement benefits are now payable at age 65, with reduced benefits available as early as age 62. Beginning in 2000, the age for full retirement benefits will gradually increase until it reaches 67 in 2027.

In Dec. 1994, 6·4m. persons were receiving Supplementary Security Income payments, including 2·1m. persons aged 65 or over and over 4·9m. disabled or blind persons, including 0·8m. children. Payments, including supplemental amounts from various states, totalled $25,900m. in 1994.

Other block grants awarded by the Administration for Children and Families included $385·5m. for community services block grant programmes for 1993–94, and $1,300m. for the low income home energy assistance programme (LIHEAP). During 1989, the Public Health Services awarded a total of $554·3m. for maternal and child health services, $465·3m. as block grants to the States, $82·1m. for special projects of regional and national significance, and $6·9m. for genetic screening.

Other block grants awarded by the Public Health Service in 1988 included $88m. for preventive health; $487m. for alcohol, drug abuse and mental health; $155m. for alcohol and drug abuse treatment and rehabilitation. In 1989, $414·8m. was awarded for community health centres; $45·6m. for migrant health centres; $20·6m. for efforts to reduce infant mortality; $3·2m. for black lung clinics; and $135·1m. for family planning.

Berkowitz, E. D., *America's Welfare State from Roosevelt to Reagan.* Johns Hopkins Univ. Press, 1991
Marmor, T. R. *et al. America's Misunderstood Welfare State.* New York, 1990

DIPLOMATIC REPRESENTATIVES

Of the USA in Great Britain (Grosvenor Sq., London, W1A 1AE)
Ambassador: Adm. William J. Crowe.

Of Great Britain in the USA (3100 Massachusetts Ave., Washington, DC, 20008)
Ambassador: Sir John Kerr, KCMG.

Of the United States to the United Nations
Ambassador: Dr Madeleine Albright.

Further Reading

Official Statistical Information

The Office of Management and Budget, Washington, D.C. 20503 is part of the Executive Office of the President; it is responsible for co-ordinating all the statistical work of the different Federal Government agencies. The Office does not collect or publish data itself. The main statistical agencies are as follows:

(1) Data User Services Division, Bureau of the Census, Department of Commerce, Washington, D.C. 20233. Responsible for decennial censuses of population and housing, quinquennial census of agriculture, manufactures and business; current statistics on population and the labour force, manufacturing activity and commodity production, trade and services, foreign trade, state and local government finances and operations. (*Statistical Abstract of the United States*, annual, and others).

(2) Bureau of Labor Statistics, Department of Labor, 441 G Street NW, Washington, D.C. 20212. (*Monthly Labor Review* and others).

(3) Information Division, Economic Research Service, Department of Agriculture, Washington, D.C. 20250. (*Agricultural Statistics*, annual, and others).

(4) National Center for Health Statistics, Department of Health and Human Services, 3700 East-West Highway, Hyattsville Md. 20782. (*Vital Statistics of the United States*, monthly and annual, and others).

(5) Bureau of Mines Office of Technical Information, Department of the Interior, Washington, D.C. 20241. (*Minerals Yearbook*, annual, and others).

(6) Office of Energy Information Services, Energy Information Administration, Department of Energy, Washington, D.C. 20461.

(7) Statistical Publications, Department of Commerce, Room 5062 Main Commerce, 14th St and Constitution Avenue NW, Washington, D.C. 20230; the Department's Bureau of Economic Analysis and its Office of Industry and Trade Information are the main collectors of data.

(8) Center for Education Statistics, Department of Education, 555 New Jersey Avenue NW, Washington, D.C. 20208.

(9) Public Correspondence Division, Office of the Assistant Secretary of Defense (Public Affairs P.C.), The Pentagon, Washington, D.C. 20301-1400.

(10) Bureau of Justice Statistics, Department of Justice, 633 Indiana Avenue NW, Washington, D.C. 20531.

(11) Public Inquiry, APA 200, Federal Aviation Administration, Department of Transportation, 800 Independence Avenue SW, Washington, D.C. 20591.

(12) Office of Public Affairs, Federal Highway Administration, Department of Transportation, 400 7th St. SW, Washington, D.C. 20590.

(13) Statistics Division, Internal Revenue Service, Department of the Treasury, 1201 E St. NW, Washington, D.C. 20224.

Statistics on the economy are also published by the Division of Research and Statistics, Federal Reserve Board, Washington, D.C. 20551; the Congressional Joint Committee on the Economy, Capitol; the Office of the Secretary, Department of the Treasury, 1500 Pennsylvania Avenue NW, Washington, D.C. 20220.

OTHER OFFICIAL PUBLICATIONS

Economic Report of the President. Annual. Bureau of the Census. *Statistical Abstract of the United States.* Annual. *Historical Statistics of the United States, Colonial Times to 1970.*

United States Government Manual. Washington. Annual.

The official publications of the USA are issued by the US Government Printing Office and are distributed by the Superintendent of Documents, who issued in 1940 a cumulative *Catalog of the Public Documents of the... Congress and of All the Departments of the Government of the United States.* This *Catalog* is kept up to date by *United States Government Publications, Monthly Catalog* with annual index and supplemented by *Price Lists.* Each *Price List* is devoted to a special subject or type of material.

Treaties and other International Acts of the United States of America (Edited by Hunter Miller), 8 vols. Washington, 1929–48. This edition stops in 1863. It may be supplemented by *Treaties, Conventions... Between the US and Other Powers, 1776–1937* (Edited by William M. Malloy and others). 4 vols. 1909–38. A new Treaty Series, *US Treaties and Other International Agreements* was started in 1950.

Writings on American History. Washington, annual from 1902 (except 1904–5 and 1941–47).

NON-OFFICIAL PUBLICATIONS

Brewer T. L., *American Foreign Policy: a Contemporary Introduction.* 3rd ed. New York, 1991

Degler, C. N., *Out of Our Past: The Forces That Shaped Modern America.* Rev. ed. New York, 1970

Duigan, P. and Rabushka, A., (eds.) *The United States in the 1980s.* Stanford, 1980

Fawcett, E. and Thomas, T., *America and the Americans.* London, 1983

Foner, E. and Garraty, J. A. (eds.) *The Reader's Companion to American History.* New York, 1992

Herstein, S. R. and Robbins, N., *United States of America.* [Bibliography] Oxford and Santa Barbara, 1982

Lord, C. L. and E. H., *Historical Atlas of the US.* Rev. ed. New York, 1969

Brogan, H., *The Longman History of the United States of America.* London, 1985

Campbell, C. and Rockman, B. A. (eds.) *The Bush Presidency: First Appraisals.* Chatham, (NJ), 1991

Merriam, L. A. and Oberly, J. (eds.) *United States History: an Annotated Bibliography.* Manchester Univ. Press, 1995

Morison, S. E. with Commager, H. S., *The Growth of the American Republic.* 2 vols. 5th ed. OUP, 1962–63

Norton, M. B., *People and Nation: the History of the United States.* 4th ed. 2 vols. New York, 1994

Pfucha, F. P., *Handbook for Research in American History: a Guide to Bibliographies and Other Reference Works.* 2nd ed. Nebraska Univ. Press, 1994

Who's Who in America. Annual

Other more specialized titles are listed under TERRITORY AND POPULATION, CONSTITUTION AND GOVERNMENT, DEFENCE, BANKING AND FINANCE, TENNESSEE VALLEY AUTHORITY, JUSTICE, RELIGION *and* WELFARE, *above.*

National library: The Library of Congress, Independence Ave. SE, Washington DC, 20540. - *Librarian:* James H. Billington.

National statistical office: Bureau of the Census, Washington DC, 20233.

STATES AND TERRITORIES

See also the section 'State and Local Government' under UNITED STATES. Constitution and Government.

Against the names of the Governors and the Secretaries of State, (D.) stands for Democrat and (R.) for Republican.

Figures for the revenues and expenditures of the various states are those of the

Federal Bureau of the Census unless otherwise stated, which takes the original state figures and arranges them on a common pattern so that those of one state can be compared with those of any other.

Further Reading

Official publications of the various states and insular possessions are listed in the *Monthly Check-List of State Publications*, issued by the Library of Congress since 1910. Of great importance bibliographically are the publications of the Historical Records Survey and the American Imprints Inventory, which record local archives, official publications and state imprints. These publications supplement those of state historical societies which usually publish journals and monographs on state and local history. An outstanding source of statistical data is the material issued by the various state planning boards and commissions, to which should be added the annual *Governmental Finances* issued by the US Bureau of the Census.

The Book of the States. Biennial. Council of State Governments, Lexington, 1953 ff.
State Government Finances. Annual. Dept. of Commerce, 1966 ff.
Bureau of the Census. *State and Metropolitan Area Data Book.* Irregular.—*County and City Data Book.* Irregular.

Hill, K. Q., *Democracy in the 50 States.* Nebraska Univ. Press, 1995

ALABAMA

KEY HISTORICAL EVENTS. Alabama, settled in 1702 as part of the French Province of Louisiana, and ceded to the British in 1763, was organized as a Territory, 1817, and admitted into the Union on 14 Dec. 1819.

TERRITORY AND POPULATION. Alabama is bounded in the north by Tennessee, east by Georgia, south by Florida and the Gulf of Mexico and west by Mississippi. Land area, 50,750 sq. miles (131,443 sq. km). Census population, 1 April 1990, 4,040,587 (60·4% urban), an increase of 3·87% since 1980. Population estimate (1994), 4,218,733. Births, 1993, 61,588 (15·1 per 1,000 population); deaths, 41,232 (10·1); infant deaths (under 1 year), 636 (10·3 per 1,000 live births); marriages, 40,156 (9·8); divorces, 27,126 (6·6).

Population in 5 census years was:

	White	*Black*	*Indian*	*Asiatic*	*Total*	*Per sq. mile*
1930	1,700,844	944,834	465	105	2,646,248	51·3
1960	2,283,609	980,271	1,726	915	3,266,521	64·0
			All others			
1970	2,533,831	903,467	6,867		3,444,165	66·7
1980	2,872,621	996,335	24,932		3,893,888	74·9
1990	2,975,797	1,020,705	44,085		4,040,587	79·6

Of the total population in 1990, 47·9% were male, 66% were urban and 68·7% were 21 years or older.

The large cities (1990 census) were: Birmingham, 265,968 (metropolitan area, 907,810); Mobile, 196,278 (476,923); Montgomery (the capital), 187,106 (292,517); Huntsville, 159,789 (238,912); Tuscaloosa, 77,759 (150,522).

CLIMATE. Birmingham. Jan. 46°F (7·8°C), July 80°F (26·7°C). Annual rainfall 54" (1,346 mm). Mobile. Jan. 52°F (11·1°C), July 82°F (27·8°C). Annual rainfall 63" (1,577 mm). Montgomery. Jan. 49°F (9·4°C), July 81°F (27·2°C). Annual rainfall 53" (1,321 mm). The growing season ranges from 190 days (north) to 270 days (south). Alabama belongs to the Gulf Coast climate zone (*see* UNITED STATES: Climate).

CONSTITUTION AND GOVERNMENT. The present constitution dates from 1901; it has had 578 amendments (as at Nov. 1995). The legislature consists of a Senate of 35 members and a House of Representatives of 105 members, all elected for 4 years. The Governor and Lieut.-Governor are elected for 4 years.

The state is represented in Congress by 7 representatives. Applicants for registration must take an oath of allegiance to the United States and fill out a questionnaire to the satisfaction of the registrars. In the 1992 presidential election Bush polled 804,283 votes; Clinton, 690,080; Perot, 183,109.

Montgomery is the capital.

Governor: Forrest H. (Fob) James, Jr. (R.), 1995–99 ($87,643).
Lieut.-Governor: Don Siegelman (D.), ($3,780).
Secretary of State: Jim Bennett (D.) ($61,779.44).

BUDGET. The total net revenue for the fiscal year ending 30 Sept. 1990 was $9,041m. ($3,820m. from tax, $2,060m. from federal payments); total net expenditure was $7,400m. ($3,380m. on education, $1,049 on public welfare, $298m. on health, $716m. on highways).

The outstanding debt on 30 Sept. 1991 amounted to $4,214m.

Per capita income (1994) was $18,010.

NATURAL RESOURCES

Minerals. Principal minerals, 1993 (in net 1,000 tons): Limestone, 21,692; coal, 24,629; sand and gravel, 8,015; oil and condensates (18·48m. bbl.) and natural gas (361,197m. cu. ft.). Total mineral output (1986) was valued at $2,001m.; non-fuel minerals (1990) $562m.

Agriculture. The number of farms in 1995 was some 47,000, covering 10·2m. acres; the average farm had 217 acres and was valued at $1,262 per acre in 1995.

Cash receipts from farm marketings, 1994: Crops, $745,700,000m.; livestock and poultry products, $2,159,400,000m.; and total, $2,905,100,000m. Principal sources: broilers, cattle and calves, eggs, hogs, dairy products, greenhouses and nurseries, peanuts, soybeans, cotton, and vegetables. In 1994, broilers accounted for the largest percentage of cash receipts from farm marketings; cattle and calves were second, eggs third, cotton fourth.

Forestry. Area of national forest lands, Oct. 1990, 651,200 acres. Area of commercial timberland, 1990, 21,931,600 acres, of which 1,161,700 acres were public forests and 20,769,900 acres private forests. In 1990, 23,075m. cu. ft of timber was inventorized. Harvest volumes in 1994, 294·12m. cu. ft softwood saw timber, 78·63m. cu. ft hardwood saw timber, 744·47m. cu. ft paper fibre and 11·74m. cu. ft poles. Total harvest, 1994, was $1,128·9m. cu. ft. The estimated delivered timber value of forest products in 1994 was $1,359m.

INDUSTRY. Alabama is both an industrial and service-oriented state. The chief industries are textiles, paper, food products and primary metals. In Nov. 1995 (preliminary) government establishments employed 349,300 workers; trade, 414,900; services, 386,400; transport and public utilities, 86,400 (total non-agricultural workforce 1994 was 1,737,100).

TOURISM. In 1994, 19,088,935 tourists stayed at least one night in hotels, motels and resorts, spending some $4,300m.

COMMUNICATIONS

Roads. Paved roads of all classes in 1994 totalled 69,554 miles; total highways, 93,608 miles. Registered motor vehicles, 1994, 4,065,251.

Railways. At Oct. 1995 the railways had a length of 5,089 miles including side and yard tracks.

Civil Aviation. In 1995 the state had 97 public-use airports. Eight airports are for commercial service, three are relief airports for Birmingham and the rest, general aviation.

Shipping. There are 1,600 miles of navigable inland water and 50 miles of Gulf Coast. The only deep-water port is Mobile, with a large ocean-going trade; total tonnage (1995), 42,067,640 tons. The Alabama State Docks also operates a system of 10 inland docks; there are several privately-run inland docks.

SOCIAL INSTITUTIONS

Justice. In 1994 there were 391 law enforcement agencies employing 8,973 sworn and 4,015 civilian people. There were 203,802 offences reported of which 21% were cleared by arrest. Total property value stolen was $183,866,185 of which 20% was recovered. In total, for past and present felony and misdemeanour crimes, there were 38,949 people arrested for Part I offences, 168,703 for Part II offences, 11,610 for drug violations, and 44,029 for alcohol violations. As of 30 Sept. 1994, there were 19,269 people in prison or community-based facilities of which 134 were awaiting execution. There were also 35,302 people on probation and/or parole. Chain gangs were reintroduced into prisons in 1995.

Following the reinstatement of the death penalty by the US Supreme Court in 1976, death sentences have been awarded since 1983.

In 41 counties the sale of alcoholic beverage is permitted, and in 26 counties it is prohibited; but it is permitted in 8 cities within those 26 counties. Draught beverages are permitted in 22 counties.

Religion. Membership in selected religious bodies (in 1993): Southern Baptist Convention (1,049,441), Black Baptist (estimated 315,331), United Methodist Church, 264,968, African Methodist Episcopal Zion Church (134,305), Roman Catholic (137,834 adherents), Churches of Christ (91,660), Assemblies of God (38,442).

Education. In the school year 1995–96 the 1,333 public elementary and high schools required 43,796 teachers to teach 735,912 students enrolled in grades K–12. In 1994-95 there were 16 public senior institutions with 126,940 students and 4,930 faculty members. In 1994–95 the average salary of public school teachers was $31,144. As of autumn 1994–95 the 20 community colleges had 88,512 students and 4,340 faculty members; 2 public junior colleges had 3,903 students and 191 faculty members; 9 public technical colleges had 8,362 students and 565 faculty members.

Health. In 1995 there were 125 hospitals licensed by the State Board of Health, 7 exempt from licensure with a total of 20,856 beds. In 1992 there were 5,281 patients in hospitals for mental illness and 1,449 residents in facilities for the mentally retarded.

Welfare. In July 1995 Alabama paid supplements (to federal welfare payments) to 1,064 recipients of old-age assistance, receiving an average of $49·83 each; 956 permanently and totally disabled, $54·76; 22 blind, $49·91. Combined state–federal aid to dependent children was paid to 43,784 families, average $149·32 per family.

Further Reading

Alabama Official and Statistical Register. Montgomery. Quadrennial
Alabama County Data Book. Alabama Dept. of Economic and Community Affairs. Annual
Directory of Health Care Facilities. Alabama State Board of Health
Economic Abstract of Alabama. Center for Business and Economic Research, Univ. of Alabama, 1992
McCurley, R. L., Jr., ed., *The Legislative Process.* Alabama Law Institute, 3rd ed., 1984
Thigpen, R. A., *Alabama Government Manual.* Alabama Law Institute, 7th ed., 1986
Wiggins, S. W., (ed.) *From Civil War to Civil Rights, 1860–1960.* Univ. of Alabama Press, 1987

ALASKA

KEY HISTORICAL EVENTS. Discovered in 1741 by Vitus Bering, its first settlement, on Kodiak Island, was in 1784. The area known as Russian America with its capital (1806) at Sitk was ruled by a Russo-American fur company and vaguely claimed as a Russian colony. Alaska was purchased by the United States from Russia under the treaty of 30 March 1867 for $7·2m. It was not organized until

1884, when it became a 'district' governed by the code of the state of Oregon. By Act of Congress approved 24 Aug. 1912 Alaska became an incorporated Territory; its first legislature in 1913 granted votes to women, 7 years in advance of the Constitutional Amendment.

Alaska officially became the 49th state of the Union on 3 Jan. 1959.

TERRITORY AND POPULATION. Alaska is bounded north by the Beaufort Sea, west and south by the Pacific and east by Canada. The land area is 570,374 sq. miles (1,477,268 sq. km). Census population, 1 April 1990, was 550,043 (67·5% urban), including military personnel, an increase of 37·4% over 1980. Population estimate (1992), 586,900. Births, 1992, 11,714 (20 per 1,000 population); deaths, 2,317 (3·9); infant deaths, 99 (9·8 per 1,000 live births); marriages, 5,771 (9·8); divorces, 3,639 (6·2).

Population in 5 census years was:

	White	*Black*	*All Others*	*Total*	*Per sq. mile*
1950	92,808	...	35,835	128,643	0·23
1960	174,649	...	51,518	226,167	0·40
1970	236,767	8,911	54,704	300,382	0·53
1980	309,728	13,643	78,480	401,851	1·00
1990	415,492	22,451	112,100	550,043	1·00

Of the total population in 1990, 52·7% were male, 67·5% were urban and 68·7% were aged 18 years or over.

The largest city is the borough of Anchorage, which had a 1990 census population of 226,338. Census populations of the other 13 boroughs, 1990: Aleutians East, 2,464; Bristol Bay, 1,410; Fairbanks North Star, 77,720; Haines, 2,117; Juneau, 26,751; Kenai Peninsula, 40,802; Ketchikan Gateway, 13,828; Kodiak Island, 13,309; Lake and Peninsula, 1,668; Matanuska-Susitna 39,683; North Slope, 5,979; Northwest Arctic, 6,113; Sitka, 8,588. Other Census Area populations, 1990: Aleutians West, 9,478; Bethel, 13,656; Dillingham, 4,012; Nome, 8,288; Prince of Wales-Outer Ketchikan, 6,278; Skagway-Yakutat-Angoon, 4,385; Southeast Fairbanks, 5,913; Valdez-Cordova, 9,952; Wade Hampton, 5,791; Wrangell-Petersburg, 7,042; Yukon-Koyukuk, 8,478. In 1995 there were 16 boroughs and 145 incorporated cities.

CLIMATE. Anchorage. Jan. 12°F (–11·1°C), July 57°F (13·9°C). Annual rainfall 15" (371 mm). Fairbanks. Jan. –11°F (–23·9°C), July 60°F (15·6°C). Annual rainfall 12" (300 mm). Sitka. Jan. 33°F (0·6°C), July 55°F (12·8°C). Annual rainfall 87" (2,175 mm). Alaska belongs to the Pacific Coast climate zone (*see* UNITED STATES: Climate).

CONSTITUTION AND GOVERNMENT. The state has the right to select 103·55m. acres of vacant and unappropriated public lands in order to establish 'a tax basis'; it can open these lands to prospectors for minerals, and the state is to derive the principal advantage in all gains resulting from the discovery of minerals. In addition, certain federally administered lands reserved for conservation of fisheries and wild life have been transferred to the state. Special provision is made for federal control of land for defence in areas of high strategic importance.

The constitution of Alaska was adopted by public vote, 24 April 1956. The state legislature consists of a Senate of 20 members (elected for 4 years) and a House of Representatives of 40 members (elected for 2 years). The state sends 1 representative to Congress. The franchise may be exercised by all citizens over 18.

The capital is Juneau.

In the 1992 presidential election Bush polled 102,000 votes; Clinton, 78,294; Perot, 73,481.

Governor: Tony Knowles (D.), 1995–98 ($81,648).
Lieut.-Governor: Fran Ulmer (D.) ($76,188).

ECONOMY

Budget. Total state government revenue for the year ended 30 June 1994 (Annual Financial Report figures) was $2,692m. Total expenditure was $3,361m.

In 1976 a Permanent Fund was set up for the deposit of at least 25% of all mineral-related revenue; total assets at 30 June 1994, $14,977m.

General obligation bonds, 30 June 1994, $178m.

Per capita income (1994) was $23,788.

NATURAL RESOURCES

Oil and Gas. Commercial production of crude petroleum began in 1959 and by 1961 had become the most important mineral by value. Production: 1991, 672m. bbls, value $2,572m.; 1992, 627m. bbls, value $2,624m.; 1994, 569m. bbls. Oil comes mainly from Prudhoe Bay, the Kuparuk River field and several Cook Inlet fields. Natural gas (liquid) production, 1991, 20·4m. bbls; 1992 production, 26·91m. bbls; 1994 production, 19·3m. bbls. Revenue to the state from petroleum in 1993 was $2,684·8m. (87% of general fund revenues). General fund unrestricted revenues, 1993: Severance taxes, 33%; oil and gas royalties, 25%; investment earnings, 2%; other oil and gas, 27%; non-petroleum, 13%.

Oil from the Prudhoe Bay Arctic field is now carried by the Trans-Alaska pipeline to Prince William Sound on the south coast, where a tanker terminal has been built at Valdez.

Minerals. Estimated value of production, 1994, in $1,000: Gold, 70,291; silver, 10,391; lead, 25,513; zinc, 296,103; industrial minerals (including sand, gravel and building stone), 68,009; platinum, 2·07; coal, 36,750; peat, 439·5. Total 1994 value, $507·5m.

Agriculture. In some parts of the state the climate during the brief spring and summer (about 100 days in major areas and 152 days in the south-eastern coastal area) is suitable for agricultural operations, thanks to the long hours of sunlight, but Alaska is a food-importing area. In 1994 about 0·93m. acres was farmland and there were 520 farms and ranches with annual sales of $1,000 or more; crops covered 28,940 acres. In 1991 the average farm had 1,768 acres. At 1 Jan. 1995 there were 9,900 cattle and calves and 1,700 sheep and lambs; at 1 Dec. 1994, 2,000 hogs and pigs and 2,000 poultry.

Total value of agricultural products in 1994: $27,766,000 of which $2,828,000 was from feed crops, $2,738,000 from vegetables (including potatoes), $6·1m. from livestock and poultry, $2,465,000 from dairy products and $15,833,000 from greenhouse and nursery industries.

There were about 33,000 reindeer in western Alaska in 1994. Sales of reindeer meat and by-products in 1994 were valued at $1,366,000.

Forestry. Of the 129m. forested acres of Alaska, 21m. acres are classified as timberland or commercial forest. The interior forest covers 115m. acres; more than 13m. acres are considered commercial forest, of which 3·4m. acres are in designated parks or wilderness and unavailable for harvest. The coastal rain forests provide the bulk of commercial timber volume; of their 13·6m. acres, 7·6m. acres support commercial stands, of which 1·9m. acres are in parks or wilderness and unavailable for harvest. In 1992, 590m. bd ft of timber were harvested from private land for a total value of $548·9m., and in 1993 9·38m. bd ft from state land for $342·6m.

Fisheries. The catch for 1993 was 2·7m. lbs of fish and shellfish having a value to fishermen of $905m. The most important species are salmon, crab, herring, halibut and pollock.

INDUSTRY. The largest manufacturing sectors are wood processing, seafood products and printing and publishing.

Labour. Total non-agricultural employment, 1995, 280,000. Employees by branch, 1995 (in 1,000): Government service, 69; trade, 58·1; services, 63·4; construction, 15·5; manufacturing, 26·2; mining including oil and gas, 9·9; transport, communication and utilities, 25·3; finance, insurance and property, 12·6.

TOURISM. About 1·05m. tourists visited the state in 1993.

COMMUNICATIONS

Roads. Alaska's highway and road system, 1991, totalled 13,485 miles. Registered motor vehicles, 1994, 631,465.

The Alaska Highway extends 1,523 miles from Dawson Creek, British Columbia, to Fairbanks, Alaska. It was built by the US Army in 1942, at a cost of $138m. The greater portion of it, because it lies in Canada, is maintained by Canada.

Railways. There is a railway of 111 miles from Skagway to the town of Whitehorse, the White Pass and Yukon route, in the Canadian Yukon region (this service operates seasonally). The government-owned Alaska Railroad runs from Seward to Fairbanks, a distance of 471 miles. This is a freight service with only occasional passenger use. A passenger service operates from Anchorage to Fairbanks via Denali National Park in the tourist season.

Civil Aviation. Commercial passengers by air from Alaska's largest international airports Anchorage and Fairbanks in fiscal year 1994 numbered 4,358,437 at Anchorage and 721,496 at Fairbanks. General aviation aircraft in the state per 1,000 population is about 10 times the US average.

Shipping. Regular shipping services to and from the US are furnished by 2 steamship and several barge lines operating out of Seattle and other Pacific coast ports. A Canadian company also furnishes a regular service from Vancouver, B.C. Anchorage is the main port.

A 1,435 nautical-mile ferry system for motor cars and passengers (the 'Alaska Marine Highway') operates from Bellingham, Washington and Prince Rupert (British Columbia) to Juneau, Haines (for access to the Alaska Highway) and Skagway. A second system extends throughout the south-central region of Alaska linking the Cook Inlet area with Kodiak Island and Prince William Sound.

SOCIAL INSTITUTIONS

Justice. There is no death penalty in Alaska. In Oct. 1994 there were 3,340 adults and 245 juveniles in state and federal institutions.

Religion. Many religions are represented, including the Russian Orthodox, Roman Catholic, Episcopalian, Presbyterian, Methodist and other denominations.

Education. Total expenditure on public schools in fiscal year 1994 was $896,307,252. In 1994 there were 7,195 teachers; average salary, fiscal year 1994, $46,263. In 1994 there were 121,396 pupils enrolled at public schools. The University of Alaska (founded in 1922) main campuses had (autumn 1993) 33,087 students. Other colleges had 2,718 students in autumn 1993.

Health. In 1993 there were 27 acute care hospitals with 1,892 beds, of which 7 were federal public health hospitals and 1 mental hospital. Many hospitals offer mental health services and most communities have mental health services and/or centres.

Welfare. Old-age assistance was established under the Federal Social Security Act; in 1993 aid to dependent children covered a monthly average of 11,300 households; payments, an average of $834 per month; aid to the disabled was given to a monthly average of 4,698 persons receiving on average $348 per month. An average of 3,666 aged per month received $351.

Further Reading

Statistical Information: Department of Commerce and Economic Development, Economic Analysis Section, POB 110804 Juneau 99811. Publishes *The Alaska Economy Performance Report.*

Alaska Industry–Occupation Outlook to 1995, Department of Labor, Juneau.
Annual Financial Report, Department of Administration, Juneau.
Falk, M., *Alaska.* [Bibliography]. Oxford and Santa Barbara (CA), 1995

Gardey, J., *Alaska: The Sophisticated Wilderness.* London, 1976
Hulley, Clarence C., *Alaska Past and Present.* Portland, Oregon, 1970
Hunt, W. R., *Alaska: a Bicentennial History.* New York, 1976
Naske, C.-M. and Slotnick, H. E., *Alaska: a History of the 49th State.* 2nd ed. Univ. of Oklahoma Press, 1995
Thomas, L., Jr., *Alaska and the Yukon.* New York, 1983
Tourville, M., *Alaska: a Bibliography, 1570–1970.* 1971

State library: POB 110571, Juneau, Alaska 99811-0571.

ARIZONA

KEY HISTORICAL EVENTS. Arizona's first permanent White settlement was made by the Spaniards in 1752. It was granted territorial status on 24 Feb. 1863 and became the 48th state on 14 Feb. 1912.

TERRITORY AND POPULATION. Arizona is bounded north by Utah, east by New Mexico, south by Mexico, west by California and Nevada. Area, 114,006 sq. miles (295,276 sq. km), including 364 sq. miles (943 sq. km) of inland water. Of the total area in 1992, 28% was Indian Reservation, 17% was in individual or corporate ownership, 19% was held by the US Bureau of Land Management, 15% by the US Forest Service, 13% by the State and 8% by others. Census population on 1 April 1990 was 3,665,228 (87·5% urban), an increase of 34·92% over 1980. Population estimate (1994), 4,071,650. In 1993: Births, 69,037; deaths, 33,295; infant deaths, 531; marriages, 39,650; dissolutions of marriages, 24,198.

Population in 5 census years:

	White	*Black*	*Indian*	*Chinese*	*Japanese*	*Total*	*Per sq. mile*
1910	171,468	2,009	29,201	1,305	371	204,354	1·8
1930	378,551	10,749	43,726	1,110	879	435,573	3·8
1960	1,169,517	43,403	83,387	2,937	1,501	1,302,161	11·3
				All others			
1980	2,260,288	74,159	162,854	383,768		2,718,215	23·9
1990	2,963,186	110,524	203,527	387,991		3,665,228	32·3

Of the population in 1990, 1,810,691 (49·4%) were male, 3,206,973 (87·5%) were urban and 2,684,109 (73·2%) were aged 18 and over.

The 1994 estimated population of Phoenix was 1,051,515; Tucson, 440,335; Mesa, 318,885; Glendale, 164,890; Scottsdale, 154,145; Tempe, 150,615; Chandler, 115,095; Peoria, 65,500; Yuma, 60,150.

CLIMATE. Phoenix. Jan. 53·6°F (12°C), July 93·5°F (34°C). Annual rainfall 7·66" (194 mm). Yuma. Jan. 56·5°F (13·6°C), July 93·7°F (34·3°C). Annual rainfall 3·17" (80 mm). Arizona belongs to the Mountain States climate zone (*see* UNITED STATES: Climate).

CONSTITUTION AND GOVERNMENT. The state constitution (1911, with 116 amendments) placed the government under direct control of the people through the initiative, referendum and the recall provisions. The state Senate consists of 30 members, and the House of Representatives of 60, all elected for 2 years. Arizona sends to Congress 6 representatives. In the 1992 presidential election Bush polled 572,086 votes; Clinton, 543,050; Perot, 353,741.

The state capital is Phoenix. The state is divided into 15 counties.

Governor: J. Fife Symington III (R.), 1995–99 ($75,000).
Secretary of State: Jane Dee Hull (R.) ($54,000).

BUDGET. General revenues, year ending 30 June 1995, were $4,057·6m.; general expenditures, $3,951·6m. (education, $2,190·8m.; transport $69·6m., and public health and welfare, $1,050·4m.).

Per capita income (1995) was $20,418.

NATURAL RESOURCES

Minerals. The mining industry historically has been and continues to be a significant part of the economy. By value the most important mineral produced is copper. Production (1994) 1,254,000 tons. Most of the state's silver and gold are recovered from copper ore. Other minerals include sand and gravel, molybdenum, coal and gemstones. Total value of minerals mined in 1994 was $3,625m.

Agriculture. Arizona, despite its dry climate, is well suited for agriculture along the water-courses and where irrigation is practised on a large scale from great reservoirs constructed by the US as well as by the state government and private interests. Irrigated area, 1991, 913,841 acres. The wide pasture lands are favourable for the rearing of cattle and sheep, but numbers are either stationary or declining compared with 1920.

In 1994 Arizona contained 7,400 farms and ranches and the total farm and pastoral area was 35·4m. acres. In 1992 there were 1,344,091 acres of crop land. The average farm was estimated in 1994 at 4,784 acres. Farming is highly commercialized and mechanized and concentrated largely on cotton picked by machines operated by Indian, Mexican and migratory workers.

Area under cotton (1994): Upland cotton, 313,000 acres (782,000 bales harvested); American Pima cotton, 48,000 acres (80,400 bales harvested).

Cash income, 1994, from crops, $1,043,691,000 from livestock and products, $824,021,000. Most important cereals are wheat, corn and barley; most important crops include cotton, citrus fruit, lettuce, broccoli, grapes, cauliflower, melons, onions, potatoes and carrots. In 1994 there were 0·87m. cattle, 0·2m. sheep, 0·14m. hogs, 82,000 goats and 0·35m. chickens.

Forestry. The national forests in the state had an area (1994) of 11,246,000 acres.

INDUSTRY. In 1992 the state had an average of 4,742 manufacturing employers with an average of 171,860 employees earning total wages of $5,503,240,352.

TOURISM. In 1994, 26·3m. tourists visited Arizona; tourism-related jobs, direct and indirect (1994), 283,647; state tax revenue (1994), $312m.

COMMUNICATIONS

Roads. As of 31 Dec. 1994 there were 54,380 miles of public roads and streets and 3,082,900 motor vehicles were registered.

Civil Aviation. Registered landing facilities, 1995, numbered 294, of which 79 were for public use; 5,076 aircraft were registered.

SOCIAL INSTITUTIONS

Justice. A 'right-to-work' amendment to the constitution, adopted 5 Nov. 1946, makes illegal any concessions to trade-union demands for a 'closed shop'.

The Arizona state prison 30 June 1995 held 19,375 male and 1,367 female prisoners. Chain gangs were reintroduced into prisons in 1995. The death penalty is authorized; the last execution was in 1993.

Religion. The leading religious bodies are Roman Catholics and Mormons (Latter Day Saints); others include United Methodists, Presbyterians, Baptists, Lutherans, Episcopalians, Eastern Orthodox, Jews and Moslems.

Education. School attendance is compulsory between the ages of 6 and 16. In 1993–94 there were 762,863 pupils enrolled in grades K-12. There are 222 school districts containing 941 elementary schools and 178 high schools. In 1993–94, the total fund appropriation for all education including the Board of Regents and community colleges was $2,190,821,200. The state maintains 3 universities: The University of Arizona (Tucson) with an enrolment of 34,777 in autumn 1995;

Arizona State University (3 campuses) with 46,920; Northern Arizona University (Flagstaff) with 20,131.

Health. In 1994 there were 86 hospitals; capacity 11,547 beds; 12,852 physicians and 2,974 dentists, 65,640 registered nurses and 20,507 licensed practical nurses.

Social Security. Old-age assistance (maximum depending on the programme) is given to needy citizens 65 years of age or older through the federal supplemental security income (SSI) programme. In June 1995, SSI payments went to 13,496 aged (average $216·97 each), 57,066 disabled (average $376·26 each) and 880 blind people (average $362·08 each). In Oct. 1995, 176,394 people (average $109·84 each) in 65,452 families (average $296·01 each) received aid for families with dependent children.

Further Reading

Statistical information: College of Business and Public Administration, Univ. of Arizona, Tucson 85721. Publishes *Arizona Statistical Abstract.*

Office of the Secretary of State. *Arizona Blue Book, 1993–94.* 1994

1993–1994 Arizona Yearbook. Phoenix, 1993

Goff, J., *Arizona: an Illustrated History of Grand Canyon State.* Northridge (CA), 1988

Luey, B. and Stowe, N. J. (eds.) *Arizona at Seventy-Five: the Next Twenty-Five Years.* Arizona State Univ., 1987

Richards, J. M., *History of the Arizona State Legislature, 1912–1967.* Phoenix, 1990

Trimble, M., *Arizona: a Panoramic History of a Frontier State.* New York, 1977.—*Arizona: a Cavalcade of History.* Tucson, 1989

State Library: Department of Library, Archives and Public Records, Capitol, Phoenix 85007.

ARKANSAS

KEY HISTORICAL EVENTS. Arkansas was settled in 1686, made a territory in 1819 and admitted into the Union on 15 June 1836. The name originated with the Quapaw Indian tribe. The constitution, which dates from 1874, has been amended 59 times.

TERRITORY AND POPULATION. Arkansas is bounded north by Missouri, east by Tennessee and Mississippi, south by Louisiana, south-west by Texas and west by Oklahoma. Area, 53,187 sq. miles (137,754 sq. km), 1,109 sq. miles being inland water. Census population on 1 April 1990 was 2,350,725 (53·5% urban), an increase of 2·8% from that of 1980. Population estimate (1993), 2,424,000. Births, 1992, were 34,803; deaths, 24,941 (infant deaths, 363); marriages, 37,164; divorces 17,999.

Population in 5 census years was:

	White	*Black*	*Indian*	*Asiatic*	*Total*	*Per sq. mile*
1910	1,131,026	442,891	460	72	1,574,449	30·0
1930	1,375,315	478,463	408	296	1,854,482	35·2
1960	1,395,703	388,787	580	1,202	1,786,272	34·0
			All others			
1980	1,890,332	373,768	22,335		2,286,435	43·9
1990	1,944,744	373,912	32,069		2,350,725	45·1

Of the total population in 1990, 48·2% were male and 68·9% were 21 years of age or older.

Little Rock (capital) had a population of 175,795 in 1990; Fort Smith, 72,798; North Little Rock, 61,741; Pine Bluff, 57,140; Fayetteville, 42,099; Hot Springs, 32,462; Jonesboro, 46,535; West Memphis, 28,259. The population of the largest standard metropolitan statistical areas: Little Rock–North Little Rock, 513,117; Fayetteville, 113,409; Fort Smith (Arkansas portion), 142,083; Pine Bluff, 85,487; Memphis (Arkansas portion), 49,939; Texarkana (Arkansas portion), 38,467.

CLIMATE. Little Rock. Jan. 39·9°F, July 84°F. Annual rainfall 52·83 inches. Arkansas belongs to the Gulf Coast climate zone (*see* UNITED STATES: Climate).

GOVERNMENT. The General Assembly consists of a Senate of 35 members elected for 4 years, partially renewed every 2 years, and a House of Representatives of 100 members elected for 2 years. The sessions are biennial and usually limited to 60 days. The Governor and Lieut.-Governor are elected for 4 years. The state is represented in Congress by 4 representatives.

In the 1992 presidential election Clinton polled 505,823 votes; Bush, 337,324; Perot, 99,137.

The state is divided into 75 counties; the capital is Little Rock.

Governor: Jim Guy Tucker (D.), 1995–99 ($60,000).
Lieut.-Governor: Mike Huckabee (R.) ($29,000).
Secretary of State: Sharon Priest (D.) ($37,500).

FINANCE

Budget. The state and local government revenue for the fiscal year 1992 was $6,749m., of which taxation furnished $3,172m. and federal aid, $1,292m. General expenditure was $6,441m., of which education took $2,321m.; highways, $542m., and public welfare, $955m.

Long-term debt (state and local governments) for the financial year 1991 was $14,817m.

Per capita income (1994) was $16,898.

Banking. In 1993–94 total bank deposits were $22,107·8m.

NATURAL RESOURCES

Minerals. In 1988 crude petroleum amounted to 13,455,729 bbls; natural gas, 146,894,144m. cu. ft. The U.S. Bureau of Mines estimated Arkansas' mineral value in 1992 at $287m. Mining employment totalled 3,600 in Oct. 1992. Crushed stone was the leading mineral commodity produced, in terms of value, followed by bromine.

Agriculture. In 1991, 46,000 farms had a total area of 16·0m. acres; average farm was 337 acres. In 1993, 8·2m. acres were harvested cropland. In 1990, 2,406,338 acres were irrigated.

In 1993, Arkansas ranked first in the production of broilers (1,050m. birds) and in the acreage and production of rice (40% of US total production) and third in turkeys (25m. birds). 1,081,000 bales of cotton were harvested in 1991; soybean production yielded 90·4m. bu. in 1990. Dairy farmers received $122·6m. for the sale of milk in 1990.

Livestock in Jan. 1989 included 1·75m. all cattle and calves, total value (1990), was $425·9m.

INDUSTRY. In Aug. 1991 total employment averaged 1,039,100 (50,900 agricultural, 239,600 manufacturing, 215,200 wholesale and retail trade, 152,000 government). The Arkansas Department of Labor estimated that 196,700 factory production workers earned an average $370.77 per week (41·8 hours). In the manufacturing group, food and kindred products employed 52,400, electric and electronic equipment, 20,500 and lumber and wood products, 21,500. In Aug. 1994 estimated employment was 1,153,700, including 1,025,300 non-agricultural waged and salaried jobs.

COMMUNICATIONS

Roads. Total road mileage, 84,442 miles. State-maintained highways (1993) total 16,234 miles; local county highways, 51,157 miles; city streets, 9,807 miles; federal roads, 1,760 miles; roads not publicly maintained, 5,484 miles. In 1993 there were 2,097,872 registered motor vehicles.

Railways. In 1991 there were in the state 3,169 miles of commercial railway. In 1994 rail service was provided by 4 Class I and 23 short-line railways.

Civil Aviation. In Oct. 1994, 7 air carriers and 2 commuter airlines served the state; there were 175 airports (96 public-use and 79 private).

Waterways. There are about 1,000 miles of navigable streams, including the Mississippi, Arkansas, Red, White and Ouachita Rivers. The Arkansas River/Kerr-McClellan Channel flows diagonally eastward across the state and gives access to the sea *via* the Mississippi River.

SOCIAL INSTITUTIONS

Justice. State prisons in Oct. 1994 had 8,999 inmates. The death penalty is authorized. The last execution took place in 1994.

Religion. Main Protestant churches in 1990: Southern Baptist (617,524), United Methodist (197,402), Church of Christ (86,502), Assembly of God (55,438). Roman Catholics (1990), 72,952.

Education. In the school year 1992–93 public elementary and secondary schools had 440,682 enrolled pupils and 25,771 classroom teachers. Average salary of teachers in elementary schools was $25,771, junior high $27,492 and high $27,760.

An educational TV network provides a full 18-hour-day telecasting; it has 5 stations (1994).

Higher education is provided at 34 institutions: 9 state universities, 1 medical college, 12 private or church colleges, 12 community or 2-year branch colleges and 12 technical colleges. Total enrolment in institutions of higher education in the autumn of 1993 was 99,344.

There were in the autumn of 1993, 2 vocational-technical schools and 9 technical institutes with 28,261 students.

Health. There were 99 licensed hospitals (13,329 beds) in 1994, and 273 nursing facilities (25,888 licensed beds), excluding private facilities.

Social Welfare. In Dec. 1993, 481,910 persons drew social security payments; 271,510 were retired workers; 53,240 were disabled workers; 68,920 were widows and widowers; 36,050 were spouses. Monthly payments were $251·5m., $159·6m. to retired workers and their dependants and $31·6m. to disabled workers.

Further Reading

Statistical information: Arkansas Institute for Economic Advancement, Univ. of Arkansas at Little Rock, Little Rock, 72204. Publishes *Arkansas State and County Economic Data.*
Agricultural Statistics for Arkansas. Arkansas Agricultural Statistics Service, Little Rock, 1993
Current Employment Developments. Dept. of Labor, Little Rock, 1994
Statistical Summary for the Public Schools of Arkansas. Dept. of Education, Little Rock, 1990-92

CALIFORNIA

KEY HISTORICAL EVENTS. California, first settled in July 1769, was from its discovery until 1846 politically associated with Mexico. On 7 July 1846 the American flag was hoisted at Monterey, and a proclamation was issued declaring California to be a portion of the US. On 2 Feb. 1848, by the treaty of Guadalupe–Hidalgo, the territory was formally ceded by Mexico to the US, and was admitted to the Union 9 Sept. 1850 as the thirty-first state, with boundaries as at present.

TERRITORY AND POPULATION. Land area, 155,973 sq. miles (403,971 sq. km). Census population, 1 April 1990, 29,760,021 (92·6% urban), an increase of 25·7% over 1980. Population estimate (1994), 32m. Births in 1994, 585,000 (18·3 per 1,000 population); deaths, 224,000 (7 per 1,000 population); infant deaths (1990), 4,622 (7·5 per 1,000 live births); marriages (1990), 236,693; divorces (1990), 127,967.

Population in 5 census years was:

	White	*Black*	*Japanese*	*Chinese*	*Total (incl. all others)*	*Per sq. mile*
1910	2,259,672	21,645	41,356	36,248	2,377,549	15·0
1930	5,408,260	81,048	97,456	37,361	5,677,251	35·8
1960	14,455,230	883,861	157,317	95,600	15,717,204	99·0

	White	*Black*	*Asian/other*	*Hispanic*	*Total*	*Per sq. mile*
1980	15,763,992	1,783,810	1,575,769	4,544,331	23,667,902	149·1
1990	17,029,126	2,092,446	2,950,511	7,687,938	29,760,021	190·8

Of the 1990 population 50·1% were male, 92·6% were urban and 69% were 21 years old or older.

The largest cities with 1994 estimated population are:

Los Angeles	3,620,543	San Bernardino	184,397	Irvine	121,173
San Diego	1,184,814	Modesto	180,320	Salinas	119,840
San José	835,529	Oxnard	151,856	Orange	117,956
San Francisco	751,732	Garden Grove	151,807	Escondido	116,938
Long Beach	436,776	Chula Vista	149,347	Vallejo	116,148
Fresno	402,122	Oceanside	145,404	Lancaster	115,524
Sacramento	393,457	Ontario	143,887	Rancho Cucamonga	115,010
Oakland	384,097	Pomona	138,624	Concord	113,934
Santa Ana	310,417	Torrance	136,747	Inglewood	113,623
Anaheim	290,712	Pasadena	134,824	El Monte	110,965
Riverside	244,191	Moreno Vally	134,724	Thousand Oaks	110,263
Stockton	228,733	Santa Clarita	128,766	Berkeley	104,923
Bakersfield	201,769	Santa Rosa	124,913	Simi Valley	103,722
Glendale	190,192	Sunnyvale	124,230	Fontana	103,232
Huntington Beach	189,159	Hayward	122,384		
Fremont	184,590	Fullerton	121,456		

Urbanized areas (1990 census): Los Angeles, 11,402,946; San Francisco–Oakland, 3,629,516; San Diego, 2,348,417; San José, 1,435,019; Sacramento, 1,097,005; Riverside–San Bernardino, 1,170,196; Oxnard–Ventura, 480,482; Fresno, 453,388.

CLIMATE. Los Angeles. Jan. 55°F (12·8°C), July 70°F (21·1°C). Annual rainfall 15" (381 mm). Sacramento. Jan. 45°F (7·2°C), July 74°F (23·3°C). Annual rainfall 19" (472 mm). San Diego. Jan. 55°F (12·8°C), July 69°F (20·6°C). Annual rainfall 10" (259 mm). San Francisco. Jan. 50°F (10°C), July 59°F (15°C). Annual rainfall 22" (561 mm). Death Valley. Jan. 52°F (11°C), July 100°F (38°C). Annual rainfall 1·6" (40 mm). California belongs to the Pacific Coast climate zone (*see* UNITED STATES: Climate).

CONSTITUTION AND GOVERNMENT. The present constitution became effective from 4 July 1879; it has had numerous amendments since 1962. The Senate is composed of 40 members elected for 4 years—half being elected each 2 years—and the Assembly, of 80 members, elected for 2 years. Two-year regular sessions convene in Dec. of each even-numbered year. The Governor and Lieut.-Governor are elected for 4 years.

California is represented in Congress by 52 representatives.

In the 1992 presidential election Clinton polled 5,121,325 votes; Bush, 3,630,574; Perot, 2,296,006.

The capital is Sacramento. The state is divided into 58 counties.

Governor: Pete Wilson (R.), 1995–99 ($120,000).
Lieut.-Governor: Gray Davis (D.) ($90,000).
Secretary of State: Bill Jones (R.) ($90,000).

ECONOMY

Budget. For the year ending 30 June 1995 total General Fund revenues and transfers were $42,710m.; total General Fund expenditures were $41,961m. in fiscal year 1995 ($20,635m. for education, $13,960m. for health and welfare).

The long-term state debt (general obligation bonds outstanding) was $18,305m. on 31 Dec. 1995.

Per capita personal income (1994) was $22,353.

Banking and Finance. In 1988 there were more than 440 banks, of which 18 were foreign-owned, 11 out-of-state and 400 independent. Total loans, 31 Dec. 1994 (preliminary), $199,914m., of which real estate loans were $118,111m. All insured commercial banks had demand deposits of $67,942m. and time and savings deposits of $166,848m. Savings and loan associations had savings capital of $178,987m. at 31 Dec. 1994.

NATURAL RESOURCES

Minerals. Crude oil output was estimated at 286m. bbls in 1994. Output of natural gas was 260,550m. cu. ft; of natural gas liquids from wells, 73,250 bbls in 1994. Gold output was 33,000 kg (1994 preliminary); asbestos, boron minerals, diatomite, tungsten, sand and gravel, salt, magnesium compounds, clays, cement, copper, silver, gypsum, calcium chloride and iron ore are also produced. The value of non-fuel minerals produced was $2,500m. in 1994. Mining employed 32,400 in 1994.

Agriculture. Based on the 1992 Census, there were some 77,669 farms, comprising 29m. acres; average farm, 373 acres. Cotton, fruit, livestock and vegetables are important. Cash receipts, 1992, $18,147m. Dairy products, horticultural products, grapes, cattle, and cotton lint were the main sources of farm cash receipts.

Production of cotton lint, 1993, was 754,500 short tons; other field crops included (in 1m. short tons): Sugar-beet, 4; hay and alfalfa, 7·6; rice, 1·8; wheat, 1·3. Principal fruit, nut and vegetable crops 1993 (in 1,000 short tons): Wine, table and raisin grapes, 5,385; tomatoes, 9,458; lettuce, 3,163; almonds, 245. Citrus fruit crops 1993, were (in 1,000 short tons): Oranges, 2,505; lemons, 775; grapefruit, 308·2.

On 1 Jan. 1995 the farm animals were: 1·3m. milch cows, 4·7m. all cattle, 0·54m. sheep and 0·26m. swine.

Forestry. There are about 16·3m. acres of productive forest land, from which about 2,900m. bd ft are harvested annually. Lumber production, 1994, 2,300m. bd ft.

Fisheries. The catch in 1994 was 330m. lb.; leading species in landings were squid, mackerel, sardine, tuna, urchin, rockfish and crab.

INDUSTRY. The fastest-growing industries are business services, motion pictures and engineering and management consulting. In 1994 the civilian labour force was 15·47m., of whom 14,141,000 were employed (1,770,800 in manufacturing).

Tourism. In 1993 there were 191m. tourists, 14% from other states and 4% from abroad.

COMMUNICATIONS

Roads. In 1994 California had 66,525 miles of roads inside cities and 102,607 miles outside. In 1994 there were about 17·1m. registered cars and about 5·6m. commercial vehicles.

Railways. In addition to Amtrak's long-distance trains, local and medium-distance passenger trains run in the San Francisco Bay area sponsored by the California Department of Transportation, and a network of commuter trains around Los Angeles opened in 1992. There are metro and light rail systems in San Francisco and Los Angeles, and light rail lines in Sacramento, San Diego and San José.

Civil Aviation. In 1986 there were 283 public airports and 739 private airstrips.

Shipping. The chief ports are San Francisco and Los Angeles.

SOCIAL INSTITUTIONS

Justice. State prisons, 1 Jan. 1994, had 112,370 male and 7,581 female inmates.

The death penalty has been authorized following its reinstatement by the US Supreme Court in 1976. Death sentences have been passed since 1980. The last execution was in 1993.

Religion. There is a strong Roman Catholic presence. There were 719,000 Mormons in 1994.

Education. Full-time attendance at school is compulsory for children from 6 to 18 years of age for a minimum of 175 days per annum. In autumn 1994 there were 5·9m. pupils enrolled in both public and private elementary and secondary schools. Total state expenditure on public education, 1994–95, was $20,635m.

Community Colleges had 1,357,615 students in autumn 1994.

California has two publicly supported higher education systems: The University of California (1868) and the California State University and Colleges. In autumn 1994, the University of California with campuses for resident instruction and research at Berkeley, Los Angeles, San Francisco and 6 other centres, had 162,304 students. California State University and Colleges with campuses at Sacramento, Long Beach, Los Angeles, San Francisco and 15 other cities had 319,368 students. In addition to the 28 publicly supported institutions for higher education there are 117 private colleges and universities which had a total estimated enrolment of 212,752 in the autumn of 1994.

Health. In 1994 there were 503 general acute care hospitals; capacity, 105,885 beds. On 30 June 1995 state hospitals for the mentally disabled had 4,135 patients.

Social Security. On 1 Jan. 1974 the federal government (Social Security Administration) assumed responsibility for the Supplemental Security Income/State Supplemental Program which replaced the State Old-Age Security. The SSI/SSP provides financial assistance for needy aged (65 years or older), blind or disabled persons. An individual recipient may own assets up to $2,000; a couple up to $3,000, subject to specific exclusions. There are federal, state and county programmes assisting the aged, the blind, the disabled and needy children. In 1994, 11,485 families per month were receiving an average of $403 per family in General Relief.

Further Reading

California Almanac. Pacific Data Resources, Santa Barbara
California Government and Politics. Hoeber, T. R., et al, (eds.) Sacramento, Annual
California Statistical Abstract. 36th ed. Dept. of Finance, Sacramento, 1995
Economic Report of the Governor. Dept. of Finance, Sacramento, Annual
Bean, W. and Rawls, J. J., *California: an Interpretive History.* 6th ed. New York, 1993
Gerston, L. N. and Christensen, T., *California Politics and Government: a Practical Approach.* 3rd ed. New York, 1995
Lavender, D. S., *California.* New York, 1976

State Library: The California State Library, Library-Courts Bldg, Sacramento 95814.

COLORADO

KEY HISTORICAL EVENTS. Colorado was first settled in 1858, made a Territory in 1861 and admitted into the Union on 1 Aug. 1876.

TERRITORY AND POPULATION. Colorado is bounded north by Wyoming, north-east by Nebraska, east by Kansas, south-east by Oklahoma, south by New Mexico and west by Utah. Land area, 103,729 sq. miles (268,658 sq. km).

Census population, 1 April 1990, was 3,294,394 (82·4% urban), an increase of 14·04% since 1980. Population estimate (1993), 3,565,959. Births, 1991, were 53,968 (16·1 per 1,000 population); deaths, 22,334 (6·7); infant deaths, 419 (7·7 per 1,000 live births); marriages, 33,619 (10·0); divorces, 19,105 (5·7).

Population in 5 census years was:

	White	Black	Indian	Asiatic	Total	Per sq. mile
1910	783,415	11,453	1,482	2,674	799,024	7·7
1930	1,018,793	11,828	1,395	3,775	1,035,791	10·0
1950	1,296,653	20,177	1,567	5,870	1,325,089	12·7
			All others			
1980	2,571,498	101,703	216,763		2,889,964	27·7
1990	2,658,945	128,057	22,068	56,773	3,294,394	00·0

Of the total population in 1990, 1,631,295 were male, 1,663,099 were female; 69·4 were aged 20 years or older and 424,302 were of Hispanic origin. Large cities with 1990 census population: Denver City, 467,610; Colorado Springs, 281,140; Aurora, 222,103; Lakewood, 126,481; Pueblo, 98,640; Arvada, 89,235; Fort Collins, 87,758; Boulder, 83,312; Westminster, 74,625; Greeley, 60,536; Thornton, 55,031; Longmont, 51,555.

Main metropolitan areas (1990): Denver, 1,622,980; Colorado Springs, 397,014; Boulder, 225,339; Fort Collins, 186,136; Greeley, 131,821; Pueblo, 123,051; Front Range Urban Area, 2,686,341.

CLIMATE. Denver. Jan. 31°F (–0·6°C), July 73°F (22·8°C). Annual rainfall 14" (358 mm). Pueblo. Jan. 30°F (–1·1°C), July 83°F (28·3°C). Annual rainfall 12" (312 mm). Colorado belongs to the Mountain States climate zone (*see* UNITED STATES: Climate).

CONSTITUTION AND GOVERNMENT. The constitution adopted in 1876 is still in effect with (1989) 115 amendments. The General Assembly consists of a Senate of 35 members elected for 4 years, one-half retiring every 2 years, and of a House of Representatives of 65 members elected for 2 years. Sessions are annual, beginning 1951. Qualified as electors are all citizens, male and female (except convicted, incarcerated criminals), 18 years of age, who have resided in the state and the precinct for 32 days immediately preceding the election.

The state sends 6 representatives to Congress.

In the 1992 presidential election Clinton polled 629,681 votes; Bush, 562,850; Perot, 366,010.

The capital is Denver. There are 63 counties.

Governor: Roy Romer (D.), 1995–99 ($70,000).
Lieut.-Governor: Gail Schoettler (D.) ($48,500).
Secretary of State: Vicky Buckley (R.) ($48,500).

BUDGET. Total budget, 1993–94, $6,294m., of which taxation furnished $3,407m. and federal grants $1,655m. Expenditure on education, $1,637m.; health, social services and public safety, $2,151m., and transport, $655m. Total state and local taxes *per capita* (1994) were $513.

The state has no general obligation debt. The state revenue bond debt on 30 June 1991 was $2,659m.

Per capita personal income (1994) was $22,333.

NATURAL RESOURCES

Minerals. Colorado has a variety of mineral resources. Among the most important are crude oil and coal and gas (valued in 1992 at $1,080·6m.), non-fuel minerals ($388·5m.) and others ($307·6m.). Total value of mineral production in 1992, $1,776·7m. In 1990, 19,600 people were employed in mining: 12,500 in extracting oil and natural gas; 3,400 in metals; 2,900 in coal and 800 other.

Agriculture. In 1991 farms numbered 26,000, with a total area of 32·8m. acres. 5,580,000 acres were harvested crop land; average farm, 1,262 acres. Average value of farmland and buildings per acre in 1995 was $520. Farm income, 1992, from crops $1,099m.; from livestock, $2,906m. In 1990 there were 1,574,000 acres under irrigation.

Production of principal crops in 1990: Corn for grain, 128·65m. bu.; wheat for grain, 84·95m. bu.; barley for grain, 12m. bu.; hay, 3,805,000 tons; dry beans, 4,275,000 cwt; oats and sorghum, 12·59m. bu.; sugar beets, 944,000 tons; potatoes, 24,032,000 cwt; vegetables, 10,683 tons; fruits, 39,000 tons.

In 1987 the number of farm animals was: 76,285 milch cows, 708,070 sheep, 258,725 swine. In 1991 there were 2,800 cattle and calves. The wool clip in 1987 yielded 3·9m. lb. of wool.

INDUSTRY. In 1994, 1,749,600 were employed in non-agricultural sectors, of which 426,400 were in trade; 502,400 in services; 299,700 in government; 190,800 in manufacturing; 96,800 in construction; 107,300 in transport, communication and public utilities; 15,700 in mining; 110,500 in finance, insurance and property. In manufacturing in 1993 the biggest employers were 26,100 in food and kindred products; 25,400 in printing and publishing; 20,300 in instruments and related products.

COMMUNICATIONS

Roads. In 1990 there were 77,361 miles of road. In 1991 there were 3,045,240 motor vehicle registrations.

Railways. In 1982 there were in the state 4,500 miles of main-track and branch railway.

Civil Aviation. There were (1990) 81 airports open to the public; 14 with commercial service, 53 public non-commercial (general aviation) and 14 private non-commercial.

SOCIAL INSTITUTIONS

Justice. At 30 June 1991 there were 7,720 prisoners in state correctional institutions. The death penalty is authorized.

Religion. In 1984 the Roman Catholic Church had 550,300 members; the ten main Protestant denominations had 350,900 members; the Jewish community had 45,000 members. Buddhism is among other religions represented.

Education. In 1992 the public elementary and secondary schools had 593,030 pupils, 33,418 teachers; teachers' salaries averaged $33,418. Enrolments in 4-year state universities and colleges, 1994, were: University of Colorado (Boulder), 24,548 students; University of Colorado (Denver), 10,538; University of Colorado (Colorado Springs), 5,801; Colorado State University (Fort Collins), 21,461; Colorado School of Mines (Golden), 3,092; University of Northern Colorado (Greeley), 10,594; University of Southern Colorado (Pueblo), 4,500; Western State College (Gunnison), 2,442; Adams State College (Alamosa), 2,284; Mesa College (Grand Junction), 4,626; Fort Lewis College (Durango), 4,110; Metropolitan State College (Denver), 16,976; University of Colorado Health Sciences Centre (Denver), 2,286. 1994 total enrolments: Private 4-year universities and colleges, 27,899; 2-year colleges, 65,882; all universities and colleges, 207,039.

Health. Approved hospitals, 1993, numbered 101.

Social Security. A constitutional amendment, adopted 1956, provides for minimum old age pensions of $100 per month, which may be raised on a cost-of-living basis; for a $5m. stabilization fund and for a $10m. medical and health fund for pensioners. In 1984 the maximum monthly retirement pension (for citizens of 65 and older) was $703; maximum monthly benefit for a disabled worker, $854.

Further Reading

Statistical information: Business Research Division, Univ. of Colorado, Boulder 80309. Publishes *Statistical Abstract of Colorado.*

Griffiths, M. and Rubright, L., *Colorado: a Geography.* Boulder, 1983
Sprague, M., *Colorado: A History.* New York, 1976

State Library: Colorado State Library, State Capitol, Denver, 80203.

CONNECTICUT

KEY HISTORICAL EVENTS. Connecticut, first settled in 1634, was one of the 13 original states and has been an organized commonwealth since 1637. In 1629 a written constitution was adopted which, it is claimed, was the first in the history of the world formed under the concept of a social compact. This constitution was confirmed by a charter from Charles II in 1662, and replaced in 1818 by a state constitution, framed that year by a constitutional convention.

TERRITORY AND POPULATION. Connecticut is bounded in the north by Massachusetts, east by Rhode Island, south by the Atlantic and west by New York. Land area, 4,844 sq. miles (12,547 sq. km).

Census population, 1 April 1990, 3,287,116 (79·1% urban), an increase of 5·78% since 1980. Population estimate (1994), 3,275,251. Births (1993) were 46,658 (14·1 per 1,000 population); deaths, 28,905 (8·9); infant deaths (1990), 398 (7·9 per 1,000 live births); marriages, 26,046 (15·8); divorces, 11,617 (7·1).

Population in 5 census years was:

	White	*Black*	*Indian*	*Asian*	*Total*	*Per sq. mile*
1910	1,098,897	15,174	152	533	1,114,756	231·3
1930	1,576,700	29,354	162	687	1,606,903	328·0
1980	2,799,420	217,433	4,533	18,970	3,107,576	634·3

	White	*Black*	*Indian*	*Asian*	*Others*	*Total*	*Per sq. mile*
1990	2,859,353	274,269	6,654	50,698	96,142	3,287,116	678·6

Of the total population in 1993, 242,572 persons (of any race) were of Hispanic origin, 1,589,000 persons were male. 2,601,534 persons were urban in 1990. Those 18 years old or older numbered 2,497,836. There were 183 residents in 5 Indian Reservations.

The chief cities and towns are (1994 state estimates):

Bridgeport	136,693	Waterbury	107,831	Bristol	60,268
Hartford	135,359	Norwalk	79,106	Meriden	58,562
New Haven	125,089	New Britain	72,365	West Hartford	58,036
Stamford	109,950	Danbury	66,464	Greenwich	57,816

CLIMATE. New Haven: Jan. 25°F (–3·8°C), July 74°F (23·4°C). Annual rainfall 45" (1,143 mm). Connecticut belongs to the New England climate zone (*see* UNITED STATES: Climate).

CONSTITUTION AND GOVERNMENT. The 1818 Constitution was revised in 1955. On 30 Dec. 1965 a new constitution went into effect, having been framed by a constitutional convention in the summer of 1965 and approved by the voters in Dec. 1965.

The General Assembly consists of a Senate of 36 members and a House of Representatives of 151 members. Members of each House are elected for the term of 2 years. Legislative sessions are annual.

The state sends 6 representatives to Congress.

In the 1992 presidential election Clinton polled 682,318 votes; Bush, 578,313; Perot, 348,771. The state capital is Hartford. There are 8 counties.

Governor: John G. Rowland (R.), 1995–99 ($78,000).
Lieut.-Governor: M. Jodi Rell (R.) ($55,000).
Secretary of State: Miles S. Rapoport (D.) ($50,000).

BUDGET. For the year ending 30 June 1992 (state government figures) general revenues were $10,200m. (taxation, $5,800m., and federal aid, $2,300m.); general expenditures were $10,100m. (education, $2,500m., transport, $900m., public welfare, $2,400m.).

Per capita income, 1994, was $29,402.

NATURAL RESOURCES

Minerals. The state has some mineral resources: crushed stone, sand, gravel, clay, dimension stone, feldspar and quartz; total production in 1991 was valued at $60m.

Agriculture. In 1992 the state had 3,427 farms with annual sales of at least $1,000 having a total area of 358,743 acres; the average farm size was 105 acres, valued at $5,959 per acre. Farm income (1992): Crops, $183m. and livestock, $153m. Principal crops are grains, hay, tobacco, vegetables, maize, melons, fruit, nuts, berries and greenhouse and nursery products.

Livestock (1993): 77,000 all cattle (value $59·3m.), 10,900 sheep ($1·1m.), 6,000 swine ($630,000) and 4·6m. poultry ($11·5m.).

Forestry. The state had (1993) 143,067 acres of state forest land.

INDUSTRY. Total non-agricultural labour force in Oct. 1995 was 1,563,500. The main employers are manufacturers (280,300 workers mainly in transport equipment, machinery, computer, electronic and electrical equipment and fabricated metals); trade (262,400 workers); services (464,400) and government (220,600). There were 89,100 unemployed.

COMMUNICATIONS

Roads. The state maintains 4,073 miles of highways, all surfaced. Motor vehicles registered in 1994 numbered 1,484,254.

Railways. In 1994 there were 570 miles (912 km) of railway route length the state owns 171 km of route used by passenger trains, some of which it subsidises.

Civil Aviation. In 1995 there were 61 airports (20 commercial, 6 state-owned and 35 private), 63 heliports and 8 seaplane bases.

Telecommunications (1994). There were 75 broadcasting stations and 11 television stations.

Press. In 1994 there were 141 daily, Sunday, weekly and monthly newspapers.

SOCIAL INSTITUTIONS

Justice. In 1995 there were 14,246 inmates in 19 state correctional institutions and centres. There were 57,000 adults under state correctional supervision. The death penalty for murder has been authorized.

Religion. The leading religious denominations (1990) in the state are the Roman Catholic (1,374,000 members), United Churches of Christ (135,000), Protestant Episcopal (78,000), Jewish (115,000), Methodist (56,000), Black Baptist (64,000), Presbyterian and Greek Orthodox.

Education. Elementary instruction is free for all children between the ages of 4 and 16 years, and compulsory for all children between the ages of 7 and 16 years. In 1993 there were 978 public local schools, 3 academies, 17 state vocational-technical schools, 30 state or state-aided schools, 6 regional educational service centres and 334 non-public schools. In 1994 there were 507,825 pupils and 39,816 public elementary and secondary teachers. Expenditure of the state on public schools, 1994, $4,000m. Mean salary of teachers in public schools, 1993, $48,300.

Connecticut has 42 colleges, of which one state university, 4 state colleges, and 12 community-technical colleges are state funded. The University of Connecticut at Storrs, founded 1881, had 1,502 faculty and 23,649 students in 1994. Yale University, New Haven, founded in 1701, had 2,358 faculty and 10,916 students; Wesleyan University, Middletown, founded 1831, 261 faculty and 3,270 students; Trinity College, Hartford, founded 1823, 166 faculty and 2,146 students; Connecticut College, New London, founded 1915, 175 faculty and 1,919 students; The University of Hartford, founded 1877, 331 faculty and 7,241 students. The state colleges faculty was 1,087 and the number of students was 35,111. The technical colleges had 718 faculty and 45,542 students. There were 18 independent (4-year course) colleges with 4,219 faculty and 55,234 students; 6 independent (2-year course) colleges and 74 faculty and 1,790 students and 1 US Coastguard Academy with 43 faculty and 930 students.

Health. Hospitals listed by the American Hospital Association, 1993, numbered 62. The state operated 1 general hospital (252 beds), 7 hospitals for the mentally ill (891 patients), 1 training school for the mentally retarded, and 6 regional centres (5,705 clients in residential settings). There were 12,387 physicians and surgeons, 3,059 dentists and 49,864 registered nurses.

Social Security. Disbursements in 1992 amounted to $42m. in aid to the aged and disabled, (with an average payment per month of $664·82). In other areas of welfare, there was an average of 57,000 cases for aid to families with dependent children comprising 162,000 recipients.

Further Reading

State Register and Manual. Secretary of State. Hartford (CT). Annual
The Structure of Connecticut's State Government. Connecticut Public Expenditure Council. Hartford, 1973
Halliburton, W. J., *The People of Connecticut.* Norwalk, 1985
Van Dusen, Albert E., *Connecticut.* New York, 1961

State Library: Connecticut State Library, 231 Capitol Avenue, Hartford (CT), 06105; Tel. 860-566-4971.
State Book Store: Dept. of Envrionmental Protection, 79 Elm St., Hartford (CT), 06106; Tel. 860-424-3555.
Business Incentives: Connecticut Economic Resource Center, 805 Brook St., Rocky Hill (CT), 06067; Tel. 860-571-7136.
Connecticut Tourism: Dept. of Economic and Community Development, 865 Brook St., Rocky Hill (CT), 06067; Tel. 860-258-4355.

DELAWARE

KEY HISTORICAL EVENTS. Delaware, permanently settled in 1638, is one of the original 13 states of the Union, and the first one to ratify the Federal Constitution.

TERRITORY AND POPULATION. Delaware is bounded north by Pennsylvania, north-east by New Jersey, east by Delaware Bay, south and west by Maryland. Land area 1,982 sq. miles (5,133 sq. km). Census population, 1 April 1990 was 666,168 (73% urban), an increase of 12·1% since 1980. Population estimate, (1994), 709,278. Births in 1994, 10,550 (16·1 per 1,000 population); deaths, 6,152 (5·5); infant deaths, 94 (10·4 per 1,000 live births); marriages, 5,023 (8·0); divorces, 3,175 (4·6).

Population in 5 census years was:

	White	*Black*	*Indian*	*Asiatic*	*Total*	*Per sq. mile*
1910	171,102	31,181	5	34	202,322	103·0
1930	205,718	32,602	5	55	238,380	120·5
1960	384,327	60,688	597	410	446,292	224·0
			All others			
1980	488,002	96,157	10,179		594,338	290·8
1990	535,094	112,460	18,614		666,168	325·9

Of the total population in 1990, 48·5% were male and 70·4% were 21 years old or older.

The 1990 census figures show Wilmington with population of 71,529; Newark, 25,098; Dover, 27,630; Elsmere Town, 5,935; Milford City, 6,040; Seaford City, 5,089.

CLIMATE. Wilmington. Jan. 32°F (0°C), July 75°F (23·9°C). Annual rainfall 43" (1,076 mm). Delaware belongs to the Atlantic Coast climate zone (*see* UNITED STATES: Climate).

CONSTITUTION AND GOVERNMENT. The present constitution (the fourth) dates from 1897, and has had 51 amendments; it was not ratified by the electorate but promulgated by the Constitutional Convention. The General Assembly consists of a Senate of 21 members elected for 4 years and a House of Representatives of 41 members elected for 2 years.

The state sends 1 representative to Congress.

In the 1992 presidential election Clinton polled 126,054 votes; Bush, 102,313; Perot, 59,213.

The state capital is Dover. Delaware is divided into 3 counties.

Governor: Thomas R. Carper (D.), 1993–97 ($95,000).
Lieut.-Governor: Ruth Ann Minner (D.), ($40,700).
Secretary of State: Edward J. Freel (D.) ($85,600).

FINANCE. For the year ending 30 June 1994 total revenue was $1,448·9m., of which federal grants were $260·8m. Total expenditure, 1994, was $1,345·3m.

On 30 June 1994 the total debt was $577·7m.

Per capita income (1994) was $22,828.

NATURAL RESOURCES

Minerals. The mineral resources of Delaware are not extensive, consisting chiefly of clay products, stone, sand and gravel and magnesium compounds.

Agriculture. Delaware is mainly an industrial state, with agriculture as its main industry. There were 0·57m. acres in 2,500 farms in 1994; 0·48m. acres of this is harvested annually. The average farm was valued (land and buildings) at $580,936 in 1994. The major product is broilers, accounting for $459m. in cash receipts, out of total farm cash receipts of $660m. in 1994.

The chief field crops are soybeans and corn for feed.

INDUSTRY. In 1994 manufacturing establishments employed 63,700 people; main manufactures were chemicals, transport equipment and food.

COMMUNICATIONS

Roads. The state in 1994 maintained 4,993·56 miles of roads and streets including 1,587·25 miles of federally-aided highways. There were also 658·26 miles of municipal maintained streets. Vehicles registered in year ended 31 Dec. 1994, 618,074.

Railways. In 1994 the state had 288·5 miles of active rail line, 23·2 miles of which is part of Amtrak's high speed Northeast corridor. In 1994 there were 1,072,430 passenger trips beginning or ending in Delaware (597,390 intercity (Amtrak) and 475,040 commuter). 10·9m. tons of freight were carried.

Civil Aviation. Delaware had 9 airports, all of which were for general use in 1994.

SOCIAL INSTITUTIONS

Justice. State prisons, 30 Sept. 1994–30 Sept. 1995, had daily average of 4,623 inmates. The death penalty has been authorized; the last execution was in 1996.

Religion. Membership, 1979–80: Methodists, 60,489; Roman Catholics, 103,060; Episcopalians, 18,696; Lutherans, 10,000.

Education. The state has free public schools and compulsory school attendance. In Sept. 1994 the elementary and secondary public schools had 106,813 enrolled pupils and 6,366 classroom teachers. Another 23,968 children were enrolled in private and parochial schools. State appropriation for public schools (financial year 1994–95) was about $496·1m. Average salary of classroom teachers (financial year 1994–95), $39,076. The state supports the University of Delaware at Newark (1834) which had 901 full-time faculty members and 20,921 students in Sept. 1994, Delaware State University, Dover (1892), with 205 full-time faculty members and 3,381 students, and the 4 campuses of Delaware Technical and Community College (Wilmington, Stanton, Dover and Georgetown) with 244 full-time faculty members and 10,351 students.

Health. In 1995 there were 7 short-term general hospitals. During fiscal year 1995 the average daily census in state mental hospitals was 337.

Social Security. In 1974 the federal Supplemental Security Income (SSI) programme lessened state responsibility for the aged, blind and disabled. Total SSI payments in Delaware (1994 fiscal year), $33,852,316. Provisions are also made for the care of dependent children; in fiscal year 1994 there were 26,925 recipients in 10,073 families (average monthly payment per family, $300). The total state programme for the year ending 30 June 1994 was $36,292,952 for the care of dependent children.

Further Reading

Statistical information: Delaware Economic Development Office POB 1401, Dover 19903. Publishes *Delaware Data Book.*
State Manual, Containing Official List of Officers, Commissions and County Officers. Secretary of State, Dover. Annual
Hoffecker, C. E., *Delaware: a Bicentennial History.* New York, 1977
Smeal, L., *Delaware Historical and Biographical Index.* New York, 1984
Weslager, C. A., *Delaware Indians, a History.* Rutgers Univ. Press, 1972
Topical History of Delaware. Division of Historical and Cultural Affairs. Dover, 1977

DISTRICT OF COLUMBIA

KEY HISTORICAL EVENTS. The District of Columbia, organized in 1790, is the seat of the Government of the US, for which the land was ceded by the states of Maryland and Virginia to the US as a site for the national capital. It was established under Acts of Congress in 1790 and 1791. Congress first met in it in 1800 and federal authority over it became vested in 1801. In 1846 the land ceded by Virginia (about 33 sq. miles) was given back.

TERRITORY AND POPULATION. The District forms an enclave on the Potomac River, where the river forms the south-west boundary of Maryland. The land area of the District of Columbia is 61 sq. miles (159 sq. km).

Census population, 1 April 1990, was 606,900 (100% urban), a decrease of 4·82% from that of 1980. Metropolitan statistical area of Washington, D.C.–Md–Va. (1980), 3m. Density of population in the District, 1990, 9,884 per sq. mile. Population estimate (1993), 578,448. Births, 1991, in the District were 9,971 (17 per 1,000 population); deaths, 6,961 (11·9); infant deaths, 183 (18·7 per 1,000 live births); marriages, 5,031 (8·6); divorces, 2,290 (3·9).

Population in 5 census years was:

	White	*Black*	*Indian*	*Chinese and Japanese*	*Total*	*Per sq. mile*
1910	236,128	94,446	68	427	331,069	5,517·8
1930	353,981	132,068	40	780	486,869	7,981·5
1960	345,263	411,737	587	3,532	763,956	12,523·9
			All others			
1970	209,272	537,712	9,526		756,510	12,321·0
1980	171,768	448,906	17,659		638,333	10,184·0

CLIMATE. Washington. Jan. 34°F (1·1°C), July 77°F (25°C). Annual rainfall 43" (1,064 mm). The District of Columbia belongs to the Atlantic Coast climate zone (*see* UNITED STATES: Climate).

GOVERNMENT. Local government, from 1 July 1878 until Aug. 1967, was that of a municipal corporation administered by a board of 3 commissioners, of whom 2 were appointed from civil life by the President, and confirmed by the Senate, for a term of 3 years each. The other commissioner was detailed by the President from the Engineer Corps of the Army. The Commission form of government was abolished in 1967 and a new Mayor Council instituted with officers appointed by the President with the advice and consent of the Senate. On 24 Dec. 1973 the appointed officers were replaced by an elected Mayor and councillors, with full legislative powers in local matters as from 1974. Congress retains the right to legislate, to veto or supersede the Council's acts. The 23rd amendment to the federal constitution (1961) conferred the right to vote in national elections. The District has 2 delegates in Congress who may vote in committees but not on the House floor. In the 1992 presidential election Clinton polled 192,619 votes; Bush, 20,698; Perot, 9,681.

BUDGET. The District's revenues are derived from a tax on real and personal property, sales taxes, taxes on corporations and companies, licences for conducting various businesses and from federal payments.

The District of Columbia has no bonded debt not covered by its accumulated sinking fund.

INDUSTRY. The District's main industries are government service; services; wholesale and retail trade; finance, real estate, insurance, communications, transport and utilities.

TOURISM. About 17m. visitors stay in the District every year and spend about $1,000m.

COMMUNICATIONS

Roads. Within the District are 340 miles of bus routes. There are 1,102 miles of streets maintained by the District; of these, 673 miles are local streets, 262 miles are major arterial roads. In 1991, 246,390 motor vehicles were registered.

Railways. There is a metro in Washington extending to 130 km, and 2 commuter rail networks.

Civil Aviation. The District is served by 3 general airports; across the Potomac River in Arlington, Va., is National Airport, in Chantilly, Va., is Dulles International Airport and in Maryland is Baltimore—Washington International Airport.

SOCIAL INSTITUTIONS

Justice. The death penalty was declared unconstitutional in the District of Columbia on 14 Nov. 1973. In 1991 there were 10,095 prisoners in state correctional institutions.

The District's Court system is the Judicial Branch of the District of Columbia. It is the only completely unified court system in the United States, possibly because of the District's unique city-state jurisdiction. Until the District of Columbia Court Reform and Criminal Procedure Act of 1970, the judicial system was almost entirely in the hands of Federal Government. Since that time, the system has been similar in most respects to the autonomous systems of the states.

Religion. The largest churches are the Protestant and Roman Catholic Christian churches; there are also Jewish, Eastern Orthodox and Islamic congregations.

Education. In 1992 there were 80,092 pupils and 6,014 teachers in public secondary and elementary schools. State and local government expenditure on public schools, 1991, $721,495,000. Higher education is given through the Consortium of Universities of the Metropolitan Washington Area, which consists of six universities and three colleges: Georgetown University, founded in 1795 by the Jesuit Order; George Washington University, non-sectarian founded in 1821; Howard University, founded in 1867; Catholic University of America, founded in 1887; American University (Methodist) founded in 1893; University of D.C., founded 1976; Gallaudet College, founded 1864; Trinity College, founded 1897. There are altogether 18 institutes of higher education.

Social Security. The District government provides primary health care for residents, mainly through its Department of Human Services. In 1983 there were 17 hospitals with 8,700 beds. The welfare programme of aid to families with dependent children gave money to 55,900 recipients in 21,600 families in 1985; 4,100 aged and 11,600 disabled also received aid, total payments $43·8m.

Further Reading

Statistical Information: The Metropolitan Washington Board of Trade publications.
Reports of the Commissioners of the District of Columbia. Annual. Washington
Bowling, K. R., *The Creation of Washington D.C.: the Idea and the Location of the American Capital.* Washington (D.C.), 1991

FLORIDA

KEY HISTORICAL EVENTS. European men, probably Spaniards but possibly English, saw Florida for the first time in the period 1497–1512. John Cabot first charted the cape now called Florida in 1498. Juan Ponce de Leon sighted Florida on 27 March 1513. Going ashore between 2 and 8 April in the vicinity of what is now St Augustine, he named the land 'Pasqua de Flores' because his landing was 'in the time of the Feast of Flowers'. The first permanent settlement was Spanish and was made at St Augustine, 8 Sept. 1565; it is the oldest permanent settlement in the US. In 1763 Florida was ceded to England; back to Spain in 1783, and to the US in 1821. Florida became a Territory in 1821 and was admitted into the Union on 3 March 1845.

TERRITORY AND POPULATION. Florida is a peninsula bounded west by the Gulf of Mexico, south by the Straits of Florida, east by the Atlantic, north by Georgia and north-west by Alabama. Land area, 53,937 sq. miles (139,697 sq. km). Census population, 1 April 1990, 12,937,926, an increase of 32·8% since 1980. Estimate (1994), 13,834,040. Births in 1994 were 190,923; deaths, 147,261; infant deaths, 1,567; marriages, 142,895; divorces and other dissolutions, 81,628.

Population in 5 federal census years was:

	White	*Black*	*All Others*	*Total*	*Per Sq. Mile*
1950	2,166,051	603,101	2,153	2,771,305	51·1
1960	4,063,881	880,168	7,493	4,952,788	91·5
1970	5,719,343	1,041,651	28,449	6,789,443	125·6
1980	8,319,448	1,342,478	84,398	9,746,324	180·1
1990	10,749,285	1,759,534	429,107	12,937,926	238·9

Of the population in 1990, 84·8% were urban, 48·4% male and 73·8% were 20 years of age or over.

The largest cities in the state, 1990 census (and 1994) are: Jacksonville, 672,971 (676,718); Miami, 358,548 (365,498); Tampa, 280,015 (285,153); St Petersburg, 238,629 (241,563); Hialeah, 188,004 (203,911); Orlando, 164,693 (170,307); Fort Lauderdale, 149,377 (149,491); Tallahassee, 124,773 (137,057); Hollywood, 121,697 (125,342); Clearwater, 98,784 (101,162); Gainesville, 84,770 (96,052); Coral Springs, 79,443 (93,439); Miami Beach, 92,639 (91,775); Pembroke Pines, 65,452 (87,948); Cape Coral, 74,991 (85,807); West Palm Beach, (76,418); Plantation, (75,484); Lakeland, 70,576 (74,626); Pompano Beach, 72,411 (73,950).

Population of the largest metropolitan areas (1994): Tampa-St Petersburg-Clearwater, 2,163,509; Miami, 1,990,445; Orlando, 1,359,001; Fort Lauderdale, 1,340,220.

CLIMATE. Jacksonville. Jan. 55°F (12·8°C), July 81°F (27·2°C). Annual rainfall 54" (1,353 mm). Key West. Jan. 70°F (21·1°C), July 83°F (28·3°C). Annual rainfall 39" (968 mm). Miami. Jan. 67°F (19·4°C), July 82°F (27·8°C). Annual rainfall 60" (1,516 mm). Tampa. Jan. 61°F (16·1°C), July 81°F (27·2°C). Annual rainfall 51" (1,285 mm). Florida belongs to the Gulf Coast climate zone (*see* UNITED STATES: Climate).

CONSTITUTION AND GOVERNMENT. The 1968 Legislature revised the constitution of 1885. The state legislature consists of a Senate of 40 members, elected for 4 years, and House of Representatives with 120 members elected for 2 years. Sessions are held annually, and are limited to 60 days.

The state sends 23 representatives to Congress.

In the 1992 presidential election Bush polled 2,171,781 votes; Clinton, 2,071,651; Perot, 1,052,481.

The state capital is Tallahassee. The state is divided into 67 counties.

Governor: Lawton Chiles (D.), 1995–99 ($104,817).
Lieut.-Governor: Kenneth 'Buddy' MacKay (D.), ($100,403).
Secretary of State: Sandra Mortham (R.), ($103,757).

FINANCE. There is no state income tax on individuals. For the fiscal year 1993–94 the state had a total revenue of $33,215m. and total expenditure of $30,103m. General revenue fund expenditure was $27,653m.

Net long-term debt, 30 June 1994, amounted to $13,634m.

Per capita personal income (1994) was $21,651.

NATURAL RESOURCES

Minerals. Chief mineral is phosphate rock, of which marketable production in 1992 was 36·2m. tonnes. This was approximately 75% of US and 25% of the world supply of phosphate in 1992.

Agriculture. In 1994, area under crops, 3,937,292 acres; pasture and ranges, 6,324,067 acres. In 1995, there were 39,000 farms; net income per farm averaged $57,941. Total value of all farm land and buildings (1994), $25,297·6m. There were 10·3m. acres in farms and ranches in 1994, including 853,742 (of which 667,521 were orange) acres in citrus groves. Total cash receipts from crops and livestock (1994), $5,977·97m., of which crops provided $4,786·34m. Major crop contributors were oranges, grapefruit, tomatoes, peppers, other winter vegetables, indoor and landscaping plants and sugar-cane. Poultry farms produced 132·7m. chickens and 2,538m. eggs in 1994. On 1 Jan. 1995 the state had 2·02m. cattle, including 176,000 milch cows (1994), and about 0·1m. swine.

Forestry. The national forests area in 1994 was 1·1m. acres. There were 16,548,922 acres of commercial forest and 33 state forests of 596,137 acres.

Fisheries. Florida has extensive fisheries for oysters, shrimp, red snapper, crabs, mackerel and mullet. Catch (1990), 180m. lb. valued at $203m.

INDUSTRY. In 1994 there were 15,831 manufacturers. They employed 483,754 persons. The printing and publishing, machinery and computer equipment, apparel and finished products, fabricated metal products, and lumber and wood products industries are important.

TOURISM. During 1994, 39·8m. tourists visited Florida. They spent $33,390m. making tourism one of the biggest industries in the state. There were (1993) 148 state parks, 33 state forests, 3 national parks, 8 national memorials, monuments, seashores and preserves and 3 national forests. The state parks were visited by 11,586,999 people in 1992–93.

COMMUNICATIONS

Roads. The state (1993) had 0·11m. miles of highways, roads, and streets all of which were in the state and local system (67,903 miles being county roads); in 1992, 19,814·8 miles were federally-aided roads (1,444 miles interstate).

In 1992–93, there were 11,963,764 vehicle registrations.

Railways. In 1993 there were 2,988 miles of railway and 14 rail companies. There is a metro of 20 miles (33 km), a peoplemover and a commuter rail route in Miami.

Civil Aviation. In 1993 Florida had 133 public use airports (12 international) of which 20 have scheduled commercial service, and 28 seaplane bases.

SOCIAL INSTITUTIONS

Justice. The death penalty is authorized, and there have been 33 executions since 1979. State prisons, 1994, had 56,275 inmates. Chain gangs were introduced in 1995.

Religion. The main Christian churches are Roman Catholic, Baptist, Methodist, Presbyterian and Episcopalian. There were 0·1m. Mormons in 1995.

Education. Attendance at school is compulsory between 7 and 16.

In the 1994–95 school year the public elementary and secondary schools had 2,107,514 pupils enrolled in grades K–12. Total expenditure on public schools (1994) was $17,035m. The state maintains 28 community colleges, with a full-time equivalent enrolment of 192,698 in 1995.

There are 9 universities in the state system, with a total of 207,812 students in 1995: The University of Florida at Gainesville (founded 1853) with 39,417 students; the Florida State University (founded at Tallahassee in 1857) with 30,268; the University of South Florida at Tampa (founded 1960) with 36,146; Florida A. & M. University at Tallahassee (founded 1887) with 10,267; Florida Atlantic University (founded 1964) at Boca Raton with 18,240; the University of West Florida at Pensacola with 8,250; the University of Central Florida at Orlando with 26,555; the University of North Florida at Jacksonville with 10,463; Florida International University at Miami with 28,206.

Health. State-licensed general hospitals, 1993, numbered 325 with 61,302 beds.

Social Security. From 1974 aid to the aged, blind and disabled became a federal responsibility. The state continued to give aid to families with dependent children and general assistance. Monthly payments, 1991–92: Aid to 3,220 blind averaged $275·40; aid to 142,071 dependent children averaged $251·59; aid to 135,735 disabled averaged $260·17; aid to 82,161 aged averaged $194·04.

Further Reading

Statistical information: Bureau of Economic and Business Research, Univ. of Florida, Gainesville 32611. Publishes *Florida Statistical Abstract.*

Denslow, D. A. *et al., The Economy of Florida.* Florida Univ. Press, 1990

Fernald, E. A. (ed.) *Atlas of Florida.* Florida State Univ., 1981

Huckshorn, R. J. (ed.) *Government and Politics in Florida.* Florida Univ. Press, 1991

Morris, A., *The Florida Handbook.* Tallahassee. Biennial

Shermyen, A. H. (ed.), *1991 Florida Statistical Abstract.* Florida Univ. Press, 1991

State Library: Gray Building, Tallahassee.

GEORGIA

KEY HISTORICAL EVENTS. Georgia (so named from George II) was founded in 1733 as the 13th original colony; she became the 4th original state.

TERRITORY AND POPULATION. Georgia is bounded north by Tennessee and North Carolina, north-east by South Carolina, east by the Atlantic, south by Florida and west by Alabama. Land area, 58,910 sq. miles (152,577 sq. km). Census population, 1 April 1990, was 6,478,216 (63·2% urban), an increase of 18·56% since 1980. Population estimate (1994), 7,055,000. Births, 1993, were 110,489 (16·1 per 1,000 population); deaths, 56,038 (8·2); infant deaths, 1,150 (10·4 per 1,000 live births); marriages, 61,635 (9·0); divorces and annulments, 38,273 (5·6).

Population in 5 census years was:

	White	*Black*	*Indian*	*Asiatic*	*Total*	*Per sq. mile*
1910	1,431,802	1,176,987	95	237	2,609,121	44·4
1930	1,837,021	1,071,125	43	317	2,908,506	49·7

			All others		
1970	3,391,242	1,187,149	11,184	4,589,575	79·0
1980	3,948,007	1,465,457	50,801	5,464,265	92·7
1990	4,600,148	1,746,565	131,507	6,478,216	110·0

Of the 1990 population, 3,144,503 were male, 4,097,339 were urban and those 20 years of age and over numbered 4,534,963.

The largest cities are: Atlanta (capital), with population, 1990 census, of 394,017 (urbanized area, 2,833,511); Columbus, 179,278 (243,072); Savannah, 137,560 (242,622); Macon, 106,612 (281,103); Albany, 78,122 (112,561).

CLIMATE. Atlanta. Jan. 43°F (6·1°C), July 78°F (25·6°C). Annual rainfall 49" (1,234 mm). Georgia belongs to the Atlantic Coast climate zone (*see* UNITED STATES: Climate).

CONSTITUTION AND GOVERNMENT. A new constitution was ratified in the general election of 2 Nov. 1976, proclaimed on 22 Dec. 1976 and became effective 1 Jan. 1977. The General Assembly consists of a Senate of 56 members and a House of Representatives of 180 members, both elected for 2 years. Legislative sessions are annual, beginning the 2nd Monday in Jan. and lasting for 40 days.

Georgia was the first state to extend the franchise to all citizens 18 years old and above.

The state sends 11 representatives to Congress.

At the 1992 presidential election Clinton polled 1,002,433 votes; Bush, 985,682; Perot, 306,489.

The state capital is Atlanta. Georgia is divided into 159 counties.

Governor: Zell Miller (D.), 1995–99 ($91,092).
Lieut.-Governor: Pierre Howard (D.) ($59,145).
Secretary of State: Max Cleland (D.) ($72,966).

BUDGET. For the fiscal year ending 30 June 1995 revenue was $9,814m.; general expenditure was $9,785m.

Per capita personal income (1994), was $20,251.

NATURAL RESOURCES

Minerals. Georgia is the leading producer of kaolin. The state ranks first in production of crushed and dimensional granite, second in production of fuller's earth and marble (crushed and dimensional).

Agriculture. In 1995, 45,000 farms covered 12m. acres; average farm was of 267 acres. In 1994 the average value of farmland and buildings was $983 per acre. For 1994 cotton output was 1,537m. bales (of 480 lbs). Other major crops include tobacco, corn, wheat, soybeans, peanuts and pecans. Cash income, 1994, $5,000m.: from crops, $2,050m.; from livestock, $2,673m.

In 1995 farm animals included 1·56m. all cattle, 0·930m. swine and 1,005m. (1994) poultry.

Forestry. The forested area in 1994 was 24·1m. acres.

INDUSTRY. In 1994 the state's 10,523 manufacturing establishments had 573,643 workers; the main groups were textiles, apparel, food and transport equipment. Trade employed 804,475, services, 711,220, government, 552,526.

TOURISM. In 1994 tourists spent $12,330m. There are 44 state parks.

COMMUNICATIONS

Roads. In 1994 there were 110,794 miles of public roads, including 1,244 miles of interstate highways. In 1994 there were 6,556,500 motor vehicles registered.

Railways. In 1994 there were 5,059 miles of railways and a metro in Atlanta.

Civil Aviation. In 1995 there were 103 public airports, 9 with scheduled commercial service.

Shipping. There are deepwater ports at Savannah, the principal port, and Brunswick.

SOCIAL INSTITUTIONS

Justice. In 1994, state prisons had 33,383 inmates. The death penalty is authorized for capital offences.

Under a Local Option Act, the sale of alcoholic beverages is prohibited in some counties.

Religion. An estimated 57·6% of the population are church members. Of the total population, 45·6% are Protestant, 3·2% are Roman Catholic and 1·1% are Jewish.

Education. Since 1945 education has been compulsory; tuition is free for pupils between the ages of 6 and 18 years. In 1994 there were 1,766 public elementary and public secondary schools with 1·2m. pupils and 75,602 teachers. Teachers' salaries averaged $30,712 in 1994. Expenditure on public schools (1992–93), $5,277m. or $750 per capita and $4,115 per pupil.

The University of Georgia (Athens) was founded in 1785 and was the first chartered State University in the US (29,469 students in 1994–95). Other institutions of higher learning include Georgia Institute of Technology, Atlanta (12,901), Emory University, Atlanta (10,367), Georgia State University, Atlanta (23,776) and Mercer University, Macon (6,729). The Atlanta University Center, devoted primarily to Black education, includes Clark Atlanta University (5,128) and Morris Brown College (1,877) co-educational, Morehouse (3,005), a liberal arts college for men, Interdenominational Theological Center (387), a co-educational theological school, and Spelman College (2,028), the first liberal arts college for Black women in the US. Atlanta University serves as the graduate school centre for the complex. Wesleyan College (460) near Macon is the oldest chartered women's college in the US.

Health. In 1993, general hospitals licensed by the Department of Human Resources numbered 159 with 25,086 beds.

Social Security. In Dec. 1993, 47,024 persons were receiving SSI old-age assistance and 117,190 receiving benefits for blind and disabled persons. In 1994, there were 139,889 families receiving aid to dependent children.

Further Reading

Statistical information: Selig Center for Economic Growth, Univ. of Georgia, Athens 30602. Publishes *Georgia Statistical Abstract.*

Georgia History in Outline. Univ. of Georgia Press, Athens, 1978

Bonner, J. C. and Roberts, L. E. (eds.) *Studies in Georgia History and Government.* Reprint Company, Spartanburg, 1940 Repr.

Pound, M. B. and Saye, A. B., *Handbook on the Constitution of the U.S. and Georgia.* Univ. of Georgia Press, Athens, 1978

Rowland, A. R., *A Bibliography of the Writings on Georgia History.* Hamden, Conn., 1978

Saye, A. B., *A Constitutional History of Georgia, 1732–1968.* Univ. of Georgia, Athens, Rev. ed., 1970

State Library: Judicial Building, Capital Sq., Atlanta.

HAWAII

KEY HISTORICAL EVENTS. The Hawaiian Islands, formerly known as the Sandwich Islands, were discovered by Capt. James Cook in Jan. 1778. During the greater part of the 19th century the islands formed an independent kingdom, but in 1893 the reigning Queen, Liliuokalani (died 11 Nov. 1917), was deposed and a provisional government formed; in 1894 a Republic was proclaimed, and in accordance with the request of the Legislature of the Republic, and a resolution of the US Congress of 6 July 1898 (signed 7 July by President McKinley), the islands were on 12 Aug. 1898 formally annexed to the US. On 14 June 1900 the islands were constituted as the Territory of Hawaii.

Statehood was granted to Hawaii on 18 March 1959, effective 21 Aug. 1959.

TERRITORY AND POPULATION. The Hawaiian Islands lie in the North Pacific Ocean, between 18° 56' and 28° 25' N. lat. and 154° 49' and 178° 22' W. long., about 2,090 nautical miles south-west of San Francisco. There are 136 named islands and islets in the group, of which 7 major and 8 minor islands are inhabited. Land area, 6,423 sq. miles (16,636 sq. km). Census population, 1 April 1990, 1,108,229 (51% male, 89% urban), an increase of 14·84% since 1980; density was 172·5 per sq. mile. Estimated population (1993), 1,171,592.

The principal islands are Hawaii, 4,028 sq. miles and population, 1990, 120,317; Maui, 727 and 91,361; Oahu, 600 and 836,231; Kauai, 552 and 50,947; Molokai, 260 and 6,717; Lanai, 141 and 2,426; Niihau, 70 and 230; Kahoolawe, 45 (uninhabited). The capital Honolulu, on the island of Oahu, had a population in 1980 of 365,048 and Hilo on the island of Hawaii, 37,808 in 1990.

Figures for racial groups, 1980, were: 331,925 White, 239,734 Japanese, 132,075 Filipinos, 118,251 Hawaiian, 55,916 Chinese, 17,453 Korean, 17,687 Black, 51,650 all others. In 1989, 35% of the population (outside barracks and other institutions) was of mixed race. Of the total, 92·3% were citizens of the US.

Inter-marriage between the races is common. Of the 9,709 resident marriages in 1988, 42·9% were between partners of different race. Births, 1991, were 20,014 (17·5 per 1,000 population); deaths, 6,715 (5·9); infant deaths in 1992, 131 (6·5 per 1,000 live births); marriages, 17,669 (15·4); divorces and annulments, 5,134 (4·5).

CLIMATE. All the islands have a tropical climate, with an abrupt change in conditions between windward and leeward sides, most marked in rainfall. Temperatures vary little. Honolulu. Jan. 71°F (21·7°C), July 78°F (25·6°C). Annual rainfall 31" (775 mm).

CONSTITUTION AND GOVERNMENT. The constitution took effect on 21 Aug. 1959. Amended 1968 and 1978. The Legislature consists of a Senate of 25 members elected for 4 years, and a House of Representatives of 51 members elected for 2 years. The constitution provides for annual meetings of the legislature with 60-day regular sessions.

The state sends 2 representatives to Congress.

In the 1992 presidential election Clinton polled 179,310 votes; Bush, 136,822; Perot, 53,003.

The state capital is Honolulu. There are 5 counties.

Governor: Benjamin Cayetano (D.), 1994–98 ($94,780).
Lieut.-Governor: Mazie Hirono (D.) ($90,041).

BUDGET. Revenue is derived mainly from taxation of sales and gross receipts, real property, corporate and personal income, and inheritance taxes, licences, public land sales and leases. For the year ending 30 June 1990 state general fund receipts amounted to $3,841·8m. and federal grants, $610·4m. State expenditures were $3,546·7m. (education, $1,113·5m.; highways, $201·7m.; public welfare, $431·3m.).

Net long-term debt, 31 Dec. 1991, amounted to $4,202m.

Estimated *per capita* personal income (1994) was $24,057.

NATURAL RESOURCES

Minerals. Total value of non-fuel mineral production, 1991, $100m., mainly crushed stone ($48m.) and cement ($49m.).

Agriculture. Farming is highly commercialized, and highly mechanized. In 1991 there were about 5,000 farms with an acreage of 2m. Average number of acres per farm, 372. Sugar and pineapples are the staple crops. Farm income, 1991, from crop sales, was $489m., and from livestock and products $89m. The sugar crop was valued at $209·9m.; pineapples, $107·4m.; other crops, $168·2m. in 1988.

Forestry. In 1991 there were 1·7m. acres of forest and 0·7m. acres of timber land.

Fisheries. In fiscal year 1991 the commercial fish catch was 22m. lbs with a value of $53m. to primary producers. There were 4,043 fishermen.

INDUSTRY. In 1987 manufacturing establishments employed 15,300 production workers who earned an estimated $254·6m. Defence is the second-largest industry; US armed forces spent $1,892m. in Hawaii in 1988.

COMMERCE. In 1988 imports were $1,118m.; exports, $131m.

TOURISM. Tourism is outstanding in Hawaii's economy. Tourist arrivals numbered 1·1m. in 1967, and reached 6·1m. in 1988. Tourist expenditures, $380m. in 1967, contributed $10,900m. to the state's economy in 1989.

COMMUNICATIONS

Roads. In 1990 there were 4,082 miles of roads (2,663 miles rural). In 1991 there were 785,004 registered motor vehicles.

Civil Aviation. There were 7 commercial airports in 1990; passengers arriving from overseas in 1988 numbered 6·65m., and there were 9m. passengers between the islands.

Shipping. Several lines of steamers connect the islands with the mainland USA, Canada, Australia, the Philippines, China and Japan. In 1989, 2,024 overseas and 3,101 inter-island vessels entered the port of Honolulu.

Telecommunications. There were 530,022 telephone access lines at 31 Dec. 1988. In 1989, Hawaii had 47 commercial and 2 other radio stations, 17 commercial and 2 other TV stations.

SOCIAL INSTITUTIONS

Justice. There is no capital punishment in Hawaii. In 1991 there were 2,616 prisoners in state correctional institutions.

Religion. The residents are mainly Christians, though there are many Buddhists. A sample survey in 1979 showed that 31% were Roman Catholic, 34% Protestant, 12% Buddhist, 2·5% Latter Day Saints.

Education. Education is free, and compulsory for children between the ages of 6 and 18. The language in the schools is English. In 1988–89 there were 235 public schools and 141 private schools. In 1992, there were 174,249 pupils and 9,189 teachers in public elementary and secondary schools. In 1991 state and local government expenditure was $1,269m. The University of Hawaii-Manoa, founded in 1907, had 18,477 day students in 1988; total attendance at all campuses of the University of Hawaii system, 42,767; 9,612 at private colleges.

Social Security. During 1991, 5,646 people were receiving old-age assistance of an average $273 per month; 14,672 families, $590 in aid to dependent children; 8,005 disabled people, $372.

Further Reading

Statistical information: Hawaii State Department of Business, POB 2359, Honolulu 96804. Publishes *The State of Hawaii Data Book.*

Legislative Reference Bureau. *Guide to Government in Hawaii.* 8th ed. Honolulu, 1989

Atlas of Hawaii. Rev. ed. Hawaii Univ. Press, 1983

Bell, R. J., *Last Among Equals: Hawaiian Statehood and American Politics.* Honolulu, 1984

Kuykendall, R. S. and Day, A. G., *Hawaii: a History.* Rev. ed. New Jersey, 1961

Morgan, J. R., *Hawaii.* Boulder, 1982

Morris, N. J. and Dean, L. *Hawai'i* [Bibliography]. Santa Barbara and Oxford, 1992

IDAHO

KEY HISTORICAL EVENTS. Idaho was first permanently settled in 1860, although there was a mission for Indians in 1836 and a Mormon settlement in 1855. It was organized as a Territory in 1863 and admitted into the Union as a state on 3 July 1890.

TERRITORY AND POPULATION. Idaho is bounded north by Canada, east by the Rocky Mountains of Montana and Wyoming, south by Nevada and Utah, west by Oregon and Washington. Land area, 82,751 sq. miles (214,325 sq. km). Census population, 1 April 1990, 1,006,749 (57·4% urban), an increase of 6·65% since 1980. Population estimate (1993), 1,099,096. Births, 1991, 16,789 (16·2 per 1,000 population); deaths, 7,678 (7·4); marriages, 14,352 (13·8); divorces, 6,619 (6·4); infant deaths, 1992, 122 (7·0 per 1,000 live births).

Population in 5 census years was:

	White	*Black*	*Indian*	*Asiatic*	*Total*	*Per sq. mile*
1910	319,221	651	3,488	2,234	325,594	3·9
1930	438,840	668	3,638	1,886	445,032	5·4
1960	657,383	1,502	5,231	2,958	667,191	8·1
1980	901,641	2,716	10,521	5,948	943,935	11·3
1990	950,451	3,370	13,780	9,365	1,006,749	12·2

Of the total 1990 population, 500,956 were male, 578,214 were urban and those 20 years of age or older 665,889.

The largest cities are: Boise, with 1990 census population of 125,738; Pocatello, 46,117; Idaho Falls, 43,929; Nampa, 28,365; Lewiston, 28,082; Twin Falls, 27,591; Coeur d'Alene, 24,563.

CLIMATE. Boise. Jan. 29°F (–1·7°C), July 74°F (23·3°C). Annual rainfall 12" (303 mm). Idaho belongs to the Mountain States climate zone (*see* UNITED STATES: Climate).

CONSTITUTION AND GOVERNMENT. The constitution adopted in 1890 is still in force; it has had 105 amendments. The Legislature consists of a Senate of 35 members and a House of Representatives of 70 members, all the legislators being elected for 2 years. It meets annually.

The state sends 2 representatives to Congress.

In the 1992 presidential election Bush polled 202,645 votes, Clinton, 137,013; Perot, 130,395.

The state is divided into 44 counties. The capital is Boise.

Governor: Phil Batt (R.), 1995–99 ($85,000).
Lieut.-Governor: C. L. 'Butch' Otter (R.) ($22,500).
Secretary of State: Pete T. Cenarrusa (R.) ($67,500).

BUDGET. For the year ending 30 June 1993 general revenues were $1,028·3m. and general expenditures, $1,028·4m.

Per capita personal income (1994) was $18,231.

NATURAL RESOURCES

Minerals. Principal non-fuel minerals are phosphate rock, silver, gold, and sand and gravel. Value of total mineral output, 1992, was $338·6m.

Agriculture. Agriculture is the leading industry, although a great part of the state is naturally arid. Extensive irrigation works have been carried out, bringing an estimated 4m. acres under irrigation, and there are over 50 soil conservation districts.

In 1992 there were 21,000 farms with a total area of 13·5m. acres (25% of the land area); average value per acre (1995), $836. In 1991 average farm was 631 acres.

Farm income, 1991, from crops, $1,566m., and livestock, $1,099m. The most important crops are potatoes and wheat. Other crops are sugar-beet, alfalfa, barley, field peas and beans, onions and apples. In 1993 there were 1·68m. cattle, 230,000 sheep, 60,000 hogs and 1·22m. poultry.

Forestry. In 1990 a total of 21,818,000 acres was in forests.

INDUSTRY. In 1992 105,800 were employed in trade, 87,600 in government, 90,500 in services, 65,600 in manufacturing.

TOURISM. Money spent by travellers in 1991 was about $1,500m.

COMMUNICATIONS

Roads. In 1992 there were 61,317 miles of roads (58,911 miles rural) and 1,071,430 registered motor vehicles.

Railways. The state had (1991) 1,910 miles of railways (including 2 Amtrak routes).

Civil Aviation. There were 68 municipally owned airports in 1991.

Shipping. Water transport is provided from the Pacific to the port of Lewiston, by way of the Columbia and Snake rivers, a distance of 464 miles.

SOCIAL INSTITUTIONS

Justice. The death penalty may be imposed for first degree murder or aggravated kidnapping, but the judge must consider mitigating circumstances before imposing a sentence of death. The last execution was in 1994. The state prison system, Nov. 1992, had 2,483 inmates.

Religion. The leading religious denominations are the Church of Jesus Christ of Latter Day Saints (Mormon Church, 321,000 adherents in 1994), Roman Catholics, Methodists, Presbyterians, Episcopalians and Lutherans.

Education. In 1991–92, public elementary schools (grades K to 6) had 127,959 pupils and (1992–93) 6,234 teachers; secondary schools had 5,588 pupils and (1990–91) 5,138 classroom teachers.

Average salary, 1992–93, of elementary and secondary teachers, $27,011. The University of Idaho, founded at Moscow in 1889, in 1993 had 546 full-time instructional faculty, and a total enrolment of 11,543. There are 9 other institutions of higher education; 5 of them are public institutions with a total enrolment in autumn 1993 of 33,110 (excluding vocational-technical colleges).

Social Welfare. Old-age assistance is granted to persons 65 years of age and older if they meet needs qualifications. In 1992, 4,909 aged, blind or disabled persons received an average monthly payment of $116.94; aid to families with dependent children averaged $286.56 per month to 7,463 families with 13,439 children.

Health. In Sept. 1992 there were 3,463 licensed beds in hospitals and 5,727 in nursing homes.

Further Reading

Statistical information: Department of Commerce, 700 West State St., Boise 83720. Publishes *Idaho Facts.*

ILLINOIS

KEY HISTORICAL EVENTS. Illinois was first discovered by Joliet and Marquette, two French explorers, in 1673. In 1763 the country was ceded by the French to the British. In 1783 Great Britain recognized the United States' title to the land that became Illinois; it was organized as a Territory in 1809 and admitted into the Union on 3 Dec. 1818.

TERRITORY AND POPULATION. Illinois is bounded north by Wisconsin, northeast by Lake Michigan, east by Indiana, south-east by the Ohio River (forming the boundary with Kentucky), west by the Mississippi River (forming the boundary with Missouri and Iowa). Land area 55,646 sq. miles (144,123 sq.

km). Census population, 1990, 11,430,602 (84·6% urban), an increase of 0·36% since 1980. Population estimate (1993), 11,697,336. Births in 1991 were 17,233 (16·6 per 1,000 population); deaths, 104,389 (8·9); 1992, infant deaths under 1 year, 2,013 (10·4 per live births); marriages 100,632; divorces and annulments, 45,977.

Population in 5 census years was:

	White	*Black*	*Indian*	*All others*	*Total*	*Per sq. mile*
1910	5,526,962	109,049	188	2,392	5,638,591	100·6
1930	7,295,267	328,972	469	5,946	7,630,654	136·4

			All others		
1970	9,600,381	1,425,674	87,921	11,113,976	199·4
1980	9,233,327	1,675,398	517,793	11,426,518	203·0

	White	*Black*	*American Indian, Eskimo or Aleut*	*Asian or Pacific Islander*	*Other*	*Total*	*Per sq. mile*
1990	8,952,978	1,694,273	21,836	285,311	476,204	11,430,602	205·6

Of the total population in 1980, 5,537,737 were male, 9,518,039 persons were urban and 5,597,360 were 18 years of age or older.

The most populous cities with population (1992 estimate), are: Chicago, 2,768,483; Rockford, 141,679; Peoria, 113,983; Springfield, 106,429; Aurora, 105,929; Naperville, 91,928; Decatur, 84,273; Elgin, 81,108; Joliet, 78,917; Arlington Heights, 76,518.

Primary Metropolitan Statistical Area population, 1990 census: Chicago, 6,069,974; East St Louis, 588,995; Peoria, 339,172; Rockford, 283,719; Springfield, 189,550; Decatur, 117,206.

CLIMATE. Chicago. Jan. 28·0°F (–2·2°C), July 76·4°F (24·7°C) average mean. Average annual rainfall 37·38". Illinois belongs to the Great Lakes climate zone (*see* UNITED STATES: Climate).

CONSTITUTION AND GOVERNMENT. The present constitution became effective 1 July 1971. The General Assembly consists of a House of Representatives of 118 members, elected for 2 years and a Senate of 59 members who are divided into 3 groups; in one, they are elected for terms of 4 years, 4 years, and 2 years; in the next, for terms of 4 years, 2 years, and 4 years; and in the last, for terms of 2 years, 4 years, and 4 years. Sessions are annual. The state is divided into legislative districts, in each of which 1 senator is chosen; each district is divided into 2 representative districts, in each of which 1 representative is chosen.

The state sends 20 representatives to Congress.

In the 1992 presidential election Clinton polled 2,453,350 votes; Bush, 1,734,096; Perot, 840,575.

The capital is Springfield. The state has 102 counties.

Governor: Jim Edgar (R.), 1995–99 ($119,439).
Lieut.-Governor: Bob Kustra (R). ($84,310).
Secretary of State: George H. Ryan (R.) ($105,387).

BUDGET. For the year ending 30 June 1993 total revenues were $1,820m. and total expenditures were $1,860m.

Debt administration, 30 June 1993 (in $1m.): Outstanding general and special obligation bonds, 914 and 517; revenue bonds, 4,526; notes/general obligation certificates payable, 127; additional long-term obligations, 1,327.

Per capita personal income (1994) was $23,784.

NATURAL RESOURCES

Minerals. Chief mineral product is coal; 37 operative mines had an output (1993) of 42,143,821 tons. Mineral production also included: Crude petroleum, fluorspar, tripoli, lime, sand, gravel and stone; total estimated value in 1993, $2·1m.

Agriculture. In 1993, 80,000 farms had an area of 28·3m. acres; the average farm was 354 acres, and the average value of farmland and buildings per acre was $1,500.

Cash receipts, 1992, from crops, $5,431,346,000; from livestock and livestock products, $2,202,346,000. Illinois is a large producer of maize and soybeans, the state's leading cash commodities. Output, 1993: Soybeans, 374·19m. bu; wheat, 68·2m. bu; maize, 1,300m. bu. In Jan. 1993 there were 186,000 milch cows, 2m. cattle and calves; 105,000 sheep and lambs and 5·9m. swine. The wool clip was 681,000 lbs in 1993.

Forestry. National forest system land in 1990 was 264,000 acres. Gross area was 0·84m. acres. Total forest land, 4·29m. acres (1985).

INDUSTRY. In 1990 there were 272,738 establishments with 4,647,094 employees. The annual payroll was $107,724,031,000. Largest industries were services and non-electrical machinery. Gross state product, $291,900m.

LABOUR. In 1993 there were 5,316,000 employees, of whom 933,000 were in manufacturing, 1,245,000 in trade, 1,645,000 in services, 768,000 in government, 382,000 in finance, insurance and real estate and 0·31m. in transport, communications and utilities.

TOURISM. Tourism revenue in 1993 was $14,900m.

COMMUNICATIONS

Roads. In 1993 there were 6,548,939 passenger cars, 1,249,630 pickup trucks, 253,532 recreational vehicles, buses and trucks, 697,933 trailers and semi-trailers and 195,717 motor cycles registered in the state, and 120,473 Interstate Registration Plan vehicles. At 31 Dec. 1992 there were 13,298·35 miles of state primary roads, 3,519·6 miles of state supplementary roads and 284·72 miles of toll roads and toll bridges.

Railways. There were, in 1990, more than 7,000 miles of Class I railway. Chicago is served by Amtrak long-distance trains on several routes, and by a metro (CTA) system, and by 7 groups of commuter railways controlled by the Northeast Illinois Railroad Corporation (now called METRA).

Civil Aviation. There were (1993) 138 public airports, 662 restricted landing areas and 280 heliports.

Shipping. In 1992 the seaport of Chicago handled 7m. tons of cargo.

SOCIAL INSTITUTIONS

Justice. In June 1993 the inmate population in state prisons was 33,060. The death penalty is authorized, and executions began in 1990 following the US Supreme Courts reinstatement of capital punishment in 1976. The last execution took place in 1994.

A Civil Rights Act (1941), as amended, bans all forms of discrimination by places of public accommodation, including inns, restaurants, retail stores, railroads, aeroplanes, buses, etc., against persons on account of 'race, religion, colour, national ancestry or physical or mental handicap'; another section similarly mentions 'race or colour.'

The Fair Employment Practices Act of 1961, as amended, prohibits discrimination in employment based on race, colour, sex, religion, national origin or ancestry, by employers, employment agencies, labour organizations and others. These principles are embodied in the 1971 constitution.

The Illinois Human Rights Act (1979), prevents unlawful discrimination in employment, real property transactions, access to financial credit, and public accommodations, by authorizing the creation of a Department of Human Rights to enforce, and a Human Rights Commission to adjudicate, allegations of unlawful discrimination.

Religion. Among the larger religious denominations are: Roman Catholic (3·6m.), Jewish (257,000), Presbyterian Church, USA (0·2m.), Lutheran Church in America (0·2m.), Lutheran Church Missouri Synod (325,000), American Baptist (105,000), Disciples of Christ (75,000), and United Methodist (505,000), Southern Baptist (265,000), United Church of Christ (192,000), Church of Nazarene (50,000), Assembly of God (63,000).

Education. Education is free and compulsory for children between 7 and 16 years of age. In 1993–94 public school elementary enrolments were 1,355,890 pupils and (1992–93) 81,587 teachers; secondary enrolments, 537,187 pupils and (1992–93) 29,874 teachers. Enrolment (1993–94) in non-public schools was 317,102 pupils and 17,685 teachers elementary and 66,933 pupils and (1992–93) 3,930 teachers secondary. Total number of special education teachers (1992–93), 1,082. Public school teachers' salaries, 1993–94, averaged $39,473. Total enrolment in 184 institutions of higher education (autumn 1993) was 740,185.

Major colleges and universities (autumn 1993):

Founded	*Name*	*Place*	*Control*	*Enrolment*
1851	Northwestern University	Evanston	Independent	17,551
1857	Illinois State University	Normal	Public	20,610
1867	University of Illinois	Urbana/Champaign and Chicago	Public	64,357
1867	Chicago State University	Chicago	Public	9,507
1869	Southern Illinois University	Carbondale and Edwardsville	Public	35,074
1890	Loyola University	Chicago	Roman Catholic	14,361
1891	University of Chicago	Chicago	Independent	11,226
1895	Eastern Illinois University	Charleston	Public	11,395
1895	Northern Illinois University	DeKalb	Public	23,177
1897	Bradley University	Peoria	Independent	6,024
1899	Western Illinois University	Macomb	Public	12,877
1940	Illinois Institute of Technology	Chicago	Independent	7,027
1945	Roosevelt University	Chicago	Independent	6,587
1961	Northeastern Illinois University	Chicago	Public	10,306

Health. In 1992 there were 246 hospitals with 56,402 beds. At June 1993, 21 institutions served 18,456 patients.

Social Security. State-administered Supplemental Security Income (SSI) was paid to 189,355 recipients (monthly average) in financial year 1993; approximate total payments $773·87m.; medical payments, $3,109·58m. In 1992, aid to families with dependent children was paid to 232,419 families, average monthly payment per family, $312·53; total payments, $1,581·7m.; medical payments, $709·9m.

Further Reading

Statistical information: Department of Commerce and Community Affairs, 620 Adams St., Springfield 62701. Publishes *Illinois State and Regional Economic Data Book.* Bureau of Economic and Business Research, Univ. of Illinois, 1206 South 6th St., Champaign 61820. Publishes *Illinois Statistical Abstract.*

Blue Book of the State of Illinois. Edited by Secretary of State. Springfield. Biennial

Angle, P. M. and Beyer, R. L., *A Handbook of Illinois History.* Illinois State Historical Society, Springfield, 1943

Clayton, J., *The Illinois Fact Book and Historical Almanac 1673–1968.* Southern Illinois Univ., 1970

Howard, R. P., *Illinois: A History of the Prairie State.* Grand Rapids, 1972.—*Mostly Good and Competent Men: Illinois Governors, 1818–1988.* Springfield, 1989

Pease, T. C., *The Story of Illinois.* 3rd ed. Chicago, 1965

The Illinois State Library: Springfield, Il.62756.

INDIANA

KEY HISTORICAL EVENTS. Indiana, first settled in 1732–33, was made a Territory in 1800 and admitted into the Union on 11 Dec. 1816.

TERRITORY AND POPULATION. Indiana is bounded west by Illinois, north by Michigan and Lake Michigan, east by Ohio and south by Kentucky across the Ohio River. Land area, 35,870 sq. miles (92,903 sq. km). Census population, 1 April 1990, was 5,544,159 (64·9% urban), an increase of 0·98% since 1980. Population estimate (1994), 5,752,151. In 1993 live births were 83,665 (15 per 1,000 population); deaths, 51,975 (9·0); infant deaths (under 1 year) in 1992, 795 (9·4 per 1,000 live births); marriages (1992), 50,480 (8·9).

Population in 5 census years was:

	White	*Black*	*Indian*	*Asiatic*	*Total*	*Per sq. mile*
1930	3,125,778	111,982	285	458	3,238,503	89·4
1960	4,388,554	269,275	948	2,447	4,662,498	128·9
			All others			
1970	4,820,324	357,464	15,881		5,193,669	143·9
1980	5,004,394	414,785	71,045		5,490,224	152·8
1990	5,020,700	432,092	91,367		5,544,159	154·6

Of the total in 1990, 2,688,281 were male and 3,545,431 were 21 years of age or older.

The largest cities with census population, 1990, are: Indianapolis (capital), 741,952; Fort Wayne, 173,072; Evansville, 126,272; Gary, 116,646; South Bend, 105,511; Hammond, 84,236; Muncie, 71,035; Bloomington, 60,633; Anderson, 59,459; Terre Haute, 57,483.

CLIMATE. Indianapolis. Jan. 29°F (–1·7°C), July 76°F (24·4°C). Annual rainfall 41" (1,034 mm). Indiana belongs to the Mid-West climate zone (*see* UNITED STATES: Climate).

CONSTITUTION AND GOVERNMENT. The present constitution (the second) dates from 1851; it has had (as of Nov. 1983) 34 amendments. The General Assembly consists of a Senate of 50 members elected for 4 years, and a House of Representatives of 100 members elected for 2 years. It meets annually.

In the 1992 presidential election Bush polled 989,375 votes; Clinton, 848,420; Perot, 455,934.

The state sends 10 representatives to Congress.

The state capital is Indianapolis. The state is divided into 92 counties and 1,008 townships.

Governor: Evan Bayh (D.), 1993–97 ($77,200).
Lieut.-Governor: Frank O'Bannon (D.) ($64,000).
Secretary of State: Sue Ann Gilroy (R.) ($46,000).

BUDGET. In the fiscal year 1991 total revenues were $12,288,307,000, ($6,182,409,000 from taxes); total expenditures were $11,547,519,000 ($4,404,473,000 for education, $2,271,725,000 for public welfare and $1,044,286,000 for highways). Revenue from Federal Government, 1993, $3,732,487,000.

Total long-term debt, on 30 June 1991, was $4,624m.

Per capita personal income (1994) was $20,378.

NATURAL RESOURCES

Minerals. The state produced 36,862,000 metric tons of crushed stone and 155.62m. metric tons of dimension stone in 1993; the output of coal was 36·3m. short tons in 1990. Value of non-fuel mineral production, 1991, $403·29m.

Agriculture. Indiana is largely agricultural, about 75% of its total area being in farms. In 1992, 62,778 farms had 15,618,831 acres (average, 249 acres, average market value, $1,395 per acre). Cash income, 1992, from crops, including nursery and greenhouse crops, $2,698,335,000; from livestock, poultry and their products, $1,934,755,000. Acreage harvested in 1992 was 11·83m., with a market value of $4,633m.

The chief crops (1992) were corn for grain or seed (805,637,216 bu.), corn for silage or green crop (1,944,771 tons), wheat for grain (25,048,728 bu.), oats for grain (2,603,270 bu.), soybeans for beans (195,049,717 bu.), hay (alfalfa, other tame small grain, wild, grass silage, etc.) (1,712,613 tons, dry).

The livestock on 1 Jan. 1992 included 1,113,473 all cattle, 144,532 milch cows, 72,386 sheep and lambs, 4,618,663 hogs and pigs, 22,256,785 chickens, 12,648,219 turkeys. In 1992 the wool clip yielded 440,768 lbs of wool from 65,775 sheep and lambs.

Forestry. In 1990 there were 4·56m. acres of forest and (1995) 9 state forests (145,000 acres) and Hoosier National Forest (192,000 acres).

INDUSTRY. In 1993, 9,440 manufacturing establishments employed 636,495 workers, earning $20,690,996,000. The steel industry is the largest in the country.

COMMUNICATIONS

Roads. In 1992 there were 92,054 miles of road (72,945 miles rural). In 1993 there were 4,953,250 registered motor vehicles.

Railways. In 1989 there were 3,796 miles of mainline railway and 861·5 miles of secondary track.

Civil Aviation. Of airports, 1990, 115 were for public use and 486 were for private use.

SOCIAL INSTITUTIONS

Justice. Following the US Supreme Court's reinstatement of the death penalty in 1976, death sentences have been awarded since 1980. State correctional institutions, financial year 1987–88, had an average daily population of 11,889.

The Civil Rights Act of 1885 forbids places of public accommodation to bar any persons on grounds not applicable to all citizens alike; no citizen may be disqualified for jury service 'on account of race or colour'. An Act of 1947 makes it an offence to spread religious or racial hatred.

A 1961 Act provided 'all ... citizens equal opportunity for education, employment and access to public conveniences and accommodations' and created a Civil Rights Commission.

Religion. Religious denominations include Methodists, Roman Catholic, Disciples of Christ, Baptists, Lutheran, Presbyterian churches, Society of Friends.

Education. School attendance is compulsory from 7 to 16 years. In autumn 1993 public and parochial schools and nursery schools had 965,599 pupils and 55,107 teachers. Teachers' salaries averaged $36,516 (1994–95). Total expenditure for public schools, 1992–93, $4,797,946,000.

The principal institutions for higher education are (1989–90):

Founded	*Institution*	*Control*	*Students (full-time)*
1801	Vincennes University	State	10,139
1824	Indiana University, Bloomington	State	34,863
1837	De Pauw University, Greencastle	Methodist	2,415
1842	University of Notre Dame	R.C.	9,700
1850	Butler University, Indianapolis	Independent	4,187
1859	Valparaiso University, Valparaiso	Evangelical Lutheran Church	3,858
1870	Indiana State University, Terre Haute	State	12,005
1874	Purdue University, Lafayette	State	35,817
1898	Ball State University, Muncie	State	18,993
1902	University of Indianapolis, Indianapolis	Methodist	3,119
1963	Indiana Vocational Technical College, Indianapolis	State	5,117
1985	University of Southern Indiana	State	5,713

Health. Hospitals listed by the Indiana State Board of Health (1989) numbered 145, with 27,650 beds. In 1993 there were 3,568 patients in state mental hospitals.

Social Security. In 1994, under the Federal SSI programme and federally administered State Supplementary programme, payments to 15,546 aged persons, 56,502 disabled adults and 18,305 disabled children totalled $27·97m.

Further Reading

Statistical information: Indiana Business Research Center, Indiana Univ., Indianapolis 46202. Publishes *Indiana Factbook.*

Gray, R. D. (ed.) *Indiana History: a Book of Readings.* Indiana Univ. Press, 1994

Martin, J. B., *Indiana: an Interpretation.* Indiana Univ. Press, 1992

State Library: Indiana State Library, 140 North Senate, Indianapolis 46204.

IOWA

KEY HISTORICAL EVENTS. Iowa, first settled in 1788, was made a Territory in 1838 and admitted into the Union on 28 Dec. 1846.

TERRITORY AND POPULATION. Iowa is bounded east by the Mississippi River (forming the boundary with Wisconsin and Illinois), south by Missouri, west by the Missouri River (forming the boundary with Nebraska), northwest by the Big Sioux River (forming the boundary with South Dakota) and north by Minnesota. Land area, 55,875 sq. miles (144,716 sq. km). Census population, 1 April 1990, 2,776,755 (60·6% urban), a decrease of 4·7% since 1980. Population estimate (1995), 2,842,000. Births, 1994, 37,057; deaths, 27,651; infant deaths, 273; marriages, 22,924; dissolutions of marriages, 10,885.

Population in 5 census years was:

	White	*Black*	*Indian*	*Asiatic*	*Total*	*Per sq. mile*
1870	1,188,207	5,762	48	3	1,194,020	21·5
1930	2,452,677	17,380	660	222	2,470,939	44·1
1960	2,728,709	25,354	1,708	1,022	2,757,537	49·2
			All others			
1970	2,782,762	32,596	10,010		2,825,368	50·5
1980	2,839,225	41,700	32,882		2,913,808	51·7
1990	2,683,090	48,090	45,575		2,776,755	49·7

At the census of 1990, 1,344,802 were male, 1,683,065 were urban and 2,057,875 were 18 years of age or older.

The largest cities in the state, with their estimated population in 1994 are: Des Moines (capital), 193,965; Cedar Rapids, 113,438; Davenport, 96,964; Sioux City, 82,735; Waterloo, 66,537; Iowa City, 60,655; Dubuque, 59,084; Council Bluffs, 54,850; Ames, 46,562; Cedar Falls, 33,908; Clinton, 28,966; Mason City, 28,817; Burlington, 27,537; Fort Dodge, 25,299; Ottumwa, 24,629.

CLIMATE. Cedar Rapids. Jan. 23·7°F, July 72·6°F. Annual rainfall 34". Des Moines. Jan. 22·6°F, July 72·4°F. Annual rainfall 32·1". Iowa belongs to the Mid-West climate zone (*see* UNITED STATES: Climate).

CONSTITUTION AND GOVERNMENT. The constitution of 1857 still exists; it has had 45 amendments. The General Assembly comprises a Senate of 50 and a House of Representatives of 100 members, meeting annually for an unlimited session. Senators are elected for 4 years, half retiring every second year: Representatives for 2 years. The Governor and Lieut.-Governor are elected for 4 years. The state is represented in Congress by 5 representatives. Iowa is divided into 99 counties; the capital is Des Moines.

In the 1992 presidential election Clinton polled 586,353 votes; Bush, 504,891; Perot, 253,468.

Governor: Terry Branstad (R.), 1995–99 ($76,700).
Lieut.-Governor: Joy Corning (R.), ($60,000).
Secretary of State: Paul Pate (R.) ($60,000).

BUDGET. For fiscal year 1994-95 state tax revenue was $3,819m. General fund expenditures were $2,134·8m. for education, $801·7m. for health and human services, and $111·2m. for economic development, transportation and commerce.

On 30 June 1994 the net general long-term debt was $233·3m.

Per capita personal income (1994) was $20,265.

NATURAL RESOURCES

Minerals. Production in 1994: Crushed stone, 31m. tons; sand and gravel, 18·5m. tons; gypsum, 2,175,000 tonnes; cement, 2,504,000 tonnes; coal, 33,173 short tons. The value of mineral products in 1994 was $424·4m.

Agriculture. Iowa is the wealthiest of the agricultural states, partly because nearly the whole area (92·8%) is arable and included in farms. Large-scale commercial farming has not developed; the average farm at 1 June 1995 was 332 acres.

Cash receipts from farm markets (1994) were $10,071,325,000; from livestock, $5,119,889,000, and from crops, $4,951,436,000. Production of corn was 1,930m.[1] bu., value $2,640m. and soybeans, 442·9m.[1] bu., value $2,392·9m. In 1995 livestock included swine, 14·5m.[1]; milch cows, 265,000; all cattle, 4·25m., and sheep and lambs, 294,000. The wool clip (1994) yielded 1·64m. lbs of wool.

[1] More than any other state.

LABOUR. In 1994 manufacturing establishments employed 251,600 people; trade, 340,400; services, 343,500.

COMMUNICATIONS

Roads. On 1 Jan. 1995 there were 113,008 miles of streets and highways. In 1994 there were 1,896,518 licensed drivers and 3,224,016 registered vehicles.

Railways. The state, as of 31 Dec. 1995, had 4,326 miles of track, 5 Class I, 3 Class II and 14 Class III railways.

Civil Aviation. Airports (1995), numbered 236, which consisted of 104 publicly-owned, 122 privately-owned (of which 7 were for public use) and 10 commercial facilities. As of 31 Dec. 1995 there were 2,250 private aircraft registered.

SOCIAL INSTITUTIONS

Justice. There is now no capital punishment in Iowa. State prisons, 1995, had 5,906 inmates.

Religion. Chief religious bodies: Roman Catholic, (1994–95) 509,541 members; United Methodists, (1994) 203,243; Evangelical Lutheran in America, (1994) 266,546 baptised members; USA Presbyterians, (1994) 63,073; United Church of Christ, (1994) 43,957.

Education. School attendance is compulsory for 24 consecutive weeks annually during school age (7–16). In 1994–95, 500,592 pupils were attending primary and secondary schools; 47,137 pupils attending non-public schools; classroom teachers numbered 31,883 for public schools with average salary of $31,511. In 1994–95 the state spent an average $5,139 on each elementary and secondary school student. Leading institutions for higher education (1995) were:

Founded	*Institution*	*Control*	*Full-time Professors* [1]	*Students*
1843	Clarke College, Dubuque	Independent	10	927
1846	Grinnell College, Grinnell	Independent	42	1,243
1847	University of Iowa, Iowa City	State	398	28,000
1851	Coe College, Cedar Rapids	Independent	27	1,200
1852	Wartburg College, Waverly	Evangelical Lutheran	26	1,450
1853	Cornell College, Mount Vernon	Independent	29	1,100
1858	Iowa State University, Ames	State	316	25,263
1876	Univ. of Northern Iowa, Cedar Falls	State	161	13,045
1881	Drake University, Des Moines	Independent	100	5,800
1894	Morningside College, Sioux City	Methodist	20	1,400

[1] 1992–93.

Health. In 1995, the state had 120 community hospitals (11,604 beds).

Social Security. Iowa has a Civil Rights Act (1939) which makes it a misdemeanour for any place of public accommodation to deprive any person of 'full and equal enjoyment' of the facilities it offers the public.

Supplemental Security Income (SSI) assistance is available for the aged (65 or older), the blind and the disabled. As of June 1995, 6,168 elderly persons were drawing an average of $151.76 per month, 1,026 blind persons $321 per month, and 34,586 disabled persons $333·53 per month. As of July 1995, aid to dependent children (ADC) was received by 34,806 cases representing 95,768 recipients.

Further Reading

Statistical Information: Iowa Department of Economic Development Research Bureau, 200 East Grand Ave., Des Moines 50309. Publishes *Statistical Profile of Iowa.*
Annual Survey of Manufactures. US Department of Commerce
Government Finance. US Department of Commerce
Official Register. Secretary of State. Des Moines. Biennial
Petersen, W. J., *Iowa History Reference Guide.* Iowa City, 1952
Smeal, L., *Iowa Historical and Biographical Index.* New York, 1984
Vexler, R. I., *Iowa Chronology and Factbook.* Oceana, 1978

State Library of Iowa: Des Moines 50319.

KANSAS

KEY HISTORICAL EVENTS. Kansas, settled in 1727, was made a Territory (along with part of Colorado) in 1854, and was admitted into the Union with its present area on 29 Jan. 1861.

TERRITORY AND POPULATION. Kansas is bounded north by Nebraska, east by Missouri, with the Missouri River as boundary in the north-east, south by Oklahoma and west by Colorado. Land area, 81,823 (211,922 sq. km). Census population, 1 April 1990, 2,477,574 (69·1% urban), an increase of 4·84% since 1980. Population estimate (1993), 2,530,746. Vital statistics, 1991: Births, 37,300 (14·6 per 1,000 population); deaths, 22,511 (8·8); infant deaths (1992), 316 (8·6 per 1,000 live births); marriages, 22,074 (8·7); divorces 13,897 (5·5).

Population in 5 federal census years was:

	White	*Black*	*Indian*	*Asiatic*	*Total*	*Per sq. mile*
1870	346,377	17,108	914	—	364,399	4·5
1930	1,811,997	66,344	2,454	204	1,880,999	22·9
1960	2,078,666	91,445	5,069	2,271	2,178,611	26·3
			All others			
1970	2,122,068	106,977	17,533		2,249,071	27·5
1980	2,168,221	126,127	69,888		2,364,236	28·8

Of the total population in 1980, 1,156,941 were male, 1,575,899 were urban and those 20 years of age or older numbered 1,620,368.

Cities, with 1990 census population: Wichita, 304,011; Kansas City, 149,767; Topeka (capital), 119,883; Overland Park, 111,790; Lawrence, 65,608; Olathe, 63,352.

CLIMATE. Dodge City. Jan. 29°F (–1·7°C), July 78°F (25·6°C). Annual rainfall 21" (518 mm). Kansas City. Jan. 30°F (–1·1°C), July 79°F (26·1°C). Annual rainfall 38" (947 mm). Topeka. Jan. 28°F (–2·2°C), July 78°F (25·6°C). Annual rainfall 35" (875 mm). Wichita. Jan. 31°F (–0·6°C), July 81°F (27·2°C). Annual rainfall 31" (777 mm). Kansas belongs to the Mid-West climate zone (*see* UNITED STATES: Climate).

CONSTITUTION AND GOVERNMENT. The year 1861 saw the adoption of the present constitution; it has had 78 amendments. The Legislature includes a

Senate of 40 members, elected for 4 years, and a House of Representatives of 125 members, elected for 2 years. Sessions are annual.

The state sends 4 representatives to Congress.

In the 1992 presidential election Bush polled 449,951 votes; Clinton, 390,434; Perot, 312,358.

The capital is Topeka. The state is divided into 105 counties.

Governor: Bill Graves (R.), 1995–99 ($80,340).
Lieut.-Governor: Sheila Frahm (D.) ($81,600).
Secretary of State: Ron Thornburgh (R.) ($62,412).

BUDGET. For the year ending 30 June 1991 general revenue was $5,249m. General expenditures were $5,126m.

Per capita personal income (1994) was $20,896.

NATURAL RESOURCES

Minerals. Important fuel minerals are coal, petroleum and natural gas. Non-fuel minerals, mainly cement, salt and crushed stone, were worth $366·5m. in 1990.

Agriculture. Kansas is pre-eminently agricultural, but sometimes suffers from lack of rainfall in the west. In 1991 there were some 69,000 farms with a total acreage of 48m. Average number of acres per farm was 694. 21·71m. acres were harvested, with a farm value of $2,529m. Average value of farmland and buildings per acre, in 1995, was $535. Farm income, 1991, from livestock and products, $4,731. Chief crops: Wheat, sorghum, maize, hay. Wheat production was 472m. bu. in 1990. There is an extensive livestock industry, comprising, in 1990, 5·7m. cattle, 887,000 sheep, 1·45m. pigs and 1·4m. poultry.

INDUSTRY. Employment distribution (1985): Total workforce 975,000, of which 245,000 were in trade; 191,000 in government; 187,000 in services; 174,000 in manufacturing; 65,000 in transport and utilities; 53,000 in finance, insurance and real estate; 44,000 in construction. The slaughtering industry, other food processing, aircraft, the manufacture of transport equipment and petroleum refining are important.

COMMUNICATIONS

Roads. In 1990 there were 133,156 miles of roads (124,169 miles rural). In 1991 there were 1,879,442 registered motor vehicles.

Railways. There were 7,273 miles of railway in Jan. 1982.

Civil Aviation. There is an international airport at Wichita.

SOCIAL INSTITUTIONS

Justice. There were 5,607 prisoners in state institutions, 30 June 1991. The death penalty is not authorized.

Religion. The most numerous religious bodies are Roman Catholic, Methodists and Disciples of Christ.

Education. In 1992 there were 445,774 public elementary and secondary pupils and 30,808 teachers. There were 20 independent colleges, 20 community colleges, 2 Bible colleges, 1 municipal university in 1992.

Kansas has 6 state-supported institutions of higher education: Kansas State University, Manhattan (1863); The University of Kansas, Lawrence, founded in 1865; Emporia State University, Emporia; Pittsburg State University, Pittsburg; Fort Hays State University, Hays and Wichita State University, Wichita. The state also supports a two-year technical school, Kansas Technical Institute, at Salina.

Education expenditure by state and local governments in 1991 was $3,080·5m.

Health. In 1983 the state had 165 hospitals (18,300 beds) listed by the American Hospital Association; hospitals had an average daily occupancy rate of 70·3%.

Social Security. In Dec. 1985, 20,900 persons received state and federal aid under programmes of aid to the aged or disabled, and 66,800 in 22,700 families received aid to dependent children. Average monthly payment to the aged, $121; the disabled, $206, per family with dependent children, $303 (1984).

Further Reading

Statistical information: Institute for Public Policy and Business Research, Univ. of Kansas, 607 Blake Hall, Lawrence 66045. Publishes *Kansas Statistical Abstract.*
Annual Economic Report of the Governor. Topeka
Drury, J. W., *The Government of Kansas.* Lawrence, Univ. of Kansas, 1970
Zornow, W. F., *Kansas: A History of the Jayhawk State.* Norman, Okla., 1957

State Library: Kansas State Library, Topeka.

KENTUCKY

KEY HISTORICAL EVENTS. Kentucky, first settled in 1765, was originally part of Virginia; it was admitted into the Union on 1 June 1792 and its first legislature met on 4 June.

TERRITORY AND POPULATION. Kentucky is bounded in the north by the Ohio River (forming the boundary with Illinois, Indiana and Ohio), north-east by the Big Sandy River (forming the boundary with West Virginia), east by Virginia, south by Tennessee and west by the Mississippi River (forming the boundary with Missouri). Land area, 39,732 sq. miles (102,907 sq. km). Census population, 1990, 3,685,296 (51·8% urban), an increase of 0·7% since 1980. Population estimate (1994), 3,826,794. Births in 1994, 52,900 (13·8 per 1,000 population); deaths, 36,919 (9·6); infant deaths, 393 (7·4 per 1,000 live births); marriages, 47,063 (12·3); divorces, 21,777 (5·7).

Population in 5 census years was:

	White	*Black*	*All others*	*Total*	*Per sq.mile*
1930	2,388,364	226,040	185	2,614,589	65·1
1950	2,742,090	201,921	795	2,944,806	73·9
1960	2,820,083	215,949	2,124	3,038,156	76·2
1980	3,379,006	259,477	22,294	3,660,777	92·3
1990	3,391,832	262,907	30,557	3,685,296	92·8

Of the total population in 1990, 1,785,235 were male and 1,136,272 were 21 years old or older.

The principal cities with census population in 1990 are: Louisville, 269,555 (urbanized area, 654,870); Lexington-Fayette, 225,336; Owensboro, 53,577; Covington, 43,646; Bowling Green, 41,688; Hopkinsville, 29,818; Paducah, 27,256; Frankfort (capital), 25,535; Henderson, 25,945.

CLIMATE. Kentucky is in the Appalachian Mountains climatic zone (*see* UNITED STATES: Climate). It has a temperate climate. Temperatures are moderate during both winter and summer, precipitation is ample without a pronounced dry season, and winter snowfall amounts are variable. Lexington. Jan. 33°F (0·6°C), July 76°F (24·4°C). Annual rainfall 43" (1,079 mm). Louisville. Jan. 34°F (1·1°C), July 78°F (25·6°C). Annual rainfall 43" (1,079 mm).

CONSTITUTION AND GOVERNMENT. The constitution dates from 1891; there had been 3 preceding it. The 1891 constitution was promulgated by convention and provides that amendments be submitted to the electorate for ratification. The General Assembly consists of a Senate of 38 members elected for 4 years, one half retiring every 2 years, and a House of Representatives of 100 members elected for 2 years. It has biennial sessions. All citizens of 18 or over are qualified as electors. Registered voters, May 1995, 2,248,246. In the 1992 presidential election Clinton polled 661,059 votes; Bush, 617,419; Perot, 203,587.

The state sends 6 representatives to Congress.

The capital is Frankfort. The state is divided into 120 counties.

Governor: Paul E. Patton (D.), 1995–99 ($88,645).
Lieut.-Governor: Steve D. Henry (D.) ($75,374).
Secretary of State: John Y. Brown III (D.) ($75,374).

BUDGET. For the fiscal year ending 30 June 1995 revenues received within the five major operating funds amounted to $10,631·9m. Included in this figure are $5,154·1m. General Fund revenues and $2,927·1m. Federal Fund revenues. Total expenditures amounted to $9,731·8m. including education, $2,729·4m.; human resources benefits payments, $2,375·1m.; and transport, $691·6m.

The general obligation bonded indebtedness on 30 June 1995 was nil.

Per capita personal income (1994) was $17,753.

NATURAL RESOURCES

Minerals. The principal mineral is coal: 161m. short tons were mined in 1994, value $4,021·7m. Output of petroleum, 4m. bbls (of 42 gallons); natural gas, 73,081m. cu. ft; stone, 53·5m. short tons, value $256·8m.; clay, 0·76m. tonnes, value $3m.; sand and gravel, 8·9m. short tons, value $35·6m. Total value of non-fuel mineral products in 1994 was $431·29m. Other minerals include fluorspar, ball clay, lead, zinc, silver, cement and lime.

Agriculture. In 1995, 89,000 farms had an area of 14m. acres. The average farm was 157 acres. In 1995 the average value of farmland and buildings per acre was $1,250.

Cash income, 1994, from crops, $1,584·8m., and from livestock, $1,645·4m. The chief crop is tobacco: Production, in 1994, 420m. lbs, ranking second to North Carolina in the USA. Other principal crops include corn, soybeans, wheat, hay, fruit and vegetables, sorghum grain and barley.

Stock-raising is important in Kentucky, which has long been famous for its horses. The livestock in 1995 included 165,000 milch cows, 2·65m. cattle and calves, 27,000 sheep, 0·78m. swine.

Forestry. Total forest area, 1988, 12·7m. acres. Total commercial forest land, 1988, 12·3m. acres; 93% was privately owned.

INDUSTRY. In 1994 the state's approximately 4,400 manufacturing plants had 238,600 production workers; value added by manufacture in 1991 was $23,713·8m. The leading manufacturing industries (by employment) are apparel, industrial machinery, electrical machinery, and transportation equipment.

TOURISM. In 1994 tourist expenditure was $7,095m., producing over $731·6m. in tax revenues and generating 144,691 jobs. The state had (1994) 927 hotels and motels, 253 camping grounds and 48 state parks.

COMMUNICATIONS

Roads. In 1995 the state had about 73,000 miles of federal, state and local roads. There were 2·9m. motor vehicle registrations in 1994.

Railways. In 1995 there were 2,900 miles of railway, with 2,447 miles of Class I track.

Civil Aviation. There were (1995) 71 publicly-used airports and (1992) 2,294 registered aircraft.

Shipping. There is barge traffic on the 1,100 miles of navigable rivers. There are 6 public river ports.

SOCIAL INSTITUTIONS

Justice. There are 12 adult prisons within the Department of Corrections Adult Institutions and 3 privately-run adult institutions; average daily population

(1994–95), 9,225 in prisons, 504 in jails awaiting incarceration, and 1,439 in local community centres. There were also 15,377 individuals on probation or parole.

The death penalty is authorized for murder and kidnap. As of July 1995 there were 28 persons under sentence of death. The last execution was in 1962.

Religion. The chief religious denominations in 1990 were: Southern Baptists, with 770,425 members, Roman Catholic (365,270), United Methodists (182,302), Christian Churches and Church of Christ (90,520) and Christian (Disciples of Christ) (66,798).

Education. Attendance at school between the ages of 5 and 15 years (inclusive) is compulsory, the normal term being 175 days. In 1994–95, 22,200 teachers were employed in public elementary and 9,885 in secondary schools. In 1991 there were 439,595 pupils in public elementary and 194,503 in secondary schools. Expenditure on elementary and secondary day schools in 1994–95 was $3,700m.; public school classroom teachers' salaries (1994–95) averaged $32,651.

There were also 4,800 teachers working in private elementary and secondary schools with some 66,000 students in 1994–95.

The state has 27 universities and senior colleges, 1 junior college and 14 community colleges, with a total (autumn 1994) of 177,454 students. Of these universities and colleges, 23 are state-supported, and the remainder are supported privately. The largest of the institutions of higher learning are (autumn 1994): University of Kentucky, with 24,217 students; University of Louisville, 21,377; Eastern Kentucky University, 16,060; Western Kentucky University, 14,765; Northern Kentucky University, 11,978; Morehead State University, 8,697; Murray State University, 7,960; Kentucky State University, 2,564. Five of the several privately endowed colleges of standing are Berea College, Berea; Centre College, Danville; Transylvania University, Lexington; Georgetown College, Georgetown; and Bellarmine College, Louisville.

Health. In 1995 the state had 128 licensed hospitals (19,961 beds). There were 408 licensed long-term care facilities (34,556 beds), 380 family care homes, 115 home health agencies and 1,514 miscellaneous health facilities.

Welfare. In Nov. 1995 there were 350,796 persons receiving financial assistance; 168,615 of these persons received the Federal Supplemental Security Income (SSI); 26,480 were aged, 142,135 blind or disabled. Also, in the all state funded Supplementation programme, payments were made in Nov. 1995 to 5,913 persons, of whom 2,985 were aged, 63 blind and 2,865 disabled. The average State Supplementation payment was $233·93 to aged, $141·24 to blind and $232·89 to disabled.

In the Aid to Families with Dependent Children Program as of Nov. 1995, aid was given to 176,268 persons in 71,676 families. The average payment per person was $82·12, per family $201·94.

In addition to money payments, medical assistance, food stamps and social services are available.

Further Reading

Kentucky Deskbook of Economic Statistics. Cabinet for Economic Development, Frankfort

Lee, L. G., *A Brief History of Kentucky and its Counties.* Berea, 1981

Miller, P. M., *Kentucky Politics and Government: Do We Stand United?* Nebraska Univ. Press, 1994

LOUISIANA

KEY HISTORICAL EVENTS. Louisiana was first settled in 1699. That part lying east of the Mississippi River was organized in 1804 as the Territory of New Orleans, and admitted into the Union on 30 April 1812. The section west of the river was added very shortly thereafter.

TERRITORY AND POPULATION. Louisiana is bounded north by Arkansas, east by Mississippi, south by the Gulf of Mexico and west by Texas.

Land area, 43,566 sq. miles (112,836 sq. km). Census population, 1 April 1990, 4,219,973 (68·1% urban), an increase of 0·38% since 1980. Population estimate (1994), 4,315,085. Births, 1993, 69,328; marriages, 39,365; divorces, 15,042. Deaths, 1992, 38,040; infant deaths, 555.

Population in 5 census years was:

	White	*Black*	*Indian*	*Asiatic*	*Total*	*Per sq. mile*
1930	1,322,712	776,326	1,536	1,019	2,101,593	46·5
1960	2,211,715	1,039,207	3,587	2,004	3,257,022	72·2
			All others			
1970	2,541,498	1,086,832	12,976		3,641,306	81·1
1980	2,911,243	1,237,263	55,466		4,205,900	93·5
1990	2,839,138	1,299,281	81,554		4,219,973	97·0

Of the 1990 total, 2,031,386 were male, 2,872,038 were urban; those 20 years of age or older numbered 2,852,363.

The largest cities with their 1990 census population are: New Orleans, 496,938; Baton Rouge, 219,531; Shreveport, 198,525; Lafayette, 94,440; Kenner, 72,033; Lake Charles, 70,580; Monroe, 54,909; Bossier City, 52,721.

CLIMATE. New Orleans. Jan. 54°F (12·2°C), July 83°F (28·3°C). Annual rainfall 58" (1,458 mm). Louisiana belongs to the Gulf Coast climate zone (*see* UNITED STATES: Climate).

CONSTITUTION AND GOVERNMENT. The present constitution dates from 1974. The Legislature consists of a Senate of 39 members and a House of Representatives of 105 members, both chosen for 4 years. Sessions are annual; a fiscal session is held in odd years.

The state sends 7 representatives to Congress.

In the 1992 presidential election Clinton polled 815,971 votes; Bush, 733,386; Perot, 211,478.

Louisiana is divided into 64 parishes (corresponding to the counties of other states). The capital is Baton Rouge.

Governor: Murphy J. Foster (R.), 1996–2000 ($95,000).
Lieut. Governor: Kathleen Blanco (D.), ($85,000).
Secretary of State: Fox McKeithen (R.), ($85,000).

BUDGET. For the year ending 30 June 1993 total revenues were $12,019·1m.; total expenditures were $11,189m. (education, $2,428·8m.; transport, $220·6m.; health and welfare, $4,660·5m.).

Per capita personal income (1994) was $17,615.

NATURAL RESOURCES

Minerals. Production in 1992 of crude oil was 105·4m. bbls; production of natural gas, 1,620·5m. cu. ft. Principal non-fuel minerals are sulphur, salt and sand and gravel. Value of 1991 output, $352m.

Agriculture. The state is divided into two parts, the uplands and the alluvial and swamp regions of the coast. A delta occupies about one-third of the total area. Manufacturing is the leading industry, but agriculture is important. The number of farms in 1992 was some 32,000 covering 9m. acres; the average farm had 290 acres. Average value of farmland and buildings per acre in 1995 was $1,082. Farm income, 1993: Crops, $2,198·7m.; livestock and products, $728·3m. Principal crops, with 1993 production, are: Soybeans, 29·1m. bu.; sugar-cane, 1,872m. lbs sugar and 56·1m. gallons molasses; rice, 24·7m. cwt; maize, 18·8m. bu.; cotton, 539·6m. lbs lint and 863·4m. lbs seed; sweet potatoes, 5m. bu.; pecans, 24m. lbs; grain sorghum, 4·3m. cwt. Livestock in 1990: Cattle, 0·84m.; pigs, 50,000; sheep, 16,000; poultry, 2·1m.

Fisheries. The value of the 1993 catch of marine and freshwater fish was $244·4m.; of aquaculture, $97·1m.

Forestry. Forests, 13,782,000 acres in 1991. Income from manufactured products exceeds $2,500m. annually. Production, 1993: Sawtimber, 1,563,828,236 board feet; pulpwood, 4,980,160 standard cords.

INDUSTRY. The manufacturing industries are chiefly those associated with petroleum, chemicals, lumber, food, paper. In 1995, 10·9% of the workforce were employed in manufacturing, 24·2% in trade and 37·9% in service industries.

TOURISM. Travellers spent an estimated $5,240m. in 1993. Tourism is the second most important industry for state income.

COMMUNICATIONS

Roads. In 1995 there were 59,599 miles of roads (46,268 miles rural in 1991) and, in Oct. 1994, 4,926,387 registered motor vehicles.

Railways. In 1992 there were about 3,219 miles of main line track in the state. There is a tramway in New Orleans.

Civil Aviation. In 1991 there were about 400 commercial and private airports.

Shipping. There are ports at New Orleans, Baton Rouge and Lake Charles. The Mississippi and other waterways provide 7,500 miles of navigable water.

SOCIAL INSTITUTIONS

Justice. There were 24,194 prisoners in state correctional institutions in 1995. The death penalty is authorized; the last execution was in 1995.

Religion. The Roman Catholic Church is the largest denomination in Louisiana. The leading Protestant Churches are Southern Baptist and Methodist.

Education. School attendance is compulsory between the ages of 7 and 15, both inclusive. In 1993–94 there were 1,438 public elementary and secondary schools with 771,379 registered students, and 46,837 teachers paid an average salary of $26,285. There are 20 four-year and 5 two-year public colleges and universities and 12 non-public four-year institutions of higher learning. There are 45 state trade and vocational-technical schools. In 1991 there were 158,119 students in public, and 25,757 in private colleges and universities. Enrolment, 1995, in Louisiana State University, Baton Rouge was 23,780; University of Southwestern Louisiana, 15,840; University of New Orleans, 14,625; Southeastern Louisiana University, 13,447; Northeast Louisiana University, 10,956; Tulane University, 10,840; Southern University, Baton Rouge, 9,420; Northwestern State University, 8,505; McNeese State University, 8,135; Grambling State University, 7,325; Nicholls State University, 6,992; Loyola University, 5,634; Louisiana State University in Shreveport, 3,949; Southern University of New Orleans (1993), 4,456; Xavier University, 3,419; Dillard University, 1,566.

Health. In 1992 the state had 171 licensed hospitals with 23,438 beds.

Social Security. In Dec. 1992, assistance was being given to 404,620 retired workers and dependants, 158,590 survivors and 115,980 disabled workers and dependants. Total annual payments, 1992, $4,263m.

Further Reading

Statistical information: Division of Business and Economic Research, Univ. of New Orleans, New Orleans 70148. Publishes *Statistical Abstract of Louisiana.*

Davis, E. A., *Louisiana, the Pelican State.* Louisiana State Univ. Press, 1975

Kniffen, F. B., *Louisiana, its Land and People.* Louisiana State Univ. Press, 1968

State library: The State Library of Louisiana, Baton Rouge, Louisiana.

MAINE

KEY HISTORICAL EVENTS. After a first attempt in 1607, Maine was settled in 1623. From 1652 to 1820 it was part of Massachusetts and was admitted into the Union on 15 March 1820.

TERRITORY AND POPULATION. Maine is bounded west, north and east by Canada, south-east by the Atlantic, south and south-west by New Hampshire. Land area, 30,865 sq. miles (79,931 sq. km). Census population, 1 April 1990 1,127,928 (44·6% urban), an increase of 9·18% since 1980. Population estimate (1993), 2,239,448. Births, 1991, 16,581 (13·2 per 1,000 population); deaths, 10,952 (8·7); infant deaths, 1992, 109 (6·8 per 1,000 live births); marriages, 11,077 (8·8); divorces 5,816 (4·6).

Population for 5 census years was:

	White	*Black*	*Indian*	*Asiatic*	*Total*	*Per sq. mile*
1910	739,995	1,363	892	121	742,371	24·8
1930	795,185	1,096	1,012	130	797,423	25·7
1950	910,846	1,221	1,522	185	913,774	29·4
			All others			
1970	985,276	2,800	3,972		992,048	31·0
1980	1,109,850	3,128	12,049		1,125,027	36·3

Of the total population in 1980, 48·5% were male, 40·7% were urban and 60·5% were 21 years or older.

The largest city in the state is Portland with a census population of 61,572 in 1980. Other cities (with population in 1980) are: Lewiston, 40,481; Bangor, 31,643; Auburn, 23,128; South Portland, 22,712; Augusta (capital), 21,819; Biddeford, 19,638; Waterville, 17,779.

CLIMATE. Average maximum temperatures range from 56·3°F in Waterville to 48·3°F in Caribou, but record high (since *c.* 1950) is 103°F. Average minimum ranges from 36·9°F in Rockland to 28·3°F in Greenville, but record low (also in Greenville) is –42°F. Average annual rainfall ranges from 48·85" in Machias to 36·09" in Houlton. Average annual snowfall ranges from 118·7" in Greenville to 59·7" in Rockland. Maine belongs to the New England climate zone (*see* UNITED STATES: Climate).

CONSTITUTION AND GOVERNMENT. The constitution of 1820 is still in force, but it has been amended 153 times. In 1951, 1965 and 1973 the Legislature approved recodifications of the constitution as arranged by the Chief Justice under special authority.

The Legislature consists of the Senate with 35 members and the House of Representatives with 151 members, both Houses being elected simultaneously for 2 years. Sessions are annual.

The state sends 2 representatives to Congress.

In the 1992 presidential election Clinton polled 263,420 votes; Perot, 206,820; Bush, 206,504.

The capital is Augusta. The state is divided into 16 counties.

Governor: Angus King (ind.), 1995–99 ($69,992).
Secretary of State: G. William Diamond (D.) ($49,587).

BUDGET. For the financial year ending 30 June 1991 general revenue was $3,222m. and expenditure was $3,515m.

Per capita personal income (1994) was $19,663.

NATURAL RESOURCES

Minerals. Minerals include sand and gravel, stone, lead, clay, copper, peat, silver and zinc. Mineral output, 1990, was valued at $56m.

Agriculture. In 1991, some 7,000 farms occupied 1·42m. acres; the average farm was 203 acres. Average value of farmland and buildings per acre in 1995 was $1,245. Farm income, 1991: Crops, $203m.; livestock and products, $215m. Principal crops are potatoes, apples, hay and blueberries. Livestock in 1986: Cattle, 135,000; pigs, 79,000; sheep, 17,000; poultry, 4·9m.

Forestry. There are some 17·5m. acres of commercial forest, mainly pine, spruce and fir. Wood products industries are of great economic importance. 714m. board feet were cut in 1989.

Fisheries. In 1990 the commercial catch was valued at $129·9m.

INDUSTRY. Total non-agricultural workforce, 1985, 459,000. Manufacturing employed 106,000; trade, 108,000; services, 95,000; government, 86,000; the main manufacture is paper at 47 plants, producing about 34% of manufacturing value added.

TOURISM. Earnings were $2,000m. in 1989.

COMMUNICATIONS

Roads. In 1990 there were 22,240 miles of roads (19,781 miles rural). In 1991 there were 978,849 registered motor vehicles.

Railways. In 1984 there were 1,516 miles of mainline railway tracks.

Civil Aviation. There are international airports at Portland and Bangor.

SOCIAL INSTITUTIONS

Justice. In 1991 there were 1,614 prisoners in state correctional institutions. There is no capital punishment.

Religion. The largest religious bodies are: Roman Catholic (270,283 members), Baptists (36,808 members) and Congregationalists (40,750 members), and other Christian Churches (34,066 members).

Education. Education is free for pupils from 5 to 21 years of age, and compulsory from 7 to 17. In 1992 there were 216,887 pupils and 15,269 teachers in public elementary and secondary schools. Education expenditure by state and local government in 1991, $1,580·6m.

The state University of Maine, founded in 1865, has 7 locations; Bowdoin College, founded in 1794 at Brunswick; Bates College at Lewiston; Colby College at Waterville; Husson College, Bangor; Westbrook College at Westbrook; Unity College at Unity, and the University of New England (formerly St Francis College) at Biddeford.

Health. In 1984 the state had 42 general hospitals (4,571 beds for acute care); 3 hospitals for mental diseases, acute and psychiatric care (541 beds); 144 nursing homes (10,220 beds).

Social Security. Supplemental Security Income (SSI) is administered by the Social Security Administration. It became effective on 1 Jan. 1974 and replaces former aid to the aged, blind and disabled, administered by the state with state and federal funds. SSI is supplemented by Medicaid for nursing home patients or hospital patients. Aid to families with dependent children is granted where one or both parents are disabled or absent and income is insufficient. There is a programme of assistance for catastrophic illness. Child welfare services include basic child protective services, enforcing child support, establishing paternity and finding missing parents, foster home placements, adoptions; services in divorce cases and licensing of foster homes, day care and residential treatment services, and public guardianship. There are also protective services for adults.

Further Reading

Statistical information: Maine Department of Economic and Community Development, State House Station 59, Augusta 04333. Publishes *Maine: a Statistical Summary.*

Maine Register, State Year-Book and Legislative Manual. Tower Publishing, Portland. Annual
Banks, R., *Maine Becomes A State.* Wesleyan U.P., 1970
Clark, C., *Maine.* New York, 1977
Palmer, K. T. *et al., Maine Politics and Government.* Univ. of Nebraska Press, 1993

MARYLAND

KEY HISTORICAL EVENTS. Maryland, first settled in 1634, was one of the 13 original states.

TERRITORY AND POPULATION. Maryland is bounded north by Pennsylvania, east by Delaware and the Atlantic, south by Virginia and West Virginia, with the Potomac River forming most of the boundary, and west by West Virginia. Chesapeake Bay almost cuts off the eastern end of the state from the rest. Land area, 9,775 sq. miles (25,316 sq. km). Census population, 1 April 1990, 4,781,468 (81·3% urban), an increase since 1980 of 564,535 or 13·4%. Population estimate (1992), 4,917,569. In 1991 births were 84,452 (17·5 per 1,000 population); deaths, 37,982 (7·9); infant deaths, 1988, 856 (11·2 per 1,000 live births); marriages, 44,399 (9·2); divorces, 16,576 (3·4).

Population for 5 federal censuses was:

	White	*Black*	*Indian*	*Asiatic*	*Total*	*Per sq. mile*
1920	1,204,737	244,479	32	400	1,449,661	145·8
1930	1,354,226	276,379	50	857	1,631,526	165·0
1960	2,573,919	518,410	1,538	5,700	3,100,689	314·0
			All others			
1990	3,393,964	1,189,899	197,605		4,781,468	489·3

Of the total population in 1990, 2,318,671 were male, 3,888,429 persons were urban and those 20 years old or older numbered 3,484,455.

The largest city in the state (containing 15·4% of the population) is Baltimore, with 736,014 in 1990 (and 786,741 in 1980); Baltimore metropolitan area, 2·4m. Maryland residents in the Washington, D.C., metropolitan area total more than 1·8m. Other cities (1990) are Dundalk (65,800); Towson (49,445); Silver Spring (76,046); Columbia (75,883); Bethesda (62,936). Incorporated places, 1990: Rockville, 44,835; Bowie, 37,589; Hagerstown, 35,445; Frederick, 40,148; Annapolis, 33,187; Gaithersburg, 39,542; Cumberland, 23,706; College Park, 21,927; Loreenbelt, 21,096; Salisbury, 20,592; Cambridge, 11,514.

CLIMATE. Baltimore. Jan. 36°F (2·2°C), July 79°F (26·1°C). Annual rainfall 41" (1,026 mm). Maryland belongs to the Atlantic Coast climate zone (*see* UNITED STATES: Climate).

CONSTITUTION AND GOVERNMENT. The present constitution dates from 1867; it has had 125 amendments. The General Assembly consists of a Senate of 47, and a House of Delegates of 141 members, both elected for 4 years, as are the Governor and Lieut.-Governor. Voters are citizens who have the usual residential qualifications. At the 1992 presidential election Clinton polled 988,571 votes; Bush, 707,094; Perot, 281,414.

Maryland sends to Congress 8 representatives.

The state capital is Annapolis. The state is divided into 23 counties and Baltimore City.

Governor: Parris N. Glendening (D.), 1995–99 ($120,000).
Lieut.-Governor: Kathleen K. Townsend (D.) ($100,000).
Secretary of State: John Willis (D.) ($70,000).

BUDGET. For the fiscal year ending 30 June 1990 general revenues were $9,106,363,000 ($6,518,272,000 from taxation). General expenditures, $9,375,548,000, including $2,052,303,000 for education and $2,744,025,000 for public welfare and health; $1,686,072,000 for transport.

Total authorized long-term state debt, 30 June 1990 was $2,979·8m. (Issued and outstanding, $1,986·9m.; authorized but not issued, $992·9m.)

Per capita personal income (1994) was $24,933.

NATURAL RESOURCES

Minerals. Value of non-fuel mineral production, 1990, was $354m. Sand and gravel (17·1m. short tons) and stone (31·4m. short tons) account for 72% of the total value. Coal is the leading mineral commodity by value followed by, stone, sand and gravel and Portland cement. Output of coal was 3.5m. short tons, valued at about $90m. Natural gas is produced from 1 field in Garrett County; 22m. cu. ft in 1990. A second gas field in the same county is used for natural gas storage.

Agriculture. Agriculture is an important industry in the state. In 1991 there were approximately 15,400 farms with an area of 2·3m. acres (36% of the land area). The average number of acres per farm in 1991 was 146. The average value per acre in 1995 was $3,707. In 1992, 16,960 people were employed in agriculture.

Farm animals, 1 Jan. 1990, were: Milch cows, 103,000; all cattle, 320,000; swine, 162,000; sheep, 30,000; chickens (not broilers), 4·5m. The most important crops, 1990, were: Corn for grain, 53·1m. bu.; soybeans, 17·8m. bu.; tobacco, 9·7m. lbs, and hay, 678,000 tons.

Farm income, 1991: $1,294m.; from livestock and livestock products, $785m., and crops, $509m. Dairy products and broilers are important.

INDUSTRY. In 1992 manufactories had 183,113 employed. Total value added by manufacture, $15,241·8m. Chief industries are food and kindred products ($2,431), instruments and related products ($2,163·5), chemicals and products ($1,879·3), printing and publishing ($1,865·1) and transportation equipment ($1,584·3).

Total employment, 1992: 2,041,720.

TOURISM. Tourism is one of the state's leading industries. In 1989 tourists spent over $4,366m.

COMMUNICATIONS

Roads. The state highway department maintained, 1 Jan. 1991, 5,210 miles of highways, of which 89 miles were toll roads. The 23 counties maintained 18,785 miles of highways, and the 159 municipalities (including the city of Baltimore) maintained 4,143 miles of streets and alleys. Total mileage, 1 Jan. 1991, of public highways, streets and alleys, 28,317 miles. As of March 1991, an estimated 3·5m. automobiles were registered.

Railways. Railways, in 1990, had 1,068 miles of line. There are metro and light rail lines in Baltimore.

Civil Aviation. There were, 1992, 48 commercially licensed aiports.

Shipping. In 1990 Baltimore was the ninth largest US seaport in value of trade, twelfth in tonnage handled.

SOCIAL INSTITUTIONS

Justice. Prisons on 21 Feb. 1992 had about 18,577 men and 939 women; the total equalled 401 per 100,000 population, a high rate, which may be explained by the fact that Maryland incarcerates domestic relations law violators in state prisons; state prisons also receive a considerable number of persons committed for misdemeanours by magistrates' courts of the counties as well as from Baltimore's court system.

The death penalty is authorized.

Maryland's prison system has conducted a work-release programme for selected prisoners since 1963. All institutions have academic and vocational training programmes.

Religion. Maryland was the first US state to give religious freedom to all who came within its borders. Present religious affiliations of the population are approximately: Protestant, 32%; Roman Catholic, 24%; Jewish, 10%; remaining 34% is non-related and other faiths.

Education. Education is compulsory from 6 to 16 years of age. In Sept. 1993 the public elementary schools (including kindergartens and secondary schools) had 753,379 pupils. In Sept. 1990 teachers, principals and therapists in the elementary and secondary schools numbered 44,974. Teachers' average salary in 1990–91 was $38,312. Current expenditure by local school boards on education, 1989–90, was $3,827·8m., of which the state's contribution was $1,504·8m.

In 1991 there were 34 degree-granting 4-year institutions and 23 2-year colleges. The largest was the University of Maryland system, with 106,514 students (Sept. 1991), consisting of 11 campuses with the highest enrolment at College Park (34,623) and Towson State University (15,403).

Health. In Nov. 1991, 78 hospitals (19,526 beds) were licensed by the State Department of Health and Mental Hygiene.

The Maryland State Department of Health, organized in 1874, was in 1969 made part of the Department of Health and Mental Hygiene which performs its functions through its central office, 23 county health departments and the Baltimore City Health Department. For the financial year 1990 the department's budget was $1,985·8m., of which $1,327·5m. were general funds and $46.4m. special funds appropriated by the General Assembly. The balance of the budget, $611·9m., derives from federal funds.

During financial year 1991 Maryland's programme of medical care for indigent and medically indigent patients covered about 442,100 persons. The programme, which covers in-patient and out-patient hospital services, laboratory services, skilled nursing home care, physician services, pharmacy services, dental services and home health services, cost approximately $1,357m.

Social Security. Under the supervision of the Department of Human Resources, local social service departments administer public assistance for needy persons. In March 1990 families with dependent children received $29,217,254 (218,342 recipients, average actual monthly payment $133.81); general public assistance payments were $5,394,836 (25,443 recipients, average actual monthly payments $212.04).

Further Reading

Statistical Information: Maryland Department of Economic and Employment Development, 217 East Redwood St., Baltimore, 21202. Publishes *Maryland Statistical Abstract.*

DiLisio, J. E., *Maryland.* Boulder, 1982

Rollo, V. F., *Maryland's Constitution and Government.* Maryland Hist. Press, Rev. ed., 1982

State Library: Maryland State Library, Annapolis.

MASSACHUSETTS

KEY HISTORICAL EVENTS. The first permanent settlement within the borders of the present state was made at Plymouth in Dec. 1620, by the Pilgrims from Holland, who were separatists from the English Church, and formed the nucleus of the Plymouth Colony. In 1628 another company of Puritans settled at Salem, forming eventually the Massachusetts Bay Colony. In 1630 Boston was settled. In the struggle which ended in the separation of the American colonies from the mother country, Massachusetts took the foremost part, and on 6 Feb. 1788 became the sixth state to ratify the US constitution.

TERRITORY AND POPULATION. Massachusetts is bounded north by Vermont and New Hampshire, east by the Atlantic, south by Connecticut and Rhode Island and west by New York. Land area, 7,838 sq. miles (20,300 sq. km).

Population estimate (1993), 6,012,268. Vital statistics: Births, 86,321 (14·5 per 1,000 population); deaths, 51,366 (8·6); infant deaths in 1992, 529 (6); marriages, 43,429 (7·3); divorces, 13,547 (2·3).

Population at 5 federal census years was:

	White	*Black*	*Other*	*Total*	*Per sq. mile*
1950	4,611,503	73,171	5,840	4,690,514	598·4
1960	5,023,144	111,842	13,592	5,148,578	656·8
1970	5,477,624	175,817	35,729	5,689,170	725·8
1980	5,362,836	221,279	152,922	5,737,037	732·0
1990	...	...	...	6,016,425	...

Of the total population in 1980, 47·6% were male, 83·8% were urban and 32% were 21 years old or older.

Population of the largest cities at the 1990 census: Boston, 574,283; Lowell, 103,439; Springfield, 156,983; Worcester, 169,759; New Bedford, 99,922; Cambridge, 95,802; Brockton, 92,788; Fall River, 92,703; Quincy, 84,985; Newton, 82,585; Lynn, 81,245.

CLIMATE. Boston. Jan. 28°F (–2·2°C), July 71°F (21·7°C). Annual rainfall 41" (1,036 mm). Massachusetts belongs to the New England climate zone (*see* UNITED STATES: Climate).

CONSTITUTION AND GOVERNMENT. The constitution dates from 1780 and has had 116 amendments. The legislative body, styled the General Court of the Commonwealth of Massachusetts, meets annually, and consists of the Senate with 40 members and the House of Representatives of 160 members, both elected for 2 years.

The state sends 10 representatives to Congress.

At the 1992 presidential election Clinton polled 1,318,639 votes; Bush, 805,039; Perot, 630,731.

The capital is Boston. The state has 14 counties.

Governor: William F. Weld (R.), 1995–99 ($75,000).
Lieut.-Governor: A. Paul Cellucci (R.) ($60,000).
Secretary of State: William F. Galvin (D.) ($60,000).

BUDGET. For the fiscal year ending 30 June 1990 the total revenue of the state was $15,773·7m. ($9,369·1m. from taxes, $3,306·6m. from federal aid); total expenditures, $17,039m. ($3,495·8m. for education, $615·8m. for highways and $4,603·7m. for human services).

Per capita personal income (1994) was $25,616.

NATURAL RESOURCES

Minerals. Total mineral output in 1990 was valued at $111·3m., of which most came from sand, gravel, crushed stone and lime.

Agriculture. In 1991 there were approximately 6,900 farms with an average area of 99 and a total area 0·68m. acres. Average value per acre in 1995 was $5,398. Farm income: Crops, $337m.; livestock and products, $116m.

Principal crops include cranberries and greenhouse products.

Forestry. About 68% of the state is forest. State forests cover about 256,000 acres. Total forest land covers about 3m. acres. Commercially important hardwoods are sugar maple, northern red oak and white ash; softwoods are white pine and hemlock. 85m. board feet of timber were cut in 1989.

Fisheries. The 1990 catch totalled 328m. lbs and was valued at $303m.

INDUSTRY. In 1991, manufacturing establishments employed an average of 484,500 workers, service industries employed 889,900 and trade, 649,500; total non-agricultural employment, 2,817,000.

COMMUNICATIONS

Roads. In 1990 there were 33,807 miles of public roads (13,201 miles rural). In 1991 there were 3,663,843 registered motor vehicles.

Railways. In 1984 there were 1,310 miles of mainline railway. There are metro, light rail, tramway and commuter networks in and around Boston.

Civil Aviation. There is an international airport at Boston.

Shipping. The state has 3 deep-water harbours, the largest of which is Boston. Other ports are Fall River and New Bedford.

SOCIAL INSTITUTIONS

Justice. In 1991 state correctional institutions held 8,817 prisoners. The death penalty is not authorized.

Religion. The principal religious bodies are the Roman Catholics, Jewish Congregations, Methodists, Episcopalians and Unitarians.

Education. School attendance is compulsory for ages 6–16. In 1991–92 expenditure by cities and towns on public schools was $3·5m. or $600 per capita, including debt retirement and service payments. In 1991–92 there were 56,000 classroom teachers and approximately 900,000 pupils.

Some leading higher education institutions are:

Year opened	*Name and location of universities and colleges*	*Students 1988*
1636	Harvard University, Cambridge [1]	16,871
1839	Framingham State College	4,303
1839	Westfield State College	6,053
1840	Bridgewater State College	6,539
1852	Tufts University, Medford [1,3]	6,297
1854	Salem State College	6,364
1861	Mass. Institute of Technology, Cambridge [1]	9,158
1863	University of Massachusetts, Amherst [1]	26,233
1863	Boston College (RC), Chestnut Hill [1]	12,858
1865	Worcester Polytechnic Institute, Worcester [1]	4,022
1869	Boston University, Boston [1]	22,373
1874	Worcester College	4,899
1894	Fitchburg State College	5,212
1894	University of Lowell [1]	10,445
1895	Southeastern Massachusetts University	5,031
1898	Northeastern University, Boston [1,4]	20,618
1899	Simmons College, Boston [2]	2,594
1905	Wentworth Institute of Technology	3,350
1906	Suffolk University	5,978
1917	Bentley College	5,611
1919	Western New England College	3,686
1919	Babson College	3,163
1947	Merrimack College	2,300
1948	Brandeis University, Waltham [1]	3,484
1964	University of Massachusetts, Boston	8,027

[1] Co-educational. [2] For women only.
[3] Includes Jackson College for women. [4] Includes Forsyth Dental Center School.

Health. In 1990 there were 157 state hospitals with 33,500 beds and 125,300 personnel.

Social Security. In 1990 the Department of Public Welfare paid $647m. in aid to families with dependent children (some 282,000 recipients received an average monthly payment of $510). Medicare enrolments were 0·87m. and total payments $3,152m.; Medicaid, 0·59m. recipients, total payments $2,730m. 0·73m. persons received retirement, 0·15m. survivors' and 91,000 disability benefits.

Further Reading

Hart, Albert B., (ed.) *Commonwealth History of Massachusetts, Colony, Province and State.* 5 vols., New York, 1966

Levitan, D. with Mariner, E. C., *Your Massachusetts Government.* Newton, Mass., 1984

MICHIGAN

KEY HISTORICAL EVENTS. Michigan, first settled by Marquette at Sault Ste Marie in 1668, became the Territory of Michigan in 1805, with its boundaries greatly enlarged in 1818 and 1834; it was admitted into the Union with its present boundaries on 26 Jan. 1837.

TERRITORY AND POPULATION. Michigan is divided into two by Lake Michigan. The northern part is bounded south by the lake and by Wisconsin, west and north by Lake Superior, east by the North Channel of Lake Huron; between the two latter lakes the Canadian border runs through straits at Sault Ste Marie. The southern part is bounded in the west and north by Lake Michigan, east by Lake Huron, Ontario and Lake Erie, south by Ohio and Indiana. Area, 58,110 sq. miles (150,544 sq. km). Census population, 1 April 1990, 9,295,297 (70·5% urban), an increase of 0·4% since 1980. Population estimate (1993), 9,478,000. In 1992 births were 143,827; deaths, 78,916; infant deaths, 1,460 (10·2 per 1,000 live births); marriages, 71,322; divorces, 40,425.

Population of 5 federal census years was:

	White	*Black*	*Indian*	*Asiatic*	*Total*	*Per sq. mile*
1910	2,785,247	17,115	7,519	292	2,810,173	48·9
1930	4,663,507	169,453	7,080	2,285	4,842,325	84·9
1960	7,085,865	717,581	9,701	10,047	7,823,194	137·2
			All others			
1980	7,872,241	1,199,023	190,814		9,262,078	162·6
1990	7,756,086	1,291,706	247,505		9,295,297	160·0

Of the total population in 1990, 4,512,781 were male, 6,554,846 persons were urban and those 20 years old or older numbered 6,540,323. 201,596 were Hispanic.

Population of the chief cities (census of 1 April 1990) was: Ann Arbor, 109,592; Detroit, 1,027,974; Flint, 140,761; Grand Rapids, 189,126; Lansing, 127,321; Livonia, 100,850; Sterling Heights, 117,810; Warren, 144,864.

CLIMATE. Detroit. Jan. 22·1°F (–5·5°C), July 72°F (22·2°C). Annual rainfall 32" (813 mm). Grand Rapids. Jan. 23·8°F (–4·6°C), July 72·6°F (22·5°C). Annual rainfall 33·6" (833 mm). Lansing. Jan. 21·7°F (–5·7°C), July 71°F (21·7°C). Annual rainfall 30·8" (782 mm). Michigan belongs to the Great Lakes climate zone (*see* UNITED STATES: Climate).

CONSTITUTION AND GOVERNMENT. The present constitution became effective on 1 Jan. 1964. The Senate consists of 38 members, elected for 4 years, and the House of Representatives of 110 members, elected for 2 years. Sessions are biennual.

The state sends 16 representatives to Congress.

At the 1992 presidential election Clinton polled 1,871,182 votes; Bush, 1,554,940; Perot, 824,813.

The capital is Lansing. The state is organized in 83 counties.

Governor: John Engler (R.), 1995–99 ($112,025).
Lieut.-Governor: Connie Binsfeld (R.) ($84,315).
Secretary of State: Candice Miller (R.) ($109,000).

BUDGET. For the financial year ending 30 Sept. 1994, the general revenue was $18,133m. (taxation, $10,360m.); general expenditures, $18,038m.

Per capita personal income (1994) was $22,333.

NATURAL RESOURCES

Minerals. Output of petroleum, 1992, 16m. bbls; natural gas, 195,000m. cu. ft. Non-fuel mineral output in 1993 was valued at $1,408m., mainly iron ore, cement, stone, sand and gravel.

Agriculture. The state, formerly agricultural, is now chiefly industrial. In 1992 it contained 46,562 farms with a total area of 10·1m. acres; the average farm was 217 acres. Average value per acre in 1995 was $1,329. Principal crops are maize, oats, wheat, sugar-beet, soybeans and hay. 6,584m. acres were harvested in 1992, at a total farm value of $3,028m. In 1994 there were 335,000 milch cows, 5·5m. chickens and 4·5m. turkeys. Farm income, 1992: Crops, $1,671m.; livestock and products, $1,356m.

Forestry. The forests in 1990 covered 18·22m. acres. About 17·5m. acres of this total is commercial forest. Three-fourths of the timber volume is hardwoods, principally hard and soft maples, aspen, oak and birch. Christmas trees are another important forest crop. 323m. board feet of timber were cut in 1989.

INDUSTRY. Manufacturing is important; among principal products are motor vehicles and trucks, machinery, fabricated metals, primary metals, cement, chemicals, furniture, paper, foodstuffs, rubber, plastics and pharmaceuticals. Total non-agricultural labour force, 1994, 4,797,000, of which 954,000 were in manufacturing.

COMMUNICATIONS

Roads. In 1993 there were 118,468 miles of roads (88,742 miles of country roads, 20,118 miles of municipal roads). In 1993 there were 8,338,188 registered motor vehicles.

Railways. On 1 Jan. 1986 there were 4,770 miles of railway and 67 miles of active car-ferry routes.

Civil Aviation. There are international airports at Detroit, Sault Ste Marie, Grand Rapids and Kalamazoo.

SOCIAL INSTITUTIONS

Justice. A Civil Rights Commission was established, and its powers and duties were implemented by legislation in the extra session of 1963. Statutory enactments guaranteeing civil rights in specific areas date from 1885. The legislature has a unique one-person grand jury system. In 1994 there were 38,145 prisoners in state correctional institutions. The death penalty is authorized.

Religion. Roman Catholics make up the largest body; largest Protestant denominations, Lutherans, United Methodists, United Presbyterians, Episcopalians.

Education. Education is compulsory for children from 6 to 16 years of age. Education expenditure by state and local governments in 1994 was $10,080m. In 1994–95 there were 1,603,535 pupils and 80,476 teachers in public elementary and secondary schools.

In 1993 there were 96 institutes of higher education with 572,391 students.

Universities and students (autumn 1992):

Founded	*Name*	*Students*
1817	University of Michigan	36,543
1849	Eastern Michigan University	27,597
1855	Michigan State University	40,047
1884	Ferris State College	12,134
1885	Michigan Technological University	6,961
1868	Wayne State University	34,945
1892	Central Michigan University	16,349
1889	Northern Michigan University	8,897
1903	Western Michigan University	27,282
1946	Lake Superior State College	3,503
1959	Oakland University	13,068
1960	Grand Valley State College	12,867
1965	Saginaw Valley College	6,869

Social Welfare. Old-age assistance is provided for persons 65 years of age or older who have resided in Michigan for one year before application; assets must not exceed various limits. In 1974 federal Supplementary Security Income (SSI) replaced the adults' programme. In Nov. 1995 aid was supplied to a monthly average of 365,169 dependent children in 184,249 families at $417 per family.

Health. In 1992 the state had 197 hospitals (37,871 beds) licensed by the state and 19 psychiatric hospitals, 7 centres for developmental disabilities, 5 centres for emotionally disturbed children.

In the fiscal year 1993–94 the Medicaid programme disbursed (with federal support) $3,274m. to 1,186,621 persons.

Further Reading

Michigan Manual. Dept of *Management and Budget.* Lansing. Biennial
Bureau of Business Research, Wayne State University. *Michigan Statistical Abstract, 1986–87*
Bald, F. C., *Michigan in Four Centuries.* 2nd ed. New York, 1961
Browne, W. P. and Verburg, K., *Michigan Politics and Government: Facing Change in a Complex State.* Nebraska Univ. Press, 1995
Catton. B., *Michigan—a Bicentennial History.* Norton, New York, 1976
Lewis, F. E., *State and Local Government in Michigan.* Lansing, 1979
Dunbar, W. F. and May, G. S., *Michigan: A History of the Wolverine State.* Grand Rapids, 1980
Sommers, L. (ed.), *Atlas of Michigan.* East Lansing, 1977

State Library Services: Library of Michigan, Lansing 48909.

MINNESOTA

KEY HISTORICAL EVENTS. Minnesota, first explored in the 17th century and first settled in the 20 years following the establishment of Fort Snelling (1819), was made a Territory in 1849 (with parts of North and South Dakota), and was admitted into the Union, with its present boundaries, on 11 May 1858.

TERRITORY AND POPULATION. Minnesota is bounded north by Canada, east by Lake Superior and Wisconsin, with the Mississippi River forming the boundary in the south-east, south by Iowa, west by South and North Dakota, with the Red River forming the boundary in the north-west. Land area, 79,617 sq. miles (206,207 sq. km). Census population, 1 April 1990, 4,375,099 (69·9% urban), an increase of 7·31% since 1980. Population estimate (1993), 4,517,416. Births in 1991, 67,020 (15·1 per 1,000 population); deaths, 35,270 (7·9); infant deaths in 1992, 494 (7·4 per 1,000 live births); marriages, 32,848 (7·4); divorces, 15,968 (3·6).

Population in 5 census years was:

	White	*Black*	*Indian*	*Asiatic*	*Total*	*Per sq. mile*
1910	2,059,227	7,084	9,053	344	2,075,708	25·7
1930	2,542,599	9,445	11,077	832	2,563,953	32·0
			All others			
1970	3,736,038	34,868	34,163		3,805,069	47·6
1980	3,935,770	53,344	86,856		4,075,970	51·4
1990	4,130,395	94,944	149,760		4,375,099	55·0

Of the 1990 population, 2,145,183 were male; 3,056,474 were urban; those 21 years of age or older numbered 3,015,507.

The largest cities (with 1990 census population) are Minneapolis (368,383), St Paul (272,253), Bloomington (86,335) and Duluth (85,931).

CLIMATE. Duluth. Jan. 8°F (–13·3°C), July 63°F (17·2°C). Annual rainfall 29" (719 mm). Minneapolis-St. Paul. Jan. 12°F (–11·1°C), July 71°F (21·7°C). Annual rainfall 26" (656 mm). Minnesota belongs to the Great Lakes climate zone (*see* UNITED STATES: Climate).

CONSTITUTION AND GOVERNMENT. The original constitution dated from 1857; it was extensively amended and given a new structure in 1974. The Legislature consists of a Senate of 67 members, elected for 4 years, and a House of

Representatives of 134 members, elected for 2 years. It meets for 120 days within each 2 years.

The state sends 8 representatives to Congress.

In the 1992 presidential election Clinton polled 1,020,997 votes; Bush 747,841; Perot, 562,506.

The capital is St Paul. There are 87 counties.

Governor: Arne Carlson (R.), 1995–99 ($114,506).

Lieut.-Governor: Joanell Dyrstad (ind. R.) ($62,980).

Secretary of State: Joan A. Growe (Democratic-Farmer-Labor) ($62,980).

BUDGET. The general fund budget for the 1989–91 2-year period was $13,686m.; tax relief $1,966m., education $7,121m., public welfare $1,940m., transport $207m.

Net long-term debt, 30 June 1991, was $3,941m.

Per capita personal income (1994) was $22,453.

NATURAL RESOURCES

Minerals. The iron ore and taconite industry is the most important in the USA. Production of usable iron ore in 1988 was 42m. tons, value $1,278m. Other important minerals are sand and gravel, crushed and dimension stone, lime and manganiferous ore. Total value of mineral production, 1990, $1,470m.

Agriculture. In 1991 there were some 88,000 farms with a total area of 30m. acres; the average farm was of 341 acres. Average value of land and buildings per acre, (1995) $936. Farm income, 1991, from crops, $3,386m.; from livestock, $3,485m. Important products: Sugar-beets, spring wheat, processing sweet corn, oats, dry milk, cheese, mink, turkeys, wild rice, butter, eggs, flaxseed, milch cows, milk, corn, barley, swine, cattle for market, soybeans, honey, potatoes, rye, chickens, sunflower seed and dry edible beans. In 1991 there were 2·76m. cattle (0·71m. milch cows) and 4·5m. hogs and pigs. In 1988 the wool clip amounted to 1·89m. lb. of wool from 255,000 sheep.

Forestry. Forests of commercial timber cover 14m. acres, of which 53% is government-owned. The value of forest products in 1987 was $4,400m.: $1,300m. from primary processing, of which $901m. was from pulp and paper; and $3,100m. from secondary manufacturing. Logging, pulping, saw-mills and associated industries employed 53,700 in 1987.

INDUSTRY. In 1986 manufacturing establishments employed 369,000 workers; value added by manufacture was $19,800m. Largest manufacturing industry is computers and non-electric machinery (81,000 employees); then food products and kindred products (45,000), printing and publishing (43,000).

TOURISM. In 1987, travellers spent about $5,500m. The industry employed about 108,000.

COMMUNICATIONS

Roads. In 1990 there were 129,553 miles of roads (115,458 miles rural). In 1991 there were 3,273,153 registered motor vehicles.

Railways. There are 3 Class I and 16 Class II and smaller railroads operating, with total mileage of 5,044.

Civil Aviation. In 1989 there were 141 airports for public use and 12 public seaplane bases.

SOCIAL INSTITUTIONS

Justice. In 1991 there were 3,136 prisoners in state correctional institutions. There is no death penalty.

Religion. The chief religious bodies are: Lutheran with 1,088,304 members in 1980; Roman Catholic, 1,041,781; Methodist, 146,422. Total membership of all denominations, 2,653,161.

Education. In 1992, there were 775,567 students and 44,200 teachers in public elementary and secondary schools. In 1988 there were 1,511 public schools, and 82,165 kindergarten, elementary, and secondary students enrolled in 572 private schools. The University of Minnesota, chartered in 1851 and opened in 1869, had a total enrolment in 1988 of 54,515 students on all campuses. The 18 public community colleges (2-year) had a total enrolment of 49,589. There are seven state universities (4-year) at Bemidji, Mankato, Marshall, Moorhead, St Cloud, Winona, Minneapolis and St Paul. Enrolment in all institutions of higher education, 1988, 251,304.

Health. In 1989 the state had 163 general acute hospitals with 19,229 beds. Patients resident in institutions under the Department of Human Services in Aug. 1989 included 1,343 people with mental illness, 1,405 people with mental retardation, 265 with chemical dependency and 486 in state nursing homes.

Social Security. Programmes of old age assistance, aid to the disabled, and aid to the blind are administered under the federal Supplemental Security Income (SSI) Programme. Minnesota has a supplementary programme, Minnesota Supplemental Aid (MSA) to cover individuals not eligible for SSI, to supplement SSI benefits for others whose income is below state standards, and to provide one-time payments for emergency needs such as major home repair, essential furniture or appliances, moving expenses, fuel, food and shelter.

Further Reading

Statistical Information: Department of Trade and Economic Development, 900 American Center Building, St Paul 55101. Publishes *Compare Minnesota: an Economic and Statistical Factbook.—Economic Report to the Governor.*

Legislative Manual. Secretary of State. St Paul. Biennial
Minnesota Agriculture Statistics. Dept. of Agric., St Paul. Annual

MISSISSIPPI

KEY HISTORICAL EVENTS. Mississippi, settled in 1716, was organized as a Territory in 1798 and admitted into the Union on 10 Dec. 1817. In 1804 and in 1812 its boundaries were extended, but in March 1817 a part was taken to form the new Territory of Alabama, leaving the boundaries substantially as at present.

TERRITORY AND POPULATION. Mississippi is bounded north by Tennessee, east by Alabama, south by the Gulf of Mexico and Louisiana, west by the Mississippi River forming the boundary with Louisiana and Arkansas. Area, 47,689 sq. miles (123,515 sq. km), 457 sq. miles (1,184 sq. km) being inland water. Census population, 1 July 1990, 2,573,216 (47·1% urban), an increase of 2·09% since 1980. Population estimate (1993), 2,642,748. Births, occurring in the state, 1994, were 41,319; deaths, 25,959; infant deaths, 409; marriages, 22,872; divorces, 13,302.

Population of 5 federal census years was:

	White	*Black*	*Indian*	*Asiatic*	*Total*	*Per sq. mile*
1910	786,111	1,009,487	1,253	263	1,797,114	38·8
1930	998,077	1,009,718	1,458	568	2,009,821	42·4
1950	1,188,632	986,494	2,502	1,286	2,178,914	46·1
			All others			
1980	1,615,190	887,206	18,242		2,520,638	53·0
1990	1,633,461	915,057	24,698		2,573,216	54·8

Of the population in 1990, 1,230,617 were male, 1,210,729 were urban and 1,729,749 were 20 years old or older.

The largest city (1990) is Jackson, 196,637. Others are: Biloxi, 46,369; Greenville, 45,226; Hattiesburg, 41,882; Meridian, 41,036; Gulfport, 40,775; Tupelo, 30,685; Pascagoula, 25,899; Columbus, 23,799; Clinton, 21,847; Vicksburg, 20,908.

CLIMATE. Jackson. Jan. 47°F (8·3°C), July 82°F (27·8°C). Annual rainfall 49" (1,221 mm). Vicksburg. Jan. 48°F (8·9°C), July 81°F (27·2°C). Annual rainfall 52" (1,311 mm). Mississippi belongs to the Central Plains climate zone (*see* UNITED STATES: Climate).

CONSTITUTION AND GOVERNMENT. The present constitution was adopted in 1890 without ratification by the electorate; 103 amendments by 1990.

The Legislature consists of a Senate (52 members) and a House of Representatives (122 members), both elected for 4 years. Electors are all citizens who have resided in the state 1 year, in the county 1 year, in the election district 6 months before the election and have been registered according to law. In the 1992 presidential election Bush polled 487,793 votes, Clinton, 400,258; Perot, 85,626.

The state sends 5 representatives to Congress.

The capital is Jackson; there are 82 counties.

Governor: Kirk Fordice (R.), 1996–2000 ($83,160).
Lieut.-Governor: Ronnie Musgrove (D.) ($40,800).
Secretary of State: Eric Clark (D.) ($59,400).

BUDGET. For the fiscal year ending 30 June 1995 the general revenues were $7,706,056,556 (taxation, $3,356,284,154; federal aid, $2,239,091,752; other state revenues, $2,110,680,650), and general expenditures were $7,335,051,879 ($2,077,676,620 for education, $520,844,028 for highways and $2,180,715,540 for public welfare).

On 30 June 1995 the total net long-term debt was $1,188,323,524.

Per capita personal income (1994) was $14,088.

NATURAL RESOURCES

Minerals. Petroleum and natural gas account for about 90% (by value) of mineral production. Output of petroleum, 1994, was 20,124,303 bbls and of natural gas 120,502,946m. cu. ft. There are 5 oil refineries. Taxable value of oil and gas products sold in 1994 was $422,137,126.

Agriculture. Agriculture is the leading industry of the state because of the semi-tropical climate and a rich productive soil. In 1995 there were 82 soil conservation districts covering 25·6m. acres of co-operators. In 1995 farms numbered 40,000 with an area of 12·9m. acres. Average size of farm was 323 acres. This compares with an average farm size of 138 acres in 1960. Average value of farm per acre in 1993 was $757.

Cash income from all crops and livestock during 1994, including government payments, was $3,148,159,000. Cash income from crops was $1,210,043,000 and from livestock and products, $1,706,316,000. The chief product is cotton, cash income (1994) $743,983,000 from 1·5m. acres producing 2,132,700 bales of 480 lbs. Soybeans, rice, corn, hay, wheat, oats, sorghum, peanuts, pecans, sweet potatoes, peaches, other vegetables, nursery and forest products continue to contribute.

On 1 Jan. 1995 there were 1·34m. head of cattle and calves on Mississippi farms. In June 1995 milch cows totalled 56,000, beef cows, 683,000; (1994) hogs and pigs, 166,000. Of cash income from livestock and products, 1994, $242,662,000 was credited to cattle and calves. Cash income from poultry and eggs, 1994, totalled $1,046,158,000; dairy products, $102·95m.; swine, $24,112,000.

Forestry. In 1994 income from forestry amounted to $1,078,747,371; output of logs, lumber, etc., was 1,836,233,000 bd ft; pulpwood, 7,989,701 cords; distillate wood, 20,801 tons. There are about 18·6m. acres of forest (62% of the state's area). National forest area, 1994, 1·1m. acres.

INDUSTRY. In 1994 the 3,718 manufacturing establishments employed 261,416 workers, earning $5,906,148,961. The average annual wage was $22,593.

TOURISM. Total receipts in fiscal year 1994, $3,800m.; an estimated 3·5m. overnight tourists visted the state in 1994.

COMMUNICATIONS

Roads. The state as of 1 July 1995 maintained 10,480·7 miles of highways, of which all miles were paved. In 1995, 2,150,214 cars were registered.

Railways. The state in 1995 had 2,841·46 main-line miles of railway.

Civil Aviation. There were 76 public airports in 1995, 69 of them general aviation airports. There were also 44 privately owned airports.

SOCIAL INSTITUTIONS

Justice. The death penalty is authorized; the last execution took place in 1989. As of 6 Oct. 1995, the state prisons had 12,901 inmates.

Religion. Southern Baptists in Mississippi (1994), 693,194 members, including some Black members; Negro Baptists (1994), 0·32m.; United Methodists (1994) 186,185; Roman Catholics (1995), 108,044 in Biloxi and Jackson dioceses.

Education. Attendance at school is compulsory as laid down in the Education Reform Act of 1982. The public elementary and secondary schools in 1994–95 had 503,301 pupils and 29,113 classroom teachers.

In 1995, teachers' average salary was $26,801. The expenditure per pupil in average daily attendance, 1994–95, was $4,211.

There are 21 universities and senior colleges, of which 8 are state-supported. In 1994–95, the University of Mississippi, Oxford had 412 instructors and 10,435 students; Mississippi State University, Starkville, 587 instructors and 14,215 students; Mississippi University for Women, Columbus, 111 instructors and 3,023 students; University of Southern Mississippi, Hattiesburg, 578 instructors and 13,047 students; Jackson State University, Jackson, 305 instructors and 6,224 students; Delta State University, Cleveland, 176 instructors and 3,917 students; Alcorn State University, Lorman, 128 instructors and 2,742 students; Mississippi Valley State University, Itta Bena, 101 instructors and 2,182 students. State support for the universities (1994–95) was $333,580,759.

Junior colleges had (1994–95) 76,934 students and 2,739 full-time instructors. The state appropriation for junior colleges, 1994–95, was $131,199,913.

Health. In 1994 the state had 103 acute general hospitals (11,666 beds) listed by the State Department of Health; 17 hospitals with facilities for care of the mentally ill had 638 licensed beds; 7 rehabilitation hospitals had 265 beds.

Social Security. The Division of Medicaid paid (fiscal year 1995) $1,442,688,608 for medical services, including $161,081,776 for drugs, $242,043,645 for skilled nursing home care, and $369,623,902 for hospital services. There were 37,827 persons eligible for Aged Medicaid benefits at 30 June 1995 and 116,037 persons eligible for Disabled Medicaid benefits. In June 1995, 52,067 families with 104,712 dependent children received $6,156,323 in the Aid to Dependent Children programme. The average monthly payment was $118.99 per family or $43.54 per recipient.

Further Reading

Statistical information: College of Business and Industry, Mississippi State Univ., Mississippi State 39762. Publishes *Mississippi Statistical Abstract.*

Secretary of State. *Mississippi Official and Statistical Register.* Biennial

Bettersworth, J. K., *Mississippi: A History.* Rev. ed. Austin, Tex., 1964

Mississippi Library Commission: PO Box 10700 Jackson, MS. 39289–0700. *Executive Director:* Mary Ellen Pellington.

MISSOURI

KEY HISTORICAL EVENTS. Missouri, first settled in 1735 at Ste Genevieve, was made a Territory on 1 Oct. 1812, and admitted to the Union on 10 Aug. 1821. In 1837 its boundaries were extended to their present limits.

TERRITORY AND POPULATION. Missouri is bounded north by Iowa, east by the Mississippi River forming the boundary with Illinois and Kentucky, south by Arkansas, south-east by Tennessee, south-west by Oklahoma, west by Kansas and Nebraska, with the Missouri River forming the boundary in the north-west. Land area, 68,898 sq. miles (178,446 sq. km).

Census population, 22 April 1990, 5,117,073 (68·7% urban), an increase since 1980 of 4·1%. Population estimate (1994), 5,278,000. Births, 1994, were 73,279; deaths, 53,611; infant deaths, 597 (8·1 per 1,000 live births); marriages, 45,070 (8·5 per 1,000 population); divorces, 26,441 (5).

Population of 5 federal census years was:

	White	*Black*	*Indian*	*Asiatic*	*Total*	*Per sq. mile*
1930	3,403,876	223,840	578	1,073	3,629,367	52·4
1960	3,922,967	390,853	1,723	3,146	4,319,813	62·5
			All others			
1970	4,177,495	480,172	19,732		4,677,399	67·0
1980	4,345,521	514,276	56,889		4,916,686	71·3
1990	4,486,228	548,208	82,637		5,117,073	74·3

Of the total population in 1990, 2,464,315 were male. In 1990, 3,515,882 persons were urban and those 18 years of age or older numbered 3,939,284.

The principal cities at the 1990 census are:

Kansas City	435,146	Columbia	69,101
St Louis	396,685	St Charles	54,555
Springfield	140,494	Florissant	51,206
Independence	112,301	Joplin	40,961
St Joseph	71,852	University City	40,087

Metropolitan areas, 1990: St Louis, 2,444,099; Kansas City, 1,566,280.

CLIMATE. Kansas City. Jan. 30°F (–1·1°C), July 79°F (26·1°C). Annual rainfall 38" (947 mm). St Louis. Jan. 32°F (0°C), July 79°F (26·1°C). Annual rainfall 40" (1,004 mm). Mississppi belongs to the Central Plains climate zone (*see* UNITED STATES: Climate).

CONSTITUTION AND GOVERNMENT. A new constitution, the fourth, was adopted on 27 Feb. 1945; it has been revised 9 times with over 100 amendments. The General Assembly consists of a Senate of 34 members elected for 4 years (half for re-election every 2 years), and a House of Representatives of 163 members elected for 2 years. The Governor and Lieut.-Governor are elected for 4 years.

The state sends 9 representatives to Congress.

In the 1992 presidential election Clinton polled 1,053,873 votes; Bush, 811,159; Perot, 518,741.

Jefferson City is the state capital. The state is divided into 114 counties and the city of St Louis.

Governor: Mel Carnahan (D.), 1995–97 ($94,563).
Lieut.-Governor: Roger Wilson (D.) ($57,145).
Secretary of State: Rebecca McDowell Cook (D.) ($75,854).

BUDGET. For the year 1993 the total revenues from all funds were $12,559m. (federal revenue, $2,732·6m., general revenue, $4,674·5m.).

Total outstanding debt, 1993, was $6,516m.

Per capita personal income (1994) was $20,717.

NATURAL RESOURCES

Minerals. The 3 leading mineral commodities are lead, portland cement and crushed stone. Value of production (1992) $897·2m.

Agriculture. In 1995 there were 2,073 farms in Missouri producing crops and livestock on 30m. acres; the average farm had 283 acres and in 1994 was valued at $762 per acre. Production of principal crops, 1994: Corn, 273·7m. bu.; soybeans, 173·3m. bu.; wheat, 49·5m. bu.; sorghum grain, 49·5m. bu.; oats, 1·77m. bu.; rice, 6·5m. cwt; cotton, 615,000 bales (of 480 lbs). Cash receipts from farming, 1994, $2,450m. to which livestock and products contributed $2,300m. and soybeans $95·54m.

Forestry. Forest land area, 1993, 3·06m. acres.

INDUSTRY. The largest employer in 1992 was manufacturing, in which the transport equipment industry employed 57,748 workers. Other large industries are food and kindred products, electronic and other electronic equipment, apparel and other textile products, industrial machinery and equipment, leather products, chemicals, paper, primary metal industries and metal products, printing and publishing, stone, clay, glass, rubber and plastic products, instruments, lumber and wood products. Wholesale and retail trade employed 561,001 as of March 1992.

LABOUR. The State Board of Mediation has jurisdiction in labour disputes involving only public utilities. The Prevailing Wage Law (1959) provides that no less than the local hourly rate of wages for work of a similar character shall be paid to any workmen engaged in public works. The Industrial Commission has authority to inspect records and to institute actions for penalties described in the Act. There is a state programme for industrial safety in hand, under the Federal Occupational and Health Act. In 1994 the annual average number of employed was 2,564,000, and 131,000 were unemployed; the unemployment rate was 4·9%.

COMMUNICATIONS

Roads. At 31 Dec. 1993 there were 121,787 miles of roads (105,637 miles rural) and 4,065,686 registered motor vehicles.

Railways. The state has 8 Class I railways; approximate total mileage, 6,645. There are 9 Class II and Class III railways (switching, terminal or short-line), total mileage 435, in 1993. There is a light rail line in St Louis.

Civil Aviation. In 1994 there were 114 public airports and 359 private airports.

Shipping. Two major barge lines (1993) operated on about 1,050 miles of navigable waterways including the Missouri and Mississippi Rivers. Boat shipping seasons: Missouri River, April–end Nov.; Mississippi River, all seasons.

Post and Broadcasting. There were 196 commercial radio stations and 29 TV stations in 1995.

Press. There were (1995) 46 daily and 260 weekly newspapers.

SOCIAL INSTITUTIONS

Justice. State prisons in 1994 had an average of 18,346 inmates including 886 females. The median age was 33·3 in 1994. The death penalty was reinstated in 1978, and first execution since 1965 was in 1989. The Missouri Law Enforcement Assistance Council was created in 1969 for law reform. With reorganization of state government in 1974 the duties of the Council were delegated to the Department of Public Safety. The Dept. of Corrections was organised as a separate department of State by an Act of the Legislature in 1981.

Religion. Chief religious bodies (1990) are Catholic, with 802,434 members, Southern Baptists (789,183), United Methodists (255,111), Christian Churches (166,412), Lutheran (142,824), Presbyterian (45,341). Total membership, all denominations, about 2·3m. in 1990.

Education. School attendance is compulsory for children from 7 to 16 years for the full term. In the 1993–94 school year, public schools (kindergarten through grade 12) had 851,086 pupils. Total expenditure for public schools in 1993–94, $3,563,419,000. Salaries for teachers (kindergarten through grade 12), 1993–94, averaged $30,227. Institutions for higher education include the University of Missouri, founded in 1839 with campuses at Columbia, Rolla, St Louis and Kansas City, with 3,469 accredited teachers and 48,072 students in 1994–95. Washington University at St Louis, founded in 1857, is an independent co-ed university with 11,655 students in 1994–95. St Louis University (1818), is an independent Roman Catholic co-ed university with 10,365 students in 1994–95. Seventeen state colleges had 129,466 students in 1994–95. Private colleges had (1994–95) 34,548 students. Church-affiliated colleges (1994–95) had 41,420 students. Public junior colleges had 66,853 students. There are about 90 secondary and post-secondary institutions offering vocational courses, and about 294 private career schools. There were 265,186 students in higher education in autumn 1994.

Health. There were 14 state mental health hospitals and centres and 5 children's hospitals in 1994, admitting 41,109 patients.

Social Security. The number of actual recipients of medicaid for the last 5 months of 1994 averaged 346,873; eligible to receive medicaid, 559,331. The number of recipients of Aid to families with Dependent Children was 259,048 with an average monthly payment per family of $264.79.

Further Reading

Statistical information: Business and Public Administration Research Center, Univ. of Missouri, Columbia 65211. Publishes *Statistical Abstract for Missouri.*
Missouri Area Labor Trends, Department of Labor and Industrial Relations, monthly
Missouri Farm Facts, Department of Agriculture, annual
Report of the Public Schools of Missouri. State Board of Education, annual

MONTANA

KEY HISTORICAL EVENTS. Montana, first settled in 1809, was made a Territory (out of portions of Idaho and Dakota Territories) in 1864 and was admitted into the Union on 8 Nov. 1889.

TERRITORY AND POPULATION. Montana is bounded north by Canada, east by North and South Dakota, south by Wyoming and west by Idaho and the Bitterroot Range of the Rocky Mountains. Land area, 145,556 sq. miles (336,991 sq. km). US Bureau of Indian Affairs (1990) administered 5,574,835 acres, of which 2,663,385 were allotted to tribes. Census population, 1 April 1990, 799,065 (52·5% urban), an increase of 2% since 1980. Population estimate (1993), 839,422. Births in 1991, 11,544 (14·3 per 1,000 population): deaths, 7,071 (8·8); infant deaths, 106 (9·1 per 1,000 live births); marriages, 7,175 (8·9); divorces, 4,385 (5·4).

Population in 5 census years was:

	White	*Black*	*Indian*	*Asiatic*	*Total*	*Per sq. mile*
1910	360,580	1,834	10,745	2,870	376,053	2·6
1930	519,898	1,256	14,798	1,239	537,606	3·7
1950	572,038	1,232	16,606	—	591,024	4·1
1980	740,148	1,786	37,270	2,503	786,690	5·3
1990	741,111	2,381	47,679	4,259	799,065	5·4

Of the total population in 1990, 395,769 were male, 419,826 persons were urban. Persons 18 years of age or older numbered 576,961. Median age, 33·8 years. Households, 306,163.

The largest cities, 1990 are Billings, 81,151; Great Falls, 55,097. Others: Missoula, 42,918; Butte-Silver Bow, 33,336; Helena (capital), 24,569; Bozeman, 22,660; Kalispell, 11,917; Anaconda-Deer Lodge County, 10,278; Havre, 10,201.

CLIMATE. Helena. Jan. 18°F (–7·8°C), July 69°F (20·6°C). Annual rainfall 13" (325 mm). Montana belongs to the Mountain States climate zone (*see* UNITED STATES: Climate).

CONSTITUTION AND GOVERNMENT. A new constitution came into force on 1 July 1973. The Senate consists of 50 senators, elected for 4 years, one half at each biennial election. The 100 members of the House of Representatives are elected for 2 years.

The state sends 1 representative to Congress.

In the 1992 presidential election Clinton polled 154,507 votes; Bush, 144,207; Perot, 107,225.

The capital is Helena. The state is divided into 56 counties.

Governor: Marc Racicot (R.), 1993–97 ($59,310).
Lieut.-Governor: Dennis Rehberg (R.), ($43,242).
Secretary of State: Mike Cooney (D.), ($40,101).

BUDGET. Total state revenues for the year ending 30 June 1990 were $2,225,000,000; total expenditures were $2,007,000,000.

Total net long-term debt on 30 June 1990 was $396m.

Per capita personal income (1994) was $17,865.

NATURAL RESOURCES

Minerals. 1990 nonfuel mineral production value was $568m. Copper was the leading commodity in terms of value, followed by gold, platinum-group metals, molybdenum and silver.

Agriculture. In 1991 there were 24,800 farms and ranches (50,564 in 1935) with an area of 60,300,000 acres (47,511,868 acres in 1935). Large-scale farming predominates; in 1991 the average size per farm was 2,431 acres, and in 1995 the average value per acre was $277. The farm population in 1991, was 67,546 (2·8% people per farm). Irrigated area harvested in 1986 was 1·6m. acres; non-irrigated, 7·8m. acres.

The chief crops (cash receipts, 1990) are wheat, amounting in 1986 to 138·5m. bu. ($435,788); barley, 85m. bu. ($125,436); oats, 4·1m. bu.; sugar-beet, hay ($81,996), potatoes, corn, dry beans and cherries. Farm income, 1991: crops, $746m.; livestock and products, $854m. In 1986 there were 24,000 milch cows, 2·4m. all cattle; 190,000 swine and 423,000 sheep. In 1990 the cash receipts for cattle and calves were $725,476; dairy products, $45,292; hogs and pigs, $42,150; sheep and lambs, $18,655.

Forestry. Total forest area (1986), 22·6m. acres. In 1990 there were 16·8m. acres within 11 national forests.

INDUSTRY. In 1987 manufacturing establishments numbering 1,223 had 20,900 production workers; value added by manufacture was (1986) $907·4m.

LABOUR (March 1991). Work force, 401,400; total employed, 369,600; total non-agricultural workers, 291,800. Workers employed by major industry group: Mining, 5,900 (average net weekly earnings, $592.18); construction, 7,700 ($499.56); manufacturing, 20,200 ($442.37); transport and public utilities, 20,000 ($468.43; trade industry, 76,500 ($388.90); finance/insurance/real estate, 13,270; services, 75,500 ($258.34); government, 71,400 (no income figures available). Average weekly earnings for all workers in private non-agricultural industries $295.45. During 1990, 56 mass layoff events involved 5,001 workers laid off from their jobs (separations), 50% more separations than in 1989.

COMMUNICATIONS

Roads. In March 1992 there were a total of 70,806 miles of roads and in 1991, 765,754 registered motor vehicles.

Railways. In Feb. 1992 there were 3,329 route miles of railway in the state.

Civil Aviation. In 1992 there were 122 publicly owned airports.

Telecommunications. In 1992 there were 51 radio stations, 18 TV stations and 10 cable systems.

Press. In 1992 there were 12 daily newspapers and 74 semi-weekly, weekly, or shopper-type papers.

SOCIAL INSTITUTIONS

Justice. At 31 Dec. 1991 the Montana State Prison at Deer Lodge held 1,188 inmates and the Women's Correctional Facility at Warm Springs, 62. The death penalty is authorized, but there have been no executions since 1943.

Religion. The leading religious bodies are (1987): Roman Catholic with 162,000 members; Lutheran, 68,654; Methodist (Yellowstone Conference, including N. Wyoming, Montana, and Salmon, Idaho), 21,609 (church estimates).

Education. In 1992 public elementary and secondary schools had 153,075 pupils and 9,599 teachers. Expenditure on public school education by state and local governments in 1991 was $1,055·1m.

The Montana University system consists of the Montana State University, at Bozeman (autumn 1992 enrolment: 10,111 students), the University of Montana, at Missoula, founded in 1895 (10,788), the Montana College of Mineral Science and Technology, at Butte (1,881), Northern Montana College, at Havre (1,973), Eastern Montana College, at Billings (3,631) and Western Montana College, at Dillon (1,106).

Social Security. In June 1991, 5,241 persons over age 65 were receiving in medical assistance an average of $980 per year per person; 52 blind persons, $700, 7,000 totally disabled, $833; 9,937 families received in aid-to-dependent children assistance an average of $342. Aid was from state and federal sources.

Health. In Sept. 1990 the state had 60 hospitals (3,359 beds) and 102 licensed long-term care facilities (7,487 beds).

Further Reading

Statistical information. Census and Economic Information Center, Montana Department of Commerce, 1425 9th Ave., Helena 59620.

Lang, W. L. and Myers, R. C., *Montana, Our Land and People.* Pruett, 1979

Malone, M. P. and Roeder, R. B., *Montana, A History of Two Centuries.* Univ. of Washington Press, 1976

Spence, C. C., *Montana: a History.* New York, 1978

NEBRASKA

KEY HISTORICAL EVENTS. The Nebraska region was first reached by Europeans from Mexico under the Spanish general Coronado in 1541. It was ceded by France to Spain in 1763, retroceded to France in 1801, and sold by Napoleon to the US as part of the Louisiana Purchase in 1803. Its first settlement was in 1847, and on 30 May 1854 it became a Territory and on 1 March 1867 a state. In 1882 it annexed a small part of Dakota Territory, and in 1908 it received another small tract from South Dakota.

TERRITORY AND POPULATION. Nebraska is bounded in the north by South Dakota, with the Missouri River forming the boundary in the north-east and the boundary with Iowa and Missouri to the east; south by Kansas, south-west by Colorado and west by Wyoming. Land area, 76,878 sq. miles (199,113 sq. km). Census population, 1990: 1,578,385 (66·1% urban), an increase of 0·53% since 1980. Population estimate (1993), 1,607,199. Births, 1991, were 23,933 (14·7 per 1,000 population); deaths, 14,665 (9); infant deaths in 1992, 186 (7·9 per 1,000 live births); marriages, 12,695 (7·8): divorces, 6,496 (4).

Population in 5 census years was:

	White	Black	Indian	Asiatic	Total	Per sq. mile
1910	1,180,293	7,689	3,502	730	1,192,214	15·5
1920	1,279,219	13,242	2,888	1,023	1,296,372	16·9
1960	1,374,764	29,262	5,545	1,195	1,411,330	18·3
			All others			
1970	1,432,867	39,911	10,715		1,483,791	19·4
1980	1,490,381	48,390	31,054		1,569,825	20·5

Of the total population in 1980, 48·8% were male, 62·9% were urban 65·6% were 21 years of age or older. The largest cities in the state are: Omaha, with a census population, 1990, of 335,795; Lincoln, 191,972; Grand Island, (1986 estimate) 39,100; North Platte, 22,490; Fremont, 23,780; Hastings, 22,990; Bellevue, 32,200; Kearney, 22,770; Norfolk, 20,260.

The Bureau of Indian Affairs in 1990 administered 64,932 acres, of which 21,742 acres were allotted to tribal control.

CLIMATE. Omaha. Jan. 22°F (–5·6°C), July 77°F (25°C). Annual rainfall 29" (721 mm). Nebraska belongs to the High Plains climate zone (*see* UNITED STATES: Climate).

CONSTITUTION AND GOVERNMENT. The present constitution was adopted in 1875; it has been amended 184 times. By an amendment of 1934 Nebraska has a single-chambered legislature (elected for 4 years) of 49 members elected on a non-party ballot and classed as senators—the only state in the USA to have one. It meets annually.

The state sends 3 representatives to Congress.

In the 1992 presidential election Bush polled 343,678 votes; Clinton, 216,864; Perot, 174,104.

The capital is Lincoln. The state has 93 counties.

Governor: Ben Nelson (R.), 1995–99 ($65,000).
Lieut.-Governor: Kim Robak (D.) ($47,000).
Secretary of State: Scott Moore (R.) ($52,000).

BUDGET. For the fiscal year ending 1990 the state's revenues were $2,855·5m. (taxation, $1,512·9m. and federal aid, $681·4m.); general expenditures were $2,815m. ($906·9m. for education, $409·5m. for highways and $498·5m. for public welfare).

Total outstanding debt, 1991, was $1,596m.

Per capita personal income (1994) was $20,488.

NATURAL RESOURCES

Minerals. The total output of non-fuel minerals, 1990, was valued at $106·4m., sand and gravel being the most important. 6·1m. bbls of petroleum were produced in 1987. Other minerals include limestone, potash, pumice, slate, shale and clay.

Agriculture. Nebraska is one of the most important agricultural states. In 1991 it contained approximately 56,000 farms, with a total area of 47m. acres. The average farm was 841 acres and in 1995 the average value per acre was $596. In 1990, 8m. acres were irrigated, 70% receiving water from irrigation wells.

Cash income from crops (1991), $3,724m., and from livestock (1991), some $5,000m. Principal crops, with estimated 1987 yield: Maize, 812·2m. bu.; wheat, 85·8m. bu.; sorghums for grain, 109·2m. bu.; oats, 17·3m. bu.; soybeans, 81·9m. bu. Livestock, 1990: Cattle, 6m.; pigs, 4·2m.; sheep, 0·16m.; chickens, 2·1m.; turkeys, 2·1m.

Forestry. There were 722,000 acres of forest in 1990.

INDUSTRY. In 1986 there were 1,800 manufacturing establishments; 62,600 production workers earned $1,141·2m. and value added by manufacturing was

$5,362·6m. The chief industry is meat-packing. Pork products were worth $878m. in 1991.

In 1991, 186,582 workers were employed in trade, 179,730 in services, 145,503 in government, 99,267 in manufacturing, 48,479 in finance, insurance and real estate, 47,505 in transport, communication and utilities and 29,105 in construction and mining.

COMMUNICATIONS

Roads. In 1990 there were 92,459 miles of roads (87,509 miles rural). In 1991 there were 1,404,444 registered motor vehicles.

Railways. In 1988 there were 4,013 miles of railway.

Civil Aviation. Airports (1988) numbered 354, of which 101 were publicly owned.

SOCIAL INSTITUTIONS

Justice. A 'Civil Rights Act' revised in 1969 provides that all people are entitled to a full and equal enjoyment of public facilities.

In 1991 there were 2,436 prisoners in state correctional institutions. The death penalty is authorized. The last execution was in 1994.

Religion. The Roman Catholics had 337,855 members in 1985; Protestant Churches, 737,361; Jews, 7,865 members. Total, all denominations, 1,083,081.

Education. School attendance is compulsory for children from 7 to 16 years of age. Public elementary and secondary schools, in 1992, had 277,652 enrolled pupils and 18,358 teachers. Teachers' salaries, 1987–88, averaged $23,246. Public school expenditure by state and local government, in 1991 was $2,142·6m. Total enrolment in 27 institutions of higher education, autumn 1987, was 100,454 students. The largest institutions were (1987):

Opened	*Institution*	*Students*
1867	Peru State College, Peru (State)	1,396
1869	Univ. of Nebraska, Lincoln (State)	25,722
1872	Doane College, Crete (UCC)	796
1878	Creighton Univ., Omaha (RC)	5,827
1882	Hastings College (Presbyterian)	894
1883	Midland Lutheran College, Fremont (Lutheran)	836
1887	Nebraska Wesleyan Univ. (Methodist)	1,359
1891	Union College, Lincoln (Seventh Day Adventist)	578
1894	Concordia Teachers' College, Seward (Lutheran)	816
1905	Kearney State College, Kearney (State)	9,075
1908	Univ. of Nebraska, Omaha (State)	14,210
1910	Wayne State College, Wayne (State)	2,899
1911	Chadron State College, Chadron (State)	2,250
1923	College of St. Mary	1,256
1966	Bellevue College, Bellevue (Private)	1,922

The state holds 1·52m. acres of land as a permanent endowment of her schools; permanent public school endowment fund in Aug. 1988 was $94·9m.

Health. In 1988 the state had 114 hospitals and 565 patients in mental hospitals.

Social Security. The administration of public welfare is the responsibility of the County Divisions of Welfare with policy-forming, regulatory, advisory and supervisory functions performed by the State Department of Public Welfare. In 1987 public welfare provided financial aid and/or services as follows: for 7,680 individuals who were aged, blind or disabled, with an average state supplement of $58.65; for 16,315 families with dependent children, with an average payment of $318.31 per family; for 88,390 individuals who had medical needs, $1,937.02, per individual; for 3,280 children in need of child welfare services; $1·8m. was spent on medically-handicapped children. The amount of aid is based on need in accordance with State assistance standards; the programme of aid to families with dependent children is limited to a maximum maintenance payment of $300 for 1 child plus $75 for each additional child.

Further Reading

Statistical information: Department of Economic Development, Box 94666, Lincoln 68509. Publishes *Nebraska Statistical Handbook.*
Agricultural Atlas of Nebraska. Univ. of Nebraska Press, 1977
Climatic Atlas of Nebraska. Univ. of Nebraska Press, 1977
Economic Atlas of Nebraska. Univ. of Nebraska Press, 1977
Nebraska. A Guide to the Cornhusker State. Univ. of Nebraska Press, 1979
Nebraska Blue-Book. Legislative Council. Lincoln. Biennial
Olson, J. C., *History of Nebraska.* Univ. of Nebraska Press, 1955

State Library: State Law Library, State House, Lincoln.

NEVADA

KEY HISTORICAL EVENTS. Nevada, first settled in 1851, when it was a part of the Territory of Utah (created 1850), was made a Territory in 1861, enlarged in 1862 by an addition from Utah Territory and admitted into the Union on 31 Oct. 1864 as the 36th state. In 1866 and 1867 the area of the state was significantly enlarged at the expense of the Territories of Utah and Arizona.

TERRITORY AND POPULATION. Nevada is bounded north by Oregon and Idaho, east by Utah, south-east by Arizona, with the Colorado River forming most of the boundary, south and west by California. Land area, 105,540 sq. miles (273,349 sq. km). The federal government in 1995 owned 56,854,307 acres, or 80·4% of the land area.

Census population on 1 April 1990, 1,201,833 (88·3% urban), an increase of 401,325 since 1980. Population estimate (1995), 1,582,280. Births, 1994, were 24,226; deaths, 11,680; marriages, 139,867; divorces, 12,969; infant deaths, 155; abortions, 6,736.

Population in 5 census years was:

	White	*Black*	*Indian*	*All others*	*Total*	*Per sq. mile*
1910	74,276	513	5,240	1,846	81,875	0·7
1930	84,515	516	4,871	1,156	91,058	0·8
1970	449,850	27,579	7,329	3,980	488,738	4·4
1980	700,360	50,999	13,308	35,841	800,508	7·2
1990	1,012,695	78,771	19,637	90,730	1,201,833	10·9

Of the total population in 1990, 611,880 were male, 1,061,312 were urban and 364,109 were under 21 years of age.

The largest cities (with 1995 estimated population) are: Las Vegas, 368,360; Reno, 150,620; Henderson, 115,380; North Las Vegas, 77,820; Sparks, 59,880; Carson City (the capital), 46,770.

CLIMATE. Las Vegas. Jan. 44°F (6·7°C), July 85°F (29·4°C). Annual rainfall 4·13" (105 mm). Reno. Jan. 32°F (0°C), July 69°F (20·6°C). Annual rainfall 7·53" (191 mm). Nevada belongs to the Mountain States climate zone (*see* UNITED STATES: Climate).

CONSTITUTION AND GOVERNMENT. The constitution adopted in 1864 is still in force, with 119 amendments by 1994. The Legislature meets biennially (and in special sessions) and consists of a Senate of 21 members elected for 2 years, half their number retiring every 2 years, and an Assembly of 42 members elected for 4 years. The Governor may be elected for 2 consecutive 4-year terms.

The state sends 2 representatives to Congress.

In the 1992 presidential election Clinton polled 189,148 votes; Bush, 175,828; Perot, 132,580.

The state capital is Carson City. There are 16 counties, 18 incorporated cities and 44 unincorporated communities and 1 city-county (the Capitol District of Carson City).

Governor: Bob Miller (D.), 1995–99 ($90,000).
Lieut.-Governor: Lonnie Hammargren (R.) ($20,000).
Secretary of State: Dean Heller (R.) ($57,000).

BUDGET. For the fiscal year ending 30 June 1994, state general fund revenues were $1,076·7m.; budget expenditures were $1,007·8m. from the general fund. Education (56·5% of the total), followed by human services (24·3%), received the largest appropriations.

State bonded indebtedness on 30 June 1994, was $423m. The state has no franchise tax, capital stock tax, special intangibles tax, stock transfer tax, admissions tax, gift tax, or income tax. Taxes on gambling and the state's 2% share of the sales tax represent nearly 76% of the general fund revenues.

Per capita personal income (1994) was $23,817.

NATURAL RESOURCES

Minerals. Value of total production, 1994, $3,054m., including: Gold ($2,610m.), silver ($120m.), sand and gravel ($126m.), barite ($20m.). Petroleum produced, 4m. bbls. Other minerals are iron ore, mercury, lime, lithium, gemstones, lead, molybdenum, fluorspar, perlite, pumice, clays, talc, salt, tungsten, magnesite, diatomite and zinc.

Agriculture. In 1992, an estimated 2,890 farms had a farm area of 9,263,684 acres under cultivation. Farms averaged 3,205 acres. Average value per acre in 1995 was $289. Area under irrigation (1989) was 569,800 acres compared with 542,976 acres in 1959.

Total farm income, 1993, from crops, $345·1m., including from marketing crops and livestock, $186·2m. Cattle, hay, dairy products, potatoes and sheep are the principal commodities in order of cash receipts. In 1995 there were 0·5m. cattle and 107,500 sheep. In 1994, 722,000 lbs. of wool were produced with a total value of $527,000.

Forestry. The National Forests Wilderness area in 1995 was 5,169,587 acres. National forests: Toiyabe (322,000 acres); Humboldt (466,200).

INDUSTRY. The main industry is the service industry (43·1% of employment), especially tourism and legalized gambling. In 1994 there were 1,475 manufacturing establishments with 30,546 employees, and 3,937 construction firms with 49,894 employees.

Gaming industry gross revenue for 1994 was $6,723m. generated by 361 non-restricted licensed casinos. There are 2,468 licences in force.

LABOUR. In 1994, industries employed a total of 736,675 workers. Main industries and employees, 1994: Service industries, 327,550 (including gaming and tourism, 193,508); retail trade, 116,692; government, 92,158; finance, insurance and real estate, 34,142; transport, communications and public utilities, 37,833; mining, 12,350; manufacturing, 33,575. There were 48,000 unemployed in 1994.

COMMUNICATIONS

Roads. Highway mileage (federal, state and local) totalled 52,548 in 1990, of which 9,898 miles were paved; motor vehicle registrations in 1991 numbered 881,274.

Railways. In 1995 there were 1,275 miles of main-line railway. Nevada is served by the Southern Pacific, Union Pacific and Northern Nevada railways, and Amtrak passenger service for Las Vegas, Elko, Reno, Caliente, Lovelock, Stateline, Winnemucca and Sparks.

Civil Aviation. There were 98 civil airports and 24 heliports in Jan. 1996. During 1994 McCarran International Airport (Las Vegas) handled 26,850,486 passengers and Reno-Cannon International Airport handled 5,331,786 passengers.

Telecommunications. In Sept. 1995 there were 84 telephone exchanges, and 981,941 telephones in service (not including cellular).

SOCIAL INSTITUTIONS

Justice. Capital punishment was reintroduced in 1978, and executions began in 1979. In 1994 there were 6,911 persons in state and federal prisons.

Religion. Roman Catholics are the most numerous religious group, followed by members of the Church of Jesus Christ of Latter-day Saints (Mormons) and various Protestant churches.

Education. School attendance is compulsory for children from 7 to 17 years of age. Numbers of pupils in public schools, 1994–95: Pre-kindergarten, 1,424; kindergarten, 20,462; elementary, 124,371; secondary grades 7–9, 57,090; secondary grades 10–12, 46,708. Numbers of teachers in public schools, 1994–95: Elementary, 6,642; secondary, 4,605; special education, 17,434; occupational, 239. Numbers of pupils in private schools, 1994–95: Kindergartens, 1,779; elementary, 5,390; secondary grades 7–9, 2,085; secondary grades 10–12, 1,296.

The University of Nevada System comprises campuses at Las Vegas and Reno and 4 community colleges. In 1994–95 it had 35,428 students and 1,710 academic staff.

Health. At 30 June 1993 the state had 29 hospitals (4,300 beds). In Jan. 1996 there were 36 nursing units (3,676 beds).

Social Security. In 1993 benefits were paid to 205,000 persons: 152,000 retired (aged 62 and over) workers (average payment $638 per month); 28,000 widows and widowers ($658); 25,000 disabled workers ($643).

Further Reading

Statistical information: Budget and Planning Division, Department of Administration, Capitol Complex, Carson City, Nevada, 89710. Publishes *Nevada Statistical Abstract* (Biennial).

Bushnell, E. and Driggs, D. W., *The Nevada Constitution: Origin and Growth.* 5th ed. Univ. of Nevada Press, 1980
Hulse, J. W., *The Nevada Adventure: a History.* 6th ed. Univ. of Nevada Press, 1990
Laxalt, R., *Nevada: a History.* New York, 1977
Mack, E. M. and Sawyer, B. W., *Here is Nevada: a History of the State.* Sparks, 1965
Paher, S. W., *Nevada: an Annotated Bibliography.* Carson City, 1980

State Library: Nevada State Library, Carson City.

NEW HAMPSHIRE

KEY HISTORICAL EVENTS. New Hampshire, first settled in 1623, is one of the 13 original states of the Union.

TERRITORY AND POPULATION. New Hampshire is bounded in the north by Canada, east by Maine and the Atlantic, south by Massachusetts and west by Vermont. Land area, 8,993 sq. miles (23,292 sq. km). Census population, 1 April 1990, 1,109,252 (51% urban), an increase of 20·49% since 1980. Estimated population (1993), 1,125,310. Births, 1991, were 16,324 (14·7 per 1,000 population); deaths, 8,382 (7·6); infant deaths, 1992, were 89 (5·5 per 1,000 live births); marriages, 9,805 (8·5); divorces, 4,927 (4·3).

Population at 5 federal censuses was:

	White	*Black*	*Indian*	*Asiatic*	*Total*	*Per sq. mile*
1910	429,906	564	34	68	430,572	47·7
1960	604,334	1,903	135	549	606,921	65·2
			All others			
1970	733,106	2,505	2,070		737,681	81·7
1980	910,099	3,990	6,521		920,610	101·9
1990	1,087,433	7,198	14,621		1,109,252	123·7

The largest city in the state is Manchester, with a 1992 population of 99,490. The capital is Concord, with 36,364. Other cities are: Nashua, 79,666; Rochester,

26,640; Portsmouth, 25,342; Dover, 25,114; Keene, 22,373; Laconia, 15,743; Claremont, 13,779; Lebanon, 12,231; Berlin, 11,734; Somersworth, 11,239; Franklin, 8,213. There are also 221 towns.

CLIMATE. New Hampshire is in the New England climate zone (*see* UNITED STATES: Climate). Manchester. Jan. 22°F (–5·6°C), July 70°F (21·1°C). Annual rainfall 40" (1,003 mm).

CONSTITUTION AND GOVERNMENT. While the present constitution dates from 1784, it was extensively revised in 1792 when the state joined the Union. Since 1775 there have been 16 state conventions with 49 amendments adopted to amend the constitution.

The Legislature (called the General Court) consists of a Senate of 24 members, elected for 2 years, and a House of Representatives, of 400 members, elected for 2 years. It meets annually. The Governor and 5 administrative officers called 'Councillors' are also elected for 2 years.

The state sends 2 representatives to Congress.

In the 1992 presidential election Clinton polled 209,040 votes; Bush, 202,484; Perot, 121,337.

The capital is Concord. The state is divided into 10 counties.

Governor: Stephen Merrill (R.), 1995–97 ($86,235).
Secretary of State: William M. Gardner (D.) ($68,768).

BUDGET. New Hampshire has no general sales tax or state income tax but does have local property taxes. Other government revenues come from rooms and meals tax, business profits tax, motor vehicle licences, fuel taxes, fishing and hunting licences, state-controlled sales of alcoholic beverages, cigarette and tobacco taxes. The state government's general revenue for the fiscal year ending 1990 was $1,563·3m. ($595·3m. from taxes, $430·1m. from federal aid); general expenditures, $1,676·3m. ($401·4m. on education, $328·2m. on public welfare, $206·8m. on highways).

Per capita personal income (1994) was $23,434.

NATURAL RESOURCES

Minerals. Minerals are little worked; they consist mainly of sand and gravel, stone, and clay for building and highway construction. Value of non-fuel mineral production, 1990, $37·4m.

Agriculture. In 1991, there were some 2,900 farms covering 480,000 acres; average farm was 166 acres. Average value per acre in 1995, $2,486. The US Soil Survey estimates that the state has 164,167 acres of excellent soil, 486,615 acres of fair soil, 530,630 of poor soil and 3,843,798 of non-arable soil. Only 636,195 acres (11% of the total area) show moderate erosion.

Farm income, 1991, from crops, $70m., and livestock and products, $63m. The chief field crops are hay and vegetables; the chief fruit crop is apples. Livestock, 1992: Cattle, 46,000; pigs, 9,000; sheep, 11,600; poultry, 273,000.

Forestry. In 1990 forest land totalled 5,021,000 acres; national forest, 735,000 acres.

Fisheries. The 1990 catch was worth $10m.

INDUSTRY. Principal manufactures: Electrical and electronic goods, machinery, and metal products.

Labour. In 1990, 632,298 persons were in employment (excluding agriculture), of whom 182,754 worked in services, 123,218 in retail trade and 113,489 in manufacturing.

COMMUNICATIONS

Roads. In 1990 there were 14,803 miles of roads (12,387 miles rural). In 1991 there were 906,464 registered motor vehicles.

Railways. In 1991 the length of railway in the state was 626 miles.

Civil Aviation. In 1992 there were 14 public and 18 private airports.

Telecommunications. Across the state there were 42 radio and 5 TV stations in 1993.

Press. In 1993 there were 11 daily and 57 weekly newspapers.

SOCIAL INSTITUTIONS

Justice. The state prison held 1,565 persons on 15 June 1992. The death penalty is authorized, but there have been no executions since 1939.

Religion. The Roman Catholic Church is the largest single body. The largest Protestant churches are Congregational, Episcopal, Methodist and United Baptist Convention of N.H.

Education. School attendance is compulsory for children from 6 to 14 years of age during the whole school term, or to 16 if their district provides a high school. Employed illiterate minors between 16 and 21 years of age must attend evening or special classes, if provided by the district.

In 1992 the public elementary and secondary schools had 173,881 pupils and 10,677 teachers. Public school salaries, 1990, averaged $28,939. Education expenditure on public schools by state and local governments in 1991 was $1,251·58m.

Of the 4-year colleges, the University of New Hampshire (founded in 1866) had 13,853 students in 1992–93; New Hampshire College (1932), 7,000; Keene State College (1909), 4,882; Rivier College (1933), 2,765; Dartmouth College (1769), 5,090. Total enrolment, 1992-93, in the 30 institutions of higher education, was 62,207.

Health. In 1992 the state had 36 hospitals and 11 institutional infirmaries.

Social Security. The Division of Human Services handles public assistance for (1) aged citizens 65 years or over, (2) needy aged aliens, (3) needy blind persons, (4) needy citizens between 18 and 64 years inclusive, who are permanently and totally disabled, (5) needy children under 18 years, (6) Medicaid and the medically needy not eligible for a monthly grant.

In May 1988, 1,298 persons were receiving old-age assistance of an average $87 per month; 2,761 permanently and totally disabled, $133 per month; 4,003 families with dependent children, $439 per month.

Further Reading

Delorme, D. (ed.) *New Hampshire Atlas and Gazetteer.* Freeport, 1983
Morison, E. E. and E. F., *New Hampshire.* New York, 1976
Squires, J. D., *The Granite State of the United States: A History of New Hampshire from 1623 to the present.* 4 vols. New York, 1956

NEW JERSEY

KEY HISTORICAL EVENTS. New Jersey, first settled in the early 1600s, is one of the 13 original states in the Union.

TERRITORY AND POPULATION. New Jersey is bounded north by New York, east by the Atlantic with Long Island and New York City to the north-east, south by Delaware Bay and west by Pennsylvania. Land area, 7,419 sq. miles (19,210 sq. km). Census population, 1 April 1990, 7,730,188 (89·4% urban), an increase of 4·96% since 1980. Population density, 1990, 1,042·2 per sq. mile. Population estimate (1994), 7,904,000. Vital statistics, 1992 (per 1,000): Births, 120,437 (15·5); deaths, 70,847 (9·1); infant deaths in 1993, 989 (8·2); marriages, 55,296 (7·1); divorces in 1992, 25,405 (3·3).

Population at 5 federal censuses was:

	White	*Black*	*Indian*	*Asiatic*	*Others*	*Total*
1910	2,445,894	89,760	168	1,345	—	2,537,167
1930	3,829,663	208,828	213	2,630	—	4,041,334
1960	5,539,003	514,875	1,699	8,778	2,427	6,066,782
1980	6,127,467	925,066	8,394	103,848	200,048	7,364,823
1990	6,130,465	1,036,825	14,970	272,521	275,407	7,730,188

Of the population in 1990, 3,735,685 were male, 6,910,220 persons were urban, 5,718,136 were 20 years of age or older and 739,861 were Hispanic.

Census population of the larger cities and towns in 1990 was:

Newark	275,221	East Orange	73,552	Vineland	54,780
Jersey City	228,537	Clifton	71,742	Gloucester	53,797
Paterson	140,891	Cherry Hill	69,348	Union Township	50,024
Elizabeth	110,002	Middletown	68,183	Parsippany-Troy Hills	48,478
Woodbridge	93,086	Brick	66,473	North Bergen	48,414
Edison	88,680	Bayonne	61,444	Piscataway	47,089
Trenton (capital)	88,675	Irvington	61,018	Wayne	47,025
Camden	87,492	Passaic	58,041	Plainfield	46,567
Hamilton	86,553	Union City	58,012	Bloomfield	45,061
Dover	76,371	Old Bridge	56,475		

Largest metropolitan areas (1990) were: Newark, 1,824,321; Bergen-Passaic, 1,278,440; Jersey City, 553,099; Trenton, 325,824.

CLIMATE. Jersey City. Jan. 31°F (–0·6°C), July 75°F (23·9°C). Annual rainfall 41" (1,025 mm). Trenton. Jan. 32°F (0°C), July 76°F (24·4°C). Annual rainfall 40" (1,003 mm). New Jersey belongs to the Atlantic Coast climate zone (*see* UNITED STATES: Climate).

CONSTITUTION AND GOVERNMENT. The present constitution, ratified by the registered voters on 4 Nov. 1947, has been amended 45 times. There is a 40-member Senate and an 80-member General Assembly. Assembly members serve 2 years, senators 4 years, except those elected at the election following each census, who serve for 2 years. Sessions are held throughout the year.

The state sends 13 representatives to Congress.

In the 1992 presidential election Clinton polled 1,436,206 votes; Bush, 1,356,865; Perot, 521,829.

The capital is Trenton. The state is divided into 21 counties, which are subdivided into 567 municipalities—cities, towns, boroughs, villages and townships.

Governor: Christine Todd Whitman (R.), 1994–98 ($85,000).
Secretary of State: Lonna R. Hooks ($100,225).

BUDGET. For the year ending 30 June 1993 (budget figures) general revenues were $25,943m., general expenditures were $26,192m.

Outstanding general obligation bonded debt, 30 June 1993, was approximately $3,595m.

Per capita personal income (1994) was $27,742.

NATURAL RESOURCES

Minerals. In 1992 the chief minerals were stone (17·1m. short tons, value $126m.) and sand and gravel (17,934,000, $104,717,000); others are clays, peat and gemstones. New Jersey is a leading producer of greensand marl, magnesium compounds and peat. Total value of non-fuel mineral products, 1992, was $240,439,000.

Agriculture. Livestock raising, market-gardening, fruit-growing, horticulture and forestry are pursued. In 1994 there were some 8,500 farms averaging 101 acres. Average value per acre in 1995 was $8,052.

Market value (preliminary) of agricultural products sold, 1993: Crops, including nursery and greenhouse, $507,581,000; livestock, poultry and their products, $198·68m.

Leading crops are tomatoes (value, $18·9m., 1993), corn for grain ($15·1m.), peaches ($25·3m.), blueberries ($26·4m.), soybeans ($25·7m.), sweet corn ($15·9m.), peppers ($21·8m.), cranberries ($18·8m.). Livestock, 1993: 25,000 milch cows, 75,000 all cattle, 13,000 sheep and lambs and (Dec. 1992) 28,000 swine.

INDUSTRY. In 1993 the top 100 corporate employers employed 501,908, listed by New Jersey Business and Industry Association. The unemployment rate in Sept. 1994 was 6·7%.

In Aug. 1995 there were 3,629,100 employees on non-agricultural payrolls; 2,000 in mining, 136,400 in construction, 497,400 in manufacturing, 242,200 in transportation and public utilities, 867,600 in wholesale and retail trade, 232,000 in finance, insurance and real estate, 1,097,200 in services, 551,300 in government.

COMMUNICATIONS

Roads. In 1994 there were about 2,297 miles of state and interstate highways. At 9 Sept. 1994 there were 6,789 miles of county highways, 25,057 miles of municipal roads and 941 miles of other road. In 1992 there were 5,135,703 motor vehicle registrations.

Railways. In Oct. 1994, the state had 1,321 route miles of railway. There is a metro link to New York (22 km), a light rail line (7 km), and extensive commuter railways around Newark.

Civil Aviation. There is an international airport at Newark.

SOCIAL INSTITUTIONS

Justice. State prisons in Aug. 1994 had 25,443 inmates. The death penalty is authorized.

Religion. In 1994 the Roman Catholic population of New Jersey was 3·25m., and there were 436,000 Jews. Among Protestant sects were United Methodists, 132,000; United Presbyterians (1993), 106,700; Episcopalians, 64,200; Lutherans, 82,200; American Baptists (1992), 66,000.

Education. Elementary instruction is compulsory for all from 6 to 16 years of age and free to all from 5 to 20 years of age. In 1993–94 public elementary schools had 830,628 and secondary schools had 320,982 enrolled pupils; public colleges in autumn 1993 had 278,306 students, including 139,915 in community colleges; independent colleges had 63,051. Average salary of 83,289 elementary and secondary classroom teachers in public schools 1993–94 was $45,880.

In autumn 1993: Rutgers, the State University (founded as Queen's College in 1766) had, 48,062 students; Princeton (founded in 1746) had 6,592; Fairleigh Dickinson (1941), had 10,751; Montclair State College, 13,214; Rowan College (formerly Glassboro State College), 9,368; Trenton State College, 7,063.

Health. In 1992 the state had 119 hospitals (37,619 beds), listed by the American Hospital Association.

Social Security. In the calendar year 1993, total Old Age, Survivors and Disability Insurance benefits were $10,239,000. Average monthly Title II social security payment was $739.30.

Further Reading

Statistical information: New Jersey State Data Center, Department of Labor, CN 388, Trenton 08625. Publishes *New Jersey Statistical Factbook.*

Legislative District Data Book. Bureau of Government Research. Annual

Manual of the Legislature of New Jersey. Trenton. Annual

Boyd, J. P. (ed.) *Fundamentals and Constitutions of New Jersey, 1664–1954.* Princeton, 1964

Cunningham, J. T., *New Jersey: America's Main Road.* Rev. ed. New York, 1976

Kull, I. Stoddard (ed.) *New Jersey: a History.* New York, 1930

State Library: 185 W. State Street, Trenton, CN 520. N.J. 08625.

NEW MEXICO

KEY HISTORICAL EVENTS. The first European settlement was established in 1598. Until 1771 New Mexico was the Spanish kings' 'Kingdom of New Mexico'. In 1771 it was annexed to the northern province of New Spain. When New Spain won its independence in 1821, it took the name of Republic of Mexico and established New Mexico as its northernmost department. When the war between the US and Mexico was concluded on 2 Feb. 1848 New Mexico was recognized as belonging to the US, and on 9 Sept. 1850 it was made a Territory. Part of the Territory was assigned to Texas; later Utah was formed into a separate Territory; in 1861 another part was transferred to Colorado, and in 1863 Arizona was disjoined, leaving to New Mexico its present area. New Mexico became a state in Jan. 1912.

TERRITORY AND POPULATION. New Mexico is bounded north by Colorado, north-east by Oklahoma, east by Texas, south by Texas and Mexico and west by Arizona. Land area, 121,365 sq. miles (314,334 sq. km). Public lands, administered by federal agencies (1975) amounted to 26·7m. acres or 34% of the total area. The Bureau of Indian Affairs held 7·3m. acres; the State of New Mexico held 9·4m. acres; 34·4m. acres were privately owned.

Census population, 1 April 1990, 1,515,069 (73% urban), an increase of 211,767 or 16·2% since 1980. Population estimate (1994), 1,653,537. Vital statistics, 1994: Births, 27,981 (16·9 per 1,000 population); marriages, 12,159 (7·4); divorces, 9,882 (6·0); deaths, 12,305 (7·4); infant deaths, 250 (8·9 per 1,000 live births).

The population in 5 census years was:

	White	*Black*	*Indian*	*Asian and Pacific Island*	*Other*	*Total*	*Per sq. mile*
1910	304,594	1,628	20,573	506		327,301	2·7
1940	492,312	4,672	34,510	324		531,818	4·4
1960	875,763	17,063	56,255	1,942		951,023	7·8
1980	977,587	24,020	106,119	6,825	188,343	1,302,894	10·7
1990	1,146,028	30,210	134,355	14,124	190,352	1,515,069	12·5

Of the 1990 total, 745,253 were male, 1,068,328 were 18 years of age or older, 163,062 were 65 years of age or older.

Before 1930 New Mexico was largely a Spanish-speaking state, but since 1945 an influx of population from other states has reduced the percentage of persons of Spanish origin or descent to 38·2% (1990).

The largest cities are Albuquerque, with estimated population, 1994, 411,994; Las Cruces, 71,043; Santa Fé (capital), 62,514; Roswell, 47,395; Rio Rancho, 41,492.

CLIMATE. Santa Fé. Jan. 26·4°F (–1·6°C), July 68·4°F (20°C). Annual rainfall 15·2" (386 mm). New Mexico belongs to the Mountain States climate zone (*see* UNITED STATES: Climate).

CONSTITUTION AND GOVERNMENT. The constitution of 1912 is still in force with 105 amendments. The state Legislature, which meets annually, consists of 42 members of the Senate, elected for 4 years, and 70 members of the House of Representatives, elected for 2 years.

The state sends 3 representatives to Congress.

In the 1992 presidential election Clinton polled 261,617 votes; Bush 212,824; Perot, 91,895.

The state capital is Santa Fé. The state is divided into 33 counties.

Governor: Gary Johnson (R.), 1995–99 ($90,000).
Lieut.-Governor: Walter Bradley (R.) ($65,000).
Secretary of State: Stephanie Gonzales (D.) ($65,000).

BUDGET. For the year ending 30 June 1993 (US Census Bureau figures) the state's general revenues were $5,376m. ($2,777m. from taxation and $1,257m. from federal government); general expenditures, $5,190m. (education, $1,977m.; highways, $823m., and public welfare, $758m.).

Per capita personal income (1994) was $17,025.

NATURAL RESOURCES

Minerals. New Mexico is one of the largest energy producing states in the US. Production in 1993: Potassium salts, 1,445,000 short tons; copper, 247,000 short tons; petroleum, 68,422,000 bbls (of 42 gallons); natural gas, 1,409,000m. cu. ft; coal, 28,268,000 short tons. The value of the total mineral output (1993) was $5,090m. An average of 15,900 persons were employed in the mining industry in 1993, 10,100 in oil and gas extraction.

Agriculture. New Mexico produces grains, vegetables, fruit, livestock, cotton and nuts. Dry farming and irrigation have proved profitable in periods of high prices. In 1992 there were some 13,500 farms covering 44·2m. acres; average farm size, 3,274 acres. In 1995 average value of farmland and buildings per acre was $225.

Cash receipts, 1994, from crops, $428m., and from livestock products, $1,099m. Principal crops are wheat (5·5m. bu. from 0·23m. acres), hay (1·5m. tons from 0·33m. acres) and sorghum/grains (6·8m. bu. from 0·18m. acres). Farm animals in 1993 included 165,000 milch cows, 1·5m. all cattle, 315,000 sheep and 45,000 swine. National forest area (1991) covered 9·3m. acres.

INDUSTRY. Average monthly non-agricultural employment during 1994 was 658,100: 45,000 were employed in manufacturing, 163,100 in government. Value of manufactures shipments, 1992, $9,491·5m.; leading industries, food and kindred products, electrical and electronic equipment, petroleum and coal products.

COMMUNICATIONS

Roads. In 1992 there were 61,195 miles of roads and (1994) 1,603,580 registered motor vehicles.

Railways. In 1993 there were 1,893 miles of railway in operation.

Civil Aviation. There were 65 public-use airports in Oct. 1994.

SOCIAL INSTITUTIONS

Justice. The number of state prison inmates in Jan. 1996 was 4,209, and there was an average of 540 in state-operated juvenile centres in the fiscal year 1995. The death penalty is authorized.

Since 1949 the denial of employment by reason of race, colour, religion, national origin or ancestry has been forbidden. A law of 1955 prohibits discrimination in public places because of race or colour. An ‘equal rights’ amendment was added to the constitution in 1972.

Religion. There were (1975) approximately 356,530 Protestant Church members and 315,470 Roman Catholics.

Education. Elementary education is free, and compulsory between 6 and 17 years or high-school graduation age. In 1994–95 the 89 school districts had an estimated enrolment of 355,358 students in elementary and secondary schools of which private, parochial and state supported schools had 30,058. In 1992–93 there were 16,939 FTE teachers receiving an average salary of $26,532. Total revenue for public elementary and secondary schools was $1,626·7m. (1993–94).

The state-supported 4-year institutes of higher education are (autumn 1994 [1]):

	Students
University of New Mexico, Albuquerque	30,668
New Mexico State University, Las Cruces	23,327
Eastern New Mexico University, Portales	7,206
New Mexico Highlands University, Las Vegas	2,795
Western New Mexico University, Silver City	2,494
New Mexico Institute of Mining and Technology, Socorro	1,663

[1] Figures include branches outside main campus in cities listed.

Health. In 1993 the state had 61 federal and non-federal hospitals (6,621 beds).

Social Security. In 1993, 29,550 persons were receiving federal supplemental security income for the disabled (total annual payments, $117·0m.); 9,823 persons were receiving old-age assistance (total, $20·1m.); 620 persons were receiving aid to the blind (total, $2·2m.). In the fiscal year 1995 a monthly average of 34,497 cases received $156·2m. from aid to families with dependent children funds and 86,441 cases received $195·4m. in food stamp funds.

Further Reading

New Mexico Business (monthly; annual review in Jan.–Feb. issue). Bureau of Business and Economic Research, Univ. of N.M., Albuquerque
Economic Review (annual). Sunwest Bank, Albuquerque
Census in New Mexico (Continuing series. Vols. 1–5 to date). Bureau of Business and Economic Research, Univ. of New Mexico, Albuquerque, 1992–
Beck, W., *New Mexico: a History of Four Centuries.* Univ. of Oklahoma Press, 1979
Etulain. R., *Contemporary New Mexico, 1940–1990.* Univ. of New Mexico Press, 1994
Garcia, C., Haine, P. and Rhodes, H., *State and Local Government in New Mexico.* Albuquerque, 1979
Jenkins, M. and Schroeder, A., *A Brief History of New Mexico.* Univ. of New Mexico Press, 1974
Muench, D. and Hillerman, T., *New Mexico.* Portland (OR), 1974
Williams, J. L., *New Mexico in Maps.* Univ. of New Mexico Press, 1986

NEW YORK STATE

KEY HISTORICAL EVENTS. From 1609 to 1664 the region now called New York was claimed by the Dutch; then it came under the rule of the English, who governed the country until the outbreak of the War of Independence. On 20 April 1777 New York adopted a constitution which transformed the colony into an independent state; on 26 July 1788 it ratified the constitution of the US, becoming one of the 13 original states. New York dropped its claim to Vermont after the latter was admitted to the Union in 1791. With the annexation of a small area from Massachusetts in 1853, New York assumed its present boundaries.

TERRITORY AND POPULATION. New York is bounded west and north by Canada with Lake Erie, Lake Ontario and the St Lawrence River forming the boundary; east by Vermont, Massachusetts and Connecticut, south-east by the Atlantic, south by New Jersey and Pennsylvania. Land area, 47,224 sq. miles (122,310 sq. km). Census population, 1 April 1990, 17,990,455 (84·3% urban), an increase of 2·47% since 1980. Population estimate (1993), 18,197,154. Births in 1991 were 292,400 (16·2 per 1,000 population); deaths, 166,795 (9·2); infant deaths in 1989, 3,076 (10·6 per 1,000 live births); marriages in 1989, 162,782 (9·1); divorces, 55,610 (3·1).

Population in 5 census years was:

	White	*Black*	*Indian*	*Asiatic*	*Total*	*Per sq. mile*
1910	8,966,845	134,191	6,046	6,532	9,113,614	191·2
1930	12,143,191	412,814	6,973	15,088	12,588,066	262·6
1960	15,287,071	1,417,511	16,491	51,678	16,782,304	350·2
			All others			
1980	13,961,106	2,401,842	1,194,340		17,557,288	367·0
1990	12,460,189	2,569,126	2,961,140		17,990,455	381·0

Of the 1990 population, 8,625,673 were male, 14,857,202 (1980) were urban; those 20 years of age or older numbered 13,186,381. Aliens registered in Jan. 1980 numbered 801,411.

The population of New York City, by boroughs, census of 1 April 1990 was: Manhattan, 1,487,536; Bronx, 1,203,789; Brooklyn, 2,291,664; Queens, 1,951,598;

Staten Island, 378,977; total, 7,322,564. The New York metropolitan statistical area had, in 1990, 8,546,846.

Population of other large cities and incorporated places census, April 1990, was:

Buffalo	328,123	Troy	54,269	Elmira	33,724
Rochester	231,636	Binghampton	53,008	Auburn	31,258
Yonkers	188,082	Hempstead	49,453	Waterdown	29,429
Syracuse	163,860	White Plains	48,718	Poughkeepsie	28,844
Albany (capital)	101,082	Rome	44,350	Lindenhurst	26,879
Utica	68,637	Freeport	39,894	Newburgh	26,454
New Rochelle	67,265	N. Tonawanda	34,989	Rockville Center	24,727
Mount Vernon	67,153	Jamestown	34,681	Garden City	21,686
Schenectady	65,566	Valleystream	33,946	Massapequa Park	18,044
Niagara Falls	61,840				

Other large urbanized areas, census 1990; Buffalo, 968,532; Rochester, 1,002,410; Albany–Schenectady–Troy, 874,304.

CLIMATE. Albany. Jan. 24°F (–4·4°C), July 73°F (22·8°C). Annual rainfall 34" (855 mm). Buffalo. Jan. 24°F (–4·4°C), July 70°F (21·1°C). Annual rainfall 36" (905 mm). New York. Jan. 30°F (–1·1°C), July 74°F (23·3°C). Annual rainfall 43" (1,087 mm). New York belongs to the Atlantic Coast climate zone (*see* UNITED STATES: Climate).

CONSTITUTION AND GOVERNMENT. The present constitution dates from 1894; a later constitutional convention, 1938, is now legally considered merely to have amended the 1894 constitution, which has now had 93 amendments. A proposed new constitution in 1967 was rejected by the electorate. The Senate consists of 60 members, and the Assembly of 150 members, both elected every 2 years. The state capital is Albany. For local government the state is divided into 62 counties, 5 of which constitute the city of New York. There were state parks and recreation areas covering 260,198 acres in 1990.

In the 1992 presidential election Clinton polled 3,444,350 votes; Bush, 2,346,649; Perot, 1,090,721.

Each of the state's 62 cities is incorporated by charter, under special legislation. The government of New York City is vested in the mayor (David Dinkins), elected for 4 years, and a city council, whose president and members are elected for 4 years. The council has a President and 51 members, each elected from a district wholly within the city. The mayor appoints all the heads of departments, except the comptroller, who is elected. Each of the 5 city boroughs (Manhattan, Bronx, Brooklyn, Queens and Staten Island) has a president, elected for 4 years. Each borough is also a county bearing the same name except Manhattan borough, which, as a county, is called New York, and Brooklyn, which is Kings County.

The state sends 31 representatives to Congress.

Governor: George E. Pataki (R.), 1995–99 ($130,000).
Lieut.-Governor: Elizabeth McGaughey (D.) ($110,000).
Secretary of State: Alexander F. Treadwell (D.) ($87,338).

BUDGET. The state's general revenues for the financial year ending 31 March 1990 were $52,441·3m. ($28,614·6m. from taxes); general expenditures were $49,967·5m. ($14,266·2m. for education, $14,820·4m. for social services, $2,227·8m. for transport).

Per capita personal income was $25,999 in 1994.

NATURAL RESOURCES

Minerals. Production of principal minerals in 1988: Sand and gravel (28·7m. short tons), salt (4,614 short tons), oil (495,000 bbls), natural gas (25,447m. cu. ft). The state is a leading producer of titanium concentrate, talc, abrasive garnet, wollastonite and emery. Quarry products include trap rock, slate, marble, limestone and sandstone. Value of mineral output in 1990, $773m.

Agriculture. New York has large agricultural interests. In 1991 it had some 38,000 farms, with a total area of 8·3m. acres; average farm was 218 acres. Average value per acre in 1995 was $1,380.

Farm income, 1991, from crops $1,089m. and livestock, $1,766m. Dairying is an important type of farming. Field crops comprise maize, winter wheat, oats and hay. New York ranks second in US in the production of apples, and maple syrup. Other products are grapes, tart cherries, peaches, pears, plums, strawberries, raspberries, cabbages, onions, potatoes, maple sugar. Estimated farm animals, 1990, included 1,540,000 all cattle, 966,000 milch cows, 92,000 sheep and lambs, 124,000 swine and 5·1m. chickens.

INDUSTRY. The main employers (1987 census) are service industries (1,293,000), trade (1,150,000) and manufacture (1,267,500). Leading industries were clothing, non-electrical machinery, printing and publishing, electrical equipment, instruments, food and allied products and fabricated metals.

COMMUNICATIONS

Roads. In 1990 there were 110,965 miles of roads (73,263 miles rural). The New York State Thruway extends 559 miles from New York City to Buffalo. The Northway, a 176-mile toll-free highway, is a connecting road from the Thruway at Albany to the Canadian border at Champlain, Quebec.

Motor vehicle registrations in 1991 were 9,771,437.

Railways. There were in 1981, 3,891 miles of Class I railways. New York City has NYCTA and PATH metro systems, and commuter railways run by Metro-North, New Jersey Transit and Long Island Rail Road.

Civil Aviation. There were 489 airports and landing areas in 1989.

Shipping. The canals of the state, combined in 1918 in what is called the Improved Canal System, have a length of 524 miles, of which the Erie or Barge canal has 340 miles. In 1981 the canals carried 807,925 tons of freight.

SOCIAL INSTITUTIONS

Justice. The State Human Rights Law was approved 12 March 1945, effective 1 July, 1945. The State Division of Human Rights is charged with the responsibility of enforcing this law. The division may request and utilize the services of all governmental departments and agencies; adopt and promulgate suitable rules and regulations; test, investigate and pass judgment upon complaints alleging discrimination in employment, in places of public accommodation, resort or amusement, education, and in housing, land and commercial space; hold hearings, sub-poena witnesses and require the production for examination of papers relating to matters under investigation; grant compensatory damages and require repayment of profits in certain housing cases among other provisions; apply for court injunctions to prevent frustration of orders of the Commissioner.

In 1991, 56,530 prisoners were in state correctional institutions.

The death penalty is authorized.

In 1988 murders reported in New York were 2,239. Police strength (sworn officers) in 1988 was 61,204 (43,218 New York City).

Religion. The churches are Roman Catholic, with 6,367,576 members in 1981, Jewish congregations (about 2m. in 1981) and Protestant Episcopal (299,929 in 1980).

Education. Education is compulsory between the ages of 7 and 16. In 1992 the public elementary and secondary schools had 2,645,000 pupils and 188,400 teachers. State and local government expenditure on public schools in 1991 was $27,821·3m. Teachers' salaries, 1989, averaged $43,300.

The state's educational system, including public and private schools and secondary institutions, universities, colleges, libraries, museums, etc., constitute (by legislative act) the 'University of the State of New York', which is governed by Board of Regents consisting of 15 members appointed by the Legislature. Within the framework of this 'University' was established in 1948 a 'State University' which controls 64 colleges and educational centres, 30 of which are locally operated community colleges. The 'State University' is governed by a board of 16 Trustees, appointed by the Governor with the consent and advice of the Senate.

Higher education in the state is conducted in 296 institutions (627,676 full-time and 375,690 part-time students in autumn 1989).

In autumn 1990 the institutions of higher education in the state included:

Founded	*Name and place*	*Teachers*	*Students*
1754	Columbia University, New York	2,305	18,242
1795	Union University, Schenectady and Albany	228	2,877
1824	Rensselaer Polytechnic Institute, Troy	375	6,692
1831	New York University, New York	2,386	32,813
1846	Colgate University, New York	255	2,710
1846	Fordham University, New York	703	13,158
1847	University of the City of New York, New York	9,065	200,700
1848	University of Rochester, Rochester	1,250	9,291
1854	Polytechnic Institute of New York	261	3,701
1856	St Lawrence University, Canton	189	2,091
1857	Cooper Union Institute of Technology, New York	108	1,036
1861	Vassar College, Poughkeepsie	235	2,453
1863	Manhattan College, New York	234	3,794
1865	Cornell University, Ithaca	1,779	17,171
1870	Syracuse University, Syracuse	990	21,900
1948	State University of New York	18,852	403,028

The Saratoga Performing Arts Centre (5,100 seats), a non-profit, tax-exempt organization, which opened in 1966, is the summer residence of the New York City Ballet and the Philadelphia Orchestra—two groups which present special educational programmes for students and teachers.

Health. In 1981 the state had 278 hospitals (67,798 beds), 585 skilled nursing homes (62,435 beds) and 241 other institutions (24,302 beds). In 1986 mental health facilities had 21,836 patients and institutions for the mentally retarded had 10,581 patients.

Social Security. The federal Supplemental Security Income programme covered aid to the needy aged, blind and disabled from 1 Jan. 1975. In the state programme for 1980, $4,543m. was paid in Medicaid to 2,288,000 people; aid to dependent children in 1985 went to 1,109,610 recipients, average benefits $371 per family per month.

Further Reading

Statistical information: Nelson Rockefeller Institute of Government, 411 State St., Albany 12203. Publishes *New York State Statistical Yearbook.*

Governing the Empire State: an Insider's Guide. Albany, Rockefeller Institute, 1988

New York Red Book. Albany. Biennial.

Legislative Manual. Department of State. Biennial.

Managing Modern New York: the Carey Era. Albany, Rockefeller Institute, 1985

The Modern New York State Legislature: Redressing the Balance. Albany, Rockefeller Institute, 1991

Rockefeller in Retrospect: the Governor's New York Legacy. Albany, Rockefeller Institute, 1987

Connery, R. and G. B., *Governing New York State: The Rockefeller Years.* New York, 1974

Ellis, D. M., *History of New York State.* Cornell Univ. Press, 1967

Flick, A. (ed.) *History of the State of New York.* Columbia Univ. Press, 1933–37

Zimmerman, J. F., *The Government and Politics of New York.* New York Univ. Pres, 1981

State Library: The New York State Library, Albany 12230.

NORTH CAROLINA

KEY HISTORICAL EVENTS. North Carolina, first settled in 1585 by Sir Walter Raleigh and permanently settled in 1663, was one of the 13 original states of the Union.

TERRITORY AND POPULATION. North Carolina is bounded north by Virginia, east by the Atlantic, south by South Carolina, south-west by Georgia and west by Tennessee. Land area, 48,718 sq. miles (126,180 sq. km). Census population, 1 April 1990, 6,628,637 (50·4% urban), an increase of 12·84% since 1980. Population estimate (1993), 6,945,180. Births, 1991, were 102,442 (15·2 per 1,000 population); marriages, 48,966 (7·3); deaths, 58,909 (8·7); infant deaths in 1992, 1,073 (10·4 per 1,000 live births); divorces, 33,763 (5).

Population in 5 census years was:

	White	*Black*	*Indian*	*Asiatic*	*Total*	*Per sq. mile*
1910	1,500,511	697,843	7,851	82	2,206,287	45·3
1930	2,234,958	918,647	16,579	92	3,170,276	64·5
1950	2,983,121	1,047,353	3,742	—	4,061,929	82·7
			All others			
1970	3,901,767	1,126,478	53,814		5,082,059	104·1
1980	4,453,010	1,316,050	105,369		5,874,429	111·5

Of the total population in 1980, 2,852,012 were male, 2,818,794 were urban and 3,976,359 were 20 years old or older.

The principal cities (with census population in 1990) are: Charlotte, 395,934; Raleigh, 207,951; Greensboro, 183,521; Winston-Salem, 143,485; Durham, 136,611; Fayetteville, 75,695; High Point, 69,496; Asheville, 61,607; Wilmington, 55,530.

CLIMATE. Climate varies sharply with altitude; the warmest area is in the south east near Southport and Wilmington; the coldest is Mount Mitchell (6,684 ft). Raleigh. Jan. 42°F (5·6°C), July 79°F (26·1°C). Annual rainfall 46" (1,158 mm). North Carolina belongs to the Atlantic Coast climate zone (*see* UNITED STATES: Climate).

CONSTITUTION AND GOVERNMENT. The present constitution dates from 1971 (previous constitution, 1776 and 1868/76); it has had 19 amendments. The General Assembly consists of a Senate of 50 members and a House of Representatives of 120 members; all are elected by districts for 2 years. It meets in odd-numbered years in Jan.

The Governor and Lieut.-Governor are elected for 4 years. The Governor may succeed himself but has no veto. There are 19 other executive heads of department, 8 elected by the people and 9 appointed by the Governor.

The state sends 12 representatives to Congress.

In the presidential election of 1992 Bush polled 1,134,661 votes; Clinton, 1,114,042; Perot, 357,864.

The capital is Raleigh. There are 100 counties.

Governor: James B. Hunt Jr (D.), 1993–97 ($98,576).
Lieut.-Governor: Dennis Wicker (D.) ($87,000).
Secretary of State: Rufus Edmisten (D.) ($87,000).

BUDGET. General revenue for the year ending 30 June 1990 was $12,345·2m. General expenditure was $12,555·3m.

On 30 June 1991 the net total long-term debt amounted to $3,490m.

Per capita personal income (1994) was $19,669.

NATURAL RESOURCES

Minerals. Mining production in 1990 was valued at $578·4m. Principal minerals were stone, sand and gravel, phosphate rock, feldspar, lithium minerals, olivine, kaolin and talc. North Carolina is a leading producer of bricks, making more than 1,000m. bricks a year.

Agriculture. In 1991 there were some 60,000 farms covering 9·6m. acres; average size of farms was 160 acres and average value per acre in 1995 was $1,749.

Farm income, 1991, from crops, $2,272m. and from livestock and products, $2,554m. Main crop production: flue-cured tobacco, maize, soybeans, peanuts, wheat, sweet potatoes and apples.

Livestock, 1990: Cattle, 0·9m.; pigs, 2·6m.; chickens, 19·6m.

Forestry. Commercial forest covered 18,891,000 acres in 1990. Main products are hardwood veneer and hardwood plywood, furniture woods, pulp, paper and lumber.

Fisheries. Commercial fish catch, 1990, had a value of approximately $71·5m. The catch is mainly of menhaden, crabmeat, bay scallops, flounder, croaker, shrimps, sea trout, spots and clams.

INDUSTRY. North Carolina's manufacturing establishments in 1985 had 827,400 workers. The leading industries by employment are textiles, clothing, furniture, electrical machinery and equipment, non-electrical machinery, and food processing. In 1985 investment in new and expanded industry was $2,758m. About 576,200 were employed in trade, 422,800 in government and 427,600 in services.

TOURISM. Total receipts of the travel industry, $6,400m. in 1990.

COMMUNICATIONS

Roads. In 1990 there were 94,228 miles of roads (75,165 miles rural). In 1991 there were 5,216,177 registered motor vehicles.

Railways. The state in 1986 contained 3,682 miles of railway operating in 91 of the 100 counties. There are 22 Class I, II and III rail companies.

Civil Aviation. In 1986 there were 82 public airports of which 14 are served by major airlines.

Shipping. There are 2 ocean ports, Wilmington and Morehead City.

SOCIAL INSTITUTIONS

Justice. Following the US Supreme Court's reinstatement of the death penalty in 1976, capital punishment has been authorized. There was an execution in 1986. In 1991 there were 18,708 prisoners in state correctional institutions.

Religion. Leading denominations are the Baptists (48·9% of church membership), Methodists (20·7%), Presbyterians (7·7%), Lutherans (3%) and Roman Catholics (2·7%). Total estimate of all denominations in 1983 was 2·6m.

Education. School attendance is compulsory between 6 and 16.

In 1985–86 there were 1,968 public elementary and secondary schools. In 1992 there were 1,092,447 pupils and 64,435 teachers. State and local government expenditure in 1991 was $7,949·4m.

In autumn 1985–86 state-supported colleges and universities included 58 community and technical colleges with 654,000 full and part time students. The 16 senior universities are all part of the University of North Carolina system, the largest campus being North Carolina State University and Raleigh, with 23,400 students. The university system was founded in 1789 at Chapel Hill and first opened in 1792. Its 1986 autumn enrolment was 130,000 students.

In addition to the state-supported institutions there were 7 private junior colleges with an enrolment of 2,585 and 31 private senior institutions with a total enrolment of 19,009. The total undergraduate enrolment in private institutions for 1985 was 21,594.

Health. In Oct. 1986 the state had 160 hospitals (34,438 beds).

Social Security. In June 1982 there were 900,070 persons receiving $300·4m. in social security benefits. Of that number 496,020 were retired, receiving $186·67m.; 85,640 were disabled ($34·7m.); 318,410 others received $79m.

Further Reading

Statistical information: Office of State Planning, 116 West Jones St., Raleigh 27603. Publishes *Statistical Abstract of North Carolina Counties.*

North Carolina Manual. Secretary of State. Raleigh. Biennial
Clay, J. W. *et al* (eds.), *North Carolina Atlas: Portrait of a Changing Southern State.* Univ. of North Carolina Press, 1975
Corbitt, D. L., *The Formation of the North Carolina Counties.* Raleigh, 1969
Fleer, J. D., *North Carolina: Government and Population.* Univ. of Nebraska Press, 1995
Lefler, H. T. and Newsome, A. R., *North Carolina: The History of a Southern State.* Univ. of North Carolina Press, 1973

NORTH DAKOTA

KEY HISTORICAL EVENTS. North Dakota was admitted into the Union, with boundaries as at present, on 2 Nov. 1889; previously it had formed part of the Dakota Territory, established 2 March 1861.

TERRITORY AND POPULATION. North Dakota is bounded north by Canada, east by the Red River (forming a boundary with Minnesota), south by South Dakota and west by Montana. Land area, 68,994 sq. miles (178,695 sq. km). The Federal Bureau of Indian Affairs administered (1992) 841,295 acres, of which 214,006 acres were assigned to tribes. Census population, 1 April 1990, 638,800 (53·3% urban), a decrease of 2·13% since 1980. Population estimate (1993), 634,935. Births in 1992 were 8,935 (14 per 1,000 population); deaths, 5,797 (9·1); infant deaths in 1993, 56 (6·4 per 1,000 live births); marriages, 4,809 (7·6); divorces, 2,305 (3·6).

Population at 5 census years was:

	White	*Black*	*Indian*	*Asiatic*	*Total*	*Per sq. mile*
1910	569,855	617	6,486	98	577,056	8·2
1930	671,851	377	8,617	194	680,845	9·7
			All others			
1970	599,485	2,494	15,782		617,761	9·0
1980	625,557	2,568	24,692		652,717	9·5
1990	604,142	3,524	31,134		638,800	9·3

Of the total population in 1990, 318,201 were male, 340,490 were urban and 436,665 were 21 years old or older. Estimated outward migration, 1980–90, 110 per 1,000 population.

The largest cities are Fargo with population, census 1990, of 74,111; Grand Forks, 49,425; Bismarck (capital), 49,256, and Minot, 34,544.

CLIMATE. Bismarck. Jan. 8°F (–13·3°C), July 71°F (21·1°C). Annual rainfall 16" (402 mm). Fargo. Jan. 6°F (–14·4°C), July 71°F (21·1°C). Annual rainfall 20" (503 mm). North Dakota belongs to the High Plains climate zone (*see* UNITED STATES: Climate)

CONSTITUTION AND GOVERNMENT. The present constitution dates from 1889; it has had 95 amendments. The Legislative Assembly consists of a Senate of 53 members elected for 4 years, and a House of Representatives of 106 members elected for 2 years. The Governor and Lieut.-Governor are elected for 4 years.

The state sends 1 representative to Congress.

In the 1992 presidential election Bush polled 136,244 votes; Clinton, 99,168; Perot, 71,084.

The capital is Bismarck. The state has 53 organized counties.

Governor: Edward Schafer (R.), 1993-97 ($69,650).
Lieut.-Governor: Rosemarie Myrdal (R.) ($57,238).
Secretary of State: Alvin A. Jaeger (R.) ($52,787).

FINANCE. General fund revenues for the fiscal year ending 30 June 1993 were $544m.; taxation provided $525m. General fund expenditures for the fiscal year ending 30 June 1994 were $444m.; education took $319m.; health and human services, $531m.; highways, $177m.

Per capita personal income (1994) was $18,546.

NATURAL RESOURCES

Minerals. The mineral resources of North Dakota consist chiefly of oil which was discovered in 1951. Production of crude petroleum in 1990 was 35,895,278 bbls; of natural gas (1991), 54·8m. cu. ft. Output of lignite coal in 1991 was 26·3m. tons. Total value of mineral output, 1991, $1,016,622,000.

Agriculture. Agriculture is the chief pursuit of the population. In 1993 there were 33,000 farms (61,963 in 1954) with an area of 40·4m. acres (41,876,924 in 1954); the average farm was of 1,224 acres. In 1992 per farm net farm income was $33,067. In 1994 the average value of farmland and buildings per acre was $409.

Cash income, 1993, from crops, $2,264·1m. and from livestock, $770·8m. In 1993, North Dakota led in the production of barley, sunflowers, flaxseed, spring wheat, durum wheat and oats. Other important products are navy beans, all beans, pinto beans, all wheat, rye and honey.

The state has also an active livestock industry, chiefly cattle raising. Livestock, 1994: Cattle, 1·9m.; pigs (1993), 0·32m.; sheep, 165,000; poultry (1993), 255,000.

Forestry. Forest area, 1990, 0·46m. acres.

INDUSTRY. In July 1994, 75,900 were employed in trade, 62,900 in government, 80,250 in services, 18,100 in transport, communications and utilities, 20,800 in manufacturing.

COMMUNICATIONS

Roads. The state maintained, in 1993, 7,385 miles of road; local authorities, 75,056 miles. Motor vehicle registrations in 1992 numbered 655,335.

Railways. In 1994 there were 4,143 miles of railway.

Civil Aviation. In 1994 there were 100 public airports and 350 private airports.

SOCIAL INSTITUTIONS

Justice. The state penitentiary, in Oct. 1994, held 460 inmates. The Missouri River Correctional Center, a minimum custody institution, held 132 inmates. There is no death penalty.

Religion. In 1980, the leading religious denominations were: Combined Lutherans, 288,500 members; Roman Catholics, 230,660; Methodists, 36,500; Presbyterians, 19,500, and the United Church of Christ, 15,000.

Education. School attendance is compulsory between the ages of 7 and 16, or until the 17th birthday if the eighth grade has not been completed. In 1993–94 the public elementary schools had 83,505 pupils; secondary schools, 34,995 pupils. State expenditure per pupil in elementary and secondary schools, 1994, $4,497. Teachers (4,208 in elementary and 2,208 in secondary schools in 1994) earned an average $25,506 in 1993–94 school year.

The University of North Dakota in Grand Forks, founded in 1883, had 11,499 students in autumn 1994; North Dakota State University in Fargo, 9,665 students. Total enrolment in the 11 public institutions of higher education, autumn 1994, 34,948; in the 2 private, 2,850.

Health. In 1994 the state had 46 general hospitals (3,571 beds), and 86 nursing facilities (7,125 beds).

Social Security. In 1992, 113,810 people received $736m. in SSI payments. Monthly average, 18,300 recipients.

Further Reading

Statistical information: Bureau of Business and Economic Research, Univ. of North Dakota, Grand Forks 58202. Publishes *Staistical Abstract of North Dakota.*
North Dakota Blue Book. Secretary of State. Bismarck
Glaab, C. L. et al, *The North Dakota Political Tradition.* Iowa State Univ. Press, 1981
Jelliff, T. B., *North Dakota: A Living Legacy.* Fargo, 1983
Robinson, E. B., *History of North Dakota.* Univ. of Nebraska Press, 1966

OHIO

KEY HISTORICAL EVENTS. The first organized European settlement was in 1788; Ohio unofficially entered the Union on 19 Feb. 1803; entrance was made official, retroactive to 1 March 1803, on 8 Aug. 1953.

TERRITORY AND POPULATION. Ohio is bounded north by Michigan and Lake Erie, east by Pennsylvania, south-east and south by the Ohio River (forming a boundary with West Virginia and Kentucky) and west by Indiana. Land area, 40,952 sq. miles (106,067 sq. km). Census population, 1 April 1990, 10,847,115 (74·1% urban), an increase of 89,695 or 0·8% since 1980. Population estimate (1994), 11,102,000. In 1993, births numbered 158,773 (14·6 per 1,000 population); deaths, 102,573 (9·5); infant deaths, 1,444 (9·1 per 1,000 live births); stillbirths, 1,204 (7·6 per 1,000 live births); marriages, 88,796 (8·2); divorces, 51,070 (4·7).

Population at 6 census years was:

	White	*Black*	*Indian*	*Asiatic*	*Total*	*Per sq. mile*
1910	4,654,897	111,452	127	645	4,767,121	117·0
1930	6,335,173	309,304	435	1,785	6,646,697	161·6
1960	8,909,698	786,097	1,910	8,692	9,706,397	236·9
			All others			
1970	9,646,997	970,477	34,543		10,652,017	260·0
1980	9,597,458	1,076,748	123,424		10,797,630	263·2
1990	9,521,756	1,154,826	170,533		10,847,115	264·5

Of the total population in 1990, 5,226,340 were male. Those 18 years old or older numbered 8,047,371 in 1990.

Census population of chief cities on 1 April 1990 was:

Columbus	632,910	Hamilton	61,368	Middletown	46,022
Cleveland	505,616	Kettering	60,569	Lima	45,549
Cincinnati	364,040	Lakewood	59,718	Newark	44,389
Toledo	332,943	Elyria	56,746	Lancaster	34,507
Akron	223,019	Euclid	54,875	North Olmsted	34,204
Dayton	182,044	Cleveland Heights	54,052	Upper Arlington	34,128
Youngstown	95,753	Warren	50,793	Marion	34,075
Parma	87,876	Mansfield	50,627	East Cleveland	33,096
Canton	84,161	Cuyahoga Falls	48,950	Garfield Heights	31,793
Lorain	71,245	Mentor	47,358	Zanesville	26,788
Springfield	70,487				

Urbanized areas, 1990 census: Cleveland, 1,831,122; Cincinnati, 1,452,645; Columbus (the capital), 1,377,419; Dayton, 951,270; Akron, 657,575; Toledo, 614,128; Youngstown-Warren, 492,619; Canton, 394,106.

CLIMATE. Cincinnati. Jan. 39·1°F, July 77·1°F). Annual rainfall 43·82". Cleveland. Jan. 35°F, July 72·4°F. Annual rainfall 43·9". Columbus. Jan. 36·6°F, July 73·9°F. Annual rainfall 43·76". Ohio belongs to the Great Lakes climate zone (*see* UNITED STATES: Climate).

CONSTITUTION AND GOVERNMENT. The question of a general revision of the constitution drafted by an elected convention is submitted to the people every 20 years. The constitution of 1851 had 142 amendments by 1994.

The Senate consists of 33 members and the House of Representatives of 99 members. The Senate is elected for 4 years, half each 2 years; the House is elected for 2 years; the Governor, Lieut.-Governor and Secretary of State for 4 years. Qualified as electors are (with necessary exceptions) all citizens 18 years of age who have the usual residential qualifications. Ohio sends 19 representatives to Congress.

In the 1992 presidential election Clinton polled 1,984,942 votes; Bush, 1,894,310; Perot, 1,036,426.

The capital (since 1816) is Columbus. Ohio is divided into 88 counties.

Governor: George Voinovich (R.), 1995–99 ($115,763).
Lieut.-Governor: Nancy Hollister (R.) ($59,861).
Secretary of State: Bob Taft (R.) ($85,517).

BUDGET. For the year ending 30 June 1994 general revenue fund income was $14,952,841,000 and expenditure, $12,771,191,000.

The bonded debt on 30 June 1994 was $4,728,903,000.

Per capita personal income (1994) was $19,627.

NATURAL RESOURCES

Minerals. Ohio has extensive mineral resources, of which coal is the most important by value: Output (1993) 27,585,575 short tons. Production of crude petroleum, 1993, 8,282,023 bbls; natural gas, 135,938,848 cu. ft. Other minerals include stone, clay, sand and gravel. Value of all non-fuel industrial minerals, 1993, $511,650,285.

Agriculture. Ohio is extensively devoted to agriculture. In 1994, 75,000 farms covered 15·2m. acres; average farm value per acre, $1,800 in 1995. In 1994 the average size of farm was 203 acres.

Cash income 1993, from crop and livestock and products, $4,940m. The most important crops in 1994 were: Maize (487m. bu.), wheat (68m. bu.), oats (7m. bu.), soybeans (176m. bu.). In 1994 there were 1·64m. pigs, 1·46m. cattle and 198,000 sheep.

Forestry. State forest area, 1994, 179,338 acres. In 1994 there were 72 state parks covering 242,144 acres.

INDUSTRY. In March 1993, 18,395 manufacturing establishments employed 1,046,039 persons out of a total workforce of 4,263,248. The largest industries were manufacturing of transport equipment, industrial machinery and equipment, and fabricated metal products.

COMMUNICATIONS

Roads. In 1994 there were 113,565 miles of roads and 8·69m. registered motor vehicles.

Railways. In 1994 there were 6,458 miles of track used by 4 Class I freight railways, 1 regional railway and several short line railways. Amtrak also serves parts of Ohio.

Civil Aviation. In 1994 there were 8 major passenger airports and 1 cargo airport. There were also 177 public use general aviation airports and 28 heliports. There were 13·4m. passenger emplanements in 1991.

SOCIAL INSTITUTIONS

Justice. On 31 June 1993 there were 23 adult correctional institutions with 37,219 male and 2,235 female inmates. The death penalty is authorized; the last execution was in 1963.

Religion. Many religious faiths are represented, including (but not limited to) the

Baptist, Jewish, Lutheran, Methodist, Moslem, Orthodox, Presbyterian and Roman Catholic.

Education. School attendance during full term is compulsory for children from 6 to 18 years of age. In 1994–95 public schools had 1,806,981m. enrolled pupils and 103,929 full-time equivalent classroom teachers. Teachers' salaries (1994) averaged $35,907. Operating expenditure on elementary and secondary schools for 1994 was $3,910m., 33·8% of the state budget. Universities and colleges had a total enrolment (1994) of 312,466 students. State appropriation to state universities 1990–91, $1,711,034. Average annual charge (undergraduate) at 4-year institutions: $3,405 (state); $11,782 (private).

Main campuses, 1994–95:

Founded	*Institutions*	*Enrolments*
1804	Ohio University, Athens (State)	19,758
1809	Miami University, Oxford (State)	15,348
1819	University of Cincinnati (State)	22,589
1826	Case Western Reserve University, Cleveland	9,569
1850	University of Dayton (R.C.)	1,709
1870	University of Akron (State)	17,175
1870	Ohio State University, Columbus (State)	44,900
1872	University of Toledo (State)	17,824
1908	Youngstown University (State)	10,329
1910	Bowling Green State University (State)	15,288
1910	Kent State University (State)	16,894
1964	Cleveland State University (State)	11,556
1964	Wright State University (State)	11,783
1986	Shawnee State University, Portsmouth (State)	2,571

Health. In 1994 the state had 224 hospitals listed by the American Hospital Association with 48,541 beds. State facilities for the severely mentally retarded had 12 developmental centres serving 1,995 residents.

Social Security. Public assistance is administered through 7 basic programmes (with number of recipients as at Aug. 1995): Aid to dependent children (618,848), family emergency assistance (10,691), Medicaid (807,523), general assistance (48,544), food stamps (1,164,568) and foster care (16,440); 55·83% of the costs (except general relief and adult emergency assistance) are met by the federal government.

In the fiscal year 1994–95 Medicaid cost $5,417·2m. Aid to dependent children cost $856m. Food stamps cost $1,029·6m. General assistance cost $57m. Optional State Supplement is paid to aged, blind or disabled adults. Free social services are available to those eligible by income or circumstances.

Further Reading

Official Roster: Federal, State, County Officers and Department Information. Secretary of State, Columbus. Biennial

Rosebloom, E. H. and Weisenburger, F. P., *A History of Ohio.* Columbus, State Archive and Historical Society, 1953

Shkurti, W. J. and Bartle, J. (eds.) *Benchmark Ohio.* Ohio State Univ. Press, 1991

OKLAHOMA

KEY HISTORICAL EVENTS. An unorganized area in the centre of the present state was thrown open to white settlers on 22 April 1889. The Territory of Oklahoma, organized in 1890 to include this area and other sections, was opened to white settlements by runs or lotteries during the next decade. In 1893 the Territory was enlarged by the addition of the Cherokee Outlet, which fixed part of the present northern boundary. On 16 Nov. 1907 Oklahoma was combined with the remaining part of the Indian Territory and admitted to the Union as the 46th state with boundaries substantially as now.

TERRITORY AND POPULATION. Oklahoma is bounded north by Kansas, north-east by Missouri, east by Arkansas, south by Texas (the Red River forming part of the boundary) and, at the western extremity of the 'panhandle', by New Mexico and Colorado. Land area, 68,679 sq. miles (177,877 sq. km). Census population, 1 April 1990, 3,189,456 (67·7% urban), an increase of 5·42% since 1980. Population estimate (1994), 3,258,000. Births, 1994, 46,711 (14·8 per 1,000 population); deaths, 32,574 (10·3); marriages, 30,495 (9·7); divorces, 22,784 (7·2). Infant deaths, 1992, 450 (9·6 per 1,000 live births).

The population at 5 federal censuses was:

	White	*Black*	*Indian*	*Other*	*Total*	*Per sq. mile*
1930	2,130,778	172,198	92,725	339	2,396,040	34·6
1960	2,107,900	153,084	68,689	1,414	2,328,284	33·8
1970	2,280,362	171,892	97,179	10,030	2,559,253	37·2
1980	2,597,783	204,658	169,292	53,557	3,025,486	43·2
1990	2,583,512	233,801	252,420	119,723	3,189,456	44·5

In 1980, 1,476,719 were male, 2,035,082 were urban and those 20 years of age or older numbered 2,052,729. The US Bureau of Indian Affairs is responsible for 1,097,004 acres (1990), of which 96,839 acres were allotted to tribes.

The most important cities with population, 1990 are Oklahoma City (capital), 444,719; Tulsa, 367,302; Lawton, 80,561; Norman, 80,071; Broken Arrow, 58,043; Edmond, 52,315; Midwest City, 52,267; Enid, 45,309; Moore, 40,318; Muskogee, 37,708; Stillwater, 36,676; Bartlesville, 34,252.

CLIMATE. 1988: Oklahoma City. Jan. 34·2°F (1·2°C), July 81·6°F (27·5°C). Annual rainfall 31·94" (8,113 mm). Tulsa. Jan. 34·8°F (1·5°C), July 82·6°F (27·5°C). Annual rainfall 33·22" (8,438 mm). Oklahoma belongs to the Central Plains climate zone (*see* UNITED STATES: Climate).

CONSTITUTION AND GOVERNMENT. The constitution, dating from 1907, provides for amendment by initiative petition and legislative referendum; it has had 155 amendments (as of Jan. 1995).

The Legislature consists of a Senate of 48 members, who are elected for 4 years, and a House of Representatives elected for 2 years and consisting of 101 members. The Governor and Lieut.-Governor are elected for 4-year terms; the Governor can only be elected for two terms in succession. Electors are (with necessary exceptions) all citizens 18 years or older, with the usual qualifications.

The state sends 6 representatives to Congress.

In the 1992 presidential election Bush polled 592,929 votes; Clinton, 473,066; Perot, 319,978.

The capital is Oklahoma City. The state has 77 counties.

Governor: Frank Keating (R.), 1995–99 ($70,000).
Lieut.-Governor: Mary Fallin (R.) ($62,500).
Secretary of State: Tom J. Cole (R.) ($42,500).

BUDGET. Total revenue for the year ending 30 June 1994 was $7,851,967,335. Total expenditure, $7,424,444,072.

General obligation debt, 1994, was $414·82m.

Per capita personal income (1994) was $17,744.

NATURAL RESOURCES

Minerals. Production of mineral fuels, 1993: Petroleum, 97m. bbls of oil; natural gas, 2,020,000m. cu. ft.; coal, 1,796,000m. tons. At the end of 1993 there were 122,094 oil and gas wells in production. Value of leading non-fuel minerals produced in 1993 (in $1m.): Crushed stone, 111; cement, 59; sand and gravel, 27; iodine, 20; glass sand, 18; gypsum, 16. Other principal minerals are helium, clay and sand; other minerals include zinc, lead, granite, tripoli, bentonite, lime and volcanic ash. Total value of non-fuel mineral production, 1993, $282m.

Agriculture. In 1994 the state had some 70,000 farms and ranches with a total area of 34m. acres; average size was 486 acres; average value per acre was $494. Area harvested, 1992, 8,272,889 acres. Livestock, 1992: Cattle, 4,736,594; sheep and lambs, 103,732; hogs and pigs, 260,682.

Market value of agricultural products sold, 1992: Crops, $778·8m.; livestock, poultry and products, $2,783·8m. The major cash grain is winter wheat (value, 1990, $492m.). In 1992, 138,121,986 bu. of wheat for grain were harvested from 5,197,545 acres. Other crops include barley, oats, rye, grain, corn, soybeans, grain sorghum, cotton, peanuts and peaches. Value of cattle and calves produced, 1990, $3,080m.; catfish, $1m.; racehorses, $63m.

The Oklahoma Conservation Commission works with 91 conservation districts, universities, state and federal government agencies. The early work of the conservation districts, beginning in 1937, was limited to flood and erosion control: since 1970, they include urban areas also.

Irrigated production has increased in the Oklahoma 'panhandle'. The Ogalala aquifer is the primary source of irrigation water there and in western Oklahoma, a finite source because of its isolation from major sources of recharge. Declining groundwater levels necessitate the most effective irrigation practices.

Forestry. There are 7·5m. acres of forest, one half considered commercial. The forest products industry is concentrated in the 18 eastern counties. There are 3 forest regions: Ozark (oak, hickory); Ouachita highlands (pine, oak); Cross-Timbers (post oak, black jack oak). Southern pine is the chief commercial species, at almost 80% of saw-timber harvested annually. Replanting is essential.

INDUSTRY. In 1994 there were 3,858 industrial firms: Major commodities produced include transportation equipment (accounting for 15·3% of manufactured goods), petroleum and coal products (14·1%), non-electrical machinery (12·2%), food products (9·7%), electronic and electrical equipment (9·2%).

Labour. Total labour force, May 1989, 1,513,600. Establishment employment, 1989, 1,139,000: Manufacturing (1993), 167,900; construction (1988), 32,000; mining (1993), 33,500. Average unemployment rate, 1989, 5·9%.

TOURISM. In 1989, 16,816,546 tourists visted the 72 state parks and 10 museums and monuments. Travellers spent almost $3,000m.

COMMUNICATIONS

Roads. In 1995 there were 112,035 miles of roads and in 1991, 2,669,312 registered motor vehicles.

Railways. In 1995 Oklahoma had 3,867 miles of railway operated by 21 companies.

Civil Aviation. Airports, 1995, numbered 421, of which 127 were publicly owned. 5 cities were served by commercial airlines.

Shipping. The McClellan-Kerr Arkansas Navigation System provides access from east central Oklahoma to New Orleans through the Verdigris, Arkansas and Mississippi rivers. In 1991, 63m. tons were shipped inbound and outbound on the Oklahoma Segment. Commodities shipped, 1989 were mainly chemical fertilizer, farm produce, petroleum products, iron and steel, coal, sand and gravel.

Telecommunications. In 1995 there were 172 radio and 25 television broadcasting stations, and 16 cable-TV companies.

Press. In 1995 there were 49 daily and, in 1990, 190 weekly newspapers.

SOCIAL INSTITUTIONS

Justice. There were 12,831 prisoners in state correctional institutions in 1991. In 1990 there were 15 penal institutions, 8 community treatment centres and 7 probation and parole centres.

The death penalty was suspended in 1966 and re-imposed in 1976. The last execution was in 1995.

Religion. The chief religious bodies in 1980 were Baptists, 674,766; United Methodists, 248,635; Roman Catholics, 122,820; Churches of Christ, about 80,000; Assembly of God, 63,992; Disciples of Christ, 45,070; Presbyterian, 38,605; Lutheran, 33,664; Nazarene, 22,090; Episcopal, 21,500.

Education. In 1991 there were over 0·61m. pupils enrolled in grades Kindergarten–12. In 1992 there were 579,200 pupils at public elementary and secondary school. In 1992–93 there were 38,290 teachers; the average teacher salary per annum was $27,726. In 1992 total expenditure on the 554 school districts was $2,146,698,604. There were 32,945 students enrolled in 1992.

Institutions of higher education include:

Founded	*Name*	*Place*	*1994 Enrolment*
1890	University of Oklahoma	Norman	21,373
1890	Oklahoma State University	Stillwater	18,290
1890	University of Central Oklahoma	Edmond	16,039
1894	The University of Tulsa	Tulsa	4,579
1897	Northeastern State University	Tahlequah	9,374
1897	Northwestern Oklahoma State University	Alva	1,870
1897	Southwestern Oklahoma State University	Weatherford	5,289
1908	Cameron University	Lawton	5,863
1909	East Central University	Ada	4,468
1909	Southeastern Oklahoma State University	Durant	4,104
1909	Rogers State College	Claremore	3,404
1950	Oklahoma Christian University of Science and Arts	Oklahoma City	1,505
1969	Rose State College	Midwest City	9,234
1970	Tulsa Junior College	Tulsa	21,055
1972	Oklahoma City Community College	Oklahoma City	11,185

Health. In 1989 there were 148 hospitals; 59 alcoholism treatment centres, 25 end state renal disease facilities, 80 home health agencies, 8 hospices, 58 independent laboratories, 19 ambulatory surgical centres, 10 HIV laboratories, 25 outpatient physical therapy/speech pathology facilities, 40 physical therapists in independent practice and 4 portable X–ray units.

Welfare. In 1990–91 the Oklahoma Department of Human Services provided for medical services, $828·33m.; assistance payments and services, $321·94m.; field services, $20,167,000; Oklahoma Medical Center, $183,099,000; children and youth services, $102·55m.; mentally retarded and developmental disability, $53,849,000; rehabilitation, $137,392,000; the ageing, $30,597,000; administration, $36,452,000; management information, $16,432,000; construction and special projects, $9,708,000.

In 1988–89, payments and benefits were: Grants and energy, $184,399,170; medical payments, $685,839,185; food stamps and commodities, $181,185,160; payroll and rent, $353,472,861; day care, $18,918,539. In 1990 there were 401,000 military veterans.

Further Reading

Center for Economic and Management Research, Univ. of Oklahoma, 307 West Brooks St., Norman 73019. *Statistical Abstract of Oklahoma.*

Oklahoma Department of Libraries. *Oklahoma Almanac*. Biennial

Gibson, A. M., *The History of Oklahoma.* Rev. ed. Oklahoma Univ. Press, 1984

Morris, J. W. *et al.*, *Historical Atlas of Oklahoma.* 3rd ed. Oklahoma Univ. Press, 1986

Strain, J. W., *Outline of Oklahoma Government.* Rev. ed. Central State Univ., 1983

State library: Oklahoma Department of Libraries, 200 Northeast 18th Street, Oklahoma City 73105.

OREGON

KEY HISTORICAL EVENTS. Oregon was first settled in 1811 by the Pacific Fur Co. at Astoria, a provisional government was formed on 5 July 1843; a Territorial government was organized, 14 Aug. 1848, and on 14 Feb. 1859 Oregon was admitted to the Union.

TERRITORY AND POPULATION. Oregon is bounded in the north by Washington, with the Columbia River forming most of the boundary, east by Idaho, with the Snake River forming most of the boundary, south by Nevada and California and west by the Pacific. Land area, 97,060 sq. miles (251,385 sq. km). The federal government owned (1994) 32,132,581 acres (51·73% of the state area). Census population, 1 April 1990, 2,842,321 (70·5% urban), an increase of 8% since 1980. Population estimate (1993), 3,038,000. In 1992 births numbered 41,941 (14·1 per 1,000 population); deaths, 25,714 (8·6); infant deaths, 297 (7 per 1,000 live births); marriages, 24,866 (8·3), and divorces, 16,067 (5·4).

Population at 5 federal censuses was:

	White	*Black*	*Indian*	*Asiatic*	*Total*	*Per sq. mile*
1930	938,598	2,234	4,776	8,179	953,786	9·9
1960	1,732,037	18,133	8,026	9,120	1,768,687	18·4
1970	2,032,079	26,308	13,510	13,290	2,091,385	21·7
1980	2,490,610	37,060	27,314	34,775	2,633,105	27·3
1990	2,636,787	48,178	38,496	69,269	2,842,321	29·6

Of the total population in 1990, 1,397,073 were male. In 1980 1,788,354 persons were urban, and those 18 years and older numbered 1,910,048.

The US Bureau of Indian Affairs (area headquarters in Portland) administers (1994) 783,227·13 acres, of which 627,615·54 acres are held by the US in trust for Indian tribes and 138,950·05 acres for individual Indians, and 16,661·54 acres of mineral tracts.

The largest towns, according to 1990 census figures, are: Portland, 437,319; Eugene, 112,669; Salem (the capital), 107,786; Gresham, 68,235; Beaverton, 55,310; Medford, 46,951; Corvallis, 44,757; Springfield, 44,683; Albany, 29,462. Metropolitan areas (1990): Portland, 577,571; Eugene-Springfield, 199,009; Salem, 162,887.

CLIMATE. Jan. 32°F (0°C), July 66°F (19°C). Annual rainfall 28" (710 mm). Oregon belongs to the Pacific coast climate zone (*see* UNITED STATES: Climate).

CONSTITUTION AND GOVERNMENT. The present constitution dates from 1859; some 250 items in it have been amended. The Legislative Assembly consists of a Senate of 30 members, elected for 4 years (half their number retiring every 2 years), and a House of 60 representatives, elected for 2 years. The Governor is elected for 4 years. The constitution reserves to the voters the rights of initiative and referendum and recall.

The state sends 5 representatives to Congress.

In the 1992 presidential election Clinton polled 621,314 votes; Bush, 475,757; Perot, 354,091.

The capital is Salem. There are 36 counties in the state.

Governor: John Kitzhaber (D.), 1995–99 ($80,000).
Secretary of State: Phil Keisling (D.) ($61,500).

BUDGET. Oregon has 2-year financial periods. The total budget for the biennium 1993–95 was $20,016·8m. (federal funds, $3,370m.; general funds, $6,400m.). Budget allocations 1993–95 were: Education, $6,170m.; economic and community development, $3,808m.; human resources, $4,362m.

In 1991 the outstanding debt was $6,451m.

Per capita personal income (1994) was $20,419.

NATURAL RESOURCES

Minerals. Mineral resources include gold, silver, nickel copper, lead, mercury, chromite, sand and gravel, stone, clays, lime, silica, diatomite, expansible shale, scoria, pumice and uranium. There is geothermal potential. Mineral production value (1993), $233·5m.

Agriculture. Oregon, which has an area of 61,557,184 acres, is divided by the Cascade Range into two distinct zones as to climate. West of the Cascade Range there is a good rainfall and almost every variety of crop common to the temperate zone is grown; east of the Range stock-raising and wheat-growing are the principal industries and irrigation is needed for row crops and fruits. In 1993 the monthly average employed in agriculture was 22,500.

There were, in 1993, 37,000 farms with an acreage of 17·5m.; average farm size was 473 acres; most are family-owned corporate farms. Average value per acre (1995), $844.

Cash receipts from crops in 1992 amounted to $1,657·05m. and from livestock and livestock products, $795·31m. of which cattle made most. Principal crops: Greenhouse and nursery products ($415·8m.), hay ($104·4m.), farmforest products, wheat, potatoes, grass seed (ryegrass and fescue), Christmas trees, pears, onions ($255·8m.).

Livestock, 1 Jan. 1993: Milch cows (1992), 0·1m.; cattle and calves, 1·4m.; sheep and lambs, 415,000; swine (1992), 75,000.

Forestry. About 28·2m. acres is forested, almost half of the state. Of this amount, 22·4m. is commercial forest land suitable for timber production; ownership is as follows (acres): US Forestry Service, 13·1m.; US Bureau of Land Management, 2·7m.; other federal, 165,000; State of Oregon, 907,000; other public (city, county), 123,000; private owners, 10·8m., of which the forest industry owns 5·8m., non-industrial private owners, 4·6m., Indians, 399,000. Oregon's commercial forest lands provided a 1992 harvest of 5,742m. bd ft of logs, as well as the benefits of recreation, water, grazing, wildlife and fish. Trees vary from the coastal forest of hemlock and spruce to the state's primary species, Douglas-fir, throughout much of western Oregon. In eastern Oregon, ponderosa pine, lodgepole pine and true firs are found. Here, forestry is often combined with livestock grazing to provide an economic operation. Along the Cascade summit and in the mountains of northeast Oregon, alpine species are found.

Total covered payroll in lumber and wood products industry in 1991 was $1,475m.

Fisheries. All food and shellfish landings in the calendar year 1992 amounted to a value of $74·4m. The most important are: Ground fish, shrimp, crab, tuna, salmon.

INDUSTRY. Forest products manufacturing is Oregon's leading industry, and in 1992 employed 64,000. The second most important industry is high technology. Gross State product, 1991, $50,618m. Manufacturing employed 208,831 in 1992; trade, 328,824; services, 295,006; government, 214,659.

TOURISM. In 1992, the total income from tourism was estimated to be $3,100m.

COMMUNICATIONS

Roads. The state maintains (1994) 7,485 miles of paved highways; counties maintain 27,139 miles, and cities 8,174 miles. Federal agencies maintain (1994) 44,119 miles of roads. Registered motor vehicles, 31 Dec. 1993, totalled 3m.

Railways. The state had (1994) 21 railways with a total mileage of 2,572 (4,115 km). There is a light rail network in Portland.

Civil Aviation. In 1994 there were 1 public-use and 93 personal-use heliports; 248 personal-use and 101 public-use airports of which 34 were state-owned airports, and 2 sea-plane bases, 1 public-use and 1 personal-use.

Shipping. Portland is a major seaport for large ocean-going vessels and is 101 miles inland from the mouth of the Columbia River. In 1993 Portland handled 11·7m. short tons of cargo and other Columbia River ports 13·7m. short tons, the main commodities being grain, petroleum and wood products; the ports of Coos Bay and Newport handled 2·7m. short tons of cargo, chiefly logs, lumber and wood products.

Telecommunications. In 1993 there were 194 commercial radio stations and 37 educational radio stations. There were 24 commercial television stations and 26 educational television stations. There were also 24 cable companies.

Press. In 1994 there were 21 daily newspapers with a circulation of more than 676,000 and 111 non-daily newspapers.

SOCIAL INSTITUTIONS

Justice. There are (1993) 12 correctional institutions in Oregon. Total inmates, Sept. 1994, 6,669, including those in treatment in mental hospitals. The sterilization law, originally passed in 1917, was amended in 1967 and abolished in 1993. Some categories of euthanasia were legalized in Dec. 1994.

The death penalty is authorized.

Religion. The chief religious bodies are Catholic, Baptist, Lutheran, Methodists, Presbyterian and Mormon.

Education. School attendance is compulsory from 7 to 18 years of age if the twelfth year of school has not been completed; those between the ages of 16 and 18 years, if legally employed, may attend part-time or evening schools. Others may be excused under certain circumstances. In Oct. 1993 the public elementary and secondary schools had 516,611 students. Total expenditure on elementary and secondary education (1993–94) was $2,492,796,476; teachers' average salary (1993–94), $37,589.

Leading state-supported institutions of higher education (1993–94) included:

	Students
University of Oregon, Eugene	16,680
Oregon Health Sciences University:	1,396
Oregon State University, Corvallis	14,131
Portland State University, Portland	14,428
Western Oregon State College, Monmouth	3,871
Southern Oregon State College, Ashland	4,535
Eastern Oregon State College, La Grande	1,931
Oregon Institute of Technology, Klamath Falls	2,444

Total enrolment in state colleges and universities, 1993–94, 59,416. Largest of the privately endowed universities are Lewis and Clark College, Portland, with 3,132 students; University of Portland, 2,700 students; Willamette University, Salem, 2,451 students; Reed College, Portland, 1,277 students; Linfield College, McMinnville, 2,354 students; Marylhurst College, 1,183 students and George Fox College, 1,557 students. In 1993–94 there were 314,926 students (full-time equivalent) in community colleges.

Health. In 1993 there were 73 licensed hospitals, 2 state hospitals for the mentally ill (798 beds), 1 for the mentally retarded (400) and 1 with both programmes (133).

Social Security. The State Adult and Family Services Division provides cash payments, medical care, food stamps, day care and help in finding jobs. As of July 1994 there were an estimated 495,000 people on low incomes. Many of them were children in single-parent families, benefiting from the Aid to Families with Dependent Children Programme; 282,500 people were receiving food stamps; an estimated 376,000 were below the poverty level. There is also a Children's Services Division.

A system of unemployment benefit payments, financed by employers, with administrative allotments made through a federal agency, started in 1938.

Further Reading

Oregon Blue Book. Issued by the Secretary of State. Salem. Biennial

Carey, C. H., *General History of Oregon, prior to 1861.* 2 vol. (1 vol. reprint, 1971) Portland, 1935

Conway, F. D. L., *Timber in Oregon: History and Projected Trends.* Oregon State Univ., 1993

Corning, H. M. (ed.), *Dictionary of Oregon History.* Rev. ed. New York, 1989

Dicken, E. F. and S. N., *Oregon Divided: A Regional Geography.* Portland, 1982

Dodds, G. B., *Oregon: A Bicentennial History.* New York, 1977.—*American North-West: a History of Oregon and Washington.* Arlington Heights, (Ill.), 1986

Friedman, R., *The Other Side of Oregon.* Caldwell (ID), 1993

Highsmith, R. M. Jr. (ed.), *Atlas of the Pacific Northwest.* Rev. ed. Corvallis, 1985

McArthur, L. A., *Oregon Geographic Names.* 6th ed., rev. and enlarged. Portland, 1992
Orr, E. L. *et al.*, *Geology of Oregon.* Dubuque (IA), 1992
Patton, Clyde P., *Atlas of Oregon.* Univ. Oregon Press, Eugene, 1976
Ronda, J. P., *Astoria and Empire.* Univ. of Nebraska Press, 1990

State Library: The Oregon State Library, Salem.

PENNSYLVANIA

KEY HISTORICAL EVENTS. Pennsylvania, first settled in 1682, is one of the 13 original states in the Union.

TERRITORY AND POPULATION. Pennsylvania is bounded north by New York, east by New Jersey, south by Delaware and Maryland, south-west by West Virginia, west by Ohio and north-west by Lake Erie. Land area, 44,820 sq. miles (116,083 sq. km). Census population, 1 April 1990 (68·9% urban), 11,881,643, an increase of 0·13% since 1980. Population estimate (1993), 12,048,000. Births, 1992, 163,523 (13·6 per 1,000 population); deaths, 122,759 (10·2); infant deaths, 1,490 (9 per 1,000 live births); marriages, 79,361 (6·6); divorces, 40,796 (3·4).

Population at 5 census years was:

	White	*Black*	*Indian*	*All others*	*Total*	*Per sq. mile*
1910	7,467,713	193,919	1,503	1,976	7,665,111	171·0
1930	9,196,007	431,257	523	3,563	9,631,350	213·8
1960	10,454,004	852,750	2,122	10,490	11,319,366	251·5
			All others			
1980	10,652,320	1,046,810	164,765		11,863,895	264·3
1990	10,520,201	1,089,795	271,647		11,881,643	265·1

Of the total population in 1990, 47·9% were male, 68·9% were urban and 76·5% were 21 years of age or older.

The population of the larger cities and townships, 1992 estimate, was:

Philadelphia	1,552,572	Scranton	79,746	Harrisburg	53,430
Pittsburgh	366,852	Reading	79,028	Altoona	52,477
Erie	109,267	Bethlehem	72,373		
Allentown	106,429	Lancaster	57,171		

CLIMATE. Philadelphia. Jan. 32°F (0°C), July 77°F (25°C). Annual rainfall 40" (1,006 mm). Pittsburgh. Jan. 31°F (–0·6°C), July 74°F (23·3°C). Annual rainfall 37" (914 mm). Pennsylvania belongs to the Appalachian Mountains climate zone (*see* UNITED STATES: Climate).

CONSTITUTION AND GOVERNMENT. The present constitution dates from 1968. The General Assembly consists of a Senate of 50 members chosen for 4 years, one-half being elected biennially, and a House of Representatives of 203 members chosen for 2 years. The Governor and Lieut.-Governor are elected for 4 years. Every citizen 18 years of age, with the usual residential qualifications, may vote. Registered voters in May 1993, 5,918,871.

The state sends 21 representatives to Congress.

In the 1992 presidential election Clinton polled 2,239,164 votes; Bush, 1,791,841; Perot, 902,667.

The state capital is Harrisburg. The state is organized in counties (numbering 67), cities, boroughs, townships and school districts.

Governor: Tom Ridge (R.), 1995–99 ($105,000).
Lieut.-Governor: Mark Schweiker (D.), ($83,000).
Secretary of the Commonwealth: Yvette Kane (D.), ($72,000).

BUDGET. Total general fund revenues for fiscal year 1992-93 were $14,633m.; general fund expenditure, $13,935m. (transport, $1,377m.; public welfare, $4,628m.).

In 1993, outstanding long-term debt was $7,833m.
Per capita personal income (1994) was $22,324.

NATURAL RESOURCES

Minerals. Pennsylvania is almost the sole producer of anthracite coal. Production, 1993: Anthracite coal, 5,170,398 tons, with 2,158 employees; bituminous coal, 57,903,913 tons, with 10,336 employees; crude petroleum (1992), 1·2m. bbls; natural gas (1992), 138,000m. cu. ft. Non-fuel mineral production was worth $844m. in 1991.

Agriculture. Agriculture, market-gardening, fruit-growing, horticulture and forestry are pursued within the state. In 1992 there were 52,000 farms with a total farm area of 8m. acres (4·5m. acres in crops in 1988). Average number of acres per farm in 1992 was 154 and average value per acre in 1995 was $2,339. Cash receipts, 1992 (preliminary), from crops, $1,074·2m., and from livestock and products, $2,561·2m.

In 1992, Pennsylvania ranked first in the production of mushrooms (350·3m. lbs, value $255·6m.) and third in corn for silage (6·3m. tons, value $144·7m.); other crops were sweet corn (15,210 tons) and tomatoes for processing (34,200 tons). Pennsylvania is also a major fruit producing state; in 1992 apples totalled 500m. lbs, peaches 90m. lbs and grapes, 78,000 tons. In 1992 milk production was 10,364m. lbs; the state ranked second in eggs, numbering 5,510m. (value $197·1m.) and third in chickens (except broilers), 25·7m.; other products included 79·18m. lbs of butter and 312·67m. lbs of cheese.

On 1 Jan. 1992 there were on farms: 1·85m. cattle and calves, including 659,000 milch cows; 139,000 sheep, and 0·95m. swine.

Forestry. In 1994 state forest land totalled 1,969,923 acres as of Jan.; state park land, 281,206 acres as of Nov.; state game lands, 1,366,706 acres as of Oct.

INDUSTRY. Output of steel, 1993, 8,318,122 net tons.

In 1992, manufacturing employed 949,000 workers; services, 1,488,000; trade, 1,154,000; government, 698,000.

COMMUNICATIONS

Roads. Highways and roads in the state (federal, local and state combined) totalled (1994) 119,506 miles. Registered motor vehicles for 1992 numbered 8,915,621.

Railways. In 1993, 58 railways operated within the state with a line mileage of 5,352. There are metro, light rail and tramway networks in Philadelphia and Pittsburg, and commuter networks around Philadelphia.

Civil Aviation. There were (Nov. 1994) 141 public airports, 315 private and 8 public heliports, 353 airports for personal use and 5 seaplane bases.

Shipping. Trade at the ports of Philadelphia (1989): Imports, 60,651,352 short tons of bulk cargo and 5,581,840 of general cargo; exports, 3,182,266 of bulk cargo and 2,342,100 of general cargo.

Telecommunications. Broadcasting stations in 1993 included 45 television stations and 394 radio stations.

Press. There were (1993) 95 daily and 253 weekly newspapers.

SOCIAL INSTITUTIONS

Justice. The death penalty is authorized. The last execution was in 1995. There were 24,990 prisoners in state correctional institutions in 1992.

Religion. In 1990 there were 6,961,000 Christians and, in 1992, 329,000 Jews.

Education. School attendance is compulsory for children 8–17 years of age. In 1993–94 there were 1,744,082 pupils and 102,405 teachers in public elementary and secondary schools. In 1993–94 the public kindergartens and elementary schools had 968,465 pupils (Grades K–6) and 775,617 pupils (Grades 7–12). Non-public schools had 254,968 pupils (Grades K–8) and 79,616 pupils (Grades 9–12). Average salary, public school professional personnel in 1993–94 was 43,636; classroom teachers it was 42,411. In fiscal year, 1992–93, state and local government expenditure for elementary and secondary schools was $11,210m.

Leading senior academic institutions included:

Founded	*Institutions*	*Faculty (Autumn 1989)*	*Students (Autumn 1993)*
1740	University of Pennsylvania (non-sect.)	1,007	22,469
1787	University of Pittsburgh	1,326	33,756
1832	Lafayette College, Easton (Presbyterian)	159	2,244
1833	Haverford College	83	1,084
1842	Villanova University (R.C.)	534	11,272
1846	Bucknell University (Baptist)	226	3,694
1851	St Joseph's University, Philadelphia (R.C.)	164	6,915
1852	California University of Pennsylvania	317	6,330
1855	Pennsylvania State University	1,704	68,623
1855	Millersville University of Pennsylvania	333	7,382
1863	LaSalle University, Philadelphia (R.C.)	208	5,714
1864	Swarthmore College	151	1,522
1866	Lehigh University, Bethlehem (non-sect.)	393	6,443
1871	West Chester University of Pennsylvania	465	11,344
1875	Indiana University of Pennsylvania	660	14,062
1878	Duquesne University, Pittsburgh (R.C.)	280	8,644
1884	Temple University, Philadelphia	1,194	30,040
1885	Bryn Mawr College	136	1,810
1888	University of Scranton (R.C.)	231	4,916
1891	Drexel University, Philadelphia	448	10,205
1900	Carnegie-Mellon University, Pittsburgh	489	7,259

Health. In fiscal year 1992–93, the state had 286 acute care and specialty (including federal) hospitals, and 66,714 beds licensed and approved by the Department of Health.

Social Security. During the year ending 30 June 1993 the monthly average number of cases receiving public assistance included: Aid to families with dependent children, 604,710; blind pension, 1,891; general assistance, 170,281.

Payments for medical assistance (state and federal) in fiscal year 1993–94 totalled $5,691m., including outpatient care, $1,386m.; inpatient care, $1,672m.; capitation, $766m., and long-term care, $1,866m.

Further Reading

Statistical information: Pennsylvania State Data Center, 777 West Harrisburg Pike, Midellcton 17057. Publishes *Pennsylvania Statistical Abstract.*

Encyclopaedia of Pennsylvania, New York, 1984

Cochran, T. C., *Pennsylvania,* New York, 1978

Downey, D. B. and Bremer, F. (eds.) *Guide to the History of Pennsylvania.* London, 1994

Klein, P. S. and Hoogenboom, A., *A History of Pennsylvania.* New York, 1973

Majumdar, S. K. and Miller, E. W., *Pennsylvania Coal: Resources, Technology and Utilisation.* Pennsylvania Science, 1983

Weigley, R. F., (ed.) *Philadelphia: A 300-year History.* New York, 1984

Wilkinson, N. B., *Bibliography of Pennsylvania History.* Harrisburg, 1957

RHODE ISLAND

KEY HISTORICAL EVENTS. The earliest settlers in the region which now forms the state of Rhode Island were colonists from Massachusetts who had been driven forth on account of their non-acceptance of the prevailing religious beliefs. The first of the settlements was made in 1636, settlers of every creed being welcomed. In 1647 a patent was executed for the government of the settlements, and on 8 July 1663 a charter was executed recognizing the settlers as forming a body corporate and politic by the name of the 'English Colony of Rhode Island and

Providence Plantations, in New England, in America'. On 29 May 1790 the state accepted the federal constitution and entered the Union as the last of the 13 original states.

TERRITORY AND POPULATION. Rhode Island is bounded north and east by Massachusetts, south by the Atlantic and west by Connecticut. Land area, 1,045 sq. miles (2,707 sq. km). Census population, 1 April 1990, 1,003,464 (86% urban) a decrease of 5·95% since 1980. Population estimate (1993), 1,000,012.

Births, 1991, were 14,591 (14·5 per 1,000 population); deaths, 9,294 (9·2); infant deaths in 1992, 110 (7·5 per 1,000 live births); marriages, 7,496 (7·4); divorces, 3,314 (3·3).

Population of 5 census years was:

	White	*Black*	*Indian*	*Asiatic*	*Total*	*Per sq. mile*
1910	532,492	9,529	284	305	542,610	508·5
1930	677,026	9,913	318	240	687,497	649·3
1960	838,712	18,332	932	1,190	859,488	812·4
			All others			
1980	896,692	27,584	22,878		947,154	903·0
1990	917,375	38,861	4,071	18,325	1,003,164	960·3

Of the total population in 1990, 481,496 were male, 777,474 were 18 years of age or older and 45,752 were of Hispanic origin. 824,004 were urban in 1980.

The chief cities and their population (census, 1990) are Providence, 160,728; Warwick, 85,427; Cranston, 76,060; Pawtucket, 72,644; East Providence, 50,380.

CLIMATE. Providence. Jan. 28°F (–2·2°C), July 72°F (22·2°C). Annual rainfall 43" (1,079 mm). Rhode Island belongs to the New England climate zone (*see* UNITED STATES: Climate).

CONSTITUTION AND GOVERNMENT. The present constitution dates from 1843; it has had 42 amendments. The General Assembly consists of a Senate of 50 members and a House of Representatives of 100 members, both elected for 2 years, as are also the Governor and Lieut.-Governor. Every citizen, 18 years of age, who has resided in the state for 30 days, and is duly registered, is qualified to vote.

The state sends 2 representatives to Congress.

At the 1992 presidential election Clinton polled 213,299 votes; Bush, 131,601; Perot, 105,045.

The capital is Providence. The state has 5 counties but no county governments. There are 39 municipalities, each having its own form of local government.

Governor: Lincoln C. Almond (R.), 1995–99 ($69,900).
Lieut.-Governor: Robert A. Weygand (D.) ($52,000).
Secretary of State: James R. Langerin (D.) ($52,000).

BUDGET. For the fiscal year 1990 total revenues were $2,484·4m. (taxation, $1,233·3m., and federal aid, $667·2m.); general expenditures were $2,657·7m. (education, $781·9m.; and public welfare, $547·3m.)

Total net long-term debt on 30 June 1991 was $11,640m.

Per capita personal income (1994) was $22,251.

NATURAL RESOURCES

Minerals. The small mineral output, mostly stone, sand and gravel, was valued (1990) at an estimated $12·7m.

Agriculture. Agriculture contributed $141m. to the general cash income in 1990. In 1991 there were 700 farms with an area of some 66,000 acres. The average size of farm was 94 acres. In 1995 the average value per acre was $6,947. In 1990 60% of production value was in nursery and turf products. Farm income 1991: Crops, $58m.; livestock and products, $13m.

Fisheries. In 1990 the catch was 13·2m. lb (mainly lobster and quahang) valued at $72·9m.

INDUSTRY. Manufacturing is the chief source of income and the largest employer. Total non-agricultural employment in 1989 was 459,100, of which 112,300 were manufacturing (99,500 in 1990). Average weekly earnings for production workers in 1989 was $359.99. Principal industries are jewellery and silverware, electrical machinery, electronics, plastics, metal products, instruments, chemicals and boatbuilding.

COMMUNICATIONS

Roads. In 1990 there were 5,884 miles of roads (1,484 miles rural). In 1991 there were 628,407 registered motor vehicles.

Railways. Amtrak's New York-Boston route runs through the state, serving Providence

Civil Aviation. In 1988 there were 6 state-owned airports. Theodore Francis Green airport at Warwick, near Providence, is served by 8 airlines, and handled over 2m. passengers and 20m. lb. of freight in 1988.

Shipping. Waterborne freight through the port of Providence (1988) totalled 10·6m. tons.

Telecommunications. There are 24 radio stations and 5 television stations; there are 8 cable television companies.

SOCIAL INSTITUTIONS

Justice. The state's correctional institutions, in 1991, had 2,734 prisoners.

The death penalty is illegal, except that it is mandatory in the case of murder committed by a prisoner serving a life sentence.

Religion. Chief religious bodies are (estimated figures Sept. 1988): Roman Catholic with 550,000 members; Protestant Episcopal (baptized persons), 50,000; Baptist, 22,500; Congregational, 12,000; Methodist, 10,000; Jewish, 24,000.

Education. In 1992 there were 140,915 pupils and 9,500 teachers in public elementary and secondary schools. In 1987–88 there were 240 public elementary schools; about 25,000 pupils were enrolled in private and parochial schools. The 58 senior and vocational high schools had 3,678 teachers and 59,011 pupils. Teachers' salaries (1987) averaged $23,400. State and local government expenditure, for schools in 1991 totalled $1,212·7m.

There are 11 institutions of higher learning (3 public and 8 private). The state maintains Rhode Island College, at Providence, with 600 faculty members, and 5,600 full-time students (1987), and the University of Rhode Island, at South Kingstown, with over 900 faculty members and over 14,000 students (including graduate students). Brown University, at Providence, founded in 1764, is now non-sectarian; in 1987 it had over 600 full-time faculty members and 7,000 full-time students. Providence College, at Providence, founded in 1917 by the Order of Preachers (Dominican), had (1987) 210 professors and 5,400 students. The largest of the other colleges are Bryant College, at Smithfield, with 160 faculty and 5,000 students, and the Rhode Island School of Design, in Providence, with about 155 faculty and 1,800 students.

Health. In 1990 the state had 14 general and 7 psychiatric hospitals (with about 5,600 beds).

Social Security. In 1987 aid to dependent children was granted to 44,000 children in 15,000 families at an average payment per family of $380 per month, and the state also had a general assistance programme. (All other aid programmes were taken over by the federal government.)

Further Reading

Statistical information: Department of Economic Development, 7 Jackson Walkway, Providence 02903. Publishes *Rhode Island Basic Economic Statistics.*
Rhode Island Manual. Prepared by the Secretary of State. Providence
Providence Journal Almanac: A Reference Book for Rhode Islanders. Providence. Annual
McLoughlin, W. G., *Rhode Island: a History.* Norton, 1978
Wright, M. I. and Sullivan, R. J., *Rhode Island Atlas.* Rhode Island Pubs., 1983

State Library: Rhode Island State Library, State House, Providence 02908.

SOUTH CAROLINA

KEY HISTORICAL EVENTS. South Carolina, first settled permanently in 1670, was one of the 13 original states of the Union.

TERRITORY AND POPULATION. South Carolina is bounded in the north by North Carolina, east and south-east by the Atlantic, south-west and west by Georgia. Land area, 30,111 sq. miles (77,988 sq. km). Census population, 1 April 1990, 3,486,703 (54·6% urban), an increase of 11·73% since 1980. Population estimate (1994), 3,664,000. Births, 1994, were 51,904 (14·2 per 1,000 population); deaths, 32,223 (8·8); marriages, 51,564 (14·1); divorces and annulments, 15,802 (4·3); infant deaths in 1994, 486 (9·4 per 1,000 live births).

The population in 5 census years was:

	White	*Black*	*Indian*	*Asiatic*	*Total*	*Per sq. mile*
1910	679,161	835,843	331	65	1,515,400	49·7
1930	944,049	793,681	959	76	1,738,765	56·8
			All others			
1970	1,794,432	789,040	3,588		2,587,060	83·2
1980	2,150,507	948,623	22,703		3,121,833	100·3
1990	2,406,974	1,039,884	39,845		3,486,703	115·8

Of the total population in 1990, 1,905,378 (54·6%) were urban and 2,159,970 (61·9%) were 25 years old or older. Median age, 32.

Population estimate of large towns in 1994 (with those of associated metropolitan areas): Columbia (capital), 104,101 (486,339); Charleston, 76,854 and North Charleston, 66,431 (522,276); Greenville, 59,808; Spartanburg, 45,721 (Greenville–Spartanburg, 572,953).

CLIMATE. Columbia. Jan. 44·7°F (7°C), Aug. 80·2°F (26·9°C). Annual rainfall 49·12" (1,247·6 mm). South Carolina belongs to the Atlantic Coast climate zone (*see* UNITED STATES: Climate).

CONSTITUTION AND GOVERNMENT. The present constitution dates from 1895, when it went into force without ratification by the electorate. The General Assembly consists of a Senate of 46 members, elected for 4 years, and a House of Representatives of 124 members, elected for 2 years. It meets annually. The Governor and Lieut.-Governor are elected for 4 years.

The state sends 6 representatives to Congress.

At the 1992 presidential election Bush polled 577,507 votes; Clinton 479,514; Perot, 138,872.

The capital is Columbia. There are 46 counties.

Governor: David Beasley (R.), 1995–99 ($101,959).
Lieut.-Governor: Robert L. Peeler (R.), ($44,737).
Secretary of State: Jim Miles (R.), ($88,434).

BUDGET. For the fiscal year ending 30 June 1995 general revenues were $4,233·5m.; general expenditures were $3,984·6m.

Per capita personal income (1994) was $17,695.

NATURAL RESOURCES

Minerals. Gold is found, though non-metallic minerals are of chief importance: Value of non-fuel mineral output in 1994 was $415m., chiefly from limestone for cement, clay, stone, sand and gravel. Production of kaolin, vermiculite, scrap mica and fuller's earth is also important.

Agriculture. In 1994 there were 24,000 farms covering a farm area of over 5·15m. acres. The average farm was of 213 acres. The average value of farmland and buildings per acre was $923.

Farm income in 1994, $639m. for crops and $603·1m. for livestock and products. Chief crops are tobacco, soybeans, and corn. Production, 1993: Cotton, 204,000 bales; peaches, 165m. lbs; soybeans, 7·8m. bu.; tobacco, 111m. lbs; eggs, 1,282,000m. Livestock on farms, 1993: 650,000 all cattle, 420,000 swine.

Forestry. The forest industry is important; total forest land (1993), 12·2m. acres. National forests amounted to 609,000 acres in 1993.

INDUSTRY. A monthly average of 378,470 workers were employed in manufacturing in 1994. Major sectors are textiles (24·4%), apparel (9·1%) and chemicals (10·4%). Tourism is important.

COMMUNICATIONS

Roads. Total highway mileage in the combined highway system in Dec. 1994 was 41,497 miles. Motor vehicle registrations numbered 2,771,509 in 1994.

Railways. In 1993 the length of railway in the state was 2,354·25 miles.

Civil Aviation. In 1989 there were 161 aircraft facilities (74 public) including 139 airports, 22 heliports and 1 seaplane base. Registered general aviation numbered 2,085 in 1989.

Shipping. The state has 3 deep-water ports.

SOCIAL INSTITUTIONS

Justice. As of June 30, 1994 there were 19,800 prisoners in state correctional institutions. The death penalty is authorized. The last execution was in 1995.

Education. In 1994 there were 647,475 pupils and 45,027 teachers in public elementary and secondary schools. In 1993–94 the average teaching salary was $29,299.

For higher education the state operates the University of South Carolina (USC), founded at Columbia in 1801, with (autumn 1994), 26,754 enrolled students; USC Aiken, with 3,245 students; USC Coastal, with 4,452 students; USC Spartanburg, with 3,443 students; USC 2-year regional campuses, with 5,124 students; Clemson University, founded in 1889, with 16,290 students; The Citadel, at Charleston, with 4,441 students; Winthrop University, Rock Hill, with 5,164 students; Medical University of S. Carolina, at Charleston, with 2,256 students; S. Carolina State University, at Orangeburg, with 4,693 students, and Francis Marion University, at Florence, with 3,898 students; the College of Charleston has 9,869 students and Lander University, Greenwood, 2,779. There are 17 technical institutions (56,016).

There are also 324 private kindergartens, elementary and high schools with total enrolment (1994–95) of 45,561 pupils, and 23 private and denominational colleges and 4 junior colleges with (autumn 1994) enrolments of 25,967 and 1,348 students respectively.

Health. In July 1995 the state had 463 non-federal health facilities with 36,234 beds licensed by the South Carolina Department of Health and Environmental Control. There were 6,141 physicians and 23,435 registered nurses in 1994.

Social Security. In 1993 there were 591,000 recipients of social security benefits. The annual payment in benefits was $3,949m. and the average monthly benefit was $601.

Further Reading

Statistical information: Budget and Control Board, R.C. Dennis Bldg., Colmbia 29201. Publishes *South Carolina Statistical Abstract.*
South Carolina Legislative Manual. Columbia. Annual
Edgar, W. B., *South Carolina in the Modern Age.* Univ. of South Carolina Press, 1992
Graham, C. B. and Moore, W. V., *South Carolina Politics and Government.* Univ. of Nebraska Press, 1995
Jones, L., *South Carolina: A Synoptic History for Laymen.* Lexington, 1978

State Library: South Carolina State Library, Columbia.

SOUTH DAKOTA

KEY HISTORICAL EVENTS. South Dakota was first visited by Europeans in 1743 when Verendrye planted a lead plate (discovered in 1913) on the site of Fort Pierre, claiming the region for the French crown. Beginning with a trading post in 1794, it was settled from 1857 to 1861 when Dakota Territory was organized. It was admitted into the Union on 2 Nov. 1889.

TERRITORY AND POPULATION. South Dakota is bounded in the north by North Dakota, east by Minnesota, south-east by the Big Sioux River (forming the boundary with Iowa), south by Nebraska (with the Missouri River forming part of the boundary) and west by Wyoming and Montana. Land area, 75,898 sq. miles (196,576 sq. km). Area administered by the Bureau of Indian Affairs, 1985, covered 5m. acres (10% of the state), of which 2·6m. acres were held by tribes. The federal government, 1993, owned 2,807,000 acres.

Census population, 1 April 1990, 696,004 (50% urban), an increase of 2·4% since 1980. Population estimate (1994), 721,164. In 1994: Births, 10,504 (15·1 per 1,000 population); deaths, 6,724 (9·7); infant deaths, 100 (9·5 per 1,000 live births); stillbirths, 42 (4); marriages, 7,528 (10·8); divorces, 2,969 (4·3).

Population in 5 federal censuses was:

	White	*Black*	*American Indian*	*Asiatic*	*Total*	*Per sq. mile*
1910	563,771	817	19,137	163	583,888	7·6
1930	669,453	646	21,833	101	692,849	9·0
1960	653,098	1,114	25,794	336	680,514	8·9
			All others			
1980	638,955	2,144	49,079		690,178	9·0
				Asian/ other		
1990	637,515	3,258	50,575	4,656	696,004	9·2

Of the total population in 1990, 497,942 were 18 years of age and over and 5,252 were of Hispanic origin.

Of the total population in 1980, 340,370 were male and 320,223 were urban.

Population of the chief cities (census of 1990) was: Sioux Falls, 100,814; Rapid City, 54,523; Aberdeen, 24,927; Watertown, 17,592; Mitchell, 13,798; Brookings, 16,270; Pierre, 12,906; Yankton, 12,703; Huron, 12,448; Vermillion, 10,034; Spearfish, 6,996; Madison, 6,257; Sturgis, 5,330; Belle Fourche, 4,335; Hot Springs, 4,325.

CLIMATE. Rapid City. Jan. 25°F (–3·9°C), July 73°F (22·8°C). Annual rainfall 19" (474 mm). Sioux Falls. Jan. 14°F (–10°C), July 73°F (22·8°C). Annual rainfall 25" (625 mm). South Dakota belongs to the High Plains climate zone (*see* UNITED STATES: Climate).

CONSTITUTION AND GOVERNMENT. Voters are all citizens 18 years of age or older. The people reserve the right of the initiative and referendum. The Senate has 35 members, and the House of Representatives 70 members, all elected for 2 years; the Governor and Lieut.-Governor are elected for 4 years.

The state sends 1 representative to Congress.

In the 1992 presidential election Bush polled 136,718 votes; Clinton, 124,888; Perot, 73,295.

The capital is Pierre. The state is divided into 66 organized counties.

Governor: William J. Janklow, (R.), 1995–99 ($82,271).
Lieut.-Governor: Carole Hillard, (R.) ($59,740).
Secretary of State: Joyce Hazeltine, (R.) ($55,900).

BUDGET. For the fiscal year ending 30 June 1997 the estimated general fund revenues were $624,416,792 ($365,688,310 from sales and use tax); estimated expenditure was $624,146,738 ($233,229,921 on state aid to education and local government, 37·4% to the latter).

Per capita personal income (1994) was $19,577.

NATURAL RESOURCES

Minerals. In 1993 the mineral products included gold, 19,241 kg (fourth largest yield of all states), silver, 5 tonnes. Mineral products, 1993, were valued at $337,156,000, including gold and silver.

Agriculture. In 1993 there were 34,057 farms, average size 1,316 acres. Average value of farmland and buildings per acre in 1995 was $302. Farm income, 1992: Crops, $1,072,895; livestock and products, $2,170,659. 15,543 farms sold produce valued at over $50,000 in 1992.

South Dakota is a major producer of rye (1·3m. bu. in 1994), sunflower seed (1,427·2m. bu.), flaxseed (0·3m. bu.), and oats (31·4m. bu.). The other important crops are all wheat (95·3m. bu.), sorghum for grain (12·4m. bu.), corn for grain (367·2m. bu. in 1992) and soybeans for beans (94·4m. bu.). The farm livestock on 1 Jan. 1995 included 4m. cattle, 0·53m. sheep and (1 Dec. 1994) 1·74m. hogs. 26m. lbs of honey were produced in 1994.

Forestry. National forest area, 1992, 2,013,000 acres.

INDUSTRY. In 1994, 1,067 manufacturing establishments had 43,649 employees. Food and kindred industries had 144 establishments employing 8,286 workers. Construction had 2,786 companies employing 13,947 workers. Also significant were transport, communications and public utilities (1,698 establishments employing 14,847 workers). Mining establishments were 79 and employed 2,352 workers.

COMMUNICATIONS

Roads. In 1995 there were 83,313 miles of roads (in 1990, 71,622 miles rural). In 1994 there were 859,503 registered motor vehicles, including 699,508 cars and lorries, 127,022 trailers, 25,822 motorcycles and 5,508 snowmobiles.

Railways. In 1994 there were 1,976·4 miles of track of which 874·6 miles were state-owned.

Civil Aviation. In 1995 there were 73 general aviation airports and 9 commercial airports.

SOCIAL INSTITUTIONS

Justice. The State prisons had, in 1995, 1,733 inmates under state and 500 under federal correction. The death penalty is authorized.

Religion. The chief religious bodies are: Lutherans, Roman Catholics, Methodist, Disciples of Christ, Presbyterian, Baptist and Episcopal.

Education. Elementary and secondary education are free from 6 to 21 years of age. Between the ages of 6 and 16, attendance is compulsory. In 1994–95, 156,773 elementary and high school students attended public, private and alternative schools.

Teachers' salaries (1993–94) averaged an estimated $25,259. Total expenditure on public schools (1993–94), $498,354,704.

Higher education (spring 1994): The School of Mines at Rapid City, established 1885, had 2,373 students; the State University at Brookings, 8,467; the University of South Dakota, founded at Vermillion in 1882, 7,274; Northern State University, Aberdeen, 2,684; Black Hills State University at Spearfish, 2,751; Dakota State University at Madison, 1,213. The 10 private colleges including 2 Indian colleges had 7,550 students in 1994.

Health. In 1996 there were 57 licensed hospitals (3,486 beds).

Social Security. In financial year 1994 there were on average 9,562 disabled persons receiving $33,505,392 in benefits; 148 blind persons received $526,968. Aid to dependent families with children was $24,550,248, to 13,751 children.

Further Reading

Statistical information: State Data Center, Univ. of South Dakota, Vermillion 57069.

Governor's Budget Report. South Dakota Bureau of Finance and Management. Annual
South Dakota Historical Collections. 1902–82
South Dakota Legislative Manual. Secretary of State, Pierre, S.D. Biennial
Berg, F. M., *South Dakota: Land of Shining Gold.* Hettinger, 1982
Karolevitz, R. F., *Challenge: the South Dakota Story.* Sioux Falls, 1975
Milton, John R., *South Dakota; a Bicentennial History.* New York, 1977
Schell, H. S., *History of South Dakota.* 3rd ed. Lincoln, Neb., 1975
Vexler, R. I., *South Dakota Chronology and Factbook.* New York, 1978

State Library: South Dakota State Library, 800 Governor's Drive, Pierre, S.D., 57501–2294.

TENNESSEE

KEY HISTORICAL EVENTS. Tennessee, first settled in 1757, was admitted into the Union on 1 June 1796.

TERRITORY AND POPULATION. Tennessee is bounded north by Kentucky and Virginia, east by North Carolina, south by Georgia, Alabama and Mississippi and west by the Mississippi River (forming the boundary with Arkansas and Missouri). Land area, 41,220 sq. miles (106,759 sq. km). Census population, 1 April 1990, 4,877,185 (60·9% urban), an increase of 6·2% since 1980. Population estimate (1993), 5,098,798. Vital statistics, 1994: Births, 72,126 (14·4 per 1,000 population); deaths, 49,444 (9·9); infant deaths, 635 (8·8 per 1,000 live births); marriages, 81,674 (32·7); divorces, 34,064 (13·6).

Population in 5 census years was:

	White	*Black*	*Indian*	*Asiatic*	*Total*	*Per sq. mile*
1910	1,711,432	473,088	216	53	2,184,789	52·4
1930	2,138,644	477,646	161	105	2,616,556	62·4
			All others			
1970	3,293,930	621,261	8,496		3,923,687	95·3
1980	3,835,452	725,942	29,726		4,591,120	111·6
1990	4,048,068	778,035	51,082		4,877,185	115·7

Of the population in 1990, 2,348,928 were male, 2,969,948 were urban and those 21 years of age or older numbered 3,421,633.

The cities, with population, 1994, are Memphis, 614,289; Nashville (capital), 504,505; Knoxville, 169,311; Chattanooga, 152,259; Clarksville, 92,116; Jackson, 52,343; Johnson City, 51,573; Murfreesboro, 56,194; Kingsport, 38,476; Oak Ridge, 28,209. Standard metropolitan areas 1994 (1992): Memphis, 1,056,096 (1,033,183); Nashville, 1,069,648 (1,023,315); Knoxville, 631,107 (610,482); Chattanooga, 439,189 (430,848); Johnson City–Bristol–Kingsport, 450,641 (444,625); Clarksville, 186,017 (178,155); Jackson, 82,557 (80,230).

CLIMATE. Memphis. Jan. 41°F (5°C), July 82°F (27·8°C). Annual rainfall 49" (1,221 mm). Nashville. Jan. 39°F (3·9°C), July 79°F (26·1°C). Annual rainfall 48" (1,196 mm). Tennessee belongs to the Appalachian Mountains climate zone (*see* UNITED STATES: Climate).

CONSTITUTION AND GOVERNMENT. The state has operated under 3 constitutions, the last of which was adopted in 1870 and has been since amended 22 times (first in 1953). Voters at an election may authorize the calling of a convention limited to altering or abolishing one or more specified sections of the constitution. The General Assembly consists of a Senate of 33 members and a House of Representatives of 99 members, senators elected for 4 years and representatives for 2 years. Qualified as electors are all citizens (usual residential and age (18) qualifications). Tennessee sends 9 representatives to Congress.

In the 1992 presidential election Clinton polled 933,521 votes; Bush, 841,300; Perot, 199,968.

The capital is Nashville. The state is divided into 95 counties.

Governor: Don Sundquist (R.), 1995–99 ($85,000).
Lieut.-Governor: John Wilder (D.), ($49,500).
Secretary of State: Riley C. Darnell (D.), ($76,068).

BUDGET. For 1993–94 total revenue was $10,260m.; general expenditure, $9,401m.

Total net long-term debt on 30 June 1994 amounted to $826·4m.

Per capita personal income (1994) was $19,446.

NATURAL RESOURCES

Minerals. Non-fuel mineral production was worth $663m. in 1990.

Agriculture. In 1994, 84,000 farms covered 12·3m. acres. The average farm was of 146 acres valued, land and buildings, at $151,925.

Farm income (1993) from crops was $1,026·9m.; from livestock, $1,011·6m. Main crops were cotton, tobacco and soybeans.

On 1 Jan. 1994 the domestic animals included 160,000 milch cows, 2·55m. all cattle, 12,600 sheep, 0·58m. swine.

Forestry. Forests occupy 13,258,000 acres. The forest industry and industries dependent on it employ about 0·04m. workers. Wood products are valued at over $500m. per year. National forest system land (1991) 626,000 acres.

INDUSTRY. The manufacturing industries include iron and steel working, but the most important products are chemicals, including synthetic fibres and allied products, electrical equipment and food. In 1992, manufacturing establishments employed 504,000 workers; value added by manufactures was $35,799m.

TOURISM. In 1992, 30·9m. out-of-state tourists spent $6,366m.

COMMUNICATIONS

Roads. In 1991 there were 84,852 miles of roads (69,376 miles rural) and 5,072,084 registered motor vehicles.

Railways. The state had (1988) 2,475 miles of track. There is a tramway in Memphis.

Civil Aviation. The state is served by 11 major airlines. In 1985 there were 74 public airports and 78 private; there were 71 heliports and 2 military air bases.

SOCIAL INSTITUTIONS

Justice. The death penalty is authorized, but there has been no execution since 1960.

Prison population, 30 June 1994, 12,382.

Religion. In 1990 there were 1,086,680 Southern Baptists, 320,724 United Methodists, 199,698 Black Baptists, 168,933 members of the Church of Christ, 137,203 Catholics and 18,377 members of the African Methodist Episcopal Zion.

Education. School attendance has been compulsory since 1925 and the employment of children under 16 years of age in workshops, factories or mines is illegal.

In 1993–94 there were 1,554 public schools with a net enrolment of 923,673 pupils; 47,378 teachers earned an average salary of $30,514. Total expenditure for operating schools was $3,633m. Tennessee has 49 accredited colleges and universities, 16 2-year colleges and 27 vocational schools. The universities include the University of Tennessee, Knoxville (founded 1794), with 26,122 students in 1993–94; Vanderbilt University, Nashville (1873) with 9,853, Tennessee State University (1912) with 7,851, the University of Tennessee at Chattanooga (1886) with 8,325, University of Memphis (1912), 20,375 and Fisk University (1866) with 854.

Health. In 1992 the state had 135 hospitals with 21,643 beds. State facilities for the mentally retarded had 1,789 resident patients and mental hospitals had 1,142 in 1994.

Social Security. In 1993 Tennessee paid $5,957m. to retired workers and their survivors and to disabled workers. Total beneficiaries: 575,200 retired; 169,160 survivors; 146,240 disabled. 908,943 people received $1,977m. in Medicaid. Supplemental Security Income ($566m.) was paid to 167,590. 276,931 people (1992) received aid to dependent children ($204m.).

Further Reading

Statistical information: Center for Business and Economic Research, Univ. of Tennessee, Knoxville 37996. Publishes *Tennessee Statistical Abstract*

Tennessee Blue Book. Secretary of State, Nashville

Corlew, R. E., *Tennessee: a Short History.* 2nd ed. Univ. of Tennessee, 1981

Davidson, D., *Tennessee: Vol. I, The Old River Frontier to Secession,* Univ. of Tennessee, 1979

Dykeman, W., *Tennessee.* Rev. ed., New York, 1984

State Library: State Library and Archives, Nashville.

TEXAS

KEY HISTORICAL EVENTS. In 1836 Texas declared its independence of Mexico, and after maintaining an independent existence, as the Republic of Texas, for 10 years, it was on 29 Dec. 1845 received as a state into the American Union. The state's first settlement dates from 1686.

TERRITORY AND POPULATION. Texas is bounded north by Oklahoma, northeast by Arkansas, east by Louisiana, south-east by the Gulf of Mexico, south by Mexico and west by New Mexico. Land area, 261,914 sq. miles (678,358 sq. km). Census population, 1990, 16,986,510 (80·3% urban). Population estimate (1994), 17,957,266. Vital statistics for 1992: Births, 320,714 (18·2 per 1,000 population); deaths, 126,409 (7·3); infant deaths, 2,478 (7·7 per 1,000 live births); marriages, 178,070 (10·1); divorces, 96,629 (5·5).

Population for 5 census years was:

	White	Black	American Indian	Asian	Total	Per sq. mile
1910	3,204,848	690,049	702	943	3,896,542	14·8
1930	4,967,172	854,964	1,001	1,578	5,824,715	22·1
			All others			
1970	9,717,128	1,399,005	80,597		11,196,730	42·7
1980	11,197,663	1,710,250	1,320,470		14,228,383	54·2
				Asian/ other		
1990	12,774,762	2,021,632	65,877	2,124,239	16,986,510	64·9

Of the population in 1980, 6,998,301 were male, 11,327,159 persons were urban. Persons of Hispanic origin were also identified in the last 2 censuses, numbering 2,985,643 in 1980 and 4,339,905 in 1990.

The largest cities, with census population in 1993, are:

Houston	1,700,672	Garland	187,439	Mesquite	108,960
Dallas	1,036,309	Irving	166,523	Waco	107,191
San Antonio	991,861	Amarillo	163,569	Grand Prairie	103,913
El Paso	554,496	Plano	153,624	Wichita Falls	98,356
Austin (capital)	501,637	Laredo	140,688	Midland	95,003
Fort Worth	459,085	Pasadena	127,843	Odessa	92,257
Arlington	277,939	Beaumont	118,289	McAllen	91,184
Corpus Christi	266,958	Brownsville	117,326	Carrollton	90,934
Lubbock	193,194	Abilene	110,661	San Angelo	87,980

Metropolitan statistical areas, 1993: Houston, 3,544,601; Dallas, 2,731,503; Fort Worth-Arlington, 1,379,539; San Antonio, 1,387,618.

CLIMATE. Dallas. Jan. 45°F (7·2°C), July 84°F (28·9°C). Annual rainfall 38" (945 mm). El Paso. Jan. 44°F (6·7°C), July 81°F (27·2°C). Annual rainfall 9" (221 mm). Galveston. Jan. 54°F (12·2°C), July 84°F (28·9°C). Annual rainfall 46" (1,159 mm). Houston. Jan. 52°F (11·1°C), July 83°F (28·3°C). Annual rainfall 48" (1,200 mm). Texas belongs to the Central Plains climate zone (*see* UNITED STATES: Climate).

CONSTITUTION AND GOVERNMENT. The present constitution dates from 1876; it had been amended 364 times as of Nov. 1995. The Legislature consists of a Senate of 31 members elected for 4 years (half their number retire every 2 years), and a House of Representatives of 150 members elected for 2 years. It meets in odd-numbered years in January. The Governor and Lieut.-Governor are elected for 4 years.

The state sends 30 representatives to Congress.

In the 1992 presidential election Bush polled 2,496,701 votes; Clinton, 2,281,815; Perot, 354,781.

The capital is Austin. The state has 254 counties.

Governor: George W. Bush (R.), 1995–99 ($99,122).
Lieut.-Governor: Bob Bullock (D.) ($7,200).
Secretary of State: Antonio Garza (D.) ($76,966).

BUDGET. In the fiscal year ending 31 Aug. 1995 general revenues were $38,681,997,985 ($18,858,790,042 from taxes, $11,408,108,057 federal aid, $3,767,949,578 from licences, fees and permits, $1,714,969,342 from interest and investment income and $2,430m. from other sources); total expenditures were $39,337,381,101.

Per capita personal income (1994) was $19,857.

NATURAL RESOURCES

Minerals. Production, 1993: Crude petroleum, 576m. bbls, natural gas 5,620m. cu. ft; other minerals include natural gasoline, butane and propane gases, helium, crude gypsum, granite and sandstone, salt and cement. Total value of non-fuel mineral products in 1992, $1,380m.

Agriculture. Texas is one of the most important agricultural states. In 1993 it had 185,000 farms covering 130m. acres; average farm was of 703 acres. In 1995, land and buildings were valued at $550 per acre. Large-scale commercial farms, highly mechanized, dominate in Texas; farms of 1,000 acres or more in number far exceed that of any other state. But small-scale farming persists.

Soil erosion is serious in some parts. For some 97,297,000 acres drastic curative treatment has been indicated and for 51,164,000 acres, preventive treatment.

Production, 1992: Corn (202m. bu., value $496m.), barley, beans, cotton, hay, oats, peanuts, rye, sorghum, soybeans, sunflowers, wheat, oranges, grapefruit, peaches, sweet potatoes.

Farm income, 1991, from crops was $4,496m.; from livestock, $7,693m.

The state has a very great livestock industry, leading in the number of all cattle, 14·3m. on 1 Jan. 1992, and sheep, 2m.; it also had 0·53m. milch cows, and 0·54m. swine.

Forestry. There were (1993) 22,032,000 acres of forested land.

INDUSTRY. In 1993 manufacturing establishments employed 985,600 workers; trade employed 1,793,700; government, 1·3m.; services, 1,758,600; construction, 351,400; finance, insurance and real estate, 409,400; transport and public utilities, 426,200. Chemical industries along the Gulf Coast, such as the production of synthetic rubber and of primary magnesium (from sea-water), are increasingly important.

Texas has adopted (1993) a labour code which includes laws concerning protection of labourers, employer-employee relations, employment services and unemployment, and workers' compensation.

COMMUNICATIONS

Roads. In 1993 there were 0·3m. miles of roads (including 3,200 miles of interstate highways, 12,300 miles of US highways and 14,900 miles of state highways) and 14,496,096 registered motor vehicles.

Civil Aviation. In 1993 there were 307 public and 1,308 private airports.

Shipping. The port of Houston, connected by the Houston Ship Channel (50 miles long) with the Gulf of Mexico, is a large cotton market. Total cargo handled by all ports, 1990, 335,311,608 short tons.

SOCIAL INSTITUTIONS

Justice. In 1993 there were 47,728 men and women in state prisons. Since the US Supreme Court's reinstatement of the death penalty in 1976 there have been 105 executions, the latest in 1996.

Religion. Religious bodies represented include Roman Catholics, Baptists, Methodists, Churches of Christ, Lutherans, Presbyterians and Episcopalians. There were 176,000 Mormons in 1994.

Education. School attendance is compulsory from 6 to 17 years of age.

In 1992–93 public elementary and secondary schools had over 3·5m. students; there were 219,344 teachers whose salaries averaged $27,796. State and Federal support for public shools, 1992, $7,800m.

In 1993 there were 137 higher education institutions (35 public, 38 independent colleges and universities, 49 public community college districts and 15 others). The largest institutions with student enrolment, (1995–96), were:

Founded	*Institutions*	*Control*	*Students*
1845	Baylor University, Waco	Baptist	12,202
1852	St Mary's University, San Antonio	R.C.	4,202
1869	Trinity University, San Antonio	Presb.	2,482
1873	Texas Christian University, Fort Worth	Christian	7,050
1876	Texas A. and M. Univ., College Station	State	38,636
1878	Prairie View Agr. and Mech. Coll., Prairie View	State	5,999
1879	Sam Houston State University	State	12,439
1883	University of Texas System (every campus)	State	136,597
1890	University of North Texas, Denton	State	25,122
1891	Hardin-Simmons University, Abilene	Baptist	2,373
1889	East Texas State University, Commerce	State	7,629
1899	South West Texas State University, San Marcos	State	20,929
1901	Texas Woman's University, Denton	State	9,827
1906	Abilene Christian University, Abilene	Church of Christ	4,436
1911	Southern Methodist University, Dallas	Methodist	8,986
1912	Rice University	Independent	4,099

Founded	*Institutions*	*Control*	*Students*
1923	Lamar University, Beaumont	State	8,419
1923	Stephen F. Austin State University	State	11,781
1923	Texas Technical University, Lubbock	State	24,185
1925	Texas A&M University, Kingsville	State	6,061
1927	University of Houston, Houston	State	30,358
1947	Texas Southern University, Houston	State	9,458

Health. In 1994, the state had 474 hospitals (73,067 beds) listed by the Texas Hospital Association. In the fiscal year 1989, the average daily census of patients was: State hospitals, 3,629; state schools, 7,265 and state centres, 331.

Social Security. Aid is from state and federal sources. Number of Social Security beneficiaries in 1990: 2,193,000 who received an average of $583 (for retired workers), $579 (for disabled workers) and $538 (for widows/widowers) per month.

Further Reading

Texas Almanac. Dallas. Biennial
Cruz, G. R. and Irby, J. A. (eds.) *Texas Bibliography.* Austin, 1982
Fehrenbach, T. R., *Lone Star: A History of Texas and the Texans.* London, 1986
Jordan, T. G. and Bean, J. L., Jr., *Texas.* Boulder, 1983
Kingston, M. *Texas Almanac's Political History of Texas.* Austin, 1992
Kraemer, R. and Newell, C. *Essentials of Texas Politics.* 5th ed. Austin, 1992
MacCorkle, S. A. and Smith, D., *Texas Government.* 7th ed. New York, 1974
Marten, J., *Texas* [Bibliography]. Santa Barbara and Oxford, 1992

Legislative Reference Library: Box 12488, Capitol Station, Austin, Texas 78711-2488.

UTAH

KEY HISTORICAL EVENTS. Utah, which had been acquired by the US during the Mexican war, was settled by Mormons in 1847, and organized as a Territory on 9 Sept. 1850. After the Mormons had renounced polygamy in 1890 it was admitted as a state into the Union on 4 Jan. 1896 with boundaries as at present.

TERRITORY AND POPULATION. Utah is bounded north by Idaho and Wyoming, east by Colorado, south by Arizona and west by Nevada. Land area, 82,168 sq. miles (212,816 sq. km). The Bureau of Indian Affairs in 1990 administered 2,317,604 acres, 2,284,766 acres of which were allotted to Indian tribes.

Census population, 1 April 1990, 1,722,850 (87% urban), an increase of 17·92% since 1980. Population estimate (1993), 1,859,582. Births in 1991 were 35,070 (20·1 per 1,000 population); deaths, 9,199 (5·3); infant deaths in 1992, 226 (6·1 per 1,000 live births); marriages, 18,788 (10·8); divorces, 8,407 (4·8).

Population at 5 federal censuses was:

	White	*Black*	*Indian*	*Asiatic*	*Total*	*Per sq. mile*
1910	366,583	1,144	3,123	2,501	373,851	4·5
1930	499,967	1,108	2,869	3,903	507,847	6·2
1960	873,828	4,148	6,961	5,207	890,627	10·8
1970	1,031,926	6,617	11,273	6,230	1,059,273	12·9
1980	1,382,550	9,225	19,256	15,076	1,461,037	17·7

Of the total in 1980, 724,501 were male, 1,232,908 persons were urban; 860,304 were 20 years of age or older.

The largest cities are Salt Lake City, with a population (census, 1990) of 159,936; West Valley City, 86,976; Provo, 86,835; Sandy City, 75,058; Orem, 67,561; Ogden, 63,905.

CLIMATE. Salt Lake City. Jan. 29°F (–1·7°C), July 77°F (25°C). Annual rainfall 16" (401 mm). Utah belongs to the Mountain States climate region (*see* UNITED STATES: Climate).

CONSTITUTION AND GOVERNMENT. Utah adopted its present constitution in 1896 (now with 61 amendments). The Legislature consists of a Senate (in part renewed every 2 years) of 29 members, elected for 4 years, and of a House of Representatives of 75 members elected for 2 years. It sits annually in Jan. The Governor is elected for 4 years. The constitution provides for the initiative and referendum.

The state sends 3 representatives to Congress.

The capital is Salt Lake City. There are 29 counties in the state.

In the 1992 presidential election Bush polled 322,632 votes; Clinton, 183,429; Perot, 203,400.

Governor: Mike Leavitt (R.), 1993–97 ($77,250).
Lieut.-Governor: Olene S. Walker (R.), ($60,000).

BUDGET. For the year ending 30 June 1990 general revenue was $3,529·8m. ($1,768m. from taxes, $966·3m. from federal aid); general expenditures were $3,470·9m. ($1,663·8m. on education, $348·7m. on highways, $458m. on public welfare).

Per capita personal income (1994) was $17,043.

NATURAL RESOURCES

Minerals. The principal minerals are: Copper, gold, magnesium, petroleum, lead, silver and zinc. The state also has natural gas, clays, tungsten, molybdenum, uranium and phosphate rock. The value of non-fuel mineral production in 1990 was $1·2m.

Agriculture. In 1991 Utah had some 13,300 farms covering 11·3m. acres. In 1985 about 2m. acres were crop land, and about 300,000 acres pasture and about 1m. acres had irrigation. In 1991 the average farm was of 850 acres and the average value per acre in 1995 was $606.

Of the total surface area, 9% is severely eroded and only 9·4% is free from erosion; the balance is moderately eroded.

Farm income, 1991, from crops, $167m. and from livestock, $555m. The principal crops are: Barley, wheat (spring and winter), oats, potatoes, hay (alfalfa, sweet clover and lespedeza), maize. Livestock, 1990: Cattle, 855,000; pigs, 34,000; Sheep 0·6m.; poultry, 3·8m.

Forestry. Area of national forests, 1991, was 9,128,000 acres, of which 8,014,000m. acres were under forest service administration.

INDUSTRY. In 1985 manufacturing establishments had 94,000 workers. Leading manufactures by value added are primary metals, ordinances and transport, food, fabricated metals and machinery, petroleum products. Service industries employed 132,000; trade, 148,000; government, 138,000.

COMMUNICATIONS

Roads. In 1990 there were 42,971 miles of roads (37,430 miles rural). In 1991 there were 1,229,730 registered motor vehicles.

Railways. On 1 July 1974 the state had 1,734 miles of railways.

Civil Aviation. There is an international airport at Salt Lake City.

SOCIAL INSTITUTIONS

Justice. In 1991 there were 2,466 prisoners in state correctional institutions. The death penalty is authorized.

Religion. Latter-Day Saints (Mormons) numbered 1,458,000 in 1994. World membership was 9,025,000. The President of the Mormon Church is Howard Hunter (born 1908). The Roman Catholic church and most Protestant denominations are represented.

Education. School attendance is compulsory for children from 6 to 18 years of age. There are 40 school districts. Teachers' salaries, 1986, averaged $22,550. There were in 1992, 454,218 pupils and 17,941 teachers in public elementary and secondary schools. In 1991 education expenditure by state and local government was $2,254·3m.

The University of Utah (1850) (24,770 students in 1985–86) is in Salt Lake City; the Utah State University (1890) (11,804) is in Logan. The Mormon Church maintains the Brigham Young University at Provo (1875) with 26,894 students. Other colleges include: Westminster College, Salt Lake City (1,302); Weber State College, Ogden (11,117); Southern Utah State College, Cedar City (2,587); College of Eastern Utah, Price (1,132); Snow College, Ephraim (1,328); Dixie College, St George (2,234).

Health. In 1983, the state had 44 hospitals (5,400 beds) listed by the Utah Department of Social Services.

Social Security. In Dec. 1985 the state department of public welfare provided assistance to 37,800 persons receiving aid to dependent children at an average $322 per family per month; aid to the aged, the blind and disabled is provided from federal funds; there were 1,900 aged recipients in 1985 (average $150 per month), 6,600 disabled ($224).

Further Reading

Statistical information: Bureau of Economic and Business Research, Univ. of Utah, 401 Kendall D. Garff Bldg., Salt Lake City 84112. Publishes *Statistical Abstract of Utah.*

Utah Foundation. *Statistical Review of Government in Utah.* Salt Lake City; 1991

Arrington, L., *Great Basin Kingdom: An Economic History of the Latter-Day Saints, 1830–1900.* Cambridge, Mass., 1958

Petersen, C. S., *Utah: a History.* New York, 1977

VERMONT

KEY HISTORICAL EVENTS. Vermont, first settled by Europeans in 1724, was admitted into the Union as the fourteenth state on 4 March 1791. The first constitution was adopted by convention at Windsor, 2 July 1777, and established an independent state government.

TERRITORY AND POPULATION. Vermont is bounded in the north by Canada, east by New Hampshire, south by Massachusetts and west by New York. Land area, 9,614 sq. miles (23,955 sq. km). Census population, 1 April 1990, 562,758 (32·2% urban), an increase of 10% since 1980. Population estimate (1994), 580,209. Births, 1993, were 7,148 (12·9 per 1,000 population); deaths, 5,001 (8·6); infant deaths, 42 (6·7 per 1,000 live births); marriages, 5,945 (10·3); divorces, 2,877 (5).

Population at 5 census years was:

	White	*Black*	*Indian*	*Asiatic*	*Total*	*Per sq. mile*
1910	354,298	1,621	26	11	355,956	39·0
1930	358,966	568	36	41	359,611	38·8
1960	389,092	519	57	172	389,881	42·0
1980	506,736	1,135	984	1,355	511,456	55·1
1990	555,088	1,951	1,696 [1]	3,215 [2]	562,758	60·8

[1] Includes Eskimo and Aleut. [2] Includes Pacific Islander.

Of the population in 1990, 275,494 were male; 180,904 were urban; those 20 years of age or older numbered 400,019. The largest cities are Burlington, with a population (1990) of 39,127; Rutland, 18,230; Essex, 16,498; Bennington, 16,451.

CLIMATE. Burlington. Jan. 17°F (–8·3°C), July 70°F (21·1°C). Annual rainfall 33" (820 mm). Vermont belongs to the New England climate zone (*see* UNITED STATES: Climate).

CONSTITUTION AND GOVERNMENT. The constitution was adopted in 1793 and has since been amended. Amendments are proposed by two-thirds vote of the Senate every 4 years, and must be accepted by two sessions of the legislature; they are then submitted to popular vote. The state Legislature, consisting of a Senate of 30 members and a House of Representatives of 150 members (both elected for 2 years), meets in Jan. every year. The Governor and Lieut.-Governor are elected for 2 years. Electors are all citizens who possess certain residential qualifications and have taken the freeman's oath set forth in the constitution.

The state sends 1 representative to Congress.

In the 1992 presidential election Clinton polled 133,590 votes; Bush, 88,122; Perot, 65,985.

The capital is Montpelier (8,254, 1990). There are 14 counties and 251 cities, towns and other administrative divisions.

Governor: Howard Dean (D.), 1995–97 ($80,724).
Lieut.-Governor: Barbara W. Snelling (R.) ($33,654).
Secretary of State: Jim Milne (R.) ($50,794).

BUDGET. The total revenue for the year ending 30 June 1993 was $1,543·9m.; total disbursements, $1,610·6m.

Total net long-term bonded debt, 30 June 1993, was $339,494,838.

Per capita personal income (1994) was $20,224.

NATURAL RESOURCES

Minerals. Stone, chiefly granite, marble and slate, is the leading mineral produced in Vermont, contributing about 60% of the total value of mineral products. Other products include asbestos, talc, peat, sand and gravel. Total value of non-fuel mineral products, 1990, $82m.

Agriculture. Agriculture is the most important industry. In 1993 the state had some 6,500 farms covering 1·47m. acres; the average farm was of 226 acres and in 1995 the average value per acre was $1,479. Farm income, 1993, from livestock and products, $379m.; from crops, $35m. The dairy farms produced about 2,337,000 lbs of milk in 1989. The chief agricultural crops are hay, apples and silage. In 1992 Vermont had 310,518 cattle and calves, 17,145 sheep and lambs, 3,738 hogs and pigs, and (1993) 71,000 poultry.

Forestry. In 1993 the harvest was 251,245,000 bd ft hardwood and softwood sawlogs, and 420,272 cords of pulpwood and boltwood.

The state is 76% forest, with 10% in public ownership. National forests area (1986), 355,534 acres. State-owned forests, parks, fish and game areas, 250,000 acres; municipally-owned, 38,500 acres.

INDUSTRY. In 1988 service industries employed 62,150; trade, 59,750; manufacturing, 49,700; government, 40,850; construction, 17,400.

COMMUNICATIONS

Roads. The state had 13,987 miles of roads in 1995, including 7,376 miles of gravel, graded and drained, or unimproved roads. Motor vehicle registrations, 1991, 446,819.

Railways. There were, in 1988, 793 miles of railway, 291 of which was leased by the state to private operators.

Civil Aviation. There were 18 airports in 1990, of which 11 were state operated, 1 municipally owned and 6 private. Some are only open in summer.

SOCIAL INSTITUTIONS

Justice. In financial year 1994 prisons and centres had 1,285 inmates. The death penalty is not authorized.

Religion. The principal denominations are Roman Catholic, United Church of Christ, United Methodist, Protestant Episcopal, Baptist and Unitarian–Universalist.

Education. School attendance during the full school term is compulsory for children from 7 to 16 years of age, unless they have completed the 10th grade or undergo approved home instruction. In 1992 the public elementary and secondary schools had 96,802 pupils and 7,170 teachers. Teachers' salaries, 1990–91, average salary $34,569. State and local governments expenditure on public schools, 1991, $900·4m.

In autumn 1993 there were 36,528 students in higher education. The University of Vermont (1791) had 10,617 students in 1993–94; Norwich University (1834, founded as the American Literary, Scientific and Military Academy in 1819), had 2,687; St Michael's College (1904), 2,486; there are 5 state colleges.

Health. In Sept. 1990 the state had 18 general hospitals (2,383 beds).

Social Security. Old-age assistance (SSI) was being granted in 1993 to 3,654 (including aged, blind and disabled) persons, drawing an average of $320.42 per month; aid to dependent children was being granted to 26,986 persons, drawing an average of $194.25 per month; and aid to the permanently and totally disabled was being granted to 10,177 persons, drawing an average of $355.36.

Further Reading

Statistical information: Office of Policy Research and Coordination, Montpelier 05602
Legislative Directory. Secretary of State, Montpelier. Biennial
Vermont Annual Financial Report. Auditor of Accounts, Montpelier. Annual
Vermont Year-Book, formerly *Walton's Register.* Chester. Annual
Bassett T. (ed.) *Vermont: A Bibliography of its History,* Boston, 1981
Vermont Atlas and Gazetteer, Rev. ed., Freeport, 1983
Morrissey, C. T., *Vermont,* New York, 1981

State Library: Vermont Dept.of Libraries, Montpelier.

VIRGINIA

KEY HISTORICAL EVENTS. The first English Charter for settlements in America was that granted by James I in 1606 for the planting of colonies in Virginia. The state was one of the 13 original states in the Union. Virginia lost just over one-third of its area when West Virginia was admitted into the Union (1863).

TERRITORY AND POPULATION. Virginia is bounded north-west by West Virginia, north-east by Maryland, east by the Atlantic, south by North Carolina and Tennessee and west by Kentucky. Land area, 39,598 sq. miles (102,558 sq. km). Census population, 1 April 1990, 6,187,358 (69·4% urban), an increase of 15·73% since 1980. Population estimate (1994), 6,551,500. In 1994 there were 94,355 births (14·6 per 1,000 population), 51,466 deaths (7·9) and 778 infant deaths under 1 year (9·1 per 1,000 live births); in 1993 there were 68,559 marriages (10·7 per 1,000 population) and 29,504 divorces (4·6).

Population for 5 federal census years was:

	White	*Black*	*Indian*	*Asian/Other*	*Total*	*Per sq. mile*
1910	1,389,809	671,096	539	168	2,061,612	51·2
1930	1,770,441	650,165	779	466	2,421,851	60·7
1960	3,142,443	816,258	2,155	4,725	3,966,949	99·3
			All others			
1980	4,230,000	1,008,311	108,517		5,346,818	134·7
1990	4,791,739	1,162,994	15,282	217,343	6,187,358	155·9

Of the total population in 1990, 49% were male, 69·4% were urban and 70·7% were 21 years of age or older.

The population (census of 1990) of the principal cities was: Virginia Beach,

393,069; Norfolk, 261,229; Richmond, 203,056; Newport News, 170,045; Chesapeake, 151,976; Hampton, 133,793; Alexandria, 111,183; Portsmouth, 103,907.

CLIMATE. Average temperatures in Jan. are 41°F in the Tidewater coastal area and 32°F in the Blue Ridge mountains; July averages, 78°F and 68°F respectively. Precipitation averages 36" in the Shenandoah valley and 44" in the south. Snowfall is 5-10" in the Tidewater and 25-30" in the western mountains. Norfolk. Jan. 41°F (5°C), July 79°F (26·1°C). Annual rainfall 46" (1,145 mm). Virginia belongs to the Atlantic Coast climate zone (*see* UNITED STATES: Climate).

CONSTITUTION AND GOVERNMENT. The present constitution dates from 1971. The General Assembly consists of a Senate of 40 members, elected for 4 years, and a House of Delegates of 100 members, elected for 2 years. It sits annually in Jan. The Governor and Lieut.-Governor are elected for 4 years.

The state sends 11 representatives to Congress.

In the 1992 presidential election Bush polled 1,150,517 votes; Clinton, 1,038,650; Perot, 348,639.

The state capital is Richmond; the state contains 95 counties and 40 independent cities.

Governor: George F. Allen (R.), 1994–98 ($110,000).
Lieut.-Governor: Donald S. Beyer (D.), 1994–98 ($32,000).
Secretary of the Commonwealth: Elizabeth Beamer (R.) ($73,023).

BUDGET. General revenue for the year ending 30 June 1993 was $13,972·7m. (taxation, $7,571·8m., and federal aid, $2,883m.); general expenditures, $14,721·1m. ($5,265·2m. for education, $2,448·6m. for public welfare and $1,380·7m. for transport).

Total debt, 1993, was $7,438·4m.

Per capita personal income (1994) was $22,594.

NATURAL RESOURCES

Minerals. Coal is the most important mineral, with output (1993) of 39,317,000 short tons. Lead and zinc ores, stone, sand and gravel, lime and titanium ore are also produced. Total non-fuel mineral output was valued at $515m. in 1993.

Agriculture. In 1995 there were 47,000 farms with an area of 8·6m. acres; the average farm had 183 acres, and the average value per acre was $1,338. Income, 1994, from crops, $772·9m.; from greenhouse and nursery produce, $128·7m.; from vegetables, $98·1m.; and from livestock and livestock products, $1,386·2m. The chief crops are tobacco, soybeans, peanuts, winter wheat, maize, tomatoes, apples, potatoes and sweet potatoes. Livestock, 1995: Cattle, 1·75m.; hogs and pigs, 0·39m.; sheep and lambs, 95,000; (1992) poultry, 48,881,300.

Forestry. Forests covered 16,026,874 acres in 1992 (63·1% of the total land area).

INDUSTRY. The manufacture of cigars and cigarettes and of rayon and allied products and the building of ships lead in value of products.

TOURISM. Tourists spent about $8,086m. in 1990.

COMMUNICATIONS

Roads. In 1993 there were 68,429 miles of roads (52,848 miles rural). In 1991 there were 5,022,000 registered motor vehicles.

Railways. In 1985 there were 3,693 miles of railways including commuter services to Washington.

Civil Aviation. There are international airports at Norfolk, Dulles, Richmond and Newport News.

SOCIAL INSTITUTIONS

Justice. Prison population, 1993, 22,850 in federal and state prisons. The death penalty is authorized. The last execution was in 1995.

Religion. The principal churches are the Baptist, Methodist, Protestant-Episcopal, Roman Catholic and Presbyterian.

Education. Elementary and secondary instruction is free, and for ages 6–17 attendance is compulsory.

In 1994–95 the 133 school districts had, in primary schools, 684,000 pupils and 43,000 teachers and in public high schools, 377,000 pupils and 28,000 teachers. Teachers' salaries averaged $32,700 (primary school) and $35,300 (high school). Total expenditure on education, 1994–95, was $6,435m.

In 1993–94 there were 87 higher education institutions (48 private) including:

Founded	*Name and place of college*	*Staff 1994–95*	*Students 1994*
1693	College of William and Mary, Williamsburg (State)	479	7,547
1749	Washington and Lee University, Lexington	166	1,990
1776	Hampden-Sydney College, Hampden-Sydney (Pres.)	84	970
1819	University of Virginia, Charlottesville (State)	987	21,421
1832	Randolph-Macon College, Ashland (Methodist)	79	1,093
1832	University of Richmond, Richmond (Baptist)	228	4,258
1838	Virginia Commonwealth University, Richmond	777	21,523
1839	Virginia Military Institute Lexington (State)	97	1,179
1865	Virginia Union University, Richmond	83	1,525
1868	Hampton University	303	5,769
1872	Virginia Polytechnic Institute and State University	1,466	25,842
1882	Virginia State University, Petersburg	168	4,007
1908	James Madison University, Harrisonburg	520	11,680
1910	Radford University (State)	394	9,105
1930	Old Dominion University, Norfolk	634	16,490
1956	George Mason University (State)	677	21,774

Health. In 1993 the state had 111 hospitals listed by the American Hospital Association.

Social Security. In 1993 there were 901,000 Social Security beneficiaries (average monthly grant $642); 118,000 Supplemental Security Income beneficiaries (average monthly grant $279); 779,000 Medicare beneficiaries (average monthly grant $259); 576,000 recipients of Medicaid; 195,000 recipients of aid to families with dependent children (average monthly payment per family $262); 11,399 persons receiving Black Lung benefits (average monthly payment $373), and 10,650 children enrolled in the Head Start programme. In 1994 there were 232,000 households (547,000 persons) participating in the federal Food Stamp programme and 601,000 students participating in the National School Lunch programme; a total of 210,116 persons received some form of state-sponsored public assistance.

Further Reading

Statistical information: Cooper Center for Public Service, Univ. of Virginia, 918 Emmet St. N., Suite 300, Charlottesville 22903-4832. Publishes *Virginia Statistical Abstract. – Population Estimates of Virginia Cities and Counties.*

Dabney, V., *Virginia, the New Dominion.* 1971
Gottmann, J., *Virginia in our Century.* Charlottesville, 1969
Morton, R. L., *Colonial Virginia.* 2 vols. Univ. Press of Virginia, 1960
Rouse, P. *Virginia: a Pictorial History.* New York, 1975
Rubin, L. D. Jr., *Virginia: a Bicentennial History.* Norris, 1977

State Library: Virginia State Library, Richmond 23219.

WASHINGTON

KEY HISTORICAL EVENTS. Washington, formerly part of the then Oregon Territory, was created a Territory in 1853, and was admitted into the Union as a state on 11 Nov. 1889. Its settlement dates from 1811.

TERRITORY AND POPULATION. Washington is bounded north by Canada, east by Idaho, south by Oregon with the Columbia River forming most of the boundary, and west by the Pacific. Land area, 66,582 sq. miles (172,447 sq. km). Lands owned by the federal government, 1993, were 12·7m. acres or 29·8% of the total area. Census population, 1 April 1990, 4,866,663 (76·4% urban), an increase of 17·83% since 1980. Population estimate (1995), 5,429,900. Births, 1994, were 77,315; deaths, 39,829. Marriages, 1994, were 43,315 (8·1 per 1,000 population); divorces, 29,292 (5·5).

Population in 5 federal census years was:

	White	*Black*	*Indian*	*Asian/Other*	*Total*	*Per sq. mile*
1910	1,109,111	6,058	10,997	15,824	1,141,990	17·1
1930	1,521,661	6,840	11,253	23,642	1,563,396	23·3
1960	2,751,675	48,738	21,076	31,725	2,853,214	42·8
1980	3,779,170	105,574	60,804	186,608	4,132,156	62·1
1990	4,308,937	149,801	81,483	326,471	4,866,663	73·1

Of the total population in 1990, 2,413,747 were male; 3,387,546 were 20 years of age or older.

There are 27 Indian reservations. Indian reservations in 1990 covered 2,718,516 acres, of which 2,250,731 acres were tribal lands.

Leading cities are Seattle, with a population in 1990 (and 1995 estimate) of 516,259 (532,900); Spokane, 177,165 (188,800); Tacoma, 176,664 (184,500); Bellevue, 86,872 (102,000). Others : Everett, 69,974; Federal Way, 67,449: Yakima, 54,843; Bellingham, 52,179; Vancouver, 46,380; Kennewick, 42,152; Renton, 41,688; Kirkland, 40,059; Bremerton, 38,142; Kent, 37,960; Redmond, 35,800.

CLIMATE. Seattle. Jan. 40°F (4·4°C), July 63°F (17·2°C). Annual rainfall 34" (848 mm). Spokane. Jan. 27°F (–2·8°C), July 70°F (21·1°C). Annual rainfall 14" (350 mm). Washington belongs to the Pacific Coast climate zone (*see* UNITED STATES: Climate).

CONSTITUTION AND GOVERNMENT. The constitution, adopted in 1889, has had 63 amendments. The Legislature consists of a Senate of 49 members elected for 4 years, half their number retiring every 2 years, and a House of Representatives of 98 members, elected for 2 years. The Governor and Lieut.-Governor are elected for 4 years.

The state sends 9 representatives to Congress.

In the 1992 presidential election Clinton polled 993,037 votes; Bush, 731,234; Perot, 541,780.

The capital is Olympia. The state contains 39 counties.

Governor: Mike Lowry (D.), 1993–97 ($121,000).
Lieut.-Governor: Joel Pritchard (D.) ($62,700).
Secretary of State: Ralph Munro (R.) ($64,300).

BUDGET. For the biennium 1993–95 unaudited final All Budgeted expenditures were $32,895m. and unaudited final All Budgeted Fund revenues were $33,563m.

Total General Obligation Bonded Indebtedness at the end of the 1993–95 biennium was $5,650·7m.

Per capita personal income (1994) was $22,542.

NATURAL RESOURCES

Minerals. Mining and quarrying are not as important as forestry, agriculture or manufacturing. Uranium is mined but figures are not disclosed; other minerals include sand and gravel, stone, coal and clays. Non-fuel mineral output in 1994 was valued at $556·5m.

Agriculture. Agriculture is constantly growing in value because of more intensive and diversified farming and because of the 1m.-acre Columbia Basin Irrigation Project.

In 1992 there were 30,264 farms with an acreage of 15·7m.; the average farm was 520 acres. Average value of farmland and buildings per acre in 1995 was $1,065. Wheat, cattle and calves, milk and apples are important. On 1 Jan. 1992 livestock included 242,787 milch cows, 310,554 beef cows, 63,584 sheep and lambs, and 56,171 hogs and pigs.

Value of agricultural products sold in 1994 (in $1m.): Field crops, 1,598·8; vegetables, 302·8; livestock, poultry and their products, 1,459·8.

Forestry. Forests cover 21,856,000 acres, of which 9m. acres are national forest. In 1994, timber harvested was an estimated 4,086m. bd ft. Acres planted or seeded, 1993, 163,442, not including natural re-seeding. Production of wood residues, 1992, included 2,671,000 tons of pulp and board.

Fisheries. Salmon and shellfish are important; total fish catch, 1993, was worth an estimated $159,035,000.

INDUSTRY. In 1994 manufacturing employed 337,300 workers, of whom 91,900 were in aerospace and 53,900 in the forest products industry. Principal manufactures: Aircraft, pulp and paper, lumber and plywood, aluminium, processed fruit and vegetables. In 1994 trade employed 565,400, service industries, 599,500 and government, 437,900.

COMMUNICATIONS

Roads. In 1994 there were 79,038 miles of roads. In 1994 there were 5,207,531 registered motor vehicles.

Railways. In 1993 there were 2,979 route miles.

Civil Aviation. There are international airports at Seattle/Tacoma, Spokane and Boeing Field.

SOCIAL INSTITUTIONS

Justice. The adult inmates in state prisons on 30 June 1995 numbered 11,443. The death penalty is authorized. The last execution was in 1994.

Religion. Religious faiths represented include the Roman Catholic, United Methodist, Lutheran, Presbyterian and Episcopalian. There were 206,000 Latter Day Saints (Mormons) in 1994.

Education. Education is given free to all children between the ages of 5 and 21 years, and is compulsory for children from 8 to 15 years of age. In Oct. 1995 there were 951,696 pupils in elementary and secondary schools. In Oct. 1993 there were 45,456 classroom teachers, average salary, $37,777.

The University of Washington, founded 1861, at Seattle, had, autumn 1995, 35,185 students, and Washington State University at Pullman, founded 1890, for science and agriculture, had 19,229 students. Eastern Washington University had 8,078; Central Washington University, 8,512; The Evergreen State College, 3,625; Western Washington University, 10,708. Community colleges had (1992) a total of 175,445 state-funded and excess enrolment students.

Health. In fiscal year 1995 the 2 state hospitals for mental illness, the 2 mental health facilities and the child study and treatment centre had, together, a daily average of 1,320 patients.

In 1994 there were 91 licensed private general hospitals (11,484 beds) and 2 private psychiatric hospitals (175 beds). In 1995 there were 16,344 doctors, 4,262 dentists, 55,407 registered nurses and 5,751 pharmacists.

Social Security. Old-age assistance is provided for persons 65 years of age or older without adequate resources (and not in need of continuing home care) who are residents of the state. In July 1995 the following assistance was provided: 932 blind persons received a monthly average of $355·10; 13,057 aged, $277·80; 76,981 disabled, $391·12. Aid was also given to 179,199 children in 99,659 families, averaging $382·98 per family monthly.

Further Reading

Statistical information: State Office of Financial Management, POB 43113, Olympia 98504. Publishes *Washington State Data Book*

Dodds, G.B., *American North-West: a History of Oregon and Washington.* Arlington (Ill), 1986

Swanson, T., *Political Life in Washington.* Pullman, 1985

State Library: Washington State Library, Olympia.

WEST VIRGINIA

KEY HISTORICAL EVENTS. In 1862, after the state of Virginia had seceded from the Union, electors from the western counties ratified an ordinance providing for the formation of a new state. West Virginia was admitted into the Union by presidential proclamation on 20 June 1863. Voters, in an almost unanimous decision, had adopted the constitution on 26 March 1863.

TERRITORY AND POPULATION. West Virginia is bounded north by Pennsylvania and Maryland, east and south by Virginia, south-west by the Big Sandy River (forming the boundary with Kentucky) and west by the Ohio River (forming the boundary with Ohio). Total area, 24,232 sq. miles (62,761 sq. km). Census population, 1 April 1990, 1,793,477 (36·1% urban), a decrease of 8·01% since 1980. Population estimate (1993), 1·82m. Births, 1993, 20,722 (11·5 per 1,000 population); deaths, 19,762 (11); infant deaths, 183 (8·8 per 1,000 live births); marriages, 11,671 (6·5); divorces, 9,799 (5·4).

Population in 5 federal census years was:

	White	*Black*	*Indian*	*Asiatic*	*Total*	*Per sq. mile*
1910	1,156,817	64,173	36	93	1,221,119	50·8
1940	1,614,191	114,893	18	103	1,729,205	71·8
1960	1,770,133	89,378	181	419	1,860,421	77·3
1970	1,673,480	67,342	751	1,463	1,744,237	71·8
1980	1,874,751	65,051	1,610	5,194	1,949,644	80·3

Of the total population in 1980, 945,408 were male, 705,319 were urban; those 20 years of age or older numbered 1,319,566.

The 1990 census population of the principal cities was: Huntington, 58,844; Charleston, 57,287. Others: Wheeling, 38,882; Parkersburg, 33,882; Morgantown, 25,879; Weirton, 22,124; Fairmont, 20,210; Clarksburg, 18,059.

CLIMATE. Charleston. Jan. 34°F (1·1°C), July 76°F (24·4°C). Annual rainfall 40" (1,010 mm). West Virginia belongs to the Appalachian Mountains climate zone (*see* UNITED STATES: Climate).

CONSTITUTION AND GOVERNMENT. The present constitution was adopted in 1872; it has had 62 amendments. The Legislature consists of the Senate of 34 members elected for a term of 4 years, one-half being elected biennially, and the House of Delegates of 100 members, elected biennially. The Governor is elected for 4 years and may serve 1 successive term.

The state sends 3 representatives to Congress.

In the 1992 presidential election Clinton polled 331,001 votes; Bush, 241,974; Perot, 108,829.

The state capital is Charleston. There are 55 counties.

Governor: Gaston Caperton (D.), 1993–97 ($72,500).
Secretary of State: Ken Hechler (D.), ($43,200).

FINANCE. Total revenues for the year ending 30 June 1993 were $5,088m. ($2,043m. from taxes, $1,715m. from federal funds, $411m. from highway funds,

$918m. from special revenues); general expenditures were $6,102m. (education, $1,970m.; highways, $592m.; health and welfare, $2,710m.).

Gross tax-supported debt for 1993 was $1,232,000m., net tax-supported debt was $1,026,000m., and gross non-tax-supported debt was $1,617,000m.

Estimated *per capita* personal income (1994) was $17,208.

NATURAL RESOURCES

Minerals. 38% of the state is underlain with mineable coal; 163·8m. short tons of coal were produced in 1992. Petroleum output (1991), 2m. bbls; natural gas production (1991), 179,178m. cu. ft. Salt, sand and gravel, sandstone and limestone are also produced. The total value of non-fuel mineral output in 1990 was $132m.; total output in 1992, 11m. tons.

Agriculture. In 1993 the state had 20,000 farms with an area of 3·7m. acres; average size of farm was 185 acres and valued at $696 per acre. Livestock farming predominates.

Cash income, 1992, from crops was $75·5m.; from government payments, $6·9m., and from livestock and products, $267·1m. Main crops harvested, 1992: Hay (1·07m. tons); all corn (5·4m. bu.); tobacco (3,623,000 lb). Area of main crops, 1992: Hay, 0·54m. acres; corn, 85,000 acres. Apples (225m. lb in 1992) and peaches (20m. lb.) are important fruit crops. Livestock on farms, 1993, included 0·52m. cattle, of which 23,000 were milch cows; sheep, 76,000; 1992: Hogs, 32,000; chickens, 1·23m. excluding broilers. Production, 1992, included 46·6m. broilers, 180m. eggs; 4·1m. turkeys.

Forestry. State forests, 1992, covered 73,646 acres; national forests, 1,673,700 gross acres; 79% of the state is woodland.

INDUSTRY. In 1993, 1,906 manufactories had 83,018 production workers who earned $2,503m. Leading manufactures are primary and fabricated metals, glass, chemicals, wood products, textiles and apparel, machinery, plastics, speciality chemicals, aerospace, electronics, medical and related technologies and industrial products recycling.

In 1993 non-agricultural employment was 651,700 of whom 148,600 were in trade, 132,500 in government and 166,500 in service industries.

COMMUNICATIONS

Roads. In 1993 there were 37,246 miles of roads (34,563 miles rural) and 1,321,902 registered motor vehicles.

Railways. In Feb. 1994 the state had 1,828 miles of railway.

Civil Aviation. There were 36 licensed airports in 1993.

Shipping. There are some 300 miles of navigable rivers.

Telecommunications. In 1994 there were 155 commercial radio stations. Television stations number 12 commercial and 3 public.

Press. In 1994 daily newspapers numbered 25, weekly and college newspapers 84.

SOCIAL INSTITUTIONS

Justice. The state court system consists of a Supreme Court, 31 circuit courts, and magistrate courts in each county. The Supreme Court of Appeals, exercising original and appellate jurisdiction, has 5 members elected by the people for 12-year terms. Each circuit court has from 1 to 7 judges (as determined by the Legislature on the basis of population and case-load) chosen by the voters within each circuit for 8-year terms.

There are 11 penal and correctional institutions which had, on 30 June 1994, 2,400 inmates. The death penalty is authorized. The last execution was in 1995.

Religion. Chief denominations in 1992 were United Methodist (143,000 members, estimate), Baptists (108,824) and Roman Catholics (105,645).

Education. Public school education is free for all from 5 to 21 years of age, and school attendance is compulsory for all between the ages of 7 and 16 (school term, 200 days—180–185 days of actual teaching). The public schools are non-sectarian. In 1993 public elementary and secondary schools had 314,768 pupils and 20,987 classroom teachers. Average salary of teachers in 1993, $31,245. Total 1992–93 expenditures for public schools, $1,603,057,554.

Leading institutions of higher education in 1993:

Founded		*Full-time students*
1837	Marshall University, Huntington	12,687
1837	West Liberty State College, West Liberty	2,397
1867	Fairmont State College, Fairmont	6,613
1868	West Virginia University, Morgantown	22,712
1872	Concord College, Athens	5,689
1872	Glenville State College, Glenville	1,898
1872	Shepherd College, Shepherdstown	3,591
1895	West Virginia State College, Institute	4,896
1895	West Virginia Institute of Technology, Montgomery	3,051
1895	Bluefield State College, Bluefield	2,645
1901	Potomac State College of West Virginia Univ., Keyser	1,100
1961	West Virginia Univ. at Parkersburg, Parkersburg	3,979
1972	West Virginia Graduate College, Institute	3,332
1976	School of Osteopathic Medicine, Lewisburg	260

In addition to the universities and state-supported schools, there are 2 community colleges (6,496 students in 1993), 11 denominational and private institutions of higher education (11,603 students in 1993) and 11 business colleges.

Health. In 1993 the state had 65 licensed hospitals and 65 licensed personal care homes, 105 skilled-nursing homes and 3 mental hospitals.

Social Security. The Department of Health Human Resources, originating in the 1930s as the Department of Public Assistance, is both state and federally financed. In the year ending 30 Sept. 1994, day care for an average of 12,259 children per month was provided; as of 30 June 1994, aid was given to 33,475 families with dependent children (average award, $232.19 per month); 128,182 families per month received food stamps.

Further Reading

West Virginia Blue Book. Legislature, Charleston. Annual, since 1916
Statistical Handbook, 1993. West Virginia Research League, Charleston, 1993
West Virginia History. Charleston. Quarterly, from 1939. Annual, from 1985
Conley, P. and Doherty, W. T., *West Virginia History.* Charleston, 1974
Davis, C. J. *et al.*, *West Virginia State and Local Government.* West Virginia Univ., 1963
Doherty, W. T., *West Virginia: Our Land, Our People.* Charleston, 1990
Forbes, H. M., *West Virginia History: a Bibliography and Guide to Research.* Morgantown, 1981
Rice, O. K., *West Virginia: A History.* 2nd ed. Univ. Press of Kentucky, Lexington, 1994
Williams, J. A., *West Virginia: A Bicentennial History.* New York, 1976

State Library: Archives and History, Division of Culture and History, Charleston.

WISCONSIN

KEY HISTORICAL EVENTS. Wisconsin was settled in 1670 by French traders and missionaries. Originally a part of New France, it was surrendered to the British in 1763 and in 1783, when ceded to the US, became part of the North-west Territory. It was then contained successively in the Territories of Indiana, Illinois and Michigan. In 1836 it became part of the Territory of Wisconsin, which also included the present states of Iowa, Minnesota and parts of the Dakotas. It was admitted into the Union with its present boundaries on 29 May 1848.

TERRITORY AND POPULATION. Wisconsin is bounded north by Lake Superior and the Upper Peninsula of Michigan, east by Lake Michigan, south by Illinois, west by Iowa and Minnesota, with the Mississippi River forming most of the boundary. Area, 56,154 sq. miles (145,439 sq. km), including 1,439 sq. miles of inland water, but excluding any part of the Great Lakes. Census population, 1 April 1990, 4,891,769 (65·7% urban), an increase of 4% since 1980. Estimated population (1995), 5,101,581. Births in 1994 were 68,265 (13·4 per 1,000 population); deaths, 43,982 (8·7); infant deaths, 537 (7·9 per 1,000 live births); marriages, 36,375 (7·2); divorces and annulments, 17,569 (3·5).

Population in 5 census years was:

	White	*Black*	*All others*	*Total*	*Per sq. mile*
1910	2,320,555	2,900	10,405	2,333,860	42·2
1930	2,916,255	10,739	12,012	2,939,006	53·7
1960	3,858,903	74,546	18,328	3,951,777	72·2
1980	4,443,035	182,592	80,015	4,705,642	86·4
1990	4,512,523	244,539	134,767	4,891,769	90·1

Of the total population in 1990, 49% were male, 65·7% were urban and 73·7% were 18 years old or older.

Population of the larger cities, 1990 census, was as follows:

Milwaukee	628,088	Waukesha	56,958	Fond du Lac	37,757
Madison	191,262	Eau Claire	56,856	Wausau	37,060
Green Bay	96,466	Oshkosh	55,006	Beloit	35,573
Racine	84,298	Janesville	52,133	Brookfield	35,184
Kenosha	80,352	La Crosse	51,003	Neenah	33,592
Appleton	65,695	Sheboygan	49,676	Greenfield	33,403
West Allis	63,221	Wauwatosa	49,366		

Population of larger metropolitan areas, 1990 census: Milwaukee, 1,432,149; Madison, 367,085; Appleton-Neenah, 315,121; Duluth–Superior (Minn.–Wis.), 239,971; Green Bay, 194,594; Racine, 175,034.

CLIMATE. Milwaukee. Jan. 19°F (–7·2°C), July 70°F (21·1°C). Annual rainfall 29" (727 mm). Wisconsin belongs to the Great Lakes climate zone (*see* UNITED STATES: Climate).

CONSTITUTION AND GOVERNMENT. The constitution, which dates from 1848, has 132 amendments. The legislative power is vested in a Senate of 33 members elected for 4 years, one-half elected alternately, and an Assembly of 99 members all elected simultaneously for 2 years. The Governor and Lieut.-Governor are elected for 4 years.

The state sends 9 representatives to Congress.

In the 1992 presidential election Clinton polled 1,041,066 votes; Bush, 930,855; Perot, 544,479.

The capital is Madison. The state has 72 counties.

Governor: Tommy G. Thompson (R.), 1995–99 ($101,861).
Lieut.-Governor: Scott McCallum (R.) ($54,795).
Secretary of State: Douglas La Follette (D.) ($49,719).

BUDGET. For the year ending 30 June 1995 (Wisconsin Bureau of Financial Operations figures) total revenue for all funds was $23,083,582,000 ($8,576,556,000 from taxation and $3,776,043,000 from federal aid). General expenditure from all funds was $18,058,003,000 ($5,630,754,000 for education, $5,504,309,000 for human resources).

Per capita personal income (1994) was $20,887.

NATURAL RESOURCES

Minerals. Construction sand and gravel, crushed stone, industrial or specialty sand and lime are the chief mineral products. Mineral production in 1993 was valued at $203m. This value included $77·5m. for construction sand and gravel, $89m. for crushed stone and $29m. for lime. Value of other minerals including industrial or specialty sand, dimension stone, crushed trap rock, peat and gemstones, $7·5m. The only metal mine (copper and gold) produced values estimated at over $50m.

Agriculture. On 1 Jan. 1995 there were 78,000 farms (29,000 dairy farms) with a total acreage of 16·9m. acres and an average size of 216·7 acres, compared with 142,000 farms with a total acreage of 22·4m. acres and an average of 158 acres in 1959. In 1994 the average value per acre was $949. Cash receipts from products sold by Wisconsin farms in 1994, $5,370m.; $4,034m. from livestock and livestock products and $1,336m. from crops.

Dairy farming is important, with 1·5m. milch cows. Production of cheese accounted for 30% of the USA's total. Production of the principal field crops in 1994 included: Corn for grain, 437·1m. bu.; corn for silage, 9·5m. tons; oats, 25·4m. bu.; all hay, 6·5m. tons. Other crops of importance: 25·7m. cwt of potatoes, 5·9m. lbs of tobacco, 1·5m. bbls of cranberries, 1·8m. cwt of carrots and the processing crops of 1,001,800 tons of sweet corn, 109,100 tons of green peas, 286,200 tons of snap beans, 49,900 tons of cucumbers for pickles, 6·8m. lbs of tart cherries, 60,500 tons of beets for canning, 100,800 tons of cabbage for kraut and 1·3m. cwt of cabbage for fresh market.

Wisconsin is also a major producer of mink pelts.

Forestry. Wisconsin has an estimated 15·3m. acres of forest land, though lumbering is of declining importance. Of 14·7m. acres of commercial forest (June 1988) national forests covered 1·2m. acres; state forests, 0·6m.; county and municipal forests, 2·3m.; forest industry, 1·2m.; private land, 9·1m.

Growing stock (1985), 15,500m. cu. ft, of which 11,900m. cu. ft is hardwood and 3,600m. cu. ft, softwood. Main hardwoods, aspen, maple, oak and birch; main softwoods, red pine, white pine, balsam fir, jack pine.

INDUSTRY. Wisconsin has much heavy industry, particularly in the Milwaukee area. Three fifths of manufacturing employees work on durable goods. Industrial machinery is the major industrial group (18% of all manufacturing employment) followed by food processing, fabricated metals, paper and paper products, printing and publishing, electrical machinery and rubber and miscellaneous plastics. Manufacturing establishments in 1994 provided 23% of non-farm wage and salary workers, 28·5% of all earnings. The total number of establishments was 10,033 in 1992; the biggest concentration is in the south-east.

TOURISM. The tourist-vacation industry ranks among the first three in economic importance. The Department of Tourism of the Department of Development budgeted $11,083,800 to promote tourism in financial year 1996–97.

COMMUNICATIONS

Roads. The state had on 1 Jan. 1994, 110,976 miles of highway. 76% of all roads in the state have a bituminous (or similar) surface. There are 11,816 miles of state trunk roads and 19,620 miles of county trunk roads.

On 1 July 1995 Wisconsin registered 4,268,619 motor vehicles.

Railways. On 31 Dec. 1993 the state had 4,227 track-miles of railway.

Civil Aviation. There were, in 1994, 96 publicly operated airports. Eleven scheduled air carrier airports were served by 17 regional and national air carriers.

Shipping. Lake Superior and Lake Michigan ports handled 44·9m. tons of freight in 1992; 88% of it at Superior, one of the world's biggest grain ports, and much of the rest at Milwaukee and Green Bay.

SOCIAL INSTITUTIONS

Justice. The state's penal, reformatory and correctional system on 5 Jan. 1996 held 10,399 men and 468 women in 11 state-owned and other institutions for adult offenders; the probation and parole system was supervising 58,769 adults, 393 males and 40 females were being supervised under intensive sanctions. Average daily population in the state's 3 juvenile institutions as of Dec. 1995 was 923 males and 90 females. Wisconsin does not impose the death penalty.

Religion. Wisconsin church affiliation, as a percentage of the 1990 population, was estimated at 31·8% Catholic, 20·1% Lutheran, 3·2% Methodist, 9·5% other churches and 35·4% un-affiliated.

Education. All children between the ages of 6 and 18 are required to attend school full-time to the end of the school term in which they become 18 years of age. In 1994–95 the public school grades kindergarten–8 had 582,684 pupils and 36,449 (full-time equivalent) teachers; school grades 9–12 had 259,471 pupils and 19,046 teachers. Private schools enrolled 138,125 students grades kindergarten–12. Public pre-schools enrolled 18,531 children, and private, 9,877. Public elementary teachers' salaries, 1993–94, averaged $34,865; secondary, $37,171.

In 1993–94 vocational, technical and adult schools had an enrolment of 438,396 and 4,351 (full-time and part-time) teachers and 2 community colleges enrolled 886. There is a school for the visually handicapped and a school for the deaf.

The University of Wisconsin, established in 1848, was joined by law in 1971 with the Wisconsin State Universities System to become the University of Wisconsin System with 13 degree granting campuses, 13 2-year campuses in the Center System, and the University Extension. The system had, in 1994–95, 7,424 full-time professors and instructors and 2,487 student assistants. In autumn 1995, 150,114 students enrolled (10,316 at Eau Claire, 5,444 at Green Bay, 8,787 at La Crosse, 40,005 at Madison, 22,342 at Milwaukee, 10,453 at Oshkosh, 4,851 at Parkside, 4,871 at Platteville, 5,259 at River Falls, 8,414 at Stevens Point, 7,060 at Stout, 2,589 at Superior, 10,441 at Whitewater and 9,282 at the Center System freshman-sophomore centres). UW-Extension enrolled 263,237 students in its continuing education programmes in 1993–94. There are also several independent institutions of higher education. These (with autumn 1995 enrolment) include 3 universities (15,683), 16 colleges (30,800), 4 technical and professional schools (4,972), and 5 theological seminaries (437).

The total expenditure, 1993–94, for all public education (except capital outlay and debt service) was $8,445m. ($1,668 per capita).

The state maintains an educational broadcasting and television service.

Health. In fiscal year 1994 the state had 125 general medical and surgical hospitals (14,575 beds), 14 psychiatric hospitals (886 beds), 3 treatment centres for alcohol and drug abuse (99 beds) and 2 physical rehabilitation hospitals (138 beds). There were 2 state mental hospitals (625 beds) and 3 US Veterans' Administration hospitals. Patients in state mental hospitals and institutions for the developmentally disabled averaged 2,062 in 1994. On 31 Dec. 1994 the state had 460 licensed nursing homes with 46,938 residents.

Social Security. On 1 Jan. 1974 the US Social Security administration assumed responsibility for financial aid (Supplemental Security Income) to persons 65 years old and over, blind persons and totally disabled persons, who satisfy requirements as to need. Recipients receive a federal payment plus a federally administered state supplementary payment, except for those who reside in a medical institution. In Dec. 1995, there were 107,450 SSI recipients in the state; payments (1996) were $554 for a single individual, $600 for an eligible individual with an ineligible spouse, and $837 for an eligible couple. A special payment level of $650 for an individual and $1,182 for a couple may be paid with special approval for SSI recipients who are developmentally disabled or chronically mentally ill, living in a non-medical living arrangement not his or her own home. All SSI recipients receive state medical assistance coverage.

Under the Aid to Families with Dependent Children programme, 65,917 households of 186,175 persons received aid in Dec. 1995. Medicaid cost $2,293m. (state share was $843·3m.) in financial year 1994–95.

Further Reading

Dictionary of Wisconsin Biography. Wis. Historical Society, Madison, 1960

Wisconsin Blue Book. Wisconsin Legislative Reference Bureau, Madison. Biennial
Current, R. N., *Wisconsin, a History.* New York, 1977
Danziger, S. and Witte, J. F., *State Policy Choices: The Wisconsin Experience.* Univ. Wisconsin Press, 1988
Martin, L., *The Physical Geography of Wisconsin.* Univ. Wisconsin Press, 3rd ed., 1965
Nesbit, R. C., *Wisconsin, A History.* State Historical Society of Wisconsin, Madison, rev. ed., 1989
Robinson, A. H. and Culver, J. B., (eds.) *The Atlas of Wisconsin.* Univ. Wisconsin Press, 1974
Vogeler, I., *Wisconsin: A Geography.* Boulder, 1986

State Historical Society of Wisconsin: *The History of Wisconsin.* Vol. I [Alice E. Smith], Madison, 1973.—Vol. II [R. N. Current], Madison, 1976.—Vol. III [R. C. Nesbit], Madison, 1985.—Vol. VI [W. F. Thompson], Madison, 1988.—Vol. V (P. W. Glad), Madison, 1990

State Information Agency: Legislative Reference Bureau, 100 N. Hamilton St., P.O. Box 2037, Madison, WI 53701-2037. *Acting Chief:* Peter J. Dykman.

WYOMING

KEY HISTORICAL EVENTS. Wyoming, first settled in 1834, was admitted into the Union on 10 July 1890 as the 44th state.

TERRITORY AND POPULATION. Wyoming is bounded north by Montana, east by South Dakota and Nebraska, south by Colorado, south-west by Utah and west by Idaho. Land area, 97,105 sq. miles (251,501 sq. km). The Yellowstone National Park occupies about 2·22m. acres; the Grand Teton National Park has 307,000 acres. The federal government in 1986 owned 49,838 sq. miles (50·9% of the total area of the state). The Federal Bureau of Land Management administers 17,546,188 acres.

Census population, 1 April 1990, 453,588 (65% urban), a decrease of 3·66% since 1980. Population estimate (1994), 475,981. Births in 1993 were 6,550; deaths, 3,488; marriages, 4,667; divorces, 3,048; infant deaths, 52 (7·9 per 1,000 live births).

Population in 5 census years was:

	White	*Black*	*American Indian*	*Asiatic*	*Total*	*Per sq. mile*
1910	140,318	2,235	1,486	1,926	145,965	1·5
1930	221,241	1,250	1,845	1,229	225,565	2·3

			All others		
1970	323,619	2,568	6,229	332,416	3·4
1980	446,488	3,364	19,705	469,557	4·8

	White	*Black*	*American Indian*	*Asian/ Pacific Islands*	*Other*	*Total*	*Per sq. mile*
1990	427,061	3,606	9,479	2,806	10,636	453,588	4·7

Of the total population in 1990, 227,007 were male and those over 18 years of age numbered 318,063.

The largest towns (with 1990 census population) are Cheyenne, 50,008; Casper, 46,742; Laramie, 26,687; Rock Springs, 19,050; Gillette, 17,635; Sheridan, 13,900; Green River, 12,711.

CLIMATE. Cheyenne. Jan. 25°F (–3·9°C), July 66°F (18·9°C). Annual rainfall 15" (376 mm). Yellowstone Park. Jan. 18°F (–7·8°C), July 61°F (16·1°C). Annual rainfall 18" (444 mm). Wyoming belongs to the Mountain States climate region (*see* UNITED STATES: Climate).

CONSTITUTION AND GOVERNMENT. The constitution, drafted in 1890, has since had 43 amendments. The Legislature consists of a Senate of 30 members elected for 4 years, 15, retiring every 2 years, and a House of Representatives of 60 members elected for 2 years. It sits annually in Jan. or Feb. The Governor is elected for 4 years.

The state sends 1 representative to Congress.

In the 1992 presidential election Bush polled 79,347 votes; Clinton, 68,160; Perot, 51,263.

The capital is Cheyenne. The state contains 23 counties.

Governor: Jim Geringer (R.), 1995–99 ($95,000).

Secretary of State: Diana J. Ohman (R.) ($77,000).

ECONOMY

Budget. In the fiscal year ending 1 July 1993 total receipts were $2,563,796,156; disbursements were $2,327,868,866.

Per capita personal income (1994) was $20,436.

Banking and Finance. In June 1995 there were 19 national and 34 state banks with a total of $6,017,799,000 deposits.

NATURAL RESOURCES

Minerals. Wyoming is largely an oil-producing state. In 1994 the output of oil was 80·2m. bbls; natural gas, 959,200m. cu. ft. In 1992 there were 620 mining establishments. 1994 production: Coal, 236·9m. short tons; trona, 16·1m. short tons; uranium, 1·2m. lbs; bentonite, 2·8m. short tons. Total value of non-fuel mineral production, 1994, $219·6m.

Agriculture. Wyoming is semi-arid, and agriculture is carried on by irrigation and dry farming. In 1994 there were 9,200 farms and ranches; total farm area in 1994 was 34·7m. acres; average size of farm in 1994 was 3,761 acres, and average value per acre in 1995 was $192. In 1993, 13,432 people were employed on farms.

Total value, 1994, of crops produced, $289m.; of livestock and products, $463m. Crop production in 1994 (1,000 bushels): Corn for grain, 5,856; wheat, 4,949; oats, 1,344; barley, 7,600; sugar-beet, 1,107 tons. Animals on farms in 1994 included 1·39m. cattle, 0·79m. sheep and 45,000 hogs and pigs. Total egg production in 1994 was 2·9m.

Forestry. In 1989 there were 35,379 acres of timberland.

Fisheries. In 1991 the production of fish hatchery was 522,388 lbs.

INDUSTRY. In 1992 there were 581 manufacturing establishments. A large portion of the manufacturing in the state is based on natural resources, mainly oil and farm products. Leading industries are food, wood products (except furniture) and machinery (except electrical). The Wyoming Industrial Development Corporation assists in the development of small industries by providing credit.

LABOUR. In July 1995 the mining industry employed 17,800 wage and salary workers; construction, 16,100; manufacturing, 9,900; transportation and public utilities, 14,200. The total civilian labour force in July 1995 was 259,332, of whom 248,815 were employed; non-agricultural wage and salary employment, 223,000. The unemployment rate was 4·1% in July 1995. Total wages paid in covered employment in 1990, $3,825m.

Trade Unions. There were 21,694 working members in trade unions (10·2% of total employment) in 1989 (the last year for which official data were collected).

TOURISM. There are over 7m. tourists annually, mainly outdoor enthusiasts. The state has large elk and pronghorn antelope herds, 10 fish hatcheries and numerous wild game. In 1994, 7,748,593 people visited the 6 national areas; 2,139,690 people visited state parks and historic sites. In 1990 811,183 fishing, game and bird licences were sold. There were (1994) 9 operational ski areas.

COMMUNICATIONS

Roads. In 1995 there were 2,298 miles of urban roads and 32,911 miles of rural roads, the latter including (1990, in miles): Federal, 3,882; state, 6,226; county, 13,636. There were 590,750 motor vehicle registrations in 1994.

Railways. In 1995, 1,795 miles of Class I railway were operated.

Civil Aviation. There were 10 towns with commuter air services and 2 towns on jet routes in 1995.

Telecommunications. In 1995 there were 29 AM, 35 FM radio stations and 9 television stations.

Press. (1995) there were 9 daily newspapers.

SOCIAL INSTITUTIONS

Justice. In the third quarter of 1995 there were 1,190 prisoners in state adult correctional institutions. The death penalty is authorized.

Religion. Chief religious bodies in 1990 were the Roman Catholic (with 59,565 members), Mormon (45,793) and Protestant churches (110,375). There were 5,000 members of the Eastern Orthodox Church in 1972.

Education. In 1994–95 public elementary and secondary schools had 100,314 pupils and 6,748 teachers. In 1990–91 enrolment in the parochial elementary and secondary schools was about 3,500. The average expenditure per pupil for 1994–95 was $5,392. State and local government expenditure in 1991 was $839·2m.

The University of Wyoming, founded at Laramie in 1887, had in academic year 1994–95, 12,020 students. There were 7 community colleges in 1991–92 with 20,517 students.

Social Welfare. In 1993 fiscal year, $26·5m. was distributed in food stamps; $27m. in aid to families with dependent children; and $129m. in Medicaid. Total expenditure on public assistance and social services programmes, fiscal year 1992, $190·1m.

Health. In 1993 the state had 29 general hospitals with 1,998 beds, and 37 registered nursing homes with 2,899 beds.

Further Reading

Statistical information: Department of Administration and Information, 327 E. Emerson Bldg., Cheyenne 82002. Publishes *Wyoming Data Handbook*

Equality State Almanac. Wyoming Department of Administration and Information, Cheyenne, annual

Wyoming Official Directory. Secretary of State. Cheyenne, annual

Wyoming Data Handbook. Dept. of Administration and Information. Division of Economic Analysis. Cheyenne, annual

Brown, R. H., *Wyoming: A Geography.* Boulder, 1980

Larsen, T. A., *History of Wyoming.* Rev. ed. Univ. of Nebraska, 1979

Treadway, T., *Wyoming.* New York, 1982

OUTLYING TERRITORIES

GUAM

KEY HISTORICAL EVENTS. Magellan is said to have discovered the island in 1521; it was ceded by Spain to the US by the Treaty of Paris (10 Dec. 1898). The island was captured by the Japanese on 10 Dec. 1941, and retaken by American forces from 21 July 1944. Guam is of great strategic importance; substantial numbers of naval and air force personnel occupy about one-third of the usable land.

TERRITORY AND POPULATION. Guam is the largest and most southern island of the Marianas Archipelago, in 13° 26' N. lat., 144° 43' E. long. Total area, 571 sq. miles (1,478 sq. km). Agaña, the seat of government is about 8 miles from the anchorage in Apra Harbour. The census on 1 April 1990 showed a population of

133,152, an increase of 27,173 since 1980 (50,801 urban; 62,207 female); density, 637·1 per sq. mile; estimate, 1992, 140,200. In 1990 those of Guamanian ancestry numbered 63,504; density was 637 per sq. mile. Vital statistics, 1988: Births, 3,509; deaths, 464; infantile deaths, 27. The Malay strain is predominant. The native language is Chamorro; English is the official language and is taught in all schools.

CLIMATE. Tropical maritime, with little difference in temperatures over the year. Rainfall is copious at all seasons, but is greatest from July to Oct. Agaña. Jan. 81°F (27·2°C), July 81°F (27·2°C). Annual rainfall 93" (2,325 mm).

CONSTITUTION AND GOVERNMENT. Guam's constitutional status is that of an 'unincorporated territory' of the US. Entry of US citizens is unrestricted; foreign nationals are subject to normal regulations. In 1949–50 the President transferred the administration of the island from the Navy Department (who held it from 1899) to the Interior Department. The transfer conferred full citizenship on the Guamanians, who had previously been 'nationals' of the US. There was a referendum on status, 30 Jan. 1982. 38% of eligible voters voted; 48·5% of those favoured Commonwealth status.

The Governor and his staff constitute the executive arm of the government. The legislature is a 21-member *Senate*; its powers are similar to those of an American state legislature. At the general election of Nov. 1991, the Democratic Party won 14 seats and the Republicans 7. Guam returns 1 non-voting delegate to the House of Representatives.

Governor: Carl Gutierrez (D.), 1995–99.
Lieut.-Governor: Frank Blas.

ECONOMY

Budget. Total revenue (1989) $378m.; expenditure $369m.

Banking. Banking law makes it possible for foreign banks to operate in Guam.

NATURAL RESOURCES

Water. Supplies are from springs, reservoirs and groundwater; 65% comes from water-bearing limestone in the north. The Navy and Air Force conserve water in reservoirs. The Water Resources Research Centre is at Guam University.

Agriculture. The major products of the island are sweet potatoes, cucumbers, water melons and beans. In 1982 there were 140 full-time and 1,904 part-time farmers. Livestock (1988) included 2,000 cattle, 14,000 pigs, and (1984) 36,430 poultry. Commercial productions (1983) amounted to 6·6m. lb. of fruit and vegetables ($3·4m.), 567,000 doz. eggs ($811,093). There is an agricultural experimental station at Inarajan.

Fisheries. Fresh fish caught in 1982, 319,300 lb. Offshore fishing produced 100,687 lb., including 6,080 lb. of shrimps.

INDUSTRY AND TRADE

Industry. Guam Economic Development Authority controls three industrial estates: Cabras Island (32 acres); Calvo estate at Tamuning (26 acres); Harmon estate (16 acres). Industries include textile manufacture, cement and petroleum distribution, warehousing, printing, plastics and ship-repair. Other main sources of income are construction and tourism.

Labour. In 1990 there were 90,990 persons of employable age, of whom 66,138 were in the workforce (54,186 civilian). 2,042 were unemployed.

Trade. Guam is the only American territory which has complete 'free trade'; excise duties are levied only upon imports of tobacco, liquid fuel and liquor. In the year ending 31 Dec. 1980 imports were valued at $544·1m. and accounted for 90% of trade.

Tourism. Tourism is developing; there were 1,900 visitors in 1964 and 407,100 in 1986. Visitors' receipts were $550m. in 1990.

COMMUNICATIONS

Roads. There are 419 miles of all-weather roads.

Civil Aviation. There is an international airport at Tamuning. 7 commercial airlines serve Guam.

Telecommunications. Overseas telephone and radio dispatch facilities are available. In 1983 there were 23,442 telephones. There are 4 commercial stations, a commercial television station, a public broadcasting station and a cable television station with 24 channels. In 1993 there were 105,000 radio and 75,000 TV sets (colour by NTSC).

Press. There is 1 daily newspaper, a twice-weekly paper, and 4 weekly publications (all of which are of military or religious interest only).

SOCIAL INSTITUTIONS

Justice. The Organic Act established a District Court with jurisdiction in matters arising under both federal and territorial law; the judge is appointed by the President subject to Senate approval. There is also a Supreme Court and a Superior Court; all judges are locally appointed except the Federal District judge. Misdemeanours are under the jurisdiction of the police court. The Spanish law was superseded in 1933 by 5 civil codes based upon California law.

Religion. About 80% of the Guamanians are Roman Catholics; others are Baptists, Episcopalians, Bahais, Lutherans, Mormons, Presbyterians, Jehovah's Witnesses and members of the Church of Christ and Seventh Day Adventists.

Education. 8 years of primary education to the age of 16 are compulsory. There are Chamorro Studies courses and bi-lingual teaching programmes to integrate the Chamorro language and culture into elementary and secondary school courses. In 1988-89 there were 18,713 pupils in primary schools and 7,223 in secondary schools. There were 1,403 teachers in 1986. There is a University of Guam.

Social Welfare. There is a hospital, 8 nutrition centres, a school health programme and an extensive immunization programme. Emphasis is on disease prevention, health education and nutrition. In 1990 $83·2m. was paid in Federal direct payments for individuals, including $1·91m. Medicare, $1·91m. disability insurance and $11·37m. retirement insurance.

Further Reading

Report (Annual) of the Governor of Guam to the US Department of Interior
Guam Annual Economic Review. Economic Research Center, Agaña

Carano, P. and Sanchez, P. C., *Complete History of Guam*. Rutland, (VT), 1964
Rogers, R. F., *Destiny's Landfall: a History of Guam*. Hawaii Univ. Press, 1995
Wuerch, W. L. and Ballendorf, D. A., *Historical Dictionary of Guam and Micronesia*. Metuchen (NJ), 1995

COMMONWEALTH OF THE NORTHERN MARIANA ISLANDS

KEY HISTORICAL EVENTS. In 1889 Spain ceded Guam (largest and southernmost of the Marianas Islands) to the US and sold the rest to Germany. Occupied by Japan in 1914, the islands were administered by Japan under a League of Nations mandate until occupied by US forces in August 1944. In 1947 they became part of the US-administered Trust Territory of the Pacific Islands. On 17 June 1975 the electorate adopted a covenant to establish a Commonwealth in association with the US; this was approved by the US government in April 1976 and came into force on 1 Jan. 1978. In Nov. 1986 the islanders were granted US citizenship. The UN terminated the Trusteeship status on 22 Dec. 1990.

TERRITORY AND POPULATION. The Northern Marianas form a single chain of 16 mountainous islands extending north of Guam for about 560 km, with a total area of 5,050 sq. km (1,950 sq. miles) of which 464 sq. km are dry land and a population (1990 Census) of 43,345 (urban, 12,151; female, 20,543); density, 235·6 per sq mile. 16,752 persons were born in the Islands. Population estimate (1995) 47,200.

The areas and populations of the islands are as follows:

Island(s)	*Sq. km*	*1980 Census*	*1990 Census*
Northern Group [1]	171	104	36
Saipan	122	14,585	38,896
Tinian (with Aguijan)	101 [2]	899	2,118
Rota	83	1,274	2,295

[1] Pagan, Agrihan, Alamagan and 9 uninhabited islands. [2] Including uninhabited Aguijan.

In 1980, 55% spoke Chamorro, 11% Woleaian and 13% Filipino languages, but English remains the official language. The largest town is Chalan Kanoa on Saipan. In 1987 births numbered 958 and deaths 115.

CONSTITUTION AND GOVERNMENT. The Constitution was approved by a referendum on 6 March 1977 and came into force on 9 Jan. 1978. The legislature comprises a 9-member *Senate*, with 3 Senators elected from each of the main 3 islands for a term of 4 *years*, and an 18-member *House of Representatives*, elected for a term of 2 years. At the elections of Nov. 1991 the Republican Party won 8 seats and the Democratic Party 1 in the Senate; the Republicans won 10, the Democrats 6 and independents 2 in the House of Representatives.

The Commonwealth is administered by a Governor and Lieut.-Governor, elected for 4 years.

Governor: Froilan C. Tenorio (D.), 1994–98.

Lieut.-Governor: Benjamin Manglona.

Flag: Blue, with a five-pointed white star superimposed on a grey latte stone in the centre.

LABOUR. In 1990 there were 32,522 persons of employable age, of whom 26,589 were in the workforce. 616 were unemployed.

COMMERCE. In 1988 imports totalled US$242m.; exports in 1985 were US$12·3m.

TOURISM. In 1984 there were 104,156 vistors.

COMMUNICATIONS

Roads. There are about 300 km of roads (54 km paved).

Civil Aviation. Air Micronesia provides inter-island services.

Telecommunications. In 1989 there were 10,500 radio and 4,100 television receivers, 3 radio stations and a 15-channel cable TV station in Saipan. Telephones (1987), 4,900.

SOCIAL INSTITUTIONS

Religion. The population is predominantly Roman Catholic.

Education. In 1989 there were 18 primary schools with 4,882 pupils and 9 secondary schools with 2,075 pupils. The tertiary college on Saipan had 1,097 students.

Health. In 1986 there were 23 doctors, 4 dentists, 103 nursing personnel, 2 pharmacists and 2 midwives. In 1988 there was 1 hospital with 70 beds.

AMERICAN SAMOA

KEY HISTORICAL EVENTS. The Samoan Islands were first visited by Europeans in the 18th century; the first recorded visit was in 1722. On 14 July 1889 a treaty between the USA, Germany and Great Britain proclaimed the Samoan islands neutral territory, under a 4-power government consisting of the 3 treaty powers and the local native government. By the Tripartite Treaty of 7 Nov. 1899, ratified 19 Feb. 1900, Great Britain and Germany renounced in favour of the US all rights over the islands of the Samoan group east of 171° long. west of Greenwich, the islands to the west of that meridian being assigned to Germany (now the independent state of Western Samoa). The islands of Tutuila and Aunu'u were ceded to the US by their High Chiefs on 17 April 1900, and the islands of the Manu'a group on 16 July 1904. Congress accepted the islands under a Joint Resolution approved 20 Feb. 1929. Swain's Island, 210 miles north of the Samoan Islands, was annexed in 1925 and is administered as an integral part of American Samoa.

TERRITORY AND POPULATION. The islands (Tutuila, Aunu'u, Ta'u, Olosega, Ofu and Rose) are approximately 650 miles east-north-east of Fiji. The total area is 1,511 sq. km (583 sq. miles), of which 200 sq. km are dry land; population (1990 Census), 46,773, nearly all Polynesians or part-Polynesians, of whom 25,573 were born in American Somoa (urban, 15,599; female, 22,750); density, 607·4 per sq. mile; estimate (1993), 52,860. The island's 3 Districts are Eastern (population, 1980, 17,311), Western (13,227) and Manu'a (1,732). There is also Swain's Island, with an area of 1·9 sq. miles and 29 inhabitants (1980), which lies 210 miles to the north west. Rose Island (uninhabited) is 0·4 sq. mile in area. In 1990 some 85,000 American Samoans lived in the USA.

CLIMATE. A tropical maritime climate with a small annual range of temperature and plentiful rainfall. Pago-Pago. Jan. 83°F (28·3°C), July 80°F (26·7°C). Annual rainfall 194" (4,850 mm).

CONSTITUTION AND GOVERNMENT. American Samoa is constitutionally an unorganized unincorporated territory of the US administered under the Department of the Interior. Its indigenous inhabitants are US nationals and are classified locally as citizens of American Samoa with certain privileges under local laws not granted to non-indigenous persons. Polynesian customs (not inconsistent with US laws) are respected.

Fagatogo is the seat of the Government.

The islands are organized in 15 counties grouped in 3 districts; these counties and districts correspond to the traditional political units. On 25 Feb. 1948 a bicameral legislature was established, at the request of the Samoans, to have advisory legislative functions. With the adoption of the Constitution of 22 April 1960, and the revised Constitution of 1967, the legislature was vested with limited law-making authority. The lower house, or House of Representatives, is composed of 20 members elected by universal adult suffrage and 1 non-voting member for Swain's Island. The upper house, or Senate, is comprised of 18 members elected, in the traditional Samoan manner, in meetings of the chiefs.

Governor: A. P. Lutati (D.), 1993–97.
Lieut.-Governor: Galeá I. Poumele.

ECONOMY

Policy. The first formal Economic Development and Planning Office completed its first year in 1971. Much has been done to promote economic expansion within the Territory and a large amount of outside investment interest has been stimulated.

The Office initiated the first Territorial Comprehensive Plan. This plan when completed will, with periodic updating, provide a guideline to territorial development for 20 years. The planning programme was made possible under a Housing and Urban Development '701' grant programme, and Economic Development Administration '302' planning programmes.

The focus will be on physical development and the problems of a rapidly increasing population with severely limited labour resources.

Budget. The chief sources of revenue are annual federal grants from the US, and local revenues from taxes, and duties, and receipts from commercial operations (enterprise and special revenue funds), utilities, rents and leases and liquor sales. During the financial year 1983–84 the Government had a revenue of $76·6m. including local appropriations of $9·5m., federal appropriations of $39·6m. and enterprise funds of $17·5m.

Banking. The American Samoa branch of the Bank of Hawaii and the American Samoa Bank offer all commercial banking services. The Development Bank of American Samoa, government-owned, is concerned primarily through loans and guarantees with the economic advancement of the Territory.

ENERGY AND NATURAL RESOURCES

Electricity. Net power generated (financial year 1981) was 72·2m. kWh., of which 23·1m. kWh. was supplied to large power users and 20·2m. kWh. to householders. All the Manu'a islands have electricity.

Agriculture. Of the 48,640 acres of land area, 11,000 acres are suitable for tropical crops; most commercial farms are in the Tafuna plains and west Tutuila. Principal crops are taro, bread-fruit, yams, bananas and coconuts. Production (1988 in 1,000 tonnes): Taro, 4; bananas, 1; fruit, 1; coconuts, 5.

Livestock (1988): Pigs, 11,000; (1984) goats, 8,000; poultry, 45,000.

INDUSTRY AND TRADE

Industry. Fish canning is important, employing the second largest number of people (after government). Attempts are being made to provide a variety of light industries. Tuna fishing and local inshore fishing are both expanding. In 1990 there were 27,991 persons of employable age, of whom 14,198 were in the workforce. There were 726 unemployed.

Commerce. In 1982 American Samoa exported goods valued at $186,782,060 and imported goods valued at $119,416,918. Chief exports are canned tuna, watches, pet foods and handicrafts. Chief imports are building materials, fuel oil, food, jewellery, machines and parts, alcoholic beverages and cigarettes.

COMMUNICATIONS

Roads. There are (1983) about 76 miles of paved roads and 16 miles of unpaved within the Federal Aid highway system. There are 21 miles of other unpaved roads. Motor vehicles registered, 1983, 3,657.

Civil Aviation. South Pacific Island Airways and Polynesian Airlines operate daily services between American Samoa and Western Samoa. South Pacific Island Airways also operates between Pago Pago and Honolulu, and between Pago Pago and Tonga. The islands are also served by Air Nauru which operates between Pago Pago, Tahiti and Auckland, and Air Pacific (Fiji and westward). South Pacific and Manu'a Air Transport run local services.

Shipping. The harbour at Pago Pago, which nearly bisects the island of Tutuila, is the only good harbour for large vessels in Samoa. By sea, there is a twice-monthly service between Fiji, New Zealand and Australia and regular service between US, South Pacific ports, Honolulu and Japan.

Telecommunications. A commercial radiogram service is available to all parts of the world. Commercial phone and telex services are operated to all parts of the world. Number of telephones (Sept. 1983), 6,029; telex subscribers, 78. In 1993 there were about 20,000 radio and 8,000 TV (colour by NTSC) sets in use.

SOCIAL INSTITUTIONS

Justice. Judicial power is vested firstly in a High Court. The trial division has original jurisdiction of all criminal and civil cases. The probate division has jurisdiction of estates, guardianships, trusts and other matters. The land and title division decides cases relating to disputes involving communal land and Matai title court rules on questions and controversy over family titles. The appellate division hears appeals from trial, land and title and probate divisions as well as having original jurisdiction in selected matters. The appellate court is the court of last resort. Two American judges sit with 5 Samoan judges permanently. In addition there are temporary judges or assessors who sit occasionally on cases involving Samoan customs. There is also a District Court with limited jurisdiction and there are 69 village courts.

Religion. In 1992 about 55% of the population belonged to the Congregational Church and 19% were Roman Catholics. Methodists and Mormons are also represented.

Education. Education is compulsory between the ages of 6 and 18. In 1988-89 there were 8,313 pupils in elementary and 2,935 in secondary schools. There were 674 teachers in 1986.

Welfare. In 1990 Federal direct payments to individuals totalled $14·62m., of which $2·41m. were disability, and $4·33m. were retirement, insurance.

OTHER PACIFIC TERRITORIES

Johnston Atoll. Two small islands 1,150 km south-west of Hawaii, administered by the US Air Force. Area, under 1 sq. mile; population (1990 census) 173.

Midway Islands. Two small islands at the western end of the Hawaiian chain, administered by the US Navy. Area, 2 sq. miles; population (1980 census) 453.

Wake Island. Three small islands 3,700 km west of Hawaii, administered by the US Air Force. Area, 3 sq. miles; population (1980 census) 302.

COMMONWEALTH OF PUERTO RICO

KEY HISTORICAL EVENTS. Puerto Rico, by the treaty of 10 Dec. 1898 (ratified 11 April 1899), was ceded by Spain to the US. The name was changed from Porto Rico to Puerto Rico by an Act of Congress approved 17 May 1932. Its territorial constitution was determined by the 'Organic Act' of Congress (2 March 1917) known as the 'Jones Act', which ruled until 25 July 1952, when the present constitution of the Commonwealth of Puerto Rico was proclaimed.

TERRITORY AND POPULATION. Puerto Rico is the most easterly of the Greater Antilles and lies between the Dominican Republic and the US Virgin Islands. The total area is 13,791 sq. km (5,325 sq. miles), of which 8,875 sq. km are dry land; population, according to the census of 1990, of 3,522,037 (1,816,395 females), an increase of 10·2% over 1980; density, 1,027·9 per sq. mile. Urban population (1990) 2,508,346 (71·2%). Population estimate (1993), 3,552,037.

A law of April 1991 made Spanish the sole official language, replacing a law of 1902 establishing Spanish and English as joint official languages.

Vital statistics (1992): Births, 64,481 (18 per 1,000 population); deaths, 26,397 (7·4); deaths under 1 year, 822 (12·7 per 1,000 live births).

Chief towns, 1990 are: San Juan, 437,745; Bayamón, 220,262; Ponce, 187,749; Carolina, 177,806; Caguas, 133,447; Mayaguez, 100,371; Arecibo, 93,385.

The Puerto Rican island of Vieques, 10 miles to the east, has an area of 51·7 sq. miles and 8,602 (1990) inhabitants. The island of Culebra, between Puerto Rico and St Thomas, has an area of 10 sq. miles and 1,542 (1990) inhabitants. It has a good harbour.

CONSTITUTION AND GOVERNMENT. Puerto Rico has representative government, the franchise being restricted to citizens 18 years of age or over, residence (1 year) and such additional qualifications as may be prescribed by the Legislature of Puerto Rico, but no property qualification may be imposed. Puerto Ricans do not vote in the US presidential elections, though individuals living on the mainland are free to do so subject to the local electoral laws. The executive power resides in a Governor, elected directly by the people every 4 years. Fourteen heads of departments form the Governor's advisory council, also designated as his Council of Secretaries. The legislative functions are vested in a Senate, composed of 27 members and the House of Representatives, composed of 53 members. Both houses meet annually in Jan. Puerto Rico sends to Congress a Resident Commissioner to the US, elected by the people for a term of 4 years, but he has no vote in Congress. Puerto Rican men are subject to conscription in US services.

On 27 Nov. 1953 President Eisenhower sent a message to the General Assembly of the UN stating 'if at any time the Legislative Assembly of Puerto Rico adopts a resolution in favour of more complete or even absolute independence' he 'will immediately thereafter recommend to Congress that such independence be granted'.

For an account of the constitutional developments prior to 1952, *see* THE STATESMAN'S YEAR-BOOK, 1952, p. 742. The new constitution was drafted by a Puerto Rican Constituent Assembly and approved by the electorate at a referendum on 3 March 1952. It was then submitted to Congress, which struck out Section 20 of Article 11 covering the 'right to work' and the 'right to an adequate standard of living'; the remainder was passed and proclaimed by the Governor on 25 July 1952.

At the election on 4 Nov. 1988 the Popular Democratic Party, headed by Rafael Hernández Colón, polled 871,858 votes (48·7% of the total); the New Progressive Party, headed by Baltazar Corrada del Rió, polled 820,342 votes (45·8% of the total); the Independence Party (full independence by constitutional means), headed by Rubén Berrios Martínez, polled 99,206 votes (5·5% of the total).

At a referendum on 8 Dec. 1991 in advance of an impending plebiscite on Puerto Rico's future status (status quo, 51st state of the USA or full independence), 53% of votes cast were against proposals emphasizing independence.

Governor: Dr. Pedro Rossello (New Progressive Party).

ECONOMY

Budget. Central Government budget, year ending 30 June 1991: Balance at 1 July 1992, $254,458,000; receipts, $7,106,323,000; disbursements, $6,851,865,000.

Assessed value of property, 30 June 1993, was $7,410m. Bonded indebtedness for the commonwealth and municipalities, 30 June 1993, was $4,517m.

The US administers and finances the postal service and maintains air and naval bases. US payments in Puerto Rico, including direct expenditures (mainly military), grants-in-aid and other payments to individuals and to business totalled: 1989–90, $4,891·7m.; 1990–91, $5,036·5m; 1991–92, $5,344·4m.

Per capita personal income (1992) was £6,360.

Banking and Finance. Banks on 30 June 1993 had total deposits of $23,468·3m. Bank loans were $15,298·8m. This includes 18 commercial banks, 2 government banks and 4 trust companies.

ENERGY AND NATURAL RESOURCES

Electricity. Production in 1992-93 was 16,743m. kWh.

Minerals. There is stone, and some production of cement (1·44m. tons in 1992–93).

Agriculture. Farming is mainly of sugar-cane. Production of raw sugar, 96 degrees basis, 1993 crop year, was 64,215 tons (preliminary).

Livestock (1992, preliminary): Cattle, 428,778; pigs, 0·21m.; poultry, 12,450,346.

LABOUR. In 1993 the total labour force was 1,201,000, with 999,000 employed. 202,000 persons were unemployed.

COMMERCE. In 1992–93 (preliminary) imports amounted to $16,385·8m., of which $11,385·8m. came from US; exports were valued at $19,790·7m., of which $17,049·7m. went to US.

In financial year 1993 the US took: Cigarettes, cigars and cheroots, 1,457,056,000 units; other tobacco products (1992), 388,581 kg; rum, 79,827,847 proof litres.

Puerto Rico is not permitted to levy taxes on imports.

Total trade between Puerto Rico and UK (British Department of Trade returns, in £1,000 sterling):

	1990	*1991*	*1992*	*1993*	*1995*
Imports to UK	123,087	109,295	103,463	107,113	81,961
Exports and re-exports from UK	69,593	81,637	156,118	188,417	466,196

COMMUNICATIONS

Roads. The Department of Public Works had under maintenance at 31 Dec. 1992, 21,772 km of paved road. Motor vehicles registered 30 June 1992, 1,650,709.

Shipping. In financial year 1992–93, 9,440 American and foreign vessels of 74,876,870 gross tons entered and cleared Puerto Rico.

Telecommunications. In Oct. 1991 there were 105 broadcasting stations and 20 television companies. There were (Sept. 1992) 1,166,231 telephones.

Press. In 1993 there were 3 main newspapers: *El Nuevo Día* had a daily circulation of 225,118; *El Vocero,* 250,006; *San Juan Star,* 48,000.

SOCIAL INSTITUTIONS

Justice. The Commonwealth judiciary system is headed by a Supreme Court of 7 members, appointed by the Governor, and consists of a Superior Tribunal with 11 sections and 92 superior judges, a District Tribunal with 38 sections and 99 district judges, and 60 municipal judges all appointed by the Governor.

Religion. Over 85% of the population are Roman Catholic.

Education. Education was made compulsory in 1899, but in 1981, 3·6% of the children still had no access to schooling. The percentage of illiteracy in 1990 was 10·6% of those 10 years of age or older. Total enrolment in public day schools, Aug. 1991, was 642,579 (first school month). All private schools had a total enrolment of 123,712 pupils in Dec. 1990. All instruction below senior high school standard is given in Spanish only.

The University of Puerto Rico, in Río Piedras, 7 miles from San Juan, had 53,290 students in 1991–92 of which 13,603 were in 6 Regional Colleges and 39,687 in other colleges. Higher education is also available in the Inter-American University of Puerto Rico (42,673 students in 1991–92), the Catholic University of Puerto Rico (12,366), the Sacred Heart College (5,024) and the Fundación Ana G. Méndez (17,658). Other private colleges and universities had 30,071 students.

Further Reading

Statistical Information: The Area of Economic Research and Social Planning of the Puerto Rico Planning Board publishes: *(a)* annual *Economic Report to the Governor; (b) External Trade Statistics* (annual report); *(c) Reports on national income and balance of payments; (d) SocioEconomic Statistics* (since 1940); *(e) Puerto Rico Monthly Economic Indicators.*

Annual Reports. Governor of Puerto Rico. Washington

Bloomfield, R. J., *Puerto Rico: the Search for a National Policy.* Boulder (Colo.), 1985

Carr, R., *Puerto Rico: a Colonial Experiment.* New York Univ. Press, 1984

Cevallos, E., *Puerto Rico.* [Bibliography], Oxford and Santa Barbara, 1985

Crampsey, R. A., *Puerto Rico.* Newton Abbot, 1973

Dietz, J. L., *Economic History of Puerto Rico: Institutional Change and Capital Development.* Princeton Univ. Press, 1987

Falk, P. S., (ed.) *The Political Status of Puerto Rico.* Lexington, Mass., 1986

Commonwealth Library: Univ. of Puerto Rico Library, Rio Piedras.

VIRGIN ISLANDS OF THE UNITED STATES

KEY HISTORICAL EVENTS. The Virgin Islands of the United States, formerly known as the Danish West Indies, were named and claimed for Spain by Columbus in 1493. They were later settled by Dutch and English planters, invaded by France in the mid-17th century and abandoned by the French *c.* 1700, by which time Danish influence had been established. St Croix was held by the Knights of Malta between two periods of French rule.

They were purchased by the United States from Denmark for $25m. in a treaty ratified by both nations and proclaimed 31 March 1917. Their value was wholly strategic, inasmuch as they commanded the Anegada Passage from the Atlantic Ocean to the Caribbean Sea and the approach to the Panama Canal. Although the inhabitants were made US citizens in 1927, the islands are, constitutionally, an 'unincorporated territory'.

TERRITORY AND POPULATION. The Virgin Islands group, lying about 40 miles due east of Puerto Rico, comprises the islands of St Thomas (31 sq. miles), St Croix (83 sq. miles), St John (20 sq. miles) and 65 small islets or cays, mostly uninhabited. The total area is 1,910 sq. km (738 sq. miles), of which 346 sq. km are dry land.

The population, according to the census of 1 April 1990, was 101,809, a decrease of 8,991 since 1985 (52,599 females); density, 760·9 per sq. mile. Population (1990 census) of St Croix, 50,139; St Thomas, 48,166; St John, 3,504. About 45% (1990) were native-born, 29% from other Caribbean islands, 13% from mainland USA and 5% from Puerto Rico. St Croix has over 40% of Puerto Rican origin or extraction, Spanish speaking. In 1988, live births were 2,216 and deaths, 501.

The capital and only city, Charlotte Amalie, on St Thomas, had a population (1990 census) of 12,331; there are two towns on St Croix. Christiansted (2,555) and Frederiksted (1,064).

CLIMATE. Average temperatures vary from 77°F to 82°F throughout the year; humidity is low. Average annual rainfall, about 45 inches. The islands lie in the hurricane belt; tropical storms with heavy rainfall can occur in late summer, but hurricanes rarely.

CONSTITUTION AND GOVERNMENT. The Organic Act of 22 July 1954 gives the US Department of the Interior full jurisdiction; some limited legislative powers are given to a single-chambered legislature, composed of 15 senators elected for 2 years representing the two legislative districts of St Croix and St Thomas-St John.

The Governor is elected by the residents. Since 1954 there have been four attempts to redraft the Constitution, to provide for greater autonomy. Each has been rejected by the electorate. The latest was defeated in a referendum in Nov. 1981, 50% of the electorate participating.

For administration, there are 14 executive departments, 13 of which are under commissioners and the other, the Department of Justice, under an Attorney-General. The US Department of the Interior appoints a Federal Comptroller of government revenue and expenditure.

The franchise is vested in residents who are citizens of the United States, 18 years of age or over. In 1986 there were 34,183 voters, of whom 26,377 participated in the local elections that year.

They do not participate in the US presidential election but they have a non-voting representative in Congress.

The capital is Charlotte Amalie, on St Thomas Island.

Governor: Roy Schneider (ind), 1995–99 ($62,400).
Lieut.-Governor: Derek M. Hodge ($57,000).
Administrator St Croix: Richard Roebuck, Jr.

Administrator St John: William Lomax.
Administrator St Thomas: Harold Robinson.

ECONOMY

Budget. Under the 1954 Organic Act finances are provided partly from local revenues—customs, federal income tax, real and personal property tax, trade tax, excise tax, pilotage fees, etc.—and partly from Federal Matching Funds, being the excise taxes collected by the federal government on such Virgin Islands products transported to the mainland as are liable.

Per capita income, 1990, $8,717.

Budget for financial year 1988, $303,575,186.

Currency and Banking. United States currency became legal tender on 1 July 1934. Banks are the Chase Manhattan Bank; the Bank of Nova Scotia; the First Federal Savings and Loan Association of Puerto Rico; Barclays Bank International; Citibank; First Pennsylvania Bank; Banco Popular de Puerto Rico, and the First Virgin Islands Federal Savings Bank.

ENERGY AND NATURAL RESOURCES

Electricity. The Virgin Islands Water and Power Authority provides electric power from generating plants on St Croix and St Thomas; St John is served by power cable and emergency generator. 426,521 kWh were produced in 1990.

Water. There are 6 de-salinization plants with maximum daily capacity of 8·7m. gallons of fresh water. Rain-water remains the most reliable source. Every building must have a cistern to provide rain-water for drinking, even in areas served by mains (10 gallons capacity per sq. ft of roof for a single-storey house).

Agriculture. Land for fruit, vegetables and animal feed is available on St Croix, and there are tax incentives for development. Sugar has been terminated as a commercial crop and over 4,000 acres of prime land could be utilized for food crops.

Livestock (1988): Cattle, 11,000; goats, 4,000; pigs, 3,000; sheep, 3,000, poultry (1986), 18,345.

Fisheries. There is a fishermen's co-operative with a market at Christiansted. There is a shellfish-farming project at Rust-op-Twist, St Croix.

INDUSTRY AND TRADE

Industry. The main occupations on St Thomas are tourism and government service; on St Croix manufacturing is more important. Manufactures include rum (the most valuable product), watches, pharmaceuticals and fragrances. Industries in order of revenue: Tourism, refining oil, watch assembly, rum distilling, construction.

Labour. In 1990 the total labour force was 45,990, of whom 13,640 were employed in government, 8,450 in retail trades, 9,030 in hotels and other lodgings, 3,550 self-employed and unpaid family workers, 2,290 in transportation and public utilities, 2,420 in manufacturing, 4,140 in construction, 930 in banking, 2,090 in finance, insurance and real estate, 970 in wholesale trades, 920 in business services, 350 in legal services, and 2,330 in gift shops.

Commerce. Exports, calendar year 1990, totalled $2,820·7m. and imports $3,294·6m. The main import is crude petroleum, while the principal exports are petroleum products.

Total trade between the US Virgin Islands and UK (financial years, British Department of Trade returns, in £1,000 sterling):

	1990	*1991*	*1992*	*1993*	*1995*
Imports to UK	317	384	48	488	95
Exports and re-exports from UK	26,725	4,393	8,744	5,311	4,018

Tourism. Tourism accounts for 60% of GDP. 522,900 tourists stayed and 1,311,200 day visitors arrived in 1990 spending $700·9m.; 697,800 came by air and 1,136,800 on cruise ships, mainly to St Thomas.

COMMUNICATIONS

Roads. The Virgin Islands have (1986) 660 miles of roads, and 48,800 motor vehicles registered.

Civil Aviation. There is a daily cargo and passenger service between St Thomas and St Croix. Alexander Hamilton Airport on St Croix can take all aircraft except Concorde. Cyril E. King Airport on St Thomas takes 727-class aircraft. There are air connexions to mainland USA, other Caribbean islands, Latin America and Europe. In 1991 1,023,055 passengers were handled.

Shipping. The whole territory has free port status. There is an hourly boat service between St Thomas and St John.

Telecommunications. All three Virgin Islands have a dial telephone system. In 1990 there were about 60,000 telephones. Direct dialling to Puerto Rico and the mainland, and internationally, is now possible. Worldwide radio telegraph service is also available.

There are 8 radio stations and 1 public and 1 commercial TV station. In 1993 there were some 90,000 radio and 31,500 TV (colour by NTSC) receivers in use.

Press. In 1991 there were 2 dailies, 1 fortnightly paper and 1 magazine.

SOCIAL INSTITUTIONS

Religion. There are churches of the Protestant, Roman Catholic and Jewish faiths in St Thomas and St Croix and Protestant and Roman Catholic churches in St John.

Education. In 1988 there were 13,359 pupils and 873 teachers in elementary schools, and 10,661 pupils and 723 teachers in secondary schools; 33 non-public schools had 5,079 pupils. In autumn 1991 the University of the Virgin Islands had 924 full-time students, 1,538 part-time students and 254 graduate students. The College is part of the United States land-grant network of higher education.

Welfare. In 1990 Federal direct payments for individuals totalled \$95·4m., including: Medicare, \$4·98m.; supplemental medical insurance, \$3·72m.; disability insurance, \$5·69m.; retirement insurance, \$31·6m.; Food Stamps, 18·4m.

Further Reading

Boyer, W. W., *America's Virgin Islands.* Durham, N.C., 1983
Dookhan, I., *A History of the Virgin Islands of the United States.* Caribbean Univ. Press, 1974
Moll, V. P., *Virgin Islands.* [Bibliography]. Oxford and Santa Barbara, 1991

URUGUAY

República Oriental del Uruguay

Capital: Montevideo
Population: 3·12m. (1992)
GNP per capita: US$4,650 (1994)
HDI/world rank: 0·881/32 (1992)

KEY HISTORICAL EVENTS. The Republic of Uruguay, formerly a part of the Spanish Viceroyalty of Río de la Plata and subsequently a province of Brazil, declared its independence 25 Aug. 1825 which was recognized by the treaty between Argentina and Brazil signed at Rio de Janeiro 27 Aug. 1828. The first constitution was adopted 18 July 1830.

TERRITORY AND POPULATION. Uruguay is bounded on the north-east by Brazil, on the south-east by the Atlantic, on the south by the Río de la Plata and on the west by Argentina. The area is 176,215 sq. km (68,037 sq. miles). The following table shows the area and the population of the 19 departments at census 1985:

Departments	*Sq. km*	*Census 1985*	*Capital*	*Census 1985*
Artigas	11,928	68,400	Artigas	34,551
Canelones	4,536	359,700	Canelones	17,316
Cerro-Largo	13,648	78,000	Melo	42,329
Colonia	6,106	112,100	Colonia	19,077
Durazno	11,643	54,700	Durazno	27,602
Flores	5,144	24,400	Trinidad	18,271
Florida	10,417	65,400	Florida	28,560
Lavalleja	10,016	61,700	Minas	34,634
Maldonado	4,793	93,000	Maldonado	33,498
Montevideo	530	1,309,100	Montevideo	1,247,920
Paysandú	13,922	104,500	Paysandú	75,081
Río Negro	9,282	47,500	Fray Bentos	20,431
Rivera	9,370	88,400	Rivera	56,335
Rocha	10,551	68,500	Rocha	23,910
Salto	14,163	107,300	Salto	80,787
San José	4,992	91,900	San José	31,732
Soriano	9,008	77,500	Mercedes	37,110
Tacuarembó	15,438	82,600	Tacuarembó	40,470
Treinta y Tres	9,529	45,500	Treinta y Tres	30,956

Total population, census (1985) 2,940,200 and estimate 1992 was 3,116,802 (87·3% urban). Population density, 1992, 17·7 per sq. km. In 1985 Montevideo (the capital) had a census population of 1,246,500 (1992 estimate: 1,383,660); Las Piedras, 58,221.

Vital statistics rates (per 1,000 population), 1991: Birth, 17·3; death, 10; growth, 7·3; infant mortality (per 1,000 live births), 23·8. Life expectancy was 72·4 years in 1991.

The official language is Spanish.

CLIMATE. A warm temperate climate, with mild winters and warm summers. The wettest months are March to June, but there is really no dry season. Montevideo. Jan. 72°F (22·2°C), July 50°F (10°C). Annual rainfall 38" (950 mm).

CONSTITUTION AND GOVERNMENT. Congress consists of a *Senate* of 30 members and a *Chamber of Deputies* of 99 members, both elected by proportional representation for 5-year terms. The electoral system provides that the successful presidential candidate be a member of the party which gains a parliamentary majority. Electors vote for deputies on a first-past-the-post system, and simultaneously vote for a presidential candidate of the same party. The winners of the second vote are credited with the number of votes obtained by their party in the parliamentary elections. Referendums may be called at the instigation of 10,000 signatories.

Presidential, parliamentary and gubernatorial elections were held on 27 Nov. 1994. The electorate was 2·4m. Julio Sanguinetti was elected President with 31·36% of votes cast against 18 opponents.

President: Julio Maria Sanguinetti (b. 1939; Colorado Party; sworn in 1 March 1995).

Vice President: Dr Hugo Batalla.

A new government took office in March 1995, which in Nov. 1995 comprised:

Minister of the Interior: Dr Didier Operti. *Foreign Affairs:* Alvaro Ramos. - *Economy and Finance:* Luis Mosca. *Transport and Public Works:* Lucio Caceres. *Health:* Dr Alfredo Solari. *Labour and Social Security:* Dr Ana Lia Piñeyrua. *Livestock, Agriculture and Fisheries:* Carlos Gasparri. *Education and Culture:* Samuel Lichtensztejn. *Defence:* Dr Raul Iturria. *Industry, Energy and Mining:* Federico Slinger. *Tourism:* Benito Stern. *Territorial Regulation and Environment:* Juan Chiruchi. *Planning and Budget Office:* Ariel Davrieux.

National flag: Nine horizontal stripes of white and blue, a white canton with the 'Sun of May' in gold.

National anthem: 'Orientales, la patria o la tumba' ('Easterners, the fatherland or the tomb'); words by F. Acuña de Figueroa, tune by F. J. Deballi.

Local Government. The 19 departments are each administered by a governor, elected for 5-year terms simultaneously with the presidential and parliamentary elections.

DEFENCE

Army. The Army consists of volunteers who enlist for 1-2 years service. There are 4 military regions with divisional headquarters. The Army is organized in 5 infantry, 1 engineer, 1 artillery and 3 cavalry brigades and 3 artillery and 4 combat engineer battalions. Equipment includes 17 M-24, 29 M-3A1 and 22 M-41A1 light tanks. Strength (1996) 17,600.

Navy. The navy consists of 3 ex-French frigates, 3 fast inshore patrol craft, 7 other inshore patrol vessels and 4 ex-German inshore minesweepers. Auxiliaries comprise 1 freighting tanker, 1 sail training ship, 1 ex-German support ship; 1 salvage ship and 2 service vessels. There are 4 small landing craft.

A naval aviation service 300 strong operates 6 S-2 Tracker anti-submarine aircraft, 1 King Air for maritime reconnaissance, 6 training aircraft and 6 general purpose helicopters. Personnel in 1995 totalled 5,000 including 400 naval infantry. The main base is at Montevideo.

An integrated coastguard operates 8 inshore patrol craft.

Air Force. Organized with US aid, the Air Force had (1995) about 3,000 personnel and 20 combat aircraft, including 2 counter-insurgency squadrons with 6 IA 58 Pucara, 8 AT-33 armed jet trainers and 6 A-37B light strike aircraft, a reconnaissance and training squadron with 6 PC-7 Turbo-Trainers, 3 transport squadrons with 2 turboprop F.27 Friendships, 3 turbo-prop C-130s, 4 Brazilian-built EMB-110 Bandeirantes (1 equipped for photographic duties), 2 CASA C-212 Aviocars and 5 Queen Airs, a search and rescue squadron with Cessna U-17A aircraft and Bell helicopters, and a number of Cessna 182 light aircraft for liaison duties. Basic training types are the T-41 and T-34.

INTERNATIONAL RELATIONS

Membership. Uruguay is a member of the UN, OAS, Mercosur and LAIA.

ECONOMY

Policy. A referendum of Dec. 1992 rejected large-scale privatization.

Budget. Central government finance (in 1m. pesos):

	1988	*1989*	*1990*	*1991*	*1992*
Revenue	456,675	753,573	1,738,704	3,714,341	6,771,250
Expenditure	510,651	918,442	1,746,224	3,636,941	6,654,107

Components of 1991 revenue: VAT, 42·2%; customs duties, 11·7%; fuel tax, 9·9%; income tax, 6%; capital gains tax, 5·8%. Expenditure included: Social welfare and salaries, 56·7%; interest on public debt, 9·5%; capital expenditure, 9·4%.

Currency. The unit of currency is the *Uruguayan peso* (UYP), of 100 *centésimos*, which replaced the nuevo peso in March 1993 at 1 Uruguayan peso = 1,000 nuevos pesos. There are notes of 0·50, 1, 2, 5, 10, 20, 50, 100, 200, 500 and 1,000 pesos. In 1993 foreign exchange reserves were US$509m.; gold reserves were US$522m. Inflation was 52·9% in 1993. In March 1996, £1 = 11·23; US$1 = 7·35; DM1 = 4·98 pesos.

Banking and Finance. The Central Bank was inaugurated on 16 May 1967. It is the bank of issue and supreme regulatory authority. In 1994 there were 22 commercial banks, 3 state-supported and 18 foreign-owned. Savings banks deposits were 358,322m. pesos in 1991.

The State Insurance Bank has a monopoly of new insurance business. There is a stock exchange in Montevideo.

Weights and Measures. The metric system is in use.

ENERGY AND NATURAL RESOURCES

Electricity. Power output in 1991 was 5,868m kWh.

Agriculture. Uruguay is primarily a pastoral country. In 1993, 11·7% of GDP was produced by agriculture. Some 41m. acres are devoted to farming, of which 90% to livestock and 10% to crops. Some large *estancias* have been divided up into family farms; the average farm is about 250 acres. In 1991 agriculture accounted for 9·8% of GDP.

Livestock, 1993 (in 1,000): cattle, 10,093; sheep, 25,702; pigs, 223; goats, 15; horses, 475; chickens, 9m.

Livestock products, 1993 (in 1,000 tonnes): Beef and veal 317; cow's milk, 1·1 m.

Main crops (in 1,000 tonnes), 1993: Barley, 140; maize, 128; oats, 35; rice, 700; sugar-beet, 40; wheat, 300; sugar-cane, 350; potatoes, 170. Wine is produced for domestic consumption (107,000 tonnes in 1993). The country has some 6m. fruit trees, principally peaches, oranges, tangerines and pears.

Forestry. In 1992 the forest area was 26,000 ha, mainly eucalyptus and pine.

Fisheries. In 1991, the total catch was 193,800 tonnes.

INDUSTRY. In 1993 services accounted for 38·1% of GDP and manufacturing and building, 24·6%. Industries include meat packing, oil refining, cement manufacture, foodstuffs, beverages, leather and textile maufacture, chemicals, light engineering and transport equipment. 1991 output (in 1,000 tonnes): Wool, 94; cement, 436; sugar, 86; motor cars, 11,794 units; lorries, 567 units; meat-packing, 1,132,000 head (1,408,000 head in 1990); petroleum, 1,587,000 cu. metres.

Labour. Retirement age is 55 for women and 60 for men. In 1994 the workforce was 1·1m. In 1991 40·2% of the workforce was engaged in services, 21·8% in manufacturing, 16·7% in trade, 6·9% in building and 5·6% in transport and communications.

FOREIGN ECONOMIC RELATIONS. External debt was US$7,890m. in 1993.

Commerce. The foreign trade (officially stated in US dollars, with the figure for imports based on the clearance permits granted and that for exports on export licences utilized) was as follows (in US$1m.):

	1989	*1990*	*1991*	*1992*	*1993*
Imports	1,202·8	1,342·9	1,636·5	2,045	2,324
Exports	1,598·8	1,692·9	1,604·7	1,702	1,645

Principal exports in 1993 (in US$1,000): Textiles, 388·5 (including washed wool, 33·4); meat, live animals and by-products, 355·5; agricultural produce, 250·1 (including rice, 150·1); leather, hides and manufactures, 176·9; footwear, 25·6.

Main export markets in 1993 (in US$1m.): Argentina, 316·4; Brazil, 282·9; USA and Canada, 148·8; Germany, 104·4. Main import suppliers: Brazil, 635·7; Argentina, 482·6; USA and Canada, 222·5; Italy, 97·2.

Total trade between Uruguay and UK (British Department of Trade returns, in £1,000 sterling):

	1991	*1992*	*1993*	*1994*	*1995*
Imports to UK	47,894	49,492	47,394	52,173	62,379
Exports and re-exports from UK	33,303	31,462	45,674	51,546	56,833

Tourism. There were 1,168,000 tourists in 1986.

COMMUNICATIONS

Roads. There were (1991) about 52,000 km of roads including 12,000 km of motorways. In 1989 there were some 175,000 private cars and 85,000 commercial vehicles.

Railways. The total railway system open for traffic was (1992) 2,073 km of 1,435 mm gauge, which carried 1m. tonnes of freight. Passenger service, which had been abandoned in 1988, was resumed on a limited basis in 1993.

Civil Aviation. There is an international airport at Montevideo (Carrasco). The national carrier is Pluna, which in 1995 operated 1 B-707-320B, 3 B-737-200 Advs and 1 DC-10-30. It maintains routes to Argentina, Bolivia, Brazil and Paraguay. Services were also provided by Aeroflot, Aerolíneas Argentinas, Air France, Iberia, KLM, Ladeco, Lan-Chile, LAPSA, Lloyd Aéreo Boliviano, United Airlines and Varig.

Shipping. In 1995, sea-going shipping totalled 150,296 GRT; including oil tankers, 93,297 GRT and container ships, 28,153 GRT. Navigable inland waterways total 1,270 km.

Telecommunications. The telephone system in Montevideo is controlled by the State; small companies operate in the interior. Telephones, 1990, numbered 390,000. There were 1,277 post offices in 1986. There were (1990) about 1·8m. radio and 0·65m. television receivers (colour by PAL). There are 4 TV networks (3 commercial) and about 100 radio stations.

Cinemas (1980). Cinemas numbered 85 with seating capacity of 47,000.

Press (1994). There were 6 daily newspapers in Montevideo and 5 weeklies. There were also 30 provincial newspapers, many bi-weekly.

SOCIAL INSTITUTIONS

Justice. The Supreme Court is elected by Congress; it appoints all other judges. There are 4 courts of appeal, each with 3 judges. There are civil and criminal courts. Each department has its court, and there are 224 lower courts.

Religion. State and Church are separated, and there is complete religious liberty. In 1992 there were 1·83m. Roman Catholics.

Education. In 1992 95·4% of the population over 10 years old were literate. Primary education is obligatory; both primary and secondary education are free. In 1985–86 there were 356,002 primary school pupils, and 188,176 secondary school pupils.

There is 1 state university, 1 independent Roman Catholic university and 1 private institute of technology. In 1994–95 there were 71,379 students and 6,683 academic staff.

Health. Hospital beds, 1983, numbered (estimate) 23,400; physicians numbered (1984) 5,736.

Social Security. The welfare state dates from the beginning of the 1900s. In 1994 there were 0·5m. recipients of pensions and benefits.

DIPLOMATIC REPRESENTATIVES

Of Uruguay in Great Britain (140 Brompton Rd., London, SW3 1HY)
Ambassador: Juan Enrique Fischer.

Of Great Britain in Uruguay (Calle Marco Bruto 11300, Montevideo)
Ambassador: Robert Hendrie.

Of Uruguay in the USA (1918 F. St., NW, Washington, D.C., 20006)
Ambassador: Dr Alvaro de Medina.

Of the USA in Uruguay (Lauro Muller 1776, Montevideo)
Ambassador: Thomas Dodd.

Of Uruguay to the United Nations
Ambassador: Dr Jorge Pérez Otermín.

Further Reading

Finch, H., *Uruguay:* [Bibliography]. Oxford and Santa Barbara (CA), 1989
González, L. E., *Political Structures and Democracy in Uruguay.* Univ. of Notre Dame Press, 1992
Sosnowski, S. (ed.) *Repression, Exile and Democracy: Uruguayan Culture.* Duke Univ. Press, 1993
Weinstein, M., *Uruguay: Democracy at the Crossroads.* Boulder (CO), 1988

National library: Biblioteca Nacional del Uruguay, Guayabo 1793, Montevideo.

UZBEKISTAN

Uzbekiston Respublikasy

Capital: Tashkent
Population: 22·2m. (1994)
GNP per capita: US$950 (1994)
HDI/world rank: 0·706/94 (1992)

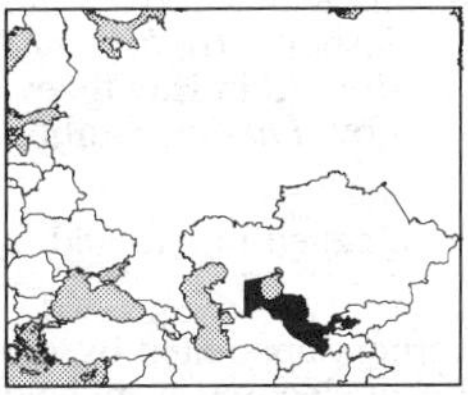

KEY HISTORICAL EVENTS. In Oct. 1917 the Tashkent Soviet assumed authority, and in the following years established its power throughout Turkestan. The semi-independent Khanates of Khiva and Bokhara were first (1920) transformed into People's Republics, then (1923–24) into Soviet Socialist Republics and finally merged in the Uzbek SSR and other republics.

The Uzbek Soviet Socialist Republic was formed on 27 Oct. 1924 from lands formerly included in Turkestan. It included a large part of the Samarkand region, the southern part of the Syr Darya, Western Ferghana, the western plains of Bukhara, the Kara-Kalpak ASSR and the Uzbek regions of Khorezm. In 1963 40,000 sq. km were transferred from Kazakhstan.

On 20 June 1990 the Supreme Soviet adopted a declaration of sovereignty, and in Aug. 1991, following the unsuccessful coup, it declared itself independent as the 'Republic of Uzbekistan', which was confirmed by referendum in Dec. In Dec. 1991 Uzbekistan became a member of the CIS.

TERRITORY AND POPULATION. Uzbekistan is bordered in the north by Kazakhstan, in the east by Kyrgyzstan and Tajikistan, in the south by Afghanistan and in the west by Turkmenistan. Area, 447,400 sq. km (172,741 sq. miles). At the 1989 census the population was 19,810,077 (71·4% Uzbek, 8·4% Russian, 4·7% Tajik, 4·1% Kazakh, 3·2% Tatar and 2·1% Karakalpak). The population in Jan. 1994 was 22,199,000 (50·6% female; 39·4% urban). Vital statistics rates, 1993 (per 1,000 population): Birth, 31·5; death 6·6; infant mortality (per 1,000 live births), 32. Natural increase, 2·49%.

The country comprises the following regions: Andizhan, Bukhara, Dzhizak, Ferghana, Kashkadar, Khorezm, Namangan, Navoi, Samarkand, Surkhan-Darya, Syr-Darya, Tashkent and the Karakalpak Autonomous Republic. The capital is Tashkent (2·1m. population in 1994); other large towns are Samarkand, Andizhan and Namangan. There are 124 towns, 97 urban settlements and 155 rural districts.

The Roman alphabet (in use 1929–40) was re-introduced in 1994 to be completely phased in by 2000. Arabic script was used prior to 1929 and Cyrillic, 1940–94.

CONSTITUTION AND GOVERNMENT. A new constitution was adopted on 8 Dec. 1992 which states that Uzbekistan is a pluralist democracy. Presidential elections were held on 29 Dec. 1991. Islam Karimov was elected against a single opponent with over 80% of the vote. A referendum on 26 March 1995 proposed the cancellation of elections due in 1997 and the extension of President Karimov's term of office to 2000. The electorate was 11m.; turn-out was reported to be 99·3%, with 99·62% of votes cast in favour.

Parliament has 250 seats. Parliamentary elections were held in 3 diminishing rounds in Dec. 1994 and Jan. 1995. The electorate was 11m.; turn-out was 70% at the first round. The People's Democratic Party (former Communists) won 213 seats, the National Progress Party 12.

President: Islam Karimov (b. 1938).

Prime Minister: Abdulhashim Mutalov.

First Deputy Prime Minister: Ismail Djurabekov. *Deputy Prime Minister:* Kamiljan Rahimov. *Deputy Prime Minister:* Rustan Yunusov. *Deputy Prime Minister,*

Minister of Finance: Bakhtiar Hamidov. *Deputy Prime Minister:* Saidmukhtar Saidqasimov. *Deputy Prime Minister, Minister of Foreign Economic Relations:* Otkir Sultanov. *Deputy Prime Minister:* Mirabror Usmaov. *Deputy Prime Minister, Chair of State Property Committee:* Viktor Chzehen. *Deputy Prime Minister, Chair of Women's Committee:* Dilbar Ghulomova. *Minister of Interior:* Zokirjon Almatov. *Defence:* Maj.-Gen. Rustan Ahmadov. *Foreign Affairs:* Abdulaziz Komilov. *Justice:* Alisher Mardiev. *Power and Electrification:* Valeri Otaev. *Agriculture:* Rasulmat Husanov. *Water Resources and Land Improvement:* Rim Ginjyatullin. *Communications:* Tahir Rahimov. *Education:* Jora Yoldoshev. *Higher and Secondary Specialized Education:* Oqil Salimov. *Cultural Affairs:* Erkin Hayitboev. *Health:* Shavkat Karimov. *Social Security:* Bakhodir Umurzoqov. *Labour:* Oqiljon Obidov. *Municipal Economy:* Viktor Mikhailov.

National flag: Blue, white and green stripes, with the white edged in red, and in the upper stripe a white crescent and 12 white stars.

Local Government: Local authorities are headed by governors appointed by the President of the Republic and directly responsible to him. Local elections were held on 25 Dec. 1994.

DEFENCE. Conscription is for 18 months.

Army. The Army comprises 3 motor rifle, 1 airborne, 1 artillery and 1 special forces brigade and 1 tank and 2 artillery regiments. Equipment includes 179 T-62 main battle tanks. Personnel, 1996, 20,400. There are paramilitary forces totalling 16,000.

Air Force. Aviation units include a regiment of MiG-27 fighter-bombers and a regiment of An-12 transports, as well as some armed helicopters.

ECONOMY

Budget. Budgetary income in 1993 was 1,843,200m. som-coupons; expenditure was 199,500m. som-coupons.

Currency. A coupon for a new unit of currency, the *som* (UKS), was introduced alongside the rouble on 15 Nov. 1993. This was replaced by the *som* proper at 1 som = 1,000 coupons on 1 July 1994. Inflation was 270% in 1994 (1,100% in 1993). Exchange controls were abolished on 1 July 1995. In March 1996, no exchange rates were available.

ENERGY AND NATURAL RESOURCES

Electricity. Output was 49,100m. kWh in 1993.

Oil and Gas. Crude oil production (including gas concentrate) was 4m. tonnes in 1993; natural gas, 45m. cu. metres.

Minerals. Of its mineral resources, in addition to oil and coal, copper and building materials and ozocerite deposits are now also exploited. 3·8m. tonnes of coal were produced in 1993. Some 70 tonnes of gold are produced annually.

Agriculture. Uzbekistan is a land of intensive farming, based on artificial irrigation. It is a major cotton-growing area. In 1993, 25·5m. ha were under cultivation, of which 428,500 ha were accounted for by private subsidiary agriculture and 149,900 ha by commercial agriculture, in 7,500 farms. Private and commercial agriculture accounted for 38% of output by value in 1993. Total output was valued at 10,300m. roubles (in constant 1983 prices) in 1993, 99·7% of the 1992 figure.

Fruit, silk and rice are also cultivated, particularly in the well-watered, warm oases areas. In the higher-lying plains grain is grown; the wide desert and semi-desert area of Western Uzbekistan is mainly given to pasture land and the breeding of the Karakul sheep.

Livestock on 1 Jan. 1994: 5·3m. cattle, 10·2m. sheep and goats, and 0·4m. pigs.

Output of main agricultural products (in 1,000 tonnes) in 1993: Grain, 2,098; cotton, 4,234; potatoes, 463; vegetables, 2,941; fruit and berries, 486; meat, 452; milk, 3,566; and 1,663m. eggs.

Forestry. Afforestation over an area of 50,000 ha has been carried out to protect the Bokhara and Karakul oases from the advancing Kzyl-Kum sands and to stop the sand-drifts in a number of districts of Central Ferghana. Output of sawn timber, 1989, 563,000 cu. metres.

INDUSTRY. Output was valued at 4,905,000m. roubles in 1993. Output, 1993 (in tonnes): Rolled ferrous metals, 0·6m.; cement, 5·3m.; mineral fertilizer, 1·3m.; chemical fibre, 22,600; paper, 13,100; fabrics, 632m. sq. metres; footwear, 39·6m. pairs; 11,500 tractors; 10,000 TV sets; 81,700 refrigerators and freezers; 10,300 washing machines.

Labour. In 1993 the population of working age was 10·55m., of whom 8·2m. were employed, 57·8% in the state sector, 19·7% in the private sector and 22·1% in co-operatives. In Jan. 1994 there were 13,300 registered unemployed (0·2% of the labour force), of whom 7,600 were receiving benefits. Average monthly salaries in 1993 were 27,161 rubles. A minimum wage of 70,000 som-coupons a month was imposed on 1 June 1994.

FOREIGN ECONOMIC RELATIONS. In Jan. 1994 an agreement to create a single economic zone was signed with Kazakhstan and Kyrgyzstan. Foreign investors are entitled to a 2-year tax holiday and repatriation of hard currency.

Commerce. In 1993 imports were valued at US$947·3m. and exports at US$706·5m. In 1995, cotton fibre made up 50% of exports, and gold, 15%. Total trade between Uzbekistan and UK (British Department of Trade returns, in £1,000 sterling):

	1993	*1994*	*1995*
Imports to UK	282	3,493	1,611
Exports and re-exports from UK	8,363	17,297	15,073

COMMUNICATIONS

Roads. Total length of motor roads in Jan. 1990 was 73,100 km (hard surface, 62,600 km). In 1993, 2,347m. passengers and 217·2m. tonnes of freight were carried.

Railways. The total length of railway in 1993 was 3,380 km of 1,520 mm gauge (300 km electrified). In 1993, 18·6m. passengers and 59·8m. tonnes of freight were carried.

Civil Aviation. The national carrier is the state-owned Uzbekistan Airlines, which in 1996 operated 3 A310-300s and 105 ex-Soviet aircraft, and flew services to Amsterdam, Athens, Bahrain, Bangladesh, Beijing, Delhi, Frankfurt, Istanbul, Jakarta, Jeddah, Karachi, Kuala Lumpur, London, Manchester, New York, Riga, Seoul and Tel Aviv. In 1993, 1·4m. passengers and 16,800 tonnes of freight were carried.

Inland Waterways. Total length in 1990 was 1,100 km.

Telecommunications. Broadcasting is under the aegis of the State Teleradio Broadcasting Company. The government-controlled Uzbek Radio transmits 2 national and several regional programmes, Radio Moscow and Voice of America relays and a foreign service, Radio Tashkent (Uzbek, Arabic, English, Dari, Farsi, Hindi, Pushtu, Uighur).

Press (1989). There were 185 newspapers in the Uzbek language out of a total of 279. Daily circulation of Uzbek-language newspapers, 4·9m.; in all languages, 6·6m.

SOCIAL INSTITUTIONS

Religion. The Uzbeks are predominantly Sunni Moslems.

Education. In 1993–94 there were 9,000 elementary and secondary schools with

4,789,000 pupils, 55 higher educational establishments with 272,300 students and 248 technical colleges with 240,100 students. There are universities and medical schools in Tashkent and Samarkand. In Jan. 1994, 1·2m. children (21% of those eligible were attending pre-school institutions.

Health. In Jan. 1994 there were 77,700 doctors, 255,000 junior medical personnel and 1,361 hospitals with 208,000 beds.

Welfare. In Jan. 1994 there were 1,726,000 age pensioners and 1,007,000 other pensioners.

DIPLOMATIC REPRESENTATIVES

Of Uzbekistan in Great Britain (72 Wigmore St., London, W1H 9DL)
Ambassador: Vacant.

Of Great Britain in Uzbekistan (6 ul. Murtazaeva, Tashkent)
Ambassador: Barbara Hay, MBE.

Of Uzbekistan in the USA
Ambassador: Fatikh Teshabaev.

Of the USA in Uzbekistan (82 Chilanzarskaya, Tashkent)
Ambassador: Stanley T. Escudero.

Of Uzbekistan to the United Nations
Ambassador: Fatikh Teshabaev.

Further Reading

Kangas, R. D., *Uzbekistan in the Twentieth Century: Political Development and the Evolution of Power.* New York, 1994

KARAKALPAK AUTONOMOUS REPUBLIC (KARAKALPAKSTAN)

Area, 164,900 sq. km (63,920 sq. miles); population (Jan. 1990), 1,244,700. Capital, Nukus (1989 census population, 174,000). The Karakalpaks are first mentioned in written records in the 16th century as tributary to Bokhara, and later to the Kazakh Khanate. In the second half of the 19th century they came under Russian rule. On 11 May 1925 the territory was constituted within the then Kazakh Autonomous Republic (of the Russian Federation) as an Autonomous Region. On 20 March 1932 it became an Autonomous Republic within the Russian Federation, and on 5 Dec. 1936 it became part of the Uzbek SSR. At the 1989 census Karakalpaks were 32·1% of the population, Uzbeks, 32·8% and Kazakhs, 26·3%.

170 deputies were elected to its Supreme Soviet in Feb. 1990.

Its manufactures are in the field of light industry—bricks, leather goods, furniture, canning, wine. In Jan. 1990 cattle numbered 336,000 and sheep and goats, 518,100. There were 38 collective and 124 state farms in 1987. The total cultivated area in 1985 was 350,400 ha.

In 1990–91 there were 313,500 pupils at schools, 22,100 student at technical colleges, and 7,800 at Nukus University. There is a branch of the Uzbek Academy of Sciences.

There were 2,600 doctors and 12,800 hospital beds in 1987.

VANUATU

Ripablik blong Vanuatu—
Republic of Vanuatu

Capital: Vila
Population: 160,000 (1996)
GNP per capita: US$1,150 (1994)
HDI/world rank: 0·541/119 (1992)

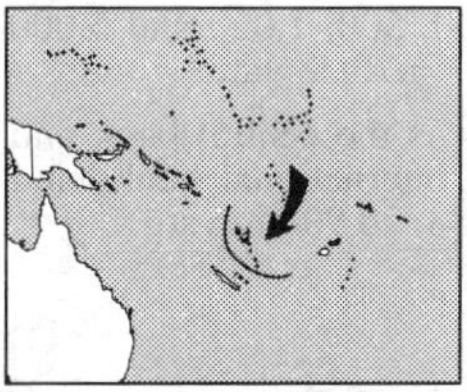

KEY HISTORICAL EVENTS. The group was administered for some purposes jointly, for others unilaterally, as provided for by Anglo-French Convention of 27 Feb. 1906, ratified 20 Oct. 1906, and a protocol signed at London on 6 Aug. 1911 and ratified on 18 March 1922. On 30 July 1980 the Condominium of the New Hebrides achieved independence and became the Republic of Vanuatu.

TERRITORY AND POPULATION. Vanuatu comprises 80 islands, which lie roughly 500 miles west of Fiji and 250 miles north-east of New Caledonia. The estimated land area is 4,706 sq. miles (12,190 sq. km). The larger islands of the group are: (Espiritu) Santo, Malekula, Epi, Pentecost, Aoba, Maewo, Paama, Ambrym, Efate, Erromanga, Tanna and Aneityum. They also claim Matthew and Hunter islands. 67 islands were inhabited in 1990. Population at the census (1989), 142,630. Vila (the capital) 19,400. Estimate, 1996, 160,000 (30% urban); density, 12·7 per sq. km.

The national language is Bislama (spoken by 82% of the population); English and French are also official languages; about 50,000 speak French.

CLIMATE. The climate is tropical, but moderated by oceanic influences and by trade winds from May to Oct. High humidity occasionally occurs and cyclones are possible. Rainfall ranges from 90" (2,250 mm) in the south to 155" (3,875 mm) in the north. Vila. Jan. 80°F (26·7°C), July 72°F (22·2°C). Annual rainfall 84" (2,103 mm). A cyclone hit Vila in Feb. 1987.

CONSTITUTION AND GOVERNMENT. Legislative power resides in a 50-member unicameral Parliament elected for a term of 4 years. The President is elected for a 5-year term by an electoral college comprising Parliament and the presidents of the 11 regional councils. Executive power is vested in a Council of Ministers, responsible to Parliament, and appointed and led by a Prime Minister who is elected from and by Parliament.

There is also a *Council of Chiefs,* comprising traditional tribal leaders, to advise on matters of custom. Parliamentary elections were held on 30 Nov. 1995. The United Front gained 20 seats; the Union of Moderate Parties (UPM), 17; the National United Party (NUP), 9; others, 4.

President: Jean-Marie Leyé (b. 1932; UPM; elected 2 March 1994).

A UPM-NUP coalition government was formed in Dec. 1995.
Maxine Carlot (UPM) was elected *Prime Minister* on 23 Feb. 1996.

National flag: Red over green, with a black triangle in the hoist, the three parts being divided by fimbriations of black and yellow, and in the centre of the black triangle a boar's tusk overlaid by two crossed fern leaves.

National anthem: 'Yumi yumi yumi i glat blong talem se, yumi, yumi yumi i man blong Vanuatu' ('We we we are glad to tell, we we we are the people of Vanuatu'); words and tune by F. Vincent.

DEFENCE. There is a paramilitary force with about 300 personnel. The Vanuatu Police naval service operates 1 inshore patrol craft, and a former motor yacht, both lightly armed. Personnel numbered about 50 in 1995.

INTERNATIONAL RELATIONS

Membership. Vanuatu is a member of the UN, the Commonwealth and the South Pacific Forum and is an ACP state of the EU.

ECONOMY

Budget. The budget for 1988 balanced at 3,938m. vatu.

Currency. The unit of currency is the *vatu* (VUV) with no minor unit. There are coins of 1, 2, 5, 10, 20, 50 and 100 vatu, and notes of 100, 500, 1,000 and 5,000 vatu. In March 1996, £1 = 172 vatu; US$1 = 113 vatu; DM1 = 76·38 vatu.

Banking and Finance. The Reserve Bank blong Vanuatu is the central bank and bank of issue. The Finance Centre in Vila consists of 4 international banks and 6 trust companies. Commercial banks' assets at 31 Dec. 1988, 20,900m. vatu.

Weights and Measures. The metric system is in force.

ENERGY AND NATURAL RESOURCES

Electricity. Production (1986) 20m. kWh.

Agriculture. The main commercial crops are copra, cocoa and coffee. Production, (1993, in tonnes): Copra, 35,000; cocoa, 3,000. 80% of the population are engaged in subsistence agriculture; yams, taro, cassava, sweet potatoes and bananas are grown for local consumption. A large number of cattle are reared on plantations, and a beef industry is developing.

Livestock (1993): Cattle, 128,000; goats, 11,000; pigs, 59,000.

Forestry. In 1987 some 1,900 ha of plantation had been established. In 1990 there were 914,000 ha of forest and woodland.

Fisheries. The principal catch is tuna (1985, 3,962 tonnes) mainly exported to the USA. Small-scale commercial fishing (1985) over 200 tonnes.

INDUSTRY. Industries in 1987 included copra processing, meat canning and fish freezing, a saw-mill, soft drinks factories and a print works. Building materials, furniture and aluminium were also produced, and in 1984 a cement plant opened.

FOREIGN ECONOMIC RELATIONS

Commerce. In 1990 imports were valued at US$93m. and exports at US$14m. Main export markets: Federal Republic of Germany, US$29m.; Japan, US$20·8m; Italy, US$15·5m. Main import suppliers: Japan, US$56·8m.; Italy, US$16·6m.

The main exports are copra, beef, timber, cocoa.

Total trade between Vanuatu and UK (British Department of Trade returns, in £1,000 sterling):

	1991	*1992*	*1993*	*1994*	*1995*
Imports to UK	202	448	1,484	1,618	1,162
Exports and re-exports from UK	381	569	220	383	277

Tourism. In 1988 there were 17,544 visitors to Vanuatu. In addition there were 50,932 tourists from cruise ships. Earnings from tourism 2,000m. vatu.

COMMUNICATIONS

Roads. In 1984 there were 1,062 km of roads, about 250 km paved, mostly on Efate Island and Espiritu Santo. There were 3,784 registered cars in 1988.

Civil Aviation. There is an international airport at Bauerfield Port Vila. The state-owned Air Vanuatu had 1 B-737-400 and 1 other aircraft in 1995. It provides services to Australia. Services are also provided by Air Calédonie, Air Pacific, Qantas and Solomon Airlines.

Shipping. Sea-going shipping totalled 2·57m. GRT in 1995, including oil tankers, 21,833 GRT, and container ships, 29,890 GRT. Several international shipping lines serve Vanuatu, linking the country with Australia, New Zealand, other Pacific territories, Hong Kong, Japan, North America and Europe. The chief ports are Vila and Santo. Small vessels provide frequent inter-island services.

Telecommunications. Services are provided by the Posts and Telecommunications and Radio Departments. There are automatic telephone exchanges at Vila and Santo; rural areas are served by a network of tele-radio stations. In 1983 there were 6 post offices and 3,000 telephones.

External telephone, telegram and telex services are provided by VANITEL, through their satellite earth station at Vila. There are direct circuits to Noumea, Sydney, Hong Kong and Paris and communications are available on a 24-hour basis to most countries. Air radio facilities are provided. Marine coast station facilities are available at Vila and Santo. The government-controlled Radio Vanuatu broadcasts in French, English and Bislama. In 1991 there were about 20,000 radio receivers.

SOCIAL INSTITUTIONS

Justice. A study was begun in 1980 which could lead to unification of the judicial system.

Religion. Over 80% of the population are Christians, but animist beliefs are still prevalent.

Education. There were (1988) 260 primary schools with 24,634 pupils, 11 government and denominational secondary schools with 2,000 pupils and Matevulu College. Tertiary education is provided at the Vanuatu Technical Institute and the Teachers College, while other technical and commercial training is through regional institutions in the Solomon Islands, Fiji and Papua New Guinea.

Health. In 1988 there were 12 hospitals (5 rural) with 419 beds, 37 health centres, 50 dispensaries, 23 doctors and 270 nurses.

DIPLOMATIC REPRESENTATIVES

Of Vanuatu in Great Britain
High Commissioner: Vacant.

Of Great Britain in Vanuatu (KPMG Hse., Rue Pasteur, Vila)
High Commissioner: James Daly, CVO.

Of Vanuatu in the USA
Ambassador: Vacant.

Of the USA in Vanuatu
Ambassador: Richard W. Teare.

Of Vanuatu to the United Nations
Ambassador: Jean Ravou-Akii.

VATICAN CITY STATE

Stato della Città del Vaticano

KEY HISTORICAL EVENTS. For many centuries the Popes bore temporal sway over a territory stretching across mid-Italy from sea to sea and comprising some 17,000 sq. miles, with a population finally of over 3m. In 1859–60 and 1870 the Papal States were incorporated into the Italian Kingdom. The consequent dispute between Italy and successive Popes was only settled on 11 Feb. 1929 by three treaties between the Italian Government and the Vatican: (1) A Political Treaty, which recognized the full and independent sovereignty of the Holy See in the city of the Vatican; (2) a Concordat, to regulate the condition of religion and of the Church in Italy; and (3) a Financial Convention, in accordance with which the Holy See received 750m. lire in cash and 1,000m. lire in Italian 5% state bonds. This sum was to be a definitive settlement of all the financial claims of the Holy See against Italy in consequence of the loss of its temporal power in 1870. The treaty and concordat were ratified on 7 June 1929. The treaty has been embodied in the Constitution of the Italian Republic of 1947. A revised Concordat between the Italian Republic and the Holy See was subsequently negotiated and signed in 1984, and which came into force on 3 June 1985.

The Vatican City State is governed by a Commission appointed by the Pope. The reason for its existence is to provide an extra-territorial, independent base for the Holy See, the government of the Roman Catholic Church.

TERRITORY AND POPULATION. The area of the Vatican City is 44 ha (108·7 acres). It includes the Piazza di San Pietro (St Peter's Square), which is to remain normally open to the public and subject to the powers of the Italian police. It has its own railway station (for freight only), postal facilities, coins and radio. Twelve buildings in and outside Rome enjoy extra-territorial rights, including the Basilicas of St John Lateran, St Mary Major and St Paul without the Walls, the Pope's summer villa at Castel Gandolfo and a further Vatican radio station on Italian soil. *Radio Vaticana* broadcasts an extensive service in 34 languages from the transmitters in the Vatican City and in Italy.

The Vatican City has about 1,000 inhabitants.

CONSTITUTION. The Pope exercises sovereignty and has absolute legislative, executive and judicial powers. The judicial power is delegated to a tribunal in the first instance, to the Sacred Roman Rota in appeal and to the Supreme Tribunal of the Signature in final appeal.

The Pope is elected by the College of Cardinals, meeting in secret conclave. The election is by scrutiny and requires a two-thirds majority.

Name and family	*Election*	*Name and family*	*Election*
Benedict XIV *(Lambertini)*	1740	Leo XIII *(Pecci)*	1878
Clement XIII *(Rezzonico)*	1758	Pius X *(Sarto)*	1903
Clement XIV *(Ganganelli)*	1769	Benedict XV *(della Chiesa)*	1914
Pius VI *(Braschi)*	1775	Pius XI *(Ratti)*	1922
Pius VII *(Chiaramonti)*	1800	Pius XII *(Pacelli)*	1939
Leo XII *(della Genga)*	1823	John XXIII *(Roncalli)*	1958
Pius VIII *(Castiglioni)*	1829	Paul VI *(Montini)*	1963
Gregory XVI *(Cappellari)*	1831	John Paul I *(Luciani)*	1978
Pius IX *(Mastai-Ferretti)*	1846	John Paul II *(Wojtyla)*	1978

Supreme Pontiff: **John Paul II** (Karol Wojtyła), born at Wadowice near Kraków, Poland, 18 May 1920. Archbishop of Kraków 1964–78, created Cardinal in 1967, elected Pope 16 Oct. 1978, inaugurated 22 Oct. 1978.

Pope John Paul II was the first non-Italian to be elected since Pope Adrian VI (a Dutchman) in 1522.

Secretary of State: Angelo Sodano.
Secretary for Relations with Other States: Jean-Louis Tauran.

Flag: Vertically yellow and white, with on the white the crossed keys and tiara of the Papacy.

ROMAN CATHOLIC CHURCH. The Roman Pontiff (in orders a Bishop, but in jurisdiction held to be by divine right the centre of all Catholic unity, and consequently Pastor and Teacher of all Christians) has for advisers and coadjutors the Sacred College of Cardinals, consisting in Nov. 1994 of 167 Cardinals appointed by him from senior ecclesiastics who are either the bishops of important Sees or the heads of departments at the Holy See. In addition to the College of Cardinals, the Pope has created a 'Synod of Bishops'. This consists of the Patriarchs and certain Metropolitans of the Catholic Church of Oriental Rite, of elected representatives of the national episcopal conferences and religious orders of the world, of the Cardinals in charge of the Roman Congregations and of other persons nominated by the Pope. The Synod meets as and when decided by the Pope. The last Synod (on the formation of priests) met in Oct. 1990.

The central administration of the Roman Catholic Church is carried on by a number of permanent committees called Sacred Congregations, each composed of a number of Cardinals and diocesan bishops (both appointed for 5-year periods), with Consultors and Officials. Besides the Secretariat of State and the Second Section of the Secretariat of State (Section for Relations with States) there are now 9 Sacred Congregations, viz.: Doctrine, Oriental Churches, Bishops, the Sacraments and Divine Worship, Clergy, Religious, Catholic Education, Evangelization of the Peoples and Causes of the Saints. Pontifical Councils have replaced some of the previously designated Secretariats and Prefectures and now represent the Laity, Christian Unity, the Family, Justice and Peace, Cor Unum, Migrants, Health Care Workers, Interpretation of Legislative Texts, Inter-Religious Dialogue, Culture, Preserving the Patrimony of Art and History, and, a new Commission, for Latin America. There are also Offices for the Apostolic Penitentiary, the Supreme Tribunal of the Apostolic Signature, the Roman Rota, the Apostolic Camera, the Patrimony of the Holy See, Economic Affairs, the Papal Household, Liturgical Celebrations, the Secret Archives, the Apostolic Library, the Academy of Sciences, the Polyglot Press, the Publishing House, Vatican Radio, the Vatican Television Centre, the Fabric of St Peter's, Papal Charities, Translation Centre, Central Labour Office, the Consistory, Council of Cardinals, Economic Questions and the Institute for Works of Religion (the IOR). The Pontifical Academy of Sciences was revived by Pius XI in 1936 with 70 members. The director of the Vatican Bank (Istituto per le Opere di Religione) is Giovanni Bodio.

DIPLOMATIC REPRESENTATIVES

In its diplomatic relations with foreign countries the Holy See is represented by the Secretariat of State and the Second Section (Relations with States) of the Council for Public Affairs of the Church. It maintains permanent observers to the UN in New York and Geneva and to UNESCO and FAO. The Holy See is a member of IAEA and the Vatican City State is a member of UPU and ITU. It therefore attends as a member those international conferences open to State members of the UN and specialized agencies.

Of the Holy See in Great Britain (54 Parkside, London, SW19 5NE)
Apostolic Nuncio: Archbishop Luigi Barbarito, GCVO.

Of Great Britain at the Holy See (91 Via Condotti, I–00187, Rome).
Ambassador: Maureen MacGlashan.

Of the Holy See in the USA (3339 Massachusetts Ave., NW, Washington, D.C., 20008).
Apostolic Nuncio: Agostino Cacciavillan.

Of the USA at the Holy See (Villino Pacelli, Via Aurelia 294, 00165, Rome).
Ambassador: Raymond L. Flynn.

Further Reading

Acta Apostolicæ Sedis Romanæ. Rome
Annuario Pontificio. Rome. Annual
L'Attività della Santa Sede. Rome. Annual
Catechism of the Catholic Church. 1994
The Catholic Almanac. Huntingdon. Annual
The Catholic Directory. London. Annual
The Catholic Directory for Scotland. Glasgow. Annual
Code of Canon Law. London, 1983
The New Catholic Encyclopædia. New York
Osservatore Romano. Vatican. Daily with weekly editions in English and other languages
Bull, G., *Inside the Vatican.* London, 1982
Cardinale, I., *The Holy See and the International Order.* Gerrards Cross, 1976
Mayer, F. *et al, The Vatican: Portrait of a State and a Community.* Dublin, 1980
Nichols, P., *The Pope's Divisions.* London, 1981
Walsh, M. J., *Vatican City State.* [Bibliography] Oxford and Santa Barbara, 1983

VENEZUELA

República de Venezuela

Capital: Caracas
Population: 20·41m. (1993)
GNP per capita: US$2,760 (1994)
HDI/world rank: 0·859/47 (1992)

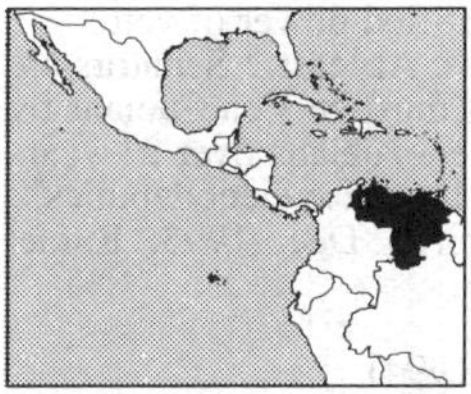

KEY HISTORICAL EVENTS. Venezuela had formed part of the Spanish colony of New Granada until 1821 when it became independent in union with Colombia. A separate, independent republic was formed in 1830. There were 2 abortive military coups in 1992. President Pérez Rodríguez was accused of embezzling public funds and suspended from his functions on 21 May 1993.

TERRITORY AND POPULATION. Venezuela is bounded in the north by the Caribbean, east by Guyana, south by Brazil, south-west and west by Colombia. The area is 912,050 sq. km (352,143 sq. miles). Population (1990) census, 19,405,429 (84% urban). Estimate (1993) 20,407,000; density, 22·4 per sq. km. The 1981 census excluded tribal Indians estimated at 53,350 (chiefly in Amazonas Territory) and illegal immigrants, estimated (1979) at about 3m. The official language is Spanish.

Area, population and capitals of the 20 states and 4 federally-controlled areas:

State	*Sq. km*	*Census 1990*	*Capital*	*Census 1990*
Anzoátegui	43,300	924,074	Barcelona	106,061
Apure	76,500	305,132	San Fernando	57,308 [1]
Aragua	7,014	1,194,982	Maracay	354,428
Barinas	35,200	456,246	Barinas	152,853
Bolívar	238,000	968,695	Ciudad Bolívar	225,846
Carabobo	4,650	1,558,608	Valencia	903,076
Cojedes	14,800	196,526	San Carlos	37,892 [1]
Falcón	24,800	632,513	Coro	124,616
Guárico	64,986	525,737	San Juan	57,219 [1]
Lara	19,800	1,270,196	Barquisimeto	602,622
Mérida	11,300	615,503	Mérida	167,992
Miranda	7,950	2,026,229	Los Teques	143,519
Monagas	28,900	503,176	Maturin	207,382
Nueva Esparta	1,150	280,777	La Asunción	10,375 [1]
Portuguesa	15,200	625,576	Guanare	64,025 [1]
Sucre	11,800	722,707	Cumaná	212,492
Táchira	11,100	859,861	San Cristóbal	220,697
Trujillo	7,400	520,292	Trujillo	31,774 [1]
Yaracuy	7,100	411,980	San Felipe	57,526 [1]
Zulia	63,100	2,387,208	Maracaibo	1,207,513
Ter. Amazonas	175,750	60,207	Puerto Ayacucho	28,248 [1]
Ter. Delta Amacuro	40,200	91,085	Tucupita	27,299 [1]
Federal District	1,930	2,265,874	Caracas	1,824,892
Federal Dependencies	120	2,245	—	—

[1] 1980 census

Other large towns (1980) are Petare (334,800), Ciudad Guyana (314,041, census 1981), Baruta (180,100), Cabimas (138,529, census 1981), Acarigua (126,000), Maiquetiá (120,200), Valera (101,981, census 1981), Chacao (101,900), Puerto Cabello (94,000), Carúpano (82,000) and Puerto La Cruz (81,800).

At the 1981 census, 69% were of mixed ethnic origin (*mestizo*), 20% white, 9% black and 2% Amerindian.

CLIMATE. The climate ranges from warm temperate to tropical. Temperatures vary little throughout the year and rainfall is plentiful. The dry season is from Dec. to April. Caracas. Jan. 65°F (18·3°C), July 69°F (20·6°C). Annual rainfall 32"

(833 mm). Ciudad Bolivar. Jan. 79°F (26·1°C), July 81°F (27·2°C). Annual rainfall 41" (1,016 mm). Maracaibo. Jan. 81°F (27·2°C), July 85°F (29·4°C). Annual rainfall 23" (577 mm).

CONSTITUTION AND GOVERNMENT. The constitution of 1961 provides for the election for a term of 5 years of a President, a National Congress, and state and municipal legislative assemblies by universal compulsory suffrage at 18 years. Voting is by proportional representation. The President must be a Venezuelan by birth and over 30 years of age and has a qualified power of veto.

Congress consists of a Senate and a Chamber of Deputies. At least 2 Senators are elected for each State and for the Federal District. Senators must be Venezuelans by birth and over 30 years of age. Deputies must be native Venezuelans over 21 years of age. The territories, on reaching the population fixed by law, also elect deputies.

Presidential and Congressional elections were held on 5 Dec. 1993. Rafael Caldera was elected President against 3 opponents.

In Feb. 1996 the government comprised:

President: Rafael Caldera (b. 1916; ind; sworn in 2 Feb. 1994).

Interior: Ramón Escobar Salóm. *Foreign Affairs:* Miguel Angel Burelli. *Finance:* Luis Matos Azócar. *Defence:* Moises Orozco Graterol. *Transport and Communications:* Ciro Zaa Alvárez. *Urban Development:* Francisco González. *Energy and Mines:* Erwin José Arrieta. *Environment and Natural Renewable Resources:* Roberto Pérez Lecuna. *Health and Social Security:* Pedro Rincón Gutiérrez. *Agriculture and Livestock:* Raúl Alegrett. *Education:* Antonio Luis Cardenas. *The Family:* Mercedes Pulido. *Justice:* Ruben Creixems. *Presidential Secretariat:* Andrés Caldera. *Decentralization:* José Guillermo Andueza. *Culture:* Oscar Sambrano. *Co-ordination and Planning:* Edgar Paredes Pisani. *Minister, Guyana Corporation of Venezuela:* Elias Nadín Inati. *Foreign Trade:* Werner Corrales. *Labour:* Juan Neporuceno Garrido. *Information:* Fernando Egaña. *Higher Education, Science and Technology:* Guido Arnal Arroyo. *Investment Fund:* Alberto Poletto. *Youth:* María de Pilar Iríbarren. *State Reform:* Ricardo Combellas. *Governor of the Central Bank:* Antonio Casas González. *National Commission against the Illicit Use of Drugs:* Guillermo Romero. *Supervision of Public Administration:* Adelso González Urdaneta. *Tourism:* Hermann Soriano.

National flag: Three horizontal stripes of yellow, blue, red, with an arc of 7 white stars in the centre, and the national arms in the canton.

National anthem: 'Gloria al bravo pueblo' ('Glory to the brave people'); words by Vicente Salias, tune by Juan Landaeta.

Local Government. The 20 states, autonomous and politically equal, have each an elected legislative assembly and governor. The states are divided into 156 districts and 613 municipalities. There are also 2 federal territories with 7 departments, and a federal district with 2 departments and 2 parishes. Each district has a municipal council. The federal district and the 2 territories are administered by the President. Elections were held on 3 Dec. 1995 to elect 22 governors, 330 mayors and several thousand councillors. Turn-out was 40%. The Democratic Action Party gained 12 governorships. State assembly elections were held on 5 Dec. 1993.

DEFENCE. There is selective conscription for 30 months.

Army. The Army consists of 6 infantry divisions, 7 infantry brigades, 1 airborne, 1 Ranger, 1 armoured and 1 cavalry brigade and 1 aviation regiment. Equipment includes 70 AMX-30 main battle tanks. Army aviation comprises 24 helicopters and 14 aircraft. Strength (1996) 34,000 (27,000 conscripts).

Navy. The combatant fleet comprises 2 German-built submarines, 2 ex-US Knox Class and 6 Italian-built Lupo class frigates, 6 fast missile craft, 4 tank landing ships and 12 craft. Auxiliaries comprise 1 logistic support, 1 survey ship, 2 transports, and a sail training ship, as well as a few harbour service craft.

The Naval Air Arm, 1,000 strong, comprises 4 shore-based C-212 Aviocars for maritime reconnaissance and transport, 8 AB-212 ship-borne anti-submarine helicopters and 4 miscellaneous transport and liaison aircraft.

Personnel in 1995 totalled 15,000 (4,000 conscripts) including the 5,000-strong Marine Corps and 1,000 in Naval Aviation. Main bases are at Caracas, Puerto Cabello and Punto Fijo.

The Coastguard, 1,000 strong in 1994, organizationally separate but under Naval operational control, is responsible for control of the economic exclusion zone and comprises 2 large frigate-type patrol craft, 1 ex-tug, 6 inshore patrol craft and a number of boats.

Air Force. Formed in 1920, the Air Force, some 7,000 strong in 1995, has about 80 combat aircraft and 15 armed helicopters. There are 6 combat squadrons. Two are equipped with 18 F-16A and 6 F-16B Fighting Falcons. Two have 9 Canadair CF-5A fighter-bombers and 9 two-seat CF-5Ds, and one has 12 Mirage 50 single-seaters and 2 Mirage 50 trainers. 2 other operational squadrons have 25 OV-10 Bronco twin-turboprop counter-insurgency aircraft and there is 1 squadron of armed Tucano trainers. A helicopter force consists of more than 40 Super Pumas, Bell 212s, 214STs and 412s, UH-1B/D/H Iroquois and Alouette IIIs. Transport units are equipped with 5 C-130H Hercules, 1 Boeing 707 tanker and 8 Aeritalia G222s. Communications aircraft are Queen Airs and other types. 12 Tucanos and 20 T-34A Mentors are used for training as well as 16 T-2D Buckeye advanced jet trainers, which have a secondary attack role. A battalion of paratroops comes within Air Force responsibility. There is a staff college and a cadet academy.

National Guard, a volunteer force of some 22,000 under the Ministry of Defence, is broadly responsible for internal security. It includes customs and forestry duties among its tasks. The Coast Guard, 1,000 strong in 1995, organizationally separate but under Naval operational control, is responsible for control of the economic exclusion zone, and comprises 2 large frigate-type patrol craft, 1 ex-tug, 6 inshore patrol craft and a number of boats.

INTERNATIONAL RELATIONS

Membership. Venezuela is a member of the UN, OAS, LAIA, OPEC and the Andean Group.

ECONOMY

Policy. In Feb. 1994 the President suspended provisions of the constitution affecting freedom of economic activity and assumed powers to issue financial and economic decrees. A 2-year economic stabilization plan was initiated in Sept. 1994. In July 1995 a revised version to cover 1995–98 was introduced.

Budget. The revenue and expenditure for calendar years were, in Bs.1m., as follows:

	1987	*1988*	*1989*	*1990*	*1991*
Revenue	182,787	175,583	354,468	604,722	799,452
Expenditure	173,232	189,045	326,869	563,394	758,636

Currency. The unit of currency is the *bolívar* (VEB) of 100 *céntimos*. There are notes of Bs 1, 5, 10, 20, 50, 100, 500, 1,000 and 5,000, and coins of 5, 25 and 50 céntimos and Bs 1, 2 and 5. Foreign exchange reserves were US$8,900m. in 1994. Exchange controls were imposed in July 1994, when the bolívar was fixed at 170 = US$1. It was devalued by 41·4% in Dec. 1995. Inflation was an annualized 70·8% in 1994. In March 1996, £1 = Bs.442·66; US$1 = Bs.289·63; DM1 = Bs.196·24.

Banking and Finance. A law of Dec. 1992 provided for greater autonomy for the Central Bank. Its governor is appointed by the President for 5-year terms. (*Governor*, Antonio Casas González). Since 1993 foreign banks have been allowed a controlling interest in domestic banks.

There is a stock exchange in Caracas.

ENERGY AND NATURAL RESOURCES

Electricity. Production (1986) 50,240m. kWh. The Guri hydroelectric plant supplies 70% of the country's needs.

Oil. Proven resources of crude were 62,650,000m. bbls. in 1992. The oil-producing region around Maracaibo, covering some 30,000 sq. miles, produces about three-quarters of Venezuelan petroleum. There are large deposits in the Orinoco region. The oil sector was nationalized in 1976, but private and foreign investment have again been permitted since 1992. Estimated crude oil production (1995) was 2,657,000 bbls. a day.

Gas. Production (1985) 33,059m. cu. metres.

Minerals. Output (in 1,000 tonnes) in 1991 (and 1990): Bauxite, 2,100 (702); alumina, 1,500 (1,405); aluminium, 605 (595); iron ore, 19,959 (20,120); coal 2,500 (1,572). Gold production was 7,700 kg in 1990.

Agriculture. Venezuela is divided into 3 zones: the agricultural, the pastoral and the forest zone. In the first are grown coffee, cocoa, sugar-cane, maize, rice, wheat (grown in the Andes), tobacco, cotton, beans and sisal; the second affords grazing for more than 6m. cattle and horses. The 1993 livestock (in 1,000): Cattle, 14,660; pigs, 2,100; goats, 1,650; sheep, 525; chickens, 74m. Over 50% of all farmers are engaged in subsistence agriculture. Government has introduced a programme of price support, tax incentives and price increases.

Production (1993, in 1,000 tonnes): Rice, 645; maize, 700; cassava, 382; sugar-cane, 6,900; bananas, 1,215; oranges, 440; potatoes, 215; tomatoes, 200; coffee, 72; sesame seed, 45; tobacco, 14; cocoa, 15.

Forestry. The forest zone covers a large portion of the country. Resources have been barely tapped; 600 species of wood have been identified.

Fisheries. Total catch (1986) was 283,600 tonnes.

INDUSTRY. Production (1985): Steel, 2·72m. tonnes; aluminium, 407,000; ammonia, 490,000; fertilizers, 650,000; cement, 5·12m.; paper, 550,000; vehicles (units) 116,000.

Labour. The labour force in 1990 was 6,655,000, of whom 758,000 worked in agriculture. Unemployment was 10% in 1995.

Trade Unions. The most powerful confederation of trade unions is the CTV (*Confederacion de Trabajadores de Venezuela*, formed 1947).

FOREIGN ECONOMIC RELATIONS. The Group of Three free trade pact with Colombia and Mexico came into effect on 1 Jan. 1995. Foreign debt was estimated at US$35,100m. in 1992.

Commerce. In 1993 imports were valued at US$11,000m. and exports at US$14,200m. Oil exports were valued at US$12,200m. in 1991. In 1990 the USA accounted for 46·1% of imports and 52% of exports. Other principal import suppliers were: Germany, 9·3%; Italy, 4·8%; Japan, 3·9%. Export markets: Germany, 5·1%; Cuba, 3·4%; Japan, 3·2%.

Total trade between UK and Venezuela (British Department of Trade returns, in £1,000 sterling):

	1991	*1992*	*1993*	*1994*	*1995*
Imports to UK	100,210	138,425	125,492	133,589	204,167
Exports and re-exports from UK	166,654	188,895	226,769	196,787	178,784

Tourism. 692,400 tourists visited Venezuela in 1988.

COMMUNICATIONS

Roads. There were, 1985, 62,601 km of road fit for traffic the year round; of these 24,036 km are paved. There are 10,097 km of high-speed 4-lane motorway type.

Railways. The Puerto Cabello to Barquisimeto and Acarigua lines (336 km–1,435 mm gauge) carried 31·3m. passenger-km and 259,000 tonnes of freight in 1994.

There is a metro in Caracas.

Civil Aviation. There is an international airport at Caracas (Simon Bolívar). The national carrier is Viasa, 40% state-owned, which operated 5 B-727-200 Advs and 5 other aircraft in 1995. Services are also provided by ALM, Aeroperú, Aerotour Dominicano, Air Aruba, Air France, Alitalia, American Airlines, Avianca, British Airways, BWIA, Compania Mexicana, Cubana, Iberia, KLM, LACSA, Lan-Chile, LIAT, Lloyd Aéreo Boliviano, Lufthansa, SAETA, Servivensa, TAP, United Airlines and Varig. Avensa provides domestic services.

Shipping. Ocean-going shipping totalled 1·37m. GRT in 1995, including oil tankers, 0·69m. GRT, and container ships, 1,180 GRT. La Guaira, Maracaibo, Puerto Cabello, Puerto Ordaz and Guanta are the chief ports. The principal navigable rivers are the Orinoco and its tributaries Apure and Arauca.

Telecommunications. There were 1,165,699 telephones in 1985. An international telex service operates in the Caracas metropolitan zone. There is a submarine telephone link with USA.

There are 2 government and 4 cultural radio stations; the remainder are commercial. There are 2 government, 3 commercial and 3 other TV channels (colour by NTSC). In 1991 there were 8·1m. radio and 3·5m. TV receivers.

Press (1983). There were 25 leading daily newspapers with a circulation of over 1·7m.

SOCIAL INSTITUTIONS

Justice. The Supreme Court, which operates in Divisions, each with 5 members, is elected by Congress for 5 years. The country is divided into 20 legal districts. They select their own President and Vice-President. The Federal Procurator-General is appointed for 5 years. There are lower federal courts.

Each state has a Supreme Court with 3 members, a superior court, or superior tribunal, courts of first instance, district courts and municipal courts. In the territories there are civil and military judges of first instance, and also judges in the municipalities.

Religion. In 1992 there were 18·49m. Roman Catholics. There are 4 archbishops, 1 at Caracas, who is Primate of Venezuela, 2 at Mérida and 1 at Ciudad Bolívar. There are 19 bishops. In the state primary schools instruction is given only to those children whose parents expressly request it. Protestants number about 20,000.

Education. In 1987–88 there were 13,500 primary schools with 115,000 teachers and 2,900,000 pupils, 2,000 secondary schools with 63,000 teachers and 1,100,000 pupils.

In 1995–96 there were in the public sector 16 universities, 1 polytechnic university and 1 open (distance) university; and in the private sector, 12 universities, 2 Roman Catholic universities and 1 technological university.

Health. In 1983 there were 21,502 doctors and 43,650 beds in hospitals and dispensaries in 1979.

DIPLOMATIC REPRESENTATIVES

Of Venezuela in Great Britain (1 Cromwell Rd., London, SW7)
Ambassador: Vacant.

Of Great Britain in Venezuela (Torre Las Mercedes, Avenida La Estancia, Chuao, Caracas 1060)
Ambassador: John Flynn, CMG.

Of Venezuela in the USA (1099 30th St., NW, Washington, D.C., 20007)
Ambassador: Pedro Luís Echeverria.

Of the USA in Venezuela (Avenida Francisco de Miranda and Avenida Principal de la Floresta, Caracas)
Ambassador: Jeffrey Davidow.

Of Venezuela to the United Nations
Ambassador: Dr Enrique Tejera-Paris.

Further Reading

Dirección General de Estadística, Ministerio de Fomento, *Boletín Mensual de Estadística.—Anuario Estadístico de Venezuela.* Caracas, Annual
Ewell, J., *Venezuela: A Century of Change.* London, 1984
Hellinger, D.V., *Tarnished Democracy.* Boulder (Colo.), 1991
Lombard, J., *Venezuelan History: A Comprehensive Working Bibliography.* Boston, 1977.—*Venezuela: The Search for Order, the Dream of Progress.* OUP, 1982
Martz, J. D. and Myers, D. J., *Venezuela: The Democratic Experience.* New York, 1986
Naim, M., *Paper Tigers and Minotaurs: the Politics of Venezuela's Economic Reforms.* Washington (DC), 1993

VIETNAM

Công Hòa Xã Hôi Chu Nghĩa Viêt Nam

(Socialist Republic of Vietnam)

Capital: Hanoi
Population: 74m. (1995)
GNP per capita: US$190 (1994)
HDI/world rank: 0·539/120 (1992)

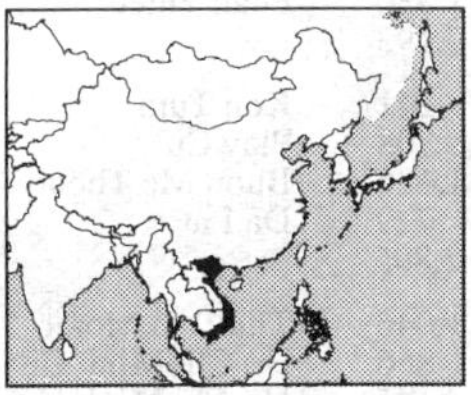

KEY HISTORICAL EVENTS. Conquered by the Chinese in B.C. 111, Vietnam broke free from Chinese domination in 939, though at many subsequent periods it was a nominal Chinese vassal. (For subsequent history until the cessation of hostilities with the US in Jan. 1973 *see* THE STATESMAN'S YEAR-BOOK, 1989–90).

After the US withdrawal, hostilities continued between the North and the South until the latter's defeat in 1975. A Provisional Revolutionary Government established an administration in Saigon. A general election was held on 25 April 1976 for a National Assembly representing the whole country. Voting was by universal suffrage of all citizens of 18 or over, except former functionaries of South Vietnam undergoing 're-education'. The unification of North and South Vietnam into the Socialist Republic of Vietnam took place formally on 2 July 1976.

TERRITORY AND POPULATION. Vietnam is bounded in the west by Cambodia and Laos, north by China and east and south by the South China Sea. It has a total area of 329,566 sq. km and is divided into 53 provinces grouped in 7 regions. Areas and populations (in 1,000):

Province/*Region*	*Sq. km*	*Census, 1989*	*Estimate, 1992*	*Capital*
Lai Chau	17,140	438	482	Lai Chau
Son La	14,210	682	754	Son La
Lao Cai [1]	8,050		515	Lao Cai
Yen Bai [1]	6,802		617	Yen Bai
Hoa Binh [1]	4,612		699	Hoa Binh
Ha Giang [2]	7,831	1,026	506	Ha Giang
Tuyen Quang [2]	7,801		614	Tuyen Quang
Cao Bang	8,445	566	614	Cao Bang
Lang Son	8,167	611	656	Lang Son
Bac Thai	6,503	1,033	1,119	Thai Nguyen
Quang Ninh	5,939	814	874	Hai Duong
Vinh Phu	4,836	1,806	2,164	Viet Tri
Ha Bac	4,614	2,061	2,222	Bac Giang
North Mountain and Midland	102,949	11,909	11,823	
Hanoi [3]	921	3,057	2,106	Hanoi
Ha Tay [3]	2,153		2,170	
Hai Phong	1,504	1,448	1,542	Hai Phong
Hai Hung	2,552	2,440	2,612	Hai Duong
Thai Binh	1,524	1,632	1,738	Thai Binh
Nam Ha [4]	2,419	3,157	2,531	Nam Ha
Ninh Binh [4]	3,387		819	Ninh Binh
Red River Delta	12,457	11,734	13,518	
Thanh Hoa	11,168	2,991	3,233	Thanh Hoa
Nghe An [5]	16,381	3,582	2,623	Vinh
Ha Tinh [5]	6,054		1,265	Ha Tinh
Quang Binh [6]	7,983	1,995	716	Dong Hoi
Quang Tri [6]	4,592		505	Dong Ha
Thua Thien (Hue) [6]	5,009		945	Hue
Central North Region Coast	51,187	8,568	9,287	

[1] Created mainly from former Hoang Lien Song province (1,032,000 inhabitants in 1989) and Ha Son Binh province (1,840,000 inhabitants in 1989). [2] Created by division of former Ha Tuyen province. [3] Ha Tay province created from Hanoi province. [4] Created by division of former Ha Nam Ninh province. [5] Created by division of former Nghe Tinh province. [6] Created by division of former Binh Tri Thien province.

Province/*Region*	*Sq. km*	*Census, 1989*	*Estimate, 1992*	*Capital*
Quang Nam (Da Nang)	11,988	1,739	1,811	Da Nang
Quang Ngai [7]	5,856	2,288	1,120	Quang Ngai
Binh Dinh [7]	6,076		1,137	Quy Nhon
Phu Yen [8]	5,223	1,463	689	Tuy Hoa
Khanh Hoa [8]	5,258		897	Nha Trang
Ninh Thuan [9]	3,430	1,170	438	
Binh Thuan [9]	7,992		830	Phan Thiet
Central Coast of North Region	45,823	6,660	7,193	
Kon Tum [10]	9,934	873	241	Kon Tum
Gia Lai [10]	15,662		708	Play Cu
Dac Lat	19,800	974	1,126	Buon Me Thoat
Lam Dong	10,173	639	729	Da Lat
Central Highlands	55,569	2,486	2,805	
Song Be	9,546	939	1,046	Thu Dau Mot
Tay Ninh	4,024	791	856	Ho Chi Minh City
Thanh Pho Ho Chi Minh	2,090	3,934	4,145	Ho Chi Minh City
Dong Nai [11]	5,865		1,721	Bien Hoa
Ba Ria (Vung Tau) [11]	1,957		637	Ba Ria
North Eastern South Region	23,481	7,807	8,406	
Long An	4,338	1,121	1,197	Tan An
Dong Thap	3,276	1,337	1,433	Cao Lamh
Tien Giang	2,339	1,484	1,591	My Tho
Ben Tre	2,246	1,214	1,285	Ben Tre
Tra Vinh [12]	2,247	1,812	924	Tra Vinh
Vinh Long [12]	1,487		1,025	Vinh Long
An Giang	3,424	1,793	1,896	Long Xuyen
Can Tho [13]	3,054	2,682	1,739	Can Tho
Soc Trang [13]	3,107		1,152	Soc Trang
Kien Giang	4,243	1,198	1,299	Rach Gia
Minh Hai	7,689	1,562	1,681	Bac Lieu
Mekong River Delta	39,575	14,203	15,221	

[7] Created by division of former Nghia Binh province. [8] Created by division of former Phu Khahn province. [9] Created by division of former Thuan Hai province. [10] Created by division of former Gai Lai-Kon Tum province. [11] The existing province of Dong Nai (7,585 sq. km with 2,007,000 population in 1989) and the special area of Vung Tau-Con Dao (237 sq. km with 136,000 population in 1989) were reorganized into the 2 new provinces of Dong Nai and Ba Ria-Vung Tau. [12] Created by division of former Cuu Long province. [13] Created by division of former Hau Giang province.

At the 1989 census the population was 64,411,713 (20·1% urban); density, 195 per sq. km.

Estimated population (1992), 69,306,000 (33,555,000 females; 20·2% urban); (1995), 74m. density, 209·4 per sq. km. (Ho Chi Minh 4m.; Hanoi, 2m. (1979); growth rate (1992) 2·47% per annum. Infant mortality per 1,000 live births was 36 in 1992. Expectation of life was 67 years in 1992. Sanctions are imposed on couples with more than two children.

Cities with over 0·2m. inhabitants at the 1989 census: Ho Chi Minh City (3,169,135), Hanoi (1,088,862), Haiphong (456,049), Da Nang (370,670), Long Xuyen (217,171), Nha Trang (213,687), Hue (211,085), Can Tho (208,326).

87% of the population are Vietnamese (Kinh). There are also 53 minority groups thinly spread in the extensive mountainous regions. The largest minorities are: Tay, Khmer, Thai, Muong, Nung, Meo, Dao. The USA in Jan. 1990 began the phased immigration of some 94,000 families of former South Vietnamese soldiers and officials.

In 1975–84 554,000 illegal emigrants ('boat people') succeeded in finding refuge abroad. By 1989 there were 57,000 'boat people' in camps in Hong Kong, and the UK government announced it would embark on a programme of mandatory repatriation. In 1991 and 1992 Vietnam and the UK signed agreements providing for the forcible return of almost all the 55,700 'boat people' remaining. (For a fuller account *see* THE STATESMAN'S YEAR-BOOK, 1992-93, p. 1593). Following the lifting of the US trade embargo in Feb. 1994 the UN began phasing out its special treatment of 'boat people'. By the end of 1995, 37,000 'boat people' remained in Hong Kong and other south-east Asian countries' camps, and 75,000 had been repatriated. Vietnam agreed to accept the return of all of them in 1996.

CLIMATE. The humid monsoon climate gives tropical conditions in the south, with a rainy season from May to Oct., and sub-tropical conditions in the north, though real winter conditions can affect the north when polar air blows south over Asia. In general, there is little variation in temperatures over the year. Hanoi. Jan. 62°F (16·7°C), July 84°F (28·9°C). Annual rainfall 72" (1,830 mm).

CONSTITUTION AND GOVERNMENT. The National Assembly unanimously approved a new constitution on 15 April 1992. Under this the Communist Party retains a monopoly of power and the responsibility for guiding the state according to the tenets of Marxism-Leninism and Ho Chi Minh, but with certain curbs on its administrative functions. The powers of the National Assembly are increased. The 395-member *National Assembly* is elected for 5-year terms. Candidates may be proposed by the Communist Party or the Fatherland Front (which groups various social organizations), or they may propose themselves as individual Independents. The Assembly convenes 3 times a year and appoints a prime minister and cabinet. It elects the *President*, the head of state. The latter heads a *State Council* which issues decrees when the National Assembly is not in session.

President (titular head of state): Gen. Le Duc Anh (b. 1920; elected Sept. 1992).
Vice-President: Nguyen Thi Dinh (b. 1927; elected Sept. 1992).

At the National Assembly elections of 19 July 1992 the electorate was 37·41m. There were 601 candidates (90% Communists).

The ultimate source of political power is the Communist Party of Vietnam, founded in 1930; it had 3m. members in 1995. Its Politburo in Oct. 1995 consisted of Do Muoi (b. 1917; *Secretary General)*; Gen. Le Duc Anh; Vo Kan Kiet; Gen. Dao Dui Tung; Gen. Doan Khue; Pham The Duyet; Vo Tran Chi; Le Phuoc Tho; Buy Thien Ngo; Nguyen Duc Binh; Nong Duc Manh; Phan Van Khai; Vu Oanh; Gen. Le Kha Phieu; Nguyen Manh Cam; Do Quang Thang; Nguyen Ha Phan.

In Oct. 1995 the government comprised:
Prime Minister: Vo Van Kiet (b. 1923).
First Deputy Prime Minister: Phan Van Khai.
Deputy Prime Ministers: Nguyen Kanh, Tran Duc Luong. *Foreign:* Nguyen Manh Cam. *Defence:* Gen. Doan Khue. *Interior:* Buy Thien Ngo. *Head of State Planning Commission:* Do Quoc Sam. *Justice:* Nguyen Dinh Loc. *Finance:* Ho Te. *Commerce and Tourism:* Le Van Triet. *Heavy Industry:* Tran Lum. *Head, State Inspectorate:* Nguyen Ky Cam. *Head, Ethnic Minorities and Mountain Region Commission:* Hoang Duc Nghi. *Population and Family Planning:* Mai Ky. *Governor of the State Bank:* Cao Si Kiem. *Labour, War Invalids and Social Affairs:* Tran Dinh Hoan. *Construction:* Ngo Xuan Loc. *Communications and Transport:* Buy Danh Luu. *Energy:* Thai Phung Ne. *Light Industry:* Dang Vu Chu. *Agriculture:* Nguyen Cong Tan. *Forestry:* Nguyen Quang Ha. *Water Conservation:* Nguyen Canh Dinh. *Marine Products:* Nguyen Tan Trinh. *Culture and Information:* Tran Hoan. *Health:* Nguyen Trong Nhan. *Education and Training:* Tran Hong Quan. *Children:* Tran Thi Thanh. *Without Portfolio:* Phan Van Tiem, Ha Quang Du.
Speaker of the National Assembly: Nong Duc Manh.

National flag: Red, with a yellow 5-pointed star in the centre.
National anthem: 'Doàn quân Viêt Nam di chung lòng cúú quôc' ('Soldiers of Vietnam, we are advancing'); words and tune by Van Cao.

Local Government is administered by people's councils, which appoint executive committees. Local elections were held with the National Assembly elections in July 1992.

DEFENCE. Men between 18 and 35 and women between 18 and 25 are liable for conscription of 2 years, specialists 3 years. Since 1989 troops have been permitted to engage in economic activity.

Army. There are 8 military regions and 2 special areas. The Army consists of 14 corps headquarters, 50 infantry, 3 mechanized, 8 engineer and 10 to 16 economic construction divisions, 10 armoured, 10 field artillery and 20 independent engineer brigades and 15 independent infantry regiments. Special forces include an airborne brigade and a demolition engineer regiment. Equipment includes some 1,000 T-34/-54/-55, 200 T-62 and 100 Chinese Type-59 and M-48A3 main battle tanks. Strength, (1996), 0·5m. Paramilitary forces number 4·5m. and consist of the Peoples' Self-Defence Force (urban), a People's Militia (rural) and a rear force (reserves).

Navy. The fleet currently includes 5 ex-Soviet 'Petya' class frigates, 2 ex-US frigates (built 1943 and 1944), 2 ex-Soviet missile corvettes, 8 Soviet-built fast missile craft, 16 fast torpedo craft, 3 patrol hydrofoils, 28 inshore patrol craft, 4 coastal and 7 inshore minesweepers, 7 landing ships, and some 20 smaller amphibious craft.

In 1995 personnel were estimated to number 12,000 plus an additional Naval Infantry force of 30,000.

Air Force. The Air Force, built up with Soviet and Chinese assistance, had (1995) about 15,000 personnel and 190 combat aircraft and 33 armed helicopters. There are reported to be 3 squadrons of variable-geometry MiG-23s, 6 squadrons of Su-22s, 150 MiG-21 interceptors; An-2, An-24 and An-26 transports; and a strong helicopter force with Ka-25, Mi-6, Mi-8/17 and Mi-24 helicopters. The 15,000 strong air defence force is organized in 14 divisions and deploys 66 surface-to-air missile sites.

INTERNATIONAL RELATIONS

Membership. Vietnam is a member of the UN and ASEAN.

ECONOMY

Policy. Long-term forward planning gives priority to self-sufficiency in agriculture and stimulating regional industry. The fourth 5-year plan covered 1986–90.

Small family businesses were legalized in 1986, and a law of April 1991 sanctions and protects all private business.

A reform programme (*Doi Moi*) injecting free enterprise principles and reducing central control has been implemented. The 'Draft Strategy for Socio-Economic Stabilization and Development to 2000' aims to double GDP through the 'socialist-oriented commodity economy, a market economy under state management' in which the state and collective sectors will play a 'predominant role'.

The 1992 constitution embodies the market-oriented reforms of recent years, recognizing citizens' right to engage in private business. A bankruptcy law was passed in Jan. 1994.

Budget. Revenue in 1991 (in 1,000m. dong), 8,210; expenditure, 9,230.

Currency. The unit of currency is the *dong* (VND). A currency reform of 1985 substituted a new *dong* at a rate of 1 new *dong* = 10 (old) *dong*. There are notes of 100, 1,000, 2,000, 5,000, 10,000, 20,000 and 50,000 dong. In a currency reform of March 1989 the dong was brought into line with free market rates. The direct use of foreign currency was made illegal in Oct. 1994. Foreign exchange reserves were US$830m. at the end of 1995. Currency in circulation, 1991, 5,340,000m. dong. Inflation was 15% in 1995. Gold reserves were 98,300 troy oz. in June 1991. In March 1996, £1 = 16,831 dong; US$1 = 11,012 dong; DM1 = 7,462 dong.

Banking and Finance. The central bank and bank of issue is the National Bank of Vietnam (founded in 1951; *Governor*, Cao Si Kiem). There are 12 commercial banks (some private) normally specializing in one sector of the economy but also carrying out commercial banking. Vietcombank is the foreign trade bank. 18 foreign banks had branches in 1995.

ENERGY AND NATURAL RESOURCES

Electricity. Installed capacity in 1995 was 3,500 MW, of which 325 MW were hydroelectric. In 1990, 6,300m. kWh. of electricity were produced. A hydro-electric power station with a capacity of 2m. kW. was opened at Hoa-Binh in 1989.

Oil. Offshore exploration for oil near Da Nang started in 1989. Estimated crude oil production in 1992, 5·40m. tonnes.

Minerals. North Vietnam is rich in anthracite, lignite and hard coal: Total reserves are estimated at 20,000m. tonnes. Coal production was 4·8m. tonnes in 1992. There are deposits of iron ore, manganese, titanium, chromite, bauxite and a little gold. Reserves of apatite are some of the biggest in the world. 1992 output (in 1,000 tonnes): Sand, 13,260; limestone, 667; salt, 542.

Agriculture. Ownership of land is vested in the state, but since 1992 farmers may inherit and sell plots allocated on 20-year leases. In 1989 the Government abandoned virtually all its controls on the production and sale of agricultural produce, and switched to encouraging the household as the basic production unit. Peasants may market their produce, or deal through the co-operatives. Rice cultivation was deregulated in 1989.

Production in 1,000 tonnes in 1993: Coffee, 135; tea, 35; rubber, 76; coconut, 1,207; (1994) rice, 24,500. Other crops include sugar-cane and cotton.

Livestock, 1993 (in 1,000): Cattle 3,320; pigs, 14,861; goats, 300; poultry, 113m.

Livestock products (1993): Eggs, 115,000 tonnes; meat, 1,126,000 tonnes.

37,627 tractors were in use in 1992.

Forestry. In 1995, forests covered 9·2m. ha (13·5m. ha in 1943). It is planned to reafforest 0·2m. ha annually. Timber exports were prohibited in 1992. Timber production was 4,846,000 cu. metres in 1991. 24,679,000 cu. metres were cut for fuel.

Fisheries. In 1992 there were 32 fishing vessels over 100 GRT with a total tonnage of 13,956 GRT. Total catch, 1990, 0·85m. tonnes, of which 0·24m. tonnes were freshwater fish.

INDUSTRY. 1992 production (in 1,000 tonnes): Crude steel, 175·2; cement, 3,727; fertilizers, 507; sulphuric acid, 8; dyestuffs, 4·3; glass and glassware, 32·3; textile fibre, 42·5; processed fish, 627·4; sugar, 304; tea, 20·1; (in units): Bricks, 3,675m.; tiles, 410m.; machine tools, 2,316; hydraulic pumps, 500; threshing machines, 40,125; diesel motors, 3,300; ventilators, 257,000; batteries, 68m.; lamps, 9·6m.; textiles, 276m. metres; beer, 162·1m. litres; cigarettes, 1,524m. packets.

Labour. In 1991 the workforce (in 1,000) was 30,974, of whom in agriculture, 22,276; forestry, 207; manufacturing, 3,394; building, 820; transport, 480; communications, 46; trade, 1,749; services, 296; research, 49; education, 804; culture, 46; health, social welfare and sport, 310; finance, 118; public administration, 240. In 1993, 32% of the workforce was female. In 1991, 58% of the workforce worked in co-operatives, 31% in the private sector and 11% in the state sector. 0·6m. Vietnamese worked abroad. There were some 3m. unemployed in 1990.

FOREIGN ECONOMIC RELATIONS. In Feb. 1994 the USA lifted the trade embargo it had imposed in 1975. The EEC established relations in Oct. 1990. In 1991 Vietnam's total indebtedness was estimated at US$14,600. In 1978 the IMF approved a virtually interest-free loan of US$90m. repayable over 50 years, but in April 1985 suspended all further credits to Vietnam. Sweden has given annual aid of US$47m. The 1992 constitution regulates joint ventures with Western firms; full repatriation of profits and non-nationalization of investments are guaranteed. In 1992 there were 390 joint ventures with a total capital of US$2,973·7m. 34% of this was in industry, 25% in gas and oil exploitation and 20% in tourism. Foreign debt was US$19,600m. in 1994.

Commerce. Trade is conducted through the state import-export agencies. Value of exports in 1994, US$3,600m.; imports, US$5,000m. Main export markets in 1992 (in US$1m.): Japan, 912·5; Singapore, 502·5; Hong Kong, 275·3; Germany, 237·7; France, 119·5. Main import suppliers: Singapore, 881; Hong Kong, 281; Japan, 192; South Korea, 185; France, 158; Taiwan, 120. Main exports are coal, farm produce, sea produce and livestock. Imports: Oil, steel, artificial fertilizers. Following the removal of rice cultivation from state control, Vietnam moved from being a net importer of rice to the world's third largest exporter in 1989. Rice exports in 1992 were some 1·4m. tonnes, coal, 0·78m. tonnes (0·23m. in 1987), mainly to Japan and South Korea.

Trade between Vietnam and UK (British Department of Trade returns, in £1,000 sterling):

	1991	*1992*	*1993*	*1994*	*1995*
Imports to UK	6,440	11,921	22,104	66,389	106,943
Exports and re-exports from UK	6,916	21,373	16,950	62,915	60,442

Tourism. Since 1992 Vietnamese have been permitted to travel abroad freely with exit visas. There were 0·67m. visitors in 1993 and 1·02m. in 1994.

COMMUNICATIONS

Roads. In 1994 there were about 90,000 km of roads, of which 9,000 km were hard-surfaced. In 1994 there were 0·2m. 4-wheeled vehicles. 373·7m. passengers and 39·57m. tonnes of freight were transported in 1991.

Railways. Route length was 2,205 km of metre gauge and 172 km of 1,435 mm gauge in 1994, 80% of it narrow-gauge. Rail links with China were reopened in Feb. 1996. 20% of trains were steam-hauled in 1992. In 1994, 9m. passengers and 4m. tonnes of freight were carried.

Civil Aviation. There are international airports at Hanoi (Noi Bai) and Ho Chi Minh City (Tan Son Nhat) and 2 domestic airports. The national carrier is Vietnam Airlines, which operated 7 A320-200s, 1 B-767-200ER, 1 B-767-300ER, 23 ex-Soviet and 4 other aircraft in 1995. Services are also provided by Air France, British Airways, Cathay Pacific, Japan Airlines, KLM, Lufthansa and Qantas. 89,000 passengers (18,000 international) were flown in 1991.

Shipping. In 1995, sea-going vessels totalled 1·21m. GRT, including oil tankers, 0·19m. GRT. The major ports are Hai Phong, which can handle ships of 10,000 tons, Ho Chi Minh City and Da Nang. There are regular services to Hong Kong, Singapore, Thailand, Cambodia and Japan. 0·7m. passengers and 4·88m. tonnes of freight were carried in 1991. In 1987 there were some 6,000 km of navigable waterways. 120·2m. passengers and 16·36m. tonnes of freight were transported in 1991.

Telecommunications. Vietnam Posts and Telecommunications and the military operate telephone systems with the assistance of foreign companies. In 1994, telephone provision was 3·3 per 1,000 population. Broadcasting is controlled by the state Vietnam Radio and Television Committee. There are 2 national radio programmes from Hanoi and 1 from Ho Chi Minh City, 14 provincial programmes and an external service, the Voice of Vietnam (11 languages). There is a national and 2 provincial TV services. There were 6m. radio and 2·5m. TV sets in 1993 (colour by NTSC and SECAM).

Cinemas. 116 films were produced in 1980 (including 10 full-length).

Press. In 1994 there were some 350 newspaper and periodical titles. There are 2 national dailies, the Communist Party's *Nhan Dan* ('The People'), circulation, 0·2m., and the Army's *Quan Doi Nhan Dan*, 60,000. There are 3 major regional dailies with a combined circulation of 155,000. There were 10 titles in English, including 2 dailies in 1995. 3,043 book titles were published in 1991 totalling 62·4m. copies.

SOCIAL INSTITUTIONS

Justice. A new penal code came into force 1 Jan. 1986 'to complete the work of the 1980 Constitution'. Penalties (including death) are prescribed for opposition to the people's power, and for economic crimes. The judicial system comprises the

Supreme People's Court, provincial courts and district courts. The president of the Supreme Court is responsible to the National Assembly, as is the Procurator-General, who heads the Supreme People's Office of Supervision and Control.

Religion. Taoism is the traditional religion but Buddhism is widespread. At a Conference for Buddhist Reunification in Nov. 1981, 9 sects adopted a charter for a new Buddhist church under the Council of Sangha. The Hoa Hao sect, associated with Buddhism, claimed 1·5m. adherents in 1976. Caodaism, a synthesis of Christianity, Buddhism and Confucianism founded in 1926, has some 2m. followers. In 1992, there were 38·2m. Buddhists and 4·84m. Roman Catholics. There is an Archbishopric of Hanoi and 13 bishops. There were 2 seminaries in 1989. In 1983 the Government set up a Solidarity Committee of Catholic Patriots.

Education. Adult literacy was 88% in 1992. Primary education consists of a 10-year course divided into 3 levels of 4, 3 and 3 years respectively. In 1991–92 there were 16,076 primary schools with 11·8m. pupils and 389,000 teachers and 1,113 secondary and tertiary schools with 568,000 pupils and 35,100 teachers. In 1995–96 there were 7 universities, 2 open (distance) universities and 9 specialized universities (agriculture, 3; economics, 2; technology, 3; water resources, 1).

Health. In 1991 there were 1,550 hospitals with 118,100 beds, 10,710 medical centres with 73,500 beds and 115 sanatoria. There were 74,600 doctors, 68,300 nurses, 13,600 midwives and 12,400 pharmacists.

DIPLOMATIC REPRESENTATIVES

Of Vietnam in Great Britain (12–14 Victoria Rd., London, W8)
Ambassador: Huynh Ngoc An.

Of Great Britain in Vietnam (16 Pho Ly Thuong Kiet, Hanoi)
Ambassador: Peter Williams, CMG.

US-Vietnamese diplomatic relations were established on 11 July 1995.

Of Vietnam in the USA
Ambassador: Vacant.

Of the USA in Vietnam (7 Lang Ha, Ba Dinh District, Hanoi)
Ambassador: Vacant.

Of Vietnam to the United Nations
Ambassador: Ngo Quang Xuan.

Further Reading

Trade and Tourism Information Centre with the General Statistical Office. *Economy and Trade of Vietnam* [various 5-year periods]
Beresford, M., *National Unification and Economic Development in Vietnam.* London, 1989
Dellinger, D., *Vietnam Revisited.* Boston (Mass.), 1986
Ho Chi Minh, *Selected Writings, 1920–1969.* Hanoi, 1977
Karnow, S., *Vietnam: A History.* 2nd ed. London, 1992
Leitenberg, M. and Burns, R. D., *War in Vietnam.* 2nd ed. Oxford and Santa Barbara, 1982
Norlund, I. (ed.) *Vietnam in a Changing World.* London, 1994
Post, K., *Revolution, Socialism and Nationalism in Vietnam.* vol. 1. Aldershot, 1989
Smith, R. B., *An International History of the Vietnam War.* London, 1983

National statistical office: General Statistical Office, Hanoi.

BRITISH VIRGIN ISLANDS

Capital: Road Town
Population: 17,000 (1993)
GNP per capita: US$16,775 (1994)

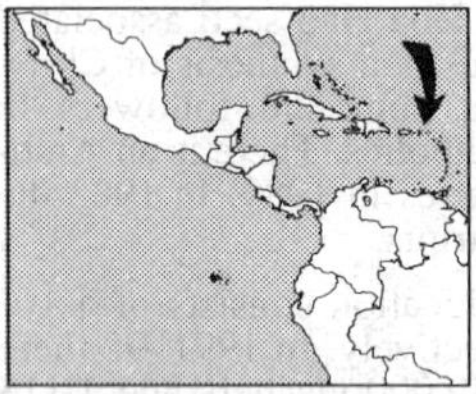

KEY HISTORICAL EVENTS. The Virgin Islands were discovered by Columbus on his second voyage in 1493. The British Virgin Islands were first settled by the Dutch in 1648 and taken over in 1666 by a group of English planters. In 1774 constitutional government was granted. The Islands became a largely self-governing dependent territory of the UK in 1967.

TERRITORY AND POPULATION. The British Virgin Islands form the eastern extremity of the Greater Antilles and number 70, of which 16 are inhabited. The largest, with population (1991 census), are Tortola, 13,568, Virgin Gorda, 2,495, Anegada, 156 and Jost Van Dyke, 141. Other islands had a total population (estimate 1990) of 183; marine population (estimate 1989), 124. Total area 59 sq. miles (130 sq. km); total population (1991 census), 16,749; (1993 estimate, 17,000). Road Town, on the south-east of Tortola, is a port of entry; population (estimate, 1991), 6,330.

CLIMATE. A pleasantly healthy sub-tropical climate with summer temperatures lowered by sea breezes. Nights are cool and rainfall averages 50" (1,250 mm).

CONSTITUTION AND GOVERNMENT. The Constitution dates from 1967 as amended in 1977 and 1994. The head of State is Queen Elizabeth II, represented by a *Governor* who is responsible for defence and internal security, external affairs, the public service, and the courts. The Executive Council consists of the Governor, the Chief Minister, the Attorney-General *ex officio* and 3 ministers. The ministers are appointed by the Governor. The *Legislative Council* consists of the 4 ministers, 5 directly elected members from constituencies and 4 members from 'at large' seats covering the territory as a whole. The Speaker is elected from outside the Council. At the elections of Feb. 1995 the Virgin Islands Party gained 6 seats, the Independent People's Movement, 3, the United Party, 2, and the Concerned Citizens' Movement, 2.

Governor: David P. MacKilligin, CMG.
Chief Minister: Ralph T. O'Neal (Virgin Islands Party; sworn in 25 May 1995).

Flag: The British Blue Ensign with the arms of the Territory in the fly is used for distinguishing purposes.

INTERNATIONAL RELATIONS

Membership. The Islands are an associate member of CARICOM and the Organization of Eastern Caribbean States.

ECONOMY

Budget. In 1994 revenue (estimate) was US$72·6m.; expenditure, US$65·5m.

Currency. The unit of currency is the US dollar.

Banking and Finance. Bank of Nova Scotia, Barclays Bank PLC, Chase Manhattan Bank NA, London International Bank and Trust Company Ltd, Guyerzeller Bank (BVI) Ltd, Banco Popular De Puerto Rico, Crorebridge Bank Ltd, Disa Bank BVI Ltd, Rathbone Bank (BVI) Ltd, Bank of East Asia (BVI) Ltd and VP Bank (BVI) Ltd hold valid banking licences. As of 14 Dec. 1995 total deposits recorded amounted to US$1,875m. There are a large number of trust companies providing financial services other than banking. Financial services are the most important industry after tourism.

ENERGY AND NATURAL RESOURCES

Electricity. Production, 1994, 74·9m. kWh.

Agriculture. In 1994: Total land suitable for agriculture, 5,324 acres; crops, 1,767 acrres and pastures, 3,557 acres. Agricultural production is limited, with the chief products being livestock (including poultry), fish, fruit and vegetables. Production, 1994, in tonnes: Fruits, 525; vegetables/root crop, 153; beef, 172; mutton, 29; pork, 39; and 1,535 cases of eggs.

Livestock (1994, in 1,000): Cattle, 3·5; pigs, 2·8; sheep, 5 and goats, 6.

INDUSTRY. The construction industry is a significant employer. There are a rum distillery, ice-making plants and cottage industries producing tourist items.

FOREIGN ECONOMIC RELATIONS

Commerce. There is a very small export trade almost entirely with the Virgin Islands of the USA. In 1993 imports were US$122·9m. and exports US$5·5m.

Total trade between the British Virgin Islands and UK (British Department of Trade returns, in £1,000 sterling):

	1991	*1992*	*1993*	*1994*	*1995*
Imports to UK	545	139	1,316	3,716	994
Exports and re-exports from UK	8,619	4,097	2,597	5,935	5,399

Tourism. Tourism is the most important industry and accounts for some 75% of economic activity. In 1993 there were 200,174 tourist arrivals, of whom 113,245 were cruise ship visitors and 46,217 day visitors. Total tourist expenditure for 1993 was US$186·4m.

COMMUNICATIONS

Roads. In 1994 there were 107 km of surfaced roads. In 1994 there were 6,265 registered vehicles on Tortola and 760 on Virgin Gorda.

Civil Aviation. Beef Island Airport, about 16 km from Road Town, is capable of receiving 80-seat short-take-off-and-landing jet aircraft. American Eagle and LIAT provide scheduled flights to Puerto Rico and the Eastern Caribbean.

Shipping. There is a deep water harbour at Port Purcell (Road Town). There are services to the Netherlands, UK, USA and other Caribbean islands, and daily services by motor launches to the US Virgin Islands.

Telecommunications. There were (1995) 9,282 telephones, 21 telex subscribers, 582 fax machine subscribers and an external telephone service links Tortola with Bermuda and the rest of the world. Radio ZBVI transmits 10,000 watts and British Virgin Islands Cable TV operates a cable system of 19 television channels and 8 pay-per-view channels.

Press. In 1994 there were 2 weekly newspapers and a periodical.

SOCIAL INSTITUTIONS

Justice. Law is based on UK common law. There are courts of first instance. The appeal court is in the UK.

Religion. There are Anglican, Methodist, Seventh-Day Adventist, Roman Catholic, Baptist, Pentecostal and other Christian churches in the Territory. There are also Jehovah's Witness and Hindu congregations.

Education. In 1994 adult literacy was 95%. Primary education is provided in 16 government schools, 3 with secondary divisions, and 16 private schools. Total number of pupils in primary and pre-primary schools (31 Dec. 1994) 2,855.

Secondary education to GCSE level and Caribbean Examination Council level is provided by the BVI High School and the secondary divisions of the schools on Virgin Gorda and Anegada. Total number of secondary level pupils (31 Dec. 1994) 1,363.

Government expenditure, 1994 (estimate), US$14m. In 1994 the total number of classroom teachers in all Government schools was 232. In 1986 a branch of the Hull University (England) School of Education was established.

Health. As of 31 Dec. 1995 there were 17 doctors, 67 nurses, 50 public hospital beds and 1 private hospital with 10 beds. Expenditure, 1994 (estimate) was US$5·3m.

Further Reading

Dookham, I., *A History of the British Virgin Islands.* Epping, 1975
Harrigan, N. and Varlack, P., *The Virgin Islands Story.* Road Town, 1975
Moll, V. P., *Virgin Islands.* [Bibliography] Oxford and Santa Barbara, 1991
Pickering, V. W., *Early History of the British Virgin Islands.* London, 1983

WESTERN SAMOA

Malo Tutoatasi o Samoa i Sisifo—Independent State of Western Samoa

Capital: Apia
Population: 163,000 (1994)
GNP per capita: US$970 (1994)
HDI/world rank: 0·651/102 (1992)

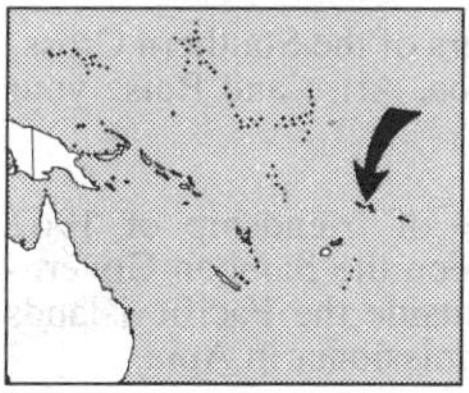

KEY HISTORICAL EVENTS. Western Samoa, a former German protectorate (1899–1914), was administered by New Zealand from 1920 to 1961, at first under a League of Nations Mandate and from 1946 under a UN Trusteeship Agreement. In May 1961 a plebiscite voted overwhelmingly in favour of independence on the basis of a Constitution which a Constitutional Convention had adopted in 1960. The UN terminated the trusteeship agreement as from 1 Jan. 1962, on which date Western Samoa became an independent sovereign state.

TERRITORY AND POPULATION. Western Samoa lies between 13° and 15° S. lat. and 171° and 173° W. long. It comprises the two large islands of Savai'i and Upolu, the small islands of Manono and Apolima, and several uninhabited islets lying off the coast. The total land area is 1,093 sq. miles (2,830·8 sq. km), of which 659·4 sq. miles (1,707·8 sq. km) are in Savai'i, and 431·5 sq. miles (1,117·6 sq. km) in Upolu; other islands, 2·1 sq. miles (5·4 sq. km). The islands are of volcanic origin, and the coasts are surrounded by coral reefs. Rugged mountain ranges form the core of both main islands. The large area laid waste by lava-flows in Savai'i is a primary cause of that island supporting less than one-third of the population of the islands despite its greater size than Upolu.

Population at the 1991 census, 161,298. The population at the 1986 census was 112,228 in Upolu (including Manono and Apolima) and 44,930 in Savai'i. The capital and chief port is Apia in Upolu (population 32,196 in 1986). Expectation of life was 66 years in 1989.

The official languages are Samoan and English.

CLIMATE. A tropical marine climate, with cooler conditions from May to Nov. and a rainy season from Dec. to April. The rainfall is unevenly distributed, with south and east coasts having the greater quantities. Average annual rainfall is about 100" (2,500 mm) in the drier areas. Apia. Jan. 80°F (26·7°C), July 78°F (25·6°C). Annual rainfall 112" (2,800 mm).

CONSTITUTION AND GOVERNMENT. HH Malietoa Tanumafili II is the sole Head of State for life. Future Heads of State will be elected by the Legislative Assembly and hold office for 5-year terms.

The executive power is vested in the *Head of State*, who swears in the Prime Minister (who is appointed by members of the Legislative Assembly) and, on the Prime Minister's advice, the Ministers to form the Cabinet. The Constitution also provides for a *Council of Deputies* of 3 members, of whom the chairman is the Deputy Head of State.

Before 1991 the 47-member *Legislative Assembly* was elected exclusively by *matai* (customary family heads). At the elections of April 1991 the suffrage was universal, but only the approximately 20,000 *matai* could stand as candidates. The electorate was 56,000. The Human Rights Protection Party won 30 seats, the Samoan National Development Party, 16 and an independent, 1.

Head of State: HH Malietoa Tanumafili II, GCMG, CBE.
Deputy Head of State: Mataafa Faasuamaleaui Puela.

The cabinet in March 1996 was composed as follows:

Prime Minister, Minister of Foreign Affairs, Broadcasting, Police and Prisons, Attorney General, Public Service Commission Public Relations and Official Information: Tofilau Eti Alesana.

Finance: Tuilaepa Sailele. *Agriculture:* Misa Telefoni. *Works:* Leafa Vitale. *Health:* Sala Vaimili. *Education:* Fiame Naomi. *Post Office and Telecommunications:* Toi Aukuso. *Lands and Environment:* Fasootauloa Pati. *Justice:* Fuimaono Lotomau. *Civil Aviation:* Jack Netzler. *Sport and Culture:* Pule Lameko. *Women's Affairs:* Polataivao Fosi.

National flag: Red with a blue quarter bearing 5 white stars of the Southern Cross.

National anthem: 'Samoa, tula'i ma sisi ia laufu'a/Samoa, Arise and Raise your Banner'; words and tune by S. I. Kuresa.

INTERNATIONAL RELATIONS. Under a treaty of friendship of 1962 New Zealand acts as the channel of communication between the Samoan Government and governments and international organizations outside the Pacific islands area. Liaison is maintained by the New Zealand High Commissioner in Apia.

Membership. Western Samoa is a member of the UN, the Commonwealth, the South Pacific Forum and is an ACP state of the EU.

ECONOMY

Budget. In 1989 budgeted revenue was $WS101·7m.; expenditure, $WS81·6m.

Currency. The unit of currency is the *tala* (WST) of 100 *sene.* There are coins of 1, 2, 5, 20 and 50 sene and 1 tala, and notes of 2, 5, 10, 20, 50 and 100 talas. In March 1996, £1 = 3.81 talas; US$1 = 2·50 talas; DM1 = 1·69 tala.

Banking and Finance. The Central Bank of Samoa (founded 1984) is the bank of issue.

ENERGY AND NATURAL RESOURCES

Electricity. Production (1995) 69m. kWh.

Agriculture. The main products (1993, in 1,000 tonnes) are coconuts (130), taro (37), copra (11), bananas (10), papayas (10), mangoes (5), pineapples (6) and cocoa beans (1, in 1991).

Livestock (1993): Horses, 3,000; cattle, 25,000; pigs, 178,000; poultry 1m. (1991).

Fisheries. The total catch (1983) was 3,150 tonnes, valued at 5·1m. talas.

INDUSTRY. Some industrial activity is being developed associated with agricultural products and forestry.

FOREIGN ECONOMIC RELATIONS

Commerce. In 1992, exports were valued at $WS44,384,000. Principal exports in 1994 were coconut cream ($WS3·82m.); beer ($WS1·19m.) and cigarettes ($WS0·8m.).

Total trade between Western Samoa and UK (British Department of Trade returns, in £1,000 sterling):

	1991	*1992*	*1993*	*1994*	*1995*
Imports to UK	16	12	23	12	16
Exports and re-exports from UK	671	471	1,297	1,115	567

Tourism. There were 47,007 visitors in 1994 (45,109 in 1993).

COMMUNICATIONS

Roads. In 1987 there were 2,085 km of roads, 400 km surfaced, and 1,200 km plantation roads. In 1993 there were 1,269 private cars, 1,936 pick-up trucks, 472 trucks, 334 buses, 936 taxis and 67 motor cycles.

Civil Aviation. There is an international airport at Apia (Faleolo). The national carrier is Polynesian Airlines, which in 1995 operated 1 B-737-300 and 1 other aircraft. Services are also provided by Air New Zealand and Air Pacific. Samoa Air provides domestic services to Upolu and Savai'i.

Shipping. Sea-going shipping totalled 6,501 GRT in 1995. Western Samoa is linked to Japan, USA, Europe, Fiji, Australia and New Zealand by regular shipping services.

Telecommunications. There are 3 radio communication stations at Apia. Radio telephone service connects Western Samoa with American Samoa, Fiji, New Zealand, Australia, Canada, USA and UK. Telephone subscribers numbered 3,452 in 1985. Broadcasting is the responsibility of the government-run commercial Western Samoa Broadcasting Department, which transmits radio programmes in Samoan and English. In 1991 there were 75,000 radio receivers and about 2,500 television sets.

Cinemas. In 1995 there were 3 cinemas.

Press. In 1989, there were 4 weeklies, circulation 12,000 and 2 monthlies (8,000); all were in Samoan and English.

SOCIAL INSTITUTIONS

Religion. At the 1991 census, 43% of the population were Congregationalist, 21% Roman Catholic, 17% Methodist, 10% Mormon and 3% Seventh Day Adventist.

Education. In 1991 the total number of pupils in primary, junior and secondary schools was 53,600. The University of the South Pacific School of Agriculture is in Western Samoa. A National University was established in 1984. In 1994–95 it had 614 students and 30 academic staff. The University of the South Pacific has a School of Agriculture at Apia.

Health. In 1994 there were 2 national hospitals, 14 district hospitals, 9 health centres and 22 subcentres. There were 44 doctors in 1990.

DIPLOMATIC REPRESENTATIVES

Of Western Samoa in Great Britain
High Commissioner: Afamasaga Faamatala Toleafoa (resides in Brussels).

Of Great Britain in Western Samoa
High Commissioner: Robert Alston, CMG (resides in Wellington)

Of the USA in Western Samoa
Ambassador: Josiah H. Beeman (resides in Wellington).

Of Western Samoa in the USA and to the United Nations (1115 15th St., NW, Washington D.C. 20005)
Ambassador: Tuiloma Neroni Slade.

Further Reading

Fox, J. W. (ed.) *Western Samoa.* Univ. of Auckland, 1963

YEMEN

Jamhuriya al Yamaniya

(Republic of Yemen)

Capital: Sana'a
Commercial capital: Aden
Population: 15·8m. (1995)
GNP per capita: US$280 (1994)
HDI/world rank: 0·424/137 (1992)

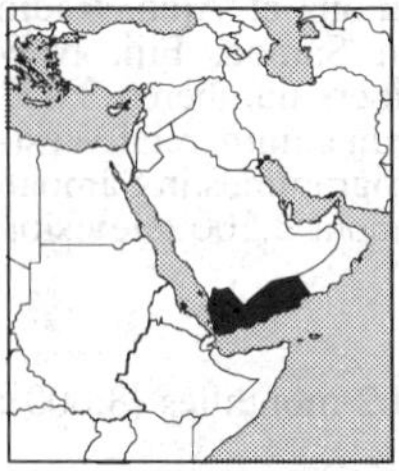

KEY HISTORICAL EVENTS. Following an agreement reached in Dec. 1989 on a constitution for a unified state, the (northern) Yemen Arab Republic and the (southern) People's Democratic Republic of Yemen were united as the Republic of Yemen on 22 May 1990.

In Aug. 1993 Vice-President Ali Salem Albidh withdrew to Aden and demanded the implementation of a reform programme as a condition of re-joining President Saleh in Sana'a. Albidh agreed to a modified reform programme at an agreement brokered by King Hussein of Jordan in Feb. 1994, but clashes between north and south escalated into full civil war at the beginning of May. Southern officials announced their secession from Yemen on 21 May 1994. Aden was captured by northern forces on 7 June 1994. The former vice-president and prime minister went into exile abroad.

TERRITORY AND POPULATION. Yemen is bounded in the north by Saudi Arabia, east by Oman, south by the Gulf of Aden and west by the Red Sea. The territory includes 112 islands including Kamaran (181 sq. km) and Perim (300 sq. km) in the Red Sea and Socotra (3,500 sq. km) in the Gulf of Aden. The island of Greater Hanish is claimed by both Yemen and Eritrea. On 15 Dec. 1995 Eritrean troops occupied it, and Yemen retaliated with aerial bombardments. A ceasefire was agreed at presidential level on 17 Dec. On 20 Dec. the UN resolved to send a good offices mission to the area. The area is 555,000 sq. km excluding the desert Empty Quarter (Rub Al-Khahi). A dispute with Saudi Arabia broke out in Dec. 1994 over some 1,500–2,000 km of undemarcated desert boundary. A memorandum of understanding signed on 26 Feb. 1995 reaffirmed the border agreement reached at Taif in 1934. An agreement of June 1995 completed the demarcation of the border with Oman.

The population was estimated at 15·8m. in 1995; density, 21 persons per sq. km. At the census of 1986 in the north and 1988 in the south the population was 9,664,939 (4,938,318 females; 1,793,861 urban). There were 1,168,199 citizens working abroad mainly in Saudi Arabia and the United Arab Emirates not included in the census total. Since 1990 Saudi Arabia has compulsorily repatriated almost all Yemeni workers. In 1988 there were 17 governorates:

	1986/88 census population		*1986/88 census population*
Sana'a (city)	427,502	Shabwah	192,324
Sana'a	1,237,016	Hajjah	720,000
Aden	326,919	Bayda	295,439
Ta'iz	1,419,708	Hadhramant	537,095
Hodeida	1,052,086	Sa'adah	323,124
Lahej	458,385	Mahwit	260,836
Ibb	1,254,128	Mahrah	44,225
Abyan	279,241	Marib	95,326
Dhamar	698,823	Jawf	42,762

The population of the capital, Sana'a, was estimated at 972,000 in 1995. The commercial capital is the port of Aden, with a population of (1995) 562,000. Other important towns are the port of Hodeida (population, 155,110), Mukalla (154,360), Ta'iz (178,043), Ibb and Abyan.

CLIMATE. A desert climate, modified by relief. Sana'a. Jan. 57°F (13·9°C), July

71°F (21·7°C). Aden, Jan. 75°F (24°C), July 90°F (32°C). Annual rainfall 20" (508 mm) in the north, but very low in coastal areas: 1·8" (46 mm).

CONSTITUTION AND GOVERNMENT. There is a 301-member *House of Representatives* which after the elections of April 1993 was composed of: General People's Congress (GPC), 123 seats; Islah, 62; Yemen Socialist Party, 56; ind, 47; others, 13.

On 28 Sept. 1994 the 302-member House of Representatives unanimously adopted a new constitution founded on Islamic law. This abolishes the former 5-member Presidential Council and instals a *President* elected by parliament for 5-year terms. Lieut.-Gen. Ali Abdullah Saleh was elected President on 1 Oct. 1994 and a new government was formed.

President: Ali Abdullah Saleh (GPC; sworn in 2 Oct. 1994).

Vice-President: Abd Rabbah Mansour Hadi.

In Oct. 1995 the government comprised:

Prime Minister: Lieut.-Gen. Abdalaziz Abdalghani (b. 1939; GPC). *Deputy Prime Minister:* Abdalwahab Al-Anisi (Islah). *Deputy Prime Minister and Minister of Foreign Affairs:* Dr Abdalkareem Al-Eryani (GPC). *Deputy Prime Minister and Minister for Industry, Oil and Minerals:* Dr Mohamed Saeed Al-Attar (GPC). *Deputy Prime Minister and Minister for Development and Planning:* Abdalkader Bajammal (GPC). *Minister of the Interior:* Hussein Mohamed Arab (GPC). *Finance:* Mohamed Ahmed Al-Gonaid (GPC). *Information:* Abdalrahman Al-Akwa'a (GPC). *Transport:* Ahmed Musaed Hussein (GPC). *Communications:* Ahmed Mohamed Al-Anisi (GPC). *Culture and Tourism:* Yahya Hussein Al-Arashi. *Social Security and Social Affairs:* Mohamed Abdallah Al–Battani (GPC). *Legal Affairs and Council of Deputies' Affairs:* Abdallah Ahmed Ghanem. *Civil Service and Administrative Reform:* Sadeq Amin Aburaas (GPC). *Commerce and Provisions:* Mohamed Ahmed Afandi (Islah). *Health:* Dr Nagib Ghanem (Islah). *Local Government:* Mohamed Hassan Dammai (Islah). *Religious Endowments:* Ghaleb Al-Kirshi (Islah). *Fisheries:* Abdalrahman Bafadhl (Islah). *Justice:* Abdalwahab Addailami (Islah). *Defence:* Abdalmalik Al-Sayyani (ind). *Agriculture:* Ahmed Salem Al-Gabali (GPC). *Housing and Urban Planning:* Ali Hameed Sharaf. *Sports and Youth:* Abdalwahab Raweh. *Education:* Abdo Ali Qubati (Islah). *Electricity and Water:* Abdullah Mohsen Al-Akwa'a (Islah).

The *Speaker* is Sheikh Abdullah Al-Ahmar (Islah).

National flag: 3 horizontal stripes of red, white and black.

National anthem: 'Raddidi Ayyatuha ad Dunya nashidi' ('Repeat, O World, my song'); words by A. Noman, tune by Ayub Tarish.

Local Government. The country is administratively divided into 27 governorates and the capital city.

DEFENCE. Conscription is for 3 years.

Army. The Army comprises 7 armoured, 18 infantry, 5 mechanized, 2 airborne commando, 5 militia, 4 artillery, 1 special forces and 1 surface-to-surface missile brigade. Equipment includes 250 T-34, 675 T-54/-55, 150 T-62 and 50 M-60A1 main battle tanks. Strength (1996) 37,000 (some 25,000 conscripts) with 39,500 reserves. There are paramilitary tribal levies numbering at least 20,000 and a Central Security Organization of 10,000.

Navy. The Navy comprises 5 ex-Soviet fast missile craft, 3 inshore patrol craft, 3 inshore minesweepers, 2 tank landing ships and 2 craft. Forces are based at Aden and Hodeida, with other facilities at Mokha, Mukalla and Perim. Personnel in 1995 were estimated at 1,500.

Air Force. The unified Air Forces of the former Arab Republic and People's Democratic Republic are now under one command, although this unity was broken by the attempted secession of the south in 1994 which resulted in heavy fighting between the air forces of Sana'a and Aden. The status of the Air Force now is not known. Prior to the civil war, it had about 60 MiG-21 fighters, 50 Su-22 attack aircraft, 15 Mi-24 gunship helicopters, 7 An-24 and 6 An-26 twin-turboprop transports, 15 other transports (including 2 C-130H Hercules) and about 40 Mi-8 and 12 other helicopters. Personnel (1993) about 3,000.

INTERNATIONAL RELATIONS

Membership. Yemen is a member of the UN and the Arab League.

ECONOMY

Policy. A 5-year plan is running from 1996 to 2000. It includes some privatization proposals.

Budget. Government revenue and expenditure (in 1,000 riyals):

	1990	*1991*	*1992*
Revenue			
Current	19,407,442	27,237,585	36,368,700
Tax	13,733,075	20,077,282	27,109,200
Services	500,702	522,434	988,700
State property	5,173,665	6,637,869	8,270,800
Capital	6,604,184	10,761,244	9,408,900
Loans and aid	2,070,848	4,853	3,177,500
Expenditure			
Administration, defence and social	...	40,301,813	49,573,916
Economic	...	3,768,042	8,539,684

There were no budgets in 1993 and 1994. Estimates for 1995: Revenue, 87,000m. riyals; expenditure, 124,100m. riyals.

Currency. The unit of currency is the *riyal* (YER) of 100 *fils*. There are notes of 1, 2, 5, 10, 20, 50 and 100 riyals. During the transitional period to north-south unification the northern *riyal* of 100 *fils* and the southern *dinar* of 1,000 *fils* coexisted. Inflation was an annualized 175% in 1995. There were 3 foreign exchange rates operating: an internal clearing rate, an official rate and a commercial rate. In 1996 the official rate was abolished. In March 1996, the commercial rate was £1 = 214 riyals; US$1 = 140 riyals; DM1 = 94·86 riyals.

Banking and Finance. Total assets of the Central Bank were 109,497m. riyals in 1992. There were 6,616m. riyals in savings deposits.
A stock exchange is scheduled to open in 1998.

ENERGY AND NATURAL RESOURCES

Electricity. Production (1992) 1,953m. kWh.

Oil and Gas. The first large-scale oilfield and pipeline was inaugurated in 1987. There are reserves of 2,000m. bbls on the former north-south border. Further major oil finds were announced in 1991. Estimated crude oil production (1992) 9·96m. tonnes. Gas reserves are some 7,000m. cu. metres.

Minerals. 107,000 tons of salt were produced in 1992. Reserves (estimate) 25m. tonnes. In 1992 647,000 cu. metres of stone and 77,898 tons of gypsum were extracted.

Agriculture. In 1992 the cultivable area was 1,630,972 ha, of which 1,040,254 ha were cultivated. In the south, agriculture is largely of a subsistence nature, sorghum, sesame and millet being the chief crops, and wheat and barley widely grown at the higher elevations. Cash crops include cotton. Fruit is plentiful in the north.

Owing to the meagre rainfall, cultivation is largely confined to fertile valleys and flood plains on silt. Irrigation schemes with permanent installations are in progress. Production (1993, in 1,000 tonnes): Wheat, 160; seed cotton, 14; sesame seeds, 11; millet, 60; maize, 75; sorghum, 465; barley, 66; pulses, 76; potatoes, 213; tomatoes, 204; onions, 61; watermelons, 120; melons, 35; alfalfa, 149,087 (1992); coffee, 9; dates, 22; grapes, 144; bananas, 62.

Livestock in 1993 (in 1,000): Cattle, 1,163; camels, 173; sheep, 3,715; goats, 3,297; poultry, 21m. Livestock produce, 1993 (in 1,000 tonnes): Meat, 124; milk, 155.

Fisheries. Fishing is a major industry. Total catch (1992) 86,514 tonnes.

INDUSTRY. In 1992 there were 211 industrial firms (142 private, 48 public, 13 mixed and 8 co-operative). 64 of these were producing foodstuffs, 50 chemicals and petroleum products, 27 textiles and leather goods and 27 metal goods. Output (in 1,000 tons), 1992: Edible oils, 102; flour, 247; cement, 820; cartons, 17; petrol, 947; fuel oil, 1,782; fuel gas, 160; jet fuel, 643; asphalt, 48.

Labour. In 1992 there were 30,381 industrial employees, of whom 13,139 were in the public sector. Unemployment was 36% at the end of 1993.

FOREIGN ECONOMIC RELATIONS. Foreign debt was US$7,800m. in 1992.

Commerce. Trade (in 1,000 riyals):

	1990	*1991*	*1992*
Exports	8,315,504	6,075,948	5,693,349
Imports	18,867,090	24,314,326	31,075,611

Main import suppliers, 1992 (in 1,000 riyals): USA, 2,858,220; UAE, 2,559,581; Saudi Arabia, 2,311,965; Japan, 2,172,044; UK, 1,713,618. Main export markets: USA, 1,396,053; Japan, 666,689; Germany, 470,723; Saudi Arabia, 268,769.

Cotton and fish are major exports, the largest imports being food and live animals. A large transhipment and entrepôt trade is centred on Aden, which was made a free trade zone in May 1991. Oil income (exports and concessions) was US$1,150m. in 1992.

Total trade between Yemen and the UK (British Department of Trade returns, in £1,000 sterling):

	1991	*1992*	*1993*	*1994*	*1995*
Imports to UK	16,770	56,871	16,065	5,081	4,113
Exports and re-exports from UK	65,572	78,409	85,484	74,177	66,825

Tourism. In 1992 72,164 tourists stayed 360,820 nights and spent 56,287,900 riyals.

COMMUNICATIONS

Roads. There were (1992) 7,264 km of roads, including 2,344 km paved. In 1992 there were 105,175 private cars, 35,472 taxis, 4,061 buses, 223,028 lorries and 20,423 motorcycles. In 1992 there were 9,267 road accidents with 1,290 fatalities.

Civil Aviation. There are international airports at Sana'a and Aden. There are 2 national carriers: The former southern state-owned Alyemda Yemen Airlines, which in 1995 operated 1 A310-300, 1 B-707-320C, 2 B-737-200C Advs and 2 other aircraft; and the former northern Yemenia Yemen Airways, 51% state-owned which had 1 A310-200, 3 B-727-200 Advs, 1 B-737-200 Adv and 2 other aircraft. Services are also provided by Aeroflot, Egyptair, Ethiopian Airlines, Gulf Air, KLM, Lufthansa, Qatar Airways, Royal Jordanian, Saudia, Sudan Airways and Syrian Airlines. 1·16m. passengers and 14·42m. tons of freight were handled in 1992.

Shipping. In 1995, sea-going shipping totalled 26,431 GRT, including oil tankers, 3,185 GRT. There are ports at Aden, Mokha, Hodeida, Mukalla and Nashtoon. 449,621 tons of cargo were discharged in 1992, and 7,697 tonnes of oil at the Ras Issa terminal.

Telecommunications. In 1992 there were 208 post offices. There were 131,655 telephones in 1992. Broadcasting is managed by the government-controlled Yemen Radio and Television Corporation. Programmes are transmitted from Sana'a and Aden. In 1993 there were 325,000 radio and 0·1m. TV receivers (colour by PAL and NTSC).

Cinemas. In 1992 there were 45 cinemas with 43,265 seats. Attendance was 8,319,805.

Press. In 1995 there were 3 daily (1 in English), 5 weekly and 4 monthly newspapers and 15 periodicals.

SOCIAL INSTITUTIONS

Justice. A civil code based on Islamic law was introduced in 1992.

Religion. In 1989 there were some 5·3m. Shiite and 5,925,000 Sunni Moslems.

Education. In 1991–92 there were 61 kindergartens (18 private) with 10,283 children and 645 teachers. There were 9,348 schools with 2,214,292 pupils (553,685 girls) and 63,670 teachers. There are universities at Sana'a (founded 1974) and Aden (1975). The former had 3,520 students, 330 academic staff and in 1994–95, the latter 4,800 and 470.

Health. In 1992 there were 75 hospitals with 8,150 beds, 370 health centres with 1,777 beds, 912 primary health units and 2 maternity centres. There were 3,065 doctors, 163 dentists and 231 pharmacists with 1,137 pharmacies.

DIPLOMATIC REPRESENTATIVES

Of Yemen in Great Britain (57 Cromwell Rd., London, SW7 2ED)
Ambassador: Dr Hussein Abdullah Al-Amri.

Of Great Britain in Yemen (129 Haddah Rd., Sana'a)
Ambassador: Douglas Scrafton.

Of Yemen in the USA (2600 Virginia Ave., NW, Washington, D.C., 20037)
Ambassador: Mohsin A. Alaini.

Of the USA in Yemen (Dhahr Himyar Zone, Sheraton Hotel District, POB 22347, Sana'a)
Ambassador: David G. Newton.

Of Yemen to the United Nations
Ambassador: Abdalla Saleh Al-Ashtal.

Further Reading

Central Statistical Organization. *Statistical Year Book*
Bidwell, R., *The Two Yemens.* Boulder and London, 1983
El Mallakh, R., *The Economic Development of the Yemen Arab Republic*. London, 1986
Ismael, T. Y. and Ismael, J. S., *The People's Democratic Republic of Yemen.* London, 1986
Smith, G. R., *The Yemens.* [Bibliography] Oxford and Santa Barbara, 1984

National statistical office: Central Statistical Organization, Ministry of Planning and Development

YUGOSLAVIA

Capital: Belgrade
Population: 10·51m. (1994)

Savezna Republika Jugoslavija

(Federal Republic of Yugoslavia)

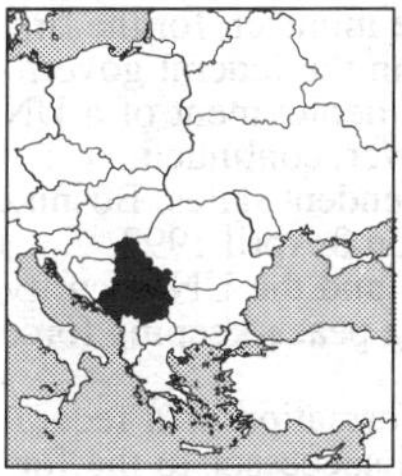

KEY HISTORICAL EVENTS. In 1917 the Yugoslav Committee in London drew up the Pact of Corfu, which proclaimed that all Yugoslavs would unite after the first world war to form a kingdom under the Serbian royal house. The Kingdom of Serbs, Croats and Slovenes was proclaimed on 1 Dec. 1918. In 1929 the name was changed to Yugoslavia. During the Second World War Tito's partisans set up a provisional government which was the basis of a Constituent Assembly after the war. On 29 Nov. 1945 Yugoslavia was proclaimed a republic.

The peace treaty with Italy, signed in Paris on 10 Feb. 1947, stipulated the cession to Yugoslavia of the greater part of the Italian province of Venezia Giulia, the commune of Zara and the island of Pelagosa and the adjacent islets.

By an agreement of 10 Nov. 1975 the city of Trieste ('Zone A') was recognized as Italian and the Adriatic coastal portion of the former Free Territory of Trieste ('Zone B') as Yugoslav.

Dissensions in Kosovo between Albanians and Serbs, and in parts of Croatia between Serbs and Croats brought inter-ethnic tensions into prominence after 1988. With the election of new national assemblies in all 6 republics during 1990, several of the latter came increasingly into conflict with the federal government. At the end of 1990 both Croatia and Slovenia proclaimed their right to secede from federal Yugoslavia.

In May 1991, following escalating Serb-Croat violence and demands for secession from predominantly Serb-inhabited areas of Croatia, the federal army was given powers to restrict the movement of unofficial armed groups. On 12 May the Krajina area held a self-styled referendum resulting, it was claimed, in an overwhelming vote for union with Serbia. Croatia rejected the poll.

On 15 May 1991 Croatia's representative in the state presidency, Štipe Mesić, failed to secure the 5 votes needed to become president in the annual election, hitherto a mere formality. Serbia, Kosovo and Vojvodina voted against and Montenegro abstained, leaving Yugoslavia without a head of state.

On 25 June Croatia and Slovenia made declarations of independence. On 27 June federal forces moved into Slovenia to secure Yugoslavia's external frontiers. An EC mission presented a 3-point peace plan, viz. that Mesić should be elected president, Slovenia and Croatia should suspend their declarations of independence for 3 months, and federal forces should leave Slovenia. The first points were agreed on 30 June, but attempts by federal troops to leave with their tanks were alleged by Slovenia to contravene the truce terms and blocked. On 2 July federal forces launched another attack to rescue these beleaguered troops, and there were also clashes between federal and Croatian forces. Fighting continued during the summer in Croatia between Croatian forces and Serb irregulars from predominantly Serbian areas of Croatia backed by federal forces. All federal forces eventually left Slovenia by July 1991.

On 25 Sept. the UN Security Council imposed a mandatory arms embargo on Yugoslavia.

By Oct. fighting had broken out again. On 4 Oct. the Serbian and Croatian presidents met the EC negotiators at The Hague and came to an agreement recognizing

Croatia's independence within a loose Yugoslav confederation as a basis for peace, but despite this and several other ceasefire attempts fighting continued.

The 3-month moratorium agreed at the EC peace talks on 30 June having expired, both Slovenia and Croatia declared their complete independence from the Yugoslav federation on 8 Oct.

In Oct. the EC put forward a plan for the orderly dissolution of the Yugoslav federation which Serbia rejected. The 12 EC foreign ministers then issued an ultimatum that trade sanctions would be imposed if any republic did not comply with the plan by 5 Nov., which Serbia again rejected. Sanctions on the whole of Yugoslavia were applied from 8 Nov., but restricted to Serbia after 2 weeks.

After 13 ceasefires had failed to be observed, a fourteenth was signed on 23 Nov. by the presidents of Croatia and Serbia and the federal defence minister, for the first time under UN auspices. Following a request on 26 Nov. from the federal government, a Security Council resolution of 27 Nov. proposed the deployment of a UN peace-keeping force if the ceasefire were kept. Fighting, however, continued.

On 15 Jan. the EC recognised Croatia and Slovenia as independent states. Bosnia-Hercegovina was recognized on 7 April 1992 and Macedonia on 8 April 1993.

A UN delegation began monitoring the ceasefire on 17 Jan. and the UN Security Council on 21 Feb. voted unanimously to send a 14,000-strong peace-keeping force to Croatia and Yugoslavia.

On 27 April 1992 Serbia and Montenegro announced the formation of a federal republic of Yugoslavia constituted by themselves as the legal successor to the former Socialist Federal Republic of Yugoslavia (SFRY).

On the grounds of continuing Serbian military activities in Bosnia and Croatia on 30 May the UN Security Council voted the imposition of sanctions. These involved a total ban on trade, the suspension of air links, the withdrawal of diplomats, the seizure of financial assets and the cancellation of sporting and cultural exchanges.

In mid-1992 WEU countries began to commit air, sea and eventually land forces to enforce sanctions and protect humanitarian relief operations in Bosnia.

At a joint UN-EC peace conference on Yugoslavia held in London on 26–27 Aug. some 30 countries and all the former republics of Yugoslavia endorsed a plan to end the fighting in Croatia and Bosnia, instal UN supervision of heavy weapons, recognize the borders of Bosnia-Hercegovina and return refugees. At a further conference at Geneva on 30 Sept. the Croatian and Yugoslav presidents agreed to make efforts to bring about a peaceful solution in Bosnia, but fighting continued.

On 22 Sept. the UN resolved (by 127 votes to 6 with 26 abstentions) that the self-proclaimed Federal Republic of Yugoslavia of Serbia and Montenegro could not automatically assume the seat of the former SFRY and excluded it from the General Assembly.

On 16 Nov. the UN Security Council voted for sanctions against Yugoslavia to be made more effective, and NATO and the WEU agreed to lend naval support to their enforcement.

Further peace talks were held in Geneva in Jan. 1993, and transferred to the UN in Feb. On 22 Feb. the UN Security Council resolved to set up a war crimes tribunal for alleged violations of human rights in the former SFRY. A court was inaugurated at The Hague on 17 Nov. 1993. The Chief Prosecutor and his office began work in Aug. 1994. The tribunal is funded subject to review, and in 1995 was merged into the International Penal Tribunal for Yugoslavia and Rwanda sitting at The Hague.

Following the Serbian President Milošević's announcement that Yugoslavia would no longer send supplies to Bosnian Serbs and would accept international monitors on its borders, on 24 Sept. 1994 the UN Security Council lifted the non-trade sanctions against Yugoslavia affecting civil aviation, culture and sport.

TERRITORY AND POPULATION. Yugoslavia is bounded in the north by Hungary, north-east by Romania, east by Bulgaria, south by Macedonia and Albania, and west by the Adriatic Sea, Bosnia-Hercegovina and Croatia. Area, 102,173 sq. km. Population (1991 census), 10,394,026 (5,236,906 females). Population density, 101·7 per sq. km. Estimate, 1994, 10,513,710.

Yugoslavia is a federation of 2 republics: Montenegro and Serbia and 2 former autonomous provinces within Serbia: Kosovo and Metohija, and Vojvodina. The federal capital is Belgrade (Beograd). Population (1991 census) of principal towns:

Belgrade	1,168,454	Subotica	100,386
Novi Sad	179,626	Zrenjanin	81,316
Nis	175,391	Pančevo	72,793
Kragujevac	147,305	Smederevo	63,884
Podgorica	117,875	Leskovac	62,053

The 1991 census was not carried out in Kosovo and Metohija. 1991 estimated population: Priština, 108,083; Prizren, 92,303; Peć, 68,163; Kosovska Mitrovica, 64,323.

Ethnic groups at the 1991 census: Serbs, 6,504,048; Albanians, 1,714,768; Montenegrins, 519,766; Hungarians, 344,147; Moslems, 336,025; Gypsies, 143,519; Croats, 111,650; Slovaks, 66,863; Macedonians, 47,118; Romanians, 42,364; Bulgarians, 26,922; Valachians, 17,810; Turks, 11,263. At the 1981 census, 239,756 nationals worked abroad.

Vital statistics, 1994: Births, 138,980; deaths, 105,757; marriages, 59,596; divorces, 6,498. Rates, 1994 (per 1,000 population): Births, 13·2; death, 10·1; marriage, 5·7; growth, 3·2; infant mortality, 18·9 (per 1,000 live births). Expectation of life in 1993: Males, 69·1; females, 74·5.

The official language is Serbian, the Eastern variant (Croatian is the Western) of Serbo-Croat, which was regarded as constituting one language in the Socialist Federal Republic of Yugoslavia. Serbian is written in the Cyrillic alphabet. There are also substantial Albanian and Hungarian-speaking minorities.

CLIMATE. Most parts have a central European type of climate, with cold winters and hot summers. Belgrade. Jan. 4·3°C, July 22·5°C. Annual rainfall 590 mm. Podgorica, Jan. 7·5°C, July 28·7°C. Annual rainfall 1,460 mm.

CONSTITUTION AND GOVERNMENT. The head of state is the *Federal President*, elected by both chambers of the federal parliament. Zoran Lilić was elected unopposed on 25 June 1993.

The federal parliament consists of 2 chambers: The *Chamber of the Republics* has 40 members, 20 each elected from the assemblies of Montenegro and Serbia. Its assent is necessary to all legislation. The *Chamber of Citizens* has 138 members, elected by universal suffrage.

At the elections to the Chamber of Citizens on 31 May 1992 turn-out was 56·62%. The Socialist Party of Serbia (SPS; former Communists) gained 73 seats, the Radical Serb Party 33, the Montenegrin Socialist Democratic Party (SDP; former Communists) 23, the Democratic Hungarian Community of the Vojvodina 2, the League of Communists-Movement for Yugoslavia 2 and others 3.

Federal President: Zoran Lilić (b. 1954).

In Jan. 1996 the government comprised:

Prime Minister: Radoje Kontić (b. 1936; SPS).

Deputy Prime Ministers: Jovan Zebić (*and Finance*) Nikola Sainović (*and Economy*); Uroš Klikovac (*and Justice*). *Foreign Minister:* Milan Milutinović. *Interior:* Vukašin Jokanović. *Defence:* Pavle Bulatović. *Trade:* Djordje Siradović. *Transport and Communication:* Zoran Vujović. *Labour, Health and Social Affairs:* Miroslav Ivanišević. *Development, Science and Environment:* Janko Radulović. *Information:* Dragutin Brčin. *Agriculture:* Kiviljko Lovre. *Sport:* Zoran Bingulac. *Human and Minority Rights:* Margit Savović. *Without portfolio:* Tomislav Rajičević, Vuk Ognjanović. *Government Secretary-General:* Mladen Vukčevič.

The *Speaker* is Radoman Božović (SPS).

National flag: Three horizontal stripes of blue, white and red in the proportions 1:2.

National anthem: 'Hej, Slaveni, jošte živi reč naših dedova' ('O Slavs, our ancestors' words still live'); words by S. Tomašik, tune anonymous.

Local Government. Within the federal framework of republics Yugoslavia is administratively divided into 29 districts, 210 communes, 7,401 localities, 233 urban localities and 4,819 local communities.

DEFENCE. Military service for 12 to 15 months is compulsory.

Army. The Army comprises 3 tank, 7 motorized infantry, 6 artillery, 1 anti-tank artillery, 8 mechanized, 1 airborne and 1 special forces brigades, 9 air defence and 5 surface-to-air missile regiments and 2 task forces. Equipment includes 407 T-54/-5 and 232 M-84 main battle tanks. Personnel (1996) were about 90,000 (37,000 conscripts).

Navy. The Navy comprises 4 small diesel submarines, 5 midget submarines, 2 Soviet and 2 locally built missile-armed frigates, 9 fast missile craft, 4 fast torpedo craft, 6 inshore patrol craft, 4 inshore minesweepers and 18 small landing craft. Auxiliaries include 3 transports and 1 headquarters ship.

The Air Force operates 4 Mi-14, 4 Ka-25 Hormone and 2 Ka-27 Helix anti-submarine helicopters. A Marine force of 900 is divided into 2 'brigades'.

Personnel in 1995 totalled 6,000 including Coastal Defence and Marines. The force is based at Kotor.

Air Force. There are 2 fighter divisions equipped primarily with about 100 Russian-built MiG-21s and 15 MiG-29s, 2 ground-attack divisions of locally-built Jastreb and Orao jet attack aircraft, and 2 squadrons of Jastreb jet reconnaissance aircraft. Transport units fly An-26 twin-engined aircraft, 4-turboprop An-12s, and a few other types in small numbers, notably CL-215 amphibians, Turbo-Porters and Yak-40s, Falcon 50s and Learjets for VIP duties. Training types are the nationally-designed UTVA-75 primary trainer, Galeb jet basic trainer and the Super Galeb jet advanced trainer. About 120 Gazelle, Agusta-Bell 205 and Mi-8 helicopters are in service. 'Guideline' and 'Goa' surface-to-air missiles have been supplied by the USSR. Personnel (1995) 29,000 (3,000 conscripts), with 282 combat aircraft and 110 armed helicopters.

INTERNATIONAL RELATIONS. Relations with Croatia were established in Jan. 1994 with the opening of mutual representative offices.

Membership. The former Yugoslavia (SFRY) was a member of the UN but its self-proclaimed successor state (Federal Republic of Yugoslavia) is excluded from the General Assembly, while retaining access to other bodies.

ECONOMY

Budget. The federal budget for 1994 was set at 1,673,433,931 dinars; 76·6% of expenditure was on defence.

Currency. The unit of currency is the *new dinar* (YUD) of 100 *para.* There are notes of 1, 5, 10 and 20 dinars. The currency became convertible on 1 Jan. 1990 and a new 'heavy' dinar was introduced worth 10,000 old dinars. Following the creation of the Croatian dinar on 23 Dec. 1991 the National Bank on 25 Dec. issued new dinars replacing the former notes of denominations of 100, 500, 1,000 and 5,000 dinars. The dinar was devalued by 80% in Jan. and by 85% in July 1992, when another new dinar was introduced pegged to the US dollar. By 1993 hyper-inflation had set in, with notes of up to 10,000m. dinars being issued. The dinar was devalued in June 1993 in line with unofficial prices, and by 98·65% in Nov. 1993, pegged at 0·7m. dinars = US$1. On 24 Jan. 1994 a new convertible 'super-dinar' was introduced equivalent to 1,000m. previous dinars, at parity with, and pegged to, the Deutschmark. This was devalued by 69·7% in Nov. 1995. Foreign exchange reserves were 225,130m. dinars in 1992. In March 1996, £1 = 7·46 dinars; US$1 = 4·88 dinars; DM1 = 94·86 dinars.

Banking and Finance. The National Bank is the bank of issue (*Governor*, Dragoslav Avramović (b. 1920). There are also republican banks. A reform programme which started in Feb. 1989 has transformed banks into shareholding companies, empowers the National Bank to impose solvency ratios on financial institutions and strengthens its control of the money supply. Total assets of commercial banks at the end of 1992, 12,827,870m. dinars. There is a stock exchange at Belgrade.

Weights and Measures. The metric weights and measures have been in use since 1883. The *wagon* of 10 tonnes is used as a unit of measure for coal, roots and corn. The Gregorian calendar was adopted in 1919.

ENERGY AND NATURAL RESOURCES

Electricity. Output in 1994, 35,328m. kWh, of which 24,201m. kWh were thermal and 11,127m. kWh hydro-electric.

Oil and Gas. Crude oil production (1994), 1,078,000 tonnes; natural gas, 824 cu. metres.

Minerals. Lignite production (1994), 37·74m. tonnes; coal, 38,351,000 tonnes; brown coal, 529,000 tonnes; copper ore, 17,935,000 tonnes.

Agriculture. In 1994 there were 6,243,000 ha of agricultural land, of which 3,729,000 ha were arable (2,504,000 ha cereals; 307,000 ha industrial crops), 0·79m. ha meadow and 1,327,000 ha pasture. 4,777,000 ha of land were in private farms and 1,466,000 ha in agricultural organizations. The economically active agricultural population was 1,061,488 in 1994.

Crop production, 1994 (in 1,000 tonnes): Maize, 4,724; sugar beet, 2,238; wheat, 3,249; potatoes, 844; grapes, 464; plums, 430; soya beans, 83.

Livestock, 1994 (in 1,000): Cattle, 1,809m.; pigs, 3,693; sheep, 2,635m.; horses, 82; poultry, 22,111.

Livestock products, 1994: Meat, 504,000 tonnes; milk, 1·84m. litres; wool, 3,928,000 tonnes; eggs, 1,464m. 174,337,000 litres of wine were produced in 1994.

Forestry. Forest area, 1993, 2,858,000 ha, of which 1,341,000 ha were in private hands. 3·11m. cu. metres of timber were cut in 1994.

Fisheries. In 1994 the landings of fish were (in tonnes): Salt-water, 264; freshwater, 6,229.

INDUSTRY. In Sept. 1995 there were 217,654 enterprises, including 152,854 private enterprises, 644 public enterprises, 4,701 co-operatives and 3,395 social enterprises.

Industrial output (in 1,000 tonnes) in 1994: Pig-iron, 17; crude steel, 137; steel castings, 18; tractors, 4,500 units; lorries, 698 units; passenger cars, 8,400 units; sugar, 210; TV sets, 40,000 units; refrigerators, 41,000 units; cement, 1,612; sulphuric acid, 24; artificial fertilizers, 291; plastics, 17.

Labour. In 1994 there were 2,178,000 workers in the social sector, including 895,000 in industry, 267,000 in trade, catering and tourism, 175,000 in education and culture, 147,000 in transport and communications, 90,000 in communities and organizations, 104,000 in agriculture, 83,000 in commercial services. In the private sector there were 355,700 self-employed and employed, including 43,196 in arts and crafts, 52,961 in catering and tourism, 27,098 in transport and communications, 135,286 in trade. In Sept. 1995 there were 784,000 unemployed. Average monthly wage in Sept. 1995 was 283 dinars.

FOREIGN ECONOMIC RELATIONS. In joint ventures the foreign partner may own up to 98% of the equity. 379 foreign-owned companies were operating in 1992.

UN sanctions against Yugoslavia were lifted in Nov. 1995 following the Bosnian-Croatian-Yugoslav (Dayton) agreement on Bosnia.

Commerce. Foreign trade, in US$1m., for calendar years:

	1989	*1990*	*1991*	*1992*
Imports	5,383	7,460	5,548	3,859
Exports	4,461	5,816	4,704	2,539

Exports, 1992 (in US$1m.): Manufactures and minerals (including machinery, 117; transport equipment, 130; electrical goods, 155; chemicals, 129; iron and steel, 123; textiles, 45; leather goods, 4); agricultural produce, 225; other, 24. Imports:

Transport equipment, 195; electrical goods, 212; machinery, 354; agricultural produce, 178; foodstuffs, 186.

Main trading partners, 1992 (exports and imports in US$1m.): Germany, 683 and 483; CIS, 321 and 242; Italy, 393 and 255; USA, 141 and 110.

Total trade between Yugoslavia and UK (British Department of Trade returns, in £1,000 sterling):

	1991	*1992*	*1993*	*1994*	*1995*
Imports to UK	147,876	123,797	2	44	560
Exports and re-exports from UK	193,836	123,061	3,652	4,253	9,970

Tourism. In 1994, 906,000 foreign tourists (156,000 from former Yugoslav republics) spent 11·79m. nights.

COMMUNICATIONS

Roads. In 1994 there were 48,961 km of roads comprising 6,477 km of main roads, 12,590 km of regional roads and 29,894 km of local roads. In 1994 there were 1,903,149 registered motor vehicles, including 1,731,444 private cars, 92,874 lorries and (1993) 13,133 buses. Passenger-km, 1994, 3,371m.; tonne-km of freight carried, 910m. There were 2,031 deaths in road accidents in 1993.

Railways. In 1993 there were 3,960 km of railway, of which 1,341 km were electrified. In 1994, 26,472,000 passengers and 4,738,000 tonnes of freight were carried.

Civil Aviation. There are 5 airports, the chief at Belgrade and Podgorica. The national carrier is JAT (Jugoslovenski Aero Transport) which in 1995 operated 6 B-727-200 Advs, 5 B-737-300s and 16 other aircraft. In 1992, 876,000 passengers and 4,873 tonnes of freight were carried.

Shipping. In 1994 Yugoslavia possessed 27 sea-going passenger vessels and 26 cargo vessels totalling 432,000 GRT.

Length of navigable waterways (1994), 588 km. In 1994 there were 530 cargo vessels and 2·77m. tonnes of freight were transported.

Telecommunications. There were 1,606 post offices and 2,315,000 telephones in 1994. Alongside the state-run Serbian Radio and Television and Montenegrin Radio and Television there were 3 independent radio and TV networks in 1993. The state-run Kosovar Radio and Kosovar Television broadcast a few hours a week in Albanian. In 1994 there were 77 broadcasting and 7 TV stations. There were 2·39m. TV and 1,412,000 radio receivers in use in 1994.

Cinemas. In 1994 there were 137 cinemas. 7 full-length films were made. Attendances in 1994: Cinema, 1,491,000.

Press. In 1994 there were 16 dailies with a circulation of 296,156,000, 520 other newspapers and 411 periodicals. 2,799 book titles (412 by foreign authors) were published in 1994 in a total of 11,975,000 copies.

SOCIAL INSTITUTIONS

Justice. In 1994 there were 2 supreme courts, 32 district courts and 153 communal courts, with 2,242 judges and 9,601 lay assessors. There were also 19 economic courts with 263 judges.

In 1994, 38,976 criminal sentences were passed.

Religion. Religious communities are separate from the State and are free to perform religious affairs. All religious communities recognized by law enjoy the same rights.

Serbia has been traditionally Orthodox. Moslems are found in the south as a result of the Turkish occupation. The Serbian Orthodox Church with its seat in Belgrade has 27 bishoprics within the boundaries of former Yugoslavia and 12 abroad (5 in the USA and Canada, 5 in Europe and 2 in Australia). The Serbian Orthodox Church numbers about 2,000 priests. Its *Patriarch* is Pavle (enthroned 22 May 1994).

The Serbian Orthodox Church is the official church in Montenegro, the

Montenegrin church having been banned in 1922, but in Oct. 1993 a breakaway Montenegrin church was set up under its own patriarch.

Relations with the Vatican are regulated by a 'Protocol' of 1966.

The Moslem Religious Union has Superiorates in Podgorica and Priština.

The Jewish religion has 9 communities making up a common league of Jewish Communities with its seat in Belgrade.

Education. Compulsory primary education lasts 8 years, secondary 3–4 years. In 1994 there were 1,674 nursery schools with 166,586 pupils and 17,657 teachers. In 1993–94 there were 4,420 primary schools with 914,585 pupils and 51,575 teachers and 544 secondary schools with 334,616 pupils and 26,271 teachers. There were 53 institutions of tertiary education with 26,542 students and 1,617 teachers and 91 institutes of higher education with 115,045 full-time students and 9,896 academic staff.

Health. In 1993 there were 20,690 doctors, 4,278 dentists, 2,209 pharmacists and 57,307 hospital beds.

Social Security. In 1994 there were 1,194,750 pensioners, including 461,103 age, 445,463 disability and 288,184 widowed pensioners. 13,259,269 working days were lost through sickness. In 1994 health expenditure totalled 1,978,915,000 dinars, age, 796,836,000 dinars and disability, 627,656,000 dinars. In 1994, 207m. dinars were paid in child allowances.

DIPLOMATIC REPRESENTATIVES

Of Yugoslavia in Great Britain (5 Lexham Gdns., London, W8 5JJ)
Ambassador: Vacant.

Of Great Britain in Yugoslavia (46 Generala Ždanova, Belgrade)
Ambassador: Vacant.

Of Yugoslavia in the USA (2410 California St., NW, Washington, D.C., 20008)
Chargé d'affaires: Zoran Popović.

Of the USA in Yugoslavia (Belgrade)
Ambassador: Vacant.

Of Yugoslavia to the United Nations
Ambassador: Vacant.

Further Reading

Federal Statistical Office. *Statistički godišnjak Jugoslavije*, annual since 1954 with a separate volume of captions and editorial matter in English; *Statistical Yearbook of Yugoslavia*; *Statistical Pocket-Book of Yugoslavia*, annual since 1955; *Statistics of Foreign Trade of the Federal Republic of Yugoslavia*, annual since 1946.

Banac, I., *The National Question in Yugoslavia*. Cornell Univ. Press, 1985

Bennett, C., *Yugoslavia's Bloody Collapse: Causes, Course and Consequences*. Farnborough, 1995

Cohen, L. J., *Broken Bonds: the Disintegration of Yugoslavia*. Boulder (CO), 1993

Dedijer, V., *et al., History of Yugoslavia*. New York, 1974

Djilas, A., *The Contested Country: Yugoslav Unity and Communist Revolution, 1919–1953*. Harvard Univ. Press, 1991

Djilas, M., *Memoir of a Revolutionary*. New York, 1973.—*Rise and Fall*. London, 1985

Friedman, F. (ed.) *Yugoslavia: a Comprehensive English-Language Bibliography*. London, 1993

Garde, P., *Vie et Mort de la Yougoslavie*. Paris, 1992

Glenny, M., *The Fall of Yugoslavia*. London, 1992

Horton, J. J., *Yugoslavia*. [Bibliography] Oxford and Santa Barbara, 1978

Magaš, B., *The Destruction of Yugoslavia: Tracking the Break-up, 1980–92*. London, 1993

Singleton, F., *Twentieth Century Yugoslavia*. London, 1976.—*A Short History of the Yugoslav Peoples*. CUP, 1985

Tito, J. B., *The Essential Tito*. New York, 1970

Woodward, S. L., *Balkan Tragedy: Chaos and Dissolution after the Cold War*. Brookings Institution (Washington), 1995

Zimmerman, W., *Open Borders, Non-Alignment and the Political Evolution of Yugoslavia.* Princeton Univ. Press, 1987

National statistical office: Federal Statistical Office, Kneza Miloša 20, Belgrade. *Director:* Milovan Živković.

REPUBLICS AND PROVINCES

In Dec. 1992 the new self-styled Federal Republic of Yugoslavia comprised the 2 republics of Montenegro and Serbia, and the 2 formerly autonomous provinces of Kosovo and Metohija, and Vojvodina within Serbia.

Each republic has its own constitution and parliament.

MONTENEGRO

KEY HISTORICAL EVENTS. Montenegro emerged as a separate entity on the break-up of the Serbian Empire in 1355. It was never effectively subdued by Turkey. It was ruled by Bishop Princes until 1851, when a royal house was founded. The remains of King Nicholas I, who was deposed in 1918, were returned to Montenegro for reburial in Oct. 1989.

TERRITORY AND POPULATION. Montenegro is a mountainous region which opens to the Adriatic in the south-west. It is bounded in the west by Croatia, north-west by Bosnia-Hercegovina, in the north-east by Serbia and in the south-east by Albania. The capital is Podgorica (population, 1993 estimate, 135,000). Its area is 13,812, sq. km. Population at the 1991 census was 615,035, of which the predominating ethnic groups were Montenegrins (380,467), Moslems (89,614), Serbs (57,453) and Albanians (40,415). Population density per sq. km, 45. Estimate, 1994, 630,925.

Vital statistics:

	Live births	*Marriages*	*Deaths*	*Growth rate per 1,000*
1992	9,524	4,041	4,393	8·3
1993	8,922	3,873	4,471	7·1
1994	8,887	3,753	4,660	6·7

CONSTITUTION AND GOVERNMENT. There is an 85-member single-chamber National Assembly. At the second round of the presidential elections on 10 Jan. 1993 Momir Bulatović (b. 1956; Socialist) was re-elected against one opponent with 63·3% of votes cast. Parliamentary elections were held on 20 Dec. 1992.

A referendum was held on 29 Feb.–1 March 1992 to determine whether Montenegro should remain within a common state, Yugoslavia, as a sovereign republic. The electorate was 412,000, of whom 66% were in favour.

Prime Minister: Milo Djukanović (b. 1962).

ECONOMY

Agriculture. In 1994 the cultivated area was 186,067 ha. Yields (in 1,000 tonnes): Wheat, 13·6; maize, 12·9; potatoes, 48·8. Livestock in 1994 (1,000 head): Cattle, 173; sheep, 430; pigs, 22. Timber cut in 1994: 591,138 cu. metres.

Industry. Production (1994): Electricity, 1,998m. kWh; lignite, 1,194,000 tonnes; 1993: Bauxite, 101,929 tonnes; 1992: Pig-iron, 4,024 tonnes; cotton, 4·98m. sq. metres.

Labour. Population of working age (males, 15–64 years; females, 15–59), 1993: 399,977 (190,948 females). Non-agricultural workforce, 216,491 (84,850 females) at the 1991 census.

SERBIA

KEY HISTORICAL EVENTS. The Serbs received Orthodox Christianity from the Byzantines. They threw off the latter's suzerainty to become a large prosperous medieval state, which was destroyed by the Turks at the Battle of Kosovo in 1389. After revolutions in 1804 and 1815 Serbia won increasing degrees of autonomy from Turkey; complete independence came with the Treaty of Berlin in 1878. Its prince took the title of king in 1881.

TERRITORY AND POPULATION. Serbia is bounded in the north-west by Croatia, in the north by Hungary, in the north-east by Romania, in the east by Bulgaria, in the south by Macedonia and in the west by Albania, Montenegro and Bosnia-Hercegovina. It includes the 2 provinces (formerly autonomous) of Kosovo and Metohija in the south and Vojvodina in the north. With these Serbia's area is 88,361 sq. km; without, 55,968 sq. km. The capital is Belgrade. Population at the 1991 census was (with Kosovo and Vojvodina) 9,778,991, of which the predominating ethnic group was Serbs (6,446,595). Population density per sq. km: 111; (without Kosovo and Vojvodina) 5,824,211, of which the predominating ethnic group was Serbs (5,108,682). Population density per sq. km, 104. Estimate, 1994 (with Kosovo and Vojvodina), 9,884,657; (without) 5,809,245.

Vital statistics *(without Kosovo and Vojvodina):*

	Live births	*Marriages*	*Deaths*	*Growth rate per 1,000*
1992	64,828	34,271	65,569	–0·1
1993	65,913	33,338	67,131	–0·2
1994	63,698	33,338	65,493	–0·3

CONSTITUTION AND GOVERNMENT. In Sept. 1990 a new constitution was adopted by the National Assembly. It defines Serbia as a 'democratic' instead of a 'socialist' republic, lays down a framework for multi-party elections, and describes Serbia as 'united and sovereign on all its territory', thus stripping Kosovo and the Vojvodina of the attributes of autonomy granted by the 1974 federal constitution.

There is a 250-member single-chamber National Assembly. At the elections on 20 Dec. 1992 Slobodan Milošević was re-elected *President* of Serbia with 56·32% of the votes cast against 34·05% for Milan Panić, the then prime minister.

Parliamentary elections were held on 19 Dec. 1993. The electorate was 7·1m. The Serbian Socialist Party (former Communist) gained 123 seats, the Democratic Opposition of Serbia (DEPOS) 45, the Serbian Radical Party 39, the Democratic Party 29, the Democratic Party of Serbia 7, the Democratic Community of Hungarians in the Vojvodina 5, Albanian parties' coalition 2.

ECONOMY [1]

Agriculture. In 1994 the cultivated area was 4,688,894 ha. Yields (in 1,000 tonnes): Wheat, 3,236; maize, 4,711; potatoes, 785; sugar-beet, 2,238; plums, 421; grapes, 437. Livestock in 1994 (in 1,000): Cattle, 1,777; sheep, 2,241; pigs, 4,170. Timber cut in 1994: 2,500,105 cu. metres.

Industry. (1994): Electricity, 29,464m. kWh.; lignite, 30,259,000 tonnes; steel, 40,000 tonnes; copper ore, 17,935,000 tonnes; lorries, 669 units; cars, 7,639 units; sulphuric acid, 21,806 tonnes; plastics, 13,821 tonnes; cement, 0·92m. tonnes; sugar, 25,853 tonnes; cotton fabrics, 24,282 sq. metres.

Labour. Population of working age (males, 15–64 years; females, 15–59), 1993, 6,243,225 (2,964,496 females). Non-agricultural workforce, 3,131,208 (1,209,436 females) at the 1991 census.

[1] Figures include Kosovo and Vojvodina.

KOSOVO AND METOHIJA

KEY HISTORICAL EVENTS. Following Albanian-Serb conflicts the Kosovo and Serbian parliaments adopted constitutional amendments in March 1989 surrendering much of Kosovo's autonomy to Serbia. Renewed Albanian rioting broke out in 1990. The Prime Minister and 6 other ministers resigned in April 1990 over ethnic conflicts. In July 1990, 114 of the 130 Albanian members of the National Assembly voted for full republican status for Kosovo, but the Serbian National Assembly declared this vote invalid and unanimously voted to dissolve the Kosovo Assembly. Direct Serbian rule was imposed. The *President* is Hisen Kajdomci.

TERRITORY AND POPULATION. Area: 10,887 sq. km. The capital is Priština. The 1991 census was not taken. Population estimate, 1991, 1,956,196 (1,596,072 Albanians, 194,190 Serbs); density, 179·7 per sq. km. Estimate, 1994, 2,079,234; density, 191 per sq. km.

Vital statistics:

	Live births	*Marriages*	*Deaths*	*Growth rate per 1,000*
1992	44,418	13,367	8,004	18·1
1993	44,132	13,372	7,804	17·8
1994	43,450	11,959	7,667	17·2

ECONOMY

Agriculture. The cultivated area in 1994 was 400,459 ha. Yields in 1994 (in 1,000 tonnes): Wheat, 289; maize, 228; potatoes, 75·9; plums, 15·5; grapes, 43·1. Livestock in 1994 (in 1,000): Cattle, 423; sheep, 389; pigs, 84; poultry, 2,528. Timber cut in 1994, 219,926 cu. metres.

Industry. Production (1994): Electricity, 3,800m. kWh; lignite, 6,287,000 tonnes; sulphuric acid (1993), 1,550 tonnes; cement, 22,000 tonnes.

Labour. Population of working age, 1991, 1,058,522 (512,716 females). Non-agricultural workforce, 1993, 127,000 (38,000 females).

VOJVODINA

TERRITORY AND POPULATION. Area: 21,506 sq. km. The capital is Novi Sad. Population at the 1991 census, 2,013,889 (1,143,723 Serbs, 339,491 Hungarians). Density, 93·6 per sq. km. Estimate, 1994, 1,996,178; density, 92·8 per sq. km.

Vital statistics:

	Live births	*Marriages*	*Deaths*	*Growth rate per 1,000*
1992	22,049	11,884	27,906	−2·9
1993	22,018	11,462	27,990	−3·0
1994	21,595	11,048	27,518	−3·0

CONSTITUTION AND GOVERNMENT. The 1990 Serbian constitution deprived Vojvodina of its autonomy. Serbo-Croat was declared the only official language in 1991. In March 1993 the provincial assembly comprised 7 members of the Socialist Party of Serbia and 5 of the Serbian Radical Party. The *Prime Minister* was Boško Perošević.

ECONOMY

Agriculture. The cultivated area in 1994 was 1,643,083 ha. Yields (in 1,000 tonnes): Wheat, 1,716; maize, 2,657; potatoes, 202; sugar-beet, 1,987. Livestock in 1994 (in 1,000): Cattle, 221; sheep, 297; pigs, 1,640; poultry, 8,354. Timber cut in 1994: 583,753 cu. metres.

Industry. Production (1994): Electricity, 92m. kWh; crude petroleum, 1,069 tonnes; sulphuric acid, 1,050 tonnes; plastics, 3,629 tonnes; cement, 0·67m. tonnes.

Labour. Population of working age, 1991, 1,273,356 (608,146 females). Non-agricultural workforce, 1993, 458,000 (202,000 females).

ZAÏRE

République du Zaïre

Capital: Kinshasa
Population: 43·8m. (1994)
GNP per capita: US$220 (1990)
HDI/world rank: 0·384/143 (1992)

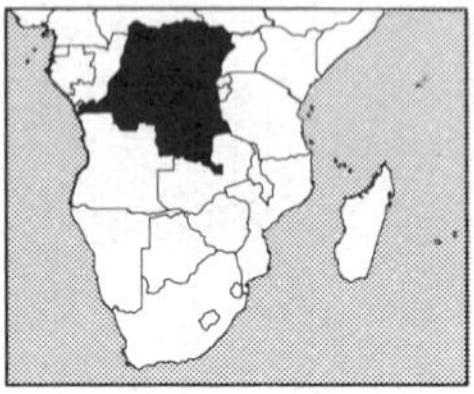

KEY HISTORICAL EVENTS. When the explorer Henry Stanley reached the mouth of the Congo in 1877, King Leopold II of the Belgians took the lead in exploring and exploiting the Congo Basin. The Berlin Conference of 1884–85 recognized King Leopold II as the sovereign head of the Congo Free State.

In 1908 the country was annexed to Belgium as the Belgian Congo, until the country became independent on 30 June 1960. The country's name was changed from Congo to Zaïre in Oct. 1971. For subsequent history to 1977 *see* THE STATESMAN'S YEAR-BOOK, 1980–81, p. 1613.

Following a week of rioting and looting by unpaid soldiers and discontented citizens at the end of Sept. 1991, President Mobutu agreed that the political opposition should form a government. Further rioting took place at the beginning of 1993, and dissensions appeared between the president and the government.

TERRITORY AND POPULATION. Zaïre is bounded north by the Central African Republic, north-east by Sudan, east by Uganda, Rwanda, Burundi and Lake Tanganyika, south by Zambia, south-west by Angola, north-west by Congo. There is a 37-km Atlantic coastline separating Angola's province of Cabinda from the rest of that country.

The area is estimated at 2,344,885 sq. km (905,365 sq. miles). At the 1984 census the population was 29,671,407 (44% urban). A further census in 1988 gave a figure of 34·7m. Estimate (1995) 43,814,000 (29·1% urban). Population growth rate, 1984, 3%. Infant mortality, 1995, 93 per 1,000 live births. Life expectancy, 1995: Males, 50 years; females, 53·2.

Area, populations (1991 estimate) and chief towns of the regions:

Region	*Area (sq. km)*	*Population (in 1,000)*	*Chief town*	*Population*
Bandundu	295,658	4,817	Bandundu (Banningville)	96,841 [2]
Bas-Zaïre	53,920	2,485	Matadi	172,926
Equateur	403,293	4,312	Mbandaka (Coquilhatville)	165,623
Haut-Zaïre	503,239	5,073	Kisangani (Stanleyville)	373,397
Kasai Occidental	156,967	2,982	Kananga (Luluabourg)	371,862
Kasai Oriental	168,216	3,338	Mbuji-Mayi (Bakwanga)	613,027
Kinshasa City	9,965	3,804	Kinshasa (Leopoldville)	3,804,000
Kivu [1]	256,662	6,728	Bukavu (Costermansville)	209,566
Shaba	496,965	5,207	Lubumbashi (Elizabethville)	739,082

[1] Now divided into 3 regions: Nord-Kivu (chief town, Goma), Sud-Kivu (Bukavu) and Maniema (Kindu). [2] 1984 census.

Other large cities (with estimated 1991 population): Kolwezi (544,497), Likasi (279,839), Boma (246,207), Kikwit (182,850).

The population is composed almost entirely of Bantu groups, with minorities of Sudanese (in the north), Nilotes (northeast), Pygmies and Hamites (in the east).

French is the only official language, but of more than 200 languages spoken, 4 are recognized as national languages. Of these, Kiswahili is used in the east, Tshiluba in the south, Kikongo in the area between Kinshasa and the coast, while Lingala is spoken widely in and around Kinshasa and along the river; Lingala has become the *lingua franca* after French.

CLIMATE. Because of the size and the relief of the country, the climate is very varied, the central region having an equatorial climate, with year-long high temperatures and rain at all seasons. Elsewhere, depending on position north or south of the Equator, there are well-marked wet and dry seasons. The mountains of the east and south have a temperate mountain climate, with the highest summits having considerable snowfall. Kinshasa. Jan. 79°F (26·1°C), July 73°F (22·8°C). Annual rainfall 45" (1,125 mm). Kananga. Jan. 76°F (24·4°C), July 74°F (23·3°C). Annual rainfall 62" (1,584 mm). Kisangani. Jan. 78°F (25·6°C), July 75°F (23·9°C). Annual rainfall 68" (1,704 mm). Lubumbashi. Jan. 72°F (22·2°C), July 61°F (16·1°C). Annual rainfall 50" (1,237 mm).

CONSTITUTION AND GOVERNMENT. Under the Constitution of 1978 (as amended in 1980) the sole political party was the *Mouvement Populaire de la Révolution* (MPR), whose leader and President was automatically Head of State, of the National Executive Council and of the National Legislative Council. His nomination by the Political Bureau of the MPR (whose 38 members were all nominated by him) was confirmed for a 7-year term (renewable once) by election by universal adult suffrage (all Zaïreans acquiring automatic membership of the MPR at birth).

Parliament consisted of a unicameral National Legislative Council comprising People's Commissioners (one per 150,000 inhabitants) elected by universal suffrage for a 5-year term. At the latest elections (Sept. 1987) 210 People's Commissioners were elected from a list of candidates presented by the MPR.

In April 1990 President Mobutu announced the end of the Second Republic and the transition to a multi-party state. A national conference of 2,850 delegates to debate the country's political future held proceedings from Aug. 1991 (being more than once suspended by the President) until it wound itself up in Dec. 1992, having nominated a 443-member High Council of the Republic as a provisional government, with Etienne Tshisekedi as Prime Minister. On 17 March 1993 President Mobutu announced the appointment of Faustin Birindwa as Prime Minister, but Etienne Tshisekedi refused to step down. On 2 April 1993 the President's nominee Faustin Birindwa formed a transitional government. This resigned in Jan. 1994; at the same time the National Legislative Council and the High Council of the Republic were dissolved and a new High Council of the Republic-Transitional Parliament formed to prepare a new government. On 14 June 1994 this body elected Joseph Kengo wa Dondo as Prime Minister against 6 opponents.

President: Marshal Mobutu Sésé Séko Kuku Ngbendu wa Zabanga (took office 25 Nov. 1965, elected 1 Nov. 1970 and re-elected Dec. 1977 and July 1984).

A new government was formed on 26 Feb. 1996.

Prime Minister: Joseph Kengo wa Dondo (b. 1935; Union for the Republic and Democracy).

National flag: Green, with a yellow disc bearing an arm holding a flaming torch.

National anthem: 'Zaïrois, dans la paix retrouvée, peuple uni, nous sommes zaïrois' ('Zaïreans, in peace found again, a united people, we are Zaïreans'); words and tune by Boka Di Mpasi Londi.

Local government: Zaïre is composed of Kinshasa (administered by a Governor) and 10 regions, each under a Regional Commissioner and 6 Councillors; all are appointed by the President. The regions are divided into 41 sub-regions.

DEFENCE

Army. The Army is divided into 8 Military Regions and comprises 1 Presidential Guard division and 3 infantry, 1 parachute, 1 special forces, 1 independent armoured and 2 independent infantry brigades. Equipment includes 40 Chinese Type-62 and 20 Type-59 main battle tanks. Strength (1996) 25,000. There is a paramilitary gendarmerie responsible for security which numbered about 21,000, and a Civil Guard 10,000 strong.

Navy. The navy comprises 2 ex-Chinese and 2 US-built inshore patrol craft and some 6 small boats divided among coastal, river and lake flotillas. Personnel in 1995 numbered 1,300 including 600 marines. The coastal base is at Banaua.

Air Force. The Air Force has been built up with training assistance from Italy, but serviceability is low. In 1995 it operated 9 Aermacchi MB.326GB and 3 MB.326K armed jet trainers, 4 C-130 Hercules and 2 DHC-5 Buffalo turboprop transports, 6 C-47 piston-engined transports, 12 Alouette, Puma and Super Puma helicopters, 6 SIAI-Marchetti SF.260MC basic trainers and 20 other transport and training aircraft. Personnel (1995) 1,800, with 22 combat aircraft.

INTERNATIONAL RELATIONS

Membership. Zaïre is a member of the UN, OAU and is an ACP state of the EU.

ECONOMY

Policy. The 5-year Development Plan, 1986–90, envisaged expenditure of US$5,000m. Emphasis is placed on food production and agricultural exports.

Budget. Revenue was 2,914,022,000m. zaïres in 1993, and expenditure, 14,492,134,000m. zaïres.

Currency. The unit of currency is the *zaïre* (ZRZ) notionally of 100 *makuta* replacing the former zaïre in Oct. 1993 at 1 new zaïre = 3m. old zaïre. There are notes of 1, 5, 10 and 50 makuta and 1, 5, 10, 20, 50, 100, 200 and 500 new zaïres. Foreign exchange reserves were US$151·77m. in 1993; gold reserves were US$6·99m. in 1992. In March 1996, £1 = 30,415 zaïres; US$1 = 19,900 zaïres; DM1 = 13,483 zaïres.

Banking and Finance. The central bank is Banque du Zaïre. A development bank with state backing is the Société Financière de Développement (SOFIDE). Commercial banks operating in Zaïre are Banque de Paris et des Pays-Bas, Banque de Kinshasa, National & Grindlays Bank, Barclays Bank SZPRL, First National City Bank, Union Zaïroise de Banques, Banque Commerciale Zaïroise, Banque du Peuple, Caisse Nationale d'Epargne et de Crédit Immobilier and Banque Internationale pour L'Afrique au Zaïre.

Since Aug. 1991 commercial banks have been able to trade foreign exchange freely at their own rates.

Weights and Measures. The metric system is in force.

ENERGY AND NATURAL RESOURCES

Electricity. Production (1991), 6,168m. kWh. A dam at Inga, on the Zaïre River near Matadi, has a potential capacity of 39,600 MW.

Oil. Offshore oil production began in Nov. 1975; estimated crude production (1992) was 1·35m. tonnes.

Minerals. Production in 1993 (in 1,000 tonnes): Copper, 48; zinc, 30; cobalt, 2·4; gold, 1,400 kg; diamonds, 15·6m. carats. Coal, tin and silver are also found. The most important mining area is in the region of Shaba (formerly Katanga).

Agriculture. There were (1992) 7·28m. ha of arable land and 15·0m. ha of permanent pasture. The main food crops (1993 production in 1,000 tonnes) are: Cassava, 20,835; plantains, 2,224; sugar-cane, 1,400; maize, 1,201; groundnuts, 604; bananas, 406; yams, 315; rice, 458. Cash crops (1993) include palm oil, 181; coffee, 78; palm kernels, 72; rubber, 5; seed cotton, 77. There are also pineapples, 145; mangoes, 212; oranges, 156; papayas, 210.

Livestock (1993, in 1,000): Cattle, 1,650; sheep, 985; goats, 4,120; pigs, 1,130; poultry, 35m.

Forestry. Equatorial rain forests cover 55% of the country. In 1991 290,700 cu. metres of logs were produced.

Fisheries. The catch for 1991 was 160,000 tonnes, almost entirely from inland waters.

INDUSTRY.

The main manufactures are foodstuffs, beverages, tobacco, textiles, rubber, leather, wood products, cement and building materials, metallurgy and metal extraction, metal items, transport vehicles, electrical equipment and bicycles.

Labour. In 1990 the workforce was 13·08m. (4·65m. females; 0·82m. persons aged 10–15).

FOREIGN ECONOMIC RELATIONS. With Burundi and Rwanda, Zaïre forms part of the Economic Community of the Great Lakes. External debt was US$9,800m. in 1992.

Commerce. Exports in 1993 (and 1992) totalled US$1,144m. (US$1,246m.), imports, US$614m. (US$935m.). Main exports, 1993 (in US$1m.): Copper, 127·1; diamonds, 312; crude oil, 130·8; coffee, 61·5. Principal export markets, 1992: Belgium, 46·5%; USA, 18·9%. Principal import suppliers: Belgium, 19·2%; France, 5·5%; Germany, 6·4%; South Africa, 7·6%.

Total trade between Zaïre and UK (British Department of Trade returns, in £1,000 sterling):

	1991	*1992*	*1993*	*1994*	*1995*
Imports to UK	4,733	3,022	7,138	10,973	11,350
Exports and re-exports from UK	15,040	16,820	16,941	12 058	15,671

Tourism. There were some 46,000 foreign visitors in 1991.

COMMUNICATIONS

Roads. In 1991 there were almost 68,000 km of main, and 77,000 km of secondary, roads.

Railways. There are two railway operators, the Zaïre National Railways (SNCZ) and the National Office of Transport and Communications (ONATRA), which leases two lines from SNCZ. Length in 1990 was 5,118 km on 3 gauges, of which 858 km is electrified. In 1988 SNCZ and ONATRA carried 4m. passengers and 5·8m. tonnes of freight.

Civil Aviation. There is an international airport at Kinshasa (Ndjili). The national carrier is Air Zaïre, 80% state-owned, which in 1995 operated 1 B-737-200C Adv and 2 other aircraft. Services are also provided by Air France, Air Gabon, Cameroon Airlines, Ethiopian Airlines, Nigeria Airways, SAA, Sabena, Swissair, TAAG and TAP.

Shipping. The Zaïre River and its tributaries are navigable to 300-tonne vessels for about 14,500 km. Regular traffic has been established between Kinshasa and Kisangani as well as Ilebo, on the Lualaba (*i.e.*, the river above Kisangani), on some tributaries and on the lakes. Zaïre has only 40 km of sea coast. The merchant marine in 1993 comprised 27 vessels over 100 GRT with a total tonnage of 14,900 GRT. Matadi, Kinshasa and Kalemie are the main seaports; in 1993, Matadi handled 0·6m. tonnes of freight.

Telecommunications. In 1983 there were 362 post offices. Length of telegraph lines, 2,459 km. There were 15 broadcasting stations, 161 stations of wireless telegraphy and 206 telegraph offices; telephones numbered 31,855 in 1985. There is a ground satellite communications station outside Kinshasa. Broadcasting is provided by the government-controlled Voix du Zaïre and Télévision Zaïre (colour by SECAM). There is also an educational radio station. In 1991 there were 3·7m. radio and about 41,000 TV receivers.

Press. There were (1989) 4 dailies: *Salongo* (mornings) and *Elima* (evenings) in Kinshasa; *Njumbe* in Lubumbashi and *Boyoma* in Kisangani. Since 1990 several independent newspapers have been founded.

SOCIAL INSTITUTIONS

Justice. There is a Supreme Court at Kinshasa, 11 courts of appeal, 36 courts of first instance and 24 'peace tribunals'.

Religion. In 1992 there were about 17·32m. Roman Catholics, 10·38m. Protestants, and 6·12m. Kimbanguistes (African Christians). In 1988 there were some 450,000 Moslems. The remaining inhabitants chiefly adhere to animist beliefs.

Education. In 1990 28·2% of the population over 15 were illiterate. In 1987 there were 4,356,515 pupils in 10,819 primary schools and 1,066,351 pupils in 4,276 secondary schools. Secondary schools combine schools of general education, teacher training colleges and technical schools. In higher education there were in 1994–95 3 universities (Kinshasa, Kisangani and Lubumbashi), 14 teacher training colleges and 18 technical institutes in the public sector; and 13 university institutes, 4 teacher training colleges and 49 technical institutes in the private sector. In 1994–95 there were 20,130 university students and 1,630 academic staff.

Health. In 1986 there were 210 state and 190 private hospitals with 68,508 beds, about 4,000 health centres and 15 leprosy centres. There were about 2,000 doctors in 1982.

DIPLOMATIC REPRESENTATIVES

Of Zaïre in Great Britain (26 Chesham Pl., London, SW1X 8HH)
Ambassador: Vacant.

Of Great Britain in Zaïre (Ave. de Trois Z, Gombe, Kinshasa)
Ambassador: Marcus Hope.

Of Zaïre in the USA (1800 New Hampshire Ave., NW, Washington, D.C., 20009)
Ambassador: Tatanene Manata.

Of the USA in Zaïre (310 Ave. des Aviateurs, Kinshasa)
Ambassador: David H. Simpson.

Of Zaïre to the United Nations
Ambassador: Vacant.

Further Reading

Leslie, W. J., Zaïre: Continuity and Political Change in an Oppressive State. Boulder (CO), 1993

MacGaffey, J., *Entrepreneurs and Parasites: the Struggle for Indigenous Capitalism in Zaïre.* CUP, 1988

Williams, D. B. *et al. Zaïre:* [Bibliography] 2nd ed. Oxford and Santa Barbara (CA), 1995

Young, C. and Turner, T., *The Rise and Decline of the Zaïrian State*. Univ. of Wisconsin Press, 1985

ZAMBIA

Republic of Zambia

Capital: Lusaka
Population: 8·94m. (1993)
GNP per capita: US$350 (1994)
HDI/world rank: 0·425/136 (1992)

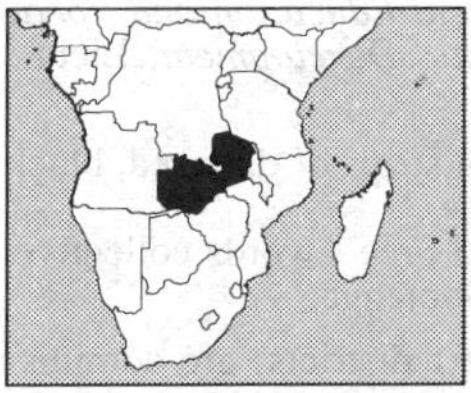

KEY HISTORICAL EVENTS. The independent Republic of Zambia (formerly Northern Rhodesia) came into being on 24 Oct. 1964 after 9 months of internal self-government following the dissolution of the Federation of Rhodesia and Nyasaland on 31 Dec. 1963.

TERRITORY AND POPULATION. Zambia is bounded by Zaïre in the north, Tanzania in the north-east, Malaŵi in the east, Mozambique in the south-east and by Zimbabwe and Namibia in the south. The area is 290,586 sq. miles (752,614 sq. km). Population (1990 census) 7,818,447 (3,975,014 females); estimate (1993), 8·94m. (55·6% urban); population density, 11·7 per sq. km.

The republic is divided into 9 provinces. Area, population and chief towns:

Province	*Area (in sq. km)*	*Population (1990 census)*	*Chief Town*
Central	94,395	725,611	Kabwe
Copperbelt	31,328	1,579,542	Ndola
Eastern	69,106	973,818	Chipata
Luapula	50,567	526,705	Mansa
Lusaka	21,898	1,207,980	Lusaka
Northern	147,826	867,795	Kasama
North-Western	125,827	383,146	Solwezi
Southern	85,283	946,353	Livingstone
Western	126,386	607,497	Mongu

Major towns (with estimated 1989 population in 1,000) are: Lusaka, 921; Kitwe, 495; Ndola, 467; Kabwe, 210; Mufulira, 206; Chingola, 201; Luanshya, 171; Livingstone, 102; Kalulushi, 100; Chililabombwe, 85.

The official language is English and the main ethnic groups are the Bemba (34%), Tonga (16%), Malawi (14%) and Lozi (9%).

CLIMATE. The climate is tropical, but has three seasons. The cool, dry one is from May to Aug., a hot dry one follows until Nov., when the wet season commences. Frosts may occur in some areas in the cool season. Lusaka. Jan. 70°F (21·1°C), July 61°F (16·1°C). Annual rainfall 33" (836 mm). Livingstone. Jan. 75°F (23·9°C), July 61°F (16·1°C). Annual rainfall 27" (673 mm). Ndola. Jan. 70°F (21·1°C), July 59°F (15°C). Annual rainfall 52" (1,293 mm).

CONSTITUTION AND GOVERNMENT. On 13 Dec. 1972 President Kaunda signed a new Constitution based on one-party rule. In Dec. 1990 the National Assembly unanimously passed a constitutional amendment permitting opposition parties, and in Aug. 1991 it adopted a new constitution by 107 votes to 15 permitting multi-party elections for a new wholly-elected parliament of 150 members.

At the Oct. 1991 presidential and parliamentary elections the registering electorate was 2·9m. Turn-out was about 40%. Frederick Chiluba (b. 1943; MMD) was elected President by 75% of votes cast against President Kenneth David Kaunda (UNIP) with 24%. The Movement for Multiparty Democracy (MMD) won 125 seats, the United Nationalist Independent Party (UNIP), 25.

President: Frederick Chiluba.
Vice-President: Vacant.
In Dec. 1995 the government comprised:

Defence: Ben Mwila. *Foreign:* Gen. Christon Tambo. *Finance:* Ronald Penza. *Home Affairs:* Chitalou Sampa. *Local Government and Housing:* Ben Mwiinga. *Health:* Michael Sata. *Education:* Alfeyo Hambayi. *Labour and Social Security:* Newstead Zimba. *Commerce, Trade and Industry:* Dipak Patel. *Communications:* Dawson Lupunga. *Energy and Water Development:* Edith Nawakwi. *Agriculture, Foods and Fisheries:* Suresh Desai. *Lands:* Dr Luminzu Shimaponda. *Legal Affairs:* Dr Remmy Mushota. *Environment and Natural Resources:* William Harrington. *Mines and Mineral Development:* Kelly Walubita. *Technical Education and Vocational Training:* Kabunda Kayongo. *Sport, Youth and Child Development:* Lieut.-Col. Patrick Kafumnkache. *Tourism:* Gabriel Maka.

National flag: Green, with in the fly a panel of 3 vertical strips of dark red, black and orange, and above these a soaring eagle in gold.

National anthem: 'Stand and Sing of Zambia, Proud and Free'; words collective, tune (same as that for Tanzania and Zimbabwe) by M. E. Sontanga.

Local Government. The 9 provinces (sub-divided into 61 districts) are administered by deputy ministers appointed by the President from elected or nominated members of parliament and with the Permanent Secretary as head of the civil service in each province. Elections are normally held every 3 years. Elections were held in Nov. 1992. Turn-out was 10%. The MMD won a majority of seats.

DEFENCE

Army. The Army consists of 1 armoured and 1 artillery regiment and 1 engineer and 9 infantry battalions. Equipment includes 10 T-54/-55 and 20 Chinese Type-59 main battle tanks. Strength (1995) 20,000. There are also paramilitary police units numbering 1,400.

Air Force. Creation of the Zambian Air Force was assisted initially by an RAF mission. Training and expansion of the Air Force was next taken over by Italy, with the purchase of 23 Aermacchi M.B.326G armed jet basic trainers (of which 12 remain in service), 8 SIAI-Marchetti SF.260M piston-engined trainers and 16 Agusta-Bell 47G, 10 AB.205 and 2 AB.212 helicopters. Twelve F-6 (MiG-19) jet fighter-bombers and some BT-6 primary trainers have been acquired from China, a squadron of 12 MiG-21 fighters, 3 Yak-40 light jet transports, 4 An-26 twin-turboprop transports and 6 Mi-8 helicopters from the Soviet Union, 4 DHC-5 Buffalo twin-turboprop transports from Canada, 7 DO 28D Skyservant light transports from Germany, 15 Supporter armed light trainers from Sweden. Serviceability of most types is reported to be low and a number have been written off. Personnel (1995) 1,600, with 32 combat aircraft.

INTERNATIONAL RELATIONS

Membership. Zambia is a member of the UN, the Commonwealth, SADC, OAU and is an ACP state of the EU.

ECONOMY

Policy. There is a privatization programme of 130 state-owned companies.

Budget. Revenue and expenditure for 1989 (in K1m.): Envisaged expenditure of 24,503 and revenue of 20,366.

Currency. The unit of currency is the *kwacha* (ZMK) of 100 *ngwee*. There are coins of 50, 20, 10, 5, 2 and 1 ngwee and banknotes of K500, K100, K50, K20, K10, K5 and K2. Gold reserves in 1989 were 13,000 troy oz. Foreign currency reserves were US$135m. K5,749·9m. were in circulation in 1991. In Dec. 1992 the official and free market exchange rates were merged and the kwacha devalued 29%. Annualized inflation was 29% in 1994. In March 1996, £1 = 1,604·82 kwacha; US$1 = 1,050 kwacha; DM1 = 711·43 kwacha.

Banking and Finance. The central bank is the Bank of Zambia (*Governor,* Jacob Mwanza), which had deposits of K12,332m. in 1991 and assets of K33,393·4m. In

1994 there were some 30 licensed banks, of which 20 were operating. Total assets of domestic and foreign commercial banks were K71,216·6m. in 1991. Assets of the Zambia National Building Society were K1,683·2m.

The Finance Development Corporation (FINDECO) controls the building societies, all insurance companies, one commercial bank and has shares in a second one. The Agricultural Finance Corporation provides loans to farmers, co-operatives, farmers' associations and agricultural societies.

There is a stock exchange at Lusaka.

ENERGY AND NATURAL RESOURCES

Electricity. Installed capacity, 1986, was 1,729 MW (1,538 MW hydro-electric). Output in 1990 was 7,923·2m. kWh.

Minerals. Minerals produced (in 1,000 tonnes) in 1990: Copper, 127; zinc, 10·2; lead, 5·4; silver, 7·5 tonnes; gold (1985), 7,903 oz. Zambia is well-endowed with gemstones, especially emeralds, amethysts, aquamarine, tourmaline and garnets. In 1990 the government freed the gemstones trade from restrictions.

Agriculture. 70% of the population is dependent on agriculture and 18·2% of GDP was provided by it and fishing in 1990. Principal agricultural products (1993, in 1,000 tonnes): Maize, 1,598; sugar-cane, 1,300; seed cotton, 58; tobacco, 7; groundnuts, 42.

Livestock (1993, in 1,000): Cattle, 3,204; pigs, 293; sheep, 67; goats, 600 and 21m. poultry.

Forestry. Forests covered (1990) 28·8m. ha, about 39% of the total land area. Roundwood removals (1988) 12·2m. cu. metres (11·6m. cu. metres for fuel).

Fisheries. Total catch (1987) 68,000 tonnes.

INDUSTRY. In 1990 manufacturing accounted for 31·9% of GDP.

Labour. In 1990 the workforce was 2,644,000 (767,000 female; 161,000 aged 10–15). In 1990 there were 111,630 employees in services, 56,810 in mining, 50,940 in manufacturing and 30,740 in catering. In 1989 there were 44 reported work stoppages with 58,434 workdays lost.

Trade Unions. There is a Zambia Congress of Trade Unions.

FOREIGN ECONOMIC RELATIONS. In 1993 foreign debt was some US$6,900m. Incentives introduced by the 1991 Investment Act include tax holidays and exemptions, remittance of 75% of after-tax profits and guarantees against expropriation.

Commerce. In 1993 exports were valued at US$950m. and imports at US$974m.

Exports (in tonnes) in 1990: Copper, 441,200; zinc, 9,489; lead, 40 (1,180 in 1989); cobalt, 4,931; tobacco, 2,027. In 1990, copper provided 90% of all exports (by value), cobalt 6%, zinc 2%. Official emerald exports in 1989 were valued at US$10m., but unofficial sales may have been a further US$200m. Main export markets are USA, Japan, UK and Germany; main import suppliers, South Africa, Japan, USA and Germany.

Total trade between Zambia and UK (British Department of Trade returns, in £1,000 sterling):

	1991	*1992*	*1993*	*1994*	*1995*
Imports to UK	22,468	7,279	12,056	13,038	19,460
Exports and re-exports from UK	62,655	65,127	73,548	44,523	49,819

Tourism. There were 108,300 visitors in 1988, of whom 10,900 were tourists (15·6% from Europe, 3·5% from America).

COMMUNICATIONS

Roads. There were (1988) 37,359 km of roads (6,444 km paved) including 56 km of motorway and 6,387 km of main road. In 1990 there were 9,473 road accidents with 888 fatalities.

Railways. In 1993 there were 1,273 km of Zambia Railways and 891 km of the Tanzania-Zambia (Tazara) Railway, both on 1,067 mm gauge. The state railway carried 1·1m. passengers and 3·4m. tonnes of freight in 1993.

Civil Aviation. The national carrier, Zambia Airways, went into voluntary liquidation in 1995; some of its services have been taken over by Aero Zambia and Zambia Express. Lusaka is the principal international airport. Services are also provided by Aeroflot, Air Botswana, Air France, Air Malaŵi, Air Namibia, Air Tanzania, Air Zimbabwe, British Airways, Kenya Airways, Royal Swazi, SAA, TAAG and Uganda Airlines.

Telecommunications. In 1987 there were 80,900 telephones. In 1995 there were direct connections to 16 countries. The telex network had 2,800 lines in 1995. The Zambia National Broadcasting Corporation is an independent statutory body which oversees 4 radio networks. There is also a religious radio station. Television is run by the government-controlled Television-Zambia (colour by PAL). In 1991 there were 1,660,360 radio and about 0·2m. TV receivers.

Press. There were (1996) 2 state-owned daily papers, *The Times of Zambia* and *Zambia Daily Mail* and 3 weeklies. There were also 5 privately-owned newspapers in 1995.

SOCIAL INSTITUTIONS

Justice. The Judiciary consists of the Supreme Court, the High Court and 4 classes of magistrates' courts; all have civil and criminal jurisdiction.

The Supreme Court hears and determines appeals from the High Court. Its seat is at Lusaka. The High Court exercises the powers vested in the High Court in England, subject to the High Court ordinance of Zambia. Its sessions are held where occasion requires, mostly at Lusaka and Ndola. All criminal cases tried by subordinate courts are subject to revision by the High Court.

Religion. In 1993 the President declared Zambia to be a Christian nation, but freedom of worship is a constitutional right. In 1992 there were 5·98m. Christians.

Education. Schooling is for 9 years. In 1986 there were 1·4m. pupils in 3,100 primary schools, secondary schools, 150,000 in 276 schools.

There are 2 universities, 3 teachers' colleges and 1 Christian college. In 1994–95 there were 6,139 university students and 640 academic staff.

Health. In 1987 there were 42 state, 29 mission and 11 mining company hospitals with a total of 15,846 beds and 912 health centres with 7,081 beds. In 1984 there were 798 doctors.

DIPLOMATIC REPRESENTATIVES

Of Zambia in Great Britain (2 Palace Gate, London, W8 5LS)
High Commissioner: Love Mtesa.

Of Great Britain in Zambia (Independence Ave., Lusaka)
High Commissioner: Patrick Nixon, CMG, OBE.

Of Zambia in the USA (2419 Massachusetts Ave., NW, Washington, D.C., 20008)
Ambassador: Dunstan Weston Kamana.

Of the USA in Zambia (PO Box 31617, Lusaka)
Ambassador: Roland K. Kuchel.

Of Zambia to the United Nations
Ambassador: Peter Kasanda.

Further Reading

Central Statistical Office. *Monthly Digest of Statistics.*

Bliss, A. M. and Rigg, J. A., *Zambia.* [Bibliography] Oxford and Santa Barbara, 1984
Burdette, M. M., *Zambia: between Two Worlds.* Boulder, 1988

De Waal, V., *The Politics of Reconciliation: Zambia's First Decade.* London, 1990
Kaunda, K. D., *Zambia Shall be Free.* London, 1962.—*Humanism in Zambia.* Lusaka. 2 vols. 1967 and 1974.—*Zambia's Economic Revolution.* Lusaka, 1968.—*Zambia's Guidelines for the Next Decade.* Lusaka, 1968.—*Letter to my Children.* Lusaka, 1973
Roberts, A., *A History of Zambia.* London, 1977

National statistical office: Central Statistical Office, Lusaka

ZIMBABWE

Republic of Zimbabwe

Capital: Harare
Population: 11·5m. (1995)
GNP per capita: US$490 (1994)
HDI/world rank: 0·539/121 (1992)

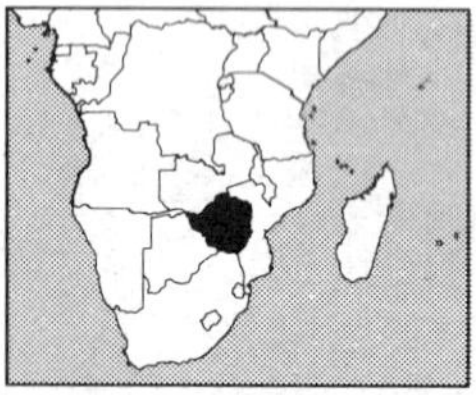

KEY HISTORICAL EVENTS. Southern Rhodesia, like Northern Rhodesia, was originally under the administration of the British South Africa Company, but following a vote in favour of responsible government on 12 Sept. 1923 it was annexed by the UK as a self-governing colony. For the history of the period 1961–1979 including the period of unilateral declaration of independence *see* THE STATESMAN'S YEAR-BOOK, 1980–81, pp. 1623–25.

At the Commonwealth Conference held in Lusaka in Aug. 1979 agreement was reached for a new Constitutional Conference to be held in London and this took place between 10 Sept. and 15 Dec. 1979. It was attended by the various factions in Zimbabwe-Rhodesia, including Abel Muzorewa, Robert Mugabe and Joshua Nkomo, and was chaired by Lord Carrington. It achieved 3 objectives: (*i*) the terms of the Constitution for an independent Zimbabwe; (*ii*) terms for a return to legality: and (*iii*) a ceasefire. Lord Soames became Governor of Southern Rhodesia in Dec. 1979 and elections took place in March 1980, resulting in victory for the Zimbabwe African National Union-ZANU (PF). Rhodesia (Southern Rhodesia) became the Republic of Zimbabwe on 18 April 1980. The state of emergency in force since 1965 was lifted in July 1990. In June 1991 the ZANU (PF) renounced Marxism.

TERRITORY AND POPULATION. Zimbabwe is bounded in the north by Zambia, east by Mozambique, south by South Africa and west by Botswana and the Caprivi Strip of Namibia. The area is 150,872 sq. miles (390,759 sq. km). The population was (1992 census) 10,401,767 (51·2% female). Estimate, 1995, 11,536,000 (50·4% female); density, 29·5 per sq. km.

Vital statistics (1990–95): Birth rate, 40·5 per 1,000; death rate, 11 per 1,000; infant mortality, 59 per 1,000 live births; growth rate, 2·96%. Life expectancy in 1994: Males, 54·4 years; females, 57·3.

There are 8 provinces and 2 cities, Harare and Bulawayo, with provincial status. Area and population (1992 census):

	Area (sq. km)	*Population*		*Area (sq. km)*	*Population*
Bulawayo	479	620,936	Mashonaland West	57,441	1,116,928
Harare	872	1,478,810	Masvingo	56,566	1,221,845
Manicaland	36,459	1,537,676	Matabeleland North	75,025	640,957
Mashonaland Central	28,374	857,318	Matebeleland South	54,172	591,747
Mashonaland East	32,230	1,033,336	Midlands	49,166	1,302,212

The chief cities (with 1992 census populations) were Harare, the capital (1,184,169), Bulawayo (620,936), Chitungwiza (274,035), Mutare (131,808) and Gweru (124,735). The main ethno-linguistic groups are the Shona (71%), Ndebele (16%) and Nyanja (3%).

The official language is English.

CLIMATE. Though situated in the tropics, conditions are remarkably temperate throughout the year because of altitude, and an inland position keeps humidity low. The warmest weather occurs in the three months before the main rainy season, which starts in Nov. and lasts till March. The cool season is from mid-May to mid-Aug. and, though days are mild and sunny, nights are chilly. Harare. Jan. 69°F (20·6°C), July 57°F (13·9°C). Annual rainfall 33" (828 mm). Bulawayo. Jan. 71°F

(21·7°C), July 57°F (13·9°C). Annual rainfall 24" (594 mm). Victoria Falls. Jan. 78°F (25·6°C), July 61°F (16·1°C). Annual rainfall 28" (710 mm).

CONSTITUTION AND GOVERNMENT. The Constitution provides for a single-chamber 150-member Parliament (*House of Assembly*), universal suffrage for citizens over the age of 18, an *Executive President* (elected for a 5-year term of office by Parliament), an independent judiciary enjoying security of tenure and a Declaration of Rights, derogation from certain of the provisions being permitted, within specified limits, during a state of emergency.

The House of Assembly is elected for 5 year terms: 120 members are elected by universal suffrage, 10 are chiefs elected by all the country's tribal chiefs, 12 are appointed by the President and 8 are provincial governors. The constitution can be amended by a two-thirds parliamentary majority.

Presidential elections were held on 17 March 1996. The electorate was 4·9m.; turn-out was 35%. President Mugabe was re-elected unopposed.

At the elections of 8–9 April 1995 turn-out was 54%. ZANU-PF gained 118 seats of the electable seats with 82% of votes cast (55 seats wre uncontested), ZANU (Ndonga) 2 with 6·5%. Parliamentary party composition: ZANU-PF, 148 seats; ZANU (Ndonga), 2.

Executive President: Robert G. Mugabe (b. 1924; sworn in on 30 Dec. 1987, re-elected April 1990; re-elected again March 1996).

The Cabinet in Nov. 1995 comprised:

Vice-Presidents: Simon Muzenda, Dr Joshua Nkomo. *Minister of Foreign Affairs:* Dr Stanislaus Mudenge. *Justice, Legal and Parliamentary Affairs:* Emmerson Mnangagwa. *Defence:* Moven Mahachi. *Home Affairs:* Dumiso Dabengwa. *Lands and Water Resources:* Kumbirai Kangai. *Information, Posts and Telecommunications:* David Karimanzira. *Public Service, Labour and Social Welfare:* Dr Nathan Shamuyarira. *Industry and Commerce:* Dr Herbert Murerwa. *Mines:* Dr Eddison Zvogbo. *Transport and Energy:* Simon Moyo. *Health and Child Welfare:* Dr Timothy Stamps. *Public Construction and National Housing:* Enos Chikowore. *Environment and Tourism:* Chen Chimutingwende. *Higher Education:* Ignatius Chombo. *Education:* Thenjive Lesabe. *National Security:* Dr Sidney Sekeramayi. *Finance:* Ariston Chambati. *Planning:* Richard Hove. *National Affairs, Employment Creation and Co-operatives:* Florence Chitauro. *Local Government, Rural and Urban Development:* John Nkomo. *Agriculture:* Denis Norman. *Home Affairs:* Dumiso Dabengwa. *Sports, Recreation and Culture:* Dr Witness Mangwende. *President's Office:* Ceplas Msipa.

National flag: Seven horizontal stripes of green, yellow, red, black, red, yellow and green; on a white black-edged triangle in the hoist a red star surmounted by the Zimbabwe Bird in yellow.

National anthem: 'Ishe Komborerai Afrika' ('God Bless Africa'); words collective, tune (same as that for Tanzania and Zambia) by M. E. Sontanga.

Local government: Municipal elections were held on 28 Oct. 1995.

DEFENCE

Army. The Army consists of 1 air defence, 1 engineer and 1 field artillery regiment, 26 infantry battalions, 1 armoured car and 1 tank squadron. Equipment includes 30 Chinese T-59 and 10 Chinese T-69 main battle tanks. Strength was (1996) 41,000, and there are a further 19,500 paramilitary police and a national militia of 1,000.

Air Force. The Air Force (ZAF) has a strength of (1995) about 4,000 personnel and 50 combat aircraft. Headquarters ZAF and the main ZAF stations are in Harare; the second main base is at Gweru, with many secondary airfields throughout the country. Equipment includes 1 squadron of F-7 (MiG-21) interceptors, 1 squadron of Hunter fighter-bombers and 1 squadron of Hawk training and light attack aircraft, a transport squadron with 11 turbo-prop CASA Aviocars and 6 twin-engined Islanders; a squadron with 14 Reims/Cessna 337 Lynx attack aircraft; a squadron with 14 SIAI-Marchetti SF.260W Gennet and 15 SF.260C Gennet trainers; a helicopter liaison/transport squadron with 20 Alouette IIIs, a helicopter casualty evacuation/transport squadron with 9 Bell 412s.

INTERNATIONAL RELATIONS

Membership. Zimbabwe is a member of UN, the Commonwealth, OAU and SADC and is an ACP state of the EU.

ECONOMY

Policy. A donor-funded Structural Adjustment Policy is running, 1991–95, aimed at promoting a market economy by economic stabilization, liberalization of trade, deregulation, reform of the public sector and social reform.

Budget. Revenue and expenditure (in Z$1,000):

	1991–92	*1992–93*	*1993–94*	*1994–95*
Revenue	9,428	10,763	13,677	15,477
Expenditure	11,178	13,657	15,979	16,909

Since April 1992 corporate tax has been 42·5% and the top rate of income tax (comes into effect at Z$45,000) 55%.

Currency. The unit of currency is the *Zimbabwe dollar* (ZWD) divided into 100 *cents*. There are coins of 1, 5, 10, 20 and 50 cents and Z$1, and notes of Z$1, 2, 5, 10, 20, 50 and 100. Gold reserves were 0·6m. troy oz. in 1994; foreign exchange reserves were US$532·6m. Z$1,226·8m. were in circulation. The currency was devalued 17% in Jan. 1994 and made fully convertible. Inflation was 18·7% in 1993. In March 1996, £1 = Z$14·54; US$1 = Z$9·51; DM1 = Z$6·45.

Banking and Finance. The Reserve Bank of Zimbabwe is the central bank (established 1965; *Governor*, Dr Leonard Tsumba). It acts as banker to the Government and to the commercial banks, is the note-issuing authority and co-ordinates the application of the Government's monetary policy. The Zimbabwe Development Bank, established in 1983 as a development finance institution, is 51% Government-owned.

In 1994 there were 5 commercial and 4 merchant banks. There are 5 registered finance houses, 3 of which are subsidiaries of commercial banks.

There is a stock exchange.

Weights and Measures. The metric system is in use but the US short ton is also used.

ENERGY AND NATURAL RESOURCES

Electricity. Production (1993) 7,185m. kWh.

Minerals. The total value of all minerals produced in 1993 was Z$3,026·3m.

1993 production: Gold, 18·6 tonnes, value Z$1,393m., (46% of all mineral production); nickel, value Z$369·1m. (12%); asbestos, 0·16m. tonnes; coal, some 5m. tonnes.

Agriculture. Replacing a constitutional provision that permitted the government to acquire land on a 'willing-seller willing-buyer' basis, legislation of March 1992 provides for its compulsory purchase at a fixed price for peasant resettlement. The possibility of compensation is not excluded. 52,000 peasants have been resettled on 3m. ha of land purchased from white farmers. In 1990 some 4,000 farmers owned 12m. ha while 0·75m. peasants occupied 15m. ha of communal agricultural areas.

The most important food crop is maize, the staple food of a large proportion of the population.

Both citrus and deciduous fruit production are well established.

Tobacco is the most important single product. In 1993 production was 205,000 tonnes.

Production, 1993 in 1,000 tonnes: Maize, 2,562; sorghum, 90; barley, 24; millet,

95; soyabeans, 65; groundnuts, 64; fruit, 153; vegetables and melons, 140; seed cotton, 187; wheat, 300; tea, 14; coffee, 4; sugar-cane, 700.

The commercially-owned beef cattle herd was 1·8m. in 1991 (3·2m. in 1975). Livestock (1993): Cattle, 4m.; pigs, 270,000; sheep, 530,000; goats, 2·5m. Milk production (1993): 400,000 tonnes.

Fisheries. Trout, prawns and bream are farmed to supplement supplies of fish caught in dams and lakes.

INDUSTRY. Metal products account for over 20% of industrial output. Important agro-industries include food processing, textiles, furniture and other wood products.

Labour. The labour force (1986–87) was 3·3m. Unemployment was 1·2m. in 1990.

Trade Unions. There is a Zimbabwe Congress of Trade Unions.

FOREIGN ECONOMIC RELATIONS. Since 1 Jan. 1995 foreign companies have been permitted to remit 100% of after-tax profits. The Customs Agreement with South Africa was extended in 1982.

Commerce. Imports and exports (in US$1m.):

	1988	*1989*	*1990*	*1991*	*1993*
Imports	871	1,061	1,168	1,800	1,425
Exports	1,385	1,465	1,411	1,765	1,543

Principal exports in 1993 (in US$1m.): Tobacco, 365; ferrochrome, 142; clothing and textiles, 122; nickel, 56; cotton lint, 26; steel, 16.

In 1993, 10·8% of exports went to the UK, 6·1% to the Federal Republic of Germany, 12·9% to the Republic of South Africa and 7·2% to the USA, while the Republic of South Africa provided 40% of imports, the UK 8·8%, the USA 5·9% and the Federal Republic of Germany 5%.

Total trade between Zimbabwe and UK (British Department of Trade returns, in £1,000 sterling):

	1991	*1992*	*1993*	*1994*	*1995*
Imports to UK	103,291	86,254	121,500	145,640	149,344
Exports and re-exports from UK	135,309	100,856	83,114	104,690	87,696

Tourism. In 1993, 0·88m. visitors visited Zimbabwe, bringing foreign exchange revenue of US$95m. The main tourist areas are Victoria Falls, Kariba, Hwange, the Eastern Highlands and Great Zimbabwe. The Zimbabwe Tourist Development Corporation is in Harare and Victoria Falls.

COMMUNICATIONS

Roads. The total length of roads is almost 86,000 km including surfaced, 12,900; gravel, 47,000; earth, 25,800.

Number of motor vehicles, 1992: Passenger cars, 310,400; commercial vehicles, 30,200; motor cycles, 29,100; tractors, 7,200.

Railways. Zimbabwe is served by the National Railways of Zimbabwe, which connect with the South African Railways to give access to the South African ports, with the Mozambique Railways to give access to the ports of Beira and Maputo and with the Zambia railway system. In 1994 there were 2,836 km (1,067 mm gauge) of railways including 457 km electrified. In 1994 the railways carried 10·8m. tonnes of freight and 2·1m. passengers.

Civil Aviation. There are 3 international airports: Harare, Bulawayo and Victoria Falls. Air Zimbabwe, the state-owned national carrier, operated 4 B-707-320Bs, 3 B-737-200 Advs, 2 B-767-200ERs and 3 other aircraft in 1995. The country is also served by British Airways, Kenya Airways, Ethiopian Airlines, Air Tanzania, Air Malawi, Zambian Airways, Balkan Bulgarian Airlines, Mozambique Airlines, South African Airways, Air Botswana, the Royal Swazi Airlines, TAP Air Portugal, Qantas, Lesotho Airways and Air India.

Shipping. Zimbabwe's outlets to the sea are Maputo and Beira in Mozambique, Dar-es-Salaam, Tanzania and the South African ports.

Telecommunications. At 31 Aug. 1986 there were 170 full post offices, 47 postal telegraph agencies and 86 postal agencies. At 30 June 1986 there were 251,344 telephones in Zimbabwe served by 96 exchanges; 2,102 telex connexions, served by 2 telex exchanges. Zimbabwe Broadcasting Corporation is an independent statutory body broadcasting a general service in English, Shona, N'debele, Nyanja, Tonga and Kalanga. There are 3 national semi-commercial services, Radio 1, 2 and 3, in English, Shona and N'debele. Radio 4 transmits formal and informal educational programmes. Zimbabwe Television broadcasts on 2 channels (colour by PAL). In 1992 there were 280,000 television and in 1993 522,000 radio sets in use.

SOCIAL INSTITUTIONS

Justice. The general common law of Zimbabwe is the Roman Dutch law as it applied in the Colony of the Cape of Good Hope on 10 June, 1891, as subsequently modified by statute. Provision is made by statute for the application of African customary law by all courts in appropriate cases.

The death penalty is authorized. The last execution took place in 1995.

The Supreme Court consists of the Chief Justice and at least 2 Supreme Court judges. It is the final court of appeal. It exercises appellate jurisdiction in appeals from the High Court and other courts and tribunals; its only original jurisdiction is that conferred on it by the Constitution to enforce the protective provisions of the Declaration of Rights. The Court's permanent seat is in Harare but it sits regularly in Bulawayo also.

The High Court is also headed by the Chief Justice, supported by the Judge President and an appropriate number of High Court judges. It has full original jurisdiction, in both Civil and Criminal cases, over all persons and all matters in Zimbabwe. The Judge President is in charge of the Court, subject to the directions of the Chief Justice. The Court has permanent seats in both Harare and Bulawayo and sittings are held three times a year in 3 other principal towns.

Regional courts, established in Harare and Bulawayo but also holding sittings in other centres, exercise a solely criminal jurisdiction that is intermediate between that of the High Court and the Magistrates' courts. Magistrates' courts, established in 20 centres throughout the country, and staffed by full-time professional magistrates, exercise both civil and criminal jurisdiction.

Primary courts consist of village courts and community courts. Village courts are presided over by officers selected for the purpose from the local population, sitting with two assessors. They deal with certain classes of civil cases only and have jurisdiction only where African customary law is applicable. Community courts are presided over by presiding officers in full-time public service who may be assisted by assessors. They have jurisdiction in all civil cases determinable by African customary law and also deal with appeals from village courts. They also have limited criminal jurisdiction in respect of petty offences.

Religion. Some of the population adhere to traditional animist religion. In 1989, 5·29m. persons were Christian: Anglicans, Roman Catholics, Methodists and Presbyterians.

Education. Education is compulsory. 'Manageable' school fees were introduced in 1991; primary education had hitherto been free to all. All instruction is given in English. There are also over 3,800 private primary schools and over 950 private secondary schools, all of which must be registered by the Ministry of Education. In 1993 there were 2,376,000 pupils at primary schools and, in 1992, 657,300 pupils at secondary schools. In 1992 69% of the population (aged 15 years and over) was classed as literate.

There are 10 teachers' training colleges, 8 of which are in association with the University of Zimbabwe. In addition, there are 4 special training centres for teacher trainees in the Zimbabwe Integrated National Teacher Education Course. In 1990 there were 17,873 students enrolled at teachers' training colleges, 1,003 students at agricultural colleges and 20,943 students at technical colleges.

There are 2 universities. In 1994–95 there were 8,205 students and 944 academic staff.

Health. In 1985 there were 162 hospitals, 1,062 static rural clinics and health centres and 32 mobile rural clinics operated by the Ministry of Health. All mission health institutions get 100% government grants-in-aid for recurrent expenditure. There is a medical school attached to the University of Zimbabwe in Harare, four government training schools attached to the 4 central hospitals for training state registered nurses, 14 training schools for medical assistants out of which 11 are administered by missions, and two for training maternity assistants, health assistants/health inspectors.

Social Services. It is a statutory responsibility of the government in many areas to provide: Processing and administration of war pensions and old age pensions; protection of children; administration of remand, probation and correctional institutions; registration and supervision of welfare organisations.

DIPLOMATIC REPRESENTATIVES

Of Zimbabwe in Great Britain (Zimbabwe Hse., 429 Strand, London, WC2R 0SA)
High Commissioner: Dr Ngoni Chideya.

Of Great Britain in Zimbabwe (Stanley Hse., Jason Mayo Ave., POB 4490, Harare)
High Commissioner: Martin Williams, CVO, OBE.

Of Zimbabwe in the USA (1608 New Hampshire Ave., NW, Washington, D.C., 20009)
Ambassador: Amos B. Muvengwa Midzi.

Of the USA in Zimbabwe (172 Herbert Chitepo Ave., Harare)
Ambassador: Johnny Carson.

Of Zimbabwe to the United Nations
Ambassador: Vacant.

Further Reading

Central Statistical Office. *Monthly Digest of Statistics.*

Akers, M., *Encyclopaedia Rhodesia.* Harare, 1973
Caute, D., *Under the Skin: The Death of White Rhodesia.* London, 1983
Cliffe, L. and Stoneman, C., *Zimbabwe: Politics, Economy and Society.* London, 1989
Hatchard, J., *Individual Freedoms and State Security in the African Context: the Case of Zimbabwe.* Ohio Univ. Press, 1993
Herbst, J., *State Politics in Zimbabwe.* Univ. of California, 1990
Keppel-Jones, A., *Rhodes and Rhodesia: The White Conquest of Zimbabwe, 1884–1902.* Univ. of Natal Press, 1983
Martin, D. and Johnson, P., *The Struggle for Zimbabwe.* London, 1981.—*Destructive Engagement.* Harare, 1986
Morris-Jones, W. H., (ed.) *From Rhodesia to Zimbabwe.* London, 1980
Nkomo, J., *Nkomo: The Story of My Life.* London, 1984
Potts, D., *Zimbabwe* [Bibliography]. 2nd ed. Oxford and Santa Barbara, 1993
Schatzberg, M. G., *The Political Economy of Zimbabwe.* New York, 1984
Skålnes, T., *The Politics iof Economic Reform in Zimbabwe: Continuity and Change in Development.* London, 1995
Stoneman, C., *Zimbabwe's Inheritance.* London, 1982.—*Zimbabwe: Politics, Economics and Society.* London, 1988
Verrier, A., *The Road to Zimbabwe, 1890–1980.* London, 1986
Weiss, R. *Zimbabwe and the New Elite.* London, 1994
Zimmerman, Z., *Zimbabwe's First Decade of Independence, 1980–1990: a Select and Annotated Bibliography.* Johannesburg, 1991

National statistical office: Central Statistical Office, POB 8063, Causeway, Harare.

Reference library: National Archives of Zimbabwe, PO Box 8043, Causeway, Harare.

INDEXES

PLACE AND INTERNATIONAL ORGANIZATIONS INDEX

Italicised page numbers refer to extended entries

PRODUCT INDEX

References are to production data

PERSON INDEX